ANNOTATED TEACHER'S EDITION

HOLT
World
History

The Human Journey

HOLT, RINEHART AND WINSTON

A Harcourt Education Company

Austin • Orlando • Chicago • New York • Toronto • London • San Diego

Staff Credits

Editorial

Sue Miller, *Director*
Robert Wehnke, *Managing Editor*
Dr. Melissa Langley-Biegert, *Project Editor*
Sue Minkler, *Assistant Editorial Coordinator*

Technology Resources

Annette Saunders, *Editor*

Art, Design & Photo

Book Design
Diane Motz, *Senior Design Director*
Lori Male, *Senior Designer*

Image Acquisitions
Joe London, *Director*

Tim Taylor, *Photo Research Supervisor*
Elaine Tate, *Art Buyer Supervisor*

Design New Media
Susan Michael, *Design Director*
Kimberly Cammerata, *Design Manager*
Michael Rinella, *Senior Designer*
Grant Davidson, *Designer*

Media Design
Curtis Riker, *Design Director*

Cover Design
Pronk & Associates

Design and Page Production
The Quarasan Group, Inc.

Pre-Press and Manufacturing

Production
Gene Rumann, *Production Manager*
Antonella Posterino, *Coordinator*
Jevara Jackson, *Manufacturing Coordinator, Book*
Rhonda Fariss, *Inventory Planning Analyst*
Kim Harrison, *Manufacturing Coordinator, Media*

Content Reviewers

Dr. Jack Balcer
Ohio State University
Ancient Greece

Dr. Lenard Berlanstein
University of Virginia
European social, modern France

Dr. Pierre Cagniart
Southwest Texas State U.
Ancient

Dr. Elton Daniel
University of Hawaii at Manoa
Islamic, West Asia, Iran

Dr. Toyin Falala
University of Texas at Austin
West Africa

Dr. Michael Hall
University of Texas at Austin
Colonial America

Dr. Arnold Krammer
Texas A&M University
Modern Europe, Germany

Dr. Julian Martin
University of Alberta
Science and medicine, early modern Britain

Dr. Alida Metcalf
Trinity University
Latin America, Brazil

Dr. Mark Parillo
Kansas State University
United States military, diplomatic, Japan

Dr. E. Bruce Reynolds
San Jose State University
Japan, China, Southeast Asia

Dr. Richard Saller
University of Chicago
Ancient, Roman

Dr. Lynn Struve
Indiana University
Premodern China, Chinese political and intellectual

Dr. Gerhard L. Weinberg
Emeritus, University of North Carolina—Chapel Hill
Modern Germany, WW I and WW II

Educational Reviewers

Peggy Altoff, Supervisor
Carroll County Public Schools
Westminster, Maryland

Laura L. Boelter
Shepherd Junior High School
Mesa, Arizona

Margaret Elaine Cox
Retired, Manatee High School
Bradenton, Florida

Alfred J. Hamel
South High Community School
Worcester, Massachusetts

Jay Harmon
Catholic High School
Baton Rouge, Louisiana

Paul Horne
Education Oversight Committee
Columbia, South Carolina

David Olson
Angola High School
Angola, Indiana

Madeleine Schmitt
St. Louis Public Schools
St. Louis, Missouri

Deanna Spring
Cincinnati Public Schools
Cincinnati, Ohio

Andy Turay
Bronx High School
Bronx, New York

Scott Whitlow
Round Rock High School
Round Rock, Texas

Laura Watkins
Acton Boxborough Regional High School
Acton, Massachusetts

It's All About

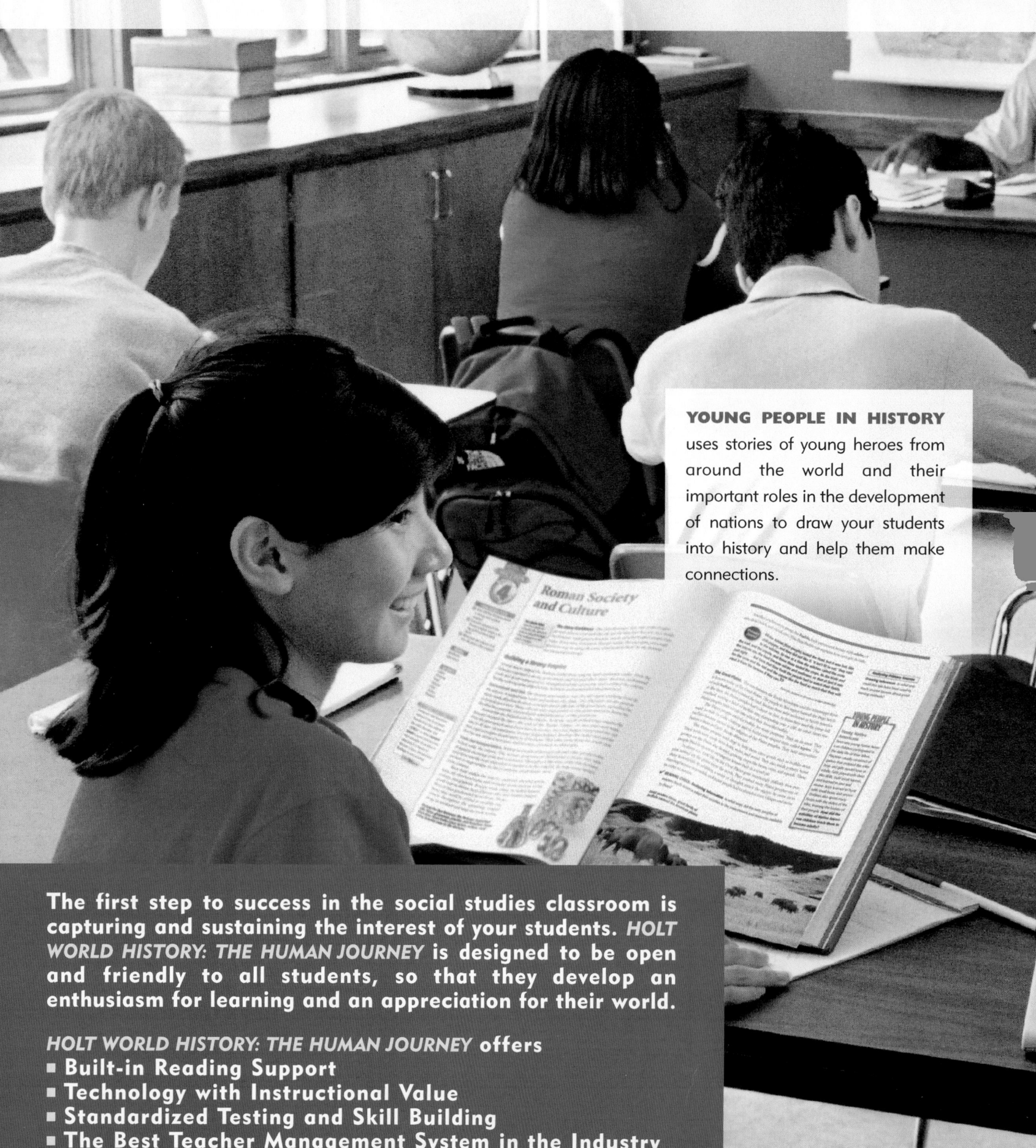

YOUNG PEOPLE IN HISTORY uses stories of young heroes from around the world and their important roles in the development of nations to draw your students into history and help them make connections.

The first step to success in the social studies classroom is capturing and sustaining the interest of your students. *HOLT WORLD HISTORY: THE HUMAN JOURNEY* is designed to be open and friendly to all students, so that they develop an enthusiasm for learning and an appreciation for their world.

HOLT WORLD HISTORY: THE HUMAN JOURNEY offers
- **Built-in Reading Support**
- **Technology with Instructional Value**
- **Standardized Testing and Skill Building**
- **The Best Teacher Management System in the Industry**

RELEVANCE

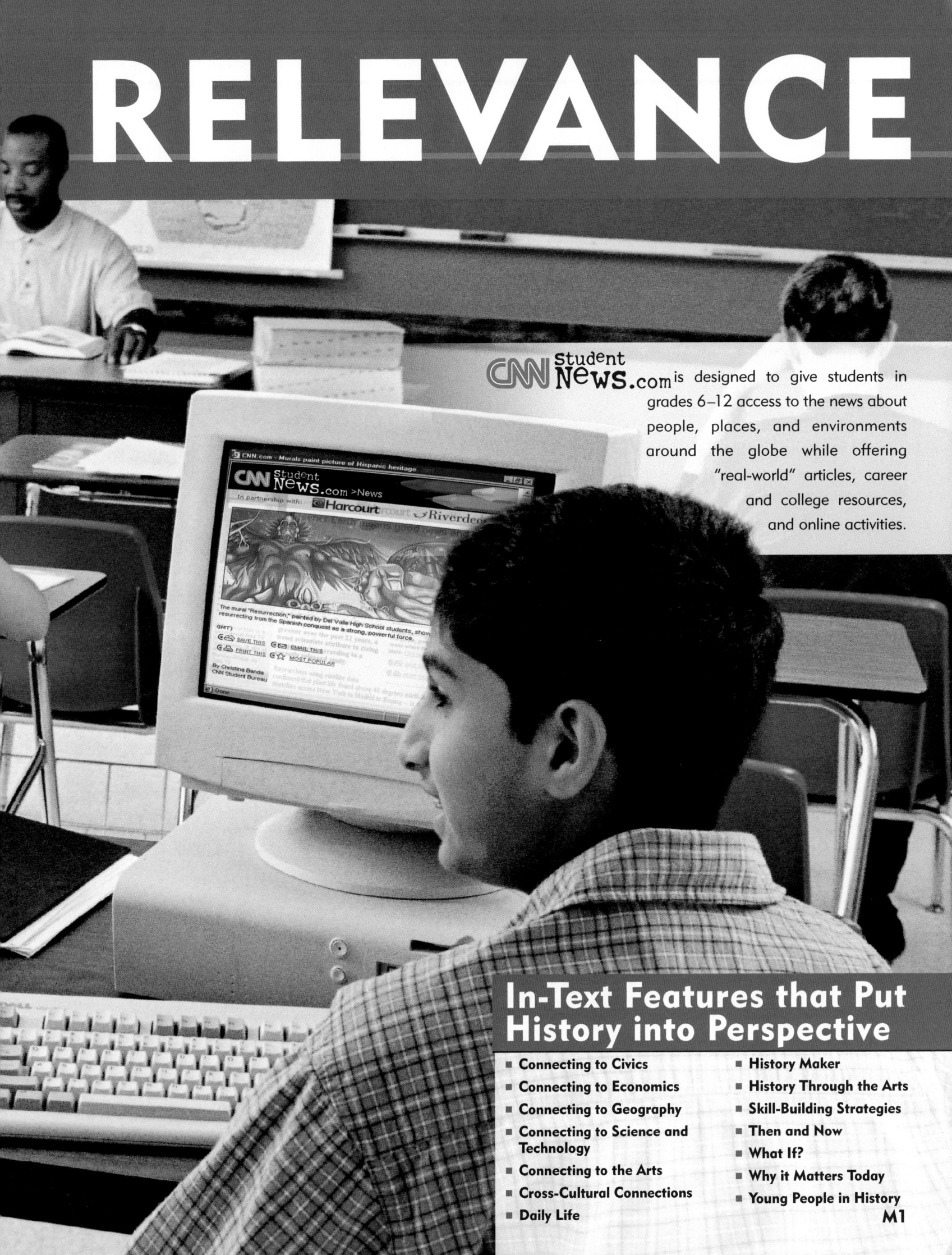

CNN Student News.com is designed to give students in grades 6–12 access to the news about people, places, and environments around the globe while offering "real-world" articles, career and college resources, and online activities.

In-Text Features that Put History into Perspective

- Connecting to Civics
- Connecting to Economics
- Connecting to Geography
- Connecting to Science and Technology
- Connecting to the Arts
- Cross-Cultural Connections
- Daily Life

- History Maker
- History Through the Arts
- Skill-Building Strategies
- Then and Now
- What If?
- Why it Matters Today
- Young People in History

Reading for

At Holt, we don't assume that students know how or have any desire to make sense of what they're reading, and we develop our programs based on that assumption. We don't just ask students questions about content, we give them strategies to get to that content. Through design, research, and the help of experts like Dr. Judith Irvin, we make sure students' reading needs are covered with our programs.

Helping Students Make Sense of What They're Reading

An Essay by Dr. Judith Irvin, Ph.D.

Who in middle and high schools helps students become more successful at reading and writing informational text? When I ask this question of a school faculty, the Language Arts/English teachers point to the social studies and science teachers because they are the ones with this type of textbook. The social studies and science teachers point to the Language Arts/English teachers because they are the ones that "do" words.

I advocate teachers taking an active role in helping students learn how to use text structure and context to understand what they read. Through consistent and systematic instruction that includes modeling of effective reading behavior, teachers can assist students in becoming better readers while at the same time helping them learn more content material.

The strategies in this book are designed to assist students with getting started, maintaining focus with reading, and organizing information for later retrieval. They engage students in learning material, provide the vehicle for them to organize and reorganize concepts, and extend their understanding through writing.

When teachers combine the teaching of reading and the teaching of content together into meaningful, systematic, and corrected instruction, students can apply what they have learned to understanding increasingly more difficult and complex texts as they progress through the school years.

READING STRATEGIES FOR THE SOCIAL STUDIES CLASSROOM

by Dr. Judith Irvin,
Ph.D. Reading Education

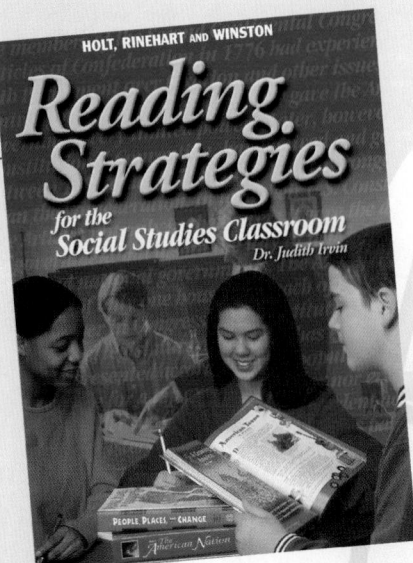

HOLT, RINEHART AND WINSTON

Reading Strategies
for the
Social Studies Classroom
Dr. Judith Irvin

Additional Reading Support

- **Main Idea Activities**
- **Graphic Organizer Activities**
- **Audio CD Program**
- **Guided Reading Strategies**

MEANING

Successful Readers must have:

1 AN ENGAGING NARRATIVE

Great care is taken in selecting and presenting content in a way that students will find motivating and engaging. Features such as **Young People in History** help students connect their own lives to those who have played a role in the development of our nation.

2 A FORECAST OF WHAT THEY WILL LEARN

Read to Discover questions give students insight into the content they will cover in the chapter to come. In features such as **What's Your Opinion?** students are encouraged to give their opinions, thus helping them develop an ownership of the material.

3 OPPORTUNITIES TO ACTIVATE PRIOR KNOWLEDGE

In the pre-reading features **Build on What You Know** and **Chapter Timelines,** students are encouraged to connect content they have covered in previous chapters or other courses to the material they will learn about in the upcoming chapter.

4 VOCABULARY DEFINED IN CONTEXT

Important new terms are identified at the beginning of every section and are defined in context so students will develop an understanding of the contextual meaning of all terms.

5 STRATEGIES FOR UNDERSTANDING WHAT THEY READ

Through the design of the text, students are led through the content using built-in reading strategies. For example, **Reading Checks** in the text are used as a comprehension tool. The checks remind students to stop and engage with what they have read, functioning as a "Tutor in the Text."

Get Your Students

Your students love activities that get them involved with the content. That's why Holt offers active-learning resources that link directly to program content and provide a multitude of different lessons for large-group, small-group, and individual projects.

CREATIVE TEACHING STRATEGIES

Customize these innovative teaching strategies and use them at various points in your lessons to motivate your students by getting them actively involved in the learning process.

ACTIVE LEARNING AND GEOGRAPHY SUPPORT

Hands-on History Activities: Classroom to Community will get your students out of their seats for group-oriented, active-learning projects that offer specific links between history and your local community.

Geography Activities help your students understand the role geography plays in history through mapping and skill-related activities.

PRIMARY SOURCES

World History and Geography Document-Based Questions Activities offers your students rich content allowing them to make intelligent, formed opinions based on their observations of a diverse range of primary sources. Important historical themes are grouped together, allowing for scaffolded instruction.

Readings in World History presents primary and secondary-source historical readings, discussing the political, cultural, social, and intellectual significance of events.

Involved in Learning

Skill-Based Ancillaries

- Guided Reading Strategies
- Visual Resources
- The Complete School Atlas
- Creative Teaching Strategies
- Hands-on History Activities: Classroom to Community
- Geography Activities
- World History and Geography Document-Based Questions Activities
- Readings in World History

Joining Forces

CNN® Presents
World Cultures: Yesterday and Today

to Enrich your Classroom

CNNStudentNews.com

At **CNNStudentNews.com**, students will love exploring news stories written by experienced journalists as well as student bureau reporters complete with links to homework help and lesson plans.

CNN PRESENTS VIDEO LIBRARY

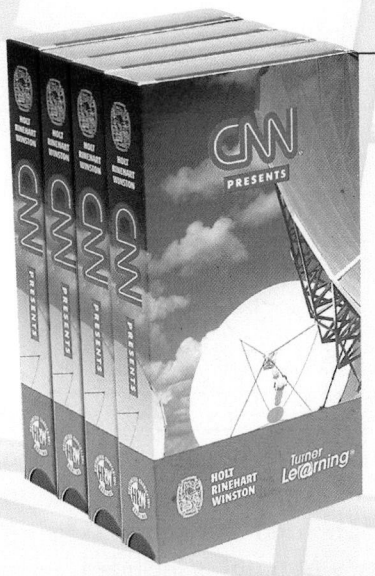

The **CNN PRESENTS** video collection tackles the issue of making content relevant to students head on. Real-world news stories enable students to see the connections between classroom curriculum and today's issues and events around the nation and the world.

CNN PRESENTS...

- **America: Yesterday and Today, Beginnings to 1914**
- **America: Yesterday and Today, 1850 to Present**
- **America: Yesterday and Today, Modern Times**
- **Geography: Yesterday and Today**
- **World Cultures: Yesterday and Today**
- **American Government**
- **Economics**
- **September 11, 2001: Part One**
- **September 11, 2001: Part Two**

Your Multi-talented Classroom

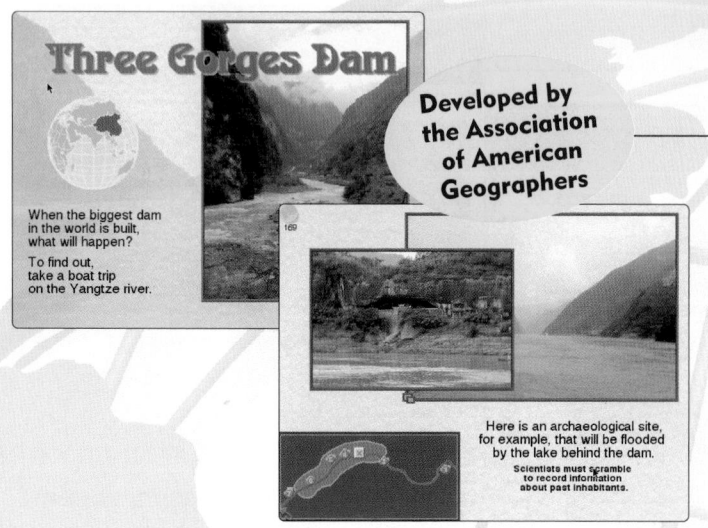

Developed by the Association of American Geographers

ACTIVITIES AND READINGS IN THE GEOGRAPHY OF THE WORLD

Integrate real geography into the topic you're studying with *Activities and Readings in the Geography of the World (ARGWorld)*. This CD-ROM features world geography case studies with a multitude of activities that focus around geographical themes, population geography, economic geography, political geography, and environmental issues. Case studies will help teachers address the National Geography Standards.

GLOBAL HISTORY RESOURCE CENTER CD-ROM

This comprehensive database includes audio and video clips, maps, photographs, and readings to be integrated with the textbook for additional study.

GLOBAL SKILL BUILDER CD-ROM

This CD-ROM is a comprehensive program containing interactive lessons that motivate your students to strengthen their map, graph, and computer skills. A **User's Guide and Teacher's Manual** is included.

needs Multimedia Tools

THE WORLD TODAY VIDEODISC PROGRAM

This unique resource offers a stimulating outlook on world geography by showing your students the different ways geographers organize the world, and challenging them to contemplate and discuss significant world issues. Compelling video segments with in-depth content cover contemporary culture in every major world region.

HOLT WORLD HISTORY AUDIO CD PROGRAM

The *Audio CD Program* provides in-depth audio section summaries and self-check activity sheets to help those students who respond to auditory learning. Available in English and Spanish.

Audio CD Program

Other Multimedia Products

- CNN Presents Geography: Yesterday and Today
- CNN Presents World Cultures: Yesterday and Today
- Holt Researcher Online: World History and Cultures
- World History and Cultures Video Program, English
- World History and Cultures Video Program, Spanish
- World History and Cultures Videodisc Program

Technology with

go.hrw.com FOR TEACHERS

Throughout the *Annotated Teacher's Edition*, you'll find **Internet Connect** boxes that take you to specific chapter activities, links, current events, and more that correlate directly to the section you are teaching. Through **go.hrw.com** you'll find a wealth of teaching resources at your fingertips for fun, interactive lessons.

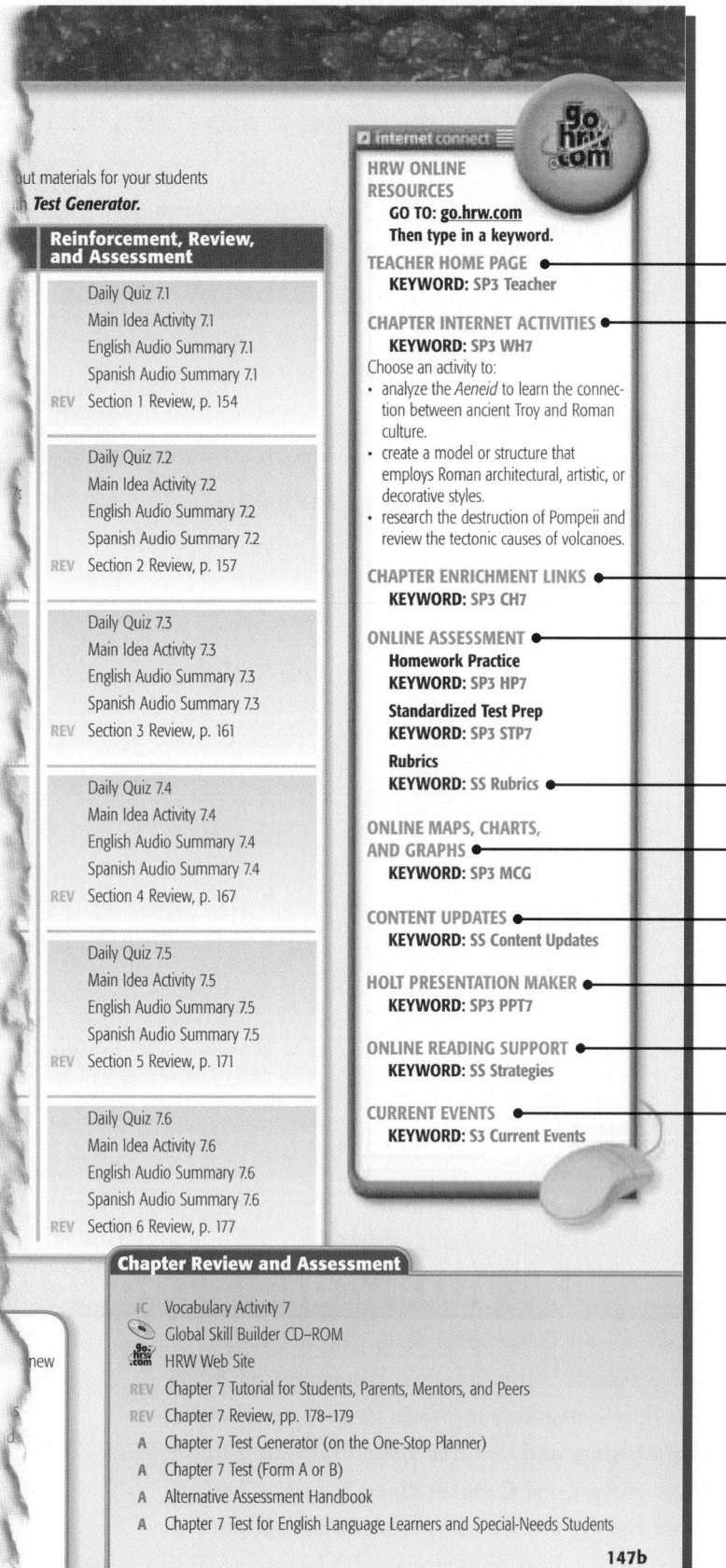

...ut materials for your students
...h *Test Generator.*

Reinforcement, Review, and Assessment

Daily Quiz 7.1
Main Idea Activity 7.1
English Audio Summary 7.1
Spanish Audio Summary 7.1
REV Section 1 Review, p. 154

Daily Quiz 7.2
Main Idea Activity 7.2
English Audio Summary 7.2
Spanish Audio Summary 7.2
REV Section 2 Review, p. 157

Daily Quiz 7.3
Main Idea Activity 7.3
English Audio Summary 7.3
Spanish Audio Summary 7.3
REV Section 3 Review, p. 161

Daily Quiz 7.4
Main Idea Activity 7.4
English Audio Summary 7.4
Spanish Audio Summary 7.4
REV Section 4 Review, p. 167

Daily Quiz 7.5
Main Idea Activity 7.5
English Audio Summary 7.5
Spanish Audio Summary 7.5
REV Section 5 Review, p. 171

Daily Quiz 7.6
Main Idea Activity 7.6
English Audio Summary 7.6
Spanish Audio Summary 7.6
REV Section 6 Review, p. 177

Chapter Review and Assessment

IC   Vocabulary Activity 7
     Global Skill Builder CD-ROM
     HRW Web Site
REV Chapter 7 Tutorial for Students, Parents, Mentors, and Peers
REV Chapter 7 Review, pp. 178–179
A   Chapter 7 Test Generator (on the One-Stop Planner)
A   Chapter 7 Test (Form A or B)
A   Alternative Assessment Handbook
A   Chapter 7 Test for English Language Learners and Special-Needs Students

147b

internet connect

HRW ONLINE RESOURCES
GO TO: go.hrw.com
Then type in a keyword.

TEACHER HOME PAGE
KEYWORD: SP3 Teacher

CHAPTER INTERNET ACTIVITIES
KEYWORD: SP3 WH7
Choose an activity to:
- analyze the *Aeneid* to learn the connection between ancient Troy and Roman culture.
- create a model or structure that employs Roman architectural, artistic, or decorative styles.
- research the destruction of Pompeii and review the tectonic causes of volcanoes.

CHAPTER ENRICHMENT LINKS
KEYWORD: SP3 CH7

ONLINE ASSESSMENT
Homework Practice
KEYWORD: SP3 HP7

Standardized Test Prep
KEYWORD: SP3 STP7

Rubrics
KEYWORD: SS Rubrics

ONLINE MAPS, CHARTS, AND GRAPHS
KEYWORD: SP3 MCG

CONTENT UPDATES
KEYWORD: SS Content Updates

HOLT PRESENTATION MAKER
KEYWORD: SP3 PPT7

ONLINE READING SUPPORT
KEYWORD: SS Strategies

CURRENT EVENTS
KEYWORD: S3 Current Events

DIRECT LAUNCH TO CHAPTER ACTIVITIES

GUIDED ONLINE ACTIVITIES

LINKS FOR EVERY SECTION

INTERACTIVE PRACTICE AND REVIEW

RUBRICS FOR SUBJECTIVE GRADING

MAPS AND CHARTS

UP-TO-DATE INFORMATION

CLASSROOM PRESENTATION SUPPORT

PRACTICE FOR READING SUCCESS

WEB RESOURCES FOR CURRENT ISSUES

GO.HRW.COM

Online Teaching Materials

Select a Resource
HRW Online Resources ▼

<u>Reading Strategies</u> written by Dr. Judith Irvin are targeted at US History and World Studies.

<u>HRW's State Handbooks</u> provide state-specific links and activities at the click of a mouse button.

Instructional Value

ONLINE TEACHING SUPPORT

Teacher materials on **go.hrw.com** offer you multiple resources for keeping content current. From **World History Maps and Charts** to **State Handbooks**, we've got it all.

CLASSROOM PRESENTATION SUPPORT

Lecture notes and animated graphic organizers help add visual support to your classroom presentations.

Technology that

go.hrw.com FOR STUDENTS

Your students can access interactive activities, homework help, up-to-date maps, and more when they visit **go.hrw.com** and type in the keywords they find in their text.

ONLINE WORLD TRAVEL

When you log on to **go.hrw.com**, you and your students gain passage to **GeoTreks**—a site with guided Internet activities that integrate program content, spark imaginations, and promote online research skills. You'll find:

Interactive templates for creating newspapers, postcards, travel brochures, guided research reports, and more

GeoMaps—Interactive satellite maps of the world's regions for content review

Drag-and-drop exercises to review chapter content in short, fun activities

Chapter Web Links for prescreened, age-appropriate Web sites and current events

HOMEWORK PRACTICE

This helpful tool allows students to practice and review content by chapter anywhere there is a computer.

HRW ONLINE ATLAS AND HISTORICAL MAPS

The helpful online atlas contains over 300 well-rendered and clearly labeled country and state maps. Available in English and Spanish, these maps are continually updated so you can rest assured that you and your students have the latest and most accurate geographical content.

Online historical maps provide fascinating visual "snapshots" of the past. Students will relish the chance to explore medieval European trade routes, explorers' routes, ancient African kingdoms, and more.

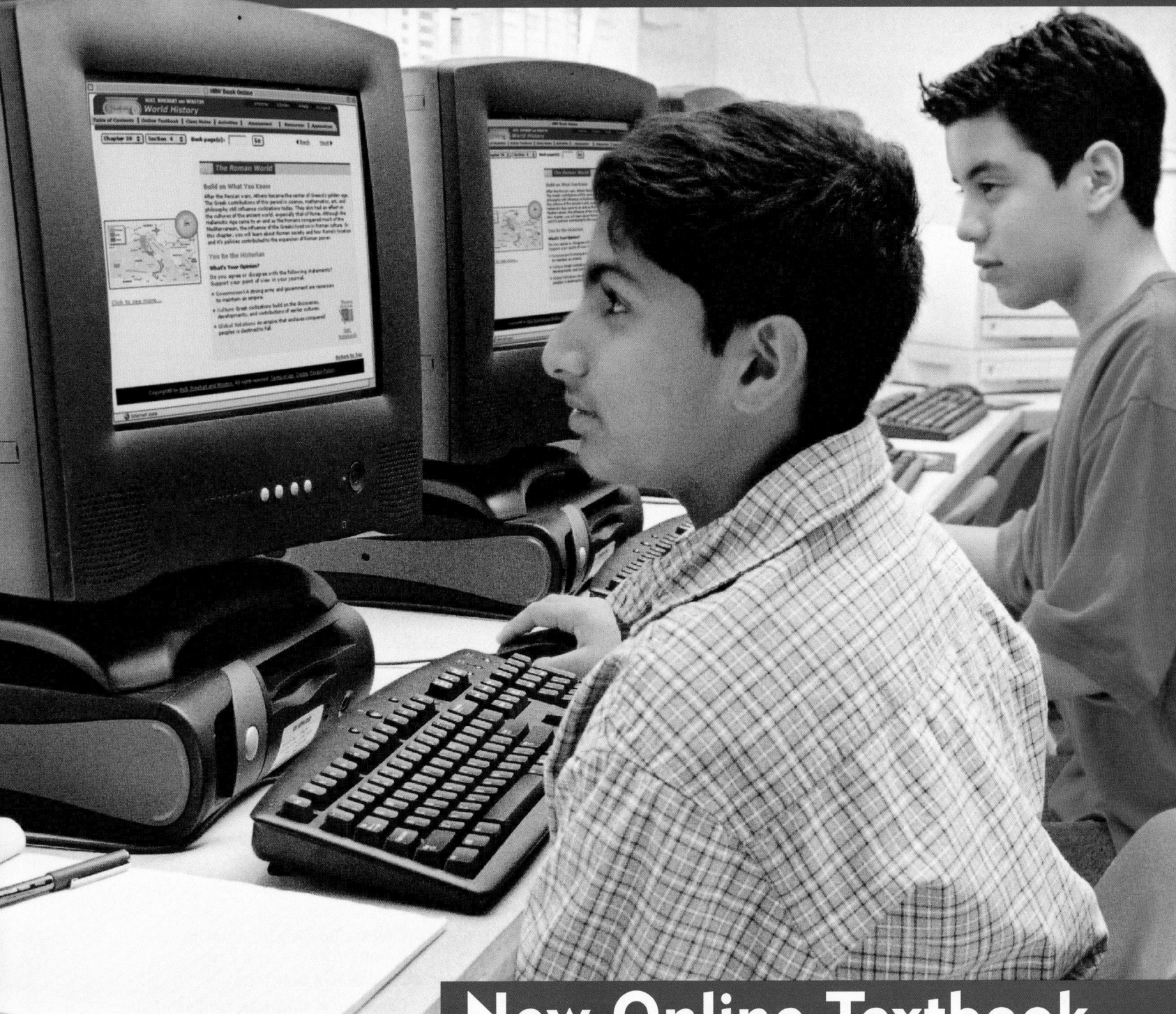

Delivers Content

New Online Textbook

You'll know what to do when you see it!
Finally, an online textbook that takes full advantage of Web technology in a way that makes sense—*HOLT WORLD HISTORY: THE HUMAN JOURNEY ONLINE EDITION*.

- **Entire student edition online formatted to match printed text**
- **User-friendly navigation**
- **Hot links to interactive activities, practice, and assessment**
- **Student Notebook for online responses**

M13

Unique Teacher's

In-Text Chapter Planning

Program Resources at Your Fingertips

READING SUPPORT

- **Graphic Organizer Activities**
- **Guided Reading Strategies**
- **Main Idea Activities for English Language Learners and Special-Needs Students**
- **Reading Strategies for the Social Studies Classroom**

PRIMARY SOURCES

- **Readings in World History**
- **Visual Resources**
- **World History and Geography Document-Based Questions Activities**
- **Visual Resources Transparency Directory**

GEOGRAPHY SUPPORT

- **The Complete School Atlas**
- **Geography Activities**
- **World and Regional Outline Maps**

ACTIVE-LEARNING SUPPORT

- **Block Scheduling Handbook with Team Teaching Strategies**
- **Creative Teaching Strategies**
- **Hands-on History Activities: Classroom to Community**

REVIEW AND ASSESSMENT

- **Daily Quizzes**
- **Chapter Tutorials for Students, Parents, Mentors, and Peers**
- **Chapter and Unit Tests**
- **Chapter and Unit Tests for English Language Learners and Special-Needs Students**
- **Alternative Assessment Handbook**
- **Social Studies Skills Review**

Management System

One-Stop Planner
with Test Generator

Everything you need is on one disc!

ONE-STOP PLANNER® CD-ROM WITH TEST GENERATOR

Holt brings you the most user-friendly management system in the industry with the *One-Stop Planner CD-ROM with Test Generator.* Plan and manage your lessons from this single disc containing all the teaching resources for *Holt World History: The Human Journey,* valuable planning and assessment tools, and more.

- **Editable lesson plans**
- **Classroom Lecture Notes and Animated Graphic Organizers**
- **Easy-to-use test generator**
- **Previews of all teaching and video resources**
- **Easy printing feature**
- **Direct launch to go.hrw.com**

BLOCK SCHEDULING HANDBOOK WITH TEAM TEACHING STRATEGIES

This is more than a pacing guide—it provides daily lesson plans that suggest practical ways to cover more than one textbook section in an extended class period and ways to make inter-disciplinary connections.

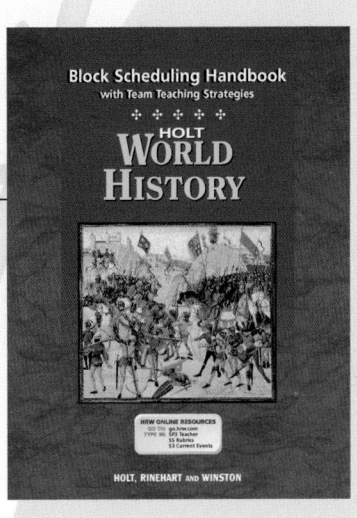

Block Scheduling Handbook
with Team Teaching Strategies
✦ ✦ ✦ ✦ ✦
HOLT
WORLD HISTORY

HOLT, RINEHART AND WINSTON

Energize

Presentations That Benefit Learning

Classroom presentations and lecture notes can be accessed with ease when you use Holt's **Presentation** tool found on the *One-Stop Planner CD-ROM*. This resource helps you spice up your presentations and gives you ideas to build on. You'll find Microsoft® PowerPoint® presentations that include lecture notes and animated graphic organizers for each chapter and section of your text.

Your Classroom Presentations

OBJECTIVE-BASED LESSON CYCLE

With lively activities and presentation strategies such as **Let's Get Started, Building Vocabulary,** and **Graphic Organizers,** your step-by-step lesson cycle makes planning your lessons easy and productive.

TEACHER TO TEACHER

These strategies are offered in the columns of your *Annotated Teacher's Edition* and provide you with valuable, classroom-tested ideas and activities that have been developed and successfully applied by your peers.

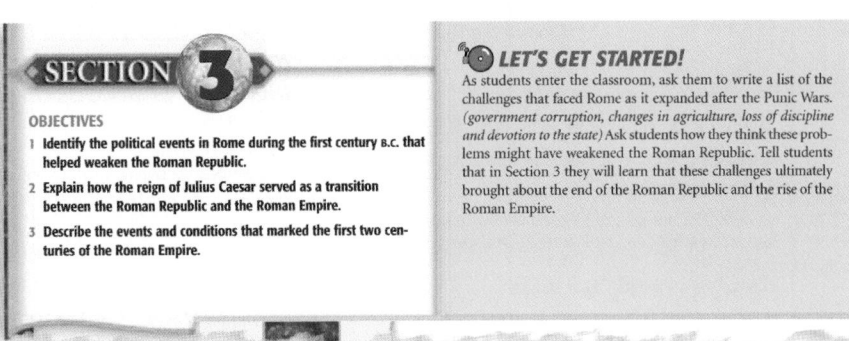

SECTION 3

OBJECTIVES

1 Identify the political events in Rome during the first century B.C. that helped weaken the Roman Republic.

2 Explain how the reign of Julius Caesar served as a transition between the Roman Republic and the Roman Empire.

3 Describe the events and conditions that marked the first two centuries of the Roman Empire.

LET'S GET STARTED!

As students enter the classroom, ask them to write a list of the challenges that faced Rome as it expanded after the Punic Wars. *(government corruption, changes in agriculture, loss of discipline and devotion to the state)* Ask students how they think these problems might have weakened the Roman Republic. Tell students that in Section 3 they will learn that these challenges ultimately brought about the end of the Roman Republic and the rise of the Roman Empire.

TEACH OBJECTIVE 1

LEVEL 1: Copy the following cause-and-effect chart on the board, omitting the italicized answers, and have students complete after reading Section 3.

ENGLISH LANGUAGE LEARNERS

Gracchus brothers introduce reforms	→ *angry senators kill both Gracchus brothers*
violence = primary tool of Roman politics	→ *leaders recruit personal armies*
Sulla marches on Rome; civil war	→ *Sulla establishes dictatorship*

In-Text Features that put History into Perspective

- **Connecting to Civics**
- **Connecting to Economics**
- **Connecting to Geography**
- **Connecting to Science and Technology**
- **Connecting to the Arts**
- **Cross-Cultural Connections**
- **Daily Life**
- **History Maker**
- **History Through the Arts**
- **Skill-Building Strategies**
- **Then and Now**
- **What If?**
- **Why it Matters Today**
- **Young People in History**

TEACH OBJECTIVE 2

ALL LEVELS: As students read the section "Caesar in Power" on page 159, have them complete a web diagram that includes characteristics and events related to Caesar. Then draw a web on the board and fill it in with students' responses.

ENGLISH LANGUAGE LEARNERS

HOMEWORK Write an essay explaining how Julius Caesar's reign was a transition between the Roman Republic and the Roman Empire. Use standard grammar, spelling, sentence structure, and punctuation.

TEACH OBJECTIVE 3

LEVEL 3: Assign pairs of students to study a Roman leader of this time and to write a profile that explains the leader's significance. Encourage students to use their textbooks, the library, the Internet, and other sources. Invite students to read their profiles aloud.

CLOSE

List characteristics of Roman politics before, during, and after the rule of Julius Caesar.

REVIEW

Have students complete the Section 3 Review on page 161.

ASSESS

Have students complete Daily Quiz 7.3. As Alternative Assessment, have students complete the cause-and-effect chart or Caesar web diagram in this section's lessons.

RETEACH

Have students complete Main Idea Activity for English Language Learners and Special-Needs Students 7.3. Have students identify three events during the time the republic fell that changed the course of Roman history.

ENGLISH LANGUAGE LEARNERS

EXTEND

Have students write a brief script and stage a mock trial of Caesar's assassins. Students should take the roles of judge, prosecutor, defense attorney, and conspirators. **BLOCK SCHEDULING**

Assessment for

REVIEW OF MAIN IDEAS

SECTION 4 REVIEW

1. **Define** and explain the significance:
   gladiators
   aqueducts

2. **Identify** and explain the significance:
   Galen
   Ptolemy
   Virgil
   Horace
   Ovid
   Tacitus
   Plutarch

3. **Summarizing** Make a chart like this to summarize the lives of the Romans.

	Description
Daily Life	
Slavery	
Roles of men and women	
Religion	
Entertainment	

Finding the Main Idea
a. What factors contributed to the strength of the Roman Empire? How?
b. What do you think are the five most important contributions the Romans made to law and government, engineering and architecture, and literature and language? Explain your answers.

5. **Writing and Critical Thinking**
Making Generalizations Imagine that you are a teenager belonging to the upper class and living in the Roman Empire during the Pax Romana. Write a short diary entry recounting the events of a typical day.
Consider:
• the importance of your family
• the kind of schooling and education you receive
• how being a boy or a girl influences your life

Homework Practice Online
keyword: SP3 HP7

CHAPTER 7 Review

Creating a Time Line

Copy the time line below onto a sheet of paper. Complete the time line by filling in the events, individuals, and dates from the chapter that you think were significant. Pick three events and explain why you think they were significant.

| 1000 B.C. | 500 B.C. | A.D. 1 | A.D. 500 |

Writing a Summary

Using standard grammar, spelling, sentence structure, and punctuation, write an overview of the events in the chapter.

Identifying People and Ideas

Identify the following terms or individuals and explain their significance:

1. republic
2. checks and balances
3. dictator
4. Punic Wars
5. Pax Romana
6. Julius Caesar
7. Augustus (Octavian)
8. aqueducts
9. Jesus
10. Constantine

Understanding Main Ideas

SECTION 1 (pp. 150–154)
Founding the Roman Republic
1. How was the Roman Republic's government organized?
2. How did the Conflict of the Orders change how the Roman Republic was governed?

SECTION (pp. 155–157)
Rome Expands Its Borders
3. What was the outcome of the Punic Wars?
4. What problems occurred as a result of Rome's expansion?

SECTION 3 (pp. 158–161)
The Birth of the Roman Empire
How did Julius Caesar rise to power?
How did the republic become the Roman Empire?

SECTION 4 (pp. 162–167)
Roman Society and Culture
7. What was the economy of the Roman Empire like?
8. In what areas did Rome make great contributions to the world? Give examples to support your answers.

SECTION 5 (pp. 168–171)
The Rise of Christianity
9. How did Christianity begin and what was unique about it?
10. What factors helped Christianity gain acceptance in the Roman Empire?

SECTION 6 (pp. 172–177)
The Fall of the Western Empire
11. How did Diocletian and Constantine try to strengthen the Roman Empire?
12. What were some causes of Rome's decline?

Reviewing Themes

1. **Government** What two major factors helped Rome unify its empire and maintain peace?
2. **Culture** What ideas and inventions did the Romans borrow and adapt from the Greeks?
3. **Global Relations** How did Rome's relationship with the people it conquered change over time?

Thinking Critically

1. **Comparing** Compare the role of citizens in Athenian democracy with that of citizens in Rome's republic.
2. **Contrasting** How did the governments of the Roman Republic and the Roman Empire differ?
3. **Sequencing** Trace the spread of Christianity in the Roman world.
4. **Identifying Cause and Effect** How did the use of written law strengthen Rome's government?

Writing About History

Analyzing Information Romans were skilled builders who developed many new ideas. Write a description of how Roman engineering ideas are used today. Use the following chart to organize your thoughts before you begin writing.

	Roman Examples	Examples Today
Ideas and Innovations in Architecture and Engineering		

Every Student

WORLD HISTORY AND GEOGRAPHY DOCUMENT-BASED QUESTIONS ACTIVITIES

This resource provides a wide variety of primary sources and thought-provoking questions to help students develop intelligent, formed opinions. Important historical and geographical themes are grouped together, allowing for scaffolded instruction.

Building Social Studies Skills

Interpreting Maps

Study the map below. Then use the information on the map to help you answer the questions that follow.

Ancient Italy, c. 600 B.C.

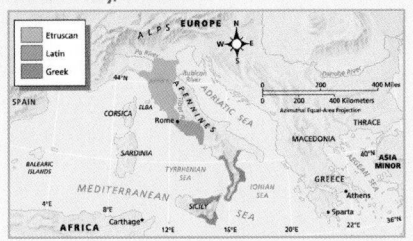

1. Which of the following statements correctly describes how geographic factors influenced Rome's rise to power?
   a. The Alps protected Italy from invasion from the north.
   b. The rugged Apennine Mountains made it difficult to unify Italy.
   c. Italy's location helped Rome control the eastern and western Mediterranean.
   d. Italy's rugged coast discouraged sea trade.

2. Using information from the map, support your choice of statements in question 1.

Analyzing Primary Sources

Read the following quote by the historian Polybius, who lived in Rome during the 100s B.C., then answer the questions.

"Having then got rid of these rulers by assassination or exile, they do not venture to set up a king again, being still in terror of the injustice to which this led before; nor dare they intrust the common interests again to more than one, considering the recent example of their misconduct: and therefore, as the only sound hope left them is that which depends upon themselves, they are driven to take refuge in that; and so changed the constitution from an oligarchy to a democracy."

3. Which of the following statements best describes the author's point of view?
   a. People cannot pick good leaders.
   b. People have no control over their leaders.
   c. Power should be limited to a few people.
   d. Democracy is a response to past abuses.

4. When interpreting a primary source, historians examine the historical context in which the source was written. What events in Rome's history might have influenced Polybius's point of view? Give specific examples.

Alternative Assessment

Building Your Portfolio

Link to TODAY

Government

America's views on the rights and responsibilities of its citizens, including the notion of equality before the law, owe much to ancient Rome and to Jewish and Christian beliefs. Compile a list of the ways in which these legal and moral traditions have influenced American practices. Then use the list to create a chart that summarizes your findings.

internet connect

Internet Activity: go.hrw.com
KEYWORD: SP3 WH7

Choose a topic on the Roman World to:
- analyze the *Aeneid* to learn the connection between ancient Troy and Roman culture.
- create a model or structure that employs Roman architectural, artistic, or decorative styles.
- research the destruction of Pompeii and review the tectonic causes of volcanoes.

THE ROMAN WORLD **179**

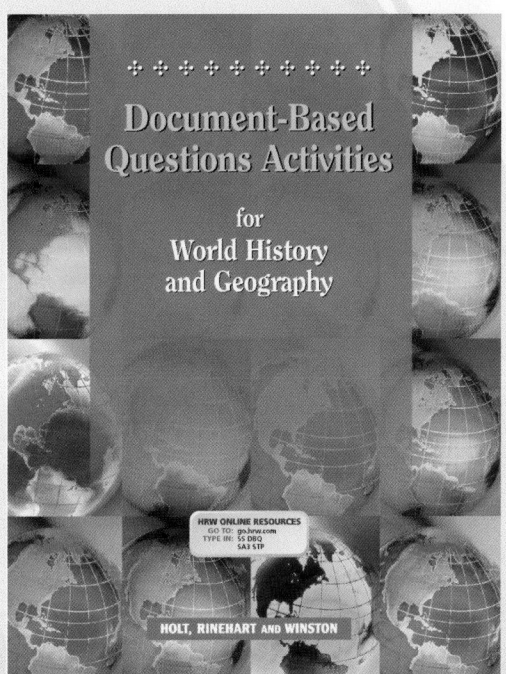

Document-Based Questions Activities for World History and Geography

HRW ONLINE RESOURCES
GO TO: go.hrw.com
TYPE IN: SS DBQ
SA3 STP

HOLT, RINEHART AND WINSTON

Additional Print and Technology Assessment Resources

- **Alternative Assessment Handbook**
- **Audio CD Program**
- **Chapter and Unit Tests**
- **Chapter and Unit Tests for English Language Learners and Special-Needs Students**
- **Chapter Tutorials for Students, Parents, Mentors, and Peers**
- **Daily Quizzes**
- **Document-Based Questions Activities for World History and Geography**
- **Main Idea Activities**
- **Test Generator (located on the One-Stop Planner CD-ROM)**

ACCESS ONLINE RUBRICS FOR GRADING PROJECTS AND PORTFOLIO ASSIGNMENTS

Contents

UNIT 1 The Beginnings of Civilization xxxv

CHAPTER 1

The Emergence of Civilization
(3,700,000 B.C.– 1200 B.C.) 4

CHAPTER 2

The First Civilizations
(c. 6000 B.C.– 587 B.C.) 18

Early castings of horseriders

CHAPTER 3

Ancient Indian Civilizations
(c. 2500 B.C.– A.D. 550) 50

CHAPTER 4

Ancient Chinese Civilization
(c. 1500 B.C.– A.D. 589) 74

Indus valley pictographic seals

v

The Parthenon of Athens

Carved mask from the African kingdom of Benin

UNIT
3
The World in Transition
Cross-Cultural Connections:
Culture

◆ **CHAPTER 10** ◆

The Byzantine Empire and Russia

◆ **CHAPTER 11** ◆

The Islamic World

◆ **CHAPTER 12** ◆

The Civilizations of East Asia

Buffalo on the American Plains

*Early Arab navigational
instrument*

The throne of Charlemagne

*Copernican model showing
planetary revolutions*

*The papal palace
at Avignon*

Glazeware from Safavid Persia

The Great Wall of China

The golden fountain at Versailles

*Sheffield, England, in the
Industrial Revolution*

Sculpture by Edgar Degas

*Irish immigrants
bound for North
America*

Hungarian independence fighters

Charles Lindbergh's The Spirit of St. Louis

Headlines announcing the U.S. entry into World War II

Scene from the Korean War

Flag of the People's Republic of China

Notes and coins of the European Union

View of Torres del Paine
National Park in Chile

Primary Sources

History Makers Speak

Primary Sources *continued*

History Makers Speak continued

Primary Source

History and Your World

YOUNG PEOPLE IN HISTORY

Young drummer of the American Revolution

▶ WHY IT MATTERS TODAY

CNN student News.com

History and Your World *continued*

Cross–Cultural Connections

*Islamic calligraphy and box of
calligrapher's tools*

CROSS-CULTURAL CONNECTIONS *Literature*

Giuseppe Garibaldi, Italy

Illustration from Chaucer's The
Canterbury Tales

Interdisciplinary Activities

Symbol of equality from the era of the French Revolution

LEGALITE

Historical Highlights

Early American stone-tipped spears

DAILY LIFE

HISTORY MAKER & Primary Source ◆ EYEWITNESS ◆

Queen Isabella

What If?

Technology Activities

internet connect

Skill-Building Activities

Economic
• High taxes
• High inflation
• Loss of war loot
• Decline of manufacturing
• Decline of agriculture

Social
• Growing divisions between rich and poor
• Loss of values
• Loss of patriotism

Military
• German invasions
• High cost of defense
• Dependence on German troops
• Loss of soldiers' loyalty to Rome
• Military interference in government

Causes of the Fall of the Western Roman Empire

Political
• Ineffective city-state system
• Division of empire
• Growing power of Eastern Empire
• Corruption and unstable leadership
• Burden of public service

Skill-Building Activities *continued*

Charts and Graphs

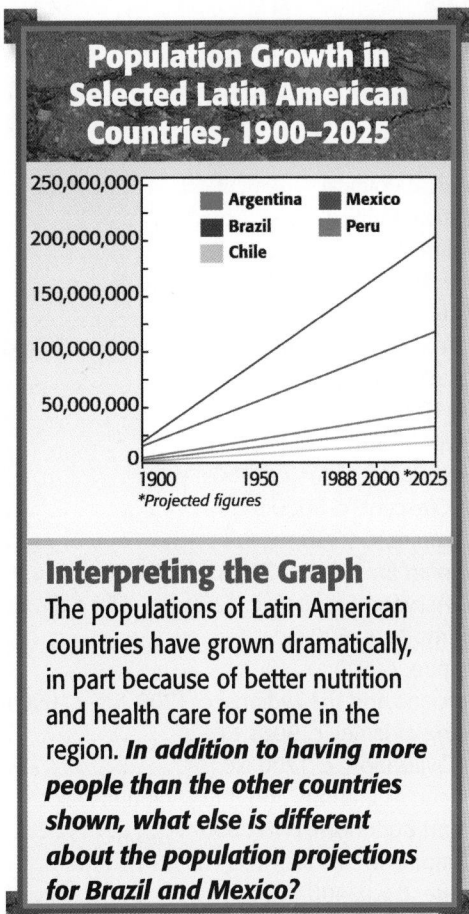

Population Growth in Selected Latin American Countries, 1900–2025

Argentina / Mexico / Brazil / Peru / Chile

*Projected figures

Interpreting the Graph

The populations of Latin American countries have grown dramatically, in part because of better nutrition and health care for some in the region. *In addition to having more people than the other countries shown, what else is different about the population projections for Brazil and Mexico?*

Skill-Building Activities *continued*

Japan under the Tokugawa Shogunate, 1603–1867

Interpreting Maps Edo was the capital of the Tokugawa shogunate.

■ **Skills Assessment: Using Geography** Why might Edo have been a good location for the capital?

Skill-Building Activities *continued*

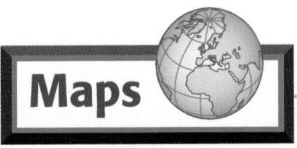

Maps *continued*

Renaissance Italy, c. 1500
Interpreting Maps During the Renaissance, Italy was a patchwork of states.
■ **Skills Assessment: Human Systems** What commercial cities became the centers of city-states?

How to Use Your Textbook

Use the chapter opener to get an overview of the time period.

The Chapter Time Line shows you selected events in world history within the timeframe of the chapter.

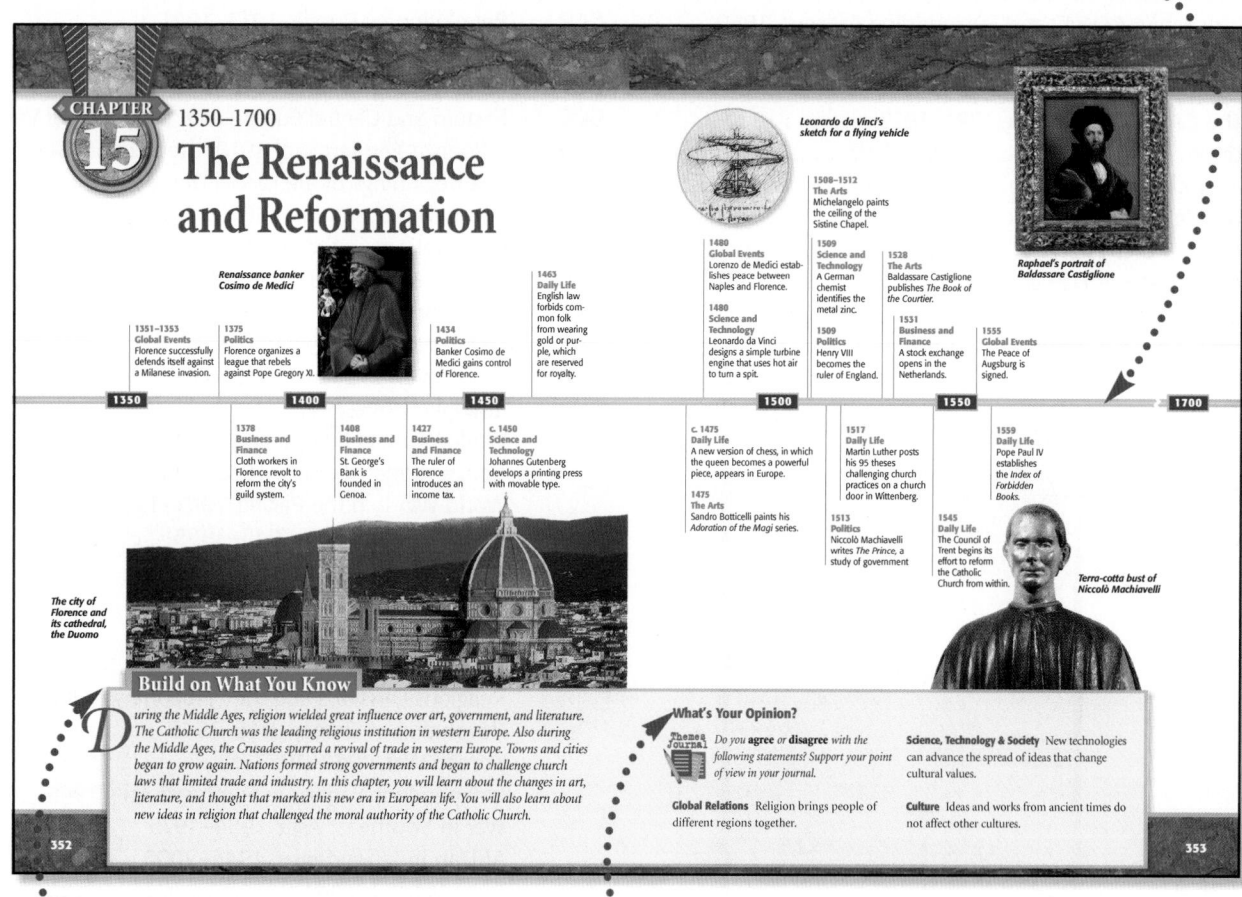

CHAPTER 15

1350–1700

The Renaissance and Reformation

Renaissance banker Cosimo de Medici

Leonardo da Vinci's sketch for a flying vehicle

Raphael's portrait of Baldassare Castiglione

1351–1353
Global Events
Florence successfully defends itself against a Milanese invasion.

1375
Politics
Florence organizes a league that rebels against Pope Gregory XI.

1434
Politics
Banker Cosimo de Medici gains control of Florence.

1463
Daily Life
English law forbids common folk from wearing gold or purple, which are reserved for royalty.

1480
Global Events
Lorenzo de Medici establishes peace between Naples and Florence.

1480
Science and Technology
Leonardo da Vinci designs a simple turbine engine that uses hot air to turn a spit.

1508–1512
The Arts
Michelangelo paints the ceiling of the Sistine Chapel.

1509
Science and Technology
A German chemist identifies the metal zinc.

1509
Politics
Henry VIII becomes the ruler of England.

1528
The Arts
Baldassare Castiglione publishes *The Book of the Courtier*.

1531
Business and Finance
A stock exchange opens in the Netherlands.

1555
Global Events
The Peace of Augsburg is signed.

1350   1400   1450   1500   1550   1700

1378
Business and Finance
Cloth workers in Florence revolt to reform the city's guild system.

1408
Business and Finance
St. George's Bank is founded in Genoa.

1427
Business and Finance
The ruler of Florence introduces an income tax.

c. 1450
Science and Technology
Johannes Gutenberg develops a printing press with movable type.

c. 1475
Daily Life
A new version of chess, in which the queen becomes a powerful piece, appears in Europe.

1475
The Arts
Sandro Botticelli paints his *Adoration of the Magi* series.

1517
Daily Life
Martin Luther posts his 95 theses challenging church practices on a church door in Wittenberg.

1513
Politics
Niccolò Machiavelli writes *The Prince*, a study of government.

1559
Daily Life
Pope Paul IV establishes the *Index of Forbidden Books*.

1545
Daily Life
The Council of Trent begins its effort to reform the Catholic Church from within.

The city of Florence and its cathedral, the Duomo

Terra-cotta bust of Niccolò Machiavelli

Build on What You Know

During the Middle Ages, religion wielded great influence over art, government, and literature. The Catholic Church was the leading religious institution in western Europe. Also during the Middle Ages, the Crusades spurred a revival of trade in western Europe. Towns and cities began to grow again. Nations formed strong governments and began to challenge church laws that limited trade and industry. In this chapter, you will learn about the changes in art, literature, and thought that marked this new era in European life. You will also learn about new ideas in religion that challenged the moral authority of the Catholic Church.

What's Your Opinion?

Themes Journal Do you **agree** or **disagree** with the following statements? Support your point of view in your journal.

Global Relations Religion brings people of different regions together.

Science, Technology & Society New technologies can advance the spread of ideas that change cultural values.

Culture Ideas and works from ancient times do not affect other cultures.

352

353

Build on What You Know bridges the material you have studied in previous chapters with the material you are about to begin. As you read the Build on What You Know feature, take a few minutes to think about the topics that might apply to the chapter you are starting.

What's Your Opinion puts you in the place of the historian looking at the past. In this section, you will be asked to respond to three general statements about the chapter. Each statement is tied to one of the key themes of the program. You should respond based on your own knowledge, and record your responses in your journal. There are no right or wrong answers, just your informed opinion.

Use these built-in tools to read for understanding.

Read to Discover questions begin each section of *The Human Journey*. These questions serve as your guide as you read through the section. Keep them in mind as you explore the section content.

Define and Identify terms are introduced at the beginning of each section. The terms will be defined in context throughout the section.

Why It Matters Today is an exciting way for you to make connections between what you are reading and the world around you. In each section, you will be invited to explore a topic that is relevant to our lives today by using **CNNStudentNews.com** connections.

Interpreting the Visual Record features accompany many of the book's rich images. Pictures are one of the most important primary sources historians can use to help analyze the past. These features invite you to examine the images and make predictions about their content.

Reading Check questions appear throughout the book to allow you to check your comprehension while you are reading. As you read each section, pause for a moment to consider each Reading Check. If you have trouble answering the question, go back and examine the material you just read.

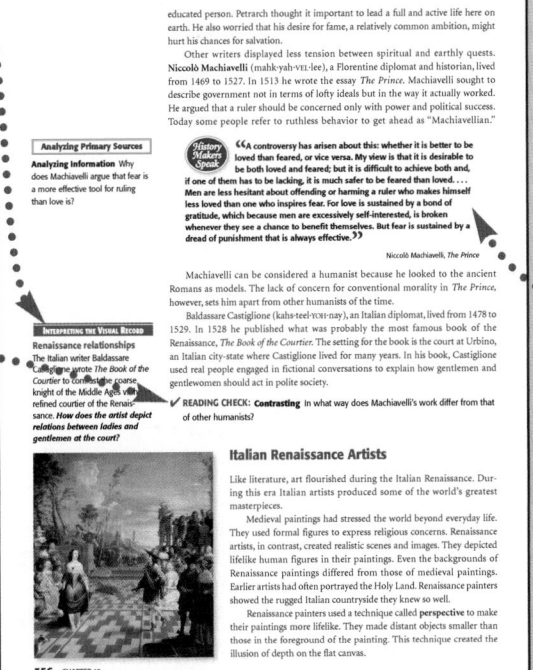

The Story Continues features an interesting episode from world history that shows you that history is not just a collection of facts, but a blend of many individual stories and adventures.

History Makers Speak quotations appear frequently throughout the book. These exciting primary source quotations give you a glimpse into the lives of the actual people who made history. Many of these quotations are accompanied by an **Analyzing Primary Sources** question to help you better interpret the sources and draw inferences about their importance.

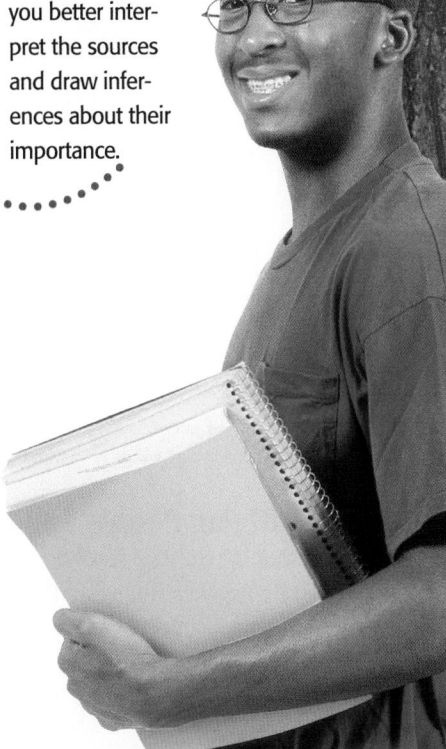

xxvii

Use these built-in tools to read for understanding.

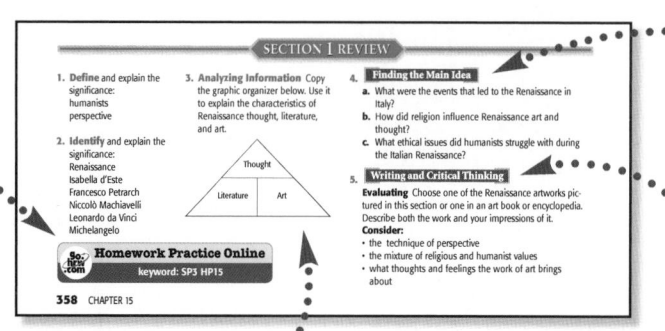

Homework Practice Online lets you log on to the **GO.hrw.com** Web site to complete an interactive self-check.

Finding the Main Idea questions help review the main points you have studied in the section.

Writing and Critical Thinking activities allow you to explore a section topic in greater depth and build your skills.

Graphic Organizers will help you pull together important information from the section. You can complete the graphic organizer as a study tool to prepare for a test or writing assignment.

Creating a Time Line and **Writing a Summary** activities help you to organize, sequence, and synthesize the chapter discussion and place major events and individuals into the historical chronology.

Reviewing Themes, Thinking Critically, and **Writing About History** activities help you to focus on key chapter ideas and enhance critical thinking and writing skills as you explore major chapter topics.

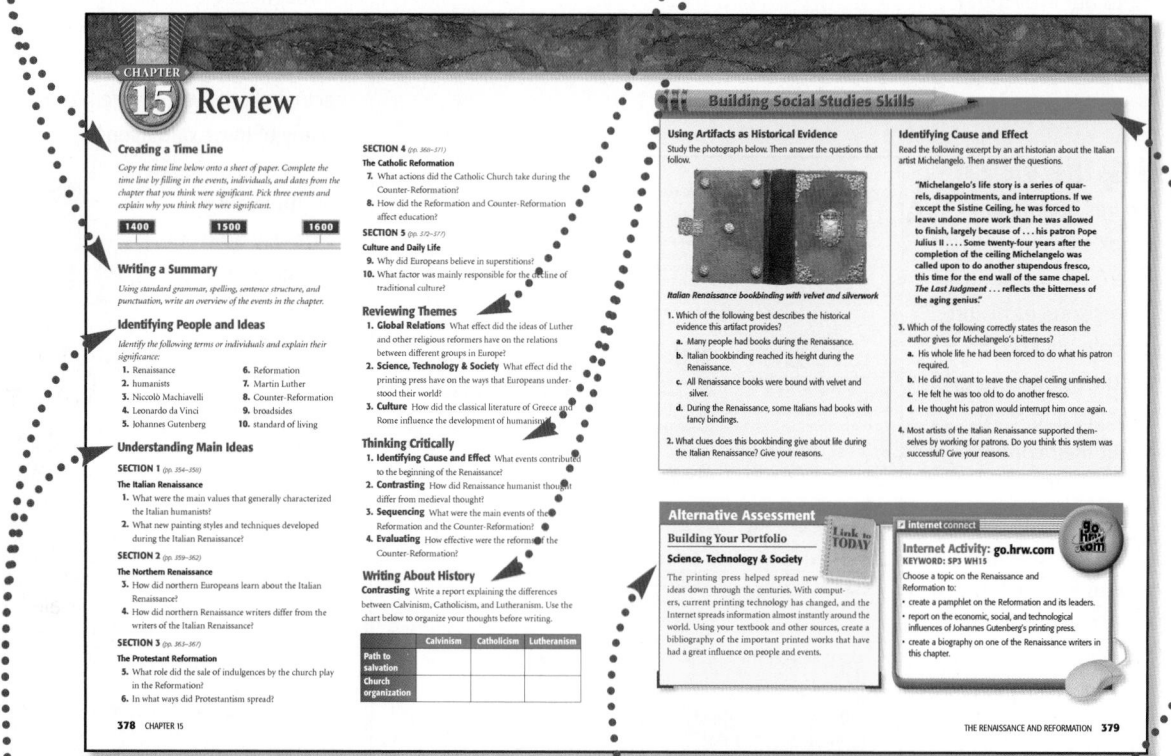

Identifying People and Ideas and **Understanding Main Ideas** reinforce learning by extending your understanding and comprehension of history-shaping people and concepts.

Building Social Studies Skills and **Building Your Portfolio** activities create exciting opportunities to practice social studies skills, to use interesting primary and secondary source materials, and to develop understanding of the connections between past and present.

Use these review tools to pull together all the information you have learned.

go.hrw.com **Homework Practice Online**
keyword: SP3 HP13

Homework Practice Online
lets you log on for review anytime. You'll find interactive activities for each section of the text.

Internet Connect
activities are just one part of the world of online learning experiences that awaits you on the GO.hrw.com Web site. By exploring these online activities, you will take a journey through some of the richest world history materials available on the World Wide Web. You can then use these resources to create real-world projects, such as newspapers, brochures, reports, and even your own Web site!

internet connect

Internet Activity: go.hrw.com
KEYWORD: SP3 WH13

Choose a topic on the Rise of the Middle Ages to:
• evaluate primary and secondary sources about Charlemagne.
• create a poster on medieval art and architecture.
• write a report on daily life in the Middle Ages.

Why History Matters Today

"History and destiny have made America the leader of the world that would be free. And the world that would be free is looking to us for inspiration."

Colin Powell

Right now, at this very second, somewhere in the world, someone is making history. It is impossible to know who, or in what way, but the actions of people today may become the history of tomorrow.

History and Your World

All you need to do is watch or read the news to see history unfolding. How many news stories do you see or hear about ordinary people doing extraordinary things? The Why It Matters Today feature beginning every section of *The Human Journey* invites you to use the vast resources of **CNNStudentNews.com** or other current event sources to examine the links between past and present. Through this feature you will be able to draw connections between what you are studying and the events that are taking place in our world today.

Anyone Can Be a History Maker

When you think of the word history, what comes to mind? Do you picture politicians sitting around a table deciding the future of the world? Or do you see a long list of dates and boring facts to be memorized? Of course, politicians, dates, and facts are part of history, but there is actually much more to understanding and exploring our past. Our world has developed through the efforts of many different people, from all backgrounds and walks of life. Many of them were teenagers like you. Did you know that teenagers have helped to shape the course of world history? It's true. For example, Joan of Arc was only about 17 when she led the French army that defeated the English at Orléans in 1429. Joan's victory was a turning point in the Hundred Years' War between France and England, a conflict that helped to build the French nation. Anne Frank, whose

cnn_fav_ref.mov

JANA JACOBS
CNN STUDENT BUREAU

Blind children share with sighted
CNN Student Bureau's Jana Jacobs reports or and blind children together (August 7)

00:00:00

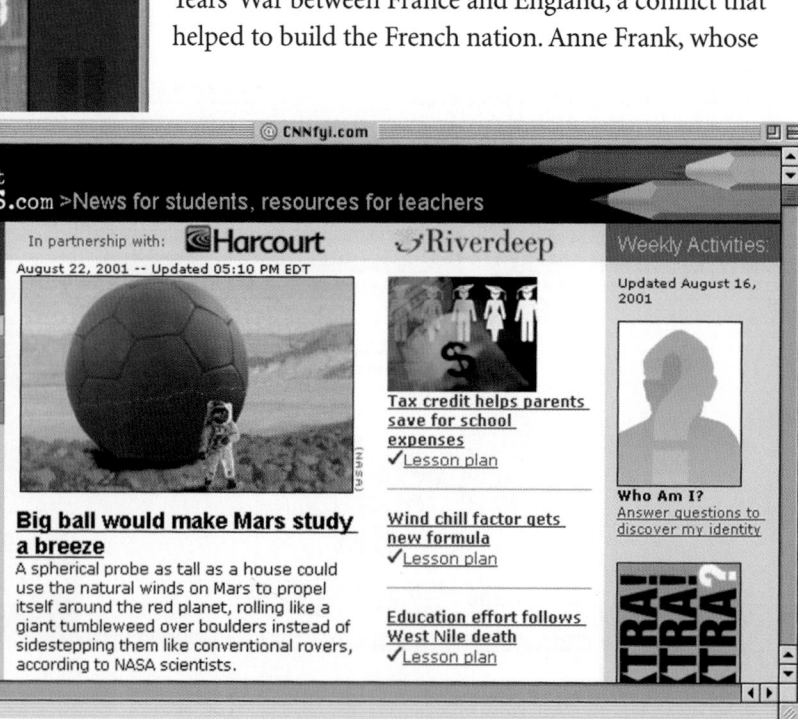

@ CNNfyi.com

CNN student News.com >News for students, resources for teachers

SEARCH
GO

Select a section:
FYI MAIN PAGE
TEACHER RESOURCES
EDUCATION NEWS
HOW TO USE THIS SITE
BACK TO CNN.com

CNN NEWSROOM

• Daily guide
• Guide Archives
• Transcript
• Program Calender
• Enroll now

CNN Newsroom is a commercial-free TV program for classrooms. It airs at 4:30 a.m. ET Monday-Friday on

In partnership with: **Harcourt** **Riverdeep**

August 22, 2001 -- Updated 05:10 PM EDT

Big ball would make Mars study a breeze
A spherical probe as tall as a house could use the natural winds on Mars to propel itself around the red planet, rolling like a giant tumbleweed over boulders instead of sidestepping them like conventional rovers, according to NASA scientists.

Tax credit helps parents save for school expenses
✓Lesson plan

Wind chill factor gets new formula
✓Lesson plan

Education effort follows West Nile death
✓Lesson plan

Weekly Activities

Updated August 16, 2001

Who Am I?
Answer questions to discover my identity

XTRA! XTRA! XTRA?

Internet zone

haunting account of Nazi persecution during World War II is an eloquent and timeless attack on all forms of political repression, was 16 years old when she died at Belsen concentration camp in 1945. Her tragic yet triumphant story has inspired people around the world. You might also be interested to know that young people in their teens helped to open and settle our own nation's frontiers long before there was a United States of America. These are just a few of the many examples of how people in their teens—people your age—have helped to shape our world's past. What contributions do you think your generation will make to world history?

History Makes Us Who We Are

There is no one single "story" in history. Instead, the combined experiences of millions of people across time have come together to form the societies and cultures of today's world.

Students of today dressed in Renaissance-era garb

Although the World War II Memorial was under construction when we visited, it was an awesome and inspiring sight.

So when someone asks you, "Why does history matter today?," you might answer, "Because in our past, we see a reflection of ourselves."

Themes in World History

A Hindu religious sculpture from early India

The Human Journey begins every chapter with a set of theme statements under the heading "What's Your Opinion?" These statements are drawn from several broad themes central to world history: Geography, Economics, Government, Citizenship, Culture, Science, Technology & Society, Constitutional Heritage, and Global Relations. As you begin each chapter of *The Human Journey,* you will be asked to respond to the theme statements in a general way on the basis of your own knowledge. At the end of the chapter, you will be asked to respond to more specific questions about the themes, based on the chapter content.

Geography

The Geography theme explores ways in which our world's vast and diverse geography has played an important role in world history. The theme examines how the development of the world's resources has

The Astronomer, by Jan Vermeer

helped shape world economies, societies, and political structures. In addition, the Geography theme traces how public and government attitudes about resources and the environment have changed over time.

Economics

The Economics theme asks you to explore the relationship between history and economics over the course of human development. The theme examines how various, often very different economic systems have developed to address changing human needs and how they have influenced the world's political and social growth.

Gold Byzantine goblet

Government

The Government theme asks you to explore the workings of different systems of government—from the earliest forms of community organization to the complex structures of the present. This theme also examines the various aspects of different types of governments utilized by various societies throughout history and how different governmental systems affect societies in different ways.

Scene of Japanese Kabuki theater

Citizenship

Throughout history, people have struggled to define the rights and responsibilities of citizenship in their societies. The Citizenship theme explores how changing social, economic, and political conditions have influenced different societies and how those societies have perceived and addressed the ideas of citizenship.

Culture

The rich, unique, and diverse cultures that have developed over the course of history have emerged from our world's many ethnic, racial, and religious groups. The Culture theme examines how people have built their diverse cultures from earliest times to the present. It also investigates how various aspects of culture, including religion, rituals and shared traditions, art, music, and literature, have influenced social and political events throughout history.

Science, Technology & Society

From the building of the Egyptian pyramids and the irrigation systems of the earliest farming peoples to the development of advanced computers and the advent of the information age, science and technology have influenced every aspect of our world's cultures and societies. The Science, Technology & Society theme explores scientific and technological developments and their impacts on economic, political, and social developments around the world.

Constitutional Heritage

No study of world history would be complete without examining how the idea of constitutionalism developed over time. This includes influences on the United States Constitution, as well as comparisons of different constitutional systems as they developed over time.

Global Relations

The Global Relations theme invites you to trace ways in which different nations, cultures, and peoples around the world and throughout history have interacted with one another. It also explores issues and events that affect large segments of the world, not just one particular country.

Essential Elements of Geography

History and geography share many elements. History describes important events that have taken place from ancient times until the present day. Geography describes how physical environments affect human events. It also examines how people's actions influence the environment around them. One way to look at geography is to identify essential elements of its study. The following six essential elements, developed as part of the National Geography Standards, will be used throughout The Human Journey:

▶ **The World in Spatial Terms** This essential element refers to the way geographers view the world. They look at where things are and how they are arranged on Earth's surface. For example, geographers might be interested to learn why certain cities developed where they did.

▶ **Places and Regions** Geographers often focus on the physical and human characteristics that make particular parts of Earth special. A region is an area with common characteristics that make it different from surrounding areas. People create regions as a convenient way to study the world. Regions can be large like Asia, or small like a neighborhood.

Early Egyptian pyramids at Giza

▶ **Physical Systems** Geographers study the physical processes and interactions among four physical systems—Earth's atmosphere, land, water, and life. Physical processes shape and change Earth's physical features and environments.

▶ **Human Systems** As with physical systems, studying human systems can tell geographers much about the world around us. For example, studying population growth, distribution, and movement helps in understanding human events and their effect on the environment.

▶ **Environment and Society** One of the most important topics in geography is how people interact with the environment. Human activities can have both positive and negative effects on Earth's environment. However, people depend on the environment's natural resources for survival.

▶ **The Uses of Geography** Historians use geography to understand the past. They look not only at when things happened but at where and why they happened. But geography is also important to the present as well as the past. People use geography every day to determine how to use Earth's limited resources, such as water and minerals, more effectively and in ways that ensure the success of future generations.

Skills Handbook

Critical Thinking and the Study of History

Throughout *The Human Journey*, you are asked to think critically about the events and issues that have shaped world history. Critical thinking is the reasoned judgment of information and ideas. The development of critical thinking skills is essential to effective citizenship. Such skills empower you to exercise your civic rights and responsibilities. Helping you develop critical thinking skills is an important goal of *The Human Journey*. The following critical thinking skills appear in the section reviews and chapter reviews of the book.

◆ **Analyzing Information** is the process of breaking something down into its parts and examining the relationships between them. Analyzing enables you to better understand the whole. For example, to analyze the outcome of the Norman invasion of England in 1066, you might study the basis for Duke William of Normandy's claims to the English throne, why Harold Godwinson opposed those claims, and how the English people viewed the issues.

Emperor Maximilian I

◆ **Sequencing** is the process of placing events in correct chronological order to better understand the historical relationships among these events. You can sequence events in two basic ways: according to *absolute* or *relative* chronology. Absolute chronology means that you pay close attention to the actual dates events took place. Placing events on a time line would be an example of absolute chronology. Relative chronology refers to the way events relate to one another. To put events in relative order, you need to know which one happened, which came next, and so forth.

A sailor's astrolabe, an early navigational instrument

◆ **Categorizing** is the process by which you group things together by the characteristics they have in common. By putting things or events into categories, it is easier to make comparisons and see differences among them.

◆ **Identifying Cause and Effect** is a part of interpreting the relationships between historical events. A *cause* is an action that leads to an event. The outcome of the action is an *effect*. To explain historical events, historians often point out multiple causes and effects. For example, economic and political differences between the United States and the

Soviet Union led to the "cold war" that characterized the post-World War II era. These differences also resulted in an arms race that posed serious threats to world peace and development.

Comparing and Contrasting is the process of examining events, situations, or points of view for their similarities and differences. *Comparing* focuses on both similarities and the differences. *Contrasting* focuses only on differences. For example, a comparison of the development of civilization in the Indus River valley or northern India and the Hwang River valley of east-central China shows that certain factors were shared by each group of early people, while other factors were unique to one emerging civilization or the other.

Stone relief from early India

Finding the Main Idea is combining and sifting through information to determine what is most important. Historical writing often uses many examples and details to support the author's main ideas. Throughout *The Human Journey,* you will find numerous Reading Checks and questions in section reviews to help you focus on the main ideas in the text.

Summarizing is the process of taking a large amount of information and boiling it down into a short and clear statement. Summarizing is particularly useful when you need to give a brief account of a longer story or event. For example, Alexander the Great's conquest of the Persian Empire is an exciting but detailed story consisting of a complex chain of conditions, actions, and situations. Many different events came together to make up this story. You could summarize these events by saying something like, "Between 334 B.C. and 333 B.C., Alexander won major victories against the Persians at Granicus and then at Issus, where he defeated the Persian emperor, Darius III. Alexander then conquered the Persian-held lands of Syria, Egypt, and Mesopotamia. He met Darius again in 331 B.C., defeated him in the Battle of Gaugamela, and won control of the once-mighty Persian Empire."

Making Generalizations and Predictions is the process of interpreting information to form more general statements and guess about what will happen next. A *generalization* is a broad statement that holds true for a variety of historical events or situations. Making generalizations can help you see the "big picture" of historical events, rather than just focusing on details. It is very important, however, that when making generalizations you try not to include situations that do not fit the statement. When this occurs, you run the risk of creating a stereotype, or overgeneralization. A *prediction* is an educated guess about an outcome. When you read history, you should always be asking yourself questions like, "What will happen next? If this person does this, what will that mean for . . . ?", and so on. These types of questions help you draw on information you already know to see patterns throughout history

Drawing Inferences and Conclusions is forming possible explanations for an event, a situation, or a problem. When you make an *inference,* you take the information you know to be true and come up with an educated guess about what else you think is true about that situation. A *conclusion* is a prediction about the outcome of a situation based on what you already know. Often, you must be prepared to test your inferences and conclusions against new evidence or arguments. For example, a historian might conclude that women's leadership roles in the abolition movement led to the development of the early women's movement. The historian would then organize the evidence needed to support this conclusion and challenge other arguments.

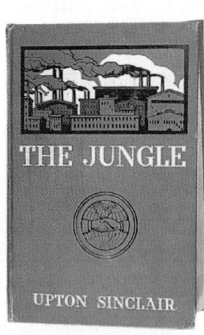
Cover from Upton Sinclair's The Jungle

Identifying Points of View is the process of identifying factors that influence the outlook of an individual or group. A person's point of view includes beliefs and attitudes that are shaped by factors such as age, gender, religion, race, and economic status. This critical thinking skill helps you examine why people see things as they do and reinforce the realization that people's views may change over time or with a change in circumstances.

◆ Supporting a Point of View involves choosing a viewpoint on a particular event or issue and arguing persuasively for that position. Your argument should be well organized and based on specific evidence that supports the point of view you have chosen. Supporting a point of view often involves working with controversial or emotional issues. For example, you might consider the points of view involved in the struggles between labor unions and business owners in Great Britain and the United States during the late 1800s. Whether you choose a position in favor of labor unions or in favor of business owners, you should state your opinion clearly and give reasons to support it.

◆ Identifying Bias is the process of evaluating the opinions of others about events or situations. *Bias* is an opinion based on prejudice or strong emotions, rather that fact. It is important to identify bias when looking at historical sources because biased sources often give you a false sense of what really happened. When looking at both primary and secondary sources, it is always important to keep the author's or speaker's point of view in mind and to adjust your interpretation of the source based on any bias you might detect.

Soap advertisement reflecting a widespread bias of the late 1800s

◆ Evaluating is assessing the significance or overall importance of something, such as the success of a reform movement, the actions of a president, or the results of a major conflict. You should base your judgment on standards that others will understand and are likely to share. For example, you might consider the outcomes of the Spanish conquests of the Aztec and Inca empires and evaluate their importance

Aztec dishware

relative to the development of Spain as a major European power. You could also evaluate the effect of the conquests on Native American peoples and civilizations.

◆ Problem Solving is the process by which you pose workable solutions to difficult situations. The first step in the process is to identify a problem. Next you will need to gather information about the problem, such as its history and the various factors that contribute to the problem. Once you have gathered information, you should list and consider the options for solving the problem. For each of the possible solutions, weigh their advantages and disadvantages and, based on your evaluation, choose and implement a solution. Once the solution is in place, go back and evaluate the effectiveness of the solution you selected.

◆ Decision Making is the process of reviewing a situation and then making decisions or recommendations for the best possible outcome. To complete the process, first identify a situation that requires a solution. Next, gather information that will help you reach a decision. You may need to do some background research to study the history of the situation, or carefully consider the points of view of the individuals involved. Once you have done your research, identify options that might resolve the situation. For each option, predict what the possible consequences might be if that option were followed. Once you have identified the best option, take action by making a recommendation and following through on any tasks that option requires.

Becoming a Strategic Reader

by Dr. Judith Irvin

Everywhere you look, print is all around us. In fact, you would have a hard time stopping yourself from reading. In a normal day, you might read cereal boxes, movie posters, notes from friends, T-shirts, instructions for video games, song lyrics, catalogs, billboards, information on the Internet, magazines, the newspaper, and much, much more. Each form of print is read differently depending on your purpose for reading. You read a menu differently from poetry, and a motorcycle magazine is read differently than a letter from a friend. Good readers switch easily from one type of text to another. In fact, they probably do not even think about it, they just do it.

When you read, it is helpful to use a strategy to remember the most important ideas. You can use a strategy before you read to help connect information you already know to the new information you will encounter. Before you read, you can also predict what a text will be about by using a previewing strategy. During the reading you can use a strategy to help you focus on main ideas, and after reading you can use a strategy to help you organize what you learned so that you can remember it later. *The Human Journey* was designed to help you more easily understand the ideas you read. Important reading strategies employed in *The Human Journey* include:

1. Methods to help you **anticipate** what is to come

2. Tools to help you **preview and predict** what the text will be about

3. Ways to help you **use and analyze visual information**

4. Ideas to help you **organize the information** you have learned

1. Anticipating Information

How can I use information I already know to help me understand what a new chapter will be about?

Anticipating what a new chapter will be about helps you connect the upcoming information to what you already know. By drawing on your background knowledge, you can build a bridge to the new material.

 Each chapter of *The Human Journey* asks you to explore the main themes of the chapter before you start reading by forming opinions based on your current knowledge.

> **What's Your Opinion?**
>
> **Themes Journal** *Do you **agree** or **disagree** with the following statements? Support your point of view in your journal.*
>
> **Government** A strong army and government are necessary to maintain an empire.
>
> **Culture** Great civilizations build on the discoveries, developments, and contributions of earlier cultures.
>
> **Global Relations** An empire that enslaves conquered peoples is destined to fall.

Create a chart like this one to help you analyze the statements.

A Before Reading Agree/Disagree		B After Reading Agree/Disagree
2	Government—A strong army and government are necessary to maintain an empire.	**4**
	Culture—Great civilizations build on the discoveries, developments, and contributions of earlier cultures.	
	Global Relations—An empire that enslaves conquered peoples is destined to fall.	

3 Read the text and discuss with classmates.

5 You can also refine your knowledge by answering the Reviewing Themes questions in the chapter review.

Anticipating Information

Step 1 Identify the major concepts of the chapter. In *The Human Journey*, these are presented in the What's Your Opinion? box at the beginning of each chapter.

Step 2 Agree or disagree with each of the statements and record your answers in your journal.

Step 3 Read the text and discuss your answers with your classmates.

Step 4 After reading the chapter, revisit the statements and answer them again based on what you have learned.

Reviewing Themes

1. **Government** What two major factors helped Rome unify its empire and maintain peace?
2. **Culture** What ideas and inventions did the Romans borrow and adapt from the Greeks?
3. **Global Relations** How did Rome's relationship with the people it conquered change over time?

2. Previewing and Predicting

How can I figure out what the text is about before I even start reading a section?

Previewing and Predicting

Step ❶ Identify your purpose for reading. Ask yourself what you will do with this information after you have finished reading.

▼

Step ❷ Determine the main idea of the text and the key vocabulary words you need to know.

▼

Step ❸ Use signal words to help identify the structure of the text.

▼

Step ❹ Connect the information to what you already know.

Previewing and **predicting** are good methods to help you understand the text. If you take the time to preview and predict before you read, the text will make more sense to you during your reading.

❶ Usually, your teacher will set the purpose for reading. After reading some new information, you may be asked to write a summary, take a test, or complete some other type of activity.

"After reading about the English Civil War, you will work with a partner to create a historical museum exhibit describing . . .".

❷ As you preview the text, use graphic signals such as headings, subheadings, and boldface type to help you determine what is important in the text. Each section of *The Human Journey* opens by giving you important clues to help you preview the material.

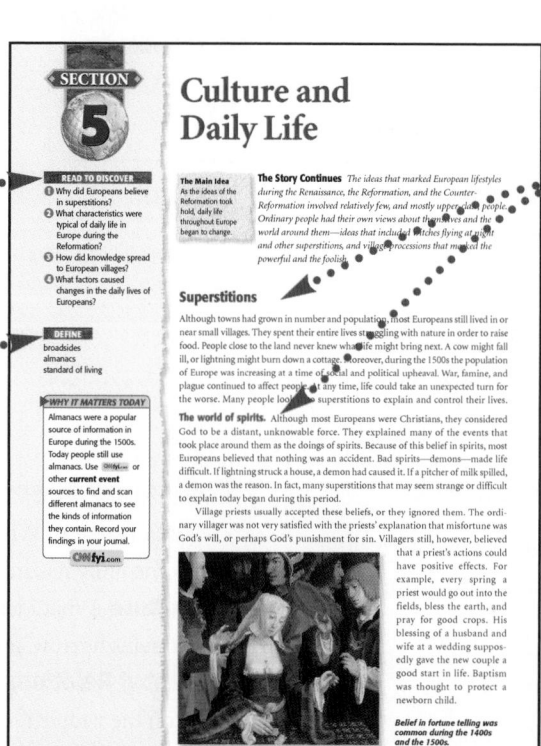

Read to Discover questions give you clues as to the section's main ideas.

Define and Identify terms let you know the key vocabulary you will encounter in the section.

Looking at the section's **main heading** and **subheadings** can give you an idea of what is to come.

3 Other tools that can help you in previewing are **signal words**. These words prepare you to think in a certain way. For example, when you see words such as *similar to, same as,* or *different from,* you know that the text will probably compare and contrast two or more ideas. Signal words indicate how the ideas in the text relate to each other. Look at the list below of some of the most common signal words grouped by the type of text structures they include.

Cause and Effect	Compare and Contrast	Description	Problem and Solution	Sequence or Chronological Order
because	different from	for instance	problem	not long after
since	same as	for example	the question is	next
consequently	similar to	such as	a solution	then
this led to . . . so	as opposed to	to illustrate	one answer is	initially
if . . . then	instead of	in addition		before
nevertheless	although	most		after
accordingly	however	importantly		finally
because of	compared with	another		preceding
as a result of	as well as	furthermore		following
in order to	either . . . or	first, second . . .		on (date)
may be due to	but			over the years
for this reason	on the other hand			today
not only . . . but	unless			when

4 Learning something new requires that you connect it in some way with something you already know. This means you have to think before you read and while you read. You may want to use a chart like this one to remind yourself of the information already familiar to you and to come up with questions you want answered in your reading. The chart will also help you organize your ideas after you have finished reading.

What I know	What I want to know	What I learned

3. Use and Analyze Visual Information

How can all the pictures, maps, graphs, and time lines with the text help me be a stronger reader?

Analyzing Information

Step ❶ As you preview the text, ask yourself how the visual information relates to the text.

▼

Step ❷ Generate questions based on the visual information.

▼

Step ❸ After reading the text, go back and review the visual information again.

Using visual information can help you understand and remember the information presented in *The Human Journey*. Good readers make a picture in their mind when they read. The pictures, charts, graphs, cartoons, time lines, and diagrams included throughout *The Human Journey* are placed strategically to increase your understanding.

❶ You might ask yourself questions like:

"Why did the author include this image with the text?"

"What details about this visual are mentioned in the text?"

After you have read the text, see if you can answer your own questions.

❷
"What seems to be happening in this illustration?"

"Why are the people, their styles of dress, and their surroundings important?"

"How does this illustration reflect the social and political conditions of the era it portrays?"

Scene from the court of King Philip IV of France

❸ After reading, take another look at the visual information.

❹ Try to make connections to what you already know.

4. Organize Information

Once I learn new information, how do I keep it all straight so that I will remember it?

To help you remember what you have read, you need to find a way of **organizing information**. Two good ways of doing this are by using graphic organizers and concept maps. **Graphic organizers** help you understand important relationships—such as cause-and-effect, compare/contrast, sequence or events, and problem/solution—within the test. **Concept maps** provide a useful tool to help you focus on the text's main ideas and organize supporting details.

Identifying Relationships

Using graphic organizers will help you recall important ideas from the section and give you a study tool you can use to prepare for a quiz or test or to help with a writing assignment. Some of the most common types of graphic organizers are shown below.

Cause and Effect Events in history cause people to react in a certain way. Cause-and-effect patterns show the relationship between results and the ideas or events that made the results occur. You may want to represent cause-and-effect relationships as one cause leading to multiple effects, or as a chain of cause-and-effect relationships.

> **Constructing Graphic Organizers**
>
> **Step ❶** Preview the text, looking for signal words and the main idea.
>
> ▼
>
> **Step ❷** Form a hypothesis as to which type of graphic organizer would work best to display the information presented.
>
> ▼
>
> **Step ❸** Work individually or with your classmates to create a visual representation of what you read.

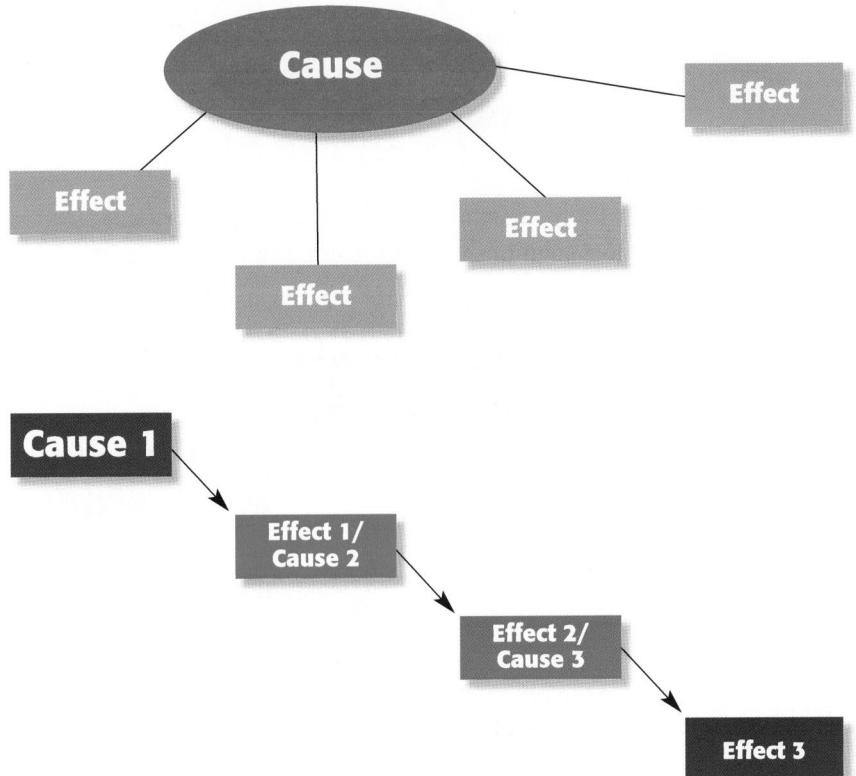

Comparing and Contrasting Graphic Organizers are often useful when you are comparing or contrasting information. Compare-and-contrast diagrams point out similarities and differences between two concepts or ideas.

Sequencing Keeping track of dates and the order in which events took place is essential to understanding history. Sequence or chronological-order diagrams show events or ideas in the order in which they happened.

Problem and Solution Problem-solution patterns identify at least one problem, offer one or more solutions to the problem, and explain or predict outcomes of the solutions.

Identifying Main Ideas and Supporting Details

One special type of graphic organizer is the concept map. A concept map, sometimes called a semantic map, allows you to zero in on the most important points of the text. The map is made up of lines, boxes, circles, and/or arrows. It can be as simple or as complex as you need it to be to accurately represent the text.

Here are a few examples of concept maps you might use.

Constructing Concept Maps

Step ❶   Preview the text looking at what type of structure might be appropriate to display a concept map.

▼

Step ❷   Taking note of the headings, bold-faced type, and text structure, sketch a concept map you think could best illustrate the text.

▼

Step ❸   Using boxes, lines, arrows, circles, or any shapes you like, display the ideas of the text in the concept map.

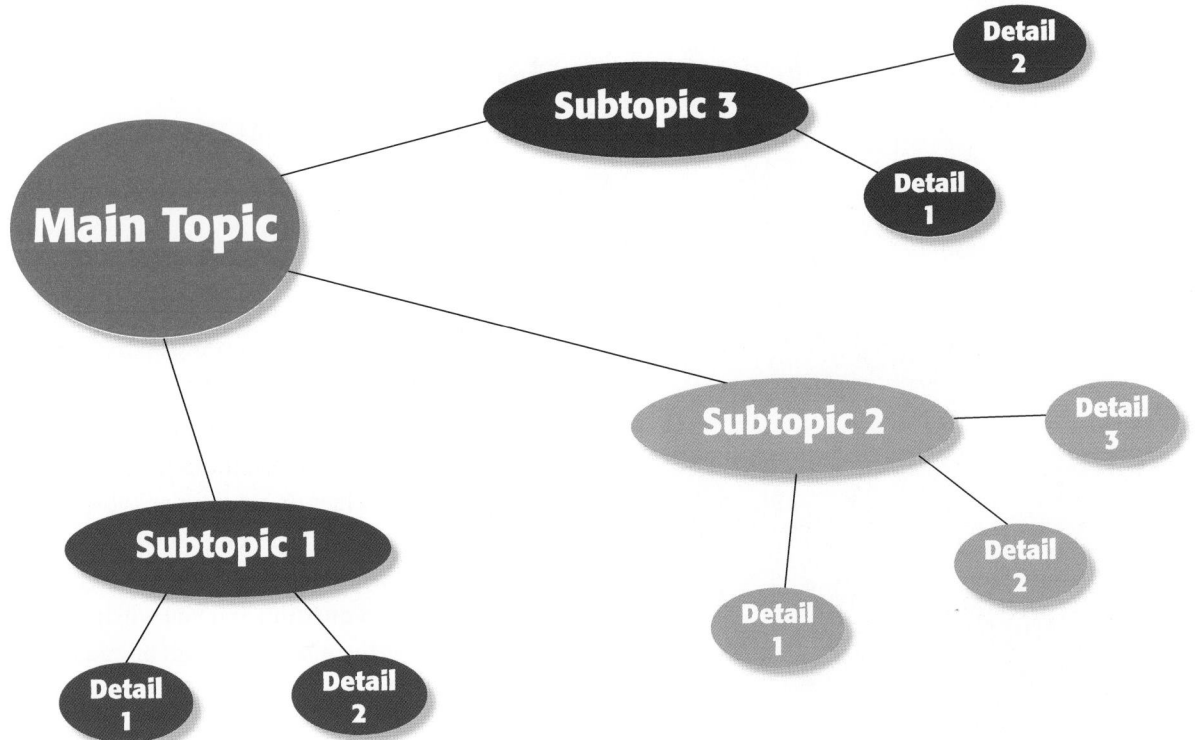

Standardized Test-Taking Strategies

A number of times throughout your school career, you may be asked to take standardized tests. These tests are designed to demonstrate the content and skills you have learned. It is important to keep in mind that in most cases the best way to prepare for these tests is to pay close attention in class and take every opportunity to improve you general social studies, reading, writing, and mathematical skills.

Tips for Taking the Test

1 Be sure that you are well rested.

2 Be on time, and be sure that you have the necessary materials.

3 Listen to the instructions of the teacher.

4 Read directions and questions carefully.

5 **DON'T STRESS!** Just remember what you have learned in class, and you should do well.

Practice the Strategies at go.hrw.com

Tackling Social Studies

The social studies portions of many standardized tests are designed to test your knowledge of the content and skills that you have been studying in one or more of your social studies classes. Specific objectives for the test vary, but some of the most common include:

1 Demonstrate an understanding of issues and events in history.

2 Demonstrate an understanding of geographic influences on historical issues and events.

3 Demonstrate an understanding of economic and social influences on historical issues and events.

4 Demonstrate an understanding of political influences on historical issues and events.

5 Use critical thinking skills to analyze social studies information.

Standardized tests usually contain multiple-choice and, sometimes, open-ended questions. The multiple-choice items will often be based on maps, tables, charts, graphs, pictures, cartoons, and/or reading passages and documents.

Tips for Answering Multiple-Choice Questions

1 If there is a written or visual piece accompanying the multiple-choice question, pay careful attention to the title, author, and date.

2 Then, read through or glance over the content of the written or visual piece accompanying the question to familiarize yourself with it.

3 Next, read the multiple-choice question first for its general intent and then reread it carefully, looking for words that give clues or can limit possible answers to the question. For example, words such as *most* or *best* tell you that there may be several correct answers to a question, but you will look for the one that is the most important or had the most effect.

4 Read through the answer choices. Always read all of the possible answer choices even if the first one seems like the correct answer. There may be a better choice farther down in the list.

5 Reread the accompanying information (if any is included) carefully to determine the answer to the question. Again, note the title, author, and date of primary-source selections. The answer will rarely be stated exactly as it appears in the primary source, so you will need to use your critical thinking skills to read between the lines.

6 Think of what you already know about the time in history or person involved and use that to help limit the answer choices.

7 Finally, reread the question and selected answer to be sure that you made the best choice and that you marked it correctly on the answer sheet.

Strategies for Success

There are a variety of strategies you can prepare ahead of time to help you feel more confident about answering questions on social studies standardized tests. Here are a few suggestions:

1 Adopt an acronym—a word formed from the first letters of other words—that you will use for analyzing a document or visual that accompanies a question.

Helpful Acronyms			
For a document, use **SOAPS** which stands for:		For a picture, cartoon, map, or other visual piece of information, use **OPTIC**, which stands for:	
S	**S**ubject	**O**	**O**verview
O	**O**ccasion (or time)	**P**	**P**arts (labels or details of the visual)
A	**A**udience	**T**	**T**itle
P	**P**urpose	**I**	**I**nterrelations (how the different parts of the visual work together)
S	**S**peaker/author	**C**	**C**onclusion (what the visual means)

2 Form visual images of maps and try to draw them from memory. The standardized test will most likely include important maps from the time period and subjects you have been studying. For example, in early Chinese history, be able to see in your mind's eye such things as the location and geographic outline of China Proper, the area's major land forms, rivers, and sea coasts, and the general geography of surrounding lands. Understand patterns of population distribution and ways in which humans interacted with the environment. Know major physical features, such as river and mountain systems, other topographic characteristics of the region, and the locations of important human systems, such as transportation routes and areas of major settlement.

3 When you have finished studying any historical era, try to think of who or what might be important enough for the test. You may want to keep your ideas in a notebook to refer to when it is almost time for the test.

4 Pay particular attention to the concept of constitutionalism. Many standardized tests contain questions dealing with this all-important idea and its historical development. Questions may test your understanding of Magna Carta, the English Bill of Rights, the American Declaration of Independence, the United States Constitution, as well as many other important historical documents. Questions may also cover the roles of various political thinkers and philosophers, such as the French *philosophes.*

5 For the skills area of the tests, practice putting major events and personalities in order in your mind. Sequencing people and events by dates can become a game you play with a friend who also has to take the test. Always ask yourself why this event is important.

6 Follow the tips under "Ready for Reading" on the next page when you encounter a reading passage in social studies, but remember that what you have learned about history can help you in answering reading comprehension questions.

Ready for Reading

The main goal of the Reading sections of most standardized tests is to determine your understanding of different aspects of a reading passage. Basically, if you can grasp the main idea and the author's purpose, and then pay attention to the details and vocabulary so that you are able to draw inferences and conclusions, you will do well on the test.

Tips for Answering Multiple-Choice Questions

1 Read the passage as if you were not taking a test.

2 Look at the big picture. Ask yourself questions like, "What is the title? What do the illustrations or pictures tell me?" and "What is the author's purpose?"

3 Read the questions. This will help you know what information to look for.

4 Reread the passage, underlining information related to the questions.

5 Go back to the questions and try to answer each one in your mind before looking at the answers.

6 Read all the answer choices and eliminate the ones that are obviously incorrect.

Types of Multiple-Choice Questions	
Main Idea	This is the most important point of the passage. After reading the passage, locate and underline the main idea.
Significant Details	You will often be asked to recall details from the passage. Read the question, and underline the details as you read, but remember that the correct answers do not always match the wording of the passage precisely.
Vocabulary	You will often need to define a word within the context of the passage. Read the answer choices and plug them into the sentence to see what fits best.
Conclusion and Inference	There are often important ideas in the passage that the author does not state directly. Sometimes you must consider multiple parts of the passage to answer the question. If answers refer to only one or two sentences or details in the passage, they are probably incorrect.

Tips for Answering Short-Answer Questions

1 Read the passage in its entirety, paying close attention to the main events and characters. Jot down information you think is important.

2 If you can't answer a question, skip it and come back later.

3 Words such as compare, contrast, interpret, discuss, and summarize appear often in short answer questions. Be sure you have a complete understanding of each of these words.

4 To help support your answer, return to the passage and skim the parts you underlined.

5 Organize your thoughts on a separate sheet of paper. Write a general statement with which to begin. This will be your topic statement.

6 When writing your answer, be precise but brief. Be sure to refer to details in the passage in your answer.

Targeting Writing

On many standardized tests, you will occasionally be asked to write an essay. In order to write a concise essay, you must learn to organize you thoughts before you begin writing the actual composition. This keeps you from straying too far from the essay's topic.

Tips for Answering Composition Questions

1 Read the question carefully.

2 Decide what kind of essay you are being asked to write. Essays usually fall into one of the following types: persuasive, classificatory, compare/contrast, or "how to." To determine the type of essay, ask yourself questions like, "Am I trying to persuade my audience? Am I comparing or contrasting ideas?," or "Am I trying to show the reader how to do something?"

3 Pay attention to keywords, such as compare, contrast, describe, advantages, disadvantages, classify, or speculate. They will give you clues as to the structure that your essay should follow.

4 Organize your thoughts on a separate sheet of paper. You will want to come up with a general topic sentence that expresses your main idea. Make sure this sentence addresses the question. You should then create an outline or some type of graphic organizer to help you organize the points that support your topic sentence.

5 Write your composition using complete sentences. Also be sure to use correct grammar, spelling, punctuation, and sentence structure.

6 Be sure to proofread your essay once you have finished writing.

Gearing Up for Math

On most standardized tests you will be asked to solve a variety of mathematical problems that draw on the skills and information you have learned in class. If math problems sometimes give you difficulty, have a look at the tips below to help you work through the problems.

Tips for Solving Math Problems

1 Determine the goal of the question. Read or study the problem carefully and determine what information must be found.

2 Locate the factual information. Decide what information represents key facts—the ones you must have to solve the problem. You may also find facts you do not need to reach your solution. In some cases, you may determine that more information is needed to solve the problem. If so, ask yourself, "What assumptions can I make about this problem?" or "Do I need a formula to help solve this problem?"

3 Decide what strategies you might use to solve the problem, how you might use them, and what form your solution will be in. For example, will you need to create a graph or chart? Will you need to solve an equation? Will your answer be in words or numbers? By knowing what type of solution you should reach, you may be able to eliminate some of the choices.

4 Apply your strategy to solve the problem and compare your answer to the choices.

5 If the answer is still not clear, read the problem again. If you had to make calculations to reach your answer, use estimation to see if your answer makes sense.

The Geographer's Tool Kit

A map is an illustration drawn to scale of all or part of Earth's surface. Knowing how to read and interpret maps is one of the most valuable tools you can use to study history.

Types of Maps

Types of maps include physical maps, political maps, and thematic (special-purpose) maps.

Physical maps illustrate the natural landscape of an area—the landforms that mark Earth's surface. Physical maps often use shading to show relief—the existence of mountains, hills, and valleys—and colors to show elevation, or the height above sea level. The map of the World on pages A2–A3 is strictly a physical map.

Political maps illustrate political units, such as states and nations, and use color variations and lines to mark boundaries, dots for major cities, and stars or stars within circles for capitals. Political maps show information such as territorial changes or military alliances. The map of the United States on page A4 is a political map.

Thematic (special-purpose) maps present specific information, such as the route of an explorer or the outcome of an election. The maps shown on page 56 ("Indo-European Migrations") and page 188 ("Trading States of Africa, c. 1230–1591") of *The Human Journey*, for example, are thematic maps.

Map Features

Most maps have a number of features in common. Familiarity with these elements makes reading maps easier.

Titles, legends, and labels

A map's title tells you what the map is about, what areas are shown, and usually what time period is being represented. The legend, or key, explains any special symbols, colors, or shadings used on the map. Labels designate political and geographic

place-names, and physical features like mountain ranges, oceans, and rivers.

The global grid The absolute location of any place on Earth is given in terms of latitude (degrees north or south of the equator) and longitude (degrees east or west of the prime meridian). The symbol for a degree is °. Degrees are divided into 60 equal parts called minutes, which are represented by the symbol ´. The global grid is created by the intersecting lines of latitude (parallels) and lines of longitude (meridians). Lines of latitude and longitude may sometimes be indicated by tick marks near the edge of the map, or by lines across an entire map. Many maps also have locator maps, which place the area of focus in a larger context, showing it in relation to a continent or to the entire world.

Directions and distance Most maps in this textbook have a compass rose, or directional indicator. The compass rose indicates the four cardinal points—*N* for north, *S* for south, *E* for east, and *W* for west. You can also find intermediate directions—northeast, southeast, southwest, and northwest—using the compass rose. This helps in

The Unification of Spain, 1479–1515

Interpreting Maps
Four kingdoms on the Iberian Peninsula were united to form Spain.

■ **Skills Assessment:**
1. **The World in Spatial Terms** Which kingdom was largest? Which was second largest?
2. **Sequencing** By 1515, what two nations were on the Iberian Peninsula?

describing the relative location of a place. (If a map has no compass rose, assume that north is at the top, east is to the right, and so on.) Many maps in this textbook include a scale, showing both miles and kilometers, to help you relate distances on the map to actual distances on Earth's surface.

Map projections Because Earth is a sphere, it is best represented by a three-dimensional globe. Although a flat map is an imperfect representation of Earth's surface, mapmakers have devised various ways of showing Earth two dimensionally. These different flat views of Earth's surface are called projections.

Every map projection, and therefore every map, distorts to some extent at least one of the following aspects: (1) the shape of land areas, (2) their relative sizes, (3) directions, or (4) distances. Mapmakers choose the projection that least distorts what they wish to show. For example, an equal-area projection shows the relative sizes of different countries or continents quite accurately but distorts shapes somewhat.

How to Read a Map

1 Determine the focus of the map. Read the map's title and labels to determine the map's focus—its subject and the geographic area it covers.

2 Study the map legend. Read the legend and become familiar with any special symbols, lines, colors, and shadings used in the map.

3 Check directions and distance. Use the directional indicator and scale as needed to determine direction, location, and distance between various points on the map.

4 Check the grid lines. Refer to lines of longitude and latitude, or to a locator map, to place the area on the map in a larger context.

5 Study the map. Study the map's basic features and details, keeping its purpose in mind. If it is a special-purpose map, study the specific information being presented.

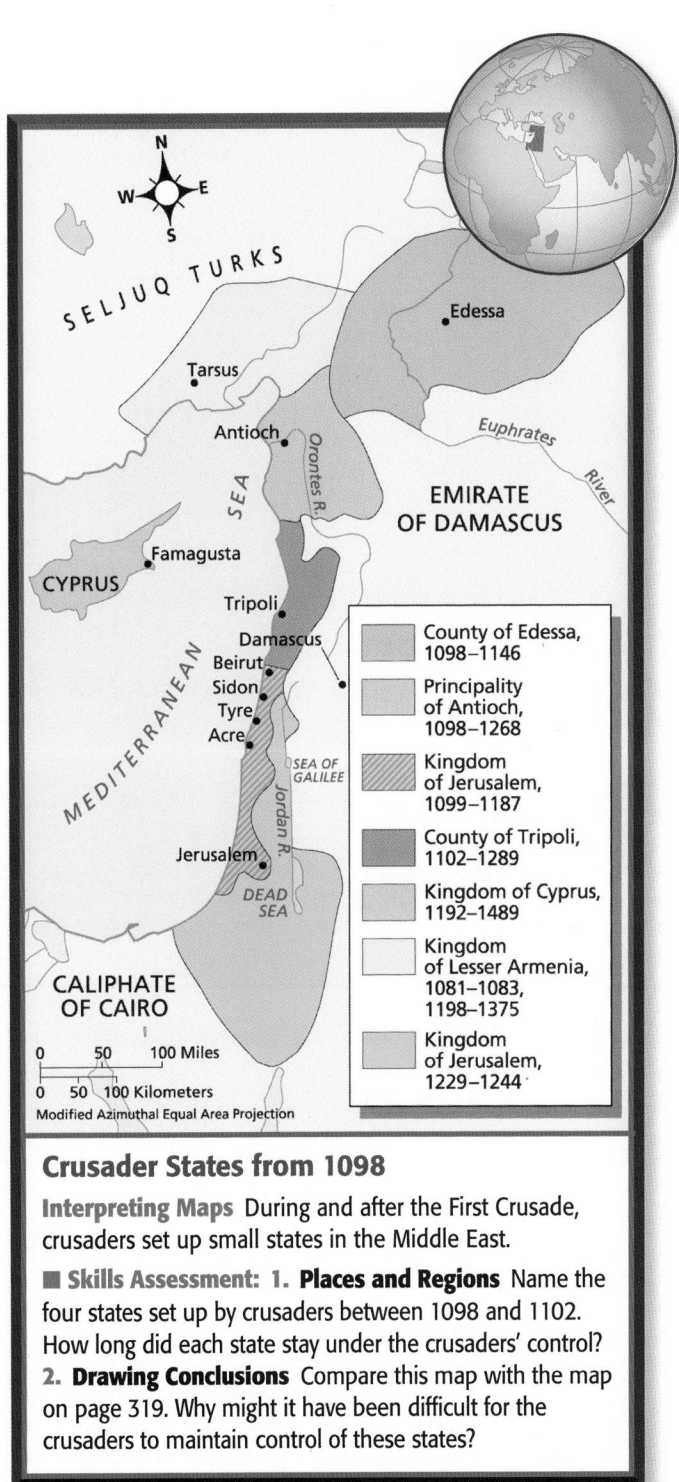

	County of Edessa, 1098–1146
	Principality of Antioch, 1098–1268
	Kingdom of Jerusalem, 1099–1187
	County of Tripoli, 1102–1289
	Kingdom of Cyprus, 1192–1489
	Kingdom of Lesser Armenia, 1081–1083, 1198–1375
	Kingdom of Jerusalem, 1229–1244

0 50 100 Miles
0 50 100 Kilometers
Modified Azimuthal Equal Area Projection

Crusader States from 1098

Interpreting Maps During and after the First Crusade, crusaders set up small states in the Middle East.

■ **Skills Assessment: 1. Places and Regions** Name the four states set up by crusaders between 1098 and 1102. How long did each state stay under the crusaders' control?
2. Drawing Conclusions Compare this map with the map on page 319. Why might it have been difficult for the crusaders to maintain control of these states?

ATLAS

World: Political

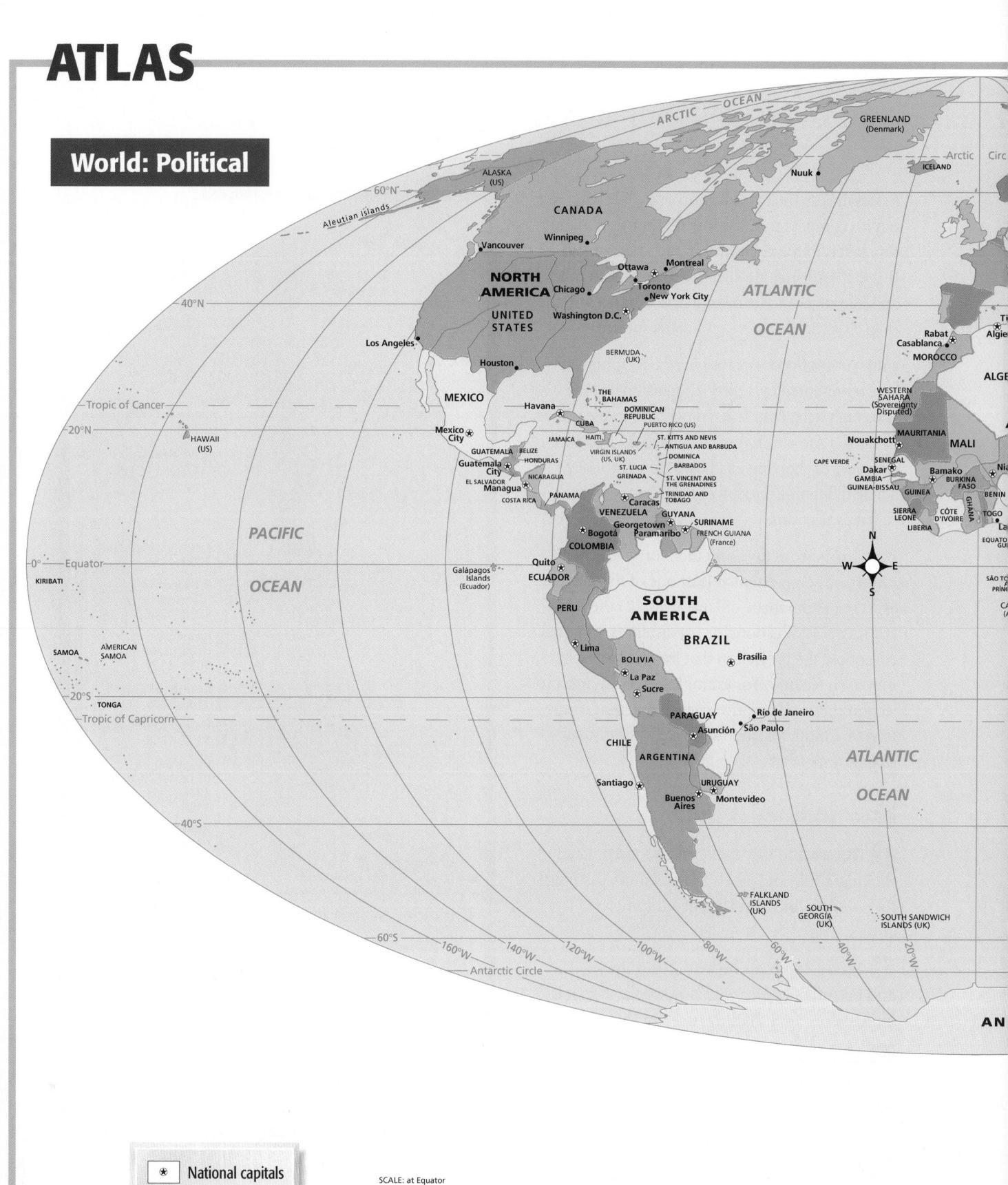

ARCTIC OCEAN

GREENLAND
(Denmark)

Arctic Circle

ICELAND

Nuuk •

ALASKA
(US)

60°N

CANADA

Aleutian Islands

Vancouver •

Winnipeg •

Ottawa • Montreal
• ✳ Toronto
• New York City

ATLANTIC

NORTH
AMERICA

Chicago •

40°N

UNITED
STATES

Washington D.C. ✳

OCEAN

Rabat
Casablanca • ✳
MOROCCO

Algie

TH

Algie

Los Angeles •

Houston •

BERMUDA
(UK)

WESTERN
SAHARA
(Sovereignty
Disputed)

ALGE

Tropic of Cancer

MEXICO

20°N

Havana ✳

THE
BAHAMAS

DOMINICAN
REPUBLIC

CUBA

PUERTO RICO (US)

Nouakchott ✳

MAURITANIA

MALI

Mexico ✳
City

HAWAII
(US)

GUATEMALA BELIZE
Guatemala ✳
City
EL SALVADOR

JAMAICA HAITI

VIRGIN ISLANDS
(US, UK)

CAPE VERDE

Dakar ✳
SENEGAL
GAMBIA
GUINEA-BISSAU

Bamako ✳
BURKINA
FASO

Nia

ST. KITTS AND NEVIS
ANTIGUA AND BARBUDA

DOMINICA

BENIN

HONDURAS

BARBADOS

NICARAGUA
Managua ✳

ST. LUCIA
GRENADA

ST. VINCENT AND
THE GRENADINES

GUINEA

SIERRA
LEONE

CÔTE
D'IVOIRE
LIBERIA

GHANA

TOGO

La

EQUATO

PANAMA

TRINIDAD AND
TOBAGO

PACIFIC

COSTA RICA

Caracas ✳

VENEZUELA

GUYANA

Bogotá ✳
Georgetown ✳
Paramaribo ✳
SURINAME

COLOMBIA

FRENCH GUIANA
(France)

N

SÃO TO
PRIN

EQUATO
GUI

OCEAN

Quito ✳
ECUADOR

W   E

CA
(A

0°   Equator

KIRIBATI

Galápagos
Islands
(Ecuador)

S

PERU

SOUTH
AMERICA

SAMOA

AMERICAN
SAMOA

BRAZIL

Brasília •

20°S

TONGA

Lima ✳

BOLIVIA

La Paz ✳
Sucre ✳

Tropic of Capricorn

Río de Janeiro •

PARAGUAY

São Paulo •

ATLANTIC

Asunción ✳

CHILE

ARGENTINA

URUGUAY

OCEAN

Santiago ✳

Buenos ✳
Aires

Montevideo ✳

40°S

FALKLAND
ISLANDS
(UK)

SOUTH
GEORGIA
(UK)

SOUTH SANDWICH
ISLANDS (UK)

60°S

160°W   140°W   120°W   100°W   80°W   60°W   40°W   20°W

Antarctic Circle

AN

✳ National capitals

• Other cities

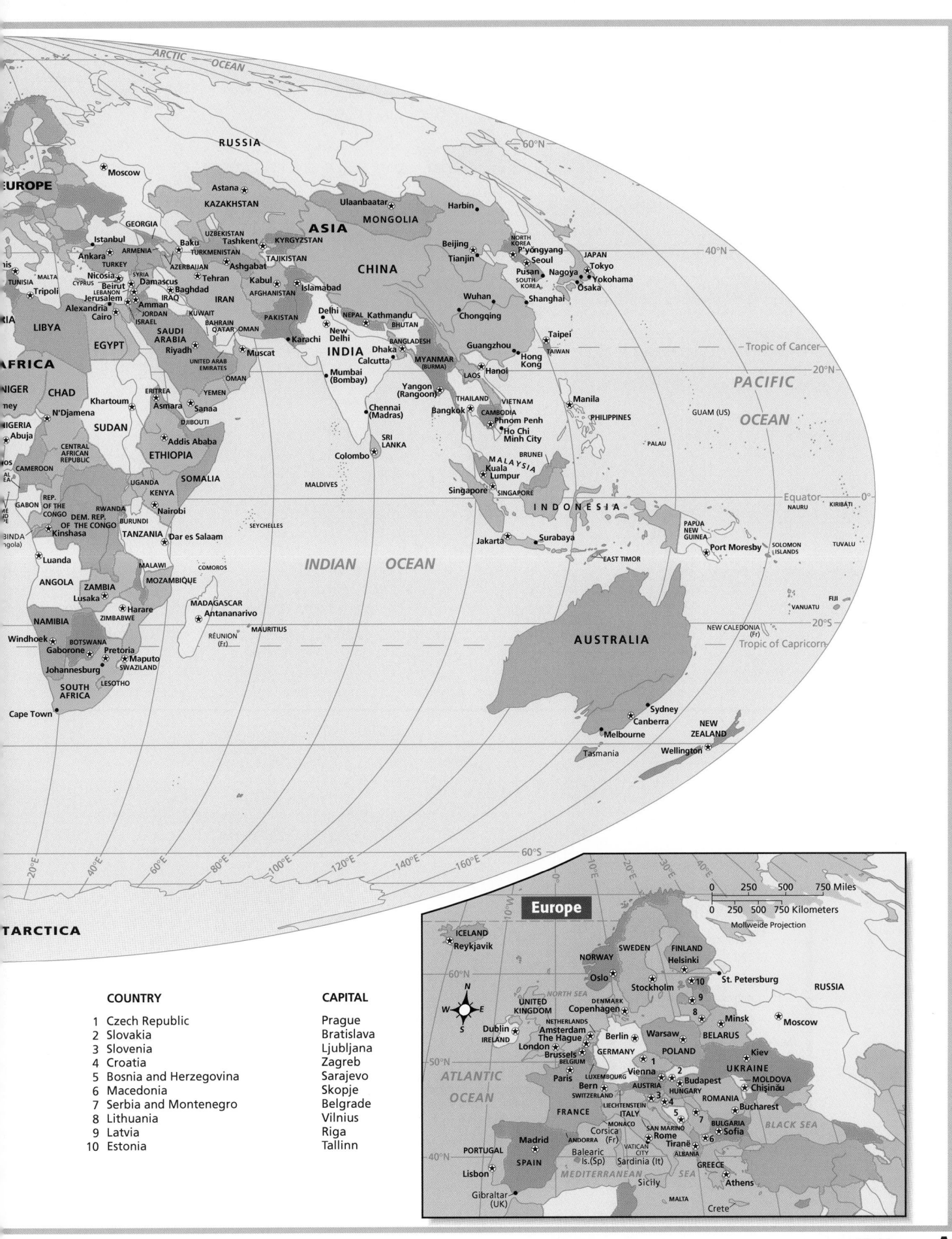

COUNTRY	CAPITAL
1 Czech Republic	Prague
2 Slovakia	Bratislava
3 Slovenia	Ljubljana
4 Croatia	Zagreb
5 Bosnia and Herzegovina	Sarajevo
6 Macedonia	Skopje
7 Serbia and Montenegro	Belgrade
8 Lithuania	Vilnius
9 Latvia	Riga
10 Estonia	Tallinn

World: Physical

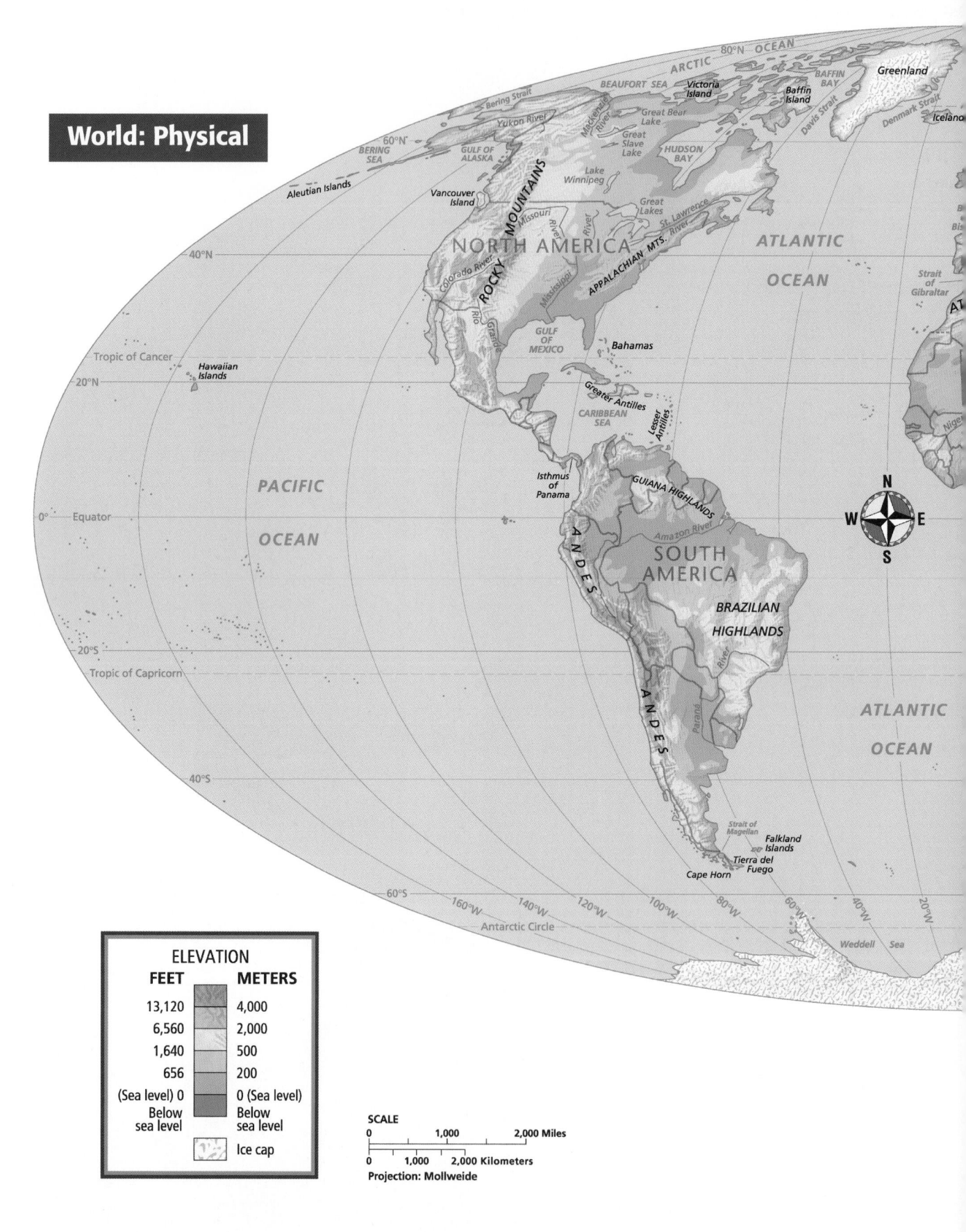

ATLANTIC OCEAN

ARCTIC OCEAN

BEAUFORT SEA

Bering Strait

Victoria Island

Baffin Island

BAFFIN BAY

Greenland

Davis Strait

Denmark Strait

Iceland

Yukon River

Mackenzie River

Great Bear Lake

Great Slave Lake

BERING SEA

GULF OF ALASKA

Aleutian Islands

Vancouver Island

Lake Winnipeg

HUDSON BAY

Great Lakes

NORTH AMERICA

ROCKY MOUNTAINS

Missouri River

St. Lawrence River

APPALACHIAN MTS.

Colorado River

Rio Grande

Mississippi

GULF OF MEXICO

Bahamas

ATLANTIC OCEAN

Strait of Gibraltar

Hawaiian Islands

Tropic of Cancer

Greater Antilles

CARIBBEAN SEA

Lesser Antilles

Niger

Isthmus of Panama

GUIANA HIGHLANDS

PACIFIC OCEAN

Amazon River

ANDES

SOUTH AMERICA

BRAZILIAN HIGHLANDS

Equator

ANDES

Paraná

ATLANTIC OCEAN

Tropic of Capricorn

Strait of Magellan

Falkland Islands

Tierra del Fuego

Cape Horn

Weddell Sea

Antarctic Circle

80°N
60°N
40°N
20°N
0°
20°S
40°S
60°S

160°W 140°W 120°W 100°W 80°W 60°W 40°W 20°W

ELEVATION

FEET		METERS
13,120		4,000
6,560		2,000
1,640		500
656		200
(Sea level) 0		0 (Sea level)
Below sea level		Below sea level
	Ice cap	

SCALE

0   1,000   2,000 Miles

0   1,000   2,000 Kilometers

Projection: Mollweide

ARCTIC 80°N OCEAN

North Cape
BARENTS SEA
KARA SEA
LAPTEV SEA
EAST SIBERIAN SEA

BALTIC SEA

EUROPE

URAL MOUNTAINS

Volga River
Ob River
Yenisey River
Lena River
Kolyma River

60°N
SEA OF OKHOTSK
KAMCHATKA PENINSULA

Sakhalin

ALPS

ARAL SEA
Lake Balkhash
ALTAY SHAN

Lake Baikal
Amur River

BLACK SEA
CASPIAN SEA

ASIA
GOBI
(Yellow) River

Hokkaidō

40°N

TS.
MEDITERRANEAN SEA
Euphrates River
Tigris River
Persian Gulf

HIMALAYAS
Chang (Yangtze) River

SEA OF JAPAN
Honshū

Shikoku
Kyūshū

SAHARA
Nile River
RED SEA
ARABIAN PENINSULA
THAR DESERT
Ganges River
Mekong River

EAST CHINA SEA

Taiwan
Tropic of Cancer

ARABIAN SEA
20°N

Bay of Bengal
SOUTH CHINA SEA
Philippine Islands

PACIFIC

OCEAN

AFRICA

Gulf of Guinea
Congo River

Sri Lanka

Strait of Malacca
MALAY PENINSULA

Borneo
Equator 0°

Lake Tanganyika
Lake Victoria

Sumatra
Java
Sulawesi (Celebes)
New Guinea
Solomon Islands

INDIAN OCEAN

CORAL SEA

Madagascar

Mozambique Channel

GREAT SANDY DESERT

New Caledonia
20°S

KALAHARI DESERT

AUSTRALIA
GREAT VICTORIA DESERT
GREAT DIVIDING RANGE
Darling River
Tropic of Capricorn

Cape of Good Hope

North Island

Denmark Strait

TASMAN SEA

Tasmania
South Island

60°S

ANTARCTICA

20°E 40°E 60°E 80°E 100°E 120°E 140°E 160°E

Iceland
20°E 30°E 40°E 50°E 60°E KARA SEA 80°E
North Cape
BARENTS SEA

SCALE
0 250 500 750 Miles
0 250 500 750 Kilometers
Projection: Mollweide

N
W E
S

KJØLEN MTS.
URAL MTS.

60°N
British Isles
NORTH SEA
BALTIC SEA
Volga River

50°N
ATLANTIC OCEAN
Rhine
Danube
EUROPE

Bay of Biscay
ALPS

BLACK SEA

40°N
MEDITERRANEAN SEA
Euphrates River

Strait of Gibraltar
Crete

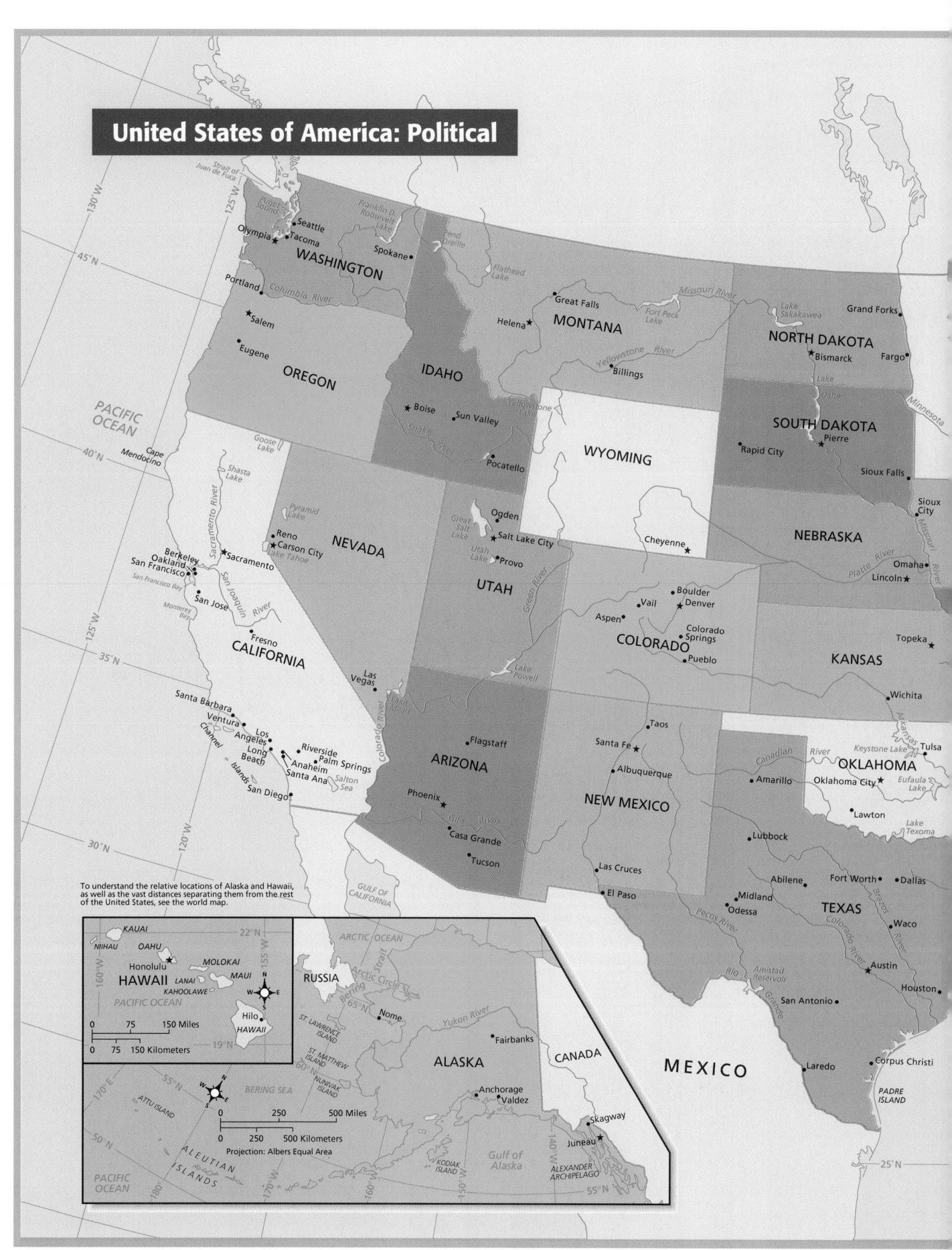

United States of America: Political

To understand the relative locations of Alaska and Hawaii, as well as the vast distances separating them from the rest of the United States, see the world map.

WASHINGTON
Olympia ★ Seattle • Tacoma • Spokane
Portland • Salem ★ Eugene •
OREGON

Strait of Juan de Fuca
Puget Sound
Columbia River
Franklin D. Roosevelt Lake
Pend Oreille
Flathead Lake

IDAHO
Boise • Sun Valley • Pocatello •

MONTANA
Great Falls • Helena ★ Billings •
Missouri River
Fort Peck Lake
Yellowstone River
Yellowstone Lake
Snake River

NORTH DAKOTA
Bismarck ★ Fargo •
Grand Forks •
Lake Sakakawea
Minnesota

SOUTH DAKOTA
Rapid City • Pierre ★
Lake Oahe
Sioux Falls •
Missouri River

PACIFIC OCEAN
Cape Mendocino
Goose Lake
Shasta Lake
Pyramid Lake

NEVADA
Reno • Carson City ★
Lake Tahoe
Sacramento River

WYOMING
Cheyenne ★

NEBRASKA
Omaha •
Lincoln ★
Platte River

Berkeley Oakland San Francisco • Sacramento
San Francisco Bay
San Jose •
San Joaquin River
Monterey Bay

Ogden • Salt Lake City ★
Utah Lake • Provo •
Great Salt Lake

UTAH
Green River

COLORADO
Aspen • Vail • Boulder • Denver •
Colorado Springs • Pueblo •

KANSAS
Topeka ★
Wichita •

CALIFORNIA
Fresno •
Las Vegas •
Santa Barbara
Ventura • Los Angeles •
Long Beach Anaheim Santa Ana
Riverside Palm Springs
San Diego •
Channel Islands
Salton Sea

Colorado River
Lake Mead
Lake Powell

ARIZONA
Flagstaff •
Phoenix ★
Casa Grande •
Tucson •
Gila River

NEW MEXICO
Taos •
Santa Fe ★
Albuquerque •
Las Cruces •
El Paso •

OKLAHOMA
Oklahoma City ★
Amarillo •
Lawton •
Canadian River
Keystone Lake
Tulsa •
Eufaula Lake
Lake Texoma
Arkansas River

TEXAS
Lubbock •
Abilene • Fort Worth • Dallas •
Midland • Odessa •
Waco •
Austin ★
San Antonio •
Houston •
Laredo •
Corpus Christi •
Pecos River
Colorado River
Brazos River
Rio Grande
Amistad Reservoir
PADRE ISLAND

GULF OF CALIFORNIA
MEXICO

To understand the relative locations of Alaska and Hawaii, as well as the vast distances separating them from the rest of the United States, see the world map.

KAUAI
NIIHAU OAHU
Honolulu ★
MOLOKAI
LANAI MAUI
KAHOOLAWE
HAWAII
Hilo •
HAWAII
PACIFIC OCEAN

0 75 150 Miles
0 75 150 Kilometers

ARCTIC OCEAN
Arctic Circle
RUSSIA
Bering Strait
Nome •
ST. LAWRENCE ISLAND
ST. MATTHEW ISLAND
NUNIVAK ISLAND
Yukon River
Fairbanks •

ALASKA
Anchorage •
Valdez •
Skagway •
Juneau ★

CANADA

BERING SEA
ATTU ISLAND
ALEUTIAN ISLANDS
KODIAK ISLAND
Gulf of Alaska
ALEXANDER ARCHIPELAGO
PACIFIC OCEAN

0 250 500 Miles
0 250 500 Kilometers
Projection: Albers Equal Area

CANADA

MINNESOTA
Duluth
Superior
Marquette
Sault Ste. Marie

Minneapolis
★ St. Paul
Green Bay

WISCONSIN

Madison
Milwaukee

IOWA
Cedar Rapids
Davenport
Des Moines

Rockford
Chicago
Gary
South Bend
Fort Wayne

MICHIGAN
Grand Rapids
Lansing ★
Saginaw
Ann Arbor
Detroit

Lake Superior
Lake Michigan
Lake Huron
Lake Erie
Lake Ontario

MAINE
Augusta

Burlington
Montpelier
VT
NH
Concord
Manchester
Portland

Buffalo
Rochester
Syracuse
Albany ★
NEW YORK

St. Lawrence River
Lake Champlain

MA
Boston
Worcester
Providence
Cape Cod

Springfield
Hartford ★
CT RI
Bridgeport
New Haven
LONG ISLAND
Long Island Sound

Peoria

ILLINOIS
★ Springfield
Indianapolis
INDIANA

Cleveland
Youngstown
Akron
Toledo

OHIO
★ Columbus
Dayton
Cincinnati

PENNSYLVANIA
Allentown
Harrisburg ★
Pittsburgh
Philadelphia
Susquehanna River

Newark
Yonkers
New York City
Jersey City
Trenton ★
Camden
NJ
Atlantic City

Kansas City
Kansas City
St. Louis
East St. Louis
Jefferson City

Louisville
Evansville

Frankfort ★
Lexington
Ohio River

KENTUCKY

WEST VIRGINIA
★ Charleston

VIRGINIA
Richmond ★

Baltimore
MD
Annapolis ★
⊛ Washington, D.C.
DE
Dover
DELAWARE BAY

ATLANTIC OCEAN

MISSOURI
Springfield

Lake Barkley
Nashville ★
TENNESSEE
Chattanooga
Knoxville

Kentucky Lake

CHESAPEAKE BAY
Newport News
Norfolk
Virginia Beach

Cape Hatteras

Fayetteville

ARKANSAS
Little Rock ★
Pine Bluff

Memphis

Huntsville

Winston-Salem
Greensboro
Durham
Raleigh ★
NORTH CAROLINA
Asheville
Charlotte

Greenville

Mississippi River

Red River

Shreveport

Vicksburg
Jackson ★
MISSISSIPPI

Meridian
Montgomery ★
ALABAMA
Birmingham

Atlanta ★
GEORGIA
Macon
Columbus

Savannah River

SOUTH CAROLINA
Columbia ★

Charleston

SEA ISLANDS

Toledo Bend Reservoir

LOUISIANA
Baton Rouge
Beaumont
New Orleans

Mobile
Biloxi
Pensacola
CHANDELEUR ISLANDS

Chattahoochee River

★ Tallahassee
Gainesville

Jacksonville

FLORIDA
Orlando
Cape Canaveral

Galveston

GULF OF MEXICO

Tampa
St. Petersburg
Lake Okeechobee

Fort Myers
Fort Lauderdale
Miami

THE BAHAMAS

Cape Sable
FLORIDA KEYS
Straits of Florida

CUBA

0   250   500 Miles
0   250   500 Kilometers
Projection: Albers Equal Area

N
W   E
S

⊛	National capital	
★	State capitals	
•	Other cities	

ARCTIC OCEAN
NORTH AMERICA
EUROPE
ASIA
ATLANTIC OCEAN
AFRICA
Equator
PACIFIC OCEAN
SOUTH AMERICA
AUSTRALIA
INDIAN OCEAN
ANTARCTICA
Robinson Projection

50° N
60° W
45° N
40° N
65° W
35° N
30° N
75° W
25° N
70° W
95° W
90° W
85° W
80° W

North America: Political

ASIA

EUROPE

NORTH POLE

BERING SEA

St. Lawrence Island

Nunivak Island

Point Barrow

ARCTIC OCEAN

BEAUFORT SEA

Banks Island

Queen Elizabeth Islands

Ellesmere Island

Arctic Circle

ICELAND

GREENLAND (Denmark)

DENMARK STRAIT

BAFFIN BAY

ALASKA (US)

Anchorage

Gulf of Alaska

Kodiak Island

Victoria Island

Great Bear Lake

Baffin Island

DAVIS STRAIT

Nuuk

Cape Farewell

Alexander Archipelago

Juneau

Great Slave Lake

Southampton Island

HUDSON STRAIT

LABRADOR SEA

Queen Charlotte Islands

Coats Island

Mansel Island

HUDSON BAY

PACIFIC OCEAN

Edmonton

CANADA

Anticosti Island

Newfoundland

ST. PIERRE AND MIQUELON (Fr)

Vancouver Island

Vancouver

Calgary

Lake Winnipeg

Prince Edward Island

GULF OF ST. LAWRENCE

Cape Breton Island

Seattle

Winnipeg

Quebec

Portland

Lake Superior

Montreal

Lake Huron

Ottawa

Lake Ontario

Boston

Cape Cod

Minneapolis

Toronto

Detroit

Lake Erie

New York City

Milwaukee

Cleveland

Philadelphia

San Francisco

Great Salt Lake

Salt Lake City

Chicago

Columbus

Baltimore

ATLANTIC OCEAN

Denver

Indianapolis

Washington, D.C.

Kansas City

St. Louis

Norfolk

UNITED STATES

Los Angeles

Memphis

Cape Hatteras

BERMUDA (UK)

San Diego

Phoenix

Atlanta

Tijuana

Birmingham

Dallas

Jacksonville

Austin

San Antonio

Houston

New Orleans

Cape Canaveral

Tropic of Cancer

Monterrey

GULF OF MEXICO

Florida Keys

Miami

THE BAHAMAS

Nassau

TURKS AND CAICOS ISLANDS (UK)

STRAITS OF FLORIDA

DOMINICAN REPUBLIC

PUERTO RICO (US)

MEXICO

Havana

CUBA

San Juan

ANTIGUA & BARBUDA

Guadalajara

Mérida

CAYMAN IS. (U.K.)

HAITI

Santo

VIRGIN IS. (US, UK)

GUADELOUPE (Fr)

Mexico City

Port-au-Prince

Domingo

ST. KITTS & NEVIS

DOMINICA

Puebla

Kingston

MARTINIQUE (Fr)

ST. LUCIA

Belmopan

JAMAICA

ST. VINCENT AND THE GRENADINES

BARBADOS

BELIZE

NETHERLANDS ANTILLES (Neth)

GRENADA

GUATEMALA

CARIBBEAN SEA

ARUBA (Neth)

TRINIDAD AND TOBAGO

Guatemala City

HONDURAS

San Salvador

Tegucigalpa

EL SALVADOR

NICARAGUA

Managua

Panama Canal

COSTA RICA

San José

Panama City

PANAMA

SOUTH AMERICA

GULF OF CALIFORNIA

Legend

⊛ National capital

• Other cities

N W E S

ARCTIC OCEAN

NORTH AMERICA

EUROPE

ASIA

ATLANTIC OCEAN

AFRICA

Equator

PACIFIC OCEAN

AUSTRALIA

SOUTH AMERICA

INDIAN OCEAN

ANTARCTICA

Robinson Projection

0   250   500   750   1,000 Miles

0   250   500   750   1,000 Kilometers

Azimuthal Equal-Area Projection

Equator 0°

South America: Political

CENTRAL AMERICA

CARIBBEAN SEA

Barranquilla
Cartagena
Caracas

Lake Maracaibo

VENEZUELA

Georgetown
Paramaribo

GUYANA

Cayenne

SURINAME
FRENCH GUIANA (Fr)

Medellín

Bogotá

COLOMBIA

Cali

Orinoco River

ATLANTIC OCEAN

Malpelo Island (Colombia)

Rio Negro

Quito

ECUADOR

Amazon River

Amazon River

Belém

Galápagos Islands (Ecuador)

Guayaquil

Equator

Equator

Marañon River

PERU

Trujillo

Ucayali River

BRAZIL

Recife

Callao
Lima

Arequipa

Lake Titicaca

BOLIVIA

La Paz

Lake Poopó

Sucre

Salvador

São Francisco River

Brasília

PACIFIC OCEAN

Belo Horizonte

PARAGUAY

Campinas
São Paulo

Río de Janeiro

Tropic of Capricorn

Asunción

Curitiba

Tropic of Capricorn

San Ambrosio Island (Chile)

Paraguay River

San Félix Island (Chile)

CHILE

Pôrto Alegre

Paraná River

Uruguay River

Córdoba

URUGUAY

Juan Fernández Islands (Chile)

Valparaíso
Santiago

Rosario
Buenos Aires
Morón
San Justo
Lomas de Zamora

Montevideo

RÍO DE LA PLATA

ATLANTIC OCEAN

ARGENTINA

N
W   E
S

⊛	National capital
•	Other cities

ARCTIC OCEAN

NORTH AMERICA

EUROPE

ASIA

ATLANTIC OCEAN

AFRICA

Equator

PACIFIC OCEAN

SOUTH AMERICA

INDIAN OCEAN

AUSTRALIA

ANTARCTICA

Robinson Projection

0   250   500   750   1,000 Miles
0   250   500   750   1,000 Kilometers
Azimuthal Equal-Area Projection

STRAIT OF MAGELLAN

FALKLAND ISLANDS (UK)

Tierra del Fuego

SOUTH GEORGIA ISLAND (UK)

Europe: Political

ATLAS

ASIA

URAL MOUNTAINS

RUSSIA

Nizhniy Novgorod

Moscow

Ural River

Don River

Volga River

CASPIAN SEA

SOUTHWEST ASIA

BARENTS SEA

WHITE SEA

St. Petersburg

BLACK SEA

Dnieper River

UKRAINE

Kiev

BELARUS

Minsk

MOLDOVA

Chişinău

Odesa

ROMANIA

Bucharest

Danube River

BULGARIA

Sofia

SERBIA & MONTENEGRO

Belgrade

Skopje

MACEDONIA

GREECE

Thessaloniki

AEGEAN SEA

Athens

Crete

Rhodes

North Cape

FINLAND

Helsinki

Tallinn

ESTONIA

LATVIA

Riga

LITHUANIA

Vilnius

RUSSIA

GULF OF FINLAND

BALTIC SEA

Stockholm

SWEDEN

Göteborg

POLAND

Warsaw

Lodz

Kraków

CZECH REPUBLIC

Prague

SLOVAKIA

Bratislava

Budapest

HUNGARY

Vienna

AUSTRIA

Zagreb

CROATIA

SLOVENIA

Ljubljana

BOSNIA & HERZEGOVINA

Sarajevo

Tirane

ALBANIA

ADRIATIC SEA

SERBIA & MONTENEGRO

NORWAY

Oslo

Bergen

DENMARK

Copenhagen

Hamburg

Berlin

GERMANY

Leipzig

Dresden

Cologne

Bonn

Munich

LIECHTENSTEIN

Vaduz

SWITZERLAND

Bern

Lake Geneva

ALPS

Milan

Turin

MONACO

Monaco

SAN MARINO

San Marino

ITALY

Rome

VATICAN CITY

Naples

Palermo

Sicily

MALTA

Valletta

MEDITERRANEAN SEA

ARCTIC OCEAN

Arctic Circle

NORTH SEA

THE NETHERLANDS

Amsterdam

The Hague

Rotterdam

Antwerp

BELGIUM

Brussels

LUXEMBOURG

Luxembourg

Elbe River

Rhine River

Danube River

Paris

Seine River

Loire River

FRANCE

Lyon

Rhône River

Marseille

Corsica (France)

Sardinia (Italy)

AFRICA

Shetland Islands

FAEROE ISLANDS (Denmark)

SCOTLAND

Edinburgh

Glasgow

NORTHERN IRELAND

Belfast

UNITED KINGDOM

Manchester

Liverpool

Leeds

Sheffield

Birmingham

WALES

ENGLAND

London

Dublin

IRELAND

British Isles

Channel Islands (UK)

ENGLISH CHANNEL

BAY OF BISCAY

PYRENEES

ANDORRA

Andorra la Vella

Barcelona

Balearic Islands (Spain)

ICELAND

Reykjavik

SPAIN

Madrid

Valencia

Seville

Tagus River

PORTUGAL

Lisbon

Gibraltar (UK)

STRAIT OF GIBRALTAR

ATLANTIC OCEAN

PACIFIC OCEAN

NORTH AMERICA

SOUTH AMERICA

ATLANTIC OCEAN

EUROPE

ASIA

AFRICA

INDIAN OCEAN

AUSTRALIA

ANTARCTICA

PACIFIC OCEAN

Equator

Robinson Projection

N E W S

National capital
Other cities

500 Miles

500 Kilometers

250

250

0

0

Azimuthal Equal-Area Projection

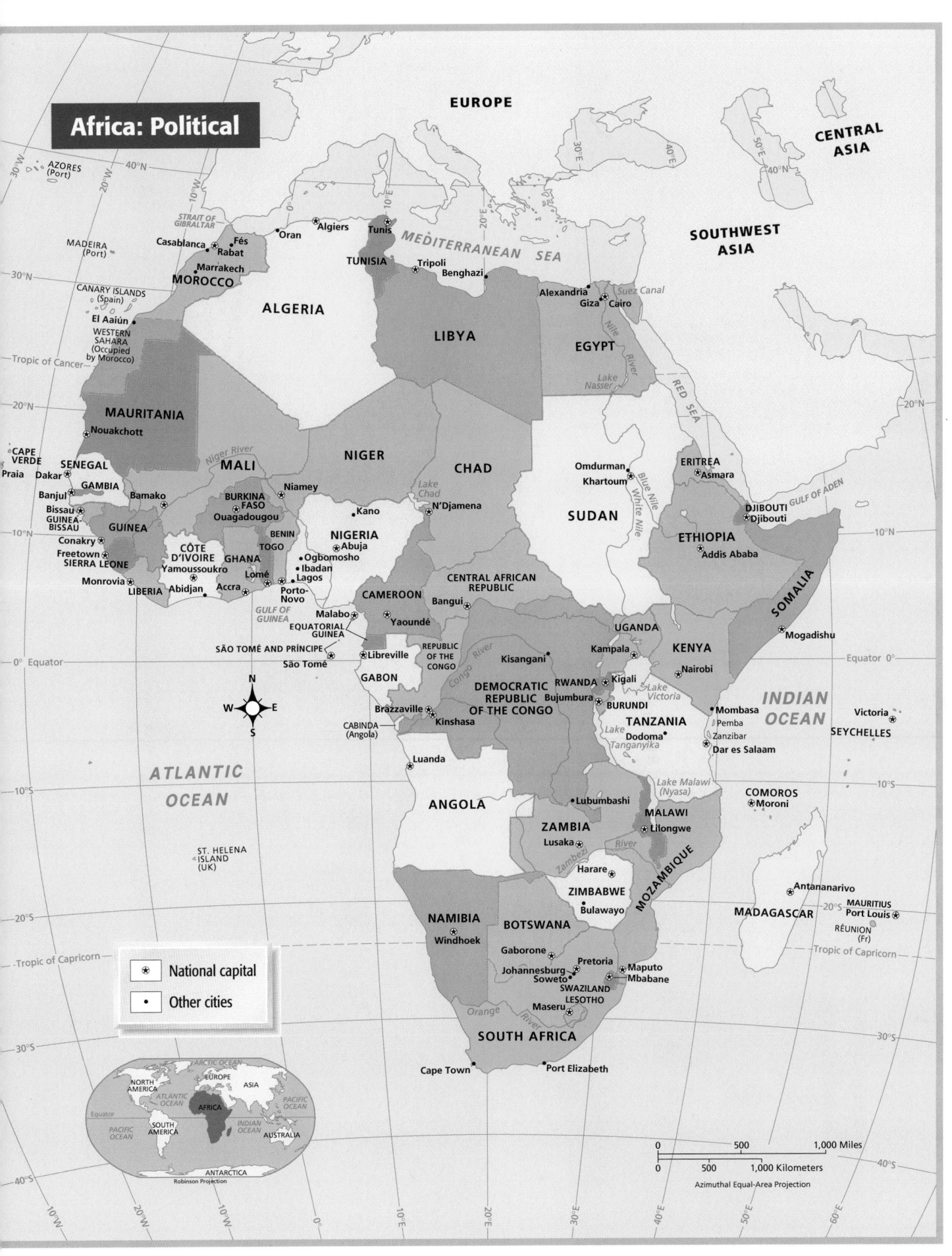

Africa: Political

EUROPE

CENTRAL
ASIA

SOUTHWEST
ASIA

MEDITERRANEAN SEA

AZORES
(Port)

STRAIT OF
GIBRALTAR

• Oran
⊛ Algiers
⊛ Tunis
TUNISIA

• Tripoli
Benghazi

MADEIRA
(Port)

Casablanca
⊛ Fés
⊛ Rabat
• Marrakech

MOROCCO

CANARY ISLANDS
(Spain)

• El Aaiún

WESTERN
SAHARA
(Occupied
by Morocco)

Tropic of Cancer

ALGERIA

LIBYA

EGYPT

Alexandria
Giza ⊛ Cairo

Suez Canal

Nile River

Lake
Nasser

RED SEA

MAURITANIA

⊛ Nouakchott

Niger River

NIGER

CHAD

Omdurman •
⊛ Khartoum

ERITREA
⊛ Asmara

Blue Nile

White Nile

GULF OF ADEN

CAPE
VERDE

Praia ⊛

SENEGAL

⊛ Dakar

GAMBIA
⊛ Banjul

Bamako ⊛

MALI

BURKINA
FASO

⊛ Niamey

Lake
Chad

Kano •
N'Djamena •

SUDAN

DJIBOUTI
⊛ Djibouti

ETHIOPIA

⊛ Addis Ababa

Bissau ⊛

GUINEA-
BISSAU

GUINEA

⊛ Ouagadougou

NIGERIA

⊛ Abuja

Conakry ⊛

Freetown ⊛
SIERRA LEONE

CÔTE
D'IVOIRE

Yamoussoukro ⊛

GHANA

BENIN
TOGO

Ogbomosho •
• Ibadan
• Lagos

Monrovia ⊛

LIBERIA

Abidjan •

Accra ⊛

Lomé ⊛
⊛ Porto-
Novo

CENTRAL AFRICAN
REPUBLIC

UGANDA

⊛ Kampala

SOMALIA

Mogadishu •

GULF OF
GUINEA

Malabo ⊛

CAMEROON

Bangui ⊛

KENYA

⊛ Nairobi

EQUATORIAL
GUINEA

• Yaoundé

SÃO TOMÉ AND PRÍNCIPE

São Tomé •

⊛ Libreville

GABON

REPUBLIC
OF THE
CONGO

Congo River

Kisangani •

RWANDA
⊛ Kigali

Bujumbura ⊛

Lake
Victoria

INDIAN
OCEAN

• Mombasa
• Pemba

Victoria ⊛

SEYCHELLES

N
W   E
S

CABINDA
(Angola)

Brazzaville ⊛
Kinshasa ⊛

DEMOCRATIC
REPUBLIC
OF THE CONGO

BURUNDI

TANZANIA

⊛ Dodoma
•

Zanzibar •
Dar es Salaam •

Lake
Tanganyika

ATLANTIC
OCEAN

Luanda ⊛

ST. HELENA
ISLAND
(UK)

ANGOLA

• Lubumbashi

Lake Malawi
(Nyasa)

COMOROS
⊛ Moroni

MALAWI
⊛ Lilongwe

ZAMBIA

Lusaka ⊛

Zambezi River

Antananarivo ⊛

MOZAMBIQUE

MADAGASCAR

MAURITIUS
⊛ Port Louis

RÉUNION
(Fr)

Harare ⊛

ZIMBABWE

• Bulawayo

Tropic of Capricorn

NAMIBIA

⊛ Windhoek

BOTSWANA

⊛ Gaborone

Johannesburg •
Soweto •

Pretoria ⊛

⊛ Maputo
⊛ Mbabane

SWAZILAND
LESOTHO

Maseru ⊛

Orange River

SOUTH AFRICA

Cape Town ⊛

• Port Elizabeth

Legend

⊛ National capital

• Other cities

NORTH
AMERICA

EUROPE

ASIA

ATLANTIC
OCEAN

Equator

AFRICA

PACIFIC
OCEAN

INDIAN
OCEAN

SOUTH
AMERICA

PACIFIC
OCEAN

AUSTRALIA

ANTARCTICA

Robinson Projection

0   500   1,000 Miles

0   500   1,000 Kilometers

Azimuthal Equal-Area Projection

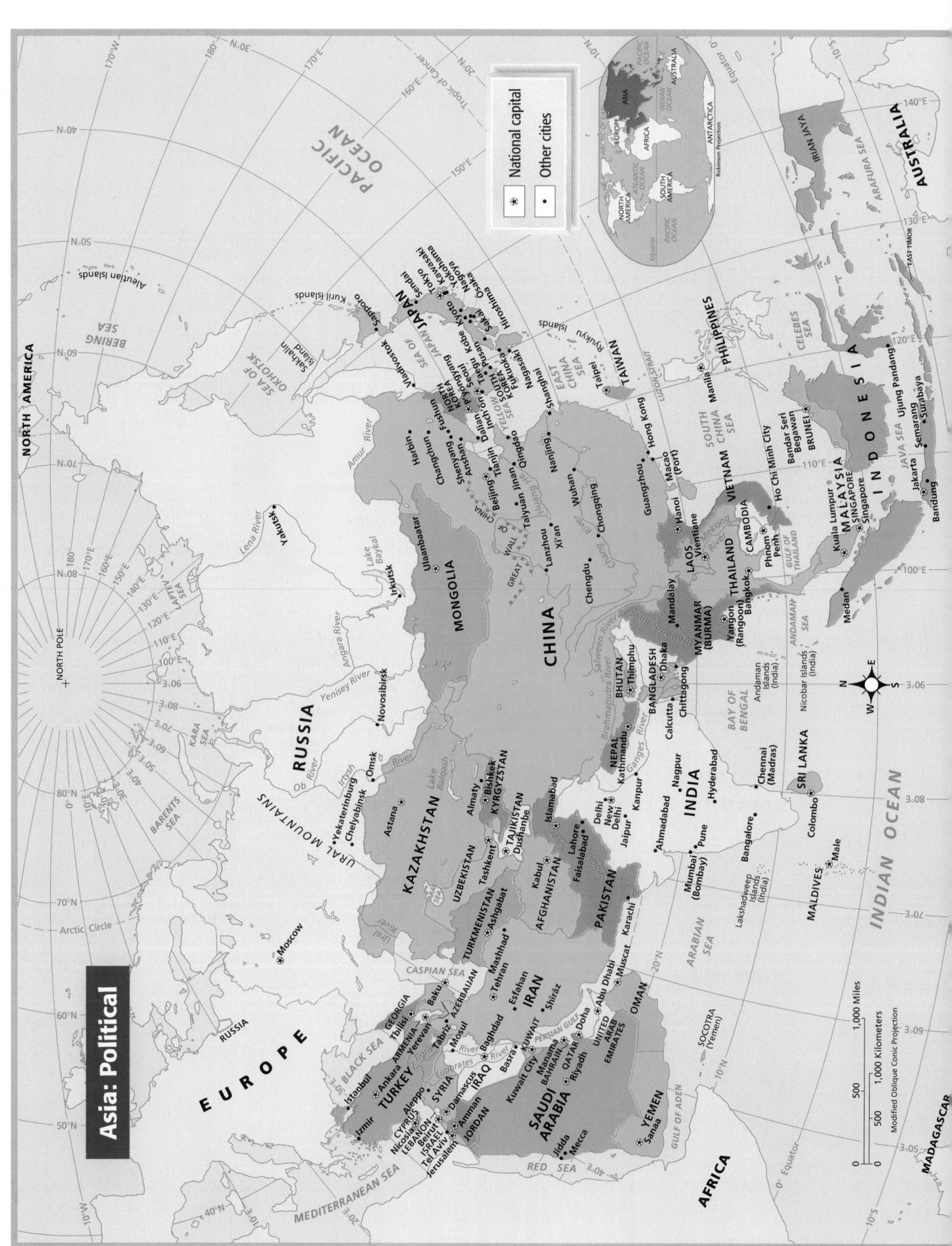

Asia: Political

National capital ⊛
Other cities •

Robinson Projection

NORTH AMERICA

PACIFIC OCEAN

BERING SEA

SEA OF OKHOTSK

Aleutian Islands

Sakhalin Island

Kuril Islands

RUSSIA

Lena River

Angara River

Yenisey River

Ob River

Irtysh River

URAL MOUNTAINS

BARENTS SEA

KARA SEA

LAPTEV SEA

NORTH POLE

Arctic Circle

Yakutsk

Irkutsk

Novosibirsk

Omsk

Yekaterinburg

Chelyabinsk

Moscow

EUROPE

RUSSIA

BLACK SEA

CASPIAN SEA

GEORGIA
Tbilisi
ARMENIA
Yerevan
AZERBAIJAN
Baku

TURKEY
Ankara
Istanbul
Izmir
Aleppo
CYPRUS
Nicosia
LEBANON
Beirut
ISRAEL
Tel Aviv
Jerusalem
SYRIA
Damascus
JORDAN
Amman

Tabriz
Mosul
Baghdad
IRAQ
Basra
Tigris River
Euphrates River

KAZAKHSTAN
Astana
Almaty

UZBEKISTAN
Tashkent
Lake Balqash

KYRGYZSTAN
Bishkek

TAJIKISTAN
Dushanbe

TURKMENISTAN
Ashgabat

IRAN
Tehran
Esfahan
Shiraz
Mashhad

AFGHANISTAN
Kabul

PAKISTAN
Islamabad
Lahore
Faisalabad
Karachi

KUWAIT
Kuwait City
BAHRAIN
Manama
QATAR
Doha
UNITED ARAB EMIRATES
Abu Dhabi
OMAN
Muscat
PERSIAN GULF

SAUDI ARABIA
Riyadh
Mecca
Jidda

YEMEN
Sanaa

RED SEA

GULF OF ADEN

SOCOTRA
(Yemen)

AFRICA

MEDITERRANEAN SEA

ARABIAN SEA

MONGOLIA
Ulaanbaatar

CHINA
Beijing
Tianjin
Jinan
Qingdao
Taiyuan
Shanghai
Nanjing
Wuhan
Chongqing
Chengdu
Lanzhou
Xi'an
Guangzhou
Hong Kong
Macao (Port)
Harbin
Changchun
Fushun
Shenyang
Anshan
Dalian
HWANG HE
YELLOW SEA
GREAT WALL OF CHINA
Huang He
Chang Jiang

NORTH KOREA
Pyongyang
SOUTH KOREA
Seoul
Inch'on
Taegu
Pusan

JAPAN
Tokyo
Yokohama
Kyoto
Osaka
Kobe
Nagoya
Sendai
Sapporo
Vladivostok
Kawasaki
Nagasaki
Fukuoka
Hiroshima
SEA OF JAPAN

EAST CHINA SEA

TAIWAN
Taipei

PHILIPPINES
Manila
LUZON STRAIT

SOUTH CHINA SEA

VIETNAM
Hanoi
Ho Chi Minh City

LAOS
Vientiane

THAILAND
Bangkok

CAMBODIA
Phnom Penh

MYANMAR (BURMA)
Yangon (Rangoon)
Mandalay

GULF OF THAILAND

Mekong River
Salween River

NEPAL
Kathmandu
BHUTAN
Thimphu
BANGLADESH
Dhaka
Chittagong

INDIA
New Delhi
Delhi
Jaipur
Kanpur
Ahmadabad
Nagpur
Hyderabad
Mumbai (Bombay)
Pune
Bangalore
Chennai (Madras)
Calcutta
Ganges River
Brahmaputra River
Indus River

SRI LANKA
Colombo

MALDIVES
Male

Lakshadweep Islands (India)

Andaman Islands (India)

Nicobar Islands (India)

ANDAMAN SEA

BAY OF BENGAL

INDIAN OCEAN

MALAYSIA
Kuala Lumpur
SINGAPORE
Singapore

BRUNEI
Bandar Seri Begawan

INDONESIA
Jakarta
Bandung
Semarang
Surabaya
Ujung Pandang
Medan
Palembang

JAVA SEA

CELEBES SEA

IRIAN JAYA

EAST TIMOR

AUSTRALIA

ARAFURA SEA

PACIFIC OCEAN

MADAGASCAR

Equator

Tropic of Cancer

500   1,000 Miles
500   1,000 Kilometers
Modified Oblique Conic Projection

Australia, New Zealand, and the Pacific Islands: Political

Scale: At Equator
1,000 Miles
1,000 Kilometers
Miller Cylindrical Projection

National capital
Other cities

A11

CHAPTER 1 — The Emergence of Civilization

Scholars study prehistoric peoples, such as Neanderthals and Cro-Magnons, by examining the objects they left behind. During the Stone Age, humans discovered how to make and use primitive tools, plant and grow food, and domesticate animals. The development of agriculture allowed the first civilizations to begin in four great river valleys in Asia and Africa.

CHAPTER 2 — The First Civilizations

The first civilizations developed more than 5,000 years ago around two river valleys—the Nile and the Tigris-Euphrates. Due to geographic differences, Egyptian civilization lasted thousands of years, while Mesopotamia rose and fell in a series of empires. These early civilizations developed complex societies with religious beliefs, systems of law and education, and artistic traditions. They also made important technological and scientific discoveries.

CHAPTER 3 — Ancient Indian Civilizations

The Harappan civilization developed in the Indus Valley about 2500 B.C. and lasted about 1,000 years,

---

UNIT 1

The Beginnings of Civilization

c. 3,700,000 B.C.–A.D. 589

until Aryans invaded India. During the Vedic Age, Indo-Aryans followed the Vedas, a religious text that defined Indian life for centuries. Hinduism and Buddhism eventually replaced the Vedic religion in India. Indian civilization developed distinctive styles of art, architecture, and literature under the Mauryan and Gupta Empires. Indian scientists also excelled in mathematics, astronomy, and medicine.

◆ CHAPTER ◆ **Ancient Chinese Civilization**

4 Chinese civilization developed in the Huang River valley. Under the first dynasty, the Shang, irrigation and flood-control systems were introduced. During the three succeeding dynasties—the Zhou, Qin, and Han—China grew into a large and powerful empire. Important philosophies, including Daoism, Legalism, and Confucianism, appeared in China. In addition, Buddhism was introduced from India. Chinese literature, medicine, science, and technology also flourished during this time.

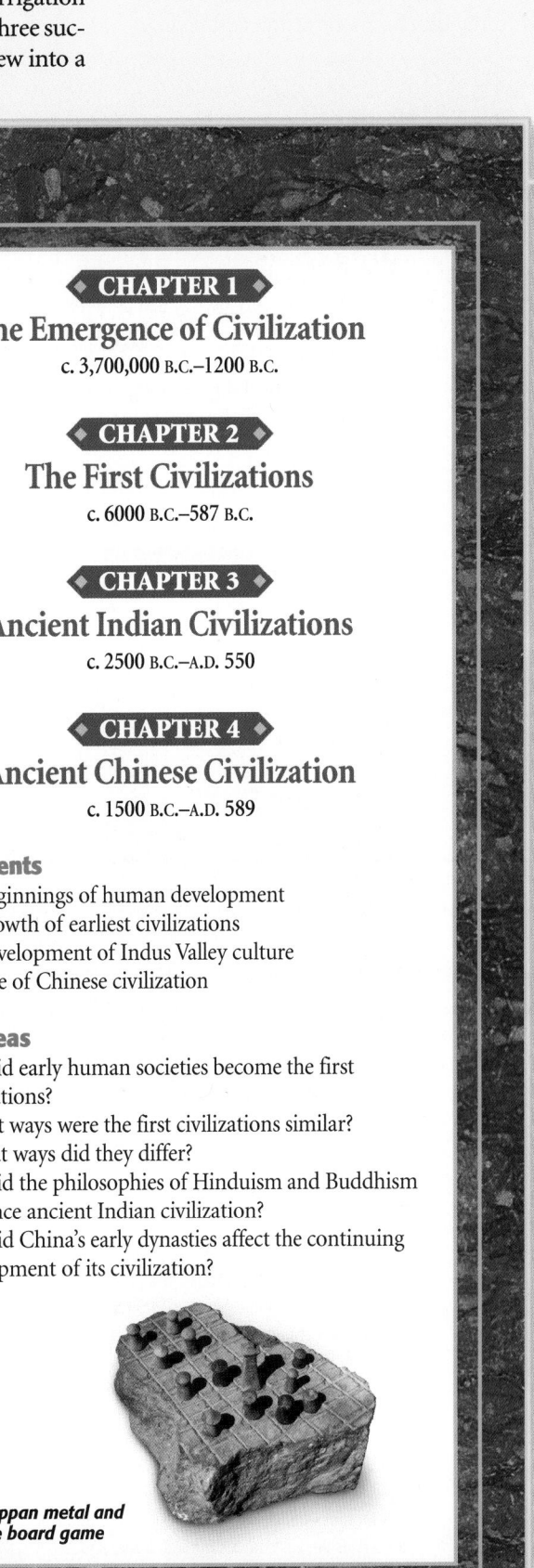

◆ **CHAPTER 1** ◆

The Emergence of Civilization

c. 3,700,000 B.C.–1200 B.C.

◆ **CHAPTER 2** ◆

The First Civilizations

c. 6000 B.C.–587 B.C.

◆ **CHAPTER 3** ◆

Ancient Indian Civilizations

c. 2500 B.C.–A.D. 550

◆ **CHAPTER 4** ◆

Ancient Chinese Civilization

c. 1500 B.C.–A.D. 589

Main Events

■ The beginnings of human development
■ The growth of earliest civilizations
■ The development of Indus Valley culture
■ The rise of Chinese civilization

Main Ideas

■ How did early human societies become the first civilizations?
■ In what ways were the first civilizations similar? In what ways did they differ?
■ How did the philosophies of Hinduism and Buddhism influence ancient Indian civilization?
■ How did China's early dynasties affect the continuing development of its civilization?

Harappan metal and stone board game

Main Events

Ask students to select two Main Events and list questions they would like to have answered about the topics. Later, when you have completed Unit 1, ask students to return to their original questions and write an answer using the information they learned in the unit.

Main Ideas

Ask each student to read the Main Ideas and write brief answers to the questions. Share the *Consider* points with students as necessary. Later, when you have completed Unit 1, ask students to analyze their original answers by comparing them to information they learned in the unit. Tell them to revise or expand their answers as necessary.

Development of the First Civilizations

Consider:

■ the effects of the Neolithic agricultural revolution
■ the characteristics of civilization

Characteristics of Ancient Civilizations in India and China

Consider:

■ the role of religion in ancient civilization
■ the influence of China's early dynasties

These Cro-Magnon cave paintings from Lascaux Cave in present-day France date from about 15,000 B.C. **1**

LET'S GET STARTED!

As students enter the classroom, have them study the map on page 12 and ask them to locate and name the four river valley civilizations. Explain that these civilizations will be the focus of this unit. Tell students that in this unit they will learn about the important changes in human life brought about by the Neolithic agricultural revolution, as well as the economic, social, and geographic factors that led to the development of the first civilizations.

TEACH

ALL LEVELS: Help students fill out the graphic organizer below with the information shown in italics. Then ask students to give examples of each influence from the text and from contemporary society.

ENGLISH LANGUAGE LEARNERS

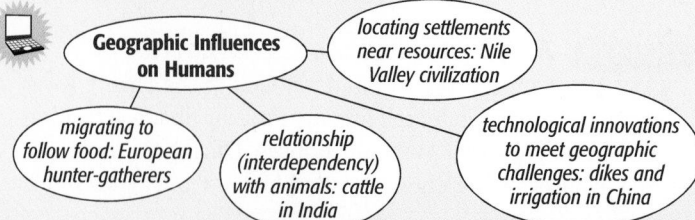

Geographic Influences on Humans
- locating settlements near resources: Nile Valley civilization
- migrating to follow food: European hunter-gatherers
- relationship (interdependency) with animals: cattle in India
- technological innovations to meet geographic challenges: dikes and irrigation in China

---

History Maker

HOWARD CARTER. One of the most famous scholars to study ancient Egypt was the British archaeologist Howard Carter (1873–1939). In 1922 Carter and his team discovered the untouched tomb of the Egyptian king, or pharaoh, Tutankhamen. King Tut–who died when he was only 18 years old–ruled Egypt about 3,300 years ago. Within the tomb, 5000 artifacts were discovered. These included a golden throne, parts of a chariot, life-sized wooden statues of King Tut, cups, jars, furniture, and a golden funeral mask that covered the king's head and shoulders. Previously, Carter had discovered the tombs of Egyptian Queen Hatshepsut and King Thutmose IV.

Critical Thinking

What do you think scholars learned from the artifacts found in King Tutankhamen's tomb?

ANSWER: Answers will vary. Students might suggest religious practices, daily life, use of local resources, and scientific achievements.

CROSS-CULTURAL CONNECTIONS

Focus On: Geography

Main Idea **How did geography affect early societies?** The early history of human beings was greatly shaped by geography. Early hunter-gatherers migrated in search of food, Egyptians relied on the mighty Nile River, Indians domesticated animals that could manage their rough terrain, and the Chinese built dikes to control annual flooding.

China
India
Egypt
Cro-Magnon

c. 33,000 B.C.   c. 8000 B.C.   c. 3200 B.C.   c. 2500 B.C.   c. 1500 B.C.   c. 300 B.C.   A.D. 550   A.D. 589

Cro-Magnon, c. 33,000 B.C.–c. 8000 B.C.

Hunter-gatherers Early hunter-gatherers traveled in search of food. In the northeastern region of Europe, where timber was scarce, people used the bones of giant mammoths to build shelters similar to the museum model shown here. Hunter-gatherer groups moved to different sites throughout the year, returning to these shelters on a regular basis. They dug oval holes in the ground and carefully arranged the bones above the holes to create a strong frame. The frames were then covered with mammoth skins. These mammoth-bone houses probably took ten people between five and six days to build.

Egyptian Civilization The presence of natural resources often determined patterns and distributions of early human settlement and activity. The annual flood cycle of Egypt's Nile River, for example, produced rich deposits of topsoil and created an excellent farming and herding environment. The river itself, moreover, provided a natural transportation highway. Early farming settlements grew along the river. Over time, some of these communities developed into religious and political centers as well as sources of food, trade, and transportation.

Egypt, c. 3200 B.C.–300 B.C.

REVIEW

Have students review the information about geographic influences on civilizations. Ask them to use standard grammar, spelling, sentence structure, and punctuation to answer the question in "Why it Matters Today" and to share their answers with the class.

ASSESS

Have students complete their answer to the question in "Why It Matters Today" and add it to their portfolio. As Alternative Assessment, you may want to use the graphic organizer in this lesson.

EXTEND

Have students choose one of the four river valley civilizations and research its geography. Tell students to use information from their textbooks, the library, computer software, and any other available resources to determine how geographic factors influenced that particular civilization. Have students present their findings in an oral report to the class. **BLOCK SCHEDULING**

Interdependence in Early India India is a land of great geographic variety. Rugged mountains, arid deserts, humid jungles, and fertile plains share the sub-continent. India's early people relied for food and labor upon strong animals that could survive the region's geographic challenges. Whether herded through rocky mountain passes or grazed on plains grasslands, cattle were a valuable resource. Cow's milk was a staple of the early Indian diet. Early farmers used cattle to pull carts and plows. Cattle became so valuable to early Indian civilization that they were used as money and were viewed as sacred beings.

India, c. 2500 B.C.—A.D. 550

Carved stone bull image, c. 2500 B.C.—1700 B.C.

China, c. 1500 B.C.—A.D. 589

Chinese Dikes and Tools The availability and use of natural resources often affects the way people live. In ancient China, people responded to the challenges of their surrounding geography by developing effective flood-control and irrigation systems. Dikes held back damaging floodwaters, while canals linked river systems and improved trade and transportation. Irrigation systems turned arid soil into rich farmland. China's early people also used other natural resources to improve their living conditions. For example, the Chinese used iron to make tools, weapons, and equipment.

Chinese iron-casting mold, c. 500—300 B.C.

Why It Matters Today

People and societies of today, like early people and civilizations, are strongly influenced by geographic factors such as landforms, weather patterns, and the availability of natural resources. **How does the influence of geography today compare with its influence on early peoples and civilizations?**

Culture

The religions that developed in early Indian civilization taught respect and even reverence for animals. Hindus and Buddhists believed all forms of life are equally important and that each creature is an incarnation of a single energy or life force. They believed that when a being died, this energy was reincarnated in another life form. Therefore, killing any other being was inconceivable, because it might be the soul of an ancestor or a friend.

Critical Thinking

How might religious beliefs have affected Indians' diets?

ANSWER: Indians following these religions probably would have been vegetarians because killing animals went against their religious beliefs.

WHY IT MATTERS TODAY ANSWER

Answers will vary, but students might say most people today do not have to migrate to find their food; geographic factors continue to influence the economic development of places and regions today; people now rely more on machines than on animals to overcome geographic obstacles; and people continue to modify their environment with mechanisms such as dikes and irrigation.

The Emergence of Civilization

CHAPTER RESOURCE MANAGER

Objectives	Pacing Guide	Reproducible Resources
SECTION 1 **Prehistoric Peoples** (pp. 6–10)		
• Describe how anthropologists, archaeologists, historians, and geographers study prehistory. • Identify the major achievements of Neanderthal and Cro-Magnon peoples. • Explain the important changes caused by the Neolithic agricultural revolution.	**Regular** 1.5 day **Block Scheduling** 1 day *Block Scheduling Handbook with Team Teaching Strategies, 1.1*	**RS** Guided Reading Strategy 1.1 **RS** Graphic Organizer Activity 1: The Prehistoric Age **SM** Geography Activity 1: Anthropology and Geology **PS** Readings in World History 1: The Task of the Archaeologist **PS** Readings in World History 2: The Nomadic Life **PS** Readings in World History 3: The First Painters **PS** Readings in World History 4: An Early Agricultural Village **E** Hands-on History Activity 1: On the Archaeological Trail **E** Creative Teaching Strategy 1: Time Lines of Prehistoric Peoples
SECTION 2 **The Foundations of Civilization** (pp. 11–15)		
• Identify the three main characteristics shared by civilizations. • Explain what other two characteristics may be shared by civilizations. • Describe the other characteristics and achievements that marked the first river valley civilizations.	**Regular** 1.5 day **Block Scheduling** 1 day *Block Scheduling Handbook with Team Teaching Strategies, 1.2*	**RS** Guided Reading Strategy 1.2

Chapter Resource Key

PS Primary Sources	**REV** Review	Video	**One-Stop** Planner CD-ROM
RS Reading Support	**ELL** Reinforcement and English Language Learners	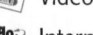 Internet	See the ***One-Stop Planner*** for a complete list of additional resources for students and teachers.
IC Interdisciplinary Connections		Holt Presentation Maker Using Microsoft® PowerPoint®	
E Enrichment	Transparencies		
SM Skills Mastery	CD-ROM		
A Assessment	Music		

One-Stop Planner CD-ROM

It's easy to plan lessons, select resources, and print out materials for your students when you use the **One-Stop Planner** CD–ROM with **Test Generator.**

Technology Resources	Reinforcement, Review, and Assessment
One-Stop Planner 1.1	Daily Quiz 1.1
Holt Researcher: World History: Mary Leakey	Main Idea Activity 1.1
CNN Presents World Cultures: Yesterday and Today Segment 1: The Kennewick Man	English Audio Summary 1.1
World History Teaching Transparencies: Geography and History 1: World Domestication	Spanish Audio Summary 1.1
World History Teaching Transparencies: Art and History 1: Hall of the Bulls, Lascaux Cave	REV Section 1 Review, p. 10
Online Maps, Charts, and Graphs: Early Agriculture in Asia	
One-Stop Planner 1.2	Daily Quiz 1.2
World History and Cultures Video Program 1: The Rise of Civilization	Main Idea Activity 1.2
Homework Practice Online	English Audio Summary 1.2
	Spanish Audio Summary 1.2
	REV Section 2 Review, p. 15

internet connect

HRW ONLINE RESOURCES
> GO TO: go.hrw.com
> Then type in a keyword.

TEACHER HOME PAGE
> KEYWORD: SP3 Teacher

CHAPTER INTERNET ACTIVITIES
> KEYWORD: SP3 WH1

Choose an activity to:
- analyze artifacts from an archaeological site.
- compare and contrast a modern calendar used in the United States with calendars of different cultures.
- list different divisions of labor in modern society.

CHAPTER ENRICHMENT LINKS
> KEYWORD: SP3 CH1

ONLINE ASSESSMENT
> **Homework Practice**
> KEYWORD: SP3 HP1
> **Standardized Test Prep**
> KEYWORD: SP3 STP1
> **Rubrics**
> KEYWORD: SS Rubrics

ONLINE MAPS, CHARTS, AND GRAPHS
> KEYWORD: SP3 MCG

CONTENT UPDATES
> KEYWORD: SS Content Updates

HOLT PRESENTATION MAKER
> KEYWORD: SP3 PPT1

ONLINE READING SUPPORT
> KEYWORD: SS Strategies

CURRENT EVENTS
> KEYWORD: S3 Current Events

Meeting Individual Needs

Ability Levels

Level 1 Basic level activities designed for all students encountering new material

Level 2 Intermediate level activities designed for average students

Level 3 Challenging activities designed for honors and gifted and talented students

English Language Learners These activities address the needs of students with Limited English Proficiency.

Chapter Review and Assessment

IC Vocabulary Activity 1

Global Skill Builder CD–ROM

HRW Web Site

REV Chapter 1 Tutorial for Students, Parents, Mentors, and Peers

REV Chapter 1 Review, pp. 16–17

A Chapter 1 Test Generator (on the One-Stop Planner)

A Chapter 1 Test (Form A or B)

A Alternative Assessment Handbook

A Chapter 1 Test for English Language Learners and Special-Needs Students

Build on What You Know

Ask students to answer the following questions:

What basic things do all humans share? What do people need to advance beyond simple survival?
Consider:

- the necessities of life
- the reasons that people form groups
- the role of technology in human survival and progress

How might early humans have met these needs?
Consider:

- the interaction between humans and their environments
- geographic factors that help to shape human standards of living
- scientific discoveries and technological innovations that enable humans to gain control of their surroundings

EXPLORING THE TIME LINE

GLOBAL EVENTS

internet connect

go.hrw.com

TOPIC: Early Human Settlement

GO TO: go.hrw.com

KEYWORD: SP3 WH1

Have students access the Internet through the HRW Go site to conduct research on the geographic patterns and factors of early human settlement. Then ask students to compose an informative report that details how geographic conditions influenced where early humans settled and how they met basic needs such as food and shelter. Students' reports should include appropriate examples and evidence drawn from their research.

CHAPTER 1

3,700,000 B.C.–1200 B.C.

The Emergence of Civilization

Prehistoric cave painting from Lascaux Cave, France

c. 1,800,000 B.C.
Global Events
Early humans migrate from Africa to Asia.

c. 3,400,000 B.C.
Global Events
The Isthmus of Panama forms as a land bridge linking the Americas.

c. 500,000 B.C.–300,000 B.C.
Science and Technology
People are using fire.

c. 33,000 B.C.
The Arts
Cro-Magnon people create cave paintings.

4,000,000 B.C. | **500,000 B.C.** | **30,000 B.C.**

c. 3,700,000 B.C.
Daily Life
Wandering Australopithecus leave footprints in volcanic ash, proving to modern anthropologists that early hominids walked upright.

c. 2,500,000 B.C.
Science and Technology
The first stone tools appear.

c. 400,000 B.C.–100,000 B.C.
Daily Life
The first *Homo sapiens* appear.

Anthropologist Mary Leakey measures prehistoric footprints near Olduvai Gorge, Tanzania.

Neolithic stone axes and carved ivory tool

Build on What You Know

History is the record of events since people first developed writing, about 5,000 years ago. People, however, have lived on earth for far more than 5,000 years. The period of time before writing was developed is called prehistory. In this chapter, you will learn about prehistory—how and why we study it, how the prehistoric record has helped to shape the present, and how prehistoric humans gradually developed the first civilized societies. You will learn, too, how and why our understanding of prehistory is continually changing as a result of scientific discoveries, new tools, and new ways of thinking about the past.

What's Your Opinion?

To help students create their Themes Journal entries, provide the following examples of appropriate **agree**/**disagree** *statements.*

Culture

Agree The development of culture enables people to live and work together based on cooperation and shared values.

Disagree Biological and physical differences and the human brain do more than culture to set humans apart from other creatures.

Geography

Agree When humans seek a place to settle, geography and climate are not of primary importance.

Disagree Physical environment is the most important factor in determining whether a civilization develops.

Economics

Agree Farming is an economic activity fundamental to all civilizations.

Disagree Manufacturing and trade form the basis of all human economies.

Cave painting of women gathering grain

Figures of horseriders found in what is now Austria

c. 9000 B.C.
The Arts
People in what is now France paint and engrave pebbles.

c. 15,500 B.C.–10,000 B.C.
Business and Finance
Industries develop using bone materials.

c. 8000 B.C.
Global Events
The last Ice Age ends.

c. 8000 B.C.
Science and Technology
Agriculture emerges.

c. 4000 B.C.
Daily Life
People in what is now Russia begin to domesticate the horse.

c. 1200 B.C.
Science and Technology
The Iron Age begins in southwestern Asia.

15,000 B.C.	10,000 B.C.	5000 B.C.	1000 B.C.

c. 15,000 B.C.
Global Events
Humans now inhabit Africa, Europe, Asia, North America, and Australia.

c. 8000 B.C.
Daily Life
Cities gradually begin to develop.

c. 8350 B.C.–7350 B.C.
Politics
Jericho, the first walled town, is established.

c. 2700 B.C.
The Arts
The first literary texts are produced.

c. 3100 B.C.
Politics
The first known king of Egypt, Menes, rules.

Ruins at the site of ancient Jericho

EXPLORING THE TIME LINE

GLOBAL EVENTS

Tell students that artistic expression seems to have been a part of human culture since prehistoric times. Ancient cave paintings give us valuable clues about prehistoric life, attitudes, and events. Have students look at the image of a prehistoric cave painting on page 4 and share their impressions of it. Tell students that through the ages art has evolved from stone carvings to oil paintings to digital images.

Critical Thinking

Why do you think humans continue to express themselves through art? Give significant examples of art that demonstrates an artistic ideal or reflects the history of the culture in which it is produced.

ANSWER: Students might suggest that humans use art to help them relate to and understand the world around them, as well as to express emotions and convey their ideas to others. They might mention cave paintings, impressionism, or modern art.

What's Your Opinion?

Do you **agree** *or* **disagree** *with the following statements? Support your point of view in your journal.*

Culture The most important factor that sets humans apart from other creatures is the development of culture.

Geography Physical environment has little, if any, influence on the development of a civilization.

Economics Farming and the domestication of animals are the most basic of human economic activities.

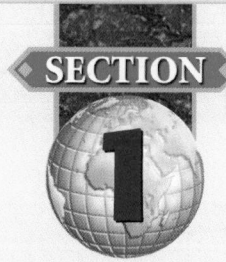

SECTION 1

OBJECTIVES

1 **Describe how anthropologists, archaeologists, historians, and geographers study prehistory.**

2 **Identify the major achievements of Neanderthal and Cro-Magnon peoples.**

3 **Explain the important changes caused by the Neolithic agricultural revolution.**

SECTION 1 RESOURCES

REPRODUCIBLE RESOURCES

▶ Guided Reading Strategy 1.1
▶ Graphic Organizer Activity 1
▶ Geography Activity 1
▶ Readings in World History 1–4
▶ Hands-on History Activity 1
▶ Creative Teaching Strategy 1

TECHNOLOGY RESOURCES

▶ One-Stop Planner 1.1
▶ Holt Researcher: World History: Mary Leakey
▶ CNN Presents World Cultures: Yesterday and Today Segment 1
▶ World History Teaching Transparencies: Geography and History 1; Art and History 1

REINFORCEMENT, REVIEW, AND ASSESSMENT

▶ Section 1 Review, p. 10
▶ Daily Quiz 1.1
▶ Main Idea Activity 1.1
▶ English Audio Summary 1.1
▶ Spanish Audio Summary 1.1

SECTION 1

READ TO DISCOVER

❶ How do anthropologists, archaeologists, historians, and geographers study prehistory?
❷ What were the achievements of Neanderthal and Cro-Magnon peoples?
❸ What important changes did the Neolithic agricultural revolution cause?

DEFINE

hominids
artifacts
culture
limited evidence
nomads
agriculture
domestication
hunter-gatherers

IDENTIFY

Donald Johanson
Lucy
Mary Leakey
Neanderthals
Cro-Magnons
Neolithic agricultural revolution

WHY IT MATTERS TODAY

How scientists study and draw conclusions from prehistoric remains and artifacts affects our understanding of humans and of our place on Earth. Use CNN or other **current event** sources to explore recent discoveries by anthropologists, archaeologists, historians, and geographers. Record your findings in your journal.

CNNstudentNews.com

🔊 LET'S GET STARTED!

As students enter the classroom, ask them to look at the picture of the archaeologists on page 6. Explain to them that anthropologists, archaeologists, historians, and geographers study the objects of earlier civilizations. Ask students what types of tools they think archaeologists might use and what kinds of difficulties they might encounter. *(Students might list digging tools and guess that archaeologists might encounter difficulties based on the geographic and environmental conditions of sites under study.)* Tell students that in Section 1 they will learn how anthropologists, archaeologists, historians, and geographers have contributed to our understanding of the human record.

Prehistoric Peoples

The Main Idea
The cultures of early peoples gradually changed as humans adapted to environmental shifts.

The Story Continues *Many researchers have long believed that human beings originated in Africa. In 1974 a team of researchers went out seeking evidence that might support this claim. In November of that year, in a place called Hadar in Ethiopia, the team found some very convincing evidence—the oldest humanlike skeleton discovered up to that time.*

Exploring Prehistory

Scientists have discovered much about prehistory by using scientific methods. For example, scientists called anthropologists study the remains of the skeletons of **hominids.** Hominids include humans as well as earlier humanlike creatures. By studying their remains, anthropologists can figure out what early hominids looked like. They can also determine how long the hominids lived.

Other scientists, called archaeologists, dig into ancient settlements to find objects made and used by early hominids. These objects—including tools, clothing, works of art, weapons, and toys—are **artifacts.** By studying artifacts, archaeologists learn about early peoples and their cultures. **Culture** is the set of beliefs, knowledge, and patterns of living that a group of people develops. Anthropologists and archaeologists use advanced technology to date remains and artifacts. Because artifacts give **limited evidence,** however, anthropologists, archaeologists, historians, and geographers must make educated guesses about the prehistoric world. Using their knowledge of geography and climate, scientists draw conclusions. They make judgments about changes that took place many thousands of years ago to describe some of the ways the first human beings lived.

Anthropologists have found evidence that humanlike creatures appeared on Earth millions of years ago. In 1974 in Ethiopia, a team led by **Donald Johanson** found the remains of a hominid skeleton.

Archaeologists carefully unearth artifacts in "digs" such as this one.

LEVEL 1: Ask a volunteer to read aloud the first two paragraphs under "Exploring Prehistory" on page 6. Then ask students to explain what anthropologists and archaeologists do. (*Anthropologists study the remains of the skeletons of hominids. Archaeologists dig into ancient settlements and study the artifacts they find.*) Have another volunteer read the next paragraph before asking students to describe how scientists date remains and artifacts. (*They use advanced technology but must also make educated guesses because artifacts give limited evidence.*) **ENGLISH LANGUAGE LEARNERS**

internet connect

Internet Activity: go.hrw.com
TOPIC: Archaeology **KEYWORD: SP3 WH1**

Have students access the Internet through the HRW Go site to learn more about archaeological finds. Have students select artifacts or archaeological sites that interest them and write a short informative article that could be published in the student science magazine. Have them describe their topic in detail: What is it? Where is it located? Who created it? If possible, have students include illustrations with their article.

The bones Johanson found belonged to a female hominid who may have lived 3 million years ago. Johanson and his team named the skeleton **Lucy** after the Beatles song "Lucy in the Sky with Diamonds." Johanson later described his remarkable discovery.

History Makers Speak 〝I spent the morning of November 30 scanning the ground for fossils . . . At midday, under a murderous sun and in temperatures topping 100 degrees, we reluctantly headed back toward camp. Along the way I glanced over my right shoulder. Light glinted off a bone. I knelt down for a closer look. This time I knew at once I was looking at a hominid elbow. . . . Everywhere we looked on the slope around us we saw more bones lying on the surface. Here was the hominid skeleton . . .〞

Donald Johanson, from *Ancestors: In Search of Human Origins,*
by Donald Johanson, Lenora Johanson, and Blake Edgar

Other researchers added to the findings of Johanson's team. In the late 1970s in Tanzania, anthropologist **Mary Leakey** found parts of a skeleton dating back about 3.7 million years. Like Lucy, this hominid belonged to a group called Australopithecus (aw·stray·lo·PI·thuh·kuhs), or "southern ape." These hominids walked upright, like humans. Other hominids lived in East Africa 2 million years ago. Tools made from chipped stone have been found near their remains.

The period of prehistory that begins with the development of stone tools is called the Stone Age. It began about 2.5 million years ago. Almost all the artifacts that have been found from this time were made of stone. The oldest part is called the Old Stone, or Paleolithic (pay·lee·uh·LI·thik), Age. The word *paleolithic* comes from two Greek words: *palaios* ("ancient") and *lithos* ("stone"). The Old Stone Age lasted for more than 2 million years—until about 12,000 years ago.

✔ **READING CHECK: Finding the Main Idea** What limited evidence did Donald Johanson and Mary Leakey examine to learn about early hominids? skeletal remains, artifacts

Early Humans

There is limited evidence from prehistory about early humans. Therefore, many scientists disagree about what conclusions can be drawn about them. Future discoveries may change the ideas that many scientists hold today.

The first people. From studying bones, anthropologists can describe what the first humans looked like. These individuals had powerful jaws, receding chins, low foreheads, and heavy eyebrow ridges. Scientists believe they sometimes used caves as shelters. They probably ate seeds, fruits, nuts, and other plants. Eventually, they hunted—first small and then large animals. To hunt successfully, they had to make tools, work together, and communicate.

As humans became successful hunters, they migrated, or moved over great distances, in search of food. Over many generations, early people migrated from Africa to Asia. At some point, probably between 100,000 and 400,000 years ago, a new human species, *Homo sapiens,* appeared. *Homo sapiens* may have developed first in Africa, then spread to Europe and Asia. All people living today belong to this species.

The Ice Age. Several times within the last 1.7 million years, Earth has had periods of extremely cold weather. Each cold period lasted from 20,000 to about 140,000 years. Together these periods are called the Ice Age. Scientists believe we live in a warm era that began about 10,000 years ago. That is when the last period of the Ice Age ended.

Analyzing Primary Sources

Drawing Conclusions What evidence might Donald Johanson have used to draw his conclusion that the bones were those of a hominid? skeletal remains

HISTORY MAKER
Lucy
(c. 3,000,000 B.C.)

After examining the hominid skeleton called Lucy, researchers concluded that the young female had walked upright, like humans do. Scientists are still not certain whether modern humans are related to Lucy and Australopithecines. An upright posture, however, leaves the hands free to use tools. Many scientists believe that this was a major step in early human development. **What evidence indicates Lucy might be related to modern humans?**

History Maker

MARY LEAKEY. Mary Leakey knew she wanted to be an anthropologist at age 11 when she visited a Cro-Magnon rock shelter containing early modern human fossils. As an adult, Leakey became an expert in early human technology and stone tools. She participated in numerous pioneering excavations in East Africa and elsewhere.

ACTIVITY: Have students find out more about Mary Leakey. Ask them to create a time line that shows her major finds.

Interdisciplinary Connection

STRATIGRAPHY. One way to verify artifacts' ages is through stratigraphy. It assumes that objects found in deeper layers of earth are older than those found above them. Stratigraphy is not very exact, however. Layers of earth can shift, and objects within them could range in age.

Critical Thinking

How might an archaeologist rely on stratigraphy to date a site or an artifact?

ANSWER: Archaeologists could use their knowledge about the age of layers of earth to guide them in their digging.

HISTORY MAKER ANSWER
her upright posture, structure of hands, feet, skull

ALL LEVELS: Tell students that a significant part of trying to understand the lives of prehistoric people is understanding the environment in which they probably lived. Using the information under "The Ice Age" on pages 7–8, point out the extreme challenges presented by the environment for many thousands of years. Help students further explore what scientists have learned about prehistoric peoples by having them complete a Venn diagram comparing and contrasting the Neanderthal and Cro-Magnon peoples. **ENGLISH LANGUAGE LEARNERS**

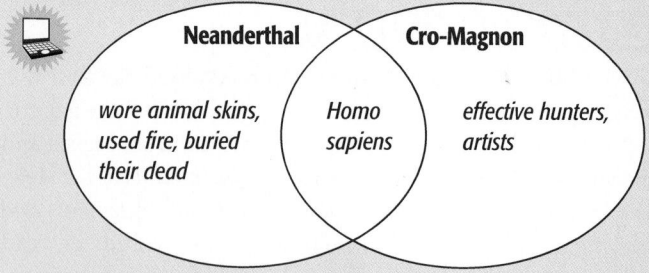

Neanderthal — *wore animal skins, used fire, buried their dead* | *Homo sapiens* | Cro-Magnon — *effective hunters, artists*

Science, Technology & Society

Hearths have been discovered with the remains of Peking man, who lived approximately 500,000 years ago. With the advent of controlled fire, prehistoric people apparently learned to cook their meat, making it easier to chew and eliminating the need for a powerful jaw and large teeth. The mastery of fire also allowed people to live in colder parts of the world.

Critical Thinking

Ask students how hominids may have learned to master fire.

ANSWER: Lightning may have started a fire, and hominids learned how to keep it burning.

WHAT IF? ANSWER

People and animals might not have migrated to the Americas. Prehistoric species of animals might have survived, and humans might not have learned to use fire or other survival techniques as quickly. Finally, Earth's geography would have been vastly different without the chiseling and grinding effects of glaciers.

CONNECTING TO ART ANSWER

Some prehistoric peoples had an appreciation of beauty similar to ours, and some groups had time for artistic creation.

What If? If there had been no Ice Age, how might prehistory have been different?

Holt Researcher
go.hrw.com
KEYWORD: Holt Researcher
FreeFind: Mary Leakey
After reading more about Mary Leakey on the Holt Researcher, draw a sketch of one of her findings and explain what conclusions she reached from it.

CONNECTING TO
Art

Sculpture: Cro-Magnon Carving

A Cro-Magnon artist in what is now France carved this ivory head of a woman thousands of years ago, during the Old Stone Age. From artifacts such as this, we learn that some prehistoric peoples had an appreciation of beauty, as we do. We also learn that some groups had time for activities other than looking for food and making tools.

Understanding the Arts

What can we learn from this Cro-Magnon art?

During the cold periods, ice covered a large part of Earth's surface. Sea levels dropped because so much seawater was locked in large ice caps. As sea levels fell, ridges that had been underwater were uncovered, forming land bridges between some regions that are today separated by water. Humans and animals migrated over some of these land bridges. However, only when prehistoric people learned to make fire and clothing could they settle in colder regions.

Neanderthal people. In caves in Europe and Southwest Asia, anthropologists have found remains of early *Homo sapiens* called **Neanderthals** (nee·AN·duhr·tawls). Neanderthals lived about 35,000 to 130,000 years ago, during the Old Stone Age. They wore animal skins as clothing and used fire for warmth and for cooking. Their tools were more efficient than the tools of earlier hominids.

Neanderthals also differed from earlier hominids in another important way— they buried their dead. What is more, they buried meat and tools with the dead. Scientists think this shows that Neanderthals believed in some form of life after death. Belief in an afterlife is basic to many of the world's religions.

Like earlier hominids, Neanderthals disappeared. No one knows why. Perhaps a new period of the Ice Age began, producing a cold, hostile environment. Or perhaps another group of *Homo sapiens*—stronger or more mentally alert—destroyed or interbred with them.

Cro-Magnon people. About 35,000 years ago, another kind of *Homo sapiens*— the **Cro-Magnons**—appeared in Europe. These new people made even better tools and weapons. Their spear-throwers, for example, made them effective hunters. Cro-Magnons were thus well equipped to survive.

Scientists know something about Cro-Magnons from their artwork. Paintings of the animals they hunted have been found. On cave walls in Spain and southern France, bulls toss their heads. Wounded bison chase a hunter. Long horses leap majestically. Scientists are not sure, however, why Cro-Magnons painted such scenes. The art might be the story of a hunt. It could be a "textbook" to teach young hunters. Or it may be a creation myth.

By about 20,000 years ago, humans had migrated to northern Asia and Australia. This movement of people into new areas marks humans' ability to adapt—to live and succeed in many different environments.

The Cro-Magnons lived on Earth for many thousands of years. By about 10,000 years ago, however, Cro-Magnons as distinct types of humans no longer existed. In appearance, people looked basically like they do today.

✔ **READING CHECK: Summarizing** What important advances did Neanderthal and Cro-Magnon peoples make? fire, clothing, better tools, artwork

The Agricultural Revolution

The Middle Stone Age and the New Stone Age followed the Old Stone Age. The dates for each age vary in different regions of the world. Generally, however, the Middle Stone Age lasted until about 10,000 years ago. The New Stone Age lasted to about 4,000 years ago. Each age is marked by a new level of tools and other artifacts. In addition, the New Stone Age is marked by a revolutionary human activity.

LEVEL 3: Have students create illustrated time lines with known facts about life during the Paleolithic, Mesolithic, and Neolithic time periods. They should include several appropriate illustrations to help clarify advancements in the lives of early humans during each time period. Have several volunteers share their time lines. Point out that the Neolithic agricultural revolution was one of the most significant turning points in human history. Ask students to explain why the rise of agriculture was so important to human development. (*It allowed people to establish permanent settlements and produce a surplus of food, paving the way for the development of civilizations.*)

HOMEWORK Assign each student to one time period: Paleolithic, Mesolithic, or Neolithic. Have each student develop a brief oral presentation about his or her time period. Encourage students to include environmental and physical challenges faced by people of their time periods and to describe the technological advances made during the era to meet these challenges.

CLOSE

Discuss the change from hunting and gathering to agriculture, including economic, social, and geographic factors. How did a hunter-gatherer society differ from an agricultural society?

The Middle Stone Age is also called the Mesolithic Age (from the Greek word *mesos,* meaning "middle"). During the Mesolithic Age, the use of the bow and arrow, fishhooks, fish spears, and harpoons made from bones and antlers was widespread. People tamed dogs, which were useful in hunting smaller animals. Humans also hollowed out logs to make dugout canoes so they could fish in deep water and cross rivers.

The New Stone Age is also called the Neolithic Age (from the Greek word *neos,* meaning "new"). During the Neolithic Age, technology continued to improve. In earlier ages, people chipped stone to produce an edge or a point. In the Neolithic Age, people shaped stone tools by polishing or grinding. They also discovered ways to make tools from many kinds of stone as well as from wood. With such new methods and materials, people were able to make more specialized tools. Even more important changes occurred during the New Stone Age. Earlier people had been **nomads,** wandering from place to place in search of food. Some Neolithic people, however, began settling in permanent villages. They began to develop **agriculture**—the raising of crops for food. They practiced **domestication**—the taming of animals such as cattle, goats, sheep, and pigs.

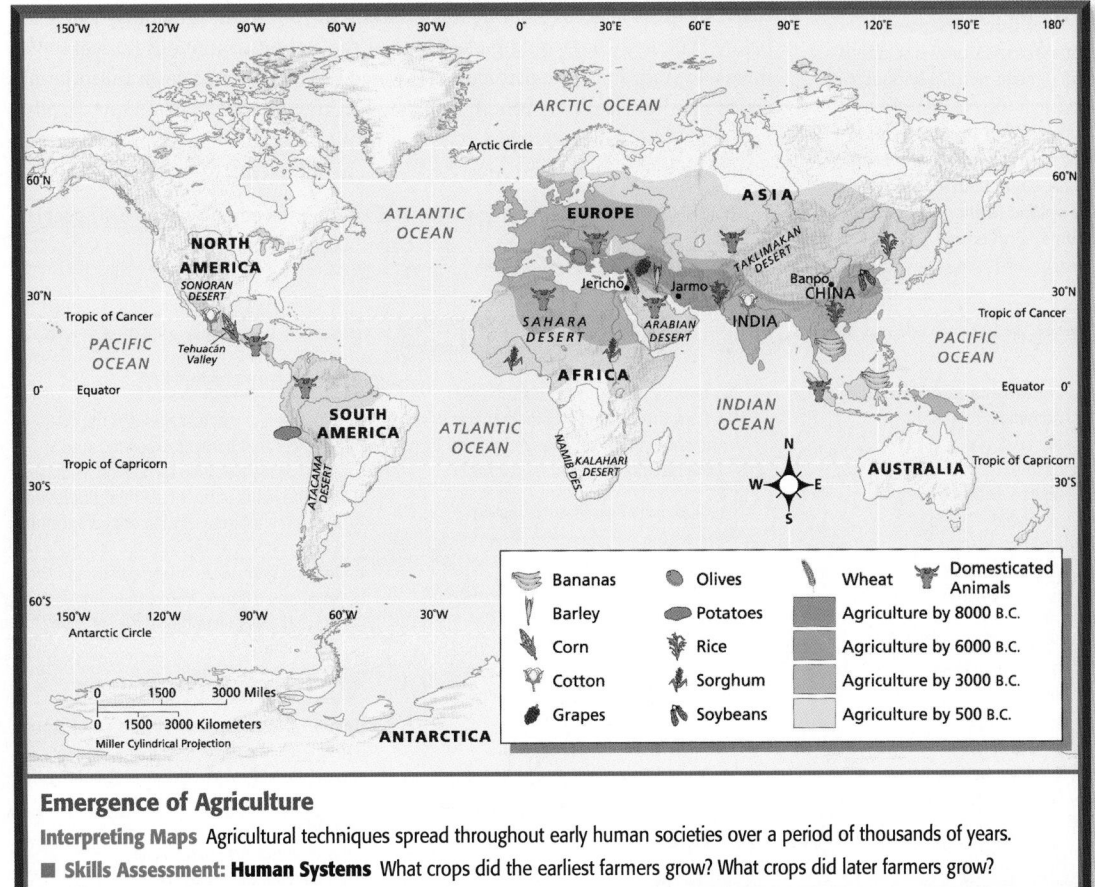

Emergence of Agriculture

Interpreting Maps Agricultural techniques spread throughout early human societies over a period of thousands of years.

■ **Skills Assessment: Human Systems** What crops did the earliest farmers grow? What crops did later farmers grow?

Culture

Many cultures throughout history—including some American Indian and African cultures—have held beliefs about life after death, as evidenced by their burial rituals. Like the Neanderthal, people of such cultures buried food, tools, and luxury items with their dead, presumably for use by the deceased in the afterlife. In modern American society, the majority of people are buried or cremated following religious or secular ceremonies of farewell.

Critical Thinking

Ask students to consider modern American burial customs. What parts, if any, of the typical American burial ritual may have been practiced by our ancestors?

ANSWER: Students might point out that we tend to bury our dead dressed in their best, with jewelry and beloved objects to accompany them into the grave.

MAP ANSWER

earliest farmers: rice, barley
later farmers: potatoes, corn

Technology Resources
 Online Maps, Charts, and Graphs: Early Agriculture in Asia

REVIEW

Have students complete the Section 1 Review on p. 10.

ASSESS

Have students complete Daily Quiz 1.1. As Alternative Assessment, you may want to use the Venn diagram or time line exercise in this section's lessons.

RETEACH

Have students complete Main Idea Activity for English Language Learners and Special-Needs Students 1.1. Then have students list the main ideas of each heading and subheading in the section. **ENGLISH LANGUAGE LEARNERS**

EXTEND

Organize the class into four groups and have each group use the process of historical inquiry to research a method of dating archaeological finds: radiocarbon dating, potassium-argon dating, dendrochronology, or stratigraphy. Have each group teach the rest of the students about the method it researched, using a visual based on written or statistical information. **BLOCK SCHEDULING, COOPERATIVE LEARNING**

VISUAL RECORD ANSWER

Students might point out that hunter-gatherers moved around; therefore they had no permanent villages.

SECTION 1 REVIEW ANSWERS

❶ Define
- hominids, p. 6
- artifacts, p. 6
- culture, p. 6
- limited evidence, p. 6
- nomads, p. 9
- agriculture, p. 9
- domestication, p. 9
- hunter-gatherers, p. 10

❷ Identify
- Donald Johanson, p. 6
- Lucy, p. 7
- Mary Leakey, p. 7
- Neanderthals, p. 8
- Cro-Magnons, p. 8
- Neolithic agricultural revolution, p. 10

❸ hunter-gatherers turned to farming; hunting-and-gathering settlements became farming settlements; development of cities

❹ a. advantages: shift from food gathering to food producing, growth of cities; disadvantages: dependence on weather, threats of crop failure

b. Australopithecus, Neanderthal, Cro-Magnon

c. They buried their dead. Cro-Magnons had more advanced tools and weapons, fire, and clothing.

❺ Scientists use technology to date artifacts. They must make educated guesses and draw conclusions.

10

INTERPRETING THE VISUAL RECORD

A Neolithic settlement
Archaeologists have discovered the remains of mud-brick houses and shrines at Çatalhüyük in Turkey. *What evidence would tell archaeologists that such a village must have been home to settled farmers rather than hunter-gatherers?*

The development of agriculture changed the basic way people lived. In prehistoric times people were **hunter-gatherers.** Men went out to hunt animals. Women remained near the campsite to care for children. Women and children gathered plants and fruit for food. Perhaps it was a woman who first realized that seeds could be planted and grown. The knowledge that grains and other plants grew from seeds was a major breakthrough in human progress.

Over time people learned to raise wheat, barley, rice, and millet. They learned to make furrows in the earth—probably first using sharpened sticks—in which to plant seeds. The invention of the plow and the use of fertilizer marked major steps in the human record. The shift from food gathering to food producing was an achievement of the greatest importance. It revolutionized human life, which is why we call this long process the **Neolithic agricultural revolution.**

Between about 9000 B.C. and about 5000 B.C., many hunting-and-gathering settlements throughout the world turned to farming. Some grew larger and more complex. In fact, many Neolithic villages developed into small cities. For example, in Jericho, on the west bank of the Jordan River, scientists have found evidence of a Neolithic walled town that may date from before 8000 B.C. That would make it one of the earliest continuous human settlements. In Iraq, archaeologists have discovered the remains of a town called Jarmo, which may have had 100 or more inhabitants in about 6500 B.C. In Turkey, scientists have dug out Çatalhüyük (chah-TUHL-hoo-YOOHK). This town, which may have had many hundreds of residents, flourished from about 6700 B.C. to about 5600 B.C.

✔ **READING CHECK: Identifying Cause and Effect** What advances were early peoples able to make as a result of the Neolithic agricultural revolution? shift from food gathering to food producing; growth of cities

SECTION 1 REVIEW

1. Define and explain the significance:
hominids
artifacts
culture
limited evidence
nomads
agriculture
domestication
hunter-gatherers

2. Identify and explain the significance:
Donald Johanson
Lucy
Mary Leakey
Neanderthals
Cro-Magnons
Neolithic agricultural revolution

Homework Practice Online
keyword: SP3 HP1

3. Identifying Cause and Effect
Copy the concept web below. Use it to show the main changes caused by the Neolithic agricultural revolution.

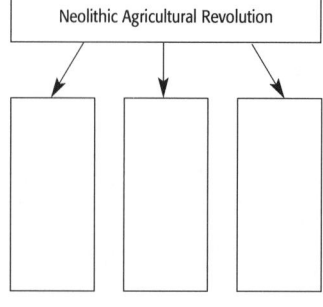

Neolithic Agricultural Revolution

4. Finding the Main Idea

a. What were the advantages and the disadvantages that humans experienced as a result of the Neolithic agricultural revolution?

b. List the kinds of hominids that developed over time in order of their appearance on Earth.

c. In what ways were Neanderthals and Cro-Magnons different from earlier hominids? In what ways were they different from each other?

5. Writing and Critical Thinking

Drawing Conclusions How do anthropologists, archaeologists, historians, and geographers draw conclusions about the prehistoric world from limited evidence?
Consider:
- the evidence researchers use
- the limits of that evidence
- the information such evidence provides

SECTION 2

OBJECTIVES

1 **Identify the three main characteristics shared by civilizations.**

2 **Explain what other two characteristics may be shared by civilizations.**

3 **Describe the other characteristics and achievements that marked the first river valley civilizations.**

LET'S GET STARTED!

As students enter the classroom, ask them to think about the economic, social, and geographic factors that define a civilization. Have them make a list of the things they think characterize a civilization. *(Students might mention groups of people living together and some form of government.)* Tell students that in Section 2 they will learn about the development of civilizations.

SECTION 2

READ TO DISCOVER

1 What three main characteristics are shared by civilizations?
2 What two other characteristics may be shared by civilizations?
3 What other characteristics and achievements marked the first river valley civilizations?

DEFINE

civilization
irrigation
division of labor
artisans
cultural diffusion

WHY IT MATTERS TODAY

Civilizations today share basic characteristics with the first civilizations. Use **CNN Student News.com** or other **current event** sources to explore a modern civilization. Record your findings in your journal.

CNN Student News.com

The Foundations of Civilization

The Main Idea
As early settlements grew, they began to show the characteristics of major civilizations.

The Story Continues *By the end of the New Stone Age, people had learned to make tools and weapons, use fire, create works of art, tame animals, and grow food. Many had established permanent settlements. The stage was set for the next level of development.*

Characteristics of a Civilization

Not all people had established permanent settlements by the end of the New Stone Age. Those who lived in climates unsuitable for farming continued their old ways of hunting and gathering. Those in permanent settlements, however, began to advance more rapidly. The settlements in four specific regions were particularly important for later human development. These four regions were (1) the Nile River valley in Africa, (2) the valley of the Tigris and Euphrates (yoo·FRAY·teez) Rivers in southwestern Asia, (3) the Indus River valley in southern Asia, and (4) the Huang, or Yellow, River valley in eastern Asia.

In these four river valleys, civilizations first developed. A **civilization** is a complex culture that has at least three characteristics. The first is that people are able to produce surplus, or extra, food. The second is that people establish large towns or cities with some form of government. The third is that people perform different jobs, instead of each person doing all kinds of work.

Surplus food and irrigation. The valleys of the Nile, Tigris and Euphrates, Indus, and Huang share a common feature. Their rivers rise and flood the valleys during periods of heavy rain. Except for these rainy periods, little if any rain falls. During much of the year, the climate is warm or hot.

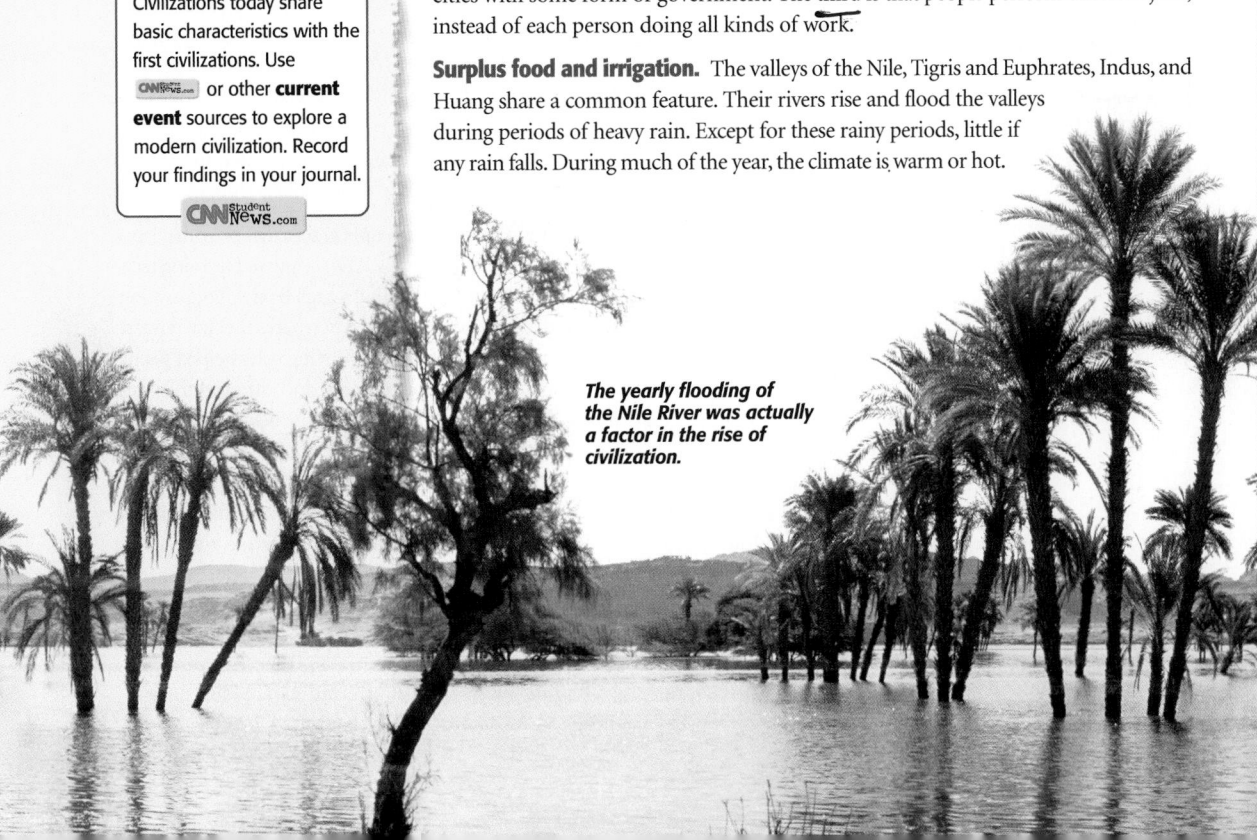

The yearly flooding of the Nile River was actually a factor in the rise of civilization.

SECTION 2 RESOURCES

REPRODUCIBLE RESOURCES

▶ Guided Reading Strategy 1.2

TECHNOLOGY RESOURCES

▶ One-Stop Planner 1.2
▶ World History and Cultures Video Program 1: The Rise of Civilization
▶ Homework Practice Online

REINFORCEMENT, REVIEW, AND ASSESSMENT

▶ Section 2 Review, p. 15
▶ Daily Quiz 1.2
▶ Main Idea Activity 1.2
▶ English Audio Summary 1.2
▶ Spanish Audio Summary 1.2

TEACH OBJECTIVE 1

 LEVEL 1: Have students list the three main characteristics shared by civilizations. *(surplus food, government, division of labor)* Ask students to write a short paragraph explaining why each characteristic is necessary. *(Answers will vary. Surplus food allows the population to grow. Government regulates people's behavior and helps to ensure order and security. A division of labor allows people to specialize in different jobs.)* **ENGLISH LANGUAGE LEARNERS**

TEACH OBJECTIVE 2

ALL LEVELS: Ask students what other two accomplishments are characteristic of civilizations. *(a calendar and some form of writing)* Have students draw a two-column chart, with one of these characteristics at the top of each column. Then, ask students to list the reasons why each characteristic is important in a civilization. *(Students might mention that a calendar was important to river valley civilizations because it told people when the yearly floods would occur. A system of writing allowed people to communicate and pass on ideas more easily.)* **ENGLISH LANGUAGE LEARNERS**

Geography

The climate around the Nile provided early Egyptians with ideal conditions for farming. The two main tributaries of the Nile, the Blue Nile and the White Nile, received heavy rainfall during the summer. When the Nile overflowed its banks, it flooded the Nile Valley and Delta. In October and November the water receded and the remaining moisture in the soil sustained the crops until harvest.

Critical Thinking

Ask students why the seasonal cycle of the Nile was ideal for farming.

ANSWER: Students might note that the Nile floods brought essential water to growing crops, yet receded in time to allow harvest.

MAP ANSWERS
1. 20° N and 40° N

2. They were located along rivers.

River Valley Civilizations

Interpreting Maps The earliest civilizations arose across Asia and Africa.

■ **Skills Assessment:**
1. Locate Between which degrees of latitude did the Indus, Nile, Tigris-Euphrates, and Huang river valleys lie?
2. Human Systems What geographic features did the four major civilization areas share?

The climate and flooding greatly influenced the development of civilizations in these river valleys. Somehow farmers had to get water to their crops during the dry season. At some point, farmers in each valley learned to dig ditches and canals to move water from the river to their fields. Thus they developed the first systems of **irrigation.** Farmers also built dikes to keep the rivers within their banks during the rainy season. These improved farming techniques led to more and better food, which then led to increases in population. As the population grew, some of the villages became cities.

Cities, government, and labor. The large number of people in the cities provided labor to build great palaces, temples, and other public buildings. Also, improved farming techniques such as irrigation and flood-control systems required a high level of cooperation. Different forms of leadership emerged to help societies run. These were the first governments. Governments made rules to guide people's behavior. Having rules helped people plan, direct, and regulate their work. Government leaders made and enforced the rules.

As methods of farming improved, fewer people had to work the fields. Some people could specialize in other kinds of work. In other words, there was a **division of labor.** For example, people skilled in making tools could devote their time to such work. They would then trade their products for food. Soon a class of skilled workers, called **artisans,** developed. Other people became merchants and traders. They made their living by buying goods from farmers or artisans and then selling them. Traders not only transported goods to be sold, but also passed along ideas. The spread of ideas and other aspects of culture from one area to another is called **cultural diffusion.**

✔ **READING CHECK: Making Generalizations** In what ways are surplus food, government, and division of labor necessary for advanced civilization? allow improved cooperation and leadership, appearance of skilled workers and trades

LEVEL 3: Organize students into four or five groups to take on the role of a museum committee that is planning an exhibit called "The Dawn of Civilization." Their job is to come up with a list of the types of artifacts they would like to display. Their exhibit should identify and explain the following:

- advances in farming and metalworking
- the rise of governments
- division of labor
- the development of calendars and alphabets

(Students' lists will vary but should include items such as tools and written documents that demonstrate the achievements of early civilizations.) **COOPERATIVE LEARNING**

 HOMEWORK Have students use their textbooks to make a list of facts about the Neolithic agricultural revolution and the economic, social, and geographic factors that led to the growth of the first civilizations in one column of a two-column chart. In the other column, tell them to write any logical conclusion they can draw regarding the significance of each fact in the first column.

Fact	Significance
People began making tools and weapons out of bronze.	*They could work more efficiently with stronger tools, produce surplus food, and make division of labor possible.*

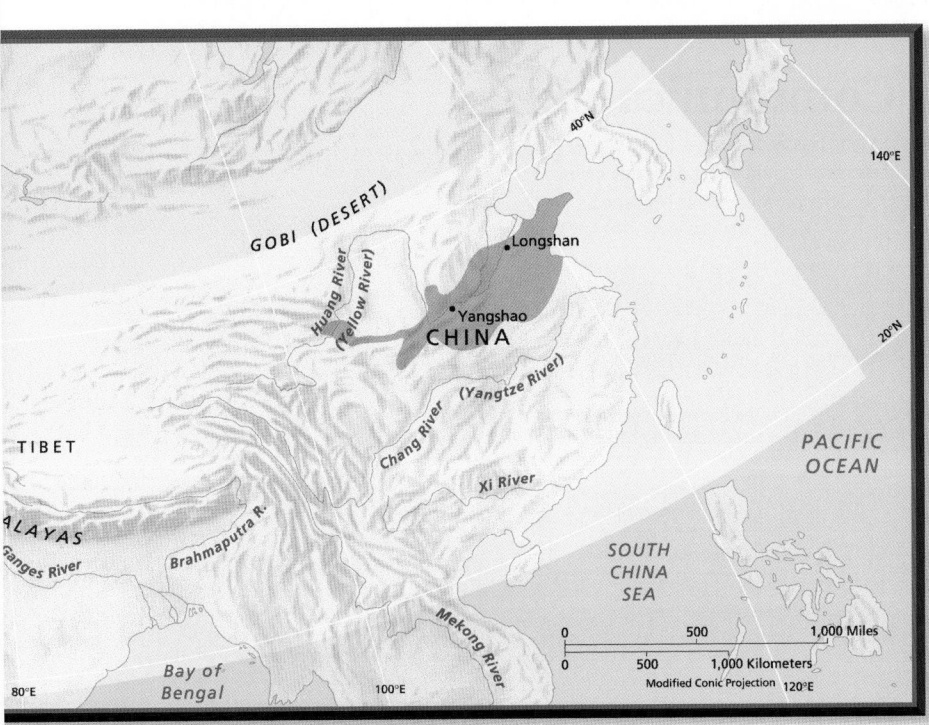

Other Characteristics

In addition to food supply, cities and government, and division of labor, some historians consider two more accomplishments to be characteristics of civilization: a calendar and some form of writing.

Early in their histories, river valley civilizations developed calendars. Because these people farmed, they needed to know when the yearly floods would start and stop. One way was to regard the time from flood to flood as a year. That year was divided according to the phases of the moon. The time from one full moon to the next full moon was a month. This system presented a major problem, however. A lunar month lasts only about 29 ½ days. Thus, 12 lunar months equal 354 days. A solar year, however, has approximately 365 ¼ days. Therefore, the moon-based calendars of the river valley civilizations fell about 11 days short of the time it took Earth to rotate around the sun. As you read about the river valley civilizations in following chapters, you will see how they coped with this problem.

Life in a civilized society is complex. Civilizations in the river valleys were trading goods and developing rules for living and working together. These developments required new forms of communication. People needed a written language to keep and pass on information and ideas. What we now define as writing began around 3000 B.C. The development of writing was a long and complex process. By developing written languages, the early river valley civilizations created records of their cultures and societies. In other words, history had begun.

✔ **READING CHECK: Identifying Cause and Effect** How did the needs of early civilizations lead to the development of calendars and systems of writing? calendar was necessary for agriculture, writing was necessary for increased communication

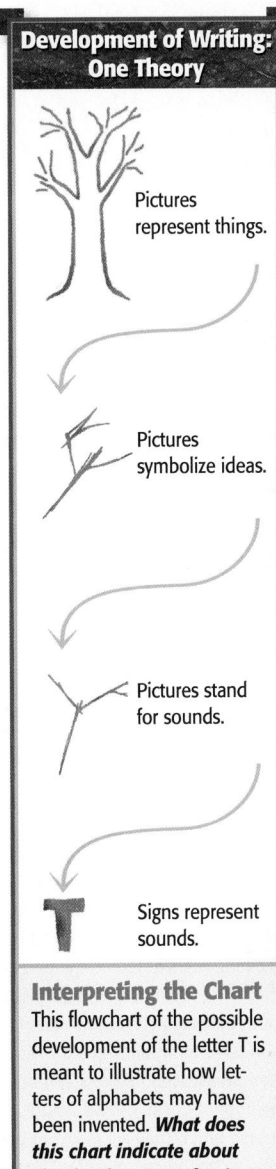

Development of Writing: One Theory

Pictures represent things.

Pictures symbolize ideas.

Pictures stand for sounds.

Signs represent sounds.

Interpreting the Chart
This flowchart of the possible development of the letter T is meant to illustrate how letters of alphabets may have been invented. *What does this chart indicate about the development of written language?*

Daily Life

Pottery discovered by scientists at Mohenjo Daro on the Indus indicates skillful artists capable of showing great detail. Most pottery varied in shape. Pieces were made of pinkish clay with a red slip, and black paint stylized features. Usual themes for pottery included animals, plants, and geometric motifs of intersecting circles and scales. Because scientists have found Indus objects on Mesopotamian sites, they believe trade existed between the two civilizations and have compared the pottery created by both populations.

Critical Thinking

Ask students why a civilization would have developed that was located beyond the flood plain of the Indus River.

ANSWER: Students should suggest that such a location would avoid flooding and destruction of crops and buildings.

INTERPRETING THE CHART ANSWER
It suggests that the characters of a written language evolve from pictures.

SKILL-BUILDING STRATEGIES — Using a Time Line

The History of Communication

The invention of writing was just one step in a long history of changes in the way people communicate. Reading a time line of events in communications history helps us to understand the absolute and relative chronology of when events happened.

Early Advances in Communication

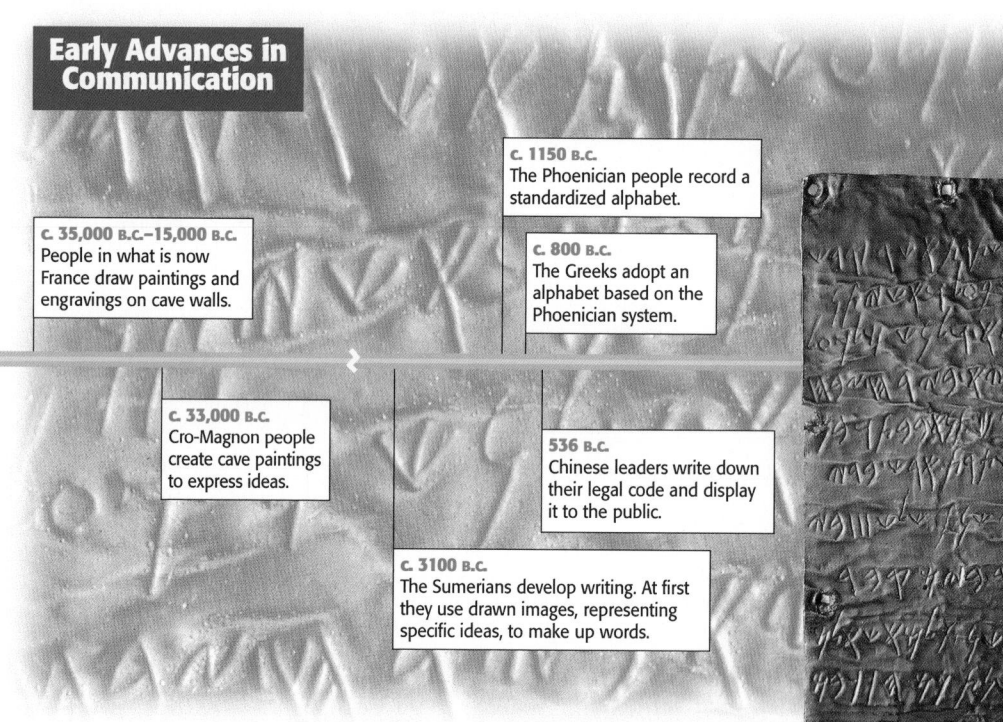

c. 1150 B.C.
The Phoenician people record a standardized alphabet.

c. 35,000 B.C.–15,000 B.C.
People in what is now France draw paintings and engravings on cave walls.

c. 800 B.C.
The Greeks adopt an alphabet based on the Phoenician system.

c. 33,000 B.C.
Cro-Magnon people create cave paintings to express ideas.

536 B.C.
Chinese leaders write down their legal code and display it to the public.

c. 3100 B.C.
The Sumerians develop writing. At first they use drawn images, representing specific ideas, to make up words.

This 7 ½-inch-high gold tablet is inscribed with characters from the Phoenician alphabet. The message details the dedication of a religious shrine to a Phoenician goddess.

Skills Reminder

A time line shows the dates events happened, or their absolute chronology, as well as when events happened relative to each other, or their relative chronology. This book follows a system of dating years based on the traditional date of birth of Jesus Christ. The Muslim, Chinese, Jewish, and Hindu calendars all count the years differently. Years following Jesus's birth are numbered in order. They start with A.D., which stands for the Latin phrase **A**nno **D**omini ("in the year of the Lord" or "since the birth of Christ"). Years before Jesus's birth are numbered in reverse order. They are followed by B.C. ("**B**efore **C**hrist"). The initial c. (for "circa," meaning "approximately") indicates that the exact date is unknown and that the one given is a good estimate.

Skills Practice

❶ Read the time line of major events in the history of communication. Approximately how many years passed between the invention of writing by the Sumerians and the Greek adoption of an alphabet?

❷ What does the passage of time between these two events imply about the development of communication? Based on the other information given, what else does the time line imply about the development of communication?

❸ Using information in your textbook and from other sources, create your own time line of events reflecting a characteristic other than writing that was crucial to the development of early civilizations.

CLOSE

Ask students to write a "recipe" for a civilization using "ingredients" such as agriculture or division of labor.

REVIEW

Have students complete the Section 2 Review on p. 15.

ASSESS

Have students complete Daily Quiz 1.2. As Alternative Assessment, you may want to use the civilization graphic organizer or the museum exercise in this section's lessons.

RETEACH

Have students complete Main Idea Activity for English Language Learners and Special-Needs Students 1.2. Then ask them to write a main idea question and answer for each subsection.

ENGLISH LANGUAGE LEARNERS

EXTEND

Alphabet letters may have evolved from pictures. A picture of a tree began to look like the letter T, which became the first letter of the word *tree*. Have students invent several original letters and create a chart to show how each evolved.

BLOCK SCHEDULING

The River Valley Civilizations

The river valley civilizations moved humans out of the Stone Age. People developed family roles and religious beliefs that related to their farming-based cultures.

The use of metals. More than 6,000 years ago, people in both the Nile and the Tigris-Euphrates river valleys were using copper to make tools and jewelry. In time people learned to make a more useful metal—bronze. A mixture of copper and tin, bronze is harder than copper. People in the Nile and the Tigris-Euphrates river valleys made objects of bronze as early as 5,000 years ago. People in India and China also used bronze at an early date. The invention of bronze tools marked the end of the Stone Age and the beginning of the Bronze Age.

Iron is stronger than copper or bronze. Making iron is a long, difficult process. We do not know when people discovered how to use iron. It may have been discovered separately in several different areas. We do know, however, that about 3,200 years ago people in southwestern Asia had learned to make iron. The Iron Age began.

Family and religion. Women managed the family. They cared for children, prepared food, made clothing, and probably invented pottery and weaving. When agriculture initially developed, women did much of the farming. The rise of goddesses during this time suggests that responsibility for the food supply increased women's authority and independence. However, when the plow was invented and animals were harnessed to pull it, men again became the primary food providers. This change shifted the power women had gained back to men, who continued to be the primary authorities in society.

People believed in many gods and goddesses and in unseen forces of nature. These controlled all aspects of human life. People worried that the rains would not come and their crops would not grow. They prayed to their gods and goddesses to provide water. Often they offered sacrifices. They gave thanks when they believed their prayers had been answered.

✔ **READING CHECK: Summarizing** What technologies and patterns of home life did the first river valley civilizations share? bronze and iron tools, women in charge of family and agriculture

This small figure represents the mother goddess of the Indus River valley civilization.

That's Interesting!

As people gathered into larger communities, their religious beliefs and practices became more formalized. They began building massive megaliths, or stone monuments, and temples. Some of these structures are astounding in their workmanship and sheer size, considering that, in most cases, the builders had nothing more than simple tools to help them.

SECTION 2 REVIEW ANSWERS

❶ **Define**
- civilization, p. 11
- irrigation, p. 12
- division of labor, p. 12
- artisans, p. 12
- cultural diffusion, p. 12

❷ villages became cities; high level of cooperation; leadership emerged; division of labor

❸ a. developed along rivers, began to use metals, developed family roles and religious beliefs

b. A calendar allowed people to know when the yearly floods would start and stop. A system of writing allowed people to pass on information and ideas.

c. (1) Stone Age: agriculture, (2) Bronze Age: bronze tools, (3) Iron Age: iron tools

❹ Students might point out that if they wanted to pass on information and ideas they would have to do it orally or pictorially.

SECTION 2 REVIEW

1. **Define** and explain the significance:
   civilization
   irrigation
   division of labor
   artisans
   cultural diffusion

2. **Drawing Conclusions** Make a flowchart like the one below. Add to it to show how a food surplus led people in four river valleys to develop other characteristics of civilization.

Food Surplus	→	Increase in Population
	→	
	→	

3. **Finding the Main Idea**
   a. What did the four main early civilizations have in common geographically and culturally?
   b. What problems did a calendar and a system of writing help solve?
   c. Identify aspects of the following eras and list them according to their relative chronology: Iron Age, Stone Age, Bronze Age.

4. **Writing and Critical Thinking**
   Making Generalizations Imagine you are living in a culture before it has developed a system of writing. Describe what everyday life would be like.
   Consider:
   - what human activities can make use of writing
   - how those same activities would be handled without writing

Homework Practice Online

keyword: SP3 HP1

REVIEW AND ASSESSMENT RESOURCES

REPRODUCIBLE RESOURCES
▶ Vocabulary Activity 1

TECHNOLOGY RESOURCES
▶ Chapter 1 Test Generator (on the One-Stop Planner)
▶ Global Skill Builder CD–ROM
▶ HRW Web Site

REINFORCEMENT, REVIEW, and ASSESSMENT
▶ Chapter 1 Review, pp. 16–17
▶ Chapter 1 Tutorial for Students, Parents, Mentors, and Peers
▶ Chapter 1 Test (Form A or B)
▶ Alternative Assessment Handbook
▶ Chapter 1 Test for English Language Learners and Special-Needs Students

REVIEW
Have students complete the Chapter 1 Review on pages 16–17.

ASSESS
Use one of the chapter tests to assess students' understanding of the content. For Alternative Assessment, see the Portfolio Activities and Alternative Assessment Handbook.

Understanding Main Ideas

1. They use advanced technology to date remains and artifacts. They also use educated guesses and assumptions to determine information about the artifacts they find.

2. wore animal skins as clothing; used fire for warmth and cooking; buried their dead with meat and tools

3. more advanced tools and weapons; better hunters; art on cave walls

4. More permanent farming settlements developed.

5. People are able to produce surplus food. People establish large towns or cities with some form of government. Division of labor occurs.

6. As cities develop, government is needed to make rules to guide people's behavior.

7. a calendar, a system of writing

8. They invented bronze and iron tools.

Reviewing Themes

1. They became successful hunters and migrated great distances in search of food.

2. They developed along rivers.

It resulted in food surpluses   caused an increase in popu-   d the development of

---

CHAPTER 1 Review

Creating a Time Line

Copy the time line below onto a sheet of paper. Complete the time line by filling in the events, individuals, and dates from the chapter that you think were significant. Pick three events and explain why you think they were significant.

3,700,000 B.C. 300,000 B.C. 20,000 B.C. 1200 B.C.

Writing a Summary

Using standard grammar, spelling, sentence structure, and punctuation, write an overview of the events in the chapter.

Identifying People and Ideas

Identify the following terms or individuals and explain their significance:

1. hominids
2. artifacts
3. culture
4. limited evidence
5. Lucy
6. Neanderthals
7. Cro-Magnons
8. Neolithic agricultural revolution
9. civilization
10. division of labor

Understanding Main Ideas

SECTION 1 *(pp. 6–10)*

Prehistoric Peoples

1. What methods do anthropologists, archaeologists, historians, and geographers use to explore prehistory?
2. What were some important characteristics of Neanderthal people?
3. What were some important characteristics of Cro-Magnon people?
4. What effect did the Neolithic agricultural revolution have on people's lives?

SECTION 2 *(pp. 11–15)*

The Foundations of Civilization

5. What are the three major characteristics of a civilization?
6. How are the development of cities and government related?
7. What other two characteristics usually mark civilizations?
8. What advances in metalworking did early river civilizations make?

Reviewing Themes

1. **Culture** What characteristics of early *Homo sapiens* most set them apart from earlier hominids?
2. **Geography** What similarities in physical environment did the first civilizations share?
3. **Economics** How did improved farming lead to the development of civilization?

Thinking Critically

1. **Comparing** Explain the economic, social, and geographic factors that led to the first civilizations.
2. **Drawing Conclusions** How did the development of towns and cities affect prehistoric peoples?
3. **Evaluating** Why was the development of bronze and iron important?
4. **Identifying Cause and Effect** How did the development of agriculture in the river valley civilizations affect the roles and influence of women?

Writing About History

Analyzing Information Imagine you are an archaeologist. You have dug up the site of one of the first human civilizations. Write a description of the artifacts you might find and what they reveal about the culture. Use the following chart to organize your thoughts before you begin writing.

Artifact	What this suggests about the culture

CLOSE

Ask students to name the three major characteristics of civilizations. Have them explain how life in the United States today meets each of these characteristics.

RETEACH

Group students who had trouble with the test into pairs. Have them use their textbook to correct their tests. Ask them to create flash cards and then quiz each other on the chapter content. Then have students take the Form B test to assess their mastery of the material. **ENGLISH LANGUAGE LEARNERS, COOPERATIVE LEARNING**

Portfolio Extensions

1. Ask students to imagine they are archaeologists excavating the site of an ancient civilization. Have them create a list of artifacts that might indicate what farming techniques people used. Have students write an explanation of each item.

2. Assign groups of students a major crop such as corn, wheat, or rice. Then have group members research where their crop is grown and identify major producers. Have groups prepare maps and/or graphs showing the results of their research.

3. Have students locate and use web sites, media and news services, and interviews to collect information about recent archaeological finds. Have them use this information to write articles on the development of agriculture.

Building Social Studies Skills

Using Art to Understand History

Study the painting below. Then answer the questions that follow.

Cro-Magnon cave painting, Lascaux Cave, France.

1. Which statement best describes what you can infer about the artist who drew this painting?
   a. The artist hunted animals like this for food.
   b. The artist was intelligent, was able to mix paints and use tools, and had carefully observed the environment.
   c. Huge herds of animals were in existence at the time the artist drew the painting.
   d. The artist drew the animal to decorate the walls of the cave.

2. Art helps historians understand the people who created it. What conclusions regarding the Cro-Magnon people can you reach on the basis of this illustration?

Analyzing a Primary Source

Read the following description by anthropologists Alan Walker and Pat Shipman. Then answer the questions.

> "First we had to clear every twig, leaf, and rock from a large area where Kamoya found the fossil. Then the whole gang would take Olduvai picks—six-inch nails embedded in curved, hand-carved wooden handles—and break up the top few inches of the surface layer of pebbles and disturbed sediment. How deep we had to go depended on how loose or consolidated the sediment was and whether or not any more pieces were recovered in the process."

3. Which of the following statements best summarizes the excerpt?
   a. Anthropologists use a tool called an Olduvai pick.
   b. The diggers cleared twigs, leaves, and rocks from a large area.
   c. Anthropologists break up the soil around an area where a fossil has been found.
   d. The diggers cleared the ground around the fossil site and carefully broke up the soil to look for more fossils.

4. Reread the excerpt. Then decide whether you would want to take part in an anthropological dig. Give specific reasons.

Alternative Assessment

Building Your Portfolio

Economics

Agriculture was a significant development in human history. The ability to produce food surpluses led to the development of early civilizations. Using your textbook and other sources, gather data about the agricultural production of the United States today. Make a graph of the data. Then write an explanation of how the food production of the United States affects its economy as well as its culture. Consider what the country would be like if it did not produce the amount of food that it does.

📶 internet connect

Internet Activity: go.hrw.com
KEYWORD: SP3 WH1

Choose a topic on the Emergence of Civilization to:
- analyze artifacts from an archaeological site.
- compare and contrast a modern calendar used in the United States with calendars of different cultures.
- list different divisions of labor in modern society.

Thinking Critically

1. Climate and flooding in river valleys produced a food surplus; population increased; villages became cities.

2. Governments emerged.

3. improved tools and weapons

4. Women initially did much of the farming. After the invention of the plow, men again became the primary food providers. The power women had gained shifted back to men.

Writing About History

Answers will vary but might include items such as jewelry, pottery, and tools. Students should describe what each item reveals about the culture.

Building Social Studies Skills

1. b

2. skilled artists, hunters

3. d

4. Answers will vary.

Building Your Portfolio

Students should describe how economy and culture are affected by the ability of the United States to produce the amount of food it does.

CHAPTER 2

The First Civilizations

CHAPTER RESOURCE MANAGER

	Objectives	Pacing Guide	Reproducible Resources
SECTION 1 **Ancient Kingdoms of the Nile** (pp. 20–25)	• Explore how geography affected the development of ancient Egypt. • Identify the events and discoveries that marked the development of Egyptian civilization. • Explain how Egyptian kingdoms developed and why they collapsed.	**Regular** 1.5 day / **Block Scheduling** 1 day *Block Scheduling Handbook with Team Teaching Strategies 2.1*	**RS** Guided Reading Strategy 2.1
SECTION 2 **Egyptian Life and Culture** (pp. 26–29)	• Describe Egyptian achievements in the arts and architecture. • Examine how the Egyptians expressed their religious beliefs. • Explain how farming and trade were carried on in Egypt.	**Regular** 1 day / **Block Scheduling** .5 day *Block Scheduling Handbook with Team Teaching Strategies 2.2*	**RS** Guided Reading Strategy 2.2 **PS** Readings in World History 5 **E** Hands-on History Activity 2
SECTION 3 **Sumerian Civilization** (pp. 30–34)	• Explore how geography affected the development of the Sumerian civilization. • Identify the achievements of the Sumerian people. • Describe what life was like in Sumerian society.	**Regular** 1.5 day / **Block Scheduling** 1 day *Block Scheduling Handbook with Team Teaching Strategies 2.3*	**RS** Guided Reading Strategy 2.3 **PS** Readings in World History 6: An Early City in the Tigris-Euphrates Valley
SECTION 4 **Empires of the Fertile Crescent** (pp. 35–40)	• Explain why Sumerians were attacked by outsiders. • Examine the characteristics of Babylonian society. • Investigate which invaders conquered Babylon and why they failed to control it. • Describe the achievements of the Persians.	**Regular** 1.5 day / **Block Scheduling** .5 day *Block Scheduling Handbook with Team Teaching Strategies 2.4*	**RS** Guided Reading Strategy 2.4 **RS** Graphic Organizer Activity 2 **PS** Readings in World History 7, 8
SECTION 5 **The Phoenicians and the Lydians** (pp. 41–43)	• Examine how trade influenced Phoenician culture. • Describe how a money economy developed in Lydia.	**Regular** 1 day / **Block Scheduling** .5 day *Block Scheduling Handbook with Team Teaching Strategies 2.5*	**RS** Guided Reading Strategy 2.5 **SM** Geography Activity 2: The End of an Island Civilization
SECTION 6 **The Origins of Judaism** (pp. 44–47)	• Explain how the migrating Hebrews found a homeland. • Explore how religious views affected Hebrew culture.	**Regular** 1 day / **Block Scheduling** .5 day *Block Scheduling Handbook with Team Teaching Strategies 2.6*	**RS** Guided Reading Strategy 2.6 **E** Creative Teaching Strategy 2: Time Capsules from the Ancient World

Chapter Resource Key

PS	Primary Sources	**A**	Assessment		Music
RS	Reading Support	**REV**	Review		Video
IC	Interdisciplinary Connections	**ELL**	Reinforcement and English Language Learners		Internet
E	Enrichment		Transparencies	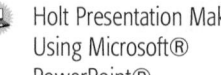	Holt Presentation Maker Using Microsoft® PowerPoint®
SM	Skills Mastery		CD–ROM		

 One-Stop Planner CD-ROM

See the ***One–Stop Planner*** for a complete list of additional resources for students and teachers.

One-Stop Planner CD-ROM

It's easy to plan lessons, select resources, and print out materials for your students when you use the **One-Stop Planner** CD–ROM with **Test Generator.**

Technology Resources

- One-Stop Planner 2.1
- Holt Researcher: World History: Ramses II
- World History Teaching Transparency: Everyday Life 1: Irrigation in Ancient Egypt
- Homework Practice Online

- One-Stop Planner 2.2
- **CNN.** Presents World Cultures: Yesterday and Today Segment 2: Restoring the Sphinx
- World History Teaching Transparency: Everyday Life 2
- Homework Practice Online

- One-Stop Planner 2.3
- Homework Practice Online
- Online Maps, Charts, and Graphs: Development of Cuneiform, 3000 B.C.– 600 B.C.

- One-Stop Planner 2.4
- Holt Researcher: World History: Cyrus, Darius I, Zoroaster
- World History and Cultures Video Program 2: The First Empires
- Homework Practice Online

- One-Stop Planner 2.5
- World History Teaching Transparency: Geography and History 2: The Eastern Mediterranean
- Homework Practice Online
- Online Maps, Charts, and Graphs: Phoenician Sea Routes

- One-Stop Planner 2.6
- Holt Researcher: World History: David, Solomon
- Religions of the World Video Series: Judaism
- Homework Practice Online

Reinforcement, Review, and Assessment

- Daily Quiz 2.1
- Main Idea Activity 2.1
- English Audio Summary 2.1
- Spanish Audio Summary 2.1
- REV Section 1 Review, p. 25

- Daily Quiz 2.2
- Main Idea Activity 2.2
- English Audio Summary 2.2
- Spanish Audio Summary 2.2
- REV Section 2 Review, p. 29

- Daily Quiz 2.3
- Main Idea Activity 2.3
- English Audio Summary 2.3
- Spanish Audio Summary 2.3
- REV Section 3 Review, p. 34

- Daily Quiz 2.4
- Main Idea Activity 2.4
- English Audio Summary 2.4
- Spanish Audio Summary 2.4
- REV Section 4 Review, p. 40

- Daily Quiz 2.5
- Main Idea Activity 2.5
- English Audio Summary 2.5
- Spanish Audio Summary 2.5
- REV Section 5 Review, p. 43

- Daily Quiz 2.6
- Main Idea Activity 2.6
- English Audio Summary 2.6
- Spanish Audio Summary 2.6
- REV Section 6 Review, p. 47

internet connect

HRW ONLINE RESOURCES
GO TO: go.hrw.com
Then type in a keyword.

TEACHER HOME PAGE
KEYWORD: SP3 Teacher

CHAPTER INTERNET ACTIVITIES
KEYWORD: SP3 WH2
Choose an activity to:
- explore Egyptian pyramids and create an illustrated brochure.
- interview the leader of an ancient civilization.
- write about ancient and modern structures in Egypt.

CHAPTER ENRICHMENT LINKS
KEYWORD: SP3 CH2

ONLINE ASSESSMENT
Homework Practice
KEYWORD: SP3 HP2
Standardized Test Prep
KEYWORD: SP3 STP2
Rubrics
KEYWORD: SS Rubrics

ONLINE MAPS, CHARTS, AND GRAPHS
KEYWORD: SP3 MCG

CONTENT UPDATES
KEYWORD: SS Content Updates

HOLT PRESENTATION MAKER
KEYWORD: SP3 PPT2

ONLINE READING SUPPORT
KEYWORD: SS Strategies

CURRENT EVENTS
KEYWORD: S3 Current Events

Meeting Individual Needs

Ability Levels

Level 1 Basic level activities designed for all students encountering new material

Level 2 Intermediate level activities designed for average students

Level 3 Challenging activities designed for honors and gifted and talented students

English Language Learners These activities address the needs of students with Limited English Proficiency.

Chapter Review and Assessment

- IC Vocabulary Activity 2
- Global Skill Builder CD–ROM
- HRW Web Site
- REV Chapter 2 Tutorial for Students, Parents, Mentors, and Peers
- REV Chapter 2 Review, pp. 48–49
- A Chapter 2 Test Generator (on the One-Stop Planner)
- A Chapter 2 Test (Form A or B)
- A Alternative Assessment Handbook
- A Chapter 2 Test for English Language Learners and Special-Needs Students

Build on What You Know

Ask students to answer the following questions:

What were some of the developments of prehistoric peoples?

Consider:

- agriculture
- government
- science and technology

Where are civilizations likely to develop?

Consider:

- geography
- climate
- science and technology

EXPLORING THE TIME LINE

GLOBAL EVENTS

internet connect

go hrw.com

TOPIC: The Arts
GO TO: go.hrw.com
KEYWORD: SP3 WH2

Have students access the Internet through the HRW Go site to conduct research on the artistic achievements of the first civilizations (e.g., Sumerians and Egyptians). Then ask students to write an article that could be published in an art history magazine. Their article should detail the artistic achievements of one of these civilizations. Students' articles should include appropriate examples and evidence drawn from their research.

CHAPTER

2

C. 6000 B.C.–587 B.C.

The First Civilizations

Egyptian scarab amulet

Relief from the palace of Sargon showing the transportation of wood in boats

c. 2600 B.C.
The Arts
The Great Pyramid is constructed at Giza.

c. 2400 B.C.
Daily Life
Egyptians begin wearing scarab beetles as amulets.

c. 2334 B.C.
Politics
Sargon's rule of the Akkadian Empire begins.

c. 2000 B.C.
Business and Finance
Assyrian merchants send caravans of goods into Asia Minor.

| 6000 B.C. | 2500 B.C. | 2000 B.C. |

c. 2675 B.C.
Business and Finance
Egypt and Sumeria import cedar wood from Phoenicia.

c. 2680 B.C.
Politics
The Old Kingdom period begins in Egypt.

c. 2330 B.C.
Global Events
The Akkadians conquer the Sumerians in Mesopotamia.

c. 1900 B.C.
The Arts
Egyptian artists decorate royal tombs with scenes from everyday life.

Sculpture of head of an Akkadian ruler, possibly Sargon

Build on What You Know

By studying the limited evidence available, anthropologists and archaeologists have learned much about the lives of early humans. During the long Stone Age, prehistoric peoples gradually learned to use stone tools and to farm. They domesticated animals and plants and established permanent settlements. From these beginnings, human beings built civilizations. People began to use metals, to irrigate their fields, and to specialize in work besides farming. Some groups developed calendars and invented increasingly complex forms of writing. In this chapter, you will learn more about some of the first civilizations and their many achievements.

What's Your Opinion?

 To help students create their Themes Journal entries, provide the following examples of appropriate **agree**/**disagree** *statements.*

Global Relations

Agree Trade can promote the exchange of cultural beliefs and ideas between civilizations.

Disagree Cultural beliefs and ideas are not exchanged between civilizations through trade.

Geography

Agree Civilizations cannot survive if they are geographically isolated.

Disagree Civilizations that are geographically isolated can survive.

Government

Agree A civilization needs strong rulers to survive.

Disagree To survive, a civilization does not need strong rulers.

Relief depicting Moses guiding the Exodus

c. 1600 B.C.
Science and Technology
Mesopotamians begin to produce glass.

c. 1600 B.C.
Science and Technology
Egyptian physicians produce what some scholars regard as the first medical handbook.

c. 1250 B.C.
The Arts
Sumerians construct the Choghā Zanbīl ziggurat in Khūzestān.

c. 1200s B.C.
Global Events
The Hebrews' Exodus from Egypt takes place.

c. 1000s B.C.
Business and Finance
Phoenicia is the Mediterranean world's great sea trading power.

c. 600 B.C.
Business and Finance
The Lydians invent coined money.

c. 600 B.C.
Daily Life
Zoroastrianism becomes the dominant religion in Persia.

c. 600 B.C.
Science and Technology
Chaldean astronomers chart movements of the stars and planets and predict eclipses.

1500 B.C.	**1000 B.C.**	**500 B.C.**

c. 1550 B.C.
Daily Life
Egyptians make cats household pets.

c. 1300 B.C.
Science and Technology
Egyptian astronomers have identified the planets Mercury, Venus, Mars, Jupiter, and Saturn.

c. 1100 B.C.
Politics
The New Kingdom period in Egypt ends.

c. 900 B.C.
Global Events
The Assyrians conquer Mesopotamia.

562 B.C.
Politics
Nebuchadnezzar's reign in Babylon comes to a close.

Egyptian cat sculpture

Relief of Assyrian soldiers with slingshots

What's Your Opinion?

 Do you **agree** *or* **disagree** *with the following statements? Support your point of view in your journal.*

Global Relations Trade between civilizations can be a way to exchange cultural beliefs and ideas.

Geography Civilizations that are isolated by geographical features such as deserts or seas cannot survive.

Government Strong rulers are needed to help a civilization survive.

EXPLORING THE TIME LINE
GLOBAL EVENTS

Living along the Nile, the Egyptians were some of the earliest developers of water transportation. An image on a pot from about 3200 B.C. shows that Egyptians were already using the sail to travel on the Nile. Early boats floated downriver, and then their captains could raise a sail and be carried back upstream by the wind, which blows most often from the north. Rafts and barges carried goods up and down, and ferries traveled across the river and along the canals.

Critical Thinking

Ask students to consider how the geography of the Nile Valley and the development of water transportation might have contributed to the rise of a unified government in Egypt.

ANSWER: Students should note that the use of boats for transportation would have enabled a leader to impose authority on places along the river. This would probably have helped a leader to dominate the entire population of Egypt.

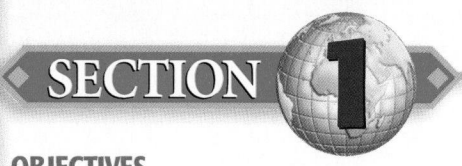

SECTION 1

OBJECTIVES

1 **Explore how geography affected the development of ancient Egypt.**

2 **Identify the events and discoveries that marked the development of Egyptian civilization.**

3 **Explain how Egyptian kingdoms developed and why they collapsed.**

🔊 LET'S GET STARTED!

As students enter the classroom, ask them to write down the reasons why they believe civilizations often develop along rivers. *(Students might mention the need for a plentiful water supply, transportation, and fertile soil.)* Have volunteers share their responses with the class. Tell students that in Section 1 they will learn about the civilization that developed along the Nile.

SECTION 1 RESOURCES

REPRODUCIBLE RESOURCES

▶ Guided Reading Strategy 2.1

TECHNOLOGY RESOURCES

▶ One-Stop Planner 2.1
▶ Holt Researcher: World History: Ramses II
▶ World History Teaching Transparency: Everyday Life 1: Irrigation in Ancient Egypt
▶ Homework Practice Online

REINFORCEMENT, REVIEW, AND ASSESSMENT

▶ Section 1 Review, p. 25
▶ Daily Quiz 2.1
▶ Main Idea Activity 2.1
▶ English Audio Summary 2.1
▶ Spanish Audio Summary 2.1

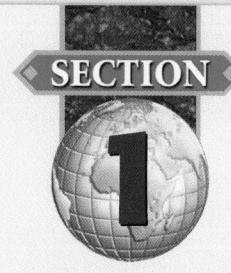

SECTION 1

READ TO DISCOVER

1 How did geography affect the development of ancient Egypt?
2 What events and discoveries marked the development of Egyptian civilization?
3 How did Egyptian kingdoms develop and why did they collapse?

DEFINE

hieroglyphics
papyrus
dynasty
pharaoh
empire
polytheism
monotheism

IDENTIFY

Rosetta Stone
Menes
Hyksos
Hatshepsut
Thutmose III
Amenhotep IV
Ramses II

WHY IT MATTERS TODAY

Water is necessary for a community to develop. Use CNNStudentNews.com or other **current event** sources to find information about a country or a community dealing with a water shortage. Record your findings in your journal.

CNN Student News.com

Ancient Kingdoms of the Nile

The Main Idea
Patterns of daily life and culture in early Egyptian empires were shaped by the features of the Nile River.

The Story Continues *"Hail to thee, O Nile! Who manifests thyself over this land, and comes to give life to Egypt!"* These lines begin *"Hymn to the Nile,"* an ancient poem celebrating the river that gave birth to and sustained the culture of the Egyptians. Without the Nile, there would be no Egypt as we know it.

The Land: Its Geography and Importance

Today desert covers large areas of Egypt. In ancient times, however, the landscape was quite different. Some 12,000 years ago, much of the area was covered by swampland that probably supported large populations of animals such as the hippopotamus and the crocodile. Even so, for the last 5,000 years one physical feature has dominated the region: the Nile River. Without this important river, the land could not have supported the great civilization that appeared in Egypt. This civilization developed in the fertile valley provided by the Nile.

The Nile River. For many thousands of years, the geography of Egypt has been dominated by the mighty Nile River. The Nile is the longest river in the world, stretching about 4,160 miles. Its main sources are the White Nile, which begins near Lake Victoria in eastern Africa, and the Blue Nile, which runs from the Ethiopian highlands. The river flows from south to north, eventually branching into a fan-shaped delta and emptying into the southern Mediterranean Sea. During ancient times, the long course of the Nile was broken by a series of six great cataracts, or rapids. At each cataract, the river was forced into a narrow channel cut through rock. The white-water rapids driving through the cataracts were difficult or nearly impossible to navigate.

The mighty Nile River gave birth to one of history's earliest and richest civilizations.

LEVEL 1: Tell students to imagine that they are members of an agricultural community and are searching for a new home. Ask students what kind of geographical features they would look for. *(rich soil, fair climate, natural resources, access to water, natural protection from invaders)* Have students identify geographical factors of the Nile River valley that meet any of these needs. *(fertile soil; a sunny, frost-free climate; deposits of minerals; the Nile River; deserts and seas)* Discuss how each geographic factor contributed to the success of the Egyptian civilization. **ENGLISH LANGUAGE LEARNERS, COOPERATIVE LEARNING**

Teacher to Teacher

Laura Watkins of Acton, Massachusetts, suggested the following activity: Create a chart listing four key characteristics of the natural environment of Egypt, with examples of how each characteristic affected the culture of Egypt. Then create a similar chart reflecting how the natural environment of your town or region has affected your local culture.

Along most of its course, however, the Nile's smooth, steady flow provided a natural route for transportation, as well as a seemingly endless supply of life-giving water.

The ancient Egyptians built their civilization along a 750-mile stretch of the Nile, roughly between the first great cataract and the delta. The Nile's south-to-north flow made it possible for early people to move goods upland. At the same time, prevailing winds blowing from north to south enabled boats to sail southward on the river. In the 400s B.C. the Greek historian Herodotus (hih·RAHD·uh·tuhs) described another remarkable feature of the Nile River—its annual cycle of months-long flooding.

> *History Makers Speak*
> **"When the Nile overflows, it floods both its banks to an average distance of forty miles. But why it does so I find it impossible to discover . . . I would particularly like to know why it starts flooding in mid-summer, of all times, and goes on doing so for over three months before sinking back to its original level. . . . "**
>
> Herodotus, from *The Histories*

Analyzing Primary Sources

Evaluating What puzzled Herodotus about the Nile? why the Nile flooded in mid-summer

We know now that heavy summer rains at the Nile's source cause the summer floods. Although Egyptian farmers could not explain the floods, they planned their work around them. They harvested crops before the floods came. When the waters receded, fertile soil was left behind.

By digging short canals to carry river water to their fields, farmers could grow two or even three crops a year. With several crops a year, the farmers could feed a large population. The planning of irrigation systems promoted cooperation among the people.

Other natural advantages. The Nile Valley offered other natural resources besides its fertile soil. Its sunny, frost-free climate made it easy to grow many kinds of crops. Another important feature of the climate was, and still is, the north wind that blows from the Mediterranean Sea upstream into the Nile Valley. Boats on the Nile can either travel upstream with the wind or row downstream with the current. This fact allowed the ancient Egyptians to use the Nile River as a pathway of travel and trade linking all parts of the Nile Valley. It also helped the ancient Egyptians unite the region into one kingdom.

The Nile Valley contains deposits of granite, sandstone, and limestone. The Egyptians used these minerals as building materials. Finally, the valley's location also created an advantage. The deserts and seas that surrounded the Nile Valley provided a natural protection against invaders. Only the Isthmus of Suez broke these natural barriers. The isthmus forms a land bridge between Africa and Asia. This land bridge provided a route for trade and for the exchange of ideas between the Egyptians and their neighbors to the east.

✔ **READING CHECK: Finding the Main Idea** How did the Nile River contribute to the development of Egyptian civilization? provided route for trade and travel, aided farming

Nile floodplain
Northern winds

0   150   300 Miles
0   150   300 Kilometers
Lambert Conformal Conic Projection

Ancient Egypt, c. 3000 B.C.

Interpreting Maps The Nile is the longest river in the world.
■ **Skills Assessment: 1. Physical Systems** Into which body of water does the Nile River flow? **2. Drawing Conclusions** How might the ability to travel both north and south along the Nile have helped early Egyptian civilizations?

Linking Past to Present

The Aswan High Dam was built to hold back the floodwaters of the Nile River, generate electricity, and to provide year-round irrigation for Egypt's agricultural fields. In these respects, the dam has been remarkably successful. Since its construction, the dam has increased the amount of land irrigated each year by about 2.25 million acres and enabled Egypt to double its agricultural production. This advancement, however, has not come without cost. The dam has had serious negative side effects on the environment, including the once fertile soil of the Nile River valley. Without the annual flooding, the land no longer is naturally fertilized by silt. Modern farmers must resort to applying millions of tons of expensive artificial fertilizers on their farmland. The absence of silt has also caused greater erosion of land along the Mediterranean coast.

ACTIVITY: Have groups of students discuss other technological advances that have produced both benefits and costs.

MAP ANSWERS
1. the Mediterranean Sea

2. Students might suggest that it made trading goods easier.

History Maker

TUTANKHAMEN. Pharaoh Tutankhamen was just nine years old when he came to the throne. He died in his late teens. Since pharaohs were buried with all the things they might need in the afterlife, scholars and historians analyzed evidence from the tomb to create a detailed picture of this "boy king." The contents of his tomb included mirror holders, elaborate shaving tools, and an array of boxes that had once contained various oils and ointments. Although much of the clothing had decayed over time, it was obvious that Tutankhamen had an extensive wardrobe. Some of the clothes were brightly colored and decorated with gold and precious stones. Many pieces of jewelry were also found in the tomb.

Critical Thinking

What do the contents of Tutankhamen's tomb say about him?

ANSWER: Students may point out that he seems to have taken great care of his personal appearance.

CONNECTING TO ART ANSWER

The beard links the pharaoh with the god Osiris; the vulture and cobra symbolize power over Upper and Lower Egypt.

CONNECTING TO
Art

Metalworking: Funeral Mask of a Pharaoh
One of the world's most beautiful treasures is this life-size funeral mask of Pharaoh Tutankhamen. The mask shows the pharaoh as he was when he died in his late teens. It is made of beaten gold, with blue glass and beads. The beard is a symbol of the god Osiris, who judged the dead. The vulture and cobra on the headdress represent the pharaoh's power over Upper and Lower Egypt.

Understanding the Arts

How does the mask show the power of the pharaoh in Egyptian life?

Early Steps Toward Civilization

Archaeological finds suggest that other ancient cultures influenced early Nile Valley civilization. Hunter-gatherer groups had moved into the Nile River valley by 12,000 B.C. or earlier. Over time, these people formed farming settlements. A Neolithic culture developed in the valley probably by about 6000 B.C. By about 3800 B.C. Nile River valley people had taken other important steps along the road to civilization. They mined copper, perhaps to make tools and jewelry. They discovered how to make bronze, a mixture of copper and tin. They may also have learned to glaze pottery.

By about 3000 B.C. Nile River valley people had developed **hieroglyphics** (hy·ruh·GLI·fiks), a form of writing. Hieroglyphic writing used more than 600 signs, pictures, or symbols to represent words and sounds. At first Egyptians carved hieroglyphics in stone or other hard materials. Carving was a long and difficult process, however, and soon the Egyptians discovered a way to make a kind of paper. They used the papyrus plant that grew in marshes near the Nile. They cut the plant stem into long, thin slices. They then moistened the strips and pressed them together to make **papyrus,** from which we get our word *paper*. Egyptians wrote on papyrus with ink made from soot, water, and plant juice, using a brush made from a rush.

Thousands of years later, scholars learned to read hieroglyphic writing. In A.D. 1798 a French army invaded Egypt. The next year a French officer discovered an unusual stone. It became known as the **Rosetta Stone** because it was found in the village of Rosetta. Carved on this stone were passages written in Greek, hieroglyphics, and an Egyptian writing style called *demotic*. Some 23 years later, a French language expert used the Rosetta Stone to solve the mystery of hieroglyphics. Modern scholars could read the Greek text, which stated that all three passages said the same thing. The language expert used the Greek text to decode the hieroglyphics. He also figured out rules for understanding all other hieroglyphics. Scholars could now read eyewitness accounts of Egypt's history.

✔ **READING CHECK: Analyzing Information** What evidence indicates that Egyptians were creating a civilization? mining metals, making alloys and pottery, writing

The Egyptian Kingdoms

Over the centuries, two distinct cultures developed along the Nile. They formed two kingdoms, Lower Egypt and Upper Egypt. Lower Egypt lay to the north in the Nile River delta. Upper Egypt lay farther south, away from the Mediterranean Sea.

Sometime after 3200 B.C., **Menes** (MEE·neez), a king of Upper Egypt, united all of Egypt into one kingdom. Menes founded a **dynasty,** or family of rulers. In a dynasty the right to rule passes on within the family, usually from father to son or daughter. A dynasty's rule ends when the family is driven from power or when no family member is left to become ruler. Menes and his successors gained new territory. They also improved irrigation and trade, making Egypt wealthier. Egypt's dynastic rulers were religious and political leaders. The people regarded them as gods, and built great temples and tombs to honor them. In later years the rulers took the title **pharaoh,** which means "great house." Pharaohs held absolute, or unlimited, power. They not only led the government, but also served as judges, high priests, and generals of the armies.

LEVEL 3: Draw a time line beginning with the date 2650 B.C. and ending with 200 B.C. and have the periods of the Old Kingdom (2650 to 2180 B.C.), Middle Kingdom (2040 to 1650 B.C.), and New Kingdom (1570 to 1100 B.C.) marked on it. Have students fill in the time line with important events in Egypt's history during each time period. *(Possible answers: Old Kingdom—pyramids, science, art, civil war; Middle Kingdom—Hyksos rule Egypt, falls into disorder; New Kingdom—empire, strict government, army, conquering of new territories)*

From the time of Menes until almost 300 B.C., some 30 dynasties ruled Egypt. Historians divide this time span into three kingdoms: the Old Kingdom, the Middle Kingdom, and the New Kingdom.

The Old Kingdom. The Old Kingdom existed from about 2680 B.C. to about 2180 B.C. Many important developments in science and the arts took place during this time. For example, Egyptians of the Old Kingdom built the Great Sphinx and the largest pyramids. These structures still stand as symbols of the glory of Egyptian civilization.

Egyptian society in the Old Kingdom was split into two classes. The lower class included peasants and farmers. These people owed the pharaoh certain services. They served in the army and worked on building projects, such as irrigation canals and pyramids. The upper class included the pharaoh, the royal family, priests, scribes, and government officials. As time passed, these upper-class officials gradually became a small but powerful hereditary group of nobles.

Toward the end of the Old Kingdom, the pharaohs grew weaker and the nobles grew stronger. For more than 100 years after the end of the Old Kingdom, civil wars divided Egypt as rivals battled for control of the land. Historians call this period of internal strife before a new line of pharaohs came to power the First Intermediate Period.

The Middle Kingdom. In about 2050 B.C. this new line of pharaohs reunited Egypt and ushered in the Middle Kingdom. Overall, this was the "golden age" for the Egyptians, marked by stability and prosperity. During the Middle Kingdom, however, nobles and priests again began to weaken the power of the pharaoh. By 1780 B.C. the Middle Kingdom was becoming unstable.

At this time a people called the **Hyksos** (HIK·sos), meaning "foreigners," arrived in Egypt from Asia, introducing new war tools such as the chariot and the compound bow. Historians disagree greatly about the history of the Hyksos. In about the 200s B.C. an Egyptian priest, Manetho, wrote an account of Egyptian history that described how people from the east had invaded Egypt. Manetho claimed that these people destroyed cities and temples, murdered Egyptians, and made women and children slaves. Based on Manetho's account and other stories, some historians believe that the Hyksos invaded and conquered Egypt.

Other historians, however, disagree. They point out that there is little evidence that Egyptian cities and temples were destroyed. They claim that tales of the Hyksos' brutality were made up. Egyptians needed an excuse to explain why foreigners were able to take over Egypt. After all, how could a land ruled by a god fall under foreign rule unless the foreigners had mighty armies? These historians believe that the nomadic Hyksos migrated to the Nile Delta in the 1700s B.C. In the confusion following the collapse of the Middle Kingdom, they became powerful. The Hyksos ruled most of Lower Egypt for more than 100 years. In about 1650 B.C. much of Egypt fell under the rule of their horse-drawn chariots, ushering in a Second Intermediate Period before the Egyptians rose to power again.

INTERPRETING THE VISUAL RECORD

The Sphinx The Great Sphinx at Giza was probably constructed during the reign of the pharaoh Khafre, c. 2540 B.C.–c. 2514 B.C. The head of the Sphinx may have portrayed Khafre. *What characteristics of Egypt's ruler does the Sphinx reflect?*

Government

Explain to students that Egypt was a monarchy when it was ruled by pharaohs. In a monarchy, there is one ruler who has absolute power. Ask students which present-day countries are monarchies. Have students discuss the problems that this type of government can cause. Then have students compare a monarchy to a democracy.

ACTIVITY: Ask students to create a chart comparing the government of ancient Egypt to the U.S. government. After students have completed their comparison chart, go over their responses as a class.

VISUAL RECORD ANSWER

Students may note that it reflects the ruler's majesty and power.

Spotlight on CULTURE

Akhenaton is considered one of the first monotheists in history because he promoted the worship of only one god—Aton. In his effort to eradicate all of the old gods, he commanded his servants to climb to the top of towering structures to erase images that were not even visible from the ground. Akhenaton's reforms failed, however, partly because of his religion's focus on the afterlife, instead of life on Earth, and its lack of traditional lavish ceremonies.

CLOSE

Organize the class into three groups representing priests of Akhenaton who want to spread the religious belief of monotheism, priests who want to maintain a polytheistic Egyptian religion, and critics of Egyptian religious society. Have the first two groups prepare and present speeches trying to convince their audience that their religious beliefs are correct. The third group should note problems with the beliefs and practices of both groups of priests. Finally, have the class discuss the ideas and critiques presented. **BLOCK SCHEDULING, COOPERATIVE LEARNING**

Geography

After the Hyksos were driven from Egypt, a new warrior tradition arose. It became the duty of Egyptian kings to lead their armies into battle. The most famous of these warrior-kings was Thutmose III, who has been called the Napoléon of Egypt. Through Thutmose's military expertise and courage, Egypt conquered land in Southwest Asia and established it as a part of the New Kingdom.

Critical Thinking

Ask students if they think the concept of a "warrior-king" applies to present-day national leaders.

ANSWER: Modern national leaders do not usually lead battles, but they must decide when military action is necessary.

MAP ANSWERS

1. approximately 1,500 miles

2. The New Kingdom did not expand far beyond the fertility of the Nile.

HISTORY MAKER ANSWER

Students might suggest that she wanted to command the same respect as her male predecessors.

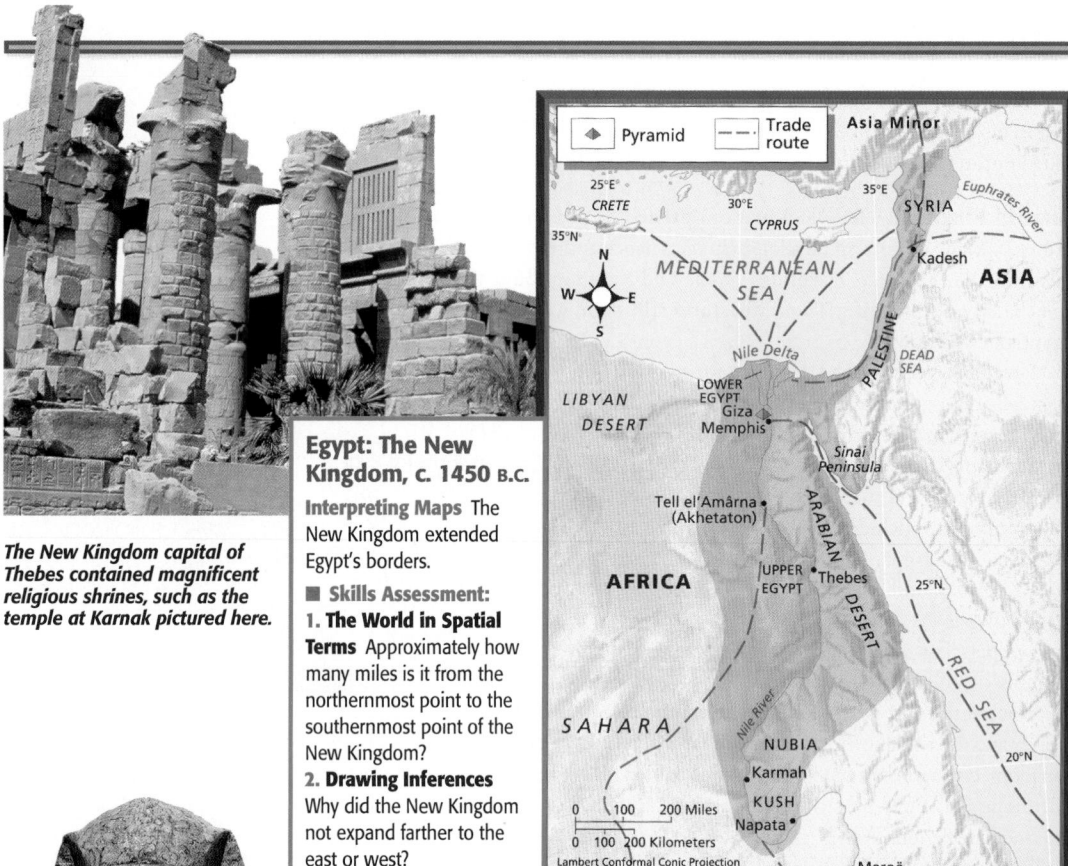

The New Kingdom capital of Thebes contained magnificent religious shrines, such as the temple at Karnak pictured here.

Egypt: The New Kingdom, c. 1450 B.C.

Interpreting Maps The New Kingdom extended Egypt's borders.

■ **Skills Assessment:**
1. The World in Spatial Terms Approximately how many miles is it from the northernmost point to the southernmost point of the New Kingdom?
2. Drawing Inferences Why did the New Kingdom not expand farther to the east or west?

HISTORY MAKER
Hatshepsut (c. 1503 B.C.–1482 B.C.)

Sometime after her husband's death, Hatshepsut became pharaoh of Egypt. This was a bold move, for only one woman, Sebeknefru, had ever held such complete power before.

Hatshepsut ruled as a male pharaoh would. She dressed like a pharaoh, too, even wearing the false beard that only kings could wear. **Why might Hatshepsut have dressed like a male pharaoh?**

The New Kingdom. Most historians agree on one thing about the Hyksos: they remained outsiders in Egypt. Eventually leaders in Upper Egypt drove the Hyksos out of the country. A line of strong pharaohs began to rule a reunited Egypt. Their base was the city of Thebes. The period in which they ruled—from about 1570 B.C. to about 1080 B.C.—is called the New Kingdom.

For a time, the pharaohs once again had absolute power. They kept strict control over the government. Adopting the horse-drawn chariots of the Hyksos, the pharaohs created a strong army. They gained land along the eastern end of the Mediterranean Sea and south into Nubia. In doing so, the New Kingdom pharaohs built an **empire,** a form of government in which an individual or a single people rules over many other peoples and their territories. Only the strongest pharaohs could hold the empire together. When weaker pharaohs ruled, some parts of the empire tried to break away.

One of the New Kingdom pharaohs was also one of the first known female rulers. After the death of her husband, **Hatshepsut** (hat·SHEP·soot) reigned as pharaoh from about 1503 B.C. to about 1482 B.C. Although technically a co-pharaoh with her young stepson, Hatshepsut was a strong ruler who kept Egypt's borders secure and built trade with other lands. Her stepson **Thutmose III** continued this trend, bringing Egypt to the height of its power through conquest and trade until his death in 1450 B.C.

From about 1380 B.C. to 1362 B.C. Egypt was ruled by the pharaoh **Amenhotep IV** (ahm·en·HOH·tep). Amenhotep tried to bring about social and religious change in Egypt. Before Amenhotep became pharaoh, Egyptians believed that many gods

REVIEW

Have students complete the Section 1 Review on p. 25.

ASSESS

Have students complete Daily Quiz 2.1. As Alternative Assessment, use the time line exercises in this section's lessons.

RETEACH

Have students complete Main Idea Activity for English Language Learners and Special-Needs Students 2.1. Then have students write the section's headings and subheadings on a sheet of paper and list the main ideas. **ENGLISH LANGUAGE LEARNERS**

internet connect

Internet Activity: go.hrw.com
TOPIC: Egyptian Structures **KEYWORD:** SP3 WH2

Have students access the Internet through the HRW Go site to research both ancient Egyptian structures and modern structures. Then tell students to find examples of a modern and ancient structure and write a paragraph contrasting these ancient and modern styles.

Eras of Egyptian History

Old Kingdom	1st Intermediate Period	Middle Kingdom	2nd Intermediate Period	New Kingdom	Post-Imperial Era
c. 2680 B.C. to c. 2180 B.C.	c. 2180 B.C. to c. 2050 B.C.	c. 2050 B.C. to c. 1650 B.C.	c. 1650 B.C. to c. 1570 B.C.	c. 1570 B.C. to c. 1080 B.C.	c. 1080 B.C. to c. 300s B.C.

existed. This belief is called **polytheism.** Amenhotep believed in only one god—a belief called **monotheism.** For Amenhotep, the one god was the sun, symbolized by a disk called the Aton. To honor Aton, the pharaoh changed his name to Akhenaton (ahk·NAHT·uhn), which means "he who is pleasing to Aton."

Akhenaton, however, could not change his people's religious beliefs. The pharaoh struggled with Egyptian priests, who did not want to lose their power and wealth. After the death of Akhenaton, the priests regained power and Egyptians returned to the old polytheistic religion.

Egypt's decline. After the death of Akhenaton, few strong pharaohs ruled Egypt. **Ramses II** was among those leaders. Ramses, who ruled from 1279 B.C. to 1213 B.C., kept the Egyptian empire together and ordered the construction of many temples and monuments. He is sometimes called Ramses the Great. The pharaohs who followed Ramses were not as successful. A series of invasions from groups called the Sea Peoples weakened Egypt. Eventually foreign empires such as the Assyrians, the Nubians, and the Persians attacked Egypt. It was no longer an imperial power. By the 300s B.C. rule in Egypt by Egyptians came to an end.

✔ **READING CHECK: Making Generalizations** What kind of rule characterized the height of each Egyptian kingdom?
strong rule by pharaohs

Holt Researcher

go.hrw.com
KEYWORD: Holt Researcher
FreeFind: Ramses II
After reading more about Ramses II on the Holt Researcher, write an essay evaluating whether he deserved the title "Ramses the Great."

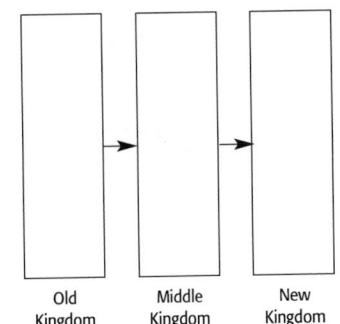

This black granite statue of Ramses II dates from between about 1300 B.C. and about 1200 B.C.

SECTION 1 REVIEW

1. Define and explain the significance:
hieroglyphics
papyrus
dynasty
pharaoh
empire
polytheism
monotheism

2. Identify and explain the significance:
Rosetta Stone
Menes
Hyksos
Hatshepsut
Thutmose III
Amenhotep IV
Ramses II

3. Comparing Copy the chart below. Use it to compare the three Egyptian kingdoms.

[ ] → [ ] → [ ]
Old Kingdom   Middle Kingdom   New Kingdom

4. **Finding the Main Idea**
a. What physical features of the Nile River valley contributed to the rise of civilization there?
b. What factors within Egyptian society contributed to the disruption of the Old Kingdom and the beginning of the First Intermediate Period between kingdoms?
c. What benefits did strong pharaohs bring to the Egyptian kingdoms?

5. **Writing and Critical Thinking**
Summarizing Write a paragraph for a travel brochure that discusses the importance of the Nile River in Egyptian history.
Consider:
• the geography and climate of the Nile River valley
• the annual Nile flood
• the natural advantages provided by the location of the Egyptian kingdoms

Homework Practice Online
keyword: SP3 HP2

SECTION 1 REVIEW ANSWERS

❶ **Define**
• hieroglyphics, p. 22
• papyrus, p. 22
• dynasty, p. 22
• pharaoh, p. 22
• empire, p. 24
• polytheism, p. 25
• monotheism, p. 25

❷ **Identify**
• Rosetta Stone, p. 22
• Menes, p. 22
• Hyksos, p. 23
• Hatshepsut, p. 24
• Thutmose III, p. 24
• Amenhotep IV, p. 24
• Ramses II, p. 25

❸ Old Kingdom: development of noble class, building of the Great Sphinx and pyramids; Middle Kingdom: pharaohs reunited Egypt; New Kingdom: Egypt became an empire

❹ a. sunny, frost-free climate; north wind enabled boats to sail upstream; deposits of granite, sandstone, and limestone; natural protection of deserts and seas

b. Pharaohs grew weaker and nobles grew stronger.

c. strict control of government, strong army, expansion

❺ Students may suggest that the annual flooding of the Nile made the surrounding land fertile, that Egyptian farmers used water from the Nile to irrigate their fields, and that the Nile also provided a natural transportation route.

SECTION 2

OBJECTIVES

1 **Describe Egyptian achievements in the arts and architecture.**

2 **Examine how the Egyptians expressed their religious beliefs.**

3 **Explain how farming and trade were carried on in Egypt.**

SECTION 2

READ TO DISCOVER

❶ What did the Egyptians achieve in the arts and architecture?

❷ How did the Egyptians express their religious beliefs?

❸ How were farming and trade carried on in Egypt?

DEFINE

scribes
mummification
caravans

WHY IT MATTERS TODAY

People still build large build-ings for many reasons. Use CNN.com or other **current event** sources to explore the construction of a new government building, sta-dium, or skyscraper. Record your findings in your journal.

CNN student News.com

Egyptian Life and Culture

The Main Idea
Egyptian culture was marked by long peri-ods of stability built around their religion and geography.

The Story Continues *According to myth, Osiris was a king of Egypt murdered by his evil brother. Osiris's wife, Isis, turned into a bird and flapped her wings until the breeze breathed life back into Osiris's body. This story reflects many of the beliefs the Egyptians held about their religion and culture. For example, many Egyptian coffins showed the wings of Isis, which bring life to the souls of the dead.*

The Achievements of Ancient Egypt

Although dynasties rose and fell, Nile Valley civilization lasted for many centuries. Ancient Egyptians lived in a stable world based on the dependability of the annual Nile floods and Egypt's geographic isolation, which protected it from frequent invasions. This stability allowed the Egyptians to create a remarkable culture.

Architecture and the arts. When people today think of Egypt, they often picture the huge stone figure of the Great Sphinx and the pyramids. The Egyptians built the pyramids as tombs for the pharaohs. About 80 pyramids still stand, most of which are clustered in groups along the west bank of the Nile. The best-known pyramids, including the Great Pyramid, tower above the sands at Giza. Built in about 2600 B.C., the Great Pyramid covers about 13 acres at its base. It was originally about 480 feet high and was constructed with more than 2 million blocks of stone, each weighing about 5,000 pounds.

The pyramids at Giza were built during the reigns of several Old Kingdom pharaohs.

TEACH OBJECTIVE 1

ALL LEVELS: On the board draw a chart like the one shown. Have students fill in the columns with achievements of ancient Egypt and comparable modern-day achievements. Possible answers are listed in italics.

ENGLISH LANGUAGE LEARNERS, COOPERATIVE LEARNING

	Then	**Now**
Architecture	*pyramids*	*skyscrapers*
The Arts	*Great Sphinx*	*monuments*
Science	*calendar*	*X-rays*
Mathematics	*number system*	*computer math programs*
Medicine	*herbal and medicinal treatments for illnesses*	*penicillin, antibiotics, vaccines, organ transplants, artificial organs*

ENGLISH LANGUAGE LEARNERS

Building the pyramids required great skill. Egyptian architects and engineers ranked among the best in the ancient world. Historians believe the engineers built ramps and levers, which were used by thousands of workers to move the heavy stones.

The Egyptians perfected other art forms as well. Sculptors crafted small, lifelike statues of rulers and animals. Buildings were decorated with paintings of everyday life. The paintings show farmers in their fields, artisans at work, and people at banquets. They provide us with colorful examples of the Egyptian way of life.

Science, math, and medicine. Early in their history the Egyptians invented a calendar based on the movements of the moon. As discussed in Chapter 1, such a calendar does not fill the entire year. Some time later, the Egyptians realized that a bright star appeared above the horizon right before the Nile floods. The time between one rising of this star and the next is 365 days. The Egyptians based their calendar on this cycle. This calendar had 12 months of 30 days each. The remaining five days were used for holidays and feasting. To keep track of the years, Egyptians counted the years of the pharaohs' reigns. For example, they might refer to the first, second, or tenth years of the reign of a certain pharaoh.

In addition to developing a calendar, the Egyptians used a number system based on ten. This system is similar to the decimal system used today. The Egyptians used fractions and whole numbers. They also used geometry to build pyramids and rebuild fields after floods.

The Egyptians made important discoveries in medicine. They knew a good deal about the human body. They used their knowledge to treat illnesses and to preserve bodies after death. Although Egyptian treatments included "magic spells," they also often involved herbs and medicines.

✔ **READING CHECK: Categorizing** What accomplishments did the Egyptians make in architecture, the arts, science, math, and medicine? *pyramids, sculptures, calendar, number system and geometry, herbal medicines*

Education and Religion

To pass on their knowledge, Egyptians developed an educational system. Education focused mainly on an elite group of people called **scribes,** or clerks. Scribes learned to read and write so that they could work for the government. Religious instruction formed an important part of Egyptian education. Schools were usually attached to temples. In fact, religion played a major role in Egyptian life.

The gods. In the early days of Egyptian civilization, many villages had their own local god or gods. These gods often had an animal symbol that people considered sacred. Sacred animals included the cat, the bull, the crocodile, and the scarab beetle.

In time, some of these gods came to be worshiped by people throughout Egypt. The most important god was Amon, or Amon-Re, the creator, identified with the sun. Osiris, who judged people after death, was also associated with the Nile River—just as

INTERPRETING THE VISUAL RECORD

Rituals Wealthy Egyptians used many herbs and ointments to protect their bodies. In this scene from the back of the ornate chair pictured below it, a wife is anointing her husband. **What does this image imply about Egyptian views toward the human body?**

LEVEL 3: Tell students that the Egyptians did not believe that their life cycle ended with death. The Egyptians felt the body needed to be preserved to make existence after death possible. Ask students what objects people with such beliefs might also consider to be important in the afterlife and why.

 HOMEWORK Have each student write a paragraph that describes ancient Egyptian religious beliefs and how these beliefs influenced Egyptian burial practices.

LEVEL 1: Tell students that in ancient Egypt most people were farmers, but the pharaohs directed and profited from their labor. Remind students that farmers grew more crops than they could use in order to have items to trade with other civilizations. Have students look at the map on page 24. Ask them how Egypt might have conducted trade with people in Europe and western and central Africa. *(build ships that would carry them across the Mediterranean, sail ships down the Red Sea, cross the desert)*
ENGLISH LANGUAGE LEARNERS

That's Interesting!

Women had economic power in ancient Egypt. Women could write their own wills, and one woman, displeased with four of her children, disinherited them. Another court document records that a wife loaned some of her silver to her husband. The contract stated that he was required to repay it over three years at a 30 percent interest rate.

VISUAL RECORD ANSWER

They were able to communicate their beliefs visually.

internet connect

TOPIC: Pyramids
GO TO: go.hrw.com
KEYWORD: SP3 WH2

Have students access the Internet through the HRW Go site to research the Egyptian Pyramids. Then have them write detailed paragraphs about the pyramids that they will use in an illustrated brochure. Tell students to include information in their brochure that gives historical background on the pyramids, how they were built, what is inside them, and how they were excavated.

INTERPRETING THE VISUAL RECORD

The ankh The ankh was a powerful religious and spiritual image in ancient Egypt. It was used to symbolize the idea of life. *What do objects such as this ankh tell us about the Egyptians' ability to communicate their beliefs?*

the Nile River regularly flooded and receded, Osiris periodically died and was reborn. Isis was Osiris's wife and the goddess of the royal throne.

The afterlife. At first, Egyptians believed that only pharaohs had an afterlife, or life after death. Later, Egyptians believed that everyone, including animals, had an afterlife. They believed that in the afterlife a person was judged. The person's heart, which would tell whether the person had lied, murdered, or been too proud, was weighed on a great scale against a sacred feather, the symbol of truth. If the scale balanced, the heart had told the truth. It could then enter a place of eternal happiness. If the scale did not balance, the heart was thrown to a horrible monster called the Eater of the Dead.

Egyptians believed that the body had to be preserved to make life after death possible. To do this, they developed a process called **mummification.** Organs were removed from the body, which was then treated with chemicals. This process preserved the body for centuries. Workers placed the mummy in a tomb stocked with clothing, food, tools, and weapons. They even included painted figures that represented servants. The number and value of the objects in the tomb depended on the importance of the dead person. The Egyptians considered the objects necessary for use in the afterlife. In later years, scrolls known as the *Book of the Dead* were placed in the tomb to serve as a kind of guide to the afterlife.

✔ **READING CHECK: Drawing Inferences** In what way can burial sites reveal information about ancient Egyptian religious beliefs? artifacts were meant for use in afterlife

Society and Economy

The pyramids reflected the greatness of the pharaohs. Most Egyptians, however, could never hope for wealth or power. Egyptian social classes were rigidly divided. People in the lower class could improve their status, but they almost never entered the ranks of the upper class. Women, however, enjoyed many legal rights. They ranked as the equals of their husbands in social and business affairs. An Egyptian woman could own property in her own right. She could leave that property to her daughter. In many ways, Egyptian women had more freedom and power than women of other cultures in the region.

Farming. Farmland in Egypt was divided into large estates. Peasants did most of the farming, using crude hoes or wooden plows. Wheat and barley were the chief grain crops. Flax was grown and then spun and woven into linen. Farmers also grew cotton—just as important to Egypt in ancient times as it is today—for weaving into cloth.

CLOSE

Ask students to list the accomplishments of the Egyptians in architecture, the arts, science, mathematics, and medicine and tell which accomplishments were the most important.

REVIEW

Have students complete the Section 2 Review on p. 29.

ASSESS

Have students complete Daily Quiz 2.2. As Alternative Assessment, use the achievements exercise in this section's lesson.

RETEACH

Have students complete Main Idea Activity for English Language Learners and Special-Needs Students 2.2. Then ask students to write a question and answer that covers the main idea for each subsection in the section. **ENGLISH LANGUAGE LEARNERS**

EXTEND

Have students work in groups to build a pyramid. They may use a problem-solving process to create a pyramid modeled after one that exists in Egypt or create a new pyramid with whatever type of materials they choose. **BLOCK SCHEDULING, COOPERATIVE LEARNING**

This mural shows Egyptian farmers processing grain.

The peasants, however, could keep just part of the crop. The rest went to the pharaoh, who legally owned all land, as rents and taxes. The life of a farmer was difficult. One Egyptian described the farmer's day:

Primary Source

"Let me set out for you the farmer's state—that other hard calling. . . . He spends the day cutting tools for cultivating barley and the night twisting ropes. His midday hour even he is in the habit of spending in farmer's work. He sets about equipping himself to sally forth in the field like any warrior [that is, the farmer is burdened with many heavy tools]. The field is parched . . . "

Lansing Papyrus, from *Pharaoh's People*

Trade. Trade was also tightly controlled by the government. Since the peasants of ancient Egypt grew more food than the country needed, Egyptians traded the extra food with other peoples. As trade developed it offered new opportunities to the growing merchant class. Merchants riding donkeys and later camels formed **caravans**— groups of people traveling together for safety over long distances. Caravans traveled from Egypt to western Asia and deep into Africa. Egyptians also traded by sea. They were among the first people to build seagoing ships. Egyptian ships sailed the Mediterranean and Red Seas and traveled the African coast.

Analyzing Primary Sources

Drawing Conclusions Why does the writer claim that farmers have a "hard calling"? farm work was labor-intensive and time-consuming

✔ **READING CHECK: Making Predictions** How might trade affect the spread of Egyptian culture? could expose people in far-off places to Egyptian ideas

---

SECTION 2 REVIEW

1. **Define** and explain the significance:
   scribes
   mummification
   caravans

2. **Categorizing** Copy the concept web below. Use it to record Egyptian achievements in architecture, the arts, education, mathematics, medicine, and the sciences.

   Architecture — Mathematics
   The Arts — Egypt — Medicine
   Education — Science

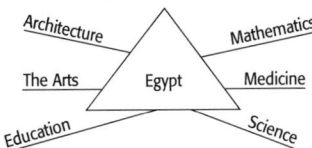

Homework Practice Online
keyword: SP3 HP2

3. **Finding the Main Idea**
   a. How did the Nile floods influence the development of the Egyptian calendar?
   b. What does the Egyptian belief in an afterlife tell about the importance they placed on having a good character?
   c. How did Egyptian success at farming lead to contact with other peoples and cultures?

4. **Writing and Critical Thinking**
   Summarizing Explain why the Egyptians buried mummies in tombs.
   Consider:
   • Egyptian beliefs regarding the afterlife
   • the process of mummification
   • the goods placed in the tombs

SECTION 2 REVIEW ANSWERS

❶ **Define**
• scribes, p. 27
• mummification, p. 28
• caravans, p. 29

❷ Architecture: pyramids; The Arts: Great Sphinx, sculpture, painting; Education: education system for the elite; Mathematics: a number system; Medicine: treatments, ways to preserve bodies after death; Science: a calendar based on 365 days

❸ a. Egyptians based their calendar on a star that appeared near the beginning of the flood cycle.

b. They believed a good character was important for having a good afterlife.

c. Because they grew more food than the country needed, they began trading with other peoples.

❹ Students might suggest that burying people in tombs allowed them to be buried with all they would need in the afterlife.

THE FIRST CIVILIZATIONS **29**

SECTION 3

OBJECTIVES

1 **Explore how geography affected the development of the Sumerian civilization.**

2 **Identify the achievements of the Sumerian people.**

3 **Describe what life was like in Sumerian society.**

SECTION 3

READ TO DISCOVER

❶ How did geography affect the development of the Sumerian civilization?

❷ What were the achievements of the Sumerian people?

❸ What was life like in Sumerian society?

DEFINE

cuneiform
arch
ziggurats
city-state

WHY IT MATTERS TODAY

The Fertile Crescent remains an area of conflict today. Use CNNstudentNews.com or other **current event** sources to explore conflicts between present-day nations in that region. Record your findings in your journal.

Sumerian Civilization

The Main Idea
The Fertile Crescent gave rise to the Sumerian civilization in the Tigris-Euphrates Valley.

The Story Continues *Almost 4,000 years ago in the town of Sumer, a father gave his son the advice that would be repeated by fathers throughout history: "Go to school, stand before your 'school-father,' recite your assignment . . . After you have finished your assignment . . . come to me. . . . Don't stand about in the public square, or wander about the boulevard." The story of the Sumerians shows how early peoples of the Fertile Crescent passed their cultures on to future generations.*

The Land: Its Geography and Importance

The story of ancient Egypt describes one people living in one place for centuries. A very different story developed in southwestern Asia, another cradle of early civilization. Unlike Egypt, this area was not geographically isolated. Wave upon wave of invaders crisscrossed the land.

A strip of fertile land begins at the Isthmus of Suez and arcs through Southwest Asia to the Persian Gulf. The land within this crescent-shaped area is so well suited to farming that it is known as the Fertile Crescent. Between 5000 B.C. and 4000 B.C., Neolithic farmers began to build an identifiable civilization in the Fertile Crescent. Their society was built around the cooperation necessary to control floodwaters and to irrigate fields.

The Fertile Crescent, c. 3000 B.C.

Interpreting Maps
Early civilizations thrived in Mesopotamia, in the heart of the Fertile Crescent.

■ **Skills Assessment: Physical Systems**
According to the map, what type of geographic feature was common to the locations of the earliest Mesopotamian cities?

ALL LEVELS: Have students compare the map of ancient Egypt on page 24 with the map of the Fertile Crescent on page 30. Ask them what similarities they find in the geography of the two civilizations. *(Both civilizations have some natural protections, such as mountains, seas, and desert.)* Then have students make up questions about the geographic distribution of peoples in these regions. Use the questions for class discussion. **ENGLISH LANGUAGE LEARNERS**

HOMEWORK Tell students that they are journalists who write for the newspaper *Sumer Today.* Their assignment is to write an article summarizing why the Fertile Crescent experienced so many invasions, what happened to the newcomers, and the result for Sumer of these invasions. Instead of writing an article, some students may draw illustrations for the newspaper and write short captions.

The Tigris and Euphrates Rivers are major geographical features of the Fertile Crescent. Both rivers begin in the hills of what is now Turkey and flow southeast. At one point the two rivers lie within 30 miles of each other. They then spread apart until the valley between them—the Tigris-Euphrates Valley—widens to about 250 miles. The Tigris-Euphrates Valley has been known by many names, including Mesopotamia. The southeastern part of the valley has usually been called Babylonia.

Both the Tigris and the Euphrates overflow often, sending floodwaters swirling over the surrounding land. People must build canals and dikes to bring water to their fields and to return water to the river after floods. Unlike the Nile flood, the flooding of the Tigris and Euphrates cannot be easily predicted. It may come anytime between the beginning of March and the end of June. The size of the flood also varies. Not surprisingly, the early people of the valley viewed nature and the gods as harsh and unpredictable.

As with the Nile Valley, the Fertile Crescent was surrounded by dry lands and mountains. They were not as barren as those around Egypt, however. Tribes of wandering herders lived off the grasses and other plant life there. They often invaded the valley, conquered it, and established empires. Over time, these invaders grew weak and new waves of invaders conquered them. This pattern makes the history of the Fertile Crescent a story of repeated migration and conquest. A priest described the results of one such invasion.

Primary Source **❝The [invading herders] have set fire to the [crop lands surrounding several Sumerian villages]. They have carried away the silver and precious stones. They have shed blood in the palace of [the local Sumerian ruler]. . . . They have removed the grain from [Sumerian fields and villages], all of it that was under cultivation.❞**

Priest of Lagash, from *The Sumerians*

✔ **READING CHECK: Contrasting** How did the geography of the Fertile Crescent differ from that of ancient Egypt? not isolated by natural barriers

Sumer and Its Achievements

As the Tigris and Euphrates flow to the Persian Gulf, they carry rich soil. In ancient times, particularly fertile soil covered the lower part of the Tigris-Euphrates Valley. Neolithic people settled in this area, called Sumer (SOO·muhr), and grew crops. Over time, they created what we call Sumerian culture. We do not know much about the origins of the Sumerians. A group of nomadic people probably migrated to Sumer and mingled with the people already there. By 3000 B.C. these people used metal and had developed a kind of writing called pictographs, or picture writing. Sumerian pictographs are one of the earliest known forms of writing.

Sumerian writing. Sumerian writing was different from Egyptian writing. Egyptian hieroglyphics were symbols carved on stone or written on paper. The papyrus reed that Egyptians used to make paper did not grow in Sumer, however. Sumerians wrote by pressing marks into clay tablets. Writers used a wedge-shaped tool called a stylus. As a result, most signs were wedge shapes. Today we call Sumerian writing **cuneiform** (kyooh·NEE·uh·fawrm), from the Latin word for wedge, *cuneus.* Cuneiform writing developed from pictographic writing. Sumerians had about 600 cuneiform signs.

Analyzing Primary Sources

Identifying Cause and Effect
How might their fear of the destruction described by the priest have affected the river valley people? might have made them suspicious of outsiders or foreigners

INTERPRETING THE VISUAL RECORD
Sumerian writing The cuneiform above, carved on a clay tablet with a stylus, dates from about 2400 B.C. *In what way does this writing reflect the tools used by the Sumerians?*

Geographically, Mesopotamia is readily accessible from almost all directions. The mountains to the north and east have many valleys and natural passes. The desert to the west and south also provides easy access. Although the area is crisscrossed by many rivers, the rivers are easy to cross. Thus, the Sumerians had few natural barriers to protect their cities and farmland from invasion by nomadic peoples.

Critical Thinking

Ask students to suggest how Mesopotamia's lack of natural boundaries might also have been an advantage.

ANSWER: Although Mesopotamia was vulnerable to invasion, the Sumerians were able to reach the areas around it to engage in trade, exchange ideas, or invade their neighbors.

VISUAL RECORD ANSWER

It involved pressing marks into clay tablets with a wedge-shaped tool.

LEVEL 3: Tell students that, like the Egyptians, the Sumerians created a successful civilization. Ask students to use their knowledge of early civilizations to predict Sumerian achievements.

As a class, have students create a set of 26 cuneiform-style wedge shapes to represent all the letters of the alphabet. Draw these shapes on the chalkboard so that students can copy them. Have each student write a word or phrase in the new alphabet that relates to an aspect of Sumerian society. Have students exchange papers and translate each other's work.

BLOCK SCHEDULING, COOPERATIVE LEARNING

Economics

Economic wealth often shifted between the major city-states throughout the history of Sumer. Just before 3000 B.C. the city-state of Uruk was extremely prosperous. During this period, Sumerians built major temples and shrines in Uruk, which were large and elaborately decorated. When archaeologists uncovered the ruins of these temples, they discovered silver and copper figurines, bowls inlaid with stones, and other carved stone objects. A three-foot-tall vase, with sculpted decorations of a religious procession, as well as a realistic sculpted head of a woman, were also found. Other objects found include the first preserved written records, which were primitive pictographs.

Critical Thinking

Ask students to suggest what the size and wealth of the temples of Uruk may tell us about the role of religion in Sumerian society.

ANSWER: Students should note that religion was important enough to control large amounts of wealth and labor. This would be consistent with the priests' great influence on the Sumerian city-states.

Builders constructed the Choghā Zanbil ziggurat in the Khūzestān province of present-day Iran in about 1250 B.C.

Architecture and science. The Sumerians may also have invented several important architectural designs. The **arch,** a curved structure over an opening, is one of the strongest forms in building. By combining several arches, the Sumerians built rounded roofs in the shape of domes or vaults.

The most striking Sumerian buildings were the temples, known as **ziggurats.** Like other Sumerian buildings, ziggurats were made of baked brick placed in layers. The ziggurats looked something like a wedding cake. Each could be up to 150 feet high. The top served as a shrine to a Sumerian god.

The Sumerians may have been the first people to develop and use the wheel. In mathematics, they used a system of numbers based on 60. For example, Sumerians divided a circle into 360 degrees (six 60s). Each degree was divided into 60 minutes, and each minute into 60 seconds. Today, when you look at a compass or a watch, you are using a system that the Sumerians developed thousands of years ago.

Like other early civilizations, the Sumerians created a lunar calendar. To keep it accurate, they added a month every few years.

✔ **READING CHECK: Finding the Main Idea** What were the main achievements of the Sumerian civilization? cuneiform writing, the arch, the wheel, math

Sumerian Society

Early in their history, Sumerians developed a form of community called the **city-state.** A city-state included a town or city and the surrounding land controlled by it. Major Sumerian city-states—such as Ur, Erech, and Kish—had thousands of residents.

Government and society. The many Sumerian city-states rarely united under a single government. The people believed that much of the land in each city-state belonged to one or more gods. Not surprisingly, priests were important figures. As city-states competed for water and land, however, war leaders became more important. Eventually these leaders ruled as kings.

Kings, high priests, and nobles were at the top of Sumerian society, followed by lower priests, merchants, and scholars. Below them were peasant farmers, then slaves who had been kidnapped from other regions or captured in war.

LEVEL 1: Distribute sheets of drawing paper to students. Tell students to draw a map of a Sumerian city-state. Explain that the maps should include symbols for places such as homes, schools, government buildings, markets, ziggurats, and farms. Students should include a map key to explain the symbols.
ENGLISH LANGUAGE LEARNERS

Have students create a chart or a Venn diagram to compare the religious beliefs of the Sumerians and the Egyptians. *(similarities: polytheism, gods identified with forces of nature and heavenly bodies, gods guarded cities, belief in afterlife; differences: Sumerians did not believe in rewards and punishments after death; Egyptians believed that people were judged after death.)*

SKILL-BUILDING STRATEGIES Evaluating Sources of Evidence

Ancient Discoveries

To learn about ancient civilizations such as the Sumerians or Egyptians, we can study both primary and secondary sources. Primary sources include items such as artifacts, diaries, letters, official documents, and eyewitness accounts. Secondary sources are accounts or histories written after the events by people who did not take part in those events. Each type of evidence offers different information. Sometimes a piece of evidence can be both a primary and a secondary source of evidence.

Howard Carter (top) and colleagues open Tutankhamen's tomb at Luxor, Egypt, 1922.

An Archaeologist's View:
Archaeologist Howard Carter found many artifacts in his lifetime. His greatest discovery was the tomb of the Egyptian pharaoh Tutankhamen. Carter described his find:

"With suppressed excitement I carefully cut the cord, removed that precious seal, drew back the bolts, and opened the doors, when a fourth shrine was revealed . . . There, filling the entire area within stood an immense yellow quartzite sarcophagus [stone coffin]. . . . The lid being suspended in mid-air, we rolled back those covering shrouds, one by one . . . so gorgeous was the sight that met our eyes: a golden effigy [image] of the young boy king.

"The hands, crossed over the breast, held the royal emblems—the Crook and the Flail. Upon the forehead of this recumbent figure . . . were two emblems delicately worked in brilliant inlay—the Cobra and the Vulture—symbols of Upper and Lower Egypt."

The Standard of Ur was found in a Sumerian royal cemetery. It is a mosaic from about 2500 B.C., made of shells and colored stones. The panel is double-sided, showing scenes of war on one side and scenes of peace (right) on the other.

Skills Reminder

To evaluate sources of evidence, you must first identify the source. For example, is it a biography, a diary, a government record, or a work of art? Then review the definitions of primary and secondary sources to determine what type of source it is. The language of a written source, comparison with other sources, and information about the origins or author of the source will also help you determine its usefulness.

Skills Practice

❶ What kind of source is *The Standard of Ur*? What does it reveal about Sumerian society?

❷ How might Howard Carter's description of the opening of King Tutankhamen's tomb be considered both a primary and a secondary source?

❸ Is a primary source always more reliable than a secondary source? Why or why not?

That's Interesting!

Artistic innovations can be found in several Sumerian temples. At the Eanna temple, builders found an innovative way to decorate the walls. Artists took tens of thousands of small clay cones with red, black, or buff tips. They then inserted these cones into the mud plaster of the walls to form triangles, zigzags, and other geometric designs.

SKILLS PRACTICE ANSWERS

1. It is a primary source. It reveals the various activities of Sumerian society.

2. The description would be considered a primary source when used to answer questions about the opening of the tomb, and it would be considered a secondary source when used to answer questions about the burial of King Tut.

3. Students might answer yes, because the writer was present during the event, or no, because the accounts may be subjective.

REVIEW

Have students complete the Section 3 Review on p. 34.

ASSESS

Have students complete Daily Quiz 2.3. As Alternative Assessment, have students complete either of the map exercises in this section's lessons.

RETEACH

Have students complete Main Idea Activity for English Language Learners and Special-Needs Students 2.3. Have students write three important Sumerian achievements and describe why each was important. (*Students may mention cuneiform, arches, ziggurats, the wheel, the city-state. Encourage students to expand on their descriptions of why each was important.*)
ENGLISH LANGUAGE LEARNERS

EXTEND

Tell students to imagine that they are social studies schoolteachers in ancient Sumer. Using social studies terminology, have them prepare a lesson to present to the class about Sumerian history, contemporary civilization, or any aspect of Sumerian society.
BLOCK SCHEDULING

YOUNG PEOPLE IN HISTORY ANSWER

Students might suggest that the Sumerians believed only intelligent and skillful boys could learn to be scribes.

SECTION 3 REVIEW ANSWERS

❶ **Define**
• cuneiform, p. 31
• arch, p. 32
• ziggurats, p. 32
• city-state, p. 32

❷ Writing: cuneiform; Religion: polytheism, did not believe in rewards and punishment after death; Architecture/Science: arches, ziggurats, the wheel, number system, calendar; Government/Society: city-state, trade, education

❸ a. It was not geographically isolated, making invasions easy.

b. They considered learning very important for intelligent, upper-class males.

c. The Sumerians did not believe in an afterlife or in rewards or punishments after death.

❹ Students should mention achievements such as cuneiform writing, ziggurats, the wheel, a number system, a calendar, and successful trade with other peoples.

YOUNG PEOPLE IN HISTORY

Ancient Schools
Sumerian boys who showed intelligence and skill were trained to be scribes. They learned to read and write in cuneiform. They also learned basic mathematics. Teachers often punished poor performance with beatings.

Schoolboys who were late for class were also punished harshly. One Sumerian boy wrote, "In school the monitor in charge said to me: 'Why are you late?' Afraid and with pounding heart, I entered before my teacher and made a respectful [bow]." History does not record the outcome of the boy's tardiness. **Why might just some Sumerian boys have been allowed to receive an education?**

Farming and trade. Most Sumerians farmed. They grew dates, grains, and vegetables, and raised domestic animals. They also grew flax for linen and wove woolen goods.

Sumerian farmers grew enough food to allow many people to work as artisans and traders. Before 3000 B.C., Sumerians had begun trading with other peoples of Southwest Asia. Some merchants had agents in faraway places. Others traveled by land or boat to sell Sumerian goods.

Education and religion. The Sumerians considered education very important. However, only upper-class boys—and no girls—attended school. Students learned to write and spell by copying religious books and songs. They also studied drawing and arithmetic.

Sheep provided wool and meat for early Sumerians. This sheep's head sculpture was crafted in Sumeria about 5,200 years ago.

Like the Egyptians, the Sumerians practiced polytheism. The Sumerian gods were identified with forces of nature and heavenly bodies, such as the sun and the moon. Important gods included An (lord of heaven), Enlil (god of air and storms), and Enki (god of water and wisdom). Sumerian gods and goddesses also guarded individual cities. The city of Nippur, for example, was overseen by the god Enlil, while his son Nanna, god of the moon, guarded the city of Ur.

The Sumerians buried food and tools with their dead. Unlike the Egyptians, however, the Sumerians did not imagine the afterlife in detail. Instead, the Sumerians believed in a kind of shadowy lower world. They did not believe in rewards and punishments after death.

✔ **READING CHECK: Identifying Bias** What did the structure of their educational system reveal about the biases in Sumerian society? only upper-class males were educated

SECTION 3 REVIEW

1. **Define** and explain the significance:
   cuneiform
   arch
   ziggurats
   city-state

2. **Summarizing** Copy the chart below. Use it to show the major characteristics of Sumerian civilization.

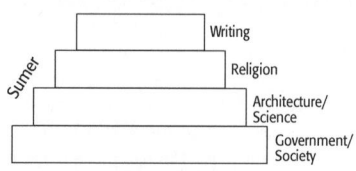

3. **Finding the Main Idea**
   a. How did geography shape life in the Fertile Crescent?
   b. What did their focus on education reveal about Sumerian values?
   c. How was society in Sumer different from society in Egypt?

4. **Writing and Critical Thinking**
   Supporting a Point of View Write a report that persuades readers that Sumerians created a successful civilization.
   Consider:
   • Sumerian achievements in math and writing
   • trade with other peoples
   • construction of large temples

Homework Practice Online
keyword: SP3 HP2

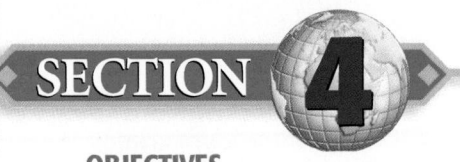

SECTION 4

OBJECTIVES

1 Explain why Sumerians were attacked by outsiders.

2 Examine the characteristics of Babylonian society.

3 Investigate which invaders conquered Babylon and why they failed to control it.

4 Describe the achievements of the Persians.

LET'S GET STARTED!

As students enter the classroom, ask them to write a short description of what they think happened to the Sumerians. *(Students might guess that their geographic vulnerability led to many attacks on them and eventually they were conquered.)* Tell students that in Section 4 they will learn about the empires of the Fertile Crescent that developed after the Sumerians were conquered.

SECTION 4

READ TO DISCOVER

❶ Why were Sumerians attacked by outsiders?

❷ What characterized Babylonian society?

❸ What invaders conquered Babylon and why did they fail to control it?

❹ What were the achievements of the Persians?

IDENTIFY

Sargon
Hammurabi
Nebuchadnezzar
Cyrus
Zoroaster

▶WHY IT MATTERS TODAY

The people who lived in the Fertile Crescent developed different legal systems. Use CNNstudentNews.com or other **current event** sources to find information about a law being proposed in the United States today and why people oppose or support it. Record your findings in your journal.

CNNstudentNews.com

Empires of the Fertile Crescent

The Main Idea
A series of invaders from both within and outside of Mesopotamia controlled the Fertile Crescent.

The Story Continues *"You dolt, numskull, school pest, you illiterate, you Sumerian ignoramus, your hand is terrible; it cannot even hold the stylus properly; it is unfit for dictation."* So wrote one Sumerian scribe about another, criticizing his writing skills. More serious infighting so weakened the Sumerians that they were left vulnerable to attack.

The Akkadians

In about 2330 B.C. the Akkadians, a people who lived in Mesopotamia, attacked and conquered the Sumerians. The Akkadians spoke a Semitic language related to modern Arabic and Hebrew. **Sargon,** who ruled from about 2334 B.C. to 2279 B.C., was the most powerful Akkadian king. He established a great empire that reached as far west as the Mediterranean Sea.

The Akkadian Empire lasted about 150 years. When it ended, Sumerian city-states once again prospered, including the important city of Ur. However, new waves of invaders swept through the eastern Fertile Crescent. Another powerful state of Semitic-speaking people arose. It was centered at a large new city called Babylon.

✔ **READING CHECK: Problem Solving** What actions might the Sumerians have taken to help fight off invaders like the Akkadians?

Akkadian Empire, c. 2330 B.C.

Interpreting Maps The Akkadian king Sargon first came to power in the city of Kish. Later, Sargon moved his capital to Akkad.

■ **Skills Assessment: Environment and Society** Why might the city of Ur have been an important center of Mesopotamian trade?

SECTION 4 RESOURCES

REPRODUCIBLE RESOURCES

▶ Guided Reading Strategy 2.4

▶ Graphic Organizer Activity 2

▶ Readings in World History 7, 8

TECHNOLOGY RESOURCES

▶ One-Stop Planner 2.4

▶ Holt Researcher: World History: Cyrus, Darius I, Zoroaster

▶ Homework Practice Online

REINFORCEMENT, REVIEW, AND ASSESSMENT

▶ Section 4 Review, p. 40

▶ Daily Quiz 2.4

▶ Main Idea Activity 2.4

▶ English Audio Summary 2.4

▶ Spanish Audio Summary 2.4

MAP ANSWER
Students might point out that it was located near other cities.

THE FIRST CIVILIZATIONS **35**

35

TEACH OBJECTIVE 1

LEVEL 3: Tell students to imagine they are Sumerians preparing for an attack by outside invaders. Have students use a problem-solving process to determine why outside invaders attack and to develop a method for defending their city-state. Ask them to develop a plan for governing the area that would unite all the city-states and prevent outside invaders from conquering them. Have students share their plans with the class.

Government

The Code of Hammurabi covered all sorts of legal issues and dealings between individuals. One important aspect of the code was that it made people think twice about bringing false charges against a neighbor. The code stated: "If a seignior came forward with false testimony in a case, and has not proved the word which he spoke, if that case was a case involving life, that seignior shall be put to death."

Critical Thinking

Ask if students see any disadvantage to this aspect of the Code of Hammurabi.

ANSWER: This rule might have discouraged people from testifying, out of fear for their own lives.

HISTORY MAKER ANSWER
his code of laws

MAP ANSWER
the mountains

Technology Resources
World History and Cultures Video Program 2: The First Empires

---

The Babylonians

In about 1792 B.C. a strong ruler named **Hammurabi** (ham·uh·RAHB·ee) came to power in Babylon. He conquered most of the Tigris-Euphrates Valley. More than just a great military leader, Hammurabi was also an outstanding political leader and lawmaker. He is best known for the Code of Hammurabi. This collection of about 282 laws was compiled under his direction. It contained some ideas that are still found in law codes today.

Code of Hammurabi. The Code of Hammurabi concerned all aspects of life in Babylon. Some laws dealt with commerce and industry, while others regulated wages, hours, working conditions, and property rights. Punishment was harsh, based as it was on the idea of "an eye for an eye."

 "[1] If a man bring[s] an accusation against a man, and charge[s] him with a [major] crime, but cannot prove it, he, the accuser, shall be put to death. [229–30] If a builder build[s] a house for a man and [does] not make its construction firm, and the house which he has built collapse[s] and cause[s] the death of the owner of the house, that builder shall be put to death."

Hammurabi, from *Code of Hammurabi*

Punishment varied according to status, however. If a wealthy man destroyed the eye of a poor man, the wealthy man did not lose his eye. Instead, he paid a fine.

Babylonian culture. In some ways Babylonian culture resembled that of the Sumerians. Most Babylonians farmed. They kept domestic animals and grew a wide variety of food crops. They also wove cotton and wool cloth. The Babylonians were very active traders. Their merchants exchanged goods with distant parts of the Fertile Crescent and with Egypt and India.

Babylonian women had some legal and economic rights, including property rights. Women could be merchants, traders, or even scribes. On the other hand, husbands could divorce their wives, but wives could not divorce their husbands. If a husband was cruel, however, a woman could leave him and take her property with her.

Religion. The Babylonians adopted many Sumerian religious beliefs. The Babylonians made sacrifices to their gods for favors like good harvests or success in business. Like the Sumerians, they believed in a shadowy life after death. Their religious practices were directed toward a successful life on Earth. Babylonians also believed that their priests could foretell the future. Therefore, Babylonian priests held great power and wealth.

✔ **READING CHECK: Drawing Conclusions** How do you think the Code of Hammurabi affected Babylonian society? people probably feared breaking the law

---

HISTORY MAKER
Hammurabi (d. 1750 B.C.)

Hammurabi was originally a king of the Amorite people, who migrated into Mesopotamia. As ruler Hammurabi built on the civilization that had begun in Sumer. Today he is best remembered for his code of laws. **What is Hammurabi best known for?**

The Babylonian Empire, c. 1750 B.C.

Interpreting Maps Like other kingdoms of the Fertile Crescent, the Babylonian Empire was centered on the Tigris and Euphrates Rivers.

■ **Skills Assessment: Using Geography** What major geographic feature may have prevented the expansion of the Babylonian Empire northward?

Other Conquerors

Many times throughout history, conquerors adopted the culture of the people they conquered. This was certainly true of the Babylonians after they conquered the Sumerians. Some conquerors, however, kept their own cultural values. This was the case with the Hittites.

The Hittites. The Hittites were a warlike people who invaded the Tigris-Euphrates Valley from Asia Minor sometime in the 1600s B.C. The Hittites were among the first people to smelt iron. Their most important achievement, however, may have been their laws and government. Under Hittite law, only major crimes received the death penalty. Hittite law called for a person to pay a fine, rather than experience retaliation, for causing damage or injury. As in some other empires of the time, the Hittite kings were regarded as chief-priests, although they allowed significant religious freedom.

When the Hittites invaded the Tigris-Euphrates Valley, they conquered and looted the city of Babylon. The Hittites were too far from their homeland to control Babylon permanently, however. They soon withdrew to the western part of the Fertile Crescent. They remained a powerful force there until about 1200 B.C., when the entire region began to be hit by invasions from the Sea Peoples.

The Assyrians. The Assyrians were a Semitic-speaking people from northern Mesopotamia. As early as the 2000s B.C. they had settled the city of Ashur on the upper Tigris River and adopted many elements of Sumerian culture. For centuries they had been dominated by others. The Assyrians briefly established an empire of their own in the 1300s B.C., but it was soon overrun by nomadic migrations. They gradually recovered, however, and began to dominate the area of southwest Asia. Between about 900 B.C. and about 650 B.C., the Assyrians expanded their power across the Fertile Crescent and into Egypt. At its height, the mighty empire included all of Mesopotamia, Syria, Palestine, and the Nile Valley.

The Assyrians were fierce, effective warriors. Not only did they use chariots in battle, but they also were the first to use cavalry—soldiers on horseback. They used terror to control their enemies. They frequently enslaved the people they conquered and killed captured enemy soldiers. Sometimes they deported whole populations to other regions. By these methods, the Assyrians added land to their empire and gained many slaves. About 700 B.C. the Assyrians captured Babylon, looted it, and then destroyed it completely.

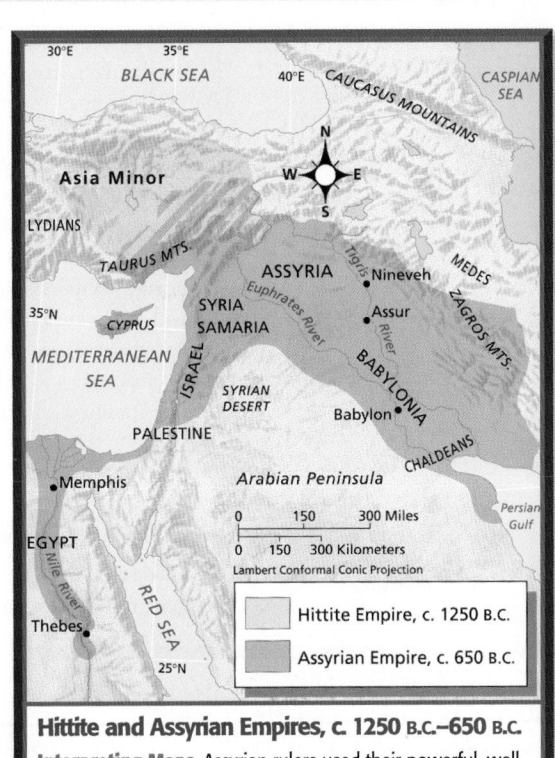

Hittite and Assyrian Empires, c. 1250 B.C.–650 B.C.

Interpreting Maps Assyrian rulers used their powerful, well-trained army to conquer new lands and to expand their empire. Captive peoples were forced by the Assyrians to work on various construction projects.

■ **Skills Assessment: The World in Spatial Terms** In terms of size, how did the Assyrian Empire compare to the earlier empires of Akkad and Babylonia?

INTERPRETING THE VISUAL RECORD

Epic of Gilgamesh Preserved by the Assyrians, the *Epic of Gilgamesh* is the story of a mythical Sumerian king. It reflects Sumerians' beliefs about life and death. Here Gilgamesh is pictured wrestling with a lion. ***In what way does this ancient relief portray Gilgamesh as a heroic, larger-than-life figure?***

Culture

A Hittite king was also the chief priest of the kingdom. On occasion, a king might even return from a military campaign to perform his religious duties. Indeed, when a Hittite king died, it was believed that he became a god. This supposed transformation, along with the Hittite custom of adopting the gods of their conquered subjects, meant that the number of Hittite gods continued to grow. At the height of their power, it is believed that the Hittites worshipped over 600 gods. Arinna, the sun goddess, was the most powerful of the deities, while Tarhunnas, the weather god, stood at her side.

Critical Thinking

Ask students why the Hittites might have adopted the gods of their conquered subjects.

ANSWER: Students might suggest that the Hittites wanted to win some acceptance from the peoples they conquered.

VISUAL RECORD ANSWER

The lion appears tiny compared to him.

MAP ANSWER
It was much larger.

LEVEL 1: Have students write their definition of the word *empire. (a government that unites different territories and people under one rule)* Then ask students what systems and skills are necessary to run an empire. *(Students might answer: strong army, good communication and transportation system, efficient government, common language, legal system.)* Then tell students to make a chart with the headings *Pros* and *Cons.* Have students list the following empires along the left side of the chart: *Akkadians, Babylonians, Hittites, Assyrians, Chaldeans, Persians.* Tell students to fill in their charts as they read the section. The *Pros* column includes characteristics that contributed to the empire's continuation, and the *Cons* column includes characteristics that contributed to its downfall.

ENGLISH LANGUAGE LEARNERS

Empire	Pros	Cons
Akkadians		
Babylonians		
Hittites		
Assyrians		
Chaldeans		
Persians		

LITERATURE. In the *Epic of Gilgamesh* the hero travels to the Land of the Dead to search out immortality. His first advice comes from a wine maiden in the Land of the Dead. To his confession that he fears death and cannot rest, she replies: "Gilgamesh, where are you hurrying to? You will never find that life for which you are looking. When the gods created man they allotted to him death, but life they retained in their own keeping. As for you, Gilgamesh, fill your belly with good things; day and night, night and day, dance and be merry, feast and rejoice. . ." An ancestor to whom Gilgamesh goes for advice on obtaining immortality replies: "There is no permanence. Do we build a house to stand for ever, do we seal a contract to hold for all time? Do brothers divide an inheritance to keep for ever, does the flood-time of the rivers endure?"

Critical Thinking

Ask students what this myth indicates about Mesopotamians' view of life and death.

ANSWER: Mesopotamians seemed to believe that there was little permanence in life and it was better to enjoy life while it lasted.

MAP ANSWERS

1. the Euphrates

2. They could transport goods easily by boat.

The Assyrians were one of the first peoples to effectively govern a large empire. The Assyrian king had absolute, or total, power. He was responsible only to the god Ashur. Priests and government officials took orders from the king and answered to him. Governors ruled conquered lands and made regular reports to the king.

After the Assyrians rose to power, they made the city of Nineveh their capital. Attempting to fortify the city as strongly as possible, they constructed a huge double wall around it. The wall was more than 70 feet high and stretched for 7.5 miles around the city. In places, it was as much as 148 feet wide and it had 15 decorated gates.

Nineveh contained a great library in which Assyrian scholars kept clay tablets filled with literature and other works collected from all over the empire. This library helped to preserve learning for future generations. Among the many texts it contained was the great *Epic of Gilgamesh*, the story of a Sumerian king and one of the oldest works of literature known. Today's historians have learned much about Sumerian beliefs and lifestyles by studying the *Epic of Gilgamesh*.

Powerful Assyria and its great capital eventually fell. In about 635 B.C. civil war broke out, weakening Assyria so that it could not resist outside invaders. Finally in 612 B.C., a group of enemies led by the Chaldeans and the Medes captured and destroyed Nineveh.

The Chaldeans. The Chaldeans took control of much of the territory that the Assyrians had ruled. Under the leadership of **Nebuchadnezzar** (neb·uh·kuhd·NEZ·uhr), the Chaldeans conquered most of the Fertile Crescent. Nebuchadnezzar governed from the rebuilt city of Babylon from 605 B.C. until his death in 562 B.C.

Under Nebuchadnezzar, Babylon once again became a large and wealthy city. Trade flourished, and within the city were impressive canals and magnificent buildings. The king's palace included beautiful terraced gardens, known as the Hanging Gardens. According to legend, Amytis, one of Nebuchadnezzar's wives, had lived in the mountains. Now, living on the drier plains of Babylonia, she missed the greenery of her homeland. To please her, the king planted thousands of brightly colored tropical trees and flowers on the palace grounds. The Greeks and other peoples of the ancient world regarded the Hanging Gardens of Babylon as one of the Seven Wonders of the World.

The Chaldeans were skilled astronomers. They kept careful records of the apparent movement of the stars and planets and could predict solar and lunar eclipses. The Chaldeans also made advances in mathematics. They calculated the length of a year with a very high degree of accuracy.

All the strength of the Chaldeans, however, lay in the leadership of Nebuchadnezzar. After he died the Chaldeans had difficulties. One of his successors quarreled with the priests, who then betrayed the city to enemies. Within 30 years of Nebuchadnezzar's death, the Chaldean empire fell.

Chaldean Empire, c. 600 B.C.

Interpreting Maps The Chaldeans under Nebuchadnezzar conquered a large part of the Assyrians' far-flung empire.

■ **Skills Assessment: 1. Locate** On what river was Babylon located? **2. Drawing Conclusions** How would this location have helped the Chaldeans improve trade?

✔ **READING CHECK: Evaluating** In what ways did the great Assyrian library at Nineveh contribute to the ancient world's store of knowledge? preserved learning from many regions for future generations

TEACH OBJECTIVES 2 and 4

LEVEL 2: Have students complete a list of the accomplishments of the empires of the Fertile Crescent. *(Babylonians: Code of Hammurabi; Hittites: less brutal system of law than the Babylonians; Assyrians: built a large library, encouraged scholarship and literature; Chaldeans: advances in astronomy; Persians: developed an effective government, developed Zoroastrianism)* You may choose to extend this activity by organizing the class into three groups: Assyrians, Chaldeans, and Persians. Tell the members of each group to prepare a debate speech explaining why their accomplishments demonstrate that they are the most advanced Fertile Crescent society. Members of the opposing groups should ask questions. **COOPERATIVE LEARNING**

HOMEWORK Have students read the section under "Persian religion" on page 40. Ask students to list similarities and differences between Zoroastrianism and the religions of ancient Egypt and Babylon. Then ask them to list similarities between Zoroastrianism and Judaism.

CLOSE

Have students write a brief summary of the achievements and political systems of the Akkadians, Babylonians, Hittites, Assyrians, Chaldeans, and Persians.

REVIEW

Have students complete the Section 4 Review on p. 40.

The Persians

The Persians conquered Babylon in 539 B.C. Like the Hittites, the Persians spoke an Indo-European language. They and another group, the Medes, had migrated into what is now Iran by about 850 B.C. The region became known as Persia and Media.

At first the Medes ruled over the Persians. In about 550 B.C., however, the Persian ruler **Cyrus** the Great rebelled against the Medes. Cyrus then captured Babylon and took over the rest of the Fertile Crescent and Asia Minor.

Cyrus and later rulers, including Darius I and his son Xerxes I (ZUHRK·seez), expanded Persian rule even more. The Persian Empire stretched between the Indus River and parts of southeastern Europe. Both Darius and Xerxes invaded Greece in the 400s B.C., but failed to conquer it. Nevertheless, the Persians still ruled the mightiest empire in history up to that time.

Government. The early Persian kings were effective rulers as well as great generals. Although all-powerful, they showed great concern for justice. They collected taxes and administered the law fairly. The Persians also treated the people they conquered better than earlier empires had. They allowed conquered peoples to keep their own religions and laws. Secret agents known as "the King's Eyes and Ears" kept the king informed. As a result, regional governors and military leaders appointed by the ruler were held in check.

Holt Researcher
go.hrw.com
KEYWORD: Holt Researcher
FreeFind: Cyrus
Darius I
After reading more about Cyrus and Darius I on the Holt Researcher, create a chart comparing and contrasting their reigns.

Government

Before weights and measures were standardized, different methods were used across the Persian Empire. This made trade difficult. To determine volume, Darius established the king's measure, which was similar to the modern bushel. The unit of length was the royal cubit, measuring 18 inches, and the standard for weight was the karsha, which equaled about one-fifth of a pound.

Critical Thinking

Ask students to imagine why standardized measures would have made trade easier.

ANSWER: Students should suggest that standardized measures would have allowed people to easily know the cost of the product, without having to convert units of measure.

MAP ANSWERS

1. Royal Road

2. It connected the widely separated cities of the realm, allowing rulers to travel between them more easily.

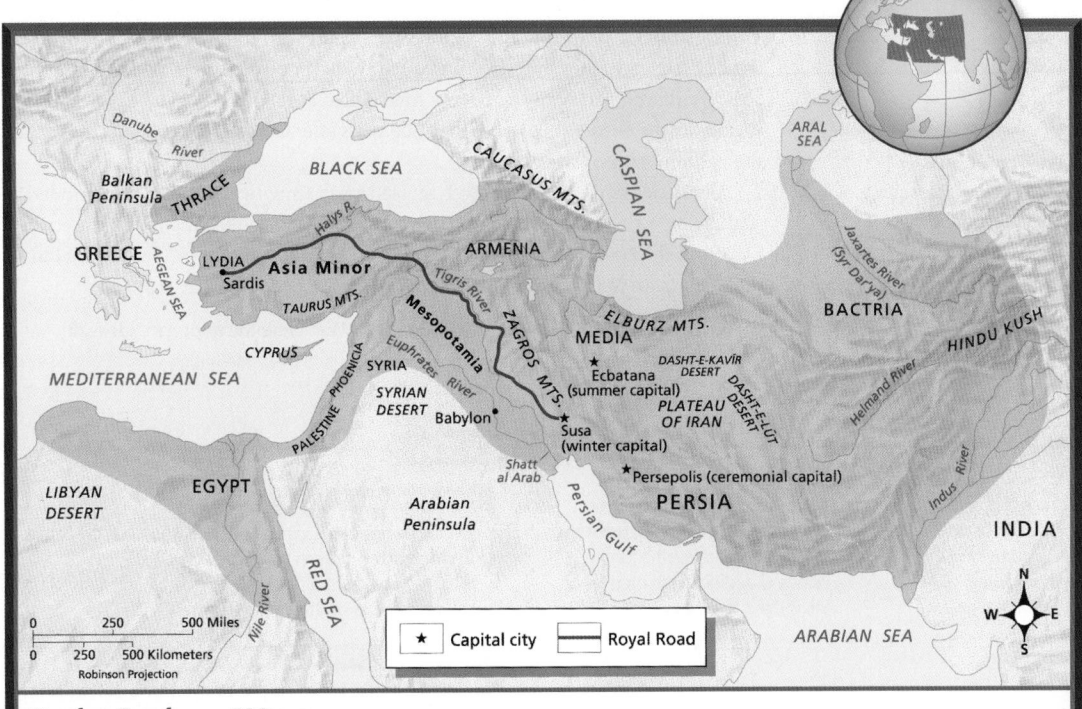

Persian Empire, c. 500 B.C.

Interpreting Maps At its height, the mighty Persian Empire stretched from southeastern Europe to the Hindu Kush plateau and the Indus River in southwestern Asia.

■ **Skills Assessment: 1. Human Systems** What road ran through the Persian Empire? **2. Drawing Inferences** How might this road have helped Persian rulers control their huge empire?

ASSESS

Have students complete Daily Quiz 2.4. As Alternative Assessment, you may want to use the empires or accomplishments exercises in this section's lessons.

RETEACH

Have students complete Main Idea Activity for English Language Learners and Special-Needs Students 2.4. Then ask them to think about what they have learned about each of the empires of the Fertile Crescent. Have them write brief journal entries describing a day in the life of a teenager in the Fertile Crescent. **ENGLISH LANGUAGE LEARNERS**

EXTEND

Divide students into six groups and assign one of the empires discussed in the section to each group. Tell students that they are to use sources such as computer software, biographies, and artifacts to produce a contemporary magazine about their empire.
BLOCK SCHEDULING, COOPERATIVE LEARNING

SECTION 4 REVIEW ANSWERS

❶ Identify
- Sargon, p. 35
- Hammurabi, p. 36
- Nebuchadnezzar, p. 38
- Cyrus, p. 39
- Zoroaster, p. 40

❷ Akkadians: conquered Sumerians, established a great empire; invaders; Babylonians: Code of Hammurabi, cotton and wool, trade, property rights for women; conquered by Hittites; Hittites: iron, legal system; too far from homeland to control Babylon, invasion from the Sea Peoples; Assyrians: chariots, cavalry, library; civil war led to invasions from outside; Chaldeans: trade, canals, buildings, advances in astronomy, sciences and mathematics; death of Nebuchadnezzar; Persians: just government, roads, Zoroaster; weak rulers

❸ a. Akkadians, Babylonians, Hittites, Assyrians, Chaldeans, Persians

b. Students answers will vary and should be supported.

❹ Students should mention the Code of Hammurabi, the legal and economic rights of women, and the focus on a successful life on Earth rather than in an afterlife.

The Persian prophet and teacher Zoroaster developed an influential religious philosophy during the 600s B.C.

Holt Researcher go.hrw.com
go.hrw.com
KEYWORD: Holt Researcher
FreeFind: Zoroaster
After reading more about Zoroaster on the Holt Researcher, make a list of the ways in which Zoroastrianism influenced world events.

The Persians built roads to connect the cities within their empire. The Royal Road, for example, stretched more than 1,250 miles. It connected Sardis in western Asia Minor with Susa, one of the imperial capitals. The Persians built these roads mainly for the army and postal riders. Some historians think that later civilizations, such as the Romans, borrowed this idea. The Persian road system helped to link the sprawling empire together. The roads also allowed different cultures in the empire to exchange customs, goods, and ideas.

Persian religion. Perhaps the greatest cultural contribution of the Persians concerned religion. At first, like other early peoples, the Persians worshiped many gods. Then, in about 600 B.C., the teachings of a great prophet named **Zoroaster** (ZOHR·uh·was·tuhr), or Zarathushtra, changed their religious outlook.

Zoroaster taught that on Earth people receive training for a future life. He said that in the world the forces of good and evil battle one another. People must choose between them. Those who chose good would be rewarded with eternal blessings; those who chose evil would face punishment. In the distant future, the forces of good would triumph. Then Earth would disappear.

The teachings of Zoroaster are known as Zoroastrianism. The central beliefs of this religion—the universal struggle between good and evil and the idea of final judgment—have had a great impact on history. Among the many great religions that Zoroastrianism probably influenced were Judaism and, later, Christianity.

The decline of the Persians. The Persian kings who followed Darius and Xerxes lacked their leadership abilities. Consequently, the empire began to lose its strength. In 331 B.C., the Persian Army suffered a final defeat at the hands of the Greek forces of Alexander the Great. Thus, more than 200 years after Cyrus's revolt against the Medes, the Persian empire was conquered.

Centuries later, Persian power revived for a time under a dynasty founded in A.D. 226 by a ruler named Ardashir, who saw himself as following in the tradition of Darius and Xerxes. Ardashir worked to rid Persia of foreign influences, including those left from the Greeks. He also revived the practice of Zoroastrianism.

✔ **READING CHECK: Finding the Main Idea** What were the important ideas of Zoroaster's teachings? struggle between good and evil, final judgment

SECTION 4 REVIEW

1. **Identify** and explain the significance:
   Sargon
   Hammurabi
   Nebuchadnezzar
   Cyrus
   Zoroaster

2. **Sequencing** Copy the graphic organizer below six times. Use it to plot the main achievements and causes of decline of the empires of the Fertile Crescent.

   Empire

   Achievements   Decline

3. **Finding the Main Idea**
   a. List the names of the various peoples who ruled the Fertile Crescent in the order in which they ruled.
   b. Which achievement of the empires of the Fertile Crescent do you believe was most important? Why?

4. **Writing and Critical Thinking**
   Finding the Main Idea Imagine that you are a traveler in the ancient world who is visiting the Tigris-Euphrates Valley from another land. Write a brief description of Babylonian society.
   Consider:
   • how society was organized
   • how people were treated under Babylonian law and the Code of Hammurabi
   • how religion affected the way people acted

Homework Practice Online

keyword: SP3 HP2

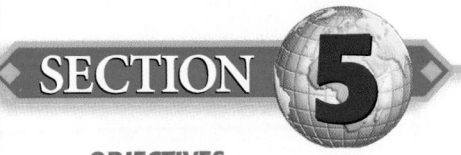
🔔 LET'S GET STARTED!

As students enter the classroom, ask them what caused elements of culture to spread between ancient civilizations. *(traveling to other areas for trade)* Tell students that in Section 5 they will learn about Phoenician trade and the cultural diffusion that resulted.

TEACH OBJECTIVE 1

ALL LEVELS: Have students work in pairs to conduct a business transaction, replacing written words with visuals. Then discuss how the development of an alphabet influenced the spread of Phoenician culture. *(Other peoples learned the alphabet from Phoenician traders who used written contracts.)*

ENGLISH LANGUAGE LEARNERS, COOPERATIVE LEARNING

READ TO DISCOVER

❶ How did trade influence Phoenician culture?

❷ How did a money economy develop in Lydia?

DEFINE

barter
commodities
money economy

IDENTIFY

Phoenician alphabet

► WHY IT MATTERS TODAY

Trade remains an important activity in the world today. Use CNN or other **current event** sources to find information about international trade. Record your findings in your journal.

CNN student News .com

The Phoenicians and the Lydians

The Main Idea
The societies of Phoenicia and Lydia made important contributions to other Mediterranean cultures.

The Story Continues *"Who was ever silenced like Tyre . . . ? When your merchandise went out on the seas, you satisfied many nations; with your great wealth and your wares you enriched the kings of the earth." This passage from the Bible evokes the splendor of the Phoenician city-state of Tyre at its height.*

The Phoenicians

The peoples in the western end of the Fertile Crescent did not create large empires, but they still had a great influence on the modern world. Today this region forms the nations of Israel, Lebanon, and Syria. In ancient times, people called part of this region Phoenicia (fi·NI·shuh).

Phoenicia consisted of a loose union of city-states, each governed by a different king. Phoenicia had little fertile land and the Lebanon Mountains made migration to the east difficult. Thus, the Phoenicians turned to trading on the sea. The Phoenician seaports of Tyre and Sidon (SYD·uhn) became world famous.

The Phoenicians and the Lydians, c. 1200 B.C.– c. 600 B.C.

Interpreting Maps The early cultures of the eastern Mediterranean inhabited lands that were characterized by many different geographic environments.

■ **Skills Assessment: Environment and Society** What two cities shown on the map would you expect to be major centers of trade and commerce?

[Map showing the Phoenicians and the Lydians region: Black Sea, Asia Minor, Lydia, Aegean Sea, Mediterranean Sea, Cyprus, Taurus Mts., Lebanon Mts., Euphrates River, Sidon, Tyre, Syrian Desert, Dead Sea, Africa, Egypt, Nile River, Sinai Peninsula, Mt. Sinai, Arabian Peninsula. Legend: Lydia c. 600 B.C., Phoenicia c. 1200 B.C. Scale: 0–150–300 Miles; 0–150–300 Kilometers. Lambert Conformal Conic Projection.]

SECTION 5 RESOURCES

REPRODUCIBLE RESOURCES

▶ Guided Reading Strategy 2.5

▶ Geography Activity 2: The End of an Island Civilization

TECHNOLOGY RESOURCES

▶ One-Stop Planner 2.5

▶ World History Teaching Transparency: Geography and History 2: The Eastern Mediterranean

▶ Homework Practice Online

REINFORCEMENT, REVIEW, AND ASSESSMENT

▶ Section 5 Review, p. 43

▶ Daily Quiz 2.5

▶ Main Idea Activity 2.5

▶ English Audio Summary 2.5

▶ Spanish Audio Summary 2.5

TEACH OBJECTIVE 2

LEVEL 1: Organize students into groups and assign each group a different product. Then have groups negotiate with one another to trade their goods. Discuss how the use of coined money simplifies trade.
ENGLISH LANGUAGE LEARNERS, COOPERATIVE LEARNING

HOMEWORK Ask students to write a short report about how salespeople conduct business today. How do these methods compare with those used by Phoenicians and Lydians?

TEACH OBJECTIVE 2

LEVEL 3: Have students work in groups to design coins and determine their values. Students should use the following chart to illustrate their money systems.

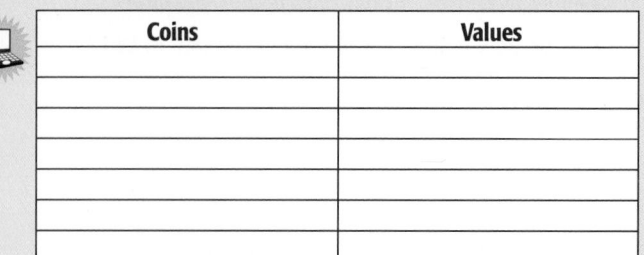

Coins	Values

COOPERATIVE LEARNING

That's Interesting!

It took about 60,000 murices to make one pound of royal purple dye. The dye came from a small gland in the murex, but each gland yielded only a drop or two of the yellowish liquid that would darken into purple when exposed to sun and air.

VISUAL RECORD ANSWER

It was far-reaching.

WHAT IF? ANSWER

Europeans might have developed an alphabet later in history, and they might have been influenced by other cultures, such as Arabic or Chinese cultures.

Technology Resources

 Online Maps, Charts, and Graphs: Phoenician Sea Routes

INTERPRETING THE VISUAL RECORD

Ivory carving Ivory—the material from which this Phoenician sculpture was carved—was highly prized in the ancient world. Phoenician merchants imported ivory from coastal North and East Africa. *What evidence does this carving provide about the extent of the Phoenicians' trading empire?*

What If? Phoenician trade helped spread the use of the alphabet throughout the Mediterranean region. **How might the history of writing have been different if the Phoenicians had not been traders?**

Phoenician trade. The Phoenicians sailed in ships that today would seem small and frail, but their sailors were highly skilled. Using sails and oars, the Phoenicians took their ships throughout the Mediterranean and beyond. Some historians believe that the Phoenicians sailed as far as Britain. They might even have sailed around the western coast of Africa. In time the Phoenicians became the greatest traders in the ancient world.

Phoenicia reached its peak as a great sea trading power in the centuries after 1000 B.C. Phoenician colonies were established throughout the Mediterranean region. The Phoenician city of Carthage in North Africa became a major regional power. Other important colonies could be found on the islands of Sicily, Sardinia, and Malta. Farther west, the Phoenicians established a colony in what is now Spain. These colonies themselves became centers for trade.

Phoenicia had one particularly important natural resource—lumber. The Lebanon Mountains had beautiful cedar forests and other trees. Many ancient peoples used this lumber for building.

The Phoenicians developed several other valuable exports as well. They became skilled workers in metal and created beautiful objects of gold and silver. To do so, the Phoenicians used methods they learned from the Egyptians. They probably imported the materials they used as well. The Phoenicians invented the art of glassblowing and made exquisite glass objects. The city of Sidon became the home of a well-known glass industry.

On their coast the Phoenicians gathered a shellfish called murex. They used the murex to make a purple dye. Sidon and Tyre became the centers of the dyeing trade. People throughout the ancient world prized cloth dyed with this purple. A favorite of the rich and of royalty, the color became known as royal purple. The Phoenicians also exported dried fish, linen, olive oil, and wine.

Phoenician culture. The Phoenicians imitated the cultures of other peoples. Their government and customs resembled those of the Egyptians and Babylonians. Through trading, the Phoenicians spread Egyptian and Babylonian culture throughout the Mediterranean area.

The religion of the Phoenician people offered few comforts. While the Phoenicians believed in an afterlife, their efforts were focused on winning the favor of one of the many gods they worshiped, sometimes going so far as to sacrifice their own children. Some scholars believe this was done just in a few places and just under extreme circumstances. Sacrifices might have taken place, for example, if a natural disaster convinced people that the gods were very angry with them.

The Phoenicians never established a major empire. Eventually, their cities were conquered by the Assyrians. The Phoenicians did, however, make one major contribution to the world: the **Phoenician alphabet.** Writing systems had been developed earlier in both Egypt and Mesopotamia. The Phoenicians, however, developed the alphabet that became the model for later Western alphabets.

The spread of the alphabet is a good example of how commerce can speed cultural diffusion. Phoenicians used writing in their businesses to draw up contracts and record bills. Their trading partners saw these written records. They probably also saw the advantages of them. Phoenician traders spread the knowledge of alphabetical writing throughout the Mediterranean world.

Relief of a Phoenician trading ship

CLOSE

Ask students how the invention of coined money made trade easier. Lead a class discussion about the benefits of coined money.

REVIEW

Have students complete the Section 5 Review on p. 43.

ASSESS

Have students complete Daily Quiz 2.5. As Alternative Assessment, you may want to use either of the coined money exercises in this section's lessons.

RETEACH

Have students complete Main Idea Activity for English Language Learners and Special-Needs Students 2.5. Ask students to summarize the achievements of the Phoenicians and Lydians. **ENGLISH LANGUAGE LEARNERS**

EXTEND

Have students draw a map to show the extent of the Phoenician trading network. **BLOCK SCHEDULING**

The Greeks adopted the Phoenician alphabet. They improved it by adding signs for vowel sounds. Later, the Etruscans and then the Romans copied this alphabet from the Greeks. Eventually, the Romans developed the alphabet we use now.

✔ **READING CHECK: Drawing Inferences** Why were the Phoenicians more likely than some ancient peoples to spread and borrow from other cultures? as traders they had more contact with other peoples

Lydians

Today Asia Minor makes up the greater part of the nation of Turkey. In ancient times the western portion of Asia Minor was called Lydia (LI·dee·uh). Like the Phoenicians, the Lydians did not create an empire. Also like the Phoenicians, however, they made an extremely important contribution. Today Lydians are remembered as the first people to use coined money. They began issuing small kidney-bean-shaped pieces of money made out of a mixture of gold and silver.

Before coins were invented in about 600 B.C., traders had to rely on barter. **Barter** is the exchange of one good or service for another; goods that have value are called **commodities.** In bartering, for example, a fisherman might trade a commodity such as a basket of fish for a farmer's extra vegetables. Barter, however, limited trade. Two people could strike a bargain only if each could offer goods or services that the other wanted.

In contrast, the use of money allowed traders to set prices for goods and services. Lydian traders developed a **money economy.** This economic system is based on the use of money as a measure of value and a unit of account. Through trade, the Lydians passed on the concept of a money economy to the Greeks and Persians. They, in turn, helped spread this concept to other parts of the world.

✔ **READING CHECK: Contrasting** How does a money economy differ from barter? in barter, goods are traded directly; in a money economy, prices are set for goods

These Greek coins show the influence of the Lydians' development of a money economy.

DAILY LIFE

Money
Money can be any object that people are willing to accept as payment for goods or services. The first form of money was called commodity money. Salt, shells, and special stones were all used as commodity money.

Later, Mediterranean countries began making coins from precious metals. These ancient coins often were stamped with images of gods or rulers. Today, coins and paper notes still bear images, but the materials themselves have little actual value. Instead, they represent a value that everyone agrees upon. **What might be some advantages of a money economy?**

SECTION 5 REVIEW

1. Define and explain the significance:
barter
commodities
money economy

2. Identify and explain the significance:
Phoenician alphabet

3. Identifying Cause and Effect
Copy the chart below. Use it to illustrate the ways in which trade influenced life in Phoenicia.

Trade →

4. **Finding the Main Idea**
   a. What effect did the trading civilization of Phoenicia have on the ancient world?
   b. What role did colonies fill for Phoenicia?
   c. What effect would the Lydians' development of a money economy have on ancient civilizations?

5. **Writing and Critical Thinking**
   Summarizing Imagine that you are a Phoenician trader. Write a journal account about traveling to a foreign land to trade.
   Consider:
   • the goods the Phoenicians traded
   • how they transported goods to other lands

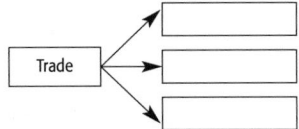
Homework Practice Online
keyword: SP3 HP2

OBJECTIVES

1 **Explain how the migrating Hebrews found a homeland.**

2 **Explore how religious views affected Hebrew culture.**

As students enter the classroom, ask them to write their own definition of *ethical.* Then have them list some guidelines for Judeo-Christian ethics and behavior. *(Students' lists may include guidelines such as: do not lie; do not cheat; do not steal.)* Tell students that in Section 6 they will learn about the origins of Judaism, which emphasizes ethical conduct.

REPRODUCIBLE RESOURCES

▸ Guided Reading Strategy 2.6

▸ Creative Teaching Strategy 2: Time Capsules from the Ancient World

TECHNOLOGY RESOURCES

▸ One-Stop Planner 2.6

▸ Holt Researcher: World History: David, Solomon

▸ Homework Practice Online

REINFORCEMENT, REVIEW, AND ASSESSMENT

▸ Section 6 Review, p. 47

▸ Daily Quiz 2.6

▸ Main Idea Activity 2.6

▸ English Audio Summary 2.6

▸ Spanish Audio Summary 2.6

LINK TO TODAY ANSWER
According to the Bible, it is where Moses received the Ten Commandments.

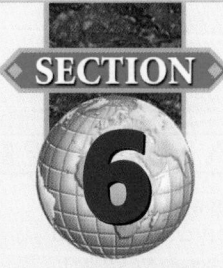

SECTION 6

■ READ TO DISCOVER

❶ How did the migrating Hebrews find a homeland?

❷ How did religious views affect Hebrew culture?

■ DEFINE

covenant
ethical monotheism

■ IDENTIFY

Abraham
Twelve Tribes of Israel
Moses
Exodus
Saul
David
Solomon
Torah
Judeo-Christian ethics

▶ WHY IT MATTERS TODAY

The ethical laws of Judaism, many of which were later adopted by Christians, still influence the beliefs of many Americans today. Use CNN🎬News.com or other **current event** sources to find recent news stories about the Ten Commandments and the impact of Judeo-Christian ethics on society today. Record your findings in your journal.

CNN Student News.com

The Origins of Judaism

The Main Idea
The Hebrews established a unique and influential religion based on ethical monotheism.

The Story Continues *"You shall not ill-treat any widow or orphan. . . . You shall not commit robbery. . . . Love your fellow [countryman] as yourself. . . You . . . must befriend the stranger . . . [Do] not harden your heart and shut your hand against your needy kinsman." These and other holy laws from the ancient culture of the Hebrews were to have a profound effect on Western civilization.*

The Hebrews

To the south of Phoenicia lay a small strip of land known as Canaan. Just as in the eastern part of the Fertile Crescent, a series of peoples inhabited Canaan. At different times the Assyrians, Babylonians, Egyptians, Persians, Syrians, and other groups all conquered this area. One group of people who lived in Canaan were the Hebrews—the ancestors of modern Jews. They had a great influence on the region and on the history of the world.

According to the Bible, the founder of the Hebrew people was **Abraham.** Abraham once lived in Sumer. He left there and led his people through the desert to the borders of northern Canaan. Modern Jews trace their heritage through Abraham's grandson Jacob (also called Israel), whose twelve sons each established a tribe. These groups were known as the **Twelve Tribes of Israel.**

The Exodus. The descendants of Abraham left Canaan and traveled west into Egypt, probably to escape drought and famine. These Hebrews lived peacefully in Egypt for some time. Eventually, however, they fell from favor with the Egyptians. Some scholars believe that one group of Hebrews may have entered Egypt with the Hyksos in the 1700s B.C. When the Egyptians expelled the Hyksos in the 1200s B.C. they enslaved the Hebrews. The Hebrews were held as slaves for 400 years, during which time they suffered greatly.

The Hebrews were led out of slavery by a great leader, **Moses.** The biblical books of Exodus, Numbers, and Deuteronomy tell the story of Moses. According to the Bible, Moses led the **Exodus,** the escape of the Hebrews from Egypt. The Hebrews fled into the deserts of the Sinai Peninsula, where they wandered in the wilderness.

INTERPRETING THE VISUAL RECORD

Mount Sinai Mount Sinai is located in the southern Sinai Peninsula. According to the Bible, this is where Moses received the written words that established the principles and beliefs of Judaism. It remains a biblical landmark today.

Link to Today Why might Mount Sinai be an important place for followers of Judaism today?

TEACH OBJECTIVE 1

LEVEL 1: Have students complete the following graphic organizer to show how the migrating Hebrews found a homeland.

| | → | Journey to Egypt | → | | → | |

(Students should include their journey to Canaan, their journey to Egypt, the Exodus from Egypt, and their journey back to Canaan.)
ENGLISH LANGUAGE LEARNERS

TEACH OBJECTIVE 2

ALL LEVELS: Ask students to think of instances in history in which people held other humans as slaves. Discuss with students how these enslaved persons reacted to this situation. Ask students how some slaves and other people who were against slavery tried to free the slaves. Close by asking students to imagine how the Hebrews felt about leaving Egypt and what their expectations for the future were. **ENGLISH LANGUAGE LEARNERS**

The Ten Commandments. As the Bible tells it, Moses climbed to the top of Mount Sinai. When he returned to the Hebrews, he carried tablets bearing the Ten Commandments. These commandments were the moral laws that the Hebrew god, Yahweh (YAH·way), had revealed to Moses.

The first four commandments establish the Hebrews' relationship with Yahweh. The rest of the commandments emphasize self-restraint and underscore the importance of family and human life. When the Hebrews agreed to follow these commandments, they entered into a **covenant,** or solemn agreement, with Yahweh.

Moses announced that Canaan was a land promised to his ancestors. He also said that Yahweh had sent him to found a holy nation. Inspired by his words, the Hebrews set out for Canaan. They wandered in the desert for many years, however, before finally entering the "promised land." They expected to find a land "flowing with milk and honey."

The founding of Israel. The Hebrews who had come from Egypt joined those who had lived on the borders of northern Canaan. They remained a loose confederation of tribes bound together in part by the need to maintain a strong central shrine for the Ark of the Covenant—the container of Moses's tablets. Leaders known as Judges ruled the various tribes in these years. Their task was to enforce God's laws and settle disputes among the tribes. The Hebrews also sometimes acknowledged the authority of holy men known as prophets, who appeared from time to time to warn people that they were incurring God's anger by straying from the terms of the covenant.

The harsh wilderness life had hardened the Hebrews into tough desert tribes. However, establishing a homeland in Canaan nonetheless proved difficult for the Hebrews. People known as Canaanites held the northern Jordan Valley. Another group, the Philistines, lived along the southern coast. Both groups resisted the Hebrews and defended their lands in a struggle that lasted more than 200 years. The Hebrews first conquered the Canaanites. The Philistines, however, proved far more difficult to overcome. Over time, the Hebrews drove them closer to the seacoast, but they never succeeded in conquering the Philistines completely.

As nomads, the Hebrews had been divided into 12 tribes. During the years of fighting, the tribes united under one king. The first king of this united kingdom called Israel was **Saul.** Saul was succeeded by **David,** who formed a new dynasty. David occupied the city of Jerusalem, making it a capital and religious center.

THE TEN COMMANDMENTS

According to the Bible, "God spoke, and these were his words:

1. I am the Lord your God who brought you out of Egypt. You shall have no other gods.*
2. You shall not make or worship idols.
3. You shall not swear falsely by the name of the Lord your God.
4. Remember the Sabbath and keep it holy.
5. Honor your father and mother.
6. You shall not murder.
7. You shall not commit adultery.
8. You shall not steal.
9. You shall not bear false witness against your neighbor.
10. You shall not covet your neighbor's belongings."

*Some translations include this sentence in the second commandment.

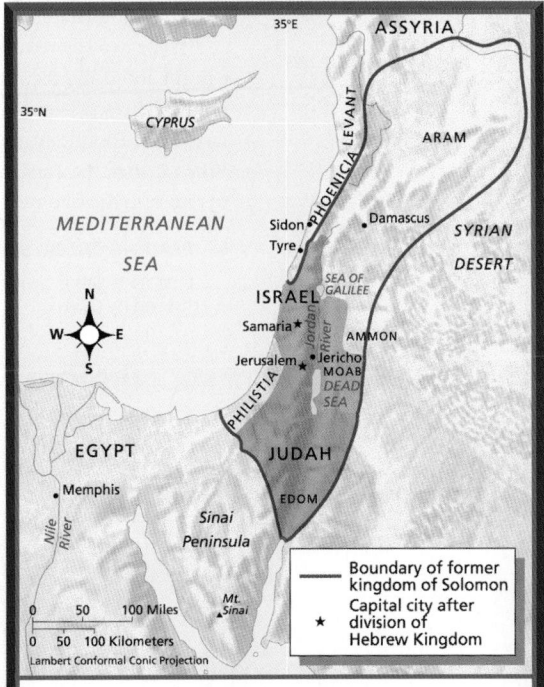

The Founding of Israel, c. 900s B.C.
The kingdom of Israel, which reached the height of its size and power under Solomon, was divided after 922 B.C.

■ **Skills Assessment: Places and Regions** After the mid-900s B.C., which of the Hebrew kingdoms probably had great access to seagoing trade and commerce?

Geography

The geography of the Fertile Crescent greatly affected the coastal towns of Canaan. To the east of Canaan were the Assyrian and Babylonian Empires (at different times), to the south was the Egyptian Empire, and to the north was the Hittite Empire, which were separated by deserts. These empires had powerful, large armies but no naval fleets. In order to attack each other, the armies of these empires could only travel by land through a few mountain passes or along the Mediterranean coast. Thus Canaan's port towns were constantly fought over, destroyed, burned, and built up again.

Critical Thinking

Ask students what one consequence of Canaan's location could be for archaeologists.

ANSWER: Answers may vary but students might suggest that there are fewer artifacts left from Canaan, making it hard to learn about its culture.

MAP ANSWER
Israel

HOMEWORK Have students carefully read through the Ten Commandments on page 45. Ask students to write a response to each commandment, explaining why such a rule would help to preserve the Hebrew community.

TEACH OBJECTIVE 2

LEVEL 3: Review with students the meaning of the word *ethics*. Have students brainstorm actions that are ethical and actions that are not ethical. Ask students how ethical they feel the laws of the Egyptians, Babylonians, Hittites, Assyrians, and Persians were. Have students discuss how ethical these civilizations' laws seem compared to those of the Hebrews. Then have students describe how basic elements of the Hebrew religion

can be seen in modern religious thought. Close by having students brainstorm how Judeo-Christian ethics influence societies and institutions today.

Culture

It is likely that Solomon's royal scribes first recorded the Hebrew narratives that would evolve into the Torah. Today, scribes still scrupulously follow a carefully defined ritual when preparing a new Torah scroll. Using ritually cleaned parchment, pen, and ink, the scribe copies from an authorized guide. The scribe will work for about 18 months to complete a single handwritten Torah.

Critical Thinking

Ask students to think of reasons why the old methods are still used to make new Torah scrolls.

ANSWER: Students might suggest that members of a religious or cultural group might preserve ancient traditions and rituals because they are part of the rules of their religion, or to strengthen their sense of group identity.

Technology Resources

 Religions of the World Video Series: Judaism

Analyzing Primary Sources

Identifying Cause and Effect
How might the covenant between the Hebrew kings and their people have helped the kings to rule? *states that they both share a common faith*

 Holt Researcher

go.hrw.com
KEYWORD: Holt Researcher
FreeFind: David
Solomon
After reading more about David and Solomon on the Holt Researcher, use a problem-solving process to evaluate how well they handled problems during their reigns.

The Torah consists of the Hebrews' most sacred writings.

Also beginning with David, the kings of Israel established a tradition of making a covenant with their people as well as with God. According to a biblical account of one king's coronation,

Primary Source **"Jehoida [the priest] solemnized the covenant between the Lord, on the one hand, and the king and the people, on the other—as well as between the king and the people—that they should be the people of the Lord."**

Benjamin Mazer, *Biblical Israel: State and People*

Under the rule of David's son and successor, **Solomon,** Israel reached the height of its wealth and power. Solomon sought to build peaceful, cooperative relations with the other leading powers of the region. One of his wives, for example, was a daughter of Egypt's pharaoh. Solomon vastly increased Israel's wealth through favorable trade policies with Arabia. The king used the riches gained from this trade to build a magnificent temple to God in Jerusalem. The temple became both the center of religious life in Israel and a symbol of the Israelite state.

Following Solomon's death, unity within the Israelite kingdom was disrupted by struggles for political power. In the late 900s B.C. the 10 northern tribes revolted, and the kingdom split in two. The northern part remained the kingdom of Israel, with its capital at Samaria. The southern part, located around the Dead Sea, became the kingdom of Judah. Its capital was Jerusalem.

These two Hebrew kingdoms lacked the strength to withstand invasions from the east. In about 722 B.C. the Assyrians conquered Israel. They captured and enslaved many Hebrews. Later, in 587 B.C., the Chaldeans conquered Judah and destroyed Jerusalem. They destroyed Solomon's temple and took the southern Hebrews captive. When Cyrus, the Persian king, conquered the Chaldeans, he allowed the Hebrews to return to their homeland. The Hebrews then rebuilt the temple in Jerusalem.

✔ **READING CHECK: Sequencing** What events led to the Hebrews making Canaan their homeland? *conquest of Hebrew kingdoms by Assyrians and Chaldeans, then freeing by Cyrus*

The Development of Judaism

The Hebrew scriptures tell of the creation of the world and the special mission of the Hebrews. About one third of these scriptures—also known as the Old Testament of the Christian Bible—is Hebrew history. The remaining scriptures include laws, poetry, prophecy, and religious instruction.

Law and ethics. The first five books of the Old Testament are known as the **Torah.** They include the Hebrew code of laws. This Mosaic law—named for Moses—includes the Ten Commandments. Like the Code of Hammurabi, it demanded an "eye for an eye." Mosaic law, however, placed a higher value on human life. The law demanded kindness toward the poor and toward slaves. It reserved the death sentence for severe crimes, such as adultery, kidnapping, treason, and sacrifices to idols. This system of law reflected the belief that all people deserved kindness and respect.

For the Hebrews, prophets were messengers sent to reveal the will of Yahweh. The prophets' messages often formed the basis for Jewish moral and ethical behavior.

CLOSE

Ask volunteers to sequence on the board the events that led up to the Hebrews settling in Canaan.

REVIEW

Have students complete the Section 6 Review on p. 47.

ASSESS

Have students complete Daily Quiz 2.6. As Alternative Assessment, you may want to have students complete the slavery or ethics exercises in this section's lessons.

RETEACH

Have students complete Main Idea Activity for English Language Learners and Special-Needs Students 2.6. Then ask each student to create an annotated time line of Hebrew history.
ENGLISH LANGUAGE LEARNERS

EXTEND

Have students create a map like the one on page 41. First, have them shade the Jordan Valley and the regions where the Canaanites and Philistines lived. Tell students to use lines and arrows to show the movement of the Hebrews from the days of Abraham up through the 500s B.C., and to label locations with dates.
BLOCK SCHEDULING

Religion. The early Hebrews worshiped Yahweh as their only god. They believed that Yahweh protected them from enemies and provided them with food and water. Those who sinned against Yahweh would suffer, and so would their children and succeeding generations. The early Hebrews therefore viewed Yahweh as a god to fear.

This understanding of Yahweh slowly changed. The Hebrews came to believe that people had a choice between good and evil. Yahweh held them responsible for their choices, but he allowed them the freedom to make those choices for themselves. The Hebrews came to think of Yahweh as a god who lived in the hearts of worshippers. Humans were not intended to be Yahweh's slaves, but to serve him out of love.

Other ancient peoples thought of their gods as being more powerful than humans but still having human qualities. In contrast, the Hebrews viewed Yahweh as a spiritual force, not as a glorified human being or part of nature. Moreover, other ancient cultures sometimes viewed their kings as gods or the representatives of gods. Among the Hebrews, however, earthly political rulers had no claims to divinity. As stated in the Ten Commandments, only Yahweh was divine.

The Hebrew religion was monotheistic based on belief in a single god. Because it emphasized ethics, or proper conduct, it is often called **ethical monotheism.** The Jewish system of ethics carried over into the founding of Christianity. Thus today many people refer to the values first established by the Hebrews as **Judeo-Christian ethics.** These ideas rank among the Hebrews' most important contributions to Western civilization.

Dating from about the 100s B.C., the Dead Sea Scrolls contain ancient manuscripts detailing the history and principles of Judaism.

✔ **READING CHECK: Contrasting** How did the Hebrews' idea of God differ from those of other ancient civilizations? viewed Yahweh as a spiritual force, not as a glorified human being or force of nature

---

SECTION 6 REVIEW

1. Define and explain the significance:
covenant
ethical monotheism

2. Identify and explain the significance:
Abraham
Twelve Tribes of Israel
Moses
Exodus
Saul
David
Solomon
Torah
Judeo-Christian ethics

Homework Practice Online
keyword: SP3 HP2

3. Sequencing Copy the time line below. Use it to organize the history of the Hebrew people.

1500 B.C.		500 B.C.
2000 B.C.	1000 B.C.	

4. **Finding the Main Idea**
   a. In what way is the history of the land of Canaan typical of the Fertile Crescent region?
   b. If you had been one of the ancient Hebrews, would you have fought to stay in Canaan or would you have moved elsewhere? Explain your answer.
   c. How did the Hebrews' ideas about people's rights, such as fair treatment before the law, differ from other ancient groups?
   d. Explain why the Hebrew or Jewish religion can be called ethical monotheism.

5. **Writing and Critical Thinking**
   Analyzing Information Why do you think that many people consider the values that came to be known as Judeo-Christian ethics to be among the Hebrews' most important contributions to Western civilization?
   Consider:
   • the meaning of those values
   • the effect they had on Jewish society
   • how they are evident in societies and institutions today

---

SECTION 6 REVIEW ANSWERS

❶ **Define**
• covenant, p. 45
• ethical monotheism, p. 47

❷ **Identify**
• Abraham, p. 44
• Twelve Tribes of Israel, p. 44
• Moses, p. 44
• Exodus, p. 44
• Saul, p. 45
• David, p. 45
• Solomon, p. 46
• Torah, p. 46
• Judeo-Christian ethics, p. 47

❸ Students should include the Exodus, the Ten Commandments, the founding of Israel, and the succession of the kings of Israel.

❹ a. It was inhabited by a series of peoples.

b. Students' answers will vary but should support their point of view.

c. believed in fairer treatment, more kindness and respect for all, than most ancient groups

d. It is based on a belief in a single god and emphasizes ethics.

❺ Students' entries will vary but should consider their enslavement in Egypt, the role of Moses, and the migration across the desert.

THE FIRST CIVILIZATIONS **47**

47

REVIEW AND ASSESSMENT RESOURCES

REPRODUCIBLE RESOURCES
▸ Vocabulary Activity 2

TECHNOLOGY RESOURCES
▸ Chapter 2 Test Generator (on the One-Stop Planner)
▸ Global Skill Builder CD–ROM
▸ HRW Web Site

REINFORCEMENT, REVIEW, and ASSESSMENT
▸ Chapter 2 Review, pp. 48–49
▸ Chapter 2 Tutorial for Students, Parents, Mentors, and Peers
▸ Chapter 2 Test (Form A or B)
▸ Alternative Assessment Handbook
▸ Chapter 2 Test for English Language Learners and Special-Needs Students

REVIEW
Have students complete the Chapter 2 Review on pages 48–49.

ASSESS
Use one of the chapter tests to assess students' understanding of the content. For Alternative Assessment, see the Portfolio Activities and Alternative Assessment Handbook.

CHAPTER 2 REVIEW ANSWERS

Understanding Main Ideas
1. It provided a transportation route, a supply of water, and fertile soil.

2. Old Kingdom: nobles grew stronger than the pharaohs, civil war; Middle Kingdom: weakening of pharaohs' power by nobles and priests; New Kingdom: weaker pharaohs and outside invasions

3. as tombs for pharaohs

4. The soul was judged and entered either a place of eternal happiness or was thrown to a horrible monster called the Eater of the Dead.

5. They were not geographically isolated.

6. It regulated all aspects of life in Babylon.

7. Akkadians, Babylonians, Hittites, Assyrians, Chaldeans, Persians

8. They lacked fertile land and the Lebanon Mountains made migration to the east difficult.

9. It viewed Yahweh as a spiritual force rather than as a glorified human or a part of nature. Earthly political rulers had no claims to divinity.

Reviewing Themes
1. Peoples often adopted aspects of the cultures of those they had contact with.

2. Egyptians could focus on developing culture because they had less chance of invasion.

48

CHAPTER 2 Review

Creating a Time Line
Copy the time line below onto a sheet of paper. Complete the time line by filling in the events, individuals, and dates from the chapter that you think were significant. Pick three events and explain why you think they were significant.

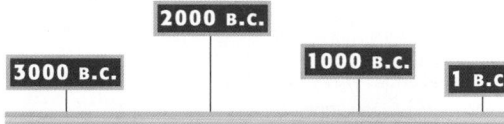

3000 B.C.   2000 B.C.   1000 B.C.   1 B.C.

Writing a Summary
Using standard grammar, spelling, sentence structure, and punctuation, write an overview of the events in the chapter.

Identifying People and Ideas
Identify the following terms or individuals and explain their significance:

1. hieroglyphics
2. dynasty
3. empire
4. ziggurats
5. city-state
6. Hammurabi
7. Zoroaster
8. money economy
9. Moses
10. ethical monotheism

Understanding Main Ideas

Section 1 *(pp. 20–25)*
Ancient Kingdoms of the Nile
1. How did the Nile River contribute to the development of ancient Egypt?
2. Why did each of the three kingdoms of ancient Egypt collapse?

Section 2 *(pp. 26–29)*
Egyptian Life and Culture
3. Why did the Egyptians build pyramids?
4. What were some Egyptian beliefs about the afterlife?

Section 3 *(pp. 30–34)*
Sumerian Civilization
5. Why were civilizations in the Fertile Crescent frequently invaded?

Section 4 *(pp. 35–40)*
Empires of the Fertile Crescent
6. What was the impact of the Code of Hammurabi?
7. Which peoples established empires in the Fertile Crescent?

Section 5 *(pp. 41–43)*
The Phoenicians and the Lydians
8. Why did the Phoenicians become traders?

Section 6 *(pp. 44–47)*
The Origins of Judaism
9. In what ways was Judaism different from the religions of other ancient civilizations?

Reviewing Themes
1. **Global Relations** How did trade promote cultural exchanges between ancient civilizations?
2. **Geography** How did geographic isolation contribute to the development of Egyptian culture?
3. **Government** Why did civilizations with strong rulers typically survive longer than other civilizations with weak rulers?

Thinking Critically
1. **Comparing** What did the governments of Babylon, Egypt, and Israel have in common?
2. **Contrasting** How did life in the Nile River valley differ from life in the Tigris-Euphrates Valley?
3. **Evaluating** What aspects of the Code of Hammurabi and of the Hebrews' laws are evident in our legal system today?
4. **Summarizing** How did slavery affect people and civilizations in the ancient world?

Writing About History
Comparing and Contrasting Write a report describing the most important similarities and differences among Egyptian, Sumerian, and Hebrew beliefs. Use the chart below to organize your thoughts before writing.

Religious beliefs	Egyptian	Sumerian	Hebrew
Number of gods			
Role of gods			
Behavior on Earth			
Belief in afterlife			

CLOSE

Have students choose two groups of people in the chapter and explain how the environment affected their ways of living.

RETEACH

Have students who had difficulty with the test compile a chapter glossary of important places, people, and concepts. Then have students take the Form B Test to assess their mastery of the material.

ENGLISH LANGUAGE LEARNERS

Portfolio Extensions

Link to TODAY

1. Ask students to imagine they are Mesopotamian travelers in the year 1500 B.C. Have them write a journal that describes the geography of the lands they visit, the people they meet, the difficulties they face, and the ideas that they will take back to Mesopotamia. Students should include a map of their routes, showing the major geographical features and civilizations they encounter.

2. Have students use encyclopedias to write a report comparing Judaism, Zoroastrianism, and the religion of ancient Egypt. Ask them to focus on beliefs about the struggle between good and evil. Tell students to discuss why the conflict between good and evil is a theme in most religions.

3. The pyramids are among the most impressive structures left by any civilization. Have students research and write a report on techniques of ancient Egyptian building. Ask them to include illustrations in their report.

Building Social Studies Skills

Using a Model

Analyze the model below. Then use the conclusions you have reached to answer the questions that follow.

The Great Pyramid at Giza, c. 2600 B.C.

Pharaoh's Chamber
Airshaft
Airshaft
Queen's Chamber
Grand Gallery
Entrance
Underground Chamber

Interior of the Great Pyramid at Giza

1. Which statement best describes the information provided by the model?
   a. The Great Pyramid was constructed of limestone blocks.
   b. Each of the blocks used in the pyramid's construction weighed about 3,000 pounds.
   c. A single entrance opened from one side of the pyramid.
   d. The pyramid's builders used log rollers to move and position its blocks.

2. Using information from the model, describe the interior of the Great Pyramid at Giza.

Sequencing

Read the sentences below about the city of Babylon. Then answer the questions that follow.

   A. Even before the Persians captured it in 539 B.C., Babylon was the target of conquerors.
   B. Hammurabi came to power in Babylon in about 1792 B.C.
   C. It was not until Nebuchadnezzar's time (605 B.C. to 562 B.C.) that the Hanging Gardens of Babylon were built.
   D. Babylon was conquered and destroyed by the Assyrians in about 700 B.C. It was later rebuilt.
   E. In the 1600s B.C. the powerful Hittites, expanding their empire from Anatolia, captured Babylon.

3. Which of the following lists shows the events in the order in which they occurred?
   a. D, E, B, C, A
   b. B, E, D, C, A
   c. A, C, D, E, B
   d. B, D, E, A, C

4. According to the information provided, which group of conquerors was the first to capture Babylon? Which group was the last?

Alternative Assessment

Building Your Portfolio

Link to TODAY

Global Relations

Just as world leaders today make important decisions about global events, early civilizations had rulers whose influence was felt throughout the ancient world. Locate and use biographies of these rulers to write a brief summary of their impact. Then locate and use interviews to learn about the activities and influence of some current world leaders. Create a chart to summarize your findings.

internet connect

go hrw .com

Internet Activity: go.hrw.com
KEYWORD: SP3 WH2

Choose a topic on the First Civilizations to:
• explore Egyptian pyramids and create an illustrated brochure.
• interview the leader of an ancient civilization.
• write about ancient and modern structures in Egypt.

3. Strong rulers were often able to unify their civilizations.

Thinking Critically
1. They were monarchies.

2. The Nile River valley was geographically isolated and thus less prone to attack than the Tigris-Euphrates Valley was.

3. Laws deal with many aspects of life; death sentence is reserved for severe crimes.

4. Hebrews, who had been held as slaves for 400 years, developed a great civilization.

Writing About History
Answers should compare and contrast the beliefs of each civilization.

Building Social Studies Skills
1. c

2. The Great Pyramid contained a Pharaoh's chamber, a Queen's chamber, an underground chamber, and a grand gallery. The interior was connected to the outside through one entrance and two airshafts.

3. b

4. Babylonians; Persians

Building Your Portfolio
Charts should show similarities and differences among leaders.

Ancient Indian Civilizations

CHAPTER RESOURCE MANAGER

Objectives	Pacing Guide	Reproducible Resources
SECTION 1 **Indus River Valley Civilizations** (pp. 52–55)	• Examine the role geography and climate played in the settlement of the Indian subcontinent. • Investigate how people in the first Indus River valley civilization lived.	**Regular** **Block Scheduling** 1 day .5 day *Block Scheduling Handbook with Team Teaching Strategies, 3.1*	**RS** Guided Reading Strategy 3.1 **SM** Geography Activity 3: Indian Trade **PS** Readings in World History 4: Everyday Life in Mohenjo-Daro and Harappa
SECTION 2 **Indo-Aryan Migrants** (pp. 56–59)	• Explain how life in northern India changed with the coming of the Indo-Aryans. • Identify the major contributions of the Indo-Aryans to ancient Indian society.	**Regular** **Block Scheduling** 1 day .5 day *Block Scheduling Handbook with Team Teaching Strategies, 3.2*	**RS** Guided Reading Strategy 3.2 **E** Creative Teaching Strategy 3: Telling the Story of India
SECTION 3 **Hinduism and Buddhism** (pp. 60–65)	• Describe the importance of religion in ancient Indian society. • Identify the principal elements of Hinduism. • Identify the basic beliefs of Buddhism.	**Regular** **Block Scheduling** 1.5 day 1 day *Block Scheduling Handbook with Team Teaching Strategies, 3.3*	**RS** Guided Reading Strategy 3.3 **RS** Graphic Organizer Activity 3: Buddhism and Hinduism **PS** Readings in World History 10: Buddhism and Equality **E** Hands-on History Activity 3: Hinduism in Indian Life
SECTION 4 **Ancient Indian Dynasties and Empires** (pp. 66–68)	• Explain how the Mauryan rulers increased their power. • Examine the reasons for the decline of Gupta rule.	**Regular** **Block Scheduling** 1 day .5 day *Block Scheduling Handbook with Team Teaching Strategies, 3.4*	**RS** Guided Reading Strategy 3.4 **PS** Readings in World History 11: Aśoka's Edicts
SECTION 5 **Ancient Indian Life and Culture** (pp. 69–71)	• Describe how women's rights were limited in ancient Indian society. • Identify the most important achievements of the Gupta period.	**Regular** **Block Scheduling** 1 day .5 day *Block Scheduling Handbook with Team Teaching Strategies, 3.5*	**RS** Guided Reading Strategy 3.5 **PS** Readings in World History 12: The Place of Women in Hindu Society

Chapter Resource Key

PS Primary Sources	**A** Assessment	Music
RS Reading Support	**REV** Review	Video
IC Interdisciplinary Connections	**ELL** Reinforcement and English Language Learners	Internet
E Enrichment	Transparencies	Holt Presentation Maker Using Microsoft® PowerPoint®
SM Skills Mastery	CD–ROM	

 One–Stop Planner CD-ROM

See the **One–Stop Planner** for a complete list of additional resources for students and teachers.

One-Stop Planner CD-ROM

It's easy to plan lessons, select resources, and print out materials for your students when you use the *One-Stop Planner* CD–ROM with *Test Generator.*

Technology Resources	Reinforcement, Review, and Assessment
One-Stop Planner 3.1 Homework Practice Online Online Maps, Charts, and Graphs: Mohenjo-Daro Online Maps, Charts, and Graphs: Sites of Harappan Civilization	Daily Quiz 3.1 Main Idea Activity 3.1 English Audio Summary 3.1 Spanish Audio Summary 3.1 REV Section 1 Review, p. 55
One-Stop Planner 3.2 Homework Practice Online Online Maps, Charts, and Graphs: Indo-Aryan Migration into India, c. 1750 B.C.	Daily Quiz 3.2 Main Idea Activity 3.2 English Audio Summary 3.2 Spanish Audio Summary 3.2 REV Section 2 Review, p. 59
One-Stop Planner 3.3 CNN Presents World Cultures: Yesterday and Today Segment 3: The Sacred Ganges World History Teaching Transparency: Everyday Life 6: Ganesha, Hindu Deity World History Teaching Transparency: Art and History 12: Seated Buddha Preaching the First Sermon Religions of the World Video Series: Hinduism Religions of the World Video Series: Buddhism Homework Practice Online Online Maps, Charts, and Graphs: The Spread of Buddhism, 500s B.C.–A.D. 600s	Daily Quiz 3.3 Main Idea Activity 3.3 English Audio Summary 3.3 Spanish Audio Summary 3.3 REV Section 3 Review, p. 65
One-Stop Planner 3.4 Holt Researcher: World History: Chandragupta Maurya Homework Practice Online	Daily Quiz 3.4 Main Idea Activity 3.4 English Audio Summary 3.4 Spanish Audio Summary 3.4 REV Section 4 Review, p. 68
One-Stop Planner 3.5 Regions of the World Music Audio CD Program 17: India: Ragas: Songs from India Homework Practice Online	Daily Quiz 3.5 Main Idea Activity 3.5 English Audio Summary 3.5 Spanish Audio Summary 3.5 REV Section 5 Review, p. 71

internet connect

HRW ONLINE RESOURCES

GO TO: go.hrw.com
Then type in a keyword.

TEACHER HOME PAGE
KEYWORD: SP3 TEACHER

CHAPTER INTERNET ACTIVITIES
KEYWORD: SP3 WH3

Choose an activity to:
- study ancient India and create a travel poster.
- write a biography of a leader of the Mauryan Empire.
- explore the geographic regions of India and create a brochure.

CHAPTER ENRICHMENT LINKS
KEYWORD: SP3 CH3

ONLINE ASSESSMENT
Homework Practice
KEYWORD: SP3 HP3

Standardized Test Prep
KEYWORD: SP3 STP3

Rubrics
KEYWORD: SS Rubrics

ONLINE MAPS, CHARTS, AND GRAPHS
KEYWORD: SP3 MCG

CONTENT UPDATES
KEYWORD: SS Content Updates

HOLT PRESENTATION MAKER
KEYWORD: SP3 PPT3

ONLINE READING SUPPORT
KEYWORD: SS Strategies

CURRENT EVENTS
KEYWORD: S3 Current Events

Meeting Individual Needs

Ability Levels

Level 1 Basic level activities designed for all students encountering new material

Level 2 Intermediate level activities designed for average students

Level 3 Challenging activities designed for honors and gifted and talented students

English Language Learners These activities address the needs of students with Limited English Proficiency.

Chapter Review and Assessment

IC Vocabulary Activity 3
Global Skill Builder CD–ROM
HRW Web Site
REV Chapter 3 Tutorial for Students, Parents, Mentors, and Peers
REV Chapter 3 Review, pp. 72–73
A Chapter 3 Test Generator (on the One-Stop Planner)
A Chapter 3 Test (Form A or B)
A Alternative Assessment Handbook
A Chapter 3 Test for English Language Learners and Special-Needs Students

CHAPTER

3

Section 1 Indus River Valley
          Civilizations

Section 2 Indo-Aryan Migrants

Section 3 Hinduism and Buddhism

Section 4 Ancient Indian Dynasties
          and Empires

Section 5 Ancient Indian Life and
          Culture

Build on What You Know

Ask students to answer the following questions:

What were some of the developments of the first civilizations?

Consider:

- art
- agriculture
- science and technology
- government

List some characteristics of the early empires of the Fertile Crescent and describe the reasons for the empires' collapse.

Consider:

- the Akkadians
- the Babylonians
- the Persians

EXPLORING THE TIME LINE

GLOBAL
EVENTS

internet connect

TOPIC: Ancient Indian
Civilization
GO TO: **go.hrw.com**
KEYWORD: **SP3 WH3**

Have students access the Internet through the HRW Go site to conduct research on the ways in which geography and climate affected the development of Indian civilization. Then ask students to compose an informative report that details how geographic and climactic conditions influenced where civilizations developed on the Indian subcontinent. Students' reports should include appropriate examples and evidence drawn from their research.

CHAPTER

3

c. 2500 B.C.–A.D. 550

Ancient Indian
Civilizations

Harappan animal sculptures

c. 2500 B.C.
Politics
The Harappan civilization appears in the Indus Valley.

c. 1500 B.C.
Global Events
The Rig-Veda is compiled.

| 2500 B.C. | 2000 B.C. | 1500 B.C. |

c. 2300 B.C.
The Arts
Indus River valley people use pictographs.

c. 2300 B.C.
Business and Finance
Indus River valley people trade with people of the Tigris and Euphrates River valleys.

c. 2000 B.C.
Science and Technology
Harappans use extensive irrigation and drainage systems.

c. 1750 B.C.
Global Events
Indo-Aryans begin migrating into the Indian subcontinent.

c. 1750 B.C.
Daily Life
The city of Mohenjo Daro begins to decline.

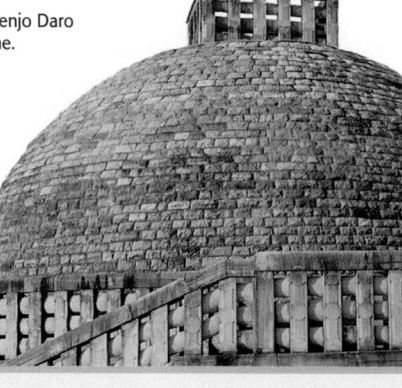

Dome of the Sanchi Stupa

Gemstone necklace from Mohenjo Daro

Build on What You Know

Scientists have learned much about the early peoples of the world. From artifacts we know that early peoples invented tools, produced beautiful art, built cities, and developed governments. Gradually the first civilizations arose in northeastern Africa and southwestern Asia. Civilizations were defined by the ability to produce food, the creation of towns with governments, and a division of labor. In this chapter, you will learn how civilizations in ancient India not only fulfilled these conditions but also went on to develop complex social and religious systems and make great advances in science and culture.

What's Your Opinion?

 To help students create their Themes Journal entries, provide the following examples of appropriate agree/disagree statements.

Geography

Agree A region's physical geography and climate greatly affect a civilization's ability to engage in successful farming, trade, and cultural development.

Disagree A civilization can develop despite a treacherous physical geography and harsh climate.

Science, Technology & Society

Agree In order for a civilization to survive, it must make many advances in science and technology.

Disagree Cultural achievements, such as religion and art, are more important than a society's scientific and technological advances.

Culture

Agree A people's culture and religion are interwoven with the activities of their daily lives.

Disagree People are generally not affected by their society's cultural and religious developments during their daily lives.

Stone relief depicting scene from the life of Siddhartha Gautama

Detail of "cloud maidens" painting from Sigiriya cave fresco, Sri Lanka

c. 800s B.C.
Science and Technology
Indo-Aryans use iron.

c. 525 B.C.
Global Events
Siddhartha Gautama becomes "the Enlightened One," or the Buddha.

c. 270 B.C.
Politics
Aśoka becomes ruler of the Mauryan Empire.

c. 200 B.C.
The Arts
The earliest Buddhist sculptures appear.

c. A.D. 100
Business and Finance
Indian traders appear in Ethiopia.

c. A.D. 550
Politics
Gupta rule in India ends.

500 B.C. **A.D. 1** **A.D. 500**

327–325 B.C.
Global Events
The armies of Alexander the Great occupy northern India.

c. 500 B.C.
Business and Finance
Indus River valley people first use coins.

c. 50 B.C.
Business and Finance
Trade between southern India and Rome begins.

c. 100 B.C.
The Arts
The western gateway of the Sanchi Stupa is erected.

c. A.D. 476
The Arts
King Kasyapa builds a palace at Sigiriya featuring the famous "cloud maidens" paintings.

A.D. 320
Politics
Chandra Gupta I founds the Gupta dynasty in India.

EXPLORING THE TIME LINE
GL◯BAL EVENTS

Religion has always played an important part in the creation of Indian art. Paintings and sculptures of the three main gods of the Hindu faith—Brahma, Vishnu, and Siva—fill numerous temples across India. Most works of Hindu art are meant to symbolize religious teachings.

Critical Thinking

Why might works of art be important tools in teaching religious ideas?

ANSWER: Students might answer that art can be interpreted by people who are illiterate or who speak different languages.

What's Your Opinion?

 Do you agree or disagree with the following statements? Support your point of view in your journal.

Geography The physical geography and climate of a region strongly affect the development of civilization there.

Science, Technology & Society A society's scientific and technological achievements are its greatest contribution to human civilization.

Culture In general, cultural and religious developments have a major influence on people's daily lives.

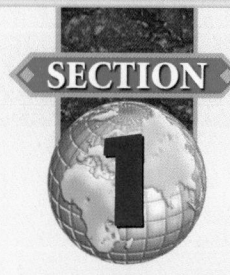
OBJECTIVES

1 **Examine the role geography and climate played in the settlement of the Indian subcontinent.**

2 **Investigate how people in the first Indus River valley civilization lived.**

SECTION 1

READ TO DISCOVER

❶ What role did geography and climate play in the settlement of the Indian subcontinent?

❷ How did people in the first Indus River valley civilization live?

DEFINE

monsoons
citadel

▶ **WHY IT MATTERS TODAY**

Despite our advanced technology, geography and climate still affect the way we live. Use CNNfyi.com or other **current event** sources to explore how the geography and climate of your region influence the way people live and work. Record your findings in your journal.

CNN student News.com

Indus River Valley Civilization

The Main Idea
The Indus River valley in the Indian subcontinent gave rise to the earliest Indian civilizations.

The Story Continues *Thousands of years ago near the Indus River valley there existed a village called Amri, whose citizens were makers of fine pottery. Indus River valley people like those in Amri helped lay the foundation for cultures in the modern countries of Bangladesh, Bhutan, India, Nepal, Pakistan, and Sri Lanka.*

The Importance of Geography and Climate

The first Indian civilization developed in the Indus River valley, in the northwestern part of the Indian subcontinent, about 4,500 years ago. Geography and climate played important roles in the development of civilization on the subcontinent.

Physical geography. The Indian subcontinent extends southward from central Asia into the Indian Ocean. It is separated in the north from the rest of Asia by towering mountain ranges. The greatest of these ranges is the Himalayas, which include the highest peaks in the world. These mountains made it difficult for immigrants and invaders to enter India by land. The famous Khyber Pass was one of a few paths that permitted people to cross the mountains into India.

Two great rivers lie south of the northern mountains. The Ganges River flows to the southeast through a fertile valley. In the west the Indus River flows southwest across a drier plain. The region drained by these two rivers is called the Indo-Gangetic Plain. To the south of these great river systems lies a high plateau called the Deccan. It makes up much of the interior of the subcontinent. To the west of the Deccan stand the Western Ghats. This mountain range rises abruptly from a narrow coastal plain along the Arabian Sea. A lower mountain range called the Eastern Ghats marks the eastern edge of the Deccan. On the eastern coast of India, another and broader coastal plain faces the Bay of Bengal. The inhabitants of the coastal plains became sea traders very early in their history.

The climate. Two features dominate India's climate: monsoons and high temperatures. **Monsoons** are winds that mark the seasons in India. Generally from November until the following March, monsoons blow from the north and northeast. Any moisture they carry falls onto the northern slopes of the Himalayas. Little rain falls on India during this season.

The wet season, called the southwest monsoon, occurs from mid-June through October, when southwesterly winds carry warm, moist air from the Indian Ocean. Water vapor in the air condenses to form clouds and rain. Heavy rains fall along the coastal plains, but sparse rainfall is typical of the land behind the Western Ghats. The lower Ganges Valley and the eastern Himalayas receive the heaviest rainfall. These regions lie directly in the path of the monsoon.

In most of India, much of the year's rainfall comes with the southwest monsoon. The timing of the monsoon is important. If it arrives late or brings little rain, crops fail. If the monsoon brings too much rain, floods may wash across the countryside.

TEACH OBJECTIVE 1

LEVEL 1: Ask students to summarize India's climate. *(They should note the seasonal monsoons and the potential for extreme heat.)* Remind the class that the first civilizations arose in four great river valleys; point out that one of these four valleys was the Indus River valley and help students locate the region on a map. Ask students why they think this civilization arose in the Indus Valley rather than in the Ganges Valley. *(Students should note that the Ganges Valley receives the heaviest rainfall during the monsoon.)* **ENGLISH LANGUAGE LEARNERS**

TEACH OBJECTIVE 2

LEVEL 3: Have students make a chart that lists 10 to 15 facts about the Harappan civilization, using the information on pages 53–55. Have them organize their charts into four columns labeled: *government, religion, technology,* and *economy.* Call on each student to share one fact from his or her chart. Ask students what causes, other than an earthquake or flood, might explain the unburied skeletons and abandoned homes at Mohenjo Daro. *(Students might suggest a plague, a drought, a deadly heat wave, and so on.)*

The other important feature of India's climate is the range of temperatures. Along the coast or on the Deccan, summers are fairly mild. In the Indo-Gangetic Plain, however, summer temperatures can reach 120°F.

✔ **READING CHECK: Making Predictions** How might geography and climate have affected early settlement in the Indian subcontinent? mountains slowed entry into India; monsoons and high temperatures made settlement difficult

Early Civilization in the Indus River Valley

A great civilization arose in the Indus River valley in about 2500 B.C. and lasted until about 1500 B.C. Much of what we know of this civilization comes from the ruins of two ancient cities, Harappa and Mohenjo Daro. Scholars have named it the Harappan civilization after the first of these cities.

Ruins – Civilization

Extensive archaeological digs at Harappa and Mohenjo Daro have revealed much about this early civilization. We know, for example, that both cities were large and carefully planned. Wide streets crossed at right angles. Each city had a water system with public baths and brick sewers. Some Harappans lived in two-story brick homes, some of which had bathrooms and garbage chutes. Each city had a strong central fortress, or **citadel,** built on a brick platform. There were also storehouses for grain. At Harappa the storehouses could hold enough to feed about 35,000 people.

The ability of Harappan leaders to store and distribute surplus food provides added evidence of careful, long-range planning. It may also suggest that Harappans were threatened by invaders or by crop-destroying floods. In any case, similar findings at Harappa, Mohenjo Daro, and other Harappan sites indicate that the civilization was probably organized around a strong central government.

Excavations at the site of Mohenjo Daro have revealed a large, well-planned city and a fortified citadel.

Harappan Civilization, c. 1700 B.C.

Interpreting Maps Rivers formed natural highways that encouraged exchange as well as unity in the Harappan civilization.

■ **Skills Assessment: 1. Locate** Identify the major waterways in the Indus River valley. **2. Drawing Conclusions** How might the location of Harappa and Mohenjo Daro have affected their relationship? Why?

Economics

In addition to the cities of Mohenjo Daro and Harappa, archaeologists have uncovered many other sites along the Indus River valley that were a part of the Harappan civilization. Among these sites are seaports that give evidence of Harappan trading and commerce. The port of Lothal, for example, had an enclosed brick shipping dock that was more than 700 feet long. There was also a sluice gate that made it possible to load ships at high or low tide. At such ports, Harappans exported gold, copper, lapis lazuli, turquoise, timber, ivory, and cotton.

Critical Thinking

Ask students what the presence of seaports tells us about a civilization.

ANSWER: Students might say that it means that the civilization had made contact with other civilizations or that trade was a major part of the society.

MAP ANSWERS
1. Indus, Sutlej, Chenab, and Ravi Rivers

2. Students might suggest that it allowed them to trade with each other.

ALL LEVELS: Have students look at the chart they created about Harappan achievements. Have them draw at least one other type of graphic organizer that could convey this information effectively. *(Students might draw cluster diagrams, branching or webbing organizers, horizontal or vertical lists, circular [pie] charts, concentric circles in a "bulls-eye" formation, and so on.)*

 HOMEWORK Have students draw a map of the Indian subcontinent showing the Indus River valley and Ganges River valley.

Teacher to Teacher

Mary Catherine Rahman of Chicago, Illinois, suggested the following activity: Give students an outline map of India. Have them locate and label the major landforms and rivers of India, as well as the two famous Harappan cities. Then have them explain what geographic factors might have helped or hurt early civilizations in India.

That's Interesting!

The Ganges River is considered sacred by the Hindus. Its soil is rich, and the crops along the Ganges have always been plentiful, irrigated by the river and the seasonal monsoons. Earthly sins are thought to be washed away by a bath in the waters of the Ganges. Many Hindus hope to make a pilgrimage to the river at some point in their lives to experience its purification.

SKILLS PRACTICE ANSWERS

1. Students might conclude that Harappan cities were planned carefully and the people were very resourceful.

2. Check students' charts to make sure they have categorized information accurately.

SKILL-BUILDING STRATEGIES — Categorizing Historical Information

Harappan Civilization

There are many different aspects to early civilizations like that of the Harappans. To help understand all of these different aspects, it sometimes helps to classify information. This involves grouping facts into categories according to the characteristics they share.

A Historian's View

Read the following description of Harappa and Mohenjo Daro by a historian who has studied the region:

"At Harappa and Mohenjo Daro the basic form of the ideal Indus city was achieved. . . . on the west a citadel mound built on a high podium of mud brick. . . and to the east, dominated by the citadel, a lower city. . . . The architects of the citadel platform were . . . troubled by the prospects of flooding and to counter this danger they protected the citadel by a mud-brick embankment. . . . [The Great Bath] occupied a central area in the citadel. . . . The Great Bath may have been part of a religious and ceremonial center, offering ritual immersion and perhaps the services of resident priesthood. . . . To the north and east of the Great Bath were other large and prestigious [important] buildings, which may have been the offices or quarters of administrators. . . . Divided into rectangular blocks by the street pattern, the individual buildings of the lower city differed considerably in size and function. . . . Nearly all the larger houses were equipped with wells, indoor bathroom platforms and seated latrines connected to sewers underneath the streets. . . . In addition to residential areas, there were many shops and workshops, producing wares for local consumption and for export: for example, potteries, dyers' vats and metalworkers', shell-ornament makers' and beadmakers' shops. . . . Wheat and barley were two staple crops. . . . The agricultural surplus made it possible to support a number of crafts and specialists. . . ."

Categories of Progress

Economic
division of labor
specialization of crafts
variety of services
products made for export
crop surplus

Technological
architectural skill
city planning
flood protection
and water drainage system

This baked-clay sculpture from Mohenjo Daro shows well-developed artistic techniques.

Skills Reminder

To classify information, first read the information and sort it into groups of related data. Assign a category name to each group to indicate the topic to which the data in that group refers. Then, place the groups into broader categories if possible. Finally, compose a statement relating the categories to each other. This should help you to clearly establish the meaning of the information.

Skills Practice

Study the chart above to see how the information in the quote about Harappan civilization can be grouped into categories.

❶ What conclusions can you draw about Harappan civilization based on this information?

❷ Build a similar chart to classify evidence of economic and technological progress in your town or city.

CLOSE

Have students explain how geography and climate affected the growth of civilization in the Indus River valley.

REVIEW

Have students complete the Section 1 Review on p. 55.

ASSESS

Have students complete Daily Quiz 3.1. As Alternative Assessment, you may want to use the map or chart exercises in this section's lessons.

RETEACH

Have students complete Main Idea Activity for English Language Learners and Special-Needs Students 3.1. Then have them write a question about the main idea for each subsection in the section.

ENGLISH LANGUAGE LEARNERS

EXTEND

Have students use primary and secondary sources, such as computer software, to conduct research on monsoons. Have them write a report explaining how monsoons affected Indian civilization.

Rich farmlands surrounded Harappa and Mohenjo Daro. Harappan farmers grew cotton, wheat, barley, and rice. They also raised cattle, sheep, pigs, and goats. To irrigate their fields, the farmers built canals and ditches. Successful farming practices allowed Harappan farmers to raise surplus crops for storage and trade.

City dwellers were involved in the production or trade of goods. As early as 2300 B.C. they traded with people of the Tigris-Euphrates River valley. Indus River valley craft workers made fine goods. Products included cotton cloth, pottery, bronze items, and gold and silver jewelry.

The early Indus River valley people also developed a written language, as evidenced by pictographs dating from about 2300 B.C. Scholars have not yet been able to read these, however. This is because most of the pictographs that have been found are personal seals that may bear the names of individuals. Writing has also been found on clay pots and fragments, but scholars have been unable to connect this writing to any other language.

No Harappan temples, shrines, or religious writings have been found. Scholars believe, however, that people of the Indus River valley worshiped a great god and used images of certain animals, such as the bull, the buffalo, and the tiger, in religious rituals. Evidence indicates that a mother goddess symbolized fertility. Harappans may have held religious ceremonies in their homes or in outdoor locations, such as around sacred trees.

We do not know why the Indus River valley civilization disappeared. There are several possible reasons. Scientists do know that the waters of the Indus River valley have changed course in the past. Floods caused by these shifts destroyed settlements and would have made life difficult for farmers. Some evidence suggests possible violence from invading forces. There is also evidence of a major earthquake striking the region in about 1700 B.C. Several unburied skeletons were found at Mohenjo Daro, and people appear to have abandoned their homes and possessions. This seems to indicate that some disastrous event occurred at Mohenjo Daro, but evidence to verify this theory has not been found.

✔ **READING CHECK: Drawing Inferences**
What does the size of Harappa's grain storehouses tell us about the city's population?
numbered in the thousands

CONNECTING TO
Economics

Industry and Trade in the Indus River Valley

Trade was an important part of life in the Indus River valley. Artisans made both decorative and practical goods to trade. Decorative articles included ceramic beads, ornaments, and gold and silver jewelry. Useful goods included bronze and copper tools, pots and pans, and stone tools.

Among the most interesting art objects are seals like the ones shown below. These Harappan seals have been found in the Tigris-Euphrates region near Sumerian sites.

Understanding Economics

What might explain the appearance of these seals so far from the Indus River valley?

The pictographs on these Harappan seals may symbolize individuals' names.

CONNECTING TO ECONOMICS ANSWER
Students might suggest that the Harappans traded with civilizations in the Tigris-Euphrates region.

🖥 **internet** connect

TOPIC: Ancient India
GO TO: go.hrw.com
KEYWORD: SP3 WH3

Have students access the Internet through the HRW Go site to research ancient India. Then have them make a poster "advertisement" on ancient India that promotes it as a vacation spot.

SECTION
1 REVIEW ANSWERS

❶ **Define**
• monsoons, p. 52
• citadel, p. 53

❷ Students should mention that the civilization's location near waterways led to sea trade, and that farmers had to adapt their practices to the monsoon climate.

❸ a. It allowed easy trade and successful farming.

b. Harappan seals have been found in the Tigris-Euphrates region.

❹ Students' paragraphs should discuss the things that were important to Harappans and the occupations of the people.

SECTION 1 REVIEW

1. **Define** and explain the significance:
   monsoons
   citadel

2. **Analyzing Information** Copy the graphic organizer below. Use it to analyze the influence of geography and climate on early Indus River valley civilization.

   Geography   Climate
          ↘   ↙
      Indus River Valley Civilization

3. **Finding the Main Idea**
   a. In what ways did the physical setting of the Indus River valley encourage the growth of civilization?
   b. What evidence suggests that people of the Indus River valley had contact with other early civilizations?

4. **Writing and Critical Thinking**
   Supporting a Point of View Write a paragraph from the point of view of a young person in Harappa describing what you like most about life in your city.
   Consider:
   • what seemed important to the people of the city
   • how the people of the city made their livings

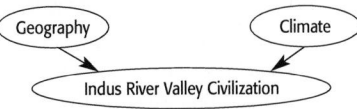

Homework Practice Online
keyword: SP3 HP3

ANCIENT INDIAN CIVILIZATIONS   **55**

OBJECTIVES

1 **Explain how life in northern India changed with the coming of the Indo-Aryans.**

2 **Identify the major contributions of the Indo-Aryans to ancient Indian society.**

🔊 *LET'S GET STARTED!*

As students enter the classroom, tell them that human migration has been an important part of society throughout history. Ask them how immigration affects the society of the United States today. *(Students might mention that immigrants bring their culture with them and that this culture often influences U.S. culture.)* Tell students that in Section 2 they will learn about nomadic people who migrated into India.

MAP ANSWER
mountains

SECTION 2

READ TO DISCOVER

❶ How did life in northern India change with the coming of the Indo-Aryans?

❷ What were the major contributions of the Indo-Aryans to ancient Indian society?

DEFINE

raja

IDENTIFY

Indo-Aryans
Vedas
Sanskrit
Vedic Age
Brahmins

▶ WHY IT MATTERS TODAY

Human migration plays a key role in our society. Use CNNstudentNews.com or other **current event** sources to explore how immigrants have influenced American society. Record your findings in your journal.

CNN student News.com

Indo-Aryan Migrants

The Main Idea
The Vedic Age of early Indian civilization was marked by Indo-Aryan migration and cultural development.

The Story Continues *As the Harappan civilization was declining, a new warrior civilization was entering India. It is possible that this group destroyed what was left of the Harappan civilization. Whether or not they did, we know that these warriors soon came to dominate the region.*

The Nomadic Indo-Aryans

In about 1750 B.C. tribes of Indo-European peoples began to cross the Hindu Kush Mountains into northwestern India. They came from north of the Black and Caspian Seas. We call these nomadic people the **Indo-Aryans.**

The Vedic Age. The Indo-Aryans, sheep and cattle herders as well as skilled warriors, were drawn into northern India by the region's rich pasturelands. In fact, the Indo-Aryan word for war meant "a desire for more cows." Their armies of archers and charioteers enabled the Indo-Aryans to conquer all of northern India.

Most of what we know of these people comes from the **Vedas.** These are the Indo-Aryans' great works of religious literature. For centuries people memorized the Vedas and retold them to their children. Later the Indo-Aryans developed writing. Scholars recorded the Vedas in **Sanskrit,** the Indo-Aryan language. We call the period of India's history from 1500 B.C. to 1000 B.C. the **Vedic Age.**

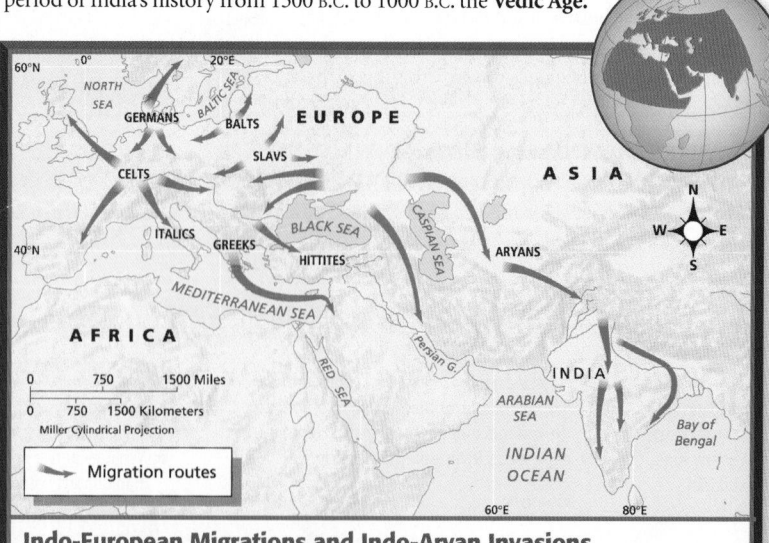

Indo-European Migrations and Indo-Aryan Invasions

Interpreting Maps The Indo-Aryan invaders of northern India were part of a larger movement of peoples westward from central Asia.

■ **Skills Assessment: Physical Systems** What geographic features determined the routes taken by the Indo-Aryans into northern India?

LEVEL 3: Tell students that throughout history urban societies have often come into conflict with their nomadic neighbors. Although the Harappan civilization was well-protected by the natural barrier presented by the northern mountains, the Khyber Pass through the Hindu Kush Mountains provided a means for the Indo-Aryans to invade India after about 1750 B.C. Ask students why they think the Indo-Aryans invaded India. If students guess that the Indo-Aryans were interested in the cities, tell them that they ignored the cities, leaving them to decay.

Indo-Aryan religion. The earliest gods mentioned in the Vedas were drawn from nature. Earth, fire, light, rain, sky, storms, sun, and water were personified. Thus the sky became a father, Earth a mother. Although the Vedas mention gods and goddesses, they also refer to one supreme god. An important hymn celebrates "That One," who created order in the universe. As Indo-Aryan views developed, the Vedic gods were portrayed as having particular characteristics. Varuna, for example, was the guardian of cosmic order. He lived in a great palace in the sky. Over time Varuna became the divine judge who punished sin. Other gods had different characteristics.

It appears that there were no temples in the early Vedic religion. Ceremonies were performed in open spaces chosen for important occasions. Fires were lit on special altars. Foods such as meat, butter, milk, and barley cakes were offered as ritual sacrifices. The juice of the soma plant was poured into the sacred fire as a special offering. The plant's juice was thought to be the drink of immortality.

It was important to the Indo-Aryans that religious ceremonies be performed properly. As time passed, their religious rituals became more and more complicated. Special priests called **Brahmins** knew the proper forms and rules. Brahmins became very important in Indo-Aryan society. No longer the language of everyday speech, Sanskrit became the language used by priests in their rituals.

✔ **READING CHECK: Finding the Main Idea** Why were Brahmins important members of Indo-Aryan society? They had specialized religious training.

Early Indo-Aryan Society

As Indo-Aryans settled in villages, they gave up the way of nomadic wanderers. They continued to herd animals, but they planted crops as well. In time Indo-Aryan settlements joined to form small independent states or territories, each of which was governed by a **raja,** or chief. The raja acted as the military leader, lawmaker, and judge. A royal council assisted him. At times states or territories would go to war against one another. Most often, however, Indo-Aryans lived in peace with neighboring groups.

Indo-Aryan society. Physical and social differences existed between the Indo-Aryan migrants and the earlier inhabitants of the Indo-Gangetic Plain. These differences were the source of the complex system of social orders that over time became very important in Indian society. The Indo-Aryans were light skinned, whereas the earlier settlers were dark skinned. The Indo-Aryans had been a nomadic people, while Indus Valley peoples lived in settled communities. Warriors, and later priests, were at the top of the Indo-Aryan social structure, with merchants, traders, farmers, and servants below them.

In addition to providing information about Indo-Aryan religion, the Vedas tell us a great deal about family life in the Vedic Age. Marriage was an important Indo-Aryan institution, and rules governed—and later limited—marriage among the social orders. Other rules outlined complicated marriage ceremonies. Parents usually arranged marriages, but marriage by purchase or capture and marriage for love were

In this relief from Gandhara, two young Brahmins raise their right hands to perform a religious gesture.

Culture

Throughout their history, the people of India have respected and revered animals. The ancient Indus Valley dwellers carved the likenesses of animals, particularly bulls, on their beautiful trading seals. The Indo-Aryans, with nomadic herding roots, valued cattle so highly that they considered them to be the basic unit of wealth and used cattle as currency to purchase items of great value. Eventually the Hindus declared cows to be sacred and forbade killing them. The Hindus believed that souls could be reincarnated as humans or animals. Killing any creature—even an insect—was forbidden because any creature might house the soul of an ancestor or friend. Other animals that were highly revered in India include birds, monkeys, and elephants.

Critical Thinking

Ask students why they think the cow has been valued so highly by Indian peoples from the earliest civilizations to the present.

ANSWER: Students might mention that the cow was a source of food and fuel, and was even used as currency by the earliest Indians. They might also point out that cow's milk was likely a major source of nutrition for Indians throughout history. They should also mention the Hindu belief that the cow is a sacred animal.

ALL LEVELS: Tell students that most of what we know about the Indo-Aryans comes from the Vedas. These are the great literature of the Indo-Aryan religion, memorized and passed on for centuries. After the development of writing, scholars wrote them in the Indo-Aryan language. Draw a three-column chart on the board. Title it *Characteristics of Indo-Aryan Society,* and label its three columns *Government, Social Life,* and *Economy.* Have students copy this chart and categorize the information as they read Section 2. **ENGLISH LANGUAGE LEARNERS**

Characteristics of Indo-Aryan Society		
Government	**Social Life**	**Economy**
• tribes formed small city-states • each state ruled by raja and his council	• complex system of social orders • elaborate rules governed marriage among the different orders • parent-arranged marriage favored • marriage by purchase, by capture, and by mutual consent recognized	• mostly farmers • wheat and barley major crops • poor transportation and trading methods sometimes limited trade • system of barter for goods

HOMEWORK Have students prepare a short oral report about Indo-Aryan society. Instruct them to use correct social studies terminology to describe the society.

Daily Life

Life in Indo-Aryan clans and families was somewhat freer and more open than in other societies. Although the Indo-Aryans were a patriarchal society, tribal chiefs did not have the absolute authority over the affairs of the group. Indo-Aryan customs and laws governed the chief's actions. When the Aryans first came to India, women were also freer to choose their own husbands, rather than being told whom they must marry. This practice, however, changed over time.

Critical Thinking

Ask students to suggest possible reasons why this freedom for women might have been taken away over time.

ANSWER: Cultural attitudes toward women might have changed, or families might have begun arranging women's marriages as a way of gaining power through family alliances.

SCIENCE AND TECHNOLOGY ANSWER

shovels, trowels, brushes, aerial photography, magnetometers, sonar scanners, computers, particle accelerators, potassium-argon dating

CONNECTING TO
Science and Technology

The Tools of Archaeology

Archaeologists have a number of tools that they use to understand ancient peoples like the Indo-Aryans. Many are simple tools, such as shovels, trowels, and brushes. Archaeologists use these and other tools to carefully uncover and preserve artifacts. Aerial photographs, magnetometers, and sonar scanners also help archaeologists find sites both visible and buried under earth or water. Once a site is found; computers aid in cataloging and classifying uncovered objects.

Since the development in the late 1940s of carbon-14 dating, archaeologists have been able to date the remains of living things from up to 50,000 years ago. A machine measures the amount of radiocarbon in the remains. This tells scientists how long ago the person, animal, or plant died.

Archaeologists have other tools for measuring the age of artifacts. Some instruments help to determine the age of tiny objects up to 60,000 years old. Recently potassium-argon dating has been used to date rock formations that are millions of years old.

> **Understanding Science and Technology**
>
> **What are some of the scientific tools that archaeologists use?**

Grid system for keeping track of location of artifacts

Screen for sifting soil samples

Brushing dirt from the artifact

Analyzing Primary Sources

Drawing Inferences What do you think the writer meant by the last line of this chant? that they strengthened their social values by following tradition

also recognized. Indo-Aryan society strongly emphasized the value of sacrificing, as this passage from the Vedas reveals:

> **Primary Source**
>
> **❝All power to our life through sacrifice!**
> **All power to our lungs through sacrifice!**
> **All power to our eyes through sacrifice!**
> **All power to our ears through sacrifice!**
> **All power to our backs through sacrifice!**
> **All power to Sacrifice through sacrifice!❞**
>
> Yajur-Veda IX, 21

The Indo-Aryan Economy. The Indo-Aryans began raising wheat and barley on the rich plains of the Indus and Ganges Rivers. Irrigation was used to grow rice. Other crops included sugarcane, leafy vegetables, gourds, peas, beans, and lentils. Although villages traded with one another, poor transportation made continuous trade difficult. Early traders bartered, since coins were not widely used in Indo-Aryan society until about 500 B.C.

The Indo-Aryan migrants had a significant impact on the civilization of northern India. They brought with them a new social order. Their language, an early form of Sanskrit, soon spread over much of India. They contributed new religious ideas of how the world works, involving many gods associated with forces of nature. Archaeologists believe that over time these migrants blended into the existing civilization of the Indus River valley people. Religious values changed as social classes became more rigid and closely identified with ritual purity. The result was a new society.

CLOSE

Ask students to explain who the Indo-Aryans were. Then have them describe how the Indo-Aryans influenced political, economic, and cultural developments in Indian civilization.

REVIEW

Have students complete the Section 2 Review on p. 59.

ASSESS

Have students complete Daily Quiz 3.2. As Alternative Assessment, you may want to use the chart exercise in this section's lessons.

RETEACH

Have students complete Main Idea Activity for English Language Learners and Special-Needs Students 3.2. Then have them write a paragraph that describes the developments of Indo-Aryan society, using standard grammar, spelling, sentence structure, and punctuation. **ENGLISH LANGUAGE LEARNERS**

EXTEND

Ask students to use computer software to locate an excerpt from the Vedas in English translation. Encourage them to make a dramatic reading from the Vedas. **BLOCK SCHEDULING**

Southern India. Early civilization in the southern portion of the Indian subcontinent followed different patterns of development. The southern part of the subcontinent was protected from invasion from the north by mountains. The rugged, forest-covered Vindhya Range separates the southern region of the subcontinent from the Indo-Gangetic Plain. The people of the south were able to hold on to their distinct ways of life. The hilly landscape of southern India made unification of its peoples difficult. As a result, people there remained divided into diverse social groups. Many of these divisions still exist today.

Many southern Indians lived as farmers, while others were hunter-gatherers. Others, living along the subcontinent's southern coastal areas, turned to trade to make a living. A few became wealthy trading cotton, spices, and ivory. Through coastal ports, southern Indians eventually made contact with the peoples of other civilizations in Southeast Asia.

✔ **READING CHECK: Summarizing** What were the major contributions of the Indo-Aryans to ancient Indian society? established a new social order, language, and religion

The rough terrain of the Deccan and the Vindhya Range slowed the flow of goods and ideas between northern and southern India.

◀ SECTION

2 REVIEW ANSWERS

❶ **Define**
• raja, p. 57

❷ **Identify**
• Indo-Aryans, p. 56
• Vedas, p. 56
• Sanskrit, p. 56
• Vedic Age, p. 56
• Brahmins, p. 57

❸ Students' analyses should include the following: gods were drawn from nature, natural elements were personified, ceremonies were performed in open spaces.

❹ a. Their language and new religious ideas resulted in a new society.

b. Students might guess that it was to prevent intermarriage between social orders.

❺ Students should contrast the social order created by the Indo-Aryans to what they know about Indian civilizations before the arrival of the Indo-Aryans.

SECTION 2 REVIEW

1. **Define** and explain the significance:
   raja

2. **Identify** and explain the significance:
   Indo-Aryans
   Vedas
   Sanskrit
   Vedic Age
   Brahmins

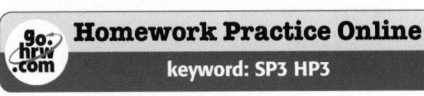
Homework Practice Online
keyword: SP3 HP3

3. **Analyzing Information** Copy the concept web below. Use it to analyze how early Indo-Aryan religious beliefs reflected the natural world.

The Natural World

4. **Finding the Main Idea**

   a. How did the early Indo-Aryans' nomadic lifestyle help them to win control of northern India?

   b. Why might the Indo-Aryans have created strict rules governing marriage among the different social orders?

5. **Writing and Critical Thinking**

   Summarizing Write a paragraph explaining the changes in ancient Indian civilization as a result of Indo-Aryan migration.
   Consider:
   • what you know about Indian civilization before the arrival of the Indo-Aryans
   • what you know about the new social order the Indo-Aryans created

SECTION 3

OBJECTIVES

1 **Describe the importance of religion in ancient Indian society.**

2 **Identify the principal elements of Hinduism.**

3 **Identify the basic beliefs of Buddhism.**

🔊 LET'S GET STARTED!

As students enter the classroom, have them think about social divisions in American society today. Ask them how structured they believe American social classes are and if it is possible for a person to move to a higher social class. *(Students might mention examples of people achieving a higher social class.)* Tell students that in Section 3 they will learn about the structure of social classes in ancient India.

SECTION 3 RESOURCES

REPRODUCIBLE RESOURCES

▸ Guided Reading Strategy 3.3

▸ Graphic Organizer Activity 3: Buddhism and Hinduism

▸ Readings in World History 10: Buddhism and Equality

▸ Hands-on History Activity 3: Hinduism in Indian Life

TECHNOLOGY RESOURCES

▸ One-Stop Planner 3.3

▸ CNN Presents World Cultures: Yesterday and Today Segment 3: The Sacred Ganges

▸ Homework Practice Online

▸ Online Maps, Charts, and Graphs: The Spread of Buddhism, 500s B.C.–A.D. 600s

REINFORCEMENT, REVIEW, AND ASSESSMENT

▸ Section 3 Review, p. 65

▸ Daily Quiz 3.3

▸ Main Idea Activity 3.3

▸ English Audio Summary 3.3

▸ Spanish Audio Summary 3.3

SECTION 3

READ TO DISCOVER

❶ How important was religion in ancient Indian society?

❷ What were the principal elements of Hinduism?

❸ What were the basic beliefs of Buddhism?

DEFINE

epics
caste system
varnas
monism
maya
reincarnation
nirvana
polytheistic

IDENTIFY

Upanishads
Bhagavad Gita
Siddhartha Gautama

WHY IT MATTERS TODAY

Religion plays an important role in world affairs today. Use CNN.com or other **current event** sources to identify news stories with religious elements. Record your findings in your journal.

Hinduism and Buddhism

The Main Idea
Hinduism and Buddhism became the dominant spiritual philosophies of ancient India.

The Story Continues *"From the unreal lead me to the real. From darkness lead me to light! From death lead me to immortality!"* These verses from a religious text reflect a growing focus on spiritualism in ancient India. Enlightenment became the goal for many Indian believers.

The Upanishads and the Epics

By the end of the Vedic Age, the social structure of India had taken shape. Over the next thousand years, many great works of religious literature were written, based on earlier Indo-Aryan religious stories and traditions. During this time two of the world's great religions—Hinduism and Buddhism—developed in India.

In about 700 B.C. several Indian religious thinkers began to question the authority of the Brahmins. These thinkers became wanderers who taught their messages in the forests of the Ganges Plain. The school of thought that grew from their teachings was known as Vedanta, or "end of the Vedas." These teachings were collected in the **Upanishads** (oo·PAH·ni·shahdz). They were the written explanations of the Vedic religion.

Ordinary people, who could neither read nor write, could not use the Upanishads. Instead they listened to religious stories that helped to explain the ideas of Vedanta. These exciting stories used tales of heroes and great events to pass along religious traditions. After generations of retelling, the stories were combined into two **epics**—long poems based on historical or religious themes. They became known as the Mahabharata (muh·HAH·BAHR·uh·tuh) and the Ramayana.

The Mahabharata tells the story of a great battle in a kingdom in what is now northern India. Part of this epic is known as the **Bhagavad Gita.** It is the most famous of Hindu scriptures. The Ramayana tells the story of Rama, a prince and an incarnation of the god Vishnu, and his wife Sita. When Sita was kidnapped by a demon, Rama rescued her and became king. Rama and Sita became role models for men and women in Indian society.

✔ **READING CHECK: Identifying Cause and Effect** In what way did the epics help to spread religious understanding among India's ordinary people? Illiterate people could still listen to the epics.

The god Vishnu is depicted in this striking Indian sculpture.

TEACH OBJECTIVE 1

LEVEL 3: Have students study the information in the sections titled "A Changing Society" and "Hinduism." Ask students to describe how the Indian caste system and Hinduism were related. (*According to Hinduism, people who fulfill their dharma gain good karma and are born into a higher social group in the next life. People who do not live moral lives will be born as members of lower groups.*)

Spotlight on CULTURE

The Puranas are a group of 18 epics made up of many myths and legends. Their plots are taken from the Mahabharata. Narratives from the Puranas have been used to teach Hindu religious ideals to the public. Ask students to list examples of stories from the Bible that have been popularized in American culture. (*Students might list stories such as creation, Adam and Eve, Noah and the Ark, and Moses.*)

A Changing Society

Two developments transformed Indian society between 1500 B.C. and A.D. 500. One of these was the establishment of the **caste system,** a complex form of social organization that began to take shape after the Indo-Aryan migration. Four distinct **varnas,** or social classes, appeared in Indian society. At the top of the social scale were the rulers and warriors. The second varna was the Brahmins, the priests and scholars. Over the centuries the Brahmins became the first varna because of their important role in society. The third class included merchants, traders, and farmers. Peasants who worked in fields owned by others, or who did menial labor, made up the fourth varna.

People in a fifth group were called Pariahs, or "untouchables." Pariahs were viewed as being outside of varnas, although still a part of the caste system. They were allowed to perform only jobs that were considered unclean, such as skinning animals or preparing the dead for funerals. According to the Indian law of the time,

Primary Source

> **❝Not only does one not take water from them [the untouchables], they may not even take water from the same well. . . . Not only does one not marry them, they may not even enter the temple or the house or stroll on the main village streets. Even their cattle may often not drink from the same pool as [others.]❞**
>
> Taya Zinkin, *Caste Today*

Over time the four varnas divided into smaller subgroups, called jati. Eventually there were some 3,000 different jati. Strict rules developed. A person was born into the jati of his or her parents and could marry only within that subgroup. People's jatis determined what jobs they could hold and who they could eat with. This complex caste system remained a part of Indian society for centuries. The constitution of today's India has abolished the caste system, but its influence remains strong in parts of Indian society.

✔ **READING CHECK: Analyzing Information** How did the caste system affect Indian society? separated people into classes

Hinduism

The other major development in ancient Indian society was the growth of Hinduism, which became deeply interwoven with the caste system. Hinduism gradually spread to become India's major religion. It developed through the Brahmin priests' explanations of the Vedas. According to the Upanishads, a divine essence called Brahman fills everything in the world. People have an individual essence, called Self or Atman. Hinduism teaches that Brahman and Atman are one and the same. This reflects the belief that all things in the universe are of the same essence as God. This belief in the unity of God and creation is called **monism** (not to be confused with *monotheism*, the belief in one god).

Hindu beliefs. Hinduism teaches that the world we see is an illusion. If people accept this illusion, called **maya,** they cannot be saved. People can gain salvation only if they learn to recognize and reject maya, but this is not easy to do. According to Hinduism it can take many lifetimes to fully recognize maya. As a result, souls must be reborn over and over again. The experience they gain as they pass through life helps them to identify maya. This belief in the rebirth of souls is called **reincarnation.** Hindus believe that the soul does not die, but rather can be reborn in the body of another human being or even an animal.

Link to Today This Indian woman's caste can be determined by her traditional clothing and facial decoration.

Analyzing Primary Sources

Identifying Bias How do the instructions regarding the treatment of untouchables reflect the view of others towards them? The instructions set them apart.

Linking Past to Present

Only in the past few decades has the system of jati begun to change. In 1950 the Indian government adopted a new constitution outlawing untouchability. It took several more years, however, before punishment for discrimination against the untouchables began to be enforced. Since the 1950s the Indian government has tried to broaden opportunities for former untouchables. Today the children of former untouchables also receive benefits, such as special scholarships to Indian universities.

Critical Thinking

Ask students why they think a society might develop a system of jati.

ANSWER: Students might suggest that a system of jati would likely provide order and stability within a society.

Technology Resources

 Religions of the World Video Series: Hinduism

ANCIENT INDIAN CIVILIZATIONS **61**

61

LEVEL 1: Remind students of the connection between Hinduism and the Indian caste system. Tell them to create a graphic organizer that clearly shows how the classes were categorized and ranked in early India. Here is one acceptable way to accomplish this:

Point out to students that these classes eventually were divided into thousands of smaller groups called jati.
ENGLISH LANGUAGE LEARNERS

Class System in Early India	
Upper Class	Brahmins: priests, scholars
	rulers, warriors
Middle Class	merchants, traders, farmers
Lower Class	peasants bound to the land
	Pariahs: untouchables

That's Interesting!

Many of the most beautiful buildings in early India were religious buildings such as Buddhist sanctuaries and Hindu temples. These buildings were frequently covered with carvings of religious symbols; images of gods, animals, and beautiful men and women; and elaborate ornamentation. Sometimes not an inch of such structures remained unadorned. Some scholars believe that the temple builders carved such images and scenes into their buildings because worshipers frequently were illiterate; the building itself therefore became a teaching tool since its images told the story of religious beliefs.

VISUAL RECORD ANSWER

The image shows three different aspects of one Hindu god.

Technology Resources
World History Teaching Transparency: Everyday Life 6: Ganesha, Hindu Deity

INTERPRETING THE VISUAL RECORD

The Hindu god This sculpture represents Brahma, Vishnu, and Siva as a three-headed creature. *How does this image reflect the Hindu belief in the oneness of the universe?*

Two important principles of Hinduism are dharma and karma. Dharma means doing one's moral duty in this life so that the soul can advance in the next life. Karma is the good or bad force created by a person's actions. According to Hinduism, people who fulfill their dharma gain good karma and are born into a higher social group in the next life. People who do not live moral lives will be born as members of lower groups or as animals. In time, souls who grow spiritually can reach **nirvana,** a perfect peace. At that point the cycle of reincarnation is complete and the individual's soul unites with Brahman.

The Hindu god Brahma can be represented as a number of gods. Brahma the Creator, Vishnu the Preserver, and Siva the Destroyer can be forms of Brahma. Other gods are represented in the spirits of trees, animals, or people, but each is a part of Brahman. For this reason, Hindus must respect all forms of life. To many outsiders, Hinduism appears **polytheistic**—based on a belief in many gods. Hindus point out, however, that their gods simply represent different aspects of creation. Thus Hinduism is actually a monistic faith.

Hindu religious practices. Hindus often practice yoga, a set of mental and physical exercises designed to bring the body and soul together. In one form of yoga, a person might sit for hours in the same position. Over time, this frees the mind of thoughts about the body.

Hindu festivals combine religious ceremonies, rituals, music, dancing, eating, and drinking. Celebrations might last for days. These festivals represent the seasonal course of nature. Originally it was believed that such festivals helped to promote the return of the seasons. Many ancient festivals are celebrated throughout India today.

Some Hindus see certain animals as particularly sacred. Cows are special because they traditionally provided power for plows and carts. They also produce milk and butter for food. For these reasons cows are protected by law.

✔ **READING CHECK: Drawing Conclusions** Why is Hinduism considered to be a monistic faith? holds that all things are of the same essence as God

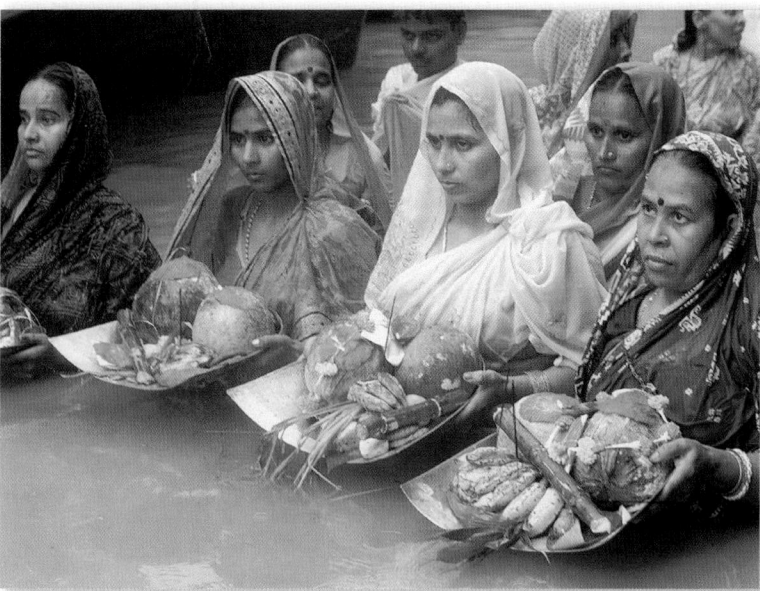

There are many festivals and celebrations in the Hindu calendar. This image shows Hindu women celebrating the Chaat Puja festival in early November.

ALL LEVELS : Have students create a Venn diagram to compare Hinduism and Buddhism. The diagram should include elements that are unique to each religion as well as elements they have in common. (*Hinduism: belief in dharma and karma, belief that the sensory world is an illusion; Buddhism: belief in the way to enlightenment, ethical guidelines—Four Noble Truths and Eightfold Path; both: belief in reincarnation, belief that progress of soul depends on life led, belief in nirvana*) **ENGLISH LANGUAGE LEARNERS**

Buddhism

Buddhism, another of the world's great religions, also arose in India. Its founder was **Siddhartha Gautama.** He became known as the Buddha, or "the Enlightened One." Born in about 563 B.C. in northern India, Siddhartha Gautama was the son of a wealthy prince of the region. During his youth he received every advantage of luxury, education, and comfort. His royal lifestyle shielded him from the harsh realities of everyday life. He knew nothing, for example, of disease, poverty, fear, or other aspects of life among ordinary people.

At the age of 29, Siddhartha Gautama ventured out of his palace and was shocked to learn of the challenges and tragedies common to everyday life. He vowed to discover the reasons for human suffering. In what is now called the Great Renunciation, he left his family and his lifestyle in search of truth and meaning. He tried many methods to discover wisdom, practicing yoga and meditation and fasting so strictly that he nearly died. None of these approaches, however, gave Siddhartha Gautama the answers that he sought.

One day, after six years of searching, Siddhartha Gautama sat meditating under a tree. Suddenly, he felt that he understood the truth that forms the basis of life. In that moment, according to his followers, Siddhartha Gautama became the Buddha. He spent the remainder of his life teaching his followers to pursue the way to enlightenment, the Way of Life.

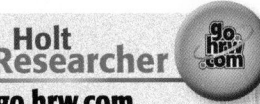

Holt Researcher

go.hrw.com
KEYWORD: Holt Researcher
FreeFind:
   Siddhartha Gautama
After reading more about Siddhartha Gautama on the Holt Researcher, write a series of interview questions that you would ask the Buddha if you could meet him.

Hinduism and Buddhism, c. A.D. 600

Interpreting Maps Buddhism and Hinduism spread along major trade routes.

■ **Skills Assessment: Places and Regions** How far had Buddhism and Hinduism spread by about A.D. 600?

Culture

A religion called Jainism arose from the questioning of the Vedas. Its founder, Varadhamana, was later called Mahavira, the "Great Hero." Mahavira accepted the ideas of karma and reincarnation as well as the concepts of Atman and Brahman. But he believed that, in order to cleanse the soul, one must abstain from any activities that would add to the impurities clinging to the soul like barnacles. This belief led to an ascetic lifestyle in which Jainists did not eat meat and avoided causing harm to other souls, including those of insects. The supreme accomplishment of a Jain was to commit suicide by starvation, which is how Mahavira died at the age of 72.

Critical Thinking

Ask students how Jainism is similar to Hinduism.

ANSWER: It embraces the ideas of karma, reincarnation, and Atman and Brahman. Students might also point out that it has its foundation in the Vedas.

MAP ANSWER
to Japan, Burma, and Siam

Technology Resources
   Religions of the World
   Video Series: Buddhism

CLOSE

Organize the class into small groups. Have each group discuss the Four Noble Truths and the principles of the Eightfold Path.

History Maker

THE BUDDHA. The Buddha's belief in the rejection of the self was one of the most important aspects of his philosophy. This belief is reflected in his sayings:

"Let a man overcome anger by love, let him overcome evil by good; let him overcome the greedy by liberality, the liar by truth...."

"The fault of others is easily perceived but that of one's self is difficult to perceive; a man winnows his neighbor's faults like chaff, but his own fault he hides, as a cheat hides the bad die from the player...."

Critical Thinking

Ask students how the Buddha's teachings might have led to better relations between members of a community.

ANSWER: Students might suggest that followers of the Buddha's teachings would have considered their own faults before criticizing other people.

Technology Resources

World History Teaching Transparency: Art and History 12: Seated Buddha Preaching the First Sermon

The Buddha's teachings. The Buddha accepted some Hindu ideas, including reincarnation. He believed that the progress of the soul depends on the life a person leads—good is rewarded and evil punished. However, he taught that salvation comes from knowing the "Four Noble Truths" and following the "Eightfold Path."

The Buddha taught ethics—a code of morals and conduct—more than ceremonies. He believed that desire causes suffering. As a result, he stressed the importance of selflessness. The Buddha did not accept the Hindu gods, but rather taught that priests should live peaceful and moral lives of poverty. He did not attack the Hindu caste system openly, but denied its importance. According to Buddhism, any person, regardless of caste, could reach nirvana. This gave Buddhism a broad appeal. Powerful Brahmins opposed these teachings.

THE FOUR NOBLE TRUTHS

All human life involves suffering and sorrow.

The desire for a life of pleasure and material gain causes suffering and sorrow.

Renouncing desire frees people from suffering and helps their souls attain nirvana.

The Eightfold Path leads to renunciation, or denial of desire and attainment of nirvana.

THE EIGHTFOLD PATH

Right Views
seeing life as it really is

Right Intentions
living a life of good will; striving toward perfection

Right Speech
avoiding lies and gossip

Right Action
trying to be law-abiding and honest

Right Living
avoiding work that harms others

Right Effort
seeking to prevent evil

Right Mindfulness
constant awareness of one's self

Right Concentration
directing the mind in meditation

Traditional stone sculpture of the Buddha near the Japanese city of Tokyo

REVIEW

Have students complete the Section 3 Review on p. 65.

ASSESS

Have students complete Daily Quiz 3.3. As Alternative Assessment, you may want to use the Venn diagram exercise in this section's lessons.

RETEACH

Have students complete Main Idea Activity for English Language Learners and Special-Needs Students 3.3. Ask students to list the main ideas of each heading and subheading in this section. **ENGLISH LANGUAGE LEARNERS**

EXTEND

Organize students into two groups to study Hinduism and Buddhism. Have students use computer software to acquire information about how the respective religions spread throughout Asia. Finally, have students from each group teach each other about the religion they studied. **BLOCK SCHEDULING, COOPERATIVE LEARNING**

The Buddha taught that the Vedas—the great works of Hindu religious literature—were not actually sacred writings. He believed that virtue could not be inherited and that all people should practice virtuous conduct, nonviolence, and poverty. He explained the cycle through which one passed to achieve wisdom and, ultimately, the state of nirvana:

 "A learned, noble hearer of the word becomes weary of body, weary of sensation, weary of perception . . . weary of consciousness. Becoming weary of all that, he divests [rids] himself of passion; by absence of passion he is made free; when he is free, he becomes aware that he is free; and he realizes that re-birth is exhausted; that holiness is completed; that duty is fulfilled; and there is no further return to this world."

The Buddha, from Max Mueller, ed., *The Sacred Books of the East*

The spread of Buddhism. The Buddha gained only a few followers in his lifetime. Over several centuries, however, his teachings won wide acceptance in Asia. Between about 200 B.C. and A.D. 200, Buddhism split into two branches. Theravada followed the traditional beliefs of Buddhism. Its followers believed that the Buddha was a great teacher and spiritual leader. Theravada Buddhism was widely accepted in Burma (now Myanmar), Siam (now Thailand), Ceylon (now Sri Lanka), Laos, and other countries. Followers of Mahayana Buddhism, on the other hand, regarded the Buddha as a god and savior. Mahayana Buddhism, which uses more elaborate ceremonies than Theravada, took hold in China, Vietnam, Korea, and Japan.

As contacts increased between India and central Asia, Buddhism developed and spread. In India it began to gain more followers, but it was strongly opposed by the Brahmins. Over time Buddhism declined in India. It was in other parts of Asia that Buddhism reached its greatest strength.

✔ **READING CHECK: Contrasting** In what way did the two branches of Buddhism that formed after about 200 B.C. differ from one another? Theravada was traditional; Mahayana viewed the Buddha as a deity

SECTION 3 REVIEW

1. **Define** and explain the significance:
   epics
   caste system
   varnas
   monism
   maya
   reincarnation
   nirvana
   polytheistic

2. **Identify** and explain the significance:
   Upanishads
   Bhagavad Gita
   Siddhartha Gautama

 Homework Practice Online
keyword: SP3 HP3

3. **Comparing and Contrasting** Build a Venn diagram like the one shown below. Use it to explain the differences and similarities between the two branches of Buddhism.

   Mahayana Buddhism / Theravada Buddhism

4. **Finding the Main Idea**
   a. Which elements of Indian religion seem most clearly reflected in the Indian social structure?
   b. In what ways can Hinduism be considered monistic?

5. **Writing and Critical Thinking**
   Identifying a Point of View Imagine that you are Siddhartha Gautama. Write a song or a poem that reflects the beliefs that you formed after experiencing enlightenment.
   Consider:
   • the early life that Siddhartha Gautama led as a wealthy prince
   • the conditions that led him to begin his search for the causes of human suffering
   • his later teachings

SECTION 3 REVIEW ANSWERS

❶ **Define**
• epics, p. 60
• caste system, p. 61
• varnas, p. 61
• monism, p. 61
• maya, p. 61
• reincarnation, p. 61
• nirvana, p. 62
• polytheistic, p. 62

❷ **Identify**
• Upanishads, p. 60
• Bhagavad Gita, p. 60
• Siddhartha Gautama, p. 63

❸ similarities: based on teachings of the Buddha; declined in India; differences: Mahayana—regarded the Buddha as a god; used elaborate ceremonies; spread in China, Vietnam, Korea, Japan; Theravada—considered the Buddha a great teacher; spread in Burma, Siam, Ceylon, Laos

❹ a. caste system and Hinduism are deeply interwoven; belief in the unity of God and creation

b. Hinduism holds that all things in the universe are of the same essence as God.

❺ Students' poems and songs should reflect the Buddha's teachings.

ANCIENT INDIAN CIVILIZATIONS **65**

65

OBJECTIVES

1 **Explain how the Mauryan rulers increased their power.**

2 **Examine the reasons for the decline of Gupta rule.**

SECTION 4

Ancient Indian Dynasties and Empires

The Main Idea
The Mauryans and Guptas established the first Indian empires to control most of the subcontinent.

The Story Continues *Geography helped protect the Indian kingdoms from foreign invaders. Yet India was not a unified country. By the early 500s B.C., some 16 kingdoms existed in northern India alone. The most powerful kingdom was that of Magadha.*

Rise of the Mauryan Empire

The rulers of the Magadha kingdom were the first to try to unify much of India. Their efforts helped protect India from a new round of invasions. The kingdom of Magadha was at its most powerful in 540 B.C., under King Bimbisara. Sometime between about 520 B.C. and 510 B.C., the Persian ruler Darius the Great sent an army to invade the Indus River valley. Darius held the area for a time as part of the Persian Empire, but Magadha soon regained control and held the area until its rule ended in about 320 B.C.

Chandragupta Maurya. As Magadha was declining, a powerful young adventurer named **Chandragupta Maurya** appeared on the scene. He established the Mauryan Empire. The Mauryans ruled for almost 150 years.

Mauryan Empire, c. 320 B.C.–185 B.C.

Interpreting Maps Chandragupta Maurya's grandson expanded the Mauryan Empire until it included all of India except the southern tip of the subcontinent.

■ **Skills Assessment:**
1. Locate What mountain range formed the northern border of the Mauryan Empire? **2. Drawing Inferences** What question might you ask about the Mauryan Empire based on this map?

TEACH OBJECTIVES 1 and 2

LEVEL 1: Have students fill in the following chart to categorize the information in Section 4.
ENGLISH LANGUAGE LEARNERS

Mauryan and Gupta Rulers	
Mauryan	**Examples:**
Chandragupta Maurya	• made Patalipura into a beautiful city • united northern India
Aśoka	• enlarged empire to include all but the southern tip of India • converted to Buddhism
Gupta	
Chandra Gupta II	• favored Hinduism • society and the arts prospered
Skanda Gupta	• last Gupta ruler • empire was weakened under his rule

TEACH OBJECTIVES 1 and 2

ALL LEVELS: Have students create a time line that shows the approximate length of time each ruler controlled India. Tell them to include Chandragupta Maurya, Aśoka, and Chandra Gupta II. Ask students which ruler mentioned in this section they think was probably the most effective leader. Encourage volunteers to justify their choices. **ENGLISH LANGUAGE LEARNERS**

HOMEWORK Ask students to write a paragraph explaining how the Gupta Empire was created.

Because a Greek diplomat at the Mauryan court kept a detailed record of his experiences, we know much about Chandragupta Maurya's rule. Chandragupta built a grand palace at Pataliputra on the Ganges River. He raised an army of 600,000 soldiers who were equipped with thousands of chariots and elephants. His army united northern India from the Ganges River to the region west of the Indus. Chandragupta conquered all of northwestern India up to the Hindu Kush.

Chandragupta Maurya was an able ruler who established a rigid bureaucracy to carry out his commands. Under his rule workers dug mines and built centers for spinning and weaving. Chandragupta standardized weights and measures throughout the empire and established standards for physicians.

Chandragupta also made many enemies. The Greek diplomat wrote that the ruler slept in a different room each night for fear of attempts on his life. Because of the dangers of assassination, strong precautions were taken for the ruler's safety. In about 300 B.C. he gave up his throne to his son, Bindusāra.

Aśoka. Chandragupta's grandson, **Aśoka,** came to power in about 270 B.C. Aśoka proved to be an even greater ruler than his grandfather. Early in his rule, Aśoka fought bloody wars to increase the size of his kingdom. He enlarged the Mauryan Empire until it included all of India except the southern tip of the subcontinent. Thus the Mauryans became the first imperial dynasty to hold nearly all of India.

In time Aśoka became sickened by the bloody battles he had fought. He ordered an end to the killing and became a Buddhist. Many other Indian people also became Buddhists about this time. Aśoka sent a relative as a missionary to Ceylon. He also sent missionaries to other countries, thus spreading the Buddhist faith. Aśoka reversed many of the policies of his father and grandfather. His laws were carved into stone pillars set up in public places. On one pillar he carved this quote reflecting his views about religious tolerance:

❝The Beloved of the Gods. . . honors members of all sects. . . . Whoever honors his own sect and disparages [speaks ill of] another man's . . . does his own sect the greatest possible harm. Concord [harmony] is best, with each hearing and respecting each other's teachings.❞

Aśoka, from William Theodore de Bary et al., *Sources of Indian Tradition*

The Mauryan conquests brought many different peoples and states under imperial control. In an effort to unite his diverse empire, Aśoka worked to improve living conditions throughout the subcontinent. He explained, "On the roads I have had banyan trees planted which will give shade to beasts and men." He also ordered wells to be dug and had rest houses built along trade routes. The later years of Aśoka's rule were remembered as a time of cultural and political advance in India.

Aśoka died in about 232 B.C. and the strength of the Mauryan Empire began a slow decline. His sons battled one another for control of the throne, and invaders from the north and east attacked the empire's northern provinces. Finally, in 184 B.C., the last Mauryan emperor was killed by one of his Brahmin generals, who declared the beginning of a new imperial dynasty. After some 140 years, the once mighty Mauryan Empire collapsed.

✔ **READING CHECK: Making Generalizations** In general, how did the Mauryan rulers increase the power and size of their empire? military conquest

Holt Researcher
go.hrw.com
KEYWORD: Holt Researcher
FreeFind:
Chandragupta Maurya
After reading more about Chandragupta Maurya on the Holt Researcher, evaluate how his political rule changed India.

HISTORY MAKER

Aśoka (unknown–c. 232 B.C.)

Aśoka became a dedicated Buddhist late in his life. His great reputation and authority helped to spread Buddhism throughout India. However, as ruler of India, Aśoka supported religious freedom for all people.

Aśoka also carried out a number of good works. For example, he built animal hospitals and passed laws punishing those who were cruel to animals. **How did Aśoka show his respect for all life?**

Government

After Aśoka enlarged the Mauryan Empire, his conversion to Buddhism and his policy of nonviolence led him to abandon military conquest. To help ensure peace, Aśoka established a group of "High Commissioners of Equity," who traveled his empire and addressed the complaints and needs of minorities and other groups. Aśoka is so revered in Indian history that today the official Indian government seal features the top of one of the pillars he erected.

🖵 internet connect

TOPIC: Mauryan Leaders
GO TO: go.hrw.com
KEYWORD: SP3 WH3

Have students access the Internet through the HRW Go site to research the leaders of the Mauryan Empire, especially the rulers Chandragupta Maurya and Aśoka. Ask students to think about what it takes to build an empire. Then ask them to choose one of these historical leaders of India and write a biography on the life and accomplishments of that leader. Instruct students to use standard grammar, spelling, sentence structure, and punctuation.

HISTORY MAKER ANSWER
He enacted changes that respected animal life.

CLOSE

Have students make a list to summarize the accomplishments of each: Chandragupta Maurya, Aśoka, Chandra Gupta I, and Chandra Gupta II.

REVIEW

Have students complete the Section 4 Review on p. 68.

ASSESS

Have students complete Daily Quiz 3.4. As Alternative Assessment, you may want to use the chart or time line exercises in this section's lessons.

RETEACH

Have students complete Main Idea Activity for English Language Learners and Special-Needs Students 3.4. Then have them write a question about the main idea for each subsection in the section. Have volunteers read their questions for the class to answer. **ENGLISH LANGUAGE LEARNERS**

EXTEND

Have students imagine that they are policy advisors in an ancient Indian kingdom. Have them use a decision-making process to compile a list of policies they would recommend to their ruler to help establish a strong, stable government. **BLOCK SCHEDULING**

MAP ANSWER
Arabian Sea, Bay of Bengal

SECTION 4
REVIEW ANSWERS

❶ Identify
- Chandragupta Maurya, p. 66
- Aśoka, p. 67
- Chandra Gupta II, p. 68

❷ Hinduism: Chandragupta Maurya; Buddhism: Aśoka; Both: Chandra Gupta

❸ a. It was the first imperial dynasty to hold nearly all of India.

b. Society prospered and great progress was made in the arts.

❹ Students' paragraphs should consider Chandragupta Maurya's rigid bureaucracy and Aśoka's wide popular appeal. Students should also imagine how the Gupta rulers may have responded to invaders from central Asia.

Gupta Empire, c. A.D. 400

Interpreting Maps The Gupta rulers united northern India, where they built temples to Hindu gods.

■ **Skills Assessment: The World in Spatial Terms** What major bodies of water bordered the Gupta Empire on the east and west?

The Gupta Rulers

The rise of a new dynasty also contributed to the relative decline of Buddhism and the growth of Hinduism in India. In the A.D. 300s the Gupta family came to power in Magadha, the old capital of the Mauryans. Chandra Gupta I, the founder of the Gupta Empire, took power in A.D. 320. The Gupta family then began to expand their territory through conquest and intermarriage. By A.D. 400 the Gupta Empire reached from the Bay of Bengal to the Arabian Sea. Eventually it included all of the northern part of India.

Under the early Gupta rulers, Indian civilization flourished. The Guptas favored Hinduism, but they also supported Buddhism. During Gupta rule Hinduism became the dominant religion of India. It remains so today.

The early years of Gupta rule have been called a golden age. Indian civilization flourished under their leadership. During the reign of **Chandra Gupta II** (A.D. 374–415) society prospered. Great progress was made in the arts as well. Under later rulers, however, this great empire became weakened. The Gupta political system was less centralized than the Mauryan government had been, and gave much power to local leaders.

Invaders from central Asia crossed into India in the late A.D. 400s. During the next century they began to take control of northern India. The last great Gupta king, Skanda Gupta, drained the treasury in an attempt to defend the empire. Gupta rule ended by about A.D. 550.

✔ **READING CHECK: Evaluating** In what way did the Guptas allow religious freedom in their empire? supported both Hinduism and Buddhism

---

SECTION 4 REVIEW

1. **Identify** and explain the significance:
   Chandragupta Maurya
   Aśoka
   Chandra Gupta II

2. **Categorizing** Copy the chart below. Use it to identify which rulers supported Hinduism, which supported Buddhism, and which supported both religions.

Hinduism	Both	Buddhism

3. **Finding the Main Idea**
   a. In what ways did the Mauryan Empire differ from previous empires and kingdoms in ancient India?
   b. Why might the period of early Gupta rule be called a "golden age" in India?

4. **Writing and Critical Thinking**
   Analyzing Information Write a paragraph explaining how the Mauryan and Gupta rulers persuaded people to support them in power.
   Consider:
   - what Chandragupta Maurya and his successors did to consolidate their power
   - how the Gupta rulers may have responded to invaders from central Asia

Homework Practice Online
keyword: SP3 HP3

🔔 *LET'S GET STARTED!*

As students enter the classroom, ask them if they think cultural advances are a good way to measure the historical significance of a nation. Have them make a list of ten achievements for which they predict the United States will be remembered in the future. *(Students might mention achievements in technology, science, or medicine.)* Tell students that in Section 5 they will learn about ancient Indian cultural achievements.

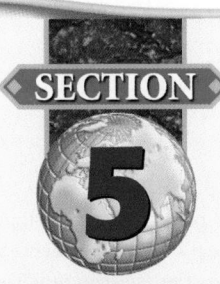

SECTION 5

Ancient Indian Life and Culture

READ TO DISCOVER

❶ In what ways were women's rights limited in ancient Indian society?

❷ What were the most important cultural achievements of the Gupta period?

DEFINE

polygyny
suttee
inoculation

IDENTIFY

Panchatantra
Nalanda
Aryabhata

▶**WHY IT MATTERS TODAY**

Cultural advances are still an important way to measure the historical significance of a nation. Use CNN or other **current event** sources to identify recent advances in art, medicine, science, and education. Record your findings in your journal.

CNNstudentNews.com

The Main Idea
Early Indian cultures made many significant advances in economics, arts, and sciences.

The Story Continues *"It is a day of festival. . . . the streets are broad rivers of people, folk of every race, buying and selling in the marketplace or singing to the music of wandering minstrels." This account recalls a day of celebration during the Gupta Empire, an era in which Indian culture and achievements flourished.*

Economy and Society

From ancient times, the land provided a living for almost all the people of northern India. Although a few members of the highest social classes enjoyed great luxury, most people barely got by. During the Indo-Aryan period, the rajas controlled the land and drew much of their wealth from farmers who worked their fields. During the time of the Mauryans, the rulers claimed one-fourth of each harvest in taxes.

In southern India many people made their living through trade with foreign nations. Foreign trade expanded to northern India under the Guptas. Traders sold silks, cottons, wool, ivory, spices, and precious gems. Indian goods appeared in the Far East, Southwest Asia, Africa, and Europe.

Hindu custom gave women in ancient Indian society some protections. Under the law, however, women did not have the same rights as men. The Hindu Laws of Manu were written between 200 B.C. and A.D. 200. According to these laws, girls were required to obey their fathers. When they married, women were forced to obey their husbands. If their husbands died, widows were supposed to obey their sons. The Laws of Manu also prohibited women from owning property or from studying sacred writings such as the Vedas.

Men were allowed to have more than one wife in ancient India. This practice, called **polygyny,** became widespread during the Gupta period. Another practice that became common later was **suttee.** Widows committed suicide by throwing themselves on top of their husbands' flaming funeral pyres. Suttee was sometimes required among the upper castes.

✔ **READING CHECK: Drawing Inferences** How much independence did women have in ancient Indian society? very little

This image from the 1600s depicts women practicing suttee.

SECTION 5 RESOURCES

REPRODUCIBLE RESOURCES

▶ Guided Reading Strategy 3.5

▶ Readings in World History 12: The Place of Women in Hindu Society

TECHNOLOGY RESOURCES

▶ One-Stop Planner 3.5

▶ Regions of the World Music Audio CD Program 17: India: Ragas: Songs from India

▶ Homework Practice Online

REINFORCEMENT, REVIEW, AND ASSESSMENT

▶ Section 5 Review, p. 71

▶ Daily Quiz 3.5

▶ Main Idea Activity 3.5

▶ English Audio Summary 3.5

▶ Spanish Audio Summary 3.5

ALL LEVELS: Ask students to imagine they are women in ancient India. Have each student write a letter to a friend explaining what life is like in Indian society.
ENGLISH LANGUAGE LEARNERS

TEACH OBJECTIVE 2

LEVEL 1: Have students draw a four-column chart in their notes with the columns labeled *Art and Architecture, Education, Mathematics and Astronomy,* and *Medicine.* Have them fill in their charts with cultural achievements during the Gupta period. (*Students' charts should include the* Panchatantra, *stu-pas, Nalanda, algebra and Arabic numerals, astronomy, and inoculation.*) **ENGLISH LANGUAGE LEARNERS**

 HOMEWORK Ask students to reflect on the advances in mathematics, science, and technology made by ancient Indians. Have them list some of the Indian achievements and trace the spread of these ideas to other civilizations.

LITERATURE. The *Panchatantra* is an anonymous collection of Buddhistic fables most likely compiled sometime before A.D. 500. The framework of the *Panchatantra* consists of one narrative thread that holds together several different stories. The stories, which combine both prose and verse, were originally intended for the instruction of the sons of royalty.

Critical Thinking

Ask students why the author of the *Panchatantra* might have used one narrative theme for several stories.

ANSWER: Students might suggest that the author used multiple stories to tell a broad, moral idea from different perspectives.

THEN AND NOW ANSWER

Students might suggest that they communicate human concerns that are similar in many different cultures.

VISUAL RECORD ANSWER

Students might suggest that its towering structure represents the quest for nirvana.

Then & Now

Fairy Tales

"Once upon a time . . ." is a phrase that we all recognize from the fairy tales that we read as children. The stories that we call fairy tales occur in many cultures around the world. Often the same basic tales can be found in several cultures.

The Jataka tales are popular Indian stories taken from Buddhist writings. They use animals as characters to teach lessons about kindness. Their theme is good versus evil. The same theme underlies the story of Cinderella. There are at least 500 different versions of the tale from various cultures. **Why do you think similar themes are found in fairy tales from different cultures?**

Cultural Achievements

In addition to the religious epics, people enjoyed the stories of the **Panchatantra,** or "Five Books." These were fables from the Gupta period—stories with morals that taught such traits as adaptability, shrewdness, and determination. They influenced stories that were already popular in other parts of the world. The *Panchatantra* has been translated into more languages than any other book except the Bible.

Indian drama developed greatly in the Gupta period. The plays might contain tragic scenes, but they always ended happily. Plays were often performed in the open air. They made little use of scenery, since there were no regular theaters.

Art and architecture. Mural paintings in caves tell us something about early Indian painters. They also offer clues about daily life in ancient India. The cave paintings at Ajanta, from the Gupta period, depict the Buddha and his followers. Less is known about other types of painting. The wood and cloth that artists used have not survived.

Early images of the Buddha show the influence of Greek and Roman art. The styles began to change during the Gupta period. Sculpture became more rigid and formal. As Hinduism grew in importance, architects designed great temples. Hindu temples were built square with heavy walls surrounding a statue of a god. The great Mauryan ruler Aśoka, who had carved his laws on stone pillars, also built thousands of stupas. A stupa was a dome-shaped shrine. Artifacts and objects associated with the Buddha were placed inside.

INTERPRETING THE VISUAL RECORD

The great dome of the Boudha Stupa in Nepal is an inspiring symbol of Buddhism. *How does the Boudha Stupa serve to inspire a spiritual response from believers?*

CLOSE

Have students describe what the early Indians achieved in the fields of literature, mathematics, astronomy, and medicine.

REVIEW

Have students complete the Section 5 Review on p. 71.

ASSESS

Have students complete Daily Quiz 3.5. As Alternative Assessment, you may want to use the letter or chart exercises in this section's lessons.

RETEACH

Have students complete Main Idea Activity for English Language Learners and Special-Needs Students 3.5. Have students identify three important Indian cultural achievements and describe why each was important. **ENGLISH LANGUAGE LEARNERS**

EXTEND

Have students use a decision-making process to plan attractions that promote an understanding and appreciation of Indian culture during the Gupta Empire. **BLOCK SCHEDULING, COOPERATIVE LEARNING**

Education. Education was very advanced for some in ancient India. Children of the higher castes received formal education in many subjects. They studied the Vedas and other literature, including the great epics. They also learned astronomy, mathematics, warfare, and government. Children of lower castes learned only crafts or trades.

Nalanda was a famous Buddhist university located in the eastern Ganges Valley. It became the center of higher learning in India during the time of the Guptas. Thousands of students attended for free. Although it was a Buddhist university, students also studied the Vedas and Hindu philosophy, along with logic, grammar, and medicine.

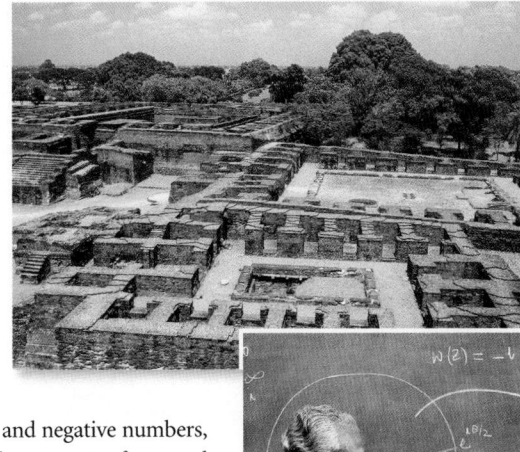

Mathematics and astronomy. Indian scientists were highly skilled. Mathematicians understood abstract numbers and negative numbers, without which algebra could not exist. They also understood the concepts of zero and infinity. **Aryabhata** was a mathematician born in the late A.D. 400s. He was one of the first people known to have used algebra and to have solved quadratic equations. Today we call the digits 1 through 9 "Arabic." However, they probably were invented by Indian mathematicians. Other scientists studied the stars. Indian astronomers identified the seven planets visible to the naked eye. They also understood the rotation of the earth and accurately predicted eclipses of the sun and moon.

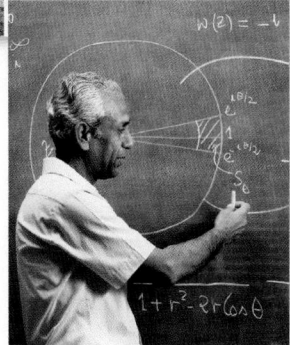

Medicine. Indian medicine was very advanced. Indian physicians understood the importance of the spinal cord. Their surgical procedures included bone setting and plastic surgery. They developed the technique of **inoculation**—the practice of infecting a person with a mild form of a disease so that he or she will not become ill with the more serious form. Early Indian physicians successfully inoculated people against smallpox. Smallpox vaccines were unknown in the Western world until the 1700s. Indian rulers built free hospitals in the A.D. 400s. Physicians practiced cleanliness before an operation and also disinfected wounds, another procedure not known in the West until modern times.

The remains of the great university at Nalanda (above) reflect the importance of this ancient center of learning. An Indian educator of today provides an important learning experience.

Link to Today What do these images tell us about educational traditions in Indian culture?

✔ **READING CHECK: Summarizing** What were the main cultural achievements of the Gupta Period? *Panchatantra, stupas, Nalanda, algebra and Arabic numerals, astronomy, medicine*

SECTION 5 REVIEW

1. **Define** and explain the significance:
   polygyny
   suttee
   inoculation

2. **Identify** and explain the significance:
   Panchatantra
   Nalanda
   Aryabhata

3. **Summarizing** Copy the table below. Use it to illustrate the cultural and artistic achievements made during the Mauryan and Gupta periods.

	Mauryan Period	Gupta Period
Cultural Achievements	▪ ▪ ▪	▪ ▪ ▪
Artistic Achievements	▪ ▪ ▪	▪ ▪ ▪

4. **Finding the Main Idea**
   a. What limitations were imposed on Indian women during the Gupta period?
   b. Describe the major literary contributions of the Gupta period.

5. **Writing and Critical Thinking**
   Drawing Conclusions Write a paragraph detailing the cultural advances of the Gupta period. Indicate which you believe to be most important.
   Consider:
   • the advances in various fields
   • how these advances may have affected people's lives

Homework Practice Online
keyword: SP3 HP3

LINK TO TODAY ANSWER
India has a strong educational tradition.

SECTION 5 REVIEW ANSWERS

❶ **Define**
• polygyny, p. 69
• suttee, p. 69
• inoculation, p. 71

❷ **Identify**
• *Panchatantra*, p. 70
• Nalanda, p. 71
• Aryabhata, p. 71

❸ Mauryan cultural achievements: standardized weights and measures, roads, built centers for spinning and weaving; Mauryan artistic achievements: stupas; Gupta cultural achievements: *Panchatantra*, Nalanda, algebra and Arabic numerals, astronomy, medicine, drama; Gupta artistic achievements: cave paintings, temples

❹ a. Women were forced to obey men and some were expected to commit suicide when their husbands died.

b. *Panchatantra*, drama

❺ Students should mention the *Panchatantra*, temples, Nalanda, algebra and Arabic numerals, astronomy, medicine and indicate which they believe was most important.

CHAPTER 3

REVIEW AND ASSESSMENT RESOURCES

REPRODUCIBLE RESOURCES
▸ Vocabulary Activity 3

TECHNOLOGY RESOURCES
▸ Chapter 3 Test Generator (on the One-Stop Planner)
▸ Global Skill Builder CD–ROM
▸ HRW Web Site

REINFORCEMENT, REVIEW, and ASSESSMENT
▸ Chapter 3 Review, pp. 72–73
▸ Chapter 3 Tutorial for Students, Parents, Mentors, and Peers
▸ Chapter 3 Test (Form A or B)
▸ Alternative Assessment Handbook
▸ Chapter 3 Test for English Language Learners and Special-Needs Students

REVIEW
Have students complete the Chapter 3 Review on pages 72–73.

ASSESS
Use one of the chapter tests to assess students' understanding of the content. For Alternative Assessment, see the Portfolio Activities and Alternative Assessment Handbook.

CHAPTER 3 REVIEW ANSWERS

Understanding Main Ideas
1. Students should mention that it allowed easy trade and successful farming.

2. Farmers raised crops for storage and trade while city dwellers were involved in the production or trade of goods.

3. Students should discuss the religion, society, and economy of the Indo-Aryans.

4. The caste system was supported by the Hindu belief in reincarnation.

5. retained: belief in reincarnation, nirvana; rejected: ceremonies, Hindu gods, caste system, the Vedas

6. All were successful in consolidating power, but each empire eventually collapsed.

7. very few

8. Society prospered and great progress was made in the arts.

Reviewing Themes
1. Waterways allowed easy trade and the climate allowed successful farming after the farmers adapted to the monsoons.

2. algebra and Arabic numerals, astronomy, medicine

3. Hinduism was reflected in India's caste system; Buddhism denied the caste system; both emphasized living a moral life.

72

CHAPTER 3 Review

Creating a Time Line
Copy the time line below onto a sheet of paper. Complete the time line by filling in the events, individuals, and dates from the chapter that you think were significant. Pick three events and explain why you think they were significant.

| 2500 B.C. | 800 B.C. | A.D. 550 |

Writing a Summary
Using standard grammar, spelling, sentence structure, and punctuation, write an overview of the events in the chapter.

Identifying People and Ideas
1. Indo-Aryans
2. Vedas
3. Sanskrit
4. Brahmins
5. Upanishads
6. Bhagavad Gita
7. Siddhartha Gautama
8. Aśoka
9. Chandra Gupta II
10. inoculation

Understanding Main Ideas

SECTION 1 *(pp. 52–55)*
Indus River Valley Civilizations
1. How did the geography and climate of the Indian subcontinent influence the development of early civilizations there?
2. What was daily life like for the people of the first Indus River valley civilization?

SECTION 2 *(pp. 56–59)*
Indo-Aryan Migrants
3. Compare and contrast the society of the first Indus River valley civilization with that of the Indo-Aryans.

SECTION 3 *(pp. 60–65)*
Hinduism and Buddhism
4. In what ways did life in ancient Indian society reflect the beliefs of Hinduism?
5. Which elements of Hinduism did the Buddha retain? Which did he reject?

SECTION 4 *(pp. 66–68)*
Ancient Indian Dynasties and Empires
6. How successful were the Mauryan and Gupta rulers in consolidating and holding on to power?

SECTION 5 *(pp. 69–71)*
Ancient Indian Life and Culture
7. What rights did women have in ancient Indian society?
8. Why was the period of Gupta rule known as a "golden age" in Indian history?

Reviewing Themes
1. **Geography** How did the physical geography and climate of the Indian subcontinent help lead to the development of a unique civilization?
2. **Science, Technology & Society** What were the particular scientific and technological achievements of ancient Indian civilization?
3. **Culture** In what ways did Hinduism and Buddhism influence daily life in ancient India?

Thinking Critically
1. **Evaluating** What sources do scholars use to find out about daily life in ancient Indian society?
2. **Supporting a Point of View** Explain why you agree or disagree with the following statement: The ancient Indus River valley civilization was superior to the Indo-Aryan society that replaced it.
3. **Drawing Inferences** How might Siddhartha Gautama's observations of the world have influenced his religious philosophy?
4. **Analyzing Information** How did Buddhism and Hinduism change the course of Indian history?

Writing About History
Evaluating The "golden age" of Gupta rule saw important advances in science, medicine, and mathematics, many of which are still valid today. Write an essay explaining how achievements in Indian science still have uses in modern life. Use the following table to organize your ideas.

	Ancient India	Today
Mathematics		
Science		
Medicine		

72 CHAPTER 3

CLOSE

Ask students to make a chart showing the major accomplishments of the Indus River valley civilization and the Indo-Aryan society.

RETEACH

Have students who had difficulty with the test develop several questions about the information in a section of the chapter. Have them trade questions with a partner and answer them. Then assign Form B Test to assess students' mastery of the material.

ENGLISH LANGUAGE LEARNERS, COOPERATIVE LEARNING

Portfolio Extensions

Link to TODAY

1. Have students work in groups to create collages depicting the importance of water as a resource. Have group members write a poem or a paragraph summarizing the ideas shown in their collage.

2. Have students research their city's water system. They should find out about the source of water, methods of storage and purification, and sewage systems. Students might create diagrams such as charts and graphs to illustrate their findings.

3. Have students use media and news services to acquire information about public health concerns related to water systems in India today.

Building Social Studies Skills

Connecting Architecture to History

Study the photograph below of the ruins of a city in the Indus Valley. Then answer the questions that follow.

Mohenjo Daro, from c. 2500–1500 B.C., Indus Valley, Pakistan

1. Which is the best general statement about the people who built this city?
   a. They took pride in a well-planned, orderly city.
   b. They valued large open spaces around their homes.
   c. They preferred architecture that used many different geometric forms.
   d. They preferred to build with materials that could be dismantled and moved quickly.
   e. Their city was constructed in a haphazard and poorly planned fashion.

2. Explain your choice of statements in question 1. Give specific examples to support your point of view.

Using Biographies

Read the following quote from *Siddhartha,* a novel about the early life of the Buddha. It was published in 1922 by Hermann Hesse. Then answer the questions.

> "Siddhartha went into the room where his father was sitting on a mat made of bast. He went up behind his father and remained standing there until his father felt his presence. . . . Siddhartha said: 'With your permission, Father, I have come to tell you that I wish to leave your house tomorrow and join the ascetics [holy men]. . . . I trust my father will not object.'"

3. Which statement best describes the main point the author is making about Siddhartha in this passage?
   a. Siddhartha wanted his father's opinion of his plan.
   b. Neither Siddhartha nor his father were ascetics.
   c. Siddhartha was a respectful and obedient son.
   d. Siddhartha's father was a kind man.
   e. Siddhartha's father was violently opposed to his son's plan to join the ascetics.
   f. Siddhartha was fearful of his father, who was harsh and heavy-handed toward his son.

4. Based on this passage, why did Siddhartha wish to leave his father's house?

Thinking Critically

1. artifacts discovered during archaeological digs

2. Students may agree or disagree, but should support their position.

3. Students might answer that leaving his life of luxury to observe poverty and suffering compelled him to create a religion with broad appeal.

4. Answers will vary but should include an emphasis on moral conduct.

Writing About History

Check students' tables to ensure they mention algebra and Arabic numerals, astronomy, and inoculation.

Building Social Studies Skills

1. a

2. Students might note the orderly arrangement of buildings grouped closely together, the use of brick or stone building materials, and the geometric style of the structures.

3. c

4. to become an ascetic

Building Your Portfolio

Charts will vary.

Alternative Assessment

Link to TODAY

Building Your Portfolio

Science, Technology & Society

Like the people of ancient India, Americans today recognize the importance of water as a resource. Using your textbook and other sources, show how modern people have developed technologies similar to those found in the early Indus River valley. Create a chart to summarize your findings.

internet connect

Internet Activity: go.hrw.com
KEYWORD: SP3 WH3

Choose a topic on Ancient Indian Civilizations to:
- study ancient India and create a travel poster.
- write a biography of a leader of the Mauryan Empire.
- explore the geographic regions of India and create a brochure.

Ancient Chinese Civilization

CHAPTER RESOURCE MANAGER

Objectives	Pacing Guide	Reproducible Resources
SECTION 1 **Geographic and Cultural Influences** (pp. 76–79)	• Explore the role that rivers played in Chinese life. • Investigate how geography influenced the development of Chinese culture.	**Regular** 1 day **Block Scheduling** .5 day *Block Scheduling Handbook with Team Teaching Strategies, 4.1*	**RS** Guided Reading Strategy 4.1
SECTION 2 **The Shang Dynasty** (pp. 80–83)	• Examine how the Chinese explained their early history. • Describe how the Shang government and economy were organized. • Identify the religious beliefs held by the Shang. • Explain why the Shang dynasty collapsed.	**Regular** 1 day **Block Scheduling** .5 day *Block Scheduling Handbook with Team Teaching Strategies, 4.2*	**RS** Guided Reading Strategy 4.2
SECTION 3 **The Zhou, Qin, and Han Dynasties** (pp. 84–88)	• Explain why the Zhou fell from power. • Describe how the Qin dynasty used power to maintain its authority. • Identify the achievements of the Han emperors.	**Regular** 1.5 day **Block Scheduling** 1 day *Block Scheduling Handbook with Team Teaching Strategies, 4.3*	**RS** Guided Reading Strategy 4.3 **SM** Graphic Organizer Activity 4 **E** Hands-on History Activity 4
SECTION 4 **Philosophies of Ancient China** (pp. 89–92)	• Examine why the Chinese valued the concept of balance. • Explore what the Chinese philosopher Confucius taught. • Analyze how Daoism and Confucianism worked together in Chinese society. • Investigate how beliefs such as Legalism and Buddhism influenced Chinese history.	**Regular** 1.5 day **Block Scheduling** .5 day *Block Scheduling Handbook with Team Teaching Strategies, 4.4*	**RS** Guided Reading Strategy 4.4 **PS** Readings in World History 13, 14, 15: The Wisdom of Confucius; The *Dao De Ching* of Laozi; Mo Tzu on Universal Love **E** Creative Teaching Strategy 4
SECTION 5 **Chinese Life and Culture** (pp. 93–95)	• Explain why the family was a central institution in Chinese society. • Describe how farmers lived in ancient China. • Identify the artistic and scientific achievements of the Chinese.	**Regular** 1 day **Block Scheduling** .5 day *Block Scheduling Handbook with Team Teaching Strategies, 4.5*	**RS** Guided Reading Strategy 4.5 **RS** Graphic Organizer Activity 4 **PS** Readings in World History 16

Chapter Resource Key

PS Primary Sources	**A** Assessment	Music
RS Reading Support	**REV** Review	Video
IC Interdisciplinary Connections	**ELL** Reinforcement and English Language Learners	Internet
E Enrichment	Transparencies	Holt Presentation Maker Using Microsoft® PowerPoint®
SM Skills Mastery	CD-ROM	

 One-Stop Planner CD-ROM

See the ***One-Stop Planner*** for a complete list of additional resources for students and teachers.

One-Stop Planner CD-ROM

It's easy to plan lessons, select resources, and print out materials for your students when you use the *One-Stop Planner* CD–ROM with *Test Generator.*

Technology Resources	Reinforcement, Review, and Assessment
One-Stop Planner 4.1 World History and Cultures Video Program 6: Confucius, Laozi, and the Buddha Homework Practice Online	Daily Quiz 4.1 Main Idea Activity 4.1 English Audio Summary 4.1 Spanish Audio Summary 4.1 REV Section 1 Review, p. 79
One-Stop Planner 4.2 CNN Presents World Cultures: Yesterday and Today Segment 4: Treasures from China Homework Practice Online	Daily Quiz 4.2 Main Idea Activity 4.2 English Audio Summary 4.2 Spanish Audio Summary 4.2 REV Section 2 Review, p. 83
One-Stop Planner 4.3 World History Teaching Transparency: Art and History 6: Han Dynasty Homework Practice Online	Daily Quiz 4.3 Main Idea Activity 4.3 English Audio Summary 4.3 Spanish Audio Summary 4.3 REV Section 3 Review, p. 88
One-Stop Planner 4.4 Holt Researcher: World History: Confucius, Laozi World History Teaching Transparency: Geography and History 6: The Rise of Buddhism and Daoism Religions of the World Video Series: Buddhism Homework Practice Online Online Maps, Charts, and Graphs: Early Confucianism c. 200 B.C.	Daily Quiz 4.4 Main Idea Activity 4.4 English Audio Summary 4.4 Spanish Audio Summary 4.4 REV Section 4 Review, p. 92
One-Stop Planner 4.5 Homework Practice Online	Daily Quiz 4.5 Main Idea Activity 4.5 English Audio Summary 4.5 Spanish Audio Summary 4.5 REV Section 5 Review, p. 95

HRW ONLINE RESOURCES
GO TO: go.hrw.com
Then type in a keyword.

TEACHER HOME PAGE
KEYWORD: SP3 Teacher

CHAPTER INTERNET ACTIVITIES
KEYWORD: SP3 WH4
Choose an activity to:
- compare and contrast Western, Arabic, and Chinese calligraphy.
- research the Qin dynasty and create a brochure on the Great Wall.
- write a report on Chinese philosophy or Chinese contributions to science.

CHAPTER ENRICHMENT LINKS
KEYWORD: SP3 CH4

ONLINE ASSESSMENT
Homework Practice
KEYWORD: SP3 HP4
Standardized Test Prep
KEYWORD: SP3 STP4
Rubrics
KEYWORD: SS Rubrics

ONLINE MAPS, CHARTS, AND GRAPHS
KEYWORD: SP3 MCG

CONTENT UPDATES
KEYWORD: SS Content Updates

HOLT PRESENTATION MAKER
KEYWORD: SP3 PPT4

ONLINE READING SUPPORT
KEYWORD: SS Strategies

CURRENT EVENTS
KEYWORD: S3 Current Events

Meeting Individual Needs

Ability Levels

Level 1 Basic level activities designed for all students encountering new material

Level 2 Intermediate level activities designed for average students

Level 3 Challenging activities designed for honors and gifted and talented students

English Language Learners These activities address the needs of students with Limited English Proficiency.

Chapter Review and Assessment

IC Vocabulary Activity 4
 Global Skill Builder CD–ROM
 HRW Web Site
REV Chapter 4 Tutorial for Students, Parents, Mentors, and Peers
REV Chapter 4 Review, pp. 96–97
A Chapter 4 Test Generator (on the One-Stop Planner)
A Chapter 4 Test (Form A or B)
A Alternative Assessment Handbook
A Chapter 4 Test for English Language Learners and Special-Needs Students

Build on What You Know

Ask students to answer the following questions:

How did religion affect ancient Indian society?

Consider:

- **Hinduism**
- **Buddhism**

How was power transferred from one government to another in ancient India?

Consider:

- **the Indo-Aryans**
- **the Mauryans**
- **the Guptas**

EXPLORING THE TIME LINE

GL○BAL EVENTS

internet connect

TOPIC: Ancient Chinese
Culture
GO TO: go.hrw.com
KEYWORD: SP3 WH12

Have students access the Internet through the HRW Go site to conduct research on the "Warring States" of ancient China. Then have students write an informative report on the progression of dynasties that evolved from the Warring States. Have students focus on the significant political and cultural developments of each dynasty. Encourage students to enhance their reports with illustrations.

CHAPTER 4

c. 1500 B.C.–A.D. 589

Ancient Chinese Civilization

Wall hanging depicting a giraffe given in tribute to China's emperor

Early Chinese coin

c. 1000 B.C.
Daily Life
Emperor Wen Wang establishes a zoo in China.

c. 500 B.C.
Business and Finance
The Chinese begin using coined money.

c. 1000 B.C.–700 B.C.
Science and Technology
Iron is in widespread use in China.

| 1500 B.C. | 1000 B.C. | 500 B.C. |

c. 1300 B.C.
Daily Life
According to tradition, the Chinese found the city of Anyang.

c. Late 1000s B.C.
Politics
The Zhou dynasty begins in China.

771 B.C.
Global Events
Invaders destroy the Zhou capital.

c. 1500 B.C.
The Arts
Chinese potters create leak-proof stoneware pottery.

Life-size terra-cotta figures from the tomb of Emperor Cheng

Build on What You Know

*T*he earliest civilizations grew along major rivers, slowly rising from Neolithic farming villages. The fertile valleys of the Nile, Tigris, Euphrates, and Indus rivers each gave birth to early cultures. The societies that grew along these great river systems shared many key characteristics, while at the same time developing their own distinct cultures and patterns of life. The river valleys of China also nurtured early civilizations. In this chapter, you will learn how China's earliest civilizations developed and how they compare with other ancient cultures.

What's Your Opinion?

To help students create their Themes Journal entries, provide the following examples of appropriate **agree**/**disagree** *statements.*

Culture

Agree In order to develop new ideas, a culture must be exposed to and influenced by many other cultures.

Disagree Isolated cultures can develop new and unique ideas independently.

Global Relations

Agree The development of philosophies, art, and government has little to do with unsuccessful foreign invasions.

Disagree Unsuccessful attacks from outsiders influence the ideas and values of a culture.

Government

Agree Rulers are successful only if they assert absolute authority in order to help their people.

Disagree Moderation is the key to becoming a successful ruler.

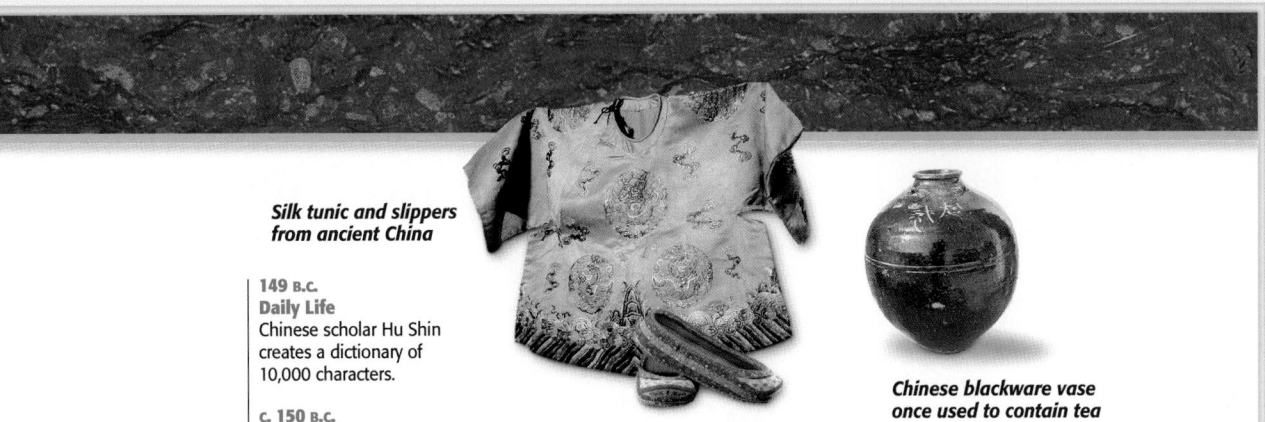

Silk tunic and slippers from ancient China

Chinese blackware vase once used to contain tea

149 B.C.
Daily Life
Chinese scholar Hu Shin creates a dictionary of 10,000 characters.

C. 150 B.C.
Science and Technology
The Chinese invent paper.

C. 100 B.C.
Business and Finance
The Silk Road stretches some 4,000 miles, linking China, central Asia, and the Mediterranean.

C. 73 B.C.
Global Events
Han emperor Xuandi conquers part of the Xiongnu's territory.

A.D. 220
Politics
The Han dynasty ends.

C. A.D. 400
Global Events
The Chinese traveler Faxian visits India.

C. A.D. 500
Daily Life
Tea becomes a popular drink in southern China.

A.D. 581
Politics
The Sui dynasty reunifies China.

1 B.C.

A.D. 500

28 B.C.
Science and Technology
Chinese astronomers observe sunspots.

C. 124 B.C.
The Arts
Liu Ch'e founds an imperial university for the study of the Five Classics.

221 B.C.
Politics
Cheng becomes China's first emperor and unifies China under Qin rule.

C. 220 B.C.
The Arts
Cheng orders artisans to sculpt thousands of life-size terra-cotta warriors for his tomb.

C. A.D. 460
The Arts
Construction begins on the Yungang temple complex, which contains a sculpture of the Buddha over 44 feet-high.

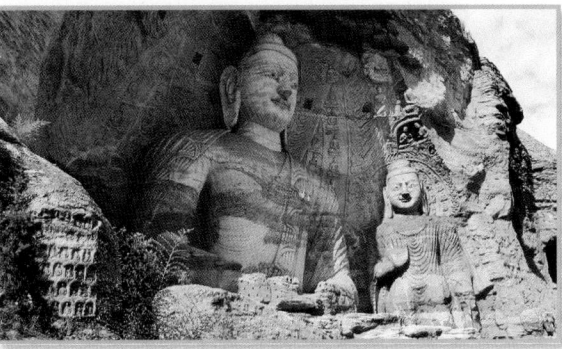

Stone-carved seated Buddha from the Yungang temple grotto in Shanxi Province, China

---

EXPLORING THE TIME LINE
GLOBAL EVENTS

The Han, one of the ancient Chinese dynasties discussed in this chapter, created an extensive government bureaucracy. The bureaucracy took care of the everyday workings of society. The structure of the Han government consisted of two parts—the central administration, located in the capital, and the offices of the outlying provinces. The officials of the central government were responsible for making decisions, in consultation with the emperor or on his behalf. They were also supposed to ensure the collection of revenue and provide for the security of the empire.

Critical Thinking

Ask students how the structure of the Han bureaucracy resembles that of the modern U.S. government.

ANSWER: Students might note that the division of government into central and provincial parts resembles the separate national and state governments of the United States, and the role of the emperor in making decisions has some resemblance to the role of the president.

What's Your Opinion?

Do you **agree** *or* **disagree** *with the following statements? Support your point of view in your journal.*

Culture Cultures that grow in isolation from other cultures generally do not develop new ideas, nor do they emphasize inquiry and innovation.

Global Relations Unsuccessful foreign invasions have little or no effect on the way that a culture grows and develops.

Government Leaders who combine harsh rule with actions to help their people are often successful.

SECTION 1

READ TO DISCOVER

❶ What role did rivers play in Chinese life?
❷ How did geography influence the development of Chinese culture?

DEFINE

loess
dikes

WHY IT MATTERS TODAY

Every year, river floods devastate different regions of the world. Use CNN fyi.com or other **current event** sources to find information about a country or a community that has recently faced severe flooding. Record your findings in your journal.

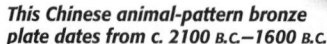

Geographic and Cultural Influences

The Main Idea
China's rivers, and isolation caused by mountains and deserts, shaped early Chinese culture.

The Story Continues *"Floodwater dashed up against the skies. . . . God issued a command allowing Yü to spread out the self-replacing soil so as to quell the floods in the Nine Provinces."* This myth from China's remote past may reflect stories about the efforts of early rulers to control the floodwaters of the Huang River—the mighty river that has been central to Chinese civilization since earliest times.

The Physical Setting

China is a land of enormous size, great geographic variety, and widely contrasting climate patterns. Rugged, snow-capped mountains range across the country's west, northwest, and southwest. These towering mountains, including some of the world's tallest and most forbidding, slope down to high, wind-swept desert or semi-desert plateaus. Moving south the plateaus give way to rolling country of low hills and valleys. In the north the plateaus slope gently down to the North China Plain, a coastal area along the Yellow Sea.

Different regions. The mountain range that cuts from west to east across China is called the Qinling (CHIN·LING) Shandi. This range separates the valleys of two great rivers—the Huang and the Chang, or Yangtze. The Qinling Shandi also marks the boundary between northern and southern China. Compared to central and southern China, the north receives less rain. Temperatures are more extreme in the north, and the growing season is shorter. Wheat is the principal crop there. In China's central and southern areas, where rainfall is more plentiful, rice is the leading farm product.

What we call China has consisted of many different geographic and political sections over time. The smaller but most historically significant section—the heart of China—is called China Proper. It stretches from the eastern seacoast inland. Three great river systems wind through China Proper. These include the Huang, Chang, and Xi (SHEE). China's other political sections have at various times included Tibet, Xinjiang (SHIN·JYAHNG), Mongolia, Manchuria, and northern Korea. These regions form a semicircle around China Proper. At different times throughout their history, the Chinese conquered and ruled these regions. On other occasions, nomads from one or another of these outlying regions conquered and ruled China's heartland.

This Chinese animal-pattern bronze plate dates from c. 2100 B.C.–1600 B.C.

ALL LEVELS: Draw a three-column chart on the chalkboard. Label the columns with the following river names: *Huang, Chang,* and *Xi.* Ask students to explain how the Chinese used each river and fill in the chart as students give their answers. (*Huang: fertile farming; Chang and Xi: commercial waterways*) Ask class members what other geographic features of China played a part in shaping its development and how they were important. (*isolating influence of mountains, deserts, vastness*) **ENGLISH LANGUAGE LEARNERS**

Huang	Chang	Xi
fertile farming	commercial waterway	commercial waterway

HOMEWORK Have students read History Makers Speak on page 78 and write a short paragraph that explains why they think the Chinese did not follow Chang Jung's advice. Remind students to use standard grammar, spelling, sentence structure, and punctuation.

SKILL-BUILDING STRATEGIES — Reviewing Map Basics

China's Geography

To understand the history of China, one must understand its geography. One of the best ways to learn about China's geography is by studying maps of the country. Maps show many different types of information, from political boundaries to military battles to climate patterns. Most maps share several characteristics, and familiarity with these elements makes reading a map easier. The map's title explains its subject or focus. The legend, or key, explains any special symbols, colors, or shadings used on a map. The directional indicator, or compass rose, indicates direction on a map——the map's "orientation." The scale compares distances on the map to actual distances on the earth's surface. Grid lines provide a frame of reference for a map in terms of latitude and longitude.

Early China, c. 5000 B.C.–c. 1000 B.C.

Legend:
- Areas of rice farming
- Spread of rice farming
- Ancient sea coast
- Ancient rivers

Skills Reminder

A map is a drawn or printed representation of all or part of the earth's surface. To accurately interpret a map's information, read the map's title and labels to determine its focus. Then study the legend to become familiar with the map's symbols, colors, and shadings. Different colors and shadings can indicate features of the landscape, such as height above sea level or climate and rainfall. Consult the directional indicator and scale to determine the map's direction and distances. You may also need to use math skills to determine distances. Analyze the map's features and details, including the location of rivers, mountains, and human settlements. Use this information to form generalizations and draw conclusions, particularly about distribution of geographic features and patterns in human history.

Skills Practice

❶ Study the map shown above. What is the subject of the map?

❷ Around what geographic feature were most of the cities built? Why might this have been so?

❸ What does the activity of rice farming shown on the map demonstrate about the geographic distribution of agriculture in early east Asia?

❹ Approximately how much farther is the trip from Wuchang to Taixicun than Wuchang to Erlitou?

❺ Trace the map above. Use an atlas to create an outline map of modern China. Locate and label important land forms and features such as major cities, rivers, and elevations. Include other items, such as types of crop, dams, weather patterns, and resources.

Geography

In early China, two patterns of agricultural development emerged as early as 5000 B.C. In northern China, people relied on drought-resistant crops like millet, and supplemented their diets with fruits and nuts. In southern China, people grew rice.

Critical Thinking

Ask students to speculate how the climates of northern and southern China might be different.

ANSWER: Based on the crops, students might suggest that southern China has a wetter climate, while northern China is drier and subject to droughts.

SKILLS PRACTICE ANSWERS

1. early China, c. 5000 B.C.– 1000 B.C.

2. rivers, which provided water and transportation

3. It spread from the coast to the river valleys.

4. about 300 miles

5. Students' maps should use appropriate labels, symbols, and a legend.

LEVEL 1: Have students read the material under the heading "The rivers of China." Ask for a volunteer to describe what purpose the earthen walls around the Huang River were supposed to serve. *(prevent flooding)* What was the result of building ever-higher dikes along the Huang River? *(The river now flows at least 12 feet above the surrounding land.)* Did the dikes stop the Huang River from flooding? *(No)*
ENGLISH LANGUAGE LEARNERS

LEVEL 3: Tell students that early Chinese called the region in which they lived "All under Heaven." Ask the class what clues this name provides about how the Chinese regarded their culture. *(Students should suggest feelings of cultural superiority, a link with the divine, a blessed land and people.)* Ask students what other name the Chinese had for their land that indicates they felt culturally superior. *(Middle Kingdom)* Then discuss what caused these feelings of superiority. *(China's geographic isolation and lack of contact with foreigners)*

Economics

The Chang is the world's third-longest river (after the Amazon and the Nile). It carries about 75 percent of China's domestic water-borne commerce and irrigates more than a third of the nation's agriculture. In addition, the river's watershed covers some 700,000 square miles, about a fifth of China's total land area.

Critical Thinking

Ask students why water transportation would be especially important to the economic development of civilizations in China.

ANSWER: Students should recognize that developing nations generally lack the sophisticated infrastructure, such as highways and railroads, of more developed nations.

That's Interesting!

The Chinese do not call their nation "China." Foreigners use this name. Instead the Chinese use the name Zhongguo (chung-kou), meaning "Middle Kingdom," a reference to the early Chinese belief that their country was at the center of the world.

VISUAL RECORD ANSWER

It is navigable.

The rivers of China. The Huang, the Chang, and the Xi rivers have played major roles in Chinese history. The Huang River flows some 2,900 miles across China before emptying into an arm of the Yellow Sea. The Huang River valley has a fertile yellow soil called **loess** (LES). So much loess washes into the Huang River that it gives the river a yellow tint. That is why the Chinese named it the Huang River, which means "Yellow River."

The Huang River has also been prone to devastating floods. These floods led the ancient Chinese to nickname the river "China's Sorrow." Early farmers built earthen **dikes**, or walls, along the Huang to protect crops from floods. The dikes had the unintended effect, however, of slowing the river's flow. This in turn caused the Huang to deposit silt on the river bottom. Over the years, the silt grew deeper, forcing the river level higher. The river level finally reached the tops of the dikes, so that even moderate rains caused the river to wash over the dikes and into the surrounding fields. In about 1 B.C., a Chinese engineer, Chang Jung, proposed a new solution to this problem.

Analyzing Primary Sources

Problem Solving What solution did Chang Jung offer to reduce flooding along the Huang River? to stop building dikes

INTERPRETING THE VISUAL RECORD

The Huang River The Huang River in northeastern China has shifted course many times over the centuries. These shifts have affected millions of acres of rich farmland. *What does the deep channel of the Huang River tell us about the river?*

 History Makers Speak

" . . . the government and the people go on building dykes until the level [of the river] becomes slightly higher than the surrounding country. . . . It would be better to follow the nature of the water . . . the water-ways would keep themselves in order and there would be much less danger from floods breaking through, with all the harm they bring about. **"**

Chang Jung, from *Science and Civilisation in China*

Chang Jung's advice was mostly ignored, however. The Chinese built ever-higher dikes. As a result, today the Huang River flows at least 12 feet above the surrounding land. The higher dikes, however, did not end the flooding. Every few years the Huang broke through the dikes. The resulting floods destroyed crops and caused great loss of life. Since the floodwater could not drain back into the higher riverbed, it tended to remain on the land until it evaporated. Moreover, rainfall in the region was unpredictable, so that floods alternated with periods of drought and famine.

CLOSE

Ask students to list the factors that led to China's relative isolation from other civilizations.

REVIEW

Have students complete the Section 1 Review on p. 79.

ASSESS

Have students complete Daily Quiz 4.1. As Alternative Assessment, you may want to use the river exercise in this section's lessons.

RETEACH

Have students complete Main Idea Activity for English Language Learners and Special-Needs Students 4.1. Then have students use standard grammar, spelling, sentence structure, and punctuation to write a paragraph that summarizes what they have learned in Section 1. **ENGLISH LANGUAGE LEARNERS**

EXTEND

Have students use computer software to conduct research on dikes and other methods of flood prevention in China. Ask them to write a short report that summarizes their findings.
BLOCK SCHEDULING

The Chang River, in central China, flows for 3,434 miles. The river cuts a deep channel through its valley. In modern times, large ocean-going ships have been able to navigate nearly 600 miles upstream. Smaller ships can travel about 1,700 miles upriver. The Xi River, in southern China, is about 1,200 miles long. Like the Chang, it forms an important commercial waterway. Large ships can navigate about one third of its length.

✔ **READING CHECK: Summarizing** What benefits do the Huang River, the Chang River, and the Xi River bring to the Chinese people? fertile soil, commercial waterways

China's Isolation

Great distances, rugged mountains, and harsh deserts, such as the Gobi, isolated China from the civilizations of India and the West. As a result, China developed its own distinctive culture. The Chinese did adopt some ideas and skills from other peoples. However, they were probably influenced less by other cultures than any other people in ancient times.

Along their northern and northwestern borders, the Chinese had regular contact with nomadic and semi-nomadic peoples. These peoples spoke their own languages and had their own cultures. Usually they traded peacefully with the Chinese. Sometimes, however, they organized bands of mounted warriors and attacked Chinese settlements. The Chinese considered these people culturally inferior and called them barbarians.

Infrequent contact with foreigners helped give the Chinese a strong sense of identity and superiority. They regarded China as the only civilized land, calling it *Zhongguo,* or "Middle Kingdom," meaning the center of the world. They believed that other people became fully civilized only by learning the Chinese language and adopting Chinese customs. In many cases, even when outsiders overran parts of China, as sometimes happened, the invaders would lose their identity over time and be absorbed into China's population.

✔ **READING CHECK: Identifying Bias** Why did the Chinese regard other peoples as inferior? lack of contact with foreigners

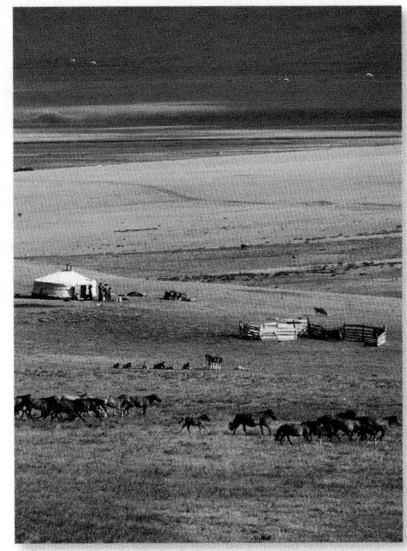

In parts of Mongolia, north of China, nomadic lifestyles continue today.

SECTION 1 REVIEW ANSWERS

❶ **Define**
- loess, p. 78
- dikes, p. 78

❷ Huang: fertile farming; Chang: commercial waterway; Xi: commercial waterway

❸ a. northern: less rain, more extreme temperatures, shorter growing season; southern: more rainfall; China Proper: most historically significant; outlying regions (Tibet, Xinjiang, Mongolia, Manchuria, northern Korea): sometimes conquered by China, sometimes ruled China

b. China's isolation led to the development of a distinctive culture.

❹ Students' outlines will vary but should include a discussion of flooding and dikes.

SECTION 1 REVIEW

1. **Define** and explain the significance:
   loess
   dikes

2. **Comparing** Copy the web diagram below. Use it to compare the uses that the Chinese have made of the Huang, the Chang, and the Xi rivers.

   Chang River — Xi River — Huang River

3. **Finding the Main Idea**
   a. How do the northern and southern regions of China differ geographically and politically?
   b. How did geography contribute to the Chinese sense of identity?

4. **Writing and Critical Thinking**
   Summarizing Imagine you are a university professor teaching a class on the history of China. Prepare an outline for a lecture in which you teach students about the role the Huang River has played in Chinese history.
   Consider:
   • the characteristics of the river and its surrounding lands
   • the problem of flooding
   • the effects of dikes on the river

Homework Practice Online
keyword: SP3 HP4

SECTION 2

OBJECTIVES

1 Examine how the Chinese explained their early history.

2 Describe how the Shang government and economy were organized.

3 Identify the religious beliefs held by the Shang.

4 Explain why the Shang dynasty collapsed.

SECTION 2 RESOURCES

REPRODUCIBLE RESOURCES

▶ Guided Reading Strategy 4.2

TECHNOLOGY RESOURCES

▶ One-Stop Planner 4.2

▶ CNN Presents World Cultures: Yesterday and Today Segment 4: Treasures from China

▶ Homework Practice Online

REINFORCEMENT, REVIEW, AND ASSESSMENT

▶ Section 2 Review, p. 83

▶ Daily Quiz 4.2

▶ Main Idea Activity 4.2

▶ English Audio Summary 4.2

▶ Spanish Audio Summary 4.2

MAP ANSWER

desert to the north and mountains to the west

SECTION 2

READ TO DISCOVER

❶ How did the Chinese explain their early history?

❷ How was the Shang government and economy organized?

❸ What religious beliefs did the Shang hold?

❹ Why did the Shang dynasty collapse?

DEFINE

bureaucracy
animism
oracle bones
dialects
calligraphy

IDENTIFY

Xia
Shang
Zhou

▶ WHY IT MATTERS TODAY

Myths and legends still play an important role in today's world. Use or other **current event** sources to find information regarding a myth or legend that remains influential today. Record your findings in your journal.

CNN student News.com

The Shang Dynasty

The Main Idea
The Shang dynasty established a model that shaped future governments of China.

The Story Continues *"To give continuance to foremothers and forefathers / We build a house, many hundred cubits of wall; . . . / Here we shall live, here rest, / Here laugh, here talk."* This ancient Shang poem—celebrating the building of a house—reflects the values of those people who gave China its first great dynasty.

Legends of Ancient China

The early Chinese placed great importance on explaining the distant past and on China's role in history. They passed on many legends about the beginnings of the world and about the origins of ancient China. For example, an early Chinese story tells of Pangu, the first man, who awoke from 18,000 years of sleep to create the universe. Another Chinese legend describes the labors of Yu, a mythological figure who drained away floodwaters so people could live in China. Yu established a line of kings called the **Xia** (SHAH). The Xia ruled over a late Neolithic people who lived in the Huang River region starting in about 2200 B.C.

Shang Dynasty c. 1750 B.C.– c. 1050 B.C.

Interpreting Maps At its height, Shang rule stretched across much of eastern and central China, from the Yellow Sea to the rich lands of the Huang River valley.

■ **Skills Assessment: Physical Systems** What geographic features characterized the western and northern borders of the Shang kingdom?

LEVEL 3: Explain that in cultures without writing, history depends on stories passed from one generation to the next. Have students write a short legend about Xia's rule. Form small groups and have one member tell his or her legend to another. That student should repeat it to a third, and so on, until it has passed through the group. Have the last person in each group tell the legend to the class. Ask the class to assess the value of legends as historical sources. Then discuss what the accuracy of China's legends suggests about the importance its people put on their past. **COOPERATIVE LEARNING**

HOMEWORK Create a chart titled *Developments under the Shang.* Head the columns *Farming Advances, Crafts Advances,* and *Government Accomplishments.* Have students copy the chart and categorize the information on their own.

Developments under the Shang		
Farming Advances	Crafts Advances	Government Accomplishments

There is little evidence to support most of these legends. Scholars agree, however, that the Xia people existed and that they made great advances over time. For example, they developed improved methods of agriculture and may have begun to use written symbols. The people lived well in good times, but may have had little centralized control over irrigation and flood-prevention measures. The early Chinese, then, could do little in the face of droughts and floods.

At some point between 1750 B.C. and 1500 B.C., invaders called the **Shang** swept into the Huang River valley. Many scholars believe that the Shang introduced simple irrigation and flood-control systems to the region. This may have strengthened Shang rule. By controlling these systems, the Shang could more easily control the region's people.

The Shang created China's first historic dynasty. Later Chinese writers wrote an account in which Tang, a Shang leader, asks the Xia people to reject their king and to follow him.

History Makers Speak **❝I would have you stand by my side . . . to bring upon him [the Xia ruler] Heaven's punishment. I will greatly reward you. Do not ye disbelieve me. I do not eat my words. If you do not follow the words of this vow, I will slay you and all your offspring and none will be forgiven.❞**

Tang, from *An Anthology of Chinese Literature*

✔ **READING CHECK: Drawing Inferences** Why would people use legends to explain their past? They placed importance on explaining their own role in history.

Government and Culture

At its height, the Shang kingdom stretched across 40,000 square miles. Apparently the Shang moved their capital several times, probably for defensive reasons or to avoid floods. During the last centuries of Shang rule, the capital was near what is today the city of Anyang.

Shang rulers created a complex **bureaucracy**—a government organized into different levels and tasks. A hereditary king ruled over all land in the kingdom. The Shang army used war chariots and bronze weapons to defend against the peoples on the kingdom's borders. Their military might and well-organized government allowed the Shang to gain territory and to spread their culture.

Economy and handicrafts. The Shang economy was based mainly on agriculture. Crops included millet and rice. Domestic animals included pigs and chickens for meat and horses for labor. During the Shang dynasty, the Chinese knew how to raise silkworms. They spun thread from the silkworms' cocoons and wove silk cloth from the thread.

Not all Chinese of the Shang period were farmers. Many merchants and artisans lived in the capital and in the towns of the Shang realm. Artisans worked in bone, ivory, and jade. Shang artisans also established the foundation for later Chinese ceramic art. They developed the forms and shapes used in Chinese ceremonial vases. Shang potters used *kaolin*, a fine white clay, and could glaze pottery to give it a shiny finish. This made the pottery more durable.

Analyzing Primary Sources

Evaluating How did Tang appeal to the people's spiritual and moral sense in his effort to overthrow the Xia ruler? by claiming that he was acting on behalf of Heaven

CONNECTING TO
Art

Metalworking: Ancient Bronze Vessel
This small vessel—just over a foot long—shows animal designs that were common in Shang dynasty bronzes. The tiger at the left becomes an owl in the middle and yet another bird on the right. The vessel was probably used for mixing and pouring wine. The head of the tiger serves as a lid. The neck of the bird at the right provides a handle for pouring.

Understanding the Arts
How was this bronze casting multi-functional?

Science, Technology & Society

Silkworms are not worms at all. Instead they are caterpillars in a family belonging to the biological order of Lepidoptera—butterflies and moths. The most commonly raised silkworms eat only the leaves of mulberry trees. The silk comes from the cocoons they spin and live in when they grow large enough to metamorphasize into moths. In the silk-making process, heat is used to kill the caterpillar inside the cocoon. Next the cocoon is carefully unwound, producing a continuous silk thread. These threads are then spun into silk cloth. About 100 cocoons are needed to make a silk tie, and more than 600 for a blouse. A silk kimono can require 3,000 silkworms, which will eat about 135 pounds of mulberry leaves before they spin their cocoons.

Critical Thinking

Garments made of silk generally cost more than similar items made of cotton, wool, or polyester. Ask students why this would be so.

ANSWER: Students should recognize the high costs involved in producing silk thread and enough cloth to make an item.

CONNECTING TO ART ANSWER
It is both beautiful and practical.

TEACH OBJECTIVE 2

ALL LEVELS: Ask students to identify two ways that the Shang dynasty maintained its power. *(force of arms, such as war chariots and bronze weapons; public works systems, such as irrigation and flood control)* Ask them to deduce the role that technology played in sustaining the dynasty. *(Both examples are technology-related.)* **ENGLISH LANGUAGE LEARNERS**

TEACH OBJECTIVE 3

LEVEL 1: Call on volunteers to name some of the religious beliefs held by the Shang. *(combination of animism and ancestor worship, Shangdi, interpretation of oracle bones)* Ask students

how Shang rulers used the religious beliefs of the early Chinese to legitimize their rule. *(They claimed that their decisions were the will of Shangdi.)* **ENGLISH LANGUAGE LEARNERS**

TEACH OBJECTIVE 4

LEVEL 1: Ask students why the Shang dynasty collapsed. *(It could not defend against the constant attacks from peoples on its borders.)* Have students explain who conquered the Shang dynasty and how they justified their conquest. *(the Zhou; claimed that the Shang were corrupt and unfit to rule)* **ENGLISH LANGUAGE LEARNERS**

Government

The belief system of the Shang religion legitimized the power of the ruling king. According to this religion, the god Shangdi could bestow bountiful harvests and victory in battle on the Shang people, and the king's ancestors could supposedly influence Shangdi in these matters. Through prayer and sacrifice, the king was believed to be able to communicate with his ancestors and ask them to intercede with Shangdi on behalf of the Shang people. Therefore it was the king himself who could produce abundant crops and ensure military triumphs, and consequently, religious and political powers were concentrated in his hands.

Critical Thinking

Ask students how the Shang beliefs about their kings could turn out to be a disadvantage for a ruler.

ANSWER: Students might suggest that a random event such as a drought could discredit a ruler.

VISUAL RECORD ANSWER

They recorded the answers in writing on the bones.

INTERPRETING THE VISUAL RECORD

Oracle bones The Shang believed that they could receive answers and advice from the spirit world through the use of oracle bones like the one shown here. *What does the writing on this bone suggest about the Shang system for interpreting these messages?*

Astronomy and the calendar. The Chinese primarily used two calendars, one based on the sun and one based on the movements of the moon. The lunar, or moon-based, calendar was probably used to record private and public events, such as the birth of a child or the death of a ruler. Each lunar month began with a new moon and was about 29 days long. Twelve lunar months made one year. To include enough days for a full 365-day year, skilled priest-astronomers employed by the government were responsible for adding days as needed. The king's popularity depended upon the success of the harvest, which in turn depended in part on the time of planting as determined by the calendar. Therefore the priest-astronomers played a very important role.

✔ **READING CHECK: Analyzing Information** What factors enabled the Shang to build and extend their kingdom? military strength, well-organized government

Religion in the Shang Period

The religion that developed during the Shang period combined **animism**—the belief that spirits inhabit everything—with ancestor worship. People believed in an all-powerful and kindly dragon that lived in the seas and rivers and that could rise into the clouds. In time, this dragon became the symbol of Chinese rulers.

The Chinese also worshiped gods of the wind, sun, clouds, and moon. Some of these gods were honored by festivals. The people held a great religious festival in the spring to ensure good crops. In an autumn religious festival, the people thanked the moon god for the harvest.

The Shang also believed in Shangdi, a great god who controlled human destiny and the forces of nature. Rulers often asked the spirits of their ancestors to plead on their behalf with Shangdi, offering them sacrifices. Rulers used Shangdi's control over destiny to justify their decisions.

Priests played an important role in Chinese religion. Some tried to predict future events or interpret divine messages, especially messages from the spirits of ancestors. The priests wrote questions on **oracle bones**—the shoulder bones of cattle or tortoise shells. The priests heated the bones and interpreted the cracks that would then appear. They marked their interpretations on the bone or shell. Some think the name of the ruler who asked the questions was also often scratched onto the bone. Thus the markings on oracle bones have helped scholars learn more about the Shang.

✔ **READING CHECK: Drawing Conclusions** How did Shang leaders use religious beliefs to build support for their rule? claimed that their decisions were the will of Shangdi

Language and Writing

The Chinese of the Shang period were among the few early peoples to develop a written language. The early Chinese—like the Chinese of today—spoke many **dialects,** or variations of their language. The Chinese developed a written language that could be used for all these dialects. They assigned special symbols, or characters, to the words in their language. At first these characters were pictographs, or drawings of objects. Later, as their language became more complex, the Chinese developed ideographs. Many ideographs consisted of two parts—a signifier, or idea sign, and a phonetic sound sign. The signifier showed the meaning of the character and the phonetic sign told how to pronounce it.

CLOSE

Ask students to name the major cultural achievements that occurred under the Shang dynasty.

REVIEW

Have students complete the Section 2 Review on p. 83.

ASSESS

Have students complete Daily Quiz 4.2. As Alternative Assessment, you may want to use the legend or religion exercises in this section's lessons.

RETEACH

Have students complete Main Idea Activity for English Language Learners and Special-Needs Students 4.2. Then ask students to use correct social studies terminology to write a question that covers the main idea for each subsection in the section.
ENGLISH LANGUAGE LEARNERS

EXTEND

Have students research and report on bronze casting and a writing system, two important technological breakthroughs that took place in Shang China. Have them create visuals such as charts and graphs to illustrate their reports. **BLOCK SCHEDULING**

This system of writing allowed the Shang to invent new characters by combining existing signs. Each character, however, had to be memorized. For many centuries the ability to read and write was limited to a small number of specialists. These people generally served the Shang rulers as clerks, scribes, and teachers. Scribes recorded special events and composed literary works. They wrote characters in lines that ran from the top to the bottom of the page, beginning on the right side. Eventually, writing became an art called **calligraphy.** Artists used the same kind of brush for calligraphy as for painting.

✔ **READING CHECK: Identifying Cause and Effect** Why were reading and writing limited to specialists in early China? required long study

Fall of the Shang Dynasty

By about 1200 B.C. herders from the harsh Gobi Desert and the Tian Shan foothills had begun to edge toward the Huang valley. These peoples were probably attracted by the wealth and lifestyles of China Proper. Over time, some seem to have begun to settle along the borders of Shang China.

During the 1100s B.C. the Shang almost continuously battled these warlike neighboring states. Their extended military efforts finally exhausted the Shang rulers. The last Shang king, Di-xin, could not protect the kingdom's northwest borders. In about 1050 B.C. a people called the **Zhou** (JOH) formed an alliance with nearby tribes and overthrew the dynasty. The Zhou justified their conquest by claiming that the Shang were corrupt and unfit to rule. This explanation for the overthrow of one dynasty by another has been used throughout China's long history.

✔ **READING CHECK: Identifying Cause and Effect** Why did the Shang dynasty collapse? constant attacks from peoples on their border

Mastery of the traditional Chinese written language demanded much study and practice. Thus most ancient Chinese people, whose working lifestyles left little time for study, were prevented from learning to write or to read.

SECTION
2 REVIEW ANSWERS

❶ Define
- bureaucracy, p. 81
- animism, p. 82
- oracle bones, p. 82
- dialects, p. 82
- calligraphy, p. 83

❷ Identify
- Xia, p. 80
- Shang, p. 81
- Zhou, p. 83

❸ Students' answers should include descriptions of the lunar calendar, the agricultural economy, bureaucracy, animism, oracle bones, and calligraphy.

❹ a. They used legends to explain how Yu drained away floodwaters in China so people could live there.

b. centralized rule under a king

c. They were under constant attack from peoples on their borders.

❺ Students' descriptions will vary but should include a discussion of Shangdi, oracle bones, and the role of priests in Shang society.

SECTION 2 REVIEW

1. **Define** and explain the significance:
   bureaucracy
   animism
   oracle bones
   dialects
   calligraphy

2. **Identify** and explain the significance:
   Xia
   Shang
   Zhou

3. **Summarizing** Copy the chart below. Use it to create a written description of the calendars, economy, government, religion, and forms of writing that developed during the Shang dynasty.

   | Calendars |
   | Economy |
   | Government | → Shang Dynasty Achievements |
   | Religion |
   | Writing |

4. **Finding the Main Idea**
   a. How did the Xia use legends about early Chinese history to explain their origins as a people?
   b. How did the Shang rulers maintain control over their large kingdom?
   c. How did poor relations with neighboring peoples help contribute to the ultimate collapse of the Shang dynasty?

5. **Writing and Critical Thinking**
   Analyzing Information The Shang believed that spirits, including those of their ancestors, continued to play an important role in daily life. Describe the method of communicating with the spirit world that was developed during the Shang dynasty.
   Consider:
   • the Shang belief in Shang di
   • the meaning and use of oracle bones
   • the role of priests in Shang society

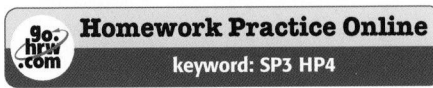
Homework Practice Online
keyword: SP3 HP4

ANCIENT CHINESE CIVILIZATION **83**

SECTION 3

OBJECTIVES

1 **Explain why the Zhou fell from power.**

2 **Describe how the Qin dynasty used power to maintain its authority.**

3 **Identify the achievements of the Han emperors.**

LET'S GET STARTED!

As students enter the classroom, have them think about the qualities of a good leader. Ask them to list some of the ways leaders can legitimize their authority. *(Students might answer that they can be honest, be fair to all, and practice moderation.)* Tell students that in Section 3 they will learn about the leaders of ancient Chinese dynasties.

SECTION 3

READ TO DISCOVER

❶ Why did the Zhou fall from power?

❷ How did the Qin dynasty use power to maintain its authority?

❸ What did the Han emperors achieve?

DEFINE

autocracy
civil service
leveling

IDENTIFY

Qin
Han
Cheng
Great Wall of China
Liu Bang
Liu Ch'e
Silk Road

WHY IT MATTERS TODAY

Some governments today still use harsh methods to control their people. Use or other **current event** sources to explore repressive governments. Record your findings in your journal.

The Zhou, Qin, and Han Dynasties

The Main Idea
Three major dynasties—the Zhou, the Qin, and the Han—built China into a powerful country.

The Story Continues *"Nothing is so strong as goodness; / On all sides men will take their lesson from it. . . . / But those that rule today / Have brought confusion and disorder into government; . . . / Therefore mighty Heaven is displeased."* These verses appear in the Book of Poetry, *one of the ancient Five Classics. During the time of China's great dynasties, these works served as a guide to good government.*

The Zhou Dynasty

The Zhou conquest of China in about 1050 B.C. marked the beginning of a dynamic era in Chinese history. Under the rule of three successive dynasties—the Zhou, the **Qin** (CHIN), and the **Han**—China gradually became a large and powerful state. The longest-lasting of the three dynasties was the Zhou, which ruled China from about 1050 B.C. until about 256 B.C.

The Zhou rulers did not create a centralized form of government following their conquest of the Shang kingdom. Instead, they granted territories to members of the royal family and their allies. The rulers of the territories had to give military service and tribute to the Zhou kings. Their positions were hereditary, but each generation had to renew its pledge of loyalty. Zhou rulers believed that the god of Heaven determined who should rule China, a right known as the "Mandate of Heaven." Throughout Chinese history, when rebels overthrew a dynasty, they claimed that the old dynasty had lost the Mandate of Heaven.

By the 700s B.C. Zhou kings were losing control as local leaders began to fight among themselves. In addition, Zhou lands were often attacked by outsiders. Chinese tradition has it that the quality of the Zhou kings also declined at this time. One legend claims that wicked King Yu abandoned his wife for another woman, Pao-Szu. To entertain themselves, Yu and Pao-Szu signaled that nomadic raiders were attacking. The false alarm led Zhou soldiers to rush to defend their capital. Later, angry troops ignored warnings when a real army attacked. Whether or not the legend is true, an invading force actually did destroy the Zhou

This bronze vessel of the Zhou dynasty reflects a high standard of technology and artistry.

TEACH OBJECTIVE 1

LEVEL 1: Ask students to explain why the Zhou fell from power. *(internal fighting and attacks by outsiders)* Then have students create an annotated time line showing significant events in the Zhou dynasty. Ask volunteers to present their time lines to the class. **ENGLISH LANGUAGE LEARNERS**

Zhou Dynasty

Zhou and Qin Dynasties

Interpreting Maps The Zhou Dynasty (left) relied heavily upon the kingdom's great river systems. Cheng extended Qin rule (right) even farther.

■ **Skills Assessment:**
1. Places and Regions What were the main rivers in the Zhou Dynasty? **2. Comparing** How did the size of the Qin Dynasty compare to that of the Zhou?

capital in 771 B.C. The Zhou ruler fled eastward and established a new capital. The Zhou dynasty lasted for 500 more years but had lost much of its former power. New powers, known as the Warring States, began to compete for control of China. By the 400s B.C. the Zhou had no real power outside their own city-state. Instead, local rulers ran things. One of the Warring States, the Qin, emerged victorious.

✔ **READING CHECK: Identifying Cause and Effect** What factors led to the decline of the Zhou dynasty? fought among themselves, attacked by outsiders

The Qin Dynasty

The Qin dynasty came to power in 221 B.C. through their military might. The ruler **Cheng** founded this new dynasty, taking for himself the title Shih Huang Ti, which means "first emperor." The Qin dynasty lasted only 15 years but produced many lasting changes in Chinese life. In fact, the Western name for "China" is derived from the name of the Qin dynasty. Cheng claimed that the founding of his dynasty marked a turning point in China's history.

History Makers Speak

❝In the . . . years of his reign
A new age is opened by [Cheng].
Rules and measures are corrected,
Everything is set in order,
Human affairs are clarified
And there is harmony between fathers and sons.❞

Cheng, from *The First Emperor*

Analyzing Primary Sources

Evaluating What benefits did Cheng claim his rule would bring to China? improved social order and family harmony

EXPLORING THE TIME LINE

GLOBAL EVENTS

Initially the Zhou were merely a minor satellite state of the powerful Shang dynasty. In about 1100 B.C., however, the Zhou began to form alliances with several smaller states to the south and the west of the Shang. In 1122 B.C., the Zhou and their allies decisively defeated the demoralized Shang. The former subjects had triumphed over the most dominant empire in ancient China.

Critical Thinking

Ask students to list the ways the Zhou, a minor power, were able to defeat the Shang.

ANSWER: Students should note that the Zhou formed alliances with other states and waited until the military power of the Shang was weakened.

MAP ANSWERS

1. Huang, Wei, and Chang

2. It was much larger.

ANCIENT CHINESE CIVILIZATION **85**

85

ALL LEVELS: Tell students to imagine they are newspaper editors during the Qin dynasty and to write an editorial about the emperor. Editorials should either charge that the emperor has lost the Mandate of Heaven or defend him as having it. Remind students that editorials explain to readers the reasons for the writer's point of view. *(has lost mandate: Qin's harsh rule, popular unrest; has mandate: dynasty's accomplishments, maintains strong power)* Have students read their editorials to the class. Then hold a discussion on whether the Qin had the Mandate of Heaven. **ENGLISH LANGUAGE LEARNERS**

🎵 internet connect

Internet Activity: go.hrw.com
TOPIC: The Great Wall of China **KEYWORD: SP3 WH4**

Have students access the Internet through the HRW Go site to do research on the Qin Dynasty and the Great Wall of China. Then have students write four paragraphs about the history of the wall, hiking along the Great Wall, interesting facts, and the myths and legends that surround the wall. Students may wish to use the interactive template provided to create an illustrated brochure on the Great Wall of China.

History Maker

QU YAN. Each year Chinese Americans gather in New York City for the Dragon Boat Festival. The event commemorates the death of Qu Yan, a poet from the 300s B.C. who drowned in China's Milo River. Dragon boat races reenact the attempt to reach Qu Yan and rescue him. The boats, each of which holds 20 paddlers, are 40 feet long and are adorned at bow and stern by a dragon's head and tail. The Dragon Boat Festival in Great Britain attracts some 20,000 participants each year.

ACTIVITY: Organize students into groups and have them write a plan for a festival that commemorates an important person from their community. Have them describe the kinds of activities they want to include in the festival as well as why the person they choose to commemorate is important.

VISUAL RECORD ANSWER
negative

MAP ANSWER
Answers should include two of the following: Kashi, Dunhuang, Xi'an

INTERPRETING THE VISUAL RECORD

Qin oppression Cheng maintained rigid control over his subjects. Here he watches as scholars are executed. *What was the artist's view of the emperor?*

From their capital near Ch'ang-an—now called Xi'an (shee·AHN)—the Qin ruled over a huge area. They maintained order by establishing an **autocracy,** in which the emperor held total power. Cheng saw dangers in allowing scholars to investigate and discuss problems freely. He suppressed and even executed scholars who criticized the government.

Like earlier rulers, the Qin guarded against invasion by building defensive walls along parts of their borders. Later dynasties added to these structures. Eventually, the connected walls became known as the **Great Wall of China.** This massive structure, much of which still stands today, was about 1,500 miles long during Qin times. The Qin employed forced labor for public works projects like the Great Wall. This policy angered many people. Discontent spread further as a great gap arose between the ruler and the mass of people. In 206 B.C. a rebel army revolted against the dynasty. In that same year **Liu Bang,** a commoner who had become a Qin general, overthrew the empire. Liu Bang founded a new dynasty known as the Han.

✔ **READING CHECK: Drawing Inferences** Why might Cheng have felt that free discussion was dangerous to his rule? Public criticism might have weakened his total power.

Han Dynasty, c. 206 B.C.–A.D. 220
Interpreting Maps Trade and commerce helped the Han to extend their control far to the west of earlier Chinese dynasties.
■ **Skills Assessment: Human Systems** Name two cities through which a merchant would have to pass while traveling along the Silk Road.

LEVEL 3: Have small groups conduct short interviews with Hsiao Yen, focusing on some aspect of his rule, such as conquest of the Xiongnu. One student takes the role of the interviewer and another of Hsiao Yen. The third student plays an imperial assistant such as a general. Have groups present their interviews to the class. **COOPERATIVE LEARNING**

 HOMEWORK Ask students to decide whether they would have preferred to live under Zhou, Qin, or Han rule. Have students write a paragraph that supports their point of view.

The Han Dynasty

The new dynasty received its name from the title that Liu Bang took—King of Han. Like the Qin, the Han ruled a centralized and growing empire. The Han were more moderate rulers than the Qin, however, and kept power for about 400 years. Han rulers had so much influence over the development of China that many Chinese today call themselves "People of Han." The longest-ruling Han emperor was **Liu Ch'e,** commonly known as Wu Ti, who ruled from about 140 B.C. to 87 B.C. From his capital at Ch'ang-an, Liu Ch'e extended Han rule north into present-day Manchuria and Korea, south into Southeast Asia, and west into central Asia. The Han ruled over an area larger than the Roman Empire.

The civil service system. Building on a foundation laid by the Qin, the Han dynasty established a centralized civil service system to govern China. A **civil service** system runs the day-to-day business of government. At first government officials recommended candidates for civil service positions on the basis of family connections. Eventually, however, the Han created a system of examinations to select the most qualified candidates. Liu Ch'e also established an imperial university to train people for government service. Theoretically the civil service was open to anyone. In practice, however, usually only those with family connections and money for schooling and books could train. The civil service was improved over the centuries and during the course of many Chinese dynasties. Over generations, it produced many effective, well-trained government workers who helped the emperors rule China's growing, increasingly complex society. The system remained important to China's government until the early A.D. 1900s.

Other accomplishments. Under earlier rulers, rising and falling prices for farm products had caused much hardship for peasants. Liu Ch'e began an economic policy, which some scholars call **leveling,** to solve this problem. Under the leveling system, the

Civil Service

The Chinese civil service was created to help run the government. The system was designed to be fair and to reward ability. Citizens had to pass a written test in order to hold civil service jobs. Those who showed strong ability were promoted to higher positions.

In today's China, entry into the civil service is based upon loyalty to the ruling political party as well as on ability. In the United States, most civil service jobs are gained by passing a written test. American laws forbid the selection of civil service workers based upon political ties. **Why might some people today consider civil service exams to be unfair?**

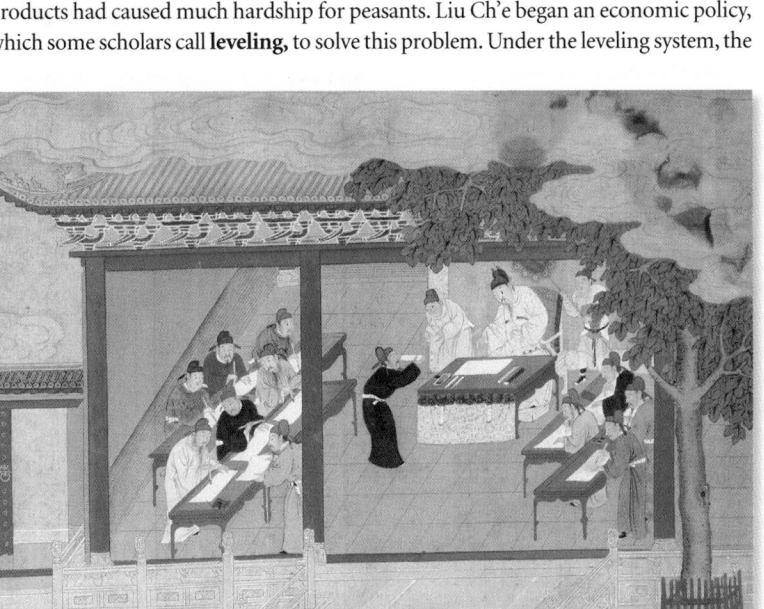

Much ceremony was involved in the administration of civil service examinations. Candidates for government positions had to thoroughly prepare for the test, which often involved years of study and training. Failure was considered a disgrace.

Culture

The establishment of the ruler as a divine power—the Son of Heaven—was extremely important to the Han dynasty. Using the Zhou dynasty's Mandate of Heaven theory of divine authority, the Han emperors legitimized their claims by saying that the Mandate of Heaven had been reborn in their new ruler. The Han religion established that the ruler should be responsible for the well-being of his subjects and for being an example of moral virtue. The emperor showed his moral virtue by performing regular rituals and ceremonies.

Critical Thinking

Ask students if they think the Han emperors' rule was an example of a pure autocracy, or an arrangement that placed obligations on both rulers and people. Have them give reasons to support their answer.

ANSWER: Students may say that the emperors held total power because there were no real checks on their rule, or that the rulers were required to consider the welfare of their subjects and show moral virtue in exchange for the people's obedience.

THEN AND NOW ANSWER

The ability to pass a test does not necessarily mean a person will be a good worker.

Ask students to name some accomplishments of each dynasty—Zhou, Qin, and Han. List their responses on the chalkboard.

REVIEW

Have students complete the Section 3 Review on p. 88.

ASSESS

Have students complete Daily Quiz 4.3. As Alternative Assessment, you may want to use the time line or interview exercises in this section's lessons.

RETEACH

Have students complete Main Idea Activity for English Language Learners and Special-Needs Students 4.3. Then have students create a chart that summarizes the characteristics/achievements and causes of decline of the Zhou, Qin, and Han dynasties.
ENGLISH LANGUAGE LEARNERS

EXTEND

Have students work in groups to diagram China's political structure under the Zhou dynasty. (*Diagrams should illustrate the hierarchy of Zhou rule and the reciprocal relationship that existed between the Zhou king and his subordinates.*) **BLOCK SCHEDULING**

HISTORY MAKER ANSWER
He brought relative peace to China after many years of fighting.

SECTION 3 REVIEW ANSWERS

❶ Define
- autocracy, p. 86
- civil service, p. 87
- leveling, p. 87

❷ Identify
- Qin, p. 84
- Han, p. 84
- Cheng, p. 85
- Great Wall of China, p. 86
- Liu Bang, p. 86
- Liu Ch'e, p. 87
- Silk Road, p. 88

❸ Students should include comparisons of military and political policies.

❹ a. Liu Ch'e brought relative peace and political and economic reform to China. Cheng executed scholars who criticized the government.

b. no centralized form of government; attacks by outsiders

c. He was a commoner.

d. They claimed the old dynasty had lost the Mandate of Heaven.

❺ Students' paragraphs will vary but should consider civil service, leveling, and the Silk Road.

HISTORY MAKER

Liu Ch'e
(Ruled c. 140 B.C.–87 B.C.)

Liu Ch'e spent much of his reign working to secure China's northern and western borders. Among the greatest threats to peace during Liu Ch'e's rule were the warlike nomadic tribes who attacked Han China from the north in search of plunder.

After years of fighting, Liu Ch'e succeeded in bringing relative peace to China. By about 104 B.C. conditions were so improved that his reign was called "the Grand Beginning." **Why was Liu Ch'e's reign called "The Grand Beginning?"**

government used price controls to balance the economic effects of farm surpluses or shortages. The program worked by storing surplus grains produced during good harvests for use during lean years.

Liu Ch'e fought many battles with the nomadic Xiongnu (shee·UNG·noo) of central and eastern Asia. Through military conquest and the establishment of military colonies, Liu Ch'e greatly expanded China's control in Asia. Because of this control, China lived in relative peace. During this period of peace, trade prospered along the famous **Silk Road.** This trade route stretched from China across central Asia to the Mediterranean region. Camel caravans carried jade, silk, and other valuable Chinese goods. These goods were ultimately sold to wealthy Greeks and Romans. The caravans returned to China with gold, silver, and wool.

China's population grew to about 50 million during the Han dynasty. In the capital city of Ch'ang-an, people could find luxury goods from lands throughout Europe and Asia. One such good was paper, a Chinese invention. Paper spread from China to the Western world, where it had a profound impact on Western cultures.

None of Liu Ch'e's Han successors matched his leadership abilities. Still, with the exception of one brief interruption, the Han dynasty ruled China until A.D. 220. After the fall of the last Han emperor, countless nomadic peoples swept across northern China. For hundreds of years, these peoples caused many Han subjects to move south. Not until A.D. 581 did a Chinese general unify China once again.

✔ **READING CHECK: Evaluating** How did the civil service system affect China? improved the effectiveness of government

This Chinese painting, dating from about A.D. 100, portrays the papermaking process.

SECTION 3 REVIEW

1. **Define** and explain the significance:
   autocracy
   civil service
   leveling

2. **Identify** and explain the significance:
   Qin
   Han
   Cheng
   Great Wall of China
   Liu Bang
   Liu Ch'e
   Silk Road

3. **Comparing** Copy the flow chart below. Use it to build a comparison of the achievements of the Zhou, Qin, and Han dynasties.

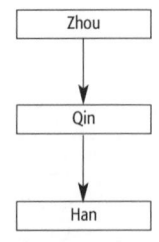

```
┌──────┐
│ Zhou │
└──────┘
   │
   ▼
┌──────┐
│ Qin  │
└──────┘
   │
   ▼
┌──────┐
│ Han  │
└──────┘
```

4. **Finding the Main Idea**
   a. In what ways did the reign of Cheng differ from the reign of Liu Ch'e?
   b. What forces led to the collapse of the early Chinese dynasties?
   c. In what way did Liu Bang's background make him a different kind of ruler than the Qin emperors had been?
   d. How did new dynasties throughout Chinese history use the idea of the "Mandate of Heaven" to justify taking power from previous rulers?

5. **Writing and Critical Thinking**
   Supporting a Point of View Write a paragraph designed to persuade readers that the achievements of the Han dynasty mark a cultural and economic high point in Chinese history.
   Consider:
   - the development of the civil service
   - Liu Ch'e's policy of leveling
   - trade along the Silk Road

Homework Practice Online
keyword: SP3 HP4

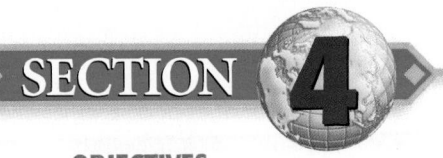
OBJECTIVES

1 Examine why the Chinese valued the concept of balance.

2 Explore what the Chinese philosopher Confucius taught.

3 Analyze how Daoism and Confucianism worked together in Chinese society.

4 Investigate how beliefs such as Legalism and Buddhism influenced Chinese history.

LET'S GET STARTED!

As students enter the classroom, ask them how a society's values are reflected in its laws. (*Students might answer that a society's values are reflected in legal concepts of right and wrong and in the way criminals are punished.*) Tell students that in Section 4 they will learn about the philosophies of ancient China and how they affected the government.

SECTION 4

READ TO DISCOVER

❶ Why did the Chinese value the concept of balance?

❷ What did the Chinese philosopher Confucius teach?

❸ How did Daoism and Confucianism work together in Chinese society?

❹ How did beliefs such as Legalism and Buddhism influence Chinese history?

DEFINE

yin
yang

IDENTIFY

Confucius
Analects
Laozi
Dao De Jing
Legalism

WHY IT MATTERS TODAY

Today, many people in the West are drawn to Eastern religious beliefs and values. Use [CNN] or other **current event** sources to find information about Westerners who study or practice an Eastern religion. Record your findings in your journal.

Philosophies of Ancient China

The Main Idea
Chinese philosophers and teachers sought ways to understand the universe and the human condition.

The Story Continues *An ancient Chinese philosopher once wrote, "To understand others is to be wise, but to understand one's self is to be illuminated [enlightened]. One who overcomes others is strong, but he who overcomes himself is mighty." Throughout early Chinese history many philosophers struggled to understand themselves and the world around them.*

Ancient Chinese Beliefs

Political conflict marked the last centuries of the Zhou dynasty. Nevertheless, this period was one of the most creative in the history of Chinese philosophy. Philosophers looked for ways to restore harmony. At the root of the many harmonizing philosophies was an ancient Chinese belief regarding the dualism, or two-sidedness, of nature. This idea states that everything in the world results from a balance between two forces. The force known as **yin** is female, dark, and passive. The opposite force, **yang**, is male, bright, and active. Yin and yang are not in conflict with each other. Instead, they depend on each other. Under the best of conditions, they maintain a balance. For example, day, which is yang, gives way to night, which is yin.

The concepts of yin and yang led to the belief that balance in human affairs is a normal condition. For example, extremes such as harsh government or anarchy (no government) should not last long.

✔ **READING CHECK: Drawing Inferences** What other natural events might be classified as yin and yang? change of seasons, weather

The yin-yang symbol was a major theme in Chinese art and literature. The balance and harmony that it represented were viewed as key elements of the natural world.

SECTION 4 RESOURCES

REPRODUCIBLE RESOURCES

▸ Guided Reading Strategy 4.4

▸ Readings in World History 13, 14, 15: The Wisdom of Confucius; The *Dao De Ching* of Laozi; Mo Tzu on Universal Love

▸ Creative Teaching Strategy 4: The All-Asian Conference on Religion and Philosophy

TECHNOLOGY RESOURCES

▸ One-Stop Planner 4.4

▸ Holt Researcher: World History: Confucius, Laozi

▸ Religions of the World Video Series: Buddhism

▸ Homework Practice Online

REINFORCEMENT, REVIEW, AND ASSESSMENT

▸ Section 4 Review, p. 92

▸ Daily Quiz 4.4

▸ Main Idea Activity 4.4

▸ English Audio Summary 4.4

▸ Spanish Audio Summary 4.4

ANCIENT CHINESE CIVILIZATION **89**

TEACH OBJECTIVE 1

 LEVEL 1: Ask students why the Chinese valued the concept of balance. *(They believed that everything in the world resulted from a balance between two forces.)* Draw a two-column chart with one column labeled *yin* and the other labeled *yang*. Have students list the characteristics of each in the chart. **ENGLISH LANGUAGE LEARNERS**

TEACH OBJECTIVE 2

ALL LEVELS: Write the following passage from the *Analects* on the chalkboard: *"To see what is right and not to do it is want of courage."* Tell students that the passage is a teaching of Confucius. Ask the class what the saying means and what effect following it would have had on the government of China. *(Students should restate the adage in their own words and realize that it would encourage good government.)* Discuss whether these are words to live by today. **ENGLISH LANGUAGE LEARNERS**

Yin	Yang
female	male
dark	bright
passive	active

☐ internet connect

TOPIC: Chinese Philosophy and Science

GO TO: go.hrw.com
KEYWORD: SP3 WH4

Have students access the Internet through the HRW Go site to conduct research on Chinese philosophy or Chinese contributions to science. Ask students to take notes on the topic they choose and then write a report. Students may wish to use the interactive report template. Students should use standard grammar, punctuation, and sentence structure in their reports.

VISUAL RECORD ANSWER

The scrolls he is carrying show that learning was very important to him.

WHAT IF? ANSWER

Answers will vary, but students should recognize that the teachings of Confucius reinforced the importance of ancestors, family, individual responsibility to society, and good government. Without Confucius, these cultural forces might have been weaker or nonexistent.

Technology Resources

 Online Maps, Charts, and Graphs: Early Confucianism c. 200 B.C.

INTERPRETING THE VISUAL RECORD

Confucius The death of his father left Confucius in poverty at the age of three. Largely self-educated, Confucius became a symbol of wisdom, learning, and great moral strength. ***What clues does this picture provide about the focus of Confucius's life?***

What If? What if Confucius had never lived? How might the history of China have been different?

Holt Researcher

go.hrw.com
KEYWORD: Holt Researcher
FreeFind: Confucius Laozi
After reading more about Confucius and Laozi on the Holt Researcher, write an imaginary dialogue between the two comparing their ideas.

Confucius and Laozi

Chinese philosophers developed new ideas and theories to explain economic, political, and social change during the Zhou era. A leading philosopher of the period was **Confucius.** He lived from 551 B.C. to 479 B.C. Confucius's followers collected his ideas and teachings in a work called the ***Analects.*** In time, Confucius's teachings became known as Confucianism.

Confucianism. The philosophy of Confucianism had more influence on Chinese life than any other philosophy. Confucius taught about the importance of family, respect for one's elders, and reverence for the past and one's ancestors. These three concepts form the basis of Confucian philosophy.

Confucius sought to end the political disorder of his time. He was not a religious prophet, and he had little to say about gods or about purely religious ideas. Confucius's teachings were not concerned with the meaning of death, ideas about life after death, or issues of faith. Instead, Confucius was concerned with the causes of political and social unrest and with how moral and ethical leadership could solve those problems.

Confucius aimed to encourage strong, positive behavior on the part of China's leaders. He believed that this could be accomplished in two ways. First, every person should willingly accept his or her role in society and should perform the duties of that role. Second, the government and its leaders should be virtuous. Virtue, according to Confucius, involved correct behavior toward others. Instead of seeking wealth and power, rulers should be honest and honorable toward those they lead. Their greatest interest should be the welfare and happiness of their people. Confucius encouraged only moral, well-educated officials to be appointed to lead the government and to administer its laws. In this way rulers would set a good example for all. The people, moreover, would willingly follow leaders who lived and governed according to these virtuous guidelines.

Over time, many of Confucius's ideas and values were adopted by other Chinese thinkers. One of the most influential of these was Mencius, who lived between about 372 B.C. and about 289 B.C. Mencius was a strong supporter of the Confucian philosophy. He taught that individuals contained much goodness. In the proper environment, Mencius argued, the best characteristics of the individual would strengthen and would benefit others.

Like Confucius, Mencius believed that rulers who governed according to strong moral and ethical guidelines would receive the willing support of their people. Mencius also believed that people had a right to rebel against weak or harsh rulers. He held that unjust rulers who oppressed their people surrendered their right to rule and should be overthrown, by force if necessary. Mencius's teachings, like those of Confucius, became part of China's classical tradition over time.

✔ **READING CHECK: Identifying a Point of View** What were Confucius's views on politics? favored strong but moral government

Daoism. At about the same time that Confucius lived and taught, another important Chinese philosophy appeared. According to legend, **Laozi** (LOWD-ZOO) founded the philosophy called Daoism (DOW-ih-zuhm). Daoism took its name from its central idea, the Dao, which is defined as "The Way." Laozi saw the Dao as an indescribable force that governed the universe and all of nature. He taught that people should withdraw from the world and contemplate nature. In this way, they could understand the Dao and live with it in harmony.

TEACH OBJECTIVES 3 and 4

LEVEL 3: Organize groups of three students with each taking one role: a Daoist, a Legalist, or a Confucian. Have them debate, in their roles, one of the following questions: (1) What should be the main goal in life? (2) Are people basically bad or good? (3) What is the best kind of government? After their discussion, ask members to describe their positions. Then have the class predict the consequences of following each philosophy.
COOPERATIVE LEARNING

HOMEWORK Present the class with the following situation: A weak, inefficient, and corrupt ruler is governing their country. Crime and disorder are rampant and a revolt is likely. Have students write the solutions a Confucian, a Daoist, and a Legalist might offer in this situation.

TEACH OBJECTIVE 4

LEVEL 2: Explain that a maxim is a saying that sets out a truth or rule of conduct. Then have pairs of students write a maxim for Buddhism with the purpose of attracting Chinese converts to the faith. Have pairs read their maxims to the class. Have the class discuss whether each maxim accurately represents Buddhism.
COOPERATIVE LEARNING

According to Laozi, people should not strive for material wealth. Unlike Confucius, Laozi shunned politics. He advised people not to seek power. Rather, they should work to bring themselves into harmony with the Dao by being humble, quiet, and thoughtful. This advice could be found in the ***Dao De Jing***, a compilation of Laozi's teachings.

“They know the world without even going out the door. They see the sky and its pattern without even looking out the window. The further out it goes, the less knowledge is; therefore sages know without going, name without seeing, complete without striving.”

Laozi, from *Dao De Jing*

Daoism became second only to Confucianism in importance to Chinese life. The Daoist ideal appealed to many peasants because of its concern with natural forces. It appealed to many artists and poets because it valued the spontaneity and freedom of artistic expression. Daoism appealed to many Confucianists as well because it encouraged balance in life. Some Confucianists believed that concerning oneself only with education, politics, and social problems was frustrating and pointless. In the Daoist contemplation of nature, officials and rulers found a way to put the pressures of governing in perspective. Like yin and yang, Daoism and Confucianism provided balance to Chinese culture; each supplied what the other lacked.

✔ **READING CHECK: Finding the Main Idea** What were the main beliefs of the Daoists?
appreciation of nature, harmony, balance

Legalism and Buddhism

Like Confucianism, the school of Chinese philosophy called **Legalism** concerned itself with politics. It differed from Confucianism, however, in that Legalists believed in power—not virtue—and in harsh laws. In their view, people were by nature selfish and untrustworthy. Peace and prosperity could be achieved only by threatening severe punishment if people did not obey the laws. One Legalist philosopher noted,

“Men have likes and dislikes; thus they can be controlled by means of rewards and punishments. . . . The ruler need only hold these handles [rewards and punishments] firmly, in order to maintain his supremacy. . . . Force is the stuff that keeps the masses in subjection [under control].”

Han-fei-tzu, quoted in *Chinese Thought from Confucius to Mao Tse-tung*

Legalism in practice. The first Qin emperor, Cheng, followed the ideas of Legalism. He succeeded in creating a very powerful empire. His dynasty ruled, however, for only a very short period. Later Chinese philosophers claimed that the Qin dynasty failed because of its cruel methods.

The government of the Han dynasty accepted many of the Legalist principles of the Qin dynasty. Han rulers, however, also followed the more moderate principles of Confucianism. Many later scholars agreed that the Han dynasty possibly lasted so long because it achieved a balance between Legalism and Confucianism.

INTERPRETING THE VISUAL RECORD

Laozi Laozi and the Daoists believed that, left to itself, the universe would proceed along a harmonious course. *What conclusions might the creator of this sculpture have wanted viewers to draw about the character of Laozi?*

Government

Cheng ruled his state on the Legalist principles of reward and punishment. As Shang Yang, his adviser, put it: "To club together and keep your mouth shut is to be good; to be alienated from and spy on each other is to be a scoundrel. If you glorify the good, errors will be hidden; if you put scoundrels in charge, crime will be punished."

Critical Thinking

Ask students to describe what it might be like to live in a society based on Legalist principles.

ANSWER: Students' answers will vary, but they might include a concentration of power in the government, laws enforced by the threat of violence, and rewards given to encourage cooperation.

VISUAL RECORD ANSWER
He was in harmony with nature.

Technology Resources

World History Teaching Transparency: Geography and History 6: The Rise of Buddhism and Daoism

ANCIENT CHINESE CIVILIZATION **91**

CLOSE

Have students work in groups to summarize the fundamental ideas of Confucianism, Daoism, or Legalism.

REVIEW

Have students complete the Section 4 Review on p. 92.

ASSESS

Have students complete Daily Quiz 4.4. As Alternative Assessment, you may want to use the Confucianism or maxim exercises in this section's lessons.

RETEACH

Have students complete Main Idea Activity for English Language Learners and Special-Needs Students 4.4. Then have students write one question and answer for each Chinese philosophy. **ENGLISH LANGUAGE LEARNERS**

EXTEND

Have students use a problem-solving process to devise a plan of government for their community based on a Chinese philosophical tradition. **BLOCK SCHEDULING**

VISUAL RECORD ANSWER

charity and compassion

SECTION 4 REVIEW ANSWERS

❶ Define
• yin, p. 89
• yang, p. 89

❷ Identify
• Confucius, p. 90
• *Analects*, p. 90
• Laozi, p. 90
• *Dao De Jing*, p. 91
• Legalism, p. 91

❸ Legalism: power without moral virtue, people naturally selfish and untrustworthy; Daoism: people should withdraw from the world and contemplate nature; Buddhism: universal charity and compassion; Confucianism: importance of family, respect for elders, reverence for past and ancestors

❹ a. The government might have been corrupt and the people rebellious.

b. The turmoil caused philosophers to look for ways to restore harmony, which led to the development of their philosophies.

c. Its teachings, temples, and ceremonies offered a sense of comfort, tranquility, and a vision for dealing with worldly problems during turbulent times.

❺ Students' poems will vary but should demonstrate an understanding of Daoist belief.

INTERPRETING THE VISUAL RECORD

Buddhism Mahayana Buddhism emphasizes the heavenly qualities of the Buddha. The figure shown here is found in the Jade Buddha Temple in Shanghai. *What aspects of the Buddha's personality and teachings do these images emphasize?*

Buddhism in China. Buddhism was another great influence on Chinese thought and religious belief. Missionaries from India first brought Buddhism to China during the Han dynasty.

Throughout the later years of the dynasty, violence and lawlessness became increasingly common in many parts of China. Military leaders, competing with one another for power, led destructive raids through many areas of the once-peaceful land. The traditional Chinese emphasis upon order and family-centered security seemed to be threatened. When the Han dynasty finally fell, many Chinese, especially peasants, turned to Buddhism. They felt that the teachings of the Buddha helped to explain the widespread disruption that accompanied the Han collapse. They found comfort, as well, in the values that Buddhism championed. Buddhist temples and ceremonies offered a sense of peace and safety during turbulent times. In addition, Buddhism emphasized universal charity and compassion, ideals that Chinese philosophy had largely overlooked. The branch of Buddhism called Mahayana Buddhism became popular in China, Japan, and Korea. Mahayana Buddhists worship the Buddha as a savior. They believe that he is committed to helping all human beings escape from the miseries of the world.

The teachings of the Buddha, Confucius, Laozi, and the Legalists had a lasting effect on Chinese attitudes. Eventually the northern nomads established kingdoms and adopted Chinese ways. Buddhism, Confucianism, and Daoism provided moral and ethical guides to right living. They strongly influenced Chinese social ideals, attitudes, and individual and group behavior. The centralizing political ideas of Legalism provided a strong foundation for Chinese government. Confucianism, with reverence for the past and emphasis on the family, won the most followers. The Chinese also absorbed Daoist and Buddhist ideas regarding values such as contentment, justice, loyalty, obedience, and wisdom.

✔ **READING CHECK: Contrasting** In what major way did Legalism differ from the teachings of Confucius? believed in power without moral virtue

SECTION 4 REVIEW

1. Define and explain the significance:
yin
yang

2. Identify and explain the significance:
Confucius
Analects
Laozi
Dao De Jing
Legalism

3. Categorizing Copy the web diagram below. Use it to illustrate the main concepts of Buddhism, Confucianism, Daoism, and Legalism.

Legalism	Daoism
Buddhism	Confucianism

4. **Finding the Main Idea**

a. What might have happened had the rulers of the Han dynasty not included Confucian philosophy in their style of governing?

b. How did the turmoil of the Zhou dynasty influence Confucianism and Daoism?

c. What factors contributed to the increased popularity of Buddhism among Chinese peasants after the fall of the Han dynasty?

5. **Writing and Critical Thinking**

Summarizing Write a poem that expresses a Daoist belief.
Consider:
• the meaning of the Dao
• Daoist attitudes toward wealth and power
• how Daoists sought to understand the Dao

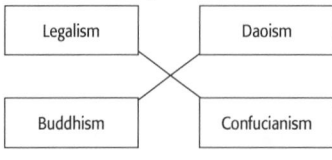
Homework Practice Online
keyword: SP3 HP4

SECTION 5

OBJECTIVES

1 Explain why the family was a central institution in Chinese society.

2 Describe how farmers lived in ancient China.

3 Identify the artistic and scientific achievements of the Chinese.

🔔 LET'S GET STARTED!

As students enter the classroom, ask them to think about the concept of family in the United States today. Have students describe various family units. (*parents and children; single parent and child; grandparents, parents, and children; blended families, etc.*) Tell students that in Section 5 they will learn about the ancient Chinese concept of family.

SECTION 5

READ TO DISCOVER
❶ Why was the family a central institution in Chinese society?
❷ How did farmers live in ancient China?
❸ What did the Chinese achieve in the arts and sciences?

DEFINE
genealogy
acupuncture

IDENTIFY
Five Classics

▶ WHY IT MATTERS TODAY
Ancient Chinese medical practices, including the use of herbs and acupuncture, have received attention in modern America. Use CNN News.com or other **current event** sources to gather information about the use of an ancient Chinese medical practice. Record your findings in your journal.

CNN Student News.com

Chinese Life and Culture

The Main Idea
The family, farming, and educational pursuits for government officials marked daily life in China.

The Story Continues *"As Yin and Yang are not of the same nature, so man and woman have different characteristics," wrote a first-century Chinese woman named Ban Zhao. "Man is honored for strength; a woman is beautiful on account of her gentleness. . . . The correct relationship is based upon harmony and . . . love is grounded in proper union." This idea greatly influenced the Chinese approach to family life.*

Family and Social Life

The ancient Chinese believed that the well-being of the state rested upon the well-being of the family. Values that governed family life included reverence for one's family, respect for age, and acceptance of decisions made by one's superiors. These values also shaped China's social and cultural life, including economics, education, literature, and science.

The family, not the individual, was the most important factor in Chinese society. Each upper-class family probably kept a careful **genealogy**, or record of its family tree. When family members died, they became honored ancestors. The Chinese expressed reverence for their ancestors as links between the family's past, present, and future. Most families constructed altars in honor of their ancestors.

Typically, an upper-class family included a father, his wife, sons with their wives and children, and unmarried daughters. Often all members of the family lived in the same house. The father ruled the family. He arranged his children's and his grandchildren's marriages. He decided how much education his sons would receive. He even chose his sons' careers.

Chinese women had fewer rights and powers than did men. They usually had no property rights of their own. On the other hand, Chinese society taught great respect for mothers and mothers-in-law. Within the household these women held much power. After she married, a young woman sometimes became almost a servant in the household of her husband's family. However, she became an important family figure after bearing children, especially sons.

✔ **READING CHECK: Comparing and Contrasting** What roles did men and women play in the family life of traditional China? men: ruled family, decided on marriages and careers; women: gained power by bearing children

SECTION 5 RESOURCES

REPRODUCIBLE RESOURCES
▶ Guided Reading Strategy 4.5
▶ Graphic Organizer Activity 4: Chinese Advances
▶ Readings in World History 16: The Book of Songs

TECHNOLOGY RESOURCES
▶ One-Stop Planner 4.5
▶ Homework Practice Online

REINFORCEMENT, REVIEW, AND ASSESSMENT
▶ Section 5 Review, p. 95
▶ Daily Quiz 4.5
▶ Main Idea Activity 4.5
▶ English Audio Summary 4.5
▶ Spanish Audio Summary 4.5

LINK TO TODAY ANSWER
It includes the extended family.

INTERPRETING THE VISUAL RECORD
The ideal of the extended family was of great importance in ancient China. Traditional households often included parents, grandparents, children, and grandchildren.

Link to Today How does the modern Chinese family pictured here reflect the concept of "family" in traditional Chinese society?

ALL LEVELS: Develop a list with the class that describes a typical family in ancient China. Then ask them to cite ways in which this family illustrates the philosophy of Confucianism. *(importance of family, respect for elders, members' acceptance and fulfillment of their roles)* **ENGLISH LANGUAGE LEARNERS**

TEACH OBJECTIVE 2

LEVEL 3: Organize the class into small groups to discuss how rural life in ancient China compares to rural life in the United States today. *(similarities: most people farmed, paid taxes, con-*

tended with nature; differences: most Chinese lived in rural areas, Chinese farmers lived in villages, often worked fields in common, had to perform public services) **COOPERATIVE LEARNING**

TEACH OBJECTIVES 3 and 4

LEVEL 1: Have students draw a chart listing Chinese achievements in the arts and sciences. **ENGLISH LANGUAGE LEARNERS**

Artistic Achievements	Scientific Achievements
Book of Poems	*astronomy*
Book of History	*seismography*

Daily Life

Grass fibers, hemp, and silk were the most common fabrics in use during the Han dynasty. While few examples of hemp cloth exist today, historians assume that the majority of the population used hemp or other fibers for clothes. Silk was very expensive and is known to have been used for imperial robes.

Critical Thinking

Ask students to suggest reasons why soldiers' uniforms might have been made from a luxury fabric like silk.

ANSWER: Students might suggest that soldiers can be considered representatives of the government, and silk uniforms would emphasize the wealth and power of the state.

LINK TO TODAY ANSWER

The design is similar to an ancient Chinese junk.

INTERPRETING THE VISUAL RECORD

Junks The early Chinese used sailboats called junks to trade throughout East Asia. The basic design of junks that sail China's rivers and coastlines today has changed little from the design of ancient Chinese junks.

Link to Today In what way does the junk pictured here reflect the importance of tradition in Chinese culture?

Analyzing Primary Sources

Finding the Main Idea What does this poem reveal about ancient Chinese courtship practices? men courted women, not vice versa

The Economy

Although Chinese towns grew in size and number, most Chinese people lived as small village farmers. Farm life was difficult. A group of families might work fields in common, using ox-drawn plows and complex systems of irrigation and flood control. If too much or too little rain fell, crops could be ruined. Also, the government required peasants to pay taxes and to perform labor on canals, roads, and other local construction projects.

Trade was not an important factor in the economy of earliest China. Trade and commerce grew quickly, however, during the Qin dynasty. Qin leaders brought many important reforms to China's economy. They standardized the currency and the system of weights and measures. Trade also increased during the Han dynasty when the Silk Road linked China with the Mediterranean region.

✔ **READING CHECK: Categorizing** What reforms helped to encourage the growth of trade during the Qin dynasty? Qin standardized currency, weights, and measures

Arts and Sciences

The Chinese education system relied upon a small number of texts to train scholars and civil servants, who tended to be dedicated and reliable. By using these books, the system emphasized respect for tradition. At the same time, the use of the same books created a common culture all across China.

The Five Classics. The texts used to train scholars and civil servants in ancient China were known as the **Five Classics.** We do not know who wrote these works or exactly when they were written. We do know, however, that they had started to become important in the time of the Zhou dynasty. The *Book of Poems* contains more than 300 songs about domestic life, joy, love, and politics. For example, the second poem of the collection is about courtship.

Primary Source

❝Plop fall the plums; but there are still seven.
Let those gentlemen who would court me
Come while it is still lucky!
Plop fall the plums; there are still three.
Let any gentleman who would court me
Come before it is too late!
Plop fall the plums; in shallow baskets we lay them.
Any gentleman who would court me
Had better speak while there is time.❞

The *Book of Poems*, from *An Anthology of Chinese Literature*

The *Book of History* contains speeches and documents about government. The *Book of Changes* is about the art of predicting the future. The *Spring and Autumn Annals* is a record of events in the city-state of Lu from 722 B.C. to 481 B.C. The *Book of Rites* deals with manners and ceremonies. Study of the Five Classics became essential for every well-educated young man in China, along with the *Analects* of Confucius.

HOMEWORK Review China's accomplishments under the Shan, Zhou, Qin, and Han rulers. Then have students write an answer to the following question: How did strong rulers encourage the development of Chinese civilization?

CLOSE

Ask students to list some of the major Chinese contributions to science, technology, and math.

REVIEW

Have students complete the Section 5 Review on p. 95.

ASSESS

Have students complete Daily Quiz 4.5. As Alternative Assessment, you may use the family exercises in this section's lessons.

RETEACH

Have students complete Main Idea Activity for English Language Learners and Special-Needs Students 4.5. Ask students to list the main ideas of each heading. **ENGLISH LANGUAGE LEARNERS**

EXTEND

Have students find out about ancient Chinese achievements in science and technology. **BLOCK SCHEDULING**

Science and technology. Education was available only to a privileged few in ancient China. However, the Qin and Han periods still saw dramatic developments in science and technology. Early Chinese astronomers learned that the year was slightly longer than 365 days. Han dynasty astronomers further refined these calculations. In 28 B.C. astronomers in China first observed sunspots; Europeans did not make similar observations until the A.D. 1600s. Sometime before A.D. 100 Chinese astronomers built instruments to track the movements of planets.

The Chinese invented a seismograph that registered even the faintest of earthquakes. They also invented paper, which was first produced in about 150 B.C. The earliest paper was made from fishing nets, hemp, old rags, and tree bark. By the middle of the A.D. 700s, the use of paper had spread throughout Central Asia and the Middle East, where it replaced papyrus as the main writing material. The Chinese also invented the sundial, the water clock, and the process of printing.

Chinese scholars, especially the Daoists, were very interested in chemistry. They discovered substances for dyeing cloth and glazing pottery. They also developed medicines based on herbs and minerals. Perhaps the most widely known Chinese contribution to medicine is the therapy known as **acupuncture.** Its development stemmed from the Daoist belief that good health depends on the movement of a life-force energy through the body. Illness or pain results when something interferes with that movement.

In acupuncture the doctor inserts needles into certain points of the body to enable the life-force energy to move properly. Some modern researchers believe that these needle insertion points may have less electrical resistance than other parts of the body and thus may affect the nervous system. Today the Chinese use acupuncture as an anesthetic in many types of surgery. Many Americans use it to relieve pains from ailments such as arthritis or cancer.

✔ **READING CHECK: Contrasting** In what areas did Chinese scientists of ancient times surpass their European counterparts? *astronomy, seismography, clocks, paper-making, and printing*

This device, developed in A.D. 132, warned of earthquakes. Ground tremors would cause metal balls to drop from the dragons' mouths to the frogs below.

SECTION 5 REVIEW

1. **Define** and explain the significance:
   genealogy
   acupuncture

2. **Identify** and explain the significance:
   Five Classics

3. **Making Generalizations** Copy the chart below. Use it to illustrate the different roles of men, women, and children in the Chinese family.

Male Family Members	Female Family Members

4. **Finding the Main Idea**
   a. What effect did Chinese philosophy have on Chinese medicine?
   b. How might the limited role of trade in ancient China have affected the development of Chinese culture?

5. **Writing and Critical Thinking**
   Evaluating Write a brief report that evaluates the different aspects of family life in ancient China.
   Consider:
   • the importance of family to the Chinese
   • respect paid to various family members
   • the roles of men and women in the traditional families of ancient China

Homework Practice Online
keyword: SP3 HP4

That's Interesting!

Paper was so valued in ancient China that it was forbidden to step on a piece that had writing on it. The Chinese closely guarded the papermaking process and were able to keep it secret for some 500 years.

SECTION 5 REVIEW ANSWERS

❶ **Define**
• genealogy, p. 93
• acupuncture, p. 95

❷ **Identify**
• Five Classics, p. 94

❸ males: ruled family, decided on marriages and careers; females: fewer rights and powers, gained power by bearing children

❹ a. Acupuncture was developed because of the Daoist belief that good health depends on the movement of a life-force energy through the body.

b. It may have caused China to be fairly culturally isolated.

❺ Students' reports will vary but should discuss the Chinese family, respect, and the roles of men and women.

CHAPTER 4

REVIEW AND ASSESSMENT RESOURCES

REPRODUCIBLE RESOURCES
▸ Vocabulary Activity 4

TECHNOLOGY RESOURCES
▸ Chapter 4 Test Generator (on the One-Stop Planner)
▸ Global Skill Builder CD–ROM
▸ HRW Web Site

REINFORCEMENT, REVIEW, and ASSESSMENT
▸ Chapter 4 Review, pp. 96–97
▸ Chapter 4 Tutorial for Students, Parents, Mentors, and Peers
▸ Chapter 4 Test (Form A or B)
▸ Alternative Assessment Handbook
▸ Chapter 4 Test for English Language Learners and Special-Needs Students

REVIEW

Have students complete the Chapter 4 Review on pages 96–97.

ASSESS

Use one of the chapter tests to assess students' understanding of the content. For Alternative Assessment, see the Portfolio Activities and Alternative Assessment Handbook.

CHAPTER 4 REVIEW ANSWERS

Understanding Main Ideas

1. problems: flooding; benefits: fertile soil

2. great distances, rugged mountains, harsh deserts

3. combination of animism and animal worship; belief in Shangdi; interpretation of oracle bones

4. consists of ideographs

5. fought among themselves; attacked by outsiders

6. civil service system, leveling, peace

7. Everything in the world results from a balance between two forces, yin and yang.

8. power without virtue; harsh laws

9. discoveries in astronomy, inventions, chemistry, medicine, acupuncture

Reviewing Themes

1. Great distances, rugged mountains, and harsh deserts isolated China geographically.

2. Some of the dynasties collapsed because of attacks from outsiders.

3. They were more moderate rulers than their predecessors.

CHAPTER 4 Review

Creating a Time Line

Copy the time line below onto a sheet of paper. Complete the time line by filling in the events, individuals, and dates from the chapter that you think were significant. Pick three events and explain why you think they were significant.

| 1500 B.C. | 1000 B.C. | 500 B.C. |

Writing a Summary

Using standard grammar, spelling, sentence structure, and punctuation, write an overview of the events in the chapter.

Identifying People and Ideas

Identify the following terms or individuals and explain their significance:

1. loess
2. dike
3. animism
4. calligraphy
5. Cheng
6. Liu Ch'e
7. Confucius
8. *Dao De Jing*
9. Five Classics
10. acupuncture

Understanding Main Ideas

Section 1 *(pp. 76–79)*
Geographic and Cultural Influences
1. What problems and benefits did the Huang River bring to the Chinese people?
2. What geographic features contributed to Chinese isolation?

Section 2 *(pp. 80–83)*
The Shang Dynasty
3. What were the main features of Shang religious beliefs?
4. How is Chinese writing different from the Western alphabet?

Section 3 *(pp. 84–88)*
The Zhou, Qin, and Han Dynasties
5. Why did the Zhou dynasty collapse?
6. What were the main achievements of Han emperor Liu Ch'e?

Section 4 *(pp. 89–92)*
Philosophies of Ancient China
7. What was the ancient Chinese belief concerning the dualism of nature?
8. What did the Legalists teach?

Section 5 *(pp. 93–95)*
Chinese Life and Culture
9. What did the ancient Chinese achieve in science and technology?

Reviewing Themes
1. **Culture** Why did Chinese culture develop in isolation?
2. **Global Relations** What effect did foreign peoples have on the success or failure of Chinese dynasties?
3. **Government** Why were Liu Ch'e and other Han dynasty rulers more effective than earlier Chinese rulers?

Thinking Critically
1. **Analyzing Information** How did the idea of the Mandate of Heaven influence Chinese government?
2. **Contrasting** How did the teachings of Confucius differ from those of Laozi?
3. **Evaluating** How did the geography of China affect the governments and dynasties in the region?
4. **Drawing Conclusions** How did literature shape Chinese thought and education?

Writing About History
Summarizing Write a report summarizing the similarities and differences between the Zhou, Qin, and Han dynasties. Use the chart below to organize your thoughts before writing.

	Zhou	Qin	Han
Period of rule			
Achievements			
Causes of decline			

Ask students which dynasty—the Zhou, the Qin, or the Han—did the most to advance Chinese culture. Have each student write a short paragraph that gives evidence to support his or her response.

Organize students who had difficulty with the test into five small groups. Have each group use correct social studies terminology to answer the Read to Discover questions in one section. Have students take the Form B Test to assess their mastery of the material.

ENGLISH LANGUAGE LEARNERS

Portfolio Extensions

Link to TODAY

1. Have students choose one of the three main Chinese philosophical traditions—Confucianism, Daoism, or Legalism—learn more about it, and use a decision-making process to devise a plan of student government for their school that is based on the tenets of this philosophy.

2. Have students use the process of historical inquiry to research pictures of bronze items from the Shang dynasty. Ask them to study the pictures to determine the religious functions and the aesthetic value of the bronzes. Have them write a report that describes their findings.

3. Have students use media and news services to find out about philosophies and beliefs in China today. Have them report on the similarities and differences between ancient and modern Chinese culture.

Building Social Studies Skills

Reading a Chart

Study the chart below. Then answer the questions that follow.

Chinese Dynasty	When	Achievements
Shang	c. 1750 B.C.–1122 B.C.	Calendar, astronomy, writing
Zhou	c. 1050 B.C.–c. 256 B.C.	Copper coins, iron tools, canals, dikes, reservoirs
Qin	c. 221 B.C.–c. 206 B.C.	Standard weights, measures, and coins, uniform writing system
Han	c. 206 B.C.–A.D. 220	Civil service system, paper

1. Which statement correctly describes a relationship shown on the chart?

a. The Shang Dynasty did not last as long as the Han Dynasty.

b. Iron tools came into use before the calendar.

c. Although writing began before 1100 B.C., paper was not invented until more than 900 years later.

d. The Zhou Dynasty adopted the uniform writing system developed during the Qin Dynasty.

2. In your opinion, which dynasty made the most important contributions? Give specific reasons for your choice.

Making Generalizations

Read the excerpt from the *Analects* by Confucius. Then answer the questions that follow.

"If you govern the people by laws, and keep them in order by penalties, they will avoid the penalties, yet lose their sense of shame. But if you govern them by your moral excellence, and keep them in order by your dutiful conduct, they will retain their sense of shame, and also live up to this standard [that is, to the ruler's standard of moral excellence and dutiful conduct]."

3. Which of the following is the best general statement of the ideas in this excerpt?

a. A ruler should lead by example.

b. People should lose their sense of shame.

c. Laws are not necessary to keep order.

d. A ruler should be moral.

e. A ruler should impose harsh laws and strict penalties to maintain order.

f. A ruler's conduct has little or no real impact on the behavior of the people.

4. In your opinion, what would be the effect on a society if a ruler did what Confucius suggested in this excerpt? Give examples.

Alternative Assessment

Building Your Portfolio

Link to TODAY

Culture

Chinese philosophy and religion remain an important influence on thought today. Using your textbook and other sources, compile a list of different Chinese philosophies and beliefs. Then prepare a pamphlet that illustrates the philosophical and religious ideas that you have studied.

internet connect

go.hrw.com

Internet Activity: go.hrw.com
KEYWORD: SP3 WH4

Choose a topic on Ancient Chinese Civilization to:

• compare and contrast Western, Arabic, and Chinese calligraphy.

• research the Qin dynasty and create a brochure on the Great Wall.

• write a report on Chinese philosophy or Chinese contributions to science.

Thinking Critically

1. Rulers believed that the gods determined who should rule.

2. Unlike Confucius, Laozi shunned politics and advised people not to seek power.

3. Isolation from India and the West caused the government to develop independently; proximity to neighboring states resulted in attack from outsiders and the fall of some dynasties.

4. The educational system emphasized respect for tradition and created a common culture.

Writing About History

Students' reports should include the information that follows. Zhou: c. 1050–256 B.C.; Mandate of Heaven; internal fighting, outside attack; Qin: 221–206 B.C.; autocracy, defensive walls; people's revolt; Han: 206 B.C.–A.D. 220; civil service system, leveling, peace; attack from nomads

Building Social Studies Skills

1. c

2. Students' answers should demonstrate knowledge of contributions and logical reasoning.

3. a

4. Students' answers will vary.

Building Your Portfolio

Students' pamphlets should include a discussion of Confucianism, Daoism, Legalism, and Buddhism.

CROSS-CULTURAL CONNECTIONS *Literature*

Spotlight on LITERATURE

Cultural epics originated as oral traditions. During ancient times, aristocratic families would recite the heroic deeds of their ancestors. In Japan, families of reciters known as *katari-be* handed down myths and legends by word of mouth. As more people became literate, oral epics were transferred to written form. Have students research the history of a cultural epic.

Spotlight on LITERATURE

The universal themes expressed in the *Epic of Gilgamesh* (c. 3000 B.C.) and the *Ramayana* (c. 300 B.C.) have made these epics meaningful far beyond the historical periods that produced them. For example, the *Odyssey*, written in the 900s or 800s B.C., contains many parallels with the *Epic of Gilgamesh*. Today, the *Ramayana* continues to be very popular in India, and recitation of the poem is considered an honored accomplishment. Have students research the literary and/or cultural influence of either the *Epic of Gilgamesh* or the *Ramayana*. Ask them to find modern references to the epics if possible.

Daily Life

After his friend Enkidu dies, Gilgamesh, in the *Epic of Gilgamesh,* wanders through the wilderness searching for immortality. Gilgamesh is told several times that it is no use trying to avoid death—everyone must die sooner or later. He is advised to live his life to the fullest—to eat well, to care for himself, and to enjoy life. This advice reflects the culture's live-for-the-day attitude. Mesopotamians did not believe in life after death. In contrast, the Hindu epic, the *Ramayana*, tells of Sita freely giving herself over to death to prove her love and faithfulness to her husband.

Critical Thinking

Why do you think Sita was able to die so willingly?

ANSWER: Students might suggest that the Hindu belief in reincarnation allowed Sita to die; knowing that she was innocent, she believed that she would come back to earth with a higher status.

UNDERSTANDING LITERATURE ANSWER

Answers will vary. Students might cite, "Then Gilgamesh wept some more for his dead friend," as expressing the value of friendship; or, "For that moment, everywhere in the whole universe, there was harmony," from the Ramayana, as showing how important peace, even for a moment, is in Hindu culture.

CROSS-CULTURAL CONNECTIONS *Literature*

Ancient Worldviews

Cultural epics are ancient stories—often myths or legends—that describe and explain a culture's origins and that shape its values. They help to express a culture's view of life and the world, and they emphasize the culture's most basic ideals. The Babylonian cultural epic, The Epic of Gilgamesh, *describes how early Mesopotamians viewed such concepts as loyalty, friendship, and death. These same theses are echoed in different ways in the Ramayana, one of ancient India's great cultural epics.*

Stone relief of Gilgamesh between two gods

The Epic of Gilgamesh

[Enkidu] is the friend who, wild heart for wild heart, will equal you and be your second self, to guard your back in battle and in peace sit by your side; to laugh when you laugh and to share your grief. He will not forsake you. . . .

[Following Enkidu's tragic death]. . . Gilgamesh wept . . . for his dead friend. He wandered over barren hills, mumbling to his own spirit: "Will you too die as Enkidu did? Will grief become your food? Will we both fear the lonely hills, so vacant? I now race from place to place, dissatisfied with wherever I am . . .

As if in sleep I come upon the mountain door at midnight where I face wild-eyed lions, and I am afraid. Then to Sin, the god of mighty light, I raise my solemn chant to beg: 'Save me, please, my god.' " [He] wandered through the woods so like a savage beast just then did he bring death again and again upon the lions' heads with an ax he drew from off his belt.

The Ramayana

[A trusted friend tells Sita,] "All the universe is a sign to be read rightly. War and peace, love and separation/ Are hidden gateways we must pass [through]/ To reach other worlds. Let us not grow old thinking that truth Is what most people see or say it is."

. . . This world is like a breath on a mirror. It does not last. Have patience.

. . . Sita approached Rama and said, "Let me prove my innocence before you/ Once and for all."

. . . Then Sita took a step back and said, "Mother earth, if I have been faithful to my husband,/ Take me home." . . . The ground rolled and moved/ Beneath Sita. With a great noise/ The ground opened and took Sita back.

. . . For that moment, everywhere in the whole universe,/ There was harmony.

Scene from the Ramayana

Understanding Literature

Explain how a cultural epic expresses the values and worldview of its culture, using examples from *The Epic of Gilgamesh* and the Ramayana.

Science, Technology & Society

Copy the following graphic organizer on the board. Ask students to work together in pairs, using their textbooks and other available resources, to fill in the graphic organizer with examples, including the appropriate dynasty. *(Possible answers include math—calendar [Shang], economic "leveling" [Han]; science— paper [Han]; technology—irrigation and flood control [Shang], sophisticated bronzework [Shang], defensive walls [Qin])*

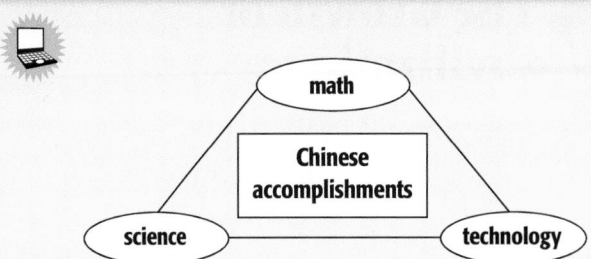

math

Chinese accomplishments

science

technology

BUILDING YOUR Portfolio

Science, Technology & Society

Social scientists learn much about ancient civilizations by studying the artifacts—or material remains— they have left behind. In many cases, works of art are especially useful in helping researchers to understand what an early civilization was like during a particular time. Imagine that you are an ancient Chinese artist. Your task is to create a series of line drawings or paintings meant to illustrate Chinese discoveries in math, science, and technology, especially ones that came to affect later cultures. What kinds of images would you show, and what would they reveal about life in China?

Egyptian tools, shards, and weapons, dating from Old or Middle Kingdom dynasties

Han dynasty line painting

Culture

To find out how ancient civilizations such Egypt interacted with other cultures, scientists often pose and answer questions from information revealed on maps, graphs, charts, models, and databases. Write a series of questions about geographic distribution and patterns that a scientist might pose about early Egyptian culture. Then, using resources on the bibliography below, as well as any maps, graphs, charts, models, or databases referenced in this unit, record any answers to your questions that you find.

Further Reading

Dersin, Denise, ed. *What Life Was Like: On the Banks of the Nile, Egypt 3050–30 B.C.* Alexandria, Virginia: Time-Life Books, 1999. A survey of daily life in ancient Egypt.

Gowlett, John A. *Ascent to Civilization: The Archaeology of Early Humans.* New York: McGraw-Hill, 1993. An overview of historical developments in the art, agriculture, and technology of early humans.

Oliphant, Margaret. *The Atlas of the Ancient World: Charting the Great Civilizations of the Past.* New York: Simon and Schuster, 1992. A comprehensive and descriptive overview of nine ancient world civilizations.

Starr, Chester G. *A History of the Ancient World.* New York: Oxford University Press, 1991. A survey of Chinese, Indian, Greek, and Mesopotamian cultures.

internet connect

go hrw .com

Internet Activity
KEYWORD: SP3 U1

In assigned groups, develop a multimedia presentation about early people and civilizations between about 3,700,000 B.C. and A.D. 589. Choose information from the chapter Internet Connect activities and the Holt Researcher that best reflects the major topics of the period. Write an outline and a script for your presentation, which may be shown to the class.

Culture

Ask students to research geographic distributions during one period in ancient Egyptian history. Have them create a thematic map that illustrates their research findings. Have students present their maps to the class and explain the physical and human characteristics of their chosen period.

Interdisciplinary Connection

ARCHAEOLOGY. In 1968 archaeologists excavated the tomb of Liu Sheng, who was king of Zhongshan province during the Han dynasty. The more than 2,800 objects in Liu Sheng's tomb offer clues into his luxurious lifestyle. Members of the Liu family—ancestors of the Han emperors—were often buried with full-body jade coverings. For Liu Sheng's body, 2,498 small plaques of the precious stone were sewn together with gold wire and his head was placed on an elaborate headrest of gilt bronze with jade inlay. The Han believed jade's durable properties could be transferred to humans to ensure immortality.

Critical Thinking

Ask students why the Han might have buried family members in jade shrouds.

ANSWER: The shroud may have been an immortal replacement of Liu Sheng's body, or a type of "armor" to protect him from evil spirits.

UNIT 2

The Growth of Civilizations

EXAMINING THE VISUAL RECORD

❶ What is the main architectural element of the building in the center of the painting?

ANSWER: marble columns

Marble columns support the roof of the Temple of Castor and Pollux in the Roman Forum. The Greeks had three styles for the capital, or top, of their columns: Doric (see Parthenon, page 130), Ionic (see Temple of Saturn, page 152), and Corinthian (this temple). The Romans added another style—Composite—that combined the curved corners of the Ionic with the leaf designs of the Corinthian. These styles of columns are still used in classical or Neoclassical architecture today.

❷ What architectural element did the designers use in the building to the right of the Temple of Castor and Pollux?

ANSWER: arches

The Romans' greatest contribution to architecture was perfecting the use of the arch. This marble building, the Basilica Julia, housed the civil courts. The U.S. Capitol, with its columns and arches, has many elements from Greco-Roman buildings.

ACTIVITY: Ask students to use primary and secondary sources, including computer software, to identify public buildings in the United States and around the world that have examples of columns and arches in their designs.

UNIT 2

The Growth of Civilizations

c. 2000 B.C.–A.D. 1500

empire, Rome's power spread throughout the Mediterranean and into northern Europe. Christianity spread throughout the empire and became the leading religion. In the late A.D. 400s, internal problems and invasions from Germanic tribes caused the decline and collapse of the Roman Empire in the West.

◆ CHAPTER ◆ **Africa**
8 Trading kingdoms of Kush and Aksum grew in the interior of eastern Africa. Swahili-speaking city-states developed on the East Coast. The Shona people of Great Zimbabwe controlled the gold trade. Control of the salt-for-gold trade in West Africa resulted in the rise and fall of the kingdoms of Ghana, Mali, and Songhai.

◆ CHAPTER ◆ **The Americas**
9 People began migrating from Asia to the Americas about 50,000 years ago. In North America many different cultures developed because of the variety of geography and climate. The Maya and the Aztecs developed advanced cultures in Mesoamerica, and the Incas controlled much of Andean South America.

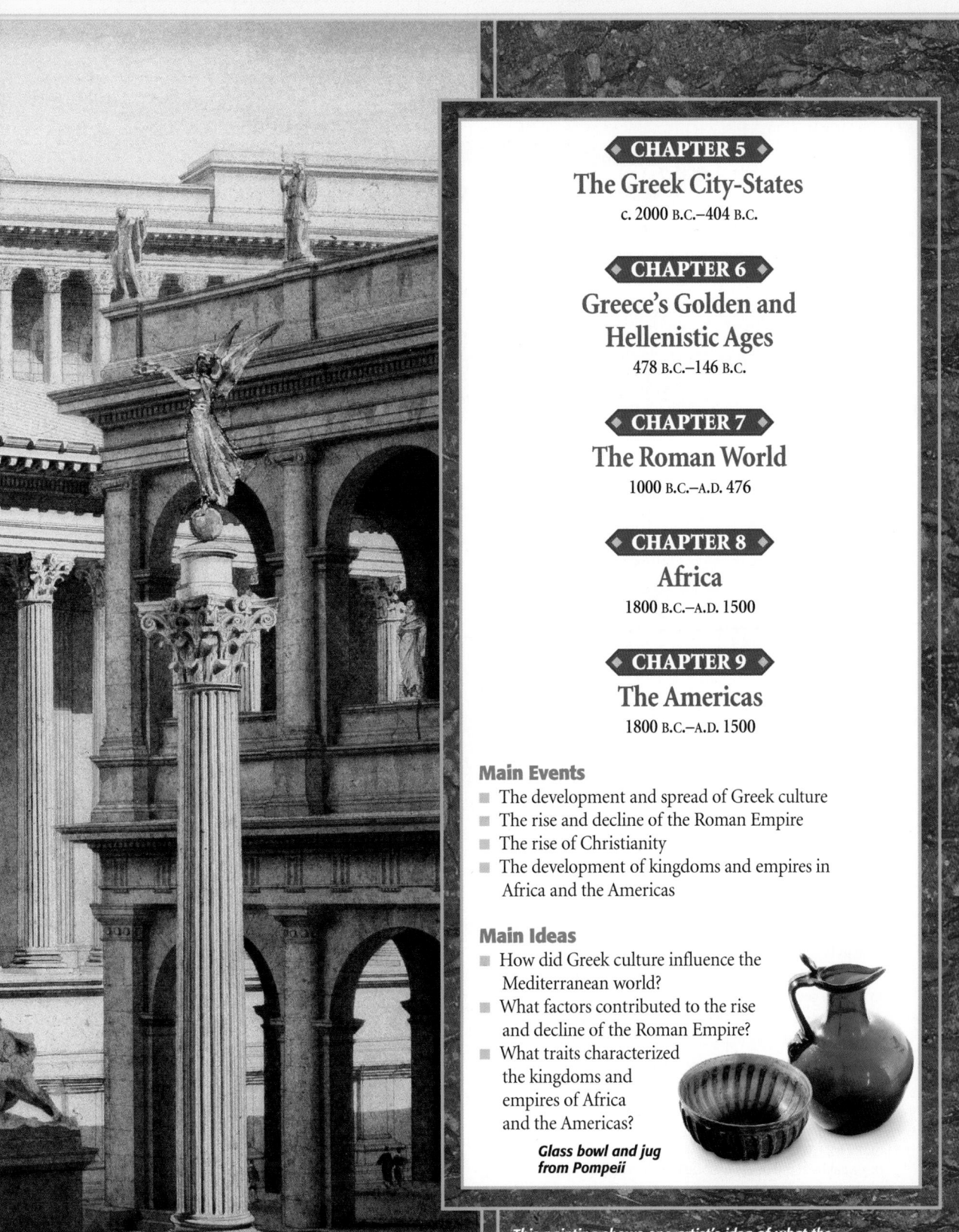

◆ **CHAPTER 5** ◆
The Greek City-States
c. 2000 B.C.–404 B.C.

◆ **CHAPTER 6** ◆
Greece's Golden and Hellenistic Ages
478 B.C.–146 B.C.

◆ **CHAPTER 7** ◆
The Roman World
1000 B.C.–A.D. 476

◆ **CHAPTER 8** ◆
Africa
1800 B.C.–A.D. 1500

◆ **CHAPTER 9** ◆
The Americas
1800 B.C.–A.D. 1500

Main Events
■ The development and spread of Greek culture
■ The rise and decline of the Roman Empire
■ The rise of Christianity
■ The development of kingdoms and empires in Africa and the Americas

Main Ideas
■ How did Greek culture influence the Mediterranean world?
■ What factors contributed to the rise and decline of the Roman Empire?
■ What traits characterized the kingdoms and empires of Africa and the Americas?

Glass bowl and jug from Pompeii

This painting shows one artist's idea of what the Forum looked like at the height of Roman power. **101**

Introduce Unit 2

Main Events
Ask students to select two Main Events and list questions they would like to have answered about the topics. Later, when you have completed Unit 2, ask students to return to their original questions and write an answer using the information they learned in the unit.

Main Ideas
Ask each student to read the Main Ideas and write brief answers to the questions. Share the *Consider* points with students as necessary. Later, when you have completed Unit 2, ask students to analyze their original answers by comparing them to information they learned in the unit. Tell them to revise or expand their answers as necessary.

The Influence of Greek Culture on the Mediterranean World
Consider:
■ the effects of colonization and conquest
■ the development of art, architecture, and political ideas

Characteristics of Kingdoms and Empires in Africa and the Americas
Consider:
■ types of governments and organization of society
■ economic factors such as farming and trade

CROSS-CULTURAL CONNECTIONS

Focus On Government

 LET'S GET STARTED!

As students enter the classroom, ask them to write definitions of *democracy* and *republic*. Have students keep their definitions to revise as they read Cross-Cultural Connections. Tell students that in this unit they will learn how democratic-republican government began in classical Greece and Rome. In later units they will trace the process by which this kind of government evolved in England and during the Enlightenment.

TEACH

 ALL LEVELS: Help students fill in the chart below with information about these governments.

ENGLISH LANGUAGE LEARNERS

	Athens	Rome	Kush	Maya
Government/ Dates	Democracy 570–322 B.C.	Republic 509–27 B.C.	Monarchy 250 B.C.– A.D. 150	Monarchy A.D. 250–900
Who ruled	all male citizens	elected officials	king or queen	kings helped by military
Power of women	none	none	queens	none

Daily Life

The toga, a distinctive white-woolen cloth garment, could be worn only by Romans. During early Roman times before the use of military uniforms, the toga was worn into battle. Men, boys, and girls wore togas. When girls married, they turned in their togas for the stola, the dress of a married woman.

Members of the upper classes and later emperors wore white togas. The lower classes wore dark colors. Colored stripes on togas symbolized various offices. A broad purple stripe was woven into the front of senators' togas. Generals wore togas with a red stripe and gold embroidery to special ceremonies. Eventually, only emperors could wear that special toga.

Critical Thinking

Compare how the use of stripes on a toga in Rome and on a U.S. military uniform reflect social and political order.

ANSWER: The colored stripes on a toga showed a man's position of power. In the same way, the number of stripes on a military uniform indicates a position of authority.

CROSS-CULTURAL CONNECTIONS

Focus On: Government

Main Idea **Who participated in government?** Within the great city-states and empires of early history, levels of public participation in government varied. Some societies were led exclusively by kings and queens, others by small groups of wealthy men. Some experimented with democracy, helping lay the foundation for the democratic systems we enjoy today.

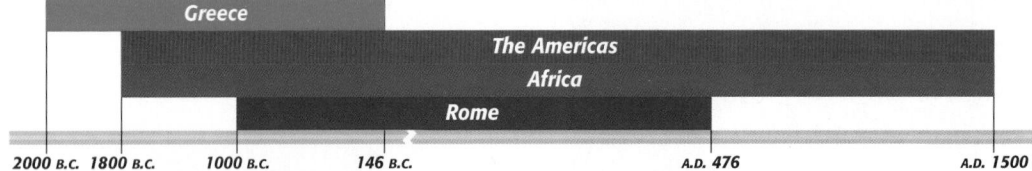

Greece					
		The Americas			
		Africa			
	Rome				
2000 B.C. 1800 B.C.	1000 B.C.	146 B.C.		A.D. 476	A.D. 1500

Greece, c. 2000 B.C.–146 B.C.

Democracy in Athens This stone carving shows Democracy, represented by a woman, crowning the people of Athens. From about 570 B.C. to 322 B.C. Athens ruled itself as a democracy. All full citizens had an equal vote in the assembly, regardless of their wealth or education. Not everyone was a citizen, however. It is estimated that at its height, Athens had approximately 50,000 full citizens out of a population of about 350,000 people. To be a full citizen you had to be a male over the age of 18 born of a citizen family.

The Roman Republic In 509 B.C. wealthy Roman landowners overthrew the king and established a republic. In a republic, voters elect officials to run the government. As in Greece, only adult male citizens could vote. Unlike in Greece, however, a person did not have to be born into a citizen family to become a citizen. Even the sons of freed slaves became citizens. Nevertheless, the first ordinary citizen was not elected to the government until 409 B.C. Even after this date, the Senate and other key parts of Rome's government remained firmly in the hands of the wealthiest members of society. This image shows the Roman Senate.

Rome, 1000 B.C.–A.D. 476

Have students review the information about the different groups that participated in government in Athens, Rome, Kush, and the Maya Empire. Ask them to use standard grammar, spelling, sentence structure, and punctuation to answer the question in "Why It Matters Today" and to share their answers with the class.

Have students work in groups of three or four to propose a new student government for their school. Tell students to use information from their textbooks, the library, computer software, and any other available resources to determine the structure of the government and who will participate directly and indirectly in it. Allow time for students to demonstrate how their various governments would work. **BLOCK SCHEDULING, COOPERATIVE LEARNING**

ASSESS

Have students complete their answer to the question in "Why It Matters Today" and add it to their portfolio. As Alternative Assessment, you may want to use the chart exercise in this lesson.

The Kingdom of Kush Located south of Egypt, the wealthy African trading kingdom of Kush reached its height between about 250 B.C. and A.D. 150. Kush patterned its government after that of the Egyptians, who were ruled by a powerful royal family. There were key differences, though. The kings and queens of Kush were not all-powerful. Rather than make laws, they followed and enforced laws established by priests. Also, when one king died, his son did not automatically inherit the throne. New monarchs were elected from among the royal family. Because the royal family traced its heritage through women and elected its rulers, more queens (like the one pictured here) ruled Kush than any other major early civilization.

Africa, 1800 B.C.–A.D. 1500

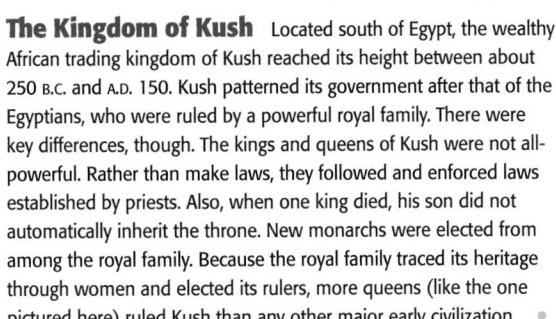

The Americas, c. 1800 B.C.–A.D. 1500

The Maya The Yucatán Peninsula was home to the great city-states of the Maya. During the Classic Period (c. A.D. 250–A.D. 900), kings ruled the Maya with assistance from military leaders and royal priests. The empire was divided into provinces, each ruled by a governor chosen from among four royal families. The governors were all-powerful, running their provinces like mini-kingdoms. Below the governors were leaders of small towns and provinces. These leaders were not members of the royal family; they were usually members of the society who had distinguished themselves somehow. The stone temple relief to the left, dating from c. A.D. 725, shows a possibly mythical Mayan ruler and his wife.

Mayan plate from A.D. 900–A.D. 1500

Why It Matters Today

Today most countries practice some form of democracy. In the United States, almost all adult citizens are allowed to vote, regardless of income, gender, or race. **How does our system of government today compare to those of ancient Greece, Rome, Africa, and the Americas?**

History Maker

PACEL. Pacel, one of the greatest Mayan leaders, ruled the city of Palenque from A.D. 615 to 683. At the age of 12, he inherited his throne from his mother, Lady Zac-Kuk. One of Pacel's important contributions was construction of the Temple of the Inscriptions. Its corridors displayed lists of the past kings and their reigns. Some scholars think that Lady Zac-Kuk held actual power until her death in 640 because Pacel did not commission inscriptions relating to his rule until after her death.

Critical Thinking

How did scholars use information from the Temple of Inscriptions to interpret Mayan political history?

ANSWER: Students might suggest that scholars could trace Mayan history through the list of kings and infer that Lady Zac-Kuk held power until her death.

WHY IT MATTERS TODAY ANSWER

Answers will vary but might include that New England town meetings are somewhat like the Assembly in Athens; that the U.S. Senate and state senates are based on the Roman Senate; that the way U.S. presidents are elected and the way they carry out laws made by Congress is similar to the government in Kush; and that the levels of U.S. government show some similarity to the levels of government of Mayan city-states.

CHAPTER 5

The Greek City-States

CHAPTER RESOURCE MANAGER

	Objectives	Pacing Guide	Reproducible Resources
SECTION 1 **Early Greeks and the Rise of City-States** (pp. 106–109)	• Analyze the role that geography played in early Greek history. • Explain the influence that Minoan and Mycenaean civilizations had on Greek civilization. • Describe the development of the Greek city-states.	**Regular** 1.5 day / **Block Scheduling** 1 day *Block Scheduling Handbook with Team Teaching Strategies, 5.1*	**RS** Guided Reading Strategy 5.1 **E** Hands-on History Activity 5: The Greek City-States
SECTION 2 **Greek Government and Society** (pp. 110–112)	• Explain the importance of Homer's works. • Identify major religious beliefs and practices of the ancient Greeks. • Describe changes that occurred in the governments of the Greek city-states.	**Regular** 1.5 day / **Block Scheduling** 1 day *Block Scheduling Handbook with Team Teaching Strategies, 5.2*	**RS** Guided Reading Strategy 5.2 **RS** Graphic Organizer Activity 5 **PS** Readings in World History 17
SECTION 3 **Sparta and Athens** (pp. 113–117)	• Analyze the society of Sparta. • Explain the development of democracy in Athens.	**Regular** 1.5 day / **Block Scheduling** 1 day *Block Scheduling Handbook with Team Teaching Strategies, 5.3*	**RS** Guided Reading Strategy 5.3 **PS** Readings in World History 18: The Making of Spartan Soldiers **PS** Readings in World History 19: A Plea for Eunomy
SECTION 4 **Daily Life in Athens** (pp. 118–120)	• Explain the basis of Athens's economy. • Describe the family life and education in Athens.	**Regular** 1.5 day / **Block Scheduling** 1 day *Block Scheduling Handbook with Team Teaching Strategies, 5.4*	**RS** Guided Reading Strategy 5.4 **E** Creative Teaching Strategy 5: Athens Today!
SECTION 5 **The Expansion of Greece** (pp. 121–125)	• Explain how the Persian Wars began and what the results of those wars were. • Analyze the effects of Pericles's leadership on Athens. • Explain how the Peloponnesian War began and its results.	**Regular** 1.5 day / **Block Scheduling** 1 day *Block Scheduling Handbook with Team Teaching Strategies, 5.5*	**RS** Guided Reading Strategy 5.5 **SM** Geography Activity 5: Greek Alliances **PS** Readings in World History 20: The Greatness of Athens

Chapter Resource Key

PS Primary Sources	**A** Assessment	Music	
RS Reading Support	**REV** Review	Video	
IC Interdisciplinary Connections	**ELL** Reinforcement and English Language Learners	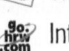 Internet	
E Enrichment	Transparencies	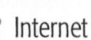 Holt Presentation Maker Using Microsoft® PowerPoint®	
SM Skills Mastery	CD-ROM		

 One-Stop Planner CD-ROM

See the *One-Stop Planner* for a complete list of additional resources for students and teachers.

One-Stop Planner CD-ROM

It's easy to plan lessons, select resources, and print out materials for your students when you use the *One-Stop Planner CD–ROM with Test Generator.*

Technology Resources	Reinforcement, Review, and Assessment
One-Stop Planner 5.1 CNN Presents World Cultures: Yesterday and Today Segment 5: Crete: Past and Present Homework Practice Online Online Maps, Charts, and Graphs: Turmoil in the Aegean Lands, c. 1250–1100 B.C.	Daily Quiz 5.1 Main Idea Activity 5.1 English Audio Summary 5.1 Spanish Audio Summary 5.1 REV Section 1 Review, p. 109
One-Stop Planner 5.2 Holt Researcher: World History: Homer World History Teaching Transparency: Art and History 3: Dipylonvase Homework Practice Online	Daily Quiz 5.2 Main Idea Activity 5.2 English Audio Summary 5.2 Spanish Audio Summary 5.2 REV Section 2 Review, p. 112
One-Stop Planner 5.3 Holt Researcher: World History: Solon World History and Cultures Video Program 3 Homework Practice Online Online Maps, Charts, and Graphs: The Long Walls of Athens	Daily Quiz 5.3 Main Idea Activity 5.3 English Audio Summary 5.3 Spanish Audio Summary 5.3 REV Section 3 Review, p. 117
One-Stop Planner 5.4 World History Teaching Transparency: Geography and History 3: The Peloponnesian War Homework Practice Online	Daily Quiz 5.4 Main Idea Activity 5.4 English Audio Summary 5.4 Spanish Audio Summary 5.4 REV Section 4 Review, p. 120
One-Stop Planner 5.5 Holt Researcher: World History: Xerxes Homework Practice Online Online Maps, Charts, and Graphs: The Battle of Salamis Online Maps, Charts, and Graphs: The Battle of Thermopylae	Daily Quiz 5.5 Main Idea Activity 5.5 English Audio Summary 5.5 Spanish Audio Summary 5.5 REV Section 5 Review, p. 125

♫ **internet** connect ▤

HRW ONLINE RESOURCES
GO TO: go.hrw.com
Then type in a keyword.

TEACHER HOME PAGE
KEYWORD: SP3 Teacher

CHAPTER INTERNET ACTIVITIES
KEYWORD: SP3 WH5
Choose an activity to:
• model ancient writing systems of the Mediterranean.
• build a map that connects modern and ancient Mediterranean cultures with pizza.
• report on Minoan civilization.

CHAPTER ENRICHMENT LINKS
KEYWORD: SP3 CH5

ONLINE ASSESSMENT
Homework Practice
KEYWORD: SP3 HP5
Standardized Test Prep
KEYWORD: SP3 STP5
Rubrics
KEYWORD: SS Rubrics

ONLINE MAPS, CHARTS, AND GRAPHS
KEYWORD: SP3 MCG

CONTENT UPDATES
KEYWORD: SS Content Updates

HOLT PRESENTATION MAKER
KEYWORD: SP3 PPT5

ONLINE READING SUPPORT
KEYWORD: SS Strategies

CURRENT EVENTS
KEYWORD: S3 Current Events

Meeting Individual Needs

Ability Levels

Level 1 Basic level activities designed for all students encountering new material

Level 2 Intermediate level activities designed for average students

Level 3 Challenging activities designed for honors and gifted and talented students

English Language Learners These activities address the needs of students with Limited English Proficiency.

 Chapter Review and Assessment

IC Vocabulary Activity 5	A Chapter 5 Test Generator (on the One-Stop Planner)
Global Skill Builder CD–ROM	A Chapter 5 Test (Form A or B)
HRW Web Site	A Alternative Assessment Handbook
REV Chapter 5 Tutorial for Students, Parents, Mentors, and Peers	A Chapter 5 Test for English Language Learners and Special-Needs Students
REV Chapter 5 Review, pp. 126–127	

103b

Build on What You Know

Ask students to answer the following questions:

How might other civilizations have influenced the development of Greek civilization?

Consider:

• the location of early civilizations

• how ideas would spread along the trade routes

• the examples that early civilizations set of what people could do

What might the Greeks have learned from China, India, Egypt, and Mesopotamia?

Consider:

• new ideas in religion, art, and science

• advances in manufacturing, ship-building, and trade

• ways in which the governments of these civilizations developed

---

EXPLORING THE TIME LINE

GLOBAL EVENTS

🖥 internet connect

go.hrw.com

TOPIC: The First Olympic Games

GO TO: go.hrw.com

KEYWORD: SP3 WH5

Have students access the Internet through the HRW Go site to conduct research on the first Olympic Games in 776 B.C. Then ask students to compose an informative report that details the origin and history of the games, what types of sports were played, and the similarities and differences between ancient Olympic games and the Olympics of today. Students' reports should include appropriate examples and evidence drawn from their research. Instruct students to use standard grammar, spelling, sentence structure, and punctuation.

CHAPTER

5

C. 2000 B.C.–404 B.C.

The Greek City-States

Greek coins, c. 500s B.C.

Minoan bull's head from Knossos, c. 1600 B.C.

c. 2000 B.C.
Global Events
Mycenaean invasions begin.

c. 2000 B.C.–1500 B.C.
Science and Technology
Minoans of the island kingdom of Crete use the decimal numbering system.

c. 900 B.C.–750 B.C.
The Arts
The Homeric Age occurs.

776 B.C.
Daily Life
First Olympic games are held.

| 2000 B.C. | 1600 B.C. | 900 B.C. | 800 B.C. | 700 B.C. |

c. 1600 B.C.–1200 B.C.
Daily Life
Mycenaean civilization reaches its height on mainland Greece.

800 B.C.–700 B.C.
Business and Finance
Greeks establish trading outposts around the Mediterranean.

800 B.C.–700 B.C.
Politics
The Greeks establish city-states.

c. 2000 B.C.–1500 B.C.
Business and Finance
Seagoing trade routes linking the growing parts of the eastern Mediterranean to coastal villages in Europe develop.

Mycenaean gold wreath

Build on What You Know

Between about 3000 B.C. and 1000 B.C., civilizations developed along river valleys in Egypt, Mesopotamia, India, and China. The people of these civilizations formed governments, built cities, and carried on trade. They also developed systems of writing, practiced religious beliefs, and invented new ways of making things. Some ideas from these early civilizations were passed on to the Greeks who lived along the eastern Mediterranean Sea. In this chapter, you will learn about early Greek history and the various forms of government that the ancient Greeks developed.

What's Your Opinion?

To help students create their Themes Journal entries, provide the following examples of appropriate **agree**/**disagree** *statements.*

Geography

Agree The geography of a region must allow for good transportation and communication in order for civilizations to develop.

Disagree A civilization can develop even if the terrain isolates towns and cities.

Citizenship

Agree A government can rule best if decisions are made by only a limited number of citizens.

Disagree A government rules best when all members of society are invited to participate as citizens.

Global Relations

Agree The development of an advanced and respected civilization often requires military dominance.

Disagree War-mongering societies are often seen as barbarians not worthy of respect.

Solon of Athens, c. 630 B.C.–560 B.C.

Relief of the Battle of Marathon, 490 B.C.

c. 650 B.C.
Daily Life
Most trees in Greece have been used for homes, ships, and fuel.

c. 650 B.C.–500 B.C.
Politics
Rule by tyrants occurs in many Greek city-states.

c. 600 B.C.
Business and Finance
Greeks begin using metal coins.

594 B.C.
Business and Finance
Solon forbids the export of Athenian farm products.

490 B.C.–479 B.C.
Global Events
The Persian Wars are fought between the Persian Empire and the Greek city-states.

431 B.C.
Science and Technology
Greek philosopher Empedocles develops the idea that matter is composed of four elements—earth, fire, water, and air.

431 B.C.–404 B.C.
Global Events
The Peloponnesian War is fought.

600 B.C. | **500 B.C.** | **400 B.C.**

621 B.C.
Politics
Draco issues Greece's first written law code.

590 B.C.
The Arts
Sappho writes poetry on the island of Lesbos.

546 B.C.
Daily Life
Peisistratus starts the cult of Dionysus.

429 B.C.
Daily Life
A devastating plague kills at least one third of Athens's population, threatening the overall collapse of the city.

GLOBAL EVENTS

The first advanced civilization to develop on the mainland of Greece was that of the Mycenaeans. Like the Greeks that followed them, the Mycenaeans were traders. They traded with Cyprus for copper, Syria for ivory, and Egypt for gold and jewelry. Mycenaean ships brought home amber that originated in the Baltic region. Archaeological evidence indicates that the Mycenaeans were active traders in southern Italy, Mesopotamia, and throughout the Mediterranean region. There is some evidence that they traded with far-off Britain.

Critical Thinking

In what ways might the widespread trading empire of the Mycenaeans have influenced the Greek city-states that succeeded them?

ANSWER: Students should recognize that when people trade goods, they also transmit ideas, language, science and technology, and other accidental cargo. The infusion of ideas undoubtedly inspired and directed some of the later development of the Greek civilization.

Terra-cotta farmer and oxen from Thebes, c. 575 B.C.

What's Your Opinion?

Do you **agree** *or* **disagree** *with the following statements? Support your point of view in your journal.*

Geography The growth of civilizations is decided by their geography.

Citizenship The best way for governments to rule is to limit the number of people who can be citizens.

Global Relations People often go to war to gain respect for their country.

OBJECTIVES

1 **Analyze the role that geography played in early Greek history.**

2 **Explain the influence that Minoan and Mycenaean civilizations had on Greek civilization.**

3 **Describe the development of the Greek city-states.**

📀 LET'S GET STARTED!

As students enter the classroom, ask them to list some advances made by civilizations they have studied. *(metalworking, calendars, religions, Arabic numerals, astronomy, writing)* Ask what basic qualities a society needs in order to grow into a civilization. *(Students might suggest a common language and religion, an interest in education and art, a common ancestry, and an economic system.)* Tell students that in Section 1 they will learn about the early Greek people and the rise of the Greek city-states.

REPRODUCIBLE RESOURCES

▶ Guided Reading Strategy 5.1

▶ Hands-on History Activity 5: The Greek City-States

TECHNOLOGY RESOURCES

▶ One-Stop Planner 5.1

▶ Homework Practice Online

▶ Online Maps: Turmoil in the Aegean Lands, c. 1250–1100 B.C.

REINFORCEMENT, REVIEW, AND ASSESSMENT

▶ Section 1 Review, p. 109

▶ Daily Quiz 5.1

▶ Main Idea Activity 5.1

▶ English Audio Summary 5.1

▶ Spanish Audio Summary 5.1

VISUAL RECORD ANSWER

Women were active athletes and participants in Minoan practices.

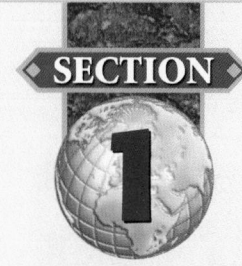
READ TO DISCOVER

❶ How did geography influence Greek history?

❷ How did the Minoans and Mycenaeans affect Greek civilization?

❸ How did Greek city-states develop?

DEFINE

frescoes
polis
acropolis
agora

IDENTIFY

Minoans
Mycenaeans

▶ WHY IT MATTERS TODAY

The United States and other democratic countries have adopted the Greek idea that citizens can govern themselves. Use **CNN**student News.com or other **current event** sources to find examples of how citizens in the United States and in other countries take part in government. Record your findings in your journal.

CNNstudent News.com

Early Greeks and the Rise of City-States

The Main Idea
The geography of Greece isolated settlements and strongpoints from one another, leading to the rise of city-states.

The Story Continues *According to legend, primitive Greeks called Dorians moved into Asia Minor, Crete, and the Peloponnesus about 1100 B.C. Modern historians now believe the Dorians never really existed. They do know, however, that some invaders did arrive at about this time, and that they influenced the development of certain Greek city-states.*

The Sea and the Land

The geography of Greece had much to do with the way the early Greeks lived. Mainland Greece lies on the southern part of the Balkan Peninsula. This peninsula is at the northeastern end of the Mediterranean Sea. The Aegean Sea to the east separates Greece from Asia Minor. To the west, the Ionian Sea divides Greece from the Italian Peninsula. Small islands dot the Aegean and Ionian Seas. Many of them are also part of Greece.

Greece's long, uneven coastline brought every part of the mainland close to the sea. The sea came to play an important part in the lives of the Greeks, many of whom became fishers, sailors, and traders. People from Egypt and the Fertile Crescent also traveled to Greece, bringing with them goods and ideas. Later, the Greeks set up colonies in other parts of the Mediterranean.

Greece's geography made it hard for its early people to develop a sense of unity. Short mountain ranges cut up the Greek mainland. These mountains kept villages apart. They also allowed invaders to enter Greece from the north. Unlike the great rivers of Egypt and Mesopotamia, rivers in Greece were short and did not aid travel and trade between villages. Instead of a large kingdom or empire forming in Greece, separate city-states arose.

✔ **READING CHECK: Identifying Cause and Effect** How did geography affect the development of ancient Greece? groups developed in isolation

INTERPRETING THE VISUAL RECORD

Early Greek frescoes *The Toreador Fresco* (c. 1500 B.C.) is the largest Minoan mural in existence. It shows athletes jumping over a bull, a Minoan religious practice. The figures with the lighter skin tones are women. *What does this fresco imply about the role women played in Greek society?*

TEACH OBJECTIVE 1

LEVEL 1: Before students read "The Sea and the Land," have them examine the maps on pages 107 and 108. Ask students what geographical features they notice on the Balkan Peninsula. *(Students should mention the numerous mountain ranges, the lack of long rivers, the long irregular coastline, and many islands.)* Guide a discussion of the advantages and disadvantages these features posed for people living in the region.

TEACH OBJECTIVE 2

ALL LEVELS: Draw a compare-and-contrast chart on the chalkboard. Guide students in filling in the chart. Then have students pose and answer questions about the influence of the Minoans and Mycenaeans on Greek civilization.

ENGLISH LANGUAGE LEARNERS , COOPERATIVE LEARNING

	Minoans	Mycenaeans
Location	Crete	Greek mainland, Crete
Dates	c. 2000 B.C.–1500 B.C.	c. 1600 B.C.–1200 B.C.
Achievements	indoor running water, art, traded network, navy, written language	built fort-like cities throughout Greece, kept written records
Reasons for collapse	volcanic eruption, tidal waves	earthquakes, war

Early Greek Peoples

People first lived in Greece about 55,000 years ago. Not until about A.D. 1900, however, did archaeologists find evidence of the earliest Greek civilization. This was the Minoan civilization. It had developed on the island of Crete by 2000 B.C. About that same time, Indo-European people entered the Greek mainland from the north.

The Minoans. The Minoan civilization was named after the legendary king of Crete, King Minos. Minos had his palace in the city of Knossos (NAHS·uhs). There the **Minoans** built a great civilization. The palace and the homes of nobles had running water. Minoan artists covered the palace walls with colorful **frescoes**—paintings made on wet plaster walls. Other artists carved beautiful figures from bronze, gold, ivory, silver, and stone. Some of the figures show the Minoans worshipping a bull and an Earth goddess.

Many Minoans became sailors and traders. They traded for food because Crete's soil was poor. It could not grow many kinds of crops. These Minoans set up trading posts on islands in the Aegean Sea and in Asia Minor. The kings of Crete maintained strong navies to support Minoan trade.

In about 1628 B.C. a volcano erupted on a nearby island. Tidal waves caused by the eruption destroyed many coastal settlements on Crete. From that time on Minoan civilization grew weak. In about 1400 B.C. **Mycenaeans** (my·suh·NEE·uhnz) from the Greek mainland conquered central Crete.

☑ internet connect

TOPIC: Minoans
GO TO: go.hrw.com
KEYWORD: SP3 WH5

Have students access the Internet through the HRW Go site to conduct research on the Minoan civilization of ancient Crete. Then ask students to write an informative report about Minoan civilization. Instruct students to use standard grammar, spelling, sentence structure, and punctuation.

That's Interesting!

Although human habitation first began in present-day Greece about 55,000 years ago, the first people to speak the language we know as Greek were the Mycenaeans.

MAP ANSWER

Greece was in a central location with access to sea trade with Europe, Asia, and Africa.

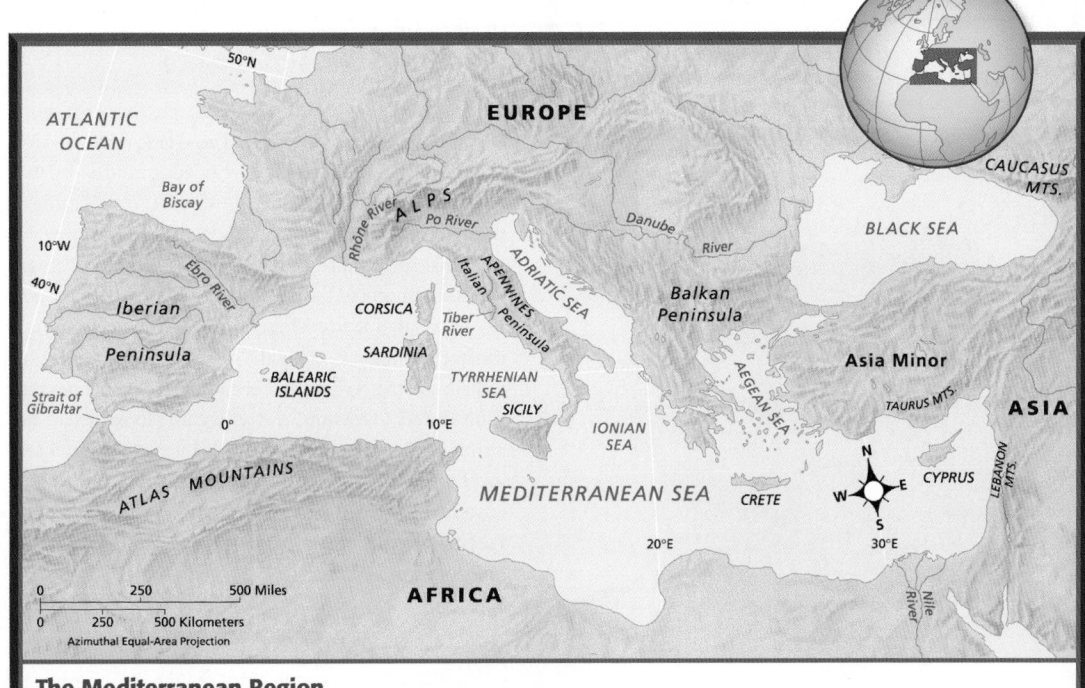

The Mediterranean Region
Interpreting Maps The geography of the Balkan Peninsula placed the Greeks in a central location in the Mediterranean, encouraging trade, colonization, and communication.

■ **Skills Assessment: Physical Systems** In what ways did the location of Greece encourage commerce and trade?

Technology Resources

CNN. Presents World Cultures: Yesterday and Today Segment 5: Crete: Past and Present

LEVEL 3: After students read the paragraphs under "The City-States of Greece," create a chart with four columns on the chalkboard. Label each column with these key features of the city-state: *small size, small population, setting on a hill,* and *public meeting place.* Have students copy the chart and list details about each key feature as it relates to the development of city-states. Then have students write details about each feature as it applies to their city or town.

HOMEWORK Have students draw a large map of the Balkan Peninsula and illustrate it with the geographic factors they have read about and discussed. Then have them make icons or models to represent how people made a living in ancient Greece and place the icons or models on the map.

CLOSE

Ask students to list ways in which all ancient Greeks were alike.

REVIEW

Have students complete the Section 1 Review on p. 109.

Interdisciplinary Connection

ARCHITECTURE. Although little is known about the earliest palaces, the later palaces of the Minoans and Mycenaeans are distinctive for the quality of their workmanship and the sophistication of their designs. The carefully laid-out palaces had wide staircases, multiple stories, vistas and facades, and storage rooms for goods and crops. Artisans painted the interior walls with scenes of everyday life. Built-in bathtubs and running water could be found inside the palaces.

Critical Thinking

Ask students what the remains of the palaces show about the societies that built them.

ANSWER: The palaces show that the societies were concerned with practical function as well as aesthetics.

MAP ANSWERS

1. Athens, Mycenae, Tiryns, Pylos, Troy, Knossos

2. They were traders. Transportation and commerce were easier by sea than across the mountains.

VISUAL RECORD ANSWER

Mycenaean artisans had highly developed, sophisticated skills.

Aegean Civilization, c. 1450 B.C.–700 B.C.
Interpreting Maps The early Greeks were great traders and warriors alike.

■ **Skills Assessment: 1. Locate** Locate cities on the Greek mainland and on Crete. **2. Drawing Conclusions** Why did the Greeks build their cities near the sea?

The Mycenaeans. The Mycenaeans controlled mainland Greece from about 1600 B.C. to about 1200 B.C. They were a warring people who grouped themselves into clans and tribes. Several related families formed a clan that was headed by a warrior. A number of clans made up a tribe that had its own chief. The Mycenaeans built fort-like cities in the Peloponnesus (pel·uh·puh·NEE·suhs), the southern part of Greece, as well as in north-central Greece. The Mycenaeans carried out raids throughout the eastern Mediterranean. However, by 1200 B.C. earthquakes and warfare had destroyed most of the Mycenaean cities.

The Mycenaeans made important contributions to the development of Greek civilization. After conquering Crete, the Mycenaeans adopted many elements of Minoan civilization. For instance, they used the Minoan system of writing. Called linear B, this writing system was an early form of Greek writing. The Mycenaeans kept records in linear B.

✔ **READING CHECK: Summarizing** In what ways did the Minoans and Mycenaeans influence Greek civilization?
Minoans made advances that the Mycenaeans passed on.

The City-States of Greece

During the 800s and 700s B.C. the Greeks formed a number of independent city-states. The Greek word for city-state is **polis.** A polis usually developed around a fort. As a city grew up around the fort, the idea of the polis came to mean the fort, its city, and the lands and small farming villages that surrounded the city and that supplied its food.

The concept of the polis was based on three basic and closely related ideas. These included the geographical territory of the city-state; the community that it represented; and the political and economic independence that it produced. Over time, the polis came to represent the center of Greek identity and its inhabitants were intensely loyal to it. The Greeks also understood the polis as an absolutely independent and self-sufficient community. Frequently, economic and political competition separated one polis from another.

INTERPRETING THE VISUAL RECORD
Mycenaean artifacts The Mycenaeans buried their dead in cone-shaped stone chambers. Silver and gold masks, cups, jewelry, and weapons were also placed in these tombs. *What do these artifacts reveal about the skills of Mycenaean artisans?*

ASSESS

Have students complete Daily Quiz 5.1. As Alternative Assessment, you may want to use the charts in this section's lessons.

RETEACH

Have students complete Main Idea Activity for English Language Learners and Special-Needs Students 5.1. Then have students create a web diagram for each section.

ENGLISH LANGUAGE LEARNERS

EXTEND

internet connect

Internet Activity: **go.hrw.com**
TOPIC: Ancient Writings KEYWORD: **SP3 WH5**

Have students access the Internet through the HRW Go site to conduct research about the writing systems of the Mediterranean. These can include linear B, cuneiform, hieroglyphics, and the early alphabet. Then ask students to construct their own model of a writing system. Ask them to create a few sentences for the class to decipher.

The Greek city-states were alike in many ways. First, they covered a small area of land. For example, Athens was smaller than the state of Rhode Island. Sparta was smaller than Connecticut. Yet these two city-states were very large compared to the others. Second, most city-states had a population of fewer than 10,000 people, most of whom were slaves and other non-citizens. Only free adult males had citizenship rights. Third, in most city-states the original fort was built on an **acropolis,** or hill. Temples and other public buildings also stood on the acropolis. Finally, each city-state had an **agora,** or marketplace. The agora also served as the main public meeting place. Citizens met in the agora to discuss common issues.

The polis gave ancient Greeks a sense of identity. Greek citizens believed that they owed loyalty to their polis. They loved their city-state and often were willing to die for it.

The Greeks placed great value on the political independence of each polis. Each city-state formed its own kind of government and laws. Each city-state also had its own calendar, money, and system of weights and measures.

However, all ancient Greeks had certain things in common. They spoke the same language; they tended to regard people who did not speak Greek as barbarians; and they shared many religious ideas, cultural characteristics, and social patterns. Great festivals also brought the Greeks together.

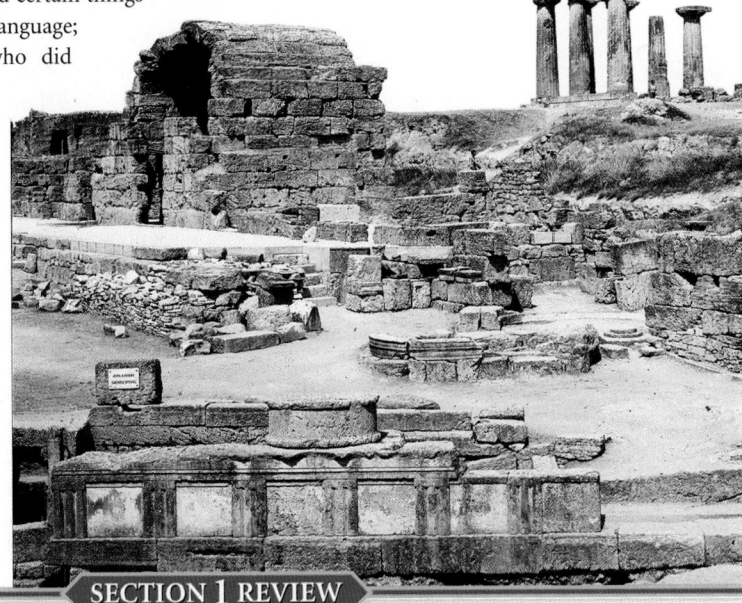

✔ **READING CHECK: Comparing and Contrasting** In what ways were the Greek city-states alike and different? all had a polis and agora, most had an acropolis; each formed its own government and laws

The agora of Corinth once bustled with marketplace and religious activity.

SECTION 1 REVIEW

1. **Define** and explain the significance:
   frescoes
   polis
   acropolis
   agora

2. **Identify** and explain the significance:
   Minoans
   Mycenaeans

Homework Practice Online
keyword: SP3 HP5

3. **Analyzing Information** Copy the outline map of ancient Greece below. Fill in and label the geographic features that made it hard for the ancient Greeks to become united.

4. **Finding the Main Idea**
   a. How did life in ancient Greece change after the fall of the Mycenaeans?
   b. Why was the development of the polis important in ancient Greece?

5. **Writing and Critical Thinking**
   Supporting a Point of View Imagine you are a citizen of a Greek city-state. Write a letter to a Greek leader explaining your reasons for wanting to open citizenship to all people in the city-state.
   Consider:
   • the qualifications for citizenship in ancient Greece
   • how Greek citizens felt about their polis
   • the things ancient Greeks had in common

◄SECTION►

1 REVIEW ANSWERS

❶ **Define**
• frescoes, p. 107
• polis, p. 108
• acropolis, p. 109
• agora, p. 109

❷ **Identify**
• Minoans, p. 107
• Mycenaeans, p. 107

❸ Students' maps should show the mountains that divided the Greek mainland and kept villages apart.

❹ a. After the fall of the Mycenaeans, the Greeks formed independent city-states. These were built around forts that were often on hilltops. They also had an agora, which was both a marketplace and a meeting place where citizens discussed common issues.

b. The polis gave Greeks a sense of identity and pride.

❺ Students' letters should express an understanding that only adult free males could vote. Slaves and women were excluded from citizenship. People of the city-states had great loyalty to their cities. They also had a great deal in common, including language, religion, and festivals, and a general arrogance toward outsiders. Students should use these details to support an argument for granting citizenship to all people in the city-state.

OBJECTIVES

1 **Explain the importance of Homer's works.**

2 **Identify major religious beliefs and practices of the ancient Greeks.**

3 **Describe changes that occurred in the governments of the Greek city-states.**

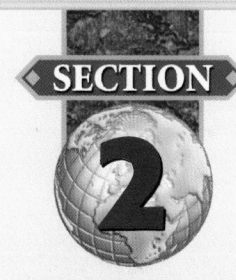

SECTION ❷

READ TO DISCOVER

❶ Why was the work of the poet Homer important?

❷ What were the main religious beliefs and practices of the ancient Greeks?

❸ How did the governments of the Greek city-states change over time?

DEFINE

myths
oracles
aristocracies
hoplite
tyrants
popular government
democracy

IDENTIFY

Iliad
Odyssey
Homer
Olympic Games

▶WHY IT MATTERS TODAY

Several nations in Europe and the Middle East have democratic monarchies somewhat like those in later Greek city-states. Use **CNN** or other **current event** sources to discover which nations still have kings and queens, as well as elected assemblies. Record your findings in your journal.

CNN StudentNews.com

Greek Government and Society

The Main Idea
Greeks sought to improve their lives through religious practices and experiments in government.

The Story Continues *Between 1000 B.C. and 700 B.C., the Greeks based their governments on the old system of tribes and chiefs. These tribal systems gradually developed into small kingdoms that were often at war with one another. By 700 B.C., however, many city-states had overthrown their kings. New forms of government began to evolve.*

Greek Culture in the Homeric Age

The Greeks of this period did not have a very advanced civilization. Few people could write, so most communication was oral, or spoken. Traveling poets sang or recited folk songs, ballads, or epics. An epic is a long poem about heroes and great events.

The *Iliad* and the *Odyssey*. Sometime during the 700s B.C. much of this oral poetry was gathered into two great epics, the *Iliad* and the *Odyssey*. According to tradition, the blind poet **Homer** wrote these epics. However, we do not really know who the author or authors were. Nevertheless, this period is often called the Homeric Age.

The *Iliad* tells the legend of the Trojan War. The story begins when a Trojan prince named Paris falls in love with Helen, the wife of a Mycenaean king. Paris kidnaps Helen and takes her with him to Troy. The Mycenaeans lay siege to Troy for 10 years but cannot capture the city. Finally, the Mycenaeans win by building a wooden horse so huge that all their best soldiers can hide inside. They give the horse to the Trojans as a "gift." Thinking they have won, the Trojans bring the horse into the city. That night the Mycenaean soldiers leap out of the horse and conquer Troy.

The *Odyssey* tells what happened after the Trojan War. It describes the adventures of the Mycenaean king Odysseus on his way home from the war. Along the way he encounters many dangers as well as interference from the gods. In the story it takes Odysseus 10 years to reach his home city-state of Ithaca. Today we use the word *odyssey* to refer to any long, adventure-filled journey.

Greek religious beliefs. The religion that the Greeks developed during the Homeric Age differed from that of the Egyptians, Hebrews, and Persians. For the most part, Greek religion did not emphasize high standards of personal morality. Instead, the ancient Greeks looked to religion for three things. First, they wanted religion to explain nature. For example, they wanted to know what caused lightning, thunder, and the change of seasons. Second, they wanted religion to explain the emotions that sometimes cause people to lose self-control. The Greeks considered self-control very important. Third, they believed religion could bring them certain benefits

Holt Researcher 🔵

go.hrw.com
KEYWORD: Holt Researcher
FreeFind: Homer
After reading more about Homer on the Holt Researcher, identify how his works transcend Greek culture to convey universal themes.

TEACH OBJECTIVE 1

ALL LEVELS: Ask students why the poems of Homer were important to the ancient Greeks. *(told about the Trojan War; form of entertainment; told about Greek history and heroes)* Then ask what modern scholars might learn about ancient Greeks from these epics. *(They would learn about the history and culture of the Greeks in the Homeric Age.)*

TEACH OBJECTIVE 2

LEVEL 3: Ask students to read a short Greek myth, such as one in Edith Hamilton's *Mythology.* Have students write a brief essay that explains Greek beliefs about natural phenomena.

HOMEWORK Have students read a myth and list the characteristics of the myth. Later, students may compare their lists to determine common characteristics of myths.

TEACH OBJECTIVE 3

LEVEL 1: Tell students that between about 700 and 500 B.C., the Greek city-states had a number of different types of government. Have students fill in a chart with heads as shown below.

ENGLISH LANGUAGE LEARNERS

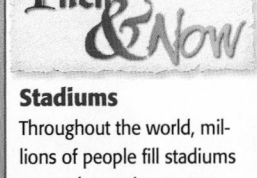

Government	Who ruled	Why rulers lost power
kingdoms	kings	overthrown by nobles
aristocracies	aristocrats	overthrown by tyrants

here and now, such as long life, good luck, or a good harvest. The Greeks did not expect their religion to save them from sin. Also, Greeks of the Homeric Age were not as concerned as other ancient peoples about what happened after death. They believed that the spirits of almost all people went to a gray, gloomy underworld ruled by the god Hades. It was not viewed as a place of either punishment or reward.

To explain their world, the Greeks created myths. **Myths** are traditional stories about gods, goddesses, and heroes. The Greeks gave human qualities and personalities to their gods, who were said to live on Mount Olympus in northern Greece. Zeus was the king of the gods. One of his daughters was the goddess Athena, protector of wisdom and womanly goodness. She was also the special protector of the great city-states. Athens was named in her honor. Apollo, one of Zeus's sons, was the god of light, music, and poetry. Dionysus was the god of fertility and wine. The Greeks believed that the gods spoke through priests and priestesses at special places called **oracles.** Greeks would often travel to oracles to ask questions about the future.

Pleasing the gods was an important part of Greek life. Showing strength and bravery in athletic contests was one way to do this. The most important contests were the **Olympic Games,** held every four years in honor of Zeus. Only men could watch or compete in these games. The Olympics were probably held for the first time in 776 B.C. Events included boxing, foot races, javelin and discus throwing, and wrestling. At the end of the games, the winners received wreaths of wild olive branches. There were no second or third prizes.

✔ **READING CHECK: Finding the Main Idea** What were the main aspects of Greek culture? epic poems, religion, myths, oracles, athletic contests

Greek Government: From Kings to Democracy

The city-states of Greece had originated as small kingdoms ruled by warrior chieftains from their hilltop fortresses. These chieftains had in turn relied on wealthy landowners to support their rule and to form their armies. This was because only wealthy landowners could afford the expensive horses, chariots, and bronze weapons necessary to discourage raiders and to maintain each kingdom's security. Over time, the small group of landowners, known as *aristocrats,* or "best men" in Greek, came to represent each city-state's noble class. Little by little, the nobles gained more land and power. By about 700 B.C. nobles in many of the Greek city-states had overthrown their kings and had taken power themselves.

Greek city-states that were controlled by nobles were known as **aristocracies.** Originally, the word *aristocracy* meant "rule by the best." Over time, however, the term came to describe a privileged social class, usually composed of the wealthiest landowners in the city-state. Aristocrats controlled virtually every aspect of Greek society during these years. They held a monopoly over the military and, as major landowners, they controlled the economy. Aristocrats acted

Then & Now

Stadiums

Throughout the world, millions of people fill stadiums to watch sporting events. Ancient Greeks built the first stadiums about 2,500 years ago. The first Olympic Games were held in a stadium especially built for them.

Today, stadiums also have more than one use. For example, Yankee Stadium in New York City has baseball games and music events. Of course, most modern stadiums are larger than the ancient ones. **How do stadiums reflect Greek influences on modern architecture?**

THEN & NOW ANSWER
They are circular with seats rising in terraces around the playing field.

Culture

Women also participated in their own Olympic Games. This competition was held in honor of Hera, wife of Zeus. It took place at a different time than the men's games. Little is known about these games, but one Greek reported that unmarried women competed in a footrace that was five-sixths as long as the men's race.

Critical Thinking

Ask students if they think the winners of the women's games were treated as enthusiastically as the winners of the men's games. Have them support their point of view.

ANSWER: No, women were not considered to be men's equals, so they most likely would not have been treated as enthusiastically.

CLOSE

Have students representing nonaristocratic male citizens, women, and slaves in Greek city-states describe how changes in government between 650 B.C. and 500 B.C. affected them.

REVIEW

Have students complete the Section 2 Review on p. 112.

ASSESS

Have students complete Daily Quiz 5.2. As Alternative Assessment, use the chart or the essay in this section's lessons.

RETEACH

Have students complete Main Idea Activity for English Language Learners and Special-Needs Students 5.2. Then ask students to create a web diagram for each of the section's main ideas.
ENGLISH LANGUAGE LEARNERS

EXTEND

Have students select a passage from the *Odyssey* to present orally. Discuss the universal themes presented in this epic.
COOPERATIVE LEARNING, BLOCK SCHEDULING

SECTION 2 REVIEW ANSWERS

❶ Define
- myths, p. 111
- oracles, p. 111
- aristocracies, p. 111
- hoplite, p. 112
- tyrants, p. 112
- popular government, p. 112
- democracy, p. 112

❷ Identify
- *Iliad*, p. 110
- *Odyssey*, p. 110
- Homer, p. 110
- Olympic Games, p. 111

❸ Government: kingdoms, aristocracies, tyrannies, democracies; Writings: *Iliad, Odyssey;* Religious Events: visits to oracles, Olympic Games

❹ a. Kings fell because the aristocrats became too strong. The aristocrats fell because nonaristocrats acquired weapons and overthrew them. Tyrants fell because they abused power.

b. Homer's work was great literature and recorded the values and history of the Greeks.

c. They used religion to explain natural events and people's emotions and to bring them benefits.

❺ A tyrant needed courage and boldness to seize power, sound business judgment, and fairness in order to keep the support of the people.

The rise of the heavily armed, well-trained Greek infantry soldier known as the hoplite did much to weaken the power of the aristocrats.

as judges and determined the city-state's laws and punishments. They even held control over religion, since the gods supposedly would not listen to commoners. Before the 600s B.C. aristocrats were the only people who participated in politics.

In time, social and economic changes took place that weakened the power of the aristocrats. By the 600s B.C. some wealthy nonaristocrats could afford the costly weapons and armor needed by the soldiers of the times. A new kind of nonaristocratic soldier called the **hoplite** emerged in many parts of Greece. Hoplites were heavy infantry who carried long spears and who fought in closely spaced rows. The cavalry and chariots of the aristocrats were no match for the powerful hoplite formations. As hoplites became more important to the defense of the city-state, they demanded more say in its daily government. Poor citizens, especially farmers, were also unhappy with the rule of the nobles. Many citizens began to look for leaders who could provide a better life.

The leaders who were able to bring a better life to the people were the **tyrants.** A tyrant was someone who illegally took power but had the people's support. Between 650 B.C. and 500 B.C. tyrants ruled many city-states. At first, many tyrants ruled well. They ended the nobles' fights for power and promoted more trade. In some cases, however, these powerful rulers became unjust. The word *tyrant* came to mean someone who uses absolute power brutally.

During the 150 years after about 650 B.C., many Greek city-states overthrew their tyrants. In some of these city-states, the idea of **popular government** began to take root. This is the idea that people can and should rule themselves. Some city-states, such as Athens, developed forms of **democracy,** or government in which citizens take part. Even in these developing democracies, however, full political rights were allowed to only a small part of the population. Women, for example, did not have political rights. Slaves, who often represented a large part of the city-state's population, also lacked political rights. Other Greek city-states, including the powerful Sparta, either maintained their aristocratic forms of government or restored rule by kings or nobles. Even in monarchies and aristocracies, however, a council of citizens now limited the individual ruler's power.

✔ **READING CHECK: Analyzing Information** How did Greek government change between the 700s B.C. and the late 500s B.C.? passed from monarchy through aristocracy and tyrants to democracy

SECTION 2 REVIEW

1. **Define** and explain the significance:
   myths   hoplite
   oracles   tyrants
   aristocracies popular government
                  democracy

2. **Identify** and explain the significance:
   Iliad
   Odyssey
   Homer
   Olympic Games

Homework Practice Online
keyword: SP3 HP5

3. **Categorizing** Copy the web diagram below. Use it to name the type of government, important pieces of writing, and religious events that were part of the Homeric Age (c. 900 B.C. to 750 B.C.).

Government
Writings
Homeric Age
Religious Events

4. **Finding the Main Idea**

   a. Why did the rulers of governments in the Greek city-states change?

   b. Why might Homer's work have been important to later generations?

   c. How did the Greeks view the role of religion in their lives?

5. **Writing and Critical Thinking**

   Making Generalizations In a paragraph, describe the qualities a tyrant needed to be successful.
   Consider:
   • how the tyrants came to power
   • what some tyrants were able to accomplish
   • the importance of the support of the public to a tyrant's rule

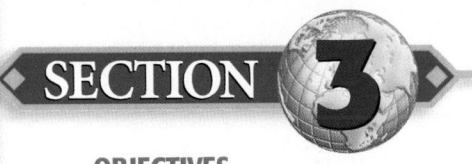

SECTION 3

OBJECTIVES

1 Analyze the society of Sparta.

2 Explain the development of democracy in Athens.

🔊 LET'S GET STARTED!

As students enter the classroom, ask them to describe the types of government that developed in the Greek city-states. (*First Greek city-states were governed by kings. The kings were overthrown by aristocrats. Eventually the aristocrats were overthrown by tyrants who, in turn, were overthrown by citizens who set up popular governments.*) Explain to students that in Section 3 they will learn about the government and society of two of the most important city-states: Sparta and Athens.

SECTION 3

READ TO DISCOVER

❶ What kind of society developed in Sparta?

❷ How did democracy develop in Athens?

DEFINE

helots
ephors
metics
archons
direct democracy
representative democracy

IDENTIFY

Draco
Solon
Peisistratus
Cleisthenes

▶ WHY IT MATTERS TODAY

The United States and other democracies trace the idea of government and people working together from Athenian democracy. Use [CNN Student News.com] or other **current event** sources to discover ways in which the United States government and ordinary citizens work together. Record your findings in your journal.

Sparta and Athens

The Main Idea
Sparta and Athens developed very different societies and systems of government.

The Story Continues *Greek city-states were both similar and different. The two most important city-states, Athens and Sparta, showed great differences. While Athens was known for its laws and government, Sparta was known for the physical strength and discipline of its people. According to legend, Spartan laws were intentionally not written down so that people would have to memorize them as a further test of discipline.*

Sparta: The Military Ideal

By the late 1100s B.C., invaders from the north had overrun most of the Peloponnesus and forced many of the people they conquered to work for them. They called these conquered people **helots.** The invaders conquered the village that became their capital, Sparta. Unlike other city-states, Sparta was located in a valley, not on a hill. Moreover, it was not surrounded by walls for defense. The Peloponnesus was isolated and mountainous. This may help to explain why Sparta developed very differently from Athens, becoming a rigid and highly militarized society.

Spartan society. Sparta had three social groups. Members of the first group, known as the equals, were descended from the invaders. They controlled the city-state. Land was divided equally among these citizens and their families. Along with the land went helots to work it. Sparta's second group was made up of half-citizens. They were free, paid taxes, and served in the army. Half-citizens, however, had no political power. Some half-citizens farmed. Others lived in the towns, where they worked in trade and industry. Some half-citizens even became rich.

Helots made up the third and lowest group in Sparta. The helots became the slaves of the Spartan city-state. The Spartans decided how the helots should work and live. However, the helots greatly outnumbered the Spartans. Therefore, the Spartans had to use force to control them. Fear of a helot uprising was one reason the Spartans created a military society. The Spartans systematically terrorized the helots to keep them from rebelling. Not surprisingly, the helots hated the Spartans.

INTERPRETING THE VISUAL RECORD

A Spartan soldier Some of Sparta's half-citizens became artisans. Much of their work also focused on Sparta's military. *How does this bronze figure of a Spartan soldier show that artisans were also involved in Sparta's military society?*

SECTION 3 RESOURCES

REPRODUCIBLE RESOURCES

▶ Guided Reading Strategy 5.3

▶ Readings in World History 18, 19

TECHNOLOGY RESOURCES

▶ One-Stop Planner 5.3

▶ Holt Researcher: World History: Solon

▶ World History and Cultures Video Program 3

▶ Homework Practice Online

▶ Online Maps, Charts, and Graphs: The Long Walls of Athens

REINFORCEMENT, REVIEW, AND ASSESSMENT

▶ Section 3 Review, p. 117

▶ Daily Quiz 5.3

▶ Main Idea Activity 5.3

▶ English Audio Summary 5.3

▶ Spanish Audio Summary 5.3

VISUAL RECORD ANSWER

Artisans helped to promote the respect for and tradition of military excellence.

THE GREEK CITY-STATES **113**

HOMEWORK Have students reread the quote from Lycurgus on page 114. Then ask them to write a paragraph describing how most Americans today would react to such treatment of children.

History Maker

LYCURGUS. Scholars are not certain whether Lycurgus was a historical or mythical figure. If he was a real person, he probably lived in the 700s or 800s B.C. According to legend, Lycurgus developed Sparta's laws and government. Legend held that Lycurgus and the Spartan people were descended from Hercules, a mythical hero of incredible strength. Lycurgus passed laws that eliminated inequalities and luxuries from Spartan life. He emphasized discipline and obedience. He banned the use of money in Sparta and redistributed land. He is most famous for creating the Spartan system of communal education for men. Laws were taught in schools so that every citizen would memorize them.

Critical Thinking

Ask students why scholars know more about the government and society of Athens than they do about Sparta.

ANSWER: Students should suggest that because Spartans emphasized military preparedness, they did not leave the large body of political, philosophical, and historical writings that the Athenians left behind.

LINK TO TODAY ANSWER
Because scholars have few ruins to study, they have little evidence of how Spartans lived or how they organized their households, businesses, government, and society in general.

114

Analyzing Primary Sources

Identifying a Point of View How did the treatment of children in Sparta reflect Spartan ideals? harsh discipline

Link to Today These ruins are all that is left of the once-thriving city-state of Sparta. How might having few ruins today limit our knowledge of Spartan society?

Government in Sparta. Sparta's government had several parts. Two kings were at the head of the government. One king led the army, while the other took care of matters at home. A Council of Elders was made up of 28 male citizens over the age of 60. These were usually wealthy, aristocratic men. The council proposed laws and served as a criminal court. The final part of Sparta's government was an assembly that included all male citizens over 30 years old. The assembly voted to accept or reject laws proposed by the Council of Elders. The assembly also elected five **ephors** for one-year terms. The ephors made sure that the kings stayed within the law. They also had complete control over the education of young Spartans.

Life in Sparta's military society. Sparta controlled the lives of its citizens from birth to death. The goal was to make every adult male citizen part of the military machine. The Spartan military worked to control the helots and to expand Spartan power.

The development of Spartan fighting men began at birth. A group of officials examined newborn babies. Any child who seemed unhealthy was left to die. One Spartan lawmaker, Lycurgus, ordered the following practices:

Primary Source

"The Spartans bathed their infants in wine rather than water, to test and toughen their bodies. Children were subject to strict discipline from the start, and were taught not to be afraid in the dark, not to be finicky about their food, and not to be peevish [moody] and tearful."

Lycurgus, as quoted by Plutarch in *Parallel Lives*

At the age of seven, boys left home to live in military barracks. Military training formed the basis of their education, along with reading and writing. From ages 18 to 20, they trained specifically for war.

At the age of 20, Spartan male citizens began their military service. They could now marry but could not live at home until they were 30. They were not allowed to engage in any trade or business. The authorities believed that the love of money interfered with military discipline. Men remained available for military service until they were 60 years old. Older men were expected to work for the public good rather than focus on their private lives.

As the future wives and mothers of Spartan soldiers, Spartan girls also had to be strong and healthy. They received strict physical training and were taught to be devoted to the city-state. Both boys and girls studied music in order to learn discipline and coordination.

This training by the Spartan state led to a strong government and an almost unbeatable army. The Spartans, however, paid a high price for their power—they gave up their individual freedom. In addition, Spartan society created little in art, literature, philosophy, or science.

✔ **READING CHECK: Identifying Bias** How did the need for defense influence the way the Spartan government ruled its people? emphasized militarism

ALL LEVELS: Have students match each of the following reforms with the Athenian who enacted them.

Descriptions	Identifications
1. developed a form of direct democracy	a. Draco
2. improved Athens's economy but clashed with nobles	b. Cleisthenes
3. created Athens's first written law code	c. Solon
4. set up a court system with citizen jurors	d. Peisistratus

(1: b, 2: d, 3: a, 4: c)

LEVEL 3: Ask students to compare the basic features of direct and representative democracies. *(All citizens participate in making the decisions in a direct democracy, while citizens elect representatives to run the government for them in a representative democracy.)* Ask students if they think a direct democracy would work well in the United States, and why or why not.

Athens: The Birth of Democracy

Athens developed very differently from Sparta. Athens is located on the Attic peninsula, one of the least fertile areas in Greece. Thus the Athenians turned to the sea, and many became sea traders. The introduction of coined money in the 600s B.C. also stimulated trade by making it easier to buy and sell goods. The Athenians built their city inland, perhaps to protect it from pirates, and constructed Piraeus (py·REE·uhs) as its special port. Athens itself was a typical polis built around the rocky hill of the Acropolis. In times of war, people took refuge inside the city's strong walls.

Athenian society. Citizens formed the top group in Athenian society. Citizens might be rich aristocrats or poor farmers. Only Athenian-born men, however, had full political rights. Female citizens could not vote or hold office.

The next group in Athenian society was the **metics.** These people were noncitizens because they had been born outside Athens. Metics usually worked as merchants or artisans. They were free and paid the same taxes as citizens. Metics, however, could not take part in government or own land.

Slaves stood at the bottom of Athenian society. Like all Greeks, Athenians considered slavery natural and necessary. Slaves were people captured in war. They were owned by masters and treated as property. Sometimes masters freed slaves, who then became metics. In time, slaves and metics made up more than half of Athens's population.

Early government in Athens. After Athens's monarchy ended, the city-state had an aristocratic government. Only citizens who owned land held office. All adult male citizens, however, met in an assembly. They elected generals in time of war. They also elected nine **archons,** rulers who served one-year terms.

At first, Athens's laws were not written down. In the late 600s B.C., many nonaristocrats complained about this. An archon named **Draco** is believed to have created Athens's first written law code around 621 B.C. Draco's laws were so harsh and severe that today we call a harsh law a Draconian law.

As time passed, nobles and metics became wealthy from trade but many farmers grew poorer. More and more citizens were sold into slavery to pay their debts. Discontent and anger spread among the poor. **Solon,** who became an archon in 594 B.C., settled the disputes between creditors and debtors by erasing the debts of the poor and outlawing slavery for debt. He freed people who had become slaves to pay their debts. Solon believed that this was the best way to help the city. He once wrote,

> **History Makers Speak**
>
> **❝These are the evils loosed upon the people:**
> **Of the poor, many, sold, in shameful chains,**
> **Take the road leading to a foreign land. . . .**
> **Thus the public evil reaches each man at home.❞**
>
> Solon, *Eunomy*

CONNECTING TO Civics

Rights and Responsibilities in Ancient Greece

The ancient Athenians took their duties seriously. All free men over the age of 18 were members of the assembly, which met regularly to make decisions and solve problems. Men could speak, make motions, and vote. The decisions of the assembly were law.

Each year 500 men were chosen by lot to serve on the Council, which attended to state business. Athenian trials were judged by juries of 101 to 1,001 people, and each year 6,000 citizens were chosen by lot to serve on the juries, whose decisions were final.

Understanding Civics

Why would the Athenian form of government be difficult to use today?

Analyzing Primary Sources

Evaluating According to Solon, how did slavery affect all Athenians, even those who were not themselves slaves? removes citizens from the community

This juror's token from the 300s B.C. symbolizes the importance of the individual citizen in the Athenian judicial system.

Government

In addition to erasing debt and outlawing slavery for debt, Solon also wanted to eliminate social pressures in Athenian society by basing citizenship on wealth rather than birth into the aristocracy.

Critical Thinking

Ask students why basing citizenship on wealth might relieve some of the social tensions in Athens. Have them support their point of view.

ANSWER: Students should note that some nonaristocrats—the metics—had become wealthy, but since they were not citizens they could neither vote nor hold office. When they were allowed to hold political office, they had less reason to resent the aristocrats' power.

CONNECTING TO CIVICS ANSWER

Students should recognize that populations are too large and society is too complex now for direct democracy to work well.

That's Interesting!

U.S. bankruptcy laws say that a person who has legally declared bankruptcy cannot be held responsible for debts previously incurred. The source of these laws is Solon's ordinance canceling the burdens of Greek debtors.

Spotlight on CITIZENSHIP

Pericles was one of the great leaders in Athenian history. In fact, the 30-year period of his rule became known as the Age of Pericles. He fought wars to expand Athens's power and influence. He restored democracy that had been lost after the death of Cleisthenes. He built Athens's navy and beautified the city with new buildings and sculptures. But his rule was not without controversy. Have students work in pairs to investigate the Age of Pericles. Urge them to assess Pericles's accomplishments both in light of the time in which he lived and of the legacy he left to Greece and Western civilization. Have students share their findings with the class. Encourage them to use visuals such as charts and time lines to enhance their presentation.
COOPERATIVE LEARNING, BLOCK SCHEDULING

CLOSE

Have students write a paragraph explaining whether they would rather have lived in Sparta or Athens. Ask them to provide at least three reasons to support their point of view.

REVIEW

Have students complete the Section 3 Review on p. 117.

Interdisciplinary Connection

LITERATURE. The poet Terpandros spent most of his life in Sparta. According to the *Suda Lexicon,* an ancient Greek work, "The Spartans were fighting amongst themselves and sent to Lesbos for the musician Terpandros; he came and made their minds tranquil and stopped the quarrel."

Critical Thinking

Ask students what they learned about Spartans from this excerpt from the *Suda Lexicon.*

ANSWER: Spartans valued music and found creative ways to manage conflict.

SKILLS PRACTICE ANSWERS

1. favors the many instead of the few; laws provide equal justice; leadership based on ability

2. Athenian democracy: equal rights to all citizens; Spartan government: most power to aristocrats; Athens: could pursue private interests; Sparta: interests of city-state above private interests

3. United States: representative; Athens: direct

4. Athenian government was advanced; citizens of surrounding city-states probably had less freedom, no participation in government

---

SKILL-BUILDING STRATEGIES — Analyzing Historical Context

Athenian Democracy

Analyzing historical context involves trying to understand events and people within the context, or circumstances, of their times. Historians take up this task because ideas and notions have meant different things at various times in history. For example, today, many people would probably consider Athenian democracy limited since it did not include women, slaves, or those born outside Athens. In analyzing historical context, historians seek to identify the beliefs and values of a particular group during a specific era. This helps them to evaluate and understand the choices and decisions that people have made throughout the different periods of history.

A Historian's View

The Greek historian Thucydides is often called the first true historian because he took a critical look at historical evidence. Partly for this reason, he is widely recognized as the greatest historian of ancient times, even though he wrote only one work. The following excerpt is his account of a speech given by Pericles about Athenian democracy.

"Our constitution does not copy the laws of neighbouring states; we are rather a pattern to others than imitators ourselves. Its administration favours the many instead of the few; this is why it is called a democracy. If we look to the laws, they afford equal justice to all in their private differences; if to social standing, advancement in public life falls to reputation for capacity [ability], class considerations not being allowed to interfere with merit.... The freedom which we enjoy in our government extends also to our ordinary life. There, far from exercising a jealous surveillance [secret observation] over each other, we do not feel called upon to be angry with our neighbor for doing what he likes. ... But all this ease in our private relations does not make us lawless as citizens. Against this fear is our chief safeguard, teaching us to obey the magistrates and the laws."

Although Athens was named after a woman—the goddess Athena—women could not participate in its government. This temple to Athena, the Erechtheion, was built between about 421 B.C. and 405 B.C.

Skills Reminder

To analyze historical context, identify the topic by determining the person or group as well as the time period you are examining. Recognize clues that explain attitudes and beliefs. Look for words, phrases, or quotes that provide reasons for a person's or group's choices and decisions. This will help you establish the historical context. Then formulate a comparison. Evaluate how the group's actions and decisions differ from those of later or present-day societies.

Skills Practice

1. According to Pericles, what were the advantages of Athenian democracy?
2. How did the Athenian government differ from that of Sparta?
3. How did Athenian democracy differ from democracy in the United States today?
4. Given the historical context of the time, was the Athenian form of government advanced? Explain your answer.

ASSESS

Have students complete Daily Quiz 5.3. As Alternative Assessment, have students complete the role-playing or the matching exercises in this section's lessons.

RETEACH

Have students complete Main Idea Activity for English Language Learners and Special-Needs Students 5.3. Instruct students to create a Venn diagram in which they use correct social studies terminology to compare and contrast the society and government of Sparta and Athens. They should use the later Athens government. (*Alike—three social groups: equals/citizens, half-citizens/metics,*

EXTEND

Organize students into groups of five and direct them to prepare a live TV broadcast about government or social conditions in Sparta or Athens. Are people satisfied? What should be changed? Who benefits? Is it fair? Students should take the roles of reporters, news anchor, and citizens and half-citizens.
COOPERATIVE LEARNING, BLOCK SCHEDULING

Democracy in Athens

621 B.C.	594 B.C.	546 B.C.–527 B.C.	508 B.C.	461 B.C.–429 B.C.
Law code attributed to Draco was drawn up.	Solon abolished enslavement for debt, defined political rights in terms of wealth rather than birth, and established court of appeals.	Peisistratus, tyrant who ruled with support of lower classes, may have divided nobles' estates among poor farmers.	Cleisthenes broke up power of aristocrats and created the Council of Five Hundred, chosen from local government units, with wide power.	Pericles opened offices to all male citizens and provided that officeholders be paid.

Solon also made changes in Athens's government. He divided all citizens into four groups based on wealth. The two richest groups could hold public office. All citizens, however, could sit in the assembly that elected those officials. Solon set up a court made up of citizen jurors. Solon's changes did not end Athens's problems, however. Between about 546 B.C. and 527 B.C., **Peisistratus** (py·SIS·truh·tuhs) ruled over Athens as a tyrant. Although Peisistratus improved Athens's economy, he clashed with the nobles. After the rule of Peisistratus's sons, the nobles returned to power.

Athenian democracy. In about 507 B.C., **Cleisthenes** (KLYS·thuh·neez) seized power in Athens and turned it into a democracy. First, he divided Athens's citizens into 10 tribes. Then he had each tribe choose 50 men. These men formed the Council of Five Hundred. Members served for one year and could not be chosen more than twice. The council proposed laws to the assembly, but the assembly had final authority. Athens's courts also became more democratic. Jurors were citizens chosen by lot. Each man could plead his own case to the jury. The jury voted on each case by secret ballot. The form of democracy Athens had under Cleisthenes is called **direct democracy.** That is, all citizens participated directly in making decisions. Present-day democracies such as the United States use **representative democracy.** That is, citizens elect representatives to govern for them.

✔ **READING CHECK: Supporting a Point of View** Which leader did the most to help lead Athens to democracy? Cleisthenes

Holt Researcher
go.hrw.com
KEYWORD: Holt Researcher
FreeFind: Solon
After reading more about Solon on the Holt Researcher, make a chart comparing Solon's government to the U.S. government today.

SECTION 3 REVIEW

1. **Define** and explain the significance:
   helots
   ephors
   metics
   archons
   direct democracy
   representative democracy

2. **Identify** and explain the significance:
   Draco
   Solon
   Peisistratus
   Cleisthenes

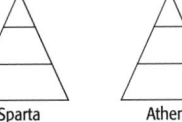
Homework Practice Online
keyword: SP3 HP5

3. **Categorizing** Copy the two pyramids below. Label one *Sparta* and the other one *Athens.* Place the different groups in Spartan and Athenian society in the correct part of the pyramid and describe what part each group played in its city-state.

Sparta   Athens

4. **Finding the Main Idea**
   a. How did Sparta build its military society?
   b. What changes led to Athens's aristocratic government becoming a democracy?
   c. How does direct democracy differ from representative democracy?

5. **Writing and Critical Thinking**
   Making Predictions Explain what the results might have been if Solon had not changed the way citizens in debt were treated and the way citizens could receive a hearing in court.
   Consider:
   • how those citizens were treated before Solon's changes
   • what effect Solon's changes had

---

❶ **Define**
• helots, p. 113
• ephors, p. 114
• metics, p. 115
• archons, p. 115
• direct democracy, p. 117
• representative democracy, p. 117

❷ **Identify**
• Draco, p. 115
• Solon, p. 115
• Peisistratus, p. 117
• Cleisthenes, p. 117

❸ Answers given in top to bottom order. Sparta: equals, half-citizens, helots; Athens: citizens, metics, slaves

❹ a. Young boys began military training at age 7 and served in the military until age 60.

b. Cleisthenes broke up the power of the aristocrats and created the Council of Five Hundred, comprised of citizens elected by their tribe. The council proposed laws, which were approved or vetoed by the Assembly made up of all citizens.

c. In a direct democracy, all citizens vote on all issues and laws. In a representative democracy, citizens vote for representatives who govern for them.

❺ If Solon had not changed the way citizens who were in debt were treated, the society would have been depleted as more and more citizens became slaves. The old policy might also have pushed poorer citizens to revolt and overthrow their government.

OBJECTIVES

1 Explain the basis of Athens's economy.

2 Describe the family life and education of Athenians.

MAP ANSWER

Olbia

READ TO DISCOVER

❶ What activities formed the basis of Athens's economy?

❷ What were Athenian family life and education like?

DEFINE

terracing
import
export
pedagogue
ethics
rhetoric

IDENTIFY

Sappho
Sophists

WHY IT MATTERS TODAY

Training in public speaking and debate helps candidates in the United States run for office, much as it helped the Greeks take part in public life. Use CNN News.com or other **current event** sources to find examples of officials with public speaking and debating skills. Record your findings in your journal.

CNN Student News.com

Daily Life in Athens

The Main Idea
Daily life in Athens consisted of simple economic and educational pursuits, and family concerns.

The Story Continues *In most city-states, private and public life were carefully balanced. As far as we know, citizens of most Greek city-states, except Sparta, lived their daily lives in much the same way as the people of Athens. Their days were filled with work, family, and educational pursuits.*

The Athenian Economy

Most Athenian citizens were farmers who grew olives, grapes, and figs, which they planted on terraced hillsides. **Terracing** means carving small, flat plots of land from hillsides.

The Athenian assembly voted to send farmers and workers to set up overseas colonies. This spread Greek culture throughout the Mediterranean and promoted trade. Colonies imported goods from, and exported goods to, Greece. An **import** is a good or service bought from another country or region. An **export** is a good or service sold to another country or region.

Trade was the mainstay of Athens's economy. The Athenians exported olive oil, wine, and household items, and imported grain and other foodstuffs. Athenian ships sailed throughout the Mediterranean world.

✔ **READING CHECK: Categorizing** What goods did Athenian farmers, metics, and traders produce or handle? vases, olives, grapes, wine

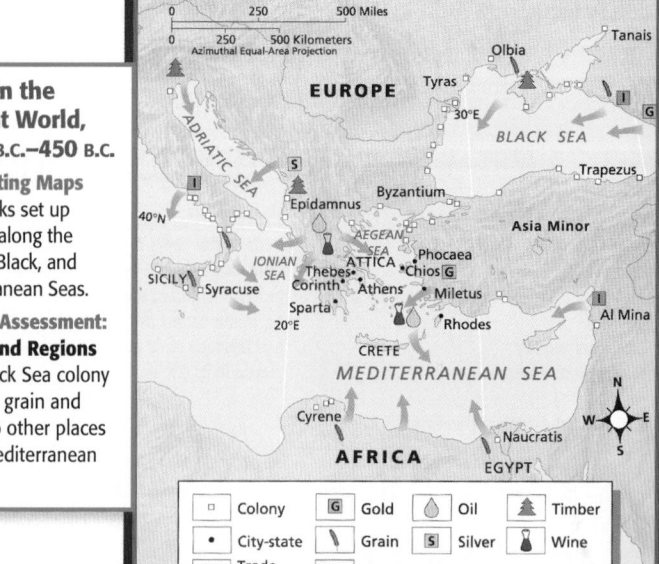

Trade in the Ancient World, c. 750 B.C.–450 B.C.

Interpreting Maps
The Greeks set up colonies along the Aegean, Black, and Mediterranean Seas.

■ **Skills Assessment: Places and Regions** What Black Sea colony exported grain and timber to other places in the Mediterranean region?

	Colony	G	Gold	🛢	Oil	🌲	Timber
•	City-state	\	Grain	S	Silver	🏺	Wine
➡	Trade route	I	Iron				

TEACH OBJECTIVE 1

ALL LEVELS: Make a web diagram on the chalkboard with *Athenian Economy* at the center. Then write *Agriculture* and *Trade*, circle each, and connect them to the first circle. Have students read the paragraphs on the Athenian economy and complete the web. (*Agriculture: poor soil; terracing; olives, grapes, figs, olive oil, wine. Trade: set up colonies; imported grain and foodstuffs; exported vases and household items*)
ENGLISH LANGUAGE LEARNERS

TEACH OBJECTIVE 2

LEVEL 3: Have students create a chart with two headings: *Female* and *Male*. Then have them fill in the columns with equivalent facts about the lives and duties of females and males in Athens. Have students combine their ideas in a class chart to be used for discussion. **COOPERATIVE LEARNING**

HOMEWORK Have students identify subjects that Greek boys learned in school at different ages and discuss why the subjects differed.

Home and Family Life

Athenians built magnificent temples and other public buildings. However, most Athenian families lived in simple homes. Generally, most Athenians believed that money should be spent on buildings to benefit the whole community, not on private homes. Their one-story houses, made of sun-dried brick, sat close to the street. The door to the home opened from the street into a courtyard. From the courtyard, doors opened into other parts of the home. These included the living room, dining room, bedrooms, storerooms, and kitchen. Lamps that burned olive oil provided dim light. The houses had no plumbing. Residents had to fill jars with water at the fountain near the agora.

Marriage and family life were very important to Athenians. Parents always arranged marriages. Girls married young, at age 13 or 14. A girl's husband might be twice her age or older. The main purpose of marriage was to have children. Sometimes, however, a family could not afford to raise a child. Then the baby was left to die, especially if it was a girl. This is not to say that Greek parents did not love their daughters. One of the most touching poems written by the ancient Greek poet **Sappho** was "Sleep, Darling," an ode to her daughter.

 Primary Source ❝Sleep, darling
I have a small daughter called Cleis, who is
like a golden flower
I wouldn't take all Croesus' kingdom with love thrown in, for her❞

Sappho, "Sleep, Darling," from *Sappho: A New Translation* by Mary Bernard

Despite such personal feelings, legally and socially Athenian women were considered inferior to men. They were citizens but could not own or inherit property. Even at home, women were expected to stay in the background. For example, they stayed out of sight when their husbands had guests. They could appear in public only with their husbands' permission. Women's duties included managing the household and slaves and raising children.

In many Athenian households, the mother took care of all children until the age of six. At about age seven, boys came under the care of their **pedagogue.** This was a male slave who taught the boy manners. The pedagogue went everywhere with the boy, including to school. Athenian girls stayed at home. They learned to run a household but usually received no other education. Some daughters of wealthy families, however, were taught to read and write.

✔ **READING CHECK: Contrasting** How did life differ for men and women and for boys and girls in Athens? men participated in public life, women were kept in the home; boys got an education, girls were trained for household

120

Education and Military Service

As part of their gymnastics training, young boys learned how to box.

Most Greeks were poor and hardworking. They labored long hours and had little leisure time. Wealthy men spent their time in the pursuit of intellectual and physical excellence. They engaged in politics, gossip in the marketplace, conversations with friends, and athletic activities.

Athenians placed great value on literacy and education. They sent their sons to elementary schools, which charged a small fee. Athenian boys studied reading, writing, grammar, poetry, music, and gymnastics. They learned poetry by heart, including Homer's *Iliad* and *Odyssey*.

The Athenian ideal stressed a sound mind in a healthy body. Grammar and music were meant to develop the minds and emotions of students. Gymnastics developed the body. In open fields at the edge of the city, boys practiced running, jumping, boxing, and throwing the discus and javelin.

In the 400s B.C. men called **Sophists** opened schools for older boys. The Sophists took their name from the Greek word *sophos,* meaning "wise." At these schools boys studied government, mathematics, ethics, and rhetoric. **Ethics** deals with what is good and bad, and moral duty. **Rhetoric** was the study of oratory, or public speaking, and debating.

Education helped spread the Greek language and civilization throughout the Mediterranean world. Greek was a second language for educated people everywhere. Even today we use many words that are derived from Greek.

At age 18 Athenian males received a year of military training. Young men who could afford armor and weapons then became hoplites and served in the army for a year. Hoplites formed the center of the infantry. Poorer men, who could not afford good equipment, served on the army's flanks. Citizens also rowed the warships in the Athenian fleet.

✔ **READING CHECK: Summarizing** How did Athenian education fulfill the Greek ideal of a sound mind in a healthy body? students exercised physically and mentally

SECTION 4 REVIEW

1. **Define** and explain the significance:
   terracing
   import
   export
   pedagogue
   ethics
   rhetoric

2. **Identify** and explain the significance:
   Sappho
   Sophists

3. **Sequencing** Copy the graphic organizer below. Use it to show what Athenian boys and young men learned at each stage of their educations.

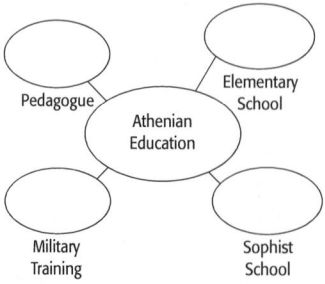

4. **Finding the Main Idea**
   a. Why did trade become the most important part of the Greek economy?
   b. What role did colonies play in the rise of Greek trade?
   c. In what ways did Greek society show the attitude that women were valued less than men?

5. **Writing and Critical Thinking**
   Summarizing In a diary entry, describe a day in the life of a young Athenian boy or girl.
   Consider:
   - how Athenians made their livings
   - what Athenian home and family life was like
   - what place education had in Athenian life

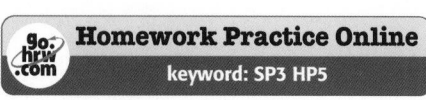
Homework Practice Online
keyword: SP3 HP5

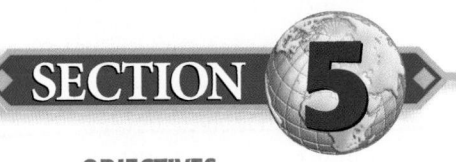

OBJECTIVES

1 **Explain how the Persian Wars began and what the results of those wars were.**

2 **Analyze the effects of Pericles's leadership on Athens.**

3 **Explain how the Peloponnesian War began and its results.**

SECTION 5

The Expansion of Greece

The Main Idea
Destructive wars that pitted Greeks against other powers and city-state against city-state weakened Greece.

The Story Continues *At first, the Greek city-states developed without interference from the nearby empires of Southwest Asia. Eventually, however, the mighty Persian Empire entered into Greek affairs. In 546 B.C. King Cyrus of Persia conquered the Greek colonies on the western coast of Asia Minor. Cyrus permitted these Greeks to keep their local governments. Later rulers, however, tightened Persian rule and raised taxes.*

READ TO DISCOVER

❶ How did the Persian Wars begin and what were their results?

❷ What effect did Pericles's leadership have on Athens?

❸ Why did the Peloponnesian War begin and what were its results?

IDENTIFY

Persian Wars
Battle of Marathon
Battle of Thermopylae
Themistocles
Delian League
Pericles
Peloponnesian War

▶ WHY IT MATTERS TODAY

The United Nations today works much like the Delian League in ancient Greece. Member nations contribute money and promise to send troops to trouble spots around the world. Use CNN.com or other **current event** sources to find examples of activities in which the United Nations is involved. Record your findings in your journal.

CNN student News.com

The Persian Wars

In about 500 B.C. Greeks in Asia Minor rebelled against the Persians. Athens helped these city-states in their uprisings. This began a series of conflicts between Greece and Persia that lasted until 479 B.C. These conflicts are known as the **Persian Wars.**

The wars under Darius and Xerxes. Persian ruler Darius easily crushed the Greek revolts in Asia Minor. However, he also wanted to punish Athens for helping the rebels. Darius hoped to gain control of the Greek mainland. In 492 B.C. his forces conquered Thrace and Macedonia. Two years later, the Persians invaded Greece itself. The Athenians, although outnumbered, defeated the Persians at the **Battle of Marathon.** The Persians withdrew, and an uneasy peace lasted for 10 years.

In 480 B.C. Darius's son Xerxes led another huge Persian army and fleet against Greece. This time, several Greek city-states united to stop the Persians. The Persians had to advance through the narrow mountain pass of Thermopylae (thuhr·MAH·puh·lee). A small force led by 300 Spartans met them there. The Greeks held the pass for three days. Then the Persians found another way through the mountains and surrounded the Greeks. The Spartans, although badly outnumbered, refused to surrender. Instead, they fought until they were all killed. The Spartans' courage at the **Battle of Thermopylae** bought the other city-states time to prepare their forces.

INTERPRETING THE VISUAL RECORD

War memorial This present-day memorial honors the Greek soldiers who fought to the death at Thermopylae. Even today, the battle symbolizes resistance against huge odds.

Link to Today What does this memorial tell us about how modern Greeks feel about the Battle of Thermopylae?

LEVEL 3: Have students create an illustrated time line showing the significant events of the Persian Wars. (*546 B.C.: Persia conquers Greek colonies in Asia Minor; c. 500 B.C.: Greek colonies rebel/Athens becomes involved; 492 B.C.: Persia conquers Thrace and Macedonia; 490 B.C.: Athens defeats Persians at Battle of Marathon; 480 B.C.: Spartans inspire Greeks in loss of Battle of Thermopylae; Persians destroy Athens; 479 B.C.: Athens and Sparta defeat Persia.*) Tell students that they should try to make their time line self-explanatory so that someone looking at it can understand the events of the Persian Wars and who took part in them.

ENGLISH LANGUAGE LEARNERS

ALL LEVELS: Ask students if the final Greek victory successfully ended the conflict with Persia. (*Students should recognize that the victory was incomplete because the threat from Persia continued.*) Have students identify the effects of the ongoing tensions between Greece and Persia. (*Greek city-states worked toward unity; Athens and other city-states formed Delian League.*)

COOPERATIVE LEARNING

Global Relations

The Persian army drew soldiers and fleets from their conquered territories, among them Phoenicia. The Phoenicians may have contributed as many as 300 ships to the Persian fleet total of about 1,000. Phoenician sailors served in the Persian army. These sailors, who were more skilled than the Persians and the Greeks at naval maneuvers, bore the brunt of the Persian defeat at Salamis.

Critical Thinking

Why do you think the Phoenician sailors served in the Persian fleet? How do you think they felt about it? Support your point of view.

ANSWER: The Phoenicians may have been forced to serve in the fleet and resented it. Some may have liked serving in a powerful army.

MAP ANSWERS

1. The valleys between the mountain ranges run in a north-south direction, so the invading Persians would not have had to cross high mountain passes.

2. Some Greek city-states may have resented the power of Athens and Sparta.

Holt Researcher

go.hrw.com
KEYWORD: Holt Researcher
FreeFind: Xerxes
After reading more about Xerxes on the Holt Researcher, write a paragraph summarizing his successes and failures as a leader.

The Persians then marched toward Athens. **Themistocles** (thuh·MIS·tuh·kleez), Athens's leader, told the Athenians to leave the city and escape. Xerxes's army entered Athens and destroyed it. However, Themistocles tricked Xerxes into attacking the Athenian fleet in the narrow Salamis Strait. The Persian navy was larger than the Greek navy, but the Greek ships were more maneuverable. In the narrow waters of the strait, the Greeks sank much of the Persian fleet. In 479 B.C. the Athenians and Spartans joined forces to defeat the Persians at Plataea, northwest of Athens. This ended the Persian Wars.

Results of the Persian Wars. Although Greek city-states in Asia Minor were now free from Persian rule, the Persian Empire still remained powerful. The Persians still meddled

The Persian Wars, c. 500 B.C.–479 B.C.

Interpreting Maps Some of the Greek city-states supported Persia or took no side in the Persian Wars.

■ **Skills Assessment: 1. Using Geography** Why was the Persian army able to march easily through northern Greece?
2. Drawing Inferences Why might some Greek city-states have remained neutral or favored Persia?

in Greek affairs and worked to prevent Greek unity. However, success against the Persians gave the Greeks confidence. The Athenians rebuilt their city and entered a period of great cultural achievement. Athens began to create its own empire in the Aegean Sea.

Although the Persians had been defeated, the threat of invasion from the Persian Empire continued. Unity among the Greek city-states seemed necessary for survival. Sparta wanted Greek unity under its own leadership, but fear of helot revolt kept the Spartans from sending troops far from home for very long. Athens was more successful, using diplomacy to form the **Delian League,** an alliance of city-states with Athens as leader. Eventually the league included 140 other city-states, who each contributed money or ships. The money was kept on the island of Delos, from which the name Delian is derived. By the 450s B.C. Athens had built an empire based on the Delian League.

✔ **READING CHECK: Drawing Conclusions** Why did the Greek city-states unite during and after the Persian Wars? to face the Persian threat

The Age of Pericles

During this time, Pericles was the leader in Athens. **Pericles** was a great general, orator, and statesman who held public office or was active in public life from 461 B.C. to 429 B.C. During those years, Athens reached its peak of power and wealth. Pericles's leadership was so important to Athenian success that this period is called the Age of Pericles.

Under Pericles, Athenian democracy reached its height. All male citizens except for the lowest class could hold public office. Officeholders were paid a salary and were chosen by lot so that no one had an advantage. Athens achieved probably the most completely democratic government in history. Remember, however, that women rarely took part in public life. Also, many other residents were not citizens or were slaves.

Pericles strengthened and extended the empire that Athens had built. He established colonies of Athenian citizens in important or rebellious areas. He used the Athenian navy to keep the Persians out of the Aegean Sea. The Athenian system of weights and measures became standard throughout the empire. The rule of Pericles brought stability and prosperity to the eastern Mediterranean region. The members of the Delian League received these benefits but lost their independence.

HISTORY MAKER

Pericles
(c. 495 B.C.–429 B.C.)

Pericles was one of the greatest Greek statesmen. He was responsible for building the Parthenon and the Acropolis. He made Athens the cultural and political capital of Greece.

Pericles came of age at a time when Greeks first used the popular vote to change politics. He defeated his enemies in war, but used trade to build unity among the Greek city-states. **How did Pericles help make Athens the center of Greece?**

INTERPRETING THE VISUAL RECORD

The Acropolis Pericles rebuilt the buildings on the Acropolis after the Persian Wars. All Athenians took pride in the new look of the Acropolis. *How did the Acropolis reflect Athenian pride?*

TEACH OBJECTIVE 2

LEVEL 2: Write *Age of Pericles* on the chalkboard and circle it. Have students use this beginning to create a web summarizing the achievements of this period. (*Athens at peak of power and wealth; officeholders were paid; Athenian empire extended; Athenian navy kept Persians from Aegean Sea; Athenian weights and measures became Greek standard; stability and prosperity; Delian League cities received benefits but lost independence*)
ENGLISH LANGUAGE LEARNERS

TEACH OBJECTIVE 3

LEVEL 1: Before students read about the Peloponnesian War, discuss with them the quotation by Thucydides on page 124. Ask students if they can think of other reasons that young Greeks might be eager to go to war. Then tell students that war finally broke out between Athens and Sparta. Lead a discussion about who students think will win the Peloponnesian War. Close by having them read about the war.

Interdisciplinary Connection

SCIENCE. The plague that broke out in Athens was devastating. Thucydides was himself a victim of it, although he survived. He gave a detailed account of the disease. Modern scientists have not been able to positively identify it from his description, however. They know it was not the bubonic plague, which rampaged through Europe in the 1300s. The strongest candidate is typhus, a disease characterized by fever, rash, and mental confusion. The plague may have killed about one-third of the Athenians and left the rest badly demoralized.

ACTIVITY: Have students use their textbooks, the library, computer software, and other available resources to research other plagues throughout history. Students should transfer any statistical information to a written or visual form.

MAP ANSWERS

1. Athens: Ionia, Rhodes, Chalcidice, Thessaly, Euboea, Attica; Sparta: Macedon

2. Sparta's allies included a major land power.

Although government in Athens was democratic, the Delian League was not. Athens made all the decisions. According to the historian Thucydides (thoo·SID·uh·deez), one citizen gave the following advice to his fellow Athenians:

Analyzing Primary Sources

Identifying Points of View
According to this passage, how did some Athenians feel about Pericles's policies? opposed them

> **Primary Source**
> **"**Your empire is a tyranny . . . over subjects who do not like it and who are always plotting against you; you will not make them obey you by injuring your own interests . . . ; your leadership depends on superior strength and not on any goodwill of theirs.**"**
>
> Thucydides, *History of the Peloponnesian War*

Pericles moved the league's treasury from Delos to Athens. He used the money for the good of Athens. Pericles also forced more city-states to join the league. Sometimes Athenian forces had to put down revolts by other city-states.

✔ **READING CHECK: Summarizing** What changes did Pericles bring to Athens and to the rest of Greece? strengthened Delian League, made other city-states subordinate to Athens

The Peloponnesian War

Pericles failed to unite Greece under Athens. Discontent grew. Quarrels over trade divided Athens and Corinth. Tensions grew between Athens and Sparta until war broke out in 431 B.C. This war is called the **Peloponnesian War.** Athens and Sparta shared responsibility for the Peloponnesian War. The city-states had been rivals for years. As Thucydides wrote, "The Peloponnesus [Sparta] and Athens were both full of young men whose inexperience made them eager to take up arms."

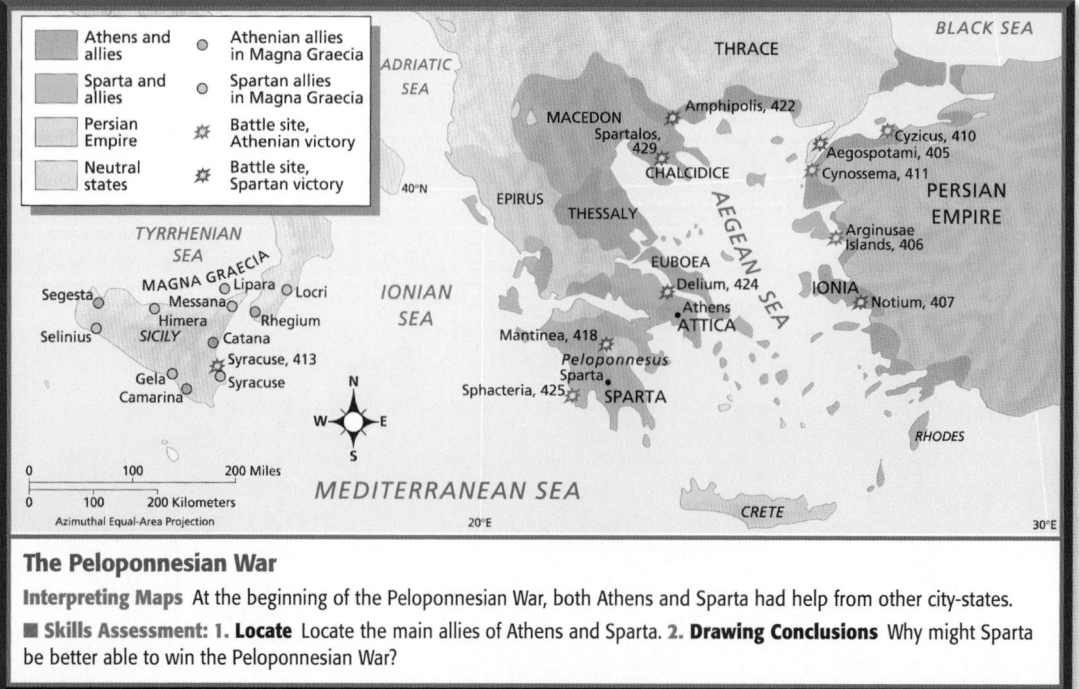

The Peloponnesian War

Interpreting Maps At the beginning of the Peloponnesian War, both Athens and Sparta had help from other city-states.
■ **Skills Assessment: 1. Locate** Locate the main allies of Athens and Sparta. **2. Drawing Conclusions** Why might Sparta be better able to win the Peloponnesian War?

CLOSE

Have students write an epitaph for Pericles. Ask them to include a summary of his major accomplishments.

REVIEW

Have students complete the Section 5 Review on p. 125.

ASSESS

Have students complete Daily Quiz 5.5. As Alternative Assessment, use the time line of the Persian Wars or the web diagram about the Age of Pericles in this section's lessons.

RETEACH

Have students complete Main Idea Activity for English Language Learners and Special-Needs Students 5.5. Have groups write the main idea and six supporting details for each of the main sub-headings of the section.

EXTEND

Organize students into groups representing Athenians and Spartans or other members of the Delian League. Have groups discuss ways to settle the disagreements among city-states and present their solutions to the class. **COOPERATIVE LEARNING, BLOCK SCHEDULING**

The Spartans had the stronger army. They started the fighting by invading the Attic peninsula, destroying fields and villages. The Athenians withdrew behind the city walls of Athens. Because Athens had the better navy and could bring in food by ship, the Spartans could not starve the Athenians out. The siege of Athens continued for years. During this time a plague broke out in Athens, killing many people, including Pericles.

The war continued for 27 years, punctuated by periods of truce and armed peace. The struggle even spilled over into the rest of the Greek world. During one truce in 415 B.C., Athens attacked the Greek city-state of Syracuse in Sicily. Syracuse was friendly to Sparta. The Athenians were driven back with great losses, which weakened the government of Athens. For a time aristocrats seized power. The Athenian people overthrew the aristocrats and restored their democracy, but the internal fighting further weakened Athens. Sparta, with the help of Persia, finally managed to block Athens's food supply. The starving Athenians finally surrendered to Sparta in 404 B.C. Athens was reduced for a time to being a second-rate power in Greece.

After the Peloponnesian War, Greece was politically unstable. First Sparta and then Thebes tried to control all of Greece. They were defeated and wars between the city-states continued. Many Greeks felt that only a foreign power could unite Greece. It would be many years before this would come to pass. However, Greek civilization still made great advances during this time.

During the Peloponnesian War, Athenians erected monuments to soldiers killed in battle.

✔ **READING CHECK: Identifying Cause and Effect** Why did the Peloponnesian War begin? old rivalries, Athenian control of Delian League

---

SECTION 5 REVIEW

1. **Identify** and explain the significance:
   Persian Wars
   Battle of Marathon
   Battle of Thermopylae
   Themistocles
   Delian League
   Pericles
   Peloponnesian War

2. **Comparing** Copy the graphic organizer below. Use it to write a brief comparison of the relationship between Athens and Sparta during the Persian Wars and the Peloponnesian War.

   Athens ⸺ Sparta
   Persian Wars

   Athens ⸺ Sparta
   Peloponnesian War

3. **Finding the Main Idea**
   a. How did the Greek victory over the Persians help bring about an Athenian empire?
   b. Why did paying officeholders a salary widen Athenian democracy during the Age of Pericles?
   c. How did the many differences between Sparta and Athens lead to the Peloponnesian War?

4. **Writing and Critical Thinking**
   Supporting a Point of View Write a letter to a friend in which you share your thoughts and feelings about Pericles's policies toward the Delian League.
   Consider:
   • why the Delian League was set up
   • how Pericles affected the Delian League

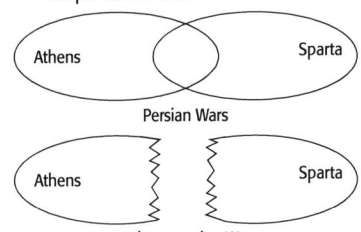

Homework Practice Online
keyword: SP3 HP5

SECTION 5 REVIEW ANSWERS

❶ **Identify**
• Persian Wars, p. 121
• Battle of Marathon, p. 121
• Battle of Thermopylae, p. 121
• Themistocles, p. 122
• Delian League, p. 123
• Pericles, p. 123
• Peloponnesian War, p. 124

❷ Students' comparisons should note that during the Persian Wars, Athens and Sparta were allies against the Persians. In the Peloponnesian War, the two cities were enemies who fought for control of Greece.

❸ **a.** The Greek victory was incomplete, leaving the Persians as a constant threat. As a result, the Greek city-states were willing to form an alliance, and Athens became dominant, turning the other city-states into an Athenian empire.

b. Paying officeholders a salary allowed poor people as well as wealthy aristocrats to hold public office.

c. Sparta and Athens were natural rivals. Discontent in Greece grew. Quarrels over trade divided cities. Young men were eager to take up arms. One had a strong army, one a strong navy. Sparta was a kingdom; Athens was a democracy. Both sought leadership of Greece.

❹ Letters will vary, but students should explain the impetus for forming the Delian League as well as how people would have responded to Pericles's strong leadership abilities.

THE GREEK CITY-STATES **125**

125

REVIEW AND ASSESSMENT RESOURCES

REPRODUCIBLE RESOURCES

▶ Vocabulary Activity 5

TECHNOLOGY RESOURCES

▶ Chapter 5 Test Generator (on the One-Stop Planner)
▶ Global Skill Builder CD–ROM
▶ HRW Web Site

REINFORCEMENT, REVIEW, and ASSESSMENT

▶ Chapter 5 Review, pp. 126–127
▶ Chapter 5 Tutorial for Students, Parents, Mentors, and Peers
▶ Chapter 5 Test (Form A or B)
▶ Alternative Assessment Handbook
▶ Chapter 5 Test for English Language Learners and Special-Needs Students

REVIEW

Have students complete the Chapter 5 Review on pages 126–127.

CLOSE

Ask students to write an outline for an encyclopedia article on the Greek city-states. Main headings and subheadings should indicate what topics the article would include.

CHAPTER 5 REVIEW ANSWERS

Understanding Main Ideas

1. Mountains isolated the early civilizations; communication and travel were difficult; people focused on the sea and trading.

2. Everything the people needed was in their polis.

3. Governments evolved from kingdoms to aristocracies to democracies.

4. *Iliad:* story of the Trojan War; *Odyssey:* tells of Odysseus's adventures as he returns home from the Trojan War

5. to be good soldiers and to defend their city-state

6. Cleisthenes made Athens a direct democracy. Solon allowed more citizens to hold office.

7. men: farmed, produced goods, engaged in trade, participated in public life; women: managed household, raised children; boys: attended school; girls: learned to run a household

8. defended the pass at Thermopylae

9. Greece became politically unstable and wars continued.

Reviewing Themes

1. Mountains isolated cities; people became sailors and traders.

2. only free, adult men

3. Both wanted to control Greece.

126

CHAPTER 5 Review

Creating a Time Line

Copy the time line below onto a sheet of paper. Complete the time line by filling in the events, individuals, and dates from the chapter that you think were significant. Pick three events and explain why you think they were significant.

| 2000 B.C. | 700s B.C. | 594 B.C. | 500 B.C. | 404 B.C. |

Writing a Summary

Using standard grammar, spelling, sentence structure, and punctuation, write an overview of the events in the chapter.

Identifying People and Ideas

Identify the following terms or individuals and explain their significance:

1. polis
2. Homer
3. myths
4. aristocracies
5. Solon
6. direct democracy
7. Sophists
8. Battle of Thermopylae
9. Delian League
10. Pericles

Understanding Main Ideas

SECTION 1 *(pp. 106–109)*

Early Greeks and the Rise of City-States

1. How did the geography of Greece affect the way its early civilizations grew?
2. Why was the polis such an important part of Greek life?

SECTION 2 *(pp. 110–112)*

Greek Government and Society

3. What kinds of governments did Greek city-states have between the 700s B.C. and the late 500s B.C.?
4. What kinds of information did Homer provide in the *Iliad* and the *Odyssey*?

SECTION 3 *(pp. 113–117)*

Sparta and Athens

5. From the Spartans' point of view, what was the purpose of life?
6. What conditions or developments helped to promote the rise of democracy in Athens?

SECTION 4 *(pp. 118–120)*

Daily Life in Athens

7. What were the main activities for men, for women, and for children in Athens?

SECTION 5 *(pp. 121–125)*

The Expansion of Greece

8. How did Sparta help Athens during the Persian Wars?
9. What happened in Greece after the Peloponnesian War?

Reviewing Themes

1. **Geography** How did Greece's landscape help determine the growth of the polis and of Greek trade?
2. **Citizenship** Who were allowed to be citizens in Athens and in Sparta?
3. **Global Relations** Why did Sparta go to war with Athens?

Thinking Critically

1. **Comparing** Compare the social classes in Spartan society with those in Athenian society.
2. **Contrasting** How did life in the city-states of Sparta and Athens differ?
3. **Sequencing** Trace the growth of Athenian democracy from Draco to Pericles.
4. **Categorizing** What were the outcomes of the Persian Wars and of the Peloponnesian War?

Writing About History

Evaluating Over a period of many years, the Athenians formed the world's first democracy. Write an explanation of how basic ideals from Athenian democracy, rules of law, and rights and responsibilities of citizens, including equality before the law, have become part of life in the United States today. Use the following chart to organize your thoughts before you begin writing.

Ideals of Democracy	
In Athens	In the United States

ASSESS

Use one of the chapter tests to assess students' understanding of the content. For Alternative Assessment, see the Portfolio Activities and Alternative Assessment Handbook.

RETEACH

Organize students into small groups and ask them to plan a children's book on the Greek city-states. Have each group develop an outline that contains chapter headings. Groups should also prepare a two-paragraph mar-keting statement that summarizes the book in an engaging way. Then have students take the Form B Test to assess their mastery of the material. **ENGLISH LANGUAGE LEARNERS, COOPERATIVE LEARNING**

Portfolio Extensions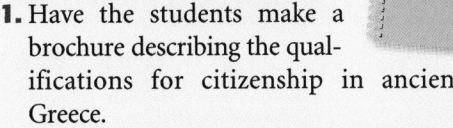

1. Have the students make a brochure describing the qualifications for citizenship in ancient Greece.
2. Have students work in groups of two or three and use their textbooks and other sources to trace the process of the democratic-republican form of government from its beginnings in classical Greece and Rome through its developments in England and during the Enlightenment. Ask students to pay particular attention to how citizens were defined and the privileges they had. Then have each group create a chart to summarize its findings.
3. Have students write a newspaper editorial explaining whether they feel that requirements for citizenship in the United States today are fair or unfair.

Building Social Studies Skills

Interpreting Artifacts

The Greek coins below date from the 500s B.C. Study the coins and consider what they reveal about the culture that made and used them. Then answer the questions that follow.

1. Using only the information that can be inferred from the image above, select the statement that best describes early Greek society and culture.
   a. The Greek city-states differed greatly from one another in terms of technological development.
   b. These coins reflect a relatively high level of technological development.
   c. There was much economic competition among the Greek city-states.
   d. The Greeks colonized and traded throughout the Mediterranean region during the 500s B.C.

2. In what ways might coined money help to promote trade and commerce across a culture?

Identifying Bias

Read the following excerpt from the work of Thucydides, an Athenian who wrote a history of the Peloponnesian War. Then answer the questions.

> "As for this present war, . . . if one looks at the facts themselves, one will see that this was the greatest war of all. . . . And with regard to my factual reporting of the events of the war . . . either I was present myself at the events which I have described or else I heard of them from eye-witnesses whose reports I have checked with as much thoroughness as possible."

3. Which of the following statements drawn from the excerpt above represents the author's opinion?
   a. "I was present myself at the events."
   b. "I heard of them [the events] from eye-witnesses whose reports I have checked."
   c. "This was the greatest war of all."
   d. "my factual reporting of the events of the war."

4. Use the information you have gained from Chapter 5 to identify important events that an Athenian such as Thucydides might have experienced during the Peloponnesian War? Give specific examples.

Alternative Assessment

Building Your Portfolio Link to TODAY

Citizenship

The ancient Greeks set up qualifications for citizenship. Today, most nations also have certain requirements that people must meet to become citizens. Using your textbook and other sources, find information about requirements for citizenship in the United States, Russia, and modern Greece. Create a chart comparing the three.

internet connect go.hrw.com

Internet Activity: go.hrw.com
KEYWORD: SP3 WH5

Choose a topic on the Greek City-States to:
- model ancient writing systems of the Mediterranean.
- build a map that connects modern and ancient Mediterranean cultures with pizza.
- report on Minoan civilization.

Thinking Critically

1. Citizens in Athens and equals in Sparta were males who could vote and own property. Metics in Athens and half-citizens in Sparta were free and paid taxes but could not take part in government or own land. Athens's slaves and Sparta's helots had no political rights.

2. Sparta: focused on military training; Athens: centered on education and culture

3. Draco: first written law; Solon: abolished enslavement for debt and established a court of appeals; Peisistratus: ruled with support of lower classes; Cleisthenes: broke up the power of aristocrats, created the Council of Five Hundred; Pericles: opened offices to all male citizens

4. Persian Wars: ended conflict with but not threat of Persia; Peloponnesian War: Athens defeated; conflicts between city-states persisted

Writing About History
Students might include individuals' rights.

Building Social Studies Skills
1. b

2. Coins could be traded instead of goods.

3. c

4. Answers will vary.

Building Your Portfolio
Students should include reasons for a country's requirements.

Greece's Golden and Hellenistic Ages

CHAPTER RESOURCE MANAGER

	Objectives	Pacing Guide	Reproducible Resources
SECTION 1 **Greek Art of the Golden Age** (pp. 130–132)	• Explain why the 400s B.C. are considered the golden age of Greek art and architecture. • Examine how Greek art of the golden age reflected the Greeks' view of themselves and the world.	**Regular** 1.5 day **Block Scheduling** 1 day *Block Scheduling Handbook with Team Teaching Strategies, 6.1*	RS Guided Reading Strategy 6.1 RS Graphic Organizer Activity 6: Greek Arts
SECTION 2 **Philosophers and Writers of the Golden Age** (pp. 133–137)	• Explain the basic ideas of Socrates, Plato, and Aristotle. • Identify the achievements of Greek mathematicians and scientists of the golden age. • Identify the important literary forms that originated or flourished during Greece's golden age.	**Regular** 1.5 day **Block Scheduling** 1 day *Block Scheduling Handbook with Team Teaching Strategies, 6.2*	RS Guided Reading Strategy 6.2 PS Readings in World History 21: The Death of Socrates PS Readings in World History 22: Aristotle's Views on Education PS Readings in World History 23: The Medical Aphorisms of Hippocrates
SECTION 3 **Alexander the Great** (pp. 138–141)	• Detail how Philip II of Macedon paved the way for cultural change. • Examine what Alexander the Great accomplished. • Identify the factors that contributed to the breakup of Alexander's empire.	**Regular** 1.5 day **Block Scheduling** 1 day *Block Scheduling Handbook with Team Teaching Strategies, 6.3*	RS Guided Reading Strategy 6.3 SM Graphic Activity 6 PS Readings in World History 24 E Creative Teaching Strategy 6
SECTION 4 **The Spread of Hellenistic Culture** (pp. 142–145)	• Describe how society changed during the Hellenistic Age. • Explain how philosophers of the Hellenistic Age viewed ethics. • Identify how Hellenistic scientists added to the existing body of knowledge.	**Regular** 1.5 day **Block Scheduling** 1 day *Block Scheduling Handbook with Team Teaching Strategies, 6.4*	RS Guided Reading Strategy 6.4 E Hands-on History Activity 6: A Hellenistic Family

Chapter Resource Key

PS	Primary Sources	**A**	Assessment	Music
RS	Reading Support	**REV**	Review	Video
IC	Interdisciplinary Connections	**ELL**	Reinforcement and English Language Learners	Internet
E	Enrichment		Transparencies	Holt Presentation Maker Using Microsoft® PowerPoint®
SM	Skills Mastery		CD-ROM	

 One-Stop Planner CD-ROM

See the ***One–Stop Planner*** for a complete list of additional resources for students and teachers.

One-Stop Planner CD-ROM

It's easy to plan lessons, select resources, and print out materials for your students when you use the **One-Stop Planner** CD–ROM with **Test Generator.**

Technology Resources	Reinforcement, Review, and Assessment
One-Stop Planner 6.1 World History teaching Transparency: Everyday Life 3: Greek Architecture Homework Practice Online	Daily Quiz 6.1 Main Idea Activity 6.1 English Audio Summary 6.1 Spanish Audio Summary 6.1 REV Section 1 Review, p. 132
One-Stop Planner 6.2 Holt Researcher: World History: Pythagoras Holt Researcher: World History: Thucydides World History and Cultures Video Program 4: A Socratic Education CNN Presents World Cultures: Yesterday and Today Segment 6: The Ancient Theaters of Epidaurus Homework Practice Online	Daily Quiz 6.2 Main Idea Activity 6.2 English Audio Summary 6.2 Spanish Audio Summary 6.2 REV Section 2 Review, p. 137
One-Stop Planner 6.3 Homework Practice Online Online Maps, Charts, and Graphs: Division of Alexander's Empire, 303 B.C.	Daily Quiz 6.3 Main Idea Activity 6.3 English Audio Summary 6.3 Spanish Audio Summary 6.3 REV Section 3 Review, p. 141
One-Stop Planner 6.4 Holt Researcher: World History: Archimedes Holt Researcher: World History: Erastosthenes World History Teaching Transparency: Art and History 3 Homework Practice Online Online Maps, Charts, and Graphs: The Hellenization of Asia Online Maps, Charts, and Graphs: The Economy of the Hellenistic Era	Daily Quiz 6.4 Main Idea Activity 6.4 English Audio Summary 6.4 Spanish Audio Summary 6.4 REV Section 4 Review, p. 145

internet connect

HRW ONLINE RESOURCES
GO TO: go.hrw.com
Then type in a keyword.

TEACHER HOME PAGE
KEYWORD: SP3 Teacher

CHAPTER INTERNET ACTIVITIES
KEYWORD: SP3 WH6
Choose an activity to:
- research Athens's golden age and create a newspaper article describing a representative political development.
- identify currents of Greek thought in art from different time periods.
- report on the scientific contributions of the ancient Greeks.

CHAPTER ENRICHMENT LINKS
KEYWORD: SP3 CH6

ONLINE ASSESSMENT
Homework Practice
KEYWORD: SP3 HP6
Standardized Test Prep
KEYWORD: SP3 STP6
Rubrics
KEYWORD: SS Rubrics

ONLINE MAPS, CHARTS, AND GRAPHS
KEYWORD: SP3 MCG

CONTENT UPDATES
KEYWORD: SS Content Updates

HOLT PRESENTATION MAKER
KEYWORD: SP3 PPT6

ONLINE READING SUPPORT
KEYWORD: SS Strategies

CURRENT EVENTS
KEYWORD: S3 Current Events

Meeting Individual Needs

Ability Levels

Level 1 Basic level activities designed for all students encountering new material

Level 2 Intermediate level activities designed for average students

Level 3 Challenging activities designed for honors and gifted and talented students

English Language Learners These activities address the needs of students with Limited English Proficiency.

Chapter Review and Assessment

IC Vocabulary Activity 6
  Global Skill Builder CD–ROM
HRW Web Site
REV Chapter 6 Tutorial for Students, Parents, Mentors, and Peers
REV Chapter 6 Review, pp. 146–147
A Chapter 6 Test Generator (on the One-Stop Planner)
A Chapter 6 Test (Form A or B)
A Alternative Assessment Handbook
A Chapter 6 Test for English Language Learners and Special-Needs Students

CHAPTER 6

Section 1 *Greek Art of the Golden Age*

Section 2 *Philosophers and Writers of the Golden Age*

Section 3 *Alexander the Great*

Section 4 *The Spread of Hellenistic Culture*

Build on What You Know

Ask students to answer the following questions:

What characteristics distinguished Greece from other early civilizations?

Consider:
- the rise of the city-states
- democratic rule
- religion and myths with humanlike gods and goddesses

How might the Greeks' victory over the Persians have affected Greek culture?

Consider:
- the confidence and sense of security it gave the Greeks
- the rise of Athens after the victory
- the strong leadership of Pericles

CHAPTER 6

478 B.C.–146 B.C.

Greece's Golden and Hellenistic Ages

400s B.C.
Global Events
The "golden age" of Greece occurs.

Greek vase showing potters at work, c. 450 B.C.

450 B.C.–401 B.C.
Daily Life
The population of Greece consists of two million citizens and one million slaves.

c. 375 B.C.
Science and Technology
Catapults are used as weapons of war.

359 B.C.
Politics
Philip II becomes king of Macedon.

336 B.C.–323 B.C.
Politics
Alexander the Great rules.

335 B.C.
Daily Life
Aristotle founds a school in Athens.

450 B.C.	400 B.C.	350 B.C.

458 B.C.
The Arts
Aeschylus, the father of Greek tragedy, presents *Agamemnon*.

470 B.C.
Global Events
Socrates is born in Athens.

c. 387 B.C.
Daily Life
Plato founds the Academy in Athens.

404 B.C.–362 B.C.
Politics
Sparta and Thebes struggle for control of Greece.

407 B.C.
Business and Finance
The town and harbor of Rhodes are built.

c. 340 B.C.
The Arts
Aristotle lays the foundations of musical theory.

Ruins of the city of Rhodes

Gold mask thought by some to portray Agamemnon

Build on What You Know

The ancient Greeks developed a civilization that greatly influenced Western history. By the 700s B.C. great Greek city-states had developed. They were led by Sparta and Athens. For years the Greek city-states fought off threats from Persian invaders. At Plataea in 479 B.C., Athens and Sparta joined to end the Persian threat. Following this victory, Greece entered an era of great cultural progress. In this chapter, you will learn about the development of Greek culture and how a rising power from outside of Greece helped to spread Greek achievements throughout the ancient world.

What's Your Opinion?

Government

Agree A powerful leader can stress common characteristics and show how unity brings strength.

Disagree A powerful leader can stir resentment and the desire for independence.

Culture

Agree A strong sense of cultural unity helps people put aside their differences and work for the common good.

Disagree A strong sense of cultural unity is not really possible when many diverse groups live in one nation.

Economics

Agree Contact with different lands introduces people to new goods and services and to the means of producing or trading for them.

Disagree Contact with different lands can make a people feel threatened and want to protect their culture and economy from outside influences.

Artist's conception of Greek women at a fountain

Greek terra-cotta oil lamp, 400s B.C.

323 B.C.
Global Events
Alexander the Great dies in Babylon.

323 B.C.
Science and Technology
Euclid writes the *Elements*.

323 B.C.–146 B.C.
Daily Life
The social status of some Hellenistic women improves.

323 B.C.–146 B.C.
Global Events
The Hellenistic Age occurs.

323 B.C.–146 B.C.
Business and Finance
Trade routes connect the Mediterranean with Asia and India.

c. 230 B.C.
Daily Life
Greeks introduce the use of molded pottery oil lamps.

146 B.C.
Global Events
The Romans conquer Greece.

300 B.C. — **250 B.C.** — **200 B.C.** — **150 B.C.**

301 B.C.
Politics
Alexander's empire is divided.

c. 307 B.C.
The Arts
The city of Alexandria founds its museum and library.

330 B.C.
Science and Technology
Greek explorer Pytheas reaches Britain.

332 B.C.
Business and Finance
Alexander the Great founds the Port of Alexandria.

c. 265 B.C.
Science and Technology
Romans have their first contact with Greek medicine.

Statue of Hippocrates

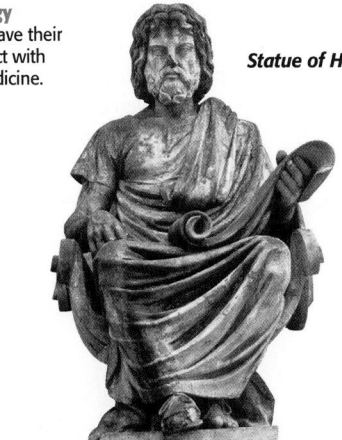

EXPLORING THE TIME LINE
GLOBAL EVENTS

Throughout most of the 400s and into the 300s B.C., the Greek city-states competed among themselves for dominance. The power that finally did unify Greece came from north of the Greek peninsula. Philip II, king of Macedon, moved his powerful army east into Thrace and beyond. When some Greeks saw Philip as a natural ally against the Persians, he was encouraged to move south into Greece. One by one, the city-states fell to his Macedonian army. Philip's conquest of Thebes and Athens came in 338 B.C. He forced the Greek city-states into a new League of Corinth, with himself at the head. The goal of Greek unity had been achieved, but not under a Greek leader.

Critical Thinking

Was Philip's conquest of Greece good or bad for the Greek people? Support your point of view.

ANSWER: Students might note that on one hand, conquest unified Greece and ended fighting between city-states. On the other hand, conquest brought loss of self-rule.

What's Your Opinion?

*Do you **agree** or **disagree** with the following statements? Support your point of view in your journal.*

Government A powerful national leader can unite local governments.

Culture A strong sense of cultural unity can help a nation that includes diverse groups of people grow.

Economics Contact with people in distant lands helps to strengthen a country's economy.

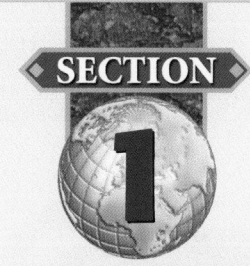
OBJECTIVES

1 **Explain why the 400s B.C. are considered the golden age of Greek art and architecture.**

2 **Examine how Greek art of the golden age reflected the Greeks' view of themselves and the world.**

SECTION 1

READ TO DISCOVER

❶ Why are the 400s B.C. considered the golden age of Greek art and architecture?

❷ How did Greek art of the golden age reflect the Greeks' view of themselves and the world?

DEFINE

golden age

IDENTIFY

Acropolis
Parthenon
Myron
Phidias
Praxiteles

▶ WHY IT MATTERS TODAY

Greek art and architecture had a lasting influence on Western culture. Use CNN Student News.com or other **current event** sources to find a current example of a building or object that is based on Greek styles. Record your findings in your journal.

CNN Student News.com

Greek Art of the Golden Age

The Main Idea
Greek artists of the golden age expressed their society's ideals in styles that combined beauty and usefulness.

The Story Continues *After the Persian Wars, the wealth and power of Athens drew artists and teachers from across Greece. These people worked to make Athens a center of learning and artistic achievement. As Pericles said to his fellow Athenians, "We are lovers of the beautiful, yet with economy, and we cultivate the mind without loss of manliness. . . . To sum up: I say that Athens is the school of Hellas [Greece]."*

The Arts of the Golden Age

In the 400s B.C. Greece entered a new era of cultural progress. Thus, we call this period the **golden age** of Greek culture. Athens stood as the symbol of Greece's golden age. The city's wealth and power drew artists and teachers from across Greece. These people worked to make Athens a center of learning and artistic achievement.

Architecture. The Athenians surrounded themselves with beauty. They showed their pride in Athens by building temples, gymnasiums, and theaters. Artists decorated these structures with their finest work, especially sculpture.

A high hill called the **Acropolis** was the center of the original city-state. This hill offered a perfect setting for special artistic creations. A magnificent gate marked the entrance to a path up the hill. Nearby stood a towering bronze statue of the goddess Athena.

At the top of the Acropolis stood the **Parthenon,** a white marble temple built in honor of Athena. The Parthenon is considered the finest example of Greek architecture. People admire it most for its perfectly balanced proportions—that is, the relation of length to width, and of length and width to height.

Construction of the Parthenon began in 447 B.C. and was completed about 15 years later.

TEACH OBJECTIVE 1

ALL LEVELS: Copy the following graphic organizer on the board, omitting the italicized answers. Ask each student to complete it. **ENGLISH LANGUAGE LEARNERS**

Examples/Artists	Characteristics
Architecture: *Parthenon*	*balanced proportions; columns; statues*
Painting: *vases*	*everyday life and myths; graceful, natural movement; light, shade show contour, depth*
Sculpture: *steles; Myron's The Discus Thrower; statues by Phidias; Praxiteles*	*showed how people lived and worked; early figures were stiff and unnatural; later figures were lifelike, natural*

TEACH OBJECTIVE 2

LEVEL 1: Have students discuss the ideals expressed in the Parthenon. **ENGLISH LANGUAGE LEARNERS**

LEVEL 3: Have each student select a piece of Greek art and explain how it expresses the four basic Greek ideals.

HOMEWORK Have students explain how the art in this section exhibits Greek characteristics.

CLOSE

Have students write a letter to Myron, Phidias, or Praxiteles explaining why they admire his work.

The Parthenon had doors but probably had few windows. This is because Greek temples were built as shrines to honor Greek gods, not as meeting places for worshippers. A series of columns, called a colonnade, surrounded the structure. Large, sculpted figures painted in bright colors decorated the marble above the columns. Inside the Parthenon stood an even larger statue of Athena. Made of ivory and gold, it rose to about 38 feet high. Today many people consider the Parthenon and its sculpture to be among the Greeks' greatest achievements.

Painting. Painting was an important form of art in ancient Greece. Unfortunately, most original artwork has been lost or badly damaged. Knowledge of Greek painting comes mainly from written descriptions and from later Roman copies. The best-preserved Greek paintings are found on vases. Greek vase painters illustrated scenes from everyday life as well as mythological events. These artists delighted in showing graceful and natural movements of their subjects. Some vase painters used light and shade on the pottery to show contour and depth.

The Greeks initially adopted styles of painting from other cultures, then transformed them into their own. Researchers believe that Greek traders were impressed by the animals they found painted on pottery in places such as Egypt. Greek artists adopted this style, but over a few centuries began to replace the animals with human figures.

Sculpture. Original works of Greek sculpture, like Greek paintings, are rare today. We know about Greek sculpture chiefly from studying copies made during Roman times. Like Greek paintings, Greek sculpture shows Egyptian influences. Early Greek sculpture was highly structured. Figures were shown in stiff, unnatural poses. Men and women were often portrayed standing with their arms straight down by their sides. By the 400s B.C., however, Greek sculptors were creating figures that were more lifelike. Many used mathematical proportions to make their works look realistic.

Myron and **Phidias** (FID·ee·uhs) were two of history's greatest sculptors. They both lived during the golden age. Myron sculpted the famous figure *The Discus Thrower*. Phidias created the statues of Athena that decorated the Acropolis and the Parthenon. His greatest work, however, was the statue of Zeus at the Temple of Olympia. In ancient times people considered this statue, which stood almost 40 feet high, to be one of the Seven Wonders of the World.

Praxiteles (prak·SIT·uhl·eez) lived about 100 years after Phidias. He created a very different kind of sculpture. Phidias had made large, formal works appropriate for the gods. Praxiteles, on the other hand, sculpted figures that were more lifelike and natural in form and size. Above all, Praxiteles expressed the Greek admiration for the beauty of the human body.

✔ **READING CHECK: Analyzing Information** What qualities defined Greek architecture, painting, and sculpture? balanced proportions; scenes from everyday life; admiration for the human form

CONNECTING TO
Art

Sculpture: Greek Funeral Stele

The ancient Greeks believed in a sort of "shadowy" existence after death. They carved steles (STEE·leez), or stone slabs, to commemorate their dead. Many steles showed how the dead person had lived and worked. The *Grave Stele of Hegeso* is from the late 400s B.C. It shows Hegeso, an Athenian woman. Hegeso is choosing a jewel from a box held by her servant.

Understanding the Arts

How does the *Grave Stele of Hegeso* show major characteristics of Greek art?

The Grave Stele of Hegeso

Interdisciplinary Connection

MATHEMATICS. The visual appeal of the Parthenon and other Greek temples results from the application of mathematical principles of proportion. The Parthenon is constructed in a ratio of 4:9, which the Greeks believed to be the ideal relationship of width to length. This ratio holds throughout the structure of the temple, from the arrangement of the columns along the ends and sides to the size and spacing of the columns themselves. Although the columns of the Parthenon are of different thicknesses, the diameter of each column is four-ninths of the space between any two of them.

ACTIVITY: Have students draw diagrams of the Parthenon in scale with its actual proportions, including 8 columns on the ends and 17 on the sides, and discuss the visual appeal of these dimensions. Discuss how this style of architecture influenced other cultures.

CONNECTING TO ART ANSWER
relief figures are physically beautiful, graceful; scene is taken from daily life

REVIEW

Have students complete the Section 1 Review on p. 132.

ASSESS

Have students complete Daily Quiz 6.1. As Alternative Assessment, you may want to use the graphic organizer in this section's lessons.

RETEACH

Have students complete Main Idea Activity for English Language Learners and Special-Needs Students 6.1. Then have

EXTEND

internet connect

Internet Activity: go.hrw.com
TOPIC: Ancient Athens **KEYWORD: SP3 WH6**
Have students access the Internet through the HRW Go site to research ancient Athens. Ask students to create a newspaper about Athens during its golden age.

VISUAL RECORD ANSWER

figure is unclothed to show body; great detail; perfectly proportioned

SECTION 1 REVIEW ANSWERS

❶ **Define**
• golden age, p. 130

❷ **Identify**
• Acropolis, p. 130
• Parthenon, p. 130
• Myron, p. 131
• Phidias, p. 131
• Praxiteles, p. 131

❸ Sculpture: grave steles, *The Discus Thrower*; Architecture: Parthenon, public buildings, religious shrines; Painting: vases

❹ a. showed perfectly balanced proportion according to mathematical principles and no nonessential details

b. Phidias: heroic in size and formal; Praxiteles: more lifelike and natural in size and form

c. glorified human beings: reflected ideals of beauty and strength; public: symbolized pride in city-state; simple, restrained: reflected ideals of harmony, balance, order, moderation; beautiful and useful: reflected belief in relationship of both to the good

❺ Letters should accurately reflect Greek views of art, their religious beliefs, and their daily activities.

INTERPRETING THE VISUAL RECORD

Greek sculpture This marble statue, entitled *The Discus Thrower,* was crafted by Myron during the mid-400s B.C. *What qualities in this statue show the artist's admiration for the human form?*

The Nature of Greek Art

Greek architecture, painting, and sculpture reflected the Greeks' view of themselves and the world. Artistic styles of the golden age expressed Greek ideals in four main ways. First, Greek art glorified human beings. Much of Greek painting and sculpture portrayed gods and goddesses. However, the Greeks also placed great importance on human qualities and actions. By the time of the golden age, Greek sculptors had begun to create detailed statues of athletes, warriors, and even ordinary citizens. Greek painters and sculptors idealized their human subjects. In other words, the faces and figures of men and women represented the Greek ideal of beauty. The statues also suggested other traits admired by the Greeks. These included strength, intelligence, pride, grace, and courage.

Second, the art of the golden age symbolized Greeks' pride in their city-states. Art was meant for public enjoyment, and the architecture of public buildings was meant to be a monument to the power and glory of the polis. Through their art the Greeks honored and thanked the gods and tried to win their favor. For example, the Athenians built the Parthenon as a beautiful shrine for Athena. This showed their love for their city and their hope for its continued good fortune.

Third, Greek art expressed Greek beliefs in harmony, balance, order, and moderation. By moderation, the Greeks meant simplicity and restraint, qualities that they emphasized in their day-to-day lives. In art and architecture these principles resulted in a search for calmness, clarity, and freedom from any details not absolutely necessary to the work.

Finally, Greek art expressed the Greek belief in combining beauty and usefulness. In Greek culture the useful, the beautiful, and the good were closely bound together. Most Greek art was functional and had a clearly defined purpose. For example, the Greeks designed vases with different shapes intended for different functions. The potters and artists adapted their decorations to the curves and shapes of their vases.

✔ **READING CHECK: Making Generalizations** How did Greeks of the golden age use art to express their ideals? used art to express ideals of harmony, order, and balance; art combined beauty and usefulness

SECTION 1 REVIEW

1. **Define** and explain the significance:
golden age

2. **Identify** and explain the significance:
Acropolis
Parthenon
Myron
Phidias
Praxiteles

3. **Categorizing** Copy the web below. Use it to list examples of Greek artistic achievements during the golden age.

Sculpture — Painting — Architecture — Greek Art

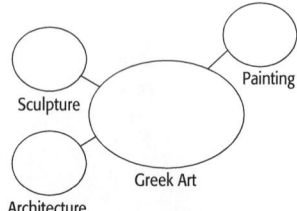
Homework Practice Online
keyword: SP3 HP6

4. **Finding the Main Idea**
a. Briefly explain how the following quotation can be applied to Greek architecture: "Nothing in excess, and everything in proportion."
b. How did the style of Phidias differ from that of Praxiteles?
c. List four characteristics of Greek art and explain how each reflected Greek ideals.

5. **Writing and Critical Thinking**
Supporting a Point of View Imagine you are a citizen of Athens during Greece's golden age. Write a letter to your fellow citizens describing what types of buildings or public works of art you feel should be added to the city.
Consider:
• the purpose or use of any new buildings, statues, or paintings
• the religious beliefs of you and your fellow citizens
• the daily activities or entertainment needs of Athenians

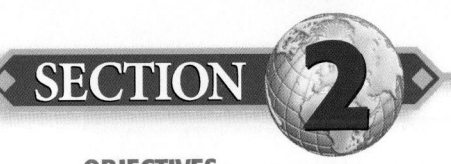

OBJECTIVES

1 **Explain the basic ideas of Socrates, Plato, and Aristotle.**

2 **Identify the achievements of Greek mathematicians and scientists of the golden age.**

3 **Identify the literary forms that originated or flourished during Greece's golden age.**

As students enter the classroom, ask them how the values of a society are expressed through its literature. *(Students should recognize that the themes that poets, playwrights, and other authors choose to write about, as well as what they have to say, in some way reflect the values of their particular society.)* Tell students that in Section 2 they will learn what types of literature the Greeks developed and how Greek writers, as well as philosophers, expressed Greek values.

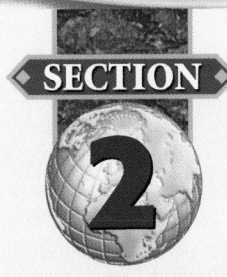

Philosophers and Writers of the Golden Age

The Main Idea
Greeks of the golden age made great advances in philosophy, the sciences, and literature.

The Story Continues *As Greece entered its golden age, philosophers and writers began to think about the nature of the universe and of human life. While the Greeks still honored the old gods, they took pride in human accomplishments. As the playwright Sophocles wrote, "Many are the wonders, none is more wonderful than what is man."*

READ TO DISCOVER

❶ What basic ideas did Socrates, Plato, and Aristotle express?

❷ What were the achievements of Greek mathematicians and scientists of the golden age?

❸ What important literary forms originated or flourished during Greece's golden age?

DEFINE

philosophy
aristocracy
dramas
tragedies

IDENTIFY

Socrates
Plato
Aristotle
Pythagoras
Hippocrates
Herodotus
Sophocles
Euripides
Aristophanes

▶ WHY IT MATTERS TODAY

Greek writers often used drama to comment on aspects of Greek society such as war or politics. Use **CNN** or other **current event** sources to find examples of writers or artists today who comment on social or political issues through their work. Record your findings in your journal.

CNN Student News.com

The Rise of Philosophy

One of the Greeks' greatest achievements was the development of **philosophy,** the study of basic questions of reality and human existence. The Greeks used philosophy to better understand themselves and the world around them. (The word *philosopher* means "lover of wisdom.") Philosophers often disagreed with one another, but most believed that all of nature is based upon certain natural laws, or truths. They believed they could discover these truths through reason.

According to tradition, the first Greek philosopher was Thales of Miletus. Thales and others like him wanted to understand the nature of the cosmos, or universe. Thus they are known as cosmologists. Parmenides of Elea set up formal rules of logic for philosophical arguments. Another cosmologist, Democritus, developed atomic theory by using logic and mathematics. Democritus stated that everything is made up of tiny bits of matter called atoms.

Socrates. One of the most important thinkers of the new era was an Athenian, Socrates (SAHK·ruh·teez). He taught that education was the key to personal growth. Unlike other teachers, Socrates did not use memorization as a teaching tool. Instead, he insisted that students be trained to think for themselves. He asked questions that forced students to test their own values and ideas. Socrates's way of teaching through questioning has become known as the Socratic Method.

Although greatly loved, Socrates had powerful enemies. His questions often made public officials look foolish. He criticized democracy, saying that unskilled people should not hold positions of power. Finally, Socrates came into conflict with the Sophists, a group of Athenian teachers. He mocked their teachings as little more than untested assumptions.

Socrates's enemies falsely accused him of denying the existence of many Greek gods. They also said his teachings corrupted the minds of Athenian youth. The leaders of Athens brought Socrates to trial. Socrates did little to defend himself. He refused to deny his teachings, although this could possibly have saved his life. Socrates was found guilty and executed.

Plato. Socrates never recorded his ideas. Later generations learned of them from the writings of **Plato,** a wealthy young aristocrat and the greatest of Socrates's students. After the death of Socrates, Plato founded the Academy, a special school in Athens for teaching philosophy.

SECTION 2 RESOURCES

REPRODUCIBLE RESOURCES

▶ Guided Reading Strategy 6.2

▶ Readings in World History 21: The Death of Socrates

▶ Readings in World History 22: Aristotle's Views on Education

▶ Readings in World History 23: The Medical Aphorisms of Hippocrates

TECHNOLOGY RESOURCES

▶ One-Stop Planner 6.2

▶ Holt Researcher: World History: Pythagoras

▶ Holt Researcher: World History: Thucydides

▶ World History and Cultures Video Program 4: A Socratic Education

▶ Homework Practice Online

REINFORCEMENT, REVIEW, AND ASSESSMENT

▶ Section 2 Review, p. 137

▶ Daily Quiz 6.2

▶ Main Idea Activity 6.2

▶ English Audio Summary 6.2

▶ Spanish Audio Summary 6.2

TEACH OBJECTIVE 1

ALL LEVELS: Organize students into three groups and assign each group to study and represent the ideas of Socrates, Plato, or Aristotle. Students may decide whether to vote on one spokesperson or to allow any member to speak as the philosopher. Ask questions such as: How do you view education? the world? What special views do you hold? What are your views on government? You may want students to role-play the philosophers discussing the last question among themselves.
ENGLISH LANGUAGE LEARNERS, COOPERATIVE LEARNING

Teacher to Teacher

Mattie P. Collins of Pine Bluff, Arkansas, suggested the following activity: Have students write an essay in answer to the question, "Whose political ideas do you like better, those of Plato or Aristotle?" Students must defend their positions in their essays. You may also divide students into groups and organize a debate around this question. Students are expected to use standard grammar, spelling, sentence structure, and punctuation.

Government

Plato was an aristocrat who had little use for democracy. In *The Republic,* Plato outlined his ideal society. Everyone would be placed according to natural skills. Most people would be workers. Above the workers would be the Guardians, who would be trained as warriors to protect the state. Those who showed the greatest intelligence and discipline would be trained as philosophers and would become the rulers of the state. Plato's ideas were never put into practice, and his efforts at political influence failed.

Critical Thinking

Ask students if they think Plato's plan for the government of society would work. Have them explain their answers.

ANSWER: Some students may say no—many would not want to stay in their assigned place. Others may say yes—everyone would be happy because all would be doing what suited them best.

HISTORY MAKER ANSWER

To be truly alive, people should seek to know themselves and carefully consider the personal meaning of values.

VISUAL RECORD ANSWER

The academy is pictured as open and informal; figures' poses suggest contemplation and seriousness; the mosaic suggests dialogue and the free exchange of ideas.

134

HISTORY MAKER

Socrates
(470 B.C.–399 B.C.)

Born in Athens, Socrates was one of the leading teachers and philosophers in Greece. His ideas and teaching methods helped to shape Western thought and education.

One of Socrates's greatest contributions was his study of ethics or "right living." Socrates felt that values such as duty and honesty should be studied and taught. "The unexamined life," Socrates held, "is not worth living." He trained his students to follow the motto "Know thyself." Socrates encouraged people to think about the personal meaning of common values. **What do you think Socrates meant by saying, "The unexamined life is not worth living"?**

INTERPRETING THE VISUAL RECORD

The teaching of philosophy
This mosaic depicts Plato's Academy, founded about 387 B.C. to instruct students in philosophy and science. *What does this scene tell you about styles of teaching and learning at the Academy?*

Plato wrote dialogues, or imaginary discussions among several people. He dealt with government, education, justice, and religion. Most of the dialogues featured Socrates teaching and asking questions, but they also expressed many of Plato's own theories. Perhaps Plato's most important idea was the "Theory of Forms." Plato believed that all material things were imperfect expressions of perfect and universal ideas, or "forms." He felt that perfection could never be reached in the physical world. Because the human senses could be fooled, Plato argued, a true philosopher pursued knowledge of the perfect form that lay beyond the senses. For example, an ideal geometrical figure, such as a square, could be expressed perfectly as a mathematical formula. But in practical terms, it was almost impossible to make a perfect physical square.

For Plato, the realm of perfect forms had been conceived by the "divine worker," or God. This realm of perfection, he believed, existed apart from the physical examples of forms. Plato also saw human beings as consisting of two parts—the soul and the body. The soul, he taught, was the creation of God. Plato believed that through reincarnation, soul and form would eventually unite.

Plato was also interested in politics. The *Republic* is a long dialogue describing Plato's view of the perfect society. Plato's ideal government was an **aristocracy**— a government ruled by an upper class. However, this would not be an aristocracy of birth or of wealth. Instead, Plato's ideal rulers were philosophers, chosen for their wisdom, ability, and high ideals.

Aristotle. One of Plato's students in the Academy was a young man named **Aristotle.** Aristotle founded his own school in Athens in 335 B.C. Aristotle believed that every field of knowledge had to be studied logically. He collected as many facts as possible and organized them into systems. Aristotle had a special skill for defining and classifying things. This process of organization is an important part of modern science.

Aristotle investigated almost every field of study known during his time. He collected, described, and classified plants and animals. In his book *Ethics,* Aristotle tried to learn what brings people happiness. In *Poetics,* he analyzed Greek drama to show what makes a good or bad play.

TEACH OBJECTIVE 2

ALL LEVELS: Copy the following graphic organizer on the board, omitting the italicized answers. Ask each student to complete it. **ENGLISH LANGUAGE LEARNERS**

Greek Science and Medicine	
Scientists	**Contribution**
Pythagoras	*Pythagorean theorem*
Aristotle	*foundations for anatomy, botany, zoology; classification*
Hippocrates	*medical studies, cures*

Spotlight on CULTURE

Engage students in a dialogue by asking such questions as: What is philosophy? With what questions is a philosopher concerned? What is the difference between philosophy and science? Tell students they have just taken part in the Socratic Method of teaching. Challenge them to carry on a short lesson on a particular theme, such as honesty or happiness, using the Socratic Method. They should take turns playing the role of Socrates.

Aristotle's political views reflected his study of Greek culture. He believed that monarchy, aristocracy, and democracy were equally good forms of government. However, he felt that they could easily be corrupted. Aristotle wanted to combine the best of all three types of government to create a limited democracy.

✔ **READING CHECK: Comparing and Contrasting** What common issues did Socrates, Plato, and Aristotle study? How did their ideas about government differ? studied social and individual values; differed on democracy

Mathematics, Medicine, and Science

For the Greeks, philosophy covered all areas of knowledge, including the fields of mathematics and science. For example, **Pythagoras** (pih·THAG·uhr·uhs) was a philosopher who believed that everything could be explained in terms of mathematics. He is best remembered for his development of the Pythagorean theorem. According to the Pythagorean theorem, the length of the longest side of a right triangle can be found if the lengths of the two shorter sides are known.

Greek philosophers did not specialize in any one field of study. This kept them from fully developing practical scientific knowledge until much later. Aristotle, for example, did little more than lay the foundations for anatomy, botany, and zoology. He also helped to pioneer important classification practices, used to group similar things together and to describe and compare them. The Greek approach to scientific thought, however, differed in very important ways from the work of the Egyptians and Mesopotamians. These earlier thinkers made little distinction between the natural and the supernatural worlds. They tended to explain natural events as the work of gods and other supernatural forces. The Greeks, in contrast, believed that the natural world could be explained in terms of natural laws. They held, too, that the rules that govern our universe could be identified, observed, and defined. This approach depended on objectivity and reason, rather than on superstition, and did much to advance scientific thought.

The Greeks excelled in medicine. **Hippocrates** (hip·AHK·ruh·teez), who lived between about 460 B.C. and about 377 B.C., is considered to be the founder of medical science. Many historians believe that Hippocrates wrote between 60 and 70 medical studies. These studies were based on observation, experiment, and experience and helped to collect medical knowledge in a usable form. Hippocrates taught that disease comes from natural causes, not as punishment from the gods. He believed that rest, fresh air, and a proper diet made the best cures. Hippocrates's ideals were passed along to other Greek physicians. Doctors who were trained in Hippocrates's methods accepted his philosophy that medical treatment should be based on reason, rather than on magic. Today, medical doctors still take the Hippocratic oath. They pledge to follow a code of ethics based on Hippocrates's teachings.

> (Primary Source) **❝I swear . . . that I will carry out, according to my ability and judgment, this oath and this indenture [contract]. . . . I will use treatment to help the sick according to my ability and judgment, but never with a view to injury and wrongdoing.❞**

✔ **READING CHECK: Contrasting** How did the Greeks' approach to medical science differ from their approach to other sciences? developed practical applications

CONNECTING TO Math

The Pythagorean Theorem

The Pythagorean theorem is one of the basic tools of geometry. Although it is named after Pythagoras, he actually built on ideas developed earlier by the Egyptians and others.

The theorem states that by squaring (multiplying by itself) the lengths of the two shorter sides of a right triangle and adding those numbers together, the sum will equal the square of the longest side.

This knowledge is useful in many fields, including architecture, engineering, manufacturing, navigation, and surveying.

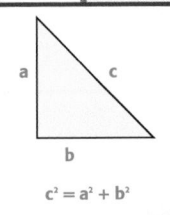

$$c^2 = a^2 + b^2$$

Understanding Math

What does the development of the Pythagorean theorem tell us about the exchange of ideas in the ancient world?

Holt Researcher

go.hrw.com
KEYWORD: Holt Researcher
FreeFind: Pythagoras
After reading more about Pythagoras on the Holt Researcher, assess his contributions to science, noting how his ideas are still used today.

Linking Past to Present

Modern scientists use various methods in their research. These methods include observing, collecting and classifying data, applying logical reasoning, experimenting, hypothesizing, and expressing their findings mathematically.

Critical Thinking

How do modern scientific methods relate to the beliefs of ancient Greeks?

ANSWER: Aristotle helped pioneer classification principles. Pythagoras believed the world could be explained mathematically.

CONNECTING TO MATH ANSWER

implies that knowledge was transmitted from culture to culture throughout the ancient world

🌐 internet connect

TOPIC: Greek Scientist
GO TO: go.hrw.com
KEYWORD: SP3 WH6

Have students access the Internet through the HRW Go site to find information about Greek contributions to science. Have them summarize their findings in a report.

HOMEWORK Have students write paragraphs about what scientific knowledge in Greece might have been like before the golden age compared to changes produced by scientific discovery during the golden age. *(unsystematic and tied to religion)* Remind them to use standard grammar, spelling, sentence structure, and punctuation.

TEACH OBJECTIVE 3

LEVEL 1: Write the following literary genres on the board: *History, Tragedy, Comedy.* Ask students what the Greeks contributed to the development of each. Conclude by asking how all three contribute to our knowledge and understanding of

ancient Greece. *(Histories record important events; tragedies and comedies give insights into values.)*
ENGLISH LANGUAGE LEARNERS

LEVEL 3: Ask students to choose and read a play written by one of the Greek dramatists discussed in this section, and report to the class on its theme, plot, and characters.

CLOSE

Have students design a chart that lists each philosopher, scientist, historian, and dramatist, and each person's major ideas, works, and/or contributions.

History Maker

THUCYDIDES. Born about 460 B.C. into a wealthy Athenian family, Thucydides served as a general for his city-state against Sparta in the Peloponnesian War. After failing to stop the Spartans from taking the city of Amphipolis in 424 B.C., he was exiled from Athens. Thucydides drew on his military experiences to write his *History of the Peloponnesian War.* He focused on how human choices and actions affected the course of the war.

Critical Thinking

How might the experiences of Thucydides have affected his writing?

ANSWER: His first-hand knowledge of the war would enable him to make the connection between human choices and outcomes. His experience might also have given him the desire to report events accurately.

VISUAL RECORD ANSWER

Students may note the theater is an open-air amphitheater with stage at bottom. Most theaters today are indoors with raised stages. Also they may note the stone seats and narrow aisles.

Technology Resources
CNN Presents World Cultures: Yesterday and Today Segment 6: The Ancient Theaters of Epidaurus

Holt Researcher
go.hrw.com
KEYWORD: Holt Researcher
FreeFind: Thucydides
After reading more about Thucydides on the Holt Researcher, identify what evidence Thucydides analyzed to make his historical study more accurate.

INTERPRETING THE VISUAL RECORD
Greek theaters The theater at Epidaurus, which dates from the mid-300s B.C., is one of the best-preserved Greek theaters. Its many rows of benches seat about 12,000 people. *How does this theater differ from present-day theaters?*

History

The Greeks became the first people to take the writing of history seriously. **Herodotus** (hih-RAHD-uh-tuhs) was the first historian of the Western world. Herodotus traveled to Babylonia, Phoenicia, and Egypt. He included his views of these countries and their people in his histories.

Herodotus was an interesting writer and a wonderful storyteller. He exaggerated at times. However, Herodotus was careful to note whether he had seen something for himself or had only been told about it. Historians still consult his writings for information about the world during his time. Herodotus is often called the Father of History.

Another Greek historian, Thucydides (thoo-SID-uh-deez), became famous for his *History of the Peloponnesian War.* Thucydides believed that studying the past helps us to understand human nature. He tried to make his own work reflect this belief. Thus, Thucydides worked to make his history accurate and fair.

✔ **READING CHECK: Drawing Inferences** Why was the approach to history developed by Herodotus and Thucydides important? This approach led to improved accuracy and objectivity.

Greek Theater

Athenian writers produced many of the world's greatest works of literature. Many of today's literary styles were first developed by the Greeks.

Drama. The Greeks were the first people to write **dramas**—plays containing action or dialogue and involving conflict and emotion. The Greeks always wrote plays in poetic form. Two or three actors spoke or sang the lines for an audience. Male actors with trained voices played women's roles. A group of singers, called the chorus, described the scene and commented on the action.

The Greeks carved outdoor theaters into hillsides. At the bottom of the hill they created a flat area called the *orchestra*, where the chorus and actors performed. Unlike many plays of today, Greek dramas featured little scenery. Instead, audiences relied on the chorus to describe the time and place.

Greek dramas were often performed in connection with religious festivals. Each spring three playwrights were invited to compete at the annual festival of Dionysus, the Greek god of fertility and wine. This festival, called the Great Dionysia, became Athens's major dramatic

REVIEW

Have students complete the Section 2 Review on p. 137.

ASSESS

Have students complete Daily Quiz 6.2. As Alternative Assessment, you may want to use the Science and Medicine graphic organizer or the literary genre exercise in this section's lessons.

RETEACH

Have students complete Main Idea Activity for English Language Learners and Special-Needs Students 6.2. Group students who are able to understand the concepts with those having difficulty.

Allow time for discussion. **ENGLISH LANGUAGE LEARNERS, COOPERATIVE LEARNING**

EXTEND

Students may want to perform scenes from plays by the dramatists discussed in this section. Suggest they make masks to use in their performances. **COOPERATIVE LEARNING, BLOCK SCHEDULING**

competition. The competition's judges were ordinary citizens chosen by lottery. They awarded prizes based on the beauty or wisdom of each play.

Tragedies. In Greek **tragedies** the main character struggled against fate, or events. Usually a combination of outside forces defeated the main character. Often, tragic heroes were punished for displaying *hubris* (HYOO·bruhs)—the sin of pride. Hubris offended the gods and doomed the hero to a tragic end.

Three well-known writers of tragedies lived during the 400s B.C. Aeschylus (ES·ke·luhs) wrote about religion and the relationship between gods and people. His three most famous plays centered on the murder of Agamemnon, the king who had led the Greeks against Troy. Another writer of tragedies, **Sophocles** (SAHF·uh·kleez), defended many traditional Greek values. Aristotle called Sophocles's most famous play, *Oedipus Rex*, a perfect example of tragedy.

The third great playwright of the golden age was **Euripides** (yoo·RIP·uh·deez). He was more of a realist than Aeschylus or Sophocles. Like Socrates, he questioned many old beliefs and ideas. Earlier writers had often honored war for its deeds of courage and heroism. In *The Trojan Women*, Euripides showed the pain and misery of war.

Comedies. Greek comedies also originated at the Great Dionysia festival. These plays made fun of ideas and people. Comedies usually included both tragic and humorous figures. Unlike characters in tragedies, however, the main characters in comedies solved their problems.

The finest writer of Greek comedies, **Aristophanes** (ar·uh·STAHF·uh·neez), was known for his sharp wit. In *Clouds* he poked fun at Socrates for his theories about education. Aristophanes also disliked war. He used comedy to make Athenians think about the causes and effects of war.

Greek actors wore masks, such as this one, to represent various characters and emotions.

✔ **READING CHECK: Analyzing Information** How did the Greeks' style of playwriting reflect their society? reflected belief in the gods, commented on social issues

---

SECTION 2 REVIEW

1. **Define** and explain the significance:
   philosophy
   aristocracy
   dramas
   tragedies

2. **Identify** and explain the significance:
   Socrates
   Plato
   Aristotle
   Pythagoras
   Hippocrates
   Herodotus
   Sophocles
   Euripides
   Aristophanes

3. **Comparing and Contrasting**
   Copy the following graphic organizer. Use it to list the ideas of Socrates and Plato that differed from those of Aristotle. Then list areas in which all three agreed.

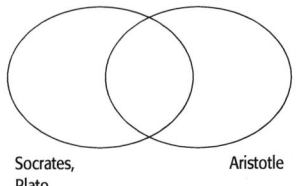

   Socrates, Plato   Aristotle

4. **Finding the Main Idea**
   a. How did Socrates's teaching method help him accomplish his purpose?
   b. What were the main characteristics of the ideal government described in Plato's *Republic*?
   c. In what ways did Aristotle's view of the principles of government differ from Plato's view?
   d. What view did the Greeks take toward the development of practical scientific knowledge?
   e. What do the dramatic styles developed by the Greeks reveal about their culture?

5. **Writing and Critical Thinking**
   Summarizing Describe how Greek ideas of good government and citizenship developed and changed during the golden age.
   Consider:
   • the different theories of government of Socrates, Plato, and Aristotle
   • public reaction to Socrates's teachings
   • the opinions about leaders expressed by Greek playwrights

Homework Practice Online
keyword: SP3 HP6

SECTION 2 REVIEW ANSWERS

❶ **Define**
• philosophy, p. 133
• aristocracy, p. 134
• dramas, p. 136
• tragedies, p. 137

❷ **Identify**
• Socrates, p. 133
• Plato, p. 133
• Aristotle, p. 134
• Pythagoras, p. 135
• Hippocrates, p. 135
• Herodotus, p. 136
• Sophocles, p. 137
• Euripides, p. 137
• Aristophanes, p. 137

❸ Socrates and Plato: did not support democracy; Aristotle: supported limited democracy, emphasized logic; shared: studied ethics and other ideals

❹ a. Questioning forced students to examine values and beliefs.

b. His long dialogue described an aristocracy in which rulers were chosen for their wisdom, ability, and high ideals.

c. Plato: emphasized an aristocracy; Aristotle: monarchy, aristocracy, and democracy

d. Greek thinkers did not specialize, did not emphasize practical applications

e. belief in gods and their relationship with humans

❺ growing acceptance of questioning authority—Socrates was executed for questioning officials; Plato advocated government by skill; Aristotle supported limited democracy; playwrights openly criticized rulers.

OBJECTIVES

1 Detail how Philip II of Macedon paved the way for cultural change.

2 Examine what Alexander the Great accomplished.

3 Identify the factors that contributed to the breakup of Alexander's empire.

REPRODUCIBLE RESOURCES

▶ Guided Reading Strategy 6.3

▶ Graphic Activity 6: Stopping Alexander the Great

▶ Readings in World History 24: Alexander's Deification at the Temple of Zeus-Ammon

▶ Creative Teaching Strategy 6: A Debate About Power

TECHNOLOGY RESOURCES

▶ One-Stop Planner 6.3

▶ Homework Practice Online

REINFORCEMENT, REVIEW, AND ASSESSMENT

▶ Section 3 Review, p. 141

▶ Daily Quiz 6.3

▶ Main Idea Activity 6.3

▶ English Audio Summary 6.3

▶ Spanish Audio Summary 6.3

VISUAL RECORD ANSWER

Soldiers stood and marched close together, and they were heavily armed and shielded.

LET'S GET STARTED!

As students enter the classroom, have them recall what they learned about the Peloponnesian War and its aftermath. *(destructive civil war; Sparta conquered Athens and fought with Thebes for domination of Greece)* Ask why such events might expose a country to conquest by an outside power. *(Responses should note a relationship between disunity and weakness.)* Tell students that in Section 3 they will learn how this happened to the disunified and politically unsettled city-states of Greece.

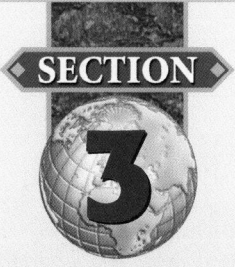

SECTION 3

READ TO DISCOVER

❶ How did Philip II of Macedon pave the way for cultural change?

❷ What did Alexander the Great accomplish?

❸ What factors contributed to the breakup of Alexander's empire?

DEFINE

phalanx
orators

IDENTIFY

Philip II of Macedon
Demosthenes
Alexander the Great
Hellenistic culture

▶ WHY IT MATTERS TODAY

Alexander the Great brought Greek ideas to other parts of the ancient world through military conquest. Use **CNN** or other **current event** sources to explore ways in which ideas pass from culture to culture in today's world. Record your findings in your journal.

CNNstudentNews.com

Alexander the Great

The Main Idea
Alexander the Great spread Greek culture and ideas throughout the Mediterranean and Near East.

The Story Continues *Through a brilliant career of military conquest, the Macedonian leader Alexander the Great built an empire that reached from the Mediterranean to the Indus River valley. To rule more efficiently, Alexander encouraged a blending of Greek culture with the customs of conquered peoples. An ancient historian wrote about Alexander, "[H]e understood that the sharing of race and customs is a great step towards softening men's hearts."*

Philip II of Macedon

Despite its great advances, Greece entered a period of struggle after its golden age. Athens declined in power. Bitter competition among the city-states weakened Greece, and the Persians worked to undermine Greek unity. Finally, in 338 B.C., peace was restored. A new era of Greek progress began. This era would eventually give rise to a new culture.

Macedon was a rising kingdom in the Macedonian region to the north of Greece. The Macedonians were a hardy, warlike people. They lived in villages, each led by a local noble. Macedonian kings could rule only with the support of the nobles.

In 359 B.C. a young man named **Philip II of Macedon** became king. As a youth Philip had been a hostage in Thebes for about three years. During that time, he had come to admire Greek ways. He had also learned about the organization of Thebes's army.

Earlier Macedonian kings had depended on nobles to supply troops for the army. Philip did not want to rely on others to secure his rule. Thus he recruited and organized the best-disciplined army in Macedonian history.

Borrowing a Greek idea, Philip organized his infantry into phalanxes. A **phalanx** (FAY·langks) contained rows of soldiers standing shoulder to shoulder. They carried pikes, or heavy spears, up to about 18 feet long. Tightly spaced, with pikes forward, these soldiers were especially effective against cavalry charges.

INTERPRETING THE VISUAL RECORD

The phalanx The Macedonian phalanx used many lines of soldiers. It was the most powerful fighting machine of its day. *Based on this drawing, why would it have been hard to attack a phalanx?*

LEVEL 2: Have students list the events that led to Philip's conquest of Greece. *(Greek city-states are weakened by war and disunited; Philip becomes king of Macedon; recruits paid army and applies Greek idea of phalanxes; takes control of northern Athenian colonies; moves into Greece; some, like Demosthenes, oppose; Athens fights, but city-states remain disunited; one by one city-states fall; Thebes and Athens defeated at Chaeronea in 338 B.C.)*

LEVEL 3: Ask students to explain the irony of Philip conquering the Greeks. *(He had been a hostage in Greece when young; he borrowed the idea of phalanxes from the Greeks.)* Then ask them to choose a point of view about Philip—whether he was a savior who could unify Greece or someone who would threaten its freedom. Have them write a paragraph identifying and supporting their point of view.

Philip's first goal after becoming king was to restore order in Macedon. He then won control of several Athenian colonies in northern Greece. Finally he turned his attention south, to the heartland of Greece.

The Greeks had differing views of Philip. Some saw him as a savior who could unify Greece, while others felt that he threatened their freedom. One of Athens's finest **orators,** or public speakers, was **Demosthenes** (di·MAHS·thuh·neez). He led Athenian opposition to Philip.

Demosthenes attacked Philip in a series of speeches. He tried to get Athens to lead Greece in a fight for liberty. Demosthenes's fiery speeches drove the Athenians to action. However, the city-states failed to follow the lead of Athens. One by one, they fell to Philip's army. In 338 B.C., Philip defeated Thebes and Athens at the Battle of Chaeronea (ker·uh·NEE·uh). With this victory Philip united Greece under his rule.

Philip organized the cities into a league and planned to invade Persia. He did not live to achieve this goal. In 336 B.C. he was assassinated. Philip's 20-year-old son, Alexander, succeeded him. He would become known to history as **Alexander the Great.**

✔ **READING CHECK: Analyzing Information** How did Philip's army differ from previous Macedonian armies? was first professional army

Many Macedonian and Greek coins of the late 300s B.C. carried images of Philip II—shown riding a chariot on this gold stater—or of his son, Alexander.

Interdisciplinary Connection

LANGUAGE ARTS. The Greeks valued rhetoric, the art of using language effectively and persuasively. As a great orator, Demosthenes was an expert at rhetoric. In one persuasive speech, he begged his fellow Athenians: "Consider the facts, gentlemen, consider the outrageous lengths to which Philip has gone. He does not offer us a choice between action and inaction. He utters threats . . . in overbearing terms. He is not content to rest on his laurels but is continually adding to the haul he collects in the net in which he ensnares our hesitant, inactive country." Demosthenes's condemnation of Philip was so extreme that today such a tirade is called a *philippic*.

ACTIVITY: Have groups of students work to prepare speeches for and against Philip. Each group should select a speaker to present its argument to the class.

MAP ANSWER
Gaugamela (331 B.C.)

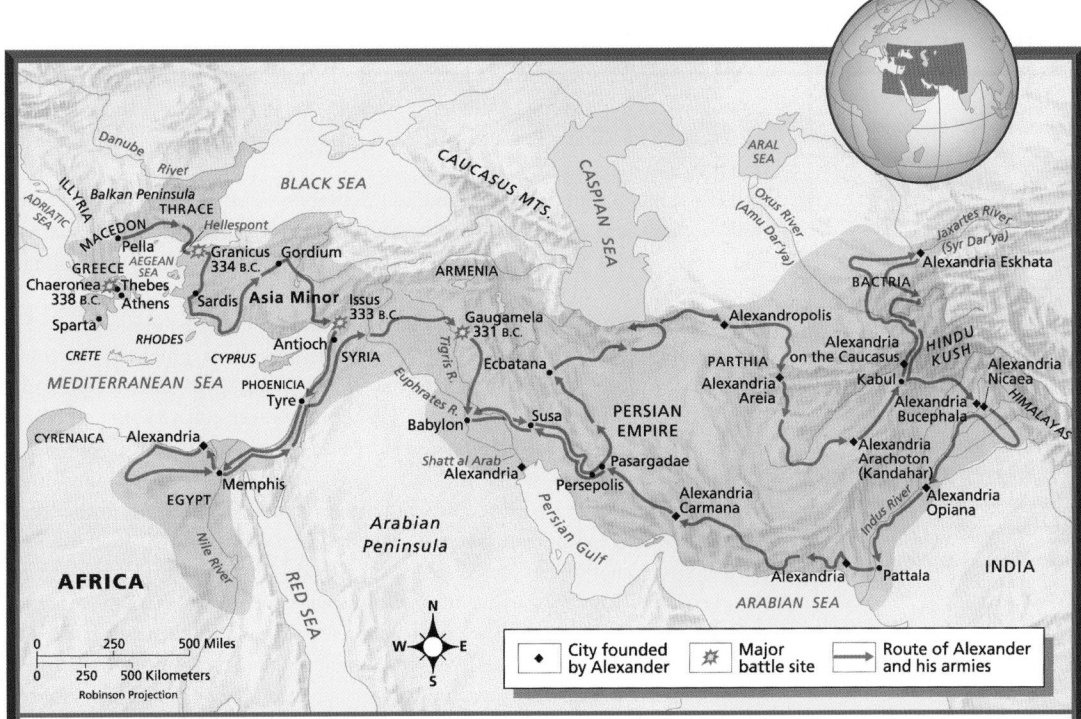

Alexander the Great's Empire, 323 B.C.

Interpreting Maps Alexander's military campaigns led him through Asia Minor, Syria, Egypt, the Persian Empire, and India.

■ **Skills Assessment: The World in Spatial Terms** Trace the route of Alexander and his armies from the Macedonian region to India. In which city did Alexander's last major battle take place?

Map legend:
- ◆ City founded by Alexander
- ✶ Major battle site
- Route of Alexander and his armies

Technology Resources

Online Maps, Charts, and Graphs: Division of Alexander's Empire, 303 B.C.

ALL LEVELS: Write the following goals of Alexander on the board: (1) conquer the world, (2) spread Greek culture, (3) manage an empire. Organize the class into pairs or triads. Have each group use these goals as a basis for a chart that records what Alexander did to accomplish each goal and that assesses whether or not he accomplished it. Call on volunteers to explain their charts to the class.

ENGLISH LANGUAGE LEARNERS, COOPERATIVE LEARNING

ALL LEVELS: Discuss whether Alexander's empire really was "one world." Ask how its size and composition may have undermined its unity. (*Its people were diverse, and ultimate authority was distant.*) Ask what other factors led to the empire's breakup. (*fighting among generals, Roman invasion*)

ENGLISH LANGUAGE LEARNERS

 HOMEWORK Have students prepare short speeches supporting or opposing Alexander the Great. Students should choose one of these perspectives: a soldier in Alexander's army, a Greek citizen, or a citizen of a land threatened with conquest.

Historical Sidelight

Many legends surround Alexander the Great. One of the best-known involves his horse, Bucephalus. According to legend, Bucephalus was a gift to Philip, but no one could ride him. The horse shied and reared whenever someone tried to mount him. Alexander noticed that the horse was merely afraid of its own shadow. He turned the horse to face the sun and mounted him easily. Acknowledging his son's wisdom, Philip gave Bucephalus to Alexander, who rode him for many years. When the horse died on a campaign, Alexander founded a city at the spot named Alexandria Bucephala.

ACTIVITY: Have students find the city named Alexandria Bucephala on the map on page 139. Then have them locate other cities that were named after Alexander.

THEN AND NOW ANSWER

Answers will vary but will likely include U.S. presidents.

Memorials

Many schools, colleges, and towns are named for famous people. In this way, we remember and honor individuals long after they have died. In the United States, two of our most famous leaders are honored in the Washington Monument and the Lincoln Memorial in Washington, D.C.

Alexander the Great has been memorialized throughout the world, both during his life and after his death. As he conquered cities and towns, he gave many of them his name. Beginning in Alexandria, Egypt, his route can be traced eastward on a map by following the towns bearing his name. The image to the right shows a view of the bustling Egyptian city of Alexandria. **Notice streets or buildings in your town that have been named after people. Can you think of other well-known people who have been memorialized in this way?**

Alexander the Great

Philip had given his son the best training and education possible. Alexander received his military training in the Macedonian army. He got his formal education from the great Greek philosopher Aristotle. This combination of military and classical education prepared Alexander well for leadership.

As a military commander, Alexander was even more skilled than his father. His military campaigns are among the most admired in history. He was physically strong and brave, and his courage in battle won the loyalty of his troops. They willingly followed him into unknown lands.

Alexander crushed the rebellions that broke out in Greece after Philip's death. He then set out to conquer the world. By 331 B.C. Alexander had completely destroyed Persia. In the process, he had conquered Asia Minor, Syria, Egypt, and Mesopotamia. Alexander now ruled a huge territory. His aim, however, was to bring all of the known world into a single empire. Beyond Persia lay India. For almost four years, Alexander led his troops east. He met little resistance and got as far as the Indus River. From there he intended to gain control of northern India. Alexander's army had seen enough fighting, however, and refused to go on. He pleaded with his tired soldiers, but they would not follow. In 326 B.C. Alexander was forced to turn back to Persia.

Alexander led his army to the Indian Ocean, where he divided his troops. A part of the army traveled west by sea. They explored the Persian Gulf and then sailed inland to meet Alexander at the city of Susa. Alexander led the rest of his army through the desert. Many of his troops died from exposure and lack of food and water. Those who survived reached Susa in 324 B.C. By the spring of 323 B.C., discontent had begun to spread through the empire. Alexander, in Babylon, became seriously ill. He struggled with a raging fever for about 10 days. Finally Alexander died in June of 323 B.C. He was not yet 33 years old.

✔ **READING CHECK: Comparing** Compare the accomplishments of Alexander the Great with those of Philip II. Philip built Macedon into a regional power; Alexander expanded conquest to known world.

CLOSE

Have students sequence the events that enabled Philip II to conquer Greece, that enabled Alexander to build his empire, and that caused the empire to break up.

REVIEW

Have students complete the Section 3 Review on p. 141.

ASSESS

Have students complete Daily Quiz 6.3. As Alternative Assessment, have students use the speech exercise in this section's lessons.

RETEACH

Have students complete Main Idea Activity for English Language Learners and Special-Needs Students 6.3. Then ask them to write a question and answer about the main idea for each subsection.
ENGLISH LANGUAGE LEARNERS

EXTEND

Organize students into small groups and have each group develop a list of qualities that make someone a great leader. From the group lists, create a master class list on the board. Then ask students to assess which of these qualities Alexander possessed.
COOPERATIVE LEARNING, BLOCK SCHEDULING

Beginnings of the Hellenistic World

In 13 years Alexander almost never lost a battle. He conquered much of the known world in that brief time. Alexander's actions during those years tell us much about his views of rule and leadership.

The spread of Greek culture. Alexander purposely spread Greek culture wherever his armies marched. He founded numerous cities, many named Alexandria in his honor. Groups of Greeks and Macedonians were settled in each of these cities.

Under Alexander's leadership, Macedonians, Greeks, and Persians often worked together to govern the empire. This enabled Alexander to rule his empire more efficiently. To set an example, Alexander married two Persian noblewomen. He required his generals to marry women of the Persian royal family and held a mass wedding in which 10,000 of his troops married Persian women. Clearly he aimed to bring Greeks and Persians together in a single culture.

Alexander failed to achieve his dream of world rule. However, his reign spread a new culture throughout much of the world. No longer purely Hellenic, or Greek, this new "Greek-like" way of life became known as the **Hellenistic culture.** It combined ideas and values drawn from the Mediterranean and Asia. This remarkable culture thrived in the time between Alexander's death and the Roman conquest of Greece in 146 B.C. We call this period the Hellenistic Age. Its achievements still influence the world today.

The breakup of Alexander's empire. After Alexander's death, his generals competed for his empire. In 301 B.C. three generals divided Alexander's empire into three main kingdoms—Macedon, Egypt, and Syria—and several smaller kingdoms. These new kingdoms were often at war with one another. Their rulers wasted much wealth and energy on war. In about 200 B.C. Roman legions invaded Macedon. Over time the Romans conquered most of the once-mighty Hellenistic empire.

✔ **READING CHECK: Identifying Cause and Effect** What actions of later rulers contributed to the decline of the Hellenistic empire? wars and internal conflicts

This gold crown found in Macedon may have belonged to Alexander the Great, whose bust appears below.

What If? Alexander the Great had not died so young? Do you think he would have continued to expand his empire? Explain your answer.

◀SECTION▶
3 REVIEW ANSWERS

❶ Define
• phalanx, p. 138
• orators, p. 139

❷ Identify
• Philip II of Macedon, p. 138
• Demosthenes, p. 139
• Alexander the Great, p. 139
• Hellenistic culture, p. 141

❸ Rise: Philip I conquering Greece, superior military organization, Alexander's background and training for leadership; Fall: power struggles between generals, resources wasted on war, Roman invasion

❹ a. founded cities that were settled by Greeks and Macedonians; encouraged cross-cultural marriage

b. his education, military skill, physical strength, and courage

c. internal power struggles; wasted resources on war; conquest by Romans

❺ Diary entries should reflect soldiers' admiration for Alexander, as well as weariness and discontent.

◤ **SECTION 3 REVIEW** ◥

1. Define and explain the significance:
phalanx
orators

2. Identify and explain the significance:
Philip II of Macedon
Demosthenes
Alexander the Great
Hellenistic culture

3. Sequencing Copy the graphic organizer below. Use it to list the factors that helped Alexander establish his empire. Then list the factors that contributed to the empire's breakup.

Hellenistic Empire

Rise   Fall

4. � **Finding the Main Idea**
a. How did the actions of Alexander the Great help to encourage the spread of Hellenistic culture?
b. What special qualities made Alexander the Great a remarkable leader?
c. Why did Alexander's empire collapse after his death?

5. **Writing and Critical Thinking**
Evaluating Imagine that you are a soldier in the army of Alexander the Great. In 323 B.C. you find out that Alexander has just died. Write a diary entry looking back on your time with Alexander the Great.
Consider:
• why Alexander was loved by his soldiers
• what the new Hellenistic culture offered for Alexander's soldiers
• how the soldiers probably felt by the time they reached Susa

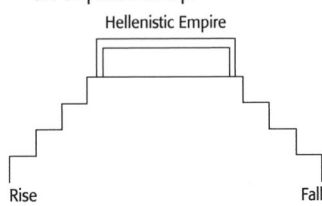
Homework Practice Online
keyword: SP3 HP6

OBJECTIVES

1 Describe how society changed during the Hellenistic Age.

2 Explain how philosophers of the Hellenistic Age viewed ethics.

3 Identify the ways in which Hellenistic scientists added to the existing body of knowledge.

LET'S GET STARTED!

As students enter the classroom, ask what it means when we say that the United States is a multicultural or pluralistic society. *(Many different ethnic and racial groups live in one nation.)* Discuss the concept of one overlying American culture in this multicultural society and how the subcultures help create it. Tell students that in Section 4 they will learn about the spread of "Greek-like," or Hellenistic, culture throughout Alexander's empire.

SECTION 4

READ TO DISCOVER

❶ How did society change during the Hellenistic Age?

❷ How did philosophers of the Hellenistic Age view ethics?

❸ In what ways did Hellenistic scientists add to the existing body of knowledge?

IDENTIFY

Zeno
Epicurus
Euclid
Archimedes
Aristarchus
Eratosthenes

WHY IT MATTERS TODAY

Western civilizations owe a great deal to advances made by philosophers and scientists of the Hellenistic age. Use CNN.com or other **current event** sources to find scientists or thinkers of today who are working in areas that Hellenistic scientists pioneered. Record your findings in your journal.

CNN studentNews.com

The Spread of Hellenistic Culture

The Main Idea
In the Hellenistic world, people looked to science, philosophy, and religion for a sense of understanding.

The Story Continues *The changing Hellenistic society created by Alexander the Great produced great achievements in the arts and sciences. Hellenistic philosophers and scientists learned a great deal about the natural world using very simple tools. The scientist and inventor Archimedes displayed this new confidence in his famous saying, "Give me a lever and a place to stand on and I will move the earth."*

Learning and Commerce

The conquests of Alexander the Great brought Greek culture to many areas, including the Nile Valley, Southwest Asia, and the lands that bordered India. Greek ways continued to influence these areas long after Alexander's death. At the same time, ideas from these other lands changed Greek culture at home.

Hellenistic society contained a small group of wealthy people and a large group of poor people. In between were small, middle-ranked groups. The spread of Greek culture helped these middle ranks thrive during the Hellenistic Age.

Many people prospered from the growth of trade in the Hellenistic world. For the most part, trade was based in the major cities. Alexandria, Egypt—the biggest Hellenistic city—became a leading commercial center. Trade routes linked the Hellenistic world. The spread of routes to China, India, and Arabia also helped to increase trade.

Alexander built many cities along the route of his conquests. Many of these grew to become centers of learning as well as trade. For example, the library at Alexandria, Egypt contained thousands of papyrus scrolls. These scrolls held much of the Hellenistic world's knowledge and literature.

As people became more prosperous, education became more widespread. Old values faded; new values brought freer lifestyles for some. For example, Hellenistic women appeared more often in public and won new rights regarding property. Another major change centered on a new idea of what it meant to be Greek. Now a Hellenized Egyptian or Syrian was considered a "Greek." The old Greek bias against "barbarians" had not actually disappeared. It was just that more of the world had become "Greek" through the spread of culture.

✔ **READING CHECK: Identifying Cause and Effect** How did the growth of the economy affect the status of women in Hellenistic society? appeared more often in public; acquired property rights

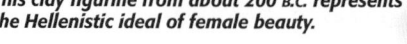

This clay figurine from about 200 B.C. represents the Hellenistic ideal of female beauty.

TEACH OBJECTIVE 1

ALL LEVELS: Call on students to identify ways in which Greek society changed during the Hellenistic Age. List responses on the board. (*growth of trade, cities as centers of trade and learning, thriving middle class, widespread education, new values, more rights for women, new idea of "Greek"*) Then explore with the class how some of the changes are related. **ENGLISH LANGUAGE LEARNERS**

HOMEWORK Have students write explanations of how the Hellenistic culture changed society. Encourage them to use their notes from the previous activity.

TEACH OBJECTIVE 2

ALL LEVELS: Copy the following chart on the board, omitting the italicized answers. Ask students to complete it, then debate the merits of each philosophy. **ENGLISH LANGUAGE LEARNERS**

Cynicism	Skepticism	Stoicism	Epicureanism
Diogenes	Pyrrho	Zeno	Epicurus
live simply; no regard for wealth, pleasure, status	*changing universe; uncertain knowledge; acceptance*	*divine reason directs world; acceptance of fate*	*seek pleasure; avoid pain; limit desires to avoid suffering*

Religion and Philosophy

In the large-scale urban civilization of the Hellenistic kingdoms, the Greek concept of the polis declined. This caused many people to feel that they had lost control over their lives. In their efforts to adapt to their changing society, many people turned to new religions and philosophies. All focused on satisfying people's need for a sense of belonging.

The Hellenistic kings in Egypt and in Asia, for example, encouraged the practice of ruler-worship. Ruler-worship provided a useful means to fill people with a new sense of civic duty as the role of the polis was replaced by that of the monarch. People found comfort in looking to these authority figures for guidance. Many also turned to the so-called mystery religions—cults that introduced worshippers to secret teachings or mysteries. These teachings usually had to do with the secrets of life after death and immortality. The rituals of the mystery religions provided members with a feeling of unity, security, and personal worth.

While some thus looked for a new sense of belonging in religion, others turned to philosophy in search of understanding. Hellenistic philosophers were mainly concerned with ethics. Four chief schools of philosophy existed—Cynicism, Skepticism, Stoicism, and Epicureanism. The Cynics taught that people should live simply and naturally, without regard for pleasure, wealth, or social status. The best-known Cynic was Diogenes (dy·AHJ·uh·neez). The Skeptics believed that because the universe is always changing, all knowledge is uncertain. By accepting this fact, however, people can achieve peace of mind. Pyrrho (PIR·oh) is credited as the founder of Skepticism.

Zeno established the Stoic philosophy in Athens in the late 300s B.C. He and his followers believed that divine reason directs the world. Thus people should accept their fate without complaint. Stoics believed that every person had some "spark" of the divine within. People could achieve happiness only by following this spark. The Stoics greatly influenced Roman and Christian thinking.

Epicurus was the founder of Epicurean philosophy. He taught that the aim of life is to seek pleasure and avoid pain. Epicurus said that people should limit their desires. This, he felt, was the best way to avoid suffering.

✔ **READING CHECK: Drawing Inferences** In what ways did Hellenistic religions and philosophies offer people comfort for changing times? helped people feel a greater sense of control and belonging

Science in the Hellenistic Age

Two features of Hellenistic science were very remarkable. First, scientists learned a great deal about the world using very simple instruments. Second, Hellenistic scientists showed little interest in turning their discoveries into labor-saving machines. Perhaps this was because slave labor was used throughout the Hellenistic world.

Mathematics and physics. Greeks of the Hellenistic Age became outstanding scientists and mathematicians. **Euclid** contributed extremely important work to the development of geometry. He showed how geometric statements flow logically from one another. Euclid's *Elements* is the basis for many of today's geometry books.

Probably the greatest scientist of the Hellenistic period was **Archimedes** (ahr·kuh·MEED·eez). He calculated the value of pi (π), the ratio of the circumference of a circle to its diameter. Archimedes also used mathematics to explain how levers work. He invented many machines, including the compound pulley. He also invented the Archimedes screw, which draws water upward. This device is still used today.

Holt Researcher
go.hrw.com
KEYWORD: Holt Researcher
FreeFind: Archimedes
After reading more about Archimedes on the Holt Researcher, assess his significance to science.

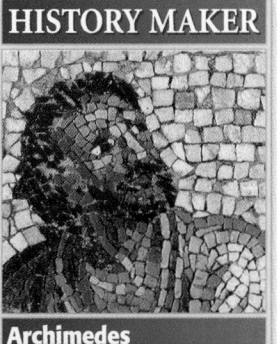

HISTORY MAKER

Archimedes
(287 B.C.–212 B.C.)

Unlike most scientists of his day, Archimedes put math and physics to practical use. For example, he used physics to build defensive weapons. When the Romans attacked Syracuse, Archimedes built devices to beat them back. According to the historian Plutarch, Archimedes's weapons were so effective that if the Romans "did but see a little rope or a piece of wood from the wall . . . they turned their backs and fled."

How did Archimedes's view of science and technology differ from that of other Hellenistic scientists?

Culture

Hellenistic society remained Greek in language and culture. Using a universal language throughout the empire improved and simplified commerce and the exchange of ideas. Education in the Greek language extended knowledge of Hellenic culture and forged a common civilization instead of separate thoughts, traditions, and customs.

Critical Thinking

What might have happened if the Greeks had not retained their language?

ANSWER: Financial and business transactions, unification of ideas, and advances in mathematics, science, and astronomy would have been slowed down.

HISTORY MAKER ANSWER

Unlike many Hellenistic scientists, Archimedes put mathematics and physics to practical use.

That's Interesting!

The Lighthouse of Alexandria is considered one of the Seven Wonders of the Ancient World. A fire burned atop this more than 400-foot sculpture to guide ships into the city's harbor.

Technology Resources

Online Maps, Charts, and Graphs: The Hellenization of Asia

LEVEL 1: Have students work in pairs to note the various scientists discussed in the text and the accomplishments of each. You might also want students to prepare questions for the presenters in the Level 3 activity for this objective. **ENGLISH LANGUAGE LEARNERS, COOPERATIVE LEARNING**

LEVEL 2: Ask students to discuss or write a paragraph describing Hellenistic science as largely "knowledge for knowledge's sake." Then have them discuss or write a second paragraph predicting how this concept might have changed if slavery were not so prevalent in the empire. Students should support their point of view.

LEVEL 3: Have students play the roles of Euclid, Archimedes, Aristarchus, Hipparchus, or Eratosthenes. Ask each to explain the scientist's work to the class and discuss how it spread to other cultures. **COOPERATIVE LEARNING**

CLOSE

Ask students to imagine they are elderly Greeks in Hellenistic society. Ask them to describe changes in the economy, society, and ways of thinking during their lifetime.

SKILLS PRACTICE ANSWERS

1. The size of the tool affects the volume of water it can move.

2. less time and manual labor spent bringing water to and away from fields

3. were spread and used hundreds of miles away and hundreds of years later

4. Answers will vary.

SKILL-BUILDING STRATEGIES — Using Models to Understand History

The Archimedes Screw

Many of Archimedes's inventions are still in use today. One of these is the Archimedes screw. It can be used in drainage, irrigation, and pump systems. Although Archimedes himself left no sketches or models of his invention, knowledge of its use became well known by word of mouth and through the writings of others. A Roman engineer named Vitruvius described the Archimedes screw in an architectural guide he wrote in the first century B.C. He provided some of the first known sketches of the device.

Historians often use models to help us understand past events or eras. In most common uses, a model is a representation of something. A scale model of a ship or a building is one example. Some researchers use models to illustrate what ancient cities once looked like. Others use models of geographic areas, such as three-dimensional maps, to illustrate conclusions regarding geographic distribution, land use, or other geography-related factors.

circular treadmill to drive screw

enclosed, water-tight outer tube

continuously revolving spiral threads

spiral threads draw water upward above original level

Skills Reminder

To use a model to understand historical developments, first identify what the model is designed to represent. If the model has been made to scale, use your mathematics skills to determine the actual size of the item represented. Make sure you understand the time frame during which the item would have been created and used. Ask yourself questions about the various ways in which the item represented by the model might have been used. Try to imagine why such an item might have been important for the daily life or work of people at the time. This will indicate what needs the item was designed to meet and will help you to evaluate what the model reveals about an event or era.

Skills Practice

Study the illustration above, picturing the use of an Archimedes screw in Europe in the 1500s.

❶ In what ways do the tool's dimensions affect its performance?

❷ How could this invention have helped save labor in Hellenistic Greece?

❸ What does the use of the Archimedes screw in Europe in the 1500s tell us about the geographic distribution of Greek ideas?

❹ Archimedes also invented the compound pulley, often called a block and tackle. Design a scale model of a compound pulley. What would the dimensions of the actual pulley be? How could such a pulley save labor?

REVIEW

Have students complete the Section 4 Review on p. 145.

ASSESS

Have students complete Daily Quiz 6.4. As Alternative Assessment, you may want to use the homework assignment or graphic organizer in this section's lessons.

RETEACH

Have students complete Main Idea Activity for English Language Learners and Special-Needs Students 6.4. Then have them create flash cards with terms from Section 4 on one side with an appropriate explanation on the other. Let pairs of students use their flash cards to reinforce section concepts.
ENGLISH LANGUAGE LEARNERS, COOPERATIVE LEARNING

EXTEND

Organize students into groups to create maps of the Hellenistic world. Each group should draw its map and add illustrations of sculptures, buildings, reliefs of rulers, and other period art and artifacts at appropriate locations. Each image should include a descriptive caption.
BLOCK SCHEDULING, COOPERATIVE LEARNING

Medicine. Hellenistic scientists added greatly to the ancient world's medical knowledge. Alexandria, Egypt was the center of medical science. As Greek and Egyptian traditions came together, Hellenistic doctors learned from the Egyptian art of embalming to examine and catalog the parts of the human body.

To learn more about anatomy, Alexandrian doctors studied the bodies of executed criminals. They learned much about the human body; for example, Herophilus (huh·RAHF·uh·luhs) concluded that the brain is the center of the nervous system. This and other medical advances allowed Hellenistic doctors to perform delicate surgery.

Astronomy and geography. Hellenistic scientists made significant advances in astronomy as they came into contact with the knowledge of the Egyptians and Babylonians. They used principles of geometry to track the movements of stars and planets. **Aristarchus** (ar·uh·STAHR·kuhs) correctly believed that the earth and other planets moved around the sun, but he failed to convince others. Hipparchus (hi·PAHR·kuhs) used trigonometry to predict eclipses. He used the sun and the moon to calculate the length of the year.

Hellenistic geographers knew that Earth was round. At Alexandria, **Eratosthenes** (er·uh·TAHS·thuh·neez) calculated the distance around the earth with amazing accuracy. He did so by finding the angle of the sun's rays from different points on the globe. Eratosthenes was considered one of the most brilliant mathematicians and astronomers of his time. He was honored by the Hellenistic ruler of Egypt to head the great Library of Alexandria.

This papyrus from the 100s B.C. contains one ancient Greek astronomer's notes on the cosmos.

Holt Researcher
go.hrw.com
KEYWORD: Holt Researcher
FreeFind: Eratosthenes
After reading more about Eratosthenes on the Holt Researcher, assess his significance to science.

✔ **READING CHECK: Supporting a Point of View** Why is it important today to study Hellenistic achievements in science? Many scientific fields of today draw basic understanding from Hellenistic discoveries.

SECTION 4 REVIEW

1. **Identify** and explain the significance:
   Zeno
   Epicurus
   Euclid
   Archimedes
   Aristarchus
   Eratosthenes

2. **Categorizing** Copy the table below. Each column lists a field of study in which Hellenistic thinkers were active. List the major Hellenistic accomplishments in each subject area. Give the names of any scientists or philosophers identified with the work.

	Philosophy	Math, Physics	Medical Science	Astronomy, Geography
Hellenistic Achievements				

3. **Finding the Main Idea**
   a. In what way did new understanding of the term "Greek" help to unify the Hellenistic world?
   b. How did the primary ideas of the four major Hellenistic philosophies differ from each other? How were they similar?

4. **Writing and Critical Thinking**
   Making Predictions Describe the possible outcomes that might have been achieved had more Hellenistic scientists put their discoveries to work.
   Consider:
   • the achievements of Greek scientists
   • the practical uses their achievements could have had
   • how these discoveries would have changed Greek life

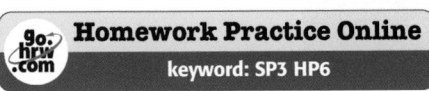
Homework Practice Online
keyword: SP3 HP6

SECTION 4 REVIEW ANSWERS

❶ **Identify**
• Zeno, p. 143
• Epicurus, p. 143
• Euclid, p. 143
• Archimedes, p. 143
• Aristarchus, p. 145
• Eratosthenes, p. 145

❷ Philosophy: Stoicism (Zeno), Epicureanism (Epicurus), Cynicism (Diogenes), Skepticism (Pyrrho); Math, Physics: *Elements* (Euclid), *pi* and lever (Archimedes); Medical Science: anatomy, surgery; Astronomy, Geography: circumference of Earth (Eratosthenes), Earth moves around sun (Aristarchus), length of year (Hipparchus)

❸ a. promoted a shared sense of cultural and social unity

b. similar: focused on ethics; different: Cynics–simple, natural lifestyles; Skeptics–knowledge is uncertain, peace comes from acceptance of change; Stoics–people must accept their fate without complaint; Epicureans–self-control and moderation

❹ Predictions should mention saving labor and making the economy more efficient. Practical devices could have led to less need and support for slavery.

REVIEW AND ASSESSMENT RESOURCES

REPRODUCIBLE RESOURCES

▸ Vocabulary Activity 6

TECHNOLOGY RESOURCES

▸ Chapter 6 Test Generator (on the One-Stop Planner)
▸ Global Skill Builder CD–ROM
▸ HRW Web Site

REINFORCEMENT, REVIEW, and ASSESSMENT

▸ Chapter 6 Review, pp. 146–147
▸ Chapter 6 Tutorial for Students, Parents, Mentors, and Peers
▸ Chapter 6 Test (Form A or B)
▸ Alternative Assessment Handbook
▸ Chapter 6 Test for English Language Learners and Special-Needs Students

REVIEW

Have students complete the Chapter 6 Review on pages 146–147.

ASSESS

Use one of the chapter tests to assess students' understanding of the content. For Alternative Assessment, see the Portfolio Activities and Alternative Assessment Handbook.

CHAPTER 6 REVIEW ANSWERS

Understanding Main Ideas

1. balanced proportions; scenes from everyday life; admiration for human form

2. glorified humans; showed harmony, balance, order, and moderation; combined beauty and usefulness

3. believed in natural laws that could be discovered

4. histories became more accurate, objective; dramas reflected belief in gods; comedies questioned beliefs, poked fun

5. expanded conquest from Greece into Africa and Asia, including Persia

6. spread Greek culture; combined Macedonians and Persians; encouraged marriage between Macedonians and Persians; actions showed he wanted a united empire

7. Women appeared in public more often and won property rights. All Greeks benefited from more widespread education.

8. trade increased; small middle class thrived

Reviewing Themes

1. brought city-states under rule of one leader

2. Anyone who adopted the Hellenistic culture would be considered Greek.

3. Increased trade and the growth of cities helped many prosper.

146

CHAPTER 6 Review

Creating a Time Line

Copy the time line below onto a sheet of paper. Complete the time line by filling in the events, individuals, and dates from the chapter that you think were significant. Pick three events and explain why you think they were significant.

| 500 B.C. | 350 B.C. | 200 B.C. |

Writing a Summary

Using standard grammar, spelling, sentence structure, and punctuation, write an overview of the events in the chapter.

Identifying People and Ideas

Identify the following terms or individuals and explain their significance:

1. Parthenon
2. Socrates
3. Plato
4. Aristotle
5. Pythagoras
6. aristocracy
7. dramas
8. Philip II of Macedon
9. Alexander the Great
10. Hellenistic culture

Understanding Main Ideas

SECTION 1 *(pp. 130–132)*

Greek Art of the Golden Age

1. What were the main features of Greek arts of the golden age?
2. How did the Greeks of the golden age use art to express their values and ideals?

SECTION 2 *(pp. 133–137)*

Philosophers and Writers of the Golden Age

3. What basic approach to knowledge did philosophers and scientists of the golden age share?
4. How did Greeks of the golden age comment on their society through literature and comedy and drama?

SECTION 3 *(pp. 138–141)*

Alexander the Great

5. In what ways did Alexander the Great build on the accomplishments of Philip II of Macedon?
6. What specific actions did Alexander take to unify the Hellenistic world, and what do these actions tell us about his view of rule and leadership?

SECTION 4 *(pp. 142–145)*

The Spread of Hellenistic Culture

7. How did the social and economic changes of the Hellenistic Age work to improve the status of women and ordinary Greeks?
8. What major economic developments took place during the Hellenistic Age?

Reviewing Themes

1. **Government** In what way did the rise of Macedon under Philip II influence unity among the Greek city-states?
2. **Culture** How did new ideas of what it meant to be Greek influence the growth of Hellenistic culture?
3. **Economics** Why was the Hellenistic Age a time of economic prosperity for many?

Thinking Critically

1. **Finding the Main Idea** Why are the 400s B.C. generally known as the golden age of Greece?
2. **Problem Solving** How did Aristotle propose to deal with the problem of corruption in government?
3. **Supporting a Point of View** Provide evidence to support the claim that the approach to history used by Herodotus and Thucydides was a good system.
4. **Drawing Conclusions** How did the cities founded by Alexander the Great influence the spread of Greek culture?

Writing About History

Analyzing Information Using a major Greek or Hellenistic figure from the 400s B.C. or 300s B.C. as a main character, create an outline for a short story. Use the graphic organizer below to help you organize your story.

Setting:	
Main Character:	
Secondary Character:	
Conflict:	
Plot:	
Resolution:	

Building Social Studies Skills

Interpreting a Time Line

Study the time line below. Then answer the questions that follow.

338 B.C.
Philip II becomes ruler of all Greece.

146 B.C.
Romans complete conquest of Greece.

336 B.C.
Philip II is assassinated; Alexander becomes king of Macedon.

1. Which statement correctly describes the span of the time line?
   a. It spans from the beginning of Philip's rule in Greece until the end of Alexander's rule in Greece.
   b. It spans from the unification of Greece under one king until the conquest of Greece by Rome.
   c. It spans events during Philip's reign through events during Alexander's reign.
   d. It spans Alexander's reign and the Roman conquest of Greece.

2. What are some other events that belong on this time line? Give specific dates for the events.

Drawing Inferences

Read the following passage from *The Republic* by Plato. Then answer the questions.

> "And so we may venture to assert that anyone who can produce the best blend of the physical and intellectual sides of education and apply them to the training of character is producing harmony in a far more important sense than any mere musician."

3. Which of the following is the best statement of what this passage implies?
   a. Physical training is more important than intellectual training.
   b. A teacher's goal should be to help a student develop character.
   c. Musical training is more important than both physical and intellectual training.
   d. A teacher's goal should be to give students more physical education than intellectual education.
   e. Harmony and character are best developed when a teacher emphasizes intellectual education.

4. What would your school day be like if it were based on the statement you chose in question 3 above? Give specific examples.

Alternative Assessment

Building Your Portfolio

Link to TODAY

Culture

The Hellenistic empire united people from different ethnic and religious groups into one common culture, much like the United States today. Compile a list of the ways in which different regions and groups of people contribute to the economy and culture of the United States. Then use the list to create a chart that summarizes your findings.

✔ internet connect

go.hrw.com

Internet Activity: go.hrw.com
KEYWORD: SP3 WH6

Ancient Athens

Choose a topic on Greece's Golden and Hellenistic Ages to:
- research Athens's golden age and create a newspaper article describing a representative political development.
- identify currents of Greek thought in art from different time periods.
- report on the scientific contributions of the ancient Greeks.

The Roman World

CHAPTER RESOURCE MANAGER

Objectives	Pacing Guide	Reproducible Resources
SECTION 1 **Founding the Roman Republic** (pp. 150–154) • Identify the role geography played in Italy's and Rome's development. • Explain the form of government in the Roman Republic. • Examine the Conflict of the Orders and how it changed the early Roman Republic. • Compare and contrast the roles of citizens and noncitizens as Rome expanded its power.	**Regular** 1.5 day | **Block Scheduling** 1 day *Block Scheduling Handbook with Team Teaching Strategies, 7.1*	RS Guided Reading Strategy 7.1 RS Graphic Organizer Activity 7 E Hands-on History Activity 7
SECTION 2 **Rome Expands Its Borders** (pp. 155–157) • Discuss the Punic Wars and how Rome gained control over Carthage. • Identify political, economic, and social changes caused by Roman expansion.	**Regular** 1 day | **Block Scheduling** .5 day *Block Scheduling Handbook with Team Teaching Strategies, 7.2*	RS Guided Reading Strategy 7.2 PS Readings in World History 25: Rome's Perfect Location
SECTION 3 **The Birth of the Roman Empire** (pp. 158–161) • Identify the political events in Rome that helped weaken the Roman Republic. • Explain how the reign of Julius Caesar served as a transition between the Roman Republic and the Roman Empire. • Describe the events and conditions that marked the first two centuries of the Roman Empire.	**Regular** 1.5 day | **Block Scheduling** 1 day *Block Scheduling Handbook with Team Teaching Strategies, 7.3*	RS Guided Reading Strategy 7.3 SM Geography Activity 7 PS Readings in World History 26
SECTION 4 **Roman Society and Culture** (pp. 162–167) • Explain how the Romans built a strong and unified empire. • Describe how Roman citizens made a living and led their daily lives. • Discuss the role played by science and the arts in the empire.	**Regular** 1.5 day | **Block Scheduling** .5 day *Block Scheduling Handbook with Team Teaching Strategies, 7.4*	RS Guided Reading Strategy 7.4
SECTION 5 **The Rise of Christianity** (pp. 168–171) • Describe how the conditions Jews faced in Judaea contributed to the rise of Christianity. • Identify the difficulties early Christians experienced while under the influence of the Roman Empire. • Discuss the changes that occurred during the late Roman Empire that helped establish Christianity and stabilize the church.	**Regular** 1 day | **Block Scheduling** .5 day *Block Scheduling Handbook with Team Teaching Strategies, 7.5*	RS Guided Reading Strategy 7.5 PS Readings in World History 27: Christians in the Roman Empire
SECTION 6 **The Fall of the Western Empire** (pp. 172–177) • Identify the problems the Roman Empire had to deal with during the A.D. 200s. • Describe how the reigns of Diocletian and Constantine slowed the decline of the empire. • List the factors that led to the final decline of the Roman Empire in the West.	**Regular** 1 day | **Block Scheduling** .5 day *Block Scheduling Handbook with Team Teaching Strategies, 7.6*	RS Guided Reading Strategy 7.6 PS Readings in World History 28 E Creative Teaching Strategy 7

Chapter Resource Key

PS	Primary Sources	A	Assessment		Music
RS	Reading Support	REV	Review		Video
IC	Interdisciplinary Connections	ELL	Reinforcement and English Language Learners		Internet
E	Enrichment		Transparencies		Holt Presentation Maker Using Microsoft® PowerPoint®
SM	Skills Mastery		CD–ROM		

 One-Stop Planner CD-ROM

See the ***One-Stop Planner*** for a complete list of additional resources for students and teachers.

One-Stop Planner CD-ROM

It's easy to plan lessons, select resources, and print out materials for your students when you use the **One-Stop Planner** CD–ROM with **Test Generator.**

internet connect

HRW ONLINE RESOURCES
 GO TO: go.hrw.com
 Then type in a keyword.

TEACHER HOME PAGE
 KEYWORD: SP3 Teacher

CHAPTER INTERNET ACTIVITIES
 KEYWORD: SP3 WH7
Choose an activity to:
• analyze the *Aeneid* to learn the connection between ancient Troy and Roman culture.
• create a model or structure that employs Roman architectural, artistic, or decorative styles.
• research the destruction of Pompeii and review the tectonic causes of volcanoes.

CHAPTER ENRICHMENT LINKS
 KEYWORD: SP3 CH7

ONLINE ASSESSMENT
 Homework Practice
 KEYWORD: SP3 HP7

 Standardized Test Prep
 KEYWORD: SP3 STP7

 Rubrics
 KEYWORD: SS Rubrics

ONLINE MAPS, CHARTS, AND GRAPHS
 KEYWORD: SP3 MCG

CONTENT UPDATES
 KEYWORD: SS Content Updates

HOLT PRESENTATION MAKER
 KEYWORD: SP3 PPT7

ONLINE READING SUPPORT
 KEYWORD: SS Strategies

CURRENT EVENTS
 KEYWORD: S3 Current Events

Technology Resources

One-Stop Planner 7.1
World History Teaching Transparency: Geography and History 4; Everyday Life 4
Homework Practice Online

One-Stop Planner 7.2
CNN Presents World Cultures: Yesterday and Today Segment 7: In the Shadow of Mt. Vesuvius
Homework Practice Online

One-Stop Planner 7.3
Holt Researcher: World History: Caesar, Augustus
Homework Practice Online

One-Stop Planner 7.4
World History and Cultures Video Program 5: What Made Rome Great?
Homework Practice Online
Online Maps, Charts, and Graphs: Roman Roads in A.D. 14

One-Stop Planner 7.5
Holt Researcher: World History: Jesus
Religions of the World Video Series: Christianity
Homework Practice Online

One-Stop Planner 7.6
Homework Practice Online
Online Maps, Charts, and Graphs: Division of the Roman Empire

Reinforcement, Review, and Assessment

Daily Quiz 7.1
Main Idea Activity 7.1
English Audio Summary 7.1
Spanish Audio Summary 7.1
REV Section 1 Review, p. 154

Daily Quiz 7.2
Main Idea Activity 7.2
English Audio Summary 7.2
Spanish Audio Summary 7.2
REV Section 2 Review, p. 157

Daily Quiz 7.3
Main Idea Activity 7.3
English Audio Summary 7.3
Spanish Audio Summary 7.3
REV Section 3 Review, p. 161

Daily Quiz 7.4
Main Idea Activity 7.4
English Audio Summary 7.4
Spanish Audio Summary 7.4
REV Section 4 Review, p. 167

Daily Quiz 7.5
Main Idea Activity 7.5
English Audio Summary 7.5
Spanish Audio Summary 7.5
REV Section 5 Review, p. 171

Daily Quiz 7.6
Main Idea Activity 7.6
English Audio Summary 7.6
Spanish Audio Summary 7.6
REV Section 6 Review, p. 177

Meeting Individual Needs

Ability Levels

Level 1 Basic level activities designed for all students encountering new material

Level 2 Intermediate level activities designed for average students

Level 3 Challenging activities designed for honors and gifted and talented students

English Language Learners These activities address the needs of students with Limited English Proficiency.

Chapter Review and Assessment

IC Vocabulary Activity 7
 Global Skill Builder CD–ROM
HRW Web Site
REV Chapter 7 Tutorial for Students, Parents, Mentors, and Peers
REV Chapter 7 Review, pp. 178–179
A Chapter 7 Test Generator (on the One-Stop Planner)
A Chapter 7 Test (Form A or B)
A Alternative Assessment Handbook
A Chapter 7 Test for English Language Learners and Special-Needs Students

147b

Build on What You Know

Ask students to answer the following questions:

How might Greek achievements have spread throughout the ancient world?

Consider:

- the effects of trade and travel
- the establishment of Greek colonies throughout the Mediterranean
- the conquests of Alexander the Great

How might Greek culture have influenced the Romans?

Consider:

- the influence of Greek culture on other societies
- Greek achievements in the arts and sciences
- Greek ideas on government, law, and citizenship

EXPLORING THE TIME LINE
GLOBAL EVENTS

internet connect

TOPIC: Ovid
GO TO: go.hrw.com
KEYWORD: SP3 WH7

Have students access the Internet through the HRW Go site to conduct research on Ovid, one of the great Roman poets. Then have students create a detailed time line of Ovid's life, including the publication of his greatest works. At the bottom of the time line, students should write a brief paragraph describing one of Ovid's works and explaining what it tells us about the Roman Empire.

CHAPTER 7

1000 B.C.–A.D. 476
The Roman World

Mosaic of a theater scene from Pompeii

c. 365 B.C.
The Arts
Etruscan actors stage the first theatrical performances in Rome.

c. 1000 B.C.– 509 B.C.
Global Events
Latins and Etruscans settle west-central Italy.

c. 800 B.C.–701 B.C.
Science and Technology
The Etruscans introduce horse-drawn chariots.

500 B.C.–451 B.C.
Business and Finance
Winemaking develops in Italy and Gaul.

c. 289 B.C.
Business and Finance
The first Roman mint is established.

| 1000 B.C. | 800 B.C. | 600 B.C. | 400 B.C. | 200 B.C. |

c. 753 B.C.
Global Events
According to legend, the city of Rome is founded.

509 B.C.
Politics
The Roman Republic is established.

264 B.C.–146 B.C.
Global Events
The Punic Wars are fought.

c. 814 B.C.
Business and Finance
Carthage becomes a trading center.

c. 312 B.C.
Daily Life
Construction of the Via Appia begins.

Carthaginian general Hannibal

Build on What You Know

After the Persian wars, Athens became the center of Greece's golden age. The Greek contributions during this period in science, mathematics, art, and philosophy still influence civilizations today. They also had an effect on the cultures of the ancient world, especially that of Rome. Although the Hellenistic Age came to an end as the Romans conquered much of the Mediterranean, the influence of the Greeks lived on in Roman culture. In this chapter, you will learn about Roman society and how Rome's location and its policies contributed to the expansion of Roman power.

What's Your Opinion?

 To help students create their Themes Journal entries, provide the following examples of appropriate agree/disagree statements.

Government

Agree A strong army and government help ensure order and peace among diverse peoples.

Disagree Cooperation among different groups and a sense of unity are more important to an empire than a strong army and government.

Culture

Agree The contributions of earlier cultures provide a foundation for a later culture's progress.

Disagree A culture that depends upon another's contributions will not be innovative and unique, characteristics that are key to greatness.

Global Relations

Agree An empire that enslaves conquered people creates hatred and resistance toward its rule.

Disagree By enslaving conquered peoples, an empire ensures control over those who might threaten its rule.

The Roman poet Ovid

Gold coin showing Roman Emperor Diocletian

133 B.C.
Politics
Tiberius Gracchus is elected tribune.

60 B.C.
Politics
The First Triumvirate is formed.

43 B.C.
Politics
The Second Triumvirate is formed.

A.D. 8
The Arts
The poet Ovid writes the *Metamorphoses.*

A.D. 96–A.D. 180
Politics
The Five Good Emperors rule Rome.

C. A.D. 124
The Arts
The rebuilding of The Pantheon is completed by Emperor Hadrian.

A.D. 284–A.D. 305
Politics
Emperor Diocletian rules Rome.

A.D. 386
The Arts
Hymns are introduced into Christian churches.

A.D. 476
Global Events
The last Roman emperor in the West is overthrown.

| A.D. 1 | A.D. 200 | A.D. 400 |

44 B.C.
Global Events
Julius Caesar is assassinated.

A.D. 79
Daily Life
Mount Vesuvius erupts and destroys the city of Pompeii.

A.D. 162
Science and Technology
The Greek doctor Galen begins practicing medicine in Rome.

A.D. 324
Politics
Emperor Constantine becomes sole Roman ruler.

A.D. 410
Global Events
Rome is attacked by the Visigoths.

C. A.D. 30
Global Events
Jesus is crucified.

Colored glassware from Judaea

Julius Caesar

EXPLORING THE TIME LINE
GLOBAL EVENTS

According to tradition, the early Romans were ruled by another Italian power–the Etruscans–who dominated central Italy during the 800s B.C. and the 700s B.C. The Etruscans themselves were culturally influenced by Greeks who had colonized southern Italy, and they passed this influence on to their Roman subjects. Etruscan women held considerable power in their society and enjoyed a more equal lifestyle than did women of many other early societies. By about 390 B.C. Etruscan power in central Italy had been broken and the kingdom had been absorbed by the Romans.

Critical Thinking

In what ways did the Etruscans' domination of central Italy help to spread classical Greek culture?

ANSWER: Students might note that Etruscan culture would have influenced those peoples–including the early Romans–who fell under Etruscan political control.

What's Your Opinion?

Themes Journal *Do you* **agree** *or* **disagree** *with the following statements? Support your point of view in your journal.*

Government A strong army and government are necessary to maintain an empire.

Culture Great civilizations build on the discoveries, developments, and contributions of earlier cultures.

Global Relations An empire that enslaves conquered peoples is destined to fall.

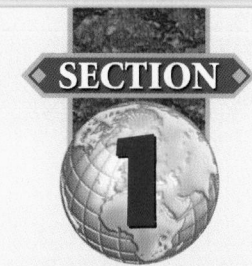
OBJECTIVES

1 **Identify the role geography played in Italy's and Rome's development.**

2 **Describe the form of government of the Roman Republic.**

3 **Explain the Conflict of the Orders and how it changed the early Roman Republic.**

4 **Compare and contrast the roles of citizens and noncitizens as Rome expanded its power.**

MAP ANSWER
Sicily

SECTION 1

READ TO DISCOVER

❶ What role did geography play in Italy's and Rome's development?

❷ How was the government of the Roman Republic set up?

❸ What was the Conflict of the Orders, and how did it change the early Roman Republic?

❹ How were the roles of citizens and noncitizens under Roman rule different?

DEFINE
republic
dictator
consuls
veto
checks and balances
praetors
censors
tribunes
patricians
plebeians

▶**WHY IT MATTERS TODAY**

The United States and other democracies are in debt to the Roman Republic for controls on government power. Use CNNnews.com or other **current event** sources to explore how the United States protects its people against abuses of government power. Record your findings in your journal.

Founding the Roman Republic

The Main Idea
The early Romans established a powerful and well-organized republic that grew and changed over time.

The Story Continues *Although the power of the Greeks waned, their culture would live on in a new civilization that grew out of western Italy. In about 750 B.C. a group of villages along the Tiber River formed what would become the center of Roman civilization.*

The Land: Its Geography and Importance

The geography of Italy had a great deal to do with the rise of Roman power. Italy looks like a giant boot. Its top is sheltered by the Alps to the north. Its toe and heel slice into the Mediterranean Sea to the south. To the east lies the Adriatic Sea. This location made it an excellent base from which to control both the eastern and the western halves of the region. The Apennine Mountains, which run the full length of the boot, are not very rugged. This made early trade and travel relatively easy.

Not everything about Italy's geography worked to its advantage, however. The Alps in the north separate Italy from the rest of Europe. Several pathways cut through the mountains, creating avenues for the movement of peoples. Over the centuries, enemy armies have streamed into Italy through these passages. Italy's long coastline has also made it open to attack from the sea.

✔ **READING CHECK: Identifying Cause and Effect** How was Italy helped and hurt by its geography? protected by mountains, helped to control Mediterranean, overland travel made easy; separated from rest of Europe; vulnerable to enemy attacks

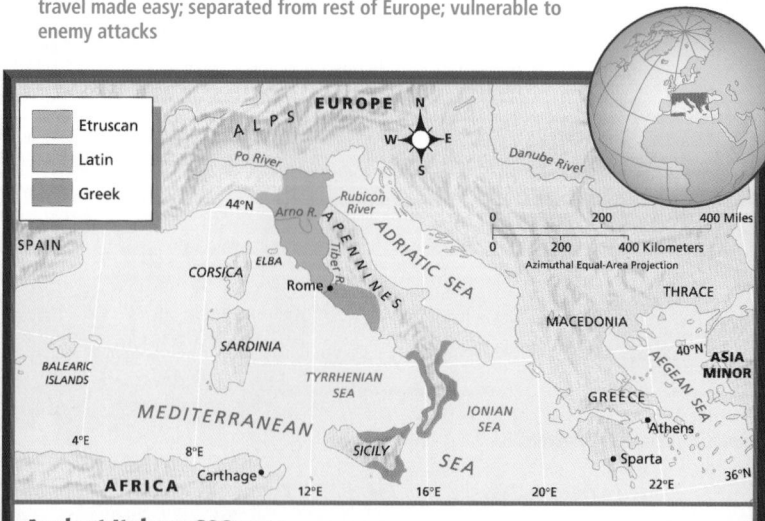

Ancient Italy, c. 600 B.C.

Interpreting Maps Rome's location on the Italian Peninsula protected the city from sea invasions and encouraged trade in all directions.

■ **Skills Assessment: Locate** On what island did the Greeks establish colonies?

TEACH OBJECTIVE 1

LEVEL 1: Ask students to list geographical advantages of the Italian peninsula. *(center of the Mediterranean region; low mountains do not hinder inland trade; access by land and sea)* Have students locate Rome on the map on page 150. Ask them to use this map and the information on page 150 to list advantages of Rome's location. *(on the Tiber, so water and transportation available; not on coast, so protected from sea invasion; near easy crossing on Tiber, so Rome became a major trading center)*

ENGLISH LANGUAGE LEARNERS

Rome and the Beginning of an Empire

People lived in Italy as early as the Paleolithic period. But it was not until after 2000 B.C. that waves of invaders swept through the mountain passes and overran the peninsula. As in Greece, these invaders came from north of the Black and Caspian Seas.

The founding of Rome. Sometime before the mid-700s B.C., a group of people called the Latins moved into west-central Italy. This plains region was called Latium (LAY·shee·uhm). Some of the Latin settlers built villages along the Tiber River. In time, these villages united to form Rome.

In the late 600s B.C., Rome came under the rule of Etruscan kings from northern Italy. The Etruscans had a written language, which the Romans adapted. The Etruscans crafted jewelry, made fine clothing, and worked skillfully in metal, pottery, and wood. These city dwellers also knew how to pave roads, drain marshes, and construct sewers. Under the Etruscans, Rome grew into a large and prosperous city. Over time the Etruscans blended into the general Roman population. Their culture, however, continued to influence the Romans.

Some Greeks also settled in ancient Italy. Greek colonies in southern Italy and on the island of Sicily became city-states. These city-states were as disunited and quarrelsome as those of Greece. Nonetheless, the Greek culture of these colonies strongly influenced the Romans. For instance, although they went by different names, many Roman gods mirrored Greek gods. Jupiter, for example, had the same traits as the Greek god Zeus. Roman myths were also similar to Greek myths.

A strategic location. Rome was built on seven hills along the Tiber River, about 15 miles inland from the coast. This location protected the city from invasion by sea. Rome's location gave its people economic advantages as well. The city lay along a shallow part of the Tiber, making it one of the easiest places for miles to cross the river. This put Rome at the center of trade routes that spread out across the land in all directions.

✔ **READING CHECK: Finding the Main Idea** How was Rome helped by its location? Its location provided defense from sea invasions. Also, Rome lay at a natural river crossing, helping to promote the city as a hub of overland trade and transportation.

The Early Roman Republic

In 509 B.C. wealthy Roman landowners overthrew the Etruscan king and vowed never again to be ruled by a monarch. In place of the monarchy, the Romans established a republic. A **republic** is a form of government in which voters elect officials to run the state. In the Roman Republic, only adult male citizens were entitled to vote and to take part in government. Three important groups of citizens helped govern the republic: the Senate, the magistrates, and a variety of popular assemblies.

Senate. The Senate was the most influential and powerful of the three governing bodies because it controlled public funds and decided foreign policy. Sometimes the Senate also acted as a court. In times of emergency, the senators could propose that a citizen be named **dictator,** or absolute ruler. A dictator could rule for up to six months. During that period, he had complete command over the army and the courts. Over time, the size of the Senate changed dramatically.

Geography

Rome's location on the Italian peninsula, slightly inland on a shallow part of the Tiber River, protected Rome from invasion from the sea, yet encouraged trade.

Critical Thinking

Look at the map on page 150. Why do you think the Greeks decided to establish colonies on the island of Sicily?

ANSWER: Answers will vary. Students might suggest that the mountains in the north protected the peninsula, its location promoted control of the Mediterranean, and its terrain made overland travel relatively easy.

That's Interesting!

The Etruscans worshiped a great variety of gods, and their religion was very important to them. The priests believed that they could discover the future by studying and interpreting natural phenomena or animal entrails.

PRIMARY SOURCE EYEWITNESS ANSWER

The gods influenced the outcome of the brothers' fight so that Romulus won.

TEACH OBJECTIVE 2

ALL LEVELS: Have students work in pairs to create an orga-nizational chart of the Roman Republic government. Instruct them to include all governing bodies *(Senate, popular assem-blies, magistrates)* and officials. *(consuls, praetors, censors, dicta-tor, tribunes)* **ENGLISH LANGUAGE LEARNERS, COOPERATIVE LEARNING**

 HOMEWORK List duties of the assemblies. Write an explanation of how the tribunes influenced assembly decisions.

Linking Past to Present

Coins can be useful in linking together a civilization's political history. Many coins used by both ancient civilizations and those today have images and/or inscrip-tions engraved on their surface. Such images frequently show powerful leaders. The inscription often states the leader's motto. Also, coins can shed light on a society by their relative abun-dance and distribution. For exam-ple, large hoards of coins might suggest political or economic instability.

Critical Thinking

Ask students what they might deduce about U.S. society based on an examination of coins used today.

ANSWER: Answers will vary, but students might suggest that for-mer presidents are revered by our society; liberty and religious prin-ciples are held in high regard; his-toric government buildings indicate the stability and impor-tance of our government.

The Forum, which was made up of many important and beautiful buildings, served as the center of all government business. Today, its ruins stand as monuments to the grand style of Roman architecture with its towering columns and graceful arches.

Magistrates. The magistrates who made up the second group of Roman leaders were elected officials. The magistrates included consuls, praetors, and censors. After the monarchy ended in 509 B.C., two individuals were elected to one-year terms to serve as **consuls,** or chief executives. The consuls ran the government, commanded the army, and could appoint dictators. Although powerful, consuls governed with the advice of the Senate. In addition, each consul could **veto,** or refuse to approve, the acts of the other consul. (The Latin word *veto* means "I forbid.") This division of power was an example of the principle of **checks and balances,** which prevents any one part of the government from becoming too powerful. The United States and many other nations of the modern world later adopted the veto and the principle of checks and balances as safeguards in their own governments.

The Romans elected the **praetors** (PREE·tuhrz) to help the consuls. In times of war, praetors commanded armies. In times of peace, they oversaw the Roman legal system. The number of praetors varied over time, but they continued to head specific Roman courts. The interpretations of legal questions made by praetors formed much of the civil law in Rome.

Censors registered citizens according to their wealth, appointed candidates to the Senate, and oversaw the moral conduct of all citizens. Censors became very powerful magistrates in the Roman Republic.

Assemblies. Several assemblies existed in the Roman Republic. Citizens in these assemblies voted on laws and elected officials, including the consuls. Some assemblies voted to make war or peace, while others served as courts. The assemblies elected 10 officials called **tribunes,** who had some power over actions by the Senate and other public officials. If the tribunes believed actions were not in the public interest, they could refuse to approve them.

✔ **READING CHECK: Analyzing Information** How did the Romans organize the gov-ernment of their republic? The government was based on a system of checks and bal-ances. Citizens elected senators and magistrates to make and execute laws and served on representative assemblies that oversaw defense and that acted as courts.

TEACH OBJECTIVE 3

ALL LEVELS: Copy the following graphic organizer on the board, omitting the italicized answers. Call on students to identify characteristics of these two groups of Romans before the Conflict of the Orders. Discuss what rights the plebeians gained over time. *(join army, hold office, form assembly, elect tribunes, Twelve Tables)*

ENGLISH LANGUAGE LEARNERS, COOPERATIVE LEARNING

TEACH OBJECTIVE 4

LEVEL 3: Have students write an essay comparing and contrasting the roles and rights of citizens and noncitizens under Roman rule and evaluating the consequences of Roman policy in this regard. Tell students to use standard grammar, spelling, sentence structure, and punctuation.

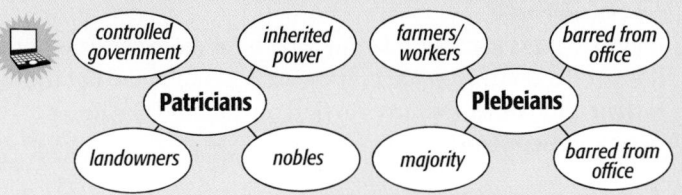

12 TABLES → written laws of Rome.

The Conflict of the Orders

The types of people who served as officials in the Roman government changed over time. These changes stemmed from the attempts of common people to win more rights. The struggles became known as the Conflict of the Orders.

In the early republic, Romans were divided into two classes of people: patricians and plebeians. **Patricians** were powerful landowners who controlled the government. As nobles, they inherited their power. **Plebeians,** who made up most of the population, were mainly farmers and workers. For many years, plebeians had few rights. They could vote, but they were barred from holding most public offices. Plebeians could not even know Roman laws because the laws were not written down. In court, a judge stated and applied the law, but only patricians served as judges.

Over time, plebeians increased their power through demands and strikes. They gained the right to join the army, hold government office, form their own assembly, and elect tribunes. In one of their greatest victories, they forced the government to write down the laws of the Roman Republic. In about 450 B.C. the Romans engraved their laws on tablets called the Twelve Tables. The laws were placed in the Forum, the chief public square, for all to view.

The first plebeians were appointed to the government in the late 400s B.C. After 342 B.C. a plebeian always held one of the consul positions. By about 300 B.C. many plebeians had become so powerful and wealthy themselves that they joined with patricians to form the Roman nobility. From that time on, the distinction between patricians and plebeians was not as important. Membership in the nobility was still very important, however. Since government officials were not paid a salary, only wealthy nobles could afford to hold office. Thus, the nobles still controlled the republic.

✔ **READING CHECK: Drawing Conclusions** What effect did the Conflict of the Orders have on the early Roman Republic? helped plebeians to gain more rights, resulted in a written code of law, weakened political distinctions between patricians and plebeians

The Republic Grows

The years of the Roman Republic were not a time of peace. For more than 200 years after the republic was founded, the Romans fought many wars against neighboring peoples. By 265 B.C. they controlled all of Italy south of the Rubicon, a river on Italy's northeast coast. The Romans extended their republic with both a well-organized, impressive army and wise political policies.

The role of the Roman army. Every adult male citizen who owned land was required by law to serve in the Roman army. In general the soldiers themselves enforced army discipline, which tended to be very strict. The major unit of the army was the legion, consisting of from 4,500 to 6,000 citizens called *legionnaires.* The Romans also later established the *auxilia,* which were units made up of noncitizens. In general during this time, Roman army units were well trained, and morale among the troops was usually high.

INTERPRETING THE VISUAL RECORD

Legionnaires Roman soldiers' helmets were made of either bronze or iron. Their body armor was first made of hardened leather. Later, overlapping bronze sections were sewn together. *What does the carved relief sculpture below reveal about the protection that a Roman soldier's uniform gave him?*

Culture

The Roman army was more than a match against most of its opponents. Legionnaires were known for their high standards of training, fighting ability, discipline, and stamina. They routinely marched 20 miles a day and were skilled bridge and road builders. Their abilities often allowed them to surprise their enemies by arriving on the battlefield with unexpected speed, strength, and organization.

Critical Thinking

What advantages did legionnaires have over enemy armies that typically maneuvered and fought as individuals?

ANSWER: The disciplined, well-trained, and cohesive Roman legions fought as a powerful unit and could concentrate their strength with overwhelming force against disorganized, poorly disciplined forces.

VISUAL RECORD ANSWER

Students should note that legionnaires' armor combined protection and mobility, and that the most vulnerable parts of the soldier's body were also the most heavily armored.

VISUAL RECORD ANSWER

(page 154)
Students should suggest that Rome, like the United States, took a periodic census, and that Roman census workers personally visited people's homes to make sure they were counted.

THE ROMAN WORLD **153**

CLOSE

Discuss how the Roman republican form of government is reflected in U.S. state and national governments.

REVIEW

Have students complete the Section 1 Review on p. 154.

ASSESS

Have students complete Daily Quiz 7.1. As Alternative Assessment, you may want to use the Roman government chart or the essay exercise in this section's lessons.

RETEACH

Have students complete Main Idea Activity for English Language Learners and Special-Needs Students 7.1. Then have students write the section's headings and subheadings on paper and list the main ideas of the section in the appropriate spaces.
ENGLISH LANGUAGE LEARNERS

EXTEND

Invite students to create a family scrapbook from the days of the Roman Republic. Have them use their textbooks, the library, the Internet, and other resources to find out about daily life.
BLOCK SCHEDULING

SECTION 1 REVIEW ANSWERS

❶ **Define**
• republic, p. 151
• dictator, p. 151
• consuls, p. 152
• veto, p. 152
• checks and balances, p. 152
• praetors, p. 152
• censors, p. 152
• tribunes, p. 152
• patricians, p. 153
• plebeians, p. 153

❷ Senate: controlled public funds, decided foreign policy; Magistrates: consuls ran government, commanded army, could appoint dictators; Assemblies: voted on laws, elected officials

❸ a. Rome lay inland, protected from sea invasion, and along an easy river crossing.

b. All adult male citizens were entitled to vote and participate in government; government was divided into branches; each consul could veto acts of the other consul.

c. strong, well-trained army projected Roman power and culture; full or partial citizenship was granted to inhabitants of other Italian cities; allies were allowed to remain independent; land policies enabled them to control conquered areas and to spread their culture

❹ Students might mention that granting citizenship encouraged loyalty to Rome, although partial citizens could not vote.

INTERPRETING THE VISUAL RECORD

The census The Romans periodically took a census—an official count of their population. Today the U.S. government takes a census by mail every 10 years. Government workers personally visit those who do not mail in forms to make sure they are counted. *What does this relief show about the ways Romans conducted their census?*

Link to Today How is the U.S. census today similar to the Roman census?

The role of wise policies. The Romans had a talent for ruling other people. Because they wanted the people they conquered to be loyal to Rome, the Romans granted full citizenship to the inhabitants of nearby Italian cities. They granted partial citizenship to the people of more-distant cities, including the Greek city-states in Italy. Although partial citizens could own property and marry, under Roman law they could not vote. As the Romans made allies in more distant areas, they allowed the allies to remain independent, but these areas had to provide soldiers for the Roman army.

The Romans also expected conquered peoples to provide land for Roman farmers. This land policy helped the Romans to maintain control over conquered areas. It also led to the spread of the Latin language, Roman law, and other aspects of Roman culture throughout Italy.

✔ **READING CHECK: Contrasting** What specific right enjoyed by full citizens was denied to partial citizens as Rome expanded? the right to vote

SECTION 1 REVIEW

1. **Define** and explain the significance:
   republic
   dictator
   consuls
   veto
   checks and balances
   praetors
   censors
   tribunes
   patricians
   plebeians

2. **Categorizing** Copy the chart below. Use it to organize the three main parts of the government of the Roman Republic.

Government Group	Functions

3. **Finding the Main Idea**
   a. How did the location of Rome help it become a seat of trade and power?
   b. How was the government of the Roman Republic an example of checks and balances?
   c. How did the military organization of the Roman army and the republic's wise policies work together to help Rome extend its power?

4. **Writing and Critical Thinking**
   Drawing Conclusions How might the granting of the rights of citizenship have affected Rome's ability to rule conquered peoples?
   Consider:
   • the rights and roles of citizens
   • the rights and roles of noncitizens

Homework Practice Online
keyword: SP3 HP7

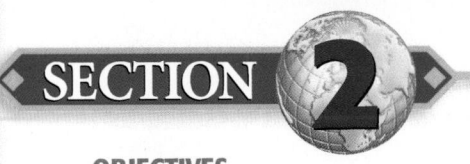

SECTION 2

OBJECTIVES

1 **Discuss the Punic Wars and how Rome gained control over Carthage.**

2 **Explain how expansion changed the Roman Republic.**

LET'S GET STARTED!

As students enter the classroom, ask them to predict some possible causes of conflict between the growing Roman Republic and surrounding Mediterranean peoples. *(Students might note that sources of conflict could include trade rivalry and economic competition, competition for land, mutual suspicion, perceptions that one culture posed a threat to the other.)* Tell students that in Section 2 they will learn how Rome confronted the gravest threat yet to its growth and, possibly, its very survival.

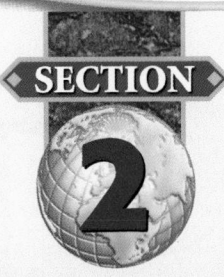

SECTION 2

READ TO DISCOVER

1 How did Rome gain control over Carthage?

2 How did expansion change the Roman Republic?

DEFINE

equites

IDENTIFY

Punic Wars
Hannibal
Scipio
Spartacus

WHY IT MATTERS TODAY

Economic factors often play an important role in conflicts between countries. Use CNN or other **current event** sources to find a current conflict in which economics plays a role. Record your findings in your journal.

Rome Expands Its Borders

The Main Idea
Through warfare and alliances, the Romans greatly expanded the lands under their control.

The Story Continues *"Our republic was not made by the genius of one man, but of many, nor in the life of one, but through many centuries and generations." This statesman's words reflected the Romans' pride in their civilization. As generations passed, the power and influence of the republic grew even more.*

Rome Fights Carthage

By the middle 200s B.C., the Roman Republic controlled all of the Italian Peninsula south of the Rubicon. Rome soon came into conflict with Carthage, a powerful city on the coast of North Africa that had once been a Phoenician colony. Carthage was now a great commercial power whose empire spanned the western Mediterranean. Carthage had colonies and markets on Sicily, an island off the southern coast of Italy. After the Romans moved into southern Italy, Carthage feared that they would also try to take Sicily. The Romans feared that the Carthaginian navy would control the Mediterranean and prevent Roman expansion overseas. These fears sparked three costly conflicts that we call the **Punic Wars** because the Latin adjective for *Phoenician* is *punicus*.

The First Punic War. The First Punic War began in 264 B.C. At first Rome had no navy, but it quickly built one. Rome used a Carthaginian ship it had captured as a model. The Romans employed land warfare tactics at sea. By equipping their ships with "boarding bridges," they could ram their vessel into a Carthaginian ship and then let down the bridge. Heavily armed soldiers then stampeded across the bridge and took the enemy. In 241 B.C., after 23 years of war, Carthage asked for peace. The Romans made Carthage pay a large sum of money for the damages it had caused and forced it to give up Sicily. Rome now had a major territory outside Italy.

The Second Punic War. The Second Punic War began in 218 B.C. In Spain, **Hannibal,** one of the greatest generals of all time, assembled a huge Carthaginian army that included foot soldiers, horse soldiers, and elephants. The army marched across the Alps into Italy. The crossing was difficult, and many in Hannibal's force died.

Despite the losses, the Romans were no match for Hannibal's army. Hannibal won several victories, causing the Romans to retreat before him. Because Hannibal

INTERPRETING THE VISUAL RECORD

Rome's navy During the First Punic War, Rome became a naval force equal to the Carthaginian fleet. *What does this relief imply about the size and strength of Roman ships?*

SECTION 2 RESOURCES

REPRODUCIBLE RESOURCES

▶ Guided Reading Strategy 7.2

▶ Readings in World History 25: Rome's Perfect Location

TECHNOLOGY RESOURCES

▶ One-Stop Planner 7.2

▶ CNN Presents World Cultures: Yesterday and Today Segment 7: In the Shadow of Mt. Vesuvius

▶ Homework Practice Online

REINFORCEMENT, REVIEW, AND ASSESSMENT

▶ Section 2 Review, p. 157

▶ Daily Quiz 7.2

▶ Main Idea Activity 7.2

▶ English Audio Summary 7.2

▶ Spanish Audio Summary 7.2

VISUAL RECORD ANSWER

Students should note that Roman ships were relatively small and crowded, heavily armed and defended, very strong, and designed to carry troops.

TEACH OBJECTIVE 1

ALL LEVELS: Discuss the Punic Wars as a class. Then have students work with a partner to complete the chart showing the causes and outcomes of each war.
ENGLISH LANGUAGE LEARNERS

TEACH OBJECTIVE 2

LEVEL 1: Have students list changes that resulted from Roman expansion. **ENGLISH LANGUAGE LEARNERS**

LEVEL 3: Ask students to identify major challenges posed to Rome by its expansion and to suggest possible solutions.

HOMEWORK Have students write a summary of how the Roman Republic acquired the territory shown on the map on page 156. Use standard grammar, spelling, sentence structure, and punctuation.

Punic Wars		
	Causes	**Results**
First Punic War	*Carthage was afraid Rome would take Sicily; Rome was afraid Carthage would close the Adriatic Sea and the Strait of Messina.*	*Carthage asked for peace; had to pay indemnity and give up control of Sicily.*
Second Punic War	*Hannibal invaded Italy.*	*Carthage asked for peace; paid an indemnity and lost the Spanish colonies.*
Third Punic War	*Some Romans passionately hated Carthage; Rome declared war.*	*Carthage was destroyed.*

MAP ANSWERS

1. Pyrenees, Alps, Apennines

2. advantages: surprise, maneuverability, allowed interior attack of Italy; disadvantages: difficult terrain, bad weather, created supply problems

Global Relations

Hannibal successfully regained several territories for Carthage in the Second Punic War, including much of what is now Spain, before his army was weakened while crossing the Alps. In Italy, Hannibal's position was further weakened when his plans to ally with free Italians, Macedonians, Spaniards, and Gauls failed. Hannibal never received reinforcements from Carthage, leaving him too weak to mount a powerful attack against Rome. His allies lost interest as victory began to fade and as the Romans became more aggressive. Although Hannibal's tactics and skills far surpassed those of most Roman generals, Rome ultimately claimed victory in the Second Punic War.

Critical Thinking

Ask students what factors cost Hannibal an early victory.

ANSWER: Students might mention Hannibal's dependence on foreign allies, distance from Carthage and reinforcements, and loss of soldiers and elephants while crossing the Alps.

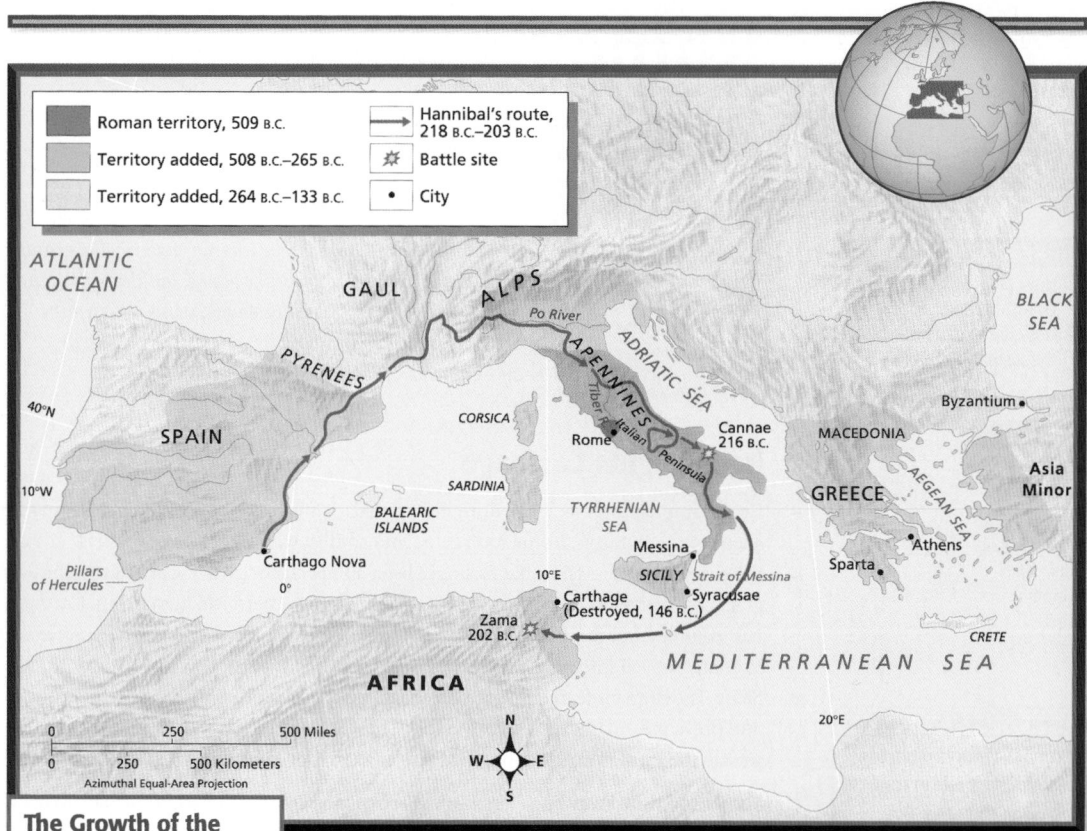

The Growth of the Roman Republic, 509 B.C.—133 B.C.

Interpreting Maps Rome and Carthage fought three Punic Wars between 264 B.C. and 146 B.C.

■ **Skills Assessment:** Trace Hannibal's route from Spain to Carthage. **1. Places and Regions** Across which mountain ranges did his army advance during the journey? **2. Comparing and Contrasting** What advantages and disadvantages did this route provide?

did not have the equipment to attack the cities, he spent years laying waste to the countryside, raiding farms and taking crops and livestock. He also tried to win away Rome's allies. The Roman policy of sharing citizenship and political power proved its value, however, as most of the republic's allies remained loyal. The historian Polybius wrote that after their defeat at Cannae in 216 B.C., the Romans vowed to conquer the enemy or die on the field of battle.

" Hannibal's joy in his victory over the Romans was exceeded by his frustration, as he saw with astonishment the endurance and greatness of the Romans when they deliberated on national policy.**"**

Polybius, *The Histories,* Vol. VI

Finally, Rome turned the tables by invading Africa and threatening Carthage. Hannibal's government ordered him home to defend the city. In Africa he met his match—the Roman general **Scipio** (SIP·ee·oh). In 202 B.C. at the battle of Zama, near Carthage, Scipio and the Romans defeated Hannibal and his army. Once more Carthage had to pay a huge sum of money. It also had to give up most of its navy and its colonies in Spain. Carthage remained independent, but it had lost all its power. Rome was now the most powerful force in the western Mediterranean.

The Third Punic War. Although Carthage was no longer a threat, some Romans still hated the city. Thus, the Roman Senate decided to crush Carthage. In 149 B.C. Rome again declared war on its old enemy. After a bitter siege, Carthage was destroyed in 146 B.C.

During the Second Punic War, Macedonia had been allied with Carthage. To get revenge, Rome started a war against Macedonia and defeated it in 197 B.C. The Greek cities came under Roman "protection." By 133 B.C. Rome had extended its control over the entire region. It was now the supreme power in the Mediterranean.

✔ **READING CHECK: Sequencing** How did Rome gain control over the Mediterranean? defeated Carthage in a series of three wars

The Problems of Expansion

Because Rome now controlled a vast area, the republic and its government had to change. It remained a republic, but the Senate gained almost complete control over the army and foreign policy. The nobles gained even more power.

The Romans governed the new territories, called provinces, loosely. They did not allow the people of the provinces to become citizens, nor did they make them allies. Instead, the Romans simply made the people of each province subjects of Rome. Each province was administered by a governor who was backed by the power of the Roman army. Some provincial governors took bribes and paid little, if any, attention to the needs of the people. In addition, tax collectors tried to squeeze as much money as they could from the provinces.

The Romans also had problems at home. The Roman farmer-soldiers who returned from the Punic Wars were sickened to find their livestock killed, their homes in ruins, and their olive groves or vineyards uprooted. The farmers did not have enough money to restore their farms and thus had little choice but to sell the land. As time passed, Rome became dependent on the provinces for grain, its chief food.

Many of the farmers who lost their land moved to the cities. Not all of them could find jobs there, however, and they depended on the government for food. In contrast, trade within Rome's vast empire had created a class of business people and landowners called **equites** (EK·wuh·teez). They had great wealth and political influence. Within the republic, the gap between rich and poor, powerful and powerless, continued to grow.

✔ **READING CHECK: Identifying Cause and Effect** What changes occurred in the Roman Republic as a result of Roman expansion? Senate gained almost complete control over the army and foreign policy; nobles gained more power

HISTORY MAKER
Spartacus
(unknown–71 B.C.)

Romans often enslaved conquered peoples. Some slaves enjoyed fairly good treatment. For example, some slaves could buy their freedom. By Roman law, a freed slave became a citizen.

Other slaves led such horrible lives that they revolted. The most brutal revolt, led by a slave named **Spartacus,** began in 73 B.C. More than 70,000 slaves took part. By 71 B.C. the Roman army had crushed the uprising. Spartacus died in battle. Some 6,000 rebels were crucified—nailed or tied to crosses and left to die. **Why do you think Spartacus and his followers revolted?**

SECTION 2 REVIEW

1. **Define** and explain the significance:
   equites

2. **Identify** and explain the significance:
   Punic Wars
   Hannibal
   Scipio
   Spartacus

3. **Comparing** Copy the chart below. Use it to detail the changes in the Roman Republic that resulted from Rome's expansion.

Changes in the Roman Republic		
Government	Agriculture	Society

4. **Finding the Main Idea**
   a. In what ways were Rome and Carthage different?
   b. What were the final results of the Punic Wars?

5. **Writing and Critical Thinking**
   Making Generalizations Write a character sketch describing what an average Roman citizen-soldier might have been like.
   Consider:
   - soldiers' actions during and after the Punic Wars
   - the changing society

Homework Practice Online
keyword: SP3 HP7

OBJECTIVES

1 **Identify the political events in Rome during the first century B.C. that helped weaken the Roman Republic.**

2 **Explain how the reign of Julius Caesar served as a transition between the Roman Republic and the Roman Empire.**

3 **Describe the events and conditions that marked the first two centuries of the Roman Empire.**

⟨((◦ LET'S GET STARTED!

As students enter the classroom, ask them to write a list of the challenges that faced Rome as it expanded after the Punic Wars. *(government corruption, changes in agriculture, loss of discipline and devotion to the state)* Ask students how they think these problems might have weakened the Roman Republic. Tell students that in Section 3 they will learn that these challenges ultimately brought about the end of the Roman Republic and the rise of the Roman Empire.

SECTION 3 RESOURCES

REPRODUCIBLE RESOURCES

▶ Guided Reading Strategy 7.3

▶ Geography Activity 7: Rome During the Reign of Augustus

▶ Readings in World History 26: Caesar's Funeral

TECHNOLOGY RESOURCES

▶ One-Stop Planner 7.3

▶ Holt Researcher: World History: Caesar, Augustus

▶ Homework Practice Online

REINFORCEMENT, REVIEW, AND ASSESSMENT

▶ Section 3 Review, p. 161

▶ Daily Quiz 7.3

▶ Main Idea Activity 7.3

▶ English Audio Summary 7.3

▶ Spanish Audio Summary 7.3

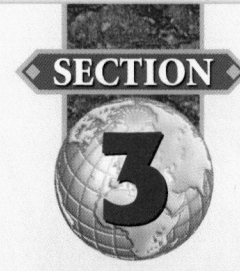

SECTION 3

READ TO DISCOVER

❶ What political events during the first century B.C. helped weaken the Roman Republic?

❷ How did the reign of Caesar serve as a transition between the Roman Republic and the Roman Empire?

❸ What events and conditions marked the first two centuries of the Roman Empire?

DEFINE

triumvirate

IDENTIFY

the Gracchi
Gaius Marius
Lucius Cornelius Sulla
Julius Caesar
Gnaeus Pompey
Cleopatra
Marc Antony
Augustus (Octavian)
Pax Romana
Julio-Claudian Emperors
Five Good Emperors

WHY IT MATTERS TODAY

The actions of political leaders can have a strong effect on a country. Use CNN or other **current event** sources to find a current country in which a leader is abusing power. Record your findings in your journal.

CNN student News.com

The Birth of the Roman Empire

The Main Idea
Bitter political power struggles within the Roman Republic led to the creation of the Roman Empire.

The Story Continues *As the Roman Republic expanded its borders, its problems increased. One Roman official noted the corruption of the government in a letter to his brother. "Remember that this is Rome," he wrote, "a city made up of many people, in which plots, lies, and all kinds of vices abound."*

A Weakening Republic

By 133 B.C. the Roman Republic faced many problems. Brave leaders attempted reform, but the days of the republic were numbered.

Two brothers, Tiberius and Gaius (GAY·uhs) Gracchus (GRAK·uhs), saw the need for reform. Together the brothers were known as **the Gracchi.** Tiberius was elected tribune in 133 B.C. He was deeply troubled by the fate of the farmer-soldier. Although his suggested land reforms made him popular with the common people, they angered and frightened many senators. A mob of senators and their supporters clubbed Tiberius and hundreds of his followers to death.

Gaius was elected tribune in 123 B.C. and again in 122 B.C. He used public funds to buy grain, which was then sold to the poor at low prices. This and other acts outraged the senators, who sought to cancel some of the laws Gaius had passed. Gaius and many of his supporters were eventually killed in a riot. The deaths of the Gracchi marked a turning point in Roman history. From this point on, violence replaced respect for the law as the primary tool of politics.

The Social War. During this period, Rome's relationship with its allies throughout the Italian Peninsula entered a crisis. Citizens of the Italian cities had served in the Roman army and had endured much hardship in defense of Rome during the Punic Wars. The ruling groups of these cities wanted to share in the benefits of Rome's growing power. Above all, they wanted the right to hold public offices in the Roman government, and they called for Roman citizenship. The Senate, however, sought to maintain its hold on power and stubbornly resisted the allies' demands.

Finally, in 91 B.C., the allies rebelled. The war that followed was called the Social War, from the Latin word *socius,* meaning "ally." Many of the allied cities' troops had served with the legions and were as well trained and disciplined as the Romans themselves. Thus, the war that followed was one of the bloodiest in Rome's history. Ultimately, Rome won. The Senate, however, finally agreed to the allies' calls for citizenship and political participation. With this decision, people throughout Italy began to view themselves as Romans, and the Roman state grew to include all of the peninsula.

Gaius Marius, a Roman general who was elected consul in 107 B.C., brought major changes to the Roman political scene. He created an army of volunteers who were well rewarded with money, newly conquered land, and war loot. As more generals followed suit, troops became more loyal to them than to the government.

LEVEL 1: Copy the following cause-and-effect flow-chart on the board, omitting the italicized answers, and have students complete it after reading Section 3.

ENGLISH LANGUAGE LEARNERS

Gracchus brothers introduce reforms	→ *angry senators kill both Gracchus brothers*
violence = primary tool of Roman politics	→ *leaders recruit personal armies*
Sulla marches on Rome; civil war	→ *Sulla establishes dictatorship*

In 88 B.C. **Lucius Cornelius Sulla** was elected consul. After his term expired, he wanted to take a military command that promised to gain him great fame and fortune. His enemies in Rome, led by Marius, tried to prevent him from doing so. Sulla responded by marching on Rome, an action that led to civil war. Sulla triumphed, and from 82 B.C. to 79 B.C. he ruled as dictator. Sulla tried to restore power to the Senate, enlarging it by 300 members and giving it complete control over the government. More and more, however, an army commander with loyal troops could force the Senate to do his bidding.

✔ **READING CHECK: Identifying Cause and Effect** In what ways did political events help weaken the Roman Republic? The republic was weakened by civil violence, loss of respect for law, civil war, and the rise of private armies.

Caesar in Power

Julius Caesar, a nephew of Marius, was becoming a popular general during this time. Caesar was a powerful public speaker who spent a great deal of money to win support. As a result, Caesar built a huge following among Rome's poor.

The First Triumvirate. In 60 B.C. Caesar joined with two other popular generals, **Gnaeus Pompey** (PAHM·pee) and Licinius Crassus. The three formed a political alliance called the First Triumvirate. **Triumvirate** means "rule of three." With the support of Pompey and Crassus, Caesar became consul in 59 B.C.

Caesar knew he could not win power without a loyal army, so he obtained a special command in Gaul, a region that is now France. During the next 10 years, Caesar brought all of Gaul under Roman rule. Meanwhile, Crassus died in battle in 53 B.C. Pompey was made sole consul in 52 B.C. Jealous of Caesar's rising fame, he ordered Caesar home without his army. Caesar refused to give up his military command and take second place to Pompey. Instead, he marched his army toward Rome in 49 B.C.

On January 10 Caesar led his troops across the Rubicon into Italy. With this act, he declared war on the republic. Pompey and his followers fled to Greece, where Caesar defeated him and then marched into Egypt. He put **Cleopatra,** a daughter of the ruling Ptolemy family, on the throne as a Roman ally. In 46 B.C. Caesar returned triumphant to Rome. Two years later, the Senate declared him dictator for life.

The rule of Caesar. Caesar increased the Senate to 900 members but reduced its power. Many senators, fearing Caesar's ambition and popularity, formed a conspiracy against him. Two were men Caesar considered friends: Gaius Cassius and Marcus Brutus. On March 15—the Ides of March—44 B.C., the conspirators killed Caesar in the Senate. Suetonius, a Roman historian, described the scene.

History Makers Speak

❝As soon as Caesar took his seat the conspirators crowded around him. . . . Tillius Cimber came up close, pretending to ask a question. . . . Cimber caught hold of his shoulders. This is violence!' Caesar cried, and at that moment . . . one of the Casca brothers with a sweep of his dagger stabbed him just below the throat. . . . Confronted by a ring of drawn daggers, he drew the top of his gown over his face and did not utter a sound . . . though some say that when he saw Marcus Brutus . . . he reproached him in Greek with: 'You, too, my child?'❞

Gaius Suetonius Tranquillus, *The Twelve Caesars*

✔ **READING CHECK: Sequencing** What steps did Julius Caesar take to gain and keep power over the Roman Republic? reduced power of the Senate; assumed role of dictator

HISTORY MAKER

JULIUS CAESAR. Caesar's shrewdly calculated rise to power echoed his boldness on the battlefield. His brilliant conquest of Gaul made him extremely popular. Pompey, fearing Caesar's popularity, persuaded the Senate to order Caesar to disband his army and return to Rome. Caesar disobeyed and led his army toward Rome, which resulted in civil war across the Roman world. When Caesar crossed the Rubicon River—the border between Gaul and Italy south of which no Roman general could lead an army—he said "the die is cast," meaning that there was no turning back from rebellion. Today, people use the phrase "crossing the Rubicon" to describe a momentous and irreversible decision.

Critical Thinking

How might Rome's history have differed had Caesar balked at crossing the Rubicon with his army?

ANSWER: The Roman Republic may have continued, and Rome's drive toward empire may have faltered.

Julius Caesar (100 B.C.–44 B.C.)

One of Caesar's greatest qualities was his willingness to show mercy toward his defeated enemies. True to form, once in power, Caesar forgave Pompey's supporters in the Senate. These men were among those who murdered Caesar.

What If? How might the history of the Roman Republic have been different if Caesar had shown less mercy?

HISTORY MAKER ANSWER

Students might suggest that if Caesar had not shown mercy toward his defeated enemies and freed them, he might not have been murdered.

TEACH OBJECTIVE 2

ALL LEVELS: As students read the section "Caesar in Power" on page 159, have them complete a web diagram that includes characteristics and events related to Caesar. Then draw a web on the board and fill it in with students' responses.

ENGLISH LANGUAGE LEARNERS

HOMEWORK Write an essay explaining how Julius Caesar's reign was a transition between the Roman Republic and the Roman Empire. Use standard grammar, spelling, sentence structure, and punctuation.

TEACH OBJECTIVE 3

LEVEL 3: Assign pairs of students to study a Roman leader of this time and to write a profile that explains the leader's significance. Encourage students to use their textbooks, the library, the Internet, and other sources. Invite students to read their profiles aloud.

CLOSE

List characteristics of Roman politics before, during, and after the rule of Julius Caesar.

Interdisciplinary Connection

LANGUAGE. Forms of Julius Caesar's name—the Russian word *czar* and the German word *kaiser*—have been adapted by later cultures to express imperial power and supreme rule.

Critical Thinking

How have Roman names influenced calendars used today?

ANSWER: Students might suggest the months of July (named for Julius Caesar) and August (Augustus Caesar).

Linking Past to Present

Emperor Hadrian was famous for his military defenses. He had great walls built in many places across the empire to protect its borders. Parts of his walls still exist today.

Critical Thinking

Why do you think Hadrian spent so much money and effort on the defense of Rome's borders?

ANSWER: Students should note that Rome's borders were extensive and required continuous patrolling to maintain.

HISTORY MAKER ANSWER

Students might point out that Augustus is shown in towering proportions, indicating his greatness and supremacy.

HISTORY MAKER

Augustus (63 B.C.–A.D. 14)

Augustus's funeral followed Roman tradition. His body was burned on a funeral pyre and his ashes were buried with great ceremony. After a senator reported seeing Augustus's spirit rise through the flames, the Senate declared that the Divine Augustus should be made a god of the state. **How does this sculpture demonstrate a new Roman view of a divine ruler?**

Holt Researcher

go.hrw.com
KEYWORD: Holt Researcher
FreeFind: Caesar
        Augustus
After reading more about Caesar and Augustus on the CD-ROM, create political campaign posters comparing the qualities of each man.

The Roman Empire

Caesar had chosen his grandnephew, Octavian, as his heir. A struggle for power, however, broke out after Caesar's death.

The Second Triumvirate. Octavian was 19 years old when Caesar was murdered. **Marc Antony,** a general and an ally of Caesar's, drove out the conspirators and took control in Rome. Then Octavian and Antony—along with Lepidus, Caesar's second-in-command—formed the Second Triumvirate. Marc Antony led an army east, reconquering Syria and Asia Minor from the armies of Brutus and Cassius. Then he joined his ally Cleopatra in Egypt. Meanwhile, Octavian forced Lepidus to retire and built his own power in Italy.

Antony and Octavian divided the Roman world. Antony took the east, and Octavian the west. In time, however, Octavian persuaded the Senate to declare war on Antony and Cleopatra. In 31 B.C., in a naval battle at Actium in Greece, Octavian defeated their fleet. Within a year, Octavian captured Alexandria. Seeing that they could not escape, Antony and Cleopatra committed suicide.

Octavian: the first Augustus. Octavian was determined to avoid Julius Caesar's fate. When the Senate appointed him consul, Octavian did not present himself as king or emperor. Instead, he called himself *princeps,* or "first citizen." In 27 B.C. the Senate gave Octavian the title *Augustus,* or "the revered one." He has been known ever since as Augustus Caesar, or simply **Augustus.**

Although Augustus never used the title *emperor,* historians generally refer to him as the first Roman emperor. This is because beginning with the reign of Augustus, the Roman Republic became the Roman Empire. Augustus began a series of military conquests that greatly expanded the empire's frontiers. Under his rule, the empire stretched from Spain in the west to Syria in the east, and from Egypt and the Sahara in the south to the Rhine and Danube Rivers in the north. Augustus hoped to push the borders of Rome even further. He ordered his legions to drive north of the Rhine River. Roman forces moved into Germany as far as the Elbe River. In A.D. 9, however, German tribes defeated the invaders. The Germans' victory forced Rome to accept the Rhine River as the boundary of its northern frontier.

The reign of Augustus began a period known as the **Pax Romana,** or "Roman Peace." This period of peace would last for more than 200 years. Peace came at a price, however. The political system that Augustus created greatly reduced the traditional powers of the Senate, assemblies, and magistrates. Thus, there was always a threat that an emperor would abuse his power. Over the years, some did.

The Pax Romana emperors. Augustus died in A.D. 14. For the next 54 years, relatives of Julius Caesar, called the **Julio-Claudian Emperors,** ruled the empire. Tiberius, who reigned from A.D. 14 to A.D. 37, was the adopted son of Augustus. Tiberius proved to be an adequate, but disliked, ruler. Caligula, his brutal and insane successor, was murdered in A.D. 41. Claudius, an intelligent man who administered the empire wisely, followed Caligula. During his rule the Roman legions conquered Britain. But even Claudius could not escape the violence that often ended an emperor's reign. It is believed that his wife, Agrippina, poisoned him in A.D. 54. Nero, the last of the Julio-Claudians, also came to an untimely end. Blamed for a disastrous fire that swept Rome, Nero killed himself rather than face certain assassination.

REVIEW

Have students complete the Section 3 Review on p. 161.

ASSESS

Have students complete Daily Quiz 7.3. As Alternative Assessment, have students complete the cause-and-effect chart or Caesar web diagram in this section's lessons.

RETEACH

Have students complete Main Idea Activity for English Language Learners and Special-Needs Students 7.3. Have students identify three events during the time the republic fell that changed the course of Roman history. **ENGLISH LANGUAGE LEARNERS**

EXTEND

Have students write a brief script and stage a mock trial of Caesar's assassins. Students should take the roles of judge, prosecutor, defense attorney, and conspirators. **COOPERATIVE LEARNING, BLOCK SCHEDULING**

Emperors of the Pax Romana 27 B.C.–A.D. 180				
27 B.C.–A.D. 14* Augustus	**A.D. 14–A.D. 68 Julio-Claudian Emperors** Tiberius (14–37) Caligula (37–41) Claudius (41–54) Nero (54–68)	**A.D. 68–A.D. 69 Army Emperors** Galba, Otho, Vitellius (Chosen by various legions during a succession crisis)	**A.D. 69–A.D. 96 Flavian Emperors** Vespasian (69–79) Titus (79–81) Domitian (81–96)	**A.D. 96–A.D. 180 The Five Good Emperors** Nerva (96–98) Trajan (98–117) Hadrian (117–138) Antoninus Pius (138–161) Marcus Aurelius (161–180)

*Dates of reign

Because the Romans never developed a rule for selecting a new emperor, many emperors named their successors. The Roman army, however, often refused to accept the new emperors. In A.D. 69 alone, four different emperors ruled Rome.

Vespasian, the last emperor to come to power in A.D. 69, was the first of the Flavian emperors. The Flavians ruled the empire until A.D. 96, when Emperor Nerva came to power. He was the first of a series of rulers known as the **Five Good Emperors.** Together, they ruled Rome for almost 100 years. Hadrian and Marcus Aurelius were among this notable group of Roman emperors. Hadrian, who ruled from A.D. 117 to A.D. 138, was born in Spain. Thus, he understood the provinces and spent a great deal of time trying to Romanize them. To help protect the boundaries of the empire, Hadrian built fortifications along the frontier. In northern Britain, for example, he built Hadrian's Wall, which stretched from sea to sea. Marcus Aurelius, the last of the Good Emperors, began his reign in A.D. 161. He was a well-educated man who preferred studying Stoic philosophy to fighting wars. Nevertheless, he had to defend the empire against invaders from the north and the east. These invaders would play a key role in the future of Rome.

Marcus Aurelius was forced to begin military activity on the frontiers almost immediately after he came to power.

✔ **READING CHECK: Finding the Main Idea** What characterized the first two centuries of the Roman Empire? territorial expansion, loss of senatorial power, decline of representative government, the Pax Romana

SECTION 3 REVIEW

1. **Define** and explain the significance:
   triumvirate

2. **Identify** and explain the significance:
   the Gracchi
   Gaius Marius
   Lucius Cornelius Sulla
   Julius Caesar
   Gnaeus Pompey
   Cleopatra
   Marc Antony
   Augustus (Octavian)
   Pax Romana
   Julio-Claudian Emperors
   Five Good Emperors

Homework Practice Online
keyword: SP3 HP7

3. **Sequencing** Make a time line like the one below. Complete it by showing the main events in Julius Caesar's rise to power.

   [78 B.C.]—[44 B.C.]

   returns to Rome — made dictator; murdered

4. **Finding the Main Idea**
   a. What political changes during the first century B.C. helped lead to the end of the Roman Republic?
   b. In what ways did Julius Caesar's rule mark a shift from a republic to an empire?
   c. Contrast the rule of the Julio-Claudians with the rule of the Five Good Emperors.

5. **Writing and Critical Thinking**
   Identifying a Point of View Explain how the Roman view of power and authority changed from the first century B.C. through the first two centuries of the Roman Empire.
   Consider:
   • the earlier vow by Romans never to be ruled by a king
   • Rome's republican government, with its checks and balances
   • the murder of Julius Caesar
   • the establishment of the empire

SECTION 3 REVIEW ANSWERS

❶ **Define**
• triumvirate, p. 159

❷ **Identify**
• the Gracchi, p. 158
• Gaius Marius, p. 158
• Lucius Cornelius Sulla, p. 159
• Julius Caesar, p. 159
• Gnaeus Pompey, p. 159
• Cleopatra, p. 159
• Marc Antony, p. 160
• Augustus (Octavian), p. 160
• Pax Romana, p. 160
• Julio-Claudian Emperors, p. 160
• Five Good Emperors, p. 161

❸ First Triumvirate, 60 B.C.; elected consul, 59 B.C.; Crassus dies, 53 B.C.; Pompey sole consul, 52 B.C.; marches on Rome, 49 B.C.; named dictator for life, 44 B.C.; assassinated, 44 B.C.

❹ a. death of the Gracchi, leaders buying loyalty of soldiers, generals using their armies to control the Senate

b. established First Triumvirate, seized sole power, weakened Senate, used army to enforce his personal will, expanded boundaries of the republic

c. Julio-Claudian: rule inconsistent; Five Good Emperors: wise policies and effective measures to defend the empire

❺ Students should mention that Romans of the Republic held that political power should be shared among citizens. This view gradually changed as Romans came to accept a more autocratic, centralized, and exclusive form of government in return for peace and stability.

THE ROMAN WORLD **161**

OBJECTIVES

1 **Explain how the Romans built a strong and unified empire.**

2 **Describe the daily lives and occupations of Roman citizens.**

3 **Explain the role of science and the arts in the Roman Empire.**

📻 *LET'S GET STARTED!*

As students enter the classroom, invite them to look carefully at the pictures in Section 4. Ask students what assumptions they can make about imperial Roman life and culture based on these pictures. *(technological advancements, great architectural achievements, prosperity, enjoyment of the arts, luxurious life for some, leisure time)* Tell students that in Section 4 they will learn about Roman society and culture during the empire.

SECTION 4

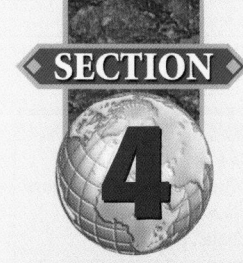

READ TO DISCOVER

❶ How did the Romans build a strong and unified empire?

❷ How did citizens of the Roman Empire make a living and lead their daily lives?

❸ What part did science and the arts play in the empire?

DEFINE

gladiators
aqueducts

IDENTIFY

Galen
Ptolemy
Virgil
Horace
Ovid
Tacitus
Plutarch

WHY IT MATTERS TODAY

European and American cultures have borrowed heavily from the culture of the early Romans. Use CNN.com or other **current event** sources to find a current example of an idea or object that is based on Roman culture. Record your findings in your journal.

CNN Student News.com

Roman Society and Culture

The Main Idea
Over the course of centuries, the Romans built a cultural heritage that continues to influence us today.

The Story Continues *The Pax Romana was one of the longest periods of peace and stability the world has ever known. As a result, the Romans made great advances, many of which affect people even today. If you were to travel to Europe today, for example, you could find your way by using the same road system built by the Romans two thousand years ago.*

Building a Strong Empire

Several factors helped the Romans build their empire and maintain order. First, the Romans organized a strong government and revised their laws. Second, widespread trade and good transportation strengthened the economy and unified the empire. Finally, a strong army defended the frontiers and controlled the provinces.

Government and law. The Roman government was the strongest unifying force in the empire. It helped keep order and enforce the laws. The emperor ran the government, made all policy decisions, and appointed officials of the provinces, including the provincial governors. These officials were responsible to the government in Rome for the effective, peaceful, and profitable administration of the provinces.

Roman law also helped unify the empire. To fit the needs of their huge empire, the Romans changed the laws—the code of the Twelve Tables—in two important ways. First, the government passed new laws as needed. Second, judges interpreted the old laws to fit new circumstances. Roman judges helped develop the belief that certain basic legal principles should apply to all humans. This idea came from the Greek view that law was dictated by nature and therefore common to all people.

Trade and transportation. Widespread trade of farm goods and other products also helped unify the empire. The Roman government developed policies that were designed to encourage trade and commerce. Throughout the time of the Pax Romana, agriculture was the most important occupation in the empire. In Italy many farmers worked on large estates. In the provinces, small farms were fairly common.

Most trade within the empire centered around grain, wine, oil, other food items, and everyday items such as cloth, pottery, and glassware. Foreign trade often included luxury goods such as African ivory, Chinese silk, and Indian pepper. Most of these goods ended up in Rome. From there, they could be carried to wealthy customers throughout the sprawling empire along its overland and seagoing trade routes.

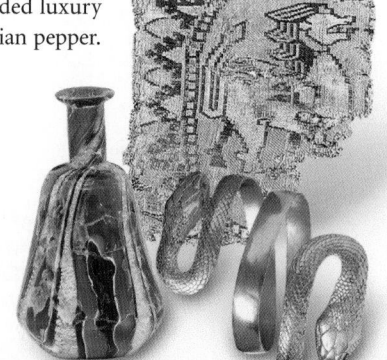

During the Pax Romana, the Romans imported silk, linen, glassware, jewelry, and furniture from East Asia. From India came spices, cotton, and many luxuries new to the Romans.

LEVEL 1: Discuss ways the Romans built a strong empire. Then copy the following graphic organizer on the board, omitting the italicized answers. Have students complete it to understand why the Roman Empire was strong.

ENGLISH LANGUAGE LEARNERS

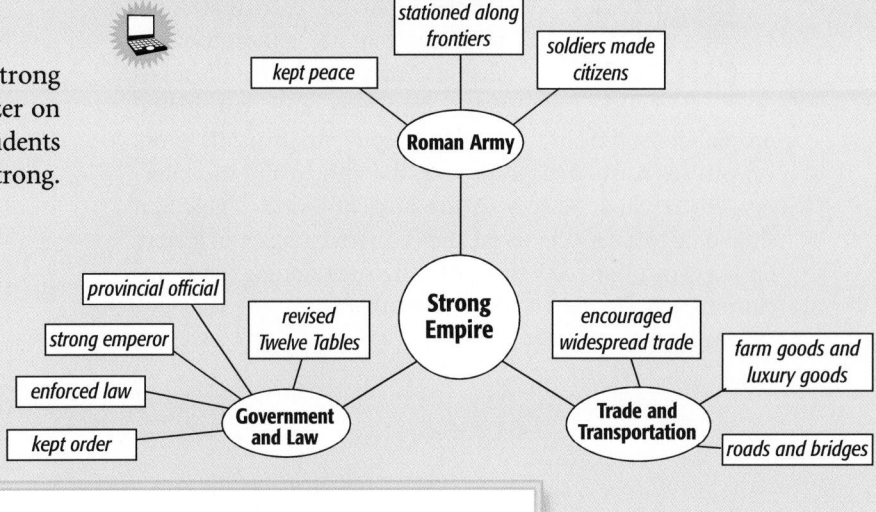

Roman Army
- kept peace
- stationed along frontiers
- soldiers made citizens

Strong Empire

Government and Law
- provincial official
- strong emperor
- revised Twelve Tables
- enforced law
- kept order

Trade and Transportation
- encouraged widespread trade
- farm goods and luxury goods
- roads and bridges

Trade goods:
- ◎ Olive oil
- Ⓜ Metals
- ㋐ Grains
- ㏖ Meat
- ㏒ Spices
- △ Glassware
- △ Leather
- ══ Trade route

Trade in the Roman Empire, A.D. 117

0   400   800 Miles
0   400   800 Kilometers
Azimuthal Equal-Area Projection

Nearly everywhere it went during the Pax Romana, the Roman army built roads and bridges. These well-constructed road systems served to move reinforcements and supplies quickly. They also promoted trade, travel, and communication throughout the empire. About 60,000 miles of paved highways extended to army outposts. Bridges spanned rivers, and highways linked all provincial cities to Rome. These roads were built to last. The top pavement rested on several layers of broken stone and crushed chalk. The good surfaces made travel fast. This was especially true of Rome's major road systems, which were designed to carry heavy military and trade traffic.

The Roman army. The Roman army, too, helped strengthen the empire by keeping peace. Citizen soldiers served for 16 to 20 years in the Roman legions. They were stationed in large fortified camps along the frontiers. People often settled around these camps, which eventually grew into cities. Often men from the provinces or from border areas enlisted in the Roman army. In return they were promised Roman citizenship at the end of their enlistment. Thus a vast army of veterans guarded the frontiers.

If necessary, the army used force to maintain peace in the provinces. In A.D. 60, for example, an uprising in Britain left some 70,000 Romans and their allies dead. The army soon crushed the rebels and destroyed their lands. More often, however, provincial governors aligned themselves with local leaders. This helped ensure that the locals would work to keep the peace.

✔ **READING CHECK: Summarizing** What aspects of Roman rule helped unify and strengthen the Roman Empire? growing trade, good transportation, strong government, revised laws, and strong army

Trade in the Roman Empire, A.D. 117

Interpreting Maps Although an improved system of roads made it easier to transport goods across land, most goods still traveled by sea or river in the A.D. 100s. Historians estimate that it was 28 times more expensive to move goods by land than by sea.

■ **Skills Assessment:**
1. The World in Spatial Terms How far would it have been to move goods from Rome to Alexandria by sea? By land? **2. Drawing Conclusions** Why might the land route have been more expensive?

MAP ANSWERS
1. approximately 1,250 miles by sea; about 3,100 miles by land

2. Overland travel was often longer, more difficult, and time-consuming, and goods could more easily be lost, stolen, or damaged.

That's Interesting!

Despite the Romans' remarkable road system, overland travel throughout most of the empire was difficult, expensive, time-consuming, and sometimes dangerous. Goods were hauled overland by two- or four-wheeled carts drawn by horses or oxen. Traffic in each direction may have kept to one side of the road, although historians are uncertain which side was held. An edict from the reign of Emperor Diocletian in A.D. 301 indicates that bulk shipments of grain could be carried by sea from Spain to Syria at less than the cost of moving the same cargo overland a distance of 75 miles.

Point out to the class that some practices that we abhor today—such as slavery and forced labor—were common and considered normal in the time of the Roman Empire. Ask students to use various sources—their textbooks, the library, and the Internet—to research slavery in the ancient world. Their aim should be to assess the social and economic impact of slavery on Roman culture. Ask them to share their findings and conclusions with the class. **BLOCK SCHEDULING, COOPERATIVE LEARNING**

Historical Sidelight

Slavery was an enduring institution on the Italian peninsula and throughout much of the ancient world. Among the Etruscan city-states, slave unrest had become a major issue as early as the 300s B.C. and may have contributed to the decline of Etruscan power. Slavery was widespread throughout the Roman Empire and was relied upon to provide essential skills and labor in virtually every area of social and economic activity. A considerable body of Roman law was devoted to the regulation and treatment of slaves.

Critical Thinking

How would the Romans benefit by passing laws to protect slaves?

ANSWER: Students might suggest a well-treated slave would be less rebellious, and slave owners would be protecting their own investment.

A ROMAN BANQUET MENU

Appetizers
+ Jellyfish and eggs
+ Sow's udders stuffed with salted sea urchins
+ Broiled tree fungi with peppered fish-fat sauce
+ Sea urchins with spices, honey, oil and egg sauce

Main Course
+ Fallowed deer roasted with onion sauce, rue, Jericho dates, raisins, oil and honey
+ Boiled ostrich with sweet sauce
+ Turtle dove boiled in its feathers
+ Roasted parrot
+ Dormice stuffed with pork and pine kernels
+ Ham boiled with figs and bay leaves, rubbed with honey, baked in pastry crust
+ Flamingo boiled with dates

Dessert
+ Stewed roses with pastry
+ Stoned dates stuffed with nuts and pine kernels, fried in honey
+ Hot African sweet-wine cakes with honey

Bowl with remains of eggs recovered from a Roman site

Life in the Empire

The Pax Romana was a time of great prosperity throughout the empire. Citizens did not share equally in this wealth, however. While the rich enjoyed great luxuries, the majority of Romans were poor. Many of the free poor lived on the land. Some owned their own small plots, but many were laborers or tenant farmers. Others crowded into the cities. Slavery was also widespread in the empire.

Daily life. Rich citizens usually had both a city home and a country home. Each home had many conveniences, such as running water and baths. The rich had much time for recreation and leisure. They attended huge banquets, at which exotic foods, such as jellyfish or boiled ostrich, were often served. The historian Ammianus Marcellinus noted with contempt that the rich held dinner parties primarily to impress one another.

 History Makers Speak

❝Sometimes too at their dinner-parties scales are called for to weigh the fish, birds and dormice that are served. The guests are bored to death by repeated expressions of wonder at the unheard-of size of the creatures, especially when some thirty secretaries are in attendance with writing-cases and notebooks to take down the statistics.❞

Ammianus Marcellinus, quoted in *Readings in the Classical Historians* by Michael Grant

In contrast, many of Rome's residents lived in crowded multistory apartment houses made of wood. The average Roman home was sparsely furnished with simple, very basic furniture made of wood. These pieces offered little style or comfort. Rome's working people could barely make a living. The government provided free grain to city residents, but food was still scarce. Most Romans ate simple meals that included bread, cheese, and fruit.

Slaves and slavery. Slaves were among the least fortunate of the empire's population. Historians estimate that by the time Augustus took power, there were several million slaves in Italy representing a large fraction of the entire population. Slavery was also common in the eastern empire, where it had existed for centuries. It was much less common in Britain and other parts of the western empire. Life could be cruel for slaves. Until the mid-second century A.D., there was nothing to stop masters from treating slaves in any way they wished. Records indicate that slaves who worked the mines or large farms were often treated with extreme harshness and brutality. Life was probably better for household slaves. Often, skilled slaves held positions of trust, serving as doctors, teachers, or secretaries. Unlike slaves in Greece, Roman slaves could buy their freedom or be freed by order of their masters. Nevertheless, Roman slaves enjoyed few legal rights or protections and were dependent on the good will of their masters.

Historians do not believe that slavery was essential to the Roman economy. With so many poor workers available, the labor of a free worker would have been as cheap as—or cheaper than—slave labor. A person gained status, as well as an easier lifestyle, by owning slaves.

ALL LEVELS: Group students and inform them that they are creative consultants for a movie to be set in the Roman Empire during the Pax Romana. Tell them that creative consultants advise filmmakers on the historical aspects of a movie. Their job is to check for historical accuracy and to offer plot advice. Each group is to work together on one aspect of daily life or contribution to the arts and sciences in the Roman Empire. Groups should put together a portfolio of images, diagrams, and narrative descriptions. Encourage students to be creative by building models or developing illustrative materials and costume designs. Detailed information should be included to help the prop and set builders, make-up artists, wardrobe specialists, and others working on the film. **COOPERATIVE LEARNING**

The roles of men, women, and children. The family was at the heart of Roman society. The father held most of the power. He made all important decisions, controlled family property, and conducted religious ceremonies. Women were not without power, however. The mother managed the household, did the buying of food and household needs, and helped her husband entertain guests. Evidence indicates that women also participated in family decision-making. By the end of the republic, moreover, women—especially among the patrician class—had political influence. Women could also own property and accept inheritances.

Early education took place at home. Fathers taught their sons the duties of citizenship, while mothers taught their daughters to manage a household. Children from the richest families continued their formal education at home. Other children attended schools throughout the empire. Boys and girls entered elementary school at a relatively early age to study reading, writing, arithmetic, and music. If their families could afford it, boys went on to secondary school, where they studied grammar, Greek, literature, composition, and expressive speech. In most cases, girls did not receive as lengthy an education as did boys.

Religion. The early Romans sought to achieve harmony with their gods. These included the *lares* (LAIR·eez), who were ancestral spirits. Family worship focused on Vesta, the spirit who guarded fire and hearth. Over time, Roman religious beliefs were increasingly influenced by Greek thought.

By the time of the empire, a state religion had evolved. Based on the old family religion, this state religion had its own temples, ceremonies, and processions. Its purpose was to promote patriotism and loyalty to the state. In 12 B.C. Augustus became its chief priest. Since the Romans believed that gods and spirits were everywhere, it was necessary to please them through rituals and sacrifice. Thus, religious ritual was a part of daily and state life.

Fun and games. The Romans enjoyed many types of amusements and entertainment. They liked the theater, particularly comedies and satires. Mimes, jugglers, dancers, acrobats, and clowns were all popular. Romans also enjoyed brutal sports. Many spectators watched chariot racing in the huge Circus Maximus of Rome, a racetrack that could hold thousands of spectators. Romans also flocked to the Colosseum, the great arena in Rome. Wild beasts, made more fierce by hunger, fought humans or other animals in the arena. Combat between **gladiators**—trained fighters who were usually slaves—drew the largest crowds. A gladiator fight most often ended in death for one or both men. Public executions of criminals also drew large crowds and served as a warning to would-be lawbreakers. Sometimes these executions took the form of public combat between two or more condemned criminals. The Roman senator Seneca described one such public execution.

History Makers Speak
❝The combatants have absolutely no protection. Their whole bodies are exposed to one another's blows and thus each never fails to injure his opponent.... The spectators demand that combatants who have killed their opponents be thrown to combatants who will in turn kill them.... For every combatant, therefore, the outcome is certain death.❞

Seneca, quoted in *Egypt, Greece and Rome* by Charles Freeman

✔ **READING CHECK: Summarizing** What was daily life like for the Romans? growing contrast between rich and poor; family-centered society; daily religious practice; varied forms of entertainment

DAILY LIFE

Baths

The Romans were fond of bathing, and they built baths wherever they settled. The baths were often filled with water of different temperatures. Bathers would go from one pool to another. They combined the dips with exercises followed by massages with fine oils. Romans used public baths as social gathering places. Here people could meet, gossip, and even carry on business.

Today public baths are popular gathering places throughout Japan and other countries. In the United States, public swimming pools serve the same purpose as the Roman baths.

What role did public baths serve in Rome?

Daily Life

All classes of people in the Roman Empire loved spectacular entertainment. Rome's largest race course, the Circus Maximus, hosted chariot races. The chariots thundered around an oval track, making dangerously tight turns at either end. Fans loved to bet on their favorite teams, and successful charioteers were considered heroes.

Gladiator contests were even more popular. Many of the gladiators were slaves who had been trained to fight. In the arena, they battled singly or in groups. A skilled gladiator might even win his freedom.

The emperors paid for these amusements with taxes collected from the empire. In much the same spirit, emperors also provided free grain to feed the poor. Critics warned against this "bread and circuses" policy, but were largely ignored.

ACTIVITY: Have students create a political cartoon about daily life in Rome during the Pax Romana. Encourage them to use their cartoons to point out subtle signs of decay and decline of Roman culture.

DAILY LIFE ANSWER
social gathering places

TEACH OBJECTIVE 3

LEVEL 2: Have students discuss how life in the Roman Empire presented a complex picture of great progress and achievement contrasted against corruption, injustice, and violence. Be sure they support their views with specific examples.

LEVEL 3: Tell students that the Romans renamed the Greek gods but changed the myths themselves very little. Encourage students to read a Roman myth and summarize it for the class, comparing it with the Greek counterpart.

HOMEWORK Make a two-column chart to identify positive and negative aspects of life during the Roman Empire.

CLOSE

Write a short summary of life during the Pax Romana.

REVIEW

Have students complete the Section 4 Review on p. 167.

CONNECTING TO SCIENCE AND TECHNOLOGY ANSWER
system was sloped from mountain areas down to cities

Science, Technology & Society

The finest surviving example of a Roman aqueduct is the Pont du Gard in Nimes, France. It is 885 feet long and 185 feet high. It has three tiers of arches that are constructed of stone blocks. It was built about A.D. 14 to bring water to Nimes from higher ground north of the city. Surviving aqueducts and roads demonstrate the enduring nature of Roman engineering and construction.

internet connect

TOPIC: Roman Art
GO TO: go.hrw.com
KEYWORD: SP3 WH7

Have students access the Internet through the HRW Go site to conduct research on how the art and architecture of Rome reflected the empire's power and glory. Then ask students to create a model of a structure that employs Roman architectural, artistic, or decorative styles.

Science and the Arts

The Romans were a practical people who were not much interested in learning just to learn. Rather, they wanted to collect and organize information and put it to use.

Science, engineering, and architecture. During the A.D. 100s, the physician **Galen** wrote several volumes that summarized all the medical knowledge of his day. For centuries people thought he was the greatest authority on medicine. People also accepted **Ptolemy**'s theories of astronomy for almost 1,500 years. Ptolemy, a scientist and scholar from the great Egyptian city of Alexandria, developed a system of astronomy and geography—the Ptolemaic system—based on the belief that the sun, the planets, and the stars revolved around the earth. Ptolemy's studies in geography contributed to the classical world's understanding of the earth's physical features.

The Romans used scientific knowledge from the Greeks to plan cities, build water and sewage systems, and improve farming and livestock breeding. Roman engineers were masters at building roads, bridges, arenas, and public buildings. In most cities, the Romans built **aqueducts.** These bridgelike structures carried water from the mountains.

The Romans, unlike the Greeks, knew how to build the arch and the vaulted dome. The most important contribution of Roman architects, however, was the use of concrete, which made large buildings possible. Roman architects designed great public buildings—courthouses, palaces, temples, arenas, and triumphal arches—for the emperor and the government. Their buildings were large as well as pleasing to the eye.

CONNECTING TO
Science and Technology

The Roman Aqueducts

The Roman aqueduct system carried water from the mountains to the city, often by aboveground channels. These channels occasionally ran over valleys on stone arches. Other parts of the aqueduct system were made of underground stone or terra-cotta pipes. Waterproof cement lined the pipes to stop leaks. The Romans carefully sloped the aqueduct system to allow gravity to move water along its path. An aqueduct not only carried water, it also purified it. Reservoirs were constructed along the aqueduct course. Sediment carried in the water was deposited in these reservoirs.

Understanding Science and Technology

How does the structure of the aqueduct system enable gravity to cause water to flow?

Many Roman aqueducts contained filtering systems. Water flowed through the filter's upper chambers. Dirt and sediment dropped into lower chambers, which were periodically cleaned.

Have students complete Daily Quiz 7.4. As Alternative Assessment, you may want to use the graphic organizer or homework exercise in this section's lessons.

RETEACH

Have students complete Main Idea Activity for English Language Learners and Special-Needs Students 7.4. Have partners make cards labeled *Strong Empire, Daily Life,* and *Achievements.* Tell them to write supporting details of each concept on each card.

EXTEND

◢ **internet** connect

Internet Activity: go.hrw.com
TOPIC: *Aeneid* **KEYWORD: SP3 WH7**

Have students access the Internet through the HRW Go site to conduct research on Virgil's *Aeneid*. Ask students to select certain passages of the *Aeneid* and draw connections between Virgil's work and ancient Troy and Roman culture. Then ask students to summarize their findings in a one-page essay.

Literature. Augustus and several of the Good Emperors encouraged the development of art and literature. **Virgil,** who lived during Augustus's reign, was the greatest of the Roman poets. His epic poem, the *Aeneid,* tells the story of Aeneas, a prince of Troy. Another Roman poet, **Horace,** wrote of human emotions in odes, satires, and epistles (letters). A third poet, **Ovid,** wrote love lyrics and the *Metamorphoses,* a collection of myths written in verse. The great Roman historian **Tacitus** wrote *Annals,* a history of Rome under the Julio-Claudian emperors. In this work, Tacitus expresses his criticism of the government set up by Augustus. Tacitus was especially concerned with the growing gap between rich and poor and with the decline of Roman moral standards. He strongly criticized the pampered and luxurious lifestyles of the wealthy and the loss of public virtue and respect for the rule of law. Tacitus called for a return to the simpler, more straightforward and traditional behavior that he believed had characterized the republic. **Plutarch,** a Greek, wrote *Parallel Lives,* a collection of Greek and Roman biographies. Each description of a famous Greek is followed by a description of a Roman whose life is similar to the Greek's life in some important way.

Language. Romans learned the alphabet from the Etruscans, who had adapted the Greeks' alphabet. Later they changed some of the letters. Today we use the Roman, or Latin, alphabet of 23 letters, plus *J, Y,* and *W,* which the English added after Roman times.

Long after the end of the Roman Empire, the Latin language continued to be used in most of Europe. The Roman Catholic Church held services in Latin until the A.D. 1960s. Latin is the parent of the modern Romance (from the word *Roman*) languages. These include Italian, French, Spanish, Portuguese, and Romanian. Many of the scientific terms we use today have either Greek or Latin origins. In fact, a large fraction of all English words have Latin origins.

✔ **READING CHECK: Analyzing Information** In what ways did the Romans contribute to science, architecture, literature, and language? They collected and organized knowledge in these fields and applied it to practical situations.

INTERPRETING THE VISUAL RECORD

Latin Nearly all medieval European universities used Latin in their classes. *What does this page tell us about the impact of the Latin language over time?*

VISUAL RECORD ANSWER

Latin was used in written texts for centuries.

SECTION 4 REVIEW ANSWERS

❶ **Define**
• gladiators, p. 165
• aqueducts, p. 166

❷ **Identify**
• Galen, p. 166
• Ptolemy, p. 166
• Virgil, p. 167
• Horace, p. 167
• Ovid, p. 167
• Tacitus, p. 167
• Plutarch, p. 167

❸ Daily Life: homes varied for rich and poor; Slavery: widespread; Roles: men made important decisions, controlled property; women managed households; Religion: numerous gods and goddesses; Entertainment: theater, chariot racing, gladiatorial contests, athletic events

❹ a. government unified empire and helped enforce the law; widespread trade; army kept peace

b. law and government: laws, role of judges, belief that certain basic legal principles apply to all humans, role of emperor, rights of citizens to appeal decisions of leaders; engineering and architecture: plan cities, water and sewage systems, arch and vaulted dome, use of concrete; literature and language: poetry, history, biographies, alphabet

❺ Students might want to include a description of family or daily events.

SECTION 4 REVIEW

1. **Define** and explain the significance:
   gladiators
   aqueducts

2. **Identify** and explain the significance:
   Galen
   Ptolemy
   Virgil
   Horace
   Ovid
   Tacitus
   Plutarch

3. **Summarizing** Make a chart like this to summarize the lives of the Romans.

	Description
Daily Life	
Slavery	
Roles of men and women	
Religion	
Entertainment	

4. **Finding the Main Idea**
   a. What factors contributed to the strength of the Roman Empire? How?
   b. What do you think are the five most important contributions the Romans made to law and government, engineering and architecture, and literature and language? Explain your answers.

5. **Writing and Critical Thinking**
   Making Generalizations Imagine that you are a teenager belonging to the upper class and living in the Roman Empire during the Pax Romana. Write a short diary entry recounting the events of a typical day.
   Consider:
   • the importance of your family
   • the kind of schooling and education you receive
   • how being a boy or a girl influences your life

go.hrw.com **Homework Practice Online**
keyword: SP3 HP7

OBJECTIVES

1 **Describe how the conditions Jews faced in Judaea contributed to the rise of Christianity.**

2 **Identify the difficulties early Christians experienced in the Roman Empire.**

3 **Explain the changes that helped establish Christianity and stabilize the church during the late Roman Empire.**

SECTION 5

READ TO DISCOVER

1 How did the conditions Jews faced in Judaea contribute to the rise of Christianity?

2 What difficulties did early Christians experience while under the influence of the Roman Empire?

3 What changes occurred during the late Roman Empire that helped establish Christianity and stabilize the church?

DEFINE

rabbis
martyrs
bishops
patriarchs
pope

IDENTIFY

Jesus

WHY IT MATTERS TODAY

The Roman government at first tried to stop the spread of Christianity. Use CNN.com or other **current event** sources to find examples of religious groups around the world that currently face government opposition. Record your findings in your journal.

CNN Student News.com

The Rise of Christianity

The Main Idea
The rise of Christianity and its gradual spread across the empire changed the culture of the Romans.

The Story Continues *Although the Pax Romana was marked by a lack of military conflicts, the Romans still faced challenges. Unifying a vast empire that included many different peoples with varying cultures and beliefs was often difficult. Most Roman officials considered their culture and beliefs superior to all others. One of their greatest challenges would come from a group of people whose ideals and values soon threatened those of the empire.*

The Beginning of Christianity

To keep peace, the Romans allowed people in the provinces to practice their different religions, as long as the people honored the gods of Rome and the "divine spirit" of the emperor. Since most people of the time were polytheistic, worshipping more gods did not present a great problem.

Jews and the Roman Empire. In Roman times many Jews lived in Judaea, which became a Roman province in A.D. 6. At first, Jews were not required to honor Roman gods or the "divine spirit" of the emperor because the Romans did not want to violate the Jewish belief in one God. Still, some Jews, known as the Zealots, feared Judaism would be weakened by outside influences and therefore supported rebellion against Rome to establish their own independent state. Other Jews believed that God would soon send a Messiah, or savior, to lead the Jews to freedom.

In A.D. 66 to A.D. 70 the Jews revolted against Rome. Afterward, the Romans sacked the Jewish holy city of Jerusalem and destroyed all but the western retaining wall of the Second Temple. The Jewish historian Josephus recounted the attack on the temple:

History Makers Speak

❝As the flames shot into the air the Jews sent up a cry that matched the calamity and dashed to the rescue, with no thought now of saving their lives or husbanding their strength; for that which hitherto they had guarded so devotedly was disappearing before their eyes.❞

Josephus, quoted in *Readings in the Classical Historians* by Michael Grant

Today what remains of the wall is known as the Wailing Wall. Jews consider it a sacred site of their faith. The destruction of the Second Temple marked a turning point in Jewish history. With the temple gone, the priests' role weakened. **Rabbis**—Jewish scholars who interpreted scripture and were learned in Jewish law—became the leaders of Jewish congregations.

In A.D. 70 Roman soldiers destroyed the Second Temple and removed many of its sacred objects as spoils of war.

TEACH OBJECTIVE 1

LEVEL 1: Have students draw time lines and enter the events that signaled increasing problems between the Roman government and the Jews of Judaea. *(Jews excused from honoring Roman gods; Jews revolted; Jerusalem sacked by Romans; Second Temple destroyed; rabbis became religious leaders; Jews revolted again; Hadrian suppresses revolt; Jews banned from Jerusalem.)* **ENGLISH LANGUAGE LEARNERS**

TEACH OBJECTIVES 1 and 2

LEVEL 3: Have students write an analysis of the message of Christianity and relate it to the spread of the religion. Remind them to use standard grammar, spelling, sentence structure, and punctuation.

In A.D. 135 the Roman army, under the emperor Hadrian, brutally put down the last Jewish revolt. Afterward, Hadrian banned all Jews from the holy city of Jerusalem. Jews built communities outside Jerusalem, however. Here they carried on their Jewish faith and culture. About a century earlier, Christianity arose. This new religion was founded by the followers of the Jewish teacher **Jesus** of Nazareth.

The teachings of Jesus. Jesus had begun teaching around A.D. 27. He wandered the countryside with his disciples, or followers. According to the Gospels, Jesus created great excitement wherever he went. He performed miracles of healing and defended the poor. The teachings of Jesus as he traveled through the Judaean countryside have become one of the greatest influences on the Western world. His life and teachings are recorded in the Gospels of Matthew, Mark, Luke, and John. The Gospels make up the first four books of the New Testament of the Christian Bible.

Jesus's teachings were grounded in Jewish traditions. He emphasized that people must love God above all else, and they must love others as they love themselves. Jesus taught that there is only one true God. He also taught that God cares more for people, especially those who are suffering, than he does for laws and rituals. Jesus explained these views in the Sermon on the Mount.

Primary Source

> **❝Blessed are you who are poor, for yours is the kingdom of God.**
> **Blessed are you who hunger now, for you will be satisfied.**
> **Blessed are you who weep now, for you will laugh.**
> **Blessed are you when men hate you, when they exclude you and insult you.❞**
>
> Luke 6:20–22, N.I.V.

Jesus's teachings were for all people. They promised forgiveness and eternal life for those who accepted by faith what God had already done for them.

The death of Jesus. Jewish religious leaders who opposed Jesus gained the cooperation of the Roman authorities in Judaea to have him arrested. Jesus was put on trial before Pontius Pilate, the Roman governor. Soon afterward, Jesus was crucified.

According to the New Testament, Jesus arose from the dead after his crucifixion. He remained on Earth for 40 more days. Then he ascended into heaven. His followers believed that the resurrection and the ascension proved that Jesus was the Messiah. They called him Jesus Christ, after the Greek word for Messiah—*Christos*. They believed Christ had died for the sins of human beings. Through his death, all people could be redeemed, or saved, from God's final judgment. The resurrection became the central event of a new religion—Christianity.

✔ **READING CHECK: Identifying Cause and Effect** What factors and events in Judaea contributed to the rise of Christianity? Jesus's teachings grounded in Jewish traditions; teachings were for all people; Jewish revolts against Roman rule led to their expulsion from Jerusalem

The Spread of Christianity

Jesus's disciples believed that the day of God's final judgment was coming soon. They set out to spread this message, working mainly in the Jewish communities of Palestine. At first Christianity spread slowly. Its appeal increased, however, as life in the empire became more difficult. Christianity accepted everyone, poor and rich alike. It promised hope and freedom from the penalties of sin and death.

Holt Researcher

go.hrw.com
KEYWORD: Holt Researcher
FreeFind: Jesus
After reading more about Jesus on the CD-ROM create an illustration or collage that describes something about his life or teachings.

INTERPRETING THE VISUAL RECORD

Jesus and children Jesus often used children as examples in his teachings. According to the Gospel of Matthew, Jesus once said, "Unless you change and become like children, you will never enter the kingdom of heaven." *Why do you think Jesus suggested his followers become like children?*

Culture

During Roman times, many Jews left their homeland of Judaea and settled around the Mediterranean region. Many of those who migrated began to speak Greek instead of Hebrew. Two Greek words became an important part of Jewish history and tradition.

The Greek word *diaspora*, which means "scattering," refers to the fact that some Jews migrated and settled in other parts of the world. The Greek word *synagogue*, or "a bringing together," was used for the places where Jews gathered to read the sacred Torah. By meeting in synagogues, Jews were able to share ideas, hold their communities together, and preserve their ancient traditions. Today, synagogues can be found in most major cities of the world.

Critical Thinking

How did synagogues help Jewish culture to survive the diaspora?

ANSWER: Synagogues helped Jews come together to share ideas, develop communities, and preserve traditions.

VISUAL RECORD ANSWER

Students might suggest that Jesus was referring to children's faithfulness, trust, innocence, and lack of worldly skepticism.

ALL LEVELS: Copy the following flowchart on the board, omitting the italicized answers. Have students enter the major events in the development of Christianity.
ENGLISH LANGUAGE LEARNERS

Jesus	Spread of Christianity	Acceptance and Organization
personally taught in Judaea *gained followers* *crucified* *believed risen from dead*	*disciples deliver message* *spreads slowly through empire* *outlawed by Romans* *Christians persecuted*	*accepted by Romans, Constantine* *made official religion* *priests, bishops, patriarchs, pope* *church councils set down beliefs*

HOMEWORK Use the graphic organizer to write a paragraph about the development of Christianity. Remember to use standard grammar, spelling, sentence structure, and punctuation.

Linking Past to Present

Religious persecution has occurred throughout history and still continues today. In the 1990s, religious differences and intolerance ignited conflicts around the world. In the Balkan states of southeastern Europe, for example, various religious groups were embroiled in civil wars based on centuries-old animosities. In Israel, conflict between Jews and Palestinian Arabs continued. After the Persian Gulf war of 1991, thousands of Shiite Muslims fled Iraq to escape the army of Iraq's Sunni government. In Tibet, Buddhists were persecuted by the Chinese government, which continued to be intolerant of Tibetan religious beliefs.

ACTIVITY: Assign students to research these or other examples of modern religious conflict, using primary and secondary sources such as media and news services.

MAP ANSWERS
1. Mediterranean Sea

2. Students should note that it allowed easy travel between the cities.

One person who did much to spread Christianity was the martyr Paul, who founded churches throughout the eastern Mediterranean.

At first the Roman government viewed Christians as a Jewish sect and thus freed them from the obligation to worship the emperor. By the A.D. 100s, however, Rome recognized that Christians were different. Christians often spoke out against the idea of worshiping more than one god. They also tried to convert others to their point of view. The Romans came to view these actions as an attack on Roman religion and law and soon outlawed Christianity. The Romans occasionally seized Christian property and executed Christians. Many Christians became **martyrs,** meaning they were put to death for their beliefs. These Roman efforts, however, failed to stop the spread of Christianity.

In the A.D. 200s, after the era of the Five Good Emperors, violence and unrest again shook the Roman Empire. Many people turned to Christianity for hope. By the A.D. 300s, the Christian church had become so large that the government could not punish all its members. In response, Roman law accepted Christianity as a religion.

✔ **READING CHECK: Analyzing Information** What difficulties did Christians experience under Roman rule? persecution, property seizures, execution

The Spread of Christianity, A.D. 300–A.D. 600
Interpreting Maps Christianity spread throughout the Roman Empire.
■ **Skills Assessment: 1. Places and Regions** Around which physical features did the church establish the five Christian cities of Rome, Constantinople, Alexandria, Antioch, and Jerusalem? **2. Evaluating** Why might this have been so?

CLOSE

Discuss the influence of Jesus Christ on history.

REVIEW

Have students complete the Section 5 Review on p. 171.

ASSESS

Have students complete Daily Quiz 7.5. As Alternative Assessment, use the time line exercise or the development of Christianity graphic organizer in this section's lessons.

RETEACH

Have students complete Main Idea Activity for English Language Learners and Special-Needs Students 7.5. Ask students to explain how the structure of the Roman Empire helped spread Christianity. **ENGLISH LANGUAGE LEARNERS**

EXTEND

Assign various groups of students to one major religion studied so far to review its historical origins, central ideas, and how it spread. Have each group represent its religion during a panel discussion to compare those three factors. **COOPERATIVE LEARNING, BLOCK SCHEDULING**

The Romans Adopt Christianity

The situation of Christians improved greatly in A.D. 312. In that year, the Roman emperor Constantine declared his support for Christianity. Constantine promoted Christianity throughout the empire and was baptized on his deathbed in A.D. 337. In A.D. 391 the emperor Theodosius made Christianity the official religion of the empire. Within 400 years Christianity had spread across the Roman Empire.

During the later years of the Roman Empire, the Christian church became well organized. Priests conducted local services and ceremonies. Above the priests were **bishops,** who headed the church in each city. Rome, Constantinople, Alexandria, Antioch, and Jerusalem became centers of the church. The bishops of these empire cities were called **patriarchs.** Over time the patriarch of Rome took the title of **pope** (from a Latin word meaning "father"). The pope claimed to be supreme over the other patriarchs. The bishops traced their authority from Jesus's disciples, mainly Peter, who was considered the first pope. Any decisions made by the bishops and the pope were equivalent to those coming directly from the disciples, who had received their authority straight from Jesus.

Church councils also helped strengthen the Christian church. In A.D. 325 the council at Nicaea (ny·SEE·uh) wrote down the main beliefs of the church. It claimed the existence of the Trinity—three persons, or forms, in one God (Father, Son, and Holy Spirit). Today the Trinity is a central belief of Christians.

✔ **READING CHECK: Sequencing** What changes and events occurred during the late Roman Empire that helped establish Christianity and stabilize the church? *Christianity became empire's official religion; church became better organized; church councils collected and spread main beliefs*

INTERPRETING THE VISUAL RECORD **The Trinity** This stained glass window from a modern Christian church in Chicago, Illinois, portrays the idea of the Trinity.

Link to Today What does this window tell us about the strength of the Christian church over time?

SECTION 5 REVIEW

1. **Define** and explain the significance:
   rabbis
   martyrs
   bishops
   patriarchs
   pope

2. **Identify** and explain the significance:
   Jesus

3. **Sequencing** Make a flow chart like the one below to sequence the main events that led to the rise of Christianity in the Roman Empire.

   | Second Temple destroyed |
   ↓
   | |
   ↓
   | |
   ↓

4. **Finding the Main Idea**
   a. Review the information about Judaism in Chapter 2. In what ways was Christianity the same as Judaism? In what ways was it different?
   b. What caused the church to become stronger and more established during the later years of the Roman Empire?

5. **Writing and Critical Thinking**
   Identifying a Point of View Write a paragraph explaining why the Romans feared Jesus and considered Christianity a threat.
   Consider:
   • what Jesus said and taught
   • how people responded to Jesus and his teachings

Homework Practice Online
go.hrw.com
keyword: SP3 HP7

LINK TO TODAY ANSWER
Students should note that this modern window suggests the continuity of the Christian faith, enduring as it has over 2,000 years.

SECTION 5 REVIEW ANSWERS

❶ Define
• rabbis, p. 168
• martyrs, p. 170
• bishops, p. 171
• patriarchs, p. 171
• pope, p. 171

❷ Identify
• Jesus, p. 169

❸ Suggestions: more Jews move away from Jerusalem, teachings and execution of Jesus, Christian persecution, internal strife, legal acceptance of Christianity, conversion of Constantine, Rome's official religion

❹ a. similarities: roots in the Old Testament (the Torah), similar ethical codes and belief in one God, persecuted by the Romans; differences: Christians believe that Jesus was the Messiah, followers redeemed by Jesus's resurrection

b. unrest throughout the Roman Empire; Emperor Constantine supported Christianity; Theodosius made it the official religion of the empire; church structure; church councils recorded Christian belief

❺ Students may note that the Romans considered him an enemy of the state and feared he would lead an uprising.

OBJECTIVES

1 **Identify the problems the Roman Empire had to deal with during the A.D. 200s.**

2 **Explain how the reigns of Diocletian and Constantine slowed the decline of the empire.**

3 **List the factors that led to the final decline of the Roman Empire in the West.**

🔊 *LET'S GET STARTED!*

As students enter the classroom, write *The Decline and Fall of the Roman Empire* on the board. Ask students to speculate about the kinds of problems that could have caused the fall and write down three possible causes. Tell students that in Section 6 they will learn about the fall of the Western Roman Empire.

REPRODUCIBLE RESOURCES

▶ Guided Reading Strategy 7.6

▶ Readings in World History 28: A Description of the Barbarians

▶ Creative Teaching Strategy 7: Documentary Newscast on the Fall of Rome

TECHNOLOGY RESOURCES

▶ One-Stop Planner 7.6

▶ Homework Practice Online

▶ Online Maps, Charts, and Graphs: Division of the Roman Empire

REINFORCEMENT, REVIEW, AND ASSESSMENT

▶ Section 6 Review, p. 177

▶ Daily Quiz 7.6

▶ Main Idea Activity 7.6

▶ English Audio Summary 7.6

▶ Spanish Audio Summary 7.6

READ TO DISCOVER

❶ What problems did the Roman Empire have to deal with during the A.D. 200s?

❷ How did the reigns of Diocletian and Constantine slow the decline of the empire?

❸ What factors led to the final decline of the Roman Empire in the West?

DEFINE

inflation

IDENTIFY

Diocletian
Constantine
Goths
Vandals
Huns
Attila

▶ WHY IT MATTERS TODAY

In many countries today, governments depend upon military power to control their citizens. Use CNN or other **current event** sources to identify modern governments that use armed force to maintain political power. Record your findings in your journal.

CNN Student News.com

The Fall of the Western Empire

The Main Idea
Internal conflicts and invading forces weakened the Roman Empire and led to its decline.

The Story Continues *One Roman leader who strongly supported Christianity was Empress Galla Placidia (c. A.D. 390–A.D. 450). The era in which she lived was not a good one for the Romans, however. Years of poor leadership and conflicts with other peoples began to take their toll. Eventually such problems would result in the collapse of the Roman Empire.*

Troubled Times Arise

The last of the Good Emperors, Marcus Aurelius, died in A.D. 180. His son, Commodus, proved to be an unpopular emperor who was killed in his bed on the last day of A.D. 192. Within a few years the empire began to slide into crisis. Between A.D. 235 and A.D. 284, many ambitious men competed for the title of emperor. Throughout this period invaders threatened the borders and civil war tore at the empire.

Rising inflation. In an effort to collect more taxes, the government had granted citizenship to all free people of the empire in A.D. 212. But defense of the frontiers and civil wars were costly, and the end of expansion meant wealth was no longer pouring into the empire. The result was a shortage of silver for coins—the main form of official currency. Emperors responded by decreasing the amount of silver in each coin so that they could mint more money. By A.D. 270 a silver coin contained little actual silver. To receive the same amount of silver as before, merchants raised prices. A rise in prices caused by a decrease in the value of money is called **inflation.**

Increasing insecurity. As the economic crisis deepened and attacks on the borders continued, daily life became harder for many people. Many small farmers were forced to sell their farms to land speculators and large landowners. During the A.D. 250s and 260s, Athens and Antioch were both sacked by invaders. The rich were able to escape the cities for the countryside, but city workers were not so lucky. They were unable to leave their jobs and, in any case, they had no other place to go.

✔ **READING CHECK: Identifying Cause and Effect** How did events and government policies contribute to the empire's economic problems in the A.D. 200s? policies led to inflation, growing insecurity

Inflation became so severe that some people stopped using money and traded goods and services with others.

TEACH OBJECTIVE 1

 LEVEL 1: Draw a chart on the board titled *Problems in Roman Empire* and have students complete it as they read "Troubled Times Arise" on page 172. Then ask students to use a problem-solving process to determine whether they think these problems were insurmountable.

ENGLISH LANGUAGE LEARNERS

 HOMEWORK Ask students to imagine the Western Roman Empire during its last days and to describe this image in words or pictures, using computer software as appropriate.

Two Able Emperors Attempt Reform

By A.D. 284 the Romans had made some progress in pushing back the invaders. Things were far from secure, however, and the economy was still shaky. It would take the efforts of two emperors—**Diocletian** and **Constantine**—to slow the empire's decline.

Diocletian. Diocletian (dy·uh·KLEE·shuhn), a general in the Roman army, was made emperor in A.D. 284. An able administrator, he realized that the empire had grown too large for one person to manage. He appointed a co-emperor and two assistants, or caesars. Diocletian ruled in the East, his co-emperor in the West. Under Diocletian the government controlled almost every aspect of life. Defense and security of the empire came first. Individual freedom was second. Diocletian ended lawlessness within the empire by driving out the invading barbarian tribes. He also tried, although unsuccessfully, to improve the economy by controlling prices and wages.

Diocletian and his co-emperor retired in A.D. 305. Their caesars now became co-emperors, with their sons as caesars. When Constantius, the new emperor in the West, died suddenly in A.D. 306, his son Constantine took his place as emperor. The emperor in the East, however, refused to recognize Constantine as co-emperor. The divided rule Diocletian had created quickly broke down. Civil war once again racked the empire.

Constantine. In the end Constantine won out and became sole emperor in A.D. 324. Constantine is remembered for many things, including supporting Christianity throughout the empire. According to the historian Eusebius, Constantine began supporting Christianity after receiving a vision the day before his victory over his rival for emperor:

 History Makers Speak **❝Around noontime, when the day was already beginning to decline, he saw before him in the sky the sign of a cross of light. He said it was above the sun and it bore the inscription, 'Conquer with this.' The vision astounded him, as it astounded the whole army that was with him.❞**

Eusebius, quoted in *Readings in the Classical Historians* by Michael Grant

Constantine is also remembered for creating a new capital city in the East called Constantinople. The new capital served as a base from which to defend the eastern empire.

After Constantine died in A.D. 337, the empire was stable for about 50 more years. The government, however, was inefficient and corrupt. By A.D. 400, two empires existed, one in the West and one in the East. As the western empire grew weaker and weaker, the eastern empire became the center of power and wealth.

✔ **READING CHECK: Analyzing Information** What reforms and other actions did Diocletian and Constantine introduce that helped delay the decline of the Roman Empire? divided rule; imposed strong government controls; drove out barbarian invaders

Diocletian's Wage and Price Controls

Wages per day

Farm laborer . . . . 24 denarii
Sewer cleaner . . . 25 denarii
Carpenter . . . . . . 50 denarii
Wall painter . . . . . 75 denarii
Picture
 painter . . . . 150 denarii
Baker . . . . 50 denarii

Prices per pound

Pork . . . . 12 denarii
Beef . . . . 8 denarii
Sea fish . . . . 24 denarii
Second-
 quality fish . . . . 15 denarii

Interpreting the Chart
Diocletian passed wage and price controls in an attempt to curb inflation. The move did not work. People hoarded goods and prices soared. *What can you tell about Roman society from the amounts set for various jobs and goods?*

Economics

During the A.D. 200s and 300s large landowners on the Roman frontiers began to hire their own armies and build fortifications to protect their holdings.

Landowners took displaced farmers, craftspeople, and entire villages under their protection in exchange for servitude, leading to the development of the "villa economy." Some historians contend that the feudal system that dominated much of Western Europe for the next 1,000 years had its roots in the villa economy of the late Western Roman Empire.

Critical Thinking

Ask students why people were willing to surrender their freedom to serve landowners.

ANSWER: Students might point out that the growing instability and insecurity that characterized the late empire frightened the people.

INTERPRETING THE CHART ANSWER

Students might suggest that Roman society valued artists and skilled workers over general laborers. They might also note that many Romans could barely afford food prices.

Constantinople, the empire's new capital city, was built on the site of the former Greek city of Byzantium. Today it is the Turkish city of Istanbul.

LEVEL 2: Have students list the accomplishments and policies of Diocletian and Constantine. Then compare and contrast the lists in a group discussion.
ENGLISH LANGUAGE LEARNERS

LEVEL 3: Discuss using a problem-solving process. Then have students write edicts for both Diocletian and Constantine to deliver to the Roman people announcing new policies and reforms that the emperor hopes will solve the problems facing the Roman Empire. If time permits, have some of the students give their speeches to the class.

ALL LEVELS: Discuss the role that the barbarian invasions played in the fall of Rome. Have students compare the map on page 174 with the map on page 170. *(Much of the spread of Christianity coincided with the barbarian invasions.)* Ask students for the results of the invasions. *(separate tribal kingdoms rather than one united empire, people left cities, farm fields destroyed, learning declined)* **ENGLISH LANGUAGE LEARNERS**

Global Relations

In the A.D. 500s a Goth named Jordanes wrote *On the Origins and History of the Goths,* in which he claimed that the Amazons, a group of female warriors from Roman myths, were in fact Goths. According to Jordanes, when the men of the Gothic army were away, "a neighboring tribe attempted to carry off women of the Goths as prizes. But they made a brave resistance, . . . and routed in disgrace the enemy who had come upon them." Inspired by this victory, the Goths chose two women to lead them in the conquest of new territories.

Critical Thinking

Why would this tale be considered inspirational to the Goths?

ANSWER: The women are shown as brave warriors, capable of defeating the enemy and bringing glory to the Goths.

MAP ANSWERS
1. Adrianople, A.D. 378

2. The Roman Army was no longer assured of defeating its barbarian opponents.

Invasions into the Roman Empire, A.D. 340–A.D. 481

Interpreting Maps By the A.D. 300s, invading tribes were attacking the Roman Empire on most of its frontiers. This contributed greatly to the collapse of the Western Roman Empire.

■ **Skills Assessment:**
1. Locate Locate the place and date of the major battle that took place in the Eastern Roman Empire. **2. Analyzing Information** How did this attack reflect the weakening of Roman forces?

The Final Invasions

Diocletian and Constantine were able to hold the empire together through their efforts and reforms. The threat of invasion from the north and east never disappeared, however. The most troublesome of the invaders were the Germans. These tribes—the **Goths** (made up of the western Visigoths and eastern Ostrogoths), **Vandals,** Franks, and others—lived north of the Rhine and Danube Rivers.

The Goths and the Vandals. By the late A.D. 300s large numbers of Goths were flooding into the empire in an attempt to escape invaders from the east. The Romans treated them badly. In response, the Goths revolted in A.D. 378. The heavily armed Goths quickly crushed the large Roman army when they met in battle at Adrianople. Among the dead was the eastern emperor Valens. The Romans no longer had the upper hand against the invaders. In the wake of the defeat, the Romans allowed the Goths to settle in the empire under their own leaders. In return, the Goths agreed to join the Roman army. The peace this brought was short-lived. In A.D. 410 the Visigoth king Alaric and his troops sacked Rome. It was the first time Rome had been sacked in 800 years.

While the Romans were busy defending themselves against the Visigoths, the Vandals crossed the border with little opposition. They proved to be a serious threat to the empire. In A.D. 429 the Vandals invaded North Africa, quickly conquering the area. In A.D. 455 they returned to Europe to sack Rome. Today's use of the word "vandal" suggests the terror and destruction that accompanied these continuing invasions.

Decline of the Roman Empire		
Political/Military	**Economic**	**Social**
• *inadequate government for size of empire* • *competition for power* • *army interference made government unstable* • *dependence on German troops*	• *expense of defending and maintaining empire* • *heavy taxes* • *loss of income* • *decline of manufacturing and agriculture*	• *too many poor* • *loss of patriotism, interest in government, and political honesty*

The Huns. The Goths had moved into the empire to escape the advancing Huns. The **Huns** were nomadic peoples from Asia who lived by raiding and plundering. The Greek historian Ammianus Marcellinus described the Huns in vivid detail:

History Makers Speak

❝They have squat bodies, strong limbs, and thick necks. . . . They wear garments of linen or of the skins of fieldmice stitched together, and there is no difference between their clothing whether they are at home or abroad.

Once they have put their necks into some dingy shirt they never take it off or change it until it rots and falls to pieces from incessant [constant] wear. . . . Buying or selling, eating or drinking, are all done by day or night by horseback, and they even bow forward over their beasts' narrow necks to enjoy a deep and dreamy sleep.❞

Ammianus Marcellinus, quoted in *Readings in the Classical Historians* by Michael Grant

---

Analyzing Primary Sources

Identifying Bias What evidence of bias is there in Ammianus Marcellinus's description of the Huns? Ammianus shows bias by using disparaging language to describe the Huns' appearance, dress, and habits.

By the mid-400s the Huns were led by the fierce **Attila.** In A.D. 451 Attila launched an attack on Gaul. His troops were defeated by an army of Romans and Visigoths in a great battle near Châlons-sur-Marne. After invading Italy, Attila's army withdrew and broke up, but the Western Roman Empire soon fell. In A.D. 476 a barbarian commander overthrew Romulus Augustulus, the last Roman emperor in the West.

Results of the invasions. The Germans who invaded the West were made up of many different tribes. Thus, they set up separate tribal kingdoms once they were in power. This made it impossible for them to rule a united empire. In many areas, people left the cities in search of food and greater safety. In the country, soldiers often trampled crops during battles, and weeds choked the fields. Learning declined as schools and libraries were destroyed. Over time, knowledge of the world and the past declined.

✔ **READING CHECK: Drawing Inferences** What roles did the Goths, Vandals, and Huns play in the decline of the Roman Empire in the West? invasions displaced people, caused instability and destruction

Causes of the Decline

People sometimes refer to the overthrow of Romulus Augustulus as the "fall" of the Roman Empire. Actually, no such thing as a single fall occurred. Instead, the empire in the West gradually declined. The empire in the East would remain until A.D. 1453.

For centuries historians have debated how this mighty empire could disappear. The most obvious cause of the final collapse is the mass of German invasions triggered by the Huns pushing westward from Asia. This put a terrible strain on Roman resources, already spread too thin. Overwhelmed and short on Roman recruits, the army became dependent on German troops, who gained more and more power and freedom. But this was simply the last blow. It took centuries to set the stage for the final outcome. Between the A.D. 200s and the A.D. 400s almost no part of Roman life—political, military, economic, or social—escaped decay.

Political and military weaknesses. In an age of slow transportation, the Roman Empire grew too fast and too large. Rome tried to control this vast empire with a government designed for a small city-state. Faced with governing the entire Mediterranean world, the system failed. Competition for power, oppressive public service, and corrupt courts added to the problems. The army also contributed to the decline by interfering with the choice of emperor and making the government unstable.

Continuous conflict with nomadic peoples from central and southwestern Asia posed an ever-growing threat to Rome during the late empire.

History Maker

ATTILA. Attila was notorious for his ruthlessness. In about A.D. 445 he murdered his brother to become sole ruler of the Huns. Attila invaded Italy, sacked several cities, and may have taken the entire peninsula had his army not been decimated by the plague.

ACTIVITY: Have students use the library or other resources to write a short research report on Attila the Hun and present their findings to the class.

Government

One of Rome's legacies came from the empire's policy of recognizing the legal rights of noncitizens and foreigners. The Romans developed the *ius gentium*, a body of international law, to help them deal with people from beyond the empire. They also understood that circumstances were constantly changing, so they left the law open to interpretation by jurisprudents, or judges.

Critical Thinking

In what way might the establishment of noncitizens' rights have affected their role in the empire?

ANSWER: Students might suggest that by having certain rights protected, noncitizens might be more willing to share in the support of the empire.

Spotlight on ECONOMICS

The costs of defending Rome's borders against invaders such as the Huns and the Goths had a severe and escalating impact on the Roman economy. Funds used in the empire's defense could no longer be dedicated to meeting internal needs, and the imperial infrastructure in the West—roads, ports, communication networks, and essentials such as public water supplies—could no longer be maintained. Ask pairs of students to use their texts, the library, and the Internet to search for information on Rome's economic decline during the fourth and fifth centuries. They should aim to identify links between growing defense costs and declining living standards in the West. Ask them to share their findings and conclusions with the class.

BLOCK SCHEDULING, COOPERATIVE LEARNING

Linking Past to Present

Edward Gibbon was one of the first historians to study the past with the aim of linking historical events and developments to the present. His six-volume *History of the Decline and Fall of the Roman Empire* presents a model of exceptional scholarship, wide-ranging analysis, and relevance that continues to influence today's writers and students. In addition, Gibbon was an outstanding stylist whose work reflects literary mastery, as well as profound knowledge and insight. In many ways his work is as applicable today as it was when first published in 1788.

Critical Thinking

Why might Gibbon's approach to the writing of history be considered as important as the knowledge he contributed?

ANSWER: Students might suggest that Gibbon's pioneering approach—a conscious effort to link and relate the past and the present—greatly enhanced the meaning and importance of historical study.

SKILLS PRACTICE ANSWERS

1. combined economic, social, political, and military causes

2. Essays will vary, but points of view should be supported.

SKILL-BUILDING STRATEGIES   Making Generalizations and Predictions

Why the Western Empire Fell

Many factors contributed to the fall of the Western Roman Empire. It is possible to make generalizations about the causes of the fall by analyzing information about these factors. It is also possible to use the same information to make predictions about how the Romans might have prevented the decline. Examine the information below, then complete the Skills Practice.

A Historian's View:

Historian Edward Gibbon summed up his view of the causes of the fall of Rome.

"This long peace, and the uniform government of the Romans, introduced a slow and secret poison into the vitals of the empire. The minds of men were gradually reduced to the same level, the fire of genius was extinguished, and even the military spirit evaporated."

The most immediate cause of the fall of the Western Roman Empire was the series of invasions by Germanic groups. This skull shows the topknot that Germanic soldiers wore to identify themselves.

Economic
- High taxes
- High inflation
- Loss of war loot
- Decline of manufacturing
- Decline of agriculture

Social
- Growing divisions between rich and poor
- Loss of values
- Loss of patriotism

Military
- German invasions
- High cost of defense
- Dependence on German troops
- Loss of soldiers' loyalty to Rome
- Military interference in government

Causes of the Fall of the Western Roman Empire

Political
- Ineffective city-state system
- Division of empire
- Growing power of Eastern Empire
- Corruption and unstable leadership
- Burden of public service

Skills Reminder

❶ A generalization is a broad statement about a subject based on a variety of facts. The statement may not be exactly true for all cases, but represents a safe assumption given the existing facts.

❷ A prediction is a statement about what might happen based on certain events or conditions. To make predictions, examine existing information and suggest possible outcomes.

Skills Practice

❶ **Making Generalizations** Examine the written and visual information above. Based on this information, write a general statement about the causes of the fall of the Western Roman Empire.

❷ **Making Predictions** Use the same information to write a short essay predicting how the Romans might have prevented the decline by avoiding or changing one or more of the factors.

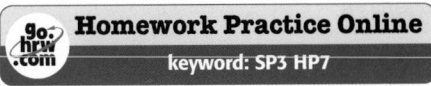

CLOSE

Debate whether the fall of the Western Roman Empire was inevitable or whether it could have been prevented.

REVIEW

Have students complete the Section 6 Review on p. 177.

ASSESS

Have students complete Daily Quiz 7.6. As Alternative Assessment, you may want to use the graphic organizer exercise in this section's lessons.

RETEACH

Have students complete Main Idea Activity for English Language Learners and Special-Needs Students 7.6. Then ask each student to create an annotated time line of the fall of the western empire.
ENGLISH LANGUAGE LEARNERS

EXTEND

Have students create collages that highlight Roman legacies in the modern world, including contributions to the arts and sciences.
BLOCK SCHEDULING

Ambitious generals often seized control, assassinated the emperor, and took the throne. The soldiers lost their loyalty to Rome. Instead, they served anyone who could pay them more. Faced with poor leadership, discipline crumbled. Also, some Roman leaders recruited whole tribes of German troops, granting them money and goods in return for their service. As a result, the Romans became too dependent upon German troops for defense.

Economic decline. Strains on the economy were possibly even more damaging. The defense and maintenance of the empire was expensive. Heavy taxes crushed the people. But even heavy taxes could not provide enough money. The problem was compounded once the empire stopped expanding. The government could no longer depend upon the gold and goods it plundered during foreign wars. As manufacturing and agriculture declined, the Roman economy grew increasingly weaker and more fragmented.

Social change. Roman wealth had always been in the hands of a small part of the population. As the empire grew, the number of poor citizens increased. The division between the rich and the poor contributed to social decay. Most early Romans were stern, honest, hardworking, and patriotic people who believed it was their duty to serve the government. Romans of the later empire lost this patriotism. Most took little interest in the government and lacked political honesty.

✔ **READING CHECK Analyzing Information** What long-term factors contributed to the decline of the Roman Empire in the West? political and military weakness; economic decline; social change

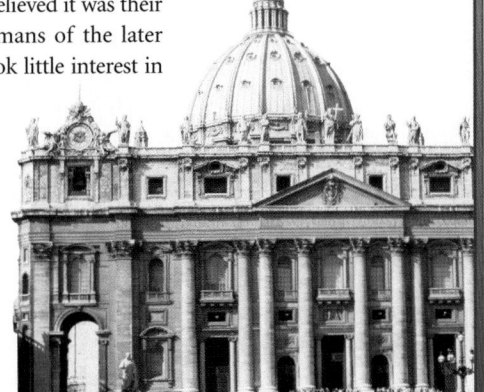

St. Peter's Basilica is an enduring example of Roman architecture.

**Rome:
An Enduring Legacy**
The Roman Empire collapsed more than 1,500 years ago. Even so, the Roman influence still survives. The letters you see on this page are a gift from the Romans. Roman numerals are still used. Also, our calendar is based on the one developed by Julius Caesar in A.D. 46.

Roman influence is also evident throughout the world. Two key influences are Roman law and Christianity. In addition, Roman bridges and Roman roads remain today. The ruins of many Roman buildings continue to inspire people. In these and many more ways, Rome lives on. **Can you identify evidence of Roman influence in the photograph of St. Peter's Basilica?**

THEN AND NOW ANSWER

Students should note the dome, the use of columns, and the massive architectural style.

SECTION
6 REVIEW ANSWERS

❶ **Define**
• inflation, p. 172

❷ **Identify**
• Diocletian, p. 173
• Constantine, p. 173
• Goths, p. 174
• Vandals, p. 174
• Huns, p. 175
• Attila, p. 175

❸ **Rise:** military power and conquest, the Republic's growing political disorder, Caesar's dictatorship and the reduction of the Senate, the birth of the Pax Romana; **Fall:** economic and political decline, division of the empire, growing division between rich and poor, growing military weakness, continuing German invasions

❹ **a.** population decline, civil unrest, barbarian invasions, inflation and economic decline, inefficiency and corruption in government

b. disunity of separate tribal kingdoms, people left the cities, armies destroyed crops, learning declined as schools and libraries were destroyed

❺ Students might suggest that a better system of succession could have been developed, taxes lowered, and expansion continued.

---

1. **Define** and explain the significance: inflation

2. **Identify** and explain the significance:
   Diocletian
   Constantine
   Goths
   Vandals
   Huns
   Attila

3. **Evaluating** Use the following graphic organizer to outline the factors that led to the rise and fall of the Western Roman Empire.

   Rome
   E   F
   S   A
   I   L
   R   L

4. **Finding the Main Idea**

   a. What problems faced the Roman Empire during the A.D. 200s?

   b. How did invasions by the Visigoths, Huns, and others contribute to the problems in the Roman Empire?

5. **Writing and Critical Thinking**

   Problem Solving Write a brief newspaper editorial expressing your opinion about what Rome might have done differently to solve some of its problems and lessen its decline.
   Consider:
   • problems within the empire
   • solutions tried by Diocletian
   • forces outside the empire

go.hrw.com **Homework Practice Online**
keyword: SP3 HP7

REVIEW AND ASSESSMENT RESOURCES

REPRODUCIBLE RESOURCES
▸ Vocabulary Activity 7

TECHNOLOGY RESOURCES
▸ Chapter 7 Test Generator (on the One-Stop Planner)
▸ Global Skill Builder CD–ROM
▸ HRW Web Site

REINFORCEMENT, REVIEW, and ASSESSMENT
▸ Chapter 7 Review, pp. 178–179
▸ Chapter 7 Tutorial for Students, Parents, Mentors, and Peers
▸ Chapter 7 Test (Form A or B)
▸ Alternative Assessment Handbook
▸ Chapter 7 Test for English Language Learners and Special-Needs Students

REVIEW
Have students complete the Chapter 7 Review on pages 178–179.

ASSESS
Use one of the chapter tests to assess students' understanding of the content. For Alternative Assessment, see the Portfolio Activities and Alternative Assessment Handbook.

CHAPTER 7 REVIEW ANSWERS

Understanding Main Ideas
1. senate, magistrates, assemblies

2. Plebeians increased power

3. Rome became supreme in Mediterranean.

4. new territories governed loosely, farmer-soldiers forced to sell lands and move to cities

5. formed the First Triumvirate and conquered new territory

6. Augustus expanded frontiers; emperor became supreme

7. widespread trade of farm goods

8. government systems, laws

9. founded on teachings of Jesus, belief in redemption due to Jesus's resurrection

10. conversion of Constantine, structure, church councils clarified Christian belief

11. Diocletian appointed a co-emperor and caesars. Constantine supported Christianity.

12. population decline, civil unrest, barbarian invasions

Reviewing Themes
1. government and legal system, powerful Roman army

2. scientific and medical knowledge, Roman alphabet

3. became rigid

CHAPTER 7 Review

Creating a Time Line
Copy the time line below onto a sheet of paper. Complete the time line by filling in the events, individuals, and dates from the chapter that you think were significant. Pick three events and explain why you think they were significant.

| 1000 B.C. | 500 B.C. | A.D. 1 | A.D. 500 |

Writing a Summary
Using standard grammar, spelling, sentence structure, and punctuation, write an overview of the events in the chapter.

Identifying People and Ideas
Identify the following terms or individuals and explain their significance:
1. republic
2. checks and balances
3. dictator
4. Punic Wars
5. Pax Romana
6. Julius Caesar
7. Augustus (Octavian)
8. aqueducts
9. Jesus
10. Constantine

Understanding Main Ideas
SECTION 1 *(pp. 150–154)*
Founding the Roman Republic
1. How was the Roman Republic's government organized?
2. How did the Conflict of the Orders change how the Roman Republic was governed?

SECTION 2 *(pp. 155–157)*
Rome Expands Its Borders
3. What was the outcome of the Punic Wars?
4. What problems occurred as a result of Rome's expansion?

SECTION 3 *(pp. 158–161)*
The Birth of the Roman Empire
5. How did Julius Caesar rise to power?
6. How did the republic become the Roman Empire?

SECTION 4 *(pp. 162–167)*
Roman Society and Culture
7. What was the economy of the Roman Empire like?
8. In what areas did Rome make great contributions to the world? Give examples to support your answers.

SECTION 5 *(pp. 168–171)*
The Rise of Christianity
9. How did Christianity begin and what was unique about it?
10. What factors helped Christianity gain acceptance in the Roman Empire?

SECTION 6 *(pp. 172–177)*
The Fall of the Western Empire
11. How did Diocletian and Constantine try to strengthen the Roman Empire?
12. What were some causes of Rome's decline?

Reviewing Themes
1. **Government** What two major factors helped Rome unify its empire and maintain peace?
2. **Culture** What ideas and inventions did the Romans borrow and adapt from the Greeks?
3. **Global Relations** How did Rome's relationship with the people it conquered change over time?

Thinking Critically
1. **Comparing** Compare the role of citizens in Athenian democracy with that of citizens in Rome's republic.
2. **Contrasting** How did the governments of the Roman Republic and the Roman Empire differ?
3. **Sequencing** Trace the spread of Christianity in the Roman world.
4. **Identifying Cause and Effect** How did the use of written law strengthen Rome's government?

Writing About History
Analyzing Information Romans were skilled builders who developed many new ideas. Write a description of how Roman engineering ideas are used today. Use the following chart to organize your thoughts before you begin writing.

	Roman Examples	Examples Today
Ideas and Innovations in Architecture and Engineering		

CLOSE

Discuss what role the Roman Empire played in world history.

RETEACH

Pair students and have them use their textbook to correct their tests. Ask them to create flash cards and then quiz each other on the chapter content. Then have students take the Form B Test to assess their mastery of the material. **ENGLISH LANGUAGE LEARNERS, COOPERATIVE LEARNING**

Portfolio Extensions

Link to TODAY

1. Have students create a time line to trace the historical development of the rule of law and rights and responsibilities, starting with the ancient world and continuing to the beginning of the first modern constitutional republics. Tell students to include entries that help summarize the worldwide influence of Greco-Roman and Judeo-Christian ideas.

2. Divide the class into small groups. Ask each group to select one aspect of Roman republican or imperial government to define and describe.

3. Have students create posters or collages in which they illustrate Roman contributions and achievements in engineering, architecture, and technology.

Building Social Studies Skills

Interpreting Maps

Study the map below. Then use the information on the map to help you answer the questions that follow.

Ancient Italy, c. 600 B.C.

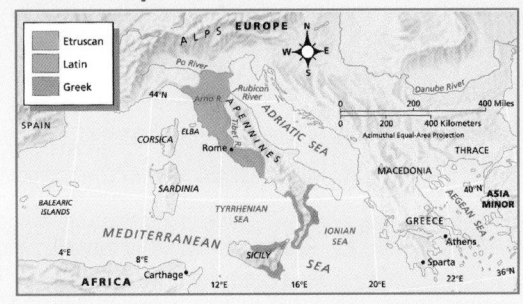

1. Which of the following statements correctly describes how geographic factors influenced Rome's rise to power?
   a. The Alps protected Italy from invasion from the north.
   b. The rugged Apennine Mountains made it difficult to unify Italy.
   c. Italy's location helped Rome control the eastern and western Mediterranean.
   d. Italy's rugged coast discouraged sea trade.

2. Using information from the map, support your choice of statements in question 1.

Analyzing Primary Sources

Read the following quote by the historian Polybius, who lived in Rome during the 100s B.C., then answer the questions.

> "Having then got rid of these rulers by assassination or exile, they do not venture to set up a king again, being still in terror of the injustice to which this led before; nor dare they intrust the common interests again to more than one, considering the recent example of their misconduct: and therefore, as the only sound hope left them is that which depends upon themselves, they are driven to take refuge in that; and so changed the constitution from an oligarchy to a *democracy*."

3. Which of the following statements best describes the author's point of view?
   a. People cannot pick good leaders.
   b. People have no control over their leaders.
   c. Power should be limited to a few people.
   d. Democracy is a response to past abuses.

4. When interpreting a primary source, historians examine the historical context in which the source was written. What events in Rome's history might have influenced Polybius's point of view? Give specific examples.

Alternative Assessment

Building Your Portfolio

Link to TODAY

Government

America's views on the rights and responsibilities of its citizens, including the notion of equality before the law, owe much to ancient Rome and to Jewish and Christian beliefs. Compile a list of the ways in which these legal and moral traditions have influenced American practices. Then use the list to create a chart that summarizes your findings.

📶 internet connect

go.hrw.com

Internet Activity: go.hrw.com
KEYWORD: SP3 WH7

Choose a topic on the Roman World to:
- analyze the *Aeneid* to learn the connection between ancient Troy and Roman culture.
- create a model or structure that employs Roman architectural, artistic, or decorative styles.
- research the destruction of Pompeii and review the tectonic causes of volcanoes.

Africa

CHAPTER RESOURCE MANAGER

Objectives	Pacing Guide	Reproducible Resources
SECTION 1 **Africa's Early History** (pp. 182–186) • Identify what geographic features of Africa affected human cultures. • Describe how historians have learned about the migrations of early African peoples. • Explain the predominant patterns of life in early African societies.	**Regular** 1.5 day / **Block Scheduling** 1 day *Block Scheduling Handbook with Team Teaching Strategies, 8.1*	**RS** Guided Reading Strategy 8.1 **E** Hands-on History Activity 8: African Festivals **E** Creative Teaching Strategy 8: Museum of Early African History
SECTION 2 **The Kingdoms of Kush and Aksum** (pp. 187–190) • Explain how Kush developed as an independent kingdom. • Analyze the factors that helped Aksum develop as an independent kingdom.	**Regular** 1.5 day / **Block Scheduling** 1 day *Block Scheduling Handbook with Team Teaching Strategies, 8.2*	**RS** Guided Reading Strategy 8.2 **RS** Graphic Organizer Activity 8: African Kingdoms
SECTION 3 **Trading States of Africa** (pp. 191–195) • Discuss how trade developed along the East African coast. • Explain how the kingdoms of West Africa became rich and powerful.	**Regular** 1.5 day / **Block Scheduling** 1 day *Block Scheduling Handbook with Team Teaching Strategies, 8.3*	**RS** Guided Reading Strategy 8.3 **SM** Geography Activity 8: The Spread of Ironworking **PS** Readings in World History 49: Blind Man and Lame Man **PS** Readings in World History 50: Mansa Musa's Pilgrimage

Chapter Resource Key

PS Primary Sources	**A** Assessment	Music	
RS Reading Support	**REV** Review	Video	
IC Interdisciplinary Connections	**ELL** Reinforcement and English Language Learners	Internet	
E Enrichment	Transparencies	Holt Presentation Maker Using Microsoft® PowerPoint®	
SM Skills Mastery	CD–ROM		

 One-Stop Planner CD-ROM

See the ***One–Stop Planner*** for a complete list of additional resources for students and teachers.

One-Stop Planner CD-ROM

It's easy to plan lessons, select resources, and print out materials for your students when you use the *One-Stop Planner* CD–ROM with *Test Generator.*

Technology Resources

 One-Stop Planner 8.1

 World History and Cultures Video Program 7: Early African Traditions

Regions of the World Music Audio CD Program 16: Southern Africa: Bantu Choral Folk Songs: Pete Seeger with the Song Swappers

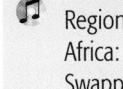 World History Teaching Transparency: Geography and History 7: North Africa and the Sahara

World History Teaching Transparency: Regional and World Map 36: Africa

 Homework Practice Online

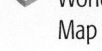 One-Stop Planner 8.2

Regions of the World Music Audio CD Program 13: North Africa: Arabic songs of Lebanon and Egypt

Homework Practice Online

One-Stop Planner 8.3

Holt researcher: World History: Sonni 'Ali, Askia the Great

CNN. Presents World Cultures: Yesterday and Today Segment 24: The Farms of Zimbabwe

CNN. Presents World Cultures: Yesterday and Today Segment 32: A Kenyan Reggae Festival

World History Teaching Transparency: Geography and History 13: African Trading Kingdoms

World History Teaching Transparency: Everyday Life 13: Great Zimbabwe

Homework Practice Online

Online Maps: Cities of Africa, A.D. 1200

Online Maps, Charts, and Graphs: African Trade, c. 1450–1600

Online Maps: African Caravan Routes

Reinforcement, Review, and Assessment

Daily Quiz 8.1

Main Idea Activity 2.1

English Audio Summary 8.1

Spanish Audio Summary 8.1

REV Section 1 Review, p. 186

Daily Quiz 8.2

Main Idea Activity 8.2

English Audio Summary 8.2

Spanish Audio Summary 8.2

REV Section 2 Review, p. 190

Daily Quiz 8.3

Main Idea Activity 8.3

English Audio Summary 8.3

Spanish Audio Summary 8.3

REV Section 3 Review, p. 195

🔀 **internet** connect 🔀

HRW ONLINE RESOURCES
GO TO: go.hrw.com
Then type in a keyword.

TEACHER HOME PAGE
KEYWORD: SP3 Teacher

CHAPTER INTERNET ACTIVITIES
KEYWORD: SP3 WH8
Choose an activity to:
- research threats to the Congo Basin's ecosystem.
- explore the ancient kingdom of Nubia.
- analyze language development in Africa.

CHAPTER ENRICHMENT LINKS
KEYWORD: SP3 CH8

ONLINE ASSESSMENT
Homework Practice
KEYWORD: SP3 HP8
Standardized Test Prep
KEYWORD: SP3 STP8
Rubrics
KEYWORD: SS Rubrics

ONLINE MAPS, CHARTS, AND GRAPHS
KEYWORD: SP3 MCG

CONTENT UPDATES
KEYWORD: SS Content Updates

HOLT PRESENTATION MAKER
KEYWORD: SP3 PPT8

ONLINE READING SUPPORT
KEYWORD: SS Strategies

CURRENT EVENTS
KEYWORD: S3 Current Events

Meeting Individual Needs

Ability Levels

Level 1 Basic level activities designed for all students encountering new material

Level 2 Intermediate level activities designed for average students

Level 3 Challenging activities designed for honors and gifted and talented students

English Language Learners These activities address the needs of students with Limited English Proficiency.

Chapter Review and Assessment

IC Vocabulary Activity 8

 Global Skill Builder CD–ROM

 HRW Web Site

REV Chapter 8 Tutorial for Students, Parents, Mentors, and Peers

REV Chapter 8 Review, pp. 196–197

A Chapter 8 Test Generator (on the One-Stop Planner)

A Chapter 8 Test (Form A or B)

A Alternative Assessment Handbook

A Chapter 8 Test for English Language Learners and Special-Needs Students

Section 1   *Africa's Early History*

Section 2   *The Kingdoms of Kush and Aksum*

Section 3   *The Trading States of Africa*

Build on What You Know

Ask students to answer the following questions:

How might scientists have learned about early human life in Africa?

Consider:

- the work of archaeologists
- the kinds of artifacts found at archaeological digs
- the study of languages and of stories passed on through storytellers

Based on your knowledge of early civilizations, how might early African civilizations have passed cultural elements on to succeeding cultures?

Consider:

- the migration of early peoples and the spread of language
- the impact of trade, travel, and conquests
- the spread of religion

EXPLORING THE TIME LINE
GL⊘BAL EVENTS

internet connect

go hrw com

TOPIC: Conquest and Diffusion
GO TO: go.hrw.com
KEYWORD: SP3 WH8

Have students access the Internet through the HRW Go site to conduct research on the conquest and cultural diffusion among the early African civilizations of Egypt, Kush, and Aksum. Then ask students to create a chart that shows the cultural effects of conquest on each of these groups of peoples. Students' charts should include appropriate examples and evidence drawn from their research.

CHAPTER

8

1800 B.C.–A.D. 1500
Africa

Funeral stele from ancient Kush

c. 1668 B.C.–1570 B.C.
Daily Life
Classic Karmah prospers.

    c. 1650 B.C.
    Science and Technology
    Hyksos invaders use horse-drawn chariots against the Egyptians.

c. 1200 B.C.
Science and Technology
The Iron Age begins in southwestern Asia and later spreads to Africa.

c. 710 B.C.
Politics
Kush rules Egypt.

c. 250 B.C.–150 B.C.
The Arts
Probably during this period, great pyramids and temples are built in Kush.

c. 250 B.C.
Science and Technology
Meroë is an important center of ironmaking in Africa.

1500 B.C.	**1000 B.C.**	**500 B.C.**

c. 1500 B.C.–1000 B.C.
The Arts
Nubians build the Great Temple of Abu Simbel.

c. 671 B.C.
Global Events
The Assyrians invade Kush.

Reliefs at Abu Simbel

Religious sculpture from Benin, West Africa, A.D. 1200s

Build on What You Know

*I*n earlier chapters you learned about the origins of human life on Earth. Human-like creatures lived and developed in the rugged highlands of East Africa almost 4 million years ago. In fact, many scientists are convinced that the continent of Africa may very well have been where our species began. You also learned that the continent gave birth to one of the world's earliest civilizations, the remarkable culture of Egypt, in North Africa. In this chapter, you will learn about early civilizations that emerged, flourished, and then gave way to succeeding cultures in other parts of the African continent.

What's Your Opinion?

Themes Journal *To help students create their Themes Journal entries, provide the following examples of appropriate agree/disagree statements.*

Economics

Agree People always trade for goods that they cannot grow or produce themselves but that are needed as basic necessities of life.

Disagree Important trade goods are often luxuries that only the rich can afford.

Geography

Agree A region's physical environment influences the kinds of economic activities that people can successfully undertake in that region.

Disagree A region's physical environment has little effect on the development of trade and commerce.

Global Relations

Agree People who lack natural resources to meet their needs often conquer others to gain those resources.

Disagree People can get what they need through trade and hard work.

Ruins of the Great Zimbabwe fortress

Mask of the queen mother of Benin, A.D. 1500s

C. A.D. 1100 Business and Finance Kilwa becomes a leading Indian Ocean port.

C. A.D. 320–A.D. 340 Daily Life King 'Ēzānā converts to Christianity.

C. A.D. 700–A.D. 1300 Business and Finance East Africa has a golden age of trade.

C. A.D. 1100s– A.D. 1400s Business and Finance Gold mining and trade thrives in Great Zimbabwe.

C. A.D. 1450–A.D. 1500 Global Events Great Zimbabwe declines.

A.D. 1	A.D. 500	A.D. 1000	A.D. 1500

C. A.D. 330 Global Events Kush is defeated by Aksum.

C. A.D. 1000 Global Events Ghana reaches its height.

C. A.D. 1468 Politics The reign of Sonni 'Alī in Songhai begins.

C. A.D. 900s Daily Life Bantu-speaking societies are established across southern Africa.

C. A.D. 1352 Science and Technology Arab geographer Ibn Battūtah explores the Sahara Desert.

C. A.D. 1307–C. A.D. 1332 Politics Mansa Mūsā rules Mali.

Brass sculpture of a hunting scene, made by the Akan people of West Africa as a weight to measure gold powder

What's Your Opinion?

Themes Journal *Do you agree or disagree with the following statements? Support your point of view in your journal.*

Economics Important trade goods always meet the essential needs of people.

Geography The physical environment of a region influences the development of trade and commerce in that region.

Global Relations People seek to get what they need by conquering others.

GLOBAL EVENTS

The Nubians, who were controlled by Egypt, acted as middlemen in trade along the Upper Nile. In time, they started asking for a tax on the goods that went through their land. In 1472 B.C. Queen Hatshepsut of Egypt had five ships carried across the desert to avoid the Nubian-controlled Upper Nile. Eventually the Nubians gained control of the trade routes from the Red Sea to the Nile and established the kingdom of Kush.

Critical Thinking

How do you think Egypt's control of the Nubians influenced the government of Kush?

ANSWER: The government was similar to the strong pharaoh-centered government of Egypt.

☑ **internet** connect

TOPIC: Nubia
GO TO: go.hrw.com
KEYWORD: SP3 WH8

Have students access the Internet through the HRW Go site to research Nubia. Ask students to imagine they are traveling back in time to ancient Nubia. Have students find information about the people, their customs, and their homes. Then ask them to write a journal entry as if they were living in ancient Nubia.

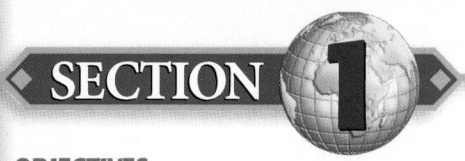

SECTION 1

OBJECTIVES

1 **Identify what geographic features of Africa affected human cultures.**

2 **Describe how historians have learned about the migrations of early African peoples.**

3 **Explain the predominant patterns of life in early African societies.**

LET'S GET STARTED!

As students enter the classroom, ask them to write some of the methods scientists use to learn about the history and culture of early civilizations. Students should also write a brief description of each method. *(excavating cities and buildings, studying artifacts, and analyzing the spread of languages)* Tell students that in Section 1 they will learn how scientists have learned about the cultures and civilizations of early Sub-Saharan Africa.

SECTION 1 RESOURCES

REPRODUCIBLE RESOURCES

▸ Guided Reading Strategy 8.1

▸ Hands-on History Activity 8: African Festivals

▸ Creative Teaching Strategy 8: Museum of Early African History

TECHNOLOGY RESOURCES

▸ One-Stop Planner 8.1

▸ World History and Cultures Video Program 7: Early African Traditions

▸ World History Teaching Transparency: Regional and World Map 36: Africa

▸ Homework Practice Online

REINFORCEMENT, REVIEW, AND ASSESSMENT

▸ Section 1 Review, p. 186

▸ Daily Quiz 8.1

▸ Main Idea Activity 8.1

▸ English Audio Summary 8.1

▸ Spanish Audio Summary 8.1

SECTION 1

READ TO DISCOVER

❶ What geographic features of Africa affected human cultures?

❷ How did historians learn about the migrations of early peoples?

❸ What were the predominant patterns of life in many early African societies?

DEFINE

savannas
tropical rain forests
jungle
linguists
oral traditions
matrilineal

IDENTIFY

Bantu

WHY IT MATTERS TODAY

Many African Americans look to Sub-Saharan Africa as the homeland of their ancestors. Use ⟨CNN news.com⟩ or other **current event** sources to find out how African Americans view and celebrate their ancestry. Record your findings in your journal.

Africa's Early History

The Main Idea
Although the geography of Africa varies, many early societies there shared common cultural traits.

The Story Continues *The African American poet Countee Cullen once asked, "What is Africa to me?" He was writing about his lost African heritage, but the question could be asked by anyone practically anywhere in the world today. Most scientists believe that human life began in Africa. Yet much about the early civilizations of Africa remains a mystery to most modern people. Within its history is the story of a great continent that housed a wealth of cultures.*

The Physical Setting

In the northeast corner of Africa, the Neolithic people of ancient Egypt had begun to move toward civilization by about 3800 B.C. Other great civilizations also thrived on the African continent. Written records, still-standing monuments, and ruins are evidence of early North African civilizations. They arose on the narrow slice of land between the Mediterranean Sea and the great Sahara. Equally important cultures developed south of the desert. This vast portion of the continent is called Sub-Saharan Africa. The physical geography of Sub-Saharan Africa strongly influenced the growth of human societies there.

The plateau. Much of Sub-Saharan Africa is a plateau. This highland is dimpled by river basins and valleys. Like a great upside-down bowl, it drops sharply to a coastal plain. The steep shoreline has few natural harbors. Most rivers—like the Congo, Niger, and Zambezi—are blocked by rapids. Therefore boats could not go far upstream from the ocean. This protected the interior from invasion, but it also made trade and communication among Africans harder.

The enormous Sahara Desert covers about one-fourth of the African continent. Thousands of years ago, the Sahara was fertile and well watered. Over the course of centuries, however, changing wind and weather patterns have caused the area to become increasingly dry and barren. The southern edge of the desert is a region known as the Sahel, from the Arabic word for "shore." Rainfall in the Sahel is both sparse and uncertain, and the area is often the scene of harsh droughts that may last for years. For this reason farming is difficult throughout the region. South of the Sahel are vast stretches of dry grasslands called **savannas.** The savannas are dotted with a few trees and thorny bushes. Farming techniques began to spread in Africa by about 3000 B.C. Savanna farmers began to grow grains such as sorghum, millet, and rice. Where the savannas met the deserts, people herded cattle.

Rainfall is much greater farther south. So too is the amount of vegetation. Some areas in central and western Africa receive more than 100 inches of rain a year. There, vast forests called **tropical rain forests** thrive. The tropical rain forests include areas of jungle. In **jungle** areas, dense tangles of plants grow wherever sunlight reaches through the tall trees to the forest floor. Early farmers in the forested regions grew root crops such as yams.

ALL LEVELS: Draw a large outline map of Africa. Divide the class into three groups and assign one of the following regions to each: desert, savanna, and tropical rain forest. Have each group choose a color to code its region on the map and design symbols to represent the natural vegetation, crops, and livestock suited to the region *(Rain forest—green/ trees and yams; savanna—brown/ grasses, sorghum, millet, rice; desert—yellow/ cattle.)* Have each group complete its part of the map.

ENGLISH LANGUAGE LEARNERS, COOPERATIVE LEARNING

LEVEL 3: Have students read pages 182–183 and locate the Congo Basin on the map on page 183. Prompt them to discuss how natural barriers such as a river that is hard to navigate, a rain forest, mountains, and deadly insects might affect the culture of a region. *(Rain forests, insects, mountains, and rapids-filled rivers can hinder trade, travel, and invasions; a farming culture could develop in the river valley.)*

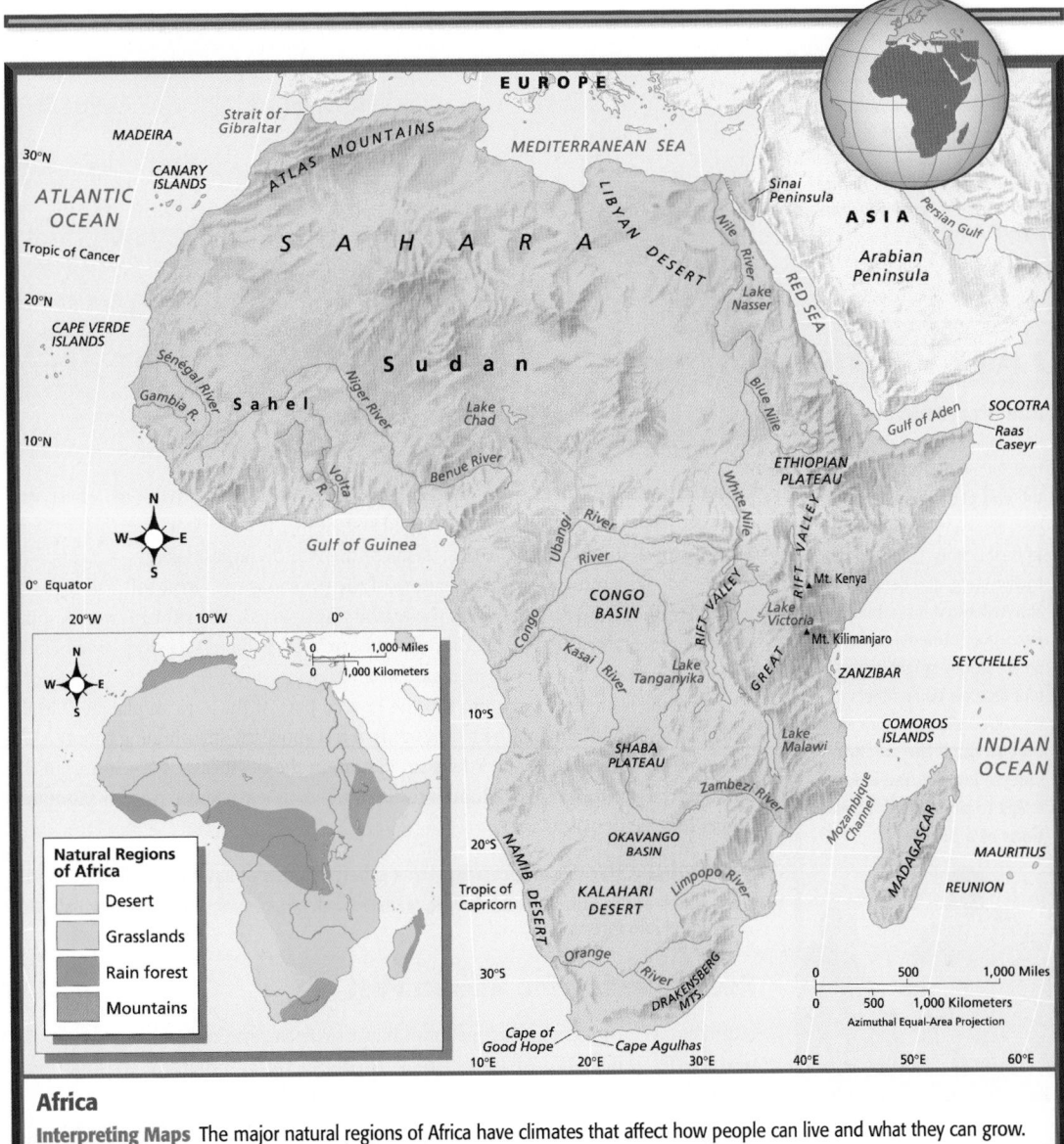

Africa

Interpreting Maps The major natural regions of Africa have climates that affect how people can live and what they can grow.

■ **Skills Assessment: 1. The World in Spatial Terms** Where does Africa lie in relation to the equator? **2. Drawing Conclusions** How might its position relative to the equator affect Africa's climate?

The hot, wet climate of the rain forests provides breeding grounds for insects. Some of them carry deadly diseases. Among the diseases are malaria and yellow fever, carried by mosquitoes, and sleeping sickness, carried by tsetse flies. Although modern medicine can treat these diseases, many Africans perished from them in earlier centuries.

Farther south of the rain forests are more dry grasslands. These are broken in the south by yet more stretches of harsh desert. The Kalahari Desert and the Namib Desert range from the center of southern Africa westward to the Atlantic coast and, like the Sahara to the north, are largely barren and desolate.

MAP ANSWERS
1. Africa lies almost equally north and south of the equator.
2. It would give Africa a hot climate.

Geography

Sub-Saharan Africa's main rivers are long but are blocked by rapids. This protected African peoples from invaders but also made it hard for Africans to carry on trade among themselves.

Critical Thinking

Look at the map on page 183. What other geographic factors kept early African peoples apart?

ANSWER: Students might suggest that mountains and rain forests acted as natural barriers between groups of African peoples.

That's Interesting!

The tsetse fly infects cattle and horses, as well as people, with sleeping sickness. In animals, sleeping sickness is called *nagana*. Because of *nagana*, African farmers have not been able to depend on livestock for plowing fields or providing fertilizer.

Technology Resources

World History Teaching Transparency: Geography and History 7: North Africa and the Sahara

TEACH OBJECTIVE 2

LEVEL 1: Have students create an inverted tree diagram that will help them to remember some of the methods scholars use to analyze limited evidence from early African civilizations. Instruct them to include examples of language, cultural exchange, and other evidence. Use the following sample diagram to help get students started.

Methods to Discover the Past

- **Language**
  - spread of languages
  - oral tradition
  - new words
  - stories songs poems
- **Cultural Exchange**
  - music
  - styles of art
- **Other**
  - spread in cultivated plants
  - changes in climate
  - excavation of artifacts

ENGLISH LANGUAGE LEARNERS, COOPERATIVE LEARNING

VISUAL RECORD ANSWER

shows mountains, plateau, and savanna

Interdisciplinary Connection

LANGUAGE. Some Bantu languages spoken today are Zulu in South Africa, Makua in Mozambique, Shona in Zimbabwe, Bemba in Zambia, Swahili in Tanzania, Ganda in Uganda, Kongo in Congo, and Fang in Cameroon.

Critical Thinking

Have students turn to the political map of Africa in the Atlas. Ask how they can determine in which directions early Bantu speakers migrated if they started in West Africa.

ANSWER: Bantu speakers migrated east and south.

DAILY LIFE ANSWER

The storyteller preserves traditions by telling stories of important events and people in a village's history.

LINK TO TODAY ANSWER

By studying modern African languages, people can learn about the migration of early groups of people who lived in Africa.

Technology Resources

 Regions of the World Music Audio CD Program 16

184

INTERPRETING THE VISUAL RECORD

Mount Kilimanjaro Mount Kilimanjaro, in Tanzania, is a dormant volcano and the tallest mountain in Africa. *How does this image reflect Africa's great geographic variety?*

DAILY LIFE

The Storytellers

Storytellers played an important role in African society. At the end of the workday, the people of a village gathered to hear a story. Using words, music, song, and dance, the storyteller told his or her tale. Each story carried a message. Some stories taught important lessons, while others described village history. **How do you think the modern storyteller pictured below helps to preserve the traditions of a people?**

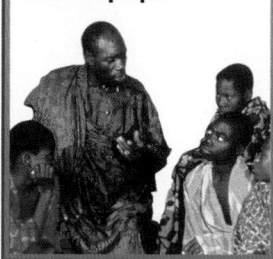

Link to Today How does the study of modern languages help us understand African history?

Other natural features. The African plateau has six large depressions. These vast drainage basins formed around Lake Chad and along the continent's five major rivers. Lake Victoria, in east central Africa, is one of the world's largest lakes.

Perhaps the most remarkable feature of the plateau is the Great Rift Valley. It was formed millions of years ago when the earth's crust parted. The rift runs north-south near the plateau's eastern edge. Many long, narrow lakes lie in this steep-sided crack. Among them are Lake Tanganyika and Lake Malawi.

Isolated mountain peaks also dot the eastern part of the African plateau. Mount Kenya and Mount Kilimanjaro jut thousands of feet above the surrounding countryside. A main highland region is the Ethiopian Plateau in the northeast. It is a source of the Nile River. The Drakensberg Mountains lie in the southeast. Some African mountain ranges have active volcanoes.

✔ **READING CHECK: Categorizing** What different kinds of landforms, climates, and features are in Sub-Saharan Africa? plateau highlands, deserts, dry savanna grasslands, tropical rain forests, and jungles

Rediscovering the African Past

Humans developed societies in Sub-Saharan Africa long before they developed writing. To understand African history before the development of writing there, scholars use many methods to analyze limited evidence.

Language. For example, **linguists**—scientists who study languages—have used computers to compare modern African words. Linguists have shown how **Bantu,** a family of closely related African languages, spread. Their study suggests to anthropologists and historians that for centuries people have migrated throughout Sub-Saharan Africa.

The "cradle land" of Bantu lies in west central Africa. This area is along the present border of Nigeria and Cameroon. From there, perhaps 2,000 years ago or earlier, Bantu-speaking people began migrating east and south into what is now Gabon. These migrations continued for about 1,000 years, possibly longer. Over time the Bantu language group became one of Africa's largest.

Information about the history and the cultural development of Africa also comes from the study of **oral traditions.** These are poems, songs, and stories passed by word of mouth from one generation to another. Often these tales hold some moral lesson or tell of the deeds of past kings and heroes. Africans have always had a strong sense

---

TEACH OBJECTIVE 3

LEVEL 2: Have students discuss the patterns of life in early Africa. Discussions should include the village as the basic unit of society, the role of women as farmers, matrilineal inheritance of property, religions with gods linked to nature and human activities, and the role of the village elders. **COOPERATIVE LEARNING**

 HOMEWORK Have students find examples of women's roles in present-day African societies. Ask them to identify those societies in which matrilineal inheritance is still practiced.

CLOSE

Have students summarize how geography influenced ways of life in early African societies.

REVIEW

Have students complete the Section 1 Review on p. 186.

---

of their own history. Some societies had oral historians, like the griots (GREE·ohz) of West Africa. Griots were highly trained speakers and entertainers who memorized the oral tradition of their village. Through their performances they amused and also taught their audiences. Kings and noble families often hired griots to keep a record of their achievements. Today individual families and villages in Africa still remember important events by telling about them in poetry and song. As stories are passed along, each generation adds events from its own time. Historians and anthropologists have now written down much of this oral African tradition.

Cultural exchange. Other scholars have also helped discover Africa's past. Among them are those who study music. They have found, for example, that the design and tuning of xylophones in East Africa are like those in Indonesia, in Southeast Asia. This similarity suggests that at an early date there was cultural exchange between Africa and Asia.

Certain languages also show that there was early contact between Africa and Asia. Malagasy is an example. This language is spoken on the Indian Ocean island of Madagascar, off eastern Africa. It has many words spoken by people in Indonesia. In addition, scholars have noted the prevalence of the banana in Africa. This crop is native to Asia.

Through such study of musical instruments, language, and plants, scholars have determined that cultural exchange between parts of Africa and Asia probably took place over thousands of years.

Other evidence. Scholars have discovered that the people of Sub-Saharan Africa were able to deal with their often harsh environment. For example, wheat and barley did not grow well south of the Sahara near sea level. Crops such as millet and sorghum did, however. The early people of the Sahel domesticated these grains. In later centuries, they became staple crops throughout Sub-Saharan Africa. Over the years, the climate in the Sahel became increasingly drier. People either migrated south or shifted more to herding.

Archaeologists have carefully excavated sites throughout Africa. Their work has added much to our understanding of African history and our knowledge of early lifestyles and social patterns. Archaeologists working today in Africa use scientific methods and tools, up-to-date technology, and detailed analysis to study the evidence they unearth. They also use knowledge drawn from many different fields of learning, such as history and other social sciences, earth sciences, and mathematics. Archaeological evidence shows that many early Sub-Saharan cultures were complex, well organized, and wealthy. We know, too, that many had contact with early cultures from other parts of the ancient world.

✔ **READING CHECK: Summarizing**
What methods have been used by scholars to learn about the history of Sub-Saharan Africa? linguistic study, oral traditions, musical studies, and archaeological methods

Then & Now

Trumpets

Trumpet music conveys universal themes that have been sounded around the world for centuries. People used trumpets to mourn at funerals. Early Africans also used horns to send messages over long distances. Today, in Nigeria, horns are still sounded at celebrations.

How did early Africans use trumpet music?

Bronze horn player from Benin

Link to Today

What does the use of trumpets in ancient Africa and modern America reflect about the universality of such music?

The great American trumpeter, Wynton Marsalis, is famed for his powerful music.

THEN AND NOW ANSWER
Students should list the following uses of early trumpets: to mourn at funerals; to send messages long distances.

LINK TO TODAY ANSWER
Students might suggest that musical instruments such as trumpets have been used for centuries and throughout all parts of the world.

Linking Past to Present

Today in many parts of Africa, women still do most of the work raising crops. They farm mainly by hand, bending over the fields all day with their babies on heir backs. Men usually look after the livestock, though in some communities they farm for prospective in-laws as part of a marriage agreement.

Critical Thinking

Why do you think African men sometimes farm for their prospective bride's family?

ANSWER: Students might note that families in Africa still pass property through the female line of the family.

AFRICA **185**

ASSESS

Have students complete Daily Quiz 8.1. As Alternative Assessment, you many want to use the hand-drawn maps or the graphic organizer.

RETEACH

Have students complete Main Idea Activity for English Language Learners and Special-Needs Students 8.1. Then have them write a diary entry describing a day in the life of an early African teenager. **ENGLISH LANGUAGE LEARNERS**

EXTEND

🔲 internet connect

Internet Activity: go.hrw.com
TOPIC: African Languages **KEYWORD:** SP3 WH8

Have students access the Internet through the HRW Go site to conduct research on African languages. Ask students to summarize one language or language group. They should include information about where the language is spoken, the current number of speakers, and information about the roots of the language.

SECTION 1 REVIEW ANSWERS

❶ Define
- savannas, p. 182
- tropical rain forests, p. 182
- jungle, p. 182
- linguists, p. 184
- oral traditions, p. 184
- matrilineal, p. 186

❷ Identify
- Bantu, p. 184

❸ Mountains—north, south, east; Desert—north, south; Grasslands—west, east, central; Tropical Rain Forest—west, central

❹ a. The natural environment determined what crops people in early African cultures grew. Grains grew best on the savannas; yams in tropical rain forests; cattle herding took place in areas between deserts and savannas.

b. Xylophones used in traditional music of East Africa are similar to such instruments in Indonesia; the Malagasy language spoken in Madagascar contains words spoken in Indonesia; and the banana plant grown in Africa is native to Asia.

c. very important because it survived even when kingdoms rose and fell

❺ Students' poems will vary.

INTERPRETING THE VISUAL RECORD

African houses This Bantu house illustrates a traditional style of building. Houses are constructed of thatch and dried mud, sometimes reinforced with woven strips of wood. *Based on this picture, what can you infer about traditional Africans' relationship with their natural environment?*

Patterns of Life

Based on their studies of limited evidence, experts have drawn conclusions about patterns of life in early Africa. Many believe that most early Africans lived in small, independent farming, herding, or fishing villages. Ties of kinship and age bound each society together.

Women in particular played a crucial role in both the African family and economy. Unlike Europe and Asia, in Africa women were the primary farmers. Historians believe that societies in many parts of Sub-Saharan Africa were **matrilineal.** In other words, people traced their ancestors and inherited property through their mothers rather than fathers.

Religion was important in many African cultures, and many shared similar religious ideas. In most African societies, people believed that spirits populated the world. These included the spirits of ancestors, who remained an important part of the ongoing life of the clan. Most religions included a supreme creator god. They linked other gods to certain aspects of nature or to human activities, such as farming.

The pace of life and the calendar of daily activity in most early African villages were set by the seasonal cycles of planting and harvesting crops. Village elders, the traditional leaders of community life in many parts of Africa, usually had authority over daily life and work. Their position in village society was respected and unquestioned. The village-centered society of traditional Africa flourished through the rise and fall of kingdoms. Over centuries, this timeless lifestyle survived as the basic unit of African social, political, and economic development. Today it remains a vital part of the African heritage.

✔ **READING CHECK: Making Generalizations** What do scholars believe about the role of women in many early African societies? played crucial roles in social and economic life as primary farmers

---

◀ **SECTION 1 REVIEW** ▶

1. **Define** and explain the significance:
savannas
tropical rain forests
jungle
linguists
oral traditions
matrilineal

2. **Identify** and explain the significance:
Bantu

3. **Analyzing Information** Copy the chart below. Use it to place check marks to show the main natural regions in various parts of Africa.

Main Natural Region	Part of Africa				
	North	West	South	East	Central
Mountains					
Desert					
Grasslands					
Tropical Rain Forest					

4. **Finding the Main Idea**
   a. How did people decide what crops to grow in early African cultures?
   b. What evidence is there of cultural exchange between early Africa and Asia?
   c. How important was the village in early African societies?

5. **Writing and Critical Thinking**
   Making Generalizations Write a short poem about a day in an early African village.
   Consider:
   • the importance of family relationships and events, such as marriage or birth
   • the importance of planting and harvesting crops
   • the role of religion in early African cultures

Homework Practice Online
keyword: SP3 HP8

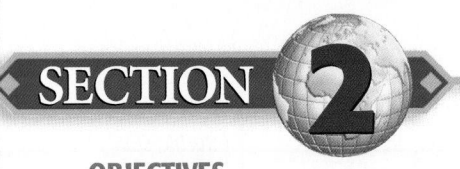

SECTION 2

OBJECTIVES

1 **Explain how Kush developed as an independent kingdom.**

2 **Analyze the factors that helped Aksum develop as an independent kingdom.**

🔊 LET'S GET STARTED!

As students enter the classroom, ask them to think about political units other than villages that might have developed in Sub-Saharan Africa. Have them write down some ideas and give a brief description of each political unit. *(Answers might include city-states, kingdoms, and empires.)* Tell students that in Section 2 they will learn how the independent kingdoms of Kush and Aksum developed.

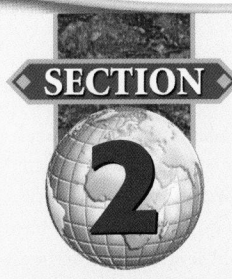

SECTION 2

READ TO DISCOVER

❶ How did Kush develop as an independent kingdom?

❷ How did Aksum develop as an independent kingdom?

IDENTIFY

King 'Ēzānā

▶ WHY IT MATTERS TODAY

Trade is an important economic activity, in early Africa and in today's world. Use CNNstudentNews.com or other **current event** sources to find out about goods traded to and from Africa today. Record your findings in your journal.

CNN Student News.com

The Kingdoms of Kush and Aksum

The Main Idea
The kingdoms of Kush and Aksum dominated much of Sub-Saharan Africa.

The Story Continues *Some Sub-Saharan African peoples continued to live in small, independent villages. Others, however, established small city-states, kingdoms, and even empires. One of these was the kingdom of Kush. Kush arose along the upper Nile River in an Egyptian area known as Nubia. Because of its close connection with Egypt, Kush's culture resembled that of the Egyptians in many ways.*

Kush Arises

Kush thrived as an important corridor of trade. Gold, ivory, ebony, and ostrich feathers were transported through Nubia. Here caravans hauled goods from the Red Sea to barges on the Nile. In about 1600 B.C. a Nubian trading center on the Nile called Karmah emerged. Recent archaeological discoveries reveal a rich cultural exchange between Karmah and Egypt. Kush may have traced its roots to the city of Karmah.

Over the next few centuries, Kush became a distinct kingdom. The capital of its ruling dynasty was located at Napata, a city that lay upstream along the Nile from Karmah. At first Kush maintained close economic and cultural ties with Egypt. In about 1520 B.C., however, the rulers of Egypt's New Kingdom brought Nubia and Kush under their control. For the next 500 years, Kush was governed by the pharaohs. During this time, however, the Nubian kingdom appears to have grown increasingly isolated from Egyptian rule. Many historians believe that in the years between about 1100 B.C. and about 1000 B.C., communication and cultural exchange between Kush and Egypt diminished. Some 300 years later, in about 710 B.C., Kush conquered Upper Egypt, and a Kush dynasty ruled a unified Egypt for about 50 years.

SECTION 2 RESOURCES

REPRODUCIBLE RESOURCES

▶ Guided Reading Strategy 8.2

▶ Graphic Organizer Activity 8: African Kingdoms

TECHNOLOGY RESOURCES

▶ One-Stop Planner 8.2

▶ Regions of the World Music Audio CD Program 13: North Africa: Arabic songs of Lebanon and Egypt

▶ Homework Practice Online

REINFORCEMENT, REVIEW, AND ASSESSMENT

▶ Section 2 Review, p. 190

▶ Daily Quiz 8.2

▶ Main Idea Activity 8.2

▶ English Audio Summary 8.2

▶ Spanish Audio Summary 8.2

The Lion Temple of ancient Kush reflects the kingdom's power and glory.

ALL LEVELS: Have students read the material titled "Kush Arises" on pages 187–188 of the text. Then have them construct a chart that lists the geographic, economic, political, and cultural factors that led to Kush's development and fall.

KUSH		
Factors	**Development of**	**Fall of**
Geographic	*Nile River, Red Sea; fertile soil near Meroë*	*Infertile soil*
Economic	*Control of trade routes to Egypt between Nile River and Red Sea*	*Lost control of trade routes*
Political	*Controlled Egypt; survived Assyrians*	*Taken over by Aksum*
Cultural	*Use of iron, pottery; built pyramids and temples; written language*	

ENGLISH LANGUAGE LEARNERS, COOPERATIVE LEARNING

Geography

Today the temple and pyramid ruins of Kush stand in desert lands. Long ago, however, huge herds of cattle grazed in the area.

Critical Thinking

Ask students what cattle grazing near Kush 2,500 years ago tells about the climate at that time.

ANSWER: A much wetter climate existed for grass to grow and to provide drinking water for cattle.

Interdisciplinary Connection

ART. The artisans of Aksum were known for their work with stone. They are perhaps best known for making massive stone obelisks called stelae. Some of these monumental pillars nearly reached 100 feet or more in height and were carved from single blocks of stone.

Critical Thinking

Ask students to speculate about the purposes Aksumite stelae might have served.

ANSWER: Stelae might have commemorated events in the lives of rulers or the community.

MAP ANSWER

cities in Kush: Karmah, Napata, Meroë; seaport in Aksum: Adulis

In 671 B.C. the Assyrians, armed with iron weapons, invaded Kush, greatly weakening the kingdom. Evidence suggests that about 80 years later, Napata was captured by an Egyptian force. The kingdom of Kush reorganized, however, and a new period of growth and cultural achievement began. The new capital city of Meroë may have been an early center of ironworking in Africa. The region's fertile soil made Meroë an ideal location for agriculture.

Kush was located across trade routes between the Red Sea and the Nile. Caravans brought cultural influences as well as goods from other peoples. The people of Meroë adapted these to their own culture. The Greek historian Herodotus wrote this description of Meroë, based on travelers' accounts:

Analyzing Primary Sources

Evaluating What evidence does Herodotus provide to suggest that the people of Meroë had contact with other peoples and cultures? mention of Greek gods and practices

 Primary Source **❝In twelve days [one] reaches a big city named Meroë, said to be the capital city of the Ethiopians [the inhabitants of the kingdom of Kush]. The inhabitants worship Zeus and Dionysus alone of the gods, holding them in great honor. There is an oracle of Zeus there, and they make war according to its pronouncements [declarations].❞**

Herodotus, quoted in *African Civilization Revisited,* by Basil Davidson

Some historians believe that Kush's civilization reached its height between about 250 B.C. and about A.D. 150. The people of Meroë built impressive pyramids and temples and crafted beautiful pottery and metal ornaments. They developed a written form of their language. A period of decline set in, however. Some historians believe the decline occurred because the land lost its fertility. Kush may also have lost control of trade routes as they were taken over by a rival state, Aksum.

✔ **READING CHECK: Drawing Inferences** What led to the growth of the kingdom of Kush? its location as a corridor of trade

Aksum

Aksum lay in the rugged Ethiopian Highlands south of Kush. The kingdom straddled the important trade routes that stretched from the Red Sea into Egypt and the interior of Africa. By about the A.D. 100s, the people of Aksum had developed an independent kingdom that boasted a thriving ivory trade. As Kush declined, Aksum increasingly competed with it for control of trade in eastern Africa. Aksum sent gold, rhinoceros horns, ivory, incense, and decorative obsidian stone to Mediterranean countries by way of Egypt. The Aksumites imported glass, metal ornaments, and pottery, as well as wine and olive oil. Aksum also minted its own coins.

By about A.D. 300 Aksum was a military power. In about A.D. 350 **King ʿĒzānā** of Aksum conquered Kush. He set up a thriving kingdom. Like other kings of Aksum, ʿĒzānā held power over surrounding chiefdoms.

The Kingdoms of Kush and Aksum

Interpreting Maps Aksum conquered Kush about A.D. 350.

■ **Skills Assessment: Human Systems** Through what river cities in Kush would goods be transported? Through what seaport in Aksum would goods be transported?

Map labels: MEDITERRANEAN SEA; EGYPT; Memphis; Nile River; Thebes; NUBIAN DESERT; Karmah; NUBIA; Napata; Meroë; RED SEA; Adulis; Atbara R.; SUDAN; Blue Nile; Aksum; Arabian Peninsula; Gulf of Aden; ETHIOPIA; ETHIOPIAN HIGHLANDS

Kush, c. 500 B.C.
Aksum, c. A.D. 400

0 300 600 Miles
0 300 600 Kilometers
Azimuthal Equal-Area Projection

TEACH OBJECTIVE 2

LEVEL 1: Make a chart titled *Aksum*, similar to the one for Kush, on the chalkboard. Have students read "Aksum" on pages 188 and 190 and study the map on page 188. Then ask students to complete the chart by working alone or in pairs to identify geographic, economic, political, and cultural factors in the development of the independent kingdom of Aksum.
ENGLISH LANGUAGE LEARNERS, COOPERATIVE LEARNING

LEVEL 3: Ask students what geographic factors are important for the growth of trade. *(location on a river, seaports, clear routes for trade)* Have students look at the map on page 188 and make a list of ways Aksum's location helped it become a trading kingdom. Have students discuss how Aksum's power increased by conquering Kush.

 HOMEWORK Have students write a brief summary of the importance of King 'Ēzānā's conversion to Christianity.

SKILL-BUILDING STRATEGIES — Using Artifacts as Historical Evidence

The Kingdom of Kush

Scientists have learned much about Kush by studying artifacts that they have found. Artifacts include everything from pottery and tools to coins and buildings. Artifacts are an important part of historical research because they allow historians to gain a more complete understanding of the past. Much like photographs, artifacts offer valuable clues about customs, beliefs, and details of daily life. In order to gain the historical insight that artifacts offer, however, historians must know how to examine them properly.

Shown here are a relief plaque of a winged, lion-headed goddess found at Meroë (left); a decorated gold cylinder, possibly used for holding papyrus, from the tomb of a Kushite king near Napata (center); and a gold plaque depicting a king of Meroë honoring the Egyptian god Horus (right).

Skills Reminder

To evaluate an artifact as historical evidence, determine what the artifact is and what purpose it might have served. If possible, find out who created it and when. Examine the artifact carefully. Study the artifact's construction and design. Note such things as what material the artifact is made from as well as what tools might have been used to create it. Consider also how the artifact might have been used. Use what you have learned from written sources about the particular people and time period surrounding the artifact to gain a better understanding of the object. Based on your examination of the artifact, as well as other information you have gathered, draw conclusions about the people who created the object or the time period in which it existed.

Skills Practice

❶ What do the artifacts show?
❷ Based on these artifacts, do you think that religion was important in Kush? Why or why not?
❸ What other conclusions might you draw about the people of Kush from these artifacts?
❹ Based on your analysis of the artifacts, their materials, and their construction, what conclusions can you draw concerning the level of Kushite technology and craftsmanship?
❺ Choose a group from this chapter and find an artifact from its culture in a book or on the Internet. Write a paragraph describing the artifact and explaining what you think that artifact says about the group.

SKILLS PRACTICE ANSWERS

1. human figures, animals, symbols

2. Answers will vary. Students might say yes because gods and goddesses appear on many artifacts.

3. People used symbols in their writing; animals were important.

4. The Kushites had a high level of craftsmanship and technology.

5. Answers should include what the construction, design, and materials tell about the level of craftsmanship and technology.

Science, Technology & Society

The Great Enclosure of Musawwarat is a Kush ruin in modern Sudan. It consists of sandstone structures surrounding a temple. The temple is on a raised platform and can be entered only by climbing a ramp. Recent work by archaeologists shows that underground pipes for irrigation supplied water to gardens within the enclosure.

Critical Thinking

Ask students what the Great Enclosure shows about the level of Kush technology.

ANSWER: suggests a high level of technology

CLOSE

Have students create a Venn diagram to compare Kush and Aksum.

ASSESS

Have students complete Daily Quiz 8.2. As Alternative Assessment, you may want to use the graphic organizers and lists of factors that led to the development of Kush and Aksum.

RETEACH

Have students complete Main Idea Activity for English Language Learners and Special-Needs Students 8.2. Then ask them to apply absolute chronology by making a time line of major events in the development of Kush and Aksum.

ENGLISH LANGUAGE LEARNERS

EXTEND

Have students work in small groups to use the process of historical inquiry to conduct research on the ivory trade in Africa in about A.D. 100. **COOPERATIVE LEARNING, BLOCK SCHEDULING**

HISTORY MAKER ANSWER
Aksum became a Christian kingdom in Africa.

◆SECTION◆

2 REVIEW ANSWERS

❶ Identify
• King 'Ēzānā, p. 188

❷ Kush: Nile River, Nubia, iron-working, pyramids, cities of Karmah, Napata, and Meroë, conquest of Egypt; Aksum: Ethiopian Highlands, city of Adulis, Christianity; Overlapping characteristics: kingdoms, trade routes between Red Sea and Nile River, ties with Egypt, written languages, lost control of trade routes, land less productive

❸ a. Both arose as trading kingdoms and retained their power as long as they controlled important trade routes.

b. Kush conquered Egypt and later was attacked by the Assyrians. This event forced the Kushites to set up a new capital in Meroë. Aksum conquered Kush and later lost control of political and economic power to Arab forces.

❹ Descriptions of Meroë will vary but should include its location on the Nile River on fertile land; its pyramids and temples; and farming, ironworking, and trade as ways of making a living.

Analyzing Primary Sources

Identifying a Point of View What does this excerpt tell us about King 'Ēzānā's approach to rule? He believed in a just and moral approach to rule.

HISTORY MAKER

King 'Ēzānā (unknown–c. A.D. 360)

King 'Ēzānā of Aksum was known as the "king of kings." Late in life he became a Christian and declared Christianity the official religion of his kingdom. Aksum thus became the first Christian kingdom in Africa. **How did Aksum differ from other African kingdoms?**

He collected tribute from neighboring rulers. At the port city of Adulis his officials collected taxes on trade goods. During his reign 'Ēzānā converted to Christianity. He made it the official religion of Aksum. 'Ēzānā's religious beliefs were reflected in his rule. He declared:

 History Makers Speak
❝I will rule the people with righteousness and justice, and will not oppress them, and may they preserve this Throne which I have set up for the Lord of Heaven.❞

King 'Ēzānā, quoted in *African Civilizations* by Graham Connah

King 'Ēzānā's conversion to Christianity was a key event in the history of eastern Africa. The form of Christianity that grew throughout the region incorporated many of the people's traditional beliefs and customs. Thus its appeal was strong and widespread. 'Ēzānā's conversion, moreover, had an impact on Christianity in eastern Africa that was similar to the effect that Constantine's conversion had on Christianity in the Roman Empire. Christianity became a powerful influence throughout the region. This development laid the foundations of the Ethiopian Church that continues to thrive today and that forms an important element of the area's cultural tradition.

Aksum became a major center of long-distance trade throughout coastal East Africa. Between the A.D. 300s and 600s, for example, it dominated the African side of the Red Sea trade. Its location and dominance brought great wealth to Aksum. The kingdom's power and prosperity began to decline, however, in the A.D. 600s. This was caused by several factors. Environmental problems such as erosion—caused by excessive land use and the destruction of forests—made the land less productive. The Persians, a trade rival, had gained control over much of the Red Sea trade. Beginning in the early A.D. 700s, moreover, the rise of Islamic Arab power led to new economic and political competition with Aksum. Arab forces won control of both the Arabian and the African sides of the Red Sea. As a result Aksum gradually lost control over most of its external trade and steadily declined as a commercial and political power.

✔ **READING CHECK: Drawing Conclusions** How would Aksum's location on the Red Sea and the Ethiopian Highlands have helped it conquer Kush? straddled trade routes from Red Sea to Egypt and African interior

---

SECTION 2 REVIEW

1. **Identify** and explain the significance:
   King 'Ēzānā

2. **Categorizing** Copy the Venn diagram below. Use the diagram to organize characteristics of Kush and Aksum. In the far left circle, list characteristics of Kush alone. In the far right circle, list characteristics of Aksum alone. In the overlapping area, list characteristics that both Kush and Aksum shared.

   Kush ⬭⬭ Aksum

3. **Finding the Main Idea**
   a. How did trade affect the development of both Kush and Aksum?
   b. What role did conquest play in the histories of Kush and Aksum?

4. **Writing and Critical Thinking**
   Summarizing Write a description of social and economic activities in Meroë, the capital city of Kush.
   Consider:
   • its location
   • the structures built there
   • the livelihoods of the people there
   • the area's geographic advantages

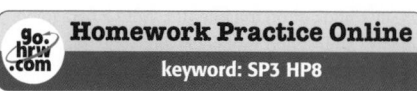 **Homework Practice Online**
keyword: SP3 HP8

OBJECTIVES

1 **Discuss how trade developed along the East African coast.**

2 **Explain how the kingdoms of West Africa became rich and powerful.**

🔔 LET'S GET STARTED!

As students enter the classroom, have them look at the map on page 192. Ask them to write the location of the areas highlighted on the map in relation to the kingdoms of Kush and Aksum. *(southeast and west)* Tell students that in Section 3 they will learn about trading kingdoms that developed along the East Coast of Africa and in West Africa.

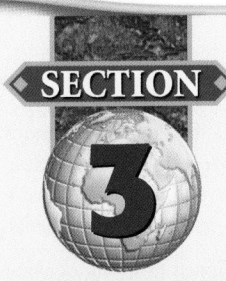

SECTION 3

READ TO DISCOVER

❶ How did trade develop along the East African coast?

❷ How did kingdoms of West Africa become prosperous and powerful?

IDENTIFY

Swahili
Shona
Tunka Manin
Mansa Mūsā
Sonni 'Alī
Mohammed I Askia

WHY IT MATTERS TODAY

The Swahili language is still used in East Africa. It is the official language of Tanzania and Kenya. Use [CNN] or other **current event** sources to learn about the Swahili language. Record your findings in your journal.

Trading States of Africa

The Main Idea
Trade strongly influenced cultures on the east and west coasts of Africa.

The Story Continues *Trade kept Africa well connected to the rest of the world. Ancient Greek traders were familiar with parts of East Africa, which they called "Azania." One sailor's handbook written by an Egyptian-Greek merchant described several trading villages along the "Azanian" coast. Traders there would swap African items such as ivory, rhinoceros horns, coconut oil, and tortoise shells for iron tools, weapons, and cotton cloth.*

East Africa and Great Zimbabwe

No kingdoms as large as Kush and Aksum emerged on the coast of East Africa. Instead, several city-states dominated coastal trade in the Indian Ocean. Sailing ships were powered by the seasonal monsoon winds. Trade routes linked all shores of the Indian Ocean. Africans exported gold, ivory, hides, and tortoise shells. They imported porcelain and weapons. They also sold slaves.

The spread of the Islamic religion from Arabia to northeastern Africa spurred trade. In fact, strong trade activity began in the A.D. 700s and lasted through the A.D. 1300s and possibly later. The opportunity to make money attracted merchant families and adventurers to Africa. Groups of Muslim settlers from Arabia and Persia began to move onto the East African coast. At the same time, people from Indonesia settled on the island of Madagascar, off the coast of East Africa. These groups, strongly influenced by the ideals of Islam, formed a new, trade-based society in coastal East Africa that combined elements of African, Asian, and Islamic cultures.

Swahili states. Over several generations a unique African culture, **Swahili,** developed in East Africa. The people of this culture spoke Swahili, a Bantu language with Arabic and Persian influences. Swahili speakers were not a single ethnic group. They were bound together by both language and their association with trade.

Among the earliest of the trading city-states along the Indian Ocean coast were Mogadishu (moh·guh·DEE·shoo), Pate, and Mombasa. These centers were in the north, but commerce gradually shifted southward. By the late A.D. 1200s the city-state of Kilwa had become a leading port.

INTERPRETING THE VISUAL RECORD

Dhow These Tanzanians are sailing a boat, called a "dhow" (DOW), similar to those that Arab traders used to visit the East African coast centuries ago. *In what way does this picture demonstrate the fact that different cultures influence and borrow from one another?*

SECTION 3 RESOURCES

REPRODUCIBLE RESOURCES
▶ Guided Reading Strategy 8.3
▶ Geography Activity 8

TECHNOLOGY RESOURCES
▶ One-Stop Planner 8.3
▶ Holt researcher: World History: Sonni 'Ali, Askia the Great
▶ CNN Presents World Cultures: Yesterday and Today Segments 24, 32
▶ Homework Practice Online

REINFORCEMENT, REVIEW, AND ASSESSMENT
▶ Section 3 Review, p. 195
▶ Daily Quiz 8.3
▶ Main Idea Activity 8.3
▶ English Audio Summary 8.3
▶ Spanish Audio Summary 8.3

VISUAL RECORD ANSWER

East Africans still use boats similar to those introduced by Arab traders.

TEACH OBJECTIVE 1

LEVEL 1: Discuss the development of the Swahili states and Great Zimbabwe. On the board, draw a circle labeled *Swahili States.* From this circle, extend lines labeled *People, Cities, Religion, Trade Partners, Goods Traded.* Draw another circle at the other end of each line. Have students fill in the circles. Then help students proceed in the same manner to learn about trade in Great Zimbabwe.

ENGLISH LANGUAGE LEARNERS

HOMEWORK Have students study the map on page 192 and refer to their notes and text to summarize the areas in which trade took place in East Africa.

Interdisciplinary Connection

ARCHITECTURE. Arab and Persian traders influenced the development of the Swahili language, introduced Islam, and brought other cultural changes to East Africans. A distinctive architecture reflected Arab and Asian elements. Traditional homes of mud and wattle were replaced by buildings made of coral rag and coral stone.

Critical Thinking

Ask students why they think East Africans were able to change the type of materials used in their buildings.

ANSWER: Students might point out that coral was easily available along the coast.

Technology Resources

 Online Maps: African Caravan Routes; Cities of Africa, A.D. 1200

Technology Resources

 World History Teaching Transparencies: Geography and History 13; Everyday Life 13

Under Kilwa's leadership the East African coast flourished. Ibn Battūtah, a famous Islamic traveler of the A.D. 1300s, praised Kilwa. He called it one of the most beautiful, well-built cities in the world. Modern archaeological digs have uncovered a massive trade center and a large mosque. They reveal Kilwa's great wealth and achievements.

Great Zimbabwe. Kilwa grew as a trade port. Gold was shipped from mines along the Zambezi River in southcentral Africa. No later than A.D. 947, gold and other goods had moved from inland to the coast. They were exchanged for such needed goods as salt, tools, and cloth.

When Indian Ocean trade grew after the A.D. 900s, the demand for gold greatly increased. Kingdoms competed for control over both mining and shipping gold. The **Shona** were a people who had migrated onto the plateau of what is today Zimbabwe. Over centuries the Shona gained control over local peoples and, with it, over the gold that they mined and traded.

Historians believe that the Shona probably attained great wealth and power. They built fortified enclosures. Great Zimbabwe was probably the largest and most important of these fortresses. It became the center of the Shona state. Excavations have been made on its 60-acre site that reveal a hilltop fortification with many rooms and mazelike passageways. Below the hill was a thick stone-block wall, stone buildings, and a tower. The building stones were cut so finely that they stayed in place without mortar.

For unknown reasons Great Zimbabwe declined in the A.D. 1400s. One explanation is that the population grew too fast. It may have outpaced dwindling supplies of food and water.

✔**READING CHECK: Identifying Cause and Effect** What factors helped make East Africa a center for trade? location, weather and wind patterns, resources

Trading States of Africa, c. A.D. 1230–1591

Interpreting Maps Prosperous kingdoms and city-states developed across Sub-Saharan Africa hundreds of years ago.

■ **Skills Assessment: Places and Regions** Compare this map with the map on page 183. In what type of region or regions did these cultures arise?

Camel caravans crossed the Sahara with salt to trade with West African kingdoms. For centuries camels were the main form of transportation across the desert.

TEACH OBJECTIVE 2

ALL LEVELS: Ask students to read the material entitled "West Africa." Divide the class into four groups. Assign the introductory paragraphs to one group; assign "Ghana," "Mali," and "Songhai" each to the other groups. Ask each group to compile a summary that includes geographic area covered; goods traded; important events in sequence; rulers; cities; cultural accomplishments. Have a representative from each group present the summary to the class. **ENGLISH LANGUAGE LEARNERS, COOPERATIVE LEARNING**

LEVEL 3: Have students discuss the role of Islamic traders in the development of trade in Ghana, Mali, and Songhai. Then assign groups of students to conduct research on trade routes, goods traded, and impact of Islam on one of the West African trading kingdoms. Have students present their research as the class takes notes. **COOPERATIVE LEARNING**

West Africa

Several important societies flourished in West Africa. They lay between Lake Chad and the Atlantic Ocean and included the kingdoms of Ghana, Mali, and Songhai. Knowledge of them comes from oral accounts and the writings of African scholars and Islamic traders.

The wealth and strength of these kingdoms depended on control of the trade routes across the Sahara. At the desert's southern edge, commerce developed. There, gold mined south of the Sahel was traded for salt mined in the desert. This trade was mutually important. The people of the Sahel needed salt to flavor and preserve their food, while the gold that they traded for salt had obvious value. Traders from the north wanted gold for coins and for buying goods from Europe. Where this gold-for-salt exchange took place, cities grew and flourished. Thus areas of West Africa became major centers of commerce.

The gold-for-salt exchange was an important part of the region's trade. Indeed, West Africa produced large amounts of gold until about A.D. 1500. In time the traders also exchanged ivory and even slaves for textiles, jewels, and copper.

Monarchs ruled the West African kingdoms. Often adorned in gold, these monarchs oversaw elaborate ceremonies. They also administered justice. One way of conducting a trial was recounted by Islamic historian al-Bakri, who traveled throughout the area and who left accurate eyewitness accounts.

> *Primary Source* **"When a man is accused of denying a debt or having shed blood or some other crime, a headman takes a thin piece of wood, which is sour and bitter to taste, and pours upon it some water which he then gives to the defendant to drink. If the man vomits, his innocence is recognized and he is congratulated. If he does not vomit and the drink remains in his stomach, the accusation is accepted as justified."**
>
> Al-Bakri, quoted in *The Horizon History of Africa*, edited by Alvin Josephy, Jr.

Below the royal family on the social scale were government officials. Then came merchants, farmers, fishers, and cattle breeders. Slaves ranked among the last.

Ghana. The earliest of the West African kingdoms was Ghana, where long-range trade networks encouraged higher levels of political organization. The kingdom of Ghana was established by the Soninke people sometime after the A.D. 300s. The Soninke lived in the western Sahel, northwest of the present-day nation of Ghana. Their kingdom began around the old trading village of Kumbi, or Kumbi Saleh, in what is now Mauritania. There the Soninke participated in and profited from the gold-for-salt exchange between North and West Africa. They used iron tools to farm and to clear more land for farming and grazing. They also probably developed agriculture along the upper Niger River.

CONNECTING TO Art

Sculpture: Royal Figure from West Africa

The Yoruba people, in what is now Nigeria, began sculpting life-sized, naturalistic heads more than 700 years ago. The heads were made in bronze, which is difficult to cast. The Yoruba, however, achieved artistic and technical excellence.

The casting shown here is of a Yoruba king. The beaded crown may have symbolized his importance. The vertical lines may represent ritual scarring.

Understanding the Arts

What do you think the artist wanted to reveal about this ruler?

Analyzing Primary Sources

Contrasting In what basic way did the West African system of justice described by al-Bakri differ from our American system of justice today? It depended upon physical demonstration rather than written law.

CONNECTING TO ART ANSWER
Students might say that the crown shows how powerful the ruler is and the scars indicate that this king took part in rituals.

Linking Past to Present

During the 1500s the gold trade shifted to the southern coast of West Africa, where Africans traded gold with Europeans for weapons. Called the Gold Coast, this part of West Africa eventually became a colony of Britain. Today the Gold Coast is the nation of Ghana. Kwame Nkrumah, the first president of Ghana, named the new nation after the ancient West African kingdom. In 1957 Ghana was the first British colony in Sub-Saharan Africa to gain independence from European control.

Critical Thinking

Ask students why Nkrumah might have chosen the name Ghana for the new country in West Africa.

ANSWER: Students might point out that he named the first independent nation after the first kingdom in West Africa as a reminder of a time when the region was not ruled by others.

Technology Resources
 Online Maps, Charts, and Graphs: African Trade, c. 1450–1600

Teacher to Teacher

Mattie P. Collins of Pine Bluff, Arkansas, suggested the following activity: Have students write an essay titled "What Is the Truth about Africa?" Students should find one common misperception about Africa and disprove it using facts from their textbook and other research sources. Essays should include an introduction that states the thesis, a body with supporting details, and a conclusion that restates the thesis. Students are expected to use standard grammar, spelling, sentence structure, and punctuation.

Spotlight on CULTURE

Have students examine the pictures on pages 194 and 195. Tell them that a unique type of architecture influenced by Islam developed in the West African kingdoms. Ask students to use the library or computer software to conduct research on traditional architecture in Islamic cultures. Have them collect pictures of buildings and structures and share their findings with the class. Encourage class discussion about basic elements of the Islam-inspired architecture.

HISTORY MAKER ANSWER

Students might point out that by showing his wealth, Mansa Mūsā was demonstrating the wealth and power of his kingdom as a way to gain respect from other countries and leaders.

VISUAL RECORD ANSWER

Students might say that a large Muslim population would have required a large mosque for religious services.

History Maker

Sonni 'Alī, the founder of the kingdom of Songhai, claimed to be a Muslim. However, he dabbled in sorcery and magic. Islamic scholars and religious leaders objected to these activities. To protect his power against the Islamic leaders, Sonni 'Alī had the Islamic scribes at Timbuktu killed. This action, however, turned many of the ruler's Muslim subjects against him.

Critical Thinking

Ask students why religion was an important element in the political strategy of Sonni 'Alī.

ANSWER: Students might point out that by controlling religion and religious leaders, Sonni 'Alī hoped to control the people.

Reproducible Resources

PS Readings in World History 49, 50

HISTORY MAKER

Mansa Mūsā (unknown–c. A.D. 1332)

In A.D. 1324 Mansa Mūsā, the king of Mali, traveled to Mecca, in what is today the country of Saudi Arabia. This trip was no ordinary journey. Mansa Mūsā traveled with a party of as many as 80,000 other people.

The group included hundreds of slaves, each carrying four-pound bars of gold. In fact, Mansa Mūsā brought a huge treasury on his journey. His entire party was richly dressed, many wearing expensive silks and gold ornaments.

The king's great display of wealth showed people the vast riches and power of Mali. It was said that Mansa Mūsā spent so much gold during his trip that the value of the precious metal fell in areas through which he passed. **Why do you think Mansa Mūsā wanted to demonstrate his great wealth?**

INTERPRETING THE VISUAL RECORD

Malian mosque As a devout Muslim, Mansa Mūsā encouraged the building of mosques. This one in Dejenné, Mali, dates from the A.D. 1300s. *What does the size of this mosque say about the influence of Islam in West Africa?*

As the Soninke settled in larger communities, kings arose to act as war leaders and to negotiate with foreign merchants. Ghanaian kings were powerful and wealthy from the gold trade. They were able to build large armies to conquer new territory. The kingdom of Ghana reached its peak around A.D. 1050. One of the most powerful Ghanaian rulers was **Tunka Manin,** who ruled in about A.D. 1067. Tunka Manin commanded an army of 200,000 warriors, well equipped with bows, arrows, and iron-pointed spears. In the late A.D. 1000s, however, Ghana began to decline. In A.D. 1076 the Berbers—who had once controlled the salt trade—invaded from the north, destroying Kumbi Saleh. The Soninke began to lose control of the salt trade to neighboring peoples. Finally, probably in about A.D. 1235, the neighboring Malinke people overthrew Ghana and established the empire of Mali.

Mali. The rise of a successor kingdom—Mali—followed the fall of Ghana. The kingdom of Mali came to power in the area that had been Ghana. It also spread over large areas to the north and west along the upper Niger River.

Mali's power reached its peak under its great ruler **Mansa Mūsā.** Mūsā reigned in the early A.D. 1300s. He was a supporter of education, the arts, and public building. Under his rule, the city of Timbuktu became a leading center of learning. Its large university attracted scholars from Egypt and Arabia.

Mūsā is famous for his historic pilgrimage to Mecca, an Islamic holy place in Arabia. He was accompanied by thousands of other pilgrims. Most notably he brought large amounts of gold with him in a great display of West African power and wealth. The Islamic traveler Ibn Battūtah visited Mali and noted:

History Makers Speak

❝[The people of Mali] are seldom unjust and have a greater abhorrence [hatred] of injustice than any other people. Their Sultan [leader] shows no mercy to any one guilty of the least act of it. There is complete security in their country. Neither traveler nor inhabitant in it has anything to fear from robbers or men of violence.❞

Ibn Battūtah, quoted in *The Horizon History of Africa,* edited by Alvin Josephy, Jr.

Disputes over Mansa Mūsā's successor weakened Mali. Rival members of the royal court fought for leadership of the empire. This conflict greatly weakened central authority within Mali. The kingdom kept control of the desert trade routes until the A.D. 1400s. Then in A.D. 1468 rebel leader **Sonni 'Alī** captured Timbuktu and built up the kingdom of Songhai. During the Songhai period the city of Gao (GAH·oh) became one of West Africa's busiest commercial centers.

CLOSE

Have students imagine they are traders in East Africa or West Africa during the time period covered in this section. Have them write an advertisement for their goods.

REVIEW

Have students complete the Section 3 Review on p. 195.

ASSESS

Have students complete Daily Quiz 8.3. As Alternative Assessment, you may want to use the graphic organizer from this section's lessons.

RETEACH

Have students complete Main Idea Activity for English Language Learners and Special-Needs Students 8.3. Then have them write the main idea for each of the section's headings.

ENGLISH LANGUAGE LEARNERS, COOPERATIVE LEARNING

EXTEND

Have students work in small groups to conduct research on the gold trade in Africa in the A.D. 900s and present the information in a written or visual form.

Songhai. The kingdom of Songhai was centered on the important trading city of Gao, on the Niger River. The new kingdom stretched from the Atlantic Ocean almost to Lake Chad. It covered an area even larger than Mali. Sonni 'Alī was both a skilled soldier and an able administrator. He kept tight control over the kingdom, dividing it into several provinces. Each province had a governor and officials who reported directly to him.

'Ali built a fleet of warships to patrol the Niger River, which had become a major shipping route. Sonni 'Alī and his successor, **Mohammed I Askia,** built Songhai into a strong kingdom. Under Askia's rule Timbuktu became a great commercial center. Goods came from Europe, India, and China. The growing number of merchants included Arabs, Jews, Italians, and many others. Timbuktu was also a thriving cultural center. As Mansa Mūsā had done, Askia supported a revival of Islamic scholarship based around the university there. Travelers reported that books and manuscripts imported to the markets of Timbuktu were sold for higher prices than any other merchandise.

Despite this prosperity, however, problems arose. The Songhai Empire began to experience a steady decline after the reign of Mohammed I Askia. For one thing, the Tuareg, Fulani, Malinke, and other subject peoples fought among themselves. The empire also had many powerful neighbors. In 1591 a Moroccan army equipped with firearms defeated Songhai troops, spelling the end of the empire.

✔ **READING CHECK: Evaluating** How important was trade in West Africa? Why? key to rise of powerful, trade-based kingdoms and to West African economy

The great cultural and commercial city of Timbuktu was a center of trade in the Songhai Empire.

Holt Researcher

go.hrw.com
KEYWORD: Holt Researcher
FreeFind: Sonni 'Ali
          Mohammed I Askia
After reading more about Sonnī 'Alī and Mohammed I Askia on the Holt Researcher, create a time line of the major events of their reigns.

SECTION 3 REVIEW

1. **Identify** and explain the significance:
   Swahili
   Shona
   Tunka Manin
   Mansa Mūsā
   Sonni 'Alī
   Mohammed I Askia

2. **Comparing** Copy the chart below. Use it to compare the various political states in Sub-Saharan Africa.

State	Location in Africa	Important Features
Swahili States		
Great Zimbabwe		
Ghana		
Mali		
Songhai		

3. **Finding the Main Idea**
   a. How did the Swahili culture develop in East Africa?
   b. How could the people of Great Zimbabwe have preserved their kingdom?
   c. How did Mansa Mūsā influence Mali?

4. **Writing and Critical Thinking**
   Analyzing Information Write a travelogue describing Mali when Mansa Mūsā ruled.
   Consider:
   • the importance of trade
   • the public buildings, art, and university Mūsā supported
   • Ibn Battūtah's account of the people of Mali

Homework Practice Online
keyword: SP3 HP8

SECTION 3 REVIEW ANSWERS

❶ **Identify**
   • Swahili, p. 191
   • Shona, p. 192
   • Tunka Manin, p. 194
   • Mansa Mūsā, p. 194
   • Sonni 'Alī, p. 194
   • Mohammed I Askia, p. 195

❷ Swahili States: eastern Africa; Swahili culture, trading ports, Muslim settlers. Great Zimbabwe: eastern Africa; Shona people, hilltop fortifications. Ghana: western Africa; trading center. Mali: western Africa; rule by Mansa Mūsā, university at Timbuktu, Islam. Songhai: western Africa; Gao, kingdom divided into provinces, Niger River shipping route

❸ a. from the Swahili language, a combination of Bantu with Arabic and Persian influences, and the activities of Swahili speakers, especially in trade

b. could have found new sources of food and water or relocated part of the population

c. made Timbuktu a center of learning; supported the arts, education, and public building; made Islam an important aspect of the culture

❹ Travelogues should mention the importance of trade, public buildings, art, the university, and people's hatred of injustice.

REVIEW AND ASSESSMENT RESOURCES

REPRODUCIBLE RESOURCES
▸ Vocabulary Activity 8

TECHNOLOGY RESOURCES
▸ Chapter 8 Test Generator (on the One-Stop Planner)
▸ Global Skill Builder CD–ROM
▸ HRW Web Site

REINFORCEMENT, REVIEW, and ASSESSMENT
▸ Chapter 8 Review, pp. 196–197
▸ Chapter 8 Tutorial for Students, Parents, Mentors, and Peers
▸ Chapter 8 Test (Form A or B)
▸ Alternative Assessment Handbook
▸ Chapter 8 Test for English Language Learners and Special-Needs Students

REVIEW
Have students complete the Chapter 8 Review on pages 196–197.

ASSESS
Use one of the chapter tests to assess students' understanding of the content. For Alternative Assessment, see the Portfolio Activities and Alternative Assessment Handbook.

CHAPTER 8 REVIEW ANSWERS

Understanding Main Ideas
1. a vast plateau

2. the Sahara

3. languages, oral traditions, musical instruments, crops, excavations

4. matrilineal societies

5. At first Kush engaged in trade and cultural exchanges with Egypt. About 1520 B.C. Kush came under Egypt's control. About 710 B.C. Kush conquered Upper Egypt and ruled all of Egypt for 50 years.

6. Control of trade routes brought control of wealth, culture, and political power.

7. Land lost fertility; Kush lost control of trade routes.

8. It incorporated many traditional beliefs and customs.

9. Muslims

10. Swahili; language and trade

11. led to power and wealth

12. the gold-for-salt trade

Reviewing Themes
1. Gold, ivory, and ebony were traded for goods people needed.

2. The land and climate limited where people could live and what crops they could grow. Access to rivers and the sea provided opportunities for trade.

3. by trade and conquest

CHAPTER 8 Review

Creating a Time Line
Copy the time line below onto a sheet of paper. Complete the time line by filling in the events, individuals, and dates from the chapter that you think were significant. Pick three events and explain why you think they were significant.

| 1800 B.C. | 1000 B.C. | A.D. 500 |

Writing a Summary
Using standard grammar, spelling, sentence structure, and punctuation, write an overview of the events in the chapter.

Identifying People and Ideas
Identify the following terms or individuals and explain their significance.

1. linguists
2. Bantu
3. oral traditions
4. matrilineal
5. King 'Ēzānā
6. Swahili
7. Shona
8. Mansa Mūsā
9. Sonni 'Alī
10. Mohammed I Askia

Understanding Main Ideas

SECTION 1 *(pp. 182–186)*
Africa's Early History
1. What is the main natural landform of Sub-Saharan Africa?
2. What geographical feature made trade and communication difficult in many parts of Africa?
3. What are some of the tools that scholars have used to uncover the history of Africa?
4. How was early African society organized?

SECTION 2 *(pp. 187–190)*
The Kingdoms of Kush and Aksum
5. What was the relationship of the kingdom of Kush to Egypt?
6. Why was control of trade routes important in the growth of Kush and Aksum?
7. What factors may have explained the decline of the kingdom of Kush?
8. How did Christianity become important in the kingdom of Aksum?

SECTION 3 *(pp. 191–195)*
Trading States of Africa
9. Who established trading centers along the East African coast?
10. What unique culture developed in coastal East Africa, and what factors bound the different peoples of this culture together?
11. Why was control of gold mining important in East Africa?
12. What general factors helped to promote the rise of West African kingdoms?

Reviewing Themes
1. **Economics** What types of goods were traded in Africa and how did they meet people's needs?
2. **Geography** How did the natural environment affect the people of Africa?
3. **Global Relations** How did the rulers of African kingdoms get what they wanted from others?

Thinking Critically
1. **Contrasting** How did early East African societies differ from the early African societies of Kush, Aksum, and West Africa?
2. **Identifying Bias** Why is it helpful to have observations of African societies from Arab travelers and historians who lived during the historical period?
3. **Making Generalizations** How were the people of Africa able to build complex civilizations and share cultural ideas with one another and with people from other lands?

Writing About History
Evaluating Write an evaluation in which you describe the major similarities and differences in the development of the kingdoms of Kush and Mali. Use the Venn diagram below to organize your thoughts before writing.

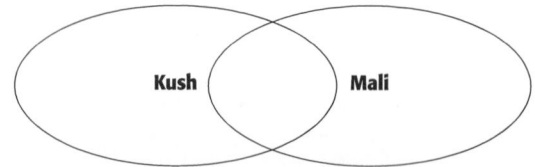

Kush   Mali

Divide students into three groups and assign one section from this chapter to each group. Have students create a summary of the main ideas in their section.

COOPERATIVE LEARNING

RETEACH

Have students who had trouble with the test use their textbooks to correct their tests. Then when they are ready, have them take the Form B Test to assess their mastery of the material. **ENGLISH LANGUAGE LEARNERS**, **COOPERATIVE LEARNING**

Portfolio Extensions

1. Ask students to imagine that they are living in a tropical rain forest about 3000 B.C. Tell them to write a letter to a friend who lives on a savanna. Have them compare the environment, foods, and diseases of their two regions.

2. Divide the class into small groups. Ask each group to select one of the early African kingdoms (Kush, Aksum, Ghana, Mali, or Songhai), the Swahili states, or Great Zimbabwe and write a television script for a documentary that describes the importance of trade to the people of their kingdom or state.

3. Have students write a story about the history of their family, school, or town that could be told orally in the manner of the African storytellers. Allow students to tell their stories to the class.

Building Social Studies Skills

Interpreting a Graph
Study the graph below. Then use the information on the graph to help you answer the questions that follow.

Average Maximum Temperatures in African Cities (in Fahrenheit)

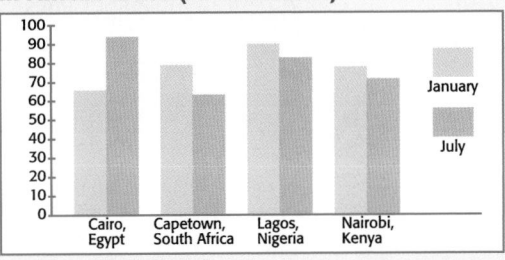

January
July

Cairo, Egypt | Capetown, South Africa | Lagos, Nigeria | Nairobi, Kenya

1. Which of the following is a correct general statement about temperatures in African cities?

   a. Lagos has a greater year-round temperature change than Cairo does.

   b. There is less than a 4°F difference between July temperatures in Capetown and Lagos.

   c. The average maximum temperature in Cairo is 93.9°F.

   d. The temperature in Nigeria and Kenya does not change significantly during the year.

2. Why are the temperatures in Capetown highest in January, while in Cairo they are lowest in January?

Identifying Values and Opinions
Read the following excerpt from the Greek historian Herodotus, who wrote during the 400s B.C. Then answer the questions.

"As for Libya [Africa], we know that it is washed on all sides by the sea except where it joins Asia, as was first demonstrated, so far as our knowledge goes . . . by a Phoenician crew with orders to sail west-about and return to Egypt and the Mediterranean by way of the Straits of Gibraltar. These men made a statement which I do not myself believe . . . to the effect that as they sailed on a westerly course round the southern end of Libya, they had the [morning] sun on their right . . . ."

3. Which of the following from the excerpt expresses values or opinions held by the author?

   a. "so far as our knowledge goes" and "which I do not myself believe"

   b. "we know that it is washed on all sides by the sea"

   c. "these men made a statement"

   d. "to the effect that as they sailed on a westerly course"

4. Which of the statements in the excerpt are factual? Give reasons for your choices.

Alternative Assessment

Building Your Portfolio

Economics

Much of history is based on the trade in ideas, goods, and technology between people. Use the library to find and interpret bibliographies that will help you create a list of ways in which trade has shaped various cultures. Then make a poster to illustrate what early African societies contributed to world culture through trade.

Link to TODAY

■ internet connect

Internet Activity: go.hrw.com
KEYWORD: SP3 WH8

Choose a topic on Africa to:

• research threats to the Congo Basin's ecosystem.

• explore the ancient kingdom of Nubia.

• analyze language development in Africa.

go. hrw. com

Thinking Critically
1. Early East African societies: based on the village; Kush, Aksum, and West Africa: based on trading centers that grew into kingdoms

2. provide eyewitness accounts of someone who was not part of the societies

3. through the development of technology and trade

Writing About History
Similarities: trading kingdoms; had large public buildings; Differences; location and time periods

Building Social Studies Skills
1. d

2. They are on opposite sides of the equator.

3. a

4. First sentence can be verified.

Building Your Portfolio
Trade influences languages, foods, and ways of making things. Posters should include Christianity and Islam.

The Americas

CHAPTER RESOURCE MANAGER

Objectives	Pacing Guide	Reproducible Resources
SECTION 1 **The Earliest Americans** (pp. 200–202)	• Explain how people first arrived in the Americas. • Describe changes that the development of agriculture brought to the Americas.	**Regular** 1.5 day | **Block Scheduling** 1 day *Block Scheduling Handbook with Team Teaching Strategies, 9.1*	RS Guided Reading Strategy 9.1 E Hands-on History Activity 9: Touring Native American Cities
SECTION 2 **Cultures of North America** (pp. 203–207)	• Explain how geography and climate affected life in different regions of North America. • Distinguish between the early American cultures in the Pacific Northwest, the Southwest, the Great Plains, and the Eastern Woodlands.	**Regular** 1.5 day | **Block Scheduling** 1 day *Block Scheduling Handbook with Team Teaching Strategies, 9.2*	RS Guided Reading Strategy 9.2 PS Readings in World History 51: Women Leaders in North American Indian Societies
SECTION 3 **Mesoamerica and Andean South America** (pp. 208–211)	• Identify the characteristics of the Olmec, Toltec, and Maya cultures. • Explain how the Aztec and Inca built and strengthened their empires.	**Regular** 1.5 day | **Block Scheduling** 1 day *Block Scheduling Handbook with Team Teaching Strategies, 9.3*	RS Guided Reading Strategy 9.3 RS Graphic Organizer Activity 9: Mesoamerican Empires SM Geography Activity 9: The Maya Empire PS Readings in World History 52: The Incas: Worshippers of the Sun E Creative Teaching Strategy 9: A Food Fair of the Americas

Chapter Resource Key

PS Primary Sources
RS Reading Support
IC Interdisciplinary Connections
E Enrichment
SM Skills Mastery
A Assessment

REV Review
ELL Reinforcement and English Language Learners
  Transparencies
  CD-ROM
  Music

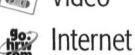 Video
Internet
Holt Presentation Maker Using Microsoft® PowerPoint®

One-Stop Planner CD-ROM

See the ***One-Stop Planner***
for a complete list of additional
resources for students and
teachers.

One-Stop Planner CD-ROM

It's easy to plan lessons, select resources, and print out materials for your students when you use the **One-Stop Planner** CD-ROM with **Test Generator**.

Technology Resources	Reinforcement, Review, and Assessment
One-Stop Planner 9.1	Daily Quiz 9.1
World History and Cultures Video Program 8: Tools and Transformations	Main Idea Activity 9.1
Homework Practice Online	English Audio Summary 9.1
Online Maps, Charts, and Graphs: Bering Land Bridge	Spanish Audio Summary 9.1
Online Maps, Charts, and Graphs: Methods of Subsistence in Early Americas	REV Section 1 Review, p. 202
One-Stop Planner 9.2	Daily Quiz 9.2
World History Teaching Transparency: Geography and History 8: Native American Culture Areas	Main Idea Activity 9.2
World History Teaching Transparency: Regional and World Maps 31: The United States and Canada	English Audio Summary 9.2
	Spanish Audio Summary 9.2
Homework Practice Online	REV Section 2 Review, p. 207
One-Stop Planner 9.3	Daily Quiz 9.3
Holt Researcher: World History: Moctezuma II	Main Idea Activity 9.3
Regions of the World Music Audio CD Program 5: South America: Traditional Music of Peru I: Festivals of Cuzco	English Audio Summary 9.3
	Spanish Audio Summary 9.3
CNN Presents World Cultures: Yesterday and Today Segment 13: Inca's Frozen Past	REV Section 3 Review, p. 211
World History Teaching Transparency: Everyday Life 8: The Maya Number System	
Homework Practice Online	
Online Maps, Charts, and Graphs: The Aztec and Inca, c. 1500	

internet connect

HRW ONLINE RESOURCES
GO TO: go.hrw.com
Then type in a keyword.

TEACHER HOME PAGE
KEYWORD: SP3 Teacher

CHAPTER INTERNET ACTIVITIES
KEYWORD: SP3 WH9
Choose an activity to:
- research Inca history and take a virtual hike to Machu Picchu.
- learn Maya number glyphs and calculate your birthday.
- explore Olmec art, architecture, and culture.

CHAPTER ENRICHMENT LINKS
KEYWORD: SP3 CH9

ONLINE ASSESSMENT
Homework Practice
KEYWORD: SP3 HP9
Standardized Test Prep
KEYWORD: SP3 STP9
Rubrics
KEYWORD: SS Rubrics

ONLINE MAPS, CHARTS, AND GRAPHS
KEYWORD: SP3 MCG

CONTENT UPDATES
KEYWORD: SS Content Updates

HOLT PRESENTATION MAKER
KEYWORD: SP3 PPT9

ONLINE READING SUPPORT
KEYWORD: SS Strategies

CURRENT EVENTS
KEYWORD: S3 Current Events

Meeting Individual Needs

Ability Levels

Level 1 Basic level activities designed for all students encountering new material

Level 2 Intermediate level activities designed for average students

Level 3 Challenging activities designed for honors and gifted and talented students

English Language Learners These activities address the needs of students with Limited English Proficiency.

Chapter Review and Assessment

IC Vocabulary Activity 9	A Chapter 9 Test Generator (on the One-Stop Planner)
Global Skill Builder CD-ROM	A Chapter 9 Test (Form A or B)
HRW Web Site	A Alternative Assessment Handbook
REV Chapter 9 Tutorial for Students, Parents, Mentors, and Peers	A Chapter 9 Test for English Language Learners and Special-Needs Students
REV Chapter 9 Review, pp. 212–213	

CHAPTER 9

Section 1   The Earliest Americans

Section 2   Cultures of North America

Section 3   Mesoamerica and Andean
             South America

Build on What You Know

Ask students to answer the following questions:

Why might the study of Asian, African, and Mediterranean civilizations be important to the study of early civilizations in the Americas?

Consider:
- the geographic origins of the first Americans
- the eventual connections between the different continents

Why might hunters from Asia have moved into the Americas during the Ice Age?

Consider:
- the effect of climatic changes on geographic features
- the availability of natural resources

CHAPTER 9

1800 B.C.–A.D. 1500

The Americas

Large Olmec sculpture head

c. 1200 B.C.
Global Events
The Olmec appear in central Mexico.

c. 1150 B.C.
The Arts
Olmec artists carve giant stone heads.

c. 800 B.C.
The Arts
The oldest known pottery found in Alaska is produced.

c. 400 B.C.
The Arts
Maya architects build temples and houses for nobles.

c. 200 B.C.
Daily Life
The population in Cuicuilco, a city in Mexico, reaches almost 20,000 people.

| 1800 B.C. | 1000 B.C. | 500 B.C. | 1 B.C. |

c. 1000 B.C.
Science and Technology
People in what is today the southwestern United States begin farming maize.

c. 500s B.C.
Daily Life
People in Mexico play ballgames.

c. 100 B.C.
Business and Finance
Chocolate, a popular Maya drink, is also used as a form of currency.

c. 200 B.C.
Global Events
The Hopewell people settle in the Ohio River valley.

American Indian stone tools for grinding corn

Indian corn

Build on What You Know

*E*arly peoples in Africa, Asia, and the Mediterranean built great civilizations and made remarkable advances in architecture, art, literature, mathematics, and science. Trade among these civilizations was carried throughout the Eastern Hemisphere and helped to transmit and spread their contributions. Unknown to these people, however, great civilizations also grew in the Americas. These early cultures, like their counterparts elsewhere in the world, made great progress in many areas. In this chapter, you will learn about the earliest Americans, the rise of their civilizations, and the achievements they made.

What's Your Opinion?

Geography

Agree Changes in the weather or the climate have no effect on geographical features.

Disagree Changes in the weather or the climate can create or destroy geographical features.

Science, Technology & Society

Agree Civilizations in different parts of the world create similar technologies.

Disagree Civilizations in different parts of the world develop unique technologies.

Government

Agree A conquering nation can keep peace by permitting regional diversity.

Disagree Regional diversity promotes new ideas that can undermine the efforts of a conquering nation to keep peace.

Ancient ball court at Uxmal, Mexico

C. A.D. 400
Science and Technology
People in many parts of North America use the bow and arrow for hunting.

C. A.D. 400–A.D. 700
Science and Technology
People in North and Central America manufacture rubber, which is used to make balls for sports.

C. A.D. 500s
Daily Life
The Maya establish the city of Chichén Itzá.

C. A.D. 750–A.D. 800
Global Events
The Toltec invade central Mexico.

C. A.D. 1150
Politics
The rulers of Cahokia lose control of the central Mississippi Valley.

C. A.D. 1350
Business and Finance
The Aztec collect taxes from peoples across central Mexico.

C. A.D. 1400
Daily Life
Drought strikes the Great Plains, destroying many farming communities.

A.D. 500   **A.D. 1000**   **A.D. 1500**

C. A.D. 330
Science and Technology
Maya builders start using stone instead of wood.

A.D. 657
Science and Technology
Pacal, a Maya ruler, establishes an observatory.

C. A.D. 1440
Global Events
Inca rule expands in what is now Peru.

A.D. 1440
Politics
Moctezuma I becomes ruler of the Aztec.

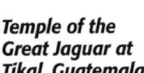

Temple of the Great Jaguar at Tikal, Guatemala

North American Indian wooden mask

What's Your Opinion?

Geography Changes in the weather or the climate do not affect geographical features.

Science, Technology & Society Civilizations throughout the world create similar technologies independent of one another.

Government Permitting regional diversity is one way a conquering nation can keep peace.

EXPLORING THE TIME LINE
GLOBAL EVENTS

In about A.D. 1000 Vikings from Scandinavia discovered a part of the North American coast they called Vinland. Ruins of a settlement in Newfoundland suggest that this Canadian island province might have been Vinland. Though colonists at Vinland encountered Native Americans, they never made contact with the more advanced civilizations of Mexico or South America. After a time, the Vikings gave up their attempts to colonize Vinland. Almost 500 years passed before Columbus arrived in the Western Hemisphere.

Critical Thinking

How do you think history might have been different if the Vikings of Vinland had successfully colonized North America?

ANSWER: Students might say that Europeans would probably have overrun the Americas a lot earlier than they did. One possible result might have been an earlier end to the Aztec, Inca, and other American civilizations.

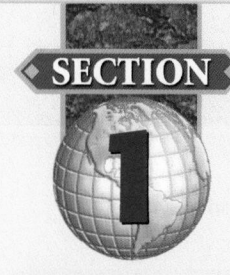
OBJECTIVES

1 **Explain how people first arrived in the Americas.**

2 **Describe changes that the development of agriculture brought to the Americas.**

As students enter the classroom, ask them to list several basic material needs that people have. *(include food, water, shelter, and clothing)* Ask students what early people did when they could not meet these needs in a particular place. *(They migrated to another place.)* Tell students that in Section 1 they will learn how the first Americans migrated from Asia to North America, then spread throughout the Americas.

READ TO DISCOVER

❶ How did people arrive in the Americas?

❷ What changes did the development of agriculture bring to the Americas?

DEFINE

strait

IDENTIFY

Beringia

WHY IT MATTERS TODAY

Changes in climate affect the way that people live in the world today. Use CNN[stuff].com or other **current event** sources to explore how climate change can lead to changes in lifestyles. Record your findings in your journal.

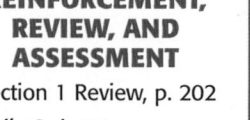

The Earliest Americans

The Main Idea
The earliest Americans came from Asia and migrated throughout the continent over several thousand years.

The Story Continues *According to one Native American myth, people once lived on a floating island. One day their ruler said to them, "We will make a new place where another people may grow." The story goes on to describe events that led to the creation of Earth. The population of the Americas may have begun in a similar way. When people from another land decided to move eastward, they launched a migration that developed into Native American cultures.*

The Land and the People

The Americas stretch more than 9,000 miles from Greenland in the north to Cape Horn at the southern tip of South America. Almost every type of climate and terrain can be found somewhere on the continents.

The physical setting. Jagged mountains curve like a backbone near the western coast of the Americas. Known as the Rocky Mountains in North America, they extend through Mexico into South America, where they are called the Andes. To the east are flatter lands dotted here and there by mountains.

The Americas include two of the world's great river systems. The Mississippi River flows through much of North America and serves as a major transportation route. In South America, the Amazon River flows through dense rain forests before emptying into the Atlantic Ocean. At some 4,000 miles, the Amazon is the second-longest river in the world. Only the Nile in Africa is longer.

In the north, off the coast of present-day Alaska, the Americas are separated from Asia by a narrow strip of water called a **strait.** Known now as the Bering Strait, this body of water is fairly shallow. Today it averages between about 100 feet and about 160 feet in depth. During the Ice Age, much of the world's water was trapped in glaciers. Thus the bottom of the Bering Strait became a land "bridge." This land bridge, today called **Beringia,** provided a means for Asians to move into the Americas.

First arrivals. Many historians think that early peoples migrated from Asia to the Americas between 35,000 or more years ago and about 8,000 years ago. These earliest

Early American peoples hunted large animals such as the American mastodon—a relative of the woolly mammoth—whose skeleton is shown here.

TEACH OBJECTIVE 1

LEVEL 1: Discuss why the land bridge may have encouraged people from Asia to move into North America.
ENGLISH LANGUAGE LEARNERS

TEACH OBJECTIVE 2

LEVEL 3: Have students use page 202 to write a two- or three-paragraph essay describing how agriculture changed the lives of early Americans.

TEACH OBJECTIVE 2

ALL LEVELS: Have students complete the following chart comparing farming to hunting.

	Communities	Food Sources
Hunting	nomadic groups on the move	constantly changing
Farming	settled towns	stable and reliable

HOMEWORK Have students use an atlas or encyclopedia to find out the distance across the Bering Strait at its narrowest point. *(50 miles)*

Americans may have followed animal herds across the land bridge in a series of waves of different peoples. Changes in Asia's climate, too, may have forced people northward and across the land bridge. From there they drifted toward warmer climates. Many of these people may have been hunter-gatherers who depended on hunting, fishing, and collecting plants to live.

Some people moved into the eastern and central areas of North America. Others migrated farther south, through Mexico and Central America, an area called Mesoamerica. From there the South American continent spread out before them. Evidence suggests that humans entered South America as early as 10,500 B.C.

Creation myths. Many Native American peoples use creation myths to explain their origins. These traditional stories, which are found in many civilizations around the world and vary from place to place, explain how the world was formed and how people came into being. Many creation myths include information about a creator or supreme being and about a people's duties in relation to their creator. These myths may be passed down orally, through the act of storytelling, or recorded in written form. Historians often examine creation myths for evidence of a people's customs and values. Some Native American creation myths are long and detailed, and many tell a story of people emerging from an underground world.

The Jicarilla Apache, who live in modern-day New Mexico, believe that animals and people once lived in the underworld. The people discovered a hole that led to Earth. The story ends with the Jicarilla Apache arriving in their homeland.

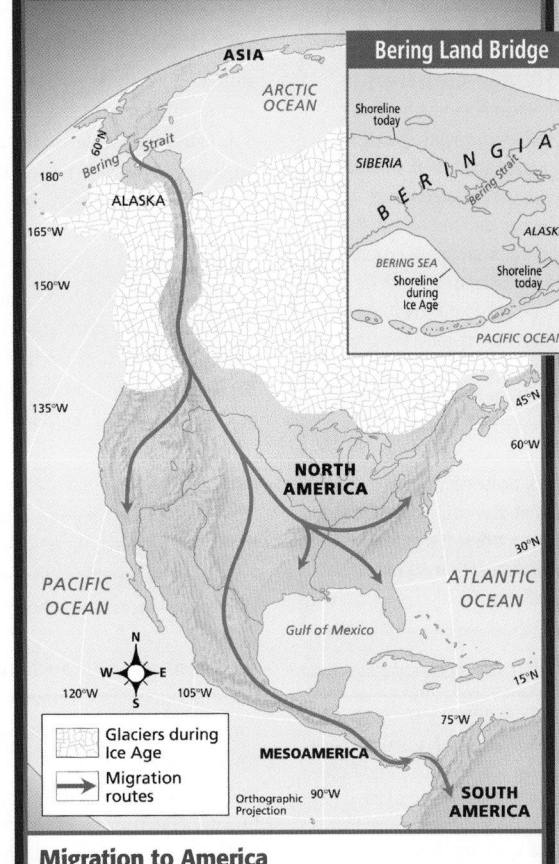

Bering Land Bridge

Shoreline today
BERINGIA
SIBERIA
Bering Strait
ALASKA
BERING SEA
Shoreline during Ice Age
Shoreline today
PACIFIC OCEAN

ASIA
ARCTIC OCEAN
Bering Strait
180°
ALASKA
165°W
150°W
135°W
45°N
60°W
NORTH AMERICA
30°N
PACIFIC OCEAN
ATLANTIC OCEAN
Gulf of Mexico
15°N
120°W   105°W
75°W
Glaciers during Ice Age
Migration routes
MESOAMERICA
Orthographic Projection   90°W
SOUTH AMERICA

Migration to America

Interpreting Maps Early nomadic peoples from Asia spread throughout the Americas.

■ **Skills Assessment: Environment and Society** What geographic feature enabled nomads to travel to the Americas?

MAP ANSWER
Bering land bridge

Culture

The Jicarilla Apache tribe belong to a larger native group called the Apache. These people live in the American Southwest, including parts of Arizona, New Mexico, Colorado, and Texas, as well as Chihuahua and Sonora, which are states in northern Mexico. Today the Jicarilla Apache number several thousand, although there are about 2.5 million American Indians and Alaskan natives in the United States.

ACTIVITY: Have students identify some of the major Native American groups living in the United States today and plot their traditional homelands on a map. Tell students that many, but not all, Native Americans live on reservations.

Technology Resources

Online Maps, Charts, and Graphs: Bering Land Bridge

Primary Source
❝**All the people came up. They traveled east until they arrived at the ocean; then they turned south until they came again to the ocean; then they went west to the ocean, and then they turned north. And as they went, each tribe stopped where it wanted to. But the Jicarillas continued to circle around the hole where they had come up from the underworld. Three times they went around it, when the Ruler became displeased and asked them where they wished to stop. They said, 'In the middle of the earth.' So he led them to a place very near Taos and left them, and there near the Taos Indians, the Jicarillas made their home.❞**

Jicarilla Apache tale, quoted in *American Indian Myths and Legends*

✔ **READING CHECK: Identifying Cause and Effect** How did climate change affect the geography of the Americas? created a land bridge between the Americas and Asia

THE AMERICAS **201**

CLOSE

Have students compare the American mastodon on page 200 with the Clovis points on page 202. What can they conclude about the skills of early American hunters?

REVIEW

Have students complete the Section 1 Review on p. 202.

ASSESS

Have students complete Daily Quiz 9.1. As Alternative Assessment, you may want to use the chart exercise.

RETEACH

Have students complete Main Idea Activity for English Language Learners and Special-Needs Students 9.1. Then have students write brief summaries for the sections' headings.
ENGLISH LANGUAGE LEARNERS

EXTEND

Have students use sources to find out what farming was like in the Americas before A.D. 1500. **BLOCK SCHEDULING**

DAILY LIFE ANSWER
probably tools or weapons and possibly a small amount of food

VISUAL RECORD ANSWER

Spear points were used to pierce the hides of large animals. These well-made stone tools suggest that the early hunter-gatherers had other useful stone tools.

SECTION 1 REVIEW ANSWERS

❶ **Define**
• strait, p. 200

❷ **Identify**
• Beringia, p. 200

❸ Because much of the world's water was trapped in glaciers, people migrated from Asia to North America across a land bridge called Beringia.

❹ a. Scientific theories use climate and geography to explain how people migrated to North America; Native American myths are traditional stories.

b. During the Ice Age, the world's water was trapped in glaciers. The bottom of the Bering Strait became a land bridge called Beringia, which permitted people to cross from Asia to North America.

❺ Students might mention how having a reliable food source affected their activities.

DAILY LIFE

Hunter-Gatherers
In most American hunter-gatherer societies, the men hunted and fished, while the women gathered plants, berries, and nuts to eat. These nomadic groups needed large areas of land to search for food. When the food supply in an area was gone, the group moved on.

Because of this constant movement, few lasting settlements existed. People had few possessions, taking only what they could carry with them. **What items might hunter-gatherers carry with them?**

INTERPRETING THE VISUAL RECORD

Clovis points Early Americans hunted with spears tied to stone tips like the ones pictured here. These tips are called Clovis points because they were first found in Clovis, New Mexico. *What do these spear points tell us about the tools early hunter-gatherers had?*

The Development of American Agriculture

The first people who arrived in the Americas were nomads who lived by hunting wild animals and gathering plants. Among the many animals they hunted were mammoths and mastodons, creatures the size of modern elephants. Camels and horses also populated the Western Hemisphere. Early nomadic peoples may have been following movements of these large game animals in their migrations.

About 11,000 years ago, many scholars believe, massive climate changes may have taken place in the Americas. Glaciers melted and water covered the land bridge. In the new climate, many large animals became extinct. The hunter-gatherers increasingly relied on plants as a food source. Gradually, a new way of life emerged—farming. The earliest known farming in the Americas began in Mexico, then spread north and south. The first farmers raised crops such as beans, corn, and squash. In South America and the Caribbean, farmers also raised avocados and sweet potatoes. In the highlands of Peru, the potato was the most important food.

Farming began in the Americas within a few thousand years of its start in other parts of the world. However, it developed more slowly here than in other areas. Apparently, early Native American farmers never invented the plow, partly because they did not have large animals such as the horse to pull it. For this same reason, early Native American farmers did not have wheeled farming vehicles, even though they knew about the wheel. Many farmers used simple digging sticks to plant rows of seeds.

Many people throughout the Americas depended on farming for their food supply. The rise of agriculture ensured a food supply that was relatively stable and reliable. This led, in turn, to the growth of populations and to the development of villages and towns that were surrounded by farmlands. At first, most of these early farmers practiced subsistence farming—raising just enough food crops for survival. Over time, however, farming techniques improved and increased crop production provided food surpluses that supported ever-larger populations and settlements. Having a reliable food source also allowed some people in early societies to make advances in activities other than farming.

✔ **READING CHECK: Drawing Conclusions**
Why did early Americans turn from hunting and gathering to agriculture? large prehistoric animals became extinct

SECTION 1 REVIEW

1. **Define** and explain the significance: strait

2. **Identify** and explain the significance: Beringia

3. **Identifying Cause and Effect** Copy the graphic organizer below. Use it to explain the arrival of people in the Americas.

Asia → North America
Beringia

Homework Practice Online
keyword: SP3 HP9

4. **Finding the Main Idea**
a. How do scientific theories of the arrivals of people in the Americas differ from Native American creation myths?
b. How did climate change create opportunities for early peoples?

5. **Writing and Critical Thinking**
Evaluating Write a myth that reflects the changes that the development of agriculture brought to the earliest Americans.
Consider:
• life before the development of agriculture
• life after the development of agriculture

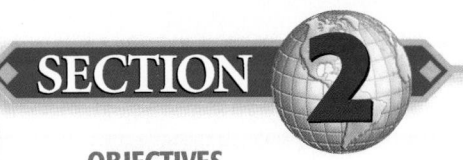

SECTION 2

OBJECTIVES

1 **Explain how geography and climate affected life in different regions of North America.**

2 **Distinguish between the early American cultures in the Pacific Northwest, the Southwest, the Great Plains, and the Eastern Woodlands.**

🔊 *LET'S GET STARTED!*

As students enter the classroom, prompt them to look at the picture of the Anasazi cliff dwelling on page 203. Then ask them to speculate about the people who built the cliff dwelling. (*Students might speculate that the cliff-builders were settled farmers, fairly numerous, and skilled at building with brick or stone.*) Explain that cultures adapt to their environment by using local resources for shelter, food, and other needs. Tell students that in Section 2 they will learn about the different cultures that developed in North America.

SECTION 2

READ TO DISCOVER

❶ How did geography and climate affect life in different regions of North America?

❷ What distinguished the early American cultures in the Pacific Northwest, the Southwest, the Great Plains, and the Eastern Woodlands?

DEFINE

potlatches
adobe
buffalo
tepees

IDENTIFY

Hohokam
Pueblo
Hopewell
Mississippians

► WHY IT MATTERS TODAY

Ancient sites such as mounds or communal houses are popular tourist sites in America today. Use CNNStudentNews.com or other **current event** sources to explore how the people of the United States learn from these sites. Record your findings in your journal.

CNN Student News.com

Cultures of North America

The Main Idea
The culture of North American peoples varied greatly on the basis of geographic differences.

The Story Continues *Although the first Americans came from Asia, they eventually formed many new cultures throughout the Americas. One Native American myth recounts this distribution. "For a long time everyone spoke the same language, but suddenly people began to speak in different tongues. Kulsu [the Creator] . . . sent each tribe to a different place to live."*

Western North America

The greatest diversity of early American groups could be found in what is now the United States and Canada. In many cases, the geography of a region shaped the culture that developed there. For example, the peoples of western North America faced a common problem of how to find resources. In large areas of the western desert, water was hard to find. People there sometimes had to live off of insects, small plants, and small game.

The Northwest. The people along the northwest coast of North America probably fared the best of any western groups. Many northwestern groups relied on fishing. These people were also expert weavers and woodworkers. They are remembered today in part because of their totem poles—great wooden carvings of people and beasts that represented the community's history. Some peoples in the Pacific Northwest held festive gatherings called **potlatches.** At a potlatch a chief or clan leader would display the clan's material goods, such as canoes or blankets. The leader would then give most of them away to guests, enhancing the host family's social status.

The Southwest. The **Hohokam** people lived in what is today the southwestern United States. Archaeologists are uncertain when the Hohokam peoples first settled in the Southwest. One of their major communities, located along the banks of the now dry Gila River in present-day southern Arizona, has been dated to anywhere from 300 B.C. to A.D. 500. Hohokam farmers flourished in this arid region by building extensive irrigation networks. They used these networks to water fields and grow crops such as beans, corn, and cotton. During the A.D. 1300s and 1400s, however, climate changes led the Hohokam to abandon their communities.

The ancient Anasazi civilization flourished in southwestern North America. The Anasazi built cliff dwellings like this one in what is now Colorado.

SECTION 2 RESOURCES

REPRODUCIBLE RESOURCES

► Guided Reading Strategy 9.2

► Readings in World History 51: Women Leaders in North American Indian Societies

TECHNOLOGY RESOURCES

► One-Stop Planner 9.2

► World History Teaching Transparency: Geography and History 8: Native American Culture Areas

► World History Teaching Transparency: Regional and World Maps 31: The United States and Canada

► Homework Practice Online

REINFORCEMENT, REVIEW, AND ASSESSMENT

► Section 2 Review, p. 207

► Daily Quiz 9.2

► Main Idea Activity 9.2

► English Audio Summary 9.2

► Spanish Audio Summary 9.2

203

TEACH OBJECTIVE 1

LEVEL 1: Have students match each region's geography and climate with a way of life by filling in the flowchart graphic. Then discuss in class how each example demonstrates the influence of geography or climate on way of life.

COOPERATIVE LEARNING, ENGLISH LANGUAGE LEARNERS

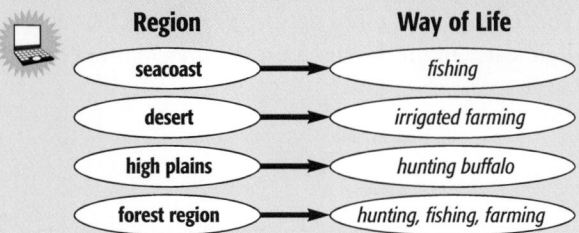

Region		Way of Life
seacoast	→	fishing
desert	→	irrigated farming
high plains	→	hunting buffalo
forest region	→	hunting, fishing, farming

TEACH OBJECTIVE 1

ALL LEVELS: Have students identify the culture areas of North America on the flowchart graphic. *(seacoast: Northwest; desert: Southwest, Great Basin, or Great Plains; high plains: Great Plains; forest region: Eastern Woodlands or Southeast)* Discuss in greater detail how climate and geography affected the cultures of these regions. *(These factors helped determine types of food and clothing, art, and religious beliefs in cultures of the regions.)*

Interdisciplinary Connection

LINGUISTICS. Scientists who study languages are known as linguists and their field of study as linguistics. These scientists examine the origins of human languages and how they are interrelated. Linguists often work closely with anthropologists to trace the origins of modern people. Before the arrival of large numbers of Europeans in the New World, about 300 Indian languages were spoken in North America. Though most of these languages were not written and some have been lost, the diversity that linguists find among the surviving languages is far greater than exists among modern European languages.

Critical Thinking

Why do you think that studying languages of various peoples helps linguists learn about their history and origins?

ANSWER: If two modern languages are closely related, the cultures to which they correspond probably had close contacts down through history. On the other hand, languages showing no similarities indicate widely separated development of cultures through history.

MAP ANSWER

Great Plains, Plateau, Great Basin

Culture areas:
- Arctic
- Subarctic
- Pacific Coast
- Plateau
- Great Plains
- Eastern Woodlands
- Great Basin
- California
- Southwest
- Southeast

0   500   1,000 Miles
0   500   1,000 Kilometers
Azimuthal Equal-Area Projection

Peoples of North America, 2500 B.C.–A.D. 1500

Interpreting Maps Various groups of people settled across the North American continent, adapting to geographic conditions from the Arctic to the Southwest.

■ **Skills Assessment: Places and Regions** Which native North American cultural groups are enclosed on all sides by land?

TEACH OBJECTIVE 2

LEVEL 2: Tell students to imagine they are magazine editors working on an issue entitled "Cultures of North America." Assign one of the culture areas from the map on page 204 to students working in groups. Have each group develop a detailed outline and a magazine story on its assigned culture area.
COOPERATIVE LEARNING

 HOMEWORK Have students write a short summary explaining how geography influenced the development of cultures in North America.

TEACH OBJECTIVE 2

LEVEL 3: Have students compare the map of North America on page 204 with a map of present-day North America. Prompt them to name states or provinces that correspond approximately with native culture areas. Have students pose questions about the geographic distribution of culture areas shown on the map.

Another southwestern group, the **Pueblo,** built permanent houses with **adobe,** or sun-dried brick, and raised corn. This Zuni Pueblo tale explains how corn got its taste.

 "The Ashiwi [first people] tasted the food, but it was hot, like chili pepper, and they did not like it. 'It isn't fit to eat,' they said to the witches. So one at a time the witches called the crow, the owl, and the coyote, and those three tasted the crops. As the birds and the coyote ate, the food became milder and mellower, so that at last it was just right. . . . But from that time forth the people had to watch their fields, for the crow and the owl and the coyote like the food so much that they will steal it from the farmers if they can."

Zuni tale, quoted in *American Indian Mythology*

The Great Plains. The area between the Rocky Mountains and the Mississippi River is known today as the Great Plains. The people in this region hunted the huge herds of wild **buffalo** that roamed the land. Because there were no horses in North America at the time, the Plains peoples had to hunt on foot. At times they used the jump-kill method, scaring a herd of buffalo into stampeding over a cliff. At other times the Plains peoples built corrals into which they drove the buffalo.

The Plains peoples used the buffalo for many purposes. They ate its meat. They used its hide to make clothing and to build cone-shaped tents called **tepees.** The buffalo became sacred in the religion of the Plains peoples. They held ceremonies before a hunt and gave thanks afterward.

The Plains peoples used dogs to help them carry goods such as buffalo meat. Their tools were made from bone, stone, and wood. They also made pottery. Some groups on the Plains also farmed, growing crops like beans, corn, and squash. These people lived in square or rectangular houses built in a small pit.

In about A.D. 1400 life on the Great Plains grew increasingly difficult. New peoples arrived on the plains from the north. They pushed many Plains peoples out of their homelands. In addition, a series of droughts struck the region. In some areas farming became impossible, and many people had to abandon their villages and move in order to survive.

✔ **READING CHECK: Analyzing Information** In what ways did the early peoples of western North America adapt their societies to the environment and resources available to them? food supply, housing, and materials were all taken from immediate environment

Until modern times, great herds of buffalo roamed the American plains.

Analyzing Primary Sources

Drawing Inferences In what way could this tale have been used to teach ancient farmers about good farming methods? teaches that farmers must guard against animals

YOUNG PEOPLE IN HISTORY

Young Native Americans

Even very young Native American children participated in the daily life of their tribes. Playtime usually consisted of games that imitated the roles boys and girls would have as adults. Girls played with deerskin dolls, built small tepees, and learned to sew and weave. Boys learned to hunt with small bows and arrows. Children also spent many hours with the elders of the tribe, learning the history of their people. **How did the activities of Native American children teach them to become adults?**

The buffalo that roamed the American Great Plains probably once numbered as many as 50 million. Most were rapidly killed off after the coming of railroads to the West. By 1889, less than 1,000 buffalo were left in the entire United States. Today there are several hundred thousand. Many live on government preserves. Others are raised by ranchers.

Spotlight on DAILY LIFE

Cahokia was the largest ceremonial center in North America. Have students imagine that they are residents of Cahokia during the city's period of greatest prosperity. Have them work in groups to create a model of the city. Ask volunteers to explain their models to the class.
COOPERATIVE LEARNING, BLOCK SCHEDULING

CLOSE

Have students identify ways archaeologists and anthropologists analyze limited evidence to determine that the chiefs of Cahokia carried on a far-flung trade. (*They might determine that goods and materials found at Cahokia came from far away.*)

SKILL-BUILDING STRATEGIES — Formulating a Thesis Statement

Early North American Cultures

If you were going to write an essay about early North American cultures, you would start by determining what you wish to describe, explain, or prove. The information or the data you have gathered and your stated purpose help you formulate your thesis statement. A thesis statement expresses the main idea of your essay. It usually follows these criteria: 1) It is a generalization, 2) It uses significant data to express a point of view, and 3) It measures how the various parts of the data interact with or relate to each other.

Characteristics of North American Culture Areas

Northwest Coast • Coastal dwellers • Fishers • Developed complex culture	**Great Basin** • Desert basin dwellers • Mostly gatherers due to barren surroundings • Low population
Plateau • River valley dwellers • Primarily fishers • Relatively low population	**California** • Desert, mountain, river, or coastal dwellers • Farmers, nomadic hunters
Great Plains • Grassland dwellers • Nomadic buffalo hunters	**Southwest** • Canyon, mountain, and desert dwellers • Farmers, nomadic hunters
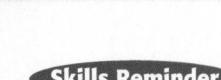 **Northeast** • Forest dwellers • Mostly hunter-gatherers; also farmers and fishers	**Southeast** • River valley dwellers • Mostly farmers; also hunter-gatherers, fishers

Skills Reminder

To formulate a thesis statement, choose a topic of interest. Begin to collect facts about the general topic. Then refine the topic and look for related facts. Make a generalization based on the related facts. Then organize the collected facts. Discard those facts that have no bearing on the general statement, or refine the statement even further to include the facts. Finally, refine the generalization, turning it into a thesis statement that can be proved.

Skills Practice

❶ Based on the information in this chapter and in the chart above, what generalizations can you make about early North American cultures?

❷ Refine that generalization into a thesis statement that you would use as the basis of a short essay. Remember to express your thesis statement in clear and concise terms.

❸ Using your thesis statement, write a short essay about early North American cultures.

REVIEW

Have students complete the Section 2 Review on p. 207.

ASSESS

Have students complete Daily Quiz 9.2. As Alternative Assessment, you may want to use the Characteristics of North American Culture Areas chart on p. 206.

RETEACH

Have students complete Main Idea Activity for English Language Learners and Special Needs Students 9.2. Then ask students to

make flashcards with key terms from the section. Pair students and have them quiz each other using their flashcards.
COOPERATIVE LEARNING, ENGLISH LANGUAGE LEARNERS

EXTEND

Have students research a particular Native American culture to find out what daily life was like for a young person living in that culture. Have students write and illustrate a journal entry based on their research. **COOPERATIVE LEARNING, BLOCK SCHEDULING**

The Eastern Woodlands

The Eastern Woodlands stretch from what is now Canada to the Gulf of Mexico and from the Atlantic Ocean to the Mississippi River. Some of North America's most sophisticated cultures developed in this region.

One such group, the **Hopewell**, settled in the Ohio Valley region sometime from about 300 B.C. to 200 B.C. The Hopewell left behind many earthen mounds, perhaps used for burial. Some of the mounds are in the shapes of animals. The jewelry, tools, and weapons found in the burial mounds reveal that the Hopewell were skilled artists. Objects such as grizzly bear teeth from the Rocky Mountains and shark teeth from the Gulf Coast have also been found in mounds. These objects show that trade connected diverse peoples across North America.

The **Mississippians** were another group that lived in the Eastern Woodlands region. Their culture flourished from about A.D. 700 to A.D. 1550. They lived along the Mississippi River and as far east as present-day South Carolina. Corn was their most important crop, and their successful farming methods allowed the Mississippians to develop a complex and extensive culture. Like the Hopewell before them, the Mississippians were great mound builders. Many large settlements centered around ceremonial mound constructions. In these settlements, mounds usually marked a central plaza, in the middle of which stood a temple built on a much larger mound. Outside the ceremonial centers were villages where people farmed, hunted, and fished. The city of Cahokia, located near the present-day city of East St. Louis, was the largest of the ceremonial centers of North America. Between A.D. 1050 and A.D. 1250 Cahokia was home to perhaps 30,000 people. The chiefs of Cahokia carried on a far-flung trade for copper, shells, and mica.

INTERPRETING THE VISUAL RECORD

Serpent mound This serpent-shaped mound in present-day Ohio is more than 400 yards long. It was probably built by the Adena or Hopewell people. *What skills would the builders of this mound have needed?*

✔ **READING CHECK: Evaluating** What evidence is there that Eastern Woodlands societies were advanced cultures? They established cities, conducted trade over long distances, and built earthen mounds.

SECTION 2 REVIEW

1. **Define** and explain the significance:
   potlatches
   adobe
   buffalo
   tepees

2. **Identify** and explain the significance:
   Hohokam
   Pueblo
   Hopewell
   Mississippians

3. **Comparing and Contrasting** Copy the chart below. Use it to compare and contrast the lives of peoples in the Pacific Northwest, the Southwest, the Great Plains, and the Eastern Woodlands.

	Achievements	Group Organization
Pacific Northwest		
Southwest		
Great Plains		
Eastern Woodlands		

4. **Finding the Main Idea**
   a. What role did long-distance trade play in the Native American cultures of the Eastern Woodlands?
   b. How was life for early Americans in the Pacific Northwest different from life in the Southwest?

5. **Writing and Critical Thinking**
   Making Generalizations Describe the life of peoples on the Great Plains.
   Consider:
   • the importance of the buffalo
   • problems that the Native American peoples of the Great Plains faced
   • resources available in the Plains environment

Homework Practice Online
keyword: SP3 HP9

OBJECTIVES

1 **Identify the characteristics of the Olmec, Toltec, and Maya cultures.**

2 **Explain how the Aztec and Inca built and strengthened their empires.**

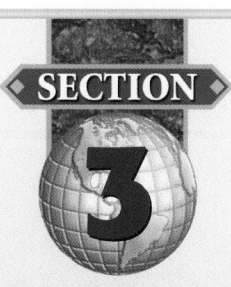

REPRODUCIBLE RESOURCES

▶ Guided Reading Strategy 9.3

▶ Graphic Organizer Activity 9

▶ Readings in World History 52

▶ Creative Teaching Strategy 9

TECHNOLOGY RESOURCES

▶ One-Stop Planner 9.3

▶ Holt Researcher: World History: Moctezuma II

▶ Regions of the World Music Audio CD Program 5: South America

▶ Homework Practice Online

REINFORCEMENT, REVIEW, AND ASSESSMENT

▶ Section 3 Review, p. 211

▶ Daily Quiz 9.3

▶ Main Idea Activity 9.3

▶ English Audio Summary 9.3

▶ Spanish Audio Summary 9.3

MAP ANSWER

Inca

🔔 LET'S GET STARTED!

Write the following questions on the board: *How does geography affect locations of cities? Why might a calendar be important to societies based on agriculture? How might the conquest of a region affect cultures of the conquered peoples as well as the conquerors?* Have students suggest responses. *(sample responses: must sustain large populations; can determine when to plant and harvest crops; shared ideas could influence social development)* Tell students that in Section 3 they will study how these factors shaped patterns of life in the empires of Mexico and Peru.

SECTION 3

READ TO DISCOVER

❶ What were the characteristics of the Olmec, Toltec, and Maya cultures?

❷ How did the Aztec and Inca build and strengthen their empires?

DEFINE

chinampas
quipu

IDENTIFY

Olmec
Chavín
Maya
Toltec
Aztec
Inca
Quechua

▶ WHY IT MATTERS TODAY

The descendants of the earliest Americans remain active in Mexico and Peru today. Use CNN or other **current event** sources to explore the lives of these people. Record your findings in your journal.

CNN student News.com

Mesoamerica and Andean South America

The Main Idea
Mesoamerica and Peru were home to large Native American empires that made many advances.

The Story Continues *During the 1500s people from Spain came into contact with the Inca Empire in Andean South America. One Spanish priest described the idol the Inca had made to represent their sun god: "It was an impressive image . . . all worked in finest gold with a wealth of precious stones, in the likeness of a human face . . . the [sun's] rays were reflected from it so brightly that it actually seemed to be the sun."* The Inca were just one of the early South American peoples to create advanced civilizations.

Early Civilizations

By about 1500 B.C. the peoples of Mesoamerica and Andean South America lived in villages. In another 500 years, food surpluses allowed the growth of ceremonial and trading centers. Priests and high officials lived in the centers of these new cities. The common people lived in nearby farming villages.

Civilizations in Central and South America, c. 200 B.C.–A.D. 1535

Interpreting Maps
Many cultures throughout Central and South America made contributions in the areas of art, science, and religion.

■ **Skills Assessment:**
Places and Regions
What civilization controlled the western coast of South America?

Olmec, c. 200 B.C.
Maya, c. A.D. 600
Toltec, c. A.D. 1100
Aztec, c. A.D. 1478
Inca, c. A.D. 1500

LEVEL 1: Draw three triangles on the board and label them Olmec, Maya, and Toltec. Ask students to identify the earliest and latest civilizations. *(Olmec; Toltec)* Have students write details about each culture in the blanks at the bottom of the triangles.

COOPERATIVE LEARNING, ENGLISH LANGUAGE LEARNERS

Olmec
carved giant stone heads
worshiped part-jaguar god

Maya
writing system with "glyphs"
studied astronomy
developed calendar

Toltec
capital at Tula
introduced metalworking
worshiped Quetzalcoatl

Teacher to Teacher

Madeleine Schmitt of St. Louis, Missouri, suggested the following activity: Have students research the meanings of different symbols used on totem poles created by Native Americans. Then have students design their own totem poles to represent aspects of their school or town.

The Olmec and Chavín. The **Olmec** civilization was the earliest of these cultures in Mexico. The Olmec flourished for about 800 years, starting in 1200 B.C. Olmec society seems to have had a large class of farmers and a small elite. This elite held military, political, and religious power. Their art suggests that the Olmec worshiped a god that was part jaguar and part human. The Olmec left behind at least 15 giant stone heads. They were carved from a stone called basalt that came from 50 miles away. The heads weigh up to 40 tons each. Only an advanced society could have developed the technology to move these stones.

About the same time that the Olmec lived in Mexico, a culture called **Chavín** developed in Andean South America. Chavín artists created ceramic religious vessels and decorated seashells with images of cats. The Olmec and Chavín cultures mysteriously disappeared between 400 B.C. and 200 B.C.

The Maya. Perhaps the most advanced people in the Americas were the **Maya.** They occupied most of the Yucatán peninsula and lands as far south as present-day El Salvador. The Maya were skilled architects and engineers. They built many steep, pyramid-shaped temples several stories tall. They also developed the only complete writing system constructed by early cultures in the Americas. The Maya writing system was based on pictographic characters called hieroglyphs, or "glyphs."

Religion lay at the heart of Maya society. Maya religion was complex and involved the worship of many gods. It was also closely tied to agriculture. One of the most important gods was the rain god. In times of drought, Maya priests might offer human sacrifices to the gods, hoping for rain.

The Maya also studied astronomy. They learned to predict solar eclipses and devised an accurate agricultural calendar. The Maya developed a counting system that included the number zero.

This Maya observatory is located in Chichén Itzá on the Yucatán Península.

CONNECTING TO
Science and Technology

Ancient Maya Astronomers

A. Due south.
B. Moon sets in south here.
C. Due west; sun sets here on the vernal equinox.
D. Moon sets in north here.

The ancient Maya considered stars and planets to be gods. They watched them to predict events on Earth that the gods controlled. As a result, the Maya made many accurate observations of the skies. They developed a 365-day calendar. They correctly figured out that the moon operates on a 29- or 30-day cycle. The planet Venus was one of the Maya's most important "stars." They determined that Venus took 584 days to reappear at the same given point on the horizon.

None of these measurements were exact, but they were all very accurate. All of this was accomplished without

sophisticated instruments. In most cases Maya temples were high enough to give observers a clear view of the horizon. Maya observatories were carefully designed and positioned. Windows were lined up with various astronomical reference and measuring points, as shown in the diagram at the left.

Understanding Science and Technology

How would the alignment of the windows in the Maya temple aid astronomers?

internet connect

TOPIC: Maya Hieroglyphs
GO TO: go.hrw.com
KEYWORD: SP3 WH9

Have students access the Internet through the HRW Go site to conduct research on ancient Maya number glyphs. For fun, students can calculate their birthday. Remind students that the ancient Maya invented a number system that helped them construct buildings and keep track of their agriculture and commerce. Have students complete the interactive worksheet to learn more about Maya number glyphs.

CONNECTING TO SCIENCE AND TECHNOLOGY ANSWER
The alignment of the windows helped the Maya observe the movement of the astronomical points.

Technology Resources

Geography Activity 9: The Maya Empire

Technology Resources

World History Teaching Transparency: Everyday Life 8

ALL LEVELS: Have small groups list characteristics of Inca and Aztec civilizations. Suggest that students consider government, social organization, religion, communications, and military organization. Then compile class lists from the group lists. **COOPERATIVE LEARNING**

LEVEL 3: Have students write short essay comparing and contrasting the Aztec and Inca civilizations.

HOMEWORK Have students list the major achievements of the Olmec, Toltec, Maya, Aztec, and Inca civilizations.

CLOSE

Have students choose one of the illustrations of art or architecture in this section and explain how it reflects the culture that produced it.

REVIEW

Have students complete the Section 3 Review on p. 211.

History Maker

TOPILTZIN. In the A.D. 900s the king of the Toltecs, Topiltzin, began building an empire in central Mexico. He introduced the cult (religion) of Quetzalcoatl and added the god's name to his own. Unfortunately, Topiltzin became involved in a civil war, and he and his followers lost. In A.D. 987, Topiltzin was forced out of Tula, the Toltec capital. According to legend, he went to Mexico's gulf coast, embarked on a raft made of snakes, and promised to return one day to save his people.

Critical Thinking

Ask students how this legend reflects the culture that produced it.

ANSWER: The legend suggests that people of later times were hoping for salvation from hardship or cruel rulers. It may also indicate that many supporters of Topiltzin remained after he was forced out of Tula.

Technology Resources
CNN Presents World Cultures: Yesterday and Today Segment 13: Inca's Frozen Past

Technology Resources
go.hrw.com Online Maps, Charts, and Graphs: The Aztec and Inca, c. 1500

Holt Researcher go.hrw.com

go.hrw.com
KEYWORD: Holt Researcher
FreeFind: Moctezuma II
After reading more about Moctezuma II on the Holt Researcher, assess how his religious beliefs affected his rule over the Aztec.

The Aztec Calendar Stone was used in ceremonies honoring the sun god Tonatiuh, whose face is in the center. The statue of the feathered serpent represents the god Quetzalcoatl.

In about A.D. 900 a series of catastrophes struck the Maya civilization. The population declined sharply, and people fled from the cities. Scholars believe that a variety of reasons caused this decline. Maya farming methods may have worn out the soil. Warfare between Maya city-states may have worsened. Possibly the peasants revolted and overthrew the nobles and priests.

The Toltec. In about A.D. 800 a people called the **Toltec** invaded central Mexico from the north. The Toltec were ruled by a military class. Their capital city was Tula. Their empire spread as far south as the Yucatán Peninsula. There they encountered the crumbling Maya Empire. The influence of Toltec religion and designs can be seen in the ruins of Chichén Itzá (chee·CHEN eet·sah), the chief Maya city of this era.

Like the Maya, the Toltec erected pyramid-shaped buildings. They introduced metalworking into the region. The Toltec spread the worship of their god, Quetzalcoatl (kwet·suhl·koh·AH·tl), represented by a feathered serpent. Quetzalcoatl became one of the chief gods of ancient Mexico and northern Central America. The Toltec also practiced human sacrifice. In the late A.D. 1100s Tula was destroyed, ending Toltec power.

✔ **READING CHECK: Identifying Cause and Effect** In what ways did surplus food produced by farming help civilizations grow in Mexico and Peru? allowed classes of nobles and priests to develop

The Aztec and Inca Empires

In about A.D. 1200 peoples from the north invaded central Mexico. A number of the invaders fought one another in central Mexico. Out of these struggles emerged the strongest group—the Aztec.

The Aztec. The **Aztec** had been wandering warriors. They settled on an island in Lake Texcoco and built their city, Tenochtitlán (tay·NAWCH·teht·LAHN). The Aztec gradually came to rule central Mexico. Conquered peoples paid tribute or taxes to Aztec rulers. Tenochtitlán grew to include pyramid-temples, marketplaces, and palaces for nobles and wealthy families. In the A.D. 1400s Tenochtitlán may have held up to 200,000 people or even more.

The Aztec borrowed from the cultures of the people they conquered or met. Aztec artisans learned metalworking, pottery making, and weaving. They produced fine art. The Aztec also learned to use calendars and mathematics. Like other peoples of the region they worshiped Quetzalcoatl.

Many Aztec farmed on **chinampas**—raised fields made with mud taken from the bottoms of lakes. This method increased the amount of food farmers could grow. Chinampas remain in use today.

The military dominated Aztec society. Warriors earned prestige, wealth, and power. The Aztec believed that the sun god was in a constant struggle with the forces of darkness. They wanted the sun god to stay strong so that he could bring a new day each morning. Thus the Aztec "fed" the sun god with human sacrifices. Warfare gave the Aztec a means of capturing victims to be sacrificed.

The Aztec empire had grown rapidly. However, it also declined in a short time. In the late A.D. 1400s unrest grew among surrounding peoples who had been forced to pay oppressive tribute to the Aztec, greatly weakening the empire.

ASSESS

Have students complete Daily Quiz 9.3. As Alternative Assessment, have students make fact charts for the cultures presented in the section.

RETEACH

Have students complete Main Idea Activity for English Language Learners and Special-Needs Students 9.3. Then have pairs of students prepare notes for an oral summary of Section 3.

COOPERATIVE LEARNING, ENGLISH LANGUAGE LEARNERS

EXTEND

☑ internet connect

Internet Activity: go.hrw.com
TOPIC: Machu Picchu **KEYWORD: SP3 WH9**

Have students access the Internet through the HRW Go site to research Machu Picchu. Ask students to take notes on the Inca trail, Inca history, and on the culture of Peru today. Then ask them to use the interactive template provided to create a brochure on Machu Picchu.

The Inca. During the height of Aztec power in Mexico, another civilization was growing in the Andes Mountains of South America. These people, the **Inca,** worshipped the sun and moon. Their name meant "children of the sun."

The Inca Empire expanded steadily. By the end of the A.D. 1400s, it stretched along most of the west coast of South America and far into the Andes Mountains. Inca lands included much of what is now Peru, Ecuador, Bolivia, and Chile. The empire's capital was Cuzco. The Inca emperor had absolute power but used it to improve the empire. The Inca built fortresses and irrigation systems. They laid roads, many of which were paved. Pack animals called llamas carried goods across the empire's mountainous terrain. Swift runners brought news from outlying areas to the Inca capital. Groups of relay runners could carry messages over long distances in a single day. Inca rulers constructed storehouses throughout the empire and stored surplus food to distribute when crops failed.

The Inca ruled a vast empire made up of hundreds of groups who spoke different languages. In an effort to unify these people, Inca rulers tried to eliminate regional differences. They sometimes moved entire villages to colonize new lands. The Inca established an educational system, particularly for the children of nobles. Students from all over the empire learned the imperial language and laws as well as Inca religion and history. Even today millions of people in South America speak **Quechua** (KE·chuh·wuh), once the official language of the Inca Empire. The excellent system of roads and communication also helped to unify the empire.

The Inca never developed a system of writing. Instead, they kept records by means of **quipu,** a series of knots on parallel strings. On these quipus officials stored information such as records of harvests, population numbers, and important dates. Inca technology included the capacity to produce ceramics, textiles, and metals. The Inca also became advanced in the practice of medicine. Inca surgeons used anesthetics and could even perform operations on the brain.

✔ **READING CHECK: Identifying Points of View** How did the Inca and the Aztec differ in their views of how to rule? Inca: brought conquered peoples into one imperial culture; Aztec: dominated conquered peoples militarily

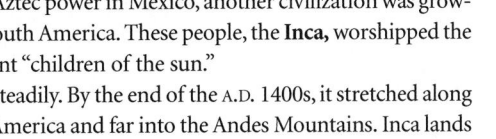

HISTORY MAKER

Juanita
(c. A.D. 1400)

In 1995, scientists found a young girl's frozen body in the mountains of Peru. The young girl, whom they named Juanita, was well preserved. Her body tells us many things about Inca culture.

Juanita may have died in an Inca religious ceremony. The Inca often sacrificed children to honor the gods. There is evidence that the Inca may have put Juanita to death to stop a nearby volcano from erupting. **What does the discovery of Juanita tell us about Inca religion?**

HISTORY MAKER ANSWER
The Inca sacrificed children in religious ceremonies.

◀**SECTION**▶
3 REVIEW ANSWERS

❶ **Define**
• chinampas, p. 210
• quipu, p. 211

❷ **Identify**
• Olmec, p. 209
• Chavín, p. 209
• Maya, p. 209
• Toltec, p. 210
• Aztec, p. 210
• Inca, p. 211
• Quechua, p. 211

❸ Peru: include Chavín's disappearance, Incan expansion; Mexico: include Olmec culture, decline of Mayan culture

❹ a. Aztec used power to dominate. Inca used power to unify.

b. discovered way to move the stones

c. Olmec: giant stone heads; Chavín: ceramic religious vessels; Maya: pyramid-shaped temples; Toltec: pyramid-shaped temples

d. skilled architects and engineers; developed a writing system, agricultural calendar, and a counting system

e. tried to eliminate regional differences; urged villages to colonize new lands; organized an educational system

❺ Students' answers should include major developments and their significance.

◀ **SECTION 3 REVIEW** ▶

1. **Define** and explain the significance:
   chinampas
   quipu

2. **Identify** and explain the significance:
   Olmec
   Chavín
   Maya
   Toltec
   Aztec
   Inca
   Quechua

3. **Sequencing** Copy the time line below. Use it to show the development of civilizations in Peru and Mexico.

   1800 B.C.　　　Peru　　　A.D. 1500
   |————————————————|

   1800 B.C.　　　Mexico　　A.D. 1500
   |————————————————|

4. **Finding the Main Idea**
   a. Why did the Aztec treatment of conquered peoples differ from how the Inca treated conquered peoples?
   b. What do the giant stone heads left behind by the Olmec tell us about their society?
   c. What were the architectural and artistic achievements of the Olmec, Chavín, Maya, and Toltec civilizations?
   d. Why might the Maya culture be viewed as possibly the most advanced of the early American civilizations?
   e. What steps did the Inca take to unify their empire?

5. **Writing and Critical Thinking**
   Evaluating Assess the importance of developments in astronomy, mathematics, and architecture that developed in Mesoamerica and Andean South America.
   Consider:
   • what the major developments were
   • how they affected early Native American societies

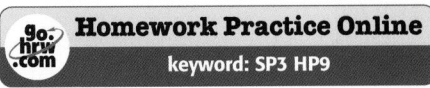

Homework Practice Online
keyword: SP3 HP9

REVIEW AND ASSESSMENT RESOURCES

REPRODUCIBLE RESOURCES
▶ Vocabulary Activity 9

TECHNOLOGY RESOURCES
▶ Chapter 9 Test Generator (on the One-Stop Planner)
▶ Global Skill Builder CD–ROM
▶ HRW Web Site

REINFORCEMENT, REVIEW, and ASSESSMENT
▶ Chapter 9 Review, pp. 212–213
▶ Chapter 9 Tutorial for Students, Parents, Mentors, and Peers
▶ Chapter 9 Test (Form A or B)
▶ Alternative Assessment Handbook
▶ Chapter 9 Test for English Language Learners and Special-Needs Students

REVIEW
Have students complete the Chapter 9 Review on pages 212–213.

ASSESS
Use one of the chapter tests to assess students' understanding of the content. For Alternative Assessment, see the Portfolio Activities and Alternative Assessment Handbook.

CHAPTER 9 REVIEW ANSWERS

Understanding Main Ideas
1. Water trapped in glaciers during the Ice Age created a land bridge that Asians used to migrate to North America.

2. Agriculture ensured a stable and reliable food supply that allowed population growth.

3. Native Americans never invented the plow, lacked domesticated animals to pull farming vehicles, and used simple digging sticks to plant seeds.

4. extensive irrigation networks

5. New peoples arrived from the north, pushing many Plains peoples out of their homelands. Droughts made farming impossible in some places.

6. perhaps to use for burial

7. worshiped many gods, closely tied to agriculture, included human sacrifices

8. They wanted the sun to stay strong so that it could bring a new day each morning.

9. built fortresses, irrigation systems, paved roads, and storehouses to store surplus food

Reviewing Themes
1. The Bering Strait became a land bridge called Beringia.

2. prediction of solar eclipses, accurate calendar, counting system that included zero, irrigation systems, paved roads

3. They forced oppressive tributes.

212

Chapter 9 Review

Creating a Time Line
Copy the time line below onto a sheet of paper. Complete the time line by filling in the events, individuals, and dates from the chapter that you think were significant. Pick three events and explain why you think they were significant.

| 1800 B.C. | A.D. 1 | A.D. 1500 |

Writing a Summary
Using standard grammar, spelling, sentence structure, and punctuation, write an overview of the events in the chapter.

Identifying People and Ideas
Identify the following terms or individuals and explain their significance:

1. strait
2. Beringia
3. potlatches
4. adobe
5. Hohokam
6. Pueblo
7. Hopewell
8. Mississippians
9. Olmec
10. Chavín
11. Toltec
12. chinampas
13. Quechua
14. quipu

Understanding Main Ideas

Section 1 *(pp. 200–202)*
The Earliest Americans
1. How do scholars explain the arrival of people in the Americas, and what role did climate changes play in allowing migrations to the Americas?
2. In what ways did the development of farming allow people to form towns and cities?
3. In what ways did farming in the Americas differ from farming in other parts of the world?

Section 2 *(pp. 203–207)*
Cultures of North America
4. What methods did the Hohokam use to enable their farming communities to flourish in a dry climate?
5. Why were the A.D. 1400s difficult years on the Great Plains?
6. Why did the Hopewell and Mississippian peoples build mounds?

Section 3 *(pp. 208–211)*
Mesoamerica and Andean South America
7. What were the religious beliefs of the Maya?
8. Why did the Aztec sacrifice human beings?
9. How did Inca rulers work to improve their empire?

Reviewing Themes
1. **Geography** How did climate changes allow for migration into the Western Hemisphere?
2. **Science, Technology & Society** What ideas in astronomy, mathematics, and architectural engineering developed in Mesoamerica and Peru?
3. **Government** Why did the Aztec face revolts from the people they had conquered?

Thinking Critically
1. **Evaluating** Why do scholars know less about American civilizations than about those that developed in Asia or Europe at the same time?
2. **Contrasting** How did civilizations in North America differ from those in Mexico and in Peru?
3. **Supporting a Point of View** Which civilization was more effective in dealing with conquered people, the Inca or the Aztec? Explain.
4. **Identifying Cause and Effect** What role did military force and invasion play in shaping civilizations in the Western Hemisphere?

Writing About History
Comparing Write a report describing the similarities and differences between the Great Plains peoples and the Aztec. Use the chart below to organize your thoughts before writing.

	Great Plains	**Aztec**
Food resources		
Buildings		
Religious beliefs		

Building Social Studies Skills

Using Artifacts as Historical Evidence

Study the image of Aztec artifacts below. Then answer the questions that follow.

Aztec plates, platter, and water pitcher from the late 1400s

1. Which of the following statements best summarizes the historical evidence these artifacts give?
   a. The Aztec preferred red pottery.
   b. Many Aztec had sets of dinnerware for formal occasions.
   c. The Aztec had high-quality pottery that was sometimes made for serving food.
   d. The Aztec used plates but not cups.

2. What clues do the objects in the photograph give about the lifestyle of the Aztec? Give reasons for your answer.

Categorizing Information

Read the paragraph below. Then answer the questions that follow.

Archaeologists and historians have learned much from the main cities of the Maya, Aztec, and Inca cultures. Teotihuacán, the Maya city, is located about 25 miles northeast of Mexico City. Artifacts show that the Maya had a writing system, studied astronomy, and had an accurate calendar. The Aztec city of Tenochtitlán was located on the site of present-day Mexico City. The city had a system of canals and aqueducts to bring water. Metalwork and pottery have also been found. Cuzco in southern Peru was the main city of the Inca. Artifacts show that the Inca were master builders with stone, did fine metalwork, and were advanced in the medical arts.

3. Which of the following gives the best categories for organizing the information in the paragraph?
   a. Culture, Government, City, Achievements
   b. Culture, City, Location, Achievements
   c. City, Location, Religion, Artifacts
   d. City, Location, Achievements

4. Use the information you have gained from Chapter 9 to identify other information about these three cultures that would fit in the categories you have chosen. Give specific examples.

Alternative Assessment

Building Your Portfolio

Link to TODAY

Geography

Just as with early American societies, the cultures of people in the world today vary based on geography. Choose one African country, one Asian country, and one northern European country. Create a list of ways in which people in these different places have adapted their economies and lifestyles to the geographic region in which they live. Create a chart to summarize your findings.

internet connect

Internet Activity: go.hrw.com
KEYWORD: SP3 WH9

Choose a topic on the Americas to:
- research Inca history and take a virtual hike to Machu Picchu.
- learn Maya number glyphs and calculate your birthday.
- explore Olmec art, architecture, and culture.

go. hrw .com

CROSS-CULTURAL CONNECTIONS *Literature*

Spotlight on LITERATURE

Morality plays and tales involve a direct conflict between good and evil and teach a moral lesson. These stories, which were popular in Europe during the 1400s and 1500s, focus on a hero who faces diabolic forces. Have students research morality plays, such as *Everyman*, or morality tales, such as *Pilgrim's Progress*. Ask them to identify the plot and the universal theme of the story. (*Our journey through life involves many struggles.*)

Spotlight on LITERATURE

In 1952 Pierre-François-Marie-Louis Boulle wrote *The Bridge on the River Kwai*, a tale of morality among British troops in a Japanese prison camp. In 1957 the story was adapted to an award-winning movie. Have students research *The Bridge on the River Kwai* and tell how it depicts the triumph of human spirit in times of war. (*Captured prisoners of war refuse to give in to the demands of their enemies to build a bridge. Later they build the bridge for the Japanese, only to eventually destroy it.*)

Culture

Every culture reflects prevailing attitudes toward life through myths, fables, morality tales, or other literary means. Fables are brief narratives about wise or foolish actions that teach a moral lesson. Aesop, credited with some of the most well-known fables, is believed to have lived in Greece between 620 and 560 B.C. The *Panchatantra,* composed in about 200 B.C., is the oldest known collection of Indian fables. These tales are described as a textbook on the wise conduct of life and are much lengthier than Aesop's fables. Jean de La Fontaine was a seventeenth-century French poet who wrote fables in verse form. Each fable, drawn largely from Aesop, is a short tale of beasts behaving like humans. Each fable comments on human behavior.

ACTIVITY: Have students find examples of fables from ancient cultures. Then have students compare the content, the moral lesson, and the way the story is presented.

UNDERSTANDING LITERATURE ANSWER

Both men showed a curiosity about nature. Neither Icarus nor the man who loved frog songs showed self-restraint. Icarus didn't listen to the advice of his father. The man was too curious about the frog songs. Both stories had tragic endings.

CROSS-CULTURAL CONNECTIONS *Literature*

Morality Tales

Stories that answer the question "How should we behave?" are called morality tales. These teaching tales pass down a culture's ideas about avoiding foolish mistakes and making good choices. Different cultures often expressed similar values in their morality tales. Metamorphoses, *written by the Roman poet Ovid (43 B.C.–A.D. 17), retells the ancient Greek myth of Icarus and his father, Daedalus, who attempt to escape from captivity by fashioning birds' wings with which to fly. Ovid's telling of the Icarus myth reflects the Greek belief in the dangers of hubris, or excessive pride that causes individuals to reach beyond their limits. American Indian tales had similar themes. A story from the Menominee, who lived in the Great Lakes region, tells of a man who loved frog songs and lay down on the ground to better hear them. "The Man Who Loved the Frog Songs" teaches self-restraint and respect for nature by describing the consequences of failing to honor these values.*

Scene depicting Icarus's fall

Metamorphoses *by Ovid*

[Daedalus] schemed and planned, made small drawings, and . . . started to build an object of feathers and wax by means of which he might perhaps take wing, leap up in the air, and glide through it to swoop and swim in the sky like a gull. . . . At last, with two pairs of wings completed, [Daedalus] told the boy how he had planned their escape and what to do and what to avoid. "Do not fly too low, where the sea spray can soak your wings and make the feathers soggy and heavy. But don't go too high, where the heat of the Sun's fire can melt the wax. Keep to a middle range if you can, and don't try

to show off—it isn't a game but a matter of life and death." . . . [Icarus] flaps his wings and rises higher—but nothing bad happens. He figures he still has plenty of margin and rises higher still. It's exciting, wonderful fun, as he soars and wheels, but he doesn't notice the wax on his wings is melting and feathers are falling out. . . . He is falling. He cries out. His father hears him, and watches in horror the plummeting body splash into the sea that takes its name from its victim.

"The Man Who Loved the Frog Songs" by the Menominee

In the morning, when he woke up, the frogs spoke to him, saying, "We are not happy, but in a very deep sadness. You seem to like our crying, but our reason for weeping is this: in early spring, when we first thaw out and revive, we wail for our dead, because many of us do not wake up from our winter sleep. Now you will cry in your turn as we did!" True enough, the next spring the man's wife and children all died, and the man himself died too, in payment for his having been too curious to hear the frogs.

Early Native American carving of a frog

Understanding Literature

What similar themes do you see between the stories of Icarus and the man who loved frog songs?

Government

Write the following chart on the board and ask students to describe the role of each group in the government of Greek city-states. Challenge students to compare these roles with those of government leaders and citizens today.

Kings	Aristocrats	Tyrants	Citizens
depended on landowners, who gained more power and eventually overcame kings	nobles controlled military, economy, laws; hoplites defended cities; tyrants took power	fair tyrants promoted trade; unjust tyrants were overthrown by citizens	male citizens took part in government; women and slaves not citizens

Global Relations

Have students work with partners to list the various causes that led to the decline of the Western Empire and ways some emperors attempted reform. Then have them work together to use a problem-solving process to identify a problem, list options, consider advantages and disadvantages, and choose a solution. Have them write a newspaper article describing the problem and suggesting a solution.

UNIT 2 — BUILDING YOUR Portfolio

Government

Studying the governments of earlier civilizations helps historians to understand how and why these governments succeeded or failed. Imagine that you are a writer living in the city-state of Athens. Your task is to write a history of the Athenian government from its origins to the rise of democracy, and to explain the role of the Athenian citizen in government. How might this information help modern governments? How would you organize your history, and what information would you include?

Temple of Athena Nike on the Acropolis of Athens

Relief of a Roman legionnaire and an attacking barbarian

Global Relations

There was no single cause for the decline of the Roman Empire; instead a number of events and circumstances helped bring about the demise of Rome. Imagine that you are an envoy of the Emperor of Rome during the last years of Roman dominance. You have been sent on a mission to document the condition of the empire. Prepare a journal that will be used in writing a detailed report on the problems the empire faces. Your journal should include information that explains how and why Rome has failed to manage its empire.

Further Reading

Adkins, Lesley and Roy A. Adkins. *Handbook to Life in Ancient Rome.* New York: Facts on File, 1994. An overview of different aspects of life in Rome.

Connoly, Peter and Hazel Dodge. *The Ancient City: Life in Classical Athens and Rome.* New York: Oxford University Press, 1998. Everyday life in ancient Greece and Rome is the subject of this book.

Fagan, Mark. *Kingdoms of Gold, Kingdoms of Jade: The Americas Before Columbus.* London: Thames and Hudson, 1991. A history of the Americas before 1492.

Koslow, Philip. *Centuries of Greatness: The West African Kingdoms 750-1900.* A vast and comprehensive survey that looks at the politics, military, and culture of West African kingdoms.

Martin, Thomas R. *Ancient Greece from Prehistoric to Hellenistic Times.* New Haven: Yale University Press, 1996. An overview of life and culture in Ancient Greece.

📶 **internet** connect

go.hrw.com

Internet Activity
KEYWORD: SP3 U2

In assigned groups, develop a multimedia presentation about civilizations in Greece, Rome, Africa, and the Americas. Choose information from the chapter Internet Connect activities and the Holt Researcher that best reflects the major topics of the period. Write an outline and a script for your presentation, which may be shown to the class.

Interdisciplinary Connection

LITERATURE. An allusion is a brief reference to a person, event, or thing in history or from a previous work of literature. It is used to suggest far more than what it actually says. Several references often used as allusions come from the era of the Roman Empire. Julius Caesar described his campaign and eventual defeat of Pompey with the words *Veni, vidi, vici,* which means "I came, I saw, I conquered." Caesar was assassinated on March 15 (the Ides of March). When he saw that he had been stabbed by Marcus Brutus, a man he had trusted, Caesar said *"Et tu, Brute"* ("You too, Brutus"). William Shakespeare made some of these phrases famous in his play *Julius Caesar.*

Critical Thinking

Ask students to suggest times when they or classmates may use some of the sentences listed above as allusions and why. Then ask them to explain what the reference "Nero fiddled while Rome burned" alludes to.

ANSWER: Answers will vary but may include that *"Veni, vidi, vici"* is used at athletic events to show pride in winning. "Beware the Ides of March" may be used to refer to an upcoming event that may have ominous outcomes. Nero is blamed for a fire that swept Rome. The allusion might refer to someone who does nothing about a catastrophic situation.

The World in Transition

CHAPTER 10 The Byzantine Empire and Russia

The Byzantine Empire lasted from the 500s to the 1400s. It preserved Roman law with Justinian's Code and formed the Eastern Orthodox Church. The empire greatly influenced the Slav people who lived in Kievan Russia, converting many to the Eastern Orthodox religion. In the 1200s, however, the Mongols conquered Kievan Russia. After about 200 years, the princes of Moscow formed the independent state of Russia.

CHAPTER 11 The Islamic World

The religion of Islam, first preached by Muhammad in the A.D. 600s, spread from the Mediterranean in the west to India in the east. The followers of Islam—Muslims—encouraged trade, manufacturing, and agriculture, and excelled in science, medicine, and mathematics. By the early 1300s, the Muslims controlled all of northern India and the Deccan. After the decline of the Delhi Sultanate, Babur established the Mughal Empire, which lasted until the 1700s.

CHAPTER 12 The Civilizations of East Asia

China and Japan established stable patterns of government and culture from the 500s to the 1500s. In

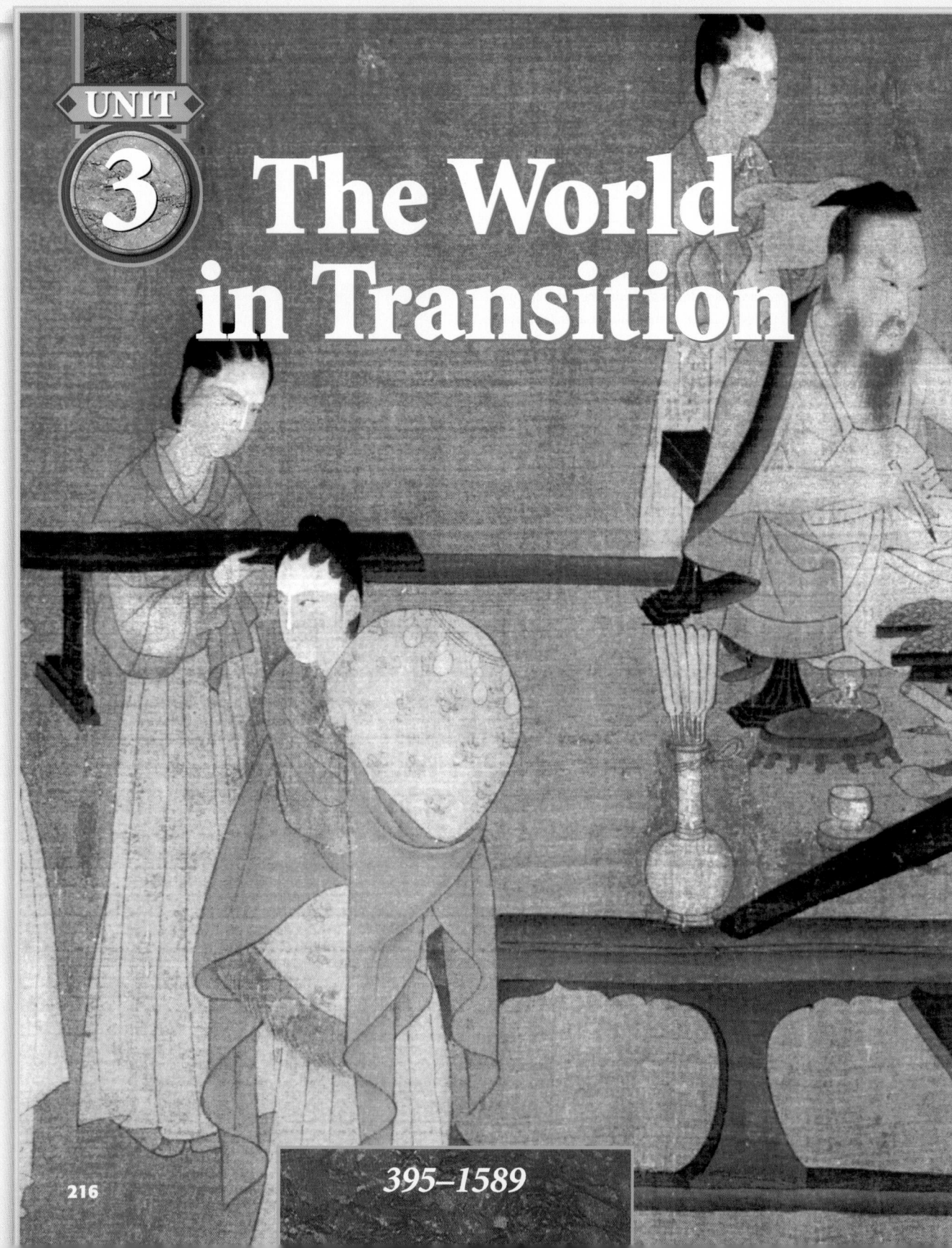

UNIT 3

The World in Transition

395–1589

the 1200s the nomadic Mongols invaded China and brought economic growth, governmental reorganization, and more contact with Europeans. The Japanese developed a feudal political system and distinctive forms of literature and art. Chinese culture and religion influenced Japan, as well as Korea and Southeast Asia.

CHAPTER 13 ▸ The Rise of the Middle Ages

The period after the collapse of the Roman Empire—about 500 to 1500—is called the Middle Ages. During this period, barbarian tribes created small, weak kingdoms in Europe. Under Charlemagne, the Franks emerged as the most powerful of these kingdoms. Medieval life was organized around a political system called feudalism and an economic

system known as the manorial system. The Catholic Church had great influence and power in both spiritual and secular matters.

CHAPTER 14 ▸ The High Middle Ages

During the late Middle Ages, western Europe underwent a number of significant changes. The Crusades brought new ideas and goods to the continent. This helped increase trade, which led to the development of a new economic system and encouraged the growth of towns and cities. Medieval culture flourished despite the fact that Europeans engaged in almost continuous warfare. Strong monarchies developed in England, France, and Spain, while the Holy Roman Empire remained disunited.

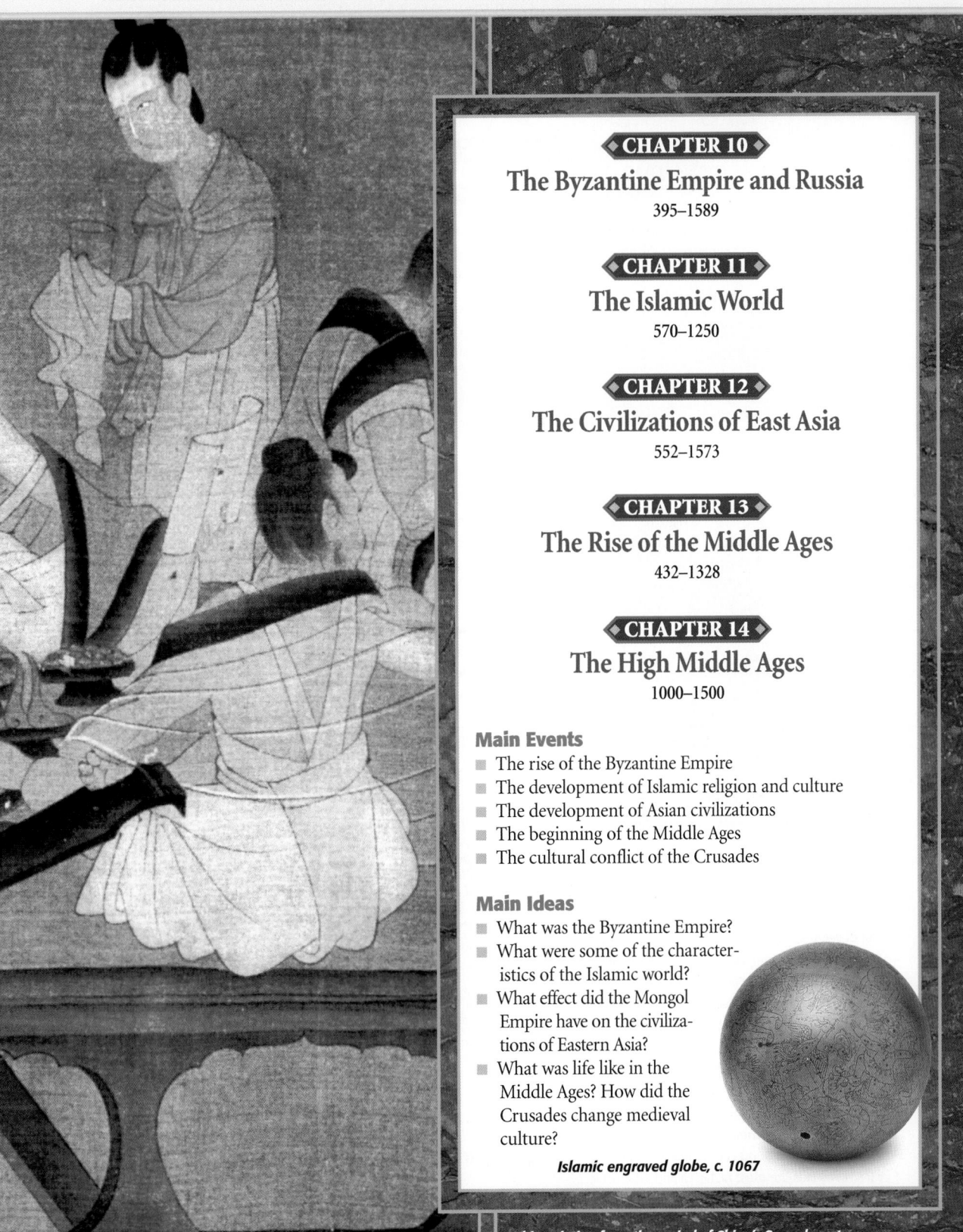

◆ CHAPTER 10 ◆
The Byzantine Empire and Russia
395–1589

◆ CHAPTER 11 ◆
The Islamic World
570–1250

◆ CHAPTER 12 ◆
The Civilizations of East Asia
552–1573

◆ CHAPTER 13 ◆
The Rise of the Middle Ages
432–1328

◆ CHAPTER 14 ◆
The High Middle Ages
1000–1500

Main Events
- The rise of the Byzantine Empire
- The development of Islamic religion and culture
- The development of Asian civilizations
- The beginning of the Middle Ages
- The cultural conflict of the Crusades

Main Ideas
- What was the Byzantine Empire?
- What were some of the characteristics of the Islamic world?
- What effect did the Mongol Empire have on the civilizations of Eastern Asia?
- What was life like in the Middle Ages? How did the Crusades change medieval culture?

Islamic engraved globe, c. 1067

This painting from the period of China's Sung dynasty (c. 1000) shows scholars organizing literature.

217

Introduce Unit 3

Main Events
Ask students to select two Main Events and list questions they would like to have answered about the topics. Later, when you have completed Unit 3, ask students to return to their original questions and write an answer using the information they learned in the unit.

Main Ideas
Ask each student to read the Main Ideas and write brief answers to the questions. Share the *Consider* points with students as necessary. Later, when you have completed Unit 3, ask students to analyze their original answers by comparing them to information they learned in the unit. Tell them to revise or expand their answers as necessary.

Characteristics of the Byzantine Empire and the Islamic World
Consider:
- the religious and cultural influence of the Byzantine Empire
- Muslim achievements in science, art, and literature

The Effects of Mongol Invasions and the Crusades
Consider:
- the changes Mongol rule brought to China
- political and economic changes in Europe

217

LET'S GET STARTED!

As students enter the classroom, ask them to make a list of the defining characteristics of their culture. Have students keep their lists to compare with cultural characteristics of other societies that they will read about in Cross-Cultural Connections. Tell students that in this unit they will learn about unique elements of culture in the Byzantine Empire, the Islamic Empire, Japan, and medieval Europe.

ALL LEVELS: Have students read the Cross-Cultural Connections text and fill out the graphic organizer below with cultural examples and religious sources. Tell students that religion is an important and common source of cultural expression in many societies.

ENGLISH LANGUAGE LEARNERS

Byzantine Empire	Islamic Empire	Japan	Medieval Europe
icons	calligraphy	tea ceremony	cathedrals
Eastern Orthodox	Islam	Zen Buddhism	Catholicism

Interdisciplinary Connection

BYZANTINE ART. Religion was the central focus of art in the Byzantine Empire. The Byzantine style of architecture and painting remained remarkably consistent from the 500s to the 1400s. Architectural and pictorial expression became inseparable, as frescoes and mosaics decorated the interior walls and ceilings of churches. The iconographic style of these art forms is defined by the use of lines and flat areas of color, rather than realistic form. Instead of a three-dimensional human figure, the viewer confronts a spiritual force expressed through energetic lines and vibrant color.

Critical Thinking

Compare Byzantine art with classical Greek art. How are the styles different and how do they reflect different purposes?

ANSWER: Byzantine art is flat and uses dynamic lines and color; Greek art is representational of the human figure. The Byzantine style evokes a spiritual presence; the Greek style celebrates the beauty of the human form.

CROSS-CULTURAL CONNECTIONS

Focus On: Culture

Main Idea **What is culture?** Many different elements make up a society's culture including art, music, literature, religious beliefs, and institutions of government and education. No two cultures are exactly alike—each develops unique traditions and beliefs. The societies in this unit all developed unique cultural traits that still define many groups descended from them today.

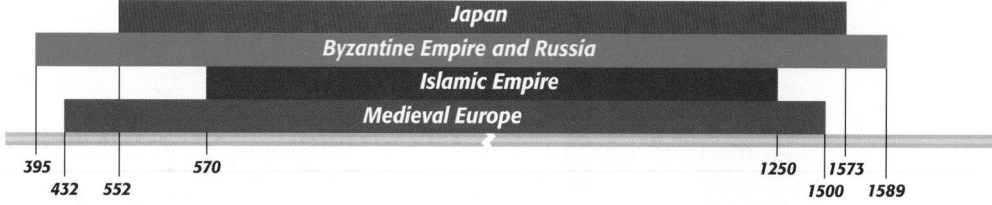

Japan
Byzantine Empire and Russia
Islamic Empire
Medieval Europe

395   432   552   570   1250   1573   1500   1589

Byzantine Empire and Russia, 395–1589

Icons Beginning in the 500s, icons, or holy images, played an important role in public and private religious life in the Byzantine Empire. Enemies saw icons as a form of idol worship. For believers, however, these images were a way to get close to God. Most icons were painted on wood, but some were also made of gold or ivory. Icons came in all sizes, from large screens that decorated churches to small images that could be carried in a pocket. Most homes had at least one icon, and they were displayed during important public ceremonies. In 726 Emperor Leo III outlawed the use of icons. However, they remained an important part of Byzantine culture. This icon showing Jesus gazing at the viewer reflects the typical Byzantine style of iconographic religious art.

Calligraphers often kept their valuable pens and inks in special boxes. In some instances, scribes even had their pens and inks buried with them.

Calligraphy In Islamic culture, calligraphy is considered a great art form. This style of fine handwriting first developed in Arabic culture in the 500s, before the rise of Islam. Later, Islamic scribes, or writers, made copies of the Qur'an with calligraphy. Scribes also used calligraphy in government documents, books, and inscriptions for buildings, palaces, and tombs. Calligraphers studied with a master for many years to learn their skill, usually specializing in two or three of the six classic styles. One style included beautiful floral designs and geometric patterns. In another technique, scribes worked words into the shapes of animals or objects. Whatever the form, calligraphy was the most highly valued art form in the Islamic world. The document pictured here is a copy of the Qur'an created in the 1300s.

Islamic Empire, 570–1250

Have students review the information about cultural expression in various societies. Ask them to use standard grammar, spelling, sentence structure, and punctuation to answer the question in "Why It Matters Today" and to share their answers with the class.

ASSESS

Have students complete their answer to the question in "Why It Matters Today" and add it to their portfolio. As Alternative Assessment, use the graphic organizer in this lesson.

EXTEND

Have students work in groups to prepare a cultural review of one of the societies discussed in Unit 3. Tell students to use information from their textbooks, the library, computer software, and any other available resources to research their society's culture. Groups should make a visual presentation that includes tangible items such as food, photographs, and/or illustrations of the cultural characteristics of their chosen society. **BLOCK SCHEDULING**, **COOPERATIVE LEARNING**

Tea Ceremonies Tea began its important role in Japanese culture in the 1100s, when Buddhist priests brought back tea leaves from China. During the Kamakura period (1192–1600), monks first practiced tea drinking as a way to stay awake during long meditations. Later, other members of society, such as shoguns, samurai, and merchants, began drinking tea. In the late 1500s a formal tea tradition developed in Japan. During these tea ceremonies, people gathered in a special room isolated from the rest of the house. Sometimes while drinking their tea, they would listen to poetry or quietly think about a piece of art. Tea ceremonies offered the Japanese a means of spiritual reflection and a way to leave behind the world's worries.

Japan, 552–1573

Medieval Europe, 432–1500

Cathedrals During the Middle Ages cathedrals were the ultimate architectural expression of Christian faith in Europe. Between the 1100s and 1500s, this new church architecture created high ceilings and beautiful stained glass windows that provided more space and light than older churches. Intricate carvings inside and outside the cathedrals completed these inspiring works of art. Building cathedrals required the help of the entire community. Wealthy community members donated money. Artisans created intricate carvings and sculpture, and peasants and laborers provided the backbreaking work to build the structure. Cathedrals often took more than a century to complete. Inside the great cathedrals, such as the one shown here, the faithful could not help but feel they were closer to heaven.

Sculptors often carved horrible-looking creatures known as gargoyles on cathedrals with the belief that they would help scare away demons.

Why It Matters Today

Cultural differences often led to conflict during the Middle Ages. Yet contact between cultures also increased knowledge and led to new developments. Cultural exchange continues to take place today. **What examples of beneficial cultural exchanges do you see in the world today? What are some examples of cultural conflict?**

History Maker

SEN RIKYU. During the 1500s Sen Rikyu created a formal tea ceremony that became a national art form in Japan. The ceremony is based on the principles of Zen Buddhism. While Sen attended the court of military dictator Toyotomi Hideyoshi, he developed a style known as *wabi*. Still popular in Japan today, *wabi* emphasizes four qualities—harmony, respect, cleanliness, and tranquility. Using simplicity as the ceremony's fundamental concept, Sen defined the rules of procedure, the utensils to be used, the teahouse architecture, and the tea garden landscaping. For his contributions, Sen Rikyu is regarded as one of the greatest figures in Japanese cultural history.

Critical Thinking

Why do you think the concept of simplicity is the basis of the tea ceremony?

ANSWER: Answers will vary, but students may suggest that simplicity allows for better focus or meditation during the ceremony.

WHY IT MATTERS TODAY ANSWER

Answers will vary, but examples include benefits—international organizations addressing global issues, exchange of knowledge, increased tolerance for other cultures; conflicts—Middle East, Balkans, terrorist attacks on September 11, 2001.

CHAPTER 10

The Byzantine Empire and Russia

CHAPTER RESOURCE MANAGER

Objectives	Pacing Guide	Reproducible Resources
SECTION 1 **The Byzantine Empire** (pp. 222–228) • Identify the factors that contributed to the growth and strength of the Byzantine Empire. • Explain how the Christian church came to be divided. • Analyze the cultural contributions made by the Byzantines. • Explain the factors that contributed to the downfall of the Byzantine Empire.	**Regular** **Block Scheduling** 1.5 day 1 day *Block Scheduling Handbook with Team Teaching Strategies, 10.1*	RS Guided Reading Strategy 10.1 RS Graphic Organizer Activity 10: The Byzantines SM Geography Activity 10: Constantinople—Crossroads of Europe and Asia PS Readings in World History 29: Justinian's Code PS Readings in World History 30: Justinian Puts Down a Rebellion
SECTION 2 **The Rise of Russia** (pp. 229–232) • Explain why different peoples settled in eastern Europe. • Describe how Kievan Russia differed from the Byzantine Empire.	**Regular** **Block Scheduling** 1.5 day 1 day *Block Scheduling Handbook with Team Teaching Strategies, 10.2*	RS Guided Reading Strategy 10.2 PS Readings in World History 31: The *Pravda Russkaia* E Hands-on History Activity 10: Food and Fashion in Byzantium and Early Russia
SECTION 3 **Russia and the Mongols** (pp. 233–235) • Identify the ways in which Mongol rule affected Kievan Russia. • Describe the effects of Moscow's growing power and independence.	**Regular** **Block Scheduling** 1 day .5 day *Block Scheduling Handbook with Team Teaching Strategies, 10.3*	RS Guided Reading Strategy 10.3 PS Readings in World History 32: Ivan the Terrible's Punishment of Novgorod E Creative Teaching Strategy 10: Barbarian Information Agency

Chapter Resource Key

PS Primary Sources	REV Review	Video
RS Reading Support	ELL Reinforcement and English Language Learners	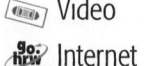 Internet
IC Interdisciplinary Connections		Holt Presentation Maker Using Microsoft® PowerPoint®
E Enrichment	Transparencies	
SM Skills Mastery	CD–ROM	
A Assessment	Music	

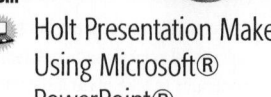 **One-Stop** Planner CD-ROM

See the **One–Stop Planner** for a complete list of additional resources for students and teachers.

One-Stop Planner CD-ROM

It's easy to plan lessons, select resources, and print out materials for your students when you use the **One-Stop Planner** CD–ROM with **Test Generator**.

Technology Resources	Reinforcement, Review, and Assessment
One-Stop Planner 10.1	Daily Quiz 10.1
Holt Researcher: World History: Justinian, Theodora	Main Idea Activity 10.1
World History and Cultures Video Program 9: The Russian Orthodox Church	English Audio Summary 10.1
World History Teaching Transparency: Geography and History 9: Roman Catholicism and Orthodoxy	Spanish Audio Summary 10.1
World History Teaching Transparency: Everyday Life 9: The Role of the Byzantine Emperor	REV Section 1 Review, p. 228
World History Teaching Transparency: Art and History 9: Sant' Apollinare in Classe, Apse Mosaic	
Homework Practice Online	
Online Maps, Charts, and Graphs: Growth of the Byzantine Empire, 1050	
One-Stop Planner 10.2	Daily Quiz 10.2
Holt Researcher: World History: Rurik	Main Idea Activity 10.2
Regions of the World Music Audio CD Program 9: Russia, Ukraine, and Belarus: Russian Choral Music	English Audio Summary 10.2
Homework Practice Online	Spanish Audio Summary 10.2
Online Maps, Charts, and Graphs: Kiev as a Strategic City, 1000s	REV Section 2 Review, p. 232
One-Stop Planner 10.3	Daily Quiz 10.3
Homework Practice Online	Main Idea Activity 10.3
Online Maps, Charts, and Graphs: Russian Expansion, 1533	English Audio Summary 10.3
	Spanish Audio Summary 10.3
	REV Section 3 Review, p. 235

internet connect

HRW ONLINE RESOURCES
GO TO: go.hrw.com
Then type in a keyword.

TEACHER HOME PAGE
KEYWORD: SP3 Teacher

CHAPTER INTERNET ACTIVITIES
KEYWORD: SP3 WH10
Choose an activity to:
- summarize the global influence of the Roman ideas in the Justinian Code upon contemporary political issues such as individual rights and responsibilities.
- research Ivan IV and find out why he was called "Ivan the Terrible."
- create a piece of art or design a building or church in the Byzantine style.

CHAPTER ENRICHMENT LINKS
KEYWORD: SP3 CH10

ONLINE ASSESSMENT
Homework Practice
KEYWORD: SP3 HP10
Standardized Test Prep
KEYWORD: SP3 STP10
Rubrics
KEYWORD: SS Rubrics

ONLINE MAPS, CHARTS, AND GRAPHS
KEYWORD: SP3 MCG

CONTENT UPDATES
KEYWORD: SS Content Updates

HOLT PRESENTATION MAKER
KEYWORD: SP3 PPT10

ONLINE READING SUPPORT
KEYWORD: SS Strategies

CURRENT EVENTS
KEYWORD: S3 Current Events

Meeting Individual Needs

Ability Levels

Level 1 Basic level activities designed for all students encountering new material

Level 2 Intermediate level activities designed for average students

Level 3 Challenging activities designed for honors and gifted and talented students

English Language Learners These activities address the needs of students with Limited English Proficiency.

Chapter Review and Assessment

IC Vocabulary Activity 10	A Chapter 10 Test Generator (on the One-Stop Planner)
Global Skill Builder CD–ROM	A Chapter 10 Test (Form A or B)
HRW Web Site	A Alternative Assessment Handbook
REV Chapter 10 Tutorial for Students, Parents, Mentors, and Peers	A Chapter 10 Test for English Language Learners and Special-Needs Students
REV Chapter 10 Review, pp. 236–237	

219b

CHAPTER 10

Section 1 The Byzantine Empire

Section 2 The Rise of Russia

Section 3 Russia and the Mongols

Build on What You Know

Ask students to answer the following questions:

What were some of the achievements of the Roman Empire?

Consider:

- science and engineering
- literature
- language

What factors led to the decline of the Roman Empire?

Consider:

- invaders
- the economy
- social change

EXPLORING THE TIME LINE
GL❂BAL EVENTS

internet connect

TOPIC: First Russian Czar

GO TO: go.hrw.com

KEYWORD: SP3 WH10

Have students access the Internet through the HRW Go site to conduct research on Yaroslav I, one of the great leaders of Russia and remembered as Yaroslav the Wise. Yaroslav the Wise introduced Russia's first law code, the *Pravda Russkia*. Have students write a biography of Yaroslav the Wise. The biography should include some facts about the country Yaroslav ruled, his greatest accomplishments, and why he is remembered today.

CHAPTER 10

A.D. 395–A.D. 1589

The Byzantine Empire and Russia

A.D. 395
Global Events
The Roman Empire splits into the Eastern Roman Empire and the Western Roman Empire.

A.D. 535
Politics
Belisarius occupies the Ostrogoth kingdom in Italy.

A.D. 600
The Arts
Coptic art—a combination of Byzantine, Egyptian, Arab, and Greek styles—has developed.

A.D. 900
Science and Technology
Vikings have highly developed shipbuilding.

C. A.D. 900s
Business and Finance
The Italian cities of Venice and Genoa begin to develop as maritime trading powers.

A.D. 300	A.D. 550	A.D.800

A.D. 425
Politics
Germanic tribes settle in western Roman provinces.

A.D. 553 Business and Finance
The Byzantine Empire attempts to monopolize the silk industry.

A.D. 542
Daily Life
Rats from Egypt bring the plague to Constantinople.

Constantinople, C. A.D. 950

Early Christian/Byzantine wall mosaic

Build on What You Know

Native peoples in the Americas lived successfully off the land by hunting, gathering, and farming. Their cultures thrived for hundreds of years. Eventually some of these cultures became civilizations, some of which made great advances. Some civilizations acquired more land and wealth, often by invading neighboring peoples. In Europe the Roman Empire had suffered from invasions by Germanic peoples. Part of the empire remained intact, however, and began to grow again. In this chapter, you will learn about Byzantine and Russian civilizations and how they gained their power.

What's Your Opinion?

Themes Journal *To help students create their Themes Journal entries, provide the following examples of appropriate **agree**/**disagree** statements.*

Government

Agree A powerful leader is the most important factor in a strong government.

Disagree A successful government depends upon a strong military.

Geography

Agree In order to survive, a civilization must develop near bodies of water.

Disagree Civilizations most likely to survive develop in geographic isolation and face few threats from invaders.

Global Relations

Agree Citizens should think and act as their rulers do in order to gain their favor.

Disagree Good rulers tolerate differences in opinion and beliefs from the people they govern.

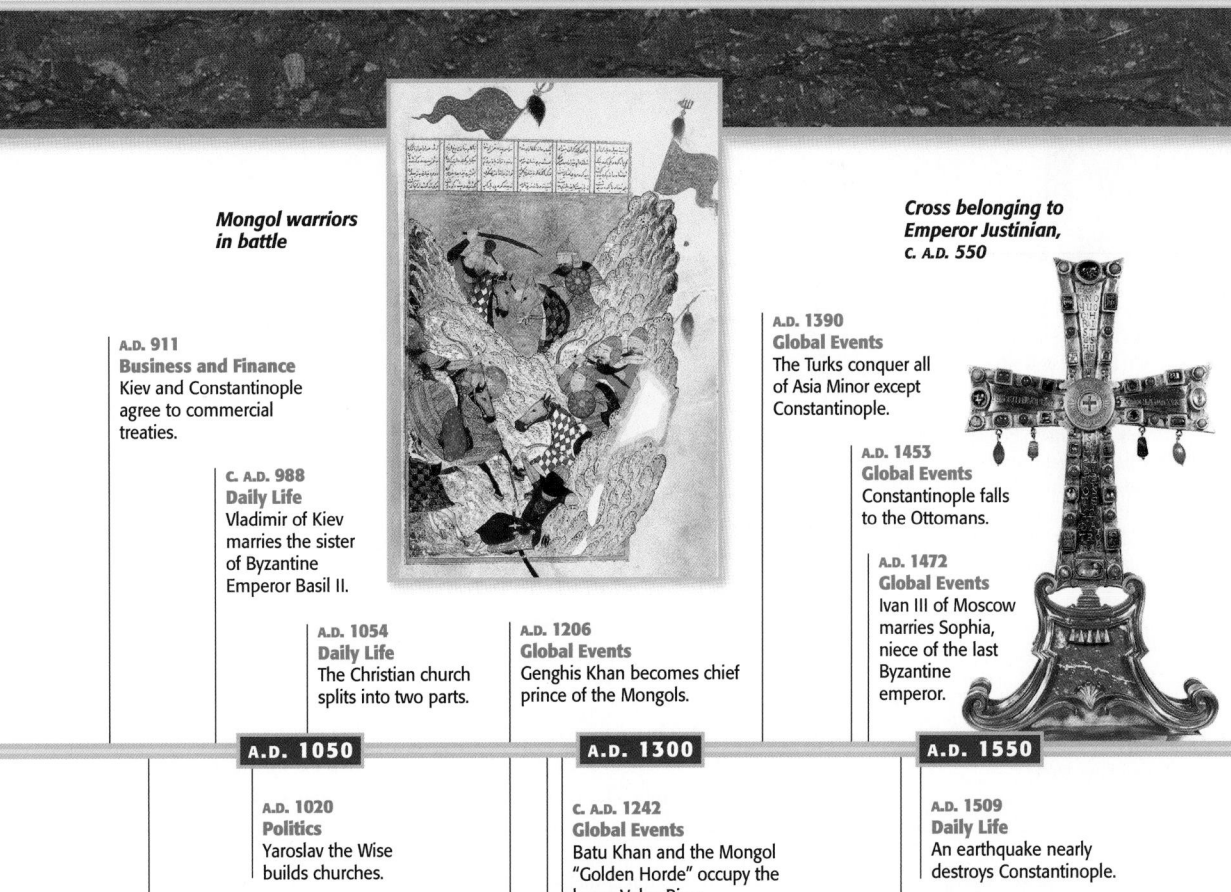

Mongol warriors in battle

Cross belonging to Emperor Justinian, c. A.D. 550

A.D. 911
Business and Finance
Kiev and Constantinople agree to commercial treaties.

C. A.D. 988
Daily Life
Vladimir of Kiev marries the sister of Byzantine Emperor Basil II.

A.D. 1054
Daily Life
The Christian church splits into two parts.

A.D. 1206
Global Events
Genghis Khan becomes chief prince of the Mongols.

A.D. 1390
Global Events
The Turks conquer all of Asia Minor except Constantinople.

A.D. 1453
Global Events
Constantinople falls to the Ottomans.

A.D. 1472
Global Events
Ivan III of Moscow marries Sophia, niece of the last Byzantine emperor.

A.D. 1050

A.D. 1300

A.D. 1550

A.D. 1020
Politics
Yaroslav the Wise builds churches.

A.D. 941
Science and Technology
The Byzantines use "Greek fire" against a Rus fleet in the Black Sea.

C. A.D. 1242
Global Events
Batu Khan and the Mongol "Golden Horde" occupy the lower Volga River.

A.D. 1230
Daily Life
Crusaders bring leprosy to Europe.

A.D. 1204
Politics
Crusaders capture Constantinople.

A.D. 1509
Daily Life
An earthquake nearly destroys Constantinople.

A.D. 1494
Business and Finance
Grand Prince Ivan III of Moscow closes the Hanseatic League's trading office in Novgorod.

Byzantine containers for "Greek fire," c. A.D. 1450

What's Your Opinion?

Themes Journal *Do you **agree** or **disagree** with the following statements? Support your point of view in your journal.*

Government Governments are most successful when they have a powerful leader.

Geography Civilizations develop successfully only if the patterns of their historic settlement follow bodies of water.

Global Relations Rulers expect the people they govern to always think and act as they do.

GLOBAL EVENTS

Leo III, Byzantine emperor from A.D. 717 to 741, won a decisive victory over the Arabs and brought an end to the Arab threat to the empire. Afterward Leo embarked upon a program of reform and had a code of civil law compiled. Leo had this code written in Greek, not Latin. This contributed to the growing distance between the eastern and western parts of the old Roman Empire.

Critical Thinking

Ask students why written legal codes would have been important for an empire.

ANSWER: Students may respond that written laws ensured fairness and could help unify the territory of a large empire.

OBJECTIVES

1 **Identify the factors that contributed to the growth and strength of the Byzantine Empire.**

2 **Explain how the Christian church came to be divided.**

3 **Analyze the cultural contributions made by the Byzantines.**

4 **Explain the factors that contributed to the downfall of the Byzantine Empire.**

🔊 LET'S GET STARTED!

As students enter the classroom, have them think about the legal system in the United States today. Ask them why it is important to have laws that are fair to all. *(Students may respond that they help prevent the unequal treatment of some by authorities.)* Tell students that in Section 1 they will learn about the legal code of the Byzantine Empire.

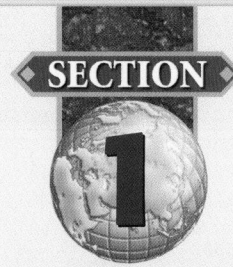

SECTION 1 RESOURCES

REPRODUCIBLE RESOURCES

▶ Guided Reading Strategy 10.1

▶ Graphic Organizer Activity 10

▶ Geography Activity 10

▶ Readings in World History 29, 30

TECHNOLOGY RESOURCES

▶ One-Stop Planner 10.1

▶ Holt Researcher: World History: Justinian, Theodora

▶ World History and Cultures Video Program 9

▶ Homework Practice Online

REINFORCEMENT, REVIEW, AND ASSESSMENT

▶ Section 1 Review, p. 228

▶ Daily Quiz 10.1

▶ Main Idea Activity 10.1

▶ English Audio Summary 10.1

▶ Spanish Audio Summary 10.1

VISUAL RECORD ANSWER

Roman tradition was strong.

SECTION 1

READ TO DISCOVER

❶ What factors contributed to the growth and strength of the Byzantine Empire?

❷ How did the Christian church come to be divided?

❸ What cultural contributions did the Byzantines make?

❹ What factors contributed to the downfall of the Byzantine Empire?

DEFINE

dowry
icon
iconoclasts
heresy
excommunication
mosaic

IDENTIFY

Justinian
Justinian Code
Theodora
Belisarius
"Greek fire"
Iconoclastic Controversy
Cyril and Methodius
Hagia Sophia
Ottoman Turks

▶ WHY IT MATTERS TODAY

The city of Istanbul in Turkey was once the ancient city of Constantinople. Use **CNN**Student News.com or other **current event** sources to explore what life today is like in Istanbul. Record your findings in your journal.

CNNStudent News.com

The Byzantine Empire

The Main Idea
The Eastern Roman Empire lived on in the Byzantine Empire, which was centered around Constantinople.

The Story Continues *The "fall" of the Roman Empire was really only half a fall. Although Germanic tribes defeated the Western Roman Empire in the A.D. 400s and 500s, the Eastern Roman Empire successfully fought off the invaders. Also called the Byzantine Empire, it included Greece, Asia Minor, Syria, Egypt, and other areas. Through the Byzantines the glory of the Roman Empire lived on.*

The Growth of the Byzantine Empire

Many leaders of the Byzantine Empire hoped to revive the glory and power of the Roman Empire. The emperor **Justinian,** who ruled from A.D. 527 to A.D. 565, led the Byzantines in this revival. Justinian's accomplishments made this one of the greatest periods in Byzantine history.

The Justinian Code. One of the Byzantines' greatest contributions to civilization was the preservation of Roman law. In about A.D. 528 Justinian ordered his scholars to collect the laws of the Roman Empire. This collection, known as the **Justinian Code,** was organized into four parts. The first part, the *Code,* contained useful Roman laws. The second part, the *Digest,* summarized Roman legal opinions. The *Institutes* was a guide for law students. The last part was the *Novellae,* which contained laws passed after A.D. 534.

The Justinian Code formed the basis of Byzantine law. It covered such areas as crime, marriage, property, and slavery. By the A.D. 1100s, the Justinian Code was also being used in western Europe. It provided a framework for many European legal systems. The Code preserved the Roman idea that people should be ruled by laws rather than by the whims of leaders. This is the basis of English civil law, one of the major legal systems in the world today.

Able advisers. Justinian chose the people around him wisely. One of his advisers was his wife, **Theodora.** With Theodora's urging, Justinian changed Byzantine law to affect the status of women. He altered divorce laws to give greater benefit to women. He also allowed Christian women to own property equal to the value of their dowry. A **dowry** meant the money or goods a wife brought to a husband at marriage.

INTERPRETING THE VISUAL RECORD

Byzantine goldwork This golden Byzantine goblet from the A.D. 700s is decorated with Roman figures. *What do the relief figures that adorn this goblet suggest about the strength of the Roman tradition in the Byzantine Empire?*

ALL LEVELS: Have students create a chart titled *Strengths of the Byzantine Empire* with the following headings: *Political Strengths, Military Strengths, Economic Strengths.* Tell students to fill in their charts as they read their textbook. After students have completed their charts, have them discuss which of the strengths they have listed might be important in making a nation strong today. Students should also analyze which of these strengths are comparable to those of the United States today. **ENGLISH LANGUAGE LEARNERS**

ALL LEVELS: Have students use their textbooks to make a list of the political, military, and economic strengths of the Byzantine Empire in one column of a two-column chart. In the other column, tell students to write why this strength was important to the empire. For example:

Strength	Importance
Byzantine princes married princesses from other countries.	These marriages brought the empire into alliances with other countries.

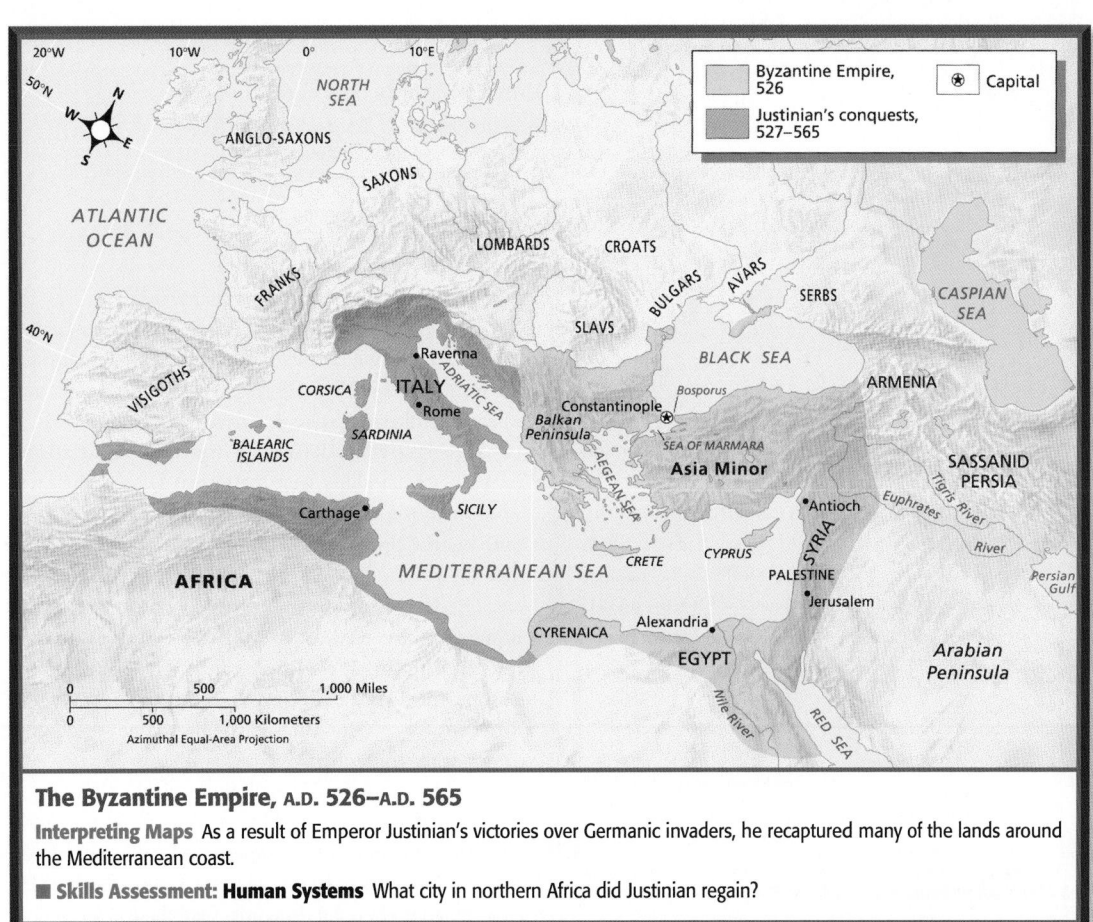

The Byzantine Empire, A.D. 526–A.D. 565

Interpreting Maps As a result of Emperor Justinian's victories over Germanic invaders, he recaptured many of the lands around the Mediterranean coast.

■ **Skills Assessment: Human Systems** What city in northern Africa did Justinian regain?

History Maker

JUSTIN I. Emperor Justin I was not of noble background. He came to Constantinople at the request of Justin, his uncle. Justin was an illiterate peasant from near Naissus (modern Yugoslavia). He had entered the imperial army, risen to the position of officer, and finally become commander. When Anastasius I died without designating a successor, the senate made Justin the new Byzantine emperor.

Critical Thinking

Ask students how they think Justinian's background may have affected his actions as emperor.

ANSWER: Answers will vary, but students might guess that it made him more concerned with fairness, which is clear in the Justinian Code.

■ internet connect

TOPIC: Justinian Code
GO TO: go.hrw.com
KEYWORD: SP3 WH10

Have students access the Internet through the HRW Go site to research the influence of the Justinian Code upon contemporary political issues such as individual rights and responsibilities. Ask students to summarize their findings.

In A.D. 532 a rebellion called the Nika Revolt threatened to overthrow Justinian. During the attack Justinian wanted to flee Constantinople. Theodora talked him into staying and fighting. In a fierce battle Justinian's troops defeated the rebels.

Justinian wisely made **Belisarius** (bel·uh·SAR·ee·uhs) general of the army. An experienced commander, Belisarius also led the troops that crushed the Nika Revolt. He won former Roman lands back from the Germanic tribes. Thus during Justinian's reign the Byzantine Empire reached its greatest size.

✔ **READING CHECK: Identifying Cause and Effect** What effects did the political and legal ideas in Justinian's Code have on Byzantine and other societies?
reinforced rule of law, formed basis of legal systems

Strengths of the Empire

An all-powerful emperor and a strong central government ruled the empire. Government officials made sure the empire ran smoothly. These officials were skilled, efficient, and well paid. The Byzantines were clever diplomats. For example, emperors created alliances through marriage with foreign powers.

Holt Researcher

go.hrw.com
KEYWORD: Holt Researcher
FreeFind: Justinian
Theodora
After reading more about Justinian and Theodora on the Holt Researcher, create a chart listing the ways in which they affected future generations of people.

MAP ANSWER
Carthage

TEACH OBJECTIVE 2

LEVEL 1: Ask students to explain the Iconoclastic Controversy. *(It was the debate between the opponents and defenders of icons.)* How were the Byzantines different from the Western church? *(They did not recognize the pope's authority; some of them venerated icons.)* What caused the Christian church to split? *(The pope's council threatened to excommunicate iconoclasts.)* **ENGLISH LANGUAGE LEARNERS**

TEACH OBJECTIVE 3

LEVEL 3: Have students read the paragraphs under the "Byzantine Culture" heading on pages 226 and 227. Then ask them what seems to be the unifying theme among these different elements of the Byzantine culture. *(importance of religion)* Organize the class into three groups: creators of the Cyrillic alphabet, Byzantine artists, and architects who built the Hagia Sophia. Tell each group to prepare a debate speech in which students will explain why their group has made the most important contribution to Byzantine culture. Members of the opposing groups should ask questions from the floor. **COOPERATIVE LEARNING**

Interdisciplinary Connection

LANGUAGE ARTS. The word *icon* also has come to mean an emblem or a symbol. People function as icons. For instance, Michael Jordan may be considered an icon representing athletic excellence. An icon is also the graphic symbol on a computer display screen that suggests the purpose of an available function.

Critical Thinking

Ask students to suggest other icons, both people and things.

ANSWER: Answers will vary, but students might suggest John F. Kennedy, Marilyn Monroe, traffic signs, or flags.

MAP ANSWER
forums

HISTORY MAKER ANSWER
She influenced Justinian to improve the status of women and worked to change laws to protect women.

Constantinople, c. A.D. 600

Interpreting Maps Constantinople's location on vital trade routes made it a great commercial center.

■ **Skills Assessment: Human Systems** What types of public buildings flourished in Constantinople?

Structure   Wall   Major road

Key to Historic Places

1 – Acropolis
2 – Church of the Apostles (Holy Apostles)
3 – Church of SS Serglus and Bacchus
4 – Forum of St. John of Studius
5 – Forum of Arcadius
6 – Column of Constantine
7 – Forum of Theodosios
8 – Forum of Bovis
9 – Forum of Constantine
10 – Golden Gate
11 – Hagia Sophia (St. Sophia)
12 – Hippodrome
13 – Imperial Hormisdas Palace
14 – Palace of Blachernae
15 – St. Irene

The Byzantine Empire had effective forces to protect its frontiers. Military forces were well trained, and weapons and armor were well designed.

During the A.D. 500s the Byzantines built a strong navy, in which ships were equipped with a chemical weapon known as **"Greek fire."** When sprayed or thrown onto enemy ships, the liquid burst into flames, setting them on fire.

The East had always been the richest part of the Roman Empire. At the heart of this wealth lay Constantinople. This grand city was strategically located where Europe meets Asia. Constantinople looked over the Bosporus Strait. This allowed the Byzantines to control the sea trade routes between Asia and Europe.

Goods from as far away as Scandinavia and China came into Constantinople. Imperial tax policies raised huge government revenues. The government used this income to pay soldiers and government officials. The emperor also paid for large, magnificent public buildings with these taxes.

✔ **READING CHECK: Making Generalizations** What kind of government did the Byzantine Empire have? *strong, centralized government*

The Christian Church

The Christian church was an important part of life in the Byzantine Empire. However, church leaders in the West and East had different ideas about church practices. These differences led to a final division in the Christian church.

The pope was the most powerful leader of the Christian church in the West. The Byzantines, however, did not recognize the pope's authority. In the East the patriarch of Constantinople was the most powerful church leader.

Byzantines differed from the Western church on many issues. They also disagreed among themselves on issues of religious practice and belief within the Byzantine Church. One important debate concerned the role of icons. An **icon** is a holy picture of Jesus, the Virgin Mary, or the saints. Many Byzantines kept icons in their homes and venerated, or honored, them in churches. However, some Byzantines were iconoclasts. **Iconoclasts** believed that having icons in church was the same as worshipping idols. They felt this was wrong.

HISTORY MAKER

Empress Theodora (c. A.D. 500–A.D. 548)

Theodora influenced Justinian to improve the status of women in society. She worked to change many laws so as to protect women. She donated money to churches and orphanages. **How did Theodora try to improve the lives of women?**

ALL LEVELS: Ask students to name social improvements benefiting women that occurred during Justinian's reign. *(Women gained greater benefit from divorce laws and could own property.)* Ask students to keep in mind other empires they have studied while generating a short written response to the following statement: *Women were better off in Justinian's time than any previous time in history.* Remind students that their responses should include details and facts. After students have completed their responses, discuss their ideas as a class.
ENGLISH LANGUAGE LEARNERS

Spotlight on CITIZENSHIP

Have students write a short story, from the perspective of a woman, that incorporates one or more of the changes Justinian made to improve the status of women. Tell students they may conduct additional research or review Chapter 5, about the Greek city-states, or Chapter 7, about the Roman Empire, to find out more about the daily life of women before Justinian's reforms. **BLOCK SCHEDULING**

SKILL-BUILDING STRATEGIES   Identifying Bias

Views of Justinian and Theodora

Justinian and Theodora did many great things for the Byzantine Empire. Yet at times they could be harsh with their enemies. Their supporters viewed them as wise rulers protecting the empire. Their enemies viewed them as tyrants who forced their beliefs on others. Interpreting different aspects of rulers can be difficult for historians. In judging the usefulness of sources, historians must recognize the biases held by the author of the source. In the simplest sense, bias means the prejudice, or slanted viewpoint, a speaker or writer holds. Pre-existing biases often shape the ways observers describe historical events, causing them to leave out important facts or make statements without much supporting evidence. Historians themselves can even present a biased view of events.

Justinian (fifth from right) and his attendants

A Historian's View:
Procopius (pruh·кон·pee-uhs) was a Byzantine historian who lived during the reign of Justinian. In *The Secret History* he described the rule of Justinian and Theodora.

"... they were a pair of blood-thirsty demons.... For they plotted together to find the easiest and swiftest means of destroying all races of men and all their works ... [Justinian] would order tens of thousands of quite innocent persons to be put to death, cities to be razed to the ground, and all their possessions to be confiscated for the Treasury.... His ambition being to force everybody into one form of Christian belief he wantonly destroyed everyone who would not conform, and that while keeping up a pretense of piety. For he did not regard it as murder, so long as those who died did not happen to share his beliefs."

Theodora (third from right) and her attendants

That's Interesting!

After Justinian's death, the Muslims made inroads in the present-day Middle East and North Africa, and many of the people in these lands welcomed their conquerors as liberators. Some of these people shared religious beliefs more in common with those of Islam than with those of Orthodox Christianity. People in Egypt, Syria, and Palestine all found their new rulers a welcome change from the Byzantines.

SKILLS PRACTICE ANSWERS

1. He felt their rule was unjust and ruthless, as indicated by phrases such as "blood-thirsty demons," and "he wantonly destroyed everyone who would not conform."

2. He described him carrying out very ruthless acts.

3. He leaves out the positive things they accomplished, leading the reader to draw a very negative conclusion about their reign.

4. Students' answers will vary.

Skills Reminder

Bias in historical sources may be either positive or negative. In either case, bias results in distortions that may mislead observers who do not carefully evaluate the source. Bias may cause observers to draw inaccurate conclusions or to misunderstand descriptions and outcomes of historical events. To identify bias, look for clues. What words or phrases convey a positive or negative meaning? Look at the evidence. Decide whether you agree or disagree with the attitude, based on the evidence presented. Analyze what information has been left out by the author. Assess how this changes the conclusions that may be drawn based on the source's description or analysis.

Skills Practice

❶ How did Procopius feel about the rule of Justinian and Theodora? What words and phrases indicate this?

❷ How does Procopius's description of Justinian's behavior support the same outlook?

❸ What information about Justinian and Theodora does Procopius leave out? How might this change the conclusions the reader draws about their reign?

❹ Read an article from a newspaper, magazine, or the Internet about a recent event and try to identify the author's bias. If possible, read another source's coverage of the same event. Do both authors have a similar or different bias?

Technology Resources
World History Teaching Transparency: Everyday Life 9: The Role of the Byzantine Emperor

LEVEL 2: Have students create a time line extending from A.D. 1000 to A.D. 1500, labeled with events that contributed to the decline of the Byzantine Empire. Under each event, have students write a statement that explains its significance. (*Possible answers: early A.D. 1000s—Saljuq Turks capture most of Asia Minor. The loss of territory weakened the empire; A.D. 1096–A.D. 1099—Western European armies recaptured western Asia Minor for the Byzantines. This action restored and ensured the stability of Constantinople; A.D. 1204—Western Europeans captured Constantinople for themselves. The empire lost its most* important city; A.D. 1261—the Byzantines recaptured Constantinople. This action ensured the existence of the empire; A.D. 1453—Ottoman Turks captured Constantinople. The Byzantine Empire came to an end.)

HOMEWORK Remind students that most people in the Byzantine Empire could not read. Have students use computer software or other means to create visual images that would help nonreaders understand important aspects of the Byzantine Empire.

Culture

In A.D. 787 the Second Council of Nicaea, called by the Byzantine empress Irene, met in an attempt to resolve the issue of iconoclasm. The council decided that icons should be revered but not worshiped and that they could remain in churches. This council–attended mostly by Byzantine delegates, although some papal legates from Rome did attend–was the last council accepted by both the Roman Catholic Church and the Orthodox Church.

Critical Thinking

Ask students if they think this compromise was a good way to deal with the conflict over icons. Have them support their point of view.

ANSWER: Some students might suggest that the compromise seemed to address the concerns of both sides. Other students might argue that the compromise happened too late, seems to have been mostly a Byzantine decision, and failed to prevent the division of the churches.

Technology Resources
World History Teaching Transparency: Geography and History 9: Roman Catholicism and Orthodoxy

Major Disagreements Between the Roman Catholic and Eastern Orthodox Churches		
	Roman Catholic	**Eastern Orthodox**
Clergy	No married priests allowed	Married priests allowed
Icons	Veneration accepted	Veneration initially rejected, later accepted
Leadership	Roman pope was supreme church authority	Rejected supremacy of Roman pope over local leaders
Trinity	Accepted the view that the Holy Spirit combines both Father and Son	Maintained supremacy of the Father in the Trinity

This debate between the opponents and defenders of icons is called the **Iconoclastic Controversy.** In A.D. 726 Emperor Leo III, an iconoclast, ordered the destruction of icons. However, many people refused to give up their icons. In the West, church leaders also condemned the use of icons. Many people in western Europe, however, could not read or write. Icons portrayed images and symbols that helped them to learn about Christianity.

In A.D. 787 the pope in Rome called bishops together to discuss the Iconoclastic Controversy. This council decided that it was a heresy *not* to allow the veneration of icons. A **heresy** is an opinion that conflicts with official church beliefs. The council threatened iconoclasts with **excommunication.** An excommunicated person cannot be a member of the church anymore.

The council's decision caused friction between the pope in Rome and the patriarch in Constantinople. Finally the Christian church split into two churches in 1054. The church in the West became the Roman Catholic Church, with the pope at its head. In the East it became the Eastern Orthodox Church, with the patriarch of Constantinople as leader. The two churches are still separate today. Ironically, the Eastern Church eventually came to accept icons, and they are now recognized as an important part of Eastern Orthodox tradition.

✔ **READING CHECK: Drawing Inferences** How did the council of bishops in Rome feel about Byzantine views of Christianity?
that they were heretical

Byzantine Culture

While western Europe struggled to find a new way of life, Constantinople was the center of a great civilization. The Byzantine Empire provided a great service for cultures that followed it. Byzantine scholars produced many original works. In addition, they passed on to future generations the learnings of ancient Greece, Rome, and the East.

The Byzantine Empire also brought Mediterranean culture to lands beyond its borders. For example, the brothers **Cyril** (SIR·uhl) **and Methodius** (muh·THOH·dee·uhs) were Christian missionaries. They tried to teach the Bible to Slavs in central and eastern Europe. The Slavs had no written language, so Cyril and Methodius created an alphabet for them. This alphabet came to be known as Cyrillic (suh·RIL·ik). Many Slavic peoples today use Cyrillic or an alphabet derived from it.

The missionary brothers Cyril and Methodius present a scroll showing the Cyrillic alphabet.

LEVEL 3: Ask students what other systems of law had been developed by early civilizations. *(Babylonians and the Code of Hammurabi, Hittites, Greece and Draco's code of laws, and Solon's reforms)* Ask students in what way each of the four parts of the Justinian Code would have contributed to the overall system of laws in the Byzantine Empire. *(The* Code *reorganized Roman law; the* Digest *could be used when a law was not fully understood; the* Institutes *could be used for making new laws; the* Novellae *contained the updated laws.)* Close by asking students how we know that the Justinian Code was successful and efficient. *(It was the basis of many European legal systems.)*

Teacher to Teacher

Scott Whitlow of Round Rock, Texas, suggested the following activity: Have students research and write reports or create presentations on some aspect of Byzantine architecture, icons, art, or symbols. These studies should explain how these items reflect Byzantine history.

Link to Today Although the Hagia Sophia was built in the A.D. 500s as a Christian church, it was used after 1453 as an Islamic mosque. How does the Hagia Sophia today reflect the history of the Byzantine Empire?

The interior of the Hagia Sophia was dramatically illuminated with natural lighting.

Government

Over time Byzantine emperors eliminated paganism from the Byzantine Empire. Emperors closed pagan temples and dismantled pagan shrines.

Critical Thinking

Ask students why Byzantine emperors might have wanted to destroy paganism.

ANSWER: Students' responses will vary, but they might answer that the Byzantine emperors wanted to be more revered than the pagan gods.

LINK TO TODAY ANSWER

It reflects the Byzantines' Christian beliefs and the importance of religion in their art.

Technology Resources

 World History Teaching Transparency: Art and History 9: Sant' Apollinare in Classe, Apse Mosaic

Art. Religion was the main subject of Byzantine art. Murals and icons covered the walls, floors, and ceilings of churches. Floors, walls, and arches glowed with mosaics. A **mosaic** is a picture or design made from small pieces of enamel, glass, or stone. The location of an image indicated its importance. For example, an image of the Father was always found in the dome of the church. To modern eyes Byzantine art may appear stiff or artificial. Byzantine artists did not try to imitate reality. They tried to inspire adoration of the religious figures and help people look toward an afterlife.

Architecture. The Byzantines created great religious architecture. One of the world's great buildings is the church of **Hagia Sophia** (meaning "holy wisdom") in Constantinople. Justinian ordered the building of the Hagia Sophia in A.D. 532. The Hagia Sophia is a huge building, considered by many to be an architectural and engineering wonder. Justinian devoted a great deal of money and energy to its completion, one reason that it was completed in the amazingly short time of about six years.

A huge dome sits on top of the church. The dome is 180 feet high and 108 feet wide. Romans and other peoples had built domes before. However, Byzantine architects were the first to solve the problem of placing a round dome over a rectangular building. The Hagia Sophia was completed in A.D. 537. The Byzantine historian Procopius described what he saw when entering the church:

 History Makers Speak “The entire ceiling is covered with pure gold, which adds to its beauty. . . . who could tell of the beauty of the columns and marbles with which the church is adorned? One would think that one had come upon a meadow full of flowers in bloom. Whoever enters there to worship perceives at once that it is not by any human strength or skill, but by the favour of God that this work has been perfected; his mind rises sublime to commune with God, feeling that He cannot be far off. . . . ”

Procopius, *The Secret History,* translated by G. A. Williamson

Analyzing Primary Sources

Identifying a Point of View
According to Procopius, how would citizens feel upon entering the Hagia Sophia? *awed, closer to God*

✔ **READING CHECK: Supporting a Point of View** What evidence would you give to show that the Byzantines built upon previous cultures and contributed to future cultures? *retained and passed on Roman legal system, Greek and Roman scholarship*

CLOSE

Ask students to summarize the achievements of Justinian. Then have them explain why the Byzantine Empire was able to survive and prosper.

REVIEW

Have students complete the Section 1 Review on p. 228.

ASSESS

Have students complete Daily Quiz 10.1. As Alternative Assessment, you may want to use one of the chart exercises in this section's lessons.

RETEACH

Have students complete the Main Idea Activity for English Language Learners and Special-Needs Students 10.1. Then have them list the main ideas of each heading and subheading in the section.
ENGLISH LANGUAGE LEARNERS

EXTEND

Have interested students locate primary and secondary sources, such as computer software, to find out what kinds of goods and merchandise came through Constantinople. Then have students plan a creative way to share their findings with the class.
BLOCK SCHEDULING

SECTION 1 REVIEW ANSWERS

① Define
- dowry, p. 222
- icon, p. 224
- iconoclasts, p. 224
- heresy, p. 226
- excommunication, p. 226
- mosaic, p. 227

② Identify
- Justinian, p. 222
- Justinian Code, p. 222
- Theodora, p. 222
- Belisarius, p. 223
- "Greek fire," p. 224
- Iconoclastic Controversy, p. 226
- Cyril and Methodius, p. 226
- Hagia Sophia, p. 227
- Ottoman Turks, p. 228

③ Eastern: patriarch of Constantinople as leader, eventually accepted icons; Western: allowed icons, became Roman Catholic Church, pope as leader

④ a. The Byzantine Empire might never have reached such a great size.

b. It might have been weakened.

c. disagreement about church leader, Iconoclastic Controversy

d. became the basis of English civil law, which still exists

e. civil wars, conflicts with outside powers, Turkish capture of Asia Minor, Ottoman capture of Constantinople

⑤ Students' tables will vary.

Technology Resources
 Online Maps, Charts, and Graphs: Growth of the Byzantine Empire, 1050

The Decline of the Empire

After Justinian died in A.D. 565, the Byzantine Empire suffered from many wars and conflicts with outside powers. To the east there was war with the Persians. The Lombards, a Germanic tribe, settled in Italy. The Avars and Slavs invaded the Balkan Peninsula. The Muslim Empire conquered Syria, Palestine, and much of North Africa. By A.D. 650 the Byzantines had lost many lands.

During the A.D. 1000s the Seljuq Turks, a nomadic people from central Asia, captured much of Asia Minor. This region was an important source of food and soldiers for the empire. Next the Turks prepared to attack Constantinople. The Byzantine emperor asked the West to help defend Constantinople. From A.D. 1096 to A.D. 1099 a western European army seized and eventually returned western Asia Minor to the Byzantines. In A.D. 1204, however, Western forces turned against the Byzantine Empire and captured Constantinople.

In A.D. 1261 the Byzantines recaptured Constantinople. The Byzantine Empire lasted for almost 200 more years. However, it never regained its former strength. In the A.D. 1300s a rising Asian power, the **Ottoman Turks,** began to threaten Byzantine territory. By the mid-1300s the Ottomans had begun to move into the Balkans. In A.D. 1361 they took Adrianople, one of the empire's leading cities. With the Ottoman capture of Constantinople in A.D. 1453, the Byzantine Empire finally came to an end.

This painting by an Italian artist dramatizes the Ottoman Turks' conquest of Constantinople in 1453.

✔ **READING CHECK: Identifying Cause and Effect** Why was the Seljuq Turks' invasion of Asia Minor so harmful to the Byzantine Empire? Asia Minor was main source of food supply and soldiers

SECTION 1 REVIEW

1. **Define** and explain the significance:
   dowry
   icon
   iconoclasts
   heresy
   excommunication
   mosaic

2. **Identify** and explain the significance:
   Justinian
   Justinian Code
   Theodora
   Belisarius
   "Greek fire"
   Iconoclastic Controversy
   Cyril and Methodius
   Hagia Sophia
   Ottoman Turks

3. **Comparing and Contrasting** Copy the Venn diagram below. Use it to organize the similarities and differences between the Eastern and Western Christian churches.

Eastern Christian church   Western Christian church

4. **Finding the Main Idea**
   a. What might have happened if Justinian had not survived the Nika Revolt?
   b. How might the Byzantine military have been affected by a bad economy?
   c. What factors contributed to the division of the Christian church?
   d. How did Justinian's interest in Roman law affect European legal systems for years to come?
   e. What events and developments led to the gradual decline of the Byzantine Empire?

5. **Writing and Critical Thinking**
   Categorizing Develop a table in which you classify the advantages and disadvantages of having an all-powerful emperor and a strong, centralized government in the Byzantine Empire.
   Consider:
   • how the Byzantine Empire grew
   • the results of collecting large tax revenues
   • the role of the emperor and the government in the development of the empire's code of law
   • the actions of the emperor and the government to manage the empire and to ensure its security from outside attack

 Homework Practice Online
keyword: SP3 HP10

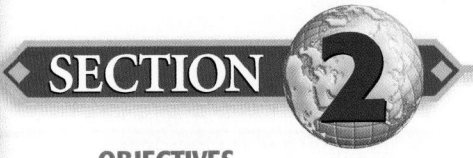

SECTION 2

OBJECTIVES

1 **Explain why different peoples settled in eastern Europe.**
2 **Describe how Kievan Russia differed from the Byzantine Empire.**

SECTION 2

READ TO DISCOVER

❶ Why did different peoples settle in eastern Europe?
❷ How did Kievan Russia differ from the Byzantine Empire?

DEFINE

steppe
boyars
taiga

IDENTIFY

Rurik
Rus
Yaroslav the Wise
Pravda Russkia
Vladimir I

▶ **WHY IT MATTERS TODAY**

The economy in Kievan Russia depended largely on agriculture. Use CNN.com or other **current event** sources to explore the Russian economy today. Record your findings in your journal.

The Rise of Russia

The Main Idea
Kievan Russia established many practices and traditions that defined Russian culture.

The Story Continues *The people who came to rule Russia were first mentioned in historical records in A.D. 860. In that year they launched a fierce surprise attack against the city of Constantinople. "The unexpectedness of the incursion [attack] and its extraordinary speed . . . ," recalled one Byzantine leader, "prove that this blow has been sent from heaven like a thunderbolt." Although the attack was unsuccessful, the Byzantines would not soon forget this fighting force.*

The Setting and People

A large plain stretches across eastern Europe and central Asia. It extends eastward from the Carpathian (kahr•PAY•thee•uhn) Mountains in Europe to the Ural (YOOR•uhl) Mountains at the western edge of Asia. In the south this plain is grassy and mostly treeless and is called the **steppe.** The steppe has black, fertile soil that is ideal for agriculture, particularly in the area that is now Ukraine.

The Ural Mountains run north and south at the eastern edge of the plain. These mountains are often considered the boundary between the continents of Europe and Asia. Europe and Asia actually form a huge landmass that is called Eurasia. Many rivers crisscross the plain and provide a network of transportation within the region. The Dniester, Dnieper, and Don Rivers are ideal for trade because they flow into the Black Sea and give access to the Mediterranean. Other major rivers, such as the Vistula, Neman, and Dvina, do not flow into the Black Sea and thus have somewhat less impact on trade. They provide important regional transportation links, however.

The southern part of eastern Europe has been inhabited since Neolithic times. Probably beginning during the very late 1500s B.C., several groups from this region invaded southwest Asia. These invasions took place over the course of centuries. After about the A.D. 400s, Slavs settled in much of eastern Europe. Other peoples, including the Avars, Huns, and Magyars, invaded the region at different times. These invaders frequently made the Slavs their subjects. From their servitude comes the word "slave."

During the A.D. 800s Vikings from Scandinavia drove into eastern Europe. Trade was the primary interest of the Vikings as they moved into the area.

INTERPRETING THE VISUAL RECORD

Viking ships Vikings from Scandinavia used longboats to conduct trade. *What design characteristics of this Viking longboat made it an excellent craft for navigating the shallow waters of coastal and inland rivers, as well as the open sea?*

SECTION 2 RESOURCES

REPRODUCIBLE RESOURCES

▶ Guided Reading Strategy 10.2
▶ Readings in World History 31: The *Pravda Russkaia*
▶ Hands-on History Activity 10: Food and Fashion in Byzantium and Early Russia

TECHNOLOGY RESOURCES

▶ One-Stop Planner 10.2
▶ Holt Researcher: World History: Rurik
▶ Homework Practice Online

REINFORCEMENT, REVIEW, AND ASSESSMENT

▶ Section 2 Review, p. 232
▶ Daily Quiz 10.2
▶ Main Idea Activity 10.2
▶ English Audio Summary 10.2
▶ Spanish Audio Summary 10.2

VISUAL RECORD ANSWER

The bottom of the boat kept it high on the surface of shallow water and the ends kept it from tipping over in the open sea.

TEACH OBJECTIVE 1

LEVEL 3: Have students look at the map on page 230. Ask them what is the most outstanding feature of Kievan Russia. *(Many Viking trade routes cut through the territory.)* Ask them what benefit this might have had for the people who lived in this region. *(It gave them access to other goods as well as an outlet for trading their own goods.)* Ask students why they think Kiev and not Novgorod became the most important city. *(Answers will vary, but students might suggest that because Kiev was closer to southern Europe and Asia Minor its inhabitants were more easily able to trade goods and learn about new ideas.)*

HOMEWORK Have students create an enlarged or three-dimensional version of the map on page 230. Then have students illustrate or decorate *(such as with spices or bits of silk)* their map to show the agricultural and trading activities that took place in Kievan Russia. Remind students that their maps should be relatively self-explanatory to viewers.

Economics

The corridor from the Baltic Sea to the Black Sea, inhabited by the Eastern Slavs, was an important trade route for furs, amber, wax, metal, slaves, and various foodstuffs. The trade route was an unsettled and often dangerous area. A Persian geographer once reported that one town along the trade route produced excellent swords, but "strangers are killed whenever they visit it."

Critical Thinking

Ask students what effect the danger of the routes might have had on trade.

ANSWER: Students might answer that the dangerous trade routes would have either prevented trade or raised the prices of goods from that area so that traders would be repaid for their risks.

MAP ANSWER

rivers

Technology Resources
Online Maps, Charts, and Graphs: Kiev as a Strategic City, 1000s

---

Holt Researcher

go.hrw.com
KEYWORD: Holt Researcher
FreeFind: Rurik
After reading more about Rurik on the Holt Researcher, create a travel log about the journeys of the Rus under Rurik, including why they chose to take over certain places.

The numerous large and small rivers of eastern Europe enabled them to build far-flung water-going trade routes.

✔ **READING CHECK: Categorizing** What groups of people lived in eastern and south-eastern Europe between the late 1500s B.C. and the A.D. 800s? Slavs, Avars, Huns, Magyars, and Vikings

Kievan Russia

Cities such as Novgorod and Kiev lay along the Viking trade routes. **Rurik,** the leader of a people called the **Rus,** took control of Novgorod in A.D. 862. Rurik and his successors soon came to rule over Kiev as well as over Slavic tribes along the Dnieper River. The region under their control came to be called the Rus. The word *Russia* probably comes from this name. Kiev prospered because of its location along the rich trade route between Constantinople and the Baltic Sea. Kiev became the most important principality in Kievan Russia and served as the capital for nearly 300 years after about A.D. 879. As early as A.D. 911, Kiev was powerful enough to win a favorable trade treaty with the Byzantine Empire. Other principalities paid tribute to Kiev. Some towns, however, remained more independent.

Kievan Russia, A.D. 879–A.D. 1240
Interpreting Maps A network of rivers crosses the plain between the Carpathian and Ural Mountains.
■ **Skills Assessment: Environment and Society** What common geographic feature did the Kievan trade routes follow?

TEACH OBJECTIVE 1

ALL LEVELS: Have students read the paragraphs under the "Religion" heading on page 231. Then have students create a cause-and-effect chart and fill it in with facts about Kievan Russia and Christianity. For example:

Cause	Effect
Religious themes dominated Kievan culture.	The majority of Kievan literature was written to serve religious purposes.

Ask students how Kievan Russia's religion differed from that of the Byzantine Empire. (*Kievan religion was both Christian and pagan.*) **ENGLISH LANGUAGE LEARNERS**

TEACH OBJECTIVE 2

LEVEL 1: Ask students to describe the Pravda Russkia. (*It was the legal code written by Yaroslav I. It combined elements of Slavic tribal customs with older laws and traditions and outlined lawful responses in cases of violence and other harmful activity.*) How was the Pravda Russkia similar to the Justinian Code? (*They both contained elements of older laws.*) How was it different? (*It also included elements of Slavic tribal customs.*) **ENGLISH LANGUAGE LEARNERS**

Government. Many areas in Kievan Russia were led by princes who governed with the advice of councils made up of **boyars,** or nobles. Another institution in Kievan Russia was the *veche,* or town meeting. When the prince requested it, all heads of households would meet in the public marketplace. They discussed important matters like wars, disputes between princes, or emergencies.

Yaroslav I ruled from A.D. 1019 to A.D. 1054, a great period in Russian history. He came to be known as **Yaroslav the Wise.** He built many churches and introduced Russia's first law code, the **Pravda Russkia** (the "Russian Justice"). Yaroslav's code seems to have combined elements of tribal customs and older laws and traditions. It outlined lawful responses in cases of violence and other harmful activity.

> *History Makers Speak*
>
> **❝If a man kills a man: the brother is to avenge his brother; the son, his father; or the father, his son. . . . If there is no avenger, [the murderer pays compensation of] 40 *grivna*. . . . If a slave runs away . . . and [if a freeman who conceals that slave] does not declare him for three days, and [the owner of the slave] discovers him on the third day, he [the owner] receives his slave back and 3 *grivna* for the offense . . . if a slave strikes a freeman and hides in [his master's] house, and his master is not willing to give him up, the master has to pay 12 *grivna*, and the offended freeman beats the slave whenever he finds him. . . .❞**

"The Pravda Russkia," from *Medieval Russian Laws,* translated by George Vernadsky

Religion. Traders and Greek missionaries brought Christianity to Kievan Russia in the A.D. 800s. However, little Christian activity took place until the mid-900s. In the A.D. 980s the ruler **Vladimir I** sent observers to Christian church services in several places. His officials were impressed with what they saw at the Hagia Sophia in Constantinople. They admired the services and rituals of Orthodox Christianity. Moreover, Vladimir wanted to marry Anna, the sister of the Byzantine emperor. In A.D. 988 he converted to Christianity. After converting he ordered all Kievans to become Christians. He also had all pagan statues destroyed.

Many Kievans still worshiped the spirits of their ancestors or gods of nature. However, the Byzantine church became a more and more important force in Kievan Russia. The patriarch in Constantinople chose the bishop of the Kievan church. Monasteries became centers of religious thought, social service, and the arts. This further strengthened the church. When the Christian church split in A.D. 1054, the Kievans followed the Eastern Orthodox Church.

Religious themes dominated Kievan culture during this period. Most writing focused on religion, in the form of hymns and sermons. Icon painting became the most distinctive Kievan art form. Artists also created mosaics and frescoes. Much of the decorative painting created by Kievan artists was designed to illustrate religious ideas and figures. The visual quality of these works was often powerful and stylized. Many Kievan mosaics, frescoes, and icons portrayed a deep and thoughtful spirituality. These art forms helped viewers to reflect on the meaning of religious ideas and values.

Economy. Kievan Russia included two major agricultural regions. North of the steppe lies the **taiga** (TY·guh). The taiga has great forests and receives much rainfall. However, winters are long and cold, and the growing season on the taiga is short. Therefore, everyone in a farm family worked long hours to grow and harvest crops. The steppe gets less rain than the taiga. However, the steppe has a milder climate and a longer growing season. People there had more time to plant and harvest crops.

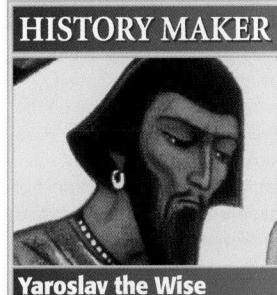

HISTORY MAKER

Yaroslav the Wise
(A.D. 980–A.D. 1054)

Yaroslav's Pravda Russkia was in use until the A.D. 1550s in some parts of Russia. Before his death he divided his kingdom among his sons with instructions on how to rule. They ignored these instructions and civil war soon broke out. **How did Yaroslav continue to affect Russia after his death?**

Then & Now

Town Meetings

All free men in Kievan Russia had the right to speak at the *veche*—a village or town meeting. Town meetings like these continue today. They have become popular in the United States, where they are used to address many issues. Citizens sometimes discuss safety concerns or hear ideas for improving neighborhoods. The U.S. government has organized town meetings to share information with communities. Presidential candidates often hold town meetings to allow voters to ask questions and state their opinions. **What situations might make a town decide to hold a meeting?**

That's Interesting!

Historians have never successfully determined the origin of the Slavs. One of the problems with tracing their ancestry is that the name Slav was not used until about A.D. 530; before that time the people who became known as the Slavs were most often referred to as the Venedi and the Antes.

HISTORY MAKER ANSWER

His Pravda Russkia was still in use well after his death.

THEN & NOW ANSWER

safety concerns; ideas for improving neighborhoods; share information; question political candidates

Technology **Resources**

Regions of the World Music Audio CD Program 9: Russia, Ukraine, and Belarus: Russian Choral Music

CLOSE

Have each student write a paragraph that describes the political, economic, and social life of Kievan Russia.

REVIEW

Have students complete the Section 2 Review on p. 232.

ASSESS

Have students complete Daily Quiz 10.2. As Alternative Assessment, you may want to use the map or chart exercises in this section's lessons.

RETEACH

Have students complete Main Idea Activity for English Language Learners and Special-Needs Students 10.2. Then ask them to use correct social studies terminology to write a question that covers the main idea for each subsection in the section.
ENGLISH LANGUAGE LEARNERS

EXTEND

Have interested students use computer software to acquire information and prepare a class report on the Pravda Russkia. Students might also report on its similarities to and differences from the Justinian Code. **BLOCK SCHEDULING**

VISUAL RECORD ANSWER

The rivers were very important to economic activity.

SECTION 2 REVIEW ANSWERS

1 Define
- steppe, p. 229
- boyars, p. 231
- taiga, p. 231

2 Identify
- Rurik, p. 230
- Rus, p. 230
- Yaroslav the Wise, p. 231
- Pravda Russkia, p. 231
- Vladimir I, p. 231

3 Students' charts should include the following from top to bottom: Political System–prince, council, *veches*; Social Classes–local princes and their families, boyars, artisans and merchants, peasants

4 a. The flat terrain allowed for invasion; the numerous rivers provided a network of transportation and enabled trade. The fertile soil was ideal for farming.

b. Kiev prospered and gained power because of its location along the rich trade route between Constantinople and the Baltic Sea.

c. They traded with each other.

5 Students' paragraphs will vary but should include how Vladimir's religion affected his policies and how the people reacted to these changes.

INTERPRETING THE VISUAL RECORD

Kievan trade This modern painting shows one Russian artist's idea of what trade on the rivers of Kievan Russia may have looked like. *Based on this image, what was the impact of geography on economic activity in Kievan Russia?*

Kievan Russia traded agricultural goods and other products with the Byzantines. These products included wood, iron, salt, furs, and honey. Kievan Russia also provided slaves for the Byzantines. In return, the Kievans received goods such as wine, silk, spices, and fruit. From western Europe they received jewelry, silver, and textiles. By the early A.D. 1000s, trade had helped Kievan Russia become a strong, wealthy power.

Several social classes emerged in Kievan Russia. At the top were the local princes and their families, followed by the boyars. Next were the town artisans and merchants, who devoted themselves to trade. The largest and lowest class, however, were the peasants. Peasants lived in small villages in the country and produced the crops that fed Kievan Russia. The clergy formed another important group. They were not directly involved in the government or economic activities. Some clergy, however, enjoyed considerable influence over daily life in Kievan Russia. Clergy performed religious ceremonies and ran hospitals and charities.

✔ **READING CHECK: Contrasting** How did Kievan Russia's government and religion differ from the Byzantine Empire's? Kievan government was based on Slavic custom and law, and followed the Orthodox Church.

SECTION 2 REVIEW

1. **Define** and explain the significance:
   steppe
   boyars
   taiga

2. **Identify** and explain the significance:
   Rurik
   Rus
   Yaroslav the Wise
   Pravda Russkia
   Vladimir I

3. **Summarizing** Copy the charts below. Use them to show the organization of the Kievan political system and the Kievan social classes.

   Kievan political system

   Kievan social classes

4. **Finding the Main Idea**

   a. What geographic features characterize the plain of eastern Europe and central Asia, and why did these features attract human settlement?

   b. What importance did geography have in the development of Kiev as a powerful city?

   c. How did Kievan Russia and the Byzantine Empire similarly increase their wealth?

5. **Writing and Critical Thinking**

   Identifying Cause and Effect Write a paragraph explaining how Vladimir I's conversion to Christianity affected Russia.

   Consider:
   - how his religion affected Vladimir's policies
   - how the people reacted to these changes

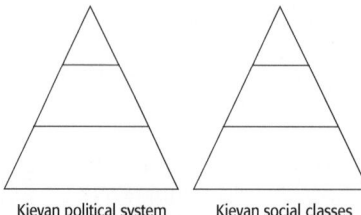
Homework Practice Online
keyword: SP3 HP10

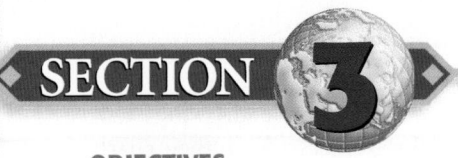
OBJECTIVES

1 Identify the ways in which Mongol rule affected Kievan Russia.

2 Describe the effects of Moscow's growing power and independence.

🔔 *LET'S GET STARTED!*

As students enter the classroom, ask them to write changes that occur in people's lives when outside invaders seize control of their region. *(Students might list changes such as a new form of government, a different dominant religion, and changes in the economic system.)* Tell students that in Section 3 they will learn about how Mongol rule affected Kievan Russia.

SECTION 3

READ TO DISCOVER

❶ In what ways did Mongol rule affect Kievan Russia?
❷ What were the effects of Moscow's growing power and independence?

DEFINE

czar
"third Rome"

IDENTIFY

Vladimir Monomakh
Polovtsy
Ivan III
Ivan the Terrible

▶WHY IT MATTERS TODAY

Eastern Europe has suffered from civil wars and internal conflicts for many years. Use CNN or other **current event** sources to explore a current conflict or political unrest in an Eastern European country. Record your findings in your journal.

CNN Student News.com

Russia and the Mongols

The Main Idea
Under Mongol rule the power of Kiev weakened while Moscow became stronger.

The Story Continues *When Yaroslav the Wise's rule ended in A.D. 1054, Kiev declined in power. During the first quarter of the A.D. 1100s, however, the city enjoyed a brief revival under the leadership of **Vladimir Monomakh**, who ruled from A.D. 1113 to A.D. 1125. In protecting the Kievan state, Vladimir was merciless against his enemies. As a result, Kiev was often at war during his reign.*

Attacks on Kiev

Kiev had declined because Kievan rulers gave the outlying towns to their sons to rule independently. Eventually these princes fought among themselves—and with Kiev itself—to expand their territory. At the same time the **Polovtsy** interfered with Kiev's trade. The Polovtsy were a Turkish people who after A.D. 1055 controlled the area south of Kiev. Vladimir Monomakh made his reputation by leading military campaigns against the Polovtsy. At one point he ordered the deaths of some 200 of their princes. Kievan trade may also have suffered from competition with Italian city-states that had developed new trade routes.

In A.D. 1169 and A.D. 1203, groups of princes sacked Kiev, ruining the city's prosperity. New invaders, the Mongols, took advantage of Kiev's weakness. The Mongols came from the Asian steppe east of the Ural Mountains. By A.D. 1240 they had conquered or destroyed almost every city in Kievan Russia. The Mongols continued across the Carpathian Mountains into Hungary and Poland. In A.D. 1242 they defeated the Hungarian and Polish armies. However, the Mongol leader Batu called off his attack to return to Russia. He wanted to influence the choice of the next Mongol leader. Thus Hungary and Poland escaped long-term Mongol rule.

Kievan Russia under the Mongols. Mongols controlled Kievan Russia until the late A.D. 1400s. This long Mongol presence had a strong influence on the Slavic way of life. The Mongols sought to gain wealth from the region. They taxed the people heavily. As long as the Slavs paid, they could keep their own government and customs. Russian peasants in the conquered lands probably paid taxes in several ways. They may have paid in money or in goods, or they may have paid their Mongol overlords with labor.

Although the Mongols formed only a small ruling class, they influenced Slavic society in several ways. They built important roads and improved methods of taxation and communication. Some Mongol words entered the language that came to be called Russian, as did some Mongol customs, traditions, and patterns of behavior.

Skilled cavalry archers like the warrior pictured here helped the Mongols seize Kievan Russia.

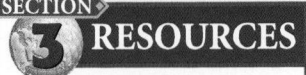
SECTION 3 RESOURCES

REPRODUCIBLE RESOURCES

▶ Guided Reading Strategy 10.3
▶ Readings in World History 32: Ivan the Terrible's Punishment of Novgorod
▶ Creative Teaching Strategy 10: Barbarian Information Agency

TECHNOLOGY RESOURCES

▶ One-Stop Planner 10.3
▶ Homework Practice Online
▶ Online Maps, Charts, and Graphs: Russian Expansion, 1533

REINFORCEMENT, REVIEW, AND ASSESSMENT

▶ Section 3 Review, p. 235
▶ Daily Quiz 10.3
▶ Main Idea Activity 10.3
▶ English Audio Summary 10.3
▶ Spanish Audio Summary 10.3

TEACH OBJECTIVE 1

ALL LEVELS: Ask students how the Mongols influenced Russian culture. (*Mongols' words became part of the Russian language; Mongols built roads and improved methods of taxation and communication.*) Then ask how these influences make sense in terms of the Mongols' goal in Russia. (*Mongols would want to have good roads, communication, and systems of taxation to ensure that the Russians delivered taxes to the Mongols.*)

TEACH OBJECTIVE 2

LEVEL 1: Have students create a chart with the following headings: *Ivan I, Ivan III, Ivan IV.* Tell students to fill in their charts with characteristics and accomplishments of each leader. After students have completed their charts, have them discuss who was the best ruler. **ENGLISH LANGUAGE LEARNERS**

HOMEWORK Have students use at least one primary or secondary source, such as computer software, to write a short report about one of the early rulers of Moscow.

Some historians have estimated that the Mongol domination of Kievan Russia slowed the development of that region by some 150 to 200 years. Records from the period show a decline from the Kievan style of life and high cultural standards. Although the Mongol invasion left Kiev in ruins, some cities, such as Moscow and Tver, grew and prospered.

**HISTORY MAKER
ANSWER**
He was ruthless, yet Russia prospered under his rule.

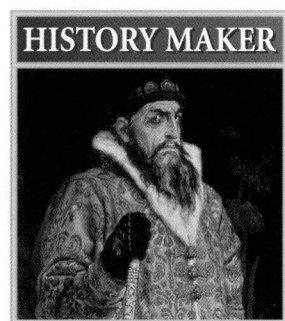

HISTORY MAKER

Ivan the Terrible
(A.D. 1530–A.D. 1584)

Ivan IV had a violent and unpredictable temper. Some people trace his violent nature to tragedies in his life. When he was very young, for example, Ivan's mother was murdered by nobles. As a ruler, he gained a reputation for cruelty toward his enemies.

Following the death of his wife in A.D. 1560, Ivan felt deep despair and became more ruthless than ever. Accusing the boyars of murdering his wife, Ivan ordered the execution of many nobles. Despite his violent behavior, Russia prospered under Ivan. In Russian, his nickname means "awe-inspiring." **How can Ivan IV's nickname be interpreted in different ways?**

Kievan Russia and its neighbors. During Mongol rule the Slavs of eastern Europe had some contact with central and western Europe. In the A.D. 1300s Lithuania and Poland took territory away from Kievan Russia. They formed a kingdom that was hostile to the eastern Slavs. There were also religious conflicts. The Poles had been converted to western Christianity, while the Slavs kept their Eastern Orthodox faith. This set the Slavs apart from both the Poles and the Mongols. To some degree, moreover, the Slavs became suspicious of western Europeans and their influence. Even today, this suspicion has not completely disappeared.

✔ **READING CHECK: Summarizing** How did society in Kievan Russia change under Mongol rule? transportation and communication improved; Mongol words entered language

The Rise of Moscow

In time Mongol rule grew weaker. The princes of the region became more independent. During the early A.D. 1300s Moscow, or Muscovy, became a major Russian principality. Moscow's leader, Prince Ivan I, achieved this by cooperating with the Mongols. In return the Mongols awarded him with the title of Great Prince in A.D. 1328. Around the same time, the leader of the Orthodox Church moved to Moscow. This increased the city's power even more.

From A.D. 1462 to A.D. 1505 **Ivan III,** also called Ivan the Great, ruled as Great Prince. By this time Moscow had begun to assert its independence from the Mongols. By A.D. 1480 Ivan III no longer acknowledged the Mongol khan as Moscow's supreme ruler. He united many principalities. Ivan III became the first ruler of the independent state called Russia. He gained more territory through military conquest. His rule began a long tradition of absolute monarchy in Russia.

Ivan the Terrible. In A.D. 1533 the three-year-old Ivan IV became ruler of Russia. Because of his youth, for many years the boyars were actually in control. In A.D. 1547 Ivan IV finally took power for himself. He considered himself to be the true heir of the Roman and Byzantine Empires. Thus he took the title of **czar,** or caesar. Ivan was an able administrator who sponsored the development of a modernized legal code. He renewed trade with western Europe and opened the vast territory of Siberia to Russian settlement. During his reign, Ivan built the power and authority of the Russian monarchy.

Ivan formed a personal group of civil servants called the *oprichniki* (aw·PREECH·nee·kee). The *oprichniki* arrested boyars and gave their land to Ivan's supporters. He also led his army in an attack on Novgorod, destroying the city. Sometimes Ivan's actions were puzzling and cruel. In A.D. 1581 he even murdered his oldest son. These acts earned him the nickname **Ivan the Terrible.** However, Ivan did lay the foundations for a new Russian state. This state included old Kievan Russia and stretched from Siberia to the Caspian Sea. The czar had absolute power.

The growth of the church. The Orthodox Church in Russia grew more powerful by acquiring land. Much land was acquired by the church through donations from the faithful. By about A.D. 1500 the church was a major Russian landowner.

During Mongol rule, the Russian Orthodox Church had become more and more independent of Constantinople. In A.D. 1448 Russian bishops chose their own leader for the Orthodox Church in Moscow. In A.D. 1589 Moscow's church leader was named patriarch. This helped to make Moscow the center of the Russian church.

CLOSE

Ask students to imagine they are teenagers living in Kievan Russia under Mongol rule. Have students write a short journal entry that describes their daily lives.

REVIEW

Have students complete the Section 3 Review on p. 235.

ASSESS

Have students complete Daily Quiz 10.3. As Alternative Assessment, you may want to use the chart exercise in this section's lessons.

RETEACH

Have students complete Main Idea Activity for English Language Learners and Special-Needs Students 10.3. Then have them write three statements about each subsection.
ENGLISH LANGUAGE LEARNERS, COOPERATIVE LEARNING

EXTEND

Have students study illustrations or slides of Russian art of the period to look for examples of Byzantine influence. Students should make a chart of elements that are common to both artistic traditions. **BLOCK SCHEDULING, COOPERATIVE LEARNING**

A turning point in the development of the Russian church took place in A.D. 1453 with the fall of Constantinople to the powerful army of the Ottoman sultan, Mehmed II. The Turks' victory over the proud and ancient city of the Byzantine emperors removed a major source of competition for church leadership in the Orthodox Christian world.

With the fall of once-mighty Constantinople, Russians proclaimed Moscow to be the **"third Rome."** A Russian churchman explained this phrase by stating that the first Rome had fallen because of heresy. The second Rome, Constantinople, had been conquered by non-Christians. The churchman then claimed that Moscow—the third Rome—would bring the spiritual light of Christian orthodoxy to the whole world.

The new sense of Russian confidence reflected in the churchman's statements is seen in the art and architecture of this period. Domed churches were built and filled with beautiful artwork. Sparkling chandeliers and candles lit every space. These churches were meant to inspire awe, religious wonder, and a mystical feeling of spirituality among the people who worshiped there.

✔ **READING CHECK: Analyzing Information** In what ways did the Russian Orthodox Church gain from Moscow's growing power? prospered financially, became politically independent of Constantinople

INTERPRETING THE VISUAL RECORD

St. Basil In keeping with the Russian Orthodox Church's growth in power, magnificent new churches were built. This photo shows the Cathedral of St. Basil the Blessed, built in Moscow between A.D. 1554 and A.D. 1560. *How does this church reflect a new Russian sense of power and confidence?*

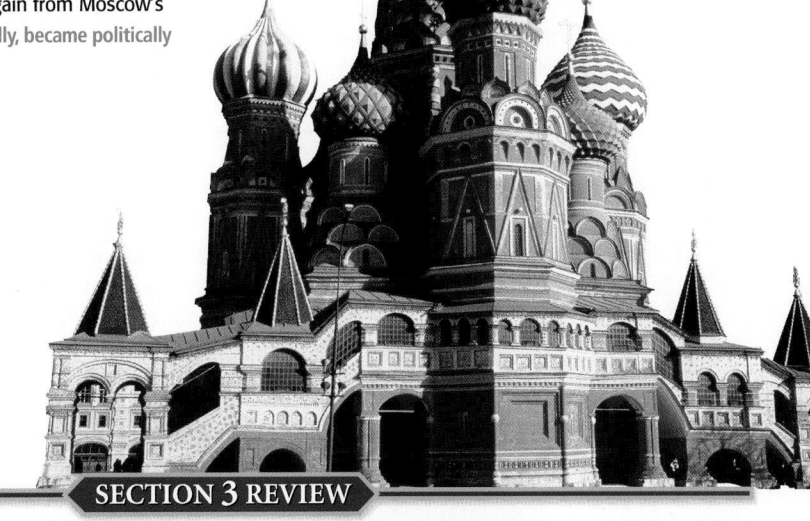

SECTION 3 REVIEW

1. **Define** and explain the significance:
   czar
   "third Rome"

2. **Identify** and explain the significance:
   Vladimir Monomakh
   Polovtsy
   Ivan III
   Ivan the Terrible

3. **Identifying Cause and Effect**
   Copy the chart below. Use it to organize the forces acting between A.D. 1054 and A.D. 1203 that caused the downfall of Kievan Russia.

4. **Finding the Main Idea**
   a. How did the distribution of land among Kievan princes help the Mongols to invade?
   b. How was Ivan IV's use of absolute rule different than Ivan III's?

5. **Writing and Critical Thinking**
   Contrasting Create a dialogue between a peasant and a prince discussing the differences in their lives and their ancestors' lives under the Mongols and Kievan Russia.
   Consider:
   • what life may have been like for a peasant during both eras
   • what life may have been like for landowners during both eras

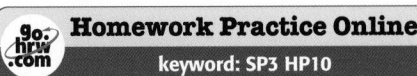
Homework Practice Online
keyword: SP3 HP10

VISUAL RECORD ANSWER
The church is very grand.

🖥 **internet** connect
TOPIC: Byzantine Art
GO TO: go.hrw.com
KEYWORD: SP3 WH10
Have students access the Internet through the HRW Go site to conduct research on Byzantine Art. Then ask them to create a piece of art or design a building or church in Byzantine style. Have students display their creation to the class.

SECTION
3 REVIEW ANSWERS

❶ **Define**
• czar, p. 234
• "third Rome," p. 235

❷ **Identify**
• Vladimir Monomakh, p. 233
• Polovtsy, p. 233
• Ivan III, p. 234
• Ivan the Terrible, p. 234

❸ Students' charts should include civil war; invasion by Polovtsians; Mongol invasion

❹ a. Towns were weakened when Kievan princes began to fight among themselves.

b. He was cruel and ruthless.

❺ Students' dialogues will vary but should consider the relationship between peasants and landowners, especially regarding taxation.

THE BYZANTINE EMPIRE AND RUSSIA **235**

REVIEW AND ASSESSMENT RESOURCES

REPRODUCIBLE RESOURCES
▸ Vocabulary Activity 10

TECHNOLOGY RESOURCES
▸ Chapter 10 Test Generator (on the One-Stop Planner)
▸ Global Skill Builder CD-ROM
▸ HRW Web Site

REINFORCEMENT, REVIEW, and ASSESSMENT
▸ Chapter 10 Review, pp. 236–237
▸ Chapter 10 Tutorial for Students, Parents, Mentors, and Peers
▸ Chapter 10 Test (Form A or B)
▸ Alternative Assessment Handbook
▸ Chapter 10 Test for English Language Learners and Special-Needs Students

REVIEW
Have students complete the Chapter 10 Review on pages 236–237.

ASSESS
Use one of the chapter tests to assess students' understanding of the content. For Alternative Assessment, see the Portfolio Activities and Alternative Assessment Handbook.

CHAPTER 10 REVIEW ANSWERS

Understanding Main Ideas

1. It provided the basis for many European legal systems and for English civil law.

2. strong centralized government and strong military

3. The Christian church split into two churches, the Eastern and Western.

4. passed on learnings of ancient Greece, Rome, and the East; Cyrillic alphabet; murals; icons; mosaics; Hagia Sophia

5. civil wars, conflicts with outside powers, Turkish capture of Asia Minor, Ottoman capture of Constantinople

6. They benefited from Viking trade.

7. Individual households had the least power, while princes had the most power.

8. taxes

9. Ivan I, Ivan III, Ivan the Terrible

10. They believed Moscow would bring spiritual light to the whole world.

Reviewing Themes

1. Yes, they participated in town meetings.

2. It allowed them both to engage in profitable trade.

3. Byzantine Empire, because of its strong central government; Mongol princes became independent, weaker.

236

CHAPTER 10

Creating a Time Line

Copy the time line below onto a sheet of paper. Complete the time line by filling in the events, individuals, and dates from the chapter that you think were significant. Pick three events and explain why you think they were significant.

| A.D. 527 | 1019 | 1480 |

Writing a Summary

Using standard grammar, spelling, sentence structure, and punctuation, write an overview of the events in the chapter.

Identifying People and Ideas

Identify the following terms or individuals and explain their significance:

1. Justinian
2. Iconoclastic Controversy
3. excommunication
4. Hagia Sophia
5. Rurik
6. Pravda Russkia
7. Polovtsy
8. Ivan the Terrible
9. czar
10. "third Rome"

Understanding Main Ideas

Section 1 *(pp. 222–228)*
The Byzantine Empire
1. Why was Justinian's Code important?
2. How was the Byzantine Empire able to last for 1,000 years?
3. What was the result of the Iconoclastic Controversy?
4. What are some cultural highlights of the Byzantine Empire?
5. What led to the decline of the Byzantine Empire?

Section 2 *(pp. 229–232)*
The Rise of Russia
6. How did Slavs benefit from the Vikings' travels in the southern part of eastern Europe?
7. Who had the least and most power in Kievan Russia?

Section 3 *(pp. 233–235)*
Russia and the Mongols
8. What demands did the Mongols make on the Kievan Russians?
9. Which rulers helped the rise of Moscow?
10. Why did the Russian Orthodox Church call Moscow the "third Rome"?

Reviewing Themes

1. **Government** Did Kievan Russia have a form of government in which citizens had a voice? Explain.
2. **Geography** What effects did access to bodies of water have on the Byzantine Empire and Kievan Russia?
3. **Global Relations** Which lasted longer, Mongol rule in Russia or the Byzantine Empire? How did the way in which these two powers ruled make a difference?

Thinking Critically

1. **Comparing** What similar factors contributed to the wealth of the Byzantine Empire and Kievan Russia?
2. **Analyzing Information** The Mongols in Russia were concerned with increasing their wealth through collecting taxes. Why did they bother improving the roads?
3. **Making Predictions** What might have happened to Kievan Russia if the Mongols had not invaded?

Writing About History

Making Predictions Write a newspaper editorial about the struggle for power following Yaroslav's death. Using the chart below, make a list of what might happen if the land is divided among the princes. Incorporate the list into an editorial. Discuss what might happen to the council of boyars, *veches*, and Russia's trade business.

If the land is divided up . . .
1.
2.
3.
4.

CLOSE

Have students draw a time line covering the time period from A.D. 300 to A.D. 1500 and add events from this chapter.

RETEACH

Have students who had difficulty with the test outline the chapter and compile a chapter glossary. When they are ready, have students take the Form B Test to assess their mastery of the material.

Portfolio Extensions

Link to TODAY

1. Have students locate primary and secondary sources, such as computer software, about the Byzantine Empire and Kievan Russia to prepare a written report about the development of trade.
2. Using pictures in encyclopedias as models, have students draw a building plan of the church of Hagia Sophia. Discuss how this building demonstrates an artistic ideal from Byzantine culture.
3. Have students imagine that they are traders in the Byzantine Empire or Kievan Russia. Have them write journal entries describing their experiences.

Building Social Studies Skills

Building and Using Chronology

Order the statements below in their correct chronological sequence. Then use the information to answer the questions that follow.

Selected Events in the History of Kievan Russia, c. A.D. 500–A.D. 1300

1. Kiev becomes the capital of Kievan Russia, c. A.D. **882.**
2. Beginning of Kievan economic and political decline, c. A.D. **1170.**
3. Kiev is destroyed by Mongols under Batu Khan, A.D. **1240.**
4. Christianity is introduced to Kiev, c. A.D. **988.**
5. Kiev is incorporated into the Kingdom of Poland, A.D. **1569.**
6. Kiev is founded, c. A.D. **550.**

1. Which of the following best represents the actual chronological order of events shown above?
   a. 1, 6, 4, 5, 2, 3
   b. 6, 1, 4, 2, 3, 5
   c. 5, 6, 1, 3, 4, 2
   d. 6, 1, 4, 2, 5, 3

2. According to the chronology you have constructed, why might the Mongols have found Kiev a relatively easy target for destruction?

Identifying a Point of View

Read the following quote. It is from the preface to the book of laws compiled by the Byzantine emperor Justinian. Then answer the questions.

> "The maintenance of . . . government depends upon two things, namely, the force of arms and the observance of the laws: and, for this reason, the fortunate race of the Romans obtained power and precedence over all other nations in former times, and will do so forever, if God should be propitious [kind] . . ."

3. Which of the following statements best describes Justinian's point of view?
   a. The Romans will continue to have power over other nations for all time.
   b. A government succeeds only if it has a strong military to maintain order.
   c. The Romans succeeded because they enforced their laws and had a strong military.
   d. Laws must be obeyed for a government to gain power.

4. An individual's background and experience often influence that person's point of view. What personal experiences might have influenced Justinian's point of view? Give specific examples.

Alternative Assessment

Building Your Portfolio

Link to TODAY

Geography

Trace a physical map of Eurasia. Locate and highlight the rivers, straits, seas, and oceans that contributed to the growth of the Byzantine Empire and Kievan Russia. You may also want to include what goods were being traded and where. Identify cities, such as Constantinople and Kiev, as well as dates when trade was occurring in these cities. Create a key to help others interpret your map.

✔ internet connect

Internet Activity: go.hrw.com
KEYWORD: SP3 WH10

Choose a topic on the Byzantine Empire and Russia to:
• summarize the global influence of the Roman ideas in the Justinian Code upon contemporary political issues such as individual rights and responsibilities.
• research Ivan IV and find out why he was called "Ivan the Terrible."
• create a piece of art or design a building or church in the Byzantine style.

Thinking Critically

1. their location along waterways and ability to engage in profitable trade

2. Better transportation would have ensured that the Russian taxes were paid and delivered to the Mongols.

3. Moscow might not have gained strength and the Russian Orthodox Church might not have become independent of Constantinople.

Writing About History

Students' editorials will vary, but lists might include: the council of boyars would be disassembled; the *veches* would end; and trade would suffer.

Building Social Studies Skills

1. b

2. Kiev was in a period of economic and political decline.

3. c

4. Justinian was successful in reviving the glory and power of the Roman Empire by using Roman laws as the basis for the Justinian Code.

Building Your Portfolio

Students should locate and trace the Black Sea, Baltic Sea, Mediterranean Sea, Bosporus, Nile River, and Volga River. Remind them to identify cities and the goods that were traded.

The Islamic World

CHAPTER RESOURCE MANAGER

Objectives	Pacing Guide	Reproducible Resources
SECTION 1 **The Rise of Islam** (pp. 240–242)	• Describe how geography affected the people of the Arabian Peninsula. • Explain how Islam began. • Identify the main beliefs of Islam.	**Regular** 1 day **Block Scheduling** .5 day *Block Scheduling Handbook with Team Teaching Strategies, 11.1*	**RS** Guided Reading Strategy 11.1 **E** Hands-on History Activity 11: Muhammad's World
SECTION 2 **The Spread of Islam** (pp. 243–247)	• Explore how the Muslims expanded their empire. • Explain why the Islamic community divided.	**Regular** 1.5 day **Block Scheduling** 1 day *Block Scheduling Handbook with Team Teaching Strategies, 11.2*	**RS** Guided Reading Strategy 11.2 **SM** Geography Activity 11: The Spread of Islam **PS** Readings in World History 33: The Muslim Conquest of Spain
SECTION 3 **Islamic Civilization** (pp. 248–253)	• Describe how the location of Arabia affected trade in the Muslim Empire. • Explain what Muslim society and family life were like. • Identify Muslim achievements in science. • Explore how Islam influenced Arab art and literature.	**Regular** 1.5 day **Block Scheduling** 1 day *Block Scheduling Handbook with Team Teaching Strategies, 11.3*	**RS** Guided Reading Strategy 11.3 **RS** Graphic Organizer Activity 11: Science and Islam **PS** Readings in World History 34, 35: Muslim Towns and Trade in North Africa; Social Classes in Muslim India **E** Creative Teaching Strategy 11: The Islamic Heritage Museum

Chapter Resource Key

PS Primary Sources
RS Reading Support
IC Interdisciplinary Connections
E Enrichment
SM Skills Mastery

A Assessment
REV Review
ELL Reinforcement and English Language Learners
 Transparencies
 CD-ROM

 Music
 Video
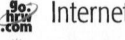 Internet
Holt Presentation Maker Using Microsoft® PowerPoint®

One-Stop Planner CD-ROM

See the ***One-Stop Planner*** for a complete list of additional resources for students and teachers.

One-Stop Planner CD-ROM

It's easy to plan lessons, select resources, and print out materials for your students when you use the *One-Stop Planner* CD–ROM with *Test Generator.*

Technology Resources	Reinforcement, Review, and Assessment
One-Stop Planner 11.1	Daily Quiz 11.1
Holt Researcher: World History: Muhammad	Main Idea Activity 11.1
World History and Cultures Video Program 10: At the Crossroads	English Audio Summary 11.1
Regions of the World Music Audio CD Program 11: The Persian Gulf and Interior: Classical	Spanish Audio Summary 11.1
CNN Presents World Cultures: Yesterday and Today Segment 9: Pilgrimage to Mecca	REV Section 1 Review, p. 242
Homework Practice Online	
One-Stop Planner 11.2	Daily Quiz 11.2
World History and Cultures Video Program 10: At the Crossroads	Main Idea Activity 11.2
World History Teaching Transparency: Geography and History 10: Islam in Spain	English Audio Summary 11.2
Religions of the World Video Series: Islam	Spanish Audio Summary 11.2
Homework Practice Online	REV Section 2 Review, p. 247
Online Maps, Charts, and Graphs: Muslim Lands in the 1100s	
One-Stop Planner 11.3	Daily Quiz 11.3
Holt Researcher: World History: Scheherazade	Main Idea Activity 11.3
World History Teaching Transparency: Art and History 10: Stoneware Bowl	English Audio Summary 11.3
Religions of the World Video Series: Islam	Spanish Audio Summary 11.3
Homework Practice Online	REV Section 3 Review, p. 253
Online Maps, Charts, and Graphs: Muslim Trade Routes	

internet connect

HRW ONLINE RESOURCES

GO TO: go.hrw.com
Then type in a keyword.

TEACHER HOME PAGE
KEYWORD: SP3 TEACHER

CHAPTER INTERNET ACTIVITIES
KEYWORD: SP3 WH11
Choose an activity to:
- research Muslim contributions to medicine and science.
- research and report on Islamic culture.
- create a chart of Islamic calligraphy designs.

CHAPTER ENRICHMENT LINKS
KEYWORD: SP3 CH11

ONLINE ASSESSMENT
Homework Practice
KEYWORD: SP3 HP11
Standardized Test Prep
KEYWORD: SP3 STP11
Rubrics
KEYWORD: SS Rubrics

ONLINE MAPS, CHARTS, AND GRAPHS
KEYWORD: SP3 MCG

CONTENT UPDATES
KEYWORD: SS Content Updates

HOLT PRESENTATION MAKER
KEYWORD: SP3 PPT11

ONLINE READING SUPPORT
KEYWORD: SS Strategies

CURRENT EVENTS
KEYWORD: S3 Current Events

Meeting Individual Needs

Ability Levels

Level 1 Basic level activities designed for all students encountering new material

Level 2 Intermediate level activities designed for average students

Level 3 Challenging activities designed for honors and gifted and talented students

English Language Learners These activities address the needs of students with Limited English Proficiency.

Chapter Review and Assessment

IC	Vocabulary Activity 11	A	Chapter 11 Test Generator (on the One-Stop Planner)
	Global Skill Builder CD–ROM	A	Chapter 11 Test (Form A or B)
	HRW Web Site	A	Alternative Assessment Handbook
REV	Chapter 11 Tutorial for Students, Parents, Mentors, and Peers	A	Chapter 11 Test for English Language Learners and Special-Needs Students
REV	Chapter 11 Review, pp. 254–255		

Build on What You Know

Ask students to answer the following questions:

What are some ways religion is spread?

Consider:

- **Buddhism**
- **Christianity**

What were some contributions made by the Byzantine Empire?

Consider:

- **the Justinian Code**
- **changes in the Christian church**
- **art and architecture**

EXPLORING THE TIME LINE
GLOBAL EVENTS

internet connect

TOPIC: Córdoba
GO TO: go.hrw.com
KEYWORD: SP3 WH11

Have students access the Internet through the HRW Go site to conduct research on present-day and 11th century Córdoba. Then have students create a travel brochure encouraging people to visit present-day Córdoba. The brochure should include a historical section that talks about when this city became the capital of the Moorish kingdom of Al-Andalus and why it was so important.

CHAPTER 11

A.D. 570–A.D. 1250
The Islamic World

A page from the Qur'an

A.D. 622
Daily Life
The hijrah occurs.

A.D. 632
Politics
Abū Bakr becomes the first Muslim caliph.

C. A.D. 661
Politics
The Islamic split between the Sunni and the Shi'ah doctrines occurs.

A.D. 711
Business and Finance
The Moors bring rice, saffron, and sugar to Spain.

A.D. 732
Global Events
The Franks defeat the Moors at the Battle of Tours.

A.D. 785
The Arts
The Moors begin to build the Mosque of Córdoba.

A.D. 810
Science and Technology
Al-Khwārizmī first uses the term *al-jabr*, which we call algebra.

Bowl of saffron spice

A.D. 550   **A.D. 650**   **A.D. 750**   **A.D. 850**

C. A.D. 570
Daily Life
Muhammad is born.

C. A.D. 642
The Arts
Muslims begin to build the Amr Mosque in Cairo.

C. A.D. 635
Business and Finance
Arabs establish the major trading center of Basra on the Persian Gulf.

A.D. 711
Politics
Tāriq leads an expedition to Spain.

C. A.D. 691
The Arts
Muslims complete the Dome of the Rock in Jerusalem.

C. A.D. 793
Business and Finance
The city of Baghdad establishes a paper mill.

The Dome of the Rock mosque in Jerusalem

Build on What You Know

By the end of the A.D. 400s, the Western Roman Empire had collapsed. In the eastern part of the empire, however, the Byzantine culture kept Roman government and traditions alive. The Byzantines also passed on for future generations much learning and scholarship from Greek and Roman antiquity. However, during this time another vast empire with its own thriving economy based on trade was developing to the south and east of the Byzantines. In this chapter, you will learn about a new religion that inspired this empire and encouraged its growth, leading to new advances in the arts and sciences.

What's Your Opinion?

Themes Journal — *To help students create their Themes Journal entries, provide the following examples of appropriate* **agree**/**disagree** *statements.*

Science, Technology & Society

Agree Scientists can achieve great advances when they build on the knowledge of other cultures.

Disagree Scientific achievements are likely to occur in a culturally isolated society.

Global Relations

Agree When one nation conquers another, both can engage in a mutually beneficial exchange of knowledge.

Disagree The ideas of a conquered people are not likely to blend well with the ideas of their conquerors.

Culture

Agree Religious beliefs have no influence on a society's government, art, or science.

Disagree A society's religion and culture are heavily dependent upon one another.

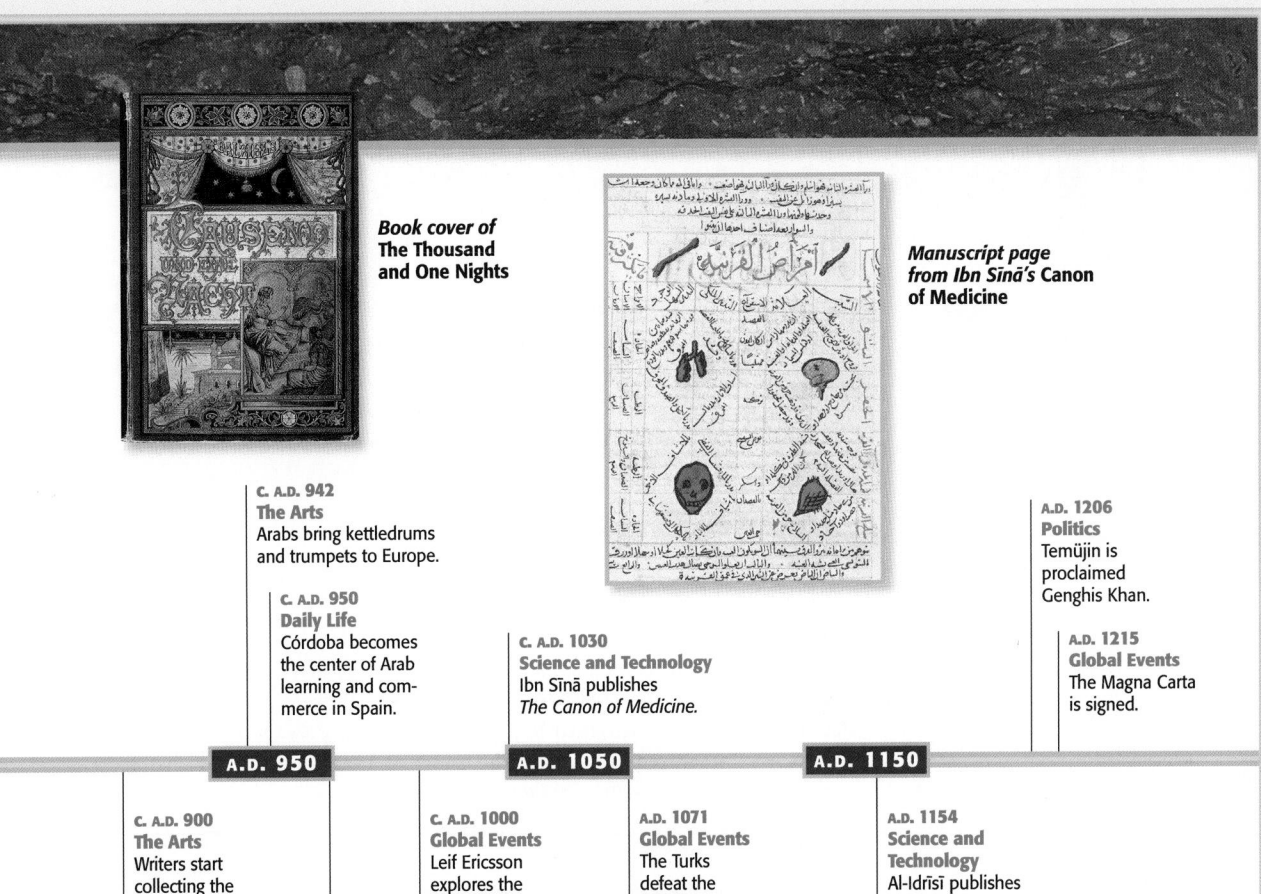

Book cover of The Thousand and One Nights

Manuscript page from Ibn Sīnā's Canon of Medicine

C. A.D. 942
The Arts
Arabs bring kettledrums and trumpets to Europe.

C. A.D. 950
Daily Life
Córdoba becomes the center of Arab learning and commerce in Spain.

C. A.D. 1030
Science and Technology
Ibn Sīnā publishes *The Canon of Medicine.*

A.D. 1206
Politics
Temüjin is proclaimed Genghis Khan.

A.D. 1215
Global Events
The Magna Carta is signed.

A.D. 950   **A.D. 1050**   **A.D. 1150**

C. A.D. 900
The Arts
Writers start collecting the tales for *The Thousand and One Nights.*

C. A.D. 1000
Global Events
Leif Ericsson explores the North American coast.

A.D. 1071
Global Events
The Turks defeat the Byzantines at the Battle of Manzikert.

A.D. 1154
Science and Technology
Al-Idrīsī publishes his book of maps.

C. A.D. 970
Science and Technology
A public hospital is founded in Baghdad.

Celestial sphere, or globe of the universe, used by Muslim astronomers

The dates attached to people and events discussed in this chapter are not the same dates that would be found in many Islamic histories. This is because most of the world uses the Gregorian calendar, in which the years are based on the date of the birth of Jesus. However, many Muslims use the Islamic calendar, which is based on the date Muhammad, the prophet of Islam, left Mecca and went to Medina. Thus dates of events according to the Islamic calendar are 622 years "younger" than dates on the Gregorian calendar.

Critical Thinking

Ask students what is similar about the Gregorian and Islamic calendars.

ANSWER: Students should realize that both are based on religiously significant events.

What's Your Opinion?

Themes Journal — *Do you* **agree** *or* **disagree** *with the following statements? Support your point of view in your journal.*

Science, Technology & Society Science flourishes in societies open to other cultures' ideas.

Global Relations The peoples of conquering and conquered nations can learn from each other.

Culture Religion and culture have very little to do with each other.

SECTION 1

OBJECTIVES

1 **Describe how geography affected the people of the Arabian Peninsula.**

2 **Explain how Islam began.**

3 **Identify the main beliefs of Islam.**

LET'S GET STARTED!

As students enter the classroom, write the following passage on the chalkboard or overhead projector: *Do unto all men as you would that they should do unto you.* Ask students to explain this statement and call on volunteers to identify its source. Many students may believe it comes from the Bible, as a similar passage is found in Matthew 7:12. Explain to the class that, in fact, the passage comes from the Qur'an, the holy book of Islam. (If students correctly attribute the passage, shift the discussion to its similarity with the biblical passage.) Tell students that in Section 1 they will discover other similarities between the teachings of Islam and Judeo-Christian principles.

MAP ANSWERS

1. many waterways

2. Red Sea

3. Arabian Desert

SECTION 1

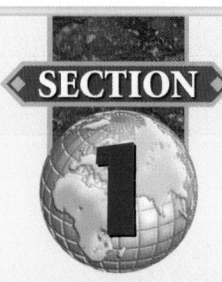

READ TO DISCOVER

❶ How did geography affect the people of the Arabian Peninsula?

❷ How did Islam begin?

❸ What were the main beliefs of Islam?

DEFINE

bedouins
hijrah
jihad
mosques

IDENTIFY

Muhammad
Islam
Muslims
Qur'an

▸WHY IT MATTERS TODAY

The largest country of the Arabian Peninsula is Saudi Arabia. Use CNN or other **current event** sources to explore the culture of Arabia today and its relationship with the United States. Record your findings in your journal.

The Rise of Islam

The Main Idea
The founding of the Islamic religion in the Arabian Peninsula changed and unified the Arab world.

The Story Continues *As the Byzantines were struggling to carry on the traditions of the Roman Empire, another empire was developing on the Arabian Peninsula based on a new religion. This faith would affect cultures and civilizations in a large part of the world. It is still one of the strongest spiritual movements in the world of today.*

Arabia: Its Geography and People

The Arabian Peninsula is bordered on the south by the Arabian Sea, on the east by the Persian Gulf, on the west by the Red Sea, and to the north by the Syrian Desert. Except for narrow strips along the coasts, most of the Arabian Peninsula is desert. Because the desert dwellers could not grow crops, many herded sheep and camels. These Arab herders, called **bedouins** (BEH·duh·wuhnz), were nomads. Whole bedouin families moved with their flocks from one grazing area to another. The bedouins were organized into tribes. The leader of a tribe was called a sheikh (SHAYK). This title was a sign of respect that was given to a man because of his knowledge or position.

Arabian Peninsula
C. A.D. 650

Interpreting Maps
The Arabian Peninsula is the most southwestern part of Asia.

■ **Skills Assessment:**
1. Human Systems
Why do you think many people in Arabia became traders?
2. Physical Systems
What body of water formed a natural trade route between the Arabian Peninsula and the east coast of Africa?
3. Evaluating What geographic feature might have prevented the growth of cities in the southeastern part of the peninsula?

TEACH OBJECTIVE 1

![clock icon] **LEVEL 1:** As a class, discuss the geography of the Arabian Peninsula. Then draw a two-column chart on the board or overhead projector. Label one column *Desert Arabs* and the other *Coastal Arabs*. Have students complete the chart by listing the differences in geography and lifestyle of each.
ENGLISH LANGUAGE LEARNERS

![worksheet icon] **HOMEWORK** Have each student use standard grammar, spelling, sentence structure, and punctuation to write a paragraph explaining why some non-Muslim peoples might readily have accepted Islam. Select students to read their paragraphs to the class.

TEACH OBJECTIVE 2

LEVEL 3: Ask students to create an annotated time line of the development of Islam. Have volunteers use their time lines to explain how Islam began.

TEACH OBJECTIVE 3

ALL LEVELS: Ask students to describe the major beliefs of Islam. Have them list the five chief obligations of a Muslim.
ENGLISH LANGUAGE LEARNERS

The areas along the coasts generally had milder climates that could support greater numbers of people. Towns grew up in these areas, and the townspeople became traders. For example, goods from Asia and Africa entered the port of Jidda on the Red Sea. From there they were transported inland to the city of Mecca (Makkah). Mecca was on a caravan route running north across the desert to Syria. Through trade, Arabs in the towns met and were influenced by people from many different cultures.

✔ **READING CHECK: Contrasting** How did the lifestyle of the desert Arabs differ from the lifestyle of the Arabs who lived along the coasts? *nomadic herders instead of traders*

The Prophet Muhammad

In Mecca in about A.D. 570, a man named **Muhammad** was born into a poor clan of Mecca's ruling tribe. Like many Arabs in Mecca, Muhammad made a living as a caravan trader. As a trader, he came in contact with a variety of people. Some, such as Christians and Jews, were monotheists. They believed in a single god. Many of them, particularly the Arabs, were polytheists who worshiped many gods.

When he was about 40 years old, Muhammad reported that the angel Jibreel (Gabriel, in English) told him that he was called to be a prophet of God (in Arabic, Allah) and revealed verses that Muhammad was to recite. A little later, he was instructed to teach others. Over the next several years Muhammad reported receiving many more revelations.

The merchant rulers at Mecca were very much against Muhammad's teaching. They thought his ideas criticized their conduct and attitudes and threatened their authority. Every year Arab pilgrims came to Mecca to worship at the Kaaba (KAH-buh). The Kaaba was a stone building filled with idols that some people worshiped. The merchant rulers may have feared that Muhammad's teachings about one god might stop such pilgrimages. Before long, they began to harass Muhammad and his followers. Eventually Muhammad looked for a more accepting place.

In A.D. 622 Muhammad and his followers settled in the town of Yathrib. This journey from Mecca to Yathrib is known as the **hijrah** (hi·JY·ruh). Hijrah means "flight" or "migration." Later, Yathrib became known as Medina, or Al-Madinah, the "City of the Prophet." Eventually the year of the hijrah became the first year of the Muslim calendar.

After the move to Yathrib, Muhammad gained followers in greater numbers. Desert tribes began to accept his ideas, increasing tensions between Mecca and Medina. Several years of war followed. Finally, Mecca submitted. Muhammad went back to Mecca in A.D. 630. The idols in the Kaaba were destroyed, and it then became a holy place for Muhammad's followers. Muhammad rededicated the Kaaba to the worship of the One God, Allah.

Soon Arabs everywhere began to accept Muhammad's ideas. Through a combination of wise policies, tolerance, and force, Muhammad converted many of the bedouin tribes to his new religion, called **Islam.** By A.D. 632, when he died, many Arab tribes had become followers of Muhammad. Within a very few years, Islam had spread across Arabia and the Middle East and into North Africa.

✔ **READING CHECK: Sequencing** What were the important events in the development of Islam? *vision of Muhammad; hijrah; conquered Mecca and destroyed idols*

Today the Kaaba in the Great Mosque at Mecca serves as a spiritual sanctuary for Muslims.

Link to Today Why might modern followers of Islam consider the Kaaba a special place?

Daily Life

Bedouins camped in tents in groups of related families. The scarcity of rainfall in the desert prevented the nomadic bedouins from staying in one place for more than a few days. By that time, the animals had exhausted the grass supply in the area. In years when rainfall was scarce, tribes often had to travel hundreds of miles to find water and grazing land. Incursions on another tribe's land inevitably led to clashes, which normally took the form of raiding the rival's herds.

Critical Thinking

Ask students to suggest how this lifestyle of scarce resources and frequent conflict might affect a culture.

ANSWER: Students might suggest that a culture would probably come to emphasize virtues such as bravery and skill in battle.

LINK TO TODAY ANSWER
It's an important part of the history of Islam.

Holt Researcher ![go.hrw.com icon]
go.hrw.com
KEYWORD: Holt Researcher
FreeFind: Muhammad
After reading more about Muhammad on the Holt Researcher, write a short essay explaining how he changed life on the Arabian Peninsula and beyond.

Technology Resources
 CNN Presents World Cultures: Yesterday and Today Segment 9: Pilgrimage to Mecca

CLOSE

Discuss with students what the origins and teachings of Islam have in common with other major world religions.

REVIEW

Have students complete the Section 1 Review on p. 242.

ASSESS

Have students complete Daily Quiz 11.1. As Alternative Assessment, you may want to use the chart or time line exercises in this section's lessons.

RETEACH

Have students complete Main Idea Activity for English Language Learners and Special-Needs Students 11.1. Then ask each student to write a paragraph about the development of Islam. **ENGLISH LANGUAGE LEARNERS**

EXTEND

Have students develop a list of questions they would ask Muhammad in a half-hour interview if they were either a bedouin or a Meccan. **BLOCK SCHEDULING**

SECTION 1 REVIEW ANSWERS

❶ Define
• bedouins, p. 240
• hijrah, p. 241
• jihad, p. 242
• mosques, p. 242

❷ Identify
• Muhammad, p. 241
• Islam, p. 241
• Muslims, p. 242
• Qur'an, p. 242

❸ Students' time lines should include the vision of Muhammad, the hijrah, and the conquest of Mecca and destruction of idols.

❹ a. Mecca was near waterways and on a caravan route, which allowed merchants to engage in profitable trade.

b. It led Muhammad to teach about a single God, Allah.

c. Followers settled in Medina and their numbers grew. Nomadic tribes began to accept Muhammed's ideas and helped spread Islam.

❺ Students' dialogues will vary but should consider the beliefs of polytheists and Muslims.

Technology Resources

Regions of the World Music Audio CD Program 11: The Persian Gulf and Interior: Classical Music of Iran

---

THE FIVE PILLARS OF ISLAM

1. **The profession of faith.**
This includes acknowledging that there is no god but God (Allah) and that Muhammad is the messenger of God. It implies belief in earlier messengers.

2. **The five daily prayers.**
This includes following a ritual of washing and prescribed movements and facing the direction of Mecca.

3. **Paying zakat.**
This is an annual tax used to help the poor and others in need.

4. **Fasting during the holy month of Ramadan.** (RAH·muh·dahn)
Muslims eat and drink nothing from dawn to sunset. This reminds them of the importance of self-discipline, dependence on the Creator, and the feelings of the poor.

5. **Making a pilgrimage to Mecca at least once, if possible.**
During the pilgrimage, which takes place during a certain time of the year, Muslims meet to pray and perform rituals to remind them of the faith of Abraham, and the unity and equality of Muslims all over the world.

The Faith of Islam

Islam is based on the central beliefs that there is only one God, and that each believer must obey God's will. In fact, in Arabic the word *Islam* means "submission to [the will of] God." Followers of Islam are called **Muslims.** Today millions of people throughout the world are Muslims. The largest Muslim communities are in Asia, North Africa, and parts of eastern Europe.

The holy book of Islam is the **Qur'an** (kuh·RAN). According to Muslims, the Qur'an is the word of God as revealed to Muhammad. This includes rules and instructions for right living. There are five basic acts of worship, called the Five Pillars of Islam, required of all Muslims. There are other rules for Muslims to follow as well, such as living humble lives, being tolerant and generous, and not eating pork or drinking alcoholic beverages. Islam also emphasizes the importance of the **jihad** (ji·HAHD), which means "the struggle to defend the faith." Some Muslims believed that anyone who died in this struggle would be rewarded in heaven.

Muhammad taught that God had revealed the Qur'an as a sacred guide for all people. First written in Arabic, the Qur'an was not rapidly translated into other languages because Muslims believed that God's revelations might be lost or changed. As a result, Arabic became the common language of Muslims in religion, law, and literature. Muslims memorize and recite the Qur'an in Arabic.

Muslims worship in **mosques.** Mosques have no furnishings, only mats or rugs on which to kneel, and they never contain images of people or even animals. There is no official clergy in Islam. Men who are trained in the Qur'an and Islamic law guide the people in worship. On Friday at noon, Muslims gather together for congregational prayer and sermons. In most Islamic cultures, women say the same prayers at home or in a section of the mosque set aside for them.

✔ **READING CHECK: Finding the Main Idea** What are the central beliefs of Islam? one God; obey God's will

---

SECTION 1 REVIEW

1. **Define** and explain the significance:
bedouins
hijrah
jihad
mosques

2. **Identify** and explain the significance:
Muhammad
Islam
Muslims
Qur'an

3. **Sequencing** Copy the time line below. Use it to organize and identify events in the rise of Islam.

C. A.D. 610 — A.D. 632

Muhammad reports receiving a revelation from God.

Muhammad dies.

4. **Finding the Main Idea**

a. In what way did the geographic location of Mecca help its early merchant rulers establish their base of power there?

b. How did belief in Muhammad's prophethood lead to the religion of Islam?

c. What role did settled and nomadic Arabs play in the spread of Islam throughout the Arabian Peninsula?

5. **Writing and Critical Thinking**

Comparing Imagine a meeting between a polytheist of Mecca and a convert to Islam. Write a dialogue between them comparing their faiths.
Consider:
• the beliefs of the polytheists
• the beliefs of Muslims

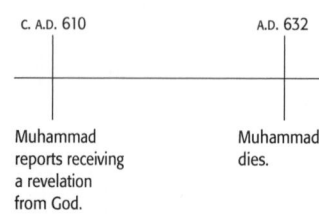

Homework Practice Online
keyword: SP3 HP11

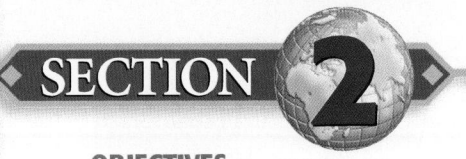

OBJECTIVES

1 Explore how the Muslims expanded their empire.

2 Explain why the Islamic community divided.

LET'S GET STARTED!

As students enter the classroom, ask who would take over if the president of the United States died suddenly. *(the vice-president)* Then ask why this provision is spelled out in the U.S. Constitution. *(so there is no question about who is the leader and the government can maintain stability)* Tell students that in Section 2 they will learn about the conflicts that arose after the death of Muhammad.

SECTION 2

READ TO DISCOVER

❶ How did the Muslims expand their empire?

❷ Why did the Islamic community divide?

DEFINE

caliph
imams
sultan

IDENTIFY

Abū Bakr
'Umar
Sunni
Shi'ah
Sufi
Rābi'ah al-'Adawīyah
Tāriq
Moors

▶ WHY IT MATTERS TODAY

Several million Muslims live in North America. Use CNN Student News.com or other **current event** sources to find out where the largest Islamic communities in North America are located. Record your findings in your journal.

CNN Student News.com

The Spread of Islam

The Main Idea
After the death of Muhammad, the Islamic world greatly expanded, but soon split into two factions.

The Story Continues *According to the Qur'an and the Hadith, or sayings of the prophet, during a journey to Jerusalem, Muhammad traveled through seven heavens to visit the throne of God. Although some followers refused to believe the story at first, one faithful convert named Abū Bakr accepted it immediately. For his faithfulness he was called "The Upright."*

Expansion Under Abū Bakr and 'Umar

When Muhammad died in A.D. 632, his followers chose **Abū Bakr** (uh·BOO BAK·uhr) as his successor. Abū Bakr was Muhammad's oldest friend and one of his early converts. He was given the title **caliph** (KAY·luhf), meaning "successor to the Prophet." During his rule, Abū Bakr helped to bring the Arabic tribes together. He also began to expand Islam's influence northward.

In A.D. 634 **'Umar** (OO·mahr) succeeded Abū Bakr as caliph. 'Umar was a strong leader with a well-run government. Under 'Umar, Muslim expansion continued and people began to share in the empire's wealth. He continued conquering neighboring territories of non-Muslims. In about A.D. 640, for example, the growing armies of Islam under 'Umar's leadership won much of the once-mighty Persian Empire and took control of Iraq. Every victory further encouraged people from across the region to accept Islam. Within 25 years of Muhammad's death, the Muslim Empire included parts of Syria, Persia, and North Africa.

The Arab policy toward conquered people made expansion easier. Fierce and fearless in war, Arabs also entered into many treaties without battle. They were often more tolerant than other conquerors. They did not demand that all conquered people convert to Islam. In the early years, Arabs were particularly tolerant of Christians and Jews.

Muslims called Christians and Jews "People of the Book." Muhammad had accepted the Torah and the Christian Bible as part of God's teachings. Christians, Jews, and some other groups could choose to accept Islam or to pay extra taxes. Some people who refused both options were killed. Many conquered people, however, either paid or converted to Islam.

The caliphs who came after 'Umar expanded Muslim influence even more as the power of other empires, such as the Byzantines, was weakening. Within about 100 years after Muhammad's death, Muslims had swept eastward through part of India and moved westward to conquer much of North Africa. During this time of expansion, the Muslims also conquered islands in the Mediterranean Sea. These gave them control of important trade routes. In A.D. 711 a powerful Muslim force invaded Spain and thus brought Islam to Europe. Muslim troops also tried to conquer Constantinople, but their attempt failed when Byzantine armies successfully defended the city.

✔ **READING CHECK: Sequencing** What steps did Abū Bakr and 'Umar take to spread Islam? unified Arabic tribes; conquered neighboring non-Muslim lands

SECTION 2 RESOURCES

REPRODUCIBLE RESOURCES

▶ Guided Reading Strategy 11.2

▶ Geography Activity 11: The Spread of Islam

▶ Readings in World History 33: The Muslim Conquest of Spain

TECHNOLOGY RESOURCES

▶ One-Stop Planner 11.2

▶ World History and Cultures Video Program 10: At the Crossroads

▶ World History Teaching Transparency: Geography and History 10: Islam in Spain

▶ Religions of the World Video Series: Islam

▶ Homework Practice Online

REINFORCEMENT, REVIEW, AND ASSESSMENT

▶ Section 2 Review, p. 247

▶ Daily Quiz 11.2

▶ Main Idea Activity 11.2

▶ English Audio Summary 11.2

▶ Spanish Audio Summary 11.2

LEVEL 1: Refer students to the map on page 244 of their textbook and ask how far Islam spread under Muhammad. *(through much of the Arabian Peninsula)* Ask how much farther it spread under Abū Bakr and 'Umar. *(throughout the Arabian Peninsula and well into North Africa and Persia)* Ask how much farther it spread in the approximate 100 years after Muhammad's death. *(throughout Persia and North Africa and into India and Europe)* Have students identify two activities that contributed to the rapid spread of Islam. *(war and trade)* **ENGLISH LANGUAGE LEARNERS**

Teacher to Teacher

Mary Catherine Rahman of Chicago, Illinois, suggested the following activity: Have students trace a political map of the present-day Middle East and North Africa. Students should then add information about the spread of Islam from page 244 of their textbook. Have students list the modern countries that were wholly or partly included in the Islamic Empire by 750. Students should then research and list the major religion of each country today.

MAP ANSWERS

1. A.D. 633–A.D. 661

2. It may have caused some people in North Africa and China to convert to Islam.

Global Relations

The period of expansion that began under Abū Bakr and continued under 'Umar was not originally intended as an organized series of military campaigns designed to create an empire. The conflicts did not become strategically organized campaigns until the first battles had been successful.

Critical Thinking

Ask students what the goals of the early fighting might have been.

ANSWER: Students might answer that the goals of the early battles might have been to obtain wealth.

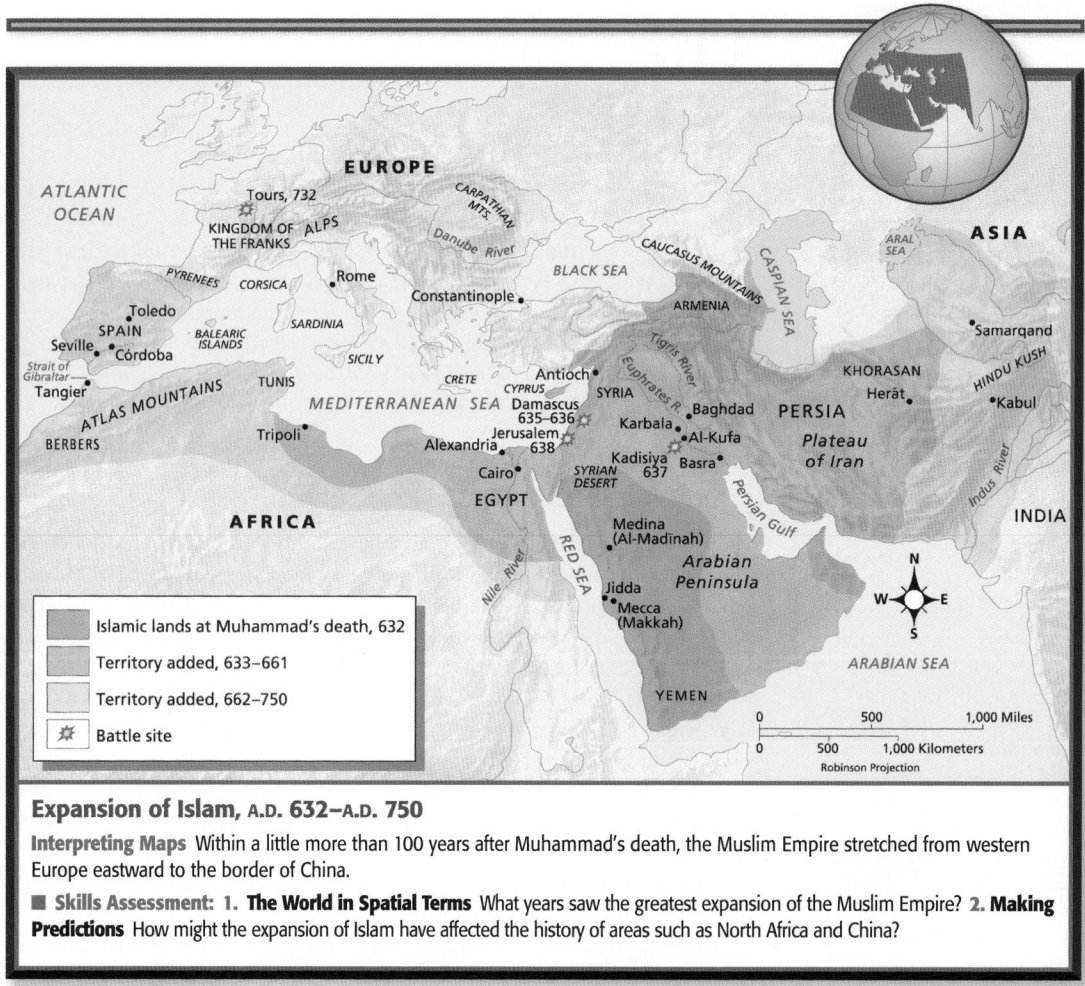

Expansion of Islam, A.D. 632–A.D. 750

Interpreting Maps Within a little more than 100 years after Muhammad's death, the Muslim Empire stretched from western Europe eastward to the border of China.

■ **Skills Assessment: 1. The World in Spatial Terms** What years saw the greatest expansion of the Muslim Empire? **2. Making Predictions** How might the expansion of Islam have affected the history of areas such as North Africa and China?

The Islamic Community Divides

The system of Islamic government allowed the caliphs to exercise great authority. From the beginning, however, people could not agree about who should be caliph. Eventually these disagreements split the Muslim community. The split began when 'Umar's successor, 'Uthmān (ooth·MAHN), was murdered. 'Uthmān was killed because rebels believed he favored his own clan. 'Alī was chosen to succeed 'Uthmān as caliph. 'Uthmān's relative Mu'awiyah (mooh·AH·wee·ya) protested. He accused 'Alī of helping the killers. War broke out between the two sides. In A.D. 661 'Alī was assassinated, and Mu'awiyah became caliph.

Most Muslims agreed to accept Mu'awiyah as caliph. These Muslims eventually became known as the **Sunni** (SOOH·nee). They were followers of the Sunna, meaning "way of the Prophet" or "habitual practice." The Sunni believed that agreement among the Muslim people should settle religious matters.

'Alī's followers insisted that only his descendants should be caliphs. This group later became known as the **Shi'ah** (SHEE·ah). The Shi'ah believed that 'Alī's descendants, called **imams** (i·MAHMZ), should decide religious and worldly matters.

TEACH OBJECTIVE 2

LEVEL 3: Form students into triads to decide whether the death of Muhammad, Abū Bakr, or 'Umar was a more critical event for Muslims. *(Students should recognize that while Islam survived after Muhammad's death, his successors were faced with maintaining Muslims' political unity.)* Use the responses to launch a discussion of the divisions that arose among Muslims after 'Umar's death. Ask whether these disputes were about power or Islamic principles. *(power)* **COOPERATIVE LEARNING**

The split between the two groups continued. The rift deepened when Mu'awiyah's descendants killed 'Alī's son Husayn. According to the Shi'ah, on a day of reckoning, Husayn's mother, Fātimah, will take her son's blood-stained shirt to God and say:

"Oh God, you have given me and my son a promise. For the sake of his sacrifice, have mercy upon the people of the Last Prophet!"

Fātimah, from *Islam in Practice: Religious Beliefs in a Persian Village,* by Reinhold Loeffler

Then, in memory of Husayn's death, God will forgive the sins of the Shi'ah and there will be peace. Today the division between the Shi'ah and the Sunni still exists. Less than 10 percent of the world's Muslims are Shi'ah.

Later another group within Islam developed. Muslim mystics known as **Sufi,** such as **Rābi'ah al-'Adawīyah,** tried to live simple lives centered on God. They turned away from worldly possessions and success. The Sufi believed that faith in God was the only mark of a person's worth.

✔ **READING CHECK: Comparing and Contrasting** What are the similarities and differences between the Sunni and the Shi'ah? both follow teachings of Muhammad, but disagree about who should be caliphs

The Empire Continues to Spread

Despite this split, the Muslim Empire continued to spread. Soon a North African people called the Berbers converted to Islam. In A.D. 711 a Berber general named **Tāriq** led a Muslim army to Spain. They crossed the Mediterranean at the great rock that guards the strait between Africa and Europe. The rock became known as *Jabal Tāriq,* or "Mount Tāriq." In English it is called the Rock of Gibraltar.

The Moors. Tāriq's Muslim army conquered Spain quickly. Those Muslims who made Spain their home were called **Moors.** Within a few years, the Moors crossed over the Pyrenees to raid central France. In A.D. 732 the Franks defeated the Moors at the Battle of Tours and the Moors eventually withdrew from France. They continued to rule parts of Spain, however, for more than 700 years.

Suleymaniye Mosque in Istanbul, Turkey

Analyzing Primary Sources

Identifying a Point of View Why might the Shi'ah consider Husayn's death a special sacrifice? died for his faith

HISTORY MAKER

Rābi'ah al-'Adawīyah
(C. A.D. 717–A.D. 801)

Rābi'ah al-'Adawīyah was one of the greatest Sufi mystics. Abandoned at a young age, she was later sold into slavery. While she filled her days with hard work, Rābi'ah spent her nights praying to Allah for help, guidance, and deliverance.

One night, a great light appeared above her head. Her master, recognizing her devotion to Allah, set her free. Rābi'ah went on to become one of the first female Sufi mystics. Her religious poetry and other writings still inspire Muslims today.

Because no known images of Rābi'ah al-'Adawīyah exist, the calligraphy above is used to symbolize her. It translates as: "In the name of Allah Most Gracious, Most Merciful." **How is Rābi'ah al-'Adawīyah important to Islam?**

Government

While 'Uthmān was thought by many to be a well-meaning man, he enraged many Arabs by appointing his relatives to important positions. In addition, 'Uthmān accepted gifts sent by his governors and their representatives. The rebellion against 'Uthmān began in al-Kufah among 'Ali's followers and grew in strength in Egypt. Five hundred rebels went to Medina in A.D. 656. They stormed 'Uthmān's home. Muhammad, son of Abū Bakr, was the first to break into the residence and attack 'Uthmān. 'Uthmān was killed by the rebels.

Critical Thinking

Ask students what factor might have compounded the tension caused by 'Uthmān appointing his relatives to power.

ANSWER: Students might answer that there was disagreement over who should be caliph.

HISTORY MAKER ANSWER
She was one of the first female Sufi mystics.

THE ISLAMIC WORLD **245**

245

ALL LEVELS: Have students work in pairs to create two diagrams that illustrate how Sunni and Shi'ah Muslims differed over where religious and secular authority originate and the proper relationship between the two types of authority. Select volunteer pairs to duplicate their diagrams on the chalkboard or overhead projector and explain them to the class.
ENGLISH LANGUAGE LEARNERS, COOPERATIVE LEARNING

 HOMEWORK Using the textbook discussion as a reference, have each student outline the issues and events that led to the split between Sunnis and Shi'ahs.

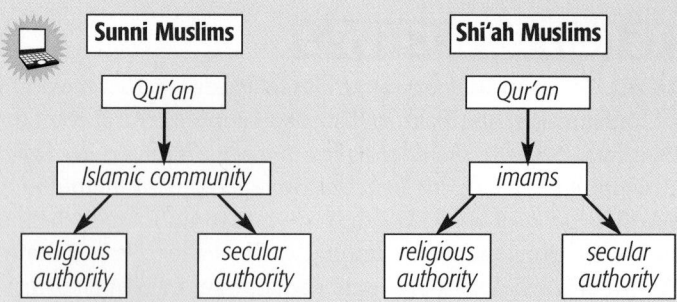

Sunni Muslims

Qur'an → Islamic community → religious authority / secular authority

Shi'ah Muslims

Qur'an → imams → religious authority / secular authority

CLOSE

Organize a class discussion about the causes and effects of the dispute between the Sunni and Shi'ah Muslims.

History Maker

MUHAMMAD. According to Islamic tradition, after Muhammad was approached by the angel Jibreel, he was afraid and confused, and he considered ending his life. He changed his mind, however, when he heard a voice telling him he was "the Messenger of God." Muhammad told Khadijah, his wife, that he was afraid he had been possessed by an evil spirit. According to tradition, Khadijah told him that she would go to the home of her cousin, who was a Christian, and ask his opinion. Khadijah's cousin said that if what she told him was true, then she and Muhammad should not worry, because Muhammad was the Prophet of his people.

Critical Thinking

Ask students why the fact that Khadijah's cousin was a Christian might have been significant.

ANSWER: This endorsement from a Christian might have made it easier to convert Christians to Islam.

SKILLS PRACTICE ANSWERS

1. Students should use dates to arrange events in order.

2. Sequence shows cause-and-effect relationships.

Technology Resources

 Online Maps, Charts, and Graphs: Muslim Lands in the 1100s

SKILL-BUILDING STRATEGIES Understanding Sequence

The Expansion of Islam

Certain events happened in a certain way to help Islam succeed. Understanding the sequence in which events happened can help us understand why some events occurred as they did.

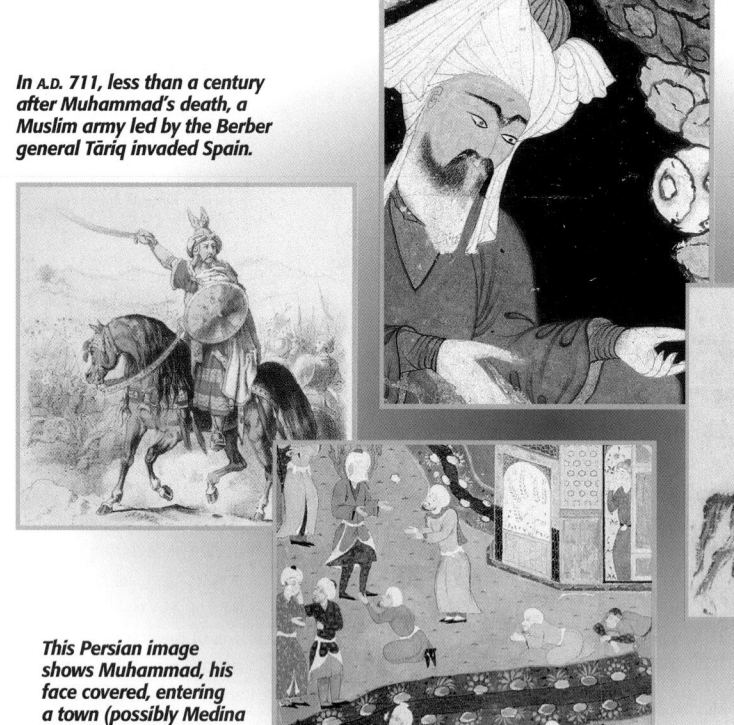

In A.D. 711, less than a century after Muhammad's death, a Muslim army led by the Berber general Tāriq invaded Spain.

Abū Bakr followed Muhammad as the leader of Islam and became the faith's first caliph in A.D. 632.

This Persian image shows Muhammad, his face covered, entering a town (possibly Medina or Mecca), probably at some point between A.D. 622 and A.D. 632.

A troop of Muslim Turkish cavalry is shown in battle formation in this image, c. A.D. 1050–c. A.D. 1100.

Skills Reminder

A sequence is an arrangement of things or events in a logical order. Creating a sequence helps you understand information. From the pattern you create, you can decide how events or things are related to each other. To help sequence information, look for calendar references; time periods; and clue words, such as *first, second, after, before, meanwhile,* or *later.* If there are no calendar references or clue words, look for an implied sequence. For example, could one event have happened without another taking place first?

Skills Practice

❶ Study the images and captions above. They show and describe historical events that occurred during the early history of Islam. These events helped lead to the rise and spread of Islam. The events described have been placed in random order. Reorganize the events to place them in their proper sequence.

❷ How does understanding the sequence in which these historical events occurred help to explain how Islam succeeded?

REVIEW

Have students complete the Section 2 Review on p. 247.

ASSESS

Have students complete Daily Quiz 11.2. As Alternative Assessment, you may want to use the map or diagram exercises in this section's lessons.

RETEACH

Have students complete Main Idea Activity for English Language Learners and Special-Needs Students 11.2. Then ask them to create a flowchart showing the succession of Islamic leaders.
ENGLISH LANGUAGE LEARNERS

EXTEND

Have students form small groups and imagine that they are Arab merchants in Medina. Tell them that they have employees traveling throughout North Africa and Persia buying, selling, and trading goods. Have each group develop a written code of conduct for these employees while away from home and in dealings with non-Muslim customers that will strengthen the perception of Islam in those regions. **BLOCK SCHEDULING, COOPERATIVE LEARNING**

The great era of Arab Muslim expansion lasted until the 1100s. After that, the Turks became the ruling force in Islam. The Islamic empire, though, continued to expand under the Turks.

The Turks and Islam. Turkish-speaking groups from the steppes of central Asia began to move west and south. These tough, nomadic people lived as much by fighting and raiding as by herding. They developed a warlike culture that encouraged expansion and conquest. The conquests brought these Turkish peoples into contact with Arab and Persian Muslims of the Middle East. By the late A.D. 900s, large numbers of Turks had converted to Islam. Many of these people settled around the great Muslim city of Baghdad, in what is now Iraq, where they served the caliph as troops. The Turks supported Islamic law, but their growing power caused political authority to gradually shift away from the caliph. A **sultan** ruled the Turks and claimed to serve the caliph, who still played an important symbolic role. By the mid-1000s the Turks had won control of Baghdad. During the next century, they became the dominant ruling force throughout much of the Islamic world.

During the A.D. 1000s, Turkish Muslims seized Syria, Mesopotamia, and much of Asia Minor. The Turks were skillful warriors. They won a major victory against the Byzantines at the Battle of Manzikert in A.D. 1071. Meanwhile, Turkish Muslims began raiding northern India. The Indians fought fiercely. The Turks, however, fought on horseback. They used their horses cleverly and succeeded. By the early A.D. 1200s they controlled most of northern India.

In the A.D. 1250s outside forces slowed Turkish Muslim expansion. Christians from the West captured cities in a series of wars. Meanwhile, Mongols from the East destroyed Baghdad.

✔ **READING CHECK: Supporting a Point of View** What evidence would you give that the Muslims had a large and well-trained army? conquered parts of Spain, Syria, Mesopotamia, and Asia Minor

INTERPRETING THE VISUAL RECORD

Flag bearers This artwork from A.D. 1237 shows the flag bearers of an Islamic caliph. *How do the flag bearers indicate the importance of the caliph, even during the reign of the Turks?*

SECTION 2 REVIEW

1. **Define** and explain the significance:
   caliph
   imams
   sultan

2. **Identify** and explain the significance:
   Abū Bakr   Sufi
   'Umar   Rābi'ah al-'Adawīyah
   Sunni   Tāriq
   Shi'ah   Moors

3. **Categorizing** Copy the chart below. Use it to organize the areas that the Muslims conquered during the expansion of the Muslim Empire.

	Arabs	Turks
Years		
Areas		

4. **Finding the Main Idea**

   a. In what ways did the geography of the Arabian Peninsula contribute to the spread of Islam?

   b. What effect might the split in the Islamic community have had on the expansion of the Muslim Empire?

5. **Writing and Critical Thinking**

   Evaluating Explain why the Muslims were able to expand their empire so rapidly.
   Consider:
   • how the Muslim government and military were organized
   • what the Muslim policies were toward conquered people
   • how conquered people reacted to Islam

Homework Practice Online
keyword: SP3 HP11

VISUAL RECORD ANSWER

There are quite a few flag bearers with many adornments.

SECTION
2 REVIEW ANSWERS

❶ **Define**
• caliph, p. 243
• imams, p. 244
• sultan, p. 247

❷ **Identify**
• Abū Bakr, p. 243
• 'Umar, p. 243
• Sunni, p. 244
• Shi'ah, p. 244
• Sufi, p. 245
• Rābi' ah al-'Adawīyah, p. 245
• Tāriq, p. 245
• Moors, p. 245

❸ **Arabs:** A.D. 637–1100s; Iraq, parts of Syria, Persia, and North Africa, Spain; **Turks:** A.D. 900s–1250; Baghdad, Syria, Mesopotamia, much of Asia Minor, northern India

❹ **a.** It borders many bodies of water, but is also connected by land to parts of Asia and Africa.

b. It may have slowed expansion.

❺ Students should consider the organization of the government and military, policies toward conquered people, and how conquered people reacted to Islam.

SECTION 3

OBJECTIVES

1 Describe how the location of Arabia affected trade in the Muslim Empire.

2 Explain what Muslim society and family life were like.

3 Identify Muslim achievements in science.

4 Explore how Islam influenced Arab art and literature.

🔔 LET'S GET STARTED!

As students enter the classroom, write the following words on the chalkboard or overhead projector: *algebra, almanac, apricot, cotton, damask, guitar, lemon, soda,* and *sofa.* Tell the class that all these words are derivations of Arab terms that over time have found their way into the English language. Ask students what this list suggests about contact between the Muslim world and Europe. *(Responses should include that a considerable trade existed between Europe and the Near East, and the Arab culture had a significant influence on Europeans.)*

SECTION 3 RESOURCES

REPRODUCIBLE RESOURCES

▶ Guided Reading Strategy 11.3

▶ Graphic Organizer Activity 11: Science and Islam

▶ Readings in World History 34: Muslim Towns and Trade in North Africa

▶ Creative Teaching Strategy 11: The Islamic Heritage Museum

TECHNOLOGY RESOURCES

▶ One-Stop Planner 11.3

▶ Holt Researcher: World History: Scheherazade

▶ Religions of the World Video Series: Islam

▶ Homework Practice Online

▶ Online Maps, Charts, and Graphs: Muslim Trade Routes

REINFORCEMENT, REVIEW, AND ASSESSMENT

▶ Section 3 Review, p. 253

▶ Daily Quiz 11.3

▶ Main Idea Activity 11.3

▶ English Audio Summary 11.3

▶ Spanish Audio Summary 11.3

SECTION 3

READ TO DISCOVER

❶ How did the location of Arabia affect trade in the Muslim Empire?

❷ What were Muslim society and family life like?

❸ What Muslim achievements were made in science?

❹ How did Islam influence Arab art and literature?

DEFINE

astrolabe
minaret

IDENTIFY

al-Rāzī
Ibn Sīnā
al-Idrīsī
The Thousand and One Nights

▶ WHY IT MATTERS TODAY

The role of women in Muslim society has changed throughout the years. Use CNNStudentNews.com or other **current event** sources to explore the role of women in Muslim societies today. Record your findings in your journal.

CNNStudentNews.com

Islamic Civilization

The Main Idea
Muslims made many advances in economics, government, education, science, and the arts.

The Story Continues *Islam became more than just a religion. It was also a great cultural movement that affected virtually every aspect of life within the Islamic Empire. As one Muslim saying expressed: "Islam, the government, and the people are like the tent, the pole, the ropes, and the pegs. The tent is Islam; the pole is the government; the ropes and pegs are the people. None will do without the others."*

A Culture of Traders

The Arabs had been traders for centuries before their empire developed. Muhammad himself had been a trader. It is not surprising, then, that trade was important to Muslim culture. The empire was at the center of a world trade network that linked Europe, Asia, and Africa. India and China sent goods to ports in Syria and Egypt.

As trade grew, other cultures increasingly demanded the quality goods that Muslims produced, such as textiles manufactured from silk, cotton, and wool, as well as beautiful woven tapestries and carpets. Muslims also made metal products from gold and silver. Steel swords from Damascus and from the Spanish city of Toledo became world famous. Luxuries such as jewelry, perfumes, and spices were in great demand. Muslim artisans produced pottery and glassware. Artisans in North Africa and Spain made fine leather goods. All this trade made the Islamic Empire wealthy.

Muslims exchanged ideas with other cultures as well. Both Córdoba and Toledo in Spain were famous centers of learning. Christian and Jewish scholars carried Muslim ideas from Spain into western Europe. Sicily under the Muslims was known for its astronomers and geographers. They, too, influenced Europeans. Many Europeans, in fact, viewed the Muslim world as a source of advanced knowledge in many scientific areas and in banking and commerce.

✔ **READING CHECK:**
Evaluating How important was the location of the Arabian Peninsula to trade in the Muslim Empire? enabled them to trade with Europe, Asia and Africa

Muslim merchants carried goods across a far-flung network of trade routes.

TEACH OBJECTIVE 1

 LEVEL 1: Have students list some items that Muslims produced and traded. *(silk, cotton, and wool textiles, woven tapestries, carpets, metal products, jewelry, perfumes, leather goods)* In addition to goods, ask students what else Muslims exchanged with other cultures. *(ideas)*
ENGLISH LANGUAGE LEARNERS

 HOMEWORK Assign each student to create a three- or four-panel cartoon strip showing how Muslim culture was spread by Muslims' interaction with other peoples.

Government and Society

Under Arab rule, the Muslim Empire was organized into provinces. At first one caliph headed the government. Disagreement over succession to the position developed, however. In time, these disputes led to the breakup of the empire into three areas, or caliphates. The caliphates were ruled by caliphs in Baghdad, Cairo, and Córdoba.

Muslims throughout the Islamic Empire lived according to the Qur'an. It guided both their religious life and daily life—there was no separation. The Qur'an gave detailed instructions about how society should be organized and how people should live. All Muslims were expected to follow the Islamic laws in public and private life.

Slavery was common in Arabia. The Qur'an urged Muslims to free their slaves. Those who chose to keep slaves were required to treat them humanely. No free Muslim could be enslaved, and the children of a female slave and her master were free.

The family was the core of Muslim daily life. Muslims showed concern for all members of their family—parents, children, grandparents, aunts, uncles, and cousins. They particularly respected the elderly. In Islamic families everyone had specific roles and duties. Men were responsible for the family's needs. Women had the right to just treatment, and they could control property, but they were not required to contribute to the family's needs. As the Qur'an stated:

This illustration from an Arabic book shows the great detail used in Islamic art.

> **Primary Source** "Women have such [as many] honourable rights as obligations, but their men have a degree [of rights and obligations] above them."
>
> The Qur'an

Parents usually arranged marriages for their children. However, the Qur'an gave a woman the right to refuse the arrangement. The groom was required to give his bride a marriage gift of property or money.

It was common in Arabia for a man to have several wives. The Qur'an restricted a Muslim man to four wives, and he had to treat them equally. In fact, the Qur'an gave women more rights than they had received under traditional Arab law. For example, if a woman got divorced, she kept her own money and was free to remarry. She could also inherit money and own property. Muslim women enjoyed more freedom than most women at the time. Later, however, women began to be secluded and lost some rights.

The government supported schools and libraries. The family and the mosque also took responsibility for education. A person who could speak and write well was thought to be educated. Students attended religious study groups at the mosque. Advanced students could attend schools established for the study of science, mathematics, or law.

✔ **READING CHECK: Identifying Bias** How did old Arab customs and Islamic law affect Muslim family life? *established custom of polygamy*

Analyzing Primary Sources

Drawing Inferences How does this passage show that the Qur'an guided more than just religious beliefs? *defines social roles of men and women*

Reproducible Resources

PS Readings in World History 35: Social Classes in Muslim India

ALL LEVELS: Ask students what rights Muslim women had. *(Women could choose their husbands; men had to treat all wives equally; women could divorce, keep their own money, and remarry; women could inherit money and own property.)* Have volunteers list some of the differences in the rights of Muslim men and women. *(Women had a clearly defined position; men were responsible for women's behavior; Muslim men engaged in polygamy.)* **ENGLISH LANGUAGE LEARNERS**

Science, Technology & Society

Among the most significant of Muslim medical innovations was the concept of the hospital. Although treatment facilities existed in other cultures and earlier times, the medieval Islamic hospital was a more elaborate institution with a much wider range of functions. It served as a treatment center, a convalescent facility, a place of confinement for the mentally ill, and a retirement home for the aged and infirm. Most Islamic hospitals treated both Muslims and non-Muslims, rich and poor alike.

Critical Thinking

Ask students why knowledge from other cultures was important to Muslim scientific advances.

ANSWER: They were able to build on the knowledge of other cultures and were able to advance more quickly than if they had had to start at the beginning.

VISUAL RECORD ANSWER

He is examining the man's arm.

LINK TO TODAY ANSWER

Doctors today also examine patients before treating them.

SCIENCE AND TECHNOLOGY ANSWER

They developed surgical techniques, wrote an illustrated surgical textbook, and made medicines.

INTERPRETING THE VISUAL RECORD

Arab physicians This medieval artwork shows Arab doctors treating a patient. ***What do you think the doctor is doing?***

Link to Today How does this technique compare with that used by doctors today?

CONNECTING TO
Science and Technology

Muslim Medicine
The Arab surgeon Abū al-Qāsim (A.D. 936–1013) developed surgical techniques in Córdoba. He wrote the first illustrated surgical textbook.

Other Arab scientists were interested in chemistry. They learned to distill substances and make medicines. Many drugs used today are of Arab origin.

Understanding Science and Technology

How did Arabs of the Muslim Empire contribute to medical science?

The Sciences

Though divided politically, the Muslim world remained united in one great civilization. As Muslims expanded their empire, they learned from the people they conquered. They also learned from the merchants with whom they traded. The Arabs adopted the best ideas, customs, and institutions they found. They combined ideas of Greece, Rome, and Asia in their culture. From India the Muslims got new ideas about astronomy and mathematics. From China they learned about papermaking. They particularly learned from the writings of the Greek philosophers and scientists.

Medicine. Some of the most important contributions that Muslims made were to medical science. They studied the work of the famous Greek physicians Hippocrates and Galen. Then they added to what the Greeks had done.

Scientific advances in the use of herbs, foods, and prepared drugs added to the Islamic world's vast store of medical knowledge. Some of this early Muslim work in the development and preparation of pharmaceutical drugs is still in use today. In some cases, techniques such as distillation that were first used by Muslim scientists to prepare medical drugs are also followed by today's manufacturers.

Muslim doctors achieved great progress in the techniques of dissection to study anatomy. They also developed improved surgical instruments and processes. The Muslim surgeon Abū al-Qāsim, for example, practiced in Islamic Spain, in the city of Córdoba. His work did much to raise the surgical standards of the time, and his illustrated book of surgical techniques, the first of its kind, was widely used in Europe for centuries.

Muslim physicians learned to correctly diagnose certain diseases. They also pioneered in the development of new ideas concerning hygiene.

Muslim doctors in Baghdad were required to pass difficult examinations in order to practice medicine. They also established the world's first school of pharmacy and created the first encyclopedia of known drugs, the preparation of drugs, and their medical effects. A great public hospital was founded in Baghdad. Physicians at this hospital learned to diagnose and treat deadly smallpox and other diseases.

One of the greatest doctors of the Islamic world was **al-Rāzī**. He was chief physician at the hospital in Baghdad in the early A.D. 900s. Al-Rāzī was best known for a paper he wrote about smallpox and measles. He was the first to clearly describe these diseases so that doctors could tell them apart. Al-Rāzī also compiled a huge medical encyclopedia. It was translated into Latin and used in Europe for centuries.

Some of the greatest Islamic thinkers and scholars were also doctors. **Ibn Sīnā** (also called Avicenna) was among the best known. One of his textbooks was the encyclopedic *Canon of Medicine*.

A page from a text on Islamic medicine illustrates the anatomy of the human eye.

Muslim Culture			
Manufactures	**Science and Medicine**	**Mathematics**	**Geography**
silk, cotton, and wool metal products from gold and silver steel swords jewelry, perfumes, and spices pottery and glassware fine leather	pharmaceutical drugs techniques of dissection to study anatomy surgical instruction and processes diagnosis of disease new ideas concerning hygiene started the world's first school of pharmacy founded public hospital compiled medical encyclopedia	developed Arabic numerals used decimals in Arab arithmetic book wrote about al-jabr, which became algebra spread mathematical ideas to Europe	developed more accurate way to measure distances on Earth made better maps improved the astrolabe

He wrote it in the early 1000s. This medical book was used in Europe until at least 1650. Ibn Sīnā's thoughts about his own training give a good picture of this extraordinary man.

History Makers Speak

❝I busied myself with the study of . . . [a treatise by al-Farabi] and other commentaries on physics and metaphysics, and the doors of knowledge opened before me. Then I took up medicine . . . Medicine is not one of the difficult sciences, and in a very short time I undoubtedly excelled in it, so that physicians of merit studied under me. I also attended the sick, and the doors of medical treatments based on experience opened before me to an extent that can not be described. At the same time I carried on debates and controversies in jurisprudence [law]. At this point I was sixteen years old.❞

Ibn Sīnā, from his autobiography

Analyzing Primary Sources

Drawing Conclusions Ibn Sīnā said that medicine is "not one of the difficult sciences." Why did he say that? in keeping with Islamic idea of modesty and humility

The Muslim conquest of Spain contributed to an expansion of learning in that country. Córdoba became the medical equal of Baghdad. From Spain, Muslim medical science spread to other European centers of learning. Christians had preserved the old medical knowledge. Now it was combined with Muslim learning. Universities throughout Europe began to teach medicine based on Arab Muslim medical advances.

Geography. Because the Muslims were traders, they traveled and explored distant places. It is not surprising that they were interested in astronomy, navigation, and maps.

At first the Muslims studied the maps the Greeks made. Then they added their own improvements. In Baghdad astronomers developed a more accurate way to measure distances on earth. Geographers used their measurements to make better maps. One Muslim geographer, **al-Idrīsī,** sent people to other countries. He asked them to draw the geographic features they saw. Al-Idrīsī then combined what they found with existing maps to make new, more accurate maps.

Muslims adopted another Greek invention. This was the small instrument called the **astrolabe,** which allowed observers to chart the positions of the stars and thus calculate their own position on Earth. Muslim astronomers improved the astrolabe several centuries later. By the 1100s, mariners throughout Europe and the Muslim Empire were using astrolabes.

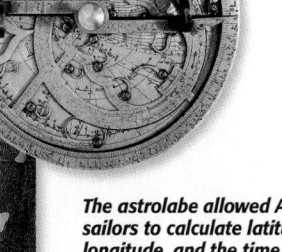

The astrolabe allowed Arab sailors to calculate latitude, longitude, and the time of day.

The maps that al-Idrīsī created in the 1100s were an important advance in geography.

Geography

One of the greatest Muslim geographers was Yaqut ibn-'Abdullah al-Hamawi, who lived from 1179 to 1229. Yaqut was a Greek slave. After he was given his freedom, Yaqut traveled from place to place, copying and selling manuscripts to support himself. He later wrote the *Dictionary of Cities*.

Critical Thinking

Ask students why they think scholars consider Yaqut to be such a good geographer.

ANSWER: Students might suggest that Yaqut based his information on observation and experience because he traveled extensively.

LEVEL 3: Read these words of Muhammad to the class: "The ink of scholars is more precious than the blood of martyrs." Ask students what they think Muhammad meant. Ask what this statement suggests about the value that Muslims put on knowledge and learning. *(Responses should suggest that writings were seen as a more permanent way of spreading the faith than was conquest, and that knowledge was highly revered in Muslim society.)* Have a volunteer explain how Islam affected Arab art. *(Religious art could not show the human form, so it emphasized geometric and floral patterns.)*

Spotlight on CULTURE

Locate a photograph of the Taj Mahal to show the class. Suggest that students use the photo as inspiration to create a poem about the Taj Mahal. Tell students that their poem may be about the structure itself, the reason it was built, or the time and effort required to build it. Call on volunteers to read their poems to the class.

☑ internet connect

TOPIC: Islamic Calligraphy
GO TO: go.hrw.com
KEYWORD: SP3 WH11

Search the Internet through the HRW Go site to gather information on Islamic calligraphy. Remind students about the special religious and artistic significance of calligraphy to Islamic culture. Ask them to create a chart showing several designs that are important to Islamic culture, and learn what they mean. Have volunteers share these designs with the class.

Technology Resources

World History Teaching Transparency: Art and History 10: Stoneware Bowl

Mathematics. In about the A.D. 800s Muslims learned a new number system from India. This system expressed any number using only 10 figures. It included a figure for zero to mean an empty place. Muslim scholars introduced the Indian number system into the Greek science of mathematics. When Europeans learned about this number system, they called the figures "Arabic". These are the same Arabic numerals in use today.

Muslims also got the idea of decimals from India. Al-Khwārizmī used them in an Arab arithmetic book. He also wrote about what he called *al-jabr*, or "restoring," which became *algebra* in English. During the A.D. 1000s scholars from Europe visited Muslim schools in Spain to learn about Muslim arithmetic and algebra. Soon the Muslim mathematical ideas spread to Europe.

✔ READING CHECK: Supporting a Point of View What evidence would you give that the Muslims were outstanding scientists? their ideas and inventions were adopted in other parts of the world

The Arts

Islamic teaching forbids the use of images to show God. In fact, Islamic religious art avoided showing human or animal forms. Instead artists created beautiful geometric and floral designs. Calligraphy, the art of fine handwriting, was the highest art form. In their nonreligious art Muslims sometimes showed people in daily life, famous battles, or other similar scenes.

Architecture became one of the greatest forms of Islamic art. Mosques, palaces, marketplaces, and libraries were designed to show the glory of Islam. They also showed the power of the ruler who sponsored their construction.

The first Islamic mosques were modeled after Muhammad's private courtyard at Medina, where he had led the community in prayer. These earliest mosques were, in many cases, simple plots of ground marked as sacred. As the Islamic Empire expanded, Muslims built mosques in the territories they conquered. During the earliest years of growth and conquest, mosques that were constructed in conquered lands beyond the Arabian Peninsula were apparently not used solely as religious centers. Rather, they often served as community centers where many kinds of group activities, in addition to prayer and religious ceremonies, were conducted. The community's treasury might have been kept at the site of the mosque, and community social, political, and educational activities and events might also have been held there.

Over time the design of many mosques became more elaborate. In the western part of the Muslim world, the beautiful mosque at Córdoba, in Spain, was a fine example of this increasingly sophisticated architectural style. Built in stages between about A.D. 785 and about A.D. 988, this mosque remains as a magnificent monument to Islam.

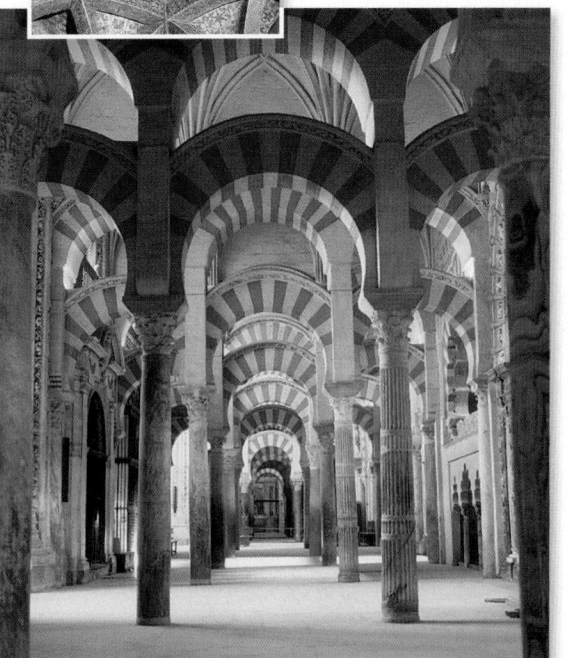

The Great Mosque of Córdoba took more than 200 years to complete. It is a masterpiece of Islamic architecture. The inset shows a part of the ceiling.

CLOSE

Ask each student to write down what he or she believes to be the most important scientific achievement of Islamic culture. Have volunteers defend their choices to the class.

REVIEW

Have students complete the Section 3 Review on p. 253.

ASSESS

Have students complete Daily Quiz 11.3. As Alternative Assessment, you may want to use the trade or chart exercises in this section's lessons.

RETEACH

Have Students complete Main Idea Activity for English Language Learners and Special-Needs Students 11.3. Then have them write down three important Islamic achievements and describe why each was important. **ENGLISH LANGUAGE LEARNERS**

EXTEND

Have interested students research Arabic music and bring in selections to play for the class. Students should explain the significance of each musical selection and describe the instruments used. **BLOCK SCHEDULING**

Mosques were designed to house the thousands of followers who gathered to worship. The main part of the mosque was a vast area for prayer. A semicircular niche faced in the direction of Mecca. There also was a pulpit for the prayer leader. Often there was a **minaret**, or tower, attached to the outside of the mosque. Five times a day, a crier in the minaret would call Muslims to worship.

The Islamic Empire also produced outstanding poetry and literature. The caliphs were great patrons of the arts. Some writers lived at the caliph's court and wrote about what they saw.

One story in Muslim literature tells of a ruler who married a new bride each night. The next morning he would order her execution because he thought no wife would remain loyal. To save herself, one wife, Scheherazade (shuh·HEHR·uh·zahd), began to tell a story one night. She promised to finish it the next night. Interested and eager for the ending, her husband delayed her execution. Night after night she charmed him with stories. Each night she left the story unfinished. After a thousand and one nights, the king was convinced she would remain faithful and he abandoned his plans to execute her.

The story of Scheherazade is the tale around which a body of Muslim folktales was organized. Today we know the collection as *The Thousand and One Nights*. It includes the familiar tales of "Sinbad the Sailor," "Aladdin," and "Ali Baba and the Forty Thieves." They are among the most widely read stories in history.

✔ **READING CHECK: Identifying Cause and Effect** How did Islamic teachings influence Muslim art and architecture? religious art cannot show human form, so emphasized geometric and floral patterns

CONNECTING TO Art

Weaving: Carpets of the Muslim World

For centuries Muslims who could afford them have knelt and prayed on beautiful rugs. A prayer rug must be placed on the floor so that the arch in the design points toward Mecca. The prayer rug shown here was woven in Turkey during the late 1600s or early 1700s. It has a border of wide and narrow stripes and various geometric designs. The parts of the carpet have specific meanings. Different colors, for example, may symbolize various attitudes or values.

Understanding the Arts

Which side of the rug pictured would be laid closest to Mecca? Why?

CONNECTING TO ART ANSWER
the top of the arch, because Muslims pray facing Mecca

SECTION 3 REVIEW ANSWERS

❶ **Define**
- astrolabe, p. 251
- minaret, p. 253

❷ **Identify**
- al-Rāzī, p. 250
- Ibn-Sīnā, p. 250
- al-Idrīsī, p. 251
- *The Thousand and One Nights*, p. 253

❸ Students' charts should show how Muslim culture was influenced by other cultures and influenced other cultures in areas of the arts and sciences.

❹ a. It played a very important role and made the empire wealthy.

b. It guided both religious and daily life.

c. medicine, geography, Arabic numerals

❺ Students' outlines will vary but should consider the daily lives and occupations of Muslim people, the importance of religion and the themes in *The Thousand and One Nights*.

SECTION 3 REVIEW

1. **Define** and explain the significance:
   astrolabe
   minaret

2. **Identify** and explain the significance:
   al-Rāzī
   Ibn Sīnā
   al-Idrīsī
   The Thousand and One Nights

3. **Identifying Cause and Effect**
   Copy the chart below. Use it to show how Muslim culture was influenced by other cultures and how it influenced other cultures.

Muslim Culture	←→	Other Cultures

4. **Finding the Main Idea**
   a. What role did trade play in the Muslim Empire?
   b. How did the Qur'an influence Muslim culture?
   c. What were the main scientific and mathematic achievements of the Muslim Empire?

5. **Writing and Critical Thinking**
   Summarizing Write an outline for a short story or folktale that takes place in the Muslim Empire.
   Consider:
   • the daily lives and occupations of men and women in various regions of the empire
   • the importance of religion in the culture
   • the themes of the folktales in *The Thousand and One Nights*

Homework Practice Online
keyword: SP3 HP11

REVIEW AND ASSESSMENT RESOURCES

REPRODUCIBLE RESOURCES
▶ Vocabulary Activity 11

TECHNOLOGY RESOURCES
▶ Chapter 11 Test Generator (on the One-Stop Planner)
▶ Global Skill Builder CD–ROM
▶ HRW Web Site

REINFORCEMENT, REVIEW, and ASSESSMENT
▶ Chapter 11 Review, pp. 254–255
▶ Chapter 11 Tutorial for Students, Parents, Mentors, and Peers
▶ Chapter 11 Test (Form A or B)
▶ Alternative Assessment Handbook
▶ Chapter 11 Test for English Language Learners and Special-needs Students

REVIEW
Have students complete the Chapter 11 Review on pages 254–255.

ASSESS
Use one of the chapter tests to assess students' understanding of the content. For Alternative Assessment, see the Portfolio Activities and Alternative Assessment Handbook.

CHAPTER 11 REVIEW ANSWERS

Understanding Main Ideas
1. Except for coastal areas, most of the Arabian Peninsula is desert. People became nomadic herders because they could not grow crops.

2. He had a religious vision and believed Allah spoke to him through Jibreel.

3. Muslims believe it is the word of God and follow its rules and instructions.

4. parts of Syria, Persia, and North Africa, Spain, Mesopotamia, much of Asia Minor, northern India

5. The Muslim army conquered Spain and the Moors began ruling.

6. They could not agree on who should be caliph and 'Uthmān was murdered for favoring his own clan.

7. Historically Arabs, including Muhammad, had been traders.

8. maps, measuring system, astrolabe

9. Islamic religious art cannot show human form, so it emphasized geometric and floral patterns.

Reviewing Themes
1. Muslims learned from the peoples they conquered.

2. The peoples they conquered were influenced by Muslim culture.

3. The Qur'an guided daily life and Islamic belief shaped the art that was created.

254

Review

Creating a Time Line
Copy the time line below onto a sheet of paper. Complete the time line by filling in the events, individuals, and dates from the chapter that you think were significant. Pick three events and explain why you think they were significant.

| A.D. 500 | A.D. 700 | A.D. 1000 | A.D. 1200 |

Writing a Summary
Using standard grammar, spelling, sentence structure, and punctuation, write an overview of the events in the chapter.

Identifying People and Ideas
Identify the following terms or individuals and explain their significance:

1. Muhammad   6. caliph
2. hijrah   7. Tāriq
3. Muslims   8. Moors
4. Qur'an   9. al-Rāzī
5. mosque   10. minaret

Understanding Main Ideas

Section 1 (pp. 240–242)
The Rise of Islam
1. Why did some Arab traders and others who lived in the Arabian Peninsula follow the lifestyles of nomadic herders?
2. Why do Muslims call Muhammad "the prophet of Islam"?
3. What role does the Qur'an play in the lives of faithful Muslims?

Section 2 (pp. 243–247)
The Spread of Islam
4. Which areas were included in the Muslim Empire by A.D. 750?
5. What was the result when the Berbers crossed into Spain?
6. What factors caused Islam to divide into two main branches?

Section 3 (pp. 248–253)
Islamic Civilization
7. What role did trade play in Muslim culture?
8. What navigational aids did the Muslims develop?
9. Why did Muslims produce the type of art they did?

Reviewing Themes
1. **Science, Technology & Society** Why was there a development and flow of scientific information in the Muslim Empire?
2. **Global Relations** How did conquest contribute to the spread of Muslim culture?
3. **Culture** In what ways did the Islamic religion shape how the Muslim culture developed?

Thinking Critically
1. **Summarizing** How did the rise of Islam change the course of Arab history?
2. **Drawing Conclusions** How was Islam linked to other faiths?
3. **Evaluating** How did *The Thousand and One Nights* reflect both the history of the culture in which it was created and universal themes?
4. **Supporting a Point of View** What do you think was the most important contribution of the Muslim Empire to the world? Why?

Writing About History
Summarizing Write a report describing how Islamic rules affected Muslim family life in the Islamic Empire. Use the chart below to organize your thoughts before you write.

	Islamic Rules	Effect
Men		
Women		
Marriage		
Slavery		

Have students explain how Muslims made advances in trade, art, mathematics, science, and education.

RETEACH

Direct students who had difficulty with the test to write a question and answer about the material in each subsection. When students are ready, have them take the Form B Test to assess their mastery of the material.

ENGLISH LANGUAGE LEARNERS

Portfolio Extensions

Link to TODAY

1. Ask students to investigate nations that today are predominantly Islamic. Have them prepare a report on the role religion plays in law, government, and daily life there.

2. Have students prepare a report on the holy places in Mecca and the religious ceremonies that take place during pilgrimage. Have them explain how these ceremonies differ from those of Buddhism, Christianity, Confucianism, Hinduism, and Judaism.

3. Have students write a journal for a Muslim trader sometime between 570 and 1000. Have them create a map showing their journey.

Building Social Studies Skills

Using Art to Understand History

Study the illustration below. Then answer the questions that follow.

Islamic illustration of weighing goods, c. A.D. 900s–A.D. 1000s

1. Which statement best describes what you can conclude about daily life during the period illustrated?

   a. The people of this time invented the scales pictured.

   b. Merchants sold goods by weight, and wore clothing similar to that shown.

   c. Merchants only sold goods in bundles like those shown in the drawing.

   d. Only men could be merchants.

2. The subject of the drawing above is taken from Islamic daily life. What other subjects were used in Islamic art? Give specific examples.

Analyzing Historical Context

Read the following excerpt from a modern historian's description of the life of Muhammad. Then answer the questions below.

> "But at this point a group of pilgrims from Yathrib [the city of Medina] . . . met him [Muhammad] . . . and some time later a deputation [group of representatives] set out to invite the Prophet to make Yathrib his home and base. This was the first big breakthrough. Muhammad eagerly accepted the offer and . . . arrived safely in Yathrib in September, 622."

3. According to the excerpt above, which of the following statements best describes the reason that Muhammad settled in Yathrib?

   a. Muhammad was invited to settle in Yathrib by representatives of the city.

   b. Muhammad settled in Yathrib because it was a major commercial and trading center in the Arabian Peninsula.

   c. Muhammad refused to accept the Yathrib deputation's offer and thus had to be forced to settle in the city.

   d. Muhammad and his followers settled in Yathrib after city officials offered to build a great mosque there.

4. Why did the author of the excerpt above describe the events surrounding Muhammad's move to Yathrib as "the first big breakthrough"? Give specific reasons for your answer.

Alternative Assessment

Building Your Portfolio

Link to TODAY

Science, Technology & Society

The contributions to science, mathematics, and technology made by early Islamic societies had a far-ranging impact on the world. Identify a scientific, mathematical, or technological discovery of Islamic societies. Then trace the spread of these ideas to other civilizations and describe the changes they produced.

internet connect

Internet Activity: go.hrw.com
KEYWORD: SP3 WH11

Choose a topic on the Islamic World to:

• research Muslim contributions to medicine and science.

• research and report on Islamic culture.

• create a chart of Islamic calligraphy designs.

Thinking Critically

1. Islam guided both religious life and daily life.

2. based on belief in one God; word of God revealed in a holy book that includes rules for right living

3. It deals with universal themes in the context of Muslim culture and history.

4. Answers will vary.

Writing About History

Men: head of household, could have no more than four wives—responsible for a woman's behavior; Women: clearly defined position, had more rights than under traditional Arab law—enjoyed more freedom than most women of the time; Marriage: woman could make her own choice—afforded women more freedom; Slavery: Qur'an urged Muslims to free their slaves—slave owners were required to treat slaves humanely

Building Social Studies Skills

1. b

2. Geometric and floral designs, famous battles

3. a

4. After the move to Yathrib, Muhammad gained many followers.

Building Your Portfolio

Students should find Islamic discoveries, trace their spread, and describe the changes produced.

CROSS-CULTURAL CONNECTIONS

World Religions

 LET'S GET STARTED!

As students enter the classroom, ask them to identify examples of religious influence in contemporary world events. (*Students might mention international visits of religious leaders or prayer services honoring the memory of victims of natural disasters or terrorist attacks.*) Tell students that in the World Religions feature they will learn about the history and importance of major world religions.

MAP ANSWER

Major religions are predominant in the following regions: Christianity—North America, South America, Europe, northern Asia, Australia; Islam—northern Africa, southwest Asia; Hinduism— India; Buddhism— central Asia and southeast Asia

INTERPRETING THE GRAPHS ANSWERS

most: Christianity, 33%; second most: Islam, 19.3%

CROSS-CULTURAL CONNECTIONS

World Religions

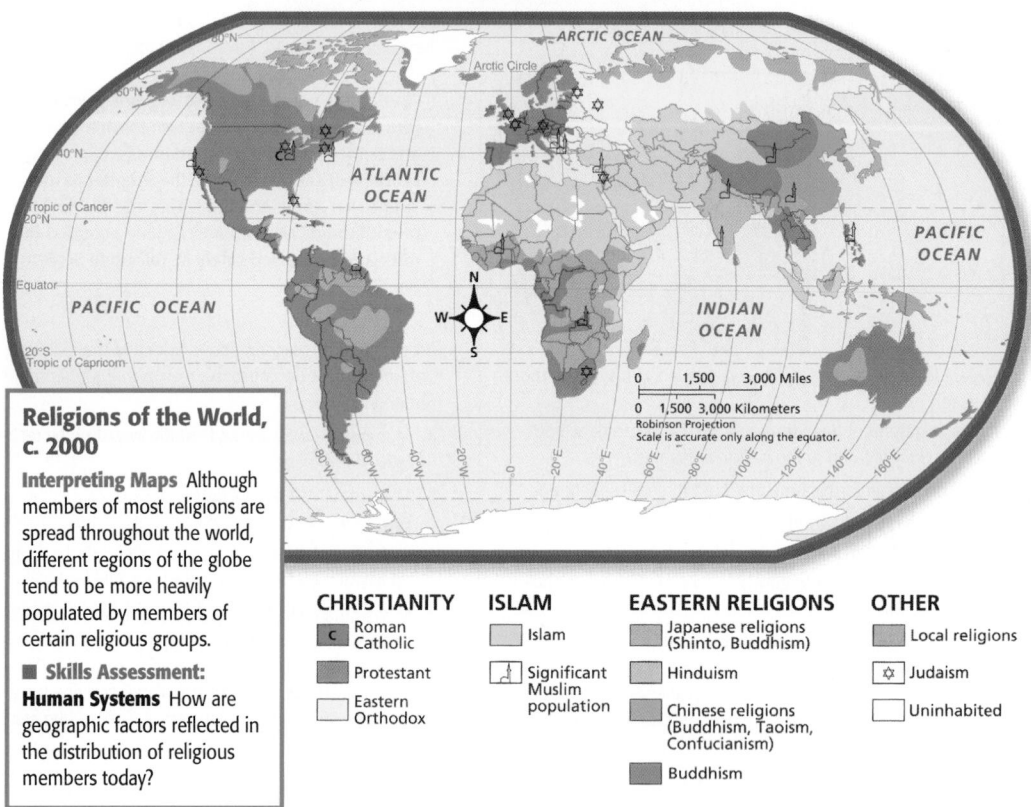

CHRISTIANITY
- C — Roman Catholic
- Protestant
- Eastern Orthodox

ISLAM
- Islam
- Significant Muslim population

EASTERN RELIGIONS
- Japanese religions (Shinto, Buddhism)
- Hinduism
- Chinese religions (Buddhism, Taoism, Confucianism)
- Buddhism

OTHER
- Local religions
- Judaism
- Uninhabited

Religions of the World, c. 2000

Interpreting Maps Although members of most religions are spread throughout the world, different regions of the globe tend to be more heavily populated by members of certain religious groups.

■ **Skills Assessment:**
Human Systems How are geographic factors reflected in the distribution of religious members today?

MEMBERSHIP IN WORLD RELIGIONS, c. 2000

Percentage of World Population

- Christianity 33%
- Islam 19.3%
- No Religion 15.3%
- Hinduism 13.4%
- Other 12.7%
- Buddhism 6%
- Judaism .2%
- Confucianism .1%

Number of Followers

- Christianity — 1,974,181,000
- Islam — 1,155,109,000
- Hinduism — 799,028,000
- Buddhism — 356,270,000
- Judaism – 14,313,000
- Confucianism – 6,253,000
- All Other Religions — 760,884,000

Source: *World Almanac and Book of Facts, 2001*

Interpreting the Graphs

The six major religions in this feature still have large followings throughout the world. *What religion has the most followers throughout the world? The second most? What percentage of the global population do they represent?*

256

TEACH

Tell students that Judaism developed in the eastern Mediterranean region. The migration of Jews to other parts of the world is known as the diaspora (dy•AS•puh•ruh). During the Babylonian Exile in 586 B.C., many Jews were forced into slavery in Babylon (modern-day Iraq). During Roman times, Jews were dispersed throughout the Mediterranean lands of the Roman Empire. Later, they moved throughout much of Europe, North Africa, and Arabia. Jews in Mediterranean lands were known as *Sephardim,* while those in central and eastern Europe were known as *Ashkenazim.* In the late 1800s and 1900s many *Ashkenazim* migrated to North America. The Holocaust in Europe forced many Jews to flee to the United States and to Palestine. The creation of the state of Israel in 1948 encouraged further migration to that area.

Have students create a map of the diaspora. The map should show routes of major migrations, dates, and numbers of migrants. Then have students create a pie graph showing the distribution of Jews today by major countries.

JUDAISM

Sacred Text:
The Torah

Sacred Symbol:
Star of David

The Wailing Wall,
Jerusalem

Sacred Site:
Jerusalem

HISTORY MAKER

**Abraham
(c. 2000 B.C.)**

According to biblical sources, Abraham was originally an inhabitant of Ur, where he was known as Abram. After establishing a covenant with God, he changed his name to Abraham, meaning "father of many." This reflected a promise that Abraham would be the leader of many peoples.

Abraham is a sacred figure to three religions: Judaism, Christianity, and Islam. All three faiths trace their heritage to Abraham through the line of prophets descended from his sons. Some people consider Abraham the first historical figure to follow a faith with one supreme deity. **How does Abraham's connection to modern religions reflect his name "father of many"?**

SPECIAL DAYS

Passover, in spring; Rosh Ha-Shanah and Yom Kippur, in autumn; and Hanukkah, in late autumn or winter

Interdisciplinary Connection

LITERATURE. The Torah, Hebrew for "law" or "doctrine," consists of the first five books of the Old Testament, also called the Pentateuch. According to tradition, they were written by Moses and are based on God's revelation to the people of Israel.

The Torah forms the cornerstone of Jewish religion and law. Every synagogue keeps a copy of the Torah on parchment scrolls handwritten in Hebrew and kept inside a special container called an ark. During religious services, the scrolls are removed from the ark, and certain passages are read aloud. Torah scrolls are always treated with great care and reverence when they are handled. In fact, the actual parchment is not supposed to be touched. Instead, a small pointer called a Yad is used to assist with readings from the Torah.

Critical Thinking

Ask students why the Torah is important in Judaism.

ANSWER: based on God's revelation, forms the cornerstone of Jewish religion and law

HISTORY MAKER ANSWER

Judaism, Christianity, and Islam trace their religious heritage to Abraham through the line of prophets descended from his sons.

Point out that Hinduism began to develop about 4,000 years ago in the Indian subcontinent. Today Hinduism is the main religion of India and is closely tied to India's history and culture. Unlike most other major world religions, Hinduism has no founder, no clear beginning, and no central authority, hierarchy, or organization. Hinduism includes the worship of many different gods that range from local deities to pan-Indian gods or even a single high God. There is no single belief that unites all followers of the religion. There are, however, several widely held beliefs that are common among Hindus. Most believe in the sanctity of the ancient religious writings known as the Vedas and in an eternal and infinite source of reality called *brahman*. Other common beliefs include *ahimsa*—noninjury to living things—and *samsara*—a continuous cycle of rebirth.

Have students work in groups to find answers to the following questions: How many people in the world are followers of Hinduism? In which countries other than India is Hinduism practiced? What are some common beliefs and practices of Hinduism?

Culture

One of the most important concepts in the study of geography and religion is the idea of sacred space. Followers of nearly all religions perceive certain places as holy or sacred. These places are visited, venerated, and respected by the religion's followers. Sacred places are usually clearly marked, and important ritual behaviors, ceremonies, and activities take place there. In fact, certain behaviors such as taking off one's shoes or not taking photographs may be required of all visitors.

Hindus believe the waters of the Ganges River have the power to cleanse sin, and hundreds of temples line the river's banks. In addition to the Ganges, other sacred rivers in India include the Indus, Narmada, and Yamuna.

ACTIVITY: Have students create a map of sacred places in India using the library and other resources. Then have them analyze the distribution of India's sacred sites.

HISTORY MAKER ANSWER

He taught that the key to enlightenment was to live apart from the material world.

HINDUISM

HISTORY MAKER

Mahavira (c. 599 B.C.–527 B.C.)

Over the years many religious leaders added to and expanded Hindu thought. One such person was Mahavira, also known as Vardhamana. He was born into a warrior clan in northeastern India. At the age of 30 he left his home and entered the forest to find spiritual fulfillment. He got rid of all his personal possessions, then spent more than 12 years wandering the countryside with nothing to his name and little contact with other people.

After he felt he had gained the answers to his questions about life, Mahavira began teaching others. He believed the key to enlightenment was to live apart from the material world as much as possible. Many early Hindus were influenced by his ideas. Eventually his beliefs became the basis of Jainism, a new religion. **How did Mahavira influence Hindus?**

Sacred Texts:
The Vedas, Bhagavad Gita

Festival of Holi

Hindus consider it a sacred duty to bathe in the holy waters of the Ganges River. This ritual cleanses the bather's mind and spirit.

Sacred Sites:
Ganges River, city of Varanas

Sacred Creature:
The cow

The cow is a particularly sacred animal in the Hindu faith in part because of the important role it has played in sustaining life.

SPECIAL DAYS

Festival of Holi, in spring; Diwali, or Deepavali (Festival of Lights) in autumn

Explain that Buddhism originated about 2,500 years ago in the foothills of the Himalayas in what is now India as an offshoot of Hinduism. The Buddha sent monks to preach the faith to others. During the Buddha's lifetime, the new religion spread throughout northern India. In the 200s B.C. missionaries introduced Buddhism to Sri Lanka. Missionaries and traders later introduced Buddhism to China (c. 100 B.C.–A.D. 200), Korea and Japan (c. A.D. 300–500), Southeast Asia (c. A.D. 400–600), Tibet (c. A.D. 700), and Mongolia (c. A.D. 1500). Buddhism developed many regional forms such as Mahayana in China, Korea, and Japan; Theravada in Sri Lanka and mainland Southeast Asia; and Lamaism in Tibet and Mongolia. While Buddhism diffused throughout much of Asia, it declined in India.

Using the information above, have students create a map showing the origin and diffusion of Buddhism in Asia. The maps should show the direction of the religion's spread and dates when it reached certain areas.

BUDDHISM

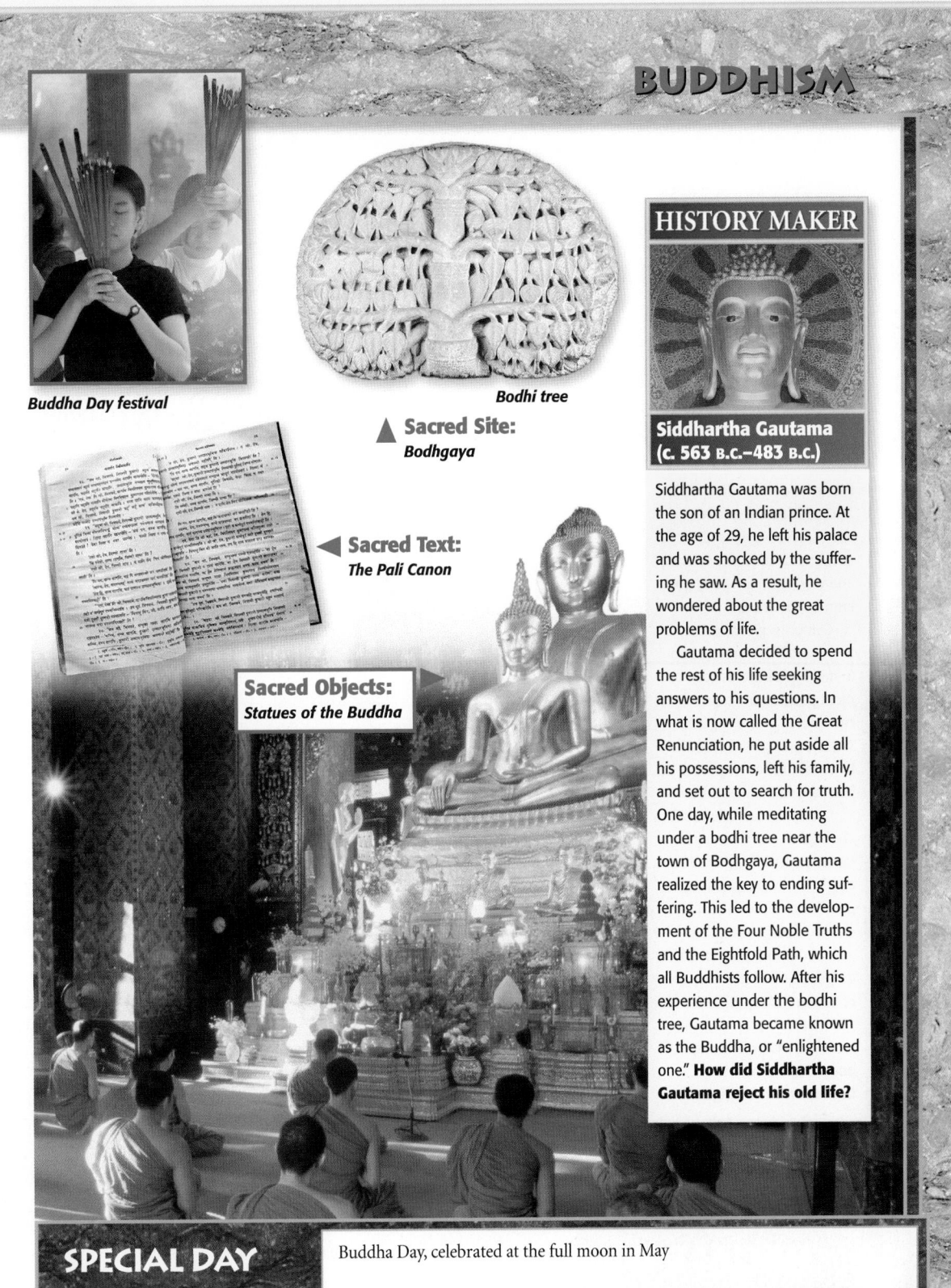

Buddha Day festival

Bodhi tree

▲ **Sacred Site:**
Bodhgaya

◄ **Sacred Text:**
The Pali Canon

Sacred Objects:
Statues of the Buddha

SPECIAL DAY

Buddha Day, celebrated at the full moon in May

HISTORY MAKER

Siddhartha Gautama
(c. 563 B.C.–483 B.C.)

Siddhartha Gautama was born the son of an Indian prince. At the age of 29, he left his palace and was shocked by the suffering he saw. As a result, he wondered about the great problems of life.

Gautama decided to spend the rest of his life seeking answers to his questions. In what is now called the Great Renunciation, he put aside all his possessions, left his family, and set out to search for truth. One day, while meditating under a bodhi tree near the town of Bodhgaya, Gautama realized the key to ending suffering. This led to the development of the Four Noble Truths and the Eightfold Path, which all Buddhists follow. After his experience under the bodhi tree, Gautama became known as the Buddha, or "enlightened one." **How did Siddhartha Gautama reject his old life?**

Interdisciplinary Connection

ART. The first Buddha statues were made in about A.D. 100 in what are now Afghanistan, Pakistan, and northern India. Later, statues were produced in nearly every location where Buddhism was practiced. They range from enormous stone carvings made in cliffs to bronze and gold statues in temples and smaller figures that occupy gardens or homes.

Statues typically show the Buddha in one of four positions: standing, walking, sitting in meditation, or lying down. In addition, certain hand gestures (mudras) are used to symbolize important ideas, events, or actions. Hands nestled in the lap symbolize meditation. The right hand raised with the palm facing outward symbolizes the dispelling of fear. A seated Buddha with one finger touching the ground symbolizes faith and resolution.

ACTIVITY: Have students use computer software to find photographs of different Buddha statues. Then have them copy the images and describe what the position and hand gestures symbolize.

HISTORY MAKER ANSWER
He put aside his possessions, left his family, and set out to search for truth.

Tell students that Confucius was China's most famous and influential teacher and philosopher. His ideas and personal views on how to live a moral and proper life have influenced Chinese culture for more than 2,000 years. In addition, Confucian ideas diffused to other countries, particularly Japan, the Koreas, and Vietnam. One of the fundamental beliefs of followers of Confucianism is that all people have the ability to learn and improve themselves. Confucius spent many years studying Chinese rituals, history, music, poetry, arithmetic, archery, and charioteering. In his 30s, Confucius began teaching. He wanted to make education widely available. As his fame spread, many people came to listen to his teachings. Confucius lectured on topics such as the ancient classics and self-improvement. He helped to establish teaching as a profession and way of life.

Have students research the life, philosophy, teachings, and influence of Confucius. Then ask them to discuss which educational philosophies of Confucius are still important concepts today.

Culture

In ancient Chinese thought there are two complementary forces contained in all things—yin and yang. Yin is thought of as Earth, female, dark, passive, and yielding. It is associated with the Moon, winter, even numbers, and valleys and streams. Yang is conceived of as heaven, male, light, active, and forceful. It is associated with the Sun, summer, odd numbers, and mountains.

According to belief, a balance of yin-yang forces is essential to universal harmony. As one of the forces increases, the other decreases. When the two forces are in balance, they are represented as the light and dark halves of a circle.

ACTIVITY: Have students draw a circle with light and dark halves representing a balance of yin-yang forces. Then have them list the ideas and symbols associated with each half of the circle.

HISTORY MAKER ANSWER

because Confucius had little to say about gods, the meaning of death, or life after death

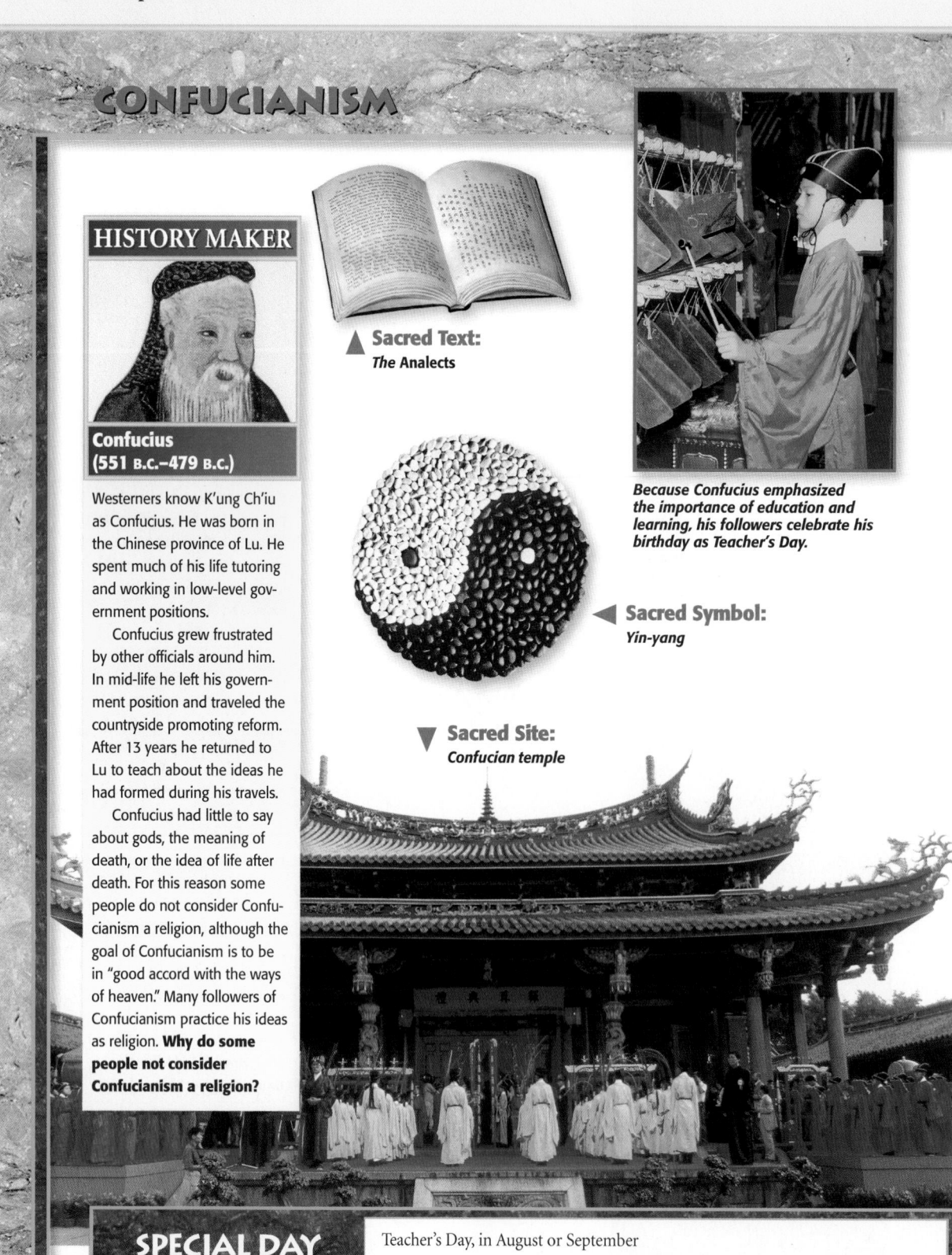

CONFUCIANISM

HISTORY MAKER

Confucius (551 B.C.–479 B.C.)

Westerners know K'ung Ch'iu as Confucius. He was born in the Chinese province of Lu. He spent much of his life tutoring and working in low-level government positions.

Confucius grew frustrated by other officials around him. In mid-life he left his government position and traveled the countryside promoting reform. After 13 years he returned to Lu to teach about the ideas he had formed during his travels.

Confucius had little to say about gods, the meaning of death, or the idea of life after death. For this reason some people do not consider Confucianism a religion, although the goal of Confucianism is to be in "good accord with the ways of heaven." Many followers of Confucianism practice his ideas as religion. **Why do some people not consider Confucianism a religion?**

▲ **Sacred Text:** *The* Analects

Because Confucius emphasized the importance of education and learning, his followers celebrate his birthday as Teacher's Day.

◀ **Sacred Symbol:** *Yin-yang*

▼ **Sacred Site:** *Confucian temple*

SPECIAL DAY

Teacher's Day, in August or September

TEACH

Point out that Christianity is the world's largest religion, both in number of followers and by area. More than 1.8 billion people are Christian—roughly one third of the world's population. Christianity is the dominant religion in most of North and South America, Europe and Russia, Australia, New Zealand, the Philippines, and many parts of sub-Saharan Africa. Despite Christianity's widespread distribution, it is fragmented into many separate denominations with different religious hierarchies and practices. In the United States, there are hundreds of different Christian groups. Some major regional patterns include an area of Baptist and other conservative denominations in the South; Lutherans in Wisconsin, Minnesota, and the Dakotas; Mormons in Utah; and Roman Catholics in southern Louisiana, the Southwest, and Northeast.

Have students create a map showing major regional patterns of Christian groups in the United States. Then ask them to identify historical and cultural factors that might explain these patterns.

CHRISTIANITY

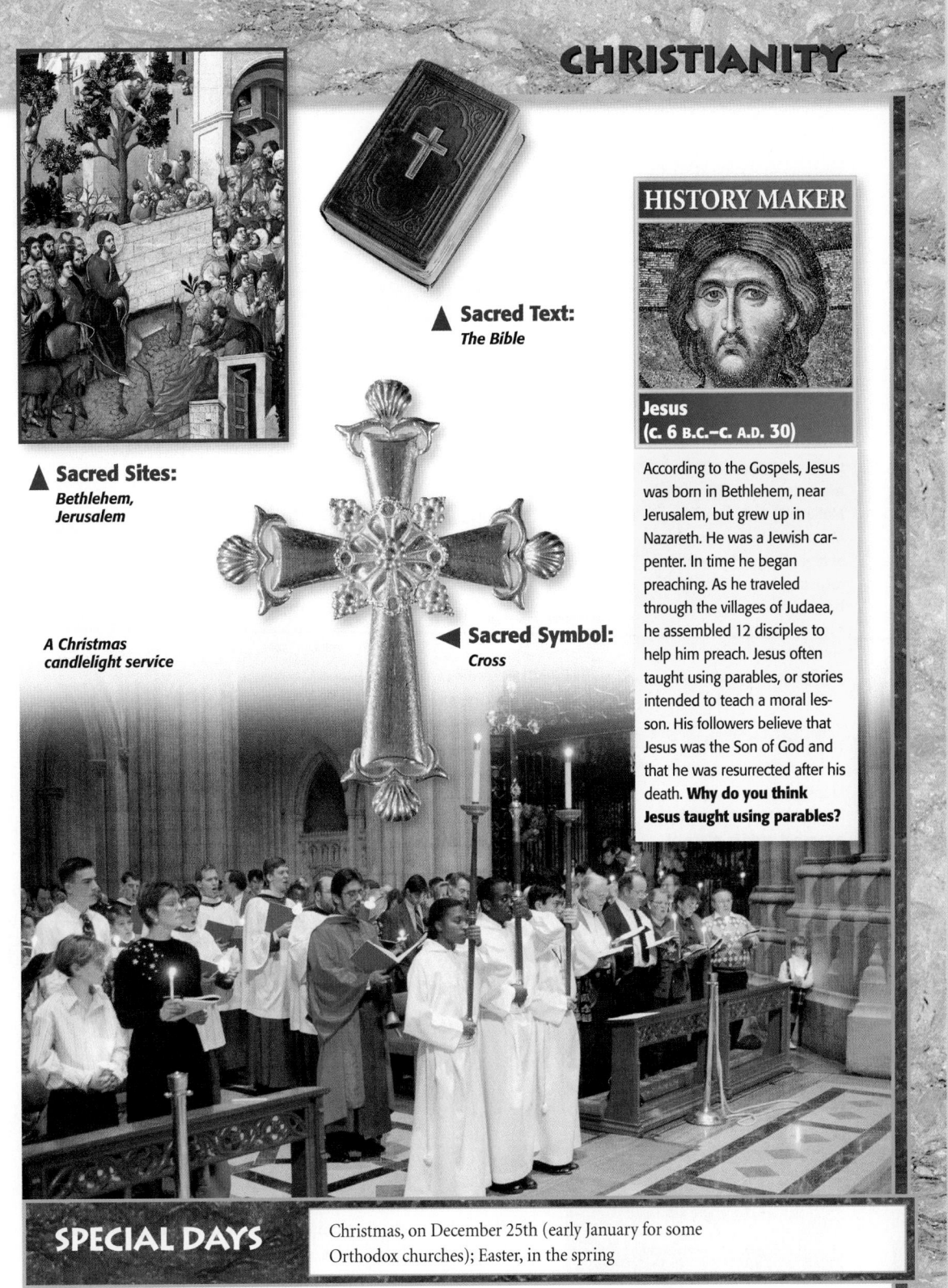

▲ **Sacred Text:**
The Bible

▲ **Sacred Sites:**
Bethlehem,
Jerusalem

A Christmas
candlelight service

◀ **Sacred Symbol:**
Cross

HISTORY MAKER

Jesus
(c. 6 B.C.–c. A.D. 30)

According to the Gospels, Jesus was born in Bethlehem, near Jerusalem, but grew up in Nazareth. He was a Jewish carpenter. In time he began preaching. As he traveled through the villages of Judaea, he assembled 12 disciples to help him preach. Jesus often taught using parables, or stories intended to teach a moral lesson. His followers believe that Jesus was the Son of God and that he was resurrected after his death. **Why do you think Jesus taught using parables?**

SPECIAL DAYS

Christmas, on December 25th (early January for some Orthodox churches); Easter, in the spring

Daily Life

Buildings such as churches can reflect the history, culture, beliefs, and regional geography of the places where they are found.

Christian churches vary greatly in architectural style, size, ornateness, building materials, and other factors. For example, Europe's gothic cathedrals are typically huge stone structures with vaulted ceilings, stained glass windows, flying buttresses, gargoyles, and other decorations. In contrast, many Protestant churches in the United States are very simple in design and decoration.

Critical Thinking

Ask students how geographers use church architecture to learn about the history, culture, and physical geography of different regions.

ANSWER: They study the distribution of such factors as the age of churches, building materials used, and cultural characteristics.

HISTORY MAKER ANSWER
to teach moral lessons to ordinary people in simple terms

Tell students that the Five Pillars of Islam provide Muslims with the basis for living a proper and moral life. The Five Pillars are 1) a profession of faith demonstrated by the statement "There is no god but Allah, and Muhammad is His messenger"; 2) daily prayer; 3) giving charity to the poor; 4) fasting from dawn to sunset during the holy month of Ramadan; and 5) making a pilgrimage to the holy city of Mecca once in a lifetime. The Five Pillars are important symbolic acts of faith. For example, fasting during the month of Ramadan is a demanding physical exercise. This practice binds members of the Muslim community together and symbolizes the importance of spiritual matters over the phys-

ical demands of the body. Every evening after dark, families and friends congregate to break their fast and celebrate their faith.

Have students research the Five Pillars of Islam. Then lead a discussion on the importance of these symbolic acts of faith in Muslim communities.

Daily Life

The use of prayer rugs developed many years after the death of Muhammad, but some Muslims use them to cover the ground on which they worship. Prayer rugs are usually 2–4 feet wide and 4–8 feet long. They are often decorated with special religious designs or prayers.

Islamic art generally does not include images of humans or animals. Therefore, prayer rugs are characterized by rich colors and detailed geometric patterns. These decorations always include the arched mihrab, or prayer place, that is pointed toward Mecca when the rug is used in prayer.

Critical Thinking

Ask students why prayer rugs are special objects for Muslims.

ANSWER: used during worship; decorated with religious designs or prayers

---

HISTORY MAKER ANSWER
Islam prohibits the use of images for Muhammad.

ISLAM

HISTORY MAKER

Muhammad
(C. A.D. 570–A.D. 632)

In Islam, Muhammad is a messenger or prophet of God. Muhammad was born in Mecca (Makkah) and orphaned at an early age. He was from a respected but poor family. They belonged to a leading tribe of caravan merchants and keepers of Abraham's shrine and pilgrimage site, the Kaaba.

Islam prohibits the use of images for Muhammad. The symbol above, which means "Muhammad is the Prophet of God," is often used in place of his picture. **Why is a symbol used in place of Muhammad's image?**

▲ **Sacred Text:**
Qur'an

▲ **Special Objects:**
Prayer rugs

Muslim woman praying during Ramadan

Thousands of Muslim pilgrims gather around the Kaaba in Mecca.

Sacred Sites:
Mecca (Makkah), Al-Madīnah, Jerusalem

SPECIAL DAYS

Fast of Ramadan, during the entire ninth month of the Islamic year; ʿĪd al-Fitr, at the end of Ramadan; and ʿĪd al-Adha, at the end of the hajj in the twelfth lunar month

Portfolio Extensions

1. Have students work in groups to create a collage for each of the major religions covered in this feature. Collages may include photocopies or drawings of buildings or other sacred places, symbols or sacred objects, and founders or other leaders. Have groups display and discuss their collages, noting similarities among the religions.

2. Have each student research one of the special days listed for a religion covered in this feature. Students should create presentations that include traditions, songs, and/or foods associated with each special day. Then have students create a class calendar showing when these special days are celebrated.

3. Discuss the information provided in the bibliography for this feature (Further Reading). Then divide students into groups and assign each group one of the religions covered in this feature. Have each group create a bibliography for its assigned religion.

BUILDING YOUR **Portfolio**

World Religions Review

Culture

The major religions of the world share many common ideas and histories. Using what you have read in this feature and in previous chapters, create a chart comparing the historical origins, central ideas, and spread of Judaism, Hinduism, Buddhism, Confucianism, Christianity, and Islam.

Global Relations

Religion has played an important role in many historical events and continues to shape events even today. Using what you have read in this book, as well as other sources, pick one of the religions covered in this feature and create a booklet identifying examples of its influence on both historic and modern world events.

A Roman Catholic patriarch and a Jewish rabbi shake hands. Christianity and Judaism, like other major religions, share many traditions and beliefs.

Further Reading

Breuilly, Elizabeth, et al. *Religions of the World: The Illustrated Guide to Origins, Beliefs, Traditions, and Festivals.* Checkmark Books, 1997.

Crim, Keith, general editor. *The Perennial Dictionary of World Religions.* Harper San Francisco, 1989.

Smith, Huston. *The Illustrated World's Religions: A Guide to Our Wisdom Traditions.* Harper San Francisco, 1995.

Sullivan, Lawrence E. *Enchanting Powers: Music in the World's Religions.* Harvard University Press, 1997.

Wilson, Andrew, editor. *World Scripture: A Comparative Anthology of Sacred Texts.* Paragon House, 1995.

internet connect

Internet Activity: go.hrw.com
KEYWORD: SP3 Religions
KEYWORD: Holt Researcher

In assigned groups, develop a multimedia presentation about one of the world religions in this feature. Choose information from the HRW Go site and from the Holt Researcher that best reflects the major historical events, ideas, and traditions of that religion.

Linking Past to Present

In conjunction with the Columbian Exposition, a Parliament of World Religions was held in Chicago in 1893. The purpose of the meeting was to promote peace and harmony among the world's religions. One hundred years later, a second meeting in Chicago brought together 8,000 people of diverse cultures to discuss the role of religion in the world. In 1999 a third Parliament of World Religions was held in Cape Town, South Africa. At this meeting, people celebrated their religious diversity and worked toward understanding and tolerance.

Critical Thinking

Ask students what common goals might be shared by people of different religions.

ANSWER: support for human rights, desire for world peace, promotion of tolerance and understanding among different cultures

The Civilizations of East Asia

CHAPTER RESOURCE MANAGER

	Objectives	Pacing Guide	Reproducible Resources
SECTION 1 **China under the Sui, Tang, and Sung Dynasties** (pp. 266–271)	• Explain how Chinese civilization advanced during the Sui and Tang dynasties. • Describe what daily life was like for the Chinese people during the Sung dynasty.	**Regular** 1.5 day / **Block Scheduling** 1 day *Block Scheduling Handbook with Team Teaching Strategies, 12.1*	RS Guided Reading Strategy 12.1 RS Graphic Organizer Activity 12: The Dynasties PS Readings in World History 45: A Woman's Hundred Years E Hands-on History Activity 12: Warriors, Writers, and Inventors
SECTION 2 **The Mongol Empire** (pp. 272–275)	• Explore how the Mongol invaders were able to conquer and rule so much of Asia. • Examine the effect Mongol rule had on China.	**Regular** 1.5 day / **Block Scheduling** 1 day *Block Scheduling Handbook with Team Teaching Strategies, 12.2*	RS Guided Reading Strategy 12.2 PS Readings in World History 46: Kublai Khan's Great Park at Shangdu
SECTION 3 **Japan, Korea, and Southeast Asia** (pp. 276–283)	• Investigate how the geography of Japan influenced its development. • Analyze how China influenced the early development of Japan. • Describe how changes in government influenced society in feudal Japan. • Examine how Southeast Asia was influenced by China and India.	**Regular** 1.5 day / **Block Scheduling** 1 day *Block Scheduling Handbook with Team Teaching Strategies, 12.3*	RS Guided Reading Strategy 12.3 SM Geography Activity 12: The Wind That Saved Japan PS Readings in World History 47: Drinking Tea for a Long Life PS Readings in World History 48: Actors and Entertainers in Feudal Japan E Creative Teaching Strategy 12: Asian Travelogues

Chapter Resource Key

PS	Primary Sources	REV	Review		Video
RS	Reading Support	ELL	Reinforcement and English Language Learners		Internet
IC	Interdisciplinary Connections				Holt Presentation Maker Using Microsoft® PowerPoint®
E	Enrichment		Transparencies		
SM	Skills Mastery		CD–ROM		
A	Assessment		Music		

One-Stop Planner CD-ROM

See the **One-Stop Planner** for a complete list of additional resources for students and teachers.

One-Stop Planner CD-ROM

It's easy to plan lessons, select resources, and print out materials for your students when you use the **One-Stop Planner** CD–ROM with **Test Generator.**

Technology Resources	Reinforcement, Review, and Assessment
💿 One-Stop Planner 12.1	Daily Quiz 12.1
🎵 Holt Researcher: World History: Empress Wu	Main Idea Activity 12.1
📼 World History and Cultures Video Program 12: The Golden Age of Asian Civilization	English Audio Summary 12.1
💾 World History Teaching Transparency: Art and History 13: Landscape on a Fan	Spanish Audio Summary 12.1
💾 World History Teaching Transparency: Everyday Life 12: Chinese Tea Processing	REV Section 1 Review, p. 271
🌐 Homework Practice Online	
🌐 Online Maps, Charts, and Graphs: Changan, 750	
🌐 Online Maps, Charts, and Graphs: Population Shifts in China, 750–1250	
💿 One-Stop Planner 12.2	Daily Quiz 12.2
🌐 Holt Researcher: World History: Genghis Khan	Main Idea Activity 12.2
🌐 Homework Practice Online	English Audio Summary 12.2
🌐 Online Maps, Charts, and Graphs: Mongol Empire, 1200s	Spanish Audio Summary 12.2
	REV Section 2 Review, p. 275
💿 One-Stop Planner 12.3	Daily Quiz 12.3
🌐 Holt Researcher: World History: Sejong	Main Idea Activity 12.3
🎵 Regions of the World Music Audio CD Program 20: Japan and the Koreas: Music of the One-String Ichigenkin	English Audio Summary 12.3
📼 CNN Presents World Cultures: Yesterday and Today Segment 12: Buddhism in Mongolia	Spanish Audio Summary 12.3
💾 World History Teaching Transparency: Geography and History 12: New Cultures in Asia, c. 670–1392	REV Section 3 Review, p. 283
🌐 Homework Practice Online	

⚡ internet connect

HRW ONLINE RESOURCES
  GO TO: go.hrw.com
  Then type in a keyword.

TEACHER HOME PAGE
  KEYWORD: SP3 Teacher

CHAPTER INTERNET ACTIVITIES
  KEYWORD: SP3 WH12
Choose an activity to:
- understand similarities and differences of Chinese, Japanese, and Korean art.
- research the early development of Korea, Vietnam, and the Khmer Empire of Southeast Asia.
- learn more about Genghis Khan.

CHAPTER ENRICHMENT LINKS
  KEYWORD: SP3 CH12

ONLINE ASSESSMENT
  Homework Practice
  KEYWORD: SP3 HP12
  Standardized Test Prep
  KEYWORD: SP3 STP12
  Rubrics
  KEYWORD: SS Rubrics

ONLINE MAPS, CHARTS, AND GRAPHS
  KEYWORD: SP3 MCG

CONTENT UPDATES
  KEYWORD: SS Content Updates

HOLT PRESENTATION MAKER
  KEYWORD: SP3 PPT12

ONLINE READING SUPPORT
  KEYWORD: SS Strategies

CURRENT EVENTS
  KEYWORD: S3 Current Events

Meeting Individual Needs

Ability Levels

Level 1 Basic level activities designed for all students encountering new material

Level 2 Intermediate level activities designed for average students

Level 3 Challenging activities designed for honors and gifted and talented students

English Language Learners These activities address the needs of students with Limited English Proficiency.

Chapter Review and Assessment

IC Vocabulary Activity 12	A Chapter 12 Test Generator (on the One-Stop Planner)
💿 Global Skill Builder CD–ROM	A Chapter 12 Test (Form A or B)
🌐 HRW Web Site	A Alternative Assessment Handbook
REV Chapter 12 Tutorial for Students, Parents, Mentors, and Peers	A Chapter 12 Test for English Language Learners and Special-Needs Students
REV Chapter 12 Review, pp. 284–285	

Section 1 *China under the Sui, Tang, and Sung Dynasties*

Section 2 *The Mongol Empire*

Section 3 *Japan, Korea, and Southeast Asia*

Build on What You Know

Ask students to answer the following questions:

What advances were made in China under the Han dynasty?

Consider:

- the government
- trade
- the arts and sciences

How did the philosophies of ancient China influence its development?

Consider:

- Confucianism
- Daoism
- Legalism

EXPLORING THE TIME LINE
GLOBAL EVENTS

internet connect

go.hrw.com

TOPIC: Marco Polo
GO TO: go.hrw.com
KEYWORD: SP3 WH12

Have students access the Internet through the HRW Go site to conduct research on Marco Polo. In about 1275, Marco Polo visited the court of Kublai Khan. Have students pretend to be Marco Polo and compose a journal entry for one of the days Polo visited Khan's court.

CHAPTER
12

A.D. 552–A.D. 1573

The Civilizations of East Asia

C. A.D. 584
Science and Technology
Work begins on the Grand Canal.

A.D. 589
Politics
The Sui dynasty reunites China.

A.D. 618
Politics
The Tang dynasty begins in China.

A ceramic Chinese vase, from between A.D. 960 and A.D. 1127

C. A.D. 750
Daily Life
About 70 million people live in China.

C. A.D. 950
Science and Technology
The Chinese first use gunpowder in warfare.

C. A.D. 960
Business and Finance
Foreign trade begins to expand in China.

C. A.D. 960
The Arts
Chinese artisans perfect the craft of porcelain making.

 A.D. 550

 A.D. 750

A.D. 950

C. A.D. 700
Global Events
Buddhism is flourishing in Korea.

A.D. 700s
Daily Life
Zen Buddhism becomes the dominant form of Buddhism in Korea.

C. A.D. 670
Politics
The Kingdom of Silla unifies Korea.

A.D. 868
The Arts
The Chinese produce the world's first known printed book, the *Diamond Sutra*.

A.D. 960–A.D. 1279
Politics
The Sung dynasty exists in China.

A figure of a Bactrian camel from the Tang dynasty

An illustration of the Buddha preaching, from the Diamond Sutra

Build on What You Know

The people of the Islamic world fashioned a unique society based on a powerful religious ideal. Their culture lay at the crossroads of many civilizations and spread with the movement of people and with trade. In little more than a century after the death of Muhammad in A.D. 632, Islamic culture and beliefs had been carried throughout much of the Middle East, through large parts of Africa, Asia, and the Mediterranean, and even into Europe. In this chapter, you will learn about the unique cultures of East Asia that, like Islamic civilization, reflected a strong spiritual influence.

What's Your Opinion?

Global Relations

Agree The government, religion, and customs of a powerful nation often influence those of other nations in the region.

Disagree A nation's society and culture develop in isolation, without influence from its neighbors.

Government

Agree The ability to maintain political power is affected by many factors in addition to the strength of a ruler.

Disagree A strong ruler should be able to maintain political power no matter what other factors or circumstances may be.

Culture

Agree Religious beliefs are often reflected in the government, art, and customs of a society.

Disagree Religion typically has little influence on the culture of a society.

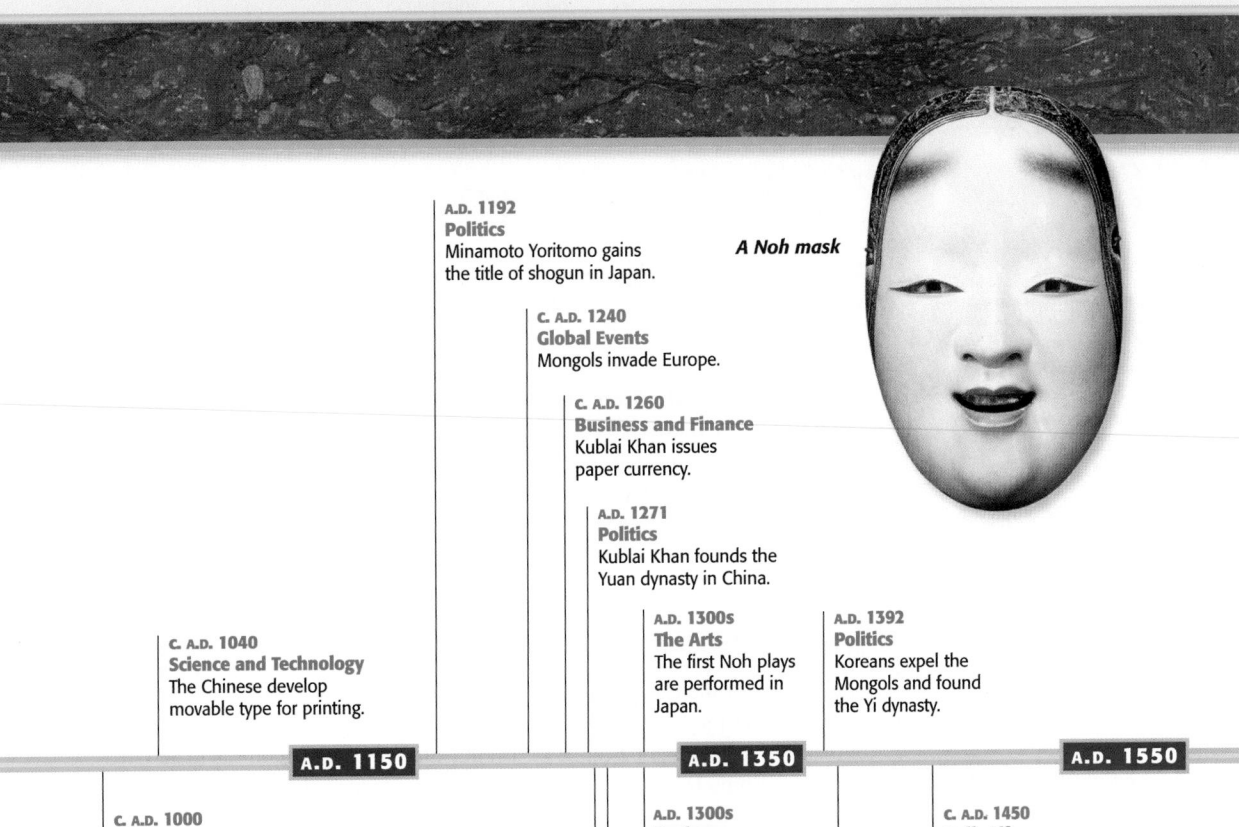

A.D. 1192
Politics
Minamoto Yoritomo gains the title of shogun in Japan.

A Noh mask

C. A.D. 1240
Global Events
Mongols invade Europe.

C. A.D. 1260
Business and Finance
Kublai Khan issues paper currency.

A.D. 1271
Politics
Kublai Khan founds the Yuan dynasty in China.

C. A.D. 1040
Science and Technology
The Chinese develop movable type for printing.

A.D. 1300s
The Arts
The first Noh plays are performed in Japan.

A.D. 1392
Politics
Koreans expel the Mongols and found the Yi dynasty.

A.D. 1150

A.D. 1350

A.D. 1550

C. A.D. 1000
The Arts
Lady Murasaki Shikibu writes *The Tale of Genji.*

A.D. 1300s
Business and Finance
State-controlled foreign trade flourishes in China.

C. A.D. 1450
Daily Life
Emperor Sejong directs the development of the Korean alphabet.

A.D. 1281
Global Events
The "Divine Wind" turns back a Mongol invasion of Japan.

C. A.D. 1400
Daily Life
The tea ceremony develops in Japan.

C. A.D. 1275
Business and Finance
European trader Marco Polo visits the court of Kublai Khan.

A Japanese tea caddy

Lady Murasaki Shikibu

EXPLORING THE TIME LINE
GLOBAL EVENTS

Vietnam was strongly influenced by China from about 100 B.C. to about A.D. 940—the period during which the Chinese occupied northern Vietnam. During this period the Chinese introduced their writing system, the Confucian religion, and their system of government. Most important, perhaps, Chinese technology continued the shift of traditional Vietnamese agriculture to intensive rice farming. For the first time in Southeast Asia, a well-defined, centralized society arose.

Critical Thinking

Ask students what effect the invasion and conquest by China had on the development of Vietnam.

ANSWER: Chinese conquest influenced Vietnamese government, culture, religion, and economy.

What's Your Opinion?

Themes Journal Do you **agree** or **disagree** with the following statements? Support your point of view in your journal.

Global Relations A powerful nation affects the societies and cultures of its neighbors.

Government It is difficult for even the strongest rulers to continuously maintain their political power for long periods of time.

Culture Religious ideas can be reflected in societies in a variety of ways.

🔊 *LET'S GET STARTED!*

As students enter the classroom, ask them to think about city and rural life in America today. Have students list some differences between city and rural life. (*Students might point out that city dwellers have easier access to many goods and services and that people who live in rural areas sometimes make a living by farming or raising livestock.*) Ask students which type of life they believe is more difficult and have them support their opinions. Tell students that in Section 1 they will learn about city and rural life in China.

SECTION 1 RESOURCES

REPRODUCIBLE RESOURCES

▸ Guided Reading Strategy 12.1

▸ Graphic Organizer Activity 12

▸ Hands-on History Activity 12

TECHNOLOGY RESOURCES

▸ One-Stop Planner 12.1

▸ Holt Researcher: World History: Empress Wu

▸ World History and Cultures Video Program 12

▸ Homework Practice Online

▸ Online Maps, Charts, and Graphs: Changan, 750

REINFORCEMENT, REVIEW, AND ASSESSMENT

▸ Section 1 Review, p. 271

▸ Daily Quiz 12.1

▸ Main Idea Activity 12.1

▸ English Audio Summary 12.1

▸ Spanish Audio Summary 12.1

VISUAL RECORD ANSWER

to accompany the dead in the afterlife

SECTION 1

READ TO DISCOVER

❶ How did Chinese civilization advance during the Sui and Tang dynasties?

❷ What was daily life like for the Chinese people during the Sung dynasty?

IDENTIFY

Grand Canal
Li Bo
Du Fu
Empress Wu
Zen
Diamond Sutra

▸ WHY IT MATTERS TODAY

The differences between city and rural life are as real today in China as they were over 1000 years ago. Use CNN **or** other **current event** sources to explore differences in the daily lives of people your age living in the cities or in the country. Record your findings in your journal.

CNNstudentNews.com

China under the Sui, Tang, and Sung Dynasties

The Main Idea
The Sui, Tang, and Sung dynasties shaped China but could not maintain control over it.

The Story Continues *The fall of the Han dynasty in the 200s led to a long era of instability and decline in China. Hordes of invaders swept in and destroyed Han cities. An observer described visiting one such city in the 300s. "At this time in the city . . . there were not more than 100 families," he wrote. "Weeds and thorns grew thickly as if in a forest."*

The Sui and Tang Dynasties

The collapse of the Han dynasty in 220 signaled a long era of social and political disruption in China. Wave after wave of invaders swept into China from beyond its borders. Over time, these peoples settled in China, set up kingdoms, and adopted Chinese customs. In the late 500s one of these groups succeeded in reuniting China under its rule. The new dynasty, known as the Sui, came into power in 589. During their brief rule, the Sui emperors began construction of the **Grand Canal.** They connected existing and newly dug waterways, linking northern and southern China for the first time. The canal was one of the engineering marvels of the ancient world.

Despite their accomplishments, however, the Sui dynasty did not last. The rulers tried to do too much at once. They tried unsuccessfully to conquer southern Manchuria and northern Korea. In 615 invading Turks defeated them. An uprising in 618 ended the Sui dynasty and brought the Tang dynasty to power.

Expansion under the Tang. The early Tang rulers defeated the invading Turks to the north and west. They extended China's frontiers farther west than ever before. The Tang rulers made contact with India and with the Muslim Empire to the south and the west. To the east, Chinese ideas greatly influenced the people of Korea and Japan. This contact with other peoples also contributed to Chinese culture.

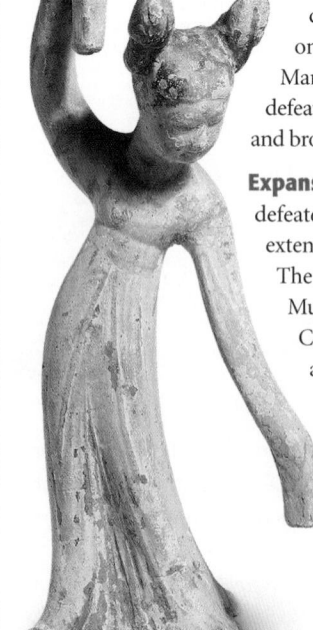

INTERPRETING THE VISUAL RECORD

Tang sculpture This ceramic figure of a girl was discovered in a Tang dynasty tomb. The Chinese also buried figures of servants, animals, and guards. *What might have been the purpose of these figures buried alongside wealthy Chinese people?*

LEVEL 1: Remind students that many cultural, political, and economic changes occurred in China under the Sui and Tang dynasties. Have students make web diagrams of these changes, filling in circles for *Arts, Economy, Government, Society,* and *Technology.* Organize students into pairs or triads to compare and discuss differences in their web diagrams and to revise their entries if necessary.

ENGLISH LANGUAGE LEARNERS , COOPERATIVE LEARNING

The Tang made Xi'an their capital. During the 700s and 800s, about 2 million people lived there. This made Xi'an the largest city in the world at that time. Xi'an was both the center of government and a center of culture. People from many parts of the world settled there. Arabs, Persians, Jews, Greeks, and native Chinese lived side by side.

China flourished under the Tang dynasty. The Tang only ruled until 907, but they began what would be another golden age in China. For many years China was the most powerful and wealthy country in the world.

Literature under the Tang. The Tang dynasty marked a high point in the development of Chinese literature. Some 2,300 known poets lived and worked during the era of the Tang dynasty. Together, these poets wrote nearly 49,000 known works. Among the best of these poets were **Li Bo** (Li Po) and **Du Fu.** They both wrote during the 700s.

Li Bo, a Daoist, spent much of his life seeking pleasure. His poems describe life's delights in light, happy, elegant terms. His love of life, however, may have caused his death. According to legend, Li Bo became tipsy after drinking too much and drowned while reaching from a boat for the moon's reflection in the water.

Du Fu, on the other hand, wrote about serious subjects. He was a devout follower of the teachings of Confucius. Du Fu's carefully written verses showed his deep concern for the suffering and tragedy of human life. Du Fu used his poet's gift to

CONNECTING TO
Science and Technology

The Grand Canal

The Grand Canal is the world's oldest and longest canal system. It connects the Chinese cities of Hangzhou and Beijing, and is almost 1,000 miles long. Before the development of railroads, the canal was a convenient way to travel and transport goods between the northern and southern parts of China.

The canal was created over many hundreds of years. It was made by digging trenches to link lakes, rivers, and other canals. Dams were built to equalize water levels.

As railroads developed, the Grand Canal's importance faded, and it fell into a state of disrepair. By 1949 only small boats were able to use it. China repaired and modernized the canal system between 1958 and 1964. Today the Grand Canal again serves as a way for boats to transport goods and passengers.

Understanding Science and Technology

Why would floods be harmful to the Grand Canal?

The Grand Canal is still an important waterway today, as this photo indicates.

Linking Past to Present

Sui emperors established a system of government departments and ministries to rule more effectively. They increased the size of the state education system, reformed the civil service system, and built upon the efforts of the Han emperors to control the independence of local officials. One result of Sui reforms was more efficient collection of taxes. The royal coffers swelled, allowing vast public works projects like the Grand Canal and extensive repairs of the Great Wall.

Critical Thinking

Limiting the terms of government officials is a historical method of reform that some states and localities have adopted today. What arguments might be advanced for and against this idea?

ANSWER: Term limits might be seen as restricting voters' freedom of choice and forcing the removal of officials who are doing a good job. On the other hand, they also keep officials from becoming entrenched and self-serving.

SCIENCE AND TECHNOLOGY ANSWER
Flooding would cause erosion of the canal walls.

LEVEL 3: Ask students to recall how Buddhism arrived in China. *(by missionaries from India)* Ask students why it flourished in Tang China. *(supported by Empress Wu and wealthy believers; similar to Daoism)* Have students explain how Buddhism's popularity caused problems for its followers. *(The government feared the growing wealth of the Buddhist monasteries.)* Ask what other religions were popular at the time. *(Daoism, Neo-Confucianism)* Have students speculate whether the government would have reacted against Buddhism if it had been a "native" religion like Daoism or Neo-Confucianism. *(Answers will vary but students should note that many Buddhist sects in China were uniquely Chinese.)*

Global Relations

During the Tang dynasty Chinese inventions flourished and spread to the outside world through China's increased contact with other peoples. The Chinese improved the manufacture of paper and porcelain, invented the wheelbarrow, and used gunpowder during this period. In addition, the use of coal as a fuel originated in northern China sometime in the 300s.

Critical Thinking

Ask students what they can conclude about how Chinese inventions reached foreign countries.

ANSWER: Trade spread new Chinese inventions throughout the world.

MAP ANSWER
the Grand Canal

call for an end to the frontier wars and destructive uprisings that tore at Tang China. One of Du Fu's greatest works was entitled "A Song of War Chariots." This poem, a classic example of descriptive poetry, creates a mood of great sadness. It tells of the sorrow of parting as a young soldier goes off to fight. The poem also suggests that the life of a Tang soldier could be brutal and harsh.

Analyzing Primary Sources

Drawing Inferences How does Du Fu's poem reflect Chinese history? reflects experiences of Chinese soldiers in battle

Primary Source

**❝The war-chariots rattle,
The war-horses whinny,
Each man of you has a bow and a quiver at his belt.
Father, mother, son, wife, stare at you going,
Till dust shall have buried the bridge beyond Xi'an,
They run with you, crying, they tug at your sleeves,
And the sound of their sorrow goes up to the clouds . . .
Men of China are able to face the stiffest battle,
But their officers drive them like chickens and dogs.
Whatever is asked of them,
Dare they complain?❞**

Du Fu, from Cyril Birch, ed., *Anthology of Chinese Literature*

Tang Dynasty, A.D. 814

Interpreting Maps The Tang rulers extended their empire westward into Central Asia and southward into Indochina.

■ **Skills Assessment: Physical Systems** Along what waterway could Tang people travel between the cities of Tianjin and Hangzhou?

TEACH OBJECTIVE 2

ALL LEVELS: Have students work in pairs to complete four-cell charts that list how urban life and rural life in Sung China was similar to urban and rural life in the United States today. Charts should be headed as follows:

	Urban Life in China	Rural Life in China
Similar in USA		
Different from USA		

ENGLISH LANGUAGE LEARNERS, COOPERATIVE LEARNING

Religion in Tang China. Missionaries from India brought Buddhism to China during the Han dynasty. Buddhism reached its peak under the Tang. **Empress Wu,** who ruled from 690 to 705, was an outspoken supporter of Buddhism. She was a strong leader and an able administrator. Empress Wu was also the only woman to hold the Chinese throne in her own name.

Wealthy Buddhists donated land for monasteries. Many different forms, or sects, of Buddhism appeared. The most famous sect is best known by its later Japanese name, **Zen.** Zen Buddhism stressed meditation as a means to enlightenment. It was similar in many ways to Daoism. Following the Buddhists' example, Daoists formed sects that appealed to the masses of peasants. In later years many Chinese adopted a mix of Buddhist and Daoist teachings.

In time the growing wealth of the Buddhist monasteries alarmed government officials. They seized the monasteries' lands and took art objects for the emperor's treasury. In the last century of the Tang dynasty, government officials persecuted Buddhists. They destroyed thousands of shrines and monasteries. They forced more than 250,000 monks and nuns to give up their duties and return to ordinary life. Buddhism continued to exist in China. However, it was never again so important a force in Chinese life.

The Tang rulers brought back Confucianism, especially its emphasis on ethics. This movement, called Neo-Confucianism, or "new Confucianism," remained the main religion of China's ruling classes until the early 1900s. Tang rulers built temples to Confucius and required government officials to study Confucian classics.

The decline of the Tang dynasty. The Tang dynasty reached its height in about 750. It then gradually declined under the rule of weak emperors. By 900 nomads had begun to invade China. In 907 a warlord who had murdered the emperor years earlier seized the throne for himself. The Tang dynasty ended.

✔ **READING CHECK: Finding the Main Idea** What were the main accomplishments in Chinese culture during the Sui and Tang dynasties? development of powerful literature, Buddhism and Confucianism

China under the Sung Dynasty

In 960 Zhao Kuangyin (JOW KWAHNG·yin) established the Sung dynasty. China continued to flourish under Sung leadership. The emperors, however, never succeeded in winning control of all China. Rulers from Tibet held a kingdom in the northwest. A powerful Mongol tribe that held Manchuria increasingly threatened northeastern China. Like the Tang rulers before them, moreover, the Sung emperors faced constant pressure from foreign invasions and civil wars. Nevertheless, China under the Sung was a land of cultural and artistic progress.

By the mid-900s the main foreign danger to China came from the north. Mongols called the Qidan (CHI·DAHN) had taken Chinese territory in southern Manchuria. In time they invaded as far south as the Huang River. Finally the Sung agreed to a treaty with the Qidan. The Sung emperors had to pay a huge tribute to the Mongol invaders to avoid war. By 1042 the Sung were paying more than 200,000 ounces of silver to the Qidan every year. This was a great economic hardship.

Another Central Asian people, the Juchen, also moved into Manchuria. They took over northern China in 1126. The Juchen established the Jin dynasty in the north. Their capital was located at what is now Beijing. Hangzhou (HANG·CHOW) in the south became the new capital of the Sung dynasty.

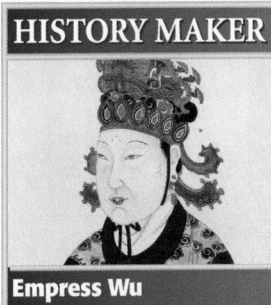

HISTORY MAKER

Empress Wu (c. 625–705)

Wu Hou first entered royal life at a young age as a member of the Tang emperor's household. She eliminated her female rivals within the palace and in A.D. 655 was made empress.

Wu Hou had her political opponents exiled or even executed. The emperor was often ill and relied on Wu Hou to manage state affairs. In 690 Wu Hou took power in her own name. Although ruthless against her opponents, Empress Wu ruled with great efficiency and she brought about needed social changes. **What did Empress Wu do once she gained power?**

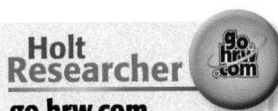

Holt Researcher

go.hrw.com
KEYWORD: Holt Researcher
FreeFind: Empress Wu
After reading more about Empress Wu on the Holt Researcher, write a newspaper article describing her political, economic, and social influence on China.

Government

The most compelling problem that Zhao Kuangyin faced was the almost absolute power held by local military leaders. In order to assert his authority, Zhao Kuangyin—himself a former general—transferred generals to other posts, coaxed them into retirement, and limited their scope of operations. As these military leaders retired or died, he replaced them with civilian administrators from the central government.

Though successful in consolidating power, Zhao Kuangyin's military reform weakened the competence and effectiveness of the fighting forces. The Sung were never able to reconquer Vietnam, any of central Asia, or the northern steppe.

Critical Thinking

Ask students what factors in Zhao Kuangyin's background might have led him to consider military leaders a threat to his rule.

ANSWER: Zhao Kuangyin had been a general and had seized power to establish the Sung dynasty.

HISTORY MAKER ANSWER
She had her political opponents exiled or executed.

Reproducible Resources
PS Readings in World History 45: A Woman's Hundred Years

HOMEWORK Ask students to imagine that they are either rural or city teenagers in Sung China. Have students write diary entries in their chosen roles for a typical day in their family lives. Read selected diary entries aloud and have the class critique how accurately they represent family life in rural or urban China.

CLOSE

Ask students to list some important changes that occurred in government and society during the Tang and Sung dynasties. Write students' responses on the chalkboard.

Economics

Under Sung government policies, China underwent a period of major economic change. International trade with Japan and Southeast Asia grew. Trade between regions remained limited to valuable commodities like porcelain and silk. The overall increase in trade created new opportunities for rural peasants, many of whom became entrepreneurs engaged in timber-growing, papermaking, weaving, and a variety of other new occupations. Villagers imported any raw materials they lacked. A cash economy also replaced the barter system during the Sung period. When copper, the common medium of exchange, was in short supply, the world's first paper money was printed in 1024.

Critical Thinking

Ask students how the introduction of paper money would affect the growth of a nation's economy.

ANSWER: Economic expansion would no longer be limited by the need to barter goods.

MAP ANSWER
about 700 miles

Technology Resources
World History Teaching Transparency: Art and History 13: Landscape on a Fan; Everyday Life 12: Chinese Tea Processing

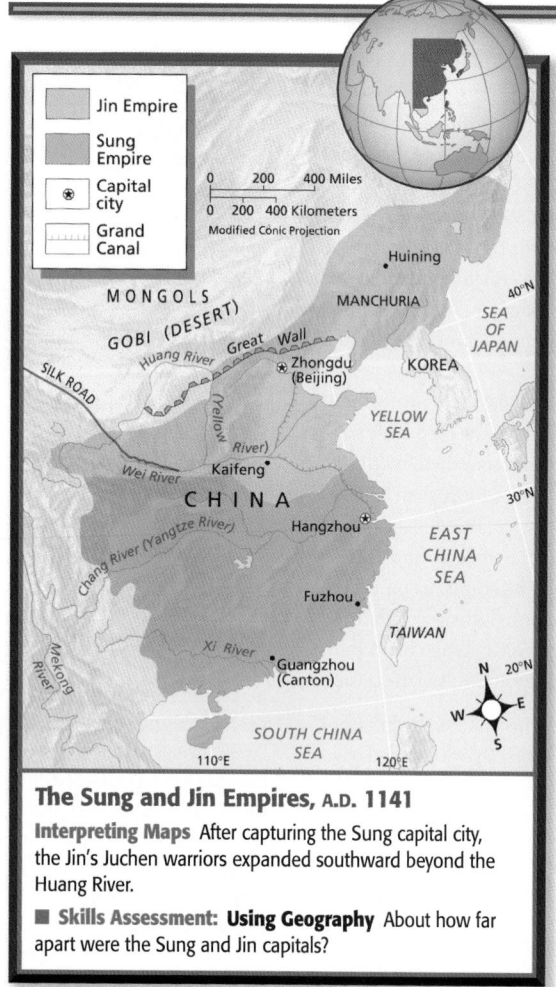

The Sung and Jin Empires, A.D. 1141

Interpreting Maps After capturing the Sung capital city, the Jin's Juchen warriors expanded southward beyond the Huang River.

■ **Skills Assessment: Using Geography** About how far apart were the Sung and Jin capitals?

Trade and arts. Despite their troubles, the Sung emperors kept Chinese civilization at a high level. Foreign trade expanded. Hangzhou and Guangzhou became key port cities. Caravans brought in goods from Central Asia and India.

Exports included gold, silver, and copper. One of China's most valuable exports was porcelain, a fine, translucent pottery. Sung artisans perfected the art of making porcelain. They created delicate vases with colorful and complex designs. Sung artists also produced beautiful landscape paintings, inspired by the Daoist love of nature.

The civil service system. The Chinese further improved their civil service system during the Sung dynasty. Examinations took place in the capital every three years. To qualify, an individual first had to pass an examination at the local level. The Sung ended the need for sponsorship. This practice had allowed only those from important families to take the examinations.

Because some people tried cheating to pass the civil service exams, a system was developed to stop corruption. Applicants were assigned numbers and did not use their names on the exams. Guards probably watched over them as they took the exams. Clerks copied their answers so that their handwriting could not be recognized. Finally, three judges read each paper.

Great inventions. The Chinese invented gunpowder during the Han dynasty. At that time it was used only for fireworks and signals. Gunpowder was first used for warfare during the 900s. Printing was another important Chinese invention. The Chinese had learned very early how to make ink and paper. By 500 artisans were making seals of metal or wood that had inscriptions carved in reverse. The images they created resembled today's block prints. The world's first known printed book was the *Diamond Sutra,* a Buddhist religious text produced in China in 868. Movable type was developed in the 1040s. However, it was not as practical to use as carved blocks.

Peasant life. By about 1050 China's population was about 100 million people. Most were peasants who lived and worked in the countryside. Two important changes took place in peasant life during the Tang and Sung dynasties.

One change was an improvement in farming methods. Water-control projects allowed farmers to irrigate more fields so that they could grow more rice. A new type of quick-ripening rice from Southeast Asia let farmers grow two crops each year instead of one. Peasants could sell surplus food in the many small market towns. Another important crop during those years was tea, which was made into a drink that was popular throughout China.

The second major change made life harder for the peasants. New taxes levied by the Tang rulers fell particularly hard on them. Peasants who could not pay their taxes had to sell their farms. They became tenant farmers, paying high rents to landlords.

REVIEW

Have students complete the Section 1 Review on p. 271.

ASSESS

Have students complete Daily Quiz 12.1. As Alternative Assessment, you may want to use the web diagram or chart exercises in this section's lessons.

RETEACH

Have students complete Main Idea Activity for English Language Learners and Special-Needs Students 12.1. Then have students

who are having difficulty work in pairs to ask each other questions based on the section subheads. **ENGLISH LANGUAGE LEARNERS**

EXTEND

Have groups of students create pamphlets on various aspects of the Tang and Sung dynasties. Pamphlets might focus on politics; famous artists or writers; scientific, mathematical, and technological advances; agriculture, industry, foreign trade, or religious developments. Suggest that groups include appropriate images to illustrate their pamphlets and use correct social studies terminology. **BLOCK SCHEDULING**

Photograph ©1978 The Metropolitan Museum of Art

This image is taken from a Chinese scroll of the 1100s. Entitled "Spring Festival on the River," the image portrays a prosperous and orderly society.

City life. During the Sung dynasty, more Chinese than ever before lived in cities and towns. Hangzhou was said to have had a population of about 2 million, with perhaps as many as 2 million more living near the city. The cities of Sung China bustled with activity. Shipments of farm produce arrived daily in the marketplaces. Shopkeepers sold embroidered silks, printed books, and handicrafts. Shoppers watched puppet shows, plays, dancers, and acrobats in the streets.

Wealthy Chinese probably lived in fine homes surrounded by gardens and artificial lakes. Ordinary people, on the other hand, probably lived in crowded apartments, often in extended families of several generations. Some people had no homes at all and had to beg for food. The Sung government set up hospitals and orphanages to help the poor, but poverty and overcrowding remained a serious problem.

During this period the status of women in Chinese society began to change. There was less work for them to do in the cities than on the farms. The custom of footbinding spread among the wealthy classes. Girls' feet would be tied tightly with strips of linen, with their toes tucked underneath. Their feet would not be allowed to grow. The result was crippling. The custom was meant to show that a man was successful. His wife did not have to do housework because he could afford servants. Eventually, small feet became viewed as a sign of feminine beauty.

✔ **READING CHECK: Categorizing** What developments during the Sung dynasty improved life for the Chinese people? Which made life worse? development of trade and arts, civil service improvements, inventions, improved farming methods; heavy taxation

The custom of footbinding survived in China for centuries, as this photograph of a Chinese woman from the 1900s reveals.

SECTION 1 REVIEW ANSWERS

❶ **Identify**
- Grand Canal, p. 266
- Li Bo, p. 267
- Du Fu, p. 267
- Empress Wu, p. 269
- Zen, p. 269
- *Diamond Sutra*, p. 270

❷ Sui: Grand Canal; Tang: expanded frontiers; Sung: foreign trade expanded, civil service and tax systems revised

❸ a. Literature flourished; Buddhism reached its peak; Neo-Confucianism began; porcelain making and landscape painting became important.

b. Farming methods improved. New taxes forced some peasants to become tenant farmers. Many people lived in cities. Status of women improved.

❹ Students' poems and lyrics will vary but should reflect information about daily life and culture in Hangzhou.

Technology Resources

 Online Maps, Charts, and Graphs: Population Shifts in China, 750–1250

SECTION 1 REVIEW

1. **Identify** and explain the significance:
   Grand Canal
   Li Bo
   Du Fu
   Empress Wu
   Zen
   Diamond Sutra

2. **Categorizing** Copy the chart below. Use it to identify the principal accomplishments of the Sui, the Tang, and the Sung dynasties.

Sui dynasty		
Tang dynasty		
Sung dynasty		

3. **Finding the Main Idea**

   a. What were the most noteworthy advances in Chinese culture during the Sui, Tang, and Sung dynasties?
   b. How did life improve for ordinary people during the Sung dynasty?

4. **Writing and Critical Thinking**

   Evaluating Imagine yourself visiting Hangzhou. Write a poem or a song lyric about your impressions of the Sung capital.
   Consider:
   • what daily life was like for individuals living in the city
   • what items you might want to trade for to take back home with you

Homework Practice Online
keyword: SP3 HP12

SECTION 2

OBJECTIVES

1 Explore how the Mongol invaders were able to conquer and rule so much of Asia.

2 Examine the effect Mongol rule had on China.

LET'S GET STARTED!

As students enter the classroom, have them recall what they learned about the Mongols in Chapter 10. Ask students what they remember about Kievan Russia under Mongol rule. *(Students may recall that Mongols wanted to gain wealth from the region and that they improved transportation and communication.)* Tell students that in Section 2 they will learn about the Mongol Empire in China.

VISUAL RECORD ANSWER

They had strong armor and powerful weapons.

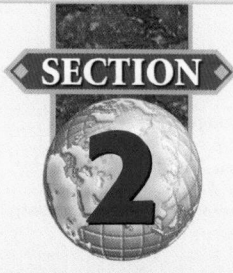

SECTION 2

READ TO DISCOVER

❶ How were the Mongol invaders able to conquer and rule so much of Asia?
❷ What effect did Mongol rule have on China?

IDENTIFY

Genghis Khan
Kublai Khan
Batu
Golden Horde
Marco Polo

WHY IT MATTERS TODAY

Changing political boundaries can have important consequences for people. Use [CNN Student News] or other **current event** sources to locate a place in the world where changing boundaries have changed peoples' lives. Record your findings in your journal.

CNN Student News.com

The Mongol Empire

The Main Idea
The powerful Mongol people established a large and strong empire in China and other areas.

The Story Continues *"The Tartars—that is, the Mongols—are the most obedient people in the world in regard to their leaders,"* noted a European traveler in the 1240s. *"They hold them [their leaders] in the greatest reverence and never tell them a lie."* The Chinese learned about Mongol leaders firsthand, as the invaders came to control the entire land.

Genghis Khan and the Mongols

The Mongols lived north of China in the rugged steppe region now called Mongolia. Although they were never a numerous people, the Mongols' culture encouraged the skills of battle. Mongol leaders could mobilize much of the population to engage in conquest. At its height, the Mongol army had about 100,000 cavalry. Mounted warriors enjoyed a great advantage over foot soldiers. Mongol cavalry could cover up to 100 miles in a day. Special saddles and iron stirrups allowed them to fire arrows accurately while riding at top speed. They made good use of their speed and mobility on horseback. In battle Mongol riders would surround their enemy like hunters surrounding wild game.

The Mongol armies were highly skilled in the use of massed firepower, rapid movement, and maneuvers. They would wear down an enemy through constant attack or threat of attack. They also used powerful weapons, possibly including catapults and

INTERPRETING THE VISUAL RECORD

Mongols This manuscript from the 1200s illustrates a battle between Mongol tribes. *What does this picture tell us about Mongol armor and weapons?*

LEVEL 2: Have students compare the map on page 273 with maps in the Reference Section to list modern nations that were once part of the Mongol Empire. (*China, Mongolia, Russia, North and South Korea, Pakistan [part], Afghanistan, Iran, Iraq, Azerbaijan, Turkey [part], Armenia, Georgia, Turkmenistan, Uzbekistan, Kazakhstan, Ukraine, Poland, Hungary*) Ask how the Mongols were able to establish and govern so vast an empire. (*well-organized armies and superior troops, military technology, and tactics; divided empire into four parts*)

LEVEL 1: Have students create a flowchart that shows important events in the Mongol conquest of Asia.
ENGLISH LANGUAGE LEARNERS

capture of Beijing → conquest of Central Asia → conquest of most of Persia → conquest of Tibet → conquest of part of Southeast Asia

Mongol Empire, A.D. 1294

Interpreting Maps Under the leadership of Genghis Khan and his grandson Kublai Khan, Mongol soldiers captured much of Asia. **Skills Assessment: Places and Regions** What country did the Mongols unsuccessfully try to invade across the East China Sea?

Science, Technology & Society

Mongol soldiers spent their lives in the saddle. During long marches they could even sleep while on their horses. At one time in Hungary, the cavalry traveled 270 miles in three days. The Mongols also used an iron stirrup and a powerful bow that could be used effectively from the saddle.

Critical Thinking

Ask students what advantages horsemanship gave the Mongols.

ANSWER: It gave them better mobility and versatility.

internet connect

TOPIC: Genghis Khan
GO TO: go.hrw.com
KEYWORD: SP3 WH12

Have students access the Internet through the HRW Go site to conduct research on Genghis Khan. Remind students that Genghis Khan ruled the largest empire in history, reaching from Korea and China to Russia and Iraq. Ask students to write a biography of Genghis Khan. Students may wish to use the interactive template to write their biographies.

---

giant crossbows mounted on stands. Battle provided a way for individual soldiers to acquire riches, honor, and personal power. The evidence suggests, too, that many of the Mongol generals were extremely capable.

The fiercest Mongol leader of all time was **Genghis Khan,** who lived from about 1162 to 1227. Originally named Temujin, he took the title Genghis Khan, meaning "Universal Ruler," in 1206. He went on to create an immense empire.

Mongol conquests. In the early 1200s, Mongols under Genghis Khan swept down from Karakorum, their capital. They captured the city now called Beijing and named it Khanbalik (kahn·buh·LEEK). They then turned westward, conquering Central Asia and most of Persia. Led by **Kublai** (KOO·bluh) **Khan,** a grandson of Genghis Khan, they conquered the rest of China. They also conquered the area now called Tibet and part of Southeast Asia. They tried but failed to capture Japan.

Another grandson of Genghis Khan, **Batu,** invaded Europe around 1240. His troops swept across Russia, Poland, and Hungary to the outskirts of Vienna. They plundered city after city, either killing the inhabitants or taking them as slaves. Frightened Europeans called the Mongolian invaders the **Golden Horde.** This name referred to the gold color of the Mongol tents in the sun. The Mongols soon left Poland and Hungary. They controlled Russia, however, for almost 200 years.

Holt Researcher
go.hrw.com
KEYWORD: Holt Researcher
FreeFind: Genghis Khan
After reading more about Genghis Khan on the Holt Researcher, create a collage that shows the changes his invasions brought to other parts of the world.

MAP ANSWER
Japan

TEACH OBJECTIVE 2

ALL LEVELS: Have students suggest headlines for a news story on the political, economic, or cultural consequences of the Mongols' rule of China. List responses on the board. (*Examples: Mongols Restore Peace and Prosperity; Khan Extends Grand Canal; New Roads Improve Trade; Heavy Taxes Burden Nation*) Then have students choose one of the headlines and write a short news article to accompany it.

 HOMEWORK Have students create editorial cartoons supporting a point of view on Mongol discrimination against the Chinese.

TEACH OBJECTIVE 2

LEVEL 3: Have students prepare to hold a mock trial of Kublai Khan for alleged crimes against the Chinese people. Pairs of students should serve as prosecution and defense teams. Other students should be witnesses for the prosecution and the defense. Remaining class members should serve as jurors, evaluating Khan's political choices and decisions and voting on the defendant's guilt or innocence. To actively involve jurors during the trial, require each to write an explanation of his or her vote, citing the testimony that influenced it. **COOPERATIVE LEARNING**

Daily Life

In spite of Kublai Khan's use of the Chinese way of governing, the Mongols did not wish to become Chinese. They kept their own values and ways of life. Mongol women did not adopt the Chinese custom of foot binding, and they continued to dress in their own styles of clothing.

Critical Thinking

Ask students to suggest reasons why the Mongols relied on Chinese administrative structures to rule.

ANSWER: Students might answer that the Mongols had no existing bureaucratic and governmental structures of their own that could control such a huge empire.

HISTORY MAKER ANSWER

conquered China; first emperor of the Mongol dynasty; use of paper money; extended Grand Canal; improved trade; improved communication system

---

Reproducible Resources

PS Readings in World History 46: Kublai Khan's Great Park at Shangdu

---

HISTORY MAKER

Kublai Khan (1215–1294)

The grandson of the great Mongol warrior Genghis Khan, Kublai Khan also proved to be a great general and ruler. He would go on to conquer China and become the first emperor of the Mongol dynasty.

Kublai Khan was known for his capable governing and his mercy toward conquered peoples. He stressed religious toleration. He was also the first ruler to use only paper money. **What were some of Kublai Khan's achievements?**

Mongol rule. The Mongol Empire was divided into four parts. These four parts remained united until the 1300s, then slowly began to drift apart.

In 1260 Kublai Khan was given the title of Great Khan. He was recognized as the head of the whole Mongol Empire. He adopted many Chinese ways and introduced Chinese ceremonies to his court. He also relied on Chinese officials in the lower and middle ranks of the government. Kublai Khan built two palaces, one in Mongolia and one near Beijing.

✔ **READING CHECK: Identifying Cause and Effect** How were the Mongol nomads able to conquer so much of Asia? powerful, well-organized army of skilled cavalry

China under the Mongols

In 1271 Kublai Khan announced the beginning of his own dynasty. Called the Yuan dynasty, it covered northern China, with its capital at Beijing. In 1279 Yuan forces defeated the Sung dynasty in southern China. The Yuan ruled China until 1368.

Under Mongol rule, China prospered in many ways. Once the Mongols secured their empire, a century of war ended. The population, which had dropped to about 60 million, began to grow again.

Kublai Khan extended the length of the Grand Canal by hundreds of miles in order to supply his new capital with food from the southern farmlands. He also fostered routes linking China with India and Persia. This greatly improved trade. Probably as many as 10,000 courier stations, each stabling hundreds of horses used by relay riders, dotted Yuan China. These stations, set about 25 miles from one another, enabled mounted couriers to carry news and imperial messages throughout the empire. The efficient Yuan system of communications connected to virtually every corner of the empire and helped to maintain unity and order. Improved trade and communication encouraged China's economic growth. At the same time, however, heavy taxes enforced by the Yuan emperors may have weakened the economy and created many hardships for farmers and merchants. Over time, the emperors' harsh taxes and frequent demands for tribute helped to undermine Yuan authority and to promote growing resentment toward Mongol rule.

Contact with Europeans. During Mongol rule, contact between China and the rest of the world increased. King Louis IX of France and the pope in Rome both sent ambassadors to China. Christian missionaries also traveled there, as did travelers from other non-European nations.

It was during the reign of Kublai Khan that the Italian **Marco Polo** traveled to China. Marco Polo was a famous merchant and explorer. At about the age of seventeen

Marco Polo, pictured here in Mongol dress, brought news of Kublai Khan's empire back to Europeans.

CLOSE

Organize a class debate in which students argue that Mongol rule was either positive or negative overall.

REVIEW

Have students complete the Section 2 Review on p. 275.

ASSESS

Have students complete Daily Quiz 12.2. As Alternative Assessment, you may want to use the map or flowchart exercises in this section's lessons.

RETEACH

Have students complete Main Idea Activity for English Language Learners and Special-Needs Students 12.2. Then have students write a paragraph that summarizes what they have learned in Section 1. **ENGLISH LANGUAGE LEARNERS**

EXTEND

Have students work together to create a comic book, storyboard, or multimedia presentation about the Mongols' conquest or rule of China, using computer software, biographies, and artifacts to acquire information. **BLOCK SCHEDULING**

he left Venice with his father and uncle. After three years of difficult travel they arrived in China. Kublai Khan was impressed with the young Marco Polo. He employed Polo as his special representative. Polo traveled around China for 17 years and became famous. In his book *The Travels of Marco Polo*, he described Kublai Khan's court to his fellow Europeans:

> **History Makers Speak**
>
> **❝When the Great Khan is holding court, the seating at banquets is arranged as follows. He himself sits at a much higher table than the rest . . . His principal wife sits next to him on the left. On the right, at a somewhat lower level, sit his sons in order of age . . . . They are placed so that their heads are on a level with the Great Khan's feet. Next to them are seated the other noblemen at other tables lower down again. . . . All the wives of the Khan's sons and grandsons and kinsmen are seated on his left at a lower level, and next to them the wives of his nobles and knights lower down still.❞**
>
> Marco Polo, *The Travels of Marco Polo*, trans. by R.E. Latham

Chinese-Mongol relations. The Yuan dynasty did much that was good for China. However, there were still tensions between the Mongols and the Chinese. For one thing, they spoke different languages. More importantly, the Mongols did not treat the Chinese as equals. Only Mongols or other non-Chinese people could hold important positions in the government. Mongol law punished Chinese criminals more harshly than non-Chinese ones. Moreover, the Mongols did not allow marriage between different groups of people.

Kublai Khan died in 1294, leaving China to weak successors. During the period after his death, the country experienced many problems. The Huang River flooded, destroying crops and causing famine. Rebellions sprang up. Finally, in 1368, the Yuan dynasty was overthrown.

The Mongols influenced China in several ways. They brought greater contact with Europe. They made local governments more responsible to the central government in Beijing. Later Chinese dynasties built on these political reforms by giving more powers to the emperor.

✔ **READING CHECK: Making Generalizations** What were the good and bad effects of Mongol rule in China? improved communication, transportation, and trade; unequal treatment, harsh taxes and laws

---

Analyzing Primary Sources

Drawing Inferences What can you infer about the society of the Yuan dynasty from the way that people were seated at Kublai Khan's banquet? organized by hierarchy, social and political status

Paper money, as well as coins like those shown here, served as currency during the reign of Kublai Khan. Eventually only paper money was used.

SECTION 2 REVIEW

1. **Identify** and explain the significance:
   Genghis Khan
   Kublai Khan
   Batu
   Golden Horde
   Marco Polo

2. **Sequencing** Copy the graphic organizer below. Use it to illustrate the events that led the Mongol nomads from the plains of Central Asia to become rulers of China.

3. **Finding the Main Idea**

   a. Why did the Mongol invaders want to conquer so much land in Asia?

   b. Overall, was Mongol rule good or bad for the average Chinese person? Explain your answer.

4. **Writing and Critical Thinking**

   Supporting a Point of View Write a letter to Kublai Khan requesting that he change some policy of his government with which you disagree.
   Consider:
   • the impact of Mongol rule on the Chinese people
   • the way you think the Great Khan might expect to be addressed

Homework Practice Online
go. hrw .com
keyword: SP3 HP12

SECTION 2 REVIEW ANSWERS

❶ **Identify**
• Genghis Khan, p. 273
• Kublai Khan, p. 273
• Batu, p. 273
• Golden Horde, p. 273
• Marco Polo, p. 274

❷ Students should include the capture of Beijing, the conquest of Tibet, and the conquest of part of Southeast Asia.

❸ **a.** Their culture encouraged battle skills. Their leaders wanted to create an empire.

b. Students might answer that Mongol rule was good because of improved communication, transportation, and trade. Students might answer that Mongol rule was bad because of unequal treatment and harsh taxes and laws.

❹ Students' letters will vary but should consider the impact of Mongol rule on the Chinese people and should address Kublai Khan formally.

THE CIVILIZATIONS OF EAST ASIA **275**

275

OBJECTIVES

1 Investigate how the geography of Japan influenced its development.

2 Analyze how China influenced the early development of Japan.

3 Describe how changes in government influenced society in feudal Japan.

4 Examine how Southeast Asia was influenced by China and India.

((•)) LET'S GET STARTED!

As students enter the classroom, ask them what effects geographic isolation can have on the development of civilizations and nations. *(Students should answer that the people may have little contact with foreigners and the nation may develop unique legal systems and culture.)* Have students name a culture they have already studied that developed in isolation. *(China)* Tell students that in Section 3 they will learn about the effects of geographic isolation on Japan.

SECTION 3 RESOURCES

REPRODUCIBLE RESOURCES

▸ Guided Reading Strategy 12.3

▸ Geography Activity 12

▸ Readings in World History 48

▸ Creative Teaching Strategy 12

TECHNOLOGY RESOURCES

▸ One-Stop Planner 12.3

▸ Holt Researcher: World History: Sejong

▸ CNN Presents World Cultures: Yesterday and Today Segment 12

▸ World History Teaching Transparency: Geography and History 12

▸ Homework Practice Online

REINFORCEMENT, REVIEW, AND ASSESSMENT

▸ Section 3 Review, p. 283

▸ Daily Quiz 12.3

▸ Main Idea Activity 12.3

▸ English Audio Summary 12.3

▸ Spanish Audio Summary 12.3

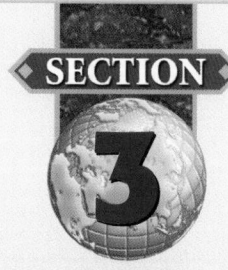

SECTION 3

READ TO DISCOVER

❶ How did the geography of Japan influence its development?

❷ How did China influence the early development of Japan?

❸ How did changes in government influence society in feudal Japan?

❹ How was Southeast Asia influenced by China and India?

DEFINE

kami
shogun
samurai
seppuku
daimyo

IDENTIFY

Shinto
The Tale of Genji
Fujiwara
Minamoto
Ashikaga
Bushido
Yi
Sejong

▶ WHY IT MATTERS TODAY

Powerful nations can have enormous influence on their smaller neighbors. Use CNN or other **current event** sources to locate a place in the world where a large nation is changing the lives of people in a smaller nation. Record your findings in your journal.

CNN Student News.com

Japan, Korea, and Southeast Asia

The Main Idea
China's culture strongly influenced other countries in eastern and southeastern Asia.

The Story Continues *Japan is a chain of islands in the western Pacific Ocean off the east coast of Asia. A Chinese observer once wrote about Japan, "The land of [Japan] is warm and mild. In winter as in summer, the people live on raw vegetables and go about barefoot." Although Japan is a country of great scenic beauty, its environment has often turned against its people.*

The Physical Setting

The modern nation of Japan consists of a string of thousands of islands in the western Pacific Ocean off the east coast of Asia. This island chain stretches over a distance of nearly 1,400 miles. The great majority of present-day Japan's large population lives on the country's four largest islands. These include Honshu (HAWN·shoo), Hokkaido (hoh·KY·doh), Kyushu (KYOO·shoo), and Shikoku (shee·KOH·koo). No place in Japan is more than about 100 miles from the ocean.

Japan is very mountainous. As a result, only a relatively small part of its land can be used for farming. Hard-working Japanese farmers still are able to produce a great deal of food. They are aided by plentiful rainfall, sunny days, and long growing seasons in some areas. Many rivers provide easy irrigation. Nature is not always kind to Japan, however. Earthquakes, tidal waves, and typhoons often strike the islands.

Until modern times, the seas surrounding Japan protected the islands from foreign influences. The Japanese people could choose whether or not they wanted to have contact with other peoples. At times in their history, they have showed interest in the outside world. At other times they have preferred to live in isolation.

The Mongols under Kublai Khan tried twice to conquer Japan without success. In 1281, a Mongol fleet carrying more than about 140,000 soldiers assembled to invade Japan. A powerful typhoon wrecked the fleet. The grateful Japanese called the storm *kamikaze*, or "Divine Wind."

✔ READING CHECK: Finding the Main Idea How did the geography of Japan affect Japanese contact with other peoples? isolated Japan, limited contact

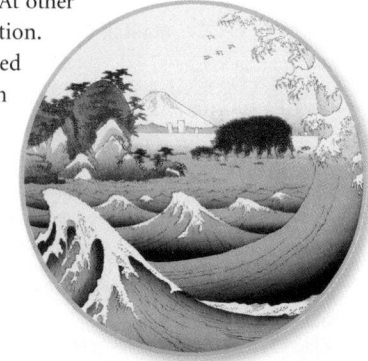

This detail from a Japanese painting is meant to depict the "Divine Wind."

Japan's Beginnings

In prehistoric times migrants from the Asian mainland settled the Japanese islands. By the first centuries A.D. these migrants had organized themselves into clans.

TEACH OBJECTIVE 1

LEVEL 1: Write the following questions on the board: *What geographic similarities do Korea and Japan share? How are Korea and Japan different geographically? How did those similarities and differences influence the development of each?* Pair students and ask them to prepare an answer to each question. Have pairs share their answers with the class.

ENGLISH LANGUAGE LEARNERS, COOPERATIVE LEARNING

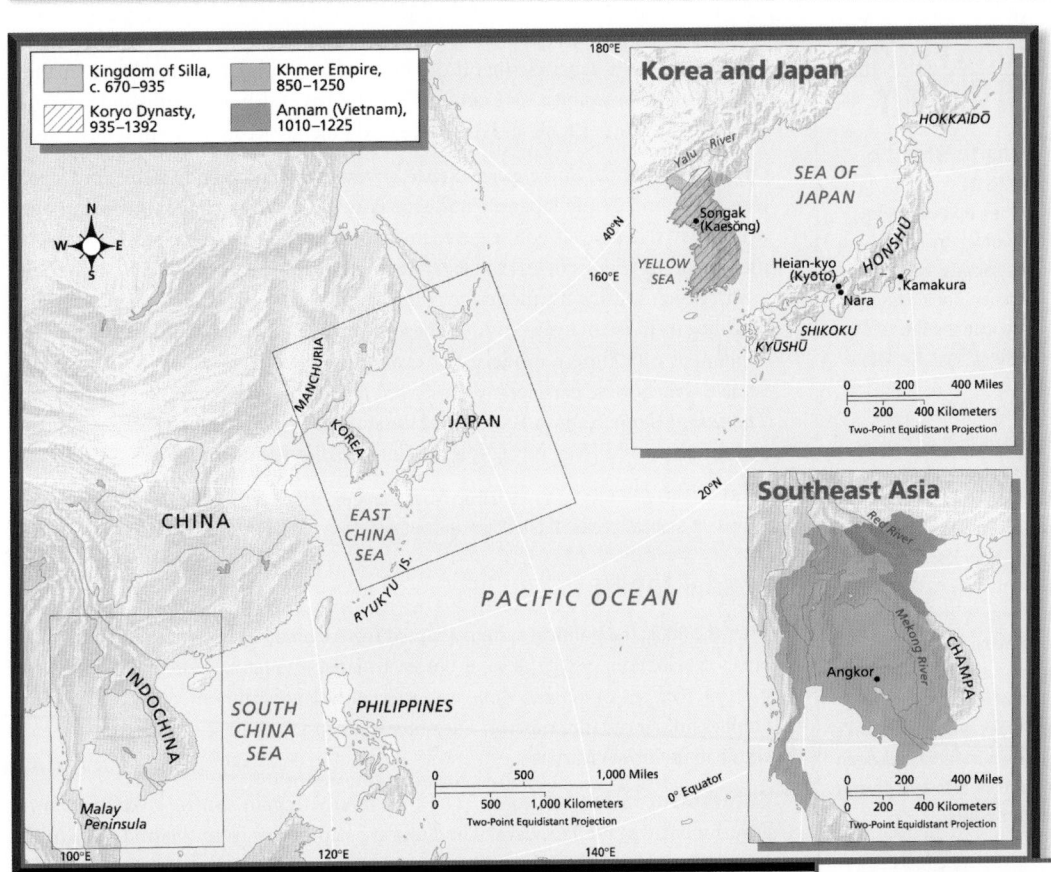

Government

In A.D. 702 the Taiho Code, based on the Chinese bureaucratic model, divided Japan into three levels of governmental administration: provinces, districts, and villages. Taxes were collected in goods, such as grain or cloth, or in labor. Furthermore, all males were liable for conscription into the military. However, a Chinese-style civil service examination system was not retained by the Japanese. Thus despite much borrowing from the mainland—religion, written language, government, laws, tax systems, and land reform—the aristocratic families retained ultimate authority.

Critical Thinking

Ask students to suggest how government positions were probably obtained in Japan in the absence of civil service examinations.

ANSWER: Students should suggest that such positions were obtained by birth into one of the powerful families or clans.

MAP ANSWERS

1. approximately 125 miles

2. They probably interact frequently and influence each other's culture.

Japan, Korea, and Southeast Asia, c. A.D. 670–1392

Interpreting Maps Japan is a long, narrow country made up of four main islands. The Korean peninsula gave birth to the country of Korea.

■ **Skills Assessment:**
1. **Using Geography** At the narrowest point, approximately how much distance separates Korea from Japan?
2. **Drawing Inferences** How might this affect the relationship between the two countries?

The most powerful clans lived on the island of Honshu. Since then the Japanese people have come together to form a strong, unified society.

Early history. Religion played an important role in helping Japanese culture form. From earliest times, the Japanese believed in gods or nature spirits called **kami.** They believed that these spirits lived in natural objects. For example, kami could be in sand, waterfalls, or trees. Many Japanese clans trace their origins to a particular kami. This religion is now called **Shinto,** meaning "way of the kami." Shinto has no established scripture or doctrine. Shinto worship involves prayers and rituals to please the kami. People might ask for many children or bountiful crops. Shinto is also concerned with ritual cleanliness.

Shinto helped unify Japan under imperial rule. Early emperors seem to have acted as Shinto priests. For all of Japan's history, probably only one imperial family has reigned—the Yamato clan. The first Yamato emperor probably came to power during the early 300s.

Few records of early Japanese history exist. The Chinese, however, knew about Japan before 100. The Japanese adapted Chinese writing by at least the early 700s, and possibly much earlier. Another Chinese influence was Buddhism, introduced in 552. At first the emperor's advisers disliked the new religion. Eventually, the rulers allowed Buddhist temples to be built. Many people in the Japanese court became Buddhists.

THE CIVILIZATIONS OF EAST ASIA **277**

277

Spotlight on CULTURE

The Japanese writing system combines Chinese characters, called *kanji*, with two syllabic or phonetic systems called *kana*. In Chinese each character represents one sound. In Japanese a character can have different pronunciations. *Kana*, believed to have been influenced by India's Sanskrit, adds inflectional endings to Chinese characters. This allows the use of Japanese words that cannot be written in Chinese alone. Today, students of Japanese must learn and memorize 1,945 *kanji* characters and the 48 *kana* modifiers. The *kana* characters distinguish words containing the same *kanji*. Have students study some examples of Japanese characters and practice writing some of them.

History Maker

LADY MURASAKI SHIKIBU.
Today every Japanese student studies passages from *The Tale of Genji*, written by Lady Murasaki Shikibu. Parts of the book's 54 chapters have been adapted for traditional Noh and Kabuki plays as well as for movies and television dramas. The book has been translated into English several times. The most exact translation was published in 1976.

ACTIVITY: Have students read parts of *The Tale of Genji* in English translation. Assign each student a passage from the book to read for the class.

YOUNG PEOPLE IN HISTORY ANSWER
They were taught martial arts skills as well as social skills.

YOUNG PEOPLE IN HISTORY

Training to Become a Samurai

Young men and even some young women trained to become samurai warriors in feudal Japan. Their training included learning the art of warfare and, later, the ways of peace.

To become a samurai demanded strict training in the martial arts. Many samurai developed great skill handling a sword. But a samurai also learned other lessons, such as the proper way to conduct a tea ceremony and how to write poetry. Above all, a samurai trained to overcome his or her fear of death. **In what ways was a samurai's training a balance between the martial arts and proper social conduct?**

Samurai suit of armor

Analyzing Primary Sources

Identifying Cause and Effect In what ways did Bushido, the "way of the warrior," help to support and strengthen the militaristic society of feudal Japan? encouraged loyalty, devotion to duty

---

In later centuries, Buddhism spread among the common people and became an important part of Japanese life. It did not replace Shinto, however. Most Japanese believed in both religions. For example, they may have celebrated births and marriages according to Shinto rituals and may have held funerals according to Buddhist rituals.

Chinese influence. Chinese art, science, government, and fashion influenced Japanese society. In 702 the Japanese emperor issued a new law code modeled on Tang dynasty laws. It centralized the government and gave the emperor more power over the lives of his people. In 794 the Japanese built a capital named Heian-kyo (HAY·ahn kyoh), which became the modern city of Kyoto (KYOH·toh). At the capital, the ruling class began to turn away from Chinese influence. Japanese culture became less dependent on Chinese models. For example, poets began to write in Japanese. Female writers were particularly important at Heian. Lady Murasaki Shikibu wrote *The Tale of Genji* in about 1000. It told the story of Prince Genji, the perfect courtier, and was the world's first novel. It is considered a literary masterpiece.

✔ **READING CHECK: Summarizing** What changes helped Japan develop its own culture?
rise of Shinto, spread of Buddhism, movement away from Chinese influence

Feudal Japan

After the 800s, the political system adapted from China began to decline. In its place, Japan developed a system of local power. In Japan the feudal system contained two general sources of power. One was the central government, where important families influenced the emperor. The other was a group of powerful local landowners who had their own warriors.

Government in feudal Japan. The first family to gain control over the central government was the **Fujiwara**. The Fujiwara had power from the mid-800s to the mid-1100s. In 1185 the **Minamoto** clan gained power. The reign of this clan marked a change in the way the government was run. In 1192 the emperor granted Minamoto Yoritomo the title of **shogun**, or general. The emperor kept his throne, but the shogun had control of the military, finances, and laws. In 1331, the Emperor Go-Daigo tried to regain power but failed. One of his generals, Ashikaga Takauji (ah·shee·KAH·gah tah·KOW·jee) claimed the shogunate for his own clan. The **Ashikaga** shoguns ruled for nearly 250 years.

At the local level, however, wealthy landlords held power. They hired warriors called **samurai** for protection. In some ways, the samurai were similar to European knights. A samurai was fiercely loyal to his lord and clan. His power rested on his skill with the sword. The samurai followed a code of behavior called **Bushido.** This means the "way of the warrior." Bushido stressed bravery, loyalty, and honor. Samurai would accept physical hardship without complaint and did not fear death. As one samurai scholar wrote,

History Makers Speak

❝The business of the samurai consists in reflecting on his own station in life, in discharging loyal service to his master . . . and with due consideration of his own position, in devoting himself to duty above all.❞

Yamaga Soko, quoted in Conrad Totman, *A History of Japan*

If samurai displeased their masters or were defeated in battle, they might practice seppuku. **Seppuku** was ceremonial suicide, also known in the West as hara-kiri. It was a way to avoid the dishonor that accompanied defeat or disobedience.

LEVEL 2: Ask students to summarize various ways in which China influenced the development of Japanese society. List responses on the board. *(artistic designs, Buddhism, fashion, government methods, writing)* Then hold a class debate over which item on the list was the most important influence. *(Positions will vary, but students should support their point of view. Buddhism was very influential, but Shinto remained popular. Chinese writing allowed literature to develop, but Japan eventually adopted its own writing system.)*

SKILL-BUILDING STRATEGIES   Reading a Chart

Japan's Feudal System

In Japan's feudal system some groups at lower levels of power actually had more influence than those at higher levels. For example, although the emperor and the shoguns held the top positions, they were often just figureheads. The daimyo had the most real power and were the most responsible for running the business of daily life for most of Japanese society. Reading an organization chart can help to show relationships within this system, using connecting lines to show who has authority over whom.

Emperor

Shogun

Daimyo

Samurai   *Samurai*

Peasant   *Peasant*

Critical Thinking

Ask students how a samurai's life and duties compare to those of the American cowboy of a later era.

ANSWER: Both worked for large landowners and lived physically demanding lives.

SKILLS PRACTICE ANSWERS

1. that it was based upon a hierarchical organization

2. Student charts should show the equality of the executive branch, the legislative branch, and the judicial branch. Cabinet posts and the federal court system should be included under the executive branch and judicial branch, respectively.

Skills Reminder

Charts are an effective way of visually organizing and communicating information to show relationships, comparisons, and contrasts. To read a chart, identify the type of chart and its purpose. Then identify the details given by the chart, such as labels and leader lines. Assess how the details relate to each other and what information this provides about a subject.

Skills Practice

❶ What can you determine about Japan's feudal system from the chart above?

❷ Using what you know about charts, draw an organization chart like the one above that shows the structure of the United States government. You may need to use an American government textbook to find the information necessary to practice this skill.

LEVEL 3: Have five students take the roles of emperor, shogun, daimyo, samurai, and peasant. Have each class member, in turn, direct a "yes" or "no" question to one of the five students. Do not allow direct questions about a student's identity, such as "Are you the peasant?" When all class members have had a chance to ask their question, have each write out his or her prediction of the identity of each role player. See how many students can correctly identify all five. Conclude the activity by discussing what each role player's answers reveal about power in feudal Japan.

That's Interesting!

Many of Japan's gardens were attached to Buddhist temples and were designed by the monks. The aesthetics of their design link them with meditation and landscape painting, both important activities of the monks. Some of these gardens are monochromatic and quite abstract, containing only rocks and raked white gravel.

VISUAL RECORD ANSWER

tranquility

Reproducible Resources

PS   Readings in World History 47: Drinking Tea for a Long Life

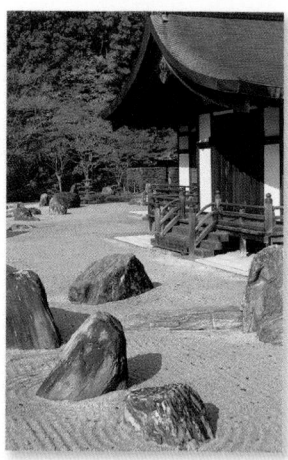

INTERPRETING THE VISUAL RECORD

Zen garden Shown above is a Zen garden in contemporary Japan. The sand has been raked into spare, clean lines to represent the Zen Buddhist values of simplicity and appreciation of nature. *What mood is suggested by the design of the landscape?*

The daimyo. In time local lords known as **daimyo** (DY·mee·oh), or "great names," gained great power. These lords and their samurai became the most powerful people in Japan during the Ashikaga shogunate. For a century, Japan had no effective central government and warfare was common. Despite this situation, Japan continued to grow economically and socially. Peasants produced greater crop yields, which meant more tax money for the daimyo. The daimyo promoted trade, which they also taxed. The taxes were very likely used to pay for the wars. Wars could offer people of lower status a chance to rise in society. Any man who could use a sword or lance could possibly join a daimyo's army. Those who fought well could be promoted to a higher rank.

Zen Buddhism. A religious awakening occurred in feudal Japan as Buddhists established new sects. Some taught that salvation could come through faith alone. Older sects asked people to give money to monasteries or study Buddhist scriptures. Therefore, the new sects appealed to ordinary people.

Zen Buddhism was introduced from China in the 1100s. It particularly interested warriors. Zen taught salvation through enlightenment, not faith. This perspective was very similar to the views embodied in Daoism. Zen Buddhism also taught that the life of the body was not important. Zen Buddhists developed self-discipline through long hours of meditation. These skills helped warriors in battle.

The Ashikaga shoguns supported Zen Buddhism. They encouraged the artistic efforts of Zen monks. New art forms inspired by Zen appeared in the late 1300s and early 1400s. One was landscape architecture, or the art of gardens. By arranging rocks, trees, and water, Zen artists tried to represent the beauty of nature. A related art form was the tea ceremony, designed to produce spiritual calm. People would gather in a simple room by a garden to quietly drink tea and admire the beauty of nature. Another important Zen art form was the Noh play. First performed in the 1300s, these were highly stylized dance dramas. Noh plays drew on religious, historical, or romantic themes. Male actors wearing masks would perform on a bare stage while a chorus chanted the story.

✔ **READING CHECK: Identifying Cause and Effect** How did the confusion in government offer new opportunities for people in Japanese society? offered ways to improve social status

Korea

Korea is a rugged, mountainous peninsula that juts south from Manchuria into the sea between China and Japan. As is true of Japan, Korea's political and cultural development was strongly shaped by China.

Korea's history. Because of its location, Korea has long served as a bridge that has allowed the passage of people and ideas from the mainland of eastern Asia to neighboring island chains. The Korean Peninsula was first settled in prehistoric times by nomadic peoples from northeastern Asia. These people enjoyed abundant sources of food, including wild deer, fish and other seafoods, and certain plant foods. Agriculture—especially rice farming—reached Korea from China, perhaps as early as about 1500 B.C. Metalworking techniques also spread from China to early Korea.

As early as 300 B.C., migrants from China began to arrive in Korea, bringing with them knowledge of metalworking and agriculture. Not long afterward, the first strong Korean kingdom, Chosŏn, emerged in the northern part of the peninsula. By the early 100s B.C. Chosŏn was strong enough to hold some control over much of the Korean Peninsula.

ALL LEVELS: Have students think about Chinese influences on the development of Japanese and Korean civilizations. Ask them to list the similarities that Vietnam's development shares with either of these countries. *(Japan and Vietnam: Buddhism, Chinese writing system, Chinese influences on government; Korea and Vietnam: conquest by China, Buddhism, Confucianism, Chinese influences on government)* **ENGLISH LANGUAGE LEARNERS**

HOMEWORK Have each student develop a diagram or chart that shows the similarities and differences in China's influence on the development of Japanese, Korean, and Vietnamese culture. Select students to copy their diagram or chart on the chalkboard and explain it.

Chinese Influences in Asia			
Influence	Japan	Korea	Vietnam
Religion	✔	✔	✔
Writing System	✔		✔
Government/Political Structure	✔	✔	✔
Technology	✔	✔	
Fashion	✔		
Literature	✔	✔	

In about 108 B.C. troops from Han China invaded Korea, conquered the kingdom of Chosŏn, and turned it into a Han colony. For the next 400 years the Chinese maintained tight control over northwestern Korea, allowing native Koreans little or no voice in their government. Elsewhere on the peninsula, however, three Korean kingdoms—Koguryo, Paekche, and Silla—arose in opposition to Chinese rule. Because these native kingdoms also fought amongst themselves, they were unable to challenge China's dominance in Korea. With the fall of the Han dynasty, Koguryo invaded the north and took over the one-time Chinese colony.

Unification under the Silla. Korea's three kingdoms continued to fight one another for the next several centuries. During the early A.D. 600s China's Sui dynasty attempted to conquer Korea but failed. Later, however, the rulers of Silla formed a strategic alliance with the Tang emperor of China. Working together, the armies of Silla and China conquered Paekche and Koguryo. Silla then turned on the Tang forces and drove them from Korea. By about 670 the kingdom of Silla had united Korea for the first time. Over time, Silla was weakened by internal rebellions and the loss of leadership. During the early 900s a new kingdom, Koryo (from which comes the name Korea), grew to challenge Silla's rule. By 935 Koryo had overthrown Silla and had taken control of the peninsula.

Korea remained independent throughout the era of the Tang dynasty. But in the mid-1200s the peninsula once again fell under the control of its powerful neighbor to the west, and Korea became part of the Mongol Empire. It was not until 1392 that Koreans regained their independence by driving out the Mongols. The **Yi** dynasty arose to rule the peninsula, lasting for centuries until Japan annexed Korea in 1910.

The growth of Korean culture. The culture and civilization of China has had a strong and lasting influence on Korea. Chosŏn, the first true kingdom in Korea, was founded in part by immigrants from China and clearly reflected many elements of Chinese culture. Korean rulers adopted Chinese as their written language, and they embraced China's Confucian traditions and ideas. They also followed the Chinese model of government. Korean rulers built dynasties controlled by hereditary kings. The rulers of Koryo used an examination process to select and train their government administrators. This process was based in large part on China's Confucian civil service system. The kings of Koryo, moreover, built Kaesong, a great capital city much like Xi'an, the imperial city of China's Tang dynasty.

During the 300s the ideals of Chinese Buddhism were brought to Korea. Many Koreans accepted the Buddhist philosophy and built magnificent temples that became major centers of learning. Buddhist teachings became part of Korean culture, philosophy, and morality. During the period of the three kingdoms, Buddhism became Korea's state religion. In the 700s Zen was introduced. It became the dominant form of Buddhism throughout the peninsula. Later, Korean scholars also studied the philosophy of Confucius and the Korean government adopted the Chinese civil service system.

Global Relations

As the ancient tribal systems broke down, Silla's government and culture were heavily influenced by China. Silla regularly sent tribute missions to the Tang capital. In addition, many students and monks from Silla pursued their education and training in China. Thus a flow of new ideas and philosophies arose. Eventually the people of Silla embraced Buddhism and duplicated the Tang political system.

Critical Thinking

Ask students why they think Silla accepted Tang systems.

ANSWER: Students might suggest that Silla wanted to replace older tribal customs.

VISUAL RECORD ANSWER

They were very advanced.

INTERPRETING THE VISUAL RECORD

Dragon's head This gold and bronze dragon's head was fashioned in Korea to decorate the top of a flagstaff. *What does this metalwork suggest about Korean artistic and technological skills during the Silla and Koryo periods?*

CLOSE

Ask students to describe the influence of China and India on the countries of mainland Southeast Asia.

REVIEW

Have students complete the Section 3 Review on p. 283.

Culture

The kingdom of Silla lacked its own writing system in which the people could transcribe their native language. Therefore they used the Chinese writing system.

This fact probably affected the degree of Chinese influence in Korea that exists even today. The most visible form of this influence may be seen in Korea's place-names and personal names. Because they were written in Chinese, original Korean names were replaced with their Chinese equivalents.

Despite the difficulty of fitting the polysyllabic Korean language into the Chinese format, there was a great deal of literary activity in Silla. Histories, poetry, and Buddhist writings were published along with Korean translations of Chinese texts, though few exist today.

Critical Thinking

Ask students how the adoption of Chinese characters to transcribe the Korean language would have encouraged the Chinese cultural influence.

ANSWER: Students might answer that the use of Chinese characters would have made it easier for Koreans to learn to read Chinese and would have introduced Chinese sounds and patterns into the Korean language.

Technology Resources

Regions of the World Music Audio CD Program 20: Japan and the Koreas

Holt Researcher

go.hrw.com
KEYWORD: Holt Researcher
FreeFind: Sejong
After reading more about Sejong on the Holt Researcher, use a problem-solving process to evaluate how his administration improved upon Chinese traditions.

Koreans learned to use movable type from the Chinese. They advanced this technology by casting type blocks in metal.

Despite the strength of China's influence, however, Korea did not become an identical copy of its huge neighbor to the west. Instead, Koreans worked to maintain the strength and identity of their culture and traditions. As one ruler of Koryo insisted in 982, "Let us follow China in poetry, history, music, ceremony, and the [principles of Confucius], but in riding and dressing let us be Koreans." Thus, the people of ancient Korea built a civilization that was, in many important ways, unique and distinct from that of China. Korean Buddhism, for example, included many elements of traditional Korean beliefs.

Another important difference between Korean and Chinese cultures was the presence of a powerful nobility in Korea. Korean aristocrats, unlike Chinese nobles, had great influence on the country's political development. As a result, the power of Korea's Confucian-style government administration was limited. Korean society differed from that of China, too, because it never developed a large, well-educated social class of merchants, government administrators, and scholars. In China, this group formed a kind of middle class between the traditional nobles and the peasant farmers. Korean society, however, was more sharply divided between its small upper class and its very large lower class.

During the 1400s the emperor **Sejong** ordered the development of a Korean alphabet. The Koreans borrowed the Chinese invention of movable wood type and then improved upon it. They designed movable type blocks made of metal, which was far more durable and produced sharper images.

✔ **READING CHECK: Contrasting** How did Korean aristocrats differ from Chinese nobles? had great influence on Korea's political development

Civilization in Southeast Asia

The mainland of Southeast Asia (also known as Indochina) is made up of the modern nations of Cambodia, Laos, Malaysia, Myanmar, Thailand (formerly Siam), and Vietnam. Like Japan and Korea, the kingdoms and peoples of ancient Southeast Asia were strongly and continuously influenced by China, which borders Southeast Asia to the north. The civilization of India, which lies to the region's northwest, also helped to shape Southeast Asian lifestyles, traditions, and beliefs. In a broader sense, however, the cultures that developed in Southeast Asia have their own distinct identities.

Northern Vietnam—known as Annam—was controlled by China throughout much of its history. By the 900s the Vietnamese had made several attempts to throw off Chinese dominance. It was not until 939, however, that the people of northern Vietnam won their independence from China. Soon after, Vietnam fell into widespread disorder and political violence. Finally, the emergence of several dynasties led to growing stability and the first steps toward the unification of the country.

The Vietnamese civilization that developed during these years was heavily influenced by contact with China. For example, Vietnam adopted Mahayana Buddhism from the Chinese. Over time, this form of Buddhism became the guiding philosophy of the Vietnamese culture. Daoism and Confucianism also contributed to the development of Vietnam's culture and society. In addition, Vietnam used the writing system and political organization of the Chinese.

Much of the rest of mainland Southeast Asia was shaped by Indian culture and tradition. Early in the history of Southeast Asia, people from India began to settle in the region, many of them perhaps Hindu and Buddhist missionaries.

ASSESS

Have students complete Daily Quiz 12.3. As Alternative Assessment, you may want to use the geography or feudal Japan exercises in this section's lessons.

RETEACH

Have students complete Main Idea Activity for English Language Learners and Special-Needs Students 12.3. Then ask them to write a question and answer that covers the main idea for each subsection in the section. **ENGLISH LANGUAGE LEARNERS**

EXTEND

🖵 **internet** connect

Internet Activity: go.hrw.com
TOPIC: Asian Art **KEYWORD:** SP3 WH12

Have students access the Internet through the HRW Go site to conduct research on art in China, Japan, and Korea. Present your findings to the class in an illustrated brochure emphasizing the similarities and differences in the art of these three cultures.

The Sanskrit language came into use, helping to spread Indian literature and thought. In present-day Cambodia, ruins of the city of Angkor Thom and the huge temple of Angkor Wat offer reminders of Indian influence. Reliefs with scenes from the Hindu epics adorn Angkor Wat, one of the architectural wonders of the Far East.

Centered in modern-day Cambodia, the Khmer Empire grew to control much of Southeast Asia in the years between about 850 and about 1250. Khmer rulers, strongly influenced by Indian culture, adopted many Hindu and Buddhist beliefs. For many years, Khmer society embraced the Indian principle of a god-king. The rulers probably used forced labor and income from taxes to build elaborate cities, government centers, and magnificent temple complexes. At the same time, Khmer leaders undertook major construction projects for the public good. These included hospitals, travelers' rest-houses, and canal and water-control systems designed to encourage rice farming throughout the region.

The Khmer kings' abuse of their royal powers eventually led to social discontent and rebellion. The ideas of Theravada Buddhism became increasingly widespread throughout much of Southeast Asia. This Buddhist philosophy had no place for splendid ceremonies, elaborate temples such as Angkor Wat, or the concept of a god-king. Over time, the all-powerful Khmer kings were overthrown and Theravada Buddhism became the predominant form of Buddhism in Southeast Asia.

✔ **READING CHECK: Categorizing** In what ways did Korea and Southeast Asia develop their own cultures despite the influences of China and India? worked to maintain their own cultures and traditions, rejected many Chinese and Indian influences over time

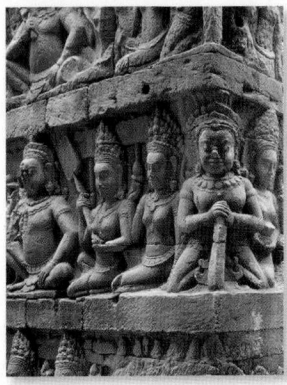

INTERPRETING THE VISUAL RECORD

Angkor Wat The temple of Angkor Wat in Cambodia is one of the architectural wonders of the Far East. It is decorated with scenes from Hindu epics.

Link to Today **How does this temple show evidence of Indian influence on Southeast Asian art and beliefs?**

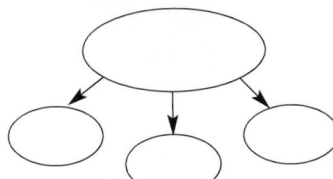

SECTION 3 REVIEW

1. **Define** and explain the significance:
   kami   seppuku
   shogun   daimyo
   samurai

2. **Identify** and explain the significance:
   Shinto   Ashikaga
   The Tale of Genji Bushido
   Fujiwara   Yi
   Minamoto   Sejong

3. **Summarizing** Copy the graphic organizer below. Label the largest oval China and the others Japan, Korea, and Southeast Asia. Use it to identify the institutions and customs that the latter three adopted from China.

4. **Finding the Main Idea**

   a. How did the breakup of the central government in Japan lead to changes in feudal Japanese society?

   b. How did China influence the societies of Japan, Korea, and Southeast Asia?

5. **Writing and Critical Thinking**

   Supporting a Point of View What are the advantages and disadvantages of Bushido—the "way of the warrior"—as a code of behavior in feudal Japan?

   Consider:
   • the nature of society in feudal Japan and the values that it emphasized
   • the skills and behaviors that could help a person to advance in feudal Japan
   • the ways a person could express bravery, loyalty, and honor in daily life

go. hrw. com **Homework Practice Online**

keyword: SP3 HP12

LINK TO TODAY ANSWER
It portrays scenes of Hindu epics.

◆**SECTION**◆
3 **REVIEW ANSWERS**

❶ **Define**
• kami, p. 277
• shogun, p. 278
• samurai, p. 278
• seppuku, p. 278
• daimyo, p. 280

❷ **Identify**
• Shinto, p. 277
• *The Tale of Genji*, p. 278
• Fujiwara, p. 278
• Minamoto, p. 278
• Ashikaga, p. 278
• Bushido, p. 278
• Yi, p. 281
• Sejong, p. 282

❸ Japan: Buddhism, writing, law code, governmental methods, artistic designs, medical knowledge, fashion; Korea: Buddhism, Confucian teachings, printing, civil service system; Southeast Asia: Chinese philosophies, writing system, political structure, Buddhism

❹ a. The breakup gave people a chance to improve their social status.

b. See response to Number 3.

❺ Opinions will vary but should be well supported and consider the nature of society in feudal Japan and the skills and behaviors that could help a person advance.

CHAPTER 12

REVIEW AND ASSESSMENT RESOURCES

REPRODUCIBLE RESOURCES
▶ Vocabulary Activity 12

TECHNOLOGY RESOURCES
▶ Chapter 12 Test Generator (on the One-Stop Planner)
▶ Global Skill Builder CD–ROM
▶ HRW Web Site

REINFORCEMENT, REVIEW, and ASSESSMENT
▶ Chapter 12 Review, pp. 284–285
▶ Chapter 12 Tutorial for Students, Parents, Mentors, and Peers
▶ Chapter 12 Test (Form A or B)
▶ Alternative Assessment Handbook
▶ Chapter 12 Test for English Language Learners and Special-Needs Students

REVIEW
Have students complete the Chapter 12 Review on pages 284–285.

ASSESS
Use one of the chapter tests to assess students' understanding of the content. For Alternative Assessment, see the Portfolio Activities and Alternative Assessment Handbook.

CHAPTER 12 REVIEW ANSWERS

Understanding Main Ideas

1. literature flourished; Zen, Confucianism revived

2. Farming methods improved, but taxes forced some peasants to become tenant farmers. Poverty and overcrowding remained problems in cities.

3. skillful warriors with powerful weapons

4. Communication, transportation, and trade improved, but citizens were subject to unequal treatment and harsh taxes and laws.

5. It was isolated and had little contact with other peoples.

6. Buddhism, writing, law code, governmental methods, artistic designs, medical knowledge, fashion

7. People had opportunities to improve their social status.

8. Chinese philosophies, writing system, political structure, Buddhism, Hinduism

Reviewing Themes
1. heavily influenced by Chinese society and culture

2. could not defend themselves against Mongol invasions

3. Buddhism, and later Zen Buddhism, became a part of Japanese culture. Korea accepted the Buddhist philosophy. Vietnam adopted Mahayana Buddhism from China.

284

CHAPTER 12 Review

Creating a Time Line
Copy the time line below onto a sheet of paper. Complete the time line by filling in the events, individuals, and dates from the chapter that you think were significant. Pick three events and explain why you think they were significant.

A.D. 552	A.D. 1000	A.D. 1573

Writing a Summary
Using standard grammar, spelling, sentence structure, and punctuation, write an overview of the events in the chapter.

Identifying People and Ideas
Identify the following terms or individuals and explain their significance:

1. Grand Canal
2. Empress Wu
3. Zen
4. *Diamond Sutra*
5. Genghis Khan
6. Kublai Khan
7. Golden Horde
8. Shinto
9. shogun
10. samurai

Understanding Main Ideas

Section 1 *(pp. 266–271)*

China under the Sui, Tang, and Sung Dynasties

1. What were the most important developments in Chinese culture during the Sui, Tang, and Sung dynasties?
2. Did life improve for ordinary people during the Sung dynasty? Explain.

Section 2 *(pp. 272–275)*

The Mongol Empire

3. How were the Mongol nomads able to gain power in China?
4. How did China change under Mongol rule?

Section 3 *(pp. 276–283)*

Japan, Korea, and Southeast Asia

5. How did Japan's geography affect its relations with its neighbors?
6. How did China influence Japanese society and culture?

7. What unique features of society in feudal Japan were the result of political confusion?
8. What were the influences of China and India on societies in Korea and Southeast Asia?

Reviewing Themes
1. **Global Relations** How did proximity to China affect the rest of Asian civilization?
2. **Government** Why were the rulers of the several Chinese dynasties unable to retain their hold on power?
3. **Culture** How were the various forms of Buddhism reflected in east Asian cultures?

Thinking Critically
1. **Drawing Inferences** How did the Sung and Yuan dynasties change China?
2. **Identifying Bias** Would Marco Polo have said that Kublai Khan's rule was good for China? Why or why not?
3. **Contrasting** How did the culture of feudal Japan differ from earlier Japanese culture?

Writing About History
Categorizing Write a report explaining the impact of Chinese culture on life in Mongol society and on Japan. Use the chart below to organize your thoughts before writing.

	Mongol society	Japanese society
Government		
Religion		
Art & literature		
Daily life		

CLOSE

Ask students to describe how the role of emperor in Japan was different from the role of emperor in China.

RETEACH

Have students who had difficulty with the test work in small groups to develop several questions about the information in the chapter. Then have each group use its questions to quiz the other groups. When they are ready, have groups take the Form B Test to assess their mastery of the material.

ENGLISH LANGUAGE LEARNERS

Portfolio Extensions

Link to TODAY

1. Have students research American products that are marketed in other nations. Have them transfer the information into a visual medium, using computer software as appropriate, to advertise one of the products.

2. Have students choose an example of American literature, drama, or music and write a paragraph or two about how it reflects the history of American culture.

3. Assign students to find out about fashions in other parts of the world. Have them determine which styles reflect the influence of American culture.

Building Social Studies Skills

Drawing Inferences

Study the chart below. Then use the information from the chart to answer the questions that follow.

The Sui Dynasty—Successes versus Problems	
Some Sui Successes	**Some Sui Problems**
• Reunited China	• Suffered defeats in Korea
• Rebuilt the Great Wall	• Constant demands for labor
• Constructed canals	• Heavy spending
• Built strong central government	• Excesses at court

1. Which statement below most accurately describes an inference that may be drawn from the chart?

   a. The Sui rulers were generally popular among the people they ruled.

   b. Military defeats in Korea probably had little effect on Sui rule at home.

   c. The people were probably willing to support heavy imperial spending, since it benefited them.

   d. Military defeats in foreign lands may have caused the Sui rulers to lose prestige among their people.

2. The Sui dynasty ruled for a relatively brief period of time. Write a short paragraph in which you analyze some of the factors in the dynasty's history that might explain why it could not maintain its rule.

Analyzing a Primary Source

Read the following quote from Ibn Battūtah, a Moroccan Muslim who traveled in China during the 1300s. Then answer the questions.

> "In regard to portraiture there is none . . . who can match . . . [the Chinese] in precision, for in this art they show a marvellous talent. This is a custom of theirs, making portraits of all who pass through their country. In fact they have brought this to such perfection that if a stranger commits any offence that obliges him to flee from China, they send his portrait far and wide. A search is then made for him and wherever the person bearing a resemblance to that portrait is found, he is arrested."

3. Which statement best describes what you can infer about the Chinese attitude toward foreigners?

   a. They wanted to impress them with their artistic ability.

   b. They respected their privacy.

   c. They disliked them.

   d. They did not completely trust them.

4. What is your opinion of how the Chinese kept track of strangers? Give reasons for your point of view.

Alternative Assessment

Building Your Portfolio

Link to TODAY

Culture

Historical China had a powerful influence on the cultures of other nations. Using your textbook and other sources, make a list of ideas, institutions, and advances in mathematics, science, and technology that originated in China. Use a poster board to prepare a map of the world or a collage to trace the spread of these ideas to other civilizations.

internet connect

go.hrw.com

Internet Activity: go.hrw.com
KEYWORD: SP3 WH12

Choose a topic on the Civilizations of East Asia to:

• understand similarities and differences of Chinese, Japanese, and Korean art.

• research the early development of Korea, Vietnam, and the Khmer Empire of Southeast Asia.

• learn more about Genghis Khan.

Thinking Critically

1. The Chinese civil service system was perfected; important innovations in the use of gunpowder and printing were made; farming methods were improved; heavy taxation was implemented.

2. Yes, because Marco Polo was a merchant and trade improved under Kublai Khan's rule.

3. A system of local power emerged.

Writing About History

Students should include: Mongol—administrative organization, ceremonies; Japan—Buddhism, writing, law code, governmental methods, artistic designs, roads, medical knowledge, fashion

Building Social Studies Skills

1. d

2. Factors include trying to do too much at once, unsuccessful attempts to conquer southern Manchuria and northern Korea, invasion by Turks, and uprising.

3. d

4. Answers will vary but students should support their point of view.

Building Your Portfolio

Students' lists may include the civil service system, gunpowder, and printing.

The Rise of the Middle Ages

CHAPTER RESOURCE MANAGER

Objectives	Pacing Guide	Reproducible Resources
SECTION 1 **The Rise of the Franks** (pp. 288–293) • Describe how Frankish rulers gained control of Europe. • Explain what caused the decline of Charlemagne's empire.	**Regular** 1.5 day / **Block Scheduling** 1 day *Block Scheduling Handbook with Team Teaching Strategies, 13.1*	RS Guided Reading Strategy 13.1 PS Readings in World History 37: Peasant Life During the Time of Charlemagne
SECTION 2 **Feudalism and the Manorial System** (pp. 294–299) • Explore how feudalism helped shape political and social development in Europe during the Middle Ages. • Identify the ways in which the manorial system influenced economic growth in Europe during the Middle Ages.	**Regular** 1.5 day / **Block Scheduling** 1 day *Block Scheduling Handbook with Team Teaching Strategies, 13.2*	RS Guided Reading Strategy 13.2 PS Readings in World History 38: The Table of a Thirteenth-Century English Lord
SECTION 3 **The Church** (pp. 300–303) • Describe how the church hierarchy fit into society. • Explain how the practices of monasticism changed. • Explore how the church influenced life in medieval Europe.	**Regular** 1 day / **Block Scheduling** .5 day *Block Scheduling Handbook with Team Teaching Strategies, 13.3*	RS Guided Reading Strategy 13.3 SM Geography Activity 14: The Structure of the Church
SECTION 4 **The Struggle for Power in England and France** (pp. 304–309) • Explain how the kingdom of England was formed. • Identify the achievements of William the Conqueror and his successors. • Describe how Parliament and common law affected political developments in England. • Explore how the French kings gained power over their nobles.	**Regular** 1.5 day / **Block Scheduling** 1 day *Block Scheduling Handbook with Team Teaching Strategies, 13.4*	RS Guided Reading Strategy 13.4 SM Geography Activity 13: England Under the Normans PS Readings in World History 39
SECTION 5 **The Clash over Germany and Italy** (pp. 310–313) • Describe how the Holy Roman emperors used their power. • Explain how the struggle between the popes and emperors developed.	**Regular** 1 day / **Block Scheduling** .5 day *Block Scheduling Handbook with Team Teaching Strategies, 13.5*	RS Guided Reading Strategy 13.5 PS Readings in World History 40 E Creative Teaching Strategy 13

Chapter Resource Key

PS Primary Sources
RS Reading Support
IC Interdisciplinary Connections
E Enrichment
SM Skills Mastery
A Assessment

REV Review
ELL Reinforcement and English Language Learners
 Transparencies
 CD–ROM
 Music

 Video
 Internet
 Holt Presentation Maker Using Microsoft® PowerPoint®

One-Stop Planner CD-ROM

See the **One-Stop Planner** for a complete list of additional resources for students and teachers.

One-Stop Planner CD-ROM

It's easy to plan lessons, select resources, and print out materials for your students when you use the **One-Stop Planner** CD–ROM with **Test Generator.**

Technology Resources	Reinforcement, Review, and Assessment
One-Stop Planner 13.1 Homework Practice Online	Daily Quiz 13.1 Main Idea Activity 13.1 English Audio Summary 13.1 Spanish Audio Summary 13.1 REV Section 1 Review, p. 293
One-Stop Planner 13.2 Homework Practice Online Online Maps, Charts, and Graphs: A Medieval Manor	Daily Quiz 13.2 Main Idea Activity 13.2 English Audio Summary 13.2 Spanish Audio Summary 13.2 REV Section 2 Review, p. 299
One-Stop Planner 13.3 Holt Researcher: World History: Benedict, Hildegard of Bingen Homework Practice Online Online Maps, Charts, and Graphs: A Monk's Day	Daily Quiz 13.3 Main Idea Activity 13.3 English Audio Summary 13.3 Spanish Audio Summary 13.3 REV Section 3 Review, p. 303
One-Stop Planner 13.4 Holt Researcher: World History: William the Conqueror World History Teaching Transparency: Art and History 11: Bayeux Tapestry Homework Practice Online	Daily Quiz 13.4 Main Idea Activity 13.4 English Audio Summary 13.4 Spanish Audio Summary 13.4 REV Section 4 Review, p. 309
One-Stop Planner 13.5 Holt Researcher: World History: Innocent III, John Paul II Homework Practice Online Online Maps, Charts, and Graphs: Holy Roman Empire at the Death of Otto I	Daily Quiz 13.5 Main Idea Activity 13.5 English Audio Summary 13.5 Spanish Audio Summary 13.5 REV Section 5 Review, p. 313

internet connect

HRW ONLINE RESOURCES
GO TO: go.hrw.com
Then type in a keyword.

TEACHER HOME PAGE
KEYWORD: SP3 Teacher

CHAPTER INTERNET ACTIVITIES
KEYWORD: SP3 WH13
Choose an activity to:
- evaluate primary and secondary sources about Charlemagne.
- create a poster on medieval art and architecture.
- write a report on daily life in the Middle Ages.

CHAPTER ENRICHMENT LINKS
KEYWORD: SP3 CH13

ONLINE ASSESSMENT
Homework Practice
KEYWORD: SP3 HP13
Standardized Test Prep
KEYWORD: SP3 STP13
Rubrics
KEYWORD: SS Rubrics

ONLINE MAPS, CHARTS, AND GRAPHS
KEYWORD: SP13 MCG

CONTENT UPDATES
KEYWORD: SS Content Updates

HOLT PRESENTATION MAKER
KEYWORD: SP3 PPT13

ONLINE READING SUPPORT
KEYWORD: SS Strategies

CURRENT EVENTS
KEYWORD: S3 Current Events

Meeting Individual Needs

Ability Levels

Level 1 Basic level activities designed for all students encountering new material

Level 2 Intermediate level activities designed for average students

Level 3 Challenging activities designed for honors and gifted and talented students

English Language Learners These activities address the needs of students with Limited English Proficiency.

Chapter Review and Assessment

IC Vocabulary Activity 13
Global Skill Builder CD–ROM
HRW Web Site
REV Chapter 13 Tutorial for Students, Parents, Mentors, and Peers
REV Chapter 13 Review, pp. 314–315

A Chapter 13 Test Generator (on the One-Stop Planner)
A Chapter 13 Test (Form A or B)
A Alternative Assessment Handbook
A Chapter 13 Test for English Language Learners and Special-Needs Students

CHAPTER 13

Section 1	The Rise of the Franks
Section 2	Feudalism and the Manorial System
Section 3	The Church
Section 4	The Struggle for Power in England and France
Section 5	The Clash over Germany and Italy

Build on What You Know

Ask students to answer the following questions:

What were some of the cultural achievements of Asia?

Consider:

- **China**
- **Japan**
- **Korea**

What were some of the reasons for the collapse of the Roman Empire?

Consider:

- **the economy**
- **social change**
- **invaders**

EXPLORING THE TIME LINE
GLOBAL EVENTS

☐ internet connect

TOPIC: Troubadours
GO TO: go.hrw.com
KEYWORD: SP3 WH13

Have students access the Internet through the HRW Go site to conduct research on troubadours. Then ask them to pretend they are modern-day troubadours. Have students write a song in one of the troubadour genres: *canso* (courtly love-song), *dansa* (mock-popular song based on a dance form), *escondig* (a lover's apologia), *gap* (a challenge), *pastorela* (an encounter between a knight and a shepherdess), *planh* (a lament), and *joc partit* (songs of debate). Have students read or sing their song to the class.

CHAPTER 13

A.D. 432–A.D. 1328
The Rise of the Middle Ages

A medieval crossbow

C. A.D. 476
Global Events
The last Western Roman emperor is deposed.

C. A.D. 542
Daily Life
A devastating plague begins to move across Europe, resulting in a decades-long population decline.

A.D. 782
Politics
Charlemagne executes Saxon hostages.

C. A.D. 797
Daily Life
French kings establish a royal messenger service.

| A.D. 425 | A.D. 525 | A.D. 725 | A.D. 825 |

A.D. 455
Global Events
Vandals attack Rome.

C. A.D. 500
Science and Technology
Architects develop the first plans for the Vatican in Rome.

C. A.D. 750
Daily Life
Beds become popular in France and Germany.

C. A.D. 787
Global Events
The first Viking raids into Britain occur.

Viking carving of a lion's head, A.D. 800s

Illustration of the invasion of England by Danish Vikings

Build on What You Know

Great civilizations flourished in East and Southeast Asia in the thousand years after about the A.D. 500s. The cultures that emerged in China, Korea, Japan, and Southeast Asia reached new heights of achievement. Change and growth also characterized the civilizations that emerged in Europe during these same years. The barbarian peoples who overran much of the Roman Empire brought with them behaviors and traditions that gradually developed into a new and distinct European civilization. In this chapter, you will learn how new European societies and cultures arose from the ashes of Rome's collapse.

286

What's Your Opinion?

Government

Agree Political leaders should deal only with matters of the state, and religious leaders should concern themselves only with church matters.

Disagree It is important for issues of church and state to be considered in relation to each other.

Constitutional Heritage

Agree It is not important to list and define individual rights in a constitution.

Disagree Citizens may be subject to the whims of their leaders if individual rights are not included and defined in a constitution.

Economics

Agree An agricultural economy is more stable and desirable than an industrial economy.

Disagree Both farming societies and industrial societies have advantages and disadvantages.

Detail from the Bayeux Tapestry depicting a battle scene between the English and the Normans

c. A.D. 900
Daily Life
European nobles begin to build fortified castles.

c. A.D. 900s
Science and Technology
The crossbow is used in Europe.

A.D. 925

c. A.D. 1110
The Arts
The earliest recorded miracle play is performed in England.

c. A.D. 1125
The Arts
The "troubadour" tradition of wandering musicians begins in France.

c. A.D. 1124
Business and Finance
Coins are first minted in Scotland.

A.D. 1125

c. A.D. 1190s
Science and Technology
The magnetic compass is used by mariners in Western Europe.

c. A.D. 1170
The Arts
Chrétien de Troyes writes the courtly love story "Lancelot."

A.D. 1215
Politics
King John I signs Magna Carta.

A.D. 1225

c. A.D. 1253
Business and Finance
Linen is made in England.

c. A.D. 1269
Business and Finance
The first English toll roads are built.

c. A.D. 1314
Politics
Scotland becomes independent under Robert I, the Bruce.

c. A.D. 1317
Politics
French law excludes women from inheriting the throne.

c. A.D. 1305
Business and Finance
Edward I standardizes measures, including the yard and the acre.

A.D. 1325

An idealized illustration of medieval knights

The castle of the Counts of Flanders

The development of local trade contributed to the growth of towns and cities in the 1000s. Rural peasants provided the towns with food and livestock, and in exchange they bought the manufactured goods produced in the towns. As peasants began to focus their economic activity on the towns, the power of feudal lords began to decrease.

Critical Thinking

Ask students what peasants may have found in the city that they found appealing.

ANSWER: Students may answer that peasants found freedom and consumer goods in the towns.

What's Your Opinion?

Themes Journal *Do you* **agree** *or* **disagree** *with the following statements? Support your point of view in your journal.*

Government Successful governments should establish a firm separation between the powers of church and state.

Constitutional Heritage Individual rights do not need to be included and defined in a constitution.

Economics Farming societies promote more secure and peaceful lifestyles than do societies that are centered upon industrial growth.

OBJECTIVES

1 **Describe how Frankish rulers gained control of Europe.**

2 **Explain what caused the decline of Charlemagne's empire.**

SECTION 1

READ TO DISCOVER

❶ How did Frankish rulers gain control of Europe?

❷ What caused the decline of Charlemagne's empire?

DEFINE

medieval

IDENTIFY

Middle Ages
Clovis
Merovingians
Charles Martel
Carolingians
Charlemagne
Louis the Pious
Magyars
Vikings

WHY IT MATTERS TODAY

The Vikings were known for their shipbuilding ability. Use or other **current event** sources to discover how ships are part of peoples' lives in Scandinavia today. Record your findings in your journal.

The Rise of the Franks

The Main Idea
A new European civilization arose based on Roman and Germanic values and traditions.

The Story Continues *"Charles was large and strong, and of lofty stature. . . . his appearance was always stately and dignified . . . His gait [stride] was firm, his whole carriage manly, and his voice clear."* This is how one observer described Charlemagne, one of the strong rulers who helped bring order to Europe in the Middle Ages.

The Frankish Rulers

For hundreds of years following the breakup of the Western Roman Empire, Europe was the scene of widespread disorder and change. Waves of barbarian invasion and settlement brought new customs and lifestyles to many parts of western Europe. Over time the social and political patterns typical of life in the empire merged with new patterns brought by barbarian peoples who settled in the West.

An age of transition. Gradually Europeans began to restore order in their lives. Many historians see the years between the 400s and about 1500 as a transition in the development of Western culture. Thus this period is generally known as the **Middle Ages,** or the **medieval** period of European development. It is the time in history between the end of the classical age and the beginnings of the modern world.

Many Germanic tribes plundered Europe and established small kingdoms. One tribe proved to have a lasting impact on European history. This group of loosely organized Germanic peoples, known as the Franks, did much to shape the new culture of post-Roman Europe.

Clovis and the Merovingians. The Franks first came into contact with the Roman Empire during the 200s, when they began moving into the lower Rhine River valley. In 481 a ruler named **Clovis** became king of one of the Frankish tribes. Clovis and his successors were called **Merovingians** because Clovis traced his family back to an ancestor named Merovech. Clovis was an able military leader. He and his troops conquered and absorbed other Frankish tribes. Soon they controlled all of northern Gaul.

Because Clovis had by this time become a Christian, the Franks received the support of the Christian church. The Franks soon seized and began to rule southwestern Gaul. This is the area that today is occupied by France, which is named for the Franks. When Clovis died, his sons divided the kingdom, as was often the Frankish custom.

INTERPRETING THE VISUAL RECORD

Frankish warrior This medallion depicts a mounted Frankish warrior with his lance at the ready. Note the lack of a stirrup, which was a later development. *Why did the Frankish artist who crafted this object show the warrior on horseback?*

TEACH OBJECTIVE 1

ALL LEVELS: Organize students into five groups and assign each group one of the following Frankish kings or mayors of the palace: Clovis, Pepin II, Charles Martel, Pepin III (Pepin the Short), or Charlemagne. Tell students to develop one-page biographical profiles of their assigned leaders. Encourage each group to find and include an image with their profile. When students have completed their profiles, arrange and display them in chronological order and have students take notes from one another's profiles. **ENGLISH LANGUAGE LEARNERS, COOPERATIVE LEARNING**

Teacher to Teacher

Rudy Martinez of San Antonio, Texas, suggested the following activity: Using what they learned in Chapter 12, as well as other information gained through research, have students develop a chart comparing and contrasting the Japanese feudal system with that of European feudalism. OR: Have students create a visual presentation comparing and contrasting the lives of Japanese samurai with those of European knights.

The Merovingian kings who ruled after Clovis were generally weak. Eventually the chief of the royal household, known as the "mayor of the palace," became the real ruler of each kingdom. One of these mayors was Pépin II, who ruled from 687 to 714. Pépin and his successors united the Frankish kingdoms.

Charles Martel and Pépin the Short. After Pépin II died, his son, **Charles Martel,** known as Charles the Hammer, became mayor of the palace. Charles Martel's cavalry defeated the Spanish Moors in 732 when they invaded France. This halted the Muslim advance in western Europe, although Muslim raids continued.

Charles Martel died in 741. His son, Pépin III, called "the Short," became the Merovingian kingdom's joint mayor of the palace with his brother, Carloman. Pépin, already king in all but name, overthrew Childeric III, the last Merovingian ruler, and claimed the Frankish throne for his own. In 751 Pépin was anointed king of the Franks. Pépin III's coronation established the **Carolingians,** a new line of Frankish rulers. The pope's confirmation of Pépin's rule, moreover, strengthened the legitimacy of the new Carolingian dynasty. This was because European Christians believed that the pope's blessing came directly from God. Over time monarchs throughout western Europe sought the church's blessing in order to support their rule.

The pope sought Pépin's help against the Lombards, a Germanic tribe that was attacking central Italy and threatening Rome. Pépin led a Frankish army into Italy and defeated the Lombards. The Franks won control of the territory around Rome and gave it to the pope. This gift of land is called the Donation of Pépin. It created the Papal States, which for centuries remained the stronghold of the church. The alliance that grew between the Franks and the church as a result of these actions made each side stronger. It also paved the way for the rise of **Charlemagne,** Pépin's son and the greatest of all Frankish kings.

Charlemagne's empire. Charlemagne inherited the Frankish throne in 768 and ruled until 814. During the 46 years of his reign, Charlemagne worked to build a "new Rome" centered in what is now France and Germany. As a devout Christian he helped to spread church teachings and Christian beliefs. His rule did much to bring civilization, order, and learning to barbarian Europe during the 800s.

Charlemagne spent much of his life at war. He defeated the Lombards in Italy, the Saxons in northern Germany, and the Avars in central Europe. He tried to conquer all of Muslim Spain, but failed. He was able, however, to drive the Moors back across the Pyrenees, a mountain range that separates Spain and France. Charlemagne's victory over the Moors added a small strip of Spanish land, called the "Spanish March," to his large empire. It also created a "buffer zone"—a kind of frontier—between Christian and Muslim Europe.

On Christmas Day of the year 800, Charlemagne was in Rome to worship at Saint Peter's Basilica. As Charlemagne knelt in prayer, Pope Leo III placed a crown on his head and declared him "Emperor of the Romans." Although the Roman Empire was long gone, the title indicates Charlemagne's importance to western Europe. He had united much of western Europe for the first time in

The simple, unadorned throne of Charlemagne, or "Charles the Great," did not reveal his power and importance.

HISTORY MAKER

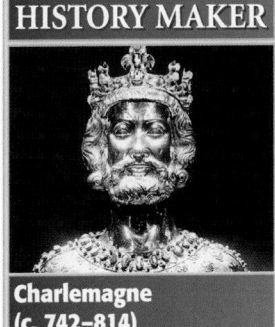

Charlemagne (c. 742–814)

As emperor, Charlemagne united most of the Christian lands in western Europe. During his reign, Charlemagne strengthened the political power of the Franks. He also set into motion a cultural rebirth throughout Europe by supporting education, creating libraries, and sponsoring the collection and copying of ancient Roman manuscripts. Charlemagne's rule became a model for later kings in medieval Europe. **What were some of Charlemagne's accomplishments as a ruler?**

TOPIC: Charlemagne
GO TO: go.hrw.com
KEYWORD: SP3 WH13

Have students access the Internet through the HRW Go site to research both primary and secondary sources about Charlemagne. Ask them to take notes on his life, accomplishments, and significance to history. Remind students that Charlemagne was so revered that he became an ideal and a legend. Ask them to evaluate the information they find and analyze whether the information is factual or exaggerated, and explain how they know. Then have them write a biography of Charlemagne.

HISTORY MAKER ANSWER

united Christian lands in western Europe, strengthened political power of the Franks, cultural rebirth

TEACH OBJECTIVE 1

LEVEL 1: Have students draw time lines that trace the Frankish rulers' involvement in the Christian faith from Clovis to Charlemagne. *(The following events should be included: Clovis converts to Christianity after victory; the pope crowns Pepin III "king by the grace of God;" Pepin aids the pope in defending Rome; Pope Leo III crowns Charlemagne "Emperor of the Romans.")* Ask students why they think this friendly relationship between church and state developed. *(Students may note that the relationship was of mutual benefit.)* **ENGLISH LANGUAGE LEARNERS**

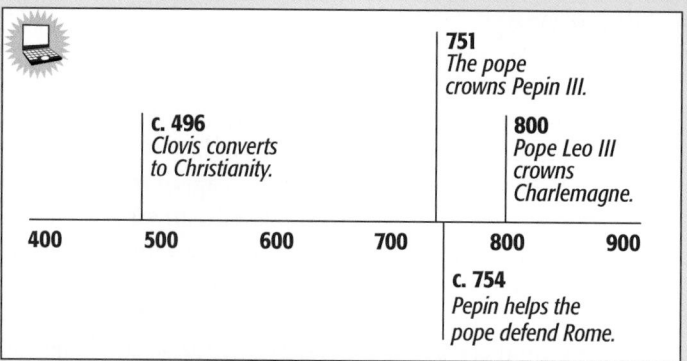

Government

Until Clovis united the Frankish tribes under his leadership, the Franks were divided into two major groups, the Salians and the Ripuarians. The Salian Franks lived along the northern Rhine River, while the Ripuarian Franks lived along the southern Rhine. In the 300s the Salian Franks became allies of the Romans, and in the next century, migrated into Gaul.

After Clovis became the leader of the Salian Franks—reputedly by murdering many of his own relatives—he overthrew the Romans in Gaul in 486. After converting to Christianity and gaining the support of the church, Clovis expanded his empire to include most of Gaul.

Critical Thinking

Ask students to explain the importance of Clovis's empire, though it did not outlast his death.

ANSWER: Students might suggest that Clovis's empire established the idea of a French monarchy. Students might also suggest that it foreshadowed the creation of Charlemagne's empire 400 years later.

VISUAL RECORD ANSWER

Pope Leo; maybe because the artist wanted to depict the church as very powerful

INTERPRETING THE VISUAL RECORD

The crowning of Charlemagne Pope Leo III crowns Charlemagne Emperor of the Romans. *Which figure—Charlemagne or Pope Leo—is depicted as more powerful in this French illustration from the 1300s? Why might that be so?*

400 years. Because of this, Europe regarded Charlemagne as the successor to the Roman emperors. The pope's coronation of Charlemagne was also significant because it showed the close ties that existed between the Franks and the Christian church.

Charlemagne was very conscious of his unique position as leader of a new western order. He saw himself, moreover, as the inheritor of Roman authority. He aimed to live up to the image of a Roman emperor in his actions, his policies, and the glory of his empire. He was greatly admired for his skills as a warrior as well as for his devotion to Christianity.

Government. Charlemagne's empire was divided into regions, each governed on the emperor's behalf by an official known as a count. Charlemagne established his capital at the northern Frankish city of Aix-la-Chapelle (EKS·LAH·shah·PEL), today the bustling German city of Aachen (AH·kuhn). The emperor used oaths of fidelity to ensure that the counts and other Carolingian officials ruled effectively under his command. Appointed officials helped Charlemagne run his empire. These officials were called *missi dominici* or "the lord's messengers." They would travel through the empire to hear complaints, investigate official misconduct, and determine the effectiveness of laws. The *missi dominici* ensured that the counts were serving the emperor and not themselves. Charlemagne viewed the *missi dominici* as his direct representatives and gave them a great deal of authority to make decisions in his name.

 History Makers Speak **❝Let the *missi* themselves make a diligent investigation whenever any man claims that an injustice has been done to him by any one . . . and they shall administer the law fully and justly in the case of the holy churches of God and of the poor, of wards [orphans] and widows, and of the whole people.❞**

Charlemagne, quoted in D.C. Munro, ed., *Translations and Reprints from the Original Sources of European History*, Vol. IV, *Laws of Charles the Great*

Education and learning. Although Charlemagne himself was not formally educated, he placed great value on education. He started schools at his palace for his own children and other young nobles. Scholars—usually monks—were invited from all over western Europe to teach at the school. Charlemagne appointed one of Europe's most respected thinkers, Alcuin (AL·kwihn) of York, to head the school and establish its course of learning. Alcuin developed a curriculum based on the Roman model, emphasizing grammar, rhetoric, logic, mathematics, music, and astronomy. Charlemagne also brought together scholars to produce a readable Bible. They used a new script called Caroline minuscule. The new Bible was used throughout Charlemagne's empire. Charlemagne also ordered the empire's bishops to create libraries.

Although some scholars claim Charlemagne never learned to write, he could read. Saint Augustine's *City of God* was one of his favorite books. Throughout his rule Charlemagne encouraged—sometimes forced—the empire's people to convert to Christianity.

✔ **READING CHECK: Summarizing** What steps did Charlemagne take to help assure that his officials ruled effectively and honestly? frequent personal inspections; appointed *missi dominici* to investigate complaints

Help students find excerpts from primary sources such as *The History of the Franks* written by Gregory of Tours or an early biography of Charlemagne. You may need to help students interpret the archaic language of such sources. When students have read an excerpt or two, have them summarize what they learned about daily life in the Middle Ages. Then discuss how these excerpts differ from the way that modern historians record events. **BLOCK SCHEDULING**

The Decline of the Frankish Empire

The proud empire that Charlemagne had built and governed so well did not long survive his death in 814. His descendants did not inherit Charlemagne's energy, his ability, or his long-range point of view. As a result, the empire's strength declined rapidly. By the mid-800s the once mighty Carolingian state had begun to divide and collapse.

The empire after Charlemagne's death. Charlemagne's only surviving son, **Louis the Pious,** proved to be a well-educated and religious king but a weak and shortsighted ruler. When Louis died in 840, his sons Lothair, Charles the Bald, and Louis the German agreed to divide the empire among themselves after much dispute. This agreement, signed in 843, became known as the Treaty of Verdun.

Instead of uniting to overcome enemies from within and beyond the splintered empire, Charlemagne's grandsons and their successors fought among themselves. By

Charlemagne's Empire, 768–814 (left) and The Frankish Kingdoms After the Treaty of Verdun, 843 (right)

Interpreting Maps The Carolingian Empire, begun under Pépin III and expanded by Charlemagne, brought much of western Europe under Frankish rule. Charlemagne's grandsons divided the empire into three separate kingdoms.

■ **Skills Assessment: 1. Human Systems** Identify the Germanic tribes that Charlemagne incorporated into his empire.
2. Analyzing Information Whose kingdom after 843 claimed the most major cities?

LEVEL 3: Ask students why Charlemagne's vast empire did not last long after his death. (*Frankish practice of dividing the kingdom among the king's sons, numerous invasions*) Have students use their textbooks to list the most prominent invading peoples. (*Muslims, Magyars, Vikings*) Have students use computer software to learn more about Vikings, the most feared invaders. Have students write short stories about Viking characters in the 800s. Stories should be creative, but settings and characters should be based on historical facts. **BLOCK SCHEDULING**

 HOMEWORK Ask students to explain how the history of the Western world might have been different if Charlemagne's descendants had been able to hold his empire together.

CLOSE

Organize the class into three groups. Have each group evaluate the accomplishments of Clovis, Charles Martel, or Charlemagne by listing the political choices and decisions they made.

The Franks were famous for their swords, which were in great demand across Europe. These swords were known for their balance and strength. Frankish foot soldiers used short swords and carried spears, bows and arrows, and shields. The cavalry carried both long and short swords, spears, and round shields. In addition, Charlemagne's mounted soldiers wore rudimentary armor and helmets, possibly the early stages of the armored knight of later centuries.

___

MAP ANSWERS
1. Muslim

2. Students might guess that it was because of Constantinople's favorable location.

870 the middle kingdom had been divided between the rulers of the eastern and western kingdoms. To make matters worse, powerful lords in these two kingdoms became increasingly independent of the Carolingian monarchs. These lords thought they could best serve their own interests by defying the weakening rule of the central monarchs.

Charlemagne's empire was further undermined by invasions of different peoples from beyond the empire's frontiers. Muslims from Africa invaded the Mediterranean coast. Slavs from the east raided central Europe. Another group from the east, the nomadic **Magyars** who settled in what is now Hungary, terrorized Europe for about 50 years before they were finally defeated.

The Vikings. The most feared invaders of western Europe during the 800s and the 900s were the **Vikings** from Scandinavia in the north. Vikings, or "Norsemen," were Germanic peoples from what are now the countries of Norway, Sweden, and Denmark. The Vikings' customs and myths centered on pagan gods. Archaeologists have excavated Viking burial mounds that include boats and tools for use in the afterlife. The Vikings would sometimes place a dead person in a boat and burn it. In about 930 an Arab, Ibn Fadlan, witnessed the funeral of a Viking chieftain. The chieftain's ship was hauled onto the land, and his body

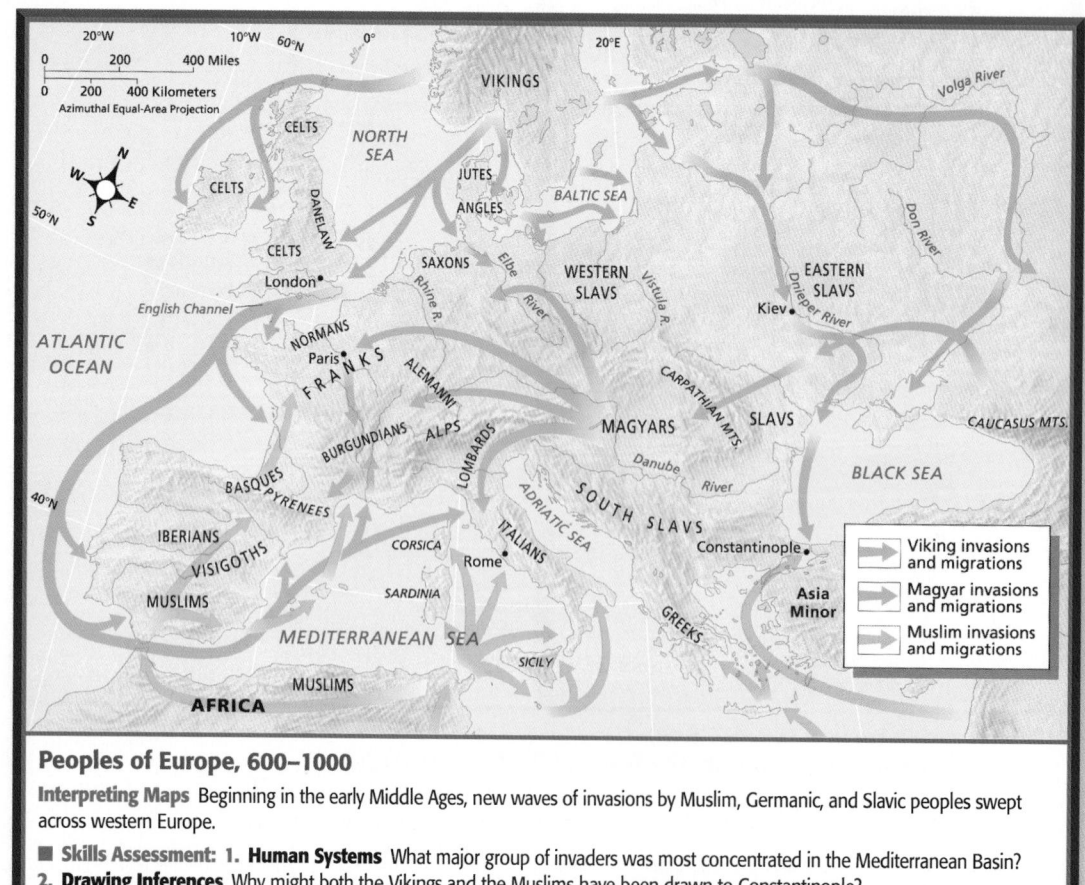

Peoples of Europe, 600–1000

Interpreting Maps Beginning in the early Middle Ages, new waves of invasions by Muslim, Germanic, and Slavic peoples swept across western Europe.

■ **Skills Assessment: 1. Human Systems** What major group of invaders was most concentrated in the Mediterranean Basin?
2. Drawing Inferences Why might both the Vikings and the Muslims have been drawn to Constantinople?

was placed on the ship along with rich grave goods. A historian, using Ibn Fadlan's account, described the Arab observer's experience:

Primary Source **"On the day of the burial, . . . the slave girl said, 'Lo, I see my lord and master he calls to me. Let me go to him.' Aboard the ship waited the old woman called the Angel of Death, who would kill her. The girl drank from a cup . . . and sang a long song. She grew fearful and hesitant. At once the old woman grasped her head and led her into the tent.**
Inside the tent the girl died beside her master by stabbing and strangling. Then the ship was fired."

Ibn Fadlan, quoted in Robert Paul Jordan, "Viking Trail East,"
National Geographic Magazine, March 1985

Although the Vikings were ruled by kings and nobles, their government was surprisingly democratic for its time. Assemblies of landowners made the laws. The Vikings were primarily farmers but also gathered, fished, and hunted. In the spring and summer the Vikings would travel south and west along the coasts of mainland Europe and the British Isles. They sailed rivers into Germany, France, and the Baltic area. The Vikings would raid and loot settlements and bring captives back to work as slaves on their farms in Scandinavia. Their way of capturing towns was often savage and cruel. Their use of axes and large dogs struck terror into people. The Vikings were also skilled in siege operations and could capture even strongly fortified towns.

Their sturdy ships carried the Vikings across the Atlantic Ocean to what is now Iceland, Greenland, and North America. In time they settled in England, Ireland, and parts of continental Europe. A large Viking settlement in northwestern France gave that region its name—Normandy, from the French word for "Northmen."

✔ **READING CHECK: Finding the Main Idea** Why were groups such as the Magyars and Vikings able to invade the Frankish Empire successfully? Charlemagne's successors fought among themselves instead of uniting to overcome invaders.

Figure of the head of a Viking from about 850

SECTION 1 REVIEW

1. **Define** and explain the significance:
   medieval

2. **Identify** and explain the significance:
   Middle Ages
   Clovis
   Merovingians
   Charles Martel
   Carolingians
   Charlemagne
   Louis the Pious
   Magyars
   Vikings

3. **Categorizing** Copy the diagram and use it to show how Charlemagne organized his government and what responsibilities were held by the various officials.

   Charlemagne's Empire
   → ☐
   → ☐

4. **Finding the Main Idea**
   a. What actions helped Charlemagne to unify his empire?
   b. In what ways did the actions of Charlemagne's grandsons cause the Carolingian Empire to become vulnerable to invaders from the north, south, and east?

5. **Writing and Critical Thinking**
   Comparing and Contrasting Imagine that you are living in Paris at the end of the 800s. Write a journal entry in which you compare daily life in the western kingdom to stories that you have heard of life in the Carolingian Empire during Charlemagne's reign.
   Consider:
   • the actions that Charlemagne took to centralize and expand the empire
   • the effects of the Treaty of Verdun on the unity and security of the empire

Homework Practice Online
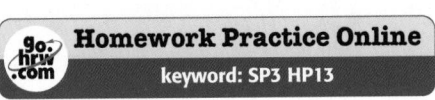
keyword: SP3 HP13

THE RISE OF THE MIDDLE AGES **293**

SECTION 2

OBJECTIVES

1 Explore how feudalism helped shape political and social development in Europe during the Middle Ages.

2 Identify the ways in which the manorial system influenced economic growth in Europe during the Middle Ages.

📀 LET'S GET STARTED!

As students enter the classroom, have them think about the importance of land ownership throughout history and in the United States today. Ask them if one must own land to prosper economically. *(no)* Have them explain how land ownership today is usually transferred between individuals. *(It is usually bought, sold, or inherited.)* Tell students that in Section 2 they will learn about land ownership in the Middle Ages.

SECTION 2

READ TO DISCOVER

❶ How did feudalism help to shape political and social development in Europe during the Middle Ages?

❷ In what ways did manorialism influence economic growth in Europe during the Middle Ages?

DEFINE

feudalism
fief
vassal
primogeniture
manorialism
serfs
chivalry

▶ WHY IT MATTERS TODAY

Feudal Europe was the scene of frequent local wars and conflicts. Use CNNfyi.com or other **current event** sources to investigate how continual conflict affects the people of a region and the lifestyles they follow. Record your findings in your journal.

CNN Student News.com

Feudalism and the Manorial System

The Main Idea
Feudalism and manorialism structured and organized European society in the Middle Ages.

The Story Continues *Society in the Middle Ages was strongly shaped by relationships of loyalty and service between higher and lower nobles. "I urge you . . . to maintain towards [your overlord] . . . a devoted and certain fealty [loyalty] both of body and soul," one mother advised her son. For centuries the nature of this binding relationship organized medieval society on the basis of military service and land ownership.*

Feudalism

Within 100 years of Charlemagne's death, organized, large-scale government in Europe all but disappeared. By the 900s most Europeans were governed by small, local, independent leaders, most often by local lords. The political organization these leaders represented is known as **feudalism.**

The system. Within the feudal system a powerful noble granted land to a lesser noble. Actual ownership of the land remained with the noble who made the grant. The noble who received the grant was entitled to use of the land and its products, but could not "own" the land. This grant of land allowed the lesser noble to "maintain" himself and his household. In return for maintenance, the lesser noble promised loyalty, military assistance, and other services to the lord who granted the land. The person who granted land was a lord and the grant of land was called a **fief.** The person who received the fief was a **vassal.** The transaction of a noble granting land and a vassal receiving land created a contract between the two. A vassal could further divide the land he had been granted and grant it to others, such as knights. Thus, a vassal could also be a lord.

Eventually the fief became hereditary, as legal possession of the land passed from a vassal to his son. By about 1100 it had become customary for the eldest son of a lord or vassal to inherit ownership or possession of the land. This system of inheritance from father to eldest son is called **primogeniture** (pry·moh·JE·nuh·choohr). Women's rights regarding legal property were limited. A woman might have had fiefs in her dowry. However, when she married, her husband gained control over her dowry. In most cases a woman regained control of the property in her dowry if her husband died.

▶ INTERPRETING THE VISUAL RECORD

Lord and vassal This stained-glass window depicts the relationship between a lord and his vassals. *How can you tell that the lord is more powerful than the vassals in this picture?*

TEACH OBJECTIVES 1 and 2

LEVEL 2: Tell students to imagine that they work for a time travel agency. They need to develop a brochure explaining feudalism and the manorial system to travelers who wish to visit medieval Europe. Students' brochures should include the following: definitions of terms such as *vassal*, *fief*, and *lord*; information about the roles various individuals play within the system; information about feudal justice and warfare; and a brief note about chivalry. Encourage students to include illustrations and graphic organizers to help clarify the system of feudalism—a graphic representation of the feudal hierarchy would be particularly helpful. Tell students to remember that the purpose of their brochure is to prepare travelers to exist within the political system they will encounter during their expedition.

Throughout the Middle Ages local lords held many of the powers associated with government. Kings were also bound by the customs and obligations of feudalism. In theory every landholder was a vassal to the king. In practice, however, the king controlled only those who lived on his feudal lands. Even the church was part of the feudal system. The medieval church owned vast amounts of land and had many vassals who were granted fiefs in return for military protection and service.

Warfare. Wars were common during the Middle Ages. Many wars grew out of private fights between feudal lords, or lords and vassals, and were local conflicts that involved only a handful of nobles and their knights. In other cases, wars could be large-scale events that involved whole regions and that could be immensely destructive.

Knights in the Middle Ages wore armor in battle and were heavily armed. In the early Middle Ages, armor was made of chain mail—small, interlocking metal links stitched to a knee-length leather shirt. The knight would also wear an iron helmet and carry a sword, a large shield, and a lance. With the introduction of gunpowder during the late Middle Ages, overlapping metal plates replaced chain mail. Often, plate armor was so heavy that knights had to be hauled onto their horses with cranes. Battle horses were much larger than today's saddle horses. The warhorses of the Middle Ages probably resembled today's Clydesdales and Percherons in size, weight, and power.

In medieval times wars had different effects on society. For nobles, wars were an opportunity for glory and wealth. For most people of the Middle Ages, however, war was a major cause of suffering and hardship. The church tried to limit the general suffering caused by war by issuing several decrees that prohibited acts of violence and private warfare near churches and other holy buildings. If the decrees were not obeyed, the church threatened punishment. The church also forbade violence against cattle and agricultural equipment as well as certain types of persons, including clergy, women, merchants, and pilgrims. The church tried to get all lords to accept another decree that forbade fighting on certain days, such as weekends and holy days. However, restrictions on fighting could almost never be enforced strictly. Private wars continued until kings became strong enough to stop them.

Feudal justice. Feudal justice differed greatly from Roman justice. A feudal trial was decided in one of three ways: trial by battle; compurgation, or oath taking; and trial by ordeal. A trial could be a duel between accuser and accused—or their representatives—in which the outcome determined innocence or guilt.

INTERPRETING THE VISUAL RECORD

The knight Technical improvements, such as the development of the stirrup and better armor, added greatly to mounted knights' effectiveness in battle. *How would stirrups help a knight's effectiveness in battle?*

Citizenship

As early as the 1000s, knights carried personal symbols mounted on banners or shields into battle. In the 1100s it became customary for sons to inherit their fathers' banners and shields. Later, three-dimensional crests, mostly of animals, were added to helmets. In time these crests became badges of nobility. By the 1200s the crest, helmet, and shield had been incorporated into a family coat of arms.

Critical Thinking

Ask students why they think knights first wore such symbols.

ANSWER: Students might suggest that knights needed something to identify them when their faces were covered with helmets.

VISUAL RECORD ANSWER

They would make it easier to stay on the horse.

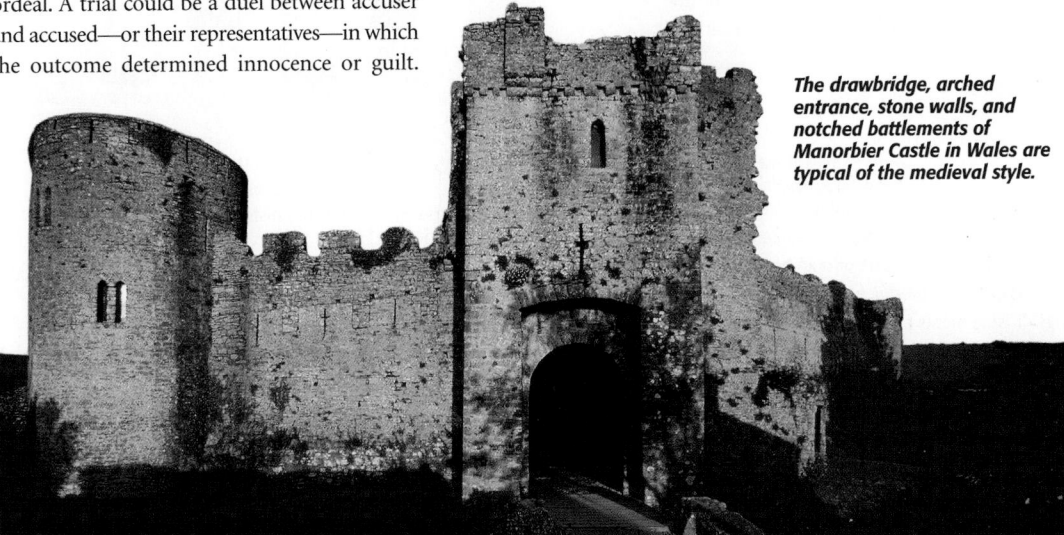

The drawbridge, arched entrance, stone walls, and notched battlements of Manorbier Castle in Wales are typical of the medieval style.

295

TEACH OBJECTIVE 2

LEVEL 3: Have students use their textbooks to create mock contracts that represent the relationship between a medieval noble and a peasant who worked his land. These contracts, which should resemble modern legal agreements, must include a list of each party's obligations to the other.

 HOMEWORK Ask students to imagine that they are the teenage sons or daughters of an English lord and have them write a journal entry from this point of view. Then have students write another journal entry from the point of view of a peasant teenager.

Economics

The most important nobles held large fiefs received directly from the king, and they in turn divided their land and granted fiefs to lesser nobles. This division continued down to the level of the lowest noble, who held a single manor. Originally the granting of fiefs was repeated whenever a lord or vassal died, but eventually control of the fief became hereditary.

Critical Thinking

Ask students what advantages hereditary control of fiefs would have held compared to redistributing the fiefs whenever a lord or vassal died.

ANSWER Students might suggest that hereditary control gave nobles further incentives to take care of their lands and protect them so their children could inherit them.

SKILLS PRACTICE ANSWERS

1. second sentence of first paragraph

2. first sentence of first paragraph, both sentences of second paragraph

3. Students' answers will vary.

The Rise of Feudalism

When reading sources on the rise of feudalism, readers should be careful to distinguish between facts and values statements. A fact can be proven true or false. A values statement is an opinion that represents a particular point of view. For example, a writer can state that Charlemagne was a successful ruler. That is a values statement because it is based on the writer's idea of success. Sometimes a fact and a values statement can be included in the same sentence. For example, a writer may state that Charlemagne spoke Greek and Latin so beautifully he could have taught both languages. Charlemagne's ability to speak the languages can be proven true or false. However, whether he spoke them beautifully is a matter of opinion.

A Historian's View

The statement below discusses one historian's view of the best way to define feudalism.

"The simplest way will be to begin by saying what feudal society was not. Although obligations arising from blood-relationship played a very active part in it, it did not rely on kinship alone...feudal ties...developed when those of kinship proved inadequate...

European feudalism should therefore be seen as the outcome of the violent dissolution of older societies. It would in fact be unintelligible without the great upheaval of the Germanic invasions which, by forcibly uniting the two societies originally at very different stages of development, disrupted both of them and brought to the surface a great many...social practices of an extremely primitive nature."

The Structure of Feudalism

King and Queen

Church Officials and Nobles

Knights

Peasants

Skills Reminder

To distinguish a fact from a values statement, review the difference between a fact and a values statement. Then identify words that suggest a value or opinion. For example, adjectives such as *great, wonderful, horrible* are words that express feelings. "I" statements can also help determine whether a statement is a point of view. *In my opinion* or *I think* express a point of view. Finally, ask questions about the sentence. Can "That meal I had was really awful" mean more than one thing? What is the fact in the statement and what is the opinion?

Skills Practice

❶ Which sentences in the historian's statement contain facts?

❷ Which sentences in the historian's statement contain values statements?

❸ While listening to a radio or TV news report, identify the factual information provided by the report. Then identify statements of opinion and values statements, and analyze how those statements are used to influence the listener's/viewer's conclusions.

TEACH OBJECTIVES 1 and 2

LEVEL 1: Have students create a graphic organizer like the one shown. Have students, either independently or with guidance, find at least three details from the text that describe peasant life. Examples are listed in italics on the chart. Then, in small groups, have students fill in the other side of the chart, comparing poverty in feudal Europe to poverty in the United States today. Discuss and debate conclusions. **ENGLISH LANGUAGE LEARNERS**

Poverty in Feudal Europe	Poverty in the Modern U.S.
"fear of my master"	
did not own their own land	
opportunity for protection from lord	
couldn't leave manor without permission ("not a free man")	

In compurgation, the accuser and the accused were supported by people who swore that the person they represented was telling the truth. The oath takers were probably similar to character witnesses in today's trials. The outcome of a trial by ordeal was determined by how the accused survived a particular ordeal. The accused had to carry a piece of hot iron, plunge his hand in a pot of boiling water, or survive extended immersion in cold water. If the accused person's wounds healed quickly and well, he was innocent; if not, he was guilty.

✔ **READING CHECK: Analyzing Information** What were some aspects of feudalism? grant of land in exchange for loyalty, military service; localized government

The Manorial System

Feudalism provided social and political structure to the culture of the Middle Ages. Similarly, **manorialism** shaped the economy of much of Europe during these years. The system took its name from the manors of the Middle Ages. Manors were large farming estates that included manor houses, cultivated lands, woodlands, pastures, fields, and villages.

Central authority and organized trade—key parts of most modern economies—were almost nonexistent during the Middle Ages. Thus people who lived on manors needed to be self-sufficient. They sought to produce everything they needed, including food, clothing, and shelter. Some items, however, such as iron, salt, wool, wine, and certain manufactured goods, were purchased.

A lord and several peasant families shared the land of the manor. Generally the lord kept about one third of the manor's lands, called the domain, for himself. The manor's peasants farmed the remaining two-thirds of the land for themselves. In return for being able to work the land, the peasants gave the lord some of their crops and helped to farm his land. The peasants also provided other services on the manor and paid many kinds of taxes.

Ideally a manor village was located along a stream or river, which provided waterpower for the village mill. For safety a small group of houses were clustered near the manor house or castle. The land surrounding the manor house included the village, vegetable plots, cultivated fields, pastures, and forests. Cultivated land was often divided into three large fields for growing grain. Only two of the three fields were planted at one time. The third field could lie fallow, or unplanted, for a season to regain its fertility. The three fields were divided into small strips distributed among the peasants. If the lord's domain was divided, he too had strips of land in each field.

Peasant life. Peasants' lives were difficult in medieval times because they spent long hours at backbreaking work in the fields. A text written during the Middle Ages described a typical workday from a peasant's point of view.

> **Primary Source** "... I work very hard. I go out at dawn, driving the oxen to the field, and I yoke them to the plough; however hard the winter I dare not stay at home for fear of my master; but, having yoked the oxen and made the plough-share ... fast to the plough, every day I have to plough a whole acre or more. ... It is hard work, because I am not a free man."

Aelfric, *Colloquy*, translated by G.G. Coulton in *The Medieval Village*

INTERPRETING THE VISUAL RECORD

Peasant farmers This stylized image from the 1400s illustrates the work of medieval peasants during harvest time. *What evidence does this illustration provide of tools and techniques used by farm workers during the Middle Ages?*

Analyzing Primary Sources

Summarizing According to this account, why did the peasant find his work to be especially hard? He was not a free man.

VISUAL RECORD ANSWER

Farmers are using handheld tools to harvest crops.

Technology Resources

 Online Maps, Charts, and Graphs: A Medieval Manor

ALL LEVELS: Have students read the subsection entitled "Chivalry" on pages 298 to 299. Discuss the characteristics of the code of chivalry. *(Knights had to be brave, fight fairly, be loyal, keep their word, treat conquered foes gallantly, be courteous to women.)* Show students sample images of medieval or modern coats of arms and point out the unique symbolism of each. Then have students create coats of arms for themselves, considering events, people, places, or animals that were or are significant in their lives or represent themselves. Encourage students to use images in their coat of arms that represent the characteristics of the code of chivalry that they feel they possess. Their family might also suggest a symbol. **ENGLISH LANGUAGE LEARNERS**

Have each student list three aspects of the feudal system and three aspects of the manorial system. Then lead a class discussion on how the two systems worked together.

Science, Technology & Society

Although castles were the homes of the aristocracy, their main purpose was to defend against attack. The strongest part of the castle was the keep, where the lord and his family lived. The keep was surrounded by a wall or a series of walls, which were flanked by towers. The outermost walls were often protected by moats or by the sheer drop of cliffs. Castles proved to be effective defensive fortifications until the use of gunpowder allowed artillery to penetrate castle walls.

Critical Thinking

Ask students to speculate on how the invention of gunpowder might have affected the manorial system.

ANSWER: Students might suggest that when castles no longer provided protection for the lord, his authority was weakened.

YOUNG PEOPLE IN HISTORY ANSWER

so that they might improve their status by learning the skills and responsibilities that were expected of high-ranking noble-women

YOUNG PEOPLE IN HISTORY

Preparing for Life as a Noblewoman

Young girls from the families of lesser nobles often went to live in the households of higher-ranking noblewomen. There they would be trained in the skills and responsibilities that were expected of women in their rank.

Generally the young noblewoman was taught to sew, to weave, to cook, to play musical instruments, and to sing. She learned, as well, the social conduct that was proper for women of the nobility. In some cases girls and young women were also instructed in the skills of household supervision. **Why might noble parents send their daughters to train in the households of higher-ranking nobles?**

Young women of the nobility serve a noblewoman.

Most peasants—called **serfs**—could not leave the land without the lord's permission. Their meals consisted mainly of black bread, lentils, some vegetables, and ale. Because livestock helped work the fields, and because peasants were generally forbidden to hunt on the lord's land, they could rarely afford to eat meat. Compared to life expectancies today, average life spans in the Middle Ages were very short. Among the factors that severely limited the life expectancies of most Europeans were disease, starvation, and frequent warfare. Very likely, peasants lived, worked, and died in the village in which they had been born.

Nobles' lifestyles. Frequently people think of the Middle Ages as a time when lords and knights lived in elegant castles. The upper classes of the Middle Ages, however, generally did not live in luxury or even in comfort by today's standards.

A castle was a fortified base from which the lord enforced his authority and protected the surrounding countryside. In the early Middle Ages, castles were simple structures made from earth and wood. Later they were made from stone.

Castles were usually built on hills or other landforms that would prevent easy attack. If a castle was on flat land that was difficult to defend, a ditch called a moat was built around it and sometimes flooded with water. A drawbridge extended across the moat to allow entry to the castle's courtyard. If the castle was attacked, the drawbridge could be raised.

A building called the "keep" was the main part of the castle. The keep was a strong tower that usually contained storerooms, workshops, and perhaps barracks and the lord's living quarters. In the great hall the lord received visitors. The castle's rooms had thick walls and small windows with no glass. As a result the rooms were usually dark and chilly. The lord spent most of his day looking after his land and dispensing justice among his vassals and serfs.

A lord or the head of a peasant family depended on his wife and children for help. Marriage was viewed as a way to advance one's fortune. Through marriage a man might acquire land. While marriage might bring a man land, it usually produced children who had to be cared for. A lord would often provide dowries for any daughters. Among peasants, children were often welcomed as a source of farm labor.

Chivalry. By the late 1100s a code of conduct known as **chivalry** had begun to bring major changes to feudal society. Chivalry was a system of rules that dictated knights' behavior towards others. The word chivalry comes from the French word *cheval*, meaning "horse," and refers to the fact that knights were mounted soldiers.

To become a knight, a boy had to belong to the noble class and had to pass through two stages of training. The first stage began at about the age of seven, when a boy would serve as a knight's page, or attendant. The page would learn knightly manners and begin to learn how to use and care for weapons. As a teenager the page would

REVIEW

Have students complete Section 2 Review on p. 299.

ASSESS

Have students complete Daily Quiz 13.2. As Alternative Assessment, you may want to use the time travel or contract exercises in this section's lessons.

RETEACH

Have students complete Main Idea Activity for English Language Learners and Special-Needs Students 13.2. Then ask them to write a question and answer that covers the main idea for each subsection. **ENGLISH LANGUAGE LEARNERS**

EXTEND

The mutual-dependency relationships basic to manorialism may remind students of a term from science class: *symbiosis*. Ask a group of students to research symbiotic relationships in nature and report on some of these to the class. Have them point out parallels with feudal-manorial society. **BLOCK SCHEDULING, COOPERATIVE LEARNING**

INTERPRETING THE VISUAL RECORD

Coats of arms The knights shown battling in this image bear coats of arms on their clothing and shields. A knight's coat of arms helped to identify him when he was fully armored. *What might the characters and symbols shown on each coat of arms represent?*

become a knight's assistant, called a squire. The squire would take care of the knight's horse, armor, and weapons. Then, probably when the knight thought that the squire was ready, the squire would accompany the knight into battle. If the squire proved himself to be a skilled and courageous fighter, he would be knighted in an elaborate religious ceremony.

A knight in full armor, wearing a closed helmet, often could be distinguished from other knights only by his coat of arms. The knight's coat of arms was a graphic symbol that identified him and that represented his personal characteristics. The coat of arms was painted or stitched onto the knight's shield or outer coat, his flag, or possibly his horse's trappings. Generally the coat of arms was passed along from one generation to the next.

According to the code of chivalry, knights were expected to be courageous in battle and to fight fairly. If a knight used tricks and strategy to overcome an opponent, he was considered a coward. A knight was expected to be loyal to his friends and to keep his word. He was required to treat his conquered foes gallantly. A knight was also expected to be courteous to women and the less powerful.

Chivalry did much to improve the rough and crude manners of early feudal lords. Behavior, however, did not become perfect by any modern standard. A knight was required to extend courtesy only to people of his own class. Toward others his attitude and actions could be coarse, bullying, and arrogant.

✔ **READING CHECK: Drawing Inferences** How did manorialism complement feudalism?
feudalism provided social and political structure; manorialism provided economic structure

---

SECTION 2 REVIEW

1. **Define** and explain the significance:
   feudalism
   fief
   vassal
   primogeniture
   manorialism
   serfs
   chivalry

2. **Making Generalizations** Copy the graphic organizer below to demonstrate the responsibilities of lords and peasants on a manor.

   Manor

   (Lords) → (Peasants)

3. **Finding the Main Idea**
   a. How was medieval Europe different from previous civilizations?
   b. What were the chief political and economic characteristics of feudalism and manorialism?

4. **Writing and Critical Thinking**
   Summarizing Imagine that you are a squire in service to a knight, or a young noblewoman in service to a lady. Compose a journal entry that describes your duties and goals.
   Consider:
   • the relationship between the squire and knight or the young noblewoman and the lady
   • the responsibilities of the servant

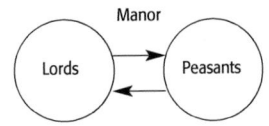

Homework Practice Online
keyword: SP3 HP13

VISUAL RECORD ANSWER

personal characteristics

SECTION 2 REVIEW ANSWERS

❶ **Define**
• feudalism, p. 294
• fief, p. 294
• vassal, p. 294
• primogeniture, p. 294
• manorialism, p. 297
• serfs, p. 298
• chivalry, p. 298

❷ Peasants: farmed the land, gave some crops to the lord, paid taxes; Lords: managed land, kept domain

❸ a. Organized, large scale government was replaced by small, local, independent leaders.

b. feudalism: powerful nobles granted land to lesser nobles in exchange for loyalty and military assistance; system of primogeniture manorialism: a lord and several peasant families shared the land of the manor; peasants farmed two thirds of the land, provided services, and paid taxes

❹ Students' journal entries will vary but should incorporate what students have read about the relationship between squires and knights or ladies and ladies-in-waiting and the responsibilities of the servant.

THE RISE OF THE MIDDLE AGES **299**

299

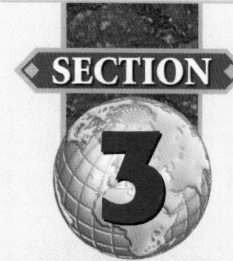
OBJECTIVES

1 **Describe how the church hierarchy fit into society.**

2 **Explain how the practices of monasticism changed.**

3 **Explore how the church influenced life in medieval Europe.**

🔊 LET'S GET STARTED!

As students enter the classroom, have them consider the separation between church and state in the United States. Ask them what this separation means. *(The government cannot attempt to control religious belief, and religion cannot control matters of the state.)* Have students state whether they think the separation is positive or negative and explain why. Tell students that in Section 3 they will learn about the role of the church in medieval society.

SECTION 3

READ TO DISCOVER

❶ How did the church hierarchy fit into society?

❷ How did the practices of monasticism change?

❸ How did the church influence life in medieval Europe?

DEFINE

sacraments
curia
cardinals
monasticism
abbot
abbess
canon law
interdict
heretics
tithe
simony

IDENTIFY

Saint Benedict
Hildegard of Bingen
Saint Patrick
Saint Augustine
Inquisition

▶ WHY IT MATTERS TODAY

Papal powers and influence today differ greatly from the powers of the medieval popes. Use **CNN** Student News.com or other **current event** sources to find examples of papal authority in today's world. Record your findings in your journal.

CNN Student News.com

The Church

The Main Idea
The Roman Catholic Church was a central part of daily life in Europe during the Middle Ages.

The Story Continues *Throughout the Middle Ages the church was one of the few sources of leadership and stability that people could rely upon. One historian has noted that "The continuity and the authority of the Church of Rome stood out in marked contrast against . . . the short-lived kingdoms which rose and fell in [the early Middle Ages]." As a result, the Catholic church became one of medieval Europe's most powerful and enduring institutions.*

The Church Hierarchy

The medieval church had broad political powers, probably because Europe's central governments were weak if they existed at all. The church filled the need for leadership by performing many of the functions that modern governments provide today. Throughout most of the Middle Ages, the church was one of the only institutions whose presence was felt throughout Europe. Its powers extended across kingdoms and through every social and political level. The church was also a great economic force during the Middle Ages. By the 1100s the medieval church was one of Europe's leading landowners, and many of its leaders were powerful feudal overlords.

The parish priest. Within the church, members of the clergy were organized according to a strict hierarchy of rank. Each rank within the clergy had different responsibilities and powers. The parish priest held the lowest rank in the church hierarchy. The parish itself was the smallest division in the church, and the priest directly served the people in his parish. He was responsible for their religious instruction and for the moral and spiritual life of the community as a whole. In some remote parishes, however, people might still have mixed pagan beliefs and superstitions with elements of Christianity.

Although he held the lowest rank in the church, the parish priest was one of its most important officers. He could administer five of the seven **sacraments.** The sacraments were ceremonies at which participants received God's direct favor, or grace, to help ward off the consequences of sin. By the 1100s the church recognized seven sacraments that are still practiced today. Parish priests could perform baptism, Holy Communion, penance, matrimony, and the anointing of the sick and dying. Bishops performed the sacraments of confirmation and the taking of holy orders.

The bishop. The bishop managed a group of parishes called a diocese. The cathedral, the bishop's official church, was usually located in the principal city of the diocese. *Cathedra* is the Latin word for the bishop's throne, or chair. The king or powerful nobles usually controlled the selection of bishops on

This jeweled silver cup was made in Germany in the 1200s for use during the sacrament of Holy Communion.

TEACH OBJECTIVE 1

ALL LEVELS: Have students create a chart that demonstrates the hierarchy of the medieval church.

ENGLISH LANGUAGE LEARNERS

HOMEWORK Ask each student to write a paragraph explaining the relationship between the church and the nobility. Have volunteers read their paragraph aloud. Encourage the class to respond to and discuss each response.

```
                    pope
              cardinals/curia:
              advisers to the pope
        archbishop: had some authority over
        bishops and other dioceses in the province
    bishop: managed a diocese, administered confirmation
    and holy orders, appointed parish priests, managed church property
  parish priest: conducted church services, supervised moral
  and religious instruction, administered five of the seven sacraments
```

the basis of family connections and political power. Many bishops were feudal lords or vassals in their own right and had vassals themselves.

Church leadership. A group of several dioceses, called an archdiocese, was managed by an archbishop. An archbishop had all the powers and responsibilities of a bishop and also had authority over the bishops of the archdiocese.

The pope held supreme authority in the church. The pope was advised by the **curia,** a group of counselors drawn from the highest ranks of the clergy. The curia's most important and powerful members were **cardinals,** the "princes of the church," who advised the pope on legal and spiritual matters. From the late 1100s on, only cardinals could elect the pope. With very few exceptions, a commoner could move up in the medieval world only by being a member of the church hierarchy. A man of great ability, regardless of birth, could rise to great heights within the church, although this did not happen often.

✔ **READING CHECK: Drawing Inferences** Why was the role of the parish priest among the most important within the hierarchy of the church? directly served the people of a parish; responsible for community's moral and spiritual life; administered five of the seven sacraments

Monasticism

The medieval church was made up of two types of clergy. Priests, bishops, and the pope were secular clergy. The word *secular* comes from the Latin word *saeculum,* which means "the present world." Secular clergy gave sacraments and preached the gospel among people in the everyday world. The second group of clergy was called regular clergy. The word *regular* comes from the Latin word *regula,* which means "rule." Male monks made up the regular clergy because they had to live in accordance with strict rules. Female nuns also lived in accordance with strict rules, but they were not considered clergy because only men could fulfill that role in the church.

Monastic lifestyles. Monks and nuns believed that they had to withdraw from the world and its temptations to live a Christian life. They chose to serve God through fasting, prayer, and self-denial. During the early centuries of Christianity, monks lived alone and practiced their devotion to God in many ways. They sometimes inflicted extreme physical suffering on themselves to prove their dedication. Eventually most monks and nuns gave up the hermit's lifestyle and formed religious communities. Monks lived in communities called monasteries, while nuns lived in convents. **Monasticism** refers to the way of life in convents and monasteries.

The Benedictine Rule. In some places efforts were made to organize the monastic communities before the 500s. Around that time a young Roman named Benedict became disgusted with the worldly corruption he witnessed. He left Rome to worship God as a hermit. Benedict's reputation for holiness spread and he attracted many followers. To accommodate his growing following, Benedict established a monastery at Monte Cassino, in the mountains of central Italy. Benedict—later **Saint Benedict**—created rules to govern monks' lives. Monasteries and convents all over Europe adopted these standards, called the Benedictine Rule.

CONNECTING TO
Art

Print Design: The Lindisfarne Gospels

As part of their monastic duties, monks copied important books, including the Bible, by hand. When they copied the Bible—considered God's sacred word—the monks sought to create particularly beautiful manuscripts. They illustrated, or *illuminated,* pages with gold leaf, colors, and detailed designs. This page from the Lindisfarne Gospels was produced in about 700 at the monastery of Lindisfarne, one of England's earliest centers of monastic learning.

Understanding the Arts

What does this print demonstrate about the monks' view of their work?

Culture

Among the most lasting and impressive architectural sites from the Middle Ages are monasteries and abbeys.

ACTIVITY: Have students use computer software to acquire images of monasteries. Have them work in groups to create a floor plan for a monastery, using information from the text and images they find.

CONNECTING TO ART ANSWER
The print demonstrates that the monks took great care to create beautiful work because they considered the Bible to be God's sacred word.

🔲 **internet** connect

TOPIC: Medieval Art
GO TO: go.hrw.com
KEYWORD: SP3 WH13

Have students access the Internet through the HRW Go site to conduct research on early medieval art and architecture. Have students find elements of medieval art and architecture that interests them and create an illustrated poster. Students may wish to use the interactive templates provided.

TEACH OBJECTIVE 2

LEVEL 3: Ask students why they think monastic life appealed to so many people during the Middle Ages. *(Monasteries and convents offered a feeling of stability.)* Have students use their textbooks to summarize the Benedictine Rule as a bulleted list in their notes.

The Benedictine Rule

- *A monk can own absolutely nothing.*
- *Everything a monk uses or wears belongs to the monastery.*
- *The abbot controls and distributes property.*

TEACH OBJECTIVE 3

LEVEL 1: Ask students to put themselves in the shoes of a medieval European. Whom might they fear more, church or king? Have students compare powers of church and king. Guide them to the idea that the powers of excommunication and interdict often seemed more mighty and frightening than the powers of the monarch. True, a king might imprison or even execute, but if the church excommunicated a person, he would not only be shunned in life but doomed for eternity.

ENGLISH LANGUAGE LEARNERS

Linking Past to Present

Among medieval nobility, marriages were usually arranged for political advantage; love was of little importance. Young people could not choose their partner. Instead, parents often betrothed their children at a young age. The bride's dowry, or inheritance, became the husband's property. It was not unusual in such arranged marriages for men to take concubines. Wives, however, were expected to remain true to their husbands, and could be put aside by their husbands if unable to bear children.

Critical Thinking

Ask students how the lot of medieval noblewomen compares to that of modern American women.

ANSWER: Some students might say that modern American women have many more freedoms, which include the right to own property, the freedom to marry, and the right to vote. Others might say that American women still suffer under the control of men.

HISTORY MAKER ANSWER

wrote religious music, founded a convent, criticized corrupt church practices

HISTORY MAKER

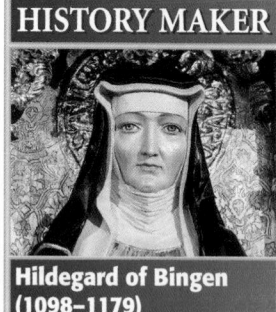

Hildegard of Bingen (1098–1179)

Nuns played an important role in the medieval church. The German nun **Hildegard of Bingen,** for example, wrote religious music and a medical text. She also founded the convent at Rubertsberg and served as its first abbess. Hildegard was a vocal critic of corrupt church practices. She was later named a saint of the church.

How did Hildegard of Bingen contribute to the church?

Holt Researcher

go.hrw.com
KEYWORD: Holt Researcher
FreeFind: Benedict
 Hildegard of Bingen
After reading more about Benedict and Hildegard of Bingen on the Holt Researcher, draw a sketch of a stained-glass window that reflects their influence on monastic life.

The Benedictine Rule was fairly strict. Everything a monk or nun used or wore belonged to their community. Even the monk's time and labor belonged to his monastery. An **abbot** was the elected head of the community and controlled and distributed all property. An **abbess** served a similar role for women in convents. Monks and nuns spent many hours of each day in prayer. The rest of their days were taken up with tasks that the abbot or abbess assigned them.

The spread of monastic influence. Monks and nuns often took care of the needy in medieval society. In time many monasteries became rich as pious nobles gave money or land to monasteries in return for spiritual favor. Convents also received some gifts, but they generally did not become as wealthy as many monasteries.

Some monks left their monasteries to become missionaries. For example, **Saint Patrick** is credited with bringing Christianity to Ireland in 432. Monastic schools in Ireland were the basis of an advanced culture that lasted from about 500 to about 800. **Saint Augustine** led a group of monks to England. Eventually all of England accepted Christianity. Augustine became the Archbishop of Canterbury, and Canterbury became the center of the Christian church in England.

✔ **READING CHECK: Identifying Cause and Effect** How did Saint Benedict change monasticism? created rules to organize and govern monks' lives

The Church and Medieval Life

The Christian clergy—secular and regular alike—played a major role in medieval institutions and everyday life. Throughout the Middle Ages the church enjoyed great political, economic, and social influence across most of Europe.

Political role. In the Papal States the pope was both political and religious leader. Many popes claimed that the church held political as well as spiritual power over all monarchs. Church leaders also held positions of power as feudal lords and as advisors to kings and nobles.

The church had its own code of law, called **canon law,** and its own courts. Members of the clergy could be tried in this court and the court would rule accordingly, perhaps excommunicating them. An excommunicated person was cut off from the church and could not receive the sacraments or be buried in sacred ground. Excommunication was greatly feared by Christians because it effectively removed an individual from society.

The court could also issue an **interdict** against an entire region. All churches in that region would be closed, and clergy would be forbidden to perform marriages, burials, or other sacraments. People in an interdicted area could be at risk of eternal punishment. In many cases the church used its power of interdiction to turn a region's people against rulers who opposed church powers and policies. The church did not allow anyone to question the basic principles of the Christian religion. People who denied the truth of the church's principles or who preached beliefs not approved by the church were considered **heretics.** They were viewed as unbelievers whose sinful beliefs attacked the church and who thus deserved eternal damnation. In a sense, heresy was a threat to the church in the way that treason is a threat to a government.

The medieval church also had the power to tax. The parish priest collected a **tithe,** or one-tenth of a Christian person's income. The church also received a large income from its own lands. By the early 1200s, when the church was at the height of its power, it was perhaps the wealthiest single institution in Europe.

Economic and social role. The spiritual teachings of the church did much to shape the European economy of the Middle Ages. For example, the church generally did not approve of people gaining wealth at the expense of others. Instead it taught that people who labored should be regarded with the dignity of free people. Monks participated in agriculture and some monasteries were involved in large-scale trade.

The church considered the family a sacred institution. It did not allow divorce and said special prayers for family members. The clergy was involved with social work and took care of the poor and needy. Some religious orders even established hospitals.

Problems of the church. The church's great wealth and influence led to many problems. One major problem concerned lay investiture—the practice of a noble, such as a king, appointing a friend or relative to be a bishop or abbot. Church leaders held that only a member of the clergy could grant spiritual authority to another member. During the Middle Ages, moreover, people could buy high positions within the church hierarchy. This practice was called **simony.** The purchaser might have expected to gain wealth through his position, either from church income or by charging high fees for performing religious services. As time went on the practice of simony came under growing criticism from inside and outside the church.

Many church leaders and lay rulers attempted to bring about church reform. Two religious groups dedicated themselves to this goal. Saint Francis of Assisi founded the order of Franciscans in 1209. Saint Dominic founded the order of the Dominicans in 1216. Members of these orders, called friars, lived and preached among the people.

In the mid-1200s the church attempted to reform itself with the help of the Dominicans. The church ordered the Dominicans to seek out heretics and to stamp out teachings that opposed church doctrines. This search for heretics is known as the **Inquisition.** Heretics who confessed to sinful teachings or practices were forced to perform penance, a ritual designed to bring forgiveness. Those who did not confess were turned over to the government for punishment or execution, which sometimes involved burning at the stake. The church believed that these severe actions were needed to stop the spread of heresy in the Christian world.

✔ **READING CHECK: Summarizing** How was the church involved in the political and economic life of the Middle Ages? enjoyed broad political power across Europe; teachings helped to shape economic activity

DAILY LIFE

The Parish Church
The parish church was an important part of a medieval town. Houses in towns and villages were sometimes little more than small wood huts. Some parish churches, however, were built of stone and were among the largest buildings in the town. **Why was a church often among the most important buildings in a medieval town or village?**

DAILY LIFE ANSWER
The church was typically the center of medieval life.

SECTION 3 REVIEW

1. **Define** and explain the significance:

sacraments	canon law
curia	interdict
cardinals	heretics
monasticism	tithe
abbot	simony
abbess	

2. **Identify** and explain the significance:

Saint Benedict	Saint Augustine
Hildegard of Bingen	Inquisition
Saint Patrick	

   Homework Practice Online
   keyword: SP3 HP13

3 **Categorizing** Construct a chart like the one below to show the organization of church hierarchy during the Middle Ages.

   Church Hierarchy

4. **Finding the Main Idea**

   a. Why was the role of the parish priest important to the church?

   b. Describe how monasticism developed during the Middle Ages.

   c. How did the church attempt to reform itself?

5. **Writing and Critical Thinking**

   Supporting Points of View Write a dialogue between two peasants who are debating whether or not to join a monastic order or convent.

   Consider:
   - the lifestyles of monks, nuns, and peasants
   - the advantages and disadvantages of monasticism
   - the purpose of monasticism

THE RISE OF THE MIDDLE AGES **303**

OBJECTIVES

1 **Explain how the kingdom of England was formed.**

2 **Identify the achievements of William the Conqueror and his successors.**

3 **Describe how Parliament and common law affected political developments in England.**

4 **Explore how the French kings gained power over their nobles.**

READ TO DISCOVER

❶ How was the kingdom of England formed?

❷ What were the achievements of William the Conqueror and his successors?

❸ How did the parliamentary system and common law affect political developments in England?

❹ How did the French kings gain power over their nobles?

DEFINE

shires
common law

IDENTIFY

Alfred the Great
Edward the Confessor
William the Conqueror
Henry II
Thomas Becket
Eleanor of Aquitaine
Magna Carta
Simon de Montfort

WHY IT MATTERS TODAY

Some challenges facing governments today are very similar to those that confronted the monarchies of the Middle Ages. Use CNNfyi.com or other **current event** sources to find examples of issues that representative governments, such as the U.S. Congress or the British Parliament, are currently discussing. Record your findings in your journal.

CNN Student News.com

The Struggle for Power in England and France

The Main Idea
Royal power gained supremacy over the power of the nobles in England and France during the Middle Ages.

The Story Continues *Kings, nobles, and church leaders sought to gain power over one another throughout the Middle Ages. King Philip II of France, for example, sought to control the election of bishops in the French church. "We warn the canons and monks," Philip ordered, "to elect someone who will be pleasing to God and useful to the realm." The struggle for power among these groups was a continuing theme in the development of medieval Europe.*

Anglo-Saxon and Norman England

In Europe before the 1000s, kings and lords often struggled for power. Some lords were as powerful as kings and served the kings when they wished. Some kings, however, tried to control the nobles. From this continual struggle for power the kingdoms of England and France emerged. Over time the power of the monarchs in these kingdoms became supreme.

Anglo-Saxon England. By about 450 Roman rule in Britain ended. Following the legions' withdrawal, Germanic tribes moved into the island, first as raiders, then as settlers. The culture that emerged from this Germanic settlement was named "Anglo-Saxon" after two of these tribes, the Angles and the Saxons. England, the "land of the Angles," refers to the eastern island of the British Isles, except for Scotland in the north and Wales in the west.

Over time the Anglo-Saxons formed several independent kingdoms in England. These kingdoms became known as Northumbria, in northern England and what is now southern Scotland; Mercia, in central England; and Wessex, in southern England. Eventually the Anglo-Saxons divided these kingdoms into governmental districts called **shires.** A shire was governed by a shire-reeve, which became the word *sheriff.*

Statue of Alfred the Great

Alfred the Great. By the early 800s the kings of Wessex controlled almost all of England. Viking raiders from the north, however (called "Danes" by the English), challenged the rule of Wessex and overran much of England. In 871 **Alfred the Great** came to the throne of Wessex determined to drive the Danes from the island. Alfred made a temporary peace after being defeated by the Danes. He spent the next five years building a powerful army and a fleet of fighting ships. In 876 Alfred attacked the Danes. By 886 the exhausted and weakened Danes had sued for peace.

TEACH OBJECTIVE 1

ALL LEVELS: Ask students to look at the series of maps on page 308, which represent the growth of France. In their textbooks, students should read about the shifting of power in England between the 400s and the 1100s. Then have students create a map progression for England. Students should create three to five rough maps appropriately colored and keyed to show major shifts in boundaries and power between the Anglo-Saxons, the Danes, and the Normans. Encourage students to consult additional sources in order to complete their maps as accurately as possible. **ENGLISH LANGUAGE LEARNERS**

The treaty that resulted allowed the Danes to live in parts of Mercia and Northumbria, where they were allowed to govern themselves.

Danish rule. During the 900s Alfred's successors were able to win more land back from the Danes. At the same time they unified the country, strengthened its government, and spread Christianity throughout the land. However, the Danes began to attack again at the end of the century. By 1013 the Danes once again controlled the entire country.

In 1016 King Canute of Denmark took the throne of England and most of Scandinavia in a combined kingdom. Canute was a wise ruler and spent much of his time in England. His sons, however, were weak rulers. By 1042 the Danish line had died out and the Anglo-Saxon nobles chose **Edward the Confessor** as their new king.

The Norman Conquest. Edward the Confessor was part Anglo-Saxon and part Norman. The powerful Duchy of Normandy was located in northwestern France. When Edward died without leaving an heir in 1066, a distant relative—Duke William of Normandy—claimed the English throne. The Anglo-Saxons refused to recognize his claim. Instead they selected Edward's brother-in-law, Harold of Wessex, to be king. William, determined to win the throne of England, crossed the English Channel with a powerful force of Norman knights. In a decisive battle William defeated Harold's Anglo-Saxon army at Hastings in October 1066. In December of that year, he was crowned King William I of England.

William, known today as **William the Conqueror,** soon overcame armed Anglo-Saxon resistance to his rule. In the years after the conquest, the Normans' laws, customs, and language were introduced in England. However, the Anglo-Saxons did not quickly accept them. Anglo-Saxon was a Germanic language. Norman French, in contrast, was based on Latin. As a result, the language of the Norman-English nobility continued to be French, while the language of most people in England continued to be Anglo-Saxon. Slowly, however, the lifestyles, laws, and customs of England grew to combine elements of both Anglo-Saxon and Norman cultures.

✔ **READING CHECK: Summarizing** Why is the year 1066 significant in English history?
It is the year of the Norman invasion of England.

The Conqueror and His Successors

William ruled England from 1066 to 1087. He brought feudalism from France to the newly conquered England. William shaped England's new feudal system, however, so that the king, not the nobles, held supreme authority. He required each feudal lord to swear personal loyalty directly to him. This meant that all English lords were vassals of the king. William also stopped the lords from uniting against him by scattering their fiefs throughout England. The new king's actions laid a strong foundation for centralized government and a strong monarchy in England.

The king also worked to determine the population, wealth, and ways that land was divided and used in his new kingdom. William sent royal commissioners to every English shire. Their task was to count each shire's people, assess landholdings, and measure type and value of property. The results of this great survey helped the king to set up an accurate, central tax system. The records that were gathered became known as the Domesday, or Doomsday, Book.

Holt Researcher
go.hrw.com
KEYWORD: Holt Researcher
FreeFind:
    William the Conqueror
After reading more about William the Conqueror on the Holt Researcher, evaluate his decision to take the throne by force, taking into account historical context. Then analyze how such a tactic would be viewed in the world today.

INTERPRETING THE VISUAL RECORD

Domesday Book This page from the Domesday Book is a record of property holdings in Bedfordshire and of boundary settlements among small tenants. *In what way was the Domesday Book evidence of the strength of William the Conqueror's monarchy?*

Economics

Besides the nobility and the peasants, another segment of feudal society began to emerge during the Middle Ages: the *burgher*, or free townsman. Burghers were merchants, craftsmen, and day laborers. In addition, runaway serfs frequently went to towns to find work. As trade between nations began to increase, the burghers started to gain some wealth and power. They built defenses for their towns and sometimes paid feudal lords for military protection.

Critical Thinking

Ask students to describe how burghers differed from peasants.

ANSWER: Students should recognize that they were not bound to the land as peasants were.

VISUAL RECORD ANSWER

It measured the monarchy's wealth and allowed the king to collect taxes centrally.

THE RISE OF THE MIDDLE AGES **305**

305

LEVEL 2: Have students read about the Norman Conquest and the policies of William the Conqueror and his successors. Then have them write letters to the editorial section of a fictional medieval newspaper evaluating the changes brought about by William and his successors. The letters should be written from the perspective of commoners who have lived under the rule of one or more of these Norman kings.

Economics

The laws put forward by Henry II to try clergy members in secular courts were called the Constitutions of Clarendon. Thomas Becket opposed the church's approval of these laws for two years before Henry ordered him arrested. Becket fled to France. With the pope's intervention, Becket returned to England. He excommunicated the bishops who had signed the Constitutions of Clarendon. Outraged, Henry was rumored to have said, "Will no one here rid me of this meddlesome priest?" Four knights consequently murdered the archbishop while he prayed at Canterbury. The Christian world was horrified. Rumors of miracles at Canterbury began to circulate. Becket was soon canonized. Henry ultimately rescinded part of the Constitutions.

Critical Thinking

What were the results of Henry II's attempt to eliminate Becket's popular influence and his opposition to Henry's wishes?

ANSWER: The murders helped martyr and immortalize Becket and caused part of the Constitutions of Clarendon to be rescinded.

HISTORY MAKER ANSWER

created a center of medieval culture, helped build a strong nation

HISTORY MAKER

Eleanor of Aquitaine (c. 1122–1204)

Eleanor of Aquitaine was wife to two kings: first to Louis VII of France, and later to Henry II of England. She was also one of the most powerful women in medieval Europe.

As queen, Eleanor played an active role in the leadership of both France and England. In France, she created a center of medieval culture at the court of Poitiers. And although Eleanor's marriage to Henry II of England was often troubled, she and the king built a strong partnership and a strong kingdom.

How did Eleanor of Aquitaine use her position as queen?

Analyzing Primary Sources

Analyzing Information What evidence does Roger of Wendover cite to show that England's nobles were prepared to support their demands with armed rebellion? arrived in "military array"; spoke in "bold tones" that threatened John

Reforms under William's successors. Henry I, one of William the Conqueror's sons, ruled from 1100 to 1135. Henry was an able ruler and administrator who set up a new department, the exchequer, to handle the kingdom's finances. This made the central government more efficient. He also made an important contribution to England's legal system. Henry sent traveling judges throughout the country to try cases. This action weakened the feudal lords because the king's royal court, not the lords' feudal courts, dispensed justice.

Henry II, who ruled from 1154 to 1189, also made decisions that increased royal authority. Instead of performing feudal military service for the king, his vassals—the nobles—could pay him a fee. He would use the money to hire mercenaries, or soldiers from different places. In this way Henry II would have an army made up of soldiers who were loyal to him because he was paying them. An army made up of nobles might not have been as loyal.

England's legal system grew under Henry II's direction. Traveling judges established routes, or circuits, and further strengthened royal law throughout England. During the late 1100s the 12-member jury developed in the court system. Juries decided civil as well as criminal cases. Trial by jury to determine guilt or innocence replaced the feudal trial by ordeal and combat.

Henry aimed to increase the authority of his royal courts at the expense of the church. Thus he sought to try certain members of the clergy who had already been judged in church courts. **Thomas Becket,** the Archbishop of Canterbury, refused to allow his clergy to be tried in royal courts. Becket and Henry, who had once been good friends, became bitter enemies over the issue. Four of the king's knights, believing that they were helping Henry, murdered the archbishop in his cathedral.

Even though Henry II denied any part in the murder, he did penance to appease the church. Henry had to abandon his attempts to reduce the power of the English church. Becket was named a saint, and his shrine in Canterbury became a popular destination for pilgrims.

The last years of Henry II's reign were troubled. His sons plotted against him and his marriage to **Eleanor of Aquitaine** was stormy. The French lands that Eleanor had brought to Henry when they married, moreover, involved England in new conflicts with the French. Nevertheless, the years of Henry's rule had strengthened the English monarchy at the feudal lords' expense. Later kings were able to build upon Henry's work.

King John and Magna Carta. One of Henry II's sons, King John, is known for his actions that led to a revolt among England's nobles. John demanded that the nobles pay more taxes to support his wars in France. In 1215 a powerful group of high nobles—barons of the kingdom—joined together against the king and his demands. Their threats of an armed uprising against the throne forced John to accept a document known as **Magna Carta** (Latin for "Great Charter"). One eyewitness described the confrontation between John and the nobles who opposed his harsh and high-handed rule:

 ❝[The] nobles came to [King John] in gay military array, and demanded the confirmation of the liberties and laws of King Edward, with other liberties granted to them and to the kingdom and Church of England . . . The King, hearing the bold tones of the barons in making this demand, much feared an attack from them . . .❞

Roger of Wendover, "An Account of Magna Carta," quoted in *Problems in Western Civilization: The Challenge of History,* Vol. I, L. F. Schaefer, D. H. Fowler, and J. E. Cooke, eds.

TEACH OBJECTIVES 3 and 4

LEVEL 3: Organize students into four groups. Assign two groups to study English politics and the other two to study French politics between 1000 and 1350. Each group will prepare a multimedia presentation outlining the evolution of royal power in their assigned kingdom. Presentations on England should include information about rulers and their policies, Magna Carta and its impact on English society, Parliament, and common law. Presentations on France should include information about rulers and their policies, the growth of royal territory, the central government, and taxation policies. Encourage students to include maps, charts, illustrations, excerpts from documents, and any other interesting items they find. **COOPERATIVE LEARNING**

TEACH OBJECTIVES 3 and 4

LEVEL 1: Ask students to list the goals of William the Conqueror and successors and the Capetian kings. Ask them to support their point of view on how well these rulers accomplished their goals. **ENGLISH LANGUAGE LEARNERS**

Magna Carta protected the liberties of the nobles. It also provided a limited outline of rights for England's ordinary people. King John agreed not to collect any new or special taxes without the consent of the Great Council, a body of important nobles and church leaders who advised the king. John also promised not to take property without paying for it. He promised not to sell, refuse, or delay justice. The king also agreed to let any accused person be judged by a jury of his or her peers. John's acceptance of Magna Carta meant that the king—like his subjects—had to obey the law or face revolt and overthrow. Magna Carta made the law the supreme power in England.

✔ **READING CHECK: Summarizing** What contributions did William the Conqueror and his successors make to England? built strong, efficient, well-financed government and monarchy; improved legal system

Parliament and Common Law

Two other major developments took place in England in the years following Magna Carta. The first was the growth of Parliament and the beginnings of representative government. The second was the growth of **common law**—law based upon customs and judges' decisions, rather than upon written codes.

Parliament. A widespread revolt of nobles against King Henry III in the 1260s rocked England and again threatened the monarchy. **Simon de Montfort,** a powerful lord who led the revolt, aimed to build middle-class support for the nobles' cause. In this way, de Montfort reasoned, both the middle class and the nobility could combine forces against the king. In 1265 de Montfort asked representatives of the middle class to meet with the nobles and clergy who made up the Great Council. The middle-class representatives included four knights from each shire and two burgesses—leading citizens—from each of several major towns.

The practice of having members of the middle class meet with the clergy and the nobles in the Great Council remained. This representative body eventually became the English Parliament. Over time Parliament was divided into two parts, called "houses." Nobles and the clergy made up the House of Lords, and knights and burgesses made up the House of Commons.

The early Parliament mainly served to advise the king, but it also had the right to refuse new taxes sought by the king. As England's centralized government grew, taxes were needed to help meet its ever-increasing costs. Parliament's power to accept or reject new taxes became more and more important.

Common law. Edward I ruled England from 1272 to 1307. Edward, one of England's greatest monarchs, divided the king's court into three branches. The Court of the Exchequer kept track of the kingdom's financial accounts and tried tax cases. The Court of Common Pleas heard cases between ordinary citizens. The Court of the King's Bench conducted trials that concerned the king or the government.

The decisions made by the new royal courts were collected and used as the basis for future court verdicts. This collection of decisions became known as common law because it was applied equally and in common to all English people. Common law differed greatly from law that was based on statutes, such as Roman law. It was a "living law" in the sense that it changed to meet changing conditions.

✔ **READING CHECK: Comparing** How are the parliamentary system and common law similar to the government and laws practiced in the United States? used as basis for future court verdicts; applied equally and in common to all

CONNECTING TO
Civics

Magna Carta

Magna Carta became a cornerstone of constitutional government and rule by law. Its original purpose was to limit the king's powers and protect the nobles' feudal rights. It included such concepts as church freedom, trial by jury, freedom from taxation without cause and consent, and due process of law. The document's final article empowered a group of barons to take up arms against the king if he violated its conditions.

Over time the freedoms guaranteed by Magna Carta spread to all citizens. Today the Charter forms part of the British Constitution, and its ideas can be found in our own United States Constitution.

Understanding Civics

What are some of the liberties ensured by Magna Carta that are also guaranteed in our United States Constitution?

Interdisciplinary Connection

LITERATURE. The murder of Thomas Becket heavily influenced literature. Throughout the Middle Ages pilgrims flocked to Becket's tomb at Canterbury. They inspired Geoffrey Chaucer to write his masterpiece, *The Canterbury Tales*. Becket's murder also inspired the English writer T.S. Eliot to dramatize Becket's last hours in his 1935 play *Murder in the Cathedral*. Similarly the playwright Jean Anouilh [ah-nwee-yuh] immortalized the archbishop's career in his 1959 play *Becket; or, The Honour of God*.

Critical Thinking

Ask students what elements of Becket's life or death might have inspired so many literary interpretations.

ANSWER: Students might answer that Becket's willingness to choose principles over politics is a virtue many cultures find important.

UNDERSTANDING CIVICS ANSWER
freedom of religion, right to a jury trial, due process, right to bear arms

THE RISE OF THE MIDDLE AGES **307**

HOMEWORK Magna Carta became the basis for England's constitution and influenced the U.S. Constitution. Ask students to make a two-column chart. In the first column, display the following excerpts from Magna Carta. Have students use the chart to compare these statements to elements of the Bill of Rights and then write a paragraph describing or evaluating the comparisons.

Magna Carta	U.S. Bill of Rights
"Scutage [a tax]…shall be levied in our kingdom only by the common counsel of our kingdom…."	
"No freeman shall be… imprisoned…except by lawful judgment of his peers or by the law of the land."	
"To no one will we sell, to no one will we deny or delay right of justice."	

CLOSE

Ask students how the rise of the Capetian kings in France illustrates the feudal struggle for power. How did the Capetians add to their power?

Constitutional Heritage

In June of 1215, King John rode to meet his angry nobles at Runnymede, a wide meadow on the banks of the Thames River. No one present on that day could have guessed that the nobles' demands, written in the form of the document we now call Magna Carta, would later become the cornerstone of constitutional government and representative democracy.

ACTIVITY: Organize the class into groups of four students and pass out copies of Magna Carta and the U.S. Constitution. Ask students to compare and contrast the two documents. Have each group list elements of the U.S. Constitution that were clearly influenced by Magna Carta.

MAP ANSWERS
1. Paris

2. Kings married women who owned lands or took control of lands of noble families that died out

Rise of the Capetian Kings in France

The last Carolingian king died in 987. In the same year a group of nobles chose Hugh Capet to be King of France. Capet and his descendants, a line known as the Capetians, ruled for more than 300 years.

Hugh Capet ruled only a small area called the Île-de-France (eel·duh·FRAHNS). Feudal lords ruled the rest of France, holding areas known as duchies. The Capetians aimed to develop a strong central government and to unite the duchies of France under the rule of the monarchy.

The growth of royal territory. The Capetians sought to increase the lands under their control in several ways. For example, some Capetian kings married noblewomen whose dowries included great fiefs. They also took control of the lands of noble families that had died out. The Capetians looked, as well, to conquer French lands held by the English kings since the days of William the Conqueror. Philip II, known as Philip Augustus, particularly favored this policy of taking English holdings in France. King Philip, who ruled from 1180 to 1223, greatly increased royal landholdings by taking large provinces, such as Normandy and Maine, from the English.

Strengthening the central government. The Capetian kings appointed well-trained officials to run the government. They also extended the jurisdiction of the royal courts. The Parliament of Paris, the highest of the royal courts, eventually became a kind of supreme court, hearing appeals from all parts of the kingdom.

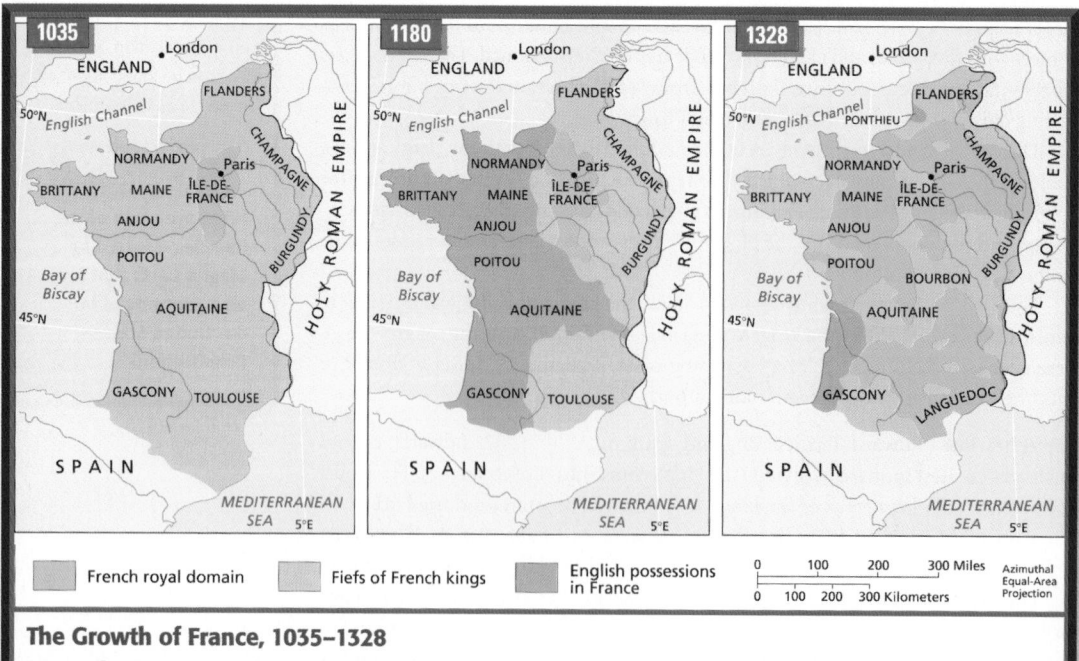

The Growth of France, 1035–1328

Interpreting Maps In 1035 the French royal domain—land that was personally owned by the French monarch—was limited to the Île-de-France. Within 300 years, the royal domain had grown many times over, and the king controlled most of France.

■ **Skills Assessment: 1. Locate** Identify the principal city of the Île-de-France. **2. Making Generalizations** How did the king control those parts of France that were not part of the royal domain?

REVIEW

Have students complete Section 4 Review on p. 309.

ASSESS

Have students complete Daily Quiz 13.4. As Alternative Assessment, use map or presentation exercises in this section's lessons.

RETEACH

Have students complete Main Idea Activity for English Language Learners and Special-Needs Students 13.4. Have partners outline the section and compile a chapter glossary, using outline and glossary to create flashcards to quiz each other on correct social studies terminology. **ENGLISH LANGUAGE LEARNERS**

EXTEND

Have each student choose and read a tale from Chaucer's *The Canterbury Tales* and prepare a shortened, modernized version for dramatic reading, using standard grammar, spelling, sentence structure, and punctuation. Encourage audience questions. **BLOCK SCHEDULING**

The Capetians' struggle for power continued under Philip IV (Philip the Fair), who ruled France from 1285 to 1314. Philip was able to increase royal power over the French church by taxing the clergy. When Pope Boniface VII opposed Philip, the king had him arrested. Following Boniface's death in 1303, Philip influenced the election of the next pope, Clement V. The shrewd king also moved to build his popularity among the French people. Philip convened the Estates General, a representative body made up of the three major social classes in France. The Estates General included commoners as well as nobles and members of the clergy. By involving the Estates General in his government, Philip secured widespread support in his struggle against the church.

Royal power in France was greatly strengthened under Philip IV and the earlier Capetian rulers. Despite the centralizing reforms they achieved, however, France remained largely feudal in its political organization. The Capetian kings had a vision of France as a united country, but the idea of unification under the monarchy had little appeal at the local level. Thus the Capetians failed to achieve their great aim. By the 1300s, moreover, the dynasty itself had reached an end, for although Philip IV had three sons, none produced an heir to the throne. In 1328 the last of the Capetian rulers, Charles IV, died. A new line of French kings— the Valois—came into power.

Philip IV was one of France's mightiest rulers during the Middle Ages. In this 15th-century illustration, Philip is shown giving an audience to a French noble.

✔ **READING CHECK: Comparing** How was the Estates General of France similar to England's Parliament? Both were representative bodies composed of the society's major classes.

SECTION 4 REVIEW

1. **Define** and explain the significance:
   shires
   common law

2. **Identify** and explain the significance:
   Alfred the Great
   Edward the Confessor
   William the Conqueror
   Henry II
   Thomas Becket
   Eleanor of Aquitaine
   Magna Carta
   Simon de Montfort

3. **Sequencing** Create a time line like the one below. Complete it to show the major events in the early development of representative government in medieval England.

   1215 — late 1200s
   1265

4. **Finding the Main Idea**
   a. How did William the Conqueror's actions in 1066 change England?
   b. In what ways did Magna Carta support the rise of representative government in England?
   c. What role did Simon de Montfort play in the development of Parliament?
   d. Why did the kings of France seek to weaken church power in their lands?

5. **Writing and Critical Thinking**
   Supporting a Point of View Write a paragraph that supports the following statement: "Americans today are governed by a constitution that traces its origins back to events in England in the 1200s."
   Consider:
   • the struggle for power between England's kings and nobles during the Middle Ages
   • the rights and freedoms that are guaranteed by our Constitution and Bill of Rights

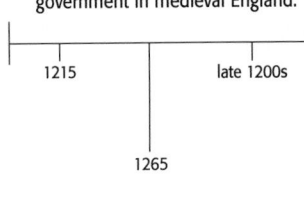

Homework Practice Online
keyword: SP3 HP13

SECTION 4 REVIEW ANSWERS

❶ **Define**
• shires, p. 304
• common law, p. 307

❷ **Identify**
• Alfred the Great, p. 304
• Edward the Confessor, p. 305
• William the Conqueror, p. 305
• Henry II, p. 306
• Thomas Becket, p. 306
• Eleanor of Aquitaine, p. 306
• Magna Carta, p. 306
• Simon de Montfort, p. 307

❸ Possible answers—1265: Simon de Montfort asks representatives of middle class to meet with nobles and clergy; 1272–1307: reign of Edward I, who divided kings' court into three branches

❹ a. led to a combination of Anglo-Saxon and Norman culture in England

b. forced the king to seek the advice of the Great Council

c. led the revolt of nobles, sought support of middle class

d. to increase royal power

❺ Students' paragraphs should support the statement with evidence from the chapter.

OBJECTIVES

1 **Describe how the Holy Roman emperors used their power.**

2 **Explain how the struggle between the popes and emperors developed.**

SECTION 5

READ TO DISCOVER

❶ How did the Holy Roman emperors use their power?

❷ How did the struggle between the popes and emperors develop?

IDENTIFY

Otto I
Henry III
Henry IV
Pope Gregory VII
Frederick Barbarossa
Innocent III

▶ WHY IT MATTERS TODAY

The Italian cities of Milan, Bologna, and Padua were great commercial centers during the Middle Ages. Use **CNN** or other **current event** sources to investigate the role of these cities in Italian and world commerce today. Record your findings in your journal.

The Clash over Germany and Italy

The Main Idea
Political conflict between the medieval popes and the German emperors weakened both sides.

The Story Continues *The struggle between church and state was particularly bitter in the Holy Roman Empire. Both the emperor and the pope held that their authority came from God. Pope Innocent III, who led the medieval church to its greatest power, claimed divine supremacy over all worldly rulers. According to Innocent, ". . . our power is not from man but from God." Ultimately the conflict between church and state weakened both.*

The Holy Roman Empire

While Charlemagne was still alive, Italy was part of his empire. However, his death in 814 caused Italy to fall into a state of disorder. Several of Charlemagne's descendants inherited the title of Holy Roman Emperor. However, they did not really rule Italy. In the years around 900, the Byzantine Empire held parts of Italy. The pope ruled the Papal States, while Arab Muslims ruled Sicily and frequently attacked the Italian mainland.

In Germany the great feudal lords elected **Otto I** their king in 936. Otto, a powerful and forceful ruler, became known as Otto the Great. Otto worked to develop a strong kingdom in Germany like that of the Capetians in France. However, the German king was also interested in Italy. In 951 Otto moved to seize territory in northern Italy. When Pope John XII struggled with Roman nobles, he begged Otto for help. The pope rewarded Otto's support by crowning him Emperor of the Romans in 962.

Otto's title was the same as that granted to Charlemagne 162 years earlier. Otto ruled Germany and northern Italy, however—a much smaller area than Charlemagne had held. Nevertheless, the empire stood as a major power in Europe for hundreds of years after Otto's crowning. It endured—in name, at least—until the early 1800s. Over time, however, the Holy Roman Empire was weakened by internal divisions, the rise of other European powers, and the ambitions of local nobles who sought to break from imperial control. Imperial power gradually declined until the emperor became little more than a figurehead. But the once mighty empire did leave an enduring legacy: a close and lasting tie between Germany and Italy.

INTERPRETING THE VISUAL RECORD

The coronation of Otto I Pope John XII placed this crown on the head of Otto I in 962, naming Otto "Emperor of the Romans." *In what way does the emperor's crown symbolize the relationship between church and state in the Holy Roman Empire of the Middle Ages?*

ALL LEVELS: Assign *An Exchange Between Pope Gregory VII and Emperor Henry IV* from **Readings in World History.** Use the Reading Review questions to launch an opening discussion about the relationship of the popes to the Holy Roman emperors. Point out the ongoing animosity between the two powerful men. Ask students what they think this escalating power struggle indicated. (*need for separation of church and state, that each leader wanted to establish the supremacy of their type of power*) **ENGLISH LANGUAGE LEARNERS**

LEVEL 1: Have students use graphic organizers to illustrate how the Concordat of Worms would divide power between popes and emperors. Discuss the division that existed between popes and emperors.

The reign of Emperor **Henry III** between 1046 and 1056 represented the height of imperial power. Henry, like Charlemagne, viewed the church as a branch of the imperial government. He expected the church to actively support the empire and its ruler. During Henry's reign, three different men claimed the papacy. Henry removed these men from office and elected a German as pope. He also chose the next three popes.

✔ **READING CHECK: Comparing** In what major way was Henry III's view of the church similar to the view of Charlemagne? Henry, like Charlemagne, viewed the church as a branch of the imperial government.

Struggles between the Papacy and European Rulers

Henry III's death in 1056 brought his five-year-old son, **Henry IV,** to the imperial throne. Powerful German nobles saw Henry's youth as an opportunity to regain their independence and feudal powers. The church, too, moved to restore the power it had lost during Henry III's reign. At the age of about 15, Henry moved to strengthen his imperial rule. Eventually Henry's actions brought him into conflict with one of the great leaders of the medieval church, **Pope Gregory VII.** The struggle between Henry and Gregory reflected the clash between church and state that was a continuing issue in the Middle Ages.

Gregory and Henry IV. Pope Gregory was both devout and able. He worked to bring spiritual reform to the church by increasing the power and authority of the papacy. Gregory believed that the church was the supreme spiritual and temporal power on the earth. He felt that rulers and ordinary people alike were subject to the will of the church and its pope. Gregory did not hesitate to use the terrible punishment of excommunication as a way to resolve conflicts of church and state.

The conflict between Henry IV and Gregory VII concerned the old issue of lay investiture—the appointment of bishops by temporal rulers. Henry believed that he had the right to appoint bishops of the German church. Gregory angrily opposed lay investiture and responded to the emperor's attempt to name bishops by excommunicating Henry. In addition, Gregory released the emperor's subjects from their vows of loyalty to their ruler and urged the nobles to elect another emperor.

Imperial submission. Fearing rebellion, Henry sought the pope's mercy. During the harsh winter of 1077, Henry traveled to meet the pope. They met at Canossa, in the mountains of northern Italy. Henry and his attendants had to make their way through treacherous, ice-covered peaks. When he finally reached Canossa, the humiliated Henry waited in the bitter cold for three days to be admitted to the pope's presence. When they finally met, Henry pleaded for the pope's mercy. As a result, the pope revoked Henry's excommunication.

The struggle over lay investiture continued, however. Finally, in 1122, representatives of both sides met in the German city of Worms to settle the conflict. The agreement they reached, known as the Concordat of Worms, limited imperial power over the German church. The emperor could appoint bishops to fiefs. Only the pope, however, had the power to name bishops, whose spiritual authority came directly from the church.

INTERPRETING THE VISUAL RECORD

Meeting at Canossa In 1077 Pope Gregory VII (left) and Emperor Henry IV (center) settled some of their differences at Canossa. Countess Matilda of Tuscany (right) helped arrange the meeting. *What visual clues does the artist provide to indicate the dominant figure in this painting?*

Interdisciplinary Connection

ART. The illustration of Charlemagne's coronation on page 290 comes from the *Grandes Chroniques de France*, a French chronicle from the 1300s. The artist shows Pope Leo III wielding supreme power over Charlemagne by bestowing on him a measure of civil power. Earlier the coronation was portrayed differently. The earliest representation, a mosaic from the 800s, shows Saint Peter bestowing equal power upon Leo and Charlemagne, with Leo in charge of spiritual and Charlemagne in charge of civil matters.

Critical Thinking

Ask students to compare effects of the representations. What may have happened between the 800s and 1300s that would cause this shift in representation?

ANSWER: Students may suggest that the shift was caused by the struggle between monarchs and the church.

VISUAL RECORD ANSWER

Henry IV is shown kneeling, while the pope, shown very large, is above him.

Reproducible **Resources**

PS Readings in World History 40: An Exchange Between Pope Gregory VII and Emperor Henry IV

THE RISE OF THE MIDDLE AGES **311**

TEACH OBJECTIVES 1 and 2

LEVEL 3: Have pairs of students prepare a staged interview of Pope Innocent III, taking on the roles of the pope and an interviewer. Together students should generate at least five intelligent questions and research the answers. Questions might deal with Innocent's background, policies concerning both the church and secular politics, and his more notable actions as pope. Questions and answers should give the audience a well-rounded picture of Innocent III and highlight his importance in the history of the church. Have students take turns staging their interview for the class. **COOPERATIVE LEARNING**

HOMEWORK Have students select one of the following topics to study in more detail: Otto I, Pope John XII, Henry III, the Concordat of Worms, Frederick Barbarossa, or the Lombard League. Then have students write two or three paragraphs about their topics, using correct social studies terminology. Call on volunteers to share their findings with the class.

CLOSE

Lead a class discussion about the conflict between Pope Gregory VII and Henry IV. Ask students to summarize how the conflict developed and how it was resolved.

Culture

During the Inquisition, inquisitors initially allowed the accused a month's grace period to renounce their heresy. If they did, they received a light penance. After the grace period, the inquisitors put all other accused heretics on trial. The inquisitors commonly tortured the accused to elicit information. Most of the accused were found guilty. While some were burned at the stake, the most common punishments were fines, penance, imprisonment, and confiscation of property.

Critical Thinking

Ask students what might be the consequences of enforcing religious doctrine in this way.

ANSWER: Students might answer that the Inquisition could have unified medieval society by forcing people into similar behavior or beliefs. However, it stifled free thought.

THEN AND NOW ANSWER

John Paul II uses the power of persuasion to influence political affairs, while Innocent III was more directly involved.

The Pope

The popes of the Middle Ages had great political power. In 1075 Pope Gregory VII said that the pope had power over all Christians and could get rid of church and political leaders. Pope Innocent III was involved in many of Europe's political affairs. He even overthrew two of Germany's kings.

Over time the papacy turned its attention to making the pope the spiritual leader of all Roman Catholics. Today the pope works to create and uphold the laws, traditions, and spiritual beliefs of the church. Officially the pope has less political power, although recent popes like John Paul II have tried to influence nations and their leaders through the power of persuasion. **How did Pope Innocent III's involvement in world political affairs differ from the approach of John Paul II?**

Holt Researcher
go.hrw.com
KEYWORD: Holt Researcher
FreeFind: Innocent III
John Paul II
After reading more about Innocent III and John Paul II on the Holt Researcher, analyze how they each influenced the eras in which they lived.

The Concordat of Worms recognized the spiritual leadership of the popes. Conflict between popes and emperors did not end in 1122, however. The German emperors continued to interfere in Italian politics and to threaten the popes' rule in the Papal States. The popes, in turn, opposed all attempts by the emperors to gain control in Italy.

Frederick Barbarossa. Frederick I, also known as **Frederick Barbarossa** (Frederick of the Red Beard), ruled Germany from 1152 to 1190. Frederick, like other emperors before him, sought to gain control of Italy.

In the northern Italian region known as Lombardy, the great trading centers of Bologna, Padua, Verona, and Milan had grown increasingly independent of imperial control. Each of these city-states had a wealthy merchant class. Frederick, seeking to strengthen his rule by gaining wealth, set out to capture the Lombard cities. Frederick sent imperial representatives to take control of the cities' governments. When Milan resisted, Frederick captured and destroyed the city and drove out the people.

The other city-states refused Frederick's demands. With the help of the pope, they united to form the Lombard League. They raised a powerful army that defeated Frederick in 1176. In the peace settlement that followed, the cities of the League recognized Frederick as overlord. In return, Frederick let the cities govern themselves. The Lombard League's success showed the growing political power of cities in medieval Europe.

Innocent III. Between 1198 and 1216, the strongest of the medieval popes—**Innocent III**—greatly strengthened the church and increased its worldly power. Innocent was a skillful political leader who, like Gregory VII before him, believed in the supreme earthly power of the papacy. To Innocent, emperors and kings were no more than servants of the church. Because of this belief Innocent felt that he had the authority to settle all political, as well as spiritual, problems. Temporal rulers and nobles could advise the pope, but they could not control him.

 ❝Just as the founder of the universe [God] established two great lights in the firmament of heaven, a greater one to preside over the day and a lesser to preside over the night, so too . . . he instituted two great dignities [pope and monarch], a greater one [the pope] to preside over souls . . . and a lesser one [the monarch] to preside over bodies . . . These are the pontifical authority and the royal power.❞

Innocent III, quoted in *The Crisis of Church & State: 1050–1300*, by Brian Tierney

Fresco portrait of Pope Innocent III

REVIEW

Have students complete Section 5 Review on p. 313.

ASSESS

Have students complete Daily Quiz 13.5. As Alternative Assessment, you may want to use the graphic organizer or interview exercises in this section's lessons.

RETEACH

Have students complete Main Idea Activity for English Language Learners and Special-Needs Students 13.5. Then direct each student to write a question about the material under each heading or subheading. **ENGLISH LANGUAGE LEARNERS**

EXTEND

Have interested students conduct further research, using primary and secondary sources including biographies, on the power struggle between Henry IV and Gregory VII. Ask them to prepare and present to the class an oral report that details their findings. **BLOCK SCHEDULING**

Innocent III involved himself in disputes all over Europe. He freely used his powers of excommunication and interdiction to settle conflicts. When he quarreled with King John of England, Innocent placed the entire realm under interdict. To have the interdict lifted, John was forced to become the pope's vassal and to pay an annual tithe to Rome. Innocent also used the interdict against the king of France, Philip Augustus, after Philip tried to have his marriage annulled. Innocent forced Philip to take his wife back and to restore her to her place as queen of France. Innocent also dominated nearly all of Italy. In Germany he overthrew two kings and put rulers of his choice on the throne.

Innocent was able to greatly increase papal authority and prestige in medieval Europe. Conditions in Europe, as well as Innocent's personal skill, helped him to build church power. Later popes, however, lacked both Innocent's abilities and the favorable conditions that had helped him to become supreme. As a result, papal power slowly declined after Innocent's death in 1216.

The great goal of uniting Germany and Italy was never achieved. During the early 1200s Emperor Frederick II tried to bring the two regions together under imperial rule. Like earlier emperors, however, Frederick failed.

Not only did imperial attempts to unify Italy and Germany fail, but each country also remained divided into small, independent cities and feudal states. The emperor had little real control over the fragmented kingdom. Italy remained divided into three regions. Northern Italy was controlled by the Lombard cities. The Papal States held power in Italy's center, and the kingdom of Sicily controlled the south. Neither Italy nor Germany were unified until the 1800s.

✔ **READING CHECK: Comparing** How were the aims of Gregory VII and Innocent III similar? Both sought to make church power superior to temporal authority.

A bitter quarrel between Pope Innocent III and King John of England, shown hunting in this image, caused England to be placed under the Church's dreaded interdict.

SECTION 5 REVIEW ANSWERS

❶ Identify
- Otto I, p. 310
- Henry III, p. 311
- Henry IV, p. 311
- Pope Gregory VII, p. 311
- Frederick Barbarossa, p. 312
- Pope Innocent III, p. 312

❷ Frederick seized control of the city-states' governments; Frederick destroyed Milan; the city-states formed the Lombard League and defeated Frederick.

❸ a. It represented a conflict over power and authority of spiritual and temporal rulers.

b. Students may suggest that each wanted supreme power.

❹ Students' letters should use information from the chapter to support their arguments.

SECTION 5 REVIEW

1. **Identify** and explain the significance:
   Otto I
   Henry III
   Henry IV
   Pope Gregory VII
   Frederick Barbarossa
   Pope Innocent III

2. **Summarizing** Copy the graphic organizer shown below. Use it to summarize the actions and events that led to Frederick Barbarossa's defeat by the Lombard League.

3. **Finding the Main Idea**
   a. Why was the issue of lay investiture considered so important by both German emperors and popes?
   b. Why do you think emperors and popes were unable to cooperate or to build alliances that would have strengthened both?

4. **Writing and Critical Thinking**
   Supporting a Point of View Imagine yourself as a literate citizen of the Holy Roman Empire during the late 1100s. Write a letter to Frederick Barbarossa with the aim of convincing him that the powers of church and state should be separate.
   Consider:
   • the extensive powers of the Holy Roman emperors
   • how Otto's empire might have benefited from a separation of church and state
   • why both the pope and the emperor might have gained by resolving their conflict for power

Homework Practice Online
keyword: SP3 HP13

THE RISE OF THE MIDDLE AGES **313**

313

REVIEW AND ASSESSMENT RESOURCES

REPRODUCIBLE RESOURCES
▸ Vocabulary Activity 13

TECHNOLOGY RESOURCES
▸ Chapter 13 Test Generator (on the One-Stop Planner)
▸ Global Skill Builder CD–ROM
▸ HRW Go Site

REINFORCEMENT, REVIEW, and ASSESSMENT
▸ Chapter 13 Review, pp. 314–315
▸ Chapter 13 Tutorial for Students, Parents, Mentors, and Peers
▸ Chapter 13 Test (Form A or B)
▸ Alternative Assessment Handbook
▸ Chapter 13 Test for English Language Learners and Special-Needs Students

REVIEW
Have students complete Chapter 13 Review on pages 314–315.

ASSESS
Use one of the chapter tests to assess students' understanding of the content. For Alternative Assessment, see the Portfolio Activities and Alternative Assessment Handbook.

CHAPTER 13 REVIEW ANSWERS

Understanding Main Ideas

1. shows the king's closeness to the church and might lead to the belief that God favors the king

2. established constitutional government, rule by law; limited power of monarchies

3. Land was inherited by the eldest son of a lord or vassal.

4. The manners of feudal lords were improved, but knights were courteous only to their own class.

5. It was organized into a hierarchy with the most powerful leader at the top.

6. He organized a monastic movement and created rules to govern monks' lives.

7. lay investiture, simony

8. 1066: Norman conquest; 1215: Magna Carta

9. through the verdicts of judges in the royal courts

10. English kings were made subject to the law.

11. He was more interested both in seizing control of Italy and building a strong kingdom in Germany.

12. Henry II tried to transfer trials of the clergy from church to royal courts. Becket refused to allow this. Henry IV insisted on the right to lay investiture, but Gregory VII disagreed.

CHAPTER 13 Review

Creating a Time Line
Copy the time line below onto a sheet of paper. Complete the time line by filling in the events, individuals, and dates from the chapter you think were significant. Pick three events and explain why you think they were significant.

| 455 | 768 | 1066 | 1215 |

Writing a Summary
Using standard grammar, spelling, sentence structure, and punctuation, write an overview of the events in the chapter.

Identifying People and Ideas
Identify the following terms or individuals and explain their significance:

1. Middle Ages
2. Charlemagne
3. feudalism
4. primogeniture
5. manorialism
6. Saint Benedict
7. Inquisition
8. Thomas Becket
9. Magna Carta
10. Eleanor of Aquitaine

Understanding Main Ideas

SECTION 1 (pp. 288–293)
The Rise of the Franks
1. Why would the pope's blessing strengthen a king's rule?
2. How did Magna Carta and the type of government that it fostered affect events in Europe?

SECTION 2 (pp. 294–299)
Feudalism and the Manorial System
3. How did the practice of primogeniture exclude women or peasants from controlling land?
4. How were feudal lords and peasants affected by the principles of chivalry?

SECTION 3 (pp. 300–303)
The Church
5. How was the church's organization similar to that of a centralized government?
6. What overall effect did Benedict have on the development of monasticism?
7. What were some of the problems the church faced in the Middle Ages?

SECTION 4 (pp. 304–309)
The Struggle for Power in England and France
8. Why are the years 1066 and 1215 significant to English history?
9. Describe how common law developed in England.
10. How did royal power in France and England differ?

SECTION 5 (pp. 310–313)
The Clash over Germany and Italy
11. Why was Otto's rule different than the Capetians' in France?
12. Contrast the conflicts between Henry II and Thomas Becket and Henry IV and Pope Gregory VII.

Reviewing Themes
1. **Government** How could religious leaders and kings have avoided many wars in the Middle Ages?
2. **Constitutional Heritage** How did Magna Carta and the type of government it fostered affect events in Europe?
3. **Economics** When would working the land for the lord of a manor not have provided a living for a peasant?

Thinking Critically
1. **Drawing Inferences** Why was it so important for kings, emperors, the church, and nobles to possess land?
2. **Analyzing Information** Why did the Concordat of Worms not end the struggles between popes and emperors?
3. **Identifying Cause and Effect** How did church officials, such as bishops, become involved in feudalism?

Writing About History
Comparing Write a report comparing the life of a present-day teenager to that of a squire or a young noblewoman in service to a higher-ranking noblewoman. Use the chart below to help you organize your thoughts.

	Squire or young noblewoman	Present-day teenager
Food		
Clothes		
Education		
Duties		
Chances for movement in society		

CLOSE

Ask students how the church became part of the feudal system in Europe. Then have them explain in what ways the church was independent of the feudal system.

RETEACH

Pair students who had difficulty with the test. Have pairs compile a chapter list of important places, people, and concepts.

Have students take the Form B Test to assess their mastery of the material.

ENGLISH LANGUAGE LEARNERS, COOPERATIVE LEARNING

Portfolio Extensions

1. Have students conduct research on agricultural economies in Europe today. Have them find out about major crops and modern technology. Have them compare current methods and products with those in medieval Europe. Then ask them to create graphs, charts, maps, or other visuals to illustrate their findings.

2. Have students use computer software to find information about Alfred the Great and present the information in the form of a time line.

3. Have students further research medieval manors and construct a scale model of a typical manor, labeling all structures and areas on their model.

Building Social Studies Skills

Interpreting Maps

Study the map below. Then use the information on the map to answer the questions that follow.

The Vikings in Britain, 700s–1100s

1. Based on the map, which of the following statements best describes how geographic factors influenced Viking settlement in England and Ireland?
   a. Britain is an island.
   b. The Vikings were in search of croplands.
   c. The Vikings settled along rivers and coastal areas.
   d. Open land for settlement was plentiful in Britain.

2. How successful do you think the Vikings were at expanding their settlements in England and Ireland? Explain your answer.

Decision Making

Read the quote below about London in the 1200s. Then answer the questions that follow.

> "In the thirteenth century, London succeeded in piping water from springs at Tyburn to a fountain in West Cheap, but there was neither pressure nor abundant quantity of water. The authorities intended the fountain to provide drinking water for the poor, and household water for the neighborhood. . . . but the chief sources of water . . . remained the wells, streams, . . . and the River Thames—the ultimate destination of most of London's garbage and sewage."

3. Which of the following statements best expresses what you think about an issue described in the quote?
   a. Piping water to a fountain was not a good idea because people would have fought over the water.
   b. The poor people in London did not have enough water and the authorities should have drilled wells for them.
   c. Dumping garbage and sewage into the Thames polluted it and the water would have been harmful to drink.
   d. The authorities should not have piped water from Tyburn because that left the people of Tyburn without water.

4. Why did you choose the statement you did in question 3? Use a decision-making process to explain your answer.

Alternative Assessment

Building Your Portfolio

Economics

The economies of modern, industrialized nations differ greatly from those of medieval societies. Research ways in which the high-technology economy of the United States functions differently than the agricultural economies of medieval Europe. Use a decision-making process to decide if you would rather live in the United States today or in medieval Europe. Write a summary of the steps you took to reach your decision.

📶 internet connect

Internet Activity: go.hrw.com
KEYWORD: SP3 WH13

Choose a topic on the Rise of the Middle Ages to:
- evaluate primary and secondary sources about Charlemagne.
- create a poster on medieval art and architecture.
- write a report on daily life in the Middle Ages.

Reviewing Themes
1. by agreeing to separate matters of church and state

2. King John demanded that the nobles pay more taxes. The threat of an armed uprising forced the king to sign Magna Carta.

3. if the lord demanded all the crops that the peasant produced

Thinking Critically
1. Land ownership created power and authority.

2. The emperors continued to threaten the popes' rule. The popes firmly opposed emperors' attempts to seize power in Italy.

3. The church granted some of its lands as fiefs. Bishops served as feudal lords and vassals.

Writing About History
Reports should compare the food, clothes, education, duties, and social mobility of each.

Building Social Studies Skills
1. c

2. Viking settlements were scattered throughout England and Ireland, but many areas had few Viking settlements.

3. Answers will vary.

4. Students should support their answers.

Building Your Portfolio
Summaries might include the importance of land ownership and education.

The High Middle Ages

CHAPTER RESOURCE MANAGER

Objectives	Pacing Guide	Reproducible Resources
SECTION 1 **The Crusades** (pp. 318–322) • Identify the main causes of the Crusades. • Describe the outcome of the First Crusade. • Describe the outcomes of the other major crusades. • Explain how the Crusades affected Europe.	**Regular** — 1.5 day / **Block Scheduling** — 1 day *Block Scheduling Handbook with Team Teaching Strategies, 14.1*	**RS** Guided Reading Strategy 14.1 **PS** Readings in World History 41: *Saladin's Courage and Steadfastness* **E** Hands-on Activity 14: The Crusaders
SECTION 2 **The Revival of Trade** (pp. 323–326) • Explain factors that led to the revival of trade in Europe. • Describe goods traded in Europe and explain why fairs began. • Identify important business developments that resulted from the growth of trade.	**Regular** — 1.5 day / **Block Scheduling** — 1 day *Block Scheduling Handbook with Team Teaching Strategies, 14.2*	**RS** Guided Reading Strategy 14.2
SECTION 3 **The Growth of Towns** (pp. 327–330) • Identify rights townspeople gained during the late Middle Ages. • Explain how merchant and craft guilds contributed to their communities. • Describe how the growth of cities helped lead to the decline of serfdom.	**Regular** — 1.5 day / **Block Scheduling** — 1 day *Block Scheduling Handbook with Team Teaching Strategies, 14.3*	**RS** Guided Reading Strategy 14.3 **RS** Graphic Organizer Activity 13: The Growth of Towns **SM** Geography Activity 14
SECTION 4 **Life and Culture in the Middle Ages** (pp. 331–335) • Analyze changes in language and literature during the Middle Ages. • Examine changes in education during the Middle Ages. • Identify developments made in philosophy and science. • Describe the characteristic architecture of the later Middle Ages.	**Regular** — 1.5 day / **Block Scheduling** — 1 day *Block Scheduling Handbook with Team Teaching Strategies, 14.4*	**RS** Guided Reading Strategy 14.4 **E** Creative Teaching Strategy 14: Power and the Pope
SECTION 5 **Wars and the Growth of Nations** (pp. 336–340) • Identify how the Hundred Years' War affected England and France. • Analyze how Spain's rulers both strengthened and weakened their nation. • Explain why the Holy Roman Empire remained weak throughout the later Middle Ages.	**Regular** — 1.5 day / **Block Scheduling** — 1 day *Block Scheduling Handbook with Team Teaching Strategies, 14.5*	**RS** Guided Reading Strategy 14.5
SECTION 6 **Challenges to Church Power** (pp. 341–343) • Identify the factors that led to the decline of the Catholic Church in the later Middle Ages. • Describe how the Babylonian Captivity and the Great Schism affected the church. • Explain why teachers and priests challenged the church during the later Middle Ages.	**Regular** — 1.5 day / **Block Scheduling** — 1 day *Block Scheduling Handbook with Team Teaching Strategies, 14.6*	**RS** Guided Reading Strategy 14.6 **PS** Readings in World History 44: The Papal Court at Avignon

Chapter Resource Key

PS Primary Sources	**A** Assessment	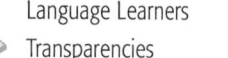 Music	
RS Reading Support	**REV** Review	Video	
IC Interdisciplinary Connections	**ELL** Reinforcement and English Language Learners	Internet	
E Enrichment	Transparencies	Holt Presentation Maker Using Microsoft® PowerPoint®	
SM Skills Mastery	CD-ROM		

One-Stop Planner CD-ROM

See the ***One-Stop Planner*** for a complete list of additional resources for students and teachers.

One-Stop Planner CD-ROM

It's easy to plan lessons, select resources, and print out materials for your students when you use the *One-Stop Planner* CD-ROM with *Test Generator*.

Technology Resources	Reinforcement, Review, and Assessment
One-Stop Planner 14.1 World History Teaching Transparency: Geography and History 11: Trade Routes in the Middle Ages Religions of the World Video Series: Islam Religions of the World Video Series: Christianity Homework Practice Online	Daily Quiz 14.1 Main Idea Activity 14.1 English Audio Summary 14.1 Spanish Audio Summary 14.1 REV Section 1 Review, p. 322
One-Stop Planner 14.2 Homework Practice Online Online Maps, Charts, and Graphs: European Trade in the 1200s	Daily Quiz 14.2 Main Idea Activity 14.2 English Audio Summary 14.2 Spanish Audio Summary 14.2 REV Section 2 Review, p. 326
One-Stop Planner 14.3 World History Teaching Transparency: Everyday Life 14: The Triumph of Death Homework Practice Online Online Graphs: Largest Cities in Africa, Asia, Europe, c. 1200	Daily Quiz 14.3 Main Idea Activity 14.3 English Audio Summary 14.3 Spanish Audio Summary 14.3 REV Section 3 Review, p. 330
One-Stop Planner 14.4 Holt Researcher: World History: Geoffrey Chaucer World History and Cultures Video Program 11: Cathedrals and Castles Homework Practice Online	Daily Quiz 14.4 Main Idea Activity 14.4 English Audio Summary 14.4 Spanish Audio Summary 14.4 REV Section 4 Review, p. 335
One-Stop Planner 14.5 Holt Researcher: World History: Joan of Arc Homework Practice Online Online Maps: England and France on the Eve of the Hundred Years' War; The Hundred Years' War by 1453	Daily Quiz 14.5 Main Idea Activity 14.5 English Audio Summary 14.5 Spanish Audio Summary 14.5 REV Section 5 Review, p. 340
One-Stop Planner 14.6 World History Teaching Transparency: Geography and History 14: The Great Schism Religions of the World Video Series: Christianity Homework Practice Online	Daily Quiz 14.6 Main Idea Activity 14.6 English Audio Summary 14.6 Spanish Audio Summary 14.6 REV Section 6 Review, p. 343

 internet connect

HRW ONLINE RESOURCES
GO TO: go.hrw.com
Then type in a keyword.

TEACHER HOME PAGE
KEYWORD: SP3 Teacher

CHAPTER INTERNET ACTIVITIES
KEYWORD: SP3 WH14
Choose an activity to:
- create a propaganda poster about the Crusades.
- learn more about the monarchies of Henry VII, Louis IX, and Ferdinand and Isabella of Spain.
- explore the effects of the Black Death on Europe in the 1300s.

CHAPTER ENRICHMENT LINKS
KEYWORD: SP3 CH14

ONLINE ASSESSMENT
Homework Practice
KEYWORD: SP3 HP14
Standardized Test Prep
KEYWORD: SP3 STP14
Rubrics
KEYWORD: SS Rubrics

ONLINE MAPS, CHARTS, AND GRAPHS
KEYWORD: SP3 MCG

CONTENT UPDATES
KEYWORD: SS Content Updates

HOLT PRESENTATION MAKER
KEYWORD: SP3 PPT14

ONLINE READING SUPPORT
KEYWORD: SS Strategies

CURRENT EVENTS
KEYWORD: S3 Current Events

Meeting Individual Needs

Ability Levels

Level 1 Basic level activities designed for all students encountering new material

Level 2 Intermediate level activities designed for average students

Level 3 Challenging activities designed for honors and gifted and talented students

English Language Learners These activities address the needs of students with Limited English Proficiency.

Chapter Review and Assessment

- IC Vocabulary Activity 14
- Global Skill Builder CD-ROM
- HRW Web Site
- REV Chapter 14 Tutorial for Students, Parents, Mentors, and Peers
- REV Chapter 14 Review, pp. 344–345
- A Chapter 14 Test Generator (on the One-Stop Planner)
- A Chapter 14 Test (Form A or B)
- A Alternative Assessment Handbook
- A Chapter 14 Test for English Language Learners and Special-Needs Students

315b

Build on What You Know

Ask students to answer the following questions:

How did feudalism and manorialism shape civilization in the Middle Ages?

Consider:

- the relationship between lords and peasants
- the relationship between kings and lords
- the self-sufficiency of a manor village

How might the Christian church have influenced the politics and economy of Europe in the later Middle Ages?

Consider:

- the church's role in education
- the church's power of taxation
- the struggles between popes and kings

EXPLORING THE TIME LINE
GLOBAL EVENTS

internet connect

TOPIC: Joan of Arc
GO TO: go.hrw.com
KEYWORD: SP3 WH14

Have students access the Internet through the HRW Go site to conduct research on Joan of Arc. Students should take notes on her life, accomplishments, and significance to history. Then have them write a biography of this French heroine. Students should use standard grammar, punctuation, and sentence structure.

CHAPTER 14

1000–1500
The High Middle Ages

Crusaders at the gates of Jerusalem

c. 1000
Politics
European feudalism begins.

c. 1000
Science and Technology
Arabs and Jews become court physicians in Germany.

c. 1050
The Arts
English monks excel at embroidery.

c. 1054
Daily LIfe
The Christian church splits.

1096–1291
Global Events
The Crusades are fought.

c. 1150
The Arts
Gothic architecture begins to develop.

1174
Daily Life
The earliest known horse races occur in England.

c. 1202
Daily Life
The first court jesters appear at European courts.

1193
Business and Finance
The first known merchant guild is formed in London.

1225
The Arts
Guillaume de Lorris writes "Roman de la Rose," a story of courtly wooing.

c. 1241
Business and Finance
The Hanseatic League is formed.

1000   **1100**   **1200**

Figure of the head of a crusader

A medieval knight with a female admirer

Build on What You Know

During the early Middle Ages, the people of western Europe gradually developed new institutions based upon a combination of Roman and Germanic traditions, values, and lifestyles. Feudalism became the primary political system, while manorialism became the primary economic system. These structures helped shape the new civilization that grew across much of Europe. The Christian church, too, played a strong role in the political and economic growth of the time. In this chapter, you will learn how changes occurred in government, economics, culture, and religion during the later Middle Ages.

What's Your Opinion?

 *To help students create their Themes Journal entries, provide the following examples of appropriate **agree**/**disagree** statements.*

Global Relations

Agree Enemies focus on destroying one another's way of life rather than learning about it.

Disagree Learning an enemy's strengths and weaknesses is a major focus during wartime.

Economics

Agree Towns serve as centers for trade, and trade generates new businesses that help towns grow.

Disagree Self-sufficiency contributes more than trade to a town's growth, and trade depends more on itinerant merchants than on populous centers.

Government

Agree The development of a new nation requires groups to relinquish power to a central government.

Disagree The development of new nations simply legitimizes leaders who are already the most powerful.

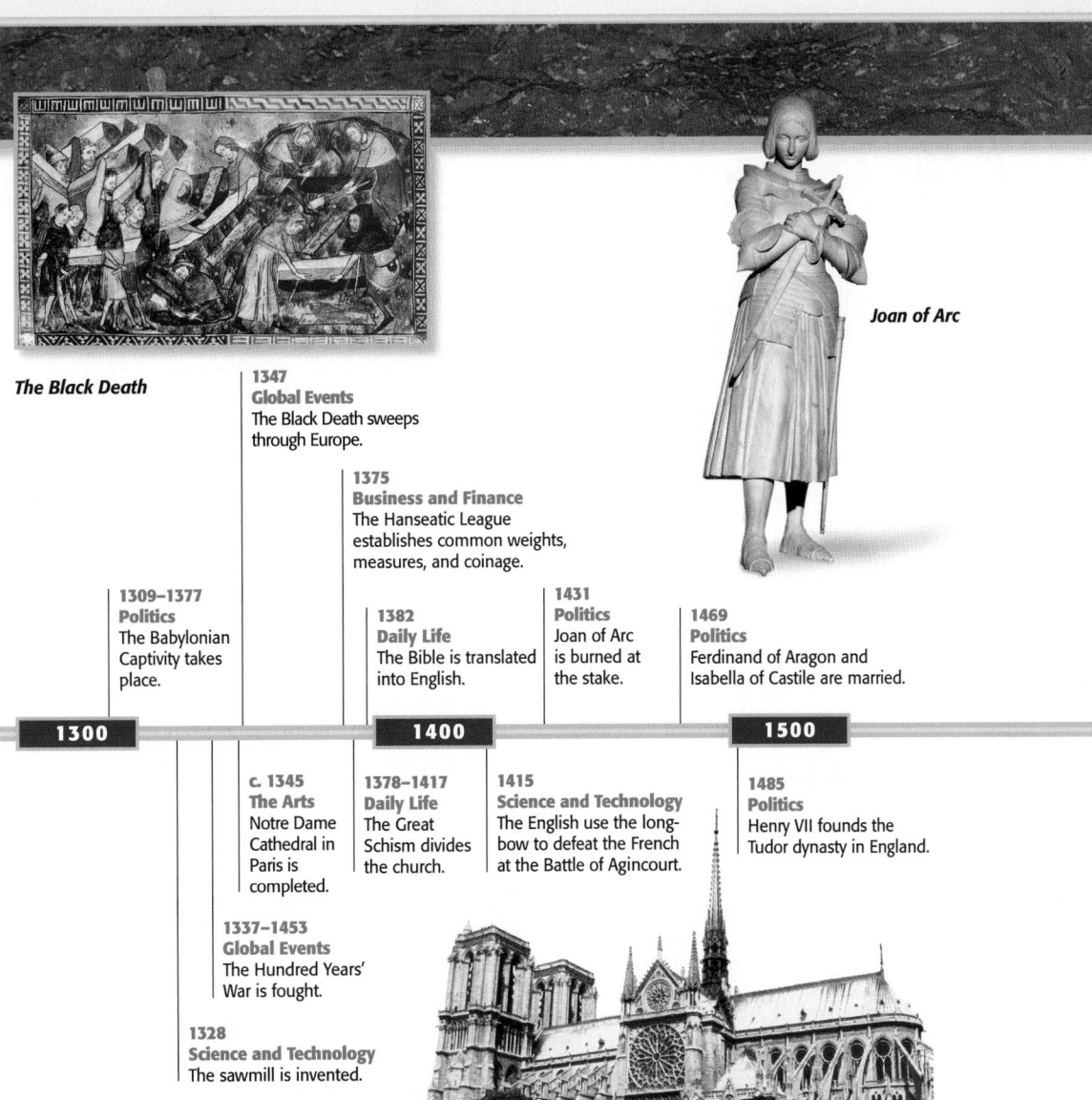

The Black Death

Joan of Arc

1309–1377
Politics
The Babylonian Captivity takes place.

1347
Global Events
The Black Death sweeps through Europe.

1375
Business and Finance
The Hanseatic League establishes common weights, measures, and coinage.

1382
Daily Life
The Bible is translated into English.

1431
Politics
Joan of Arc is burned at the stake.

1469
Politics
Ferdinand of Aragon and Isabella of Castile are married.

1300

1400

1500

c. 1345
The Arts
Notre Dame Cathedral in Paris is completed.

1378–1417
Daily Life
The Great Schism divides the church.

1415
Science and Technology
The English use the long-bow to defeat the French at the Battle of Agincourt.

1485
Politics
Henry VII founds the Tudor dynasty in England.

1337–1453
Global Events
The Hundred Years' War is fought.

1328
Science and Technology
The sawmill is invented.

Notre Dame Cathedral

What's Your Opinion?

 *Do you **agree** or **disagree** with the following statements? Support your point of view in your journal.*

Global Relations Two groups of people cannot learn from each other when they are at war because of religion.

Economics The growth of trade and the growth of towns are related and dependent upon one another.

Government Shifts in the balance of political power almost always take place as new nations develop.

In 1347 ships returning from eastern Mediterranean ports brought black rats infected with bubonic plague, or the Black Death, to Italy. When infected rats died, their fleas began biting people, thus spreading the disease.

An infected person suffered from painfully swollen lymph glands, high fever, large purple blotches on the skin, and black spots at the point of the flea bite. Death usually didn't take long. Victims lucky enough to survive the illness developed an immunity against further infection. Most estimates say that about a third of Europe's people died of the Black Death between 1347 and 1351.

Critical Thinking

Have students predict how the loss of so many people affected the economy of Europe.

ANSWER: Students may predict that employers might have had difficulty finding enough workers and that skilled workers might have charged high prices because their numbers were few.

OBJECTIVES

1 **Identify the main causes of the Crusades.**

2 **Describe the outcome of the First Crusade.**

3 **Describe the outcomes of the other major crusades.**

4 **Explain how the Crusades affected Europe.**

REPRODUCIBLE RESOURCES

▸ Guided Reading Strategy 14.1

▸ Readings in World History 41: Saladin's Courage and Steadfastness

▸ Hands-on Activity 14: The Crusaders

TECHNOLOGY RESOURCES

▸ One-Stop Planner 14.1

▸ Religions of the World Video Series: Islam

▸ Religions of the World Video Series: Christianity

▸ Homework Practice Online

REINFORCEMENT, REVIEW, AND ASSESSMENT

▸ Section 1 Review, p. 322

▸ Daily Quiz 14.1

▸ Main Idea Activity 14.1

▸ English Audio Summary 14.1

▸ Spanish Audio Summary 14.1

◆ SECTION 1

▶ READ TO DISCOVER

❶ What were the main causes of the Crusades?

❷ What was the outcome of the First Crusade?

❸ What were the outcomes of the other major crusades?

❹ How did the Crusades affect Europe?

▶ IDENTIFY

Seljuq Turks
Urban II
Crusades
Saladin
Children's Crusade

▶ WHY IT MATTERS TODAY

Conflicts continue today in the Holy Land. Use CNN Student News.com or other **current event** sources to find information on recent conflicts between the Israelis and the Palestinians. Record your findings in your journal.

CNN Student News.com

LET'S GET STARTED!

As students enter the classroom, tell them to locate Dover and Acre on the map on page 319. Have them use the scale to estimate the distance of the route crusaders took from Dover to Acre. *(about 4,000 miles)* Then have students speculate about why the crusaders might have gone to war thousands of miles from home. Tell students that in Section 1 they will learn why the crusaders went to the Holy Land.

The Crusades

The Main Idea
European Christians tried to end Islamic rule of Palestine in a series of wars called the Crusades.

The Story Continues *To Christians, as well as to Jews and Muslims, Palestine was a holy land. Jerusalem, said one pope, was "the land which the Redeemer of mankind illuminated by his coming," the land where Jesus had lived, preached, and died. In the 600s Muslim Arabs took control of Palestine. They generally let Christians and Jews there practice their religions, travel freely, and trade. During the Middle Ages, however, this situation changed.*

Causes of the Crusades

During the late 1000s, the **Seljuq Turks,** a Muslim people from Central Asia, gained control of Palestine—known among Christians as "the Holy Land." The Turks went on to attack Asia Minor, part of the Byzantine Empire. When they threatened the capital city of Constantinople, the Byzantine emperor called on Pope **Urban II** in Rome for help. Because Christian pilgrims to Palestine reported that they had been persecuted by the Turks, the Byzantine emperor's appeal met with a warm reception.

Urban was eager to regain the Holy Land from the Turks. In 1095 he called a meeting of church leaders and feudal lords. They met in Clermont, France. Urban asked the lords to stop fighting among themselves and join in a great war to win back the Holy Land. They would "wear the cross of Christ on their right shoulder or back, and with one voice . . . cry out: 'God wills it, God wills it, God wills it!'"

Thus began the **Crusades,** a series of military expeditions to regain the Holy Land. At least 10,000 Europeans took up the cause. They sewed a cross of cloth on their clothes and were called crusaders. (The Latin word *cruciata* means "marked with a cross.")

Crusaders joined the cause for different reasons. Some went to save their souls. They believed that if they died on crusade they would go straight to heaven. Some knights hoped to gain land and wealth in Palestine and southwest Asia. Some merchants saw a chance to make money. Thus the Crusades appealed to a love of adventure and the promise of rewards, both spiritual and material.

✔ **READING CHECK: Identifying Cause and Effect** Why did Pope Urban II call for a crusade? to free the Holy Land from Seljuq control

Pope Urban II called upon the nobles of western Europe to free the Holy Land from Seljuq rule.

LEVEL 1: Copy the graphic organizer on the chalk-board, omitting the italicized answers. Then work with the students to complete a chain of causes and effects that led to the First Crusade. **ENGLISH LANGUAGE LEARNERS**

HOMEWORK Have students make a chart with two columns entitled *Upside* and *Downside.* Then have them categorize what they consider the positive and negative aspects of the Crusades in the appropriate columns.

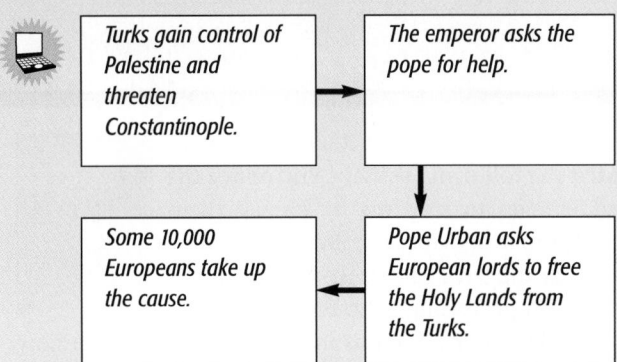

Turks gain control of Palestine and threaten Constantinople. → *The emperor asks the pope for help.*

Some 10,000 Europeans take up the cause. ← *Pope Urban asks European lords to free the Holy Lands from the Turks.*

The First Crusade

The First Crusade lasted from 1096 to 1099. French and Italian lords led several armies of crusaders from Europe to Constantinople. The Byzantine emperor, glad for help from the West against the Turks, was nonetheless suspicious of the crusaders. Seeing the crusader armies approach his city, the emperor feared they might capture and plunder the capital. After much discussion the emperor allowed the crusaders to pass through Constantinople.

Across Asia Minor the crusaders continued their long, hot march toward Palestine. In their wool and leather garments and heavy armor, the armies suffered severely from the heat. They lacked enough food and water because they had few pack animals to carry supplies. Despite such difficulties, the crusaders forged on to capture the city of Antioch.

The crusaders then marched down the coast toward Palestine and their main target—the holy city of Jerusalem. Fleets of ships from Italy brought supplies. The Turks, quarreling among themselves, were disunited and therefore unable to prevent the crusaders from surrounding the city. After a series of vicious battles, the crusaders captured Jerusalem. In a terrible massacre, they slaughtered its Muslim and Jewish inhabitants.

What If? The Byzantine emperor called for help from the pope in Rome to control the Turks in the Holy Land. **How might the history of European trade have been different if the Byzantine Christians had gained control of the Holy Land from the Turks and had not needed western Europeans' help?**

■ **internet** connect

TOPIC: Crusades
GO TO: go.hrw.com
KEYWORD: SP3 WH14

Have students access the Internet through the HRW Go site to find information on the genesis of the Crusades and the rationalizations that Europeans posed at the time for undertaking the Crusades. After researching students should draw their own opinions on whether or not Europeans were justified in their actions. Then have students create propaganda posters that could have been used during the Middle Ages to persuade people to their opinion.

WHAT IF? ANSWER
Students' answers might include that Europeans would have taken longer to forge national identities because fellow countrymen would not have fought side by side in the Crusades.

MAP ANSWERS
1. Constantinople
2. the Third Crusade

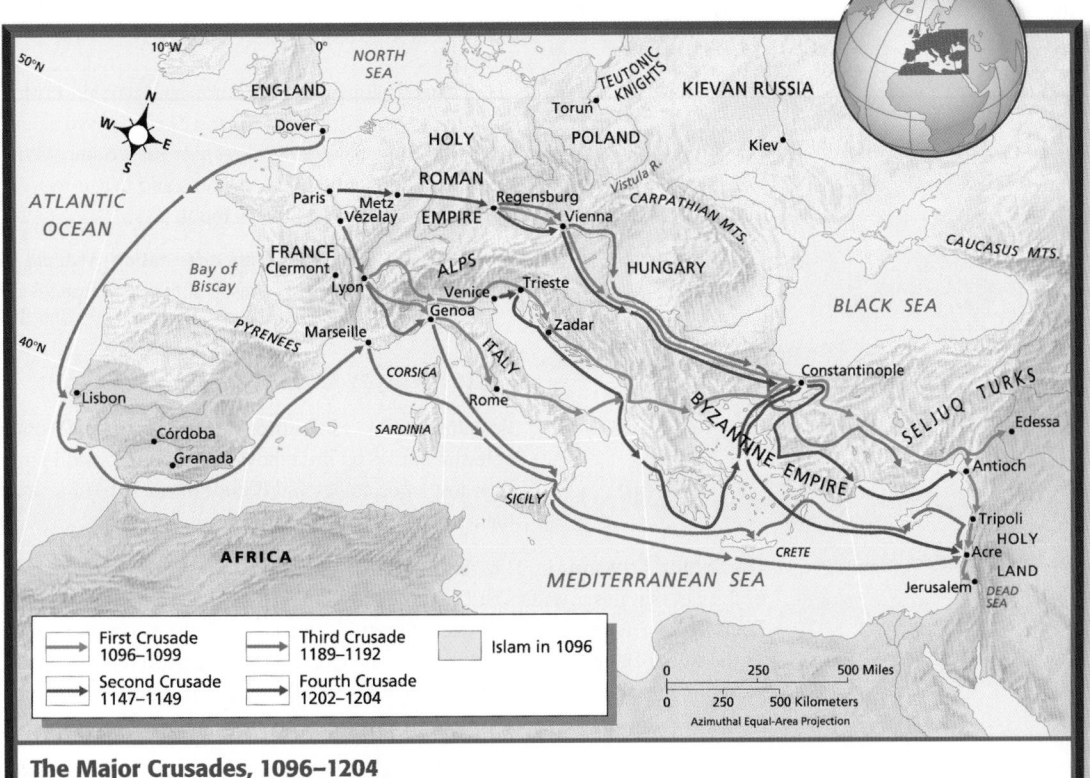

The Major Crusades, 1096–1204

Interpreting Maps The crusaders set out from many European cities to free the Holy Land from the Turks.

■ **Skills Assessment: 1. Places and Regions** Near what city did the routes of the four crusades cross? **2. Comparing** Which crusade brought armies from the farthest distance to the Holy Land?

Map legend:
- First Crusade 1096–1099
- Second Crusade 1147–1149
- Third Crusade 1189–1192
- Fourth Crusade 1202–1204
- Islam in 1096

0 250 500 Miles
0 250 500 Kilometers
Azimuthal Equal-Area Projection

TEACH OBJECTIVE 2

ALL LEVELS: Have students work in pairs to create a chart of the political, economic, and cultural effects of the First Crusade. (*political: Europeans control Holy Land, European institutions spread, crusaders set up small states; economic: feudalism spread, trade between Europe and the Holy Land, Italian shipping business grew; cultural: Europeans wore Eastern clothes and ate Eastern foods, Christians grew to respect Muslims*)
ENGLISH LANGUAGE LEARNERS, COOPERATIVE LEARNING

That's Interesting!

In the crusader states, a new type of knight developed—the monk-knight. The most famous of these orders were the Templars and the Hospitallers. The Hospitallers were founded to care for sick pilgrims in Jerusalem and the Templars to protect Christian pilgrims traveling to the Holy Land.

Both of these religious groups, however, developed into fighting forces dedicated to the defense of Christendom. They also grew wealthy from bequests, and the monk-knights lived in a world of plenty with the best horses, armor, and weapons.

The Arab historians Ibn al-Athīr and Ibn al-Qalanisi described the crusaders' actions after their conquest of Jerusalem. According to them,

Analyzing Primary Sources

Identifying Bias How might a crusader's description of the attack and capture of Jerusalem differ from those of the Muslim writers Ibn al-Athīr and Ibn al-Qalanisi? might emphasize that Jerusalem was restored to Christian control, avoid description of the inhabitants' slaughter

History Makers Speak

❝The population was put to the sword by the Franks [crusaders], who pillaged for a week. . . . the Franks slaughtered more than 70,000 people, among them a large number of Imams and Muslim scholars who had left their homelands to live in the pious seclusion of the Holy Place.❞

Ibn al-Athīr, quoted in Michael Foss, *People of the First Crusade*

❝The Jews [who lived in Jerusalem and who had been trapped by the crusaders' siege of the city] had gathered in their synagogue and the Franks burnt them alive. They also destroyed monuments of saints and the tomb of Abraham, may peace be upon him.❞

Ibn al-Qalanisi, quoted in Michael Foss, *People of the First Crusade*

The crusaders' capture of Jerusalem brought much of the Holy Land under European control. As a result, European customs and institutions were put into place in parts of southwest Asia and the Holy Land. The crusaders set up four small states. They introduced the idea of European feudalism and subdivided the land into fiefs, with lords and vassals. Trade between Europe and the Holy Land sprang up. Italian ships carried most of the trade goods.

Changes happened to the European occupiers during this time as well. The Christians and Muslims lived alongside each other and grew to respect each other. Many Europeans adopted Eastern customs and began to wear Eastern clothes and eat Eastern foods.

✔ **READING CHECK: Analyzing Information** What did the crusaders achieve as a result of the First Crusade? brought much of the Holy Land under European control

The crusaders attack Jerusalem.

Other Major Crusades

For almost 100 years, European Christians held onto Palestine. Little by little, however, the Turks won back their lost lands. Popes and European rulers tried to stop them during three more major crusades.

The Second Crusade. By 1146 the Turks had united their forces. They started taking back cities that the crusaders had captured. In 1147 the Second Crusade began. King Louis VII of France and German king Conrad III led separate armies across Europe. At the city of Damascus, the two armies joined forces. The combined forces failed to recapture the city, however. The Turks held. In 1149 the crusaders returned to Europe in disgrace.

The Third Crusade. In 1187 the Muslim leader **Saladin** gained control of Jerusalem. Three European rulers—Holy Roman Emperor Frederick Barbarossa, King Philip II of France, and King Richard I of England—then led separate armies in the Third Crusade. The crusade lasted from 1189 to 1192. It, too, failed. When Barbarossa drowned on the way to the Holy Land, his army turned back. Philip and Richard quarreled, and Philip

TEACH OBJECTIVE 3

LEVEL 2: Have students write five false statements about the outcomes of the other major crusades on a sheet of paper. Ask them to skip spaces between each statement. Then tell students to exchange papers with a partner and correct the partner's false statements in the spaces provided. **COOPERATIVE LEARNING**

TEACH OBJECTIVE 4

LEVEL 3: Ask students to imagine a reunion of elderly crusaders. Then have them write speeches that the attendees might give about their lives since the Crusades. Tell students to use information under "Results of the Crusades."

CLOSE

Ask students to write a short paragraph in which they make predictions about which changes brought about by the Crusades were most important to Europe's development. Have students share their predictions with the class.

took his army back home to seize English lands in France. Richard and the forces under his command remained in the Holy Land, but they could not recapture Jerusalem. Richard settled for a truce with Saladin. Through the truce, the crusaders received control of some towns along the Palestinian coast. The truce also allowed Christians to enter Jerusalem freely.

The Fourth Crusade. Pope Innocent III gathered a group of French knights for the Fourth Crusade. In 1202 they left on ships provided by the Italian city-state of Venice. The Venetians persuaded the crusaders to attack Zadar—a trade rival to Venice—as they moved down the Adriatic coast. Because Zadar was a Christian city, however, the crusaders who attacked it were later excommunicated by Innocent III.

Then in 1204, the crusaders attacked and looted Constantinople, another Christian city. They stole many things that were holy to the Byzantine Christians. The Venetians gained control of Byzantine trade. Constantinople remained under western European control for about 60 years. The Byzantines eventually regained the city, but they never regained their strength. The once-mighty empire collapsed when the Turks seized Constantinople in 1453.

Other crusades. In 1212 the short-lived and unfortunate **Children's Crusade** took place. Young people from across Europe decided to march to the Holy Land and regain it for Christian Europe. The young crusaders lacked adequate training, equipment, and supplies. By the time they reached the Mediterranean coast, the army of children was little more than a hungry and disorganized mob. The pope sent some of them back home. Others reached southern France, where they were tricked into boarding ships that carried them off into slavery instead of to the Holy Land. Several thousand children, most from Germany and France, were lost in the course of this tragedy.

For many years, European crusaders tried to recapture the Holy Land. The Crusades continued until 1291, when the Muslims captured the city of Acre (AH·kruh). Acre was the last Christian stronghold in the Holy Land and, with its fall, the Crusades ended.

✔ **READING CHECK: Supporting a Point of View** What evidence would you give to show that from 1147 the Crusades were a failure? Crusades in 1147 and after failed to regain European control of the Holy Land

Results of the Crusades

The goal of the Crusades was to take the Holy Land from the Turks. All the Crusades except the first failed to reach that goal. By the end of the Crusades, the Muslims again controlled Palestine. In Europe, however, the Crusades helped bring about many changes.

Crusader States from 1098

Interpreting Maps During and after the First Crusade, crusaders set up small states in the Middle East.

■ **Skills Assessment: 1. Places and Regions** Name the four states set up by crusaders between 1098 and 1102. How long did each state stay under the crusaders' control?
2. Drawing Conclusions Compare this map with the map on page 319. Why might it have been difficult for the crusaders to maintain control of these states?

Interdisciplinary Connection

LITERATURE. Since the 1800s the medieval folk hero Robin Hood has been linked with Richard the Lion-Hearted.

However, in the original tales from the 1300s, Robin treats women and the poor kindly but rebels against all authority. These early versions make no mention of Richard and were probably set in the England of the late 1300s, long after the Crusades were over.

Critical Thinking

Ask students to give reasons why the story of Robin Hood changed over the years.

ANSWER: A possible response is that different generations reshaped the story to fit their idea of heroic.

Technology Resources
World History Teaching Transparency: Geography and History 11: Trade Routes in the Middle Ages

ASSESS

Have students complete Daily Quiz 14.1. As Alternative Assessment, you may want to use the cause-and-effect chart or the Upside/Downside chart in this section's lessons.

RETEACH

Have students complete Main Idea Activity for English Language Learners and Special-Needs Students 14.1. Then have students list the names of the crusades in one column and their outcomes in a second column. **ENGLISH LANGUAGE LEARNERS**

EXTEND

Have students create historical comic books that tell the story of the Crusades. Recommend that they research the clothing and weapons of the time. Encourage students to show as much action as possible and yet convey the causes and effects of the Crusades. **BLOCK SCHEDULING**

CONNECTING TO GEOGRAPHY ANSWER

made Europeans want to see new climates, religions, societies for themselves; opened new possibilities for trade

SECTION 1 REVIEW ANSWERS

❶ **Identify**
- Seljuq Turks, p. 318
- Urban II, p. 318
- Crusades, p. 318
- Saladin, p. 320
- Children's Crusade, p. 321

❷ First Crusade: massacre of Muslims and Jews, Holy Land under European control, crusaders set up four small states, trade between Europe and Holy Land, Europeans adopt Eastern customs. Second Crusade: Crusaders fail to recapture Damascus, return home in disgrace. Third Crusade: Crusaders gain control of Palestinian coastal towns, get permission for Christians to enter Jerusalem. Fourth Crusade: Crusaders attack and loot Constantinople, Venetians control Byzantine trade. Other crusades: young children attempt to regain Holy Land.

❸ **a.** Turks captured cities in the Holy Land.

b. new methods of waging war; more powerful European kings; new ideas and culture; Italian cities became trading centers

❹ Reports might include undermining walls, using catapults, and learning about gunpowder.

CONNECTING TO GEOGRAPHY

The World of Arab Geographers

In Chapter 11 you read how Europeans learned about the geographical achievements of the Muslims. Arab geographers had published the world's first climatic atlas in the 900s. One Arab geographer, al-Muqaddasī, wrote a geographic encyclopedia in which he discussed not only physical systems such as climate and land but also human systems such as religion, society, commerce, and agriculture.

During the 1100s the great geographer al-Idrīsī completed his *Amusement for Him Who Desires to Travel Around the World*. He is also credited with creating the world's first globe.

Understanding Geography

What effect might such new geographical knowledge have had on Europeans?

Weapons and warfare. During the Crusades, the weapon of choice for many European soldiers was the crossbow. This weapon was a powerful bow that was held horizontally. It fired a short, heavy arrow called a bolt with the pull of a trigger. The crossbow required far less skill to use than did the traditional bow. Yet it was a deadly weapon that was capable of penetrating chain mail and plate armor. From the Byzantines and Muslims, Europeans also discovered new ways to wage war. For example, they learned how to undermine walls and use catapults to throw rocks. From the Muslims, they may have learned about gunpowder.

Political changes. To raise money to go on crusade, some lords had sold their land. Without land, they had no power in the feudal system. Many nobles also died fighting in the Crusades. With fewer lords, the power of European kings grew stronger. The kings placed new taxes and led armies drawn from their entire country. All these changes helped bring an end to feudalism.

During the Crusades, the Christian church became more powerful also. As organizers of crusades, the popes took on more importance. This was particularly true after the First Crusade.

Ideas and trade. Between 1096 and 1291, thousands of crusaders traveled through the Holy Land. They exchanged ideas with crusaders from other parts of Europe. They also gained knowledge from the Byzantines and Muslims whom they met. When the crusaders returned home, these new ideas helped to enrich European culture.

Changes in trade also took place. Italian cities became major trading centers. Ships from Italian cities carried crusaders to the Holy Land. The ships came back loaded with foods from southwest Asia. Europeans began buying such goods as apricots, lemons, melons, rice, and sugar.

✔ **READING CHECK: Summarizing** In what ways did the Crusades change Europe? new methods and weapons of war; strengthened monarchies; new ideas and trade patterns

Map drawn by Arab geographer al-Idrīsī

SECTION 1 REVIEW

1. **Identify** and explain the significance:
   Seljuq Turks
   Urban II
   Crusades
   Saladin
   Children's Crusade

2. **Comparing and Contrasting** Copy the web diagram below. Use it to compare and contrast the outcomes of the first four Crusades.

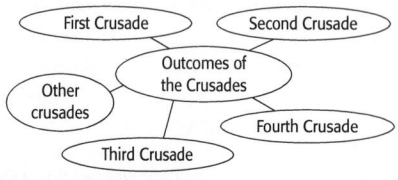

First Crusade — Second Crusade
Outcomes of the Crusades
Other crusades — Fourth Crusade
Third Crusade

3. **Finding the Main Idea**
   a. What issues led to the Crusades?
   b. What long-term importance did the Crusades have for Europe?

4. **Writing and Critical Thinking**
   Identifying Cause and Effect Imagine you are a soldier during the Crusades. Write a field report identifying how new technology is changing the way you fight.
   Consider:
   • new forms of technology used by Muslims and Europeans during the Crusades
   • how this technology affected warfare

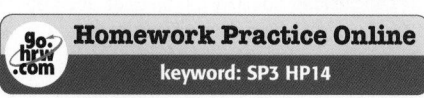

Homework Practice Online

keyword: SP3 HP14

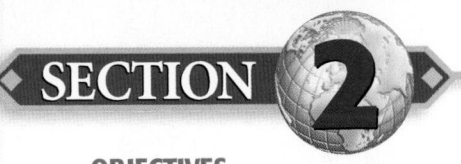

SECTION 2

OBJECTIVES

1 **Explain factors that led to the revival of trade in Europe.**

2 **Describe goods traded in Europe and explain why fairs began.**

3 **Identify important business developments that resulted from the growth of trade.**

🔔 *LET'S GET STARTED!*

As students enter the classroom, have them study the picture of the annual fair at Lendit on page 325. Ask them to find the similarities between the fair and a modern department store. *(A variety of goods are sold, the sellers advertise their wares—with flags at the fair and signs at the stores.)* Tell students that in Section 2 they will learn more about shopping in the High Middle Ages.

SECTION 2

READ TO DISCOVER

❶ What factors led to the revival of trade in Europe?

❷ What kinds of goods were traded, and why did fairs begin?

❸ What important business developments resulted from the growth of trade?

DEFINE

barter economy
domestic system
usury
capital
market economy

▶WHY IT MATTERS TODAY

Many nations have entered trade agreements with rules about prices and taxes, somewhat like the Hanseatic League. Use CNN or other **current event** sources to find examples of trade agreements among nations today. Record your findings in your journal.

CNN Student News.com

The Revival of Trade

The Main Idea
The Crusades spurred a revival of trade and led to economic growth throughout western Europe.

The Story Continues *It is fair day in a medieval town. Merchants from throughout Europe and even Asia and Africa hoist colorful tents and stalls and display their wares: spices from the East, silk from China, woolens from Flanders, cheese, leather goods, jewelry. Entertainers arrive as well—jugglers, acrobats, and musicians. Such a fair would not have been found 200 years earlier. After the Crusades, however, a fair was held somewhere on almost any given day of the year.*

Trade Routes

After the collapse of the Roman Empire in the 400s, trade almost died out in western Europe. With the rise of the Middle Ages, manors grew or made nearly everything they needed. Towns and cities, which depended on trade and manufacturing, shrank in population.

Because of the Crusades, trade began to grow again in Europe. Italy was the earliest site of this trade revival. Towns and trade had declined less there. Lying between northern Europe and southwest Asia, Italy's location also favored trade.

Trade in Italy. Northern Europeans wanted Asian goods, and those goods could be bought in southwest Asia. The Italian city-states of Genoa, Pisa, and Venice became important trading centers, acting as go-betweens for traders from Asia and northern Europe. The Crusades increased this trade. Ships from Italian city-states carried crusaders to Palestine. On their return trips, they brought back goods from Asia. These goods then traveled overland from Italy into central and northern Europe. This overland trade route led to the growth and increasing wealth of cities along its path.

Trade in northern Europe. Trade also began to grow again in northern Europe. Kiev, in what is now Ukraine, became a trading center. Before the year 1000, Viking traders from Kiev traveled to Constantinople. There they collected goods from Asia to bring back to cities in northern Europe.

Flanders became another important northern trading center. Now a part of Belgium, France, and the Netherlands, Flanders in the 1100s was the meeting point of several trade routes. Many traders came to Flanders from England, France, Germany, or countries along the Baltic Sea. They were eager to buy the fine woolen cloth made there. Flemish cities such as Bruges and Ghent grew in population and wealth.

The Hanseatic League. German cities on the Baltic and North Seas also became important trading centers. The most important were Bremen, Hamburg, and Lübeck. Germany's weak central government could not control trade. For that reason, the German trading cities joined together to form the Hanseatic League. In time, about 100 cities were members of the league. They set up trading posts in England, Flanders, Russia, and Scandinavia. During the 1300s and 1400s, the Hanseatic League increased trade in northwestern Europe.

SECTION 2 RESOURCES

REPRODUCIBLE RESOURCES

▶ Guided Reading Strategy 14.2

TECHNOLOGY RESOURCES

▶ One-Stop Planner 14.2
▶ Homework Practice Online
▶ Online Maps, Charts, and Graphs: European Trade in the 1200s

REINFORCEMENT, REVIEW, AND ASSESSMENT

▶ Section 2 Review, p. 326
▶ Daily Quiz 14.2
▶ Main Idea Activity 14.2
▶ English Audio Summary 14.2
▶ Spanish Audio Summary 14.2

THE HIGH MIDDLE AGES **323**

LEVEL 1: On the chalkboard, draw the web to the right, omitting the italicized words. Tell students to fill the ovals with reasons for the revival of trade in Europe.

ENGLISH LANGUAGE LEARNERS

Italian ships brought goods back from Asia.

The Crusades stimulated trade.

Viking ships brought Asian goods to northern Europe.

Revival of Trade

Flanders became a meeting center of different trade routes.

The Hanseatic League set up trading posts.

MAP ANSWERS

1. Italian city-states

2. The Hanseatic League controlled trading in those areas.

Culture

A noble household in the Middle Ages spent more than one-tenth its total income on clothing. Luxurious fabrics, such as some imported silk, signified the wearer's wealth and high rank.

Camlet was an especially magnificent fabric of silk and wool probably imported from the Middle East and was closely associated with nobility. In fact, the court of the legendary King Arthur was called Camelot, a name derived from camlet.

Critical Thinking

Ask students whether clothing is still a good indicator of wealth.

ANSWER: Students may think clothing is a good indicator of wealth because only wealthy people can afford high-quality fabrics. Or, they may think that clothing is no longer a good indicator of wealth because mass-produced clothing offers similar-looking styles and fabrics at a wide range of prices.

Trade Routes of the Middle Ages

Interpreting Maps Medieval overland trade routes linked eastern and western Europe.

■ **Skills Assessment: 1. Human Systems** Who controlled most of the trade routes in Europe?
2. Evaluating Why did they not control trade in the North Sea and Baltic Sea?

The rules of the Hanseatic League were strict. Any member city that did not follow the league's rules lost its trading rights. Sometimes a country's ruler took away the rights of a Hanseatic trader. When that happened, the league stopped shipping goods to that country. This placed great pressure on the ruler to restore the trader's rights. League members also waged wars to win back trading rights.

✔ **READING CHECK: Making Generalizations** How did the geographic locations of Italy, Kiev, and Flanders and the power of the Hanseatic League revive trade in Europe?
locations along major sea and overland trade routes promoted trade and manufacturing

Trade Goods and Markets

The Crusades had increased Europeans' demand for goods from Asia, especially those goods considered "exotic" or new. European merchants in the Middle Ages made their highest profits trading in luxury goods, including dyes, medicines, silks, and spices. Europeans also wanted manufactured goods such as cotton cloth, linen, and art objects. Moreover, Asia supplied Europe with fruit, grain, and rugs. In exchange Europe offered its own goods and products. Baltic countries traded fish, fur, and timber. Leather, oil, and soap came from Spain, and France produced wine. Venice exported glassware, and England and Flanders traded fine woolen cloth.

TEACH OBJECTIVE 2

ALL LEVELS: Organize the class into groups of four. Assign each group the role of either medieval merchants or rulers. Have the merchants plan how to attract more buyers for their goods. Have the rulers plan how to profit from the increased trade in their kingdoms. Have each group present its plan to the class. **ENGLISH LANGUAGE LEARNERS, COOPERATIVE LEARNING**

TEACH OBJECTIVE 3

LEVEL 3: Give students this analogy: Homes were to manufacturing in the Middle Ages as factories are to manufacturing today. Have pairs of students use the example as a model to create ten

analogies that compare manufacturing, banking, and investing in the Middle Ages to today. **COOPERATIVE LEARNING**

 HOMEWORK Have students use information in the section to create a chart comparing the characteristics of a barter economy with those of a market economy.

As trade grew, merchants needed places where they could exchange goods. Many villages held weekly market days. These local markets, however, did not attract large crowds. Then some merchants started selling goods during church festivals. Some local rulers also allowed fairs for the sale of imported goods. They placed a tax on each item that was sold. In return for the taxes, local rulers arranged special services for merchants. Armed guards protected merchants from robbery. They also kept the fairgrounds safe for everyone.

The most important and best-known fairs were held in Champagne. This section of northeastern France was on the trade route from Italy. At different times each year, four towns in Champagne held six fairs. Each fair lasted 49 days.

At first, business at fairs was done through a simple **barter economy.** Goods and services were exchanged for other goods and services without using money. As the fairs grew larger, a fixed value was placed on goods. This value could be in terms of goods, services, or money. However, local rulers each issued their own coins. Money changers placed a value on currencies from one region in relation to currencies from another region. Based on their value, money changers then exchanged coins from one region for coins of another. Little money ever changed hands at fairs. Buyers and sellers, however, started thinking of the value of a good in terms of money.

Although the major purpose of fairs was the buying and selling of goods, they became important social events as well. Fairs provided entertainment with clowns, jugglers, and musicians. People traveled from great distances to attend the large fairs. They met other travelers and shared news and ideas. In that way, fairs helped people broaden their outlook on the world.

✔ **READING CHECK: Finding the Main Idea** Why were fairs important during the Middle Ages? promoted economic growth and social activity and communication

Manufacturing, Banking, and Investment

The revival of trade in Europe during the Middle Ages led to three important business developments, each of which greatly affected economic life and progress down to the present day. During these years a new system of manufacturing began, a banking system developed, and the practice of investing wealth started.

Manufacturing. The system of manufacturing that developed during the Middle Ages was called the **domestic system.** Manufacturing took place in workers' homes rather than in a shop or factory. A good example of the domestic system was the woolen industry. An individual would buy wool and then hand it out to several workers. Each worker completed a different task, such as spinning, weaving, or dyeing. Then the owner of the wool collected the spun wool or finished cloth and sold it at the highest possible price. The domestic system began in towns but gradually spread to the countryside.

The annual fair at Lendit, France

CONNECTING TO Economics

Trade Fairs of the Middle Ages

Fairs in the Middle Ages were colorful events. They were also the main method of carrying out trade. Because of the fairs, easier ways to trade developed.

For example, some goods were sold by length or weight. Because people came from all over Europe to trade fairs, a standard system of weights and measures was needed. The troy weight was set to weigh gold and silver. This weight, named for the town of Troyes, France, is still used today.

Trade fairs also helped develop the bill of exchange. This note was a written promise to pay a sum of money at a later time.

Understanding Economics

Why did new ways of carrying on trade develop from fairs?

Economics

In the 1200s Italian traders regularly made the overland journey north to attend the international fairs at Champagne. Italian traders were thus able to sell their goods to the many inhabitants of the lands bordering the eastern part of France.

A century later, however, Italian merchants often traveled by ship instead. Ships sailed from Venice and Genoa to northern ports. This shift in travel routes made Flanders the most important location for merchants to do business.

Critical Thinking

Ask students how they think this shift in trade affected the people of Champagne.

ANSWER: Students will probably conclude that the people of Champagne suffered economically when the Italian merchants shifted their business to Flanders. Point out that regions which suffer economic setbacks often cultivate new businesses and that Champagne is now known for champagne rather than for fairs.

Banking. Another new business system of the later Middle Ages was banking. The word *bank* comes from the old Italian word *banca*, meaning "money changer's bench." Money changers were the first bankers. Besides exchanging currencies at fairs, money changers began to provide other services. Lending money was the most important service early bankers offered. Rulers, nobles, and merchants often borrowed money to pay for their activities. During the early Middle Ages, Jews, who were not allowed to own land or join most groups for skilled workers, became the main moneylenders. The Christian church did not allow **usury** (YOO·zuh·ree), or charging interest on loans. By the late Middle Ages, however, some Christians had also become moneylenders. Most law codes by then allowed the collection of interest on loans for business matters.

Bankers also made it easier to move money from one place to another. They developed special notes called bills of exchange. These notes were used in place of money. For example, a merchant might deposit money with a banker in Ghent in return for a bill of exchange in the amount of the deposit. The merchant could then cash the bill of exchange with a banker in Venice. This system was somewhat like present-day checking accounts.

Investing. In the later Middle Ages, Europeans began investing capital. **Capital** is wealth that is earned, saved, and invested to make profits. Sometimes, several people called investors formed a partnership. They put together their capital to pay for a new business. In that way, each partner shared in the cost. If the business made money, each partner would receive part of the profits.

Manufacturing, banking, and investing capital were the first steps toward the creation of a **market economy.** In a market economy, land, labor, and capital are controlled by individual persons. The medieval market economy formed the basis for our modern capitalist system.

This medieval illustration portrays aspects of banking and finance.

✔ **READING CHECK: Summarizing** What new business systems developed because of the revival of trade in Europe? *manufacturing, banking, and investment*

SECTION 2 REVIEW

1. **Define** and explain the significance:
   barter economy
   domestic system
   usury
   capital
   market economy

2. **Identifying Cause and Effect** Copy the chart below. Use it to show which cities in Italy, northern Europe, and the Hanseatic League became important trading centers and explain why each did.

Italy	Northern Europe	Hanseatic League

3. **Finding the Main Idea**
   a. What economic and social changes did fairs bring about in the Middle Ages?
   b. How did the revival of trade lead to the domestic system, a banking system, and the investing of capital?

4. **Writing and Critical Thinking**
   Analyzing Information Choose a town in Europe during the Middle Ages, and write an advertisement to attract people to its fair.
   Consider:
   - the location of the town
   - goods that will be for sale and where they are from
   - entertainment that will be provided

Homework Practice Online
keyword: SP3 HP14

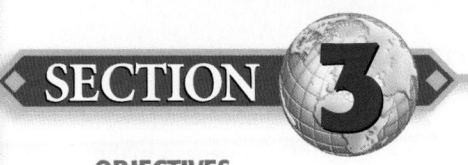

SECTION 3

OBJECTIVES

1 Identify rights townspeople gained during the late Middle Ages.

2 Explain how merchant and craft guilds contributed to their communities.

3 Describe how the growth of cities helped lead to the decline of serfdom.

🔔 LET'S GET STARTED!

As students enter the classroom, tell them that the approximate present-day populations of Paris and London are 2 million and 7 million, respectively. Have them predict their size in the 1200s. Ask volunteers to write their predictions on the chalkboard. Tell students that in Section 3 they will learn the actual size of these cities in the Middle Ages.

SECTION 3

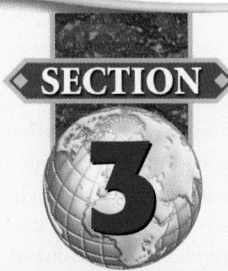

READ TO DISCOVER

❶ What rights did townspeople gain during the later Middle Ages?
❷ How did merchant and craft guilds contribute to their communities?
❸ How did the growth of cities help lead to the decline of serfdom?

DEFINE

merchant guild
craft guilds
apprentice
journeyman
middle class

IDENTIFY

Black Death

▶WHY IT MATTERS TODAY

Today different groups of workers organize into unions for many of the same reasons that medieval workers formed craft guilds. Use CNN or other **current event** sources to find information about current union activities. Record your findings in your journal.

CNN studentNews.com

The Growth of Towns

The Main Idea
The growth of European towns accompanied the revival of trade during the Middle Ages.

The Story Continues *As trade increased in the late 900s, European towns grew larger and new towns sprang up. In the 1300s, however, the populations of both town and countryside throughout Europe would be devastated by, as the Welsh called it, "death coming into our midst like black smoke."*

The Rights of Townspeople

Trade and cities generally grow together. As towns grew in the Middle Ages, townspeople saw that they did not fit into the manorial system. They played little part in the farming economy of villages. Instead, townspeople made their living by making and trading goods.

Manor lords, however, still controlled the towns. They would give up control only if given something in return. In some towns the people won self-government by peaceful means. In others, they resorted to violence. Some lords granted their towns charters of liberties. A charter was a written statement of the town's rights. In time, townspeople throughout Europe gained four basic rights.

> 1. **Freedom.** Anyone who lived in a town for a year and a day became free. This included serfs who escaped from a manor to a town.
>
> 2. **Exemption.** Townspeople won the right of being exempt, or free, from ever having to work on the manor.
>
> 3. **Town justice.** Towns had their own courts. Leading citizens tried cases that involved townspeople.
>
> 4. **Commercial privileges.** Townspeople could sell goods freely in the town market. They could also charge tolls to outsiders who wanted to trade there.

✔ **READING CHECK: Summarizing** What rights did townspeople gain? freedom, exemption from manor work, town justice, and commercial privileges

Guilds

As trade increased, towns grew larger and richer. Merchants and workers began to unite in associations called guilds.

Merchants. In each town, a **merchant guild** had the sole right to trade there. Merchants from other towns or nations could trade there only if they paid a fee. Merchant guilds also helped their members and members' families. For example, guilds looked after members who were in trouble and made loans to members. When guild members died, the guild aided the widow and children.

SECTION 3 RESOURCES

REPRODUCIBLE RESOURCES

▶ Guided Reading Strategy 14.3
▶ Graphic Organizer Activity 13
▶ Geography Activity 14

TECHNOLOGY RESOURCES

▶ One-Stop Planner 14.3
▶ World History Teaching Transparency: Everyday Life 14
▶ Homework Practice Online
▶ Online Maps, Charts, and Graphs: Largest Cities in Africa, Asia, Europe, c.1200

REINFORCEMENT, REVIEW, AND ASSESSMENT

▶ Section 3 Review, p. 330
▶ Daily Quiz 14.3
▶ Main Idea Activity 14.3
▶ English Audio Summary 14.3
▶ Spanish Audio Summary 14.3

TEACH OBJECTIVE 1

LEVEL 1: On the chalkboard, write the four basic rights of medieval townspeople. *(freedom, exemption, town justice, and commercial privileges)* Then tell students to use the reading to explain each one. Ask students to compare these rights with those of American citizens.

ENGLISH LANGUAGE LEARNERS

TEACH OBJECTIVE 2

LEVEL 3: Have students compose letters that members of a merchant or craft guild might write to townspeople who question the worth of guilds. Tell students to explain how the existence of guilds helps the entire community. Letters should contain standard grammar, spelling, sentence structure, and punctuation. Ask volunteers to share their letter with the class.

That's Interesting!

People in the Middle Ages made no distinction between fine artists and craft workers. Master painters often went from creating portraits to painting banners or designing clothes. During the late 1300s the court painter to the Duke of Burgundy also decorated chairs and did mechanical repairs.

Citizenship

The growth of towns led to the rise of the merchant class. The degree of freedom in European towns and cities varied. The lords sought the support of towns against kings, while kings sought the support of townsmen against subjects perceived as too powerful. They gave towns charters and privileges. Wealthy merchants typically became the dominant figures of the new town life and fought for their corporate privileges.

Critical Thinking

Ask students to use a problem-solving process to evaluate the merchants' solution to the problem of control by feudal lords.

ANSWER: Students might say that merchants traded control by the lords for control by a king; or, the king profited from the merchants' prosperity and so allowed them much freedom.

This illustration from about 1480 depicts medieval craft workers at their trades: an apprentice grinding colors (bottom left), a fresco painter (top), and a chest painter (bottom right).

Workers. In time, skilled workers came together in **craft guilds.** Each guild had members from a single craft, such as shoemaking or weaving. The craft guilds set rules for wages, hours, and working conditions. They also set standards for the quality of work. The guilds looked after ill members and those who could no longer work. Perhaps most important, the craft guilds controlled the training of skilled workers.

The master workers of each guild trained boys and men who wanted to join their guild. First, a boy served as an **apprentice.** His parents paid a master worker to house, feed, clothe, and train the boy. Apprentice training could take five to nine years. Next, the young man became a **journeyman,** a skilled worker who was paid wages by a master. After some time, a journeyman could become a master himself by making a masterpiece—a piece of work worthy of a master. If masters of the journeyman's guild approved his masterpiece, the journeyman could open his own shop. He was then a guild member. Some girls also served as apprentices.

The rise of the middle class. In time, towns' guild members—merchants and master workers—became the **middle class.** They were between the class of nobles and that of peasants and unskilled workers. The middle class favored kings over nobles because kings could provide stable governments that would protect trade, business, and property. In turn, kings looked to the middle class for advice. They also gave members of the middle class jobs in government. In these ways, during the later Middle Ages the middle class started to gain power.

✔ **READING CHECK: Problem Solving** If you were a young person in the Middle Ages who wanted work, how might a guild help you? under the guild's guidance a young person could become an apprentice, a journeyman, and finally a master worker and member of the guild

Medieval Towns

In the Middle Ages, most northern and western European cities had fewer than 2,000 people. A few cities were larger. By the 1200s, for example, about 150,000 people lived in Paris. Growing commercial cities like London, Ghent, and Bruges had about 40,000 residents each.

Town life. Towns offered serfs a chance to improve their lives. Some serfs escaped to towns to gain freedom. Others were pushed off the land as farming methods changed. They moved to cities to find jobs. Serfs who stayed on the manors sold their crops in town markets. They paid the manor lord with money rather than with their labor.

In the Middle Ages, cities often stood on hilltops or lay along river bends. Such locations made cities easier to defend. Most cities had little land, so houses were built several stories high. Each story extended a little beyond the one below it. At their tops, the houses almost touched over the middle of the street, darkening the narrow roadway below. Cities also had large public buildings, including churches or cathedrals, town halls, and guild halls.

TEACH OBJECTIVE 3

ALL LEVELS: Copy the following chart on the chalkboard, omitting the italicized words.

The Decline of Serfdom	
Serfs could leave for towns.	
Serfs could earn money by selling crops to townspeople.	
Changing agricultural methods pushed them off the land.	
The Black Death killed many people in Europe so the demand for workers increased.	

Have students list factors that contributed to the decline of serfdom in the left column. Then ask the class rank the importance of each factor and write the result in the right column.

ENGLISH LANGUAGE LEARNERS, COOPERATIVE LEARNING

HOMEWORK Tell students to make a Venn diagram showing the similarities and differences between merchant and craft guilds.

CLOSE

Have students write diary entries like those survivors of the Black Death might write about their experiences during the plague.

SKILL-BUILDING STRATEGIES Using Maps to Analyze Historical Patterns

The Spread of the Black Death

Between 1347 and 1351, Europe and the Mediterranean world were devastated by the "Black Death"—a deadly plague. Carried from China along sea and overland trade routes, the Black Death quickly swept through Europe's population. By studying a map that illustrates the spread of the plague, we can develop conclusions regarding its effect on the civilization of the late Middle Ages.

Spread of the Black Death, 1347–1351

Skills Reminder

To use a map to analyze historical patterns, define the map's overall topic. Then identify the historical context of the map and the events or changes it is designed to illustrate. Connect the information on the map to the historical context of the subject. Analyze the change, trend, or pattern that is illustrated by the map and build a hypothesis to explain why it took place. Finally, determine how the map helps to show the change, pattern, or trend that came to represent a new historical reality.

Skills Practice

Study the map above and answer the following questions:
1. How was the plague carried from Marseille to North Africa? From Marseille to Paris?
2. Why might Paris have been stricken by the plague earlier than London but later than Constantinople?
3. Why might the plague have been slower to reach eastern Europe than it was to reach western and northern Europe?

Geography

Plagues are not a thing of the past. An outbreak of pneumonic plague—a more serious and almost always fatal form of the Black Death—hit western India in 1994, killing scores of people. Agencies such as the Centers for Disease Control track current outbreaks of such highly infectious diseases.

ACTIVITY: Have students search the library or computer software for more information on current outbreaks of infectious diseases. Then have them use the information to create maps that show the geographic distribution of plagues. Good sources of information include the World Health Organization and the Centers for Disease Control.

SKILLS PRACTICE ANSWERS

1. carried along shipping trade routes; carried on overland trade routes
2. The plague traveled west from China.
3. Ships traveled to more places than overland traders.

REVIEW

Have students complete the Section 3 Review on p. 330.

ASSESS

Have students complete Daily Quiz 14.3. As Alternative Assessment, you might have students make an outline of the section or use the serfdom chart in this lesson.

RETEACH

Have students complete Main Idea Activity for English Language Learners and Special-Needs Students 14.3. Then have students review the section by stating the main idea of each paragraph in a sentence. **ENGLISH LANGUAGE LEARNERS**

EXTEND

Have students write short skits depicting a serf's first day in a city such as Paris or London. Suggest students research first-person accounts as well as use information from the section.
BLOCK SCHEDULING

SECTION 3 REVIEW ANSWERS

① Define
- merchant guild, p. 327
- craft guilds, p. 328
- apprentice, p. 328
- journeyman, p. 328
- middle class, p. 328

② Identify
- Black Death, p. 330

③ Apprentice: trains five to ten years; Journeyman: paid wages, creates masterpiece; Master Worker: opens own shop, joins guild

④ a. Serfs and townspeople exempted from working on manors.

b. gave loans to members, aided widows and children, trained workers, cared for ill and elderly members

c. Serfs escaped to towns. Demand for workers grew as a result of the Black Death.

⑤ Reports should include: rights of townspeople, opportunities for serfs, easily defended locations, dark streets, wastes in gutters, fear of robbers, and the spread of disease.

The devastating plague of 1347 through 1351 was carried by flea-infested rats.

Analyzing Primary Sources

Drawing Conclusions What effect would such circumstances have on people's beliefs and morale? weaken faith, promote insecurity, and reduce morale

The Black Death. The growing cities of the Middle Ages could be exciting places. However, many were also dark, unsafe, dirty, and unhealthy. There were no streetlights or police. People did not go out alone at night for fear of robbers. Waste was dumped into open gutters. For that reason, diseases spread quickly through the crowded cities.

Beginning in 1347, one such disease, a terrible plague called the **Black Death,** swept through Europe. The plague began in Asia and spread along busy trade routes. It entered ports by way of trading ships. Black rats on the ships carried the disease. The plague was spread to people by bites from fleas on the rats.

No one knows the exact number of plague deaths in Europe. They happened so rapidly and in such great numbers that often survivors could not keep up with burying the dead.

History Makers Speak
❝They died by the hundreds, both day and night, and all were thrown in . . . ditches and covered with earth. And as soon as those ditches were filled, more were dug. And I buried my five children with my own hands.❞

Angolo di Tura, quoted in *The Black Death,* by Robert S. Gottfried

Some entire villages and towns were wiped out. By some estimates, about 25 million people died in Europe from 1347 to 1351—about one-third of the entire population.

The Black Death caused many changes in Europe. People's faith in God was shaken. The church lost some of its power and importance. Relations between the upper classes and lower classes changed. Workers, now in short supply, demanded higher wages. In several European countries, peasants staged uprisings.

✔ **READING CHECK: Analyzing Information** What role did towns and cities begin to play in the lives of serfs? offered serfs a chance to improve their lives

---

SECTION 3 REVIEW

1. **Define** and explain the significance:
   merchant guild
   craft guilds
   apprentice
   journeyman
   middle class

2. **Identify** and explain the significance:
   Black Death

3. **Sequencing** Copy the flowchart below. Use it to show the sequence of steps required to become a guild member.

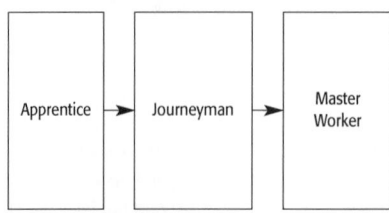

Apprentice → Journeyman → Master Worker

4. Finding the Main Idea

   a. How would the rights won by townspeople help break down manorialism?
   b. How did merchant and craft guilds help their members?
   c. How did the growth of towns and the Black Death lead to the decline of serfdom?

5. Writing and Critical Thinking

   Categorizing Write a short report that gives the advantages and disadvantages of living in a medieval city.
   Consider:
   • the rights of townspeople
   • health and safety factors
   • opportunities for work

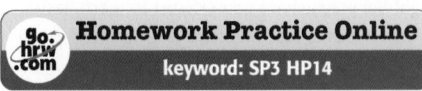

Homework Practice Online
keyword: SP3 HP14

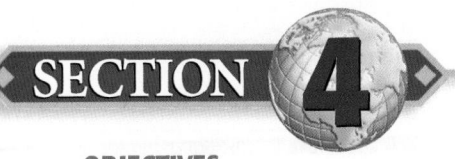
OBJECTIVES

1 Analyze changes in language and literature during the Middle Ages.

2 Examine changes in education during the Middle Ages.

3 Identify developments made in philosophy and science.

4 Describe the characteristic architecture of the later Middle Ages.

🔊 *LET'S GET STARTED!*

As students enter the classroom, write these words on the chalkboard: *culture, educate, language, literature,* and *romance.* Tell students to find each word's origin in the dictionary. *(All originated with Latin words.)* Explain that Latin was the language of educated people during the early Middle Ages. Tell students that in Section 4 they will learn how spoken languages such as Middle English became part of European literature.

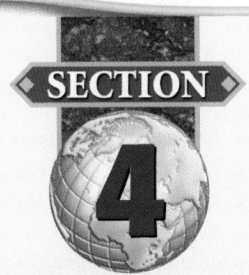

SECTION 4

READ TO DISCOVER

❶ How did languages and literature change during the Middle Ages?

❷ In what ways did education change?

❸ What developments were made in philosophy and science?

❹ What kind of architecture characterized the later Middle Ages?

DEFINE

vernacular languages
troubadours
scholasticism

IDENTIFY

Dante Alighieri
Geoffrey Chaucer
Peter Abelard
Thomas Aquinas
Gothic

▶ **WHY IT MATTERS TODAY**

Styles of architecture continue to change today, just as they did during the Middle Ages. Use CNNstudentNews.com or other **current event** sources to find examples of recent buildings designed in new styles. Record your findings in your journal.

CNNstudentNews.com

Life and Culture in the Middle Ages

The Main Idea
Much of medieval European life and culture centered on the Christian church and faith.

The Story Continues *"There was a knight, a most distinguished man, / Who from the day on which he first began / To ride abroad had followed chivalry, / Truth, honour, generousnous, and courtesy."* Early civilizations arose only after humans had settled in towns and cities. In much the same way, medieval culture—as shown in the lines of poetry above—could flourish once city life regained importance.

Language and Literature

Throughout the Middle Ages, European culture underwent many changes. Some of these changes took place in language and literature. Since the collapse of the Roman Empire, Latin had remained the written and spoken language of educated people in western Europe. However, people with little education spoke **vernacular languages.** These languages were everyday speech that varied from place to place. Present-day French, Italian, and Spanish came from early vernacular languages that were related to Latin. Present-day English and German came from other vernacular languages.

This manuscript from the 1200s shows a traveling singer performing.

SECTION 4 RESOURCES

REPRODUCIBLE RESOURCES
▶ Guided Reading Strategy 14.4
▶ Creative Teaching Strategy 14

TECHNOLOGY RESOURCES
▶ One-Stop Planner 14.4
▶ Holt Researcher: World History: Geoffrey Chaucer
▶ World History and Cultures Video Program 11
▶ Homework Practice Online

REINFORCEMENT, REVIEW, AND ASSESSMENT
▶ Section 4 Review, p. 335
▶ Daily Quiz 14.4
▶ Main Idea Activity 14.4
▶ English Audio Summary 14.4
▶ Spanish Audio Summary 14.4

TEACH OBJECTIVE 1

![clock icon] **LEVEL 1:** On the chalkboard, copy the following chart, omitting the italicized words. Help students identify the kinds of literature described in the middle column of the chart and give an example from the text.

ENGLISH LANGUAGE LEARNERS

Vernacular Literature in the Middle Ages		
Kind of Literature	**Characteristics**	**Example**
troubadour songs	poems about love and chivalry	*love songs*
romances	fictional stories, sometimes of heroes	*King Arthur and his Knights of the Round Table*
fabliaux	short comic stories written in rhymed verse	"Reynard the Fox"
national epic	long poem about a hero	The Song of Roland
miracle, morality, and mystery plays	short dramas with religious or Biblical themes	"Noah's Flood"

History Maker

DANTE ALIGHIERI. Dante first saw Beatrice when they were both nine years old. His love for her was the purely spiritual *amor amicitiae,* defined by St. Thomas Aquinas as a love in which the beloved "is loved in love of friendship . . . simply and for its own sake." Beatrice was most likely Beatrice Portinari, who wed Simone de' Bardi at age 22 and died in 1290.

Dante later married another woman but never stopped loving Beatrice. After Dante's enemies exiled him from Florence in 1302, he wrote of Beatrice as his guide through Paradise in *The Divine Comedy.*

ACTIVITY: Have students find a translation of *The Divine Comedy* at the library and look for passages about Beatrice. Ask them to note what attributes the ideal woman had in the Middle Ages.

Holt Researcher

go.hrw.com
KEYWORD: Holt Researcher
FreeFind: Geoffrey Chaucer
After reading more about Geoffrey Chaucer on the Holt Researcher, identify some of the universal themes in his works that still make them relevant today.

Analyzing Primary Sources

Identifying a Point of View How does the author of the epic poem portray Roland? heroic, heedless of pain, courageous

Dante's The Divine Comedy *masterpiece describes an imaginary journey in which he is guided through heaven by Beatrice, a woman he loves in a spiritual way.*

Early vernacular literature. During the Middle Ages writers began to use vernacular languages in their works. Troubadours' songs were one of the first forms of vernacular literature. **Troubadours** were traveling singers who wrote poems about love and chivalry. They sang their love poems in castles and in towns.

Romances, or fictional stories, written in vernacular were popular with medieval audiences. The best-known English romances were the adventures of King Arthur and his Knights of the Round Table.

Also popular were the French *fabliaux* (FA·blee·oh). These were short comic stories written in rhymed verse. The *fabliaux* laughed at the high ideals of chivalry, human foolishness, and the clergy. Animal stories, or fables, such as "Reynard the Fox," delighted medieval audiences too.

Another kind of vernacular literature was the national epic—a long poem about a hero. France's national epic was *The Song of Roland,* written in about 1100. The poem is set during the period of Charlemagne's wars with the Moors. It describes the death of Roland, one of Charlemagne's brave, loyal knights.

❝Roland with pain and anguish winds
His Olifant [horn], and blows with all his might.
Blood from his mouth comes spurting scarlet-bright.
He's burst the veins of his temples outright.
From hand and horn the call goes shrilling high:
King Carlon [Charlemagne] hears it who through
**   the passes rides . . .**
Quoth Charles: 'I hear the horn of Roland cry!
He'd never sound it but in the thick of fight.❞

From *The Song of Roland*

Drama written in vernacular languages also developed during the Middle Ages. Miracle plays, morality plays, and mystery plays were short dramas with religious or biblical themes. At Christmas and Easter, the plays were sometimes part of church services. Later, as towns grew, they were also presented in town marketplaces. A favorite play was *Noye's Fludde,* "Noah's Flood."

The flowering of vernacular literature. During the Middle Ages vernacular literature reached its height in the works of two great medieval writers, **Dante Alighieri** and **Geoffrey Chaucer.** Dante Alighieri, commonly known simply as Dante, was born in the region of Tuscany, Italy, in 1265. He wrote his poems using the Tuscan form of Italian. People throughout Italy read Dante's works. In that way, the Tuscan dialect became Italy's written language. Today Dante is thought of by many historians and other scholars as the father of the Italian language.

Many readers consider *The Divine Comedy* to be Dante's greatest work of literature. In the course of this remarkable creative piece, Dante takes an imaginary journey through the three realms where a Christian soul might go after death. The three scenes of Dante's narrative include hell, purgatory, and heaven. The author placed his friends and supporters in heaven and his political enemies in hell. Dante used his descriptive narrative to point out the faults that he saw in Italian society.

TEACH OBJECTIVE 2

LEVEL 3: Have students write a short paper in which they describe whether or not they think a university such as those in Paris or Oxford in the 1300s would provide an education appropriate for today's students. Have them give reasons for their answers.

TEACH OBJECTIVE 3

ALL LEVELS: Write the following on the chalkboard: *Thomas Aquinas argued that science and reason were in conflict with faith.* Organize students in groups and tell the groups to decide whether

they agree or disagree with Thomas Aquinas. Have each group explain its decision. **ENGLISH LANGUAGE LEARNERS, COOPERATIVE LEARNING**

HOMEWORK Have students find illustrations of two technical improvements or innovations of the Middle Ages. (*winches, pulleys, oxen plows, oxen yokes, windmills, waterwheels*) Tell them to write a paragraph explaining how these advances made life easier.

Geoffrey Chaucer's writing and imagination had a great influence on literary styles and approaches. Chaucer was born in England about 1340 and spent much of his life in service to the English crown. He fought in France and, for about 10 years, served as a diplomat throughout western Europe. He was elected to the English Parliament in 1386.

Chaucer's most famous work is *The Canterbury Tales*, a group of stories told from the point of view of about 30 pilgrims traveling to the shrine of Saint Thomas à Becket at Canterbury. Chaucer's pilgrims poke fun at English society, especially at the clergy. Many church people, Chaucer believed, had made service to the church a profitable occupation rather than a spiritual calling.

Chaucer wrote numerous works in addition to *The Canterbury Tales.* Like Dante before him, Chaucer wrote in the vernacular, in the dialect known as Middle English, a forerunner to the modern English of today. Chaucer's use of the dialect and the popularity of his works gave Middle English great literary prestige. Later writers and poets followed his example by crafting their works in the vernacular.

Pilgrims in a scene from The Canterbury Tales

✔ **READING CHECK: Summarizing** What important changes took place in language and literature in the Middle Ages? Why? The more widely spoken and written vernacular languages began to replace Latin.

Education

During the early Middle Ages, few people received an education. Those who did were mainly nobles and the clergy. Schooling was carried out at monasteries and in churches. As towns grew larger, however, other schools opened. These schools were somewhat like the schools in Athens under Plato and Aristotle. A teacher would set up a school and try to attract students. He admitted any males who wanted to study and could pay a fee.

In time, teachers and students united to form guilds to protect and gain rights for themselves. Such a guild was called a *universitas,* Latin for "association of people." Later, the word *university* came into use.

Between the late 1000s and the late 1200s, four great universities developed. The universities in Paris and at Oxford in England were best known for teaching theology, the study of religious beliefs, as well as the liberal arts—Latin, logic, rhetoric, mathematics, astronomy, and music. Students at the University of Bologna in Italy studied civil law and church law. The University at Salerno taught medicine.

A lecturer teaches at a medieval university.

By the end of the 1400s, many more universities had opened throughout Europe. By that time, all universities had the same programs. Students had to pass certain stages of study before receiving their degrees. The first degree was the bachelor of arts, which was similar to finishing an apprenticeship in a craft guild. After more studying and tests, students could receive the master of arts degree. At that point, students were admitted to the guild of teaching. Some students then went on to study law, medicine, or theology.

✔ **READING CHECK: Comparing** How were medieval universities like guilds? organized like guilds to protect and gain rights for themselves, trained people

In the 1200s the English monk Roger Bacon used detailed observation and controlled experiments to understand the natural world. He also predicted technological innovations in the future: "Machines may be made by which the largest ships, with only one man steering them, will move faster than if they were filled with rowers; wagons may be built which will move with unbelievable speed and without the aid of beasts." Have students research Roger Bacon's experiments and compare his methods to the scientific method used today.

Daily Life

Philosophers were not the only ones reading during the Middle Ages. Many noble households had collections of books, although the typical library was small.

The small number is understandable since ordering books was an expensive process. A new prayer book, for example, required purchasing more than 200 sheets of vellum—paper made from lambskin—and hiring a scribe at a university to copy the text. In addition to religious works, noble families owned romances and cookbooks.

ACTIVITY: Have students copy a paragraph from their textbook in neat print. Then ask them to discuss the drawbacks of having to write each copy of a book by hand and to reflect on changes after the introduction of the printing press.

HISTORY MAKER

Thomas Aquinas (c. 1224–1274)

Thomas Aquinas was one of the greatest scholars of the Middle Ages. His *Summa Theologiae* is among the most important works of the medieval religious philosophy known as scholasticism.

Aquinas, a Dominican friar, became the official philosopher of the medieval church. He argued that science and reason were in conflict with faith. One of his most famous arguments was his rational proof of the existence of God. Aquinas's approach to logic was based in part upon the ideas of Aristotle and of several Arab thinkers. **How did Thomas Aquinas's faith affect his scholarly work?**

Philosophy and Science

Muslim scholars had kept the works of Greek and Roman philosophers and scientists alive. During the Middle Ages, this knowledge was passed on to Europeans.

Philosophy. Medieval European philosophers tried to make Aristotle's ideas work with those of early church writers. Aristotle placed the most importance on human reason. For the church writers, however, faith was most important. This attempt to bring together faith and reason is called **scholasticism.**

Peter Abelard, an important philosopher of scholasticism, taught in Paris in the 1100s. Abelard wrote a book called *Sic et Non* ("Yes and No"), which raised many questions about the church's teachings. In it he included quotations from the Bible, statements from popes, and writings of church philosophers. Abelard showed that many of them conflicted with one another.

Probably the greatest medieval philosopher was **Thomas Aquinas,** a monk of the Dominican order. His principal work, *Summa Theologiae,* summarized medieval Christian thought.

Science. Few advances were made in science during the Middle Ages. The Bible and the church were the main sources for information about the world. Only two subjects received serious attention: mathematics and optics, the study of light. Europeans did make some technical advances that helped with everyday life, however. They designed better winches and pulleys to make lifting and pulling heavy objects easier. They made iron plows and better oxen yokes to make farming easier. Europeans also began to use windmills and waterwheels, inventions for drawing water that had been invented in Asia.

✔ **READING CHECK: Making Generalizations** How did religion affect philosophy and science during the Middle Ages? Philosophy and science were studied in the context of religious faith.

Architecture

During the Middle Ages, church architecture was the main art form. Between about 1000 and about 1150, most architects followed the Romanesque style of architecture. They used arches, domes, vaults, and low horizontal lines in their churches. This style was like that used in the Roman Empire. A Romanesque church had a heavy domed stone roof. To support the roof, the walls were low with few windows. As a result, these churches were very dark inside.

During the mid-1100s, master builders developed a different style of church architecture. Many people did not like the new style and called it **Gothic** after the barbarian Goths. Gothic churches had tall spires. On the outside walls, builders placed rows of supporting structures called flying buttresses. The flying buttresses were connected to the church's walls with arches and carried part of the roof's weight. The church's walls could therefore be high and thin. Everything in Gothic churches—pointed arches, tall spires, and high walls—reached toward heaven.

Large stained-glass windows were set in the high walls. They filled the inside of the churches with light. Statues of the holy family, saints, and rulers lined the inside of Gothic churches, and relief sculptures adorned the walls.

The Gothic church was an example of how life had changed in the later Middle Ages. This tall building towered above the growing town around it. Traders did business in the marketplace near its walls. Religious plays were presented within and

REVIEW
Have students complete the Section 4 Review on p. 335.

ASSESS
Have students complete Daily Quiz 14.4. As Alternative Assessment, you may want to use the summarizing graphic organizer or the point of view exercise at the end of this section.

RETEACH
Have students complete Main Idea Activity for English Language Learners and Special-Needs Students 14.4. Then have students make an outline of this section using the headings as main ideas. **ENGLISH LANGUAGE LEARNERS**

EXTEND
Tell students to imagine they are troubadours who will perform a poem in the court of an important noble. Have them research one of the medieval ideals of chivalry or courtly love and write the poem. **COOPERATIVE LEARNING, BLOCK SCHEDULING**

INTERPRETING THE VISUAL RECORD

Cathedral of Notre Dame in Paris The Cathedral of Notre Dame is a good example of Gothic architecture. Its high walls hold large stained-glass windows. Flying buttresses support the walls. *When looking at this cathedral, in what direction are the viewer's eyes pulled—up, down, or sideways? Why is this so?*

VISUAL RECORD ANSWER
up; height of the walls, narrow arches and windows

SECTION 4 REVIEW ANSWERS

① Define
- vernacular languages, p. 331
- troubadours, p. 332
- scholasticism, p. 334

② Identify
- Dante Alighieri, p. 332
- Geoffrey Chaucer, p. 332
- Peter Abelard, p. 334
- Thomas Aquinas, p. 334
- Gothic, p. 334

③ Language and Literature: literature in vernacular languages; Education: great universities; Architecture: style changed to Gothic

④ a. Dante wrote in Tuscan, which became the dominant Italian language; Chaucer wrote in Middle English, was emulated by later writers

b. philosophers tried to bring faith and reason together in scholasticism; the Bible and church were sources of scientific information; church architecture main art form

⑤ Students' outlines should reflect medieval culture and use of the vernacular.

outside it. The highest artistic skills of the medieval world went into the building of this monument to God.

Gothic cathedrals were constructed in many parts of Europe, including France, England, and Germany. One of the earliest of these magnificent structures, begun in about 1140, was the abbey of Saint-Denis in Paris. Construction of the towering cathedral of Notre Dame, also in Paris, began in the early 1160s and continued in stages for about a century thereafter.

✔ **READING CHECK: Contrasting** How did the Romanesque and Gothic styles of church architecture differ from each other? dark, low walls, heavy domes versus towering, light, spacious

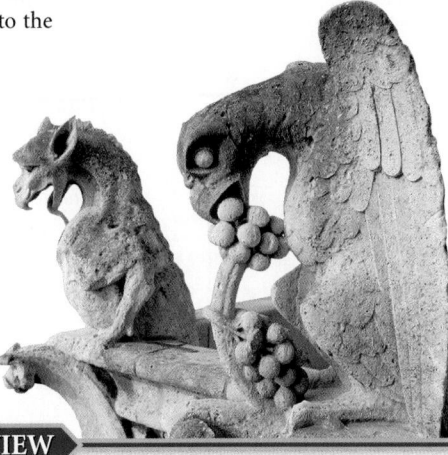

These gargoyles are found on the exterior of the Cathedral of Notre Dame.

SECTION 4 REVIEW

1. **Define** and explain the significance:
   vernacular languages
   troubadours
   scholasticism

2. **Identify** and explain the significance:
   Dante Alighieri
   Geoffrey Chaucer
   Peter Abelard
   Thomas Aquinas
   Gothic

3. **Summarizing** Copy the web diagram below. Use it to list ways in which language and literature, education, and architecture changed during the Middle Ages.

   Language and Literature

   Changes in Late Middle Ages

   Architecture   Education

4. **Finding the Main Idea**
   a. How did the writings of Dante and Chaucer reflect the history of the cultures in which they were produced?
   b. How did the church and religion influence medieval philosophy, science, and architecture?

5. **Writing and Critical Thinking**
   Making Generalizations Write an outline for a drama that might have been performed during the Middle Ages.
   Consider:
   - how medieval dramas reflected the culture of the times
   - how vernacular language influenced them

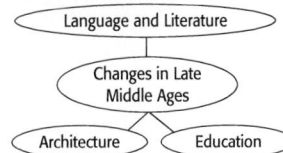
Homework Practice Online
keyword: SP3 HP14

THE HIGH MIDDLE AGES **335**

SECTION 5

OBJECTIVES

1 Identify how the Hundred Years' War affected England and France.

2 Analyze how Spain's rulers both strengthened and weakened their nation.

3 Explain why the Holy Roman Empire remained weak throughout the later Middle Ages.

LET'S GET STARTED!

As students enter the classroom, tell them to scan the section for dates. Have them arrange the dates on a time line leaving space beside each year. Tell students that in Section 5 they will learn about events that united nations during the period on their time line.

SECTION 5

READ TO DISCOVER

❶ How did the Hundred Years' War affect England and France?

❷ How did Spain's rulers both strengthen and weaken their nation?

❸ Why did the Holy Roman Empire remain weak throughout the later Middle Ages?

IDENTIFY

Hundred Years' War
War of the Roses
Henry Tudor
Joan of Arc
Louis XI
Ferdinand
Isabella
Habsburg

WHY IT MATTERS TODAY

England and France have continued to be rivals at certain times but allies at others. Use or other **current event** sources to find out how these two nations, along with other western European countries, have attempted to work together economically in recent years. Record your findings in your journal.

CNN Student News.com

Wars and the Growth of Nations

The Main Idea
The late Middle Ages saw the development of individual nations united under strong monarchs.

The Story Continues *Americans today fly the American flag and sing the national anthem to show their patriotism, or feeling of loyalty to their country. Under feudalism in the early Middle Ages, people of a country did not feel any such loyalty. This would change during the later Middle Ages, however, as states began to form and kings began to build their kingdoms as organized nations.*

England

By the late Middle Ages, England's feudal lords had lost much of their power to its king. The new class of townspeople supported a strong king. A single system of law and courts and a larger army of soldiers helped strengthen the king. In addition, as the country prospered, more taxes were paid to the king.

In the early 1300s the English king Edward III also held land in France. This made him a vassal of the French king. This fact helped lead to a series of conflicts between England and France called the **Hundred Years' War** (1337–1453).

The Hundred Years' War. In 1328 the last male member of France's Capetian dynasty died. Edward III claimed the French throne. The French assembly chose Philip VI, the Count of Flanders, as king instead. In 1337 Edward brought an army to Flanders, hoping to gain control of this rich trading area.

Thus the Hundred Years' War began. It continued for 116 years as a series of raids and battles. Sometimes there were long periods of uneasy peace. England won many battles but lost the war. By 1453 France controlled all of England's French lands except Calais.

The Hundred Years' War saw the use of new weapons in Europe. At the Battle of Agincourt (AJ·uhn·kohrt) in 1415, English foot soldiers used longbows. With these bows they could fire arrows quickly, hitting targets up to 200 yards away. French knights on horseback were no match for the English and their

INTERPRETING THE VISUAL RECORD

The longbow The six-foot longbow and its three-foot arrows, accurate over a range of 200 yards, helped the English defeat the French at Agincourt. *How does this illustration suggest that longbows were important in battle?*

TEACH OBJECTIVE 1

LEVEL 1: Make a chart on the board titled *Effects of the Hundred Years' War* and work with students to list its effects on England and on France. *(England lost all its French lands except Calais; knightly warfare was weakened by the use of longbows, cannons, and gunpowder; Parliament gained more power over the king. France: English soldiers robbed the French people and destroyed their property; the French starved even during peacetime; the French king became more powerful.)*

ENGLISH LANGUAGE LEARNERS

longbows. Both the English and the French used gunpowder and cannons in battle. Castles no longer provided protection for a feudal lord because one powerful cannon blast could break through a castle's wall. Longbows, gunpowder, and cannons further weakened knightly warfare.

Besides loss of life and land, the Hundred Years' War had another important effect on England. Parliament, particularly the House of Commons, gained more power over the king. Members of the House of Commons were angry about the way the war was going. They won the right of a special council to advise the king and the right to consider new taxes before they were discussed by the House of Lords. By the late 1300s, the king needed Parliament's consent on all special taxes.

The War of the Roses. Shortly after the Hundred Years' War ended, a war for England's throne began. In 1455 the York and Lancaster families started the **War of the Roses.** The white rose was the badge of the House of York. The red rose was used by the House of Lancaster. In 1485 **Henry Tudor** of the House of Lancaster won the war. He defeated King Richard III of York. However, Henry married a daughter from the House of York. As King Henry VII, he set up a strong monarchy in England once again.

✔ **READING CHECK: Identifying Cause and Effect** Why did the Hundred Years' War begin and what were its results? English claims to the French throne; France won all English lands in France except Calais

France

During the Hundred Years' War, France suffered more than England because the war took place on French soil. Bands of English soldiers robbed the people and destroyed their property. Even during times of peace, the French people starved.

History Makers Speak
❝And in truth when good weather came, in April, those who in the winter had made their beverages from apples and sloe plums emptied the residue of their apples and their plums into the street with the intention that the pigs of St. Antoine would eat them. But the pigs did not get to them in time, for as soon as they were thrown out, they were seized by poor folk, women and children, who ate them with great relish, . . . for they ate what the pigs scorned to eat, they ate the cores of cabbages without bread or without cooking, grasses of the fields without bread or salt.❞

Quoted in J.B. Ross and M.M. McLaughlin, eds., *The Portable Medieval Reader*

A fight for the throne. During the Hundred Years' War, a fight for power broke out within the royal family. The House of Burgundy sided with the English against the House of Orléans, preventing France from uniting against the English. Finally in 1429, with the help of a young girl named **Joan of Arc,** Charles VII of Orléans was crowned king of France. The French backed their king and drove the English out.

France and the Hundred Years' War, 1337–1453

[Map showing England, France, and surrounding regions with battle sites: Sluis 1340, Calais 1347, Agincourt 1415, Crécy-en-Ponthieu 1346, Harfleur 1415, Rouen, Reims, Paris, Verneuil 1424, Orléans 1429, Bourges, Dijon, Poitiers 1356, Bordeaux, Castillon 1453. Regions: ENGLAND, FLANDERS, NORMANDY, BRITTANY, CHAMPAGNE, HOLY ROMAN EMPIRE, BURGUNDY, AQUITAINE, GASCONY, PROVENCE, SPAIN. Bodies of water: English Channel, Bay of Biscay, MEDITERRANEAN SEA, Rhine River, Seine River, Loire River, Rhône River, Garonne River.]

Territory held in 1430 by:
- France
- England
- Burgundy
- ☼ French victory
- ☼ English victory

Interpreting Maps Until 1429 the English had won the major battles of the Hundred Years' War.

■ **Skills Assessment:**
1. Places and Regions Which of the three powers represented by the map held the least amount of physical territory?
2. Finding the Main Idea What battle marked the end of the Hundred Years' War, and who was the victor?

Government

In 1381 English peasants staged a revolt. Sir John Froissart, a French historian, reported:

"Many in the city of London envious of the rich and noble . . . said among themselves that the country was badly governed, and that the nobility had seized upon all the gold and silver. These wicked Londoners, therefore, began to . . . show signs of rebellion; they also invited all those who held like opinions in the adjoining counties to come to London; . . . in number about 60,000, were brought to London, under command of Wat Tyler . . . a bad man and a great enemy to the nobility."

Critical Thinking

Ask students to identify the bias of Froissart and to support their answer with examples.

ANSWER: Froissart is biased in favor of the nobility. He shows little sympathy for the rebels by calling them "wicked" and their leader "a bad man."

ALL LEVELS: Organize the class into two groups and plan a panel discussion. Have the members of one group defend the actions of Isabella and Ferdinand from 1479 to 1515. Ask the students in the other group to criticize the rulers' policies.
ENGLISH LANGUAGE LEARNERS, COOPERATIVE LEARNING

HOMEWORK Assign each student one of the following people: Edward III, Philip VI, Richard III, Henry VII, Joan of Arc, Charles VII, Louis XI, Ferdinand II, or Maximilian I. Have students research their assigned person to find answers to these questions: What did the person try to accomplish? How did the person influence his or her nation? Then ask students to share their information with the class.

HISTORY MAKER ANSWER
led French troops to victory at Orléans, became symbol of French patriotism

MAP ANSWERS
1. Castile, Aragon
2. Spain and Portugal

---

internet connect

TOPIC: Rulers
GO TO: go.hrw.com
KEYWORD: SP3 WH14

Have students access the Internet through the HRW Go site to find information about the monarchies of Henry VII, Louis XI, and Ferdinand and Isabella of Spain. Ask students to decide in their opinion which of these rulers developed the strongest monarchy. Then have them create a chart of that monarch's accomplishments. Ask volunteers to present their charts to the class and explain why they chose the ruler they did.

HISTORY MAKER

**Joan of Arc
(c. 1412–1431)**

Joan of Arc, the "Maid of Orléans," is a revered figure in French history. Believing that God spoke to her through visions, Joan left home to aid the French king, Charles VII, in his struggle against the English. Her strong faith persuaded thousands to follow her into battle. Her most crucial test came when the teenage Joan led French troops to victory against the English at Orléans.

A short time later, Joan was captured by English troops. She was accused of heresy, tortured, and burned at the stake. Today Joan of Arc is a Catholic saint and a symbol of French patriotism. **What was Joan of Arc's role in building the nation of France?**

Holt Researcher

go.hrw.com
KEYWORD: Holt Researcher
FreeFind: Joan of Arc
After reading more about Joan of Arc on the Holt Researcher, create a cause-and-effect chart showing how her religious faith influenced her actions, which ultimately affected political events in France.

A return of strong kings. During the Hundred Years' War, the French Estates General controlled finances and passed laws. This representative assembly was similar to the English Parliament. It took its name from the groups that assembled for its meetings: clergy (First Estate), nobles (Second Estate), and common people (Third Estate). After the war, however, the Estates General lost some of its power.

In 1461 **Louis XI** followed Charles VII as king of France. Louis made the French monarchy even stronger. He set up a harsh but efficient government with high taxes. Through diplomacy and scheming, he seized the lands of the House of Burgundy. Under Louis, France became a united country. As in England, French feudal lords lost much power to their king. They kept many rights, however, and remained wealthy and important until the mid-1700s. French peasants, unlike those in England, gained little freedom. They still owed services to the manor and its lord.

✔ **READING CHECK: Supporting a Point of View** How would you support the view that France grew as a nation after the Hundred Years' War? Feudal lords lost power to the king, who unified France under royal control

Spain

Spain became a united nation in 1479 under **Ferdinand** of Aragon and **Isabella** of Castile. In 1492 the Spanish army captured Granada, the last stronghold of the Moors, or Muslims, in Spain. In 1515 Ferdinand and Isabella added the kingdom of Navarre to their territory. Ferdinand and Isabella took powers away from church courts and from the nobles. Fervent Catholics, they did not look kindly on non-Christians in Spain. In 1492 they ordered all Jews to become Christians or leave Spain. Later, they gave the Moors the same choice. Most Jews and Moors did leave the country. As a result, Spain was robbed of many of its leaders in industry and trade.

The Unification of Spain, 1479–1515

Interpreting Maps
Four kingdoms on the Iberian Peninsula were united to form Spain.

■ **Skills Assessment:**
1. **The World in Spatial Terms** Which kingdom was largest? Which was second largest?
2. **Sequencing** By 1515, what two nations were on the Iberian Peninsula?

Legend:
- United by Ferdinand and Isabella, 1479
- Conquered by Spain, 1492
- Acquired by Spain, 1515

TEACH OBJECTIVE 3

LEVEL 3: Have students create a flowchart showing the rise of the Habsburgs. Refer them to material under "The Holy Roman Empire" for steps in the chart.

A Habsburg was elected emperor in 1273.

→

The Habsburgs used their position to arrange marriages with powerful families.

Through marriage the Habsburg family gained control of Austria and nearby lands.

→

More well-planned marriages gave the Habsburgs control of much of the empire's territory.

The Habsburgs became the most powerful family in Europe.

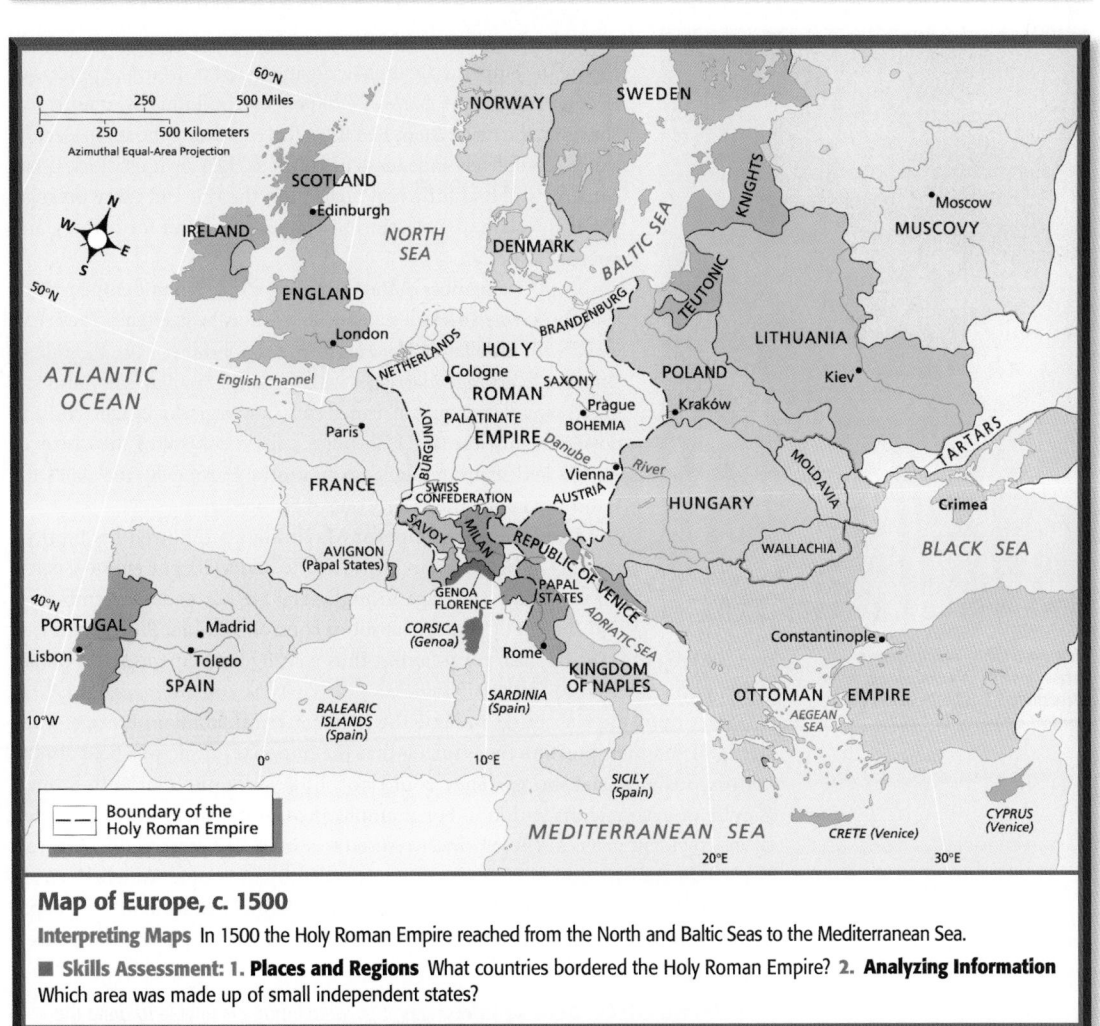

Map of Europe, c. 1500

Interpreting Maps In 1500 the Holy Roman Empire reached from the North and Baltic Seas to the Mediterranean Sea.

■ **Skills Assessment: 1. Places and Regions** What countries bordered the Holy Roman Empire? **2. Analyzing Information** Which area was made up of small independent states?

Global Relations

Several emperors attempted to reunite the Holy Roman Empire in the Middle Ages. Henry of Luxembourg, who became emperor in 1308, established control over many towns of Lombardy—the region surrounding Milan—by installing imperial vicars there.

When Henry marched to Rome, soldiers under the king of Naples blocked his path. Henry's repeated attempts to capture Florence, which led the Italian states, also failed. French and Italian kings sent their troops against him. In Italy Henry was viewed as a tyrant.

ACTIVITY: Have students create maps of Italy showing the cities that fought back against the emperor's soldiers.

✔ **READING CHECK: Comparing and Contrasting** How did Ferdinand and Isabella's policies both help and hurt Spain? gave Spain a strong monarchy but weakened business and trade through discrimination

The Holy Roman Empire

By the 1500s England, France, and Spain had each formed powerful nations. Germany and Italy, which made up the Holy Roman Empire, remained divided into states and regions ruled by princes and knights. Over time, the Holy Roman emperors had given up much of their power to these nobles in return for military support. Therefore the emperors lacked the power needed to exercise complete control.

In the early days the rulers of many German states, along with the pope, elected the Holy Roman emperor. Gradually the number who could vote for emperor decreased. Finally, by a decree issued in 1356, Emperor Charles IV ruled that only

This portrait by an unknown artist depicts the Habsburg ruler Maximilian I, who became Holy Roman emperor in 1493.

seven electors—three archbishops and four German princes—would choose the emperor. By thus removing the pope from the process of electing emperors, Charles IV hoped to rebuild his own authority. However, the new system had the effect of making the seven electors almost completely independent rulers in their own territories. The emperor still had little real power, but the title did carry prestige. For this reason, the election became an occasion for bribery and political favors.

In 1273 a member of the **Habsburg** family became emperor. The Habsburgs ruled a small state in what is now Switzerland. They were weak, with little land. The Habsburgs did, however, use the title of emperor to arrange marriages with powerful families. They also followed careful strategies of armed conquest to gradually win land and power. In this way, the Habsburgs gained control of the duchy of Austria and surrounding lands in central Europe. By the 1400s the Habsburg family was clearly one of Europe's rising stars.

The Habsburg emperor Maximilian I followed his family's strategy of marriage and conquest to add to its power and wealth. Maximilian's marriage brought The Netherlands, Luxembourg, and Burgundy under Habsburg control. His son, Philip, followed by marrying into the Spanish royal family, thus gaining large Spanish and Italian holdings for the Habsburgs.

Over time, the Habsburgs became the most powerful family in Europe. They strengthened their position by ensuring that the imperial throne was held almost continuously by Habsburgs. They could not, however, unite the Holy Roman Empire or even regions within it. For example, the German states were still ruled by independent princes. These princes refused to surrender power to the emperor. Nor could Italy be united. The Papal States, ruled by the pope, stretched across the middle of the Italian Peninsula. The geographic location of the Papal States effectively blocked efforts to bring all of Italy under centralized imperial control.

✔ **READING CHECK: Drawing Inferences** Why were emperors unable to unite the Holy Roman Empire? Independent princes in Germany and the pope in Italy refused to surrender power to the emperors.

SECTION 5 REVIEW

1. **Identify** and explain the significance:
   Hundred Years' War
   War of the Roses
   Henry Tudor
   Joan of Arc
   Louis XI
   Ferdinand
   Isabella
   Habsburg

2. **Summarizing** Copy the chart below. Use it to name important rulers in England, France, and Spain and to show how they united their nations.

England	France	Spain
↓	↓	↓
Ways Ruler United the Country		

3. **Finding the Main Idea**

   a. In what ways did the Hundred Years' War affect England and France differently?

   b. What happened in Spain in 1492 that changed the country's population?

4. **Writing and Critical Thinking**

   Analyzing Information Write a script for a newscast that describes the Battle of Agincourt and analyzes its importance.

   Consider:
   • the English use of the longbow
   • the French use of horses
   • the outcome of the battle

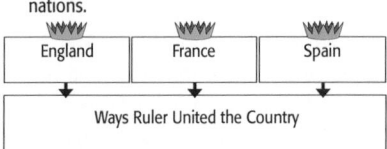

Homework Practice Online
keyword: SP3 HP14

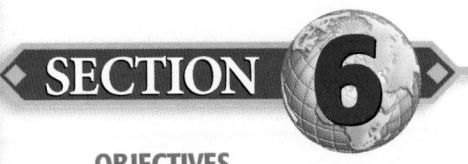

SECTION 6

OBJECTIVES

1 **Identify the factors that led to the decline of the Catholic Church in the later Middle Ages.**

2 **Describe how the Babylonian Captivity and the Great Schism affected the church.**

3 **Explain why great teachers and priests challenged the church during the later Middle Ages.**

🔔 *LET'S GET STARTED!*

As students enter the classroom, have them imagine they are screenwriters for a movie about the Catholic Church in the High Middle Ages. Encourage them to suggest ideas for scenes during the Crusades and the Black Death. Then ask them how they think their movie should end. Tell students that in Section 6 they will learn about the decline of the church's power near the end of the Middle Ages.

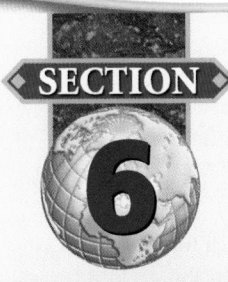

SECTION 6

READ TO DISCOVER

❶ What factors led to the decline of Catholic Church power during the late Middle Ages?

❷ How did the Babylonian Captivity and the Great Schism affect the church?

❸ Why did growing numbers of teachers and priests challenge the church during the later Middle Ages?

IDENTIFY

Babylonian Captivity
Great Schism
John Wycliffe
Jan Hus

▶ WHY IT MATTERS TODAY

Today the pope often tries to work with government leaders to improve the lives of their people. Use CNNStudentNews.com or other **current event** sources to find information about recent visits of the pope with world leaders. Record your findings in your journal.

CNN Student News.com

Challenges to Church Power

The Main Idea
During the late Middle Ages the Catholic Church lost some of its political power in many parts of Europe.

The Story Continues *A papal palace in France? Three men claiming to be pope? Europe was indeed changing. Kings were developing strong national governments with rich treasuries. Townspeople were increasing in number and importance. Such changes had to affect the one power that had unified medieval Europe—the church.*

Church Power Weakens

Innocent III was pope from 1198 to 1216. Under him the medieval papacy reached the height of its power. After Innocent, however, the worldly power of the church began to weaken. This happened for several reasons.

First, power was shifting. The kings of England, France, and Spain were forming strong governments. The increased number of townspeople gave them added importance too. Many felt that church laws limited their trade and industry. Also, people began to question some church practices. For example, they found fault with its great wealth, its method of raising money, and the worldly lives of some clergy members.

In 1294 a conflict arose between the pope and a monarch. After this conflict, King Philip IV of France ordered the clergy in France to pay taxes. This angered Pope Boniface VIII. In 1302 Boniface decreed that popes had power over worldly rulers.

Philip responded by calling the first-ever meeting of the Estates General. He wanted support against Boniface. Philip charged the pope with heresy and of selling jobs in the church. He also wanted a church council to put Boniface on trial. Philip then had his envoys in Rome take the pope prisoner. Although Boniface was quickly let go, he died soon after. For the next 100 years, the church continued to lose power.

✔ **READING CHECK: Analyzing Information** How did changes that were taking place in Europe help lead to the struggle between Philip IV and Boniface VIII? Power began shifting from the church to monarchs; people began to question church practices

This portrait shows Philip IV, sometimes called "Philip the Fair," and his family.

SECTION 6 RESOURCES

REPRODUCIBLE RESOURCES

▶ Guided Reading Strategy 14.6

▶ Readings in World History 44: The Papal Court at Avignon

TECHNOLOGY RESOURCES

▶ One-Stop Planner 14.6

▶ World History Teaching Transparency: Geography and History 14: The Great Schism

▶ Religions of the World Video Series: Christianity

▶ Homework Practice Online

REINFORCEMENT, REVIEW, AND ASSESSMENT

▶ Section 6 Review, p. 343

▶ Daily Quiz 14.6

▶ Main Idea Activity 14.6

▶ English Audio Summary 14.6

▶ Spanish Audio Summary 14.6

THE HIGH MIDDLE AGES **341**

341

TEACH OBJECTIVE 1

ALL LEVELS: Organize students into two groups to present arguments why the French clergy in 1300 should or should not pay taxes. **ENGLISH LANGUAGE LEARNERS**, **COOPERATIVE LEARNING**

TEACH OBJECTIVE 2

LEVEL 3: Have students write four cause-and-effect relationships about the Babylonian Captivity and the Great Schism. *(Example: cause—popes living in Avignon; effect—people thought French kings controlled the popes.)*

HOMEWORK Have students demonstrate how problem-solving techniques were used to end the Great Schism.

TEACH OBJECTIVE 3

LEVEL 1: Help the class complete the Venn diagram showing how John Wycliffe and Jan Hus were alike and different.

John Wycliffe | Jan Hus

- promoted English Bible
- royal court defended him
- banned, not executed
- teacher
- attacked church abuses
- accused of heresy
- angered clergy
- burned at the stake

Linking Past to Present

Perhaps no pope has more involved himself with bringing greater freedoms throughout the world than Pope John Paul II. His calls for peace and freedom have contributed to great political reform. He is considered an instrumental figure in the democratic changes in Poland and in the collapse of the Soviet Union.

More recently the pope visited Beirut, where he called for peaceful coexistence between Muslims and Christians, and Cuba, where he preached his message of love and solidarity.

ACTIVITY: Tell students to compare the role of the popes discussed in the section with that of John Paul II. Have students discuss the popes' effectiveness in promoting peace, freedom, and political reform.

The Babylonian Captivity and the Great Schism

After Boniface died, Philip had a French bishop elected pope. The new pope took the name Clement V. In 1309 Clement moved the headquarters of the church to Avignon, France. Until then, Rome had been the center of the church for 1,000 years. After Clement, the next six popes were French and lived in Avignon also.

The years that the popes lived in Avignon are called the **Babylonian Captivity** (1309–1377). The period was named for the time the ancient Hebrews were forced to live in Babylon, more than 1,800 years earlier. During the Babylonian Captivity, people in other countries lost respect for the church. They felt that the popes were being controlled by French kings.

In 1377 the French pope Gregory XI returned to Rome. A year later he died. Meeting in Rome, the cardinals elected an Italian pope to please local mobs, but later elected a French pope, who took up residence at Avignon. Until 1417 the church had two and sometimes three popes. This period of church history is called the **Great Schism** (SI·zuhm). The church was divided into opposing groups. For political reasons, each pope had the support of certain national rulers and their people and clergy.

Finally a church council met in Constance in 1414. Three years later, the Council of Constance ended the Great Schism. It removed the Italian and French popes; a third pope resigned. The council then elected a new Italian pope. It also suggested that other councils be held to correct church problems.

✔ **READING CHECK: Drawing Conclusions** How did the church become weaker during the Babylonian Captivity and the Great Schism? People lost respect for the church, and competition among opposing popes weakened papal and church authority.

More Problems for the Church

The Babylonian Captivity and Great Schism not only weakened the authority of the pope but they also increased criticism of the church. Some of this criticism came from within the church itself.

In 1324 two teachers at the University of Paris wrote *Defender of the Faith*. It claimed that the pope was the elected head of the church alone. He had no power over worldly rulers. It also stated that the church's power belonged with a council of clergy

INTERPRETING THE VISUAL RECORD

The Babylonian Captivity The popes had many enemies during the era known as the "Babylonian Captivity." The papal palace in Avignon was, in reality, a highly defensible fortress. It was built on land 190 feet above the town and surrounded by three miles of high, thick walls.

Link to Today Judging from this modern-day photograph, why might popes in Avignon have felt safe?

CLOSE

Have students draw a political cartoon illustrating a claim made in *Defender of the Faith*. Remind them to label the pictures and add a caption.

REVIEW

Have students complete the Section 6 Review on p. 343.

ASSESS

Have students complete Daily Quiz 14.6. As Alternative Assessment, you may want to use the cause-and-effect chart or Venn diagram exercise in this section's lessons.

RETEACH

Have students complete Main Idea Activity for English Language Learners and Special-Needs Students 14.6. Then have students work in pairs to list the people in the section, the actions of each, and how the actions affected the church.
ENGLISH LANGUAGE LEARNERS, COOPERATIVE LEARNING

EXTEND

Have students research and write a newspaper article about the actual trial of a heretic. Articles should contain standard grammar, spelling, sentence structure, and punctuation.
BLOCK SCHEDULING

and lay people. *Defender of the Faith* directly opposed the ideas in Pope Boniface's *Unam Sanctum*.

In the late 1300s **John Wycliffe** was a priest and teacher at Oxford University. Wycliffe attacked the wealth of the church and the immorality of some of its clergy. He also did not believe in the absolute power of the pope. Wycliffe wanted to replace the authority of the church, which he believed had been undermined, with that of the Bible. He held that individuals should be allowed to read and interpret scripture for themselves, without church intervention. This idea had great appeal among many Europeans who felt that the church and its clergy had surrendered spiritual authority. Wycliffe promoted the first translation of the Bible into English from Latin. English people could then read the Bible and

On July 6, 1415, Jan Hus was led to his death. He was burned alive at the stake for heresy.

decide for themselves what it meant. The church accused Wycliffe of being a heretic. The English royal court defended him. Because of this political support, unlike some other prominent heretics, Wycliffe was not executed. Instead he was banned from teaching and forced to retire. Wycliffe wrote to one duke: "I believe that in the end the truth will conquer."

Like many others in England and the rest of Europe, Jan Hus read Wycliffe's works. Hus was a religious reformer and teacher at the University of Prague. He also criticized abuses in the church. His attacks angered the clergy. Hus was excommunicated. In 1414 the Council of Constance declared him a heretic and ordered his death. He was burned at the stake the following year.

Despite the church's reaction to their ideas, Wycliffe and Hus would have a profound impact on many people. Their questioning of church authority set the stage for later reformers who would radically alter the history of the Christian church.

✔ **READING CHECK: Summarizing** Who was finding fault with the church in the 1300s and 1400s, and what changes did they suggest? reformers from within the church, such as John Wycliffe and Jan Hus; suggested translating Bible and eliminating church abuses

SECTION 6 REVIEW

1. **Identify** and explain the significance:
   Babylonian Captivity
   Great Schism
   John Wycliffe
   Jan Hus

2. **Sequencing** Copy the time line below. Use it to organize the events that weakened the power of the church from 1294 to 1417.

   |1300|1350|1400|1450|

3. **Finding the Main Idea**
   a. Why was the conflict between Philip IV and Boniface VIII the beginning of the weakening of church power in the late Middle Ages?
   b. According to the church's critics, where did the real power of the church come from?

4. **Writing and Critical Thinking**
   Analyzing Information Write the minutes of the meetings at the Council of Constance, which will be read at all Christian churches in Europe.
   Consider:
   • how the council ended the Great Schism
   • suggestions it made for the future of the church
   • how it dealt with Jan Hus

Homework Practice Online
keyword: SP3 HP14

◆ **SECTION** ◆
6 REVIEW ANSWERS

❶ **Identify**
• Babylonian Captivity, p. 342
• Great Schism, p. 342
• John Wycliffe, p. 343
• Jan Hus, p. 343

❷ 1294: Philip IV of France orders clergy to pay taxes; 1302: Pope Boniface declares papal power over worldly rulers; 1309: Pope Clement V moves headquarters to Avignon; 1378: cardinals elect two popes; 1378–1417: church has two, sometimes three popes

❸ **a.** first instance of a king with enough power to stand up to a pope and the church

b. a council of clergy and lay people

❹ Minutes should record that the council ended the Great Schism by removing two popes and electing a new one. They should also note that the council declared Jan Hus a heretic and sentenced him to death.

THE HIGH MIDDLE AGES **343**

REVIEW AND ASSESSMENT RESOURCES

REPRODUCIBLE RESOURCES

▸ Vocabulary Activity 14

TECHNOLOGY RESOURCES

▸ Chapter 14 Test Generator (on the One-Stop Planner)
▸ Global Skill Builder CD-ROM
▸ HRW Web Site

REINFORCEMENT, REVIEW, and ASSESSMENT

▸ Chapter 14 Review, pp. 344–345

▸ Chapter 14 Tutorial for Students, Parents, Mentors, and Peers
▸ Chapter 14 Test (Form A or B)
▸ Alternative Assessment Handbook
▸ Chapter 14 Test for English Language Learners and Special-Needs Students

REVIEW

Have students complete the Chapter 14 Review on pages 344–345.

ASSESS

Use one of the chapter tests to assess students' understanding of the content. For Alternative Assessment, see the Portfolio Activities and Alternative Assessment Handbook.

CHAPTER 14 REVIEW ANSWERS

Understanding Main Ideas

1. to recapture Holy Lands from the Turks

2. Kings grew stronger; new ideas changed culture; Italian cities became trading centers.

3. Europeans wanted Asian goods because of exposure during Crusades.

4. The domestic system developed to meet demand for goods; banks lent money and provided bills of exchange; investors wanted profits from increased trade.

5. Merchant and craft guilds formed and many serfs moved to towns.

6. Universities developed; scholars tried to bring together faith and logic in scholasticism; Romanesque church architecture gave way to Gothic.

7. Parliament gained more power over the king in England while the French king became stronger.

8. Ferdinand and Isabella united Spain, but the Holy Roman Empire remained divided in small states.

9. the conflict between the French king and the pope, the Babylonian Captivity, the Great Schism, and criticism from scholars

Reviewing Themes

1. Europeans were introduced to new ideas and goods when they traveled to the Middle East.

344

CHAPTER 14 Review

Creating a Time Line

Copy the time line below onto a sheet of paper. Complete the time line by filling in the events, individuals, and dates from the chapter that you think were significant. Pick three events and explain why you think they were significant.

| 1100 | 1200 | 1300 | 1400 | 1500 |

Writing a Summary

Using standard grammar, spelling, sentence structure, and punctuation, write an overview of the events in the chapter.

Identifying People and Ideas

Identify the following terms or individuals and explain their significance:

1. Urban II
2. Crusades
3. domestic system
4. craft guilds
5. vernacular languages
6. Dante Alighieri
7. scholasticism
8. Joan of Arc
9. Great Schism
10. John Wycliffe

Understanding Main Ideas

SECTION 1 *(pp. 318–322)*

The Crusades

1. Why did Europeans fight in the Crusades?
2. How did the Crusades affect the government, economy, and culture of Europe?

SECTION 2 *(pp. 323–326)*

The Revival of Trade

3. Why did trade begin again in Europe during the late Middle Ages?
4. How did the revival of trade help in the development of manufacturing, banking, and investing?

SECTION 3 *(pp. 327–330)*

The Growth of Towns

5. How did life for people in towns change in the late Middle Ages?

SECTION 4 *(pp. 331–335)*

Life and Culture in the Middle Ages

6. How did education, philosophy, and architecture change in the later Middle Ages?

SECTION 5 *(pp. 336–340)*

Wars and the Growth of Nations

7. How did the Hundred Years' War affect the governments of England and France?
8. Why did Spain become a strong nation and the Holy Roman Empire become weaker?

SECTION 6 *(pp. 341–343)*

Challenges to Church Power

9. What events led to the weakening of the church during the later Middle Ages?

Reviewing Themes

1. **Global Relations** How did the Crusades promote an exchange of ideas and goods?
2. **Economics** How did the growth of trade and towns bring changes to the feudal and manorial systems?
3. **Government** What groups lost power as Europe's kings established strong nations?

Thinking Critically

1. **Making Generalizations** How did the church influence life during the Middle Ages?
2. **Analyzing Information** How did trade, universities, and large churches help medieval towns grow?
3. **Comparing and Contrasting** In what ways were the development of strong central governments in England, France, and Spain alike and different?
4. **Summarizing** What were the main advances in literature during the later Middle Ages?

Writing About History

Comparing and Contrasting Medieval Europe evolved over centuries from the ruins of the Roman Empire. Compare and contrast the institutions of medieval Europe with the Roman Empire at its height. Use the compare-contrast diagram below to organize your thoughts before writing.

Roman Empire		Medieval Europe
	Government	
	Economy	
	Religion	
	Culture	
	Thought	

CLOSE

Have students choose a work of literature about or from the High Middle Ages. Ask them to select passages that describe an aspect of daily life and read those passages to the class.

RETEACH

Have students who had trouble with the test work in pairs. Ask them to outline the chapter. From the outline have the pair create flashcards and quiz each other on the chapter

content. Then have students take the Form B test to assess their mastery of the material.

ENGLISH LANGUAGE LEARNERS, **COOPERATIVE LEARNING**

Portfolio Extensions

Link to TODAY

1. Have students collect additional information on one of the Crusades. Then tell them to write a diary entry like one a crusader might write about experiences on the journey to the Holy Land.

2. Have students find one or more sources on medieval knighthood, read about the values of chivalry and the love of battle, and compare them to the values of earlier eras. Then have them present oral reports about their findings to the class.

3. Have students research and analyze the effects that the longbow and cannon had on warfare in the Middle Ages. Then ask them to write an explanation of the effects.

Building Social Studies Skills

Reading a Chart

Study the chart below. Then answer the questions that follow.

The Hundred Years' War in France

Date	BattleSite	What Happened
1346	Crécy	English king claimed French throne. English army invaded France and defeated French army.
1356	Poitiers	English won great victory over French. French king captured.
1415	Agincourt	After intervals of peace, English renewed claim to French throne. English army defeated French army.
1429	Orléans	Joan of Arc led French army. French defeated English.
1453	Castillon	French defeated English. Only Calais on English Channel remained in English hands.

1. Which statement correctly describes what you can infer from the chart?
   a. The year 1429 was a turning point in the Hundred Years' War.
   b. The Battle of Poitiers lasted for many days.
   c. In 1346 the French army was massed along the English Channel.
   d. The city of Calais is an English colony.

2. What effect did Joan of Arc have on the Hundred Years' War? Give specific examples.

Understanding Frames of Reference

Read this quote from *Sir Gawain and the Green Knight*, a romance from the 1300s about King Arthur's court. Then answer the questions.

"'Good sir,' said Gawain, 'Will you give my message to the high lord of this house, that I ask for lodging?' . . . 'Yes, by Saint Peter,' replied the porter, 'and I think you may lodge here as long as you like, sir knight.' . . . Then the prince . . . appeared from his chamber to meet in mannerly style the man in his hall. 'You are welcome to dwell here as you wish,' he said, 'treat everything as your own, and have what you please in this place.'"

3. Which of the statements below best describes how the author of *Sir Gawain and the Green Knight* might react to a short story that displayed a mocking attitude toward the manners of chivalry?
   a. He would not understand it.
   b. He would probably find it amusing.
   c. He would probably be offended by it.
   d. He would think that the story was similar to what he wrote.

4. How did the Crusades contribute to the decline of the lifestyle of chivalry portrayed in the quote? Give specific examples.

Alternative Assessment

Building Your Portfolio

Link to TODAY

Economics

Before and since the Middle Ages and even today, the shift of people from the country to towns affects not only the economy but also the government and culture of a region. Using your textbook and other sources, compile a list of previous and modern-day areas of the world where such a population shift has occurred or is occurring. Use the list to create a cause-effect chart of this shift from country to town.

✎ internet connect

Internet Activity: go.hrw.com
KEYWORD: SP3 WH14

Choose a topic on the High Middle Ages to:
• create a propaganda poster about the Crusades.
• learn more about the monarchies of Henry VII, Louis XI, and Ferdinand and Isabella of Spain.
• explore the effects of the Black Death on Europe in the 1300s.

go.hrw.com

---

2. Manors were no longer self-sufficient and power shifted from feudal lords to merchants and kings.

3. the nobles and the church

Thinking Critically

1. unified Europe and was the main source of information

2. attracted new residents and supplied jobs

3. Leaders in England and Spain brought unity through war and marriage. Louis XI united France through diplomacy and scheming.

4. vernacular literature such as poems by troubadours, romances, *fabliaux,* epics, and drama

Writing About History

Answers will vary, but might include differences in architecture, rulers, lifestyles, and religious beliefs.

Building Social Studies Skills

1. a

2. inspired French patriotism, led French to victory at Orléans

3. c

4. introduced Europeans to new ideas, revived trade, led to the growth of towns and the decline of the manorial system

Building Your Portfolio

Students should focus on the urbanization of developing nations in Latin America, Africa, and Asia.

Spotlight on LITERATURE

Epic poetry is also known as heroic poetry—literature created to celebrate acts of skill and courage by a people's warriors and rulers. For example, during the Middle Ages, the French wrote *chansons de geste* (songs of heroic deeds) that celebrated the age of Charlemagne and other legendary French figures. Have students write a poem or song that reflects heroic deeds in their country. The deeds may be historic or contemporary. (*Answers will vary.*)

Spotlight on LITERATURE

Many cultures have a tradition of epic poetry. Like cultural epics, heroic epics began as stories passed down through generations in an oral form. Heroic epics were often sung by bards, such as the *mabo* of the Fulani people in Africa's Sudan. A *mabo* would travel with a nobleman setting out on a quest for adventure. After witnessing his lord's heroic deeds, the *mabo* then composed an epic poem called *baudi*. Ask students to research epic poetry and identify a translated epic poem that conveys the universal theme of heroism. Have students recite an excerpt from their chosen epic to the class.

Linking Past to Present

In most cultures, the spread of literacy brings an end to the composition of oral epic poetry. Today, some groups still compose oral heroic poetry. Scholars have collected examples of oral epic poetry from illiterate or semiliterate peoples in Russia, Central Asia, and Greece. Scholars argue that these examples prove ancient poets like Homer also could have composed very long oral epic poems. The lengthy poems are possible because a bard blends well-known scenes with new details each time he sings a poem. In 1934 one scholar wrote down an epic poem of 12,000 lines, sung by an illiterate bard from southern Serbia.

Critical Thinking

Why do you think some cultural groups continue a tradition of oral poetry?

ANSWER: For illiterate groups, oral poetry continues to provide an effective way to preserve their history and culture.

UNDERSTANDING LITERATURE ANSWER

similarities—dying heroes killed in battle, killed by people whom they know, make speeches on their deathbeds; differences—different reactions to death, different attitudes: Siegfried expresses anger and resentment; Arcita expresses love, regret, and forgiveness

CROSS-CULTURAL CONNECTIONS *Literature*

Epic Poetry

Epics are dramatic poems that often glorify a nation's history and its heroes. Literary epics can express and even define a nation's sense of its history and destiny. The German national epic, the Nibelungenlied *(nee·buh·LOONG·uhn·LEET), was first written down in the 1100s. It was one of the first European epics to be written in the language that ordinary people spoke. In the following excerpt from the* Nibelungenlied, *the hero Siegfried (ZEEG·freed) is killed by his brother-in-law King Gunther (GOON·tuhr). Geoffrey Chaucer wrote* The Canterbury Tales *during the 1300s, when an English national identity was first forming. Chaucer's tales are told by a group of pilgrims on their way to a holy shrine at Canterbury. The following passage from the Knight's tale in* The Canterbury Tales *reflects the English ideal of chivalry. Arcita has been fatally wounded in a battle with Palamon over Emily, whom they both love. Here he bids both his foe and his lover goodbye.*

The Nibelungenlied

When lord Siegfried felt the great wound, maddened with rage he bounded back from the stream with the long shaft jutting from his heart.

The hero's face had lost its color and he was no longer able to stand. His strength had ebbed away, for in the field of his bright countenance he now displayed Death's token. Soon many fair ladies would be weeping for him. . . . "You vile cowards," he said as he lay dying. ". . . I was always loyal to you, but now I have paid for it. Alas, you have wronged your kinsmen so that all who are born in days to come will be dishonored by your deed. . . . You will be held in contempt and stand apart from all good warriors." The knights all ran to where he lay wounded to death. It was a sad day for many of them. Those who were at all loyal-hearted mourned for him, and this, as a gay and valiant knight, he had well deserved.

The Canterbury Tales *by Geoffrey Chaucer*

Farewell my sweet foe! O my Emily!
Oh take me in your gentle arms I pray,
For love of God, and hear what I will say.
"I have here with my cousin Palamon,
Had strife [conflict] and rancour [ill will] many a day that's gone,
For love of you and for my jealousy.
May Jove [the Greek god Jupiter] so surely guide my soul for me,
To speak about a lover properly,
With all the circumstances, faithfully—
That is to say, truth, honour, and knighthood,
Wisdom, humility and kinship good,
And generous soul and all the lover's art—
So now may Jove have in my soul his part
As in this world, right now, I
know of none
So worthy to be loved as
Palamon,
Who serves you and will
do so all his life.
And if you ever should
become a wife,
Forget not Palamon, the
noble man."

Understanding Literature

What similarities exist in these German and English epics? How do they differ? What attitudes are expressed in the dying words of the two soldiers?

Culture

Have students choose a non-European country and research its architecture within the period 395–1589. Students should use magazine pictures or their own drawings to create an illustrated report of their findings.

Geography

Have students study a physical map of Asia. Then ask students to map a route for traveling between east and west Asia during the 800s. Draw the following graphic organizer on the board and have students copy it as a guide. After students have completed their plans, have them work in small groups to discuss and evaluate the effectiveness of their routes.

Problem-Solving Process

Identify the problem—What are you trying to do?

↓

Gather information—What are the geographic obstacles? Where could you find supplies such as water and food?

↓

List and consider options—What routes are possible?

↓

Consider advantages and disadvantages—What are the good and bad points of various routes?

↓

Choose and implement a solution

UNIT 3 — BUILDING YOUR Portfolio

Bronze and enamel dish crafted by an Islamic artist in the 1100s

Culture

Architecture is an important expression of culture in all societies. Imagine you are an art historian preparing a lecture on church architecture during the Middle Ages in Europe. Write an outline for a lecture describing the importance of church architecture during this period and the building techniques and materials used. Explain what the churches and cathedrals of the Middle Ages reveal about religious life in medieval society. Use the bibliography below to help you in your research. When your outline is done, prepare a bibliography of the sources you used.

Further Reading

Browning, Robert. *The Byzantine Empire.* Washington, D.C.: Catholic University of America, 1992. A general overview of the Byzantine Empire.

Cantor, Norman F., ed. *The Encyclopedia of the Middle Ages.* New York: Viking, 1999. A reference work covering politics, culture, daily life, religion, and important figures of the Middle Ages.

Dersin, Denise, ed. *What Life Was Like: In the Lands of the Prophet, Islamic World A.D. 570–1405.* Alexandria, Virginia: Time-Life Books, 1999. An overview of the history and culture of the Islamic world.

Hanawalt, Barbara. *The Middle Ages: An Illustrated History.* New York: Oxford University Press, 1999. A sweeping survey of the Middle Ages from 400–1500.

Ross, Frank and Michael Goodman. *Oracle Bones, Stars, and Wheelbarrows: Ancient Chinese Science and Technology.* New York: Houghton-Mifflin, 1990. An overview of early Chinese contributions to science and technology.

Geography

Geography significantly influences historical development. Imagine you are an Arab trader living in Morocco during the mid-1100s. You have just returned from a profitable trip to Constantinople. Your task is to create a map showing your journey and a chart of the types of goods you took with you and the types of goods you brought back. Be specific about the geographic obstacles you encountered, the places you stopped, and how the items you bought and sold reflected people's needs during this time.

Examples of medieval architecture: Chartres Cathedral in France (right) and the Monastery of St. Mary the Victorious in Portugal (below).

internet connect

Internet Activity
KEYWORD: SP3 U3

In assigned groups, develop a multimedia presentation about early East Asia, the Byzantine Empire, the Islamic Empire, or medieval Europe. Choose information from the chapter Internet Connect activities and the Holt Researcher that best reflects the major topics of the period. Write an outline and a script for your presentation, which may be shown to the class.

Culture

In South India, between the 600s and 1700s, Hindu temples were built in a distinctive style. The pyramid shape of the temples' towers sets this style apart. Outer temple walls are covered with bands of floral and animal carvings as well as ornately carved sculptures. The pyramid tower is made up of layers, each holding miniature shrines. Finally, the tower is topped by a dome-shaped cupola and finial. The earliest examples of Dravida temples were cut out of rock in the 600s. However, the style is best shown in the extraordinary Brhadisvara temple at Thanjavur which was built in about 1003–10 by Rajaraja the Great. Enormous labor and skill were required to complete temples built in the South Indian style.

Critical Thinking

How is the architecture of Hindu temples similar to European cathedral architecture?

ANSWER: Both are ornately carved and required a great deal of skill and labor to produce.

The Age of Exploration

CHAPTER 15

The Renaissance and Reformation

The Renaissance began in Italy in the 1300s and later spread to northern Europe. Art, literature, and humanist thought all flourished during this period. Changes continued in the 1500s with the Protestant Reformation and the Catholic Church's Counter-Reformation. By the 1600s Europe was split across religious lines. During this period the lives of ordinary people also underwent economic, social, and cultural changes.

CHAPTER 16

Exploration and Expansion

The Scientific Revolution, which occurred during the 1500s and 1600s, profoundly changed the ways people thought about the world. Scientists made important discoveries in astronomy, medicine, physics, and other fields. Technological advances also brought an era of exploration and fostered the growth of a new economy. European exploration soon turned to colonization and the development of the Atlantic slave trade. Spain created an empire in the Americas, and the Dutch set up trading colonies in Asia and the Americas.

---

❶ *Why do you think the sun is included in this painting?*

ANSWER: It is important in navigation.

The earliest sailors used the sun, stars, and coastal landmarks to guide their vessels. In the early 1400s Prince Henry the Navigator created nautical charts and tables of the declinations of the sun (angular distance from the celestial equator). Scholars believe Columbus probably carried a compass, a cross-staff, and a table of the sun's declination to navigate his journey across the Atlantic in 1492.

❷ *How does the artist portray Columbus's ship?*

ANSWER: fast, majestic, strong

During the 1400s the Spanish and Portuguese used caravels for voyages of exploration. Caravels were relatively small, light, and agile ships that usually carried three to four masts with lateen (triangular) sails. These features allowed caravels to sail against the wind, have incredible speed, and navigate well on the open sea as well as coastal waters. In Columbus's 1492 voyage, both the *Niña* and the *Pinta* were caravels. Columbus put square sails on the *Niña* to increase the ship's ability to run before the wind.

ACTIVITY: Ask students to research shipbuilding during the 1400s and 1500s. Students should present their findings in an illustrated report that focuses on one type of ship from this period.

UNIT 4

The Age of Exploration and Expansion

1300–1868

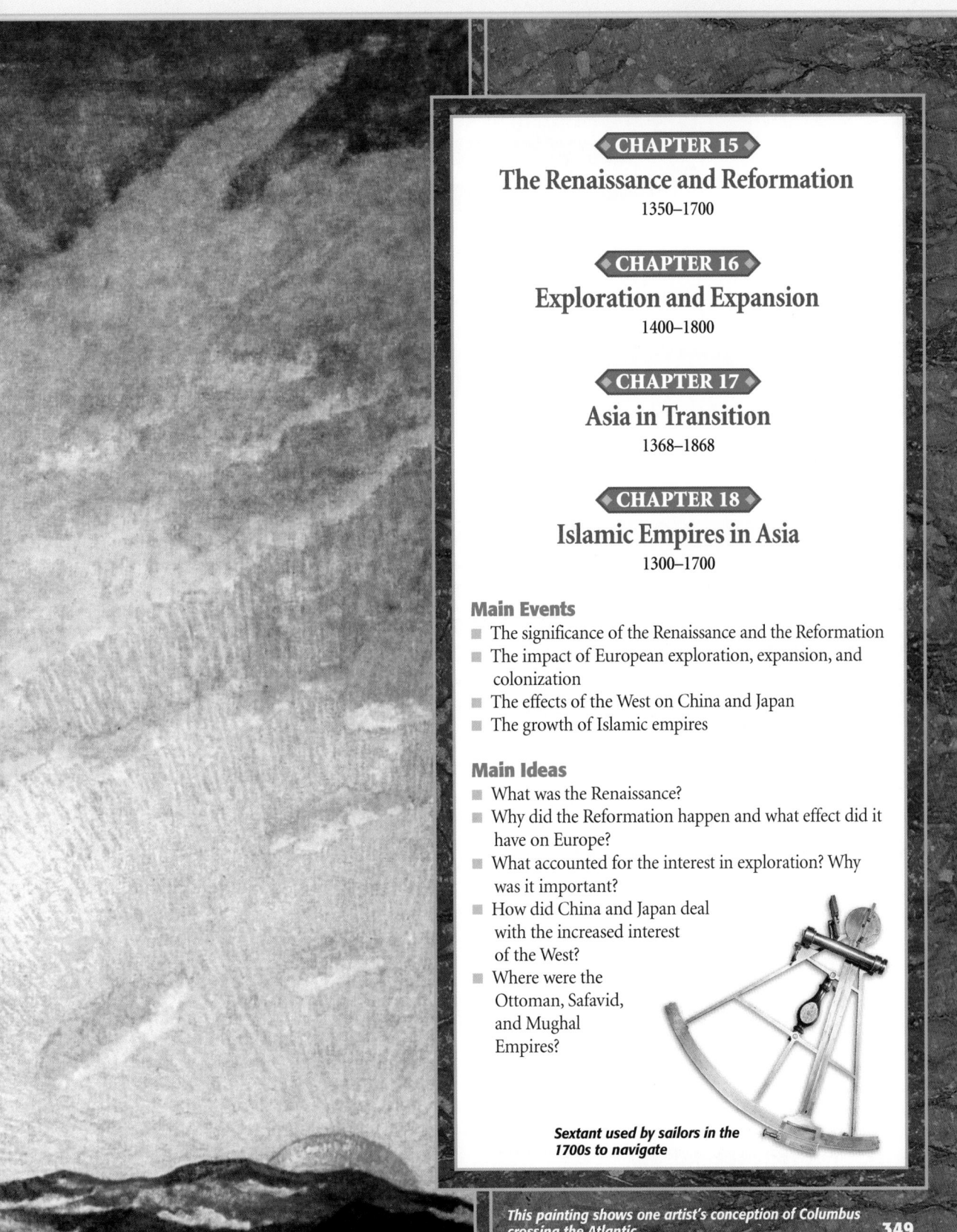

CHAPTER 17 ◆ Asia in Transition

Two powerful dynasties, the Ming and the Qing, ruled China as a self-sufficient state for more than 500 years. During this time, internal trade increased, population grew, and popular culture developed. However, growing contact with Europeans weakened the Qing dynasty and gradually undermined China's sovereignty. Despite its rulers' desire to prevent foreign contact and trade, European influence also began to be felt in Japan.

CHAPTER 18 ◆ Islamic Empires in Asia

During the 1300s and 1400s the Ottomans built a strong empire in the area of present-day Turkey.

Meanwhile, Safavid rulers created a powerful Shi'ite Muslim empire in what is today Iran. In the 1500s Mongols attacked Turkish Muslim rulers in India and established the Mughal Empire. During the following two centuries, the Mughals unified a vast and diverse Muslim empire.

◆ **CHAPTER 15** ◆

The Renaissance and Reformation
1350–1700

◆ **CHAPTER 16** ◆

Exploration and Expansion
1400–1800

◆ **CHAPTER 17** ◆

Asia in Transition
1368–1868

◆ **CHAPTER 18** ◆

Islamic Empires in Asia
1300–1700

Main Events
- The significance of the Renaissance and the Reformation
- The impact of European exploration, expansion, and colonization
- The effects of the West on China and Japan
- The growth of Islamic empires

Main Ideas
- What was the Renaissance?
- Why did the Reformation happen and what effect did it have on Europe?
- What accounted for the interest in exploration? Why was it important?
- How did China and Japan deal with the increased interest of the West?
- Where were the Ottoman, Safavid, and Mughal Empires?

Sextant used by sailors in the 1700s to navigate

This painting shows one artist's conception of Columbus crossing the Atlantic.

349

Introduce Unit 4

Main Events

Ask students to select two Main Events and list questions they would like to have answered about the topics. Later, when you have completed Unit 4, ask students to return to their original questions and write an answer using the information they learned in the unit.

Main Ideas

Ask each student to read the Main Ideas and write brief answers to the questions. Share the *Consider* points with students as necessary. Later, when you have completed Unit 4, ask students to analyze their original answers by comparing them to information they learned in the unit. Tell them to revise or expand their answers as necessary.

The Effects of Social, Economic, and Cultural Changes

Consider:
- the effects of the Renaissance and Reformation
- the global changes brought about by the Scientific Revolution and European exploration

Characteristics of Asian Empires

Consider:
- the creation of new empires in China and Japan, as well as the Ottoman, Safavid, and Mughal Empires
- the effect of Western contact on Asian empires

349

LET'S GET STARTED!

Ask students to describe the ingredients in spaghetti. *(at least noodles and tomato sauce)* Then ask them to identify the ethnic origin of the dish. *(Italian)* Explain to students that many foods that we identify with European countries actually contain ingredients that were not native to those nations. For example, both tomatoes and cocoa are native to the Americas and were introduced to Europe through the Columbian Exchange. Tell students to read page 394 for more information about the Columbian Exchange.

Daily Life

During the Renaissance the dramatic growth of European cities reflected the continent's economic resurgence. Several cities became important centers for economic activity. Lisbon was the base of the Portuguese seafaring empire. Seville became the Spanish gateway to the New World. England's cloth-making and banking activities were centered in London. Lyons, France, became an important market center and capital of the silk industry. In Belgium, Antwerp developed as a center for international banking and the primary European market for German copper and silver, Portuguese spices, and Italian alum. Antwerp more than doubled its population in the late 1400s and doubled it again by 1560.

Critical Thinking

How are economic growth and population growth related?

ANSWER: Growing populations create increased demand for goods and services. Economic growth provides the food and other services necessary for the survival of a larger population.

CROSS-CULTURAL CONNECTIONS

Focus on: Economics

Main Idea **What events changed the economies of nations throughout the world?** A changing economy set in motion a number of dramatic events during the Renaissance. Cities became vital centers of economic activity. Rich merchants and bankers used their wealth to support the arts. Hoping to gain access to the treasures of the East, European monarchs became interested in overseas exploration. Exploration brought Europeans into contact with other peoples, which at times led to conflict.

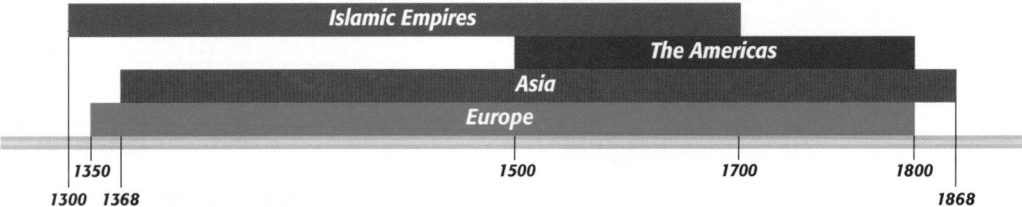

The European Marketplace The Renaissance was not simply a period of artistic rebirth, it was also a time of significant economic growth. Between the 1300s and 1600s, several factors changed the European economy. New and more efficient methods of bookkeeping improved business practices. An increase in population, the rise of cities, a greater supply of money, and advances in transportation and communication meant that more people could buy a wider variety of goods. The center of business activity was the local marketplace, such as the Naples market pictured here. People came to markets to buy and sell food, household items, livestock, and tools. Merchants offered goods made by local artisans alongside exotic items from faraway lands.

Europe, 1350–1800

During the Renaissance, monarchs and other wealthy Europeans began acquiring Eastern luxury items, such as this beautiful Persian carpet woven by highly skilled craftspeople in the late 1500s.

The Slave Trade in the Americas Overseas exploration led to increased trade between European and African countries. The Portuguese, British, and French were among the first to participate in the Atlantic slave trade. In this exchange, Europeans captured or bought enslaved Africans in West Africa and transported them to the New World. Here they were sold to planters in North and South America or the Caribbean to fill a growing need for plantation labor. As European demand for plantation products such as sugar, tobacco, and cotton increased, the demand for slaves also rose. During the 1500s and 1600s, the Atlantic slave trade became centrally important to the economies of the colonial powers. This illustration shows slaves working on a Brazilian plantation in 1662.

The Americas, 1500–1800

REVIEW

Tell students to imagine that they are traveling around the world sampling cuisine and other products from each continent that was involved in the Columbian Exchange. Have students create postcards to send back to the United States from each continent. Each postcard should identify the continent that the student is visiting and contain a brief message identifying foods he or she ate that were introduced to the continent during the Columbian Exchange. Have volunteers explain their postcards to the class.

ASSESS

Have students complete their answer to the question in "Why It Matters Today" and add it to their portfolio. As Alternative Assessment, use the graphic organizer in this lesson.

EXTEND

Have students research the economic relationship between Europe and Asia between 1350 and 1800. Tell students to address the following questions in a research paper using standard grammar, spelling, sentence structure, and punctuation: How were economic ties created between the continents? What goods were exchanged? Did one continent benefit from the exchanges more than the other? **BLOCK SCHEDULING**

Economic Growth Under the Ming China's economy grew strong during the Ming dynasty (1368-1644). Despite an official effort to discourage foreign trade, the European and Japanese demand for Chinese goods flourished. Europeans particularly prized the fine pottery Marco Polo had described as *porcellana* during his visit to China in the late 1200s. During the Ming period, Chinese artists created porcelain masterpieces with government support. Bright patterns—such as the one on this porcelain jar—became the dominant style in the late Ming period.

Asia, 1368–1868

Islamic Empires, 1300–1700

Safavid Prosperity Under the rule of Shah 'Abbās the Great in the late 1500s and early 1600s, the Safavid Empire in Persia reached new economic and cultural heights. 'Abbās encouraged manufacturing and trade, and Persian artisans produced carpets, fabrics, and ceramics that were prized around the world. This prosperity also helped Safavid arts and culture flourish, especially in the capital city of Eşfahān. Carefully planned and filled with major works of art and architecture, Eşfahān became known as one of the most beautiful cities of its day. In Eşfahān Shah 'Abbās built the Palace of Chihil Soutoun, which is where the fresco at left can be seen. In the fresco, a Persian princess writes a letter in a park while a kneeling attendant offers her a drink.

This handle in the form of a horse's head was made in the Mughal Empire sometime between about 1658 and 1710.

Why It Matters Today

Economic growth and foreign trade between the 1400s and 1800s led to a level of cultural contact most of the world had never before experienced. Today, economic factors such as trade, marketing, and advertising lead to cultural contact and cultural change. **What examples of economic influence on culture can you find today?**

Global Relations

Ming rulers worked hard to prevent Chinese contact with people from other countries. They prohibited private dealings with foreigners and did not let their subjects travel abroad. However, these restrictions were unpopular and not enforceable. As a result, widespread smuggling took place. When Europeans first visited China's coast in 1514, Ming rulers did not welcome them. As a result, Portuguese traders became involved in what the Ming called piracy and smuggling. The Spaniards soon developed an active illegal trade with China as well.

Critical Thinking

Why do you think Ming rulers prohibited foreign contact?

ANSWER: Answers may vary, but students may suggest that the Ming believed interactions with foreigners would weaken their empire.

WHY IT MATTERS TODAY ANSWER

Answers will vary but specific examples should be from the factors listed—trade, marketing, and advertising.

CHAPTER 15

The Renaissance and Reformation

CHAPTER RESOURCE MANAGER

CHAPTER 15

The Renaissance and Reformation

CHAPTER RESOURCE MANAGER

	Objectives	Pacing Guide	Reproducible Resources
SECTION 1 **The Italian Renaissance** (pp. 354–358)	• Identify the factors that led to the Italian Renaissance and describe the characteristics of Renaissance thought. • Explain how Renaissance writers combined classical teachings and Christian doctrine. • Describe how Renaissance art differed from art of the Middle Ages.	**Regular** 1.5 day / **Block Scheduling** 1 day *Block Scheduling Handbook with Team Teaching Strategies, 15.1*	RS Guided Reading Strategy 15.1 RS Graphic Organizer Activity 15: Renaissance Accomplishments PS Readings in World History 53: Advice to Princes
SECTION 2 **The Northern Renaissance** (pp. 359–362)	• Explain how the ideas of the Italian Renaissance spread to other parts of Europe. • Describe how northern Renaissance writers differed from Italian Humanists. • List the principal characteristics of northern Renaissance art.	**Regular** 1.5 day / **Block Scheduling** 1 day *Block Scheduling Handbook with Team Teaching Strategies, 15.2*	RS Guided Reading Strategy 15.2 SM Geography Activity 15: The Spread of the Renaissance
SECTION 3 **The Protestant Reformation** (pp. 363–367)	• Discuss the developments that led to the Reformation. • Describe how Martin Luther protested against the Roman Catholic Church and began a new church. • Identify the factors that caused the spread of Protestantism. • Explain the role that Calvinism played in the Reformation.	**Regular** 1.5 day / **Block Scheduling** 1 day *Block Scheduling Handbook with Team Teaching Strategies, 15.3*	RS Guided Reading Strategy 15.3 PS Readings in World History 54: Luther's Refusal at the Diet of Worms
SECTION 4 **The Catholic Reformation** (pp. 368–371)	• Describe how the Catholic Church responded to the Reformation. • Discuss the results of the Reformation and the Counter-Reformation.	**Regular** 1.5 day / **Block Scheduling** 1 day *Block Scheduling Handbook with Team Teaching Strategies, 15.4*	RS Guided Reading Strategy 15.4 E Creative Teaching Strategy 15: TV Documentary on the Renaissance and Reformation
SECTION 5 **Culture and Daily Life** (pp. 372–377)	• Explain why Europeans believed in superstitions. • Describe the characteristics of daily life that were typical in Europe during the Reformation. • Explain how knowledge spread to European villages. • Identify the factors that caused changes in the daily lives of Europeans.	**Regular** 1.5 day / **Block Scheduling** 1 day *Block Scheduling Handbook with Team Teaching Strategies, 15.5*	RS Guided Reading Strategy 15.5 PS Readings in World History 55: Sports in England E Hands-on History Activity 15: Renaissance Dining

Chapter Resource Key

PS Primary Sources
RS Reading Support
IC Interdisciplinary Connections
E Enrichment
SM Skills Mastery

A Assessment
REV Review
ELL Reinforcement and English Language Learners
 Transparencies
 CD-ROM

 Music
 Video
 Internet
 Holt Presentation Maker Using Microsoft® PowerPoint®

One-Stop Planner CD-ROM

See the *One-Stop Planner* for a complete list of additional resources for students and teachers.

One-Stop Planner CD-ROM

It's easy to plan lessons, select resources, and print out materials for your students when you use the *One-Stop Planner* CD–ROM with *Test Generator*.

Technology Resources	Reinforcement, Review, and Assessment
One-Stop Planner, Lesson 15.1	Daily Quiz 15.1
Holt Researcher: World History: Petrarch	Main Idea Activity 15.1
Holt Researcher: World History: Leonardo da Vinci & Michelangelo	English Audio Summary 15.1
CNN Presents World Cultures: Yesterday and Today Segment 14: Divinci for Sale	Spanish Audio Summary 15.1
Homework Practice Online	REV Section 1 Review, p. 358
One-Stop Planner, Lesson 15.2	Daily Quiz 15.2
World History and Cultures Video Program 14: The Renaissance Perspective	Main Idea Activity 15.2
Homework Practice Online	English Audio Summary 15.2
	Spanish Audio Summary 15.2
	REV Section 2 Review, p. 362
One-Stop Planner, Lesson 15.3	Daily Quiz 15.3
Holt Researcher: World History: John Calvin	Main Idea Activity 15.3
Religions of the World Video Series: Christianity	English Audio Summary 15.3
Homework Practice Online	Spanish Audio Summary 15.3
	REV Section 3 Review, p. 367
One-Stop Planner, Lesson 15.4	Daily Quiz 15.4
World History teaching Transparency: Everyday Life 11: A University Classroom in the Middle Ages	Main Idea Activity 15.4
Religions of the World Video Series: Christianity	English Audio Summary 15.4
Homework Practice Online	Spanish Audio Summary 15.4
Online Maps, Charts, and Graphs: European Religions, 1600	REV Section 4 Review, p. 371
One-Stop Planner, Lesson 15.5	Daily Quiz 15.5
World History and Cultures Video Program 15: A Different Way of Thinking	Main Idea Activity 15.5
Homework Practice Online	English Audio Summary 15.5
Online Maps, Charts, and Graphs: Printing Centers in Europe Before 1500	Spanish Audio Summary 15.5
	REV Section 5 Review, p. 377

internet connect

HRW ONLINE RESOURCES
GO TO: go.hrw.com
Then type in a keyword.

TEACHER HOME PAGE
KEYWORD: SP3 Teacher

CHAPTER INTERNET ACTIVITIES
KEYWORD: SP3 WH15

Choose an activity to:
- create a pamphlet on the Reformation and its leaders.
- report on the economic, social, and technological influences of Johannes Gutenberg's printing press.
- create a biography on one of the Renaissance writers in this chapter.

CHAPTER ENRICHMENT LINKS
KEYWORD: SP3 CH15

ONLINE ASSESSMENT
Homework Practice
KEYWORD: SP3 HP15
Standardized Test Prep
KEYWORD: SP3 STP15
Rubrics
KEYWORD: SS Rubrics

ONLINE MAPS, CHARTS, AND GRAPHS
KEYWORD: SP3 MCG

CONTENT UPDATES
KEYWORD: SS Content Updates

HOLT PRESENTATION MAKER
KEYWORD: SP3 PPT15

ONLINE READING SUPPORT
KEYWORD: SS Strategies

CURRENT EVENTS
KEYWORD: S3 Current Events

Meeting Individual Needs

Ability Levels

Level 1   Basic level activities designed for all students encountering new material

Level 2   Intermediate level activities designed for average students

Level 3   Challenging activities designed for honors and gifted and talented students

English Language Learners   These activities address the needs of students with Limited English Proficiency.

Chapter Review and Assessment

IC   Vocabulary Activity 15
Global Skill Builder CD–ROM
HRW Web Site
REV   Chapter 15 Tutorial for Students, Parents, Mentors, and Peers
REV   Chapter 15 Review, pp. 378–379
A   Chapter 15 Test Generator (on the One-Stop Planner)
A   Chapter 15 Test (Form A or B)
A   Alternative Assessment Handbook
A   Chapter 15 Test for English Language Learners and Special-Needs Students

CHAPTER
15

Section 1   The Italian Renaissance
Section 2   The Northern Renaissance
Section 3   The Protestant Reformation
Section 4   The Catholic Reformation
Section 5   Culture and Daily Life

Build on What You Know

Ask students to answer the following questions:

How do the art and literature of a society reflect its culture?

Consider:

- the epic poetry of Greece's Homeric Age
- the art and literature of Greece's Golden and Hellenistic Ages
- the glorification of God reflected in churches

What factors led to earlier shifts in religious thought and practice?

Consider:

- the origination of Christianity during Roman times
- the splitting of the Christian church into the Roman Catholic Church and the Eastern Orthodox Church
- the Babylonian Captivity and the Great Schism

EXPLORING THE TIME LINE
GLOBAL EVENTS

🖅 internet connect ▤▤▤

TOPIC: Baldassare Castiglione
GO TO: go.hrw.com
KEYWORD: SP3 WH15

Have students access the Internet through the HRW Go site to research *The Book of the Courtier* by Baldassare Castiglione. Using the structure of the book as a guide (four evenings of discussions addressing specific aspects of the life of a Renaissance courtier), have students write a short modern version with four people their age substituting the learned gentlemen of the Renaissance. Remind them that their peers will use this book as a strict behavior guide.

CHAPTER
15

1350–1700

The Renaissance and Reformation

Renaissance banker Cosimo de Medici

1351–1353
Global Events
Florence successfully defends itself against a Milanese invasion.

1375
Politics
Florence organizes a league that rebels against Pope Gregory XI.

1434
Politics
Banker Cosimo de Medici gains control of Florence.

1463
Daily Life
English law forbids common folk from wearing gold or purple, which are reserved for royalty.

1350   **1400**   **1450**

1378
Business and Finance
Cloth workers in Florence revolt to reform the city's guild system.

1408
Business and Finance
St. George's Bank is founded in Genoa.

1427
Business and Finance
The ruler of Florence introduces an income tax.

c. 1450
Science and Technology
Johannes Gutenberg develops a printing press with movable type.

The city of Florence and its cathedral, the Duomo

Build on What You Know

uring the Middle Ages, religion wielded great influence over art, government, and literature. The Catholic Church was the leading religious institution in western Europe. Also during the Middle Ages, the Crusades spurred a revival of trade in western Europe. Towns and cities began to grow again. Nations formed strong governments and began to challenge church laws that limited trade and industry. In this chapter, you will learn about the changes in art, literature, and thought that marked this new era in European life. You will also learn about new ideas in religion that challenged the moral authority of the Catholic Church.

What's Your Opinion?

 Themes Journal *To help students create their Themes Journal entries, provide the following examples of appropriate* **agree**/**disagree** *statements.*

Global Relations

Agree Religious practices and beliefs serve as common, unifying factors for people of different regions.

Disagree Differing opinions regarding religious practices and beliefs drive people of different regions apart.

Science, Technology & Society

Agree New technologies allow for ideas to spread more easily, leading eventually to changes in cultural values.

Disagree New technologies allow those in power to increase the flow of propaganda, thus supporting the cultural status quo.

Culture

Agree Ideas and works from ancient cultures are either lost over time or so outdated that they do not affect other cultures.

Disagree Ideas and works from ancient cultures are often revisited and reinterpreted by other cultures, providing building blocks for new thoughts and accomplishments.

Leonardo da Vinci's sketch for a flying vehicle

1508–1512
The Arts
Michelangelo paints the ceiling of the Sistine Chapel.

1480
Global Events
Lorenzo de Medici establishes peace between Naples and Florence.

1480
Science and Technology
Leonardo da Vinci designs a simple turbine engine that uses hot air to turn a spit.

1509
Science and Technology
A German chemist identifies the metal zinc.

1509
Politics
Henry VIII becomes the ruler of England.

1528
The Arts
Baldassare Castiglione publishes *The Book of the Courtier.*

1531
Business and Finance
A stock exchange opens in the Netherlands.

1555
Global Events
The Peace of Augsburg is signed.

Raphael's portrait of Baldassare Castiglione

`1500`   `1550`   `1700`

c. 1475
Daily Life
A new version of chess, in which the queen becomes a powerful piece, appears in Europe.

1475
The Arts
Sandro Botticelli paints his *Adoration of the Magi* series.

1517
Daily Life
Martin Luther posts his 95 theses challenging church practices on a church door in Wittenberg.

1513
Politics
Niccolò Machiavelli writes *The Prince,* a study of government

1545
Daily Life
The Council of Trent begins its effort to reform the Catholic Church from within.

1559
Daily Life
Pope Paul IV establishes the *Index of Forbidden Books.*

Terra-cotta bust of Niccolò Machiavelli

What's Your Opinion?

 Themes Journal *Do you* **agree** *or* **disagree** *with the following statements? Support your point of view in your journal.*

Global Relations Religion brings people of different regions together.

Science, Technology & Society New technologies can advance the spread of ideas that change cultural values.

Culture Ideas and works from ancient times do not affect other cultures.

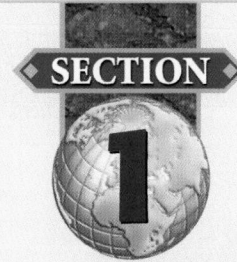
OBJECTIVES

1 **Identify the factors that led to the Italian Renaissance and describe the characteristics of Renaissance thought.**

2 **Explain how Renaissance writers combined classical teachings and Christian doctrine.**

3 **Describe how Renaissance art differed from art of the Middle Ages.**

MAP ANSWER

Turin, Genoa, Milan, Venice, Ravenna, Florence, Urbino, Rome, and Naples

---

READ TO DISCOVER

❶ How did the Renaissance begin, and what characterized the thought of this era?

❷ How were Renaissance writers able to bring classical teachings and Christian doctrine together?

❸ How did Renaissance art differ from art of the Middle Ages?

DEFINE

humanists
perspective

IDENTIFY

Renaissance
Isabella d'Este
Francesco Petrarch
Niccolò Machiavelli
Leonardo da Vinci
Michelangelo

WHY IT MATTERS TODAY

Works of Renaissance art remain popular throughout the world today. Use CNN.com or other **current event** sources to learn more about Renaissance art on display in museums. Record your findings in your journal.

The Italian Renaissance

The Main Idea
The Renaissance brought a renewed interest in Greek and Roman culture and a new way of thinking.

The Story Continues *On November 4, 1966, the Arno River in northern Italy flooded its banks and sent a torrent of water into the museums, cathedrals, and libraries of the city of Florence. News of the flood damage alarmed the world. Why? Because Florence contained the world's greatest store of Renaissance art and literature. This outpouring of creativity that began in the 1300s changed the course of Western civilization.*

An Era of Awakening

In the early 1300s, a movement began in Italy that would alter how Europeans viewed themselves and their world. The **Renaissance**—or "rebirth"—was both a philosophical and artistic movement and the era when that movement flourished. It was marked by a renewed interest in ancient Greek and Roman literature and life. Medieval scholars had studied ancient history and tried to bring everything they learned into harmony with Christian teachings.

By contrast, Italian Renaissance scholars studied the ancient world to explore its great achievements. A new emphasis on the power of human reason developed, and many advances were made in the arts and sciences.

Renaissance Italy, c. 1500

Interpreting Maps During the Renaissance, Italy was a patchwork of states.

■ **Skills Assessment: Human Systems** What commercial cities became the centers of city-states?

ALL LEVELS: Have students work in pairs to create a list of factors that led to the Renaissance (*ruins of the Roman Empire a reminder of Roman glory; contact with Byzantine civilization through Crusades and trade; knowledge of Arab and African achievements in science and medicine; an artistic awakening; the study of classical Greek and Roman literature and life; scholars' search for new knowledge*) Then ask students to copy the graphic organizer as shown, omitting the italicized answers. Work with students to fill in the ovals. Use the completed graphic organizer to discuss the nature of thought during the Renaissance. **ENGLISH LANGUAGE LEARNERS, COOPERATIVE LEARNING**

Causes. In many ways it was natural that the Renaissance would begin in Italy. Ruins of the Roman Empire reminded Italians of Roman glory. The Crusades and trade had brought them into contact with the Byzantine civilization, whose scholars had preserved Greek and Roman learning. In addition, trade with southwestern Asia and Africa helped Italians learn of Arab and African achievements in science and medicine. Over time, these and other factors helped to encourage curiosity and the search for new knowledge among some Italian thinkers.

Italian cities such as Florence, Milan, Naples, Rome, and Venice had grown rich through trade and industry. Their citizens included educated, wealthy merchants and bankers. In Florence, for example, the Medici (MED·ee·chee) family grew rich, first as bankers and then as rulers of that city-state. As leader of Florence, Lorenzo de Medici used his wealth to become a great patron of the arts. In Mantua, **Isabella d'Este** filled her palace with paintings and sculptures by the finest Renaissance artists.

The humanities. In the early Renaissance of the 1300s, Italian scholars turned to classical Greek and Roman literature to study grammar, history, poetry, and rhetoric. These studies are called the humanities, and people who specialized in them were **humanists.** Renaissance humanists searched out manuscripts written in Greek and Latin. Often, they found more than one copy of a work. If the copies differed, the humanists compared them to determine which was the most authentic. In doing so, they displayed a critical approach to learning and scholarship. That is, they sought to verify through investigation. Some Christian scholars also turned to Jewish teachers to learn Hebrew, a language of the Bible. While there were still laws that restricted Jewish life, many Jewish humanists continued to strive for knowledge and to develop new ideas.

As humanists studied classical manuscripts, they came to believe that it was important to understand how things worked. This belief led humanists to emphasize education. They also maintained that a person should lead a meaningful life. People should also become actively involved in practical affairs, such as supporting the arts.

Although fascinated by the classics, most humanists were Catholics who remained committed to Christian teachings. For that reason, they sometimes felt a tension between their studies and their religion. Humanists viewed life not only as preparation for the afterlife, but also as a joy in itself. Along with a belief in human dignity came an admiration for individual achievement. Many individuals of this period displayed a variety of talents by being, for example, both poets and scientists.

✔ **READING CHECK: Summarizing** What were the main features of Renaissance humanist thought? critical approach, studied classics, admired human achievement

Italian Renaissance Writers

One of the first humanists was **Francesco Petrarch** (PEE·trahrk), who lived from 1304 to 1374. Like many humanists, Petrarch became famous as a scholar and a teacher. He also wrote poetry. His sonnets to Laura, an imaginary ideal woman, are considered some of the greatest love poems in literature.

Petrarch's main influence grew out of his desire to continue the work of the classical writers. Petrarch believed that the classical writers were committed to virtue in public and private life. He thought these writers could best be imitated by studying their writings. The study of ancient Greek and Roman literature came to be called classical education. Knowledge of classical Greek and Latin became the mark of an

HISTORY MAKER

Isabella d'Este (1474–1539)

The court of Isabella d'Este was one of the most brilliant of the Italian Renaissance. Educated in languages and poetry, Isabella was a woman of keen intelligence and power.

Isabella used her wealth to support artists and scholars. She housed many writers, sculptors, and painters in her own court and hired famous architects to design parts of her palace. She was the subject of several paintings, including the portrait shown above. **How did Isabella d'Este support the arts?**

Holt Researcher
go.hrw.com
KEYWORD: Holt Researcher
FreeFind: Francesco Petrarch
After reading more about Francesco Petrarch on the Holt Researcher, write a sonnet that reflects the ideals of the humanists.

HISTORY MAKER ANSWER
Isabella d'Este used her wealth to house artists and hire them for their services.

Interdisciplinary Connection

HUMANITIES. Today many college students specialize in the humanities. They major in such fields as philosophy, foreign language, literature, history, or religion. Students whose major is in the humanities receive what is called a liberal arts degree.

ACTIVITY: Look through college catalogs for a list of humanities classes. Have students choose one that interests them and explain why they would like to study that subject.

☑ internet connect

TOPIC: Renaissance men
GO TO: go.hrw.com
KEYWORD: SP3 WH15

Have students access the Internet through the HRW Go site to find more information on one of the Renaissance men in this chapter. Have students write a biography about that person. Remind students to include information about the person's life, major accomplishments, and historical significance in the biography.

LEVEL 1: Ask students to name the Renaissance writers who are mentioned in this section. *(Francesco Petrarch, Niccolò Machiavelli, Baldassare Castiglione)* Ask students to explain how Renaissance writers were able to combine classical teachings with their Christian beliefs. *(showed concern for spirituality, wrote with regard for morality)* Ask students if a concern for morality was in the work of all Renaissance writers. *(not in Machiavelli's* The Prince*)* **ENGLISH LANGUAGE LEARNERS**

HOMEWORK Have students create a book jacket for one of the literature works mentioned in this section. Book jacket should include a cover, brief description of the writing, About the Author, and critical acclaim. They can look to present-day novels as examples. For information on the authors (Petrarch, Machiavelli, or Castiglione) students should use their textbooks, the library, or computer software. Remind students to use standard grammar, spelling, sentence structure, and punctuation.

Culture

This excerpt from Baldassare Castiglione's *The Book of the Courtier* describes the proper role of the gentleman: "I would have him speak not always of serious subjects but also of amusing things, such as games and jests and jokes, according to the occasion. He should always, of course, speak out fully and frankly, and avoid talking nonsense." Of gentlewomen, Castiglione wrote: "She should know how to choose topics suitable for the kind of person she is addressing.... She should not introduce... jests and jokes into a discussion about serious things. She should not... [pretend] to know what she does not know, but she should seek modestly to win credit for knowing what she does."

Critical Thinking

Ask students to compare Castiglione's ideas about gentlemen and gentlewomen.

ANSWER: Students should note that both gentlemen and gentlewomen should know how to speak appropriately for the occasion.

VISUAL RECORD ANSWER

Relations were very formal and polite as indicated by the distance between the two central figures.

Reproducible Resources
PS Readings in World History 53: Advice to Princes

educated person. Petrarch thought it important to lead a full and active life here on earth. He also worried that his desire for fame, a relatively common ambition, might hurt his chances for salvation.

Other writers displayed less tension between spiritual and earthly quests. **Niccolò Machiavelli** (mahk·yah·VEL·lee), a Florentine diplomat and historian, lived from 1469 to 1527. In 1513 he wrote the essay *The Prince*. Machiavelli sought to describe government not in terms of lofty ideals but in the way it actually worked. He argued that a ruler should be concerned only with power and political success. Today some people refer to ruthless behavior to get ahead as "Machiavellian."

Analyzing Primary Sources
Analyzing Information Why does Machiavelli argue that fear is a more effective tool for ruling than love is? love will not overcome people's self-interest

History Makers Speak

❝A controversy has arisen about this: whether it is better to be loved than feared, or vice versa. My view is that it is desirable to be both loved and feared; but it is difficult to achieve both and, if one of them has to be lacking, it is much safer to be feared than loved.... Men are less hesitant about offending or harming a ruler who makes himself less loved than one who inspires fear. For love is sustained by a bond of gratitude, which because men are excessively self-interested, is broken whenever they see a chance to benefit themselves. But fear is sustained by a dread of punishment that is always effective.❞

Niccolò Machiavelli, *The Prince*

Machiavelli can be considered a humanist because he looked to the ancient Romans as models. The lack of concern for conventional morality in *The Prince*, however, sets him apart from other humanists of the time.

Baldassare Castiglione (kahs·teel·YOH·nay), an Italian diplomat, lived from 1478 to 1529. In 1528 he published what was probably the most famous book of the Renaissance, *The Book of the Courtier*. The setting for the book is the court at Urbino, an Italian city-state where Castiglione lived for many years. In his book, Castiglione used real people engaged in fictional conversations to explain how gentlemen and gentlewomen should act in polite society.

✔ **READING CHECK: Contrasting** In what way does Machiavelli's work differ from that of other humanists? lack of concern for morality

INTERPRETING THE VISUAL RECORD
Renaissance relationships The Italian writer Baldassare Castiglione wrote *The Book of the Courtier* to contrast the coarse knight of the Middle Ages with the refined courtier of the Renaissance. *How does the artist depict relations between ladies and gentlemen at the court?*

Italian Renaissance Artists

Like literature, art flourished during the Italian Renaissance. During this era Italian artists produced some of the world's greatest masterpieces.

Medieval paintings had stressed the world beyond everyday life. They used formal figures to express religious concerns. Renaissance artists, in contrast, created realistic scenes and images. They depicted lifelike human figures in their paintings. Even the backgrounds of Renaissance paintings differed from those of medieval paintings. Earlier artists had often portrayed the Holy Land. Renaissance painters showed the rugged Italian countryside they knew so well.

Renaissance painters used a technique called **perspective** to make their paintings more lifelike. They made distant objects smaller than those in the foreground of the painting. This technique created the illusion of depth on the flat canvas.

TEACH OBJECTIVE 3

LEVEL 2: Have students list features of medieval art. Then have them list features of Renaissance art. Have them work in groups to make a comparison chart on posterboard. (*for example, Medieval Art: stressed religion and the world beyond everyday life, depicted formal and stylized figures, depicted the Holy Land; Renaissance Art: depicted religious and non-religious subjects, depicted realistic and lifelike human figures, depicted the rugged Italian countryside)* **COOPERATIVE LEARNING**

TEACH OBJECTIVES 1, 2, and 3

LEVEL 3: Ask students to write an essay describing how Italian Renaissance art, literature, and thought were reflective of the period. (*Students' essays should include a discussion of the combination of religious themes with the humanistic values of the era, and site specific examples.)*

CLOSE

Ask students to write a journal entry on the following question: Why was the Renaissance considered a time of rebirth? Encourage students to consider the rediscovery of ancient achievements, human reason, and the many advances in the arts and sciences.

SKILL-BUILDING STRATEGIES   Using Art to Understand Values

Renaissance Art

Studying works of art produced during a specific period in history can teach us a great deal about the values of the people who created the art. For example, much of the art of the Middle Ages reflects religious values. In general, medieval art developed themes of faith and religious spirituality, rather than of human individuality. In contrast, Renaissance art combined such religious themes with the humanistic values of the era. As humanity became the center of life on earth, artists placed realistic human beings at the center of their works.

Shown above is a detail from Michelangelo's Creation of Adam, part of the fresco on the ceiling of the Sistine Chapel in Rome. It portrays God touching the hand of Adam, who, according to the Bible, was the first man on Earth.

The Pietà, by Michelangelo, is both detailed and lifelike. It shows the Virgin Mary mourning over the body of her son, Jesus, after his crucifixion.

SKILLS PRACTICE ANSWERS

1. realistic and dignified depiction of the figures

2. religious themes and humanistic values

3. Answers will vary.

Skills Reminder

To understand the values reflected by a piece of art, identify when the artwork was produced and what historical period it represents. Identify the theme—is it taken from religion, mythology, or daily life? Note the subject of the work of art and the details. Then use the theme and its treatment to infer the values of the historical period in which the artist created the work.

Skills Practice

❶ What artistic ideals and visual principles are reflected in Michelangelo's works?

❷ What Renaissance values are reflected in Michelangelo's fresco and in his *Pietà?*

❸ Find and study a modern work of art. Explain how this artwork reflects the values of modern society.

REVIEW

Have students complete the Section 1 Review on p. 358.

ASSESS

Have students complete Daily Quiz 15.1. As Alternative Assessment, you may want to use the graphic organizer on Renaissance thought or the comparison of Renaissance and medieval art in this section's lessons.

RETEACH

Have students complete Main Idea Activity for English Language Learners and Special-Needs Students 15.1. Then have students write the section's headings and subheadings on a sheet of paper and list the main ideas in the appropriate space.
ENGLISH LANGUAGE LEARNERS

EXTEND

Have students create a photo essay of the 10 pieces of Renaissance art that they think have been most influential. Have them write captions for each piece, including a defense of its selection.
BLOCK SCHEDULING

SECTION 1
REVIEW ANSWERS

❶ Define
- humanists, p. 355
- perspective, p. 356

❷ Identify
- Renaissance, p. 354
- Isabella d'Este, p. 355
- Francesco Petrarch, p. 355
- Niccolò Machiavelli, p. 356
- Leonardo da Vinci, p. 358
- Michelangelo, p. 358

❸ Thought: critical approach, studied classics, admired human achievement; Literature: used classical writers as models, showed concern for morality; Art: combined religious themes with humanistic values, realistic human figures and scenes, use of perspective

❹ a. Crusades and trade led to contact with Byzantine civilization, renewed acquaintance with classical Greek and Roman literature, and knowledge of Arab and African achievements in science and medicine.

b. Renaissance art: combined religious themes with the humanistic values of the era, showed religious figures as realistic human beings; Renaissance thought: included leading a meaningful life, belief in human dignity

c. to strike a balance between spiritual and earthly quests

❺ Students should mention the use of perspective and examples of both religious and humanist values.

The works of Rafael, like Joan of Aragon, Queen of Naples *shown here, are masterworks of Renaissance art.*

Holt Researcher go.hrw.com
KEYWORD: Holt Researcher
FreeFind: Leonardo da Vinci Michelangelo
After reading more about Leonardo da Vinci and Michelangelo on the Holt Researcher, draw a sketch or write a description of an art piece that reflects their style.

Giotto (JAWT·oh), who lived from about 1276 to 1337, was a magnificent early realist painter. According to legend, a fly in one of Giotto's works looked so real that an observer tried to brush it off the painting. Another important early realist was Masaccio (mah·ZAHT·choh), who lived from 1401 to 1428. Masaccio used light and shadows to create a powerful sense of depth in his paintings.

Scholars often call the late 1400s and early 1500s the High Renaissance. There were many great painters during this period. Four made particularly outstanding contributions to the arts.

Leonardo da Vinci (dah·VEEN·chee), who lived from 1452 to 1519, was a man of many talents. He was an architect, engineer, painter, sculptor, and scientist. He made sketches of plants and animals, as well as detailed drawings of a flying machine and a submarine. Da Vinci's science improved the quality of his paintings. His studies in anatomy helped him draw realistic human figures. He used mathematics to organize the space in his paintings. People throughout the world still marvel at his mural *The Last Supper.* Perhaps his most famous painting is the portrait called the *Mona Lisa.*

Another master of Renaissance art, **Michelangelo** (mee·kay·LAHN·jay·loh), lived from 1475 to 1564. Michelangelo was a brilliant painter. Millions of people have visited the Sistine Chapel of the Vatican, the residence of the pope in Rome, to view the frescoes Michelangelo painted on the chapel ceiling. His sculptures of biblical figures such as David also continue to be admired. In addition to his art, Michelangelo wrote poetry and helped to design St. Peter's Basilica in Rome.

Rafael (RAF·ee·el), who lived from 1483 to 1520, became so popular in Florence that the pope hired him to help beautify the Vatican. Rafael painted frescoes in the papal chambers. He is also known for his madonnas, paintings of the Virgin Mary.

Titian (TISH·uhn), who lived from about 1488 to 1576, spent most of his life in Venice. His works, such as *The Assumption of the Virgin,* are known for their sense of drama and rich colors. The Holy Roman emperor was a patron of Titian. In fact, Titian was one of the first painters to become wealthy from his work.

✔ **READING CHECK: Contrasting** How did Renaissance and medieval art differ from each other? Renaissance art more realistic, showed scenes from real world

SECTION 1 REVIEW

1. **Define** and explain the significance:
   humanists
   perspective

2. **Identify** and explain the significance:
   Renaissance
   Isabella d'Este
   Francesco Petrarch
   Niccolò Machiavelli
   Leonardo da Vinci
   Michelangelo

3. **Analyzing Information** Copy the graphic organizer below. Use it to explain the characteristics of Renaissance thought, literature, and art.

   Thought / Literature / Art

4. **Finding the Main Idea**
   a. What were the events that led to the Renaissance in Italy?
   b. How did religion influence Renaissance art and thought?
   c. What ethical issues did humanists struggle with during the Italian Renaissance?

5. **Writing and Critical Thinking**
   Evaluating Choose one of the Renaissance artworks pictured in this section or one in an art book or encyclopedia. Describe both the work and your impressions of it.
   Consider:
   - the technique of perspective
   - the mixture of religious and humanist values
   - what thoughts and feelings the work of art brings about

Homework Practice Online
keyword: SP3 HP15

OBJECTIVES

1 **Explain how the ideas of the Italian Renaissance spread to other parts of Europe.**

2 **Describe how northern Renaissance writers differed from Italian humanists.**

3 **List the principal characteristics of northern Renaissance art.**

🔔 LET'S GET STARTED!

As students enter the classroom, tell them that they are going to start class by playing a game. Select a volunteer to receive a whispered message. Have that person whisper it to another, and so on, down the line. The last person in the chain will say the received message aloud. Use the game as a springboard for discussion about how ideas travel to new places, changing along the way. Explain that in Section 2 students will learn how ideas traveled from Italy to the rest of Europe during the Renaissance.

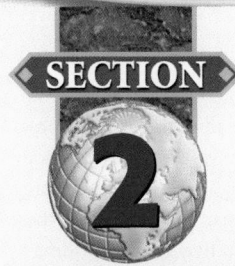

SECTION 2

READ TO DISCOVER

1 How were the ideas of the Italian Renaissance spread to other parts of Europe?
2 In what ways did northern Renaissance writers differ from Italian humanists?
3 What were the principal characteristics of northern Renaissance art?

IDENTIFY

Johannes Gutenberg
Desiderius Erasmus
Thomas More
William Shakespeare
Flemish school

WHY IT MATTERS TODAY

William Shakespeare remains perhaps the most popular playwright in the world. Use CNN.com or other **current event** sources to learn about modern plays or movies based on Shakespeare's work. Record your findings in your journal.

CNN Student News.com

The Northern Renaissance

The Main Idea
Art and literature in northern Europe also began to reflect Renaissance thought, styles, and values.

The Story Continues *"What a piece of work is a man! How noble in reason! How infinite in faculty!" Those powerful lines from Shakespeare's* Hamlet *celebrate the human potential and reflect how Renaissance humanist thought spread from Italy into northern Europe.*

The Spread of Ideas

Numerous mountain passes pierced the rugged Alps in northern Italy. These passageways allowed people and ideas to pass from Italy to northern Europe. The Danube, Rhine, and Rhone Rivers provided even easier routes. Renaissance ideas, often carried by northern European students who had studied in Italy, soon traveled to Germany, the Netherlands, France, and England. As increased commerce created new wealth and more people could afford higher education, many new universities were established in these countries.

A remarkable new process—printing—also helped spread Renaissance ideas. Hundreds of years earlier, the Chinese had learned how to etch writing or pictures onto wooden blocks. Printers put ink on the blocks and then pressed them onto paper. More ink was placed on the block, and the process was repeated. In this way writing or pictures could be reproduced many times. The Chinese also had learned how to assemble blocks from many separate pieces, or type, that could be used repeatedly. This was the beginning of movable type.

The European invention of printing appears to have been independent of the Chinese process. Scholars believe that in about 1450, **Johannes Gutenberg** of Mainz, Germany, became the first European to use movable type to print books. Gutenberg used his printing press to print copies of the Bible.

Not all Europeans were enthusiastic about Gutenberg's invention. Some complained that books printed on paper would not last long. Others noted that hand-copied manuscripts were far more beautiful than printed books. Scribes, who made a living by hand-copying manuscripts, realized that the printing press threatened their profession. The impact of Gutenberg's work was economic as well as social and technological.

This Latin version of the Gutenberg Bible was printed in Mainz in 1456.

TEACH OBJECTIVE 1

LEVEL 1: Have students imagine that no method of printing has ever been invented and that all written material must be copied by hand. Ask students how their lives might be different in this scenario. *(Getting an education would be difficult; fewer people would read; people would know less about distant places.)* Discuss how the invention of the printing press affected learning, culture, and the spread of ideas in Europe.

ENGLISH LANGUAGE LEARNERS

TEACH OBJECTIVE 2

ALL LEVELS: Help students complete a chart similar to the one shown. Tell them to include general descriptions as well as specific examples of writers and their work.

ENGLISH LANGUAGE LEARNERS, COOPERATIVE LEARNING

Italian humanist	Characteristics in common	Northern humanist
interested in human achievement	*interested in early Greek and Roman culture (classics)*	*interested in early Christian period*
Petrarch (Sonnets to Laura), Machiavelli (The Prince), Castiglione (The Book of the Courtier)	*used critical method of study*	*Erasmus (The Praise of Folly), More (Utopia), Shakespeare (Hamlet, Romeo and Juliet, Macbeth)*

Interdisciplinary Connection

LITERATURE. In *Utopia*, Sir Thomas More called for rulers to tend to the affairs of their own nations rather than make war against other Europeans. However, More did not hold out much hope that things would change. His imaginary traveler from *Utopia* explains: "Suppose I were at the court of the French king [and I could prove] that all this warmongering [would] … end in naught … what reception from my listeners … do you think this speech of mine would find?" More's reply was, "Not a very favorable one."

Critical Thinking

Ask students why More might have been interested in promoting peace.

ANSWER: Students may answer that after so much war in Europe, More, like many others, hoped for some stability.

Gutenberg's printing press with movable metal type allowed books to be printed quickly and economically.

Analyzing Primary Sources

Problem Solving How does More propose to solve the problem of poverty? Do you think it would be effective? total employment; probably not

Such obstacles did not slow the spread of the printing press. Other European publishers quickly adopted the new technology. By 1475 printing presses operated in England, France, Germany, Italy, and several other European nations. The books that these printing presses produced helped spread new humanist ideas to a large audience.

✔ **READING CHECK: Identifying Cause and Effect** How did the printing press affect life in Europe? spread Renaissance ideas

Northern Renaissance Writers

The most influential humanist of northern Europe was **Desiderius Erasmus** (i-RAZ-muhs), a Dutch scholar who lived from about 1466 to 1536. As a young man, Erasmus entered a monastery. He later left the monastery so he could pursue his studies of the classics. Erasmus learned about the ideas of the Italian humanists from printed books.

Unlike the Italian humanists, Erasmus and other northern humanists were interested in the early Christian period as well as early Greek and Roman culture. Erasmus believed that the ideas of Christianity and of classical civilization could be harmonized. He used the critical method of the Italian humanists to study the Bible. Erasmus and other northern humanists criticized the church's lack of spirituality. They believed that medieval scholars had made Christian faith less spiritual and more complicated and ceremonial. Erasmus argued for a return to the original, simple message of Jesus.

Erasmus's most famous book was entitled *The Praise of Folly*. In this book he ridiculed ignorance, superstition, and vice among Christians. He criticized fasting, pilgrimages to religious shrines, and even the church's interpretation of the Bible.

Thomas More, an English humanist and friend of Erasmus, took a similar view. Early in life More showed an interest in the classics, and in 1516 he published *Utopia*. In this work, More condemned governments as corrupt and argued that private ownership of property causes unnecessary conflicts between people. He contrasted life in Europe with his description of an imaginary, ideal society. The word *utopia* has come to mean "an ideal place or society." In More's imaginary world, all male citizens were equal. Everyone worked to support the society.

History Makers Speak

"… wherever you are, you always have to work. There's never any excuse for idleness…. Everyone has his eye on you, so you're practically forced to get on with your job, and make some proper use of your spare time. Under such a system, there's bound to be plenty of everything, and, as everything is divided equally among the entire population, there obviously can't be any poor people or beggars."

Thomas More, *Utopia*

More's *Utopia* became popular in Europe, where it was translated into German, Italian, French, English, Dutch, and Spanish. Thomas More wrote widely in both prose and verse. His work was read and generally acclaimed by humanist thinkers throughout much of Europe. Later in life More served King Henry VIII of England. Because More refused to agree that the king was the supreme head of the church in England, Henry had him executed. Some 400 years later, the Catholic Church made More a saint for his faith and service to the church.

English literature during the Renaissance reached its peak in the late 1500s and early 1600s. In classical dramas, angry gods punished humans. In English Renaissance drama, playwrights such as Christopher Marlowe wrote plays that tended to focus on human, rather than godly, actions. Marlowe used powerful language and imagery to convey his thoughts. Some of his work was composed in verse form.

William Shakespeare stands out as the leading literary figure of the time. Shakespeare built on the traditions established by Marlowe and other playwrights. Shakespeare's great strength lay in his ability to transform well-known stories into dramatic masterpieces. He portrayed personality and human emotions with a skill that few writers have matched. The moody *Hamlet,* the young lovers *Romeo and Juliet,* and the tragic *Macbeth* seem as real today as when Shakespeare created them.

✔ **READING CHECK: Contrasting** How did Erasmus and More differ from Italian humanists in their outlooks on life? interested in early Christian as well as classical culture

Northern Renaissance Artists

Northern European merchants carried Italian paintings home. Painters from northern Europe studied with Italian masters. In these ways, the dynamic new painting techniques of Italian artists inspired other artists.

In Flanders a group of painters developed their own distinct style. Known among some historians and critics as the **Flemish school,** these painters are credited with perfecting certain techniques of painting in oil on canvas.

The Flemish brothers Jan and Hubert van Eyck paid great attention to detail. Their work reveals a strong interest in facial expressions. In their masterpiece, the altar-piece they painted for a church in the city of Ghent, the faces of Adam and Eve look realistic. They are markedly different from the symbolic depictions of the Middle Ages.

William Shakespeare is probably the most widely known author in all of English literature. His insight into human nature and use of the English language mark his many plays and his poetry.

This detail from the center panel of the Ghent Altar-piece, called the Adoration of the Lamb, reveals the van Eycks' attention to detail. The face of Eve (above) is from one of the wings of the altar-piece.

Geography

Ghent is one of Belgium's oldest cities and the historic capital of Flanders. The city has retained more traces of its past than any other Belgian town. One historical highlight is a bell tower called the Belfry, crowned by a gilded (gold-covered) copper dragon forged in 1377. The feudal castle of the counts of Flanders, one of the most spectacular moated castles still standing, dates from 1180. The Cathedral of St. Bavon, which dates from the 1100s, houses Hubert and Jan van Eyck's altar-piece The Adoration of the Lamb.

Critical Thinking

What is the historical significance of Ghent?

ANSWER: It has retained many traces of its past. Some of its architecture dates from the 1100s.

THE RENAISSANCE AND REFORMATION **361**

REVIEW

Have students complete the Section 2 Review on p. 362.

ASSESS

Have students complete Daily Quiz 15.2. As Alternative Assessment, you may want to use the chart on Renaissance humanists or art in this section's lessons.

RETEACH

Have students complete Main Idea Activity for English Language Learners and Special-Needs Students 15.2. Then write the main idea of each heading in this section.
ENGLISH LANGUAGE LEARNERS

EXTEND

Have students imagine that they are living in northern Europe after studying in Florence. Ask them to write a letter to a friend back in Italy describing the Renaissance as it exists in the North. Encourage students to include their own thoughts and preferences. Remind them to use standard grammar, spelling, sentence structure, and punctuation. **BLOCK SCHEDULING**

VISUAL RECORD ANSWER

The subject matter and the human figures are realistic. By comparison, Italian Renaissance art depicted human figures as looking more like Greek gods.

SECTION 2 REVIEW ANSWERS

❶ Identify
- Johannes Gutenberg, p. 359
- Desiderius Erasmus, p. 360
- Thomas More, p. 360
- William Shakespeare, p. 361
- Flemish school, p. 361

❷ Italian: interested in human achievement, figures in artwork looked like Greek gods; Both: interested in early Greek and Roman culture (classics), use of perspective in painting, reflected ideas of Christian humanism; Northern: interested in early Christian period, more realistic figures and subject matter in artwork

❸ a. Books could be printed quickly and economically.

b. interested in early Christian culture as well as the classics, valued spirituality in the church

❹ Student responses will vary but should reflect the characteristics and use of utopian literature.

INTERPRETING THE VISUAL RECORD

Northern Renaissance art This painting by Holbein, *The French Ambassadors,* is an example of the artist's style of total control of surface and design. *In what way is this painting more realistic than an Italian Renaissance painting?*

One of the most famous Flemish artists, Pieter Brueghel (BROO·guhl) the Elder, painted in the mid-1500s. Brueghel loved the countryside and the peasants of his native Flanders. He painted lively scenes of village festivals and dances. On the other hand, Brueghel also used his paintings to criticize the intolerance and cruelty he saw around him.

The German artist Albrecht Dürer (DYUR·uhr), who lived from 1471 to 1528, was famous for his copper engravings and woodcuts. Dürer studied in Germany and Venice. He also studied the classics and humanism. Dürer became one of the first artists to see the possibilities of printed illustrations in books.

Another German artist, Hans Holbein the Younger, who lived in the early 1500s, was influenced by Italian and Flemish styles of painting. Holbein traveled through Europe painting portraits of famous people. His work includes portraits of Erasmus, Thomas More, and King Henry VIII of England. This emphasis on portrait painting reflected the Renaissance interest in the individual.

Northern European artists of the Renaissance were certainly inspired by the techniques of Italian artists, such as the use of perspective. Thus, some of the characteristics of Renaissance painting in northern Europe resemble elements of Italian painting. However, the two styles also illustrate the differences between northern and southern European artists and their societies. Many Italian paintings by artists such as Michelangelo depict human figures based on the models of Greek and Roman art. Athletic figures with rippling muscles demonstrate the artist's admiration of the human form. In the work of many northern artists, however, the figures seem more like Europeans of the 1500s—bald, frail, and imperfect—than like Greek gods. However, some northern artists did often depict the early fathers of the Christian church, emphasizing the importance of the Bible as the basis for Christianity. In this way the work of the northern European artists continued to reflect the ideas of Christian humanism.

✔ **READING CHECK: Supporting a Point of View** What evidence would you give that realism was important in northern Renaissance art? more realistic human figures, subject matter

SECTION 2 REVIEW

1. **Identify** and explain the significance:
   Johannes Gutenberg
   Desiderius Erasmus
   Thomas More
   William Shakespeare
   Flemish school

2. **Comparing and Contrasting** Copy the Venn diagram below. Use it to show which characteristics the Italian Renaissance and the northern Renaissance shared and which were unique to each.

   Italian   Northern

3. **Finding the Main Idea**
   a. Why did the printing press spread so quickly throughout Europe?
   b. What were the main ideas and values of the northern Renaissance?

4. **Writing and Critical Thinking**
   Analyzing Information Write a short story about a utopian society.
   Consider:
   - the elements of utopian literature, including its imaginary nature
   - the use of utopias to analyze governmental and social systems

Homework Practice Online
keyword: SP3 HP15

362

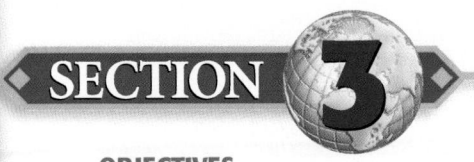
OBJECTIVES

1 **Discuss the developments that led to the Reformation.**

2 **Describe how Martin Luther protested against the Roman Catholic Church and began a new church.**

3 **Identify the factors that caused the spread of Protestantism.**

4 **Explain the role that Calvinism played in the Reformation.**

🔔 LET'S GET STARTED!

As students enter the classroom, ask them how they would feel if they had worked hard for a good grade, and then were told that they could get that grade only if they paid for it. Have students relate this system to the church's selling of indulgences in the 1500s, the practice of selling pardons for sin. Prompt students to speculate what might happen if many people became outraged about indulgences. *(They might revolt.)* Explain that in Section 3 students will learn about a religious revolution called the Reformation.

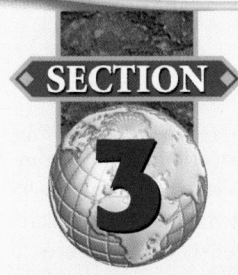

SECTION 3

READ TO DISCOVER

❶ What developments led to the Reformation?

❷ How did Martin Luther protest against the Roman Catholic Church and begin a new church?

❸ What factors caused the spread of Protestantism?

❹ What role did Calvinism play in the Reformation?

DEFINE

indulgences
sects
predestination
theocracy

IDENTIFY

Reformation
Martin Luther
Henry VIII
John Calvin
Huguenots

▶ WHY IT MATTERS TODAY

Different Christian denominations continue today in the United States and throughout the world. Use CNNfyi.com or other **current event** sources to determine the doctrines and beliefs of some of the main denominations. Record your findings in your journal.

CNN Student News.com

The Protestant Reformation

The Main Idea
The Protestant Reformation split the Catholic Church and created several new churches.

The Story Continues *In the early 1500s a young German law student was returning to school from a visit home when he got caught in a violent thunderstorm. A blinding bolt of lightning struck nearby. The young man shouted, "Saint Anne, help! I will become a monk!" Not only did he enter a monastery, but the young Martin Luther also went on to create a religious revolution.*

An Era of Reform

The humanist Erasmus was not alone in his criticism of the church and some Christian practices. In about 1500 several northern humanists argued that the Roman Catholic Church had lost sight of its spiritual mission. Their claims would lead to a reform movement that would split the church in western Europe. This religious revolution is called the **Reformation.**

Causes. Some northern humanists maintained that the church seemed more interested in its income than in saving souls. They claimed that the popes acted as political leaders and warriors instead of setting an example of moral leadership. Some priests engaged in vice and misconduct instead of encouraging spiritual and moral behavior. These northern humanists sought a new emphasis on personal faith and spirituality.

The Catholic Church, however, ignored their concerns. The humanists then urged believers who were unhappy with traditional religion to withdraw from the church and meet with like-minded people.

The beginning. The first break with the Roman Catholic Church took place in what is now Germany. The political situation there helped lay the foundation for the Reformation. Unlike some countries during the 1500s, "Germany" was not a unified nation. Although it formed the core of the Holy Roman Empire, "Germany" was made up of about 300 independent states. Weak rulers could not control independent ideas about religion, nor could they prevent abuses of power by the pope.

In Rome, as Pope Leo X was continuing the rebuilding of St. Peter's Basilica, the Vatican sent a monk named Johann Tetzel to raise funds in the northern German states. Tetzel asked people to buy **indulgences,** or pardons from punishment for sin.

This German woodcut criticizes the pope himself, showing him as a moneychanger at the sale of indulgences.

SECTION 3 RESOURCES

REPRODUCIBLE RESOURCES

▶ Guided Reading Strategy 15.3

▶ Readings in World History 54: Luther's Refusal at the Diet of Worms

TECHNOLOGY RESOURCES

▶ One-Stop Planner 15.3

▶ Holt Researcher: World History: John Calvin

▶ Religions of the World Video Series: Christianity

▶ Homework Practice Online

REINFORCEMENT, REVIEW, AND ASSESSMENT

▶ Section 3 Review, p. 367

▶ Daily Quiz 15.3

▶ Main Idea Activity 15.3

▶ English Audio Summary 15.3

▶ Spanish Audio Summary 15.3

THE RENAISSANCE AND REFORMATION **363**

ALL LEVELS: Have students work in pairs or groups to complete the graphic organizer as shown. Explain to them that Luther's excommunication is at the top of the triangle in order to represent a turning point. Events leading up to his expulsion should be written on the left side of the organizer, and events that occurred afterward, up until the formation of the Lutheran Church, belong on the right side. **ENGLISH LANGUAGE LEARNERS, COOPERATIVE LEARNING**

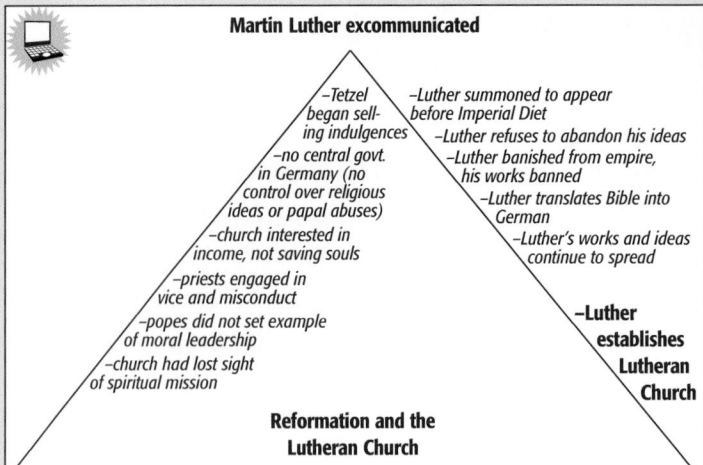

Martin Luther excommunicated

–Tetzel began selling indulgences
–no central govt. in Germany (no control over religious ideas or papal abuses)
–church interested in income, not saving souls
–priests engaged in vice and misconduct
–popes did not set example of moral leadership
–church had lost sight of spiritual mission

–Luther summoned to appear before Imperial Diet
–Luther refuses to abandon his ideas
–Luther banished from empire, his works banned
–Luther translates Bible into German
–Luther's works and ideas continue to spread

–Luther establishes Lutheran Church

Reformation and the Lutheran Church

HISTORY MAKER ANSWER

Luther disagreed with church practices such as the sale of indulgences. He claimed that the Bible was the sole religious authority and argued that salvation could not come through ceremonies or priests. Instead, he believed that God viewed all people of faith equally.

That's Interesting!

The general belief held by those Germans who bought Tetzel's indulgences was that the money raised would go to the construction of St. Peter's Basilica. What the public did not know, however, was that some of the money was going to a noble from the Hohenzollern family named Albert of Brandenburg. Albert had purchased the position of archbishop of Mainz, but because he was too young his appointment violated church law. Pope Leo decided that Albert could take the office provided he pay the church a large sum of money, which he did by borrowing. The church also authorized the sale of indulgences—with half of the money raised going to Albert to help him pay off his debt. Like the rest of the public, Luther knew nothing about this arrangement.

HISTORY MAKER

Martin Luther (1483–1546)

Martin Luther never wanted to leave the Roman Catholic Church. As a priest and teacher, he was strongly committed to his religious beliefs. He felt it necessary, however, to challenge certain church practices that he believed were unnecessary or wrong.

The church responded by throwing Luther out. As a result, Luther founded the Lutheran Church. **Why did Luther challenge the Catholic Church?**

Analyzing Primary Sources

Making Generalizations What behavior did Luther hope that Christians would engage in?
charity

Indulgences had originally been a reward for pious deeds, such as helping a poor person go on a crusade. Renaissance popes, in contrast, sold indulgences simply to raise money. This misuse of indulgences outraged northern humanists, who wanted the church to become more spiritual. The concern became particularly widespread in the German states, where rulers allowed sellers of indulgences to move freely about.

✔ **READING CHECK: Drawing Inferences** How did the sale of indulgences play a role in the beginning of the Reformation? created opposition in northern Europe

Martin Luther

One critic of Tetzel's behavior was a monk named **Martin Luther.** Luther had quit law school and entered a monastery to spend his life in search of salvation. But Luther found that the church's methods for overcoming sin gave him no comfort. He did all the things required of him. Nothing, however, relieved his feeling of inadequacy.

Through his biblical studies, Luther received a revelation. On the basis of this new insight, Luther developed beliefs that later became known as Lutheranism. Luther taught that ceremonies and good deeds made no difference in saving a sinner. The only thing that counted, Luther decided, was an inner faith in God. People could receive salvation only through the grace of God, not through their own actions. According to Luther, simple faith could lead everyone to salvation. This idea was called "justification by grace through faith."

Luther's protest. Luther claimed that Tetzel committed a grave error by asking people to give up money for false promises of forgiveness. In 1517 Luther challenged Tetzel. He posted his 95 theses, or statements, about indulgences on a church door.

 (32) **"Those who believe that they can be certain of their salvation because they have indulgence letters will be eternally [cursed], together with their teachers."** (43) **"Christians are to be taught that he who gives to the poor or lends to the needy does a better deed than he who buys indulgences."**

Martin Luther, *Luther's Works*

News rapidly spread across Europe that a monk had publicly challenged the selling of indulgences. Luther clearly considered himself a reformer who was working from within the main tradition of the church. Initially, he probably did not intend to break with Rome and the Catholic Church. Because he challenged church practices, however, church leaders denounced him.

Break with the church. By 1520 Luther openly disagreed with many church doctrines. He claimed that the Bible was the sole religious authority. Popes and bishops could not tell a person what to believe. Luther argued that ceremonies could not make up for sins and that priests had no special role in helping people to salvation. He believed that God viewed all people of faith equally. Luther considered his church "a priesthood of all believers."

Luther took advantage of the printing press to spread his ideas. In his writings, Luther continued to attack certain church practices and approaches. In 1521 Pope Leo X declared Luther a heretic. He excommunicated, or expelled, Luther from the Roman Catholic Church.

LEVEL 1: Work with students to create a list of factors that led to the spread of Protestantism. *(many Europeans' desire for a simpler, more direct religion; German rulers' establishment of Lutheran Church within their states; Charles V's inability to defeat Protestant princes; Peace of Augsburg; Henry VIII's desire for a divorce and subsequent creation of Anglican Church)* Then discuss how these events, though they took place at different times in various parts of Europe, all contributed to what has become known as the Protestant Reformation. **ENGLISH LANGUAGE LEARNERS**

HOMEWORK Have students prepare a time line of the events discussed in this section. Students may illustrate their time lines.

Holy Roman Emperor Charles V then summoned Luther to appear before the Imperial Diet, a special meeting of the empire's rulers, at the city of Worms (VOHRMZ). There Luther was commanded to abandon his ideas. He refused. After the Diet of Worms the emperor declared Luther an outlaw and banned the printing and sale of his works. However, he lacked the power to enforce this ruling. Frederick the Wise, the Elector of Saxony (Luther's home state), whisked Luther away to hide until the uproar over the confrontation at the Diet of Worms died down. While under the protection of Frederick, Luther translated the Bible into German. Now all literate Christians in the German states could read the Bible themselves.

Protestantism. Emperor Charles V continued to oppose Luther's teachings. He did what he could to keep Lutheranism from spreading. The princes who supported Luther protested the emperor's treatment of Lutheranism. Because of the protest, Luther's followers and later reformers came to be called "Protestants."

Luther's works and ideas continued to spread. In time he established a new church, the Lutheran Church. He kept the organization of the new church very simple. Based on Luther's belief in the "priesthood of all believers," Lutheran ministers were less important than Catholic priests were. According to Luther, Christians were fully capable of interpreting and understanding scripture for themselves.

✔ **READING CHECK: Sequencing** What events led to the development of Protestantism?
Luther's protest, Diet of Worms, spread of Luther's ideas

The Spread of Protestantism

Luther had touched a very deep desire among many people in Europe for a simpler, more direct religious faith. Within a short time, many German rulers established the Lutheran Church within their states. In addition, dozens of reformers appeared who criticized both the Roman Catholic Church and the Lutheran Church.

Charles V tried to stop the spread of Protestantism. At first his attention was focused on fighting the Ottoman Turks and the French. Finally, in 1546, he sent his armies against the Protestant princes in Germany. Although his armies won most of the battles, the emperor could not defeat the princes or the Lutheran Church. Charles finally reached a compromise with the princes in 1555. The Peace of Augsburg stated that each German ruler had the right to choose the religion for his state. His subjects had to either accept the ruler's decision or move away. Almost all the princes of the northern German states chose Luther's faith in opposition to Rome.

The rise of sects. During the 1520s and 1530s, hundreds of new religious groups appeared in Germany and Switzerland. These groups, known as **sects,** did not form organized churches. Many did not have clear-cut authority, discipline, membership, or rules. The sects were societies of a few people gathered together, usually with a preacher as their leader. Most of the sects later died out.

The Anglican Church. In England the Protestant Reformation came about in an entirely different way than in Germany. It was the king, **Henry VIII,** who caused the break between England and the Roman Catholic Church. The break was a political move that had

This portrait depicts Emperor Charles V on horseback at the Battle of Muhlberg in 1546.

🖥 internet connect

TOPIC: Reformation and its Leaders
GO TO: go.hrw.com
KEYWORD: SP3 WH15

Have students access the Internet through the HRW Go site to find information on the Reformation and its leaders. Ask them to create an illustrated pamphlet about some of the most prominent leaders and the roles they played in the Reformation. Students may wish to use the interactive template provided.

History Maker

ANGELA DE MERICI. Angela de Merici was at the center of the group of women who founded the Ursuline order in the Catholic Church. Merici's interest in educating women in the Christian faith began when she was about 20. In Brescia Merici recruited other women to help with her work, and in 1535 the group formed the Ursulines.

Critical Thinking

Ask students why religious reformers focused on education.

ANSWER: It might be easier to train a new generation than to change people's minds.

TEACH OBJECTIVE 4

LEVEL 3: Ask students to write an essay describing Calvinism and its role in the Reformation. Remind them to use standard grammar, spelling, sentence structure, and punctuation.

CLOSE

Ask students to respond to the following question: In what way was the sale of indulgences an important catalyst in the early stages of the Reformation? Encourage students to consider how certain events or actions can energize a particular cause.

Teacher to Teacher

Laura Watkins of Acton, Massachusetts, suggested the following activity: Using a modern Atlas or Internet sources, find a current map of religious distribution in Europe. Have students compare that map with the one of European Religions in 1600 on page 370. Have students suggest what the maps reflect about the long-term impact of the Protestant Reformation on Europe.

Linking Past to Present

Today, the population of Switzerland is approximately half Catholic and half Protestant. The country has a tiny Jewish community as well.

Critical Thinking

How does the religious makeup of Switzerland today compare to the time of the Reformation?

ANSWER: Students should recognize that Calvinism dominated Switzerland during the Reformation.

This famous portrait of Henry VIII was painted by Hans Holbein the Younger.

little to do with religious beliefs. In fact, before 1529, Henry VIII had defended the church against Luther's teachings. The pope had even granted Henry the title "Defender of the Faith."

England's break with Rome took place because Henry VIII wanted to divorce his wife, Catherine of Aragon. Henry was unhappy because Catherine had not had a son who could succeed him. The royal couple did have a daughter, Mary. However, England had no tradition of a ruling queen. Henry also wanted a divorce because he hoped to marry Anne Boleyn, a lady-in-waiting at the court.

The Catholic Church did not usually permit divorces. Although the pope was allowed to make exceptions to this general rule, Pope Clement VII refused to meet Henry's demand. This angered Henry. The king withdrew England from the Catholic Church and began a new church. Parliament passed a series of laws that created the Church of England, with the king as its head. Also known as the Anglican Church, the Church of England kept the organization and ceremonies of the Catholic Church. Over time, it also adopted some Protestant doctrines.

The Anglican Church granted Henry VIII a divorce. The king eventually married six times in all. He finally fathered a son, the future Edward VI. Of greater importance, Henry VIII's creation of the Anglican Church paved the way for the Protestant Reformation in England.

✔ **READING CHECK: Contrasting** How did the spread of Protestantism in England differ from that in the rest of Europe? resulted from the king's desire for a divorce

Calvinism

Huldrych Zwingli (TSVING·lee) was the vicar at the cathedral in Zurich, Switzerland, in the early 1500s. He was greatly influenced by the humanist writings of Erasmus. In fact, Zwingli was already calling for religious reform in Switzerland when he heard about Luther's 95 theses. Zwingli and Luther met and discovered they shared many ideas about church doctrine. They disagreed, however, about forms of worship and the use of religious images. For example, Zwingli's followers covered up wall decorations in churches. In 1531 Zwingli died in a battle between Catholics and Protestants. His work was carried on by a French Protestant named **John Calvin.**

Holt Researcher

go.hrw.com
KEYWORD: Holt Researcher
FreeFind: John Calvin
After reading more about John Calvin on the Holt Researcher, write an outline for a sermon he might have given explaining his views.

Calvin's church. In Switzerland John Calvin founded a Protestant church that had a strong following. Then in 1536 he formulated and published a complete and clear set of religious beliefs, *The Institutes of the Christian Religion.* This work explained exactly what the faithful should believe on every major religious question. Calvin's followers—called Calvinists—now had a code that united and strengthened them against opposition and persecution.

Like Luther, Calvin relied on faith and on the Bible. Calvin also emphasized **predestination,** the idea that at the beginning of time God had decided who would be saved. Predestination was a common belief among Protestant thinkers in the 1500s. Calvin explained the logic of predestination. Those who were predestined—or chosen beforehand—for salvation were called "the elect." They formed a special community of people who were expected to follow the highest moral standards. These standards placed great emphasis on self-discipline. The individual was expected to be completely dedicated to God's wishes.

REVIEW

Have students complete the Section 3 Review on p. 367.

ASSESS

Have students complete Daily Quiz 15.3. As Alternative Assessment, you may want to use the graphic organizer on the Reformation or the essay exercise in this section's lessons.

RETEACH

Have students complete Main Idea Activity for English Language Learners and Special-Needs Students 15.3. Then ask students to write a question and answer that covers the main idea for each heading and subheading in the section. Have volunteers read their questions to the class. Have the class try to answer each question. **ENGLISH LANGUAGE LEARNERS**

EXTEND

Prompt students to imagine they are John Calvin during the Reformation. Have them create pamphlets, similar to travel brochures, that encourage people to move to Geneva. Pamphlets should highlight the key characteristics of Calvinism and life in Geneva. (*predestination or "elect" status, dedication to God's wishes, strict laws governing behavior, righteous living*)
BLOCK SCHEDULING

In 1536 Calvin moved to the city of Geneva, where his doctrine of Calvinism became the official religion. In fact, Geneva became a **theocracy,** a government ruled by religious leaders who claimed God's authority. Calvinists attached great importance to righteous living. Thus citizens' lives were strongly regulated. Laws prohibited card playing, dancing, profane language, and showy dress. Breaking these laws resulted in severe punishment. Rather than being seen as a burden, however, this strictness was the heart of Calvinism's appeal. It gave its followers a sense of mission and discipline. Calvinists felt that they were setting an example and making the world fit for "the elect."

Calvinism spreads. In France many people, including high-ranking nobles, converted to Calvinism. These people were called **Huguenots** (HYOO·guh·nahts). Although France remained primarily Catholic, at one point about one third of the French nobility had become Calvinists. The Catholic French monarchs considered the Huguenots a threat to national unity. Beginning in 1562, the Huguenots defended themselves in a series of bloody civil wars with the Catholics. In 1598 King Henry IV issued the Edict of Nantes (NANTS). This proclamation gave the Huguenots freedom of worship and some political rights.

Calvinist minorities also existed in Poland and Hungary in eastern Europe. Large Calvinist populations were found in Scotland, in the northern Netherlands, and in some parts of the German states. In these areas the strength of the Calvinists among the nobility persuaded the rulers to change their views. In a form called Puritanism, Calvinism would play a vital role in England and in its North American colonies. By 1600 Calvinist churches were well established in parts of Europe.

✔ **READING CHECK: Finding the Main Idea** What role did John Calvin and Calvinism play in the Reformation? established theocracy in Geneva, led to wars in France

This German woodcut depicts the Saint Bartholomew's Day Massacre in 1572. Pro-Catholic forces in France murdered thousands of Huguenots in the massacre.

SECTION 3 REVIEW

1. **Define** and explain the significance:
   indulgences
   sects
   predestination
   theocracy

2. **Identify** and explain the significance:
   Reformation
   Martin Luther
   Henry VIII
   John Calvin
   Huguenots

Homework Practice Online

keyword: SP3 HP15

3. **Sequencing** Copy the flow chart below. Use it to illustrate the chain of events that led up to and occurred during the Reformation.

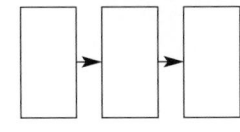

4. **Finding the Main Idea**
   a. What did Luther hope to achieve by posting the 95 theses?
   b. Would life in England have been different if the pope had granted Henry VIII a divorce?
   c. How did the views of John Calvin differ from those of the Catholic Church?

5. **Writing and Critical Thinking**
   Supporting a Point of View Imagine that you are calling for reform of the Catholic Church during the 1500s. Write several theses to persuade people that the sale of indulgences is wrong.
   Consider:
   • what indulgences were and why they were sold
   • Luther's objections to indulgences

SECTION 3 REVIEW ANSWERS

❶ **Define**
• indulgences, p. 363
• sects, p. 365
• predestination, p. 366
• theocracy, p. 367

❷ **Identify**
• Reformation, p. 363
• Martin Luther, p. 364
• Henry VIII, p. 365
• John Calvin, p. 366
• Huguenots, p. 367

❸ northern humanists express concerns about the church—church ignores concerns—humanists urge people to withdraw—Tetzel begins selling indulgences—humanists outraged by sales—Martin Luther criticizes church—Luther excommunicated—Luther establishes Lutheran Church—Henry VIII breaks with Catholic Church—Church of England created—John Calvin founds Protestant Church in Switzerland (Calvinism)—French Huguenots given freedom of worship after bloody civil wars

❹ a. Luther hoped to stop a practice he felt corrupted the church and misled the people.

b. Answers will vary; England might have remained Roman Catholic.

c. Calvin believed in predestination of the elect; the Catholic Church held that salvation was open to all through its ceremonies.

❺ Responses will vary. Remind students to use standard grammar, spelling, sentence structure, and punctuation in their writing.

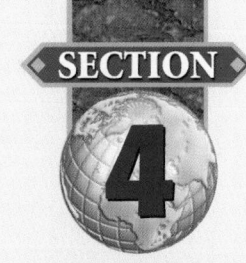

SECTION 4

OBJECTIVES

1 **Describe how the Catholic Church responded to the Reformation.**

2 **Discuss the results of the Reformation and the Counter-Reformation.**

🔊 LET'S GET STARTED!

As students enter the classroom, remind them that the Catholic Church ignored early criticism from humanists. Ask them to predict whether the church would continue to ignore threats to its dominance or respond in some manner. Have them explain the reasoning behind their predictions. Tell students that in Section 4 they will learn about the Catholic Reformation, also known as the Counter-Reformation.

SECTION 4 RESOURCES

REPRODUCIBLE RESOURCES

▶ Guided Reading Strategy 15.4

▶ Creative Teaching Strategy 15

TECHNOLOGY RESOURCES

▶ One-Stop Planner 15.4

▶ World History teaching Transparency: Everyday Life 11

▶ Religions of the World Video Series: Christianity

▶ Homework Practice Online

▶ Online Maps: European Religions, 1600

REINFORCEMENT, REVIEW, AND ASSESSMENT

▶ Section 4 Review, p. 371

▶ Daily Quiz 15.4

▶ Main Idea Activity 15.4

▶ English Audio Summary 15.4

▶ Spanish Audio Summary 15.4

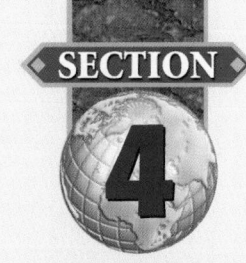

SECTION 4

READ TO DISCOVER

❶ How did the Catholic Church respond to the Reformation?

❷ What were the results of the Reformation and the Counter-Reformation?

IDENTIFY

Counter-Reformation
Council of Trent
Jesuits
Ignatius de Loyola

▶ WHY IT MATTERS TODAY

Catholic and Protestant churches have made great strides toward acceptance and toleration of each other. Yet in some places, conflict still exists. Use ~~CNN~~ or other **current event** sources to learn more about theological conflicts that continue today between Christian groups. Record your findings in your journal.

CNN student News.com

The Catholic Reformation

The Main Idea
The Catholic Church countered the Protestant Reformation by making its own reforms.

The Story Continues *Ignatius de Loyola was a Spanish soldier whose leg had been shattered fighting for Charles V. Loyola's long period of recovery gave him time to reflect. Like Martin Luther, Loyola wondered how he could attain salvation for his sins. Unlike Luther, Loyola came to believe that one could be saved by doing good deeds. He put this belief to work in one of the many steps the Catholic Church took to combat the Reformation.*

The Counter-Reformation

It took some time for the Catholic Church to recognize that Protestantism posed a serious threat. At first the pope dismissed Luther's criticisms. A number of people within the Catholic Church, including Erasmus, had called for reform even before Luther appeared. They too had been ignored. As the Protestants gained ground, reformers finally convinced the pope of the drastic need for change.

In the 1530s the Catholic Church started a major reform effort known as the **Counter-Reformation.** It is sometimes called the Catholic Reformation. The Counter-Reformation began as an attempt to return the church to an emphasis on spiritual matters. It also allowed the church to make its doctrines more clear. In addition, it was a campaign to stop the spread of Protestantism.

Counter-Reformation tactics. Pope Paul III, who reigned as pope from 1534 to 1549, worked to revive a spiritual outlook in the Catholic Church. He appointed devout and learned men as bishops and cardinals.

Pope Paul III also brought the Inquisition to Rome. Since 1478 Spanish authorities had been putting accused heretics on trial. Punishments included extreme cruelties such as burning at the stake. In the past, governments had sometimes used extreme punishments against criminals and traitors. Now the church also used them. The leaders of the Inquisition did not focus on punishing Protestants. Instead, they regarded it as their responsibility to keep Catholics within the church.

In 1559 another method of combating heresy was introduced by Pope Paul IV. He established the *Index of Forbidden Books.* Catholics were banned from reading the listed books, which were considered harmful

Pope Paul III worked to reform the Catholic Church against the threat of the Protestant Reformation.

TEACH OBJECTIVE 1

ALL LEVELS: Ask students to detail the ways in which the Catholic Church responded to the growth of Protestantism. Have them copy the graphic organizer as shown and list the main goals of the church along with the methods used to achieve those goals. Students should work in pairs or groups.
ENGLISH LANGUAGE LEARNERS, COOPERATIVE LEARNING

Goal	Methods used
revive spirituality	*ended abuses surrounding sale of indulgences, tightened discipline within clergy*
combat heresy	*brought the Inquisition to Rome, established Index of Forbidden Books*
define Catholic doctrine	*supported dependence on priests, salvation through ceremonial actions and individual faith, notion of free will in every person*
slow the spread of Protestantism	*better-educated priests worked more forcefully for the church, old and new religious orders such as Jesuits spread Catholicism*

to faith or morals. The index revealed the role of the printing press in spreading the Reformation. Before printed books, the church could easily find and burn manuscripts it regarded as dangerous. Once books could be printed, it was easier simply to forbid people to read them.

The Council of Trent. Pope Paul III knew that attacks on Protestantism would fail unless Catholic doctrines were clearly defined. However, church authorities often disagreed about complicated matters. In 1545 Paul summoned church leaders to the Italian city of Trent. The **Council of Trent** met during three different periods between 1545 and 1563. It defined the official church position on matters of doctrine.

The Council of Trent acted to end the abuses that surrounded the sale of indulgences and to tighten discipline within the clergy. In most cases the council supported the Catholic beliefs that Protestants had rejected. It emphasized the need for ceremonies, arguing that God should be worshiped with splendor. It noted that people must depend on priests because God granted forgiveness only through the church. Unlike Luther, the council claimed that salvation came from ceremonial church actions as well as from individual faith. The council also stressed that every person had free will.

The decisions made at the Council of Trent were effective for many within the Catholic Church. While some people found the simplicity of Protestantism appealing, others found the Catholic ceremonies comforting. They were moved by the beautiful churches, respected the authority of the priests, and wanted to believe that a person could gain salvation through good works.

Soldiers of the Counter-Reformation. To further strengthen support for the church, existing Catholic religious orders reformed their rules, and new religious orders formed. One such order was the Society of Jesus, known as the **Jesuits.**

Ignatius de Loyola founded the Jesuits in 1534. In 1540 Pope Paul III recognized the Jesuits as an official order of the Catholic Church. Loyola believed that salvation could be achieved, in part, by doing good deeds. His followers took vows of chastity, poverty, and obedience to the pope.

History Makers Speak

"Putting aside all private judgement, we should keep our minds prepared and ready to obey promptly and in all things the true spouse of Christ our Lord, our Holy Mother, the hierarchical church [represented by the pope]."

Ignatius de Loyola, *The Spiritual Exercises of St. Ignatius*, translated by Anthony Mottola

DAILY LIFE

Effects of the Inquisition

The Inquisition punished people who questioned the teachings of the Catholic Church. This soon came to affect the growing publishing industry that arose out of the Renaissance. In 1559 the Catholic Church published a list of books that were banned because they criticized the church. This list also identified the printers who had published these books. Catholics who possessed or helped to distribute these books could be called before the Inquisition and severely punished or excommunicated. **How did the Inquisition attempt to restrict the spread of information?**

Analyzing Primary Sources

Identifying Bias What in Loyola's statement would particularly please the pope? calls for complete obedience to pope

INTERPRETING THE VISUAL RECORD

Council of Trent Pope Paul III commissioned the Venetian painter Titian to record the Council of Trent in session. **How does this picture reflect the Catholic Church at this time?**

DAILY LIFE ANSWER
The Inquisition severely punished or excommunicated Catholics who possessed or distributed books criticizing the church.

VISUAL RECORD ANSWER

The formal setting and the ceremonial dress reflect the hierarchical (multi-level and unequal) nature of the church of that time.

That's Interesting!

The *Index of Forbidden Books* was first declared in A.D. 405, but it was under Pope Paul IV in the 1500s that it took the form in which it would remain for over 400 years. Over the years, the works of such great thinkers as Erasmus, David Hume, Thomas Hobbes, and Voltaire appeared on the list. The works of Bellarmine, a Jesuit cardinal, were even included! The *Index's* influence could be felt throughout Europe, sometimes in surprising ways. For instance, when the Bodleian library was founded at the University of Oxford in the early 1600s, its list of purchases was based on the *Index*.

THE RENAISSANCE AND REFORMATION **369**

LEVEL 1: Have students list long-term results of the Reformation and Counter-Reformation. *(many different churches in Europe, strong interest in education, growth in university enrollment, reading more important, remaining lack of tolerance for new ideas, increased power for national governments, decreased power for the pope)* **ENGLISH LANGUAGE LEARNERS**

HOMEWORK Have students create recruiting posters for the Jesuit order during the Reformation. Students can use their textbook, the library, and computer software to supplement information in their textbooks about the Jesuit order. Have students share their posters with the class.

LEVEL 3: Have students write essays comparing Protestant and Catholic churches and their respective actions throughout the Reformation and Counter-Reformation. Remind students to use standard grammar, spelling, sentence structure, and punctuation.

CLOSE

Ask students to write a journal entry on why the Catholic Reformation was also known as the Counter-Reformation. Encourage students to consider the reactionary aspect of the Catholic Reformation and the lasting effects of this era on organized religion throughout Europe.

Linking Past to Present

Today, Catholics throughout the world are launching efforts to reform the church. Some Catholics in Europe and in the United States are signing petitions calling for reforms such as the appointment of female priests and the right of a priest to marry. These Catholics also want the church to concern itself with non-religious issues, such as social justice and preservation of the environment.

ACTIVITY: Have students write an opinion paper explaining whether greater attention should be paid to social issues in the Catholic Church.

MAP ANSWERS

1. England: Anglican; Ireland: Roman Catholic; Spain: Roman Catholic; Sweden: Lutheran

2. Answers will vary. Conflict or even religious wars might occur.

Loyola organized the Jesuits like a military body, with discipline and strict obedience. The Jesuits quickly became the most effective agents in spreading Catholicism. By 1556 the order had about 1,000 members. Their missions took them as far away as China and Japan. In Europe their preaching slowed the spread of Protestantism in France, Germany, and Poland. The Jesuits stressed education, and founded some of the best colleges in Europe. They combined humanist values with Catholic doctrine to produce educated, dedicated supporters of the church.

✔ **READING CHECK: Summarizing** What reforms did the Catholic Church institute during the Counter-Reformation? clarified doctrines, established order of Jesuits

European Religions, 1600

Interpreting Maps The Reformation gained many converts in northern Europe, but southern Europe remained largely Catholic.

■ **Skills Assessment: 1. Places and Regions** What religion was dominant in England? Ireland? Spain? Sweden? **2. Making Predictions** What might result when such various religious groups come into contact?

ASSESS

Have students complete Daily Quiz 15.4. As Alternative Assessment, you may want to use the graphic organizer on the Counter-Reformation or the essay exercise from this section's lessons.

RETEACH

Have students complete Main Idea Activity for English Language Learners and Special-Needs Students 15.4. Then ask each student to create an annotated time line of the Catholic Reformation. Ask

volunteers to present their time lines to the class.
ENGLISH LANGUAGE LEARNERS

EXTEND

Have students research the Inquisition and present their findings to the class. Encourage them to use their textbooks, the library, computer software, and other sources of information on the subject. BLOCK SCHEDULING

Results of the Religious Upheaval

Some people hoped that the era of religious reformation would bring about tolerance. It did not. The period from the 1530s through the mid-1600s was a time of devastating religious wars in France, Germany, the Netherlands, and Switzerland. Not until the mid-1600s, when the wars ended, could the results of the Reformation and Counter-Reformation be seen.

The most striking result of the religious struggle was the appearance of many different churches in Europe. In Italy, where Protestantism was never a powerful force, interest in Catholic Church reform remained strong. In fact, most people in southern and eastern Europe and the native population of Ireland remained Catholic. However, France and the Netherlands had large numbers of Protestants. In England and northern Europe, including Scandinavia, various Protestant faiths became established with the backing of the central government.

Another far-reaching result of the Reformation and the Counter-Reformation was a strong interest in education. During the 1400s and 1500s, many new universities had appeared because of humanist interest in learning. After the 1500s, enrollment in these universities grew dramatically. Religious reformers supported education. Jesuits and other religious orders worked to strengthen the faith of Catholics in their schools. Protestants believed that people could find their way to Christian faith by studying the Bible. As a result, reading became increasingly important. But education did not bring greater tolerance for new ideas. Both Catholic and Protestant authorities opposed views that differed from their own.

Finally, the Reformation led to an increase in the power of national governments and a decrease in the power of the pope. In Protestant regions such as England, each government took responsibility for the leadership of the official church. In some Catholic areas such as France, rulers loyal to the pope managed to gain some degree of control over their churches.

Many schools, including the Dutch University of Leiden shown here, were established during the Reformation.

✔ **READING CHECK: Identifying Cause and Effect** How did the religious conflicts of the 1500s change life in Europe? diversity of churches appeared, education grew, national governments gained more power

---

SECTION 4 REVIEW

1. **Identify** and explain the significance:
   Counter-Reformation
   Council of Trent
   Jesuits
   Ignatius de Loyola

2. **Summarizing** Copy the graphic organizer below. Use it to record ways in which the Catholic Church made reforms in response to the Protestant Reformation.

   ```
   Reformation  →  Counter-Reformation
                →  [   ]
                →  [   ]
   ```

Homework Practice Online

keyword: SP3 HP15

3. **Finding the Main Idea**

   a. Why did Catholic leaders feel the need to launch the Counter-Reformation?

   b. Were the results of the Counter-Reformation era largely positive or negative? Support your view.

4. **Writing and Critical Thinking**

   Identifying Cause and Effect Imagine that you have lived through the religious turmoil of the 1500s. Write a journal entry about the changes you have seen in Europe.
   Consider:
   • the spread of Protestantism
   • the growth of universities
   • the growing power of national governments

SECTION
4 REVIEW ANSWERS

❶ Identify
• Counter-Reformation, p. 368
• Council of Trent, p. 369
• Jesuits, p. 369
• Ignatius de Loyola, p. 369

❷ ended abuses surrounding sale of indulgences; tightened discipline within clergy; brought Inquisition to Rome; established *Index of Forbidden Books*; reaffirmed Catholic doctrine; old and new religious orders (e.g., Jesuits) spread Catholicism

❸ a. They finally realized that Protestantism posed a threat to the Catholic Church.

b. Answers will vary. As a positive result, the Counter-Reformation solidified and improved the Catholic Church. As a negative result, it helped cause religious wars.

❹ Responses should include the spread of Protestantism, the growth of universities, and the growing power of national governments.

THE RENAISSANCE AND REFORMATION **371**

OBJECTIVES

1 **Explain why Europeans believed in superstitions.**

2 **Describe the characteristics of daily life that were typical in Europe during the Reformation.**

3 **Explain how knowledge spread to European villages.**

4 **Identify the factors that caused changes in the daily lives of Europeans.**

SECTION 5

READ TO DISCOVER

1 Why did Europeans believe in superstitions?

2 What characteristics were typical of daily life in Europe during the Reformation?

3 How did knowledge spread to European villages?

4 What factors caused changes in the daily lives of Europeans?

DEFINE

broadsides
almanacs
standard of living

WHY IT MATTERS TODAY

Almanacs were a popular source of information in Europe during the 1500s. Today people still use almanacs. Use CNN Student News.com or other **current event** sources to find and scan different almanacs to see the kinds of information they contain. Record your findings in your journal.

CNN Student News.com

Culture and Daily Life

The Main Idea
As the ideas of the Reformation took hold, daily life throughout Europe began to change.

The Story Continues *The ideas that marked European lifestyles during the Renaissance, the Reformation, and the Counter-Reformation involved relatively few, and mostly upper-class, people. Ordinary people had their own views about themselves and the world around them—ideas that included witches flying at night and other superstitions, and village processions that mocked the powerful and the foolish.*

Superstitions

Although towns had grown in number and population, most Europeans still lived in or near small villages. They spent their entire lives struggling with nature in order to raise food. People close to the land never knew what life might bring next. A cow might fall ill, or lightning might burn down a cottage. Moreover, during the 1500s the population of Europe was increasing at a time of social and political upheaval. War, famine, and plague continued to affect people. At any time, life could take an unexpected turn for the worse. Many people looked to superstitions to explain and control their lives.

The world of spirits. Although most Europeans were Christians, they considered God to be a distant, unknowable force. They explained many of the events that took place around them as the doings of spirits. Because of this belief in spirits, most Europeans believed that nothing was an accident. Bad spirits—demons—made life difficult. If lightning struck a house, a demon had caused it. If a pitcher of milk spilled, a demon was the reason. In fact, many superstitions that may seem strange or difficult to explain today began during this period.

Village priests usually accepted these beliefs, or they ignored them. The ordinary villager was not very satisfied with the priests' explanation that misfortune was God's will, or perhaps God's punishment for sin. Villagers still, however, believed

that a priest's actions could have positive effects. For example, every spring a priest would go out into the fields, bless the earth, and pray for good crops. His blessing of a husband and wife at a wedding supposedly gave the new couple a good start in life. Baptism was thought to protect a newborn child.

Belief in fortune telling was common during the 1400s and the 1500s.

TEACH OBJECTIVE 1

LEVEL 1: Have students share some common superstitions. *(Students might mention bad luck from breaking a mirror, for example.)* Ask them why they think some people believe in such things. *(Superstitions help people believe they can control fate.)* Discuss the superstitious nature of European villagers during the Renaissance and Reformation. Ask why superstitions were so widespread during this era. *(Most people were very poor and uneducated and had little control over their destinies; because science was primitive, people understood little about the natural world.)* **ENGLISH LANGUAGE LEARNERS**

HOMEWORK Have students write magazine articles about the "witch hunts" of Europe during the 1500s and 1600s. The articles should include historical data as well as students' own opinions about why the wave of witch hunting occurred. Students can use their textbooks, the library, and computer software. Remind them to use correct grammar, spelling, sentence structure, and punctuation.

The priest was not the only person to whom the villagers turned in times of trouble. They also looked to a man or woman who was considered "wise" or "cunning." This person, usually an older village member, was thought to have a special understanding of how the world worked.

Ordinary people would explain their problem—a lost ring, a cruel husband, a sick pig—to the "wise" folk. People would also report anything unusual, even something simple like a frog jumping into a boat. Such events were taken as a warning. The wise man or woman would explain what the warning meant. Sometimes wise folk recommended a remedy for warding off evil. Remedies included chanting a spell, drinking a special potion, or wearing a good-luck charm.

Belief in witchcraft. Wise people were part of a traditional belief in witchcraft. Wise people were often called "good witches." If their relationship with their neighbors turned sour, or if misfortunes began to occur, they might be accused of being "bad witches." It was believed that bad witches had made a pact with the devil. In many cases, a person accused of witchcraft was an elderly widow. Without a husband or family, she would be the most defenseless person in the community. Such a woman was an easy target to attack.

Stories about witches became more sensational as they spread through the countryside. Outrageous accusations were made. A person might be accused of flying on a broomstick, sticking pins into dolls, or dancing with the devil in the woods at night. In some of these cases, a priest might be asked to hold a ceremony to exorcise, or drive out, a demon that was thought to have taken over the witch's body. In other cases, the accused person might be dragged to a bonfire, tied to a stake, and burned, perhaps with the approval of the local lord.

An enormous outburst of "witch hunting" occurred in Europe in the mid-1500s and lasted for more than one hundred years. Those accused of being witches were put on trial. The punishment was death. Both religious and secular leaders accepted witches as an explanation for problems in the world around them. The example of Jean Bodin, a French scholar, shows that even learned people believed in witches.

History Makers Speak **❝**Now, if there is any means to appease the wrath of God, to gain his blessing, to strike awe into some by the punishment of others, to preserve some from being infected by others, to diminish the number of evil-doers . . . and to punish the most detestable crimes of which the human mind can conceive, it is to punish with the utmost rigor the witches. . . . Now it is not in the power of princes to pardon a crime which the law of God punishes with the penalty of death—such are the crimes of witches.**❞**

Jean Bodin, *Witchcraft in Europe*

Eventually fewer cases of witchcraft were reported. As the religious wars came to an end, people experienced greater security in their lives. They were less likely to worry about the influence of witches in everyday life.

✔ **READING CHECK: Identifying Cause and Effect** How did concerns about events in daily life lead to a belief in superstitions? people looked for explanations/control

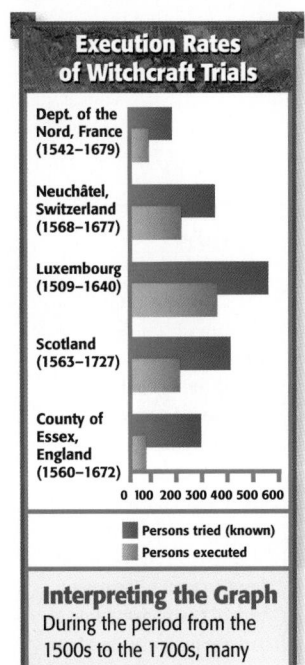

Execution Rates of Witchcraft Trials

Dept. of the Nord, France (1542–1679)	
Neuchâtel, Switzerland (1568–1677)	
Luxembourg (1509–1640)	
Scotland (1563–1727)	
County of Essex, England (1560–1672)	

0 100 200 300 400 500 600

■ Persons tried (known)
■ Persons executed

Interpreting the Graph
During the period from the 1500s to the 1700s, many Europeans were tried as witches. *What patterns of geographic distribution do you notice on this graph? What questions does the graph not answer?*

Analyzing Primary Sources

Identifying a Point of View
What is Bodin's opinion of the belief in witches? supports belief in witches

This English engraving shows a suspected witch being "swum" at a 1612 witchcraft trial.

Global Relations

The witch hunts of the 1500s and 1600s carried over to the English colonies in North America. In May 1692 a series of trials began in Salem in the Massachusetts Bay Colony. Government officials, encouraged by religious leaders, set up a special court to try women accused of practicing witchcraft. As many as 150 people were imprisoned. Suspicions fell even on the governor's wife. In all, 19 convicted "witches" were hanged. By September 1692, however, public hysteria died down, the trials were stopped, and the prisoners released. The Massachusetts legislature eventually overturned the convictions and granted payments to families of the victims.

Critical Thinking

What effect might the accusation of the governor's wife have had on the witch trials?

ANSWER: Accusations against the governor's wife probably accelerated opposition to the witch trials.

INTERPRETING THE GRAPH ANSWERS
Luxembourg tried and executed the most persons. Questions will vary but may include why different countries had various execution rates.

TEACH OBJECTIVE 2

LEVEL 2: Have students examine the painting by Pieter Brueghel the Younger on page 376. Ask them to write down what they can conclude about peasant life as they observe how the people are dressed, their facial expressions, and the activities in which they are involved. Have volunteers read their observations to the class. Then discuss characteristics of daily life during the Renaissance and Reformation era.

TEACH OBJECTIVE 3

ALL LEVELS: Ask students to identify and describe the main ways in which village people learned about the world outside of their villages. *(printed works such as broadsides, books, almanacs, and Bible translations; traveling preachers; primary schools)* Divide the class into small groups. Have each group create either a broadside, an almanac page, or the message brought by a traveling preacher. Then have the groups share their work with the class.
ENGLISH LANGUAGE LEARNERS, COOPERATIVE LEARNING

THEN AND NOW ANSWER
Answers may include tug-of-war, leap frog, and walking on stilts.

Culture

Guilds flourished in Europe between the 1000s and 1500s. They were an important part of the economic and social fabric of that time. A guild was generally one of two types: merchant guild or craft guild. Merchant guilds were associations of the merchants in a town or city. Craft guilds were associations of the artisans and craftsmen in an industry (such as weavers, masons, painters, or blacksmiths). Guilds performed a variety of important functions in the local economy, such as maintaining standards of quality and trying to bring about stable prices.

Critical Thinking

Why might a person join a merchant or craft guild?

ANSWER: Students may suggest that guilds could provide aid and protection for members and further their professional interests.

Games
People throughout the ages have played games for fun. In some cultures, games are a way for children to learn useful skills. Games provide relaxation and recreation.

Dice have been found in Egyptian tombs. The earliest form of the modern game of backgammon may date from about 3000 B.C. In recent years, people of all ages have been fascinated by the new games and twists on old games made possible by electronics and the computer.
Can you identify some games in the painting by Pieter Brueghel that people still play today?

Daily Life

For most Europeans in the 1500s and 1600s, daylight meant work and night meant sleep. Because farming was so time-consuming, people needed all the daylight hours to raise food. By evening most farmers were exhausted from working all day. Few could afford the candles needed for light. Still, people did find time for relaxation.

Forms of recreation. Every village had a gathering place where people came together to drink, sew, do simple chores, or tell stories. Some played games such as skittles, a form of bowling. Occasionally traveling companies of actors passed through and put on shows. The people also enjoyed special holidays during the year. Some were church holidays, while others honored a local saint or tradition. During some holidays, the villagers donned costumes and would often put on their own ceremonies.

One favorite holiday ceremony poked fun at village life. This ceremony went by different names in different parts of Europe. Whether it was called "rough music," "charivari," or "abbeys of misrule," the basic ceremony was much the same. The young men of the village formed a procession. They made fun of people who had behaved in unusual ways or had violated local custom.

Sometimes the marchers had more serious targets. They might want to show how things would be if the poor or the weak had power. They would dress someone like a bishop or put the poorest man in the village on a throne. At this point the jokes were no longer lighthearted. They revealed the resentment villagers felt about the privileges their rulers possessed.

Violence and protest in the village. People of this time identified closely with those of their own kind. In large towns, members of the same profession joined together in guilds and other groups. In small villages, which contained perhaps a few dozen families, whole communities tended to work and make decisions together.

Because villagers lived in close-knit communities, anyone who upset village traditions or behaved oddly was treated harshly. Quarrels between neighbors were common, and the bonds of mutual reliance that held the community together could loosen in times of stress. The strain of hardship or famine could cause villagers to respond violently. For example, if a local baker was suspected of hoarding bread or sending it elsewhere to make higher profits, villagers might band together to ransack the baker's shop.

Children's games in the 1500s

✔ **READING CHECK: Making Generalizations** What were the main features of daily life in Europe during this period?
hard work, holiday ceremonies, close-knit communities

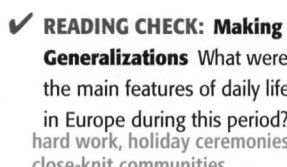

LEVEL 3: Have students create detailed before-and-after charts comparing Europe in about 1400 and Europe in about 1600. Remind students to list the differences as well as explain the reasons for them. Their graphic organizer can take the form as shown. Close by asking students what remained the same. *(Nobles and other privileged people still lived better than most peasants and the urban poor; peasants generally ate the same meals they'd been eating for centuries; peasants continued to live in thatched-roof cottages.)*

Europe c. 1400	Europe c. 1600
population decreased by Black Death, so labor in great demand resulting in higher wages	*population growing rapidly, which led to inflation*
diet consisted mainly of cheese and eggs, people rarely ate meat or fish	*new vegetables, coffee, tea, spices, and chocolate introduced*
people ate mostly with fingers	*forks and spoons came into use*
people lived in thatched-roof cottages	*in cities, houses were built with brick and stone*
peasants trapped in rural poverty	*many people moved to cities*

The Spread of Knowledge

In the 1500s the world beyond the village began to affect village life. Printed works, and in some areas traveling preachers, inspired these changes.

Books for the masses. Few ordinary villagers could read. In some cases even the village priest could not read. Nevertheless, soon after the invention of movable type, publishers started selling popular works. Single printed sheets known as **broadsides** began to appear. A broadside might include a royal decree or news of some sensational crime or other event. Books and broadsides arrived in the village, carried by peddlers who brought goods from the outside world. When the villagers gathered together, they might enjoy listening to someone read the latest broadside.

Romances and epics of the classical era appealed to nobility. Publishers also found subjects that appealed to country folk and produced cheap books for this new market. The most common books were **almanacs,** which published predictions about the weather and prospects for growing crops. Almanacs also contained calendars, maps, and medical advice. The books were best-sellers because they spoke to the beliefs and concerns of ordinary people.

Religious ideas and education. Soon after Luther's break with the church in 1521, new religious ideas began to spread beyond urban areas. Sometimes preachers came to visit. Peddlers might sell books on religious themes. Perhaps people heard stories that attacked the church. The messages of Luther and Calvin traveled in this manner, as did translations of the Bible.

As Protestants and Catholics battled for the loyalties of ordinary people, leaders of both sides encouraged the founding of primary schools in the villages and towns. Both Protestant and Catholic leaders believed that knowledge would lead a person to support the faith. In spite of this common

CONNECTING TO
Science and Technology

The Printing Press

During the Middle Ages books were written and copied by hand. The work was usually done by Christian monks, and it took a long time to produce a book. A German, Johannes Gutenberg, developed a faster way to print things by inventing the printing press in about 1450. Gutenberg developed the use of movable type. He then modified a wine press to push the paper onto the inked type, which made an impression on the paper. With the new press he could print ten sheets of paper per hour. The printing press allowed ideas and knowledge to be spread faster and farther than

ever before. Many of today's presses are computerized and can print pages at high speeds. Daily life today is filled with printed materials, from books and magazines to posters and leaflets.

screw

type form

bed

platen (flat plate)

Understanding Science and Technology

How was the Gutenberg printing technique an improvement over older techniques?

SCIENCE, TECHNOLOGY & SOCIETY ANSWER
Copying by hand took a long time and made books expensive. Printing was much quicker and reduced the costs of books.

History Maker

JOHANNES GUTENBERG. Johannes Gutenberg, the man credited with inventing the printing press, was the son of an upper-class citizen of Mainz, a German town. A skilled metalworker, Gutenberg moved to the nearby town of Strassburg between 1428 and 1430. In 1438 acquaintances of Gutenberg learned that he was working on a new invention—the printing press—which he was trying to keep secret. Gutenberg borrowed money from Johann Fust, a wealthy businessman, to finish work on his printing press. However, the two men had a falling out. Fust went to court and won a lawsuit against Gutenberg. Afterward, Gutenberg probably operated a printing shop during the 1450s and 1460s, though no one knows for sure.

Critical Thinking

Why did Johannes Gutenberg want to keep his work on the printing press a secret?

ANSWER: Students might suggest that if others learned of Gutenberg's work, they may have tried to profit by taking his idea and producing their own printing press.

The printing press, invented by Johannes Gutenberg, was a revolutionary technological advance. As the use of Gutenberg's technology spread throughout Europe, so too did new ideas and knowledge. Similarly, the Internet today can be viewed as a revolutionary technological advance. Organize the class into small groups and have each group brainstorm ideas for their own inventions that would profoundly impact our world today. Have them select one of their ideas to develop further. Each group should write a brief description of what their proposed invention would do and what long-term effects it might have on society. **BLOCK SCHEDULING, COOPERATIVE LEARNING**

Interdisciplinary Connection

SCIENCE. The depopulation caused by the Black Death had environmental as well as economic consequences. The shortage of agricultural workers meant that many marginal lands could not be farmed. As a result land that had been almost completely deforested and converted to farmland was allowed to return to its natural state.

Critical Thinking

Ask students to suggest how this reforestation might have been beneficial to Europeans.

ANSWER: These forests would have been a useful source of wood for building and heating.

concern for education, the followers of the differing religions struggled to coexist peacefully. However, because education became part of the struggle for followers, neither side included tolerance in its teachings.

✔ **READING CHECK: Summarizing** In what ways did knowledge spread to European villages? printed books became available; primary schools were founded

Changes in Daily Life

In addition to undergoing religious and political change during the Renaissance and Reformation eras, Europeans experienced other changes.

The economy. The measure of the quality of life—the **standard of living**—is affected by many factors, including environment, health, home life, income, and working conditions. During the Renaissance peasants made up as much as 85 to 90 percent of the total European population, except in the highly urbanized areas of northern Italy and Flanders. As the manorial system continued to decline, so too did medieval concepts and practices of serfdom. Increasingly, the labor dues owed by a peasant to his lord were converted into rents paid in money. By the end of the 1400s, especially in western Europe, more and more peasants were becoming legally free. Furthermore, the Black Death of the 1300s had reduced the population by at least one third. This meant that there were now fewer people to work the land. Some peasants prospered, therefore, because their labor was in demand, which often resulted in higher wages.

By 1550, when the religious wars were ravaging Europe, conditions changed again. The population was growing rapidly. With population growth came inflation, a rise in prices for goods. After 1550 wages could not keep up with the rise in prices, especially of farm goods.

The image above shows some of the foods typical of European diets in the 1500s and 1600s. In the painting below, by Pieter Brueghel the Younger, peasants of the era share a meal as they rest from their work.

Diet. During this period, white bread made from wheat was rare. Meat was scarce and expensive, and fish only a little less so. Salt had long been an important trade item because it was needed to preserve foods, but it, too, was expensive. Cheese and eggs—cheap sources of protein—were an important part of the diet everywhere in Europe. Butter was not widely used outside northern Europe until the 1700s.

Most spices introduced into Europe from the East had been considered luxury items. By the 1500s and 1600s, the importation of spices had become very competitive. Increased competition often meant a drop in prices.

In the 1500s traders introduced new vegetables to Europe. Europeans had the opportunity to try asparagus, green beans, lettuce, melons, spinach, and tomatoes. Traders also brought new luxury items such as coffee and tea. Not everyone had access to the new and varied diets, however. Wealthy people still lived better than most people did. Peasants and the urban poor usually ate the same simple meals they had eaten for centuries.

CLOSE

Have students work in pairs to summarize the main ideas presented in Section 5. Each partner should take two of the questions in "Read to Discover" and share the answer with their partner.

REVIEW

Have students complete the Section 5 Review on p. 377.

ASSESS

Have students complete Daily Quiz 15.5. As Alternative Assessment, you may want to use the before-and-after chart or magazine article exercise in this section's lessons.

RETEACH

Have students complete Main Idea Activity for English Language Learners and Special-Needs Students 15.5. Then have each student write a few questions based on Section 5 content. Ask students to take turns answering their classmates' questions.
ENGLISH LANGUAGE LEARNERS

EXTEND

Organize students into groups. Have each group create a skit depicting the life and culture of ordinary people during the Renaissance and Reformation. Encourage students to use props and costumes. **BLOCK SCHEDULING, COOPERATIVE LEARNING**

Customs and table settings that we know today were not common in the early Renaissance period. People usually ate with their fingers. They picked what they wanted to eat from a common dish. In some areas people ate from wooden plates. Guests brought their own knives. Forks did not come into use until the 1500s, and spoons were not common until the 1600s.

Housing. After the 1500s brick and stone became more common construction materials in the growing cities of Europe. In the countryside housing remained much as it had during the Middle Ages. Peasants lived in small, thatch-roofed houses. Glass was expensive and often difficult to obtain, even for the wealthy. The scarcity of glass meant that most houses had shutters instead of glass windows. Peasant houses usually contained only the necessities of rural life—a large cooking pot, a bench, a table, and some tools. The lucky few had a bed. Most people slept on sacks filled with straw.

Decline of traditional culture. Many peasants were trapped in poverty. Hoping to escape their fate, some migrated to the cities. The movement of people from countryside to city during the Renaissance and Reformation eras further changed traditional popular culture. In the city, food came from a shop rather than directly from the fields. Local governments helped out when disasters occurred. If famine struck, authorities passed out bread. If plagues broke out, the government set up hospitals and quarantined sick people.

Gradually, the residents of cities and towns became more sophisticated in their attitudes. In particular, people's understanding of how things happen in the world began to change. Superstition no longer played an important role in people's views of daily life. Instead, people sought rational explanations for day-to-day events. They had less need for magic and "wise" folk. Some scholars have called this very important development the "disenchantment" of the world—the removal of "enchantment," or magic, from nature.

✔ **READING CHECK: Contrasting** In what ways did life in Europe change during the early Renaissance? standard of living rose for some, people moved from country to cities, better diet, rational thinking more widespread

INTERPRETING THE VISUAL RECORD
Daily work This sophisticated urban couple of the 1500s are working together in their banking business. *Compare this picture with the picture of peasants on the previous page. What role did women play in the world of work?*

◆SECTION◆
5 REVIEW ANSWERS

❶ **Define**
• broadsides, p. 375
• almanacs, p. 375
• standard of living, p. 376

❷ long, hard days of work; holiday ceremonies; close-knit communities; odd behavior treated harshly; widespread belief in superstition and witchcraft

❸ a. broadsides and books, founding of new schools

b. Townspeople and city folk became more sophisticated; people sought rational explanations for everyday events.

c. Answers will vary. Factors suggesting a better life include: increase in education, movement from country to city, and better diet. Students may note that most peasants' lives remained unchanged.

❹ Responses will vary but should incorporate a mindset typical of villagers at the time.

SECTION 5 REVIEW

1. **Define** and explain the significance:
   broadsides
   almanacs
   standard of living

2. **Summarizing** Copy the concept map below. Use it to explain features of daily life in Europe during the 1500s.

   Daily Life—1500s

   go. hrw .com **Homework Practice Online**
   keyword: SP3 HP15

3. **Finding the Main Idea**
   a. What evidence would you give that the printing press had significant influence during the Renaissance?
   b. Why did urban life lead to the growing "disenchantment" of the world?
   c. Did life improve for most Europeans during the 1500s?

4. **Writing and Critical Thinking**
   Analyzing Information Imagine that you are a European villager. Prepare a broadside that explains why people believe in superstitions.
   Consider:
   • attitudes toward God and nature
   • the role of "wise" folk in village life

REVIEW AND ASSESSMENT RESOURCES

REPRODUCIBLE RESOURCES
▸ Vocabulary Activity 15

TECHNOLOGY RESOURCES
▸ Chapter 15 Test Generator (on the One-Stop Planner)
▸ Global Skill Builder CD–ROM
▸ HRW Web Site

REINFORCEMENT, REVIEW, and ASSESSMENT
▸ Chapter 15 Review, pp. 378–379
▸ Chapter 15 Tutorial for Students, Parents, Mentors, and Peers
▸ Chapter 15 Test (Form A or B)
▸ Alternative Assessment Handbook
▸ Chapter 15 Test for English Language Learners and Special-Needs Students

REVIEW
Have students complete the Chapter 15 Review on pages 378–379.

ASSESS
Use one of the chapter tests to assess students' understanding of the content. For Alternative Assessment, see the Portfolio Activities and Alternative Assessment Handbook.

CHAPTER 15 REVIEW ANSWERS

Understanding Main Ideas

1. critical approach, studied classics, admired human achievement

2. use of perspective, more realistic portrayals

3. travelers to and from Italy, printing press

4. interested in early Christian as well as classical culture

5. created opposition in northern Europe

6. Peace of Augsburg, rise of sects, creation of Anglican Church, Calvinism

7. clarified doctrines, brought Inquisition to Rome, established order of Jesuits

8. education and reading became more important, more universities

9. People looked for explanations for everyday occurrences.

10. The world beyond the village became known through the availability of printed works.

Reviewing Themes

1. They led to conflict.

2. It increased the spread of new ideas.

3. They provided one of the main features of Renaissance humanist thought.

CHAPTER 15 Review

Creating a Time Line

Copy the time line below onto a sheet of paper. Complete the time line by filling in the events, individuals, and dates from the chapter that you think were significant. Pick three events and explain why you think they were significant.

1400	1500	1600

Writing a Summary

Using standard grammar, spelling, sentence structure, and punctuation, write an overview of the events in the chapter.

Identifying People and Ideas

Identify the following terms or individuals and explain their significance:

1. Renaissance
2. humanists
3. Niccolò Machiavelli
4. Leonardo da Vinci
5. Johannes Gutenberg
6. Reformation
7. Martin Luther
8. Counter-Reformation
9. broadsides
10. standard of living

Understanding Main Ideas

SECTION 1 *(pp. 354–358)*
The Italian Renaissance
1. What were the main values that generally characterized the Italian humanists?
2. What new painting styles and techniques developed during the Italian Renaissance?

SECTION 2 *(pp. 359–362)*
The Northern Renaissance
3. How did northern Europeans learn about the Italian Renaissance?
4. How did northern Renaissance writers differ from the writers of the Italian Renaissance?

SECTION 3 *(pp. 363–367)*
The Protestant Reformation
5. What role did the sale of indulgences by the church play in the Reformation?
6. In what ways did Protestantism spread?

SECTION 4 *(pp. 368–371)*
The Catholic Reformation
7. What actions did the Catholic Church take during the Counter-Reformation?
8. How did the Reformation and Counter-Reformation affect education?

SECTION 5 *(pp. 372–377)*
Culture and Daily Life
9. Why did Europeans believe in superstitions?
10. What factor was mainly responsible for the decline of traditional culture?

Reviewing Themes

1. **Global Relations** What effect did the ideas of Luther and other religious reformers have on the relations between different groups in Europe?
2. **Science, Technology & Society** What effect did the printing press have on the ways that Europeans understood their world?
3. **Culture** How did the classical literature of Greece and Rome influence the development of humanism?

Thinking Critically

1. **Identifying Cause and Effect** What events contributed to the beginning of the Renaissance?
2. **Contrasting** How did Renaissance humanist thought differ from medieval thought?
3. **Sequencing** What were the main events of the Reformation and the Counter-Reformation?
4. **Evaluating** How effective were the reforms of the Counter-Reformation?

Writing About History

Contrasting Write a report explaining the differences between Calvinism, Catholicism, and Lutheranism. Use the chart below to organize your thoughts before writing.

	Calvinism	Catholicism	Lutheranism
Path to salvation			
Church organization			

CLOSE

Arrange a panel discussion on the following topic: The Reformation and Counter-Reformation would not have occurred if not for the invention of the printing press.

RETEACH

Group students who had trouble with the test into pairs. Have them use their textbooks to correct their tests. Ask them to create questions and answers covering chapter content. Then have students take the Form B test to assess their mastery of the material.

ENGLISH LANGUAGE LEARNERS , COOPERATIVE LEARNING

Portfolio Extension

1. During the Reformation, religious leaders created posters, called "broadsides," to persuade people to embrace their religion. The posters were composed mostly of images, because most people could not read. Have students create a broadside for either the Protestant or Catholic cause in the 1500s. Posters should include positive images and slogans to attract people to the cause.

2. Have students imagine that they are Renaissance authors or artists. Have them write a poem or short play reflecting the ideas of humanism or create an original painting, drawing, or sculpture based on Renaissance ideas. Ask them to write a short presentation for their work, explaining how it reflects the ideas of the Renaissance.

Building Social Studies Skills

Using Artifacts as Historical Evidence

Study the photograph below. Then answer the questions that follow.

Italian Renaissance bookbinding with velvet and silverwork

1. Which of the following best describes the historical evidence this artifact provides?
   a. Many people had books during the Renaissance.
   b. Italian bookbinding reached its height during the Renaissance.
   c. All Renaissance books were bound with velvet and silver.
   d. During the Renaissance, some Italians had books with fancy bindings.

2. What clues does this bookbinding give about life during the Italian Renaissance? Give your reasons.

Identifying Cause and Effect

Read the following excerpt by an art historian about the Italian artist Michelangelo. Then answer the questions.

"Michelangelo's life story is a series of quarrels, disappointments, and interruptions. If we except the Sistine Ceiling, he was forced to leave undone more work than he was allowed to finish, largely because of . . . his patron Pope Julius II . . . . Some twenty-four years after the completion of the ceiling Michelangelo was called upon to do another stupendous fresco, this time for the end wall of the same chapel. *The Last Judgment* . . . reflects the bitterness of the aging genius."

3. Which of the following correctly states the reason the author gives for Michelangelo's bitterness?
   a. His whole life he had been forced to do what his patron required.
   b. He did not want to leave the chapel ceiling unfinished.
   c. He felt he was too old to do another fresco.
   d. He thought his patron would interrupt him once again.

4. Most artists of the Italian Renaissance supported themselves by working for patrons. Do you think this system was successful? Give your reasons.

Alternative Assessment

Building Your Portfolio

Science, Technology & Society

The printing press helped spread new ideas down through the centuries. With computers, current printing technology has changed, and the Internet spreads information almost instantly around the world. Using your textbook and other sources, create a bibliography of the important printed works that have had a great influence on people and events.

internet connect

Internet Activity: go.hrw.com
KEYWORD: SP3 WH15

Choose a topic on the Renaissance and Reformation to:
- create a pamphlet on the Reformation and its leaders.
- report on the economic, social, and technological influences of Johannes Gutenberg's printing press.
- create a biography on one of the Renaissance writers in this chapter.

Thinking Critically

1. contact with Byzantine civilization, achievements in science and medicine by other cultures

2. Medieval scholars: harmonize classical culture with Christian teachings; Renaissance humanists: power of human reason and study of the classics

3. Luther's 95 theses, Luther's excommunication, establishment of Lutheran Church, Peace of Augsburg, creation of Anglican Church, founding of Calvinism, Edict of Nantes, Inquisition in Rome, *Index of Forbidden Books,* Council of Trent, establishment of order of Jesuits

4. The Catholic Church clarified doctrines and fostered spirituality, but religious conflict grew.

Writing About History

Reports should mention predestination and righteous living (Calvinism); Bible as sole religious authority, simplicity and spirituality (Lutheranism); need for ceremonies, dependence upon priests (Catholicism).

Building Social Studies Skills

1. d

2. Books were valued highly.

3. a

4. Answers will vary.

Building Your Portfolio

Students should include examples of printed works from various fields.

Exploration and Expansion

CHAPTER RESOURCE MANAGER

Objectives	Pacing Guide	Reproducible Resources
SECTION 1 **The Scientific Revolution** (pp. 382–387)	• Identify the factors that contributed to the Scientific Revolution. • Explain how Copernicus, Kepler, and Galileo challenged traditional thought. • Describe some of the important scientific discoveries of this period.	**Regular** 1.5 day / **Block Scheduling** 1 day *Block Scheduling Handbook with Team Teaching Strategies, 16.1*	**RS** Guided Reading Strategy 16.1 **PS** Readings in World History 56: On the Motion of the Heart and Blood
SECTION 2 **The Foundations of European Exploration** (pp. 388–391)	• Identify technological advances that made European exploration possible. • Describe the effect of the Commercial Revolution. • Explain the role mercantilism played in the colonies.	**Regular** 1.5 day / **Block Scheduling** 1 day *Block Scheduling Handbook with Team Teaching Strategies, 16.2*	**RS** Guided Reading Strategy 16.2 **E** Hands-on History Activity 16: A Sailor's Life **E** Creative Teaching Strategy 16: Talk Show: Changing Europe's Worldview
SECTION 3 **Voyages of Portugal and Spain** (pp. 392–399)	• Describe what the early Portuguese explorers accomplished. • Discuss how the voyages of Christopher Columbus influenced the world. • Explain why the Atlantic slave trade prospered.	**Regular** 1.5 day / **Block Scheduling** 1 day *Block Scheduling Handbook with Team Teaching Strategies, 16.3*	**RS** Guided Reading Strategy 16.3 **RS** Graphic Organizer Activity 16: Explorers and Explorations **SM** Geography Activity 16: Crossing the Atlantic **PS** Readings in World History 57: First Impressions of the New World
SECTION 4 **The Spanish and Dutch Empires** (pp. 400–407)	• Describe how Spain extended its power abroad and at home. • Explain why the Dutch were successful in the 1600s. • Analyze why the Spanish Empire declined.	**Regular** 1.5 day / **Block Scheduling** 1 day *Block Scheduling Handbook with Team Teaching Strategies, 16.4*	**RS** Guided Reading Strategy 16.4

Chapter Resource Key

PS	Primary Sources	**A**	Assessment	Music
RS	Reading Support	**REV**	Review	Video
IC	Interdisciplinary Connections	**ELL**	Reinforcement and English Language Learners	Internet
E	Enrichment		Transparencies	Holt Presentation Maker Using Microsoft® PowerPoint®
SM	Skills Mastery		CD-ROM	

 One-Stop Planner CD-ROM

See the ***One-Stop Planner*** for a complete list of additional resources for students and teachers.

One-Stop Planner CD-ROM

It's easy to plan lessons, select resources, and print out materials for your students when you use the **One-Stop Planner** CD–ROM with **Test Generator.**

Technology Resources

 One-Stop Planner 16.1

 Holt Researcher: World History: Nicolaus Copernicus, Galileo Galilei

Holt Researcher: World History: Robert Boyle

Homework Practice Online

One-Stop Planner 16.2

Homework Practice Online

Online Maps: Major European Trading Areas, c. 1500

Online Maps: European Trade Goods, c. 1500

Online Maps: European Finance and Trade, c. 1500

One-Stop Planner 16.3

Holt Researcher: World History: Isabella, Christopher Columbus

World History and Cultures Video Program 16

CNN. Presents Geography: Yesterday and Today Segment 15: Worlds Meet in the Americas

Homework Practice Online

Online Maps: European Idea of the Atlantic Before Columbus

Online Maps: Treaty of Tordesillas, 1494

 One-Stop Planner 16.4

 Homework Practice Online

Online Maps: French and Dutch Imports, 1770s

Online Maps: Portuguese Imports, 1770s

Online Maps: Spanish Imports, 1770s

Online Maps: British Imports, 1770s

Online Maps: Empires in the Americas, 1700

Online Maps: Africa in 1750

Reinforcement, Review, and Assessment

Daily Quiz 16.1

Main Idea Activity 16.1

English Audio Summary 16.1

Spanish Audio Summary 16.1

REV Section 1 Review, p. 387

Daily Quiz 16.2

Main Idea Activity 16.2

English Audio Summary 16.2

Spanish Audio Summary 16.2

REV Section 1 Review, p. 391

Daily Quiz 16.3

Main Idea Activity 16.3

English Audio Summary 16.3

Spanish Audio Summary 16.3

REV Section 3 Review, p. 399

Daily Quiz 16.4

Main Idea Activity 16.4

English Audio Summary 16.4

Spanish Audio Summary 16.4

REV Section 4 Review, p. 407

HRW ONLINE RESOURCES

GO TO: go.hrw.com
Then type in a keyword.

TEACHER HOME PAGE
KEYWORD: SP3 Teacher

CHAPTER INTERNET ACTIVITIES
KEYWORD: SP3 WH16

Choose an activity to:
- research the Scientific Revolution and create a database of scientists, dates, and contributions.
- learn more about an explorer described in this chapter.
- explain the political, economic, and cultural impact of Spanish expansion in Mesoamerica and Andean South America.

CHAPTER ENRICHMENT LINKS
KEYWORD: SP3 CH16

ONLINE ASSESSMENT
Homework Practice
KEYWORD: SP3 HP16
Standardized Test Prep
KEYWORD: SP3 STP16
Rubrics
KEYWORD: SS Rubrics

ONLINE MAPS, CHARTS, AND GRAPHS
KEYWORD: SP3 MCG

CONTENT UPDATES
KEYWORD: SS Content Updates

HOLT PRESENTATION MAKER
KEYWORD: SP3 PPT16

ONLINE READING SUPPORT
KEYWORD: SS Strategies

CURRENT EVENTS
KEYWORD: S3 Current Events

Meeting Individual Needs

Ability Levels

Level 1 Basic level activities designed for all students encountering new material

Level 2 Intermediate level activities designed for average students

Level 3 Challenging activities designed for honors and gifted and talented students

English Language Learners These activities address the needs of students with Limited English Proficiency.

Chapter Review and Assessment

IC Vocabulary Activity 16

Global Skill Builder CD-ROM

HRW Web Site

REV Chapter 16 Tutorial for Students, Parents, Mentors, and Peers

REV Chapter 16 Review, pp. 408–409

A Chapter 16 Test Generator (on the One-Stop Planner)

A Chapter 16 Test (Form A or B)

A Alternative Assessment Handbook

A Chapter 16 Test for English Language Learners and Special-Needs Students

CHAPTER
16

Build on What You Know

Ask students to answer the following questions:

How might the Italian Renaissance and the Protestant Reformation have affected how people thought about the natural world?

Consider:

- challenges to traditional authority
- study of newly-discovered ancient manuscripts
- curiosity about ideas

What changes in technology and society might have encouraged the quest for new knowledge?

Consider:

- the influence of the printing press
- the role of stronger monarchies as patrons of learning and exploration

---

EXPLORING THE TIME LINE
GLBAL EVENTS

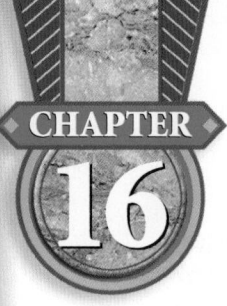

internet connect

TOPIC: Mercator projection map and other technological advances

GO TO: go.hrw.com
KEYWORD: SP3 WH16

Have students access the Internet through the HRW Go site to conduct research on the first Mercator projection map and other technological inventions that helped foster exploration and expansion in the 1500s and 1600s. Then have students create a museum display highlighting two or three of these inventions (for example, maps, navigation tools, and ships). Their display should include pictures, drawings, or models of the inventions along with text that explains how the invention aided explorers in reaching their goals.

CHAPTER
16

1400–1800

Exploration and Expansion

Woodcut from the 1500s showing Hispaniola

Coin minted during the reign of Charles V

1492
Global Events
Columbus makes his first voyage to the Americas.

c. 1503–1506
The Arts
Leonardo da Vinci paints the *Mona Lisa*.

1532
Global Events
Francisco Pizarro invades the Inca Empire.

1556
Politics
Charles V divides his lands between members of his family.

1569
Science and Technology
The first Mercator projection map makes navigation much easier.

1400

1500

1600

1431
Daily Life
Joan of Arc is burned at the stake.

1519
Global Events
The Magellan-Elcano expedition begins its voyage around the world.

1513
Global Events
Ponce de León explores and names Florida.

1543
Science and Technology
Copernicus publishes his heliocentric theory.

1588
Politics
The Spanish Armada sets sail against England.

Galileo's telescope

Build on What You Know

The Italian Renaissance of the 1300s marked a time of great change in Europe. Renaissance thinking and styles spread throughout western and northern Europe. The Protestant Reformation of the 1500s led to new social, political, and economic patterns across Europe. The Reformation challenged traditional approaches to religious thought and the individual's role in society. During this same era, new ways of studying and understanding the natural world brought about a scientific revolution. In this chapter, you will learn about the causes and effects of this revolution in thought.

What's Your Opinion?

Themes Journal *To help students create their Themes Journal entries, provide the following examples of appropriate **agree**/**disagree** statements.*

Science, Technology & Society

Agree Scientists are an educated elite who rarely discuss their ideas with ordinary people.

Disagree Most gains in standards of living result from advances in science and technology.

Economics

Agree The need for natural resources motivates governments to look for new sources.

Disagree Cultures develop around available resources; they just decide they "need" other resources they find through exploration.

Global Relations

Agree Conquering powers pursue their own interests, not those of the people they conquer.

Disagree Exploration is a quest for knowledge; conquest has different motives, such as power.

A maritime trading company's crest

Dutch ship landing slaves in colonial Jamestown

1610
Business and Finance
The Dutch East India Company introduces the term "shares" of stock.

1619
Politics
Colonists of Jamestown, Virginia, form the first representative colonial assembly in America.

1619
Global Events
A Dutch ship brings the first cargo of African slaves to Jamestown.

c. 1674
Science and Technology
Antoni van Leeuwenhoek first observes bacteria through a microscope.

1750
Daily Life
The world's population reaches approximately 750 million.

1756
The Arts
Composer Wolfgang Amadeus Mozart is born.

1776
Business and Finance
Scottish economist Adam Smith writes about mercantilism in *Wealth of Nations*.

1700

1800

1628
Science and Technology
William Harvey accurately describes the human circulatory system.

1626
Business and Finance
The Dutch purchase Manhattan Island from American Indians.

1609
The Arts
William Shakespeare publishes a book of sonnets.

1708
Business and Finance
British traders dominate trade on the coasts of India.

The Leeuwenhoek microscope, shown here, was about 3 to 4 inches high. On the back of the instrument, a screw with a needle provided a place to hold the object being viewed. The microscope was then held up to the viewer's eye.

The Dutch purchased Manhattan Island for trade goods.

What's Your Opinion?

Themes Journal *Do you **agree** or **disagree** with the following statements? Support your point of view in your journal.*

Science, Technology & Society A society's approach to scientific study has little impact upon daily lifestyles and standards of living.

Economics A nation's need for natural resources encourages national commitment to exploration and discovery.

Global Relations Exploration can lead to confrontations and mistreatment of conquered peoples.

EXPLORING THE TIME LINE
GLOBAL EVENTS

Europeans encountered Muslim culture not only through the Crusades, but also through contact with Spain. The cities of Córdoba and Toledo were famous centers of learning, and prosperous Seville was Spain's capital under Islam. Christian and Jewish scholars carried Muslim learning from Spain into western Europe. Ferdinand of Aragon and Isabella of Castile conquered the last Muslim stronghold in Spain in 1492. These and later rulers required Jews and Muslims to convert to Christianity or leave Spain.

Critical Thinking

Ask students how the Muslim presence in Spain influenced exploration and expansion by Christian Europe.

ANSWER: Students might note that it exposed Europeans to Muslim learning, particularly in geography and science, but also that it limited the money available to Ferdinand and Isabella for overseas exploration until they finished their war against Muslims in Spain.

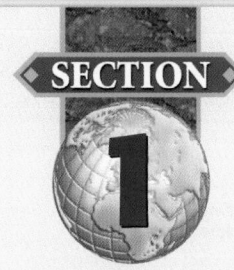
OBJECTIVES

1 **Identify the factors that contributed to the Scientific Revolution.**

2 **Explain how Copernicus, Kepler, and Galileo challenged traditional thought.**

3 **Describe some of the important scientific discoveries of this period.**

🔔 *LET'S GET STARTED!*

As students enter the classroom, ask them to divide a sheet of paper into two columns headed *Magical* and *Scientific*. In one column have them write words that describe how people who believed in magic tried to learn about nature. *(alchemy, astrology, ancient texts)* In the other column have them write words describing how scientists learn about nature. *(observation, mathematics, measurement, instruments)* Note any responses that fall in both columns. Tell students that in Section 1 they will learn how belief in magic contributed to the beginnings of the Scientific Revolution.

SECTION 1 RESOURCES

REPRODUCIBLE RESOURCES

▶ Guided Reading Strategy 16.1

▶ Readings in World History 56: On the Motion of the Heart and Blood

TECHNOLOGY RESOURCES

▶ One-Stop Planner 16.1

▶ Holt Researcher: World History: Nicolaus Copernicus, Galileo Galilei

▶ Holt Researcher: World History: Robert Boyle

▶ Homework Practice Online

REINFORCEMENT, REVIEW, AND ASSESSMENT

▶ Section 1 Review, p. 387

▶ Daily Quiz 16.1

▶ Main Idea Activity 16.1

▶ English Audio Summary 16.1

▶ Spanish Audio Summary 16.1

VISUAL RECORD ANSWER

through observation and experimentation

SECTION 1

READ TO DISCOVER

❶ What factors contributed to the Scientific Revolution?

❷ How did Copernicus, Kepler, and Galileo challenge traditional thought?

❸ What were some of the important scientific discoveries of this period?

DEFINE

scientific method
geocentric theory
heliocentric theory

IDENTIFY

Roger Bacon
Scientific Revolution
Nicolaus Copernicus
Johannes Kepler
Galileo Galilei
Isaac Newton
Andreas Vesalius
René Descartes
Francis Bacon
Robert Boyle

WHY IT MATTERS TODAY

Scientific discoveries can have both positive and negative effects on society. Use or other **current event** sources to find several social issues that involve science or technology. Record your findings in your journal.

CNN Student News.com

The Scientific Revolution

The Main Idea
The Scientific Revolution challenged and changed the way people thought about the world.

The Story Continues *In the early 1600s Spanish writer Miguel de Cervantes published a novel called* Don Quixote de la Mancha. *It told the story of an aging man stuck in the myths of the past. Cervantes's humorous tale reflected a new world that was rejecting the legends of old for a reality based on science.*

From Magic to Science

Until well into the 1500s, most Europeans saw little difference between science and magic. Alchemists used spells and magic formulas to try to change one substance to another—for example, lead into gold. Astrologers believed that the position of the stars in the sky influenced human life. People still believed many explanations of natural events proposed by Aristotle almost 2,000 years earlier. These people were called natural philosophers. They relied on religious teachings and the works of classical Greek and Roman thinkers to explain the mysteries of nature. Many scientists before the Renaissance were like **Roger Bacon,** an English philosopher and scientist of the 1200s. Bacon, a Franciscan monk who had studied at Oxford and Paris, was viewed as a leading scholar of his time. He was one of the earliest to favor a system of scientific experimentation, rather than faithful acceptance of religious ideas and ancient beliefs, as a means of finding truth. Nevertheless, he was shaped by the thinking of the time and mainly practiced alchemy. Famed for his teaching, Bacon became known as Doctor Mirabilis—wonderful teacher.

The spirit of the Renaissance encouraged curiosity, investigation, discovery, and the practical application of the knowledge of nature to everyday life. Some people felt freer to question old ideas and beliefs. They were more willing to use new approaches to answering questions about the natural world. During the era of the **Scientific Revolution,** people began using experiments and mathematics to understand these mysteries. The study of nature became more organized. They were no longer content to explain the world in terms of religious thought, magic, or the ideas of ancient writers.

INTERPRETING THE VISUAL RECORD

Alchemy Alchemists sought to understand and control the natural world through the use of magic. Some of their procedures and tools, however, were similar to those of early and later scientists. *Based on the picture, how might alchemists have contributed to the development of early scientific procedures?*

TEACH OBJECTIVE 1

LEVEL 1: Ask students to name causes of the Scientific Revolution. Write the answers in a web diagram on the board. Ask students how each cause contributed to the Scientific Revolution. **ENGLISH LANGUAGE LEARNERS**

This new approach produced answers to many questions in physics, astronomy, and anatomy. It formed the basis for what we know today as science. Before the 1600s the word science meant "to know." After the 1600s the sense of the word changed into the narrower meaning it has today.

✔ **READING CHECK: Drawing Inferences** What role did the Renaissance play in the development of science? encouraged curiosity, investigation, and discovery

The New Study of Nature

As scientists spent more time examining the world around them, they observed things that did not agree with traditional explanations. For this reason, early scientists of the 1500s began to question ancient beliefs. They learned to form conclusions based on what they could observe with their own senses. They also used three new tools—scientific instruments, mathematics, and experiments. This new approach to study and knowledge marked the beginnings of the Scientific Revolution. It was a turning point in thinking that led to a rapid increase in people's understanding of the world.

The ability to conduct experiments was key to this new approach to learning. Scientists used newly invented instruments such as the barometer, the microscope, the telescope, the air pump, and the thermometer. These tools greatly improved their ability to observe and measure. Scientists used mathematics to check and apply those measurements. Also, they repeated their experiments to make sure they got the same results. Then they drew conclusions about what they observed. This manner of study is called the **scientific method.**

✔ **READING CHECK: Drawing Conclusions** Why did the study of nature change during the 1500s and the 1600s? Scientists formed conclusions based on observation and made use of new tools and instruments to observe and measure.

Astronomy, Physics, and Anatomy

Three areas of study were especially interesting to some of the strongest thinkers of the times. Astronomy was the study of stars, planets, and other bodies in the sky. Another area, physics, focused on changes and properties of matter and energy. Scientists in the field of anatomy studied the structure of the human body, mainly by examining dead bodies. Several European scientists helped to shape the modern study of these important sciences.

Copernicus. In the A.D. 100s, the astronomer Ptolemy stated that Earth was the center of the universe. The sun and the planets, according to Ptolemy, moved around Earth. Ptolemy's theory is called the **geocentric,** or "Earth-centered," **theory.** The Greek word for Earth is *geo.* People believed this theory for many centuries.

During the early 1500s, Polish scientist **Nicolaus Copernicus** began to abandon Ptolemy's geocentric theory. Instead, he argued that the sun was the center of the universe. Copernicus developed the **heliocentric,** or "sun-centered," **theory.** *Helio* is the Greek word meaning "sun." Copernicus realized that his theory explained many of the then-known facts about astronomy.

When Copernicus's theory was published in 1543, people paid little attention. The theory seemed to deny what people's senses told them. Anyone could "see" that the sun and planets moved around Earth. Anyone could "feel" that solid Earth did not move.

HISTORY MAKER

Nicolaus Copernicus (1473–1543)

Nicolaus Copernicus, the great Polish scientist, is viewed today as the founder of modern astronomy. His heliocentric theory demonstrated that the earth is a moving planet and that it revolves around the sun. Copernicus became a symbol of the new ideas and approaches that brought about the Scientific Revolution. **How did Copernicus change our understanding of the universe?**

Model of Copernicus's theory of planetary revolutions

Science, Technology & Society

Many early alchemists devoted much of their time to creating natural remedies for illnesses. However, Paracelsus maintained that inorganic substances, such as minerals, could also be used to treat diseases. He tried to convince his colleagues that it would be beneficial to search for new inorganic medicines, rather than always searching for the "philosopher's stone," a mysterious substance they believed could change cheap materials such as lead into precious materials like gold.

Critical Thinking

Ask students why Paracelsus may have wanted alchemists to search for cures for health problems rather than the "philosopher's stone."

ANSWER: Students may answer that if alchemists found cures for health problems, they would be helping humanity and would seem less concerned with their own wealth. In addition, Paracelsus may have suspected that they might never find the "philosopher's stone."

HISTORY MAKER ANSWER

demonstrated that Earth was not at center of universe, planets revolve around sun

ALL LEVELS: Explain the difference between the geocentric theory *(sun, planets, and stars revolve around Earth)* and the heliocentric theory. *(Earth and other planets revolve around sun)* Then divide students into groups of three to six. Have each group plan and perform a short role-play about Copernicus, Kepler, or Galileo. Tell students their skit should explain the scientist's ideas in simple words and show how those ideas challenged traditional thought.

ENGLISH LANGUAGE LEARNERS, COOPERATIVE LEARNING

LEVEL 3: Have students write an essay about how changing from a geocentric to a heliocentric view of the universe might affect people's attitudes about other aspects of life. *(Essays will vary but might mention the idea that nature does not revolve around people, creation is like an impersonal machine, and what seems obvious is not necessarily true.)* Discuss the essays in class. Ask students if any modern scientific discoveries affect the ways people think about their lives. *(relativity, quantum theory, space exploration)*

CONNECTING TO MATH ANSWER

geometry of circles and ellipses; formulas about speed of objects in motion

Interdisciplinary Connection

MATH. Kepler acknowledged the difficulties that others would have understanding his work. He wrote: "It is extremely difficult nowadays to write mathematical books, especially astronomical ones. For unless use is made of an exact precision in the proportions, explanations, demonstrations and conclusion the book will not be mathematical; if such use is made, then the reading of it becomes very difficult . . . That is why nowadays there are few suitable readers; the majority generally despise and reject such works . . . . I myself, who pass for a mathematician, tire my brain in reading my own work . . . ."

Critical Thinking

Ask students to write a sentence summarizing Kepler's dilemma in their own words. Then ask them to try to suggest a way Kepler could communicate his ideas more effectively.

ANSWER: Suggestions may include making drawings or models of planetary orbits.

CONNECTING TO
Math

Kepler's Laws of Planetary Motion

Johannes Kepler tried to use mathematics to prove that the planets orbit around the sun. Kepler discovered three "laws" about how planets move in space. These laws are referred to as Kepler's laws of planetary motion.

Using the observations made by his employer, Tycho Brahe, Kepler found that planets travel around the sun in oval-shaped orbits called ellipses. Kepler's second discovery was that planets move faster when they are closer to the sun. Kepler's third law relates to the time it takes for a planet to complete an orbit around the sun.

Understanding Math

How would math help Kepler prove that his discoveries were true?

Kepler and Galileo. Copernicus had neither the instruments nor the mathematics to prove his theory. Proof came later with the work of two other scientists. **Johannes Kepler,** a German astronomer, and **Galileo Galilei,** an Italian scientist, each helped to confirm Copernicus's new understanding of the universe.

Johannes Kepler was a brilliant mathematician who used models, observation, and mathematics to test Copernicus's heliocentric theory. Some of the ideas on which Copernicus had based his theory were wrong. That slowed Kepler down, but he eventually proved the heliocentric theory correct. He published his laws of planetary motion in 1609. It took the work of an Italian scientist, however, to produce clear evidence that the earth moves around the sun.

Galileo Galilei had read of a Dutch device that made distant objects appear larger. Galileo built his own device—a telescope—and began studying the heavens. His telescope was very simple compared to those made today. However, Galileo was able to see things that no one had ever seen. He saw the mountains and valleys of the moon. He observed the rings around Saturn and spots on the sun. Galileo also observed the moons circling Jupiter. He used these observations to argue that not every heavenly body revolves around Earth. Galileo drew sketches of the things he observed through his telescope.

When Galileo published his findings in 1632, the work caused an uproar. Many scholars who still believed in Ptolemy's old geocentric theory refused to accept Galileo's findings. Church scholars disapproved because Galileo's theory seemed to contradict the Bible. Some said that the telescope was an invention of the devil.

In the central panel of this ceiling fresco, Galileo Galilei is shown demonstrating the use of his telescope. Later, Galileo was called before the Inquisition and forced to renounce his discoveries. He spent the rest of his life under house arrest.

HOMEWORK Have students choose a scientific instrument mentioned in the chapter and explain why it was important in the Scientific Revolution.

Spotlight on CULTURE Tell students that most scientific writing was in Latin, but Galileo chose to write in Italian. Ask the class how the Scientific Revolution might have been different if scientists like Copernicus (Polish) and Kepler (German) had written just in their own languages. *(They might have had less communication with scientists in other countries but more readers in their own countries.)* Ask how the growing use of national languages in place of Latin might affect society and culture. *(nationalism, less dependence on authority for information)*

BLOCK SCHEDULING

Traditional scholars in physics were also displeased with Galileo. They believed, as Aristotle had said, that heavier objects fell faster than lighter ones. Using experiments and mathematics, Galileo proved this false. If there is no friction from air, all objects fall at the same rate. Galileo's discoveries formed the basis for the modern science of mechanics—the study of objects in motion.

Newton. In 1687 English scientist **Isaac Newton** published a book building on the work of Copernicus, Kepler, and Galileo. They had shown that the planets, including Earth, revolve around the sun. They had not, however, been able to explain why these bodies moved as they did.

After many experiments and measurements, Newton realized that the force that holds the planets in their orbits and the force that causes objects to fall to Earth are one and the same. He proposed the law of universal gravitation, which states that all bodies attract each other. Moreover, the force of this attraction can be measured. Both Kepler's Proof and Galileo's discoveries about falling objects were really examples of the law of universal gravitation. Newton also explained the laws of motion and developed the mathematical means of measuring motion. In one sweeping system, Newton tied together the movement of all things in the heavens and on Earth.

Newton's work had a huge impact on the science of his time. Even today, his laws of motion and gravitation are applied in the development of everything from automobile seatbelts to space travel. Furthermore, Newton's work changed the way people viewed the world. No longer would most well-educated Europeans see the universe as a place in which everything moved according to the constant attention of God and His angels. Most Europeans still accepted God as creator of the universe. However, they now began to think of that creation as a kind of giant mechanical clock. Once wound up by the divine clockmaker, it moved according to natural and universal laws of motion. So great was Newton's influence that the English poet Alexander Pope wrote:

 "Nature and nature's laws lay hid in night; God said, 'Let Newton be!' and all was light."

Alexander Pope, epitaph intended for Sir Isaac Newton

Vesalius and Harvey. The great Renaissance artist Leonardo da Vinci was a student of the human body. To those who tried to describe the body, he once said, "I advise you not to trouble with words unless you are speaking to blind men." **Andreas Vesalius,** a Flemish scientist, heeded da Vinci's words and pioneered the study of anatomy. Vesalius refused to accept descriptions of human muscles and tissues written by Galen 1,400 years earlier. He did his own studies to see how the human body was constructed. In 1543, Vesalius published a seven-volume book called *On the Fabric of the Human Body.* The illustrations of the human body that Vesalius included in his work were amazingly detailed for the time. They helped readers to gain a visual understanding of the many complicated components of the body and of how they work together.

English physician William Harvey made equally important contributions. Using laboratory experiments, Harvey studied the circulation of blood. He described how blood moved through the veins and arteries. He also observed the working of the body's most important muscle—the heart.

✔ **READING CHECK: Making Generalizations** How did the work of early scientists during the Scientific Revolution lay the foundation for modern science? *introduced new approaches to knowledge and new methods and instruments*

HISTORY MAKER

Galileo Galilei (1564–1642)

Galileo believed that scientific study would change the way people understood themselves and their world. Science, he felt, would lead to higher standards of living at every level of society. He believed, too, that science would weaken the social and economic barriers that separated people.

Because Galileo's findings challenged the traditional beliefs of the Catholic Church, church leaders kept him from teaching or writing about his ideas. **According to Galileo, in what ways would scientific progress affect society as a whole?**

Holt Researcher **go.hrw.com**

go.hrw.com
KEYWORD: Holt Researcher
FreeFind:
   Nicolaus Copernicus
   Galileo Galilei
After reading more about Copernicus and Galileo on the Holt Researcher, write an imaginary dialogue between the two discussing their ideas about the universe.

HISTORY MAKER ANSWER
Galileo thought science would lead to higher standards of living and would weaken the social and economic barriers that separated people.

History Maker

SIR ISAAC NEWTON. The new ideas of Copernicus, Kepler, and Galileo met with either indifference or criticism. For Sir Isaac Newton, however, publishing *The Mathematical Principles of Natural Philosophy* in 1687 led to a seat in Parliament, knighthood, directorship of the royal mint, and the presidency of the Royal Society.

Critical Thinking

Ask students why the reaction to Newton's ideas was so different from the reaction to the ideas of Copernicus, Kepler, or Galileo.

ANSWER: Students may answer that by the late 1600s, people were more open to new ideas because the earlier scientists had paved the way.

That's Interesting!

Harvey explained his theories about blood circulation in a 72-page book in 1628. Many physicians accepted his argument immediately, but Harvey believed that many would not understand his work. By the time of his death in 1657, however, most people had come to believe his theories.

EXPLORATION AND EXPANSION **385**

LEVEL 2: Ask students to create a chart of discoveries made during the Scientific Revolution. Have them organize their ideas under the headings *Astronomy, Physics, Anatomy, Chemistry,* and *Mathematics.* (*heliocentric theory; all objects fall at the same speed, laws of motion and universal gravitation; construction of human body, circulation of blood; oxygen, conservation of matter; calculus*) Then have students describe the significance of as many of these discoveries as they can. (*heliocentric theory—changed basic view of the universe; objects fall at the same speed—laid the foundation for modern science of mechanics; construction of human body and circulation of blood—laid basis for modern medicine*)

Ask students which they think had greater influence, specific advances in technology or a change in the way people think about science. Have students support their arguments with specific examples of scientists, discoveries, inventions, or ways of thought.

HISTORY MAKER ANSWER

It became the basis of our view of the universe and its physical properties.

Culture

Although Descartes worked to develop a scientific worldview that would not conflict with his Christianity, the Catholic Church did not share his assessment. Descartes's works were placed on the church's *Index,* a list of prohibited books. Louis XIV refused to allow Descartes to be buried in France with a religious ceremony because he perceived the skepticism Descartes advocated as dangerous.

Critical Thinking

Why would the church object to Descartes's ideas even though he believed that the existence of God was an incontrovertible fact?

ANSWER: Students may answer that the church feared that by claiming all ideas could be doubted, Descartes might encourage others to doubt ideas he himself believed.

HISTORY MAKER

René Descartes (1596–1650)

René Descartes explained that the universe operates in a machine-like way according to the basic laws of physics. His philosophy became the basis of our modern Western view of the universe and its physical properties. **How did Descartes's view of the universe influence today's science?**

Analyzing Primary Sources

Identifying a Point of View How would Descartes view information that was assumed to be true or that was accepted as true on the basis of faith or tradition? He would doubt or reject it.

The Triumph of the New Science

The effects of discoveries made during the Scientific Revolution were felt throughout Europe. So much had been learned that scientists believed that the scientific method offered a map that could easily be followed in the search for knowledge.

During the Counter-Reformation, religious orders had helped to revive faith in church teachings. New scientific "orders" spread knowledge of the developments of the Scientific Revolution. Schools and societies devoted to science appeared in Rome, England, and France. The printing press helped scientists as it had helped religious reformers. Most of the new scientific societies published journals. Scientists everywhere could now read about scientific studies being done in Europe.

Descartes. French philosopher and mathematician **René Descartes** (day·KAHRT) was a leader of the Scientific Revolution. His ideas led to great advances in mathematics, the sciences, and philosophy.

Descartes felt that no assumptions should be accepted without question. He developed a philosophy based on his own reason. In *Discourse on Method* (1637), Descartes stated that all assumptions had to be proven on the basis of known facts. Only ideas that were true beyond all doubt could be accepted without risk. He believed, for example, that his own existence was proven by the fact that he could think. Descartes wrote, "I think, therefore I am." From this basic truth, he built a method of questioning that followed a clear, orderly progression of logical reasoning.

History Makers Speak

❝[I] was never to accept anything as true that I did not know to be evidently so: that is to say carefully to avoid precipitancy [hasty conclusions based upon assumptions, rather than observed facts] and prejudice, and to include in my judgements nothing more than what presented itself so clearly and so distinctly to my mind that I might have no occasion to place it in doubt.❞

René Descartes, *Discourse on Method*

In Descartes's view, all fields of scientific knowledge were connected, thus they should be studied together. Descartes's interests ranged across many fields. His work included studies in geometry and algebra, the scientific method, astronomy, and the physical sciences. He created a mathematical description of the way that light reflects from a smooth surface. This explanation led to the law of refraction, a basic principle in the study of optics. Much of Descartes's work challenged traditional church teachings. He was forced to live in the Protestant kingdom of Sweden, where he died in 1650.

Francis Bacon. English philosopher and scientist **Francis Bacon** lived around the same time as Descartes. Bacon believed that scientific theories could be developed only through observation. He said that no assumption could be trusted unless it could be proven by repeatable experiments. Bacon relied on truths that could be demonstrated physically, rather than through deductive thinking or reasoning. In 1620 he published *Novum Organum,* a book that outlined this new system of knowledge.

Other scientific discoveries. During the 1500s and the 1600s, scientific discoveries were made throughout Europe. German Gottfried Liebnitz (LIP·nits) and the English thinker Isaac Newton developed calculus, a new branch of mathematics. The two did not work together. They developed their mathematical ideas independent of one another.

Dutch scientist Antoni van Leeuwenhoek (LAY·ven·hook) used the microscope, invented in the late 1500s, to discover bacteria. He called them animalcules. He studied

Have students complete the Section 1 Review on p. 387.

Have students complete Daily Quiz 16.1. As Alternative Assessment, you may want to use the chart of scientific discoveries exercise in this section's lessons.

Have students complete Main Idea Activity for English Language Learners and Special-Needs Students 16.1. Then have students work in pairs to design flash cards with main ideas on one side and their meaning on the other. Have one student read the definition aloud and ask the other to name the idea.

ENGLISH LANGUAGE LEARNERS , COOPERATIVE LEARNING

Have students learn more about Robert Boyle and his significance. Have them write a dialogue between Boyle and a traditional alchemist, showing how Boyle's innovations pioneered the modern science of chemistry. **BLOCK SCHEDULING**

---

and wrote about a whole range of tiny life forms never before seen by the human eye.

An English-Irish scientist, **Robert Boyle,** helped to pioneer the modern science of chemistry. Chemistry studies the composition of matter and how it changes. In 1662, Boyle showed that temperature and pressure affect the space that a gas occupies. An English chemist, Joseph Priestley, discovered the element oxygen in 1774. Antoine Lavoisier (luhv·WAHZ·ee·ay), a French scientist, later named it.

Before Lavoisier, people believed that fire was an element. He showed that fire resulted when a substance rapidly combined with oxygen. Lavoisier also showed that steam mixes with the air and becomes invisible. In this way, Lavoisier proved that matter can change form, but that it can neither be destroyed nor created. This idea is known as the law of conservation of matter. It is one of the most important principles in the study of chemistry.

Priestley and Lavoisier made their discoveries in the late 1700s. By this time, the scientific approach had spread across Europe. The store of human knowledge and understanding had increased beyond measure and in a very brief span of time. In fact, speed of discovery and rapid spread and exchange of knowledge were important characteristics of the Scientific Revolution. These resulted, in part, from the printing press, the rise of scientific societies, and other communications improvements.

✔ **READING CHECK: Drawing Inferences** Why did so many important scientific advances take place in so brief a period of time? In part, because new developments in communication helped to speed discovery, the spread of knowledge, and the exchange of ideas.

The French Academy of Sciences was founded in 1666.

Holt Researcher

go.hrw.com
KEYWORD: Holt Researcher
FreeFind: Robert Boyle
After reading more about Robert Boyle on the Holt Researcher, write a short essay describing his contributions to science.

SECTION 1 REVIEW

1. **Define** and explain the significance:
   scientific method
   geocentric theory
   heliocentric theory

2. **Identify** and explain the significance:
   Roger Bacon
   Scientific Revolution
   Nicolaus Copernicus
   Johannes Kepler
   Galileo Galilei
   Isaac Newton
   Andreas Vesalius
   René Descartes
   Francis Bacon
   Robert Boyle

3. **Identifying Cause and Effect** Copy the web diagram below. Use it to show what factors led to the Scientific Revolution and what contribution each of the major scientists made.

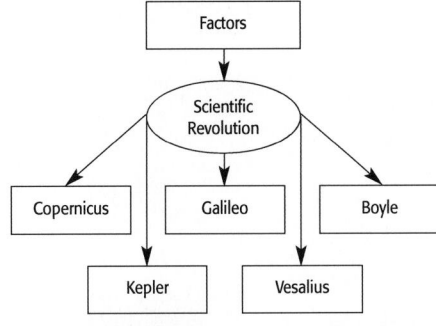

4. **Finding the Main Idea**
   a. Why were the scientific developments of the 1500s and the 1600s later called the Scientific Revolution?
   b. What did the work of Galileo, Newton, Vesalius, van Leeuwenhoek, and Lavoisier have in common?
   c. How did communications advances contribute to learning, discovery, and new scientific methods in Europe?

5. **Writing and Critical Thinking**
   Evaluating Write a short article for a science magazine describing the importance of the 1500s and the 1600s in the history of science.
   Consider:
   • how the study of science changed during this period
   • what discoveries were made that led to today's scientific and technical knowledge

Homework Practice Online
keyword: SP3 HP16

---

❶ **Define**
• scientific method, p. 383
• geocentric theory, p. 383
• heliocentric theory, p. 383

❷ **Identify**
• Roger Bacon, p. 382
• Scientific Revolution, p. 382
• Nicolaus Copernicus, p. 383
• Johannes Kepler, p. 384
• Galileo Galilei, p. 384
• Isaac Newton, p. 385
• Andreas Vesalius, p. 385
• René Descartes, p. 386
• Francis Bacon, p. 386
• Robert Boyle, p. 387

❸ Factors: Renaissance spirit, curiosity, questioning old beliefs; Copernicus: heliocentric theory; Kepler: laws of planetary motion; Galileo: observation of objects in space with telescope; Vesalius: anatomy, study of human body; Boyle: chemistry, effect of temperature and pressure on gas

❹ a. changed the way people studied nature; replaced acceptance of traditional beliefs

b. overturned old beliefs by using instruments, experiments, and mathematics

c. The printing press carried new ideas throughout Europe.

❺ Students might suggest the use of observation, instruments, experiments, and mathematics to study nature. Discoveries might include scientists' observations.

OBJECTIVES

1 Identify technological advances that made European exploration possible.

2 Describe the effect of the Commercial Revolution.

3 Explain the role mercantilism played in the colonies.

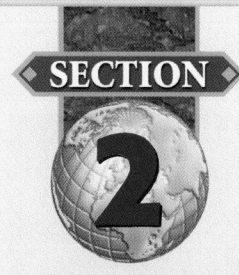

SECTION 2

READ TO DISCOVER

❶ What technological advances made European exploration possible?
❷ What effect did the Commercial Revolution have?
❸ What role did mercantilism play in the colonies?

DEFINE

compass
joint-stock company
mercantilism
favorable balance of trade
tariffs
subsidies

IDENTIFY

Commercial Revolution

WHY IT MATTERS TODAY

Social changes in one region of the world often cause people to move to other countries. Use CNNfyi.com or other **current event** sources to find out what recent social changes have caused people to leave their native countries. Record your findings in your journal.

CNN Student News.com

The Foundations of European Exploration

The Main Idea
Technological improvements led to exploration and fostered the growth of a new economy.

The Story Continues *Scientific advances would soon affect trade and the balance of political power in Europe. Rewards were offered to anyone who could invent a device for measuring longitude, since that would help ships sail more accurately and help nations compete for supremacy. It took over 100 years for someone to succeed. During that time, however, many other devices were invented that changed the global economy forever.*

Improvements in Technology

Since the time of the Crusades, Europeans had known about the riches of the East. Spices, silks, and jewels were prized as objects of trade because of their value. They came from the distant lands of India, China, and the islands of Southeast Asia. Traveling to and from these distant lands safely was essential if Europeans wished to compete with other traders. They began to focus on finding new sea routes to the East. To do this, Europeans needed better maps, navigation instruments, and ships. In short, they needed more advanced technology.

Mapmaking. Mapmaking improved during the Renaissance because of Europeans' growing interest in ancient geographers. Most scholars knew—as Ptolemy's maps had shown—that the world was round. During the Renaissance, information about Africa and Asia, unknown by Ptolemy, was added to his maps. The Americas, of course, were not yet known. Explorers believed that they could reach Asia more easily by sailing west across the Atlantic Ocean. Daring sea captains soon set out to find new trade routes to the East. Their discoveries opened whole new worlds to trade and settlement.

Navigation. Improved navigation instruments were just as important during this Age of Exploration as were more accurate maps. New navigation technology enabled ships to sail beyond sight of land without getting lost. One of the most important instruments to be developed during this time was the **compass.** In the 1100s, European navigators had learned that they could magnetize an iron needle. They rubbed the needle on a piece of lodestone—a kind of magnetic rock. When they floated the needle on water, it would point

INTERPRETING THE VISUAL RECORD

The Astronomer The Dutch artist Jan Vermeer, who worked during the 1600s, often showed his subjects in the midst of work activities. Vermeer's *The Astronomer* shows research and work connected to mapmaking. **What tools are being used by the astronomer to study the earth's surface?**

TEACH OBJECTIVE 2

ALL LEVELS: Have students create four-column charts about technology that aided overseas exploration in the 1400s. The first column should identify the technological advances. *(maps, compass, astrolabe; changes in ships, rudder, sails)* The second column should describe each advance and the third column should explain how it aided exploration. In the fourth column, students should rank the advances by their importance to exploration, from "1" (most important) to "5" (least important). Select students to explain their rankings.
ENGLISH LANGUAGE LEARNERS

HOMEWORK Have students imagine they are European sailors in the late 1400s. Have them write a letter to a friend explaining how new technology will make their voyage of exploration less dangerous.

TEACH OBJECTIVE 2

LEVEL 3: Ask volunteers to name ways expeditions were financed. *(bank loan, joint-stock company, monarch)* Have each student write and present a speech to persuade a banker, individual investor, or monarch to fund an expedition.

---

to the north. At some point during the 1200s or the 1300s, navigators created a true compass by fixing a magnetized needle to a card marked with directions.

New ships. If Europeans were to safely sail to the East, they needed better ships. Until well into the 1400s, long ships sometimes known as galleys were used by European sailors. These clumsy ships could sail using wind power only in the direction in which the wind blew. They sailed mostly along the coastlines. Sailors had to use long, heavy wooden oars to drive a galley against the prevailing winds.

In the late 1400s Spanish and Portuguese designers made important advances in ship-building technology. They built ships that were longer and larger than galleys. They also changed the size and shape of the sails. They moved the rudder—a steering device—from the side of the ship to its rear. These changes allowed ships to sail against the wind. Ships traveled more quickly and could be steered more easily. They could make way more reliably in different types of weather conditions, as well.

✔ **READING CHECK: Analyzing Information** Why did technological advances make sailors more able to explore distant lands? Mariners were better able to navigate, and ships could travel farther, faster, and under a greater variety of conditions.

Economic Changes

Improved ways of doing business also played an important part in new exploration. In some cases, banks added services to meet the needs of exploration. In other cases, Europeans changed basic economic practices. The changes were so great that many historians refer to the period between the late 1400s and the 1700s as the **Commercial Revolution.**

In many places in Europe before the 1300s and the 1400s, the value of coins could change depending on the amount of precious metal they contained. This changing value restricted European trade. Merchants and tradespeople needed a standard system of money.

As early as the mid to late 1200s, Italian cities were producing coins with fixed values. The gold florin of Florence and the ducat (DUHK·uht) of Venice were very dependable. This encouraged international trade and banking. In turn, banks could store large sums of money that they could lend governments or businesses wanting to explore overseas.

During the Commercial Revolution, individual merchants joined together into a new kind of business organization called a **joint-stock company.** Owners raised money by selling shares, or stock, in the company. Investors who bought the stock became co-owners and shared in the profits. The more shares they owned, the more of the profits they would receive. Joint-stock companies raised large sums of money from investors to finance exploration.

During the 1400s and 1500s, European monarchs supported exploration and colonization. Gaining riches through conquest and discovery would make them more powerful than rival countries. Although Italy had led the way in the Commercial Revolution, the Italians did not colonize. Instead, Portugal, Spain, and France built overseas empires. Trade shifted to these Atlantic nations.

✔ **READING CHECK: Identifying Cause and Effect** What effect did the standardization of money have on the ability of countries to trade? it encouraged international trade and banking

CONNECTING TO
Science and Technology

The Astrolabe— An Early Guidance System

Sailors of the 1500s had only a few simple tools—such as the astrolabe—to guide them. Using the position of the sun and stars, these explorers sailed the oceans of the world. They could plot and hold a course and measure their progress. Of equal importance, they could estimate where they were with respect to land.

Astrolabes were usually made of brass or iron. A sailor would sight a star along the bar shown in the picture. By lining up the bar with markings on the disk, he could figure out the latitude of his ship's position. Astrolabes were used until the invention of more accurate instruments in the 1500s and 1600s.

Understanding Science and Technology

In addition to knowing distance north or south of the equator, what other information would a sailor need to know his exact position?

Interdisciplinary Connection

LANGUAGE ARTS. The use of *port* and *starboard* to designate the sides of a ship originates from the placement of the rudder on early vessels. The long oar that served as the rudder was always on the helmsman's right side as he faced forward. Because the rudder steered the vessel, the right side became known as the "steer-board"—now starboard—side of the ship. The rudder's location also kept the right side of the ship from being brought against the dock. Thus, the left side was always the one to be tied up when the ship was in port—making it the "port" side of the vessel.

ACTIVITY: Have students identify other words related to ships and use a dictionary to learn their origins. (Words will vary but might include *gunwale, rudder, stern, tack,* and *tiller.*) Have students report to the class any word origins they find particularly interesting.

___

CONNECTING TO SCIENCE AND TECHNOLOGY ANSWER
where he was with respect to land

___

Reproducible **Resources**
E Hands-on History Activity 16: A Sailor's Life

Alfred J. Hamel of Worcester, Massachusetts, suggested the following activity: Have students use newspapers and other media sources to find modern references to mercantilism, such as tariff bills, balance of trade, free trade, etc. Have students discuss the positive and negative consequences of mercantilist policies in the modern economy.

TEACH OBJECTIVE 3

LEVEL 1: Have students draw a web diagram showing the reasons why Europeans established colonies.
ENGLISH LANGUAGE LEARNERS

VISUAL RECORD ANSWER

large port, many ships, many trade goods, much business activity

Linking Past to Present

The world's nations in 1948 launched a major effort to reduce international tensions resulting from the remnants of mercantilism. A multinational treaty called the General Agreement on Tariffs and Trade (GATT) created a mechanism to reduce tariffs and other economic barriers between nations. Average tariffs on manufactured goods fell from about 40 percent to less than 5 percent by the 1980s, and regions adopted duty-free trade arrangements like the European Union and the North American Free Trade Agreement (NAFTA). However, some nations have introduced new subsidies or import quotas for certain industries or products, in a movement called neomercantilism.

Critical Thinking

What might rulers in the 1500s have said about GATT or NAFTA?

ANSWER: Students may answer that rulers would have disapproved because free trade agreements keep nations from protecting and accumulating wealth.

INTERPRETING THE VISUAL RECORD

Lisbon Lisbon, capital of Portugal, was one of Europe's busiest seaports during the Age of Exploration. *How does this picture reflect Lisbon's role as a leading European trade center and sea power?*

Mercantilism

Economic and political changes linked to overseas expansion contributed to a new economic theory. **Mercantilism** stated that a country's government should do all it could to increase the country's wealth, which was measured by the amount of gold and silver the country possessed. According to this belief, the world contained a fixed amount of wealth. To increase its own wealth, one country had to take wealth from another country.

Balance of trade. According to mercantilists, a country could build wealth in two ways. It could mine gold and silver either at home or in its colonies. Or it could sell more goods than it bought from foreign countries, thus creating a favorable balance of trade. With a **favorable balance of trade,** a country received more gold and silver from other nations than it paid to them. This situation both strengthened the country and weakened its foreign rivals.

A favorable balance of trade was, therefore, the aim of many mercantilist countries. To achieve a favorable balance of trade, a country could do several things. First, it could reduce the amount of goods coming into it from other countries by placing **tariffs,** or import taxes, on these goods. The importer of a particular good paid the tariff and added that cost to the price of the good. The higher price discouraged people from buying it.

Second, a country could encourage exports. Manufactured goods, such as woolen cloth, were more valuable than raw materials, such as wool. Countries therefore encouraged manufacturing and the export of manufactured goods. They provided government **subsidies,** or grants of money, to help businesspeople start new industries and build ships.

Third, a country could work to gain and control overseas sources of raw materials and precious metals. A nation that controlled overseas sources of these goods would not need to import them from competing nations. Foreign countries were always considered rivals and might at any time become active enemies. The goal of winning overseas sources of materials helped fuel the race to gain colonies.

The role of colonies. Colonies played a major role in mercantilism. During the 1500s and after, European powers aimed to colonize overseas lands that were rich in gold, silver, and raw materials that could not be produced at home. A powerful nation sought to buy raw materials from its own colonies. That way, the country's wealth would remain with its own people. Most European colonial powers, moreover, forbid their colonies to sell raw materials to other countries. According to mercantilism, control of colonial markets and raw materials was key to a nation's success.

People in the home country's colonies provided strong markets for its manufactured goods. Governments passed strict laws that forbade colonies from buying foreign goods. In many cases, moreover, colonies were not allowed to manufacture goods. This forced colonies to buy manufactured goods only from their home country. Mercantilists argued that such laws were justified because colonies existed to benefit the home country.

✔ **READING CHECK: Finding the Main Idea** What was the overall aim of mercantilism?
to increase a country's wealth

CLOSE

Ask students which factor influenced European expansion most—technology, the Commercial Revolution, or mercantilism. Have them support their answers.

REVIEW

Have students complete the Section 2 Review on p. 391.

ASSESS

Have students complete Daily Quiz 16.2. As Alternative Assessment, you may want to use the persuasive speech or web diagram exercise in this section's lessons.

RETEACH

Have students complete Main Idea Activity for English Language Learners and Special-Needs Students 16.2. Then have them write brief definitions of "commercial revolution" and "mercantilism."
ENGLISH LANGUAGE LEARNERS

EXTEND

Have students draw political cartoons that illustrate one of the effects of mercantilism—such as accumulation of gold and silver, national self-sufficiency, or establishing an empire.
BLOCK SCHEDULING

Social Change

Advances in navigation and government economic policies by themselves did not lead to European exploration and overseas colonization. Certain social changes also helped create in people the desire to explore and resettle.

For one thing, the Renaissance and the Scientific Revolution had created a desire among many Europeans to learn more about the world and had added to the general store of geographic knowledge. Thus, simple curiosity and a spirit of discovery moved many people to explore the world outside Europe.

After the year 1500, moreover, the population of Europe increased. Some urban areas became very crowded. Adventurous people knew that overseas colonies might offer harsh living conditions. Some people were willing to accept these hardships, however, in return for the opportunity to gain land and possible wealth by settling in overseas colonies.

Other people went overseas hoping to reap quick profits. Tales of gold and silver and precious jewels—as well as fertile soil—persuaded thousands that easy wealth lay overseas. A few even went in search of fabulous cities with enormous riches, such as the legendary El Dorado (which means "the gilded one" in Spanish) in South America.

Finally, the Reformation and Counter-Reformation had led to the religious and political persecution of many. French Huguenots and others went overseas to seek religious freedom for themselves and to escape persecution at home. Some Christians went to spread their religion to non-Europeans.

In many cases, there was no single reason that motivated a person or group of people to explore or colonize. Rather, a combination of these hopes and aims led Europeans to leave their old lives for new and, to them, unknown lands.

✔ **READING CHECK: Summarizing** Why were some Europeans willing to explore and colonize distant lands? curiosity and spirit of discovery; hope of wealth or better way of life; escape religious persecution or spread religion

Gold and cinnamon were highly sought-after trade goods.

DAILY LIFE

The New Commercial Economy
World exploration led to a new kind of economy in Europe. Goods brought from Africa, Asia, and the New World made many countries in Europe rich. Spices, silks, gold, silver, and precious stones were some of the most sought-after items.

The Portuguese, Spanish, and Dutch were the first European powers to build trading empires. Trade and commerce eventually replaced farming as the leading economic activity in Europe. Over time, the new commercial economy generally helped to spread wealth and improve living standards.

How did European countries benefit from the changes of the Commercial Revolution?

DAILY LIFE ANSWER
Increased trade made them wealthy.

SECTION 2 REVIEW ANSWERS

❶ **Define**
• compass, p. 388
• joint-stock company, p. 389
• mercantilism, p. 390
• favorable balance of trade, p. 390
• tariffs, p. 390
• subsidies, p. 390

❷ **Identify**
• Commercial Revolution, p. 389

❸ Technological Advances: compass, astrolabe, better ships made long sea voyages safer; Economic Changes: banks and joint-stock companies funded exploration; Mercantilism: made nations want colonies for gold, silver, raw materials; Social Changes: crowding and persecution gave people reasons to settle in colonies

❹ a. Ships had to be able to sail out of sight of land without getting lost.

b. They kept colonial wealth for the home country and made colonies buy manufactured goods from the home country.

❺ Students' letters might mention overcrowding and persecution at home, dangers of sea travel, hopes for wealth, or escape from persecution.

SECTION 2 REVIEW

1. **Define** and explain the significance:
   compass
   joint-stock company
   mercantilism
   favorable balance of trade
   tariffs
   subsidies

2. **Identify** and explain the significance:
   Commercial Revolution

3. **Summarizing** Copy the table below. Fill in the ways in which each factor influenced exploration and colonization.

Factors	Influence on Exploration and Colonization
Technological Advances	
Economic Changes	
Mercantilism	
Social Changes	

4. **Finding the Main Idea**
   a. Why were technological developments necessary before nations could begin exploration and colonization?
   b. How did trade laws that limited colonies' economic freedom support the idea of mercantilism?

5. **Writing and Critical Thinking**
   Supporting a Point of View Imagine you are living in the 1500s. Write a letter to a relative explaining why you will or will not leave Europe to settle in a colony.
   Consider:
   • what conditions are like in your home country
   • what you might gain or lose by traveling to a distant land

Homework Practice Online
keyword: SP3 HP16

Reproducible Resources
E Creative Teaching Strategy 16: Talk Show: Changing Europe's Worldview

SECTION 3

OBJECTIVES

1 **Describe what the early Portuguese explorers accomplished.**

2 **Discuss how the voyages of Christopher Columbus influenced the world.**

3 **Explain why the Atlantic slave trade prospered.**

 LET'S GET STARTED!

As students enter the classroom, ask them to list products from Asia that many people in America use. *(Responses may include electronics, automobiles, watches, athletic shoes, clothing.)* Ask how these products come to the United States. *(by ship or airplane)* Ask them to imagine what would happen if everything from Asia had to come almost entirely overland, crossing from Russia to Alaska at the Bering Strait. *(goods would cost more; Russia or China could interrupt trade)* Tell students that in Section 3 they will learn how the European desire for Asian products led Europeans to try to find sea routes to Asia so they would not have to depend on overland trade.

SECTION 3 RESOURCES

REPRODUCIBLE RESOURCES

▶ Guided Reading Strategy 16.3

▶ Graphic Organizer Activity 16

▶ Geography Activity 16

TECHNOLOGY RESOURCES

▶ One-Stop Planner 16.3

▶ Holt Researcher: World History: Isabella, Christopher Columbus

▶ World History and Cultures Video Program 16

▶ CNN Presents Geography: Yesterday and Today Segment 15

▶ Homework Practice Online

REINFORCEMENT, REVIEW, AND ASSESSMENT

▶ Section 3 Review, p. 399

▶ Daily Quiz 16.3

▶ Main Idea Activity 16.3

▶ English Audio Summary 16.3

▶ Spanish Audio Summary 16.3

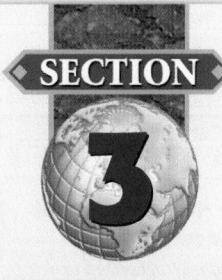

SECTION 3

READ TO DISCOVER

1 What did early Portuguese explorers accomplish?

2 How did the voyages of Christopher Columbus influence the world?

3 Why did the Atlantic slave trade prosper?

DEFINE

triangular trade

IDENTIFY

Prince Henry
Bartolomeu Dias
Vasco da Gama
Christopher Columbus
Columbian Exchange
Treaty of Tordesillas
Amerigo Vespucci
Ferdinand Magellan
Middle Passage

WHY IT MATTERS TODAY

People have always been interested in exploring what is beyond their present environment. Use or other **current event** sources to discover what kind of exploration is going on today. Record your findings in your journal.

CNN Student News.com

Voyages of Portugal and Spain

The Main Idea
Voyages sponsored by the Portuguese and Spanish led to new colonies and to the Atlantic slave trade.

The Story Continues *Life aboard a trading ship could be very difficult. "[Four galleys] were away three years, but only one galley returned and even on that galley most of the crew had died," one eyewitness recalled. "And those which survived could hardly be recognized as human." Despite such experiences, numerous sailors made voyages in search of riches for themselves and their countries.*

Portugal's First Explorers

Portuguese and Spanish explorers made the first European voyages into unknown waters. Curiosity, religion, and economic goals drove these courageous men forward. Their voyages resulted in great advances for the sponsoring governments and served as the foundation for future empires.

One man largely responsible for Portugal's interest in exploration was **Prince Henry** of the Portuguese royal family. Also known as "The Navigator," Prince Henry's first goal was to find gold for Portugal. The Portuguese also hoped to find a way to the rich spice trade of the Indies and to spread the Christian faith.

Henry gathered many of Europe's best geographers and navigators to plan expeditions. By about 1420 or earlier his navigators were exploring westward into the Atlantic, and by the 1430s they were moving southward along the west coast of Africa. These explorations taught navigators about currents, wind patterns, and climates, knowledge they needed as they ventured farther from home. Henry's explorers claimed the Azores for Portugal. In Africa, they began to trade for slaves, gold, and ivory.

The success of these early voyages of discovery and exploration created great excitement throughout Europe. Success encouraged more voyages. In 1488 **Bartolomeu Dias** sailed around the Cape of Good Hope at the southern tip of Africa. Although Dias had to turn back, he had found the route to the Indian Ocean.

Using this knowledge, **Vasco da Gama** sailed eastward across the Indian Ocean. He landed in India in 1498. Several years later, da Gama made a second voyage to India. He returned to Portugal, his ships full of valuable goods.

Thanks to Dias and da Gama, an overseas trade route from Europe to India and the East Indies was now available. Rich cargoes of spices and jewels arrived in Portugal. This direct ocean route saved the Portuguese from having to deal with middlemen traders. Now, the Portuguese could journey directly to the sources of the trade goods they sought. In many cases, too, ships could carry goods more cheaply than could overland caravans. Nor could Portuguese merchants be blocked or charged high tolls by competing powers that controlled overland routes. Overseas trade promised wealth for merchants and sailors and goods for Europe's markets.

✔ **READING CHECK: Summarizing** What did the Portuguese gain from the voyages of their early explorers? wealth and overseas trade routes

---

TEACH OBJECTIVE 1

LEVEL 1: To help students understand the economic motivations for the early voyages of exploration, lead a discussion using the following questions as a guide: What was the traditional way Asian goods moved west before the voyages of exploration? *(by various land and sea routes to the Middle East)* Why did Europeans begin to desire Asian goods? *(result of Crusades)* Before the voyages of exploration, what groups controlled the trade of these goods with Europe? *(Arab and Italian merchants)* Why did this trade process make Asian goods so expensive in Europe? *(high overland transportation costs, payments to Arab or Italian middlemen)* Have students refer to the map on pages 396–397 to answer the following questions: How did Dias and da Gama enable Portugal to trade directly with Asia? *(Dias found route to Indian Ocean; da Gama built on Dias's exploration and sailed to India.)* Why did Portugal take the lead in finding a sea route? *(location on the Atlantic; Prince Henry)* How did these explorations give Portugal a trade advantage over other European nations? *(allowed Portuguese to establish direct trade with Asian markets)* **ENGLISH LANGUAGE LEARNERS**

An idealized portrait of Vasco da Gama meeting Indian royalty.

Christopher Columbus

Spain, too, became interested in the search for new trade routes. A Genoan navigator named **Christopher Columbus** had studied the writings of Marco Polo and Ptolemy's description of a round Earth. Columbus believed that a shorter route to Asia could be found by sailing westward instead of sailing around the tip of Africa. King Ferdinand and Queen Isabella of Spain agreed to finance Columbus's voyage of exploration.

In August 1492, Columbus set sail from Palos, Spain. His three small ships—the *Niña*, the *Pinta*, and the *Santa María*—sailed westward across the Atlantic. On October 12, 1492, the small fleet landed at a tiny island that Columbus named San Salvador. It was a historic moment when Columbus and his captains planted the Spanish flag. Columbus claimed the land that he had reached for Spain. Later, in reporting his discovery, Columbus wrote:

> *History Makers Speak*
> **"It appears to me that the people [the Native Americans who met Columbus] are ingenious [clever], and would be good servants and I am of the opinion that they would very readily become Christians, as they appear to have no religion. They very quickly learn such words as are spoken to them."**
>
> Christopher Columbus, extracts from journal, quoted in *Internet Medieval Source Book*, by Paul Halsall

After exploring other islands in the area Columbus returned triumphantly to Spain in 1493. Columbus believed the islands he had found lay off the east coast of India. Thus, he called them the Indies and their inhabitants Indians. However, Columbus had actually discovered islands in the Americas. They later became known as the West Indies. Between 1493 and 1504, Columbus made three more voyages to the "Indies." For the rest of his life, he believed that he had landed off the coast of Asia.

There was a major difference between the Portuguese explorers and Columbus. The Portuguese already knew that the lands they sailed to existed. Earlier people had written of their journeys between Europe and Asia and Europe and Africa. Columbus believed he was traveling to one of these lands by a different route. Earlier Viking voyages to the Americas were unknown. When Columbus stepped ashore in what is now the Bahamas, he stepped on land that was altogether new and unknown to Europeans.

✔ **READING CHECK: Finding the Main Idea** What significant event happened in 1492?

Columbus landed at San Salvador

HISTORY MAKER

Queen Isabella (1451–1504)

Queen Isabella was one of Spain's greatest rulers. Her court was a center of learning and culture. With her husband, Ferdinand, she also helped to unify Spain.

Isabella approved the voyage of Christopher Columbus to India. Columbus found the New World and the great Spanish empire in the Americas was born. **What important events took place during Isabella's rule?**

Holt Researcher

go.hrw.com
KEYWORD: Holt Researcher
FreeFind:
  Isabella
  Christopher Columbus
After reading more about Isabella and Columbus on the Holt Researcher, create a Venn diagram that shows the similarities and differences in their beliefs about the lands and people Columbus encountered.

HISTORY MAKER ANSWER
Columbus sailed west across the Atlantic Ocean and discovered islands in the Americas; Spain was unified.

Global Relations

Even before the Europeans, the Chinese sought to establish maritime trade routes. Between 1405 and 1433 the Chinese Muslim navigator Zheng He led seven naval expeditions in Chinese ships that visited Southeast Asia, India, East Africa, and Arabia to secure trade with these regions. A change in the Chinese government's foreign policies, however, prohibited additional expeditions. China returned to using other nations' commercial fleets to carry its goods.

Critical Thinking

Ask students how European exploration and expansion might have been affected if the Chinese had continued to expand their maritime trade routes.

ANSWER: Students might suggest that Europeans would have had less access to Asian ports, so they might have concentrated even more on transatlantic exploration.

Technology Resources
Online Maps: European Idea of the Atlantic Before Columbus

EXPLORATION AND EXPANSION **393**

393

LEVEL 3: Have students imagine they are European cartographers (mapmakers) around 1500 who have been hired by the rulers of Spain or Portugal to make a map of newly-discovered territories. The rulers have asked them to illustrate the map with pictures of trade goods, scenery, or people from the regions shown. Invite students to present their maps to the class.

Interdisciplinary Connection

HEALTH. Although few European explorers had active diseases, they still carried many germs that were highly contagious to American Indians. Passing these germs to just a few Indians could rapidly infect large areas. Large, prosperous towns found by Spanish explorers in what is now the southeastern United States in the early 1540s no longer existed in 1560, when Spanish colonists in Florida tried to find them to acquire food. Diseases brought by the explorers had destroyed the towns. It is estimated that by the early 1600s, the Mesoamerican Indian population was 90 to 95 percent smaller than it had been a hundred years before.

Critical Thinking

Ask students why they think European diseases were so devastating to American Indians.

ANSWER: Students should mention that people who have never been exposed to a disease lack resistance to it.

CONNECTING TO GEOGRAPHY ANSWER
Students' answers will vary.

Technology Resources
 Online Maps: Treaty of Tordesillas, 1494

CONNECTING TO
GEOGRAPHY

The Columbian Exchange
The effects of the Columbian Exchange are still felt today. For example, diet on both sides of the Atlantic changed. Potatoes from the Andes now feed millions of people in Europe. Corn, first grown by Native Americans, is a staple around the world today. Wheat was not grown in the Americas until it was brought there by Europeans. The tomato first grew not in Italy, but in the Americas.

Horses, cattle, goats, sheep, and other animals crossed the Atlantic with Europeans. North America, in exchange, gave Europe and Asia the turkey, the gray squirrel, and the muskrat.

> **Understanding Geography**
>
> **What elements of the Columbian Exchange can you identify in your area?**

The Impact of Columbus's Voyages

In the years following Columbus's voyages, a massive exchange took place between the so-called New World and the Old World of Europe. This interaction is often called the **Columbian Exchange.** Products, plants, animals, and even diseases traveled between the Western and Eastern Hemispheres. For example, gold and silver mined in South America were shipped eastward to Spain. This helped Spain become a major world power.

The exchange affected the way people in both worlds lived. American foods such as potatoes, tomatoes, beans, and corn were introduced in Europe. The Spanish brought horses to the Americas, thus changing the lifestyles of many Native American groups forever. This was especially true in areas such as the Great Plains.

Not everything the Columbian Exchange brought to the New World was helpful. European sailors carried smallpox and other diseases westward. The native population of Spanish America had no immunity to these diseases and millions died.

✔ **READING CHECK: Drawing Conclusions** Who benefited most—Europeans or Native Americans—from the Columbian Exchange? Why? Europeans, because they gained riches, resources and new foods and exported diseases

Dividing the New Lands

During the late 1400s Spain and Portugal—Europe's most active seagoing explorers— often claimed the same newly discovered lands. To settle these conflicts, Pope Alexander VI issued an edict in 1493. The Pope's edict drew an imaginary line from north to south through the middle of the Atlantic Ocean. Alexander gave Spain the rights to all newly discovered lands west of the line. Portugal could claim discoveries east of the line. Neither country, however, could take lands already held or claimed by another Christian ruler.

A year later, the **Treaty of Tordesillas** between Spain and Portugal moved the line farther west. This soon had an important impact. In 1500 the Portuguese navigator Pedro Cabral set sail westward for India. Cabral's tiny fleet of 13 ships was blown off course, and the Portuguese made landfall on the coast of what is now Brazil. Under the Treaty of Tordesillas, Cabral was able to claim this incredibly rich land for Portugal.

Over time, Spain took control of most of Central and South America. The Spanish also claimed the Philippines. In addition to the Brazilian coast, Portugal claimed lands on the eastern and western coasts of Africa. The Portuguese also claimed lands in Asia and the East Indies.

✔ **READING CHECK: Identifying a Point of View** How might the right of Spain and Portugal to claim lands not already occupied by Christians have been viewed by the people of those lands? as arrogant and hostile

Vespucci, Balboa, and Magellan

Other European explorers followed Columbus westward. **Amerigo Vespucci** was an Italian navigator. Between 1497 and 1504, he crossed the Atlantic several times as part of Spanish and Portuguese expeditions. Unlike others, Vespucci did not think the land he saw was part of Asia. He called it a New World. A German mapmaker, impressed with Amerigo's argument, called the land America after Vespucci.

In 1513 Vasco Núñez de Balboa of Spain made an overland crossing of the Isthmus of Panama. Reaching a vast ocean, he named it the South Sea and claimed it for Spain. Balboa's discovery made it clear that the New World was not part of Asia.

HOMEWORK Have students list all the explorers mentioned in Section 3. Have them use standard grammar, spelling, sentence structure, and punctuation to write one sentence explaining why each explorer was important.

TEACH OBJECTIVE 3

LEVEL 2: Working individually or in pairs, have students create a chain-of-events chart of the origins of the transatlantic slave trade. **ENGLISH LANGUAGE LEARNERS, COOPERATIVE LEARNING**

Europeans wanted labor in the colonies

↓

Europeans enslaved Native Americans

↓

Native Americans died from European diseases

↓

Europeans imported slaves from Africa to replace them

Ferdinand Magellan, a Portuguese navigator sailing for Spain, proved Balboa was correct. In 1519 he set out from Spain with five ships to cross the Atlantic to South America. The ships sailed along its eastern shore until they reached the southernmost tip. After passing through the strait now named for him, Magellan found himself in a great ocean. He named it the Pacific Ocean because it was so calm. In Latin the word *pacificus* means "peaceful." This was Balboa's "South Sea."

Magellan sailed westward across the Pacific. He reached the Philippine Islands and died there in 1521 in a fight with the islanders. His crew, led by one of his officers, sailed on. In 1522 one ship and 18 crew members returned to Spain. They had made the first round-the-world voyage.

✔ **READING CHECK: Making Generalizations** What did Vespucci, Balboa, and Magellan contribute to Europeans' knowledge of the world? knowledge that the western lands were a New World, not a part of Asia

Portuguese Expansion

After the voyages of Dias and da Gama, the Portuguese dreamed of controlling trade with Asia. In about 1510 they conquered part of the southwest coast of India. The port of Goa (GOH·uh) became their administrative center. From India they moved on to the East Indies. They conquered Malacca (muh·LAK·uh) on the southwest coast of the Malay Peninsula and the Moluccas (muh·LUKH·uhz), a group of islands. Europeans called them the Spice Islands because of their large crops of valuable spices.

Next, the Portuguese added the island of Ceylon—now Sri Lanka—to their chain of trading bases. Ceylon was in a key location between Goa and Malacca. With its tea and spices, Ceylon helped the Portuguese control trade with the East Indies. The Portuguese also gained footholds in China and Japan. Finally, they established several armed trading posts on the East African coast. The Portuguese also established a colony in Brazil where they built huge agriculture estates.

✔ **READING CHECK: Drawing Inferences** Why did the trading posts set up by the Portuguese allow them to control trade with the East? allowed them to block others' routes to the East and gave them uncontested access to Asian goods and markets

The Slave Trade

As they did in Asia, the Portuguese went to Africa to trade. At first, they maintained friendly relations with the Africans. Christian missionaries wanted to convert the continent's residents. Friendly relations soon collapsed, however, as the economic interests of the Portuguese—in gold and, over time, in slaves—became obvious.

Despite the fact that Europeans themselves had been slaves in the Byzantine, Arab, and Turkish empires, during the 1500s they began to use slave labor in their own overseas empires. Europeans tried enslaving Native Americans, but the system did not work well due to the devastation of the Native American population caused by disease and the difficulties of enslaving people in their own land. Instead, the Europeans began to rely more heavily on enslaved Africans.

The slave trade grew quickly when the Portuguese set up sugar plantations on islands off the coast of Africa. To make a profit, large numbers of slaves were required. Plantation owners got these slaves from the African mainland. Later, the Dutch, English, and French also became active in the slave trade. By the early 1600s the slave trade was the chief focus of European relations with Africa.

HISTORY MAKER

Ferdinand Magellan (c. 1480–1521)

Ferdinand Magellan became a page in the Portuguese court at a youthful age. Over time, he grew to become an experienced navigator and sailor.

Magellan became convinced that he could reach the Spice Islands in East Asia by sailing west. The circumnavigation of the globe by his fleet was not only a great achievement of navigation and courage; it was also the first proof that the world was round. **What was the outcome of Magellan's voyage?**

HISTORY MAKER ANSWER
Magellan died, but his crew completed the journey around the world, proving it was round.

Geography

Portugal's Atlantic seacoast was not its only reason for exploring Atlantic trade routes. Economic activities between Spain and Portugal had declined. Traditional maritime routes in the Mediterranean were dominated by ships from Italian city-states.

Critical Thinking

Ask students how these other factors might have driven the Portuguese to explore the Atlantic.

ANSWER: Students may answer that the Atlantic was the only trade route open to the Portuguese.

Reproducible Resources
PS Readings in World History 57: First Impressions of the New World

ALL LEVELS: Divide students into small groups. Have each group discuss any advantages and disadvantages of the slave trade from the point of view of one of the following individuals: a plantation owner in the Americas, a slave, the owner of a slave ship, or the ruler of an African kingdom. Have each group prepare a skit or drawing about the slave trade from the character's point of view and present it to the class.

ENGLISH LANGUAGE LEARNERS, COOPERATIVE LEARNING

Geography

Because of their focus on trade with Asia, the nations that sponsored early European explorers were as interested in finding a way around or through the Americas as they were in claiming and colonizing new lands. Magellan's last voyage was intended to find a water route through South America to the ocean that Balboa had discovered six years earlier.

Later, Jacques Cartier and Henry Hudson explored the St. Lawrence and Hudson Rivers, respectively, looking for a passage to Asia. Hudson also sailed far to the north in this quest, exploring what came to be known as Hudson Bay. When he found no passage to the Pacific, his crew mutinied and left him there to die. The Northwest Passage was not successfully navigated until 1906, when the Norwegian Roald Amundsen finally accomplished the feat.

internet connect

TOPIC: Explorers
GO TO: go.hrw.com
KEYWORD: SP3 WH16

Have students access the Internet through the HRW Go site to learn more about the explorer of their choice and his voyages. Have students write a biography of the explorer they choose.

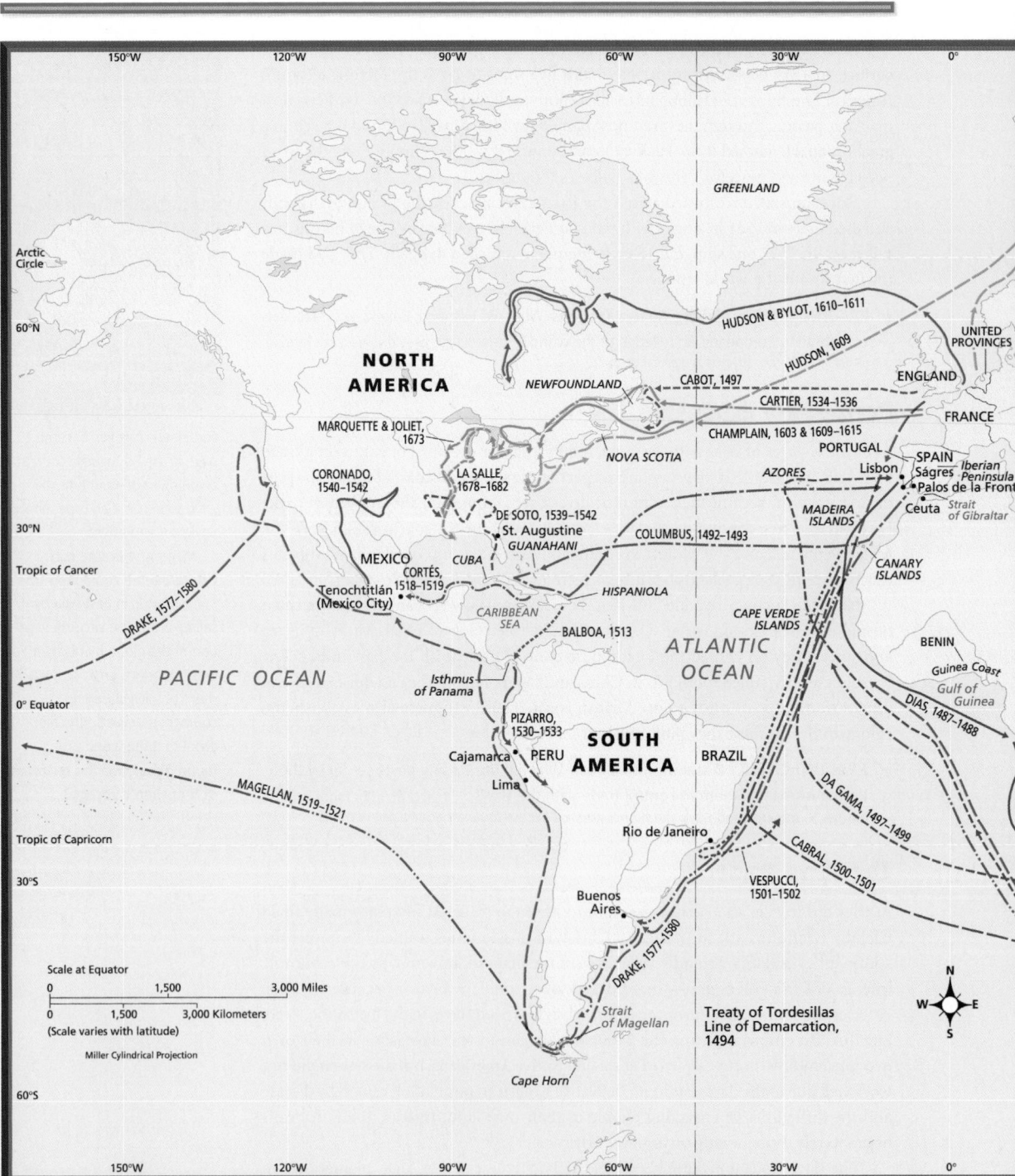

European Explorations, 1487–1682

Interpreting Maps The map shows the routes taken by Portuguese, Spanish, French, English, and Dutch explorers. They sailed both east and west to discover new lands.

TEACH OBJECTIVES 1, 2, and 3

LEVEL 2: Ask students to name the kinds of people who might be on a ship crossing the Atlantic Ocean in the 1500s. *(Answers will vary but might include explorers, mapmakers, sailors, slaves, slave merchants, settlers.)* Then have students imagine they are on a ship crossing the Atlantic. Have them write a diary of the voyage. The first entry should explain who they are and why they are on the ship.

■ **Skills Assessment: Human Systems** According to the map, what explorer duplicated Magellan's circumnavigation of the globe, and what nation did he represent?

Global Relations

The second Portuguese mission to India was led by Pedro Cabral. After his accidental visit to Brazil when he was blown off course, he eventually reached Calicut. There he and his crew encountered problems with the Arab merchants controlling the port. The Arabs attacked the Portuguese trading booths, killing some of the sailors. Cabral bombarded the city and then sailed south to the rival city of Cochin to trade.

Critical Thinking

Ask student why the Arab merchants were hostile to the Portuguese.

ANSWER: Students might suggest that the merchants realized the Portuguese threatened their monopoly on trade between Asia and Europe.

MAP ANSWER
Drake; England

Divide the class into three groups representing Asia, Africa, and America. Ask each group to discuss how Europe's interactions with its assigned region changed because of the voyages of exploration. *(Asia—established direct contact by ship; Africa—developed large-scale slave trade; America—learned it existed, gold and silver)* Have each group appoint one student to report to the class.

Economics

One cause of Portugal's decline as a trading empire was the system it set up for controlling trade. The rulers of Portugal tried to establish a monopoly over all trade within their trading sphere. Anyone trading at Asian ports was required to buy a license from Portugal and to pay duties to Portuguese officials.

Eventually this system broke down because Portugal did not have the strength to enforce it. Portugal could not prevent rivals from trading in the area, and local Asian merchants began to avoid paying for licenses.

Critical Thinking

Ask students why Portugal established such a system and why the system failed.

ANSWER: Students may suggest that Portugal wanted to control Asian trade because of mercantilist ideas, and that the system failed because Portugal was not strong enough to prevent rivals from trading in the area or to enforce the licensing requirement.

MAP ANSWER
About 7,000 miles

INTERPRETING THE VISUAL RECORD

Slave ships This sketch shows a diagram of slaves in the hold of a ship. Slaves were positioned below decks in such a way as to fit as many as possible on the ship. This helped to ensure a profitable voyage. *What does this diagram indicate about conditions on board a typical slave ship?*

Triangular trade. Slave trade in the Atlantic was part of a system known as the **triangular trade.** First, merchants shipped cotton goods, weapons, and liquor to Africa in exchange for slaves or gold. The second stage—called the **Middle Passage**—was the shipment of slaves across the Atlantic to the Americas. There, slaves were sold for goods produced on the plantations. To complete the triangle, merchants sent the plantations' products to Europe. They were used to buy manufactured products to be sold in the Americas.

The Middle Passage was brutal and degrading. Traders chained the slaves in the crowded hold of the ship. This stopped slaves from jumping overboard or causing trouble aboard ship. Slaves had little food or water and no sanitary facilities. Many died before reaching their destination.

At the height of the trade in the years between the mid-1700s and the early 1800s, European slave ships carried thousands of slaves each year. It has been estimated that some 10 million Africans survived the horrible journey to slavery in the Americas. Many perished during the horrible journey of the Middle Passage. Others died even earlier, on the hard trip from the African interior to slave ships on the coast.

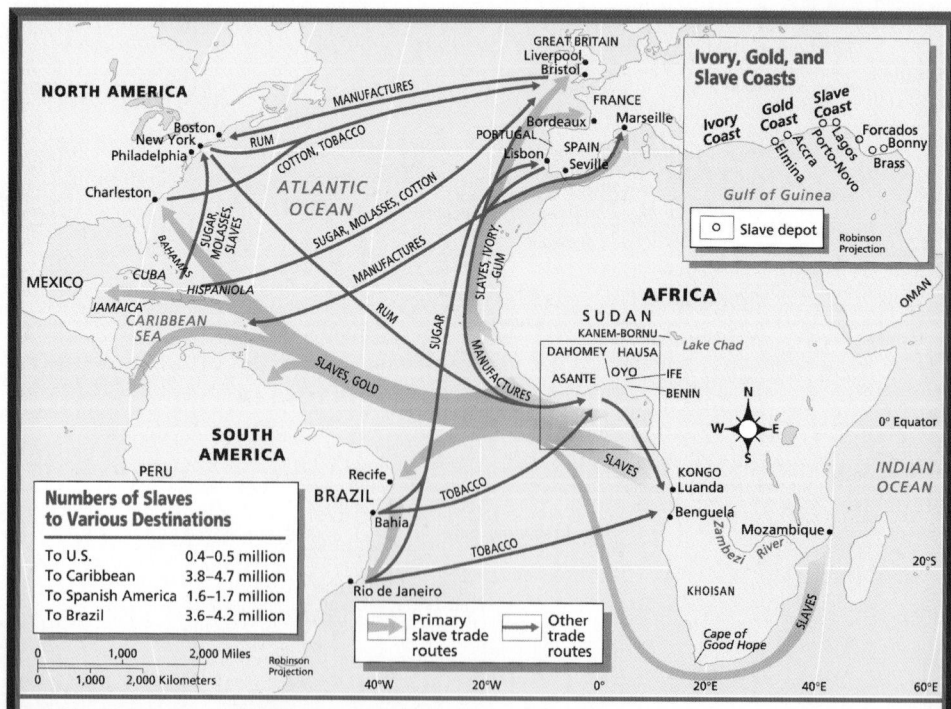

Trade Across the Atlantic, 1451–1870

Interpreting Maps Trade routes linked European ports with coastal Africa as early as the mid-1400s. By the 1700s, these routes extended to the Americas in a distinctly triangular pattern. Over the years, millions of slaves were carried along these routes.

■ **Skills Assessment: The World in Spatial Terms** Approximately how far would a trip for slaves have been if they were transported from Luanda to Charleston?

REVIEW

Have students complete the Section 3 Review on p. 399.

ASSESS

Have students complete Daily Quiz 16.3. As Alternative Assessment, you may want to use the chain-of-events activity in this section's lessons.

RETEACH

Have students complete Main Idea Activity for English Language Learners and Special-Needs Students 16.3. Then have students write one sentence summarizing the main idea for each section in the chapter. **ENGLISH LANGUAGE LEARNERS**

EXTEND

Have students imagine they are Africans recently sold to European slave traders and put on a ship with no explanation. Have them write about their thoughts and expectations.
BLOCK SCHEDULING

African kingdoms and slavery. During the 1400s and the 1500s, strong states began to rise in West Africa. Some of these kingdoms profited from the slave trade. Not all African states participated in the slave trade with Europeans. Many African societies, however, had practiced slavery well before the Europeans' arrival. Slaves were sometimes taken in war or during raids on neighboring groups. In some traditional African societies, slaves might be allowed to gain their freedom. Generally, they played a distinct role in society. Europeans, on the other hand, considered slaves as property to be bought and sold for profit.

Some Africans who lived in the interior helped the Europeans capture and move slaves. In return they received European-made arms and other goods. Neighboring groups either had to participate or be taken as slaves. During the years of the slave trade, native populations in some parts of Africa were greatly reduced. As demands for slaves increased, population losses had disastrous effects on Africa's development and progress.

✔ **READING CHECK: Supporting a Point of View** In what ways can you support the view that the slave trade slowed the development of the African continent? Talent and labor were drained and traditional lifestyles were disrupted.

The Portuguese Empire Weakens

The great Portuguese empire declined almost as rapidly as it had grown. The Portuguese government did not have the financial wealth to support so large an empire. Thousands of soldiers and sailors were needed to maintain and expand the empire, but many never returned from overseas. Shipwrecks and battles with enemies cost both money and lives. With its small population, Portugal could not replace the losses it suffered as a result of exploration and colonization.

Finally in 1580 Spain annexed Portugal. Portugal did not regain its independence until 1640. Under Spanish control, Portugal's trade was greatly restricted and its overseas colonies were neglected. Only Brazil and Angola survived as major Portuguese colonies.

✔ **READING CHECK: Drawing Conclusions** How did the relative size of Portugal and Spain influence their success in expansion and colonization? Portugal, unlike Spain, lacked the wealth and the population needed to sustain expansion and colonization.

Primary Source
◆ EYEWITNESS ◆

Olaudah Equiano was a native African who was captured and enslaved by other Africans. Eventually he was bound over to European slave traders. Years later he published an account of his experiences, which included his first impressions of the white slave traders and their ship.

"When I looked round the ship too and saw a large furnace of copper boiling and a multitude of black people of every description chained together . . . I no longer doubted my fate. . . . When I recovered a little I found some black people about me. . . . I asked them if we were not to be eaten by those white men with horrible looks, red faces, and loose hair. . .

I now saw myself deprived of all chance of returning to my native country." **What did Equiano think that the slave traders were going to do to him?**

PRIMARY SOURCE ANSWER
eat him

SECTION 3 REVIEW ANSWERS

① Define
• triangular trade, p. 398

② Identify
• Prince Henry, p. 392
• Bartolomeu Dias, p. 392
• Vasco da Gama, p. 392
• Christopher Columbus, p. 393
• Columbian Exchange, p. 394
• Treaty of Tordesillas, p. 394
• Amerigo Vespucci, p. 394
• Ferdinand Magellan, p. 395
• Middle Passage, p. 398

③ Europe to Africa: cotton goods, weapons, liquor; Africa to Americas: slaves, gold; Americas to Europe and Africa: sugar, cotton, tobacco, rum

④ a. Dias found route to Indian Ocean, 1488; da Gama reached India, 1498; Columbus reached the Americas, 1492; Magellan sailed west across the Pacific, 1521

b. There may have been more development and progress.

⑤ Students might suggest that Spain and Portugal gained wealth temporarily but lost in the long run because they did not develop industry or agriculture at home. They should note extreme negative effects for people in the Americas who died of European diseases and people from Africa who were enslaved.

SECTION 3 REVIEW

1. **Define** and explain the significance:
   triangular trade

2. **Identify** and explain the significance:
   Prince Henry
   Bartolomeu Dias
   Vasco da Gama
   Christopher Columbus
   Columbian Exchange
   Treaty of Tordesillas
   Amerigo Vespucci
   Ferdinand Magellan
   Middle Passage

3. **Analyzing Information** Copy the diagram below. Between each of the boxes, show the direction of trade in the triangular exchange and what type of cargo the ships carried.

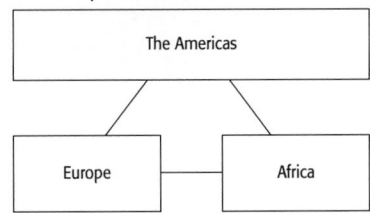

The Americas

Europe — Africa

4. **Finding the Main Idea**
   a. Sequence the important discoveries of the explorers listed in question 2.
   b. What do you think might have happened on the African continent if the European slave trade had not taken place?

5. **Writing and Critical Thinking**
   Comparing and Contrasting Write a paragraph pointing out the positive and negative effects of the explorations of the Spanish and Portuguese.
   Consider:
   • the economic benefits to both countries
   • the effects on human life and populations

go.hrw.com Homework Practice Online
keyword: SP3 HP16

OBJECTIVES

1 **Describe how Spain extended its power abroad and at home.**

2 **Explain why the Dutch were successful in the 1600s.**

3 **Analyze why the Spanish Empire declined.**

LET'S GET STARTED!

As students enter the classroom, ask them to write a list of examples of conquest or colonization, based on previous chapters or their knowledge of current events. Ask students why nations conquer places and establish colonies. *(Answers will vary but may include natural resources, wealth, power, control of strategic sites.)* Tell students that in Section 4 they will learn how the Spanish and Dutch built empires through conquest and colonization in other parts of the world.

◆ SECTION ◆
4 RESOURCES

REPRODUCIBLE RESOURCES

▶ Guided Reading Strategy 16.4

TECHNOLOGY RESOURCES

▶ One-Stop Planner 16.4

▶ Homework Practice Online

▶ Online Maps: French and Dutch Imports, 1770s

▶ Online Maps: Portuguese Imports, 1770s

▶ Online Maps: Spanish Imports, 1770s

▶ Online Maps: British Imports, 1770s

REINFORCEMENT, REVIEW, AND ASSESSMENT

▶ Section 4 Review, p. 407

▶ Daily Quiz 16.4

▶ Main Idea Activity 16.4

▶ English Audio Summary 16.4

▶ Spanish Audio Summary 16.4

VISUAL RECORD ANSWER

strong metal armor

READ TO DISCOVER

❶ How did Spain extend its power abroad and at home?

❷ Why were the Dutch successful in the 1600s?

❸ Why did the Spanish Empire decline?

DEFINE

viceroys
guerrilla warfare

IDENTIFY

Ponce de León
Hernán Cortés
Moctezuma II
Francisco Pizarro
Charles V
Philip II
William of Orange

WHY IT MATTERS TODAY

Two ways that nations increase their land are conquest and colonization. Use or other **current event** sources to find examples of both processes going on today. Record your findings in your journal.

CNN student News.com

The Spanish and Dutch Empires

The Main Idea
Spain created an empire in the Americas, while the Dutch set up trading colonies in Asia and the Americas.

The Story Continues *As Spanish explorers spread into the Americas, they came ready to conquer. "Some of them were dressed in glistening iron from head to foot," wrote one observer. "They terrified everyone who saw them." Their tactics established a powerful empire for Spain.*

Spain's Colonial Empire

Throughout the 1500s Spain was the most powerful nation in Europe, with the largest overseas empire. While Portugal focused mainly on Africa and Asia, Spain turned to the Americas. Beginning with Columbus, Spaniards explored the West Indies, Central America, and parts of North and South America. At first, they believed these lands were in the East Indies. However, the natural resources of the Americas provided riches other than spices and jewels.

Spanish explorers sailed outward from the Caribbean to the North American mainland. In 1513 **Ponce de León** sailed northward to what is now Florida. A later voyage to Florida in 1528, led by Pánfilo de Narváez, ended in disaster and shipwreck. A handful of survivors from this tragic voyage traveled overland across what is now the southwestern United States and Mexico. Their travels opened even more land to Spanish claims and settlement.

Conquests. Other Spanish explorers went to the Yucatán in Mexico. There they learned of the great Maya and Aztec civilizations. In 1519, with 11 ships and about 600 men, **Hernán Cortés** invaded Mexico. He seized the Aztec ruler **Moctezuma II,** also known as Montezuma. Cortés captured and destroyed the great Aztec city of Tenochtitlán. The Spanish later built Mexico City on its ruins. Spanish horses and guns, unknown in the Americas, helped the Spanish defeat the great Aztec armies, as did a smallpox epidemic that swept through the Aztecs.

INTERPRETING THE VISUAL RECORD

Cortés Hernán Cortés, at the head of about 600 Spanish soldiers, carved out a huge empire in Mexico and plundered the mighty Aztec civilization. Cortés is pictured here capturing the Aztec ruler Moctezuma II. *According to this picture, what advantages did the Spanish have over the Aztec?*

TEACH OBJECTIVE 1

LEVEL 1: Have students draw and color a map showing Spanish conquests in the 1500s. Then have them create a diagram showing how Spain directed colonial government. **ENGLISH LANGUAGE LEARNERS**

The Spanish also found rich civilizations in South America. In 1530 **Francisco Pizarro** led 180 men and 37 horses on an expedition. They traveled from the Isthmus of Panama to the capital of the Inca Empire in what is now Peru. In 1533 Pizarro claimed the land from present-day Ecuador to Chile for Spain.

Cortés and Pizarro destroyed many Aztec and Inca statues and temples. The gold and silver from these religious objects and buildings made the explorers and the Spanish treasury wealthy.

In time Spain controlled the West Indies, southern and western North America, Central America, and much of South America. Unlike Europeans in Africa and Asia, the Spanish established settlements throughout their vast empire.

Colonial government and society. Spain directed the colonial government. Officials called **viceroys** represented the monarchy in the colonies and reported to the Council of the Indies in Spain. The council planned and directed the empire's growth on behalf of the Spanish crown.

For a time, the colonies produced enormous wealth for Spain. There were rich silver mines in the regions that are now Peru and northern Mexico. Agriculture and trade remained important, but mineral resources were the main assets of Spain's colonies.

European diseases such as smallpox, typhus, and measles weakened the Native American societies conquered by Cortés and Pizarro. From what is now the southwestern United States through Mexico and much of Central America, millions of Native Americans died. Whole cultures that had lived and thrived for centuries were wiped out or broken up in a matter of a relatively few years. Exact losses cannot be accurately determined, but many historians believe that the numbers were enormous. This tragic outcome of expansion and colonization also promoted the growth of slavery. The Spaniards needed workers for mines and farms in the New World. To make up for the loss of native labor, they imported slaves from Africa.

✔ **READING CHECK: Analyzing Information** What were some of the factors that allowed so few Europeans to conquer large numbers of peoples in the Americas? European horses and guns, and European diseases that weakened native populations

Spain's Colonial Rivals

The Spanish government wanted to keep the wealth of the Americas to themselves. They made laws keeping foreigners out of the Spanish colonies. Only Spanish ships could carry gold and silver out of the Americas.

Making laws, however, was easier than enforcing them. The French, Dutch, and English envied Spain's American wealth. They tried various methods to capture a share of it. They traded in Spanish American ports, their monarchs encouraged pirates to attack Spanish ships, and pirates raided Spanish towns.

Spain's rivals also tried to establish colonies in the Americas, ignoring Pope Alexander's line down the middle of the ocean. Despite their efforts, these rival countries had only limited success before 1600.

✔ **READING CHECK: Making Predictions** What did Spain's rivals hope to gain by having pirates attack Spanish ships and colonial towns? a share of America's great wealth

INTERPRETING THE VISUAL RECORD

Pizarro Francisco Pizarro and a handful of Spanish conquistadores overthrew the mighty Inca Empire of Peru. Here, Pizarro is shown refusing mercy to Atahualpa, the last emperor of the Inca. *What visual technique has the artist used to depict Pizarro's dominance in this scene?*

Culture

In his letters, Hernán Cortés described Tenochtitlán: "This city has many squares where trading is done and markets are held continuously. There is also one square…where every kind of merchandise produced in these lands is found…. There are shops like apothecaries', where they sell ready-made medicines as well as liquid ointments and plasters. There are shops like barbers' where they have their hair washed and shaved, and shops where they sell food and drink."

🖳 **internet** connect

TOPIC: Mesoamericans
GO TO: go.hrw.com
KEYWORD: SP3 WH16

Have students access the Internet through the HRW Go site to learn more about the Aztec and Inca civilizations. Ask students to write an informative report on the political, economic, and cultural impact of Spanish expansion.

VISUAL RECORD ANSWER

Pizarro appears taller than the Inca. The Inca are shown in submissive poses with crossed arms and bent knees.

LEVEL 3: Ask students to imagine they are advisers to King Philip II of Spain. Have them write the advice they would give the king about how to improve the economy of Spain. As examples, suggest they consider possible changes in foreign policy, religious policy, or ways to become less dependent on imports. Have volunteers present their advice to the class, pretending that they are speaking to the king.

Government

A series of family accidents brought Charles V to the Spanish throne. He was the grandson of King Ferdinand of Aragon and Queen Isabella of Castile, who had sponsored Columbus's voyages. Isabella outlived her only son, her eldest daughter, and her first grandchild; so her second daughter, Joan, inherited her throne. Joan's husband, Philip I of the Netherlands, died when their son Charles was six years old.

Because Joan was mentally ill, her father Ferdinand ruled on her behalf. Ferdinand's death made Charles king of Spain in addition to the Netherlands. After becoming Holy Roman Emperor, Charles controlled more of Europe than any ruler since Charlemagne in the early 800s. Although Philip II received just part of that empire, he also ruled England because he was married to Queen Mary of England. The English pushed him aside after Mary's death.

ACTIVITY: Have students make a family tree from Isabella to Philip II. Lead a class discussion about the advantages and disadvantages of a system of choosing rulers based on marriage and inheritance.

Charles V

While their explorers were expanding the empire abroad, Spanish kings expanded their authority in Spain itself. One of the greatest of these kings was **Charles V.** Charles was a member of the Habsburgs, an old German family. Charles took the Spanish throne in 1516. Three years later he was elected Holy Roman Emperor.

With Charles's titles and power, he was torn between conflicting demands. As king of Spain, he had to adopt a Spanish viewpoint. As Holy Roman Emperor, he was expected to support German aims. Finally, as the political leader of Christian Europe, Charles had to defend Europe against the Ottoman Turks.

The nearly continuous religious wars during Charles's reign drained Spain's human resources and treasury. Spain lacked industries and the government did little to promote them. So much of Spain's land was devoted to raising sheep for wool that the country could not produce enough food to feed its people. Food prices increased many times over between 1500 and 1650.

Charles realized that the Spanish and Holy Roman empires had become too large for one man to rule. In 1556 he gave up his throne and divided the vast lands among members of his family. Charles's son **Philip II** received Spain and its possessions. His branch of the family became known as the Spanish Habsburgs. Charles's brother Ferdinand I was already king of Hungary and Bohemia. Now he became Holy Roman Emperor and head of the Austrian Habsburgs.

King Philip II of Spain personally managed the daily operations of the royal government.

✔ **READING CHECK: Finding the Main Idea** What were some of the factors that led Charles to split up his lands? realized that the Spanish and Holy Roman empires had become too large for one ruler to govern; was exhausted by continuing religious warfare

Philip II

Unlike his father, Philip II was born and educated in Spain. He ruled from 1556 until his death in 1598. Philip was a dedicated monarch who worked long hours at being king. His goal was to strengthen Spain's hold as Europe's leading power. Philip built a new royal residence, El Escorial, 25 miles from Madrid. From there he took control of every facet of government. This nearly paralyzed his administration. Philip also saw himself as the leader of the Counter-Reformation. A very devout Catholic, he ordered the Spanish Inquisition to stamp out heresy at home. Abroad, Philip involved Spain in wars to defend Catholicism and bring glory to Spain. These efforts were so costly that taxes could never keep up with expenses. As bankers charged more and more interest on loans to Spain, the country's financial woes increased.

Although Philip was unable to defeat all the enemies of Spain and Catholicism, he did manage to defeat the Ottoman Empire in the Mediterranean. His attempted invasion of Protestant England by the huge Spanish Armada in 1588, however, ended in disaster. An attempt to invade France to prevent a Protestant from becoming king was also an expensive failure. Yet these setbacks were not the costliest errors in Philip's policy making.

✔ **READING CHECK: Drawing Inferences** Why might the kind of control that Philip exerted over his government paralyze his administration? slowed decision-making and the flow of government business

The Rise of the Dutch

Philip II's most costly policies were those toward the Netherlands, one of Europe's great trading centers since the Middle Ages. Philip had inherited the Netherlands. Because Calvinism was becoming popular in the area, Philip treated his Dutch subjects harshly. First, he ignored the Netherlands' long tradition of self-rule. He insisted that he, rather than the local nobles, held all authority. Second, he taxed Dutch trade heavily to pay for Spanish wars. Third, he persecuted the Calvinists. These actions turned the people's distrust of Philip to outright rebellion.

The Netherlands break from Spain. In 1568 **William of Orange** led a revolt against Philip. The people of the Calvinist northern provinces lived on land below sea level. Large dikes protected the land. The people opened the dikes, flooding the countryside and leaving Philip's army helpless. William sent small bands of soldiers on quick raids to keep the Spanish army confused. Today this military technique is called **guerrilla warfare.**

In 1579 under William's leadership, the northern provinces declared their independence from Spain. William was killed in 1584, but his descendants continued the war with Spain on and off until 1648. The southern provinces were heavily Catholic and remained under Spanish control as the Spanish Netherlands.

Dutch society. Because the Netherlands lay on the North Sea, the Dutch were a seafaring people. They built very efficient ships and were expert sailors. For these reasons, they ruled European commerce throughout the 1600s. Their ships carried most of Europe's trade and the city of Amsterdam became a world financial center. All segments of Dutch business stood as models of efficiency.

Calvinists became the dominant religious group in the Netherlands. Generally, however, the Dutch followed policies of religious tolerance. Amsterdam became a lively cultural center. Scholars such as René Descartes and artists such as Rembrandt and Vermeer thrived in this comfortable setting.

The Dutch colonial empire. In 1602 the Dutch East India Company was founded. It had total control over trading between the Netherlands and the East Indies. The first Dutch overseas colony was founded on the island of Java in 1619. The Dutch took over the entire island, with its valuable crops of sugar, tea, coffee, and spices. From Java, they expanded westward to Sumatra and eastward to the Spice Islands. Their colony at the Cape of Good Hope allowed them to supply and protect their trade routes to Asia.

The Dutch also gained a foothold in Japan. Because the Dutch did not come as missionaries, the Japanese allowed them to open a trading center in Nagasaki. In the Western Hemisphere the Dutch established colonies in the West Indies, South America, and North America. In 1626 they purchased Manhattan Island from the Native Americans and built the city of New Amsterdam there.

The Dutch colonial empire was much different from that of the Spanish. The Dutch never tried to convert conquered peoples to Christianity. They did not force them to speak Dutch or live under the laws of the Netherlands. The Dutch came as traders, with the sole intention of making money. This goal reflected their businesslike society.

✔ **READING CHECK: Drawing Inferences** In what ways did the Dutch gain access to trading opportunities that other countries had missed? They made no attempt to force their culture or religious beliefs on other societies.

CONNECTING TO Art

Painting:
Young Woman with Water Jug

In the 1600s the economy of the Netherlands prospered. Dutch merchants grew rich enough to buy handsome silks and linens for their wives. Some commissioned artists to paint for them. Dutch artists such as Rembrandt and Vermeer flourished. This painting, one of Vermeer's finest works, gives us a close look at Dutch daily life.

Understanding the Arts

What does this painting tell us about life in the Netherlands in the 1600s?

CONNECTING TO ART ANSWER
Students' answers will vary but may include luxury, fine fabrics, goods from Asia such as the tablecloth, or international interests as shown in the wall map.

Geography

The Dutch entered the Asian trade in part due to a work by a Dutch writer, Jan Huyghen van Linschoten. From 1583 to 1589 Linschoten worked for the Portuguese archbishop in Goa, on the coast of India. After his return to the Netherlands, Linschoten published his *Itinerario*, which gave a geographical description of the world, sailing directions for reaching India and America, and his own observations of Asia. Up to that time the Dutch had sailed on Portuguese ships but Dutch ships had not gone to Asia. The first Dutch fleet to use Linschoten's directions sailed in 1595. Others followed, and competition between the Dutch and Portuguese grew fierce. Formation of the Dutch East India Company consolidated competing Dutch companies.

Critical Thinking

Ask students why Linschoten was particularly qualified to write the *Itinerario*.

ANSWER: Students should mention his experience in Goa.

HOMEWORK Have students study the map on pages 404–405 and identify and describe at least three patterns of distribution of European colonies in 1700.

Spotlight on GEOGRAPHY Have students identify Dutch colonies on the map on pages 404–405, then look at a modern map to identify the countries in those locations today. Ask students to use computer software to identify ways the heritage of Dutch rule influences the culture of those countries today.

Culture

In the Spanish colonies, the agricultural estate, or hacienda, was almost entirely self-contained. It was not just a source of income for its owner but also a source of pride, as status was often based on the size of the hacienda and the number of cattle or peasants on it. The owner of the hacienda had absolute control over his subjects. The peasants who lived on the hacienda existed on what they could plant on their small plots, and the rest of the hacienda was used for its main agricultural product, such as cattle, tobacco, coffee, or sugar.

Critical Thinking

Ask students how the structure of the hacienda reflects Spanish culture and political or economic thought.

ANSWER: Students may compare the power of the hacienda owner to the power of kings in Spain. In addition, they may say that mercantilist ideas encouraged colonial production of raw materials like sugar to send to the home country.

Technology Resources
 Online Maps: Empires in the Americas, 1700

Technology Resources
 Online Maps: Africa in 1750

European Overseas Empires, 1700
Interpreting Maps The map shows the territories around the globe that were held by European countries in 1700.

TEACH OBJECTIVES 1 and 2

ALL LEVELS: Organize students into small groups to present skits about life in the colonies of Spain and the Netherlands. Each group should script a scene that would have been typical in the lives and interactions of the native people and the Spanish or Dutch colonists. Suggest that groups decide on their basic story line and assign characters before developing their script. After the groups complete their scripts, have them present their skits to the class. **ENGLISH LANGUAGE LEARNERS, COOPERATIVE LEARNING**

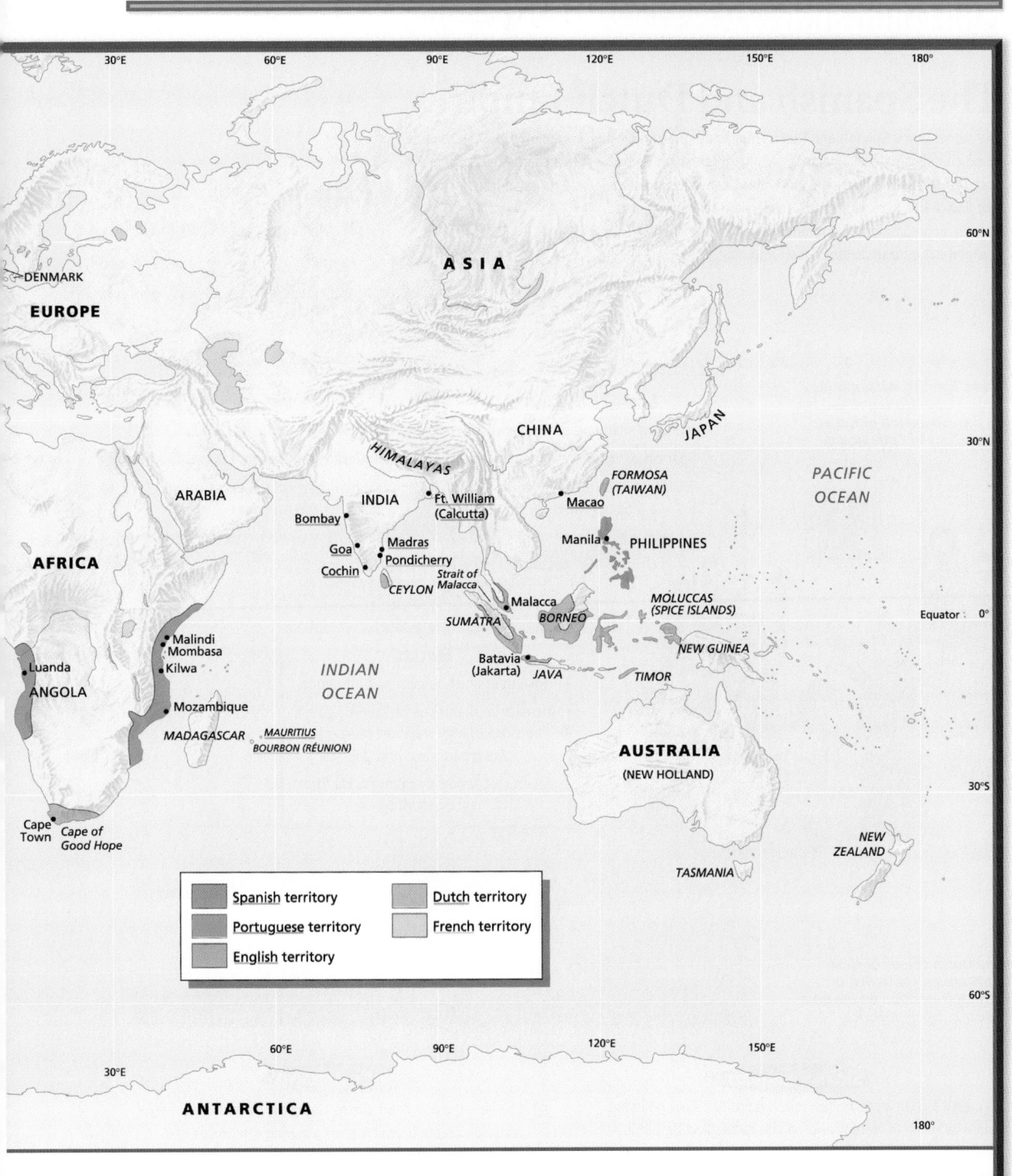

Geography

Australia was the last continent to be colonized by Europeans. Medieval European mythology tells of a Great Southland, or *Terra Australis*, but its existence and location remained a mystery. It was not near the established trade routes, and prevailing winds carried ships away from it.

A Dutch East India Company trader, Abel Tasman, finally reached Australia in 1642. For the next 100 years ships sailing to Indonesia sometimes stopped on Australia's coast. However, no European colonies were established there until the late 1700s.

Critical Thinking

Ask students why it took so long for European explorers to find Australia.

ANSWER: Students should answer that it was off the main trade routes and protected by prevailing winds.

MAP ANSWER

Spanish colonies were in North and South America and the Philippines; English and French colonies were primarily in North America; most other colonies were in coastal areas; Portuguese were primarily on east coasts of Africa and South America; Dutch were in islands of Southeast Asia, with smaller holdings in South Africa and northern South America.

■ **Skills Assessment: The World in Spatial Terms** What patterns can you identify regarding the distribution of European colonies in 1700?

ALL LEVELS: Pair students and have them develop a "Top Ten" list of reasons for Spain's decline as a world power. Select pairs to present their lists to the class, working up from the tenth reason to the number one reason. *(Lists might include ineffective rulers, Dutch revolt, defeat of Armada, expulsion of Jews and Moriscos, lack of industrial development, inflation resulting from colonial gold and silver, and so on.)* Record each pair's number one reason on the board for comparison.
ENGLISH LANGUAGE LEARNERS, COOPERATIVE LEARNING

Ask students to explain whether they would rather have lived in the Spanish Empire or the Dutch Empire. Ask them how their lives might differ if they were conquered people in the Spanish Empire or the Dutch Empire. Then ask how their lives might differ if they were Europeans in each empire.

Historical Sidelight

Unrest in the Aztec and Inca Empires contributed to their defeat by the Spanish. Both groups had built their empires in the 1400s, often through the conquest of their neighbors, and both had to put down frequent rebellions in the decades that followed. The Inca were in the midst of a civil war when the Spanish arrived in 1530. Cortés and Pizarro exploited such tensions among native peoples to gain control of both empires.

Critical Thinking

Ask students how conditions within the Aztec and Inca Empires affected Spanish conquest.

ANSWER: Both empires were weakened by internal struggles, which aided Spanish efforts to conquer them.

SKILLS PRACTICE ANSWERS

1. Long term causes: Philip II's treatment of Dutch subjects, war with Spain; Immediate causes: founding of Dutch East India Company in 1602, colony in Java in 1619, purchase of Manhattan Island in 1626; Effects: established trade throughout the world, developed businesslike society

2. Spanish tried to convert conquered peoples to Christianity; Dutch came as traders to make money. What were the long-term effects of these empires?

SKILL-BUILDING STRATEGIES   Making Charts

The Spanish and Dutch Empires

The stories of the Spanish and Dutch empires can be complicated. Sometimes in order to understand complex material it helps to organize information in the form of a chart. Charts can include such formats as time lines and family trees, as well as classification charts, organization charts, and flowcharts. In making charts, readers are able to organize, simplify, and summarize information in a way that often makes it easier to understand and remember.

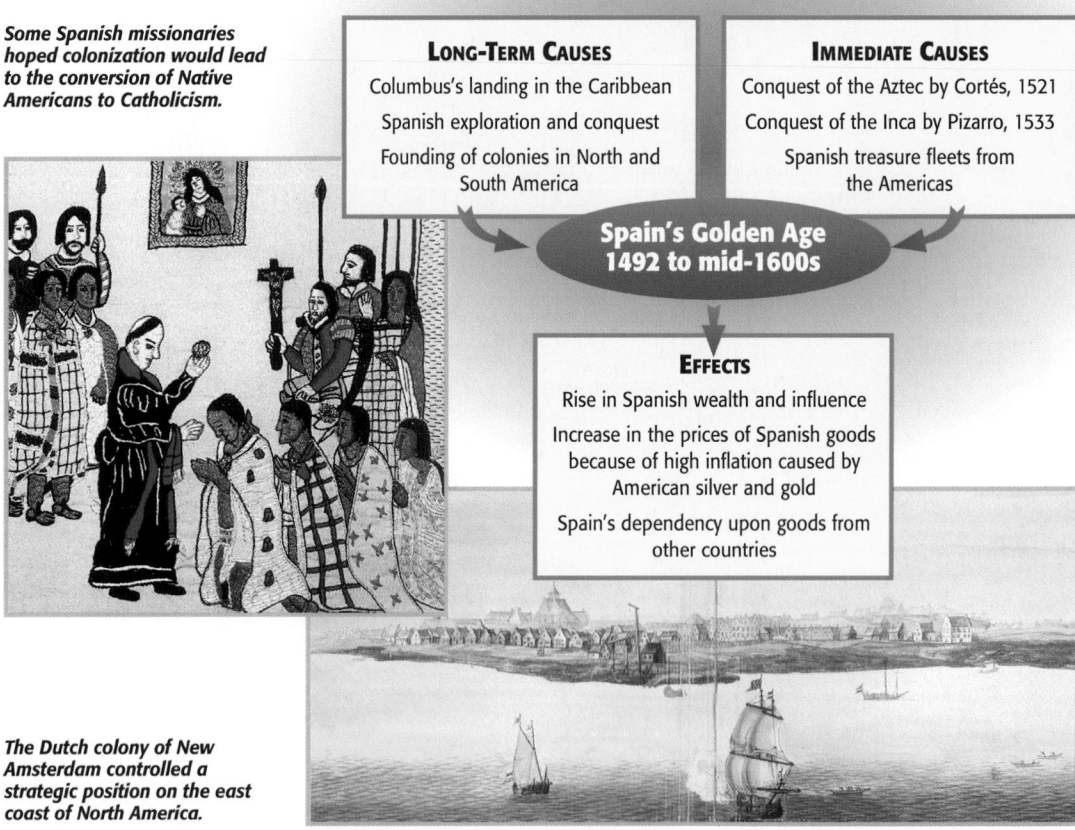

Some Spanish missionaries hoped colonization would lead to the conversion of Native Americans to Catholicism.

Causes and Effects of Spain's Age of Empire

LONG-TERM CAUSES
Columbus's landing in the Caribbean
Spanish exploration and conquest
Founding of colonies in North and South America

IMMEDIATE CAUSES
Conquest of the Aztec by Cortés, 1521
Conquest of the Inca by Pizarro, 1533
Spanish treasure fleets from the Americas

Spain's Golden Age 1492 to mid-1600s

EFFECTS
Rise in Spanish wealth and influence
Increase in the prices of Spanish goods because of high inflation caused by American silver and gold
Spain's dependency upon goods from other countries

The Dutch colony of New Amsterdam controlled a strategic position on the east coast of North America.

Skills Reminder

To create a chart from written text, it helps to follow headings and word cues to identify appropriate details and determine what facts support the chart. Make sure you present the information in a clear and easy-to-follow manner using such visual aids as heading, lines, or arrows. The final product should help to visually summarize and order information.

Skills Practice

❶ Examine the flowchart above. Using the information in your textbook, create a similar chart showing the causes and effects of the Dutch Empire.

❷ What were some of the differences in the Spanish and Dutch empires? What other questions do the charts raise?

REVIEW

Have students complete the Section 4 Review on p. 407.

ASSESS

Have students complete Daily Quiz 16.4. As Alternative Assessment, you may want to use the "Top Ten" exercise in this section's lessons.

RETEACH

Have students complete Main Idea Activity for English Language Learners and Special-Needs Students 16.4. Then have students study the "Causes and Effects of Spain's Age of Empire" chart on page 406 and restate each part of the chart in their own words. **ENGLISH LANGUAGE LEARNERS**

EXTEND

Have students make time lines that illustrate how events in Spain's European empire relate chronologically to the growth of the Spanish and Dutch Empires overseas. Suggest they plot European developments on one side of the time line and colonial developments on the other. Suggest they color-code their time lines to distinguish Dutch from Spanish events. **BLOCK SCHEDULING**

The Spanish Empire Declines

Many factors played a part in the decline of the Spanish Empire. A growing population meant that more people needed to be fed, clothed, and housed. At the same time, gold and silver flowed into Spain from the colonies. Shortages and this increase in the amount of money drove prices up in Spain. Because it cost more to produce goods in Spain than in any other country, demand for Spanish-made products declined. This loss of markets, in turn, led to a general decline in Spain's industry and commercial activity.

A capable middle class might have helped Spanish industries to develop. Many Spanish nobles, however, preferred military service. Others chose careers in the church rather than in secular life. In addition, the Spanish crown expelled first the Jews and then the Moriscos—Moorish converts to Christianity—from Spain. Unfortunately for the Spanish economy, many of those expelled were skilled bankers, businesspeople and commercial leaders, and artisans. The persecution of the Jews and the Moriscos conducted by the Spanish crown and the church further weakened Spain's economy and drained talent and capability from the country.

Much of the empire's wealth simply passed through Spain and was used to buy goods from other countries. With the gold and silver they received for goods sold in Spain, countries such as France, England, and the Netherlands grew strong. They developed their own industries at Spain's expense.

At home, people became discontented with high taxes and inflation. Along with agricultural failures, this discontent drove many people from their homes. Eventually, many people emigrated from Spain.

✔ **READING CHECK: Categorizing** What were the major problems that led to the decline of the Spanish Empire? growing population, shortages and increased costs, expulsion of Jews and Moriscos, flow of money out of Spain

Moorish rulers of Granada pay tribute to the Spanish royal couple.

SECTION 4 REVIEW

1. **Define** and explain the significance:
   viceroys
   guerrilla warfare

2. **Identify** and explain the significance:
   Ponce de León
   Hernán Cortés
   Moctezuma II
   Francisco Pizarro
   Charles V
   Philip II
   William of Orange

3. **Identifying Cause and Effect**
   Copy the web diagram below. Fill in each box to show how it contributed to the decline of the Spanish Empire.

   Economics in Spain → Decline of Spanish Empire ← Actions of Colonies
   Actions of Charles V → Decline of Spanish Empire ← Actions of Philip II

4. **Finding the Main Idea**
   a. How did the Spanish expand their colonial empire?
   b. How did the Dutch colonial empire differ from the Spanish colonial empire?
   c. What developments limited the ability of the Spanish to fully benefit from their vast and rich overseas empire?

5. **Writing and Critical Thinking**
   Making Generalizations In a diary entry, describe a day in the life of a Spanish colonist in the Americas.
   Consider:
   • ways in which things would have been better or worse than in Spain
   • what was involved in meeting and dealing with native peoples

Homework Practice Online
keyword: SP3 HP16

SECTION 4 REVIEW ANSWERS

❶ **Define**
• viceroys, p. 401
• guerrilla warfare, p. 403

❷ **Identify**
• Ponce de León, p. 400
• Hernán Cortés, p. 400
• Moctezuma II, p. 400
• Francisco Pizarro, p. 401
• Charles V, p. 402
• Philip II, p. 402
• William of Orange, p. 403

❸ Economics in Spain: inflation, high taxes, unfavorable balance of trade; Actions of Colonies: piracy, trade in Spanish ports, establish colonies in Americas; Actions of Charles V: wars, financial problems; Actions of Philip II: expensive wars, loss of Netherlands

❹ a. They conquered the Aztec and Inca and established settlements.

b. The Dutch emphasized trade and did not try to convert local people to Christianity.

c. Increases in the amount of gold and silver drove up prices. The demand for Spanish-made goods declined.

❺ Students' diaries will vary.

REVIEW AND ASSESSMENT RESOURCES

REPRODUCIBLE RESOURCES

▸ Vocabulary Activity 16

TECHNOLOGY RESOURCES

▸ Chapter 16 Test Generator (on the One-Stop Planner)
▸ Global Skill Builder CD–ROM
▸ HRW Web Site

REINFORCEMENT, REVIEW, and ASSESSMENT

▸ Chapter 16 Review, pp. 408–409
▸ Chapter 16 Tutorial for Students, Parents, Mentors, and Peers
▸ Chapter 16 Test (Form A or B)
▸ Alternative Assessment Handbook
▸ Chapter 16 Test for English Language Learners and Special-Needs Students

REVIEW

Have students complete the Chapter 16 Review on pages 408–409.

ASSESS

Use one of the chapter tests to assess students' understanding of the content. For Alternative Assessment, see the Portfolio Activities and Alternative Assessment Handbook.

CHAPTER 16 REVIEW ANSWERS

Understanding Main Ideas

1. observation, experiments, mathematics, questioning old beliefs

2. Earth moves around sun; laws of planetary motion, universal gravitation, conservation of matter; circulation of blood; calculus; bacteria; oxygen

3. compass, astrolabe, standardization of money, joint-stock companies

4. led to use of colonies for gold, silver, raw materials, letting colonies trade just with home country

5. Asia accessible by sea around southern tip of Africa

6. began contact between Europeans and people of Americas, Columbian Exchange

7. European demand for labor in colonies, devastation of American Indian population by European diseases

8. good ships and sailors, focus on trade, Dutch East India Company

9. inflation caused by influx of gold and silver, industrial decline, lack of middle class, expulsion of Jews and Moriscos

Reviewing Themes

1. new ways of thinking about the world, less acceptance of old beliefs, technology for maritime exploration

---

CHAPTER 16 Review

Creating a Time Line

Copy the time line below onto a sheet of paper. Complete the time line by filling in the events, individuals, and dates from the chapter that you think were significant. Pick three events and explain why you think they were significant.

1400   1600   1800

Writing a Summary

Using standard grammar, spelling, sentence structure, and punctuation, write an overview of the events in the chapter.

Identifying People and Ideas

Identify the following terms or individuals and explain their significance:

1. heliocentric theory
2. Galileo Galilei
3. mercantilism
4. Vasco da Gama
5. tariffs
6. Christopher Columbus
7. triangular trade
8. Middle Passage
9. Hernán Cortés
10. Philip II

Understanding Main Ideas

SECTION 1 *(pp. 382–387)*
The Scientific Revolution
1. How did the study of nature change during the Scientific Revolution?
2. What were some of the important scientific discoveries made during this period?

SECTION 2 *(pp. 388–391)*
The Foundations of European Exploration
3. What kinds of changes in science and economics made European exploration possible?
4. What role did mercantilism play in the way European countries dealt with their colonies?

SECTION 3 *(pp. 392–399)*
Voyages of Portugal and Spain
5. What new knowledge did early Portuguese explorers provide that increased successful exploration?
6. How did the voyages of Christopher Columbus influence the world?
7. What were some of the factors leading to the Atlantic slave trade?

SECTION 4 *(pp. 400–407)*
The Spanish and Dutch Empires
8. What led to the successful rise of Dutch exploration in the 1600s?
9. What factors led to the decline of the Spanish Empire?

Reviewing Themes

1. **Science, Technology & Society** How did the era known as the Scientific Revolution lead to developments in other areas of society?
2. **Economics** How did the theory of mercantilism influence nations' decisions to explore and colonize?
3. **Global Relations** What determined the kinds of relationships that European explorers formed with conquered peoples?

Thinking Critically

1. **Comparing and Contrasting** Compare and contrast the ways in which the Portuguese, Spanish, and Dutch went about exploration and colonization.
2. **Supporting a Point of View** Which European nation engaged in exploration, trade, and colonization during the age of exploration had the greatest effect on other peoples? Explain your answer.
3. **Sequencing** Trace the events leading to the rise and decline of the Spanish Empire.

Writing About History

Categorizing Many factors influenced European exploration. In turn, exploration had many effects on both Europeans and non-Europeans. Fill in the following chart, listing the political, economic, cultural, and technological influences of European expansion on both Europeans and non-Europeans.

Effects of European Conquest		
	Europeans	**Non-Europeans**
Political		
Economic		
Cultural		
Technological		

CLOSE

Have the class debate the statement: "European exploration and expansion between 1400 and 1700 lay the foundations of the modern world."

RETEACH

Have students write one or more phrases that summarize the main ideas of each heading or subheading. **ENGLISH LANGUAGE LEARNERS**

Portfolio Extensions

1. Have students make a "What If?" poster with at least five different scenes about the era of exploration and expansion. Each scene should show the short-term and long-term results if one event of the period had been different in some way. Remind them to consider what might realistically have been different in technology, exploration, politics, weather, battles, etc.

2. Organize students into groups of four or five. Have the groups locate and use biog-

raphies to research the life of one scientist, explorer, or other person in the chapter and prepare a short play to perform for the class. Plays should illustrate personality and feelings as well as why the person is important.

3. Have students imagine they are a newspaper reporter writing a feature story on an important event of exploration or expansion. Encourage them to be creative and dramatic in their writing while using correct social studies terminology.

Building Social Studies Skills

Interpreting Maps

Study the map below. Then use the information to answer the questions that follow.

Cabral's Route, April 1500

1. Which of the following correctly describes Cabral's course from Lisbon to the Cape of Good Hope?
   a. First south, then west
   b. First southwest, then southeast
   c. First northwest, then northeast
   d. First southeast, then southwest

2. Cabral did not intend to follow the course he did. He was blown off course. Why was this course change significant? Give specific reasons.

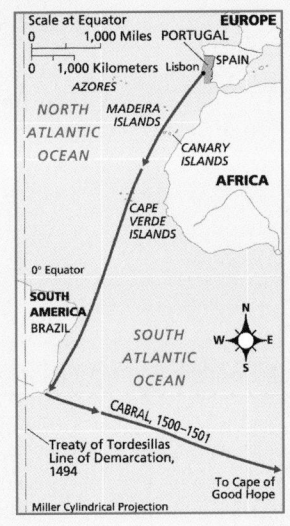

Problem Solving

Read the following quote written in 1517 by a Spanish priest in Mexico. Then answer the questions.

"As the Indians saw that the Spaniards did not attack them . . . they came . . . unarmed with kindly faces. . . . They asked the captain by signs what he wanted to which he replied 'water to drink.' The Indians showed him a round walled-up well of good water . . . where [the Spaniards] took all the water needful for the ships. . . . When day broke, all the Indians came out of their town armed with bows and arrows, shields and lances . . . to tell [the Spaniards] to go to their ships. The Spaniards obeyed their order. . . ."

3. Which of the following is the best explanation of why the Indians changed their behavior toward the Spanish?
   a. The Indians thought the Spanish had stayed too long.
   b. The Indians had only pretended to be kind.
   c. Water was scarce and the Spanish had taken too much.
   d. The Indians realized the Spanish were after their gold.

4. Why did you choose the statement you did in question 3? Explain your reasoning, using a problem-solving process.

Alternative Assessment

Building Your Portfolio

Economics

The idea of a favorable balance of trade developed during the 1500s and the 1600s. Today, most nations still take steps to keep their imports and exports balanced. Using your textbook and other sources, find statistics and other information about economic processes that countries such as the United States, Great Britain, and Japan use to maintain favorable trade balances. Summarize your findings in a poster.

internet connect

Internet Activity: go.hrw.com
KEYWORD: SP3 WH16

Choose a topic on Exploration and Expansion to:
- research the Scientific Revolution and create a database of scientists, dates, and contributions.
- learn more about an explorer described in this chapter.
- explain the political, economic, and cultural impact of Spanish expansion in Mesoamerica and Andean South America.

2. desire for gold and silver, use of colonies as source of raw materials and market for manufacturers

3. whether colonists tried to enslave conquered peoples

Thinking Critically

1. Portuguese: focus on routes around Africa to Asia for spices; Spanish: focus on Americas for gold, silver, plantation products; Dutch: emphasis on Asian spice trade

2. Spain: devastation of the Americas by diseases; Portugal: leadership in the African slave trade

3. Isabella and Ferdinand unite Spain; and sponsor Columbus; expulsion of Jews and Moriscos; Cortés conquers Aztecs; Pizarro conquers Incas; Spanish settlements established in Americas; Philip II loses Netherlands

Writing About History

Europeans: empires, trade, spread culture; non-Europeans: conquered, provided labor, changed lifestyles, new weapons

Building Social Studies Skills

1. b

2. He landed in Brazil and claimed it for Portugal.

3. Answers will vary.

4. Answers will vary.

Building Your Portfolio

Students' posters will vary.

Asia in Transition

CHAPTER RESOURCE MANAGER

Objectives	Pacing Guide	Reproducible Resources
SECTION 1 **The Ming and Qing Dynasties** (pp. 412–416) • Explain why the Chinese showed little interest in overseas trade during the Ming dynasty. • Describe how the Qing dynasty came to rule China. • Discuss changes that occurred in the Chinese economy under Qing rule. • Analyze reasons for the decline of the Qing dynasty.	**Regular** 1.5 day / **Block Scheduling** 1 day *Block Scheduling Handbook with Team Teaching Strategies, 17.1*	RS Guided Reading Strategy 17.1 E Hands-on History Activity 17: Asian Empires
SECTION 2 **China and Europeans** (pp. 417–421) • Characterize early contact between Portugal and China. • Explain why China and Great Britain went to war in the mid-1800s. • Describe how internal rebellions contributed to the decline of the Qing dynasty.	**Regular** 1.5 day / **Block Scheduling** 1 day *Block Scheduling Handbook with Team Teaching Strategies, 17.2*	RS Guided Reading Strategy 17.2 RS Graphic Organizer Activity 17: Asia and the West PS Readings in World History 69: The Treaty of Nanjing, 1842
SECTION 3 **The Tokugawa Shoguns in Japan** (pp. 422–427) • Explain how the Tokugawa shogunate came to power. • Discuss why Japan's rulers sought to isolate their nation from foreign influence. • Identify characteristics of society and culture under the Tokugawa shogunate. • Describe how Japanese isolation was brought to an end.	**Regular** 1.5 day / **Block Scheduling** 1 day *Block Scheduling Handbook with Team Teaching Strategies, 17.3*	RS Guided Reading Strategy 17.3 SM Geography Activity 17: The Struggle for Korea PS Readings in World History 70: Yoshida Shoin: Philosopher of the Meiji Restoration E Creative Teaching Strategy 17: The Way of the Shogun

Chapter Resource Key

PS Primary Sources
RS Reading Support
IC Interdisciplinary Connections
E   Enrichment
SM Skills Mastery
A   Assessment

REV Review
ELL Reinforcement and English Language Learners
 Transparencies
 CD-ROM
 Music

 Video
Internet
Holt Presentation Maker Using Microsoft® PowerPoint®

One-Stop Planner CD-ROM

See the ***One-Stop Planner*** for a complete list of additional resources for students and teachers.

One-Stop Planner CD-ROM

It's easy to plan lessons, select resources, and print out materials for your students when you use the **One-Stop Planner** CD–ROM with **Test Generator.**

Technology Resources	Reinforcement, Review, and Assessment
One-Stop Planner 17.1	Daily Quiz 17.1
Regions of the World Music Audio CD Program 19: China, Mongolia, and Taiwan: Beating the Dragon Robe: A Traditional Chinese Opera	Main Idea Activity 17.1
World History Teaching Transparency: Regional and World Map 37: East and Southeast Asia	English Audio Summary 17.1
World History Teaching Transparency: Art and History 16: Cicada on a Palm Leaf	Spanish Audio Summary 17.1
Homework Practice Online	REV Section 1 Review, p. 416
Online Maps, Charts, and Graphs: Expansion of the Manchu by 1643	

One-Stop Planner 17.2	Daily Quiz 17.2
CNN. Presents World Cultures: Yesterday and Today Segment 19: Hong Kong: Past and Present	Main Idea Activity 17.2
Religions of the World Video Series: Christianity	English Audio Summary 17.2
Homework Practice Online	Spanish Audio Summary 17.2
	REV Section 2 Review, p. 421

One-Stop Planner 17.3	Daily Quiz 17.3
Holt Researcher: World History: Oda Nobunaga	Main Idea Activity 17.3
Holt Researcher: World History: Toyotomi Hideyoshi	English Audio Summary 17.3
Holt Researcher: World History: Tokugawa Ieyasu	Spanish Audio Summary 17.3
Regions of the World Music Audio CD Program 20: Japan and the Koreas: Music of the One-String Ichigenkin	REV Section 3 Review, p. 427
Religions of the World Video Series: Christianity	
Homework Practice Online	

internet connect

HRW ONLINE RESOURCES
GO TO: go.hrw.com
Then type in a keyword.

TEACHER HOME PAGE
KEYWORD: SP3 Teacher

CHAPTER INTERNET ACTIVITIES
KEYWORD: SP3 WH17
Choose an activity to:
• analyze art of the Ming and Qing dynasties and explain how they reflect the cultures in which they were produced.
• learn more about Kabuki theater and *Bunraku,* Japanese puppet theater.
• examine an issue from the point of view of a Japanese samurai warrior.

CHAPTER ENRICHMENT LINKS
KEYWORD: SP3 CH17

ONLINE ASSESSMENT
Homework Practice
KEYWORD: SP3 HP17
Standardized Test Prep
KEYWORD: SP3 STP17
Rubrics
KEYWORD: SS Rubrics

ONLINE MAPS, CHARTS, AND GRAPHS
KEYWORD: SP3 MCG

CONTENT UPDATES
KEYWORD: SS Content Updates

HOLT PRESENTATION MAKER
KEYWORD: SP3 PPT17

ONLINE READING SUPPORT
KEYWORD: SS Strategies

CURRENT EVENTS
KEYWORD: S3 Current Events

Meeting Individual Needs

Ability Levels

Level 1   Basic level activities designed for all students encountering new material

Level 2   Intermediate level activities designed for average students

Level 3   Challenging activities designed for honors and gifted and talented students

English Language Learners   These activities address the needs of students with Limited English Proficiency.

Chapter Review and Assessment

IC Vocabulary Activity 17	A Chapter 17 Test Generator (on the One-Stop Planner)
Global Skill Builder CD–ROM	A Chapter 17 Test (Form A or B)
HRW Web Site	A Alternative Assessment Handbook
REV Chapter 17 Tutorial for Students, Parents, Mentors, and Peers	A Chapter 17 Test for English Language Learners and Special-Needs Students
REV Chapter 17 Review, pp. 428–429	

409b

Section 1   The Ming and Qing Dynasties

Section 2   China and Europeans

Section 3   The Tokugawa Shoguns in Japan

Build on What You Know

Ask students to answer the following questions:

How might changes during the Tang and Sung dynasties have affected dynasties that followed?

Consider:

• **the influence of Buddhism**

• **the structure of Chinese society**

In what ways did Chinese culture influence early Japan?

Consider:

• **forms of government**

• **language and literature**

EXPLORING THE TIME LINE
GLOBAL EVENTS

internet connect

TOPIC: Chinese Opium Wars

GO TO: go.hrw.com

KEYWORD: SP3 WH17

Have students access the Internet through the HRW Go site to research the Chinese Opium Wars. Ask students to write a letter of response from Queen Victoria to Lin Tse-Hsu's plea for England to cease its shipments of opium into China. Explain your (her) refusal to intervene on behalf of the Chinese people, and the justification for importing opium in trade for tea.

CHAPTER
17

1368–1868

Asia in Transition

Statue of King Sejong of Korea

c. 1350s–1370s
Business and Finance
In response to Japanese piracy, the Chinese ban all trade with Japan.

c. 1407
Science and Technology
The Chinese complete the "Yung Lo Ta Tien" encyclopedia.

c. 1430s
Business and Finance
Japan and China begin trading again.

c. 1514
Global Events
Portuguese ships reach the southeastern coast of China for the first time.

| **1350** | **1400** | **1450** | **1500** | **1600** |

1368
Politics
The Ming dynasty is established in China.

1420
The Arts
The Chinese build the Great Temple of the Dragon in Peking.

1415
Global Events
A Chinese fleet arrives at Aden, on the southern coast of the Arabian Peninsula.

1446
Daily Life
King Sejong of Korea introduces a phonetic alphabet to Koreans.

1598
Science and Technology
The Korean navy develops an iron-clad warship.

Great Wall of China

Build on What You Know

E ast Asia was one of the great cradles of early civilization. Over many centuries and through the course of many dynasties, China had expanded and its distinct culture had spread throughout much of Asia. Then China was conquered by the Mongols, who established the Yuan dynasty. Meanwhile, the people of Japan had developed a feudal society of their own, with a rich culture and a heritage of unique traditions and values. In this chapter, you will learn how both Chinese and Japanese rulers became increasingly concerned and threatened by the growing activity of foreigners, especially Europeans, in and around their lands.

What's Your Opinion?

To help students create their Themes Journal entries, provide the following examples of appropriate **agree**/**disagree** *statements.*

Global Relations

Agree Avoiding outside influence helps nations maintain their own cultural identity.

Disagree Isolation prevents nations from sharing and therefore benefiting from new ideas and developments.

Economics

Agree Economic growth does not depend on cultural attitudes.

Disagree Economic growth is stimulated by interaction with other peoples.

Government

Agree A strong central government can keep a nation and its culture unified.

Disagree A strong central government prevents growth and change.

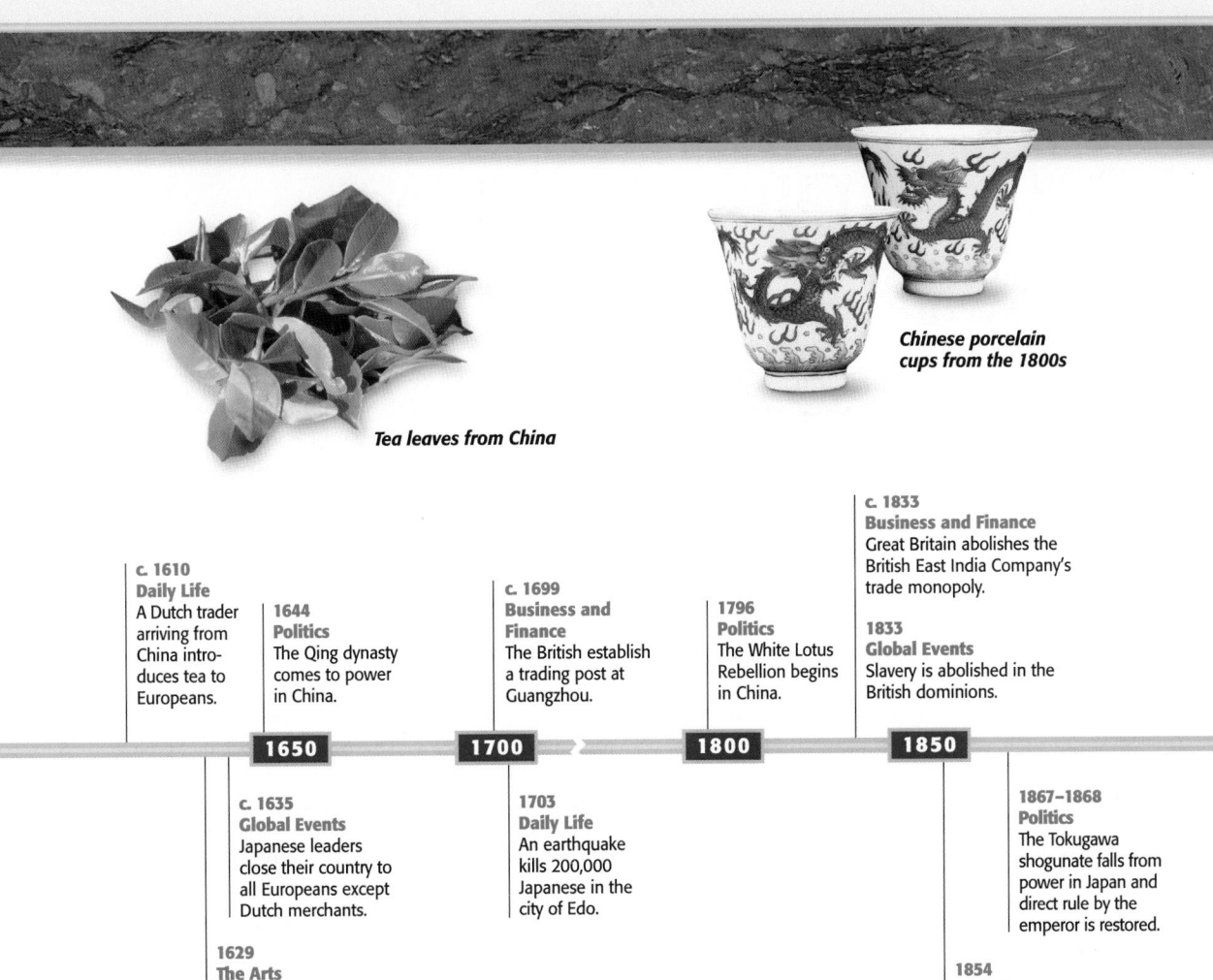

Tea leaves from China

Chinese porcelain cups from the 1800s

c. 1610
Daily Life
A Dutch trader arriving from China introduces tea to Europeans.

1644
Politics
The Qing dynasty comes to power in China.

c. 1699
Business and Finance
The British establish a trading post at Guangzhou.

1796
Politics
The White Lotus Rebellion begins in China.

c. 1833
Business and Finance
Great Britain abolishes the British East India Company's trade monopoly.

1833
Global Events
Slavery is abolished in the British dominions.

1650   **1700**   **1800**   **1850**

c. 1635
Global Events
Japanese leaders close their country to all Europeans except Dutch merchants.

1629
The Arts
The Tokugawa shogunate bans women from performing in Japanese theater.

1703
Daily Life
An earthquake kills 200,000 Japanese in the city of Edo.

1867–1868
Politics
The Tokugawa shogunate falls from power in Japan and direct rule by the emperor is restored.

1854
Global Events
American naval officer Matthew Perry forces Japan to open two ports to American trade.

Japanese city of Edo (present-day Tokyo)

The early Ming emperors restored the civil service examination system. Under the Ming, the examination system quickly became the only avenue to hold high office. At the same time, however, Ming society, despite its rigid class system, was the most open society China had yet known. One recent study of civil service exams during the Ming dynasty revealed that between 44 and 84 percent of the candidates for high office came from families where no member in the previous three generations had held any civil service job. In addition, by the late 1400s, people who had the money could buy a passing score on examinations for lesser government offices. Although this development demonstrates the growth of corruption in Ming government, it also is evidence of the fluidity of Ming society.

Critical Thinking

Ask students how this study of Chinese civil service demonstrates the openness of the Confucian class system under the Ming.

ANSWER: Students should recognize that Chinese who were not of the scholar-gentry class could rise to become officials.

What's Your Opinion?

Do you **agree** *or* **disagree** *with the following statements? Support your point of view in your journal.*

Global Relations Nations can protect themselves by isolating their people and cultures from other nations.

Economics Cultural attitudes toward trade, commerce, and interaction with other peoples do not affect a country's economic growth.

Government A country requires a strong central government to provide certain services for its citizens and to protect its culture.

SECTION 1

OBJECTIVES

1 **Explain why the Chinese showed little interest in overseas trade during the Ming dynasty.**

2 **Describe how the Qing dynasty came to rule China.**

3 **Discuss changes that occurred in the Chinese economy under Qing rule.**

4 **Analyze reasons for the decline of the Qing dynasty.**

LET'S GET STARTED!

As students enter the classroom, ask them to write a paragraph discussing whether they think the United States would be better-off or worse-off if the government prohibited all immigration and world trade. (*Most students will suggest that the nation would be worse-off.*) Have volunteers share their responses with the class. Tell students that in Section 1 they will learn how a policy of isolation affected the Ming and Qing dynasties in China.

SECTION 1 RESOURCES

REPRODUCIBLE RESOURCES

▸ Guided Reading Strategy 17.1

▸ Hands-on History Activity 17: Asian Empires

TECHNOLOGY RESOURCES

▸ One-Stop Planner 17.1

▸ World History Teaching Transparency: Regional and World Map 37

▸ Homework Practice Online

▸ Online Maps, Charts, and Graphs: Expansion of the Manchu by 1643

REINFORCEMENT, REVIEW, AND ASSESSMENT

▸ Section 1 Review, p. 416

▸ Daily Quiz 17.1

▸ Main Idea Activity 17.1

▸ English Audio Summary 17.1

▸ Spanish Audio Summary 17.1

MAP ANSWERS

1. the Great Wall

2. the Grand Canal

SECTION 1

READ TO DISCOVER

❶ Why did the Chinese show little interest in overseas trade during the Ming dynasty?

❷ How did the Qing dynasty come to rule China?

❸ What changes occurred in the Chinese economy under Qing rule?

❹ Why did the Qing dynasty decline?

DEFINE

junks
queue
philology

IDENTIFY

Hsüan-yeh
White Lotus Rebellion

WHY IT MATTERS TODAY

China remains an important trading country in the world today. Use [CNN] or other **current event** sources to learn more about China and international trade. Record your findings in your journal.

CNN Student News.com

The Ming and Qing Dynasties

The Main Idea
Two powerful dynasties, the Ming and the Qing, ruled China as a self-sufficient state for more than 500 years.

The Story Continues *The Mongol Yuan dynasty borrowed many ideas from the Chinese in order to establish an effective imperial government. They wisely followed the advice of a Chinese-trained official who said: "The [Mongol] empire was created on horseback, but it cannot be governed on horseback." In 1368, however, a former Buddhist monk named Zhu Yuanzhang (JOO YOO·en·JAHNG) overthrew the Yuan and established the Ming, or "Brilliant," dynasty. The Ming would remain in power in China for almost 300 years.*

Ming Foreign Policy

During the early period of the Ming dynasty—the late 1300s and early 1400s—the Chinese were probably the most skilled sailors in the world. For example, they built large, sturdy ships that Europeans called **junks.** Some junks were more than 400 feet long. The Chinese had been navigating their ships with the compass, which they probably invented, since the early 1100s. In 1405 the Ming emperor financed a fleet that sailed around Southeast Asia to India. Another Chinese fleet sailed across the Indian Ocean. This fleet reached the southern coast of the Arabian Peninsula in 1415.

These and other voyages of trade and discovery took place almost 100 years

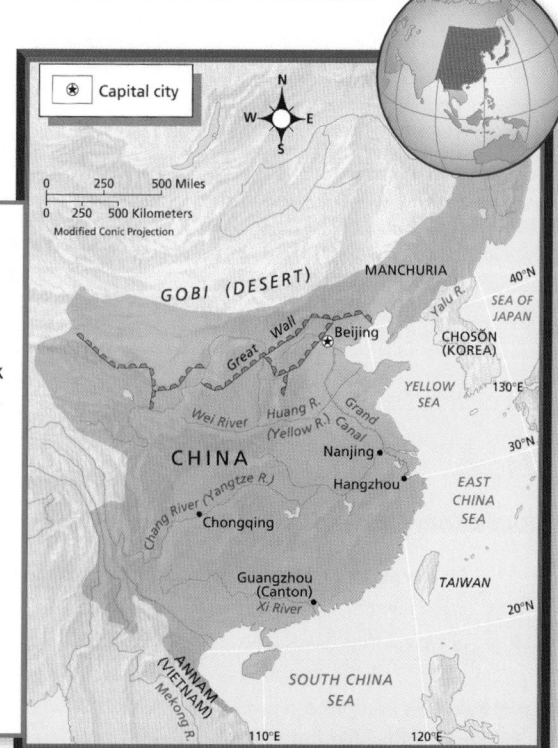

The Ming Empire, 1424

Interpreting Maps
During the Ming dynasty, the imperial capital was moved back from Nanjing to Beijing.

■ **Skills Assessment:**
1. Environment and Society What Chinese feat of engineering shown on the map would block movement from one place to another? **2. Drawing Conclusions** What feat of engineering would help movement?

LEVEL 1: Organize the class into groups. Within each group, designate a student to be the emperor and divide the remainder of the group into two factions during the Ming dynasty—one representing court officials who favor continued trade with the outside world and the other representing court officials who wish to end that trade. Each faction should present arguments in support of its position to the emperor. After hearing the arguments, the emperor must decide on a course of action regarding international trade and report his or her decision to the class. Discuss with the class the consequences each decision might have for China. **ENGLISH LANGUAGE LEARNERS, COOPERATIVE LEARNING**

before Vasco da Gama sailed from Portugal to India by going around the tip of Africa. The Chinese clearly had the ability to become a great seafaring power. However, the naval expeditions of the early Ming period did not continue for very long. Later Ming emperors had little interest in sea power or in foreign trade. They stopped financing naval expeditions. For a time they even outlawed overseas trade.

Attitudes toward trade. After defeating the Mongols in 1368, the Ming emperors tried to rid China of all Mongol influences. They wanted China to be as great as it had been during the Han, Tang, and Sung dynasties. As part of that effort, the Ming emperors restored Confucianism as the official philosophy of the government. Confucian philosophy divided society into four classes.

The Four Classes under Confucianism			
Scholar-gentry	**Farmers**	**Artisans**	**Merchants**
This landed, highly literate class helped staff the royal bureaucracy.	They produced food and paid the taxes that supported the empire.	They made beautiful and useful objects.	At the bottom of the social order, they made their living by selling objects that peasants and artisans had produced.

The Ming emperors wanted China to be self-sufficient. They refused to rely upon foreign trade as a source of government revenue. In the minds of the emperors, foreign trade did not bring enough benefits to China to make it a worthwhile endeavor. This view differed from that of European monarchs, who were strongly influenced by the ideas of mercantilism.

The northern frontier. The Ming emperors also wanted to make sure that no Central Asian people ever conquered China again. They focused their efforts on the long northern land frontier. To protect that frontier, the Ming strengthened the Great Wall of China. They encouraged soldiers to move with their families into the frontier zone by offering them free land. The Ming also encouraged peasants and city dwellers to move there. When the Ming emperors first came to power, Nanjing, in central China, was their capital. In 1421, however, the imperial capital was relocated to Beijing in the north.

The Ming emperors also tried to prevent nomadic tribes in the north from uniting into a powerful fighting force. Tribes that submitted to the Ming sent tribute to Beijing. In return, the Ming gave nomadic leaders honors, gifts, and titles.

Defending the frontier required constant attention and a great deal of money. The overseas expeditions were also extremely expensive. The Ming did not have enough revenue to do both. They chose frontier defense over trade and sea travel.

✔ **READING CHECK: Identifying Cause and Effect**
Why did the Ming emperors abandon overseas expeditions? little interest in sea power or foreign trade

What If? The Chinese had the means to become a great sea power. **What might have happened if they had used this ability as the Spanish and English did later?**

This busy festival scene provides a view of life in China during the Ming dynasty.

ALL LEVELS: Review with students how earlier Chinese dynasties fell. Then discuss with the class if the fall of the Ming dynasty and the rise of the Qing dynasty fit the pattern of Chinese political history. **ENGLISH LANGUAGE LEARNERS**

 HOMEWORK Have students write letters to the editor of a Ming-era newspaper about the government's trade policy. Select students to read their letters to the class.

Teacher to Teacher

David Olson of Angola, Indiana, suggested the following activity: Have students create compare-and-contrast charts that examine how China and Japan responded to European and American encroachment into their territories and then create a time line of crucial events.

History Maker

MATTEO RICCI. Jesuit Matteo Ricci was an early Christian missionary in China. Ricci arrived in Macao in 1582. For nearly two decades he unsuccessfully sought the emperor's support for his work. In 1601 he finally was allowed to settle in the capital. He remained there until his death in 1610. During his life in China, Ricci developed a system for spelling Chinese words using the Western alphabet and devised Chinese terms for Christian ideas.

Critical Thinking

Ask students why the emperor was reluctant to allow missionary work.

ANSWER: He wanted to maintain traditional ideas and values.

HISTORY MAKER ANSWER
He encouraged the integration of Western ideas.

🔲 **internet** connect ▤

TOPIC: Ming/Qing Art
GO TO: go.hrw.com
KEYWORD: SP3 WH17

Have students access the Internet through the HRW Go site to research the art of the Ming and Qing dynasties. Ask students to create a museum exhibit to display for the class.

HISTORY MAKER

Hsüan-yeh (1654–1722)

Hsüan-yeh was a remarkable and energetic ruler. He increased the size of the Chinese empire, presided over the civil service examination system and flood control efforts, and constructed grain storehouses in case of famine. He also sponsored literary and educational projects.

Hsüan-yeh wanted to learn more about Western ways. He opened Chinese ports to foreign trade and strongly encouraged the introduction of Western education and arts. **How did Hsüan-yeh extend Western influences in China?**

Analyzing Primary Sources

Drawing Conclusions Why was canal travel dangerous at times? *overcrowding; the lock system*

Founding the Qing Dynasty

In the early 1600s a new and serious threat to the Ming dynasty emerged. In Manchuria, to the northeast of China, a chieftain named Nurhachi unified many tribes into a single people, the Manchu. Nurhachi's son captured eastern Mongolia and Korea. He then declared the beginning of a new dynasty, the Qing.

In 1644 the Manchu captured Beijing with the help of a Chinese general. The Qing dynasty ruled China from this time until 1912. Once again, despite the efforts of the Ming, outsiders had conquered China and established their own dynasty.

The Qing emperors were not Chinese, but they adopted Chinese culture and ruled the country with traditional Chinese techniques. One such Qing ruler was the emperor **Hsüan-yeh** (shoo·AHN·yeh).

At the same time, Qing emperors tried to keep the Manchu people, a minority in the empire, separate and distinct from the far more numerous Chinese. All Manchu had to study the Manchu language and cultural traditions. The Qing emperors could marry only Manchu women. They banned further emigration of Chinese to Manchuria, which was set apart as a tribal homeland for the Manchu. Finally, the Qing required all Chinese men to wear their hair tied in a **queue** (tail), a style that was common among the Manchu. The queue symbolized Chinese submission to Manchu rule.

✔ **READING CHECK: Drawing Inferences** Why did Qing rulers strive to keep the Chinese and Manchu people separate? *as a means of keeping the Manchu minority distinct from the more numerous Chinese*

Economy, Culture, and Society

Generally life under the Ming and Qing dynasties was similar. Both Ming and Qing emperors kept traditional political institutions. Both supported traditional ideas and values. However, changes soon occurred to alter some of their traditions.

Economy. China's economy continued to grow during the Qing dynasty. Some regions of Qing China began to specialize in the manufacture or production of certain goods. The Lower Yangtze region, inland from present-day Shanghai, for example, became a center for the weaving of cotton cloth. Traders transported such goods along canals, coastal waterways, and rivers. Father Matteo Ricci, an Italian missionary to China in the late 1500s and early 1600s, described this canal traffic.

 History Makers Speak **❝So great is the number of boats that frequently many days are lost in transit by crowding each other, particularly when water is low in the canals. To prevent this, the water is held back at stated places by wooden locks, which also serve as bridges. . . . At times . . . the rush of water is so high and strong, at the exit from one lock or the entrance to another, that the boats are capsized and the whole crew is drowned.❞**

Matteo Ricci, from *China in the Sixteenth Century*

The Chinese also sent goods such as tea and silk by caravan to Central Asia and Russia. Despite government disapproval, some ships continued to sail to Southeast Asia and India to trade.

As they had during the Sung dynasty, Chinese cities continued to grow. Peace and urban growth contributed to the increase of trade within China's borders. In theory, the Chinese and their Qing rulers still looked down on merchants.

LEVEL 2: Have the class act as an advisory council to the Qing emperor and debate the following issue: Should Chinese merchants continue trading with peoples of Central and Southeast Asia, Russia, and India? How might such trade affect Chinese society? **COOPERATIVE LEARNING**

LEVEL 3: Copy the accompanying graphic organizer on the chalkboard, omitting the italicized answers. Have each student complete the diagram by filling in the effect for each cause listed.

Decline of Qing Dynasty	
Cause	**Effect**
overpopulation	*lack of food for peasants*
government inefficiency	*political unrest*
natural disasters	*social turmoil*

CLOSE

Have interested students research in greater depth the Manchu conquest of the Ming dynasty. Have them report their findings to the class.

The Qing Empire, 1760

Interpreting Maps Under the Qing dynasty, China's borders expanded to the north and to the west.

■ **Skills Assessment: 1. Using Geography** What would the Manchu have to cross to invade China and conquer Beijing?

2. Drawing Inferences Why might the Manchu first secure Korea and eastern Mongolia?

In reality, however, they needed merchants to supply city-dwellers with clothing, food, and other essential goods.

Although cities grew, most of China's people still lived in the countryside. They increased the amount of land used for farming. In addition to rice, wheat, and tea, the rural Chinese planted new crops such as peanuts, sweet potatoes, and tobacco, which had been introduced from the Americas. The sweet potato became known as "the poor man's food" in southern China because it grew well in soil unsuited for the growing of rice. It also had more nutritional value than most other food crops.

Popular culture and society. As in Europe, the growth of cities and the increasing wealth of urban people led to the growth of popular culture in China. As early as the 1300s city people read novels and plays in the common everyday language. During the Ming and Qing dynasties, these popular novels and plays increased in number. Old tales about bandits and corrupt officials, once recited by street storytellers, now appeared in novels by professional authors. The writings of this period realistically portrayed Chinese society and family life.

Scholarship also flourished under both the Ming and the Qing. Scholars wrote detailed histories of earlier dynasties and essays on Confucian ethics. They studied ancient writings, much like the Renaissance humanists in Europe had. Qing scholars studied **philology,** the history of literature and language. In the 1700s Chinese scholars began to organize a manuscript library of rare works from the past.

Culture

Although the Qing are remembered for their patronage of the arts and learning, in 1772 they began a campaign to eliminate writings the emperor's advisers thought objectionable on political or moral grounds. Especially targeted were works considered to be anti-Manchu in tone and those that dealt with security matters such as border defenses. In all, more than 2,000 works were ordered destroyed.

Critical Thinking

Have students draw conclusions about the wisdom of the Qing efforts at censorship. Would such a campaign, had it succeeded, make the nation more secure, or would it limit the growth of Chinese arts and culture?

ANSWER: Answers will vary but should demonstrate understanding that any political benefits of such censorship would be offset by cultural drawbacks.

MAP ANSWERS

1. the Great Wall

2. They could secure it without having to cross the Great Wall.

Ivory figurine depicting a Daoist, c. 1500s–1600s

REVIEW

Have students complete the Section 1 Review on p. 416.

ASSESS

Have students complete Daily Quiz 17.1. As Alternative Assessment, you may want to use the graphic organizer or the homework exercise in this section's lessons.

RETEACH

Have students complete Main Idea Activity for English Language Learners and Special-Needs Students 17.1. Then organize the class into two groups: the Ming dynasty and the Qing dynasty. Ask students in each group to prepare outlines that summarize the history of each dynasty.
ENGLISH LANGUAGE LEARNERS, COOPERATIVE LEARNING

EXTEND

Have students imagine that they are soldiers on guard at the Great Wall of China. Ask them to write diary entries describing such a life. Encourage them to think about reasons for volunteering to go to the frontier, their daily routine, and what they might do in case of an invasion. Encourage students to be as creative as possible, but to use standard grammar, spelling, sentence structure, and punctuation. **BLOCK SCHEDULING**

VISUAL RECORD ANSWER

It was done on a small scale and by hand.

SECTION 1 REVIEW ANSWERS

❶ Define
- junks, p. 412
- queue, p. 414
- philology, p. 415

❷ Identify
- Hsüan-yeh, p. 414
- White Lotus Rebellion, p. 416

❸ Stable: class structure, attitudes toward foreign trade, political institutions, ideas and values; Changed: growth of cities, growth of population, popular culture, scholarship, government inefficiency and corruption

❹ a. increased trade, increased population, growth of popular culture and scholarship

b. suspicion and distrust

❺ Answers will vary but should demonstrate understanding that governmental inefficiency and corruption would have a negative impact on the nation.

Technology Resources
Regions of the World Music Audio CD Program 19

Technology Resources
World History Teaching Transparency: Art and History 16

416

INTERPRETING THE VISUAL RECORD

Silk weaving Chinese silk weavers during the Qing dynasty worked on manual looms. *What does this image reveal about silk weaving in China?*

China's society continued to be based on the family. The family, like the state, reflected the Confucian belief that each person had a role in life. The male head of the family directed the activities of family members for the good of the family as a whole. When a daughter married, she went to live with the family of her new husband.

✔ **READING CHECK: Summarizing** How did the Chinese economy change during the eras of Ming and Qing rule? Trade and manufacturing specialization grew.

Decline of the Qing Dynasty

Under Qing rule China's population grew rapidly. Chinese farmers raised more crops, making it possible to feed more people. Peace also contributed to China's population growth. From about 1750 to the mid-1800s, China's population grew to more than 400 million people.

Qing China's rapidly growing population placed increasing pressure on the government. The Qing, however, found it increasingly difficult to meet the challenges posed by change and growth. Corruption at court and government inefficiency became more widespread. Growing numbers of bureaucrats demanded bribes in return for government services. During these years, China's enormous class of peasant farmers found it more and more difficult to hold their small farms and to support themselves and their families. Unrest spread throughout many parts of China. Disastrous floods and famine in various parts of China made the situation worse, as did growing pressure by the Western powers to gain economic control in China.

In 1796 discontent over increased taxes and growing government inefficiency led to a peasant rebellion. Members of a Buddhist cult called the White Lotus Society led the revolt, which was called the **White Lotus Rebellion.** After a difficult struggle, the government restored order in the early 1800s. Although it survived the rebellion, the Qing dynasty was seriously weakened. In addition, the basic causes of civil discontent remained. Rebellions occurred frequently after about 1850. The Qing dynasty was clearly in decline.

✔ **READING CHECK: Problem Solving** How might the Qing dynasty have brought peace to China? by maintaining higher standards of government service

SECTION 1 REVIEW

1. **Define** and explain the significance:
   junks
   queue
   philology

2. **Identify** and explain the significance:
   Hsüan-yeh
   White Lotus Rebellion

3. **Comparing and Contrasting** Copy the graphic organizer below. Use it to describe what remained stable and what changed during the Ming and Qing dynasties.

Ming and Qing Dynasties

Stable	Changed

4. **Finding the Main Idea**
   a. What changes did the growth of cities bring to China?
   b. What attitudes might Chinese rulers have had toward foreigners during the period of the Ming and Qing dynasties?

5. **Writing and Critical Thinking**
   Supporting a Point of View Imagine that you are involved in a rebellion against the Qing dynasty. Write a pamphlet that explains why you oppose Qing rule.
   Consider:
   • the spread of government inefficiency
   • the growth of corruption among officials

Homework Practice Online
keyword: SP3 HP17

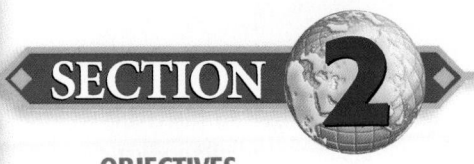
OBJECTIVES

1 **Characterize early contact between Portugal and China.**

2 **Explain why China and Great Britain went to war in the mid-1800s.**

3 **Describe how internal rebellions contributed to the decline of the Qing dynasty.**

SECTION 2

China and Europeans

READ TO DISCOVER

❶ What characterized early contact between Portugal and China?

❷ Why did China and Great Britain go to war in the mid-1800s?

❸ How did internal rebellions contribute to the Qing dynasty's decline?

DEFINE

free trade
extraterritoriality
"unequal" treaties

IDENTIFY

Opium War
Treaty of Nanjing
Taiping Rebellion

▶WHY IT MATTERS TODAY

Free trade remains an important economic concept and practice in the world today. Use CNNfyi.com or other **current event** sources to learn more about free trade in the modern world economy. Record your findings in your journal.

CNNstudentNews.com

The Main Idea
Growing contact with Europeans weakened the Qing dynasty and gradually undermined China's sovereignty.

The Story Continues *For more than 300 years after the first European trading stations were opened in China, European merchants and diplomats confronted a culture that viewed outsiders as inferior barbarians. In the early 1790s, for example, a British ambassador to the imperial Qing court offered gifts to the emperor. In turn, the emperor stated to the ambassador that "... we possess all things. I set no value on [foreign-made] objects strange or ingenious, and have no use for your country's manufactures."*

The Portuguese

In about 1514 Portuguese ships reached the southeastern coast of China. Over time the Portuguese were able to build trade ties with China. Finally, in 1557, the Chinese allowed the Portuguese to establish a trading station at Macao.

Portugal's influence, however, was not limited to trade. Jesuit missionaries also arrived on Portuguese ships. They used their knowledge of astronomy to gain admission to the emperor's inner circle. The emperor, who oversaw the prediction of eclipses and the timing of the seasons, appreciated the Jesuits' help in revising the Chinese calendar. He appointed Jesuit missionaries to official positions in his palace. He also gave them the opportunity to convert a number of high-ranking Chinese officials to Christianity. Gradually the Jesuits gained great power—economic and political, as well as spiritual—within the imperial court. Some even served as trusted advisers to the throne, quietly helping to shape imperial policies.

The Jesuits' power aroused jealousy and concern among some Chinese leaders. As a result, Qing rulers became suspicious of Christians and began to turn against them. The emperors realized that Chinese Catholics were expected to promise faith and allegiance to the pope. The Qing rulers feared that this would undermine the people's loyalty to the imperial throne and might bring about rebellion and overthrow. The emperors denounced Christianity as anti-Confucian, and the number of converts dwindled. China also deported European missionaries to Macao for a time.

✔ **READING CHECK: Summarizing** What was the initial Chinese attitude toward the Jesuits, and why did it change over time? initially positive, appreciative of their knowledge; later became suspicious, fearful of Jesuits' intentions

INTERPRETING THE VISUAL RECORD

Jesuits in China This early map of Nanjing, China, indicates the location of the Jesuit missions there. ***Who do you think produced this map—European or Chinese mapmakers? Why?***

TEACH OBJECTIVE 1

⏰ **ALL LEVELS:** Have students write essays summarizing the establishment of Portuguese trade in China and events that followed. *(Students' essays should mention the trading station at Macao established in 1557, the presence of Jesuit missionaries on Portuguese ships, the ways Jesuits gained power in the imperial court, and that Qing leaders came to fear the Jesuits' power.)* Then ask students to share and discuss their essays. **ENGLISH LANGUAGE LEARNERS**

TEACH OBJECTIVE 2

LEVEL 1: Copy the following graphic organizer on the chalkboard, omitting the italicized answers. Have students indicate above the arrows products traded between the countries. Use completed diagrams to discuss the trade imbalance between China and Great Britain. **ENGLISH LANGUAGE LEARNERS, COOPERATIVE LEARNING**

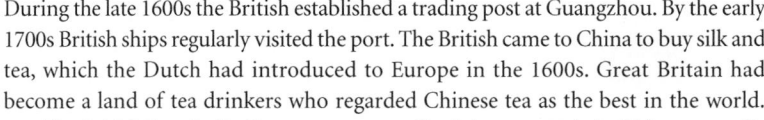

Culture

Deterioration of relations between Rome and Bejing resulted from a disagreement that developed among rival Catholic missionaries in the late 1600s over whether Chinese Christians should be allowed to continue their practice of honoring Confucius and their own ancestors. The Jesuits, who ministered mainly to the sophisticated upper classes, said yes on the grounds that such rites were not religious in nature. The Dominicans and Franciscans, who worked among the poorer and more superstitious people, strongly disagreed and appealed to the pope for a ruling in the matter. In 1704 the Vatican ruled in their favor, much to the displeasure of the emperor, who had backed the Jesuits in the dispute. When the Vatican tried to enforce its decision, relations between the missionaries and the Qing quickly deteriorated.

Critical Thinking

Ask students how a different ruling might have changed the course of relations between the Qing dynasty and Western nations.

ANSWER: Answers will vary but should show understanding that tolerance of long-standing Chinese cultural traditions on the part of the missionaries might have led to better relations.

The British were not the only admirers of Chinese tea, as the German advertisement at the top shows. Another Chinese product prized by Europeans was porcelain, like the decorative plate below it.

Analyzing Primary Sources

Identifying a Point of View
What argument did Lin make to try to persuade Britain to stop importing opium into China? asked Queen Victoria to do for China what she would want done for Britain

The British

During the late 1600s the British established a trading post at Guangzhou. By the early 1700s British ships regularly visited the port. The British came to China to buy silk and tea, which the Dutch had introduced to Europe in the 1600s. Great Britain had become a land of tea drinkers who regarded Chinese tea as the best in the world.

The British East India Company monopolized the new trade in Chinese teas. To get adequate supplies of tea, the company agreed to Chinese restrictions. Company ships could dock only at Guangzhou, and company representatives were required to stay in Guangzhou, where they lived in a special foreign settlement outside the city walls. Chinese regulations, moreover, demanded that the British trade only with a small number of officially approved Chinese merchants.

For a time, the Chinese policy worked. Contact between the British and Chinese people was kept to a minimum. In the late 1700s, however, two new developments—new ideas about trade and the sale of opium—damaged relations between the two nations.

Free trade ideas. The concept of **free trade** had developed in the West as a reaction to mercantilism. Supporters of free trade argued that governments should not restrict or interfere with international trade. British traders who did not work for the British East India Company resented the company's monopoly on the tea trade.

The British government became involved in the free trade debate. In part it did so because it hoped to gain additional overseas markets for British goods. In 1793 and again in 1816, British officials asked the Chinese government to open several more ports to British ships. Their efforts failed. In 1833 Great Britain abolished the British East India Company's monopoly on trade with China. Within a year the once-powerful company was little more than a managing agency for the British government in India.

The opium trade. The second development that came between the two countries involved the expansion of the tea trade. The British East India Company had paid for its tea purchases with cotton from India. There was a limit to Chinese demand for cotton, yet the British demand for tea kept growing. The company had to find a new product to exchange for tea. The product it chose was an addictive drug, opium.

From the late 1700s onward, British India produced opium and exported it to China. Opium addiction spread among the Chinese people. The Chinese government became alarmed, especially since China's silver supply was being used to pay for the opium. During these years, a huge trade imbalance grew, with far more silver flowing out of China than was being brought in. Chinese officials, fearing that China's economy was being undermined by the British, demanded that opium sales stop and that all opium cargoes be turned over to them. One Chinese official even pleaded with Queen Victoria of England to stop the opium trade.

 History Makers Speak

“Let us suppose that foreigners came from another country, and brought opium into England, and seduced the people of your country to smoke it. Would not you . . . look upon such a procedure with anger . . . ? Now we have always heard that your Highness possesses a most kind and benevolent [good] heart. Surely then you are incapable of doing or causing to be done unto another that which you would not wish another to do to you.”

Lin Tse-hsü, from *Commissioner Lin and the Opium War*

LEVEL 3: Have students imagine they are participants in the Taiping Rebellion. As a class, have them discuss the problems they see in Chinese society under the Qing dynasty and possible courses of action to take. On the board, list the problems and courses of action that are discussed. Then have the class vote on the best course of action to take. **COOPERATIVE LEARNING**

HOMEWORK Have students write three short editorial articles about the advantages or disadvantages of opening China to Western trade. One editorial should be from a perspective of a Western government, another from the Qing government's viewpoint, and the third from the point of view of a Chinese merchant. Select students to share their editorials with the class.

The Opium War. The British government did not respond to China's demands. When the Chinese tried to forcibly stop the opium trade, war broke out. The conflict between China and Britain, known as the **Opium War,** lasted from 1839 to 1842. Chinese army and naval forces were no match for the better-armed and better-trained British. A small British naval force that included iron-hulled steamships easily defeated Chinese forces as it sailed up the coast from Guangzhou. In 1842 the British gained control of the region near Nanjing. At that point, Qing officials agreed to negotiate on British terms.

Under the terms of the 1842 **Treaty of Nanjing,** China gave the island of Hong Kong to the British. It also opened five ports to British trade. British goods entering China through these ports were subject to a fixed, low tariff. In addition, British subjects in the ports would be governed by British, not Chinese, laws and would be tried in British courts. This requirement that foreigners must follow the laws of their home country instead of the laws of the country in which they live is called **extraterritoriality.**

More concessions. Great Britain did not keep its trade monopoly in China for long. Other Western powers, including France and the United States, also demanded trade treaties with China. Because the Chinese signed the treaties under the pressure of defeat and fear of further invasion, they called them **"unequal" treaties.** Most of the benefits of these treaties went to foreign powers. The Chinese gained little from them.

In 1856 China again went to war with Great Britain over a trade dispute. British forces, with French aid, again defeated the Chinese. The Chinese were forced to sign another "unequal" treaty. This treaty opened additional ports on the coast and along the Yangtze River. The Chinese had to allow the British to open an embassy in Beijing. Great Britain also took out a long-term lease on a small section of the Chinese mainland located opposite of Hong Kong. Finally the Chinese government had to agree to protect Christian missionaries and their converts in China.

Other foreign powers followed Britain and opened their own embassies in Beijing. In separate treaties, Russia also gained trade privileges and extraterritoriality. It received land bordering the Sea of Japan, or East Sea. The Russians established the port of Vladivostok in the southern part of this territory.

✔ **READING CHECK: Drawing Inferences** What was the British attitude toward the Chinese people and Chinese values? viewed Chinese interests, values as subordinate to British needs

The Opium War This painting from Britain's National Maritime Museum illustrates the British merchant steamer *Nemesis* attacking and destroying Chinese junks at Chuenpez, Canton. ***What do you think viewers in the 1800s were supposed to learn from examining this image?***

Western trade with China from 1760 to 1842 was considered by the Chinese to be a gracious grant by the Son of Heaven to barbarians from distant lands. However, the Chinese government would not directly involve itself in dealings with Western traders. Instead, this task was assigned to special Chinese merchants known as the *Cohong.* Foreigners were allowed to live in specified areas in the port of Canton only while engaged in trade, were not allowed the company of their wives, and were discouraged from learning Chinese. Foreign merchants could only communicate with government officials through *Cohong* intermediaries. Western traders endured these cumbersome regulations and restrictions. The end of the *Cohong* system was a major British goal in negotiating the Treaty of Nanjing.

Critical Thinking

Why did Western traders resent the Chinese trade regulations?

ANSWER: To the Westerners, the system seemed needlessly complicated and unwelcoming.

VISUAL RECORD ANSWER

British naval superiority over the Chinese

Reproducible Resources

PS Readings in World History 69: The Treaty of Nanjing, 1842

The Chinese island of Hong Kong was ceded to Great Britain after the first Opium War in 1842. Hong Kong and the peninsula of Kowloon were leased to Great Britain for 99 years. The lease expired in 1997, and the area reverted to Chinese control. Have students research the history and development of this economic power-house.

CLOSE

Ask students to summarize ways that contact with Europeans affected China. Then have them debate whether China should have remained isolated from Europeans.

The Taiping rebel force at its greatest consisted of about one million people. They captured the city of Nanjing in 1853 and made it the capital of their kingdom. They were not driven out of Nanjing until 1864.

SKILLS PRACTICE ANSWERS

1. Reports will vary but should include a bibliography, the reasons for choosing the Web sites used, and a research outline.

2. Charts or tables will vary.

Technology Resources

 CNN. Presents World Cultures: Yesterday and Today Segment 19: Hong Kong: Past and Present

---

SKILL-BUILDING STRATEGIES — Using the Internet in Historical Research

The History of China

There are a wealth of sources that can be used to learn about the history of China. Thanks to computers, that information is easier than ever to find. While the computer has revolutionized many aspects of society, it also has made a significant contribution to the field of historical research. The Internet, for example, contains numerous databases, or information organized in a way that allows you to retrieve it quickly and easily with a few strokes of the keyboard. While it is an extremely valuable research tool, not all of the information on the Internet is accurate. In using the Internet for historical research, it is important that you evaluate the quality of its content.

Navigate to a Web page that contains information that is relevant to your research topic or that can help you to find such information. Type the address of the Web page—its URL—here and press ENTER or RETURN to reach the page of your choice.

Carefully review the Web page to determine its content or whether it can direct you via links to other relevant pages. Click on links that may be of interest or that may help you to extend your research.

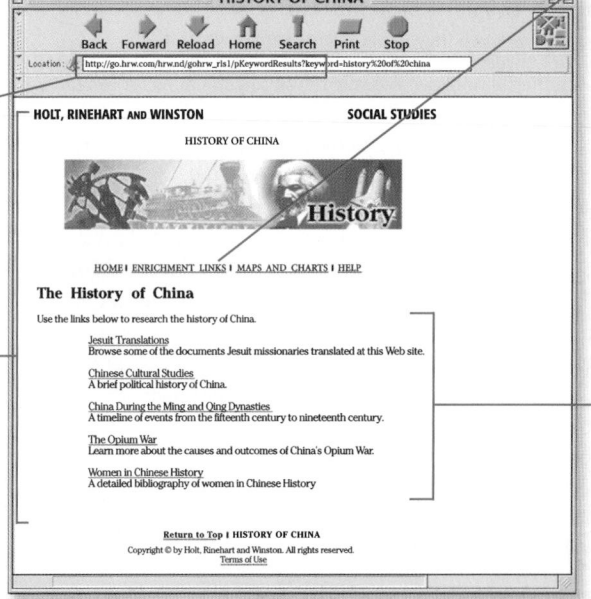

HISTORY OF CHINA

Back Forward Reload Home Search Print Stop

Location: http://go.hrw.com/hrw.nd/gohrw_rls1/pKeywordResults?keyword-history%20of%20china

HOLT, RINEHART AND WINSTON   SOCIAL STUDIES

HISTORY OF CHINA

History

HOME I ENRICHMENT LINKS I MAPS AND CHARTS I HELP

The History of China

Use the links below to research the history of China.

Jesuit Translations
Browse some of the documents Jesuit missionaries translated at this Web site.

Chinese Cultural Studies
A brief political history of China.

China During the Ming and Qing Dynasties
A timeline of events from the fifteenth century to nineteenth century.

The Opium War
Learn more about the causes and outcomes of China's Opium War.

Women in Chinese History
A detailed bibliography of women in Chinese History

Return to Top I HISTORY OF CHINA
Copyright © by Holt, Rinehart and Winston. All rights reserved.
Terms of Use

The home page of a Web site may contain useful navigational links that describe other pages within the site and that will take you to selected pages. Click on these links to move forward or backward through the site, to learn more about its content, and to evaluate the scope of its coverage. The page may also contain links to other related Web sites that may provide valuable information.

This Web page contains links and shortcuts to a broad number of other pages and activities on the Web. Explore these to determine if they will be useful as you conduct your research project. Such shortcuts may help you to sharpen the focus of your search.

Skills Reminder

To evaluate historical information on the Internet, determine if the site is published by a reputable authority or agency. In the case of individual Web publishers, try to find out if the author has credentials in the field or has a list of printed publications to his or her credit. Determine the objectivity of the site. Many Web sites are designed to sell products or to promote causes. The site's facts may be correct, but you should assess the author's point of view before deciding whether to use the information. Then evaluate the accuracy of the information. On the Internet, where anyone can be a publisher, there is a great deal of inaccurate information. Avoid sites with spelling or grammatical errors. Sites that attempt to dazzle the reader with eye-catching graphics and dramatic colors at the expense of content and substance should not be used. Also avoid sites filled with unsupported claims and undocumented arguments. Remember: a Web site's information should be as well documented as a printed page in a bound book.

Skills Practice

❶ Use the computer system at your school or library to locate one or more Web sites on one of the following:
  • the history of the Jesuits in China.
  • the geographic patterns and distribution of goods between the West and China during the 1700s and 1800s.
  • the Opium War.
  Use information from the Web sites to write a one-page report on the topic you chose. Include a bibliography of the Web sites you used and who produced them. Include also a brief explanation of why you chose these sites, including questions you asked and your research outline.

❷ Working with a partner, research the Internet and create a database in the form of a chart or table about a topic in this chapter. If you have it available, use a database management system (DBMS) to add, delete, change, or update information on the chart or table.

REVIEW

Have students complete the Section 2 Review on p. 421.

ASSESS

Have students complete Daily Quiz 17.2. As Alternative Assessment, you may want to use the graphic organizer exercise in this section's lessons.

RETEACH

Have students complete Main Idea Activity for English Language Learners and Special-Needs Students 17.2. Then have them list the steps leading to the decline of the Qing dynasty.
ENGLISH LANGUAGE LEARNERS

EXTEND

Assign students specific time periods within the Ming or Qing dynasties. Have students research and record events in China above the time line and important world events below the time line. **BLOCK SCHEDULING**

Rebellions

An event that occurred within China made the intrusion of the Western powers even easier. In the mid-1800s southern and central China were torn by a great rebellion. The leader of this revolt was Hong Xiuquan (hoohng shee·oo·choo·ahn), who had been influenced by Christian teachings. Saying that he was the younger brother of Jesus, Hong declared that his mission was to establish a new dynasty. It was to be called Taiping, meaning "Heavenly Kingdom of Great Peace." Hong's ideas attracted many followers.

The **Taiping Rebellion** lasted from 1850 to 1864. It caused terrible destruction in southern China and the Yangtze valley. Millions of people were killed. Cities and farmlands were destroyed. To make matters more difficult for Qing rulers, Muslims in central and western China launched their own rebellions at the same time. After a long struggle, the Qing finally put down these rebellions in the late 1870s.

The Taiping Rebellion and the other revolts seriously weakened both the Qing dynasty and the nation as a whole. At the same time, foreign powers in China, seeking to take advantage of the nation's internal turmoil, demanded further concessions and the opening of more treaty ports. Continuing foreign interference in China's political and economic affairs was a serious problem for the nation and its Qing rulers. It weakened China's sovereignty and undermined the emperor's prestige. It also reduced the country's control over its own economy. Increasingly, the independence of China and its rulers was viewed by the Western powers as a sham.

In this painting, soldiers in the Taiping Rebellion attack a Chinese town.

✔ **READING CHECK: Analyzing Information** What role did religion play in rebellions against the Qing?
Rebellions were motivated, in part, by Christian and Muslim teachings

---

SECTION 2 REVIEW

1. **Define** and explain the significance:
   free trade
   extraterritoriality
   "unequal" treaties

2. **Identify** and explain the significance:
   Opium War
   Treaty of Nanjing
   Taiping Rebellion

Homework Practice Online
keyword: SP3 HP17

3. **Sequencing** Copy the flowchart below. Use it to sequence the events that occurred between China and Britain between the 1600s and late 1800s. You may want to add more boxes.

   | No contact |
   | ↓ |
   | |
   | ↓ |
   | |
   | ↓ |
   | Trade with British in control |

4. **Finding the Main Idea**
   a. In what two ways did the Portuguese influence the Chinese?
   b. In what ways did unsuccessful rebellions succeed in weakening China?
   c. Why was the collection of China's customs duties by foreigners seen as a blow to Chinese sovereignty?

5. **Writing and Critical Thinking**
   Identifying Cause and Effect Imagine that you are a Chinese person who has witnessed the Opium War. Write a letter to a friend that explains the causes of the war and its effect on the Chinese.
   Consider:
   • the conflicts over free trade and the importation of opium
   • the terms of the "unequal" treaty

SECTION 2 REVIEW ANSWERS

❶ **Define**
• free trade, p. 418
• extraterritoriality, p. 419
• "unequal" treaties, p. 419

❷ **Identify**
• Opium War, p. 419
• Treaty of Nanjing, p. 419
• Taiping Rebellion, p. 421

❸ no contact, limited contact, conflict, Opium War, Treaty of Nanjing, trade with British in control

❹ a. opened up trade, introduced Christianity

b. They caused destruction and death; they forced the government to spend money and time in quelling them; they distracted the government from tending to other matters.

c. It reduced China's control over its own economy.

❺ Answers will vary but should include mention of British resentment of Chinese trade restrictions, Chinese anger at the opium trade, and the terms of the Treaty of Nanjing.

OBJECTIVES

1 **Explain how the Tokugawa shogunate came to power.**

2 **Discuss why Japan's rulers sought to isolate their nation from foreign influence.**

3 **Identify characteristics of society and culture under the Tokugawa shogunate.**

4 **Describe how Japanese isolation was brought to an end.**

LET'S GET STARTED!

As students enter the classroom, ask them to write a brief paragraph telling what they know about the nation of Japan. Have students share their knowledge of Japan in a class discussion as you write key facts on the chalkboard. Tell students that in Section 3 they will learn about the history of Japan during the time of the Tokugawa shoguns.

SECTION 3 RESOURCES

REPRODUCIBLE RESOURCES

▸ Guided Reading Strategy 17.3

TECHNOLOGY RESOURCES

▸ One-Stop Planner 17.3

▸ Holt Researcher: World History: Oda Nobunaga

▸ Holt Researcher: World History: Toyotomi Hideyoshi

▸ Holt Researcher: World History: Tokugawa Ieyasu

▸ Homework Practice Online

REINFORCEMENT, REVIEW, AND ASSESSMENT

▸ Section 3 Review, p. 427

▸ Daily Quiz 17.3

▸ Main Idea Activity 17.3

▸ English Audio Summary 17.3

▸ Spanish Audio Summary 17.3

MAP ANSWER

good harbor, centrally located, little threat of attack from Asian mainland

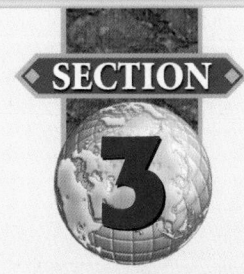

SECTION 3

READ TO DISCOVER

1 How did the Tokugawa shogunate come to power?

2 Why did Japan's rulers seek to isolate their nation from foreign influence?

3 What were society and culture like under the Tokugawa shogunate?

4 How was Japanese isolation brought to an end?

DEFINE

consulates

IDENTIFY

Oda Nobunaga
Toyotomi Hideyoshi
Tokugawa Ieyasu
Matthew Perry
Treaty of Kanagawa

▶ WHY IT MATTERS TODAY

Japan has one of the world's leading economies today. Use or other **current event** sources to learn about the Japanese economy and international trade. Record your findings in your journal.

CNN Student News.com

The Tokugawa Shoguns in Japan

The Main Idea
Despite their desire for isolation, Japan's rulers were unable to prevent foreign contact and trade.

The Story Continues *China's culture influenced that of early Japan. Over time the Japanese became increasingly isolated, especially from the rising nations of the West. By the 1850s, however, many Japanese were calling for an end to isolationism. For example, philosopher Yoshida Shoin believed that Japan would advance only if it blended Eastern thought with Western technology. Shoin urged the Japanese people to take action if their leaders failed to, arguing that "if it is true loyalty and service you seek, then you must abandon this fief and plan a grassroots uprising."*

Founding the Tokugawa Shogunate

In 1467 rival branches of the Ashikaga family in Japan became involved in a dispute over the selection of the next shogun. This conflict marked the beginning of 100 years of bitter, widespread, and almost constant warfare in Japan. Sensing the weakness and deep divisions within the Ashikaga family, local daimyo fought for control of the country. In the late 1500s a series of three daimyo emerged victorious from this long and destructive struggle. These powerful daimyo established themselves as overlords of the other daimyo and built a centralized feudal system in Japan.

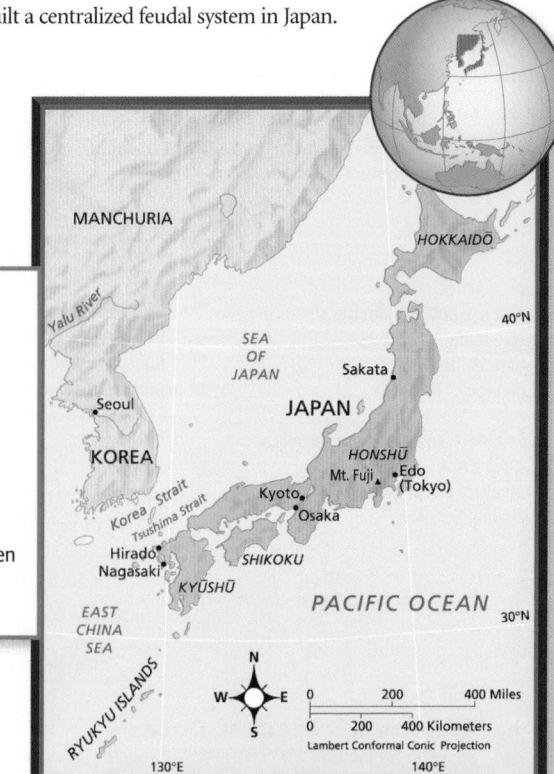

Japan under the Tokugawa Shogunate, 1603–1867

Interpreting Maps Edo was the capital of the Tokugawa shogunate.

■ **Skills Assessment:**
Using Geography
Why might Edo have been a good location for the capital?

TEACH OBJECTIVE 1

ALL LEVELS: Pair students to develop a diagram of the power structure of Japan under the Tokugawa shoguns. Select pairs to copy their diagrams on the chalkboard and explain them to the class. Ask the class how the size of the Tokugawa landholdings increased the family's political power. (*Taxes from their lands would sustain a large army of samurai.*) Then have students make changes in the chalkboard diagrams to illustrate what could have happened if the Tokugawa shoguns had permitted daimyo alliances. (*Changes could create blocks of daimyo and their samurai that could have been used against the shogun.*) Ask how the Tokugawa discouraged any such opposition.

Oda Nobunaga. The first of these overlords, **Oda Nobunaga** (ohd·ah noh·boo·NAH·gah), began his rise to power as a minor daimyo. Through conquests and alliances, Nobunaga captured the city of Kyoto in 1568. He ended the Ashikaga shogunate in 1573 and then started to strengthen his power in central Japan. Before Nobunaga could defeat his rivals, however, one of his own vassals attacked him in 1582. Wounded, Nobunaga committed suicide.

Toyotomi Hideyoshi. The second of the overlords, **Toyotomi Hideyoshi** (toh·yoh·TOH·mee HEE·day·yoh·shee), had led Nobunaga's army. After Nobunaga's death, Hideyoshi succeeded him. During the 1580s Hideyoshi defeated several powerful daimyo in battle. He forced other daimyo to pledge their loyalty to him. Hideyoshi did not totally defeat other daimyo. Instead he weakened them by reducing the size of their territories so that they could not threaten him again. He also carried out a "sword hunt" to disarm the peasants. Thereafter peasants could no longer become warriors. Only men born into warrior families could become warriors.

In 1592 and again in 1597, Hideyoshi sent his army to invade Korea. He wanted to build an empire and give Japanese warriors the chance to fight. At first the Japanese invasion of Korea succeeded. As the battles continued, however, a Chinese army that was aiding the Koreans pushed Hideyoshi's warriors back to the coast. When Hideyoshi died in 1598, the Japanese left Korea and returned home.

Tokugawa Ieyasu. Hideyoshi's most powerful vassal, **Tokugawa Ieyasu** (toh·kuh·GAH·wah ee·YAH·soo) succeeded him as overlord. Ieyasu established his capital at Edo (AY·doh), the city that is now Tokyo. Other daimyo resisted Ieyasu, but he defeated them in 1600. In 1603 Ieyasu became shogun.

Tokugawa Ieyasu crushed his defeated rivals. He did allow some 250 to 260 daimyo to keep possession of their private lands. However, Ieyasu's actions clearly demonstrated that he was prepared to expand or reduce the size of their territories in the future. The Tokugawa family would keep the title of shogun for more than 250 years. They established a government known as the Tokugawa shogunate.

Tokugawa rule. The political system established by the Tokugawa shogunate was a cross between feudalism and a central monarchy. Within his domain, each daimyo governed as an almost absolute ruler. Local peasants paid taxes to support the daimyo and those who

HISTORY MAKER

Toyotomi Hideyoshi (1536–1598)

Born to a peasant family and poorly educated, Toyotomi Hideyoshi worked hard to make up for his humble beginnings. He rose from warrior to one of the greatest generals in Oda Nobunaga's army. When he succeeded Nobunaga, Hideyoshi continued the unification of Japan. **How did Hideyoshi make up for his humble beginnings?**

Holt Researcher

go.hrw.com
KEYWORD: Holt Researcher
FreeFind: Oda Nobunaga
        Toyotomi Hideyoshi
        Tokugawa Ieyasu
After reading more about the overlords on the Holt Researcher, create a time line of the major events during their reigns.

That's Interesting!

Early Portuguese traders introduced playing cards to Japan in the late 1500s. Card playing quickly became popular throughout Japan. In response to this "barbarian" activity, a new daimyo warrior code was adopted that prohibited samurai from "gambling, cards, and other games of chance."

HISTORY MAKER ANSWER

He defeated other powerful daimyos in battle and forced them to pledge loyalty to him.

Reproducible Resources

SM Geography Activity 17: The Struggle for Korea

Reproducible Resources

PS Readings in World History 70: Yoshida Shoin: Philosopher of the Meiji Restoration

Reproducible Resources

E Creative Teaching Strategy 17: The Way of the Shogun

VISUAL RECORD ANSWER

He is wearing a sword.

INTERPRETING THE VISUAL RECORD

Preparing for war Japanese warriors regularly exercised and meditated to keep fit for battle. *What evidence suggests that at least one man who is meditating is a warrior?*

Government

One of the consequences of Tokugawa Ieyasu's defeat of his rivals and confiscation of their lands was the creation of a large number of masterless samurai, called *ronin*. Some of these samurai became retainers of other daimyo, some moved into cities, and others became teachers, physicians, and Confucian scholars. However, it is estimated that during the first 50 years of the shogunate, as many as 200,000 impoverished and dissatisfied armed warriors roamed Japan. Finding a way to deal with this potentially disruptive force was a major problem for the early Tokugawa shoguns.

Critical Thinking

How might the Tokugawa shoguns have successfully solved the problem posed by the ronin?

ANSWER: The shoguns could have added ronin warriors to their own armies, encouraged ronin to follow new vocations, or disarmed the ronin by force.

Technology **Resources**
 Religions of the World Video Series: Christianity

This mounted Japanese warrior and his horse display traditional weapons and military dress.

served him, such as the samurai. The Tokugawa family had its own private domain, which included roughly one fourth of the nation's resources. Thus the Tokugawa did not rule the entire country directly. Nor did they personally tax the entire population. In this way Japan remained politically and economically decentralized to some degree.

Because of their wealth and military power, however, the Tokugawa had considerable influence over the daimyo. Some historians believe that the Tokugawa shoguns prohibited the daimyo from making alliances with one another. Most daimyo had to spend every other year in Edo, the shogun's capital. When they returned to their own domains, the daimyo left their families in Edo as hostages. Maintaining two residences—one in Edo and one in the provinces—proved very expensive for the daimyo. Traveling to and from Edo in a grand procession also drained their financial resources. In addition, living in Edo transformed many daimyo from warriors to courtiers. In this manner the Tokugawa shoguns maintained control over the daimyo.

The Tokugawa shogunate shaped Japanese life in several ways. Its strong central government brought more than two centuries of stability to Japan. Tokugawa control of the daimyo helped to keep peace in the countryside. In addition, the Tokugawa set trade restrictions and limited contact with foreigners. By doing so, they achieved almost complete isolation from Europe by 1650. Their desire for isolation was in response to contact with foreigners that had occurred beginning in the 1500s.

✔ **READING CHECK: Sequencing** What events led to the establishment of the Tokugawa shogunate? century of warfare among competing daimyo, overthrow of Ashikaga shogun

Foreign Contact

Japanese soldiers and sailors had traveled overseas since the 1000s. In the early 1400s, during the Ashikaga shogunate, Japan's ships had sailed to China and Korea seeking trade. At times the Japanese acted as pirates, taking whatever they could from local peoples.

The Portuguese in Japan. In the mid-1500s the daimyo began to trade with the Portuguese, whose ships appeared in Japanese waters. Portuguese traders brought two items new to the Japanese: muskets and Christianity.

Apparently Oda Nobunaga had used troops armed with muskets in his battles against rival daimyo. However, some samurai did not approve of the musket. It violated the traditional samurai fighting ethic, which was based on skill. Anyone armed with a musket could overcome years of samurai training with a single shot.

In the wake of the Portuguese traders came Christian missionaries. Among the missionaries were the Jesuits, who achieved notable success during the Counter-Reformation in Europe. The Jesuits concentrated on converting the daimyo to Christianity. After a daimyo converted to Christianity, the Jesuits would seek converts in the daimyo's domain. It has been estimated that by the early 1600s the missionaries had converted as many as 300,000 Japanese to Christianity.

Closing the country. The Tokugawa shoguns concluded that Christianity was an undesirable threat to their rule. The shoguns saw Christianity as a force that might weaken their authority because it taught loyalty to a power other than the Tokugawa shogun. The shoguns also feared that Christianity would be a divisive belief in their tradition-based society. Early in the 1600s the shoguns acted on their concerns by forcing Portuguese traders and missionaries to leave the country.

LEVEL 2: Call on students to identify changes that the Tokugawa shoguns made in Japan and list responses on the chalkboard. *(expelled Portuguese, limited Dutch traders, banned shipbuilding and overseas travel, adopted Confucian ideal of social classes, educated warriors to be government officials, paid warriors' salaries, required each daimyo to live in his castle town)* Next, organize the class into small groups and assign each group one of the chalkboard changes. Have each group discuss how its assigned change would help bring stability to Japan and report its conclusions to the class. Then ask the class why cities and the arts would be more likely to grow in a stable society. *(Lack of unrest would promote commerce and culture.)* **COOPERATIVE LEARNING**

HOMEWORK Have students write an essay expressing whether they would like to live in a society where one's status is determined by heredity. Tell students to consider the advantages and disadvantages of Japan's social system under the Tokugawa shoguns. Remind students to use standard grammar, spelling, sentence structure, and punctuation.

By this time the Portuguese faced stiff competition in East Asia from Dutch traders. The Dutch had accepted a strictly controlled trading relationship with the Tokugawa shogunate. The shoguns themselves controlled the small amount of trade Japan conducted with the Dutch. In addition, a few Dutch merchants were allowed to live near Nagasaki. These Dutch merchants were the only Europeans allowed to trade in Japan after the 1630s.

The Tokugawa enforced other strict rules in order to keep Japan isolated from foreign influences. They banned most overseas trade. The Japanese people were prohibited from traveling abroad. Like China, Japan concentrated on domestic affairs and tried to ignore the outside world. Because Japan is an island nation, and because its leaders could take active steps to secure its coasts, the country was able to achieve a high degree of isolation.

✔ **READING CHECK: Decision Making** Why did the Tokugawa shogunate want to keep Japan isolated? *saw Christianity and Western technology as threats to Tokugawa rule and to Japanese traditions, values*

Life in Tokugawa Japan

The Tokugawa shoguns, like most emperors in neighboring China, did not promote change. The concept of stability was more important to the Japanese. The Confucian ideas, which the Japanese borrowed from the Chinese, supported this ideal.

Social classes. The Tokugawa shoguns adopted—with some changes—the Confucian ideal of social classes. The warrior class in Japan filled roughly the same role as the scholar-gentry in China. Therefore the samurai stood at the top of the Japanese social order. Peasants, artisans, and merchants followed in descending order of importance.

A person's social class was determined by birth. Sons followed the occupations of their fathers. For example, a person born into an artisan family in Osaka remained a member of the artisan class in Osaka for life.

The Tokugawa shoguns encouraged members of the samurai to study the Confucian classics. The shoguns established schools in the various domains to prepare young samurai for their peacetime roles as government officials. The shoguns, however, did not adopt the Chinese civil service examination system. In Japan, samurai became officials by heredity alone. Males born into low-ranking samurai families worked as low-ranking officials in their domain. Those born into high-ranking families served as high-ranking officials.

Kabuki theater is a purely Japanese art form. Often much interaction between actors and spectators takes place.

Theater: Kabuki
Kabuki, the most popular form of Japanese theater, began during the Tokugawa period. Based on street dances, Kabuki grew into a colorful art form with detailed costumes and makeup. The makeup is designed to show a character's emotions, such as anger or bravery. A Kabuki play includes song and dance. Older Kabuki plays had little speaking, but more modern ones have more. Actors use dramatic gestures to tell the story.

In 1629 women were banned from performing Kabuki. Since then, men and boys have played both male and female roles. Kabuki actors usually spend years learning the Kabuki style before being allowed to perform.

Understanding the Arts

Why do you think the Tokugawa might have banned women from Kabuki?

Interdisciplinary Connection

LANGUAGE ARTS. Tell students to imagine that they are Portuguese traders in Japan. Have them write letters home describing their life in Japan and what they have observed about its government and society.

CONNECTING TO ART ANSWER
Tokugawa codes of social conduct limited the role of women in society. Performing on stage was not considered an appropriate activity for women.

internet connect

TOPIC: Japanese Theater
GO TO: go.hrw.com
KEYWORD: SP3 WH17

Have students access the Internet through the HRW Go site to gather examples of Kabuki theater or to learn about *Bunraku,* Japanese puppet theater, which also flowered during the Tokugawa period. Have students present illustrated reports to the class.

Technology Resources
Regions of the World Music Audio CD Program 20: Japan and the Koreas: Music of the One-String Ichigenkin

LEVEL 3: Invite the class to imagine that they are daimyo in the shogun's court at Edo. Assume the role of the shogun and ask students for their advice as daimyo on how to respond to Perry's demand for U.S. trading privileges in Japan. Have the daimyo debate whether opening trade with the United States is in Japan's best interests. Have the daimyo propose courses of action that might satisfy the United States but still preserve Japan's culture and isolation. *(offer only emergency shelter, rest stop, or better treatment of shipwrecked sailors; limit the ports where trade can occur)* Then ask them to weigh all this information and suggest a response to Perry. Conclude the activity by comparing the class's proposed response to the course the shogun actually took.
BLOCK SCHEDULING

CLOSE

Have interested students locate and use biographies to find out more about Matthew Perry or one of the other people mentioned in the section. Have them report their findings to the class.

Government

The dominance of the warrior class during the Tokugawa period hurt Japan in a number of ways. Edict and Confucian prejudice forbid samurai from engaging in trade. This left them unprepared to deal with Japan's spreading commercial economy. The samurai refused to tax merchants. By the 1700s, however, government income rarely kept up with expenses. Deficits, forced loans, and currency devaluation resulted. Ironically, although they refused to tax merchants, the Tokugawa shoguns came to rely heavily on them for loans and provisions to keep their government afloat.

Critical Thinking

How did the Tokugawa refusal to tax merchants affect the development of Japanese society?

ANSWER: Growing debt may have influenced the decision to open Japan to foreign trade.

VISUAL RECORD ANSWER

The instruments and music played are probably traditional. The musicians are women; they are probably affluent; they are performing outdoors; they are reading words and/or musical notation.

The shoguns usually required a samurai to live in the castle town of his daimyo. Instead of living on income from country estates, samurai now received salaries. This policy gave the shoguns greater control over the samurai, who could not develop wealth independently. It also eliminated any opportunity for the samurai to revolt against their lords.

Change and culture. As in China, the rulers of Japan could not prevent economic, political, and social change within their country. Much of the change that took place in Japan resembled that which occurred in China. Internal trade expanded. Various regions of the country began to specialize in certain crops and handicrafts. Cities grew in size. Many artisans and merchants became well-off.

These changes did not please everyone. One writer claimed that corruption had taken root in the government and that the common people were not prospering.

History Makers Speak
 After wrenching a crop from the thin soil, they [farmers] must battle tax officers who demand sixty to seventy percent of the harvest . . . Whether soils are rich or poor, whether harvests are good or bad, farmers shiver and starve; and, ultimately, they give up farming. . . . Tillers become scarce and fields turn to wasteland . . . Those good at selling grow rich; those good at farming go hungry.

Yamagata Daini, from *A History of Japan*

There were some positive changes in Japanese life, however. As in both Europe and China, urban growth and increased wealth led to the rise of a popular culture. By the early 1700s new forms of art, literature, and theater had taken root. Many of these new forms appealed to the tastes of ordinary city residents.

✔ **READING CHECK: Categorizing** How would you classify the view of the Tokugawa shoguns and the Chinese emperors toward change—as supportive of or as resistant to change? Both were resistant to change.

Analyzing Primary Sources

Identifying a Point of View Why did Yamagata Daini criticize merchants and trading? felt that merchants took advantage of farmers, that trade drew people away from the land

INTERPRETING THE VISUAL RECORD

Popular music This musical trio from the Tokugawa period includes a singer, a lute player, and a flutist. *What information can be gathered about the music and musicians in this image?*

The End of Japan's Isolation

As part of the Tokugawa plan to keep Japan isolated, the government refused to give shelter to ships from other nations during storms. This policy angered many Westerners. Western nations that sought commercial expansion wanted Japan to follow China's lead and end its isolation.

In 1853 President Millard Fillmore of the United States sent Commodore **Matthew Perry** and a powerful naval force to Japan. Perry had orders to negotiate a treaty that would guarantee the safety of U.S. sailors and open Japanese ports to American trade. Perry's squadron of heavily armed, steam-powered warships sailed into Tokyo Bay on July 8, 1853. In a show of force and dignity, Perry ceremoniously presented a letter from President Fillmore that urged the Japanese to accept the American treaty. Perry promised to return for an answer the following year.

The American visit sparked controversy within Japan. Some powerful leaders favored military resistance and continued isolation. Others, however, believed that Japan could not hold out against the United States. The shogun, worried about the threat of a naval attack by the Americans, reluctantly agreed to negotiate when Perry returned in 1854.

The negotiations between the shogun and Perry led to the **Treaty of Kanagawa** (kah·NAH·gah·wah) in 1854. Under the treaty the Japanese opened two ports to let Americans obtain fuel, shelter, and supplies. The opening of the ports permitted trade to begin between the two nations. Within two years, Japan signed similar treaties with Great Britain, the Netherlands, and Russia. As part of the agreements, foreign nations were allowed to establish **consulates**—diplomatic offices headed by consuls.

In 1858 the governments of Japan and the United States signed a new treaty. The two countries agreed to exchange ministers. In addition, the treaty allowed foreign residence in Edo and Osaka, extraterritorial privileges, and international trade. The Japanese also opened more treaty ports to the United States. Similar agreements between Japan and other nations soon followed.

Japanese opponents of the Tokugawa shogunate criticized the government for signing treaties with foreign powers. To many samurai, the government's inability to resist Western demands cast doubt on its right to rule Japan. Many Japanese began to complain about the weakness of the government abroad and its strict rule at home. In the 1860s civil war broke out in Japan. Supporters of the Tokugawa shogunate battled its opponents. Calling for major reforms, the anti-Tokugawa forces overthrew the shogunate in 1867. They restored the power of the emperor, moving Japan toward a more centralized government. The new emperor, a teenager, named his reign Meiji, meaning "Enlightened Rule."

✔ **READING CHECK: Problem Solving** Could the Tokugawa have resisted Western demands and retained control of Japan? Students should note that Western technology and military power might have been used to overthrow the Tokugawa.

In this woodblock print, a Japanese artist recorded Commodore Perry's arrival in Edo Bay in 1853.

SECTION 3 REVIEW

1. **Define** and explain the significance:
   consulates

2. **Identify** and explain the significance:
   Oda Nobunaga
   Toyotomi Hideyoshi
   Tokugawa Ieyasu
   Matthew Perry
   Treaty of Kanagawa

3. **Categorizing** Copy the diagram. Use it to show the levels of government and classes in Japan during the era of Tokugawa rule.

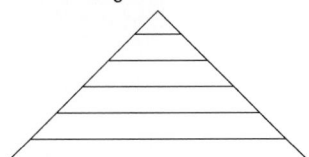

4. **Finding the Main Idea**
   a. Was the policy of isolation good for Japan and the Japanese people? Why or why not?
   b. What changes in Japanese society occurred under the Tokugawa shogunate?

5. **Writing and Critical Thinking**
   Decision Making Imagine that you are the shogun considering Matthew Perry's request for a treaty. Should you support such a treaty?
   Consider:
   • why the Americans wanted a treaty
   • how a treaty might benefit Japan
   • how a treaty might harm Japan
   • what actions a refusal might bring

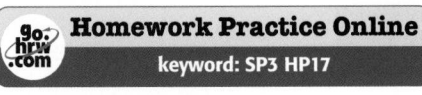
Homework Practice Online
keyword: SP3 HP17

ASIA IN TRANSITION **427**

CHAPTER 17

REVIEW AND ASSESSMENT RESOURCES

REPRODUCIBLE RESOURCES
▶ Vocabulary Activity 17

TECHNOLOGY RESOURCES
▶ Chapter 17 Test Generator (on the One-Stop Planner)
▶ Global Skill Builder CD–ROM
▶ HRW Web Site

REINFORCEMENT, REVIEW, and ASSESSMENT
▶ Chapter 17 Review, pp. 428–429
▶ Chapter 17 Tutorial for Students, Parents, Mentors, and Peers
▶ Chapter 17 Test (Form A or B)
▶ Alternative Assessment Handbook
▶ Chapter 17 Test for English Language Learners and Special-Needs Students

REVIEW
Have students complete the Chapter 17 Review on pages 428–429.

ASSESS
Use one of the chapter tests to assess students' understanding of the content. For Alternative Assessment, see the Portfolio Activities and Alternative Assessment Handbook.

CHAPTER 17 REVIEW ANSWERS

Understanding Main Ideas

1. to concentrate resources on defending borders

2. The economy grew.

3. created unrest that weakened the dynasty

4. China resented importation of opium by Great Britain.

5. China defeated, forced to allow more foreign trade

6. China had to open additional ports, allow British embassy, lease Hong Kong to Great Britain, protect Christians.

7. prohibited daimyo alliances, forced all daimyo to spend every other year at Edo, and kept daimyo family members as hostages

8. thought Christianity might weaken their authority

9. under threat of military response if they did not

Reviewing Themes

1. Western nations insisted on establishing open trade.

2. limited and regulated trade until China's defeat in the Opium Wars

3. internal rebellion and weakening of the dynasty

CHAPTER 17 Review

Creating a Time Line
Copy the time line below on a sheet of paper. Complete the time line by filling in the events, individuals, and dates from the chapter that you think were significant. Pick three events and explain why you think they were significant.

| 1400 | 1500 | 1600 |

Writing a Summary
Using standard grammar, spelling, sentence structure, and punctuation, write an overview of the events in the chapter.

Identifying People and Ideas
Identify the following terms or individuals and explain their significance:
1. Hsüan-yeh
2. free trade
3. Treaty of Nanjing
4. extraterritoriality
5. "unequal" treaties
6. Taiping Rebellion
7. Tokugawa Ieyasu
8. Matthew Perry
9. Treaty of Kanagawa
10. consulates

Understanding Main Ideas

Section 1 *(pp. 412–416)*
The Ming and Qing Dynasties
1. Why did the Chinese abandon overseas exploration?
2. How did the Chinese economy change under the Ming and Qing emperors?
3. How did government corruption affect the Qing dynasty?

Section 2 *(pp. 417–421)*
China and Europeans
4. Why did the Chinese resist free trade with Great Britain?
5. What were the effects of the Opium War on China?
6. What generally were the terms of the "unequal" treaties?

Section 3 *(pp. 422–427)*
The Tokugawa Shoguns in Japan
7. How did the Tokugawa shogunate weaken daimyo power?
8. Why did the Japanese rulers see the Jesuits as a threat?
9. Why did Japan open ports to American ships?

Reviewing Themes
1. **Global Relations** Why did Chinese and Japanese efforts to maintain isolation fail in the 1800s?
2. **Economics** How did attitudes about foreigners affect trade in China?
3. **Government** What was the result of the Qing dynasty's inability to provide services and loss of control over bureaucratic corruption?

Thinking Critically
1. **Identifying Cause and Effect** How did urban growth promote economic change in Asia?
2. **Comparing** Why did the Qing dynasty and the Tokugawa shogunate both collapse?
3. **Identifying Bias** Did British treatment of the Chinese reflect a concern for foreign peoples? Explain.
4. **Evaluating** What were the main difficulties that Asian societies faced during this period in history?
5. **Making Predictions** What might have happened if the Qing dynasty had improved tax reform and increased government services?

Writing About History
Comparing Write a report comparing China under the Qing dynasty with Japan under the Tokugawa shogunate. Use the chart below to organize your thoughts before writing.

Factors	China	Japan
Economy		
Government rule		
Popular culture		
Relations with foreign powers		

CLOSE

Have interested students research the presence and influence of American culture in China and Japan today. Have them report their findings to the class.
BLOCK SCHEDULING

RETEACH

Organize students into three groups, with each group responsible for one of the chapter's sections. Have members of each group create maps or diagrams illustrating the main events and including any relevant dates and captions. Have each group present its work to the class. **ENGLISH LANGUAGE LEARNERS, COOPERATIVE LEARNING**

Portfolio Extensions

Link to TODAY

1. Ask students to imagine that they are living during the early days of the Ming dynasty. Have them write editorials expressing the opinion that more resources should be devoted to seagoing exploration and foreign trade.
BLOCK SCHEDULING

2. Organize the class into small groups. Ask each group to select one aspect of Chinese government or culture during the Ming and Qing dynasties to define and describe.
BLOCK SCHEDULING

3. Have students create posters or collages in which they illustrate historical highlights of the Ming and Qing dynasties.
BLOCK SCHEDULING

Building Social Studies Skills

Interpreting a Time Line
Study the time line below. Then answer the questions that follow.

1557 Macao becomes a Portuguese trading station.

1842 The Treaty of Nanjing gives Hong Kong to the British.

1500 ——— 1700 ——— 1900

c. 1699 The British establish a trading post at Guangzhou.

1842 China is forced to open five ports to the British.

1. Which of the following correctly states the theme of this time line?
   a. The British and Portuguese traded with China for hundreds of years.
   b. European pressure slowly changed China's trade policies.
   c. Chinese ports were closed to the British until 1842.
   d. European pressure quickly changed China's trade policies.

2. What was the reason for the Treaty of Nanjing and what effect did it have on China? Support your answer with specific examples.

Identifying Bias
Read the following quote by Francis Xavier, a Jesuit missionary who went to Japan in 1549. Then answer the questions.

> "The people whom we have met so far are the best who have as yet been discovered, and it seems to me that we shall never find among heathens another race to equal the Japanese. They are a people of very good manners, good in general, and not malicious [mean]; they are men of honor to a marvel, and prize honor above all else in the world. . . . They have one quality which I cannot recall in any people of Christendom; this is that [they] . . . render as much honor to a poor gentleman as if he were passing rich."

3. Which of the following best describes how the author's experience influenced his viewpoint?
   a. Based on his experience, he was amazed the Japanese were so honorable.
   b. His experiences led him to believe manners were important.
   c. Since he was a poor missionary, he was surprised to be treated as if he were rich.
   d. He was surprised the Japanese were good people, because he had heard they were warriors.

4. How did the Tokugawa shoguns react to the Jesuit missionaries? Give specific examples.

Alternative Assessment

Building Your Portfolio
Link to TODAY

Economics

Opening new trade markets among nations is as topical an issue today as it was during the Qing dynasty and the Tokugawa shogunate. Using your textbook and other sources, compile a list of important trade treaties, both historical and modern day. Use the list to write a short summary of world trade.

---

internet connect

Internet Activity: go.hrw.com
KEYWORD: SP3 WH17

Choose a topic on Asia in Transition to:
- analyze art of the Ming and Qing dynasties.
- learn more about Kabuki theater and *Bunraku*, Japanese puppet theater.
- examine an issue from the point of view of a Japanese samurai warrior.

go. hrw .com

Thinking Critically
1. contributed to growth of internal trade and merchant class

2. government corruption and inefficiency, political unrest, Western intrusion

3. may suggest that the British were more concerned with gaining trade advantages

4. Western culture, isolationism, overpopulation, inability to adapt and change

5. might have retained power

Writing About History
Reports should show many similarities.

Building Social Studies Skills
1. b

2. China was defeated in Opium War, forced China to open foreign trade; examples will vary

3. a

4. The Tokugawa felt threatened by the Jesuits and eventually ejected them from Japan.

Building Your Portfolio
Lists will vary. Students should conclude that, over time, world trade continues to grow and expand.

Islamic Empires in Asia

CHAPTER RESOURCE MANAGER

Objectives	Pacing Guide	Reproducible Resources
SECTION 1 **The Ottoman Empire** (pp. 432–435) • Explain how the Ottomans built and expanded their empire. • Describe how the Ottomans organized their government and society.	**Regular** 1.5 day / **Block Scheduling** 1 day *Block Scheduling Handbook with Team Teaching Strategies, 18.1*	**RS** Guided Reading Strategy 18.1 **RS** Graphic Organizer Activity 18: Change in the Islamic Empire **PS** Readings in World History 71: Süleyman the Magnificent Captures Belgrade **E** Hands-on History Activity 18: The Ottoman World
SECTION 2 **The Safavid Empire** (pp. 436–438) • Discuss the role of religion in the development of the Safavid Empire. • Explain how 'Abbās the Great brought the empire to its height.	**Regular** 1.5 day / **Block Scheduling** 1 day *Block Scheduling Handbook with Team Teaching Strategies, 18.2*	**RS** Guided Reading Strategy 18.2 **SM** Geography Activity 18: Islam and Trade
SECTION 3 **The Mughal Empire in India** (439–443) • Explain the events that led to the beginning of the Mughal Empire. • Identify the policies that allowed for the expansion of the Mughal Empire. • Describe the Mughal Empire at its height.	**Regular** 1.5 day / **Block Scheduling** 1 day *Block Scheduling Handbook with Team Teaching Strategies, 18.3*	**RS** Guided Reading Strategy 18.3 **E** Creative Teaching Strategy 18: Training Seminar: How to Run an Empire

Chapter Resource Key

PS Primary Sources
RS Reading Support
IC Interdisciplinary Connections
E Enrichment
SM Skills Mastery
A Assessment

REV Review
ELL Reinforcement and English Language Learners
🖎 Transparencies
💿 CD–ROM
🎵 Music

📼 Video
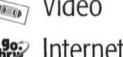 Internet
🖥 Holt Presentation Maker Using Microsoft® PowerPoint®

 One-Stop Planner CD-ROM

See the **One–Stop Planner** for a complete list of additional resources for students and teachers.

One-Stop Planner CD-ROM

It's easy to plan lessons, select resources, and print out materials for your students when you use the *One-Stop Planner* CD-ROM with *Test Generator.*

Technology Resources	Reinforcement, Review, and Assessment
One-Stop Planner 18.1 Homework Practice Online	Daily Quiz 18.1 Main Idea Activity 18.1 English Audio Summary 18.1 Spanish Audio Summary 18.1 REV Section 1 Review, p. 435
One-Stop Planner 18.2 Holt Researcher: World History: 'Abbās Homework Practice Online	Daily Quiz 18.2 Main Idea Activity 18.2 English Audio Summary 18.2 Spanish Audio Summary 18.2 REV Section 2 Review, p. 438
One-Stop Planner 18.3 World History and Cultures Video Program 13: The Mughals in India World History Teaching Transparency: Everyday Life 10: Nomadic Encampment Homework Practice Online	Daily Quiz 18.3 Main Idea Activity 18.3 English Audio Summary 18.3 Spanish Audio Summary 18.3 REV Section 3 Review, p. 443

internet connect

HRW ONLINE RESOURCES
GO TO: go.hrw.com
Then type in a keyword.

TEACHER HOME PAGE
KEYWORD: SP3 Teacher

CHAPTER INTERNET ACTIVITIES
KEYWORD: SP3 WH18
Choose an activity to:
- create an illustrated time line of the major events in the history of the Ottoman Empire.
- research life and society in the Safavid Empire.
- create a newspaper on the impact of the siege of Vienna in 1683.

CHAPTER ENRICHMENT LINKS
KEYWORD: SP3 CH18

ONLINE ASSESSMENT
Homework Practice
KEYWORD: SP3 HP18
Standardized Test Prep
KEYWORD: SP3 STP18
Rubrics
KEYWORD: SS Rubrics

ONLINE MAPS, CHARTS, AND GRAPHS
KEYWORD: SP3 MCG

CONTENT UPDATES
KEYWORD: SS Content Updates

HOLT PRESENTATION MAKER
KEYWORD: SP3 PPT18

ONLINE READING SUPPORT
KEYWORD: SS Strategies

CURRENT EVENTS
KEYWORD: S3 Current Events

Meeting Individual Needs

Ability Levels

Level 1 Basic level activities designed for all students encountering new material

Level 2 Intermediate level activities designed for average students

Level 3 Challenging activities designed for honors and gifted and talented students

English Language Learners These activities address the needs of students with Limited English Proficiency.

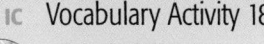

Chapter Review and Assessment

IC Vocabulary Activity 18
Global Skill Builder CD-ROM
HRW Web Site
REV Chapter 18 Tutorial for Students, Parents, Mentors, and Peers
REV Chapter 18 Review, pp. 444–445

A Chapter 18 Test Generator (on the One-Stop Planner)
A Chapter 18 Test (Form A or B)
A Alternative Assessment Handbook
A Chapter 18 Test for English Language Learners and Special-Needs Students

429b

Section 1   The Ottoman Empire

Section 2   The Safavid Empire

Section 3   The Mughal Empire in India

Build on What You Know

Ask students to answer the following questions:

How might the rulers of an empire or dynasty control their subjects?

Consider:

- military threats
- religious persecution
- rigid class system
- limited contact with outsiders and foreign books

Why might the rulers of China and Japan have wanted to avoid change while Islamic rulers were trying to expand?

Consider:

- security of power vs. growth of power and glory
- cultural stability vs. spread of new ideas
- continued economic control vs. greater wealth

EXPLORING THE TIME LINE

GLOBAL EVENTS

internet connect

go.hrw.com

TOPIC: Islamic Art
GO TO: go.hrw.com
KEYWORD: SP3 WH18

Ask students to access the Internet through the HRW Go site to conduct research on Islamic art. Have students list five key points that differentiate Islamic art from other cultures' art movements. Ask students to expand on the representation of humans and animals in Islamic art.

CHAPTER 18

1300–1700

Islamic Empires in Asia

Ottoman cavalry sword

1326
Business and Finance
The Ottomans begin to mint coins.

1398
Politics
Timur destroys Delhi.

1453
Science and Technology
The Ottomans use artillery cannons to capture Constantinople.

1453
Daily Life
The Ottomans convert the Hagia Sophia church in Constantinople into a mosque.

1458
Global Events
The Ottomans occupy the Acropolis in Athens, Greece.

| 1300 | 1375 | 1450 |

1337
Global Events
The Hundred Years' War begins.

Mongol forces invade India

1475
Daily Life
The world's first coffeehouse opens in Istanbul.

Turkish coffee urn

Build on What You Know

From the 1400s through the 1700s, rulers of China and Japan wanted to make their countries stable. They tried to prevent change by limiting contact with the outside world—particularly with the trading countries of the West. They also sought to maintain the traditions and values that had characterized their cultures for centuries. At the same time, Islamic rulers in Asia were trying to expand their empires through conquest. In this chapter, you will learn how Islamic empires grew and were organized. You will learn, too, how Islamic teachings were carried to many parts of Asia and how they influenced many traditional Asian cultures.

What's Your Opinion?

Global Relations

Agree A civilization that expands by conquest needs a large, strong military to subdue and control new lands.

Disagree A civilization that expands by conquest can maintain power through loyal citizens who can spread their culture and belief systems.

Culture

Agree The religious policies followed by a culture's leader can either unify or divide the culture.

Disagree The religious policies followed by a culture's leader will have little effect on the strength of the culture.

Government

Agree The effectiveness of a government depends upon its rulers' moral and ethical strength.

Disagree The effectiveness of a government depends upon the loyalty of its subjects.

1501
Politics
The Safavid dynasty begins rule in Persia.

1526
Politics
Bābur founds the Mughal Empire in India.

1529
Daily Life
Turkish farmers grow vast fields of American maize.

c. 1529
The Arts
Bābur finishes writing his memoirs.

1558
Global Events
Elizabeth I becomes queen of England.

1599
Daily Life
Eşfahān becomes the capital of Safavid Persia.

1600
Daily Life
Thieves smuggle coffee beans from Arabia to India.

c. 1649
The Arts
Shah Jahān completes construction of the Taj Mahal in Agra.

Safavid glazeware

1525

1600

1675

1504
Science and Technology
Venice proposes construction of a Suez Canal to the Ottomans.

1536
Science and Technology
India rubber is mentioned for the first time.

1579
Science and Technology
The Ottomans build an astronomical observatory in Constantinople.

1617
The Arts
'Abbās's Royal Mosque at Eşfahān is completed.

1611
Business and Finance
The British East India Co. establishes its first factory in India.

1658
Politics
Aurangzeb seizes power in Mughal India.

Dome and minarets of a Safavid mosque

Mughal emperor Aurangzeb at prayer

GLOBAL EVENTS

Delhi, like Constantinople, was an important political and cultural center of activity. Timur ravaged the city, left it in ruins, and took away a tremendous quantity of spoils. It took Delhi over a century to recover. The cause of the invasion, Timur claimed, was the Muslim sultans' lenience toward their Hindu subjects. Following Timur's invasion in 1398 the last of the sultan kings of Delhi moved the capital to Agra, thereby reducing Delhi's status.

Critical Thinking

In what way did Timur's destruction of Delhi reflect religious motivation and in what ways may it have been political?

ANSWER: Timur claimed to have attacked Delhi because of the sultans' tolerance for Hinduism. Students may note that Timur's political motivation may have stemmed from a desire for increased wealth and power.

What's Your Opinion?

Themes Journal *Do you **agree** or **disagree** with the following statements? Support your point of view in your journal.*

Global Relations A civilization that expands by conquest must support a large, strong military.

Culture The religious policies followed by a culture's leadership can help to unify or divide that culture.

Government The character of its rulers determines the effectiveness of a government.

SECTION 1

OBJECTIVES

1 Explain how the Ottomans built and expanded their empire.

2 Describe how the Ottomans organized their government and society.

🔊 LET'S GET STARTED!

As students enter the classroom, ask them to write down what they recall about the Ottomans. *(Muslim Turks who created an empire in Asia Minor and Europe)* Tell students that in Section 1 they will learn about the Ottoman Empire's expansion, its government, and its society.

SECTION 1

READ TO DISCOVER

1 How did the Ottomans build and expand their empire?

2 How did the Ottomans organize their government and society?

DEFINE

ghazis
reaya
millets

IDENTIFY

Osman
Janissaries
Timur
Mehmed II
Süleyman

▶ WHY IT MATTERS TODAY

The present-day country of Turkey was once the center of the Ottoman Empire. Use CNNfyi.com or other **current event** sources to find out what kind of government Turkey has today. Record your findings in your journal.

CNN Student News.com

The Ottoman Empire

The Main Idea
With their tough, disciplined army and strong rulers, the Ottomans built a powerful empire.

The Story Continues *During the 1300s and 1400s the Ottoman Empire built and expanded its power. Ottoman leaders such as Mehmed the Conqueror sought to capture the city of Constantinople. An observer described Mehmed's goals: "The empire of the world . . . must be one, one faith and one kingdom. To make this unity there is no place in the world more worthy than Constantinople."*

The Rise of the Ottomans

The first Ottomans were Turkish soldiers known as **ghazis,** or warriors for Islam. They had come to Anatolia (formerly called Asia Minor) with other Turks to escape the Mongols. In the late 1200s a ghazi leader named **Osman** had great success fighting the Byzantines. His tribe members became known as Ottomans.

During the 1300s the Ottomans took over a large part of Anatolia. Eventually Ottoman forces went to Europe. They tried to capture Constantinople but failed. In 1361 the Ottomans captured Adrianopolis, the second most important Byzantine city. They made the city their capital and renamed it Edirne. By 1396 the first Ottoman sultan had been appointed.

The elite Ottoman army. The Ottoman sultans created a highly trained troop of slave soldiers called **Janissaries.** Janissaries were young war captives and Christian slaves from Europe. First they were schooled in Islamic laws and converted to Islam, then trained as special soldiers. Janissaries belonged to the sultan, serving him for life. Eventually the Janissaries gained power and influence. They became an important political group in the Ottoman Empire.

Timur challenges the Ottomans. The Turko-Mongol leader **Timur** interrupted the Ottoman expansion. Timur was born in 1336 in what is now Uzbekistan. He claimed he was descended from the great Mongol leader Genghis Khan. Timur created an army and built his power in central Asia. Then he began a career of conquest.

By the end of the 1300s, Timur's forces were close to Ottoman territory. Several ghazi rulers fled to his court when the Ottomans conquered their states. They asked Timur to help them get their land back. In 1402 Timur invaded Anatolia. His forces defeated the Ottomans at the Battle of Ankara and captured the sultan. Timur made the Ottomans return the territory they had taken from the other ghazi rulers.

This richly decorated illustration from about 1500 shows an Ottoman sultan dining.

TEACH OBJECTIVE 1

LEVEL 1: Ask students to refer to the map on page 433 and describe how the Ottoman Empire grew from its original boundaries. *(expanded into eastern Europe, western Asia, and northern Africa)* Ask students which time period on the map was the period of greatest growth for the empire. *(1454–1519)* **ENGLISH LANGUAGE LEARNERS**

TEACH OBJECTIVE 1

ALL LEVELS: Copy the following graphic organizer on the chalkboard, omitting the italicized answers. Use it to help students organize the people responsible for the growth of the Ottoman Empire. **ENGLISH LANGUAGE LEARNERS**

Recovery and expansion. Timur's victory over the Ottomans caused a crisis in the Ottoman Empire. A civil war broke out over who should be the next sultan. Finally Murad II took power and began a new period of expansion. In 1444 Murad's army defeated the last European crusaders at the Battle of Varna. After Murad's rule, **Mehmed II** became sultan. Mehmed conquered Constantinople in 1453, renamed the city Istanbul, and made it the Ottoman capital.

The greatest Ottoman sultan was **Süleyman,** who ruled from 1520 to 1566. He brought the Ottoman Empire to its height. Known as "the Magnificent" in Europe, Süleyman was called "the Lawgiver" by his own people.

Süleyman expanded the Ottoman Empire, conquering Hungary in 1526. Three years later the Ottomans nearly captured the city of Vienna. Vienna marked the limit of Ottoman expansion in Europe. By this time, however, the Ottomans ruled most of eastern Europe, western Asia, and northern Africa.

✔ **READING CHECK: Summarizing** What important military conquests led to the expansion of the Ottoman Empire? conquests of Constantinople, Hungary

The Ottoman Empire, 1453–1683

Interpreting Maps At its height under Süleyman, the Ottoman Empire included parts of eastern Europe, western Asia, and northern Africa.

■ **Skills Assessment: The World in Spatial Terms** Which two battle sites are found at about the 40° N parallel?

Ottoman Government and Society

The sultans were the supreme rulers of Ottoman society. Those second in command to the sultan were called grand viziers (vuh·ZIRZ). Ottoman society was divided into two major groups. One group was the small ruling class of Ottomans. The other included the masses of ordinary subjects, called **reaya** or the "protected flock." People did not have to remain in one of these groups for life. Reaya with ability could become part of the ruling class. Ottomans who lacked ability became reaya.

Europeans who observed Turkish society were impressed. One observer was Ogier Ghiselin de Busbecq, the Holy Roman Emperor's ambassador to Süleyman's court. He described his view of how the system worked.

Analyzing Primary Sources

Drawing Inferences What does it mean to say, "Each man in Turkey carries in his own hand his ancestry and his position in life"? One's position in society was based on merit, not on birth.

 History Makers Speak ❝No distinction is attached to birth among the Turks; the deference to be paid to a man is measured by the position he holds in the public service. . . . it is by merit that men rise in the service, a system which ensures that posts should only be assigned to the competent. Each man in Turkey carries in his own hand his ancestry and his position in life, which he may make or mar as he will.❞

Ogier Ghiselin de Busbecq, *The Life and Letters of Ogier Ghiselin de Busbecq*

The millet system. Different groups of people made up the reaya. Muslim Turks lived in the heart of the empire in Anatolia. Christians and Jews of various ethnic groups lived in the Balkans. Muslim Arabs lived in the Fertile Crescent and along the shore of northern Africa. Religious differences caused tension among these groups.

The sultans allowed the different groups to practice their own religions. They were organized into separate religious communities called **millets.** The millets were under the general control of the sultan, but they governed themselves. Each millet operated under its own laws and customs. It had its own courts and collected taxes. It also was responsible for the education, health, and safety of its members.

Slow decline begins. Süleyman the Magnificent died in 1566. His death marked the start of a slow decline of Ottoman power and influence as European states such as France, Spain, and Poland became stronger. Although the Ottoman army and navy

HISTORY MAKER

Süleyman the Magnificent (c. 1495–1566)

As sultan of the Ottoman Empire, Süleyman was a brave and daring warrior. He is most remembered, however, for his accomplishments at home.

Süleyman surrounded himself with a group of able advisers. He built strong fortresses for defense as well as numerous roads, bridges, and mosques. He supported the arts and helped to make Constantinople the cultural and commercial center of his empire. **How did Süleyman improve the Ottoman Empire?**

This Ottoman image of the 1500s shows the Turks blockading the French port of Marseille.

CLOSE

Have students write a summary of the decline of the Ottoman Empire.

REVIEW

Have students complete the Section 1 Review on p. 435.

ASSESS

Have students complete Daily Quiz 18.1. As Alternative Assessment, you may want to use the conquests graphic organizer exercise in this section's lessons.

RETEACH

Have students complete the Main Idea Activity for English Language Learners and Special-Needs Students 18.1. Then have each student create a detailed outline covering the origin and expansion of the Ottoman empire. **ENGLISH LANGUAGE LEARNERS**

EXTEND

Have students write a dialogue with opposing opinions about the benefits of Ottoman government and social structure.

were generally strong, they suffered some defeats. In 1571, for example, Philip II of Spain led a European navy against the Ottomans. The Europeans defeated the Turks at the Battle of Lepanto, near Greece. In 1683 troops led by the Polish king John III Sobieski again stopped the Turks outside Vienna.

By the 1600s the Ottoman government and economy faced real problems as well. During these years, the empire lost control of the highly profitable silk and spice trades between Europe and Asia. European naval powers opened new sea routes to Asia that bypassed the Turks and destroyed their trade monopoly. At the same time, the power and prestige of the Ottoman sultans weakened. The government became increasingly corrupt due to internal power struggles within its growing bureaucracy. Rebellions among the Janissaries, the Ottomans' elite slave troops, added to the empire's troubles. During the late 1700s the Ottomans lost the Crimean Peninsula and lands around the Black Sea and the Sea of Azov to the Russians. The French invaded Egypt, an Ottoman possession, in 1798. Ottoman lands in the Balkans were also lost. Some sultans attempted to reform Ottoman government and military structures but had limited success. The Ottoman Empire struggled to survive, finally ending in 1923 when Turkey established itself as a republic.

✔ **READING CHECK: Analyzing Information** What problems did the Ottoman Empire face? economic problems, competition with Europe, corruption, and rebellions

INTERPRETING THE VISUAL RECORD

Ottomans in battle This painting shows Süleyman the Magnificent at the Battle of Mohács in Hungary. *What does this picture tell us about Ottoman military technology?*

VISUAL RECORD ANSWER

Students should note that the Ottomans had cannons, guns, and gunpowder.

SECTION 1 REVIEW ANSWERS

❶ **Define**
- ghazis, 432
- reaya, p. 434
- millets, p. 434

❷ **Identify**
- Osman, p. 432
- Janissaries, p. 432
- Timur, p. 432
- Mehmed II, p. 433
- Süleyman, p. 433

❸ Conquests: Anatolia in the 1300s, Adrianopolis in 1361, Constantinople in 1453, Hungary in 1526, Vienna in 1529; Defeats: Battle of Ankara in 1402, Battle of Lepanto in 1571, Vienna in 1683

❹ a. Janissaries served as highly trained slave soldiers who fought to expand the empire.

b. Religious tolerance and social mobility may have kept large numbers loyal to the empire.

❺ Answers will vary.

SECTION 1 REVIEW

1. **Define** and explain the significance:
   ghazis
   reaya
   millets

2. **Identify** and explain the significance:
   Osman
   Janissaries
   Timur
   Mehmed II
   Süleyman

3. **Sequencing** Copy the chart below. Use it to organize the major conquests and defeats that the Ottomans experienced between 1300 and 1700.

Conquests

Defeats

4. **Finding the Main Idea**
   a. What role did the Janissaries play in the success of the Ottoman Empire?
   b. How important do you think the Ottoman social system was to the success of the empire?

5. **Writing and Critical Thinking**
   Evaluating Explain your view of the Ottoman Empire's focus on military conquest.
   Consider:
   • how the people conquered were affected
   • how the Ottoman people were affected
   • the cost in both money and lives

Homework Practice Online
keyword: SP3 HP18

OBJECTIVES

1 **Discuss the role of religion in the development of the Safavid Empire.**

2 **Explain how 'Abbās the Great brought the empire to its height.**

SECTION 2

▶ READ TO DISCOVER

1 How was religion responsible for the development of the Safavid Empire?

2 How did 'Abbās the Great bring the Safavid Empire to its height?

DEFINE

kizilbash

IDENTIFY

Safī od-Dīn
Esmā'īl
Tahmāsp
'Abbās

▶ WHY IT MATTERS TODAY

The Iranian (Persian) government has kept Shi'ah Islam as the state religion from the time of the Safavids up to the present day. Use ![CNN] or other **current event** sources to explore how religious differences affect Iran's relationship with other countries. Record your findings in your journal.

![CNN Student News.com]

The Safavid Empire

The Main Idea
The Safavid rulers created a powerful Shi'ah Muslim empire with a prospering economy and culture.

The Story Continues *While the Ottomans were building their empire, the Safavid dynasty was gaining power in Persia. Shah Esmā'īl, the founder of this new empire, was driven by religious zeal. "I am committed to this action," he said. "God and the Immaculate [pure] Imams are with me, and I fear no one."*

The Rise of the Safavids

The Safavid (sah·FAH·vid) Empire was bounded on the west by the Ottoman Empire and on the east by the Mughal Empire of India. Today, much of what was the Safavid Empire is the country of Iran.

The Safavids were descended from **Safī od-Dīn,** head of the family in the 1200s. Like most Persians, the Safavids were Muslims. They belonged to the Sunni branch of Islam. In about 1399, however, the Safavids shifted from Sunni to the Shi'ah sect. As Shi'ah, they were persecuted by the Sunni.

Toward the end of the 1400s, the Safavids developed a military group to fight for political power. This army was called the **kizilbash,** meaning "Red Heads," for the red hats they wore. Other Persians killed or imprisoned many Safavids, but one of the youngest, **Esmā'īl** (is·mah·EEL), escaped into hiding. In about 1500 Esmā'īl became head of the kizilbash. In a series of victories, he brought all of modern Iran and part of present-day Iraq under his rule. In 1501 he captured the city of Tabrīz and made it the Safavid capital. Esmā'īl took the ancient Persian title of shah, or "king of kings," and reigned until 1524.

✔ **READING CHECK: Summarizing** What problems did the Safavids face during the 1400s? Sunni persecution, including murder and imprisonment

Esmā'īl's religious policy. As soon as Esmā'īl became shah, he proclaimed that Shi'ah would be the religion of the Safavid Empire. Most Persians were Sunni, but Esmā'īl forced them to convert. Many people considered Esmā'īl a Muslim saint as well as shah, which helped in the process of conversion. Shi'ah gave the Persians an identity distinct from the great number of Sunni—Turks and Arabs—

INTERPRETING THE VISUAL RECORD

Continuing conflict Until the late 1580s the Safavids were often outmatched by the stronger Ottoman army. *What generalizations can be drawn from this image?*

ALL LEVELS: Copy the following chart on the chalkboard, omitting the italicized answers. Use it to help students understand the role of religion in the development of the Safavid Empire. **ENGLISH LANGUAGE LEARNERS**

Cause		Effect
Esmā'īl's religious enthusiasm	→	*fought to control Persia*
Safavids became Shi'ah in 1399	→	*persecuted by Sunni*
forced conversion to Shi'ah	→	*gained distinction and national unity*

HOMEWORK Write a short paragraph summarizing the role of religion in the rise of the Safavid Empire.

TEACH OBJECTIVE 2

LEVEL 1: Have students list reasons why they think Shah 'Abbās was called "the Great." *(military reforms, territory recovery, improvements to Eṣfahān, economic prosperity)* Then ask students to write a paragraph telling whether they think 'Abbās's activities qualify him for his nickname. **ENGLISH LANGUAGE LEARNERS**

TEACH OBJECTIVE 2

LEVEL 3: Ask students to write a fictional interview with Shah 'Abbās. Tell them to include questions that pertain to the Shah's improvements to the Safavid Empire. Have students make their interviews interesting and creative by describing the setting of the interview, how he looks, and his personality.

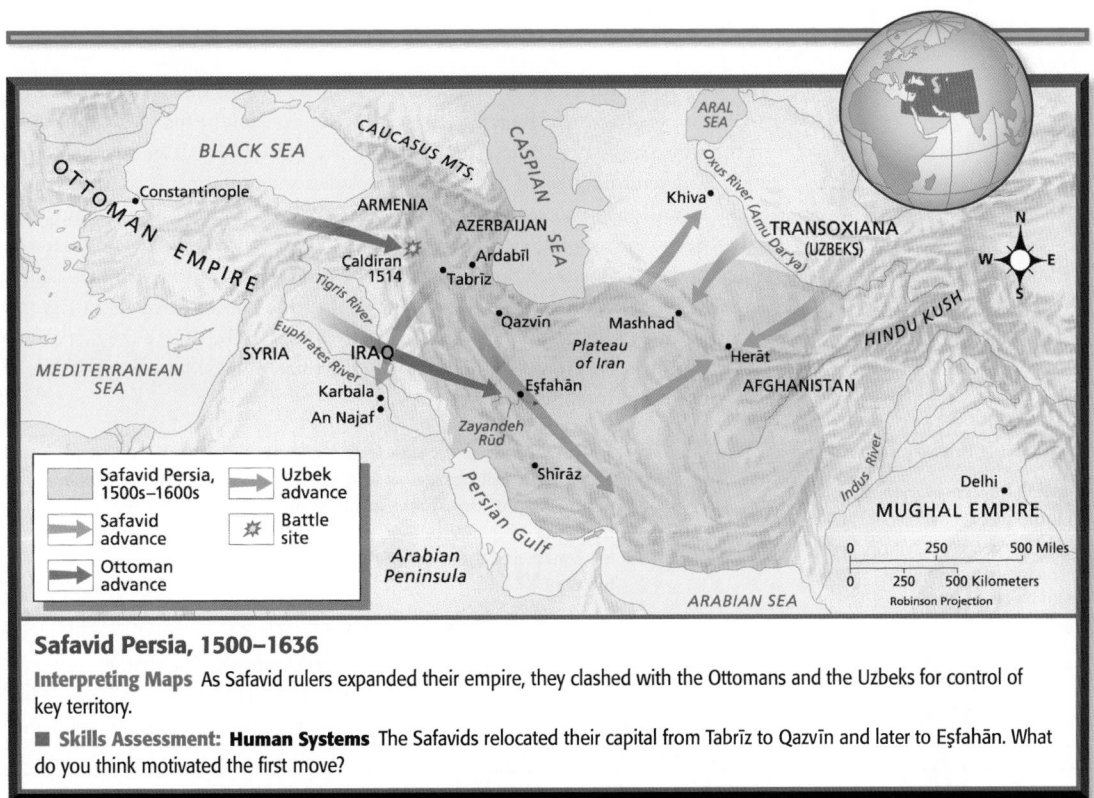

Safavid Persia, 1500–1636

Interpreting Maps As Safavid rulers expanded their empire, they clashed with the Ottomans and the Uzbeks for control of key territory.

■ **Skills Assessment: Human Systems** The Safavids relocated their capital from Tabrīz to Qazvīn and later to Eṣfahān. What do you think motivated the first move?

who lived around them. The Persian language and history also contributed to a strong sense of identity, which continues in modern Iran.

Esmā'īl's support of Shi'ah threatened Persia's neighbors—the Sunni Ottomans and Uzbek tribes to the northeast. In 1514 the Ottomans invaded northwestern Persia. They defeated the Safavids at the Battle of Çaldiran. The struggle continued through the mid-1500s. After Esmā'īl died, his son **Tahmāsp** tried to carry on the fight. However, by the 1570s the Safavids had lost territory to both the Ottomans and the Uzbeks.

✔**READING CHECK: Finding the Main Idea** Why did Esmā'īl make Shi'ah the religion of the empire? to develop distinct Persian identity, unify the nation

Shah 'Abbās the Great

When Tahmāsp died in 1576, the Safavid Empire was unstable. The kizilbash were no longer loyal to the shah. The struggles against the Ottomans and Uzbeks were going badly. Then in 1587 **'Abbās,** called "the Great," became shah.

Military reforms. 'Abbās realized he needed troops that would be loyal to him. He reformed the military, using the Ottoman army as a model. He created troops of foreign slaves who had been prisoners of war. After they were converted to Islam, they were trained for army service. These slave-soldiers belonged to the shah and were loyal only to him.

Eventually 'Abbās was ready to take on the Ottomans and Uzbeks. In 1598 his improved army defeated the Uzbeks and regained control of northeastern Persia. In a few years 'Abbās recovered all the territory the Safavids had lost.

Linking Past to Present

With a population of more than a million, Eṣfahān today is the third-largest city in Iran. Located about 200 miles south of Tehran, Eṣfahān is a major transportation center. It is also noted for its gardens and squares and its medieval mosques and ancient palaces. Eṣfahān is famous for its traditional handicrafts, such as lacework, metalwork, carpets, and hand-printed textiles. The old art of tile making also has been revived for use in restoring its many historical monuments.

Critical Thinking

Ask students what they might conclude about a society that works to restore its historical monuments.

ANSWER: Students might suggest that the society holds the monuments in high regard, has sufficient wealth to maintain its historical structures, and wishes to remember its history.

MAP ANSWER
Tabriz was too close to the Ottoman Empire and therefore vulnerable.

CLOSE

Ask students to list the effects that Esmā'īl's and Shah 'Abbās had on the Safavid Empire.

REVIEW

Have students complete the Section 2 Review on p. 438.

ASSESS

Have students complete Daily Quiz 18.2. As Alternative Assessment, you may want to use the cause-and-effect chart or the homework exercise in this section's lessons.

RETEACH

Have students complete the Main Idea Activity for English Language Learners and Special-Needs Students 18.2. Have each student write three questions and answers about the information in Section 2.

EXTEND

Have students write a rebus for children that tells the story of the Safavid Empire. Encourage students to use more than one picture on each line. **BLOCK SCHEDULING**

SECTION 2 REVIEW ANSWERS

❶ **Define**
- kizilbash, p. 436

❷ **Identify**
- Safi od-Din, p. 436
- Esmā'īl, p. 436
- Tahmasp, p. 437
- 'Abbās, p. 437

❸ Esmā'īl hidden away: because of threat from other Persians; Kizilbash formed: to fight for political power; 'Abbās reformed military: because the kizilbash was no longer loyal to the shah; Ottomans invaded Persia: because they felt threatened by Esmā'īl's support of Shi'ah religion

❹ a. gave Persians a sense of identity and unity, created conflict with the Sunni Ottomans and Uzbeks

b. 'Abbās regained all of the territory lost to the Ottomans and Uzbeks.

c. The city's beauty along with its political, commercial, and cultural life would have impressed a traveler and indicated the Safavid Empire had power and wealth.

❺ Answers will vary, but students might mention the city's design, its buildings and central park. They may also note the carpet, cloth, tile, and ceramic industries that would have signified prosperity.

The height of the empire. In about 1599 'Abbās moved the Safavid capital to Eşfahān on the Plateau of Iran. Eşfahān soon became one of the most beautiful cities in the world. 'Abbās planned his new capital city carefully. It had wide streets and a huge central square. It had splendid mosques and monuments, as well as public baths and open markets. The center of Eşfahān was an enormous rectangular park that was large enough for polo games and that was surrounded by an arcade of shops. Large inns scattered throughout the city had central courtyards where camel caravans could be housed and rested. Eşfahān became known throughout Europe and the Middle East as a political, spiritual, and commercial center of the first order.

Even 'Abbās liked to walk around his city. Christian monks who had a mission in Eşfahān kept a record of what they observed.

Analyzing Primary Sources

Drawing Inferences How do you think the shopkeepers probably reacted to 'Abbās's behavior? probably complimented by his visit, awed by his presence

Primary Source

❝He ['Abbās] will come to the greengrocers, fruiterers, and those who sell preserves and sweetmeats. Here he will take a mouthful of this, there another of that . . . . Or he will enter the shop of a shoemaker, pick up a pair of shoes that takes his fancy, put them on at the door and then continue on his way.❞

From Clive Irving, *Crossroads of Civilization: 3000 Years of Persian History*

'Abbās's reign was also a time of economic development. The shah encouraged manufacturing and foreign trade. Carpet weaving became a major industry. Fine Persian rugs began to appear in the homes of wealthy Europeans. Persian merchants exported rich fabrics such as brocade, damask, and silk. The Safavids produced beautiful tiles and ceramics for their own use as well as for trade.

'Abbās died in 1629. For a while after his death, the Safavids continued to rule. However, rulers after 'Abbās proved increasingly inept. The empire began to decline and had ended by 1736. Eventually Persia split into a number of small states.

This glazeware from about 1625 shows typical Safavid artistry.

✔ **READING CHECK: Supporting a Point of View** What evidence would you give that 'Abbās was an especially capable ruler? successful military reforms, recapture of lost territory, policies of economic growth

---

SECTION 2 REVIEW

1. **Define** and explain the significance:
   kizilbash

2. **Identify** and explain the significance:
   Safī od-Dīn
   Esmā'īl
   Tahmāsp
   'Abbās

3. **Identifying Cause and Effect** Copy the model below. Give the reasons why each event happened.

4. **Finding the Main Idea**
   a. What effect did the Safavid religious policy have on Persia?
   b. What were the results of the military reforms carried out under 'Abbās?
   c. What might a visitor to Eşfahān in the early 1600s conclude about the Safavid Empire?

5. **Writing and Critical Thinking**
   Summarizing Imagine you are a visitor to Eşfahān during Abbās's time. Write a description of your experience.
   Consider:
   • what the city looks like
   • what the people are doing in their everyday lives
   • what products and industries you see
   • in what ways the city of Eşfahān symbolizes Safavid strength and prosperity

go.hrw.com Homework Practice Online
keyword: SP3 HP18

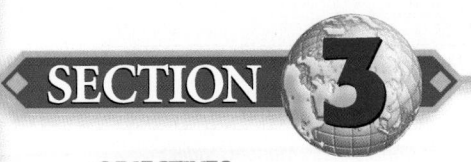

SECTION 3

OBJECTIVES

1 **Explain the events that led to the beginning of the Mughal Empire.**

2 **Identify the policies that allowed for the expansion of the Mughal Empire.**

3 **Describe the Mughal Empire at its height.**

 LET'S GET STARTED!

As students enter the classroom, ask them to list the ways in which the policies of rulers like Süleyman and Shah ʿAbbās affected their empires. *(Süleyman's aggression helped expand the Ottoman empire; he tolerated others' religions and allowed various groups to govern themselves; he supported the arts and improvements such as roads, bridges, and mosques. Shah ʿAbbās expanded his empire with a slave military force and improved the empire's capital and its economy.)* Tell students that in Section 3 they will learn how the policies of rulers in India affected the success of the Mughal Empire.

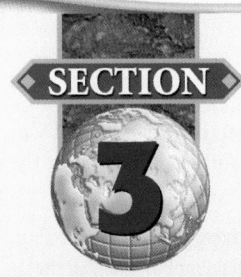

SECTION 3

READ TO DISCOVER

❶ How did the Mughal Empire begin?

❷ How did the Mughal Empire expand?

❸ What was the Mughal Empire like at its height?

IDENTIFY

Rajputs
Bābur
Akbar
Shah Jahān
Taj Mahal
Sikh
Aurangzeb

▶ WHY IT MATTERS TODAY

The Taj Mahal in Agra, India, was built by a Mughal emperor. Thousands of tourists visit it each year. Use CNN or other **current event** sources to find out more about this architectural masterpiece. Record your findings in your journal.

The Mughal Empire in India

The Main Idea
The Mughal rulers of India worked to unify and improve their vast, diverse Muslim empire.

The Story Continues *In 1605 the Mughal Empire was at the height of its glory. When Jahāngīr, son of Akbar, inherited his father's empire, his coronation ceremony reflected this splendor: "For forty days and forty nights I caused the . . . great imperial state drum, to strike up, without ceasing, the strains of joy and triumph;" he wrote, ". . . around my throne, the ground was spread by my directions with the most costly brocades [silks] and embroidered carpets. . . . Emirs of the empire, covered from head to foot in gold and jewels . . . stood round in brilliant array."*

The Origin of the Mughal Empire

During the 1300s Turkish Muslims controlled India, with Delhi as the capital of their sultanate. By the 1500s the power of the Delhi sultans had been greatly weakened. Indian warrior princes called **Rajputs** (RAHJ·poots) began to challenge them. The internal weakness of the sultanate drew the attention of India's powerful neighbors, as it had during Timur's time, and left India open to Mongol attack.

The attack came from a young leader known as "Bābur the Tiger." **Bābur** (also, Zahīr-ud-Dīn Muhammad) was a descendant of the Mongol leader Timur. He had tried to build an empire in central Asia, but the Uzbek people had driven him out. Bābur then focused on India. In 1526 he attacked the Sultanate of Delhi. A major battle took place at Panipat, a town north of Delhi. Bābur was greatly outnumbered, but he won the battle, as he described in his autobiography.

 History Makers Speak

❝**The kingdom of Hindustan [India] . . . was under the control of . . . [the sultan at Delhi] . . . His standing army was estimated at one hundred thousand. He and his commanders were said to have one thousand elephants. In such a state of affairs and with such strength, we put our trust in God . . . and faced a ruler with a huge army and vast realm. . . . God did not let our pains and difficulties go for naught and defeated such a powerful opponent and conquered a vast kingdom like Hindustan.**❞

from The Baburnama: Memoirs of Babur, Prince and Emperor

This painting from about 1590 shows the richness and ease of life at the Mughal court.

SECTION 3 RESOURCES

REPRODUCIBLE RESOURCES

▶ Guided Reading Strategy 18.3

▶ Creative Teaching Strategy 18: Training Seminar: How to Run an Empire

TECHNOLOGY RESOURCES

▶ One-Stop Planner 18.3

▶ World History and Cultures Video Program 13: The Mughals in India

▶ World History Teaching Transparency: Everyday Life 10: Nomadic Encampment

▶ Homework Practice Online

REINFORCEMENT, REVIEW, AND ASSESSMENT

▶ Section 3 Review, p. 443

▶ Daily Quiz 18.3

▶ Main Idea Activity 18.3

▶ English Audio Summary 18.3

▶ Spanish Audio Summary 18.3

TEACH OBJECTIVE 1

LEVEL 1: Ask students to draw a three-column chart entitled *Mughal Origins.* In the first column, have students list the words *who, what, when, where, why,* and *how.* The second and third columns should be labeled *Rajputs* and *Bābur.* Have students use the information on page 439 to complete their charts. **ENGLISH LANGUAGE LEARNERS**

Mughal Origins		
	Rajputs	**Babur**
who	*Indian warrior princes*	*Mongol leader, descendant of Timur*
what	*weakened power of sultans*	*attacked Sultanate of Delhi*
when	*1500s*	*1526*
where	*Delhi*	*Panipat*
why	*gain power*	*build an empire*
how	*challenged Delhi sultans*	*defeated sultan in battle*

History Maker

AKBAR. Unlike Bābur, Akbar was a native of India. Indians, whatever their religion, were his countrymen. Though he could have remained at a distance from his subjects, the young Akbar would sometimes visit anonymously with villagers to gather information about their lives. He learned about the diversity among his subjects and how different they were from their foreign rulers.

Critical Thinking

For what reasons might Akbar have instituted his tolerant religious policies?

ANSWER: His political intelligence may have prompted him to satisfy people of various religions, or he may have had respect for his subjects' beliefs.

MAP ANSWER
Goa, Calicut

Mughal Empire, 1526–1707

Interpreting Maps Many generations of Mughal emperors supported the arts and united most of India.

■ **Skills Assessment: Human Systems** What two cities on the west coast of the Indian subcontinent remained independent during Mughal rule?

After the victory at Panipat, Bābur occupied Delhi and the surrounding region. This territory became the core of the Mughal Empire.

✔ **READING CHECK: Summarizing** What role did Bābur play in establishing the Mughal Empire? founded the empire

The Growth of Mughal Power

Bābur's grandson, **Akbar,** was the greatest Mughal emperor. He took the throne at the age of 13 and reigned from 1556 to 1605. Akbar gained support for his government in various ways. He married a Rajput princess and gave other Rajputs government positions. At times he used force to maintain power. By 1605 Akbar controlled all of northern and much of central India.

Akbar introduced an improved tax system that helped him control his empire. Taxes were based on an average of what a village might produce over a 10-year period. When the harvest was poor, the tax did not have to be paid. In a good harvest, the villagers could keep anything above the tax level.

Akbar was a great supporter of the arts. He encouraged Hindu as well as Muslim artists. Mughal artists, influenced by the Persian style, created delicate, colorful miniature paintings. Akbar also encouraged the development of literature in the Hindi and Urdu languages. The Mughals made great achievements in architecture, blending Persian, Islamic, and Hindu styles.

Religious policy. Perhaps most importantly, Akbar was tolerant of all religions. He repealed the special tax that non-Muslims had been forced to pay. Over time, however, he began to think of himself as a divine ruler. In the late 1500s he established a creed called the Divine Faith. The motto for the creed was *Allahu Akbar,* meaning either "God is great" or "Akbar is God." The creed blended elements of Islam, Hinduism, Jainism, Christianity, and other religions. It attracted few followers beyond Akbar's court because Muslims strongly opposed it.

Economy and trade. During Akbar's reign the economy improved. The empire's wealth and resources, and its location along the sea routes to Asia, attracted European traders. India had impressive quantities of jewels and gold. The climate allowed the peasants to grow a variety of crops and allowed more than one harvest a year. European travelers thought India's rulers lived in greater luxury than their European kings. India's cities, such as Agra and Delhi, were filled with beautiful buildings and monuments. The Mughal cities seemed much larger than any in Europe.

✔ **READING CHECK: Making Generalizations** What role did Akbar play in the growth of the Mughal Empire? won control of all northern India, much of central India; created policies that helped to maintain Mughal strength

440

440 CHAPTER 18

Teacher to Teacher

Mary Catherine Rahman of Chicago, Illinois, suggested the following activity: After reading Section 3, have students imagine that Elizabeth I of England and Akbar were pen pals. Have students work in pairs, with one representing Elizabeth and one Akbar. Using what they have learned, have them compose a series of letters between the two leaders asking and answering questions about their cultures and how they handled issues in their countries such as religious differences and wars. **COOPERATIVE LEARNING**

TEACH OBJECTIVE 2

ALL LEVELS: Write the following terms on the chalkboard: *Rajputs, taxes, arts, religion, economy.* Pair students to develop explanations of how each item helped Akbar expand his control in India. Tell each pair to decide which of the items was most important in expanding the Mughal Empire. Then select pairs to share their judgement with the class. Discuss any differences in the pairs' assessments. **ENGLISH LANGUAGE LEARNERS, COOPERATIVE LEARNING**

The Height of the Mughal Empire

The Mughal Empire was at its height during the reign of **Shah Jahān.** He ruled from 1628 to 1658. By this time the empire had expanded to reach its greatest extent of territory, including both northern and southern India.

Shah Jahān is best known for the two famous buildings that were constructed during his reign. The magnificent **Taj Mahal** at Agra remains one of the architectural wonders of the world. Shah Jahān had the Taj Mahal built as a tomb for his beloved wife, Mumtāz Mahal. It is made of marble inlaid with semiprecious gems. The other building, the Hall of Private Audience, is in the Red Fort at Delhi. This was Shah Jahān's palace. In the Hall of Private Audience are carved these famous lines: "If there be Paradise on Earth, It is Here, It is Here, It is Here!" These great buildings were enormously expensive to build.

At the same time, the Mughals were engaged in military campaigns against Persia. Their huge armies were very expensive to maintain. They believed these armies were necessary to hold their empire together. To meet his expenses, Shah Jahān increased taxes. His subjects had to pay him half of the crops they raised. Many people suffered under this terrible burden.

A new religion. Under the Mughals, a blending of Hindu and Muslim cultures occurred. In the 1500s an Indian mystic named Nānak tried to unite the Hindu and Muslim religions. Out of Nānak's teaching arose a new religion—the **Sikh** (SEEK) faith. This faith called for devotion to one God, a lack of idols, and a less rigid social system. These ideas conflicted with Hindu beliefs. Nānak became the first guru (leader or teacher) of the Sikhs. By the late 1600s the Sikhs had become militant. They became fierce enemies of the Mughal Empire and the Muslims.

INTERPRETING THE VISUAL RECORD

The Taj Mahal Shah Jahān brought workers and materials from all over India and central Asia to build the Taj Mahal. It took more than 20,000 workers and over 20 years to finish the job. *What statement does this building make about the power of the Mughals?*

Culture

Hinduism places importance on actions rather than beliefs. It is characterized by a belief in dharma–the idea that people should behave in a manner appropriate to their station. Hindu beliefs and practices conflict with the Islamic doctrine of belief in one god, Allah, and equality among people.

Critical Thinking

Why would the Muslim and Sikh faiths appeal to the lower classes in society?

ANSWER: Both faiths opposed the rigid class system of Hinduism and supported equality and brotherhood.

That's Interesting!

Shah Jahan lived surrounded by luxury and dressed the part of absolute sovereign. He wore silk pantaloons and gold tunics and kept a jeweled dagger at his waist. The rubies on his turban alone would be worth about a half a million dollars today.

VISUAL RECORD ANSWER

They had great power and wealth.

441

HOMEWORK Tell students to imagine they are foreign ambassadors to India during the height of the Mughal Empire. Have them write a letter to an associate in their home country describing what they have seen and what is happening in the empire.

TEACH OBJECTIVE 2

LEVEL 3: Ask students to write an essay that compares and contrasts the reigns of two of the Mughal rulers in this section. Have them write their essays using a particular frame of reference. They should decide which ruler had the strongest character and how his character affected the empire. (*Students should use similar details from Section 3, though their decisions about character will vary.*)

CLOSE

Have students give their opinions about the policies of each ruler discussed in Section 3. Ask students to evaluate the success of each ruler and whether their character played a part in that success.

internet connect

go.hrw.com

TOPIC: The Safavid Empire
GO TO: go.hrw.com
KEYWORD: SP3 WH18

Have students access the Internet through the HRW Go site to research life and society in the Safavid Empire. Ask students to write a report on the Empire. They may wish to use the interactive template provided.

SKILLS PRACTICE ANSWERS

1. political, religious, social

2. Though viewed by some to be a politically effective rule, it strikes others as cruelly intolerant and inconstant.

3. Summaries will vary greatly, but students may wish to focus on religious zeal, government corruption, or economic prosperity or decline.

SKILL-BUILDING STRATEGIES Understanding Frames of Reference

The Reign of Aurangzeb

A frame of reference is a set of ideas, conditions, or beliefs. Historians use different frames of reference to analyze a person, an event, or an era. For example, a historian may examine a subject from a social, economic, legal, or political frame of reference. As a result, different scholars may tell a very different story about the same historical subject. They can come to different conclusions based on their frame of reference. Knowing a historian's frame of reference helps you to understand what you read. Understanding different interpretations about Aurangzeb's rule requires analysis of the frames of reference used by the historians.

Historians' Views

"The predominant trait of the Mughal rulers of India was their political instinct. . . . Aurangzeb displayed this character to an eminent [outstanding] degree."

Mughal Empire in India

"[The] intolerance of Aurangzeb . . . hastened the ruin of the dynasty . . . his bigotry and persecutions rendered him hateful to his Hindu subjects."

A History of the Sikhs

"Aurangzeb's government made itself ridiculous by violently enforcing for a time, then relaxing, and finally abandoning a code of puritanical morals opposed to the feelings of the entire population . . ."

The Cambridge History of India

Skills Reminder

To understand frames of reference, first identify what factors the author emphasizes, such as economics, politics, or social outcomes. Also, identify the context in which the information is given. For example, is an analysis of a leader's rule being offered in the history of a people whom he conquered? Assess how this frame of reference might influence the information. Finally, compare how authors using different frames of reference might come to different conclusions about an event.

Skills Practice

❶ Study the passages above about the reign of the Mughal ruler Aurangzeb. What frame of reference is each historian using?

❷ What conclusions can you draw about Aurangzeb's rule from these passages?

❸ Write a brief summary of the rise and fall of either the Ottoman or Safavid empires using a particular frame of reference.

REVIEW

Have students complete the Section 3 Review on p. 443.

ASSESS

Have students complete Daily Quiz 18.3. As Alternate Assessment, you may want to use the Mughal Origins chart or the letter writing exercise in this section's lessons.

RETEACH

Have students complete Main Idea Activity for English Language Learners and Special-Needs Students 18.3. Then have students work in pairs to write four facts about the Mughal Empire. Explain that three of their facts should be true and one should be false. Have each pair read their facts aloud while the rest of the class attempts to name the false one.

ENGLISH LANGUAGE LEARNERS, COOPERATIVE LEARNING

EXTEND

Have students conduct research on the art or architecture of the Mughal Empire. Ask them to recreate by drawing or sculpting one work of their choice. Encourage students to consider what the piece tells them about the Mughal Empire. Then allow students to share their works of art and descriptions with the class.

Despite his abuses Shah Jahān was an extremely vigorous ruler. During the 30 years of his rule, he put down several rebellions, built a magnificent new capital at Delhi, and conquered new territories in the Deccan. He also launched an unsuccessful attempt to recapture the old Mughal homeland in central Asia. The shah's Peacock Throne, designed to inspire awe, was the greatest symbol of Mughal splendor. The throne was encrusted with gold and the largest diamonds, emeralds, and other precious gems. Shah Jahān also sought to make Delhi the world's most beautiful capital as a means of reflecting his power.

Aurangzeb. In 1657 Shah Jahān became ill. His son Muhī-ud-Dīn Muhammad, known by his princely title of **Aurangzeb** (AWR·uhng·zeb), killed his older brother, imprisoned Shah Jahān, and declared himself emperor.

A devout Sunni Muslim, Aurangzeb followed strict Islamic law in his personal life. He dressed simply and expected his courtiers to follow his example. He ended government spending on buildings and monuments. He banned most celebrations, particularly those that included wine and music.

Aurangzeb persecuted all other faiths in the Mughal Empire. He insisted on strict observance of Islamic holy laws. He restored the hated tax on Hindus and destroyed thousands of Hindu temples. He also oppressed the Shi'ah and Sufi Muslims. When crowds gathered outside the Red Fort to protest, Aurangzeb used elephants to crush them. Religious groups rioted throughout the empire.

Under Aurangzeb the Mughal Empire was the largest it would ever be. Unfortunately, the widespread revolts and economic problems weakened the empire. Aurangzeb may have regretted the bloodshed of his reign. When he died in 1707, he wondered aloud whether his actions would please his God.

This image dating from the mid-1600s portrays Shah Jahān at the height of his power.

✔ **READING CHECK: Contrasting** How was the reign of Aurangzeb different from the reign of Shah Jahān? imposed strict Islamic law; ended government spending on buildings and monuments; persecuted other religions

---

SECTION 3 REVIEW

1. **Identify** and explain the significance:
   Rajputs
   Bābur
   Akbar
   Shah Jahān
   Taj Mahal
   Sikh
   Aurangzeb

2. **Sequencing** Copy the chart below. Use it to organize important events in the history of the Mughal Empire.

   1. Bābur wins battle at Paniput.
   2.
   3.
   4.
   5.
   6. Aurangzeb dies.

3. **Finding the Main Idea**
   a. What evidence shows that Akbar tried to unify his empire?
   b. How did Shah Jahān improve the empire?
   c. How did Shah Jahān raise funds for his ambitious building programs and his military policies?
   d. In what ways did the strict policies of Aurangzeb represent a return to intolerance in Mughal India?

4. **Writing and Critical Thinking**
   Drawing Conclusions Explain how Aurangzeb harmed the Mughal Empire.
   Consider:
   • his policies toward other religions
   • his response to protests
   • his strict observance of Islamic laws

go. hrw .com **Homework Practice Online**
keyword: SP3 HP18

SECTION 3 REVIEW ANSWERS

❶ **Identify**
• Rajputs, p. 439
• Bābur, p. 439
• Akbar, p. 440
• Shah Jahān, p. 441
• Taj Mahal, p. 441
• Sikh, p. 441
• Aurangzeb, p. 443

❷ Akbar takes the throne and gains Rajput support; Shah Jahān builds the Taj Mahal and the Hall of Private Audience; Nānak develops the Sikh religion; Aurangzeb declares himself emperor.

❸ a. married a Rajput princess and gave Rajputs government positions, improved the tax system, and tolerated all religions

b. He built a new capital at Delhi, conquered new territories, and built two famous buildings, including the Taj Mahal.

c. by imposing heavy taxes on his subjects

d. Aurangzeb, a strict Sunni Muslim, persecuted, taxed, and oppressed people from all other faiths.

❹ Answers will vary but students might mention that Aurangzeb was intolerant of other religions, responded to protests with violence, and banned celebrations. His policies angered his subjects and resulted in riots and revolts that weakened the empire.

REVIEW AND ASSESSMENT RESOURCES

REPRODUCIBLE RESOURCES
▶ Vocabulary Activity 18

TECHNOLOGY RESOURCES
▶ Chapter 18 Test Generator (on the One-Stop Planner)
▶ Global Skill Builder CD-ROM
▶ HRW Web Site

REINFORCEMENT, REVIEW, and ASSESSMENT
▶ Chapter 18 Review, pp. 444–445
▶ Chapter 18 Tutorial for Students, Parents, Mentors, and Peers
▶ Chapter 18 Test (Form A or B)
▶ Alternative Assessment Handbook
▶ Chapter 18 Test for English Language Learners and Special-Needs Students

REVIEW
Have students complete the Chapter 18 Review on pages 444–445.

ASSESS
Use one of the chapter tests to assess students' understanding of the content. For Alternative Assessment, see the Portfolio Activities and Alternative Assessment Handbook.

CHAPTER 18 REVIEW ANSWERS

Understanding Main Ideas
1. parts of eastern Europe, western Asia, and northern Africa

2. They fought for the expansion of the empire.

3. allowed the various groups to govern themselves

4. unified Persians; threatened Persia's neighbors

5. Shi'ah gave Persians an identity and helped unify them.

6. 'Abbās regained control of lands lost to the Ottomans and Uzbeks and led his people into a time of prosperity.

7. Bābur conquered the town of Panipat and then took Delhi and the surrounding region.

8. gained Rajput support, improved the tax system and the empire's economy

9. Shah Jahan spent heavily while Aurangzeb halted government spending.

Reviewing Themes
1. the histories of the Janissaries and the kizilbash

2. Tolerant policies benefited the Ottomans. Forcing subjects to accept the Shi'ah faith strengthened the Safavid Empire. In Mughal India, persecution and oppression weakened governmental control.

3. People with ability could become part of the ruling class.

CHAPTER 18 Review

Creating a Time Line
Copy the time line below onto a sheet of paper. Complete the time line by filling in the events, individuals, and dates from the chapter that you think were significant. Pick three events and explain why you think they were significant.

| 1300 | 1400 | 1500 | 1600 | 1700 |

Writing a Summary
Using standard grammar, spelling, sentence structure, and punctuation, write an overview of the events in the chapter.

Identifying People and Ideas
Identify the following terms or individuals and explain their significance:

1. millets
2. Janissaries
3. Süleyman
4. kizilbash
5. Esmāʻīl
6. 'Abbās
7. Bābur
8. Akbar
9. Shah Jahān
10. Aurangzeb

Understanding Main Ideas

Section 1 *(pp. 432–435)*
The Ottoman Empire
1. What territory was included in the Ottoman Empire at its height?
2. Why were the Janissaries important to the Ottoman sultans?
3. How did the Ottoman Turks maintain peace among the various ethnic groups within their widespread empire?

Section 2 *(pp. 436–438)*
The Safavid Empire
4. What role did the Shi'ah religion play in the strengthening of the Safavid Empire and in the empire's relations with its neighbors?
5. How did Shi'ah affect the Persians' ideas about themselves?
6. Why did the Persians of the Safavid Empire call 'Abbās "the Great"?

Section 3 *(pp. 439–443)*
The Mughal Empire in India
7. What event marks the beginning of the Mughal Empire?
8. What were Akbar's most important accomplishments?
9. How did Aurangzeb's approach to government spending differ from Shah Jahān's?

Reviewing Themes
1. **Global Relations** What evidence is there that the Islamic empires supported large, strong militaries?
2. **Culture** How did religious policies affect the Islamic empires?
3. **Government** What effect did the character of individual rulers have on the Islamic empires?

Thinking Critically
1. **Drawing Inferences** In what way did the building of the Taj Mahal contribute to the decline of the Mughal Empire?
2. **Comparing** Compare the policy toward Sunni Muslims in the Ottoman Empire to the policy in the Safavid Empire.
3. **Supporting a Point of View** What evidence would you give that in the Ottoman Empire ordinary people had an equal chance for success?

Writing About History
Comparing and Contrasting Write a report describing the similarities and differences among the Ottoman, Safavid, and Mughal empires. Use the chart below to organize your thoughts before you write.

	Ottoman	Safavid	Mughal
Title used by ruler			
Most successful ruler			
Official branch of Islam			
Policy toward other religions			
Present name of country			

CLOSE

Ask students the following question: Is the life of an empire most affected by the size and strength of its military, its leader's religious policies, or the personal character of its rulers? Divide students into groups of similar opinion and allow each group to define its position with details and examples from the text as support. **COOPERATIVE LEARNING**

RETEACH

Have students who had trouble with the test use their textbooks to correct their tests. Then have them take the Form B test to assess their mastery of the material. **ENGLISH LANGUAGE LEARNERS , COOPERATIVE LEARNING**

Portfolio Extensions

1. Ask students to summarize the effects of religion on their own community. Have them consider the divisions between doctrines, prejudice, wealth, social status, etc.

2. Put students into pairs. Ask them to select one ruler discussed in Chapter 18 and describe his religious policies.

3. Have students imagine they are living during the height of the Mughal Empire. Tell them to write a letter in which they express their opinion about the Shah's military campaigns or about the building of the Taj Mahal.

Building Social Studies Skills

Interpreting Maps

Study the map below. Then answer the questions that follow.

The Ottomans in Hungary, c. 1520–c. 1565

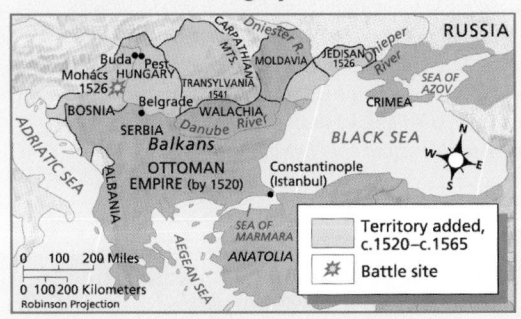

1. Which of the following statements best describes the Ottoman expansion into Hungary during the 1500s?

   a. The Ottomans' victory at Mohács had little impact on their movement into Hungary.

   b. The Ottomans' victory at Mohács allowed them to expand north, east, and west.

   c. Within ten years of their victory at Mohács, the Ottomans had taken control of all Hungary.

   d. Their victory at Mohács enabled the Ottomans to win control of the entire Mediterranean basin.

2. Why do you think the location of Mohács was important to Ottoman plans to conquer Hungary?

Sequencing

Read the sentences below about the Mughal rulers. Then answer the question that follows.

A. Shah Jahān (ruled 1628–1658) built the Taj Mahal.

B. The greatest Mughal emperor was Akbar. By the end of his reign in the early 1600s, Akbar controlled much of northern and central India.

C. Bābur occupied Delhi in 1526 and founded the Mughal Empire.

D. Economic problems had weakened the government by the time Aurangzeb died in 1707.

E. By the early years of the 1500s, the Muslim Sultanate of Delhi was suffering from internal weakness and was being increasingly challenged by the Rajput princes and their armies.

3. Which of the following shows the events listed in the order in which they occurred?

   a. B, C, A, D, E

   b. C, A, D, E, B

   c. D, E, A, B, C

   d. E, C, B, A, D

4. What were the main differences between the way Akbar and Aurangzeb ruled the Mughal Empire? Give specific examples.

Alternative Assessment

Building Your Portfolio

Link to TODAY

Culture

In the world today, religious policies still unify or divide cultures. Use your textbook and other sources to find examples of cultures that have been either unified or divided by the religious policies of governments. Then prepare a script about your findings that a television reporter could read on the evening news.

🖳 internet connect

Internet Activity: go.hrw.com
KEYWORD: SP3 WH18

Choose a topic on Islamic Empires in Asia to:

• create an illustrated time line of the major events in the history of the Ottoman Empire.

• research life and society in the Safavid Empire.

• create a newspaper article on the impact of the siege of Vienna in 1683.

CROSS-CULTURAL CONNECTIONS *Literature*

Spotlight on LITERATURE

The exact nature of poetry can be difficult to define, partly because it is written in so many different forms. *Encyclopaedia Britannica* defines poetry as "literature that evokes a concentrated imaginative awareness of experience or a specific emotional response through language chosen and arranged for its meaning, sound, and rhythm." Have students study the forms of poetic verse shown below—rhyming couplets, sonnet, and haiku—and then write a poem in one of these forms. Students may write about a subject of their choice.

Spotlight on LITERATURE

The poems below express feelings about death—a universal theme in poetry. Have students use primary and secondary sources, including computer software, to find several contemporary poems about death. Then have students use standard grammar, spelling, sentence structure, and punctuation to write a brief essay comparing the forms of their chosen poems with the ones in this feature. Which form best expresses feelings about death? Which is their favorite? Why?

Culture

Some scholars believe poetry may have been the first way people used language. Poetry probably began in rituals reciting magical spells to bring a good harvest. Humans now use poetry to affect the human spirit rather than the natural world. While poetic form is different in various cultures, the language usually follows a definite and predictable pattern. In ancient Greek poetry, the rhythm of syllables created a pattern. Rhyming patterns were first used in the poetry of the Romance languages, particularly French. The ballad, the sonnet, and blank verse all developed later in English poetry. While it is difficult to define, most people recognize poetry by the fact that it is written in lines and therefore looks different from prose on a printed page.

ACTIVITY: Ask students to research the history of poetry in a particular culture. Then have students create a time line that notes the important developments and works of poetry in that culture's history.

UNDERSTANDING LITERATURE ANSWER

similarities in purpose: all three authors talk about death and their legacies; differences in style: Shah-nameh is very long and rhymes, haiku is very short, sonnet is medium in length and has a strict pattern of rhyme and rhythm: similarities in tone: all are nostalgic

---

CROSS-CULTURAL CONNECTIONS *Literature*

Styles of Verse

Throughout the world's diverse societies, many forms of poetry have developed. Each culture's poetry has distinctive sounds and styles. The Persian poet Firdawsi (c. 935–1020) told the story of his nation's kings in an epic named Shah-nameh. This massive work contains 60,000 rhyming couplets. In the excerpt below the hero Sekander promises to care for King Dara as the king dies. William Shakespeare (1564–1616), an English writer, also wrote about death, but in a very different style. His sonnets are 14-line poems with a strict pattern of rhythm and rhyme. Japanese poet Banzan's haiku poem—written on his deathbed in 1730—follows the typical haiku form. In the original Japanese it contains five syllables in the first line, seven in the second, and five in the third.

Shah-nameh *by Firdawsi*

"I will have physicians brought for you from India and Rum [Rome] and I will cause tears of blood to flow for the pain you have suffered. . . . My heart bled and a cry issued from my lips when yesterday I heard from my elders that we two are of one stock and share a single shirt. Why should we extirpate [wipe out] our seed in rivalry?"

On hearing this, Dara said in a strong voice, ". . . Marry my pure-bodied daughter and maintain her in security in your palace. . . . It may be that by her you will have a noble son who will restore the name of Esfandiyar [an ancestor] to glory."

Shown here is the manuscript of a poem by the Japanese haiku master Bashō.

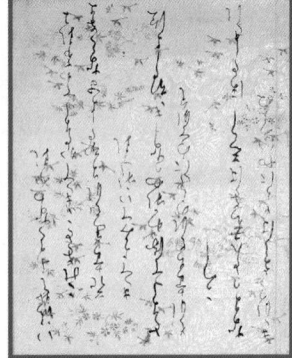

Haiku *by Banzan*

Mame de iyo
mi wa narawashi no
kusa no tsuyu.

(Translation:)
Farewell
I pass as all things do
dew on the grass.

"Sonnet 19" by William Shakespeare

Devouring time,
  blunt thou the lion's
  paws,
And make the earth
  devour her own
  sweet brood;
Pluck the keen teeth
  from the fierce
  tiger's jaws,
And burn the long-lived
  phoenix in her blood.
Make glad and sorry seasons as
  thou fleet'st,
And do whate'er thou wilt, swift-footed time,
To the wide world and all her fading sweets.
But I forbid thee one most heinous crime:
O, carve not with thy hours my love's fair brow,
Nor draw no lines there with thine antique pen.
Him in thy course untainted do allow
For beauty's pattern to succeeding men.
Yet do thy worst, old time; despite thy wrong
My love shall in my verse ever live young.

Understanding Literature

What similarities and differences do you find among these poems in their purpose, style, and tone?

Economics

During the 1500s and 1600s the Mughal Empire dominated the Indian subcontinent. Much of the empire's growth came as a result of increasing contact and trade with foreign countries. Have students research the economic history of the Mughal Empire. Then ask students to copy the graphic organizer below and complete it with their findings.

```
                  Mughal economy
    ┌────────────┬────────────┬────────────┐
  primary       primary      major
  exports       imports      trading
                             partners
```

Global Relations

Using the map on page 433 as a guide, have students create their own map of the Ottoman Empire. Encourage students to be creative in their presentation of the map's information. Remind them to include labels for important cities, bodies of water, and neighboring countries. Students should also use a key to identify relevant information. Then have students write five questions to accompany their map.

BUILDING YOUR Portfolio

UNIT 4

Economics

A search for wealth motivated European exploration of the New World. Imagine that you are an English adventurer who wishes to undertake a voyage to America in the 1500s. You will need the financial support of the Queen to make the journey. Your task is to write a proposal showing why your trip to the New World would be economically beneficial to England. What types of evidence would you use to show the importance of exploration for the economic welfare of the kingdom?

Ferdinand Magellan and his fleet setting sail from Spain in 1519

Ottoman ceramic pitcher and plate

Global Relations

During the 1400s and 1500s, the Ottoman Turks expanded the boundaries of their empire, conquering much of eastern Europe. Imagine that you are a soldier advancing with the Ottoman armies through eastern Europe in the 1520s. Create a diary in which you recount your experiences, including your impressions of European society, government, and religion. Based on your observations, discuss your view of the relations between the Ottoman Empire and the various kingdoms of eastern Europe.

Further Reading

Dersin, Denise, ed. *What Life Was Like: At The Rebirth Of Genius, Renaissance Italy 1400-1550.* Alexandria, Virginia: Time-Life Books, 1999. A survey of daily life and culture in Renaissance Italy.

Goodwin, Jason. *Lords of the Horizons: A History of the Ottoman Empire.* New York: Owl Books, 2000. A thorough survey of the Ottoman Empire from its beginnings to its collapse.

Hale, J. R., ed. *The Thames and Hudson Encyclopedia of the Italian Renaissance.* London: Thames and Hudson, 1988. A reference work on the history, politics, culture, and society of the Italian Renaissance.

Meltzer, Milton. *Columbus and the World Around Him.* New York: Watts Franklin, 1990. A history of Christopher Columbus and his four voyages.

Pilbeam, Mavis. *Japan Under The Shoguns, 1185-1868.* New York: Raintree/Steck-Vaughn, 1999. A history of the shogunates, and a look at everyday life in Japan and the role of the samurai.

internet connect

Internet Activity
KEYWORD: SP3 U4

In assigned groups, develop a multimedia presentation about the Age of Exploration and Expansion. Choose information from the chapter Internet Connect activities and the Holt Researcher that best reflects the major topics of the period. Write an outline and a script for your presentation, which may be shown to the class.

go.hrw.com

ZHENG HE. Nearly a century before the European era of exploration, the Chinese undertook extensive seafaring voyages. In the early 1400s the Chinese emperor appointed Zheng He to lead the Ming dynasty's mission to restore control over South and Southeast Asia. The Chinese had already developed an extensive maritime trade to acquire spices and raw industrial materials. Technological developments in shipbuilding and navigation allowed the Chinese to extend their influence in the region. In 1405 Zheng He set sail on his first voyage, commanding 62 ships and 27,800 men and traveling to many countries. When Zheng returned to China in 1415, he brought representatives from more than 30 states of South and Southeast Asia to pay homage to the Chinese emperor. Although Zheng He's seven expeditions did not establish the trading empires created by European explorers, his voyages did extend China's political control over maritime Asia.

Critical Thinking

How did Chinese seafaring expeditions differ from European voyages?

ANSWER: Chinese expeditions occurred a century earlier and did not establish trading empires like the European expeditions did.

UNIT 5

From Absolutism to Revolution

EXAMINING THE VISUAL RECORD

❶ *What emotions are apparent among these military recruits?*

ANSWER: excitement, concern, fear, determination, pride

The recruits pictured in Boilly's painting probably were conscripts—men drafted into military service. The French emperor Napoléon started the first nationwide system of conscription in the early 1800s. Napoléon's skill as a military leader became legendary after his death. He revolutionized military training and organization. However, the Napoléonic Wars fought between 1800 and 1815 cost France about 500,000 men. The loss of these young men also significantly reduced the French birth rate.

❷ *What do the clothing styles imply about French society in the early 1800s?*

ANSWER: reveals class distinctions, the importance of the military

The artist Louis-Leopold Boilly is best known for his paintings of everyday life in France during the Revolution and the Empire. For more than 40 years, Boilly created about 5,500 portraits and other paintings, leaving historians a wealth of visual information about French life and culture.

ACTIVITY: Have students use primary and secondary sources to locate and study other paintings by Louis-Leopold Boilly. Then have students write an essay analyzing French culture and society as reflected in Boilly's paintings.

UNIT 5

From Absolutism to Revolution

1500–1815

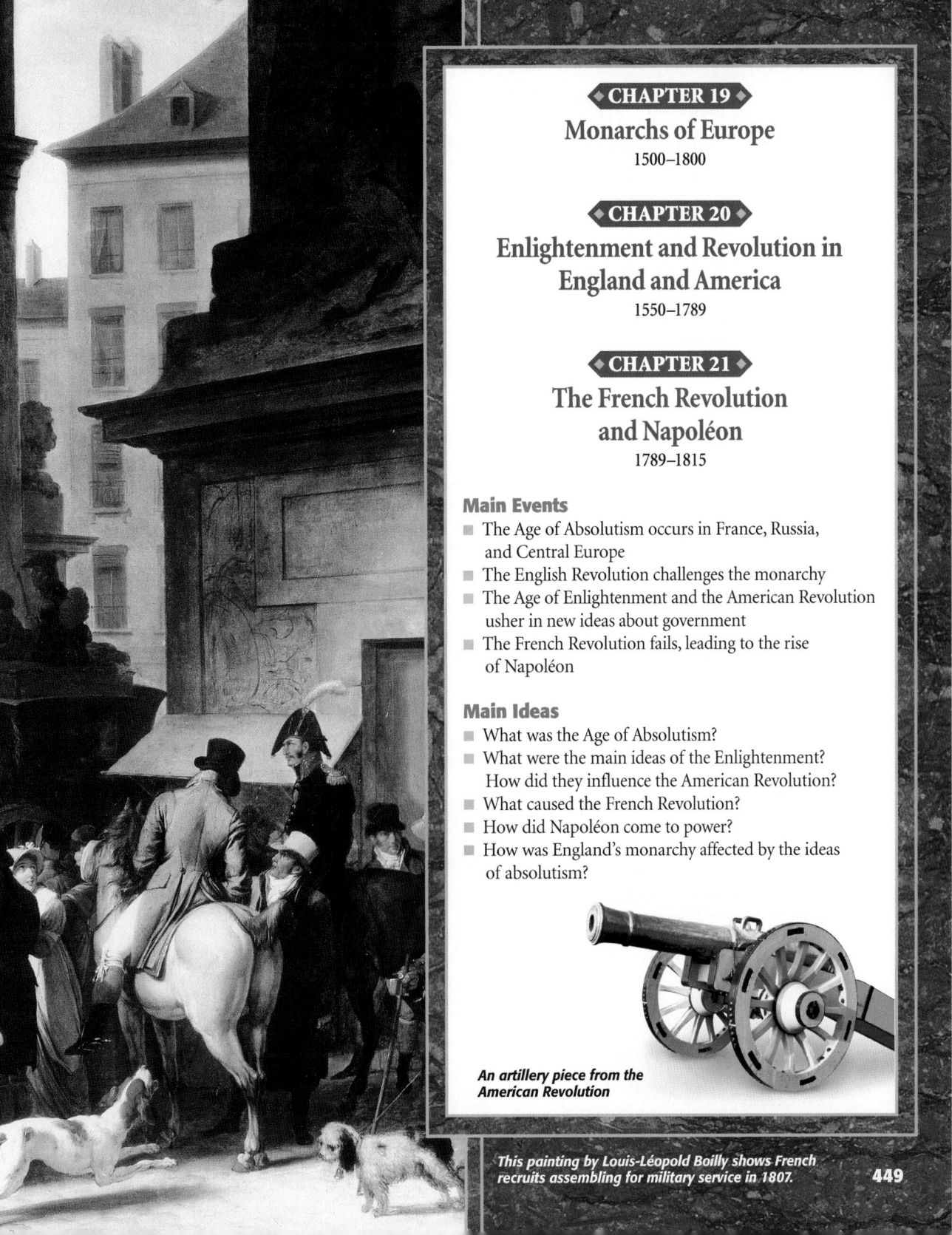

◆ CHAPTER ◆ 21
The French Revolution and Napoléon

A revolution, inspired by events in America, broke out in France in 1789. The French established a republic with a limited monarchy. Radical revolutionaries began a Reign of Terror and led France through wars with other European nations. During this chaotic period, Napoléon Bonaparte rose to power. Napoléon dominated Europe until other major states joined forces to defeat him. European countries sought to restore stability by returning to a conservative status quo.

◆ CHAPTER 19 ◆
Monarchs of Europe
1500–1800

◆ CHAPTER 20 ◆
Enlightenment and Revolution in England and America
1550–1789

◆ CHAPTER 21 ◆
The French Revolution and Napoléon
1789–1815

Main Events
■ The Age of Absolutism occurs in France, Russia, and Central Europe
■ The English Revolution challenges the monarchy
■ The Age of Enlightenment and the American Revolution usher in new ideas about government
■ The French Revolution fails, leading to the rise of Napoléon

Main Ideas
■ What was the Age of Absolutism?
■ What were the main ideas of the Enlightenment? How did they influence the American Revolution?
■ What caused the French Revolution?
■ How did Napoléon come to power?
■ How was England's monarchy affected by the ideas of absolutism?

An artillery piece from the American Revolution

This painting by Louis-Léopold Boilly shows French recruits assembling for military service in 1807. **449**

Main Events
Ask students to select two Main Events and list questions they would like to have answered about the topics. Later, when you have completed Unit 5, ask students to return to their original questions and write an answer using the information they learned in the unit.

Main Ideas
Ask each student to read the Main Ideas and write brief answers to the questions. Share the *Consider* points with students as necessary. Later, when you have completed Unit 5, ask students to analyze their original answers by comparing them to information they learned in the unit. Tell them to revise or expand their answers as necessary.

The Effects of Absolutism in Europe
Consider:

■ the nature of monarchies in France, Russia, Prussia, and Austria
■ the power of Parliament in England

The Effects of Enlightenment Ideals, Revolution, and the Rise of Constitutional Governments
Consider:

■ the development of a constitutional monarchy in England
■ the influence of Enlightenment thought on the American and French Revolutions

CROSS-CULTURAL CONNECTIONS

 LET'S GET STARTED!

As students enter the classroom, ask them what European nations exist today that did not exist in 1815. Have them verify their answer by comparing the map on page A8 with the map on page 531. *(Germany, Italy, Belgium, Hungary)* Tell students that in Unit 5 they will learn how political, social, and intellectual changes between 1500 and 1815 transformed Europe.

TEACH

ALL LEVELS: Help students fill out the following graphic organizer to show how the Enlightenment affected societies. **ENGLISH LANGUAGE LEARNERS**

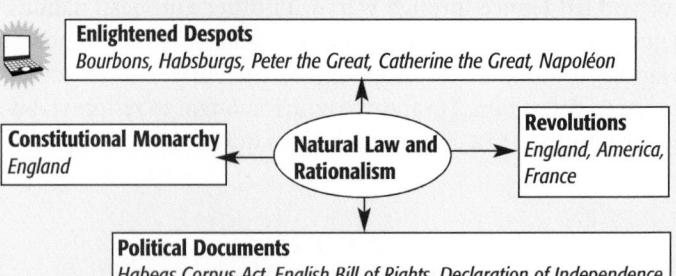

Enlightened Despots
Bourbons, Habsburgs, Peter the Great, Catherine the Great, Napoléon

Constitutional Monarchy
England

Natural Law and Rationalism

Revolutions
England, America, France

Political Documents
Habeas Corpus Act, English Bill of Rights, Declaration of Independence

---

Culture

Thomas Jefferson's ideas about architecture changed significantly after he lived in France during the 1780s. He renovated Monticello when he returned home and applied his new ideas to the design of the University of Virginia, which he founded in 1819. In addition to the Rotunda pictured here, Jefferson designed the university's "academical village" and many of its other buildings, still used and admired by students and faculty as a unique educational environment. Called the "Lawn," this central area extends out from the Rotunda and is bordered on each side by a row of classically designed buildings, walkways, and gardens.

Critical Thinking

How does Jefferson's "academical village" reflect Enlightenment ideas?

ANSWER: It is based on order, logic, function, and classic styles.

That's Interesting!

Jefferson considered his role in founding the University of Virginia as one of the greatest achievements of his life. He specified that the inscription on his tombstone should read as follows and "not a word more."
*Here was buried
Thomas Jefferson
Author of the Declaration of
American Independence
of the Statute of Virginia for religious freedom
& Father of the University of
Virginia*

450

CROSS-CULTURAL CONNECTIONS

Focus On: Constitutional Heritage

Main Idea What laws should rule? During the 1500s European political and social thinkers began a debate about the proper nature of government. Some thought the best form of government was a single ruler, such as a king, who had absolute authority. Others believed a government should represent the people, who had the right to change the government if it ruled unjustly. Increasingly, constitutional forms of government, based on the authority of law, came into being. This type of government placed even rulers under the absolute power of the constitution.

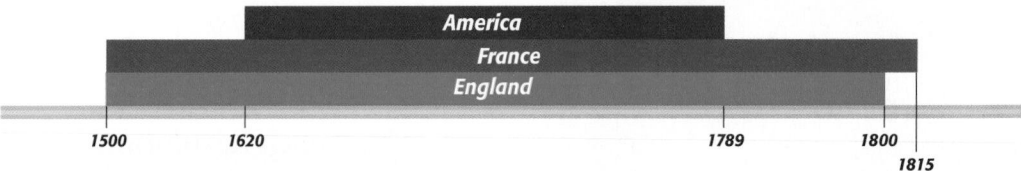

America
France
England

1500   1620   1789   1800
                                                                    1815

◀ **The Power of Parliament** Monarchs in France and Russia governed with complete authority. Government worked differently in England, however, where even the monarch was subject to the law. The English designed Parliament to act as a check on the monarch's power. In this painting England's Queen Elizabeth I is shown presiding over an opening session of Parliament. Elizabeth could not impose new taxes or pass new laws without Parliament's approval. However, she skillfully used the group to her political advantage. Later monarchs did not work as well with Parliament, however, leading to a series of upheavals that came to be known as the English Revolution. By the time the revolution had ended, the power of parliamentary law was firmly established.

England, 1500–1800

This cartoon from the period of the English Civil War shows a London woman sending her husband off to fight for the forces of Parliament.

Thomas Jefferson's Vision American leaders of the late 1700s—such as Benjamin Franklin and Thomas Jefferson—were inspired by the ideas of the European Enlightenment. Enlightenment philosophy influenced the writing of both the Declaration of Independence and the U.S. Constitution. Thomas Jefferson also used Enlightenment principles to design the University of Virginia—the University's rotunda is shown at right— and his home at Monticello. Enlightenment faith in the powers of the mind and the concepts of reason, balance, and order were the focus of Jefferson's designs. Precise geometric forms, such as the dome, embodied the principle of reason. Jefferson's architectural designs reflected classical styles from Greece and Rome, as did many of Jefferson's beliefs about government.

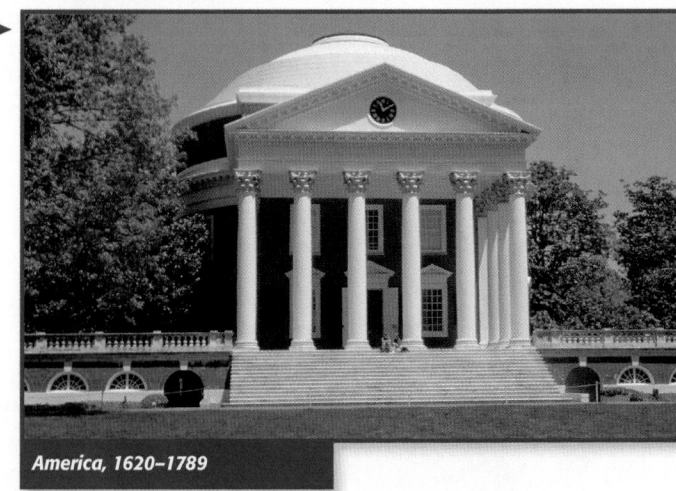

America, 1620–1789

Have students review the information about the influence of Enlightenment ideas. Then ask them to use standard grammar, spelling, sentence structure, and punctuation to answer the question in "Why It Matters Today" and to share their answers with the class.

ASSESS

Have students complete their answer to the question in "Why It Matters Today" and add it to their portfolio. As Alternative Assessment, you may want to use the graphic organizer in this lesson.

EXTEND

Have students research the causes and effects of the American and French Revolutions, including their influence on other countries. Ask students to use standard grammar, spelling, sentence structure, and punctuation to write an essay that compares and contrasts the two revolutions. **BLOCK SCHEDULING**

Citizenship

Many American women strongly supported the American Revolution. However, the Revolution failed to bring women expanded rights. In 1776 Abigail Adams wrote to her husband, John, at the Continental Congress in Philadelphia. She urged him to "remember the ladies" by sharing political power. However, neither Congress nor the state governments—with the exception of New Jersey—improved the status of their female citizens. Women could not vote. They also continued to be under their fathers' or husbands' legal control. In New Jersey, propertied women could vote under the 1776 state constitution. However, new legislation took away this right in 1807.

Critical Thinking

Why do you think rights were not extended to women?

ANSWER: Students may suggest that men viewed female political participation as inappropriate, or that men were threatened by women's potential political power.

The French Republic The idea of a constitutional republic did not appeal just to French men alone. French women also supported the Revolution, which took place between 1789 and 1793. Some women attended meetings of revolutionary groups and voiced their opinions about affairs of state. Two women in Paris started their own group in 1793, called The Society for Revolutionary Republican Women. Members of this revolutionary club thought of themselves as a family of sisters ready to rush to the defense of their country. Women in patriotic clubs, such as the one pictured here, gathered to discuss the political issues of the day. At one point during the French Revolution, men in Paris outlawed women's political clubs.

France, 1500–1815

In this portrait a French woman is wearing the "bonnet rouge" (red cap) that became a symbol of the French Revolution and of the republic it produced.

This sketch shows the planned front elevation of Jefferson's estate at Monticello, c. 1790s. The finished construction, which differs somewhat from the original design, is shown at right.

Why It Matters Today

The principles of constitutional government and the rule of law developed over centuries. The basic ideals of constitutionalism—personal liberty, representative government, and political checks and balances—continue to affect today's nations. **How does constitutionalism shape the United States today?**

WHY IT MATTERS TODAY ANSWER
Answers will vary, but students might suggest citizens' participation in a democratic form of government, the protection of personal liberties citizens have under the Bill of Rights, and the protection against governmental abuse of power through the system of checks and balances.

Monarchs of Europe

CHAPTER RESOURCE MANAGER

	Objectives	Pacing Guide	Reproducible Resources
SECTION 1 **France in the Age of Absolutism** (pp. 454–458)	• Explain how Henry IV and Cardinal Richelieu strengthened France. • Analyze Louis XIV's strategy for strengthening the central government. • Identify Louis XIV's reasons for waging war and the results.	**Regular** **Block Scheduling** 1.5 day 1 day *Block Scheduling Handbook with Team Teaching Strategies, 19.1*	**RS** Guided Reading Strategy 19.1 **SM** Geography Activity 19: The Thirty Years' War **PS** Readings in World History 58: Revolt in Bohemia **PS** Readings in World History 59: A Day in the Life of Louis XIV **E** Hands-on History Activity 19: The Royal Court
SECTION 2 **Russia in the Age of Absolutism** (pp. 459–464)	• Identify ways Russia was isolated from western Europe. • Analyze how Peter the Great used his power to change Russia. • Examine how Catherine the Great expanded Russia's territory.	**Regular** **Block Scheduling** 1.5 day 1 day *Block Scheduling Handbook with Team Teaching Strategies, 19.2*	**RS** Guided Reading Strategy 19.2 **PS** Readings in World History 60: The Great Czar
SECTION 3 **Central Europe in the Age of Absolutism** (pp. 465–469)	• Explain how the Habsburgs gained and held power. • Explain how the Hohenzollerns rose to power. • Identify the factors that contributed to conflicts between Prussia and Austria.	**Regular** **Block Scheduling** 1.5 day 1 day *Block Scheduling Handbook with Team Teaching Strategies, 19.3*	**RS** Guided Reading Strategy 19.3
SECTION 4 **The English Monarchy** (pp. 470–473)	• Describe the rule of Mary Tudor in England. • Describe the rule of Elizabeth I. • Explain the problems James I faced in ruling England.	**Regular** **Block Scheduling** 1.5 day 1 day *Block Scheduling Handbook with Team Teaching Strategies, 19.4*	**RS** Guided Reading Strategy 19.4 **RS** Graphic Organizer Activity 19: Constitutionalism **PS** Readings in World History 61: The Gunpowder Plot **E** Creative Teaching Strategy 19: Historian's Conference on European Expansion

Chapter Resource Key

PS Primary Sources
RS Reading Support
IC Interdisciplinary Connections
E Enrichment
SM Skills Mastery

A Assessment
REV Review
ELL Reinforcement and English Language Learners
 Transparencies
 CD-ROM

 Music
 Video
Internet
 Holt Presentation Maker Using Microsoft® PowerPoint®

One-Stop Planner CD-ROM

See the *One-Stop Planner* for a complete list of additional resources for students and teachers.

One-Stop Planner CD-ROM

It's easy to plan lessons, select resources, and print out materials for your students when you use the *One-Stop Planner* CD–ROM with **Test Generator.**

Technology Resources	Reinforcement, Review, and Assessment
One-Stop Planner 19.1 Homework Practice Online	Daily Quiz 19.1 Main Idea Activity 19.1 English Audio Summary 19.1 Spanish Audio Summary 19.1 REV Section 1 Review, p. 458
One-Stop Planner 19.2 Holt Researcher: World History: Catherine the Great CNN Presents World Cultures: Yesterday and Today Segment 16: Restoring St. Petersburg Homework Practice Online Online Maps, Charts, and Graphs: Russian Expansion, 1533–1689 Online Maps, Charts, and Graphs: Russian Expansion, 1533–1725	Daily Quiz 19.2 Main Idea Activity 19.2 English Audio Summary 19.2 Spanish Audio Summary 19.2 REV Section 2 Review, p. 464
One-Stop Planner 19.3 Homework Practice Online	Daily Quiz 19.3 Main Idea Activity 19.3 English Audio Summary 19.3 Spanish Audio Summary 19.3 REV Section 3 Review, p. 469
One-Stop Planner 19.4 Holt Researcher: World History: Mary I, Elizabeth I Homework Practice Online	Daily Quiz 19.4 Main Idea Activity 19.4 English Audio Summary 19.4 Spanish Audio Summary 19.4 REV Section 4 Review, p. 473

internet connect

HRW ONLINE RESOURCES
 GO TO: go.hrw.com
 Then type in a keyword.

TEACHER HOME PAGE
 KEYWORD: SP3 Teacher

CHAPTER INTERNET ACTIVITIES
 KEYWORD: SP3 WH19
Choose an activity to:
- create a pamphlet on the impact on Russian society of the reigns of Peter the Great and Catherine the Great.
- write a biography of the Sun King.
- explore the propaganda of William Shakespeare's historical plays.

CHAPTER ENRICHMENT LINKS
 KEYWORD: SP3 CH19

ONLINE ASSESSMENT
 Homework Practice
 KEYWORD: SP3 HP19
 Standardized Test Prep
 KEYWORD: SP3 STP19
 Rubrics
 KEYWORD: SS Rubrics

ONLINE MAPS, CHARTS, AND GRAPHS
 KEYWORD: SP3 MCG

CONTENT UPDATES
 KEYWORD: SS Content Updates

HOLT PRESENTATION MAKER
 KEYWORD: SP3 PPT19

ONLINE READING SUPPORT
 KEYWORD: SS Strategies

CURRENT EVENTS
 KEYWORD: S3 Current Events

Meeting Individual Needs

Ability Levels

Level 1 Basic level activities designed for all students encountering new material

Level 2 Intermediate level activities designed for average students

Level 3 Challenging activities designed for honors and gifted and talented students

English Language Learners These activities address the needs of students with Limited English Proficiency.

Chapter Review and Assessment

IC Vocabulary Activity 19
 Global Skill Builder CD–ROM
 HRW Web Site
REV Chapter 19 Tutorial for Students, Parents, Mentors, and Peers
REV Chapter 19 Review, pp. 474–475
A Chapter 19 Test Generator (on the One-Stop Planner)
A Chapter 19 Test (Form A or B)
A Alternative Assessment Handbook
A Chapter 19 Test for English Language Learners and Special-Needs Students

CHAPTER 19

Section 1   France in the Age of Absolutism

Section 2   Russia in the Age of Absolutism

Section 3   Central Europe in the Age of Absolutism

Section 4   The English Monarchy

Build on What You Know

Ask students to answer the following questions:

How might a strong centralized government be good for a nation's economy?

Consider:

- **how exploration and colonization would help trade**
- **how colonies provide resources**
- **how taxes can improve roads and support industry**

Why might individuals choose to immigrate to a newly colonized region?

Consider:

- **religious persecution back home**
- **new economic opportunities**
- **people's sense of adventure**

EXPLORING THE TIME LINE

GLOBAL EVENTS

internet connect

go.hrw.com

TOPIC: Monarchs of Europe
GO TO: **go.hrw.com**
KEYWORD: **SP3 WH19**

Have students access the Internet through the HRW Go site to learn more about Catherine the Great and Queen Elizabeth I. Have students make a chart listing both rulers and compare the two on the following five points: era of reign, main political focus, social reforms, challenges, and wars engaged in. Ask students to write a brief essay explaining which of the two rulers they would have preferred to live under and why.

CHAPTER 19

1500–1800

Monarchs of Europe

Sir Thomas More, Chancellor of England from 1529 to 1532

1535
Politics
Sir Thomas More is executed for not recognizing Henry VIII as the head of the church in England.

1556–1598
Politics
Philip II rules Spain.

1558–1603
Politics
Elizabeth I reigns in England.

1564
Politics
Russians force Ivan IV to leave Moscow.

1588
Global Events
The English navy defeats the Spanish Armada.

A locket commemorating England's victory over the Spanish Armada

1630
Business and Finance
Public advertising begins in Paris.

1632
Business and Finance
Russia begins a fur trade in Siberia.

1500

1600

1501
Daily Life
Card games increase in popularity all over Europe.

1530s
Daily Life
Henry VIII founds the Anglican Church in England.

1563
The Arts
Pieter Brueghel paints *The Tower of Babel.*

c. 1560s
Science and Technology
The first printing presses appear in Russia.

1606
The Arts
William Shakespeare writes *King Lear* and *Macbeth.*

1603
Politics
King James I founds the Stuart dynasty in England.

An oil-on-panel painting of the Tudor family

Build on What You Know

*I*n the late 1400s, European society began to change dramatically. Technological advances in mapmaking, navigation instruments, and shipbuilding, and new knowledge of Earth's geography provided Europeans with the means to explore the world beyond Europe. New methods of organizing and conducting business led to widespread economic change as well. Nations began overseas exploration and colonization, and economic and political conditions in Europe led many people to move to the newly founded overseas colonies. In this chapter, you will learn how monarchs rose to power in Europe.

What's Your Opinion?

Government

Agree A strong central government can help ensure order within a nation and peace among nations.

Disagree A single, central authority may rule through intimidation and become isolated from its people.

Culture

Agree As long as society believes in tolerance and acceptance, different religions can coexist peacefully.

Disagree People derive their social and political identity from religion.

Economics

Agree Equal wealth helps ensure equal healthcare, housing, and education, and is only fair.

Disagree Wealth should be based on ability and individual achievement.

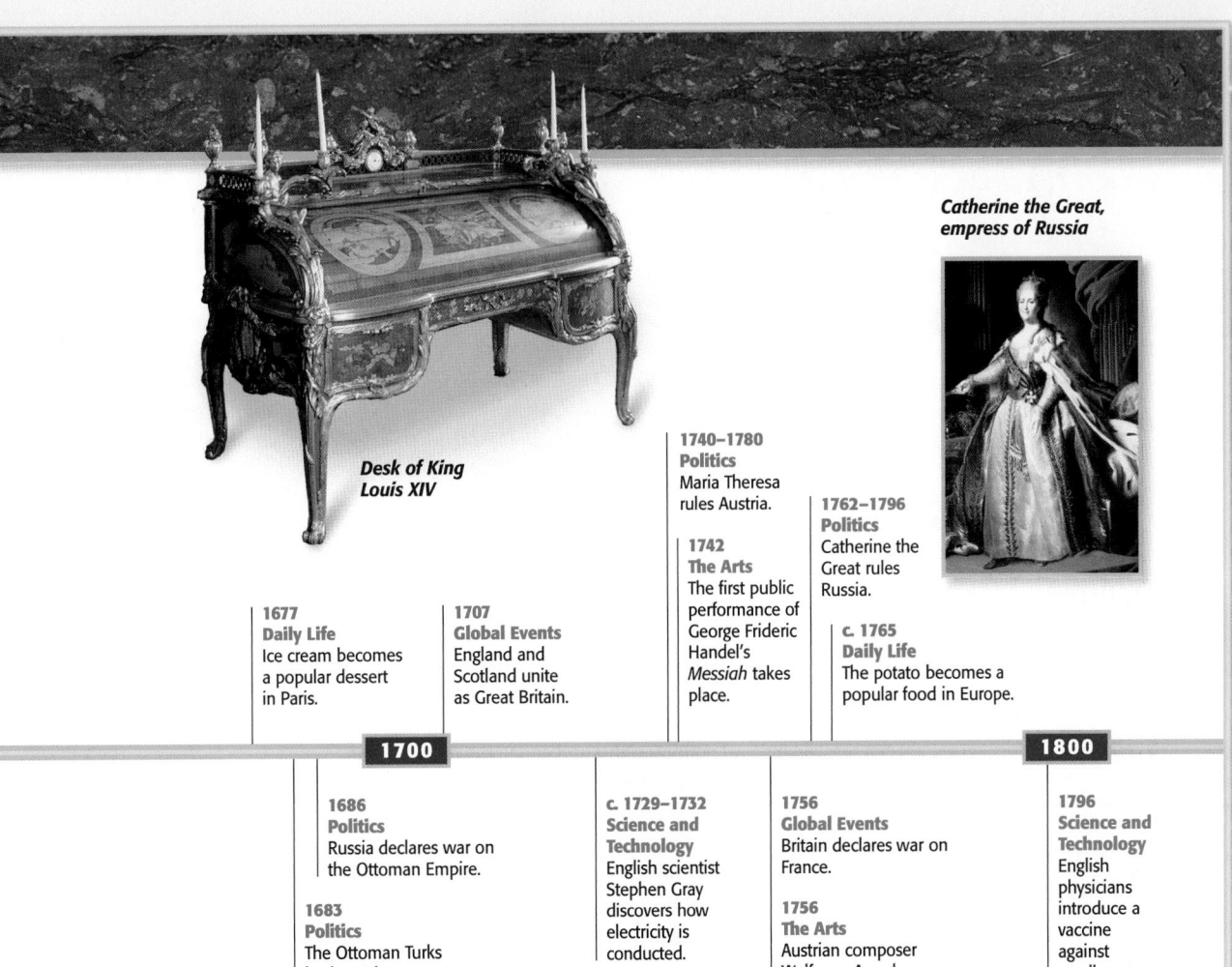

Desk of King Louis XIV

Catherine the Great, empress of Russia

1677
Daily Life
Ice cream becomes a popular dessert in Paris.

1707
Global Events
England and Scotland unite as Great Britain.

1740–1780
Politics
Maria Theresa rules Austria.

1742
The Arts
The first public performance of George Frideric Handel's *Messiah* takes place.

1762–1796
Politics
Catherine the Great rules Russia.

c. 1765
Daily Life
The potato becomes a popular food in Europe.

1700

1800

1686
Politics
Russia declares war on the Ottoman Empire.

1683
Politics
The Ottoman Turks besiege Vienna.

c. 1729–1732
Science and Technology
English scientist Stephen Gray discovers how electricity is conducted.

1756
Global Events
Britain declares war on France.

1756
The Arts
Austrian composer Wolfgang Amadeus Mozart is born.

1796
Science and Technology
English physicians introduce a vaccine against smallpox.

Section of the Catherine Palace, Russia

What's Your Opinion?

Themes Journal *Do you* **agree** *or* **disagree** *with the following statements? Support your point of view in your journal.*

Government A nation cannot survive without a strong central government.

Culture Religious beliefs have little, if any, effect on the degree of unity or disunity that characterizes a particular society.

Economics All citizens of a society should have the same amount of wealth.

EXPLORING THE TIME LINE
GL⊙BAL EVENTS

The time line lists some of the powerful monarchs of the 1500s and 1600s. These national monarchs were different from medieval monarchs, who assumed sovereign power with divine authority from the church. National monarchs held central authority and commanded the loyalties of all their citizens.

The invention of new weapons supported a monarch's control. Castles defended by archers were no defense against cannons using gunpowder. Steel crossbows were more powerful than traditional crossbows or longbows. Because such new weapons were expensive, kings were frequently the only people able to raise enough funds to buy these new instruments of war.

Critical Thinking

How would new weapons of war fuel the rise of absolute authority of monarchs?

ANSWER: New weapons would give monarchs enough force to maintain their power and defeat nobles.

OBJECTIVES

1 **Explain how Henry IV and Cardinal Richelieu strengthened France.**

2 **Analyze Louis XIV's strategy for strengthening the central government.**

3 **Identify Louis XIV's reasons for waging war and the results.**

🔔 *LET'S GET STARTED!*

As students enter the classroom, ask them to predict what would happen if there were no government. Focus thinking by listing government services such as law enforcement. Then ask students if they think people would exchange some personal liberty for security and peace. Remind them of the political and religious chaos in Europe caused by the decline of feudalism and the Reformation. Tell students that in Section 1 they will learn how a strong central government headed by a monarch then evolved in France.

◆ SECTION ◆ **1**

▰ READ TO DISCOVER

❶ How did Henry IV and Cardinal Richelieu strengthen France?

❷ How did Louis XIV strengthen the central government?

❸ Why did Louis XIV go to war, and what were the results?

▰ DEFINE

intendants
divine right of kings
balance of power

▰ IDENTIFY

Henry IV
Cardinal Richelieu
Thirty Years' War
Louis XIV
Jean-Baptiste Colbert
War of the Spanish Succession

▰ *WHY IT MATTERS TODAY*

Some nations today are still governed by a single ruler. Use CNNnews.com or other **current event** sources to find which nations are controlled by dictators or rulers with absolute power. Record your findings in your journal.

CNN student News.com

France in the Age of Absolutism

The Main Idea
Under the Bourbon kings, France became an absolute monarchy and Europe's leading power.

The Story Continues *Kings became stronger in Europe in the 1500s as the power of the church weakened. A French bishop explained just how strong monarchs were in the eyes of some: "Princes, thus, act as ministers of God, and as His lieutenants on earth. It is through them that He acts on His empire."*

Strengthening the Monarchy

From Navarre, a tiny kingdom in the Pyrenees Mountains between Spain and France, **Henry IV** came to the French throne in 1589. He was the first monarch of a new royal house—the Bourbons. Henry had been a Huguenot, a member of a Protestant minority group. However, he converted to Catholicism to help bring peace and unity to France. "Paris is well worth a mass!" he reportedly remarked. To protect the Huguenots, Henry issued the Edict of Nantes (NANTS). This order guaranteed freedom of worship and political rights and ended the religious wars.

Henry also tried to solve some of France's other major problems. Powerful nobles had weakened the central government of France in the 1500s. Henry worked to control the nobility and regain power.

However, one problem Henry could not fully solve was taxation. The burden of the French tax system was unfairly distributed, and many, including nobles and members of the clergy, were exempt from taxes altogether. People in large cities such as Paris were also exempt from the royal tax. The tax fell most heavily on members of the middle and lower classes. To improve the system, Henry placed the able Duke of Sully in charge of finances. Sully could not fix all the problems with the system, but he did end some of the abuses. More tax money thus went to the French treasury, and it was used to improve industry and trade.

Cardinal Richelieu. Henry IV was murdered in 1610. His son, Louis XIII, was just eight years old at the time. Louis's mother, Marie de Médicis, ruled as regent until Louis came to power in 1617. Louis was sickly and had trouble concentrating. To rule effectively, he chose wise advisers who provided strong leadership. Louis chose **Cardinal Richelieu** (RISH·uhl·oo) to be his chief minister.

Cardinal Richelieu ran the government of France from 1624 until 1642.

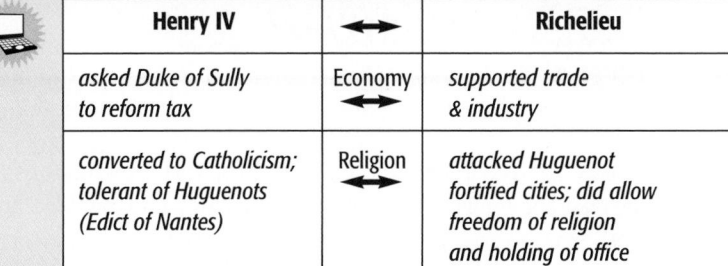

Henry IV	⟷	Richelieu
asked Duke of Sully to reform tax	Economy ⟷	*supported trade & industry*
converted to Catholicism; tolerant of Huguenots (Edict of Nantes)	Religion ⟷	*attacked Huguenot fortified cities; did allow freedom of religion and holding of office*
tried to limit power of nobles and increase power of the king	Nobles ⟷	*tried to limit power of nobles and increase power of the king*

Richelieu was a political genius who wanted to make the king supreme in France and France supreme in Europe. To strengthen the monarchy, Richelieu worked to take power away from the nobles and political rights away from the Huguenots. To strengthen France, he encouraged trade and industry.

Richelieu believed that the freedom given to the Huguenots by the Edict of Nantes was dangerous. The Huguenots lived in fortified cities that were like states within a state. They made a strong central government in France impossible. In 1627 Richelieu led military attacks on Huguenot towns. After a year the Huguenots asked for peace. Richelieu still allowed them to practice their religion and hold public office, but he took away their special rights in fortified cities.

Richelieu took further steps to centralize power under the crown. He strengthened the authority of regional representatives of the king. These officials, known as **intendants,** were the monarchy's representatives in the provinces that made up France. Over time, they took administrative and financial power away from regional governors and military leaders and concentrated it in the hands of the king.

The Thirty Years' War. In 1618 the **Thirty Years' War** began in Prague as a Protestant rebellion against the Holy Roman Empire. France, Denmark, and Sweden were all looking for ways to weaken the empire and its ruling family, the Habsburgs. Richelieu saw the war as a great opportunity to strengthen France.

Richelieu worked to keep the war going, but for the most part he kept France out of it directly. Thus, other European countries became weak from fighting while France stayed strong. Most of the war took place in Germany, ruining much of that country. France eventually joined in the fighting. By 1648 the French and their allies had accomplished most of their goals.

The war ended when the countries involved signed the Treaty of Westphalia in 1648. France was strengthened by receiving Alsace, a valuable territory along the Rhine River. The treaty also gave independence to the Netherlands and Switzerland. It made the German princes more or less independent of the Holy Roman Emperor. All these changes weakened the Holy Roman Empire and the Habsburg family.

✔ **READING CHECK: Comparing and Contrasting** How did the methods of Henry IV and Richelieu for strengthening France and the French monarchy compare? Both worked to reduce the strength of the nobles and to reform the economy.

The Sun King

In 1643 **Louis XIV** became the king of France. He ruled for 72 years, the longest reign in French history. As a boy, Louis XIV lived through the Fronde rebellions, when French nobles and peasants had attacked the central royal government. Perhaps because of this experience, Louis worked to make the king's power absolute.

Versailles. Louis built a huge palace at Versailles (ver·SY), a few miles outside of Paris, and moved the French government there. The beautiful and elaborate palace was so expensive to build that it strained the French economy. Versailles represented the grandeur and power of the monarchy and of France. This was important to Louis

INTERPRETING THE VISUAL RECORD

The Thirty Years' War This painting from the 1600s depicts the Battle of Diedenhofen, in which French troops were defeated. Eventually, however, France emerged from the war as a strong nation while much of Germany was devastated by fighting. **What modern weapons of warfare are the soldiers in the center of the picture using?**

VISUAL RECORD ANSWER

Students might suggest rifles and artillery.

Interdisciplinary Connection

LITERATURE. Alexandre Dumas's historical romance *The Three Musketeers,* written in the 1800s, is set in 1600s France. The main character, D'Artagnan, is based on an actual person, as are his three friends named by the title: Athos, Porthos, and Aramis. Cardinal Richelieu is also a character in the novel, which tells how a young D'Artagnan arrives in Paris desiring to become a guardsman of Louis XIII.

ACTIVITY: Invite students to read *The Three Musketeers* and/or watch a video of the movie (several versions have been made). Discuss how fact and fiction often become blurred when historical events are dramatized. Ask whether writers and filmmakers have an obligation to represent historical events truthfully. Why might they choose not to follow history exactly?

TEACH OBJECTIVE 2

LEVEL 2: Have students write a series of newspaper headlines that report the course of Louis XIV's policies and actions as king.

LEVEL 3: Ask students to prepare three oral presentations for the class showing how a peasant, a Huguenot, and a noble might have viewed Versailles. *(may have angered poor peasant class, may have been a symbol of excess and monarchical arrogance in the eyes of Huguenots, could have served as both palace and "prison" for nobles)*

HOMEWORK Write a paragraph that defines the phrase "divine right of kings" and explains its relationship to absolutism. Discuss whether you would like to live under an absolutist government.

Culture

Catherine de Medici introduced ballet into France in 1581, but under Louis XIV, ballet became a serious art form. He founded the first school for ballet in 1661. In 1681 female dancers first performed at the Paris Opera.

Ballet was performed during the prologue of plays such as the comedies of Molière, whom Louis XIV supported, as well as between the acts of plays. Open-air productions at Versailles for the king and his court would feature a lavishly decorated stage and a blaze of candlelight from several large chandeliers.

Louis also supported the Académie Royale des Sciences. Established in 1666, the academy promoted the exchange of new ideas.

Critical Thinking

In what ways did Louis XIV support the arts and sciences?

ANSWER: by founding school of ballet, sponsoring performances of ballet as well as plays of Molière and Royal Academy of Sciences

YOUNG PEOPLE IN HISTORY ANSWER

He was ignored by his mother, had to flee Paris, and suffered some hardship during the Fronde rebellion.

456

---

because he believed in the **divine right of kings**—that God had chosen him to rule the nation. "*L'état, c'est moi*" ("I am the state"), he proclaimed.

Louis used the palace to control the nobles. He insisted that the most important nobles live at Versailles. In this way, Louis could always keep his eye on them. The nobles could advance only by gaining Louis's favor.

Louis XIV's court at Versailles became the ideal for European royalty. Other monarchs soon took on the language and customs of France. Louis himself adopted the sun as his personal symbol. The sun's rays reached far and wide, just like his power. For this reason, Louis was nicknamed the Sun King.

Domestic and economic policies. For Louis, absolute power meant making most of the important decisions himself. As he once told his officials,

> **History Makers Speak**
> **"You will assist me with your counsels when I ask for them. I request and order you to seal no orders except by my command. I order you not to sign anything, not even a passport without my command; to render account to me personally each day and to favor no one."**
>
> Louis XIV, from *Louis XIV* by John B. Wolf

Analyzing Primary Sources

Identifying a Point of View
According to this quote, what role did Louis XIV see for his advisers and ministers? to report their actions to him and to administer fairly

YOUNG PEOPLE IN HISTORY

The Boy King
Louis XIV became the king of France at the age of four. Although he was surrounded by the luxury of the French court, the first years of his reign were not easy. When he was just nine, Louis had to flee Paris when the Fronde rebellions broke out between the French nobility and the crown. From 1648 to 1652, Louis kept moving through France, suffering from hunger, cold, and fear. The memory of that hardship stayed with Louis forever. He never again trusted the people of Paris or the nobility. **How did Louis XIV's childhood affect his rule?**

Throughout his long reign, Louis XIV was directly involved in the day-to-day operations of the French government. He also chose able advisers who, for the most part, worked under his direct supervision. One of the best of these was **Jean-Baptiste Colbert** (kawl·BAIR), an expert in finance. Colbert, a well-educated member of the middle class, followed strong policies to promote economic development in France. He aimed to increase French industry at home and to build French trade abroad. Colbert granted government subsidies to private companies to build new industries or to strengthen existing ones. He placed high tariffs on foreign imports in an effort to protect French businesses, and worked to improve transportation. Colbert also encouraged French companies to establish colonies and to carry on trade with Canada, the West Indies, and East Asia. In addition, he took strong steps to eliminate corruption and waste in the French tax-collection system.

Colbert's efforts on behalf of the crown met with varying degrees of success. He worked to reform the nation's tax system by making it more evenly distributed across the population. Colbert's aim was to make the system more fair by eliminating some of the exemptions granted to the privileged. Under his administration trade and commerce grew, and France became a leading economic power in Europe. Colbert was able to raise government income to pay for economic improvements, the large and powerful French army, and overseas exploration. At the same time France became a leading naval power and a strong force in overseas trade and colonization.

Louis XIV was concerned with religious unity. He believed that the Huguenots disturbed the unity of France and weakened the authority of the central government. Thus, in 1685 he did away with the Edict of Nantes, ending France's policy of tolerance for Protestants. More than 200,000 Huguenots fled France rather than become Catholics. Because the Huguenots had been productive citizens, their loss weakened France in the long run.

✔ **READING CHECK: Identifying Cause and Effect** How did the behavior and policies of Louis XIV strengthen the monarchy but hurt France in some ways? worked effectively to make royal power absolute, but caused France to lose many productive citizens through religious intolerance

TEACH OBJECTIVE 3

LEVEL 1: Have students write the heads *Reasons* and *Results* on a sheet of paper. Ask students what Louis XIV hoped to accomplish by going to war and list these reasons. *(increase territory, establish natural border to the east)* Then prompt them to list the results of these wars on France. *(cost in money and in lives)*
ENGLISH LANGUAGE LEARNERS

CLOSE

Ask students to explain why the Treaty of Utrecht was important for both Europe and America. *(Europe: France and Spain would never have the same ruler; America: Great Britain gained French territory in North America)* Have students point out on a map the location of settlements and territories established by French explorers in North America. *(e.g., Quebec, the St. Lawrence Valley, the Great Lakes region, Louisiana, Haiti)*

The Wars of Louis XIV

Louis reorganized and increased the size of France's military. Soldiers were well trained and discipline was strict. By the early 1700s the French had a force of about 400,000 soldiers—the most powerful army in Europe.

Fighting for new territory. Louis believed France's security depended on the country having natural frontiers. Much of France already had such borders. The Atlantic Ocean, the Pyrenees Mountains, the Alps, and the Mediterranean Sea surrounded much of France. Louis wanted to extend France's territory east to the Rhine River to form another natural border. To accomplish this, he fought four wars between 1667 and 1713.

Louis's goals alarmed other European nations, leading many to ally with one another against France. During the 1660s and the 1670s, the Netherlands, England, and Sweden formed alliances against France, as did Austria, Brandenburg, and Spain. These countries worked to achieve a **balance of power,** in which countries have equal strength in order to prevent any one country from dominating the others.

The wars took a toll on France's resources. After Louis's third war ended in 1679, France was under great financial strain.

War of the Spanish Succession. Louis XIV's last war was the **War of the Spanish Succession.** It was fought over who would become the next king of Spain. The last Spanish Habsburg king died in 1700, leaving the throne to Philip V, Louis's grandson. The other European nations did not like the idea of both France and Spain being

The golden fountain at Louis XIV's palace of Versailles symbolizes the French monarchy at its height.

The Growth of France under Louis XIV, 1643–1715

Interpreting Maps Louis XIV made France a large and powerful nation and added to its territory.

■ **Skills Assessment: 1. Physical Systems** What natural boundaries surrounded much of France? **2. Drawing Inferences** What city in southeastern France remained outside of Louis's control? Why might that be so?

France, 1643   Territory added, 1643–1715

Global Relations

Although the concept of the balance of power was directed under Louis XIV in the mid-1600s, it can be traced to Greece in the 400s and Italy in the 1400s. The success of the balance of power depended on nations agreeing to maintain equilibrium of power among many rivals. A change in alliance could be demanded of a national government at any time in order to maintain the balance. Balance of power characterized the European international system until 1914. The events of World War I and World War II caused the system to lose influence as world views and ideological differences between nations emerged.

ACTIVITY: Have students suggest examples of balance of power among nations today.

REVIEW

Have students complete the Section 1 Review on p. 458.

ASSESS

Have students complete Daily Quiz 19.1. As Alternative Assessment, you may want to use the newspaper headline exercise or homework assignment in this section's lessons.

RETEACH

Have students complete Main Idea Activity for English Language Learners and Special-Needs Students 19.1. Then have students

summarize the strengthening of the French monarchy.
ENGLISH LANGUAGE LEARNERS

EXTEND

Have students work together to draw a detailed map or build a model of the palace and gardens of Versailles. Others can research and produce illustrated displays of its art, dance, music, literature, dress, and social etiquette. **BLOCK SCHEDULING, COOPERATIVE LEARNING**

SECTION 1 REVIEW ANSWERS

① Define
- intendants, p. 455
- divine right of kings, p. 456
- balance of power, p. 457

② Identifying
- Henry IV, p. 454
- Cardinal Richelieu, p. 454
- Thirty Years' War, p. 455
- Louis XIV, p. 455
- Jean-Baptiste Colbert, p. 456
- War of the Spanish Succession, p. 457

③ In: limited nobles, tax reform, strengthened industry and commerce; Outside: strong army and navy, expanded territory, established colonies

④ a. Richelieu weakened nobility by placing intendants in provinces; Louis XIV forced nobles to live at Versailles under his watch.

b. European nations formed alliances to balance power so that France would not dominate them.

c. good: improved French security by extending to natural borders, put French monarch in Spain; not good: cost in lives and resources

⑤ Writing may suggest: Louis—a boy; Marie—her own agenda; France—needed political stability; Richelieu—personal ambition

Louis XIV encouraged improvements in much of French society, from art and literature to transportation.

under Bourbon rulers. They battled Louis's forces in Europe, in North America, and at sea. The French met defeat after defeat. Finally Louis agreed to a settlement in 1713.

The war ended with the Treaty of Utrecht, an important document for both Europe and America. The treaty recognized Louis's grandson as king of Spain, but it provided that the French and Spanish monarchies could never be united. The treaty also gave French lands in North America to Great Britain.

Louis XIV's legacy. With the Treaty of Utrecht, France began to lose some of the empire it had built up in the 1500s. Before Louis's reign, French explorers such as Jacques Cartier had already made several voyages to North America. Samuel de Champlain had founded the city of Quebec, and several other settlements were established in the St. Lawrence Valley and the Great Lakes region. The French ran a profitable fur trade and fishing industry in North America.

Under Louis XIV, the French explorer René-Robert Cavelier de La Salle sailed down the Mississippi River to the Gulf of Mexico, claiming the inland region of North America for France. He named this area Louisiana in honor of Louis XIV. The French also occupied Haiti and other West Indian islands. They set up colonies in Asia and controlled part of India.

Louis XIV's wars, however, took a toll. The continuing military effort cost many lives and placed a heavy strain on the French treasury. Yet despite his setbacks, Louis made France a very powerful nation. During these years Great Britain became a major colonial power. Within Europe, however, France was viewed by many as the leading continental power.

After Louis died in 1715, the nobles won back many of the powers he had taken from them. Louis's great-grandson, Louis XV, became king and ruled from 1715 to 1774. Louis XV and his successor, Louis XVI, were comparatively weak rulers. The French government appeared stable, but in fact the royal authority was in decline.

✔ **READING CHECK: Evaluating** In what ways did France both benefit and suffer as a result of the wars Louis XIV started? France became a leading European power; caused destruction, loss of life and resources, loss of territory

SECTION 1 REVIEW

1. **Define** and explain the significance:
   intendants
   divine right of kings
   balance of power

2. **Identify** and explain the significance:
   Henry IV
   Cardinal Richelieu
   Thirty Years' War
   Louis XIV
   Jean-Baptiste Colbert
   War of the Spanish Succession

3. **Analyzing Information** Copy the model below. Use it to list steps that Louis XIV took both within and outside of France to strengthen the country.

   In France

   Outside France

4. **Finding the Main Idea**

   a. In what ways did Louis XIV's approach to controlling the French nobility differ from that taken by Cardinal Richelieu?

   b. What role did the balance of power play in Europe when Louis XIV reigned?

   c. Were the wars that France fought under Louis XIV good for the country? Explain your answer.

5. **Writing and Critical Thinking**

   Problem Solving Write a dialogue between Cardinal Richelieu and Marie de Medici about how much power Richelieu should have as Louis XIII's chief minister.
   Consider:
   - how old Louis XIII was at that time
   - what Marie de Medici may have wanted
   - what France needed at that time
   - Richelieu's aims

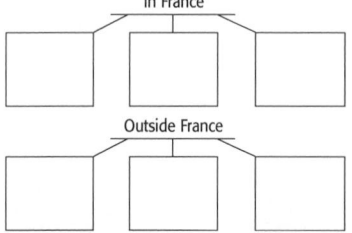

Homework Practice Online
keyword: SP3 HP19

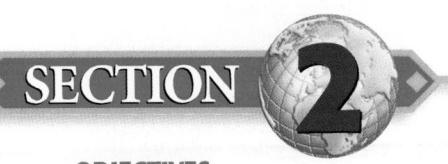

🔔 LET'S GET STARTED!

As students enter the classroom, ask them to write a player's guide for an Absolute Monarchy game by listing the goals a player should strive for, using Louis XIV and France as a model. *(Students' responses will vary but may include limiting the power of the nobility, building a strong central government, establishing a robust economy, and developing a strong military.)* Tell students that in Section 2 they will learn about two monarchs who "played this game" in Russia—Peter the Great and Catherine the Great.

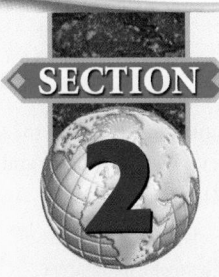

SECTION 2

Russia in the Age of Absolutism

The Main Idea
Under two great rulers, Peter and Catherine, Russia became a westernized and powerful nation.

The Story Continues *Louis XIV had his Versailles, but in 1703 the Russian czar Peter the Great had an entire city. St. Petersburg, Russia's "window to the West," was built to show how Peter modeled his government, as well as much of Russian society, after the western European monarchies. The wide boulevards, magnificent palaces, and outstanding examples of architecture and engineering characteristic of St. Petersburg make for a beautiful city even today.*

READ TO DISCOVER

❶ In what ways was Russia isolated from western Europe?

❷ How did Peter the Great use his power to change Russia?

❸ How did Catherine the Great expand Russia's territory?

IDENTIFY

Michael Romanov
Peter the Great
Catherine the Great

▶ **WHY IT MATTERS TODAY**

Peter and Catherine the Great were strong, absolutist rulers. Today Russia does not have such a strong ruler. Use CNNstudentNews.com or other **current event** sources to learn about how Russia is currently ruled. Record your findings in your journal.

Isolation and a New Dynasty

Several factors, both cultural and geographic, separated Russia from western Europe. For one, before 1480 much of Russia had been under Mongol rule for about 200 years, and thus had an Asian influence. For another, Western civilization had reached Russia through Constantinople and the Byzantine Empire, not from western Europe itself. Thus Russia's religion was Eastern Orthodox rather than Roman Catholic or Protestant. In addition, Russia used the Cyrillic alphabet. This made it hard to communicate with the rest of Europe, which used the Roman alphabet.

Most importantly, Russia's geography separated it from the rest of Europe. The country was almost entirely landlocked. The stronger kingdoms of Sweden and Poland blocked Russia off from the Baltic Sea. To the south, the Ottoman Turks controlled the coast of the Black Sea. To the west, the vast plains of Poland and eastern Europe hurt trade and commercial contact with Europeans. None of Russia's rivers flowed into the seas where trade took place.

Like some monarchs in western Europe, however, Ivan the Terrible had centered absolute power and authority on himself—the czar. After Ivan died in 1584, Russia went through a period of unrest. Nobles fought for power, and neighboring countries invaded. Then in 1613, the Russian national assembly elected **Michael Romanov** to be czar. Romanov was the grandnephew of Ivan IV. The Romanov family was large, powerful, and wealthy. It traced its origins to a nobleman who had lived in Moscow during the 1300s. Romanov czars ruled Russia for the next 300 years, during which the country became a leading European power.

The Romanovs sought to build the power of the czar. They suppressed protests by a religious group called the Old Believers, who opposed recent church reforms. The Romanovs established relations with groups of Cossack peoples who lived in southern Russia and the Ukraine. Over time, these people came under Moscow's rule.

The Cap of Monomach, pictured here, was used to crown czars from 1498 to 1682. It is studded with gems and trimmed with sable.

SECTION 2 RESOURCES

REPRODUCIBLE RESOURCES

▶ Guided Reading Strategy 19.2

▶ Readings in World History 60: The Great Czar

TECHNOLOGY RESOURCES

▶ One-Stop Planner 19.2

▶ Holt Researcher: World History: Catherine the Great

▶ CNN Presents World Cultures: Yesterday and Today Segment 16: Restoring St. Petersburg

▶ Homework Practice Online

▶ Online Maps, Charts, and Graphs: Russian Expansion, 1533–1689

▶ Online Maps, Charts, and Graphs: Russian Expansion, 1533–1725

REINFORCEMENT, REVIEW, AND ASSESSMENT

▶ Section 2 Review, p. 464

▶ Daily Quiz 19.2

▶ Main Idea Activity 19.2

▶ English Audio Summary 19.2

▶ Spanish Audio Summary 19.2

ALL LEVELS: Copy the following chart on the board, omitting the italicized answers. Have students copy it and complete it as they read the section "Isolation and a New Dynasty." Then ask volunteers to fill in details on the board.

ENGLISH LANGUAGE LEARNERS

Russian Isolation
Cultural Causes ⟶ Effects

Mongol rule ⟶	*Asian, rather than Western, influence*

Contact through Constantinople & Byzantine Empire ⟶
Eastern Orthodox, not Roman Catholic or Protestant

Cyrillic alphabet ⟶ *hindered communication*

Geographic Causes ⟶ Effect

landlocked; surrounded by powers, vast plains

no rivers flowed into seas where trade took place ⟶ *limited trade, contact*

Linking Past to Present

Peter made St. Petersburg his capital in 1712, but Russia's capital returned to Moscow after the Bolsheviks seized power in 1917. After Lenin's death in 1924, the communists renamed the city Leningrad. With the collapse of communism and the breakup of the Soviet Union, Leningrad became St. Petersburg once more in 1991.

St. Petersburg remains an important cultural center in Russia. The city is home to the world-famous Mariinsky Ballet and the Hermitage, a museum housed in the Winter Palace of Catherine the Great.

Critical Thinking

Why would a government move a capital city and rename a city?

ANSWER: Students will likely see that a name has meaning and honors who or what the city is named after. Peter would want his capital named after himself. Communists would want to reject the imperial history suggested by the name St. Petersburg.

MAP ANSWER

Sea of Azov, Black Sea, and Caspian Sea

Thus the Romanovs continued and strengthened absolutism in Russia. In 1682 Peter I became czar at the age of 10. At first he shared power with his half brother and half sister. Then in 1689 Peter became the sole leader of Russia.

✔ **READING CHECK: Summarizing** What factors kept Russia isolated from the rest of Europe in the 1500s and 1600s? Asian influence, religious differences, geographic separation

Peter the Great

Czar Peter I, or **Peter the Great,** ruled Russia until 1725. Like Ivan, he could be ruthless. Yet Peter was also a leader of great vision. Above all, he believed that Russia had to become more like the rest of Europe.

Peter's foreign mission. One of Peter's major goals was to end Russia's landlocked situation. He wanted to acquire warm-water ports on the Sea of Azov and the Black Sea. However, these areas were controlled by the Ottoman Empire. To defeat the Turks, Peter needed a stronger Russia. He also knew that he would need help from western Europe.

In 1697 Peter, disguised as a private citizen, visited several western European countries. Peter's goal was to negotiate an alliance against the Ottoman Turks. He failed in this goal, but he learned many things about the West. He met with leading scientists and artisans. He even worked as a carpenter in a Dutch shipyard to learn about shipbuilding.

Westernizing Russia. Peter reorganized Russia along western European lines. Influenced by France, Peter improved his army's training and weaponry. In 1700 he started a long war with Sweden. When Russia finally won in 1721, it gained territory on the east coast of the Gulf of Finland. Now Russia had access to the Baltic Sea. In this new territory Peter built a completely new city, St. Petersburg. He moved the capital from Moscow to St. Petersburg, closer to the nations of western Europe. St. Petersburg represented the new, westernized Russia. Peter undertook a major building program to construct the city along Western architectural styles. He wanted St. Petersburg to be viewed as the capital of a progressive nation.

Westernization included social changes. Women became less socially isolated and took a greater part in the community. Peter forced the nobles to shave off their long beards and dress in European styles. Also important were the changes Peter made to Russia's government and economy. He modernized the army and reformed the government's administration. He also encouraged manufacturing and foreign trade.

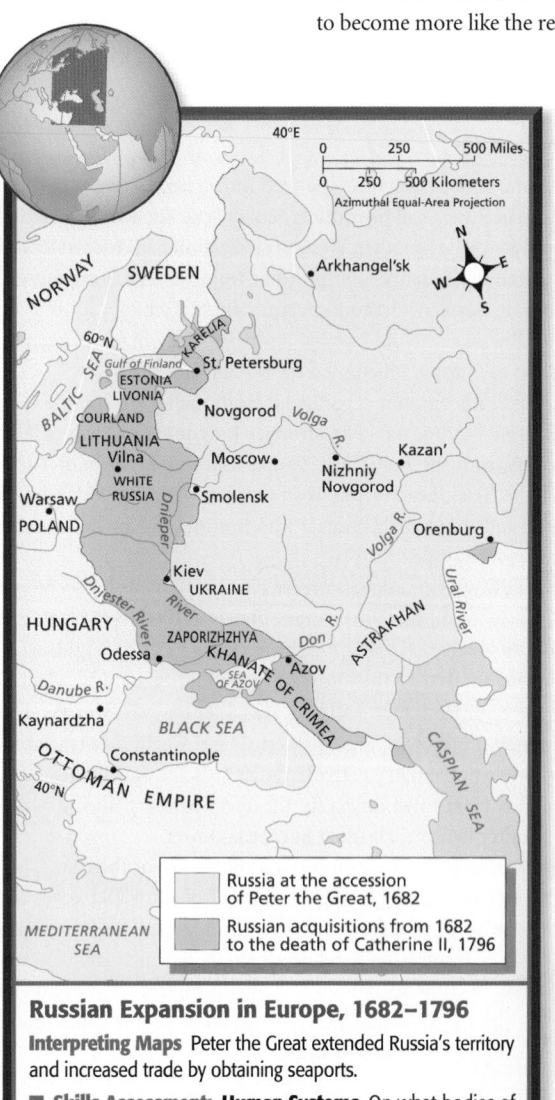

Russian Expansion in Europe, 1682–1796

Interpreting Maps Peter the Great extended Russia's territory and increased trade by obtaining seaports.

■ **Skills Assessment: Human Systems** On what bodies of water were ports established?

	Russia at the accession of Peter the Great, 1682
	Russian acquisitions from 1682 to the death of Catherine II, 1796

LEVEL 3: Invite students to imagine they are French teenagers in the 1700s visiting Russia with a grandparent. Tell them their grandparent has visited Russia in the past, but this visit is the first since Czar Peter I tried to westernize the country. Ask students to create a travel journal, recording their observations as well as any surprises their grandparent encounters. Encourage them to use the library and the Internet for research.

Spotlight on GOVERNMENT

Remind students that in *The Prince*, Niccolò Machiavelli argued that it is safer for a monarch to be feared than to be loved. Ask students whether Peter the Great was more loved or feared. Note that Peter's great accomplishments, such as St. Petersburg, contrast with his disregard for the profound human suffering he caused. Discuss whether glorious ends justify brutal means. **BLOCK SCHEDULING**

SKILL-BUILDING STRATEGIES Drawing Inferences

Understanding Peter the Great

When you study history, you read primary and secondary sources to understand the facts of an event or the actions of a historical person. Behind those facts or those actions, however, is even more information. By reading "between the lines," you can find information that is only implied. Reading between the lines involves using reasoning ability to identify something that the writer does not actually state. This identification is an inference. Such a process is often very useful in understanding a historical person's personality. You can often infer things about the person from his or her actions.

Portrait of Peter the Great dressed as a shipwright

Primary and Secondary Sources

The passage below includes both primary and secondary information about Peter the Great.

Believing that the best way to learn was by doing, Peter traveled to the West, where, for example, he worked in a Dutch shipyard to learn shipbuilding. Likewise, in England he impressed his hosts with his willingness to work with his hands. As one bishop recorded:

"He is mechanically turned, and seems designed by nature rather to be a ship carpenter than a great prince; this was his chief study and exercise while he stayed here; he wrought much with his own hands, and made all about him work at the models of ships."

This image depicts Peter the Great (front) studying the elements of shipbuilding.

Science, Technology & Society

In 1696 Peter the Great sent 50 young people from Russia to England, Venice, and Holland to study shipbuilding and fortifications. Disguised as a diplomat, Czar Peter himself went on a learning tour of Europe and worked incognito in a Dutch shipbuilding yard.

On returning to Russia, Peter introduced Arabic numerals, simplified the Cyrillic alphabet, and founded the first Russian-language newspaper.

Critical Thinking

Why do you think the young people were sent to study shipbuilding and fortifications, rather than art and music?

ANSWER: Shipbuilding would enable Russia to build naval and trading ships. Fortifications would enable Peter to protect his borders and cities.

SKILLS PRACTICE ANSWERS

1. as a man: valued learning and hard work; as a monarch: valued cultural exchange, modernization, improvement

2. Answers will vary.

Skills Reminder

To draw inferences, determine the main idea or literal interpretation of the writing. Then look for clues that suggest additional meaning. Such clues might take the form of key phrases, emotional words, or active and colorful descriptions. These may signal that additional meaning is buried "between the lines" of the document. Add these clues to your original understanding of the document to create a revised interpretation based on both the stated ideas and the implied ideas. Finally, analyze the document to develop conclusions.

Skills Practice

❶ Read the primary and secondary sources above. You might also use the images of Peter to infer additional meaning. Then write two or three descriptions about Peter the Great that are not directly stated. What type of man was he? What type of monarch was he?

❷ Read a political article in the newspaper or listen to a televised news program that focuses on a political issue. Then list several facts and any inferences you can draw from the article or program.

Government

Many of the changes introduced by Peter resulted directly from his war with Sweden. The long war required a steady supply of troops, which necessitated a conscription system and hence a census. Experts were needed to train the new troops. The need for weapons meant that mines had to be opened, forges built, and transportation systems developed.

HISTORY MAKER

Peter the Great (1672–1725)

Peter the Great used his absolute authority to change his country. Under his rule Russia became a major European power, able to compete with most western European nations. **How did Peter change Russia's standing with the rest of the world?**

Peter followed the absolutist ideas of Louis XIV of France, but because Russia was different from France, he was able to take them even further. He had complete control of a highly centralized government. Peter took measures to control the nobility, so that ultimately the nobles acted only as his agents. Even the Orthodox Church came under Peter's control.

Peter created a new system of nobility—a "service nobility"—in which the individual noble's rank depended on the performance of government service. In exchange for this service, the czar granted individual nobles large estates with thousands of serfs. He thereby increased the number of serfs in Russia and worsened their condition. Now the serfs were bound not only to the land but also to their lords. The nobles who received these grants, in turn, were bound to the czar with ties of personal dependence and loyalty. Their aristocratic lifestyles hinged entirely upon Peter's good will and appreciation, and they were much more likely to support the czar and his absolute power over the state.

Peter's reforms and his actions to achieve absolute power caused strong resentment among many Russians. The Russian Orthodox Church, for example, objected to his interference in traditional church practices and to his drive to control the clergy at every level. Many Russian nobles, moreover, were angered by Peter's moves to restructure the government and to centralize power in his own hands. During the course of his reign, Peter elevated the army, making it one of the government's most powerful institutions. Like Louis XIV in France, he sought to increase control over the nobles by restricting their freedom of movement and by isolating them from others. Peter required many of his most powerful nobles to build homes in St. Petersburg. There they were obliged to spend a great deal of time at court, where they could be kept under Peter's watchful eye. Despite the opposition of powerful Russian groups, however, the czar pushed ahead with his reforms.

Peter failed to westernize Russian society completely. However, under his leadership Russia became a great power. At Peter's funeral, the Archbishop of Novgorod—a loyal adviser to the czar—praised him in Biblical terms:

History Makers Speak

❝We are burying Peter the Great! Contrary to everybody's wishes and hopes he has come to his life's end, he who has been the cause of our innumerable good fortunes and joys; who has raised Russia as if from among the dead and elevated her to such heights of power and glory; . . . He was your Samson, Russia . . . He was your Moses . . . O Russia, he was your Solomon, who received from the Lord reason and wisdom in great plenty. . . . Most distinguished man! Can a short oration encompass his immeasurable glory?❞

Feofan Prokopovich, from *Peter the Great Changes Russia,* edited by Marc Raeff

✔ **READING CHECK: Identifying Cause and Effect** How did Peter's rule change Russia? Russia became somewhat westernized, modernized; became a major European power

Catherine the Great

Peter was succeeded by his second wife, Catherine I. Other Romanov rulers followed. Peter's grandson, Peter III, married Catherine II, a German princess. Peter III was unpopular and in 1762 was murdered by nobles who supported Catherine II. Known as **Catherine the Great,** she ruled from 1762 to 1796.

TEACH OBJECTIVE 3

LEVEL 1: Refer students to the map on this page. Note the territory that was gained under Catherine. On a world map, have students locate this same area as well as the Crimea and northern shore of the Black Sea, acquired by Catherine from the Turks. Finally, have students trace the eastern expansion of Russia across Siberia and into Alaska. **ENGLISH LANGUAGE LEARNERS**

CLOSE

Ask students whether everyone in Russia thought that Peter and Catherine were "great." Discuss the meaning of the term as used historically to denote importance, strength, and power, and not necessarily goodness or merit. Ask whether students would consider Peter and Catherine great leaders.

Catherine's policies. Catherine supported art, science, literature, and theater. These efforts meant nothing, however, to most Russians, who lived in great poverty and ignorance. In fact, Catherine extended serfdom into new Russian territories. The common people therefore remained poor. The nobles, meanwhile, thrived and became more westernized. Many began speaking French and lost touch with the Russian people.

Catherine's real greatness and her most important contributions to Russia's development lay in her foreign policy. She continued the expansion begun by Peter the Great. Russia still wanted control of the Sea of Azov and the Black Sea. In a successful war against the Turks, Catherine gained control of most of the northern shore of the Black Sea and the region of the Crimea.

Poland. Catherine also gained new territory to the west. The kingdom of Poland was large but weak. Polish nobles argued with each other over electing a king. Their legislature was not efficient. Historically, moreover, Poland had seen much conflict with people of different ethnic and religious backgrounds. This tended to promote suspicion of others. Most Poles were Roman Catholic, and their leaders often discriminated against other groups. Sometimes these minority groups would ask Prussia, Austria, or Russia for help. In 1772 these three nations took advantage of Poland's weakened condition. All three seized slices of Polish territory for themselves in an action known as the First Partition of Poland.

Polish attempts to strengthen their nation failed. In 1793 Russia and Prussia took over more Polish lands in the Second Partition. With the Third Partition in 1795, Russia, Prussia, and Austria divided what was left. Poland disappeared from the map of Europe until 1919.

Holt Researcher

go.hrw.com
KEYWORD: Holt Researcher
FreeFind:
   Catherine the Great
After reading more about Catherine the Great on the Holt Researcher, write a short essay describing her political, economic, and cultural influence on Russia.

That's Interesting!

Catherine the Great was just 16 years old when she married Peter III in 1745. It was a political marriage, and the couple soon was estranged. In 1754 she had a son, Paul, and although the public position was that Peter was the father, he was not. A coup overthrew Peter III. Although Paul was next in line to the throne, Catherine seized power, declared herself empress, and ruled ruthlessly. As an adult, Paul openly opposed his mother's policies, and Catherine tried to arrange for the throne to pass to his son. Paul successfully fought this attempt and became czar upon his mother's death in 1796.

internet connect

TOPIC: Peter the Great and Catherine the Great
GO TO: go.hrw.com
KEYWORD: SP3 WH19

Have students access the Internet through the HRW Go site to research Peter the Great and Catherine the Great. Ask them to create a pamphlet about Peter and Catherine's effects on Russian society.

MAP ANSWER
Russia

The Partitions of Poland, 1772–1795

☐ Boundary of Poland before the partitions	▨ Territory acquired by Russia
▨ Poland	▨ Territory acquired by Austria
	▨ Territory acquired by Prussia

0   150   300 Miles
0   150   300 Kilometers
Azimuthal Equal-Area Projection

Interpreting Maps Poland was divided among Russia, Austria, and Prussia in a series of three partitions.
■ **Skills Assessment: The World in Spatial Terms** By 1795, which country had acquired most of Poland?

REVIEW

Have students complete the Section 2 Review on p. 464.

ASSESS

Have students complete Daily Quiz 19.2. As Alternative Assessment, you may want to use the travel journal or homework assignment in this section's lessons.

RETEACH

Have students complete Main Idea Activity for English Language Learners and Special-Needs Students 19.2. Then ask students to list five ways in which Peter and Catherine changed Russia.
ENGLISH LANGUAGE LEARNERS

EXTEND

Louis XIV adopted the sun as his personal symbol and considered himself the Sun King. Invite students to invent appropriate symbols and slogans for Peter the Great and Catherine the Great. They might make posters or create Web site pages.
BLOCK SCHEDULING

HISTORY MAKER ANSWER
support of the Russian nobles

SECTION 2 REVIEW ANSWERS

❶ Identify
- Michael Romanov, p. 459
- Peter the Great, p. 460
- Catherine the Great, p. 462

❷ Peter–Strengths: westernized Russia, centralized government, modernized army; Weaknesses: disregard for serfs, Russian resentment of his absolute power hurt economy; Catherine–Strengths: expanded Russia's borders, supported arts; Weaknesses: extended serfdom, few social reforms

❸ a. cultural exchange, expansion of territory, importing Western ways

b. Both had absolute control of highly centralized government and monitored nobles and church.

❹ Answers will vary but should include that serfdom extended into new territories; nobles enjoyed arts, literature, theater, while no relief provided from poverty for serfs, no opportunities for basic literacy

---

HISTORY MAKER

Catherine The Great (1729–1796)

Although born in Germany, Catherine the Great dedicated herself to Russia and its growth. She was in touch with western European ideas about political reforms. She considered a new law code that would make all people equal before the law.

However, Catherine knew that her power depended on the support of the Russian nobles. Thus, instead of focusing on social reforms within Russia, Catherine concentrated on making Russia one of the great European powers. **What political factor influenced Catherine's decisions about affairs within Russia?**

With her successes in the Black Sea and Poland, Catherine added more than 200,000 square miles to her empire. Russia's borders now reached well into central Europe. Russia had become a force to consider in the European balance of power.

Expansion eastward. Russia's expansion differed from that of western European nations. Instead of expanding overseas, Russia successfully expanded overland. Even before Catherine, Russian settlers, led by Cossacks, moved eastward. In 1581 the Cossacks captured the Mongol city of Sibir. This gave Russia access to Siberia, the huge region east of the Ural Mountains. Here, a rich fur trade attracted growing numbers of settlers. Much like the pioneers of the American West, the early Russian settlers in Siberia built small posts for trade and defense. Despite the harsh climate of the region, many of these settlements thrived and became important links in Russia's continuing economic development. The opening of Siberia, with its wealth of natural resources and its vast space, added much to Russia's growing power and influence.

At the Amur River, Russians came into contact with the Chinese, who resisted Russian expansion into their lands. In 1689 the two nations signed a treaty that fixed the Amur River as the border between them and established trade relations.

By 1741 the Russians had crossed the Bering Strait to North America. They set up a colony in Alaska. Later Russian trading posts expanded southward.

✔ **READING CHECK: Drawing Inferences** In what ways was Catherine more skilled in foreign, rather than domestic, policy? domestic policies were meaningless or harmful to most Russians, but foreign policies won new territory and extended the Russian empire

Catherine the Great's horse-drawn coach reflected the luxury and wealth of the Russian court.

SECTION 2 REVIEW

1. Identify and explain the significance:
Michael Romanov
Peter the Great
Catherine the Great

2. Comparing and Contrasting Make a chart like the one below. List the strengths and the weaknesses of Peter the Great and Catherine the Great.

Peter	Catherine
Strengths	Strengths
Weaknesses	Weaknesses

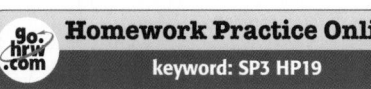
Homework Practice Online
keyword: SP3 HP19

3. � **Finding the Main Idea**

a. How did Russia overcome its isolation from Europe?

b. In what ways were Peter and Catherine the Great absolute monarchs?

4. ▕ **Writing and Critical Thinking**

Supporting a Point of View Write a brief essay from the point of view of the serfs in Russia under Catherine the Great. Explain why, in your opinion, Catherine was not "great."
Consider:
• how conditions changed for Russian serfs under Catherine's rule
• the gap between Catherine's treatment of the nobility and the serfs
• why Catherine might be considered "great"

464

464 CHAPTER 19

OBJECTIVES

1 **Explain how the Habsburgs gained and held power.**

2 **Explain how the Hohenzollerns rose to power.**

3 **Identify the factors that contributed to conflicts between Prussia and Austria.**

🔊 LET'S GET STARTED!

As students enter the classroom, ask them to write a summary in the form of a paragraph or graphic organizer of the conflicts and conquests that took place under Louis XIV, Peter the Great, and Catherine the Great. Explain that Central Europe saw struggles for territory and power similar to those that were taking place in France and Russia at about the same time. Tell students that in Section 3 they will learn how the Habsburgs of Austria and the Hohenzollerns of Prussia vied for power in Central Europe.

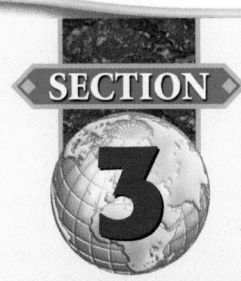

SECTION 3

READ TO DISCOVER

❶ How did the Habsburgs gain and hold power?

❷ How did the Hohenzollerns rise to power?

❸ What factors contributed to the conflicts between Prussia and Austria?

IDENTIFY

Maria Theresa
Pragmatic Sanction
Great Elector
Frederick William I
Frederick the Great
Diplomatic Revolution
Seven Years' War

▶ WHY IT MATTERS TODAY

The map of Europe has been drawn and redrawn almost countless times. Use CNNfyi.com or other **current event** sources to compare national boundaries today with those mapped in this chapter. Record your findings in your journal.

CNN Student News.com

Central Europe in the Age of Absolutism

The Main Idea
The Habsburgs of Austria and the Hohenzollerns of Prussia vied for power in Central Europe.

The Story Continues *The Habsburgs had risen from a family of local princes with little influence beyond their immediate region to become one of the most powerful families in Europe and the rulers of Austria. A typical day in the life of one Habsburg monarch of Austria, Maria Theresa, meant consulting with ministers, giving audience to courtiers and visitors, reading, and spending time with family, including her numerous children.*

Habsburg Austria

The Austrian Habsburgs lost much territory in Germany during the Thirty Years' War in the early 1600s. Over the next 100 years, however, they acquired new lands, both from the Turks and as a result of the Treaty of Utrecht. The Habsburg empire now stretched into the Balkans, Hungary, and the Italian Peninsula.

In 1740 the Holy Roman Emperor Charles VI died, leaving only his 23-year-old daughter **Maria Theresa** to inherit Austria and the other Habsburg lands. In some of these lands the law stated that the inheritance had to go to a male. Therefore, before his death Charles urged other European rulers to accept a statement called the **Pragmatic Sanction.** This agreement would allow Maria Theresa to inherit all the Habsburg lands. The laws of the Holy Roman Empire also prevented her from being elected empress. She became empress in 1745 when her husband was elected emperor.

Maria Theresa's empire was a patchwork of regions and peoples. It included Belgians, Bohemians, Croatians, Germans, Hungarians, Italians, Poles, Romanians, Serbs, and Slovenes. This variety led to many conflicts of language, religion, and nationality. Several German states became resentful of the Habsburgs' power. For example, Bavaria, which is located in southern Germany, jealously guarded its lands and independence. At times, Bavaria allied with France against the Habsburgs. Austria's chief rival was the small but rising north German state of Brandenburg-Prussia. The character and size of the Habsburg empire, with its geographic, cultural, and historic diversity, made it extremely difficult to rule effectively.

✔ **READING CHECK: Drawing Inferences**
What factors made it difficult for the Habsburgs to rule? geographic and cultural differences, jealousy and resistance to Habsburg rule among some German states

Maria Theresa made improvements in education, medicine, and military affairs.

SECTION 3 RESOURCES

REPRODUCIBLE RESOURCES

▶ Guided Reading Strategy 19.3

TECHNOLOGY RESOURCES

▶ One-Stop Planner 19.3

▶ Homework Practice Online

REINFORCEMENT, REVIEW, AND ASSESSMENT

▶ Section 3 Review, p. 469

▶ Daily Quiz 19.3

▶ Main Idea Activity 19.3

▶ English Audio Summary 19.3

▶ Spanish Audio Summary 19.3

LEVELS 1 AND 2: Have students use a map of Europe to locate the nations/regions that the Habsburgs controlled in 1740. *(includes what is now Austria, Hungary, the Czech Republic, part of the Balkans, part of the Italian peninsula, the Netherlands)* Ask students to summarize how Maria Theresa came to power over such a patchwork empire *(was only successor of Holy Roman Emperor Charles VI, who had other rulers accept the Pragmatic Sanction, allowing Maria to inherit Habsburg lands)* **ENGLISH LANGUAGE LEARNERS**

LEVEL 3: Have students list some of the problems facing Maria Theresa. *(gender prejudice, ethnic conflicts, scattered empire, resentment of power, alliances against Austria, growing rivalry with Prussia)* Ask them to imagine how a ruler in her twenties faced with such problems might feel. Invite them to write a journal entry in which Maria Theresa expresses her thoughts and feelings.

Citizenship

The marching style of the Prussian army, known as the *Paradeschritt,* put extreme demands on the human body. Soldiers pointed the toes of their jack boots and kicked their legs high, making a horizontal line. In so doing, they had to lean ahead with each step to maintain balance. Their arms swung stiffly; their chins jutted forward; their faces were grim. Every step demanded great effort.

Such a movement in mass unison communicated a clear message about the Prussian army—Prussian soldiers were disciplined athletes who would follow any order, regardless of absurdity or pain. The German and Russian armies adopted the "goose-step," as the Prussian march was called by foreign critics, and it was a feature of military parades for hundreds of years. The high-stepping march became a trademark of the Nazi army of Adolph Hitler.

Critical Thinking

What message would a goose-stepping Prussian army convey to the people of Prussia?

ANSWER: It could symbolize the might of the government, which could be used against the people as well as against enemies of the nation.

DAILY LIFE ANSWER
The clothing is a symbol of power of the monarchy.

DAILY LIFE

Dressing for Success

Frederick I was not the only monarch who tried to copy the style of Louis XIV. When France was the greatest power on the continent, Louis XIV's style of clothing was copied throughout Europe. Royalty and nobles mirrored the French king with elaborate wigs and rich fabrics. Color and pattern were very important.

How is the clothing style of Frederick I in the image at right similar to that of Louis XIV below?

Louis XIV

The Rise of the Hohenzollerns

Brandenburg-Prussia, a small north German state ruled by the Hohenzollern family, became Austria's chief rival. The Hohenzollerns were an ambitious family who had originally ruled a small territory in southern Germany. However, they wanted to increase their power and gain more land. One branch of the family settled in Brandenburg, in northern Germany. The ruler of Brandenburg eventually became an elector of the Holy Roman Empire.

Many of the Hohenzollerns were Protestants. During the Reformation they seized lands that had once belonged to the Catholic Church in their territories. By 1648 they ruled several territories in Germany, including Prussia, which bordered the Baltic Sea.

One of the greatest Hohenzollern rulers was Frederick William, called the **Great Elector.** He ruled Brandenburg-Prussia at the end of the Thirty Years' War. After the war he worked to rebuild his state. Frederick William unified the armies of all his lands into one strong force. He also improved the tax system, agriculture, industry, and transportation.

In 1688 Frederick I succeeded the Great Elector as ruler. From then on, all the Hohenzollern lands in northern Germany were unified in practice under the rule of Prussia. This greatly consolidated Hohenzollern power. Frederick I gained the title of King of Prussia. He tried to imitate Louis XIV of France, maintaining a large, lavish court.

Frederick William I. In 1713 Frederick I's son became king. **Frederick William I** did not like French ways. He ended much of his father's lavish spending. Instead, Frederick William I used the money to make Prussia stronger. He doubled the size of the Prussian army and made it the most efficient fighting force in Europe.

Prussian society in general was militarized under the king, who overhauled the government and brought the state as a whole under his control. "At the table," his daughter once wrote, "nothing else was talked of but economy and soldiers." Frederick William ensured that the Prussian army was well equipped and thoroughly trained. Discipline within the army was rigid, punishments were harsh, and soldiers were expected to obey orders instantly.

By 1740 the Prussian army was among the most powerful military forces in Europe. It had become a well-designed tool with which Prussia could both defend its borders and expand its interests.

Frederick William I also created an efficient system of government for Prussia. Tax collecting and government spending were carefully planned. Frederick William I also encouraged trade and the development of new industries. Believing that all children should have a primary education, he required that all parents send their children to school.

The coronation of Frederick I (shown holding crown)

TEACH OBJECTIVE 2

ALL LEVELS: Form students into triads to create a talk show called "Who's the Greatest?" The show's guests are Frederick William I and Frederick II. Have students compose questions to be asked by the interviewer and responses for the show's two guests. Invite triads to perform their talk shows for the class. After each performance, have the class vote to decide "Who's the Greatest?"—Frederick William I or Frederick II.
ENGLISH LANGUAGE LEARNERS, COOPERATIVE LEARNING

LEVEL 1: Have students make a concept map for each Hohenzollern ruler that details his achievements.
ENGLISH LANGUAGE LEARNERS

Frederick the Great. Frederick William I worried that his son, Frederick II, did not seem interested in military or government affairs. Instead the youth wrote poetry, played the flute, and read philosophy. The king used harsh methods, including prison, to try to change his son. Once Frederick II and a companion tried to escape Prussia, but both were caught. King Frederick William I forced his son to watch as the friend was executed.

Despite Frederick William's fears, Frederick II turned out to be an even stronger ruler than his father. He became king of Prussia in 1740, the same year Maria Theresa became the ruler of Austria. Frederick II, or **Frederick the Great,** as he came to be called, was highly intelligent and worked to expand the territory and prestige of Prussia.

✔ **READING CHECK: Finding the Main Idea** What did the Hohenzollerns hope to accomplish? Were they successful? sought to make Prussia a great power; they were generally successful

Conflict Between Prussia and Austria

Frederick William I had signed the Pragmatic Sanction allowing Maria Theresa to inherit all the Habsburg lands. Shortly after becoming king, however, Frederick II marched his powerful Prussian army into Silesia, one of Maria Theresa's most valuable territories. Prussia had only a weak claim to Silesia, but Frederick the Great wanted the territory for its farmland and iron deposits.

The Prussians seized Silesia easily. This conquest started the War of the Austrian Succession, which lasted from 1740 to 1748. On one side Bavaria, Spain, and France joined Prussia to fight Austria, Great Britain, the Netherlands, and Russia. Austria and its allies lost, and Silesia was ceded to Prussia.

The Diplomatic Revolution. After the War of the Austrian Succession, a major "reversal of alliances" occurred in Europe. This shift was known as the **Diplomatic Revolution.** Ever since the time of Louis XIV, Austria and Great Britain had been allied against the French. In 1756, however, Great Britain allied itself with Prussia. To keep Prussia from becoming too powerful, France joined with Austria and Russia. A new balance of power saw France and Austria opposed to Prussia and Great Britain.

The Hohenzollerns

1640–1688	Frederick William, the Great Elector
1688–1713	Frederick I
1713–1740	Frederick William I
1740–1786	Frederick II (the Great)

Interpreting the Chart
Between 1640 and 1786, Hohenzollern rulers added substantially to the strength and efficiency of Prussia's government. *What might be inferred about support for Hohenzollern rule on the basis of this chart?*

Culture

Frederick William I worried about the worthiness of his son to rule because of Frederick II's interest in the arts and philosophy rather than in the military or government. Yet in ancient Greece, Plato wrote in *The Republic* that the human race would never be safe from the evils of our commoner nature unless we had a philosopher king to govern us. Educated by the philosopher Aristotle, Alexander the Great focused on scholarship as well as politics and military affairs.

Critical Thinking

What do the traits deemed important in a leader tell you about the culture of a people?

ANSWER: A culture would look for the traits in its leader that it values highly.

INTERPRETING THE CHART ANSWER

Students might infer that support was strong, as there was no interruption in the line of leadership and, possibly, no challenge to its rule.

VISUAL RECORD ANSWER

proud, formal, disciplined; even the stride of the horse seems powerful and controlled

INTERPRETING THE VISUAL RECORD

Prussian troops In this painting, Frederick the Great inspects his troops. *What impression does this painting create of the Prussian army?*

ALL LEVELS: Have students make a time line, like the one at the right, of the events in Central Europe from 1740 to 1775.
ENGLISH LANGUAGE LEARNERS

HOMEWORK As an imperial adviser, write a policy memo to Maria Theresa in 1756 about the changing balance of power in Europe. Remember to use standard grammar, spelling, sentence structure, and punctuation.

| 1740 | | | | 1772 |
| Maria Theresa becomes Austrian ruler; Frederick II becomes king of Prussia; seizes Silesia | 1756 Seven Years' War begins in Europe | 1757 Prussian army defeats French forces | 1762 Russian Czar Peter makes peace with Prussia | Prussia gains land in First Partition of Poland |

| 1740s | 1750s | 1760s | 1770s |

| 1740–1748 War of Austrian Succession | 1756 Diplomatic Revolution | 1759 Austrian-Russian forces beat Prussian forces | 1763 Seven Years' War ends |

Global Relations

France and England were long-time rivals. During the 1700s, however, their rivalry took on new forms, as they began to compete for influence among the other European states in an effort to dominate the continent. They also competed for control of overseas trade routes and colonies in India, in the Caribbean, and in North America, where the French made alliances with many American Indians to prevent British settlers from expanding their colonies.

Meanwhile, the emergence of Prussia as a major military power after the War of the Austrian Succession affected the balance of power in Europe. When England allied itself with Prussia, an alarmed France allied itself with Austria. Rivalries intensified. What began as fighting between the French and British over French forts in North America led to warfare involving almost every European nation and battles on three different continents.

Critical Thinking

Why might the Seven Years' War be considered the first World War?

ANSWER: It involved many nations, spread over three continents, and shifted power throughout the world.

MAP ANSWER
Austria

The Seven Years' War. These rivalries led to another major European war called the **Seven Years' War,** which lasted from 1756 to 1763. Almost all of Europe became involved in this war. Battles took place on the continent and in European colonies overseas. In fact, the fighting actually began in North America, where it was called the French and Indian War.

Major alliances characterized the Seven Years' War. Prussia was supported by Great Britain, while Austria formed partnerships with France and Russia. In 1757 Frederick II's Prussian army defeated the French forces in Saxony and prevented Austria from reclaiming Silesia. Two years later, however, in 1759, the Prussians were badly defeated by a combined Austrian-Russian force.

Frederick struggled to regain the upper hand. His efforts met with success when mistrust and financial problems began to weaken the alliance that opposed him. At the same time, Prussia's British allies won several major victories against the French in Canada and India. A turning point was reached when the Empress of Russia, Elizabeth, died. Her successor, Czar Peter III, was a great admirer of Frederick II and had no desire to continue supporting Prussia's enemies. He broke from the alliance with Austria and France and, in 1762, made a separate peace with Prussia. At the same time, Britain's new ruler, King George III, made clear his intention to withdraw from the global conflict.

The Seven Years' War ended with no clear winner. A treaty signed in 1763 confirmed Prussia's hold on Silesia—a great loss for Austria. In that same year, the Treaty of Paris gave most of France's North American colonies to Britain, which also maintained its dominant position in India.

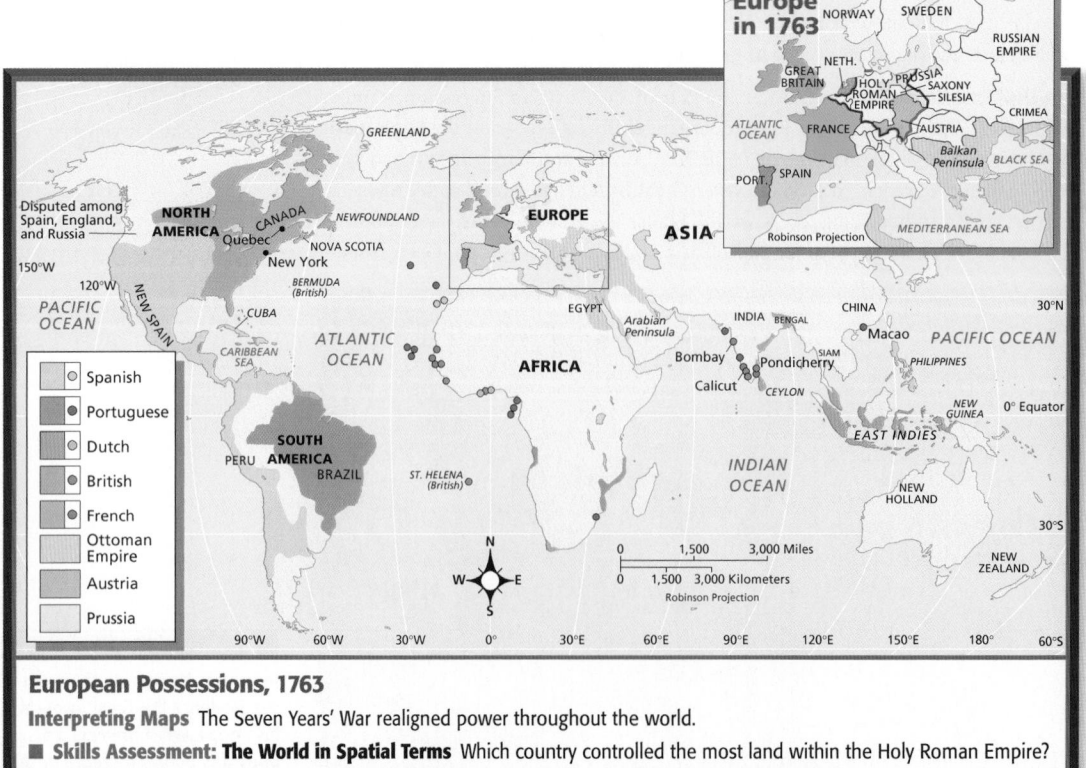

European Possessions, 1763

Interpreting Maps The Seven Years' War realigned power throughout the world.

■ **Skills Assessment: The World in Spatial Terms** Which country controlled the most land within the Holy Roman Empire?

The years of peace. The Seven Years' War had caused widespread destruction and loss of life in many parts of Europe, North America, and India. Prussia and Russia had drained their treasuries during the war. Prussia also had lost many people. As they realized the costs of war in both lives and wealth, the European powers became reluctant to fight again. A period of peace descended on a war-weary Europe that was eager to recover. Nevertheless, European monarchs continued to search for ways to expand their national boundaries, find new sources of wealth, and extend their powers.

In Prussia, Frederick the Great had spent the first 23 years of his reign at war. He spent the next 23 years working to rebuild and strengthen his kingdom. Frederick had great organizational skills and governed Prussia effectively. He expanded and improved public education and the already excellent Prussian civil service system. He also made important legal and court reforms and encouraged economic development through increased trade and manufacturing. Frederick also supported tolerance for religious minorities. Under his leadership, Prussia regained the economic prosperity it had lost during the Seven Years' War.

Prussia also continued to gain new territory during these years. Frederick the Great helped to bring about the First Partition of Poland. By acquiring Polish territory along the Baltic coast, Frederick linked Prussia with East Prussia. By the time Frederick the Great died in 1786, Prussia had emerged as a major European economic and political power.

Frederick the Great (center) and his nobles are shown here dining at the Prussian palace with the French philosopher Voltaire (leaning forward at left) as a special guest.

✔ **READING CHECK: Identifying Cause and Effect** What effect did the Prussian invasion of Silesia have on Europe? started the War of Austrian Succession

---

SECTION 3 REVIEW

1. **Identify** and explain the significance:
   Maria Theresa
   Pragmatic Sanction
   Great Elector
   Frederick William I
   Frederick the Great
   Diplomatic Revolution
   Seven Years' War

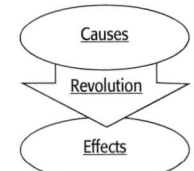

Homework Practice Online
keyword: SP3 HP19

2. **Identifying Cause and Effect**
   Copy the graphic organizer below. Use it to explain the causes and effects of the Diplomatic Revolution.

   Causes
   ↓
   Revolution
   ↓
   Effects

3. **Finding the Main Idea**
   a. In what ways were the Habsburgs and the Hohenzollerns driven by similar motives?
   b. How did Frederick William I differ from his father?

4. **Writing and Critical Thinking**
   Decision Making Write a paragraph examining whether Frederick the Great was justified in invading Silesia.
   Consider:
   • how Austria had come to possess Silesia
   • whether or not Prussia had any claim to the territory
   • why Frederick the Great wanted Silesia

OBJECTIVES

1 **Describe the rule of Mary Tudor in England.**

2 **Describe the rule of Elizabeth I.**

3 **Explain the problems James I faced in ruling England.**

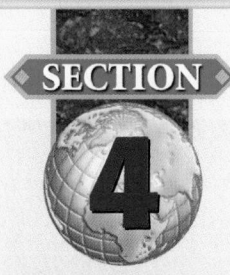

SECTION 4

READ TO DISCOVER

❶ How did Mary Tudor rule England?

❷ How did Elizabeth I rule England?

❸ Why did James I have trouble ruling England?

DEFINE

gentry
burgesses

IDENTIFY

"Bloody Mary"
Elizabeth I
Mary Queen of Scots
Spanish Armada
Puritans
James I

WHY IT MATTERS TODAY

England today maintains its monarchy, although it is different from the monarchy of Elizabeth I. Use CNN or other **current event** sources to find out how much power the British monarchy has today as compared with the 1600s. Record your findings in your journal.

CNN Student News.com

The English Monarchy

The Main Idea
Monarchs in England tried to rule with absolute power, but met with serious opposition from Parliament.

The Story Continues *"I am your anointed Queen. I will never be by violence constrained to do anything."* So goes a famous statement by Queen Elizabeth I, one of England's strongest monarchs. Yet in England, unlike countries on the continent, the absolute monarchy would never quite take hold.

The House of Tudor

In the late 1400s a new royal family, the Tudors, became England's rulers. The Tudors tried to increase their power in England just as the rulers of France and Spain had. The first Tudor king was Henry VII, who made England stable and prosperous. His son, Henry VIII, established a new official church for England, the Anglican Church, when the Roman Catholic pope would not grant him a divorce. Henry's sickly son, Edward VI, succeeded him but ruled for only six years.

Mary I, the oldest daughter of Henry VIII, took the throne in 1553 to become the first reigning queen of England. Mary, a devoted Catholic, was determined to make England a Catholic nation again. Her Protestant subjects were outraged when Mary married Philip II of Spain. Philip had helped lead the Counter-Reformation against Protestantism.

The queen did not lack courage or a sense of kindness. Nevertheless, she proved to be utterly ruthless in her aim to destroy the Anglican Church. Mary tried to do away with clergy who did not follow the laws of the Catholic Church. She had more than 300 people burned at the stake, including Thomas Cranmer, the archbishop of Canterbury. These persecutions earned Mary the nickname **"Bloody Mary"** and provoked rebellion. They also failed to destroy Protestantism in England.

✔ **READING CHECK: Problem Solving** How did Mary Tudor try to promote Catholicism in England? Why do you think her efforts failed? married Philip II of Spain, persecuted Protestant clergy; failed because persecutions were too extreme

During the reign of the Tudors, political prisoners were confined in the Tower of London.

TEACH OBJECTIVE 1

 LEVEL 1: Draw a simple family tree to help students see that Mary I was the daughter of Henry VIII's first wife, Catharine of Aragon, a devout Catholic whom he divorced to marry Anne Boleyn. Anne gave birth to Elizabeth but was later beheaded. Ask students what Mary did to earn the nickname "Bloody Mary." **ENGLISH LANGUAGE LEARNERS**

TEACH OBJECTIVES 1 and 2

ALL LEVELS: Have students complete the chart to contrast how Mary Tudor and Elizabeth dealt with religious issues.
ENGLISH LANGUAGE LEARNERS

Religion	
Mary Tudor	**Elizabeth**
wanted to restore Catholicism to England; had Protestant dissenters burned at stake	*wanted to strengthen Anglican Church; persecuted Catholics and Puritans, fined them*

The Reign of Elizabeth I

When Mary I died in 1558, her Protestant half-sister **Elizabeth I** became queen. Elizabeth was an able politician who used the monarchy and Parliament to prevent conflict and to strengthen Protestantism. Elizabeth was also in touch with the English people. As the early twentieth century writer Lytton Strachey described her,

History Makers Speak 66[T]he ordinary Englishman saw in King Hal's full-blooded daughter a Queen after his own heart. She swore; she spat; she struck with her fist when she was angry; she roared with laughter when she was amused. . . . A radiant atmosphere of humour coloured and softened the harsh lines of her destiny.99

Lytton Strachey, *Elizabeth and Essex: A Tragic History*

Elizabeth and Mary Queen of Scots. In a monarchy, the oldest child usually inherits the throne. Elizabeth, however, never married and had no children. Her closest relative and heir was Catholic—Mary Stuart, the queen of Scotland, who was also known as **Mary Queen of Scots.** The idea of another Catholic queen horrified English Protestants. However, it also delayed the plans of Philip II of Spain to invade England. He had been planning to force a Catholic ruler on the English people.

When Mary fled to England in 1568 to escape problems in Scotland, Elizabeth put her in prison. Later Mary plotted with Philip II's ambassadors in England to kill Elizabeth and seize the throne. Elizabeth found out about the plan and ordered Mary's death. In 1587 the Scottish queen was beheaded. Philip II, meanwhile, was angered by English raiders at sea and by the help Elizabeth gave to Protestants in his lands. He planned another invasion of England.

The Spanish Armada. In 1588 Philip launched a fleet of 130 ships toward England. This **Spanish Armada** was so impressive that it was called the Invincible Armada.

The English sent out their whole fleet to meet the Spanish Armada. The English ships were smaller and swifter, and their guns could shoot faster and farther than those on the Spanish ships. As a result, the English slipped through the Spanish formation of ships and damaged and sank some of the lumbering vessels. The Spanish tried to escape to the North Sea and then sail back around the British Isles. Storms, navigation errors, and lack of supplies worked against them. Many Spanish ships crashed on the shores of Scotland and Ireland. Only about half of the Invincible Armada made it back to Spain. After this defeat, Spain was no longer a threat to England, and Elizabeth's Protestant rule was secure. However, she still faced two major problems at home.

Religious problems. Religion still caused unrest in England. Henry VIII had broken with the pope when he made Anglicanism the religion of England. However, some people thought Henry had not gone far enough. They wanted to "purify" the new church even more. These people, called **Puritans,** or Separatists, objected to the fact that the Anglican Church kept some Catholic practices. For example, the Anglican Church had bishops and Anglican priests dressed in traditional vestments. Puritans thought these and other Anglican customs were too similar to those of the Catholic Church.

Elizabeth and other Tudor monarchs thought that religious disunity threatened England. They wanted to unite their subjects under the Anglican faith. Therefore, the Tudors persecuted not only Catholics but also non-Anglican Protestants, including the Puritans. For example, people who did not attend the Anglican Church had to pay fines. This angered the Puritans and failed to end the disputes. The Puritans became

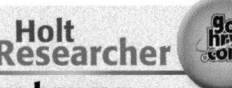

Holt Researcher
go.hrw.com
KEYWORD: Holt Researcher
FreeFind: Mary I
        Elizabeth I
After reading more about Mary I and Elizabeth I on the Holt Researcher, create a compare-and-contrast chart listing the political, economic, and cultural influence they each had on England.

HISTORY MAKER

Elizabeth I (1533–1603)

Brave and shrewd, Elizabeth I was one of the greatest rulers in English history. She changed England from an island kingdom to a world power.

Elizabeth never married because she did not want to lose her power or tie England to a foreign country. Elizabeth's self-confidence gave the English a deep sense of national pride and made her one of England's most enduring symbols. **Why did Elizabeth never marry?**

Daily Life

Although several powerful queens ruled during this time, women in general had few legal rights. Most were controlled by fathers and then by husbands. The majority of women faced a life of hard physical labor, in addition to bearing and rearing many children. In the 1640s, amid England's religious and political turbulence, two women calling themselves Mary Tattle-well and Joan Hit-him-home presented an early treatise on women's rights called *The Women's Sharpe Revenge.*

Critical Thinking

Why do you think the authors of *The Women's Sharpe Revenge* used pseudonyms? What might their pen names mean?

ANSWER: The authors probably felt that they needed to conceal their identities to express unpopular opinions safely. The name Mary Tattle-well might suggest that the author is "well" intentioned in "tattling" to expose social injustice. Joan Hit-him-home might be addressing the nature of relations between men and women.

HISTORY MAKER ANSWER

She did not want to lose her power to a husband nor tie England to a foreign country if her husband were foreign-born.

TEACH OBJECTIVE 2

LEVEL 3: Have students evaluate Elizabeth's rule in a debate. *(pros might include support of the English navy, success against the Spanish, skillful dealings with Parliament, patronage of the arts; cons might include ordering the execution of Mary Stuart, persecution of non-Anglicans, some struggles with Parliament)*
COOPERATIVE LEARNING

 HOMEWORK Write a paragraph evaluating Elizabeth's rule, using points from the debate to support your view.

TEACH OBJECTIVE 3

ALL LEVELS: As a class, list the problems James I faced. *(belief in divine right of kings, unsupported by Parliament so raised money by selling titles and granting monopoly rights, unsuccessful negotiations with Spain led to war)* Have students add James to the chart comparing/contrasting English monarchs' dealing with religion. *(supported Anglican Church, problems with Puritans, King James version of Bible)* **ENGLISH LANGUAGE LEARNERS**

THEN & NOW ANSWER
lower class stood in open area; upper class sat in boxes

Historical Sidelight

Elizabethan theater had critics among the authorities. Crowds invited thievery as well as the spread of the plague. Sometimes small riots occurred. Tensions between ruling Protestants and Catholics led to fears that the theater inspired rebellion. Puritans objected to the theater on moral grounds, claiming that the plays corrupted the people. Elizabeth and her court disagreed; in fact, Elizabeth supported the dramatic arts by licensing a company of players and later even established a company of her own.

ACTIVITY: Have students write short speeches to be delivered by Elizabeth in support of the theater.

🖉 internet connect

TOPIC: Shakespeare's Plays
GO TO: go.hrw.com
KEYWORD: SP3 WH19

Have students access the Internet through the HRW Go site to research the use of propaganda in Shakespeare's historical plays. Ask them to write a two-page report on one of Shakespeare's characters.

The Globe Theatre

In ancient Greece and Rome, plays were staged in large open-air arenas. By the time of Elizabethan England, however, special buildings—theaters—were constructed for plays. The most famous theater in history is the Globe Theatre of London, which was built in the 1500s. Most of William Shakespeare's plays were performed there. Ordinary people stood in an open area, while nobles and the wealthy sat in boxes. Although the original Globe Theatre was torn down, a new theater was recently built to reflect the original design. **How did the seating arrangement in the Globe Theatre reflect English society?**

The new Shakespeare Globe Theatre replicates the original design of the theater as much as possible.

more and more unhappy with the Anglican Church and its clergy. Elizabeth, however, refused to allow further changes to the church. Her religious policies were tolerant compared with those of other rulers at the time. However, they were still objectionable to Catholics on one side and Puritans on the other.

Relations with Parliament. England's Parliament included representatives from the entire country who had the power to pass laws and approve all taxes. In the 1530s Henry VIII had used Parliament to pass the laws that made England a Protestant nation. These acts increased the power and prestige of Parliament. Moreover, people viewed Parliament as a check on the power of the monarchy because it represented the wishes of people outside the central government.

Parliament had two houses. The House of Lords was made up of nobles and clergy. The House of Commons represented two other classes—gentry and burgesses. The **gentry** were landowners who had social position but no titles. Sometimes younger sons of nobles, who could not inherit their father's titles or positions, became gentry. The **burgesses** were merchants and professional people from towns and cities. Sometimes the line between the gentry and the burgesses became blurred. For example, a wealthy merchant who owned land might be considered gentry. Younger sons of nobles might enter a profession and be considered burgesses. Together the gentry and the burgesses had considerable power that the monarch had to respect.

Elizabeth managed Parliament skillfully. She consulted Parliament often and gave the appearance of taking its advice. She obtained the taxes she needed without letting members influence policy too directly. She usually allowed freedom of speech in Parliament. Even so, despite her skill Elizabeth could not prevent some members, particularly Puritans, from questioning her policies. Parliament became even more challenging to the monarchs who followed Elizabeth.

✔ **READING CHECK: Categorizing** What were some of Elizabeth's accomplishments and successes? What were some of her unsolved problems? victory over Spain, ability to manage Parliament, to raise taxes; Parliament continued to challenge royal power, Elizabeth provoked some Protestant groups

The image on the left illustrates the exterior of the Globe Theatre as it appeared in 1616.

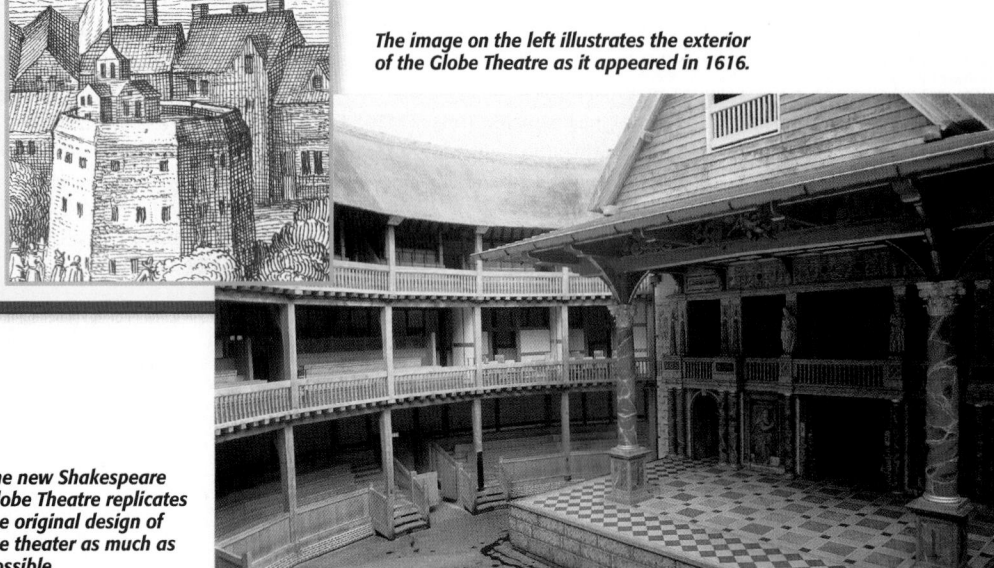

CLOSE

Ask students to summarize the relation between religion and English monarchs from Henry VIII to James I.

REVIEW

Have students complete the Section 4 Review on p. 473.

ASSESS

Have students complete Daily Quiz 19.4. As Alternative Assessment, you may want to use the compare/contrast chart or homework assignment in this section's lessons.

RETEACH

Have students complete Main Idea Activity for English Language Learners and Special-Needs Students 19.4. Then ask each student to create three concept maps showing key details for Mary Tudor, Elizabeth, and James I. **ENGLISH LANGUAGE LEARNERS**

EXTEND

Invite interested students to research some aspect of the Elizabethan Age, such as theater, politics, or historical figures. **BLOCK SCHEDULING**

James I

When Elizabeth died in 1603, she had no heir to succeed her. King James VI of Scotland, the son of Mary Queen of Scots, became King **James I** of England in 1603. Thus England and Scotland came under the rule of the same monarch.

King James was from the Stuart family, not the Tudors. He was intelligent and educated, but lacked common sense in financial and diplomatic matters. According to Henry IV of France, he was "the wisest fool in Christendom." Although James had experience ruling Scotland, many English suspected that he did not entirely understand their parliamentary system. James strongly believed in the divine right of kings and tried to intervene in the House of Commons.

James was a strong supporter of the Anglican Church. This often placed him in conflict with the Puritans, who continued to ask for religious reforms. The only change in church doctrine that James agreed to was a new translation of the Bible, the King James Version. Also known as the Authorized Version, the King James Version is still favored by some Christians today.

The main opposition to James I came from Parliament, where the Puritans had a strong voice. Because of this opposition, James could never collect enough taxes to pay for his programs. He had to raise money by other means, such as selling titles of nobility, granting monopoly rights, and raising customs duties. Parliament objected to these methods. They also opposed James's efforts to create an alliance with England's old enemy, Spain. When James's negotiations with Spain broke down, the two nations went to war. At the time of James's death in 1625, he had an uneasy relationship with the English people. The growing tension between the Stuart ruler and his English subjects would explode during the reign of James's son, Charles I.

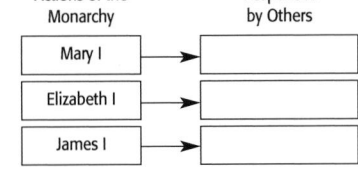

These portraits show James I of England and his wife, Anne of Denmark.

✔ **READING CHECK: Drawing Inferences** How did James I's background contribute to his problems as a ruler? lacked economic, diplomatic skill; did not fully understand English parliamentary system; belief in divine right of kings

---

SECTION 4 REVIEW

1. **Define** and explain the significance:
   gentry
   burgesses

2. **Identify** and explain the significance:
   "Bloody Mary"
   Elizabeth I
   Mary Queen of Scots
   Spanish Armada
   Puritans
   James I

3. **Categorizing** Copy the flowchart below. Use it to list actions taken by the English monarchy over religious divisions and responses to these actions by others.

Actions of the Monarchy	Responses by Others
Mary I →	
Elizabeth I →	
James I →	

4. **Finding the Main Idea**
   a. What marked Elizabeth as a strong ruler?
   b. In what ways did James I behave like an absolute monarch?

5. **Writing and Critical Thinking**
   Supporting a Point of View In a diary entry, describe the feelings of a Puritan toward the English monarchy during the reign of James I.
   Consider:
   • how the Puritans felt about Catholicism
   • what the Anglican Church was like
   • the actions of the monarchy

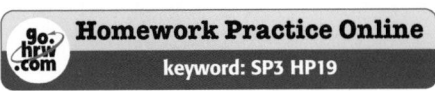

Homework Practice Online
keyword: SP3 HP19

REVIEW AND ASSESSMENT RESOURCES

REPRODUCIBLE RESOURCES
▸ Vocabulary Activity 19

TECHNOLOGY RESOURCES
▸ Chapter 19 Test Generator (on the One-Stop Planner)
▸ Global Skill Builder CD–ROM
▸ HRW Web Site

REINFORCEMENT, REVIEW, and ASSESSMENT
▸ Chapter 19 Review, pp. 474–475
▸ Chapter 19 Tutorial for Students, Parents, Mentors, and Peers
▸ Chapter 19 Test (Form A or B)
▸ Alternative Assessment Handbook
▸ Chapter 19 Test for English Language Learners and Special-Needs Students

REVIEW
Have students complete the Chapter 19 Review on pages 474–475.

ASSESS
Use one of the chapter tests to assess students' understanding of the content. For Alternative Assessment, see the Portfolio Activities and Alternative Assessment Handbook.

CHAPTER 19 REVIEW ANSWERS

Understanding Main Ideas

1. took power from nobles, attacked Huguenot towns, strengthened monarchy, improved economy

2. Louis XIV: supreme confidence, limited nobles, absolute power; Louis XV: weak ruler; nobles regained power, monarchy declined

3. strengthened army, extended territory, westernized Russia, reformed government and economy, encouraged education and science

4. gained Sea of Azov, north shore Black Sea, areas of Poland, Crimea protectorate

5. extended territory; strengthened army, government, education, trade; improved tax system, agriculture, industry, and transportation

6. War of Austrian Succession, Seven Years' War

7. enraged by English sea raiders; Elizabeth's aid to Spanish Protestants; defeat of Spanish Armada

8. Puritans in Parliament opposed James I's strong support of Anglicanism.

CHAPTER 19 Review

Creating a Time Line
Copy the time line below onto a sheet of paper. Complete the time line by filling in the events, individuals, and dates from the chapter that you think were significant. Pick three events and explain why you think they were significant.

Writing a Summary
Using standard grammar, spelling, sentence structure, and punctuation, write an overview of the events in the chapter.

Identifying People and Ideas
Identify the following terms or individuals and explain their significance:

1. Cardinal Richelieu
2. divine right of kings
3. Louis XIV
4. Peter the Great
5. Catherine the Great
6. Diplomatic Revolution
7. Frederick the Great
8. Elizabeth I
9. gentry
10. James I

Understanding Main Ideas

SECTION 1 *(pp. 454–458)*
France in the Age of Absolutism
1. How did Cardinal Richelieu strengthen France?
2. In what ways did Louis XV differ from Louis XIV?

SECTION 2 *(pp. 459–464)*
Russia in the Age of Absolutism
3. How did Peter the Great attempt to end Russian isolation?
4. What foreign policy successes did Catherine the Great have?

SECTION 3 *(pp. 465–469)*
Central Europe in the Age of Absolutism
5. How did the Hohenzollerns strengthen Prussia?
6. What wars did the Prussian invasion of Silesia trigger?

SECTION 4 *(pp. 470–473)*
The English Monarchy
7. Why did Philip II of Spain attempt to invade England? What was the result?
8. Why did James I clash with the English Parliament?

Reviewing Themes
1. **Government** How did the government of Louis XIV negatively affect the people of France?
2. **Culture** How did Elizabeth I try to control religious disunity in England?
3. **Economics** How did Peter the Great's rule affect Russian serfs?

Thinking Critically
1. **Identifying a Point of View** Why might a noble agree with Catherine's nickname of "the Great"?
2. **Identifying Cause and Effect** What happened to the French economy as a result of the construction of the palace at Versailles?
3. **Sequencing** How did Prussia prepare itself for the invasion of Silesia?
4. **Comparing** In what ways were Elizabeth I and James I similar?

Writing About History
Evaluating Absolute monarchies dominated Europe for many years. In general, do you think they affected European nations positively or negatively? Support your opinion with facts from the chapter. Use the following chart to organize your thoughts before you begin writing.

Positive effects	Negative effects

Ask what is meant by an absolute monarchy. As a class, make a chart on the board comparing and contrasting the governments of an absolute monarchy, Greek democracy, the Roman Republic, the Roman Empire, and feudalism.

RETEACH

Pair students who had trouble with the test. Have pairs write five questions about key content in the chapter, exchange questions with another pair, and discuss the answers. Then have students take the Form B Test to assess their mastery of the material.

ENGLISH LANGUAGE LEARNERS, COOPERATIVE LEARNING

Portfolio Extensions

Link to TODAY

1. Have students imagine they are foreign correspondents reporting on events taking place in one country (Russia, Austria, or Prussia) for a newspaper in their home country (France or England) and write a series of articles.

2. Have students use media and news services as well as biographies to acquire information about one of Europe's current monarchs. Have them create a report that includes a photograph of the monarch. Have students place each photograph on the appropriate country on a world map. Then have them share their reports with the class.

3. Have students create and exchange crossword puzzles using chapter content for clues.

Building Social Studies Skills

Interpreting a Graph
Study the graph below. Then use the information on the graph to answer the questions that follow.

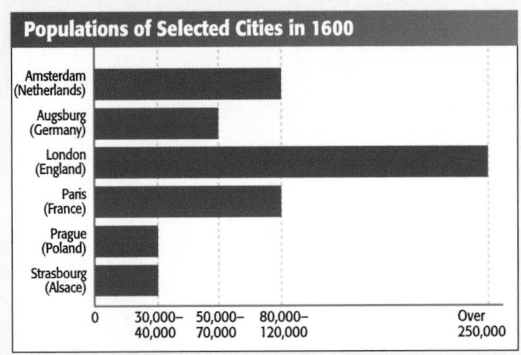

Populations of Selected Cities in 1600

Amsterdam (Netherlands)
Augsburg (Germany)
London (England)
Paris (France)
Prague (Poland)
Strasbourg (Alsace)

0   30,000–   50,000–   80,000–   Over
     40,000   70,000   120,000   250,000

1. Which of the following lists the three cities on the European continent with the largest populations in 1600?
   a. London, Amsterdam, Paris
   b. Paris, Amsterdam, Augsburg
   c. Amsterdam, Augsburg, London
   d. Paris, Augsburg, Prague

2. Which city—London or Augsburg—was probably affected most by the Thirty Years' War? Give specific reasons for your choices.

Evaluating Sources
Read the following excerpt from a travel book describing Louis XIV's palace at Versailles. Then answer the questions.

"You enter the château . . . through the gilt iron gates from huge Place d'Armes. On the first floor of the château, dead center past the Sun King's statue and across the sprawling cobbled forecourt, is Louis XIV's bedchamber. The two wings were occupied by the royal children and princes of the blood, while courtiers made do in the attics. . . . The Grands Appartements (state apartments), which flank the Hall of Mirrors, retain much of their original Baroque decoration: gilt stucco, painted ceilings, and marble sculpture."

3. Which of the following statements best describes the evidence this excerpt provides?
   a. The excerpt is a primary source of evidence.
   b. The excerpt is a secondary source of evidence.
   c. The excerpt is both a primary source and a secondary source of evidence.
   d. The excerpt is not a reliable source of evidence.

4. Explain your choice of statements in question 3. Give specific reasons to support your point of view.

Alternative Assessment

Building Your Portfolio
Link to TODAY

Government

Monarchies still exist throughout the world today, although many rulers do not have the authority of previous monarchs. Find and interpret timelines that show European monarchies beginning with the 1500s through today. Create a database with the country's name, monarch's name, and title—including a popular name such as "the Great"—their length of rule, and the scope of their power.

internet connect

go.hrw.com

Internet Activity: go.hrw.com
KEYWORD: SP3 WH19

Choose a topic on Monarchs of Europe to:
- create a pamphlet on the impact on Russian society of the reigns of Peter the Great and Catherine the Great.
- write a biography of the Sun King.
- explore the propaganda of William Shakespeare's historical plays.

Reviewing Themes
1. wars for territory and spending on luxuries such as Versailles weakened economy

2. tried to unite England under Anglican faith

3. numbers increased, conditions worsened, tied to lords

Thinking Critically
1. because she westernized life for nobles and supported art, science, literature, theater

2. it became strained

3. Pragmatic Sanction; Frederick II invades; War of Austrian Succession

4. both Protestants, warred with Spain

Writing About History
positive—supported arts and sciences, promoted trade, strengthened armies; negative—no benefits for most, luxury spending hurt economies, wars cost lives and money

Building Social Studies Skills
1. a

2. Augsburg, because Thirty Years' War was fought largely in Germany

3. a

4. It is a first-hand account.

Building Your Portfolio
Time lines will vary.

CHAPTER 20

Enlightenment and Revolution in England and America

CHAPTER RESOURCE MANAGER

	Objectives	Pacing Guide	Reproducible Resources
SECTION 1 **Civil War and Revolution** (pp. 478–482)	• Explore what led to the conflicts between Charles I and Parliament. • Examine how the rebellion in Ireland helped start the English Civil War. • Identify who would have supported the two sides in the English Revolution. • Investigate what led to the downfall of republican government in England.	**Regular** **Block Scheduling** 1.5 day 1 day *Block Scheduling Handbook with Team Teaching Strategies, 20.1*	**RS** Guided Reading Strategy 20.1 **PS** Readings in World History 62: Charles I's Speech on the Scaffold
SECTION 2 **Constitutional Monarchy in England** (pp. 483–489)	• Explain how religious attitudes affected the rules of Charles II and James II. • Describe how Parliament reduced the power of the monarchy after the Restoration. • Identify the principal features of Britain's limited constitutional monarchy.	**Regular** **Block Scheduling** 1.5 day 1 day *Block Scheduling Handbook with Team Teaching Strategies, 20.2*	**RS** Guided Reading Strategy 20.2 **PS** Readings in World History 63: The Fall of James II
SECTION 3 **English Colonial Expansion** (pp. 490–493)	• Investigate who the sea dogs were and what they accomplished. • Explore the results of the British mercantilist policy.	**Regular** **Block Scheduling** 1 day .5 day *Block Scheduling Handbook with Team Teaching Strategies, 20.3*	**RS** Guided Reading Strategy 20.3 **SM** Geography Activity 20: The Settling of the English Colonies
SECTION 4 **The Enlightenment** (pp. 494–496)	• Identify the principal characteristics of Enlightenment thinking. • Analyze the similarities and differences in the ideas of important Enlightenment philosophers.	**Regular** **Block Scheduling** 1 day .5 day *Block Scheduling Handbook with Team Teaching Strategies, 20.4*	**RS** Guided Reading Strategy 20.4 **PS** Readings in World History 64: The Colonists' View of Taxation **E** Creative Teaching Strategy 20: Enlightenment Leaders Hall of Fame
SECTION 5 **The American Revolution** (pp. 497–503)	• Explain how Americans responded to British policies after the French and Indian War. • Describe what type of government Americans set up after the American Revolution.	**Regular** **Block Scheduling** 1.5 day 1 day *Block Scheduling Handbook with Team Teaching Strategies, 20.5*	**RS** Guided Reading Strategy 20.5 **RS** Graphic Organizer Activity 20: Reasons for the Revolution **E** Hands-on History Activity 20: Revolutions in Government

Chapter Resource Key

PS	Primary Sources	**A**	Assessment		Music	
RS	Reading Support	**REV**	Review		Video	
IC	Interdisciplinary Connections	**ELL**	Reinforcement and English Language Learners		Internet	
E	Enrichment		Transparencies		Holt Presentation Maker Using Microsoft® PowerPoint®	
SM	Skills Mastery		CD-ROM			

One-Stop Planner CD-ROM

See the **One-Stop Planner** for a complete list of additional resources for students and teachers.

One-Stop Planner CD-ROM

It's easy to plan lessons, select resources, and print out materials for your students when you use the **One-Stop Planner** CD–ROM with **Test Generator**.

Technology Resources	Reinforcement, Review, and Assessment
One-Stop Planner 20.1 Homework Practice Online	Daily Quiz 20.1 Main Idea Activity 20.1 English Audio Summary 20.1 Spanish Audio Summary 20.1 REV Section 1 Review, p. 482
One-Stop Planner 20.2 Holt Researcher: World History: John Locke Homework Practice Online	Daily Quiz 20.2 Main Idea Activity 20.2 English Audio Summary 20.2 Spanish Audio Summary 20.2 REV Section 2 Review, p. 489
One-Stop Planner 20.3 Homework Practice Online	Daily Quiz 20.3 Main Idea Activity 20.3 English Audio Summary 20.3 Spanish Audio Summary 20.3 REV Section 3 Review, p. 493
One-Stop Planner 20.4 Holt Researcher: World History: Marie-Therese Geoffrin World History and Cultures Video Program 17: The Enlightenment Homework Practice Online	Daily Quiz 20.4 Main Idea Activity 20.4 English Audio Summary 20.4 Spanish Audio Summary 20.4 REV Section 4 Review, p. 496
One-Stop Planner 20.5 Holt Researcher: World History: Benjamin Franklin, Thomas Jefferson World History Teaching Transparency: Geography and History 17: The Fight for Independence, 1776–1781 Homework Practice Online	Daily Quiz 20.5 Main Idea Activity 20.5 English Audio Summary 20.5 Spanish Audio Summary 20.5 REV Section 5 Review, p. 503

internet connect

HRW ONLINE RESOURCES
GO TO: go.hrw.com
Then type in a keyword.

TEACHER HOME PAGE
KEYWORD: SP3 Teacher

CHAPTER INTERNET ACTIVITIES
KEYWORD: SP3 WH20
Choose an activity to:
- understand how the ideas of the Enlightenment have influenced institutions and societies.
- create a recruitment poster for the New Model Army.
- identify the impact of political ideas outlined in the writings of Locke and Hobbes, as well as the English Bill of Rights and the Declaration of Independence.

CHAPTER ENRICHMENT LINKS
KEYWORD: SP3 CH20

ONLINE ASSESSMENT
Homework Practice
KEYWORD: SP3 HP20
Standardized Test Prep
KEYWORD: SP3 STP20
Rubrics
KEYWORD: SS Rubrics

ONLINE MAPS, CHARTS, AND GRAPHS
KEYWORD: SP3 MCG

CONTENT UPDATES
KEYWORD: SS Content Updates

HOLT PRESENTATION MAKER
KEYWORD: SP3 PPT20

ONLINE READING SUPPORT
KEYWORD: SS Strategies

CURRENT EVENTS
KEYWORD: S3 Current Events

Meeting Individual Needs

Ability Levels

Level 1 Basic level activities designed for all students encountering new material

Level 2 Intermediate level activities designed for average students

Level 3 Challenging activities designed for honors and gifted and talented students

English Language Learners These activities address the needs of students with Limited English Proficiency.

Chapter Review and Assessment

IC Vocabulary Activity 20

Global Skill Builder CD–ROM

HRW Web Site

REV Chapter 20 Tutorial for Students, Parents, Mentors, and Peers

REV Chapter 20 Review, pp. 504–505

A Chapter 20 Test Generator (on the One-Stop Planner)

A Chapter 20 Test (Form A or B)

A Alternative Assessment Handbook

A Chapter 20 Test for English Language Learners and Special-Needs Students

Build on What You Know

Ask students to answer the following questions:

What new ideas developed in modern nation-states between 1500 and 1800?

Consider:

- new ideas concerning the nature and the organization of the state
- new relationships between the nations' people and their rulers
- monarchs' increasing desire for absolute control

What were some characteristics of countries during the Age of Absolutism?

Consider:

- **France**
- **Russia**
- **Central Europe**

EXPLORING THE TIME LINE

GLOBAL EVENTS

internet connect

TOPIC: Irish Rebellion
GO TO: go.hrw.com
KEYWORD: SP3 WH20

Have students access the Internet through the HRW Go site to research the roots of the Irish Rebellion in 1642. Students should create a time line with key events in the history of Irish/British relations from A.D. 900 to the Confederation of Kilkenny. Students should seek to develop time lines to reflect events that will help them explain why Irish national-ism has remained such a defining force in the country for hundreds of years. Which historical character do they identify with in the time line and why?

CHAPTER 20

1550–1789

Enlightenment and Revolution in England and America

1600 **Business and Finance** The British East India Company is chartered.	**c. 1619** **Business and Finance** Tobacco becomes Virginia's most valuable export.	**c. 1651** **Business and Finance** The Navigation Act is passed in England.	**1667** **The Arts** John Milton publishes *Paradise Lost.*	**1687** **Science and Technology** Isaac Newton publishes *Principia.*

1600   **1650**

1588 **Global Events** The Spanish Armada is defeated by the English navy.	**1607** **Daily Life** Jamestown, Virginia, is founded.	**1640** **Politics** The Long Parliament convenes.	**1665** **Science and Technology** Robert Hooke publishes the first significant work on microscopic observation.	**1688** **Politics** The Glorious Revolution occurs in England.

Battle of the Spanish Armada

Title page from Robert Hooke's Micrographia

Build on What You Know

*M*odern nation-states, most of which were governed by monarchs, developed first in Europe between 1500 and 1800. With the new governments came new ideas concerning the nature and the organization of the state. New relationships between the nations' people and their rulers also spread. The monarchs who led these new states increasingly sought absolute control over their governments and their subjects. A growing number of those subjects, however, had begun to dispute the ideas of absolutism. In this chapter, you will learn about revolutionary ideas that brought sweeping political and social change to England and America.

What's Your Opinion?

 To help students create their Themes Journal entries, provide the following examples of appropriate **agree**/**disagree** *statements.*

Citizenship

Agree Citizens deserve to have a say in their form of government and the actions of their leaders.

Disagree Rulers have the right to assert absolute rule over their subjects.

Constitutional Heritage

Agree Principles that clearly define the relationship between citizens and their leaders are requirements for a just government.

Disagree It is not necessary to have a written document that clearly defines the relationship between rulers and ruled.

Global Relations

Agree Colonialism is an arrangement that is mutually beneficial to a colonial power and its colonies.

Disagree A colony's citizens are almost always subject to exploitation by the colonial power.

Signing of the U.S. Constitution

Jean-Jacques Rousseau

1707
Politics
The Act of Union unites England and Scotland.

1731
Daily Life
The first colonial subscription library opens in Philadelphia.

1762
The Arts
Jean-Jacques Rousseau publishes *The Social Contract*.

1763
Global Events
The Treaty of Paris leaves the British in control of North America.

1789
Politics
The U.S. Constitution is ratified.

1700   **1750**   **1800**

c. 1742
Science and Technology
Benjamin Franklin invents the Franklin stove.

1776
Politics
The United States declares independence from Great Britain.

John Milton

American teapot with anti-Stamp Act slogan

Colonists in America gradually began to believe that they must break free of Britain. In early 1776 a recent British immigrant, Thomas Paine, published a pamphlet called *Common Sense.* He wrote:

"I challenge the warmest advocate for reconciliation to show a single advantage that this continent can reap, by being connected with Great Britain. . . . But the injuries and disadvantages we sustain by that connection are without number. . . . Any submission to, or dependence on, Great Britain, tends directly to involve this continent in European wars and quarrels, and sets us at variance [at odds] with nations who would seek our friendship, and against whom we have neither anger or complaint."

Critical Thinking

Ask students how, according to the passage by Paine, America's connection to Britain hurt its foreign relations.

ANSWER: Students should answer that, according to Paine, America's connection to Britain causes it to have unfavorable relationships with certain countries just because they are at odds with Britain.

What's Your Opinion?

 Do you **agree** *or* **disagree** *with the following statements? Support your point of view in your journal.*

Citizenship People have a right to determine their own form of government and to insist that their leaders conform to the popular will.

Constitutional Heritage Stable governments are based on clear principles that define the relationship between rulers and ruled.

Global Relations The people of both a colonial power and its colonies can benefit from their economic and political relations.

OBJECTIVES

1 **Explore what led to the conflicts between Charles I and Parliament.**

2 **Examine how the rebellion in Ireland helped start the English Civil War.**

3 **Identify who would have supported the two sides in the English Revolution.**

4 **Investigate what led to the downfall of republican government in England.**

🎵 *LET'S GET STARTED!*

As students enter the classroom, ask them to think about the issues that might divide a nation. List their responses on the board. *(Students might suggest disagreement over the form of government, who should rule, and religion.)* Tell students that in Section 1 they will learn about the issues that divided Great Britain and led to the English Civil War and Revolution.

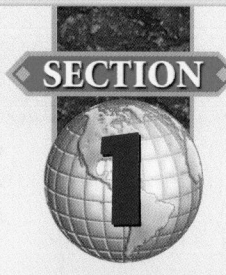

SECTION **1**

READ TO DISCOVER

1 What led to the conflicts between Charles I and Parliament?

2 How did the rebellion in Ireland help start the English Civil War?

3 Who would have supported the two sides in the English Revolution?

4 What led to the downfall of the republican government in England?

DEFINE

commonwealth
constitution

IDENTIFY

Charles I
Petition of Right
Long Parliament
Cavaliers
Roundheads
Oliver Cromwell
New Model Army
Rump Parliament
Navigation Act of 1651

WHY IT MATTERS TODAY

Constitutionalism is an important form of government in today's world. Use CNNStudentNews.com or other **current event** sources to identify countries that have a formal constitution. Record your findings in your journal.

CNN Student News.com

Civil War and Revolution

The Main Idea
Parliament's opposition to the concept of royal supremacy led to conflict and rebellion in England.

The Story Continues *Increasingly, the English monarchs of the early 1600s claimed absolute power over Parliament and the law. Their claim echoed the ideas of French philosopher Jean Bodin, who argued that "A prince is bound by no law of his predecessor, and much less by his own laws. . . . He may repeal, modify, or replace a law made by himself and without the consent of his subjects." King Charles I of England certainly held this belief. Throughout the early 1600s tensions grew between Charles and Parliament.*

Charles I and Parliament

Like his father, James I, King **Charles I** believed in the divine right of kings. This belief put Charles out of touch with the people and politics of England. His marriage to a French Catholic princess isolated him even further.

Charles I could not get funds from Parliament. He tried forcing people to loan him money and imprisoned some who refused. Parliament objected to his actions and presented Charles with a document called the **Petition of Right.** This petition stated four ancient liberties: (1) the king could not tax the people without the agreement of Parliament; (2) he could not declare martial law; (3) he could not board soldiers in private homes during peacetime; and (4) he could not imprison a person without a specific charge. Charles signed the Petition of Right, but continued to impose taxes anyway. When members of the House of Commons protested, Charles dismissed Parliament.

For 11 years Charles refused to call Parliament into session. During this time he used drastic means to collect money. The economy improved, but discontent grew over issues like religion. Charles liked the formal religious ceremonies of the Anglican Church. These ceremonies seemed too Catholic to Puritans, however. As a result of this conflict, many Puritans became determined opponents of the king. They increasingly dominated the House of Commons. These Puritans—and many others in Parliament—felt that Charles was becoming a tyrant. Charles began to use royal courts against his enemies. These courts did not guarantee civil liberties. Judges, not juries, made decisions in secret. One of these courts, called the Star Chamber, harshly punished Puritans and critics of the government. People worried that Charles was imposing absolute rule on England.

This portrait of Charles I and his queen, Henrietta, was painted by Anthony Van Dyck in about 1632.

TEACH OBJECTIVES 1 and 2

LEVEL 1: After students have read Section 1, copy the following cluster diagram on the chalkboard or overhead projector, omitting the italicized answers. Help students complete the diagram by identifying the causes of the English Civil War. **ENGLISH LANGUAGE LEARNERS**

The state religion of Scotland was a form of Protestantism called Presbyterianism. When Charles tried to force Scottish churches to follow Anglican practices, rebellion broke out. The Scots felt that the changes Charles wanted were too Catholic. In 1638 many Scots signed a statement called the National Covenant. In this solemn agreement, Scots swore that any changes to the Scottish church would violate their religion as well as their political freedom. To Scottish Presbyterians, loyalty to their church came before loyalty to the king.

Charles took troops to Scotland but could not put down the rebellion. Seeking more funds for his army, he called Parliament into session. However, the members of Parliament insisted on discussing their complaints before anything else, so Charles dismissed them again. Then the Scots handed Charles's troops a second defeat, this time within England itself. Realizing that he could not defend England without new taxes, Charles called Parliament into session once more in 1640.

✔ **READING CHECK: Summarizing** Why did Charles I close down Parliament? Parliament protested his tax measures.

The Long Parliament

Because the Parliament that Charles convened in 1640 met on and off for 20 years, it came to be known as the **Long Parliament.** Charles wanted Parliament to let him raise money to put down the rebellion in Scotland. Instead, the Puritan-controlled House of Commons ended the king's power to dissolve Parliament. It passed a law that Parliament must meet at least once every three years. It kept the king from raising taxes on his own and even forced the execution of two of his advisors for treason. When Parliament also tried to make changes in the Anglican Church, however, public support began shifting to the king.

While Charles I struggled with the Long Parliament, a rebellion broke out in Ireland. When England had conquered parts of Ireland in the late 1100s, Irish land was given to English settlers. Under James I, the mostly Anglican settlers controlled most of Ireland's wealth. Scottish Presbyterian farmers and merchants later settled in the northern region of Ulster. The native Irish Catholics worked as tenant farmers and laborers. The British treated them brutally, as a conquered people. The Irish had few rights or freedoms and lived in constant fear of being dispossessed by their English landlords. Resistance to British policies grew and, in 1641, a bloody rebellion led by Irish Catholics began against English rule.

Parliament needed a big army to put down the Irish rebellion. Not trusting the king, they proposed that Parliament be in command of the army, but Charles refused. He led troops to the House of Commons to arrest some of his opponents. With neither side compromising, a civil war began in 1642.

✔ **READING CHECK: Identifying Cause and Effect** What factors contributed to the conflict between native Irish people and British settlers in Ireland? Irish were dispossessed, treated brutally by British

Charles I opens a session of Parliament.

LEVEL 3: Have each student give a very brief oral presentation defending one of the following statements:

(a) Charles I was within his rights when he entered the House of Commons to arrest radical leaders.

(b) Parliament's cause in the civil war was just.

(c) Charles I was guilty of arrogance, not treason, and he should not have been executed.

 HOMEWORK Ask students to answer this question: Do you think the execution of Charles I was justified? Then have them support their opinions.

Government

Although he lacked military experience, Oliver Cromwell volunteered to raise military forces in his home counties. He soon played a key role in the victory of Parliament's military forces. His status as military hero allowed him to gain the support of the soldiers.

WHAT IF? ANSWER
Some students will say that the civil war could have been avoided if both sides had been willing to compromise and continue doing so. Others will say that the civil war would have happened regardless, as the next rulers clashed with Parliament over finances and religion.

English Civil War

The citizens of England were sharply divided. Those who supported the king included Anglicans, Roman Catholics, nobles, and other opponents of Parliament's reforms. They were called royalists or **Cavaliers.** Those who supported Parliament included Puritans and other non-Anglican Protestants. They were called **Roundheads,** after the close haircuts of the Puritan soldiers.

Oliver Cromwell, a rising Puritan leader, organized his troops into a powerful army. Cromwell's **New Model Army** defeated Charles in 1645. Oxford, the royalist headquarters, surrendered the next year. The king fled to Scotland, but the Scots turned Charles over to Parliament.

In November 1647 Charles escaped and rallied his Scottish supporters to fight again. Cromwell's army crushed them, however, and moved on Parliament, keeping the king's supporters out. The Cromwell-controlled Parliament, known as the **Rump Parliament,** abolished the monarchy and the House of Lords. It proclaimed England a **commonwealth,** or republic. A special court tried Charles for treason. This was its verdict:

> **Primary Source** **"Whereas Charles Stuart, King of England, is, and standeth convicted, attained, and condemned of high treason, and other high crimes; and sentence upon Saturday last was pronounced against him by this Court, to be put to death by the severing of his head from his body; of which sentence, execution yet remaineth to be done; there are therefore to will and require you to see the said sentence executed in the open street before Whitehall, upon the morrow, being the thirtieth day of this instant month of January, between the hours of ten in the morning and five in the afternoon of the same day, with full effect."**
>
> John Bradshaw, Thomas Grey, Oliver Cromwell, et al., *The Death Warrant of Charles I*

Charles was beheaded in front of the palace at Whitehall in 1649. His son fled to France, and Oliver Cromwell took control of England.

✔ **READING CHECK: Analyzing Information** What were the most significant actions of the Rump Parliament? abolished monarchy, House of Lords; proclaimed England a commonwealth; tried and executed Charles I for treason

---

Analyzing Primary Sources

Drawing Conclusions Why might Parliament have chosen to execute King Charles I "in the open street before Whitehall," an important and centrally located government building? to make a public example and a public statement

What If? Neither Charles I nor Parliament expected their differences to end in war. **What if Charles and Parliament had been able to compromise on control of the army in 1640? Do you think the civil war and revolution would have happened anyway? Why?**

The death warrant of Charles I was signed and sealed by members of Parliament.

ALL LEVELS: Using the diagram students generated about the causes of the English Civil War, have students start a second list of characteristics of Cromwell's commonwealth and its effectiveness. Ask students the following question: Why was the monarchy restored to England? *(Students' answers will vary but should include that Cromwell's experiment with republican government failed. After his death, his son was named lord protector, but his weak leadership lost the support of the army. By 1660 the English people had undergone a change of feelings and even though they had once favored the execution of Charles I, they now believed that Cromwell's commonwealth had neither settled the nation nor solved its problems.)* **ENGLISH LANGUAGE LEARNERS**

Ask students to describe the role of Oliver Cromwell after the death of Charles I. Have students consider his leadership style, his rule as lord protector, and his policies toward other countries that supported trade and manufacturing in England. Ask students to describe what eventually happened to Cromwell's republican government.

Cromwell's Commonwealth

Oliver Cromwell was an honest and devout Puritan, a powerful speaker, and a skilled leader. He was also unbending in his belief that divine providence had brought him to power. Thus, Cromwell often acted harshly to suppress resistance to his rule. Despite his dictatorial approach to leadership, however, Cromwell was fairly tolerant of others' religious views. Nevertheless, rigid Puritan followers sometimes forced Cromwell to respond to dissent with extreme force.

Cromwell ruled England as lord protector from 1653 until his death in 1658. This five-year period of English history is often known as the Protectorate. During this time, Cromwell was virtually a military dictator, since he based his rule on the support of the army. Despite his great power, however, Cromwell aimed to bring about a parliamentary republic in England. He wanted to create a representative form of government, but continuing unrest and disorder in the English commonwealth prevented this. Nevertheless, Cromwell tried twice to establish a **constitution**—a document outlining the basic laws and principles that govern a nation. The Instrument of Government of 1653 was the first written constitution of any major European nation. It provided that landowners would elect members of Parliament.

The government of the Protectorate was unpopular in England, and discontent became increasingly widespread. Cromwell's government might have been overthrown except for three factors: (1) It raised enough money from taxes and royalist land sales to support itself and its army. (2) The army was disciplined and powerful. It discouraged other groups from acting against the government. (3) Its enemies had no organized army and could never take effective action to resist the lord protector. Cromwell's control over the Irish, for example, was brutally effective, and the royalists never posed a serious threat to his rule.

Cromwell's policies toward other countries supported his aim of encouraging trade and manufacturing at home. Dutch merchants and shipowners had taken advantage of England's civil turmoil to establish a profitable oceangoing trade. Cromwell challenged the Dutch by having Parliament pass the **Navigation Act of 1651,** requiring that all goods shipped to England from other countries be carried by English ships or by ships of the producing country. This law led to war with the Dutch between 1652 and 1654. Although the war ended with no clear victor, the English navy gained prestige, and Cromwell showed that England could support its commerce with naval power.

CONNECTING TO
Civics

Constitutionalism

Constitutionalism is a form of government in which a nation follows a written constitution. No one person or group has all the power in a constitutional government. Instead, power is shared by different parts of the government. For example, the United States has a president, a two-house congress, and courts. Each of these branches has independent powers, but each is also limited by the others. Many countries today have a constitutional form of government.

Understanding Civics

What is constitutionalism and what are its advantages?

INTERPRETING THE VISUAL RECORD

Preamble This document shows the beginning of the Preamble to the U.S. Constitution. *How do the first three words of the Preamble reflect the ideas of constitutionalism?*

Constitutional Heritage

Cromwell's Instrument of Government gave the Lord Protector very broad powers where the military and foreign affairs were concerned. The republicans in Parliament did not support the document. They believed that a constitution should come from representatives of the people rather than army leaders. In their opinion, the Lord Protector was very similar to a dictator.

ACTIVITY: Pass out copies of the Instrument of Government and the U.S. Constitution to students. Organize the class into small groups and have students compare and contrast the two documents.

CONNECTING TO CIVICS ANSWER

a form of government in which a nation follows a written constitution; no one person or group has all the power; power is shared by different parts of the government

---

VISUAL RECORD ANSWER

"We the people" indicates that power is shared.

481

REVIEW

Have students complete the Section 1 Review on p. 482.

ASSESS

Have students complete Daily Quiz 20.1. As Alternative Assessment, you may want to use the web diagram or oral presentation exercises in this section's lessons.

RETEACH

Have students complete Main Idea Activity for English Language Learners and Special-Needs Students 20.1. Then ask them to create a time line that includes the major events in the English Revolution. **ENGLISH LANGUAGE LEARNERS**

EXTEND

Have interested students conduct research on Charles I or Oliver Cromwell. Ask them to prepare oral presentations from their research. Call on volunteers to present their findings to the class. **BLOCK SCHEDULING**

VISUAL RECORD ANSWER

His suit of armor indicates that he gained power through military strength.

SECTION 1 REVIEW ANSWERS

1 Define
- commonwealth, p. 480
- constitution, p. 481

2 Identify
- Charles I, p. 478
- Petition of Right, p. 478
- Long Parliament, p. 479
- Cavaliers, p. 480
- Roundheads, p. 480
- Oliver Cromwell, p. 480
- New Model Army, p. 480
- Rump Parliament, p. 480
- Navigation Act of 1651, p. 481

3 1640: Long Parliament; 1642: civil war; 1645: Cromwell defeated Charles; 1647: Cromwell gained control of Parliament; 1649: Charles beheaded; 1651: Navigation Act; 1652: war with Dutch; 1653: constitution written; 1658: Cromwell died; 1660: monarchy restored

4 a. He tried forcing people to loan him money and imprisoned some who refused.

b. Parliament wanted to control the army to put down the Irish rebellion, but Charles refused.

c. Cromwell dismissed Parliament and ruled alone.

5 Charles I: Parliament; Cromwell: English people

INTERPRETING THE VISUAL RECORD

Oliver Cromwell Cromwell ruled England as Lord Protector from 1653 to 1658. *Why might the painter of this portrait have decided to show Cromwell in military armor?*

End of the Revolution

The experiment with republican government in England eventually failed. Cromwell quarreled with Parliament, which resented his power. He eventually dissolved Parliament and ruled alone. After Cromwell died in 1658, his son Richard became lord protector. Richard was a weak leader, however, and lost the army's support.

By 1660 the English people had begun to turn against Cromwell's republican government. Many had favored Charles I's execution 11 years earlier, but they recognized that the commonwealth had failed to settle the nation or to solve its problems. In 1660, after much debate and with the army's support, Parliament invited Charles II, the Stuart son of Charles I, to return to England. Cheering crowds greeted Charles II when he reached London. People throughout the country hoped that the restoration of the monarchy would bring peace and progress to England once again. As one observer noted,

Primary Source 66This day came in his Majesty Charles the Second to London after a sad and long exile. . . . This was also his birthday, and with a Triumph of above 20,000 horse and foot, brandishing their swords and shouting with unexpressable joy. The ways strewed with flowers, the bells ringing, the streets hung with tapestry, fountains running with wine.99

John Evelyn, *Diary entry,* May 29, 1660

Some historians call the period from 1642 to 1660 the English Revolution. It includes the civil war years from 1642 to 1649, as well as the changes that continued until the monarchy was restored in 1660. Peace returned to England, but 30 years would pass before king and Parliament could work closely together.

✔ **READING CHECK: Problem Solving** What could Oliver Cromwell have done differently to have helped the republican government succeed in England? avoided conflict with Parliament, shared power, compromise

SECTION 1 REVIEW

1. **Define** and explain the significance:
   commonwealth
   constitution

2. **Identify** and explain the significance:
   Charles I
   Petition of Right
   Long Parliament
   Cavaliers
   Roundheads
   Oliver Cromwell
   New Model Army
   Rump Parliament
   Navigation Act of 1651

3. **Sequencing** Copy the time line below. Use it to identify and place into sequence the major events in the English Revolution.

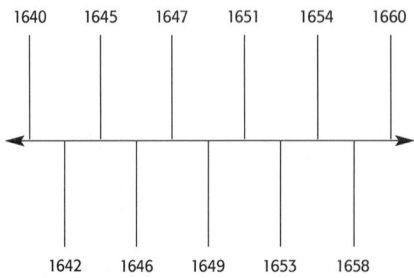

1640   1645   1647   1651   1654   1660

1642   1646   1649   1653   1658

4. **Finding the Main Idea**
   a. Why did Parliament present Charles I with the Petition of Right?
   b. How did rebellion in Ireland help trigger the English Civil War?
   c. Why did England's experiment with republican government under Cromwell fail?

5. **Writing and Critical Thinking**
   Identifying Points of View Who was likely to support Charles I in the English Revolution? Who was likely to support Oliver Cromwell?
   Consider:
   - what Charles I had done to lose the support of the English people
   - the strengths of Cromwell, his army, and his political supporters
   - how Cromwell gained control of the English government

Homework Practice Online
keyword: SP3 HP20

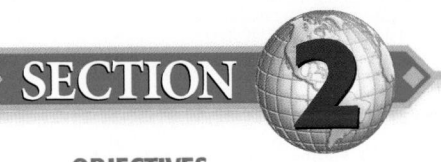

SECTION 2

OBJECTIVES

1 **Explain how religious attitudes affected the rule of Charles II and James II.**

2 **Describe how Parliament reduced the power of the monarchy after the Restoration.**

3 **Identify the principal features of Britain's limited constitutional monarchy.**

As students enter the classroom, remind them that following the failure of the commonwealth, Parliament invited Charles II back to rule England. Ask students why they think Parliament was willing to accept a king again after they had fought the English Civil War to rid themselves of the monarchy. *(Students might say that Cromwell's rule had brought confusion and resentment and the people wanted to seek refuge in the familiarity of a monarchy.)* Tell students that in Section 2 they will learn more about the restoration of the English monarchy.

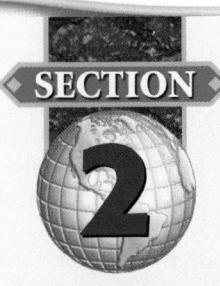

SECTION 2

READ TO DISCOVER

❶ How did religious attitudes affect the rule of Charles II and James II?
❷ How did Parliament reduce the power of the monarchy after the Restoration?
❸ What were the principal features of Britain's limited constitutional monarchy?

DEFINE

habeas corpus
cabinet
prime minister
limited constitutional monarchy

IDENTIFY

Restoration
Tories
Whigs
James II
William III
Mary II
Glorious Revolution
Thomas Hobbes
John Locke
English Bill of Rights
Toleration Act

▶ WHY IT MATTERS TODAY

Constitutional government has developed in many nations since the English Revolution. Use [CNN Student News.com] or other **current event** sources to identify a country where reformers have forced leaders to accept democratic institutions. Record your findings in your journal.

[CNN Student News.com]

Constitutional Monarchy in England

The Main Idea
Parliament gradually replaced the monarchy as the major source of political power in England.

The Story Continues *A more stable government emerged in England toward the end of the 1600s. It was fueled by new ideas about the relationship between ruler and ruled. These ideas were based, in part, upon the ideas of political thinkers such as John Locke, who wrote that "reason . . . teaches all mankind, who will but consult it, that being all equal and independent, no one ought to harm another in his life, health, liberty, or possessions."*

The Restoration and the Glorious Revolution

The reign of Charles II, when the English monarchy was restored, is called the **Restoration.** This name reflected not only the return to monarchy, but also a rebirth of English culture. Charles II loved entertainment and pleasure. Removing Puritan restrictions on the theater, he made entertainment and the arts more available to the people of England. His subjects named him the "Merry Monarch."

Despite his nickname, however, Charles II had learned much from his father's execution and from his own long years in exile. In reality, Charles was personally cynical and cautious. He avoided fights with Parliament when his policies met with opposition, but he was quite willing to use secrecy and roundabout methods to gain his ends.

Charles continued Cromwell's bold commercial policies, which eventually led to another series of conflicts with the Dutch. During these wars, England won control of the Dutch settlement of New Amsterdam in North America, renaming it New York. Charles tried, as well, to form a new alliance between England and France. Widespread protest in Parliament and throughout England, however, forced him to end his efforts. As a result, England and France began 150 years of rivalry to win control of the seas and to gain overseas colonies and resources.

Charles sought to increase toleration for Catholicism and worked to lift some of the legal restrictions that Parliament had imposed against the faith. His attempts to do so, however, met with such strong parliamentary opposition that he was forced to abandon the effort.

Charles II (shown here as a boy) became king following the fall of Cromwell's commonwealth in 1660.

SECTION 2 RESOURCES

REPRODUCIBLE RESOURCES

▶ Guided Reading Strategy 20.2

▶ Readings in World History 63: The Fall of James II

TECHNOLOGY RESOURCES

▶ One-Stop Planner 20.2

▶ Holt Researcher: World History: John Locke

▶ Homework Practice Online

REINFORCEMENT, REVIEW, AND ASSESSMENT

▶ Section 2 Review, p. 489

▶ Daily Quiz 20.2

▶ Main Idea Activity 20.2

▶ English Audio Summary 20.2

▶ Spanish Audio Summary 20.2

TEACH OBJECTIVE 1

LEVEL 1: Ask students to explain how religious attitudes affected the rule of Charles II and James II. Write their responses on the board. *(led to suspicion, conflict with Parliament, opposition to kings' policies)*

ENGLISH LANGUAGE LEARNERS

Culture

James II's son was born a month early, and though there were many witnesses present in the chamber in which he was born, rumors soon spread that he was not really Mary's son. Those who opposed the infant boy's eventual succession to the English throne, undoubtedly to rule as a Catholic monarch, claimed that Mary had never been pregnant and the child had been smuggled into the room and passed off as James's and Mary's. The rumors were eventually proved to be false, but that condition had no effect on the rising fears of the Protestant population who foresaw a never-ending succession of Catholic monarchs.

Critical Thinking

Ask students if they think the English people would have forced James II to abdicate the throne if he had not produced an heir.

ANSWER: Students' responses will vary. Some will say that James II might have been allowed to finish his reign in peace as long as he named one of his Protestant daughters as his successor. Others will say that James's arrogance and ongoing antagonization of Parliament would have resulted in the Glorious Revolution regardless.

This plate made in 1691 celebrates the coronation of William III and Mary II.

Analyzing Primary Sources

Identifying Cause and Effect
What causes did the English leaders cite for their opposition to King James II? general dissatisfaction with royal conduct toward religion, liberties, property; expectation that conditions would worsen

Political parties develop. Charles II and his Portuguese queen, Catherine of Braganza, had no children. It appeared that Charles's younger brother James, a Roman Catholic, would succeed him. The two political parties developing in Parliament at this time had opposing ideas about this royal succession.

The two parties, the **Tories** and the **Whigs,** were about equal in strength. Their names were first used as insults. In Catholic Ireland the word *tory* meant an outlaw. In England, the name was given to one who believed James had a hereditary right to rule. Tories usually supported the Anglican Church. As believers in a hereditary monarchy, however, they would be willing to accept a Roman Catholic king.

The term *Whig* originally meant horse thief. Later applied to Scottish Presbyterians, the name suggested a group that was rebellious. The Whigs claimed the right to deny the throne to James. They wanted a strong Parliament and opposed having a Catholic ruler.

The Glorious Revolution. When Charles II died in 1685, his Catholic brother came to the throne as **James II.** He was humorless and less flexible than Charles was. James's belief in absolute royal rule antagonized both Whigs and Tories. His attempts to help Catholics frightened Protestants and spurred them to resist his rule.

Succession to the throne remained an important issue during James II's reign. His daughters, Mary and Anne, had both been raised as Protestants and had married Protestant princes. When their mother died, James married Mary of Modena, who was Catholic. In 1688 she had a son, who by law would succeed his father as monarch before his older half sisters would. Protestants feared the boy would begin a whole line of Catholic rulers on the English throne.

Both the Whigs and Tories in Parliament called on James II to step down. Leaders in Parliament then invited James's daughter, Mary, and her Dutch husband, William of Orange, to replace James on the throne. In their letter of invitation to William, the English leaders described the reasons for their opposition to James's rule.

History Makers Speak

❝. . . the people are so generally dissatisfied with the present conduct of the Government in relation to their religion, liberties and properties . . . and they are in such expectation of their prospects being daily worse, that your Highness may be assured there are nineteen parts of twenty of the people throughout the kingdom who are desirous of a change and who, we believe, would willingly contribute to it.❞

"The Letter of Invitation from the Immortal Seven," quoted in *The Glorious Revolution of 1688* by Maurice Ashley

William of Orange was a famous soldier who had defeated the powerful French. When he landed in England at the head of a Dutch army in 1688, James fled to exile in France. Parliament gave the crown of England to William and Mary as joint rulers, known from that point on as **William III** and **Mary II.** The opponents of James II had combined to bring about what is known as the **Glorious Revolution,** a bloodless transfer of power in the English monarchy.

✔ **READING CHECK: Drawing Conclusions** How did religious attitudes affect the rule of Charles II and James II? led to suspicion, conflict with Parliament, opposition to kings' policies

TEACH OBJECTIVE 2

LEVEL 3: Draw this chart on the chalkboard or overhead projector, leaving the right-hand column blank for students to complete. Have students copy the chart and complete it using their textbooks. Use the italicized suggested answers to help you assess students' work.

Safeguard	Purpose
Habeas Corpus Act	*protected individuals from unfair arrest and imprisonment*
English Bill of Rights	*declared Parliament would choose who ruled the country; subjected ruler to parliamentary laws; prohibited ruler from imposing taxes or maintaining an army in peaceful times without Parliament's consent; guaranteed free speech for members of Parliament; gave citizens the right to petition the government; declared citizens should not be required to pay excessive bail or be subjected to cruel or unusual punishment*
Act of Toleration	*granted Protestant dissenters some religious freedoms*

Changes in English Government

The English Civil War and the events that followed led to important changes in the government. These events also changed the ways people thought about government. English philosopher **Thomas Hobbes,** who lived through the civil war, was disturbed by the chaos it created. He outlined his political philosophy in 1651 in a book called *Leviathan.*

Hobbes explained that the first people on Earth lived in anarchy, which he believed to be a state of nature. To avoid the resulting violence and danger, Hobbes said, people chose a leader to rule them. They made an unwritten social contract, giving the leader absolute power. The people kept only the right to protect their own lives.

Hobbes was strongly influenced by the chaos and destruction of the English Civil War. The ideas that he expressed in *Leviathan* reflected his belief that people acted from self-interest and without regard for the rights or welfare of others. In Hobbes's view, the natural world was a place in which only the strong would survive unless order was imposed by the greater power of a ruler. The social contract described by Hobbes was based on the exchange of individual liberty for group safety and social order.

John Locke, another English philosopher, disagreed. He accepted the idea of the social contract but believed that people had given up only some of their individual rights. Those they kept included the right to live, to enjoy liberty, and to own property. He said they could expect their rulers to preserve these rights. A ruler who violated these rights thus violated natural law and broke the social contract.

Locke, in contrast to Hobbes, believed that the contract between ruler and ruled could not limit the individual's natural right to enjoy life, political equality, and the ownership of property. In his *Two Treatises of Government,* Locke argued that these individual rights were superior to laws and governments. Governments existed for the sole purpose of protecting those rights. Thus, a ruler's claim to absolute power contradicted the natural order because people would not—and could not—willingly surrender their fundamental natural rights. A ruler who denied people their basic rights was a tyrant and could justly be overthrown.

Habeas Corpus Act and Declaration of Rights. Following the ideas of Locke, Parliament passed laws attempting to safeguard against arbitrary rule. In 1679 Parliament passed the Habeas Corpus Act to protect people who had been arrested. They could obtain a writ, or order, demanding to be brought before a judge. The judge would decide whether the prisoner should be released or charged and tried for a crime. The writ itself was called **habeas corpus,** Latin for "you shall have the body." The Habeas Corpus Act protected individuals against unfair arrest and imprisonment.

A document called the Declaration of Rights was read to William and Mary before they were given the throne in 1689. That year, Parliament formalized the document, calling it the **English Bill of Rights.** It declared that Parliament would choose who ruled the country. The ruler would be subject to parliamentary laws and could not proclaim or suspend any law. The ruler could not impose taxes or maintain an army in peacetime without Parliament's consent. Parliament would meet frequently and the ruler could not interfere with the election of its members. The Bill of Rights guaranteed free speech for members of Parliament.

The Bill of Rights also protected private citizens. Any citizen could petition the government for relief of injustice. No citizen could be forced to pay unfairly high bail or face cruel or unusual punishment.

HISTORY MAKER

John Locke (1632–1704)

John Locke was an important English philosopher. He believed in private property and was against taxation without representation. Locke's writings influenced the Americans who framed our Declaration of Independence and Constitution.

Locke thought that a contract existed between monarch and subjects. He said the people had the right to change their government if it became oppressive. **How did John Locke's writings affect the United States?**

Holt Researcher

go.hrw.com
KEYWORD: Holt Researcher
FreeFind: John Locke
After reading more about John Locke on the Holt Researcher, write a summary identifying the impact of the legal and political ideas contained in his *Two Treatises of Government.*

Government

Thomas Hobbes wrote that since people could not be counted on to cooperate as a society of equals, they had developed civilization as a kind of contract in which everyone agreed to give up their own power to a higher authority: "As if every man should say to every man 'I authorize and give up my right of governing myself to this man, or to this assembly of men, on this condition, that you give up your right to him and authorize all his actions in like manner.' This done, the multitude so united in one person is called a COMMON-WEALTH.... This is the generation of that great LEVIATHAN...that mortal god, to which we owe under the immortal God, our peace and defense." Like the Legalists of China, Hobbes insisted that people had to obey the ruler no matter what, or else their natural selfishness would result in disaster for everyone.

Critical Thinking

Ask students if the ideas of Hobbes supported a monarchy or a democracy.

ANSWER: Students should answer *monarchy.*

HISTORY MAKER ANSWER

They influenced the framers of the Declaration of Independence and the Constitution.

Organize the class into two large groups representing the Tories and the Whigs and have them prepare for and conduct a debate over the following topic:

The monarchy should be made as weak as possible, and under no circumstances should we accept a Roman Catholic ruler.

Before the debate, have students conduct research to find out how their party would stand on this topic and to find information to support their group's stance. Encourage students to make note cards to help them make their points during the debate. You may wish to review the rules of formal debate with students before they begin. Make sure that all students participate in some way.

BLOCK SCHEDULING, COOPERATIVE LEARNING

Government

When parliamentary leaders tried to legitimize their overthrow of James II, they turned to the ideas of one of their supporters, John Locke. In his *Two Treatises of Government,* mostly written before the revolution, Locke had argued that human beings had certain natural rights that could not be taken away, even by a monarch: "The state of nature has a law of nature to govern it, which obliges every one: and reason, which is that law, teaches all mankind, who will but consult it, that being all equal and independent, no one ought to harm another in his life, health, liberty, or possessions." Such arguments would soon have powerful effects in England and around the world.

Critical Thinking

Ask students how Locke's views of rights differed from those of Hobbes.

ANSWER: Hobbes believed that individuals gave up individual liberty in exchange for group safety and social order. Locke believed some rights could not be taken away, even by a monarch.

SKILLS PRACTICE ANSWERS

1. Hobbes believed the natural condition is one of conflict and competition. Locke believed it is freedom and equality.

2. Students' answers will vary.

3. Students' responses will vary.

SKILL-BUILDING STRATEGIES Identifying Points of View

Contrasting Views of Individual Liberty: Hobbes and Locke

The era following the English Revolution saw a continuing debate concerning the ideal form of government. Many thinkers favored centralized rule by a monarch who held absolute power over people, land, and property alike. Others, in contrast, believed that natural law gave the individual the right to govern himself or herself. Thomas Hobbes and John Locke came to symbolize opposing sides of this argument. By identifying the different points of view between Hobbes and Locke, one can better understand the political debates that led to many different experiments with government in England.

Thomas Hobbes

The natural condition of humans is one of continuous conflict and competition: "In such condition, there is no place for industry, because the fruit thereof is uncertain; and consequently no culture of the earth, ... no knowledge of the face of the earth, no account of time, no arts, no letters, no society; and which is worst of all, continual fear and danger of violent death; and the life of people, solitary, poor, nasty, brutish, and short."

John Locke

The natural condition of humans is "... a state of perfect freedom to order their actions, and dispose of their possessions and persons as they think fit, ... without asking leave or depending upon the will of any other man .... A state also of equality, wherein all the power and jurisdiction is reciprocal [shared equally], no one having more than another. ..."

Thomas Hobbes (1588–1679), above, and John Locke (1632–1704), left, were leading English political philosophers. Their strongly contrasting views concerning the nature of government and its proper limits have influenced political thought from the 1600s to the present.

Skills Reminder

To identify a writer's point of view, you should first define the topic—the central idea—on which the writer is focusing. Then, read carefully to determine the writer's position—his or her point of view—toward that idea. Think about what you have learned from the writer before accepting or rejecting the point of view. When studying sources by different authors writing about the same topic, decide if their points of view are similar or opposing. Then decide which source makes the strongest case.

Skills Practice

❶ Summarize the points of view that Hobbes and Locke held about the natural condition of human beings.

❷ Which view do you find the most convincing? Why?

❸ Search recent media sources to find two editorials that express differing views on a common political subject. Choose which view you find the most convincing and explain why. Be sure to cite specific evidence from the editorials to justify your conclusion.

Toleration Act and Act of Settlement. In 1689 Parliament passed the **Toleration Act.** It granted some religious freedoms to Dissenters, Protestants who were not members of the Anglican Church. The Toleration Act did not protect Roman Catholics or Jews, however. It also barred Dissenters from holding public office.

In 1701 Parliament passed the Act of Settlement to keep Catholics from the English throne. The act stated that should William III die with no heir, Mary's sister Anne would inherit the throne. Should Anne have no children, the throne would go to another Protestant granddaughter of James I.

✔ **READING CHECK: Analyzing Information** How did Parliament reduce the power of the monarchy after the Restoration? Habeas Corpus Act, passage of English Bill of Rights

Parliamentary Rule

The Bill of Rights and the Act of Settlement marked a turning point in the history of England. The long struggle between the monarch and Parliament over who would rule the country had finally come to an end. Parliament had emerged as clearly supreme to the monarchy. The rights of individuals, moreover, and the limits on government powers had also become better defined. The long process of political development in Britain, however, was far from complete. Views of personal liberty and of the individual's right to participate in a government that was truly representative continued to grow and change.

Growing power of Parliament. By 1700 England was still a monarchy, but Parliament held most of the power. Parliament did not represent most of the people of England, however. The House of Lords consisted only of hereditary nobles and higher clergy. Even the House of Commons, which was gradually becoming the more powerful of the two houses, represented a small minority of the population. Only the landowning male gentry and wealthy merchants and professionals could vote for representatives to the Commons.

In the 50 years following the Glorious Revolution, Parliament continued to gain importance as the real power in Britain's government. During this time, the organization and institutions characteristic of today's British government gradually emerged. Two of the most important government institutions to develop between about 1690 and about 1740 were the cabinet and the office of prime minister.

INTERPRETING THE VISUAL RECORD

William and Mary The Glorious Revolution led to Protestant rule by William III and Mary II. *Why might the artist have included so many of the trappings of monarchy in this portrait of William and Mary?*

ALL LEVELS: Review the definition of "constitutional monarchy." *(king or queen occupies the throne, but his or her powers are limited by the constitution)* Also ensure that students know how and why England became a constitutional monarchy. *(After centuries of conflict between royalty and Parliament, the English people wanted to avoid the possibility of any more tyrannical absolute rulers; however, they also wished to maintain the tradition of a monarch.)* **ENGLISH LANGUAGE LEARNERS**

Ask students why this period in English history seems particularly significant to the development of the U.S. government. Have them consider ideas concerning separation of powers, liberty, equality, democracy, popular sovereignty, human rights, constitutionalism, and nationalism that arose from the English Revolution.

That's Interesting!

During the 1600s attitudes toward children began to change. Children had commonly been treated as small adults, but during this period people began to perceive childhood as a distinct phase of life. Some people, such as John Locke, believed that education was an important tool to help children progress to adulthood.

internet connect

TOPIC: John Locke
GO TO: go.hrw.com
KEYWORD: SP3 WH20

Have students access the Internet through the HRW Go site to research the political writings of John Locke.

MAP ANSWERS

1. Cheviot Hills

2. advantages: encouraged commerce, brought wealth to both England and Scotland, major centers of learning developed; disadvantages: abolished Scotland's parliament

English monarchs always had met with advisers to discuss problems of government. After the Restoration and the Glorious Revolution, parliamentary leaders had the power to get things done for the monarchs. William III chose his officers of state from among these leaders, who were often heads of government departments. They became known as the **cabinet.**

At first cabinets included both Whigs and Tories. This changed during William III's reign. It was decided that the government would run more smoothly if cabinet ministers belonged to the majority party in Parliament. Sometimes, to make working with Parliament possible, monarchs had to accept a cabinet they did not like. During and after William's reign, Parliament continued to win more authority, including the power to declare war. The king also no longer tried to veto acts of Parliament.

Act of Union. In 1707 the parliaments of England and Scotland passed the Act of Union. This law united England and Scotland into one kingdom, known as Great Britain. It was intended as a measure to strengthen England in its growing conflict with France. Many in Scotland opposed the union. This was partly because it abolished Scotland's parliament, even though Scots now took seats in the English House of Lords and House of Commons.

The union proved beneficial, however. By removing trade barriers, it encouraged commerce and brought wealth to both England and Scotland. The Scottish town of Glasgow grew from a fishing village into a great port city. The Universities of Edinburgh and Glasgow became major centers of learning during the 1700s.

Queen Anne, who ruled from 1702 to 1714, had seventeen children. None survived her. Sophia of Hanover, granddaughter of James I, would have been next in line to the throne. She also was dead. That is how Sophia's son George, the first of the Hanoverian dynasty, became King George I of Great Britain.

Both George I and his son George II were born in Germany. Neither was familiar with British government or customs. George I, who ruled until 1727, did not even speak English. George II, who ruled until 1760, spoke fluent English, but depended heavily on cabinet ministers such as Sir Robert Walpole to manage the government's administration. Walpole served as the king's chief minister until 1742. During these years, he used his knowledge of the House of Commons to work for peace at home and overseas. Walpole also strengthened the British economy, although several of his tax measures were unpopular in Great Britain and in the kingdom's American colonies. Under Walpole's leadership, the British cabinet became increasingly important and necessary, and he is generally viewed as Great Britain's first effective **prime minister,** or first minister. His strong hand helped to stabilize the British political scene.

The British Isles, 1707

Interpreting Maps The Act of Union of 1707 united England and Scotland into one kingdom—the Kingdom of Great Britain.

■ **Skills Assessment: 1. Locate** What small mountain range separates England from Scotland? **2. Analyzing Information** What were the advantages and disadvantages of uniting England and Scotland into Great Britain?

REVIEW

Have students complete the Section 2 Review on p. 489.

ASSESS

Have students complete Daily Quiz 20.2. As Alternative Assessment, you may want to use the chart or constitutional monarchy exercises in this section's lessons.

RETEACH

Have students complete Main Idea Activity for English Language Learners and Special-Needs Students 20.2. Then have students use their textbooks to write a brief encyclopedia entry for each of the following: Charles II, Restoration, Tories, Whigs, James II, Glorious Revolution, William III and Mary II, Thomas Hobbes, John Locke, Habeas Corpus Act, English Bill of Rights, Act of Toleration, Act of Settlement, Act of Union, and constitutional monarchy. **ENGLISH LANGUAGE LEARNERS**

EXTEND

Have students write two to three paragraphs expressing their feelings about the Act of Union, first in the role of an English noble, and then in the role of a Scottish person. **BLOCK SCHEDULING**

Constitutional monarchy. From 1721 to 1742 the Whigs controlled the House of Commons, led by Walpole, the government's prime minister. Under the rule of the Hanoverian monarchs, the prime minister, who usually held the title of first lord of the treasury during these years, was the real head of government. By this point in its history, the nation had become a **limited constitutional monarchy.** The monarch remained as Britain's head of state. Royal powers, however, were clearly limited by the British constitution, which required the king or queen to consult with Parliament and which reserved certain important powers for Parliament alone. The British system of limited constitutional monarchy has changed very little since the 1700s.

Great Britain has one of the world's oldest constitutional governments. It has been a model for other nations that have wanted to end absolute monarchies. The British constitution is not a single document. Instead, it consists partly of several great documents. Among them are the Magna Carta, the Petition of Rights, the Habeas Corpus Act, the Bill of Rights, and the Act of Settlement. It also includes acts of Parliament, which can be changed by later Parliaments. Some features of the British government have never been written down. The powers of the prime minister and the cabinet are based largely on tradition. The prime minister rather than the monarch selects the other ministers. Together the prime minister and the cabinet plan and carry out government policies.

This image portrays Sir Robert Walpole, Britain's first prime minister, discussing policy with his cabinet.

✔ **READING CHECK: Summarizing** What are the principal features of Britain's limited constitutional monarchy? monarch as head of state; powers limited by constitution; monarch must consult with Parliament

---

SECTION 2 REVIEW

1. **Define** and explain the significance:
   habeas corpus
   cabinet
   prime minister
   limited constitutional monarchy

2. **Identify** and explain the significance:
   Restoration
   Tories
   Whigs
   James II
   William III
   Mary II
   Glorious Revolution
   Thomas Hobbes
   John Locke
   English Bill of Rights
   Toleration Act

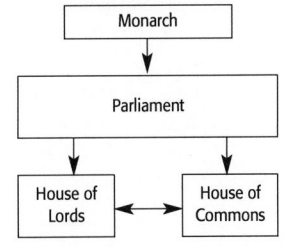
Homework Practice Online
keyword: SP3 HP20

3. **Categorizing** Copy the organizational chart below. Use it to identify the relationships between the various elements of the British government.

```
        Monarch
           │
           ▼
       Parliament
       ┌──────┴──────┐
       ▼             ▼
  House of  ◄──►  House of
   Lords          Commons
```

4. **Finding the Main Idea**

   a. In what major ways did Parliament's Tories and Whigs differ in their view of the English monarchy?
   b. What role did religion play in the reigns of Charles II and James II?
   c. What was the "social contract" of Hobbes and Locke, and how did the two thinkers disagree in their view of it?
   d. Why was the Parliament of the early 1700s not truly a "representative legislature"?

5. **Writing and Critical Thinking**

   Analyzing Information Imagine that you are a member of Parliament during the early 1700s. Write a speech for delivery to your fellow members in which you describe the progress of representative government in England after the English Revolution.
   Consider:
   • what measures Parliament took to reduce the power of the monarchy after the Restoration
   • to what degree the British constitutional system protected the rights of citizens

---

SECTION 2 REVIEW ANSWERS

❶ **Define**
- habeas corpus, p. 485
- cabinet, p. 488
- prime minister, p. 488
- limited constitutional monarchy, p. 489

❷ **Identify**
- Restoration, p. 483
- Tories, p. 484
- Whigs, p. 484
- James II, p. 484
- William III, p. 484
- Mary II, p. 484
- Glorious Revolution, p. 484
- Thomas Hobbes, p. 485
- John Locke, p. 485
- English Bill of Rights, p. 485
- Toleration Act, p. 487

❸ Monarch limited by constitution; certain powers reserved for Parliament; Parliament divided into the House of Lords and House of Commons

❹ a. Tories supported James. Whigs wanted a strong Parliament.

b. Charles sought to increase toleration for Catholicism but faced strong opposition. James attempted to help Catholics, which caused Protestants to resist his rule.

c. the exchange of individual liberty for social order; Locke: people kept some rights; Hobbes: leader had absolute power

d. House of Lords consisted only of nobles and clergy; House of Commons represented only a small minority

❺ Students' speeches will vary.

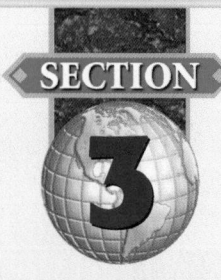

SECTION 3

OBJECTIVES

1 Investigate who the sea dogs were and what they accomplished.
2 Explore the results of the British mercantilist policy.

LET'S GET STARTED!

As students enter the classroom, tell them that Great Britain had a mercantilist economy, meaning it imported raw materials and exported manufactured goods. Ask students how the U.S. economy differs today. *(Students should point out that the U.S. imports and exports raw materials and imports and exports manufactured goods.)* Tell students that in Section 3 they will learn more about Great Britain's mercantilist economy.

SECTION 3 RESOURCES

REPRODUCIBLE RESOURCES

▶ Guided Reading Strategy 20.3
▶ Geography Activity 20: The Settling of the English Colonies

TECHNOLOGY RESOURCES

▶ One-Stop Planner 20.3
▶ Homework Practice Online

REINFORCEMENT, REVIEW, AND ASSESSMENT

▶ Section 3 Review, p. 493
▶ Daily Quiz 20.3
▶ Main Idea Activity 20.3
▶ English Audio Summary 20.3
▶ Spanish Audio Summary 20.3

SECTION 3

READ TO DISCOVER

❶ Who were the sea dogs and what did they accomplish?
❷ What were the results of British mercantilist policy?

DEFINE

sea dogs

IDENTIFY

John Cabot
Sir Francis Drake
Henry Hudson

WHY IT MATTERS TODAY

Great Britain still follows the mercantilist policy of importing raw materials and exporting manufactured goods. Use CNN or other **current event** sources to identify which four or five countries are Great Britain's main trading partners today. Record your findings in your journal.

Francis Drake was knighted by Queen Elizabeth I when he returned from his three-year voyage around the world.

English Colonial Expansion

The Main Idea
After defeating the Spanish Armada, the British began to establish a colonial empire based on trade.

The Story Continues *The defeat of the Spanish Armada in 1588 encouraged the English to compete with other European powers for control of overseas raw materials and markets. England's growing imperialism after 1588 brought criticism from other nations. ". . . I must not omit to say that the English through their rapacity [greed] and cruelty have become odious [hated] to all nations," complained a Venetian diplomat in London in 1603.*

The Beginnings of the British Empire

While Spain and Portugal were creating overseas empires during the 1500s, England was busy with problems at home. During the 1600s, however, English explorers began claiming and conquering land overseas. English merchants, who had been trading in Russia and the Baltic, now moved into the Americas and Asia. At the same time, the English navy had become a major force. English merchant shipping replaced the Dutch as a leader in foreign trade. By the 1760s Great Britain's colonial empire was the greatest in the world.

Explorers and sea dogs. Soon after Christopher Columbus sailed from Spain in 1492, King Henry VII of England entered the contest for American colonies. He hired Venetian captain **John Cabot,** who explored the coasts of Newfoundland, Nova Scotia, and possibly New England. Cabot's voyages in 1497 and 1498 gave England its first claim in North America.

During Queen Elizabeth I's reign in the second half of the 1500s, an adventurous group of English sea captains called the **sea dogs** appeared. These traders and pirates included Sir John Hawkins, **Sir Francis Drake,** and Sir Walter Raleigh. With the backing of the crown, they challenged the Portuguese and Spanish monopolies of sea trade.

TEACH OBJECTIVE 1

LEVEL 1: Have students read the section entitled "Explorers and Sea Dogs" and ask why Queen Elizabeth did nothing to stop the activities of the sea dogs. (*She profited from their piracy.*) Ask students what factors related to English naval exploits probably encouraged English rulers to establish colonies overseas. (*The navy had shown its supremacy over the Spanish Armada; adventurous captains had explored new lands overseas; and Great Britain had succeeded in challenging the Portuguese and Spanish monopolies on overseas trade.*)
ENGLISH LANGUAGE LEARNERS

TEACH OBJECTIVE 2

ALL LEVELS: Ask students to define mercantilism. (*the belief that there is a fixed amount of wealth in the world and that one country must take wealth away from another country in order to gain more*) Then have them make a diagram to show the effects of this policy. **ENGLISH LANGUAGE LEARNERS**

The sea dogs also made important voyages of exploration. Drake, for example, sailed west from England across the Atlantic Ocean. He continued around South America to the west coast of North America. He then crossed the Pacific and Indian Oceans, rounded southern Africa, and returned to England in 1580. Drake was the first English sea captain to sail around the globe.

The sea dogs were best known for plundering foreign ships. Their repeated raids of Spanish slave ships from Africa greatly angered King Philip II of Spain. However, these attacks were part of a larger effort to undermine Spain's empire in the Americas. As Richard Hakluyt, an English historian of the day, observed:

> **❝If you touch him [King Philip II of Spain] in the [West] Indies, you touch the apple of his eye; for take away his treasure . . . [and] his old bands of soldiers will soon be dissolved, his purpose defeated, his power and strength diminished, his pride abated, and his tyranny utterly suppressed . . . .❞**
>
> Richard Hakluyt, *A Discourse on Western Planting*

Philip protested to Queen Elizabeth, who claimed she was helpless to stop the raids. Secretly, Elizabeth supported the sea dogs and shared the profits from selling the slaves. Both pirates and patriots, the sea dogs helped England defeat the Spanish Armada in 1588. They strengthened the nation's seafaring tradition.

The British in India. The defeat of the Spanish Armada encouraged the British to establish colonies overseas. In 1600 Queen Elizabeth I granted a charter to a trading group that came to be known as the British East India Company. Over the course of its long life—it continued for nearly 260 years—the company played a major role in the development of Great Britain's overseas power. During its early years, the company worked to build and expand overseas trade, making no attempt to gain territory. It set up trading posts at Bombay, Calcutta, and Madras in India. These posts gradually became centers of power from which the British were able both to defend their trade interests and to expand their influence. Over time, in fact, the British East India Company became an unofficial extension of the British government. Throughout its history, the company did much to shape and apply Britain's colonial and commercial policies.

Given the decline of the once-mighty Mughal Empire by the 1600s, the British East India Company dealt mainly with local rulers during its early years. The company worked to win the support and loyalty of these rulers in several ways. It helped those who were weak, used force without hesitation against those who opposed the company's aims, and bribed those who were willing to accept its generous "gifts."

By the mid-1700s the British East India Company had established trading posts in Malaya and the East Indies, as well as in India. As it grew, the company came into increasing contact—and conflict—with French traders who had built a similar company. Increasing competition between the two trading companies, and between the British and the French in general, eventually led to open conflict. The British emerged supreme from this struggle. By the late 1750s the company had become the dominant

Analyzing Primary Sources

Finding the Main Idea What did Hakluyt think the British could accomplish by attacking Philip's ships in the West Indies? dissolve his army, defeat his purpose, diminish his strength, abate his pride, suppress his tyranny

INTERPRETING THE VISUAL RECORD

The British in India This is a painted wooden model from the early 1800s. It depicts an Indian court called the Cutcherry. *What evidence is there that officers of the British East India Company were in charge?*

Economics

While the Spanish and Portuguese explored and traded on behalf of their governments, the English and Dutch sailed for mostly commercial reasons. With the establishment of the great East India companies, they became aggressively commercial in their endeavors. Neither country showed particular interest in exploration for its own sake, for glory, or for religious reasons—the primary motivations behind many Spanish and Portuguese expeditions. Instead, they concentrated almost exclusively on profit. Consequently, England eventually supplanted Portugal as the primary trading power in India and, later, in China.

Critical Thinking

Ask students to guess why these countries might have had different motivations for exploring.

ANSWER: Answers will vary, but students might guess that the honor and glory of exploration was valued more by the cultures of Spain and Portugal.

VISUAL RECORD ANSWER

The officer is standing in front of the group in an official uniform.

LEVEL 3: Tell students that English rulers embraced the idea of mercantilism wholeheartedly and aggressively sought to acquire new territories. Before long, Great Britain established itself as one of the world's most powerful empires. Have students create one or more political cartoons commenting on the early British colonial situation in India and/or the Americas. You may wish to collect examples of modern or historical political cartoons to share with students as models or for inspiration.

 HOMEWORK Remind students of the old saying, "The sun never sets on the British Empire." Then ask them to explain what they think this old saying meant.

CLOSE

Ask students to write a paragraph explaining the results of the British mercantilist policy.

Global Relations

Approximately half the population of the new settlers in the established colonies of North America were voluntary indentured servants. The term *indentured servant* comes from the contract, called an indenture, that the servant agreed to in order to gain passage to the colonies. Although some colonizers originally hoped to establish a sort of feudal system in the new colonies in which serfs worked the land, they found that, because of the abundance of land, serfdom was not a viable option. Instead, they turned to indentured servitude.

Indentured servants were fairly expensive, but they worked the land from four to seven years. After they finished their term, they were given food, some money, clothing, and tools, and could stake a claim to land. Planters eventually discovered that importing enslaved people was more profitable, because, while initially expensive, the slaves were tied to the planters for life.

Critical Thinking

Ask students to suggest reasons why people would voluntarily become indentured servants.

ANSWER: Students might suggest that these people desired a chance to own land in the colonies but were too poor to pay for passage across the Atlantic.

VISUAL RECORD ANSWER

The Europeans appear to be peaceful, bringing supplies, and welcomed.

492

European trade interest in India. At the same time, it had become extremely powerful and wealthy and enjoyed strong support in Parliament.

✔ **READING CHECK: Evaluating** What role did the English sea dogs play in England's larger quests for power? undermined Spain's American empire, drained its wealth, added to naval strength

The British in America

England was slow to establish colonies in North America. At first, the British explored the continent in hope of finding the Northwest Passage. This would have been a northern water route to Asia through or around North America. Spain controlled the southern route around Cape Horn in South America. Unfortunately, the Northwest Passage could not be found.

Henry Hudson was one of the first to search for the Northwest Passage. In 1609 he sailed on behalf of the Dutch. He charted much of the coast of eastern North America and explored the river that now bears his name. The next year he sailed on behalf of the English. He explored the bay in northern Canada also named for him.

British settlements. As they searched for the Northwest Passage, the British began settling along the eastern coast of North America. Private companies or individuals founded the first of these colonial settlements. In 1607 they established Jamestown, in what is now Virginia. Jamestown was the first permanent English settlement in North America. In 1620 settlers founded Plymouth, in what is now Massachusetts.

The founders hoped that these settlements would make money for the home country. Few investors, however, made any profit from the colonies. The colonists themselves settled in North America for other reasons. Some came to find greater political or religious freedom. Others simply wanted better lives for their families.

Many settlers did not come voluntarily. As in other colonial empires, the English brought slaves to their colonies. Slavery was most common in the southern colonies and in the West Indies. Barbados, in the Caribbean, was a huge commercial success largely because slaves did most of the work.

The model pictured below is of Henry Hudson's ship, the Half Moon. Although they appear tiny and fragile by today's standards, ships like this carried European explorers to new lands around the world.

INTERPRETING THE VISUAL RECORD

Henry Hudson This image shows Henry Hudson landing on Manhattan Island. *How does this image reflect a European perspective?*

Most European colonies were ruled from the home country. Self-government set England's empire apart. Most English colonies had some form of representative assembly. Official control, however, remained firmly with England.

Mercantilism and the British colonies. The British government tried to make the colonies more profitable. Its policy of mercantilism held that the colonies existed for the economic benefit of the home country. Mercantilists believed that for a nation to become wealthy, it must export more goods than it imported. They saw colonies as sources of raw materials for the factories of the home country and as markets for the products of those factories.

Parliament passed laws to enforce this policy beginning in the 1650s. One law required colonists to sell certain products only to Britain—even if better prices were available in another country. Other laws discouraged colonists from manufacturing their own goods. For example, the British government forbade colonists to ship woolen cloth that they had manufactured to places outside their own colony.

Colonists resented the British trade regulations, and they found many ways to evade the laws. For example, they avoided paying taxes whenever and however they could. Smuggling became a respectable occupation in the colonies. This practice was hard to prevent because the long, indented coastline of North America had many harbors and inlets where ships could hide. Until the mid-1700s, moreover, the British government did not try very hard to enforce its colonial trade restrictions.

✔ **READING CHECK: Analyzing Information**
What were the results of British mercantilist policy? discouraged colonial manufacturing, forced colonists to sell certain products only to Britain

Britain's mercantilist policies attempted to assure a flow of gold into the nation's treasury.

CONNECTING TO
Economics

Mercantilism

Mercantilism was a theory that favored the extension of a nation's economic power beyond its borders. Mercantilists realized that a strong colonial power would benefit from having a large population to provide the workers, consumers, and soldiers needed by a growing economy. They also believed that gold and silver were important measures of national wealth.

Understanding Economics

Why might merchants in the colonies object to mercantilism?

SECTION 3 REVIEW

1. **Define** and explain the significance:
   sea dogs

2. **Identify** and explain the significance:
   John Cabot
   Sir Francis Drake
   Henry Hudson

3. **Sequencing** Copy the diagram below. Indicate with an arrow for each item the direction—to or from the home country—in which British mercantilist policy would have this item shipped.

4. **Finding the Main Idea**
   a. What was the importance of the sea dogs to British hopes for empire?
   b. What were the results of British mercantilist policy?

5. **Writing and Critical Thinking**
   Drawing Conclusions Why did Elizabeth I support the activities of the English sea dogs?
   Consider:
   • how the sea dogs attacked Spanish shipping
   • the results of the sea dogs' attacks
   • how the sea dogs supported English policies against the Spanish

Homework Practice Online
keyword: SP3 HP20

OBJECTIVES

1 **Identify the principal characteristics of Enlightenment thinking.**

2 **Analyze the similarities and differences in the ideas of important Enlightenment philosophers.**

SECTION 4

READ TO DISCOVER

❶ What were the principal characteristics of Enlightenment thinking?

❷ What were the similarities and differences in the ideas of important Enlightenment philosophers?

DEFINE

rationalism
philosophes
popular sovereignty
enlightened despotism

IDENTIFY

Enlightenment
The Encyclopedia
Denis Diderot
Baron de Montesquieu
Voltaire
Jean-Jacques Rousseau
Mary Wollstonecraft

▶ WHY IT MATTERS TODAY

The idea that science can help explain human behavior has persisted. Use CNN News.com or other **current event** sources to find an example of how the scientific method is used to give information about group behavior. Record your findings in your journal.

CNN student News.com

The Enlightenment

The Main Idea
Enlightenment thinkers examined and challenged traditional views of government.

The Story Continues *Increasingly during the 1600s and the 1700s, the ancient European social and political order, in which a small but privileged minority controlled the majority, came under attack. Critics of the old order complained that the privileged few took much and gave back little. Noted one French thinker, "If [a great lord] . . . can conceal the fact that he has nothing to do by looking busy, . . . he thinks himself the most fortunate of men."*

Crusaders of the Enlightenment

The 1700s have been called the Age of **Enlightenment.** Some people believed that reason and the scientific method could logically explain human nature. This belief that truth can be determined solely by logical thinking was called **rationalism.**

Thinkers of the Enlightenment believed in natural law. Objects in nature were expected to act in ways that were predictable. During the 1700s many people came to believe that laws of nature governed the universe and all its creatures. These beliefs formed the foundation of the modern natural sciences.

These advanced thinkers also believed that God had created the world and all living things. Just as the law of gravity governed the movement of planets, other laws governed human behavior. To live in harmony, people must live according to natural law. However, many believed that God did not act directly in human affairs and that individual human actions mattered most in determining the future. Some thinkers downplayed the importance of religion, a view that became known as secularism. Enlightenment ideas about secularism and individualism would later influence some ideas about the separation of church and state in government.

Thinkers of the Enlightenment were called **philosophes** (fee·luh·ZAWFS), after the French word for philosopher. They were not only philosophers but also critics of society. They wrote to one another and published their ideas in books, plays, pamphlets, and newspapers. Their most famous and ambitious project was ***The Encyclopedia,*** a sort of handbook describing the ideas of the Enlightenment that became the most famous publication of the period.

Shown here are a few pages from a rare first edition of **The Encyclopedia** *published by the French philosophes.*

TEACH OBJECTIVE 1

LEVEL 1: Ask students to name the major characteristics of the Enlightenment. *(belief that natural law governed human behavior, that truth could be determined by logic)* Ask students what these two characteristics have in common. *(orderliness, practicality, or interest in natural events)*

ENGLISH LANGUAGE LEARNERS

HOMEWORK Have students write an encyclopedia-style entry on a topic that would be of interest to someone studying the Enlightenment, such as one of its beliefs, characteristics, leading figures, or effects.

TEACH OBJECTIVE 2

ALL LEVELS: Have students construct a chart to list the characteristics and achievements specific to the philosophes. Then have students identify philosophies shared by them. *(wanted to change society, disliked absolute monarchy)*

ENGLISH LANGUAGE LEARNERS

Diderot	Montesquieu	Voltaire	Rousseau
edited Encyclopedia, criticized society	*wrote* Spirit of the Laws, *described "perfect" government*	*wrote* Candide, *championed freedom of thought and religion*	*wrote* The Social Contract, *believed in sovereignty*

INTERPRETING THE VISUAL RECORD

Enlightenment salons Marie-Thérèse Geoffrin's salon in the Hotel Rambouillet provided a weekly opportunity for artists and writers to meet with one another and to discuss the ideas of the Enlightenment. *How might the salon pictured to the left encourage the free exchange of ideas?*

The Encyclopedia was edited by philosopher **Denis Diderot** (dee-DROH). He and co-editor Jean d'Alembert (dah-lem-BER) published the first edition in 28 volumes between 1751 and 1772. Leading philosophes contributed articles covering nearly every possible subject. Many of the articles were very technical. Others criticized many things in society. They attacked the church, the government, the slave trade, torture, taxes, and war. The French authorities frowned on critical writings, however. They imprisoned Diderot and several other philosophes. Nevertheless, people throughout Europe read *The Encyclopedia* and adopted its ideas.

✔ **READING CHECK: Finding the Main Idea** What were the main characteristics of Enlightenment thinking? belief that natural law governed human behavior, that truth could be determined by logic, secularism, and individualism

Political Criticism

Based on the democratic-republican governments that had evolved in classical Greece and Rome, the philosophes examined the governments of their time. They criticized the power of kings and the privileges of clergy and nobles.

A number of the philosophes adopted the ideas of John Locke. One of them was **Baron de Montesquieu** (MOHN-tes-kyoo). In 1748 Montesquieu published *The Spirit of the Laws*. In this book he tried to describe the perfect government. He concluded that Great Britain had the best. He wrote that the British system's greatest strength was the division of government into three branches. He believed that the balance between the executive, legislative, and judicial branches provided checks to political power.

Although Montesquieu was wrong about how government was divided in Britain, his ideas carried great weight. His idea of checks and balances would influence the framing of the U.S. Constitution in 1787.

French writer Francois-Marie Arouet, best known as **Voltaire,** exemplified the spirit of the Enlightenment. Voltaire wrote clever and stinging satires on the French monarchy, the nobility, and the religious controls of the church. Twice imprisoned in the Bastille for his attacks on the old order, Voltaire fled for a time to Britain. He was especially critical of intolerance and of attempts to suppress personal freedoms. In defense of the freedom of speech, Voltaire wrote, "I [may] disapprove of what you say, but I will defend to the death your right to say it." In his book *Philosophical Letters*, Voltaire wrote that he, too, was impressed by the British political system.

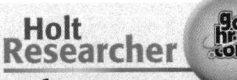

Holt Researcher

go.hrw.com
KEYWORD: Holt Researcher
FreeFind:

   Marie-Therese Geoffrin
After reading more about Marie-Thérèse Geoffrin on the Holt Researcher, write an imaginary dialogue that she might have had in her salon about political issues of the time.

Culture

Although the Enlightenment produced ideas that could be considered revolutionary for the times, the movement did not have an immediate widespread impact. In the early years of the Enlightenment, the audiences for the philosophers' ideas were relatively small, since they had to be wealthy enough to be invited to the salons or to afford the luxury of books. Many Enlightenment beliefs would later be used to defend the ideas of democracy and social equality. During the Enlightenment itself, however, the philosophers and their wealthy, educated audience remained aloof from the common people.

Critical Thinking

Ask students why it might be advantageous for the Enlightenment to be initially popular with the wealthy and educated.

ANSWER: Students might respond that rulers would be more likely to accept reforms suggested by the wealthy and educated than by common people and that the wealthy and educated would be able to spread Enlightenment ideas throughout society.

VISUAL RECORD ANSWER

The arrangement of the chairs in a semicircle may have promoted discussion from everyone present.

Ask students to note the similarities and differences among the philosophes.

REVIEW

Have students complete the Section 4 Review on p. 496.

ASSESS

Have students complete Daily Quiz 20.4. As Alternative Assessment, you may want to use the Enlightenment or philosophe exercises in this section's lessons.

RETEACH

Have students complete Main Idea Activity for English Language Learners and Special-Needs Students 20.4. Have students write one question for each subsection in the section.
ENGLISH LANGUAGE LEARNERS, COOPERATIVE LEARNING

EXTEND

Have students create a list of questions they would ask a specific Enlightenment thinker in an interview for a television current affairs program. **BLOCK SCHEDULING, COOPERATIVE LEARNING**

History Maker

equality, personal freedom, economic independence, educational opportunities, political rights

SECTION 4 REVIEW ANSWERS

❶ **Define**
- rationalism, p. 494
- philosophes, p. 494
- popular sovereignty, p. 496
- enlightened despotism, p. 496

❷ **Identify**
- Enlightenment, p. 494
- *The Encyclopedia,* p. 494
- Denis Diderot, p. 495
- Baron de Montesquieu, p. 495
- Voltaire, p. 495
- Jean-Jacques Rousseau, p. 496
- Mary Wollstonecraft, p. 496

❸ Montesquieu: checks and balances; Voltaire: freedom of speech; Rousseau: popular sovereignty; Wollstonecraft: women's rights

❹ **a.** belief that natural law governed human behavior, that truth could be determined by logic

b. Secularism and individualism led to more rights for all people, individual freedoms, and government by the people.

❺ Students' selections will vary but should include a strong argument in favor of one philosophy.

HISTORY MAKER

Mary Wollstonecraft (1759–1797)

During the Enlightenment, British author Mary Wollstonecraft argued for the equality of women with men. Wollstonecraft sought personal freedom and economic independence, working as a schoolteacher and a governess before turning to writing. In her most well-known work, *A Vindication of the Rights of Woman* (1792), Wollstonecraft argued that women should enjoy the same educational opportunities and political rights as men, including the right to vote. **What did Mary Wollstonecraft want for women?**

Back in France, Voltaire continued his criticism. He attacked everything he considered a sham or superstition. His novel *Candide* ridiculed prejudice, bigotry, and oppressive government. Voltaire became famous as a champion of religious freedom and freedom of thought.

In 1762 **Jean-Jacques Rousseau** (roo·SOH) published *The Social Contract.* He wrote that people are naturally good, but that environment, education, and laws corrupt them. He believed that people could preserve their natural state only if they could choose their own government. He wrote that good government must be based on **popular sovereignty.** By this he meant that government must be created by and controlled by the people.

 History Makers Speak ❝Man is born free; and everywhere he is in chains. One thinks himself the master of others, and still remains a greater slave than they.❞

Jean-Jacques Rousseau, *The Social Contract*

Unlike other philosophes, Rousseau did not trust reason. He believed that it brought corruption and misery. Rousseau's opposition to a strong government also set him apart. Although philosophes disliked absolute monarchy, most of them favored the idea of **enlightened despotism.** This was a system of government in which an absolute monarch would rule, but according to the principles of the Enlightenment.

By the 1780s many people had come to accept Rousseau's philosophy and his distrust of reason. His ideas on government and individual freedom became most influential during the later years of the Enlightenment.

Although most of the philosophes were men, women also participated in the Enlightenment. English author **Mary Wollstonecraft** became an early spokesperson for women's rights. Wollstonecraft argued that Enlightenment ideals of equality should be extended to women as well as men.

✔ **READING CHECK: Comparing and Contrasting** Compare and contrast the ideas of the following philosophes: Montesquieu, Voltaire, and Rousseau. Montesquieu: government divided into branches creates checks on political power; Voltaire: criticized intolerance, attempts to suppress personal freedoms; Rousseau: distrusted reason, opposed strong government, popular sovereignty

---

◁ **SECTION 4 REVIEW** ▷

1. **Define** and explain the significance:
   rationalism
   philosophes
   popular sovereignty
   enlightened despotism

2. **Identify** and explain the significance:
   Enlightenment
   The Encyclopedia
   Denis Diderot
   Baron de Montesquieu
   Voltaire
   Jean-Jacques Rousseau
   Mary Wollstonecraft

3. **Categorizing** Copy the diagram below. Draw lines to match the principles on the right with the names on the left.

Montesquieu	popular sovereignty
Voltaire	women's rights
Rousseau	checks and balances
Wollstonecraft	freedom of speech

4. **Finding the Main Idea**
   a. What were the main characteristics of Enlightenment thinking?
   b. How did the ideas of secularism and individualism that arose during the Enlightenment affect later governments?

5. **Writing and Critical Thinking**
   Evaluating Select one of the philosophes. Explain why you believe his or her views on government are correct or incorrect.
   Consider:
   • the type of government championed by the philosophe you have selected
   • whether or not his or her ideas and approaches were realistic

 Homework Practice Online
keyword: SP3 HP20

SECTION 5

OBJECTIVES

1 **Explain how Americans responded to British policies after the French and Indian War.**

2 **Describe what type of government Americans set up after the American Revolution.**

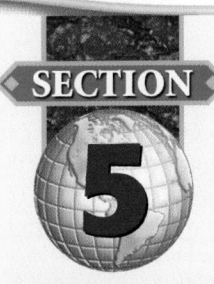

SECTION 5

READ TO DISCOVER

❶ How did Americans respond to British policies after the French and Indian War?

❷ What type of government did Americans set up after the American Revolution?

DEFINE

federal system of government
executive branch
legislative branch
judicial branch

IDENTIFY

Stamp Act
King George III
Lord North
Patriots
Loyalists
Thomas Jefferson
George Washington
Benjamin Franklin
Articles of Confederation
Bill of Rights

▶WHY IT MATTERS TODAY

In modern times people have often rebelled against tyrannical governments. Use CNN Student News.com or other **current event** sources to find several examples of recent political revolutions. Record your findings in your journal.

CNN Student News.com

The American Revolution

The Main Idea
In the late 1700s the United States of America broke from Britain to form a new kind of government.

The Story Continues *In the American colonies, Enlightenment thinking inspired new beliefs based upon the ideals of popular sovereignty. A growing number of people in Britain's North American colonies held that they should be governed by the same standards of law and liberty that governed people in Great Britain. They insisted that ". . . his majesty's subjects in these [American] colonies are entitled to all the inherent rights and privileges of his natural born subjects within the kingdom of Great Britain."*

Empire and Conflict

New ideas about government were not confined to Europe in the 1700s. In far-off North America, British colonists had developed a new way of life. They were creating a new relationship with the home country. Their first concern was with British trade laws, but they also disliked the French along their borders.

British-French rivalry. The British colonies sat along the Atlantic coast of North America. French settlements were to the north and the west, in what was called New France. In the 1700s British-American settlers moved westward across the Appalachian Mountains. Conflict with the French seemed inescapable.

France and Britain had fought in Europe for decades. The conflict spilled over into North America and in 1754 resulted in the French and Indian War. In Europe this sparked the Seven Years' War, which raged from 1756 to 1763. British victory in these conflicts was confirmed by the Treaty of Paris of 1763. The British had won control of much of North America. They ruled from the Atlantic Ocean to the Mississippi River and from the Gulf of Mexico to the Arctic Ocean. British power had reached a new height.

Increased imperial control. The war with France left Britain with a huge debt. British politicians had defended the colonists. They now expected the colonists to repay this effort.

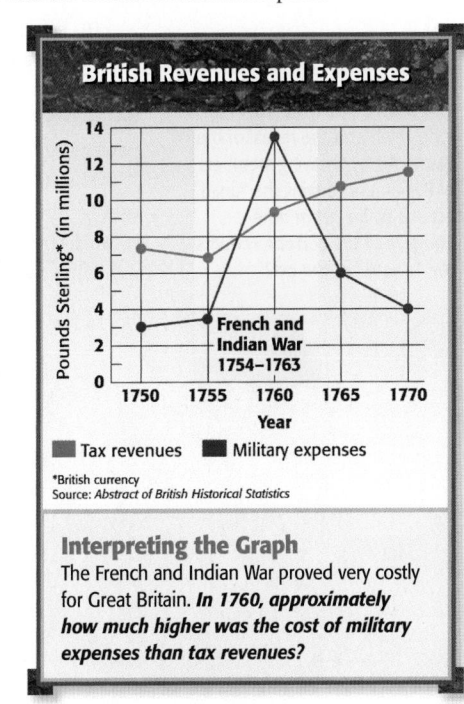

British Revenues and Expenses

French and Indian War 1754–1763

■ Tax revenues ■ Military expenses

*British currency
Source: Abstract of British Historical Statistics*

Interpreting the Graph
The French and Indian War proved very costly for Great Britain. *In 1760, approximately how much higher was the cost of military expenses than tax revenues?*

RESOURCES

REPRODUCIBLE RESOURCES
▶ Guided Reading Strategy 20.5
▶ Graphic Organizer Activity 20
▶ Hands-on History Activity 20

TECHNOLOGY RESOURCES
▶ One-Stop Planner 20.5
▶ Holt Researcher: World History: Benjamin Franklin, Thomas Jefferson
▶ Homework Practice Online

REINFORCEMENT, REVIEW, AND ASSESSMENT
▶ Section 5 Review, p. 503
▶ Daily Quiz 20.5
▶ Main Idea Activity 20.5
▶ English Audio Summary 20.5
▶ Spanish Audio Summary 20.5

INTERPRETING THE GRAPH ANSWER
$4 million

TEACH OBJECTIVE 1

LEVEL 2: Create a chart on the chalkboard. Have volunteers list British policies implemented in the mid-1700s and how the American colonists reacted to them. Students should also fill in a column explaining why they think Britain enacted such a policy, even if an explicit reason is not provided in the text. For example:

British Policy	Colonial Reaction	Possible British Cause
Colonists were forbidden to settle in the land west of the Appalachian Mountains.	Colonists felt that Britain was curbing their liberties.	Britain wanted to avoid American Indian uprisings.

After the chart is completed, ask students what actions these conflicts over policy led the American colonists to take. *(Patriot delegates met at the First Continental Congress and demanded the full rights of British people.)*

Global Relations

Previously, Britain had intervened very little in American affairs. Only governors and officials in charge of enforcing the Navigation Acts had any control. Some colonists sat in the colonial assemblies, which not only set internal policies for the colonies but also determined the salaries of the British-appointed governors.

Critical Thinking

Ask students how the colonists' experience was a factor in the revolution.

ANSWER: Students may answer that the colonists, already having political experience and structures, resented having their independence taken away and wanted to run their own government.

VISUAL RECORD ANSWER

the skulls

Stamps such as this were required by the Stamp Act to be put on all commercial and legal papers.

INTERPRETING THE VISUAL RECORD

The Stamp Act This British cartoon celebrates the repeal of the Stamp Act by showing members of Parliament carrying the "dead" act in a coffin. *What other imagery in the cartoon reflects the "death" of the act?*

British policy toward the colonies in the 1760s was uneven. In 1763 after an American Indian uprising, the British barred colonists from settling west of the Appalachians. The government also began enforcing its mercantilist trade laws. The Sugar Act of 1764, for example, imposed taxes on sugar and other imports from non-British colonies. The colonists saw this as a threat to their liberties.

In 1765 Parliament passed the **Stamp Act.** This law imposed a tax, in the form of a special stamp, on all sorts of documents, including wills, contracts, mortgages, newspapers, and pamphlets. The colonists opposed the tax. When they boycotted British goods, Parliament backed down and repealed the Stamp Act.

With each new tax law, colonial resistance increased. Some laws were repealed, but others were not. With no representatives in the British Parliament, the colonists argued against this "taxation without representation." They called it tyranny. Relations between Britain and the colonies grew steadily worse.

Intensified conflict. Reigning from 1760 to 1820, **King George III** was the first Hanoverian monarch to be born in England. He believed that Parliament had too much power. He wanted to select his own ministers. Six prime ministers came to power in just eight years. It was during this unsettled time that the final break with the American colonies occurred.

As the colonists hardened their resistance to British policies, George III was determined to force their obedience. In 1770 he found a new prime minister, **Lord North,** who was willing to carry out his policies.

Many American colonists were coming to believe that breaking away from British rule was necessary to guarantee their rights. The colonists were far from united for independence, however. About one third, called **Patriots,** wanted independence. Another third, called **Loyalists,** or Tories, opposed independence. The rest of the colonists did not take sides.

In 1773 Lord North's government gave the British East India Company a monopoly to ship tea directly to the colonies. Angry colonists threw a shipment of tea into Boston Harbor, an event that became known as the Boston Tea Party. Parliament responded by closing the port of Boston. Colonists called this and several other laws passed in 1774 the Intolerable Acts.

The Patriots took action. In the fall of 1774, delegates from 12 of the 13 colonies met in Philadelphia in the First Continental Congress. They demanded that the colonists be granted the full rights of British citizens. They agreed to meet again the following year if the British Parliament did not repeal the Intolerable Acts.

By April 1775 British troops in Boston had begun to feel threatened by the colonists' growing resistance. In response the British tried to seize colonial guns and gunpowder stored nearby. At the towns of Lexington and Concord, the British fought with groups of armed colonists. The American Revolution had begun.

✔ **READING CHECK: Evaluating** How did colonists in America respond to changing British policy in the years between 1763 and 1775? Resistance to British policies hardened.

TEACH OBJECTIVE 1

ALL LEVELS: Provide students with a copy of the Declaration of Independence. After reading the document, students should list the main reasons that the colonists demanded independence. Then call on volunteers to review key ideas of the Enlightenment. Ask students which Enlightenment principles Thomas Jefferson incorporated into the Declaration. *(All people have natural rights; governments exist by the consent of the governed; when a government ceases to serve the people, they have the right to change it.)*

ENGLISH LANGUAGE LEARNERS, BLOCK SCHEDULING

American Independence

Delegates to the Second Continental Congress met in Philadelphia in May 1775. Many still hoped to avoid conflict. When they received news of the fighting at Lexington and Concord, their attitudes quickly changed. They prepared for war.

The Declaration of Independence. Delegates met again the following year. They voted to declare their freedom from Great Britain. On July 4, 1776, they adopted the Declaration of Independence. This established the United States of America as an independent nation. **Thomas Jefferson** was the Declaration's principal author. The Declaration of Independence showed the influence of Enlightenment philosophers such as John Locke. It declared that all men are created equal and have the right to "life, liberty, and the pursuit of happiness."

In his first draft of the Declaration, Jefferson had denounced slavery. But other delegates—primarily slaveholders from the southern American colonies—objected strongly to Jefferson's attack on their rights as "property owners." In order to secure the support of slaveholders in the southern colonies, therefore, delegates to the Congress removed the passage from the Declaration. Thus the ideal of individual liberty was only applied in a limited manner. Neither women nor slaves were included in the provisions of the Declaration of Independence. Nevertheless, the Declaration represented a milestone in the struggle for broader equality and justice.

The Declaration stated that all powers of government come from the people. It said that no government can exist without the consent of its citizens and that government is created to protect individual rights. If a government fails to protect these rights, the Declaration said, the people may alter or abolish it and set up a new government. These were extreme ideas. It was one thing to reject absolute monarchy. It was quite another to say people have the right of revolution.

Primary Source

"We hold these truths to be self-evident, that all men are created equal, that they are endowed by their Creator with certain unalienable Rights, that among these are Life, Liberty, and the pursuit of Happiness. That to secure these rights, Governments are instituted among Men, deriving their just powers from the consent of the governed, That whenever any Form of Government becomes destructive of these ends, it is the Right of the People to alter or to abolish it, and to institute a new Government . . ."

The Declaration of Independence

The American Declaration of Independence was a remarkable and powerful political statement. It was also an elegant summary of many of the ideals and values that influenced Europe and America during the Enlightenment.

✔ **READING CHECK Summarizing** What new political and legal ideas were contained in the Declaration of Independence? government is created to protect individual rights and cannot exist without the consent of the governed, who can alter or abolish it

YOUNG PEOPLE IN HISTORY

Young Patriots

Patriots of all ages fought in the American Revolution. Many young boys between the ages of 14 and 16 enlisted in the American army. Other boys, some as young as six, served as drummers for the troops, like the one pictured here. Their job was to signal commands, which sometimes put them in the midst of battle.

The American navy had its share of young sailors as well. Small boys served as deckhands or "powder monkeys." They carried ammunition to the gunners during battle. **How did young boys serve during the American Revolution?**

Analyzing Primary Sources

Drawing Conclusions According to the Declaration of Independence, why are governments established, and what rights do people have when their government becomes oppressive and unjust? to secure the rights of people; people may alter or abolish oppressive governments

Culture

The British-born George III paid more attention to the American colonies than his German-born predecessors. As the crisis with the American colonies grew, and the colonists increased their resistance, George III became more determined to force them into obedience.

Critical Thinking

Ask students why they think George III was more interested in British and colonial affairs than were his predecessors.

ANSWER: Students might suggest that because he was born in Britain, George III felt more ties to the country and its affairs.

YOUNG PEOPLE IN HISTORY ANSWER
as drummers who signaled commands and deckhands who carried ammunition to the gunners

HOMEWORK Have students create a dialogue between a Patriot and a Loyalist. In the dialogue each person should explain why his or her side could expect to win the war. Students should base their arguments on their side's advantages, the other side's disadvantages, and moral strength. You may choose to have students act out several of the dialogues to the class, and then have the class vote on which side's argument is the most convincing.

That's Interesting!

In an early draft of the Declaration of Independence, Thomas Jefferson had included a paragraph that accused King George of transporting slaves from Africa to the colonies and "suppressing every legislative attempt to prohibit or to restrain this execrable commerce." Slaveholders, including Jefferson, were unsure about the desirability of ending the slave trade, however, and the Continental Congress removed the paragraph.

MAP ANSWER
Appalachian Mountains

Technology Resources

World History
Teaching Transparency:
Geography and History 17:
The Fight for Independence, 1776–1781

The war for independence. It was not clear who would win the Revolutionary War. Each side had strengths and weaknesses. The Americans were defending their own homes in well-known territory. The British, however, had a superior military force. Their army and navy were well trained. The British fleet was the strongest in the world. The British had to cross an ocean, however, and bring in most of their military supplies and equipment.

The war against the colonists was not popular in Great Britain. Some British even sympathized with the Americans. Britain had no allies to help it in the war. As a result, King George III had to hire some of his soldiers. Many of these mercenaries were Germans from Hesse, a state in the southwestern region of Germany. These mercenaries, known as Hessians, aroused a great deal of anger among the American colonists, who viewed their use by the British as especially brutal.

Military Campaigns of the American Revolution, 1775–1783

Interpreting Maps The Battle of Saratoga in October 1777 marked the first great American victory of the Revolutionary War.

■ **Skills Assessment: Physical Systems** What geographic feature marked the western boundary of the middle colonies?

LEVEL 3: Tell students to imagine that their government does not have the right to tax, coin money, or regulate trade, nor does it have a chief executive or a federal court system. Ask students what problems they can envision arising from such a situation. (*The government could run out of money; it would be difficult for merchants and consumers to conduct trade; lawmakers might have a hard time doing their jobs; punishment for crimes would differ greatly in different regions of the country.*) Tell students that such a situation existed in the early American states. Close by asking students how they would characterize the government created by the Articles of Confederation. (*ineffectual because there was no strong central government*)

Teacher to Teacher

Paul Horne of Columbia, South Carolina, suggested the following activity: Have students compare and contrast the British and U.S. constitutions. Students should identify no less than five similarities and five differences between the documents. Divide the class into groups and have the groups prepare a poster compiling their thoughts. Groups should then present their posters to the class.

At first, a lack of unity among the colonies helped the British. The weakness of the American government was a serious problem. The colonies sent representatives to the Continental Congress voluntarily. Proposals governing the conduct of the war had to be passed unanimously. These proposals involved critical issues such as the purchase of weapons and equipment, food supplies for the army, the appointment of officers, and campaign plans. At a time when speedy decisions were necessary, a single opposing voice within the Congress could halt action. Under these conditions delegates might be forced to spend much time in negotiation with one another to reach agreement and unanimity. The Congress also had to borrow money and print paper currency to finance the war. This need created many problems, however, because the Congress's credit was poor and lenders were difficult to find. In many cases troops and suppliers grumbled that they were being paid with money that was basically worthless.

Under these circumstances it was difficult to build a strong army. At first the American forces were poorly trained volunteers who did not do well in battle against the British soldiers. Fortunately they had good leaders, such as **George Washington,** commander of the American forces. Some help came from other nations, such as France, that opposed British interests on an international scale. These countries helped to provide military officers, troops, weapons, ships, and money for the colonists. Meaningful support from European powers, however, was not seen by the Americans until relatively late in the war.

War and peace. Most of the fighting took place between 1776 and 1781. A major turning point came in October 1777, when the Americans defeated a British force under General John Burgoyne at Saratoga, New York. Now that the colonists seemed to have a chance of winning, the French jumped into the fray. Eager to weaken the British Empire, France agreed to an alliance with the United States. Spain and the Netherlands also joined the colonists' efforts. In 1781 the Americans and their French allies trapped and defeated the main British army at Yorktown, Virginia. The Americans had won the Revolutionary War.

Peace negotiations between the Americans and their former British rulers lasted two years. **Benjamin Franklin** was the chief American negotiator. In 1783 the British and the Americans and their allies signed the Treaty of Paris. The Americans had won their independence. They had also won a territory much larger than the original thirteen colonies.

✔ **READING CHECK: Contrasting** What advantages and disadvantages did each side have in the American Revolutionary War? Colonists: good leaders, supported by other powers; disunity, weak government, poorly trained army. British: superior military force; long supply lines, unpopular war, no allies.

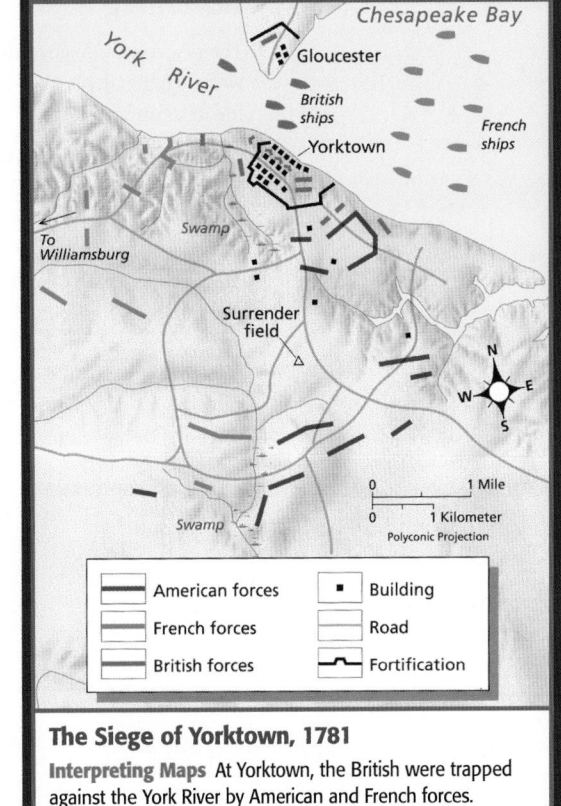

The Siege of Yorktown, 1781

Interpreting Maps At Yorktown, the British were trapped against the York River by American and French forces.

■ **Skills Assessment: 1. Human Systems** From what countries did the naval ships that engaged in battle at Yorktown sail? **2. Drawing Inferences** Why might the British forces have found it impossible to escape to their home country?

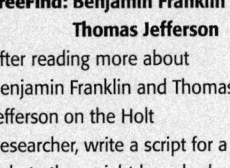

Holt Researcher

go.hrw.com
KEYWORD: Holt Researcher
FreeFind: Benjamin Franklin
Thomas Jefferson

After reading more about Benjamin Franklin and Thomas Jefferson on the Holt Researcher, write a script for a debate they might have had over the legalization of slavery in the United States.

Linking Past to Present

Many historians have pointed out that the Revolutionary War was primarily a struggle for power among members of the upper class. The men who engineered the revolt generally belonged to the wealthy ruling class; George Washington, for instance, was the richest man in the colonies. While most free men did fight in the war at some point, the majority who served were poor men. Several factors contributed to this situation. Rich men could avoid being drafted into the army by paying for substitutes, but poor men certainly did not have such means. Also, the military offered a place of promise with rewards such as a rise in rank, acquisition of money, and a change in social status.

Critical Thinking

Ask students what current issues in American society and politics tend to be split among wealthier and poorer voters.

ANSWER: Students might mention issues such as school funding, tax rates, capital gains tax, welfare, and other government spending programs.

MAP ANSWERS

1. Great Britain and France

2. Students might answer that they would have been pursued by French ships.

LEVEL 1: Ask students to describe the government created by the Constitution and why the framers so devised it. *(The government created is a democratic one in which powers are separated between the federal government and state governments and, in the federal government, between the executive, legislative, and judicial branches. The Constitution also has a Bill of Rights. The framers wanted to create a strong government in which people would be free of unfair rule, provide a system of checks and balances, and protect the freedoms of individuals.)* Then write the following words on the chalkboard: *democracy, checks and balances,* and *Bill of Rights.* Ask students how these aspects of the Constitution reflect Enlightenment thinking. *(Democracy reflects the idea that popular government is the most acceptable form of government. A system of checks and balances reflects the idea that real liberty does not exist if one branch of government is more powerful than the others. The Bill of Rights reflects the idea that individuals have certain rights and that it is the task of the government to protect these rights.)*

ENGLISH LANGUAGE LEARNERS

CLOSE

Ask students to describe the liberties that the new American democracy lacked. *(Women could not vote; voters were required to own property; those held in slavery had no rights.)*

Constitutional Heritage

Since ratification of the Bill of Rights, 17 more amendments have been added to the Constitution. These amendments have dealt with such issues as slavery, voting rights, income taxes, sale of alcohol, and presidential term limits. The 27th and most recent amendment was first proposed in 1789 by James Madison but was not ratified until 1992. This amendment states, "No law, varying the compensation for the services of the Senators and Representatives, shall take effect until an election of Representatives shall have intervened." More simply, it prohibits a sitting Congress from voting itself a pay raise—any increase in pay can only take effect after the next election.

ACTIVITY: Pass out copies of the Bill of Rights and the additional amendments to the Constitution. Ask students to study the amendments and write down the three they believe are most important to individual liberty. Discuss the students' responses as a class.

MAP ANSWER

Spain, Great Britain, Spain

Governing a New Nation

The new American government had a daunting task. It had to get the various states to work together. It also had to meet the goals of each group that had joined in winning the Revolutionary War.

The Articles of Confederation. The Second Continental Congress adopted the **Articles of Confederation** in 1777. This plan of government was ratified by the American states in 1781. The Articles set up a central government, with a one-house Congress in which each state had a single vote. Congress had the authority to declare war and make peace. It could also deal with other nations and settle disputes between the states. However, under the Articles of Confederation the central government was weak. The weakness of the new nation's government under the Articles was deliberate. Americans feared a strong central government that could quickly become repressive. They wanted to ensure that the individual rights and liberties for which they had fought were safeguarded. Thus Congress had no power to enforce its laws, which had to be approved by at least nine of the states.

Congress could not levy taxes or coin money. It could not regulate trade with foreign nations or among the states. Moreover, the Articles provided for no chief executive, and the only courts were state courts. Clearly, the Articles of Confederation were designed to place power in the hands of the individual states. State governments were seen as closer to the people and the popular will than the central government. Americans believed, too, that state governments were less likely to become repressive than the central government. Almost immediately, however, Americans began to realize that the Articles made it difficult to build an effective and stable government.

The Constitution. Many Americans were unhappy with the weakness of the new government. In May 1787 delegates from the states met again in Philadelphia to revise the Articles. The delegates soon realized, however, that a mere revision would not be enough. They decided instead to write a constitution.

After unanimously choosing George Washington as presiding officer, the delegates went to work. They wanted a strong central government. They also wanted some powers kept for the states. As a result, the Constitution they adopted provided for a **federal system of government.** The central, or federal, government was given many important powers. It could declare war, raise armies, and make treaties. It could coin money and regulate trade with foreign countries. The states and the people retained all other powers.

The federal government had three branches. The **executive branch,** headed by the president, enforced the laws. The **legislative branch,** consisting of the Congress, made the laws. The **judicial branch,** consisting of the federal courts, interpreted the laws. Each branch acted as a check on the power of the others.

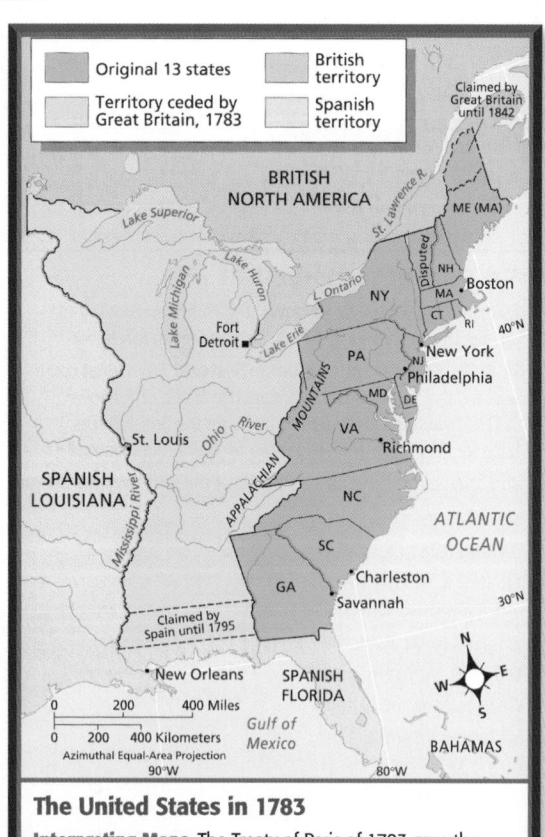

The United States in 1783

Interpreting Maps The Treaty of Paris of 1783 gave the United States a large area of land beyond the boundaries of the original 13 colonies.

■ **Skills Assessment: Places and Regions** What nation controlled the region to the south of the United States? To the north? To the west?

REVIEW

Have students complete the Section 5 Review on p. 503.

ASSESS

Have students complete Daily Quiz 20.5. As Alternative Assessment, you may want to use the Declaration of Independence or Constitution exercises in this section's lessons.

RETEACH

Have students complete Main Idea Activity for English Language Learners and Special-Needs Students 20.5. Then ask students to write a question and answer that covers the main idea for each

subsection in the section. Have volunteers read their questions to the class. Have the class try to answer each question.
ENGLISH LANGUAGE LEARNERS

EXTEND

Encourage students to imagine they are cartoonists at the time of the American Revolution. Have them draw a cartoon from the colonial viewpoint of an incident or personality mentioned in the text. Display finished cartoons in the classroom.
BLOCK SCHEDULING

Delegates to the Constitutional Convention signed the new document in September 1787. After the Constitution was ratified by the necessary nine states, it went into force in 1789.

Some Americans did not like the Constitution. They feared that it did not protect the rights of individuals. As a result, ten amendments were added in 1791. Together these amendments are known as the **Bill of Rights.** They guarantee freedom of religion, speech, the press, assembly, and petition. They also guarantee freedom from illegal search and seizure and the right to a jury trial.

Effects of American independence. The American Revolution was a major event in world history. It put into practice the ideas of John Locke and other political philosophers of the Enlightenment. The American example of democratic government was a landmark in world history and an important influence. People in other countries still suffered under absolute monarchs and privileged classes. The American Revolution gave them hope.

The American democracy of 1789 was hardly perfect. The states restricted voting to adult males. Most required that voters own property. Women could not vote. African Americans held in slavery had no political rights at all. Clearly many liberties still had to be won. Nonetheless, the American Revolution created a government with a new, democratic relationship among citizens. Not all Patriots agreed on the final form of government created by the Constitution. Still, their common beliefs and the economic and political needs of the new nation held them together. They had created a country that inspired loyalty.

✔ **READING CHECK: Summarizing** Describe the government created by the U.S. Constitution in 1789. federal system composed of three branches acting as checks on one another; states have powers not granted to central government; amendments guarantee personal rights

HISTORY MAKER

George Washington (1732–1799)

After the U.S. Constitution was ratified, George Washington was elected as the first president of the United States. Washington had led the American troops to victory in the Revolution. **Why might the American people have wanted Washington as their first president?**

HISTORY MAKER ANSWER
He was a successful leader as commander of the American forces.

SECTION 5 REVIEW

1. **Define** and explain the significance:
   federal system of government
   executive branch
   legislative branch
   judicial branch

2. **Identify** and explain the significance:
   Stamp Act
   King George III
   Lord North
   Patriots
   Loyalists
   Thomas Jefferson
   George Washington
   Benjamin Franklin
   Articles of Confederation
   Bill of Rights

3. **Comparing and Contrasting** Copy the chart below. Use it to compare and contrast the Articles of Confederation and the Constitution.

FEATURE	ARTICLES OF CONFEDERATION	CONSTITUTION
Strong executive branch	no	yes
Power to tax		
One legislative vote each state		
Bill of Rights		
Federal courts		

4. **Finding the Main Idea**
   a. How did the ideas of the Enlightenment influence the leaders of the American Revolution?
   b. How did Americans respond to changes in British colonial policy after 1763?
   c. What were the central features of the government created by the U.S. Constitution?

5. **Writing and Critical Thinking**
   Identifying Cause and Effect Imagine you are one of the signers of the Declaration of Independence. After the Revolutionary War, write a summary of the effects of the Declaration.
   Consider:
   • the legal and political ideas in the document
   • how they differed from previous systems
   • how they affected the creation of the U.S. government

Homework Practice Online
keyword: SP3 HP20

SECTION 5 REVIEW ANSWERS

❶ **Define**
• federal systems of government, p. 502
• executive branch, p. 502
• legislative branch, p. 502
• judicial branch, p. 502

❷ **Identify**
• Stamp Act, p. 498
• King George III, p. 498
• Lord North, p. 498
• Patriots, p. 498
• Loyalists, p. 498
• Thomas Jefferson, p. 499
• George Washington, p. 501
• Benjamin Franklin, p. 501
• Articles of Confederation, p. 502
• Bill of Rights, p. 503

❸ power to tax: no, yes; one legislative vote each state: yes, no; Bill of Rights: no, yes; federal courts: no, yes

❹ a. The leaders of the American Revolution were interested in securing individual rights, an important Enlightenment idea.

b. Resistance to British policies strengthened.

c. The federal system is composed of three branches acting as checks on one another; states have powers not granted to central government; amendments guarantee personal rights.

❺ Students' summaries will vary.

REVIEW AND ASSESSMENT RESOURCES

REPRODUCIBLE RESOURCES
▸ Vocabulary Activity 20

TECHNOLOGY RESOURCES
▸ Chapter 20 Test Generator (on the One-Stop Planner)
▸ Global Skill Builder CD-ROM
▸ HRW Go Site

REINFORCEMENT, REVIEW, and ASSESSMENT
▸ Chapter 20 Review, pp. 504–505
▸ Chapter 20 Tutorial for Students, Parents, Mentors, and Peers
▸ Chapter 20 Test (Form A or B)
▸ Alternative Assessment Handbook
▸ Chapter 20 Test for English Language Learners and Special-Needs Students

REVIEW
Have students complete the Chapter 20 Review on pages 504–505.

ASSESS
Use one of the chapter tests to assess students' understanding of the content. For Alternative Assessment, see the Portfolio Activities and Alternative Assessment Handbook.

CHAPTER 20 REVIEW ANSWERS

Understanding Main Ideas

1. efforts of Long Parliament to limit the monarchy's power; general rejection of changes in the church; Irish rebellion

2. Anglicans, Roman Catholics, nobles

3. Tories: supported James; believed in a hereditary monarchy; Whigs: claimed right to deny throne to James; wanted a strong Parliament

4. Charles sought to increase toleration for Catholicism, but faced opposition. James attempted to help Catholics, which caused Protestants to resist his rule.

5. English navy defeated the Spanish Armada.

6. It held that colonies existed for the economic benefit of the home country.

7. Montesquieu: balance of power; Voltaire: critical of intolerance; Rousseau: popular sovereignty

8. promoted less control by monarchs, nobles, and clergy

9. barred colonists from settling west of the Appalachians; enforced mercantilist trade laws; imposed new taxes

10. The Constitution included a strong executive branch, the power to tax, and federal courts.

CHAPTER 20 Review

Creating a Time Line

Copy the time line below onto a sheet of paper. Complete the time line by filling in the events, individuals, and dates from the chapter that you think were significant. Pick three events and explain why you think they were significant.

1550	1700	1800

Writing a Summary

Using standard grammar, spelling, sentence structure, and punctuation, write an overview of the events in the chapter.

Identifying People and Ideas

Identify the following terms or individuals and explain their significance:

1. Oliver Cromwell
2. Glorious Revolution
3. John Locke
4. habeas corpus
5. Sir Francis Drake
6. Act of Union
7. sea dogs
8. Enlightenment
9. Jean-Jacques Rousseau
10. Stamp Act
11. George Washington
12. Articles of Confederation

Understanding Main Ideas

SECTION 1 *(pp. 478–482)*

Civil War and Revolution

1. What were the immediate causes of the English Revolution?

2. Who in England was likely to oppose the execution of Charles I?

SECTION 2 *(pp. 483–489)*

Constitutional Monarchy in England

3. What were the differences between the Tories and the Whigs?

4. What role did religion play in English politics after the Restoration?

SECTION 3 *(pp. 490–493)*

English Colonial Expansion

5. How did England become the dominant naval power in the 1500s?

6. What was the British policy of mercantilism?

SECTION 4 *(pp. 494–496)*

The Enlightenment

7. What ideas did Montesquieu, Voltaire, and Rousseau contribute to political philosophy?

8. How did Enlightenment thinking affect some people's views of church and state?

SECTION 5 *(pp. 497–503)*

The American Revolution

9. What issues led to the American Revolution?

10. What were the differences between the Articles of Confederation and the United States Constitution?

Reviewing Themes

1. **Citizenship** How did many political writers and philosophers of the 1700s see the relationship between people and their government?

2. **Constitutional Heritage** What were the sources of the political ideas that led to the American Revolution and the United States Constitution?

3. **Global Relations** Why did British policy anger many Americans in the years following 1763?

Thinking Critically

1. **Identifying Cause and Effect** What features of British policy probably led Americans to design the government created by the Constitution?

2. **Supporting a Point of View** Although the United States was created with the Declaration of Independence, how could it be argued that the country was really launched in 1789?

Writing About History

Comparing and Contrasting Compare and contrast the British and American governments. Use the chart below to organize your thoughts before writing.

Elements	British Government	American Government
Constitution		
Legislature		
Executive		
Protection of individual liberties		

CLOSE

Ask students if they think the conflict between the monarchy and Parliament was more about control of government or more about religious issues. Have them explain their responses.

RETEACH

Pair students who have had difficulty with the test. Have each pair outline the chapter and compile a chapter glossary. When they are ready, have students take the Form B Test to assess their mastery of the material.

ENGLISH LANGUAGE LEARNERS

Portfolio Extensions

1. Have students conduct research on the ideas of Montesquieu, especially his idea of checks and balances. Ask them to write a report detailing how the framers incorporated his ideas into the U.S. Constitution.

2. Invite students to imagine that they are one of the great leaders mentioned in the chapter. Inform them that they have just had a long talk with an Enlightenment thinker. Direct students to write a letter to an adviser explaining the ideas the thinker expressed and how these ideas have affected their views on government.

3. Ask students to research an event from the American Revolution, such as the Boston Tea Party or the Battle of Saratoga. Have them write a fictional account of the event from the point of view of a participant of the same age as themselves.

Building Social Studies Skills

Reading a Chart

Study the chart below. Then answer the questions that follow.

Great Britain's Constitutional Monarchy

MONARCH
Hereditary head of state
Limited power

PRIME MINISTER
Leader of majority party (by custom)

CABINET
Chosen by prime minister (by custom)

HOUSE OF LORDS
Hereditary or appointed by monarch

HOUSE OF COMMONS
Elected by the people

1. Which general statement correctly describes a relationship shown on the chart?
   a. The members of the cabinet choose the prime minister.
   b. The monarch has direct power over the prime minister.
   c. Members of the House of Lords are direct representatives of the people.
   d. The prime minister is a member of the majority party in the House of Commons.

2. Which branch of government has the most power in Great Britain? Give specific reasons for your choice.

Summarizing

Read the paragraph below. Then answer the questions that follow.

> During the Enlightenment, the ideas of philosophers were widely read. Montesquieu published *The Spirit of the Laws* in 1748, describing what he thought was a perfect government. From 1751 to 1772 the *Encyclopedia* was published in France. Edited by Diderot and d'Alembert, it examined government, war, taxes, human rights, and the church. In 1759, Voltaire published *Candide,* which satirized oppressive government and prejudice. *The Social Contract,* published in 1762 by Rousseau, argued that government should be created by and subject to the will of the people.

3. The statement that best summarizes this reading is:
   a. Voltaire was more popular than was Rousseau.
   b. The *Encyclopedia* collected all the knowledge that was available during the 1700s.
   c. Rousseau and Montesquieu held opposing ideas regarding the best form of government.
   d. Some Enlightenment writers were concerned with issues of government and society.

4. What effect did the ideas of these thinkers have on the people of their time? Give specific examples.

Alternative Assessment

Building Your Portfolio

Link to TODAY

Constitutional Heritage

The ideas about democratic-republican government that inspired the Enlightenment and the revolutions in England and its colonies had many of their roots in ancient Greece and Rome. Using your textbook and other sources, create a flowchart that traces the process by which democratic-republican government evolved from its beginnings in classical Greece and Rome.

internet connect

Internet Activity: go.hrw.com
KEYWORD: SP3 WH20

Choose a topic on Enlightenment and Revolution in England and America to:
- understand how the ideas of the Enlightenment have influenced institutions and societies.
- create a recruitment poster for the New Model Army.
- identify political ideas in John Locke's *Two Treatises of Government* and its influence on the Declaration of Independence.

Reviewing Themes
1. one of mutual benefit

2. Locke, Montesquieu, Voltaire, Rousseau

3. The British began asserting stronger imperial control over the colonies.

Thinking Critically
1. lack of representation in government

2. The Constitution went into effect in 1789.

Writing About History
Charts should indicate understanding of similarities and differences.

Building Social Studies Skills
1. d

2. prime minister; chooses the cabinet

3. d

4. Students might answer that the ideas of Rousseau strongly influenced the U.S. Constitution.

Building Your Portfolio
Presentations will vary.

The French Revolution and Napoléon

CHAPTER RESOURCE MANAGER

Objectives	Pacing Guide	Reproducible Resources
SECTION 1 **The Roots of Revolution** (pp. 508–511) • Describe how the Old Regime was structured. • Analyze why discontent began to grow in the mid-1700s. • Explain why Louis XVI wanted to call the Estates General. • Describe how the meeting of the Estates General pushed France toward revolution.	**Regular** 1.5 day **Block Scheduling** 1 day *Block Scheduling Handbook with Team Teaching Strategies, 21.1*	**RS** Guided Reading Strategy 21.1 **PS** Readings in World History 65: The People State Their Grievances
SECTION 2 **The French Revolution** (pp. 512–516) • Explain why and how the French Revolution spread. • Analyze how a constitution changed French government. • Explain why the monarchy and the Legislative Assembly came to an end.	**Regular** 1.5 day **Block Scheduling** 1 day *Block Scheduling Handbook with Team Teaching Strategies, 21.2*	**RS** Guided Reading Strategy 21.2
SECTION 3 **The French Republic** (pp. 517–522) • Explain how the National Convention ruled France. • Describe how the Reign of Terror affected France. • Identify the Directory and explain how it ruled. • Analyze why Napoléon was able to come to power.	**Regular** 1.5 day **Block Scheduling** 1 day *Block Scheduling Handbook with Team Teaching Strategies, 21.3*	**RS** Guided Reading Strategy 21.3 **RS** Graphic Organizer Activity 21 **PS** Readings in World History 66, 67 **E** Creative Teaching Strategy 21: A Jacobin Strategy Session
SECTION 4 **The Napoléonic Era** (pp. 523–528) • Identify the ways in which Napoléon's government was successful. • Explain how France became an empire. • Describe how Napoléon reorganized Europe. • Analyze the events that led to Napoléon's final defeat at Waterloo.	**Regular** 1.5 day **Block Scheduling** 1 day *Block Scheduling Handbook with Team Teaching Strategies, 21.4*	**RS** Guided Reading Strategy 21.4 **PS** Readings in World History 68: A View of Napoléon's Character **E** Hands-on History Activity 21: Napoléon's France
SECTION 5 **A Return to Peace** (pp. 529–533) • Describe how the Congress of Vienna attempted to restore stability to Europe. • Explain why politicians practiced conservative policies. • Analyze how Metternich influenced conservative politics and stopped revolution.	**Regular** 1.5 day **Block Scheduling** 1 day *Block Scheduling Handbook with Team Teaching Strategies, 21.5*	**RS** Guided Reading Strategy 21.5

Chapter Resource Key

PS Primary Sources	**A** Assessment	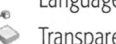 Music
RS Reading Support	**REV** Review	Video
IC Interdisciplinary Connections	**ELL** Reinforcement and English Language Learners	Internet
E Enrichment	Transparencies	Holt Presentation Maker Using Microsoft® PowerPoint®
SM Skills Mastery	CD-ROM	

One-Stop Planner CD-ROM

See the ***One-Stop Planner*** for a complete list of additional resources for students and teachers.

One-Stop Planner CD-ROM

It's easy to plan lessons, select resources, and print out materials for your students when you use the **One-Stop Planner** CD–ROM with **Test Generator**.

Technology Resources	Reinforcement, Review, and Assessment
One-Stop Planner 21.1 World History Teaching Transparency: Regional and World Map 33: Europe World History Teaching Transparency: Art and History 17: Marie Antoinette and Her Children Homework Practice Online Online Maps, Charts, and Graphs: Europe on the Eve of the French Revolution	Daily Quiz 21.1 Main Idea Activity 21.1 English Audio Summary 21.1 Spanish Audio Summary 21.1 REV Section 1 Review, p. 511
One-Stop Planner 21.2 Holt Researcher: World History: Olympe de Gouges Homework Practice Online	Daily Quiz 21.2 Main Idea Activity 21.2 English Audio Summary 21.2 Spanish Audio Summary 21.2 REV Section 2 Review, p. 516
One-Stop Planner 21.3 Holt Researcher: World History: Maximilien Robespierre Homework Practice Online Online Maps, Charts, and Graphs: Revolutionary France Expands, 1789–1799	Daily Quiz 21.3 Main Idea Activity 21.3 English Audio Summary 21.3 Spanish Audio Summary 21.3 REV Section 3 Review, p. 522
One-Stop Planner 21.4 Holt Researcher: World History: Napoléon Bonaparte, Josephine de Beauharnais Homework Practice Online Online Maps, Charts, and Graphs: The Spread of Napoléonic Institutions	Daily Quiz 21.4 Main Idea Activity 21.4 English Audio Summary 21.4 Spanish Audio Summary 21.4 REV Section 4 Review, p. 528
One-Stop Planner 21.5 World History Teaching Transparency: Everyday Life 20: A Ball During the Congress of Vienna	Daily Quiz 21.5 Main Idea Activity 21.5 English Audio Summary 21.5 Spanish Audio Summary 21.5 REV Section 5 Review, p. 533

---

internet connect

HRW ONLINE RESOURCES
GO TO: go.hrw.com
Then type in a keyword.

TEACHER HOME PAGE
KEYWORD: SP3 Teacher

CHAPTER INTERNET ACTIVITIES
KEYWORD: SP3 WH21
Choose an activity to:
- analyze artistic renderings and evaluate the historical accuracy of key events in Napoléon's life.
- evaluate the differences among the American, French, and Russian Revolutions.
- research the rise and fall of the Jacobins.

CHAPTER ENRICHMENT LINKS
KEYWORD: SP3 CH21

ONLINE ASSESSMENT
Homework Practice
KEYWORD: SP3 HP21
Standardized Test Prep
KEYWORD: SP3 STP21
Rubrics
KEYWORD: SS Rubrics

ONLINE MAPS, CHARTS, AND GRAPHS
KEYWORD: SP3 MCG

CONTENT UPDATES
KEYWORD: SS Content Updates

HOLT PRESENTATION MAKER
KEYWORD: SP3 PPT21

ONLINE READING SUPPORT
KEYWORD: SS Strategies

CURRENT EVENTS
KEYWORD: S3 Current Events

Meeting Individual Needs

Ability Levels

Level 1   Basic level activities designed for all students encountering new material

Level 2   Intermediate level activities designed for average students

Level 3   Challenging activities designed for honors and gifted and talented students

English Language Learners   These activities address the needs of students with Limited English Proficiency.

Chapter Review and Assessment

IC   Vocabulary Activity 21

  Global Skill Builder CD-ROM

  HRW Web Site

REV   Chapter 21 Tutorial for Students, Parents, Mentors, and Peers

REV   Chapter 21 Review, pp. 534–535

A   Chapter 21 Test Generator (on the One-Stop Planner)

A   Chapter 21 Test (Form A or B)

A   Alternative Assessment Handbook

A   Chapter 21 Test for English Language Learners and Special-Needs Students

CHAPTER 21

Section 1   The Roots of Revolution

Section 2   The French Revolution

Section 3   The French Republic

Section 4   The Napoléonic Era

Section 5   A Return to Peace

Build on What You Know

Ask students to answer the following questions:

How might the ideas of the Enlightenment have led to social unrest in France?

Consider:

- Voltaire's criticisms of government and religious intolerance
- Rousseau's ideas about government by consent of the people

How might the American Revolution have influenced the French Revolution?

Consider:

- French assistance to the American revolutionaries
- French admiration for the ideas embodied in the Declaration of Independence

---

EXPLORING THE TIME LINE
GLOBAL EVENTS

🖥 internet connect

TOPIC: French Revolution
GO TO: go.hrw.com
KEYWORD: SP3 WH21

Have students access the Internet through the HRW Go site to learn more about the abolition of slavery in the French colonies. Who was Toussaint L'Ouverture? Was the abolition of slavery in the colonies a humanitarian gesture or was it a pragmatic one? Though slavery was abolished in French colonies in 1794, did it really end then? Have students write a journal entry about a day in the life of a freed slave living in the new nation of Haiti after the revolt.

CHAPTER 21

1789–1815

The French Revolution and Napoléon

Rosetta Stone

c. 1790
Science and Technology
Antoine-Laurent Lavoisier publishes *Table of Thirty-One Chemical Elements.*

1792
Global Events
Denmark is the first nation to abolish slavery.

1795–1799
Politics
The Directory rules France.

1796
Science and Technology
An English physician introduces a small pox vaccine.

1785	1790	1795	1800

1789
Global Events
The first U.S. Congress meets in New York.

1794
Global Events
France abolishes slavery in French colonies.

1794
Science and Technology
France establishes the world's first telegraph communications line.

1793
The Arts
The Louvre in Paris becomes France's national art gallery.

1793
Politics
The French government bans Roman Catholicism.

1799
Global Events
French soldiers in Egypt find the Rosetta Stone.

1799
Science and Technology
A perfectly preserved mammoth is found in Siberia.

1799
Science and Technology
The first gas lighting fixture is patented by French chemist Philippe Lebon.

Model of guillotine

Model of the French inventor Claude Chappe's overhead telegraph

Build on What You Know

*I*nspired by Enlightenment ideas as well as trade concerns, the American Revolution forever changed the course of history for the colonies in North America. However, the revolution's influence did not end there. Across the Atlantic in France, people were growing more and more dissatisfied with the monarchy and with how their society was structured. Drawing from the Enlightenment, people continued to call for changes to combat inequalities and injustice. In this chapter, you will learn how the success of the American Revolution inspired similar efforts in France, and how a powerful new empire rose and fell there.

What's Your Opinion?

Themes Journal *To help students create their Themes Journal entries, provide the following examples of appropriate* **agree**/**disagree** *statements.*

Government

Agree A few wise leaders who are concerned about the people can govern effectively and represent citizens' interests.

Disagree When power is concentrated in the hands of a few people, they tend to use it for their own interests.

Constitutional Heritage

Agree To guarantee a stable government, constitutions should not be changed.

Disagree Constitutions should be changed to reflect the changing times.

Citizenship

Agree Only the government can decide whether people should be allowed to speak about anything they choose.

Disagree People have a natural right to freedom of speech, which should be respected by the government.

Portrait of Napoléon as emperor of France

1804
Politics
The French uncover a plot to assassinate Napoléon in Paris.

1805
The Arts
French author François-Auguste-René de Chateaubriand publishes the romantic novel *René*.

1806
The Arts
Construction begins on the Arc de Triomphe in France.

1810
Science and Technology
Nicolas-François Appert develops techniques for canning foods.

1810
Business and Finance
The French government gives itself a monopoly on the sale of tobacco.

1815
Science and Technology
French scientist Jean-Baptiste de Monet de Lamarck publishes *Natural History of Animals*.

1805   **1810**   **1815**

1807
Politics
England prohibits the slave trade.

1813
Daily Life
The waltz is popular in European ballrooms.

1812
Politics
Napoléon enters Russia with the Grand Army.

Arc de Triomphe in Paris

Pearl and diamond tiara of Empress Joséphine

EXPLORING THE TIME LINE
GLOBAL EVENTS

One of the French colonies in the Western Hemisphere was Saint-Domingue (now called Haiti). Saint-Domingue occupied the western third of the island of Hispaniola in the Caribbean. The eastern two-thirds of the island was occupied by Santo Domingo, which was then a Spanish colony.

In 1789, Saint-Domingue had about 500,000 black slaves, who worked mainly on the large plantations. In 1791, inspired by the events of the French Revolution, the black slaves revolted. A former slave, Toussaint-L'Ouverture, became the revolt's military leader. When in 1793 France went to war with Spain, the black commanders supported Spain and nearly drove the French out of Saint-Domingue. In 1794 the French National Convention formally abolished slavery in the colonies. Toussaint-L'Ouverture then went over to the French side and helped defeat the Spanish.

Critical Thinking

Ask students how they think Toussaint L'Ouverture contributed to the French National Convention's decision to free slaves.

ANSWER: Students may suggest that Toussaint L'Ouverture's success in leading the rebellion made the French National Convention free the slaves in hopes that the slave army would stop supporting the Spanish.

What's Your Opinion?

Themes Journal *Do you* **agree** *or* **disagree** *with the following statements? Support your point of view in your journal.*

Government A government that represents the people can be run by only a few people.

Constitutional Heritage Once it has been written, the constitution of a nation should never be changed.

Citizenship Freedom of speech can be granted only by a government.

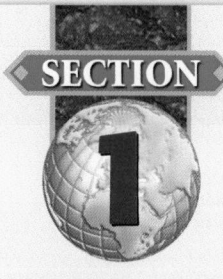

SECTION 1

OBJECTIVES

1 Describe how the Old Regime was structured.

2 Analyze why discontent began to grow in the mid-1700s.

3 Explain why Louis XVI wanted to call the Estates General.

4 Describe how the meeting of the Estates General pushed France toward revolution.

SECTION 1

READ TO DISCOVER

❶ How was the Old Regime structured?

❷ Why did discontent begin to grow in the mid-1700s?

❸ Why did Louis XVI want to call the Estates General?

❹ How did the meeting of the Estates General push France toward revolution?

DEFINE

bourgeoisie

IDENTIFY

Louis XV
Louis XVI
Marie-Antoinette

WHY IT MATTERS TODAY

The French government started to go through many changes in the 1700s. Use CNN or other **current event** sources to investigate how the French people are represented in government today. Record your findings in your journal.

CNN Student News.com

The Roots of Revolution

The Main Idea
The French Revolution was a struggle between a powerful monarch and the people.

The Story Continues *As Americans gained independence from Great Britain, the people of France were also struggling against oppression. As Thomas Jefferson observed after visiting France in the 1780s, "Out of a population of twenty millions of people . . . there are nineteen millions more wretched [poor], more accursed in every circumstance of human existence, than the most conspicuously wretched individual of the whole United States."*

The Old Regime

For more than 100 years, France had been the largest and most powerful nation in Europe, ruled by a monarch who claimed absolute power. When the French Revolution began in 1789, however, the king lost all power within months. The great changes brought by the Revolution made the French feel that they were living in a whole new society. People began to refer to the time before 1789 as the Old Regime. Under the Old Regime, society had been divided into three estates, or classes.

The privileged estates. The First Estate was made up of the clergy of the Roman Catholic Church, less than 1 percent of the French population. The church had been powerful and wealthy ever since the Middle Ages. By the late 1700s the church owned about 15 percent of all the land in France, and so collected vast amounts of money from rents, taxes, and fees. Most of this wealth was held by the higher clergy—bishops, archbishops, and abbots—who did not have to pay taxes themselves. Many of these higher church officials became materialistic and neglected their spiritual duties. The lower clergy, such as parish priests, performed most of the church's work and received little pay.

The nobility, less than 2 percent of the population, made up the Second Estate. These nobles enjoyed many privileges left over from feudal times. They paid few if any taxes, collected dues from peasants, and held the highest positions in the army and government. Eldest sons had the right to inherit titles and lands. Although some nobles cared about the welfare of France, as a group they were irresponsible.

This drawing shows one artist's representation of French society during the Old Regime—the clergy, nobles, peasants, and bourgeoisie (from left to right).

TEACH OBJECTIVE 2

ALL LEVELS: Copy the following graphic organizer on the chalkboard, omitting the italicized answers. Have students list factors that caused each estate to feel discontent.
ENGLISH LANGUAGE LEARNERS

First Estate	*changing economic conditions, political power in hands of kings*
Second Estate	*changing economic conditions, desire to protect their privileges*
Bourgeoisie	*taxes, lack of political power*
Third Estate (except bourgeoisie)	*high prices, taxes*

The Third Estate. The rest of the people of France, about 97 percent, belonged to the Third Estate. At the top of the Third Estate were the **bourgeoisie** (boorzh·wah·ZEE), or urban middle class. The bourgeoisie included merchants, manufacturers, and professional people such as doctors and lawyers. Many were educated and wealthy.

Below the bourgeoisie in the Third Estate came three groups who were usually very poor: city workers, artisans, and rural peasants. Peasants made up the largest group. In the 1700s most peasants still owed feudal dues and labor services. They paid heavy taxes as well as rent for the land they worked. They were also forced to pay a tithe—that is, one tenth of their income—to the church. Although they worked long and hard, peasants had no voice in making or changing laws. They remained under the absolute control of their landlords and king.

✔ **READING CHECK: Finding the Main Idea** How was French society organized in the Old Regime? First, Second, and Third Estates

Growing Discontent

In the mid-1700s discontent in France began to grow. Several factors explain this discontent. The first resulted from the growth of the French population. Families had more children to support, and they needed more food and money. Changing economic conditions in France also spurred discontent. The nobles, clergy, and some of the bourgeoisie who owned land pressed the peasants for higher rents. In the cities, laborers found food prices rising higher and higher, but wages were not going up as quickly. The artisans and peasants resented the rich, who collected their rents, lived in big houses, and had plenty to eat. The poor blamed the king for allowing prices to get so high. They hated having to pay taxes when the nobles and clergy did not. Sometimes the poor took to the streets and rioted against these higher prices and taxes. The worsening economic conditions also reinforced the determination of the first two estates to protect their most important privilege: freedom from taxation.

The bourgeoisie prospered during the 1700s, and now they wanted political power to go with their economic strength. Merchants and manufacturers resented paying taxes when nobles and clergy did not. They wanted to be able to conduct business without interference from the government. The bourgeoisie also wanted their sons to have important positions in the church, army, and government—positions that only nobles were allowed to hold.

Although the peasants, workers, and bourgeoisie had different complaints, they shared the same ideas and used the same words to express them. They spoke of "liberty" and "equality" as their natural rights. These ideas may have meant different things to different people, but they were enough to unify France's various groups in a challenge to the king's power.

✔ **READING CHECK: Summarizing** Why did discontent grow in France during the mid-1700s? increases in population and cost of living

INTERPRETING THE VISUAL RECORD

Peasants This picture is meant to show an idealized view of peasant life in France. *What things in the picture might be different if it were a true representation of peasant life?*

This political cartoon from about 1790 illustrates the growing conflict between "The Powers"—the nobles, clergy, and bourgeoisie—and the National Assembly.

Daily Life

The typical peasant under the Old Regime had to pay a tithe, rent fees for the upkeep of the lord's pigeons, fees for the use of the manorial mill and bakery, tolls, duties when crossing provincial and territorial boundaries, a poll tax, income taxes, and taxes on goods such as salt, wine, playing cards, and soap.

Critical Thinking

Ask students how cost of living increases might affect rural peasants.

ANSWER: Peasants were already overburdened with taxes; cost of living increases would make them suffer even more.

VISUAL RECORD ANSWER

People probably would not be as nicely dressed; they probably would be shown working.

Technology **Resources**

 Online Maps, Charts, and Graphs: Europe on the Eve of the French Revolution

TEACH OBJECTIVE 3

LEVEL 1: Ask students to create a flowchart showing how Louis XIV, Louis XV, and Louis XVI all contributed to financial crisis in France. (*Louis XIV: engaged in wars that left France with huge debts; Louis XV: increased debt by borrowing money from bankers and not economizing; Louis XVI: increased debt by giving aid to colonists in the American Revolution*) Close by asking students how Louis XVI attempted to resolve the situation in 1789. (*Louis XVI unsuccessfully attempted to tax the first two estates, and banks refused to lend the government more money. He hoped to get approval for new taxes by calling a meeting of the Estates General.*)
ENGLISH LANGUAGE LEARNERS

TEACH OBJECTIVE 4

LEVEL 3: Have students read the statement of Sieyès, "What is the Third Estate?" on page 510 and write a brief essay providing evidence to support it. Have students write a statement that a member of each of the estates and King Louis XVI might have made at the meeting of the Estates General and indicate how these differing viewpoints pushed France toward revolution.

CLOSE

Ask students to write a brief essay describing the differences between the goals of the king and those of the members of each of the three estates.

Linking Past to Present

The palace of Versailles impoverished France and was a striking example of extravagance at the taxpayers' expense. While Louis XVI ruled, 10,000 people lived or worked in his household. The palace could also accommodate thousands of courtiers, and there were special rooms for a clock, the king's throne, and the gilt-draped royal billiard table. The gardens at Versailles covered 250 acres and included miles of wide pathways, 1,400 fountains, and thousands of exotic plants. The palace was sacked during the Revolution, and although only a portion of its grandeur has been restored, today it is a popular tourist attraction.

Critical Thinking

Ask students how the palace of Versailles contributed to the Revolution.

ANSWER: The cost of maintaining it contributed to the financial crisis; people resented paying taxes to support so many idle courtiers; people who lived in poverty resented the lavish luxury of Versailles.

HISTORY MAKER ANSWER
her extravagant spending; her refusal to support reforms

HISTORY MAKER

Marie-Antoinette (1755–1793)

As the wife and queen of Louis XVI, Marie-Antoinette became the most hated woman in France. Her wild spending and refusal to support reforms made her many enemies. During the French Revolution, she spent several months in prison. Finally in October 1793 she was put to death at the guillotine. **Why did the French people dislike Marie-Antoinette?**

Analyzing Primary Sources

Finding the Main Idea What does Sieyès mean when he says nothing will go well without the Third Estate? Third Estate provides labor and services for French society

---

This building in Paris, the Conciergerie, was used as a prison and housed Marie-Antoinette during the French Revolution.

The Financial Crisis

The actions of French monarchs stoked the fires of public anger. The 59-year reign of **Louis XV** was one of the longest in France's history. While the country enjoyed nearly 20 years of peace under Louis XV, debts inherited from Louis XIV continued to grow, creating an economic crisis. Louis XV's expensive habits also turned the people against him. When taxes did not provide enough money to meet expenses, Louis XV borrowed more and more from bankers. Warned that his actions were harming France, he is said to have replied, "It will survive for my time. After me, the deluge."

In 1774 **Louis XVI** succeeded Louis XV as king. To strengthen an alliance with Austria, Louis XVI married **Marie-Antoinette,** the daughter of the Austrian empress Maria Theresa. The French people soon came to resent Marie-Antoinette's Austrian connection and her involvement in French politics.

Under Louis XVI France's debts continued to grow, due in large part to the country's assistance to the United States during the American Revolution. To raise money, Louis tried to tax the first two estates. Whenever new taxes were proposed, however, the nobles refused to cooperate and sometimes led riots. By 1787 bankers resisted lending the government more money. France faced financial disaster. In August of 1788 Louis called for a meeting of the Estates General to be held at Versailles. He hoped that by calling together the representatives of all three estates he could get approval for new taxes.

✔ **READING CHECK: Identifying Cause and Effect** What events led to the meeting of the Estates General? Louis XVI tried to raise taxes; banks refused to loan the French government more money

The Meeting of the Estates General

The French people hoped their problems would finally be addressed at the planned meeting of the Estates General. Emmanuel-Joseph Sieyès (syay·YES), a clergyman who became a revolutionary, expressed the complaints of the Third Estate:

> *History Makers Speak*
> **"What then is the Third Estate? All. But an 'all' that is fettered [chained] and oppressed. What would it be without the privileged order? It would be all; but free and flourishing. Nothing will go well without the Third Estate; everything would go considerably better without the two others."**
>
> Joseph Sieyès, from *What Is the Third Estate?*, quoted in *Sources of the Western Tradition*, edited by Marvin Perry, Joseph R. Peden, and Theodore H. Von Laue

In the past the three estates had always met separately, and each estate had cast one vote. Thus the First and Second Estates could always get together and outvote the Third Estate. The Third Estate had as many representatives as the other two estates combined. Therefore, to have a real voice in government, the Third Estate wanted representatives to vote as individuals.

The Estates General met on May 5, 1789. Louis XVI then instructed the delegates to follow the old custom of meeting separately and voting as one body. The representatives of the Third Estate refused to obey. They argued that the Estates General represented the French people, not the three classes. When Louis failed to respond, the Third Estate declared itself to be the National Assembly and invited the other two estates to work with it. This act marked the real beginning of the French Revolution. The representatives declared that they would not stop meeting until they had written a constitution for France and seen it adopted. Finally Louis XVI allowed the estates to meet together.

✔ **READING CHECK: Analyzing Information** Why did the Third Estate refuse to follow the tradition of each estate having one vote? to give more representation to the French people

When the Third Estate was locked out of the Estates General meeting, its representatives gathered nearby in an indoor tennis court. The oath they took there to continue meeting until a constitution was written became known as the Tennis Court Oath.

SECTION 1 REVIEW

1. **Define** and explain the significance:
   bourgeoisie

2. **Identify** and explain the significance:
   Louis XV
   Louis XVI
   Marie-Antoinette

3. **Summarizing** Copy the diagram and use it to show whom the three estates represented and how power was distributed.

   Most Power

   Least Power

Homework Practice Online
keyword: SP3 HP21

4. **Finding the Main Idea**

   a. How did France's social structure lead to discontent and financial crisis?

   b. Why did Louis XVI take the unusual step of calling all three estates together?

5. **Writing and Critical Thinking**

   Drawing Inferences Imagine you are a representative from the Third Estate at the Estates General meeting. Write a letter to a friend explaining what the Third Estate representatives want.

   Consider:
   • how peasants, noble, and clergy lived
   • how the Third Estate differed from the other two estates

THE FRENCH REVOLUTION AND NAPOLÉON **511**

OBJECTIVES

1 Explain why and how the French Revolution spread.

2 Analyze how a constitution changed French government.

3 Explain why the monarchy and the Legislative Assembly came to an end.

SECTION 2

READ TO DISCOVER

❶ Why and how did the French Revolution spread?

❷ How did a constitution change French government?

❸ Why did the monarchy and the Legislative Assembly come to an end?

DEFINE

émigrés
departments
conservatives
radicals
moderates

IDENTIFY

Olympe de Gouges

▶ WHY IT MATTERS TODAY

Monarchs still exist in Europe today. Use CNN Student News.com or other **current event** sources to investigate which European countries still have monarchs and what powers they have. Record your findings in your journal.

CNN Student News.com

The destruction of the Bastille prison, a symbol of royal oppression, marked the spread of revolutionary fervor.

The French Revolution

The Main Idea
The French Revolution spread quickly and violently, and it changed the government dramatically.

The Story Continues *Early in the morning of July 15, 1789, King Louis XVI was awakened by an official. The king was told that the Bastille prison had fallen to rioters. "Is this a rebellion?" the king is said to have asked. "No Sire," replied the official. "It is a revolution."*

The Spread of the Revolution

King Louis XVI allowed the Estates General to meet together, but during the meeting he moved troops into Paris and Versailles. Fearing that Louis was going to drive out the National Assembly by force, the people of Paris took action. On July 14, 1789, they captured the Bastille prison, a symbol of royal oppression. The crowd looted the Bastille for weapons, then destroyed it.

This outbreak of violence led to the formation of a new government in Paris. General Lafayette—the French hero who had fought in the American Revolution—formed a people's army called the National Guard. A new flag of red, white, and blue stripes replaced the old flag of France.

Events in Paris were repeated all over France as the "Great Fear" swept across the land. The peasants believed that the nobles were planning to crush them and stop the revolution. They also became angry as food shortages worsened. As rumors and fear spread, the peasants attacked local manor houses and monasteries. They destroyed possessions and burned documents recording rents, feudal dues, and other obligations.

✔ **READING CHECK: Identifying Cause and Effect** How did the events of July 14, 1789, change France? led to formation of new government and people's army, helped trigger "Great Fear"

LEVEL 3: Have students work in small groups using a problem-solving process to determine whether the people of France were justified in using violence. Encourage students to consider the king's action, the people's fears and beliefs, and the National Assembly's response to the violence. Have each group make a list of reasons for and against the issue and report their solutions to the class. **COOPERATIVE LEARNING**

HOMEWORK Tell students to imagine they are émigrés. Ask them the following questions: *How would you describe the events that have occurred through the summer of 1789? How do you view these events? What are your hopes for the future?* Then as a homework assignment, have students write a first-person narrative answering these questions.

Women march This engraving shows a mob of angry Parisian women marching to Versailles on October 5, 1789. They demanded relief from Louis XVI for the nationwide food shortage. *What items are the women carrying and why?*

The End of The Old Regime

Many members of the National Assembly believed that they could stop the violence through reforms. The assembly outlawed the tithe, canceled all feudal dues and services owed by peasants, and removed the privileges that the First and Second estates had previously enjoyed. By August 4, 1789, the National Assembly had formally done away with feudalism in France.

The Declaration of the Rights of Man. Following these reforms, the assembly adopted the Declaration of the Rights of Man and of the Citizen. This document dealt with basic human rights and political powers.

The Declaration of the Rights of Man and of the Citizen stated that men are born equal and remain equal before the law. It granted freedom of speech, of the press, and of religion. It guaranteed the right to take part in government, declaring that all men had an equal right to hold public office. The document also guaranteed the right to a fair trial. The declaration embodied the principles that became the slogan of the French Revolution: "liberty, equality, fraternity."

These rights, however, did not apply to women. A group of women led by Parisian playwright **Olympe de Gouges** wrote their own document, the Declaration of the Rights of Women and Citizenesses. The National Assembly rejected it. The leaders of the Revolution believed in equality for men, but did not believe that women were the equals of men.

Émigrés and royalists. The Old Regime did not die easily. Many nobles fled to Great Britain, Switzerland, and Germany. There they plotted constantly to overthrow the Revolution. These **émigrés**—French for "emigrants"—became a source of trouble for France in years to come.

Some nobles remained at Versailles with the king. They sided with Louis XVI in favor of a return to the Old Regime. They held a banquet at which they praised the king and queen and insulted the National Assembly. When the people learned of this banquet, a crowd led by angry women stormed the palace and forced Louis XVI, Marie Antoinette, and their family to return to Paris with them.

Reforms in government. Between 1789 and 1791 the National Assembly passed more laws aimed at correcting past abuses and setting up a new government. First, it reformed France's administrative structure by dividing the country into 83 equal districts, called **departments.** It called for the election of all local officials. In 1789 the

Holt Researcher
go.hrw.com
KEYWORD: Holt Researcher
FreeFind: Olympe de Gouges
After reading more about Olympe de Gouges on the Holt Researcher, write a letter she might have written to the National Assembly urging support for the Declaration of the Rights of Women and Citizenesses.

LITERATURE. In 1859 English author Charles Dickens wrote *A Tale of Two Cities,* a vivid and dramatic depiction of the French Revolution. In the novel, Dickens describes the "Great Fear" that swept the countryside and encouraged the National Assembly to make reforms. In the following scene a noble's chateau has been set on fire: "The mender of roads, and two hundred and fifty particular friends stood with folded arms at the fountain, looking at the pillar of fire in the sky. 'It must be forty feet high,' said they, grimly; and never moved.... The rider from the chateau, and the horse in a foam, clattered away through the village, and galloped up the stony steep, to the prison on the crag. At the gate, a group of officers were looking at the fire; removed from them, a group of soldiers. 'Help, gentlemen-officers! The chateau is on fire; valuable objects may be saved from the flames by timely aid! Help, help!' The officers looked towards the soldiers who looked at the fire; gave no orders; and answered, with shrugs and biting of lips, 'It must burn.'"

ACTIVITY: Have students write a newspaper article summarizing the event.

They have axes, spears, pitchforks, and swords. They plan to attack the palace.

ALL LEVELS: Have students read the paragraphs under "The Constitution of 1791" on page 514. Copy the following graphic organizer on the board, omitting the italicized answers. Have volunteers fill in the chart. Then discuss how the constitutional monarchy established by the Constitution of 1791 differed from France's previous government under the king. *(Students should note that the monarch was not limited in powers; the powers rested in the king and his advisors, not branches of government; there was no voting.)* **ENGLISH LANGUAGE LEARNERS**

Constitution of 1791	
type of government	*limited monarchy*
division of powers	*three branches—legislative, judicial, executive*
legislature	*consists of one house*
voters	*only taxpaying males may vote*

That's Interesting!

The royal family spent months making careful preparations for their escape from France. Despite their plans, they were captured at the town of Varennes, just a few miles from the French border. They were escorted back to Paris. During the heat and humiliation of the two days' journey, the queen's hair reportedly turned white.

CONNECTING TO CIVICS ANSWER

similar: both influenced by John Locke; different: American document explained colonies' actions to outside world; French document reminded people of the "sacred rights of man"

CONNECTING TO

Civics

Two Declarations of Freedom

In the last decades of the 1700s, revolutions shook both sides of the Atlantic. Two documents expressed the political changes brought on by these revolutions.

Both documents were influenced by the English philosopher John Locke. Almost a hundred years earlier, Locke had argued that men are "by nature, all free, equal, and independent."

In America, the Declaration of Independence was written when the colonies were rebelling against British rule. The document explained the colonies' actions to the outside world. The French document, the Declaration of the Rights of Man and of the Citizen, reminded people of the "sacred rights of man."

Understanding Civics

How were the American and French declarations both similar and different?

National Assembly also seized lands owned by the Catholic Church. This property was sold to the public; some of it was bought by the peasants who had formerly rented it. The proceeds were used for paying down the national debt.

The leaders of the Revolution saw the Catholic Church as a part of the Old Regime, and so they sought to reform it as well. In 1790 the National Assembly issued the Civil Constitution of the Clergy. This law stated that people in parishes and dioceses would elect their own clergy. In return for seizing church lands, the government would pay the salaries of priests and bishops. The pope, however, forbade the clergy to accept this arrangement, and most obeyed him. Because the Civil Constitution of the Clergy placed the church under the control of the French government, many Catholics came to oppose the Revolution.

✔ **READING CHECK: Summarizing** How did the National Assembly try to put the Revolution's ideas into practice? embodied them in the Declaration of the Rights of Man and of the Citizen

The Constitution of 1791

In 1791 the National Assembly finished writing a constitution for France. This constitution limited the authority of the king and divided the government into three branches—executive, legislative, and judicial.

The constitution greatly limited the powers of the king. He could no longer make or block laws on his own. Tax-paying male voters elected members to a new legislative body called the Legislative Assembly. The National Assembly was dissolved, and no one who had been a member could run for election to the Legislative Assembly. However, despite these reforms, wealthy men still held most of the political power under France's new system.

Louis XVI reluctantly agreed to his new limited powers. At the same time, he secretly plotted with émigrés to overthrow the new government and restore the Old Regime. Some of Louis's advisers urged him to flee and seek help from foreign governments friendly to the monarchy. In 1791 Louis and his family did try to escape. Even though he wore a disguise, Louis was recognized. He and his family were arrested and sent back to Paris.

People had hoped that under the new constitutional monarchy, France could recover without further disturbances. The king's attempted escape, however, marked a turning point. People no longer trusted Louis, and they publicly discussed creating a republic.

✔ **READING CHECK: Analyzing Information** What kind of government did the Constitution of 1791 provide? constitutional monarchy

This illustration, possibly from an early printing of the Declaration of the Rights of Man and of the Citizen, dramatically portrays a symbol of one of the Declaration's key ideals—equality.

LEGALITE

LEVEL 1: Have students construct a flowchart indicating events that led to the end of the monarchy. *(France declared war on Austria, commune seized control of Paris government, revolutionary troops arrived to defend Paris against invasion, Legislative Assembly voted itself out of existence and suspended the monarchy)*

Suggest to students that sometimes it is easier to state a goal than to achieve it. Ask students how the ideals of both the Declaration of the Rights of Man and the Citizen and of the Constitution of 1791, and the events that followed them, illustrate the truth of this suggestion.

The Legislative Assembly and War

The new government outlined in the Constitution of 1791 went into effect in October, but lasted less than a year. The revolutionaries had not created a sound government. They had set up a weak executive branch and a powerful but inexperienced legislature elected by only a minority of the population. Moreover, not all the French people supported the Revolution. Catholic priests and nobles opposed the new order. There was also discontent among the poorest members of French society, who had been hurt by a rise in the cost of living. These groups, along with the continuing activities of émigrés, added to the new government's troubles.

The Legislative Assembly became divided into three groups with differing attitudes. One of these groups, the **conservatives,** felt the revolution had gone far enough. Their ideal government was one in which the king had limited authority. The group known as **radicals** wanted more drastic changes than those proposed by the National Assembly. They wanted to get rid of the king, set up a republic, and make broad reforms. The third group, the **moderates,** had no extreme views. They sided with either conservatives or radicals depending on the issue at hand. In the hall where the Legislative Assembly met, each group sat in its own section. The conservatives sat on the right, the moderates in the center, and the radicals on the left. Today we still use the terms *right* to describe a conservative opinion, *center* for a moderate opinion, and *left* for a liberal opinion.

These three groups within the Legislative Assembly frequently deadlocked on domestic issues. They united, however, when they were faced with the threat of attack from other European powers that sought to restore the French monarchy. Marie-Antoinette's brother was Emperor Leopold II of Austria, and together with King Frederick William II of Prussia he issued the Declaration of Pillnitz. This declaration invited other European rulers to support the return of royal rule in France.

The threat of foreign invasion brought the Legislative Assembly to attention. Many groups within France were in favor of going to war. Each group in the assembly hoped that a successful foreign war would increase its own influence. Louis XVI favored war because he hoped that foreign armies would defeat the French army and restore him to power. Some people may have worried that war would lead to dictatorship. In April 1792, with only a few members opposing, the Legislative Assembly voted to declare war on Austria. The Assembly had hoped to keep Prussia and the other German states out of the war, but it failed in that objective. Other European monarchies, including Prussia and Sardinia, came to Austria's support. Soon afterward an army of Austrian and Prussian troops invaded France.

✔ **READING CHECK: Making Generalizations** In what ways was the first government after the revolution a weak one? executive branch was weak, legislature was inexperienced

Paris, 1789

Interpreting Maps Louis XVI and his family were imprisoned in the Temple.

■ **Skills Assessment: Locate** In which direction is the Temple from the Tuileries?

MUSIC. The French national anthem, "La Marseillaise," was composed by Claude-Joseph Rouget de Lisle, an amateur musician who was a captain in the French army. When the French declared war on Austria in 1792, Rouget de Lisle recognized the need for a marching song for the troops. It was originally titled "War Song of the Army of the Rhine." It began to be called "La Marseillaise" because of its popularity with volunteer units from Marseilles.

The song was officially made the French national anthem by a decree of the National Convention passed on July 14, 1795.

Critical Thinking

Ask students why they think it was important to have a marching song and a national anthem.

ANSWER: A marching song gave the troops a sense of camaraderie. A national anthem helped inspire patriotism and nationalism in citizens.

MAP ANSWER
The Temple is northeast of the Tuileries.

This poster summarizes the French Revolution's message of liberty, equality, and fraternity— or death.

The End of the Monarchy

The French did not do well in the initial fighting with the Austrian and Prussian armies. French citizens grew alarmed and searched for someone to blame for the defeats. As one observer noted,

Primary Source
"Everywhere you hear the cry that the king is betraying us, the generals are betraying us, that nobody is to be trusted; ... that Paris will be taken in six weeks by the Austrians ... we are on a volcano ready to spout flames."

Quoted in William Doyle, *The Oxford History of the French Revolution*

Failures in war, along with economic shortages at home, led to mass uprisings in Paris. A group of radicals seized control of the Commune, Paris's city government.

The Prussians vowed to destroy Paris and punish the revolutionaries if any harm came to the royal family. Upon hearing this the Commune demanded that the Legislative Assembly abolish the monarchy. The Commune rightly accused Louis XVI of plotting with foreign powers to overthrow the Constitution of 1791. Revolutionary troops arrived from the city of Marseilles to defend Paris against the invading armies. Their marching song, "La Marseillaise," became France's national anthem.

Finally on August 10, 1792, the Legislative Assembly suspended the office of king. Armed Parisians marched on the Tuileries Palace, the Paris home of the royal family. They killed many of the king's guards and imprisoned Louis and his family in the Temple. The Commune now ruled Paris, and the Legislative Assembly tried to govern France.

With the monarchy suspended, France needed a new constitution. The Legislative Assembly voted itself out of existence and set a date for election of delegates to a National Convention. These delegates would draw up a new constitution. Thus, in the midst of a foreign war and political turmoil, France faced a complete change of government.

✔ **READING CHECK: Drawing Inferences** Why did the Legislative Assembly exist for so short a period of time? Constitution of 1791 was no longer valid

SECTION 2 REVIEW

1. **Define** and explain the significance:
   émigrés
   departments
   conservatives
   moderates
   radicals

2. **Identify** and explain the significance:
   Olympe de Gouges

3. **Analyzing Information** Copy the diagram and use it to show the factions in the Legislative Assembly.

Left	Center	Right

4. **Finding the Main Idea**
   a. What did the assemblies accomplish?
   b. Why is the year 1789 significant in French history?

5. **Writing and Critical Thinking**
   Supporting a Point of View The French Revolution was based on the ideas of liberty, equality, and fraternity. Write a political pamphlet encouraging fellow Parisians to support the Commune and abolish the monarchy.
   Consider:
   - the actions of Louis XVI
   - the constitutional monarchy established by the Constitution of 1791

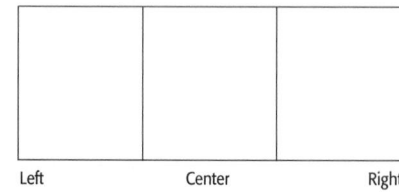
Homework Practice Online
keyword: SP3 HP21

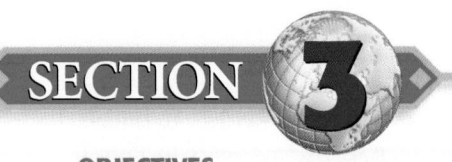

SECTION 3

OBJECTIVES

1 **Explain how the National Convention ruled France.**

2 **Describe how the Reign of Terror affected France.**

3 **Identify the Directory and explain how it ruled.**

4 **Analyze why Napoléon was able to come to power.**

🔊 *LET'S GET STARTED!*

As students enter the classroom, ask them to write responses to the following questions: What happened after the U.S. Constitution was written? How did the government function? Did any one person or small group of persons attempt to take control of the government? Remind students that France's National Assembly wrote a Constitution similar to that of the United States. Then tell students that in Section 3 they will learn how France took a very different turn after its new Constitution.

SECTION 3

READ TO DISCOVER

❶ How did the National Convention rule France?

❷ How did the Reign of Terror affect France?

❸ What was the Directory and how did it rule?

❹ Why was Napoléon able to come to power?

DEFINE

universal manhood suffrage
conscription
counterrevolutionary
coup d'état

IDENTIFY

Georges-Jacques Danton
Maximilien Robespierre
Jean-Paul Marat
Reign of Terror
Napoléon Bonaparte
Joséphine de Beauharnais

▶**WHY IT MATTERS TODAY**

Napoléon seized control of power with a coup d'état. Use CNN.com or other **current event** sources to investigate whether coups d'état are happening or have recently happened in other countries. Record your findings in your journal.

CNNstudentNews.com

The French Republic

The Main Idea
Radical revolutionaries led France through terror and war, while Napoléon rose to power.

The Story Continues *"During the greater part of the day, the guillotine had been kept busy at its ghastly work; all that France had boasted of in the past centuries of ancient names and blue blood had paid toll to her desire for liberty and fraternity."* These lines from the novel The Scarlet Pimpernel *capture the terror of those days when the French Revolution turned bloody.*

The National Convention

The National Convention held its first meeting in September 1792. Delegates were elected to this convention by **universal manhood suffrage.** This meant every adult male could vote, whether he owned property or not.

As in the Legislative Assembly, delegates in the National Convention were divided into three main groups. This time, however, fewer supported the king. The Girondins, republicans named for the department of the Gironde in southwestern France, feared the domination of France by Paris. The second group was the Jacobins, republicans who favored domination by Paris. **Georges-Jacques Danton** and **Maximilien Robespierre** were two of the most powerful Jacobins. Some of the Jacobins were extreme radicals and wanted reforms that would benefit all classes of society. **Jean-Paul Marat,** a doctor from Paris, led these radicals. The third group in the National Convention consisted of delegates who had no definite views. Later, most of these delegates came to favor the Jacobins.

The National Convention governed France for three years. Its first act was to declare the end of the monarchy and the beginning of a republic. The delegates also had to write a new constitution while trying to keep order at home and fight foreign invaders.

The National Convention brought Louis XVI to trial, charging him with plotting against the security of the nation. It found him guilty and sentenced him to death. On January 21, 1793, Louis XVI was beheaded by the guillotine. The rest of Europe found this execution of a monarch shocking. Even in the United States, people were disturbed by the National Convention's radical methods.

✔ **READING CHECK: Comparing and Contrasting** In what ways was the National Convention similar to and different from the Legislative Assembly? was divided into three main groups, but no one supported the king

At the time of the French Revolution, the guillotine was a new device that republicans believed would allow a quick and humane execution.

SECTION 3 RESOURCES

REPRODUCIBLE RESOURCES

▶ Guided Reading Strategy 21.3

▶ Graphic Organizer Activity 21: The Rise and Fall of the French Republic

▶ Readings in World History 66: The Sentencing of Louis XVI

▶ Creative Teaching Strategy 21: A Jacobin Strategy Session

TECHNOLOGY RESOURCES

▶ One-Stop Planner 21.3

▶ Holt Researcher: World History: Maximilien Robespierre

▶ Homework Practice Online

REINFORCEMENT, REVIEW, AND ASSESSMENT

▶ Section 3 Review, p. 522

▶ Daily Quiz 21.3

▶ Main Idea Activity 21.3

▶ English Audio Summary 21.3

▶ Spanish Audio Summary 21.3

517

TEACH OBJECTIVE 1

LEVEL 1: Have students form small groups to discuss the establishment and work of the National Convention. Have each group develop a list of ways in which the National Convention supported democracy. *(Students should include items such as elected by universal manhood suffrage, encouraged good citizenship, supported universal education, abolished slavery.)* **ENGLISH LANGUAGE LEARNERS, COOPERATIVE LEARNING**

HOMEWORK Lead a discussion about the apparent contradictions within the National Convention. *(Students might suggest that it was a fairly elected government that made important reforms such as freeing slaves in French colonies, but that it used extreme means to silence dissenters in French society.)* As a homework assignment, have students create a political cartoon that demonstrates some of the contradictions discussed in class.

Historical Sidelight

Robespierre and many Jacobins wanted death for the king, but most of the Girondins wanted to save his life; the final tally was 361 to 319. The remaining deputies voted for either life imprisonment in irons, execution after the war, or a death sentence to be carried out after more debate. One of the deputies who voted for death was the king's own cousin, Philippe Egalité. Before the Revolution, he had been the Duke of Orléans and an enemy of the king. During the Revolution he renounced his noble title and took the name Philippe Egalité. Despite his renunciation and his vote against the king, Philippe Egalité became a victim of the guillotine in 1793.

🔲 internet connect

TOPIC: Rise and Fall of the Jacobins
GO TO: go.hrw.com
KEYWORD: SP3 WH21

Have students access the Internet through the HRW Go site to research the rise and fall of the Jacobins. Ask students to write a report using the information they find. They may wish to use the interactive template provided.

CONNECTING TO ART ANSWER
The details give a sense of the story of Marat's assassination.

Exporting the Revolution

Even before Louis XVI's execution, the National Convention had some good news. The French army had defeated the Austrian and Prussian forces, stopping the foreign invasion. The French built on these victories by invading the Austrian Netherlands.

The monarchs of Europe now feared that the French would try to overthrow royalty outside France. Great Britain, the Netherlands, Spain, and the kingdom of Sardinia joined Austria and Prussia in an alliance against France. Together they drove the French out of the Austrian Netherlands and invaded France again.

Committee of Public Safety. In 1793 the National Convention took steps to meet the threat of invaders. It set up the Committee of Public Safety to direct the army in crushing foreign invaders. The National Convention also established a special court, the Revolutionary Tribunal, to try "enemies of the Revolution."

To prepare itself against foreign invasion, the Committee of Public Safety adopted **conscription**—the draft. All unmarried, able-bodied men between 18 and 25 were subject to military service. As a force of patriotic young men, the French army took on a new, nationalistic spirit. In the new army, men from any class who proved their ability could become officers. During the 1800s conscription became common in Europe.

Opposition. Some French people rose up against the revolutionary government. In western France the "Royal and Catholic" army fought against the revolutionary army. We call their activities **counterrevolutionary,** meaning their aim was counter to, or against, the Revolution. Counterrevolutionary groups supported the Old Regime.

Jacobins, including Danton and Robespierre, controlled the National Convention. They arrested many Girondin delegates who opposed their policies. Meanwhile Charlotte Corday, a young woman influenced by Girondin ideas, assassinated Marat.

CONNECTING TO *Art*

Painting:
The Death of Marat

French art reflected changes caused by the French Revolution. Artists began to use different subjects, moods, and techniques.

This painting by Jacques-Louis David demonstrates this new style. Traditionally an assassination would not have been considered a suitable subject for a painting. However, the artist succeeded in painting a moving portrayal of Marat's death. In Marat's hand is a letter from his assassin, Charlotte Corday. On the floor lies the knife that she plunged into his chest.

Understanding the Arts

How do the details such as the knife and letter add to the drama of Jacques-Louis David's painting?

She stabbed him to death as he was bathing. The Revolutionary Tribunal sent her to the guillotine for her crime.

✔ **READING CHECK: Analyzing Information** What happened when the new French government tried to invade other countries? monarchs outside of France joined together to drive the French back

The Reign of Terror

The National Convention worked to suppress all opposition and revolts within France. The **Reign of Terror,** as it became known, lasted from September 1793 to July 1794. As Robespierre wrote, "It is necessary to annihilate [completely destroy] both the internal and external enemies of the republic or perish with its fall." The Law of Suspects issued in 1793 defined these suspected enemies:

Primary Source

❝Those who have shown themselves the enemies of liberty, those who cannot justify their means of existence and the performance of their civic duties, . . . those of the former nobles who have not constantly manifested their attachment to the revolution, and those who have emigrated during the interval between July 1, 1789, to April 8, 1792.❞

quoted in *The Law of Suspects,* 1793

As leader of the Committee of Public Safety, Robespierre helped to lead the Reign of Terror.

The Revolutionary Tribunal punished the enemies of the Republic and occasionally executed people who were simply suspected of counterrevolution. Marie-Antoinette became an early victim of the Reign of Terror. However, the Jacobins directed the Reign of Terror not only against the nobility, but also against anyone suspected of disloyalty. Robespierre and Danton began by sending their Girondin opponents to the guillotine, along with Olympe de Gouges. In fact, the revolutionaries executed twice as many bourgeoisie as nobles, and more than twice as many peasants and workers as bourgeoisie.

By the spring of 1794, the French army had gained the advantage in the war against the foreign powers. With the republic thus out of danger, Danton declared that he thought the Reign of Terror had met its goal and should be relaxed. In contrast Robespierre became even more fanatical and accused Danton of disloyalty to the Revolution. He had Danton and his followers put to death. This caused even Robespierre's colleagues to fear for their own safety.

For several months Robespierre continued the brutal suppression. He believed that only he could protect the Revolution from its enemies. Finally a few members of the National Convention called a halt. In July 1794 they arrested Robespierre and guillotined him.

With Robespierre's death, the Reign of Terror came to an end. People throughout Paris felt a sense of relief. The Jacobins lost power, and in fact a reaction began against their ideas. The wealthy middle class took control of the National Convention. Fashions changed as people rebelled against the strict Jacobin values. People went back to wearing luxurious dresses and hats. However, prices again rose sharply, causing hardship for the poor. Riots were put down by the army but feelings of unrest persisted. By 1794 many French people even favored a return to monarchy.

✔ **READING CHECK: Summarizing** What did the supporters of the Reign of Terror hope to accomplish? eliminate all enemies of the republic

Holt Researcher

go.hrw.com
KEYWORD: Holt Researcher
FreeFind:
    Maximilien Robespierre
After reading more about Maximilien Robespierre on the Holt Researcher, create a political tract explaining why he supported the Reign of Terror.

Constitutional Heritage

The arrest warrant for Danton came on the last day in March. When his trial opened on April 2, Danton began his testimony despite attempts to stop him. In his majestic, booming voice he addressed the public: "People, you will judge me when you have heard me; my voice will not only be heard by you but throughout all of France." Danton demanded the right to call witnesses to his defense and attacked the "present dictatorship." He intended to finish presenting his case on the second day of trial, but the prosecutor was afraid his arguments would win him a not guilty verdict. The next day the Convention, acting on a false report that Danton and his fellow prisoners were plotting against the Revolutionary Tribunal, decreed that the trial should continue in their absence. Danton's enforced silence thus ensured the verdict that the Committee wanted.

Critical Thinking

Ask students how the proceedings at Danton's trial went against the ideals of the Declaration of the Rights of Man and of the Citizen.

ANSWER: Danton was not given freedom of speech or equality before the law.

Reproducible Resources
PS Readings in World History 67: Robespierre and Saint-Just Defend the Arrest of Danton

	National Convention	Directory
Voters	*universal manhood suffrage*	*male property owners only*
Executive Branch	*committees*	*5 directors*
Length of rule	*3 years*	*4 years*
Use of terror	*yes*	*no*

Citizenship

The National Convention declared that the French armies should spread the Revolution and liberate all the peoples of Europe. In 1793 the entire nation mobilized for war: "Young men shall go forth to battle; married men shall forge weapons and transport munitions; women shall make tents and clothing, and shall serve in hospitals; children will make lint from old linen; and old men shall be bought to public places to arouse the courage of soldiers."

Critical Thinking

Ask students how they think the monarchs of Europe responded to the French desire to export the Revolution.

ANSWER: They were probably upset; they may have joined forces to fight the French.

VISUAL RECORD ANSWER

Many men are enlisting. The scene suggests interest and excitement among citizens.

Technology Resources

 Online Maps, Charts, and Graphs: Revolutionary France Expands, 1789–1799

The French adopted a new calendar in 1793. The year was broken into twelve months of three "decades" (instead of weeks) each. A decade equaled ten days. Five or six extra days were added at the end of each year.

INTERPRETING THE VISUAL RECORD

The people's army The National Convention created a revolutionary army to defend France. This painting shows French citizens enlisting in the new army. *How does the artist show that the recruits are enthusiastic about joining the army?*

Work of the National Convention

Despite the dangers and difficulties of the time, the National Convention met from 1792 to 1795 and made many democratic reforms. These changes affected every level of French society. The Convention created a body called the Committee of Public Safety. Controlled by Jacobins, this committee tried to establish what it called a "Republic of Virtue." By this it meant a democratic republic in which people would act according to the principles of good citizenship. To accomplish this the Committee opened new schools and supported the idea of universal elementary education. To aid the economy the Committee established wage and price controls intended to stop inflation. Even during the Reign of Terror, the Committee worked to address human rights concerns. It abolished slavery in France's colonies and encouraged religious toleration.

In addition, the National Convention replaced the monarchy's confusing system of weights and measures with the metric system. Based on the number ten, this system reflected the interest in rational thinking of the era. Today most parts of the world use the metric system. The Convention also created a new calendar, naming September 22, 1792—the date of the republic's creation—as the first day of the First Year of Liberty. This calendar used colorful names that reflected the seasons. For example, *Thermidor* indicated the warm month (roughly July) and *Ventôse* was the windy month (roughly March). This calendar also increased the number of days in a week, or "decade", from seven to ten. The calendar did not survive, but it does reflect the French people's hope that their republic would mark the dawn of a new era.

Meanwhile the French army went on to victory. By 1795 the French had driven invaders from French soil and conquered territory as far as the Rhine River in Germany. Even more important, the coalition of European countries against France began to break up. A new militaristic spirit swept the country. The National Convention used the army to quell opposition at home. It crushed an uprising in Paris in October 1795. This demonstrated that the new government would not accept any opposition.

✔ **READING CHECK: Summarizing** What were some of the changes the National Convention put into effect? abolished slavery, planned public education, adopted metric system

TEACH OBJECTIVE 4

ALL LEVELS: Have students list Napoléon Bonaparte's important achievements prior to 1799. *(suppressed a Paris uprising; demonstrated military genius in battle; forced Sardinians to make peace; defeated Austrians four times and gained control of northern Italy from them)* Then have students explain how they think Napoléon's military victories helped him come to power. *(Students may suggest that his military victories made people see him as a hero, a strong man, and an able leader.)*
ENGLISH LANGUAGE LEARNERS

CLOSE

Have students create a time line showing events beginning with the first meeting of the National Convention through Napoléon's coup d'état.

The Directory

In 1795 the National Convention completed another constitution. The government established by the new constitution took office in November of that year. It included a two-house legislature. The 500-member lower house proposed laws, while the smaller but more powerful 250-member upper house accepted or rejected the proposed legislation. The upper house also had the power to select the new government's executive branch, which consisted of five individuals known as directors. This gave the new government its name—the Directory. The nation's new constitution also eliminated universal manhood suffrage. Only male property owners could vote. In effect, then, the wealthy once again controlled France's government, as they had under the National Assembly.

The Directory governed France for four years. However, neither radicals nor conservatives were pleased with it. The economy improved somewhat but peasants, workers, and poor people still suffered. The five directors quarreled among themselves and were weak, corrupt rulers. When crowds protested, the directors used the army to stop the unrest.

The Directory was soon as unpopular as the Old Regime had been. Like the Old Regime, it had financial difficulties. Its failure paved the way for a military dictatorship in France.

✔ **READING CHECK: Comparing** How was the National Convention similar to the previous National Assembly? the wealthy had control

Napoléon Bonaparte

Under the Directory, ongoing wars with Great Britain, Austria, and Sardinia offered opportunities for able military leaders. Between 1795 and 1799 a young general named **Napoléon Bonaparte** came to the public's attention. Born in 1769 on the French island of Corsica, Napoléon attended military school in France. Already a general at age 26, Napoléon had stopped an uprising in Paris that would have prevented the creation of the Directory.

Napoléon was only five feet two inches tall but had an extremely strong personality. He was ambitious and energetic. He had great organizational skills and was a good manager of both political and military affairs. One of his smartest personal moves was marrying **Joséphine de Beauharnais,** a leader of French society, in 1796. Two days after the marriage, Napoléon won command of the French army that was fighting the Austrians in Italy.

Rise of Napoléon. Napoléon Bonaparte is considered one of the greatest generals of all time. Because of the dominant role that he played starting in 1796, the wars that France fought from then until 1815 are called the Napoléonic Wars. Napoléon's genius lay in his ability to move troops rapidly to the most critical points on the battlefield. His opponents' tactics were older and slower.

Napoléon proved his ability in Italy. The French army there was weak and poorly equipped. Napoléon improved conditions for the troops, gaining their support and boosting morale. With these newly inspired soldiers, Napoléon forced the Sardinians to make peace. He then went on to defeat the Austrians four times. In 1797 Napoléon forced the Austrians to sign a treaty that gave France control of all of northern Italy.

HISTORY MAKER

Napoléon Bonaparte (1769–1821)

Napoléon Bonaparte defeated the most powerful armies in Europe and established a vast empire. He was known for his military skills as well as for his charm and intelligence.

After his death, Napoléon was often memorialized in French art and literature. He was usually shown standing proudly, with one hand resting inside his jacket. **Why is Napoléon popular in French art and literature?**

Historical Sidelight

The Battle of Austerlitz was one of Napoléon's most brilliant victories. His force of 68,000 troops defeated a Russian and Austrian allied force of 90,000.

Napoléon laid a trap for his enemies by deliberately vacating a high plateau. At the base of the plateau, Napoléon had a force of 20,000 infantry, hidden from sight by a thick fog. When the allied forces descended to attack Napoléon's forces on the right and left, the hidden French forces charged up the slopes to capture the plateau. The plateau was occupied by the weakened allied forces, thus splitting the allied forces in half. When the allies began a retreat, the entire French army attacked and pursued them. In the end 15,000 allied soldiers were killed or wounded, and 11,000 were taken prisoner. Napoléon lost 9,000 men, but his position as the most powerful figure in Europe was established.

Critical Thinking

Ask students how Napoléon's victory at Austerlitz helped establish his reputation as Europe's most powerful figure.

ANSWER: It showed his skill as a military leader.

HISTORY MAKER ANSWER

had great military skills, charm, and intelligence; defeated Europe's most powerful armies; established a vast empire

REVIEW

Have students complete the Section 3 Review on p. 522.

ASSESS

Have students complete Daily Quiz 21.3. As Alternative Assessment, you may want to use the time line activity or the opinion piece activity in this section's lessons.

RETEACH

Have students complete Main Idea Activity for English Language Learners and Special-Needs Students 21.3. Then have students write a brief essay summarizing the achievements of the National Convention, the organization of the Directory, and the achievements of Napoléon. **ENGLISH LANGUAGE LEARNERS**

EXTEND

Have students research how the Law of Suspects and the Revolutionary Tribunal was used during the Reign of Terror. Have them write an essay describing their findings. **BLOCK SCHEDULING**

VISUAL RECORD ANSWER

Napoléon is in dress uniform, carrying the flag and with a sword in hand; the artist shows him with a handsome and noble face.

SECTION 3 REVIEW ANSWERS

❶ Define
- universal manhood suffrage, p. 517
- conscription, p. 518
- counterrevolutionary, p. 518
- coup d'état, p. 522

❷ Identify
- George-Jacques Danton, p. 517
- Maximilien Robespierre, p. 517
- Jean-Paul Marat, p. 517
- Reign of Terror, p. 519
- Napoléon Bonaparte, p. 521
- Joséphine de Beauharnais, p. 521

❸ executive branch made up of 5 directors, only male property owners could vote; peasants, workers, and poor people had no voice in government

❹ a. established schools, wage and price controls, abolished slavery in colonies, set up metric system, created a new calendar

b. All opposition was suppressed, people lived in fear, and all citizens were required to help with the foreign wars.

c. Napoléon built his popularity as military leader and staged a coup d'état against a weak and ineffective Director.

❺ The dialogue should give detailed reasons for and against conscription.

522

INTERPRETING THE VISUAL RECORD

Napoléon the hero Napoléon had a great talent for seizing public attention and for making himself popular with the French people. *How does this painting show an idealized view of Napoléon?*

The Directory worried that the popular Napoléon might try to seize power. Meanwhile, Napoléon continued to make new conquests, keeping his name before the French people. He proposed attacking the British in Egypt to cut off British trade with India. The Directory quickly agreed, as this would keep Napoléon out of Paris.

At first Napoléon won victories on land against Egyptian forces. However, Napoléon's military campaign in Egypt ended in disaster. The British destroyed the French fleet near Alexandria, isolating the French army in Egypt. Napoléon left his army to take care of itself and returned to France. He hid the truth and exaggerated his victories in Egypt.

Napoléon takes power. Although Napoléon became a hero, France was in a dangerous situation. The British had organized an alliance of nations to oppose France, including Austria and Russia. These forces drove the French armies out of Italy, and French control over other conquered territories slipped.

Napoléon's supporters believed that only he could win victories abroad and restore order at home. Fearing that royalists might seize control, they developed a plan to overthrow the government and put Napoléon in power. These supporters wanted France to be stable because they feared losing the property and power they had gained during the Revolution.

In 1799 the legislature did away with four out of the five directors. Armed troops surrounded the legislature and forced most of its members to leave. Those who stayed turned the government over to Napoléon and his fellow plotters. Seizing power by force like this is referred to as a **coup d'état,** French for a "stroke of state." As Napoléon later said, "I found the crown of France lying on the ground, and I picked it up with my sword."

✔ **READING CHECK: Summarizing** How did Napoléon seize power? coup d'état due to unstable government

SECTION 3 REVIEW

1. **Define** and explain the significance:
   universal manhood suffrage
   conscription
   counterrevolutionary
   coup d'état

2. **Identify** and explain the significance:
   Georges-Jacques Danton
   Maximilien Robespierre
   Jean-Paul Marat
   Reign of Terror
   Napoléon Bonaparte
   Joséphine de Beauharnais

 Homework Practice Online
keyword: SP3 HP21

3. **Analyzing Information** Copy the diagram and use it to show the balance of power under the Directory.

   Hall of Legislative Assembly

4. **Finding the Main Idea**
   a. How did the National Convention change France?
   b. How did the Reign of Terror and foreign wars affect the people of France?
   c. How did Napoléon Bonaparte rise to power?

5. **Writing and Critical Thinking**
   Identifying Points of View Conscription is one way to provide a military with soldiers. Write a dialogue between a teenager who is against the draft and a representative of France hoping to make conscription a policy.
   Consider:
   • what the teenager's life could be like as a soldier
   • how conscription could help the country

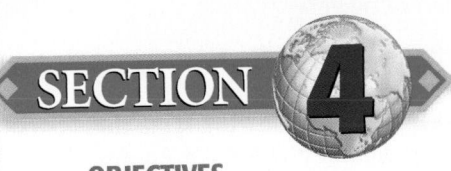

SECTION 4

OBJECTIVES

1 Identify the ways in which Napoléon's government was successful.

2 Explain how France became an empire.

3 Describe how Napoléon reorganized Europe.

4 Analyze the events that led to Napoléon's final defeat at Waterloo.

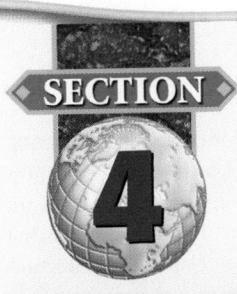

SECTION 4

READ TO DISCOVER

❶ In what ways was Napoléon's government successful?

❷ How did France became an empire?

❸ How did Napoléon reorganize Europe?

❹ What events led to Napoléon's final defeat at Waterloo?

DEFINE

plebiscite
nationalism
scorched-earth policy

IDENTIFY

Napoléonic Code
Concordat
Horatio Nelson
Duke of Wellington

▶ WHY IT MATTERS TODAY

Napoléon's conquest of Europe stirred up feelings of nationalism in European countries. Use CNN Student News or other **current event** sources to investigate how feelings of nationalism affect world affairs today. Record your findings in your journal.

CNN Student News.com

LET'S GET STARTED!

As students enter the classroom, have them read the paragraph "The Story Continues" at the top of page 523 and examine the painting of Napoléon. Ask students to volunteer opinions they have of Napoléon, based on what they have read and heard about him. List their responses on the board. After the list is complete, tell students that in Section 4 they will learn more about Napoléon, his achievements, and how he affected Europe.

The Napoléonic Era

The Main Idea
As emperor, Napoléon dominated Europe until other major powers joined forces to defeat him.

The Story Continues *After meeting Napoléon in person, French author Madame de Staël analyzed the source of his greatness: "He did not hate any more than he loved; for him nothing existed but himself; . . . His successes depended as much on the qualities which he lacked as on the talents which he possessed. Neither pity, nor religion, nor attachment to any idea whatsoever, could [deflect] him from his principal direction."*

Napoléon as Dictator

Although Napoléon's government kept the form of a republic, the coup d'état of 1799 made him dictator of France. The period from 1799 to 1814 is known as the Napoléonic Era, or Age of Napoléon, because his influence in France and the rest of Europe was so great during this time.

The Consulate. The people of France accepted Napoléon's dictatorship. Many people wanted stability after the years of chaos. Others were simply afraid to protest. Napoléon supported many of the changes brought by the Revolution. He respected the ideals of the Declaration of the Rights of Man and did not restore any feudal practices. However, while Napoléon allowed freedom of opportunity, he firmly believed that the people should obey orders given by their leader.

Napoléon reorganized and centralized the government to give himself unlimited power. The first five years of Napoléon's rule were called the Consulate. This name comes from the executive branch of the government, which was made up of three consuls with Napoléon as First Consul. Napoléon commanded the army and navy. He had the power to appoint or dismiss most officials and to propose all new laws. All the Consulate's legislative bodies could do was approve or reject Napoléon's decisions.

Napoléon put the constitution of his new government before the people for a vote. Under this procedure, called a **plebiscite,** people could vote only yes or no and could not suggest any changes. Even so, the vast majority of French voters approved the new constitution.

This painting by Jacques-Louis David captures the glory of Napoléon's military victories.

SECTION 4 RESOURCES

REPRODUCIBLE RESOURCES

▶ Guided Reading Strategy 21.4

▶ Readings in World History 68: A View of Napoléon's Character

▶ Hands-on History Activity 21: Napoléon's France

TECHNOLOGY RESOURCES

▶ One-Stop Planner 21.4

▶ Holt Researcher: World History: Napoléon Bonaparte, Josephine de Beauharnais

▶ Homework Practice Online

REINFORCEMENT, REVIEW, AND ASSESSMENT

▶ Section 4 Review, p. 528

▶ Daily Quiz 21.4

▶ Main Idea Activity 21.4

▶ English Audio Summary 21.4

▶ Spanish Audio Summary 21.4

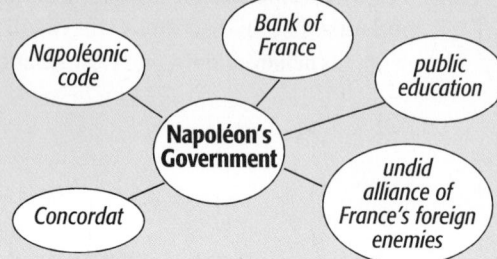

- Napoléonic code
- Bank of France
- public education
- Napoléon's Government
- Concordat
- undid alliance of France's foreign enemies

TEACH OBJECTIVE 2

LEVEL 1: Have students work in pairs to list the steps that Napoléon took to establish and enlarge the French Empire. *(crowned himself emperor; blockaded the British Isles; crushed Russian and Austrian forces and destroyed their coalition; forced Austria and Prussia to sign peace treaties; ruled the Netherlands and Spain directly and formed alliance with Denmark and the Papal States)*

ENGLISH LANGUAGE LEARNERS, COOPERATIVE LEARNING

VISUAL RECORD ANSWER

Napoléon, not the pope, is holding the crown and preparing to crown Joséphine.

Linking Past to Present

The United States has also attempted to influence international trade, though for different reasons than Napoléon's Continental System. In recent decades the United States has instituted economic boycotts and embargoes against Cuba and South Africa. In the 1960s the United States placed a trade embargo on Cuba in an attempt to change its communist government. Americans could not do business with or travel to Cuba. This situation persisted throughout the 1990s. In 1986 the U.S. Congress responded to South Africa's racist regime by passing a Comprehensive Anti-Apartheid Act, which banned new American investments or loans to South Africa, cut air links, and prohibited the importation of many goods. The United States hoped to pressure South Africa into improving its racial policies.

Critical Thinking

Ask students how they think economic boycotts affect the countries against which they are instituted.

ANSWER: They keep countries from selling their goods to others and from buying goods from others. They keep tourists out of the country.

INTERPRETING THE VISUAL RECORD

The coronation This painting shows Napoléon crowning his wife Joséphine empress after crowning himself emperor, while behind him the pope and clergy look on. The coronation ceremony took place in Notre Dame Cathedral, Paris. *How does the artist suggest that power rested with Napoléon and not with the church?*

Holt Researcher

go.hrw.com
KEYWORD: Holt Researcher
FreeFind:
Napoleon Bonaparte
Josephine de Beauharnais
After reading more about Napoléon and Joséphine on the Holt Researcher, describe how their coronation marked the end of the French Revolution.

Accomplishments in government.

While Napoléon is remembered most for his military leadership, his work in government had a more lasting effect. Under Napoléon's direction scholars organized all French law into a system called the **Napoléonic Code.** Napoléon established the Bank of France to act as a central financial institution. He also put into effect the system of public education planned by the National Convention. This system included high schools, universities, and technical schools. Elementary education was left in the control of churches and local governments.

The Civil Constitution of the Clergy in 1790 had strained relations between the French government and the Roman Catholic Church. In 1801 Napoléon ended this conflict by reaching an agreement with the pope called the **Concordat.** The Concordat recognized that most French citizens were Catholic, but it still allowed religious freedom. Most important, the church gave up claims to the property that the government had seized and sold during the Revolution.

Using skillful diplomacy Napoléon undid the alliance of France's foreign enemies. By 1802 Russia, Austria, and Great Britain had either deserted the alliance or made peace with France. It looked as though Napoléon had brought France peace, a stable government, and economic prosperity.

✔ **READING CHECK: Summarizing** What were some of Napoléon's achievements in government? Napoléonic Code, Bank of France, public education, Concordat

Napoléon as Emperor

Napoléon's supporters wanted to make his power permanent and hereditary. In another plebiscite in 1804, the French people voted to declare France an empire. Napoléon became Emperor Napoléon I and his wife became Empress Joséphine. To mark the beginning of the empire the pope came to Paris to crown the couple. However, just as he was about to place the crown on Napoléon's head, Napoléon took the crown and put it on himself. Thus Napoléon showed that the power and authority he had were not given to him by anyone but himself.

The empire extended far beyond France's old borders. The British now felt that France threatened their own empire and their control of the seas. Great Britain renewed war with France in 1803. Austria, Russia, and Sweden joined with Great Britain. Spain sided with France. Napoléon aimed to defeat the British navy and invade Great Britain.

However, in 1805 a British fleet led by Vice Admiral **Horatio Nelson** defeated a combined French and Spanish fleet off the coast of Spain. Vice Admiral Nelson was killed in the battle, but he had saved Britain from invasion. Napoléon did win great victories in land battles against Austria and Russia.

Napoléon ordered a blockade of the British Isles and forbade the French Empire and its allies from trading with Britain. This blockade was known as the Continental

ALL LEVELS: Have students study the map on page 525 and describe their general impression of Europe in the early 1800s. *(France controlled or influenced much of the continent.)* Then have them compile a list of the positive and negative aspects of Napoléon's conquests in Europe. *(positives: established the Napoléonic Code, abolished feudalism and serfdom, introduced modern military techniques, awakened the spirit of nationalism; negative: took power away from conquered peoples)*

ENGLISH LANGUAGE LEARNERS

Laura Watkins of Acton, Massachusetts, suggested the following activity: If available, have students listen to Russian composer Pyotr Ilich Tchaikovsky's 1812 Overture, which was written in 1880 to commemorate Russia's defeat of Napoléon. As students listen to the piece, ask them to think about how it reflects the historical event and era it commemorates. Afterwards, have students share their thoughts in a group discussion.

System, because Napoléon controlled so much of the continent of Europe. The British responded with a blockade against the French. The blockade hurt France, but Napoléon continued to win battles on land. In December 1805 he crushed Russian and Austrian forces, leading to the collapse of the coalition against France.

✔ **READING CHECK: Sequencing** What steps did Napoléon take as emperor? defeated Austria and Russia, ordered blockade of British Isles

The Reorganization of Europe

By 1809 Napoléon dominated Europe. He forced Austria and Prussia to sign peace treaties that benefited France, while Russia and Denmark allied themselves with Napoléon. He directly ruled the Netherlands and Spain and forced the Papal States into an alliance. He abolished the Holy Roman Empire and unified the northern Italian states into the Kingdom of Italy, under his control.

The Napoléonic Empire, 1805–1815

Interpreting Maps Napoléon gained control over most of western Europe through a series of conquests and alliances.

■ **Skills Assessment: Places and Regions** What area was neutral in 1812?

MAP ANSWER
the Ottoman Empire

That's Interesting!

On January 6, 1809, Napoléon left Spain without personally completing its conquest. The British military leader, the future Duke of Wellington, led a British force that was successful in helping the Spanish expel the French from Spain. Wellington, who would soon meet Napoléon in a final decisive battle, had a healthy respect for Napoléon's talents, and counted himself lucky in his success in Spain. He later wrote that if Bonaparte had been there, the British would have been beaten.

internet connect

TOPIC: Napoléon
GO TO: go.hrw.com
KEYWORD: SP3 WH21

Have students access the Internet through the HRW Go site to find an artistic rendering of a key event or person in Napoléon's life. Have students select an image and then write a short essay describing its significance to Napoléon.

Napoléon secured his power by placing members of his large family as monarchs of the countries he conquered. However, he felt that the best way to secure the empire was to produce an heir. When he and Joséphine failed to have a child by 1809, he had their marriage annulled. He quickly married Austrian princess Marie-Louise, who gave birth to a son, Napoléon II, in 1811.

Increased nationalism. Napoléon made far-reaching changes in the lands he controlled. Wherever he conquered he put the Napoléonic Code into effect, abolishing feudalism and serfdom. He also introduced modern military techniques throughout Europe.

Without intending to, the French increased feelings of nationalism in the people they conquered. **Nationalism** refers to love of one's country rather than one's native region. In France the Revolution, as well as the Declaration of the Rights of Man, made people think of their country and ideals as things worth fighting for. Now these same feelings of loyalty and patriotism appeared among the people Napoléon had conquered. In some places this increased opposition to French rule. Over time, the armies of Napoléon's opponents' grew stronger.

The Peninsular War. To the south of France, on the Iberian Peninsula, lay Spain and Portugal. In 1807 Portugal refused to follow the Continental System because its economy depended upon trade with Great Britain. Napoléon responded by sending his armies into Portugal and driving out its king. He also conquered Spain and forced the Spanish king to step down. Napoléon then made his brother Joseph king of Spain.

The Spanish people revolted against this foreign rule in 1808. The British sent an army led by the future **Duke of Wellington** to help the Spanish and Portuguese people rise up against the French. This war, known as the Peninsular War, lasted from 1808 to 1814. During this time Napoléon still controlled Spain's government, but the war drained France's military resources. In 1813 the Spanish, with British help, finally drove out Joseph Bonaparte. They then wrote a new constitution that set up a limited monarchy. The revolt in Spain, and this new constitution, show the influence of the ideas of the French Revolution.

✔ **READING CHECK: Finding the Main Idea** What changes did Napoléon put into place in countries he conquered? enforced Napoléonic Code, modernized military

Catastrophe in Russia

Czar Alexander I of Russia was alarmed by Napoléon's domination of Europe. Moreover, Russia had long depended on trade with Great Britain for manufactured goods. In 1812 the czar began trading again with Great Britain. Because the blockade was Napoléon's only way of striking at the British, he was angry that Russia, an ally of France, would openly ignore it. He decided to invade Russia, and he called on all parts of his empire to supply soldiers.

The Grand Army. Napoléon recruited a Grand Army of 600,000 soldiers from all over his empire. In 1812 this army began a long march east to Russia. The Russian defenders slowly retreated,

This painting from 1808 shows Napoléon commanding his forces at the Battle of Eylau.

HOMEWORK Have students create a comic strip with dialogue that depicts the French army's attack on Russia in 1812 and subsequent events. In class, have students exchange comic strips and imagine they are historians looking at the comic strip as an artifact from which they can learn about Napoléon's disastrous defeat. Have students write a few sentences telling what they learned from the comic strip.

CLOSE

Have students write a brief essay describing the advantages and the disadvantages that Napoléon brought to France and to the Europeans.

---

drawing Napoléon's army deep into their country. As the Russians retreated they practiced a **scorched-earth policy,** burning or destroying crops and everything else the Grand Army might need.

The French eventually captured Moscow, but it was a hollow victory. As soon as the French entered the city, the Russians set it on fire. The fire destroyed so many buildings that the French troops had no housing, and the harsh Russian winter was coming. Napoléon had already lost many soldiers to disease, cold, and hunger, as well as battle. He finally ordered a retreat on October 19, 1812.

Napoléon's retreat from Moscow remains one of the greatest military disasters of all time. Napoléon's troops tried to make their way back to France through the bitter Russian winter without proper clothing and supplies. Many soldiers died from cold and starvation. Furthermore, the French were constantly under attack from Russian soldiers as they passed through the destroyed countryside. By the time the Grand Army reached Prussia, it had lost two thirds of its troops. The Russians followed and invaded the French Empire.

Final defeat. Monarchs in western Europe took advantage of Napoléon's defeat in Russia. They quickly broke their alliances with Napoléon. Prussia, Austria, and Great Britain joined Russia in a final alliance to crush France. In October 1813 Napoléon's army met these allied forces in Leipzig in Saxony. The allies won, and Napoléon retreated into France. The allies captured Paris in March 1814.

Napoléon agreed to give up all claims to the throne for himself and his family. The allies gave him a pension and allowed him to retire to the small island of Elba off the west coast of Italy.

The allies wanted to make sure that France would no longer disrupt Europe's affairs. They agreed that France could keep the boundaries of 1790. They also restored the Bourbon monarchy. Louis XVIII, the brother of Louis XVI, came to the throne. France had a king again.

✔ **READING CHECK: Identifying Cause and Effect** What factors led to Napoléon's defeat in Russia? lack of proper housing and supplies, Russian winter

The Hundred Days

During 1814 and early 1815, the restored king and his family made many enemies among the French people. Learning of this discontent, Napoléon escaped from Elba and landed in France on March 1, 1815. Louis XVIII sent soldiers to capture Napoléon. Napoléon met them saying, "If there be one among you who wishes to kill his Emperor, he can. I come to offer myself to your assaults." The soldiers' resistance disappeared, and Napoléon led the army into Paris on March 20, beginning a period called the Hundred Days. Frightened, Louis XVIII fled into exile. Napoléon once again ruled France.

Napoléon hoped that disputes among his opponents would keep them from opposing his return, but he was wrong. Prussia, Great Britain, and the Netherlands sent armies toward France. Napoléon assembled an army to stop them.

Government of France, 1774–1814

1774	Louis XVI became king.
1789	Third Estate, as National Assembly, assumed power.
1791	Legislative Assembly, with Louis XVI as constitutional monarch, began rule.
1795	Directory took control.
1799	Consulate was established, with Napoléon as First Consul.
1804	Napoléon was crowned emperor.
1814	Napoléon was defeated and Bourbon monarchy was restored.

Interpreting the Chart
After being ruled as a republic and then an empire, France returned to monarchy in 1814. *What can you tell about political stability in France during this time?*

King Louis XVIII retained many of Napoléon's reforms in the law, church, and education.

INTERPRETING THE CHART ANSWER
France was unstable because a new government took over every few years.

Daily Life

During the Grand Army's bitter winter retreat from Russia, the common soldier suffered terribly. One soldier describes the retreat across Russia:

"The carriages, drawn by tired and underfed horses, were traveling fourteen and fifteen hours of the twenty-four.... Having left Moscow with us,...[the carriages] had had to take up the men wounded.... They were put on the top seats of the carts.

...At the least jolt those who were most insecurely placed fell; the drivers took no care. The driver following...for fear of stopping and losing his place... would drive pitilessly on over the body of the wretch who had fallen."

Critical Thinking

Ask students why they think Napoléon did not make provisions for a more orderly retreat from Russia.

ANSWER: He probably thought he could defeat the Russians and did not plan to have to retreat. He did not plan to be in Russia during the winter.

THE FRENCH REVOLUTION AND NAPOLÉON **527**

On June 18, 1815, the allied and the French armies met at Waterloo. The British—under the command of the Duke of Wellington—and their Prussian allies dealt Napoléon his final defeat. Napoléon gave up the throne, and the Bourbon monarchs once again took power.

Napoléon asked to be allowed to go to the United States. However, the British sent him to St. Helena, a small, lonely island in the South Atlantic, where he lived under constant guard. In 1821 Napoléon died there.

As the years passed, Napoléon's legend grew. People forgot his failures and remembered his glories and victories. Napoléon and his achievements came to be memorialized in French literature and art. In 1840 the British allowed the French to bring Napoléon's remains back to Paris, where they lie to this day.

✔ **READING CHECK: Summarizing** How was Napoléon finally defeated? Britain, Prussia, and Netherlands united against him

INTERPRETING THE VISUAL RECORD

Waterloo Scottish troops clash with charging French cavalry in this painting of Napoléon's defeat at Waterloo. *How does this painting create a sense of the confusion and chaos of battle?*

SECTION 4 REVIEW

1. **Define** and explain the significance:
   plebiscite
   nationalism
   scorched-earth policy

2. **Identify** and explain the significance:
   Napoléonic Code
   Concordat
   Horatio Nelson
   Duke of Wellington

3. **Analyzing Information** Copy the model and use it to show the allies who joined forces against Napoléon in Leipzig.

Leipzig

4. **Finding the Main Idea**
   a. Describe Napoléon's achievements through 1804.
   b. How did Napoléon establish an empire?
   c. How and by whom was Napoléon finally defeated?

5. **Writing and Critical Thinking**
   Drawing Inferences In a short script for a play, have Napoléon saying goodbye to his troops before he is taken to St. Helena.
   Consider:
   - Napoléon's triumphs
   - the loyalty and patriotism of his troops
   - the great change from being emperor to living on a small island

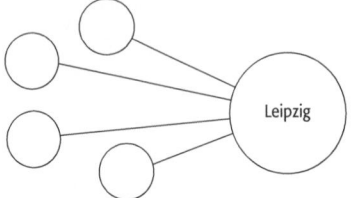

Homework Practice Online
keyword: SP3 HP21

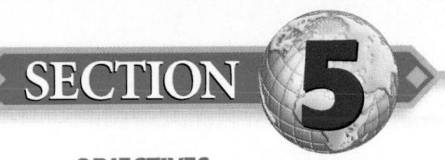
🔊 *LET'S GET STARTED!*

As students enter the classroom, have them list some of the changes that France and Europe underwent between 1789 and 1815. *(the downfall of the monarchy, several new constitutions, a period of terror, the introduction of democratic principles and ideas of nationalism, dictatorship, war, and conquest)* Then ask students what European monarchs and leaders might hope for after that period of turmoil. *(a return to peace and stability; to regain control of lost territory)* Tell students that in Section 5 they will learn how European leaders tried to restore Europe and ensure a lasting peace.

READ TO DISCOVER

❶ How did the Congress of Vienna attempt to restore stability to Europe?

❷ Why did politicians practice conservative policies?

❸ How did Metternich influence conservative politics and stop revolution?

DEFINE

legitimacy
indemnity
reaction
reactionaries
liberalism

IDENTIFY

Charles-Maurice de Talleyrand-
Périgord
Prince Metternich

▶ WHY IT MATTERS TODAY

Alliances in Europe helped to uphold the Congress of Vienna. Use CNN*fyi.com* or other **current event** sources to investigate alliances between countries today and what goals they have. Record your findings in your journal.

CNN*student*
News.com

A Return to Peace

The Main Idea
After 1815 European governments took a conservative approach in restoring stability to Europe.

The Story Continues *After defeating Napoléon, the major European powers wanted to stamp out the ideas of the French Revolution. Nevertheless, the words from the Declaration of the Rights of Man and of the Citizen—"men are born and remain free and equal in rights"—still echoed in people's minds throughout Europe.*

The Congress of Vienna

Napoléon had not always upheld the ideals of the French Revolution—liberty, equality, and fraternity—but he did extend their influence throughout Europe. This led other governments to fear that rebellions against monarchy might spread beyond France. Having defeated Napoléon, the major European powers wanted to restore order, keep the peace, and suppress the ideas of the Revolution.

The principles of the Congress of Vienna. Stability could not be achieved until territorial questions were settled. To resolve these questions hundreds of delegates met at the Congress of Vienna, in Austria. Most decision-making authority rested with Great Britain, Austria, Prussia, and Russia. However, the representative of France, **Charles-Maurice de Talleyrand-Périgord,** also played an important role.

Three principles guided the decisions of the Congress of Vienna. (1) The countries that had suffered the most at the hands of Napoléon had to be paid back for what they had lost. (2) The balance of power had to be restored in Europe, so that no single nation would become too powerful. (3) All decisions would follow the rule of **legitimacy,** which meant that all former ruling families should be restored to their thrones.

Compensations. Countries were reshuffled in an attempt to gain back losses. The Netherlands, conquered early on by French forces, received the Austrian Netherlands. In return, Austria gained two northern Italian states. Because Sweden had fought against Napoléon, it received Norway, formerly a Danish possession. This was also intended to punish Denmark for cooperating with Napoléon. Prussia received some territory along the Rhine River. Although Great Britain did not receive any lands in Europe, it did gain several islands in the French West Indies and in the Mediterranean.

INTERPRETING THE VISUAL RECORD

Restoring order The work of the Congress of Vienna continued throughout the Hundred Days of Napoléon's return to power and after his final defeat at Waterloo. *What does the presence of military officers in this painting say about politics at the time?*

5 RESOURCES

REPRODUCIBLE RESOURCES

▶ Guided Reading Strategy 21.5

TECHNOLOGY RESOURCES

▶ One-Stop Planner 21.5

▶ World History Teaching Transparency: Everyday Life 20: A Ball During the Congress of Vienna

REINFORCEMENT, REVIEW, AND ASSESSMENT

▶ Section 5 Review, p. 533

▶ Daily Quiz 21.5

▶ Main Idea Activity 21.5

▶ English Audio Summary 21.5

▶ Spanish Audio Summary 21.5

VISUAL RECORD ANSWER

The military had a say in politics since they were the ones who finally stopped Napoléon. Leaders were interested in establishing a safe, secure Europe in which there would be no more wars.

THE FRENCH REVOLUTION AND NAPOLÉON **529**

LEVEL 1: Ask students to list the guiding principles of the Congress of Vienna. (*The countries that suffered most at the hands of France should be compensated for their losses; the balance of power in Europe had to be restored; former ruling families should be restored to their thrones.*) Then have students explain the ways in which the leaders at the Congress of Vienna upheld the three principles. (*Many victorious countries received territory that had been under French domination; no European state received so much land that it became too strong or powerful, and a ring of strong states surrounded France; monarchies such as the Bourbons were returned to power.*)

ENGLISH LANGUAGE LEARNERS

HOMEWORK Ask students to imagine that they are a delegate to the Congress of Vienna either from France, from one of the countries conquered by France, or from one of the countries that fought France. From that perspective, have them write a journal entry explaining what they hope to gain for their country and for Europe at the Congress of Vienna.

History Maker

TALLEYRAND. As a statesman, Talleyrand had influenced French policy since the beginning of the Revolution. A member of the National Assembly, Talleyrand had first proposed confiscating church lands to help raise funds to pay off government debts, even though he was at the time a bishop of the Catholic Church. He also served as Napoléon's chief adviser until he openly criticized the emperor's foreign policy.

Talleyrand was one of the most influential diplomats at the Congress of Vienna, helping France achieve a satisfactory peace settlement.

Critical Thinking

Ask students to predict what kind of peace settlement France might have had if Talleyrand had not worked so hard on France's behalf.

ANSWER: France might have had to pay a heavier indemnity. France may have been divided among the other nations.

The winning powers also argued over territory. Napoléon had once given part of Poland to his allies in the German state of Saxony. Now Russia and Prussia both claimed parts of Poland. Other countries feared that either outcome would upset the balance of power, and for a time tensions increased. Finally Talleyrand resolved the dispute with a distribution of land that everyone could accept.

In the end France was surrounded by a ring of strong states so that it could not again threaten the peace of Europe. France's boundaries were returned to where they had been in 1790. France also had to pay a large **indemnity**—a financial reward to other countries for the damages it had caused.

At Talleyrand's urging the Congress of Vienna made settlements based on legitimacy. The Bourbon monarchy, already restored in France, also regained power in Spain and in the Kingdom of the Two Sicilies. This principle was not applied everywhere, however. The Austrian Habsburgs, for example, now dominated Italy because of new territorial gains.

✔ **READING CHECK: Summarizing** What were the three principles that guided the Congress of Vienna? compensation, balance of power, legitimacy

Reactionary Alliances

A time of **reaction** followed the Napoléonic Era, meaning that people in authority wanted a return to the way things had been before. **Reactionaries** are people who not only oppose change but would also like to actually undo certain changes. After 1815 the victors in Europe attempted to restore a balance of power, or stability, and to emphasize a conservative view toward politics.

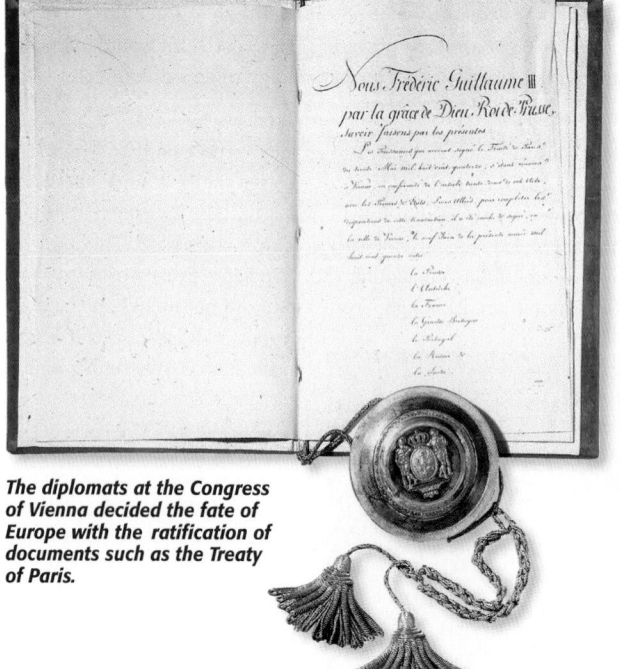

The diplomats at the Congress of Vienna decided the fate of Europe with the ratification of documents such as the Treaty of Paris.

In Spain and the Two Sicilies, the restored monarchs abolished existing constitutions and gave themselves absolute power. Switzerland alone kept its constitutional government but had to promise to remain neutral in European wars.

Napoléon's conquests had resulted in the spread of new political ideas and the rise of nationalism. Groups that shared a common language, history, and culture now wanted to unite under their own governments. Reactionary powers considered this nationalism dangerous and tried to halt it. Therefore European governments took special steps to prevent revolution, and the Congress of Vienna left nationalist groups disappointed.

The four allies that had defeated Napoléon —Austria, Great Britain, Prussia, and Russia— agreed in 1815 to continue their alliance. Known as the Quadruple Alliance, they agreed to hold periodic conferences to discuss common interests. In 1818 France was allowed to join the Quadruple Alliance, making it the Quintuple Alliance.

ALL LEVELS: Copy the following chart on the chalkboard, omitting the italicized answers. Have students fill in the boxes answering the questions. Then lead a discussion about why politicians of Europe wanted to form these alliances. *(to restore and maintain peace and stability)* **ENGLISH LANGUAGE LEARNERS**

	Main purpose	Members	Organization
Quadruple/ Quintuple Alliance	*discuss common interests, keep peace*	*Britain, Austria, Russia, Prussia, France*	*Members met at conferences.*
Holy Alliance	*monarchs rule as Christians*	*all European rulers except British king, Turkish sultan, and the pope*	*Members met at conferences.*
Concert of Europe	*keep peace and status quo*	*nations of Europe*	*Members signed pledges.*

Czar Alexander of Russia held strong religious ideals and urged the other leaders to sign an agreement called the Holy Alliance. By signing they promised to rule as Christians. Most rulers signed this reactionary document—evidence of the extreme conservatism that existed at the time.

Out of these alliances grew what was called the Concert of Europe—a form of international governance by concert, or agreement. The aim of the Concert was to maintain the balance of power set up by the Congress of Vienna. The Concert of Europe proved effective until 1848.

✔ **READING CHECK: Drawing Conclusions** In what ways were alliances after 1815 helpful to Europe? maintained balance of power

Global Relations

Whether or not the Congress of Vienna achieved a balance of power was, and still is, subject to doubt. The long-standing peace among European nations may have been due not to an achieved balance of power, but to other factors: the stability of the restored monarchy in France, changing political and economic interests, a wide-spread desire to avoid war, and a growing interest in settling differences at the conference table and not on the battlefield.

Critical Thinking

Given the history of revolution, ask students why the restored monarchy in France remained a stable government.

ANSWER: People were tired of war and upheaval and did not want to oppose the government. People preferred a king over a dictator such as Napoléon.

Europe After the Congress of Vienna, 1815

Interpreting Maps The Congress of Vienna, meeting between 1814 and 1815, attempted to settle political and territorial questions arising from the Napoléonic Wars.

■ **Skills Assessment: Locate** France's territory was greatly reduced by the actions of the Congress of Vienna. What island remained under French rule?

LEVEL 3: Ask students to suggest some effects that Metternich's system of suppression and the ideas of liberalism had on Europe. *(Metternich: suppressed freedoms, preserved absolutism, set up secret police system, suppressed revolutions; liberalism: raised ideas of individual freedoms and civil liberties, tried to secure constitutions, worked against absolute rule)* Then lead a discussion about which of these systems prevailed at first. *(Metternich's system)*
ENGLISH LANGUAGE LEARNERS

CLOSE

Have students write several paragraphs explaining what settlements European leaders reached at the Congress of Vienna and how Metternich's conservative system helped maintain peace and stability in Europe.

SKILLS PRACTICE ANSWERS

1. Congress of Vienna

2. A. 2. c.

3. Outlines should reflect appropriate format.

SKILL-BUILDING STRATEGIES Using Outlines

Europe after Napoléon

The Congress of Vienna succeeded in addressing the concerns of the major European powers after the defeat of Napoléon. Afterward, the Concert of Europe continued to enforce the terms agreed to by delegates at the Congress. Using an outline can help you to understand the terms of a complex document like the Concert of Europe.

An Eyewitness's View:
Prince Metternich, who coordinated much of this diplomatic cooperation, described his main goals in the following way:

"Liberty for every Government to watch over the well-being of its own people; a league between all Governments against factions in all States; . . . respect for the progressive development of institutions in lawful ways . . . such are happily the ideas of the great monarchs: the world will be saved if they bring them into action—it is lost if they do not."

I. Congress of Vienna addresses three main issues
   A. Compensating countries for losses
      1. France pays indemnity for damages caused
      2. Congress awards territories
         a. Austria gains two northern Italian states
         b. Great Britain gains island possessions
   B. Restoring a balance of power
      1. Officials strip France of conquests
         a. Congress restores French borders to 1792 status
         b. France surrounded by strong states
      2. Prussia and Russia reach a compromise
   C. Maintaining legitimacy of ruling families
      1. Louis XVIII rules France
      2. Bourbon monarchs restored in Spain and Two Sicilies

Much of Europe's royalty came to Vienna during the winter of 1814–15. They carried on a lively social life while diplomats and rulers discussed the state of Europe after Napoléon.

Skills Reminder

Most writers follow a standard format to create an outline. They label main heads with Roman numerals, subheads with capital letters, and details with Arabic numerals and lowercase letters. The information in the details should be more specific than at any other level. Each level should have at least two entries and be indented from the level above. Organized in such a way, an outline serves as a blueprint to help you keep track of important information and write a more well-structured research paper.

Skills Practice

❶ Study the partial outline above. What is the main topic of this outline?
❷ Suppose you wanted to add a fact about how Denmark was penalized for cooperating with Napoléon. Where would you place it in the outline?
❸ Choose one section from this chapter and outline it using the format shown above. Your thesis statement should be the main idea of the section. The section's main headings could serve as the major ideas in the outline.

REVIEW

Have students complete the Section 5 Review on p. 533.

ASSESS

Have students complete Daily Quiz 21.5. As Alternative Assessment, you may want to use the graphic organizer in this section's lessons.

RETEACH

Have students complete Main Idea Activity for English Language Learners and Special-Needs Students 21.5. Then have students

create a chart showing the three principles of the Congress of Vienna and how each was implemented by the Congress.
ENGLISH LANGUAGE LEARNERS

EXTEND

Assign students one of the following leaders: Metternich, Czar Alexander I, or Talleyrand. Tell students to use primary and secondary sources such as computer software to find out more about these individuals. Then have students write a newspaper article based on an imaginary interview with their leader.
BLOCK SCHEDULING

The Age of Metternich

For 30 years after the Congress of Vienna, **Prince Metternich** of Austria influenced European politics so strongly that this period is sometimes known as the Age of Metternich. A reactionary, Metternich believed in absolute monarchy. He feared the movement known as **liberalism,** which extended the ideas of the American and French revolutions. Liberals believed in individual rights and the rule of law. Metternich believed in suppressing such ideas as freedom of speech and of the press. He aimed to prevent war or revolution and to preserve absolutism. Metternich had little difficulty achieving these goals in Austria. He set up a central investigating commission to spy on revolutionary organizations and individuals. He also persuaded the rulers of most German states to adopt the same methods. In France King Louis XVIII was cautious in domestic affairs, but joined in suppressing revolutions elsewhere.

Liberals reacted strongly to the Congress of Vienna and to Metternich's actions. A number of uprisings occurred in Europe, and the Concert of Europe worked to suppress them. Austria, Russia, and Prussia, in particular, were very determined in their efforts to thwart revolutions. Great Britain, however, did not want to intervene in other nations' affairs. Having a representative form of government themselves, the British were sympathetic to liberal movements in other countries. For this and other reasons, Great Britain did not join the Holy Alliance.

For a time Metternich's system of suppression worked well. As repression increased, however, underground movements of resistance began. In the early 1820s allied armies had to put down popular uprisings in the Two Sicilies. In 1821 nationalism flared again as the Greeks revolted against their Ottoman Turk rulers. Under Metternich's influence European rulers ignored Greek calls for aid. Many individuals across Europe, however, supported Greece and even fought as volunteers. Finally Russia, Great Britain, and France brought pressure on the Ottomans. With the signing of the treaty of Adrianople in 1829 Greece won its independence. This successful uprising showed that feelings of nationalism could not be suppressed forever.

✔ **READING CHECK: Summarizing** How did Metternich try to stop liberalism? secret police, military suppression

Prince Metternich, shown here, used harsh means to stop revolutionary movements. He encouraged governments to place university students and faculty members under strict watch, to censor newspapers and magazines, and to search for secret revolutionary activities.

SECTION 5 REVIEW ANSWERS

❶ **Define**
• legitimacy, p. 529
• indemnity, p. 530
• reaction, p. 530
• reactionaries, p. 530
• liberalism, p. 533

❷ **Identify**
• Charles-Maurice de Talleyrand-Périgord, p. 529
• Prince Metternich, p. 533

❸ Countries that suffered most had to be paid back. Balance of power had to be restored. All former ruling families had to be restored to their thrones.

❹ a. The Congress did not want any country to become too powerful and invade other nations.

b. People of the same cultural group were not willing to have things go back to the way they were before Napoléon.

c. Metternich was a reactionary who wanted to suppress people, while Great Britain believed in representative government.

❺ Letters should include an explanation of Metternich's policy.

SECTION 5 REVIEW

1. **Define** and explain the significance:
   legitimacy
   indemnity
   reaction
   reactionaries
   liberalism

2. **Identify** and explain the significance:
   Charles-Maurice de Talleyrand-Périgord
   Prince Metternich

Homework Practice Online
keyword: SP3 HP21

3. **Summarizing** Copy the model and use it to show the three principles guiding the Congress of Vienna.

Congress of Vienna

4. **Finding the Main Idea**
   a. Why was the Congress of Vienna so concerned with the balance of power?
   b. Why was nationalism a threat to reactionaries?
   c. How were Metternich's ideas different from Great Britain's?

5. **Writing and Critical Thinking**
   Analyzing Information Write a letter from Metternich to Austria's allies explaining his system to keep the peace.
   Consider:
   • what monarchs had to fear from liberalism
   • the effectiveness of the Metternich system

REVIEW AND ASSESSMENT RESOURCES

REPRODUCIBLE RESOURCES
▸ Vocabulary Activity 21

TECHNOLOGY RESOURCES
▸ Chapter 21 Test Generator (on the One-Stop Planner)
▸ Global Skill Builder CD-ROM
▸ HRW Web Site

REINFORCEMENT, REVIEW, and ASSESSMENT
▸ Chapter 21 Review, pp. 534–535
▸ Chapter 21 Tutorial for Students, Parents, Mentors, and Peers
▸ Chapter 21 Test (Form A or B)
▸ Alternative Assessment Handbook
▸ Chapter 21 Test for English Language Learners and Special-Needs Students

REVIEW
Have students complete the Chapter 21 Review on pages 534–535.

ASSESS
Use one of the chapter tests to assess students' understanding of the content. For Alternative Assessment, see the Portfolio Activities and Alternative Assessment Handbook.

CHAPTER 21 REVIEW ANSWERS

Understanding Main Ideas

1. the injustice of the social structure and methods of taxation; the growing financial crisis; the desire of the Third Estate to have political power

2. It insisted one person-one vote and formed a National Assembly to write a constitution.

3. did away with feudalism, wrote the Declaration of the Rights of Man, reformed government administration, reformed the church in France, wrote a constitution that established a new government

4. declared war, suspended the office of the king

5. to spread revolutionary ideas and protect France from those who wanted to overturn the Revolution; to create a Republic of Virtue

6. He was a military genius and had a powerful and charming personality.

7. He invaded and conquered countries, formed alliances, and placed his family on the thrones of conquered countries.

8. Russia, Leipzig, Waterloo

9. Nations of the Concert worked together to spy on revolutionary organizations, suppress free speech, and suppress uprisings.

Review

Creating a Time Line

Copy the time line below onto a sheet of paper. Complete the time line by filling in the events, individuals, and dates from the chapter that you think were significant. Pick three events and explain why you think they were significant.

1789	1799	1815

Writing a Summary

Using standard grammar, spelling, sentence structure, and punctuation, write an overview of the events in the chapter.

Identifying People and Ideas

Identify the following terms or individuals and explain their significance:
  1. bourgeoisie
  2. Marie-Antoinette
  3. Napoléon Bonaparte
  4. radicals
  5. conscription
  6. coup d'état
  7. Horatio Nelson
  8. plebiscite
  9. Duke of Wellington
  10. Prince Metternich

Understanding Main Ideas

SECTION 1 *(pp. 508–511)*
The Roots of Revolution
  1. List three underlying causes of the French Revolution.
  2. What role did the meeting of the Estates General in 1789 play in bringing about the Revolution?

SECTION 2 *(pp. 512–516)*
The French Revolution
  3. Describe the accomplishments of the National Assembly.
  4. What effect did the Legislative Assembly have on France?

SECTION 3 *(pp. 517–522)*
The French Republic
  5. What was the purpose of France's foreign wars and the Reign of Terror?
  6. What abilities helped Napoléon rise to power?

SECTION 4 *(pp. 523–528)*
The Napoléonic Era
  7. How did Napoléon build his empire?
  8. List three of Napoléon's most important defeats.

SECTION 5 *(pp. 529–533)*
A Return to Peace
  9. How did the Concert of Europe become an instrument of suppression?

Reviewing Themes
  1. **Government** Was the National Convention truly a representative form of government?
  2. **Constitutional Heritage** How did the Constitution of 1791 change the status of the French monarchy?
  3. **Citizenship** Compare and contrast the attitude of the Jacobins, Napoléon, and Prince Metternich toward freedom of speech.

Thinking Critically
  1. **Drawing Inferences** How did the structure of French society lend itself to a revolution?
  2. **Making Generalizations** How did Napoléon gain control over Europe?
  3. **Contrasting** How was the French Revolution different from the American Revolution?

Writing About History
Categorizing In a paragraph, describe what were the lasting social, political, and cultural effects of the French Revolution. Use the chart below to help you organize your thoughts before writing.

Social Effects	Political Effects	Cultural Effects

Have students list the lasting social, cultural, and political effects of the French Revolution. Then have them debate whether the French Revolution was successful.

RETEACH

Have students who had difficulty with the test work in small groups to compile a chapter outline and glossary. When they are ready, have students take the Form B Test to assess their mastery of the material.

ENGLISH LANGUAGE LEARNERS, COOPERATIVE LEARNING

Portfolio Extensions

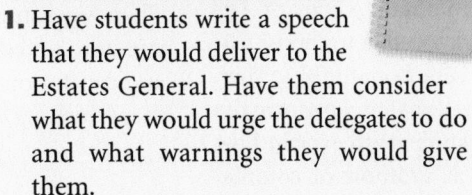

1. Have students write a speech that they would deliver to the Estates General. Have them consider what they would urge the delegates to do and what warnings they would give them.
2. Have students choose one period discussed in this chapter—the Revolution, the Napoléonic Age, or the Congress of Vienna and its aftermath. Ask them to define and describe the major events or ideas from that period.
3. Have students choose an event from this chapter, such as the meeting of the Estates General, some scene from the Reign of Terror, Napoléon's rise to power or one of his battles, or a scene from the Congress of Vienna. Encourage students to conduct research on the event to find out more details. Then have them create an illustration of the scene and write a paragraph identifying and explaining it.

Building Social Studies Skills

Interpreting Maps

Study the map below. Then use the information from the map to answer the questions that follow.

Napoléon in Russia

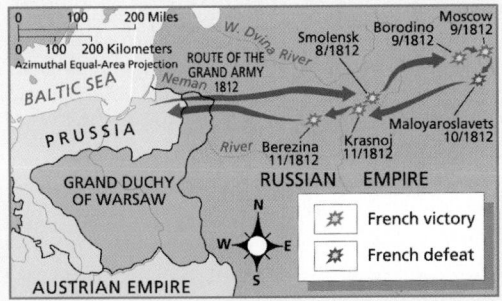

1. Which of the following statements accurately reflects the information shown on the map?
   a. Napoléon's march into Russia reached as far east as Moscow.
   b. Napoléon's army moved from east to west during its march into Russia.
   c. Napoléon's army was well supplied throughout its campaign in Russia.
   d. Weather was never an issue during the French invasion of Russia.

2. Napoléon's campaign in Russia was viewed with horror by many in the years after 1812. Why was this so? Give specific reasons.

Analyzing Historical Context

Read the following quote from Comte de Mirabeau, who was trying to calm the people of Marseille after a riot in March, 1789. Then answer the questions.

> "My good friends, I have come to tell you what I think about the events of the past three days in your proud city. . . . Let us first consider bread. . . . At the present time, dear friends, since wheat is expensive everywhere, how could it be cheap at Marseille? . . . The town of Marseille, like every other town, pays something toward the expenses of the kingdom and the support of our good king. Money is taken from this source and a little from that. . . ."

3. Which of the following statements best summarizes the situation in Marseille at the time Mirabeau spoke these words?
   a. The people of Marseille were unhappy because the price of wheat was rising.
   b. Marseille paid more taxes than other cities in France at the time.
   c. Food was scarce and very expensive, and the people of the Third Estate had begun to rebel.
   d. The people of Marseille were glad to help support France and the king.

4. What was the main point that Mirabeau was making in this quote?

Alternative Assessment

Building Your Portfolio

Link to TODAY

Constitutional Heritage

The French Revolution took many of its ideas from previous revolutions. Using your textbook and other sources, create a chart summarizing the ideas from the English, American, and French Revolutions concerning separation of powers, liberty, equality, democracy, popular sovereignty, human rights, constitutionalism, and nationalism.

internet connect

Internet Activity: go.hrw.com
KEYWORD: SP3 WH21

Choose a topic on the French Revolution and Napoléon to:
- analyze artistic renderings and evaluate the historical accuracy of key events in Napoléon's life.
- evaluate the differences among the American, French, and Russian Revolutions.
- research the rise and fall of the Jacobins.

Reviewing Themes

1. delegates elected by universal manhood suffrage, but some people disliked radical methods

2. limited the monarch's power, established a constitutional monarchy

3. believed in repressing free speech; Jacobins: to prevent opposition to the Revolution; Napoléon: to prevent opposition to his rule; Metternich: to silence revolutionary ideas

Thinking Critically

1. few people held wealth and power; most were heavily taxed and excluded from government

2. through conquests and alliances

3. Americans fought against foreign control; French overthrew monarchy

Writing About History

Paragraphs should include freedom and equality in society, representative governments, and artistic expression.

Building Social Studies Skills

1. a

2. It was a great military disaster.

3. a

4. Everyone pays something toward the support of the country.

Building Your Portfolio

Charts should show similarities among the revolutions.

Spotlight on LITERATURE

Ask students to obtain a copy of *The Group* and work together to choose a 5- to 10-minute scene from the play. Then have students rehearse and perform the scene. After their performance, ask the students to explain how Warren developed certain characters as symbols of colonial resentment toward British colonial policies. Ask the students to use the scene they have just performed to analyze and identify major causes of this resentment.

Spotlight on LITERATURE

Jonathan Swift wrote many well-known social and political satires, including *A Tale of a Tub* and *Gulliver's Travels*. Have students research Swift and his writing. Then have students use standard grammar, spelling, sentence structure, and punctuation to write an essay that draws inferences and conclusions regarding how Swift's writing reflects Enlightenment thinking.

Linking Past to Present

Political satire continues to be an effective literary form in contemporary society. Satire has spread to many forms of media, including political cartoons and motion pictures. In the United States the editorial cartoonist Herblock (by name of Herbert L. Block) used caricature and insight to create pointed commentaries on political life in the 1900s. Film director Stanley Kubrick also provided a biting—though humorous—critique of political and military leadership in his motion picture *Dr. Strangelove; or, How I Learned to Stop Worrying and Love the Bomb*. In the film, as nuclear bombs threaten to annihilate the world, Kubrick finds a way to make the audience laugh. In one scene, the president of the United States says, "You can't fight in here. This is the War Room."

ACTIVITY: Have students identify a contemporary work of political satire (for example, political cartoons). Then ask students to explain how the contemporary work compares with the works of Swift and Warren.

UNDERSTANDING LITERATURE ANSWER

Swift—poverty; Swift and Warren—greed, poor political leadership; answers may vary

CROSS-CULTURAL CONNECTIONS *Literature*

Political Satire

The pointed humor of political satire makes fun of politicians' behavior and the failings of social institutions. By making leaders and institutions look ridiculous, satirists hope to inspire people to attack social problems. To shock readers into taking action, satirists often use exaggeration and irony—saying the opposite of what is meant. When he worked in Ireland during the early 1700s, Jonathan Swift (1667–1745) saw many people, particularly children, living in dreadful conditions. Swift proposed several ways to address poverty and lack of political rights in Ireland. After his straightforward suggestions were ignored, Swift wrote the savagely ironic A Modest Proposal. Mercy Otis Warren (1728–1814) wrote some of the first plays to attack England's "imperialistic rule" in America. Her characters in The Group, all based on recognizable British officials and their Tory supporters, have names like Dupe, Spendall, Hum-bug, and Hateall. Warren's stage directions compare them to a swarm of locusts eating everything in its path. Warren's satiric plays, published in newspapers instead of being produced in the theater, contributed to Thomas Hutchinson's removal as governor of Massachusetts.

A Modest Proposal *by Jonathan Swift*

I HAVE been assured by a very knowing American of my Acquaintance in London; that a young healthy Child, well nursed, is, at a Year old, a most delicious, nourishing, and wholesome Food; whether Stewed, Roasted, Baked, or Boiled....I DO therefore humbly offer it to publick Consideration, that of the Hundred and Twenty Thousand children, already computed, Twenty thousand may be reserved for Breed.... That the remaining Hundred thousand, may, at a Year old, be offered in Sale to the Persons of Quality and Fortune, through the Kingdom; always advising the Mothers to . . . render them plump, and fat for a good Table. A child will make two Dishes at an Entertainment for Friends; and when the Family dines alone, the fore or hind Quarter will make a reasonable Dish; and seasoned with a little Pepper or Salt, will be very good boiled on the fourth Day, especially in Winter.... I GRANT this Food will be somewhat dear [expensive], and therefore very proper for Landlords; who, as they have already devoured most of the Parents, seem to have the best Title to the Children.

The Group *by Mercy Otis Warren*

The Group enter attended by a swarm of court sycophants [insincere flatterers], hungry harpies [predators who relentlessly pursue their prey], and unprincipled danglers [hangers-on] . . . hovering over the stage in the shape of locusts; led by Massachusettensis in the form of a basilisk [a fierce, sharp-toothed lizard]; the rear brought up by Proteus [someone who allies with a side in a conflict for money], bearing a torch in one hand and a powder flask in the other, the whole supported by a mighty army and navy from Blunderland, for the laudable [admirable—used here in a satirically sarcastic way] purpose of enslaving its best friends.

Understanding Literature

What are the problems that Swift and Warren attack? Do you think they use effective techniques to bring about change? Explain your answer.

Government

Napoléon Bonaparte has been both highly praised and harshly criticized for his rule as emperor of France. Have students identify primary and secondary sources that are biased either for or against Napoléon. Then ask students to write a speech either praising or criticizing Napoléon's leadership. In either case, students should address all aspects of his rule, including governmental reforms and military exploits.

Constitutional Heritage

Copy the graphic organizer below onto the board. Tell students that it illustrates the effect of parliamentary and constitutional systems of government on significant world political developments. Then ask students to work in groups to list historical and contemporary examples for each triangle.

World Political Developments

Parliamentary   Constitutional

UNIT 5

BUILDING YOUR Portfolio

Government

The English, American, and French Revolutions shared many of the same principles, even though all three had different outcomes. Create a chart summarizing the ideas from these three revolutions concerning separation of powers, liberty, equality, democracy, popular sovereignty, human rights, constitutionalism, and nationalism.

The Battle of Marston Moor in 1644 was a turning point in the English Civil War. The development of constitutionalism in England had a long and sometimes violent history.

Further Reading

Erickson, Carroly. *Great Catherine.* New York: St. Martin's Press, 1995. The life and times of Russia's Catherine the Great.

Hibbert, Christopher. *The Days of the French Revolution.* New York: Quill, 1999. An overview of people and events during the French Revolution.

Sweetman, John. *The Enlightenment and the Age of Revolution, 1700–1850.* New York: Addison Wesley, 1998. A survey of politics, people, culture, and society during the Ages of Enlightenment and Revolution.

Wheeler, Richard, ed., and Bruce Catton. *The Voices of 1776: The Story of the American Revolution in the Words of Those Who Were There.* New York: Meridian, 1996. First person accounts from both sides by men and women who witnessed the Revolutionary War.

Zienert, Karen. *Those Remarkable Women of the American Revolution.* Brookfield, CT: Millbrook Press, 1996. An overview of the role women played during the war.

The Boston Massacre in the American colonies, March 1770 (above), and the storming of the Bastille by French revolutionaries, July 1789 (right), symbolized the power of Enlightenment ideas.

Constitutional Heritage

Many of the ideas that influenced constitutional governments had roots in ancient civilizations. Create a time line tracing the historical development of the rule of law and of rights and responsibilities, beginning in the ancient world and continuing to the first modern constitutional republics. The time line should include the influence of ideas about rights and responsibilities, such as equality before the law, that originated in Greco-Roman and Judeo-Christian ideals.

internet connect

go hrw .com

Internet Activity
KEYWORD: SP3 U5

In assigned groups, develop a multimedia presentation about the era from Absolutism to Revolution. Choose information from the chapter Internet Connect activities and the Holt Researcher that best reflects the major topics of the period. Write an outline and a script for your presentation, which may be shown to the class.

Government

After ratifying the Constitution, Americans elected George Washington as their first president in 1789. In the history of the world, no other country had been led by a president. Therefore, Washington had to define the style of this new form of leadership without a model. For his inauguration, Washington wore a brown suit made in the United States. He also wore white stockings and a sword, as was the style in European courts. Great crowds of cheering supporters greeted Washington and his wife, Martha, at the inauguration. However, the Washingtons were publicly criticized for traveling as monarchs did in a coach led by four richly outfitted horses. The president used other manners of royalty such as greeting people with a formal bow rather than shaking hands. He also met guests on state occasions while standing on a raised platform and wearing his sword. In contrast, it was decided that he would be addressed with the simple title of "Mr. President." In addition, he resisted public pressure to serve a third term as president, setting a precedent for the peaceful transfer of power.

Critical Thinking

Why do you think Washington incorporated the style of European monarchs into his presidency?

ANSWER: Answers may vary; students may suggest that this was the only example he had to follow and that these symbols of leadership were familiar to Americans.

Industrialization and Nationalism

♦ **CHAPTER 22** ♦ **The Industrial Revolution**

The discoveries during the Scientific Revolution led people to apply scientific advances in a practical way. New machines and land practices led to the Agricultural Revolution in the 1700s. The Industrial Revolution followed with advances in industry, transportation, and communication. Cities grew as people flocked to the thriving new centers of industry. Lifestyles and living standards changed as a result of the Industrial Revolution.

♦ **CHAPTER 23** ♦ **Life in the Industrial Age**

Advances such as electricity, the telephone, and the combustible engine transformed the ways in which people lived, worked, and thought. Changes in occupations and living conditions brought more leisure time as well as new social problems. Artists and writers wrestled with the ever-changing industrialized society. Interest in a new field of study, the social sciences, grew. Concern about health and education led to calls for reform to make life better, as well.

EXAMINING THE VISUAL RECORD

❶ *In what ways might the ironworks in the painting be compared to a blacksmith's shop?*

ANSWER: Both are involved in making things out of iron.

Until the Industrial Revolution, most iron objects were made by hand by blacksmiths, who worked with a furnace, an anvil, tongs, hammers, or other tools to cut, shape, or flatten the iron. The ironworks is a much larger version of a blacksmith's shop. It has more people using more advanced tools making more products in a shorter amount of time.

❷ *How might a steam engine be used in an ironworks such as the one in the picture?*

ANSWER: A steam engine could pump the bellows.

A blast furnace uses bellows to infuse air into a furnace, thus increasing the heat of the fire in order to liquefy and separate iron from iron ore. The advent of the steam engine meant more air could be pumped into the furnace. In 1828 James Beaumont Neilson introduced the use of a hot-air blast instead of a cold-air blast, greatly advancing the technology of iron production.

ACTIVITY: Ask students to use primary and secondary sources, including computer software, to learn more about the processing and manufacture of iron and steel.

UNIT 6

Industrialization and Nationalism

1600–1928

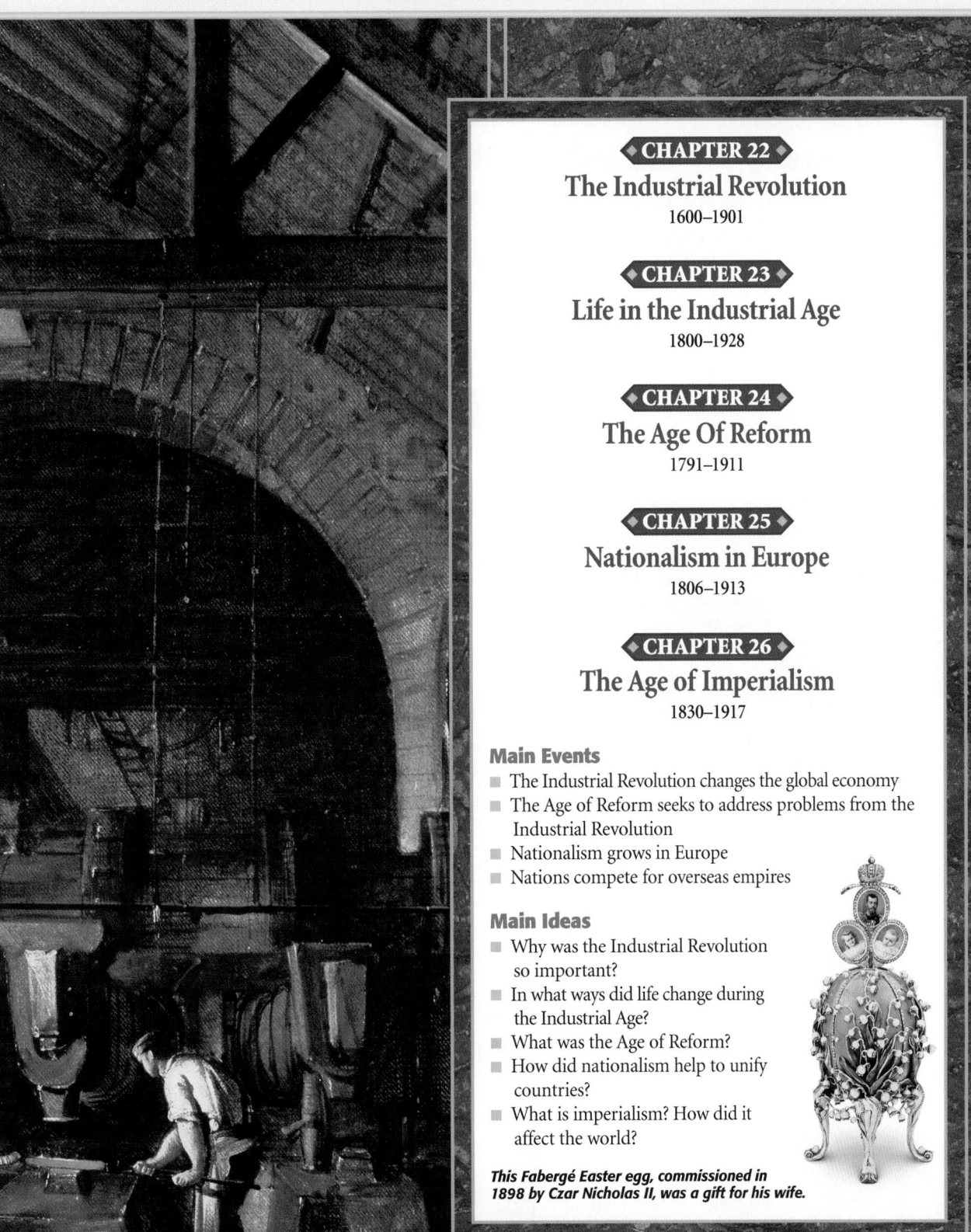

CHAPTER 24 **The Age of Reform**
During the 1800s Great Britain became more democratic. Grounded in a political philosophy of the Enlightenment, the government moved toward the protection of individual rights and civil liberties. The United States expanded its territory and fought a Civil War. Changes in France led to a republic governed by a coalition of parties. Latin American countries won independence from Spain.

CHAPTER 25 **Nationalism in Europe**
During the 1800s nationalism became a driving force for change in European regions. Italy, unified for a time under Napoléon, was divided into several states as the result of the Congress of Vienna. Nationalists began a campaign for liberation and unification. People in Germany, too, thought the unified nation-state was the best way to gain individual rights. By the late 1800s both Italy and Germany had achieved unification.

CHAPTER 26 **The Age of Imperialism**
As the ideas of nationalism swept through Europe, the countries that accepted change emerged as stronger and more unified states. Growing industries created competition for new sources of raw materials. The years between 1870 and 1914 were the height of the Age of Imperialism. By 1914 the great powers of Europe, Japan, and the United States controlled a large part of the world.

◆ **CHAPTER 22** ◆
The Industrial Revolution
1600–1901

◆ **CHAPTER 23** ◆
Life in the Industrial Age
1800–1928

◆ **CHAPTER 24** ◆
The Age Of Reform
1791–1911

◆ **CHAPTER 25** ◆
Nationalism in Europe
1806–1913

◆ **CHAPTER 26** ◆
The Age of Imperialism
1830–1917

Main Events
- The Industrial Revolution changes the global economy
- The Age of Reform seeks to address problems from the Industrial Revolution
- Nationalism grows in Europe
- Nations compete for overseas empires

Main Ideas
- Why was the Industrial Revolution so important?
- In what ways did life change during the Industrial Age?
- What was the Age of Reform?
- How did nationalism help to unify countries?
- What is imperialism? How did it affect the world?

This Fabergé Easter egg, commissioned in 1898 by Czar Nicholas II, was a gift for his wife.

This 1850 painting by Godfrey Sykes of the interior of an ironworks captures the spirit of the Industrial Revolution. **539**

Introduce Unit 6

Main Events
Ask students to select two Main Events and list questions they would like to have answered about the topics. Later, when you have completed Unit 6, ask students to return to their original questions and write an answer using the information they learned in the unit.

Main Ideas
Ask each student to read the Main Ideas and write brief answers to the questions. Share the *Consider* points with students as necessary. Later, when you have completed Unit 6, ask students to analyze their original answers by comparing them to information they learned in the unit. Tell them to revise or expand their answers as necessary.

The impact of the Industrial Revolution and the Age of Reform
Consider:
- economic changes
- social changes
- religious aspects
- scientific developments

The Results of the Rise of Nationalism and Imperialism
Consider:
- global politics
- monarchy and democracy
- cultural effects
- political effects

CROSS-CULTURAL CONNECTIONS

Focus On: Science, Technology, and Society

 LET'S GET STARTED!

As students enter the classroom, ask them to write definitions of the word *technology.* Have students keep their definitions to revise as they read Cross-Cultural Connections. Tell students that in this unit they will learn how, during the Industrial Revolution, new technologies developed and spread, leading to the rise of imperialism and nationalism.

TEACH

ALL LEVELS: Have students read Cross-Cultural Connections and the time line on pages 542–543. Help students fill in the chart below with the information shown in italics. Then have them pose and answer questions about these inventions. **ENGLISH LANGUAGE LEARNERS**

Invention	Inventor	Date	Purpose
modern steam engine	*James Watt*	*1769*	*industry*
high-pressure steam engine	*Richard Trevithick*	*1804*	*locomotives*
machine gun	*Hiram Maxim*	*1884*	*warfare*
cotton gin	*Eli Whitney*	*1793*	*agriculture*

History Maker

HENRY FORD. Henry Ford was born in Dearborn, Michigan, in 1863. When he was 15 or 16 he went to Detroit and trained as a machinist. There he came into contact with the internal combustion engine. Henry began to experiment with a horseless carriage and completed his first gasoline-powered car in 1896. In 1903 he started the Ford Motor Company. By this time he had developed an idea about making all automobiles alike. He introduced the Model T Ford in 1908. The car was a great success and in 1913 was produced on a moving assembly line.

Critical Thinking

How did Henry Ford's development of the assembly line influence the production of goods other than cars?

ANSWER: The assembly line allowed mass production of identical goods. This created a more vigorous economy but led to a decline in the creation of unique handcrafted items.

CROSS-CULTURAL CONNECTIONS

Focus On: Science, Technology, and Society

Main Idea How did new technologies of the Industrial Revolution change the world? The Industrial Revolution transformed economies and societies throughout the world. Beginning in England, the technology that started the movement quickly spread throughout Europe and the United States. To support their new industries, many nations began to seek overseas empires for raw materials. The competition for empires fueled already growing nationalism within Europe.

Africa

Greece

United States

England

1600   1806   1830   1917
             1800   1913   1928

England, 1600–1928

In 1829, the "Rocket" won a competition sponsored by the Liverpool and Manchester Railroad in England. The steam-powered locomotive pulled three times its own weight at 12.5 mph. It carried passengers at about 24 mph.

◀ **The Power of Steam** The steam engine was one of the most important inventions of the Industrial Age. The first steam engines, developed in the late 1600s, simply pumped water. Scottish engineer James Watt developed the first modern steam engine in 1769. Then British inventor Richard Trevithick designed a high-pressure steam engine to power the first railroad locomotive in 1804. In 1829 the first locomotive carried passengers and freight. Soon after, railroad construction took off at an rapid pace in Britain and the United States. Railways quickly became an important source of transportation for both goods and passengers. British artist William Frith captured the noise and bustle of a British railway station in this painting from 1862.

Increased Mobility The development of steamship travel during the second half of the 1800s allowed for an enormous increase in immigration to the United States and Canada. Some people called steamship transportation between Europe and North America "the Atlantic Ferry." Faster travel times meant that shipping companies had to provide little more than minimal living space in steerage for poorer passengers, who were required to supply their own food, bedding, and other necessities. In this image from the late 1800s, immigrants in search of new opportunities and a better life come ashore at Ellis Island, New York.

United States, 1800–1928

REVIEW

Have students review the information about the different inventions listed in the chart on page 540. Ask them to use standard grammar, spelling, sentence structure, and punctuation to answer the question in "Why It Matters Today" and to share their answer with the class.

ASSESS

Have students complete their answer to the question in "Why It Matters Today" and add it to their portfolio. As Alternative Assessment, you may want to use the invention chart exercise in this lesson.

EXTEND

Have students work in groups of three or four to create a model of an invention from the time of the Industrial Revolution. Tell students to use information from their textbooks, the library, computer software, and any other available resources to determine how the invention was constructed, how it functioned, and what its purpose was. Allow time for students to demonstrate their model for the class.

Global Nationalism Throughout the 1800s and continuing uninterrupted into the 1900s, the forces of nationalism increasingly shaped world events. In Europe, Latin America, the Middle East, and Asia, rising nationalism led to major change, in many cases sweeping away centuries-old political and social structures. Nationalism was stimulated, in part, by the material and technological progress of the Industrial Revolution, and by the general economic growth that resulted. Increased global communication and contact, also products of industrialization, helped to spread ideas of national identity and opposition to the "old order." The English poet Lord Byron, pictured here, championed nationalistic movements in Italy and in Greece, where he died of a fever in 1824.

Greece, 1806–1913

Africa, 1830–1917

Tools of Imperialism One result of technological growth in the 1800s was a rapid change in the weapons of warfare. The invention of the machine gun by Hiram Maxim in 1884 gave imperialistic countries a significant advantage over less-developed nations. Advanced weapons allowed European countries to establish colonial empires in Asia and Africa during this period. German imperialism in Africa, for example, began in the early 1880s. In this painting, created by an East African artist, German officers watch the slaughter of native Africans in the German protectorate of Tanganyika [present-day Tanzania], as German-trained African soldiers use modern weapons to defeat native warriors armed with shields and spears.

The invention of the machine gun in 1884 made for a more portable weapon that could fire 11 rounds per second.

Why It Matters Today

Historically, new technology has had the power both to help and to hurt societies. As a result, people sometimes greet technological growth with mixed emotions.
In what ways does modern technology both help and harm society? How have people in your society reacted to recently developed technology?

Interdisciplinary Connection

MEDICINE. A major contribution to the future of health care occurred in 1844 when Dr. Horace Wells, a Connecticut dentist, observed the pain-killing properties of nitrous oxide during a laughing-gas road show. He began the use of nitrous oxide inhalation to reduce or eliminate pain during dental treatments. The medical community eventually used anesthesia as a standard surgical pain management procedure.

Critical Thinking

How might the use of nitrous oxide have contributed to an improvement in people's dental health?

ANSWER: Eliminating the pain associated with dental treatments would make people less reluctant to receive proper dental care.

WHY IT MATTERS TODAY ANSWER

Answers will vary but should show understanding that technology helps society by providing new and improved ways of doing things. At the same time, new technologies often have unforeseen consequences that can be harmful to individuals and society as a whole.

The Industrial Revolution

CHAPTER RESOURCE MANAGER

Objectives	Pacing Guide	Reproducible Resources
SECTION 1 **Origins of the Industrial Revolution** (pp. 544–550) • Explain why the Industrial Revolution began in Great Britain. • Describe how inventions in the textile industry led to other new inventions. • Analyze the effects that developments in transportation and communication had on the spread of the Industrial Revolution.	**Regular** 1.5 day **Block Scheduling** 1 day *Block Scheduling Handbook with Team Teaching Strategies, 22.1*	**RS** Guided Reading Strategy 22.1 **RS** Graphic Organizer Activity 22: The Flow of Industry **SM** Geography Activity 22: Manchester: Growth of an Industrial Giant **PS** Readings in World History 73: An Accident at the Opening of a Railroad Line
SECTION 2 **The Factory System** (pp. 551–554) • Explain how the increased use of machinery affected workers and working conditions. • Identify the differences between the middle class and the working class. • Analyze how the lives of women changed during the Industrial Revolution.	**Regular** 1.5 day **Block Scheduling** 1 day *Block Scheduling Handbook with Team Teaching Strategies, 22.2*	**RS** Guided Reading Strategy 22.2 **PS** Readings in World History 74: A Working Day in a Manchester Cotton Mill **E** Hands-on History Activity 22: Inside the Factory
SECTION 3 **New Methods and Business Organizations** (pp. 555–558) • Explain how and why the methods of production changed during the Industrial Revolution. • Identify what caused corporations to emerge and the effects they had on business. • Define the business cycle and explain how it affected society.	**Regular** 1.5 day **Block Scheduling** 1 day *Block Scheduling Handbook with Team Teaching Strategies, 22.3*	**RS** Guided Reading Strategy 22.3 **E** Creative Teaching Strategy 22: The Great Business Exposition
SECTION 4 **Living and Working Conditions** (pp. 559–563) • Identify Adam Smith's ideas and explain how they affected people's views of industrialism. • Explain the causes of reform movements. • Analyze how workers tried to improve their lives.	**Regular** 1.5 day **Block Scheduling** 1 day *Block Scheduling Handbook with Team Teaching Strategies, 22.4*	**RS** Guided Reading Strategy 22.4 **PS** Readings in World History 75: The Trail of the Tolpuddle Martyrs
SECTION 5 **Socialism** (pp. 564–567) • Describe the type of society that early socialists wanted to establish. • Explain how Robert Owen put his socialist beliefs into action. • Explain what Karl Marx believed would happen to the capitalist world of the 1800s. • Identify some of the competing ideas that arose out of Marxism.	**Regular** 1.5 day **Block Scheduling** 1 day *Block Scheduling Handbook with Team Teaching Strategies, 22.5*	**RS** Guided Reading Strategy 22.5 **PS** Readings in World History 76: A Visit to New Lanark

Chapter Resource Key

PS Primary Sources	**A** Assessment	Music	
RS Reading Support	**REV** Review	Video	
IC Interdisciplinary Connections	**ELL** Reinforcement and English Language Learners	Internet	
E Enrichment	Transparencies	Holt Presentation Maker Using Microsoft® PowerPoint®	
SM Skills Mastery	CD–ROM		

One-Stop Planner CD-ROM

See the ***One–Stop Planner*** for a complete list of additional resources for students and teachers.

One-Stop Planner CD-ROM

It's easy to plan lessons, select resources, and print out materials for your students when you use the *One-Stop Planner* CD–ROM with *Test Generator*.

Technology Resources	Reinforcement, Review, and Assessment
One-Stop Planner 22.1 Holt Researcher: World History: James Watt, Robert Fulton World History and Cultures Video Program 18: The Industrial Revolution World History Teaching Transparency: Art and History 18: The Gare Saint-Lazare, Paris; Everyday Life 17, 18: European Clothing Styles, 1700s; Traditional Farming Methods Homework Practice Online Online Maps, Charts, and Graphs: European Industrialization, Mid–1800s; Railroads Link British Industries, c. 1850	Daily Quiz 22.1 Main Idea Activity 22.1 English Audio Summary 22.1 Spanish Audio Summary 22.1 REV Section 1 Review, p. 550
One-Stop Planner 22.2 Holt Researcher: World History: Elizabeth Gaskell Homework Practice Online	Daily Quiz 22.2 Main Idea Activity 22.2 English Audio Summary 22.2 Spanish Audio Summary 22.2 REV Section 2 Review, p. 554
One-Stop Planner 22.3 Homework Practice Online	Daily Quiz 22.3 Main Idea Activity 22.3 English Audio Summary 22.3 Spanish Audio Summary 22.3 REV Section 3 Review, p. 558
One-Stop Planner 22.4 Homework Practice Online	Daily Quiz 22.4 Main Idea Activity 22.4 English Audio Summary 22.4 Spanish Audio Summary 22.4 REV Section 4 Review, p. 563
One-Stop Planner 22.5 Homework Practice Online	Daily Quiz 22.5 Main Idea Activity 22.5 English Audio Summary 22.5 Spanish Audio Summary 22.5 REV Section 5 Review, p. 567

internet connect

HRW ONLINE RESOURCES
GO TO: go.hrw.com
Then type in a keyword.

TEACHER HOME PAGE
KEYWORD: SP3 Teacher

CHAPTER INTERNET ACTIVITIES
KEYWORD: SP3 WH22
Choose an activity to:
- identify the historic origins of capitalism and socialism.
- compare and contrast modern labor unions with early unions.
- write a biography of a female writer who lived and wrote during the Victorian Age.

CHAPTER ENRICHMENT LINKS
KEYWORD: SP3 CH22

ONLINE ASSESSMENT
Homework Practice
KEYWORD: SP3 HP22
Standardized Test Prep
KEYWORD: SP3 STP22
Rubrics
KEYWORD: SS Rubrics

ONLINE MAPS, CHARTS, AND GRAPHS
KEYWORD: SP3 MCG

CONTENT UPDATES
KEYWORD: SS Content Updates

HOLT PRESENTATION MAKER
KEYWORD: SP3 PPT22

ONLINE READING SUPPORT
KEYWORD: SS Strategies

CURRENT EVENTS
KEYWORD: S3 Current Events

Meeting Individual Needs

Ability Levels

Level 1 Basic level activities designed for all students encountering new material

Level 2 Intermediate level activities designed for average students

Level 3 Challenging activities designed for honors and gifted and talented students

English Language Learners These activities address the needs of students with Limited English Proficiency.

Chapter Review and Assessment

- IC Vocabulary Activity 22
- Global Skill Builder CD-ROM
- HRW Web Site
- REV Chapter 22 Tutorial for Students, Parents, Mentors, and Peers
- REV Chapter 22 Review, pp. 568–569
- A Chapter 22 Test Generator (on the One-Stop Planner)
- A Chapter 22 Test (Form A or B)
- A Alternative Assessment Handbook
- A Chapter 22 Test for English Language Learners and Special-Needs Students

Build on What You Know

Ask students to answer the following questions:

How did technological discoveries and developments of the Scientific Revolution change society?

Consider:

- scientific discoveries
- the invention of new machines
- the spread of new ideas

How did major developments in technology affect society?

Consider:

- the effects of the printing press
- technological influences on exploration

EXPLORING THE TIME LINE

GLOBAL EVENTS

internet connect

TOPIC: Combination Acts
GO TO: go.hrw.com
KEYWORD: SP3 WH22

Have students access the Internet through the HRW Go site to learn more about the Combination Acts of 1799–1800. Why did the government pass laws to prevent the formation of unions? Why were workers intent on forming those unions? Create a poster advocating the formation of a union after the passing of the Combination Acts.

CHAPTER 22

1600–1901

The Industrial Revolution

Early hand-cranked cotton gin

1600
Daily Life
The enclosure movement in England continues.

1675
Science and Technology
The Royal Observatory at Greenwich, England, is founded by King Charles II.

1713
Politics
The Treaty of Utrecht is signed.

c. 1733
Science and Technology
John Kay invents the flying shuttle.

1600

1700

c. 1633–1637
Business and Finance
Wild speculation in tulip bulbs ultimately ruins many Dutch investors.

c. 1701
Science and Technology
Jethro Tull invents the seed drill.

1721
The Arts
Johann Sebastian Bach's *Brandenberg Concertos* are completed.

1769
Science and Technology
Richard Arkwright patents a water-powered spinning frame.

Painting of a tulip by a Dutch artist

Portrait of Johann Sebastian Bach

Build on What You Know

The discoveries of Galileo Galilei, Sir Isaac Newton, and other pioneering thinkers of the Scientific Revolution led to a deeper understanding of the natural world. By the early 1700s people began to apply these scientific advances in a practical way. This led to the creation of new machines and businesses. Major developments in technology were aimed at producing and moving goods. These products were designed to meet the needs of a fast-growing population. In this chapter, you will learn about how industrial developments took place and what effect they had on society.

What's Your Opinion?

 To help students create their Themes Journal entries, provide the following examples of appropriate **agree**/**disagree** *statements.*

Science, Technology & Society

Agree New machines and inventions can make a person's work much easier and faster.

Disagree New machines and inventions can make a worker feel useless or threatened.

Citizenship

Agree Industrial society tends to emphasize class differences.

Disagree All people, regardless of wealth, are responsible for defining and protecting human rights.

Economics

Agree Public ownership and control of certain industries ensures a better distribution of wealth.

Disagree Even workers who have a say in how wealth is distributed do not have much influence.

---

c. 1785
Science and Technology
Englishman Edmund Cartwright patents the power loom.

c. 1794
Science and Technology
The American inventor Eli Whitney patents the cotton gin, a machine for cleaning seeds from cotton fibers.

c. 1814
Science and Technology
George Stephenson invents the locomotive.

c. 1817
Business and Finance
The New York Stock Exchange opens.

c. 1838
The Arts
Charles Dickens publishes *Oliver Twist*.

c. 1866
Daily Life
The first transatlantic cable is completed.

c. 1889
The Arts
The Eiffel Tower is completed in Paris.

Steam locomotive

Portrait of Charles Dickens

1800

1900

c. 1801
Politics
Great Britain and Ireland form the United Kingdom.

1848
Politics
Karl Marx and Friedrich Engels publish the *Communist Manifesto*.

1901
Business and Finance
United States Steel is founded.

c. 1790
Business and Finance
The U.S. patent office is established.

1828
The Arts
Noah Webster publishes *An American Dictionary of the English Language* in two volumes.

1776
Business and Finance
Adam Smith publishes *Inquiry into the Nature and Causes of the Wealth of Nations*.

This sequence of images shows various stages in the construction of the Eiffel Tower in Paris.

EXPLORING THE TIME LINE
GLOBAL EVENTS

The word *revolution* is used to describe the Industrial Revolution because it changed society rapidly and in significant ways. In fact, only the Neolithic agricultural revolution, which took place in the later part of the Stone Age, has produced changes as significant as the Industrial Revolution. A major change produced by the Neolithic agricultural revolution included people moving from social systems based on hunting and gathering to complex systems that depended on agriculture and the domestication of animals. This was a significant change because it allowed people to settle permanently, which eventually created urban civilizations. With the dawn of the Industrial Revolution, these agricultural societies shifted to modern industrial societies.

ACTIVITY: Have students research the Neolithic agricultural revolution and write brief reports. Ask them to compare and contrast this revolution to the Industrial Revolution.

What's Your Opinion?

Do you **agree** *or* **disagree** *with the following statements? Support your point of view in your journal.*

Science, Technology & Society A society's development depends on its ability to understand and use science and technology.

Citizenship The roles that people play in society are related to the distribution of wealth in that society.

Economics The workers who produce goods and services, and so create wealth, deserve a say in how that wealth is distributed.

SECTION 1

OBJECTIVES

1 Explain why the Industrial Revolution began in Great Britain.

2 Describe how inventions in the textile industry led to other new inventions.

3 Analyze the effects that developments in transportation and communication had on the spread of the Industrial Revolution.

LET'S GET STARTED!

Discuss with students the meaning of the word *revolution*. Tell students that the one thing all revolutions have in common is change. Ask students to list the types of long-term and short-term changes that revolution can bring about. (*Examples might include peace, improved human rights, better living conditions.*) Ask students why the Industrial Revolution is called a revolution. (*extreme changes in economy and society*) Tell students that in Section 1 they will learn about changes in the textile, transportation, and communication industries that occurred during the Industrial Revolution.

SECTION 1 RESOURCES

REPRODUCIBLE RESOURCES

▶ Guided Reading Strategy 22.1

▶ Graphic Organizer Activity 22

▶ Geography Activity 22

▶ Readings in World History 73

TECHNOLOGY RESOURCES

▶ One-Stop Planner 22.1

▶ Holt Researcher: World History: James Watt, Robert Fulton

▶ World History and Cultures Video Program 18

▶ Homework Practice Online

REINFORCEMENT, REVIEW, AND ASSESSMENT

▶ Section 1 Review, p. 550

▶ Daily Quiz 22.1

▶ Main Idea Activity 22.1

▶ English Audio Summary 22.1

▶ Spanish Audio Summary 22.1

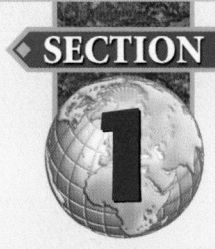

SECTION 1

READ TO DISCOVER

❶ Why did the Industrial Revolution begin in Great Britain?

❷ How did inventions in the textile industry lead to other new inventions?

❸ What effects did developments in transportation and communication have on the spread of the Industrial Revolution?

DEFINE

enclosure movement
crop rotation
Industrial Revolution
factors of production
mechanization
factory system
vulcanization

IDENTIFY

Jethro Tull
Richard Arkwright
Eli Whitney
James Watt
Henry Bessemer
Robert Fulton
Samuel Morse

▶WHY IT MATTERS TODAY

Increased demand for some product or service often promotes the development of new technology. Use CNN or other **current event** sources to find some type of new technology that developed to meet a need of society. Record your findings in your journal.

CNN student News.com

Origins of the Industrial Revolution

The Main Idea
Conditions in Great Britain led to revolutionary new methods of agriculture and manufacturing.

The Story Continues *A new era of peace after 1815 brought growing prosperity to western Europe. New agricultural methods and improved systems of transportation and communication helped to stimulate progress. One well-known writer noted that "The benefit of . . . Turn-pikes [toll roads] appears now to be so great, and the People in all Places begin to be so sensible of it, that it is incredible what Effect [turnpike construction] has already had upon Trade in the Countries where it is more completely finish'd . . ."*

The Agricultural Revolution

Before the 1600s most European villagers worked their own plots of land in order to grow food for their families. They also used common public lands for grazing animals such as sheep and cattle. In the 1500s and 1600s common lands in England began to be enclosed, or fenced off, into individual plots. At the same time, smaller landholdings were being combined into more efficient, larger holdings. This **enclosure movement** continued into the 1700s. It reached its height by the early 1800s in Great Britain, as a growing population increased demand and raised prices for agricultural products. Wealthy landholders benefited from this movement, while many small landowners lost their lands and their traditional livelihood.

The enclosure movement had several effects. As large landowners added to their holdings, former small-plot owners were forced to become tenant farmers or move to the cities. Also, with the common lands vanishing, farmers no longer had to get permission from other villagers to try new farming methods. In the early 1700s, for example, landowner **Jethro Tull** was concerned about the amount of seed wasted by hand-scattering it over the fields. Tull invented a seed drill that made it possible to plant seeds in straight rows. He also made a horse-drawn hoe to dig up weeds between the rows and break up soil before planting.

Another English landowner, Charles "Turnip" Townshend, copied a successful Dutch practice. English farmers usually left some fields unplanted for a year to let the soil rebuild its nutrients. Townshend found that planting different crops in the fields each year had the same result. For example, he planted wheat or barley one year and root crops such as turnips the next. This system, called **crop rotation,** helped farmers to produce more crops using the same amount of land.

During this Agricultural Revolution, other improvements increased production and made farm labor easier. Iron plows replaced wooden ones. An American, Jethro Wood, invented a plow with a replaceable blade, which eliminated the need to buy a whole new plow. Some of these improvements were very expensive. Only wealthy farmers could afford them. By the 1800s many farm workers, replaced by machines and forced off the land, were moving to the cities. They formed a huge labor force.

✔ **READING CHECK: Identifying Cause and Effect** How did the enclosure movement lead to the development of improved technology in agriculture? bronze and iron tools, women in charge of family and agriculture

544 CHAPTER 22

544

TEACH OBJECTIVE 1

![clock icon] **LEVEL 1:** Have students list the factors of production as you write them on the chalkboard or overhead projector. *(land, capital, labor)* Have students explain what physical and human geographic factors during the Agricultural Revolution gave Great Britain each of its factors of production. *(for example: natural resources, enclosure movement created wealth, and large labor force in centralized area)* Ask students to identify some parts of the world that remain nonindustrialized and to explain why this is so. *(Students should identify missing factors of production.)* **ENGLISH LANGUAGE LEARNERS**

TEACH OBJECTIVE 2

ALL LEVELS: Have students work in pairs to create an illustrated and captioned time line of the major events and technological advancements that contributed to the development of the textile industry. **ENGLISH LANGUAGE LEARNERS, COOPERATIVE LEARNING**

Factors of Production

An era of rapid industrial development known as the **Industrial Revolution** followed the Agricultural Revolution. It began in Great Britain, which had a favorable combination of needed factors—land, capital, and labor. Economists call these the **factors of production.** Land refers to all natural resources. Great Britain had a rich supply of such resources, particularly coal and iron ore. Its many rivers provided waterpower and inland shipping routes, and its many harbors encouraged trade both within and beyond the British Isles. Great Britain also had rich sources of capital, including the tools, machinery, equipment, and inventory used in production. Capital also included money, which those who had grown rich during the 1700s used to invest in new businesses. Great Britain also had a large supply of labor for industry, fueled by the growth in population and migration into cities.

✔ **READING CHECK: Finding the Main Idea** Why did the Industrial Revolution begin in Great Britain?
had the right factors of production

The Industrial Revolution in Great Britain, 1715–1851

Interpreting Maps In most cases, industrial centers in Britain developed around rich coal deposits and navigable rivers. Canal systems helped to link these areas to markets and shipping points.

■ **Skills Assessment: Physical Systems** What geographical factors may have helped to speed industrial development in the city of Liverpool?

Economics

The enclosure movement was not limited to Great Britain. Enclosure movements took place with varying results in Japan and Sri Lanka (Ceylon). In addition, serfdom in Russia and eastern Europe inhibited industrialization. Economic relationships and social classes created by the plantation system throughout colonial Asia and Africa complicated industrialization efforts in the 1900s.

Critical Thinking

Which factor of production was missing from Russia, eastern Europe, and colonial Asia and Africa that inhibited industrialization?

ANSWER: labor

MAP ANSWER

coal, location on the coast, availability of water

Technology Resources

World History Teaching Transparency: Everyday Life 18: Traditional Farming Methods

LEVEL 3: Discuss with students the concept of supply and demand. Have students select one invention from those listed on pages 546–547. Tell them to write a report that explains how that invention created a new need and describes how human ingenuity met that need. Students should use standard grammar, spelling, sentence structure, and punctuation.

HOMEWORK Have students complete the parts of the chart shown in italics to represent the inventors and their inventions.

Inventor	Invention	Function of invention	Industry
Jethro Tull	*seed drill, horse-drawn hoe*	*planted seeds in straight rows; dug up weeds and broke up soil*	agriculture
Eli Whitney	*cotton gin*	*cleaned more cotton in a day than hand laborers could*	textile
James Watt	*modern steam engine*	*powered engines for factories and transportation of goods*	textile and transportation
Samuel Morse	*Morse code/telegraph*	communication	communication
Richard Arkwright	*water power to drive spinning wheel*	*increased level of production*	textile
Henry Bessemer	*Bessemer process*	*used to make steel*	textile and transportation

Linking Past to Present

Originally, factory owners managed their own factories. However, as factories grew and employed more people, one person could no longer oversee so many alone. So management positions were created and many administrative responsibilities fell to managers, sometimes called "foremen." Managers took instruction from owners and were responsible for overseeing day-to-day operations. The role of managers has grown steadily until now they are an integral part of virtually all industries. People in management positions are usually well-paid, highly respected professionals.

Critical Thinking

Why were foremen so important in factories?

ANSWER: Without them, growth of an industry would be limited.

DAILY LIFE ANSWER

Players had specific positions that required specific skills, they followed standard rules of conduct, and they used new technologies.

Technology Resources

World History Teaching Transparency: Everyday Life 17: European Clothing Styles, 1700s

Analyzing Primary Sources

Drawing Conclusions According to Defoe's account, what source of power was used to drive the silk-spinning machine that he described? water power

DAILY LIFE

Industrialization and Sports

By the late 1800s, sports and industry had much in common. Like work, sports became more specialized. Players had specific positions that required specific skills. Players, like factory workers, followed standard rules of conduct. Organized sports also made use of new technologies. New types of sporting equipment, for example, became available as a result of industrialization. **How were organized sports like industry?**

The Textile Industry

In the 1600s men and women in England spun thread and wove cloth by hand in their homes. It was a slow process. England could not meet the growing demand for cloth. As a result, automatic machinery was used to increase production. This was known as **mechanization.** Author Daniel Defoe, writing in the early 1700s, described an enormous silk-spinning machine that automatically performed in minutes operations that took many workers days to complete by hand.

History Makers Speak

❝This engine contains 22,586 wheels and 97,746 movements, which work 73,726 yards of silk thread every time the wheel goes round, which is three times in one minute, and 318,504,960 yards in 24 hours. The water-wheel gives the motion to all the rest of the wheels and movements, of which any one may be stopped separately.❞

Daniel Defoe, from *The British Revolution, 1750–1970: A Social and Economic History*, by Michael St. J. Parker and D. J. Reid

New inventions. A first step toward mechanization was the invention of a mechanized loom for weaving cloth. A loom is a frame with threads stretched lengthwise from top to bottom. These threads are known as "warp" threads. A worker pushed a shuttle holding another thread—the "weft" thread—over and under the warp threads to weave cloth. In about 1733 British engineer John Kay invented the flying shuttle, which moved the weft-carrying shuttle quickly across the loom. Weavers could now make cloth so fast they outran the supply of thread from the old-fashioned spinning wheels.

In the 1760s British weaver James Hargreaves invented the spinning "jenny." This machine could produce eight times more thread than a single spinning wheel. **Richard Arkwright** later invented a way to drive the machine by waterpower. Arkwright brought workers and waterpower together and opened a spinning mill during the 1780s. Workers put in a certain number of hours each day for a fixed pay. This spinning mill was the beginning of the modern **factory system.**

Improvements in the spinning process followed, but workers still could not meet the demand for cloth. In about 1785 English minister Edmund Cartwright invented a water-powered loom. One person could now weave as much cloth as 200 hand-loom operators. This rapid change in spinning and weaving showed how inventions built on one another. The flying shuttle created a need for more thread, which faster spinning produced. This was followed by improved weaving machines. Each invention created a new need, and human ingenuity filled the gap.

Effects of mechanization. As supply increased, the price of cotton cloth went down. As a result, demand increased and so did the need for more raw cotton. Raw cotton imports by England went from 4 millions pounds in 1761 to 100 million pounds in 1815. Most of it came from the southern United States. Cleaning seeds from the cotton fiber was slow, manual work. In 1793 American **Eli Whitney** invented the cotton gin, a machine that could clean much more cotton in a day than hand laborers could. With Whitney's invention, the southern United States became the cotton-producing center of the world. As production soared, so did the profits made by using slave labor to plant and pick cotton. Thus, the cotton gin had the unintended side effect of helping to expand slavery in the United States.

✔ **READING CHECK: Analyzing Information** Why were there so many new inventions in the textile industry in such a short period of time? to meet growing demand

TEACH OBJECTIVE 3

LEVEL 1: Have students identify the developments in transportation and communication during the Industrial Revolution. *(cotton gin, steam engine, and telegraph, for example)* Then discuss the changes these technological innovations produced. *(increased production to meet increased demand, use of more labor, spread of ideas)* **ENGLISH LANGUAGE LEARNERS**

ALL LEVELS: Discuss with students the impact of new transportation technologies on society of the 1700s and 1800s. Ask them to write a paragraph or two in which they analyze the effects of these technologies on society. To help students generate ideas and to understand the bewildering rate of change during the 1700s and 1800s, ask students to name five areas of modern technology that are undergoing rapid change, such as computers, the Internet, communications, and aeronautics. Discuss with the class the level of technology in these areas ten years ago and today. Then ask students to project advancements in ten more years. **ENGLISH LANGUAGE LEARNERS**

Steam Engines, Iron, and Steel

Early machines in the Industrial Revolution were driven by waterpower. Although much better than human, animal, and wind power, waterpower had its drawbacks. A factory had to be located on a stream or river, preferably next to a waterfall or dam. Often this site was not near raw materials, a labor supply, overland transportation, or markets. Water flow also varied from season to season. A more portable and dependable power supply was needed. It was found in steam.

The power of steam had been known since ancient times. Not until about 1712, however, did English engineer Thomas Newcomen harness that power in an engine. The first, crude steam engines were expensive to operate. Scotsman **James Watt** studied and improved on Newcomen's machine. In about 1769 he patented the modern steam engine. British engineer Matthew Boulton financed the first factory to manufacture steam engines. Industry quickly adapted the engine to drive the new spinning and weaving machines. Steam replaced water as industry's major power source.

Iron and steel. More machines meant more iron was needed to make them. From early times, people in Britain had separated iron from its ore using wood or charcoal to fuel the forges. Coal worked even better because it generated more heat. Iron and coal became the two major raw materials of modern industry. Great Britain had plenty of both.

Early steam engines often exploded, however, because iron could not withstand high steam pressure. Steel, an iron alloy, was much stronger, but it was expensive to produce. In the 1850s American William Kelly and Englishman **Henry Bessemer,** working independently, developed what came to be known as the Bessemer process—a cheaper and more efficient method of making steel. The process injected air into molten pig iron, the material from which steel was produced, in order to remove impurities. The injection of air also increased the temperature at which the conversion of pig iron into steel took place. This prevented the molten metal from solidifying during production.

✔ **READING CHECK: Identifying Cause and Effect** How did developments in the textile industry result in inventions in steelmaking? mechanization meant that more iron was needed

Other Industrialization

British manufacturers applied new technology to other industries. Production of shoes, clothing, ammunition, and furniture was mechanized. Machines were used for printing, papermaking, lumber and food processing, and making other machines. Some new processes had important by-products. Gases released from coal were burned to give light. In the 1810s London was one of the first cities to burn gas in street lamps. By the 1850s gaslight was common in city streets.

American Charles Goodyear discovered how to make rubber less sticky. This **vulcanization** process is the basis of the modern rubber industry. The oil industry began around the mid-1800s, when people began using crude oil to make paraffin for candles, lubricating oil for machinery, and kerosene for lighting and heating.

✔ **READING CHECK: Drawing Conclusions** What were several ways in which industrialization spread? machines came to be used in printing, papermaking, and lumber and food processing

Holt Researcher

go.hrw.com
KEYWORD: Holt Researcher
FreeFind: James Watt
After reading more about James Watt on the Holt Researcher, write a summary of his contributions to science and technology.

A Bessemer furnace changed molten iron into steel by forcing air through the iron to burn away carbon and other impurities.

History Maker

JAMES WATT. James Watt (1736–1819) was born in Greenock, Scotland. As a young man, Watt made mathematical instruments, but as he turned his attention to steam engines, his natural curiosity took over. By figuring out the properties of steam, Watt was able to design a condensing chamber that would prevent loss of steam in steam engines. This kept steam engines from losing as much power as they had in the past. Watt patented his condensing chamber in 1769 and went on to patent other inventions, such as the rotary engine, the double-action engine, and the steam indicator.

Critical Thinking

What would have been the result if the condensing chamber had not been designed?

ANSWER: less efficiency and productivity, maybe slower advancement of other related inventions

Technology Resources
 Online Maps, Charts, and Graphs: Railroads Link British Industries, c. 1850

The effects of industrialization on society were not all good. Loss of status, wages, and legal protection, for example, were the ill effects most protested by a group of disaffected British workers and artisans called the Luddites. Luddites smashed machinery and led riots against factory owners during the Industrial Revolution in attempts to gain better wages and improved working conditions. When union activities were banned in Great Britain, Luddism reached its peak as dissatisfied workers turned to violence. The momentum of the movement threatened the government. Rioters were dispersed with armed troops and some Luddites were hanged, which suppressed the momentum of the movement.

Have students watch the classic silent film *Metropolis*, which contains imagery symbolic of life during the Industrial Revolution. Tell students to write an in-depth analysis of the film, concentrating on its imagery and symbolism. For example, students might point out that the workers all dress identically in dark, drab outfits; this might symbolize the laborers' loss of individuality in an impersonal world. Or they might note the huge machinery that seems to indicate the dominance of technology over humanity. **COOPERATIVE LEARNING**

Science, Technology & Society

One of the great canal-builders in Britain was Thomas Telford. He built the Ellesmere Canal in Wales, which included two great aqueducts. Telford also built the Caledonian Canal, a waterway that connects the east coast of Scotland to the west coast.

Critical Thinking

What other canals have you heard of or read about that have improved transportation for trade and travel?

ANSWER: Students might suggest the Panama Canal, noting that it allows ships to travel quickly between the Atlantic and Pacific Oceans.

Technology Resources
World History Teaching Transparency: Art and History 18: The Gare Saint-Lazare, Paris

This scene of steamboats on the Mississippi River was produced in the mid-1800s.

Holt Researcher
go.hrw.com
KEYWORD: Holt Researcher
FreeFind: Robert Fulton
After reading more about Robert Fulton on the Holt Researcher, create a time line of how he developed his inventions and what impact they had on society.

Transportation

Transportation had changed little between the Middle Ages and the beginning of the Industrial Revolution. Stagecoaches, packhorses, and heavy, clumsy horse-drawn wagons were common. As industrial production increased, factories needed more raw materials and finished goods had to reach markets quickly. Improvements such as stone-topped roadways were built. Canals were dug to link rivers. The newer canals had locks to regulate the level of water.

Watt's steam engine was used to speed transportation, both on land and water. In about 1814 English engineer George Stephenson perfected a steam locomotive that ran on rails. About 15 years later, a locomotive pulled a line of railway cars from Liverpool to Manchester. Railways soon were being built all over the world.

American engineer **Robert Fulton** was the first to build a profitable steamboat. In 1808 his boat, the *Clermont*, began regular trips on the Hudson River between New York City and Albany. Soon steamboats appeared on rivers and lakes all over the world. In the 1830s a steam-powered ship crossed the Atlantic Ocean. The voyage took about 17 days, less than half the time of a sailing ship. Soon Samuel Cunard of Great Britain was providing regular steamboat service across the Atlantic. Ships built of iron and steel now moved goods all over the world quickly and cheaply.

✔ **READING CHECK: Making Generalizations** What invention stimulated the rapid improvement of transportation around the world? steam engine

The Communications Revolution

Early inventions such as the steam engine were mainly the work of amateur engineers. In communications technology, however, scientific research played a more important role.

Prior to the 1800s people may have known that electricity and magnetism were related, but they had not found a practical use for this knowledge. Then in about 1800 Italian scientist Alessandro Volta built the first battery, providing a steady flow of electric current for the first time. In the 1820s André Ampère of France worked out principles governing the magnetic effect of electricity. American **Samuel Morse** put this work to practical use. Morse sent an electric current through a wire, causing a machine at the other end to click. By about 1838 Morse had worked out a system of dots and dashes—the Morse code—by which these clicks could be translated into letters of the alphabet. By 1844 Morse's invention, the telegraph, had become a practical communications device. Telegraph wires soon stretched across continents and oceans, spreading ideas at the speed of electricity.

✔ **READING CHECK: Contrasting** What was a major difference between new inventions in textiles and transportation and new inventions in communication? communications required more scientific training

SKILL-BUILDING STRATEGIES   Determining Cause and Effect

Effects of Industrialization on Lancashire

Industrialization in Great Britain had many effects. The economic and social life of some regions of the country were forever changed by new technologies and industries. Lancashire County in northwest England experienced some of the greatest change. Anchored by the manufacturing towns of Manchester and Liverpool, Lancashire became a major industrial center.

Identifying the causes of historical events and determining their effects helps us understand history. Historical events usually have several causes. Underlying causes are long term. Immediate causes lead directly to the event. Cause-and-effect relationships can be shown in many different kinds of diagrams including concept maps, sequences, and webs.

Lancashire County and Surrounding Areas, c. 1850s

Canal
Railroad
Cotton factories
Coalfield

Skills Reminder

To determine cause and effect, identify the focus of your study—for example, the outcome of an election. This is the effect in question. Then determine the underlying, or most basic, causes. For example, how satisfied were voters with the present office holder? Next, identify the immediate causes—those occurring near at hand. For example, did the weather affect who voted? Form a conclusion about the relative importance of the various causes you have identified.

Skills Practice

Study the information above.
1. What factors of physical geography may have been underlying causes of industrial development in Lancashire County?
2. What were the probable immediate causes of railroad and canal construction in Lancashire County?
3. Draw a diagram that summarizes the probable short-term and long-term causes and effects of industrialization in Lancashire County.

REVIEW

Have students complete the Section 1 Review on p. 550.

ASSESS

Have students complete Daily Quiz 22.1. As Alternative Assessment, you may want to use the time lines or Inventors graphic organizer in this section's lessons.

RETEACH

Have students complete Main Idea Activity for English Language Learners and Special-Needs Students 22.1. Then have

groups prepare a visual representation of the changes that occurred in an industry during the Industrial Revolution. **ENGLISH LANGUAGE LEARNERS**

EXTEND

Have students create a graphic short story set during the Industrial Revolution of Great Britain. Students' stories should be fictional but historically accurate in their settings and details. Students should tell their stories mainly through imagery and dialogue, much like a comic book. **BLOCK SCHEDULING**

SECTION 1 REVIEW ANSWERS

❶ Define
- enclosure movement, p. 544
- crop rotation, p. 544
- Industrial Revolution, p. 545
- factors of production, p. 545
- mechanization, p. 546
- factory system, p. 546
- vulcanization, p. 547

❷ Identify
- Jethro Tull, p. 544
- Richard Arkwright, p. 546
- Eli Whitney, p. 546
- James Watt, p. 547
- Henry Bessemer, p. 547
- Robert Fulton, p. 548
- Samuel Morse, p. 548

❸ Agriculture: seed drill; Textiles: mechanized loom; Transportation: railroads; Communication: Morse code; Power: gas

❹ a. Answers will vary but should note how the invention increased the amount of goods produced and decreased production time.

b. It provided all three factors of production (land, capital, and labor) in abundance.

❺ Students' articles will vary.

At Promontory Point, Utah, on May 10, 1869, the Union Pacific and Central Pacific railroads met, joining East Coast to West.

The Spread of Industry

Industrial growth in other European countries lagged behind Great Britain. They had not developed their raw materials or markets for their products. The wars following the French Revolution also disrupted their economies.

The French government helped local industry by imposing high tariffs on foreign goods. They also encouraged the building of railroads. However, in the 1800s, most French workers were still farmers and peasants. Germany did not have a central government to aid industrial growth. Not until the 1870s did German industrialization approach that of Great Britain.

The United States had both a strong central government and rich natural resources. It also had a rapidly increasing population. British inventions and methods were adopted in the United States. Inventions like the cotton gin and mechanical reaper boosted agricultural production. Canals and railroads were built, and the steel and machinery industries boomed. By 1869 a railroad stretched from the East Coast to the West Coast. America had joined the Industrial Revolution.

✔ **READING CHECK: Sequencing** List some of the principal developments that led to industrialization in the United States. cotton gin, mechanical reaper, canals, railroads, steel industry

SECTION 1 REVIEW

1. **Define** and explain the significance:
   enclosure movement
   crop rotation
   Industrial Revolution
   factors of production
   mechanization
   factory system
   vulcanization

2. **Identify** and explain the significance:
   Jethro Tull
   Richard Arkwright
   Eli Whitney
   James Watt
   Henry Bessemer
   Robert Fulton
   Samuel Morse

3. **Categorizing** Copy the web diagram below. In each box, list some of the advances made during the Industrial Revolution.

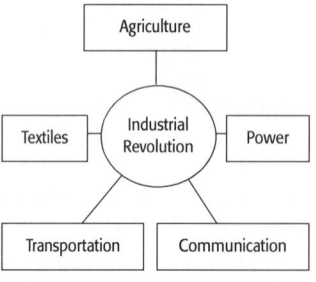

4. **Finding the Main Idea**
   a. Which inventions of the late 1600s and the 1700s do you think had the greatest influence on industrialization? Why?
   b. Why was Great Britain an ideal place for the start of the Industrial Revolution?

5. **Writing and Critical Thinking**

   Analyzing Information Imagine that you are a journalist on the staff of a magazine for young people. Write a 150-word article explaining the factors of production that influenced the start of the Industrial Revolution.
   Consider:
   • the great variety of resources included in the factors of production: land, capital, and labor
   • how the absence or shortage of some of these resources would have made industrialization more difficult

Homework Practice Online
keyword: SP3 HP22

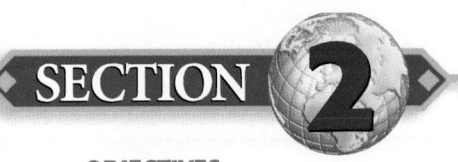
OBJECTIVES

1 Explain how the increased use of machinery affected workers and working conditions.

2 Identify the differences between the middle class and the working class.

3 Analyze how the lives of women changed during the Industrial Revolution.

As students enter the classroom, ask them to write down the following terms: *working conditions*, *middle class*, *working class*, and *women's lives*. Ask students how they would describe each of these terms in reference to the Industrial Revolution. Tell students that in Section 2 they will learn how industrialization changed people's lifestyles and living and working conditions.

SECTION 2

READ TO DISCOVER

❶ How did the increased use of machinery affect workers and working conditions?

❷ How did the middle class differ from the working class?

❸ How did the lives of women change during the Industrial Revolution?

DEFINE

tenements

WHY IT MATTERS TODAY

When women first went to work in factories, they earned much less than men. Use CNN Student News.com or other **current event** sources to find out how the wages of women compare with those of men today. Record your findings in your journal.

CNN Student News.com

The Factory System

The Main Idea
New lifestyles and living conditions grew out of the Industrial Revolution as society began to change.

The Story Continues *During the 1700s new factory jobs lured thousands of British farm workers to the cities. Many critics feared that urban growth and changing labor patterns would create dangerous social injustice. In 1848 John Stuart Mill wrote, "[Industrialization has] enabled a greater proportion [of workers] to live the same life of drudgery and imprisonment and an increased number of manufacturers and others to make fortunes."*

How Machines Affected Work

The introduction of steam-powered machinery made work easier to do. Instead of spending several years as an apprentice learning a trade, a person could learn to perform a task or operate a machine in a few days.

Employers now wanted people who could learn a few simple tasks. They soon discovered that women and children could operate machines as efficiently as men. Employers preferred to hire young men and women rather than older, skilled people. Young people did not have set working habits and did not expect high wages. Women and children would work for lower wages than men. As a result the early textile factories employed mainly children and young women.

As machines became more widely used, older, skilled workers often found themselves unemployed. Factories no longer needed their abilities as weavers or spinners and would not hire them for simpler work. To make up for their lost income, many of these people sent their children to look for work in textile factories. They themselves were reduced to looking for odd jobs in cities or on farms.

✔ **READING CHECK: Finding the Main Idea** How did the production of goods change as work became mechanized? made jobs simpler and less skilled

The Wage System

The factory system differed significantly from the domestic system. Under the domestic system, workers had usually worked unsupervised in their homes. They turned over finished products, such as thread or cloth, perhaps once a week, and were paid for the number of items completed. In factories, instead of working on a product from beginning to end, each worker performed only a small part of the entire job. Under the factory system, dozens or hundreds of laborers worked in the same room under the watchful eyes of supervisors. Everyone was employed by the factory owners. The owners paid their workers wages based on the number of hours worked or the amount of goods produced.

Several factors determined workers' wages. First and foremost, factory owners wanted to produce goods as cheaply as possible. Thus employers set wages in relation to other costs of production. For example, if the cost of land or capital increased, the owners lowered wages.

SECTION 2 RESOURCES

REPRODUCIBLE RESOURCES

▶ Guided Reading Strategy 22.2

▶ Readings in World History 74: A Working Day in a Manchester Cotton Mill

▶ Hands-on History Activity 22: Inside the Factory

TECHNOLOGY RESOURCES

▶ One-Stop Planner 22.2

▶ Holt Researcher: World History: Elizabeth Gaskell

▶ Homework Practice Online

REINFORCEMENT, REVIEW, AND ASSESSMENT

▶ Section 2 Review, p. 554

▶ Daily Quiz 22.2

▶ Main Idea Activity 22.2

▶ English Audio Summary 22.2

▶ Spanish Audio Summary 22.2

Working Class
- worked in factories for low wages
- lived in tenements
- industrializing England
- most children did not attend school
- lifestyles and living conditions similar to lower middle class

Middle Class
- were bankers, lawyers, doctors, etc.
- gained social influence and political power
- rising social status
- well-educated

TEACH OBJECTIVE 2

ALL LEVELS: Ask students to complete the following web diagram by adding additional ovals that identify the characteristics of the middle class and the working class in England.
ENGLISH LANGUAGE LEARNERS , COOPERATIVE LEARNING

Interdisciplinary Connection

LITERATURE. Charles Dickens wrote several novels, including *Hard Times*, that greatly appealed to the public during his lifetime. In his books, Dickens criticized the problems caused by the Industrial Revolution and described the life of the very poor in Great Britain.

Critical Thinking

Why do you think Dickens's writing appealed to the public?

ANSWER: Answers will vary. Students might suggest that the public felt that Dickens understood their problems.

CONNECTING TO SCIENCE AND TECHNOLOGY ANSWER

It could be produced at a much faster rate and at a lower cost of production.

CONNECTING TO
Science and Technology

Thonet Rocker
Michael Thonet, a cabinet-maker living in Austria in the mid-1800s, invented a process that revolutionized furniture making. He made the bentwood rocker shown here. Thonet bent solid wood by steaming it and clamping a thin strip of steel along one side. Complex joining and carving were no longer needed. Thonet was able to hire local people rather than costly artisans. By 1870 Thonet's factory was making about 1,300 pieces of furniture a day. With six-day work-weeks, this was an incredible 400,000 pieces a year.

Understanding Science and Technology

What was the technological significance of the Thonet rocker?

In addition, the number of workers available affected wages. An oversupply of workers brought wages down. By the same token, wages often rose when there were not enough workers to do a particular job.

Also, wages often depended on what people could expect to earn at other kinds of work. For example, early employers in textile factories wanted to attract young women as workers. Therefore they offered a wage higher than what women could earn as household servants.

Wages, moreover, were higher for men than for women. For example, in cotton mills and the London clothing trades in Great Britain, men were paid as much as twice what women earned. It was generally thought that women went to work merely to add "a little something" to their family's income. In reality, however, a woman was sometimes the only wage earner for her family.

Factory workers acquired skills and were paid accordingly. However, they had little else to show for their work. They did not own their tools or equipment, as domestic workers had. Furthermore, there were few opportunities for workers to advance within the factory.

✔ **READING CHECK: Summarizing** What four factors generally determined a factory worker's wages? costs of production, labor supply, wages for other work, gender

The Lives of Factory Workers

Factory workers had many rules to follow. They had to arrive at the factory on time. They could eat or take breaks only at set times. They could leave only with permission. They worked whether it was hot or cold, summer or winter, day or night. Breaking any rules could result in heavy fines, pay cuts, or even job loss.

Factories were cold and damp in winter and steamy in summer. Sanitary facilities were poor. Early machines had no safety devices, so accidents occurred frequently. Employers provided no compensation if a worker was hurt on the job. Workers spent up to 14 hours a day, six days a week, on the job. They had to adjust their lives to the demands of machines that never needed to rest. Some people may have thought that they were expected to become machines themselves.

Abuses in factories soon scandalized Great Britain. In about 1832 a parliamentary committee investigated working conditions for children. One worker that the committee spoke to was 23-year-old Elizabeth Bently, who began to work in a flax mill when she was six years old. Bently described how she and other children had been forced to work from five in the morning until nine at night and had been beaten for being late or working too slowly. Parliament then passed the Factory Act of 1833, which allowed for factory inspection and enforcement of child labor laws.

Life in workers' homes was not much better than in the factories and mines. Workers lived in shabby apartment buildings called **tenements.** A dozen people might be crammed into a single room. As late as 1840, up to 50,000 workers in Manchester, England, lived in cellars. A popular British novelist of the

LEVEL 3: Tell students to write a persuasive speech to be given to the British Parliament in which they argue for human rights for the working class, with supporting reasons. Students may use topics of child labor, unsafe working conditions, wages and hours, and living conditions. Tell students to use standard grammar, spelling, sentence structure, and punctuation in their speech.

TEACH OBJECTIVE 3

LEVEL 3: Have students create a collage of images representing women's work during the Industrial Revolution. Discuss with the class their impressions of what women's lives were like and what political, economic, and social influence women had during the Industrial Revolution. **ENGLISH LANGUAGE LEARNERS**

HOMEWORK Write a paragraph describing the economic influence of women and children on the Industrial Revolution.

CLOSE

Ask students to summarize the major ideas provided in Section 1.

---

mid-1800s described the below-ground dwelling in which a fictitious working-class Manchester family lived.

> **History Makers Speak**
>
> **❝It was very dark inside. The window-panes many of them were broken and stuffed with rags. . . . the smell was so fetid [foul] as almost to knock the two men [observers who were shocked by these living conditions] down. . . . they began to penetrate the thick darkness of the place, and to see three or four little children rolling on the . . . wet brick floor, through which the stagnant, filthy moisture of the street oozed up.❞**
>
> Elizabeth Gaskell, *Mary Barton*, 1848

Over time, conditions improved slightly as consumer goods became cheaper and more available to workers. Wages increased somewhat, but the lower economic classes continued to suffer.

✔ **READING CHECK: Analyzing Information** What were the living conditions of factory workers like during the Industrial Revolution? poor, cramped, dirty

Development of the Middle Class

During the Industrial Revolution, the balance of economic and political power shifted from agriculture to manufacturing. As industries and cities grew, a new, well-educated middle class thrived. It consisted of bankers, manufacturers, merchants, lawyers, doctors, engineers, professors, and their families. Many members of this middle class served in management or other types of administrative jobs that helped keep industries running. Over time, this class—based upon economic standing, rather than upon birth—gained increasing social influence and political power. To many workers, the middle class represented a social

stepladder. Each generation hoped that the next one would be able to rise a rung higher than they had been. As the middle class expanded, many families were able to do just that.

Lifestyles and living conditions at the lower levels of the middle class often differed very little from those of working-class people. As the finances of middle-class families improved, their lifestyles began to reflect their rising social status. Many middle-class families could afford to live in larger homes and less-crowded neighborhoods. Middle-class men wore business suits and women wore frills and lace. Many people in the upper tiers of the middle class owned property, hired servants, and ate well. Their children attended good schools, where they were trained for higher-level jobs. Middle-class children might also inherit money and social position from their parents. Aristocratic government leaders sought the advice of middle-class economists. Soon government leaders became as concerned about the future of industry as they were about agriculture.

✔ **READING CHECK: Drawing Inferences** What factors led to the rise of the middle class? growth of industries and cities

YOUNG PEOPLE IN HISTORY

Young Factory Workers
For many people in industrial England, working for a living began at an early age. Children as young as six worked in factories for 12 to 16 hours a day, six days a week. At lunchtime, children often ate food covered with factory dust. In general, factory conditions for children in industrializing England were brutal and often hazardous. **What were working conditions like for the youngest factory workers?**

That's Interesting!

A report written by Edwin Chadwick, the Secretary of Commission, and published in 1842, stated that in his research of the living conditions in poor neighborhoods, he found that 43,000 women had become widows and 112,000 children had become orphans as a result of poor sanitary conditions.

YOUNG PEOPLE IN HISTORY ANSWER
Working conditions were very difficult—young workers spent long hours doing hard labor in dirty, dusty environments.

🔲 **internet** connect

TOPIC: Victorian Age Writers
GO TO: go.hrw.com
KEYWORD: SP3 WH22

In 1836, 20-year-old Charlotte Brontë sent Robert Southey, the poet laureate of Great Britain, some of her poems. In return, he replied: "Literature cannot be the business of a woman's life, and it ought not to be." Have students access the Internet through the HRW Go site to find information on female writers of the Victorian Age. Have students write a biography of one of the writers. Students should include information about the writer's life, accomplishments, and significance to history.

Holt Researcher
go.hrw.com
KEYWORD: Holt Researcher
FreeFind: Elizabeth Gaskell
After reading more about Elizabeth Gaskell on the Holt Researcher, assess how her writings about the working class might have affected views of factory life by middle-class readers.

REVIEW

Have students complete the Section 2 Review on p. 554.

ASSESS

Have students complete Daily Quiz 22.2. As Alternative Assessment, you may want to use the Young People in History feature in this section's lessons.

RETEACH

Have students complete Main Idea Activity for English Language Learners and Special-Needs Students 22.2. Then ask each student to create a web diagram that shows the effects of the factory system on women, the working class, the middle class, and children.

ENGLISH LANGUAGE LEARNERS

EXTEND

Have students do research to identify primary sources that describe or discuss topics covered in this section.

BLOCK SCHEDULING

SECTION 2 REVIEW ANSWERS

① Define
• tenements, p. 552

② Working-class children: worked in factories, low wages, poor working conditions, lived in tenements, had to work to help support families; Middle-class families: better jobs that paid better wages, greater economic status, social influence, and political power; Women: worked in factories or in domestic service out of necessity or to gain independence, eventually took jobs as teachers, secretaries, nurses, and telephone operators

❸ a. Answers will vary. Many women today work outside the home; people accept women who do work outside the home.

b. Factory owners wanted to produce as much product for as much profit as possible. Hiring women and children at lower wages than men helped them reach this goal.

❹ Students' lyrics should suggest that a young person who worked in a factory worked very long hours in hazardous conditions and should indicate how the person feels or what he or she thinks about the future.

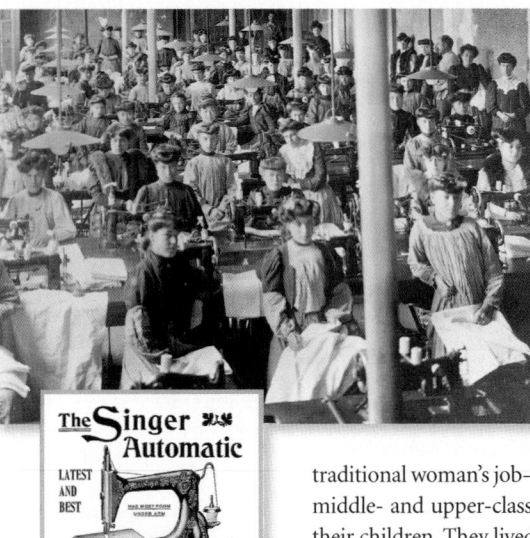

Inventions like the sewing machine eased work for many women.

Effect of Industrialization on Women's Lives

Throughout history, women had worked hard. They worked in the fields, spun yarn, made clothing, and prepared meals. They produced goods for sale and worked with their husbands in family businesses. As the Industrial Revolution moved production into factories, many working families moved to cities. As city dwellers, many women no longer had the resources or the need to grow food or make clothing.

As the need for farm labor decreased due to improved farming methods and equipment, some women took jobs in textile mills or factories. Many young women, however, continued to work at a traditional woman's job—domestic service. Moving to the cities, they found jobs with middle- and upper-class families, who hired them as maids, cooks, and nannies for their children. They lived with the families and were provided food and shelter. Some of these women later took jobs in shops or factories.

Many middle-class families had enough money so that women did not need to work outside the home. They stayed at home and, often with hired help, cleaned, cooked, and took care of the children. It was often said that a woman's nature equipped her only for these tasks. In the mid-1800s, however, middle-class women began speaking out for roles outside the home.

For some women a life outside the home meant independence. It was also a way to earn a living. During the late 1800s, jobs as nurses, secretaries, and telephone operators opened up to women. Women's colleges were founded to improve their educational levels. With the growth of public schools, many women became teachers. By the end of the 1800s, most elementary school teachers were women.

✔ **READING CHECK: Identifying Points of View** What might each of the following groups have thought about women's roles in society: working-class men, working-class women, middle-class men, middle-class women? answers will vary, but middle-class men and women may have been less accepting of women in the workplace

---

SECTION 2 REVIEW

1. Define and explain the significance:
tenements

2. Contrasting Copy the table below. List and contrast the ways in which the rise of the factory system affected each of these groups.

Factory System		
Working-class children	Middle-class families	Women

Homework Practice Online
keyword: SP3 HP22

3. **Finding the Main Idea**
a. How might some of the changes that affected women in the 1800s have affected the roles that women play in society today?
b. What factors led to the increased hiring of women and children in factories?

4. **Writing and Critical Thinking**
Summarizing Choose a well-known melody that you think suits the conditions of early factories. Write lyrics for the music expressing the feelings of a young person working in one of those factories.
Consider:
• details of the worker's daily life
• what the future might hold for them

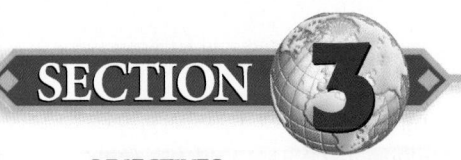

SECTION 3

OBJECTIVES

1 **Explain how and why the methods of production changed during the Industrial Revolution.**

2 **Identify what caused corporations to emerge and the effects they had on business.**

3 **Define the business cycle and explain how it affected society.**

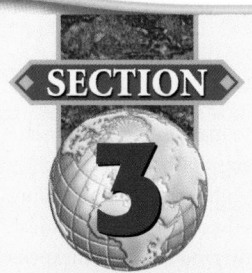

SECTION 3

READ TO DISCOVER

❶ How and why did methods of production change during the Industrial Revolution?

❷ Why did corporations emerge and how did they affect business?

❸ What is the business cycle and how did it affect society?

DEFINE

capitalism
commercial capitalism
industrial capitalism
interchangeable parts
mass production
corporations
monopoly
cartels
business cycle
depression

IDENTIFY

Henry Ford
J. P. Morgan

►WHY IT MATTERS TODAY

Today's corporations are often engaged in many different types of business. Use CNN**StudentNews**.com or other **current event** sources to identify the different businesses owned by large corporations. Record your findings in your journal.

CNN**Student News**.com

New Methods and Business Organizations

The Main Idea
Improved production methods helped to speed industrialization during the late 1800s.

The Story Continues *The 1800s were marked by new inventions and new methods of production and distribution. At the same time, new approaches to organizing businesses led to great wealth for some and to poverty for others. Some viewed the gulf between rich and poor as a danger, while others argued that, "The price which society pays for the law of competition . . . is . . . great; but the advantages of this law are . . . greater still, for it is to this law that we owe our wonderful material development . . . ."*

Capitalism and Changing Production Methods

The late 1800s in western Europe and the United States were characterized by a growing spirit of individual enterprise that we know today as capitalism. The term **capitalism** describes an economic system in which individuals or corporations, rather than governments, control the factors of production. In a capitalist system, businesses and the means of production are privately owned and operated. Before the Industrial Revolution, most capitalists were merchants who bought and sold goods. This was called **commercial capitalism.** During the Industrial Revolution, capitalists became more involved in producing and manufacturing goods. This was called **industrial capitalism.**

Division of labor and interchangeable parts. Industrialization changed the way people worked. Factory owners divided the manufacturing process into steps. They hired unskilled labor and assigned a step to each worker. This division of labor increased production. The use of machines in many of the steps helped the workers produce more in a shorter time. The lowered cost of production made more profit for the owners.

This painting of a factory shows one artist's view of the Industrial Revolution.

LEVEL 1: Divide the class into three groups and have each group create a picture that illustrates the effects of the three methods of production. *(Illustrations will vary. Effects of all three methods were increased production, lower cost of production, higher profits for owners, and lower cost to consumers. An additional effect of the assembly line was that it saved time and energy.)* **ENGLISH LANGUAGE LEARNERS**

LEVEL 3: Ensure that students understand the terms *sole proprietorship, partnership,* and *corporation.* Then have students apply this knowledge by identifying one or more businesses in their community for each category. Finally, have them write two or three paragraphs about why corporations have been so important to the U.S. economy since the Industrial Revolution.

History Maker

HENRY FORD. In about 1914 Henry Ford found himself facing a high turnover rate in his labor force. Rather than continue to hire new employees to offset these turnovers, Ford doubled the daily wage of his workers from about $2.50 to $5.00. His tactic paid off in more ways than one. Not only did his labor force stabilize, his operating costs also decreased. These positive factors allowed Ford to increase production.

Critical Thinking

Why was it a good tactic for Ford to double the daily wages of the workers?

ANSWER: Skilled and reliable workers stayed, reducing operating costs.

VISUAL RECORD ANSWER

The assembly line allowed the workers to perform a task in less time and with less energy.

American inventor Eli Whitney used division of labor to make muskets in the late 1700s. Previously, an entire gun was made by skilled artisans. Each gun was slightly different. If a part broke, a new one had to be handmade. Whitney invented machines that made parts that were all alike. Unskilled workers could now turn out identical, **interchangeable parts.** Whitney's system resulted in speedy production of inexpensive muskets that could be easily repaired. Other factory owners soon saw the benefit of interchangeable parts. They adopted the idea for their own products.

The assembly line. The system of producing large numbers of identical items is known as **mass production.** Division of labor, the use of interchangeable parts, and an assembly line are essential for mass production. Into the 1800s each part of an item was made in a different location in the factory. All the parts were brought together and assembled at a single location. Manufacturers then devised the assembly line, by which the parts were carried from worker to worker. Each worker performed a certain task on the part. This saved time and energy. The number of times per hour that a worker could perform a task increased.

Henry Ford saw a great potential in the assembly line. He used a conveyor belt to carry automobile frames from one worker to the next. Each worker added one or more of the numerous parts in the finished automobile. By using the assembly line for the production of automobiles, he founded one of the largest industries in the world.

American and European industrialists began to mass-produce many other items, such as clothing, furniture, and machinery. By reducing production costs, manufacturers were able to lower prices. More and more people could afford to buy a greater variety of goods and enjoy a higher standard of living.

✔ **READING CHECK: Making Generalizations** How did changes in production methods lead to an improved standard of living? goods became more affordable

INTERPRETING THE VISUAL RECORD

Assembly line This image shows a Ford assembly line in the early 1900s. *How do you think the assembly line might have made work easier for these Ford employees?*

ALL LEVELS: Direct students' attention to the chain of causes and effects described in the second paragraph on page 558. Provide students with a copy of the circular flowchart shown here and tell them to fill in the empty boxes to complete the business cycle chain of events. **ENGLISH LANGUAGE LEARNERS**

HOMEWORK Define and describe a corporation. Have students identify factors that affect a corporation's profits. *(the ability to sell what it makes and competition)* How are corporations today similar to corporations that existed during the Industrial Revolution? *(They have stockholders who elect directors to run them.)*

THE BUSINESS CYCLE

- factories increase orders for iron and hire more workers
- falling demand for goods
- large firm reduces orders for iron & lays off workers
- more machines and workers needed
- iron supplies cut production & lay off workers
- production increases to meet demand
- PROSPERITY
- DEPRESSION
- many workers competing for jobs
- wages go up & people buy more
- employers pay less
- new factory opens & hires many workers
- rising demand for goods
- prices go up to cover the cost of production
- workers buy less

Rise of the Corporation

Before the Industrial Revolution, most businesses were very small. A business owned and run by just one person was called a sole proprietorship. One owned and run by two or more people was called a partnership. Owners of both types of businesses were free to make business decisions. Each owner was personally responsible, however, for any debts the business had. In addition, sole proprietorships and partnerships usually remain small. Small companies with few workers typically cannot afford mass-production methods or the machinery necessary for large-scale production.

As businesses grew during the 1800s, another form of business organization became common. Businesses formed groups called **corporations** and allowed people to buy stock in their companies. This made it much easier to raise the money needed to run and expand a business. Stockholders elected directors to run the corporation. They shared in its profits, depending on how many shares of stock they owned. A stockholder's financial responsibility was limited to the amount he or she had invested. This made corporations attractive to investors. Banks played an increasingly important role in financing corporations. By the late 1800s some corporations had become very large and powerful. In 1901 American financier **J. P. Morgan** founded the United States Steel Company, one of the first of many billion-dollar corporations.

Increasing the size of a corporation did not necessarily increase its profits, however. To take advantage of mass production, factories attempted to work at full capacity. Sometimes they produced more goods than they could sell. Competition for customers was very keen between corporations making the same product. Cutting prices to sell more products could mean smaller profits. Smaller businesses often sold out to larger ones or even failed.

As a result, although the size of individual corporations increased steadily, the number of individual corporations in some industries decreased. Sometimes a corporation gained almost complete control of the production or sale of a single good or service. This was called a **monopoly.** During the late 1800s and the early 1900s, several gigantic corporations in the United States grew into monopolies or near-monopolies.

By 1900 several giant corporations in Germany had combined to control every stage of entire industries. They did this in the steel industry, for example, by owning coal and iron mines, steel mills, and factories. Such business combinations were known as **cartels.** French novelist Émile Zola described the growing size and complexity of such organizations in a dialogue in which one character describes his investment in a coal-mining cartel to another character.

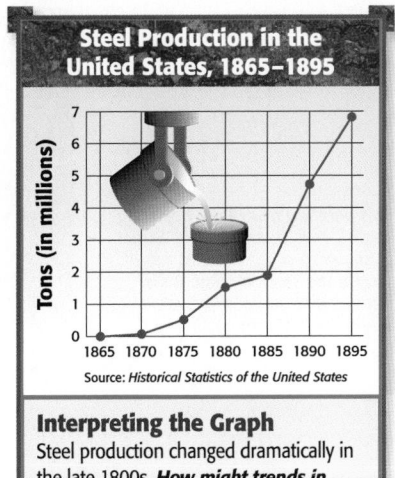

Steel Production in the United States, 1865–1895

Tons (in millions) — 1865 1870 1875 1880 1885 1890 1895

Source: *Historical Statistics of the United States*

Interpreting the Graph
Steel production changed dramatically in the late 1800s. *How might trends in steel production have affected investment in J.P. Morgan's company?*

> *Primary Source*
> **❝'And is your company rich?' asked Étienne.... 'Ah! yes.... Ten thousand workers, concessions reaching over sixty-seven towns, an output of five thousand tons a day, a railway joining all the pits, and workshops, and factories! Ah, yes! Ah, yes! There's money there!'❞**
>
> Émile Zola, *Germinal*

Analyzing Primary Sources

Drawing Conclusions What evidence does the character give to show that he has made a wise investment? *the large scale of production and output*

✔ **READING CHECK: Comparing** What advantages did corporations have over sole ownerships and partnerships? *easier to raise money, create monopoly*

This painting from 1879 depicting "bulls" and "bears" in Wall Street is meant to suggest the forces at play in the stock market. Bulls implied a strong market, while bears implied a sluggish one.

Business Cycles

As industry became more and more important, it influenced the economies of many nations. The Industrial Revolution brought alternating periods of prosperity and decline—a pattern that came to be called the **business cycle.**

The success or failure of one industry often affected others. For example, a rising demand for goods increased the demand for machines to make the goods. Factories making machines then required more steel. This increased the need for coal and iron to make steel. To keep up with the cascading demand for goods, more workers were needed. This led to higher wages and increased purchasing power and demand. On the other hand, a falling demand for goods had the opposite result. Industries laid off workers, who, with less money to buy goods, further reduced demand. Many factories might close. When this happened, the entire economy would sink into a **depression.** Eventually demand rebounded, closed factories often reopened, and workers were rehired. The economy then moved back toward prosperity, completing the business cycle.

✔ **READING CHECK: Identifying Cause and Effect** How did the business cycle work after the Industrial Revolution? *entered alternating periods*

SECTION 3 REVIEW

1. **Define** and explain the significance:
   capitalism
   commercial capitalism
   industrial capitalism
   interchangeable parts
   mass production
   corporations
   monopoly
   cartels
   business cycle
   depression

2. **Identify** and explain the significance:
   Henry Ford
   J. P. Morgan

Homework Practice Online
keyword: SP3 HP22

3. **Summarizing** Copy the diagram below. In the boxes, list and describe the three factors that made mass production possible.

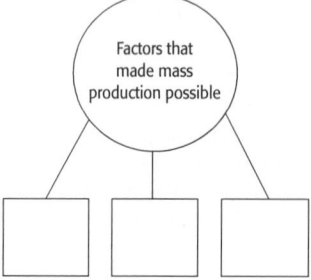

Factors that made mass production possible

4. **Finding the Main Idea**
   a. What role did the division of labor play in helping to increase production during the Industrial Revolution?
   b. In what way did the use of the assembly line allow Henry Ford to reach a new level of mass production?
   c. How might monopolies and cartels have affected a nation's economy?
   d. Draw a diagram that shows the steps in the business cycle.

5. **Writing and Critical Thinking**
   Making Generalizations Write an essay explaining how mass production affected people's lives.
   Consider:
   - changes in working conditions
   - changes in economic opportunities
   - changes in what people valued

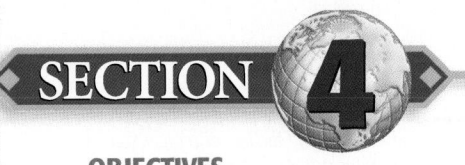

SECTION 4

OBJECTIVES

1 Identify Adam Smith's ideas and explain how they affected people's views of industrialism.

2 Explain the causes of reform movements.

3 Analyze how workers tried to improve their lives.

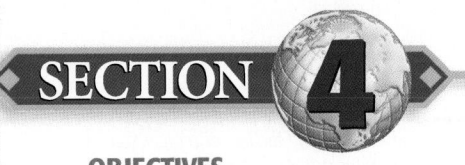 already placed; now the LET'S GET STARTED box.

SECTION 4

READ TO DISCOVER

❶ What were Adam Smith's ideas and how did they affect people's views of industrialism?

❷ Why did reform movements arise?

❸ How did workers try to improve their lives?

DEFINE

free enterprise
laissez-faire
humanitarians
utilitarianism
strike
unions
collective bargaining

IDENTIFY

Adam Smith
Thomas Malthus
David Ricardo
Charles Dickens
Jeremy Bentham
John Stuart Mill

▶ WHY IT MATTERS TODAY

Labor disputes and strikes are common in today's businesses. Use **CNN** Student News.com or other **current event** sources to find examples of a current or recent labor dispute. Record your findings in your journal.

CNN Student News.com

Living and Working Conditions

The Main Idea
New theories helped shape the Industrial Revolution and its impact upon society.

The Story Continues *As industrialization continued, some thinkers argued that business should be free to grow and change without any sort of government restrictions. Others, however, wanted workers to be granted the political and economic power needed to shape their own lives. British reformer J. R. Stephens held that ". . . every working man in the land has the right to have a good coat . . . a comfortable abode . . . a good dinner . . . and so much wages . . . as should keep him in plenty . . . ."*

Economic Theories

During the Enlightenment of the 1700s, a group of economists called the Physiocrats attacked the ideas of mercantilism. Mercantilism was the economic theory based on the belief that the world contained only a fixed amount of wealth. In order to increase its wealth, mercantilists argued, a country had to take some wealth away from another country. The Physiocrats disagreed with this. They believed that natural laws should be left to govern economic life. Any attempt to interfere with these natural economic laws, they felt, was certain to bring disaster. Scottish economist **Adam Smith** accepted some of the ideas of the Physiocrats. He stated his views in his book *Inquiry into the Nature and Causes of the Wealth of Nations,* which was published in 1776. In this book Smith focused on the creation of wealth, noting the importance of manufacturing as well as agriculture. Today Smith is considered the founder of classical economics.

Laws of economics. Smith reasoned that two natural laws governed all business and economic activity. The first was the law of supply and demand. Smith said that prices and profits depended on both the amount of available goods and the demand for those goods. If an item was scarce and in great demand, people would pay a high price for it and profits would rise. As manufacturers then invested money to make more of the product, supplies would soon exceed the demand.

The result of this supply-and-demand system was tied to Smith's second natural law—the law of competition. He said that as manufacturers compete with each other to sell their products, they must reduce prices. Manufacturers who cut prices too much, however, might lose money and even go out of business. Supply then tends to go down and prices rise. The most efficient manufacturers will survive.

This Scottish penny, bearing the words "Wealth of Nations," is a memorial to Adam Smith.

History Makers Speak

❝Every individual is continually exerting himself to find out the most advantageous employment for whatever capital he can command. It is his own advantage, indeed, and not that of the society, which he has in view. But the study of his own advantage, naturally, or rather necessarily, leads him to prefer that employment which is most advantageous to the society.❞

Adam Smith, *Inquiry into the Nature and Causes of the Wealth of Nations*

SECTION 4 RESOURCES

REPRODUCIBLE RESOURCES

▶ Guided Reading Strategy 22.4

▶ Readings in World History 75: The Trail of the Tolpuddle Martyrs

TECHNOLOGY RESOURCES

▶ One-Stop Planner 22.4

▶ Homework Practice Online

REINFORCEMENT, REVIEW, AND ASSESSMENT

▶ Section 4 Review, p. 563

▶ Daily Quiz 22.4

▶ Main Idea Activity 22.4

▶ English Audio Summary 22.4

▶ Spanish Audio Summary 22.4

ALL LEVELS: Organize students into five groups and assign each group one of the following economists or philosophers: Adam Smith, Thomas Malthus, David Ricardo, Jeremy Bentham, or John Stuart Mill. Have each group use the process of historical inquiry to create a multimedia presentation focusing on the economic theories of its assigned individual. Have students make their presentations in front of the class and tell the other students to take notes. Draw the following chart on the board and tell students to complete it. **ENGLISH LANGUAGE LEARNERS , COOPERATIVE LEARNING**

Economist	Theories
Adam Smith	*creation of wealth; manufacturing and agriculture both important; the law of supply and demand and the law of competition govern all business and economic activity; free enterprise*
Thomas Malthus	*population increase is the greatest obstacle to human progress; human misery and poverty are inevitable*
David Ricardo	*working-class poverty is inevitable; supply and demand determine wages (the iron law of wages)*
Jeremy Bentham	*utilitarianism; a good and useful law should lead to "the greatest happiness of the greatest number" of people; people should be educated so they could decide what was good for them; reform of the justice and prison systems*
John Stuart Mill	*government should work for the good of all its citizens; protection of working children; improvements in housing and factory conditions; full democracy; equality*

HISTORY MAKER ANSWER

His work emphasized the importance of supply and demand and the law of competition, and argued the need for a system of free enterprise—a system which became the basis of classical economics.

Interdisciplinary Connection

MATHEMATICS. Thomas Malthus is perhaps best known for his theory that population can expand geometrically, but food production can expand only arithmetically. In a geometric progression, each number after the first is formed by multiplying the preceding number by a constant factor. For example: 1, 3, 9, 27 is a geometric progression with a factor of 3. An arithmetic progression is a series in which a constant quantity is added to each number to form the next. For example: 1, 4, 7, 10 is an arithmetic progression in which the constant is 3.

ACTIVITY: Have students create a geometric progression and an arithmetic progression.

HISTORY MAKER
Adam Smith (1723–1790)

Adam Smith was interested in how countries create wealth through industry and farming. He also noted that the division of labor was important to the increase of wealth. In his book, *Inquiry into the Nature and Causes of the Wealth of Nations*, Smith argued that the economy worked best when government involvement was limited. He favored free economic competition. Smith's ideas formed the basis of classical economics.

Why was Adam Smith's work important?

Laissez-faire economic policies helped transform the small city of Sheffield, England into a major center of industry and production.

Smith also believed that people should be free to engage in whatever business they chose. They should be able to run the business for their greatest advantage. The result would be that investors and owners would make profits, laborers would have jobs, and consumers would buy better goods at lower prices. Smith argued that mercantilist laws and regulations hindered natural economic forces. His system was one of complete **free enterprise.** Many industrialists were attracted to Smith's ideas. In the system he described, economic forces worked automatically and naturally. Free enterprise justified competition unrestricted by laws, regulations, or government controls. Producers were free—in fact, were *required*—to do business solely for their own gain.

✔ **READING CHECK: Making Predictions** What might be some outcomes of implementing Adam Smith's theories about free enterprise? sharper competition, lower prices, higher profits, controlled supplies

Malthus and Ricardo. Smith's ideas received strong support from other economists. One was **Thomas Malthus,** an Anglican clergyman who became a professor of economics. In his book *An Essay on the Principle of Population*, published in 1798, Malthus wrote that population increases present the greatest obstacle to human progress. Despite famines, epidemics, and wars, he argued, people still multiply more rapidly than the food supply increases. Thus, Malthus believed that human misery and poverty are inevitable.

British economist **David Ricardo** wrote that working-class poverty is inevitable. In his book *Principles of Political Economy and Taxation*, published in 1817, Ricardo stated that supply and demand determine wages. When labor is plentiful, wages remain low. When labor is scarce, wages rise. As population grows, Ricardo wrote, more and more workers become available, and wages drop. Ricardo's idea became known as the iron law of wages.

Malthus and Ricardo painted a grim picture of workers as inevitably poor and suffering. Not surprisingly, the new social science of economics became known as the "dismal science."

Laissez-faire. The theories of economists such as Smith supported employers, who wanted to buy labor as cheaply as possible. They also wanted government not to meddle in the operations of business. These ideas were summed up in the French phrase **laissez-faire** (leh·say·FAR). This meant "let it be," or "leave things alone."

LEVEL 2: Ask students what motivated humanitarians to try to reform the workplace. *(novels that revealed the terrible conditions in factories and mills; church ministers, philosophers and economists sympathetic to the poverty-stricken laborers)* Ask students to suggest their own ideas for reform of specific current working conditions.

LEVEL 3: Have students take on the roles of reform activists in the 1800s to create handbills urging the government to pass laws regulating labor and the workplace. Encourage students to use their textbooks, the library, the Internet, and other sources to come up with statistics, meaningful images, and other persuasive items to include in their handbills.

In Great Britain, craft and merchant guilds had regulated the quality of goods—and in many cases, their prices—until well into the 1800s. Working hours and wages were also controlled. Beginning in the early 1800s, however, most regulations were dropped. Tariffs were eliminated and trade became almost completely unregulated. Laissez-faire economic ideas spread to the rest of Europe and to the United States.

✔ **READING CHECK: Summarizing** What does the theory of laissez-faire say should be done to achieve the most successful economy? no government regulation of business

Reformers Arise

Some people argued that businesses could not be left entirely alone. **Humanitarians**—people who work to improve the conditions of others—urged reforms. Ministers preached against the selfish practices of business people. Famous writers of the day made the public aware of the terrible working conditions in mines and factories. English writer **Charles Dickens** used his novels to attack greedy employers. In *David Copperfield*, Dickens described his own wretched childhood experiences. Other writers such as Thomas Carlyle and John Ruskin, and artists such as Gustave Doré, criticized society's obsession with money and neglect of spiritual values.

Many people argued that laws were needed to regulate work hours and set basic standards for wages and working conditions. They insisted such laws would not interfere with the economy.

In Great Britain, some reformers adopted the theory of **utilitarianism** put forth by philosopher **Jeremy Bentham.** Bentham argued that a law was useful, and therefore good, if it led to "the greatest happiness of the greatest number" of people. He believed that people should be educated so that they could decide what things were good for them or would make them happy. Bentham and his followers also called for reform of the nation's justice and prison system.

English philosopher **John Stuart Mill** also believed that a government should work for the good of all its citizens. He rejected economic systems that left workers trapped in poverty. Mill called for government to protect working children and to improve housing and factory conditions. Mill argued for full democracy and for equality for all men and women, regardless of their social class or economic power. In about 1869 he wrote *On the Subjection of Women*, a ground-breaking call for support of women's rights. Mill believed that government should promote education and guarantee individual liberty. This included the right to think as one pleased and to freely express one's views. In about 1861 Mill wrote that all human beings "have equal need of a voice in [government] to secure their share of its benefits."

✔ **READING CHECK: Identifying Cause and Effect** Why would improving education and guaranteeing individual liberty help the working class? help protect their rights and voice in government

This illustration from an early edition of Dickens's David Copperfield *gives a view of urban life in Great Britain during the Industrial Revolution.*

LEVEL 1: Ask students why the first labor unions were formed. *(to try to get better wages and working conditions through force of numbers)* What impediments were there to the formation of unions throughout much of Europe? *(Gatherings of workers were illegal in many countries.)* What changed this situation in Great Britain? *(Parliament repealed the Combination Acts and then made strikes legal.)*
ENGLISH LANGUAGE LEARNERS

LEVEL 3: Mention to students that strikes and collective bargaining are still very much a part of the management/union relationship in the United States today. Tell students to write a one-page report that answers this question: Are unions as necessary today as they were during the Industrial Revolution? Students should support their answers with specific reasons and details and provide a list of the resources they used.

 HOMEWORK List and describe the reforms that improved the lot of factory workers in Great Britain.

internet connect

TOPIC: Labor Unions
GO TO: go.hrw.com
KEYWORD: SP3 WH22

Through the HRW Go site, have students access sites on the Internet that have information about modern labor unions. Have them use the information they find to compare and contrast modern unions with the very first unions described in their textbooks. Then ask students to create a strike or boycott poster that might have been used by early labor unions and one that could be used by labor unions today. Ask them to write a one-page essay that compares and contrasts the early unions with the modern unions.

INTERPRETING THE VISUAL RECORD

Child labor Young people made up a large part of the labor force in many areas. Many early reforms centered on children. *What reforms are these young workers demanding?*

Early Reform Laws

Working conditions, particularly for women and children, greatly troubled the British public. Parliament began reform efforts with the Factory Act of 1802, which shortened hours and improved conditions for children working in cotton mills. It proved ineffective, however, because it had no means of enforcement. The Factory Act of 1833 corrected this omission and extended the law to all textile mills.

The laws prohibited mills from employing children under 9 years of age. Children between the ages of 9 and 13 could work no more than 8 hours a day, 6 days a week. Older children could work no more than 12 hours a day. A later law said coal mines could not employ any women or any children under the age of 10. A great advance came with the Ten Hours Act in 1847, which set a 10-hour working day for women and for children under the age of 18. Because most workers were women and children, factory owners extended the 10-hour day to everyone. The laws were poorly enforced, however, and conditions remained harsh. Moreover, the reform laws did nothing to improve wages. That would have to be up to the workers themselves.

✔ **READING CHECK: Drawing Inferences** Why did children in the 1800s work long hours in factories when the same is not true today? laws were passed preventing it

Collective Action

To improve their own lives, many workers banded together to demand reform. Such efforts are known as collective action.

Strikes. Workers protested working conditions and low wages by refusing to work. When a large group of workers stops working, it is called a **strike.** Workers often made a list of their demands, refusing to work until the demands were met. Employers sometimes gave in to the workers. Other times they fired the workers and hired new ones. Often they waited until economic needs forced the strikers to return to work.

Numerous strikes took place in industrial countries during the 1800s. The workers usually demanded higher wages and better working conditions. Some strikes

CLOSE

Ask students to explain how and why workers fought for better working conditions and wages. Then lead a class discussion on how the reforms strengthened society.

REVIEW

Have students complete the Section 4 Review on p. 563.

ASSESS

Have students complete Daily Quiz 22.4. As Alternative Assessment, you may want to use the Economist/Philosophers chart activity in Section 4.

RETEACH

Have students complete Main Idea Activity for English Language Learners and Special-Needs Students 22.4. Then ask each student to create an outline of the information provided in this section. **ENGLISH LANGUAGE LEARNERS**

EXTEND

Have students create collages that highlight the reality of life in London during the Industrial Revolution. **BLOCK SCHEDULING**

began over wages but spread to general working and living conditions of the working class. Some strike leaders called for reorganizing society to end the differences between rich and poor. Strikes grew to large protest movements in the textile and mining areas of England, France, and eastern Europe. These demonstrations often were put down when governments used troops to arrest protesting workers.

Unions. Workers felt that their protests would be more successful if they were organized. They began to form associations called **unions.** These unions would collect dues from members and then use that money to pay workers if they went on strike. The unions planned actions and combined the demands of different kinds of workers in the same factory.

Workers' associations were considered illegal by British, French, and German law. When workers organized anyway, the British Parliament passed the Combination Acts of 1799 and 1800. These laws said that workers who united to demand higher wages, shorter hours, and better working conditions could be imprisoned.

Eventually workers began to make some progress. In about 1825 the Combination Acts were repealed, and in the 1870s Parliament passed laws legalizing strikes. Now unions had real power. In some cases, factory owners began to acknowledge that unions spoke for all the workers. Management and union representatives began to discuss wages, hours, and working conditions. Agreements were written into contracts lasting for a fixed period of time. This process of negotiation is called **collective bargaining.**

✔ **READING CHECK: Finding the Main Idea** How were workers able to get higher wages and better working conditions by forming unions? could negotiate collectively as a group

This Italian painting entitled The Human Tide *depicts workers banding together to voice their protests.*

SECTION 4 REVIEW

1. **Define** and explain the significance:
   free enterprise
   laissez-faire
   humanitarians
   utilitarianism
   strike
   unions
   collective bargaining

2. **Identify** and explain the significance:
   Adam Smith
   Thomas Malthus
   David Ricardo
   Charles Dickens
   Jeremy Bentham
   John Stuart Mill

3. **Problem Solving** Copy the web diagram below. Fill in the top boxes by listing what employers and workers wanted regarding wages and working conditions. Then fill in the compromise box by suggesting how agreements could have been reached through collective bargaining.

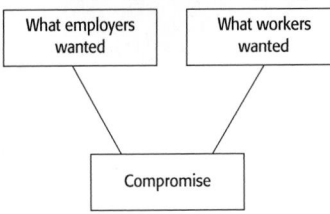

4. **Finding the Main Idea**
   a. How did Adam Smith's ideas influence employers' treatment of workers?
   b. Why was it easier for the government to pass laws about working hours than about wages?

5. **Writing and Critical Thinking**
   Evaluating Write a brief article in which you identify the strong and weak points in the ideas of economist Adam Smith or reformer Jeremy Bentham.
   Consider:
   • the advantages and disadvantages of allowing business and the economy to go unregulated
   • the advantages and disadvantages of government trying to create conditions to ensure justice for workers

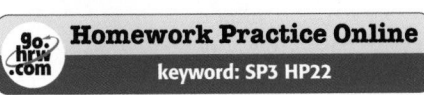

Homework Practice Online
keyword: SP3 HP22

SECTION 4 REVIEW ANSWERS

❶ **Define**
• free enterprise, p. 560
• laissez-faire, p. 561
• humanitarians, p. 561
• utilitarianism, p. 561
• strike, p. 562
• unions, p. 563
• collective bargaining, p. 563

❷ **Identify**
• Adam Smith, p. 559
• Thomas Malthus, p. 560
• David Ricardo, p. 560
• Charles Dickens, p. 561
• Jeremy Bentham, p. 561
• John Stuart Mill, p. 561

❸ Employers: profits; Workers: higher wages, better working conditions; Compromise: discussions between management and union representatives about wages, hours, and working conditions; agreements written into contracts lasting for a fixed period of time

❹ a. suggested to employers that it was okay to ignore workers' needs in the interest of making a profit

b. Opposition to laws regarding working hours was not as great as it was to laws regarding wages.

❺ Students' articles should clearly identify the advantages and the disadvantages in the ideas of either Adam Smith or Jeremy Bentham.

THE INDUSTRIAL REVOLUTION **563**

SECTION 5

OBJECTIVES

1 Describe the type of society that early socialists wanted to establish.

2 Explain how Robert Owen put his socialist beliefs into action.

3 Explain what Karl Marx believed would happen to the capitalist world of the 1880s.

4 Identify some of the competing ideas that arose out of Marxism.

SECTION 5

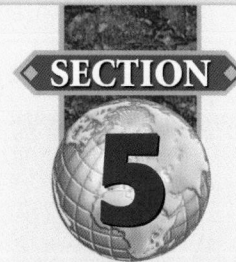

READ TO DISCOVER

❶ What type of society did early socialists want to establish?

❷ How did Robert Owen put his socialist beliefs into action?

❸ What did Karl Marx believe would happen to the capitalist world of the 1800s?

❹ What were some competing ideas that arose out of Marxism?

DEFINE

means of production
socialism
utopian socialists
proletariat
communism
democratic socialism

IDENTIFY

Robert Owen
Karl Marx
Friedrich Engels

▶ WHY IT MATTERS TODAY

Some countries of the world have socialist governments. Use CNN Student News.com or other **current event** sources to find examples of socialist countries. Record your findings in your journal.

CNN Student News.com

Socialism

The Main Idea
The Industrial Revolution gave rise to new ideas about economic, political, and social justice.

The Story Continues *As the Industrial Revolution progressed, a growing number of people became concerned with economic and social injustice. Many believed that the interests and needs of employers naturally conflicted with those of workers. As early as 1798, one writer noted that: "The increasing wealth of the nation has had little or no tendency to better the conditions of the labouring poor." As industrialization continued, demands for reform and justice based upon the new realities of the marketplace became stronger.*

Socialism

In the economy that resulted from the Industrial Revolution, a few people became enormously rich. Most, however, remained poor, including the workers whose labor drove the economy. This uneven distribution of wealth disturbed many people. Some reformers became convinced that laissez-faire capitalism was not the best economic system. They argued that laws could not do enough to remedy inequalities. The only way to distribute wealth more evenly, they felt, was to change the ownership and operation of the means of production. The **means of production** include the capital and equipment used to produce and exchange goods—for example, land, railroads, mines, factories, stores, banks, and machines.

Some of these reformers advocated a political and economic system called **socialism.** Under socialism, governments own the means of production and operate them

The political cartoon above satirizes German leader Otto von Bismarck, who passed a law trying to contain socialism. At right is a poster urging workers of the world to unite under international socialism.

TEACH OBJECTIVE 1

LEVEL 1: Ask students what the means of production are (*capital and equipment used to produce and exchange goods*) and why socialists believed that government should control the means of production.
ENGLISH LANGUAGE LEARNERS

TEACH OBJECTIVE 2

LEVEL 3: Have students apply different methods that historians use to interpret the past (such as point of view and frame of reference) to create a summary plan for a planned community similar to those proposed by Robert Owen. Students should consider how many people would live in the community, how it might be governed, and who would do what types of work.
COOPERATIVE LEARNING

TEACH OBJECTIVE 3

ALL LEVELS: Have students write papers expressing their opinions about communism. Tell them to justify their opinions with facts, examples, and evidence. **ENGLISH LANGUAGE LEARNERS**

---

for the benefit of all people, rich or poor. These reformers, called socialists, wanted to establish an economic system that would do away with the profit motive and competition. They believed everyone, not just capitalists and factory owners, had a right to share in the profits.

Utopian socialists. Early socialists believed that people could live peacefully with each other in small cooperative settlements in which everyone would work for the common good. They would own all the means of production in common and share the products. Socialists worked out plans for model towns and encouraged people to set them up. Some were modeled after the ideal community described in 1516 in Sir Thomas More's *Utopia.* For this reason, early socialists were sometimes called **utopian socialists.**

✔ **READING CHECK: Contrasting** How did socialism differ from capitalism? socialism calls for the means of production to be owned by the state, not corporations, and operated for benefit of all, not just employers

Owen. In Great Britain, the most influential utopian socialist was **Robert Owen,** who lived from 1771 to 1858. He quit school at age 10 and went to work. By 19, he managed a large cotton mill and later purchased a spinning mill. In 1814 Owen entered a partnership with Jeremy Bentham.

Owen believed that people who lived in a good environment would stop acting selfishly. He felt responsible for his workers and spent much time and money to make their lives happier and more secure. Owen built good homes for them, set up schools for their children, and made inexpensive food and clothing available. Owen believed, however, that workers should not be dependent on their employers. He encouraged them to form unions. He proposed the formation of "villages of cooperation" in which the unemployed would be self-supporting instead of relying on aid. From 1825 to about 1829 Owen lived in the United States, where he tried unsuccessfully to set up cooperative communities run along socialist lines. Only later in the 1800s and early 1900s did the cooperative movement spread in Europe and America.

✔ **READING CHECK: Drawing Conclusions** What do you think Owen hoped to gain by making his employees' lives more secure? loyalty, better workers

The Theories of Karl Marx

Some thinkers, such as **Karl Marx,** believed that utopian socialism was impractical. They said that the entire capitalist system should be destroyed. Marx believed that all great changes in history had come from changes in economic conditions. With fellow German **Friedrich Engels,** Marx published *The Communist Manifesto* in 1848. Marx and Engels summed up their view of human history in one sentence: "The history of all hitherto existing society is the history of class struggles." Marx and Engels went on to support their view:

 ❝Free man and slave, patrician and plebeian, lord and serf, guild master and journeyman, in a word, oppressor and oppressed, stood in constant opposition to one another, carried on an uninterrupted, now hidden, now open fight, a fight that each time ended either in a revolutionary reconstitution of society at large or in the common ruin of the contending classes.❞

Karl Marx and Friedrich Engels, *The Communist Manifesto,* 1848

HISTORY MAKER

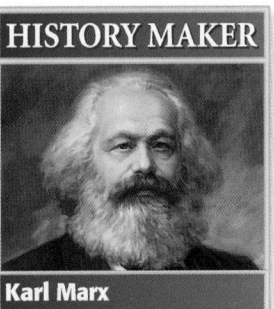

**Karl Marx
(1818–1883)**

As a young man, Karl Marx became involved with socialist political groups in Germany and France. Marx's radical views and his attacks on government led to his expulsion from several European countries. He eventually settled in London and lived there the rest of his life.

Marx believed that economics was central to human life. He dreamed of a revolution in which the workers of the world would unite to gain political power. Marx's theories inspired the communist movements of the 1900s. **What did Marx hope for?**

Global Relations

While Marx might have approved of the technological and scientific advances made during the Industrial Revolution, he did not accept the conditions of capitalism. According to Marx, revolution was inevitable. His theory of class struggle involved the middle class seizing power from the aristocracy. Eventually, the growing proletariat would rise up and take control. After the proletariat established a dictatorship and eliminated middle-class culture in the society, the state would gradually decline.

Critical Thinking

Why would Marx have predicted that the revolution of the proletariat was most likely to occur first in countries like England and Germany?

ANSWER: Students might suggest that those countries were the most highly industrialized and therefore were further along in the process that Marx believed would lead to revolution.

HISTORY MAKER ANSWER

Marx hoped for a revolution in which the workers of the world would unite to gain political power.

LEVEL 1: Draw the following web diagram on the board. Ask students to complete the diagram by identifying the competing ideas that arose out of Marxism and their characteristics. Students' diagrams should include information that identifies the roles of both people and government.
ENGLISH LANGUAGE LEARNERS

HOMEWORK Have students use a problem-solving process to come up with their own idea for social reform for the Industrial Revolution. Students should give their idea a name, identify its characteristics, and explain how their theories would solve the social problem.

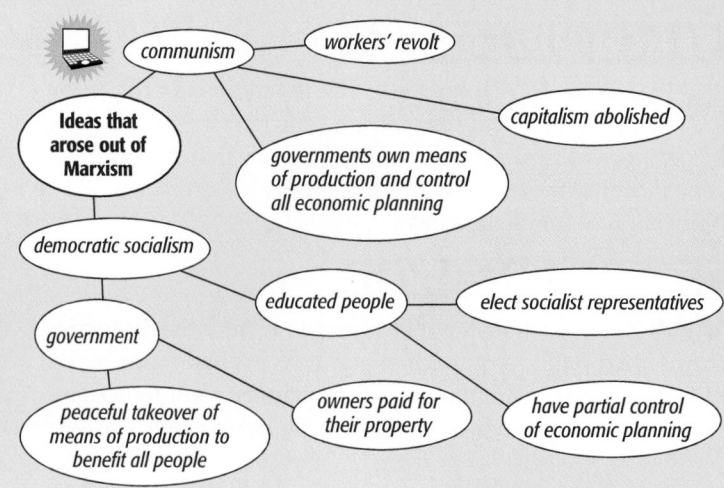

That's Interesting!

In about 1845 Karl Marx participated in the correspondence and activities of a group of émigrés, most of whom were German artisans and intellectuals. These revolutionaries contributed to and participated in the Communist Correspondence Committee and the Communist League. The first published statement of the League's principles and objectives was the *Communist Manifesto*, which ends with the call for unity, "Workers of All Countries, Unite!" It has become the most widely read of Marx's works and the most influential work on socialist views.

Karl Marx predicted that socialist revolutionaries would clash violently with government forces. This 1905 painting shows the aftermath of one such conflict.

Marx said that each stage of history involved inequality, and therefore struggle, between those who owned property and those who did not. In the capitalist stage of the 1800s, for example, the struggle existed between the owners, or bourgeoisie, and the working class, or **proletariat.** Marx argued that all wealth is created by labor. Under capitalism, however, labor receives only a small fraction of the wealth it creates. Most of the wealth goes to the owners in the form of profits. As a result of this unequal distribution of wealth, Marx thought the time would soon come when society would divide into two classes—a few capitalists and a vast mass of workers. Marx predicted that the capitalists would continue to amass wealth while driving the proletariat deeper and deeper into poverty. Finally, the proletariat in the most advanced and industrialized nations would unite and seize power in a socialist revolution.

At first the revolutionaries would have to control the government by force, Marx said, because many people would not accept socialism. He called this the "dictatorship of the proletariat." Eventually, after people learned the benefits of working together cooperatively, the state would "wither away." Marx called this truly classless society "pure communism." He believed it was the inevitable outcome of human history. In this society, Marx believed, each person would contribute what he or she could, and would receive what he or she needed. Marx said, "From each according to his abilities, to each according to his needs."

✔ **READING CHECK: Analyzing Information** What do you think Marx meant when he said that all wealth was created by labor? production would stop without workers

Variations of Socialism

In the mid-1800s socialists in several European countries formed political parties. They were influenced by the ideas of Marx and Engels. Marxist socialists often believed that violent revolution was required to get rid of capitalism. They believed this was probably the only way to establish governments that owned the means of production and controlled all economic planning. Today, this economic and political system is called authoritarian socialism, or **communism.**

CLOSE

Have students identify what caused the need for reform and the reform ideas proposed by Robert Owen, Karl Marx, and Friedrich Engels.

REVIEW

Have students complete the Section 5 Review on p. 567.

ASSESS

Have students complete Daily Quiz 22.5. As Alternative Assessment, you may want to use the web diagram for ideas that arose out of Marxism in this section's lessons.

RETEACH

Have students complete Main Idea Activity for English Language Learners and Special-Needs Students 22.5. Then ask students to create a compare-and-contrast chart on capitalism, democratic socialism, and communism. **ENGLISH LANGUAGE LEARNERS**

EXTEND

Have students create a visual that illustrates a topic covered in this lesson. Visuals can include charts, diagrams, maps, collages, etc., and can be computer-generated. **BLOCK SCHEDULING**

Another group of socialists, though influenced by Marx, believed that socialism could develop gradually through education and democratic forms of government. These moderate socialists believed that when enough people became educated about socialism, they would elect socialist representatives to their government. Then government would take over the means of production peacefully. The owners would be paid for their property and government would operate the means of production in the interests of all people. Today this type of socialism is called **democratic socialism.** Under democratic socialism, unlike communism, the people retain partial control over economic planning through the election of government officials. Individuals may own private property, but the government owns at least some of the means of production. The ideas of democratic socialism went on to influence many governments in northern and western Europe.

Marx believed that workers had to unite to fight capitalism successfully. During the 1800s several organizations for workers emerged. In 1864 Marx helped establish the International Working Men's Association, or First International. This organization disbanded, however, in 1876. A Second International was formed in 1889, after Marx's death. Torn by disagreements between moderate and radical socialists, the Second International survived only into the early 1900s. However, elsewhere, particularly in Russia, Marx's ideas would go on to have profound effects.

✔ **READING CHECK: Contrasting** How did democratic socialism differ from communism? people elect officials and retain some control over economy

Friedrich Engels's socialist activism is evidenced by his membership in the International Working Men's Association.

SECTION 5 REVIEW

1. **Define** and explain the significance:
   means of production
   socialism
   utopian socialists
   proletariat
   communism
   democratic socialism

2. **Identify** and explain the significance:
   Robert Owen
   Karl Marx
   Friedrich Engels

3. **Evaluating** Copy the table below. Complete the table by listing the effects of socialism on each sector of society.

Working people	Business or factory owners	Factors of production	Government

4. **Finding the Main Idea**
   a. According to Karl Marx, what causes conflict within a society?
   b. How did the political and economic system of communism develop?

5. **Writing and Critical Thinking**
   Comparing Write a brief comparison of Marxist socialism with moderate socialism.
   Consider:
   • how each wanted to change capitalism to socialism
   • what effects each might have on the rights of individuals
   • how each proposed to solve the problems of unequal distribution of wealth

go. **Homework Practice Online**
hrw keyword: SP3 HP22
.com

SECTION 5 REVIEW ANSWERS

❶ **Define**
• means of production, p. 564
• socialism, p. 564
• utopian socialists, p. 565
• proletariat, p. 566
• communism, p. 566
• democratic socialism, p. 567

❷ **Identify**
• Robert Owen, p. 565
• Karl Marx, p. 565
• Friedrich Engels, p. 565

❸ Working people—would share in profits; Business or factory owners—would be paid for their property; Factors of production—would be controlled by governments; Government—would control and operate means of production and economic planning to benefit all people

❹ a. uneven distribution of wealth, inequality between classes

b. from socialists who were influenced by the ideas of Marx and Engels

❺ Students' comparisons should note how Marxist socialism and moderate socialism wanted to change capitalism to socialism, the effects of each on the rights of individuals, and how each would solve unequal distribution of wealth.

REVIEW AND ASSESSMENT RESOURCES

REPRODUCIBLE RESOURCES

▶ Vocabulary Activity 22

TECHNOLOGY RESOURCES

▶ Chapter 22 Test Generator (on the One-Stop Planner)
▶ Global Skill Builder CD-ROM
▶ HRW Web Site

REINFORCEMENT, REVIEW, and ASSESSMENT

▶ Chapter 22 Review, pp. 568–569
▶ Chapter 22 Tutorial for Students, Parents, Mentors, and Peers
▶ Chapter 22 Test (Form A or B)
▶ Alternative Assessment Handbook
▶ Chapter 22 Test for English Language Learners and Special-Needs Students

REVIEW

Have students complete the Chapter 22 Review on pages 568–569.

ASSESS

Use one of the chapter tests to assess students' understanding of content. For Alternative Assessment, see the Portfolio Activities and Alternative Assessment Handbook.

CHAPTER 22 REVIEW ANSWERS

Understanding Main Ideas

1. examples: crop rotation, cotton gin, steamboats, railroads, telegraph

2. took factory jobs or jobs in homes, became teachers, secretaries, nurses, and telephone operators

3. labor divided into steps, interchangeable parts, assembly line

4. They initiated the process of negotiation called collective bargaining.

5. reform movements based on the belief that everyone should share in economic profits

Reviewing Themes

1. It helped to create a middle class, put women and children in the work force, created a capitalist economy, gave rise to corporations, and spawned ideas of social, political, and economic reform.

2. working class: did most work and received least money, began to fight for change; middle class: got social and political status; wealthy: continued to operate to ensure a profit, regardless of the plight of their workers, until unions stepped in

3. gave rise to the business cycle—alternating periods of prosperity and decline

---

CHAPTER 22 Review

Creating a Time Line

Copy the time line below onto a sheet of paper. Complete the time line by filling in the events, individuals, and dates from the chapter that you think were significant. Pick three events and explain why you think they were significant.

| 1600 | 1776 | 1901 |

Writing a Summary

Using standard grammar, spelling, sentence structure, and punctuation, write an overview of the events in the chapter.

Identifying People and Ideas

Identify the following terms or individuals and explain their significance:

1. Industrial Revolution
2. factors of production
3. James Watt
4. Robert Fulton
5. capitalism
6. mass production
7. laissez-faire
8. Adam Smith
9. socialism
10. Karl Marx

Understanding Main Ideas

Section 1 *(pp. 544–550)*

Origins of the Industrial Revolution

1. What were some of the important inventions and scientific discoveries of the Industrial Revolution?

Section 2 *(pp. 551–554)*

The Factory System

2. How did the lives of women change during the Industrial Revolution?

Section 3 *(pp. 555–558)*

New Methods and Business Organizations

3. How did methods of production change during the Industrial Revolution?

Section 4 *(pp. 559–563)*

Living and Working Conditions

4. What role did unions play in improving wages and working conditions?

Section 5 *(pp. 564–567)*

Socialism

5. What led to the development of socialism and communism?

Reviewing Themes

1. **Science, Technology & Society** How did the Industrial Revolution influence other areas of society?
2. **Citizenship** How did the distribution of wealth affect the roles that people played in society?
3. **Economics** How did the needs of different groups influence the development of economics?

Thinking Critically

1. **Sequencing** Trace the events leading to the mechanization of the textile industry.
2. **Drawing Inferences** What factors influenced the rise of capitalism?
3. **Making Generalizations** What factors forced employers to improve wages and working conditions?
4. **Comparing and Contrasting** Compare and contrast capitalist and socialist economies.

Writing About History

Evaluating American companies sometimes have goods assembled in other countries in order to cut their production costs. American workers protest that this is unfair to them. Use a problem-solving and decision-making process to decide what, if any, action you believe the government should take to address these issues. Write an editorial arguing for that action. Use the following chart to organize your thoughts before you begin writing.

Possible government action	Effect on businesses	Effect on consumers	Effect on workers
No action			
Working with other governments			
Tariffs or subsidies			
Other			

CLOSE

Divide the class into five groups. Assign each group a section from the chapter and ask them to prepare an oral summary of their assigned section. Have students present their summaries to the class.
COOPERATIVE LEARNING

RETEACH

Have students who had difficulty with the test rewrite each question that they missed and then use their textbooks and notes to answer the questions in complete sentences. Have them study their completed sentences and answers. Then pair students and allow them to quiz each other on the chapter content. **ENGLISH LANGUAGE LEARNERS , COOPERATIVE LEARNING**

Portfolio Extensions

1. Provide students with samples of kids' magazines so they can review certain aspects of articles in those magazines, such as design, illustrations and photographs, subheads, charts, and diagrams. Ask students to identify elements of the magazine articles that appeal to them the most.

2. Divide the class into two groups. Ask one group to define and describe the law of supply and demand as it relates to one product or service. You may wish to identify this product or service for them, for example: groceries, clothing, automobiles. Ask the other group to define and describe the law of competition as it relates to the same product or service.

Building Social Studies Skills

Using Artifacts as Historical Evidence
Study the photograph and then answer the questions below.

Hand-cranked sewing machine from the 1850s

1. Which of the following most accurately describes the historical significance of this artifact?
   a. The artifact probably represents a significant technological advance.
   b. The artifact was probably too cumbersome to be used effectively.
   c. The artifact proves that electrical power was available to some as early as the 1850s.
   d. The existence of this artifact proves that sewing machines were widely used during the 1850s.

2. What can you infer about life in the 1850s from this artifact? Give specific examples.

Distinguishing Fact from Opinion
Read the following quote from the American industrialist, Andrew Carnegie. Then answer the questions.

"This, then, is held to be the duty of the man of wealth: To set an example of modest, unostentatious [simple] living, shunning display or extravagance . . . the man of wealth thus becoming the mere trustee and agent for his poorer brethren . . . . In bestowing [giving] charity, the main consideration should be to help those who will help themselves; . . . to give those who desire to rise the [assistance] by which they may rise."

3. Which of the following statements best describes an opinion held by Carnegie?
   a. Charity should be given by the wealthy to all who are less financially fortunate.
   b. In a capitalist society, one must look out for oneself, without regard for others.
   c. Those who are wealthy owe nothing to their society or to the people around them.
   d. Wealth brings a responsibility to set a positive example for other, less wealthy people.

4. What is your opinion of the views described in this quote? Give specific reasons to support your point of view.

Alternative Assessment
Building Your Portfolio

Economics

Adam Smith said that the law of supply and demand and the law of competition automatically determined business and economic trends. Use your textbook, the Internet, and other sources to identify examples of how the two laws operate today. Write an article for a young people's magazine that uses examples of products and services in today's world to explain Smith's ideas.

internet connect

Internet Activity: go.hrw.com
KEYWORD: SP3 WH22

Choose a topic on the Industrial Revolution to:
• identify the historic origins of capitalism and socialism.
• compare and contrast modern labor unions with early unions.
• write a biography of a female writer who lived and wrote during the Victorian Age.

Thinking Critically

1. invention of mechanized loom for weaving cloth, flying shuttle, spinning jenny, driving machines by waterpower, spinning mill, water-powered loom

2. growth of businesses in the 1800s, need to raise money to run and expand those businesses, limited financial responsibility of investors

3. strikes, protests, competition, profit loss, unions

4. capitalist: based on law of supply and demand and law of competition, businesses independently owned; socialist: based on all working for good of all regardless of wealth or status, government controls means of production and economic planning

Writing About History
Answers will vary but should include effect on businesses, workers, and consumers.

Building Social Studies Skills
1. a
2. answers will vary; life changing due to technology
3. d
4. Answers will vary.

Building Your Portfolio
Articles will vary but should include an explanation of how those products and services represent Smith's ideas.

Life in the Industrial Age

CHAPTER RESOURCE MANAGER

Objectives	Pacing Guide	Reproducible Resources
SECTION 1 **Advances in Technology and Communication** (pp. 572–575)	• Examine how the development of electricity led to other technological advances. • Identify the inventions that improved communications. • Analyze the importance of the internal combustion engine.	**Regular** 1 day **Block Scheduling** .5 day *Block Scheduling Handbook with Team Teaching Strategies, 23.1*	**RS** Guided Reading Strategy 23.1 **PS** Readings in World History 77: The First Flight Across the English Channel
SECTION 2 **Advances in Science and Medicine** (pp. 576–582)	• Explain how cell theory changed over time. • Investigate why Darwin's theory was so significant and controversial. • Describe how scientific discoveries changed the nature of medicine and surgery. • Identify the advances made in the field of physics.	**Regular** 1.5 day **Block Scheduling** 1 day *Block Scheduling Handbook with Team Teaching Strategies, 23.2*	**RS** Guided Reading Strategy 23.2 **PS** Readings in World History 78: Two Testimonials for Albert Einstein **PS** Readings in World History 79: Edward Jenner's Case Studies
SECTION 3 **Social Sciences in the Industrial Age** (pp. 583–585)	• Explore how science influenced the study of politics, economics, and history. • Examine how archaeology, anthropology, and sociology explored cultures. • Investigate how the study of the human mind developed.	**Regular** 1 day **Block Scheduling** .5 day *Block Scheduling Handbook with Team Teaching Strategies, 23.3*	**RS** Guided Reading Strategy 23.3
SECTION 4 **Society and Culture in the Industrial Age** (pp. 586–591)	• Explain why people emigrated. • Analyze why cities grew and how they changed as they grew. • Identify the ways in which public education changed society. • Describe how the leisure activities we know today began to develop.	**Regular** 1.5 day **Block Scheduling** 1 day *Block Scheduling Handbook with Team Teaching Strategies, 23.4*	**RS** Guided Reading Strategy 23.4 **RS** Graphic Organizer Activity 23: Effects of Industrialization **SM** Geography Activity 23: New York: The New Industrial City **E** Hands-on History Activity 23: Outside the Factory
SECTION 5 **Literature, Music, and Art in the Industrial Age** (pp. 592–597)	• Explore the ideas that drove the romantic movement. • Identify the artists, writers, and musicians of the romantic movement. • Explain how realism differs from romanticism. • Explore the other artistic movements that emerged during this time.	**Regular** 1.5 day **Block Scheduling** 1 day *Block Scheduling Handbook with Team Teaching Strategies, 23.5*	**RS** Guided Reading Strategy 23.5 **PS** Readings in World History 80: Beethoven's Heiligenstadt Testament **E** Creative Teaching Strategy 23: The Great Exposition of Industrial Culture

Chapter Resource Key

PS Primary Sources
RS Reading Support
IC Interdisciplinary Connections
E Enrichment
SM Skills Mastery

A Assessment
REV Review
ELL Reinforcement and English Language Learners
 Transparencies
 CD-ROM

 Music
 Video
Internet
Holt Presentation Maker Using Microsoft® PowerPoint®

 One-Stop Planner CD-ROM

See the ***One-Stop Planner*** for a complete list of additional resources for students and teachers.

One-Stop Planner CD-ROM

It's easy to plan lessons, select resources, and print out materials for your students when you use the *One-Stop Planner* CD–ROM with *Test Generator.*

Technology Resources	Reinforcement, Review, and Assessment
One-Stop Planner 23.1 Holt Researcher: World History: Thomas Edison CNN Presents World Cultures: Yesterday and Today: Segment 21: Endangered Edison Homework Practice Online	Daily Quiz 23.1 Main Idea Activity 23.1 English Audio Summary 23.1 Spanish Audio Summary 23.1 REV Section 1 Review, p. 575
One-Stop Planner 23.2 Holt Researcher: World History: Louis Pasteur Holt Researcher: World History: Marie Curie, Albert Einstein Homework Practice Online	Daily Quiz 23.2 Main Idea Activity 23.2 English Audio Summary 23.2 Spanish Audio Summary 23.2 REV Section 2 Review, p. 582
One-Stop Planner 23.3 Homework Practice Online Online Maps, Charts, and Graphs: Growth of London, 1600–1900	Daily Quiz 23.3 Main Idea Activity 23.3 English Audio Summary 23.3 Spanish Audio Summary 23.3 REV Section 3 Review, p. 585
One-Stop Planner 23.4 Holt Researcher: World History: Jane Addams, Emily Davis Homework Practice Online	Daily Quiz 23.4 Main Idea Activity 23.4 English Audio Summary 23.4 Spanish Audio Summary 23.4 REV Section 4 Review, p. 591
One-Stop Planner 23.5 Homework Practice Online	Daily Quiz 23.5 Main Idea Activity 23.5 English Audio Summary 23.5 Spanish Audio Summary 23.5 REV Section 5 Review, p. 597

internet connect

HRW ONLINE RESOURCES

GO TO: go.hrw.com
Then type in a keyword.

TEACHER HOME PAGE
KEYWORD: SP3 Teacher

CHAPTER INTERNET ACTIVITIES
KEYWORD: SA3 WF23
Choose an activity to:
- explore Thomas Edison's inventions.
- research the immigrant experience in America during the nineteenth century.
- learn about contemporary women's colleges.

CHAPTER ENRICHMENT LINKS
KEYWORD: SP3 CH23

ONLINE ASSESSMENT
Homework Practice
KEYWORD: SP3 HP23
Standardized Test Prep
KEYWORD: SP3 STP23
Rubrics
KEYWORD: SS Rubrics

ONLINE MAPS, CHARTS, AND GRAPHS
KEYWORD: SP3 MCG

CONTENT UPDATES
KEYWORD: SS Content Updates

HOLT PRESENTATION MAKER
KEYWORD: SP3 PPT23

ONLINE READING SUPPORT
KEYWORD: SS Strategies

CURRENT EVENTS
KEYWORD: S3 Current Events

Meeting Individual Needs

Ability Levels

Level 1 Basic level activities designed for all students encountering new material

Level 2 Intermediate level activities designed for average students

Level 3 Challenging activities designed for honors and gifted and talented students

English Language Learners These activities address the needs of students with Limited English Proficiency.

Chapter Review and Assessment

IC Vocabulary Activity 23
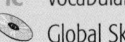 Global Skill Builder CD-ROM
HRW Web Site
REV Chapter 23 Tutorial for Students, Parents, Mentors, and Peers
REV Chapter 23 Review, pp. 598–599
A Chapter 23 Test Generator (on the One-Stop Planner)
A Chapter 23 Test (Form A or B)
A Alternative Assessment Handbook
A Chapter 23 Test for English Language Learners and Special-Needs Students

Build on What You Know

Ask students to answer the following questions:

What were some important advances made during the Industrial Revolution?

Consider:

- inventions
- scientific advances

How did society change during the Industrial Revolution?

Consider:

- the factory system
- the middle class
- the lives of women

EXPLORING THE TIME LINE

GLOBAL EVENTS

internet connect

TOPIC: Anesthesia
GO TO: go.hrw.com
KEYWORD: SP3 WH23

Ask students to access the Internet through the HRW Go site to conduct research on the introduction of anesthesia to surgery. Have them imagine they were one of the doctors in the surgical theatre on the day ether was demonstrated as an anesthesia for the first time. Each should write a letter to a colleague describing the event and the changes its arrival will bring for patients undergoing surgery. Be sure to mention William T. G. Morton, the dentist who did the demonstration.

CHAPTER 23

1800–1928

Life in the Industrial Age

Charles Darwin

1803
Science and Technology
John Dalton outlines a method of "weighing" atoms.

1805
Politics
Thomas Jefferson begins his second term as U.S. president.

1817
Daily Life
Construction begins on the Erie Canal in Buffalo, N.Y.

1831
Science and Technology
Michael Faraday produces an electric current in wire.

1835
Science and Technology
Halley's Comet reappears.

1859
Science and Technology
Charles Darwin publishes *On the Origin of Species by Means of Natural Selection.*

1800	1820	1840	1860

1808
Business and Finance
Captain S. Brown of the British Royal Navy receives a patent for a design of iron anchor chains.

1819
The Arts
Ludwig van Beethoven goes deaf but continues to compose.

1830
Daily Life
Ladies' skirts get shorter, sleeves become wider, hats are very large.

1845
Politics
Texas and Florida become states.

1842
Global Events
Riots and strikes occur in industrial areas of northern England.

1841
Daily Life
P.T. Barnum opens his "American Museum" to exhibit curiosities.

1865
Daily Life
George Pullman introduces the first railroad sleeping cars.

1865
Business and Finance
Thaddeus Lowe invents an ice machine.

1865
The Arts
Yale University opens the first Department of Fine Arts.

Circus producer P. T. Barnum (left) is shown here with Charles Stratton, who became known as Tom Thumb.

Build on What You Know

The Industrial Revolution's effects did not begin and end with inventions. Advances in technology led to new advances in all sciences. New sources of power fueled factories and forever changed the way we live and how we communicate. Cities grew as people from all over the world flocked to the thriving new centers of industry. The world of ideas also moved into the modern age as artists and writers wrestled with the ever-changing industrialized society. In this chapter, you will learn how lifestyles and living standards changed as a result of the Industrial Revolution.

What's Your Opinion?

Citizenship

Agree Equal education creates equality among all people in a society.

Disagree To achieve equality, there must also be equal access to healthcare, employment, and government office for everyone in a society.

Science, Technology & Society

Agree The sciences advance in isolation from one another; a discovery in physics has little or no impact on the field of chemistry.

Disagree Advances in one area of the sciences often have a significant impact on many other scientific fields.

Culture

Agree Artistic expression often reflects larger social, political, and economic trends.

Disagree Artists typically create in isolation from other elements of society.

Wilbur Wright pilots a glider in 1902.

1874
The Arts
The first impressionist exhibition takes place in Paris.

1875
Politics
The Public Health Act is passed in Britain.

1876
Science and Technology
Alexander Graham Bell patents the telephone.

1876
The Arts
Mark Twain publishes *The Adventures of Tom Sawyer*.

1893
Daily Life
Americans build the first successful gasoline-powered automobile.

1903
Daily Life
First World Series of baseball is held with more than 100,000 fans in attendance.

1928
Science and Technology
Alexander Fleming discovers penicillin.

1870   **1890**   **1910**   **1930**

1888
Business and Finance
George Eastman markets a box camera.

1879
Science and Technology
American inventor Thomas Edison produces an electric light bulb that burns for two days.

1905
Science and Technology
Albert Einstein develops the special theory of relativity.

1903
Science and Technology
The Wright Brothers make the first successful airplane flight.

1902
Daily Life
Coal strikes occur in the United States.

c. 1900
The Arts
Ragtime jazz develops in the United States.

The electric light bulb invented by Thomas Edison

1910 Chicago White Sox baseball card

What's Your Opinion?

Citizenship Equality of education is all that is necessary to make people within a society equal.

Science, Technology & Society Advances in one area of the sciences do not affect other fields of study.

Culture Changes in the arts reflect what is happening in society.

OBJECTIVES

1 **Examine how the development of electricity led to other technological advances.**

2 **Identify the inventions that improved communications.**

3 **Analyze the importance of the internal combustion engine.**

SECTION 1

READ TO DISCOVER

❶ How did the development of electricity lead to other technological advances?

❷ What inventions improved communications?

❸ What was the importance of the internal combustion engine?

DEFINE

dynamo
aerodynamics

IDENTIFY

Michael Faraday
Thomas Edison
Alexander Graham Bell
Guglielmo Marconi
Wilbur and Orville Wright

▶ WHY IT MATTERS TODAY

Petroleum provides power for the machines that we use every day. However, petroleum is a non-renewable resource. Use **CNN** or other **current event** sources to investigate renewable resources that could someday replace petroleum. Record your findings in your journal.

CNN student News.com

Advances in Technology and Communication

The Main Idea
Significant inventions in communications and technology followed the first wave of the Industrial Revolution.

The Story Continues *"The telephone is a curious device that might fairly find place in the magic of Arabian Tales. Of what use is such an invention?"* This was one newspaper reporter's reaction to the invention of the telephone in 1876. Although some inventions of the Industrial Revolution seemed odd at first, they soon had a great effect on how people lived, worked, and thought.

Electricity

Beginning in the early 1800s, manufacturers increasingly applied the findings of science to their businesses, thus generating new industrial growth. The application of scientific solutions to industrial problems had three main results. First, it encouraged the development and use of new sources of power. This was necessary for industry to grow. Second, it gave rise to inventions that could provide rapid communication over long distances. Finally, it led to the creation of new products and materials and the improvement of old ones.

Development of electricity. As industry grew during the 1800s, manufacturers continued to search for new and better sources of power. In the 1870s a tremendous new power source—electricity—was developed.

The English scientist **Michael Faraday** made key discoveries about electricity in the 1820s and 1830s. Faraday concentrated mainly on exploring the nature of electricity. Before Faraday, many scientists had believed that electricity was a sort of fluid that flowed through wires like water through a pipe. Faraday rejected this traditional view and argued that electricity was a form of force or vibration that passed from one particle of matter to another.

From the work of André Ampère and other scientists, Faraday already knew that electricity could produce magnetism. However, Faraday wanted to find out whether magnetism could produce electricity. He discovered that by moving a magnet through a coil of wire, he could generate an electric current in the wire. Using this research Faraday developed the first **dynamo,** or electric generator. This was the direct ancestor of all electric motors. Driven either by a steam engine or by waterpower, the dynamo transformed mechanical power into electrical energy. In turn, this energy could generate power to run machines in factories. By the late 1800s, other inventors had found ways to use electricity as a new power source for industry and even to light up whole cities.

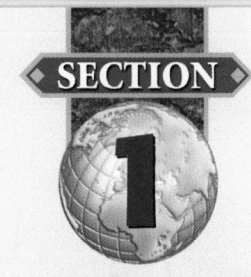

All electric generators and transformers work on the principle of Faraday's dynamo, shown here.

TEACH OBJECTIVE 1

LEVEL 1: Ask students what important scientific discovery Michael Faraday made in the early 1800s. *(He found that magnetism could be used to generate electricity.)* Then ask students to briefly chronicle the sequence of events that followed in the history of electricity. Close by asking students what this sequence of events shows about the discovery of new power sources. *(Just one new source of power can lead to many important developments.)* **ENGLISH LANGUAGE LEARNERS**

HOMEWORK Have students create an annotated time line showing the technological advances they learn about in this section.

| Other scientists developed the dynamo |
| ↓ |
| Edison invented a practical light bulb and the electrical powerhouse and transmission system |
| ↓ |
| Electric lighting replaced other methods of illumination |
| ↓ |
| Hydroelectric power was used |
| ↓ |
| Electric motors replaced steam engines in factories |

Edison and the light bulb. British and American inventors worked on developing another practical use of electricity. They knew that an electric current passing through certain kinds of wire made the wire glow. This could be a new source of light for streets, homes, and factories. Electric light bulbs were first produced in the 1840s, but they burned out in a matter of minutes. In 1879 American inventor **Thomas Edison** created a bulb that glowed for two days before burning out. As it improved over the next few decades, electric lighting came to replace other sources of illumination.

To make electricity practical, it had to be transmitted efficiently from where it was generated to where it would be used. Edison developed a system for successfully transmitting electricity from a central powerhouse. In 1882 this transmission system was put into use in New York City and London. Other places soon followed.

The electrical industry quickly grew. Waterfalls were used to power huge dynamos. This water-generated power, called hydroelectric power, was sent long distances through wires. Dams were built in many countries to provide artificial sources of waterpower. In the late 1800s large-scale production and transmission of electricity became a reality. Electric motors replaced steam engines in factories. Steam engines were likely used only in those places where hydroelectric power was unavailable or too expensive.

✔ **READING CHECK: Problem Solving** How were Thomas Edison's light bulbs an improvement over the ones that came before? *glowed longer*

Holt Researcher
go.hrw.com
KEYWORD: Holt Researcher
FreeFind: Thomas Edison
After reading more about Thomas Edison on the Holt Researcher, write a paragraph identifying which of his inventions you think was most important and explain why.

internet connect
TOPIC: Thomas Edison
GO TO: go.hrw.com
KEYWORD: SP3 WH23
Remind students that Thomas Edison's many inventions had an enormous effect on people's daily lives. Have students access the Internet through the HRW Go site to find information about these inventions. Ask students to list what they consider to be Edison's five most important inventions in ranking order. Then ask them to complete the explore activity to learn more about these inventions.

MAP ANSWERS
1. Regions include West Coast, Northwest, and East.

2. It probably caused economic growth.

The Spread of Electricity in the United States
Interpreting Maps During the 1920s annual electrical production in the United States rose dramatically until, by 1930, more than two thirds of American homes had electricity. An abundant supply of energy as well as a large network of power plants led to this expansion.
■ **Skills Assessment: 1. The World in Spatial Terms** Which regions of the United States were among the earliest to receive electrical lines? **2. Human Systems** How do you think this probably affected the economies of those regions?

TEACH OBJECTIVE 2

LEVEL 3: Ask students what advances were made in the field of communications in the late 1800s. (*the development of the telephone and wireless telegraph*) Then ask students to imagine they are average Americans who are witnessing one of these developments being used for the first time. How do they regard it? How will it affect their lives? What do they think such a development might foreshadow for the future? Then have students write a letter in which they describe the development and their thoughts about it.
ENGLISH LANGUAGE LEARNERS

TEACH OBJECTIVE 3

ALL LEVELS: Have students explain how the internal combustion engine differed from the electric motor and what inventions the internal combustion engine led to. Then have students create a before-and-after chart, describing changes that resulted from the invention of the internal combustion engine. (*Before: horse-drawn carriages and gas-filled balloons; After: gasoline-driven automobiles and airplanes*) **ENGLISH LANGUAGE LEARNERS**

Science, Technology & Society

In 1894 after studying the electromagnet wave technique at technical school, Marconi began experimenting at his father's estate near Bologna. His apparatus was crude: an induction coil for increasing voltages, a spark discharger controlled by a Morse key at the sending end, and a simple coherer (a device for detecting radio waves). He discovered that signaling was increased by using a vertical aerial with a metal plate at the top of a pole. Later, he used balloons and kites to obtain greater height for his aerials.

ACTIVITY: Have students work in small groups to develop explanations for the various equipment seen in the photograph of Marconi on page 574. You may choose to assign one group the task of investigating the devices and have them present their findings after other groups have presented their hypotheses.

Communications

The development of electrical power inspired other inventions. In the 1870s American inventor **Alexander Graham Bell** made an important advance in the field of communications. Bell transmitted the human voice over a long distance by means of an electrical circuit through a wire. Bell patented his telephone in 1876. Then in 1895 an Italian named **Guglielmo Marconi** developed a way to send messages through space without wires.

Marconi's invention was based on the work of two earlier scientists, James Clerk Maxwell of Great Britain and Heinrich Rudolph Hertz of Germany. Maxwell had made a mathematical study of electricity and magnetism. In 1873 he asserted the existence of invisible electromagnetic waves that travel through space at the speed of light. In the 1880s Hertz proved the existence of such waves by sending and receiving them. Hertz also measured the length and speed of the electromagnetic waves.

Marconi invented instruments for sending and receiving these radio waves, as they came to be called. His wireless telegraph became very important for ship-to-ship and ship-to-shore communication. In 1901 Marconi sent the first wireless message across the Atlantic ocean. This is how he later described the event:

> **Analyzing Primary Sources**
>
> **Finding the Main Idea** According to Marconi, in what way did this wireless transmission represent more than just a successful experiment? made him certain that wireless messages would be sent anywhere on Earth

 History Makers Speak

❝Shortly before mid-day I placed the single earphone to my ear and started listening.... The answer came at 12:30 when I heard, faintly but distinctly, pip-pip-pip.... The result meant much more to me than the mere successful realization of an experiment.... I now felt for the first time absolutely certain that the day would come when mankind would be able to send messages without wires not only across the Atlantic but between the farthermost ends of the earth.❞

Guglielmo Marconi, from *Scrapbook 1900–1941*

✔ **READING CHECK: Drawing Conclusions** How did Marconi's method of communication build on that of Alexander Graham Bell? Bell used wires to transmit messages; Marconi used electromagnetic waves to transmit messages without wires.

Italian electrical engineer and inventor Guglielmo Marconi is shown here in 1896 with his wireless telegraph machine.

The Internal Combustion Engine

Electricity was not the only type of power that became important in the 1800s. The electric motor, although useful, was limited because it had to remain connected to its power supply. This made electric motors impractical for moving vehicles.

Automobiles. In the late 1800s several European inventors developed engines that carried their own supply of oil or gasoline to power a vehicle. These devices were called internal combustion engines because the combustion, or burning, of fuel took place inside a closed cylinder. Thus they differed from the steam engine, in which combustion takes place outside the cylinder. Pioneers in this field included Gottlieb Daimler and Karl Benz of Germany and Etienne Lenoir of France. In 1893 Charles and Frank Duryea built the first successful gasoline-driven automobile in the United States. Fifteen years later American inventor Henry Ford produced his first commercially successful automobile, the Model T.

Airplanes. Since the 1700s people had been using balloons filled with gases lighter than air to float above the ground. Beginning in the 1800s, inventors tried to create a heavier-than-air machine that would actually fly. The first people to achieve a sustained, controlled flight in a powered airplane were **Wilbur and Orville Wright.** Their historic flight took place in Kitty Hawk, North Carolina, in 1903.

The Wright brothers succeeded by combining science with technology. They had studied **aerodynamics**—the scientific principles governing the movement of air around objects. They then used the technology of the internal combustion engine to propel their plane through the air.

✔ **READING CHECK: Contrasting** How was the internal combustion engine different than engines that came before it?
carried its own power source; combustion of fuel took place inside a closed cylinder

Petroleum represented a new industry in the 1870s, when John D. Rockefeller organized the Standard Oil Company. It quickly became an essential element of American and worldwide industrialization.

CONNECTING TO Science and Technology

Petroleum and the Industrial Age

Petroleum—that is, crude oil—and its products have been in use for thousands of years. Ancient Egyptians occasionally used pitch, a thick, sticky form of oil, as a coating for mummies. The Babylonians used pitch to build walls and pave streets.

During the 1800s the kerosene lamp and the internal combustion engine created a great demand for petroleum. Today petroleum powers cars, airplanes, and ships. It generates heat and electricity. Petroleum products include detergents, plastics, cosmetics, and fabrics.

Understanding Science and Technology

In what ways did new technologies create a demand for petroleum?

SECTION 1 REVIEW

1. **Define** and explain the significance:
   dynamo
   aerodynamics

2. **Identify** and explain the significance:
   Michael Faraday
   Thomas Edison
   Alexander Graham Bell
   Guglielmo Marconi
   Wilbur and Orville Wright

3. **Sequencing** Copy the diagram below. Use it to identify the pioneers of the internal combustion engine and the inventors who built on their work.

   | Daimler, Benz, Lenoir |
   | Internal combustion engine |

   | Ford | Wright Brothers |
   | Automobile | Airplane |

4. **Finding the Main Idea**
   a. In what way did Faraday further the development of electrical power?
   b. In what ways were Bell's and Marconi's inventions similar and different?
   c. How do new sources of power assist in the development of inventions?

5. **Writing and Critical Thinking**

   Making Predictions Write an editorial about possible uses of the telephone and wireless telegraph from the point of view of someone living at the time these inventions were new.
   Consider:
   • how the telephone allowed the human voice to be transmitted
   • how communication changed because of the wireless telegraph

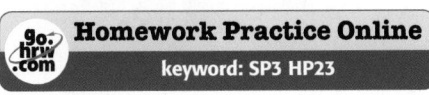

Homework Practice Online
keyword: SP3 HP23

LIFE IN THE INDUSTRIAL AGE **575**

SECTION 2

OBJECTIVES

1 Explain how cell theory changed over time.

2 Investigate why Darwin's theory was so significant and controversial.

3 Describe how scientific discoveries changed the nature of medicine and surgery.

4 Identify the advances made in the field of physics.

SECTION 2 RESOURCES

REPRODUCIBLE RESOURCES

▶ Guided Reading Strategy 23.2

▶ Readings in World History 78: Two Testimonials for Albert Einstein

▶ Readings in World History 79: Edward Jenner's Case Studies

TECHNOLOGY RESOURCES

▶ One-Stop Planner 23.2

▶ Holt Researcher: World History: Louis Pasteur

▶ Holt Researcher: World History: Marie Curie, Albert Einstein

▶ Homework Practice Online

REINFORCEMENT, REVIEW, AND ASSESSMENT

▶ Section 2 Review, p. 582

▶ Daily Quiz 23.2

▶ Main Idea Activity 23.2

▶ English Audio Summary 23.2

▶ Spanish Audio Summary 23.2

SECTION 2

READ TO DISCOVER

❶ How did cell theory change over time?

❷ Why was Darwin's theory so significant and controversial?

❸ How did scientific discoveries change the nature of medicine and surgery?

❹ What advances were made in the field of physics?

DEFINE

biological sciences
physical sciences
evolution
genetics
pasteurization
antisepsis
radioactivity
quantum theory
special theory of relativity

IDENTIFY

Charles Darwin
Louis Pasteur
Alexander Fleming
Dmitry Mendeleyev
Wilhelm C. Röntgen
Pierre and Marie Curie
Max Planck
Albert Einstein

▶WHY IT MATTERS TODAY

Many advances in the biological and physical sciences were made in the late 1800s and early 1900s. Use CNN.com or other **current event** sources to investigate what current research is happening in these sciences today. Record your findings in your journal.

CNN Student News.com

Advances in Science and Medicine

The Main Idea
During the Industrial Age advances were made in the biological, physical, and medical sciences.

The Story Continues *"Einstein is one of the most original thinkers I have ever met. . . . He does not remain attached to classical principles, and when presented with a problem in physics he quickly envisages [imagines] all its possibilities. . . . This is exactly how one should proceed."* This is how a colleague described the work of physicist Albert Einstein. In the 1800s and early 1900s, Einstein was just one of many innovative thinkers exploring new frontiers in science and medicine.

Cell Theory in Biology

The **biological sciences,** such as biology and genetics, deal with living organisms. The **physical sciences** are concerned with the properties of nonliving matter and of energy. Physical sciences include astronomy, geology, physics, and chemistry. During the 1800s and early 1900s, scientists made great strides in both of these branches of science, as well as in medicine.

Scientists of the 1800s were as interested in explaining the nature of life as they were in exploring the nature of nonliving matter. Biologists had long been familiar with the idea of cells, tiny units of living matter. Scientists in the 1600s examined living matter under their microscopes and saw what we now know to be plant and animal cells. Those early observers noticed that the cells of different species are of different shapes and sizes. However, they did not fully understand what they saw and did not draw any general conclusions about cells. It was not until 1838 that German botanist Mathias Schleiden and biologist Theodor Swann clearly expressed cell theory. They stated that all living things are made up of these tiny units of living matter. They also discovered that all cells divide and multiply, causing organisms to grow and mature.

In the 1850s the work of German scientist Rudolf Virchow expanded cell theory. Virchow showed that disease in living organisms came about when cells were changed or destroyed by some outside force. From his study of cells, Virchow also came to the important conclusion that every new cell must come from some older cell. Therefore only living matter can produce new living matter. Thus, by the late 1800s, scientists generally accepted the cell as the basic unit of living matter.

✔ **READING CHECK: Analyzing Information** What had scientists before Virchow noticed about cells? cell sizes and shapes varied for different species

Scientists of the 1800s used microscopes like the one shown here to study cell structure.

LEVEL 3: Ask students to name the major theories and ideas proposed in the biological sciences in the 1800s. *(cell theory, theory of inheritance, theory of evolution, genetics)* Then have students create and complete a chart with their four answers as column headings. Students should use the following row headings: Who, When, Basic Outline of Theory, and How It Was Received. *(cell theory: Rudolf Virchow; 1850s; cell is the basic unit of living matter; by late 1800s, scientists generally accepted theory; theory of inheritance: Jean-Baptiste Lamarack; early 1800s; living things changed their form in response to their environment; theory was disproven; theory of evolution: Charles Darwin; mid-1800s; creatures that are best adapted to their envi-* ronments will survive to reproduce and pass on their advantageous traits to their offspring; theory was controversial because it stated that human beings developed from other animals and it contradicted the Bible; genetics: Gregor Mendel; mid- to late 1800s; inborn characteristics are inherited as if they were separate particles; other scientists did not learn about genetics until later.) After charts are completed, ask students which two theories are most closely related. *(theory of inheritance and theory of evolution).*

Evolution and Genetics

Cell theory did not explain the rich variety of plants and animals on Earth. The religious beliefs of many cultures hold that a divine being or beings created all things on Earth. One group of scientists, however, argued that modern plants and animals had evolved, or developed, from common ancestors long ago. This kind of development through change is called **evolution.**

Lamarck's theory of inheritance. In the early 1800s French biologist Jean-Baptiste Lamarck suggested that living things changed their form in response to their environment. For example, giraffes developed long necks because they always had to stretch to eat leaves high up in trees. Such changes were then passed on by inheritance to descendants. Other characteristics might gradually disappear if they were never used. Lamarck thought that these kinds of changes, over millions of years, could have produced present-day plants and animals. Most of Lamarck's ideas were later proved wrong and did not become a part of modern biology. However, Lamarck did influence other scientists, including a British naturalist named **Charles Darwin.**

Darwin's theory of evolution. By 1859 Darwin had spent 30 years studying plant and animal life. He published his theory of evolution in a book called *On the Origin of Species by Means of Natural Selection.*

Darwin began with a well-known biological fact: no two living things are exactly alike, not even a parent and its offspring. Darwin combined this fact with the idea that as a result of natural dangers and limits, there were always more creatures born than could survive. Those who survive will, in general, be those whose characteristics are best adapted to their environment. This idea is known as survival of the fittest, or natural selection. The strongest survivors will live to produce offspring, who will tend to possess the same advantages as their parents. These offspring can in turn pass successful characteristics on to a new generation. In this way, Darwin thought, one could explain the evolution of all forms of life from earlier forms.

Darwin's theory inspired a great deal of activity as scientists worked to either prove or disprove it. Some looked for evidence in fossils as well as living organisms. The theory of natural selection was controversial, however, for two reasons. First, it stated that human beings developed from animals. This idea offended some people. Also, many people thought that Darwin's theory contradicted the story of creation told in the Bible. However, Darwin felt that the theory of evolution did not necessarily challenge the existence of God.

> **History Makers Speak**
>
> **❝There is grandeur in this view of life . . . having been originally breathed by the Creator into a few forms or into one; and that . . . from so simple a beginning endless forms most beautiful and most wonderful have been, and are being evolved.❞**
>
> Charles Darwin, *On the Origin of Species by Means of Natural Selection*

Genetics. Darwin's theory left an important question unanswered: why were offspring not exactly like their parents? Unknown to Darwin, an Austrian monk named Gregor Mendel had been gathering evidence that would answer this question. Mendel founded **genetics**—the study of how the inborn characteristics of plants and animals are inherited by their descendants. Mendel did much of his research in the 1850s and 1860s, working with plants. He mated tall plants with short ones. Instead of producing

THE ORIGIN OF SPECIES

BY MEANS OF NATURAL SELECTION,

OR THE

PRESERVATION OF FAVOURED RACES IN THE STRUGGLE FOR LIFE.

By CHARLES DARWIN, M.A.,

FELLOW OF THE ROYAL, GEOLOGICAL, LINNEAN, ETC., SOCIETIES;
AUTHOR OF 'JOURNAL OF RESEARCHES DURING H. M. S. BEAGLE'S VOYAGE
ROUND THE WORLD.'

LONDON:
JOHN MURRAY, ALBEMARLE STREET.
1859.

The right of Translation is reserved.

Charles Darwin gathered most of the material for his theory of evolution during a five-year expedition off the coast of South America and in the Pacific Islands. Upon his return to England, he spent 20 years writing his theory. Shown here is the book's title page.

Science, Technology & Society

Darwin collected a large number of animal specimens on the Galapagos Islands, a group of islands off the coast of Ecuador. After analyzing the specimens back in England, he realized that several Galapagos birds, which he had first thought to be totally different kinds of birds, were actually closely related species of finches. The beaks of the different birds varied greatly in size and shape. Darwin realized the beaks were specialized according to what the birds ate. For example, the ground finch, with its strong, crushing beak, eats large seeds; the warbler finch has a small, pointed beak and eats small insects.

Critical Thinking

Ask students what explanation they might pose for the difference in the shapes and sizes of the beaks.

ANSWER: Students should suggest that, originally, slight beak variations within the same species might have helped finches obtain different types of food. Through natural selection, those birds whose beaks helped them survive produced offspring that possessed the beak variations of their parents. Over many generations, the variations became greater and the different types of finches became more specialized.

TEACH OBJECTIVES 1 and 2

LEVEL 2: Ask students to compare and contrast the theory of inheritance and the theory of evolution. *(The theory of inheritance stated that living forms changed in response to their environment, but the theory of evolution stated that creatures were born with different characteristics and those that were best adapted to their environment survived to reproduce offspring that shared their characteristics.)*

Linking Past to Present

The study of genetics has come a long way since the days of Mendel. Because of genetic engineering, Australian sheep grow more wool, Scottish ewes produce a chemical in their milk that makes human blood clot, and Dutch cattle have extra proteins so they can better fight infection. Genetic engineering has raised many debates, however, particularly as genetic engineers continue their work on cloning. In 1997 a scientist cloned the first sheep, and the following year scientists announced that they had cloned multiple generations of mice.

Critical Thinking

Ask students why they think the idea of cloning humans is so controversial in the United States today.

ANSWER: Students might answer that some people worry that such technology might be abused.

THEN & NOW ANSWER
It was a time of great scientific and technological advances.

Science Fiction

The spirit of discovery of the scientific and industrial ages was reflected in a type of literature that we today call science fiction.

Stories similar to today's science fiction were popular in the 1700s and 1800s. The French philosopher Voltaire imagined a visit to Earth by a native of the star Sirius. Mary Shelley imagined a medical student named Victor Frankenstein, who created a living monster out of dead bodies. In the late 1800s French writer Jules Verne wrote about incredible journeys by balloon, rocket, and submarine. British novelist H. G. Wells wrote tales of time machines, invisible men, and invaders from Mars. **Why did science fiction grow during the scientific and industrial ages?**

medium-sized plants, this combination produced tall plants. Then Mendel fertilized these tall offspring with their own pollen. To his surprise, this produced a new mixed generation of tall and short plants.

From his experiments, Mendel concluded that inborn characteristics, or traits, were not necessarily blended or mixed together. Instead, he believed, they were all inherited as if they were separate particles. In some cases a trait could be carried but not expressed. For example, tall plants could carry and pass on to the next generation the particles that would cause shortness.

✔ **READING CHECK: Finding the Main Idea** How did the theory of evolution change science? explained the rich variety of living things

The Fight Against Disease

During the Industrial Age remarkable breakthroughs in medicine helped to prolong human life. Until the late 1800s as many as 50 percent of all people born died within the first five years after birth. Disease likely killed more people than did wars, famines, or natural disasters. Little was known about the causes of disease. Scientists had seen bacteria under the microscope as early as the 1600s but did not connect them with disease.

The smallpox vaccine. Smallpox was one of the deadliest diseases of the time. It often swept through cities in epidemics. English physician Edward Jenner investigated smallpox in the late 1700s in hopes of finding a way to prevent it. He learned that milkmaids who had once had cowpox—a disease similar to smallpox but milder—did not get smallpox even when there was an epidemic. After years of experimenting, Jenner developed a safe way to prevent smallpox. In 1796 Jenner made a vaccine from the fluid in cowpox sores and scratched it into a boy's arm. The boy developed a mild case of cowpox but quickly recovered. When the boy was later exposed to smallpox, he did not contract the disease.

Still from War of the Worlds, *a movie based on a story from H.G. Wells*

Illustration for Jules Verne's A Trip from the Earth to the Moon, *1865*

TEACH OBJECTIVE 3

LEVEL 1: Create the following chart on the chalkboard and have students fill in information about the major medical advances of the 1800s, what triggered these advances, and the effects they had on society.

Major Medical Advance	What Triggered the Advance	Effect on Society
Edward Jenner developed a vaccine for smallpox.	Jenner learned that people who had once had cowpox, a disease similar to smallpox, did not contract smallpox.	Fewer people contracted and died of smallpox.

ENGLISH LANGUAGE LEARNERS

Bacteria and germs. Although Jenner had developed a vaccine for preventing smallpox, he did not know why it worked. Later, French chemist **Louis Pasteur** discovered the scientific principle at work. Pasteur identified microorganisms called bacteria. His experiments showed that bacteria reproduce like other living things. They can travel from place to place in the air or on peoples' hands.

Pasteur also discovered that bacteria cause fermentation—the process that turns grape juice into wine and makes milk go sour. In the 1860s Pasteur developed a process of heating liquids to kill bacteria and prevent fermentation. This process was named **pasteurization** in his honor. Pasteur also discovered that some bacteria cause illness in animals and humans. These harmful bacteria are called germs or microbes.

In 1881 Pasteur experimented with the germ that causes anthrax, a disease that can kill animals and humans. He made a vaccine that contained weakened anthrax germs and injected it into animals. The vaccine prevented the animals from catching anthrax. Pasteur determined that when weakened germs enter the body, the system builds up substances called antibodies to fight them. These antibodies remain in the body and can then defend against the more deadly germs. Thus Pasteur showed why Jenner's vaccine had worked. Pasteur used this same technique to fight rabies, a fatal disease that humans can catch from dogs or other infected animals.

✔ **READING CHECK: Identifying Cause and Effect** How did Jenner's vaccine work?
used weakened germs to encourage growth of antibodies that could defend against more deadly germs

Advances in Surgery and Other Areas

Through the centuries, surgery had always been a last resort. It was always painful and often fatal. Surgeons usually performed only operations that could be completed in a few minutes, such as tooth extractions and limb amputations. Sometimes more complicated procedures were attempted. During many surgical operations patients had to be held down or have their senses dulled with liquor or opium.

The development of surgery. In the 1840s it was discovered that ether and chloroform could cause unconsciousness and eliminate pain. These anesthetics made longer operations possible. Even after anesthetics came into use, however, people still frequently died from infections soon after an operation. Pasteur's discoveries about germs helped here too. Joseph Lister, an English surgeon, studied Pasteur's findings. Lister developed **antisepsis**—the use of chemicals to kill disease-causing germs. The use of such chemicals, called antiseptics, helped to reduce infections in surgery, childbirth, and the treatment of battle wounds.

Other medical advances. The work of German physician Robert Koch further confirmed Pasteur's findings. He found the germs that cause tuberculosis and cholera. He developed sanitary measures, such as water filtration, to prevent disease.

Holt Researcher

go.hrw.com
KEYWORD: Holt Researcher
FreeFind: Louis Pasteur
After reading more about Louis Pasteur on the Holt Researcher, create a cause-and-effect chart showing how Pasteur's discoveries have affected life in the United States today.

INTERPRETING THE VISUAL RECORD

Operations In the 1800s physicians began to use nitrous oxide, ether, and chloroform to deaden pain during surgery.

Link to Today How does this image differ from operating rooms in the United States today?

Daily Life

Smallpox has had a universal impact on civilization since before recorded history. It affected all ages and socioeconomic classes, bringing down at least three empires. During the 1700s four European monarchs died of the disease. In the late 1700s in Europe, about 400,000 people died of smallpox each year. In 1796 Edward Jenner developed a vaccine effective against smallpox.

Critical Thinking

Ask students to predict how society might be different if the smallpox vaccine and vaccines effective against other diseases had been available earlier.

ANSWER: Answers will vary, but students might suggest the population would have begun to grow earlier and fewer people would have been affected by various diseases.

LINK TO TODAY ANSWER
Today operating rooms are much more sterile; doctors would be wearing medical smocks, gloves, and masks.

Read to the class the following description of Civil War conditions: "Few medical men then knew why wounds became infected or what causes disease; the treatment of wounds and disease, consequently, ranged from the inadequate through the useless to the downright harmful.... The idea that a surgical dressing ought to be sterilized never entered anyone's head.... If a surgeon's instruments were so much as rinsed off between operations at a field hospital, the case was an exception. In a camp, diseases like typhoid, dysentery, and pneumonia were dreaded killers." Then lead the class in a discussion about the ways that medicine has improved since then and how doctors have been able to put a stop to once-fatal diseases.

Science, Technology & Society

In the 1990s historians revealed that they had learned from Pasteur's notebooks that the scientist had committed several misdeeds. He "borrowed" a technique from a competitor who was also working on an anthrax vaccine; he lied in his published paper about the kind of vaccine he used in his anthrax experiment; and he used his newly developed rabies vaccine on a human subject when it had not yet been tested on animals. Historians believe that Pasteur and other great scientists of his day, such as Michael Faraday, regularly violated scientific ethics.

Critical Thinking

Ask students if they think Pasteur should be criticized for his violations of scientific ethics.

ANSWER: Students might answer yes, because he should not have committed such misdeeds, or no, because the benefits of his discoveries are more important than these violations.

The discoveries of Pasteur, Lister, and Koch were the starting point for an international fight against disease. Now that scientists could identify the causes of illness, they could develop vaccines. For example, scientists were able to trace malaria and yellow fever to germs carried in mosquitoes and transmitted by their bites. So the battle against these diseases could now extend to the mosquitoes that carried them. Bubonic plague was found to be carried by fleas on rats. Rat-extermination programs brought this disease under control.

During this time scientists invented and tested many new medicines. Aspirin, which became available in the late 1800s, reduced pain and fever. Insulin, isolated in the 1920s, helped people with diabetes survive and lead more normal lives. Other medicines were developed to fight bacterial infections. **Alexander Fleming** of Great Britain discovered penicillin in 1928. Sulfa drugs were developed in Europe in the 1930s. However, neither penicillin nor sulfa drugs became widely available until about the 1940s.

✔ **READING CHECK: Drawing Conclusions** How did advances in medicine help to fight disease worldwide? helped scientists to identify causes of illness and to develop vaccines against them

The Atom and Its Structure

According to modern atomic theory, all matter in the universe is made up of very small particles called atoms. The various arrangement and structure of these atoms yields all the different materials that make up our world. The beginning of atomic theory can be traced back to ancient Greek philosophers such as Democritus. During the Scientific Revolution of the 1500s and 1600s atomic theory became widely accepted, although it had yet to be proven.

Atomic weight and the periodic table. An English chemist and schoolteacher named John Dalton was the first scientist to obtain convincing data about atoms. In 1803 Dalton designed a method for "weighing" atoms. First he studied the ratios of elements in different gases. As a starting point Dalton assigned the weight of "1" to the lightest gas, hydrogen. He then expressed the weights of all other known elements in relation to how much heavier they were than hydrogen. Dalton opened up paths for other scientists to explore. In 1869 the Russian chemist **Dmitry Mendeleyev** (men·duh·LAY·uhf) made the first workable classification of the elements. A modified version of Mendeleyev's periodic table is still used in chemistry today.

Modern atomic theory originated in the study of chemistry. However, it soon became a part of physics—the science

Dmitry Mendeleyev's classification of the elements—the periodic table—is engraved on a wall of the Mendeleyev Institute in St. Petersburg, Russia.

ALL LEVELS: Have students match up each of the scientists listed below with one of his or her findings in the second column.

(1-g, 2-c, 3-e, 4-b, 5-d, 6-a, 7-h, 8-f)
ENGLISH LANGUAGE LEARNERS

Column 1	Column 2
1. J.J. Thomson	a. developed the quantum theory
2. Dmitri Mendeleyev	b. concluded that no particles of matter move faster than the speed of light
3. Pierre and Marie Curie	c. produced the first periodic table
4. Albert Einstein	d. discovered X-rays
5. Wilhelm C. Röntgen	e. discovered the process of radioactivity
6. Max Planck	f. outlined a method for "weighing" atoms
7. Ernest Rutherford	g. discovered electrons
8. John Dalton	h. found that an atom's nucleus contained protons

HOMEWORK Assign each student to one of the following: biological sciences, medicine, and physical sciences. Then have each student create a list of the significant advancements made in their field along with a brief summary of why the advancement was important. Ask students to share their lists with the rest of the class, and invite the class to discuss and challenge others' explanations.

---

of matter and energy. Scientists came to explain their findings about heat and gases in terms of atoms in motion. In the 1800s scientists began to think of heat as the result of the motion of atomic particles. In a cold substance, such as ice, atoms move relatively slowly. In a hot substance, such as hot water, atoms move much faster, even colliding with one another. When water boils, its atoms move so fast that the water turns into a gas—steam, or water vapor.

Structure of the atom. In 1895 German physicist **Wilhelm C. Röntgen** (RENT·guhn) discovered a new form of ray. These rays could go through many substances, including human skin and tissue. The rays could also leave an impression on photographic paper. Because he did not know what caused this powerful penetrating radiation, Röntgen named the rays X-rays. These rays became widely used in medicine as a diagnostic tool. The existence of this radiation raised more questions about the physical world.

The English physicist J.J. Thomson further studied the nature of matter. In 1897 he discovered the electron—a tiny particle with a negative electrical charge. Thomson found that the electron was 1,000 times lighter than the smallest known atom. From this he concluded that all atoms contained electrons. Therefore subatomic particles—particles inside atoms—must be the true building blocks of all matter in the universe.

Most physicists gradually accepted the electron's existence. However, a French husband-and-wife chemist team, **Pierre and Marie Curie,** provided evidence that atoms were not as simple as earlier scientists had thought. The Curies experimented with the elements polonium and radium. They found that these elements constantly break down and release energy on their own. This process is called **radioactivity.** Elements that release energy in this way are called radioactive elements.

Based on the work done by Thomson and the Curies, Ernest Rutherford of Great Britain developed a new theory of the atom. Rutherford held that at the center of every atom lay a very small but very heavy core, called a nucleus. Electrons orbit around the nucleus. Rutherford then discovered that the nucleus is made up of positively-charged particles, which he called protons. After this, scientists no longer thought of the atom as a solid piece of matter. Later scientists also found a particle inside the nucleus, which they called the neutron. Many more subatomic particles were eventually discovered.

✔ **READING CHECK: Drawing Inferences** What do the discoveries about the structure of the atom imply about the scientific process? It is a building process in which discoveries proceed from earlier discoveries.

Planck and Einstein

Before 1900 many scientists believed that energy was a continuous substance and that it could be divided into any number of smaller units. In 1900 the German physicist **Max Planck** disproved this commonly held idea. Through his research Planck proved that energy could be released only in definite "packages." He called these units *quanta,* based on *quantum,* the Latin word meaning "how much." Planck's **quantum theory** formed the basis for a completely new approach to the study of matter and energy. However, even this groundbreaking theory was not Planck's only contribution to the field of physics. In another important work, he put forth the theory that light was a continuous wave-like phenomenon.

HISTORY MAKERS

Pierre Curie (1859–1906)
Marie Curie (1867–1934)

Pierre and Marie Curie headed one of the most famous families in modern science. Their work on radioactivity defined the field. In fact Marie Curie invented the term "radioactivity" in 1898. In 1903 the Curies shared the Nobel Prize in physics. In 1911 Marie won the Nobel Prize in chemistry.

The Curies' daughter, Irene, formed a similar partnership with her husband. In 1935 they shared the Nobel Prize in chemistry for their work on radioactive materials. **What contributions did Pierre and Marie Curie make to the history of modern science?**

Holt Researcher go hrw com

go.hrw.com
KEYWORD: Holt Researcher
FreeFind: Marie Curie
Albert Einstein
After reading more about Marie Curie and Albert Einstein on the Holt Researcher, explain how they contributed to the history of science in the 1900s.

That's Interesting!

Joseph Lister was undoubtedly influenced by the findings of Ignaz Semmelweis, a Hungarian doctor. In the 1850s Semmelweis reduced deaths from a certain type of fever in maternity wards in Vienna from 16 percent to 1 percent merely by insisting that surgeons wash their hands. Semmelweis, however, was driven out of the city by a jealous professor. Sent to an asylum, he died after a wound on his hand went untreated and became infected.

HISTORY MAKER ANSWER
radioactivity, physics, chemistry

CLOSE

Ask students to list Einstein's major contributions to physics.

REVIEW

Have students complete the Section 2 Review on p. 582.

ASSESS

Have students complete Daily Quiz 23.2. As Alternative Assessment, you may want to use the medical advances chart or the matching exercise in this section's lessons.

RETEACH

Have students complete Main Idea Activity for English Language Learners and Special-Needs Students 23.2. Then tell students to think about the achievements of the Industrial Age. Have students write down three important advances and describe why each was important. **ENGLISH LANGUAGE LEARNERS**

EXTEND

Have interested students conduct additional research into one aspect of the work of Albert Einstein, such as how it has been studied, received, and expanded upon by later scientists. Have students write a brief report. **BLOCK SCHEDULING**

SECTION 2 REVIEW ANSWERS

❶ Define
- biological sciences, p. 576
- physical sciences, p. 576
- evolution, p. 577
- genetics, p. 577
- pasteurization, p. 579
- antisepsis, p. 579
- radioactivity, p. 581
- quantum theory, p. 581
- special theory of relativity, p. 582

❷ Identify
- Charles Darwin, p. 577
- Louis Pasteur, p. 579
- Alexander Fleming, p. 580
- Dmitry Mendeleyev, p. 580
- Wilhelm C. Röntgen, p. 581
- Pierre and Marie Curie, p. 581
- Max Planck, p. 581
- Albert Einstein, p. 582

❸ Newton: length, breadth, depth; Einstein: length, breadth, depth, time

❹ a. showed that disease resulted when cells were changed by an outside force

b. Many scientists worked to either prove or disprove it.

c. developed pasteurization, identified germs, made advances in fighting anthrax and rabies

d. Many subatomic particles were discovered.

❺ Students' editorials will vary.

CONNECTING TO MATH ANSWER

equal sign shows relationship between mass and energy

CONNECTING TO Math

$E = mc^2$

One of the most famous mathematical equations in history, $E = mc^2$ means that a little bit of mass can be transformed into an enormous amount of energy. This idea laid the groundwork for the development of the atomic bomb. The bomb explodes when a tiny atom is split, releasing a great amount of energy. Einstein's research showed that such weapons were possible, but he refused to take part in the building of the bomb.

Understanding Math

How does $E = mc^2$ show that mass and energy can each be transformed into the other?

In 1905 **Albert Einstein,** a young German scientist, published four papers that forever changed physics. His first paper examined some of the basic concepts of mechanics and tried to prove the existence of atoms. In his second paper, Einstein built on Planck's theory to describe the nature of light. In his third paper, Einstein developed his **special theory of relativity.** He concluded that no particles of matter can move faster than the speed of light. Einstein also stated that motion can be measured only relative to some particular observer. According to Einstein's theory, then, it does not make sense to speak of absolute motion, space, or time.

In the fourth paper Einstein developed his famous equation $E = mc^2$. This equation expresses the relationship between energy and mass. According to the formula, energy (E) equals mass (m) multiplied by the speed of light squared (c^2). This means that mass can be transformed into energy, and energy into mass.

Einstein's theories overturned long-held ideas. Isaac Newton and other scientists of the past had thought of the universe in terms of three dimensions: length, breadth, and depth. Einstein's theory of relativity declared that all events occur not only in these three dimensions of space but also in a fourth dimension— time. Einstein called this four-dimensional system the space-time continuum. Einstein's theories, as well as Planck's, paved the way for much important work.

Albert Einstein joined the Institute for Advanced Study in Princeton, New Jersey, in 1933.

✔ **READING CHECK: Summarizing** What were Einstein's major contributions to physics? overturned long-held ideas, extended understanding of the physical universe by identifying the space-time continuum

---

SECTION 2 REVIEW

1. Define and explain the significance:
biological sciences	antisepsis
physical sciences	radioactivity
evolution	quantum theory
genetics	special theory of
pasteurization	relativity

2. Identify and explain the significance:
- Charles Darwin
- Louis Pasteur
- Alexander Fleming
- Dmitry Mendeleyev
- Wilhelm C. Röntgen
- Pierre and Marie Curie
- Max Planck
- Albert Einstein

3. Comparing and Contrasting Copy the diagram and use it to show the contrast between how Newton and Einstein thought about the universe.

The Physical Universe

Newton	Einstein
length	length
breadth	breadth
depth	depth
	time

4. Finding the Main Idea

a. In what way were Virchow's ideas about cells different than the ideas that had existed before?

b. Why did Darwin's theory inspire so much scientific activity?

c. In what ways do Pasteur's discoveries affect life today?

d. How did scientific theories about atoms change ideas about the universe?

5. Writing and Critical Thinking

Supporting a Point of View From the point of view of a doctor in the mid-1800s, write a newspaper editorial explaining why surgery at that time was safer than ever before.

Consider:
- what surgical procedures were like up until the 1800s
- the advances in surgery and medicine made during the 1800s

Homework Practice Online
keyword: SP3 HP23

LET'S GET STARTED!

As students enter the classroom, write the following quotations on the chalkboard: "[The job of history] is to show what actually happened.... The strict presentation of the facts...is undoubtedly the supreme law," (Leopold von Ranke); "History is nothing more than a tableau of crimes and misfortunes," (Voltaire); "The history of the world is but the biography of great men," (Carlyle). Ask students which of the statements they agree with and why. If they do not agree with any of the statements, challenge students to create their own definition of history. Tell students that in Section 3 they will learn that an interest in social sciences grew rapidly during the 1800s.

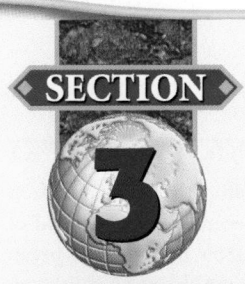 **SECTION 3**

Social Sciences in the Industrial Age

The Main Idea
Scientists studied human societies and the human mind in an effort to understand human behavior.

The Story Continues *"The decisive moment had arrived.... At first I could see nothing ... but ... as my eyes grew accustomed to the light, details of the room within emerged slowly from the mist, strange animals, statues, and gold—everywhere the glint of gold." This is how Howard Carter described his first glimpse of the tomb of King Tutankhamen in 1922. Carter's discovery was just one of the exciting events that brought new insight into human societies during the Industrial Age.*

READ TO DISCOVER

❶ How did science influence the study of politics, economics, and history?

❷ How did archaeology, anthropology, and sociology explore cultures?

❸ How did the study of the human mind develop?

DEFINE

social sciences
social Darwinism
psychoanalysis
psychiatry

IDENTIFY

E.B. Tylor
James George Frazer
Auguste Comte
Herbert Spencer
Ivan Pavlov
Sigmund Freud

▶ **WHY IT MATTERS TODAY**

Archaeology has always made use of new scientific methods to better explore and record the past. Use CNN Student News.com or other **current event** sources to investigate current archaeological finds and the techniques used to discover them. Record your findings in your journal.

SECTION 3 RESOURCES

REPRODUCIBLE RESOURCES

▶ Guided Reading Strategy 23.3

TECHNOLOGY RESOURCES

▶ One-Stop Planner 23.3
▶ Homework Practice Online
▶ Online Maps, Charts, and Graphs: Growth of London, 1600–1900

REINFORCEMENT, REVIEW, AND ASSESSMENT

▶ Section 3 Review, p. 585
▶ Daily Quiz 23.3
▶ Main Idea Activity 23.3
▶ English Audio Summary 23.3
▶ Spanish Audio Summary 23.3

Rise of the Social Sciences

During the 1800s interest in a new field of study, the **social sciences,** grew rapidly. The social sciences are those branches of knowledge that scientifically study people as members of society. The social sciences cover such topics as economics, history, political institutions, and human relations. The idea of making the study of these subjects objective and factual—of treating them like sciences—was new in the 1800s.

The study of politics dates back to the Greek philosophers Plato and Aristotle. Later it became a subject for thinkers like Machiavelli, Locke, and Rousseau. In the 1800s the study of politics became known as political science. Scholars attempted to study law and politics with the same scientific manner that physicists and biologists brought to their own fields of study.

Another social science, economics, had already been well developed in the work of Adam Smith and others. It was not until the late 1800s, however, that economists began to follow the practice of scientists by collecting and arranging statistics in order to test their theories.

The study of history, like political science, dates back to the ancient Greeks. As with political science and economics, the study of history changed in the 1800s. Influenced by nationalism, many scholars wrote histories detailing the accomplishments and glories of their native countries. In addition, historians increasingly based their writings on the systematic study of original materials and the careful organization of facts. They began a massive search for evidence of the past in documents, diaries, letters, and other written sources. New views of history began to emerge from their research.

One of these new trends in history was the study of all people in a society. The French philosopher Voltaire influenced this type of research. In the 1700s Voltaire became known for his attention to social and intellectual history. His work inspired historians to focus less on wars and great leaders and more on the study of ordinary people and how they lived. Another trend at this time—influenced by Darwin—was the interpretation of historical events in terms of evolution.

✔ **READING CHECK: Comparing** How was the development of history like that of political science? Why? both influenced by nationalism, use scientific methods to collect and organize information, study people as members of society

TEACH OBJECTIVE 1

LEVEL 1: Ask students to explain how science influenced the study of politics, economics, and history in the 1800s. *(Scholars attempted to study law and politics with the same scientific manner that physicists and biologists used.)* **ENGLISH LANGUAGE LEARNERS**

TEACH OBJECTIVES 2 and 3

ALL LEVELS: Ask students which social sciences focus on human behavior. *(anthropology, sociology, psychology)* Have students write a statement about the new theories that each of these sciences produced. *(different societies share certain beliefs and behaviors; human society evolved from lower to higher forms through natural selection; all habits constitute a series of conditioned reflexes; the unconscious is a determining factor in behavior)* Then have students choose one of their statements and create a flow-chart showing how this idea developed.
ENGLISH LANGUAGE LEARNERS

HOMEWORK Have students write a paragraph comparing the ways that archaeologists and anthropologists analyze limited evidence.

That's Interesting!

The Greeks were the first people to systematically practice the social sciences—in fact, the terms *economics, politics,* and *history* all derive from their language. During the time of Aristotle, the problem of city government dominated the field of social science. Aristotle and his researchers collected and compared the constitutions of various cities. Their goal was to find a system that would provide social harmony but still maintain class divisions and privileges.

VISUAL RECORD ANSWER

She had face-to-face interaction with the Lumbwa people.

INTERPRETING THE VISUAL RECORD

Anthropology In 1925 the American anthropologist Osa Johnson conducted field work in Kenya, in East Africa, to study the society of the Lumbwa people. On-site observation is a basic method of anthropological research. *What value might Johnson's on-site observation have added to her research?*

Analyzing Primary Sources

Drawing Inferences What did Spencer mean by saying that nature has to be a little cruel to be very kind? only best-adapted individuals would succeed

---

Archaeology, Anthropology, and Sociology

Archaeology is the study of human culture through the artifacts people leave behind. Archaeology became a separate field of study in the mid-1800s. It was in the 1800s that scientists began to learn how old Earth was and how long humans had lived on it. Archaeologists found prehistoric cave paintings in Spain and France. Careful digging of sites uncovered remains of Egyptian, Sumerian, and Assyrian cultures. Excavation techniques allowed scientists to determine the sequence of events in such ancient cities as Troy and Mycenae.

Anthropology. Anthropology is the study of different societies, both past and present. Anthropologists in the 1800s began to explore similarities in the attitudes of human societies and in the ways people relate to one another. The British anthropologist **E.B. Tylor** adopted the German term *kultur* to describe the set of beliefs and behaviors that a society shares. Tylor discussed the concept of *kultur* in his book *Primitive Culture* (1871), in which he looked at religion and how it evolved in all human cultures.

Another British anthropologist, **James George Frazer,** took this approach further in 1890 with his book *The Golden Bough.* Frazer compared the customs of different societies and tried to show links between those societies. The study of similarities and differences among various societies is still a major interest of anthropologists.

Sociology. Sociology—the study of human relationships in society—also first appeared in the 1800s. The French philosopher **Auguste Comte** (KOHNT) was one of the founders of sociology. Comte argued that society, like nature, operated by certain laws. Therefore sociologists should follow scientific methods by using objective facts, not personal interpretations.

In the 1800s sociologists became very interested in adopting the theories of the biological sciences. **Herbert Spencer,** for example, used evolution as the basis for studying human communities. Spencer applied Darwin's theory of natural selection to human societies, coining the phrase "survival of the fittest." Spencer believed that human society, like plant and animal life, had evolved from lower to higher forms through natural selection. He wrote,

❝The individuals best adapted to the conditions of their existence shall prosper most, and the individuals least adapted to the conditions of their existence shall prosper least. . . . Pervading all Nature we may see at work a stern discipline which is often a little cruel that it may be very kind.❞

A History of Civilization, 2nd ed., edited by Crane Brinton, John B. Christopher, and Robert Lee Wolff

Spencer's theory became known as **social Darwinism.** According to this theory, those who had acquired wealth and power had done so because of their superior abilities. Poverty, on the other hand, supposedly proved that people or groups were unfit. Spencer's view came to be seen as simplistic, however, as society became more complex. As people became more aware of how social problems occur, social Darwinism lost much influence.

✔ **READING CHECK: Contrasting** How do archaeology, anthropology, and sociology differ? Archaeology studies human culture through artifacts; anthropology studies different societies; and sociology studies human relationships in society.

584

584 CHAPTER 23

Psychology

Another new science of the 1800s, psychology, studies the mind and human behavior. In the mid-1800s scientists began to approach psychology as an experimental science like biology.

Influenced by Darwin, some psychologists studied animal behavior and applied the results to humans. In the 1890s Russian physiologist **Ivan Pavlov** discovered the conditioned reflex. Psychologists had long known that some behavior is automatic. For example, a dog does not have to be taught to salivate, or water at the mouth, when eating food. Psychologists call this kind of response a reflex action. By experimenting with dogs, Pavlov concluded that human actions are responses to outside stimuli and can be changed by training.

In the early 1900s **Sigmund Freud** (FROID), an Austrian doctor, introduced the idea of the unconscious as a determining factor in human behavior. The unconscious mind contains the mental processes of which a person is unaware. Freud learned that under hypnosis, some of his patients could remember past experiences that they otherwise could not recall. Freud believed that these early experiences had led to their illnesses. Freud treated his patients by identifying their unconscious fears or desires. To do this, he studied their dreams and encouraged them to talk freely about whatever came into their minds.

Freud called this process of revealing and analyzing unconscious motivations **psychoanalysis.** Freud founded modern **psychiatry,** the study and treatment of mental illness. People working in other social sciences also borrowed from Freud's theories. They began to see certain social behaviors and cultural attitudes as driven by unconscious psychological motives.

✔ **READING CHECK: Analyzing Information** According to Freud, how can one's unconscious fears and desires be revealed and examined by means of psychoanalysis? by studying one's dreams, encouraging person to talk freely about whatever comes to mind

HISTORY MAKER

Sigmund Freud (1856–1939)

Sigmund Freud was one of the most important thinkers of his time. Because of Freud's pioneering studies, doctors could better understand the causes of mental illness.

Freud believed that dreams express unconscious fears or desires. Even now, Freud's work continues to be influential, although some people believe his findings to be old-fashioned. **Why was Sigmund Freud's work important?**

SECTION 3 REVIEW ANSWERS

1 Define
- social sciences, p. 583
- social Darwinism, p. 584
- psychoanalysis, p. 585
- psychiatry, p. 585

2 Identify
- E.B. Tylor, p. 584
- James George Frazer, p. 584
- Auguste Comte, p. 584
- Herbert Spencer, p. 584
- Ivan Pavlov, p. 585
- Sigmund Freud, p. 585

3 economics, sociology, political science, psychology

4 a. Historians increasingly based their writing on the systematic study of original materials and the careful organization of facts.

b. He argued that sociologists should follow scientific methods by using objective facts, not personal interpretations.

c. Freud analyzed unconscious motivations, while Pavlov was interested in responses to outside stimuli.

5 Students' letters will vary.

SECTION 3 REVIEW

1. **Define** and explain the significance:
   social sciences
   social Darwinism
   psychoanalysis
   psychiatry

2. **Identify** and explain the significance:
   E.B. Tylor
   James George Frazer
   Auguste Comte
   Herbert Spencer
   Ivan Pavlov
   Sigmund Freud

3. **Summarizing** Copy the diagram and use it to show the fields of study that came to use scientific methods.

4. **Finding the Main Idea**

   a. In what way did the study of history become more scientific during the Industrial Age?

   b. What was Auguste Comte's contribution to sociology?

   c. How were Pavlov's ideas about the basis of human behavior different from Freud's?

5. **Writing and Critical Thinking**

   Supporting a Point of View Write a letter to Freud expressing doubt about his theories.
   Consider:
   • Freud's argument that the unconscious mind controls much human behavior
   • Freud's reliance on dreams and hypnosis to reveal unconscious feelings

Homework Practice Online
keyword: SP3 HP23

LIFE IN THE INDUSTRIAL AGE **585**

OBJECTIVES

1 Explain why people emigrated.

2 Analyze why cities grew and how they changed as they grew.

3 Identify the ways in which public education changed society.

4 Describe how the leisure activities we know today began to develop.

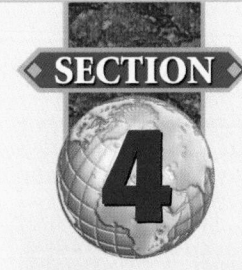

LET'S GET STARTED!

As students enter the classroom, ask them to list some of the reasons that people from other countries emigrate to the United States today. *(Students' responses will vary but may include education, economic prosperity, and jobs.)* Tell students that in Section 4 they will learn about large groups of people who came to the United States from their native lands in the late 1800s and early 1900s.

SECTION 4

READ TO DISCOVER

❶ Why did people emigrate?

❷ Why was the growth of cities so great and how did they change as they grew?

❸ In what ways did public education change society?

❹ How did the leisure activities we know today begin to develop?

DEFINE

emigrations
bobbies
suburbs

IDENTIFY

Jane Addams
Sir Robert Peel
Walter Camp

WHY IT MATTERS TODAY

Cities and suburbs continue to experience change. Use CNN fyi.com or other **current event** sources to investigate a city near you and how it interacts with surrounding suburbs. Record your findings in your journal.

CNN student News.com

Society and Culture in the Industrial Age

The Main Idea
During the 1800s increases in population changed the nature of cities, education, and leisure activities.

The Story Continues *During the Industrial Age, improved living conditions caused the populations of metropolitan areas to boom as never before. This rapid growth prompted newspaper editor Horace Greeley to comment that "We cannot all live in cities, yet nearly all seem determined to do so."*

Emigration

During the 1800s improvements in medicine, sanitation, and food distribution helped lead to an increase in population. In the United States and Europe, population growth was fastest in the more industrialized regions. As the population grew, it also became more mobile. Large numbers of people began to move across national boundaries and oceans to foreign lands.

Such movements of people away from their native lands are called **emigrations.** The largest emigrations were from Europe to North and South America, Africa, Australia and New Zealand. Between 1870 and 1900 more than 10 million people left Europe for the United States alone. This was one of the greatest mass movements of people in history. Many people fled from countries with poor economic conditions, such as Ireland and Italy. Other people, such as Jews, Armenians, and Slavs, fled oppression and discrimination.

Within Europe, large numbers of people moved to the areas of greatest industrialization. Rapid industrialization in northern and western Europe had created a great demand for factory labor. In these areas higher wages attracted workers. Also steamships and trains made travel safer and more affordable.

✔ **READING CHECK: Analyzing Information** What characterized many of the people who emigrated during the 1800s?
desire to improve economic or political standards

Between 1892 and 1943, approximately 17 million people with hopes of a better life entered the United States at New York's Ellis Island.

LEVEL 1: Ask students to list the reasons why people emigrated to the United States and Europe. List their responses on the chalkboard. *(fled from countries with poor economic conditions, fled oppression and discrimination)*

ENGLISH LANGUAGE LEARNERS

The Growth of Cities

As the population increased, changes in agriculture and industry led to the rapid growth of cities. Employment on farms declined as developing industries in or near cities offered new jobs. The factory system became the greatest cause of city growth.

Many factories were located in already established cities, which then grew greatly. Manchester, England, for example, grew from 10,000 people in 1717 to 303,000 in 1851. When factories were built in rural areas, cities grew up around them.

Before the Industrial Revolution, most people lived in rural areas or small villages. By the early 1900s, however, in many nations more people lived in or near cities than in the countryside. No city in the Western

Population Growth in Great Britain, 1751–1851

Interpreting Maps The population of industrialized countries like Great Britain ballooned in the 1800s.

■ **Skills Assessment: 1. Places and Regions** How many British counties saw a population increase of more than 200 percent? **2. Drawing Inferences** What might you guess about industrialization in these counties?

☑ internet connect ≣

TOPIC: Immigrant Voices
GO TO: go.hrw.com
KEYWORD: SP3 WH23

Have students access the Internet through the HRW Go site to find information about immigrant experiences in America in the 1800s. Ask students to imagine they have just arrived in the country. Have students choose a creative format—such as a short story, illustration, song, or poem—to describe their feelings. Students' work may reflect on their experiences coming to America and at the immigration centers, impressions of their new homes, reasons for leaving their homeland, and hopes for the future.

MAP ANSWERS
1. 12

2. Students might suggest that they were highly industrialized.

LEVEL 2: Have students read the introductory paragraph to the section and then list the factors that led to the rapid growth of population in the 1800s. Ask students what demands this enormous growth in population would place on society. *(Answers will vary, but students might suggest more food would need to be available, people would have to move to less inhabited lands, or any social services would have to be expanded.)*

Science, Technology & Society

The development of ice-making machines and the subsequent refrigeration of foods opened up a new worldwide industry. By the mid-1800s both Australia and Argentina had begun sending meat to Europe by ice ship. The first transatlantic refrigerated ship sailed from Buenos Aires to Rouen in 1877. It was called the SS *Frigorifque*.

Critical Thinking

Ask students what other changes the refrigeration of food probably brought.

ANSWER: Students might mention the ability to store food for longer periods of time.

HISTORY MAKER ANSWER
opened Hull House, crusaded for world peace

HISTORY MAKER

Jane Addams (1860–1935)

Jane Addams grew up in a wealthy Illinois family, but she dedicated her life to helping the poor. In 1889 she helped open Hull House in an immigrant neighborhood of Chicago. Hull House, which provided education, job training, and cultural events, soon became the model for community service centers throughout the United States.

Addams also crusaded for world peace. In 1915 she became chairwoman of the Women's International League. She later went on a peace mission to Europe. In 1931 she became the second woman ever to win the Nobel Peace Prize. **What were some of Jane Addams's accomplishments?**

Holt Researcher
go.hrw.com
KEYWORD: Holt Researcher
FreeFind: Jane Addams
        Emily Davies
After reading more about Jane Addams and Emily Davies on the Holt Researcher, write an imaginary dialogue between the two that reflects their political, economic, and cultural contributions to the world.

world had a population of 1 million in 1800. Yet just 100 years later, cities such as New York, London, Paris, and Berlin each had more than 1 million residents.

Sanitation and public order. European and American cities of the 1800s were very different than they are today. Houses did not have running water. Until the late 1800s most cities did not have sewers. People dumped garbage in the streets. This pollution combined with the smoke from factories made cities foul smelling and unhealthy.

After the 1870s technological advances brought improvements, such as iron pipes, flush toilets, and running water. Cities installed public sewers, paved streets, and street lights. Governments passed laws requiring better heating systems and better construction. Through the efforts of reformers like **Jane Addams,** cities began to provide social services.

Growing cities also needed a new kind of law enforcement. Police officers had to direct crowds and protect the lives and property of city dwellers. In London in 1829 **Sir Robert Peel,** a leader of the House of Commons, organized a permanent police force. The police were called "**bobbies**" after Peel's first name, Robert. Other major cities soon followed London's lead.

The development of suburbs. As cities grew, people moved to residential areas on the outskirts called **suburbs.** In the United States, suburbs connected to the city by streetcar or ferry transportation began to appear in the 1800s. Later suburbs developed along railroad and horse-drawn bus lines. Suburbs were less noisy and crowded than cities. Working people from suburban families traveled each day to jobs in the city.

Suburbs spread during the mid-to-late 1800s, as more cities created public transportation systems. At first only merchants, managers, and professionals could afford the fare for trains and buses. They could afford to live a long distance from work, in the new suburbs. Ordinary factory workers usually had to live within walking distance of their jobs. In time, however, lower fares made it possible for more people to ride trolleys or other public transportation to work.

Improvements in diet and food storage. Science and technology provided better methods of preserving and transporting food. Pasteurization was one important step. So was refrigeration, which appeared in the late 1800s. Refrigerators helped prevent the growth of harmful bacteria. Refrigerated railroad cars were first used in the 1870s to transport meats, fruit, and vegetables. These developments helped make a balanced diet available year-round.

Scientists were also learning more about the relationship of food to health. In the early 1900s scientists discovered the importance of vitamins and minerals in the diet. Diseases resulting from vitamin deficiencies were soon wiped out in many industrialized societies. Life expectancy as well as population increased.

✔ **READING CHECK: Identifying Cause and Effect** What triggered the growth of cities in the 1800s? changes in agriculture and industry

Growth of Public Education

To many people, the ideas of the American and French Revolutions about liberty, equality, and representative government made it important to provide education for all citizens. At first there was resistance to this idea from people who feared that the cost of education would mean increased taxes. However, other factors encouraged the

ALL LEVELS: Ask students what positive effects the spread of education had. *(People became better informed about current issues; people took an active interest in government activities; more people could read; more newspapers, magazines, and books were published.)* Then create the following chart on the chalkboard, and have students fill it in. **ENGLISH LANGUAGE LEARNERS**

Changes in Newspapers	Effects of New Technology	Ways of Expanding Circulation
expanded their coverage to include politics, foreign affairs, and art and science	linotype allowed newspapers to be set by machine	lower prices

HOMEWORK Ask each student to list some of the reasons people supported free public education and education for women. Then have each student choose one of the reasons listed and create a political cartoon or a letter to a newspaper editor expressing and expanding upon the reason they chose.

development of free public education. Industrialists wanted workers who could read and write. They needed engineers, scientists, and skilled technicians. Other people believed that state-sponsored schools would produce patriotic citizens. Military leaders wanted educated soldiers. Ordinary people thought that an education would improve their children's chances for a better life.

After 1870 governments in western Europe and the United States passed laws requiring education for all children. In some European nations, the central government controlled schools. In the United States, individual states administered schools and levied taxes to support them. Also many school systems grew to include kindergarten for young children and state universities for advanced study. New subjects, particularly in the sciences, were offered. Vocational and technical training were also introduced.

In general, children of the lower classes attended school only for as long as the law required. They then went to work to help support their families. Middle-class children usually went on to high school and often attended college.

Education for women. By the end of the 1800s, many countries offered elementary education for girls but secondary education was limited. Some people argued that many subjects were not necessary or proper for women. In the United States, Great Britain, and France, secondary education for girls focused on languages, literature, and home economics—not on the sciences, mathematics, or philosophy. Some people objected to these differences. A British woman named Emily Davies urged her government to prepare women to attend universities. In 1865 she argued,

> *History Makers Speak*
>
> **❝We are not encumbered [burdened] by theories about equality and inequality of mental power in the sexes. All we claim is that the intelligence of women, be it great or small, shall have full and free development. And we claim it not specially in the interest of women, but as essential to the growth of the human race.❞**
>
> *Thoughts on Some Questions Relating to Women, 1860–1908, by Emily Davies*

Few colleges admitted women as students during the 1800s. Therefore during the 1800s colleges just for women began to appear in Great Britain and the United States.

Effects of education. The spread of education had many positive results. People knew more about current issues and could participate more in government. Because people of all ages could read, more newspapers, magazines, and books were published.

Newspapers, which were not widely read before 1800, became popular and important. During the 1800s they began to cover such topics as politics, foreign affairs, art, and science. Sometimes newspapers supported or criticized certain political parties or government figures. Political cartoons began to appear. New communications technology, such as the telegraph, allowed papers to print the latest news. Newspapers began to send reporters to distant places to get important stories from far away.

Education for women changed greatly during the 1800s. The women shown in this classroom are studying geography and science.

Analyzing Primary Sources

Drawing Conclusions According to Emily Davies, who would benefit from increased education for women? the human race

As greater numbers of people learned to read, newspapers competed for their attention with sensational stories and cartoons.

Daily Life

The introduction of linotype in the United States and Europe led to a vast increase in the sale of newspapers—at least in those countries that enjoyed freedom of the press. For example, when Napoléon of France conquered Italy in the early 1800s, he suppressed 60 out of 73 papers and then turned over the job of censorship to the police. In 1815 people in northwestern Italy had to obtain a permit to read foreign newspapers. The Russian czar also initiated censorship in 1826 after nobles and officers staged an uprising in an attempt to secure a constitution. The czar also introduced a law stating that all publications had to meet the government's approval and contribute to public morals.

Critical Thinking

Ask students what types of ideas they think these governments hoped to suppress.

ANSWER: These governments hoped to suppress ideas of freedom and democratic government.

LEVEL 3: Ask students what types of activities they enjoy doing in their spare time. *(Answers will vary, but students may suggest playing and watching sports, going to concerts, going to the movies, listening to music, and reading.)* Then tell students that people in the 1800s did some of these same activities for fun. Ask students which activities they think these are. *(Answers will vary.)* After students have read the section under "Leisure and Cultural Activities," have them list ways in which people in the 1800s spent their spare time. *(playing and watching sports; going to concert halls, museums, and libraries; going to public parks)* Close by asking students to speculate on how the

activities in the 1800s differed from the same activities in the 2000s. *(Answers will vary, but students might suggest there are more sports teams now, and people listen to many different kinds of music. Technology has made electronic music such as radio and CDs possible, whereas people in the 1800s listened to live music.)*

CLOSE

Ask students to list the new forms of leisure and cultural activities that were developed in the 1800s and discuss how industrialization made more of these activities possible.

Linking Past to Present

The teams of the earliest football games usually consisted of whole villages, and the field could cover more than a dozen square miles. The ball was advanced by kicking, punching, and carrying. The game was very violent and could lead to injury and even death. In the 1600s a less violent form of football was played in England in schools, although many authorities thought it too rowdy for young gentlemen.

Critical Thinking

Ask students to describe the types of safety precautions taken by football players today to reduce the risk of injury.

ANSWER: Students should mention precautions such as wearing helmets, padding, and mouth guards.

DAILY LIFE ANSWER
It allowed people to work shorter hours.

DAILY LIFE

Leisure Time
In the Industrial Age shorter workdays and higher wages gave people more free time. Team sports, reflected in the detail from Henri Rousseau's *The Football Players,* shown below, quickly became favorite pastimes. As these sports became more popular, increased numbers of people came to cheer their team. Families played games together or went bicycling. Trips to the beach, parks, and museums were also popular activities. **How did higher wages contribute to the increase in leisure activities?**

As newspapers grew, jobs for editors and writers increased. In the past, writing was something people did in addition to work. Now it became full-time work. Journalism—writing and editing for newspapers and magazines—became an accepted profession.

✔ **READING CHECK: Drawing Conclusions** What effects did increased education have on society? people became better informed and could participate more in government; more books, newspapers, and magazines were published

Leisure and Cultural Activities

Many of today's popular forms of entertainment developed during the 1800s. People had long enjoyed concerts, games, plays, and sports. But as cities grew during the industrial age, the number and types of entertainment activities increased. Large audiences now paid to hear professional musicians perform or to watch professional athletes compete.

Sports. People had participated in athletic events since ancient times. However, during the 1800s many games became more organized. In Great Britain, "football"—known as soccer in the United States—was among the first games to become a professional spectator sport. Rugby and American football evolved from soccer.

In the 1860s the London Football Association drew up rules for the games of soccer and rugby. By the mid-1880s many soccer and rugby players in England were full-time athletes. Football clubs for working-class people were created in the 1870s. By that time, laws in England granted factory workers Saturday afternoon and Sunday as rest days. In the 1880s an American named **Walter Camp** adapted rugby into an early form of the game known as football in the United States. A professional league was set up in 1920.

In the 1890s bicycling began to experience great popularity in the United States. By 1896 there were hundreds of manufacturers of bicycles. These manufacturers used machine technology and assembly-line systems. In the late 1800s New York City introduced a traffic code to regulate bicycle and horse traffic.

Baseball also became popular in the late 1800s in the United States. English children's games using a bat and ball dated back to the 1700s. However, it was not until 1845 that a written set of rules gave baseball its modern form. The game became popular with troops in the Civil War. In the late 1860s the first professional baseball team, the Cincinnati Red Stockings, was formed. Baseball quickly grew in popularity at both the amateur and professional levels.

Concert halls, museums, and libraries. Before the 1800s individuals and private groups sponsored most cultural activities. Musicians performed concerts in the homes of the rich or as part of religious services. Artists and sculptors produced works for wealthy families or individuals. Religious and civic organizations sometimes commissioned artwork for display in churches or clubs.

During the 1800s art and music became available to more people. Forms of popular entertainment had been available in taverns in England for many years. The growing population in cities created a greater demand for such entertainment, and music and concert halls began to appear. Music halls combined musical and comic entertainment. In the late 1800s in the United States, a light entertainment known as vaudeville became popular in cities as well as frontier towns. Vaudeville consisted of light, often comical skits that combined music, dialogue, dancing, and singing.

REVIEW

Have students complete the Section 4 Review on p. 591.

ASSESS

Have students complete Daily Quiz 23.4. As Alternative Assessment, you may want to use the education or leisure exercises in this section's lessons.

RETEACH

Have students complete Main Idea Activity for English Language Learners and Special-Needs Students 23.4. Then have students

describe what positive results occurred as a result of the spread of education. **ENGLISH LANGUAGE LEARNERS**

EXTEND

Organize students into small groups to create bulletin board displays comparing leisure and cultural activities that people enjoyed in the 1800s and in the 2000s. Use the displays to discuss the similarities and differences between activities of the two time periods. **BLOCK SCHEDULING**

During the 1800s some art collections displayed in private homes or churches were moved to public museums. The Louvre museum in Paris, for example, had originally contained the art collections of French kings. After the French Revolution it became a public museum and began to collect artwork from all over the world.

Public libraries also began to appear in such cities as London and Paris. In the United States, the wealthy industrialist Andrew Carnegie donated money to open free public libraries in many cities.

Public parks and urban planning. Crowded cities had few places for outdoor recreation. When railroads were built, people often rode trains out into the country for a day. People began to demand that city governments provide parks in cities for recreation.

By the end of the 1800s, many cities had playgrounds for children. Private lands were donated or purchased by city governments and given to the people. Large areas inside city limits, such as Central Park in New York, were set aside as public parks.

✔ **READING CHECK: Sequencing** What conditions made the rise of leisure activities possible in the 1800s? growth of cities, paying audiences, publicity, written rules for games, development of parks for recreation

This painting of a croquet game in a public park reflects the increased participation in leisure activities during the late 1800s.

SECTION 4 REVIEW ANSWERS

❶ Define
- emigrations, p. 586
- bobbies, p. 588
- suburbs, p. 588

❷ Identify
- Jane Addams, p. 588
- Sir Robert Peel, p. 588
- Walter Camp, p. 590

❸ children: required attendance, kindergarten, new subjects; women: expanded opportunities, colleges; journalists: more jobs, accepted profession

❹ a. They were attracted by the demand for factory labor and higher wages.

b. Some art collections displayed in private homes or churches were moved to public museums.

❺ Students' letters will vary but should contain a strong, well-supported argument.

SECTION 4 REVIEW

1. **Define** and explain the significance:
   emigrations
   bobbies
   suburbs

2. **Identify** and explain the significance:
   Jane Addams
   Sir Robert Peel
   Walter Camp

3. **Sequencing** Copy the chart below and use it to show how changing educational opportunities affected different groups in society.

	Children	Women	Journalists
Public education			
College education			

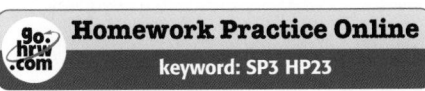

Homework Practice Online

keyword: SP3 HP23

4. **Finding the Main Idea**
   a. Why did people move from one place to another within Europe?
   b. How did public museums' collections grow?

5. **Writing and Critical Thinking**
   Supporting a Point of View Imagine that you are a resident of a large city during the Industrial Age. Write a letter to your mayor arguing for the need for public parks.
   Consider:
   • what living conditions were like as cities grew rapidly
   • the need for recreation

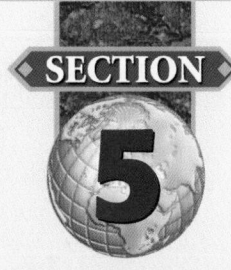

OBJECTIVES

1 **Explore the ideas that drove the romantic movement.**

2 **Identify the artists, writers, and musicians of the romantic movement.**

3 **Explain how realism differs from romanticism.**

4 **Explore the other artistic movements that emerged during this time.**

🔊 *LET'S GET STARTED!*

As students enter the classroom, have them think about the connection between art and social and economic conditions. Ask them if they think that art typically reflects or responds to social and economic conditions and have them support their point of view. *(Students' responses will vary.)* Tell students that in Section 5 they will learn about the literature, music, and art created during the Industrial Age.

SECTION 5

READ TO DISCOVER

❶ What ideas drove the romantic movement?

❷ Who were the artists, writers, and musicians of the romantic movement?

❸ How does realism differ from romanticism?

❹ What other artistic movements emerged during this time?

DEFINE

romanticism
realism
regionalism
naturalists
impressionists

IDENTIFY

Sir Walter Scott
Grimm brothers
James Fenimore Cooper
Ludwig van Beethoven
Pyotr Ilich Tchaikovsky
Mark Twain
Emile Zola
Paul Cézanne

WHY IT MATTERS TODAY

The art produced in the late 1800s is still valued today. Use or other **current event** sources to investigate how artists like Cézanne and Matisse are considered today. Record your findings in your journal.

CNN student News.com

Literature, Music, and Art in the Industrial Age

The Main Idea
Some artists of the 1800s glorified the past, while others embraced modern industrial life.

The Story Continues *During the Industrial Age some artists turned away from the modern world in favor of the imagination. Romantic poet Samuel Taylor Coleridge, in his famous poem "Kubla Khan," displays this fascination with exotic places and ancient times: "In Xanadu did Kubla Khan / A stately pleasure-dome decree; / Where Alph, the sacred river, ran / Through caverns measureless to man / Down to a sunless sea."*

Romanticism

Literature, music, and art reflected the dramatic social and economic changes of the Industrial Age. Many writers of the early 1800s, reacting against the age of reason and science, joined an artistic movement known as **romanticism.** The work of these artists appealed to the imagination and a spirit of individuality. These artists were interested in showing the life as they thought it should be rather than as it really was. Romantics valued emotion and instinct above reason.

In Great Britain, the most famous romantics were a group of young poets, including William Wordsworth, John Keats, and Lord Byron. Their works were filled with a love for beauty and nature. As Wordsworth wrote in one verse,

Primary Source

**❝One impulse from a vernal wood
May teach you more of man,
Of Moral Evil and of good,
Than all the sages can.❞**

William Wordsworth, "The Tables Turned," from *Poems of Wordsworth*, edited by Matthew Arnold

Other writers concentrated on the glories of the past, especially medieval times. For example, in *Ivanhoe* the Scottish author **Sir Walter Scott** wrote about the days of knighthood. Inspired by the growing nationalism of the times, other writers turned to the folklore, songs, and history of their own countries. In Germany the **Grimm brothers** collected fairy tales that continue to be well known. German author Johann Wolfgang von Goethe (GUHR·tuh) was a master of poetry, drama, and the novel. His drama *Faust*, the story of a man's bargain with the devil, is his most famous work. Romanticism also influenced American writers of the early 1800s. **James Fenimore Cooper** wrote adventure stories that idealized the American Indian and the frontier. Washington Irving used New York's Hudson River valley as the setting for his romantic stories, such as *The Legend of Sleepy Hollow*.

✔ **READING CHECKS: Making Generalizations** What themes did most romantic literature share? appealed to imagination and individuality, valued emotion and instinct above reason

TEACH OBJECTIVE 1

LEVEL 1: Ask students to list characteristics of romantic art including artistic ideals and visual principles. Have them give you specific examples. *(appealed to sentiment and imagination and dealt with the "romance" of life, glorified emotion and instinct, idealized nature and the golden past)*

ENGLISH LANGUAGE LEARNERS

Teacher to Teacher

Madeleine Schmitt of St. Louis, Missouri, suggested the following activity: Have students listen to a piece of music written by a composer of the romantic period. Have them list elements of the music that would define it as "romantic." Then have them compare how the "romantic" mood of such music differed from the real lives of most people of the era.

Romantic Music, Painting, and Architecture

In music, like in literature, the 1800s began with a shift toward romanticism. Although romantic music was inspired by the cultures from which the composers arose, the beauty of the music is still universally appreciated. Romantic music is still heard today throughout the world. One of the inspirations for this transition was the German composer **Ludwig van Beethoven** (BAYT·hoh·vuhn). Beethoven brought to music some of the same aims that the British poets of his time brought to literature. He expressed his love of nature in the *Pastoral Symphony.* A call for liberty and freedom dominates his one opera, *Fidelio,* as well as the final movement of his ninth, and last, symphony. Beethoven's music became known for its powerful and passionate emotions.

The romantic movement produced a great outpouring of musical composition, especially in Austria and Germany. Johannes Brahms composed powerful symphonies and concertos that surge with rich, intensely emotional music. Franz Schubert, Robert Schumann, and Felix Mendelssohn brought to their music the lyric quality of romantic poetry. Frédéric Chopin (SHOH·pan), a Polish-born composer who lived in France, wrote expressive and beautiful piano works. Franz Liszt of Hungary used gypsy songs and dances in some of his compositions. He also developed the tone poem, a symphonic piece based on a theme from literature or philosophy.

In Russia **Pyotr Ilich Tchaikovsky** (chy·KAHF·skee) wrote ballet music, operas, and symphonies. His works were often built around stories, such as the ballet *The Sleeping Beauty* and the overture fantasy *Romeo and Juliet.* His *1812 Overture* commemorates Napoléon's defeat in Russia.

Perhaps the greatest composer of operas in the 1800s was Giuseppe Verdi. His best operas, such as *Othello* and *Aïda,* contain some of the most beautiful and dramatic vocal music ever written. The stories and themes of his operas were very nationalistic. Verdi's music inspired nationalist feelings in Italians even before Italy itself became politically united.

La Scala opera house in Milan, Italy, opened in 1778. Many romantic operas of the 1800s, including Giuseppe Verdi's, are still heard there today.

Interdisciplinary Connection

LITERATURE. One of Washington Irving's most famous works is *A History of New York … by Diedrich Knickerbocker.* The book purports to be a collection of the papers of the deceased Knickerbocker, a New York gentleman with a keen interest in the history of the region. Several different tales make up the book and are preceded and followed by an authorial explanation of where Knickerbocker first heard the story and how others reacted to it. *Rip Van Winkle* tells about a man who fell asleep in the Catskill Mountains only to wake up 20 years later. Knickerbocker's postscript reads: "The story of Rip Van Winkle may seem incredible to many, but nevertheless I give it my full belief…. I have even talked with Rip Van Winkle myself, who, when I last saw him, was a very venerable old man, and so perfectly rational and consistent on every other point, that I think no conscientious person could refuse to take this into the bargain; nay, I have seen a certificate on the subject taken before a country justice and signed with a cross, in the justice's own handwriting. The story, therefore, is beyond the possibility of doubt."

Critical Thinking

Ask students how they would analyze Irving's inclusion of the postscript.

ANSWER: Some students might suggest it validates the tale, while others might suggest it draws attention to the improbability of the story.

TEACH OBJECTIVE 2

ALL LEVELS: Construct the following chart on the chalkboard, and fill in the headings. Then tell students to fill in the chart with the romantic artists they learn about as they continue their study of the section.

ENGLISH LANGUAGE LEARNERS

Artist	Type of art/ example	Why romantic?
William Wordsworth, Percy Bysshe Shelley, John Keats, Lord Byron, Samuel Taylor Coleridge	poetry	poems filled with emotion and a strong love for beauty and nature
Sir Walter Scott	novel–Ivanhoe	concerned the days of knighthood

Interdisciplinary Connection

ART. With his photographs of the American Civil War, Mathew Brady pioneered photojournalism. People could see the brutality of war through his photos. In the same way, people could see the plight of the poor in the photos taken by Jacob Riis.

Critical Thinking

Ask students to explain how the goals of these photographers differed from those of other romantic artists.

ANSWER: Students should realize that they aimed to incorporate realism into their photography.

VISUAL RECORD ANSWER

interest in nature

Richard Wagner (VAHG·nuhr) was the best known composer of operas in Germany. He referred to his operas as music dramas. His work combined singing, dancing, costumes, and scenery to create a very intense experience for his audience. Like others at the time, Wagner was very nationalistic. Many of his operas are based on Germanic myths.

In the 1820s and 1830s, romantic painters, like romantic writers, chose subjects from the past. Their paintings were full of drama and action. Eugène Delacroix (del·uh·KRWAH) of France painted this way. John Constable and J.M.W. Turner of Great Britain were landscape painters whose works reflected the romantic interest in nature. They often painted outdoors instead of in a traditional artist's studio. As a result, their work shows intense color and vitality.

Romanticism in architecture expressed itself in the so-called Gothic revival of the mid-1800s. The Gothic revival was an attempt to recreate the great architectural style of the Middle Ages. The British houses of Parliament reflect a Gothic style, as do many churches, colleges, and public buildings in the United States.

✔ **READING CHECK: Summarizing** In what ways did other arts reflect the same themes as romantic literature? expressed love of nature, ideals such as liberty and freedom, emphasized emotion and drama

Photography

The age of photography began in 1839 when Louis-Jacques-Mande Daguerre introduced his daguerreotype, an early type of photograph. Photography has since had a great impact on society. In the 1800s photographs showed the world to people in new ways. Photographs taken by William Jackson influenced Congress to make Yellowstone the first national park. Mathew Brady's Civil War photographs showed the realities of war. Like the novels of Charles Dickens, the photographs of Jacob Riis showed the lives of poor people in very dramatic ways. The camera's ability to capture such scenes helped give rise to a movement known as realism.

✔ **READING CHECK: Making Generalizations** In what ways did the goals of early photographers differ from those of romantic artists? aimed to show people and the world in realistic ways

INTERPRETING THE VISUAL RECORD

Romantic art This painting by artist Hans Dahl, entitled *Girl with Goats by a Fiord,* is typical of the romantic style. *What characteristics of romanticism can you identify in this painting?*

LEVEL 2: Write the headings *Romanticism* and *Realism* on the chalkboard. Then have students list characteristics of each artistic movement. *(Romanticism: appealed to sentiment and imagination, glorified emotion and instinct, idealized nature and the golden past, nationalistic; Realism: dealt with the realities of everyday life, expressed a keen observation of social settings, emphasized social and economic conditions)* Then lead students in a discussion about which artistic movement is more beneficial to society.

SKILL-BUILDING STRATEGIES — Using Art as a Historical Document

Art of the Industrial Age

Works of art always reflect in some way not only the values of the artist, but also the society in which the artist lives. The artist may agree or disagree with the rules of his or her society, or its political beliefs. By paying close attention to detail and the themes in a painting, you can better understand the historical period in which the artist was working, such as the Industrial Age.

An Artist's View
Honoré Daumier's painting *The Washerwoman* was created during the Industrial Revolution. Daumier rebelled against the romantic notions of art. Instead of dreaming about nature or the past, his art reflected social realities of the Industrial Revolution, which had created an urban working class that worked long and hard.

Paint box of an artist of the 1800s

Culture

At the outbreak of the American Civil War in 1861, Mathew Brady decided to record the conflict through photographs. He hired a staff of photographers. Brady supervised the operation from his studio but probably photographed battlefields such as Bull Run, Antietam, and Gettysburg himself.

ACTIVITY: Have students search the library or computer software for photographs by Mathew Brady and other Civil War photographers. Then have each student select one image that he or she feels is particularly interesting or creates a strong emotional impact. Have each student write a paragraph discussing the elements of the photograph that makes it so interesting or powerful to them. [Note: some photos may contain graphic material.]

SKILLS PRACTICE ANSWERS
1. poor, working people; carrying a bundle of clothes to wash

2. Students might answer that it is harsh.

3. Students might answer that the Industrial Revolution created an urban working class that labored long and hard but had humanity and dignity.

4. Students' responses will vary.

Skills Reminder

To use art as a historical document, first identify the historical period in which the art was created. Try to identify some major trends affecting daily life during that time. Then determine the theme of the painting. Connect the theme to the historical period. What forces in society might the artist have been responding to? Finally, think about what the artwork is saying about society.

Skills Practice

❶ Who are the subjects of the painting? What are they doing?
❷ What is the mood of the painting?
❸ What is Daumier saying about the Industrial Revolution and the people involved in it?
❹ Using library or Internet resources, find a painting by another famous artist. Try to determine how the work of art could be used as a historical document.

LEVEL 3: Write the following headings on the chalkboard: Naturalism, Impressionism, Postimpressionism. Then organize students into three groups and assign one heading to each group. Have groups write a paragraph in which they explain where the name for each school of art was derived from and give a description of the artistic technique and aims of each of the schools.

HOMEWORK Ask each student to select one of the artists discussed in this section. Then have each student write up a series of interview-style questions that explore pertinent topics they would like to discuss with the artist. Then have them locate and use biographies to find answers to their questions.

History Maker

GEORGE ELIOT. In the 1800s, Mary Ann Evans wrote realistic novels under the name George Eliot. Her novel *Middlemarch* analyzed different classes in Victorian society.

Critical Thinking

Ask students to guess why Evans chose the name George Eliot.

ANSWER: Students should recognize that George is typically a man's name. They might guess that she believed she would be taken more seriously if her readers believed she was a man.

The Rise of Realism

The subject matter of romantic art and literature had little to do with the lives of ordinary people. In the mid-1800s some writers and artists began to deal with everyday life and social settings, an approach called **realism.** One of the most important realists was Gustave Flaubert (floh·BAIR) of France. His novel *Madame Bovary* described the life of an ordinary woman with very close attention to detail. In Great Britain, Mary Ann Evans wrote realistic novels under the name George Eliot. Her greatest work, *Middlemarch,* analyzed different classes in Victorian society.

Realists often dealt with social and economic themes. In *War and Peace,* Russian writer Leo Tolstoy showed war not as a romantic adventure but as misery and death. The Norwegian playwright Henrik Ibsen brought human problems to the stage. His play *A Doll's House* argued for equality between a husband and wife in marriage.

In the United States one form of realism was **regionalism,** which focused on everyday life in particular places. For example, in his novels *The Adventures of Tom Sawyer* and *The Adventures of Huckleberry Finn,* **Mark Twain** described life along the Mississippi River.

In the late 1800s the **naturalists** took realism even further. They showed the ugly or unpleasant aspects of everyday life. The French novelist **Emile Zola** was a leader of this approach. He wrote as if he were a scientist carefully studying human activity. Although some people objected to his frankness, his exposure of social problems helped bring about reform. Another realist was the British novelist Charles Dickens, who often wrote about the poor in London.

In painting, artists such as Gustave Courbet (koor·BAY) and Honoré Daumier (dohm·YAY) tried to depict the everyday realities of life in the Industrial Age. Another type of realism was attempted by a group of painters called the **impressionists.** Impressionist painting flourished during the 1860s and 1870s in France. Impressionist

This painting by Pierre-Auguste Renoir, depicting an outdoor café scene in Paris, demonstrates the impressionists' attention to light and color.

CLOSE

Ask students to explain how the ideas and works of the realists differed from those of the romantics.

REVIEW

Have students complete the Section 5 Review on p. 597.

ASSESS

Have students complete Daily Quiz 23.5. As Alternative Assessment, you may want to use the romanticism and realism exercise in this section's lessons.

RETEACH

Have students complete Main Idea Activity for English Language Learners and Special-Needs Students 23.5. Then ask each student to write a paragraph that briefly summarizes each of the artistic movements discussed in the chapter. **ENGLISH LANGUAGE LEARNERS**

EXTEND

Have students write a poem or create an illustration in one of the artistic styles discussed in the section. Then display these works and ask the students to identify which style the piece of art represents. **BLOCK SCHEDULING**

painters tried to paint vivid impressions of people and places. To do this they carefully studied light and color. Claude Monet (moh·NAY) and Pierre-Auguste Renoir (ren·WAHR) were leading impressionist painters. Painters in England and the United States also took up the style.

✔ **READING CHECK: Finding the Main Idea** With what were the realists concerned? everyday life and social settings

Experiments in Art Forms

Like writers and musicians, painters and sculptors often rebelled against the industrial world. There was less nationalism in art than in literature and music. There was also more individual experimentation.

The landscapes and still lifes of painter **Paul Cézanne** explored the form and shapes of his subjects. He moved away from recognizable, realistic scenes. Cézanne's work influenced a group of painters who are often called the postimpressionists. Another artist, Paul Gauguin (goh·GAN), left Europe to live in Tahiti. His art stressed color and simple, flat shapes. French artist Henri-Émile-Benoît Matisse and Dutch painter Vincent Van Gogh (van·GOH) also emphasized color design over realism. Edgar Degas (deh·GAH), Henri de Toulouse-Lautrec (too·LOOZ·loh·TREK), and Édouard Manet all painted scenes of Parisian life in very personal styles.

The sculptor Auguste Rodin (roh·DAN) also broke with tradition. Some of his statues included unworked portions of marble to give the work an unfinished quality. Like many artists of the time, Rodin rejected the idea that art had to show things as they appear in real life.

✔ **READING CHECK: Analyzing Information** How did the work of Cézanne, Gauguin, and Rodin show their individual styles? through experimentation, movement away from realistic portrayals

Edgar Degas worked with the human form in both paintings and sculpture. Shown here is his Little Fourteen-Year-Old Dancer.

SECTION 5 REVIEW

1. **Define** and explain the significance:
   romanticism
   realism
   regionalism
   naturalists
   impressionists

2. **Identify** and explain the significance:
   Sir Walter Scott
   Grimm brothers
   James Fenimore Cooper
   Ludwig van Beethoven
   Pyotr Ilich Tchaikovsky
   Mark Twain
   Emile Zola
   Paul Cézanne

3. **Sequencing** Copy the diagram and use it to chart the progression of artistic styles during the Industrial Age.

   Romanticism → Realism, Regionalism, Naturalism, Impressionism → Post-impressionism, individual experimentation

4. **Finding the Main Idea**
   a. How did music of the 1800s express romanticism?
   b. In what way was realism in art and literature a departure from romanticism?
   c. In what ways did Cézanne and the postimpressionists rebel against industrialism?

5. **Writing and Critical Thinking**
   Identifying Points of View Write a dialogue between a romantic artist or writer and a realist, expressing what each one hoped to accomplish.
   Consider:
   • what the romantics felt we could learn from nature
   • the ways in which realist authors and artists could sometimes bring about social change by exposing harsh conditions

Homework Practice Online
keyword: SP3 HP23

SECTION 5 REVIEW ANSWERS

❶ **Define**
• romanticism, p. 592
• realism, p. 596
• regionalism, p. 596
• naturalists, p. 596
• impressionists, p. 596

❷ **Identify**
• Sir Walter Scott, p. 592
• Grimm brothers, p. 592
• James Fenimore Cooper, p. 592
• Ludwig van Beethoven, p. 593
• Pyotr Ilich Tchaikovsky, p. 593
• Mark Twain, p. 596
• Emile Zola, p. 596
• Paul Cézanne, p. 597

❸ Romanticism, Realism, Regionalism, Naturalism, Impressionism, Post-Impressionism, Individual experimentation

❹ a. It expressed intense emotion.

b. It aimed to show people and the world in realistic rather than idealistic ways.

c. They painted landscapes and still lifes, and moved away from showing things as they appear in real life.

❺ Students' dialogues will vary.

REVIEW AND ASSESSMENT RESOURCES

REPRODUCIBLE RESOURCES
▶ Vocabulary Activity 23

TECHNOLOGY RESOURCES
▶ Chapter 23 Test Generator (on the One-Stop Planner)
▶ Global Skill Builder CD-ROM
▶ HRW Web Site

REINFORCEMENT, REVIEW, and ASSESSMENT
▶ Chapter 23 Review, pp. 598–599
▶ Chapter 23 Tutorial for Students, Parents, Mentors, and Peers
▶ Chapter 23 Test (Form A or B)
▶ Alternative Assessment Handbook
▶ Chapter 23 Test for English Language Learners and Special-Needs Students

REVIEW
Have students complete the Chapter 23 Review on pages 598–599.

ASSESS
Use one of the chapter tests to assess students' understanding of the content. For Alternative Assessment, see the Portfolio Activities and Alternative Assessment Handbook.

Understanding Main Ideas

1. development of electric generator, invention of the light bulb, invention of the wireless telegraph

2. They used the technology of the internal combustion engine to propel their plane through the air.

3. cell theory

4. allowed doctors to fight disease; longer and safer operations became possible

5. atomic weight, periodic table, atomic structure, radioactivity, quantum theory, theory of relativity

6. Spencer applied Darwin's theory of natural selection to human societies.

7. changes in agriculture and industry

8. made people healthier by preventing the growth of harmful bacteria, made a balanced diet available year-round

9. They rejected the idea that art had to show things as they appear in real life.

Reviewing Themes
1. growth of free, public education; education offered for women

2. It allowed the human voice to be transmitted over long distances.

3. It rejected reason and science and valued emotion and instinct above reason.

CHAPTER 23 Review

Creating a Time Line
Copy the time line below onto a sheet of paper. Complete the time line by filling in the events, individuals, and dates from the chapter that you think were significant. Pick three events and explain why you think they were significant.

| 1800 | 1840 | 1880 | 1928 |

Writing a Summary
Using standard grammar, spelling, sentence structure, and punctuation, write an overview of the events in the chapter.

Identifying People and Ideas
Identify the following terms or individuals and explain their significance:

1. Alexander Graham Bell
2. pasteurization
3. antisepsis
4. Pierre and Marie Curie
5. social sciences
6. Sigmund Freud
7. psychoanalysis
8. romanticism
9. realism
10. Paul Cézanne

Understanding Main Ideas

SECTION 1 *(pp. 572–575)*

Advances in Technology and Communication
1. Record the sequence of events that followed Faraday's discovery that magnetism could generate electricity.
2. Why did Orville and Wilbur Wright succeed where others failed?

SECTION 2 *(pp. 576–582)*

Advances in Science and Medicine
3. What progress was made in the area of biological sciences?
4. Explain how advances in medicine benefited society.
5. What advances were made in atomic theory?

SECTION 3 *(pp. 583–585)*

Social Sciences in the Industrial Age
6. How did Darwin's theory of evolution influence the field of sociology?

SECTION 4 *(pp. 586–591)*

Society and Culture in the Industrial Age
7. What factors led to the rapid growth of cities in the 1800s?
8. What effect did improved food storage have on population growth?

SECTION 5 *(pp. 592–597)*

Literature, Music, and Art in the Industrial Age
9. How did the work of the postimpressionist sculptors and painters step away from realism?

Reviewing Themes
1. **Citizenship** How did education change during the 1800s?
2. **Science, Technology & Society** How did electricity affect communication?
3. **Culture** How was romanticism a response to industrialized society?

Thinking Critically
1. **Drawing Inferences** How did the public education systems that developed in France and the United States help to fulfill the ideas of equality and a representative government?
2. **Making Predictions** How might innovations in transportation and communication affect social mobility?
3. **Comparing and Contrasting** How did the ideas and works of realists differ from those of the romantics?

Writing About History
Summarizing The 1800s saw great changes in the sciences and arts and in where and how people lived. Write a page from a memoir of a person who has lived through some of these significant changes. Use the following chart to organize your thoughts before you begin writing.

Advances of the Industrial Age	Technology	Medicine	Social sciences	Arts
Effect on daily life				

Ask students to list and describe four of the technological advances made during the last half of the 1800s.

RETEACH

Pair students who have had difficulty with the test. Have each pair compile a chapter glossary. From the glossary, have the students prepare flash cards with a definitional sentence on the back, and quiz each other. When they are ready, have students take the Form B

Test to assess their mastery of the material.
ENGLISH LANGUAGE LEARNERS

Portfolio Extensions

1. Have students read one of the following novels and explain how it reflects the ideas of the romantic movement: Sir Walter Scott's *Ivanhoe* (Pocket Books); Rafael Sabatini's *Scaramouche* (Houghton Mifflin); Baroness Emmuska Orczy's *The Scarlet Pimpernel* (Macmillan).

2. Using books on the history of art, have students choose a painting by a particular artist and answer the following questions: What is the subject? What was the artist trying to convey? What techniques did he or she use? In what way does this artist represent romanticism?

3. Have interested students conduct additional research into Gregor Mendel and his work on genetics. Suggested topics include Mendel's two laws of heredity, recessive and dominant genes, heterozygous and homozygous organisms, and hereditary diseases. Students should present their findings to the class.

Building Social Studies Skills

Connecting Architecture to History

Study the glass building shown. It was built to house an exhibition celebrating new industrial products. Then answer the questions.

Interior of the Crystal Palace, built for the Great Exhibition, London, 1851

1. Which is the best general statement about this building's place in history?

  a. It was the first modern building, and from then on all buildings were built in a similar style.

  b. The design of the building and the materials used in its construction were intended to celebrate the spirit of "progress."

  c. The building's architectural style and construction materials were typical of the times.

  d. Not many people saw the building in 1851 because they weren't interested in an industry exhibition.

2. Explain your choice of statements in question 1. Give specific examples to support your point of view.

Understanding Frames of Reference

Read this quote from Mark Twain's *Life on the Mississippi*, published in 1883. Then answer the questions.

> "When I was a boy, there was but one permanent ambition among my comrades in our village on the west bank of the Mississippi River. That was, to be a steamboatman. . . . By and by one of our boys went away. At last he turned up as an apprentice engineer . . . on a steamboat. . . . And whenever his boat was laid up he would come home and swell around the town in his blackest and greasiest clothes, so that nobody could help remembering that he was a steamboatman; . . . If ever a youth was cordially admired and hated by his comrades, this one was."

3. Which is the best statement of what this quote implies about Twain's social class when he was a boy?

  a. He and his friends were from families of steamboat workers.

  b. He and his friends were from families that worked hard and had very little money.

  c. He was from a wealthy family that traveled often.

  d. He was from a middle-class family that valued cleanliness.

4. Do you think any of the "comrades" mentioned in this quote were girls? Give specific reasons for your answer.

Alternative Assessment

Building Your Portfolio

Culture

Writers and artists can often help bring about social reform by exposing harsh conditions through their works. Compile a list of realist writers and artists who addressed such themes during the Industrial Age. Create a chart to summarize your findings.

☑ internet connect

Internet Activity: go.hrw.com
KEYWORD: SP3 WH23

Choose a topic on Life in the Industrial Age to:

• explore Thomas Edison's inventions.

• research the immigrant experience in America during the 1800s.

• learn about contemporary women's colleges.

Thinking Critically

1. People knew more about current issues and could participate more in government.

2. emigration might increase, suburbs might develop

3. Romanticism: appealed to sentiment and imagination, glorified emotion and instinct, idealized nature and the golden past, nationalistic; Realism: dealt with the realities of everyday life, expressed a keen observation of social settings, emphasized social and economic conditions

Writing About History

Students' memoir pages will vary.

Building Social Studies Skills

1. b

2. Students' responses will vary.

3. b

4. Probably not, because girls were unlikely to become steamboat operators.

Building Your Portfolio

Students' charts will vary.

The Age of Reform

CHAPTER RESOURCE MANAGER

Objectives	Pacing Guide	Reproducible Resources
SECTION 1 **Liberal Reforms in Great Britain and Its Empire** (pp. 602–608) • Describe ways the British government and social welfare changed in the 1800s. • Explain the policies that Disraeli and Gladstone followed. • Describe changes in British government and social welfare in the early 1990s. • Identify changes that occurred in other areas of the British Empire during the 1800s and 1900s.	**Regular** 1.5 day | **Block Scheduling** 1 day *Block Scheduling Handbook with Team Teaching Strategies, 24.1*	**RS** Guided Reading Strategy 24.1 **RS** Graphic Organizer Activity 24: Reform Movements **PS** Readings in World History 81: A Suffragette Goes to Prison **E** Hands-on History Activity 24: Building a Better World
SECTION 2 **Expansion and Reform in the United States** (pp. 609–614) • Describe how the United States expanded westward. • Explain why the United States fought a civil war. • Describe ways the United States changed after the Civil War.	**Regular** 1.5 day | **Block Scheduling** 1 day *Block Scheduling Handbook with Team Teaching Strategies, 24.2*	**RS** Guided Reading Strategy 24.2 **SM** Geography Activity 24: The Slave Trade in the United States **PS** Readings in World History 82: The Death of President Lincoln
SECTION 3 **Revolution and Reform in France** (pp. 615–620) • Explain why the rule of Louis Philippe led to a revolution in 1848. • Describe how Louis-Napoléon started a second empire in France. • Summarize France's relations with Germany and other countries. • Explain how the Third Republic maintained political stability in France.	**Regular** 1.5 day | **Block Scheduling** 1 day *Block Scheduling Handbook with Team Teaching Strategies, 24.3*	**RS** Guided Reading Strategy 24.3 **PS** Readings in World History 83: The Last Day of the Paris Commune
SECTION 4 **Latin Americans Win Independence** (pp. 621–627) • Describe what life was like in the Spanish and Portuguese colonies of Latin America. • Explain why Latin Americans began to oppose colonial rule. • Explain how Latin American colonies won their independence. • Summarize how the new Latin American nations fared after independence.	**Regular** 1.5 day | **Block Scheduling** 1 day *Block Scheduling Handbook with Team Teaching Strategies, 24.4*	**RS** Guided Reading Strategy 24.4 **PS** Readings in World History 84: The Great Liberator **E** Creative Teaching Strategy 24: An Era of Expansion and Reform: Scored Discussion

Chapter Resource Key

PS Primary Sources	**A** Assessment	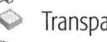 Music	
RS Reading Support	**REV** Review	Video	
IC Interdisciplinary Connections	**ELL** Reinforcement and English Language Learners	Internet	
E Enrichment	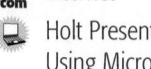 Transparencies	Holt Presentation Maker Using Microsoft® PowerPoint®	
SM Skills Mastery	CD–ROM		

 One-Stop Planner CD-ROM

See the **One–Stop Planner** for a complete list of additional resources for students and teachers.

One-Stop Planner CD-ROM

It's easy to plan lessons, select resources, and print out materials for your students when you use the *One-Stop Planner* CD–ROM with *Test Generator.*

Technology Resources	Reinforcement, Review, and Assessment
One-Stop Planner 24.1 World History and Cultures Video Program 19: An Era of Reform World History Teaching Transparency: Regional and World Map 33; Everyday Life 19 Homework Practice Online Online Maps, Charts, and Graphs: British Electoral Reforms	Daily Quiz 24.1 Main Idea Activity 24.1 English Audio Summary 24.1 Spanish Audio Summary 24.1 REV Section 1 Review, p. 608
One-Stop Planner 24.2 Holt Researcher: World History: Abraham Lincoln Holt Researcher: World History: Lucretia Mott, Elizabeth Cady Stanton CNN. Presents World Cultures: Yesterday and Today Segment 22: Honoring Women's Suffrage Homework Practice Online	Daily Quiz 24.2 Main Idea Activity 24.2 English Audio Summary 24.2 Spanish Audio Summary 24.2 REV Section 2 Review p. 614
One-Stop Planner 24.3 World History Teaching Transparency: Everyday Life 20: A Ball During the Congress of Vienna World History Teaching Transparency: Art and History 19: Derby Day Homework Practice Online Online Maps, Charts, and Graphs: War and Peace in the Crimea, 1843–1858	Daily Quiz 24.3 Main Idea Activity 24.3 English Audio Summary 24.3 Spanish Audio Summary 24.3 REV Section 3 Review, p. 620
One-Stop Planner 24.4 Holt Researcher: World History: Simon Bolivar Regions of the World Music Audio CD Program 3: Mexico: Mariachi Music of Mexico Homework Practice Online Online Maps, Charts, and Graphs: Bolivar and San Martin Fight for Independence	Daily Quiz 24.4 Main Idea Activity 24.4 English Audio Summary 24.4 Spanish Audio Summary 24.4 REV Section 4 Review, p. 627

internet connect

HRW ONLINE RESOURCES
GO TO: go.hrw.com
Then type in a keyword.

TEACHER HOME PAGE
KEYWORD: SP3 Teacher

CHAPTER INTERNET ACTIVITIES
KEYWORD: SP3 WH24
Choose an activity to:
- create a scrapbook that highlights the history of Mexico, El Salvador, Nicaragua, Colombia, Chile, or Argentina since independence.
- collect information on the status of native peoples today.
- search letters and diary entries from soldiers who served in the U.S. Civil War.

CHAPTER ENRICHMENT LINKS
KEYWORD: SP3 CH24

ONLINE ASSESSMENT
Homework Practice
KEYWORD: SP3 HP24
Standardized Test Prep
KEYWORD: SP3 STP24
Rubrics
KEYWORD: SS Rubrics

ONLINE MAPS, CHARTS, AND GRAPHS
KEYWORD: SP3 MCG

CONTENT UPDATES
KEYWORD: SS Content Updates

HOLT PRESENTATION MAKER
KEYWORD: SP3 PPT24

ONLINE READING SUPPORT
KEYWORD: SS Strategies

CURRENT EVENTS
KEYWORD: S3 Current Events

Meeting Individual Needs

Ability Levels

Level 1   Basic level activities designed for all students encountering new material

Level 2   Intermediate level activities designed for average students

Level 3   Challenging activities designed for honors and gifted and talented students

English Language Learners   These activities address the needs of students with Limited English Proficiency.

Chapter Review and Assessment

IC   Vocabulary Activity 24
Global Skill Builder CD-ROM
HRW Web Site
REV   Chapter 24 Tutorial for Students, Parents, Mentors, and Peers
REV   Chapter 24 Review, pp. 628–629

A   Chapter 24 Test Generator (on the One-Stop Planner)
A   Chapter 24 Test (Form A or B)
A   Alternative Assessment Handbook
A   Chapter 24 Test for English Language Learners and Special-Needs Students

Build on What You Know

Ask students to answer the following questions:

How might the effects of the Industrial Revolution have spurred calls for social and political reforms?

Consider:

- changes in living and working conditions
- the development of an urban middle class
- the hopes and expectations of the working class

What methods might groups in society use to achieve change?

Consider:

- how workers tried to improve their lives and those of their children
- the distribution of wealth and power in society
- the teachings of Karl Marx and other radical reformers

EXPLORING THE TIME LINE

GLOBAL EVENTS

internet connect

TOPIC: The early history of Australia

GO TO: go.hrw.com

KEYWORD: SP3 WH24

Have students access the Internet through the HRW Go site to research the settling of Australia as an English penal colony. Students should then write a letter to their families in England from the perspective of a penal colony inmate. Describe the land, the conditions, and what serving their sentence entails. Keep in mind that there was a large female convict population as well as the more publicized male group.

CHAPTER 24

1791–1911

The Age of Reform

Immigrants to the United States in the mid-1800s

**1804
Global Events**
Haiti becomes the first independent nation in Latin America.

**1814
Global Events**
The Treaty of Ghent ends the War of 1812.

**1831
Daily Life**
German immigrants to America number about 15,000.

1790   **1815**   **1840**

**1797
Politics**
John Adams becomes president of the United States.

**1828
Business and Finance**
Construction begins on the Baltimore and Ohio Railroad, the first railroad to carry passengers and freight.

**1838
Politics**
Chartists in Great Britain demand universal suffrage and vote by ballot.

The second president of the United States, John Adams, and wife, Abigail

An early passenger train

Build on What You Know

The Industrial Revolution that began in England in the mid-1700s marked a major turning point for European society. It soon transformed the ways in which people in Europe and America lived, worked, and thought. Changes in occupations and living conditions brought more leisure time as well as social problems. Life had become very different. These major changes led to calls for reform to make life better as well. In time, those calls would spread beyond Europe. In this chapter, you will learn how people in various nations worked to reform their governments and societies in the name of Enlightenment ideals.

What's Your Opinion?

 To help students create their Themes Journal entries, provide the following examples of appropriate **agree**/**disagree** *statements.*

Citizenship

Agree A society cannot be truly democratic unless all people in it can have a voice.

Disagree People who do not make a useful contribution to society should have no say in how it is governed.

Government

Agree Individual rights are the foundation of democracy and should never be limited by government.

Disagree The need for all people to be protected and secure is more important than any person's rights.

Constitutional Heritage

Agree Just government cannot exist unless the law applies equally to all its people.

Disagree Some people are more fit to lead and should not be bound by the same restrictions as others.

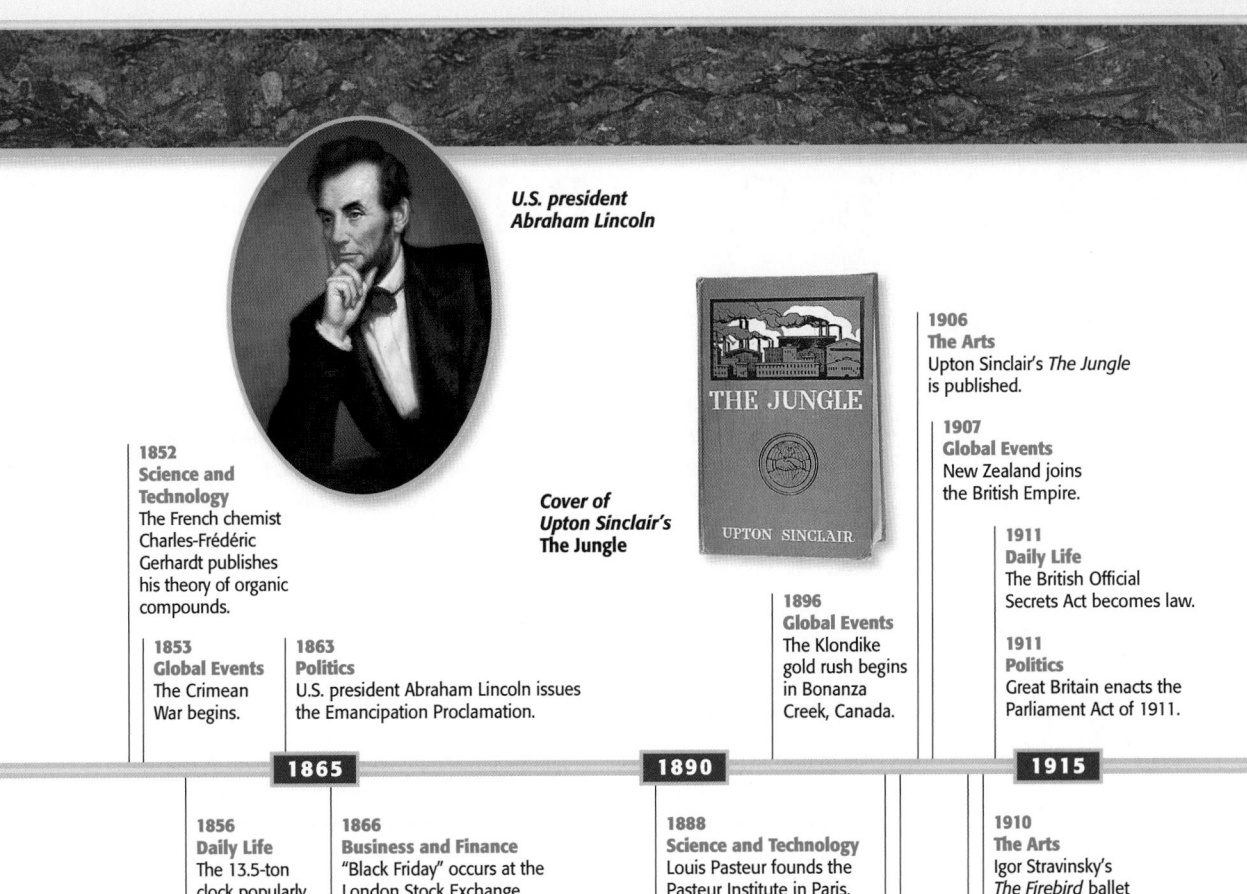

U.S. president Abraham Lincoln

Cover of Upton Sinclair's The Jungle

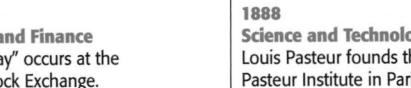

1852
Science and Technology
The French chemist Charles-Frédéric Gerhardt publishes his theory of organic compounds.

1853
Global Events
The Crimean War begins.

1863
Politics
U.S. president Abraham Lincoln issues the Emancipation Proclamation.

1896
Global Events
The Klondike gold rush begins in Bonanza Creek, Canada.

1906
The Arts
Upton Sinclair's *The Jungle* is published.

1907
Global Events
New Zealand joins the British Empire.

1911
Daily Life
The British Official Secrets Act becomes law.

1911
Politics
Great Britain enacts the Parliament Act of 1911.

1865

1890

1915

1856
Daily Life
The 13.5-ton clock popularly known as Big Ben is crafted for the British Parliament.

1856
Science and Technology
The Bessemer converter changes the steel-making process.

1866
Business and Finance
"Black Friday" occurs at the London Stock Exchange.

1888
Science and Technology
Louis Pasteur founds the Pasteur Institute in Paris.

1910
The Arts
Igor Stravinsky's *The Firebird* ballet debuts in Paris.

1909
Daily Life
London hairdressers give the first permanent waves.

1904
Science and Technology
Work begins on the Panama Canal.

1903
Business and Finance
Henry Ford founds the Ford Motor Company.

Louis Pasteur in his laboratory

What's Your Opinion?

 Do you **agree** *or* **disagree** *with the following statements? Support your point of view in your journal.*

Citizenship There should be no restrictions on who may vote in a society.

Government The interests of private individuals in a society cannot come before the interests of the government.

Constitutional Heritage Established laws, not powerful individuals, should guide a nation.

Britain and France expected a quick victory over Russia in the Crimean War. But the war was poorly managed and commanded on both sides. The British cavalry charge at the Battle of Balaklava in October 1854, immortalized in Alfred Tennyson's famous poem "The Charge of the Light Brigade," was one of the most infamous mistakes in British military history. More than 600 mounted troops, without any other support, attacked a battery of Russian guns. Nearly half the men died.

A lack of fuel, clothing, and supplies during the long winter that followed the battle cost many more French and British troops their lives. In all, more than 250,000 men were lost by each side during the 30-month war.

Critical Thinking

Ask students to predict how these developments affected British public opinion about the war.

ANSWER: These developments turned the British people against the war.

OBJECTIVES

1 **Describe ways the British government and social welfare changed in the 1800s.**

2 **Explain the policies that Disraeli and Gladstone followed.**

3 **Describe changes in British government and social welfare in the early 1900s.**

4 **Identify changes that occurred in other areas of the British Empire during the 1800s and 1900s.**

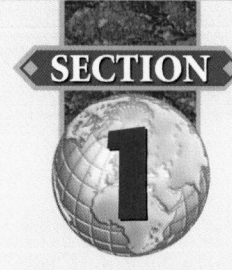

READ TO DISCOVER

❶ How did British government and social welfare change in the 1800s?

❷ What policies did Disraeli and Gladstone follow in Britain?

❸ How did British government and social welfare change in the early 1900s?

❹ What changes occurred in other areas of the British Empire during the 1800s and 1900s?

DEFINE

suffrage
suffragettes

IDENTIFY

Queen Victoria
Benjamin Disraeli
William Gladstone
Emmeline Pankhurst
Lord Durham
Aborigines
Maori

WHY IT MATTERS TODAY

Liberalism continues to be a key political philosophy in the United States and elsewhere in the world. Use CNN or other **current event** sources to see what issues liberals are interested in today. Record your findings in your journal.

CNN Student News.com

Liberal Reforms in Great Britain and Its Empire

The Main Idea
Reform movements arose in Great Britain in response to the problems of the Industrial Revolution.

The Story Continues *During the 1800s and 1900s, reformers in Britain worked to extend civil rights. Women especially fought hard for the right to vote and were often arrested. Emmeline Pankhurst, one of the leaders of this movement, noted that "Over one thousand women . . . have suffered their imprisonment . . . weakened in body, but not in spirit. We are . . . convinced that this is the only way in which we can win power to alter what for us are . . . absolutely intolerable conditions."*

Reforms of the 1800s

The Industrial Revolution had brought wealth and power to Great Britain. It had also created many economic and social inequalities. As the Industrial Revolution spread, a political philosophy grounded in the Enlightenment and the French Revolution emerged. In general this philosophy, called liberalism, supported government protection of individual rights and civil liberties.

During the 1800s individuals who believed in liberalism were very active in politics. British liberals helped enact numerous reforms to protect individuals' political and civil liberties. Some reforms were aimed at extending **suffrage,** or the right to vote. Others focused on correcting social and economic problems. The abolition of slavery and the slave trade was among these reforms.

Voting restrictions. Great Britain was one of the first European nations to limit the power of the monarchy. Since the Glorious Revolution of 1688, Parliament was the real ruler of Great Britain. The House of Commons was supposed to represent all British people. Voters in each district elected a representative to serve them.

There were many restrictions, however, on the right to vote and hold office. Only people who owned property could vote. People voted in the open, so that others could see how they voted. Therefore, voters could be bribed or intimidated. In some districts the nobles controlled who would be the representative in the House of Commons. District boundaries no longer represented how the population was distributed. Only men who owned a great deal of property could be elected to the House of Commons. No Catholics, Jews, or Dissenters—non-Anglican Protestants—could hold political office.

The Reform Bill of 1832. Workers and the middle class began to demand changes in this voting system. The members of the upper class resisted because they feared political reform would not only take power away from them, but could also bring about a reign of terror, as it had in France.

In 1829, however, Parliament passed the Catholic Emancipation Act. This law allowed Roman Catholics to serve in Parliament if they recognized the Protestant monarch as the ruler of Great Britain. By 1830 the middle class and laborers were

Social and Political Reforms of the 1800s		
Inequalities	**How Remedied**	**Results of Change**
restrictions on the right to hold office and vote	*Catholic Emancipation Act, Reform Bill of 1832*	*Catholics could run for office, people with less property could vote*
horrible working conditions for women and children	*Factory Act of 1833*	*working conditions improved*
slavery and slave trade existed	*slavery abolished in the colonies, 1833*	*individual rights improved*

HOMEWORK Have students write an editorial that supports either a Liberal or Conservative point of view of one of the British reforms in the 1800s.

demanding more wide-ranging reforms. Several times in the past the House of Commons had passed a bill that extended voting rights and redrew district boundaries more fairly. However, the House of Lords refused to let the bill pass until 1832.

This Reform Bill of 1832 took seats in the House of Commons away from less populated areas and gave them to the industrial cities. It also gave people with less property the right to vote. The middle class now had a voice in Great Britain's government and power in Parliament.

By forcing passage of the Reform Bill of 1832, the Whig Party had won the strong support of these new voters. Now the Whigs joined with some Radicals, and with liberals from the Tory Party, to form the Liberal Party. The Tory Party of wealthy landowners became known as the Conservative Party.

Social and economic change. Major social and economic changes took place in Great Britain after 1832. The Factory Act of 1833 and other laws were aimed at reforming the horrible working conditions of women and children. Slavery was abolished in all British colonies in 1833. That same year the Liberal Party took a first step toward free public education by winning financial support for private and church schools.

The Liberal Party also helped eliminate the unpopular Corn Laws. These laws placed high taxes on grain imported by Britain, enabling British landowners to sell their grain at high prices. As a result, British workers had to pay high prices or starve. After a bitter fight, Parliament repealed the Corn Laws in 1846. This was Britain's first step toward free trade.

The Chartist movement. As the spirit of reform began to spread in Great Britain during the 1830s, members of the working class felt that their voices had gone unheard. In response, a cabinetmaker named William Lovett founded the London Workingmen's Association in 1836. Among the reforms that Lovett and his group demanded were universal male suffrage and a secret ballot. The group called for electoral districts in Great Britain to be redrawn in order to equalize parliamentary representation throughout the country. It also wanted salaries for members of Parliament so that workers could afford to enter politics. These reforms were proposed in a document known as the People's Charter. Supporters of Lovett and his calls for reform were called Chartists.

The Chartist movement became widely popular among British workers. As social and economic conditions gradually improved, however, its power declined. By the late 1840s, the Chartist movement had effectively ended, but over time, many of the reforms it had backed became law. In 1867, for example, a major reform bill was passed, nearly doubling the number of British voters. Yet while most urban industrial workers could now vote, women and many lower-class workers still could not.

✔ **READING CHECK: Making Generalizations** What was the overall aim of the liberal reforms of the 1800s? *suffrage, solving social/economic problems, ending slavery*

In 1844 a London hatter placed this illustration inside his hats to show his support for free trade and the Anti-Corn-Law League.

Primary Source
◆ EYEWITNESS ◆

Suffrage and the Chartists

Some people believed that liberal movements such as the Chartists threatened the foundations of British society. To ease these fears, one Chartist explained why the group supported greater voting rights:

"Universal suffrage means meat and drink and clothing, good hours, and good beds, and good substantial furniture for every man and woman and child who will do a fair day's work." **How important was the right to vote for the Chartists? Why?**

Technology Resources
Online Maps, Charts, and Graphs: British Electoral Reforms

ALL LEVELS: Organize students into groups to discuss whether Disraeli or Gladstone made the more important contribution to British history. Have each group report its conclusions and reasoning to the class. Then ask students how Gladstone's emphasis might have differed if he had been a leader of the Conservative Party. How might being a Liberal leader have changed Disraeli's focus? *(Responses should recognize the constituencies to which each of these parties appealed and how that shaped the focus and priorities of their leaders.)* **COOPERATIVE LEARNING**

Spotlight on CULTURE

Queen Victoria's reign, the longest in British history, was marked not only by political reforms and industrial progress, but also by cultural changes. Have students use primary and secondary sources including computer software to search for information about English life and culture during the Victorian Age. Then have students work in groups to make collages or multimedia presentations about their findings. Presentations might focus on topics such as fashions, furniture, architecture, morals, or literature. **BLOCK SCHEDULING, COOPERATIVE LEARNING**

That's Interesting!

Queen Victoria had 9 children and 40 grandchildren, who eventually populated most of the thrones of Europe. When her husband, Prince Albert, died in 1861, she remained in mourning and dressed in black for 40 years, until her own death in 1901.

Constitutional Heritage

The U.S. Constitution requires that House seats be reapportioned every 10 years. In 1872 Congress required House districts to be equal in population, but that requirement was rescinded in 1929. In 1964, nearly 80 years after Britain equalized Parliament's districts, the Supreme Court ruled in *Westberry* v. *Saunders* that congressional districts with unequal numbers of people were unconstitutional.

Critical Thinking

Ask students to explain why unequal electoral districts are undemocratic.

ANSWER: Each person in a crowded congressional district would have less political power and influence than a person in a sparsely populated one.

CONNECTING TO GEOGRAPHY ANSWER
Many Irish emigrated to the United States.

Benjamin Disraeli was Queen Victoria's favorite prime minister.

CONNECTING TO GEOGRAPHY

The Irish Potato Famine

Both Ireland and the United States were changed forever when a fungus struck the Irish potato crop in 1845. The fungus returned year after year, causing plants to wilt and rot. In the already poor nation, hunger led to disease and starvation.

Unable to work or pay rent, many families were evicted from their homes. Many died in the streets or countryside as relief efforts proved insufficient. Famine and disease probably killed more than 1 million people. More than 2 million people left Ireland between 1845 and 1855, many for the United States.

Understanding Geography

How did a crop fungus in Ireland affect the United States?

Disraeli and Gladstone

When King William IV died in 1837 with no heirs, his 18-year-old niece Victoria became queen. The rule of **Queen Victoria** lasted 63 years and is known as the Victorian Age. Victoria gave her prime ministers a free hand and did not interfere. Between 1868 and 1894, two prime ministers dominated British affairs.

A leader of the Conservative Party, **Benjamin Disrael**i twice served as prime minister. He was a master politician interested in guiding foreign affairs and expanding Britain's empire. Disraeli first became prime minister in 1868, but his term lasted only a few months before the Liberal Party defeated his party in a general election. During his second term, from 1874 to 1880, Britain gained control of the Suez Canal and Queen Victoria became the Empress of India.

A leader of the Liberal Party, **William Gladstone** served four terms as prime minister. Gladstone was concerned mainly with domestic and financial affairs. Under his leadership, Parliament made many reforms. Gladstone first became prime minister in 1868. One of his achievements was passage of the Education Act of 1870, which created a national elementary education system. Working-class children could now receive a basic education for a small fee. Elementary education became free in 1891. Also under Gladstone, in 1872 Britain began to use a secret ballot. This reform reduced bribery and political pressure on voters. In 1884 Gladstone and the Liberal Party passed a third reform bill that gave the vote to male agricultural workers. In 1885 voting districts were redrawn to be approximately equal in population.

Despite their many reforms, Gladstone and the Liberal Party failed to solve the "Irish question." In 1801 the Act of Union had linked Ireland to Great Britain and disbanded Ireland's Parliament. Most Irish people hated British rule. The Irish had little representation in the British Parliament. Because most Irish were Catholic, they were upset at having to pay taxes that supported the Anglican Church. The Liberals wanted Ireland to have home rule, which would allow the Irish people to rule themselves. Conservatives, however, did not want Britain to give up control.

British policies that were designed to help British industry hurt Irish farmers. The poor were left to suffer. When the Irish potato crop failed in the mid-1800s, famine swept Ireland. Many Irish fled to the United States. Gladstone unsuccessfully fought for home rule. To ease tensions Conservatives agreed to some land reforms in the 1890s.

✔ **READING CHECK: Contrasting** How did the positions of Gladstone and the Liberals differ from those of Disraeli and the Conservatives? liberals took greater interest in domestic and financial policy, favored home rule for Ireland

TEACH OBJECTIVES 1 and 2

LEVEL 3: Have students choose two of the following questions to answer in a short essay: Why did Gladstone and the Liberals do more to reform education in England than Disraeli and the Conservatives? *(Explanations should focus on the social agenda and attitudes of each party.)* Why did the expansion of public education accompany the expansion of suffrage in Great Britain? How did the reforms in education broaden educational opportunities in Great Britain? Do you think a well-educated populace is essential to the long-term success of a democratic government?

TEACH OBJECTIVE 3

ALL LEVELS: Have pairs of students imagine a dialogue between a suffragette and a member of Parliament in 1919. The suffragette should make arguments to convince the member to vote for universal women's suffrage. The member of Parliament should respond as a Conservative would have. Select pairs to recreate their dialogues for the class. Then ask students to suggest how the response might have differed if the member belonged to the Liberal Party or the Labour Party. **COOPERATIVE LEARNING, ENGLISH LANGUAGE LEARNERS**

Reforms of the Early 1900s

Political reform was accompanied by social reform. During the late 1800s and early 1900s, the labor union movement grew stronger in Great Britain. Socialism, too, attracted more and more followers. In 1884 a group of intellectuals formed the Fabian Society. This organization aimed to improve society through socialist ideas and education. The Fabians tried to spread their ideas through established political parties. In 1906 they helped workers, who were frustrated with the Liberal and Conservative parties, form the British Labour Party.

In 1905 the Liberal Party returned to power. Under Prime Minister Herbert Asquith, the Liberals passed numerous social welfare laws. New laws provided for old-age pensions, health insurance, and unemployment insurance. To pay for these new programs, Parliament raised taxes. In 1909 Parliament's budget called for higher taxes on the wealthy. This angered the House of Lords, which fought against the plan. Liberals then took steps to limit the power of the lords. The Parliament Act of 1911 took away the lords' power to veto any tax or spending bills. It allowed them only to delay other bills. Many nobles bitterly opposed the act. George V, however, who had become king in 1910, supported the Liberals. He suggested he would create enough new Liberal lords to pass the act. The House of Lords gave in and reluctantly passed it.

Less than a month later, a law was passed that gave members of the House of Commons a salary of 400 pounds a year. That was a good salary at the time. It meant that a person without an independent income could serve in Parliament.

Beginning in the late 1800s, many women in Great Britain became **suffragettes**—women who campaigned for their right to vote. They were led by energetic and outspoken women like **Emmeline Pankhurst** and her daughter Christabel.

HISTORY MAKER

Emmeline Pankhurst (1858–1928)

For forty years Emmeline Pankhurst worked on behalf of the women's suffrage movement in Great Britain. Among her accomplishments was the passage of a bill allowing married women to vote in local elections. She also established the Women's Social and Political Union.

The Union's early tactics included demonstrations and marches. Later it became more militant. Pankhurst went to jail numerous times and suffered ill health from her many hunger strikes. Shortly before her death, women won the right to vote in Britain. **How did Emmeline Pankhurst work to achieve the vote for women?**

	Reforming the British Parliamentary System
1829	The Catholic Emancipation Act permitted Roman Catholics to be elected to Parliament.
1832	The Reform Bill of 1832 redistributed seats in Parliament and lowered property qualifications for voting.
1867	The Reform Bill of 1867 further lowered property qualifications, almost doubling the electorate.
1872	The secret ballot was adopted.
1884	The Reform Bill of 1884 gave the right to vote to most farmworkers.
1885	The Redistribution Bill divided Britain into approximately equal electoral districts.
1911	The Parliament Act of 1911 took away the power of the House of Lords to veto parliamentary bills.
1928	All British women over age 21 were granted voting rights.

Interpreting the Chart
Over the course of 100 years, many changes took place in Britain's parliamentary system. *What general trend does this chart indicate?*

LEVEL 2: Draw a time line on the board running from 1830 to 1900. Have the class fill in the time line with dates and events in Canada's expansion and movement toward self-rule. Then highlight events that are related to self-government. Ask students why there were such strong efforts by Parliament to make home rule successful in Canada. (*Regional suspicions made Canadian unity difficult; Parliament was determined to avoid repeating mistakes it had made with the American colonies.*)
ENGLISH LANGUAGE LEARNERS

LEVEL 1: Remind students that despite a strong commitment to democracy today, there have been times in Australia's and New Zealand's history when some of their people acted in ways that suggested this commitment was limited. Organize the class into small groups. Have half the groups create posters that illustrate limits on Australia's commitment to democracy in the 1800s. Have the other groups design posters that show limits on democracy in New Zealand during the same period.
COOPERATIVE LEARNING, ENGLISH LANGUAGE LEARNERS

Linking Past to Present

The differences between French and British Canadians remain strong today. A separatist movement exists in Quebec, where more than 80 percent of the population is French-speaking. In 1976 a separatist political party won control of Quebec's provincial government.

In recent years, Quebec voters have narrowly defeated referendums calling for the province's independence from the rest of Canada.

Critical Thinking

Ask students why a French-speaking region of a country might want to separate from the English-speaking majority.

ANSWER: French speakers might feel threatened because their heritage, culture, and values are different from those of the majority.

WHAT IF? ANSWER

Britain may have lost Canada and other colonies. It might not have granted self-government.

MAP ANSWER

through purchase

The suffragettes petitioned Parliament and demonstrated. They became increasingly determined and disruptive. Women's suffrage, however, was not won until after World War I.

✔ **READING CHECK: Summarizing** How was Parliament changed during the 1900s?
Lords lost veto power; House of Commons members got salary

Changes in the British Empire

Settlers in other areas of the British Empire—Canada, Australia, and New Zealand—also benefited from the liberal reforms in Great Britain.

Canada. In the early 1800s, Canadians were not happy with British rule. British settlers in Upper Canada—now part of Ontario—wanted more self-rule. French Canadians in Lower Canada—now part of Quebec—disliked being controlled by the British.

What If? What if Great Britain had not experienced the American Revolution? How might its policies toward Canada and other colonies have differed?

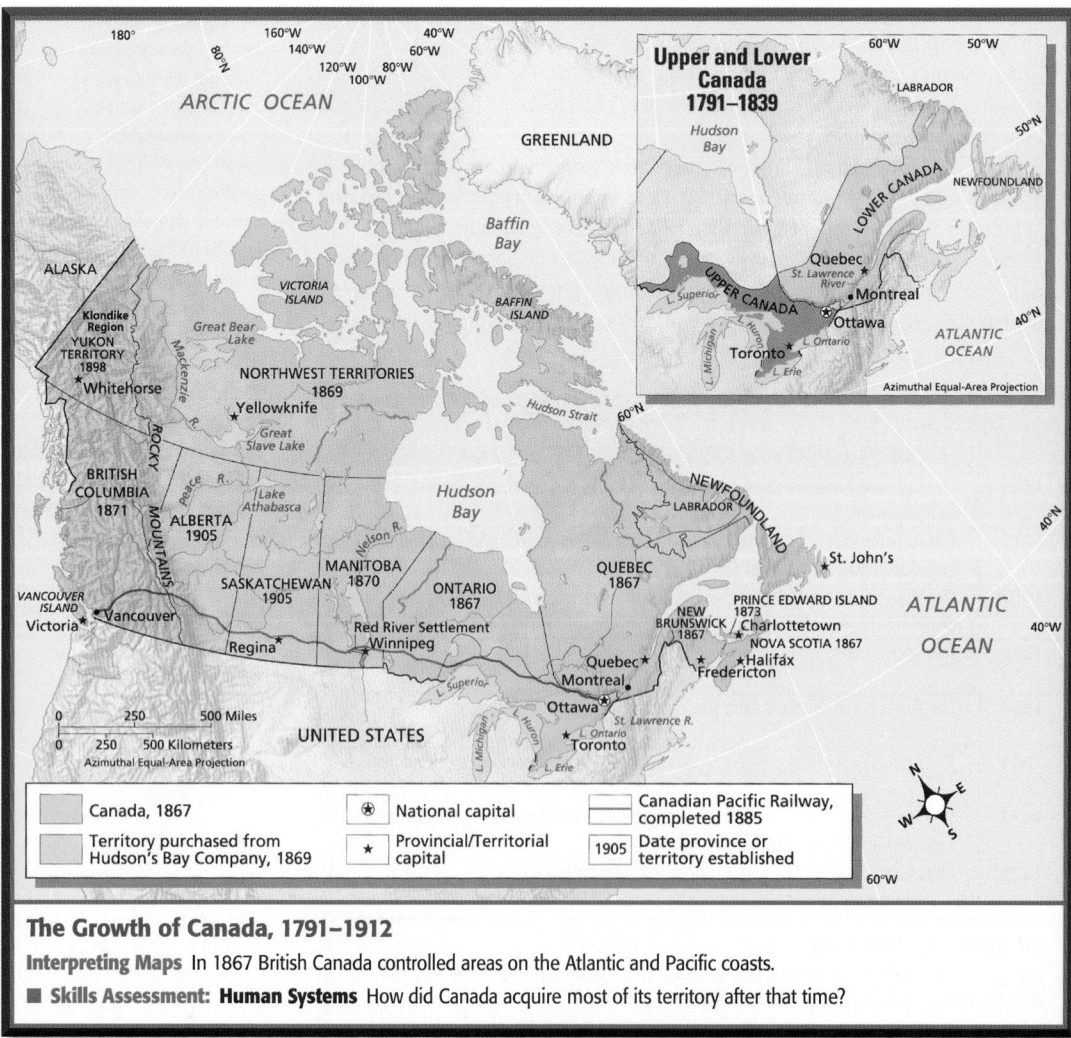

The Growth of Canada, 1791–1912
Interpreting Maps In 1867 British Canada controlled areas on the Atlantic and Pacific coasts.
■ **Skills Assessment: Human Systems** How did Canada acquire most of its territory after that time?

CLOSE

Have the class summarize the contributions Great Britain has made to the growth of democracy in the world. *(Responses should cite the movements to end slavery and extend voting rights to women, the establishment of parliamentary government in nations of the British Empire.)* Then lead students in a discussion of how these trends have affected the United States. *(Students should recognize the British foundations of American government and the influence of British reform movements on the end of slavery and the expansion of women's rights in the United States.)*

During the 1830s a depression, unemployment, and crop failures led to failed uprisings in both parts of Canada.

Britain was anxious not to repeat the mistake that had cost it the American colonies, in which the British government had not treated the colonists as full citizens. It had been too far away to fully understand their situation or enforce its authority.

In 1838 the British government sent **Lord Durham** to Canada. A member of the Liberal Party, Durham was given broad powers to reform Canada's government. Durham suggested that Great Britain could keep colonies such as Canada in the empire by granting them self-government and that Canada be united into one state. In 1841 the British Parliament unified British Upper Canada and French Lower Canada by passage of the Act of Union. A parliament was formed in which both regions were represented equally. From 1846 to 1848, the British expanded the power of Canada's Parliament and granted Canada self-government.

Uniting Upper and Lower Canada was a failure. The equally divided Parliament resulted in gridlock. This problem was solved when the British Parliament passed the British North America Act of 1867, creating the Dominion of Canada with four provinces—Ontario, Quebec, Nova Scotia, and New Brunswick. Each province had its own legislature for local affairs. A federal Parliament dealt with national issues.

Canada expanded by purchasing the Northwest Territories in 1869 and 1870 from the Hudson's Bay Company, creating the province of Manitoba. In the 1870s British Columbia and Prince Edward Island became provinces. In the late 1890s the discovery of gold brought many people to northwestern Canada, leading to the organization of the Yukon Territory in 1898. The Canadian Pacific Railway opened western Canada to immigration, and Alberta and Saskatchewan joined the Dominion in 1905.

Australia. While early history is obscure, scientists believe the earliest settlers of Oceania, which includes Australia and New Zealand, came from Asia over 40,000 years ago and lived simply off the land. In 1770 Captain James Cook, a British sailor, claimed the eastern shore of Australia for Great Britain. This area is now known as New South Wales. After the American Revolution, Britain began to use Australia as a penal colony. The first convicts arrived in 1788 and soon founded the town of Sydney. Free settlers arrived shortly thereafter. Convicts who served their sentences could stay in Australia and own land, but the two groups of settlers did not always get along.

These women and men working a Canadian mine in about 1900 dreamed of finding fortunes in gold.

Australia and New Zealand, c. 1800s

Interpreting Maps Britain established six colonies across the Australian continent.

■ **Skills Assessment: Places and Regions** What island off the southern coast of Australia did the British also colonize? ⊛TEKS

Constitutional Heritage

A miner's revolt in Australia in 1854 forced British officials to introduce democratic reforms there that were decades from accomplishment in Britain. For example, Australians gained the secret ballot in 1856 and adult male suffrage the following year. Australian parliamentarians were paid beginning in 1870 and women gained the vote in 1908—also well before similar reforms were won in Britain.

Critical Thinking

Ask students what effect these events in Australia likely had on the reform movement in Britain.

ANSWER: Students should recognize that gaining these reforms in Australia likely encouraged British reformers.

MAP ANSWER
Tasmania

REVIEW

Have students complete the Section 1 Review on p. 608.

ASSESS

Have students complete Daily Quiz 24.1. As Alternative Assessment, you may want to use the Condition and Reform chart or the homework assignment in this section's lessons.

RETEACH

Have students complete the Main Idea Activity for English Language Learners and Special Needs Students 24.1. Then have students create a time line showing the reforms in Great Britain in the 1800s and 1900s. **ENGLISH LANGUAGE LEARNERS, COOPERATIVE LEARNING**

EXTEND

Have groups research one of the political or social issues confronting Great Britain in the 1800s or early 1900s. Then have each group make an oral presentation about the issue from the point of view of Conservatives or Liberals. **BLOCK SCHEDULING, COOPERATIVE LEARNING**

VISUAL RECORD ANSWER

They valued their traditional culture.

1 **REVIEW ANSWERS**

❶ **Define**
- suffrage, p. 602
- suffragettes, p. 605

❷ **Identify**
- Queen Victoria, p. 604
- Benjamin Disraeli, p. 604
- William Gladstone, p. 604
- Emmeline Pankhurst, p. 605
- Lord Durham, p. 607
- Aborigines, p. 608
- Maori, p. 608

❸ Charts should accurately summarize conditions and reforms.

❹ a. boundaries no longer represented population distribution, only property owners could vote or hold office; gave cities and the middle class more voice in government

b. Disraeli: interested in expanding the empire; Britain gained control of the Suez Canal and Queen Victoria became empress of India; Gladstone: focused on domestic reforms; national elementary education system created, secret ballot adopted, voting rights expanded

c. granted political and social reforms, including self-government

❺ Statements will vary.

INTERPRETING THE VISUAL RECORD

The Maori A New Zealand photographer captured this image of a Maori chief in about 1880. *What does this image tell you about the chief and his people?*

The early 1800s were a lawless period in Australia. Immigrants, ex-convicts, and gangs of escaped convicts clashed. The original inhabitants of Australia, the **Aborigines,** were pushed into the interior of the country. The Aborigines population was greatly reduced by British settlement. Many died from new diseases brought by the Europeans. British ideas of racial superiority also led to brutal violence against the Aborigines.

Britain claimed the entire continent of Australia in 1829. By 1836 the colonies of Tasmania, Western Australia, and South Australia had been organized. Victoria was formed in 1851, and Queensland was added in 1859. The colonies developed independently of each other. However, to guard against territorial expansion by other European powers the colonies united in 1901 as the Commonwealth of Australia, a self-governing part of the British Empire. As Australia's economy grew, trade unions and the Labor Party influenced Parliament. Social welfare laws were passed concerning issues such as old-age pensions and wage fixing.

New Zealand. Like Australia, New Zealand had been sighted by Captain James Cook. Private companies developed the islands in the 1820s and 1830s. In 1840 the British took control of New Zealand when they signed a treaty with the **Maori** (MOW·ree), the original inhabitants. The British Parliament granted New Zealand a constitution in 1852, and the islands became a self-governing colony.

Like the Aborigines in Australia, however, the Maori were hurt by European settlement. British settlers and the native inhabitants fought over land, and several wars took place in the 1860s and early 1870s. Many Maori died from warfare and disease.

The discovery of gold in 1861 brought new waves of immigrants. In 1893 New Zealand became the first country in the world to grant women the right to vote. In 1907 New Zealand joined the British Empire as a dominion.

✔ **READING CHECK: Identifying Cause and Effect** How were the original inhabitants of Australia and New Zealand affected by European settlement? their population was pushed off land, reduced by war and disease

---

SECTION 1 REVIEW

1. **Define** and explain the significance:
   suffrage
   suffragettes

2. **Identify** and explain the significance:
   Queen Victoria
   Benjamin Disraeli
   William Gladstone
   Emmeline Pankhurst
   Lord Durham
   Aborigines
   Maori

3. **Categorizing** Copy the chart below. Use it to organize the conditions and reforms in Great Britain in the 1800s and 1900s.

Condition	Reform

4. **Finding the Main Idea**
   a. Why was the Reform Bill of 1832 needed? How did it affect British government?
   b. Compare the views and achievements of British prime ministers Benjamin Disraeli and William Gladstone.
   c. What steps did Britain take in Canada, Australia, and New Zealand to ensure that the colonists there would not rebel?

5. **Writing and Critical Thinking**
   Supporting a Point of View Write a policy statement that expresses the Conservative Party's point of view on reforms in Britain in the 1800s.
   Consider:
   • what conditions existed that prompted the reforms
   • what reforms were enacted
   • the cost of the reforms

Homework Practice Online
keyword: SP3 HP24

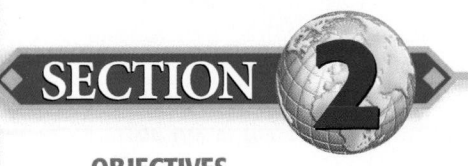

OBJECTIVES

1 **Describe how the United States expanded westward.**

2 **Explain why the United States fought a civil war.**

3 **Describe ways the United States changed after the Civil War.**

🔊 LET'S GET STARTED!

As students enter the classroom, have them each make a list of methods by which nations have expanded their land holdings throughout history. (*Likely responses will include annexation, war, and founding colonies.*) Then ask how expansion can change a nation. (*Responses will likely center on consequences of new peoples and resources.*) Tell students that in Section 2 they will learn about expansion and other types of "growth" that took place in the United States during the age of reform.

SECTION 2

READ TO DISCOVER

❶ How did the United States expand westward?

❷ Why did the United States fight a civil war?

❸ In what ways did the United States change after the Civil War?

DEFINE

sectionalism
secede
total war

IDENTIFY

Northwest Ordinance
Abraham Lincoln
Emancipation Proclamation
Lucretia Mott
Elizabeth Cady Stanton

▶ WHY IT MATTERS TODAY

The extension of suffrage and civil rights that began in the 1800s affects elections, job opportunities, housing, and education to this day. Use CNN or other **current event** sources to see how the "equal protection" clause has affected policies such as affirmative action. Record your findings in your journal.

CNNstudentNews.com

Expansion and Reform in the United States

The Main Idea
During the 1800s the United States expanded greatly, but a civil war divided the nation.

The Story Continues *As the United States gained more territory in North America, people argued bitterly over whether to abolish or continue slavery. President Abraham Lincoln promised to both stop slavery and keep the country together, saying, "I believe this government cannot endure permanently half slave and half free. I do not expect the Union to be dissolved; . . . but I do expect it will cease to be divided."*

Territorial Growth

While Great Britain was reforming its social, economic, and political systems, the United States was growing larger and more populated. In 1788 the United States was made up of 13 states and had a population of almost 4 million people, most living in small farming communities in the east. Most Americans wanted to avoid European affairs and focused on building their lives within the new country. By 1900 the United States had grown to almost four times its original size and its population was about 60 million.

The Northwest Territory. Individual colonies had once claimed the land bordered by the Appalachian Mountains, Mississippi and Ohio Rivers, and Great Lakes. When the Articles of Confederation were ratified, this land—called the Northwest Territory—was turned over to the United States. Thousands of settlers moved into the territory, and in 1787 Congress passed the **Northwest Ordinance** to provide some form of government for them.

The ordinance guaranteed that the settlers would receive the same rights as the citizens in the original 13 states. It also stated that the Northwest Territory would be divided into states that would be admitted into the Union. Once 5,000 males lived in a territory, it could start its own legislature. When 60,000 people lived there, it could

This painting shows people from Connecticut moving to the Northwest Territory in the late 1700s.

SECTION 2 RESOURCES

REPRODUCIBLE RESOURCES

▶ Guided Reading Strategy 24.2

▶ Geography Activity 24: The Slave Trade in the United States

▶ Readings in World History 82: The Death of President Lincoln

TECHNOLOGY RESOURCES

▶ One-Stop Planner 24.2

▶ Holt Researcher: World History: Abraham Lincoln

▶ Holt Researcher: World History: Lucretia Mott, Elizabeth Cady Stanton

▶ CNN Presents World Cultures: Yesterday and Today Segment 22: Honoring Women's Suffrage

▶ Homework Practice Online

REINFORCEMENT, REVIEW, AND ASSESSMENT

▶ Section 2 Review, p. 614

▶ Daily Quiz 24.2

▶ Main Idea Activity 24.2

▶ English Audio Summary 24.2

▶ Spanish Audio Summary 24.2

LEVEL 1: Copy the following chart on the board, omitting the italicized answers. Ask students to copy the chart and complete it. Tell them to include: the name of each new territory added after 1800; when, how, and from whom each territory was obtained; and the states that eventually were wholly or partly created from each new territory. Have students exchange and review one another's completed charts for accuracy. **ENGLISH LANGUAGE LEARNERS**

The Expansion of the United States			
Territory	**How obtained**	**Date**	**States created**
Louisiana Purchase	*bought from France*	*1803*	*MN, IA, MO, AR, LA, OK, KS, NE, SD, ND, CO, WY, MT*
Florida	*bought from Spain*	*1819*	*FL, AL, MS, LA*
Texas	*annexed by United States*	*1845*	*TX, OK, NM, KS, CO, WY*
Oregon Country	*treaty with Britain*	*1846*	*OR, WA, ID, MT, WY*
Mexican Cession	*war with Mexico*	*1848*	*CA, NV, UT, CO, WY, NM, AZ*
Gadsden Purchase	*bought from Mexico*	*1853*	*AZ, NM*

Geography

The Adams-Onís Treaty, which formalized the United States' acquisition of Florida in 1819, also settled a 16-year-old dispute between the United States and Spain over the western boundary of the Louisiana Purchase.

In return for Spain's cession of Florida, the United States gave up its claim to parts of what are now Texas, New Mexico, Colorado, Kansas, and Oklahoma. Since the treaty set the boundary between American and Spanish territory from the Gulf of Mexico to British Canada, it is also known as the Transcontinental Treaty.

ACTIVITY: Ask students to research the circumstances by which Alaska or Hawaii became part of the United States and to summarize their findings in a written report.

MAP ANSWER

13

adopt a constitution and apply for statehood. Many people left their homes on the east coast to settle the Northwest Territory. Of the ten new states that were added to the United States between 1791 and 1836, three were part of the Northwest Territory.

Continued expansion. In 1803 the French emperor Napoléon sold the United States the vast Louisiana Territory, which almost doubled the size of the nation. The country also purchased Florida from Spain in 1819. In 1836 American settlers in Mexican territory declared themselves independent and formed the Republic of Texas. When the United States took control of Texas, war with Mexico began. The United States won and received the Mexican Cession, a huge tract of land.

The nation continued to expand. An 1846 treaty with Great Britain gave the United States the Oregon Territory. In 1853 the country completed the Gadsden Purchase,

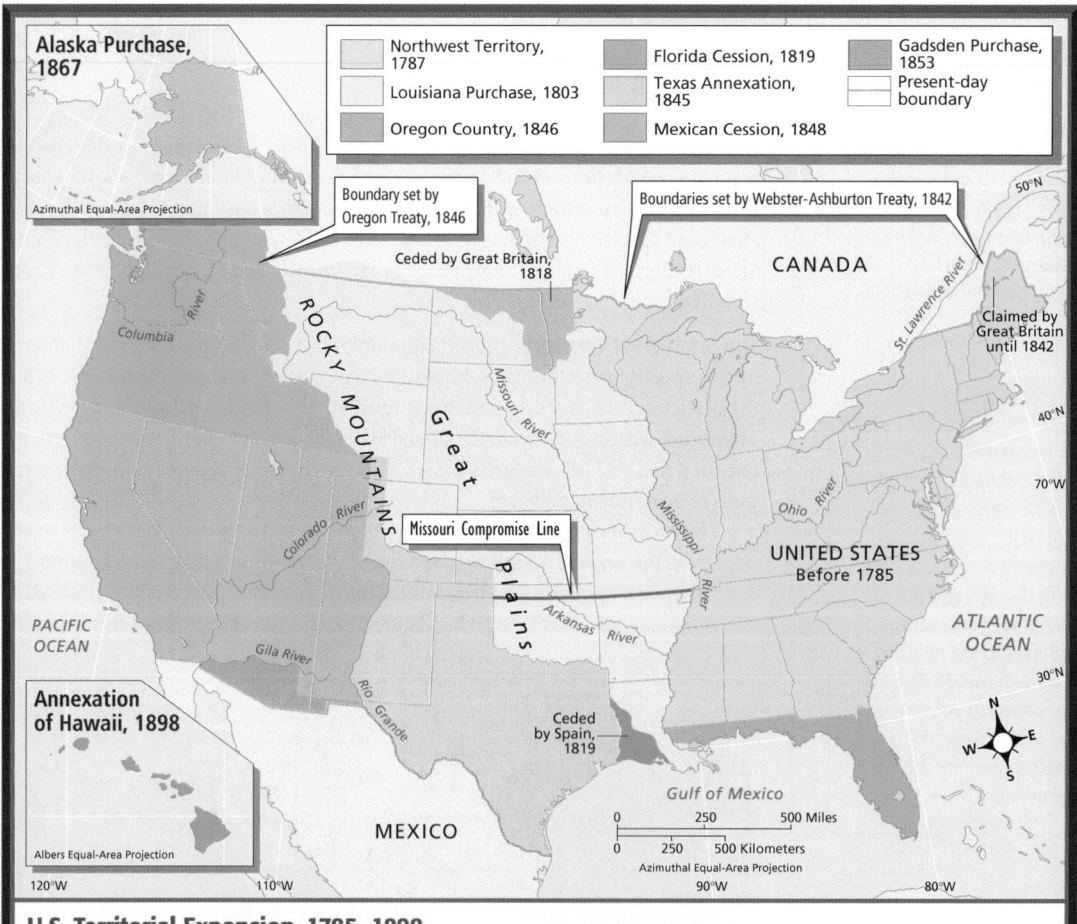

U.S. Territorial Expansion, 1785–1898

Interpreting Maps By the 1850s the nation stretched from Mexico to Canada and from one ocean to the next. This expansion led to conflicts with the Mexicans as well as American Indians.

■ **Skills Assessment: Physical Systems** How many present-day states were entirely or partially included in the Louisiana Purchase?

which expanded its southern border. Over the next 50 years Americans would move west to search for gold or to settle the land as farmers or ranchers. Their movements pushed American Indians off most of the land and onto reservations.

✔ **READING CHECK: Summarizing** In what ways did the United States acquire western lands? treaties, wars, purchases

Slavery and Civil War

Although unified politically, the United States was hurt by **sectionalism,** or competition among sections or regions of the country. In the early 1800s three major sections emerged: the industrial Northeast, the agricultural South, and the largely frontier West. People from these three regions had different ways of life and different views on issues. The issue that divided them most was slavery.

Slavery was legal in the United States, but each individual state could allow or abolish it. Some southerners believed they needed African American slaves to harvest their cotton and tobacco crops. As the nation expanded, Americans began to question whether slavery should be allowed in the new territories. Southerners said that Congress had no power to prohibit it. Northerners disagreed. In time, however, more and more people began to think that slavery should be abolished altogether. Throughout the early 1800s these arguments led to bitter sectional quarrels. Southern states sometimes threatened to **secede,** or withdraw from the Union.

In 1860 **Abraham Lincoln** was elected president. His Republican Party had already vowed to stop the spread of slavery to new territories. In response to the election South Carolina seceded from the Union. Other southern states followed, and together they formed the Confederate States of America.

President Lincoln argued that these states had no constitutional right to secede. Therefore they were rebelling, and the federal government had a constitutional duty to end all rebellions. In 1861 the Union and the Confederacy began a bloody war that continued for four long years. Military leaders employed the new strategy of **total war,** in which both the enemy's military and civilian resources were targets of destruction. The use of new and vastly more lethal weapons made this the first "modern" war.

As the war continued, it became clear that the South lacked the troops and industrial resources needed to overcome the power of the North. In April 1865 the Confederacy surrendered, ending the war. The Civil War was the most costly conflict in which the United States has ever been involved. More than 600,000 people lost their lives. Families were torn apart, property was destroyed, and bitterness endured well into the 1900s.

In 1863 President Lincoln had issued the **Emancipation Proclamation,** freeing slaves in those parts of the country still in rebellion. Although it had little immediate effect, the proclamation signaled that slavery would end everywhere with the end of the war. Following the war, Congress passed three amendments to the Constitution, abolishing slavery and guaranteeing rights to former slaves. In many places, however, the law was not followed. Freedom did not necessarily ease the lives of the former slaves.

✔ **READING CHECK: Identifying Cause and Effect** How did the election of Abraham Lincoln influence the start of the Civil War? spurred southern states to secede

---

CONNECTING TO Civics

The Civil War Amendments

The Thirteenth, Fourteenth, and Fifteenth Amendments—called the Civil War amendments—protect all Americans from abuses of power by state governments. The Thirteenth Amendment abolished slavery in all states. The Fourteenth Amendment gave former slaves citizenship rights and guaranteed everyone "equal protection" under the law. The Fifteenth Amendment provided that the right to vote could not be denied on the basis of race or former enslavement.

Understanding Civics

Why were the Civil War amendments important?

Holt Researcher go.hrw.com

go.hrw.com
KEYWORD: Holt Researcher
FreeFind: Abraham Lincoln
After reading more about Abraham Lincoln on the Holt Researcher, write a short speech he might have given explaining why the Emancipation Proclamation was needed.

TEACH OBJECTIVE 2

ALL LEVELS: Organize the class into groups to discuss whether sectionalism, slavery, or Lincoln's election was the most important cause of the Civil War. Ask spokespersons from each group to report its conclusion to the class. If no agreement exists among the groups, lead a discussion that explores the reasons for each group's evaluation of the causes and arrive at a class consensus about which was most important. **COOPERATIVE LEARNING**

Spotlight on GEOGRAPHY

Have the class study the map on page 612. Ask students why the locations of Kentucky, Maryland, Missouri, and West Virginia made their loyalty important to both sides in the Civil War. *(Kentucky, Missouri, and West Virginia: control of the Ohio and Upper Mississippi rivers; Maryland: control of Washington, D.C.)* Then ask them to deduce what role geography played in limiting the scope of Lincoln's Emancipation Proclamation. *(exempted these states in order to keep them in the Union)* **BLOCK SCHEDULING**

Global Relations

The American Civil War, in which one part of the nation fought for independence from the other, illustrates one kind of civil war. More common is the kind that occurs when factions within a country struggle for control of the entire nation. For example, in the English Civil War, fought in the 1640s and 1650s, Parliament established the supremacy over the monarchy that it enjoys today.

In recent times, the secession of Bosnia from Yugoslavia in 1992, and the struggle between Tutsis and Hutus for supremacy in Rwanda in 1994 both precipitated civil wars.

ACTIVITY: Have students find primary and secondary sources of visual materials about the American Civil War and then create a collage of the images.

MAP ANSWERS

1. Delaware, Maryland, West Virginia, Kentucky, Missouri

2. to take control of the Mississippi River

3. about 100 miles

4. the South, because most of the battles were fought there

Major Civil War Battles

Interpreting Maps Not all the states that permitted their citizens to hold slaves moved to secede from the Union after the election of Abraham Lincoln.

■ **Skills Assessment: 1. Places and Regions** Which slave states remained in the Union?
2. Using Geography Why did Union forces aim to capture Vicksburg, Mississippi?
3. The World in Spatial Terms About how far apart from one another were the capital cities of the two opposing sides?
4. Making Generalizations Which side, the North or the South, likely sustained more property damage from the war? Explain your answer.

LEVEL 3: Ask students to identify the three major social changes that resulted from the Civil War. *(end of slavery, citizenship and equal protection for African Americans, African American voting rights)* Then ask if these changes would have affected the women's rights movement and why or why not. *(Students should recognize they would have intensified it. If necessary, have students review the mention of the Fifteenth Amendment on page 611 and note that it does not prohibit denying the right to vote on the basis of gender.)*

Ask students to list all the ways they can think of that the United States "expanded" as a nation between 1865 and 1920. *(addition of new states, expansion of equality, extension of voting rights and the growth of cities, immigration, transportation)* Record responses on the board and ask students to judge if this period was as much an "age of reform" for the United States as it was for Great Britain. *(Opinions will vary.)*

SKILL-BUILDING STRATEGIES Reading Graphs

Growth through Immigration

As the United States expanded during the 1800s, patterns of immigration changed. From 1800 to 1880 more than 10 million people came to the United States. Many of these immigrants were from northwestern Europe, including Great Britain, Ireland, and Germany. Later in the century, the rate of immigration increased. Between 1891 and 1910, some 12 million immigrants arrived, mainly from southern or eastern Europe. Most of these newer immigrants were Czech, Greek, Hungarian, Italian, Polish, Russian, and Slovak. People from the Middle East, Asia, and North and South America arrived in smaller numbers. Reading graphs can help in understanding these changes in immigration trends.

An Immigrant's View
Most immigrants came to America either to seek economic opportunities or to escape religious or political persecution at home. Romanian immigrant Esther Gidiwicz recalled her feelings upon arriving in the United States:

"All of a sudden, we heard a big commotion and we came to America and everybody started yelling—they see the Statue of Liberty. . . . I remember my father putting his arms around my mother and the two of them standing and crying and my father said to my mother, 'You're in America now. You have nothing to be afraid of.'"

Total Immigration to the United States, 1860–1900

Source: *Historical Statistics of the United States*

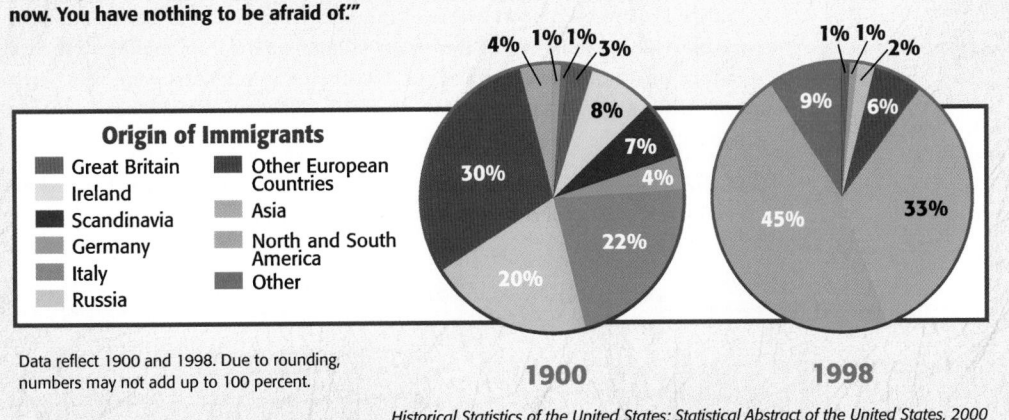

Origin of Immigrants
- Great Britain
- Ireland
- Scandinavia
- Germany
- Italy
- Russia
- Other European Countries
- Asia
- North and South America
- Other

Data reflect 1900 and 1998. Due to rounding, numbers may not add up to 100 percent.

1900   1998

Historical Statistics of the United States; Statistical Abstract of the United States, 2000

That's Interesting!

From 1892 to 1954, over twelve million immigrants entered the United States through Ellis Island.

SKILLS PRACTICE ANSWERS

1. line graph, pie graph

2. line graph: change in number of immigrants over time; pie graph: change in origin of immigrants over time

3. sample answers: Immigration to the United States increased sharply between 1860 and 1880 and then leveled off. Between 1900 and 2000, the main source of immigration shifted from Europe to the Americas and Asia.

4. Graphs and questions will vary.

Skills Reminder

To accurately interpret a graph, first read the title. The title of the graph indicates the graph's main idea and focus. Then study the labels to identify the type of information presented in each section or along each axis. Analyze the information in the graph carefully. Take note of time intervals, increases or decreases in quantities, and proportions. Use appropriate math skills as needed. Look for trends and changes in the data. Use the results of your analysis, along with your knowledge of the historical period, to sum up the data, identify trends, and draw conclusions.

Skills Practice

Examine the graphs shown above. Based on the information shown, answer the following questions.
1. What types of graphs are represented?
2. What does each graph show about immigration?
3. Write one conclusion you can draw from the graphs.
4. Using information from the library or the Internet, create a graph that shows other trends in the population of the United States over time. Write a series of questions to go with it.

HISTORY MAKER

Elizabeth Cady Stanton (1815–1902)

At the Seneca Falls Convention in 1848, Elizabeth Cady Stanton asked women to organize themselves and assert their rights. Her efforts helped launch the women's suffrage movement in the United States. **What impression of Stanton does this photograph create?**

A Changing Nation

After the Civil War, immigration and territorial expansion brought political and social change to the United States.

Suffrage and political growth. In the original 13 states, only white males who owned property could vote. However, states carved from new territories had few property requirements for voters. In time the eastern states also dropped their property restrictions. In the 1820s and 1830s, more and more political officials were elected rather than appointed. Political candidates came to be chosen by party conventions rather than a small group of legislators. More voters than ever before decided elections.

Those voters did not include women, however. In 1848 a women's rights convention was held in Seneca Falls, New York, organized by **Lucretia Mott** and **Elizabeth Cady Stanton.** The delegates drew up a list of demands, including the right to vote. Many women who campaigned for the abolition of slavery also insisted on equality for women. Their efforts gained strength after African American men were granted the right to vote. In the 1890s and early 1900s, the movement for women's suffrage grew stronger. Finally, in 1920, the ratification of the Nineteenth Amendment gave women the right to vote.

Growth in diversity. Between 1865 and 1900, cities doubled or tripled in size, connected by a network of railroads. Part of this growth was due to immigration. For decades many people had come to America from England and Scotland. In the mid-1800s, however, heavy waves of immigrants reached the United States from Ireland and Germany. During the late 1800s immigration from southern and eastern Europe greatly increased. By about 1900 many immigrants were also arriving from Latin America. Large-scale immigration during these years helped make the population of the United States more diverse.

✔ **READING CHECK: Categorizing** In what ways did the United States change after the Civil War? growth of cities and railroads, more immigration, expanded voting rights

---

SECTION 2 REVIEW

1. **Define** and explain the significance:
   sectionalism
   secede
   total war

2. **Identify** and explain the significance:
   Northwest Ordinance
   Abraham Lincoln
   Emancipation Proclamation
   Lucretia Mott
   Elizabeth Cady Stanton

3. **Sequencing** Copy the time line below. Use it to list three events that helped expand the borders of the United States.

   1775 1800 1825 1850 1875

Event	Territory gained

4. **Finding the Main Idea**

   a. Why did a growing number of Americans choose to relocate to the western regions of the country throughout the 1800s?

   b. What factors prompted the South to secede from the Union in 1860?

   c. In what significant ways did patterns of immigration to the United States change during the course of the 1800s?

5. **Writing and Critical Thinking**

   Decision Making Write a letter from the point of view of a U.S. senator in the late 1800s considering whether to support suffrage for women.

   Consider:
   - why women wanted suffrage
   - why some men might have opposed female suffrage

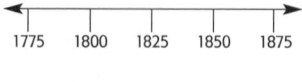

Homework Practice Online

keyword: SP3 HP24

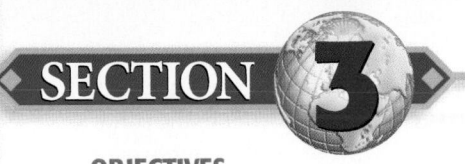

SECTION 3

OBJECTIVES

1 **Explain why the rule of Louis Philippe led to a revolution in 1848.**

2 **Describe how Louis-Napoléon started a second empire in France.**

3 **Summarize France's relations with Germany and other countries.**

4 **Explain how the Third Republic maintained political stability in France.**

 LET'S GET STARTED!

As students enter the classroom, invite them to assume the role of French citizens during the mid-1800s. Ask them to write a paragraph in support of or opposition to the following statement: *It is acceptable for the government to limit civil liberties if more jobs and a stronger France are the result.* After some students have shared their paragraphs, ask if their position would be the same if "United States" were substituted for "France" in the statement. Tell students that in Section 3 they will learn about the clashes of values that characterized the Age of Reform in France.

SECTION 3

READ TO DISCOVER

❶ Why did the rule of Louis Philippe lead to a revolution in 1848?

❷ How did Louis-Napoléon start a second empire in France?

❸ What characterized France's relations with Germany and other countries?

❹ How did the Third Republic maintain political stability in France?

DEFINE

anarchists
coalitions

IDENTIFY

Louis Philippe
Louis-Napoléon
Crimean War
Florence Nightingale
Otto von Bismarck
Franco-Prussian War
Communards
Alfred Dreyfus

▶**WHY IT MATTERS TODAY**

Socialism continues to be a force in today's French government. Use CNNStudentNews.com or other **current event** sources to see how much power socialists have in the French legislature. Record your findings in your journal.

CNN Student News.com

Revolution and Reform in France

The Main Idea
Constitutionalism was an underlying force in the turmoil that characterized France during the 1800s.

The Story Continues *"To arms, citizens! / Form your battalions, / Let us march, let us march!" These lyrics from "The Marseillaise"—the anthem of the French revolution—first called French citizens to battle in 1792. In 1879 the song once again became France's national anthem, as the French continued their long fight for political and social change.*

Discontent and Revolution

As the United States expanded its borders and endured a costly civil war, France was experiencing its own troubles. The Congress of Vienna had restored Louis XVIII to the throne after Napoleon's second exile. Louis accepted a constitution that limited his power and kept many of the reforms set from 1789 to 1815. He tried to balance between those who wanted a return to absolute monarchy and those who wanted a more liberal government.

When Louis XVIII died in 1824, his brother Charles X became king of France. Charles believed in absolute monarchy and abolished most of the liberal reforms. He also taxed the people in order to pay back nobles whose estates had been seized and sold to the peasants. When the French people revolted in July 1830, Charles gave up his throne.

The "Citizen King." The leaders of the revolution of 1830 could not agree on what kind of government to set up once Charles X left. Those who favored a republic did not have the power to create one. Eventually all groups agreed to choose another king. They decided on **Louis Philippe,** a member of the Bourbon family whom they believed to be liberal.

Louis Philippe was king of France, but one approved of by the French Parliament. To help win the support he needed from the people, he called himself the "citizen king." In reality, Louis Philippe's actions helped the upper middle class most of all. Although the number of people allowed to vote had more than doubled after the revolution of 1830, landowners still held most of the power. Workers were not allowed to organize, and labor unions were illegal. High tariffs placed on imported goods kept the prices of domestic goods high. These high prices benefited industrialists but hurt workers and peasants.

Louis Philippe sought to secure his position as France's elected king with policies that favored powerful, conservative interests.

SECTION 3 RESOURCES

REPRODUCIBLE RESOURCES

▶ Guided Reading Strategy 24.3

▶ Readings in World History 83: The Last Day of the Paris Commune

TECHNOLOGY RESOURCES

▶ One-Stop Planner 24.3

▶ World History Teaching Transparency: Everyday Life 20: A Ball During the Congress of Vienna

▶ World History Teaching Transparency: Art and History 19: Derby Day

▶ Homework Practice Online

▶ Online Maps, Charts, and Graphs: War and Peace in the Crimea, 1843–1858

REINFORCEMENT, REVIEW, AND ASSESSMENT

▶ Section 3 Review, p. 620

▶ Daily Quiz 24.3

▶ Main Idea Activity 24.3

▶ English Audio Summary 24.3

▶ Spanish Audio Summary 24.3

THE AGE OF REFORM **615**

615

LEVEL 1: Ask students to list grievances that various French groups had with Louis Philippe, identifying the source of each grievance. Then ask them to explain how the king responded in each situation and why he took those measures. *(extended voting rights, called himself "citizen king," cultivated middle class and industrialists, finally suppressed dissent and called on troops)* Conclude by problem-solving with students about what they would have done if they had been ruler of France during this period. **ENGLISH LANGUAGE LEARNERS**

HOMEWORK Have each student choose the role of a member of a French group that had a grievance with Louis Philippe. Ask students to write a letter to the editor of a French newspaper explaining why he or she supports or opposes Louis Philippe as king. Remind students to check their letters for standard grammar, spelling, sentence structure, and punctuation. Call on students to share their letters with the class.

History Maker

LOUIS-NAPOLÉON. A liberal who was influenced by his uncle Napoléon I's ideas, Louis-Napoléon was deeply involved in revolutionary activities. In 1836 he attempted a military coup against King Louis Philippe and was exiled to the United States. Returning to France in 1840, he launched another uprising against the king, for which he was sentenced to life in prison.

Escaping to Britain in 1846, he returned to France again during the revolution of 1848. This time he attracted a large following and easily won the presidency. After his capture by the Prussians in 1870, he was exiled to Britain.

Critical Thinking

Ask students to consider whether Louis-Napoléon's liberalism was compatible with being emperor.

ANSWER: As emperor, his emphasis on economic progress and development were compatible, but his censorship and harsh repression of opponents were incompatible with liberalism.

PRIMARY SOURCE EYEWITNESS ANSWER

fixed elections to favor his supporters

RÉPUBLIQUE FRANÇAISE.

Combat du peuple parisien dans les journées des 22, 23 et 24 Février 1848.

INTERPRETING THE VISUAL RECORD

Revolution Discontented French citizens rose up to battle the government of Louis Philippe and set up a republic. ***What mood does this image reflect?***

Primary Source
◆ EYEWITNESS ◆

Republicanism under Louis-Napoléon
Louis-Napoléon fixed many elections so that most of the candidates directly supported his government. His half-brother remarked:

"In voting for the friends of Louis-Napoléon, one will have a second chance to vote for the prince himself."
How did Louis-Napoléon undermine the idea of republicanism?

Monarchists who wanted a direct descendant of Charles X to be king opposed Louis Philippe. The Bonapartists also opposed Louis Philippe, because they wanted to revive Napoléon's empire. At the same time, republicans believed that France should become a republic, grant political rights, and make reforms. Most French workers agreed. Food shortages and unemployment between 1846 and 1848 heightened tension and discontent.

The revolution of 1848. France finally erupted in 1848 after Louis Philippe issued a decree that, in effect, restricted citizens' free speech. The decree led to rioting in the streets. When National Guard troops were summoned to restore order, they joined the rioters. Louis Philippe decided he had no choice but to give up the throne. He abdicated and left for England.

The people of Paris established a temporary government and proclaimed the Second French Republic. Active in the new government were urban workers who believed in socialism. To combat widespread unemployment and end economic depression, the government organized "national workshops" that gave people work. This action was an early instance of a modern government trying to remedy chronic unemployment in a country.

The Second Republic allowed all men in France to vote. Elections were held to choose a National Assembly that would write a new constitution. Conservative members of that National Assembly, however, voted to end the national workshops. Violent rioting erupted in Paris in response. The army was called in, and Paris became a battlefield. Within three days the rebellion was crushed, and its socialist leaders were executed, imprisoned, or exiled. The founder of modern socialism, Karl Marx, was expelled from France.

✔ **READING CHECK: Finding the Main Idea** Which groups divided France during the early 1800s? monarchists, Bonapartists, republicans

Louis-Napoléon and the Second French Empire

The new constitution written by the National Assembly gave France a republican form of government. A president would be elected to serve one, and only one, four-year term. The legislature would be elected by all French males of voting age.

Louis-Napoléon. The first election was held in December 1848. Rather than electing someone who had been part of the Second Republic, however, the voters chose **Louis-Napoléon,** the nephew of Napoléon Bonaparte. Louis hoped to restore the empire eventually. He tried to build support all over France, particularly among the military and French Catholics.

The republic's constitution did not allow Louis-Napoléon to serve more than one term. He hoped the National Assembly would amend the constitution to change this law. When he saw that he did not have enough votes to pass the amendment, he decided to take matters into his own hands. The writer Victor Hugo described the night of December 2, 1851, when "Paris slumbered, like a sleeping eagle caught in a black snare."

LEVEL 1: Copy the following chart on the board, omitting the italicized answers. Tell students to imagine that this is Louis-Napoléon's plan for becoming emperor of France. Then have them copy the chart in their notebooks and complete its right column with the actions he took to achieve his goals. Have students explain how achieving each goal helped Louis-Napoléon increase his power. **ENGLISH LANGUAGE LEARNERS**

Louis-Napoléon Increases His Power	
Goals	**How to achieve them**
get middle class support	*develop railroads and manufacturing*
get lower class support	*set up public works programs*
change constitution	*overthrow legislature, conduct plebiscite*
eliminate opposition	*censor newspapers, eliminate free speech*
restore French empire	*take control of Cambodia and Mexico, strengthen control in Algeria, build canal in Egypt*

That night Louis-Napoléon's troops marched into Paris and arrested 70 members of the National Assembly who had opposed his aims. Widespread rioting both in opposition to and in support of Louis-Napoléon's actions broke out in the streets of Paris. Promising to put the issues to a plebiscite—a yes-or-no vote on his actions—and to create a new constitution for France, Louis-Napoléon portrayed himself as a defender of order. Because of Louis-Napoléon's famous name and his promises of order, the people voted almost 12 to 1 in his favor. Like his uncle before him, Louis-Napoléon's coup d'état and plebiscite enabled him to win control of France.

The Second French Empire. A new constitution for France was written, giving Louis-Napoléon a ten-year term as president. He now had great power but had an even greater goal in mind: to restore the empire of his uncle, Napoléon I. In 1852 another plebiscite was held for yet another constitution. The Senate passed a resolution to restore the empire, and Louis-Napoléon was elected Emperor Napoléon III.

Although Napoléon III pretended to champion democracy, he acted to crush those who opposed him. He censored and exiled his critics. The Second French Empire appeared to be a parliamentary regime, with wide voting rights and an elected legislature. In reality, it was an authoritarian regime. The legislature could pass only laws proposed by the emperor. People lost many of their rights. Newspapers were censored and could be shut down. Liberal university professors lost their jobs. Freedom of speech did not exist, and it was impossible to organize political opposition against the government.

On the other hand, Napoléon III did try to develop France by modernizing it. He encouraged the development of railroads and manufacturing, which helped the middle class. He set up public works programs, which helped the lower class. Domestic affairs became more stable.

✔ **READING CHECK: Summarizing** What actions did Louis-Napoléon take to gain absolute power in France? built support among military and Catholics, arrested members of assembly, passed plebiscites

Foreign Conflicts

Napoléon III wanted Europe to recognize him as the head of France. He also wanted to improve relations with Britain. To achieve these ends, he involved France in a foreign dispute that ultimately led to war.

The Crimean War. Russia claimed authority over certain holy places in Palestine, an area that was part of the Ottoman Empire. France disputed this claim. At the same time, Russia claimed the right of protection over Orthodox Christian subjects within the Ottoman Empire. These disputes among Russia, the Ottomans, and France became increasingly heated during the early 1850s. In 1854 France, Great Britain, and the Ottoman Empire formed an alliance and declared war on Russia. The fighting took place mostly in the Crimea, a peninsula in southern Russia. Over the course of two years, both sides in the **Crimean War** suffered massive losses. In the end Russia was defeated and France won glory—but little else.

ALL LEVELS: Have students work in pairs to prepare a memo to Louis-Napoléon about whether France should or should not go to war with Russia or with Germany. After pairs representing both positions on each issue have presented their memos, have the class act as the National Assembly and debate Louis-Napoléon's decision in each instance. Conclude by discussing with students what Louis-Napoléon and France each had to gain by involvement in these conflicts. **COOPERATIVE LEARNING**

LEVEL 3: Call on volunteers to define the following terms: *monarchists, republicans, socialists, factions,* and *coalition.* Ask students if monarchists, republicans, and socialists are examples of factions. *(yes)* Ask students why factionalism necessitated coalition governments in France during the Third Republic. Ask if coalition government is a better form of government than majority government. *(Coalitions may establish temporary stability by sharing power, but they are unstable in the long term because they can easily fall apart.)*

Global Relations

Permission to build the Suez Canal was obtained by Ferdinand de Lesseps, a French diplomat in Egypt. Although the French provided more than half of its nearly $84 million construction cost, the canal was owned by a private company of international investors.

Just six years after its completion in 1869, the ruler of Egypt, whose government had fallen deeply in debt, sold his holdings in the company to Great Britain. This gave the British majority control of the canal. Seven years later they occupied all of Egypt. Loss of the canal, and of their influence in Egypt, was another blow to French pride.

Critical Thinking

Ask students what events caused France to lose influence in Egypt.

ANSWER: Britain gained control of the Suez Canal and then occupied Egypt.

HISTORY MAKER ANSWER

reformed hospital conditions, started professional training for nurses and a nursing school, established nursing as a profession

Analyzing Primary Sources

Identifying Bias Based on the quote in the text, is Smith's biography of Nightingale most likely negative or positive? positive

HISTORY MAKER

Florence Nightingale (1820–1910)

In 1854 Florence Nightingale headed a group of nurses sent to the Crimean War. For the next two years she worked tirelessly to care for the wounded, control the spread of disease, and improve morale. Her reports about bad conditions in the hospitals led to reforms.

Nightingale later achieved professional training for nurses and established a nursing school. She is credited with creating the modern profession of nursing. **What were Florence Nightingale's contributions to nursing?**

Two important developments grew out of the Crimean War. Modern field hospitals to care for those wounded in battle came into use, and **Florence Nightingale** introduced professional nursing of the wounded. Cecil Woodham Smith described the admiration Nightingale received from doctors and soldiers.

> **Primary Source**
> **❝She was the rock to which everyone clung. . . . Her calmness, her resource, her power to take action raised her to the position of a goddess. The men adored her. . . . The doctors came to be absolutely dependent on her.❞**
>
> From *Florence Nightingale,* by Cecil Woodham Smith

An overseas empire. After the war Napoléon III turned to building a French colonial empire. In North Africa he strengthened French control over the nation of Algeria. French engineers began constructing the Suez Canal in Egypt in 1859. In Asia France took control of Cambodia. Napoléon III also tried to control Mexico, but his appointed emperor there, Archduke Maximilian of Austria, was overthrown by Mexicans led by Benito Juárez and executed in 1867.

Back home in France, Napoléon III faced mounting pressure. Although he had relaxed controls on the press and public and had begun other reforms, the elections of 1869 showed that his opponents were growing stronger. Napoléon III had to choose between becoming more liberal or more authoritarian. He chose to be more liberal, and the voters approved. Meanwhile, a crisis with Prussia was looming.

The Franco-Prussian War. Prussia was working to unite all German states under its leadership. Napoléon III and the French people were against a union because they did not trust Prussia's motives. To prepare for war, Napoléon III tried but failed to draft army troops. Meanwhile, the head of Prussia's government, **Otto von Bismarck,** decided that a war with France would help him unite the German states. Bismarck made a series of clever diplomatic moves to insult the French and goad them into war. The plan worked. In July 1870 France declared war on Prussia.

The **Franco-Prussian War** was a disaster for France from the start. Its troops suffered defeat after defeat. Napoléon III took control of the army himself and was promptly captured. The National Assembly immediately proclaimed the fall of the Second French Empire and established the Third Republic. The new government tried to defend the nation, but the Prussians invaded France and began a siege of Paris. In January 1871 Paris fell to the Prussians, and the war was over.

Artist Richard Woodville captured the ferocity of fighting during the "Charge of the Light Brigade" at the Battle of Balaclava in 1854.

TEACH OBJECTIVE 2

ALL LEVELS: Form the class into four groups to present five-minute "live radio news broadcasts" covering the abdication of Louis Philippe, the coronation of Napoléon III, the Paris Commune, and the Dreyfus trial. Broadcasts should include background information for listeners about the event, delivered by the news anchor or reporter on the scene. In addition, the broadcasts should contain interviews with event participants, descriptions of the event in progress, and sound effects as the event takes place.
BLOCK SCHEDULING, COOPERATIVE LEARNING

CLOSE

Tell students to imagine that the class is the Chamber of Deputies in the National Assembly of France. Designate groups of students to represent monarchists, radical socialists, and conservative republicans. Then act as Chamber leader and moderate a discussion about what policies should be followed in France. Have the "deputies" present their views on the topics covered in this section: republican government versus monarchy, foreign policy and the French empire, and reform of French society.
COOPERATIVE LEARNING

France under German domination. Bismarck presented France with the Treaty of Frankfurt, which dictated harsh terms. It forced France to give up Alsace and the eastern part of Lorraine, two regions on the French-German border. Also, German troops would not leave until France made large payments to Germany. A new National Assembly was elected to decide whether to accept the terms. Most republicans wanted to continue to fight; most monarchists did not. Because the French people wanted peace, they elected a majority of monarchists, and the National Assembly voted to accept the treaty.

The surrender angered the people of Paris, who were strongly republican. They had fought almost alone to defend themselves against the Prussians. In March 1871 socialists and radical republicans in Paris set up a council to govern the city. It was called the Commune, and its members, called **Communards,** proposed to change France. The Communards wanted a decentralized government, separation of church and state, and other reforms.

The French government, now in Versailles, decided to disarm the Parisians. Troops entered the city and fought the Communards from street to street. By May 1871 the Communards were defeated, but in the process of retreat they executed their hostages. In the end, more than 20,000 Communards were killed by government troops. France borrowed the money to pay Germany, and German soldiers left France in 1873.

✔ **READING CHECK: Problem Solving** How could the French have avoided war with Prussia? *by ignoring Bismarck's insults*

The Communards destroyed famous Parisian buildings such as the Tuileries royal palace, shown burning in this illustration, during the fighting of 1871.

The Third Republic

The National Assembly was not able to agree on a new constitution until 1875. The Constitution of 1875 officially made France a republic. Under the Third Republic, a president would be elected by the legislature for a term of seven years. The legislature was made up of the Senate, whose members were elected indirectly, and the Chamber of Deputies, whose members were elected by male voters. Although there were many changes of government over time, the Constitution of 1875 stood for nearly 70 years.

In the late 1800s the legislature was made up of various factions, or opposing sides. One group wanted to strengthen the military in case another conflict broke out with Germany. Another faction wanted to weaken the powers of the Catholic Church. Still another wanted France to expand its overseas empire, as Napoléon III had been doing. The conservative republicans managed to steer a course that avoided extremes. They legalized trade unions and expanded education by establishing free, required schools for children under 13, but they did not really address the country's most serious social problems.

Another threat to the government came from extremists in the labor movement. Boycotts, strikes, and sabotage disrupted the economy. In addition, political extremists called **anarchists,** who opposed all government, waged terrorist campaigns in France and throughout Europe.

ASSESS

Have students complete Daily Quiz 24.3. As Alternative Assessment, you may want to use the homework assignment or the chart in the lessons for this section.

RETEACH

Have students complete the Main Idea Activity for English Language Learners and Special-Needs Students 24.3. Then have students work in pairs to write answers to each of the Read To Discover questions at the beginning of this section.
ENGLISH LANGUAGE LEARNERS, COOPERATIVE LEARNING

EXTEND

Ask students to draw two political cartoons, one about France and one about Great Britain. The cartoons should depict a way political change was commonly achieved in the 1800s.
ENGLISH LANGUAGE LEARNERS, BLOCK SCHEDULING

VISUAL RECORD ANSWER

destroying his sword

SECTION 3 REVIEW ANSWERS

❶ Define
• anarchists, p. 619
• coalitions, p. 620

❷ Identify
• Louis Philippe, p. 615
• Louis-Napoléon, p. 616
• Crimean War, p. 617
• Florence Nightingale, p. 618
• Otto von Bismarck, p. 618
• Franco-Prussian War, p. 618
• Communards, p. 619
• Alfred Dreyfus, p. 620

❸ elected president; stages coup against National Assembly; voters approve a new constitution to restore empire; elected Emperor Napoléon III

❹ a. monarchists wanted a strong king, opposed civil rights and liberal reforms; republicans wanted a republic, political rights, and reforms

b. give up territory and pay Germany to withdraw troops

c. legalized trade unions, expanded education, and avoided extreme measures such as weakening the Church, preparing for war, or expanding overseas empire

❺ The statement would likely have come from a monarchist. Points of view should reflect understanding of the events and reasons behind the positions.

INTERPRETING THE VISUAL RECORD

The Dreyfus case Alfred Dreyfus was not only wrongfully convicted, but he was also forced to endure public humiliation. *What are the soldiers doing to symbolically strip Dreyfus of his power?*

Scandals. In the 1890s a financial scandal rocked the nation. A French company had started work on building the Panama Canal, and thousands of French citizens had invested money in the project. When the project failed, the resulting accusations of bribery threatened the French government.

Another serious danger to the Third Republic arose in 1894. French army Captain **Alfred Dreyfus** was accused and convicted of giving French military secrets to Germany. Dreyfus, a Jew, was sentenced to life in prison, even though evidence surfaced that he was innocent. The French army would not allow anyone to criticize its actions. Monarchists and anti-Semites—people who are prejudiced against Jews—supported the army. Even when the real traitor was discovered, the army cleared him rather than admit it had the wrong man. Émile Zola, a French author, wrote an open letter, "*J'accuse*" ("I accuse"), in which he blamed the army and its supporters for covering up the truth. Finally in 1906 Dreyfus's name was cleared. By then, the case had increased tensions between the republicans and conservatives in France.

Reform and coalition. After the Dreyfus case, French republicans began to make more reforms. They ended the favored position of the Catholic Church. In 1905 church and state were separated, and the French had complete religious freedom.

Different factions still caused friction in the country. Groups ranged from monarchists on the far right to radical socialists on the far left. No one party ever had complete control of the government. In order to get things done, parties would temporarily unite to form **coalitions.** These were political groups organized to support a common cause.

✔ **READING CHECK: Summarizing** What political problems hurt France during the Third Republic? conflict between factions in government, labor unrest, anarchists, scandals, Dreyfus Affair

---

SECTION 3 REVIEW

1. **Define** and explain the significance:
   anarchists
   coalitions

2. **Identify** and explain the significance:
   Louis Philippe
   Louis-Napoléon
   Crimean War
   Florence Nightingale
   Otto von Bismarck
   Franco-Prussian War
   Communards
   Alfred Dreyfus

3. **Sequencing** Copy the flowchart below. Use it to list the events that led to Louis-Napoléon becoming Emperor of France.

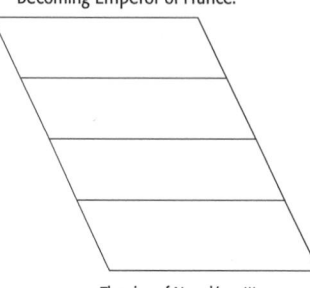

The rise of Napoléon III

4. **Finding the Main Idea**
   a. How did monarchists and republicans differ on their visions for France?
   b. What did the Treaty of Frankfurt force France to do?
   c. How did French conservative republicans help the Third Republic remain politically stable?

5. **Writing and Critical Thinking**
   Identifying Points of View Consider the following opinion: "We need a king to maintain the peace and control the nation." Write a paragraph explaining whether a monarchist or republican would make such a statement, and whether you agree with it.
   Consider:
   • what monarchists believed
   • what republicans believed
   • what you believe about how a nation should be governed

Homework Practice Online
keyword: SP3 HP24

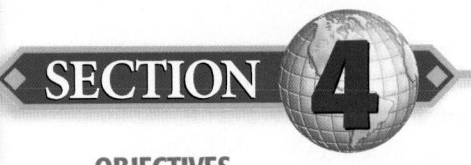

SECTION 4

OBJECTIVES

1 **Describe what life was like in the Spanish and Portuguese colonies of Latin America.**

2 **Explain why Latin Americans began to oppose colonial rule.**

3 **Explain how Latin American colonies won their independence.**

4 **Summarize how the new Latin American nations fared after independence.**

 LET'S GET STARTED!

As students enter the classroom, ask them to think of reasons why people who live in a colony might want to become free of their home country. Students may wish to consider causes of the American Revolution in framing their responses. List student responses on the board. Tell students that in Section 4 they will learn what motivated people in Latin America to seek independence from Spain and Portugal.

SECTION 4

READ TO DISCOVER

❶ What was life like in the Spanish and Portuguese colonies of Latin America?

❷ Why did Latin Americans begin to oppose colonial rule?

❸ How did Latin American colonies win their independence?

❹ How did the new nations fare after independence?

DEFINE

haciendas
peninsulares
creoles
mestizos
mulattoes

IDENTIFY

Simón Bolívar
Toussaint-Louverture
Miguel Hidalgo y Costilla
Monroe Doctrine

WHY IT MATTERS TODAY

Some nations in Central and South America continue to have political instability. Use CNNStudentNews.com or other **current event** sources to see which regions or nations are in the midst of political turmoil. Record your findings in your journal.

Latin Americans Win Independence

The Main Idea
Inspired by revolutions in North America and France, Latin Americans overthrew European rule.

The Story Continues *Inspired by political reforms in Europe and North America, Venezuelan general Simón Bolívar dreamed of an independent, united South America. As one French observer commented, "The ideas of the Liberator [Bolívar] are like his imagination: full of fire, original, and new. . . . He is a lover of truth, heroism, and honor and of the public interest and morality."*

Life in Colonial Latin America

By the 1800s the American and French Revolutions were inspiring people in Latin American colonies to consider freedom of their own. In time, a series of independence movements swept the entire region, from Mexico to the tip of South America.

Colonial economy. Portugal had colonized the region of Brazil. Spain controlled most of the rest of South America, Central America, and southwestern North America. Over several centuries, a distinct colonial life in Latin America developed and thrived. Both Spain and Portugal based their colonial empires on the principle of mercantilism. They believed that a nation gained wealth by obtaining gold and silver. As a result, the two nations took these precious metals from their colonies and used the areas as markets for their own goods. The colonies could not trade freely with other nations.

Certain colonists, usually conquistadors or favorites of the monarch, were given huge estates on which they set up large, self-sufficient farms. These were called **haciendas** (hah·see·EN·duhz) in Spanish America and *fazendas* in Brazil. The estates produced a variety of goods, such as meat, hides, and sugar.

American Indians were used as slave farm workers, miners, or servants. They were often overworked and mistreated. In addition, European diseases wiped out whole Indian settlements in some areas and led to drastic population declines in others. As the Indian population decreased and the need for labor increased, the Spanish and Portuguese began to import slaves from Africa.

Meanwhile Spanish wealth in the colonies grew. Mexico City, Lima, and other cities became centers of commerce. Imposing public buildings, cathedrals, and palaces were constructed. Fortresses protected cities from pirates and sea dogs.

INTERPRETING THE VISUAL RECORD

Slavery Africans were brought to Latin America to work as slaves, as on this sugar plantation. *How does the sugar-cane-processing machine being used by the man work?*

SECTION 4 RESOURCES

REPRODUCIBLE RESOURCES

▶ Guided Reading Strategy 24.4

▶ Creative Teaching Strategy 24: An Era of Expansion and Reform: Scored Discussion

TECHNOLOGY RESOURCES

▶ One-Stop Planner 24.4

▶ Holt Researcher: World History: Simon Bolivar

▶ Regions of the World Music Audio CD Program 3

▶ Homework Practice Online

REINFORCEMENT, REVIEW, AND ASSESSMENT

▶ Section 4 Review, p. 627

▶ Daily Quiz 24.4

▶ Main Idea Activity 24.4

▶ English Audio Summary 24.4

▶ Spanish Audio Summary 24.4

VISUAL RECORD ANSWER

Stalks are pressed between geared rollers turned by human power.

LEVEL 1: List the following terms on the board: *hacienda, peninsulare, creole, mestizo, mulatto,* and *missionary.* Call on students to define each term and ask another class member to use it correctly in a sentence. Then conduct a class discussion about the role that each item on the list played in the society that developed in colonial Latin America.
ENGLISH LANGUAGE LEARNERS

HOMEWORK Have students take the roles of peninsulare, creole, mestizo, mulatto, Indian, or African men or women and write journal entries reflecting on the life they lead in their colony. Entries should indicate why they are content with their lot in life or why they wish it were different. Remind students to use standard grammar, spelling, sentence structure, and punctuation in their journal entries. Call on volunteers to read their journal entries to the class.

HISTORY MAKER ANSWER

Locke, Hobbes, and the French writers of the Enlightenment

Daily Life

Unlike the other Latin American racial labels, *mestizo* was an official designation recorded on birth certificates and marriage licenses. The first mestizos were children of Spanish men and Indian women.

Faced with the dilemma of whether to tax mestizos as Indians or to grant them the exemption given Spaniards, the crown chose the latter course. However, regulations were adopted that barred mestizos from the priesthood, universities, most political offices, and the most prestigious craft guilds, such as gold- and silversmiths guilds.

Although they rarely became wealthy or powerful, most mestizos worked at skilled jobs, lived in Spanish-style houses, and dressed like Spaniards. These characteristics distinguished them from the Indian population.

Critical Thinking

Ask students why mestizos rarely rose to positions of wealth or power in colonial society.

ANSWER: Spain imposed occupational and educational restrictions on mestizos.

Technology Resources

 Online Maps, Charts, and Graphs: Bolivar and San Martin Fight for Independence

---

HISTORY MAKER

**Simón Bolívar
1783–1830**

Simón Bolívar was born into an aristocratic Venezuelan family of Spanish descent. Raised in wealth and privilege, Bolívar received an excellent education, in the course of which he was influenced by the thinking of Locke, Hobbes, and the French writers of the Enlightenment. He led popular revolutions against Spanish rule in what is now Bolivia, Colombia, Ecuador, Peru, and Venezuela. Today Bolívar is known throughout Latin America as *El Libertador*—"The Liberator." **What factors helped to shape Simón Bolívar's revolutionary thinking?**

Holt Researcher

go.hrw.com
KEYWORD: Holt Researcher
FreeFind: Simon Bolivar
After reading more about Simón Bolívar on the Holt Researcher, write a newspaper article identifying the changes that resulted from the revolutions he helped lead.

Colonial society. In the highest ranks of colonial society were royal officials and owners of large estates and mines. At the lower end were the workers, peasants, and slaves. An enormous social gap existed between the two groups.

Racial discrimination was a fact of colonial life. Society was ruled by **peninsulares,** Europeans who were born on the Iberian Peninsula—Spain or Portugal. White people born in the colonies were called **creoles.** Although some creoles enjoyed great wealth, most suffered social and job discrimination from the peninsulares. By the 1700s the majority of the colonial population was of mixed ancestry. **Mestizos** were of American Indian and European background; **mulattoes** were of European and African ancestry. Both groups faced racial and social barriers but still had more opportunities than Africans or American Indians.

The Catholic Church had great power and influence in the colonies. Missionaries converted American Indians to Catholicism. While some missionaries helped exploit the Indians, others took an interest in their cultures and tried to prevent abuses by the government and individuals.

Women's roles were determined by ethnic or family background. Spanish women—a relatively small segment of the colonial population—enjoyed some economic freedom because they could own property. In addition, some Spanish women managed family businesses, ranches, and estates with their husbands or, if widowed, by themselves.

✔ **READING CHECK: Contrasting** What was life in the colonies like for peasants and workers compared with life for the peninsulares? labored under poor conditions, faced discrimination; peninsulares held power

Discontent and the First Rebellion

In the 1600s and 1700s, Spain began to relax its control of the colonies. As a result, creoles began to assume more power, both politically and economically. When King Charles III of Spain tried to regain control, many colonists objected.

Causes of discontent. When Charles III took the Spanish crown in 1759, he had several goals in mind. The new king wanted to establish royal control over the Catholic Church in Spain and its overseas lands. In particular, Charles sought to weaken the wealthy and powerful Jesuits. By 1767 the king had succeeded in expelling the Jesuits from Spain, Portugal, and Latin America.

Charles moved to restore Spanish authority in Latin America by creating an intendancy system. He appointed peninsulares as intendants, or governors, in the colonies. As royal appointees, these officials were loyal to the Spanish crown rather than to the colonial viceroys. Their policies were designed to benefit the home country of Spain, and its ruler, at colonial expense. This system greatly angered many colonists in Latin America, as did Charles's economic policies. The king moved to strengthen the Spanish economy by limiting competing colonial industries. Charles also forced the colonists in Latin America to pay heavy taxes in support of Spain's European wars. These policies caused bitter resentment throughout the colonies.

Colonists responded to Charles's actions with calls for independence. Growing feelings of nationalism were fueled by the revolutionary events in France and in the British colonies in North America. **Simón Bolívar,** who would go on to lead several revolutions in Latin America, said, "The hatred that the Peninsula [Spain and Portugal] has inspired in us is greater than the ocean between us."

ALL LEVELS: Organize the class into groups. Ask students to imagine they are creoles. Each group should determine how creoles would feel about one of the following policies of their home country's government: (1) the hacienda system; (2) the labor system; (3) the class system; (4) peninsulares in top colonial jobs; (5) trade restrictions. After groups have reported on their opinions, have the class summarize Spain's early policy toward its colonies and how policy changed in the mid-1700s.

COOPERATIVE LEARNING

HOMEWORK Have students write letters to the king in the role of peninsulares, mestizos, mulattoes, or Indians, supporting their point of view about one of the policies discussed in the lesson. Remind students to check their letters for use of standard grammar, spelling, sentence structure, and punctuation. Select letters to share with the class.

Historical Sidelight

Among the first serious rebellions against Spain's rule was an Indian uprising in the Viceroyalty of Peru in 1780. Led by Tupac Amarú, who claimed descent from an Inca emperor of the same name, a poorly armed force of more than 10,000 Indians overran the Peruvian highlands and attacked the city of Cuzco. Although Tupac was captured and executed by the Spanish in 1781, the revolt continued and spread to Bolivia, where La Paz was attacked twice before the Indians were finally crushed in 1782.

Critical Thinking

Tell students that the Spanish were exceptionally brutal in putting down this revolt. Ask why they reacted in this way.

ANSWER: Students may suggest that all European colonists, both peninsulare and creole, would have had great fear of a threat that was not European-based.

MAP ANSWERS

1. four viceroyalties (New Spain, New Granada, Peru, Rio de la Plata) and three captaincies-general (Cuba, Guatemala, Venezuela)

2. Portugal

Latin America, 1784

Interpreting Maps By 1784 Spain controlled most of Latin America.

■ **Skills Assessment: 1. Human Systems** What governments ruled the Spanish colonies in Latin America?
2. Evaluating Which European colonial power controlled the Amazon River basin in 1784?

Reproducible Resources

PS Readings in World History
84: The Great Liberator

LEVEL 1: Copy the following flowchart on the board, omitting the italicized answers. Work with students to diagram the steps by which Brazil gained its independence from Portugal. Then discuss with the class the similarities and differences between the way Brazil and Spain's colonies gained independence. *(similarities: class structure and social development; difference: Brazilian independence was accomplished without war)*
ENGLISH LANGUAGE LEARNERS

How Brazil Gained Independence

1807 Napoléon invades Portugal	*future king flees to Brazil*	*Napoléon is overthrown*	*king rules Portugal from Brazil*
1822 king's son in Brazil declares independence	*king tries to rule Brazil from Portugal*	*king returns to Portugal*	*1820 revolt breaks out in Portugal*

History Maker

AGUSTÍN DE ITURBIDE. An officer in the colonial forces in Mexico, Iturbide supported the Spanish government after his hacienda was sacked by Hidalgo's Indian army. However, he was denied a promotion because he was a creole.

Iturbide rethought his loyalties and switched to the rebel side, where he quickly rose to a leadership position. After he was overthrown in 1823, he was bribed to accept exile in Europe. When the payments were not made, he disguised himself and slipped back into Mexico, ignoring the advice of fellow exile José de San Martín to not return. Despite Iturbide's disguise, a soldier recognized him by his style of mounting a horse. He was arrested, tried, and shot.

Critical Thinking

Ask students to speculate about why Iturbide returned to Mexico.

ANSWER: He likely hoped to return to power.

DAILY LIFE ANSWER
Most land was owned by powerful rancheros.

HISTORY MAKER

Toussaint-Louverture (c. 1743–1803)

Haitian patriot Toussaint-Louverture was the self-educated son of slave parents. Between 1791 and 1793 he led a series of campaigns that drove the French from Saint Domingue. He also persuaded British and Spanish forces to withdraw. In 1800 he became governor-general of the newly independent country. However, when France attacked in 1802 Toussaint-Louverture was betrayed and captured. He died in prison in France. **How did Toussaint-Louverture gain independence for Haiti?**

DAILY LIFE

Rancheros
In the 1800s in Mexican California, a small group of landowners owned most of the land. Called *rancheros,* these families lived on large ranches where they raised sheep and horses and grew grain and wine grapes. Ownership of land gave the *rancheros* social and political power. It is estimated that at one time more than 8 million acres of land were controlled by only 800 *rancheros.* **How would the *ranchero* system make it hard to acquire land?**

Haiti's slave revolution. By the early 1800s the Spanish colonies were ripe for revolution. Yet the first successful revolt occurred in the French colony of Saint Domingue, the western half of the island of Hispaniola in the West Indies.

French settlers in Saint Domingue owned plantations worked by African slaves. When the French Revolution broke out, free mulattoes in the colony demanded the same rights as French settlers. The settlers resisted. In 1791 mulattoes and slaves joined together under the leadership of **Toussaint-Louverture** (TOO·san LOO·ver·toor), a freed slave, and staged a bloody revolt. They won control of Saint Domingue. It was the only successful revolution led by slaves anywhere in the world.

In 1802 Napoléon I sent an army to regain control of the island, but in 1804 the rebels again defeated the French. Saint Domingue proclaimed its independence under the ancient name of Haiti. It became the first independent country in Latin America.

✔ **READING CHECK: Identifying Cause and Effect** What prompted Spanish colonists to think of rebelling against colonial rule? religious and economic discontent, nationalism

The Spanish and Portuguese Colonies Rebel

In the early 1800s the desire for independence began to fuel outright rebellion in Spanish and Portuguese colonies. When Napoléon attacked Spain in 1808 and the Spanish fought back, the Latin American colonists had a golden opportunity to declare their independence.

Mexico and Central America. Creoles, mestizos, and American Indians in Mexico all began to participate in revolutionary activities. In 1810 **Miguel Hidalgo y Costilla,** a local priest, led an army of Indian peasants against Spanish peninsulares and creoles. Hidalgo's army won some early victories, but the Spanish eventually captured and executed him. His army was dispersed in 1811. The independence movement did not die with Hidalgo, however. Another priest, José María Morelos y Pavón, assumed leadership of the rebels and began to fight for independence, land reform, and the end of slavery. Upper-class Mexican creoles feared Morelos and remained loyal to Spain. In 1815 Morelos was executed by the authorities.

In 1820 liberals in Spain stripped the king of some of his powers, leading upper-class Mexican creoles to fear that the Spanish government would also make liberal changes in their colonies. The creoles therefore staged an independence movement of their own, led by General Agustín de Iturbide (ee·toor·BEE·day). Iturbide proclaimed himself Emperor Agustín I. His dictatorial rule did not last long, however. In 1823 generals overthrew him and Mexico became a republic.

Central America was briefly part of Iturbide's Mexican empire. In 1823 however, representatives from Guatemala, El Salvador, Honduras, Nicaragua, and Costa Rica met to form a federal union called the United Provinces of Central America.

Spanish South America. The leaders of the fight for independence in Spanish South America were three men—Simón Bolívar, José Francisco de San Martín, and Bernardo O'Higgins—who had traveled or studied in North America or Europe. They knew the ideas of the Enlightenment and the French Revolution.

One of the first revolts against Spain was in the southern region of La Plata in 1810. Creole rebels there seized control of the government. General San Martín led the fighting against the Spanish. Six years later the colonials declared the

TEACH OBJECTIVES 2 and 3

LEVEL 3: Have students speculate about why revolution originated with the creoles and not among the lower classes. *(Responses should recognize the frustrations of the powerful creole class and the lower classes' inability to sustain a revolution.)* Then have them write a short paragraph explaining how the revolutionary experience in Mexico was both similar to and different from other Latin American countries. *(The revolt in Mexico originated among Indians but did not succeed until it had creole support.)*

Teacher to Teacher

Paul Horne of Columbia, South Carolina, suggested the following activity: Have students write a short paper comparing and contrasting the revolutions in Latin America with the American Revolution. After students have turned in their papers, conduct a class discussion of the topic.

independence of what would later be called Argentina. Paraguay, another region of La Plata, achieved its independence from Spain in a bloodless revolution in 1811.

Independence for the rest of South America came only after a long, bloody civil war. Simón Bolívar—nicknamed "the Liberator"—started the revolt in Venezuela in 1810, destroying Spanish power there by 1821. Bolívar became the president of a new nation called Gran Colombia, which included the present-day countries of Colombia, Venezuela, Ecuador, and Panama. Meanwhile, San Martín gathered troops and made a difficult crossing of the Andes into Chile. There he joined with forces led by Bernardo O'Higgins to defeat the Spanish in 1818.

San Martín and his army then sailed north to capture the city of Lima in Peru. The Spanish government there fled, and San Martín declared Peru independent in 1821. However, royalist forces remained in some parts of Peru until Simón Bolívar took charge and drove the Spanish out for good in 1824. The following year the northern territory of Upper Peru became a separate republic, named Bolivia in honor of Bolívar.

José Francisco de San Martín (left), an Argentine general, led independence movements in Argentina, Chile, and Peru.

Brazil. When Napoléon's army invaded Portugal in 1807, the prince regent Dom João and his family fled to Brazil. His rule in the colony benefited Brazil, as he opened ports to trade and encouraged industry. After Napoléon was overthrown, Dom João—now called King John VI and monarch of both Brazil and Portugal—at first remained in Brazil. When a revolt broke out in Portugal in 1820, however, Dom João returned home. He tried to control Brazil from across the ocean, angering many Brazilians. They encouraged Dom João's son, who had stayed in Brazil, to declare independence. Dom Pedro did so in 1822 and ruled as emperor until 1831. His son, Dom Pedro II, succeeded him, ruling until 1889.

The new nations of Brazil and Argentina began to argue over land that lay between them. Settlers in this disputed territory gained its independence in 1825 and called their new nation Uruguay.

By this point, almost all of Latin America was independent. Portugal lost its entire empire, and Spain held only Cuba and Puerto Rico. Very little land in the region remained under colonial rule.

✔ **READING CHECK: Drawing Inferences** Why was Simón Bolívar nicknamed "the Liberator"? led successful revolts against Spanish rule

Latin America After Independence

Independence opened Latin American markets to trade, but the United States at first paid little attention to the region. However, when in the 1820s Spain tried to regain its lost colonies, the United States took note. In 1823 President James Monroe issued the **Monroe Doctrine.** The doctrine stated that the United States would not interfere in European affairs or with Europe's remaining colonies in the Western Hemisphere. At the same time, it would oppose any attempts by European nations to take back former colonies, create new ones, or interfere with any government in the hemisphere. European nations denounced the doctrine, but none challenged it.

That's Interesting!

San Martín's success in moving his entire army through 10,000- to 12,000-foot mountain passes to cross the Andes in January and February of 1817 is ranked alongside Hannibal's legendary crossing of the Alps in 218 B.C. as one of the greatest military maneuvers in history.

🖳 **internet** connect

TOPIC: LA History
GO TO: go.hrw.com
KEYWORD: SP3 WH24

Organize students into six groups to create booklets that highlight the history of each of the following countries since independence: Mexico, El Salvador, Nicaragua, Colombia, Chile, and Argentina. Groups should do library research and access the Internet through the HRW Go site for information to include in their booklets.

ALL LEVELS: Have students compare the map on page 626 with modern maps of Central and South America. Ask what the differences between the 1830 map and the modern maps suggest about Latin America in the years following independence. *(Responses should suggest internal divisions and revolts and international rivalries over borders.)* Discuss why Latin America's internal situation might have encouraged European intervention and how that possibility was avoided. **ENGLISH LANGUAGE LEARNERS**

The United States won independence through revolution, as did many Latin American countries. Ask students for possible reasons why the United States does not also have a history of military dictatorship. *(Latin American colonies had different social environments and a lack of democratic traditions.)*

Linking Past to Present

In 1833 Great Britain seized the Falkland Islands, some 300 miles east of Argentina, and expelled the Argentine settlers. Suddenly, in 1982, Argentine forces invaded and reoccupied the islands. Argentina's defeat in the short war with Britain that followed discredited Argentina's military rulers and brought democratic government to that nation.

Critical Thinking

Ask students whether the Argentines or the British had the better claim to the Falklands.

ANSWER: Argentina: Falklands closer to Argentina than Britain and Argentina held them until 1833; Britain: possession for almost 150 years by 1982

MAP ANSWERS

1. Spanish: Cuba, Puerto Rico; British: Jamaica, Trinidad

2. fears that a European nation might try to reconquer Latin America

In addition to expanded trade, independence brought some social benefits. Some groups, particularly mestizos, were better able to advance socially. Tribute payments by Indians were ended. Slavery was abolished throughout Latin America by 1888.

Latin American unity. It was difficult for the states of Latin America to unite because of vast distances, geographical barriers, and regional rivalries. Only Brazil managed to maintain national unity. Ecuador and Venezuela broke away from Gran Colombia. The United Provinces of Central America crumbled into five separate countries. Argentina was threatened by divisions within its own territory. In 1826 Bolívar called a congress of Latin American nations to meet in Panama to promote unification. Although the Panama Congress failed, many Latin Americans cherished the idea of unity.

Latin America, 1830

Interpreting Maps Within 50 years, the huge Spanish empire in Latin America had broken into many independent nations.

■ **Skills Assessment: 1. Places and Regions** What islands remained under Spanish or British rule in 1830?

2. Drawing Inferences Why might the United States have felt the need to issue the Monroe Doctrine?

Internal problems. Conflict between liberals and conservatives kept many countries in a state of turmoil. The conflict tended to follow class lines. Upper-class creoles were usually conservative. They wanted to keep as much of their European heritage as possible, including a strong Catholic Church and government control of the economy. Mestizos had liberal values. They favored separation of church and state, democratic republics, and a laissez-faire economy.

These conflicts made it hard to establish orderly rule. Latin American governments came to power through rebellion as often as through election. Creoles often retreated to their haciendas while *caudillos*—ambitious mestizo military leaders—became presidents. *Caudillo*-led governments gave the people stability but not freedom, and usually lasted only as long as the dictator lived.

Liberals and conservatives also battled over the role of the Catholic Church. Republican governments often took positions against the church. However, educational systems that had been run by the church were neglected, and there was little public education to replace them. Upper-class conservatives opposed the loss of church power, and the lower classes remained solidly Catholic in faith. This conflict added to Latin America's internal difficulties.

The first 50 or 60 years, then, of Latin American independence were difficult. By the late 1800s growing industry and trade helped distribute wealth more evenly. Development was rapid, and cities grew. Political unrest was still common, but over time many nations began to achieve stability and economic growth.

✔ **READING CHECK: Contrasting** How did creoles and mestizos differ politically in the new Latin American countries? creoles were usually conservative, mestizos liberal

INTERPRETING THE VISUAL RECORD

Hacienda owners This early-1800s watercolor shows the wealthy creole owners of a hacienda meeting with a laborer. *How does the artist indicate the hacienda owners' high status?*

SECTION 4 REVIEW

1. **Define** and explain the significance:
   haciendas
   peninsulares
   creoles
   mestizos
   mulattoes

2. **Identify** and explain the significance:
   Simón Bolívar
   Toussaint-Louverture
   Miguel Hidalgo y Costilla
   Monroe Doctrine

3. **Categorizing** Copy the pyramid below. Use it to explain the social classes that existed in Latin America.

   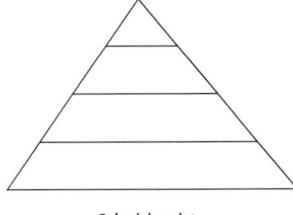

   Colonial society

4. **Finding the Main Idea**
   a. What were some of the causes of the discontent that led to revolutions in Latin America?
   b. How would you describe the revolutions for independence in Latin America?
   c. What problems did Latin Americans face after independence?

5. **Writing and Critical Thinking**
   Problem Solving Take the viewpoint of a Spanish official living in a colony. Write a letter to the king explaining what he should do to prevent the colonists from fighting for independence.
   Consider:
   • what life was like in the colony
   • what options the Spanish had for governing the colonies

Homework Practice Online
keyword: SP3 HP24

REVIEW AND ASSESSMENT RESOURCES

REPRODUCIBLE RESOURCES
▶ Vocabulary Activity 24

TECHNOLOGY RESOURCES
▶ Chapter 24 Test Generator (on the One-Stop Planner)
▶ Global Skill Builder CD–ROM
▶ HRW Go Site

REINFORCEMENT, REVIEW, and ASSESSMENT
▶ Chapter 24 Review, pp. 628–629
▶ Chapter 24 Tutorial for Students, Parents, Mentors, and Peers
▶ Chapter 24 Test (Form A or B)
▶ Alternative Assessment Handbook
▶ Chapter 24 Test for English Language Learners and Special-Needs Students

REVIEW
Have students complete the Chapter 24 Review on pages 628–629.

ASSESS
Use one of the chapter tests to assess students' understanding of the content. For Alternative Assessment, see the Portfolio Activities and Alternative Assessment Handbook.

CHAPTER 24 REVIEW ANSWERS

Understanding Main Ideas
1. suffrage, equal electoral districts, secret ballots, social welfare laws, trade relaxed

2. lost land, many deaths from warfare and disease

3. by purchase, treaty, and war

4. sectional differences, slavery dispute, Lincoln's election

5. republicans: president, democracy, political and social rights; monarchists: emperor, authoritarian, absolute power

6. coalition governments

7. opposed peninsulares, Spanish taxes, economic controls

8. benefits: expanded trade, social reforms; problems: class conflict, unrest, caudillo dictatorships

Reviewing Themes
1. male suffrage and abolitionism encouraged suffragettes

2. resisted loss of power, began to call for independence

3. republic; wanted labor unions and democracy

CHAPTER 24 Review

Creating a Time Line
Copy the time line below onto a sheet of paper. Complete the time line by filling in the events, individuals, and dates from the chapter that you think were significant. Pick three events and explain why you think they were significant.

1790	1830	1870	1910

Writing a Summary
Using standard grammar, spelling, sentence structure, and punctuation, write an overview of the events in the chapter.

Identifying People and Ideas
Identify the following terms or individuals and explain their significance:
1. Queen Victoria
2. suffrage
3. William Gladstone
4. Northwest Ordinance
5. total war
6. Louis-Napoléon
7. Communards
8. creoles
9. Simón Bolívar
10. Monroe Doctrine

Understanding Main Ideas

SECTION 1 (pp. 602–608)
Liberal Reforms in Great Britain and Its Empire
1. What were some of the governmental and economic changes that took place in Great Britain in the 1800s and 1900s?
2. How did European settlement change the lifestyles of the original inhabitants of New Zealand and Australia?

SECTION 2 (pp. 609–614)
Expansion and Reform in the United States
3. After 1783, how did the United States acquire most of its territory?
4. What factors led to the Civil War?

SECTION 3 (pp. 615–620)
Revolution and Reform in France
5. In what ways were French republicans and monarchists different?
6. What helped the Third Republic last for about 70 years despite its many problems?

SECTION 4 (pp. 621–627)
Independence Movements in Latin America
7. Why did creoles want independence from Spain?
8. What benefits and what problems resulted from independence?

Reviewing Themes
1. **Citizenship** How did the reform movement in Britain and the anti-slavery movement in the United States influence women's suffrage?
2. **Government** How did the creoles in Latin America respond when Spain tried to regain control of its colonies there?
3. **Constitutional Heritage** How did most workers in France want the government to be structured? Why?

Thinking Critically
1. **Comparing and Contrasting** Compare the changes that took place in Great Britain and France during the first half of the 1800s.
2. **Decision Making** Should the French people have voted for Louis-Napoléon? Why do you think they did?
3. **Sequencing** What major territories were gained by the United States during the 1800s, and in what order were they obtained?
4. **Problem Solving** Would it have been possible for the newly formed Latin American nations to unify? If so, how? If not, why not?

Writing About History
Comparing Write a dialogue between a republican and a monarchist in France or between a mestizo and a creole in Latin America in which the two debate the way they believe government should be structured. Use the following chart to organize your thoughts before you begin writing.

	Republican or Mestizo	Monarchist or Creole
Government structure		
Leader		
Voting rights		

CLOSE

Organize students into small groups to consider and answer this question: How might governments best be persuaded to include more people in the political process? Ask each group to report its conclusion to the class. **COOPERATIVE LEARNING**

RETEACH

Have students who had difficulty with the test work in pairs. Have each pair use their textbooks to correct their tests. When they are ready, have students take the Form B Test to assess their mastery of the material. **ENGLISH LANGUAGE LEARNERS, COOPERATIVE LEARNING**

Portfolio Extensions

Link to TODAY

1. Ask students to write editorials in support of or in opposition to extending the right to vote to a segment of society in Britain, France, the United States, or Latin America in the 1800s.

2. Invite students to create posters or political cartoons that support the extension of democracy in present-day China.

3. Have students investigate the current status of democratic government in a Latin American country of their choice and summarize their findings for the class.

Building Social Studies Skills

Interpreting a Time Line

Study the time line below. Then answer the questions that follow.

1838 Lord Durham becomes governor-general of the two Canadian provinces.

1898 The Yukon Territory is organized.

1800 — 1850 — 1900

1867 The British North America Act creates the Dominion of Canada.

1. Which statement correctly summarizes the time line?

   a. It runs from when Canada becomes a Dominion to when the Yukon Territory is formed.

   b. It runs from when Lord Durham recommends self-government to when the Yukon becomes a province.

   c. It runs from when Britain passes the Act of Union to when Canada is divided into territories.

   d. It runs from when Canada consisted of two provinces to Canada's expansion into the Yukon.

2. What are some other events in Canadian history that could be placed on this time line? Give specific dates for the events.

Making Generalizations

Read the following quote by Thomas Carlyle about Queen Victoria at age 18. Then answer the questions.

"Yesterday, going through one of the Parks, I saw the poor little Queen. She was in an open carriage, preceded by three or four swift red-coated troopers. . . . It seemed to me the poor little Queen was a bit modest, nice sonsy [sweet] little lassie; blue eyes, light hair, fine white skin; of extremely small stature: she looked timid, anxious, almost frightened; for the people looked at her in perfect silence; one old livery-man alone touched his hat to her: I was heartily sorry for the poor bairn [child] . . . It is a strange thing to look at the fashion of this world!"

3. Which is the best general statement about why Carlyle felt sorry for Queen Victoria?

   a. He thought she looked shy and uncomfortable, and it was only fate that she had become a public figure.

   b. He thought people along her route should have waved or bowed to her.

   c. He thought she looked ill.

   d. He thought she was too young and inexperienced to be Queen.

4. How would you evaluate Queen Victoria's reign? Give specific reasons to support your answer.

Alternative Assessment

Building Your Portfolio

Link to TODAY

Citizenship

During the 1800s people fought for the extension of suffrage to include more and more different groups in the population. Using your textbook and other sources, find out about other groups that have more recently won the right to vote, in the United States and elsewhere. Look also for problems that arise when the right to vote has been denied or hindered. Present your findings in the form of an oral report to your classmates.

internet connect

go.hrw.com

Internet Activity: go.hrw.com
KEYWORD: SP3 WH24

Choose a topic on The Age of Reform to:

• create a scrapbook that highlights the history of Mexico, El Salvador, Nicaragua, Colombia, Chile, or Argentina since independence.

• collect information on the status of native peoples today.

• search letters and diary entries from soldiers who served in the U.S. Civil War.

Thinking Critically

1. Britain: social and economic reforms before 1850, change from within system; France: people acted against existing system to cause changes

2. Opinions will vary.

3. Louisiana Purchase, Oregon Country, Florida, Texas, Mexican Cession, Gadsden Purchase, Alaska, Hawaii

4. Opinions will vary but should consider geographic obstacles, social tensions, political unrest.

Writing About History

Dialogues should recognize that monarchists and creoles resisted change, while republicans and mestizos wanted major reforms.

Building Social Studies Skills

1. d

2. 1841: Upper and Lower Canada; 1869: Northwest Territories purchased; 1870: Manitoba province created; 1871: British Columbia province created

3. b

4. Answers should include social and political reforms and the roles of Disraeli and Gladstone.

Building Your Portfolio

Students might look at events in Africa and Southeast Asia during independence and after, political events in China since World War II, and the voting rights movement in the United States in the 1960s.

Nationalism in Europe

CHAPTER RESOURCE MANAGER

Objectives	Pacing Guide	Reproducible Resources
SECTION 1 **The Unification of Italy** (pp. 632–636) • Describe the events that led to nationalistic movements for unification in Italy. • Identify the important leaders in the fight for the unification of Italy. • Explain the problems Italy faced after unification.	**Regular** 1.5 day **Block Scheduling** 1 day *Block Scheduling Handbook with Team Teaching Strategies, 25.1*	**RS** Guided Reading Strategy 25.1 **RS** Graphic Organizer Activity 25: Nationalism **PS** Readings in World History 85: A Volunteer's View of Garibaldi at the Battle of the Volturno **E** Hands-on History Activity 25
SECTION 2 **The Unification of Germany** (pp. 637–642) • Explain how Prussia replaced Austria as the leading German state in Europe. • Identify the ways in which German unification differed from Italian unification. • Describe the changes in German government that occurred as a result of unification.	**Regular** 1.5 day **Block Scheduling** 1 day *Block Scheduling Handbook with Team Teaching Strategies, 25.2*	**RS** Guided Reading Strategy 25.2 **SM** Geography Activity 25: Connecting Eastern and Western Russia **PS** Readings in World History 86: Bismark "Edits" the Ems Dispatch
SECTION 3 **Opposition to Bismarck** (pp. 643–646) • Explain the problems Bismarck faced as chancellor of the German Empire. • Describe how Germany became industrialized under Bismarck's leadership. • Identify the factors that led to the decline of Bismarck's power as chancellor.	**Regular** 1.5 day **Block Scheduling** 1 day *Block Scheduling Handbook with Team Teaching Strategies, 25.3*	**RS** Guided Reading Strategy 25.3
SECTION 4 **Reform and Revolution in Russia** (pp. 647–652) • Explain the geographical and cultural factors that made Russia different from the rest of Europe. • Describe the characteristics of Russian domestic and foreign policies. • Identify the reform movements that occurred in Russia and their results.	**Regular** 1.5 day **Block Scheduling** .5 day *Block Scheduling Handbook with Team Teaching Strategies, 25.4*	**RS** Guided Reading Strategy 25.4 **PS** Readings in World History 87: Czar Nicholas I's Approach to Government–Orthodoxy, Autocracy, Nationality **PS** Readings in World History 88: An Official Report on "Bloody Sunday" in St. Petersburg
SECTION 5 **Unrest in Austria-Hungary** (pp. 653–657) • Explain what led to the formation of the Dual Monarchy and what problems it faced. • Describe how the decline of the Ottoman Empire affected European politics. • Discuss how ethnic clashes in southern Europe set the stage for a showdown among the major powers.	**Regular** 1.5 day **Block Scheduling** 1 day *Block Scheduling Handbook with Team Teaching Strategies, 25.5*	**RS** Guided Reading Strategy 25.5 **E** Creative Teaching Strategy 25: An Opinion Piece on Nationalism and Liberalism in Europe

Chapter Resource Key

PS Primary Sources
RS Reading Support
IC Interdisciplinary Connections
E Enrichment
SM Skills Mastery

A Assessment
REV Review
ELL Reinforcement and English Language Learners
 Transparencies
CD–ROM

 Music
Video
Internet
Holt Presentation Maker Using Microsoft® PowerPoint®

One-Stop Planner CD-ROM

See the **One-Stop Planner** for a complete list of additional resources for students and teachers.

One-Stop Planner CD-ROM

It's easy to plan lessons, select resources, and print out materials for your students when you use the **One-Stop Planner** CD–ROM with **Test Generator.**

Technology Resources	Reinforcement, Review, and Assessment
One-Stop Planner 25.1 Holt Researcher: World History: Camillo Benso di Cavour World History and Cultures Video Program 20: Nationalism in Europe Homework Practice Online	Daily Quiz 25.1 Main Idea Activity 25.1 English Audio Summary 25.1 Spanish Audio Summary 25.1 REV Section 1 Review, p. 636
One-Stop Planner 25.2 World History Teaching Transparency: Art and History 20: Departure of King William I for the Army, July 31, 1870 Homework Practice Online	Daily Quiz 25.2 Main Idea Activity 25.2 English Audio Summary 25.2 Spanish Audio Summary 25.2 REV Section 2 Review, p. 642
One-Stop Planner 25.3 Religions of the World Video Series: Christianity Homework Practice Online	Daily Quiz 25.3 Main Idea Activity 25.3 English Audio Summary 25.3 Spanish Audio Summary 25.3 REV Section 3 Review, p. 646
One-Stop Planner 25.4 Holt Researcher: World History: Carl Fabergé Regions of the World Music Audio CD Program 9: Russia, Ukraine, and Belarus: Russian Choral Music CNN. Presents World Cultures: Yesterday and Today Segment 23: Fabergé World History Teaching Transparency: Art and History 15: Peter I at the Founding of St. Petersburg Homework Practice Online	Daily Quiz 25.4 Main Idea Activity 25.4 English Audio Summary 25.4 Spanish Audio Summary 25.4 REV Section 4 Review, p. 652
One-Stop Planner 25.5 World History Teaching Transparency: Geography and History 20: Ethnic Groups in Austria-Hungary, 1867 Homework Practice Online Online Maps, Charts, and Graphs: The Ottoman Empire, 1800 Online Maps, Charts, and Graphs: The Ottoman Empire, 1914	Daily Quiz 25.5 Main Idea Activity 25.5 English Audio Summary 25.5 Spanish Audio Summary 25.5 REV Section 5 Review, p. 657

Meeting Individual Needs

Ability Levels

Level 1   Basic level activities designed for all students encountering new material

Level 2   Intermediate level activities designed for average students

Level 3   Challenging activities designed for honors and gifted and talented students

English Language Learners   These activities address the needs of students with Limited English Proficiency.

Chapter Review and Assessment

IC   Vocabulary Activity 25
Global Skill Builder CD–ROM
HRW Web Site
REV   Chapter 25 Tutorial for Students, Parents, Mentors, and Peers
REV   Chapter 25 Review, pp. 658–659
A   Chapter 25 Test Generator (on the One-Stop Planner)
A   Chapter 25 Test (Form A or B)
A   Alternative Assessment Handbook
A   Chapter 25 Test for English Language Learners and Special-Needs Students

Build on What You Know

How did government in Great Britain become more democratic during the 1800s?

Consider:

- **the impact of the Industrial Revolution**
- **demands of workers and the middle class**
- **political and social reforms**

How did efforts to bring about democratic reforms in France differ from those in Great Britain?

Consider:

- **revolution of 1830 and 1848**
- **political problems during the Third Republic**

EXPLORING THE TIME LINE

GLOBAL EVENTS

🖥 **internet** connect

TOPIC: Giuseppe Garibaldi
GO TO: go.hrw.com
KEYWORD: SP3 WH25

Have students access the Internet through the HRW Go site to learn more about Giuseppe Garibaldi and his career as a revolutionary. Ask the students to write an editorial, taking a strong stand either supporting or opposing Garibaldi's efforts to unify Italy. Then ask students to write another editorial taking the opposite position. Discuss how personal biases can shape history and what historical figures might not be considered heroes if the outcome of their struggle had ended differently (i.e., if Italy had not been unified, and had remained kingdoms and states). Finally, ask what role the press has in shaping history. Excerpts from a speech given by Garibaldi appear on page 690.

CHAPTER

25

1806–1913
Nationalism in Europe

This Penny Black stamp shows Queen Victoria in profile

1808
The Arts
Johann Wolfgang von Goethe's *Faust, Part I* is published.

1811
Science and Technology
Luddites riot against English textile mills that have replaced people with machines.

1815
Global Events
Napoléon I is defeated at Waterloo.

1828
Daily Life
Noah Webster publishes the first *American Dictionary of the English Language.*

1840
Daily Life
The world's first adhesive postage stamp, the Penny Black, goes on sale in Great Britain.

1849
Politics
Hungary enjoys a brief period of independence.

1800		1820		1840	

1807–1813
Global Events
Napoléon I dominates Prussia.

1818
The Arts
Mary Wollstonecraft Shelley publishes her novel *Frankenstein.*

1831
Business and Finance
The McCormick reaper allows one person to do the work of five.

1848
Global Events
Revolutions break out in Italy, France, Germany, and the Austrian Empire.

Mary Wollstonecraft Shelley

The original McCormick reaper

Build on What You Know

uring the 1800s reforms in Great Britain made the government more democratic. Changes in France led to a republic that was governed by a coalition of parties. Monarchist, liberal, and socialist beliefs were all represented. During the same period, other European countries were having their own problems. Nationalism became a driving force for change in Italy, Germany, Russia, and other European regions. In this chapter, you will learn about those developments and what effects they had on the people and political futures of those countries.

What's Your Opinion?

Government

Agree Political groups with different goals and ideals may have difficulty when trying to unify under one government.

Disagree Different political groups can combine their goals and ideals, and they will be able to unify under one government.

Global Relations

Agree States that are threatened by the same outside force do not necessarily have geographic, cultural, or economic bonds that would make them want to unify.

Disagree States that are threatened by the same outside force often become unified to protect one another despite geographic, cultural, or economic diversity.

Culture

Agree States that share a long history will want to be a unified nation.

Disagree States that share a long history may have a history of conflict and will not want to be a unified nation.

This emblem bears the symbol of the International Red Cross.

Egg-shaped clock by Peter Carl Fabergé

1861 Politics
The serfs are emancipated in Russia.

1862–1890 Politics
Otto von Bismarck serves as prime minister of Prussia.

c. 1863 Global Events
The International Red Cross is founded in Switzerland.

1873 Science and Technology
Scottish physicist James Clerk Maxwell describes electromagnetism.

1878 Global Events
The Congress of Berlin takes place.

1893 Politics
New Zealand becomes the first country to grant women suffrage.

1905 Politics
The Revolution of 1905 occurs in Russia.

1912–1913 Global Events
The Balkan Wars take place.

1860

1880

1900

1859 Business and Finance
Construction on the Suez Canal begins, funded by French and Egyptian investors.

1867 Politics
The Austrian Empire forms the Dual Monarchy.

1872 The Arts
James Whistler paints a famous portrait of his mother.

1882 Science and Technology
Robert Koch discovers the tuberculosis bacillus.

1901 Science and Technology
The first Nobel prizes are awarded.

1896 The Arts
Puccini's *La Bohème* is produced in Turin, Italy.

1908 Business and Finance
Henry Ford introduces the Model T.

Gold coin of Emperor Francis Joseph I of Austria-Hungary

The Artist's Mother by James Whistler

Government The goals and ideals of different political groups often make a move toward unification difficult.

Global Relations Threats from outside forces are not usually a factor in the unification of a country.

Culture A shared history and common traditions may lead to a desire for the establishment of a unified nation.

Cyrus Hall McCormick manufactured grain reapers in Chicago in the late 1840s and sold them to thousands of farmers in the United States. In 1851 McCormick introduced the reaper into England and into other European countries. McCormick's invention changed the scale of agriculture dramatically. Before the reaper, a farmer with a sickle could harvest only about a half an acre of wheat per day. With a McCormick reaper, two people could harvest twelve acres a day.

Critical Thinking

Ask students what would happen to small farms and farmers as a result of the introduction of the reaper.

ANSWER: Students might predict that farms would become less labor-intensive. Since farms required more money for machinery and less manual labor, smaller farmers would sell their land to wealthier farmers. These poor farmers might become itinerant laborers or go to urban areas to work in factories.

OBJECTIVES

1 **Describe the events that led to nationalistic movements for unification in Italy.**

2 **Identify the important leaders in the fight for the unification of Italy.**

3 **Explain the problems Italy faced after unification.**

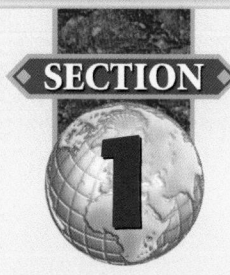

SECTION 1

READ TO DISCOVER

❶ What events led to nationalistic movements for unification in Italy?

❷ Who were the important leaders in the fight for the unification of Italy?

❸ What problems did Italy face after unification?

DEFINE

risorgimento

IDENTIFY

Carbonari
Giuseppe Mazzini
Young Italy movement
King Victor Emmanuel II
Camillo Benso di Cavour
Napoléon III
Giuseppe Garibaldi

▶ WHY IT MATTERS TODAY

In the 50 years following Italian unification, more than 5 million people emigrated from Italy to the United States. Use CNN or other **current event** sources to identify recent problems in the world that have led to similar emigrations. Record your findings in your journal.

CNN Student News.com

The Unification of Italy

The Main Idea
During the 1800s liberal and nationalist leaders established a unified and independent Italy.

The Story Continues *Throughout most of the 1800s, Italy was shaken by turmoil as its citizens struggled to throw off foreign rule and establish a free, united nation. As revolutionary leader Giuseppe Mazzini wrote, the Italians were fighting for "the eternal right which God has implanted in the peoples, that of appreciating and defining for themselves their own life, and governing themselves in accordance with their own appreciation of it."*

Liberals and Nationalists in Italy

In the 1790s many Italians had been inspired by the ideals of the French Revolution. Conquest by Napoléon had unified Italy for a brief time. However, the Congress of Vienna again divided Italy into several large and small states. Austria ruled the territories of Lombardy and Venetia, and reactionary monarchs in other states tried to undo the reforms made during Napoléon's time.

Despite this division, nationalism continued to grow. In the early 1800s many thinkers and writers tried to revive interest in Italy's traditions. This nationalist movement became known as **risorgimento**—the Italian word for "resurgence." Its goals were liberation and unification. Nationalists could not work openly and had to form secret societies. One such group was the **Carbonari.** One of the most famous Carbonari was **Giuseppe Mazzini.** In 1831 Mazzini called for all Italian patriots to join his **Young Italy movement,** dedicated to spreading the ideas of the risorgimento. Mazzini insisted that "neither pope nor king," but rather a republic, should rule Italy.

In 1848 liberals and nationalists led revolts in several Italian states. They overthrew Austrian rule in Lombardy and Venetia and forced some rulers in other states to agree to constitutions. In 1849 the revolutionaries seized Rome, setting up a republic governed by Mazzini and two other leaders. However, these victories did not last long. In 1849 Austria recaptured some of its former possessions in the north. Monarchs in the other states returned to power, revoking the new constitutions. Only the Kingdom of Sardinia remained a completely independent state.

After the failure of the revolts of 1848 and 1849, Italian liberals had little success. Conservative and clerical elements among the nationalists called for a federation of Italian states ruled by the pope. Liberals opposed this, partly because the pope had not supported their revolt in 1849. Other Italians

King Victor Emmanuel II of Sardinia sought to add to his kingdom's territory.

TEACH OBJECTIVE 1

LEVEL 1: Have students work in pairs to make visual representations of the events leading to Italian unification. Encourage students to use visual symbolism such as stair steps up to or highways converging toward unification. (*Young Italy movement, 1831; Cavour enlists Napoléon III, 1858; war with Austria, 1859; Garibaldi's rise, 1860; final unification, 1860*) **ENGLISH LANGUAGE LEARNERS, COOPERATIVE LEARNING**

TEACH OBJECTIVE 2

ALL LEVELS: Ask each student to prepare for and give an oral presentation on one of the following individuals and his role in the Italian unification: Cavour, Garibaldi, Mazzini, or Victor Emmanuel II. **ENGLISH LANGUAGE LEARNERS, COOPERATIVE LEARNING**

HOMEWORK Have students use the process of historical inquiry to find at least two sources of information for their biography. Ask them to evaluate their sources based on language, corroboration, and information about the author. Students should use standard grammar, spelling, sentence structure, and punctuation.

wanted a constitutional monarchy under **King Victor Emmanuel II** of Sardinia. This king was not especially sympathetic to the liberals, but he did want to expand Sardinian territory. His chief minister, **Camillo Benso di Cavour** (kahv·OOHR), was a republican and an Italian patriot. Cavour and the Sardinian parliament supported the goals of the liberals.

✔ **READING CHECK: Drawing Conclusions** How effective were the efforts of Italians to nationalize in the first part of the 1800s? had little success; revolts failed

Sardinia, France, and Austria

As chief minister it was Cavour, and not King Victor Emmanuel II, who actually governed the kingdom of Sardinia. Cavour admired the British system of parliamentary government. He wanted Sardinia to lead the way in uniting and industrializing Italy.

Cavour's Sardinia. Cavour reorganized and strengthened the Sardinian army. He helped to establish banks, factories, and railroads and improved trade with other countries. Believing in the separation of church and state, Cavour tried to reduce the political influence of the church. He even tried to suppress the politically powerful Jesuit order. He increased Sardinia's political influence by siding with France and Great Britain during the Crimean War and participating in the 1856 peace conference that ended that war.

Napoléon III. Cavour saw Austria as the greatest barrier to Italian unification. He proposed an alliance of France and Sardinia against Austria. French emperor **Napoléon III** wanted to increase French influence. He thought that if the Austrians were driven from Italy, France might be able to dominate the Italian states. Cavour, on the other hand, hoped that with Austria out of Italy, other Italian states might join Sardinia in a strong alliance against both France and Austria.

In 1858 Cavour and Napoléon III met secretly to plan their strategy against Austria. Napoléon III agreed that if Austria could be provoked into declaring war on Sardinia, France would send troops to help drive the Austrians from Lombardy and Venetia. In return Cavour promised to give the French-speaking regions of Nice and Savoy—then Sardinian possessions—to France.

War with Austria. In 1859 Cavour began military preparations for war. In response Austria declared war, just as Cavour had hoped. At first the war went according to plan. Sardinian and French forces drove the Austrians out of Lombardy and marched into Venetia. Italian patriots in Tuscany, Modena, and Parma overthrew their Austrian rulers and asked to be annexed to the kingdom of Sardinia.

Napoléon III had not expected the Italians to unite in this way. Fearing that Prussia might join with Austria and not wishing to fight their combined forces, Napoléon III signed an armistice with Austria. According to this agreement, Sardinia received Lombardy, but Austria kept Venetia. Austrian rulers were also returned to power in Tuscany, Modena, and Parma. Although he had delivered on only part of his bargain, Napoléon III insisted on receiving Nice and Savoy. Afraid of losing what gains Sardinia had made, Victor Emmanuel II agreed to the French terms.

A well-educated and widely traveled aristocrat, Camillo Benso di Cavour had once edited a nationalist newspaper, El Risorgimento, a page of which is shown below. Cavour also took part in the revolt of 1848.

Holt Researcher

go.hrw.com
KEYWORD: Holt Researcher
FreeFind:
   Camillo Benso di Cavour
After reading more about Camillo Benso di Cavour on the Holt Researcher, write an editorial about Sardinia that might have appeared in his newspaper.

Geography

Camillo Benso di Cavour strengthened Sardinia as the leader of the republican movement in Italy by siding with France and Great Britain during the Crimean War. The Crimea encompassed most of the north shore of the Black Sea. Sardinia is an island in the western Mediterranean Sea.

Critical Thinking

Look at the map on page 656 and find the Crimea. How would you compare and contrast Sardinia's geography with that of the Crimea? Why do you think the Sardinian military were helpful to the British and French against the Russians in the Crimea? What city would have blocked the Sardinians from traveling to the Crimea entirely by sea?

ANSWER: Both Sardinia and the Crimea have long coastlines, so the Sardinian military would probably excel at naval warfare. The sea route they might otherwise have taken was blocked by Constantinople.

That's Interesting!

During the unstable years following Italian unification, there was a massive emigration: within 50 years, more than 5 million people had left Italy for the Americas.

Teacher to Teacher

Madeleine Schmitt of St. Louis, Missouri, suggested the following activity: Divide students into groups and have them research an area that has recently experienced conflict due to national or cultural alliances, such as India and Pakistan, Malaysia, or Rwanda. Suggest that they use a variety of sources, including computers. The groups should create charts listing similarities and differences between their assigned region and the nationalist conflict in Italy.

TEACH OBJECTIVE 2

LEVEL 3: Have students use information from the text to fill in this chart.

Problem: *Garibaldi could take power from Cavour*	
Option 1 *attack Garibaldi*	**Option 2** *allow Garibaldi to take power*
Advantage: *reasserts the leadership of Sardinia*	**Advantage:** *increases likelihood of taking northern Italy from Austria*
Disadvantage: *decreases likelihood of capturing northern Italy*	**Disadvantage:** *gives Emmanuel II's power to Garibaldi*

HISTORY MAKER ANSWER

He led a volunteer army that conquered southern Italy and helped lead to the unification of Italy.

VISUAL RECORD ANSWER

The artist was probably a supporter of the Red Shirt cause. Students should notice that the Red Shirts are moving forward and are in poses indicating strength and courage, whereas King Francis II's troops are falling backward in poses of weakness and fear.

HISTORY MAKER

Giuseppe Garibaldi (1807–1882)

Born in Nice, Giuseppe Garibaldi joined the Young Italy movement while in his twenties. He was forced to flee Italy several times because of his revolutionary activities. Garibaldi spent 12 years in South America, learning the art of guerrilla warfare.

With help from Cavour, Garibaldi was able to return to Italy in 1854. He then formed an army of volunteers, called "Red Shirts" because of their colorful uniforms. This army conquered southern Italy, helping to unite the country. The feat made Garibaldi a national hero. **Why is Garibaldi important in Italian history?**

INTERPRETING THE VISUAL RECORD

The Red Shirts Giuseppe Garibaldi and his supporters, known as Red Shirts, conquered the Kingdom of the Two Sicilies in 1860, adding this area to the kingdom of Italy. *Was the artist who created this illustration a supporter or an opponent of the Red Shirt cause? Explain.*

The Italian people, however, would not abandon the idea of unity. Rebellions in Parma, Modena, and Tuscany again expelled the Austrian rulers. The people of Romagna, a province in the Papal States, also revolted. Each of these areas held a plebiscite, in which the people overwhelmingly voted to join the kingdom of Sardinia.

✔ **READING CHECK: Finding the Main Idea** How did Cavour work to unite and industrialize Sardinia? strengthened army; established banks, factories, and railroads; improved trade

Garibaldi and the Thousand

The southern half of the Italian Peninsula, together with the island of Sicily, made up the kingdom of the Two Sicilies. This area now became the target of the Italian nationalists. **Giuseppe Garibaldi,** a man devoted to Italian freedom, led the way.

With Cavour's knowledge, Garibaldi recruited an army of more than 1000 soldiers. In the spring of 1860, Garibaldi and his "Expedition of the Thousand" invaded and captured Sicily. Crossing to Italy's mainland, Garibaldi's forces seized Naples, the capital city. They then drove King Francis II and his troops north to the border of the Papal States. Celebrated for his military skill, Garibaldi became a hero both within and outside of Italy.

Garibaldi planned to continue north to capture Rome and then Venetia. Cavour, however, now feared that Garibaldi might displace Victor Emmanuel II as Italy's leader and set up a republic of his own. Therefore Cavour sent an army south to stop Garibaldi's advance. In the process, Sardinia annexed most of the territory of the Papal States.

In the fall of 1860 Garibaldi and Emmanual II met in Naples. Garibaldi promised to support the establishment of the kingdom of Italy, with Victor Emmanuel II as king. He asked only to serve as governor of Naples. Fearing Garibaldi's great popularity, the king refused.

✔ **READING CHECK: Drawing Conclusions** Why did Cavour send an army to stop Garibaldi? feared Garibaldi might displace Victor Emmanuel II

TEACH OBJECTIVE 3

LEVEL 2: Have students list the problems Italy faced after unification. *(little experience with self-government, regions divided by cultural traditions, tensions between industrialized north and agricultural south, low standard of living, labor problems, disagreements about colonial war)* **ENGLISH LANGUAGE LEARNERS**

CLOSE

Ask students to discuss the causes of Italy's unification movement. *(resurgence of interest in Italian traditions, inspiration of the French Revolution, memory of Italy's brief unification under Napoléon, reactionary monarchs, liberal ideas opposing papacy and monarchy, independence of Sardinia)*

SKILL-BUILDING STRATEGIES   Using a Problem-Solving Process

Financing a New Nation

Problem solving is the process of reviewing a troubling situation and then making decisions and recommendations for resolving that situation. Throughout history leaders have had to solve problems faced by their countries. Generally they do not develop solutions out of thin air. Rather, resolutions are developed through the use of problem-solving processes. The leaders of Italy faced many problems in the early 1800s. One of the biggest was how to raise money. The building of a new nation is an expensive process, and Italy was poor. Italian leaders arrived at a solution to this problem by working through a problem-solving process.

The Italian Process

To raise revenue, Italy's leaders knew they had to continue collecting taxes. Some officials argued for a tax system based on wealth, which would lessen the economic burden placed on the poor. Others argued that such a system would take too long to implement, because it meant determining the value of everyone's property. Instead, they called for continuing to tax food and other basic goods. While such taxes hurt the poor, they provided the government with money much more quickly. The minister of finance chose this option. As a result, many citizens accused him of insensitivity to the poor. However, the minister replied that by putting the new nation on solid financial footing, he was serving the interest of all citizens.

Problem:
Italy's lack of finances necessary to build a nation

Option 1
Tax each person based on wealth
Advantage: alleviates the burden placed on the poor
Disadvantage: takes too long to generate revenue

Option 2
Tax food and other necessities
Advantage: provides government with money more quickly
Disadvantage: hurts the poor

Solution Decided Upon:
Tax on food and other goods

Result:
Criticism from some; solid financial footing for nation

Southern Italy was a rural and agricultural land in which people led simple, traditional lives as peasants or artisans. Some leaders feared such people would be unfairly burdened by a tax on food and other similar items.

Skills Reminder

To use a problem-solving process, first identify the problem. Then gather information and examine the options. Note what steps the group or person is considering to solve the problem. Analyze the advantages and disadvantages of each action the group is considering. Note that different members of the group may hold differing opinions about an option. Then choose and implement the solution. Recognize what solution the group implemented and evaluate its success based on the results.

Skills Practice

❶ Based on the results, was the solution chosen by the minister of finance a wise one?
❷ What might have happened if he had chosen the other option?
❸ Choose a problem that another group in this chapter faced. Use the problem-solving process to describe how the group determined a solution. Consult library materials or the Internet if necessary.

SKILLS PRACTICE ANSWERS
1. yes, because it gave solid financial footing to a new nation; no, because it showed insensitivity to the poor

2. Unification would have taken longer, if at all.

3. Students' answers will vary.

REVIEW

Have students complete the Section 1 Review on page 636.

ASSESS

Have students complete Daily Quiz 25.1. As Alternative Assessment, you may want to use the stairsteps exercise or the problem listing activity in this section's lessons.

RETEACH

Have students complete Main Idea Activity for English Language Learners and Special-Needs Students 25.1. Then have students write the section's headings and subheadings on a sheet of paper, leaving a space between each. Ask students to list the main ideas of each heading and subheading in the appropriate space.
ENGLISH LANGUAGE LEARNERS

EXTEND

Have students imagine they are farmers in southern Italy. Tell students to use their textbooks, biographies, computer software, and any other available resources to find out about daily life for Italian farmers in the early 1800s. Then have them write a dialogue between a farmer and his wife about their problems and their hopes. **BLOCK SCHEDULING**

MAP ANSWER
Savoy, Nice

◆ SECTION ◆
1 REVIEW ANSWERS

❶ **Define**
- risorgimento, p. 632

❷ **Identify**
- Carbonari, p. 632
- Giuseppe Mazzini, p. 632
- Young Italy movement, p. 632
- King Victor Emmanuel II, p. 633
- Camillo Benso di Cavour, p. 633
- Napoléon III, p. 633
- Giuseppe Garibaldi, p. 634

❸ lack of experience with self-government, regions divided by cultural traditions, conflicting interests of industrial north and agricultural south, labor problems due to low standard of living

❹ a. French Revolution and Congress of Vienna

b. Giuseppe Mazzini, Camillo Benso di Cavour, Giuseppe Garibaldi

c. only independent state, influential with France and Britain because of military strength and previous alliance, similar goals of Cavour and Napoléon III

❺ Answers will vary.

Unification and its Problems

During 1860 people everywhere in Italy, except Venetia and Rome, held plebiscites. They voted overwhelmingly for national unity under the king of Sardinia. Meeting in Turin in 1861, representatives of the various states confirmed Victor Emmanuel II as king of Italy. In 1866 Italy gained Venetia in a war with Austria, and in 1870 Rome's citizens voted for union with Italy. The following year Rome was proclaimed the capital of the kingdom of Italy.

Although politically united, Italy still faced many problems. Few Italians had experience with self-government. Regions of the country remained divided by cultural traditions, and tensions grew between the industrialized north and the agricultural south. The standard of living of most Italians was low and labor problems arose.

Attempting to build a colonial empire, Italy engaged in several military ventures in Africa in the 1880s. A brief war against the Ottoman Empire in 1911 brought little gain. The conquest of Libya in 1912 strengthened Italy's position in the Mediterranean region but divided the nation.

Unification of Italy, 1858–1870

Interpreting Maps
Italy was united into a single kingdom over a 12-year period.

■ **Skills Assessment:**
The World in Spatial Terms What territories did Italy cede to France in 1860?

✔ **READING CHECK: Analyzing Information** What was a major reason that unification did not result in political stability for Italy right away?

north/south tensions

◆ SECTION 1 REVIEW ◆

1. **Define** and explain the significance:
risorgimento

2. **Identify** and explain the significance:
Carbonari
Giuseppe Mazzini
Young Italy movement
King Victor Emmanuel II
Camillo Benso di Cavour
Napoléon III
Giuseppe Garibaldi

3. **Categorizing** Make a cluster drawing like the one below. Fill in the cluster drawings by identifying the different problems of a unified Italy.

Problems of a unified Italy

4. **Finding the Main Idea**

a. What two events led to new nationalist movements for unification in Italy?

b. Who were the important leaders in the fight for Italian unification?

c. Why did the kingdom of Sardinia take the lead in Italian unification?

5. **Writing and Critical Thinking**

Supporting a Point of View Decide whether you agree with Napoléon III's actions during the Italian movement for unification. Write arguments supporting your point of view.
Consider:
- the agreement Napoléon III made with Cavour
- Napoléon III's failure to achieve his goals in his alliance against Austria
- Napoléon III's fear of having to fight both Austria and Prussia

Homework Practice Online
keyword: SP3 HP25

OBJECTIVES

1 Explain how Prussia replaced Austria as the leading German state in Europe.

2 Identify the ways in which German unification differed from Italian unification.

3 Describe the changes in German government that occurred as a result of unification.

SECTION 2

READ TO DISCOVER

❶ How did Prussia replace Austria as the leading German state in Europe?

❷ In what ways did German unification differ from Italian unification?

❸ What changes in German government occurred as a result of unification?

DEFINE

kaiser

IDENTIFY

Junkers
Zollverein
William I
Treaty of Prague
Bundesrat
Reichstag

The Unification of Germany

The Main Idea
Prussian leader Otto von Bismarck used war to bring his own brand of nationalism to Germany.

The Story Continues *In the 1800s nationalist feelings grew in Germany as the liberal ideas of the French Revolution swept across Europe. As one German student explained, "We want Germany to be considered one land and one people. . . . We want a constitution for the people that fits in with the spirit of the times and with the people's own level of enlightenment, rather than what each prince gives his people." However, the type of nationalism that emerged in Germany did not include the liberal reforms for which people had hoped.*

Prussia as Leader

In the mid-1800s Germany remained what it had been for centuries—a patchwork of independent states. Each had its own laws, currency, and rulers. In the late 1800s Prussia led the fight for unification of these states.

Prussia had become strong in the 1700s during the reigns of Frederick William I and his son Frederick the Great. However, Napoléon I defeated Prussia in 1806 and dominated the country for seven years. He seized Prussian lands, limited the size of Prussia's army, and forced Prussia to contribute money and soldiers to France.

The Prussians found ways around Napoléon's restrictions. The army drafted soldiers for short periods of intensive training. These soldiers then went into the reserves and a new group took their place. In this way Prussia trained a large force while still observing the limits Napoléon had placed on their standing army. These Prussian troops helped to defeat the French at Leipzig in 1813 and fought at Waterloo in 1815. Prussia became one of the four great powers at the Congress of Vienna and joined the Quadruple Alliance.

In 1815 the Congress of Vienna created the German Confederation, a group of states that included Prussia. The Congress granted Prussia important territories in Saxony and along the lower Rhine River. Prussia absorbed these regions into its efficient government and strong economy. Austria was Prussia's greatest German rival. An Austrian Habsburg had held the position of Holy Roman Emperor since the 1400s, giving Austria influence over the German states. Napoléon, however, had abolished the Holy Roman Empire, and the Congress of Vienna did not restore it.

This German illustration from 1850 depicts the Prussian cavalry in action.

TEACH OBJECTIVE 1

LEVEL 1: Ask students to tell how Prussia became the leading German state in Europe. *(Prussia trained a large army and defeated the French, becoming one of the four great powers at the Congress of Vienna.)*

LEVEL 2: Copy the following chart on the board, omitting the italicized answers. Have students work in groups to complete the chart and then lead a class discussion about unification in Germany. **COOPERATIVE LEARNING, ENGLISH LANGUAGE LEARNERS**

State within country that led unification process
Prussia

Means by which unification was achieved
Bismarck built strong Prussian military machine, defeated Austria and her hold over Bavaria by fighting 3 successful wars

Acquisition of land in unification process
Schleswig, Holstein, the North German Confederation, independent states of southern Germany, Alsace, and Lorraine

Major factors leading to unification
German nationalism
Zollverein
Bismarck's Prussian army

Economics

The Zollverein, a customs union established in 1834, was an important step toward German unification. Years before, in 1818, Prussia had enacted a law abolishing internal customs dues. In 1828 it established free trade with Hesse-Darmstadt. Also in 1828 customs unions were set up in the central German states and in the southern German states. These were among the 18 states that joined in the Zollverein in 1834. Because tariffs were abolished in many German states, farm products could be sold profitably across state borders. After the Zollverein, most of the German states could trade freely with one another, but not with Austria.

Critical Thinking

Ask students why the German states were able to achieve economic unity while the Austrian state could not.

ANSWER: Students might suggest that Austria was a country of many languages, but the German states spoke one language. They might also suggest that elimination of tariffs under the Zollverein promoted economic unity and free exchange.

Moreover, Napoléon's rule had inspired nationalism in the German states. German nationalism favored Prussia more than Austria. In Prussia almost everyone was German. Austria, although ruled by Germans, contained many other nationalities, such as Hungarians, Romanians, Italians, and Slavs. After Prussia's gains at the Congress of Vienna, Austria's focus moved south and east, toward Italy and the Balkans.

✔ **READING CHECK: Finding the Main Idea** What factors influenced Prussia's rise to power over the German states more than Austria? large army, efficient government, strong economy, German nationalism

The Zollverein

After the Congress of Vienna, the first major step in German unification involved the economy. Tariffs imposed by the German states made trade between states costly, forcing up the price of goods. Prussians even placed tariffs on goods moving from one Prussian possession to another.

A class of aristocratic landowners called the **Junkers** (YOOHNG·kuhrz) complained that tariffs were hurting sales of farm products. Joining with tradespeople, intellectuals, financiers, and manufacturers, the Junkers campaigned for freer movement of goods. In 1818 they persuaded the king of Prussia to abolish tariffs within his territories. By 1834 German states had agreed to treaties that resulted in a customs union called the **Zollverein** (TSOHL·fer·yn). By 1854 the Zollverein included most of the German states, but not Austria.

The Zollverein made prices lower and more uniform. Industrialization spread in the German Confederation due to free markets for goods and protection from foreign competition. The states adopted uniform systems of weights, measures, and currency. Manufacturers produced and sold more goods. The German economy moved toward unification.

Politically, however, each state in the German Confederation continued to act independently. Strong nationalistic and democratic movements emerged within the Confederation. When uprisings broke out in France in 1848, demands for liberal reforms followed throughout the German states. Elections were held for representatives to a National Assembly in Frankfurt to try to unify Germany. The National Assembly drafted a constitution that provided for a hereditary monarchy with powers limited by a popularly elected legislature. However, liberal demands for a representative government were not met, so that the German system remained absolutist. German unification would be accomplished by a king and his aggressive prime minister.

✔ **READING CHECK: Identifying Cause and Effect** How did the formation of the Zollverein move the German states toward economic unity? adopted uniform weights, measures, and currency

Powerful German aristocrats promoted the customs union known as the Zollverein to abolish trade barriers within the German Confederation. The union did much to encourage industrial growth and economic unity among its member German states.

ALL LEVELS: Have students create a chart to compare and contrast nationalism and unification in Germany and Italy. (*Italian states: shared history, economic oppression, common enemies, led by Cavour and Garibaldi, kingdom under Victor Emmanuel II; German states: shared history and language, economic unity, common enemy, led by Bismarck, empire under William I.*)

ENGLISH LANGUAGE LEARNERS

HOMEWORK Have students go to the library and use historical inquiry to find at least two sources of information about each of these two nationalist movements. They should try to find a primary source, such as a copy of a letter or flier from the period. Ask them to evaluate their sources based on language, corroboration, and information about the author. Remind students to use terminology correctly.

Bismarck and Prussian Strength

In 1861 **William I** became king of Prussia. The next year he appointed Otto von Bismarck to head the Prussian cabinet. A conservative Junker politician, Bismarck built the Prussian army into a powerful war machine.

Bismarck opposed democracy and the idea of a parliament. He believed that the state, not the people, should hold authority. Bismarck wanted to expand Prussia. He may also have believed it was Prussia's destiny to lead the German people to unification.

❝Prussia must build up and preserve her strength for the favorable moment which has already come and gone many times. Her borders under the treaties of Vienna are not favorable to the healthy existence of the state. The great questions of the day will not be settled by speeches and majority decisions—that was the great mistake of 1848 and 1849—but by blood and iron.❞

Otto von Bismarck, quoted in
The Origins of the Wars of German Unification, by William Carr

Bismarck and William faced opposition from the Prussian parliament. When the parliament refused to approve money for a military buildup, Bismarck simply collected the taxes without their approval. Claiming that the government had to keep functioning even without agreement, he ignored the constitution, outraging the liberals. As protests grew Bismarck hoped that successful foreign policy would calm an increasingly hostile public.

✔ **READING CHECK: Analyzing Information** In what ways did Bismarck act to undermine the power of Prussia's parliament? collected taxes without approval, ignored the constitution

Wars of Unification

To increase the power and size of Prussia, Bismarck first had to drive Austria from its position of leadership in the German confederation. Second, Prussia had to overcome Austria's influence over the southern German states, which opposed Prussian leadership. He accomplished these objectives in three wars.

The Danish War. On the border between Denmark and Germany lay two small states—the duchies of Schleswig and Holstein. The population of Holstein was entirely German. Schleswig's population included a mixture of Germans and Danes. The Danish king ruled the two duchies even though their constitutions made them separate from Denmark. In 1863 King Christian IX took the Danish throne. At the insistence of many Danes, he proclaimed a new constitution in which he tried to annex Schleswig for Denmark.

Both Prussia and Austria protested the new Danish constitution. Together they demanded that it be revoked. When Denmark refused, Prussia and Austria declared war on Denmark. Denmark hoped for help from France and Great Britain, but neither of those countries acted. In 1864, after three months of fighting, Denmark surrendered.

The peace treaty gave the two duchies to Prussia and Austria jointly. That arrangement produced conflict between Austria and Prussia. Austria wanted the two duchies to form a single independent state within the German Confederation. Prussia opposed the idea. After a bitter quarrel, Prussian and Austrian leaders decided that Prussia would control Schleswig and Austria would control Holstein.

Analyzing Primary Sources

Summarizing How would you describe Bismarck's approach to German unification? favored use of force

HISTORY MAKER

**Otto von Bismarck
(1815–1898)**

Known for his strong will and determination, Bismarck worked hard to unite Germany. However, he was always against any form of popular government.

Bismarck introduced a number of reforms that helped bring together the German states. Bismarck also went to war to win territory that he believed belonged to Germany. Because of Bismarck, Germany became a major power. **How did Bismarck help to unify Germany?**

Historical Sidelight

The term *realpolitik* is a German term meaning "of reality." It is generally used to describe an artful, shrewd approach to politics that completely disregards ideology. Bismarck has been characterized as a master of *realpolitik*.

Critical Thinking

Ask students what actions taken by Bismarck could be considered examples of *realpolitik*.

ANSWER: Students might mention that he collected taxes without parliamentary approval, ignored the constitution, edited the telegram from the king, and provoked more than one war to achieve German unification.

HISTORY MAKER ANSWER

He built a strong Prussian army and used political tactics to incite strategic wars.

LEVEL 3: Have students make a two-column chart showing the positions and branches of government in the German Empire and the powers of each position or branch. *(kaiser: emperor, head of government, commanded military in war, could declare defensive war without approval, appointed chancellor and Bundesrat; chancellor: under kaiser, over legislature; Bundesrat: federal council, approved or vetoed budgets; Reichstag: legislative assembly, approved military budgets every seven years after Bundesrat)*

LEVEL 2: Ask students to compare and contrast the German Empire's government with that of the United States today. *(German Empire: upper branch appointed, lower branch elected by male landowners, elected branch couldn't create laws, kaiser and chancellor could ignore legislature; United States today: upper branch elected, lower branch elected by all citizens, elected branches can create laws, executive branch cannot ignore legislature)*

Global Relations

An important political theory for students to understand in relation to Bismarck is Machiavellianism. Based on Niccoló Machiavelli's beliefs about political power, Machiavellianism is best summarized by the often-quoted statement, "The end justifies the means." This statement demonstrates a belief that rulers should maintain their power by whatever means necessary; considerations of honesty, justice, or honor should not hamper them in this.

Critical Thinking

Ask students to give some examples of how Bismarck demonstrated Machiavellian beliefs or actions.

ANSWER: Students might mention how Bismarck edited the Prussian king's description of a meeting with the French ambassador, how he provoked more than one war to achieve German unification, or how he manipulated political situations to his own or Prussia's advantage.

CONNECTING TO CIVICS ANSWER

Many Germans expected nationalism to advance representative government and individual freedoms, whereas Bismarck believed that nationalism would increase the power of the kaiser and himself.

CONNECTING TO
Civics

Nationalism
In the early 1800s Germans began to take a new interest in their national traditions, language, and customs. This spirit expressed itself in art, literature, and music, and helped inspire political steps toward unification.

Many Germans associated nationalism with liberalism. They believed that representative government and individual freedoms would advance along with nationalistic principles. However, Bismarck used nationalism mainly as a tool to help Prussia gain control over the rest of Germany.

Understanding Civics

How did different people view the connection between nationalism and government rule in Germany?

The Seven Weeks' War. As Prussian influence expanded, Bismarck prepared for conflict with Austria. He first persuaded Napoléon III of France to remain neutral, then formed an alliance with the new nation of Italy. Finally Bismarck provoked Austria into declaring war on Prussia in 1866 over the ongoing Schleswig and Holstein dispute.

Prussia's efficient conduct during the war startled the whole world. Prussian forces took advantage of technology—moving by train, communicating by telegraph, and using modern weaponry. They defeated the once-powerful Austrians in only seven weeks. The balance of European power dramatically shifted.

The **Treaty of Prague** ended the Seven Weeks' War in 1866. Under the terms of the treaty, the German Confederation was dissolved. Austria surrendered Holstein to Prussia, and Italy gained Venetia. A year later several north German states united with Prussia to form the North German Confederation. The king of Prussia was president of this confederation, but each state had self-government. As the largest and most powerful state, Prussia dominated the legislature of the Confederation.

The Franco-Prussian War. To complete the unification of Germany, Bismarck had to persuade the independent states in southern Germany to join the North German Confederation. His opportunity came in 1870 when he received a telegram from King William. Bismarck edited the telegram so that it sounded as though the king had insulted the French ambassador. When the telegram was published, it so enraged the French that in July of 1870 they declared war on Prussia.

As Bismarck had expected, the southern German states united against the French threat. No outside nation came to France's aid. The Franco-Prussian War was short but decisive. The superb Prussian army defeated the French in a few months of hard fighting. Napoléon III surrendered in September, and his government fell. Paris remained under siege until it surrendered in January 1871. A treaty followed in May. Much of France was occupied by German troops. France lost Alsace and part of Lorraine, and had to pay a huge indemnity.

✔ **READING CHECK: Making Generalizations** What was Bismarck's primary method of achieving unification? provoked war with France

King William I of Prussia (above right) helped Bismarck create a form of nationalism that suppressed democratic and liberal activities.

Prussian soldiers with cannons (right) quickly defeated the French.

Ask students to use their texts, the library, and computer software to find out about the technology available to Bismarck in 1866. Give them the following questions: Where were the railroads in Prussia and Germany? In Austria? Where were telegraph operations available in Prussia? In Austria? What modern weaponry was used by the Prussians? Ask students to discuss their findings and conclusions with the class. Have them address the influence of technology on Europeans. **BLOCK SCHEDULING**

CLOSE

Ask students to discuss the causes of Germany's unification movement. *(ideas of the French Revolution—liberty, democracy, constitutionalism; increase in nationalism under Napoléon's rule; opposition to French rule; rivalry between two most powerful German states, Prussia and Austria; Prussian military strength, efficient government, and strong economy)* Ask students to predict the likelihood of liberal reforms in Germany, considering the leadership of the unification movement. Ask them to discuss the possible reactions of Germany's people.

MAP ANSWER
Metz

Government

During the rise of German nationalism, German liberals were frustrated by Bismarck's militarism and lack of support for representative government. Some used political cartoons to express their anger and disappointment with the oppressive government.

ACTIVITY: Have students create a series of at least five cartoons in chronological order beginning in 1815 with the Congress of Vienna and ending with the 1871 proclamation of the German Empire. Consider bringing some examples of political cartoons to use as models.

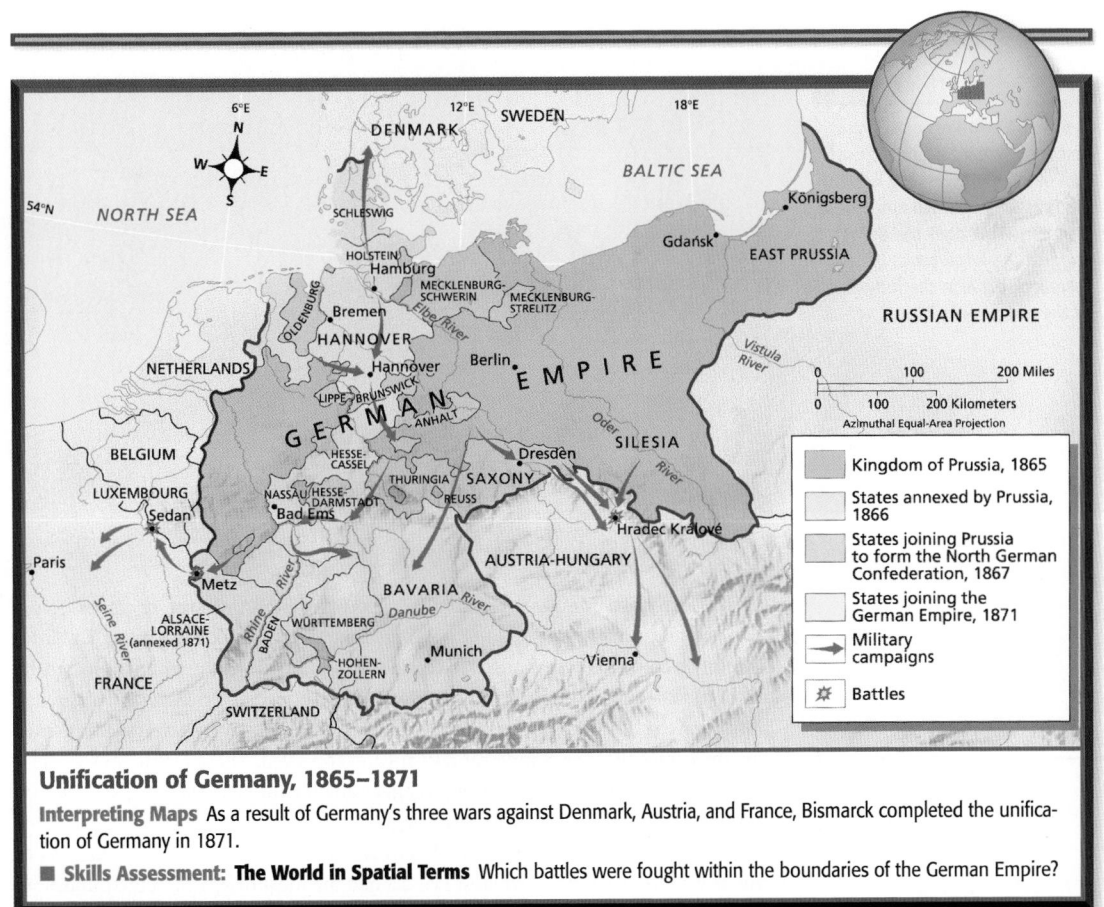

Unification of Germany, 1865–1871

Interpreting Maps As a result of Germany's three wars against Denmark, Austria, and France, Bismarck completed the unification of Germany in 1871.

■ **Skills Assessment: The World in Spatial Terms** Which battles were fought within the boundaries of the German Empire?

Formation of the German Empire

For Germany the treaty ending the Franco-Prussian War was not as important as an event that took place before its signing. On January 18, 1871, representatives of the allied German states met in the Hall of Mirrors at the Palace of Versailles near Paris. There they declared the formation of the German Empire, including all German states except Austria. The Prussian capital of Berlin became the empire's capital. King William I of Prussia was proclaimed German emperor. Bismarck was named chancellor, or chief minister, of the empire, and continued as prime minister of Prussia as well. His nickname became the "Iron Chancellor."

Although he disliked constitutions, Bismarck accepted a constitution that united the 25 German states in a federal form of government. Each state had its own ruler as well as the right to handle its own domestic matters, such as education, law enforcement, and local taxation. Southern states had some special rights, such as Bavaria's right to control its own military. The federal government controlled all common matters, such as national defense, foreign affairs, and commerce. The emperor, called the **kaiser,** headed the government. The kaiser held tremendous power. He appointed the chancellor and commanded the military in times of war. He could declare a defensive war on his own and an offensive war with legislative approval.

REVIEW

Have students complete the Section 2 Review on page 642.

ASSESS

Have students complete Daily Quiz 25.2. As Alternative Assessment, you may want to use the compare-and-contrast chart or the branches of government exercise in this section's lessons.

RETEACH

Have students complete Main Idea Activity for English Language Learners and Special-Needs Students 25.2. Then have students

write the section headings and subheadings on a sheet of paper, leaving a space between each. Ask students to list the main ideas of each heading and subheading in the appropriate space.
ENGLISH LANGUAGE LEARNERS

EXTEND

Have students imagine they are Red Cross volunteers accompanying Bismarck's soldiers to war. Tell students to use their textbooks, biographies, computer software, and any other available resources to find out about wartime medicine in the 1860s and 1870s. Then have them write journal entries.
BLOCK SCHEDULING

VISUAL RECORD ANSWER

The lighting makes him the focal point of the painting.

◈ SECTION ◈
2 REVIEW ANSWERS

❶ Define
• kaiser, p. 641

❷ Identify
• Junkers, p. 638
• Zollverein, p. 638
• William I, p. 639
• Treaty of Prague, p. 640
• Bundesrat, p. 642
• Reichstag, p. 642

❸ The Danish War: increased Prussian territory and military prestige; The Seven Weeks' War: defeated the Austrians and shifted the balance of power to Prussia; The Franco-Prussian War: united the southern German states with Prussia

❹ a. with warfare

b. less democratic, more based on military strength

c. kaiser, chancellor, legislative branch with two houses, one appointed, one elected

❺ Answers will vary but should include how he ignored parliament's refusal of taxes for military, edited the king's memo to provoke war with France, provoked Austria into war over Schleswig and Holstein, and did not allow liberals a voice in government.

INTERPRETING THE VISUAL RECORD

A new German empire In this painting, Bismarck stands at the foot of the throne as King William I of Prussia is crowned emperor of Germany. *How does the artist suggest the importance of Bismarck's role in the founding of the new empire?*

The legislative branch consisted of two houses. The **Bundesrat,** or upper house, was a federal council made up of 58 appointed members. The **Reichstag,** or legislative assembly, was the lower house. It consisted of almost 400 members elected by universal male suffrage. Supposedly a representative body, the Reichstag, however, had limited powers. It could approve military budgets only once every seven years and saw only those bills that the Bundesrat had already approved. These restrictions made it almost impossible for the Reichstag to effect any liberal or democratic change not supported by the emperor or the Bundesrat.

The German constitution strongly favored the interests of Prussia. The king of Prussia was also kaiser of Germany. Prussia had the most delegates in the Bundesrat. They were appointed by Prussia's state government. As the most populous state, it also had the most representation in the Reichstag.

✔ **READING CHECK: Categorizing** In what ways did Prussia remain the most powerful force in the German Empire? Prussian king ruled Germany; had most representatives in legislature

---

SECTION 2 REVIEW

1. Define and explain the significance:
kaiser

2. Identify and explain the significance:
Junkers
Zollverein
William I
Treaty of Prague
Bundesrat
Reichstag

3. Analyzing Information
Copy the table below. Identify how each of the wars fought by the Prussians contributed to the unification of Germany.

Unification of Germany	
The Danish War	
The Seven Weeks' War	
The Franco-Prussian War	

4. **Finding the Main Idea**
a. How did Prussia replace Austria as the leading German state in Europe?
b. Contrast the ways in which German unification differed from Italian unification.
c. After unification, what was the makeup of the German government?

5. **Writing and Critical Thinking**
Identifying Bias Explain how Bismarck's policies supported his belief in action rather than words.
Consider:
• the way he dealt with the Prussian parliament
• the way he provoked other countries into war
• how he kept liberals from carrying out reforms in the new German Empire

Homework Practice Online
keyword: SP3 HP25

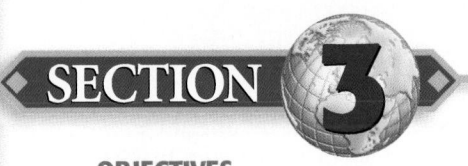
OBJECTIVES

1 Explain the problems Bismarck faced as chancellor of the German Empire.

2 Describe how Germany became industrialized under Bismarck's leadership.

3 Identify the factors that led to the decline of Bismarck's power as chancellor.

As students enter the classroom, tell them that they are poor German factory workers oppressed by wealthy, powerful German businessmen. Ask the workers what they can do to improve their lives. *(protest publicly and/or complain to the legislature)* Tell students that in Section 3 they will learn how economic factors and liberal ideas led to the fall of Bismarck and an increase in popular representation in government.

SECTION 3

Opposition to Bismarck

READ TO DISCOVER

❶ What problems did Bismarck face as chancellor of the German Empire?

❷ How did Germany become industrialized under Bismarck's leadership?

❸ What factors led to the decline of Bismarck's power as chancellor?

IDENTIFY

Kulturkampf
Social Democratic Party
William II

▶ WHY IT MATTERS TODAY

Germany has gone on to become a highly respected industrial nation. Use CNNfyi.com or other **current event** sources to find out in what industries and technologies Germany has taken the lead. Record your findings in your journal.

CNN Student News.com

The Main Idea
Bismarck encountered opposition from groups within the German Empire and a new monarch.

The Story Continues *When William II became kaiser of the German Empire, he regarded it as his sacred duty to help the German people prosper. "Those who are willing to help me in this work will be heartily welcomed by me, no matter who they be," William II declared. "But those who should oppose me in this work I will crush." The new kaiser's words were put to the test when he soon came into conflict with Otto von Bismarck.*

Problems for the Empire

Because the constitution did not give Bismarck the absolute monarchy he wanted, he tried to achieve it in other ways. However, after the formation of the German Empire, he had to compromise to make the political system work. The constitution gave the people little voice, and dissatisfied groups formed political parties that opposed Bismarck's policies. Bismarck's government was increasingly forced to attend to these demands. Some groups demanded a more liberal and democratic government. Others feared Bismarck's military policy and the ever-growing army.

Representatives in the Prussian legislature were conservative. They were elected by a special system that gave more representation to voters from the upper class. However, politicians from other areas of the empire were more likely to oppose Bismarck. The growing power of political groups in other parts of the empire increased tension between Prussia and the other German states.

Relations with the Catholic Church presented special problems for Bismarck. He was a Protestant and did not trust the loyalty of Catholics to the empire. Many Catholics were also members of the Centre Party, which Bismarck regarded as an enemy.

Bismarck began the anti-Catholic program of **Kulturkampf**—German for "culture struggle." Germany passed strict laws to control Catholic clergy and schools. The laws expelled the Jesuits and forbade political expression from the pulpit. They required that all Catholic clergy be Germans educated in German schools. Diplomatic relations with the Vatican were broken as part of the Kulturkampf. Eventually even church property was confiscated.

These policies created opposition. The Centre Party doubled in size, and many non-Catholic liberals joined the opposition. By 1878 Bismarck began to

INTERPRETING THE VISUAL RECORD

Bismarck's enemies This French political cartoon shows Bismarck as his enemies saw him. *What qualities of Bismarck does this drawing emphasize?*

SECTION 3 RESOURCES

REPRODUCIBLE RESOURCES
▶ Guided Reading Strategy 25.3

TECHNOLOGY RESOURCES
▶ One-Stop Planner 25.3
▶ Religions of the World Video Series: Christianity
▶ Homework Practice Online

REINFORCEMENT, REVIEW, AND ASSESSMENT
▶ Section 3 Review, p. 646
▶ Daily Quiz 25.3
▶ Main Idea Activity 25.3
▶ English Audio Summary 25.3
▶ Spanish Audio Summary 25.3

VISUAL RECORD ANSWER

greed, ruthlessness, militarism

TEACH OBJECTIVE 1

ALL LEVELS: Have students complete a graphic organizer like the one below.

Bismarck's problems:	Bismarck's solutions:
liberal and democratic ideas	help industry
non-Prussian politicians	repress socialism
Social Democratic Party	social reforms
Catholics/Centre Party	Kulturkamf
new kaiser	threaten to resign

Outcome: resignation accepted

TEACH OBJECTIVE 2

LEVEL 1: Have students read the subsection "Industrial Development under Bismarck." Then ask them to name factors that led to rapid industrialization for Germany. *(rich iron and coal deposits, good transportation, standardized money laws, centralized postal and telegraph, cartels to control prices, high tariffs to protect industries)* **ENGLISH LANGUAGE LEARNERS**

Science, Technology & Society

The Industrial Revolution began in Great Britain in the 1700s. In 1712 Thomas Newcomen invented the steam engine, which was later perfected by James Watt. The industrial revolution continued with Sir Henry Bessemer's 1856 invention of a new steel making process, and spread through the United States, France, and Germany. The Wright brothers' flight in 1903 was part of the Industrial Revolution.

Critical Thinking

Ask students to explain why Great Britain did not benefit as much as Germany from the Industrial Revolution.

ANSWER: Germany was able to industrialize more rapidly and efficiently by building on the innovations of other nations.

As chancellor of the German Empire, Bismarck started several industrial reforms, including the standardization of money and improved transportation. This photo shows the German industrial city of Dresden in 1875.

modify the Kulturkampf because he needed the support of the Centre Party against a growing socialist presence. He reestablished diplomatic relations with the pope and had laws against Catholics eased or repealed. Kulturkampf ended in failure in 1887.

✔ **READING CHECK: Identifying Cause and Effect** Why did Kulturkampf fail? laws changed to win support of the Centre Party

Industrial Development under Bismarck

During Bismarck's time the German Empire changed into an industrial giant. Germany had rich stores of natural resources, including great coal and iron deposits. The German government managed railroads to promote industrial development, and a system of canals provided cheaper transportation.

Industrialization came later in Germany than in Great Britain or France, which proved to be an advantage. German industries could use the best methods and most advanced machinery that had been developed elsewhere. German scientists then worked out further improvements.

Under Bismarck's leadership the government helped industry in many ways. Money and banking laws were standardized throughout the empire. Postal services, by which so much business was conducted, were centralized. The government encouraged German industrialists to form cartels—groups of companies that combine together for greater power in the marketplace—to control prices. The government adopted a high-tariff policy to protect industries from foreign competition. Germany soon rivaled Great Britain and France as an industrial power.

✔ **READING CHECK: Finding the Main Idea** How did Germany's government under Bismarck help Germany to become industrialized? standardized money and banking laws, centralized postal and telegraph services, encouraged cartels

Socialism in Germany

With the growth of German industry, cities grew rapidly, and a class of factory workers appeared. German laborers, like those in other nations, wanted decent working conditions. Some people believed that the actions of the cartels led to lower wages for workers and higher prices for consumers. Many felt that these problems required government action to regulate industry.

Some social reformers, as they had in other countries, went further. They called for government ownership of major industries. German socialists banded together in 1869 to form what would become the **Social Democratic Party** (SDP). The party grew quickly, most of its members coming from the ranks of urban workers. By 1877 the SDP had elected 12 members to the Reichstag.

Even if the SDP had gained a much greater representation, it would have accomplished very little. The Reichstag could not pass any laws that the Bundesrat opposed. Because the Bundesrat represented aristocratic rulers, they were unlikely to support or pass any laws that the socialists wanted. The Reichstag, however, served as a limited public forum in which socialist members could express grievances. Socialists explained what they would do if they were given power, thus catching the interest and support of the workers.

✔ **READING CHECK: Drawing Inferences** Why were socialists unable to get reform laws passed? Bundesrat did not support reforms

TEACH OBJECTIVE 3

LEVEL 3: Have students use biographical sources and then discuss a post-resignation career plan for Bismarck. Make sure they give quotations. (*Answers will vary but could include military advisor, political mentor, public speaker*)

 HOMEWORK List some citizen responsibilities of Bismarck's reign. (*reading newspapers, voting*)

CLOSE

Ask students to describe Bismarck's rise and fall as chancellor of the German Empire. (*rise—1871: named chancellor under Kaiser William I, standardized money laws, centralized postal/telegraph, encouraged cartels, opposition from urban workers, liberals, democrats, Catholics, non-Prussian citizens; 1877: support for industry, workers, concessions to Catholics, liberals, democrats; fall—1888: opposition from the new kaiser, William II*)

Bismarck's Antisocialist Campaign

Every gain in socialist voting strength—and every socialist demand for reform—alarmed Bismarck. When the SDP won more than 490,000 votes in 1877, Bismarck decided to use all his power to fight them. He got his opportunity in 1878 when two assassination attempts were made against the emperor.

Bismarck knew that neither of the would-be assassins had any connection with socialism. However, he took advantage of public concern by accusing the Social Democrats of plotting the attempts. The emperor and the Bundesrat dissolved the Reichstag and called for new elections. A widespread campaign against socialists and their ideas followed.

The election did not change the strength of the SDP in the Reichstag. However, Bismarck pushed through laws that prohibited newspapers, books, or pamphlets from spreading socialist ideas. He banned public meetings of socialists. Despite such restrictive laws, socialists increased their support with each election. As he had done with the Kulturkampf, Bismarck changed tactics to keep control in the face of growing opposition.

Bismarck decided to grant many of the reforms the socialists proposed, so that fewer people would have reason to support the socialists. Beginning in 1883 he endorsed laws that gave workers insurance against sickness, then against accidents—both paid for by employers. Other laws limited working hours, provided for certain holidays, and guaranteed pensions for disabled and retired workers. Thus Germany initiated a pioneering program of government-directed social reforms. The reforms did not end socialism in Germany, but they did reduce the workers' grievances. Many other industrial nations later adopted similar programs.

✔ **READING CHECK: Identifying a Point of View** What did Bismarck think that government-directed social reforms would accomplish? reduce support for socialists

What If? What if Bismarck had not begun a program of social reform in Germany in the 1880s? How might the history of Germany and other industrial nations have been different?

The Reichstag building in Berlin, Germany

WHAT IF? ANSWER
possible responses: revolution, instability, breakup of nation

Daily Life

During the years following unification, Germany enjoyed economic growth largely due to the rapid industrialization Bismarck encouraged. A stock market was established, and upper- and middle-class Germans entered into the frenzy of acquisition that industrialized Europe was already experiencing. Many people became wealthy, and there was corruption and exploitation.

Critical Thinking

Ask students to explain why there was corruption and exploitation.

ANSWER: Students might suggest that stock traders would bribe politicians to get business information, business owners would collaborate to increase stock prices, and owners would exploit workers to maximize profits.

That's Interesting!

In May 1873, Germany experienced a market crash similar to that of the Great Depression in the United States in October 1929.

DEM DEUTSCHEN VOLKE

REVIEW

Have students complete the Section 3 Review on page 646.

ASSESS

Have students complete Daily Quiz 25.3. As Alternative Assessment, you may want to use the graphic organizer or the rise and fall exercise in this section's lessons.

RETEACH

Have students complete Main Idea Activity for English Language Learners and Special-Needs Students 25.3. Then have students draw a time line and label it with major events of the section.
ENGLISH LANGUAGE LEARNERS

EXTEND

Tell students they can write a constitution for an imaginary new country. Suggest they find examples of constitutions in textbooks, the library, computer software, or any other available resources. Have them use correct social studies terminology and standard grammar, spelling, sentence structure, and punctuation.
BLOCK SCHEDULING

SECTION 3 REVIEW ANSWERS

❶ **Identify**
• Kulturkampf, p. 643
• Social Democratic Party, p. 644
• William II, p. 646

❷ positive: built military, helped industry, helped workers (1883), negative: attacked democratic movements and other countries, supported cartels

❸ a. liberal opposition, Austria, France, the Vatican

b. managed railroad, standardized banking, centralized postal and telegraph systems

c. opposition from parliament, reformists, Catholics, new emperor

❹ German scientists refined advanced technology from other countries; had coal for energy, iron for machines, railroads, canals, and communication

The Resignation of Bismarck

Kaiser William I died in 1888 at the age of 91. Crown Prince Frederick III, who was more sympathetic to liberalism, succeeded him. However, Frederick III died after only a few months in office. As a result Frederick's son, **William II,** became emperor in 1888. He was 29 years old at the time of his coronation.

William II held strongly conservative opinions. He believed in the absolute authority of the emperor. This soon brought the young monarch into conflict with Bismarck. William II felt that Bismarck had too much power. Bismarck resented the way the young emperor reduced powers that the chancellor had wielded effectively for years. He also resented William II's involvement in political affairs that previously had been under his control.

In 1890 the socialists scored huge gains in the elections. Bismarck considered convening the Bundesrat to come up with a new constitution. William II realized that this would create governmental chaos at the beginning of his reign. Under William I, Bismarck had often gotten his way by threatening to resign. When Bismarck offered his resignation in 1890, however, the kaiser accepted it. With great bitterness Bismarck resigned.

Bismarck's policies had left Germany strong, but had frustrated the German people. Bismarck had never allowed the development of a parliamentary democracy. With Bismarck gone, William II was able to pursue his own policies. He set out to expand Germany's influence in the world, and during his reign Germany became a leading industrial and military power. William II increased the size and strength of the German army and expanded the German navy. He signed new agreements with neighboring nations. By the early 1900s Germany was stronger than ever before. However, this soon brought Germany into conflict with Great Britain, the world's leading naval power at the time.

Shortly after becoming emperor of Germany, William II (left) forced Bismarck to resign as chancellor.

✔ **READING CHECK: Contrasting** How did William II's relationship with Bismarck differ from that of his grandfather, William I? *William II asked Bismarck to resign.*

SECTION 3 REVIEW

1. **Identify** and explain the significance:
   Kulturkampf
   Social Democratic Party
   William II

2. **Categorizing** Copy the diagram below. On the left side, indicate the actions of Bismarck that resulted in positive effects for the German Empire. On the right side, indicate Bismarck's actions that resulted in opposition to his actions.

```
  ┌──────┐        ┌──────┐
  │      │──────┐ │      │
  └──────┘   Actions of  └──────┘
             Bismarck
  ┌──────┐──────┘ ┌──────┐
  │      │        │      │
  └──────┘        └──────┘
```

3. **Finding the Main Idea**
   a. What problems did Bismarck face as chancellor of the German Empire?
   b. What did Bismarck do to help Germany become industrialized?
   c. What factors led to the decline of Bismarck's power as chancellor?

4. **Writing and Critical Thinking**
   Analyzing Information Explain why it was an advantage for Germany to industrialize after Great Britain and France.
   Consider:
   • what resources a country needs to industrialize
   • what machinery and processes a country needs when it industrializes
   • the role that scientists played in industrialization

Homework Practice Online
keyword: SP3 HP25

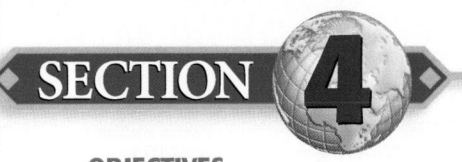

OBJECTIVES

1 **Explain the geographical and cultural factors that made Russia different from the rest of Europe.**

2 **Describe the characteristics of Russian domestic and foreign policies.**

3 **Identify the reform movements that occurred in Russia and their results.**

🔔 LET'S GET STARTED!

As students enter the classroom, tell them that they are the czar or czarina of Russia. Ask them what they can do to improve economic and social conditions. *(develop resources and technology, expand borders toward east, introduce land and labor reforms and free serfs)* Tell students that in Section 4 they will learn how conflicts between the Russian monarchy and radical liberals led to revolution.

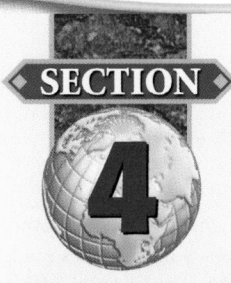

SECTION 4

READ TO DISCOVER

1 What geographical and cultural factors made Russia different from the rest of Europe?

2 What were the characteristics of Russian domestic and foreign policies?

3 What types of reform movements occurred in Russia, and what were their results?

DEFINE

autocrat
nihilists
terrorism
pogroms

IDENTIFY

"Russification"
Pan-Slavism
Alexander II
Emancipation Edict
People's Will
Social Democratic Labor Party
Duma

▶ WHY IT MATTERS TODAY

Since the fall of communism in Russia, the country has experienced new economic problems. Use CNN or other **current event** sources to find out what those problems are. Record your findings in your journal.

CNN Student News.com

Village life in many parts of Russia reflected centuries-old Slavic customs and traditions.

Reform and Revolution in Russia

The Main Idea
A series of conflicts between the monarchy and radical liberals led to revolution in Russia.

The Story Continues *In the 1800s liberal ideas from western Europe stirred up unrest among the Russian people. The Russian czars tried to shut the door to Western influence and preserve their own power. As one official wrote, "[I]n view of the sad occurrences that surround us on all sides, it was necessary to fortify our Fatherland. . . . Russia lives and is preserved by the spirit of a strong, humane, enlightened autocracy." This autocracy would soon clash with a new wave of political radicals.*

The Russian Empire

By the mid-1800s Russia had the largest territory and population of any European nation. Yet industrial development, which so strengthened the West, lagged in Russia. Most of Russia's extensive natural resources lay undeveloped. Ports were blocked by ice for much of the year and exits from the seas were controlled by other countries. This left Russia virtually landlocked. Efforts to win access to the Mediterranean led to conflicts with the Ottoman Empire.

Unlike Great Britain or France, the huge Russian Empire included a great variety of peoples and national groups. The largest ethnic groups in the European part of Russia were the Belorussians or White Russians in the west, the Ukrainians in the agricultural south, and the Great Russians in north and central Russia. These groups were descended from common Slavic ancestors, but each had its own language, customs, and history. These main Slavic groups were also divided by geography.

Scattered throughout the empire were various minorities who spoke many languages. Many of these groups, such as the Poles and Finns, had been conquered by the Russians and disliked Russian rule. Russia had also conquered peoples of Central Asia and Caucasia. This diversity of ethnic, national, and religious groups made unification difficult.

✔ **READING CHECK: Finding the Main Idea** What were some issues that made industrialization and unification difficult for Russia in the 1800s? undeveloped resources, lack of ports, diversity of population

SECTION 4 RESOURCES

REPRODUCIBLE RESOURCES

▶ Guided Reading Strategy 25.4

▶ Readings in World History 88: An Official Report on "Bloody Sunday" in St. Petersburg

TECHNOLOGY RESOURCES

▶ One-Stop Planner 25.4

▶ Holt Researcher: World History: Carl Fabergé

▶ Regions of the World Music Audio CD Program 9: Russia, Ukraine, and Belarus: Russian Choral Music

▶ World History Teaching Transparency: Art and History 15: Peter I at the Founding of St. Petersburg

▶ Homework Practice Online

REINFORCEMENT, REVIEW, AND ASSESSMENT

▶ Section 4 Review, p. 652

▶ Daily Quiz 25.4

▶ Main Idea Activity 25.4

▶ English Audio Summary 25.4

▶ Spanish Audio Summary 25.4

LEVEL 1: Have students read "The Russian Empire" and locate the map on page 651. Have them list reasons why Russia, though the largest in land and population of any European nation, remained weak. *(lagging industrial development, undeveloped natural resources, lack of access to the seas and oceans, conflict with other nations, lack of unity)*

LEVEL 3: Have students evaluate Russia's problems by using the text to complete the following chart.

Problem: *lagging industry, underdeveloped natural resources, lack of ports, external and internal conflict*	
Option 1 *expand military force*	**Option 2** *develop resources*
Advantage: *adds resources and ports, unifies populace*	**Advantage:** *avoids external conflict, supports economy*
Disadvantage: *risks loss of ports and resources, popular opposition*	**Disadvantage:** *requires unavailable technology, labor, and capital*

Geography

Just as the western United States is divided from the eastern United States by the Rocky Mountains, western Russia is divided from eastern Russia by the Ural Mountains.

ACTIVITY: Ask students to draw a map of the Russian Empire in 1900, using the map on page 651 as a guide. Have them use colored pencils to show where different groups of people were located. Ask them to pose questions about geographic distribution patterns as shown on the map.

Reproducible Resources

PS Readings in World History 87: Czar Nicholas I's Approach to Government— Orthodoxy, Autocracy, Nationality

---

Czar Nicholas I ordered Russian soldiers to imprison the sons of a Polish fugitive.

Statue of Czar Alexander II in Helsinki, Finland

Russian Domestic and Foreign Policies

The liberal movement that influenced other European nations so strongly in the 1800s made little progress in Russia. The czar ruled the huge Russian empire as an **autocrat,** one who holds absolute power. Although the czars tried to maintain autocracy, liberal political developments in Europe affected Russia.

Russia had struggled with the influence of the West from before the time of Peter the Great a century earlier. Nationalistic ideas appealed to the ethnic minorities within the Russian Empire, especially to the strongly patriotic Poles and Finns. By the early 1800s liberalism had also begun to attract some of the educated members of the Russian aristocracy.

Faced with problems caused by liberal ideas and restless nationalities, the czars took harsh measures. To counteract liberalism the government strictly censored speech and the press and rejected all demands for a constitution. In the 1830s Czar Nicholas I began a program of **"Russification."** This program forced non-Russian peoples in the empire to use the Russian language, accept the Orthodox religion, and adopt Russian customs in place of their traditional ones.

Russian foreign policy had two primary features. The first branch of Russian foreign policy was designed to increase Russian influence among the Slavic peoples of the Balkans, to the west of Russia. In this sometimes troubled region, Russia promoted **Pan-Slavism,** the union of all Slavic peoples under Russian leadership. The second main feature of Russian foreign policy addressed Russian interests to the south and east. Russia sought to continue the expansion that had begun under the first czars, pushing east into Asia and south toward the Ottoman Empire. Expansion southward, however, was halted with a defeat in the Crimean War in the 1850s. In that disastrous war, Russia lost crucial border territory.

✔ **READING CHECK: Drawing Inferences** Why did Russian foreign policy focus on expanding their territory to the east? Southward expansion led to defeat in the Crimean War.

Alexander II and Reforms

In 1855 **Alexander II** became czar. Although basically conservative and autocratic, Alexander paid attention to public opinion. He responded, although cautiously, to the movement for freedom for all serfs. His actions were the first steps toward modernization for a country that had realized its backwardness with its defeat in the Crimean War.

Emancipation for the serfs. Serfdom took a different form in Russia than it had in the rest of Europe. After the time of Peter the Great, serfs were bound to persons and not to the land. They could not leave their villages or masters' homes without their owners' permission or a government order.

ALL LEVELS: Have a group of students design a visual, such as a collage, that shows the characteristics of the domestic and foreign policies of Russia. They could also write a song/rap or produce a skit to present their information. (*Responses will vary but should indicate that domestic policy was repressive, and foreign policy was focused on expansion.*) **ENGLISH LANGUAGE LEARNERS, COOPERATIVE LEARNING**

Toward the middle of the 1800s, reform of serfdom became clearly necessary. Serfdom obstructed development by restricting the labor pool. Factory owners would benefit if the serfs were freed. The industrialists did not believe in liberal ideas; they simply needed workers for their factories. Moreover, some nobles felt that a great nation should not allow the ownership of people. These nobles began to support a campaign against serfdom. Another group of government officials, most notably in the ministry of the interior, sought reform for the serfs. They persuaded Alexander II to consider abolishing the institution.

Finally in 1861 Alexander II issued the **Emancipation Edict,** which freed all serfs. The czar decided that "It is better to abolish serfdom from above than to wait until the serfs begin to liberate themselves from below." The terms of the Emancipation Edict compensated nobles for land, which peasants could buy in small tracts from the government.

However, emancipation did not solve all problems for the former serfs. Land was sold to them in tiny plots at high prices. Most serfs could not afford enough land to earn the payments for the land, pay taxes, and still make a living. Therefore they had to rent more land from their former owners, at high rents. As one British observer wrote,

 Primary Source 66The Emancipation Law did not confer on [give] the peasants as much land as they require, and consequently the peasant who has merely his legal portion has neither enough of work nor enough of revenue.99

from *Russia in Revolution,* by Stanley W. Page

Some former serfs were unable to either buy or rent land. These people and their families moved from the country to growing towns and cities. There they became cheap sources of labor for factories.

Alexander II's other reforms. Alexander II attempted other liberal reforms, looking to modernize his nation. Because the Emancipation Edict took control of the provinces away from the landowners, it also created the need for a new system of local government. An 1864 law created this new system. Beginning in that year, Alexander allowed rural districts to elect *zemstvos.* These were councils at the provincial and county levels. Three groups had the right to vote in the *zemstvo* elections: the nobles, the middle class, and the peasants. However, the votes were still counted in a way that allowed the nobles and rich taxpayers to dominate the elections. *Zemstvos* could levy taxes and controlled programs such as public health, education, assistance for the poor, local crafts, and some public works programs. Alexander also reformed the courts. He modeled civil and criminal courts after European courts. He created courts of appeal and local justices of the peace. This helped reduce delays and corruption. In political cases, however, the ministry of the interior still held power beyond the reach of the courts. Alexander limited the powers of the secret police, gave the press greater freedom, and expanded education. He also reorganized the military, reducing the period of active service from 25 years to 6 years.

It was customary for the czar and his family to exchange eggs like this one on Easter.

 Holt Researcher
go.hrw.com
KEYWORD: Holt Researcher
FreeFind: Peter Carl Fabergé
After reading about Peter Carl Fabergé on the Holt Researcher, sketch a design for an egg that would have special significance to you.

CONNECTING TO Art

Metalworking: Fabergé Egg
This unusual piece of art is an enameled gold egg containing an accurate model of the Gatchina Palace near St. Petersburg. Only inches in height, it even includes a tiny flag flying from the palace tower. The egg is decorated with pearls and diamonds.

The Gatchina egg was created in the jewelry firm of Peter Carl Fabergé in St. Petersburg. Founded in 1842 the company employed the finest jewelers and goldsmiths in all of Europe. In 1918 the house of Fabergé was closed by officials of a new government. To raise money the government sold many of the eggs. Many of these priceless eggs are now housed in private collections and museums.

Understanding the Arts

Why are Fabergé eggs so valuable today?

LITERATURE. In his 1842 novel *Dead Souls,* Nikolai Gogol criticized the practice of buying and selling peasants. Chichikov, the main character in the novel, comes up with a scheme to buy dead peasants still listed on the census as living. He then uses these peasants as collateral for loans.

Critical Thinking

Ask students how the scheme of buying dead peasants is a criticism of Russian society.

ANSWER: It reflects the fact that peasants were considered property, rather than human beings, and that people would still try to profit from them even after their deaths.

CONNECTING TO ART ANSWER
They are exquisite antiques, valuable because they are no longer being made.

Technology Resources
 CNN. Presents World Cultures: Yesterday and Today Segment 23: Fabergé

ALL LEVELS: Ask students what event finally triggered a revolution in Russia. *(defeat in war with Japan)* Now ask students what the outcome of the revolution was. *(The czar yielded to the revolutionaries' demands and issued the October Manifesto, which guaranteed individual liberties and provided for the election of the Duma.)* Then ask students how the czar got around these concessions. *(increased representation of large landowners to create a conservative Duma)* Finally, have students write a paragraph or two summarizing why the Revolution of 1905 failed. *(the army remained loyal, French lent money to government, revolutionary groups were divided in their goals)*

Government

When news of Czar Alexander's death reached his family, his brother Nicholas declared loyalty to their other brother, Konstantin, as the new emperor. However, Alexander had named Nicholas heir apparent in a manifesto. Konstantin had married a Polish woman not of royal blood and had renounced his rights to the throne. Nevertheless, Nicholas swore allegiance to Konstantin but eventually took the throne anyway because the threat of revolt was spreading.

Critical Thinking

Ask students why the lack of an emperor would lead Russians to revolt.

ANSWER: Students might answer that Russians could seize more power and rights for themselves during the chaos.

Alexander's reform policies did not please everyone. Conservatives tried to convince the czar that such actions threatened the position of the ruler and the nobles. In their minds, this endangered the stability of the nation. Liberals considered Alexander's reforms to be mere first steps. They pointed out the need for further changes. Radicals criticized Alexander even more strongly.

✔ **READING CHECK: Making Generalizations** Why did the Emancipation Edict fail to solve the problems of serfdom? land prices too high for serfs to afford

Radicals and Government Reaction

Several radical political groups were active in Russia. In the 1860s some middle-class and upper-class intellectuals became **nihilists**—from the Latin word *nihil*, meaning "nothing." They believed a just society could be created only by building a completely new Russia. This meant abolishing the existing political, economic, and social structures.

Terrorist attacks. In the 1870s another group, the Populists, urged their followers to live among peasants as teachers and doctors. Some believed that the large estates of nobles should be seized and the land divided among the peasants. After the government arrested many Populists, some Russian radicals turned to violent action, forming a movement called **People's Will.** This group used **terrorism**—bombings and assassinations by political groups—to try to force the government to grant its demands.

Radical activity made Alexander II more conservative. After an attempt on his life in 1866, he repressed radical groups but continued his reforms. In 1870 major cities were granted limited elected government, followed by military reforms in 1874. After repeated assassination attempts, which Alexander faced with great courage, he was finally killed in a bomb attack by People's Will in 1881.

On March 1, 1881, a bomb thrown at Alexander II's coach injured several of his attendants. Alexander was killed by a second bomb thrown at the coach.

HOMEWORK Have students use historical inquiry at the library to research the following statement from page 651: "The government's repressive policies had backfired." *(Answers will vary but should include the idea that the government's violent methods of blocking change had resulted in the formation of a radical party and increased terrorism.)*

CLOSE

Ask students to create a time line showing the causes of reform and revolution in Russia. *(1830s: Russification; 1850s: undeveloped resources, few ports, population diversity, defeat in Crimean War; 1860s: high land prices for freed serfs; 1880s: assassination of Alexander II, severe government repression; 1905: defeat by Japan)*

Time of repression. The assassination of Alexander II ended liberal reform and led to an era of intense repression. Alexander III and his successor, Nicholas II, used every available means to stamp out liberalism. Many of Alexander II's reforms were overturned. His successors used censorship, control of the church and education, spies and informers, and imprisonment and exile. Discriminating against minority groups, they revived and intensified Russification. Jews were massacred in riots called **pogroms** (POH·gruhmz). In the pogroms of 1881, the government failed to intervene as more than 100 Jewish villages and towns were pillaged and many residents were murdered or forced to flee.

This attempt to preserve the old order met with much opposition. Industrialization in Russia had produced a class of workers who wanted the right to form unions and to strike. Liberals and radicals found ready support from these often-exploited workers.

The Russian government's attempts to block all change produced an explosive situation. Terrorism increased. In 1898 socialists formed the **Social Democratic Labor Party,** modeled after the German SDP. This group grew increasingly radical. The government's repressive policies had backfired.

✔ **READING CHECK: Identifying Cause and Effect** What were the effects of the Russian government's actions after the assassination of Alexander II? increased terrorism

MAP ANSWER
Trans-Siberian Railway

🖳 **internet** connect

TOPIC: Radical Writers
GO TO: go.hrw.com
KEYWORD: SP3 WH25

Have students access the Internet through the HRW Go site to research radical groups and writers in Russia in the 1800s. Ask them to take notes on why and how these people were suppressed. Ask volunteers to lead a class discussion.

The Russian Empire by 1900

Interpreting Maps The expansion of the Russian Empire in the late 1800s brought more problems than unity.

■ **Skills Assessment: The World in Spatial Terms** What did the Russians build to try to connect their empire?

INTERPRETING THE VISUAL RECORD

Bloody Sunday On Bloody Sunday, January 22, 1905, Russian troops fired shots at a group of peaceful demonstrators. The Revolution of 1905 had begun. ***Based on the picture, why do you think the attack angered the Russian people so much?***

The Revolution of 1905

In 1904 and 1905 Russia went to war with Japan over territories in China and Korea. To the surprise of the world, the Japanese dealt the Russians a humiliating defeat. The defeat spurred discontented groups into action. Russia's loss exposed a government that was corrupt and inefficient, as well as oppressive. Renewed pogroms against Jews were rampant.

On January 22, 1905—"Bloody Sunday"—the dissent came to a head. The czar's troops shot unarmed strikers on their way to deliver a petition to him. This incident triggered the Revolution of 1905. Workers struck and held demonstrations. Street fighting was especially violent in non-Russian areas. There were mutinies in the army and navy. Finally the czar issued a decree called the October Manifesto, which promised individual liberties. The decree also called for the election of a parliament called the **Duma.** After more bloody fighting, the government finally halted the revolution with severe repression and executions.

Despite the October Manifesto, autocracy continued. The czar dismissed a session of the Duma because members insisted that the czar's ministers answer to them. A 1907 law increased the representation of large landowners and restricted the voting rights of others. This resulted in a more conservative Duma.

The revolutionary movement of 1905 failed to overthrow the czar for three main reasons. First, much of the army remained loyal and would not end the czar's regime. Second, the French, bound to Russia by a military alliance, lent money to the government. Third, the many revolutionary groups were divided in their goals. Moderates feared radical demands and radicals disagreed among themselves. The autocracy continued to resist change and to use repressive measures to preserve the thousand-year-old monarchy.

✔ **READING CHECK: Identifying Bias** Why was a law passed in 1907 giving greater representation in the Duma to large landowners? to provide more control to the czar

SECTION 4 REVIEW

1. **Define** and explain the significance:
   autocrat
   nihilists
   terrorism
   pogroms

2. **Identify** and explain the significance:
   "Russification"
   Pan-Slavism
   Alexander II
   Emancipation Edict
   People's Will
   Social Democratic Labor Party
   Duma

3. **Categorizing** Copy the web diagram below. Fill in the circles by identifying the actions of the Russian government during the period of reform and revolution.

Domestic and foreign policy

The serfs

Russian government actions

Reaction to radicals

Reaction to the revolution

4. **Finding the Main Idea**
   a. Why did Russia's geography and culture make industrialization difficult?
   b. How did Russia try to force its non-Russian citizens to be more "Russian"?
   c. What types of reform did Alexander II attempt?

5. **Writing and Critical Thinking**
   Decision Making If you had been czar of Russia at the beginning of the 1800s, how might you have dealt with the issue of industrialization? Explain the actions you would have taken.
   Consider:
   - the historical way in which Russia had been ruled
   - the problem of Russia falling behind the rest of the world
   - calls for reform from different parts of Russian society

Homework Practice Online
keyword: SP3 HP25

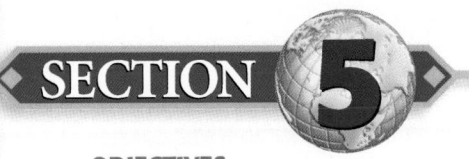

OBJECTIVES

1 Explain what led to the formation of the Dual Monarchy and what problems it faced.

2 Describe how the decline of the Ottoman Empire affected European politics.

3 Discuss how ethnic clashes in southern Europe set the stage for a showdown among the major powers.

🔔 LET'S GET STARTED!

As students enter the classroom, tell them that they are Greek nationalists under the Ottoman Empire. They are non-Muslims and have no voice in government. Ask the Greeks what they can do to promote nationalism. (*protest publicly, use terrorist tactics, align with a powerful military force against the Turks*) Tell students that in Section 5 they will learn how strategic factors, nationalism, economic factors, and religious diversity brought down the Ottoman Empire by 1913.

SECTION 5

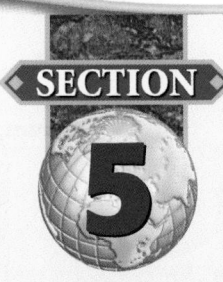

READ TO DISCOVER

1 What led to the formation of the Dual Monarchy and what problems did it face?
2 How did the decline of the Ottoman Empire affect European politics?
3 How did ethnic clashes in southern Europe set the stage for a showdown among the major powers?

IDENTIFY

Francis Joseph I
Treaty of San Stefano
Balkan League

▶ WHY IT MATTERS TODAY

In recent years, several Balkan countries have reasserted their independence. Use CNN🔴News.com or other **current event** sources to find out which Balkan countries have changed their names or manner of government in the past several decades. Record your findings in your journal.

CNN🔴News.com

Unrest in Austria-Hungary

The Main Idea
Nationalist groups in Austria-Hungary and the Balkans struggled violently for independence.

The Story Continues *"A troubled, sinister mood prevails here in all circles. The Paris revolution has illuminated the obscurity of our position like a thunderbolt. The suburbs are said to be in a very irritated state. . . . Discontent is general, and I only fear it is not recognized by the authorities as it ought to be."* This is how one observer described the mood in Vienna as demands for liberal reforms swept the Austrian Habsburg Empire.

Results of the Uprisings

By 1848 uprisings in France had set off revolts in almost every other European nation. In the city of Vienna demonstrators and the army clashed. A concerned Emperor Ferdinand ordered Prince Metternich, his chief minister, to resign. After dominating European affairs for more than 30 years, Metternich fled the country. "When France sneezes, all Europe catches cold," he remarked. Later in the year, Emperor Ferdinand himself stepped down, turning over the throne to his 18-year-old nephew.

Uprisings also occurred in Hungary, one of the largest parts of the Austrian Empire. The people of this region resented Austrian rule. A significant portion were Magyars (MAG·yahrz), descendants of nomadic warriors who had migrated to Hungary from Russia and Romania in the 900s. The Magyars spoke a language unlike most other European languages and had their own culture. A strong nationalist movement centered on throwing off Austrian rule and making the Magyars dominant in Hungary.

Hungarian patriot Lajos Kossuth led a revolt in 1848. For a time it looked as if Hungary would gain its independence. Kossuth was elected "responsible governor president" by the Hungarian Diet in 1849. However, Austria soon drove out the

These Hungarian troops fought for independence against Austrian and Russian forces in 1849.

SECTION 5 RESOURCES

REPRODUCIBLE RESOURCES

▶ Guided Reading Strategy 25.5

▶ Creative Teaching Strategy 25: An Opinion Piece on Nationalism and Liberalism in Europe

TECHNOLOGY RESOURCES

▶ One-Stop Planner 25.5

▶ World History Teaching Transparency: Geography and History 20: Ethnic Groups in Austria-Hungary, 1867

▶ Homework Practice Online

▶ Online Maps, Charts, and Graphs: The Ottoman Empire, 1800

▶ Online Maps, Charts, and Graphs: The Ottoman Empire, 1914

REINFORCEMENT, REVIEW, AND ASSESSMENT

▶ Section 5 Review, p. 657
▶ Daily Quiz 25.5
▶ Main Idea Activity 25.5
▶ English Audio Summary 25.5
▶ Spanish Audio Summary 25.5

TEACH OBJECTIVE 1

LEVEL 3: Have students write encyclopedia entries about the dual monarchy of Austria-Hungary. Students should complete the following outline to structure the entries.

I. Structure

    A. Francis Joseph I *(emperor of Austria, king of Hungary)*

    B. Ministries *(war, finance, and foreign affairs)*

    C. Parliament of Austria *(Vienna)* and Hungary *(Budapest)*

II. Problems

    A. Economy *(Austria wanted high tariffs;)*

    B. Ethnic Minorities *(did not benefit from unification)*

    C. Balkans/Ottoman Empire *(Balkan nationalists wanted to break up the Ottoman Empire.)*

Culture

The Pan-Slav movement, which advocated the union of all Slavic peoples under Russian rule, had a strong effect on the sociopolitical atmosphere of Austria-Hungary. It caused conflict within the empire and between Austria-Hungary and Russia. Francis Joseph I tried to suppress the movement by imposing Magyarization on all the people in order to force social unity.

Critical Thinking

Ask students why they think Francis Joseph's attempt to enforce Magyarization failed.

ANSWER: Ethnically based nationalist movements only strengthened in resistance to government enforcement of cultural homogeneity.

Ethnic Groups in Austria-Hungary, 1867

Interpreting Maps While Austria and Hungary joined together under the Dual Monarchy, they kept separate parliaments and languages.

■ **Skills Assessment: Human Systems** Which non-Slavic peoples lived throughout Austria-Hungary?

revolutionaries. Czar Nicholas I of Russia sent troops to help because he feared that revolution might spread to Russian-controlled Poland. Kossuth fled to Turkey, ending for a time Hungarian attempts at independence.

✔ **READING CHECK: Drawing Inferences** How did the French revolts in 1848 influence the resignation of Metternich and the abdication of Ferdinand? set off revolts in Vienna

Formation of the Dual Monarchy

After its defeat by Prussia in 1866, Austria responded to Hungarian demands for independence in 1867 by forming the Dual Monarchy—also called Austria-Hungary. The Dual Monarchy had a common ruler, **Francis Joseph I.** His title was Emperor of Austria and King of Hungary. Three ministries controlled war, finance, and foreign

TEACH OBJECTIVE 2

LEVEL 1: On the chalkboard or overhead projector, draw the beginning of a cause-and-effect model covering the events that led to the decline of the Ottoman Empire. Have students complete second and third boxes. **ENGLISH LANGUAGE LEARNERS**

> religious differences and unfair tax system in Ottoman Empire → rise of nationalism in the Balkans → Greece won independence; Serbia won some self-rule

affairs for the whole empire, but Austria and Hungary each had its own parliament. The Austrian Parliament met in Vienna; the Hungarian one met in what became the city of Budapest.

The Dual Monarchy was also a practical economic arrangement. Hungary, chiefly agricultural, furnished raw materials and food. Austria, strongly industrial, produced manufactured goods. Each provided a market for the other.

The Dual Monarchy did not solve all problems, however. Austria wanted high tariffs for its manufactured goods. Division by nationalities also remained. Austrian Germans and Hungarian Magyars spoke different languages. Ethnic minorities such as the Czechs, Slovaks, Serbs, Croats, Romanians, Poles, Slovenes, Ukrainians, and Italians existed in both Austria and Hungary. These people benefited little from the Dual Monarchy and continued to press for self-government.

The defeat in the Seven Weeks' War in 1866 also forced Austria from its leadership of Europe. Hoping to gain influence and territory, the Dual Monarchy turned toward the Balkans, a region to the southeast controlled by the Ottoman Empire.

✔ **READING CHECK: Drawing Conclusions** In what way did the Dual Monarchy fail to solve some of the problems in Austria and Hungary? *Different economic needs and division by nationalities continued.*

The Ottoman Empire and the Balkans

By the 1800s the once-powerful Ottoman Empire had declined substantially. Military defeats had decreased the empire's territory. Ottoman rulers could no longer afford many improvements in agriculture, roads, or hospitals. Many people living in the empire were Christians and Jews. The Turks granted religious and cultural freedom to these non-Muslim minorities, but did not make them social or political equals.

In the early 1800s the rise of nationalism increased discontent in the Balkan area of the Ottoman Empire. This region contained Serbs, Bulgarians, Romanians, Albanians, and Greeks. All of these diverse peoples wanted to govern themselves. Despite Turkish efforts to suppress nationalism, Greeks and Serbs revolted during the 1820s. Helped by outside powers, Greece gained independence in 1829. Serbia achieved a degree of self-rule.

Foreign countries stepped in to promote their own interests. Russia supported Balkan nationalists, many of whom were fellow Slavs and Orthodox Christians. Also, Russia stood to gain a water route from the Black Sea to the Mediterranean if the Ottoman Empire collapsed. Great Britain did not want the Russians in the Mediterranean, so they supported the Turks. It was a strange arrangement. Autocratic Russia promoted independence for the Balkans, while Great Britain, although democratic, supported the Turks in suppressing self-rule.

✔ **READING CHECK: Analyzing Information** What was unusual about the support of other countries for the Balkan nationalists and Ottoman Turks? *Russia supported independence, Great Britain supported suppression of self-rule.*

The Balkans
For centuries the Balkans have been an area of conflict. This is because they are strategically located where Europe and Asia meet. Since 300 B.C., they have been invaded and controlled by many different groups. The Roman, Byzantine, Slav, and Ottoman empires have all ruled the region. Only a few times in their history have the people there ruled themselves.

Today, the Balkans are still a region in conflict. They are no longer controlled by foreign powers. Instead, different ethnic groups struggle to control territory there.

What has contributed to a history of conflict in the Balkans?

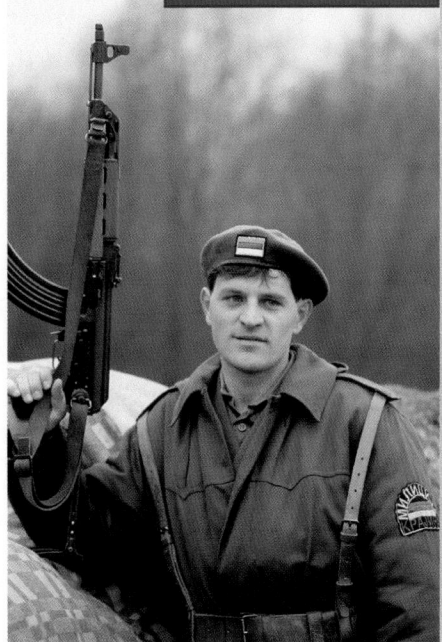

A well-armed Serbian soldier holds a defensive position in the area of Panonia, Serbia, in March 1992.

Global Relations

The Balkan region has often been at the center of conflict over the centuries because it is strategically located at the southern crossroads of Europe and Asia, just across the Adriatic Sea east of Italy. From the 300s B.C. until modern times, the Balkans have been invaded and conquered or contested by the Roman, Byzantine, Slav, Bulgar, Venetian, Ottoman, and Austro-Hungarian Empires.

Critical Thinking

Have students look at the map on page 654 and describe the isolation of the Croats, Serbs, and Slovenes.

ANSWER: They are separated from other Slavs in the north by Germans, Magyars, and Romanians.

ALL LEVELS: Organize the class into four groups. Have each group present to the class a press conference that explains how the ethnic clashes in Southern Europe set the stage for a showdown among major powers. *(Presentations will vary but should creatively indicate the impact of ethnic clashes.)*
COOPERATIVE LEARNING

HOMEWORK Have students compare and contrast the Congress of Vienna in 1815 with the Congress of Berlin in 1878. *(both called to reduce one nation's power; reactionary movements following Vienna versus aggression and expansion following Berlin)*

Ask students to explain why the western nations feared Russia gaining a Mediterranean coast. *(Russia could challenge British sea power; Russian support of Pan-Slavism threatened the traditional balance of power.)*

MAP ANSWER
41° N, 29° E

History Maker

FLORENCE NIGHTINGALE.
Florence Nightingale was born in Florence, Italy, in 1820. Her aristocratic British parents at first blocked her ambition to become a nurse, but at age 31 she went to Germany to study nursing. She was so valuable at organizing a London hospital that she was asked to head a group of nurses sent to the Crimean War. There she found crowded, filthy hospitals and hopeless, dying men. By the end of her first year in the Crimea, the mortality rate had decreased from 42 percent to 22 percent because of her reforms in hygiene and the supplies she donated. Before her death in 1910, Nightingale received the British Order of Merit for her work.

Critical Thinking

Ask students why Nightingale was able to save so many lives using simple good hygiene.

ANSWER: There were no antibiotics then, and infectious diseases could spread rapidly in hospitals and kill patients.

The Congress of Berlin and the Balkan Wars

In 1875 revolts broke out in several Turkish provinces in the Balkans. Two years later Russia, in support of the rebels, declared war on the Ottoman Empire. The Turks were defeated and forced to sign the **Treaty of San Stefano** in 1878. The treaty granted independence to Romania, Serbia, and Montenegro. It also gave self-rule to Bulgaria, which Russia then occupied for some years. Bulgaria extended to the Aegean Sea in the eastern Mediterranean.

This sudden increase of Russian influence in the Balkans alarmed other European nations. Before the Treaty of San Stefano went into effect, the major European powers forced Russia to meet with them at the Congress of Berlin in 1878. The Congress dealt with several territorial issues. Serbia, Montenegro, and Romania retained their independence.

Decline of the Ottoman Empire, 1699–1913

Interpreting Maps Throughout the 1800s and early 1900s many territories of the Ottoman Empire became independent or were annexed by other countries.

■ **Skills Assessment: Using Geography** What are the approximate latitude and longitude coordinates for the capital of the Ottoman Empire?

REVIEW

Have students complete the Section 5 Review on page 657.

ASSESS

Have students complete Daily Quiz 25.5. As Alternative Assessment, you may want to use the encyclopedia articles or the cause-and-effect chain in this section's lessons.

RETEACH

Have students complete Main Idea Activity for English Language Learners and Special-Needs Students 25.5. Then have students draw a time line and label it with major events of the section.
ENGLISH LANGUAGE LEARNERS

EXTEND

Tell students they are Muslim Turks in the Ottoman Empire. Have them explain their religious beliefs and give a rationale for not allowing Christians equality. Have them use correct terminology and standard English. **BLOCK SCHEDULING**

Bulgaria was granted self-government, but it was divided and reduced in size. Moreover, Bulgaria was kept within the Ottoman Empire, thus removing Russia's access to the Aegean Sea. Austria continued to govern Bosnia and Herzegovina but was not permitted to add them to its own territory. Great Britain won the right to occupy the island of Cyprus. This gave the British a naval base in the eastern Mediterranean and kept Russia out of the region. Over time, Great Britain and Italy each seized Ottoman territories in Africa.

In 1908 Austria broke the agreement of the Congress of Berlin by annexing Bosnia and Herzegovina. In 1912 and 1913 two wars between independent Balkan nations and the Ottomans further altered national boundaries. Bulgaria, Serbia, Greece, and Montenegro, known together as the **Balkan League,** declared war on the Ottoman Empire and won. However, the winners quarreled over division of the lands, leading to a second war. This time Serbia, Greece, Montenegro, Romania, and the Ottoman Empire attacked Bulgaria. Bulgaria suffered humiliating losses in this second war and was left with only a small outlet on the Aegean Sea.

By the end of 1913, the Ottoman Empire in Europe included only the city of Constantinople and enough land to control the water route from the Black Sea to the Mediterranean. Other important outcomes of the Balkan Wars included Bulgaria's new alignment with Austria, and Serbia's growing hostility toward Austria. These greatly contributed to heightened political tension in the Balkans.

✔ **READING CHECK: Identifying Cause and Effect**
Why did the European nations force Russia to accept changes in the Treaty of San Stefano?
to keep Russia from gaining power

INTERPRETING THE VISUAL RECORD

Violence in the Balkans This 1913 illustration shows an artillery crew preparing to fire during the Balkan Wars. *What does this picture suggest about the way the wars were fought?*

> ### SECTION 5 REVIEW

1. **Identify** and explain the significance:
   Francis Joseph I
   Treaty of San Stefano
   Balkan League

2. **Sequencing** Copy the diagram below. Create as many boxes as you need. In the boxes, sequence the actions that led to the loss of territory and power in the Ottoman Empire during the 1800s.

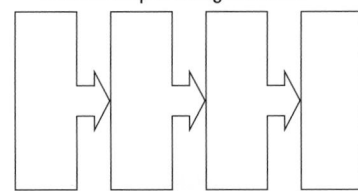

3. **Finding the Main Idea**
   a. What were the strengths and weaknesses of the Dual Monarchy?
   b. How did the decline of the Ottoman Empire influence European politics?
   c. How did ethnic clashes in the Balkans increase tensions toward the end of the 1800s?

4. **Writing and Critical Thinking**
   Contrasting Explain why revolts in Russia failed to produce reforms while those in the Ottoman Empire resulted in the decline of the empire.
   Consider:
   • the reasons why the revolution of 1905 failed in Russia
   • the difficulty of ruling an empire the size of the Ottoman Empire
   • involvement of other nations in the revolutions

Homework Practice Online
keyword: SP3 HP25

ground warfare; heavy artillery

SECTION
5 **REVIEW ANSWERS**

❶ **Identify**
• Francis Joseph I, p. 654
• Treaty of San Stefano, p. 656
• Balkan League, p. 657

❷ military defeats; lack of money for agriculture, roads, hospitals; nationalism in Balkans; Greek independence 1829; defeat by Russia and Balkan nationalists in 1878 (Congress of Berlin and Treaty of San Stefano); defeat of Ottoman Empire by Balkan League in two wars 1912–1913

❸ a. strength: agriculture/industry synergy; weakness: minorities didn't benefit from Dual Monarchy.

b. common fear of Russia among western nations, new independent nations formed in Balkans

c. undermined power of Austria-Hungary and the Ottoman Empire

❹ Sample response: Russian revolutionaries had no support from other nations as did Balkan nationalists; their government was extremely brutal and repressive, unlike the government of the Ottoman Empire.

NATIONALISM IN EUROPE **657**

CHAPTER 25

REVIEW AND ASSESSMENT RESOURCES

REPRODUCIBLE RESOURCES
▶ Vocabulary Activity 25

TECHNOLOGY RESOURCES
▶ Chapter 25 Test Generator (on the One-Stop Planner)
▶ Global Skill Builder CD–ROM
▶ HRW Web Site

REINFORCEMENT, REVIEW, and ASSESSMENT
▶ Chapter 25 Review, pp. 658–659
▶ Chapter 25 Tutorial for Students, Parents, Mentors, and Peers
▶ Chapter 25 Test (Form A or B)
▶ Alternative Assessment Handbook
▶ Chapter 25 Test for English Language Learners and Special-Needs Students

REVIEW
Have students complete the Chapter 25 Review on pages 658–659.

ASSESS
Use one of the chapter tests to assess students' understanding of the content. For Alternative Assessment, see the Portfolio Activities and Alternative Assessment Handbook.

CHAPTER 25 REVIEW ANSWERS

Understanding Main Ideas

1. Mazzini spread ideas of risorgimento (1830s); Cavour made war on Austria (1859); Garibaldi captured Sicily and Naples (1860)

2. little experience with self-government; north/south tensions; labor, poverty problems

3. three wars

4. new constitution made King William I emperor of 25 German states under federal government; Bismarck was chancellor over two legislative branches

5. opposition from non-Prussians, Catholics, liberals, SDP in Reichstag, workers, William II

6. his unpopularity, socialist gains in elections, conflict with William II

7. czar an autocrat, censorship, severe government repression, no constitution

8. secret police, executions, exile, pogroms (although Alexander II accepted a few reforms)

9. strengths: agriculture/industry synergy, Hungarian independence; weaknesses: minority groups that did not benefit from alliance with Austria because of language/cultural barriers

10. frequent external wars to extend imperial borders for resources, ports, political power; frequent internal struggles for individual rights; turmoil that resulted from industrial revolution's impact on economies, labor force

---

CHAPTER 25 Review

Creating a Time Line
Copy the time line below onto a sheet of paper. Complete the time line by filling in the events, individuals, and dates from the chapter that you think were significant. Pick three events and explain why you think they were significant.

1806		1913

Writing a Summary
Using standard grammar, spelling, sentence structure, and punctuation, write an overview of the events in the chapter.

Identifying People and Ideas
Identify the following terms or individuals and explain their significance:

1. Young Italy movement
2. Giuseppe Garibaldi
3. Zollverein
4. William I
5. Bundesrat
6. Social Democratic Party
7. "Russification"
8. terrorism
9. Francis Joseph I
10. Balkan League

Understanding Main Ideas

SECTION 1 *(pp. 632–636)*
The Unification of Italy
1. Who were some of the important leaders in Italy's fight for unification, and what did they do to achieve the goal of Italian unity?
2. What were some of the problems faced by Italy after unification?

SECTION 2 *(pp. 637–642)*
The Unification of Germany
3. What actions allowed Prussia to replace Austria as the leading German state in Europe?
4. What changes in German government occurred as a result of unification?

SECTION 3 *(pp. 643–646)*
Opposition to Bismarck
5. What problems did Bismarck have to overcome as chancellor of the German Empire?
6. What factors led to Bismarck's decline in power and to his subsequent resignation?

SECTION 4 *(pp. 647–652)*
Reform and Revolution in Russia
7. Why did the liberal movement make little progress in Russia during the 1800s?
8. How did the Russian government deal with reform movements?

SECTION 5 *(pp. 653–657)*
Unrest in Austria-Hungary
9. What were the strengths and weaknesses of the Dual Monarchy?
10. Why were the early 1900s filled with tension among nations of Europe?

Reviewing Themes
1. **Government** How did differences in the goals of different political groups affect the unification and nationalization of countries such as Germany and Russia?
2. **Global Relations** To what extent did threats from other countries influence unification movements?
3. **Culture** In what countries did common cultural backgrounds play a role in unification efforts?

Thinking Critically
1. **Comparing** Compare the way the Italians and Germans went about unification.
2. **Summarizing** Explain how liberalism affected Russia's domestic policy.
3. **Drawing Inferences** Why did Western nations fear Russian influence in the Balkans?

Writing About History
Supporting a Point of View As nationalist movements increased in countries such as Prussia and Russia, they were met with repression. Write an article that presents arguments for or against the use of repression to silence protests. Use the following chart to organize your thoughts before you begin writing.

Effects of repression on reform movements in Prussia and Russia	
Positive	**Negative**

CHAPTER 25

CLOSE

Divide the class into four groups, one for each of the nationalist movements. Have each group prepare a speech in which they tell the citizens of the empire or nation what has happened to their people over the next hundred years.

RETEACH

Group students who had trouble with the test into pairs. Have them use their textbook to correct their tests. Ask them to create flash cards and then quiz each other on the chapter content. Then have students take the Form B test to assess their mastery of the material. **ENGLISH LANGUAGE LEARNERS, COOPERATIVE LEARNING**

Portfolio Extensions

1. Imagine that it is 1870 and you are the pope. Write a letter to Bismarck complaining about Kulturkampf's harsh measures against Catholic clergy and his diplomatic break with the Vatican.

2. Divide the class into small groups. Ask each group to choose one government from this section to describe and define.

Building Social Studies Skills

Interpreting Maps

Study the map below. Then use the information to answer the questions that follow.

Prussia in 1815

Kingdom of Prussia, 1815

1. Which of the following areas might Prussia annex to gain two rivers with direct access to the North Sea?
  a. Hesse
  b. Hannover
  c. Saxony
  d. Schleswig

2. Why might it be important for Prussia to have direct access to the North Sea? Give specific reasons.

Identifying Point of View

Read the excerpt below, from an account of the Italian nationalist leader Giuseppe Garibaldi's actions as he led his Red Shirt army to victory at the Battle of the Volturno in 1860.

> "Nothing but the genius of Garibaldi in that terrible hour could have turned his fortunes so far . . . I saw Garibaldi, with his red shirt wringing wet with perspiration, his eye sternly gleaming, his face flushed with the heat of conflict, and blackened by the smoke and dust. I heard his voice commanding—but it was no longer now the calm, clear voice of quieter times. It was hoarse and guttural, and choked with emotion. For the good general saw his gallant band unfalteringly pouring out their life-blood."

3. Which of the following statements best describes the writer's point of view?
  a. Garibaldi's actions had little effect on the battle.
  b. The Red Shirts were little more than bandits.
  c. Garibaldi's actions turned the tide of battle in favor of the Red Shirt cause.
  d. Garibaldi was a poor leader who failed to inspire his followers.

4. Is this account a primary or a secondary source? What evidence can you cite to justify your answer?

Alternative Assessment

Building Your Portfolio   Link to TODAY

Culture

The Balkan countries continue to struggle over territory and independence. Cultural and religious differences fuel many of these struggles. Use the Internet and other sources to identify Balkan countries that are still in conflict with one another. Make a chart showing the countries and what each country is trying to achieve.

internet connect

Internet Activity: go.hrw.com
KEYWORD: SP3 WH25

Choose a topic on Nationalism in Europe to:
- compare and contrast modern nationalist movements with a nationalist movement discussed in the chapter.
- write a biography of a leader of a nationalist movement in Italy or Germany.
- research the suppression of radical groups and writers in Russia in the 1800s.

Reviewing Themes

1. caused internal struggles against the autocratic leadership

2. to the extent that external threats unified the populace

3. Italy, Germany, Russia

Thinking Critically

1. Cavour led the movement from a strong state, Sardinia; Bismarck led the movement from a strong state, Prussia; both used military strategies

2. drew some concessions from Alexander II for serfs, laborers, and soldiers, but brought brutal repression from other czars and the Duma

3. Russia would gain Mediterranean access.

Writing About History

Positive: maintain strong central government, powerful military for defensive and offensive warfare; Negative: government violence against civilians, popular unrest, terrorism, revolution

Building Social Studies Skills

1. b

2. naval access to Great Britain, France, Netherlands, Denmark; trade access to coastal countries

3. c

4. primary; writer was present

Building Your Portfolio

Students' answers will vary.

The Age of Imperialism

CHAPTER RESOURCE MANAGER

	Objectives	Pacing Guide	Reproducible Resources
SECTION 1 **The Roots of Western Imperialism** (pp. 662–665)	• Explain what imperialism is and how imperialists sought to control other peoples. • Identify the economic causes of Western imperialism. • Explore the ways in which Western imperialism was a product of cultural differences.	**Regular** 1.5 day / **Block Scheduling** 1 day *Block Scheduling Handbook with Team Teaching Strategies, 26.1*	**PS** Guided Reading Strategy 26.1 **RS** Graphic Organizer Activity 26 **PS** Readings in World History 89 **E** Hands-on History Activity 26
SECTION 2 **European Claims in North Africa** (pp. 666–669)	• Explain why the French wanted to gain control of North Africa. • Identify the events and aims that promoted British expansion in North and East Africa.	**Regular** 1 day / **Block Scheduling** .5 day *Block Scheduling Handbook with Team Teaching Strategies, 26.2*	**RS** Guided Reading Strategy 26.2
SECTION 3 **European Claims in Sub-Saharan Africa** (pp. 670–674)	• Describe what patterns of colonization Europeans followed in West Africa. • Identify what Europeans gained by colonizing central and East Africa. • Explain why South Africa was so important to the colonial powers. • Examine the effect imperialism had on all of Africa.	**Regular** 1.5 day / **Block Scheduling** 1 day *Block Scheduling Handbook with Team Teaching Strategies, 26.3*	**RS** Guided Reading Strategy 26.3 **SM** Geography Activity 26: Migration Patterns in Southern Africa
SECTION 4 **Expansion in Asia** (pp. 675–681)	• Describe the role Great Britain played in the development of India. • Explain how Japan changed its ancient and tradition-based culture in response to Western imperialism. • Explain how Western imperialism affected the peoples of Southeast Asia. • Explain why European and American imperialists were interested in the Pacific islands.	**Regular** 1.5 day / **Block Scheduling** 1 day *Block Scheduling Handbook with Team Teaching Strategies, 26.4*	**RS** Guided Reading Strategy 26.4 **PS** Readings in World History 72 **PS** Readings in World History 90 **PS** Readings in World History 91
SECTION 5 **Imperialism in Latin America** (pp. 682–687)	• Explain how economic pressure was used by imperialist powers to control Latin America. • Identify the causes and outcomes of the Spanish-American War of 1898. • Explain why the Panama Canal was important. • Describe the "Roosevelt Corollary" to the Monroe Doctrine.	**Regular** 1.5 day / **Block Scheduling** 1 day *Block Scheduling Handbook with Team Teaching Strategies, 26.5*	**RS** Guided Reading Strategy 26.5 **PS** Readings in World History 92: A Change in United States Policy Toward Nicaragua **E** Creative Teaching Strategy 26: The "New" Imperialism

Chapter Resource Key

PS	Primary Sources	**A**	Assessment
RS	Reading Support	**REV**	Review
IC	Interdisciplinary Connections	**ELL**	Reinforcement and English Language Learners
E	Enrichment		Transparencies
SM	Skills Mastery		CD-ROM

 Music

 Video

Internet

 Holt Presentation Maker Using Microsoft® PowerPoint®

One-Stop Planner CD-ROM

See the ***One-Stop Planner*** for a complete list of additional resources for students and teachers.

One-Stop Planner CD-ROM

It's easy to plan lessons, select resources, and print out materials for your students when you use the *One-Stop Planner* CD–ROM with *Test Generator.*

Technology Resources

One-Stop Planner 26.1

Homework Practice Online

Online Maps, Charts, and Graphs: The New Imperialism, 1900

One-Stop Planner 26.2

Holt Researcher: World History: Muhammad Ahmad

World History and Cultures Video Program 21

Regions of the World Music Audio CD Program 13

Homework Practice Online

One-Stop Planner 26.3

Holt Researcher: World History: Shaka

Regions of the World Music Audio CD Program 14, 15, 16

CNN. Presents World Cultures: Yesterday and Today Segment 24: The Farms of Zimbabwe

Homework Practice Online

One-Stop Planner 26.4

Holt Researcher: World History: Mongkut

Regions of the World Music Audio CD Program 17, 21, 22, 24

Homework Practice Online

One-Stop Planner 26.5

Holt Researcher: World History: Carlos Juan Finlay

World History Teaching Transparency: Geography and History 19, 24

Homework Practice Online

Online Maps: The United States Expands Its Influence

Reinforcement, Review, and Assessment

Daily Quiz 26.1

Main Idea Activity 26.1

English Audio Summary 26.1

Spanish Audio Summary 26.1

REV   Section 1 Review, p. 665

Daily Quiz 26.2

Main Idea Activity 26.2

English Audio Summary 26.2

Spanish Audio Summary 26.2

REV   Section 2 Review, p. 669

Daily Quiz 26.3

Main Idea Activity 26.3

English Audio Summary 26.3

Spanish Audio Summary 26.3

REV   Section 3 Review, p. 674

Daily Quiz 26.4

Main Idea Activity 26.4

English Audio Summary 26.4

Spanish Audio Summary 26.4

REV   Section 4 Review, p. 681

Daily Quiz 26.5

Main Idea Activity 26.5

English Audio Summary 26.5

Spanish Audio Summary 26.5

REV   Section 5 Review, p. 687

internet connect

HRW ONLINE RESOURCES
GO TO: go.hrw.com
Then type in a keyword.

TEACHER HOME PAGE
KEYWORD: SP3 Teacher

CHAPTER INTERNET ACTIVITIES
KEYWORD: SP3 WH26
Choose an activity to:
- create an annotated time line on the political changes experienced by the territory once known as the Congo.
- write a report on the impact of colonization on the African people.
- write a series of journal entries from the point of view of Dr. Livingstone.

CHAPTER ENRICHMENT LINKS
KEYWORD: SP3 CH26

ONLINE ASSESSMENT
Homework Practice
KEYWORD: SP3 HP26
Standardized Test Prep
KEYWORD: SP3 STP26
Rubrics
KEYWORD: SS Rubrics

ONLINE MAPS, CHARTS, AND GRAPHS
KEYWORD: SP3 MCG

CONTENT UPDATES
KEYWORD: SS Content Updates

HOLT PRESENTATION MAKER
KEYWORD: SP3 PPT26

ONLINE READING SUPPORT
KEYWORD: SS Strategies

CURRENT EVENTS
KEYWORD: S3 Current Events

Meeting Individual Needs

Ability Levels

Level 1   Basic level activities designed for all students encountering new material

Level 2   Intermediate level activities designed for average students

Level 3   Challenging activities designed for honors and gifted and talented students

English Language Learners   These activities address the needs of students with Limited English Proficiency.

Chapter Review and Assessment

IC   Vocabulary Activity 26

Global Skill Builder CD–ROM

HRW Web Site

REV   Chapter 26 Tutorial for Students, Parents, Mentors, and Peers

REV   Chapter 26 Review, pp. 688–689

A   Chapter 26 Test Generator (on the One-Stop Planner)

A   Chapter 26 Test (Form A or B)

A   Alternative Assessment Handbook

A   Chapter 26 Test for English Language Learners and Special-Needs Students

Build on What You Know

Ask students to answer the following questions:

Why had Europe reached a turning point by 1815?

Consider:

- the defeat of Napoléon
- ideas of nationalism

How did the idea of a unified nation-state gain support?

Consider:

- the desire for individual rights
- unrest and revolutions
- the benefits to European countries that accepted change and reform

---

internet connect

TOPIC: U.S. and Cuba
GO TO: go.hrw.com
KEYWORD: SP3 WH26

Have students access the Internet through the HRW Go site to research U.S.-Cuba relations. Have each student create a time line of the history of United States involvement in Cuba. Using the time line and the background of political and social interests as reference, they should write a letter to their local Senator expressing why they believe the U.S. should or should not continue the embargo against Cuba.

CHAPTER 26

1830–1917

The Age of Imperialism

A commemorative plate portraying Queen Victoria of Great Britain

1830
Politics
France occupies Algiers.

1830
Business and Finance
Chile begins to export nitrates for gunpowder.

1834
The Arts
Eugène Delacroix paints *Algerian Women at Home*.

1848
The Arts
Japanese printmaker Katsushika Hokusai finishes *Mount Fuji Seen Below a Wave at Kanagawa*.

1854
Global Events
The Crimean War begins.

1867
Global Events
Canada becomes a self-governing dominion.

1871
Daily Life
Sir Henry Stanley finds Dr. Livingstone in Africa.

1830

1837
Global Events
Queen Victoria begins her reign.

1835
Politics
The Boers begin the Great Trek in Africa.

1831
Daily Life
The French Foreign Legion is formed.

1845

1849
Daily Life
Cape Colony forbids the landing of convicts.

1860

1869
Science and Technology
The Suez Canal is completed.

1868
Politics
The Meiji era begins in Japan.

1866
Science and Technology
The first transatlantic telegraph cable is laid.

The Great Wave of Kanagawa, by the Japanese artist Katsushika Hokusai

Build on What You Know

In 1815 Europe reached a turning point. Napoléon had been defeated. The rulers hoped to return their empires to the old ways. The ideas of nationalism, though, swept through Europe. Many people thought the unified nation-state was the best way to gain individual rights. This nationalism led to unrest and revolutions. Those European countries that accepted change and reform emerged as stronger and more unified states. The strongest of these began to expand their empires across the globe. In this chapter, you will learn how the great European powers and the United States came to control a large part of the world.

What's Your Opinion?

Themes Journal To help students create their Themes Journal entries, provide the following examples of appropriate **agree**/**disagree** statements.

Global Relations

Agree Industrialization makes it easier for a country to become an imperial power.

Disagree The military strength of a country allows it to become an imperial power.

Geography

Agree The ability to transport goods and raw materials determines where imperialist expansion occurs.

Disagree Imperialists are interested in expanding into areas with large populations so they can recruit indigenous peoples into their military.

Economics

Agree An abundant supply of natural resources makes an area attractive to imperialists.

Disagree Imperial expansion is motivated by the climate and geography of an area.

Pineapples were a major crop in Hawaii during the late 1800s.

British writer Rudyard Kipling

1898 Politics
The United States annexes Hawaii.

1899 Global Events
The Boer War between the British and the Transvaal's Dutch settlers starts in South Africa.

1890 Daily Life
Influenza epidemics occur worldwide.

1907 The Arts
Rudyard Kipling wins the Nobel Prize for literature.

1901 Science and Technology
Mosquito controls rid Havana of yellow fever.

1877 Business and Finance
Frozen meat is shipped from Argentina to Europe for the first time.

1891 The Arts
French painter Paul Gauguin settles in Tahiti.

1910 Global Events
The Mexican Revolution begins.

1916 The Arts
Frank Lloyd Wright designs the Imperial Hotel in Tokyo.

1875　　　**1890**　　　**1905**　　　**1920**

1886 Business and Finance
Gold is discovered in the Transvaal in Africa.

1904 Politics
The Roosevelt Corollary is adopted.

1914 Science and Technology
The Panama Canal opens, linking the Caribbean and Pacific Oceans.

1913 Science and Technology
Dr. Albert Schweitzer opens a hospital in the French Congo.

Self-Portrait With Palette by French artist Paul Gauguin

The U.S.S. Maine

EXPLORING THE TIME LINE
GLOBAL EVENTS

Imperialists from Britain and France held vastly different views about the future of their African colonies. Britain expected them to mature into independent nations. French imperialists, on the other hand, wanted to merge the colonies with their home country. Colonized peoples were later represented in France's legislature.

Critical Thinking

Ask students why Britain and France might have had such different views on their colonies.

ANSWER: Students might suggest that France was interested in expanding the borders of its nation, but Britain was not.

What's Your Opinion?

Themes Journal Do you **agree** or **disagree** with the following statements? Support your point of view in your journal.

Global Relations An industrialized country can easily control a country that is not industrialized.

Geography Imperialists should expand into locations that benefit their need to transport goods and raw materials.

Economics Imperialists should expand into areas that have natural resources they can use.

SECTION 1

OBJECTIVES

1 **Explain what imperialism is and how imperialists sought to control other peoples.**

2 **Identify the economic causes of Western imperialism.**

3 **Explore the ways in which Western imperialism was a product of cultural differences.**

LET'S GET STARTED!

As students enter the classroom, write the following quotation from Winston Churchill on the chalkboard: "What enterprise is more noble and more profitable than the reclamation from barbarism of fertile regions and large populations." Ask students what this quotation can tell them about Europeans' attitudes toward foreign nations that have not become westernized. *(Students might suggest that Europeans do not value these people highly, that the Europeans thought that becoming involved in these people's affairs was admirable, or that the Europeans were aware of the natural resources of some of these nations.)* Tell students that in Section 1 they will learn more about Western attitudes toward foreign nations.

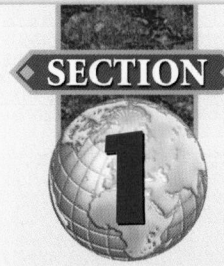

SECTION 1 RESOURCES

REPRODUCIBLE RESOURCES

▸ Guided Reading Strategy 26.1

▸ Graphic Organizer Activity 26: Imperialist Goals

▸ Readings in World History 89: A Justification of British Colonialism in Africa

▸ Hands-on History Activity 26: Life in the Colonies

TECHNOLOGY RESOURCES

▸ One-Stop Planner 26.1

▸ Homework Practice Online

▸ Online Maps, Charts, and Graphs: The New Imperialism, 1900

REINFORCEMENT, REVIEW, AND ASSESSMENT

▸ Section 1 Review, p. 665

▸ Daily Quiz 26.1

▸ Main Idea Activity 26.1

▸ English Audio Summary 26.1

▸ Spanish Audio Summary 26.1

SECTION 1

READ TO DISCOVER

❶ What is imperialism, and how have imperialists sought to control other peoples?

❷ What were the economic causes of Western imperialism?

❸ In what ways was Western imperialism a product of cultural differences?

DEFINE

imperialism
settlement colonies
dependent colonies
protectorates
spheres of influence

IDENTIFY

"The White Man's Burden"

WHY IT MATTERS TODAY

Imperialism is still common in the world today. Use CNN.com or other **current event** sources to find three instances of one country taking control of another country. Record your findings in your journal.

CNN student News.com

Imperialism often started with the merchant trade. These foreign merchant ships are arriving at a harbor in China.

The Roots of Western Imperialism

The Main Idea
Imperialism among the great powers grew out of a complex mixture of political, economic, and social forces.

The Story Continues *During the 1800s, Europeans continued their expansion. At first the Europeans had little influence in the places where they settled. In about 1870, though, they began to take control of these new areas, viewing expansion as a right and a responsibility. "It is our duty," explained a famous supporter of expansionism, "to seize every opportunity of acquiring more territory. . . ."*

Modern Imperialism

The years between 1870 and 1914 were the height of the age of **imperialism.** Imperialism is when one country takes control of another country. One country might control the other's government, trade, or culture. This was not a new idea. Empires had controlled other countries before the 1800s. What was new was the strength of the modern nations. By 1914 the great powers of Europe, Japan, and the United States controlled almost the entire world.

In the beginning, major European governments such as France, Germany, and Great Britain did not plan their imperialism. Often it started when merchants or explorers went to foreign lands. Sometimes the Europeans were not welcome. Then European soldiers would arrive to protect their citizens. After a while, engineers and builders would come. They would open mines, build roads, and make other improvements. The area would be developed, but only for the benefit of the Europeans. The local people had very little say in this process.

Types of control. In some places Europeans had **settlement colonies.** These were large groups of people from one country living together in a new place. For example, Australia was a settlement colony of Great Britain. In other areas Europeans set up **dependent colonies.** In these, a few European officials ruled the non-European people. India, for example, was a dependent colony of Great Britain.

LEVEL 1: Ask students to define imperialism. *(when one country takes control of another country)* Then have students list and describe the different types of European imperialism. *(settlement colonies: people from one country lived together in a new place; dependent colonies: a few European officials ruled the non-European people; protectorates: local rulers kept their title, but Europeans really controlled area; spheres of influence: other nations agreed to respect one nation's special interest in area)*
ENGLISH LANGUAGE LEARNERS

LEVEL 3: Ask students why European leaders and industrial leaders began to worry about the future of their industries in the late 1800s. *(got raw materials from other countries; Western countries would not buy all goods they could produce.)* Ask students why Europeans thought imperialism would solve these problems. *(If Europeans controlled countries that had the raw materials, they knew they would always have access to materials. If Europeans controlled foreign markets, they could encourage local inhabitants to buy their goods.)*

Europeans set up **protectorates** in some areas. Here, the local ruler kept his title. The Europeans, however, really controlled the area. Other nations were kept out. Areas that were not colonies or protectorates were often in **spheres of influence.** A sphere of influence was an area in which one nation had a special interest. Other nations agreed to respect those special interests.

National rivals. Nationalism was a powerful force between 1870 and 1914. Nations believed that others would respect them more if they had colonies. They also saw colonies as places to get troops for bigger armies. Gurkhas, soldiers from Nepal, joined Australians and New Zealanders in British armies. Troops from West Africa fought for the French.

Nations thought a large navy was as important as a large army. Navies protected widely scattered colonies as well as the nation's merchant ships. During this time, steam-powered ships burned coal. The range of a steamship was "from coal to coal." That made a coaling station, a place where ships could refuel, very important. Tiny islands with nothing to offer except their strategic locations became coaling stations or naval bases. Often these islands became objects of fierce competition among naval powers.

By 1914 there were bitter rivalries among the imperial powers. Nations had colonies all over the world. They had huge armies and navies. They had also created hatred among the colonized people. Eventually this led to world conflict.

✔ **READING CHECK: Comparing and Contrasting** What were the similarities and differences among the four ways imperialists controlled their colonies? settlement colonies, dependent colonies, protectorates, spheres of influence

Economic Motives for Imperialism

Industrialization spurred imperialism. After 1850 technology grew rapidly. There were new kinds of energy, new machines, and new industries. The industrialized nations needed a lot of raw materials, such as copper and rubber, to make products. None of the nations wanted to depend on others for raw materials. Their leaders were afraid that in the event of war their countries would not be able to fight off an enemy. To protect themselves, the countries tried to control regions that had the raw materials they needed.

New technology also brought a need for new markets. It was now possible to produce huge amounts of goods. There was also an increased demand for products, particularly in Europe and the United States. Even so, Europe and the United States could not use all the goods produced. Industrialists began to look for new markets in Asia, Africa, and Latin America.

INTERPRETING THE VISUAL RECORD

U.S. imperialism This political cartoon represents the United States gathering the fruits of imperialism. *What does the image imply about the ability of Western powers to take the countries they wanted?*

The desire for raw materials and trade goods fueled colonization among many European powers. This advertisement for Indian tea appeared in Britain.

BUY INDIAN TEA

Economics

Whether their colonial holdings were of substantial economic value to the imperialist powers remains unclear. A look at three Western countries provides an interesting counterargument. Before the height of imperialism, in the 1890s, Britain had reached its economic peak. Despite continued imperial expansion throughout the early twentieth century, Britain continued to lose its economic lead. Germany, which held barely any important colonies, was ready to surpass Britain and become Europe's richest power. Meanwhile, the United States, with fewer overseas colonial possessions, was richer still than Germany.

Critical Thinking

Ask students if they can draw any conclusions from these statements.

ANSWER: Students might suggest that the statements show little correlation between imperial holdings and wealth. They might also suggest that no accurate conclusions can be drawn because the statements are too scanty and do not take into account contributing factors.

VISUAL RECORD ANSWER

They had great ability and could pick and choose what they wanted.

Cultural Reasons	Political Reasons	Economic Reasons
• *Missionaries wanted to spread Christianity.*	• *Imperialists viewed colonies as sources of troops.*	• *European leaders wanted stable sources of raw materials.*

TEACH OBJECTIVE 3

ALL LEVELS: Have students create a chart with the column headings *Cultural Reasons, Political Reasons,* and *Economic Reasons.* Then have students fill in the chart with the different reasons that Europeans established colonies in foreign empires.

ENGLISH LANGUAGE LEARNERS

Global Relations

A leading cause of Britain's move toward imperialism was its loss of domination over the developing world. While still a major industrial power, Britain experienced a slight economic depression from 1873 to 1896. Once Britain felt the effects of its decline, the country's leaders intensified the policies of imperialism. They hoped to map out Britain's realm of influence before other nations had the chance to carve out their own empires.

Critical Thinking

Have students offer reasons why this economic depression might have driven England to intensify its imperialistic policies.

ANSWER: Students might suggest that the colonies could provide new markets for British goods, provide the natural resources Britain needed, and reassure Britain of its greatness.

VISUAL RECORD ANSWER

It supports forcing Western values and ideas upon other peoples.

INTERPRETING THE VISUAL RECORD

Advertising This soap advertisement appeared in the 1800s. *How does this advertisement reflect the ideas of "The White Man's Burden"?*

The first step towards lightening

The White Man's Burden

is through teaching the virtues of cleanliness,

Pears' Soap

is a potent factor in brightening the dark corners of the earth as civilization advances, while amongst the cultured of all nations it holds the highest place—it is the ideal toilet soap.

Analyzing Primary Sources

Finding the Main Idea What did Kipling mean by the phrase, "Go bind your sons to exile"?
Europeans would live among the native peoples of overseas colonies as they worked to spread Western ideas and behaviors.

Europeans and Americans believed that if other people knew their goods were available, they would buy them. Some imperialists went further. They believed they could create new markets by changing people's habits. For example, they would convince the people of central Africa to wear shirts and ties. This would create more business for European and American clothes factories. The factories would hire more people and everyone would make more money.

Industrialists thought they should control their new markets, just as they controlled the sources of their raw materials. They wanted their governments to give them exclusive rights to sell in these markets. At the same time, they demanded protective tariffs to ensure that they would not lose their home markets to foreign competition.

Rapid population growth accompanied industrialism. This provided another economic motive for imperialist expansion. Some historians estimate that the world's population doubled between 1800 and 1900. Industrial development created many jobs, but in Europe there was not enough work to employ all the new job seekers. Displaced farmers and laborers often found it necessary or desirable to go elsewhere. As a result, Europeans left their home countries in record numbers in the 1880s. For Great Britain, France, and Germany, overseas migration was not a new phenomenon. For such countries as Italy, Spain, and Austria-Hungary, however, the emigrations of the 1880s marked the first mass movements of their peoples. The populations of North America, South America, and Australia swelled with settlers from Europe.

✔ **READING CHECK: Summarizing** What were the two main economic motives for Western imperialism? need for raw materials and new markets

Cultural Motives for Imperialism

Many people in the industrialized nations thought they had a duty to spread Western ideas and knowledge around the world. People were considered lacking if their religion or culture differed from that of the West.

"The White Man's Burden." British poet Rudyard Kipling is widely considered to be the most powerful voice in favor of British imperialism. The title of one of his best-known poems is **"The White Man's Burden."** This phrase is often used to sum up the Western attitude toward non-Western people. This is the first stanza of the poem.

❝Take up the White Man's burden—
Send forth the best ye breed—
Go bind your sons to exile
To serve your captives' need;
To wait in heavy harness,
On fluttered folk and wild—
Your new-caught, sullen peoples,
Half devil and half child.**❞**

from "The White Man's Burden," by Rudyard Kipling

CLOSE

Have groups of students use words or illustrations from the text-book to describe what the imperialist's "fantasy world" might look like. Students may reflect the world of industrialists, nationalists, or missionaries. **COOPERATIVE LEARNING**

REVIEW

Have students complete the Section 1 Review on p. 665.

ASSESS

Have students complete Daily Quiz 26.1. As Alternative Assessment, you may want to use the chart in this section's lessons.

RETEACH

Have students complete Main Idea Activity for English Language Learners and Special-Needs Students 26.1. Then have students summarize the main idea for each section in the chapter.
ENGLISH LANGUAGE LEARNERS

EXTEND

Have students select a specific settlement, dependent, or protectorate colony and research the history of its colonization.
BLOCK SCHEDULING

Many Europeans agreed with Kipling's poem. They thought non-Western people were primitive—"half devil and half child." These wrong ideas caused Europeans to change the way of life for countless people. They were "helping" or "improving" them. Europeans also used the idea of their "burden" to justify imposing their own values and cultural ideas on other peoples.

People who were against imperialism claimed that the only burden the white man wanted to take up was the burden of colonial wealth. Such opponents, however, had very little effect on the imperialist policies of Western nations.

Missionaries. Christian missionaries were very active throughout many areas of the world during the age of imperialism. Churches in Europe and the United States sent a growing number of people to the colonies. Although they hoped to convert people to Christianity, the missionaries did other work as well. Many had been trained as teachers. They helped build schools and taught in them. Others had medical training. They cared for the sick and helped to establish and operate hospitals. Through the efforts of these missionaries, knowledge of medicine, hygiene, and sanitation spread along with Christianity.

✔ **READING CHECK: Identifying Bias** How did the attitudes and beliefs of Western people affect imperialism? Westerners aimed to spread their ideas, knowledge, and culture around the world.

This photo shows a missionary classroom in the Philippines. Missionaries spread learning and modern medical practices, as well as Christianity, during the age of imperialism.

SECTION 1 REVIEW ANSWERS

1 Define
- imperialism, p. 662
- settlement colonies, p. 662
- dependent colonies, p. 662
- protectorates, p. 663
- spheres of influence, p. 663

2 Identify
- "The White Man's Burden," p. 664

3 Types of control: settlement colonies, dependent colonies, protectorates, spheres of influence; Economic effects: raw materials, new markets; Cultural effects: "The White Man's Burden," religious conversion

4 a. Imperialists were taking wealth away from colonized areas.

b. Imperial powers used colonies as a source of raw materials; they sold their goods to people in the colonies.

c. Imperialists considered colonized peoples primitive and in need of improvement, and they imposed their values and cultural ideas on those they colonized.

5 Students' responses will vary but should include economic causes, national rivalries, and cultural motives.

SECTION 1 REVIEW

1. **Define** and explain the significance:
   imperialism
   settlement colonies
   dependent colonies
   protectorates
   spheres of influence

2. **Identify** and explain the significance:
   "The White Man's Burden"

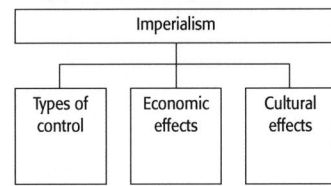

Homework Practice Online
keyword: SP3 HP26

3. **Categorizing** Copy the chart below. Use it to organize the economic and cultural effects of imperialists and the types of control they used.

4. **Finding the Main Idea**
   a. Why did imperialism lead to dissent among colonized people?
   b. What evidence would you give that the most important motive of imperialists was economic?
   c. How did the ideas expressed in "The White Man's Burden" affect the lives of colonized people?

5. **Writing and Critical Thinking**
   Identifying Cause and Effect Explain the factors that caused the Western imperialists to take over other areas of the world.
   Consider:
   - economic causes
   - national rivalries
   - cultural motives

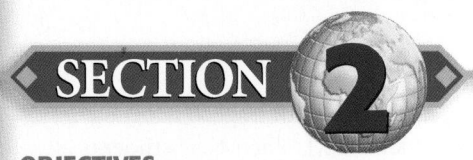
OBJECTIVES

1 **Explain why the French wanted to gain control of North Africa.**

2 **Identify the events and aims that promoted British expansion in North and East Africa.**

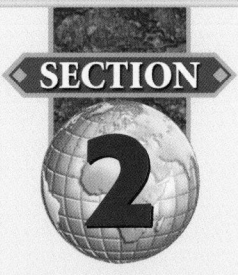
SECTION 2

READ TO DISCOVER

❶ Why did the French want to gain control of North Africa?

❷ What events and aims promoted British expansion in North and East Africa?

IDENTIFY

Suez Canal
al-Mahdī
Fashoda crisis

WHY IT MATTERS TODAY

The Suez Canal has been very important to world shipping. It is used just as much today as it was in the 1800s. Use CNN or other **current event** sources to find out about the canal and what has happened to it since 1900. Record your findings in your journal.

CNNStudentNews.com

European Claims in North Africa

The Main Idea
Imperialism motivated both France and Great Britain to establish colonies in North Africa.

The Story Continues *Some European nations sought to expand overseas not only out of a concern for national security but also from a sense of national identity and pride. Jules-François-Camille Ferry, who became France's Minister of Foreign Affairs in 1883, explained his motives for empire-building. "France . . . cannot be merely a free country. . . ," Ferry insisted. "She ought to propagate [spread] [her] influence throughout the world and carry everywhere that she can her language, her customs, her flag, and her genius."*

The French in North Africa

The French looked toward North Africa to expand their empire. In 1830 a French force occupied Algiers, a Muslim state of the Ottoman Empire. The Algerians did not want French rule. For more than 40 years, the French fought against almost continuous local rebellions. The French thought Algiers was worth the trouble. Many French people and other Europeans moved there. French officials took over Algerian land and settled many colonists there.

The small state of Tunis was east of Algiers. Tunis was also part of the Ottoman Empire, but it had an independent government. In 1881 France found a weak excuse to stage a military action against Tunis, which became a French protectorate. The Turkish governor stayed as ruler, but the French controlled the country. Like the Algerians, the Tunisians resented French control. Many people were inspired to work toward independence.

Morocco's strategic location on the Strait of Gibraltar made it another appealing prize. In 1904 France made an agreement with Britain, Spain, and Italy. According to the agreement, France took control of Morocco. In return, France promised not to get in the way of Britain's plans for Egypt or Italy's plans for Libya. Spain was allowed to keep a sphere of influence in northern Morocco for trading purposes. In 1909 Morocco became a French protectorate.

✔ **READING CHECK: Making Generalizations** How did the people of North Africa react to the French expansion? In general, they resisted.

France held Tunis (now Tunisia) as a protectorate from 1881 until granting it independence in 1956. This illustration shows French troops storming Tunis in 1881.

LEVEL 1: Have students list various regions in North Africa that European nations claimed. *(Algiers, Tunis, Morocco, Egypt, the Sudan)* Ask students why Europeans wanted these regions. Then ask students which of the regions studied in this section they find most valuable and why. **ENGLISH LANGUAGE LEARNERS**

ALL LEVELS: Tell students that France expanded its influence in North Africa by taking control of Algiers, Tunis, and Morocco. Have students create a Venn diagram to include characteristics of each region. **ENGLISH LANGUAGE LEARNERS**

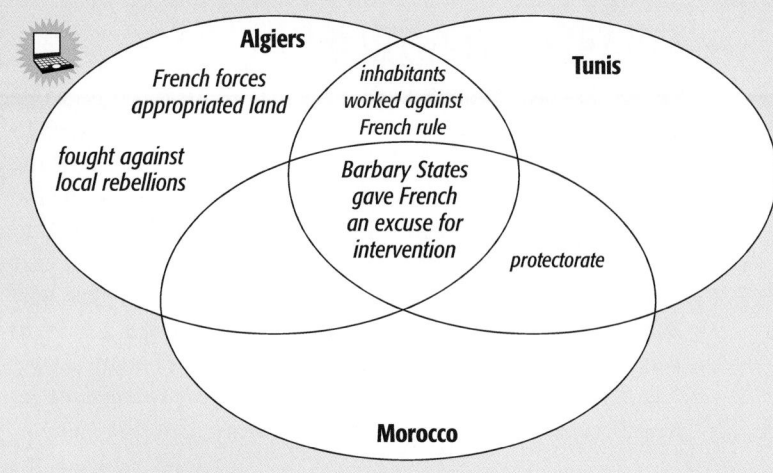

Algiers
French forces appropriated land

fought against local rebellions

inhabitants worked against French rule

Tunis

Barbary States gave French an excuse for intervention

protectorate

Morocco

SKILL-BUILDING STRATEGIES — Using a Decision-Making Process

Morocco and France

France's takeover of Morocco was not an invasion by force. Rather, the leader of Morocco, facing enormous pressure from many sides, made the decision to ask for French intervention. Making decisions like this one involves choosing between two or more courses of action. The decisions that people and nations make have played a significant role in the shaping of history. Thus, an important part of understanding the events of the past is the ability to analyze and evaluate the decisions that historical figures have made. The factors that go into choosing a course of action make up what is known as the decision-making process. Familiarity with such a process will not only help you to better understand history, but may also help you improve your own decision-making skills.

A Historian's Account
The text below describes the events that led to Moroccan sultan Moulay Abd al-Hafid asking for French control of his country.

In 1911 Moulay Abd al-Hafid found himself besieged in his capital, Fez, by hostile tribesmen. He quickly considered appealing to France for assistance. If he brought in the French to help restore order, they would seize control of the country—something for which his countrymen would never forgive him. As one prominent Moroccan put it, "Foreigners are the original cause of all our troubles." If the sultan did not seek French help, however, he might lose his throne and the country might sink deeper into violence and turmoil. In the end, Moulay Abd al-Hafid decided to invite the French in. As a result, France made Morocco a protectorate and set about governing the nation's affairs. Moroccans responded by branding the sultan a traitor and embarking on a years-long rebellion against French rule.

Sultan Moulay Abd al-Hafid (above, right) appealed to the French to help restore order in Morocco. At the left, French and Spanish delegates are shown at the signing of the treaty that made Morocco a French protectorate.

Skills Reminder
To use a decision-making process, identify the decision by determining the situation that calls for a decision to be made. Recognize the options. Note what different courses of action the person, group, or nation may choose. Then assess the possible outcomes of the different courses of action. Take into consideration the advantages and disadvantages of each option. Analyze the decision. Determine what course of action the person or group chose and evaluate it based on the actual consequences it brought about.

Skills Practice
❶ Read the account of Moulay Abd al-Hafid's decision. Identify the situation, the options, and possible outcomes.
❷ Identify the decision he made and evaluate its wisdom based on the outcomes it produced.
❸ Choose another situation from this chapter in which a person, group, or nation had to make a decision. Consult the library or Internet for more information if necessary. Using the decision-making process, write a paragraph analyzing and evaluating the decision.

Geography

For the most part, Africa's interior remained a mystery to early explorers. The Niger and Zambezi Rivers were swampy and full of sandbars. The hot river valleys also posed the threat of diseases. For these reasons the majority of the African interior remained unexplored by Europeans following the first expeditions to the coast.

Critical Thinking

Ask students how a geographer might theorize a way these natural barriers might have affected European attitudes toward Africa.

ANSWER: Students might suggest that Africa and Africans may have seemed even more alien and mysterious.

SKILLS PRACTICE ANSWERS

1. situation: Moulay Abd al-Hafid is besieged in his capital; options: ask France for help or not; outcomes: France would seize control of the country, or he could lose the throne and more violence would erupt.

2. appealed to the French for help; students might suggest an unwise decision because Morocco became a protectorate and his people turned against him.

3. Students' paragraphs will vary but should use the decision-making process and analyze the decision.

LEVEL 3: Have students look at the map of Africa on page 672 and point out the location of the Suez Canal. Ask students to write hypotheses about why Britain would want control of the Suez Canal. Then have students return to the map and locate the Sudan. Again, ask students to hypothesize why Britain would want control of this area. Finally, have students read the text under "The British in North Africa" on page 668 and ask why Britain wanted control of the Suez Canal *(provided a shortcut between Indian Ocean and Mediterranean)* and the Sudan. *(Upper Nile flows through the Sudan, and Britain wanted to build dams for irrigation water and control the flow of water in the lower Nile.)*

HOMEWORK Have each student write a short paragraph that describes the French presence in North Africa. Students' paragraphs should be written using standard grammar, spelling, sentence structure, and punctuation.

Culture

One imperialist had the following to say about Egypt: "We don't want to stay in your country forever. We don't despair of leaving you to manage your own affairs. [But] if we were to go away tomorrow, you would not succeed in doing so, because you have not shaken off the old tradition."

Critical Thinking

Ask students what belief about Western civilization this statement implies.

ANSWER: It implies that Western civilization is better than Egypt's and that Egyptians cannot manage without help.

☐ internet connect

TOPIC: David Livingstone
GO TO: go.hrw.com
KEYWORD: SP3 WH26

Through the HRW Go site, have interested students access sites on the Internet that have information about Dr. David Livingstone. Have students write a series of journal entries as if they were Livingstone, describing the new people he meets, the places he sees, and his feelings about his role in Africa.

VISUAL RECORD ANSWER

with bitterness; building the canal added to their debt

668

The British in North Africa

Egypt had been part of the Ottoman Empire for centuries. By the mid-1800s, though, the empire was weakening. The Ottoman rulers in Egypt had become nearly independent.

Egypt and the Suez Canal. In 1854 the Egyptian government allowed a French company to start building a canal. The **Suez Canal** would go through the Isthmus of Suez to connect the Mediterranean Sea and the Red Sea. Egypt bought almost half of the stock in the company.

Building the canal cost Egypt a lot of money. At the same time, the Egyptian ruler had an extravagant lifestyle. Soon Egypt was deeply in debt. To avoid bankruptcy, Egypt decided to sell its stock in the Suez Canal. This action gave the British a great opportunity. They wanted to control the canal. It would give them a more direct sea route to their colonies in India, Australia, and New Zealand. In 1875 Great Britain bought the Egyptian stock. Because the British now owned so much stock, they gained control of the canal.

At about the same time, an international committee was set up to manage Egypt's huge debt. Many Egyptians did not want to be controlled by foreigners. Egyptian army leader 'Urabi Pasha tried to explain their view to a European.

Analyzing Primary Sources

Supporting a Point of View
How does Pasha appeal to the Europeans' sense of fairness in explaining the Egyptian viewpoint?
by emphasizing common aims and needs

History Makers Speak

❝Without doubt it will please every free man to see men free . . . truthful in their sayings and doings, and determined to carry out their high projects for the benefit of mankind generally, and the advantage of their own country in particular.❞

'Urabi Pasha, from *Secret History of the Occupation of Egypt* by Wilfred Scawen Blunt

'Urabi Pasha's words fell on deaf ears, however, and in 1882 a rebellion began. The British navy attacked Alexandria to put down the rioting. Britain then sent troops to stop another rebellion near the Suez Canal. Although Egypt seemed to be independent, the British actually ruled it for many years.

INTERPRETING THE VISUAL RECORD

Suez Canal This illustration shows the first voyage through the Suez Canal on November 17, 1869. *How might the Egyptian people in the crowd have viewed the opening of the Suez Canal?*

CLOSE

Have students explain why the British wanted to take control of Egypt and the Sudan.

REVIEW

Have students complete the Section 2 Review on p. 669.

ASSESS

Have students complete Daily Quiz 26.2. As Alternative Assessment, you may want to use the Venn diagram or Suez Canal exercises in this section's lessons.

RETEACH

Have students complete Main Idea Activity for English Language Learners and Special-Needs Students 26.2. Ask students in groups representing Britain and France to prepare outlines of their country's claims in North Africa. **ENGLISH LANGUAGE LEARNERS**

EXTEND

Have students research the ways in which European political dominance affected the daily life of Africans in a particular colony. **BLOCK SCHEDULING**

The Fashoda crisis. To the south of Egypt was the Sudan. The Sudan was an Egyptian colony. Both Great Britain and France were interested in controlling this area. The upper Nile River flowed through the Sudan. The British wanted to build dams along the river. They hoped to store water for irrigation and to manage the flow of water into the lower Nile. The French wanted to add the Sudan to the colonies they already controlled in the area.

Before the Europeans could act, there was a revolution in the Sudan. In 1881 a Muslim leader named Muhammad Ahmad led a revolt against Egyptian rule. He called himself **al-Mahdī**, a title meaning "the expected one." Followers of the Mahdi gained control of several major cities. In early 1885 they captured Khartoum, the capital of the Sudan. The British decided to act to stop the Mahdists. They also wanted to prevent the French from gaining control in the Sudan. In 1898 Great Britain invaded the Sudan. Under General Horatio Herbert Kitchener, British troops quickly defeated a large Mahdist army.

Meanwhile, the French had also decided to act. Two years earlier they had sent an expedition to Africa under Captain Jean-Baptiste Marchand. Their goal was to gain control of the upper Nile at Fashoda. Starting from the French Congo, Marchand and his small force of Senegalese soldiers made a daring 3,000-mile journey through tropical Africa. In July 1898 Marchand reached Fashoda. Kitchener's British forces arrived at Fashoda two months later. The French and British troops waited for orders from their governments. Both countries prepared for war. Finally, France realized that neither its army nor navy could defeat the British. France yielded the Sudan to Great Britain.

These events became known as the **Fashoda crisis.** The outcome was that Great Britain and Egypt won joint control of the area, with Great Britain clearly the dominant partner. The region became known as Anglo-Egyptian Sudan.

✔ **READING CHECK: Finding the Main Idea** What was the main reason Great Britain and France became involved in the Fashoda crisis? Both wanted to win control of the Sudan.

Holt Researcher
go.hrw.com
KEYWORD: Holt Researcher
FreeFind:
    Muhammad Ahmad
After reading more about Muhammad Ahmad on the Holt Researcher, write an outline for a speech he might have given to his followers explaining why they should oppose the British.

The powerful British lion forces the game but weaker French rooster to withdraw from Fashoda in this 1898 cartoon.

DOINGS IN THE DESERT.

SECTION 2 REVIEW ANSWERS

❶ **Identify**
- Suez Canal, p. 668
- al-Mahdī, p. 669
- Fashoda crisis, p. 669

❷ Isthmus of Suez: 1854, connected to the Red Sea by the Suez Canal; Tunis: 1881, became a French protectorate; Khartoum: 1885, captured by followers of the Mahdī; Algiers: 1830, occupied by the French; Fashoda: 1898, France yielded the Sudan to Great Britain

❸ **a.** They saw them as a means to expand their empire.

b. Egypt: a more direct sea route to their colonies; Sudan: to store water for irrigation and manage the flow of water into the lower Nile

❹ Students' letters will vary but should be persuasive and consider how North Africans reacted to the French, how Egyptians reacted to the British, and who benefited from the Suez Canal.

SECTION 2 REVIEW

1. **Identify** and explain the significance:
   Suez Canal
   al-Mahdī
   Fashoda crisis

2. **Sequencing** Copy the organizer below. Use it to place into sequence the important events in the record of British imperialism in North and East Africa.

	Date	Describe
Isthmus of Suez		
Tunis		
Khartoum		
Algiers		
Fashoda		

3. **Finding the Main Idea**
   a. What attitude did the French seem to have toward the people of North Africa?
   b. Why was Great Britain interested in controlling Egypt and the Sudan?

4. **Writing and Critical Thinking**
   Supporting a Point of View Imagine it is the 1800s. You are against imperialism in North Africa. Write a letter to your local newspaper persuading others to support your views.
   Consider:
   • the rights of colonists
   • how North Africans reacted to the French
   • how Egyptians reacted to the British
   • who benefited from the Suez Canal

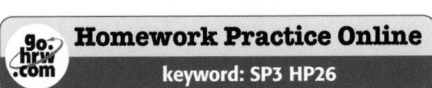
Homework Practice Online
keyword: SP3 HP26

Technology Resources
 Regions of the World Music Audio CD Program 13: North Africa: Arabic Songs of Lebanon and Egypt

OBJECTIVES

1 Describe the patterns of colonization that Europeans followed in West Africa.

2 Identify what Europeans gained by colonizing central and East Africa.

3 Explain why South Africa was so important to the colonial powers.

4 Examine the effect imperialism had on all of Africa.

SECTION 3

READ TO DISCOVER

❶ What patterns of colonization did Europeans follow in West Africa?

❷ What did Europeans gain by colonizing central and East Africa?

❸ Why was South Africa so important to the colonial powers?

❹ What effect did imperialism have on all of Africa?

DEFINE

paternalism
assimilation

IDENTIFY

Samory Touré
Sir Henry Stanley
Leopold II
Boers
Afrikaans
Shaka
Cecil Rhodes
Boer War
Menelik II

▶ WHY IT MATTERS TODAY

Today, Africa is still struggling with problems that are a result of imperialism. Use CNNstudentNews.com or other **current event** sources to identify one of these problems and explore how one African country is trying to solve that problem. Record your findings in your journal.

CNNstudentNews.com

European Claims in Sub-Saharan Africa

The Main Idea
By 1914 most of the major European industrial powers had colonies in sub-Saharan Africa.

The Story Continues *By about 1900, European powers had carved most of sub-Saharan Africa into colonies and settlements. They justified colonization as a humanitarian need, rather than a drive for profit. ". . . Europe was impelled to the development of Africa primarily by the necessities of her people, and not by the greed of the capitalists," explained one British observer.*

Competition for West Africa

West Africa had been a major center of the slave trade. Europeans had slave trading posts along the coast. In the early 1800s, however, most European countries abolished the slave trade. These former slaving centers turned to other types of trade, such as palm oil, feathers, ivory, rubber, and other products from the interior. By the late 1800s, the Europeans had started to push inland. They were eager to control the sources of the products they traded.

Europeans did not gain African land easily. Often they met with fierce resistance. For example, the French fought for control of Senegal for several years. **Samory Touré** led a revolt against the French in Senegal. He continued fighting off and on from 1883 until 1898 when he was finally captured. By 1900 the French had claimed not only Senegal but also a vast area called French West Africa.

Great Britain also met resistance. When the British moved inland from the Gold Coast (modern Ghana), they came up against the powerful African kingdom of Ashanti. The Ashanti fought hard to keep their land. In the end Great Britain ruled all Ashanti territory, and the Gold Coast became a British colony.

By the early 1900s, France, Great Britain, Germany, Spain, and Portugal had claimed almost all of West Africa. Liberia, which had become a republic in 1847, was the only independent state in that area. Because former slaves from the United States had settled Liberia, the United States helped keep the country from becoming a European colony.

✔ **READING CHECK: Finding the Main Idea** Why did the Europeans want to control the interior of West Africa? They wanted to gain control of the region's raw materials.

Competition for Central and East Africa

Journalist **Henry Stanley** fueled interest in central Africa. In 1869 the *New York Herald* hired Stanley to find Dr. David Livingstone, a missionary who had disappeared in central Africa. In 1871 Stanley finally found him, with a greeting that became famous throughout the world: "Dr. Livingstone, I presume?"

Stanley wrote many newspaper articles about his search for Dr. Livingstone. Stanley thought Europeans should develop the huge area he had explored. He tried but failed to interest the British government. Then he turned to King **Leopold II** of Belgium. Leopold, acting as a private citizen, carved out a personal colony of 900,000 square miles.

TEACH OBJECTIVE 1

ALL LEVELS: Ask students to summarize the claims in West Africa by the early 1900s. *(European nations claimed all of it, except Liberia.)* **ENGLISH LANGUAGE LEARNERS**

TEACH OBJECTIVE 2

LEVEL 1: Ask students to explain European interest in colonizing central and East Africa. *(They were interested in gaining access to raw materials, including natural rubber.)* **ENGLISH LANGUAGE LEARNERS**

Teacher to Teacher

Laura L. Boelter of Mesa, Arizona, suggested the following activity: Have students pick scraps of paper with an assigned character from the imperial era, such as a British soldier, a European missionary, an African chief, a native mine worker, a native servant, a European factory owner. Have students write a short character study describing their assigned person, including how that person might have felt about imperialist policies and what role they might have played in the imperialist era.

Leopold's rule of the Congo is an example of imperialism at its worst. His only interest was in getting as much wealth as possible. He sold business people the rights to take raw materials. They took great amounts of the Congo's natural rubber. Leopold also used slave labor. Other countries were outraged by what was happening in the Congo. Leopold finally turned over his private colony to the Belgian government and it became the Belgian Congo in 1908.

Just as in West Africa, the European nations divided East Africa into colonies. A famine helped the Europeans colonize East Africa. In the 1890s most of the cattle in East Africa died from rinderpest, a disease carried by cattle imported from Europe. After the disease killed their herds, the East Africans began to starve. The people were too weak to resist the Europeans.

✔ **READING CHECK: Identifying Cause and Effect** What did Sir Henry Stanley's writing have to do with the colonization of the Congo? *fueled interest in central Africa*

Competition for Southern Africa

European settlement in South Africa began in 1652. Dutch settlers founded Cape Town as a supply station for ships sailing to the East Indies. The Dutch settlement grew into a large colony called Cape Colony. In the early 1800s the British seized Cape Colony and it became a British possession.

African Boundaries, 1883–1914

Interpreting Maps Between the 1880s and 1914 European powers divided Africa among themselves without regard for native rights.

■ **Skills Assessment:**
Human Systems What native African state had direct access to the Red Sea coastal trade in 1883?

HISTORY MAKER

Samory Touré (c. 1830–1900)

Samory Touré was a Muslim reformer and great military leader. As a member of the Mandingo tribe in Guinea, Touré proclaimed himself a religious chief and set about building a great empire. Through his able administration and military leadership, Touré's kingdom became one of the largest empires in West Africa.

For 15 years, Touré fought against the French who wished to establish colonies in West Africa. In the end, his armies were defeated and Touré died in exile. **Why did Touré fight the French?**

Global Relations

At the battle of Isandhlwana, the British assumed that the Zulu would easily be defeated by modern artillery and the well-trained British soldiers. Thus when they set out to attack the Zulu forces, they did nothing to reinforce their camp. A force of 20,000 Zulu warriors overran the camp, destroyed the small British force, and stole the British supplies, winning a significant battle.

Critical Thinking

Ask students why the British might have made such a serious blunder.

ANSWER: Students might suggest that the British were overconfident and underestimated the Zulu military strength and tactical skills.

HISTORY MAKER ANSWER

He had founded a great empire in West Africa, and the French wished to establish colonies there.

MAP ANSWER
the Mahdist State

TEACH OBJECTIVE 3

LEVEL 2: Ask half the students to create a flowchart of events in southern Africa beginning with the British seizure of Cape Colony and ending with the competition among Western nations for land in South Africa. Ask the other half of the students to create a flowchart beginning with this competition and ending with the creation of the Union of South Africa. Have one student from each group write the flowchart on the chalkboard.

Flowchart 1:

The Boers formed three colonies to the north.

↓

They fought against the native Zulu tribe for the land.

↓

The British joined the war and helped the Boers win.

↓

Diamonds and gold were found in the Boer states.

↓

Germany declared a protectorate, and Britain tried to increase its land holdings.

Flowchart 2:

Germany declared a protectorate, and Britain tried to increase its land holdings.

↓

An attempt to overthrow the Transvaals' government led to hostility between the British and the Boers.

↓

War broke out.

↓

Britain defeated the Boers and united Cape Colony and the Boer states into the Union of South Africa.

🔲 **internet** connect

TOPIC: The Congo
GO TO: go.hrw.com
KEYWORD: SP3 WH26

Have students access the Internet through the HRW Go site to find information about the governmental and political changes that the territory that was once the Congo has experienced. Students should use this information to create an annotated time line.

MAP ANSWERS

1. Ethiopia, Liberia

2. French Somaliland

3. It may have provided access to an important waterway for trade and military operations.

Africa in 1914

Interpreting Maps By about 1914, most of the major European countries held colonies throughout Africa.

■ **Skills Assessment: 1. Human Systems** What native African states remained independent of European control during the colonial era? **2. Using Geography** What colony along the African coast of the Red Sea was held by France?
3. Drawing Inferences Why might the location of this French colony along the Red Sea coast have had great economic and military importance?

Map labels: 40°N, EUROPE, ASIA, SPANISH MOROCCO, TUNISIA, MEDITERRANEAN SEA, Suez Canal, MADEIRA (Port.), MOROCCO, IFNI, CANARY IS., ALGERIA, LIBYA, EGYPT, Nile River, RED SEA, Arabian Peninsula, RIO DE ORO, 20°N, MAURITANIA, FRENCH WEST AFRICA, Sudan, EQUATORIAL AFRICA, ANGLO-EGYPTIAN SUDAN, ERITREA, FRENCH SOMALILAND, Niger River, Lake Chad, SENEGAL, GAMBIA, PORTUGUESE GUINEA, TOGOLAND, FRENCH GUINEA, NIGERIA, BRITISH SOMALILAND, ETHIOPIA, SIERRA LEONE, GOLD COAST, LIBERIA, IVORY COAST, FERNANDO PÓO (Sp.), CAMEROONS, ITALIAN SOMALILAND, MBINI, UGANDA, 0° Equator, PRÍNCIPE (Port.), SÃO TOMÉ (Port.), FRENCH, Congo River, BELGIAN CONGO, BRITISH EAST AFRICA, Lake Victoria, PEMBA (Br.), ZANZIBAR (Br.), ATLANTIC OCEAN, CABINDA, Lake Tanganyika, GERMAN EAST AFRICA, SEYCHELLES (British), Lake Malawi, COMORO IS., ANGOLA, NORTHERN RHODESIA, NYASALAND, MADAGASCAR, Caprivi Strip, Zambezi River, MOZAMBIQUE, GERMAN SOUTHWEST AFRICA, SOUTHERN RHODESIA, 20°S, BECHUANALAND, WALVIS BAY (British), Limpopo R., TRANSVAAL, SWAZILAND, UNION OF SOUTH AFRICA (Self-governing dominion), BASUTOLAND, INDIAN OCEAN, Cape of Good Hope

Territory:
- German
- Portuguese
- Belgian
- Italian
- British
- French
- Spanish
- Independent

0   500   1,000 Miles
0   500   1,000 Kilometers
Azimuthal Equal-Area Projection

20°W   0°   40°S   20°E   40°E

LEVEL 3: Create a chart that lists the costs and benefits of European imperialism in Africa. Encourage students to use specific examples from Section 3 to fill in the chart. Ask students to judge whether imperialism had an overall positive or negative effect on Africa.

HOMEWORK Assign each student one of the following countries: Great Britain, France, Belgium, and Germany. Have students create a three-column chart that details the role that their assigned nation(s) took in Africa during the 1800s with the headings *Territory, Acquired, Why Interested in Territory,* and *Major Territorial Conflicts.*

The Boers. When the British government took over, many people left the colony. They moved to the north and east in a mass migration. The move is known as the Great Trek. These people were descendants of the original Dutch settlers. They were called the **Boers.** The Boers spoke their own language, known as **Afrikaans.** In the new territories, the Boers carved out three colonies—Natal (nuh·TAHL), on the southeast coast, the Orange Free State to the west, and the Transvaal to the north.

As the Boers moved into the new territories, they came in contact with the Zulu who lived in the region. Under the great leader **Shaka,** the Zulu had created a thriving empire with a strong army. For years this army fought the Boers for control of the region. In 1879 the British joined in the war, defeating the Zulu and destroying their empire.

Rhodes and his influence. The discovery of diamonds in the Orange Free State and gold in the Transvaal increased competition in southern Africa. Germany hoped to find rich mineral reserves. In 1884 Germany declared a protectorate over the territory of South-West Africa. In the same year, Great Britain began moving inland from Cape Colony. British businessman **Cecil Rhodes** led this inland move.

Rhodes arrived in Cape Colony in 1870. He was a sickly young man who hoped the climate would improve his health. A short time later, Rhodes moved to the diamond fields in the Boer-controlled Orange Free State. He showed a great talent for business. Within 20 years of his arrival, Rhodes completely controlled South African diamond production. Later, Rhodes organized a huge colony farther north. This area was named Rhodesia (now Zimbabwe) after him. Rhodes hoped that one day Britain's control would extend from Cape Colony in South Africa to Cairo, Egypt, in the north.

The Boer War. In 1895 Rhodes sponsored a group who tried to overthrow the Transvaal government. The Boers in the Transvaal had kept the British from opening mines. The attempt failed, and relations between the Boers and the British became openly hostile. In 1899 the **Boer War,** known to modern South Africans as the South African War, broke out. After three years of costly fighting, the British defeated the Boers. As part of the settlement, the British were allowed to begin mining in the Transvaal.

To make sure the Boers stayed peaceful, the British allowed them to keep using the Afrikaans language in their schools and courts. The British also provided funds for Boers—though not for Africans—to rebuild their destroyed farms. In 1910 the British united Cape Colony and the three Boer colonies. It became the Union of South Africa. The new constitution made it almost impossible for nonwhites to ever get voting rights. This was the beginning of South Africa's system of racial segregation.

✔ **READING CHECK: Contrasting** In what ways did the British treat the Boers differently from the way they treated Africans? allowed the Boers to keep their own language and provided funding for postwar reconstruction

The Effect of Imperialism on Africa

Imperialism was a difficult experience for all of Africa. In most areas, Europeans controlled all levels of government. This meant they controlled the lives of the people. Europeans based this type of government on their belief that Africans were not able to rule themselves. This way of ruling is called **paternalism.** Europeans governed their colonies in the same way that parents guide their children.

It is true that Africa did get some benefit from imperialism. New crops and new ways of farming were introduced in many areas. European medicine helped people live longer and healthier lives. Roads and railroads were built all over Africa.

INTERPRETING THE VISUAL RECORD

Zulu warrior This drawing from about 1875 depicts a Zulu warrior with shield, spears, and traditional dress. *Based on this drawing, how effective do you think Zulu weapons were against European firearms?*

Holt Researcher

go.hrw.com
KEYWORD: Holt Researcher
FreeFind: Shaka
After reading more about Shaka on the Holt Researcher, create a time line of the significant events in his battle against the British.

History Maker

CECIL RHODES. In 1877 Cecil Rhodes drew up a will that dedicated his fortune to the formation of a "secret society" that would extend British rule to all parts of the world. Rhodes's goal was to expand British dominion into all of Africa, Australia, and the Middle East, as well as into both North and South America. He believed British control of so much of the world would promote the best interests of all people and make wars impossible.

Critical Thinking

Ask students how other countries might have responded to Cecil Rhodes's will.

ANSWER: Students might suggest that most countries would have been outraged at the suggestion that their people might be happier as British subjects.

VISUAL RECORD ANSWER

not very effective against more advanced firearms

CLOSE

Ask students to describe the differing European interests in West, Central, and East Africa.

REVIEW

Have students complete the Section 3 Review on p. 674.

ASSESS

Have students complete Daily Quiz 26.3. As Alternative Assessment, you may want to use the flowchart or cost/benefit exercises in this section's lessons.

RETEACH

Have students complete Main Idea Activity for English Language Learners and Special-Needs Students 26.3. Then have each student write three specific questions and discuss their answers in small groups. **ENGLISH LANGUAGE LEARNERS**

EXTEND

Discuss Africa under the imperialists and then have students write descriptive sentences making general statements about imperialism in Africa. **BLOCK SCHEDULING**

CONNECTING TO GEOGRAPHY ANSWER

conflicts among ethnic groups

SECTION 3 REVIEW ANSWERS

❶ **Define**
- paternalism, p. 673
- assimilation, p. 674

❷ **Identify**
- Samory Touré, p. 670
- Sir Henry Stanley, p. 670
- Leopold II, p. 670
- Boers, p. 673
- Afrikaans, p. 673
- Shaka, p. 673
- Cecil Rhodes, p. 673
- Boer War, p. 673
- Menelik II, p. 674

❸ Samory Touré: fought to prevent French control of Senegal, was defeated; Ashanti: fought to keep their land, were defeated

❹ a. Imperial powers involved in both; Liberia was an independent republic.

b. Former slaving centers turned to other types of trade, and Europeans were eager to control these areas.

c. years of war, European control of African trade, forced labor, improved health care and roads

❺ Students' columns will vary but should consider British treatment of Africans, British attitudes toward Boers, and how British aimed to exploit Africa's natural resources.

CONNECTING TO GEOGRAPHY

The Berlin Conference

In 1884 European leaders met in Germany to resolve potential conflicts over African colonies. With no regard for the boundaries the Africans already had in place (which were often based on the location of ethnic groups), the Europeans carved up Africa among themselves. The decisions made at the Berlin Conference continue to hamper the continent's development.

Understanding Geography

How might the boundaries created by European leaders at the Berlin Conference have caused problems for the nations and people of Africa?

Even though the roads were mostly for European use, they did make it possible to get African products to the world markets. To some degree, too, this helped to improve communication in parts of Africa. It also helped to break down some of the barriers that had traditionally separated African peoples.

Some African leaders even sought out alliances with Europeans to benefit their countries. Often, however, the Europeans tried to take advantage of these alliances to the detriment of the Africans. For example, in 1889 Emperor **Menelik II** of Ethiopia negotiated a treaty with Italy. Menelik discovered, however, that the Italians were trying to trick him by showing him a copy of the treaty in his language that was different from the treaty in Italian, which gave the Europeans more power. Menelik's wife, Taitu, summed up her response to the Italians, "You wish Ethiopia to be represented before the other Powers as your protectorate, but this shall never be." When Italy tried to invade Ethiopia in 1896, Menelik's forces successfully fought them off.

Most other African nations were unable to stop the advance of outsiders. Instead, many resisted imperialism by insisting on maintaining their own identity. In spite of many years of control, most Africans never accepted European culture, even though Europeans hoped they would do so. The French even hoped for **assimilation,** which happens when people give up their own culture completely and adopt another culture.

It is not so surprising that the Africans did not accept European culture. After all, nearly everything the Europeans did was for their own benefit, not that of the Africans. Europeans did not think the Africans deserved to be treated equally. For their part, the Africans continued to live much as they had lived for centuries.

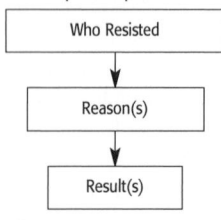

Emperor Menelik II of Ethiopia successfully resisted European imperialism.

✔ **READING CHECK: Making Generalizations** What effect did European colonization have on the African people? received some benefits, such as new medicines and new ways of farming, but lost their freedom

---

SECTION 3 REVIEW

1. **Define** and explain the significance:
   paternalism
   assimilation

2. **Identify** and explain the significance:
   Samory Touré
   Sir Henry Stanley
   Leopold II
   Boers
   Afrikaans
   Shaka
   Cecil Rhodes
   Boer War
   Menelik II

3. **Categorizing** Copy the model below. Use it to organize examples of African resistance to European expansion.

   Who Resisted
   ↓
   Reason(s)
   ↓
   Result(s)

4. **Finding the Main Idea**

   a. What were the similarities and differences between Senegal and Liberia?

   b. What role did slavery play in the colonizing of Africa?

   c. How did imperialism affect Africa?

5. **Writing and Critical Thinking**

   Identifying a Point of View Imagine that you are a European correspondent assigned to cover events in South Africa during the Boer War. Write a newspaper column in which you explain Great Britain's views of the actions and policies that led to war in South Africa.
   Consider:
   • British treatment of native Africans
   • British attitudes toward the Boers
   • how the British aimed to exploit Africa's natural resources

 Homework Practice Online

keyword: SP3 HP26

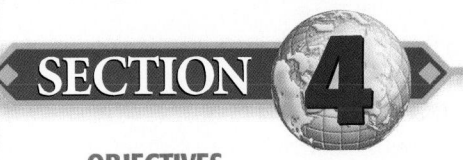
OBJECTIVES

1 Describe the role Great Britain played in the development of India.

2 Explain how Japan changed its ancient and tradition-based culture in response to Western imperialism.

3 Explain how Western imperialism affected the peoples of Southeast Asia.

4 Explain why European and American imperialists were interested in the Pacific islands.

SECTION 4

Expansion in Asia

READ TO DISCOVER

❶ What role did Great Britain play in the development of India?

❷ How did Japan change its ancient and tradition-based culture in response to Western imperialism?

❸ How did Western imperialism affect the peoples of Southeast Asia?

❹ Why were European and American imperialists interested in the Pacific islands?

IDENTIFY

Meiji Restoration
Diet
Sino-Japanese War
Treaty of Shimonoseki
Mongkut
Liliuokalani
Emilio Aguinaldo

▶ WHY IT MATTERS TODAY

The culture of modern India shows the effects of British imperialism. Use CNN student News.com or other **current event** sources to explore the ways that Indian culture has been influenced by British rule. Record your findings in your journal.

CNN student News.com

The Main Idea
Western imperialism affected Asia and the Pacific in a variety of ways during the 1800s and 1900s.

The Story Continues *As Western imperialism reached into Asia and the Pacific during the 1800s, native peoples often responded with resistance and conflict. One Indian writer described the nationalist ideals that grew in his country in the face of British imperialism: "The double policy of self-development and defensive resistance [against British colonial rule] is the common standing-ground of the new spirit all over India."*

British Imperialism in India

During the early to mid-1800s, the British East India Company controlled a large area of India. This trading company treated India as a private colony. In 1857 Indian soldiers rebelled against the company. After that, the British government took direct control. Great Britain ruled about three-fifths of the Indian subcontinent. The rest was divided up into more than 550 states. An Indian prince headed each of these states.

The nature of British rule. Great Britain wanted to control both British India and the Indian states. The British used the old Roman method of divide and rule. It granted favors to those princes who cooperated with British rule and dealt harshly with those who did not. It treated Hindus and Muslims equally but did little to ease religious hatred between them.

The British were active rulers in India. They kept public order and ended the many local wars among the other states. They built roads, bridges, and railroads, established factories, hospitals, and schools, and tried to improve Indian farming methods. Many British families went to India and made it their permanent home.

By the early 1900s, British rule in India had created an unusual situation, with the people of two very different cultures living side by side. However, the two groups had little social contact with each other. The British had put themselves above Indian society.

INTERPRETING THE VISUAL RECORD

British colonials in India Members of an aristocratic British family in India, surrounded by their Indian servants, pose before their elegant estate. *How might an image such as this provoke feelings of resentment and nationalism among native Indians?*

SECTION 4 RESOURCES

REPRODUCIBLE RESOURCES

▶ Guided Reading Strategy 26.4

▶ Readings in World History 72

TECHNOLOGY RESOURCES

▶ One-Stop Planner 26.4

▶ Holt Researcher: World History: Mongkut

▶ Regions of the World Music Audio CD Program 17, 22

▶ Homework Practice Online

REINFORCEMENT, REVIEW, AND ASSESSMENT

▶ Section 4 Review, p. 681

▶ Daily Quiz 26.4

▶ Main Idea Activity 26.4

▶ English Audio Summary 26.4

▶ Spanish Audio Summary 26.4

VISUAL RECORD ANSWER

They are depicted as subservient and below the British.

TEACH OBJECTIVE 1

LEVEL 2: On the chalkboard create a chart showing the positive and negative effects of British rule in India. For example:

Positive Effects	Negative Effects
The British ended many local wars and massacres.	*The British treated the Indians as if they were inferior.*

After students have completed the chart, ask them if they can see why a nationalist movement developed in India when it was under British rule. Then have them read the text under "The rise of Indian nationalism." Ask students to write a few sentences explaining how British rule led to Indian nationalism. *(Britain's harsh treatment of opponents and attitude of superiority and Indians' exposure to Western ideas in British schools)*

These Indian and British teachers worked together at a school in India in the late 1800s.

They thought they were a superior race. They had private social circles that were open to any European, but closed to any Indian. For many years Indians were treated this way, regardless of their social status, education, or abilities.

Although the British did not socialize with Indians, the British system of education had a powerful impact on India. From 1899 on, the British colonial administration worked to establish Western-style schools of all levels throughout India. The classes were mostly taught in English. Students learned about Western ideas, such as democracy and socialism, along with the regular school subjects.

The rise of Indian nationalism. A movement for Indian self-rule began in the late 1800s. Not all Indian nationalists supported the same approach. Some wanted to move toward independence gradually. These were usually people who had been educated in British schools. They also wanted to keep certain aspects of Western culture that they thought could benefit India.

Other Indians wanted to break all ties with Great Britain and sweep away the Western influence. The views of this second group alarmed Indian Muslims, who were a minority in the land. British rule protected them from violence. They feared that if British rule were removed their future might be in danger. The independence movement in India gathered strength very slowly. The British kept the country under a tight rein.

✔ **READING CHECK: Identifying Bias** How did the attitudes of the British affect the way they ruled in India? British sense of superiority prevented social or political contact with Indians

Japanese Responses to Imperialism

While Britain was firmly in control of India, Japan was taking a different course. Westerners did not rule in Japan. Japan controlled its own government. However, the Japanese had been influenced by Western ideas. In response, Japan changed its form of government and began to industrialize.

The Meiji Restoration. In 1868 a group of samurai overthrew the Tokugawa shogunate. Then they returned the emperor to power. This change is called the **Meiji Restoration.** The samurai took action because they had grown impatient with Japan's old ways. They wanted a government and social system more like those in the West. They convinced the Meiji government to make broad changes.

One of the most important changes was to do away with the old system of social classes. Now all Japanese were free to choose what kind of work they wanted to do. The government also required that everyone should go to school. With this program, Japan almost wiped out illiteracy.

In 1899 the Japanese put into effect a new constitution that gave the Japanese people a say in their country's government by giving voting rights to some Japanese. However, only those people who owned a large amount of property were allowed to vote. Although the constitution gave the emperor supreme power, he did not use it. The new constitution also created a two-house national assembly called the **Diet.** One house of the Diet was made up of people who were elected. In the beginning, the elected house had very limited power. A small group of leaders acting in the name of the emperor held the real power in Japan.

LEVEL 3: Ask students to identify the main factor that encouraged Japan to embark on a course of imperialist expansion. (*Japan's leaders wanted to prevent Western imperialist expansion in Asia.*) Then present to students the following statements about Japan's imperialist attempts in Asia. Have students write a result that stemmed from the action expressed in each statement.

a. A rebellion broke out in Korea that called for freedom from Chinese control. (*Japan fought a war against China.*)
b. Japan won the Sino-Japanese War. (*China was forced to give Korea its independence; Japan gained control of Taiwan and won the right to trade in China.*)

Industrialization. Japan modernized very quickly. The government bought new factory machinery from Western countries and passed laws to encourage private citizens to start businesses. Also, in the 1880s the government sent students and leaders to the Western countries. They were to learn as much as they could about Western ideas. One of these leaders was Prince Itō Hirobumi. He was an outstanding statesman during this period. One trip he made was to the United States. While he was in San Francisco, he described Japan's hopes for the future.

> *History Makers Speak* ❝Today it is the earnest wish of both our Government and people to strive for the highest points of civilization enjoyed by more enlightened countries. Looking to this end, we have adopted their military, naval, scientific, and educational institutions, and knowledge has flowed to us freely in the wake of foreign commerce.... Japan cannot claim originality as yet, but it will aim to exercise practical wisdom by adopting the advantages and avoiding the errors....❞
>
> Prince Itō Hirobumi from an 1880s speech given in San Francisco

By 1900 Japan had become the first country in Asia to industrialize. Japanese cities were linked together by railroads and telephones. Factories were making goods that could be sold to other countries. The textile industry was particularly strong. Japan exported machine-made cotton cloth and silk. The money the Japanese got from these exports paid for the imports they needed. They bought raw materials such as iron ore and crude oil. Japan used these raw materials to make steel and build ships. The country was much stronger than it had been before the Meiji Restoration.

The Sino-Japanese War. Even though Japan had modernized, it feared the imperialists in Asia. This fear led the Japanese to become imperialists themselves.

The area that most interested Japan was nearby Korea, which had been a dependent colony of China for a long time. China did not allow other countries to enter Korea. However, Russia, France, and the United States were all interested in trading there. Japan did not want these Western countries to have control of a country so near to their own.

In 1894 a rebellion broke out in Korea. The rebels wanted their people to be free from Chinese control. Both Japan and China sent armed forces to Korea. The situation exploded into the **Sino-Japanese War** (*sino* means Chinese). Foreigners predicted an easy victory for the large Chinese army. The Japanese, however, had done a better job of modernizing than China. They were well equipped and prepared. Japanese troops scored quick victories on both land and sea. In a surprisingly short time, Japan had defeated China.

In 1895 the **Treaty of Shimonoseki** ended the Sino-Japanese War. China was forced to give Korea its independence. Japan gained control of the island of Taiwan (Formosa) and some other small islands next to it. Japan also gained control of an area along the coast of Manchuria. In addition, Japan won the right to trade in China. This war between Japan and China marked the beginning of Japan as a major world power.

✔ **READING CHECK: Summarizing** How did Japan respond to Western imperialism? by modernizing rapidly

Analyzing Primary Sources

Drawing Inferences What did Prince Itō mean when he said Japan "cannot claim originality as yet"? Japan relied on Western knowledge and technology.

This was the scene at Yokohama in 1871 as Prince Iwakura left on Japan's foreign mission to learn about Western countries.

Economics

In the late 1800s Japan acquired Western techniques and machinery to mechanize its silk industry. Using steam or water power instead of turning the reel by hand produced silk filaments of uniform size and greater strength at faster speed. A large labor force was still required to prepare cocoons and tend the machines. Most of the employees were women. Under Meiji rule, the silk industry progressed due to the use of more advanced methods of production and numerous mills.

ACTIVITY: Have students use computer software to acquire information about the textile industry in India in the late 1800s and early 1900s. Have them create visuals, such as charts, to compare the textile industries in India and Japan.

Reproducible Resources

RS Readings in World History 91: The Living Conditions of Japanese Industrial Workers During the Meiji Period

ALL LEVELS: Have students look at the map on page 678 and list the imperialist countries and their territory in Southeast Asia. *(Britain: Burma, North Borneo, Malay States, parts of New Guinea; France: French Indochina; Netherlands: Netherlands East Indies)* Write *Britain*, *France*, *Netherlands*, and *Siam* on the board. Then have students match each of the following statements to the correct country.

a. gained several small nations and combined them into one territory *(France)*

b. built the city of Singapore; created an important naval base in the region *(Britain)*

c. revolts; gradual changes and reforms in colonial policies *(Netherlands)*

d. had a stable government; operated as a buffer zone for other countries *(Siam)* **ENGLISH LANGUAGE LEARNERS**

Economics

The new Japanese government abolished feudalism. Most of the feudal lords willingly gave up their privileges, but those who resisted were ruthlessly crushed. As compensation for their losses, former lords were awarded European titles and public offices. Thus counts, barons, and marquis began to appear as key figures in the Japanese government.

Critical Thinking

Ask students why they think the Japanese government wanted to eliminate feudalism.

ANSWER: Students might suggest that the Japanese government did not want the existence of feudal lords to undermine its authority.

MAP ANSWERS

1. Great Britain

2. They provided important access to trade.

Imperialism in East Asia to 1914

Interpreting Maps Western imperial powers controlled much of East and Southeast Asia by the early 1900s.

■ **Skills Assessment: 1. The World in Spatial Terms** Which European power controlled the most area in this region? **2. Analyzing Information** Why were China's treaty ports important to the Western powers?

LEVEL 1: Ask students to list reasons why Western countries were interested in the Pacific islands. *(need for coaling stations and naval bases, valuable natural resources)* Then ask students to detail the problems that developed as Western nations expanded in the Pacific islands. *(The United States, Britain, and Germany all wanted control of the Samoa Islands; American businesspeople exerted increasing influence in the Hawaiian Islands, which led the queen to abdicate; the United States went to war with Spain, and victory resulted in gaining territory in the Pacific.)*
ENGLISH LANGUAGE LEARNERS

Imperialism in Southeast Asia

In the late 1800s, European imperialism made its way to Southeast Asia as it did to nearby India. The area became an important source of spices and tea. Later, valuable products such as tin and oil came from this area.

British colonies. Great Britain had control of two important colonies in Southeast Asia—Burma and Singapore. It was natural that the British should take an interest in Burma, as it was on the eastern border of India. By 1886 all of Burma had come under British control.

The island of Singapore is on the tip of the Malay Peninsula. It guards the entrance to the Strait of Malacca. This is one of the world's most vital trade routes. Britain's first recorded contact with Singapore was in 1819, when a ship belonging to the British East India Company landed there. When the company representative learned that there were only a few residents he decided to purchase land for a factory site. The spot grew into the city of Singapore, which became an important naval base in the British Empire.

French gains. The eastern part of Southeast Asia contained three small nations, none of which had stable governments. At times they were under the influence of neighboring Siam (modern-day Thailand). In the 1800s, the French military took over the region and claimed it for France. Under French rule the governments of the three nations became more stable and their economies improved. The area became known as French Indochina. The original three nations regained their independence in the 1950s. Today they are the nations of Laos, Cambodia, and Vietnam.

The kingdom of Siam had a more stable government than the other parts of Southeast Asia. The country was well organized and well run. However, Siam had to deal with two European powers on its borders. The British had interests on one border and the French had interests on another. Both Great Britain and France nibbled at the borders of Siam. To keep their independence, Siamese rulers skillfully played British interests against French interests. King **Mongkut,** who ascended to power in 1851, was particularly good at such diplomacy. Mongkut studied Western ideas to understand his enemies and help modernize his country.

The British and French finally agreed that an independent Siam was useful as a buffer state between them. A buffer state is a country located between two hostile powers that serves to decrease the chance of war between the two powers.

The Dutch East Indies. The Dutch East Indies, now Indonesia, are a series of islands that run from the East Asian mainland 3,200 miles to the coast of Australia. The islands of Java, Sumatra, and Borneo are the largest of these islands. The Dutch first colonized the East Indies in the 1600s. In the late 1800s, several revolts convinced the government of the Netherlands to change the way they governed their richest colony. The Netherlands gradually reformed their colonial policies. The Dutch East Indies became the nation of Indonesia in 1949.

✔ **READING CHECK: Drawing Conclusions**
Why was Siam able to remain independent during the age of imperialism? Siam skillfully played Britain against France.

Holt Researcher
go.hrw.com
KEYWORD: Holt Researcher
FreeFind: Mongkut
After reading more about Mongkut on the Holt Researcher, write an evaluation of his best and worst policies as king.

INTERPRETING THE VISUAL RECORD

King Mongkut Siam's King Mongkut worked hard to protect his country's independence in the 1800s. *How does this painting reflect the king's acceptance of some aspects of Western society?*

Chinese porcelain was imported to Europe, where it was considered quite valuable. This punch bowl depicts trading centers in Canton.

Geography

Vietnam is long and narrow, and at the time of the French takeover, its two major centers of development were located at the extreme north and south. Its capital, Hue, was in the middle. France unified Vietnam in 1887 by creating a single governor-generalship. The northern and southern regions were then linked by a rail and road system.

Critical Thinking

Ask students how geography may have played a role in the French colonization of Vietnam.

ANSWER: Students might suggest that Vietnam's coastline made it easy to invade and its power and social order were decentralized.

VISUAL RECORD ANSWER

wearing Western-style clothing

Technology Resources

Regions of the World Music Audio CD Program 21: Mainland Southeast Asia: Vietnam: Songs of Liberation

THE AGE OF IMPERIALISM **679**

Spotlight on GEOGRAPHY

Have students read the text under "U.S. Interests in the Pacific Islands" beginning on page 680 and then look at the map on page 680. Ask students the following questions: Which nations were involved in the Pacific? *(Britain, France, Germany, Netherlands, United States)* Which European nation seems to dominate the region? *(Great Britain and British Commonwealth)*

HOMEWORK Write the following names of territories in the Southeast and the Pacific islands on the board: *Samoa Islands, Pago Pago, Hawaiian Islands, Philippines, Guam, Wake Island, French Indochina, Singapore, Netherlands East Indies, Siam, Burma.* Then have each student create two questions about Western interest and expansion in the Pacific islands that can be answered by one (or more) of the names on the board. Collect the questions from students. Then read them aloud and call on volunteers to provide the answers.

Global Relations

In the late 1800s and early 1900s, European countries carved out empires in Africa, Asia, and the Pacific.

Critical Thinking

Ask students how they think world history would have been different if the Europeans had not established these empires.

ANSWER: Answers will vary, but students might suggest that Africa, Asia, and the Pacific islands would have retained more of their traditional societies and cultures.

MAP ANSWER
Philippines

Technology Resources

Regions of the World Music Audio CD Program 24: The Pacific Islands: Music from Western Samoa: From Conch Shell to Disco

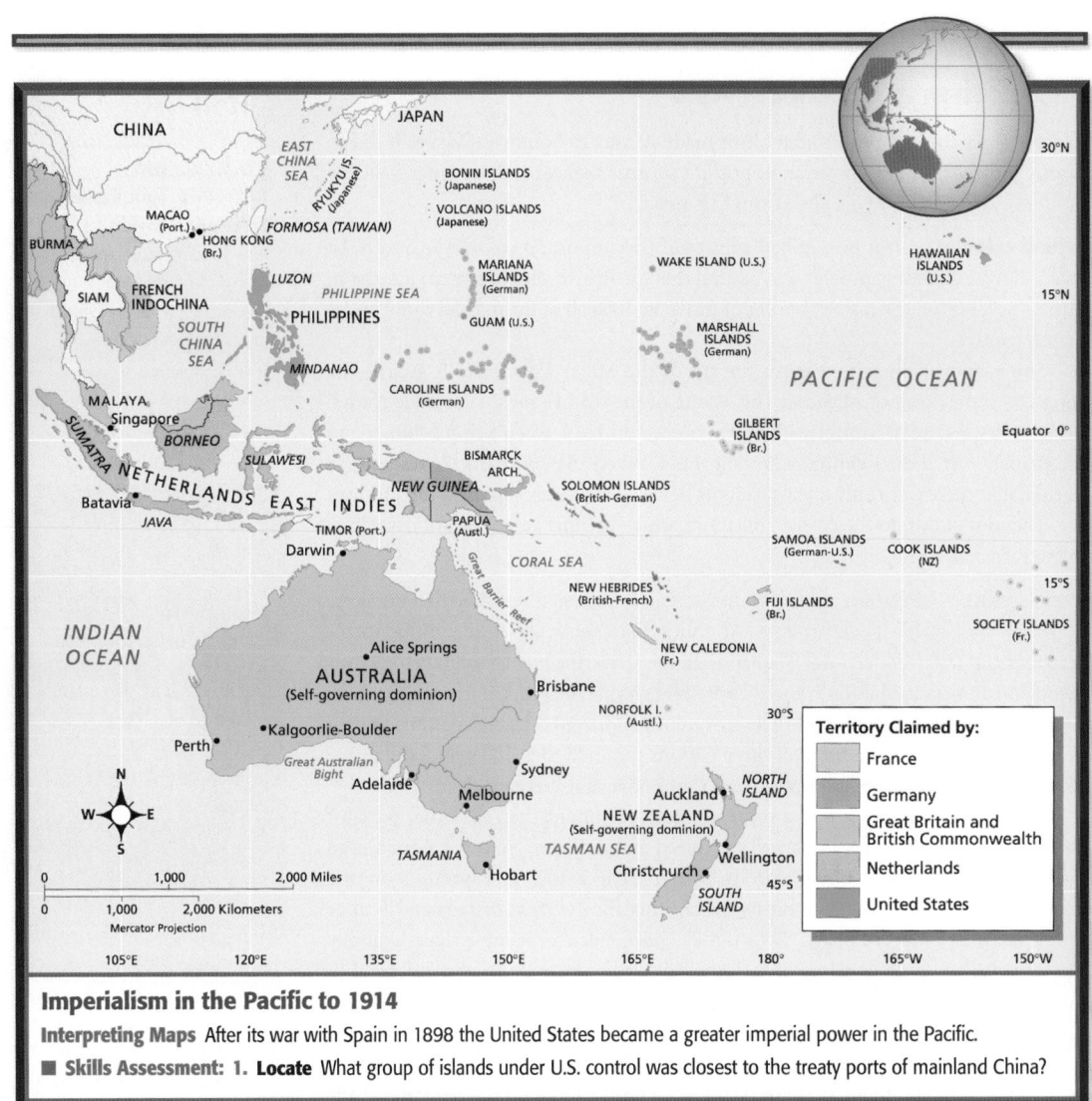

Imperialism in the Pacific to 1914

Interpreting Maps After its war with Spain in 1898 the United States became a greater imperial power in the Pacific.

■ **Skills Assessment: 1. Locate** What group of islands under U.S. control was closest to the treaty ports of mainland China?

U.S. Interests in the Pacific Islands

The imperialist powers were interested in only a few of the Pacific islands. Some islands had valuable natural resources. However, the Western powers mostly wanted islands for coaling stations and naval bases.

The Samoa Islands. In the late 1800s, a serious rivalry developed in the Samoa Islands. The United States had gained the right to use the harbor city of Pago Pago (PAHNG·oh PAHNG·oh) on the island of Tutuila (too·too·WEE·luh). Americans used it as a trading post, coaling station, and naval base. Great Britain and Germany had gotten similar rights in other parts of the Samoa Islands.

The rivalry among the three foreign powers continued for a number of years until the three came close to going to war. Finally, in 1899 the rivals signed a treaty. Great Britain, preoccupied with the Boer War, withdrew its interests. The United States

CLOSE

Ask students to explain which Pacific islands the United States controlled and why these were important possessions.

REVIEW

Have students complete the Section 4 Review on p. 681.

ASSESS

Have students complete Daily Quiz 26.4. As Alternative Assessment, you may want to use the map or Pacific islands exercises in this section's lessons.

RETEACH

Have students complete Main Idea Activity for English Language Learners and Special-Needs Students 26.4. Then have students create an annotated time line of imperialism in India and Southeast Asia. **ENGLISH LANGUAGE LEARNERS**

EXTEND

Have students conduct research to find out what effects of colonization are still evident in Indian society today.
BLOCK SCHEDULING

received firm control of Tutuila and six other small islands. Together these islands became American Samoa. Germany gained control of all the other islands in the Samoan group. They eventually became known as Western Samoa.

The Hawaiian Islands. The Hawaiian Islands were very important to the United States. They had an excellent harbor for a naval base, as well as rich soil, good rainfall, and a mild climate. After 1865 business people from the United States and other nations began to arrive. They started huge sugarcane and pineapple plantations. Soon they wanted more control over the island's government.

Hawaii's Queen **Liliuokalani** did not want foreigners to control Hawaii. She tried to change the treaties that allowed them to stay. In 1893 the business leaders gained enough power to end the queen's reign. The United States took over Hawaii in 1898.

The Philippines, Guam, and Wake Island. When Spain and the United States went to war in 1898 (see section 5), U.S. naval forces all over the world were ordered into action. The first battle of the war took place in the Spanish-controlled Philippines. Six ships under the command of Commodore George Dewey steamed from Hong Kong to Manila, the capital of the Philippines. Dewey's ships attacked the Spanish fleet in Manila harbor. The Spanish fleet was in poor repair and was destroyed in just a few hours. United States land forces followed. Within a few months, the Philippine Islands came under the control of the United States. At about this time, U.S. forces also took Guam, a small island east of the Philippines that Spain also controlled.

Some Filipinos welcomed the Americans. Some even fought with them against the Spanish. Many Filipinos, though, saw no reason to change one master for another. **Emilio Aguinaldo** led the Filipinos in a fight for independence. The Filipinos used guerrilla warfare against the better-equipped United States army. The war lasted for three hard years. The Filipinos were finally defeated in 1902.

Besides taking over the Philippine Islands and Guam, the United States also took control of Wake Island. This gave the United States a chain of islands running from its west coast across the Pacific to Asia.

✔ **READING CHECK: Making Predictions** What benefit do you think the United States gained from its Pacific islands later in the 1900s? The Hawaiian Islands brought great wealth to the nation and eventually became a state.

HISTORY MAKER

Queen Liliuokalani (1838–1917)

Queen Liliuokalani was the first woman ever to become ruler of the Hawaiian Islands. She was also the last.

As queen, Liliuokalani faced increasing pressure from American businessmen who wanted the islands to be a part of the United States. In order to avoid bloodshed, she agreed to step down from the throne. In so doing, she opened the way for the United States to annex Hawaii, a move she bitterly opposed. After leaving the throne, she withdrew from public life. **Why did Liliuokalani give up control of Hawaii?**

HISTORY MAKER ANSWER
to avoid bloodshed

◆**SECTION**◆
4 REVIEW ANSWERS

❶ **Identify**
- Meiji Restoration, p. 676
- Diet, p. 676
- Sino-Japanese War, p. 677
- Treaty of Shimonoseki, p. 677
- Mongkut, p. 679
- Liliuokalani, p. 681
- Emilio Aguinaldo, p. 681

❷ India: factories, hospitals, and schools established; farming methods improved, Indians excluded from European social circles; Japan: old system of social classes eliminated, decrease in illiteracy, new constitution, small group held power; Southeast Asia: nations more stable and economies improved; Siam became a buffer state; Pacific Islands: rivalry developed in Samoa Islands; U.S. took control of Hawaii, Philippine Islands, and Guam

❸ a. introduced Indians to Western culture through schools established by British

b. They were heavily influenced by Western ideas.

c. There was little fighting.

❹ Students' paragraphs will vary but should include both positive and negative effects.

◆ **SECTION 4 REVIEW** ◆

1. **Identify** and explain the significance:
   Meiji Restoration
   Diet
   Sino-Japanese War
   Treaty of Shimonoseki
   Mongkut
   Liliuokalani
   Emilio Aguinaldo

2. **Evaluating** Copy the web below. Use it to analyze and evaluate the ways in which each Asian region was affected by Western imperialism.

   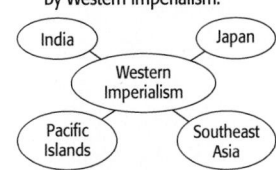

   India — Western Imperialism — Japan — Pacific Islands — Southeast Asia

3. **Finding the Main Idea**
   a. How did British rule affect India?
   b. Why were the Japanese able to reform and industrialize their nation so quickly?
   c. How did United States expansion in Hawaii differ from its expansion in the Philippines?

4. **Writing and Critical Thinking**
   Comparing and Contrasting Write two paragraphs about Western and Japanese imperialism in Asia. In the first paragraph describe the positive effects of imperialism in Asia. In the second paragraph describe the negative aspects of imperialism in the region.
   Consider:
   • improvements in Asia during the age of imperialism
   • the effects of imperialism on Asian people
   • how the imperialist powers exploited Asian land and resources

Homework Practice Online
go.hrw.com
keyword: SP3 HP26

OBJECTIVES

1 **Explain how economic pressure was used by imperialist powers to control Latin America.**

2 **Identify the causes and outcomes of the Spanish-American War of 1898.**

3 **Explain why the Panama Canal was important.**

4 **Describe the "Roosevelt Corollary" to the Monroe Doctrine.**

📻 *LET'S GET STARTED!*

As students enter the classroom, have them think about how a country with a strong economy can influence a country with a weaker economy. Ask them to list policies that might make this possible. *(Students might point out that the country with a strong economy could offer financial aid to the country with the weaker economy or take advantage of it.)* Tell students that in Section 5 they will learn how the United States and Europe asserted economic control over the countries of Latin America.

SECTION 5 RESOURCES

REPRODUCIBLE RESOURCES

▶ Guided Reading Strategy 26.5

▶ Creative Teaching Strategy 26: The "New" Imperialism

TECHNOLOGY RESOURCES

▶ One-Stop Planner 26.5

▶ Holt Researcher: World History: Carlos Juan Finlay

▶ World History Teaching Transparency: Geography and History 19: Independence in Latin America

▶ Homework Practice Online

▶ Online Maps: The United States Expands Its Influence

REINFORCEMENT, REVIEW, AND ASSESSMENT

▶ Section 5 Review, p. 687

▶ Daily Quiz 26.5

▶ Main Idea Activity 26.5

▶ English Audio Summary 26.5

▶ Spanish Audio Summary 26.5

SECTION 5

READ TO DISCOVER

❶ How was economic pressure used by imperialist powers to control Latin America?

❷ What were the causes and outcomes of the Spanish-American War of 1898?

❸ Why was the Panama Canal important?

❹ What was the "Roosevelt Corollary" to the Monroe Doctrine?

IDENTIFY

Maine
Platt Amendment
Panama Canal
Carlos Juan Finlay
Roosevelt Corollary
Porfirio Díaz
Victoriano Huerta
Venustiano Carranza
Emiliano Zapata
Pancho Villa

WHY IT MATTERS TODAY

Because of its policies toward Latin America, the United States regularly gets involved in Latin American affairs. Use CNN News.com or other **current event** sources to find examples of United States involvement in Latin America. Record your findings in your journal.

CNN Student News.com

Imperialism in Latin America

The Main Idea
Imperialist powers controlled Latin America with economic influence and political intervention.

The Story Continues *The Monroe Doctrine kept European powers from colonizing Latin America. The United States flexed its military muscle to support its interests in Latin America. "In the Western Hemisphere the . . . Monroe Doctrine may force the United States . . . to the exercise of an international police power," President Theodore Roosevelt once threatened.*

Economic Imperialism

By the end of the 1800s, the United States and Europe were buying many products from Latin America. Americans ate bananas from Central America, drank coffee from Brazil, and smoked Cuban cigars. Great Britain bought large amounts of wool and beef from Argentina. Any Latin American country with products to trade found people to buy them.

Europeans and Americans began to invest money in Latin America. They built factories and textile mills; bought ranches, plantations, and mines; and even owned railroads. Latin American governments thought it was a good idea to allow foreigners to buy land and spend money in their countries. They hoped these businesses would help their economies. The foreign investors, however, usually did not keep their money in Latin America. Instead they sent the money they made back to their own countries. This limited growth in the Latin American countries.

Some Latin American countries borrowed money from Europe or the United States. They used the money to make public improvements or strengthen their armies and navies. Sometimes a country could not pay back its loans. Foreign banks and business leaders persuaded their own governments to pressure any country that did not pay. Sometimes they sent ships and troops to force a country to pay.

✔ **READING CHECK: Finding the Main Idea** How did the Europeans and Americans control the economies of Latin American countries? gained economic control through investment

Britain and the United States funded many railroads in Latin America. This railroad was constructed through a banana plantation in Costa Rica.

LEVEL 3: Have students read the opening paragraphs of Section 5. Then ask them how early nineteenth-century imperialism in Latin America differed from imperialism in Africa, Asia, and the Pacific. *(Foreign countries did not attempt to colonize Latin America; instead, they dominated economic affairs.)* Then divide the class in two. Have half the students prepare an argument stating that the form of imperialism practiced in Latin America was better than imperialism in the rest of the world, and the native inhabitants had no cause for complaint. Have the other students prepare the argument that imperialism, no matter what form it takes, is a terrible experience for the native inhabitants, who had every right to demand their independence.

The Spanish-American War

In 1898 the United States became deeply involved in Latin America. The problem grew out of disagreements with Spain over Cuba. The Caribbean island had been a Spanish colony for many years, but the Cubans were unhappy under Spanish rule. A rebellion had failed, and the situation was tense. This alarmed Americans who had businesses in Cuba. Also, many Americans thought Cuba should be free.

Anger boiled over in 1898. The *Maine,* an American battleship, exploded in Havana harbor, killing some 260 Americans. The *Maine* had been sent to Cuba to protect American citizens and their property. No one knew the cause of the explosion. Many in the United States assumed that the Spanish were to blame.

This painting depicts Theodore Roosevelt leading the Rough Riders into battle during the Spanish-American War.

Spain wanted to avoid war, but it would not withdraw from Cuba. The United States declared war in April 1898. Congress stated that the United States was fighting only on behalf of Cuban independence and that America had no intention of taking the island for itself.

By May the war had started. The first battle ended with the defeat of the Spanish fleet in the Philippines. In July U.S. troops arrived in Cuba. With Cuban help, U.S. troops quickly defeated the Spanish. American writer Stephen Crane reported on the war for the *New York World* newspaper. Here he sums up the battle in which Theodore Roosevelt and his Rough Riders took part.

History Makers Speak
❝No doubt when history begins to grind out her story we will find that many a thundering, fine, grand order was given for that day's work; but after all there will be no harm in contending that the fighting line, the men and their regimental officers, took the hill chiefly because they knew they could take it, some having no orders and others disobeying whatever orders they had. . . . It will never be forgotten as long as America has a military history.❞

Stephen Crane in the *New York World*, July 14, 1898

The Treaty of Paris ended the war in December 1898. By the terms of the peace treaty, Spain gave up its claim to Cuba. It also gave the United States another of its colonies, Puerto Rico, which became a commonwealth of the United States. In the Pacific, Spain gave up the Philippines and Guam.

Following the war, United States troops controlled Cuba. Americans started schools, built roads, and tried to improve health care. Doctors and nurses worked to wipe out yellow fever. After two years the United States allowed Cubans to elect their own government. A new Cuban assembly wrote a constitution, which included the **Platt Amendment**. This amendment said that Cuba could not transfer any land except to the United States. In addition, it gave the United States the right to intervene in Cuba. This could happen whenever the United States thought the stable government was in danger. The United States also insisted on having a permanent naval base in Cuba at Guantánamo Bay. In this way the United States continued to exert influence over Cuba.

✔ **READING CHECK: Identifying Cause and Effect** What were the effects of the Spanish-American War? The United States controlled Cuba and won Puerto Rico, while Spain lost its holdings in the Caribbean and Pacific.

History Maker

ROUGH RIDERS. Theodore Roosevelt was put in charge of recruiting the First United States Volunteer Cavalry, which was the official title of the regiment. The public referred to them as the "Rough Riders," a cowboy cavalry who wore slouch hats, blue flannel shirts, brown trousers, leggings and boots, and handkerchiefs loosely knotted around their necks. The men in the ranks were a diverse group composed of Harvard graduates, professional gamblers, clergymen, cowboys, and Indians. Most were young, but officers often had prior experience while serving in army Indian campaigns. The riders were trained in mounted drill while using a weapon such as a rifle or revolver. However, Roosevelt believed the horse was really the weapon to strike the first blow, and he trained the men to hit their enemies with their horses.

Critical Thinking

What could be a challenge in training such a diverse group of men?

ANSWER: Students might suggest the need to teach them to act together and to obey orders.

Analyzing Primary Sources

Drawing Inferences What did Stephen Crane imply when he said the Americans "took the hill chiefly because they knew they could"? that they were more determined than were the Spanish defenders

TEACH OBJECTIVE 2

ALL LEVELS: Ask students to list the causes and the outcomes of the Spanish-American War of 1898.

Then have students create a time line of the Spanish-American War. Display completed time lines around the room so other students may examine them. **ENGLISH LANGUAGE LEARNERS**

Spanish-American War of 1898	
Causes	**Outcomes**
U.S. disagreements with Spain over Cuba	the U.S. controlled Cuba and won Puerto Rico while Spain lost its holdings in the Caribbean and Pacific
explosion of the Maine	

Holt Researcher
go.hrw.com
KEYWORD: Holt Researcher
FreeFind: Carlos Juan Finlay
After reading more about Carlos Juan Finlay on the Holt Researcher, write a summary of his contributions to medicine.

The Panama Canal

Before the war, the American battleship *Oregon* had been stationed on the Pacific coast of the United States. When war became likely, the *Oregon* was sent to the Caribbean Sea. To reach the Caribbean, the battleship had to race around the entire South American continent. This was a distance of almost 13,000 miles. The United States realized it had a problem. It would either have to build two complete navies or find a quicker way to move ships between the Atlantic and Pacific Oceans.

The idea of a canal across the Isthmus of Panama was not new. The French company that built the Suez Canal had tried to build a canal across Panama, but their attempt had failed. In the late 1800s, the United States began talks with Colombia, which controlled Panama at that time. The United States wanted to lease a strip of land across the isthmus, but the Colombian government would not approve the lease. This angered people in the United States and Panama. Some business leaders in Panama led a revolt to gain freedom from Colombia.

American naval forces prevented Colombia from putting down the revolt in Panama. The revolution succeeded. In 1903 the new government gave the United States the rights to build the canal. Work began in 1904.

The **Panama Canal** opened in 1914. It was one of the world's great engineering feats. It might have been impossible to build without new power shovels and other machines. Science, too, played an important part. A Cuban doctor named **Carlos Juan Finlay** discovered that mosquitoes carry yellow fever. The disease had killed many workers attempting to build the canal. By destroying the mosquitoes, scientists controlled the spread of the disease. This allowed construction crews to work in the Panamanian jungles.

The new canal shortened the sea route from New York to San Francisco by about 8,000 miles. Merchant ships of all nations paid a toll to use the canal. However, the greatly shortened route saved time and operating costs.

✔ **READING CHECK: Making Generalizations**
Why was the Panama Canal important for the United States? greatly reduced travel times and shipping costs

Over a period of 15 to 20 hours, oceangoing vessels moving through the Panama Canal pass through a series of locks and lakes as they move from the Atlantic Ocean to the Pacific Ocean.

LEVEL 1: Ask students to describe why the Panama Canal was important for the United States. *(Without it the United States would have needed two navies. It greatly reduced travel times and shipping costs.)* What factors hindered the building of the canal? *(the Colombian government's refusal to approve the lease; the death of workers who caught yellow fever)*

ENGLISH LANGUAGE LEARNERS

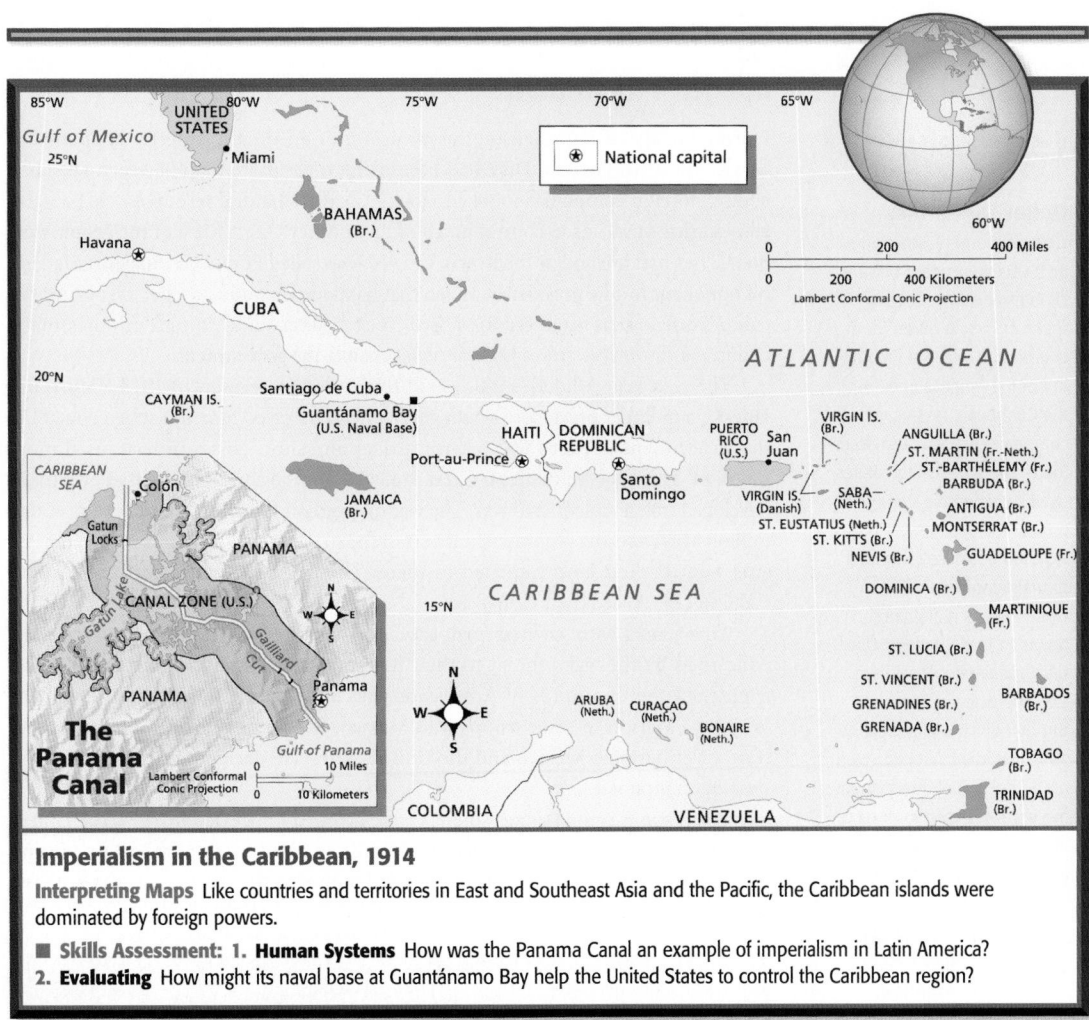

Imperialism in the Caribbean, 1914

Interpreting Maps Like countries and territories in East and Southeast Asia and the Pacific, the Caribbean islands were dominated by foreign powers.

- **Skills Assessment: 1. Human Systems** How was the Panama Canal an example of imperialism in Latin America?
- **2. Evaluating** How might its naval base at Guantánamo Bay help the United States to control the Caribbean region?

The Roosevelt Corollary

The United States knew it would have to protect the Panama Canal. It also knew Europeans might send armed forces to Latin America. To prevent this, the United States took a strong stand.

In 1904 President Theodore Roosevelt said that if the independence of any country in the Western Hemisphere were in danger, the United States would act to prevent other countries from entering. Also, the United States would make sure that Latin American countries would repay their loans. This is known as the **Roosevelt Corollary**. The corollary angered Latin Americans. To them, it sounded as if they could not manage their own governments. They were also against Americans forcing them to pay back their loans. In spite of this, the United States acted several times. It maintained a nearly continuous military presence in Nicaragua from 1912 to 1933. It did the same in Haiti and the Dominican Republic at about the same time. American troops were in Cuba from 1906 to 1909 and also intervened on other occasions.

✔ **READING CHECK: Drawing Conclusions** What effect do you think the Roosevelt Corollary had on relations between the United States and Latin America? caused anger and resentment

---

Economics

The Roosevelt Corollary contributed to a large increase in investment in the Caribbean. In 1900 American investment in the region only amounted to a little more than $100 million. Within two years this figure had risen to $500 million. A decade later it had tripled. By 1913, American businesses made up at least 50 percent of the foreign trade in Central America and the larger Caribbean nations.

Critical Thinking

Ask students why they think American investment in the region increased so greatly.

ANSWER: Students might guess that American investors took advantage of a new market for trade.

MAP ANSWERS

1. Imperialists used Panama to get what they wanted, and they employed Western technology.

2. It provides easy naval access to the region.

Technology Resources

World History Teaching Transparency: Geography and History 24: Central America and the Caribbean

LEVEL 2: Write the words *Roosevelt Corollary* on the board. Underneath write *who? what? where? when? why?* and *how?* Tell students that these are the questions that reporters often ask themselves when writing a story. Then have students write a short news report about the Roosevelt Corollary that answers all of the questions. Select students to read their report aloud. As they are doing so, fill in the answers to each question under the proper heading on the board.

HOMEWORK Have students create a research outline for a proposed paper on foreign intervention in Latin America. Students may choose to give an overall view of intervention in their proposed papers, or they may focus on one important event. Outlines should mention specific examples of intervention as well as provide pertinent details. Then have students write an introductory paragraph, including a thesis statement, for their proposed paper. Paragraphs should use correct social studies terminology, standard grammar, spelling, sentence structure, and punctuation.

Global Relations

At different times, the United States created military governments in Nicaragua, Haiti, the Dominican Republic, and Cuba. The United States intervened in these countries for several reasons. During the early 1900s, the economies of several nations in the area almost collapsed. The United States feared that governments would refuse to pay debts owed to foreign banks. European nations might have used a refusal to pay debts as a pretext for large-scale intervention in the region.

Critical Thinking

Ask students if these interventions were justified.

ANSWER: Students might say yes, because the United States wanted to prevent large-scale European intervention. Students might say no, because these interventions were motivated by economic interests.

CONNECTING TO ECONOMICS ANSWER

A country might be able to start its own businesses and increase its economic strength.

Reproducible Resources

PS   Readings in World History 92: A Change in United States Policy Toward Nicaragua

---

CONNECTING TO Economics

Dollar Diplomacy

Dollar diplomacy was started in 1909 by President William H. Taft to help Americans make money in other countries. It was used mainly in Central America and the Caribbean. American companies started businesses there. Then, the United States used its economic strength to protect the businesses. In this way, the business continued to make money and the United States maintained power in these nations. Over time, many people resisted U.S. efforts to control them through dollar diplomacy. By 1912 President Taft had given up on dollar diplomacy. Today the phrase is used to describe efforts by one country to control another through money.

Understanding Economics

How might American loans help a foreign country today?

Mexico's Revolution

During the age of imperialism, the greatest unrest in Latin America happened in Mexico. By 1910 **Porfirio Díaz** had been dictator for more than 30 years. Díaz had allowed foreign companies to take many of Mexico's natural resources. He had also allowed rich Mexicans to control much of the country's land. Most of the people were poor. They had no land of their own. In 1910 Díaz jailed Francisco Indalécio Madero, his opponent for the presidency. When that happened, a popular rebellion against the rule of Porfirio Díaz broke out in Mexico. The rebellion quickly spread throughout the country and soon became a general revolt against the government.

The next year Madero's followers brought him to power. In 1913 **Victoriano Huerta,** a member of Madero's own government, betrayed him and seized control of the government. Madero was taken prisoner and shot. This murder caused more rebellion. This time **Venustiano Carranza** led a revolt against Huerta that eventually developed into a violent civil war. The war dragged on for several years, and over one million lives were lost. An important part of the struggle was over land. Mexican peasants wanted their land returned to them. The peasant leader **Emiliano Zapata** (sah·PAH·tah) voiced their demands.

Americans who owned property and businesses in Mexico were very concerned by the war's threat to their investments. The continuing conflict also frightened the thousands of Americans who lived there. They wanted President Woodrow Wilson to send troops into Mexico. President Wilson did not want to start a war between Mexico and the United States. He decided instead to wait and see what happened.

When some United States soldiers were arrested in Mexico in 1914, the United States finally decided to act. Marines took control of Veracruz, an important port on the Gulf of Mexico. This cut off supplies and money to the Huerta government. The action helped Carranza's forces win the war.

Mexican artist Diego Rivera painted murals dealing with the history and social problems of his country. Struggle of the Classes *is in Mexico City.*

CLOSE

Ask students to describe imperialism in Latin America and to explain why foreign powers intervened.

REVIEW

Have students complete the Section 5 Review on p. 687.

ASSESS

Have students complete Daily Quiz 26.5. As Alternative Assessment, you may want to use the Spanish-American War or Panama Canal exercises in this section's lessons.

RETEACH

Have students complete Main Idea Activity for English Language Learners and Special-Needs Students 26.5. Then ask students to list the main ideas of each heading.
ENGLISH LANGUAGE LEARNERS

EXTEND

Have two groups prepare a debate discussing if imperialism practiced in Latin America was less harmful or equally harmful to its inhabitants than that practiced in Africa and Asia.
BLOCK SCHEDULING

Women played an important role in Mexico's revolution, as this photograph from 1911 illustrates.

The colorful rebel leader **Pancho Villa** (VEE·yah) continued to fight Carranza for control of the revolution. Villa led effective guerrilla attacks against the new government. He also attacked large landowners in Mexico, taking property and money to finance and supply the revolutionary army. In 1916, for reasons that are still not clearly understood, Villa moved his troops across the border into the United States. He raided the small town of Columbus, New Mexico, killing more than a dozen Americans. President Woodrow Wilson reluctantly sent troops under the command of General John Pershing into Mexico to capture Villa. As the U.S. force went deeper into Mexico, Carranza's government became more and more concerned. For a time there was a threat of war between Mexico and the United States. In 1917, however, the United States withdrew its troops from Mexico. Americans had started to pay attention to the world war that was taking place in Europe.

Pancho Villa was a Mexican revolutionary and guerrilla leader.

✔ **READING CHECK: Summarizing** What were the main causes of unrest and revolution in Mexico? economic, social, and political inequality

SECTION 5 REVIEW

1. **Identify** and explain the significance:
   Maine
   Platt Amendment
   Panama Canal
   Carlos Juan Finlay
   Roosevelt Corollary
   Porfirio Díaz
   Victoriano Huerta
   Venustiano Carranza
   Emiliano Zapata
   Pancho Villa

2. **Identifying Cause and Effect**
   Copy the chart below. Use it to identify the causes and effects of United States military interventions in Latin America from 1898 to about 1933.

   Where → Reason → What Happened

3. **Finding the Main Idea**
   a. Why were European and American investments no help to the economies of Latin American countries?
   b. What evidence shows that the United States wanted control over Cuba after the Spanish-American War?
   c. How might the United States and Mexico be different if the two countries had gone to war in 1916?

4. **Writing and Critical Thinking**
   Summarizing Imagine you are a reporter in Panama during the building of the Panama Canal. Write an article describing what you observe.
   Consider:
   • working and living conditions in the Panamanian jungle
   • physical health of the workers
   • purposes of the canal

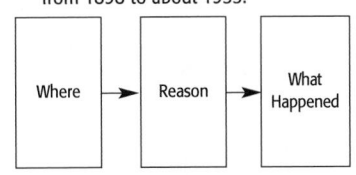
Homework Practice Online
keyword: SP3 HP26

SECTION 5 REVIEW ANSWERS

❶ Identify
• *Maine*, p. 683
• Platt Amendment, p. 683
• Panama Canal, p. 684
• Carlos Juan Finlay, p. 684
• Roosevelt Corollary, p. 685
• Porfiro Díaz, p. 686
• Victoriano Huerta, p. 686
• Venustiano Carranza, p. 686
• Emiliano Zapata, p. 686
• Pancho Villa, p. 687

❷ Cuba: cause—disagreements with Spain over Cuba; effects—war, U.S. victory, United States gained Puerto Rico; Mexico: cause—U.S. businesses and citizens were threatened by Mexico's revolution; effect—helped Carranza's forces win the war

❸ a. Foreign investors usually sent the money they made back to their own countries instead of keeping it in Latin America.

b. built roads, started schools, tried to improve health care, Platt Amendment

c. Their borders might be different.

❹ Students' articles will vary but should summarize working and living conditions in the Panamanian jungle, physical health of the workers, and purposes of the canal.

REVIEW AND ASSESSMENT RESOURCES

REPRODUCIBLE RESOURCES
▸ Vocabulary Activity 26

TECHNOLOGY RESOURCES
▸ Chapter 26 Test Generator (on the One-Stop Planner)
▸ Global Skill Builder CD–ROM
▸ HRW Web Site

REINFORCEMENT, REVIEW, and ASSESSMENT
▸ Chapter 26 Review, pp. 688–689
▸ Chapter 26 Tutorial for Students, Parents, Mentors, and Peers
▸ Chapter 26 Test (Form A or B)
▸ Alternative Assessment Handbook
▸ Chapter 26 Test for English Language Learners and Special-Needs Students

REVIEW
Have students complete the Chapter 26 Review on pages 688–689.

ASSESS
Use one of the chapter tests to assess students' understanding of the content. For Alternative Assessment, see the Portfolio Activities and Alternative Assessment Handbook.

Understanding Main Ideas

1. No nations wanted to depend on others for raw materials.

2. needed to fuel their ships

3. The British would favor trade with their colonies.

4. He led a revolt against Egyptian rule; his followers captured Khartoum.

5. only interested in amassing wealth; sold rights to raw materials; used forced labor

6. He helped to extend Britain's control in South Africa.

7. Classes were mostly taught in English and students learned about Western ideas along with regular school subjects.

8. bought new factory machinery from Western countries; passed laws to encourage private citizens to start businesses; sent students to Western countries to learn about Western ideas

9. the murder of Madero

Reviewing Themes

1. Europe, Japan, and the United States controlled many countries that were not industrialized.

2. British control of the Suez Canal; U.S. control of the Panama Canal

3. Leopold's rule of the Congo; Rhodes's control of South African diamond production

---

26 Review

Creating a Time Line

Copy the time line below onto a sheet of paper. Complete the time line by filling in the events, individuals, and dates from the chapter that you think were significant. Pick three events and explain why you think they were significant.

 1830   **1875**   **1917**

Writing a Summary

Using standard grammar, spelling, sentence structure, and punctuation, write an overview of the events in the chapter.

Identifying People and Ideas

Identify the following terms or individuals and explain their significance:

1. imperialism
2. dependent colonies
3. Fashoda crisis
4. paternalism
5. Leopold II
6. Boers
7. Meiji Restoration
8. *Maine*
9. Roosevelt Corollary
10. Venustiano Carranza

Understanding Main Ideas

Section 1 (pp. 662–665)
The Roots of Western Imperialism

1. Why did the imperialists want to control regions with raw materials?
2. Why were coaling stations important to the imperialists?

Section 2 (pp. 666–669)
European Claims in North Africa

3. How would British control of the Suez Canal affect world trading patterns?
4. What role did the al-Mahdt play in the history of the Sudan?

Section 3 (pp. 670–674)
European Claims in Sub-Saharan Africa

5. Why was Leopold's rule in the Congo an example of imperialism at its worst?
6. What role did Cecil Rhodes play in South Africa?

Section 4 (pp. 675–681)
Expansion in Asia

7. What effect did British schools have in India?

8. What did the Japanese do to industrialize their country?

Section 5 (pp. 682–687)
Imperialism in Latin America

9. Why did Venustiano Carranza lead a revolt in Mexico?

Reviewing Themes

1. **Global Relations** What evidence is there that an industrialized country can control a country that is not industrialized?
2. **Geography** What evidence is there to show that areas were colonized because they met the transportation needs of other, more powerful countries?
3. **Economics** What evidence is there to show that areas were colonized for natural resources?

Thinking Critically

1. **Summarizing** Why did the industrialized nations of the West move to become imperialist powers?
2. **Comparing and Contrasting** What are the similarities and differences between the Platt Amendment and the Roosevelt Corollary?
3. **Drawing Inferences** How did the Sino-Japanese War mark Japan's growth as a world power?
4. **Supporting a Point of View** What evidence would you give that money was an effective means of control in Latin America?

Writing About History

Identifying a Point of View Write a report explaining the reasons for Western expansion into Africa, Asia, Latin America, and the Pacific, and describe what happened as a result of this expansion. Use the chart below to organize your thoughts before you write.

	Africa	Asia	Latin America	Pacific
Raw materials and products				
Resistance and rebellions				
Imperialist competition				

CLOSE

Ask students how economic imperialism differs from political imperialism. Why did one often lead to the other during the late 1800s?

RETEACH

Pair students who have had difficulty with the test. Have each pair compile a chapter glossary and a list of key events in the history of imperialism since the 1800s. When they are ready, have students take the Form B Test to assess their mastery of the material.

ENGLISH LANGUAGE LEARNERS

Portfolio Extensions

Link to TODAY

1. Have students work in small groups to prepare a debate on the following topic: Resolved: The Europeans exploited Africa and severely damaged indigenous cultures.
2. Have students use books or computer software to prepare a report on missionary activities in colonial areas.
3. Have students create a map showing the partition of Africa by the European imperial powers. Maps should also include important events in the division of Africa, such as battles. Ask students to write a brief description of each event and place each of these annotations on the map.

Building Social Studies Skills

Reading a Chart
Study the chart below. Then answer the questions that follow.

**Foreign Investment in 1914
(in millions of U.S. dollars)**

Area	British Investments	French Investments	American Investments
North America	7,000	500	900
Latin America	3,700	1,600	1,200
Africa	2,400	900	–
Asia	3,500	1,200	100

1. Which statement correctly describes a relationship shown on the chart?
   a. In 1914, the British and French invested more in North America than any other area.
   b. In 1914, British investments worldwide were less than they had been in 1900.
   c. French and American investments in Asia were increasing in 1914.
   d. In 1914, Americans invested more in Latin America than all other areas combined.

2. Why do you think British investments were greater worldwide than those of the French or the Americans? Give specific reasons for your viewpoint.

Categorizing Information
Read the paragraph below. Then answer the questions that follow.

> As the great powers expanded their influence, scientists and adventurers explored uncharted territories. Arctic explorer Robert Edwin Peary from the United States is thought to be the first to reach the North Pole (April 6, 1909). Norwegian explorer Roald Amundsen was the leader of the first expedition to reach the South Pole, accomplished on December 14, 1911. In 1912, American archaeologist Hiram Bingham discovered the lost cities of the Inca in the Andes Mountains of Peru. Between 1875 and 1915, Prince Albert I of Monaco conducted surveys of the world's oceans. He collected marine specimens and took soundings.

3. Which of the following gives the best categories for organizing the information in the paragraph?
   a. Place Explored, Date Explored, Type of Exploration
   b. Name, Where From, Place Explored, Date Explored
   c. Name, Profession, Place Explored
   d. Place Explored, Date Explored, Importance

4. Do you think these explorations and others like them were important? Give specific reasons to support your point of view.

Alternative Assessment

Building Your Portfolio

Link to TODAY

Global Relations

Imperialism still exists in the world today. Use your textbook and other sources to find examples of imperialism today. Then, using knowledge you have gained by evaluating the actions of individuals, groups, and nations during the Age of Imperialism, write an analysis of why some nations still maintain colonies and how the colonized peoples have reacted to it.

☑ internet connect

Internet Activity: go.hrw.com
KEYWORD: SP3 WH26

Choose a topic on the Age of Imperialism to:
• create an annotated time line on the political changes experienced by the territory once known as the Congo.
• write a report on the impact of colonization on the African people.
• write a series of journal entries from the point of view of Dr. Livingstone.

Thinking Critically

1. They sought raw materials and new markets for their goods.

2. similarity: both provided for U.S. intervention and military presence; difference: Platt Amendment became part of Cuba's constitution, and the Roosevelt Corollary angered Latin Americans

3. Japan defeated China and gained control of Taiwan.

4. Latin American countries borrowed money from Europe and the United States and were often forced to repay.

Writing About History
Students' reports will vary but should include information about Western expansion.

Building Social Studies Skills
1. d

2. Britain had the strongest economy.

3. b

4. Students should include reasons for their opinions.

Building Your Portfolio
Students' analyses will vary.

CROSS-CULTURAL CONNECTIONS *Literature*

Spotlight on LITERATURE

A novel is a unique form of literature that has evolved from earlier forms such as the epic and the romance. Novels such as *War and Peace* by Leo Tolstoy seek to re-create everyday experience or to represent the world as it is rather than to create something farfetched or fantastic. Novels are often limited to facts and events that could actually happen and try to convince readers that the world they describe is real. Some novels concentrate on characters, while others concentrate on plot. Still others may present a highly detailed picture of life and the way characters are influenced as life events unfold.

Spotlight on LITERATURE

An important aspect of nationalism is pride: pride in one's heritage, pride in one's culture, pride in one's place in the world. One prominent form of expressing such nationalistic pride is through song. Have students locate the entire lyrics to the song "America" ("My country, 'tis of thee . . .") by Samuel Francis Smith and tell how the words to the song express pride in being an American. (*Pride is explicitly mentioned in the line, "Land of the pilgrims' pride.")*

Culture

One major problem caused by imperialism was the conflict of cultures. In many cases, imperialist European nations knew little about the cultures of the non-European countries they were attempting to bring within their sphere of influence. At the same time, the subjects of their imperial designs resented having foreign cultures foisted upon them.

ACTIVITY: Have students choose an imperial power and one of the nations it attempted to bring under its sway (such as Great Britain and India) and compare and contrast their cultures. Then have students conclude how cultural differences may have led to conflict.

UNDERSTANDING LITERATURE ANSWER

Both writers attempt to unite their readers by pointing out the threats from foreign nations—France for the Russians. Both writers remind their readers of their common heritage and suggest that it is necessary for people to stand together and fight together to preserve that heritage from outside influence.

CROSS-CULTURAL CONNECTIONS *Literature*

Nationalism and Literature

Literature gives historians insight into past events and into people's feelings about those events. Leo Tolstoy (1828–1910) wrote about Napoléon's 1812 invasion of Russia in his novel War and Peace. *He described how the Russians reacted to Napoléon's capture of their capital. In contrast, Giuseppe Garibaldi (1807-1882) used a speech to inspire troops, known as Red Shirts, fighting for Italian independence. He urged Italians to unite and fight for the new kingdom of Italy under King Victor Emmanuel II.*

War and Peace *by Leo Tolstoy*

When half of Russia was conquered, and the inhabitants of Moscow were fleeing to remote provinces, and one levy of militia after another was being raised for the defense of the country, we not living at the time cannot help imagining that all the people in Russia, great and small alike, were engaged in doing nothing else but making sacrifices, saving their country, or weeping over its downfall. . . . In reality, it was not at all like that. . . . The majority of the people of that period took no heed of the general progress of public affairs, and were only influenced by their immediate personal interests. . . . The significance of the drama taking place in Russia at that time was the less easy to grasp, the closer the share a man was taking in it. In Petersburg, and in the provinces remote from Moscow, ladies and gentlemen in volunteer uniforms bewailed the fate of Russia and the ancient capital, and talked of self-sacrifice, and so on.

But in the army, which had retreated behind Moscow, men scarcely talked or thought at all about Moscow, and, gazing at the burning city, no one swore to be avenged on the French, but every one was thinking of the next quarter's pay due to him, of the next halting-place, . . . and so on.

Giuseppe Garibaldi speaks to his soldiers

We must now consider the period which is just drawing to a close as almost the last stage of our national resurrection, and prepare ourselves to finish worthily the marvelous design of the elect of twenty generations, the completion of which Providence has reserved for this fortunate age.

Yes, young men, Italy owes to you an undertaking which has merited the applause of the universe. You have conquered and you will conquer still. . . . To this wonderful page in our country's history another more glorious still will be added, and the slave shall show at last to his free brothers a sharpened sword forged from the links of his fetters.

To arms, then, all of you! all of you! And the oppressors and the mighty shall disappear like dust. . . .

Providence has presented Italy with Victor Emmanuel. Every Italian should rally round him. By the side of Victor Emmanuel every quarrel should be forgotten. Once more I repeat my battle-cry: "To arms, all—all of you."

Understanding Literature

How do both Tolstoy and Garibaldi attempt to inspire feelings of nationalism in people?

---

690 UNIT 6

690

Science, Technology, and Society

Write the following chart on the board and have students fill in the boxes to correctly show the sequence of events in Unit 6. Then challenge students to explain how the events are related by cause and effect.

| Industrial Revolution | → | reform | → | nationalism | → | imperialism |

Government

Have students work with partners to list the main characteristics of nationalism and imperialism. Then have them work together to use a problem-solving process to identify problems caused by the conflicts between these two ideologies. Students should list options, consider advantages and disadvantages, and choose a solution. Have them write a newspaper article describing the problems and suggesting solutions.

UNIT 6

BUILDING YOUR Portfolio

Science, Technology, and Society

The Industrial Revolution brought about a number of important developments in technology, communications, science, and medicine. Imagine that you are a student of history at Cambridge University in England during the late 1880s. You and your friends are making a "time capsule" that will contain artifacts, drawings, and descriptions of industrial life in the late 1800s. Your task is to create a list of the different items you would include. What would these items reveal about the role of technology and industry in the late 1800s? Use the bibliography below to help you.

This cartoon caricature shows Bismarck "sweeping away" German opposition to his policies of unification.

Further Reading

Corrick, James. *The Industrial Revolution.* San Diego: Lucent Books, 1998. A survey of the Industrial Revolution and its effects on Europe and the United States.

Dersin, Denise, ed. *What Life Was Like: In the Jewel of the Crown, British India, A.D. 1600–1905.* Alexandria, Virginia: Time-Life Books, 1999. A broad survey of political, social, and cultural life in British India.

Shelston, Dorothy and Alan Shelston. *The Industrial City, 1820–1870.* New York: Macmillan, 1990. A look at how industrialization changed the city.

Smith, Bonnie G. *Imperialism: A History in Documents.* New York: Oxford University Press, 2000. First-person accounts and political documents outlining the history of imperialism during the period 1850–1945.

Tilly, Louise A. and Joan W. Scott. *Women, Work and Family.* New York: Routledge, 1987. Discusses how the Industrial Revolution affected women in France and England.

Artifacts of the Industrial Age: a typewriter of 1874 (above) and a telegraph receiver of 1840 (right)

Government

During the second half of the nineteenth century a number of European countries underwent dramatic political change. Imagine that you are a newspaper editor in Berlin in 1870. You are a strong supporter of Otto von Bismarck and the cause of German national unification. Write an editorial in which you answer Bismarck's critics and those who oppose unification of the German states under Prussian leadership. Explain why you support unification and admire Bismarck.

🖉 internet connect

Internet Activity
KEYWORD: SP3 U6

In assigned groups, develop a multimedia presentation that describes lifestyles of the Industrial Revolution. Choose information from the chapter Internet Connect activities and the Holt Researcher that best reflects the major topics of the period. Write an outline and a script for your presentation, which may be shown to the class.

go.
hrw
.com

LITERATURE. Aristotle defined *rhetoric* as language that is used to persuade. In Aristotle's time rhetoric was concerned with the practice of oratory, or formal public speaking, and was considered one of the two main forms of expression, the other being poetry. Aristotle's *Rhetoric* (c. 330 B.C.) is the oldest complete text on the subject. It contains most of the principles that rhetoric and oratory have been based on since. Aristotle defined three kinds of persuasive oratory: forensic, which is intended to prove the justice or injustice of a past action; deliberative, which is intended to move an audience to action; and epideictic, which is intended to display sentiments for such occasions as funerals, inaugurations, and dedications. Aristotle also identified three means of persuasion: appealing to reason, emotion, and ethics.

Critical Thinking

How could reformers during the Age of Reform have used Aristotle's ideas about rhetoric to promote their causes?

ANSWER: They could have used rhetoric in writing and speech to appeal to the reason, emotion, and ethics of their audience in order to persuade people of the rightness of a certain cause and to sway them to act in certain ways.

UNIT 7

World War in the Twentieth Century

CHAPTER 27 World War I and the Russian Revolution

Tensions among the world's industrialized powers increased rapidly during the last half of the 1800s. At the turn of the 20th century, tension was particularly high in Europe, where nations such as Great Britain, France, and Germany vigorously pursued economic expansion. This tension exploded in World War I (1914–1918). At about the same time, years of war and poverty in Russia led to the Russian Revolution.

CHAPTER 28 The Great Depression and the Rise of Totalitarianism

The Treaty of Versailles forced defeated European countries to pay enormous reparations and limited their freedom to rebuild. Meanwhile, the economic damage caused by the war led to the Great Depression—an almost total collapse of the global economy. In some parts of Europe, totalitarian governments used the economic chaos as a means to gain power.

UNIT 7 World War in the Twentieth Century

c. 1880–1945

692

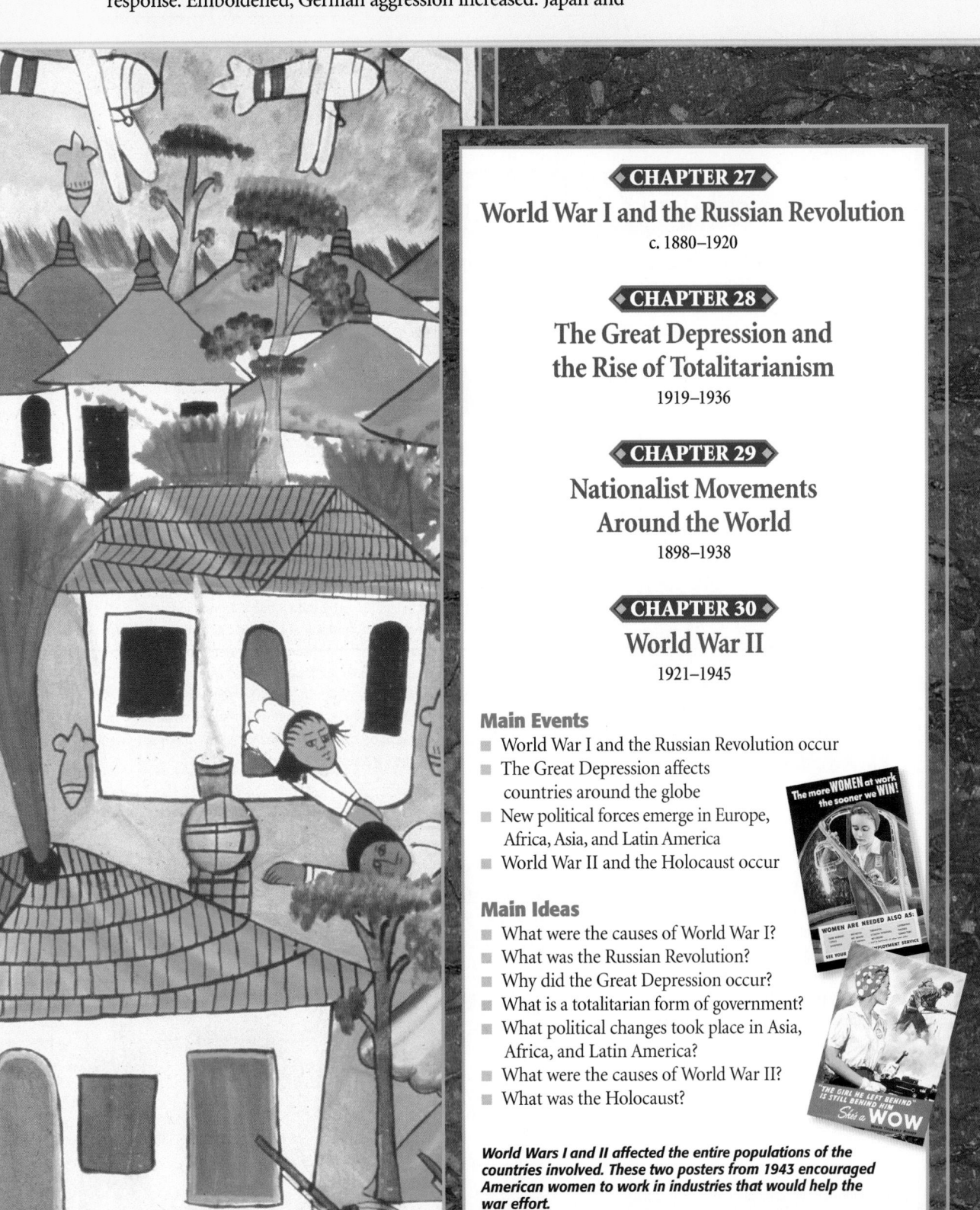

CHAPTER 29 ◆ Nationalist Movements Around the World

Just as the economic turmoil of the 1930s helped lead to the rise of dictatorships in some European nations, it led to revolutionary movements taking place in other parts of the world. Empires began to crumble as nationalist movements in Asia, Africa, and the Middle East gained momentum.

CHAPTER 30 ◆ World War II

Under the leadership of the dictator Adolf Hitler, Germany finally began breaking the terms of the Treaty of Versailles. Great Britain and France took no action in response. Emboldened, German aggression increased. Japan and Italy joined Germany in its campaign of fascist aggression, and World War II erupted. The war lasted from 1939–1945 and ended with the defeat of the Axis powers and the dawn of the nuclear age.

◆ CHAPTER 27 ◆
World War I and the Russian Revolution
c. 1880–1920

◆ CHAPTER 28 ◆
The Great Depression and the Rise of Totalitarianism
1919–1936

◆ CHAPTER 29 ◆
Nationalist Movements Around the World
1898–1938

◆ CHAPTER 30 ◆
World War II
1921–1945

Main Events
- World War I and the Russian Revolution occur
- The Great Depression affects countries around the globe
- New political forces emerge in Europe, Africa, Asia, and Latin America
- World War II and the Holocaust occur

Main Ideas
- What were the causes of World War I?
- What was the Russian Revolution?
- Why did the Great Depression occur?
- What is a totalitarian form of government?
- What political changes took place in Asia, Africa, and Latin America?
- What were the causes of World War II?
- What was the Holocaust?

World Wars I and II affected the entire populations of the countries involved. These two posters from 1943 encouraged American women to work in industries that would help the war effort.

Introduce Unit 7

Main Events
Ask students to select two Main Events and list questions they would like to have answered about the topics. Later, when you have completed Unit 7, ask students to return to their original questions and write an answer using the information they learned in the unit.

Main Ideas
Ask each student to read the Main Ideas and write brief answers to the questions. Share the *Consider* points with students as necessary. Later, when you have completed Unit 7, ask students to analyze their original answers by comparing them to information they learned in the unit. Tell them to revise or expand their answers as necessary.

The Impact of World War I and the Russian Revolution
Consider:
- political and cultural identities
- differences between communism and capitalism

The Causes for the Great Depression and the Rise of Totalitarianism
Consider:
- economic causes
- political developments

The Causes and Effects of Nationalist Movements and of World War II
Consider:
- creation of national identities
- the use of the atomic bomb

Fascist Italy used aircraft and other modern weapons to invade Ethiopia during the mid-1930s.

LET'S GET STARTED!

As students enter the classroom, ask them to think about their understanding of relationships between the world's nations as they stand today. Have students keep their thoughts in mind as they read Cross-Cultural Connections. Tell students that in this unit they will learn how, during the 20th century, tense relationships between nations caused wars and led to changes that still affect our lives.

ALL LEVELS: Help students fill in the chart below with the information shown in italics. Then have them discuss how the events are related through cause and effect.

ENGLISH LANGUAGE LEARNERS

World War I	**Great Depression**	**Totalitarianism**	**World War II**
• *destroyed European nations* • *damaged global economy*	• *total financial collapse* • *high unemployment* • *hunger and poverty*	• *loss of rights* • *expansionism* • *global tension*	• *Holocaust* • *defeat of Axis powers* • *beginning of nuclear age*

Daily Life

Some of the lesser-known stories of the Great Depression involve the thousands of teenagers who left their homes and hopped freight trains to look for work. Many of them wrote letters that described their experiences. In 1929 Berkeley N. Hackett, 13, rode an empty boxcar with his stepfather from Flint, Michigan, to Kalamazoo to work in a coal yard at 25 cents an hour. Claude Franklin, 13, his brother Charles, 16, and Robert Brookshire, 13, left their home in Fort Worth, Texas, to pick cotton in Mississippi. They were paid 75 cents for 100 pounds of cotton picked. Out of that came payment for their room and board. Norma Darrah, 18, hopped freight trains with her husband, Curly, and his nephew, 13. They traveled from Minnesota to Wyoming, where Curly's brother had offered Curly a job.

ACTIVITY: Ask students to imagine that they have to find a job in order to support their family. Have them write a letter telling their family where they will try to find a job and what they will be doing.

CROSS-CULTURAL CONNECTIONS

Focus On: Global Relations

Main Idea **How did conflicts between countries lead to two world wars?** Relations between countries during the late 1800s and early 1900s were marked by distrust, hostility, and war. Internal conflicts also plagued many nations, as various groups struggled to control national governments. In some places, new political forces arose that worsened, rather than strengthened, relations with other nations. This led to more international conflicts.

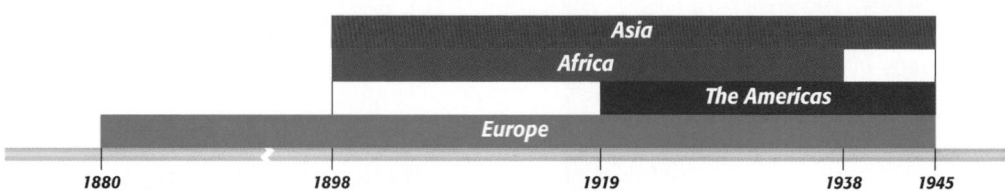

Asia

Africa

The Americas

Europe

1880   1898   1919   1938   1945

World War I in Europe, 1914–1918

World War I In 1914 Europe exploded into a war of unprecedented devastation and fearsome new weapons. The effects of poison gas, illustrated in this painting by John Singer Sargent, indicated a new level of brutality. It affected not only soldiers on the front but also civilians, who were bombarded from the air. In addition, the production of new weapons required the output of factories in industrial nations throughout the world. The devastation caused by these weapons affected postwar economic recovery.

The Great Depression The financial collapse of the Great Depression was a global crisis that shattered national economies and brought hardship to millions. Nations and markets around the world experienced drastically reduced banking, manufacturing, and commercial activity and consumer spending. Unemployment became widespread. Some countries sought to help their citizens by providing government-supported jobs, food, and other essentials, but many of these programs did little to correct the basic economic causes of the depression. Soup kitchens and breadlines became common sights in many industrialized nations, such as Austria, where this busy kitchen served people from all walks of life and all social levels.

The Great Depression, 1929–1939

Have students review the information about the historical events listed in the chart on page 694. Ask them to use standard grammar, spelling, sentence structure, and punctuation to answer the question in "Why It Matters Today" and to share their answer with the class.

Have students complete their answer to the question in "Why It Matters Today" and add it to their portfolio. As Alternative Assessment, you may want to use the chart exercise in the lesson.

Have students work in small groups to extend the cause-and-effect chart up to the present day. Students' charts should begin with World War II and include major global conflicts that have occurred since then. Charts should briefly summarize each conflict and how it is related to ones preceding and following. Tell students to use information from their textbooks, the library, computer software, and any other available resources to create their chart. Allow time for students to share their chart with the class.

Global Relations

Iwo Jima is a Japanese island in the western Pacific. Early in 1945 it was under the control of Japanese soldiers who had entrenched themselves in caves. Initial bombing had failed to weaken the Japanese resistance as U.S. Marines landed on the island, hoping to capture it and use it as a base for fighter planes flying to Japan. The struggle lasted for weeks before the island was officially captured. The photograph of the raising of the American flag is one of the best-known images of the Pacific war. It has been recreated in statues, in paintings, and on a U.S. postage stamp.

Critical Thinking

Why do you think the image is so popular and was used as the basis of a memorial in Arlington National Cemetery?

ANSWER: It appeals to national patriotism and pride.

WHY IT MATTERS TODAY ANSWER

Most students will answer that the most serious threats to current global security are terrorism and unrest in the Middle East.

Expansion in Africa The Italian fascist dictator Benito Mussolini believed overseas expansion could ease his country's economic problems during the Great Depression. Mussolini's expansionist plans led to a dispute between Italy and Ethiopia in 1934. One year later, Italy invaded the poorly armed country and defeated its army. This photograph shows Ethiopia's Emperor Haile Selassie seated in the center, surrounded by Ethiopian dignitaries and supporters. In 1936 Selassie went into exile in England, where he began planning a campaign with the British to defeat the Italians. He and the Allies accomplished this goal in 1942 when Selassie returned to power.

Ethiopia, 1934–1942

Fascist dictators Benito Mussolini (left) and Adolf Hitler (right) formed a partnership called the Rome-Berlin Axis.

World War II in the Pacific, 1939–1945

World War II The war continued in the Pacific after it had ended in Europe. The capture of Iwo Jima by U.S. Marines, memorialized in the sculpture shown here, followed some of the most intense fighting of the war. The war ended less than six months later, but its effects would shape the future of the world. World War II was not only the most destructive war in history, but it also marked the beginning of the nuclear age.

Why It Matters Today

The hostilities that provoked World War I led to future wars. They also helped spark a revolution, a push for overseas empires, and the redrawing of boundaries that affected peoples throughout the world. Global relations are still affected by these events. **What current international conflicts still threaten global security?**

CHAPTER 27

World War I and the Russian Revolution

CHAPTER RESOURCE MANAGER

Objectives	Pacing Guide	Reproducible Resources
SECTION 1 **Setting the Stage for War** (pp. 698–703) • Explain why rivalries increased among European nations. • Identify the military alliances that existed at the beginning of World War I and explain how they changed by late 1915. • Explain why the Balkans were a "powder keg."	**Regular** 1.5 day **Block Scheduling** 1 day *Block Scheduling Handbook with Team Teaching Strategies, 27.1*	**RS** Guided Reading Strategy 27.1 **RS** Graphic Organizer Activity 27: Choosing Sides **PS** Readings in World History 94: Songs of a Campaign
SECTION 2 **World War I: A New Kind of War** (pp. 704–710) • Identify the advantages that each side had in World War I. • Explain how new technology affected the way in which World War I was fought. • Explain what led the United States to join the Allied Powers.	**Regular** 1.5 day **Block Scheduling** 1 day *Block Scheduling Handbook with Team Teaching Strategies, 27.2*	**RS** Guided Reading Strategy 27.2 **SM** Geography Activity 27: World War I **PS** Readings in World History 93, 94: The Home Front in Germany; Songs of a Campaign **E** Hands-on History Activity 27: Fighting the Great War
SECTION 3 **The Russian Revolution** (pp. 711–713) • Identify the events that led to the Russian Revolution. • Explain how the Communists came to power. • Explain how Russia's revolution affected its participation in World War I.	**Regular** 1.5 day **Block Scheduling** 1 day *Block Scheduling Handbook with Team Teaching Strategies, 27.3*	**RS** Guided Reading Strategy 27.3 **PS** Readings in World History 95: The Storming of the Winter Palace
SECTION 4 **The Terms of Peace** (pp. 714–717) • Define the Fourteen Points. • Explain how the war ended. • Identify the disagreements that the peacemakers faced.	**Regular** 1.5 day **Block Scheduling** 1 day *Block Scheduling Handbook with Team Teaching Strategies, 27.4*	**RS** Guided Reading Strategy 27.4
SECTION 5 **Creating a "New" Europe** (pp. 718–723) • Identify the terms of the Treaty of Versailles. • Explain how territories were redivided after the war. • Explain how the League of Nations was structured.	**Regular** 1.5 day **Block Scheduling** 1 day *Block Scheduling Handbook with Team Teaching Strategies, 27.5*	**RS** Guided Reading Strategy 27.5 **PS** Readings in World History 96: The Germans are Informed of the Terms of the Treaty of Versailles **E** Creative Teaching Strategy 27: Reflections on the Great War

Chapter Resource Key

PS Primary Sources   **A** Assessment   Music

RS Reading Support   **REV** Review   Video

IC Interdisciplinary Connections   **ELL** Reinforcement and English Language Learners   Internet

E Enrichment   Transparencies   Holt Presentation Maker Using Microsoft® PowerPoint®

SM Skills Mastery   CD-ROM

 One-Stop Planner CD-ROM

See the ***One–Stop Planner*** for a complete list of additional resources for students and teachers.

One-Stop Planner CD-ROM

It's easy to plan lessons, select resources, and print out materials for your students when you use the *One-Stop Planner* CD–ROM with *Test Generator.*

Technology Resources	Reinforcement, Review, and Assessment
One-Stop Planner 27.1 Regions of the World Music Audio CD Program 7: Central Europe: Folk Songs of Hungary Homework Practice Online Online Maps, Charts, and Graphs: The Schlieffen Plan, 1905	Daily Quiz 27.1 Main Idea Activity 27.1 English Audio Summary 27.1 Spanish Audio Summary 27.1 REV Section 1 Review, p. 703
One-Stop Planner 27.2 Holt Researcher: World History: Manfred von Richthofen Holt Researcher: World History: Woodrow Wilson World History and Cultures Video Program 22: The Great War CNN Presents World Cultures: Yesterday and Today Segment 26: The Killer Flu of 1918 World History Teaching Transparency: Everyday Life 22: American Posters from World War I Homework Practice Online	Daily Quiz 27.2 Main Idea Activity 27.2 English Audio Summary 27.2 Spanish Audio Summary 27.2 REV Section 2 Review, p. 710
One-Stop Planner 27.3 Holt Researcher: World History: Vladimir Lenin CNN Presents World Cultures: Yesterday and Today Segment 25: Recovering Russia's Royalty Regions of the World Music Audio CD Program 9: Russia, Ukraine, and Belarus: Russian Choral Music Homework Practice Online	Daily Quiz 27.3 Main Idea Activity 27.3 English Audio Summary 27.3 Spanish Audio Summary 27.3 REV Section 3 Review, p. 713
One-Stop Planner 27.4 Homework Practice Online Online Maps, Charts, and Graphs: World War I Troop Strength and Casualties	Daily Quiz 27.4 Main Idea Activity 27.4 English Audio Summary 27.4 Spanish Audio Summary 27.4 REV Section 4 Review, p. 717
One-Stop Planner 27.5 World History Teaching Transparency: Geography and History 22: Europe and the Middle East After World War I Homework Practice Online Online Maps, Charts, and Graphs: The Polish Corridor After World War I	Daily Quiz 27.5 Main Idea Activity 27.5 English Audio Summary 27.5 Spanish Audio Summary 27.5 REV Section 5 Review, p. 723

internet connect

HRW ONLINE RESOURCES
GO TO: go.hrw.com
Then type in a keyword.

TEACHER HOME PAGE
KEYWORD: SP3 Teacher

CHAPTER INTERNET ACTIVITIES
KEYWORD: SP3 WH27
Choose an activity to:
- create a propaganda poster supporting the Allies or the Central Powers.
- learn about social issues and events that were causes or effects of the war.
- understand the strengths and weaknesses of the Versailles treaty.

CHAPTER ENRICHMENT LINKS
KEYWORD: SP3 CH27

ONLINE ASSESSMENT
Homework Practice
KEYWORD: SP3 HP27
Standardized Test Prep
KEYWORD: SP3 STP27
Rubrics
KEYWORD: SS Rubrics

ONLINE MAPS, CHARTS, AND GRAPHS
KEYWORD: SP3 MCG

CONTENT UPDATES
KEYWORD: SS Content Updates

HOLT PRESENTATION MAKER
KEYWORD: SP3 PPT27

ONLINE READING SUPPORT
KEYWORD: SS Strategies

CURRENT EVENTS
KEYWORD: S3 Current Events

Meeting Individual Needs

Ability Levels

Level 1 Basic level activities designed for all students encountering new material

Level 2 Intermediate level activities designed for average students

Level 3 Challenging activities designed for honors and gifted and talented students

English Language Learners These activities address the needs of students with Limited English Proficiency.

Chapter Review and Assessment

- IC Vocabulary Activity 27
- Global Skill Builder CD–ROM
- HRW Web Site
- REV Chapter 27 Tutorial for Students, Parents, Mentors, and Peers
- REV Chapter 27 Review, pp. 724–725
- A Chapter 27 Test Generator (on the One-Stop Planner)
- A Chapter 27 Test (Form A or B)
- A Alternative Assessment Handbook
- A Chapter 27 Test for English Language Learners and Special-Needs Students

695b

CHAPTER
27

Section 1 *Setting the Stage for War*

Section 2 *World War I: A New Kind of War*

Section 3 *The Russian Revolution*

Section 4 *The Terms of Peace*

Section 5 *Creating a "New" Europe*

Build on What You Know

Ask students to answer the following questions:

How might the conflicting interests of nations help set the stage for war?

Consider:

• the interests of different nations

• the possible causes of war

• the things about your country that you would not want changed

In what ways might technology affect warfare?

Consider:

• the usefulness of non-technological strategies

• the effect new technology can have on tactics

EXPLORING THE TIME LINE
GLOBAL EVENTS

🔲 internet connect

TOPIC: Women's Suffrage
GO TO: go.hrw.com
KEYWORD: SP3 WH27

Have students access the Internet through the HRW Go site to research women's suffrage during WWI. Women made tremendous contributions to the economies of many countries involved in World War I, yet few enjoyed the right to vote. Ask students to make a list of the countries involved in the war and to include whether or not their female citizens were able to vote during the war. Which was the first nation in the world to grant women suffrage?

CHAPTER
27

C. 1880–1920

World War I and the Russian Revolution

Impressionist painting by French artist Edgar Degas

1884
Science and Technology
The modern machine gun is invented.

1891
Science and Technology
Construction begins on the Trans-Siberian railroad.

1900
Daily Life
The "Cake Walk" becomes a popular dance.

| **1880** | | **1890** | | **1900** |

1882
Politics
The Triple Alliance affects the balance of power in Europe.

1882
Global Events
The British occupy Cairo, Egypt.

1886
The Arts
The eighth impressionist art exhibition opens in Paris.

1895
The Arts
Pyotr Ilich Tchaikovsky's *Swan Lake* is performed in St. Petersburg.

Workers building a section of the central Siberian railway

Build on What You Know

Tensions among the world's advanced industrialized powers increased rapidly during the last half of the 1800s. These nations sought new sources of raw materials for their growing industries and competed with one another for control of overseas markets. In some cases competition among the industrialized powers reached the point of military threats and confrontations. Tension was particularly high in Europe, where major nations such as Great Britain, France, and Germany vigorously pursued economic expansion. In this chapter, you will learn about how these developments led to a global war and to great social changes.

What's Your Opinion?

Government

Agree A national government cannot adequately respond to the needs of different ethnic groups.

Disagree A national government can meet the needs of all citizens, regardless of ethnic differences.

Global Relations

Agree Each country has the right to determine its own destiny.

Disagree A group of nations has the right to determine what is good for all countries within its realm of control.

Economics

Agree Governmental guidelines can help ensure fairness and safety within and between independently owned businesses.

Disagree Independent industries should not have to follow governmental guidelines to produce and distribute their goods.

Artist's conception of Grand Central Terminal, New York

A naval airship in the Dardanelles, World War I

1913
Daily Life
The Grand Central Terminal is completed in New York.

1913
Business and Finance
Henry Ford's assembly line makes the Model T.

1918
Global Events
Millions die of influenza in America, Europe, and Asia.

1915
Science and Technology
Germany becomes the first nation to use poison gas in a war.

1920
Politics
The League of Nations holds its first meeting.

1920
Daily Life
Women win the right to vote in the United States.

1908
Global Events
Austria-Hungary annexes Bosnia and Herzegovina.

1910

1920

1905
Global Events
Japan wins the Russo-Japanese War.

German U-boat poster from World War I

1919 Politics
The major powers sign the Treaty of Versailles.

1917
Global Events
The Russian Revolution begins.

1914
Global Events
World War I begins in Europe.

1914
Science and Technology
Germans introduce submarine warfare.

Women vote in the United States, c. 1920.

1913
The Arts
Charlie Chaplin begins making movies.

EXPLORING THE TIME LINE
GLOBAL EVENTS

Tell students that the years 1880 to 1920 marked a period of great economic, political, and technological change around the globe. Have students study the time line on these pages. Use it as a guide to lead a class discussion about some of the changes that took place.

Critical Thinking

Ask students how economic, political, and technological changes affect the way people view their government.

ANSWER: Students should note that the way people view their government depends on how much control government has over economic, political, and technological changes taking place. Too much or too little control can lead to unrest or dissatisfaction.

What's Your Opinion?

 Do you **agree** *or* **disagree** *with the following statements? Support your point of view in your journal.*

Government Every ethnic group, no matter how small, should have its own independent government.

Global Relations No group of nations should have the right to tell another country what it can and cannot do.

Economy A nation's government should control the production and distribution of goods within that nation.

OBJECTIVES

1 **Explain why rivalries increased among European nations.**

2 **Identify the military alliances that existed at the beginning of World War I and explain how they changed by late 1915.**

3 **Explain why the Balkans were a "powder keg."**

 LET'S GET STARTED!

As students enter the classroom, ask them to discuss the meaning of the term *world war*. *(a military conflict between many nations)* Ask them to list conditions that might turn a small, local conflict between two countries into a world war. *(Students might mention fighting between the distant colonies of hostile nations, alliances that drag other nations into the war, or meddling by other countries in the affairs of warring nations.)* Tell students that in Section 1 they will learn how conflict between Austria-Hungary and Serbia led to World War I.

VISUAL RECORD ANSWER

large size, the use of steel, gun turrets, no smokestacks for steam, antennae for communications

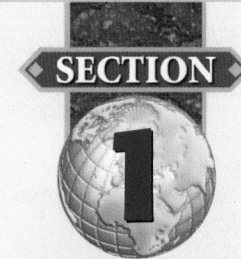

SECTION 1

READ TO DISCOVER

❶ Why did rivalries increase among European nations?

❷ What military alliances existed at the beginning of World War I? How did they change by late 1915?

❸ Why were the Balkans a "powder keg"?

DEFINE

militarism
mobilize
ultimatum
belligerents

IDENTIFY

Triple Alliance
Triple Entente
Balkan "powder keg"
Francis Ferdinand

WHY IT MATTERS TODAY

The Balkans continue to be an area of major conflict. Use CNN News.com or other **current event** sources to investigate how international military involvement has been used to keep the peace there recently. Record your findings in your journal.

CNN student News.com

Setting the Stage for War

The Main Idea
In the late 1800s and early 1900s, conflicting interests in Europe set the stage for war.

The Story Continues *European monarchs came together in 1910 for the funeral of the king of England. This unity, however, would soon be shattered by rivalry. "So gorgeous was the spectacle . . . when nine kings rode in the funeral of Edward VII of England . . . Together they represented seventy nations in the greatest assemblage of royalty and rank ever gathered in one place and, of its kind, the last."*

Nationalism, Imperialism, and Militarism

For a time after the Congress of Vienna in 1815, relations among European countries were relatively harmonious. Beginning in the mid-1800s, however, cooperation broke down. Growing rivalries were especially keen in the Balkan region of Europe and in the competition for overseas colonies. By the early 1900s the great powers of Europe were plunging toward war. Four factors fueled this: nationalism, imperialism, militarism, and the system of alliances.

Nationalism in Europe had emerged in the 1800s as various ethnic groups tried to gain more political unity. This desire was an explosive one in a Europe where several nationalities were often ruled by a single regime. The European imperialist states had already come close to war as they competed for control of Africa, Asia, and other parts of the world.

The glorification of armed strength, or **militarism,** was very important to many European leaders before World War I. They believed they could achieve their goals through the threat or use of force. By the late 1800s European nations had built large, well-trained armies. If one nation were to **mobilize,** or prepare its army for war, other nations would mobilize in self-defense.

As rivalries among European nations grew, armies also grew. In the 1890s Germany began enlarging its navy to rival Great Britain's. In 1906 Great Britain launched the *Dreadnought*, the world's first modern battleship. Germany rushed to build similar ships.

✔ **READING CHECK: Making Generalizations** How did militarism grow out of the conflicts among European nations? thought that their goals could only be achieved by force

INTERPRETING THE VISUAL RECORD

Battleships The *Dreadnought* was the first battleship to feature turbine power and rotating batteries of guns. *How does this photograph suggest the technical achievement that the Dreadnought represented?*

LEVEL 1: Discuss with students the concepts of nationalism and militarism. Ask students how nationalistic countries might come into conflict with militaristic countries. *(by attempting to gain political unity, by resisting militaristic countries attempting to gain power by force)* Then ask students how nationalistic countries might protect themselves against militaristic countries. *(by increasing the strength of their own armies)*
ENGLISH LANGUAGE LEARNERS

ALL LEVELS: Draw a word web on the board with *World War I* at the center and the terms *Rivalries, Alliances, Nationalism,* and *Militarism* around it. Form the class into four groups and assign one of the board terms to each group. Tell the groups to define their term and determine how it was a factor in the events that led to World War I. Have each group report its conclusions to the class. **ENGLISH LANGUAGE LEARNERS, COOPERATIVE LEARNING**

The System of Alliances

In the period from 1861 to 1871, the unification of Germany and that of Italy had changed the balance of power in Europe. The unification of Germany, especially, created an entirely new situation. In place of a group of relatively weak states, a powerful German Empire, under the leadership of Prussia, emerged. Otto von Bismarck, the skillful and strong-willed German chancellor, shaped its ambitious foreign policy.

The Triple Alliance. Bismarck had reason to fear that France would seek revenge for its 1871 defeat in the Franco-Prussian War. Perhaps France would do this by trying to regain Alsace-Lorraine, the region it had lost to Germany in that war. Bismarck therefore set his foreign policy to keeping France diplomatically isolated and without allies. Bismarck particularly wanted to prevent an alliance between France and Russia. Such an alliance would isolate Germany diplomatically. At worst, it could even mean that Germany would have to fight a war on both its eastern and western borders.

In 1881 Bismarck formed an alliance with Austria-Hungary and Russia. Known as the Three Emperors' League, it bound each member to remain neutral if any one of them went to war. The next year Bismarck persuaded Italy to join Germany and Austria-Hungary in the **Triple Alliance.** In this move to isolate France, he had now secured Germany's eastern and southern flanks.

The Three Emperors' League ended due to rivalry between Austria-Hungary and Russia over the Balkans. Bismarck managed to make a new agreement with Russia. In this Reinsurance Treaty of 1887, both countries again promised neutrality.

The Triple Entente. In 1888 William II became kaiser of Germany. By 1890 he had dismissed Bismarck as chancellor and abandoned Bismarck's policies. In the meantime, France had been trying to avoid diplomatic isolation. France helped Russia out of a financial crisis, and the two countries had signed a military alliance by 1894. Germany now faced enemies to both the east and the west.

During this time competition for overseas colonies grew between Germany and Great Britain. Troubled by the German naval buildup, the British searched for allies. After settling their conflicting claims in Africa, France and Great Britain soon became allies. In 1907, after agreeing to recognize each other's spheres of influence in Asia, Russia and Great Britain also became allies. The alliance between France, Russia, and Great Britain was called the **Triple Entente.**
Both France and Russia also had secret understandings with Italy, giving the Italians a foot in both rival camps.

By 1907 the powers of Europe had divided into two armed camps. These rival alliances threatened world peace. Should fighting break out between two rival powers, all six nations were almost certain to become involved.

✔ **READING CHECK: Summarizing**
Why did European nations form alliances? to maintain the balance of power

Kaiser William II surveys German troops in 1916.

Government

By the outbreak of war in 1914 the Central Powers were able to put nearly 8 million troops in the field, and the Allies more than 11 million. Russia's army was the largest at nearly 6 million men. Germany had 4.5 million under arms, followed closely by France at some 4 million. Austria-Hungary's army stood at 3 million. With a troop strength of 975,000, Great Britain was dwarfed by the armies of both its nearby friend and its rivals.

Critical Thinking

Ask students why the Triple Entente was especially important to Great Britain.

ANSWER: By forming alliances with France and Russia, Great Britain could be reasonably assured that, should war break out, its small army would have support from stronger military powers.

Technology Resources

go.
hrw
.com Online Maps, Charts, and Graphs: The Schlieffen Plan, 1905

ALL LEVELS: Copy the graphic organizer on the board, omitting the italicized answers. Work with students to fill in countries and dates of alliances that existed in Europe at the outbreak of World War I. Then have students explain how the alliances had changed by late 1915. *(Germany and Austria-Hungary allied with the Ottoman Empire and Bulgaria, and Great Britain and France allied with Japan and Italy; Germany opposed Russia; Russia supported Serbia.)* **ENGLISH LANGUAGE LEARNERS**

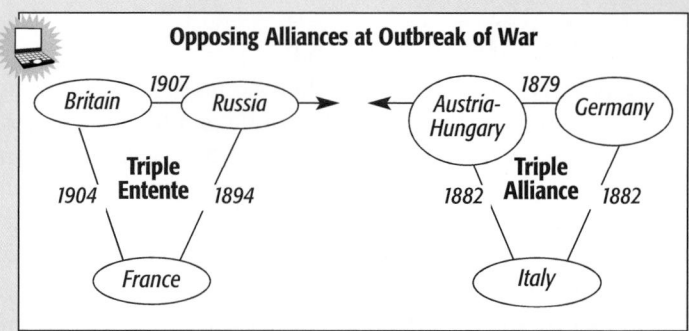

Opposing Alliances at Outbreak of War

Geography

The Berlin-Baghdad Railroad was virtually complete by the outbreak of the war. Germany hoped the railroad would provide important economic and political influence in Turkey and Persia. Except for 175 miles in Serbia, its 1,875 miles of track passed through countries friendly to Germany. Although British companies had unrestricted access to moving goods on the railroad, Great Britain viewed it as evidence of German and Austrian imperialist ambitions.

Critical Thinking

Ask students why Great Britain viewed the Berlin-Baghdad railroad as evidence of German imperialist ambitions.

ANSWER: It gave Germany access to and possible control of a large area of land within many different countries.

MAP ANSWERS

1. Triple Entente

2. Triple Alliance: German Empire, Austria-Hungary, Italy, Bosnia and Herzegovina; Triple Entente: Russia, France, Great Britain; Neutral Countries: Norway, Sweden, Belgium, Switzerland, Romania, Serbia, Bulgaria, Greece, Ottoman Empire, Spain, Portugal, Albania, Montenegro, Luxembourg, Denmark, Netherlands; Triple Alliance

Europe and the Middle East on the Eve of World War I, 1914

Interpreting Maps The Triple Alliance and the Triple Entente divided Europe into two hostile camps.

■ **Skills Assessment: 1. Places and Regions** Which military alliance was split by the territory of the other?

2. Categorizing Copy the following graphic organizer and fill in the names of the members of the Triple Alliance, the Triple Entente, and the neutral countries of Europe in 1914. Which alliance had more European members?

Triple Alliance	Triple Entente	Neutral Countries

TEACH OBJECTIVE 3

LEVEL 3: Ask pairs of students to develop a paragraph explaining why the Balkans could be considered a "powder keg" in 1914. *(rivalries between Great Britain, Russia, Austria-Hungary, and Germany in the Balkans; the alliance system; and Austria-Hungary's ultimatum)* **COOPERATIVE LEARNING**

Teacher to Teacher

Laura L. Boelter of Mesa, Arizona, suggested the following activity: Have students list all the historical people mentioned in the chapter. As a review, have each student choose one character and write a short statement, in first person, that describes the role the person played in or provides the person's opinion about some facet of World War I and/or the Russian Revolution. As students read their statements, tell the other students to try to guess who is speaking.

The Balkan "Powder Keg"

Serbia's independence from the Ottoman Empire had been recognized by the Congress of Berlin in 1878. Now, nationalists in Serbia hoped to make their country the center of a larger Slavic state. The Serbian nationalists especially wanted to gain the provinces of Bosnia and Herzegovina, because Serbia was landlocked and these two territories would provide an outlet on the Adriatic Sea. However, the Congress of Berlin had made these two provinces protectorates of Austria-Hungary. This bitterly disappointed the Serbs. After Austria-Hungary went one step further by annexing Bosnia and Herzegovina in 1908, angry Serbian nationalists increased their activities.

Russia, the largest Slavic country, saw itself as the protector of the Balkan Slavs. Russia supported Serbia's goals. The nationalist movement that pressed for the political and cultural unity of all Slavs under Russian leadership was called Pan-Slavism. This contributed to a rivalry between Great Britain and Russia. The British did not want the Russians to gain access to the Mediterranean Sea.

Kaiser William II failed to take advantage of the Anglo-Russian rivalry. Instead, he tried to bring the Ottoman Empire, an old enemy of Russia, into the Triple Alliance. He planned to extend German influence into the Balkans and the Middle East by building a railroad from Germany through Constantinople to Baghdad. Both Great Britain and Russia were alarmed by possible German expansion. As a result, British-Russian ties were strengthened. Germany, on the other hand, supported Austria-Hungary in its opposition to Slavic nationalism.

The spark that ignited the **Balkan "powder keg"** came on June 28, 1914. The heir to the Austro-Hungarian throne, Archduke **Francis Ferdinand,** and his wife were visiting Sarajevo, the capital of Bosnia and Herzegovina. As they rode in an open automobile, Gavrilo Princip, a member of a Serbian nationalist group, assassinated them both. Some Serbian officials were implicated in the terrorist plot.

Austria-Hungary angrily vowed to punish the Serbs. Afraid that Russia would support Serbia, however, it first secured the support of Germany. Austria-Hungary then sent an ultimatum to the Serbian government. In an **ultimatum** one party threatens harmful action if the demands it has made are not met. The Austro-Hungarian ultimatum included these demands: 1) The Serbian government must suppress all groups that opposed the Austro-Hungarian government; 2) Serbia must dismiss school teachers and ban books that did not support Austria-Hungary; 3) Serbia must dismiss government officials who spoke out against Austria-Hungary; and 4) Austro-Hungarian officials must be allowed to participate in the trials of those accused in the assassination. If Serbia did not agree to the ultimatum's terms, Austria-Hungary would use military action.

The Serbian government accepted the first three of these terms. It rejected the last term, but offered to submit it to the International Court at The Hague. Expecting a rejection of its offer, however, the Serbian government mobilized its troops. When the ultimatum deadline expired on July 28, Austria-Hungary declared war on Serbia. Austro-Hungarian leaders expected a quick victory.

✔ **READING CHECK: Finding the Main Idea** Why were the Balkans at the center of the conflict between European powers? provided outlet to the sea, played a part in Pan-Slavism

In 1914 this illustration of the assassination of Archduke Francis Ferdinand and his wife appeared in French newspapers.

Global Relations

Due largely to the vast mineral wealth of its Ruhr region, Germany's industrial growth between 1880 and 1913 was the fastest in the world. Coal production quadrupled, steel output increased tenfold, and large chemical and arms industries developed. The German population grew by more than 50 percent, and by 1913 some 40 percent of Germany's labor force was employed in industry.

Critical Thinking

Ask students why Germany's rivals might view such growth as a threat.

ANSWER: Students should recognize the military applications of this growth, and the security and trade concerns it posed for rival nations.

HOMEWORK Have students draw a political cartoon or write a poem that illustrates how nationalism, militarism, or the alliance system led to the outbreak of World War I. Ask students to share their creations with the class.

CLOSE

Lead a class discussion to compare and contrast how relations among European countries changed from the Congress of Vienna in 1815 to the outbreak of World War I in 1914.

Global Relations

In the early 1900s the Central Powers experienced large population growth that included a diverse mix of ethnic groups. By 1910 Germany's population had increased to 65 million. Austria-Hungary's population included 10 million Germans and 9 million Hungarians as well as Poles, Croats, Bosnians, Serbians, Italians, Czechs, Ruthenes, Slovenes, and Romanians. By 1914 the Ottoman Empire had a population of 25 million that included 14 million Turks as well as Arabs, Assyrians, Armenians, Kurds, Greeks, and Circassions.

Critical Thinking

Ask students how Europe's rapid population growth added to its growing rivalries.

ANSWER: Many different ethnic groups lived within the same country or empire, competing for social, political, and economic rights.

Mobilization of Europe

Attempts to persuade Austria-Hungary to continue negotiating with Serbia were useless. Russia prepared to support Serbia by moving troops toward its border with Austria-Hungary. Since Germany had mobilized in support of Austria-Hungary, Russia also sent troops to its border with Germany.

Germany demanded that Russia stop its mobilization or face war. Russia ignored this ultimatum. On August 1, 1914, Germany declared war on Russia. Convinced that France would side with Russia, and hoping to gain an advantage, Germany declared war on France two days later. A former president of the United States, William Howard Taft, expressed the surprise and fear many Americans felt at the news of war in Europe.

Analyzing Primary Sources

Drawing Inferences Why might former president Taft have thought that the war would spread to all of Europe? because it did in the time of Napoléon

History Makers Speak

❝As I write, Germany is reported to have declared war against Russia and France. . . . Nothing like it has occurred since the great Napoleonic wars. . . . All of Europe is to be a battle-ground. . . . The future looks dark indeed.❞

William Howard Taft, "A Message to the People of the United States"

In 1839, shortly after Belgium's independence, the great powers of Europe had guaranteed its neutrality. Under terms of the guarantee, Belgium agreed to stay out of any European war. It agreed not to help any **belligerents,** or warring nations. In turn, the great powers agreed not to attack Belgium.

When war began in 1914, however, Belgium's location between Germany and France became important. The Germans wanted to defeat France quickly so that they could then focus on Russia. The border between France and Germany was heavily fortified, so the Germans demanded to cross Belgian territory. The British protested, insisting that Germany honor the 1839 guarantee of Belgian neutrality. Germany scoffed at this "scrap of paper." On August 4, 1914, German soldiers marched into Belgium. Great Britain declared war on Germany later that day.

✔ **READING CHECK: Summarizing** What event led to Great Britain's entering the war against Germany? Germany disregarded Belgian neutrality.

This photo shows Belgian volunteers mobilizing to resist Germany.

REVIEW
Have students complete the Section 1 Review on p. 703.

ASSESS
Have students complete Daily Quiz 27.1. As Alternative Assessment, you may want to use the word web exercise in this section's lessons.

RETEACH
Have students complete Main Idea Activity for English Language Learners and Special-Needs Students 27.1. Then have them write a one-sentence summary of the main ideas under each heading and subheading in the section. **ENGLISH LANGUAGE LEARNERS**

EXTEND
Have students work in small groups to write radio news bulletins describing one of the events in this section. Students should include the announcement of a breaking story and the reporter's description of the event. Writing should demonstrate the correct use of social studies terminology, standard grammar, spelling, sentence structure, and punctuation. **COOPERATIVE LEARNING**

The War Expands

Later in August, Japan entered the war on the side of Great Britain and France. Japan was motivated by a desire to gain German possessions in China and the Pacific. In Europe all the nations of the Triple Alliance and the Triple Entente except Italy were now at war. The Italian government took the position that the Austro-Hungarians had acted as aggressors when they declared war on Serbia. Thus, the Triple Alliance, which was meant for defense only, did not require Italy to give aid to its allies.

Italy remained neutral for 10 months. Finally, it signed a secret treaty with Great Britain, France, and Russia. This treaty guaranteed Italy a share of the spoils after the expected defeat of Germany and Austria-Hungary. In May 1915, Italy entered the war against Germany and Austria-Hungary, its former allies in the Triple Alliance.

Meanwhile, Germany had been trying to gain other allies. In October 1914 the Ottoman Empire entered the war on the side of Austria-Hungary and Germany. The Ottoman Turks were not a strong military power but occupied a strategic position. They controlled the Dardanelles, the strait between the Black Sea and the Mediterranean. Turkish control of this important waterway meant that now Germany and Austria-Hungary could keep Russia's Black Sea fleet bottled up. They could also block the allies from sending supplies to Russia through the Mediterranean and the Black Sea. Germany also persuaded Bulgaria, a Slavic rival of Serbia, to enter the war on its side in October 1915.

✔ **READING CHECK: Analyzing Information**
Why did Italy join the war against Germany and its allies? *for a share of the spoils*

Turkish soldiers pose with their rifles, c. 1910; above right, a French magazine cover from 1915

SECTION 1 REVIEW ANSWERS

❶ Define
- militarism, p. 698
- mobilize, p. 698
- ultimatum, p. 701
- belligerents, p. 702

❷ Identify
- Triple Alliance, p. 699
- Triple Entente, p. 699
- Balkan "powder keg," p. 701
- Francis Ferdinand, p. 701

❸ Triple Entente: Great Britain, France, Russia, Serbia, Japan, Italy; Triple Alliance: Germany, Austria-Hungary, Ottoman Empire, Bulgaria

❹ a. rivalries between European nations, nationalism, militarism, imperialism, and the system of alliances

b. because the conflicting interests of Germany, Serbia, Austria-Hungary, Russia, and Great Britain caused a potentially explosive situation

❺ Students' speeches should include the ideals of Pan-Slavism, and should identify what they want the Congress of Berlin to do.

SECTION 1 REVIEW

1. **Define** and explain the significance:
   militarism
   mobilize
   ultimatum
   belligerents

2. **Identify** and explain the significance:
   Triple Alliance
   Triple Entente
   Balkan "powder keg"
   Francis Ferdinand

3. **Comparing and Contrasting** Copy the diagram and use it to show which countries belonged to the Triple Entente and which to the Triple Alliance by October 1915.

   Triple Entente   Triple Alliance

4. **Finding the Main Idea**
   a. What underlying factors led to World War I?
   b. Why were the Balkans called a "powder keg"?

5. **Writing and Critical Thinking**
   Identifying a Point of View Write a short speech, expressing the view of a Serbian nationalist, to the Congress of Berlin in 1878.
   Consider:
   • the ideals of the Pan-Slavism movement
   • the result of Bosnia and Herzegovina becoming protectorates of Austria-Hungary

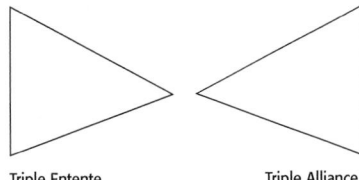
Homework Practice Online
keyword: SP3 HP27

SECTION 2

OBJECTIVES

1 Identify the advantages that each side had in World War I.

2 Explain how new technology affected the way in which World War I was fought.

3 Explain what led the United States to join the Allied Powers.

LET'S GET STARTED!

As students enter the classroom, ask them to write the words *Advantages*, *Technology*, and *United States*. Then ask them to answer the following questions: What geographic or military advantages might a country have in wartime? What are some examples of how technology can affect the way a war is fought? What circumstances would lead you to support your government's decision to enter a war? Tell students that in Section 2 they will learn about the advantages of both sides in World War I, how technology affected the war, and why the United States entered the war.

SECTION 2 RESOURCES

REPRODUCIBLE RESOURCES

▸ Guided Reading Strategy 27.2

▸ Geography Activity 27

▸ Hands-on History Activity 27

TECHNOLOGY RESOURCES

▸ One-Stop Planner 27.2

▸ Holt Researcher: World History: Manfred von Richthofen; Woodrow Wilson

▸ CNN Presents World Cultures: Yesterday and Today Segment 26

▸ Homework Practice Online

REINFORCEMENT, REVIEW, AND ASSESSMENT

▸ Section 2 Review, p. 710

▸ Daily Quiz 27.2

▸ Main Idea Activity 27.2

▸ English Audio Summary 27.2

▸ Spanish Audio Summary 27.2

MAP ANSWER

Both countries needed access to the Atlantic Ocean and to the western coasts of France and Belgium.

SECTION 2

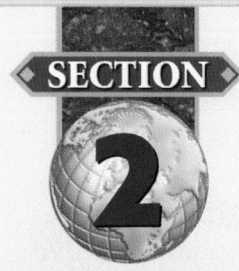

READ TO DISCOVER

1 What advantages did each side have in World War I?

2 How did new technology affect the way in which World War I was fought?

3 What led the United States to join the Allied Powers?

DEFINE

propaganda
war of attrition
contraband
atrocities

IDENTIFY

Central Powers
Allied Powers
U-boats
Woodrow Wilson
Arthur Zimmermann

WHY IT MATTERS TODAY

With advancements in technology, innovations in warfare continue to this day. Use CNN or other **current event** sources to investigate what new weapons are being developed and used today. Record your findings in your journal.

CNN student News.com

World War I: A New Kind of War

The Main Idea
World War I dragged on in Europe and other regions of the world for four long, bloody years.

The Story Continues *Writer Erich Maria Remarque vividly described the horror of an artillery bombardment during World War I. "The thunder of the guns swells to a single heavy roar and then breaks up again into separate explosions. The dry bursts of the machine-guns rattle. Above us the air teems with invisible swift movement, with howls, pipings, and hisses. They are the smaller shells;—and amongst them, booming through the night like an organ, go the . . . heavies [largest, most explosive artillery shells]."*

The Belligerents

The soldiers who marched off to war in the summer of 1914 thought they would win a quick victory. However, the war lasted four years and was filled with horrors never before seen.

The warring countries formed two powerful sides. Germany, Austria-Hungary, Bulgaria, and the Ottoman Empire became known as the **Central Powers.** Their territory extended from the North Sea to the Middle East. This helped them with both easy communication and rapid troop

Europe in 1916–1917

Interpreting Maps
Britain set up a blockade of Germany's North Sea coast. Germany countered with a U-boat blockade off Britain's west coast.

■ Skills Assessment: **The World in Spatial Terms** Why was control of the North Sea critical for both Germany and Great Britain?

	Legend	
Central Powers	Neutral nations	British blockade
Allied Powers		German U-boat blockade

ALL LEVELS: Have students create a two-column chart labeled *Advantages of the Central Powers* and *Advantages of the Allied Powers.* Students should list the advantages of each side in the appropriate column.

ENGLISH LANGUAGE LEARNERS

Advantages of the Central Powers	Advantages of the Allied Powers
• territory that extended from the North Sea to the Middle East • Germany's army	• more soldiers • greater industrial capacity • Britain's navy

Spotlight on SCIENCE

One German weapon in World War I was a dirigible called a zeppelin. Early in the war, zeppelins flew over battlefields and bombed enemy positions. Slow and vulnerable to ground fire and plane attack, zeppelins proved ineffective for such missions. By 1917 their primary use had changed to long-range, high-altitude bombing raids on Britain. On October 19, 1917, a formation of 11 zeppelins dropped 275 bombs on London and other parts of England. Have students write journal entries as Londoners describing the attack.

---

movement. The Central Powers also had the advantage of Germany's well-trained and well-equipped army.

Great Britain, France, Russia, and their partners became known as the **Allied Powers,** or the Allies. They had more soldiers and a greater industrial capacity than the Central Powers. They also had the advantage of Britain's navy, the largest in the world. This allowed the Allies to get food and raw materials from around the world more easily. It also gave them the ability to blockade the Central Powers. Eventually, 32 countries made up the Allied Powers.

✔ **READING CHECK: Comparing and Contrasting** How did the military capabilities of the Central Powers and Allied Powers differ? Central Powers had more rapid communications and movement and better army; Allied Powers had more soldiers, better industry, and better navy

Innovations in Warfare

World War I was an industrialized war. Its weapons were mass-produced by the same efficient methods used for manufacturing other products of the new industrial age. Both sides used weapons that had never been tried before. Germany became the first nation to effectively use submarines in naval warfare. **U-boats** (from the German word *Unterseebooten,* meaning "underwater boats") caused extensive losses to Allied shipping. The Germans also introduced poison gas as a weapon against enemy infantry.

Among the new weapons were machine guns and long-range artillery. A machine gun had the firepower of many rifles. It fired rapidly and almost without interruption. Although by the end of the war lighter machine guns had been developed, the first ones were very heavy. They could be fired by

CONNECTING TO Science and Technology

U-boats

U-boats greatly strengthened German sea power. U-boats armed with torpedoes sank hundreds of Allied ships during World War I. They reduced the amount of supplies being shipped to the Allies from overseas and allowed Germany to make surprise attacks on surface shipping.

A U-boat had two hulls. The inner hull protected the ship from the pressure of the sea. The outer hull fit around it. The space between the two hulls held water. Pumping water in and out of this space made the ship dive and rise.

U-boats fired torpedoes, which exploded when they hit an enemy ship. Torpedoes were stored in tubes between the two hulls of a U-boat. A door at each end of the tube allowed the crew to fire and reload torpedoes without taking on water.

Forward torpedo tubes

Mine tubes

Understanding Science and Technology

How did the crew control the depth of a U-boat under the ocean surface?

Science, Technology & Society

At the beginning of World War I, planes were generally unarmed. Aerial combat consisted of pilots shooting at each other with rifles and pistols. Air warfare was revolutionized in May 1915, however, by Germany's introduction of an "interrupter gear" that allowed a machine gun mounted near the front of a plane to fire forward without hitting its own propeller. This invention was quickly copied by the Allies and led directly to the development of specialized "fighter" planes. By 1917, lone observer planes had been replaced by formations of 50 or more aircraft that conducted bombing and strafing raids on enemy infantry, artillery, supply bases, roads, and railroad lines.

Critical Thinking

Ask students why dogfights were limited before the interrupter gear was introduced.

ANSWER: Pilots could not fire at enemy planes without destroying their own propellers.

CONNECTING TO SCIENCE AND TECHNOLOGY ANSWER
by pumping water in and out of the space between the U-boat's inner and outer hulls

ALL LEVELS: Ask students to identify new weapons and tactics that were introduced during World War I and list them on the board. *(weapons: U-boats, poison gas, machine guns, long-range artillery, airplanes, and tanks; tactics: trenches, drafted civilians, propaganda)* Then form students into groups and assign each group one item from the list. Tell each group to imagine that they are a strategic task force in the British War Office. Their task is to analyze how the enemy is likely to use the innovation and to suggest strategies for combating its anticipated effects. Have each group report its conclusions and suggestions.

ENGLISH LANGUAGE LEARNERS, COOPERATIVE LEARNING

HOMEWORK Have students write letters home in the role of World War I soldiers. They should describe an experience such as life in the trenches or an encounter with the enemy.

Daily Life

In addition to working at critical jobs and serving in Europe, American women contributed to the Allies' war effort in another important way by conserving food. Some 20 million homemakers signed pledge cards distributed by the government, promising not to serve meat on Mondays or bread on Wednesdays, to conserve other foodstuffs, and to grow their own vegetables in "Victory Gardens."

In return, they received stickers to display in the windows of their homes, indicating that they were cooperating with the war effort. Their voluntary rationing efforts helped the United States double its badly needed shipments of food to the Allies.

internet connect

TOPIC: World War I
GO TO: go.hrw.com
KEYWORD: SP3 WH27

Have students access the Internet through the HRW Go site to investigate a World War I battle, weapon, political event, social development, or other topic that interests them. Ask students to present the results of their research to the class.

THEN AND NOW ANSWER

replaced men in factories and offices, ran farms

Holt Researcher

go.hrw.com
KEYWORD: Holt Researcher
FreeFind:
   Manfred von Richthofen
After reading more about Manfred von Richtofen on the Holt Researcher, write a summary of how the airplane changed warfare.

Analyzing Primary Sources

Drawing Inferences Based on this observer's description, how effective were tanks in trench warfare? worked well to provide cover for troops

Women in Wartime
When war began in 1914, the countries of Europe desperately needed war materials. Women poured into the work force, replacing the men who had gone off to war. Many women ran farms and worked in factories or offices. This experience gave women a new sense of confidence and economic independence. *What roles did women play in the wartime economy?*

These English women worked in a factory making arms and ammunition during World War I.

---

one man, but a team of several men was needed to move and load them. Machine guns killed in great numbers. They made infantry attacks on strongly defended positions very costly. To counter both machine guns and artillery, protective trenches were dug.

Another new weapon was the airplane. Airplanes were mainly used for observing enemy troop movements. At this early stage in their development, they were neither fast nor easy to maneuver. However, they were sometimes used against enemy airplanes in air battles called dogfights. They were also used for dropping bombs on enemy targets. Several skilled dogfight pilots, called aces, became legends. The most famous flying ace was Baron Manfred von Richthofen of Germany, who was nicknamed "The Red Baron." He reportedly shot down some 80 enemy aircraft during the war.

In 1916 Britain introduced the tank, a heavily armored vehicle with guns mounted on it. Running on treads, it could move easily over rough ground. Tanks enabled troops to tear through barbed wire and cut into enemy defenses. One British observer recalled seeing a tank in action for the first time:

> *History Makers Speak*
> **❝Instead of going on to the German lines the three tanks assigned to us straddled our front line, stopped and then opened up a murderous machine-gun fire, enfilading [covering] us left and right. There they sat, squat monstrous things, noses stuck up in the air, crushing the sides of our trench out of shape with their machine-guns swiveling around and firing like mad.❞**
>
> Bert Chaney, quoted in *People at War, 1914–1918*, edited by Michael Moynihan

Even the types of soldiers in the war changed. Previously in Europe wars were fought mainly by professional soldiers. Their only source of income was their military pay and rations of food and clothing. In contrast, soldiers in World War I were mostly drafted civilians. Men who were not drafted worked at home to help their country's war effort. Many women, too, worked in arms factories. A war in which nations turn all their resources to the war effort became known as "total war."

To stir the patriotism of their people, governments made wide use of **propaganda.** This was the use of selected bits of information, both true and false, to get people to back their country's war effort. Governments set up agencies whose only purpose was to control news about the war. Newspapers and popular

LEVEL 3: Have students write an explanation of how they think the two sides would have fought World War I without airplanes and tanks. Tell students to base their writing on a thinking process similar to the following:

Problem-solving process

1. Identify a situation that requires a decision.
2. Gather information.
3. List and consider options.
4. Consider advantages and disadvantages.
5. Choose a solution.
6. Evaluate the effectiveness of the solution.

HOMEWORK Have students use computer software to create a time line showing the events of the early years of World War I. Tell students to add visuals to their time lines that illustrate two or more of the events.

magazines, especially those of the Allies, showed the enemy as brutal and sub-human while praising their own countries.

✔ **READING CHECK: Analyzing Information** What new weapons had been developed as a result of technological advances? machine gun, U-boat, poison gas, airplane, tank

Early Years of the War

Germany launched its main attack on France across neutral Belgium. By September 1914 German troops had reached the Marne River near Paris. The French and British armies fought back. In fierce battles they managed to hold the line. Paris was saved.

France's success in the Battle of the Marne changed the entire nature of the war. Germany's hope of a quick victory ended. Both sides dug in. Trenches lined the western front, which stretched from Switzerland to the English Channel and the North Sea.

On the eastern front, the Russians had mobilized their troops. The French asked Russia to help divert the German forces from the western front. The Russians launched an attack into East Prussia from the east and the south.

Late in August 1914 the Russians battled a German force at the Battle of Tannenberg. The Russian army suffered a humiliating defeat. About half its force was lost, including more than 90,000 prisoners. The German losses were less than 15,000. With this victory, the Germans launched an offensive, moving into Russian Poland.

Fighting on Gallipoli. Although Russia had a huge army, it lacked the guns and ammunition to equip its soldiers properly.

That's Interesting!

The day before German forces invaded Belgium at the beginning of World War I, two German cruisers shelled ports in French Algeria. Pursued by the British navy, the ships escaped to Turkey, where the German government sold them. The arrival and purchase of these two powerful warships strongly influenced the decision of Ottoman officials to side with the Central Powers.

MAP ANSWER
Riga

Reproducible Resources
PS Readings in World History 93, 94: The Home Front in Germany; Songs of a Campaign

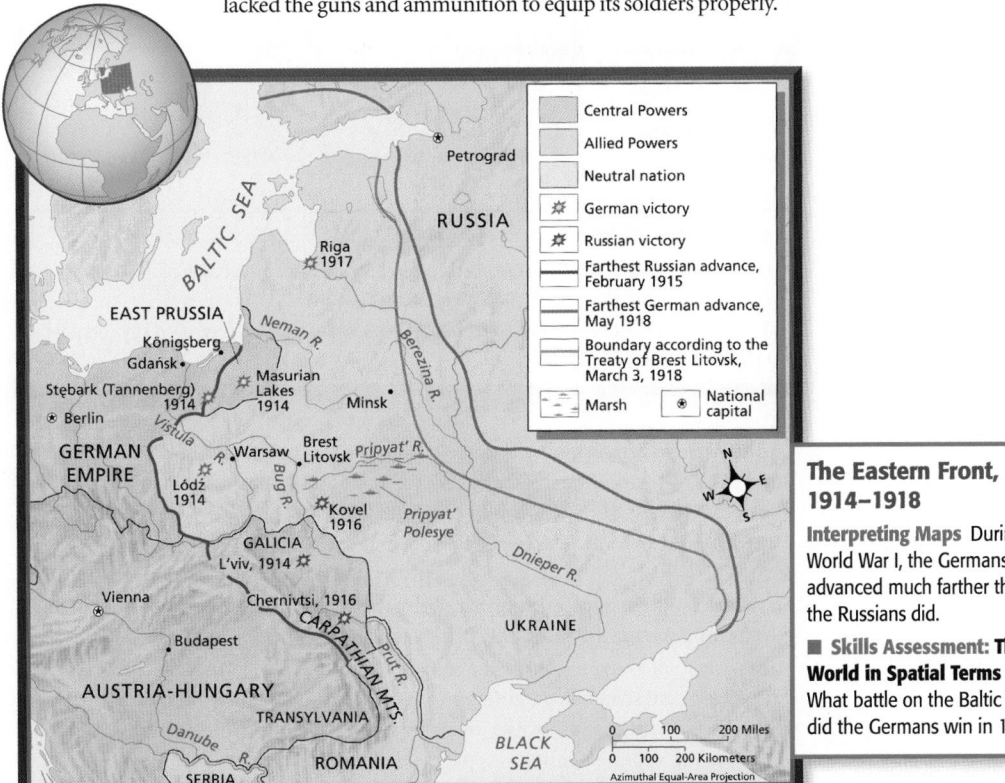

The Eastern Front, 1914–1918

Interpreting Maps During World War I, the Germans advanced much farther than the Russians did.

■ **Skills Assessment: The World in Spatial Terms** What battle on the Baltic Sea did the Germans win in 1917?

LEVEL 1: Have students create a research outline for the information on page 710. Then discuss with students what led the United States to join the Allied Powers.
ENGLISH LANGUAGE LEARNERS

LEVEL 2: Have students work in pairs to determine what factors influenced American opinion about World War I. *(sinking of the Lusitania, effect of German blockade on American trade, British propaganda, Zimmermann telegram, Germany's unrestricted submarine warfare)* Tell pairs to summarize these factors and then state why they would or would not support the decision of the United States to enter the war. Remind students to use standard grammar, spelling, sentence structure, and punctuation.
COOPERATIVE LEARNING

Science, Technology & Society

Allied difficulties in the Gallipoli Peninsula were compounded by the presence of underwater mines. Although minesweepers were able to eliminate some of the weapons, not all were discovered in time. On March 18, 1915, three Allied ships were sunk and others badly damaged by mines. Not until the British realized that they could not avoid the dangers these mines posed to ships did they decide to take the Gallipoli Peninsula by land.

Critical Thinking

Ask students how capturing the Gallipoli Peninsula would have helped Allied ships.

ANSWER: If Allied troops could destroy the Ottoman guns at Gallipoli, then Allied ships would have been able to pass through the Dardanelles.

MAP ANSWER
Great Britain

Technology Resources

World History and Cultures Video Program 22: The Great War

War in the Middle East, 1914–1918

Interpreting Maps When the Ottomans entered World War I on the side of the Central Powers, their once-powerful empire was close to collapse.

■ **Skills Assessment: Human Systems** Which European power controlled key countries in the Persian Gulf?

In 1915 Great Britain and France tried to change this situation. They decided to try to force their way through the Dardanelles so they could capture Constantinople. They hoped to remove the Ottoman Empire from the war. Then they would be able to get needed supplies to the Russians.

The British and French sent heavily armed battleships to bombard Ottoman artillery on the Gallipoli Peninsula. When after several days the bombardment failed to destroy the enemy positions, British and French troops were sent in. However, they were able to gain only a shallow foothold inland. Heavy resistance from the Turks brought the bloody fighting to a stalemate. After eight months and the loss of hundreds of thousands of lives on both sides, the Allies withdrew from Gallipoli. The plan to capture Constantinople had failed, largely due to mismanagement and bad timing.

HOMEWORK Have students create a propaganda poster, cartoon, song, speech, or editorial on one of the following topics: the British blockade of Germany, American trade with the Allies, or German submarine warfare. Advise students that their propaganda piece should be crafted from either a British or a German point of view. Tell them that it could be directed at winning American support for the war or at encouraging Americans to remain neutral.

CLOSE

Ask students to explain why World War I was considered a "new kind of war." *(Countries from all over the world formed alliances to fight the war and turned all their resources to the war effort.)* What new weapons and tactics did the countries that fought in World War I use that made the war different from other wars? *(U-boats, tanks, machine guns, poison gas, long-range artillery, drafted civilians, and propaganda)*

Naval warfare. The British decided to blockade the North Sea to keep merchant ships from reaching Germany. At first the blockade was aimed at cutting off the flow of raw materials to German factories. Eventually the blockade became an attempt to ruin the German economy and starve the German people.

Germany also set up a blockade. It used U-boats to sink ships that were carrying food and arms to the British. In May 1915 a German submarine sank the British passenger liner *Lusitania* off the coast of Ireland. The *Lusitania* was carrying a cargo of war materials as well as passengers to England. Nearly 1,200 people were killed, including 128 Americans. **Woodrow Wilson,** the U.S. president, denounced the attack. He warned Germany that the United States would not tolerate another such incident. Wary of provoking the neutral Americans into entering the war, Germany cut back its submarine attacks.

In May 1916 the only large naval battle of the war was fought, at the Battle of Jutland, in the North Sea off the coast of Denmark. Both Germany and Great Britain claimed victory. However, the German navy remained in port for the rest of the war.

The stalemate. By late 1915 the war in the west had become a stalemate on land as well as on sea. Military leaders on both sides began to wonder whether they could ever break through the other's line of trenches. As both armies continued their attacks, small areas of land changed hands again and again. Thousands and thousands of lives were snuffed out. The conflict had become a **war of attrition**—a slow wearing-down process in which each side was trying to outlast the other.

✔ **READING CHECK: Sequencing** Describe the progress of the war from 1914 to 1916. western front, eastern front, blockade, stalemate

The Western Front, 1914–1918

Interpreting Maps During World War I, the Central Powers pushed deeply into France, but fighting soon stalled out along the western front.

■ **Skills Assessment: Using Geography** Between 1914 and the end of 1917, approximately how far were the Central Powers pushed back from their farthest point of advance?

Map legend:
- Central Powers
- Allied Powers
- Neutral nations
- ⊛ National capital
- Farthest Central Powers' advance, 1914
- Front at end of 1917
- Front, November 11, 1918
- ✿ Battle site

Historical Sidelight

In addition to the blockade of Germany, British fleets assisted by the French and Italian navies patrolled the entire Mediterranean. The Allies also stopped goods from reaching neutral countries that would not agree to prevent these imports from reaching the Central Powers. So effective was the Allies' blockade that in 1916 food riots broke out in German cities. By 1918, overseas imports of meat and fish were less than 20 percent of 1916 levels. It is estimated that nearly 800,000 Germans died as a result of the blockade.

Critical Thinking

Ask students why the Allies wanted to prevent imports from reaching the Central Powers.

ANSWER: to weaken the Central Powers

MAP ANSWER
between 75 and 100 miles

Technology Resources
World History Teaching Transparency: Everyday Life 22: American Posters from World War I

REVIEW

Have students complete the Section 2 Review on p. 710.

ASSESS

Have students complete Daily Quiz 27.2. As Alternative Assessment, you may want to use the chart or the time line in this section's lessons.

RETEACH

Have students complete Main Idea Activity for English Language Learners and Special-Needs Students 27.2. Then ask each student to create a research outline of the section's main idea and supporting details. **ENGLISH LANGUAGE LEARNERS**

EXTEND

Organize the class into two groups representing the Central Powers and the Allied Powers. Have the groups research the position that their side took in the war. Then have the groups support their point of view in a class debate. **BLOCK SCHEDULING, COOPERATIVE LEARNING**

SECTION 2 REVIEW ANSWERS

❶ Define
- propaganda, p. 706
- war of attrition, p. 709
- contraband, p. 710
- atrocities, p. 710

❷ Identify
- Central Powers, p. 704
- Allied Powers, p. 705
- U-boats, p. 705
- Woodrow Wilson, p. 709
- Arthur Zimmermann, p. 710

❸ Central Powers: advantages–territory from the North Sea to the Middle East, Germany's army; disadvantages–fewer soldiers, less industrial capacity, weaker navy; Allied Powers: advantages–more soldiers, greater industrial capacity, Britain's navy; disadvantages–less strategic territory, poorly-trained, poorly-equipped army

❹ a. Both sides used weapons that had never been tried before. Machine guns killed in great numbers. Protective trenches were dug. Airplanes, tanks, and submarines also changed ways of fighting.

b. democracy and world safety

❺ Students' posters should clearly represent their points of view.

Holt Researcher

go.hrw.com
KEYWORD: Holt Researcher
FreeFind: Woodrow Wilson
After reading more about Woodrow Wilson on the Holt Researcher, write an analysis of his influence on political events of the 20th century.

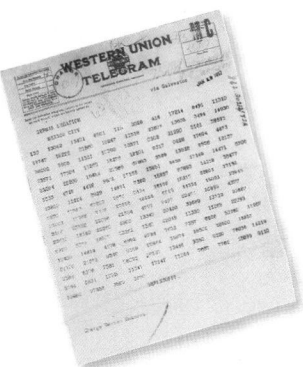

This coded telegram from Berlin to the German embassy in Mexico proposed an alliance between Mexico and Germany.

The United States and World War I

Most Americans had agreed with President Wilson's declaration in 1914 that the United States should be neutral and that the war was strictly a European affair. Nevertheless, the war soon affected the United States. As the most highly industrialized neutral nation, it supplied food, raw materials, and munitions to both sides. According to international law, however, if a ship carried **contraband**—war materials supplied by a neutral nation to a belligerent one—the goods could be seized. At first American investors and business people dealt with both sides. As the British blockade of Germany tightened, however, Americans traded more and more with the Allies.

British propaganda had a great influence on Americans. Stories about German **atrocities**—brutal acts against defenseless civilians—angered Americans. They did not realize that many of the stories were exaggerated or not true.

Early in 1917 several developments pushed the United States toward war. One incident involved a high official in the German foreign ministry, **Arthur Zimmermann**. In January, Zimmermann sent a secret telegram to the German ambassador in Mexico proposing an alliance between Germany and Mexico. Germany offered to help Mexico regain Arizona, New Mexico, and Texas if it would fight on Germany's side. The British intercepted the telegram and decoded it. It was then published in American newspapers. Americans were enraged.

Another development was the resumption of unrestricted submarine warfare by the Germans, who declared a "war zone" around Britain. German U-boats sank many ships. Many Americans died as a result of these attacks.

Then, in March, revolutionaries in Russia overthrew the autocratic czarist government. All the major Allied countries had now moved toward democracy, while none of the Central Powers had. Americans were more likely to participate in a war fought for democratic ideals. President Wilson addressed Congress, saying that "the world must be made safe for democracy." On April 6, 1917, Congress voted to declare war on Germany.

✔ **READING CHECK: Analyzing Information** How was the United States affected by the war before 1917? traded with both sides, influenced by British propaganda

---

SECTION 2 REVIEW

1. **Define** and explain the significance:
   propaganda
   war of attrition
   contraband
   atrocities

2. **Identify** and explain the significance:
   Central Powers
   Allied Powers
   U-boats
   Woodrow Wilson
   Arthur Zimmermann

3. **Comparing and Contrasting** Copy the diagram and use it to show the advantages and disadvantages each side had at the beginning of the war.

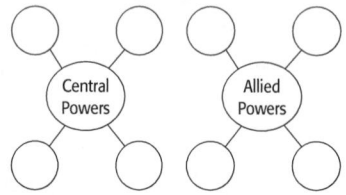

4. **Finding the Main Idea**

   a. How did new technology change the way the war was fought?

   b. What principles were proclaimed by the United States for declaring war?

5. **Writing and Critical Thinking**

   Supporting a Point of View Design a poster encouraging Americans to support the war.
   Consider:
   - the atrocities committed, such as the sinking of the *Lusitania*
   - the idea of making the world "safe for democracy"

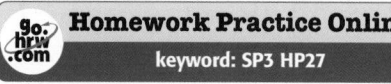
Homework Practice Online
keyword: SP3 HP27

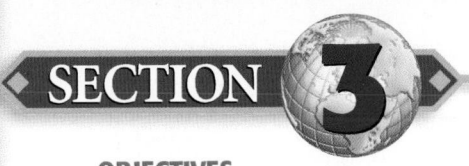

🔊 LET'S GET STARTED!

As students enter the classroom, ask them to write down what they know about Russia during the war up to 1917. *(was originally part of the Triple Alliance; supported Serbia; Germany declared war on Russia in 1914, which led to Russia's alliance with the Allied Powers; lost half its army and was defeated at the Battle of Tannenberg; army lacked guns and ammunition)* Tell students that in Section 3 they will learn why the Russian Revolution occurred and how it affected Russia's future.

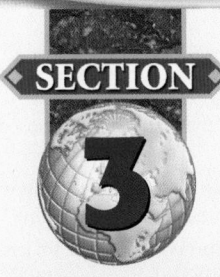

SECTION 3

READ TO DISCOVER

❶ What events led to the Russian Revolution?

❷ How did the Communists come to power?

❸ How did its revolution affect Russia's participation in World War I?

IDENTIFY

Mensheviks
Bolsheviks
Vladimir Lenin
Communist Party
Red Army

WHY IT MATTERS TODAY

Russia continues to undergo dramatic changes. Use CNNfyi.com or other **current event** sources to investigate what Russia's government is like today. Record your findings in your journal.

CNN Student News.com

The Russian Revolution

The Main Idea
Growing problems in Russia came to a crisis during World War I, finally leading to revolution.

The Story Continues *Years of war, poverty, and class struggle had brought an end to the czarist regime in Russia. One Russian described how the revolution began for him. "The streets were full of people. The trams [streetcars] weren't running, overturned cars lay across the tracks. I did not know it then, I did not understand what was happening. I yelled along with everyone, 'Down with the czar!' . . . I yelled again and again. . . . I felt that all of my familiar life was falling apart, and I rejoiced in its destruction."*

Russia in World War I

World War I showed Russia's economic weaknesses. The huge country did not have sufficient food, appropriate armaments, or adequate roads to supply its army. When the Ottoman Empire entered the war on the side of the Central Powers, supplies from outside Russia were sharply cut. The Allies had counted on the large number of Russian soldiers. However, Russia's army was not only poorly equipped but also poorly led. The corrupt, inefficient government could not deal with the problems of modern warfare. Russian war losses were enormous.

By the spring of 1917 the Russian people had lost faith in their government and in the czar. The elected legislative body, the Duma, had little power. Although serfdom had been abolished in 1861, debts, rents, and taxes kept most Russian peasants poor. Strikes and street demonstrations broke out in Petrograd, the capital. When the Duma demanded government reforms, the czar dissolved it.

In the past the government had always been able to use the army against disturbances. This time, however, the soldiers sided with the demonstrators. Encouraged by the army's defiance of the czar, the Duma refused to disband. In March 1917 the czar abdicated, giving up the throne. He and his family were soon imprisoned. The Russian monarchy, and with it the rule of the Russian aristocracy, had come to an end.

✔ **READING CHECK: Identifying Cause and Effect** What were the problems that led to the Russian Revolution? *poverty, suppression of democracy, weak Duma*

Lenin and the Bolsheviks

With the overthrow of the czar a temporary government was set up. It would rule Russia until a constitutional assembly could be elected. While the new rulers of Russia tried to restore order, however, another group was working for more radical change.

The Petrograd Soviet of Workers' and Soldiers' Deputies had been organized when unrest had begun in Russia. *Soviet* is the Russian word for "council." The leaders of the Petrograd Soviet were socialists. They believed that political equality must be coupled with economic equality. Similar soviets were organized elsewhere in Russia. Radical members called for immediate peace and land reforms.

SECTION 3 RESOURCES

REPRODUCIBLE RESOURCES

▶ Guided Reading Strategy 27.3

▶ Readings in World History 95: The Storming of the Winter Palace

TECHNOLOGY RESOURCES

▶ One-Stop Planner 27.3

▶ Holt Researcher: World History: Vladimir Lenin

▶ CNN Presents World Cultures: Yesterday and Today Segment 25: Recovering Russia's Royalty

▶ Regions of the World Music Audio CD Program 9: Russia, Ukraine, and Belarus: Russian Choral Music

▶ Homework Practice Online

REINFORCEMENT, REVIEW, AND ASSESSMENT

▶ Section 3 Review, p. 713

▶ Daily Quiz 27.3

▶ Main Idea Activity 27.3

▶ English Audio Summary 27.3

▶ Spanish Audio Summary 27.3

TEACH OBJECTIVES 1 and 2

ALL LEVELS: Work with students to create a diagram that shows the events leading to the Russian Revolution and the creation of the Communist Party.
ENGLISH LANGUAGE LEARNERS

TEACH OBJECTIVE 3

LEVEL 1: Help students identify the main idea of the subsection "Peace and the Civil War." *(treaty with Central Powers and civil war ended Russia's participation in World War I)*
ENGLISH LANGUAGE LEARNERS

LEVEL 3: Have students create a cause-and-effect chart that shows the relationship among the events that ended Russia's participation in World War I.

HOMEWORK Have students research and prepare a brief oral presentation about Vladimir Lenin that evaluates his political choices and decisions and analyzes his influence on political events of the 1900s.

CLOSE

Discuss why Russia signed the peace treaty.

Global Relations

The Bolsheviks made unsuccessful attempts to seize control of Russia during the spring and summer of 1917. Even after the October Revolution brought them to power, their control was targeted at major cities and industrial areas of Russia.

Critical Thinking

Ask students why the Bolsheviks focused on urban areas.

ANSWER: Urban areas had larger concentrations of industries, workers, and weapons. Control of these areas would give the Bolsheviks greater power.

MAP ANSWER
Petrograd, Pskov, Moscow, Kaluga, and Saratov

Holt Researcher

go.hrw.com
KEYWORD: Holt Researcher
FreeFind: Vladimir Lenin
After reading more about Vladimir Lenin on the Holt Researcher, write an analysis of his influence on political events of the 20th century.

The provisional government, however, pledged to continue the war. It also opposed the changes demanded by the more radical revolutionaries.

Two factions fought for control of the soviets. The moderate **Mensheviks** lost out to the more radical **Bolsheviks.** The leader of the Bolsheviks was **Vladimir Lenin,** a revolutionary socialist. Lenin demanded that all governing power be turned over to the soviets. The Bolsheviks' slogan of "peace, bread, and land" appealed to the war-weary and hungry Russian people. Lenin was a Marxist—a follower of Karl Marx. However, Russia had comparatively little industry and only a small working class. Lenin believed, therefore, that social forces in Russia might not move as Marx had predicted. He set up a small group of leaders to train Russian workers to become a revolutionary force. Lenin's version of Marxism formed the basis of communism.

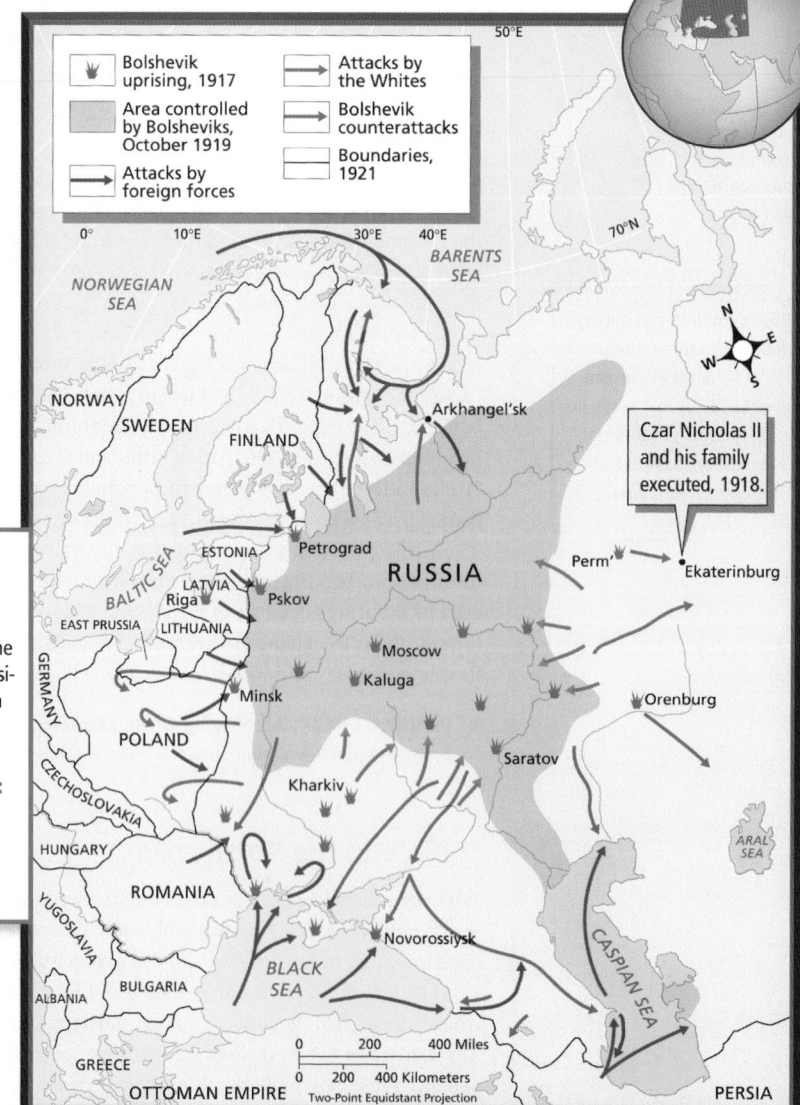

Revolutionary Russia, 1917–1921

Interpreting Maps The Bolsheviks faced opposition from some foreign forces as well as from internal opponents.

■ **Skills Assessment: Locate** What major cities were in the area controlled by the Bolsheviks?

REVIEW

Have students complete the Section 3 Review on p. 713.

ASSESS

Have students complete Daily Quiz 27.3. As Alternative Assessment, you may want to use the Reading Checks in this section's lessons.

RETEACH

Have students complete Main Idea Activity for English Language Learners and Special-Needs Students 27.3. Then have them write a main idea question and answer for each subsection. **ENGLISH LANGUAGE LEARNERS**

EXTEND

Ask students to research the events of the October Revolution, including causes and effects, and write a brief report of their findings. **BLOCK SCHEDULING**

On November 7, 1917, the Bolsheviks overthrew the provisional government and took control of Russia. This is sometimes called the October Revolution for the month that it happened in the Russian calendar. In 1918 the Bolsheviks renamed themselves the **Communist Party** and dissolved the constitutional assembly because they did not have a majority in it.

✔ **READING CHECK: Finding the Main Idea** Why did the Bolsheviks come to power?
appealed to the poor Russian masses

Peace and Civil War

Despite continuing losses, the provisional government had kept Russia in the war. Lenin's new government, however, signed a peace treaty with the Central Powers in March 1918 at the city of Brest Litovsk. Desperate for peace, the Russians accepted the harsh terms dictated by the Germans. Russia agreed to give up a lot of territory.

The new regime then turned its attention to Russia's internal political problems. The Communists faced great opposition. Their opponents included the Mensheviks and other socialist factions, and groups who wanted to restore the monarchy. Civil war broke out early in 1918. To prevent any chance of the monarchy coming back to power, the Communists executed the imprisoned czar and his entire family in July 1918.

The civil war lasted about three years. The Communists forces were called the **Red Army,** adopted from the symbolic color of the European socialist revolutionaries. Their right-wing, counter-revolutionary opponents were known as the Whites. The destruction of the civil war mirrored that caused by World War I.

The Allies were angered by the separate peace treaty Communist Russia had signed with the Central Powers. They tried to get Russia to renew fighting Germany, but the Communists stood by the treaty they had signed. The Allies also feared that the Communists would encourage the spread of revolution to their own countries. The Allies sent troops to Russia and finacial support to the White forces. By 1921, however, the Communists had won. In 1922 the Communists renamed the land they ruled the Union of Soviet Socialist Republics, or the Soviet Union.

✔ **READING CHECK: Evaluating** Why did the peace treaty between Communist Russia and the Central Powers anger the Allies? lost an ally

HISTORY MAKER

**Vladimir Lenin
(1870–1924)**

Vladimir Lenin's life changed when his older brother was executed for conspiring to overthrow the emperor. Throwing himself into revolutionary activities, Lenin was arrested and exiled. After his return he became the first leader of the new Soviet Union, which championed the ideals of socialism. Considered one of the greatest revolutionaries of all time, Lenin became a hero for many later communist leaders. **Why is Lenin important?**

HISTORY MAKER ANSWER
He was the first leader of the new Soviet Union and became a hero for later communist leaders. He helped establish many of the basic practices of communism.

◆SECTION◆
3 REVIEW ANSWERS

❶ **Identify**
• Mensheviks, p. 712
• Bolsheviks, p. 712
• Vladimir Lenin, p. 712
• Communist Party, p. 713
• Red Army, p. 713

❷ poverty, weakened army, suppression of democracy, weak Duma

❸ a. defeated the Mensheviks and overthrew the temporary government

b. because of peace treaty with Central Powers and civil war

❹ Students should consider who might attend a Bolshevik rally and what type of flyer would appeal to the potential audience.

◆ SECTION 3 REVIEW ◆

1. **Identify** and explain the significance:
   Mensheviks
   Bolsheviks
   Vladimir Lenin
   Communist Party
   Red Army

2. **Sequencing** Copy the diagram and use it to show what led to the czar's abdication.

   □ → □ → □ → □
   ↓   ↓   ↓   ↓
   Czar Nicholas II abdicates

3. **Finding the Main Idea**
   a. How did Lenin and the Bolsheviks come to power in Russia?
   b. Why did the Russians pull out of the war?

4. **Writing and Critical Thinking**
   Analyzing Information Design a flyer that the Bolsheviks might have used to organize a rally during 1917.
   Consider:
   • what issues they thought were important
   • the conditions in Russia during World War I

Homework Practice Online
keyword: SP3 HP27

OBJECTIVES

1 Define the Fourteen Points.

2 Explain how the war ended.

3 Identify the disagreements that the peacemakers faced.

SECTION 4

READ TO DISCOVER

❶ What were the Fourteen Points?
❷ How did the war end?
❸ What disagreements did the peacemakers face?

DEFINE

armistice
reparations

IDENTIFY

Fourteen Points
Ferdinand Foch
Paris Peace Conference
League of Nations

WHY IT MATTERS TODAY

After World War I many territories were transferred from one power to another. Alsace-Lorraine is a region in France that before World War I was part of Germany. Use CNN or other **current event** sources to describe life in Alsace-Lorraine today. Record your findings in your journal.

CNNstudentNews.com

The Terms of Peace

The Main Idea
With the end of World War I, the United States and European nations worked to ensure peace.

The Story Continues *Americans did not have to be soldiers to join the war effort. One woman noted, "Billy, my nephew, is twelve years old.... They call the suburb in which Billy lives one hundred percent patriotic. Everybody is in war work.... Billy's crowd is indefatigable [tireless] in its labors.... The boys usher at meetings, assist in parades, deliver bundles and run errands. They are tireless collectors of nutshells, peach pits [for gas masks] and tinsel paper."*

The Fourteen Points

President Woodrow Wilson's idea that by joining the war America was helping to safeguard democracy established a high, idealistic purpose for World War I. Russia's separate peace with the Central Powers, however, dampened Allied morale. The bloody stalemate on the western front continued. Many people feared that the war would last for many more years.

In January 1918 President Wilson spoke to Congress. He outlined a set of ideas for a more just world once the war ended. His plan became known as the **Fourteen Points.** Six of the points contained plans of a general nature. The eight remaining points dealt with specific countries and regions, such as Russia, Belgium, Alsace-Lorraine, and the Balkans.

The six general points could be summarized as follows: 1) no secret treaties; 2) freedom of the seas for all nations; 3) removal of all economic barriers, such as tariffs; 4) reduction of national armaments; 5) adjustment of colonial claims so they were fair to both the imperialist powers and the colonial peoples; 6) establishment of "a general association of nations" to guarantee political independence and protection to small and large states alike.

The Fourteen Points caught the imagination of people everywhere. Even some people of Germany, tired of the hardships of war, were impressed by Wilson's proposals.

✔ **READING CHECK: Making Generalizations** What was the overall purpose of the Fourteen Points? a just and safer world

More than 2 million American soldiers served in France in World War I. Some are seen here marching through the Arc de Triomphe in Paris.

Defeat of the Central Powers

The Treaty of Brest Litovsk with Russia allowed the Germans to pull troops from the eastern front. They now could concentrate on a huge offensive on the western front in the spring and summer of 1918. This was a last attempt to break through the Allied lines and capture Paris. Meanwhile Allied forces held out for U.S. troops to arrive.

At the end of May the Germans again reached the Marne River. They were just 37 miles from Paris. By this time, however, thousands of American troops were landing every day in France.

An Allied force under the command of French marshal **Ferdinand Foch** (FAWSH) stopped the Germans at Château-Thierry. In July the Allies began a counterattack. Major offensives in August and September forced the Germans back toward their own border. It also became worse elsewhere for the Central Powers. Bulgaria surrendered at the end of September. The Turks, too, soon asked for peace. By October the old Habsburg empire in Austria-Hungary had broken up. Austria and Hungary stopped fighting and formed separate governments.

President Wilson had told the German leaders that he would deal only with a government that truly represented the German people. In the face of growing German military and civilian unrest, the kaiser gave up the throne in early November and a German republic was announced.

In November 1918 a German delegation signed an **armistice,** an agreement to stop fighting. The armistice provided that at 11:00 A.M. on November 11, 1918, all fighting would cease. Under the terms of the armistice, Germany canceled the Brest Litovsk treaty with Russia. Germany had to give up a large part of its fleet, including all submarines. It had to turn over much of its munitions and release war prisoners. The Allies would occupy German territory west of the Rhine River.

The costs of World War I were very high. It is estimated that the war left more than 8.5 million (perhaps 10 million) soldiers dead. About 21 million more were wounded, many crippled for life. Militarily, Germany suffered the most severely, losing more than 1.8 million soldiers. Russia lost almost as many, and France and its colonies lost over 1.4 million. Austria and Hungary counted over 1 million dead, and Great Britain lost almost 1 million. The United States lost over 110,000 soldiers. Civilian deaths and injuries were also very high. Naval blockades, military encounters, famine, and disease had all taken their toll. The financial loss, too, was enormous. Historians have estimated that the total cost was more than $300 billion, a huge amount for the time.

✔ **READING CHECK: Identifying Cause and Effect** What events in Europe helped end the war? arrival of American troops, revolution in Austria-Hungary

What If? How might world history have been different if the United States had not fought in World War I?

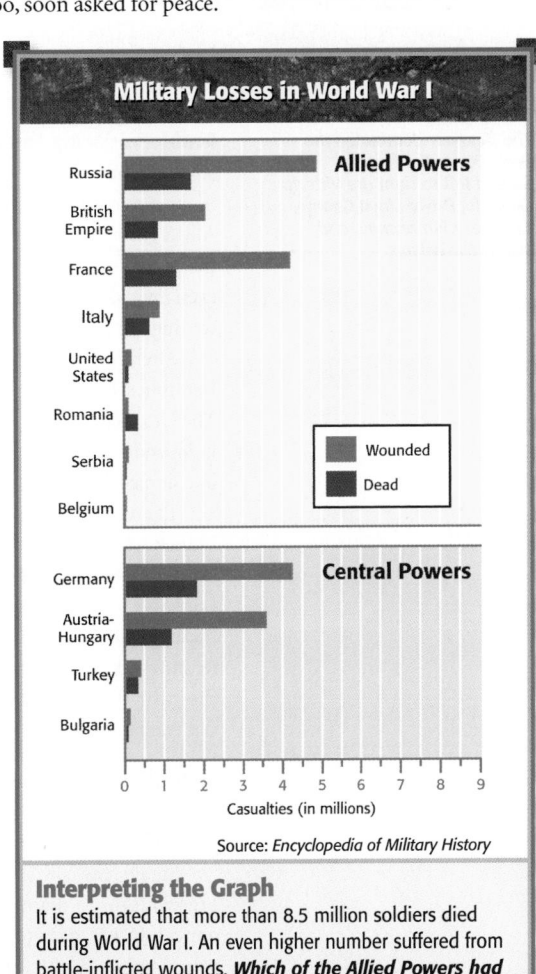

Military Losses in World War I

Allied Powers

Russia
British Empire
France
Italy
United States
Romania
Serbia
Belgium

Central Powers

Germany
Austria-Hungary
Turkey
Bulgaria

Wounded
Dead

0 1 2 3 4 5 6 7 8 9
Casualties (in millions)

Source: *Encyclopedia of Military History*

Interpreting the Graph
It is estimated that more than 8.5 million soldiers died during World War I. An even higher number suffered from battle-inflicted wounds. *Which of the Allied Powers had the highest number of total casualties? Which of the Central Powers had the highest casualties?*

LEVEL 3: Have groups of students role-play radio interviews with representatives of the Big Four. The program's host should ask the guests their opinions of the Fourteen Points, what they hope to gain for their countries, and how the Central Powers should be punished. *(There should be clear differences of opinion among the guests.)* Select one group to recreate its role-play for the class. **COOPERATIVE LEARNING**

HOMEWORK Have students write a paragraph explaining why European leaders might have resented Wilson's attempts to shape the nature of the peace treaty with his Fourteen Points.

Have students work in pairs to complete a two-column chart about the Paris Peace Conference. Students should list the goals each nation hoped to achieve in one column, and problems the peacemakers faced in the second column.
COOPERATIVE LEARNING

That's Interesting!

During World War II, Adolf Hitler gained revenge for his country's humiliation in World War I. In June 1940, he accepted France's surrender at a meeting in the forest of Compiègne, in the very same railroad car where the Germans had surrendered 22 years before.

The Big Four dominated the Paris Peace Conference. Seated left to right are Vittorio Orlando, David Lloyd George, Georges Clemenceau, and Woodrow Wilson.

The Paris Peace Conference

After the armistice in November 1918, the Allies faced the task of arranging peace terms. In January 1919 the victorious Allied nations met at Versailles, outside Paris, for what came to be known as the **Paris Peace Conference.** The meeting was dominated by the leaders of the four major Allied Powers. The group—which included U.S. President Woodrow Wilson, British Prime Minister David Lloyd George, French Premier Georges Clemenceau, and Italian Prime Minister Vittorio Orlando—came to be known as the Big Four.

Problems facing the peacemakers. Problems began almost immediately when some countries were excluded from the peace process. President Wilson had spoken of a peace conference that would write a treaty that was fair to all, but the European Allied governments were not very forgiving of their losses. They insisted on dictating the peace settlement. Russia, under Communist rule and beset by civil war, was not even invited. Representatives of the defeated Central Powers were allowed little role in writing the peace terms.

After World War I Europe faced a radically new and confusing political situation. Republics had replaced monarchies in Austria-Hungary, Germany, and Russia. The Ottoman Empire was on the brink of collapse. Various ethnic groups pressed for independence, self-government, and unified states. The spirit of nationalism also grew in colonies overseas.

The victorious nations had many conflicting territorial demands. Above all, France wanted security against another German attack. It insisted on moving its border eastward to the Rhine River. It wanted the return of the region of Alsace-Lorraine. It also wanted the coal-rich Saar valley. Italy claimed the Tirol region and the cities of Fiume and Trieste. Belgium wanted two small portions of German territory along the border. Great Britain wanted Germany's African colonies and the near destruction of the German navy. Japan wanted German colonies in the Pacific.

Reparations and peacekeeping. The destruction caused by the war also brought up questions about **reparations**—payment for war damages. Who should pay? And how much? Many Allied leaders wanted Germany to bear the cost of the war.

Finally, the conference considered President Wilson's plan for setting up a world organization to maintain peace—a **League of Nations.** This idea had widespread appeal. It was dear to Wilson's heart but many people doubted how practical it would be.

✔ **READING CHECK: Drawing Inferences** Why did the European Allies insist on setting the terms of the peace settlement? because the war had cost them so much in lives and property

REVIEW

Have students complete the Section 4 Review on p. 717.

ASSESS

Have students complete Daily Quiz 27.4. As Alternative Assessment, you may want to use the chart in this section's lessons.

RETEACH

Have students complete Main Idea Activity for English Language Learners and Special-Needs Students 27.4. Then have students write a main idea question and answer for each subheading in the section. **ENGLISH LANGUAGE LEARNERS**

EXTEND

Have students use the process of historical inquiry to research the effect the armistice had on Germany. Ask students to write short reports of their findings. **BLOCK SCHEDULING**

What Kind of Peace?

Early in the Paris Peace Conference, two very different, conflicting viewpoints surfaced. Wilson believed the peace settlement should be fair and not so harsh that it would kindle future wars. On the other hand, many of the Allies felt hatred toward Germany. They believed that Germany had started the war and should pay for it. The British, French, and Italian governments did not officially object to Wilson's Fourteen Points. Yet they had never given up the aims of their secret treaties—to divide territory taken from the Central Powers among themselves after the war. Many Allied leaders believed the only way to ensure a lasting peace was to prevent Germany from ever being powerful again.

Some countries, particularly France, wanted concrete guarantees that Germany would never again be able to threaten their security. Georges Clemenceau, the premier of France, admired Wilson's ideals, but believed the U.S. president was being naive in trusting Germany. "Hopes without certainty cannot suffice to those who suffered the aggression of 1914," he said. Clemenceau argued that the only way to ensure France's future security was to break up Germany and have Allied forces occupy its various regions. The future of Germany would rest on the decisions made at the Paris Peace Conference.

✔ **READING CHECK: Finding the Main Idea** Why did some victors in the war want to break up Germany? to eliminate Germany as a threat

INTERPRETING THE VISUAL RECORD

The costs of war European nations wanted Germany to pay reparations for damages suffered in the war. Seen here are the ruins of Houplines, France. *What do these ruins suggest about the state of Europe at the end of World War I?*

SECTION 4 REVIEW

1. **Define** and explain the significance:
   armistice
   reparations

2. **Identify** and explain the significance:
   Fourteen Points
   Ferdinand Foch
   Paris Peace Conference
   League of Nations

Homework Practice Online
keyword: SP3 HP27

3. **Summarizing** Copy the diagram and use it to show the six general ideas in the Fourteen Points.

FOURTEEN POINTS			

4. **Finding the Main Idea**
   a. How did World War I come to an end in 1918?
   b. What were some problems facing the peacemakers?

5. **Writing and Critical Thinking**
   Supporting a Point of View Write a letter to a newspaper editor supporting Wilson's view or Clemenceau's view at the Paris Peace Conference.
   Consider:
   • the cost of the war to both the Allied and Central Powers
   • how Wilson proposed to prevent future global wars
   • why Clemenceau feared German power

VISUAL RECORD ANSWER
that European cities had been devastated

SECTION 4 REVIEW ANSWERS

❶ **Define**
• armistice, p. 715
• reparations, p. 716

❷ **Identify**
• Fourteen Points, p. 714
• Ferdinand Foch, p. 715
• Paris Peace Conference, p. 716
• League of Nations, p. 716

❸ no secret treaties; freedom of the seas for all nations, removal of all economic barriers such as tariffs, reduction of national armaments, adjustment of colonial claims so they were fair to both the imperialists and the colonials, establishment of a "general association of nations" to guarantee political independence and protection to small and large states

❹ a. the Allies stopped Germany's advance, other Central Powers stopped fighting, Germany signed armistice

b. deciding the terms of peace; new and confusing political situations in Europe; conflicting territorial demands of the victors; deciding who would pay for the war; what to do with Germany

❺ Students' letters should clearly indicate whose view they are supporting and use details to support their opinions.

SECTION 5

OBJECTIVES

1 **Identify the terms of the Treaty of Versailles.**

2 **Explain how territories were redivided after the war.**

3 **Explain how the League of Nations was structured.**

LET'S GET STARTED!

As students enter the classroom, ask them to list the countries that lost World War I. *(Germany, Austria-Hungary, Bulgaria, and Russia)* Ask students what they think happened to these countries after the war. *(Students might suggest that they lost territory, as well as military, economic, and political power.)* Tell students that in Section 5 they will learn what happened to the nations involved in World War I.

SECTION 5 RESOURCES

REPRODUCIBLE RESOURCES

▸ Guided Reading Strategy 27.5

▸ Readings in World History 96: The Germans are Informed of the Terms of the Treaty of Versailles

▸ Creative Teaching Strategy 27: Reflections on the Great War

TECHNOLOGY RESOURCES

▸ One-Stop Planner 27.5

▸ Homework Practice Online

▸ Online Maps, Charts, and Graphs: The Polish Corridor After World War I

REINFORCEMENT, REVIEW, AND ASSESSMENT

▸ Section 5 Review, p. 723

▸ Daily Quiz 27.5

▸ Main Idea Activity 27.5

▸ English Audio Summary 27.5

▸ Spanish Audio Summary 27.5

SECTION 5

READ TO DISCOVER

❶ What were the terms of the Treaty of Versailles?

❷ How were territories redivided after the war?

❸ How was the League of Nations structured?

DEFINE

genocide
economic sanctions
mandate

IDENTIFY

Treaty of Versailles
World Court

WHY IT MATTERS TODAY

The League of Nations was the forerunner of the United Nations. Use CNN or other **current event** sources to investigate the structure and work of the United Nations. Record your findings in your journal.

Creating a "New" Europe

The Main Idea
The Treaty of Versailles rearranged territories and brought great changes to Europe after World War I.

The Story Continues *After World War I, world leaders gathered to try to arrive at a settlement that would keep such a war from happening again. As one participant described the proceedings, "We were preparing not Peace only, but Eternal Peace. There was about us the halo of some divine mission. . . . For we were bent on doing great, permanent and noble things."*

The Treaty of Versailles

After six months of negotiations, the delegates to the peace conference finally hammered out an agreement. The victorious Allied Powers made separate peace treaties with each of the five Central Powers—Germany, Bulgaria, the Ottoman Empire, and Austria and Hungary (now two separate nations).

In May 1919 representatives of the new German Republic were called in and presented with a peace treaty. The treaty with Germany was signed at Versailles, near Paris. It was known as the **Treaty of Versailles.** To Wilson's disappointment, the treaty dealt very harshly with Germany. The Germans complained bitterly that the treaty did not follow the Fourteen Points. The treaty made Germany admit that it was guilty of starting the war and must alone pay reparations. The Treaty of Versailles carved large chunks of territory from Germany and placed many restrictions on the German government. However, it also provided for the formation of the League of Nations. Wilson hoped this dream of his would still help create a lasting peace.

The Germans strongly objected to paying reparations. They denied that Germany alone was responsible for starting the war. Moreover, the treaty did not even state the total amount of reparations that Germany would have to pay. The defeated Germans had no choice, however. In late June 1919 they signed the treaty. One witness described the scene as the German delegates arrived to sign the treaty:

Primary Source ❝Through the door . . . isolated and pitiable, come the two German delegates. . . . The silence is terrifying. . . . They keep their eyes fixed away from those two thousand staring eyes, fixed upon the ceiling. They are deathly pale.❞

Harold Nicolson, *Peacemaking 1919*

As a result of the Versailles treaty, many territorial changes were made at Germany's expense. Alsace-Lorraine was returned to France. Belgium gained some small territories along its borders. Germany agreed not to fortify the Rhineland, which Allied troops would occupy for an unspecified period of time. Moreover, Poland was restored as an independent nation. An area called the Polish Corridor cut off East Prussia from the rest of Germany and gave Poland an outlet to the Baltic Sea. The port of Danzig became a free city under the League of Nations. Some territory of the new Polish state also had been part of Russia.

ALL LEVELS: Have students work in groups to create a newspaper page about the Treaty of Versailles. Assign the groups different countries or regions to represent, such as France, Germany, Serbia, Syria, or Africa. Each group's page should contain at least two columns expressing how the terms of the treaty affected its country or region.

ENGLISH LANGUAGE LEARNERS, COOPERATIVE LEARNING

HOMEWORK Have students write letters to the editor of a French or British newspaper expressing how they feel about the Treaty of Versailles and about Germany's lack of voice in negotiating its terms. Students should write from the point of view of a German citizen and support their views with specific reasons and details.

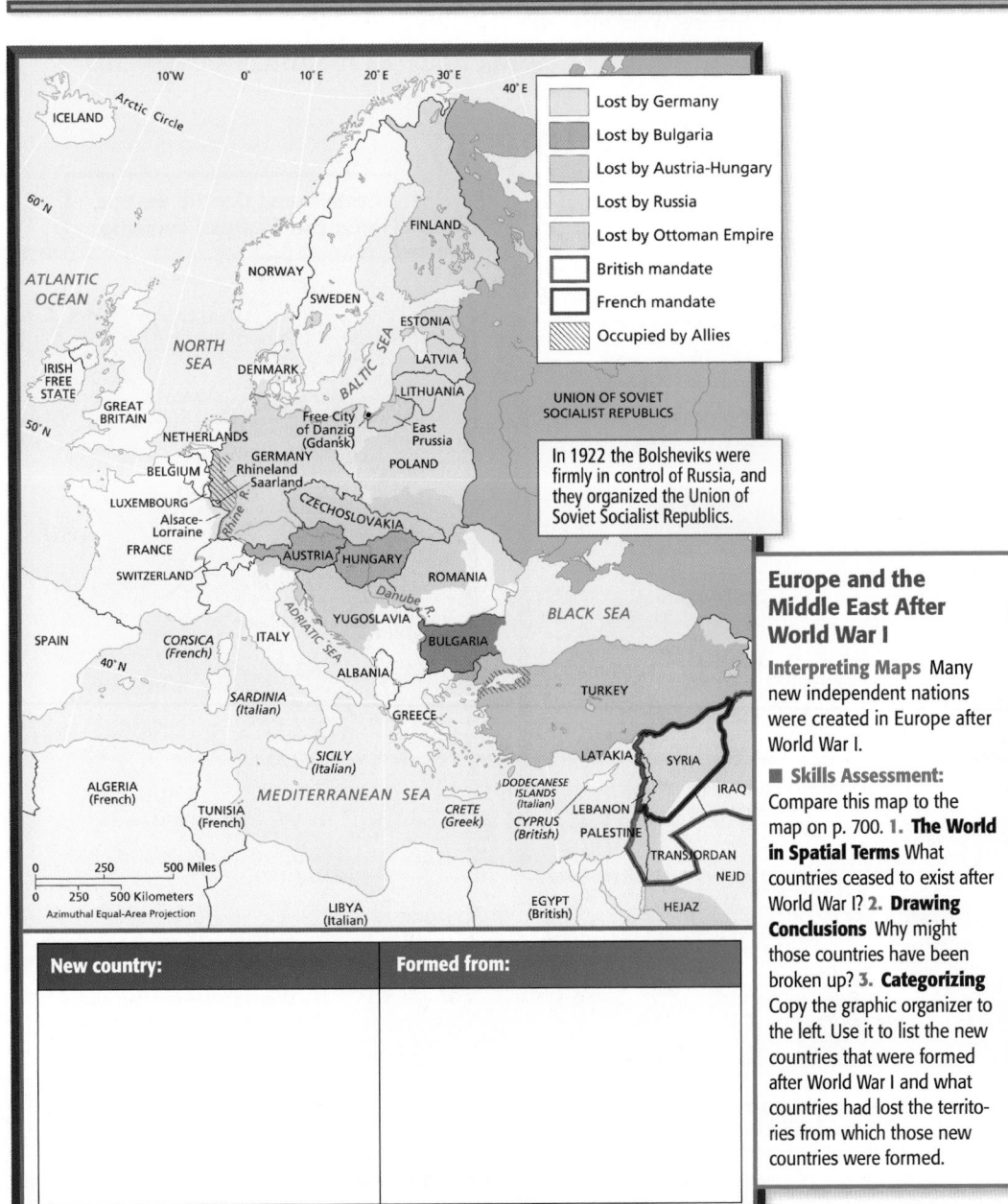

In 1922 the Bolsheviks were firmly in control of Russia, and they organized the Union of Soviet Socialist Republics.

Legend:
- Lost by Germany
- Lost by Bulgaria
- Lost by Austria-Hungary
- Lost by Russia
- Lost by Ottoman Empire
- British mandate
- French mandate
- Occupied by Allies

New country:	Formed from:

Europe and the Middle East After World War I

Interpreting Maps Many new independent nations were created in Europe after World War I.

■ **Skills Assessment:** Compare this map to the map on p. 700. **1. The World in Spatial Terms** What countries ceased to exist after World War I? **2. Drawing Conclusions** Why might those countries have been broken up? **3. Categorizing** Copy the graphic organizer to the left. Use it to list the new countries that were formed after World War I and what countries had lost the territories from which those new countries were formed.

MAP ANSWERS

1. Serbia, Austria-Hungary, Ottoman Empire, German Empire, Montenegro

2. to satisfy territorial disputes of victorious nations and to punish the nations who allied with the Central Powers

3. Estonia, Latvia, Lithuania, Finland (from Russia); East Prussia (from Germany); Poland (from Germany, Russia, and Austria-Hungary); Austria, Czechoslovakia, Hungary (from Austria-Hungary); Turkey, Syria, Iraq, Lebanon, Palestine (from Ottoman Empire); Yugoslavia (from Austria-Hungary, Serbia, and Montenegro)

Technology Resources

World History Teaching Transparency: Geography and History 22: Europe and the Middle East After World War I

Germany had to abolish its military draft. It was allowed an army of just 100,000 men. The Germans were not allowed to manufacture heavy artillery, tanks, or military airplanes. The German navy could have a few warships but no submarines. These peace terms were meant to ensure that Germany would be unable to start a war. The Allies, however, lacked the ability to enforce them.

✔ **READING CHECK: Categorizing** What limits were placed on the German military by the peace treaty? no draft, maximum 100,000 men, no heavy artillery, military planes, or submarines

LEVEL 1: Have pairs of students take turns asking and answering questions about the geographic distribution of nations and territory as it is shown on the maps on pages 719 and 720. *(example: Which country lost the area now known as Czechoslovakia? answer: Austria-Hungary)* Have students record their questions and answers in a two-column chart with the columns labeled *Questions* and *Answers.* **ENGLISH LANGUAGE LEARNERS, COOPERATIVE LEARNING**

LEVEL 3: Distribute two copies of an outline map of Europe to each student. On one map, students should show the countries of Europe before World War I. On the other map, they should show Europe after World War I. Tell students to label each map, and on a separate sheet of paper write a paragraph explaining how and why their maps differ. Students should use standard grammar, spelling, sentence structure, and punctuation to write their paragraphs.

Global Relations

Before World War I, Poland was a Russian province. At the beginning of the war, however, Polish armies fought with Austria-Hungary against Russia. By 1916 both Germany and Austria-Hungary occupied Poland. The next year the Polish National Committee was formed in Paris to win Allied support for independence. Poland was proclaimed an independent nation in 1918 and regained large amounts of land under the terms of the Treaty of Versailles in 1919.

Critical Thinking

Ask students which three countries controlled Poland at various times before World War I.

ANSWER: Russia, Austria-Hungary, and Germany

SKILLS PRACTICE ANSWERS

1. Yugoslavia

2. Budapest

3. The map of eastern Europe was redrawn, creating new boundaries and new nations.

4. changed; that it continued to be a source of conflict after World War I

720

SKILL-BUILDING STRATEGIES

Interpreting Visuals: Using Maps as Historical Documents

Changes in Austria-Hungary

From 1867 until 1919 the Austro-Hungarian Empire, ruled by the Habsburg monarchs, covered much of eastern and central Europe. After the Treaty of Versailles, however, the empire was broken up and a number of smaller countries were created. Studying maps of this area before and after the Treaty of Versailles helps you to understand the impact of World War I on political and historical developments in Europe.

The peace settlement that ended World War I was drafted by the Allies at Versailles beginning in December 1918.

Skills Reminder

To use a map as a historical document, first identify the subject of the map. You can gain more information from the map by identifying its historical context. Using the key that is given with the map will help explain the information about the subject included on the map and connect that information to the historical context of the subject. Determine how the map helps to show a particular historical pattern, change, or event. Finally, compare the map with other maps—what are some of the differences between the maps? This will help you build an overall understanding of how the pattern, change, or event that it shows produced a new historical reality.

Skills Practice

Study the maps above and answer the following questions:
❶ What new nation included the former Serbia and the former province of Bosnia and Herzegovinia?
❷ What city functioned as the capital of the new nation of Hungary?
❸ Compare the two maps. Then write a general statement describing the historical patterns, changes, or events revealed by your analysis.
❹ Using an atlas or other map sources, find a current map of this region of Europe. Has it changed or stayed the same? What might that indicate about the political situation of the region since World War I?

LEVEL 1: Call on volunteers to state the League of Nation's two main goals. *(to promote international cooperation; to maintain peace)* Have students identify methods the League used to accomplish these goals. *(such as arms reductions)* Ask how the mandate process related to the League's goals. *(protected nations until ready for independence)* **ENGLISH LANGUAGE LEARNERS**

ALL LEVELS: Copy the organization chart on the board, omitting the italicized answers. Work with students to fill in the structure of the League of Nations and its relationship to the World Court.

League of Nations	World Court
Secretariat	
Council *Permanent Members* *Rotating Members*	
Assembly	

Fates of Former Territories

The Allied victors wrote separate peace treaties with the new nations of Austria and Hungary. The treaty with Austria was signed in September 1919, with Hungary in June 1920. The two countries kept only a small part of the pre-war Austro-Hungarian Empire. Austria surrendered the southern Tirol and the city of Trieste to Italy. Hungary lost some of its territory to the newly independent nations of Czechoslovakia and Yugoslavia. Brought together in Yugoslavia were Serbia, Slovenia, Croatia, Montenegro, and Bosnia and Herzegovina. Hungary also lost territory to Romania, Poland, and Russia.

Ethnic populations. The peace treaties solved many problems but also created new ones. One of the most difficult problems was that of national self-determination. This was especially true in Austria and Hungary, where nationalist movements had been encouraged by Wilson's Fourteen Points. Often the new boundaries did not match natural ethnic divisions. For example, the new national frontiers left about 3 million Germans in Czechoslovakia and Hungarians in Romania. Poland also gained access to the Baltic Sea through the Polish Corridor, a section of land inhabited by Germans. This angered many Germans in the area. Ferdinand Foch predicted that the Polish Corridor would be "the root of the next war."

Some ethnic groups, like the Armenians in Turkey, were brutally oppressed. During World War I the Turks had launched a **genocide,** or systematic extermination, of the Armenians in the Ottoman Empire. Foreign outcry against these atrocities caused a halt to the practice once the war ended, but the Turks resumed their repression in 1920. In 1915 the Armenian population of the Ottoman Empire had stood at some 2 million. About 1.5 million were killed, the rest deported. By 1923 the Armenian population of Asia Minor was almost nonexistent.

Bulgaria, the Ottoman Empire, and Russia. The victors also punished Bulgaria. In its 1919 treaty with the Allies, Bulgaria ceded territory to Greece, losing its outlet to the Aegean Sea.

The Ottoman Empire also paid a high price for being on the losing side. By the treaty of 1920, it was stripped of almost all territory but Turkey itself. Several new

Wagons loaded with supplies, these Armenian refugees are shown here fleeing from Turkish persecution in 1920.

A great deal of time was spent debating the need for Germany to pay war costs. Two main groups emerged: those who believed Germany should pay all war costs, and those who felt the Germans should pay only for civilian losses. Wilson supported the latter, although he believed Belgium was entitled to full reimbursement. French and British interests prevailed, however, and required huge reparations. Have students research this debate, and state in an opinion paper which side they agree with. Students should support their opinions with reasons and details.

CLOSE

Form two panels of three to five students each to debate the provisions of the Treaty of Versailles. Have one panel represent the French position, and the other the German position. Have the rest of the class represent the American public. After weighing the points made in the debate, the "public" should decide whether or not the U.S. Senate was right in refusing to ratify the treaty.
COOPERATIVE LEARNING

Government

The Covenant began, "THE HIGH CONTRACTING PARTIES, In order to promote international co-operation and to achieve international peace and security . . . Agree to this Covenant of the League of Nations." The Covenant then presented the League's goals in 26 articles. The Covenant was followed by a list of the original signatories, and a list of thirteen countries that were invited to accede to the Covenant.

internet connect

TOPIC: Treaty of Versailles
GO TO: go.hrw.com
KEYWORD: SP3 WH27

Have students search the Internet through the HRW Go site for additional information on the Treaty of Versailles. Then have them list the strengths and weaknesses of the treaty.

nations were formed from the Ottoman lands east of the Mediterranean. They included Palestine, Transjordan, Syria, and Iraq. They were to be administered by Great Britain and France for the League of Nations. The Dardanelles and Bosporus remained in Turkey. However, these strategic waterways could not be fortified and were to be under international control.

Although it had fought for the Allies, Russia also suffered territorial losses. Its early withdrawal from the war and the rise of the Bolsheviks isolated Russia from the rest of the Allies. By 1918 the Baltic states of Finland, Estonia, Latvia, and Lithuania had declared their independence from Russia. The Allies recognized them as independent. In addition, Russia not only lost land to Poland but also lost the province of Bessarabia to Romania.

✔ **READING CHECK: Drawing Conclusions** What were some problems created by the peace treaties? divided ethnic populations, stirred nationalist feelings

The League of Nations

During talks among Allied leaders over the peace settlements, President Wilson made some compromises in the Fourteen Points. He realized that the treaties themselves did not fully provide a "peace of justice." He thought, however, that the new League of Nations would be able to fix any injustices the treaties created. A special commission, which included Wilson, wrote the Covenant of the League of Nations. This agreement, adopted by the Paris Peace Conference, became part of the Versailles treaty.

Organization. According to the Covenant, the League of Nations had two main aims: (1) to promote international cooperation and (2) to keep peace among nations, by settling disputes and reducing armaments. Three main agencies would conduct League business: an assembly, a council, and a secretariat. The League was to work closely with a related but independent body, the Permanent Court of International Justice, or **World Court.** This court would determine cases involving international law. Today the court is located at The Hague in the Netherlands.

The Assembly would be composed of representatives of all member nations. Regardless of size, each nation would have one vote. The Council, the main peacekeeping body, would consist of 9 member nations (later increased to 14). Five members would be permanent—Great Britain, France, Italy, Japan, and the United States—the victors in the war. The remaining seats on the Council were to be filled by the other member nations on a rotating basis.

The members of the League of Nations agreed not to go to war over any disputes. Instead they would submit a dispute to the World Court or other special commission. If a nation broke this agreement, the League could

This was the first public session of the League of Nations, in 1920.

REVIEW

Have students complete the Section 5 Review on p. 723.

ASSESS

Have students complete Daily Quiz 27.5. As Alternative Assessment, you may want to use the interpreting maps feature in this section's lessons.

RETEACH

Have students complete Main Idea Activity for English Language Learners and Special-Needs Students 27.5. Then have students write a two-paragraph summary of the section.
ENGLISH LANGUAGE LEARNERS

EXTEND

Have students write a short paper explaining why they agree or disagree with the opinion that the settlement of World War I made another major war in Europe almost inevitable.
BLOCK SCHEDULING

impose penalties such as breaking diplomatic relations. They also could impose **economic sanctions,** such as blocking trade with the offending nation. Military force would be only a last resort.

Mandates. The League of Nations provided a way to deal with the overseas colonies of the defeated powers. Until the people of a colony were considered "ready for independence," the League would hold the colony in trust and take responsibility for it. The League set aside the colony as a **mandate,** to be ruled by the government of an "advanced" nation. The ruling nation would promise to "prepare" the people there for independence. It would make annual reports to the League about the mandate's progress.

German possessions in Africa and the Pacific and Ottoman territories in the Middle East were given as mandates to Great Britain, France, Australia, New Zealand, Belgium, or Japan. The mandate for South-West Africa was given to South Africa.

The start of the League. Although the League of Nations had been strongly promoted by President Wilson, the United States never became a member. Some Americans were wary of the League's powers. Some wanted changes in the Versailles treaty, which included the League Covenant. Because of the League's peacekeeping commitments, some Americans feared being dragged into another war over issues that did not concern them. As a result of this strong opposition, the U.S. Senate did not ratify the Versailles treaty. Instead the United States eventually signed a separate peace treaty with Germany.

Despite the absence of the United States, the 42 member nations at the League's first meeting in Geneva in November 1920 were hopeful for the future. Germany joined in 1926. The Soviet Union became a member in 1934. By the 1940s some 59 nations had joined the League of Nations.

✔ **READING CHECK: Identifying Bias** What did the system of mandates reveal about the Allies' attitude toward colonial peoples? that they weren't ready for self-rule

INTERPRETING THE VISUAL RECORD

Postwar protests After World War I some Americans opposed further involvement in European affairs, including membership in the League of Nations. They wanted to focus on their own concerns. *What issue are the war veterans in this picture concerned about?*

VISUAL RECORD ANSWER

bonus payments

SECTION
5 REVIEW ANSWERS

❶ **Define**
• genocide, p. 721
• economic sanctions, p. 723
• mandate, p. 723

❷ **Identify**
• Treaty of Versailles, p. 718
• World Court, p. 722

❸ Secretariat, Council, Assembly

❹ **a.** gave most of them to other nations

b. to promote international cooperation and peace among nations

❺ Students should decide their purpose (for example, informative or persuasive) before they begin writing.

SECTION 5 REVIEW

1. **Define** and explain the significance:
   genocide
   economic sanctions
   mandate

2. **Identify** and explain the significance:
   Treaty of Versailles
   World Court

3. **Analyzing Information** Copy the diagram and use it to show the organizational structure of the League of Nations.

   League of Nations

4. **Finding the Main Idea**
   a. How did the Treaty of Versailles deal with Germany's colonies?
   b. What were the aims of the League of Nations?

5. **Writing and Critical Thinking**
   Drawing Inferences Write a speech to the U.S. Senate opposing joining the League of Nations. Use the Armenian genocide as an example of the weaknesses of the League.

   Consider:
   • what happened in the Armenian genocide
   • how the League was limited in its ability to respond to it

Homework Practice Online
keyword: SP3 HP27

CHAPTER 27

REVIEW AND ASSESSMENT RESOURCES

REPRODUCIBLE RESOURCES
▶ Vocabulary Activity 27

TECHNOLOGY RESOURCES
▶ Chapter 27 Test Generator (on the One-Stop Planner)
▶ Global Skill Builder CD–ROM
▶ HRW Web Site

REINFORCEMENT, REVIEW, and ASSESSMENT
▶ Chapter 27 Review, pp. 724–725
▶ Chapter 27 Tutorial for Students, Parents, Mentors, and Peers
▶ Chapter 27 Test (Form A or B)
▶ Alternative Assessment Handbook
▶ Chapter 27 Test for English Language Learners and Special-Needs Students

REVIEW
Have students complete the Chapter 27 Review on pages 724–725.

ASSESS
Use one of the chapter tests to assess students' understanding of content. For Alternative Assessment, see the Portfolio Activities and Alternative Assessment Handbook.

CHAPTER 27 REVIEW ANSWERS

Understanding Main Ideas
1. to isolate France and secure Germany's borders

2. the assassination of Archduke Ferdinand and his wife

3. to create new weapons

4. Zimmermann telegram and German naval attacks

5. poverty, suppression of democracy, and weak Duma

6. The regime could focus its attention on internal political problems.

7. no secret treaties, freedom of the seas, removal of all economic barriers, reduction of national armaments, adjustment of colonial claims, an association of nations to guarantee political independence and protection to all states

8. deciding the terms of peace, new and confusing political situations in Europe, conflicting territorial demands of victors, paying for the war, dealing with Germany

9. it dealt harshly with Germany

10. an Assembly, a Council, and a Secretariat; worked with the World Court

Reviewing Themes
1. convinced people to support the war effort

2. formation of alliances

3. increased due to need for war supplies and equipment

CHAPTER 27 Review

Creating a Time Line
Copy the time line below onto a sheet of paper. Complete the time line by filling in the events, individuals, and dates from the chapter that you think were significant. Pick three events and explain why you think they were significant.

| 1882 | 1916 | 1920 |

Writing a Summary
Using standard grammar, spelling, sentence structure, and punctuation, write an overview of the events in the chapter.

Identifying People and Ideas
Identify the following terms or individuals and explain their significance:

1. belligerents
2. Allied Powers
3. propaganda
4. Woodrow Wilson
5. Vladimir Lenin
6. Communist Party
7. armistice
8. League of Nations
9. Treaty of Versailles
10. economic sanctions

Understanding Main Ideas

SECTION 1 (pp. 698–703)
Setting the Stage for War
1. What was Bismarck's purpose in forming the Triple Alliance of 1882?
2. What event exploded the Balkan "powder keg" and began World War I?

SECTION 2 (pp. 704–710)
World War I: A New Kind of War
3. How was new technology used in World War I?
4. What led the United States to declare war?

SECTION 3 (pp. 711–713)
The Russian Revolution
5. What were the conditions in Russia that led to revolution?
6. How did signing the Treaty of Brest Litovsk help the Communist regime in Russia?

SECTION 4 (pp. 714–717)
The Terms of Peace
7. What were the six general proposals of the Fourteen Points?
8. What problems did the peacemakers try to solve?

SECTION 5 (pp. 718–723)
Creating a "New" Europe
9. Why was President Wilson disappointed with the Treaty of Versailles?
10. How was the League of Nations organized?

Reviewing Themes
1. **Government** What role did propaganda play in World War I?
2. **Global Relations** How did World War I affect relations between the world's great powers?
3. **Economy** How was industry affected by World War I?

Thinking Critically
1. **Analyzing Information** What role did economic conditions play in World War I?
2. **Making Predictions** What did the Armenian genocide indicate about human rights after World War I?
3. **Drawing Conclusions** How did the period from 1914 to 1918 mark the end of the old world and the beginning of a new world?
4. **Identifying Cause and Effect** What effect might the March 1917 revolution in Russia have had on the decision of the United States to join the war?

Writing About History
Summarizing World War I greatly affected the borders of many countries in and near Europe. Write a description of the changes for Germany, Russia, Austria-Hungary, Turkey (Ottoman Empire), and Poland. Refer to the maps in the chapter and use the following chart to organize your thoughts before you begin writing.

Countries that gained territory	Countries that lost territory	Countries that ceased to exist

CLOSE

Ask students to list and explain the general causes and effects of World War I. Then lead a class discussion on how these causes and effects changed the world.

RETEACH

Group students who had difficulty with the test into pairs. Ask them to create flash cards and then quiz each other on the chapter content. Then have students take the Form B Test to assess their mastery of the material.

ENGLISH LANGUAGE LEARNERS, COOPERATIVE LEARNING

Portfolio Extensions

Link to TODAY

1. Have students write a report on how the rise of militarism/fascism in Japan and the rise of communism in the Soviet Union were both among the effects of World War I and among the causes of World War II.

2. Assign groups of students to investigate a weapon that was introduced during World War I. Then have group members research how the weapon was created, by whom, and where and when the weapon was used in World War I.

3. Have students evaluate how the Russian Revolution differed from the French Revolution, including the long-term effects on political developments around the world.

Building Social Studies Skills

Analyzing Historical Statistics

Study the bar graph below. Then use the information to answer the questions that follow.

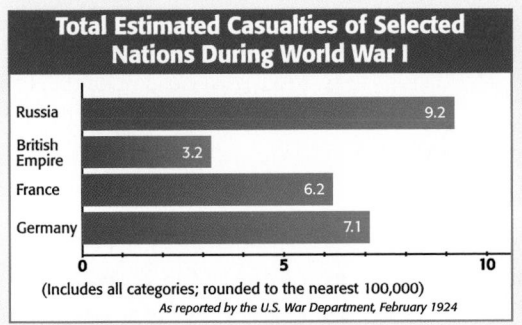

Total Estimated Casualties of Selected Nations During World War I

Russia — 9.2
British Empire — 3.2
France — 6.2
Germany — 7.1

(Includes all categories; rounded to the nearest 100,000)
As reported by the U.S. War Department, February 1924

1. Which of the following statements is most accurate?
   a. Total Russian casualties were more than three times the number of total British Empire casualties.
   b. France suffered 1 million more total casualties than did Germany.
   c. Russia suffered nearly as many total casualties as did France and the British Empire combined.
   d. Total German and Russian casualties were about equal.

2. Use the statistical information shown in the graph to write a paragraph about the war's impact on postwar recovery and development. Be sure to use correct grammar, spelling, punctuation, and writing style.

Evaluating Sources

Read the following advertisement. On May 1, 1915, the German government placed it in several American newspapers. On May 7, 1915 a German submarine sank the *Lusitania,* a British passenger liner. Then answer the questions.

> "NOTICE! Travellers intending to embark on the Atlantic voyage are reminded that a state of war exists between Germany and her allies and Great Britain and her allies; that the zone of war includes the waters adjacent to the British Isles; that, in accordance with formal notice given by the Imperial German Government, vessels flying the flag of Great Britain, or of any of her allies, are liable to destruction in those waters and that travellers sailing in the war zone on ships of Great Britain or her allies do so at their own risk."

3. Which of the following describes the type of evidence this advertisement provides?
   a. This is a secondary source of evidence.
   b. This is an unreliable source of evidence.
   c. This is a primary source of evidence.
   d. This is both a primary source and a secondary source of evidence.

4. The attack on the *Lusitania* killed 1,198 people, including 128 Americans. Do you think the U.S. had a basis for protesting the attack? Explain your reasoning.

Alternative Assessment

Building Your Portfolio

Link to TODAY

Government

The United States and Russia have often conflicted over ideological issues rooted in their respective revolutions. Write an evaluation of how the American Revolution differed from the Russian Revolution. Then create a compare-and-contrast chart that summarizes the ideas of both revolutions concerning separation of powers, liberty, equality, democracy, popular sovereignty, human rights, constitutionalism, and nationalism.

internet connect

go.hrw.com

Internet Activity: go.hrw.com
KEYWORD: SP3 WH27

Choose a topic on World War I and the Russian Revolution to:

• create a propaganda poster supporting the Allied Powers or the Central Powers.

• learn about social issues and events that were causes or effects of the war.

• understand the strengths and weaknesses of the Versailles treaty.

CHAPTER 28

The Great Depression and the Rise of Totalitarianism

CHAPTER RESOURCE MANAGER

Objectives	Pacing Guide	Reproducible Resources
SECTION 1 **The Postwar Era** (pp. 728–733) • Explain how scientific theories affected thinking in other areas of life. • Identify ways in which writers, musicians, painters, and architects experimented with new forms. • Describe how popular culture and consumerism affected societies.	**Regular** 1.5 day / **Block Scheduling** 1 day *Block Scheduling Handbook with Team Teaching Strategies, 28.1*	**RS** Guided Reading Strategy 28.1 **SM** Geography Activity 28: The Failure of World Revolution, 1917–1927
SECTION 2 **Postwar Prosperity Crumbles** (pp. 734–737) • Identify the weaknesses that appeared in the global economy during the postwar era. • Describe how nations initially responded to the Great Depression. • Explain how the New Deal marked a shift in the U.S. government's relationship with its citizens and the economy.	**Regular** 1.5 day / **Block Scheduling** 1 day *Block Scheduling Handbook with Team Teaching Strategies, 28.2*	**RS** Guided Reading Strategy 28.2 **PS** Readings in World History 97: Eleanor Roosevelt's Contribution to the New Deal **E** Hands-on History Activity 28: Facing Hard Times
SECTION 3 **Political Tensions After World War I** (pp. 738–742) • Describe the difficulties that France faced during the postwar years. • Explain how the British government dealt with its domestic problems. • Identify the problems that weakened eastern European governments.	**Regular** 1.5 day / **Block Scheduling** 1 day *Block Scheduling Handbook with Team Teaching Strategies, 28.3*	**RS** Guided Reading Strategy 28.3 **PS** Readings in World History 98: The Jarrow Crusade
SECTION 4 **Fascist Dictatorships in Italy and Germany** (pp. 743–748) • Describe how Benito Mussolini transformed Italy into a fascist state. • Explain why the Weimar Republic failed. • Trace how Adolf Hitler became an important figure in Germany. • Describe how the Nazis used power in Germany.	**Regular** 1.5 day / **Block Scheduling** 1 day *Block Scheduling Handbook with Team Teaching Strategies, 28.4*	**RS** Guided Reading Strategy 28.4 **RS** Graphic Organizer Activity 28: The Rise of Dictators **PS** Readings in World History 99: The Burning of the Books
SECTION 5 **Dictatorship in the Soviet Union** (pp. 749–753) • Identify the terms of the New Economic Policy. • Describe how Stalin shaped the Soviet economy. • Explain why Stalin imprisoned and executed millions of Soviet people.	**Regular** 1.5 day / **Block Scheduling** 1 day *Block Scheduling Handbook with Team Teaching Strategies, 28.5*	**RS** Guided Reading Strategy 28.5 **PS** Readings in World History 100: The Trial of Nikolai Bukharin **E** Creative Teaching Strategy 28: A News Magazine Looks Back

Chapter Resource Key

PS	Primary Sources	**A**	Assessment	Music	
RS	Reading Support	**REV**	Review	Video	
IC	Interdisciplinary Connections	**ELL**	Reinforcement and English Language Learners	Internet	
E	Enrichment		Transparencies	Holt Presentation Maker Using Microsoft® PowerPoint®	
SM	Skills Mastery		CD-ROM		

One-Stop Planner CD-ROM

See the *One-Stop Planner* for a complete list of additional resources for students and teachers.

One-Stop Planner CD-ROM

It's easy to plan lessons, select resources, and print out materials for your students when you use the *One-Stop Planner* CD–ROM with *Test Generator.*

Technology Resources	Reinforcement, Review, and Assessment
One-Stop Planner 28.1 Holt Researcher: World History: Pablo Picasso, Salvador Dali Homework Practice Online	Daily Quiz 28.1 Main Idea Activity 28.1 English Audio Summary 28.1 Spanish Audio Summary 28.1 REV Section 1 Review, p. 733
One-Stop Planner 28.2 CNN Presents World Cultures: Yesterday and Today Segment 27: The Great Depression World History Teaching Transparency: Geography and History 23: Major Currency Blocs, 1930s Homework Practice Online Online Maps, Charts, and Graphs: Unemployment in Europe, 1932	Daily Quiz 28.2 Main Idea Activity 28.2 English Audio Summary 28.2 Spanish Audio Summary 28.2 REV Section 2 Review, p. 737
One-Stop Planner 28.3 Homework Practice Online Online Maps, Charts, and Graphs: Irish Nationalism, 1916–1921	Daily Quiz 28.3 Main Idea Activity 28.3 English Audio Summary 28.3 Spanish Audio Summary 28.3 REV Section 3 Review, p. 742
One-Stop Planner 28.4 Holt Researcher: World History: Benito Mussolini, Adolf Hitler World History and Cultures Video Program 23: Germany Between the Wars World History Teaching Transparency: Art and History 23: Merz 19 Homework Practice Online Online Maps, Charts, and Graphs: European Democracies, 1925	Daily Quiz 28.4 Main Idea Activity 28.4 English Audio Summary 28.4 Spanish Audio Summary 28.4 REV Section 4 Review, p. 748
One-Stop Planner 28.5 World History Teaching Transparency: Regional and World Map 34: Russia and Northern Eurasia; Everyday Life 23: Nazi Promotional Materials for Sale Homework Practice Online Online Maps, Charts, and Graphs: European Democracies, 1933	Daily Quiz 28.5 Main Idea Activity 28.5 English Audio Summary 28.5 Spanish Audio Summary 28.5 REV Section 5 Review, p. 753

internet connect

HRW ONLINE RESOURCES
GO TO: go.hrw.com
Then type in a keyword.

TEACHER HOME PAGE
KEYWORD: SP3 Teacher

CHAPTER INTERNET ACTIVITIES
KEYWORD: SP3 WH28
Choose an activity to:
- create a pamphlet on the Spanish Civil War.
- create a graph and database on U.S. economic cycles.
- write journal entries from the point of view of a teenager living in the Great Depression.

CHAPTER ENRICHMENT LINKS
KEYWORD: SP3 CH28

ONLINE ASSESSMENT
Homework Practice
KEYWORD: SP3 HP28
Standardized Test Prep
KEYWORD: SP3 STP28
Rubrics
KEYWORD: SS Rubrics

ONLINE MAPS, CHARTS, AND GRAPHS
KEYWORD: SP3 MCG

CONTENT UPDATES
KEYWORD: SS Content Updates

HOLT PRESENTATION MAKER
KEYWORD: SP3 PPT28

ONLINE READING SUPPORT
KEYWORD: SS Strategies

CURRENT EVENTS
KEYWORD: S3 Current Events

Meeting Individual Needs

Ability Levels

Level 1   Basic level activities designed for all students encountering new material

Level 2   Intermediate level activities designed for average students

Level 3   Challenging activities designed for honors and gifted and talented students

English Language Learners   These activities address the needs of students with Limited English Proficiency.

Chapter Review and Assessment

- IC   Vocabulary Activity 28
- Global Skill Builder CD–ROM
- HRW Web Site
- REV   Chapter 28 Tutorial for Students, Parents, Mentors, and Peers
- REV   Chapter 28 Review, pp. 754–755
- A   Chapter 28 Test Generator (on the One–Stop Planner)
- A   Chapter 28 Test (Form A or B)
- A   Alternative Assessment Handbook
- A   Chapter 28 Test for English Language Learners and Special-Needs Students

CHAPTER 28

Section 1   *The Postwar Era*

Section 2   *Postwar Prosperity Crumbles*

Section 3   *Political Tensions After World War I*

Section 4   *Fascist Dictatorships in Italy and Germany*

Section 5   *Dictatorship in the Soviet Union*

CHAPTER 28

1919–1936

The Great Depression and the Rise of Totalitarianism

Striking dockworkers in Great Britain, c. mid-1920s

1920
Daily Life
The first commercial radio broadcasting station goes on the air in the United States.

1922
Politics
Benito Mussolini heads a coalition government in Italy.

1924
Politics
Lenin's death leads to a political struggle for leadership in the Soviet Union.

1926
Business and Finance
A general strike brings Great Britain to a halt, May 3–12.

1919

1924

1919
Science and Technology
The influenza pandemic responsible for more than 20 million deaths finally begins to subside.

1921
Business and Finance
Vladimir Lenin announces the New Economic Policy, which allows for some free enterprise in communist Russia.

1922
The Arts
T. S. Eliot publishes the poem *The Waste Land.*

1923
Business and Finance
Germany informs the Allies that it cannot make war reparations payments on schedule.

1923
Global Events
France and Belgium occupy the Ruhr Valley in Germany.

1925
The Arts
Czech writer Franz Kafka's novel *The Trial* is published.

1925
Science and Technology
German chemists discover the element rhenium.

1927
Daily Life
Charles Lindbergh becomes a worldwide celebrity after completing a solo flight across the Atlantic Ocean.

T. S. Eliot's **The Waste Land**

Charles Lindbergh's airplane **Spirit of St. Louis**

Build on What You Know

World War I destroyed lives, property, and national identities on a scale never before experienced. The Treaty of Versailles forced defeated European countries to pay enormous reparations to the victors and limited their freedom to rebuild. This drained their resources, destabilized their governments, and affected their sense of national pride. New governments created under the treaty were particularly fragile. In this chapter, you will learn how the war's aftermath led to anxiety, conflict, and, in some parts of Europe, the rise of totalitarian governments.

What's Your Opinion?

 To help students create their Themes Journal entries, provide the following examples of appropriate **agree/disagree** *statements.*

Global Relations

Agree A treaty is like a promise. Nations have a moral and ethical duty to uphold treaties.

Disagree Nations should be free to break treaties when it is in their best interest.

Government

Agree As long as a democracy is strong, no dictator can assume control.

Disagree Democratic practices may be overcome by a dictator with cunning and a strong military.

Culture

Agree Changes in culture are based on other factors, such as economics and politics.

Disagree Advances in science and technology change the way we live and think and thus affect culture.

The Persistence of Memory by Salvador Dalí

1929
Global Events
The Great Depression begins.

1929
The Arts
Ernest Hemingway's novel *A Farewell to Arms,* expressing postwar disillusionment, is published.

1931
The Arts
Salvador Dalí's painting *The Persistence of Memory* illustrates the surrealistic style.

1933
Business and Finance
A world economic conference held in London fails to solve the Great Depression.

1933
Politics
Adolf Hitler becomes chancellor of Germany.

1935
Global Events
Italian forces invade the African nation of Abyssinia (Ethiopia).

1936
Global Events
Germany occupies the Rhineland.

1936
Politics
Léon Blum becomes premier of France.

1936
The Arts
Charlie Chaplin's motion picture *Modern Times,* a satire on industrialization, is released.

1929

1934

1930
Science and Technology
U.S. astronomer Clyde Tombaugh discovers the planet Pluto.

1933
Daily Life
The Eighteenth Amendment, which bans the sale of alcoholic beverages in the United States, is repealed.

1935
Science and Technology
A British inventor develops a wearable hearing aid.

1936
Daily Life
African American Jesse Owens wins four gold medals in the Olympics in Berlin.

A relief line in New York City during the Great Depression

Jesse Owens in the 1936 Olympics

What's Your Opinion?

 Do you **agree** *or* **disagree** *with the following statements? Support your point of view in your journal.*

Global Relations Nations should always defend international treaties.

Government Democratic practices can always be relied on to prevent dictators from coming to power.

Culture Scientific and technological advances do not affect culture.

OBJECTIVES

1 **Explain how scientific theories affected thinking in other areas of life.**

2 **Identify ways in which writers, musicians, painters, and architects experimented with new forms.**

3 **Describe how popular culture and consumerism affected societies.**

LET'S GET STARTED!

As students enter the classroom, ask them to write a list of ways recent wars or international conflicts have influenced life in the United States (*terrorism, effects on trade and travel, families in the military*) Have volunteers share their responses with the class. Tell students that in Section 1 they will learn how World War I changed society in Europe and the United States.

SECTION 1

READ TO DISCOVER

❶ How did scientific theories affect thinking in other areas of life?

❷ How did writers, musicians, painters, and architects experiment with new forms?

❸ How did popular culture and consumerism affect societies?

DEFINE

influenza pandemic
surrealism
jazz
cubism
dadaists
functionalism
international style
flappers
prohibition

IDENTIFY

Gertrude Stein
Lost Generation
Franz Kafka
James Joyce
T. S. Eliot
Igor Stravinsky
Pablo Picasso
Salvador Dali
Ch'i Pai-shih
Louis Sullivan
Frank Lloyd Wright

▸ WHY IT MATTERS TODAY

Motion pictures remain important to popular culture in the world today. Use CNN_{student}news.com or other **current event** sources to learn more about the types of films that are popular with audiences today. Record your findings in your journal.

CNN student News.com

The Postwar Era

The Main Idea
The work of artists, musicians, and writers in the postwar era reflected global anxieties.

The Story Continues *World War I profoundly disrupted European and American society. The mass destruction caused by the war changed ideas about nations and people. Many people felt a sense of anxiety and concern for the future. New scientific discoveries added to the concern. A journalist writing in 1938 noted that, "Marx, Freud, [and] Einstein all conveyed the same message to the 1920s: the world was not what it seemed. The senses [that] shaped our ideas of time and distance, right and wrong, law and justice, and the nature of man's behaviour in society, were not to be trusted."*

The Effects of Scientific Events and Ideas

In the wake of World War I, with its mass destruction and wholesale slaughter, many people lost faith in the Enlightenment ideal of ongoing human progress. They felt a sense of disconnection and doubt about the future. New events and ideas in science raised even stronger doubts about the predictable nature of the world.

A global epidemic. Although the death and destruction of World War I was difficult for many people to accept, at least they understood what had caused most battlefield deaths. In the midst of the fighting, however, the world was hit by a mysterious illness that caused more deaths than the war itself and showed how little doctors still understood about disease.

In the spring of 1918 many soldiers fighting in France began to complain of flu-like symptoms. The disease spread, but few patients died from it. Then, in the summer and fall of 1918, a second, more deadly wave of this flu appeared and quickly became global in nature. In all, three waves of the **influenza pandemic** hit the world between 1918 and 1919. A pandemic is an epidemic that occurs over a large geographic area and affects a significant portion of the population. The disease spread with terrifying speed, in part because of the rapid movement of people during the global war. At the time, many doctors referred to it as the "Spanish influenza" because news of the deadly disease spread quickly throughout Spain, where wartime censorship was limited.

No inhabited continent was safe from this flu, which quickly spread into the civilian population. It could kill some victims within two or three days of the first sign of symptoms. Doctors still knew relatively little about how such illnesses developed and spread. They were unable to overcome the deadly disease. Then, just as mysteriously as it had appeared, this strain of influenza disappeared, and the pandemic stopped. It is uncertain exactly how many people died from the influenza pandemic, but most estimates put the death toll well above 20 million.

Scientific and social theories. Events like the influenza pandemic increased many people's feelings that the world was a frightening and unpredictable place. Some looked to the ideas of Sigmund Freud, founder of the modern field of psychology, to ease some of this uncertainty. Freud's claim that the unconscious—not the rational mind—often controlled people's actions seemed to explain many confusing and irrational events in life.

TEACH OBJECTIVE 1

LEVEL 1: Ask students what new developments in science occurred during the 1920s and how they affected people's understanding of their world. *(Freud, the founder of psychology, claimed unconscious motives explained irrational events, such as World War I devastation. Einstein's theory of relativity claimed that motion, space, and time are relative.)* Have students discuss Freud's theories and then write two or three paragraphs expressing their thoughts about Freudian psychology. **ENGLISH LANGUAGE LEARNERS, COOPERATIVE LEARNING**

TEACH OBJECTIVE 2

ALL LEVELS: Read aloud brief selections from Charles Dickens and Mark Twain. Ask students to describe these writings. Then read brief selections from James Joyce and Franz Kafka and ask students how they differ from the earlier literature. *(do not portray objective reality, depend on subjective interpretation)* Tell students that much of the art, architecture, music, and literature after World War I had these qualities. **ENGLISH LANGUAGE LEARNERS, COOPERATIVE LEARNING**

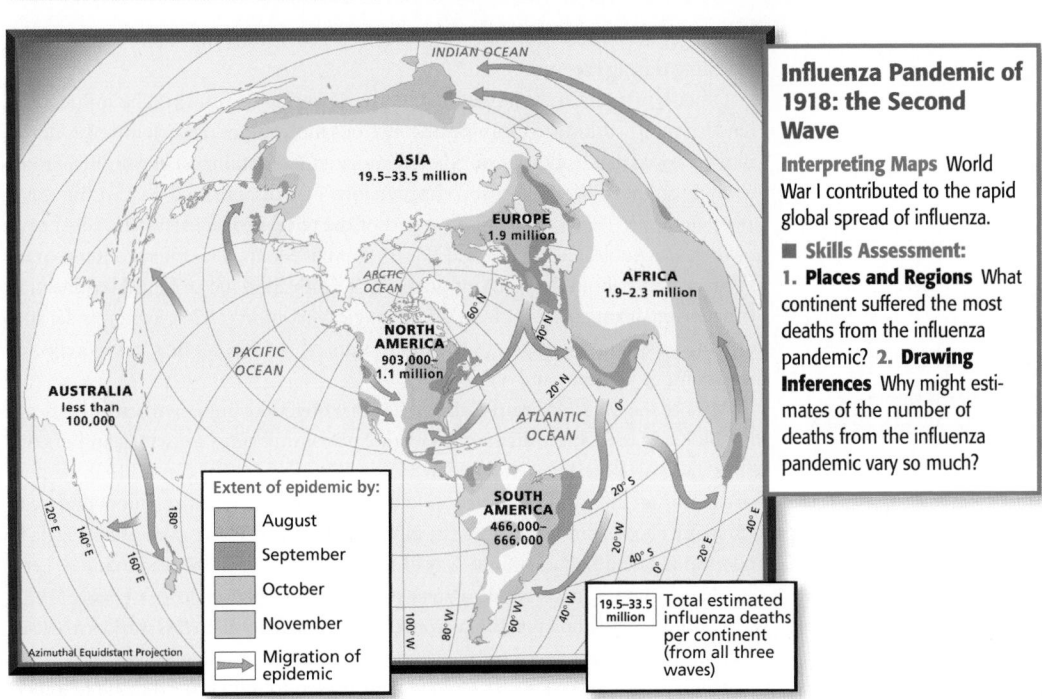

Influenza Pandemic of 1918: the Second Wave

Interpreting Maps World War I contributed to the rapid global spread of influenza.

■ **Skills Assessment:**

1. **Places and Regions** What continent suffered the most deaths from the influenza pandemic? 2. **Drawing Inferences** Why might estimates of the number of deaths from the influenza pandemic vary so much?

Some people used Freud's ideas to understand the dreadful destruction of World War I and the continued uneasiness that confronted people around the world.

Other people looked to scientific theories to support their disillusion with the attitudes that some felt had led to war. People who believed that social standards of morality or artistic taste were not absolute pointed to Albert Einstein's argument that even such definite concepts as motion, space, and time were relative. These people argued that values differ greatly in different societies. No one could say that one set of principles was good for all groups. This idea became known as moral relativism.

✔ **READING CHECK: Identifying Cause and Effect** How did scientific events and ideas shape views in the postwar era? raised doubts about the predictable nature of the world

New Directions in Literature

The major writings of World War I and the postwar years show dissatisfaction with traditional ideas. Some writers tried to offer a new vision. German historian and philosopher Oswald Spengler expressed one mood of the era in his *Decline of the West.* Spengler argued that civilizations pass from youth to maturity to old age and then to death. Spengler claimed that European civilization would disintegrate. His view matched the sense of disillusionment of the era.

One group of Americans who expressed such disillusionment included several writers who continued to live in Europe after the war. American **Gertrude Stein** hosted many of these authors in her Paris home. "All of you young people who served in the war, you are all a lost generation," she once said. After that, this group, which included Ernest Hemingway, F. Scott Fitzgerald, and John Dos Passos, became known as the **Lost Generation.** Their novels, such as Hemingway's *The Sun Also Rises*

The "Lost Generation" of American writers included such literary giants as Ernest Hemingway (top) and F. Scott Fitzgerald (bottom).

Culture

The slang of a period in history can reveal much about the popular culture of the time. In the 1920s and 1930s in the U.S., "the cat's meow" described something wonderful, "glad rags" were a person's fancy clothes, and "in a pig's eye" was a sarcastic way of saying something will never happen. The many terms for women included "doll," "dame," "babe," "broad," "dish," and "skirt."

Critical Thinking

What might the words used to refer to women indicate about women's position in American society in the 1920s and 1930s?

ANSWER: Students may suggest that women were subordinate to men and treated as objects.

That's Interesting!

The original Model T Ford was released in 1908 and sold for $850. Like most new technologies, however, the price dropped precipitously; a 1927 Model T sold for a mere $290.

MAP ANSWERS

1. Asia

2. perhaps the movement of people during the global war, poor reporting of information, illnesses not recognized as influenza at the time

TEACH OBJECTIVE 2

LEVEL 2: Show students a Renaissance painting and one from the baroque or rococo period. Ask students to describe what they see. Now show them paintings by Picasso, Kandinsky, and Dali. Again ask students to describe what they see. Ask how modern art was different from earlier art. Help them understand that the move away from straightforward representation in the arts was similar to changes in literature about the same time.
COOPERATIVE LEARNING

HOMEWORK Ask students to write one to three paragraphs telling why they think postwar artists seemed so willing to part with past traditions.

🖬 internet connect

TOPIC: U.S. Economy
GO TO: go.hrw.com
KEYWORD: SP3 WH28

Through the HRW Go site, have interested students access sites on the Internet that have information about economic cycles in the United States. Have them use the data they collect to make a graph plotting the rises and falls of the U.S. economy from the end of World War I to the present. Students may wish to use the Holt Grapher to complete their graphs. On their completed graphs, have students highlight the highs and lows, including the 1920s, the Great Depression of the 1930s, and the postwar prosperity of the 1950s. Tell them to write a few paragraphs about what they have learned. What factors contributed to extreme highs and lows? Where is the economy now in comparison to where it has been in the past 20 or 30 years?

CONNECTING TO SCIENCE AND TECHNOLOGY ANSWER

Radios were inexpensive, so most households had one. People could listen to music and other types of entertainment.

CONNECTING TO
Science and Technology

The Development of Radio

Up to the end of World War I, radio technology had been used mainly to send Morse code. In 1920 the Radio Corporation of America (RCA) began manufacturing "radio music boxes." These inexpensive radios were easily affordable for most families. Almost overnight, the radio became a popular consumer item in industrialized nations. In the United Kingdom, radio ownership soared, with a radio in three of every four households by the late 1930s.

Understanding Science and Technology

How did the radio affect the culture of industrialized countries?

An early radio system

---

and Fitzgerald's *The Great Gatsby*, reflected a generation that had lost its moral grounding during the war.

Other writers reflected a new era by experimenting with form. The influence of Freud led many authors to examine unconscious motivations. French novelist Marcel Proust believed that reality is a world of memory and sensation lost in daily life. Proust vividly brought to life the sensory impressions of a disappeared past in the novel *Remembrance of Things Past*. This first part of the novel appeared in 1913. Most of it, however, was published after World War I. Thomas Mann, a German contemporary of Proust, wrote about the constant presence of death amid life and the disconnection of the writer from society. Mann's *The Magic Mountain* (1924), which is set in a hospital, deals symbolically with the moral state of Europe. Mann's novels reflected the era's mood of decay and sadness.

Most of the works of **Franz Kafka,** a Czech writer, were unknown before his death in 1924. Kafka used **surrealism** in his work. Surrealism brings conscious and unconscious ideas together to portray life in a dreamlike way. In *The Castle* (1926), a man searches for an authority in a castle. He travels through endless corridors and deals with many people, but never finds the authority he seeks. These stories of struggle to find meaning, and Kafka's unique way of telling them, later influenced many writers.

Ireland's **James Joyce** caused a great stir during this period. Joyce's *Ulysses* (1922) was a revolutionary book that broke from the traditional novel. In this work, Joyce used a technique called "stream of consciousness." This technique attempts to record everything that comes into a character's mind. Many readers found *Ulysses* difficult to understand. It lacks normal punctuation and the story seems to skip about. Joyce's experimentation with language and form was characteristic of post-World War I artists.

Similarly, many poets of this period abandoned traditional forms such as rhyming lines. Instead they wrote poetry without rhyme that had lines of varying lengths. They also experimented with punctuation and even with the physical appearance of their poems. American-born poet **T. S. Eliot** expressed the negative outlook of the postwar years. In his long poem *The Waste Land* (1922), Eliot described a world without faith, where moral and spiritual values could not be restored.

✔ **READING CHECK: Summarizing** How did the work of leading writers reflect changes in society during the postwar era? dissatisfaction with traditional ideas, disillusionment

New Directions in Music, Painting, and Architecture

Musicians and painters of this period, like novelists and poets, experimented with creative new forms and styles. Some new artistic ideas were developed before World War I. These ideas, however, did not take hold until the unsettled postwar years.

Music. One of the pioneers of a new direction in music was Russian-born composer **Igor Stravinsky.** His ballet *The Rite of Spring* (1913) caused a major uproar at its first performance. It broke completely with traditional musical composition. This musical piece featured different instruments playing in different keys at the same time. Many people found the sound disturbing. The Austrian Arnold Schoenberg and his students were more revolutionary than Stravinsky. Schoenberg abandoned the usual eight-tone musical scale, using instead a twelve-tone scale. In addition, Schoenberg and his followers avoided traditional forms such as the large symphony. They wrote pieces for unusual groups of instruments, such as *Quartet for Violin, Clarinet, Tenor Saxophone, and Piano*.

TEACH OBJECTIVES 1 and 2

LEVEL 3: Copy this graphic organizer onto the chalkboard, omitting the italicized answers. Have each student complete the chart.

Science and Art in the Postwar Era	
Cause	**Effect**
Freudian psychology	*helped people understand the devastation of World War I*
surrealism	*combined conscious and unconscious to portray life in a dreamlike way*
functionalism	*buildings designed for particular use instead of following style*

Technology influenced music during this time. In industrialized countries a growing number of households had radios in the 1920s and 1930s. Music aimed at a mass audience filled the airwaves. This medium helped give rise to the popularity of new music such as **jazz.** This form of music originated among the African American community in New Orleans. It fused styles from West Africa and Latin America with sounds from African American folk music and some European styles. The lively music soon swept the United States and Europe, giving rise to numerous "jazz clubs." Jazz performers like Louis Armstrong, Billie Holiday, and "Jelly Roll" Morton became famous throughout the world.

Painting. Like writers and musicians, painters also experimented with forms and styles. Two artists working in Paris, **Pablo Picasso** and Georges Braque, created a new style called **cubism.** This style, which was influenced by traditional African art, emphasized geometric designs, using shapes such as cubes, flat planes, and spheres. Cubist painters often showed objects from several different viewpoints at the same time. For example, a painting might show half a face in profile and half from the front.

Other artists moved beyond traditional forms in various ways. Surrealistic painters attempted to represent the unconscious. Their works featured objects that did not seem to relate to one another. The Spanish surrealist **Salvador Dali** painted *The Persistence of Memory* (1931). It is a dreamlike landscape that appears to consist of liquid clocks draped over a tree branch and the edge of a shelf. Other artists, such as Russian painter Wassily Kandinsky and Dutch painter Piet Mondrian, created purely abstract designs. One group of painters called the **dadaists** used random images to reflect what they considered the insanity of the war.

Some places like China witnessed a struggle between modern and more traditional artists. While some Chinese artists embraced new experimental forms, others, like **Ch'i Pai-shih,** praised traditional Chinese art. Ch'i Pai-shih was the last great painter of the older school of Chinese art.

Architecture. Advances such as the use of structural steel caused remarkable changes in architecture. American **Louis Sullivan** pioneered the new architecture. Sullivan helped develop the skyscraper. He also created a new style called **functionalism.** With functionalism, a building is designed for its specific use instead of in a particular style. **Frank Lloyd Wright,** a student of Sullivan, adopted many of Sullivan's ideas and added his own. Wright believed that buildings should fit into their environment. In the 1920s Wright completed the Imperial Hotel in Tokyo, Japan. Adapting the hotel to its location, he designed a way to "float" the building's foundation, rather than to anchor it in rock. Thus, the Imperial Hotel was one of the few large buildings in Tokyo to survive a major earthquake in 1923.

Holt Researcher

go.hrw.com
KEYWORD: Holt Researcher
FreeFind: Pablo Picasso
Salvador Dali
After reading more about Pablo Picasso and Salvador Dali on the Holt Researcher, create a comparison chart noting similarities and differences in their artistic styles, including universal themes in their art.

INTERPRETING THE VISUAL RECORD

Prairie house Between 1900 and 1910, Frank Lloyd Wright developed many prairie houses in the American Midwest. This image shows an example of the outside of Wright's prairie house design. *Why might the prairie house be considered an example of functionalism?*

TEACH OBJECTIVE 2

LEVEL 3: Organize students into groups of five. Tell them that each group will complete a multimedia presentation covering the literature, art, music, popular culture, and architecture of the 1920s. Suggest that each member of the group specialize in one topic. Have students use their textbooks, the library, computer software, and interviews of senior citizens, if possible. Encourage students to include audio and video clips, images of artwork and buildings, and other images of popular culture. **COOPERATIVE LEARNING**

TEACH OBJECTIVE 3

ALL LEVELS: Have students select some aspect of the popular culture of the 1920s and 1930s to study in more depth. They might investigate the rise of the motion picture industry, sports, popular music, the Temperance Movement, radio entertainment, and so on. Ask each student to find out something interesting about their chosen topic and share it with the class in a three- to five-minute presentation. **ENGLISH LANGUAGE LEARNERS, COOPERATIVE LEARNING**

That's Interesting!

Increasingly popular dances like the Charleston and the Shimmy in the 1920s and 1930s led one critic to say, "The outstanding objection to the modern dance is that it is immodest and lacking in grace. It is based on a craving for abnormal excitement....The dance in its process of degradation has passed from slight impropriety to indecency, and now threatens to become brazenly shameless."

CONNECTING TO ART ANSWER

Chaplin is aware of the danger of being caught in the spinning gears. At the same time, he retains his humanity by making light of the situation.

CONNECTING TO Art

Film: *Modern Times*

Mechanization probably made some people uneasy. The comedian Charlie Chaplin viewed mechanization as a development that dehumanized people and their world. Chaplin used the motion picture to portray both loneliness and humor in life. One of his most famous films was *Modern Times*, released in 1936. The movie shows Chaplin at work in a huge factory. In pursuit of one bolt, Chaplin knocks other workers over, upsets the entire factory routine, and ends up as a captive of the machinery.

Understanding the Arts

What does this image from the film *Modern Times* reveal about Chaplin's attitude toward mechanization?

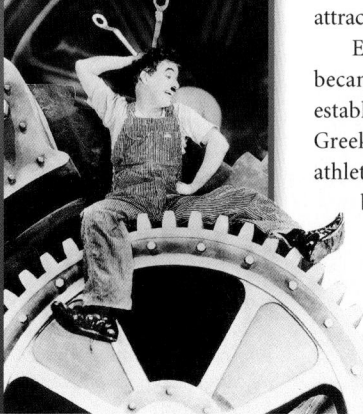

European architects, influenced by Sullivan and Wright, also developed a new style of architecture called the **international style.** This style included uninterrupted sheets of steel and glass. German architect Walter Gropius later described changes in architecture.

History Makers Speak
❝The great technical inventions and social developments of the last hundred years set off a stream of changes in our way of living and producing. . . . [T]here has been a steady movement toward a less rigid . . . style of living and building. The skeleton structures enabled us to introduce large window openings and the marvel of glass curtain walls . . . which transformed the rigid compartmental character of buildings into a transparent fluid one.❞

Walter Gropius, from *Four Great Makers of Modern Architecture*

✔ **READING CHECK: Finding the Main Idea** How did architecture change after the war?
use of structural steel; functional style

Popular Culture and Consumerism

The era of the 1920s was marked by the rise of leisure activities and purchases of consumer goods in industrialized nations. Shorter workdays and slowly improving economies gave people more money and free time. After years of war, many were ready to enjoy life. Feats like Charles Lindbergh's first solo flight across the Atlantic in 1927 seemed to many to signal a new era of progress.

Entertainment. The chief entertainment for popular audiences of the 1920s and 1930s was the motion picture. Developed in about 1900, motion pictures were first shown publicly about 10 years later. By the 1920s millions of moviegoers regularly flocked to theaters to see their favorite films. By the late 1930s, for example, 40 percent of British adults said they went to the movies once a week. Some 25 percent said they went twice a week. While some films reflected the darker feelings of the postwar years, most movies offered viewers escape and entertainment. Slapstick comedies were among the most popular films of the era. The 1927 film *The Jazz Singer* further revolutionized film by introducing sound.

Playing and watching sports became very popular throughout the world. Baseball was popular in the United States and Japan. Golf was widely played and followed in both countries, as well as in parts of Europe. Tennis was another popular sport, attracting players and spectators throughout the United States and Europe.

Europe and Latin America enjoyed soccer, also called football. The game became so popular internationally that the World Cup soccer tournament was established in 1930. The modern Olympics also grew in popularity. The ancient Greek athletic contest was revived in 1896 and held every four years. Amateur athletes from around the world competed in the games. Many Olympic athletes became instant heroes in their home countries. Countries around the world vied for the privilege of hosting the games, which brought revenue and great prestige to the sponsoring nation.

Consumer culture. The decade of the 1920s brought enormous changes to people's lifestyles. As economies improved, more people began to purchase consumer goods. The price of many goods once considered luxury items, like automobiles, dropped significantly.

As more people purchased such items, the whole structure of society began to change. One woman described how owning a car had affected her family.

 History Makers Speak ❝We'd rather do without clothes than give up the car. We used to go to [my husband's] sister's to visit, but by the time we'd get the children shoed and dressed there wasn't any money left for carfare. Now no matter how they look, we just poke 'em in the car and take 'em along.❞

from *Middletown: A Study in Modern American Culture,* by Robert S. Lynd and Helen Merrell Lynd

Companies came up with new techniques to get consumers to buy more goods. Radio advertising brought commercials right into people's homes. Companies also began offering to sell more goods on credit. Buying on credit allowed people to instantly purchase goods they wanted instead of saving up for them, as they had in the past.

The expanded use of credit reflected a gradual change in attitudes and values of the times. Increasingly people were focused on the present moment instead of planning for the future. At the same time, the questioning of traditional values was bringing other changes. Increasingly the younger generation began to challenge "proper" societal norms. For example, in industrialized nations many women started wearing short hair and skirts and going out to public places like jazz clubs. These young women were nicknamed "**flappers.**" Women were also asserting their independence by voting and joining the work force in greater numbers than ever before.

Some younger people rebelled against the older generation's efforts to curb their behavior. In the United States, the Eighteenth Amendment of the Constitution established **prohibition,** making alcoholic beverages illegal, in 1920. Many people ignored prohibition, however, and it proved too difficult to enforce. The amendment was repealed in 1933.

✔ **READING CHECK: Drawing Conclusions** How did popular culture and consumerism in industrialized nations reflect a shift in values? more leisure time, desire for luxury items

---

Analyzing Primary Sources

Identifying Cause and Effect
According to this woman, how did owning an automobile change the social life of her family? made it less formal

A stylishly dressed woman of the flapper era

SECTION 1 REVIEW

1. **Define** and explain the significance:
   influenza pandemic
   surrealism
   jazz
   cubism
   dadaists
   functionalism
   international style
   flappers
   prohibition

2. **Identify** and explain the significance:
   Gertrude Stein
   Lost Generation
   Franz Kafka
   James Joyce
   T. S. Eliot
   Igor Stravinsky
   Pablo Picasso
   Salvador Dali
   Ch'i Pai-shih
   Louis Sullivan
   Frank Lloyd Wright

3. **Categorizing** Copy the web diagram below. Use it to explain how each discipline reflected the anxieties and experimentation of the postwar years.

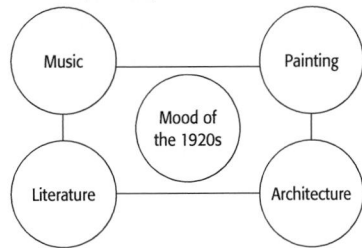

4. **Finding the Main Idea**
   a. How were popular culture and architecture affected by new technology following the end of the war?
   b. How did people's social behavior reflect a change in values in many societies?

5. **Writing and Critical Thinking**
   Analyzing Information Write an essay that explains how science and art reflected the uncertainty of the postwar years.
   Consider:
   • the ideas of Freud and Einstein
   • the work of novelists such as Mann and Kafka
   • the music of Stravinsky and Schoenberg

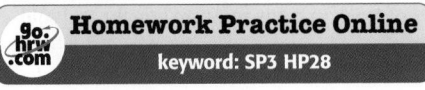
Homework Practice Online
keyword: SP3 HP28

OBJECTIVES

1 **Identify the weaknesses that appeared in the global economy during the postwar era.**

2 **Describe how nations initially responded to the Great Depression.**

3 **Explain how the New Deal marked a shift in the U.S. government's relationship with its citizens and the economy.**

🎵 LET'S GET STARTED!

As students enter the classroom, ask them to use their own words to define an economic depression. Ask them if there has been a depression during their lifetime. Encourage them to consider ways a serious depression might affect their lives. List responses on the chalkboard as you discuss them. Tell students that in Section 2 they will learn what a depression is and how the Great Depression affected the lives of people all over the world.

SECTION 2 RESOURCES

REPRODUCIBLE RESOURCES

▶ Guided Reading Strategy 28.2

▶ Readings in World History 97: Eleanor Roosevelt's Contribution to the New Deal

▶ Hands-on History Activity 28: Facing Hard Times

TECHNOLOGY RESOURCES

▶ One-Stop Planner 28.2

▶ CNN Presents World Cultures: Yesterday and Today Segment 27: The Great Depression

▶ World History Teaching Transparency: Geography and History 23: Major Currency Blocs, 1930s

▶ Homework Practice Online

REINFORCEMENT, REVIEW, AND ASSESSMENT

▶ Section 2 Review, p. 737

▶ Daily Quiz 28.2

▶ Main Idea Activity 28.2

▶ English Audio Summary 28.2

▶ Spanish Audio Summary 28.2

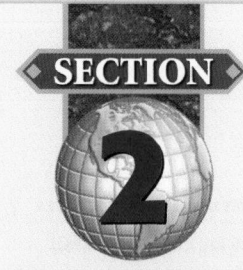

SECTION 2

READ TO DISCOVER

❶ What weaknesses appeared in the global economy during the postwar era?

❷ How did nations initially respond to the Great Depression?

❸ How did the New Deal mark a shift in the U.S. government's relationship with its citizens and the economy?

DEFINE

economic nationalism
market speculations

IDENTIFY

Black Tuesday
Great Depression
Herbert Hoover
Franklin D. Roosevelt
New Deal
Social Security Act

WHY IT MATTERS TODAY

The stock market remains an important indicator of economic well-being. Use CNN or other **current event** sources to learn more about the stock market today. Record your findings in your journal.

Postwar Prosperity Crumbles

The Main Idea
Nations responded to the global economic crisis of the 1930s by protecting their own economies.

The Story Continues *Postwar prosperity turned to worldwide economic depression by the end of the 1920s. Unemployment soared around the world. On the high plains of the United States, overcultivation and drought turned farmlands into one large Dust Bowl. In this excerpt from* The Grapes of Wrath, *author John Steinbeck describes dust bowl families as they abandon their homes. "In the little houses the tenant people sifted their belongings and the belongings of their fathers and of their grandfathers. . . . They piled up the goods in the yards and set fire to them. They stood and watched them burning, and then frantically they loaded up the cars and drove away, drove in the dust."*

Signs of Economic Troubles

Many nations never fully recovered from the economic effects of World War I. Others relied heavily on Western industrialized nations like the United States. Although Western industrialized nations generally prospered during the 1920s, some economic problems existed. As the decade of the 1920s continued, therefore, the global economy became increasingly vulnerable to disaster.

Farmers. Much of the prosperity of the 1920s was fueled by industry. Meanwhile, many farmers were suffering. Much European farmland had been destroyed during the war. During that time farmers in other areas, such as Africa, Australia, India, New Zealand, North America, and South America, increased food production to sell to Europe. American farmers took out loans to buy modern machinery and additional land. With the return of peace in 1918, the worldwide demand for certain crops like grain fell, and agricultural prices dropped. Farmers made very little money. Those who had borrowed money to expand now had problems paying their debts.

Protectionism. In the postwar world the economies of different countries were linked more closely together than at any time before. In this situation the promotion of **economic nationalism,** or protectionism, caused problems. This occurred when nations tried to protect domestic industries by limiting trade with others. To protect their industries from foreign competition, nations established tariffs on the import of goods. This policy usually failed. For example, high American tariffs made it hard for Europeans to sell their goods in the United States. Thus, they could not purchase goods from the United States or pay off their debts. American bankers and business leaders loaned money to Europeans to buy American goods. This practice, however, drove the Europeans further into debt.

Speculation and panic. During the 1920s millions of Americans engaged in **market speculations,** or risky investments, in the stock market. The stock market is an organization through which shares of stock in companies are bought and sold. A company issues shares of stock to raise money for its business. Investors who buy the stock are actually buying shares of the company. As long as investors hold the shares

TEACH OBJECTIVE 1

 LEVEL 1: Have each student fold a sheet of paper in half and write *Social Life in the United States After World War I* at the top. Have students write and define these words or phrases on the top half of the folded sheet: *economic boom, Roaring Twenties, Prohibition, economic nationalism,* and *market speculations.* Then, on the bottom half of the sheet, have students write sentences using these words or phrases to describe U.S. social life after World War I. **ENGLISH LANGUAGE LEARNERS**

TEACH OBJECTIVE 2

LEVEL 2: Have pairs of students choose one country and research how its government responded to the Great Depression. Select pairs to report to the class. **COOPERATIVE LEARNING**

 HOMEWORK Have students write three short articles about the stock market crash of 1929 from the perspectives of a world leader, a wealthy business owner, and a typical worker.

of stock, they can share in the company's earnings. They can also profit by selling the shares at prices above their original purchase cost if the company's stock increases in value.

During the 1920s stock prices soared. Many investors made large profits and believed that stock prices would continue to rise. This confidence led investors to borrow money to buy more stock. When the stock's value rose, the stock could be sold at a higher value. The investor could then repay the loan and still enjoy a profit. If the value of the stock fell, however, problems arose. By the late 1920s the stock prices of many companies had become wildly overvalued.

On October 29, 1929—**Black Tuesday**—investors on the New York Stock Exchange panicked in the face of bad economic news. Fearing a drop in stock prices that were artificially high, investors rushed to sell their shares. The sudden sell-off drove stock prices tumbling. Many stocks on the exchange became virtually worthless overnight. At the same time, many of the economy's underlying problems and weaknesses surfaced as investor confidence fell. Savers rushed to their banks to withdraw their savings, only to find that the banks had not maintained adequate cash reserves to honor mass withdrawals. Banks, in turn, demanded that borrowers repay their loans, but borrowers had no money. A major financial crunch resulted. In a very short time, thousands of banks and their customers—factories, farms, and individuals—were forced into bankruptcy.

✔ **READING CHECK: Finding the Main Idea** What economic weaknesses appeared in the global economy during the 1920s? drop in agriculture, protectionism, stock panic

The Great Depression

The collapse of the New York Stock Exchange marked the beginning of the worldwide **Great Depression.** Prices and wages fell, business activity slowed, and unemployment rose, all in a very brief period of time. By 1932 more than 30 million workers in countries throughout the industrialized world could not find jobs. Poverty during the depression, however, occurred in the midst of great productivity. Goods were available and their prices fell to very low levels, but people had no money to buy them. Some countries tried to force prices up by destroying farm surpluses. For example, Brazil burned excess coffee for years.

Most nations, including the United States, initially tried to protect themselves from the Great Depression through economic nationalism. In reality, however, this usually made economic recovery more difficult.

Great Britain tried to create jobs by granting low-interest loans to its industries. In 1931 the British government raised tariffs against foreign goods. Great Britain also formed a system of economic cooperation within its empire. France was less industrialized than Great Britain. This helped protect it from the effects of the Great Depression for a couple of years. French trade eventually declined, however, while unemployment rose and industrial production dropped sharply. The uncertainty of the depression years caused political instability in France. In 1933 alone there were three changes of government. Elsewhere in the world, the Great Depression caused unrest and violence. In Germany it helped destroy the Weimar Republic.

✔ **READING CHECK: Summarizing** How did some nations deal with the onset of the Great Depression? destroyed surpluses, tried economic nationalism

INTERPRETING THE VISUAL RECORD

The crash Crowds gather along Wall Street during the Stock Market crash. *What does this gathering reflect about the crash?*

TEACH OBJECTIVES 1 and 2

ALL LEVELS: Have students complete a flowchart showing how economic weaknesses led to the Great Depression.

ENGLISH LANGUAGE LEARNERS, COOPERATIVE LEARNING

TEACH OBJECTIVE 3

LEVEL 3: Have students use the library or computer software to make a chart identifying the main provisions of each of these New Deal programs: Civilian Conservation Corps (CCC), Federal Emergency Relief Administration (FEMA), Agricultural Adjustment Act of 1933, Tennessee Valley Authority (TVA), Federal Deposit Insurance Corporation (FDIC), Works Progress Administration (WPA), National Labor Relations Act (Wagner-Connery Act), Social Security Act.

CLOSE

Have students compare and contrast everyday life in the 1920s with that in the 1930s.

Economics

The stock market crash of 1929 set in motion a chain of events that led to the Great Depression. Investors panicked and sold their stocks. Savers rushed to banks to withdraw their savings only to find that banks did not have adequate cash reserves. Banks demanded that borrowers repay their loans, but the borrowers did not have the money. Soon the entire world economy was in crisis.

Critical Thinking

Organize a class debate about whether the Great Depression would have occurred if the stock market had not crashed in 1929.

ANSWER: Yes, because economic conditions were primed for a fall. No, because without the crash, people would not have panicked, sold their stocks, and tried to withdraw their savings from banks; the banks would not have been forced to close, and industries would have continued to produce goods.

MAP ANSWER
Norway, Denmark, Germany

The New Deal

The United States lagged behind most other industrialized nations in creating social programs to help its citizens in troubled times. Americans did not have publicly funded unemployment insurance or government relief programs that could help during periods of economic struggle. As a result, when the Great Depression began, American workers who lost their jobs had to rely on personal savings, if any, or on charity. People who could not afford to buy food stood in breadlines to receive a bowl of soup. Some people sold apples on street corners to earn money.

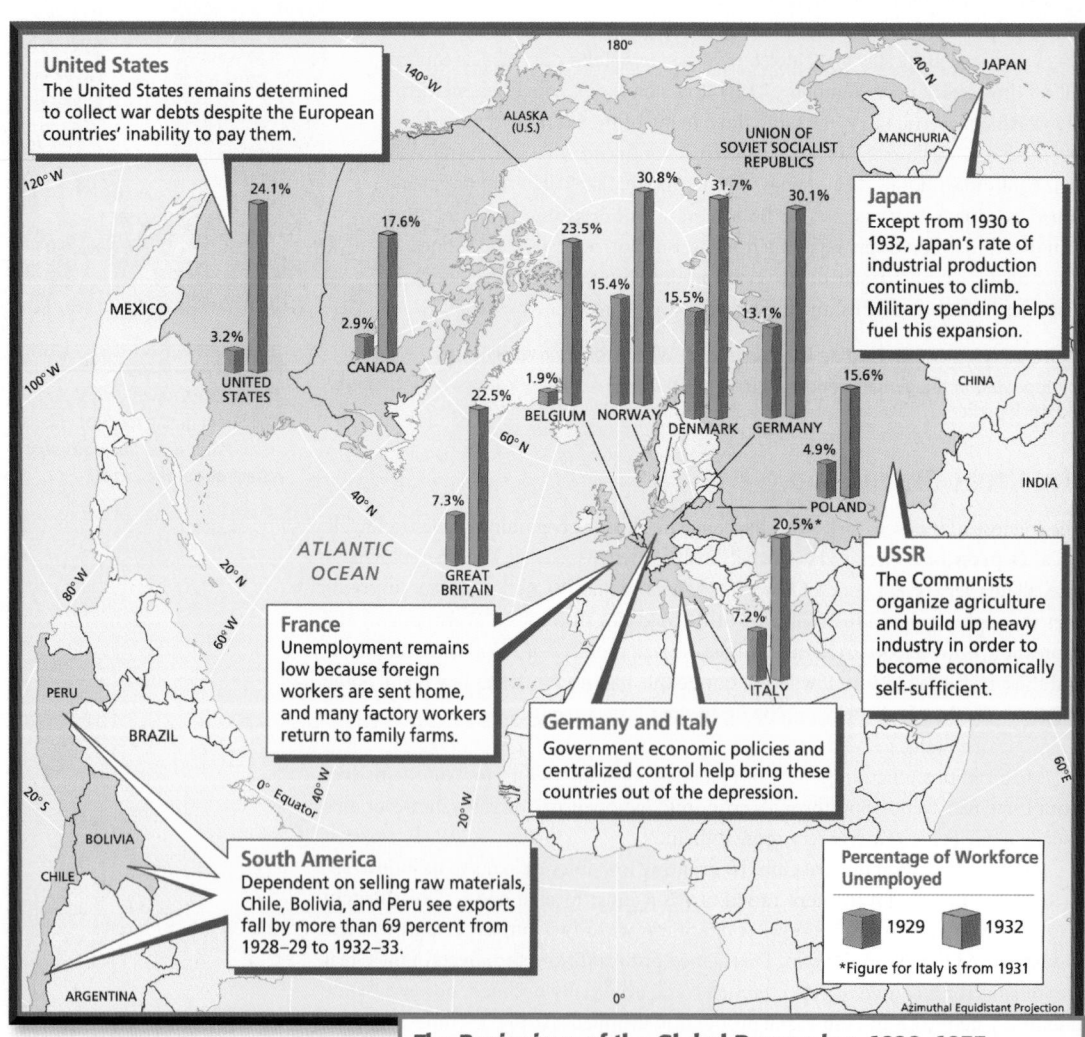

The Beginnings of the Global Depression, 1928–1933

Interpreting Maps The Great Depression created record levels of unemployment in most countries.

■ **Skills Assessment: Human Systems** Which countries had unemployment rates above 30 percent by 1932?

REVIEW

Have students complete the Section 2 Review on p. 737.

ASSESS

Have students complete Daily Quiz 28.2. As Alternative Assessment, have students make a flowchart like the chalkboard chart in this section's lessons.

RETEACH

Have students complete Main Idea Activity for English Language Learners and Special-Needs Students 28.2. Then ask students to

write three lists about the Great Depression: *causes, effects,* and *government responses.* **ENGLISH LANGUAGE LEARNERS**

EXTEND

▶ **internet** connect

Internet Activity: **go.hrw.com**
TOPIC: Great Depression **KEYWORD:** SP3 WH28
Search the Internet through the HRW Go site for information about the Great Depression. Then write a journal entry as if you were a teenager living at that time.

President **Herbert Hoover** was said to believe that prosperity was "just around the corner." Hoover tried to revive the American economy, but his efforts had little effect in the face of so massive an economic collapse. In 1932 the American people elected a new president, **Franklin D. Roosevelt.** The new president immediately created a program of relief and reform called the **New Deal.** The federal government granted money to each state to provide the needy with clothing, food, and shelter. To create jobs, the government began a program of public works. The program hired people to construct public buildings, roads, and other projects.

Congress followed Roosevelt's emergency relief program by reforming the economic system. Banks and stock exchanges were placed under stricter regulation. The **Social Security Act** of 1935 provided for unemployment and old-age benefits. Congress established a 40-hour workweek and minimum wages. It also guaranteed workers the right to form unions.

Under the New Deal, the United States became deeply involved in the welfare of its citizens. The New Deal did not, however, completely end the Great Depression in the United States. Government efforts to restore prosperity were not enough to solve the economic crisis.

✔ **READING CHECK:**
Problem Solving How did the New Deal mark a dramatic change in the U.S. government's approach to economic crisis? U.S. had not previously had extensive social programs

This migrant child rides in the backseat of the family car as his parents travel to look for work in 1939.

YOUNG PEOPLE IN HISTORY

Growing Up During the Depression
During the Great Depression, young people faced special problems. In some cases, parents expected children to work when the parents themselves could not.

Children were often a burden in poor families. For many youngsters, running away seemed the only solution. At one point, almost 250,000 teenaged "hoboes" were roaming the United States. Many of these young people searched for any kind of work or odd job that they could find. **What special concerns faced many young people during the Great Depression?**

YOUNG PEOPLE IN HISTORY ANSWER
needed to work to support families

◆SECTION◆
2 REVIEW ANSWERS

❶ **Define**
• economic nationalism, p. 734
• market speculations, p. 734

❷ **Identify**
• Black Tuesday, p. 735
• Great Depression, p. 735
• Herbert Hoover, p. 737
• Franklin D. Roosevelt, p. 737
• New Deal, p. 737
• Social Security Act, p. 737

❸ strained international relations, increased human suffering, led to drastic government reactions

❹ a. destruction of European farmland, decrease in demand for farm products, excessive buying on credit, protectionism, market speculation

b. helped many people but did not totally end the depression

❺ Journals should suggest that the New Deal was an attempt to ease American people's suffering.

SECTION 2 REVIEW

1. **Define** and explain the significance:
   economic nationalism
   market speculations

2. **Identify** and explain the significance:
   Black Tuesday
   Great Depression
   Herbert Hoover
   Franklin D. Roosevelt
   New Deal
   Social Security Act

3. **Identifying Cause and Effect**
   Copy the graph below. Use it to describe the effects of the Great Depression.

   International relations
   Human suffering
   Government reactions

4. **Finding the Main Idea**
   a. What weaknesses in the global economy led to the Great Depression?
   b. How effective was the New Deal in responding to the problems of the Great Depression?

5. **Writing and Critical Thinking**
   Drawing Inferences Imagine that you are a young American living during the Great Depression. Write a journal entry discussing President Roosevelt's approach to correcting the problems of the economy and explaining why Roosevelt called his package of legislation a "New Deal" for Americans.
   Consider:
   • the underlying problems that contributed to the Great Depression in America
   • the hardships that the depression caused
   • government efforts to assist Americans

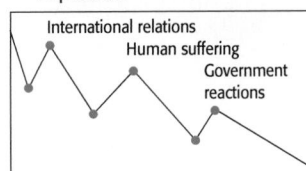
Homework Practice Online
keyword: SP3 HP28

OBJECTIVES

1 Describe the difficulties that France faced during the postwar years.

2 Explain how the British government dealt with its domestic problems.

3 Identify the problems that weakened eastern European governments.

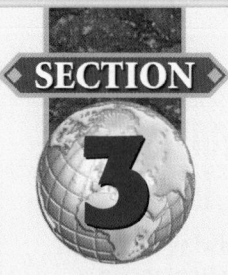

READ TO DISCOVER

❶ What difficulties did France face during the postwar years?

❷ How did the British government deal with its domestic problems?

❸ What problems weakened eastern European governments?

DEFINE

general strike
nationalization

IDENTIFY

Maginot Line
Locarno Pact
Popular Front
Léon Blum
Ramsay MacDonald
Easter Rising
Sinn Fein
Irish Republican Army

WHY IT MATTERS TODAY

Northern Ireland remains a region troubled by violence today. Use or other **current event** sources to learn about the conflict in Northern Ireland. Record your findings in your journal.

LET'S GET STARTED!

As students enter the classroom, ask them to list problems that usually follow a war. *(need to rebuild, pay war debts, return soldiers to civilian life, change wartime to peacetime economy)* Lead a discussion on how the nations of Europe could have solved these problems. Tell students that in Section 3 they will learn how the nations of Europe attempted to cope with these problems.

Political Tensions After World War I

The Main Idea
Western Europe weathered the crisis of the 1920s, but eastern Europe did not fare as well.

The Story Continues *At war's end, European lands and economies were in ruins. France was especially hard hit. One observer described the landscape of northern France: "For mile after mile nothing was left. No building was habitable and no field fit for the plow. . . . One devastated area was exactly like another—a heap of rubble, a morass [jumble] of shell-holes, and tangle of wire." The unparalleled destruction caused by World War I, and the need to rebuild in the face of rapidly changing political, social, and economic conditions, strained many European nations.*

France's Postwar Difficulties

France emerged from World War I victorious but weakened. During the four years of war, northern France had been a major battleground. At war's end, farmland and even entire cities lay in ruins. Trenches and shell holes scarred the land. The most modern parts of France's agriculture and industry had been destroyed. Most tragic of all, a large number of France's young men had died in the war.

The economy. France also faced severe economic problems. High prices hurt industrial workers and the lower middle class. At the same time, the expenses of the French government rose. After the war France owed money to its citizens and to the United States for war materials. The government had to pay the war debt and the interest on the debt. It also financed a rebuilding program for the war-damaged areas.

Military security was another major expense for the French. Twice in less than 50 years, Germany had invaded France. The French were determined to prevent another invasion from the east. France rebuilt its army and constructed a series of steel and concrete fortifications. This system, called the **Maginot** (MA·zhuh·noh) **Line,** stretched nearly 200 miles along the borders of Germany and Luxembourg. Construction of the Maginot Line was enormously costly, further weakening the French economy.

The Maginot Line was an enormously costly defense system that was ultimately useless. When World War II broke out, Germany invaded France from the vantage point shown here, north of the Maginot Line.

SECTION 3 RESOURCES

REPRODUCIBLE RESOURCES

▶ Guided Reading Strategy 28.3

▶ Readings in World History 98: The Jarrow Crusade

TECHNOLOGY RESOURCES

▶ One-Stop Planner 28.3

▶ Homework Practice Online

▶ Online Maps, Charts, and Graphs: Irish Nationalism, 1916–1921

REINFORCEMENT, REVIEW, AND ASSESSMENT

▶ Section 3 Review, p. 742

▶ Daily Quiz 28.3

▶ Main Ideas Activity 28.3

▶ English Audio Summary 28.3

▶ Spanish Audio Summary 28.3

ALL LEVELS: After students read about postwar France, have them list France's main problems while you record them on the chalkboard. (*land in ruins, technology destroyed, young men killed in war, inflation, war debt, cost of Maginot Line, political unrest*) Group students into pairs or triads to brainstorm ways French leaders might have tried to solve these problems. Have groups compare suggested solutions.
ENGLISH LANGUAGE LEARNERS, COOPERATIVE LEARNING

LEVEL 2: Draw a circle on the board and write *France: World War I* in the circle. Have students make a web diagram showing problems the war caused for postwar France. For example:

International affairs. The political situation in Europe improved during the mid-1920s. In 1925 Belgium, Czechoslovakia, France, Germany, Great Britain, Italy, and Poland met at a conference held at Locarno in Switzerland. Delegates to the conference signed a number of treaties that together became known as the **Locarno Pact.** Delegates pledged that their countries would peacefully settle all future disputes. They also guaranteed the existing boundaries between France and Germany.

France also signed mutual assistance treaties with Czechoslovakia and Poland. These defensive alliances soon weakened, however. In the mid-1930s, Belgium declared that it would be neutral in any war. Italy, a wartime ally with France, returned to its traditional opposition to France. The French formed a shaky alliance with Russia, now under a communist government. To encircle Germany, France also made alliances with Romania and Yugoslavia. Along with Czechoslovakia and Poland, these nations shared France's mistrust of Germany.

Political unrest. As the Great Depression began to affect France, many people lost confidence in the government. In early 1934 rioters in Paris called for an end to republican government. They favored a strong government headed by a dictator who would protect the nation. French trade unions responded to these right-wing demands by calling for a **general strike.** Workers in various industries refused to work until their demands were met. Left-wing parties in France then organized a government called the **Popular Front.** Its leader, the socialist **Léon Blum,** became premier of France in 1936.

To prevent the conservatives from seizing power by force, Blum's government carried out many reforms. The Popular Front first persuaded leaders of French industries to grant pay increases to end the strike. The government then established a 40-hour workweek and guaranteed workers the right to paid vacations. It also set up a system to negotiate labor disagreements. The Bank of France came under government control. The weapons industry underwent partial **nationalization,** meaning that it was placed under government control. Prices, however, continued to rise. Wage increases did little to help French workers. Divisions within the Popular Front also made governing difficult. Blum's government lasted only a year.

After the fall of the Popular Front, the new French government canceled many of the reforms that had helped labor. As a result, many workers came to oppose the government. Many new political and social groups developed, some of which followed extreme approaches. Although France remained a democracy, traditional French systems of government and society were questioned. Bitter divisions grew among the French people.

✔ **READING CHECK: Summarizing** What economic and political problems did France experience after World War I? depression, rising prices, strikes, extremist groups

Léon Blum's short-lived Popular Front government tried to cope with the effects of the Great Depression.

Citizenship

Many women in Europe had suspended movements for women's rights and suffrage to help with the war effort. After World War I these movements resurfaced as women demanded recognition for their wartime contributions. They gained voting rights in many countries, including Germany, Sweden, Spain, Austria, Poland, and Canada. Women gained a stronger legal position in Great Britain. Although many women stopped working outside the home after the war, a greater variety of job opportunities opened to them.

Critical Thinking

How did the war contribute to the success of movements for women's rights around the world?

ANSWER: During the war women had opportunities to show they could fill roles traditionally reserved for men.

That's Interesting!

In response to the Bolshevik Revolution in Russia, there were worker uprisings in most of the western European nations as well. Attempts at large-scale general strikes failed in Great Britain, France, Italy, and Germany.

LEVEL 1: After students read about postwar Great Britain, have them write letters to the editor of a fictional 1920s British newspaper expressing an opinion about an issue covered in their textbook, such as labor troubles or the Irish independence movement. Encourage students to peer-edit one another's letters before they submit their final drafts.

ENGLISH LANGUAGE LEARNERS, COOPERATIVE LEARNING

HOMEWORK Have students write an essay reviewing the major economic and political problems confronting Europe after World War I and discussing how each country in this section dealt with these situations.

Global Relations

Great Britain ruled Ireland for centuries, although Irish nationalists felt that they should be an independent nation. This conflict led to much violence and hostility over a long period of time. During the 1920s Irish nationalists made a serious attempt to win independence. Finally, Ireland was split in two, with Catholic southern Ireland becoming the Irish Free State and Protestant Northern Ireland remaining in the United Kingdom.

Critical Thinking

Ask students if they think Great Britain was right in refusing to grant independence to Ireland.

ANSWER: Answers will vary.

VISUAL RECORD ANSWER

loyalty of Irish people to Ireland rather than Britain or Germany

The Irish nationalist Padraic Pearse was executed by the British following the Easter Rising of 1916.

INTERPRETING THE VISUAL RECORD

Easter Rising A citizen army parades outside Liberty Hall during the Easter Rising of 1916. *What does the banner on Liberty Hall mean?*

Great Britain After World War I

Like France, Great Britain faced serious economic problems after World War I. The money it had used to finance industrial expansion was gone and the government had to borrow money. After the war Britain's outdated factories and machinery had trouble competing with newer American and Japanese technology. In addition, high tariffs due to economic nationalism damaged British trade.

Labor troubles. British workers suffered after the war. Disarmament left many factory workers without jobs. By 1921 nearly a quarter of Great Britain's work force was unemployed. The government provided unemployment benefits, but the high unemployment rate led to labor unrest. Labor unions tried to keep the high wages and employment rates of the war years. Industry leaders opposed these union demands.

Ramsay MacDonald, leader of the Labour Party, spoke out for the workers, but the Labour Party did not have a majority in the House of Commons. MacDonald formed a coalition government with the Liberal Party. A coalition government is made up of several parties that agree to work together. The government set a tight budget. It also protected British industry from foreign competitors and helped the construction industry. These measures helped the economy recover. They also helped Britain avoid the social unrest that toppled democratic governments elsewhere.

Ireland. In the 1920s Great Britain faced serious problems in Ireland, a country it had ruled for centuries. During the 1800s Irish nationalists demanded the right to rule themselves. By 1914 the demand for Irish independence was still not met, although the British government promised Ireland home rule once World War I was over. Many Irish nationalists, however, wanted complete independence from Great Britain. During the war Irish nationalists revolted in the **Easter Rising** on Easter Monday, April 24, 1916. The British ended the bloody revolt and executed many of its leaders.

TEACH OBJECTIVE 2

LEVEL 3: Tell students to imagine that they are members of Sinn Fein, fighting for Irish nationhood. Have them write speeches giving reasons why Ireland should be free from British rule, and exhorting others to join the cause. Some students may also wish to write speeches giving the opposing point of view.

TEACH OBJECTIVE 3

LEVEL 2: Have students review challenges facing Austria, Hungary, and Poland after World War I. *(Austria: weak economy, private armies; Hungary: succession of weak governments, new boundaries interrupted trade; Poland: political conflicts, high German tariffs)* Then have them create a series of three political cartoons about the postwar political situations in Austria, Hungary, and Poland. Encourage students to share their finished cartoons with the class.

Michael Collins, an Irish nationalist, explained the importance of the 1916 uprising. Collins noted that the execution of the Easter Rising's leaders fueled Irish nationalism.

❝It [the Easter Rising of 1916] appeared at the time of the surrender to have failed, but that valiant effort and the martyrdoms [killings] which followed it finally awoke the sleeping spirit of Ireland.**❞**

Michael Collins, from *The Path to Freedom*

In 1918 members of an Irish nationalist party called **Sinn Fein** (SHIN·FAYN) dominated the election for Irish seats in the British Parliament. Instead of taking their seats in Parliament, the Sinn Fein representatives declared themselves the representative government for an independent Irish republic. When Britain refused to recognize this new government, fighting broke out again. For several years Sinn Fein's military, the **Irish Republican Army** (IRA), battled British troops in a series of violent and bitter struggles. The British received little support from the Irish people.

Finally, with a full-scale war looming, British officials offered to compromise. A settlement was ratified in 1922, dividing Ireland in two. Catholic southern Ireland became the self-governing Irish Free State, with loose ties to Great Britain. Six northern counties with a Protestant majority remained in the United Kingdom. They were known as Northern Ireland. Many Irish nationalists refused to accept this arrangement, and civil war raged again. Just a few months after the settlement was finalized, Michael Collins, who had helped negotiate the agreement, was assassinated by nationalists who felt he had betrayed his people.

In the 1930s nationalist Eamon de Valera was elected prime minister of the Irish Free State. Under his leadership, the Free State began to break away from Great Britain. By 1949 the Irish Free State had become completely independent, calling itself the Republic of Ireland. For many nationalists, however, Ireland would only be free when both north and south were reunited.

✔ **READING CHECK: Finding the Main Idea** What kinds of domestic unrest affected Great Britain during and after the war? outdated industry, unemployment, revolt in Northern Ireland

Eastern Europe

As western European nations tried to recover from the war, new nations in eastern Europe built new governments. Instability and cultural tensions in eastern Europe had led to World War I. These problems had not disappeared with the end of the war. They reappeared in new political conflicts among nations that had little experience with democracy. In addition, these nations suffered severe economic problems. The breakup of the Austro-Hungarian and Russian Empires disrupted old trading patterns. Policies of economic nationalism further weakened eastern European economies. Several of the new governments formed in eastern and southeastern Europe after World War I angered the land-owning classes by breaking up some estates owned by the old aristocracy and redistributing the land to peasants. However, despite cultural, economic, and political problems, many of the new nations kept democratic governments.

Postwar Austria was a small, poor nation. Many Austrians wanted to unite with Germany, but peace treaties prohibited the union. Conflicts between socialists and conservatives weakened efforts to create a democracy. A third of Austria's population

---

Analyzing Primary Sources

Drawing Inferences Why would Michael Collins regard the failed Easter Rising as a victory for the Irish people? motivated and inspired people

Northern Ireland

The division of Ireland in 1922 did little to resolve tensions between pro-British Protestants and nationalist Catholics in Northern Ireland. Conflict grew in the late 1960s, when civil rights groups demanded voting reforms to eliminate discrimination against Catholics. Ongoing violence caused Great Britain to impose direct rule over Northern Ireland in 1972, but the shooting and bombing continued. In 1998 the British agreed to let Northern Ireland govern itself. Despite the 1998 peace accord, political unrest continues. **What issue led to increased violence in Northern Ireland during the 1960s and after?**

Global Relations

Austria, Hungary, and Poland were new nations created by treaty after the defeat of Germany in World War I. While established nations such as France and Great Britain had much rebuilding to do, the new nations of eastern Europe had to start from scratch.

Critical Thinking

How did being new countries make things more difficult for the nations of eastern Europe?

ANSWER: Students should note that new nations lacked democratic traditions and had to establish new governments, choose new leaders, and deal with unfamiliar political conflicts.

THEN AND NOW ANSWER
civil rights groups demanding voting reforms to eliminate discrimination

---

Have students discuss which countries were in the most precarious position and why.

REVIEW

Have students complete the Section 3 Review on p. 742.

ASSESS

Have students complete Daily Quiz 28.3. As Alternative Assessment, have students complete the web diagram exercise in this section's lessons and make similar diagrams for other countries.

RETEACH

Have students complete Main Idea Activity for English Language Learners and Special-Needs Students 28.3. Then organize a class discussion of possible solutions to problems in postwar Europe. Encourage students to explain and justify their answers.

ENGLISH LANGUAGE LEARNERS, COOPERATIVE LEARNING

EXTEND

Have students write a letter about the postwar political situation in Great Britain, France, or Eastern Europe, in the role of an American visitor to Europe writing to a friend back home.

BLOCK SCHEDULING

SECTION 3 REVIEW ANSWERS

❶ Define
- general strike, p. 739
- nationalization, p. 739

❷ Identify
- Maginot Line, p. 738
- Locarno Pact, p. 739
- Popular Front, p. 739
- Léon Blum, p. 739
- Ramsay MacDonald, p. 740
- Easter Rising, p. 740
- Sinn Fein, p. 741
- Irish Republican Army, p. 741

❸ Great Britain: labor troubles, Irish independence movement; France: land in ruins, technology destroyed, young men killed in war, inflation, war debt, cost of Maginot Line, political unrest; Austria: weak economy, private armies; Hungary: succession of weak governments, new boundaries interrupted trade; Poland: political conflicts, high German tariffs

❹ a. Great Britain: labor troubles, Irish independence movement; France: land in ruins, technology destroyed, young men killed in war, inflation, war debt; cost of Maginot Line, political unrest

b. Those that failed were unable to establish democratic governments. Most of those that survived were led by kings or strong dictators.

❺ Broadsheets should mention the inspiration of the Bolshevik Revolution, poor working conditions, and dreams of a better life.

---

lived in Vienna. They struggled for control against the rest of the country's people, who saw the nation's needs differently. Opposing groups created private armies, leading many people to desire authoritarian rule. Austria gradually became less democratic.

Hungary became a republic in November 1918. In March 1919, Béla Kun, a Hungarian communist, overthrew the weak republic. Kun had embraced communism while in Russia during the war. Now he tried to establish a system modeled on Russia's new government. He nationalized the land, which made many Hungarians angry. He also failed to distribute food to the people. When Russia did not provide promised assistance, Kun's government fell.

Admiral Miklós Horthy, a member of the military class, then ruled Hungary. He found postwar reconstruction very difficult. Parts of Hungary's prewar empire had been given to Austria, Italy, Poland, and Romania. The new boundaries cut off factories from supplies and markets. During the Great Depression, Hungary sought economic help from the League of Nations, and then from Germany and Italy. Hungary found itself with less and less control over its destiny.

Poland was located between Germany and Russia. Faced with serious economic troubles, Poland had little chance at becoming a democracy. Despite the new Polish democratic constitution, many groups bitterly opposed the government. High German tariffs crippled the Polish economy. The government became more and more unstable. In 1926 Marshal Józef Pilsudski (peel·SOOT·skee) installed a military dictatorship. By that time Bulgaria, Romania, and Yugoslavia had all replaced their democratic governments with conservative military dictatorships or monarchies.

✔ **READING CHECK: Analyzing Information** What role did geography play in the problems that eastern European nations faced? boundaries had been redrawn in a way that caused unrest

Soldier-statesman Józef Pilsudski ruled Poland with an iron hand.

SECTION 3 REVIEW

1. **Define** and explain the significance:
   general strike
   nationalization

2. **Identify** and explain the significance:
   Maginot Line
   Locarno Pact
   Popular Front
   Léon Blum
   Ramsay MacDonald
   Easter Rising
   Sinn Fein
   Irish Republican Army

3. **Analyzing Information** Copy the chart below. Use it to explain the problems each nation faced after World War I.

Country	Problems
Great Britain	
France	
Austria	
Hungary	
Poland	

4. **Finding the Main Idea**
   a. What problems did France and Great Britain face during the years following World War I?
   b. Why did some new European governments survive and others fail during the 1920s?

5. **Writing and Critical Thinking**
   Supporting a Point of View Imagine you are a laborer in Paris in 1934. Write a broadsheet that explains why you want people to strike.
   Consider:
   • France's economic troubles during the Great Depression
   • political threats to stability

Homework Practice Online
keyword: SP3 HP28

SECTION 4

OBJECTIVES

1 **Describe how Benito Mussolini transformed Italy into a fascist state.**

2 **Explain why the Weimar Republic failed.**

3 **Trace how Adolf Hitler became an important figure in Germany.**

4 **Describe how the Nazis used power in Germany.**

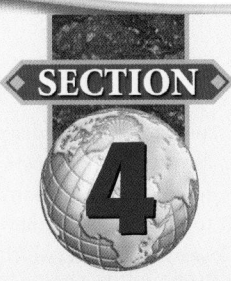

SECTION 4

READ TO DISCOVER

❶ How did Benito Mussolini transform Italy into a fascist state?

❷ Why did the Weimar Republic fail?

❸ How did Adolf Hitler become an important figure in Germany?

❹ How did the Nazis use power in Germany?

DEFINE

fascism
corporatist state

IDENTIFY

Benito Mussolini
Black Shirts
Adolf Hitler
Nazi Party
Third Reich
Rome-Berlin Axis

▶ WHY IT MATTERS TODAY

Fascist and pro-Nazi groups still exist in Germany, the United States, and other nations today. Many people oppose these groups, and keep track of their activities. Use CNNstudentNews.com or other **current event** sources to learn more about opposition to such hate groups. Record your findings in your journal.

CNN student News.com

Fascist Dictatorships in Italy and Germany

The Main Idea
Political and economic crises after World War I helped totalitarian regimes take control in Germany and Italy.

The Story Continues *After World War I, high unemployment and economic problems helped to pave the way for the rise of totalitarian dictatorships. In Italy, Benito Mussolini played upon his country's problems to gain power, becoming the first of Europe's fascist leaders. One writer compared Mussolini to Napoleon:*
". . . like Napoleon, he [Mussolini] could strike fear into men twice his size with a direct glance from those astonishing eyes."

The Rise of Fascism in Italy

As it did elsewhere, the war and its aftermath took its toll in Italy. The Italian government, a constitutional monarchy, seemed unable to respond effectively to these problems. One person who did offer a clear response to Italy's troubles was **Benito Mussolini.** As a young man, Mussolini had edited a socialist newspaper. During World War I, however, his views changed, and he became an extreme nationalist. When Mussolini returned from the war, he organized his own political party. He called it the Fascist Party and called its doctrine **fascism** (FASH·iz·uhm). The words *fascist* and *fascism* come from the Latin word *fasces*. It refers to a bundle of rods bound tightly around an ax that symbolized the authority of the government.

Fascist doctrine. Fascism relied on dictatorship and totalitarianism. It was strongly nationalistic and militaristic and opposed to communism as well as most democratic principles. In practice, fascist and communist governments seemed much alike, in that both tried to control people through force and censorship. There were important differences between fascism and communism, however. Communism appealed to workers and promised ultimately to achieve a society without social classes in which all property is shared communally. Fascism, on the other hand, appealed to the upper and middle class. Fascism promised to preserve existing social classes and the ownership of private property. The difference in views of private property placed fascism and communism in direct opposition to one another.

Mussolini criticized democracy as a weak and ineffective form of government. When he became dictator, he took the title Il Duce (il DOO·chay), Italian for "the leader."

TEACH OBJECTIVES 1 and 2

LEVEL 1: Have students write a list of the problems that faced Italy and Germany after World War I. Have students brainstorm ways that Italy and Germany might have addressed these common conditions. Tell students that they will find out as they study this section that both countries seemed unable to effectively respond to these problems.

ENGLISH LANGUAGE LEARNERS, COOPERATIVE LEARNING

TEACH OBJECTIVE 1

LEVEL 2: Ask students what personal characteristics would help a person gain power in postwar Italy. Lead a class discussion about how events might have been different if Mussolini had not lived.

Historical Sidelight

After losing fair elections, Mussolini's Fascists turned to violence. They began engaging communists and socialists in street brawls. They beat up union organizers and broke strikes by force. These vigilante methods soon gained Mussolini's Fascists the support of the police, the military, and many of the people.

Critical Thinking

Why did the military, the police, and many of the people support Mussolini's violent tactics?

ANSWER: The Fascists seemed to be restoring order, suppressing communists, and getting food production back on track.

VISUAL RECORD ANSWER

to indoctrinate people from an early, impressionable age

Technology Resources

Online Maps, Charts, and Graphics: European Democracies, 1925

This illustrated cover of Le Petit Journal *portrays fighting between communists and fascists in Florence, Italy, in 1921.*

Among Mussolini's first followers were discontented nationalists and soldiers returning from the war. Gradually, however, the Fascists attracted shopkeepers, artisans, and wealthy landowners. Large manufacturers interested in blocking communist gains among workers were especially drawn to fascism. These new supporters provided financial assistance to the Fascists. The lower middle class, which had been hurt by inflation, and the unemployed also supported the Fascists.

Mussolini recognized the appeal of anticommunism. He emphasized it in his programs and promised to prevent a communist revolution. Fascism began to stand for the protection of private property and the middle class. Mussolini proposed cooperation between labor and management to restore and protect the Italian economy. He stressed national pride, pledging to return Italy to the military glories of the Roman Empire.

Mussolini's rise to power. The Fascists conducted a violent campaign against their opponents, especially communists and socialists. Known as **Black Shirts** for the color of their uniforms, Fascists broke up strikes, intimidated voters, and drove elected socialist officials from office. In October 1922, Black Shirt groups from all over Italy met in Rome. They claimed their purpose was to defend Italy against a communist revolution. In response, liberal members of the Italian parliament called upon the king to declare martial law. When the king refused, the cabinet resigned. Conservative advisers then persuaded the king to appoint Mussolini premier and to ask him to head a coalition government.

Once in office Mussolini began to destroy democracy in Italy and to set up a dictatorship. He appointed Fascists to all official positions in the central government and pushed a new election law through parliament. Under it, the party receiving the most votes would automatically gain two thirds of the seats in the lower house of parliament.

The Fascists won the election of 1924. In 1925 Mussolini was made "head of the government." While the king was allowed to reign as a figurehead, real power was held by the Fascist Party. Mussolini took over the Ministry of War and controlled the police. A Grand Council of the Fascist Party set government policy, but it usually deferred to Mussolini.

With Mussolini firmly in control, outward signs of dictatorship appeared. Parties opposed to Fascist rule were disbanded. The government suspended basic liberties, such as freedom of speech, freedom of the press, and trial by jury. Labor unions came under government control. Strikes were outlawed. Uniformed and secret police spied on everyone. Under Fascist rule, Italy rapidly became a police state.

INTERPRETING THE VISUAL RECORD

Sons of the Wolf Mussolini established an organization for young people called "Sons of the Wolf," in which children were taught fascist ideas. *Why might Mussolini think it was important to recruit youths to the fascist movement?*

Ask the class how fascism and communism are alike and how they are different. Tell the class that one of the differences between the Fascist Party in Italy and the Socialist Party in Europe was that when the Fascist Party came to power, it effectively broke up agricultural strikes in Italy. More than a million farm workers went on strike in 1920, but by 1921 Fascist attacks had reduced the number of striking farm workers to only 80,000. Ask students why this added to the Fascists' popularity. (*people wanted order and food*)

Teacher to Teacher

Jay Harmon of Baton Rouge, Louisiana, suggested the following activity: Have the class prepare and act out a radio news broadcast from the 1930s. Students should research the news topics they are going to present and may want to research old movies, newsreels, and documentaries to examine the news style of the era.

The corporatist state. Mussolini introduced a new and complicated system of government called corporatism, making Italy a **corporatist state.** Representation was determined by area of economic activity. Major economic activities including agriculture, commerce, manufacturing, and transportation were formed into organizations similar to corporations. By about 1934 Italy had 22 of these corporations. Within each corporation, representatives of government, labor, and management met to establish wages and prices and to agree to working conditions.

Labor unions and business leaders were expected to submit to Mussolini's government and to cooperate with one another for the goals of the state. Private property and limited profits were permitted, however.

✔ **READING CHECK: Finding the Main Idea** What are some aspects of fascism and corporatism? both preserve social classes, control through force

The Weimar Republic

As in Italy, Germany underwent great political change after World War I. In early 1919, following the kaiser's abdication, Germany became a republic. The following year, an assembly met in the city of Weimar (VY·mar) and drafted a constitution. The German federal republic became known as the Weimar Republic.

The German people were unhappy with the Weimar Republic because it had signed the humiliating Treaty of Versailles. Many Germans considered the Weimar Republic to be a traitor to Germany's interests. The government faced some of the same economic, political, and social problems that all Europe faced after World War I. Unemployment was extremely high, and inflation soared. Money lost value so rapidly that printers stopped putting numbers on bills.

Both right-wing groups and communist groups tried to overthrow the republic. For example, in 1923 an uprising known as the Beer Hall Putsch occurred in Munich. It was led by a group of extreme nationalists. Although the government put down the uprising and jailed its leaders, the Beer Hall Putsch highlighted the weaknesses of the government and the growing frustrations of the German people. **Adolf Hitler,** a leader of the Beer Hall Putsch, seized on these frustrations to gain support for his political party—the Nazis.

✔ **READING CHECK: Identifying Cause and Effect** Why was the Weimar Republic so weak? had signed the unpopular Treaty of Versailles

The Nazis and Hitler

Many political parties formed in Germany after World War I. One was the National Socialist German Workers' Party, or **Nazi Party.** The party was extremely nationalistic, anti-Semitic, and anticommunist. It promised to protect Germany from communism. As a result, the Nazis eventually attracted the support of some wealthy business leaders and landowners. One of the first Nazi recruits was Adolf Hitler. By 1921 he was head of the Nazi Party. In 1923, while imprisoned for his role in the Beer Hall Putsch, Hitler wrote *Mein Kampf* (*My Struggle*). The book expressed the spirit of the Nazi movement. In it, Hitler outlined his plan for racial purity through the total elimination of all Jews and

Holt Researcher

go.hrw.com
KEYWORD: Holt Researcher
FreeFind: Benito Mussolini
Adolf Hitler
After reading more about Benito Mussolini and Adolf Hitler on the Holt Researcher, create a Venn diagram comparing the ideology and actions of the two leaders.

INTERPRETING THE VISUAL RECORD

Inflation in Germany Inflation soared in Germany during the early 1920s. The value of the German mark fell so low that people bundled the money and sold it by weight as wastepaper instead of using it as currency. *What does this picture reveal about economic conditions in Germany during the 1920s?*

Historical Sidelight

The *Schutzstaffel,* better known as the SS, was Hitler's secret police force. The SS was separate from the storm troopers; members of the SS were bound by a personal oath of loyalty to Hitler himself. The head of the SS, Heinrich Himmler, was a former agronomist known for his extreme cruelty and willingness to carry out even the most brutal of Hitler's plans with ruthless precision.

Critical Thinking

Ask students why the loyalty of the SS was crucial to Hitler's rapid rise to power.

ANSWER: Their unquestioning loyalty and willingness to perform brutal acts, including murder, let Hitler use them like a weapon, striking fear into the hearts of his opposition—or eliminating his opposition for him.

VISUAL RECORD ANSWER

The children seem to be playing with bundles of money as if they were wooden blocks. This shows that the currency had very little value.

ALL LEVELS: Assign half the class to study Mussolini and the other half to study Hitler. Tell the two large groups to organize themselves into subgroups of two, three, or four students to do research. Have subgroups organize their findings onto a time line of events by which their assigned leader achieved dominance and established totalitarian rule. Encourage students to include even minor events and to add illustrations.

ENGLISH LANGUAGE LEARNERS, COOPERATIVE LEARNING

LEVEL 3: Copy the following graphic organizer on the chalkboard, omitting the italicized answers. Have each student complete the chart.

Reasons People Embraced Totalitarianism	
Italy	**Germany**
internal turmoil	*internal turmoil*
weak government	*weak government*
crippled economy	*crippled economy*
dreams of former glory	*dreams of former glory*
restoration of order	*restoration of order*
Mussolini	*Hitler*

Daily Life

The Hitler Youth was founded in 1933 as a hiking and sporting organization, but its true purpose was to educate young Germans about National Socialism. By 1932 there were more than 100,000 members of the Hitler Youth. In 1936 all young Germans had to join either the Hitler Youth or the Society of German Maidens. Boys were trained in physical fitness while they learned about doctrines of racial purity. Girls also learned Nazi beliefs while developing skills to be wives and mothers.

Critical Thinking

Why might Hitler have required young people to join these clubs?

ANSWER: Students should suggest that by forcing people to learn Nazi ideas, Hitler hoped to form a corps of life-long believers in his ideology.

HISTORY MAKER ANSWER

crowd manipulation, fiery speaking ability, emotional appeal to German fears

others that he considered "impure." By 1927 Hitler's anti-Semitic ideology, shared by the Nazi Party, began to be transformed into active discrimination against Jews, which soon grew increasingly violent. Hitler left no doubt as to his goals for the German nation.

Analyzing Primary Sources

Drawing Conclusions What was Hitler's primary goal for Germany? more territory

 ❝If the National Socialist movement really wants to be consecrated [honored] by history with a great mission for our nation . . . it must find the courage to gather our people and their strength for an advance along the road that will lead this people from its present restricted living space to new land and soil.❞

Adolf Hitler, from *Mein Kampf*

Hitler's emotional speeches attracted many listeners. He promised to repeal the Treaty of Versailles and to restore Germany's military power. He pledged, too, to lead the nation in the recovery of its lost territory and to build a "Greater Germany." To these promises Hitler added his racial doctrine. According to Hitler the Germans were the "master race." All others were inferior. Many Germans were eager to follow a leader who pledged to restore their country's lost glory.

✔ **READING CHECK: Drawing Conclusions** What does the popularity of Hitler's message reveal about the attitudes of many German people during the 1920s? strong nationalist, anti-Semitic, and anticommunist feelings

The Nazis in Power

In 1925 the Nazi Party had just 25,000 members. By 1929 the party had grown to 180,000 members. In the 1930 election, the Great Depression and continuing social and civil unrest caused many workers and middle-class voters to turn to the Nazi Party. In 1932 the party won 230 seats in the Reichstag, one house of the German parliament.

By late 1932 the Nazis held more seats in the Reichstag than any other party. They did not have enough votes to claim a majority, however. In January 1933 the president of the republic appointed Hitler as chancellor. Hitler then used the private Nazi army to frighten members of the Reichstag. In 1933 someone set fire to the Reichstag building. Hitler blamed the communists and received emergency powers to deal with the supposed communist revolt. He used these powers to make himself a dictator.

HISTORY MAKER

Adolf Hitler (1889–1945)

Following Germany's humiliating defeat in World War I, Adolf Hitler set out to establish an iron dictatorship that would rule Germany and the world "for a thousand years." Like Mussolini in Italy, Hitler rose to power through a combination of masterful crowd manipulation, fiery speaking ability, and emotional appeal to German fears. He twisted facts and used Germans' frustrations over World War I to convince Germans that they were victims of international injustice and conspiracy. **What tactics did Hitler use to gain power?**

A formation of uniformed German workers gives the Nazi salute to Adolf Hitler, standing in the open automobile, at Nürnberg, Germany, in 1937.

TEACH OBJECTIVE 4

LEVEL 2: Tell students that in November of 1938, more than 7,500 Jewish-owned businesses and more than 170 synagogues were set on fire in a single night: *Kristallnacht,* or "night of broken glass." Have students take on the roles of people who witnessed the horrors of *Kristallnacht* and write personal letters to friends or relatives in the United States describing the event and their feelings.

CLOSE

Select student volunteers to role-play members of a German family discussing whether to leave Germany, stay and try to stop the growth of Nazi power, or simply go along with the regime. Help students to see the difficult choices faced by Germans who did not like Hitler.

SKILL-BUILDING STRATEGIES   Analyzing Documents

Adolf Hitler's Rise to Power

Adolf Hitler rose from obscurity during the bleak postwar period in Weimar Germany to become an all-powerful dictator. Hitler was expert at creating "the big lie," claiming that the greater the falsehood, the more likely it would be accepted without question. He sought to destroy Germany's postwar parliamentary democracy from within, through policies of intimidation and violence and by using the republic's laws and practices against it. Hitler learned to cover his drive for absolute power at any cost with a thin cloak of legality. A careful study of documents from the period of Hitler's rise to power reveals how he used the law to undermine Germany's democratic institutions in order to control the political system.

The Historical Background

The documents below include a chart showing the results of elections for seats in Germany's Reichstag (representative parliament) in 1932 and 1933. Document 2 is an excerpt from Hitler's Emergency Decree, which was based on the burning of the Reichstag in 1933. The Nazis blamed the fire on the Communists. The Decree played on Germans' fear of disorder and revolution, which many believed was caused by the Communists. The Emergency Decree placed severe restrictions on the Communists, who were the Nazis' biggest rivals and to whom they had lost seats in the Reichstag in the election of 1932.

THE NAZI TAKEOVER OF GERMANY'S GOVERNMENT, 1932–1933
Seats in the German Reichstag by Political Party

Party Name	Nov. 1932	Mar. 1933
National Socialists (Nazis)	196	288
Nationalists	52	52
People's Party and Bavarian People's Party	31	21
Catholic Center	90	92
Socialists	121	120
Communists	100	81

Excerpt from The Emergency Decree:

"The following is decreed as a defensive measure against Communist acts of violence, endangering the state: Sections 114, 115, 117, 118, 123, 124, and 153 of the Constitution of the German Reich are suspended until further notice. Thus, restrictions on personal liberty, on the right of free expression of opinion, including freedom of the press, on the right of assembly . . . association . . . warrants for house-searches, . . . are also permissible beyond the legal limits otherwise prescribed."

Adolf Hitler delivers an impassioned speech to the Reichstag in 1939. Hitler frequently provoked Germans' anger and resentment toward the international community by claiming that Germany was "stabbed in the back" by cowardly, hidden enemies during World War I.

Skills Reminder

Historians use documents as basic sources of information and evidence. Documents answer questions, support or disprove assumptions, and help historians to build theories concerning the historical record. They take many forms— written, printed, and visual. To analyze documents, first identify the opinion, fact, or issue that is the document's subject. Then determine the document's source, validity, and bias. Finally, place the document in its historical context and draw conclusions based upon the information that it provides.

Skills Practice

❶ Study the statistical data shown in the chart above. Recognize that for any single party to gain control of the German Reichstag, it had to have a clear majority of seats. Write a paragraph describing the trends shown by the chart and what the Nazis might have done to win control of the legislature.

❷ Analyze the excerpt from Hitler's Emergency Decree. Write a general explanation of the meaning of the excerpt, including its effects on individual rights and liberties. Then describe how this document might have used German laws to reinforce Hitler's totalitarian rule.

That's Interesting!

As a youth, Adolf Hitler wanted to become a great painter. Realizing that he had little artistic talent, he worked as a postcard artist before beginning his rise to ultimate power in Germany.

SKILLS PRACTICE ANSWERS

1. Students may suggest that the Nazis could have recruited more members of other parties, especially the Socialists.

2. Students should identify the restrictions of personal rights and liberties. The German government had a history of suppressing and jailing dissidents.

Linking Past to Present

Historians make an important distinction when studying historical documents. They categorize documents as either primary sources or secondary sources. Primary sources are documents created by eyewitnesses to or participants in the events being discussed. Secondary sources are documents created by people who were not directly involved. Primary sources are generally considered to be more reliable and accurate than secondary sources.

ACTIVITY: Have students find primary sources that tell about someone's experiences before or during World War II.

ASSESS

Have students complete Daily Quiz 28.4. As Alternative Assessment, you may want to use the graphic organizer chart or political cartoons exercise in this section's lessons.

RETEACH

Have students complete Main Idea Activity for English Language Learners and Special-Needs Students 28.4. Then have students prepare research outlines of how Mussolini and Hitler came to power. **ENGLISH LANGUAGE LEARNERS, COOPERATIVE LEARNING**

EXTEND

Have students imagine that they are living in the United States when Hitler and Mussolini rise to power. Ask them to write letters to the editor of a local newspaper suggesting how the U.S. government should respond to Hitler and Mussolini. Encourage them to consider what the results of the two leaders' policies will be. **BLOCK SCHEDULING**

VISUAL RECORD ANSWER

They approve.

SECTION 4 REVIEW ANSWERS

❶ **Define**
• fascism, p. 743
• corporatist state, p. 745

❷ **Identify**
• Benito Mussolini, p. 743
• Black Shirts, p. 744
• Adolf Hitler, p. 745
• Nazi Party, p. 745
• Third Reich, p. 748
• Rome-Berlin Axis, p. 748

❸ Class: Fascism—preserve existing social classes; Communism—abolish social classes; Property: Fascism—encourage ownership of private property; Communism—share all property communally; Government Power: Fascism—control through force and censorship; Communism—control through force and censorship

❹ a. weak governments, poor economies, internal dissent, social frustration

b. crush all opposition, rebuild military, prepare for world domination

❺ Columns should include such Nazi activities as attacking minorities and using troops on citizens.

Once in power, Hitler took the title *der Führer* (FYOOR-ur), German for "the leader." He turned Germany into a police state, banning labor unions, opposition newspapers, and opposition political parties. He gave the Gestapo, a secret police force, wide-ranging powers. Members of so-called inferior races, especially Jews, suffered persecution. In some places the Nazis forced the Jews to live in separate neighborhoods called ghettos. Many Jews were forced to wear the Star of David, a six-pointed star that is the symbol of Judaism, on their clothing. The Nazis' political opponents were harshly suppressed or sent to concentration camps. In Nazi Germany, concentration camps were initially set up to isolate all people suspected of opposing Hitler's regime. However, in accordance with Hitler's plan to rid Germany of its Jewish population, the camps soon developed into a network for the systematic suppression and extermination of millions of Jews and other so-called "impure" population groups in Nazi-occupied countries.

Like Mussolini, Hitler promised to revive his nation's economy. He also reminded Germans of their nation's former glory. He called his rule the **Third Reich.** *Reich* is the German word for "empire." The first German empire had been the Holy Roman Empire. The second was the German Empire of the Hohenzollerns. Hitler declared that the Third Reich would last 1,000 years.

During the early 1930s Germany began secretly rebuilding its military. In early 1936 Hitler ordered troops into the Rhineland. This act violated the Treaty of Versailles, which prohibited Germany from keeping troops there. Neither France nor Great Britain reacted to this treaty violation. In part, this was because neither of the two powers believed that the violation was worth going to war. Hitler was encouraged by his easy success in the Rhineland. He sought an alliance with Mussolini. In the fall of 1936, the two dictators formed the **Rome-Berlin Axis.**

✔ **READING CHECK: Summarizing** How did Hitler come to power in Germany, and how did he use that power to become a dictator? became chancellor, created anticommunist hysteria

INTERPRETING THE VISUAL RECORD

Book burnings Nazis and German students carry books and pamphlets to be burned during a demonstration against literature they believed to be anti-Germanic. *What do the participants' physical actions in this image reveal about their attitude toward the burning of books?*

SECTION 4 REVIEW

1. **Define** and explain the significance:
   fascism
   corporatist state

2. **Identify** and explain the significance:
   Benito Mussolini
   Black Shirts
   Nazi Party
   Adolf Hitler
   Third Reich
   Rome-Berlin Axis

3. **Comparing and Contrasting** Copy the chart below. Use it to compare and contrast fascism with communism.

Fascism	Communism	
		Class
		Property
		Government power

4. **Finding the Main Idea**

   a. How did World War I contribute to the rise of fascism in Italy and Germany?

   b. How did the dictators use their power in Italy and Germany?

5. **Writing and Critical Thinking**

   Supporting a Point of View Imagine that you are an American journalist in Germany during the 1930s. Write a newspaper column persuading readers that the Nazis are determined to destroy democracy.

   Consider:
   • the Nazis' use of military troops
   • Nazi attacks on minority groups

Homework Practice Online
go.hrw.com
keyword: SP3 HP28

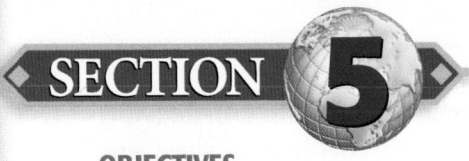

SECTION 5

OBJECTIVES

1 Identify the terms of the New Economic Policy.

2 Describe how Stalin shaped the Soviet economy.

3 Explain why Stalin imprisoned and executed millions of Soviet people.

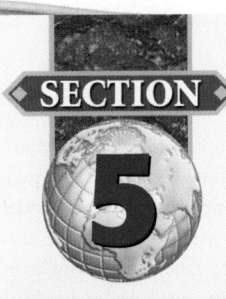

SECTION 5

READ TO DISCOVER

❶ What were the terms of the New Economic Policy?

❷ How did Stalin shape the Soviet economy?

❸ Why did Stalin imprison and execute millions of Soviet people?

DEFINE

collective farms
command economy
purge

IDENTIFY

New Economic Policy
Leon Trotsky
Joseph Stalin
Five-Year Plan
Politburo
Comintern

▶ WHY IT MATTERS TODAY

Communism remains a powerful political force in what was once the Soviet Union. Use CNN or other **current event** sources to learn more about communism's influence in the former Soviet Union. Record your findings in your journal.

CNN student News.com

Dictatorship in the Soviet Union

The Main Idea
Under the leadership of Joseph Stalin, the Soviet Union became a powerful police state.

The Story Continues *In 1917 the Communists seized power and imprisoned Czar Nicholas II, his wife Alexandra, and their five children. On the night of July 18, 1918, the royal family was taken to the basement of the house where they were being held. There, the entire family was shot to death. Many Communists thought they had ended centuries of oppression under czarist rule. Within a few years, however, Russia was once again at the mercy of an absolute ruler. Joseph Stalin would prove to be one of the most brutal dictators Russia had ever experienced.*

Russia Under Lenin

In 1922 the Communist leaders renamed Russia the Union of Soviet Socialist Republics (USSR). The people of the USSR became known as the Soviet people. The country's name indicated that the soviets, or revolutionary councils, now held power. The USSR was divided into separate political republics joined in a federal union. Eventually the USSR included 15 of these republics.

Between 1918 and 1921, Russian leader Vladimir Lenin followed a policy known as War Communism. This policy nationalized Russian industries. Social and economic measures were not based on a long-range plan, however. Communist leaders had to develop a program to build their new society in Russia.

War Communism did little to improve the Russian economy. In 1920 Russian farmers produced significantly less grain than they had grown before World War I. Factory production was less than one-sixth of its prewar levels. By 1921 the Communist leadership faced economic collapse and social disorder. In response, Lenin announced the **New Economic Policy** (NEP). The major industries—heavy industry, communications, transportation, and the credit system—remained under government control. The NEP allowed some free enterprise, however. Individuals could buy, sell, and trade farm products. Some private business, especially among peasants, was allowed. A new class of small businessmen, the Nepmen, arose. The Nepmen traded in domestic goods and helped manufacturers secure needed materials.

Soviet agriculture made important changes in this period. During the revolution farmlands had been seized from wealthy landlords and divided among the peasants. The government tried to persuade peasants to form **collective farms.** Land was pooled into large farms on which people worked together as a group. On a collective farm, peasants shared the scarce modern farm machinery.

The flag of the USSR was bright red to symbolize revolution. The hammer and sickle symbolized worker and peasant unity, while the star stood for the Communist Party.

TEACH OBJECTIVE 1

 ALL LEVELS: Ask students what economic policy was in effect in Russia before Lenin introduced the New Economic Policy. *(War Communism, command economy)* Ask what problems occurred under that system. *(low production, economic collapse, social disorder)* What changes did Lenin introduce with the New Economic Policy? *(allowed some small-scale private business)* Ask students why he made that change. *(to boost production)* **ENGLISH LANGUAGE LEARNERS**

TEACH OBJECTIVE 2

LEVEL 1: Have students summarize characteristics of the Soviet economy under Stalin. *(Five-Year Plan, command economy, farm collectivization, growth of heavy industry, suffering of the common people)* **ENGLISH LANGUAGE LEARNERS**

 HOMEWORK Have students write an essay, draw a picture, or compose a song or skit to compare and contrast Lenin's and Stalin's economic policies.

History Maker

LEON TROTSKY. Lev Bronstein was exiled to Siberia in 1898 for his Marxist ideas. By 1902 he had adopted the name Leon Trotsky and escaped. While traveling to London, Trotsky met Lenin, and when Lenin died in 1924 many expected Trotsky to become the next Soviet leader. Stalin outmaneuvered Trotsky, however, and exiled him in 1929. Trotsky moved to Mexico, where Mexican artist Diego Rivera befriended him. Trotsky was assassinated there in 1940.

Critical Thinking

How might Trotsky's two periods in exile have affected his revolutionary ideas?

ANSWER: Students may say that Trotsky became either more revolutionary or more cynical about the power of revolution.

Soviet women served in Red Army combat units in the 1920s.

Women's roles. The Communists claimed to believe that men and women in Soviet society should be equal. In 1917 they declared that women should receive equal pay for work equal to that of men. Women were also granted time off from work to take care of newborn babies. In addition, the Soviet government made it much easier to obtain a divorce. As a result, the Soviet Union had one of the highest divorce rates in Europe.

Many male Communist Party members and peasants who preferred traditional values tried to limit women's gains, however. Many women still received lower pay than men. They faced higher rates of unemployment. Few women held positions of authority within the Communist Party and the Soviet government.

Education. Soviet leaders emphasized education. They hoped to increase literacy rates and to teach socialist doctrine in the schools. In addition, they established technical schools to train industrial workers. Educators had limited success, however, partly because they lacked funds. Students lacked supplies such as pencils and notebooks. Some schools closed in the winter because they lacked heat. Moreover, the government emphasized higher education, often ignoring the needs of elementary schools. As a result, in 1925 Soviet students averaged fewer than three years in school.

✔ **READING CHECK: Finding the Main Idea** What reforms took place in the USSR under Lenin? nationalized industries, collectivized farms, gave women more rights, emphasized education

The Five-Year Plan

When Lenin died in 1924, a power struggle took place within the Communist Party. The main rivals for power were **Leon Trotsky** and **Joseph Stalin.** Trotsky was a talented party organizer. He had almost single-handedly created the Red Army that defended the Bolshevik Revolution. Stalin was a leader of the party.

Trotsky and Stalin had differing views regarding the best way to make Communism succeed. Trotsky followed the strict Marxist belief that revolution should take place among workers all over the world. Stalin broke with this doctrine and advocated "socialism in one country." Stalin argued that after socialism succeeded in the Soviet Union, revolution would spread to the rest of the world. A merciless struggle began between Trotsky and Stalin and their followers within the Communist Party. By 1928 Stalin had emerged as the leader. Trotsky, in turn, was exiled from the Soviet Union. He was later murdered in Mexico on Stalin's orders.

Stalin believed the economy was not growing quickly enough. Peasants were refusing to sell wheat at the low prices set by the government. In 1928 Stalin ended the NEP. He returned to a **command economy,** in which the government controlled all economic decisions. Stalin wanted to make government control of the economy a permanent part of Soviet life.

In 1928 the government released the first **Five-Year Plan** for economic growth. The plan set ambitious agricultural, industrial, and social goals for the next five years. Stalin wanted to double the production of oil and coal, and triple the output of steel.

Early Communist leader Leon Trotsky was killed in 1940 following a power struggle with Joseph Stalin.

TEACH OBJECTIVES 1 and 2

ALL LEVELS: Copy this chart onto the chalkboard, omitting the italicized answers. Call on students to help you fill it in. Encourage students to copy the information into their notes.
ENGLISH LANGUAGE LEARNERS, COOPERATIVE LEARNING

Problems of the New Soviet Union		
Problem	**Attempted Solution**	**Results**
near economic collapse in 1921	*Lenin's New Economic Policy allowed some free enterprise*	*moderately successful*
agriculture	*collective farms*	*failed: famine resulted*
power struggle between Trotsky and Stalin	*savage and brutal competition*	*Stalin emerged as victor*
little economic growth	*Stalin's first Five-Year Plan*	*succeeded in reviving industry somewhat*
no increase in consumer goods or food	*second Five-Year Plan*	*industry continued growing, but the people starved*

Stalin intended the Five-Year Plan to turn the Soviet Union into a modern, industrialized society. The planners hoped that collective farming would produce enough food for the Soviet people as well as a surplus for export. Money received from farm exports would help pay for modern machinery. This new machinery would advance the growth of Soviet industry.

The Five-Year Plan caused hardships for the Soviet people. Government efforts to have peasants voluntarily join collective farms failed. The government then forced people to accept the policy. All farms were to be merged into collectives. Peasants had to join or suffer severe punishment. Those who tried to keep their lands faced execution, exile, or imprisonment. The government turned about 90 percent of the productive farmland into collective farms. The Five-Year Plan actually decreased agricultural production, however, and millions of people died as a result of famine and crop failure.

Despite such failures, the Soviet economy grew under the Five-Year Plan. For example, steel production increased dramatically. A second Five-Year Plan, even broader than the first, went into effect in 1933. Soviets who expected an increase in consumer goods or food supply as a reward for their hard work were disappointed. Production of consumer goods actually decreased. The government focused its efforts on expanding heavy industry, especially military production. Rather than a reward, the Soviet people faced harder times as consumer goods and food became scarcer.

✔ **READING CHECK: Evaluating** What effect did Stalin's Five-Year Plan have on Soviet life? *caused hardship*

Stalin's Dictatorship

Before communism, the czars had used secret police and spies to maintain their absolute rule. Stalin, like Lenin, used similar tactics. Under Stalin the Soviet people were ruled by fear. People had to obey the demands of the Communist Party without complaint or face punishment such as imprisonment or death.

Religion and art were two areas of Soviet life that the government attempted to control. Soviet officials discouraged religious worship and seized the property of the Orthodox Church. Churches and Jewish houses of worship were destroyed or converted into public buildings. Government officials ordered the imprisonment and execution of many ministers, priests, and rabbis. They outlawed religious instruction in schools. The works of artists, musicians, and writers were subjected to government control and censorship. Artists were ordered to produce works of "socialist realism" as proof of their loyalty to the state.

HISTORY MAKER

Joseph Stalin (1879–1953)

Joseph Stalin was one of the major political figures of the 1900s. Under Stalin's totalitarian rule, the Soviet Union grew to become one of the world's two super powers.

Because of government propaganda, Stalin was viewed by many Soviet citizens as a great hero and patriot. Some remembered him as a "great teacher and friend," and as the savior of his nation. But others will always think of Stalin as a ruthless power-monger and the brutal murderer of millions of Russians for often-imagined "crimes against the state." **How did Stalin use violence as a political weapon?**

Economics

Under Lenin's New Economic Policy, major industries remained under government control, but free enterprise was permitted on a small scale. When Stalin took control of the government, he ended the NEP and returned to a command economy.

Critical Thinking

Why did Stalin end the NEP and return to a command economy?

ANSWER: He did not believe the economy was growing fast enough. He wanted to make government control of the economy a permanent part of Soviet life.

HISTORY MAKER ANSWER
Stalin murdered millions of Russians for "crimes against the state," thus suppressing any disagreement or opposition.

The Great Kremlin Palace in Moscow, once the sprawling home of the Romanov czars, became a government office building under the Communists.

LEVEL 3: Have students imagine living in a society where they might be imprisoned or executed at any time for even the slightest infraction. Ask them to write a diary entry describing the situation and why they think the government leaders created the situation. Remind students that, depending on what they write, their diary could lead to serious consequences if found by government officials.

CLOSE

Ask students whether allowing citizens to express opposition to government policies strengthens or weakens a nation. Have students compare and contrast policies for dealing with political opposition in closed societies such as the Soviet Union and open societies such as the United States.

Global Relations

The Communist Revolution in Russia had a serious impact on other nations throughout the world. Communist parties were formed in the United States, Great Britain, France, China, and many other nations. In most of these nations, communism failed to take hold. In some, such as China and Cuba, it succeeded.

Critical Thinking

Ask students why some nations were able to stop the spread of communism while others adopted it as their form of government.

ANSWER: The people of nations with strong governments were unwilling to change. People in nations with serious problems looked to communism as a way of improving their lives.

MAP ANSWER
Leningrad, Stalingrad

Government under Stalin. In 1936 Stalin proclaimed a new Soviet constitution. This constitution kept the basic framework of government that had existed under Lenin. The Supreme Soviet, the parliamentary body, met twice a year. The Council of People's Commissars, which later was renamed the Council of Ministers, held executive and administrative authority. On paper the Soviet government appeared to be democratic. In reality, however, most power lay in the hands of the **Politburo** (Political Bureau) of the Communist Party. The Supreme Soviet elected members to the Politburo, which was a small committee. Stalin controlled the Politburo. He was a dictator with almost complete authority.

Stalin's dictatorship grew harsher over time. In 1934 an important official in the Communist Party was assassinated. Stalin responded with a **purge**—a large-scale elimination—of party members who were supposedly disloyal to him. He used brutality, intimidation, and public trials staged for show to rid the party of members who he claimed were disloyal or were working against the interests of the state. The purge expanded to include the general population. People could be imprisoned without a trial for the most minor offenses.

The Soviet Union in 1936
Interpreting Maps The USSR included Russia, as well as as Azerbaijan, Uzbek, Kirghiz, and Georgia, among others.
■ **Skills Assessment: Human Systems** What cities' names show the influence of the Revolution?

REVIEW
Have students complete the Section 5 Review on p. 753.

ASSESS
Have students complete Daily Quiz 28.5. As Alternative Assessment, you may want to use the "Problems of the New Soviet Union" chart exercise in this section's lessons.

RETEACH
Have students complete Main idea Activity for English Language Learners and Special-Needs Students 28.5. Then have them write

Lenin, Trotsky, and *Stalin* with space between the names and use their textbooks to list as many facts as they can about each.
ENGLISH LANGUAGE LEARNERS

EXTEND
Have students review the time period from 1919 to 1936. Have students research the time period, recording events in the Soviet Union on one side of a time line and important world events on the other side. Invite students to illustrate their time lines with drawings or other art. Display the completed time lines in the classroom. **BLOCK SCHEDULING**

Scholars estimate that by 1939 more than 5 million people had been arrested, deported, imprisoned in forced labor camps, or executed. One Soviet author recalled the injustice that a peasant experienced.

❝Another peasant, with six children, met a different fate. Because he had six mouths to feed he devoted himself whole-heartedly to collective farm work, and he kept hoping he would get some return for his labor. And he did—they awarded him a decoration. They awarded it at a special assembly, made speeches. In his reply, the peasant got carried away. He said, 'Now if I could just have a sack of flour instead of this decoration! Couldn't I somehow?' A wolflike laugh rocketed through the hall, and the newly decorated hero went off to exile, together with all six of those dependent mouths.❞

Aleksandr I. Solzhenitsyn, from *The Gulag Archipelago*

Foreign policy. The Soviet Union's foreign policy during the 1920s and 1930s was confusing. On the one hand, the new Communist government wanted other established nations to accept it. On the other hand, the Soviets supported the Communist International or **Comintern.** Lenin had founded this organization to spread the Communist revolution throughout the world. The Comintern worked to overthrow democracies by urging workers in other countries to rebel. These open calls for revolution caused fear and suspicion outside the Soviet Union.

✔ **READING CHECK:**
Summarizing What was the relationship between the ordinary Soviet citizen and the state during the era of Stalin's rule? people ruled by fear, closely controlled

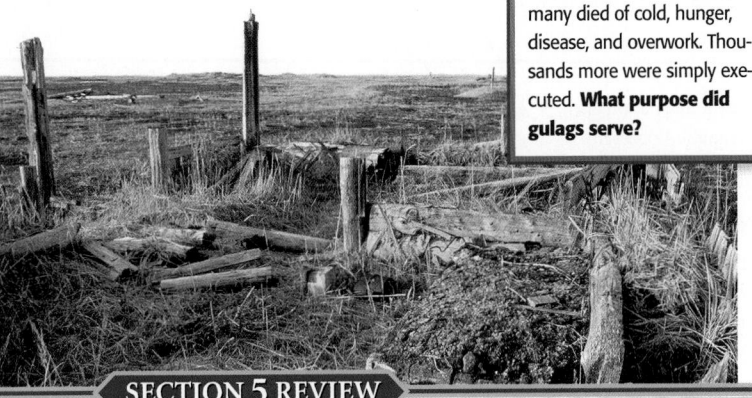

Remains of a Soviet gulag

DAILY LIFE

The Gulags
From 1934 to 1947, millions of Russians were sent to labor camps known as "gulags." Many of these brutal camps were located in the barren, frozen stretches of the Siberian frontier. Inmates included political prisoners and dissidents who dared speak out against Stalin's dictatorial rule. Many others faced extreme and unjust punishments for petty crimes. Many innocent people were also sent to the camps. Prisoners were forced to work on road-building projects or in mines. In the terrible conditions of the gulags, many died of cold, hunger, disease, and overwork. Thousands more were simply executed. **What purpose did gulags serve?**

DAILY LIFE ANSWER
punish political prisoners, dissidents, petty criminals

◆ **SECTION** ◆

5 REVIEW ANSWERS

❶ **Define**
- collective farms, p. 749
- command economy, p. 750
- purge, p. 752

❷ **Identify**
- New Economic Policy, p. 749
- Leon Trotsky, p. 750
- Joseph Stalin, p. 750
- Five-Year Plan, p. 750
- Politburo, p. 752
- Comintern, p. 753

❸ Consumer Goods: NEP limited free trade, 5-Year Plan no free trade; Economic Freedom: NEP limited, 5-Year Plan none; Agriculture: NEP voluntary collective farms, 5-Year Plan forced collectivization; Successes: NEP equality for women, improved education, 5-Year Plan economic growth; Failures: NEP little or no economic growth, 5-Year Plan hardship for people

❹ a. gained control of Communist Party after Lenin's death

b. Even before communism, the czars used secret police and spies to maintain absolute control of the people.

❺ Letters should mention economic hardship and constant fear of government forces.

SECTION 5 REVIEW

1. **Define** and explain the significance:
   collective farms
   command economy
   purge

2. **Identify** and explain the significance:
   New Economic Policy
   Leon Trotsky
   Joseph Stalin
   Five-Year Plan
   Politburo
   Comintern

3. **Comparing** Copy the chart below and use it to compare the NEP and the first Five-Year Plan.

	NEP	5 Yr. Plan
Consumer goods		
Economic freedom		
Agriculture		
Successes		
Failures		

4. **Finding the Main Idea**
   a. How did Joseph Stalin rise to power?
   b. Why did the Soviet system of government make the development of a police state possible?

5. **Writing and Critical Thinking**
   Drawing Inferences Imagine that you are a Soviet citizen living under Stalin's rule. Write a letter that you secretly smuggle to a friend in the United States. Your smuggled letter describes Soviet life.
   Consider:
   • Stalin's economic policies
   • life in the Stalinist police state

go.hrw.com Homework Practice Online
keyword: SP3 HP28

REVIEW AND ASSESSMENT RESOURCES

REPRODUCIBLE RESOURCES
▶ Vocabulary Activity 28

TECHNOLOGY RESOURCES
▶ Chapter 28 Test Generator (on the One–Stop Planner)
▶ Global Skill Builder CD–ROM
▶ HRW Web Site

REINFORCEMENT, REVIEW, and ASSESSMENT
▶ Chapter 28 Review, pp. 754–755
▶ Chapter 28 Tutorial for Students, Parents, Mentors, and Peers
▶ Chapter 28 Test (Form A or B)
▶ Alternative Assessment Handbook
▶ Chapter 28 Test for English Language Learners and Special-Needs Students

REVIEW
Have students complete the Chapter 28 Review on pages 754–755.

ASSESS
Use one of the chapter tests to assess students' understanding of the content. For Alternative Assessment, see the Portfolio Activities and Alternative Assessment Handbook.

CHAPTER 28 REVIEW ANSWERS

Understanding Main Ideas

1. helped it confront many confusing and irrational events in life

2. new building materials

3. start of worldwide Great Depression

4. public works programs, economic reforms, the Social Security Act, 40-hour workweek, minimum wage, right to form unions

5. land in ruins; agricultural and industrial technology destroyed; many young men killed in war; inflation; heavy war debt; expenses for Maginot Line; political unrest

6. Austria: weak economy, divided between socialists and conservatives, desire for order weakened democracy; Hungary: communist dictatorship, distribution of food failed, deepening economic crisis, loss of independence; Poland: bitter political conflicts prevented success of democracy

7. Fascism was a reaction to the perceived threat of communism.

8. eliminated independent labor unions, opposition newspapers, opposition parties; gave Gestapo wide powers

9. to turn the Soviet Union into a modern, industrialized society

10. through fear and intimidation

CHAPTER 28 Review

Creating a Time Line

Copy the time line below on to a sheet of paper. Complete the time line by filling in the events, individuals, and dates from the chapter that you think were significant. Pick three events and explain why you think they were significant.

| 1920 | 1929 | 1936 |

Writing a Summary

Using standard grammar, spelling, sentence structure, and punctuation, write an overview of the events in the chapter.

Identifying People and Ideas

Identify the following terms or individuals and explain their significance:

1. Igor Stravinsky
2. cubism
3. economic nationalism
4. Franklin Roosevelt
5. general strike
6. Popular Front
7. fascism
8. Third Reich
9. collective farms
10. command economy

Understanding Main Ideas

Section 1 (pp. 728–733)
The Postwar Era

1. How did Freud's notion of the irrational and the subconscious influence postwar literature?
2. How did technology lead to advances in architecture?

Section 2 (pp. 734–737)
Postwar Prosperity Crumbles

3. What was the effect of the U.S. stock market crash in 1929?
4. What New Deal programs led to reforms in the American economy?

Section 3 (pp. 738–742)
Political Tensions After World War I

5. What economic and political problems did France face after World War I?
6. What economic and political problems did eastern European nations face after World War I?

Section 4 (pp. 743–748)
Fascist Dictatorships in Italy and Germany

7. What role did communism play in Mussolini's rise to power?

8. How did Hitler turn Germany into a police state after 1933?

Section 5 (pp. 749–753)
Dictatorship in the Soviet Union

9. What was the goal of the first Five-Year Plan?
10. How did Stalin insure loyalty from government and party officials and from the Soviet people?

Reviewing Themes

1. **Global Relations** Why did western European nations and the United States fail to respond to Germany's violations of the Treaty of Versailles?
2. **Government** How did Hitler use Germany's democratic system to gain control over the country?
3. **Culture** How did the work of Freud and Einstein influence culture during the 1920s?

Thinking Critically

1. **Evaluating** Why were Allied nations in western Europe more successful at remaining democratic after World War I?
2. **Drawing Conclusions** Why did nations practice economic nationalism if this policy only prolonged the depression?
3. **Identifying Cause and Effect** Why might there be a relationship between communist or fascist doctrines and the development of a police state?
4. **Finding the Main Idea** What was life like for the average Soviet citizen during the 1930s?

Writing About History

Comparing and Contrasting Use the chart below to explain similarities and differences between communism and fascism.

	Fascism	Communism
Class		
Private property		
Government authority		
Individual rights		

CLOSE

Have interested students research the collapse of communism and the breakup of the Soviet Union. Have them report their findings to the class.

RETEACH

Organize students into five groups and assign each group one section of the chapter. Have members of each group create maps or diagrams illustrating the main events in their assigned section. Ask them to illustrate each event and to include any relevant dates and captions. Have each group present its work to the class. **ENGLISH LANGUAGE LEARNERS, COOPERATIVE LEARNING**

Portfolio Extensions

1. Ask students to imagine that they have been sent to a gulag for some petty crime. Have them write a secret diary entry telling what happened and what life in the gulag is like.

2. Divide the class into small groups. Ask each group to select one aspect of the art and culture of the 1920s and 1930s to define and describe.

3. Have students create posters or collages in which they illustrate historical highlights of the career of one of the leaders mentioned in this chapter.

Building Social Studies Skills

Using Artifacts as Historical Evidence

Study the photograph below. Then answer the questions that follow.

Classic 1920s U.S. touring car

1. Which of the following statements best summarizes the historical evidence this artifact gives?
   a. Some automobiles of this period were meant to be driven over long distances.
   b. All automobiles of this period were large.
   c. Only very wealthy people could afford to own an automobile.
   d. Some automobiles of this period may have been designed to be symbols of comfort and luxury.

2. What can you infer about 1920s lifestyles in the United States from this artifact? Give specific examples.

Linking Literature to History

Read the following excerpt from the 1934 "Ballad of Roosevelt" by poet Langston Hughes, a leader of the Harlem Renaissance. Then answer the questions.

"Sister got sick
And the doctor wouldn't come
Cause we couldn't pay him
The proper sum—
A-waitin' on Roosevelt,
Roosevelt, Roosevelt,
A-waitin' on Roosevelt.
Then one day
They put us out o' the house.
Ma and Pa was
Meek as a mouse
Still waitin' on Roosevelt,
Roosevelt, Roosevelt."

3. Which statement best describes the author's main point?
   a. Many families lost their homes during the depression.
   b. Roosevelt's relief programs did not do enough to help.
   c. Even though many people were poor during the depression, they did not complain.
   d. Medical services were almost nonexistent during the depression.

4. How does the author's view of the depression compare with what really happened? Give specific examples.

Alternative Assessment

Building Your Portfolio

Life for many during the years of the Great Depression was a struggle to survive in the face of nearly overwhelming economic hardship. Use the library, the Internet, and other sources to research living conditions in the United States, Great Britain, France, or another industrialized nation during the depression. Then use pictures, drawings, or other visual images to build a collage that reflects your findings.

internet connect

Internet Activity: go.hrw.com
KEYWORD: SP3 WH28

Choose a topic on the Great Depression and the Rise of Totalitarianism to:
- create a pamphlet on the Spanish Civil War.
- create a graph and database on U.S. economic cycles.
- write journal entries from the point of view of a teenager living in the Great Depression.

Reviewing Themes
1. violation did not seem worth war
2. by being appointed chancellor after the Nazis won more seats than any other party in the election of 1932
3. influenced moral relativism

Thinking Critically
1. They already had democratic systems in place.
2. They were attempting to protect their own economic interests.
3. Both advocate complete government control of citizens.
4. difficult and dangerous

Writing About History
Fascism: retain class system, retain private property, total government authority, limited individual rights; Communism: end class system, end private property, total government authority, limited individual rights

Building Social Studies Skills
1. d
2. prosperity, conspicuous consumption, freedom to travel independently
3. b
4. It is accurate in describing the experience of many people.

Building Your Portfolio
Collages should show various forms of hardship and struggle.

CHAPTER
29
Nationalist Movements Around the World

CHAPTER RESOURCE MANAGER

	Objectives	Pacing Guide		Reproducible Resources

SECTION 1
The British Empire in the Postwar Era
(pp. 758–761)

- Identify what caused the end of British rule in Egypt and the Middle East.
- Describe how the people of India pursued independence.
- Explain the British response to calls for change in other parts of the empire.

Regular	Block Scheduling
1.5 day	1 day

Block Scheduling Handbook with Team Teaching Strategies, 29.1

- **RS** Guided Reading Strategy 29.1
- **SM** Geography Activity 29: The Philippine War
- **PS** Readings in World History 101: Gandhi Emerges as India's New Leader
- **E** Hands-on History Activity 29: Challenging Colonial Rule

SECTION 2
Turkey, Persia, and Africa
(pp. 762–764)

- Explain Turkey's development into a modern republic.
- Identify the ideas regarding modern nationalism adopted by Persia.
- Describe the effect of World War I on African attitudes toward colonialism.

Regular	Block Scheduling
1.5 day	1 day

Block Scheduling Handbook with Team Teaching Strategies, 29.2

- **RS** Guided Reading Strategy 29.2
- **PS** Readings in World History 102: The New Africa

SECTION 3
Unrest in China
(pp. 765–769)

- Describe how resentment of foreign interests led to the downfall of the Qing dynasty.
- Identify the ways the nationalist movement in China changed under the leadership of Sun Yixian and Chiang Kai-shek.
- Explain the development of communism in China.

Regular	Block Scheduling
1.5 day	1 day

Block Scheduling Handbook with Team Teaching Strategies, 29.3

- **RS** Guided Reading Strategy 29.3
- **RS** Graphic Organizer Activity 29: Conflict in China
- **PS** Readings in World History 103: Portrait of Mao Zedong

SECTION 4
Imperialism in Japan
(pp. 770–773)

- Explain the Japanese pursuit of expansion that began in the late 1800s.
- Describe the changes in Japanese life during rapid modernization.
- Identify the effects of the military on Japan during the 1920s and the 1930s.

Regular	Block Scheduling
1.5 day	1 day

Block Scheduling Handbook with Team Teaching Strategies, 29.4

- **RS** Guided Reading Strategy 29.4
- **PS** Readings in World History 104: A Justification of Japanese Expansion

SECTION 5
Latin America Between the Wars
(pp. 774–777)

- Describe the significant changes in Latin American nations after World War I.
- Explain why authoritarian regimes gained power in many Latin American nations.
- Describe the relationship between Latin America and the United States.

Regular	Block Scheduling
1.5 day	1 day

Block Scheduling Handbook with Team Teaching Strategies, 29.5

- **RS** Guided Reading Strategy 29.5
- **E** Creative Teaching Strategy 29: Nationalist Manifestos

Chapter Resource Key

PS	Primary Sources	**A**	Assessment		Music
RS	Reading Support	**REV**	Review		Video
IC	Interdisciplinary Connections	**ELL**	Reinforcement and English Language Learners		Internet
E	Enrichment		Transparencies		Holt Presentation Maker Using Microsoft® PowerPoint®
SM	Skills Mastery		CD-ROM		

One-Stop Planner CD-ROM

See the *One-Stop Planner* for a complete list of additional resources for students and teachers.

One-Stop Planner CD-ROM

It's easy to plan lessons, select resources, and print out materials for your students when you use the **One-Stop Planner** CD–ROM with **Test Generator.**

Technology Resources	Reinforcement, Review, and Assessment
One-Stop Planner 29.1 Holt Researcher: World History: Mohandas Gandhi World History and Cultures Video Program 24 Homework Practice Online Online Maps: Nationalist Violence in India, 1908–1939	Daily Quiz 29.1 Main Idea Activity 29.1 English Audio Summary 29.1 Spanish Audio Summary 29.1 REV Section 1 Review, p. 761
One-Stop Planner 29.2 Holt Researcher: World History: Nnamdi Azikiwe, Jomo Kenyatta Regions of the World Music Audio CD Program 11 Homework Practice Online	Daily Quiz 29.2 Main Idea Activity 29.2 English Audio Summary 29.2 Spanish Audio Summary 29.2 REV Section 2 Review, p. 764
One-Stop Planner 29.3 Holt Researcher: World History: Mao Zedong Regions of the World Music Audio CD Program 19: China, Mongolia, and Taiwan: Beating the Dragon Robe: A Traditional Chinese Opera Homework Practice Online	Daily Quiz 29.3 Main Idea Activity 29.3 English Audio Summary 29.3 Spanish Audio Summary 29.3 REV Section 3 Review, p. 769
One-Stop Planner 29.4 Regions of the World Music Audio CD Program 20: Japan and the Koreas: Music of the One-String Ichigenkin CNN. Presents World Cultures: Yesterday and Today Segment 28: Japan's Royal Family Homework Practice Online	Daily Quiz 29.4 Main Idea Activity 29.4 English Audio Summary 29.4 Spanish Audio Summary 29.4 REV Section 4 Review, p. 773
One-Stop Planner 29.5 World History Teaching Transparency: Art and History 24: Murals for the New School for Social Research Homework Practice Online	Daily Quiz 29.5 Main Idea Activity 29.5 English Audio Summary 29.5 Spanish Audio Summary 29.5 REV Section 5 Review, p. 777

internet connect

HRW ONLINE RESOURCES
GO TO: go.hrw.com
Then type in a keyword.

TEACHER HOME PAGE
KEYWORD: SP3 Teacher

CHAPTER INTERNET ACTIVITIES
KEYWORD: SP3 WH29
Choose an activity to:
- write a biography of Mustafa Kemal.
- investigate the British Commonwealth of Nations and how the member nations interact.
- create a poster on wars of independence in the Philippines and Nicaragua.

CHAPTER ENRICHMENT LINKS
KEYWORD: SP3 CH29

ONLINE ASSESSMENT
Homework Practice
KEYWORD: SP3 HP29
Standardized Test Prep
KEYWORD: SP3 STP829
Rubrics
KEYWORD: SS Rubrics

ONLINE MAPS, CHARTS, AND GRAPHS
KEYWORD: SP3 MCG

CONTENT UPDATES
KEYWORD: SS Content Updates

HOLT PRESENTATION MAKER
KEYWORD: SP3 PPT29

ONLINE READING SUPPORT
KEYWORD: SS Strategies

CURRENT EVENTS
KEYWORD: S3 Current Events

Meeting Individual Needs

Ability Levels

Level 1   Basic level activities designed for all students encountering new material

Level 2   Intermediate level activities designed for average students

Level 3   Challenging activities designed for honors and gifted and talented students

English Language Learners   These activities address the needs of students with Limited English Proficiency.

Chapter Review and Assessment

IC   Vocabulary Activity 29
Global Skill Builder CD-ROM
HRW Web Site
REV   Chapter 29 Tutorial for Students, Parents, Mentors, and Peers
REV   Chapter 29 Review, pp. 778–779
A   Chapter 29 Test Generator (on the One-Stop Planner)
A   Chapter 29 Test (Form A or B)
A   Alternative Assessment Handbook
A   Chapter 29 Test for English Language Learners and Special-Needs Students

Build on What You Know

Ask students to answer the following questions:

Why do some countries want to expand their influence to other parts of the world?

Consider:

- new markets
- natural resources
- prestige and power
- spread philosophical or religious beliefs

What are some of the positive and negative effects of imperialism on the colonized peoples?

Consider:

- governmental control
- economic gains and losses
- violent control tactics
- new agricultural techniques, medicines, infrastructure

EXPLORING THE TIME LINE

GLOBAL EVENTS

internet connect

TOPIC: King Tut
GO TO: go.hrw.com
KEYWORD: SP3 WH29

Have students access the Internet through the HRW Go site to learn about the tomb of King Tutankhamen. Have each student write a feature article for a newspaper or magazine about King Tut, his tomb, and the men who found it. Students should choose the year in which their article will be published, and then consider what information would have been available at that time. Have students share their articles with the class.

CHAPTER 29

1898–1938

Nationalist Movements Around the World

Empress Dowager Tz'u-hsi

**c. 1906
Politics**
Mohandas Gandhi begins his first campaign of non-violent resistance to British colonial rule.

**1909
Business and Finance**
The Anglo-Persian Oil Company is formed.

Cartoon depicting European countries dividing China

**1900
Global Events**
The Boxer Rebellion is suppressed.

**1910
Global Events**
Japan annexes Korea.

1900

1910

**1898
Politics**
Empress Dowager Tz'u-hsi begins her rule of China.

**c. 1898
Science and Technology**
Japanese scientist Kiyoshi Shiga discovers the bacteria responsible for dysentery.

**1902
Science and Technology**
The Aswan Dam in Egypt opens.

**1904–1905
Global Events**
The Russo-Japanese War occurs.

**1908
Daily Life**
Cairo University opens.

**1912
Politics**
The Republic of China is formed.

Aswan Dam, Egypt

Build on What You Know

The world struggled to recover after World War I. However, just as the economies of many countries were beginning to fully recover from the war, the Great Depression struck. The United States dealt with the Depression by instituting President Franklin Roosevelt's New Deal. In some European countries the economic turmoil of the 1930s helped lead to the rise of dictatorships. In this chapter, you will learn about revolutionary movements that took place in other parts of the world and what effects they had on the politics and economies of the countries.

What's Your Opinion?

Government

Agree A military's active role in government provides the unity and stability necessary for progress.

Disagree When the military takes an active role in government, freedoms are lost and dissenting voices are hushed through violence and fear.

Culture

Agree Shared traditions, values, and beliefs intensify feelings of nationalism.

Disagree The intensity of nationalistic feelings is mostly affected by economic progress.

Economics

Agree An economic crisis has no effect on government.

Disagree An economic crisis will spark uprisings against the government.

Reza Shah Pahlavi of Persia

Red and green coffee beans still on the branch

1921
Politics
Reza Shah Pahlavi takes control of Persia.

1923
Politics
Transjordan is proclaimed an independent state under the British Mandate.

1923
Daily Life
Mustafa Kemal begins a program of sweeping civil and cultural change in Turkey.

c. 1928
Business and Finance
Overproduction of coffee disrupts Brazil's economy.

1931
Politics
The Statute of Westminster grants autonomy within the British Commonwealth to Australia, New Zealand, Canada, and South Africa as independent nations.

1935
Global Events
Great Britain grants India a constitution.

1920

1930

1940

1919
Global Events
Nationalist uprisings against British rule begin in Egypt.

1919
Politics
British troops kill 400 Indian demonstrators for self-government at Amritsar.

1922
Science and Technology
The tomb of King Tutankhamen is discovered.

1922
The Arts
Mori Ogai, creator of modern Japanese literature, dies.

c. 1922
The Arts
Diego Rivera begins his first mural, *Creation.*

1922–1930
Science and Technology
Dinosaur fossils are found in the Gobi Desert.

1925
Politics
Universal men's suffrage is granted in Japan.

Mao's statue in Kashgar, China

1938
Business and Finance
Oil companies in Mexico are nationalized.

1936
Global Events
King Farouk begins ruling Egypt under a newly established constitutional monarchy.

1934–1935
Politics
Mao Zedong emerges as a leader during the Long March in China.

EXPLORING THE TIME LINE
GLOBAL EVENTS

In 1921 Transjordan was separated from Palestine to placate angry Arabs who opposed British control. In 1946 the former British mandate of Transjordan became independent. Three years later, it adopted the name of the Hashemite Kingdom of Jordan. The territory gradually grew larger as Jordan annexed Palestinian land on the west side of the Jordan River, known as the West Bank. However, this land came under Israeli military occupation after the Arab-Israeli War in 1967. Arabs and Jews are still fighting over the West Bank today.

ACTIVITY: Have students locate Jordan, Israel, the Jordan River, and the West Bank on a map. Ask them to indicate the changes that have taken place in the area since 1921.

What's Your Opinion?

Themes Journal *Do you **agree** or **disagree** with the following statements? Support your point of view in your journal.*

Government The military should have an active role in government.

Culture The intensity of people's nationalistic feelings can be influenced by their culture.

Economics An economic crisis in a nation is distinct from a political crisis.

SECTION 1

OBJECTIVES

1 **Identify what caused the end of British rule in Egypt and the Middle East.**

2 **Describe how the people of India pursued independence.**

3 **Explain the British response to calls for change in other parts of the empire.**

SECTION 1 RESOURCES

REPRODUCIBLE RESOURCES

▶ Guided Reading Strategy 29.1

▶ Geography Activity 29

▶ Hands-on History Activity 29

TECHNOLOGY RESOURCES

▶ One-Stop Planner 29.1

▶ Holt Researcher: World History: Mohandas Gandhi

▶ Homework Practice Online

▶ Online Maps: Nationalist Violence in India, 1908–1939

REINFORCEMENT, REVIEW, AND ASSESSMENT

▶ Section 1 Review, p. 761

▶ Daily Quiz 29.1

▶ Main Idea Activity 29.1

▶ English Audio Summary 29.1

▶ Spanish Audio Summary 29.1

VISUAL RECORD ANSWER

to control trade with the Middle East

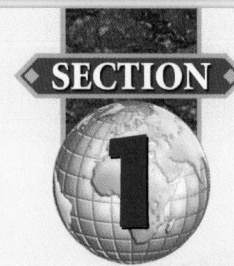

SECTION 1

READ TO DISCOVER

❶ What caused British rule in Egypt and the Middle East to end?

❷ How did the people of India pursue their desire for independence?

❸ How did the British respond to calls for change in other parts of the empire?

DEFINE

passive resistance

IDENTIFY

Wafd Party
Anglo-Egyptian Treaty
Zionism
Balfour Declaration
Mohandas Gandhi

▶ WHY IT MATTERS TODAY

The Suez Canal remains an important pathway for international trade. Use **CNN** or other **current event** sources to identify the role of the Suez Canal in the world economy today. Record your findings in your journal.

CNN student **news** .com

The British Empire in the Postwar Era

The Main Idea
After World War I, British colonies in many parts of the world began to demand more freedom.

The Story Continues *During the height of British imperialism a popular expression said, "The sun never sets on the British Empire." In the late 1800s and early 1900s, that statement was true. The British Empire was so widespread that, at any given moment, some part of the empire somewhere in the world was having daylight. This fact, however, would begin to change after World War I, as Britain began to lose control over parts of its vast empire.*

Egypt and the Middle East

After World War I many of Britain's colonies began demanding self-rule. Dealing with these nationalist movements was difficult because of the vastness of the empire.

Independence for Egypt. Although the Ottoman Empire officially ruled Egypt, the British had in fact controlled the country since 1882. When the Ottomans joined the Central Powers in 1914, the British declared Egypt a protectorate. After World War I a strong nationalist movement developed in Egypt, led by the **Wafd Party.** In 1919 the party led a popular revolt against the British. Although the British quickly put down this revolt, calls for independence continued. Finally, in 1922, the British declared Egypt independent. However, the British government would leave military forces there to defend Egypt and the Suez Canal. Britain also maintained administrative control over the Sudan, which included the Upper Nile, and wanted to oversee Egypt's foreign policy.

During the 1920s and early 1930s, the Egyptian independence movement grew stronger. Egyptian nationalists wanted complete freedom from Britain. After Italy invaded Ethiopia, an alarmed Egypt and Britain forged the **Anglo-Egyptian Treaty** of 1936, which gave Egypt greater independence. The treaty provided the British military with a garrison in Egypt for 20 years. The two nations pledged to support each other if war broke out in the Middle East, and Britain sponsored Egypt's membership in the League of Nations. Many Egyptians, however, were not satisfied because British troops were still stationed throughout Egypt.

INTERPRETING THE VISUAL RECORD

The Suez Canal The Suez Canal (circled in the photo at the left) connects the Mediterranean Sea and the Red Sea. *Based on this picture, why would the British consider it important to retain control of the Suez Canal?*

TEACH OBJECTIVE 1

LEVEL 1: Write the words *Egypt, Transjordan, Iraq,* and *Palestine* on the chalkboard. Ask students what these places had in common in the early 1900s and how they differed. *(all under British control after World War I; Egypt, Transjordan, and Iraq gained independence, although Britain kept military presence; Palestine was retained due to its location)*
ENGLISH LANGUAGE LEARNERS

TEACH OBJECTIVE 2

ALL LEVELS: Copy the following graphic organizer on the chalkboard, omitting the italicized answers. Use it to help students explore the British reaction to the Indian independence movement's policies of passive resistance.
ENGLISH LANGUAGE LEARNERS

Passive Resistance	British Reaction
boycotts	*restricted civil liberties*
nonpayment of taxes	*disrupted political gatherings*

SKILL-BUILDING STRATEGIES — Making Graphs

The Size of the British Empire

Graphs, as you have learned, are visual presentations of information. Just as interpreting graphs is an important part of reading and comprehending history, so too is the ability to create them. The ability to make graphs allows you to organize material in a way that often makes it easier to understand and remember. Making graphs out of information, such as the population of the British Empire, can help you gain a better understanding of the topic.

The British Empire was vast not only in territory, but also in population. The mandates following World War I increased the empire to its fullest extent. But the British government and military was not as strong as it had been during the buildup of its empire. As nationalist movements arose in its colonies, the British were unable to maintain their grasp on the empire.

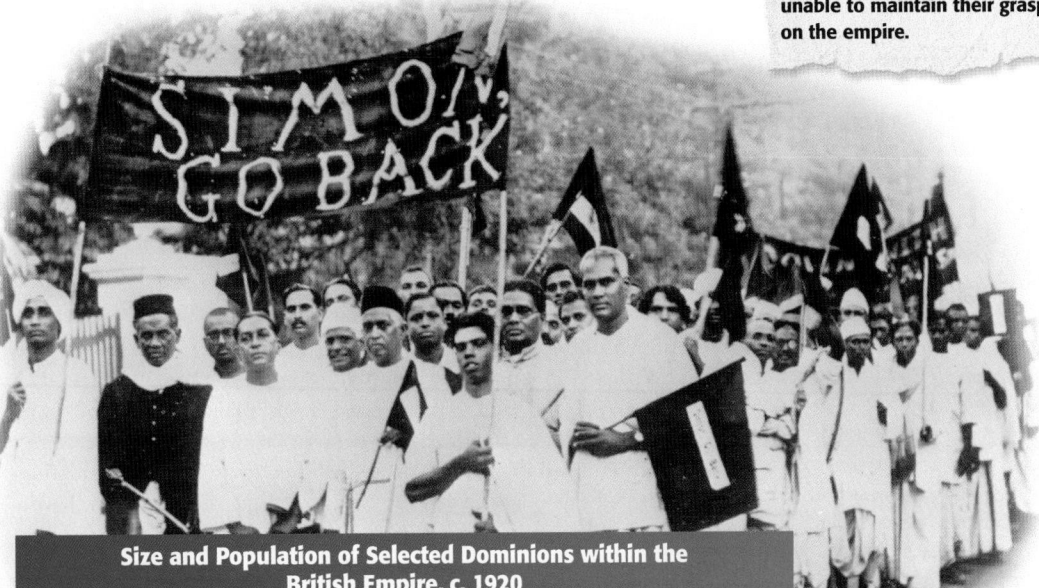

Size and Population of Selected Dominions within the British Empire, c. 1920		
Country	**Area under British control (in square miles)**	**Population under British control (approximate)**
India	1,802,629	306,000,000
Australia	2,967,909	5,000,000
Canada	3,851,809	8,788,000
South Africa	471,445	6,250,000
Rest of empire	3,006,208	69,962,000
British Empire total	**12,100,000**	**396,000,000**

Shown above are Indians protesting the Simon Commission, which was appointed by the British government to examine British rule in India. The commission met with opposition because it included no Indians.

Skills Reminder

To create a graph from written text, determine the focus and title of the graph. Then decide which type of graph will provide the best visual summary of the material. A line graph plots changes in quantities over time. A bar graph is most often used to compare amounts within categories. A pie graph, or circle graph, divides a circular whole into sections, with the whole equaling 100 percent. Identify the necessary data. Create the graph.

Skills Practice

❶ Using the data above, build a graph showing the percentage of the land area of the British Empire represented by each country. Build another graph showing the percentages of the empire's population by country.

❷ Using your library or the Internet, research other statistical data about one of the countries discussed in this chapter and use that information to create a graph.

Government

In 1928 Britain sent Sir John Simon with a parliamentary commission to India. The commission served to unite the divided Muslim and Hindu nationalists—a division not encouraged by the British—and its members were met with tremendous protests throughout India. The lack of Indian representation in the commission was at times referred to as an "oversight." In reaction to the "oversight" and expectation of the commission's report, the Indian National Congress quickly convened to demand dominion status for India. Shortly after, they met again to insist on complete self-rule, and one year later congress displayed India's current tri-colored flag to represent complete resistance to British rule.

Critical Thinking

Why would the British encourage divisions between Muslims and Hindus?

ANSWER: A lack of unity among the people would hamper efforts for independence.

SKILLS PRACTICE ANSWERS

1. land area: India 15%, Australia 24%, Canada 32%, South Africa 4%, Rest 25%; population: India 77%, Australia 1.2%, Canada 2.2%, South Africa 1.6%, Rest 18%

2. Answers will vary.

Teacher to Teacher

Laura L. Boelter of Mesa, Arizona, suggested the following activity: Have students think of a rule or law that they find unfair. Have them brainstorm what they could do to change this law. Discuss which suggestions, if any, that Mohandas Gandhi would endorse. Have students develop strategies that Gandhi might suggest and evaluate how effective these strategies might be.

TEACH OBJECTIVE 3

LEVEL 3: Have students conduct further research on the Statute of Westminster.

HOMEWORK Have students prepare a chart listing the colonies and Britain's response to each of their nationalist movements.

CLOSE

Have students consider the role culture played in India's independence movement.

HISTORY MAKER ANSWER
selfless and committed

Reproducible Resources

PS Readings in World History 101: Gandhi Emerges as India's New Leader

Technology Resources

World History and Cultures Video Program 24: Roads to Independence

HISTORY MAKER

Mohandas Gandhi (1869–1948)

A member of an Indian merchant class family, Mohandas Gandhi became a lawyer. While practicing law in South Africa, however, he confronted racist attitudes. Beginning in about 1906 Gandhi began his first campaign of non-violent resistance to achieve justice.

In 1914 Gandhi returned to India. A massacre of Hindus by British authorities convinced him that India must strive for complete independence. As a leader in the Indian National Congress, Gandhi worked toward that goal. His humble manner and attire inspired millions and earned him great respect. His followers called him Mahatma, or "Great Soul." Gandhi was assassinated in 1948. **How would you characterize Gandhi's life and work?**

The Middle East. Middle Eastern Arabs had helped the British during World War I. They therefore felt betrayed when both Britain and France imposed control on them after the war. Britain eventually recognized the independence of both Transjordan and Iraq, but maintained a strong military presence in both kingdoms. Meanwhile, the British kept complete control over Palestine because of its strategic location. Events in Palestine, however, soon presented Britain with a serious problem.

Since the late 1800s, Jews from Europe had been establishing small colonies in Palestine. A nationalist movement called **Zionism** aimed to build a Palestinian homeland for Jews. In 1917 Britain was seeking support among Jews for the Allied war effort. To win it, British foreign secretary Arthur Balfour wrote to a Zionist leader, expressing British support for a Jewish homeland. Balfour's statement later became known as the **Balfour Declaration.** It became the basis of Great Britain's mandate for Palestine and, for the next 30 years, strongly shaped British policies in the region.

 ❝His Majesty's Government view with favour the establishment in Palestine of a national home for the Jewish people, . . . it being clearly understood that nothing should be done which may prejudice the civil and religious rights of existing non-Jewish communities in Palestine. . . .❞

Lord Balfour, Balfour Declaration

The British had also promised to allow the creation of an independent Arab state that included parts of Palestine in exchange for helping defeat the Ottomans. After World War I, both the Jews and Arabs expected Great Britain to make good on its promises. Tensions rose and clashes erupted between the two groups. To calm Arab fears, the British limited the number of Jews allowed to immigrate to Palestine. The Jews resented this policy. When the Nazis began persecuting them, Jewish immigration to Palestine increased. In 1937 the British declared that a Zionist homeland and Arab independence were incompatible. It recommended dividing the land between the groups. World War II delayed action on this plan.

✔ **READING CHECK: Analyzing Information** Why did the British make promises to both the Arabs and Jews? an effort to satisfy both sides

The Independence Movement in India

India was Great Britain's largest colony. In return for Indian troops and money during World War I, Britain had promised India more self-government. After the war, however, the British were divided on the issue. Some felt that Indian self-rule would lead to the empire's destruction. Others believed that self-rule should be granted to India as it had been to other parts of the British Empire.

Indians, too, disagreed on independence. Some Indians, including some who had been educated in the West, wanted to continue under British rule. Indian nationalists called for complete independence. Any settlement would have to accommodate the diverse views in India—of both Muslims and Hindus, of both upper castes and lower castes, and of different regions.

The leader of the Indian nationalist movement was **Mohandas Gandhi.** Many Indians revered Gandhi as a spiritual as well as a political leader. Gandhi opposed violence. He urged the people to gain independence by nonviolently refusing to cooperate with the government, a form of civil disobedience called **passive resistance.** Gandhi described his feelings about passive resistance as follows:

History Makers Speak

❝I believe in the doctrine of non-violence as a weapon of the strongest. I believe that a man is the strongest soldier for daring to die unarmed with his breast bare before the enemy.❞

Mohandas Gandhi, quoted in *The Story of a Nation,* by Gulam Ali Alanna

Passive resistance included boycotting British goods and refusing to pay taxes. To control this nationalist movement, the British restricted civil liberties and forcibly broke up political gatherings. Many moderate Indians turned against British rule.

In 1935 Great Britain allowed India to elect representatives. However, it still controlled India's defense, revenue, and foreign policy. The British could also veto laws proposed by the representatives. Efforts for complete independence continued.

✔ **READING CHECK: Drawing Inferences** What factors within Indian society contributed to diverse views on Indian independence? differences in caste, religion, and education

The Commonwealth Expands

Even in parts of the British Empire that had some self-government, the people sought more. After World War I, the dominions of Canada, Australia, New Zealand, and South Africa wanted complete self-government. Great Britain agreed and in 1931 granted these four dominions autonomy. They joined with Great Britain as equal partners in the British Commonwealth of Nations. Each member became responsible for its own policies. Over the years, other British colonies became independent and joined the Commonwealth. Favorable trade agreements among member nations helped their economies during the depression that faced many countries after World War I. The Commonwealth, therefore, worked well economically for both Great Britain and its former colonies.

✔ **READING CHECK: Identifying Cause and Effect** Why did colonies that had achieved independence agree to join in the British Commonwealth? Favorable trade agreements among Commonwealth member nations helped their economies.

Analyzing Primary Sources

Making Predictions How might a nonviolent refusal to cooperate with a ruling government produce victory for nationalists? Without the participation of the people the government could not function.

Holt Researcher
go.hrw.com
KEYWORD: Holt Researcher
FreeFind: Mohandas Gandhi
After reading more about Mohandas Gandhi on the Holt Researcher, write an analysis of his influence on events of the 20th century.

SECTION 1 REVIEW

1. Define and explain the significance:
passive resistance

2. Identify and explain the significance:
Wafd Party
Anglo-Egyptian Treaty
Zionism
Balfour Declaration
Mohandas Gandhi

3. Sequencing Make a flowchart like the one below. Use it to list the important stages of Egypt's national status after World War I.

1919   1922   1920s–30s   1936

Homework Practice Online
keyword: SP3 HP29

4. **Finding the Main Idea**
   a. How did Great Britain's relationship with Egypt change over time?
   b. What role did Zionism play in Palestine's efforts toward independence?
   c. How did the people of India work for self-rule?
   d. How did the British respond to calls for change in other parts of their empire?

5. **Writing and Critical Thinking**
   Identifying Bias Write a brief explanation of what various groups might gain or lose by making India independent or by having it remain under British rule.
   Consider:
   • how independence would benefit citizens of India
   • why the existence of different religious and social groups presented a problem for independence

OBJECTIVES

1 Explain Turkey's development into a modern republic.

2 Identify the ideas regarding modern nationalism adopted by Persia.

3 Describe the effect of World War I on African attitudes toward colonialism.

🔊 LET'S GET STARTED!

As students enter the classroom, ask them to write down the role the Ottomans played during World War I and the effects of the war on that empire. *(Central Powers, lost territory)* In light of what was happening in the Middle East, ask students to predict what will happen in Turkey. *(nationalist movements may arise; country may modernize)* Tell students that in Section 2 they will learn about a new leader's modernization of Turkey.

SECTION 2 RESOURCES

REPRODUCIBLE RESOURCES

▶ Guided Reading Strategy 29.2

▶ Readings in World History 102: The New Africa

TECHNOLOGY RESOURCES

▶ One-Stop Planner 29.2

▶ Holt Researcher: World History: Nnamdi Azikiwe, Jomo Kenyatta

▶ Homework Practice Online

REINFORCEMENT, REVIEW, AND ASSESSMENT

▶ Section 2 Review, p. 764

▶ Daily Quiz 29.2

▶ Main Idea Activity 29.2

▶ English Audio Summary 29.2

▶ Spanish Audio Summary 29.2

VISUAL RECORD ANSWER

They were preferable and necessary to the modernization of Turkey.

SECTION 2

▶ READ TO DISCOVER

❶ How did Turkey become a modern republic?

❷ What ideas regarding modern nationalism were adopted by Persia?

❸ How did World War I change African attitudes toward colonialism?

▶ IDENTIFY

Mustafa Kemal
Reza Shah Pahlavi
Nnamdi Azikiwe
Jomo Kenyatta
Léopold Senghor

▶ WHY IT MATTERS TODAY

Countries have taken different approaches and attitudes toward independence, modernization, and Westernization. Use **CNN** or other **current event** sources to compare the present state of modernization in several former colonies. Record your findings in your journal.

CNN Student News.com

Turkey, Persia, and Africa

The Main Idea
After World War I nationalist movements gained political influence in Turkey, Persia, and Africa.

The Story Continues *The nationalist ideas that swept the Middle East and India after World War I did not stop there. New political forces began to stir in other colonies and remnants of old empires. Change would not come easily, however. As one new leader would declare, "We must teach our people to be free."*

Turkey Under Kemal

After its defeat in World War I, the once mighty Ottoman Empire was stripped of all its land except Turkey. Greek troops arrived to impose the peace treaty's terms, and the weak Ottoman government could do nothing to prevent their increasing grip on the country.

Then **Mustafa Kemal,** a hero of the fighting at Gallipoli, stepped forward. Kemal and his nationalist followers took control of the assembly. Declaring that the sultan was controlled by Turkey's enemies, the assembly appointed a council headed by Kemal to run the country. Kemal's forces drove the Greeks from Turkey in 1922. That same year the assembly did away with the sultanate. In 1923 it established the Republic of Turkey and moved the capital to Ankara. Kemal became the republic's first president. The government became a one-party system led by the president.

Kemal believed that the war had shown the superiority of Western technology and Western ideas of nationalism. He worked to modernize and westernize Turkey. Believing that Islam was a roadblock to modernization, he drew up a new constitution that ended the long union of Islam and the government. He abolished the position of caliph, imposed broad civil and social reforms, and abandoned the Islamic calendar.

Kemal ordered the Turkish people to adopt Western ways. He prohibited the wearing of traditional clothing and decreed that all Turks take surnames. He himself took the name Atatürk, meaning "father of the Turks." Kemal also established secular schools and colleges and replaced the Arabic-based Turkish alphabet with the Latin alphabet. He supported laws that gave women the right to vote and hold office. His economic programs included state-run industries and subsidized farming. Under Kemal, Turkey became more prosperous.

✔ **READING CHECK: Drawing Inferences** Why did Mustafa Kemal feel it was necessary to separate the government from Islam in order to carry out his programs? to keep separate the functions of religion and government

INTERPRETING THE VISUAL RECORD

Mustafa Kemal It was Mustafa Kemal who declared that the people must be taught to be free. *What does Kemal's appearance here tell you about his view of Western things?*

TEACH OBJECTIVE 1

LEVEL 1: Have students list Atatürk's reforms. Then, ask them what effect his reforms had on Turkey.
ENGLISH LANGUAGE LEARNERS

TEACH OBJECTIVE 2

LEVEL 3: Have students write an essay that compares and contrasts the nationalist reforms of Mustafa Kemal and Reza Khan and evaluates qualities of each leader.

HOMEWORK Have students create an organizational chart summarizing the changes Reza Khan implemented in Persia.

TEACH OBJECTIVE 3

ALL LEVELS: Have students examine the changes in African attitudes toward colonialism by completing the result column.
ENGLISH LANGUAGE LEARNERS

Experience	Result
World War I	*ideas about freedom and nationalism*
colonial education	*ideas about equality and self-rule*
racism and political repression	*work toward reform and independence*

Modernizing Persia

Turkey's neighbor, Persia, had never been under the control of the Ottoman Empire. Shahs of the Qajar dynasty had ruled Persia since the 1700s. By about 1900, however, both Great Britain and Russia had begun to exert a strong influence on the Persian government.

In 1921 Reza Khan, a Persian army officer with strong nationalist feelings, seized control of the government. Four years later, he deposed the ruling shah and took the throne, taking the title **Reza Shah Pahlavi.**

Like Mustafa Kemal, Reza Shah wanted to modernize his country and free it from foreign domination. He strengthened the army and broke the power of rebellious tribes. Under a massive reform program, he built roads and hospitals, established a university, and gave women more rights. Transportation and communication were improved, and new industries were begun. In 1935 Reza Shah announced that the country would be officially called what its people called it—Iran.

Iran's constitution called for a limited monarchy, but Reza Shah held most of the power. He strictly controlled the press and suppressed political parties. His secret police ruthlessly put down any opposition to his government. Reza Shah's foreign policy of balancing British and Russian interests led him to seek closer ties with Germany. This alliance would eventually cause his downfall.

✔ **READING CHECK: Supporting a Point of View** How would you support the view that Reza Shah was effective in modernizing Persia?
transportation and communication improved, new industries began

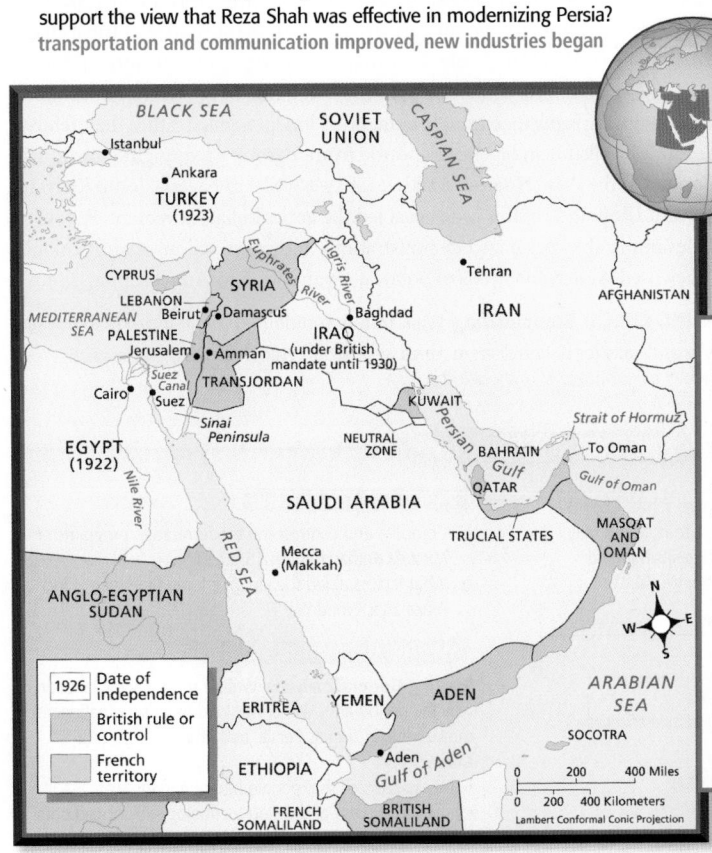

New Nations in the Middle East, 1922–1939

Interpreting Maps With the formation of new countries in the Middle East, control over vital areas, such as the Strait of Hormuz, became important.

■ **Skills Assessment:**
1. **The World in Spatial Terms** What two countries controlled the land surrounding the Strait of Hormuz?
2. **Analyzing Information** Why would the Strait of Hormuz be important?

Global Relations

During World War II, despite Reza Shah's proclamations of Iran's neutrality, Britain demanded that Iran expel all German citizens. Britain and the USSR eventually invaded Iran, exiled Reza Shah, and replaced him with his son.

Critical Thinking

What might you deduce about the son's leadership role?

ANSWER: influenced by Britain

🖵 **internet** connect

TOPIC: Mustafa Kemal
GO TO: go.hrw.com
KEYWORD: SP3 WH29

Have students access the Internet through the HRW Go site to find information on Mustafa Kemal and the reforms that occurred in Turkey under his rule. Ask students to write a biography of Mustafa Kemal that includes information about his life, accomplishments, and significance to history.

MAP ANSWERS
1. Britain and Iran

2. strategic significance for trade shipments and military

Technology Resources
Regions of the World Music Audio CD Program 11

CLOSE

Ask students to explain why it is ironic that Western ideas influenced the nationalist movements in Turkey, Persia, and Africa after World War I.

REVIEW

Have students complete the Section 2 Review on p. 764.

ASSESS

Have students complete Daily Quiz 29.2. As Alternative Assessment, you may want to use the African attitudes graphic organizer or the essay exercise in this section's lessons.

RETEACH

Have students complete Main Idea Activity for English Language Learners and Special-Needs Students 29.2. Then ask students to create, trade, and solve riddles, using words in Section 2.

EXTEND

Have students research a leader and write a one- to two-page scene relating to the leader's nationalist ideas.

YOUNG PEOPLE IN HISTORY ANSWER

to read and write in English; Christian faith

REVIEW ANSWERS

❶ **Identify**
- Mustafa Kemal, p. 762
- Reza Shah Pahlavi, p. 763
- Nnamdi Azikiwe, p. 764
- Jomo Kenyatta, p. 764
- Léopold Senghor, p. 764

❷ Turkey: Mustafa Kemal and followers take control of Turkey and institute reforms; Persia: Reza Khan declares himself shah, strengthens army, and brings about reforms; Africa: nationalists demand reforms, leaders of anticolonial movement attract support with Western methods of political organization

❸ a. Similarities: imposed civil reforms; Differences: Mustafa Kemal separated Islam from government while Reza Shah Pahlavi did not

b. soldier's experiences, Western education, racism, and repression

❹ Answers will vary but students may note that the war left soldiers with new ideas about freedom and nationalism and that people wanted the same success for their countries that so many in the West had experienced.

YOUNG PEOPLE IN HISTORY

Missionary Schools
The first experience that many Africans had with Western ideas and culture came from Christian missionary schools. Students learned to read and write in English and were taught the Christian faith with stories from the Bible. Many missionaries learned the languages and the customs of the Africans in order to live and work among them. **What did students learn in missionary schools?**

Holt Researcher
go.hrw.com
KEYWORD: Holt Researcher
FreeFind: Nnamdi Azikiwe
Jomo Kenyatta
After reading more about Azikiwe and Kenyatta on the Holt Researcher, create a time line marking the major events in their anticolonial movements.

Africans Call for Change

The many Africans who fought in the armies of Great Britain and France during World War I expected to be rewarded. They wanted greater political freedom after the war. Like the Indians, they were disappointed.

Increased political activity. The war had broadened the experience of many Africans. For the first time, they encountered the world beyond their villages and families. When these former soldiers returned home, they brought with them new ideas about freedom and nationalism. In time, they put these ideas to work organizing anticolonial protest movements. Colonial education also moved many Africans to become politically active. Missionary and government schools taught African students Western ideals of equality and self-rule. At the same time, the colonial governments denied Africans these rights. More and more Africans personally experienced the contradiction between Western teaching and their lives under colonialism. They became determined that change must come. Racism and political repression made many Africans actively seek reform and even independence.

New political associations and leaders. Africans began to organize. Tanganyika, for example, was a former German colony whose mandate had been given to Britain. Tanganyikans formed a civil servants' association. Open to all Africans, it overcame traditional ethnic barriers and became a center of anticolonial protest. Other labor unions and workers' associations also became important forums for African complaints. In response, colonial governments strengthened the authority of tribal chiefs, who generally favored colonial rule. Colonial rulers also agreed to some reforms. However, these small efforts could not stem the rising tide of opposition to colonialism. By the 1930s Africans increasingly demanded independence rather than reform.

The loudest calls for independence came from a group of young men who had been educated in the West. **Nnamdi Azikiwe** (ah-ZEEK-wah) of Nigeria, **Jomo Kenyatta** of Kenya, and **Léopold Senghor** of Senegal led the anticolonial movement. Following Gandhi's example, they organized demonstrations and other actions against colonial rulers. They used Western methods of political organization to attract support.

✔ **READING CHECK: Summarizing** What factors contributed to the increase in political activity and calls for nationalism in Africa after World War I? increased education, Western ideas of nationalism and equality

---

SECTION 2 REVIEW

1. **Identify** and explain the significance:
   Mustafa Kemal
   Reza Shah Pahlavi
   Nnamdi Azikiwe
   Jomo Kenyatta
   Léopold Senghor

2. **Analyzing Information** Copy the chart below. Use it to note the main steps toward nationalization and modernization after World War I.

Turkey	Persia	Africa

   ↓ ↓ ↓
   Nationalization and modernization

3. **Finding the Main Idea**
   a. Compare and contrast the modernization programs of Mustafa Kemal and Reza Shah Pahlavi.
   b. What factors aided the struggle for independence in Africa after World War I?

4. **Writing and Critical Thinking**
   Making Generalizations Write a summary explanation of why the period after World War I led to a rise in nationalist movements in Turkey, Persia, and Africa.
   Consider:
   • the experiences that people had during the war
   • how the success of Western technology influenced both citizens and leaders

Homework Practice Online
keyword: SP3 HP29

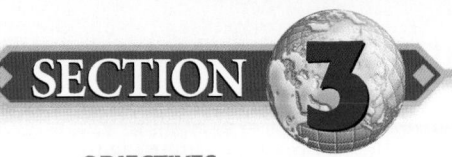

SECTION 3

OBJECTIVES

1 Describe how resentment of foreign interests led to the downfall of the Qing dynasty.

2 Identify the ways the nationalist movement in China changed under the leadership of Sun Yixian and Chiang Kai-shek.

3 Explain the development of communism in China.

SECTION 3

READ TO DISCOVER

❶ How did resentment of foreign interests lead to the downfall of the Qing dynasty?

❷ In what ways did the nationalist movement in China change under the leadership of Sun Yixian and Chiang Kai-shek?

❸ How did communism develop in China?

IDENTIFY

Open Door Policy
Empress Dowager Tz'u-hsi
Boxer Rebellion
Kuomintang
Sun Yixian
Chiang Kai-shek
Long March
Mao Zedong

WHY IT MATTERS TODAY

Today the Nationalist Chinese occupy the island of Taiwan off the coast of mainland China. Use CNN Student News.com or other **current event** sources to identify the issues that exist between the People's Republic of China and Taiwan. Record your findings in your journal.

CNN Student News.com

Unrest in China

The Main Idea
In the early 1900s Chinese nationalists fought foreign influence in their country and then each other.

The Story Continues *The increasing influence of Western powers in China caused divisions within the country. Increasingly dissatisfied with the monarchy, some Chinese launched a nationalist movement to regain Chinese power and glory through Western ideals of government. "In comparison with other nations, we have the greatest population and the oldest culture, of four thousand years' duration," noted one nationalist leader. The nationalists hoped that their movement would continue this great tradition.*

The End of the Qing Dynasty

By about 1900 the imperialist powers of France, Germany, Great Britain, Japan, and Russia enjoyed substantial spheres of influence in China. The foreign powers stayed mainly on the coast and along the Chang River. At the turn of the century, however, foreign traders increasingly moved deeper into China's interior.

The United States was concerned that American merchants would be excluded from Chinese trade. In 1899 the U.S. government appealed to other nations to recognize what it called the **Open Door Policy.** Under this policy, all nations would have equal rights to trade in China. Other countries, however, were vague in their responses to the U.S. appeal. The scramble for trade privileges continued.

The Boxer Rebellion. By the end of the 1800s, foreign powers had won numerous trade concessions and privileges. Foreign interests dominated the Chinese economy and government. Traders and missionaries traveled the country at will. China's fate as a secondary nation seemed sealed.

In 1898 the young Qing emperor hoped to reduce foreign interference by revitalizing his government and modernizing China. The country's conservative leaders were offended by these drastic cultural changes. The emperor's aging aunt, the **Empress Dowager Tz'u-hsi** (TSOO·SHEE), took action. The emperor was imprisoned, and for the next ten years Tz'u-hsi ruled China.

Tz'u-hsi 's officials encouraged anti-foreigner movements that were breaking out, including a group called the Society of the Righteous and Harmonious Fists. In the English language the members of this group became known simply as Boxers. The Boxers attacked first Chinese Christians and, later, foreign missionaries. When they began attacking foreigners throughout China, the uprising became known as the **Boxer Rebellion.** The Boxers destroyed churches, railways, mines—anything connected with outsiders. Many foreigners fled to embassies in Beijing. There they came under siege by an army of angry Boxers.

Determined to protect their interests in China, imperialist nations sent an army to Beijing. Soldiers from Great Britain, France, Germany, Russia, Japan, and the United States put down the Boxer Rebellion in 1900. The foreign powers then imposed heavy penalties on the Chinese, including fines for destroyed property. They also claimed the right to maintain troops in Beijing and along the Beijing-Tianjian

SECTION 3 RESOURCES

REPRODUCIBLE RESOURCES

▶ Guided Reading Strategy 29.3

▶ Graphic Organizer Activity 29: Conflict in China

▶ Readings in World History 103: Portrait of Mao Zedong

TECHNOLOGY RESOURCES

▶ One-Stop Planner 29.3

▶ Holt Researcher: World History: Mao Zedong

▶ Regions of the World Music Audio CD Program 19: China, Mongolia, and Taiwan: Beating the Dragon Robe: A Traditional Chinese Opera

▶ Homework Practice Online

REINFORCEMENT, REVIEW, AND ASSESSMENT

▶ Section 3 Review, p. 769

▶ Daily Quiz 29.3

▶ Main Idea Activity 29.3

▶ English Audio Summary 29.3

▶ Spanish Audio Summary 29.3

TEACH OBJECTIVE 1

ALL LEVELS: Use the following graphic organizer to help students list the steps that led to the downfall of the Qing dynasty. **ENGLISH LANGUAGE LEARNERS**

Qing downfall

imperialist powers trade in China

Qing emperor imprisoned

Tz'u-hsi supports Boxer Rebellion

foreigners put down rebellion; take more control in China

Kuomintang formed

revolts lead to end of Qing

TEACH OBJECTIVE 2

LEVEL 1: Ask students to describe Sun Yixian and Chiang Kai-shek's backgrounds before leading the Nationalists. Discuss with students how a person's background affects their point of view and ask them how these leaders' points of view affected the nationalist movement in China. (*Sun Yixian supported modernization and republican government; Chiang Kai-shek strengthened the army and supported the conservatives.*) **ENGLISH LANGUAGE LEARNERS**

Culture

Toward the end of the 1800s, many Chinese scholars shifted from traditional to modern ideas and practices. Western religious texts were translated, along with a variety of other written works. The 1870s brought newspapers and magazines that circulated information about current events and change—a distinct break from Confucianism's restrictive focus on the past. Large numbers of people were able to read the same periodicals at the same time. The press included satirical and critical pieces aimed at the government and foreign nations, which provoked reactions from the mass populace.

Critical Thinking

In what way might the press have contributed to the downfall of the Qing dynasty?

ANSWER: by allowing great numbers of Chinese to have access to new ideas

HISTORY MAKER ANSWER

Answers will vary, but students may note that Western ideas would challenge her policies.

MAP ANSWER

France

HISTORY MAKER

Empress Dowager Tz'u-hsi (1835–1908)

As a young girl growing up in the imperial court, Tz'u-hsi witnessed the effects of the Opium War and the Taiping Rebellion. She was also present when the British and French occupied Beijing in 1860 and destroyed the emperor's summer palace. She became a bitter opponent of Western influence.

As regent for Chinese emperors, Tz'u-hsi dominated China for decades. Called "Old Buddha" by Westerners, she prevented many reforms. For example, she diverted funds for a new navy to rebuild the summer palace. **Why might the Empress Dowager Tz'u-hsi have opposed Western reform?**

Railway to the coast. The crushing of the Boxer Rebellion brought China completely under foreign domination.

Overthrow of the dynasty. The Boxer Rebellion failed to drive foreigners from Chinese soil. It did, however, encourage nationalist sentiment among the Chinese people, especially the young and well educated. A new political party, the **Kuomintang,** or Chinese Nationalist Party, grew out of the nationalists' desire for reform. The party's director was **Sun Yixian** (also known as Sun Yat-sen). He had lived in the United States, attended school in Hawaii, and studied medicine at two medical schools in Hong Kong. Sun Yixian described the necessity of nationalism to his fellow Chinese:

❝The Chinese people have only family and clan groups; there is no national spirit. Consequently, . . . we are the poorest and weakest state in the world. . . . If we do not earnestly promote nationalism and weld together . . . we face a tragedy—the loss of our country and the destruction of our race.❞

Sun Yixian, quoted in *A Treasury of the World's Great Speeches,* edited by Houston Peterson

The nationalists were influenced by the Western ideas of Sun Yixian and others. They wanted a constitutional government with civil liberties guaranteed by a bill of rights. They also wanted China to become industrialized so that it could defend itself economically against imperialist powers. The nationalists believed that China could protect itself against foreign control only if it became a modern nation.

Foreign Influence in China, 1839–1912

Interpreting Maps European powers claimed control over large portions of China.

■ **Skills Assessment: Human Systems** Which country with a sphere of influence in China was least likely to be affected by the Boxer Rebellion?

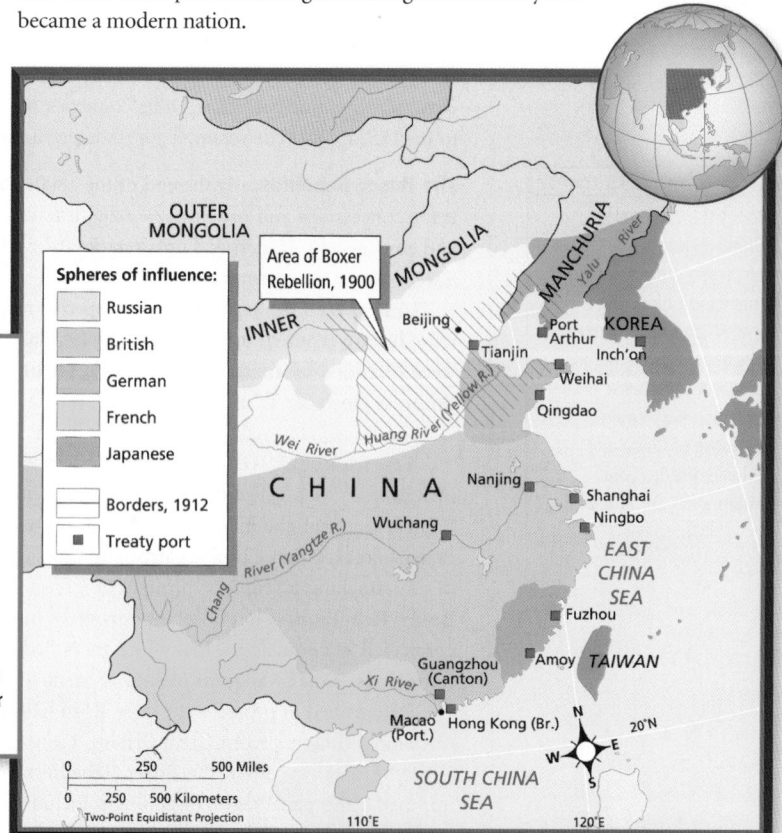

Spheres of influence:
- Russian
- British
- German
- French
- Japanese

— Borders, 1912

■ Treaty port

TEACH OBJECTIVE 2

LEVEL 3: Have students prepare and enact a court trial with the Qing dynasty as defendants and the Kuomintang as witnesses for the prosecution.

 HOMEWORK: Have students write a list of the changes Sun Yixian and the Nationalist Party wanted to make in China and reasons why they wanted to make those changes.

TEACH OBJECTIVE 3

LEVEL 2: Have students work in pairs to create a storyboard with captions underneath representing the key events that led to the rise of communism in China. **COOPERATIVE LEARNING**

ALL LEVELS: Ask students to imagine they are supporters of Chiang Kai-shek, Henry P'u-i, or Mao Zedong. Ask them to write a letter to a Chinese student outside of the country describing the development of communism in China.
ENGLISH LANGUAGE LEARNERS

Pressured by the nationalists, the Qing rulers attempted reforms, including the promise of a new constitution. Nationalists, merchants, and powerful rural families, however, wanted a complete break from "Old China" and an end to the Qing dynasty. In 1911 army officers supporting Sun Yixian led a series of revolts in southern China. The leader of the imperial army, Yuan Shikai, did not respond with force. Instead he negotiated, hoping for a new dynasty with himself in a position of power. No agreement was reached, however, and the 268-year Qing dynasty ended.

✔ **READING CHECK: Drawing Inferences** Why might Chinese nationalists have wanted a leader who had been educated by the Western nations from which they wanted freedom? wanted to modernize China

Sun Yixian, pictured here with his wife, worked to create a national spirit among the Chinese.

Forming the Chinese Republic

In February 1912 the Kuomintang forced the last Qing emperor to abdicate. It then proclaimed China a republic. Sun Yixian described the Kuomintang philosophy as the "Three Principles of the People"—the people's government, the people's rights, and the people's livelihood. The principles called for (1) political unification and an end to foreign influence; (2) a gradual change to democratic government, with full personal liberties and rights for all Chinese people; and (3) economic improvements that included industrialization and a more equal distribution of land.

Problems with the warlords. Revolution and assassination marked the early years of the Republic of China. Yuan Shikai became president, and Sun Yixian fled to Japan. Yuan tried to start his own imperial dynasty. He failed, but China was in turmoil. Powerful warlords ruled most of the country with their personal armies.

The Nationalists—as members of the Kuomintang called themselves—hoped to defeat the warlords and establish a strong central government for the Republic of China. They asked for help from foreign powers, but only the Soviet Union responded. In the early 1920s, the Soviets sent technical, political, and military advisers to help build a modern Chinese army.

A split in the Kuomintang. When Sun Yixian died in 1925, military commander **Chiang Kai-shek** (CHANG KY·SHEK) took over leadership of the Nationalists. Under Chiang the Nationalist army grew stronger. In 1926 Chiang began a military campaign against the warlords called the Northern Expedition. Warlord resistance collapsed against the efficient, highly motivated Nationalist troops. The Nationalists quickly gained control of Hunan province and the cities of the Wuhan area.

Not all members of the Kuomintang were satisfied. The left wing of the party, made up of socialists and Communists, wanted more power for the peasants and workers. The conservative right wing opposed such radical change, particularly redistributing land to the peasants. Chiang became leader of the right wing.

Under Chiang Kai-shek, the Nationalist army slowly unified China, but political forces split.

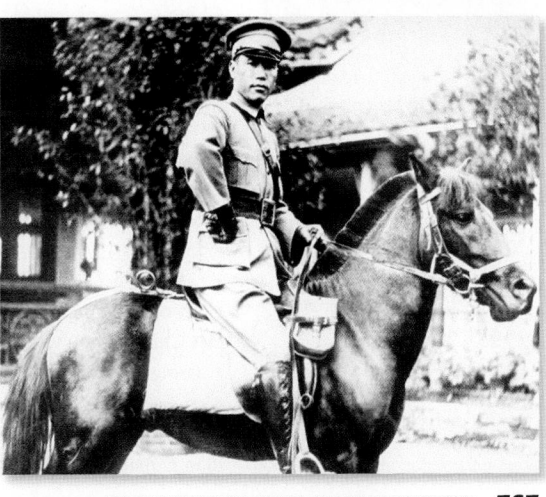

Historical Sidelight

The period from 1916 to 1928 in China is often referred to as the warlord period. A warlord was a person who commanded a personal army and controlled or wanted to control territory. Warlords had many different characteristics—some had formal military training, while others came from peasant backgrounds. One warlord was known as "the Christian General"; he baptized his troops with fire hoses. One trait shared by the warlords was their control of personal armies that followed only their command. Warlord armies were primarily comprised of peasants. Peasants joined the armies for many reasons; some saw it as a way to get ahead.

Critical Thinking

Ask students what kind of strategy the new Chinese leaders might have used to defeat the warlords.

ANSWER: Answers will vary but students might suggest that leaders could find ways to employ peasants and relieve their poverty and suffering.

Unhappy with traditional methods and betrayed by the West, many Chinese intellectuals were drawn to Marxism—a philosophy that purported the eventual demise of capitalism, the succession of socialism, and finally communism. Have students use their texts, the library, and the Internet to search for information about Marxism. Encourage students to find details about the philosophy and its history and decide why it appealed to a large number of Chinese. Ask them to share their findings and conclusions with the class.

BLOCK SCHEDULING, COOPERATIVE LEARNING

CLOSE

Ask students to list causes leading to the decline of the Qing dynasty and the rise of communism in China. Put these ideas on the chalkboard and have students decide which item is related to Chinese culture. Ask the class to make a generalization about the effect of culture and economics on the nationalist movement in China.

History Maker

MAO ZEDONG. Mao Zedong had rebellious tendencies from an early age. He went to school against his father's wishes and later served as a soldier in the 1911 revolt against the Qing dynasty. He published articles criticizing Confusionism and continued to challenge traditional doctrines as a member of the Chinese Communist party. In conflict with Marxist teachings, Mao asserted first that the peasant class rather than industrial workers would lead the Communist revolution. Second, the party needed protection from its army. Mao's Red Army followed strict rules that would earn peasant support and trust. Third, Mao believed that human will could overcome almost any obstacle.

Critical Thinking

How did Mao's early behavior foretell his reshaping of Marxist doctrine?

ANSWER: He made a habit of challenging tradition.

CONNECTING TO CIVICS ANSWER

He had a rightful claim to the throne.

CONNECTING TO
Civics

P'u-i: The Last Emperor of China
For thousands of years, the Chinese people were ruled by emperors. The last emperor, a boy of six named Henry P'u-i (also known as Pu Yi) formally abdicated on February 12, 1912. For many years afterward he lived in exile. In his adulthood, P'u-i was imprisoned for 14 years as a war criminal by the Communists.

Understanding Civics

Why might the Communists have viewed P'u-i as dangerous?

Holt Researcher
go.hrw.com
KEYWORD: Holt Researcher
FreeFind: Mao Zedong
After reading more about Mao Zedong on the Holt Researcher, write an analysis of his influence on political events of the 20th century.

In 1927 Chiang expelled all Soviet advisers from the country and moved against the party's left-wing members. Troops loyal to Chiang attacked the Communist stronghold of Shanghai. They arrested and executed large numbers of Communists. Chiang now believed that the Communists were no longer a threat to his leadership. He established a Nationalist government in Nanjing.

The Nanjing government. Chiang and his followers wanted a strong, efficient government. They did not, however, want a democratic one. They set up a one-party system with Chiang as virtual dictator.

Chiang's attempts to promote industrialization were limited by a lack of capital. Much government revenue was spent on defense. Foreign control of China's natural resources also slowed economic development. Even so, the areas of China under Nationalist control made progress. Massive construction projects of roads and railroads were begun. A national bank was established, and education was improved.

The Nationalists failed to deal with two crucial problems, however. They did not change the oppressive system of land ownership because they wanted the support of landowners and merchants. They also failed to change tax collection methods. In short, they did little to eliminate the suffering and discontent of Chinese peasants.

✔ **READING CHECK: Making Predictions** How might the peasants react to the Nationalists' failure to help them? might lead to unrest

The Growth of Chinese Communism

In July 1921 a small group of Chinese intellectuals met in Shanghai and founded the Chinese Communist Party. They were inspired by the example of the Russian Revolution and the ideas of Marx and Lenin. The founders of Chinese communism hoped to free their country from foreign domination and economic backwardness. At first, they set about building strong party organizations and labor unions in the cities. They cooperated with the Kuomintang to defeat the regional warlords.

When the Kuomintang was weak and in need of support, the Nationalists welcomed Communists. As the Communist Party grew stronger, however, conservative Nationalists became alarmed. The 1927 executions of the Shanghai Communists by Chiang's troops ended the alliance. In the early 1930s, when Chiang realized that he had failed to destroy the Communists, he undertook several large-scale military operations to eliminate communism for good.

The Long March. The Communists who escaped the purge of 1927 fled first to Jiangxi province in southeastern China. There they set up their own government, modeled after the Russian communist regime. Nationalist forces repeatedly attacked the Communists in 1934. As the Nationalists' assaults became more destructive, the Communists were forced to evacuate from Jiangxi.

In the now-famous **Long March,** which lasted more than a year, about 100,000 Communists made their way on foot from Jiangxi to Shaanxi province in northwestern China. They were chased by Nationalist troops and strafed by aircraft while crossing 18 mountain ranges and 24 rivers. Many died on the 6,000-mile trip. Those who survived, along with Communists already in Shaanxi, established their headquarters in the isolated mountain town of Yenan. On this trip, a charismatic young man named **Mao Zedong** (MAOOH ZUH-DUHNG) established himself as a leader.

REVIEW

Have students complete the Section 3 Review on p. 769.

ASSESS

Have students complete Daily Quiz 29.3. As Alternative Assessment, you may want to use the Qing downfall graphic organizer or the letter activity in this section's lessons.

RETEACH

Have students complete Main Idea Activity for English Language Learners and Special-Needs Students 29.3. Then have students write quiz questions about the section. Allow students to trade their unanswered questions with others to complete.

EXTEND

Divide students into small groups and have them conduct research on one of the leaders discussed in this section. Have each group prepare a map, model, or chart; a visual such as a photo; and a short oral presentation about their findings.

BLOCK SCHEDULING

Mao Zedong. Mao was born in the countryside of southeastern Hunan province. He had long argued that Chinese peasants, not the urban proletariat, could provide the best basis for a communist revolution in China. Finally, in a rural area far from the major cities of China, he had a chance to prove his argument. In Shaanxi province, Mao and his followers put the programs of land and tax reform advocated by the Communists into practice. To help ensure success, they met with peasants and listened to their problems. The Communists also explained China's problems at a national level to the peasants and urged them to support the revolution.

At first the peasants, suspicious of outsiders, did not trust the Communists. When they found that the Communists were trying to understand and help them, however, the peasants joined their cause. Many volunteered to serve in the Communist army, called the Red Army. Others provided useful information about the location and movement of Nationalist troops. With peasant support, the Communists rebuilt their strength and resisted Nationalist attempts to destroy them.

In addition, there was a growing threat from Japanese militarism. Many Chinese felt that Chiang Kai-shek should face this threat instead of fighting other Chinese. Support for communism grew among those who believed that Japan was the true enemy.

✔ **READING CHECK: Identifying Cause and Effect** What problems helped the Communists take hold in China? bad conditions for Chinese peasants, Japan's rising military power

Civil War in China, 1925–1935

Interpreting Maps In the cities and countryside, the Chinese people suffered tremendous upheaval as Nationalists, Communists, and warlords vied for control.

■ **Skills Assessment: Human Systems** What does the difficult and indirect path of the Long March suggest about the conditions the Communists faced?

Map legend:
- Area controlled by Kuomintang, 1925
- The Long March, 1934–1935
- Kuomintang victories over the warlords
- Kuomintang strikes against the Communists
- Japanese territory

MAP ANSWER
They were being chased and were basically running for their lives.

SECTION 3 REVIEW ANSWERS

❶ **Identify**
- Open Door Policy, p. 765
- Empress Dowager Tz'u-hsi, p. 765
- Boxer Rebellion, p. 765
- Kuomintang, p. 766
- Sun Yixian, p. 766
- Chiang Kai-shek, p. 767
- Long March, p. 768
- Mao Zedong, p. 768

❷ Tz'u-hsi: ruled China, supported Boxer Rebellion; Sun Yixian: spread Western ideas, supported modernization; Chiang Kai-shek: strengthened Kuomintang army, persecuted Communists; Mao Zedong: led Communist revolution and Long March

❸ a. few reforms, inability to resist foreign influences

b. grew more militant, resisted changes in favor of lower classes

c. foreign domination, suffering of lower classes, Japanese threat

❹ Speeches will vary but should include the desire for uniting China and the use of military force.

SECTION 3 REVIEW

1. **Identify** and explain the significance:
   Open Door Policy
   Empress Dowager Tz'u-hsi
   Boxer Rebellion
   Kuomintang
   Sun Yixian
   Chiang Kai-shek
   Long March
   Mao Zedong

2. **Summarizing** Copy the diagram below. Use it to summarize the roles and actions of Chinese leaders in the early 1900s.

   Tz'u-hsi — Sun Yixian
   Chinese leaders
   Chiang Kai-shek — Mao Zedong

3. **Finding the Main Idea**
   a. What were some of the factors that led to the fall of the Qing dynasty?
   b. How did the Nationalist movement grow and change under the leadership of Chiang Kai-shek?
   c. What factors led to the rise of communism in China?

4. **Writing and Critical Thinking**
   Supporting a Point of View Imagine that you are a member of either the Nationalist or Chinese Communist Party. Write a speech to convince others of the value of what you are working for.
   Consider:
   • what each party wanted to accomplish
   • the methods each party used to achieve its goals

Homework Practice Online
keyword: SP3 HP29

OBJECTIVES

1 Explain the Japanese pursuit of expansion that began in the late 1800s.

2 Describe the changes in Japanese life during rapid modernization.

3 Identify the effects of the military on Japan during the 1920s and the 1930s.

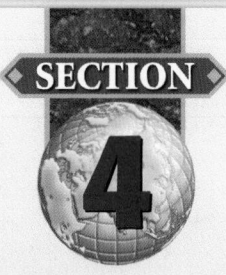

SECTION 4

READ TO DISCOVER

❶ Why and how did the Japanese pursue a policy of expansion beginning in the late 1800s?

❷ How did Japanese life change during rapid modernization?

❸ What effect did the military begin to have on Japan during the 1920s and the 1930s?

IDENTIFY

Russo-Japanese War
Treaty of Portsmouth

WHY IT MATTERS TODAY

The success of Japan's military in the early 1900s led to further attempts at expansion and aggression. Their defeat in World War II forced them to change direction. Use CNN or other **current event** sources to find out what Japan's goals are today. Write your findings in your journal.

CNN student News.com

Imperialism in Japan

The Main Idea
A policy of expansion, along with a growing militarism, marked Japan in the early 1900s.

The Story Continues *Dancing the fox trot. Listening to jazz. Playing baseball. This was Japan in the 1920s. Japan had begun to modernize as early as the late 1800s. Over the next 50 years many Japanese adopted Western ideas concerning industry, democracy, and society, as well as arts and entertainment. They would also take on imperialist ideas of their own.*

Japanese Expansion

The reforms begun by the Meiji Restoration changed Japan into a modern industrial and military power. This power allowed Japan to begin a policy of expansion in the late 1800s. Japan wanted to extend its influence for two reasons. First, new territory would provide both raw materials for Japan's growing industries and markets for its products. Second, expansion would show Western nations just how far Japan had progressed.

Korea and Manchuria. Japan had long been interested in Korea. The Treaty of Shimonoseki that ended the Sino-Japanese War in 1895 provided for Korean independence. Soon, however, Japan dominated the Korean government.

Japan then looked to Manchuria. After the Boxer Rebellion, most foreign powers withdrew their troops from China. However, many Russian troops stayed in Manchuria. Russia had forced a lease from the Chinese to extend a railway line across Manchuria. It had leased a port from China as well. To Japan, the Russians looked set to dominate Manchuria.

In 1902, believing that war with Russia was likely, Japan signed an alliance with Great Britain. They agreed that both countries had the right to protect their interests in China, Manchuria, and Korea against a third power. If either country went to war with a single power, the other would remain neutral. If a third power joined the conflict, they would aid each other. Russia was the obvious target of the alliance.

The Japanese 1st Infantry in battle

TEACH OBJECTIVE 1

 ALL LEVELS: Copy the following graphic organizer on the board, omitting the italicized answers. Use it to help students understand the methods and reasons for Japanese expansion.

Japanese Expansion	
How	**Why**
alliance with Great Britain	*support against Russia*
war with Russia	*take Russian control in Korea*
Treaty of Portsmouth	*end of war, gave Japan control in China and Korea*

 HOMEWORK Have students create flashcards with questions and answers about the important details of Japanese expansion.

TEACH OBJECTIVE 2

LEVEL 1: Write *increased population, economic trouble,* and *social tensions* on the chalkboard. Have students write one-sentence summaries describing each problem with Japan's rapid modernization.

The Anglo-Japanese alliance meant great prestige for Japan. It now had the support of one of the world's great powers. The alliance increased pressure on Russia to withdraw from Manchuria. Diplomatic attempts failed, however. In January 1904 Japan issued an ultimatum to Russia. Russia refused to answer Japan's demands.

The Russo-Japanese War. In February 1904, without declaring war, Japan attacked and badly damaged the Russian fleet at Port Arthur in Manchuria. Soon after, the Japanese military overran Korea and, throughout the summer of 1904, pushed the Russians back through Manchuria. In February and March of 1905, some 330,000 Russian troops and 270,000 Japanese troops fought a great battle at Mukden. Losses were heavy on both sides, and the Russians pulled back. Then in May 1905 the Japanese navy stunned the world when it completely destroyed the Russian Baltic fleet at the Battle of Tsushima.

Although the Japanese were winning the **Russo-Japanese War,** the costs of the war—in lives and money—were a strain. They asked U.S. president Theodore Roosevelt to mediate the conflict. Roosevelt reluctantly agreed. In 1905 he invited Japanese and Russian representatives to negotiations at Portsmouth, New Hampshire.

The Treaty of Portsmouth. Late in 1905, the **Treaty of Portsmouth** ended the Russo-Japanese War. Under the agreement, Russia ceded to Japan its lease on the Liaodong Peninsula, including Port Arthur. They also gave Japan the southern half of the Russian island of Sakhalin, north of Japan. Russia gave up control of the southern branch of the Beijing-Tianjian Railway and recognized Japan as the dominant power in Korea. In addition, Russia agreed to withdraw all troops, except for railway guards, from Manchuria.

The Treaty of Portsmouth eliminated Japan's competition in Manchuria. It forced other powers to respect Japan's strength. When Japan annexed Korea in 1910, none of the other imperialist powers protested.

✔ **READING CHECK: Finding the Main Idea** How did Japan position itself to be an important power during the early 1900s? by destroying the Russian Baltic fleet and obtaining favorable terms in the Treaty of Portsmouth

Problems of Modernization

In less than 50 years, Japan had gone from a feudal agricultural nation to one of the world's leading industrial and military powers. This leap created problems for the island nation.

Increasing population. Industrialization and scientific development brought higher standards of living and new forms of medical care to Japan. These spurred population growth. Cities grew rapidly, and every inch of suitable land was cultivated.

Even so, the increased food supply could not match the rapid increase in population. Japanese people emigrated to Korea and Taiwan, as well as to Hawaii and other Pacific islands. Thousands more left for the United States. In time, the United States prohibited the immigration of Asians but still allowed Europeans to enter the country. Japan deeply resented this policy.

INTERPRETING THE VISUAL RECORD
The Russo-Japanese War In this painting, the Japanese navy attacks Russian forces at Port Arthur. *What is happening in the picture that shows Japanese bravery?*

What If? **Japan's startling victory in the Russo-Japanese War made it the equal of other imperialist powers competing in the Pacific. How might history have changed if Russia, not Japan, had won the war in 1905?**

Economics

Control of the southern branch of the Chinese Eastern Railway, known as the South Manchuria Railway (SMR), meant a great deal more than simply tracks and trains. The SMR was a source of friction between China, Japan, and Russia for many years. Located on the Liaotung Peninsula in southern Manchuria, the SMR was constructed by Russia after control of the Liaotung Peninsula was taken from China in 1898. Following the Russo-Japanese War, Japan took possession of the Liaotung Peninsula. The Japanese considered the SMR as their chief instrument for economic exploitation of Manchuria.

Critical Thinking

Ask students to compare the Railway Zone in Manchuria to the Canal Zone in Panama.

ANSWER: Students should note that both zones were under foreign control— the Railway Zone by Japan and the Canal Zone by the United States.

WHAT IF? ANSWER
Russia would have been considered the stronger power and Japan would have kept out of China and Korea.

TEACH OBJECTIVE 2

LEVEL 3: Ask students to write a radio news segment discussing the positive and negative effects of modernization in Japan following the period of the Meiji Restoration. Have them personalize their stories with short fictional interviews from different people in Japanese society.

TEACH OBJECTIVE 3

LEVEL 2: Ask students to write a persuasive speech from the point of view of a top-ranking Japanese military official. In the speech, students should explain the changes the military wants in Japan and include reasons for those changes.

CLOSE

Have students debate whether they think Japan's military had legitimate reasons for asserting control over the country's social, economic, and political development or if a country's military should have a more limited role.

Linking Past to Present

Kabuki, a form of Japanese theater incorporating song, dance, and mime, portrays historical and contemporary events during performances that can last an entire day. The first Kabuki performance took place in the early 1600s when a dancer named Okuni created a show that included a number of other female dancers and actors. By the mid-1600s, however, older men played all Kabuki roles, a tradition that continues to the present day. Kabuki appealed to the common people of Japan, and many of its themes were derived from historical incidents. Today, the Kabuki Theatre and the National Theatre, both in Tokyo, host regular performances.

Critical Thinking

What does the endurance of Kabuki theater indicate about the relationship between tradition and change in Japan?

ANSWER: Regardless of Western influence, many Japanese still respect and enjoy Japan's cultural history.

DAILY LIFE ANSWER
new ways of thinking and behaving

DAILY LIFE

The Westernization of Japan

Beginning in the late 1800s, the Japanese became more interested in the ways of the West. As a Japanese prince explained: "We sent talented young students to Europe and America to master various fields of science and technology." The Japanese also borrowed and adapted elements of American popular culture, in particular sports such as baseball and entertainment such as music, dance, and films. Women's roles became more westernized too, and a feminist movement, though unsuccessful, began. **What effect do you think Western ideas might have on a traditional society such as Japan's?**

Economic trouble. Japan's industrialization created another problem. Because of its small size, Japan did not have many of the raw materials needed in modern industry. It had to import them. To pay for these raw materials, it had to sell goods abroad. In trying to export its goods, however, Japan met with restrictions in the rough world of international trade. Many countries passed tariff laws to protect their own products and markets against Japanese competition. They argued that Japanese goods had an unfair advantage because cheap labor in Japan allowed Japanese manufacturers to charge lower prices. The Japanese economy had to expand or collapse.

Social tensions. The Meiji era was a time of social and political stability. Customs and law allowed for little dissent. By the 1920s, however, economic development, universal education, and new ideas from the West had changed Japanese attitudes. Many believed it was time for the people to benefit from Japan's economic advances.

Industrial workers organized labor unions. They called strikes for higher wages and better working conditions. Tenant farms demanded lower agricultural rents. Urban intellectuals and students were inspired by the victory of the Western democracies in World War I. They argued that democracy was the wave of the future. Universal men's suffrage was granted in 1925, but women would not win the right to vote until years later. Other Japanese turned to socialism or communism.

Some young Japanese began to question the traditional values of their society. The center of Japanese society, once agricultural, became the modern city. New ideas and arts entered Japan from the West. Work roles shifted as well. People from farm villages now worked in factories. Women took jobs in manufacturing, textile, and office work. These changes did not come without resistance. When world financial markets collapsed in 1929, many felt that the focus away from traditional Japanese interests had corrupted the country economically and morally.

✔ **READING CHECK: Categorizing** What types of problems did modernization produce in Japan? *increased population, a lack of raw materials, and social tension*

Growing Influence of the Military

Japan's political leaders of the 1920s had difficulty answering the concerns of the Japanese people. Opposition to westernization grew. This atmosphere of turmoil and dissatisfaction on the part of many Japanese provided opportunities for Japan's military to increase its influence.

The constitution of 1889 had given top-ranking military officers great power. Civilian authorities had almost no control over military affairs. Until the 1920s military ministers usually cooperated with civilian members of government. However, during World War I, the military had seen a new kind of war. Victory had depended not only on troops, but also on controlling the entire spiritual and material resources of the nation. Because military ministers believed that victory in any future war would require the same unity, they saw discontent in Japan as a serious problem. As a result, throughout the 1920s and the 1930s, Japan was increasingly influenced by attitudes of militarism, a point of view in which military needs, values, and goals shape a nation's civil lifestyles and its domestic and international policies. Much like the rising fascist governments in Europe, Japan's increasingly militaristic government ever more strongly influenced Japanese social, economic, and political development.

REVIEW

Have students complete the Section 4 Review on p. 773.

ASSESS

Have students complete Daily Quiz 29.4. As Alternative Assessment, you may want to use the Japanese Expansion chart or the speech exercise from this section's lessons.

RETEACH

Have students complete Main Idea Activity for English Language Learners and Special-Needs Students 29.4. Then have students write review questions and exchange with a partner to answer.

EXTEND

Have students find and read a translated literary work from a Japanese author of the early 1900s such as Akutagawa Ryunosuke or Tanizaki Junichiro. Ask students to give brief presentations, discussing the plot of each work. Encourage them to take notice of Western and traditional Japanese influences that appear in the work.

Japan's economic problems in the late 1920s also drove the military officers to take a greater role in government. Army and navy officers believed that Western nations would never treat Japan as an equal. They pointed to Western restrictions on Japanese immigration and exports as proof. Groups that believed in the "purity" of Japanese culture influenced young officers. They felt that Japan should pursue a more independent course, particularly in Asia.

In time, the military insisted that the Japanese people return to traditional values. They called for a larger army and a stronger navy. In addition, they supported a Japanese "Monroe Doctrine" that gave them powers in Asia similar to those exercised by the United States in the Western Hemisphere. In particular, they looked to Manchuria as a target for future expansion. The growing influence of the military would have far-reaching consequences, not only for Japanese society but for the rest of the world as well.

✔ **READING CHECK: Analyzing Information** How did World War I contribute to the rise of military influence over the Japanese government? victory had depended on giving the military complete control over the nation's resources

Japanese Emperor Hirohito salutes as he rides past his troops.

SECTION 4 REVIEW ANSWERS

❶ **Identify**
- Russo-Japanese War, p. 771
- Treaty of Portsmouth, p. 771

❷ Russo-Japanese War: launched Japan's status as a world power; Modernization: created population, economic, and social problems; Social tensions: traditional values questioned; Military: tight control of society and a return to traditional values

❸ a. for territory and prestige

b. Japan envied Russia's power in China and Korea; Japan attacked Russian fleet at Port Arthur.

c. Civilians had no control over military affairs; military needs, values, and goals shaped the nation's lifestyle and policies.

❹ Students might focus on new jobs and independence for many, fair government, and new forms of expression in contrast with the unity and strength derived from traditional Japanese values.

SECTION 4 REVIEW

1. **Identify** and explain the significance:
   Russo-Japanese War
   Treaty of Portsmouth

2. **Categorizing** Copy the web diagram below. Use it to identify the influence of each factor on Japan from 1900 through the 1920s.

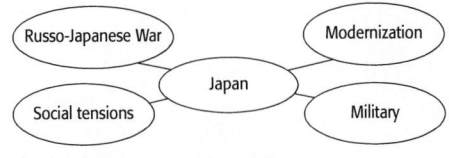

3. **Finding the Main Idea**
   a. Why did Japan pursue a policy of expansionism?
   b. What were the causes of the Russo-Japanese War?
   c. How was Japan's militaristic government similar to fascist governments in Europe?

4. **Writing and Critical Thinking**
   Supporting Points of View Write a dialogue between a young Japanese student who favors Western ideas and a young Japanese soldier who does not.
   Consider:
   • the benefits of industrialization, democracy, and new ideas in the arts
   • the benefits of traditional Japanese values

Homework Practice Online
keyword: SP3 HP29

OBJECTIVES

1 **Describe the significant changes in Latin American nations after World War I.**

2 **Explain why authoritarian regimes gained power in many Latin American nations.**

3 **Describe the relationship between Latin America and the United States.**

As students enter the classroom, ask students to name the major change that took place in Latin American countries just prior to World War I. *(gained their independence from European nations)* Ask students how the United States reacted and what the nature of its interest in these countries was. *(began asserting influence; economic)*

SECTION 5

READ TO DISCOVER

❶ In what significant ways did Latin American nations change after World War I?

❷ Why were authoritarian regimes able to come to power in many Latin American nations?

❸ What kind of relationship did Latin America have with the United States?

IDENTIFY

Diego Rivera
Rafael Trujillo Molina
Anastasio Somoza
Good Neighbor Policy
Fulgencio Batista
Lázaro Cárdenas

WHY IT MATTERS TODAY

Relations between the United States and Latin American countries are an important focus of U.S. foreign policy. Use CNN or other **current event** sources to find out recent developments in U.S. policy toward Mexico, Cuba, or some other Latin American nation. Record your findings in your journal.

CNN student NEWS.com

Latin America Between the Wars

The Main Idea
General prosperity in Latin America gave way to economic and political crises in the 1930s.

The Story Continues *Nationalism had blossomed and borne fruit in Latin America in the 1800s, when nations gained their independence from Spain and Portugal. Democracy, however, had not as yet gained as strong a hold. In fact, many Latin Americans would find themselves under the strong-arm rule of military dictators when the Great Depression threw their countries into turmoil.*

Economic, Social, and Political Developments

After World War I Latin America appeared to be headed for prosperity. The area's growing economic strength led to changes in other areas of Latin American life, as well.

Economic changes. As the 1920s began, agricultural products dominated Latin American economies. Beef, wheat, sugar, coffee, and fruits were the principal exports. Yet during the early 1900s, Mexico also became a leading oil exporter. Oil was discovered in Venezuela, Peru, Bolivia, and Colombia. The mining of copper in Chile and Peru, tin in Bolivia, and bauxite in Guiana grew rapidly, too. Most of the oil and mining operations, however, were owned by British and American companies.

The 1920s also saw a rapid expansion in electric and hydroelectric power generation in Latin America. Foreign investors financed these industries too. The energy allowed many Latin American countries to industrialize. Larger countries began producing textiles, construction materials, machinery, and automobiles. Oil refining and food processing became important. Heavy industrialization, however, would not come to Latin America until after World War II.

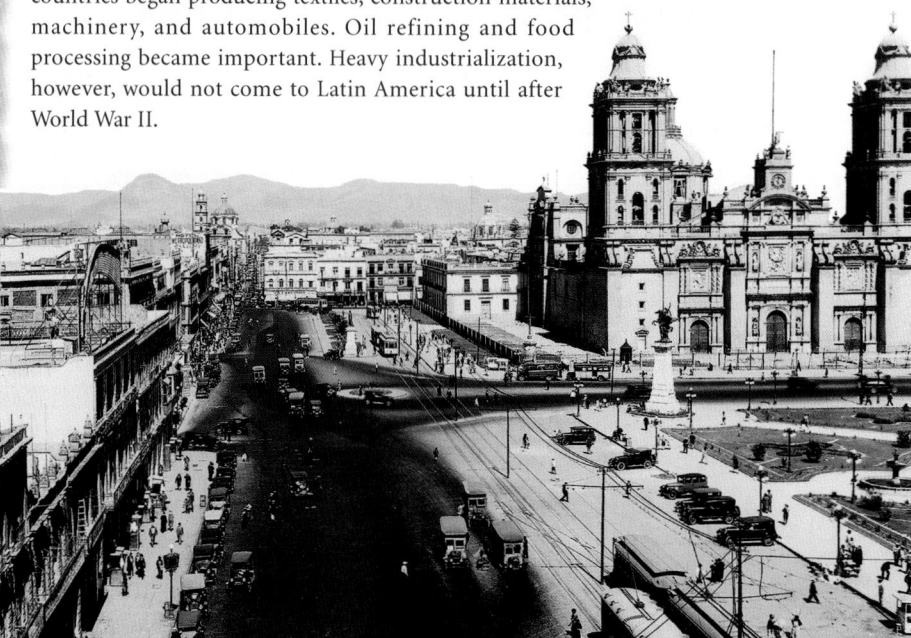

The growth of Mexico City in the 1920s and 1930s reflected the increasing economic strength of Latin America.

TEACH OBJECTIVE 1

LEVEL 1: Put students in pairs to list the changes that took place in Latin America after World War I. *(growth in industries and populations, foreign investments, labor union activity, professional jobs, education, middle class power, attempts at stability, reforms)* Have students explain whether the changes were positive or negative.

ENGLISH LANGUAGE LEARNERS, COOPERATIVE LEARNING

TEACH OBJECTIVE 2

ALL LEVELS: Ask students to fill in a web diagram showing major factors that led to the rise of authoritarian regimes in Latin America in the 1930s.

Social changes. Industrialization contributed to the growth of cities. By 1935 Mexico City, Rio de Janeiro, São Paulo, and Buenos Aires each had 1 million or more people.

Industrialization also helped change the social-economic structure. To provide labor for growing industries, countries such as Argentina, Brazil, and Chile had encouraged immigration from Europe since the late 1800s. The number of Latin American workers swelled.

With growth in the working class came an increase in labor union activity. The 1920s saw a surge in union membership. Latin American unions were largely socialist or anarchist in their views. They used strikes as the primary way to achieve their goals. As a result, by the late 1920s, many cities in Latin America had been hit by general strikes. Many governments called out police and army troops to put down strikes violently. Some governments outlawed both strikes and labor unions.

The middle class, too, began to grow as new jobs opened up in the professions, government service, and commerce. Changes in university programs created opportunities for middle-class youths in engineering, business, and public administration. Such developments gave the middle class greater access to power.

Political changes. Political life in Latin America underwent sweeping changes in the early 1900s. For example, political parties backed by the middle class emerged in Chile, Argentina, Peru, and Brazil. Torn by regional disputes, Mexico went to a single-party political system in hopes of guaranteeing stability. In Uruguay, leaders enacted a broad reform program that included free elections, social security, and nationalization of railroads and public utilities.

Democracy still eluded most Latin American nations. Concerns of the growing working class could not be ignored, however. Many Latin American artists, such as Mexico's **Diego Rivera,** addressed these concerns in their work. Middle-class politicians, struggling for control with upper-class landowners, turned to the working class for support in elections. An election did not always mean a smooth transition of power, however. In some countries, the way to change the government was still to overthrow it.

✔ **READING CHECK: Summarizing** How did Latin American nations change after World War I? *industrialization, immigration from Europe, and the rise of labor unions*

Economic Crisis and Authoritarianism

At the end of the 1920s, prices began to fall for Latin America's major agricultural exports, such as sugar and coffee. Chile's major export was nitrates, used in fertilizers and explosives. When German scientists developed a process for making synthetic nitrates, Chile's export economy suffered a crippling blow.

The effects of the Great Depression. Prices fell even more during the worldwide economic depression in the 1930s. Because they received little for their exports, many Latin American nations found it impossible to import any but the most essential goods. Some countries stopped paying their foreign debts. As national economies faltered, unemployment spread. So too did worker unrest.

Economic crisis led to political crisis. Coup d'états overthrew constitutional governments that had existed for 30 or 40 years. Most of the nations of Latin America experienced major political upheaval. Planters and exporters lost not only their fortunes to the depression but also their political power as middle classes rebelled.

CONNECTING TO
Art

Painting: *Fruits of Labor*

One of Mexico's finest artists, Diego Rivera recorded the dramatic changes in his country after World War I. A follower of the art movement known as social realism, Rivera produced paintings that dealt with contemporary problems. Among his best are works that show the plight of Mexican peasants. The Mexican government commissioned Rivera to paint many murals for schools and government buildings. Shown here is a detail from his fresco *Fruits of Labor* in Mexico City, which honors working people and their children. The fresco took Rivera and his assistants six years to complete.

Understanding the Arts

In what ways did the work of Diego Rivera reflect Latin American social issues during the 1920s and the 1930s?

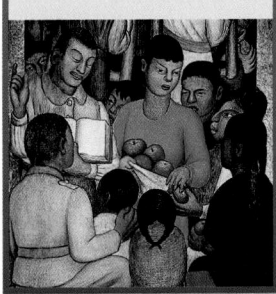

Daily Life

Originally of Basque origin, the Spanish game of jai alai was introduced in Cuba at about the turn of the twentieth century. It became a national pastime in many Latin American countries. This form of handball requires opposing individuals or teams to bounce a small, hard ball against one to three walls and catch it upon its return. Players catch and throw the ball, or *pelota*, with a scoop-shaped wicker basket called the *cesta*. The ball must stay in continual motion and can travel at speeds beyond 150 mph. To excel at this fast-paced game, players must be extremely agile and coordinated. Although most professionals come from Spain, others come from Cuba, Mexico, and the Philippines. The United States also has a small number of professionals. A world championship is sponsored every four years in South America, France, or Spain.

Critical Thinking

How was the inclusion of jai alai in the daily life of Latin Americans an indication of continued European influence?

ANSWER: The game was imported from Spain.

CONNECTING TO ART ANSWER
His work, like the social issues, involved the working classes.

LEVEL 3: Have students conduct research on one Latin American country's relationship with the United States. Ask them to focus on changes in the relationship from the early 1900s to today. Have students create a chart that displays the changes they uncover in their research.

HOMEWORK Remind students that the nature of the United States' interest in Latin America was still economic after World War I, but new policies promised less interference by the United States. Have students explore U.S. relations with Latin America by considering the Good Neighbor Policy, the Pan American Conference, Fulgencio Batista, and the Platt Amendment.

CLOSE

Discuss the relationship between economics and politics in a country. Ask students whether the economy in Latin America had an effect on political changes in that area.

History Maker

LÁZARO CÁRDENAS. A man of humble beginnings, Lázaro Cárdenas served in the Mexican revolutionary army and became a brigadier general in 1925. From 1928 to 1932 he served as governor in his birth state, Michoacán. During his term as governor, he became president of the National Revolutionary Party—the dominant party in Mexican politics. In 1934, Cárdenas found himself president of Mexico and began instituting revolutionary reforms. He expropriated large portions of land to give to peasants and converted several industries to worker cooperatives. He also nationalized the railways in Mexico and secularized education. His reforms made him one of Mexico's most popular presidents.

ACTIVITY: Have students locate information on another Latin American reformer and write a short compare and contrast paper describing the reforms of Lázaro Cárdenas and the leader of their choice.

Authoritarian regimes. The military strongly influenced or controlled many new governments. In some countries, U.S.-trained military leaders ruled. In the Dominican Republic, General **Rafael Trujillo Molina** began a dictatorship in 1930 that would last 31 years. In Nicaragua, General **Anastasio Somoza** seized power in 1936, two years after assassinating his chief rival.

Many of the new authoritarian governments suppressed any attempt at dissent. They limited the influence of landowners and broke the power of labor unions. Some simply abolished workers' organizations, jailing their leaders. In Brazil, President Getúlio Vargas dismantled any framework of democracy. In El Salvador, the army massacred more than 10,000 peasants to destroy a popular communist movement.

Some military leaders tried to gain support through persuasion rather than terror. They gave favors just to union members loyal to the military. Some even responded to the needs of the people by enacting land reforms and passing minimum wage and pension laws. These actions limited the appeal of left-wing movements.

✔ **READING CHECK: Categorizing** In what two ways did military leaders attempt to gain control and support in Latin American nations? by suppressing dissent and granting favors to their loyal supporters

Relations with the United States

Earlier United States intervention in Latin America had created ill will and suspicion. President Franklin D. Roosevelt tried to undo these feelings. During the 1930s, Roosevelt began a program he called the **Good Neighbor Policy.** It stressed cooperation and noninterference by the United States in Latin American affairs.

In 1933 the Pan American Conference met in Montevideo. There the United States pledged not to interfere in the internal or external affairs of Latin American nations. It recalled army units that had occupied Haiti since 1915. It also surrendered its right to interfere in the affairs of Panama.

The Cuban test. That same year a situation in Cuba tested Roosevelt's commitment to the Montevideo agreement. A group of radical reformers overthrew Cuban dictator Gerardo Machado. The new government declared a socialist revolution and nationalized some American-owned companies. In response the United States refused to give diplomatic recognition to the new government, but it did not intervene directly. When Cuban army sergeant **Fulgencio Batista** decided to overthrow the reformers, however, the U.S. envoy to Cuba encouraged him.

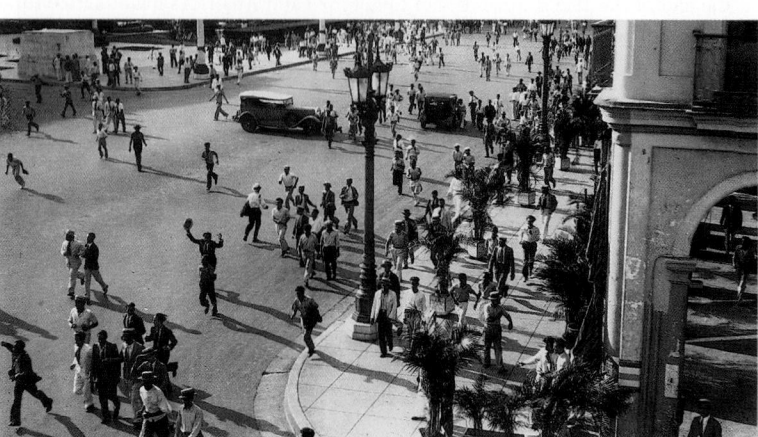

Social and political disorder spread throughout Cuba in 1933. Here citizens in Havana celebrating the rumor that President Machado has resigned react to police gunfire.

Although the United States no longer directly intervened in Latin American affairs, it still held considerable influence. In Cuba, Batista remained the power in the background while a series of civilian governments ruled in name only. In 1934 the United States recognized the stability that Batista had brought to Cuba. It canceled the Platt Amendment, which had given the United States the right to interfere in Cuban affairs.

Economic nationalism. During the 1930s, most Latin American governments worked to make their countries more self-sufficient by encouraging industry. Given the dismal economic picture caused by the global depression of the 1930s, international markets for their goods were weak. Imported goods, moreover, were generally costly. Countries therefore had no choice but to develop their own industries for manufactured goods. This economic nationalism joined with growing feelings of political nationalism. The middle class, in particular, no longer wanted to be dependent on the United States or Europe.

The most important example of economic nationalism occurred in Mexico in 1938. American- and British-owned oil companies in Mexico had become involved in a wage dispute with their workers. They refused to accept a Mexican Supreme Court ruling in favor of the workers. As a result, President **Lázaro Cárdenas** intervened and nationalized the oil industry.

The British angrily broke off diplomatic relations. The United States, however, tried to get Mexico to pay the oil companies what they claimed their holdings were worth. The two governments eventually reached a compromise. Mexicans regard March 13, 1938—the day when President Cárdenas nationalized the oil companies—as the birth date of Mexican economic independence.

✔ **READING CHECK: Making Generalizations** How did Latin American countries generally view the United States and Europe? with ill will and suspicion

Mexican president Lázaro Cárdenas, a revolutionary general and son of a poor family, carried out promises of economic reform and nationalized Mexico's petroleum industry in the 1930s.

SECTION 5 REVIEW ANSWERS

❶ Identify
- Diego Rivera, p. 775
- Rafael Trujillo Molina, p. 776
- Anastasio Somoza, p. 776
- Good Neighbor Policy, p. 776
- Fulgencio Batista, p. 776
- Lázaro Cárdenas, p. 777

❷ Effects: ability to industrialize; growth of cities; backed parties in Chile, Argentina, Peru, and Brazil; Causes: ill will and suspicion; economic crisis

❸ a. oil and foreign investments in energy industries

b. Economic crisis led to government overthrows and new governments with military backing.

c. promised cooperation and noninterference but still held influence

❹ Students should note that socialist reforms cost the United States some of its economic interest in Cuba and that the United States had agreed not to interfere with the internal or external affairs of Latin American nations.

SECTION 5 REVIEW

1. **Identify** and explain the significance:
   Diego Rivera
   Rafael Trujillo Molina
   Anastasio Somoza
   Good Neighbor Policy
   Fulgencio Batista
   Lázaro Cárdenas

2. **Identifying Cause and Effect** Copy the table below. Use it to show the causes or effects of each factor on Latin America.

Cause	Effect
Increase in exports and generation of electricity	
Industrialization	
Middle-class access to greater political power	
	The Good Neighbor Policy
	Economic nationalism

3. **Finding the Main Idea**
   a. What caused a change in the economies of Latin American countries after World War I?
   b. How did authoritarian regimes come to power in many Latin American countries?
   c. How did the United States react to events in Latin American countries in the 1930s?

4. **Writing and Critical Thinking**
   Decision Making Use a decision-making process to determine whether President Roosevelt honored the Montevideo agreement when he supported Batista's revolt in Cuba.
   Consider:
   • how United States economic interests were affected by socialist reforms
   • what the United States had agreed to in the Montevideo agreement

Homework Practice Online
keyword: SP3 HP29

REVIEW AND ASSESSMENT RESOURCES

REPRODUCIBLE RESOURCES
▶ Vocabulary Activity 29

TECHNOLOGY RESOURCES
▶ Chapter 29 Test Generator (on the One-Stop Planner)
▶ Global Skill Builder CD–ROM
▶ HRW Web Site

REINFORCEMENT, REVIEW, and ASSESSMENT
▶ Chapter 29 Review, pp. 778–779
▶ Chapter 29 Tutorial for Students, Parents, Mentors, and Peers
▶ Chapter 29 Test (Form A or B)
▶ Alternative Assessment Handbook
▶ Chapter 29 Test for English Language Learners and Special-Needs Students

REVIEW
Have students complete the Chapter 29 Review on pages 778–779.

ASSESS
Use one of the chapter tests to assess students' understanding of the content. For Alternative Assessment, see the Portfolio Activities and Alternative Assessment Handbook.

CHAPTER 29 REVIEW ANSWERS

Understanding Main Ideas
1. He encouraged them to practice passive resistance.

2. Exposure to different ideas and ways of life left soldiers wanting more authority in their country's government.

3. The United States did not want to be cut off from trade in China.

4. foreign domination, suffering of lower classes, Japanese threat

5. for territory and prestige

6. They grew with the discovery of oil and industrialization; foreign investments increased.

Reviewing Themes
1. pushed buildup of military, expansionism

2. people wanted to be ruled by government that respected and shared their culture

3. led to unrest and often revolt against governments

Review

Creating a Time Line
Copy the time line below onto a sheet of paper. Complete the time line by filling in the events, individuals, and dates from the chapter that you think were significant. Pick three events and explain why you think they were significant.

 1898   1913   1938

Writing a Summary
Using standard grammar, spelling, sentence structure, and punctuation, write an overview of the events in the chapter.

Identifying People and Ideas
Identify the following terms or individuals and explain their significance:
1. Zionism
2. Mohandas Gandhi
3. passive resistance
4. Mustafa Kemal
5. Open Door Policy
6. Chiang Kai-shek
7. Mao Zedong
8. Long March
9. Treaty of Portsmouth
10. Good Neighbor Policy

Understanding Main Ideas

SECTION 1 *(pp. 758–761)*
The British Empire in the Postwar Era
1. What influence did Mohandas Gandhi have on the way the people of India sought independence?

SECTION 2 *(pp. 762–764)*
Turkey, Persia, and Africa
2. In what way did World War I change the attitude of Africans about colonial government?

SECTION 3 *(pp. 765–769)*
Unrest in China
3. Why was the United States concerned about the influence of imperialist powers in China?
4. What factors led to the development of communism in China?

SECTION 4 *(pp. 770–773)*
Imperialism in Japan
5. Why did Japan pursue a policy of expansionism after World War I?

SECTION 5 *(pp. 774–777)*
Latin America Between the Wars
6. How did the economies of Latin American countries change after World War I?

Reviewing Themes
1. Government How did the military affect Japan's government?
2. Culture How did cultural issues affect nationalistic movements in Africa?
3. Economics How did economic issues influence political events in Latin America?

Thinking Critically
1. Contrasting Contrast the British reaction to demands for Indian independence with their reaction to similar demands from Canada, Australia, and New Zealand.
2. Evaluating How would you evaluate the effectiveness of Mustafa Kemal's attempt to modernize Turkey?
3. Sequencing Trace the events leading to the rise of communism in China.
4. Identifying Cause and Effect What factors influenced the expansionist efforts of Japan after World War I?

Writing About History
Categorizing The United States has tried to influence the political and economic activities of other countries. Some argue that the United States must do this to protect its own interests, while others believe that every nation has the right to make its own decisions. Write an informative article presenting both sides of this issue. Use the following chart to organize your thoughts.

U.S. action	Effects—U.S.	Effects—other country
Supporting revolution		
Imposing economic sanctions		
Conducting military action		
Other types of action		

CLOSE

Ask students what the sections in Chapter 29 have in common. Have them discuss the role of economics and culture in these similarities.

RETEACH

Put students who had trouble with the test into pairs. Have them use their texts to correct their tests. Then put students into two teams and draw a large tic-tac-toe grid on the chalkboard. Ask review questions to alternating groups, placing an *X* or *O* as needed. **ENGLISH LANGUAGE LEARNERS, COOPERATIVE LEARNING**

Portfolio Extensions

1. Ask students to imagine they are leaders of a country that is still working toward industrialization and economic independence. Put them in small groups to use a problem-solving process to gather information, list and consider options, consider advantages and disadvantages, and then draft a list of goals and an improvement plan for their country. **COOPERATIVE LEARNING**

2. Have groups choose an underdeveloped country and create a large map illustrating major geographic characteristics of the area. Have them explain the positive and negative aspects of each characteristic. **COOPERATIVE LEARNING**

Building Social Studies Skills

Analyzing Statistical Data

Study the information provided below. Then use the information to answer the questions that follow.

The Population of Palestine in 1914 (Estimated)

- About 535,000 Muslims
- About 70,000 Christians (mostly Arabs)
- About 85,000 Jews
- Estimated total population: 690,000

1. Which of the following best describes the population of Palestine in 1914?
   a. Muslims greatly outnumbered Christians and Jews in Palestine in 1914.
   b. Most Christians in Palestine in 1914 were immigrant farmers from Europe.
   c. Christians and Jews together slightly outnumbered Muslims in 1914 Palestine.
   d. Farmers represented the largest segment of the Palestinian population in 1914.

2. Convert the statistics above into a pie graph on the population of Palestine. How might this information have influenced Palestinian views in 1914 on who should rule the area?

Problem Solving

Read the following quote from an essay by a commentator published in 1936. Then answer the questions.

> "Negotiation between two Western states is the mutual attempt to approach common ground. Its essence is compromise. But the concept of compromise is quite foreign to the Japanese. To them, diplomatic negotiation means the effort of each national representative to put over his own plan intact, the end in view being that one shall win and the other shall lose. The Naval Conference this year has been an illustration of Japan's attitude. Arriving at London with a fixed determination to obtain parity or nothing, the Japanese were not prepared to yield a single ton, regardless of what was proposed."

3. Which of the following is the best statement of the problem described in the excerpt?
   a. There was no word for "compromise" in the Japanese language.
   b. All the Western countries had a common goal.
   c. The Japanese thought of themselves as superior.
   d. Japan and the West had very different understandings of the word "negotiate."

4. In today's world, Japan and the Western powers have become allies and active trading partners. How do you think the problem described in the quote was solved?

Alternative Assessment

Building Your Portfolio

Global Relations

Great Britain's efforts to try to direct the future of Palestine led to increased tensions in the region after World War I. Use the Internet and other sources to identify how other countries, such as the United States, have tried to assist in recent disputes within this region. Using what you have learned from Britain's example, evaluate the effectiveness of these efforts in bringing a peaceful resolution to conflict.

internet connect

Internet Activity: go.hrw.com
KEYWORD: SP3 WH29

Choose a topic on Nationalist Movements Around the World to:
- write a biography of Mustafa Kemal.
- investigate the British Commonwealth of Nations and how the member nations interact.
- create a poster on wars of independence in the Philippines and Nicaragua.

Thinking Critically

1. The British resisted changes in India but granted independence to others and admitted them to the Commonwealth of Nations.

2. Students may note that Turkey became independent and prosperous.

3. CCP formed; Long March; Mao Zedong as leader; Japanese threat

4. Russian power in China and Korea, alliance with Great Britain, Russo-Japanese War, Treaty of Portsmouth

Writing About History

Answers will vary but might mention economic prosperity and depression, loss of life, government stability.

Building Social Studies Skills

1. a

2. Muslims were in the majority.

3. d

4. Answers will vary.

Building Your Portfolio

Answers will vary but should compare the effectiveness of efforts to bring resolutions to Palestine to Britain's example.

World War II

CHAPTER RESOURCE MANAGER

Objectives	Pacing Guide	Reproducible Resources
SECTION 1 **Threats to World Peace** (pp. 782–785)	• Analyze why Japan and Italy were able to carry out aggressive territorial policies in the 1930s. • Explain why the League of Nations was unable to stop international aggression. • Describe how Spain's civil war led to a fascist dictatorship there.	**Regular** 1.5 day | **Block Scheduling** 1 day *Block Scheduling Handbook with Team Teaching Strategies, 30.1*	**RS** Guided Reading Strategy 30.1 **SM** Geography Activity 30: Japan's Drive to Expand in Manchuria
SECTION 2 **Hitler's Aggressions** (pp. 786–790)	• Explain how Hitler took over Austria and Czechoslovakia. • Discuss how and why Great Britain and France attempted to avoid another war. • Describe how Great Britain and France prepared for war. • Discuss why Hitler and Stalin created the Nazi-Soviet Pact, and how Western nations responded to Hitler's invasion of Poland.	**Regular** 1.5 day | **Block Scheduling** 1 day *Block Scheduling Handbook with Team Teaching Strategies, 30.2*	**RS** Guided Reading Strategy 30.2
SECTION 3 **Axis Gains** (pp. 791–795)	• Explain how German control of Norway, Denmark, and the Low Countries benefited Hitler. • Describe the success of German forces in France. • Identify the Battle of Britain and the reasons the Germans could not win it. • Describe the role of the United States at the beginning of the war and how that role changed.	**Regular** 1.5 day | **Block Scheduling** 1 day *Block Scheduling Handbook with Team Teaching Strategies, 30.3*	**RS** Guided Reading Strategy 30.3 **RS** Graphic Organizer Activity 30: Fighting the War **PS** Readings in World History 106: The Evacuation of Dunkirk **E** Hands-on History Activity 30: Soldiers and Civilians in War
SECTION 4 **The Soviet Union and the United States** (pp. 796–800)	• Identify the steps the Axis Powers took to gain control of eastern Europe, the Middle East, and North Africa. • Describe how Germany planned to gain control of the Soviet Union, and evaluate the Soviets' defense. • Explain how Japan's goals in the Pacific led to war with Britain and the United States.	**Regular** 1.5 day | **Block Scheduling** 1 day *Block Scheduling Handbook with Team Teaching Strategies, 30.4*	**RS** Guided Reading Strategy 30.4
SECTION 5 **The Holocaust** (pp. 801–803)	• Explain how the Final Solution was developed. • Describe conditions in the concentration camps. • Identify ways different people resisted the Holocaust.	**Regular** 1.5 day | **Block Scheduling** 1 day *Block Scheduling Handbook with Team Teaching Strategies, 30.5*	**RS** Guided Reading Strategy 30.5 **PS** Readings in World History 107: The Discovery of Anne Frank's Hiding Place
SECTION 6 **The End of the War** (pp. 804–809)	• Identify the outcomes of Allied military actions in the Soviet Union, North Africa, Italy, and the Atlantic. • Describe how the Allies were able to achieve victory in Europe. • List the steps the Allies took to end the war with Japan.	**Regular** 1.5 day | **Block Scheduling** 1 day *Block Scheduling Handbook with Team Teaching Strategies, 30.6*	**RS** Guided Reading Strategy 30.6 **PS** Readings in World History 108: The Morning of the 500-Ton Bomb **E** Creative Teaching Strategy 30: Mapping a Global War

Chapter Resource Key

PS Primary Sources	**A** Assessment	Music
RS Reading Support	**REV** Review	Video
IC Interdisciplinary Connections	**ELL** Reinforcement and English Language Learners	Internet
E Enrichment	Transparencies	Holt Presentation Maker Using Microsoft® PowerPoint®
SM Skills Mastery	CD-ROM	

 One-Stop Planner CD-ROM

See the ***One-Stop Planner*** for a complete list of additional resources for students and teachers.

One-Stop Planner CD-ROM

It's easy to plan lessons, select resources, and print out materials for your students when you use the *One-Stop Planner* CD–ROM with *Test Generator.*

Technology Resources	Reinforcement, Review, and Assessment
One-Stop Planner 30.1 Regions of the World Music Audio CD Program 19: China, Mongolia and Taiwan: Beating the Dragon Robe: A Traditional Chinese Opera Homework Practice Online Online Maps, Charts, and Graphs: Japan Invades Manchuria, 1931	Daily Quiz 30.1 Main Idea Activity 30.1 English Audio Summary 30.1 Spanish Audio Summary 30.1 REV Section 1 Review, p. 785
One-Stop Planner 30.2 Regions of the World Music Audio CD Program 7: Central Europe: Folk Songs of Hungary Homework Practice Online	Daily Quiz 30.2 Main Idea Activity 30.2 English Audio Summary 30.2 Spanish Audio Summary 30.2 REV Section 2 Review, p. 790
One-Stop Planner 30.3 Holt Researcher: World History: Winston Churchill, Franklin Roosevelt Homework Practice Online	Daily Quiz 30.3 Main Idea Activity 30.3 English Audio Summary 30.3 Spanish Audio Summary 30.3 REV Section 3 Review, p. 795
One-Stop Planner 30.4 World History Teaching Transparency: Art and History 25: Inside an Internment Camp, World War II Homework Practice Online Online Maps, Charts, and Graphs: Operation Barbarossa Online Maps, Charts, and Graphs: Attack on Pearl Harbor, December 7, 1941	Daily Quiz 30.4 Main Idea Activity 30.4 English Audio Summary 30.4 Spanish Audio Summary 30.4 REV Section 4 Review, p. 800
One-Stop Planner 30.5 Holt Researcher: World History: Fania Fenelon Religions of the World Video Series: Judaism Homework Practice Online	Daily Quiz 30.5 Main Idea Activity 30.5 English Audio Summary 30.5 Spanish Audio Summary 30.5 REV Section 5 Review, p. 803
One-Stop Planner 30.6 World History and Cultures Video Program 25: The Lessons of World War II CNN Presents World Cultures: Yesterday and Today Segment 29: Rosie the Riveter World History Teaching Transparency: Geography and History 25: World War II in the Pacific, 1941–1945 Homework Practice Online Online Maps, Charts, and Graphs: Invasion of Normandy, June 6, 1944	Daily Quiz 30.6 Main Idea Activity 30.6 English Audio Summary 30.6 Spanish Audio Summary 30.6 REV Section 6 Review, p. 809

internet connect

HRW ONLINE RESOURCES
GO TO: go.hrw.com
Then type in a keyword.

TEACHER HOME PAGE
KEYWORD: SP3 Teacher

CHAPTER INTERNET ACTIVITIES
KEYWORD: SP3 WH30
Choose an activity to:
- write a biography on Raoul Wallenberg.
- write a report on the historical information and legacy of Anne Frank.
- write a report on a landing beach on D-Day that includes a map, a description of what happened there, photographs, and eyewitness accounts.

CHAPTER ENRICHMENT LINKS
KEYWORD: SP3 CH30

ONLINE ASSESSMENT
Homework Practice
KEYWORD: SP3 HP30
Standardized Test Prep
KEYWORD: SP3 STP30
Rubrics
KEYWORD: SS Rubrics

ONLINE MAPS, CHARTS, AND GRAPHS
KEYWORD: SP3 MCG

CONTENT UPDATES
KEYWORD: SS Content Updates

HOLT PRESENTATION MAKER
KEYWORD: SP3 PPT30

ONLINE READING SUPPORT
KEYWORD: SS Strategies

CURRENT EVENTS
KEYWORD: S3 Current Events

Meeting Individual Needs

Ability Levels

Level 1 Basic level activities designed for all students encountering new material

Level 2 Intermediate level activities designed for average students

Level 3 Challenging activities designed for honors and gifted and talented students

English Language Learners These activities address the needs of students with Limited English Proficiency.

Chapter Review and Assessment

IC   Vocabulary Activity 30
Global Skill Builder CD–ROM
HRW Web Site
REV Chapter 30 Tutorial for Students, Parents, Mentors, and Peers
REV Chapter 30 Review, pp. 810–811
A   Chapter 30 Test Generator (on the One-Stop Planner)
A   Chapter 30 Test (Form A or B)
A   Alternative Assessment Handbook
A   Chapter 30 Test for English Language Learners and Special-Needs Students

Build on What You Know

Ask students to answer the following questions:

How might the Treaty of Versailles have contributed to bitterness and distrust?

Consider:

- the effect of war damages on German attitudes
- limitations on Germany's size and military forces
- German response to being blamed for the war

Why might Great Britain and France have failed to respond to aggression by Germany, Japan, and Italy?

Consider:

- unwillingness to repeat the horrors of World War I
- reluctance to cooperate with the Soviet Union
- the influence of the Great Depression

EXPLORING THE TIME LINE

GLOBAL EVENTS

internet connect

TOPIC: U.S. Neutrality Acts

GO TO: go.hrw.com

KEYWORD: SP3 WH30

Have students access the Internet through the HRW Go site to conduct research on U.S. Neutrality Acts as they affected entry and participation in World War II. Have students create time lines showing the acts and their amendments. Have each student write a short paragraph describing the reasons a country might try to maintain neutrality. Should the United States have maintained its neutrality at all costs? Or was entering WWII the right thing for the country to do?

CHAPTER

30

1921–1945

World War II

Adolf Hitler

The cover and the sheet music to George Gershwin's "Rhapsody in Blue"

1921
Business and Finance
The German mark falls rapidly and inflation begins.

1923
The Arts
American composer George Gershwin writes "Rhapsody in Blue."

1926
Science and Technology
American scientist Robert H. Goddard fires the first liquid fuel rocket.

1929
Business and Finance
A world economic crisis begins after the U.S. stock market crashes.

1933
Politics
Adolf Hitler is appointed chancellor of Germany.

1933
The Arts
Books by Jewish and other non-Nazi authors are burned in Germany.

1920

1925

1930

1922
Politics
Benito Mussolini forms a fascist government in Italy.

1924
Daily Life
More than two million radios are in use in the United States.

1926
The Arts
Ernest Hemingway publishes his novel *The Sun Also Rises*.

1928
Global Events
The Kellogg-Briand Pact is signed, making war "illegal."

1928
Science and Technology
American aviator Amelia Earhart becomes the first woman to fly across the Atlantic.

1931
Global Events
The Japanese attack Manchuria.

A radio from the 1920s

Amelia Earhart

Build on What You Know

After World War I, bitterness and distrust continued to divide Europe. Under the Treaty of Versailles, Germany and its allies had to accept blame for starting the war and pay for damages to the countries they had invaded. The treaty also greatly reduced Germany's size and put limits on the size of its military. These measures were designed to keep Germany from waging another war. When Germany began violating the terms of the treaty, however, Great Britain and France took no action. In this chapter, you will learn how German, Japanese, and Italian aggression led to the outbreak of a new world war. You will also learn how the Allies fought this aggression and defeated the Axis Powers.

What's Your Opinion?

*To help students create their Themes Journal entries, provide the following examples of appropriate **agree**/**disagree** statements.*

Global Relations

Agree International alliances can involve a nation in the conflicts of an ally in a different region of the world.

Disagree Conflicts often stay within a region because they relate to borders or other regional issues.

Government

Agree Leaders may encourage racial prejudice to gain popularity and blame someone else for national problems.

Disagree Uniting citizens in patriotism strengthens a government more than dividing them through racism.

Science, Technology & Society

Agree Military technology used to destroy an enemy in wartime can be used to benefit society after the war.

Disagree Advances in technology during wartime have no benefits to society.

These suitcases were taken from prisoners upon their arrival at the Auschwitz-Birkenau concentration camp.

A page from a child's sugar ration book from Great Britain

EXPLORING THE TIME LINE
GLOBAL EVENTS

After World War I, many people in the United States and Europe thought that the war's unsettled issues made another war virtually inevitable. At the same time, horrible memories of that war made many people anxious to prevent another one.

ACTIVITY: Ask students to identify events before 1939 on the time line that reflect unresolved issues *(inflation in Germany),* efforts to avoid war *(Kellogg-Briand Pact, Neutrality Act),* and intimations of future war *(Mussolini, Japanese in Manchuria, Hitler, Spanish Civil War, Axis).*

1935
Science and Technology
Robert Watson-Watt builds radar equipment to detect aircraft.

1937
Politics
President Franklin Roosevelt signs the U.S. Neutrality Act.

1937
The Arts
Pablo Picasso paints *Guernica* for the Paris World Exhibition.

1940
Daily Life
Bacon, butter, and sugar are rationed in Great Britain.

1941
Politics
Hitler orders the "Final Solution"—a program to kill the entire Jewish population in Europe.

1941
Global Events
The United States and Great Britain sign the Atlantic Charter.

1945
Politics
Roosevelt, Churchill, and Stalin meet at the Yalta Conference.

1945
Global Events
The Allies achieve victory in Europe on May 8, V-E Day.

1945
Science and Technology
The first atomic bomb is exploded near Alamogordo, New Mexico, on July 16.

1935	**1940**	**1945**

1934
Global Events
The Soviet Union is admitted to the League of Nations.

1936
Politics
The Spanish Civil War begins.

1936
Global Events
Mussolini and Hitler form the Rome-Berlin Axis.

1939
Global Events
Germany invades Poland.

1939
Business and Finance
The U.S. economy begins to boom from European orders for arms and war equipment.

1941
Global Events
The Japanese make a surprise attack on the U.S. naval base at Pearl Harbor, Hawaii.

1941
Science and Technology
The U.S. "Manhattan Project" of intensive atomic research begins.

1943
The Arts
Casablanca wins the Academy Award™ for best film.

1945
Business and Finance
Black—or illegal—markets for food, clothing, and cigarettes develop throughout Europe.

BOGART · BERGMAN · HENREID
Presented by WARNER BROS.
"*Casablanca*"
RAINS · VEIDT · GREENSTREET · LORRE
A HAL B. WALLIS PRODUCTION Directed by MICHAEL CURTIZ

Poster for the movie Casablanca

What's Your Opinion?

*Do you **agree** or **disagree** with the following statements? Support your point of view in your journal.*

Global Relations Regional conflicts in one part of the world can spread to affect the rest of the world.

Government Racial prejudice within a nation can be used as a political weapon by the government of that nation.

Science, Technology & Society Technology developed during wartime can be both beneficial and destructive.

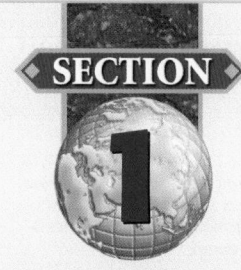
OBJECTIVES

1 Analyze why Japan and Italy were able to carry out aggressive territorial policies in the 1930s.

2 Explain why the League of Nations was unable to stop international aggression.

3 Describe how Spain's civil war led to a fascist dictatorship there.

📀 *LET'S GET STARTED!*

As students enter the classroom, ask them to list characteristics of a bully. Lead class discussion of ways to deal with bullies (*give in, refuse to give in, join with others to resist, ask someone with authority to intervene*) and the advantages and disadvantages of each. Tell students that in Section 1 they will learn how some nations in the 1930s acted as bullies and how other nations reacted.

◆ SECTION ◆
1 RESOURCES

REPRODUCIBLE RESOURCES

▶ Guided Reading Strategy 30.1

▶ Geography Activity 30: Japan's Drive to Expand in Manchuria

TECHNOLOGY RESOURCES

▶ One-Stop Planner 30.1

▶ Regions of the World Music Audio CD Program 19: China, Mongolia and Taiwan: Beating the Dragon Robe: A Traditional Chinese Opera

▶ Homework Practice Online

▶ Online Maps, Charts, and Graphs: Japan Invades Manchuria, 1931

REINFORCEMENT, REVIEW, AND ASSESSMENT

▶ Section 1 Review, p. 785

▶ Daily Quiz 30.1

▶ Main Idea Activity 30.1

▶ English Audio Summary 30.1

▶ Spanish Audio Summary 30.1

◆ SECTION ◆ 1

▶ READ TO DISCOVER

❶ Why were Japan and Italy able to carry out aggressive territorial policies in the 1930s?

❷ Why was the League of Nations unable to stop international aggression?

❸ How did Spain's civil war lead to a fascist dictatorship there?

▶ IDENTIFY

Kellogg-Briand Pact
Osachi Hamaguchi
Falange
Spanish Civil War
Francisco Franco
International Brigades

▶ WHY IT MATTERS TODAY

Today the United Nations works to keep international peace. Use **CNN** or other **current event** sources to find out what recent peace efforts the UN has undertaken. Record your findings in your journal.

CNN Student News.com

Threats to World Peace

The Main Idea
During the 1930s aggression by Japan and Italy and civil war in Spain threatened world peace.

The Story Continues *After World War I, the role of the League of Nations as an international peacekeeper was challenged. When Italy invaded Ethiopia in 1935, Ethiopia's former leader Haile Selassie explained the threat to international peace. "It is not merely a question of a settlement in the matter of Italian aggression. It is a question of collective security; of the very existence of the League . . . ."*

Japanese Aggression in Asia

In 1928 the U.S. secretary of state, Frank B. Kellogg, and the French foreign minister, Aristide Briand, met in Paris. Together they created an agreement that made war "illegal." Eventually more than 60 nations signed the **Kellogg-Briand Pact.** During the 1930s, however, it became clear that world powers would not be able to put such an agreement into effect. Japan made one of the first challenges to this pact.

The Japanese military began gaining power in the late 1920s. Then in 1930 Japan's liberal prime minister, **Osachi Hamaguchi,** was fatally shot. Political chaos followed the assassination. Within two years, a group of military leaders controlled the Japanese government. In September 1931 a small group of Japanese army officers staged a fake attack on the railway near Mukden, in China's province of Manchuria. Blaming the attack on China, Japanese forces in Manchuria quickly took control of the entire province. The major nations in the League of Nations condemned Japan's aggression but were not willing to take military action to protect China. Japan responded to the condemnation by withdrawing from the League of Nations.

The lack of enforceable opposition encouraged Japan, which announced its intention of extending its influence not only to all of China, but also throughout East Asia and the western Pacific. Six years later, in 1937, the Japanese army captured the city of Beijing. While Chinese forces fought hard to protect their country, Japan slowly gained more territory. By 1939 the Japanese controlled about one fourth of China, including all seaports.

✔ **READING CHECK: Finding the Main Idea** What was the result of Japanese aggression during the 1930s? controlled part of China, including seaports

Victorious Japanese troops celebrate the conquest of Manchuria.

LEVEL 1: Tell students that Japan had critical shortages of raw materials. Explain that Italy had economic problems and resented not getting more territory after World War I. Ask what the military leaders of Japan and Mussolini in Italy did to solve their problems. *(aggression against others: Japan conquered part of China, Italy conquered Ethiopia)*

ENGLISH LANGUAGE LEARNERS

LEVEL 3: Have students write a brief essay comparing and contrasting aggression by Italy and Japan in the 1930s. *(essays should mention motives, actions, international response)*

HOMEWORK Have students draw a cartoon comparing the behavior of Japan or Italy to that of a bully. The cartoon should indicate how other nations responded.

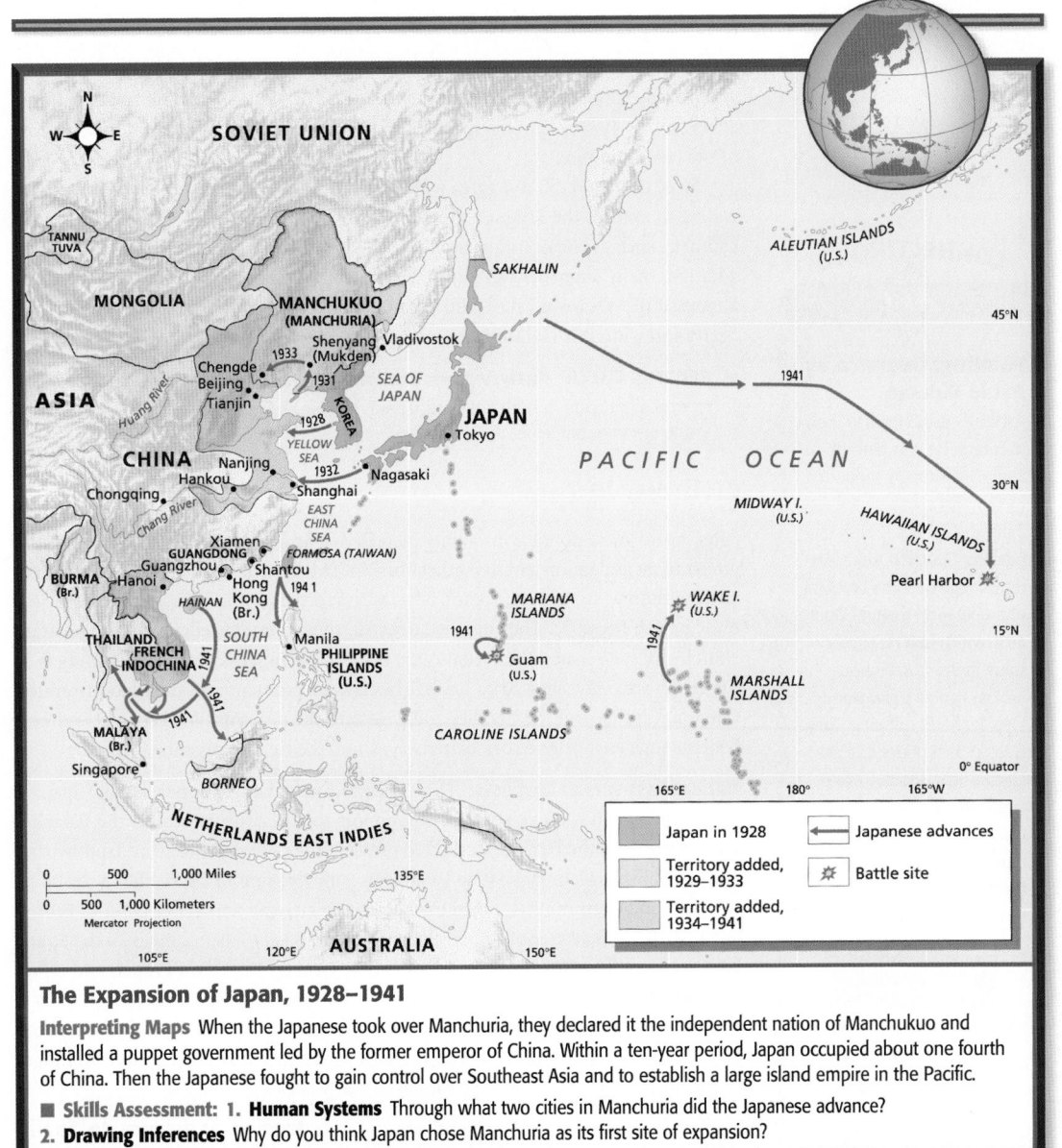

The Expansion of Japan, 1928–1941

Interpreting Maps When the Japanese took over Manchuria, they declared it the independent nation of Manchukuo and installed a puppet government led by the former emperor of China. Within a ten-year period, Japan occupied about one fourth of China. Then the Japanese fought to gain control over Southeast Asia and to establish a large island empire in the Pacific.

■ **Skills Assessment: 1. Human Systems** Through what two cities in Manchuria did the Japanese advance?
2. Drawing Inferences Why do you think Japan chose Manchuria as its first site of expansion?

Historical Sidelight

The Japanese assault on China interrupted that country's civil war between Nationalist government forces and the Communists. Although both groups fought the Japanese, Mao Zedong never lost sight of his goals. By organizing anti-Japanese resistance behind enemy lines, he recruited fighters to be used later against the Nationalists.

Critical Thinking

Remind students of the mutual hostility between fascists and communists. Then ask how the Japanese invasion might have strengthened popular support for the communists in China.

ANSWER: Many people condemned Japanese aggression.

MAP ANSWERS

1. Shenyang (Mukden), Chengde

2. near Japan, not well-defended

Italy's Conquest of Ethiopia

Benito Mussolini came to power in Italy in 1922 and ruled as a fascist dictator. Mussolini worked to improve the nation's economy. He may have believed that overseas expansion would help ease some of Italy's economic problems. Ethiopia, one of the few independent nations in Africa, became the target of Mussolini's aggressive goals.

When a border dispute with Italy broke out in 1934, Ethiopia called on the League of Nations to help. The League could not offer military protection to Ethiopia, however, because it maintained no armed forces. A year later Italian forces invaded and

TEACH OBJECTIVE 2

ALL LEVELS: Have small groups of students, acting as Chinese and Japanese officials, present their side in the Asian crisis to the League of Nations. Then have the rest of the class, as the League, debate what to do. As the debate nears resolution, announce that Japan has withdrawn from the League and ask how that changes the options. **ENGLISH LANGUAGE LEARNERS**

TEACH OBJECTIVE 3

ALL LEVELS: Have students work in pairs to chart the opposing sides in the Spanish Civil War. Then ask students to deduce from their charts why the Nationalists won.
ENGLISH LANGUAGE LEARNERS, **COOPERATIVE LEARNING**

Nationalists	Loyalists
Spain: army leaders, church leaders, landowners, nobles	*Spain: workers, peasants, socialists, communists*
Germany: fully equipped military units	*Soviet Union: airplanes, technicians, military advisors*
Italy: fully equipped military units, 50,000 troops	*International Brigades: about 70,000 volunteer fighters*

History Maker

ERNEST HEMINGWAY. Among the Americans in Spain during its civil war was author Ernest Hemingway, who covered the war as a reporter for American newspapers. One of his most famous novels, *For Whom the Bell Tolls* (published in 1940), tells the story of an American schoolteacher who is killed while fighting for the Loyalist cause. The book suggests that the loss of liberty in Spain was a threat to liberty everywhere. Hemingway himself narrowly escaped death when a shell exploded inside his hotel room during a battle.

Critical Thinking

Ask students how Hemingway's experiences influenced his work.

ANSWER: He used his experience during the Spanish Civil War as the basis for one of his novels.

CONNECTING TO ART ANSWER
distorted figures, stark light

CONNECTING TO
Art

Painting: *Guernica* by Pablo Picasso
Although Pablo Picasso lived in France, he was born in Spain. He strongly supported the Loyalist cause during the Spanish Civil War. Picasso's painting *Guernica* expresses his outrage over the bombing of the Spanish town of Guernica, which had no strategic value in the war. Picasso's broken figures show war victims' fear and suffering. They twist in pain under a bright electric light. Picasso asked that *Guernica* be kept in the United States until democracy returned to Spain. In 1981 the painting was placed in a museum in Madrid.

Understanding the Arts

What techniques does Picasso use to express the pain and horror of war?

defeated the poorly equipped Ethiopian army. The League declared Italy an aggressor and placed economic sanctions on the country. The weak boycott on trade had little effect on Italy, however. In the spring of 1936, Mussolini announced Ethiopia was part of the Italian Empire.

Most countries did not agree with Italy's actions. However, no major power was willing to enforce the League's sanctions. Horrible memories of World War I made countries such as Great Britain and the United States unwilling to risk another war. In addition, many countries were busy dealing with the problems created by the Great Depression. As a result, Italy and Japan realized they could continue their acts of aggression with little real threat of opposition.

✔ **READING CHECK: Analyzing Information** Why was the League of Nations unable to stop aggression in both Italy and Japan? had no armed forces, major powers unwilling to enforce sanctions

Civil War in Spain

After World War I political instability increased in Spain. In 1923 rebels overthrew the government and set up a military dictatorship. This government fell in 1931 when the army withdrew its support. Spain's new leaders formed a government called the Second Spanish Republic. They planned to establish freedom of religion and to separate church and state issues. Education came under government control and members of the clergy were not allowed to teach. The new government also took land from the Catholic Church and the nobility and gave it to the peasants. Workers received new benefits such as shorter hours, better wages, and the right to organize.

Nationalists versus Loyalists. These dramatic new changes angered many Spanish conservatives. They quickly gave their support to a fascist party called the **Falange.** Using terrorism, the Falange worked to preserve the power of the army, landowners, and the church. Members of the Falange became even more active after a group of socialists and Communists, called the Popular Front, won a major election in February 1936. In the summer of 1936, Falangist uprisings led to the outbreak of the **Spanish Civil War.** The Falangist rebels were led by General **Francisco Franco** and called themselves Nationalists. Those who supported the republic were known as Loyalists, or Republicans. By the end of 1936, the Nationalists controlled most of northern Spain. The Loyalists controlled the east and southeast. They also had power over most of the northern coastline and the capital city of Madrid.

Foreign assistance to Spain. The Spanish Civil War soon grew into a small European war. Germany and Italy saw a fascist Spain as a part of their plan to surround France with unfriendly powers and threaten Great Britain. They sent fully equipped military units to bolster Nationalist forces. The Soviet Union sympathized with the republican government. Soviets sent planes, technicians, and military advisers

REVIEW

Have students complete the Section 1 Review on p. 785.

ASSESS

Have students complete Daily Quiz 30.1. As Alternative Assessment, you may want to use the Spanish Civil War chart exercise in this section's lessons.

RETEACH

Have students complete Main Idea Activity for English Language Learners and Special-Needs Students 30.1. Then have students draw an illustrated time line of events mentioned in Section 1.
ENGLISH LANGUAGE LEARNERS, COOPERATIVE LEARNING

EXTEND

Have students work in groups to present radio news programs about aggression in China, Ethiopia, or Spain in the 1930s.
BLOCK SCHEDULING, COOPERATIVE LEARNING

---

to Spain. Their support, however, was not nearly as great as what Franco received from his fascist allies.

Volunteers from France, Great Britain, and the United States also rushed to help the Spanish Republic. These idealistic antifascist volunteers became known as the **International Brigades.** The French and British feared that the Spanish Civil War might spread to the rest of Europe. Spain's civil war illustrated a wider conflict between communism and fascism throughout Europe. English writer George Orwell described the antifascist city of Barcelona.

«Practically every building of any size had been seized by the workers and was draped with red flags . . . ; every wall was scrawled with the hammer and sickle and with the initials of the revolutionary parties; almost every church had been gutted and its images burnt.»

George Orwell, *Homage to Catalonia*

Nationalist forces defeated the Loyalists in the spring of 1939. Franco set up a fascist dictatorship. He became Spain's head of state and had unlimited power. Franco's government and economic structure began to look a lot like Mussolini's in Italy. Franco brought an end to all free elections and most civil rights. Spain's old ruling groups—the army, the landowners, and the Roman Catholic Church—all held positions of power under Franco's rule.

During the three years of the Spanish Civil War, Spain and its people suffered greatly. The war caused considerable destruction and loss of life. Estimates of Spain's war dead during these years range from 500,000 to 1 million. Over the course of the war, moreover, the bitter differences that had separated the various opposing groups in 1936 became deeper and even more divisive.

✔ **READING CHECK: Sequencing**
How did Spain become a fascist dictatorship? *Franco's Nationalists defeated the Loyalists.*

Analyzing Primary Sources

Identifying a Point of View Why would antifascists in Spain have destroyed churches? *to weaken the power of the Catholic Church*

INTERPRETING THE VISUAL RECORD

Spanish Civil War Europe's larger conflict between communism and fascism was demonstrated in the Spanish Civil War. *Why do you think these antifascists barricaded the streets of Barcelona?*

VISUAL RECORD ANSWER
to keep fascist troops and tanks from advancing

SECTION 1 REVIEW ANSWERS

❶ **Identify**
• Kellogg-Briand Pact, p. 782
• Osachi Hamaguchi, p. 782
• Falange, p. 784
• Spanish Civil War, p. 784
• Francisco Franco, p. 784
• International Brigades, p. 785

❷ Militarism: Japan—rule by military officers, rearmament; Italy—rearmament; Spain—political power of army under Franco; Fascism: Japan—overthrow of elected government; Italy—nationalistic, dictatorial, anticommunist; Spain—Franco ended free elections and civil rights, modeled economy on Italy

❸ a. no army, fear of another war

b. led successful revolt against government of Spanish republic

❹ Students might suggest the League would have stopped Japan in China or Italy in Ethiopia, reducing their later roles in World War II.

SECTION 1 REVIEW

1. **Identify** and explain the significance:
   Kellogg-Briand Pact
   Osachi Hamaguchi
   Falange
   Spanish Civil War
   Francisco Franco
   International Brigades

2. **Identifying Cause and Effect** Copy the chart below. Use it to explain how militarism and fascism affected Japan, Italy, and Spain in the 1930s.

	Japan	Italy	Spain
Militarism and Fascism			

3. **Finding the Main Idea**
   a. Why was the League of Nations unable to stop the aggression of Japan and Italy?
   b. How did Francisco Franco become a fascist dictator in Spain?

4. **Writing and Critical Thinking**
   Making Predictions Describe what might have happened differently during the 1930s if the League of Nations had been a more effective international peacekeeper.
   Consider:
   • Japan's aggression in the 1930s
   • Italy's aggression in the 1930s
   • the effects of not opposing such aggression

Homework Practice Online
go.hrw.com
keyword: SP3 HP30

SECTION 2

OBJECTIVES

1 **Explain how Hitler took over Austria and Czechoslovakia.**

2 **Discuss how and why Great Britain and France attempted to avoid another war.**

3 **Describe how Great Britain and France prepared for war.**

4 **Discuss why Hitler and Stalin created the Nazi-Soviet Pact, and how Western nations responded to Hitler's invasion of Poland.**

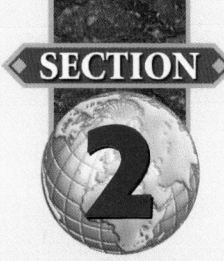

LET'S GET STARTED!

As students enter the classroom, ask them to think of situations when they have had to choose whether to appease or confront someone. Ask what *appeasement* means (*to give in to another's demands*) and why people sometimes try to appease others. (*fear, to keep the peace, issue not worth trouble*) Have the class evaluate appeasement as a strategy for living. Tell students that in Section 2 they will learn how French and British leaders tried to appease Germany.

That's Interesting!

Mussolini originated the term *Axis Powers.* He claimed that an imaginary line drawn from Rome to Berlin formed the "axis" on which the world would turn from that time forward.

SECTION 2

READ TO DISCOVER

❶ How was Adolf Hitler able to take over Austria and Czechoslovakia?
❷ How and why did Great Britain and France attempt to avoid another war in Europe?
❸ How did Great Britain and France prepare for war in the face of German aggression?
❹ Why did Hitler and Stalin create the Nazi-Soviet Pact, and how did Western nations respond to Hitler's invasion of Poland?

DEFINE

appeasement

IDENTIFY

Axis Powers
Anti-Comintern Pact
Munich Conference
Neville Chamberlain
Édouard Daladier
German-Soviet nonaggression pact

WHY IT MATTERS TODAY

Today, world powers often get involved when one country acts aggressively against another. Use CNNfyi.com or other **current event** sources to find an aggressive act during recent years that the United States has taken action against. Record your findings in your journal.

CNN Student News.com

Hitler's Aggressions

The Main Idea
Adolf Hitler led Germany in its aggressive acts to expand the territory of the German empire.

The Story Continues *Militarism and fascism also grew in Germany. Under Adolf Hitler's leadership, Germany began a plan to acquire "living space" for the "superior" German race. "An additional 500,000 kilometers [almost 200,000 square miles] in Europe can provide new homesteads for millions of German peasants . . . ," Hitler wrote.*

Austria and Czechoslovakia

In 1933 Adolf Hitler announced that he would rearm the country. He then took Germany out of the League of Nations. In March 1936 German troops marched into the Rhineland, violating the Treaty of Versailles. In October 1936, Hitler and Mussolini created an alliance called the Rome-Berlin Axis. They began calling themselves the **Axis Powers.** Shortly afterward, Japan and Germany promised to work together. They signed an agreement called the **Anti-Comintern Pact,** pledging to stop the spread of communism. Italy later signed the pact. By the end of 1936, the three nations who would later enter World War II as the Axis Powers had hidden their aggressive intentions under the cover of fighting communism.

Annexing Austria. A Nazi Party had been formed in Austria in the late 1920s. By the early 1930s, the extremely conservative Austrian government was doing little to resist Nazi inroads. By 1938 threats from both Hitler and Mussolini forced the Austrian government to include Nazi members in its cabinet.

Although the Austrian chancellor had made an agreement with Hitler on union with Germany, he regretted the agreement and suggested that the Austrian people be allowed to vote on the issue. Hitler refused, preferring instead to take Austria with a show of force. The Austrian chancellor resigned, and a German army marched into Austria unopposed. In March 1938 Hitler declared Austria to be part of the Third Reich. This was in violation of the Treaty of Versailles, which had specifically forbidden any union between Germany and Austria. Even so, Great Britain and France did nothing more than send protests to Hitler, which he ignored. The League of Nations took no action.

Mussolini and Hitler at a 1937 conference in Munich.

LEVEL 1: Have students locate Austria and Czechoslovakia on the map on page 788. Ask students to identify factors that made those countries prime targets for German expansion. *(border with Germany, link to Italy, large ethnic German populations, Nazi parties)* **ENGLISH LANGUAGE LEARNERS**

ALL LEVELS: Have students work in pairs to create chain-of-events charts of Hitler's aggression against Czechoslovakia.

Nazi growth in Sudetenland	Munich Conference
region put under martial law	Germany occupied Sudetenland
Hitler said he would invade	Germany occupied Czechoslovakia

Lead a discussion of how the Munich Conference affected events. **ENGLISH LANGUAGE LEARNERS, COOPERATIVE LEARNING**

The addition of Austria increased the size of Germany's population, territory, and resources. It also increased Hitler's power in Europe. Strategically, Germany controlled the heart of central Europe. Germany now had a common border with its ally Italy and it nearly encircled Czechoslovakia. Hitler identified this country as his next area of expansion.

Crisis in the Sudetenland. More than 3 million Germans lived in the Sudetenland (soo·DAYT·uhn·land), a region around the western rim of Czechoslovakia. The Sudetenland included a chain of mountains that provided a natural defense for Czechoslovakia. They were heavily fortified as a very important defensive line.

The Czech government tried to protect the rights of Germans living in this area. However, many still wanted union with Germany. As a result the Nazi Party grew in strength there. When riots broke out in September 1938, Czechoslovakia placed the region under martial law. Hitler then announced he would invade and annex the Sudetenland to protect fellow Germans. The loss of this heavily armed mountain region would mean disaster for Czechoslovakia since it would leave the country defenseless against Germany.

Appeasement. As tensions grew in Europe, Hitler held a meeting on September 29, 1938, called the **Munich Conference.** He invited British prime minister **Neville Chamberlain** and French premier **Édouard Daladier** (dah·lahd·yay). Also in attendance was Mussolini. Chamberlain and Daladier accepted Hitler's demand that the Sudetenland be joined with Germany. Britain and France feared Germany's military strength. In addition, they knew their own countries were not prepared for war. This policy of trying to keep the peace by accepting some of the demands of the aggressor is called **appeasement.**

Upon returning to London, Chamberlain spoke triumphantly to a cheering crowd. He announced that he had achieved "peace in our time." France announced it would not honor its agreement to defend Czechoslovakia. Germany began to occupy the Sudetenland. Abandoned by its allies, Czechoslovakia was left defenseless. The United States also tried to avoid the conflict. Famous pilot Charles Lindbergh expressed the feelings of many Americans.

These Sudeten women express strong emotions as they salute German troops in Czechoslovakia.

> **History Makers Speak**
>
> **"If we are forced into a war against the wishes of an overwhelming majority of our people, we will have proved democracy such a failure at home that there will be little use fighting for it abroad."**
>
> Charles A. Lindbergh, *The New York Times,* April 24, 1941

In March 1939 German troops invaded Czechoslovakia. Within six months this independent republic had been erased from Europe's map. Germany also gained the port city of Memel, Lithuania, in the spring of 1939. Yet another country lost its independence when Mussolini invaded Albania in April 1939. The Italians took this small country on the east coast of the Adriatic Sea in only a few days. Once again the League of Nations had failed to be effective. Its complete helplessness in the face of aggression was now obvious.

✔ **READING CHECK: Summarizing** How did Hitler conquer Austria and Czechoslovakia, and what role did Great Britain and France play? invaded and annexed; sent protests, accepted demands

---

Citizenship

Ethnic Germans comprised over 20 percent of Czechoslovakia's population and were concentrated in the Sudetenland. The Sudeten German Party that demanded autonomy there was financed and controlled by the Nazi Party in Germany. In seizing Czechoslovakia, Hitler gained control of a country that had one of the largest armaments industries in Europe, and he treated the country relatively well throughout the war.

Although organized resistance to German control was slow to develop, anti-German backlash followed the end of the war. After the Sudetenland was returned to Czechoslovakia, its government expelled most of the ethnic German population from the region.

ACTIVITY: Have students debate whether or not Czechoslovakia was justified in expelling ethnic Germans. Remind them to consider military, political, and ethical issues.

Analyzing Primary Sources

Finding the Main Idea According to Lindbergh, in what sense would democracy have failed if the United States went to war? War was against the wishes of the majority.

TEACH OBJECTIVE 2

ALL LEVELS: Have students work in groups to create editorial pages that might have appeared in French or British newspapers after the Munich Conference. Each group's page should include views for and against appeasement, a feature article providing background, letters to the editor, and a political cartoon. Post the finished pages around the room. **ENGLISH LANGUAGE LEARNERS, COOPERATIVE LEARNING**

HOMEWORK Have students imagine they are residents of the Sudetenland of either Czech or German descent. Have them write a letter to American relatives about how they feel when German troops invade.

TEACH OBJECTIVE 3

LEVEL 1: Tell students to imagine they are British or French leaders who have decided to prepare for war. Ask students how they would prepare. *(rearmament, draft, international agreements)* **ENGLISH LANGUAGE LEARNERS**

Geography

Hitler's plans for German expansion owed much to theories of geopolitics, or the relationship between geographic space and foreign policy. In the early 1900s Englishman Sir Halford Mackinder had argued that a nation's power rested on its control of large areas of land.

Mackinder believed the most important area was Eurasia and Africa, a vast connected landmass that he called the World Island. Whoever managed to control the central regions of Eurasia that included Germany and Russia—the Heartland, as he called it—could control the rest of the World Island as well.

Critical Thinking

Ask students how Mackinder's ideas about a country's greatness and the World Island may have affected Hitler's plans.

ANSWER: These theories may have influenced Hitler's desire to control central Europe and Russia.

MAP ANSWERS

1. most of Europe and North Africa

2. Switzerland, Sweden, Spain, Turkey, Ireland, Egypt, Yemen

Preparations for War

After Hitler took over Czechoslovakia, British and French leaders could no longer ignore the fascist dictators. Britain and France therefore began to prepare for war. Neville Chamberlain ordered that Britain's rearmament program be stepped up. He also rushed through Parliament a law drafting men into the military. Great Britain joined France in a promise to protect Poland if Germany attacked.

Negotiating with Stalin. Great Britain and France asked Soviet leader Joseph Stalin to become part of an alliance against Germany. The Soviet Union had joined the League of Nations while Japan, Germany, and Italy had

German and Italian Expansion, 1935–1941
Interpreting Maps Within six years of expansion, Germany and Italy controlled much of Europe and North Africa.
■ **Skills Assessment: 1. Places and Regions** What regions did Germany and Italy control by December 1941?
2. Analyzing Information What countries remained neutral during this period?

TEACH OBJECTIVE 4

ALL LEVELS: Organize the class into four groups to represent the military high commands of Germany, France, Great Britain, and Poland. Have the groups discuss what course a war in Europe might take and how the Soviet Union might be a factor. Then have each group draft a memorandum for its national leaders about the importance of the Soviet position. Discuss each group's memo. **ENGLISH LANGUAGE LEARNERS, COOPERATIVE LEARNING**

TEACH OBJECTIVES 2, 3, and 4

LEVEL 3: Have students act as journalists interviewing other students playing the roles of Chamberlain, Daladier, and Hitler at three different points in time: just after the Munich agreement, after Germany invades Czechoslovakia, and after Germany invades Poland. The journalists need to prepare two or three in-depth questions for the leaders. The leaders should consider how their opinions might change over time. **COOPERATIVE LEARNING**

CLOSE

Have students debate whether buying time through appeasement was an advantage or a disadvantage to Britain and France.

dropped out. However, Soviet leaders still did not trust the Western democracies. Western nations were fearful of communism. Until this time they had kept the Soviet Union out of all major decisions. Soviet leaders in turn feared that the Western powers would welcome a chance to turn Hitler loose on them.

The Soviets required that any agreement with the West guarantee the independence of Poland, Finland, and the Baltic countries of Estonia, Latvia, and Lithuania. All but Lithuania had common borders with the Soviet Union. The Soviets also wanted a military alliance with these countries. This would allow an immediate response if Germany attacked. The Baltic states immediately protested the Soviets' idea. A military agreement would mean that Soviet armies would have the right to move into their countries to fight off a German attack. As a result the talks dragged on without any agreement.

✔ **READING CHECK: Summarizing** What preparations did Great Britain and France make for war when Hitler's plans became clear? *rearmament, draft*

The Nazi-Soviet Pact. At the same time that Stalin was negotiating with Great Britain and France, he was carrying on secret talks with Germany. In August 1939 the Western democracies received a huge shock when Hitler proudly announced a **German-Soviet nonaggression pact.** Also called the Nazi-Soviet Pact, this agreement publicly stated that Germany and the Soviet Union would never attack each other. Each would remain neutral if the other went to war.

The reasons for this agreement were not clear at the time. Both Hitler and Stalin may simply have been playing for time. Hitler wanted to make sure the Soviets would be neutral if Great Britain or France took action against Germany. Stalin hoped that Hitler's attention would be focused on events in the West. This would give the Soviet Union enough time to prepare for a conflict with Germany.

Secretly, however, Hitler and Stalin had agreed to divide eastern Europe into spheres of influence. Germany was to take western Poland. The Soviet Union was to have a free hand in the Baltic countries. It would also control eastern Poland and the province of Bessarabia. Little doubt existed as to the meaning of the agreement. The Western nations had lost a possible ally in the East, and Germany had arranged for the Soviet Union to be neutral. This gave Germany a huge military advantage.

✔ **READING CHECK: Finding the Main Idea** Why did Hitler and Stalin create the Nazi-Soviet Pact? *secretly agreed to divide eastern Europe*

YOUNG PEOPLE IN HISTORY

Edelweiss Pirates

Hitler established youth groups to train young Germans in Nazi ideology. Not every German youngster joined the Hitler Youth, however. Many teenagers formed their own neighborhood groups. Some groups, such as the Edelweiss Pirates of Cologne-Ehrenfield, became involved in anti-Nazi activities. The Edelweiss Pirates provided shelter to concentration camp escapees and carried out secret attacks on Nazi leaders. The Nazis caught and executed several members of the group. **Who were the Edelweiss Pirates, and how did they resist Nazism?**

The Nazis hanged Bartholomäus Schink on November 10, 1944, for being a member of the Edelweiss Pirates.

Shown here is Joseph Stalin (second from right) with other Russian and German diplomats concluding the German-Soviet nonaggression pact.

YOUNG PEOPLE IN HISTORY ANSWER

anti-Nazi youth organization; sheltered escapees, secretly attacked Nazi leaders

Interdisciplinary Connection

LITERATURE. After World War I, many novelists wrote books exposing the horrors of the war. *All Quiet on the Western Front* portrays the experiences of a young German soldier on the western front. The author, Erich Maria Remarque, had fought for Germany during the war and was wounded several times. In describing the miserable experience of ordinary soldiers, he hoped to convince his readers never to let it happen again.

When the Nazis came to power, they burned Remarque's books. In 1938 they revoked his German citizenship. After living in Switzerland, Remarque moved to the United States in 1939 and in 1947 he became a U.S. citizen. He continued to write about the suffering of war in several later novels about the Nazis and World War II.

Critical Thinking

Why did Germany react so harshly against *All Quiet on the Western Front?*

ANSWER: Students may suggest that pro-war leaders in Germany objected to the novel's views.

REVIEW

Have students complete the Section 2 Review on p. 790.

ASSESS

Have students complete Daily Quiz 30.2. As Alternative Assessment, you may want to use the newspaper pages exercise in this section's lessons.

RETEACH

Have students complete Main Idea Activity for English Language Learners and Special-Needs Students 30.2. Then have students make a chart to sequence the events in this section.
ENGLISH LANGUAGE LEARNERS

EXTEND

Have students research the history of Gdańsk (Danzig), then write a dialogue between imaginary advocates of German and Polish ownership of the Polish Corridor. **BLOCK SCHEDULING**

VISUAL RECORD ANSWER

encouraged nationalism and support for German expansion

•SECTION•
2 REVIEW ANSWERS

❶ Define
• appeasement, p. 787

❷ Identify
• Axis Powers, p. 786
• Anti-Comintern Pact, p. 786
• Munich Conference, p. 787
• Neville Chamberlain, p. 787
• Édouard Daladier, p. 787
• German-Soviet nonaggression pact, p. 789

❸ Austria: 1 Nazis in cabinet, 2 chancellor suggests vote, 3 German troops in Austria; Czechoslovakia: 1 annex Sudetenland, 2 Munich Conference, 3 invade the rest of Czechoslovakia

❹ a. used appeasement because they were not ready for war

b. German leaders realized nobody would stop them.

c. They declared war on Germany.

❺ Students' essays should mention rearmament, the draft, and negotiations with Stalin.

INTERPRETING THE VISUAL RECORD

Nazi schools The government of Nazi Germany wanted children to share the military mood and master-race philosophy of the Nazi party. Here, a teacher points out the location of the Polish Corridor to a classroom full of students. *What effect do you think lectures like the one shown here had on children?*

Danzig and the Polish Corridor. The crisis that finally touched off World War II began in Poland. Hitler wanted Germany to control the seaport city of Danzig—modern day Gdańsk. Danzig was a free city, protected by the League of Nations. Poland and Germany both had rights to use the busy and strategically important port of Danzig, located at the mouth of the Vistula River on the coast of the Baltic Sea. A strip of land about 90 miles long and between 25 and 55 miles wide allowed Poland access to the port of Danzig. This land ran through what had been German Prussia. It had been granted to Poland in 1919 by the Treaty of Versailles in order to provide Poland with a direct opening to the Baltic. This strip of land, known as the Polish Corridor, became a growing source of conflict between Poland and Germany during the years following World War I. After Hitler came to power in 1933, he acted to claim Danzig for Germany because it had a large German population. It also had a strong and growing Nazi Party that by 1937 had taken control of the city government.

On September 1, 1939, Hitler announced the annexation of Danzig to the German Reich. At the same time, without warning, his air force began a massive attack on Poland. Nazi tanks sped across the border and swiftly drove toward Warsaw and the Polish heartland. The Poles were relentlessly attacked by German forces equipped with modern weapons and technology, and a strategy of total war. Polish troops made a courageous but hopeless defense against the German onslaught. Two days later Great Britain and France decided that they would not stand for any further Nazi aggression. They kept their promises to Poland and declared war on Germany. Within 48 hours the unannounced attack on Poland had become the beginning of World War II.

✔ **READING CHECK: Drawing Conclusions** How did the Nazi-Soviet Pact and Hitler's attack on Poland lead to World War II? kept Soviets neutral when France and Britain honored promise to Poland

◄ SECTION 2 REVIEW ►

1. **Define** and explain the significance:
   appeasement

2. **Identify** and explain the significance:
   Axis Powers
   Anti-Comintern Pact
   Munich Conference
   Neville Chamberlain
   Édouard Daladier
   German-Soviet nonaggression pact

3. **Summarizing** Copy the graphic organizer below. Use it to identify the steps Hitler took to annex Austria and Czechoslovakia.

   | 3 | Annexation of Czechoslovakia |
   2
   1

   | 3 | Annexation of Austria |
   2
   1

4. **Finding the Main Idea**
   a. How and why did France and Great Britain try to avoid war with Hitler?
   b. Why might British and French policies during the 1930s have encouraged German aggression?
   c. How did the Western powers react to Hitler's invasion of Poland?

5. **Writing and Critical Thinking**
   Identifying Cause and Effect Explain how Great Britain and France prepared for war after Hitler overtook Czechoslovakia.
   Consider:
   • building their military strength
   • the protection of Poland
   • negotiating with Stalin

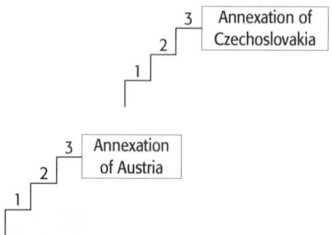

Homework Practice Online
keyword: SP3 HP30

SECTION 3

OBJECTIVES

1 **Explain how German control of Norway, Denmark, and the Low Countries benefited Hitler.**

2 **Describe the success of German forces in France.**

3 **Identify the Battle of Britain and the reasons the Germans could not win it.**

4 **Describe the role of the United States at the beginning of the war and how that role changed.**

SECTION 3

READ TO DISCOVER

1 How did German control of Norway, Denmark, and the Low Countries benefit Hitler?
2 What success did German forces experience in France?
3 What was the Battle of Britain, and why were the Germans unable to achieve victory?
4 What role did the United States play at the beginning of the war, and how did that role change?

DEFINE

blitzkrieg
"phony war"
collaborators
maquis
isolationists

IDENTIFY

Winston Churchill
Philippe Pétain
Charles de Gaulle
Luftwaffe
Battle of Britain
Neutrality Acts
Lend-Lease Act
Atlantic Charter

▶ WHY IT MATTERS TODAY

Great Britain and the United States continue to work together on international issues. Use CNNfyi.com or other **current event** sources to find a recent issue that these two countries have addressed. Record your findings in your journal.

CNN Student News.com

Axis Gains

The Main Idea
Striking quickly and forcefully, the Axis Powers gained military control over most of Europe.

The Story Continues *After France and Great Britain agreed to Hitler's demands at the Munich Conference, the German leader believed he had little to fear from the Western leaders. "I saw them at Munich," he said. "They are little worms." Germany's invasion of Poland brought declarations of war from Great Britain and France. Hitler already had the advantage, however, and continued his conquest of European nations.*

The "Phony War"

Hitler's invasion of Poland introduced the world to a new kind of warfare. The attack was a **blitzkrieg** (German for "lightning war"), meaning it took place with great speed and force. After a month of fighting, Poland surrendered to Hitler. While Germany attacked Poland, France moved its army up to its chain of fortifications along the Maginot Line. British forces landed on the northern coast of France and the British navy blockaded Germany's ports. The Germans placed troops in the Siegfried Line, the system of fortifications they had built in the Rhineland. There were a few attacks on British battleships. Otherwise, however, there was little action on the western front. While there was an increase in troop movement and arms production, newspapers began to speak of the **"phony war"** in western Europe. Some people still hoped that an all-out war could be avoided.

As the Germans marched into Poland from the west, the Soviet army built up on the Soviet-Polish border. Then following the secret deal made in the Nazi-Soviet Pact, the Soviets invaded eastern Poland on September 17. Once again Poland disappeared from the map of Europe. The Soviets also took control of Estonia, Latvia, and Lithuania. On November 30, 1939, the Soviet Union attacked Finland. The Finns appealed to the League of Nations. However, the League could do nothing more than expel the Soviet Union for its aggression against another member nation. Although the Finns fought bravely, their struggle ended in March 1940.

Scandinavia and the Low Countries. On April 9, 1940, the "phony war" ended with a sudden German invasion of Denmark and Norway. The Germans sometimes depended on help from **collaborators,** people who were willing to help their country's enemies. A leader of the Norwegian Fascist Party named Quisling proved to be an important collaborator for Germany. He provided information to the Germans before the invasion and aided the occupying forces. In a single day German troops took control of some of Norway's strategic ports. Both Norway and Denmark fell to German control.

By taking these countries, Germany gained an outlet to the Atlantic Ocean. The Scandinavian coastline and landscape gave Germany very good submarine bases and airfields. This put shipping to France and Great Britain in serious danger. The British realized that Hitler was now an immediate threat to their safety. In May 1940 **Winston Churchill** replaced Neville Chamberlain as prime minister. Churchill had been one of the few politicians to speak out against the policy of appeasement in the 1930s.

SECTION 3 RESOURCES

REPRODUCIBLE RESOURCES

▶ Guided Reading Strategy 30.3
▶ Graphic Organizer Activity 30: Fighting the War
▶ Readings in World History 106: The Evacuation of Dunkirk
▶ Hands-on History Activity 30: Soldiers and Civilians in War

TECHNOLOGY RESOURCES

▶ One-Stop Planner 30.3
▶ Holt Researcher: World History: Winston Churchill, Franklin Roosevelt
▶ Homework Practice Online

REINFORCEMENT, REVIEW, AND ASSESSMENT

▶ Section 3 Review, p. 795
▶ Daily Quiz 30.3
▶ Main Idea Activity 30.3
▶ English Audio Summary 30.3
▶ Spanish Audio Summary 30.3

TEACH OBJECTIVE 1

LEVEL 2: Have students draw and illustrate maps showing the pattern of German invasions in western Europe and why Germany wanted to control Norway, Denmark, and the Low Countries. Maps should show how occupation of the Low Countries let Germany bypass the Maginot Line to attack France, and how occupying those countries plus the Atlantic coast of France gave Germany control of all the Atlantic seaports and bases for attacking Britain.

TEACH OBJECTIVE 2

ALL LEVELS: Have students work in pairs to complete Venn diagrams to compare and contrast Vichy France and occupied France. **ENGLISH LANGUAGE LEARNERS, COOPERATIVE LEARNING**

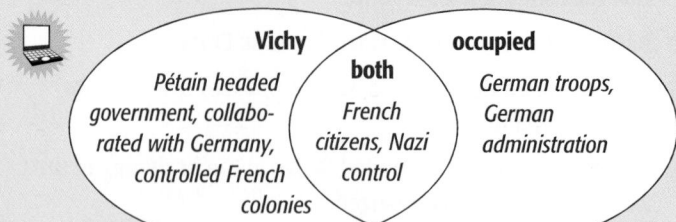

Science, Technology & Society

The defensive structure known as the Maginot Line cost the French millions of francs. It consisted of a vast series of underground bunkers and fortresses, connected by underground tunnels and underground railways that could be used to defend the entire frontier against any attack from Germany. However, the Maginot Line proved virtually useless against the German attack in 1940.

Critical Thinking

Ask students why the French believed the Maginot Line would be a useful defense.

ANSWER: In building the Maginot Line the French had prepared themselves to defend against the type of trench fighting of World War I.

That's Interesting!

Many maquis were young French men who fled into the forests and mountains to avoid forced labor service in Germany. Some were intent only on avoiding capture. However, those who were willing to fight were secretly armed and trained by the British secret service and later by the American OSS, the forerunner of today's CIA.

Citizens of Warsaw, Poland, flee the German Blitzkreig as fire consumes their neighborhood.

In June 1940 northern France became a scene of absolute confusion. Carrying whatever belongings they could, civilians crowded roads as they tried to escape to the south.

Hitler, meanwhile, continued to attack. On May 10, 1940, German armored units invaded the Low Countries—the Netherlands, Belgium, and Luxembourg. By the end of May, all three countries had surrendered. Hitler's forces were now in a position to outflank France's Maginot Line. German armored units drove westward toward the English Channel. Reaching the coast, they cut off a large number of British, Belgian, and French troops from the main French force to the south. Outnumbered and with no room to change their position, the encircled Allied troops tried to escape from the French seaport of Dunkerque.

Evacuation of Dunkerque. The British air force, badly outnumbered, struggled to help the trapped forces in Dunkerque. Fortunately the German ground forces stopped their advance. Every available ship and boat in Britain was ordered to Dunkerque. Even fishing and rowboats fell under attack by aircraft, submarines, and artillery as they picked up forces from the beaches. Between about May 27 and June 4, about 338,000 men were safely transported across the channel to England. However, they did lose all their heavy equipment.

The reason why Hitler did not attack the retreating Allies is not known for certain. He may have believed his air force could finish off the Allied forces. This decision would later be seen as a costly mistake. It allowed Britain to regain its strength. Although the Allies were defeated at Dunkerque, the success of the rescue effort helped raise British spirits.

✔ **READING CHECK: Evaluating** How did Hitler benefit from taking control of Norway, Denmark, and the Low Countries? could outflank France's Maginot Line

The Fall of France

After the evacuation of Dunkerque, the French were left to fight alone on the European continent. The Maginot Line was useless. Having taken Belgium, the Germans were in a position to attack France from the north, where there were few fortifications. Germany turned southward to attack the heart of France early in June 1940. The French fought a difficult, losing battle. The French army expected stationary battles such as those in World War I. They were not trained or equipped for this new kind of war. German planes bombed and machine-gunned civilians who tried to escape the attack, causing great panic and disorder.

ALL LEVELS: Form students into groups to discuss whether the Battle of Britain should be considered a turning point of World War II. Ask a spokesperson for each group to explain its determination to the class. *(Students should recognize that Britain was the last free county in western Europe.)* Then have students work individually to create poems, song lyrics, raps, or political cartoons or posters about the RAF's saving of Great Britain. Select students to present their creations to the class.
ENGLISH LANGUAGE LEARNERS, COOPERATIVE LEARNING

HOMEWORK Have students imagine they are Luftwaffe pilots, RAF pilots, or London civilians. Have them write a letter to a family member describing their experiences, emotions, and observations during the Battle of Britain.

Spotlight on CULTURE

Ask students why Germany's method of attack was called *Blitzkrieg* or "lightning war." Compile a class list of other German terms related to warfare. *(Panzer, Luftwaffe, U-boat, Blitz)* Have volunteers use a German dictionary to research the origins of these terms and report to the class.

Mussolini quickly took advantage of France's weakness. He declared war on France and Great Britain on June 10, and Italian forces attacked southern France. On June 14 the Germans entered Paris, and the French armed resistance in the north fell apart. Rather than surrender, the French cabinet resigned.

Some French leaders, however, were willing to surrender. **Philippe Pétain** (PAY·tan), a hero of World War I, formed a government and assumed dictatorial powers. Late in June, Hitler forced the Pétain government to sign a peace agreement with Germany and Italy. The terms of the agreement were severe. German troops were to occupy northern France, including Paris, and a strip of territory along the Atlantic coast southward to Spain. France had to pay the costs of this occupation. The French navy was to be disarmed and not allowed out of French ports. Pétain's government moved to the city of Vichy (VISH·ee), in the south. Thus France was divided into occupied France, administered by the Germans, and Vichy France, which collaborated with the Germans. The Vichy government also controlled most French possessions in North Africa and the Middle East.

The French Resistance. Some of the French who wanted to continue to fight against Germany escaped to Africa or to Britain. Under the leadership of General **Charles de Gaulle** (duh·GOHL), they formed the Free French government. It set up headquarters in London, Britain, and later the United States, equipped the Free French army. As the war went on, this army played a part in several campaigns.

In France itself a resistance movement worked underground, or in secret. Similar movements developed in other German-occupied countries as well. Members of some of these groups were called **maquis** (mah·KEE)—the French term for the scrubby undergrowth common in the areas where resistance fighters hid. The maquis fought the Germans from within their occupied lands. They undermined the Nazi war effort by engaging in acts of sabotage such as blowing up bridges, wrecking trains, and cutting telephone and telegraph lines.

✔ **READING CHECK: Summarizing** What success did Hitler have in France? occupied France, collaborated with Vichy government

The Battle of Britain

After France fell, many predicted that Britain would prove to be even weaker than France. Little by little, Hitler began scattered bombing raids on Great Britain, gradually increasing them in intensity. When he offered to negotiate a peace settlement, Churchill refused. At the end of June 1940, Churchill braced the British people for the dangerous battle that he felt sure would come.

History Makers Speak
❝Hitler knows that he will have to break us in this island or lose the war. If we can stand up to him, all Europe may be free and the life of the world may move forward into broad, sunlit uplands. But if we fail, then the whole world, including the United States, including all that we have known and cared for, will sink into the abyss of a new Dark Age. . . . Let us therefore brace ourselves to our duties, and so bear ourselves that, if the British Empire and its Commonwealth last for a thousand years, men will say, 'This was their finest hour.'❞

Winston Churchill, quoted in *A Treasury of the World's Great Speeches,* edited by Houston Peterson

Hitler ordered his air force, the **Luftwaffe,** to soften up Britain for invasion. He moved the Luftwaffe units to airfields in France and Belgium, closer to their targets.

HISTORY MAKER

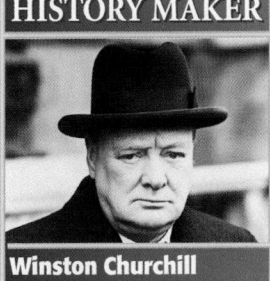

Winston Churchill (1874–1965)

Winston Churchill is generally considered to be one of Great Britain's most outstanding leaders. As prime minister during World War II, Churchill is best remembered for helping to boost British hopes of victory.

Churchill also recognized the importance of maintaining close ties with the United States. Throughout the war, he worked hard to promote good relations between the two countries. His distrust of Stalin and the Soviet Union emphasized his concern about the spread of communism. **What were Churchill's goals and concerns?**

Analyzing Primary Sources

Evaluating Why do you think Churchill's speech made a difference in the war? inspired British people to withstand Hitler's attacks

---

Citizenship

The Vichy regime not only collaborated with the Germans but also sought to replace the weak Third Republic with conservative authoritarian rule. Although some French people joined the resistance or Charles de Gaulle's Free French government in exile, most French people acquiesced in the Vichy regime and the German occupation. Vichy officials rounded up laborers for the German war effort and Jews for transportation to death camps. After the war Pétain and other Vichy leaders were tried and executed or imprisoned. Collaboration remained a touchy subject in postwar France, as most people tried to forget or deny the extent to which they had cooperated with the Germans.

Critical Thinking

Ask students why the French wanted to forget or deny collaboration with the Vichy government.

ANSWER: Students may suggest that the French did not want to admit they had willingly helped the Nazis.

HISTORY MAKER ANSWER
boost hopes of victory, close ties with the United States, distrust of Stalin and the Soviet Union

LEVEL 1: Ask students how the Neutrality Acts were intended to prevent a recurrence of the circumstances that drew the United States into World War I. *(avoid trade involvement, U-boat sinkings)* Ask how and why American policy changed toward the war in Europe. *(German victories, fear of Nazi world domination, sympathy for Britain)* Then draw a horizontal continuum line on the chalkboard and work with students to plot changes in U.S. foreign policy along it, from the Neutrality Acts at one end to undeclared naval warfare at the other. **ENGLISH LANGUAGE LEARNERS**

CLOSE

Ask students what might have happened if the United States had maintained its isolationist position. Then ask whether the United States could have succeeded in staying out of the war altogether if it had not been attacked.

Daily Life

As early as September 1939, fearing potential air attacks, British authorities began preparations to evacuate children from parts of London. Thousands of children were relocated from the city to temporary homes in the countryside beyond the reach of German bombers. Although moving children to the countryside separated families, it also saved many lives as London underwent persistent German bombing during the Blitz.

Critical Thinking

Ask students how World War II affected British children.

ANSWER: Separation from their families may have made children feel insecure or taught them independence.

INTERPRETING THE VISUAL RECORD

The Battle of Britain Between about September 1940 and May 1941, Britain suffered regular nighttime air raids by German bombers. Some 43,000 civilians died and thousands were left homeless. *Why might this British family need the wooden shutters that they are making?*

Holt Researcher

go.hrw.com
KEYWORD: Holt Researcher
FreeFind: Winston Churchill
Franklin Roosevelt
After reading more about Winston Churchill and Franklin Roosevelt on the Holt Researcher, create a Venn diagram comparing their accomplishments in office. Then assess which one you think had the greatest impact on the 20th century.

The first German air attacks were on British military sites. Later they struck railroads and civilian and industrial targets. These raids, along with British efforts to counter them, became known as the **Battle of Britain.** This fighting continued non-stop during September and October. Hitler believed his airforce would destroy the people's will to fight. The British, however, dug out of their ruins and carried on. The Royal Air Force—or RAF—continued fighting to defend the island country. The growing success of these fighter planes gave the British hope.

Outnumbered by the Luftwaffe, British pilots flew combat missions day after day, night after night. The RAF also had a new electronic tool called radar. This helped identify enemy aircraft or ships as they came near. The early warning provided by radar gave British fighters time to counterattack and kept the Germans from making surprise attacks. The RAF's control of the air also meant that Germany could not invade across the English Channel.

The Germans continued their night bombing for many months. At the same time, British bombers made stronger and heavier attacks on German cities. By the middle of 1941, air warfare had peaked. Germany began sending some of its war resources to the east. However, Germany's blockade of British shipping meant there was a chance that Great Britain could be starved into surrendering. This might have happened had it not been for the United States.

✔ **READING CHECK: Finding the Main Idea** Why was Germany unable to win the Battle of Britain? success of RAF fighter planes

United States Involvement

In the **Neutrality Acts** passed between 1935 and 1937, the United States had stated its wish to stay neutral in future wars. These laws said Americans could not sell war equipment to warring nations. Americans could not make loans to these nations or sail on their ships. In addition, American ships were restricted from entering war zones.

Many people worried that Nazi Germany would hurt not only Europe, but also civilization itself. Most Americans, however, believed that Europe's wars should not concern the United States. These **isolationists,** as they were called, had come to power at the end of World War I. Their power began to fade as fears grew that the Nazis would take over the world. In 1939 a revised Neutrality Act allowed American firms to sell munitions to warring nations on a cash-and-carry basis. Great Britain still controlled sea routes between the United States and Great Britain. Therefore, the effect of this law was to allow the sale of arms only to Great Britain.

After the rescue from Dunkerque and the fall of France, American sympathy for the British grew. President Franklin D. Roosevelt believed that Britain was the front line of a war that would involve the United States sooner or later. In September 1940 President Roosevelt moved 50 old American warships to Great Britain. In exchange Great Britain gave the United States use of several naval and air bases. In that same month Congress passed the first national draft law in the United States during peacetime. Early in 1941 Churchill said to the United States: "Give us the tools, and we will finish the job." In March Congress passed the **Lend-Lease Act,** authorizing the president to supply war materials to Great Britain on credit. Now the direction of America's involvement became clear.

✔ **READING CHECK: Sequencing** What was the U.S. position on foreign wars during the 1930s and how did it begin to change? neutrality; sold arms to Britain, passed draft law

The Atlantic Charter

President Roosevelt and Prime Minister Churchill met in August 1941. Together they created a statement that became known as the **Atlantic Charter.** This document stated that the United States and Great Britain (1) sought no territorial gain, (2) would allow no territorial changes without the consent of the people concerned, (3) respected the right of all people to choose their own form of government, (4) believed that all nations should have equal rights to trade and to raw materials, (5) wanted nations to cooperate on economic matters to ensure everyone a decent standard of living, (6) believed people everywhere should have the right to security and freedom from want and fear, (7) believed freedom of the seas should be guaranteed, and (8) believed that nations must abolish the use of force and establish a system of general security, suggesting the creation of an international organization.

During the fall of 1941, the United States Navy helped the British in many ways. It fought against German submarines and protected ships in the western Atlantic. Isolationist opinion was still strong in the United States. By November 1941, however, the United States was giving the British all aid short of joining the war.

In August 1941 Roosevelt and Churchill met aboard a British battleship off the coast of Newfoundland. Their Atlantic Charter publicly announced the democratic goals shared by Great Britain and the United States.

✔ **READING CHECK: Summarizing** In what ways did the United States become involved in the war? fought against German submarines, protected ships in western Atlantic

SECTION 3 REVIEW

1. **Define** and explain the significance:
   blitzkrieg
   "phony war"
   collaborators
   maquis
   isolationists

2. **Identify** and explain the significance:
   Winston Churchill
   Philippe Pétain
   Charles de Gaulle
   Luftwaffe
   Battle of Britain
   Neutrality Acts
   Lend-Lease Act
   Atlantic Charter

3. **Sequencing** Copy the time line below. Use it to describe German progress in the war through the first half of 1941.

```
              April      June
              1940       1940
    |_____|_____|_____|
 September     May        mid-
   1939       1940       1941
```

4. **Finding the Main Idea**
   a. How did Hitler gain control over France and how did some French people continue to resist German rule?
   b. How was British airpower able to prevent a German invasion across the English Channel?

5. **Writing and Critical Thinking**
   Sequencing Describe the progression of the involvement of the United States in World War II.
   Consider:
   • the original Neutrality Acts and the revised Neutrality Act of 1939
   • why Americans sympathized with the British
   • the Atlantic Charter and U.S. aid to the British in the fall of 1941

Homework Practice Online
keyword: SP3 HP30

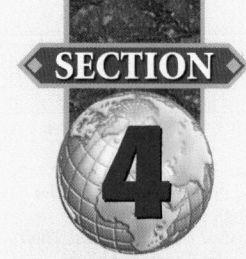

SECTION 4

OBJECTIVES

1 **Identify the steps the Axis Powers took to gain control of eastern Europe, the Middle East, and North Africa.**

2 **Describe how Germany planned to gain control of the Soviet Union, and evaluate the Soviets' defense.**

3 **Explain how Japan's goals in the Pacific led to war with Britain and the United States.**

🔔 LET'S GET STARTED!

As students enter the classroom, ask them why some people might believe their country is superior to others. (*Answers may include culture, economy, ethnicity, military conquests, accomplishments.*) Ask how a national leader who attributes his or her country's greatness to race or ethnicity might treat countries with citizens of a different ethnicity. (*Students should suggest poor treatment.*) Tell students that in Section 4 they will learn how Hitler's beliefs about his nation's superiority affected world history.

SECTION 4 RESOURCES

REPRODUCIBLE RESOURCES

▶ Guided Reading Strategy 30.4

TECHNOLOGY RESOURCES

▶ One-Stop Planner 30.4
▶ World History Teaching Transparency: Art and History 25: Inside an Internment Camp, World War II
▶ Homework Practice Online
▶ Online Maps, Charts, and Graphs: Operation Barbarossa
▶ Online Maps, Charts, and Graphs: Attack on Pearl Harbor, December 7, 1941

REINFORCEMENT, REVIEW, AND ASSESSMENT

▶ Section 4 Review, p. 800
▶ Daily Quiz 30.4
▶ Main Idea Activity 30.4
▶ English Audio Summary 30.4
▶ Spanish Audio Summary 30.4

SECTION 4

READ TO DISCOVER

❶ What steps did the Axis Powers take to gain control of eastern Europe, the Middle East, and North Africa?
❷ How did Germany plan to gain control of the Soviet Union, and how successful was the Soviets' defense?
❸ How did Japan's goals in the Pacific lead to war with Britain and the United States?

IDENTIFY

Erwin Rommel
Hideki Tōjō

WHY IT MATTERS TODAY

After two world wars, the Soviets and Germans continued to be fearful of each other. Use or other **current event** sources to find information about the relationship between Russia and Germany today. Record your findings in your journal.

The Soviet Union and the United States

The Main Idea
The Soviet Union entered the war against Germany, while the United States fought Germany and Japan.

The Story Continues *In the Atlantic Charter, Franklin D. Roosevelt and Winston Churchill called for the destruction of "Nazi tyranny." They pledged to create a postwar world in which "all men in all the lands may live out their lives in freedom from fear and want." The loyalty of the United States to the Allied cause now was obvious.*

Eastern Europe and the Mediterranean

In the fall of 1940, Germany held almost all of western Europe. It controlled the Atlantic coastline from the tip of Norway to southern France. Spain, under Franco's rule, remained neutral but allowed German submarines to use its ports. Italy and Germany also controlled much of the western Mediterranean coastline. This was an important advantage. Great Britain still held Gibraltar, on the southern coast of Spain. It also held the islands of Malta and Cyprus, in the Mediterranean, and Alexandria in Egypt. British troops were stationed in Palestine and in Egypt, protecting the Suez Canal. In September Japan joined the Rome-Berlin Axis, allying itself with Hitler and Mussolini.

Mussolini hoped to build a Mediterranean empire for Italy. In the fall of 1940 he sent his troops into Egypt and Greece. The decision proved to be unwise. Italy's attack on Greece did not go well. The British stopped the Italians' advance into Egypt and took Tobruk, a port city of Libya. They also liberated Ethiopia and turned the Italians back from British Somaliland.

The Axis powers had more success in and around the Balkans. By April 1941, Hungary, Romania, Slovakia, and Bulgaria had all joined the Axis side. That same spring, Germany took Yugoslavia, Greece, and the island of Crete. This gave the Germans control over the Balkan Peninsula except for European Turkey. In June 1941 Germany and Turkey signed a treaty that said Turkey would remain neutral. The Balkan victories put Germany in a position to attack the Soviet Union and the Middle East. Controlling the region's rich oil fields would give Hitler a huge advantage. If Britain lost the Suez Canal, its position in India, Southeast Asia, and the Pacific would be threatened.

The Axis Powers had the support of many citizens in Iraq and Egypt who wanted to be rid of their British occupiers. The French Vichy government controlled Lebanon and Syria. In May 1941 British and Indian troops crushed a pro-Axis coup d'etat in Iraq. In July British and Free French forces drove the Vichy French out of Lebanon and Syria. Meanwhile, the Allied situation in Africa grew worse.

An Ethiopian chief addresses his troops before battle.

TEACH OBJECTIVE 1

LEVEL 2: On the chalkboard, create a table of countries under Axis or Allied control in eastern Europe and the Mediterranean from 1940 through 1942.

1940		1941		1942	
Allies	*Axis*	*Allies*	*Axis*	*Allies*	*Axis*

Call on students to add a country to the chalkboard table. Discuss the steps Axis Powers took to gain control of each area.
ENGLISH LANGUAGE LEARNERS, COOPERATIVE LEARNING

TEACH OBJECTIVE 2

ALL LEVELS: Split the class into two groups representing German and Soviet perspectives. Ask the German group to discuss why Hitler invaded the Soviet Union (*living space for Germans*) and how the invasion progressed. (*German troops pushed deep into Russia but did not reach Moscow before winter set in.*) Ask the Soviet group to discuss how the Soviets defended themselves. (*scorched earth, guerrilla attacks, winter counterattack*) Have the groups compare perspectives. **ENGLISH LANGUAGE LEARNERS, COOPERATIVE LEARNING**

German troops commanded by General **Erwin Rommel** moved across the Mediterranean to take control of Libya in early 1941. However, by the summer of 1942, the British were having success in the naval and air war in the Mediterranean. This allowed the British to build up troops and equipment in North Africa. They also were able to cut off Axis supplies. In October Rommel's forces were soundly beaten at the Battle of El Alamein. Now the Axis forces, unable to make up their losses, retreated to Tunisia.

✔ **READING CHECK: Comparing** What were the results of Axis Powers trying to take control of eastern Europe, the Middle East, and North Africa? *driven back by Allied victories*

World War II in Europe and North Africa, 1939–1945
Interpreting Maps World War II made Europe and North Africa one huge battlefield.
■ **Skills Assessment: 1. The World in Spatial Terms** What two battles took place along the 50° N parallel in Europe?
2. Drawing Conclusions What physical feature affected fighting in southern Europe and North Africa?

Map legend:
- Allied countries
- Axis countries
- Axis-controlled territory, 1942
- Neutral countries
- Allied advance
- Axis advance
- ⊛ National capital
- • Other city

Major battles:
- Britain, July–Oct. 1940
- Leningrad, Sept. 1941–Jan. 1944
- El Alamein, Oct.–Nov. 1942
- Stalingrad, Sept. 1942–Feb. 1943
- Kursk, July 1943
- Anzio, Jan.–Mar. 1944
- D-Day, June 6, 1944
- Minsk, July 1944
- The Bulge, Dec. 1944–Jan. 1945
- Warsaw, Aug.–Oct. 1944
- Berlin, Apr.–May 1945

History Maker

RAOUL WALLENBERG. As the Nazis took control across Europe, many people acted with extraordinary courage to resist Nazi domination and persecution of Jews. Many risked their lives to hide their Jewish neighbors or help them escape Nazi-occupied Europe to other countries.

One was the Swedish diplomat Raoul Wallenberg, who helped save as many as 100,000 Hungarian Jews. He provided many of them with passports from neutral Sweden. He hid many in houses he had bought or rented. Toward the end of the war he persuaded the Nazis to spare the lives of thousands of Jews living in a Budapest ghetto.

After the Soviet army captured Budapest in late 1944, Wallenberg pressed the Soviets to provide adequate care for the city's Jews. In January 1945 he was summoned to the Soviet army headquarters and then disappeared without a trace.

ACTIVITY: Have students discuss how and why some Europeans in Nazi-occupied countries resisted the Nazis, and why others acquiesced.

MAP ANSWERS
1. D-Day, Battle of the Bulge

2. Mediterranean Sea

Have students create a short story, diary entry, or political cartoon about Hitler's invasion of the Soviet Union. A short story might tell an invasion-related event through the eyes of a German or Soviet soldier, a guerrilla fighter, or a Russian civilian. A diary entry might express the feelings of a German soldier far from home in the harsh Russian winter or a Soviet soldier defending his homeland. A cartoon might portray the changing relationship between Hitler and Stalin.

TEACH OBJECTIVE 3

LEVEL 1: Remind students what they learned in Section 1 about Japanese militarism and expansion in China in the 1930s. Tell them that Japan continued to bully its neighbors in 1940, moving troops into French Indochina. Ask why Japan bombed Pearl Harbor *(to knock out United States capability to challenge their expansion in the Pacific)* and how Americans responded. Then have students write two newspaper headlines that might have appeared after the bombing of Pearl Harbor.
ENGLISH LANGUAGE LEARNERS

Science, Technology & Society

Soon after invading the Soviet Union, the Nazis began to experiment on Russian Jews and other Soviet prisoners to determine the most efficient way to kill large numbers of people. The first method tried—machine-gunning massed groups of prisoners—was rejected as labor-intensive, inefficient, and hard to keep secret. The first experiment with gas—confining prisoners in trucks with altered exhaust systems until they were overcome by carbon monoxide fumes—was also rejected as too slow. In September 1941, some 600 Soviet POWs were placed in a sealed area with crystals of Zyklon B, a commercial pesticide. The victims quickly died of asphyxiation. The Germans thus discovered the means they would later use to kill millions of Jews.

Critical Thinking

What does the experimentation on Soviet prisoners suggest about Nazi attitudes?

ANSWER: Nazis committed atrocities and had no respect for human life.

DAILY LIFE ANSWER
Germans suffered from the cold Russian winter.

Germany's Attack on the Soviet Union

The Soviet Union reacted to German victories in the Balkans with alarm and anger. It believed the Balkans should be within the Soviet sphere of influence. The Soviet Union demanded that certain parts of this region be kept in their sphere of influence. Hitler suggested instead that Germany should have Europe and the Soviet Union should create a sphere in Asia. The Soviets rejected this idea.

On June 22, 1941, the war began a new phase. Without declaring war, German armies invaded the Soviet Union. Hitler had opened a huge new front in the east. It was 2,000 miles long from north to south. Churchill offered aid to the Soviet Union. The United States also said it was willing to help. Sending aid to the Soviets, however, was very difficult. Shipping across the Mediterranean ran the risk of submarine and air attacks. The route through the Baltic Sea was impossible. Reaching Soviet ports on the Arctic required passing the long, German-held coast of Norway. As a result, the Allies started a new route. They moved supplies from the Persian Gulf across Iran by train and truck to the southern part of the Soviet Union.

The Soviet defense. The Germans' first movements into the Soviet Union had great success. Everywhere the Soviet armies were driven back. Soviet defenders used the same scorched-earth methods against Hitler that their ancestor had used against Napoléon. The retreating soldiers and civilians carried away what they could. They destroyed everything else. Many Soviet soldiers stayed hidden in forests, making daring guerrilla attacks on railroads, bridges, and trains.

Soon, however, Moscow and Leningrad were under attack. Hitler had expected the Soviet Union to surrender quickly. The Soviets were able to hold off German control of Moscow and Leningrad, however. As a result, the German army had to stay longer than expected. The delay forced the Germans to fight during the bitterly cold Russian winter. When the Soviets chose the winter for a counterattack, the Germans were forced to retreat.

In the spring of 1942, Hitler ordered a new offensive to the south. He hoped to take the oil-producing area around Baku, on the shore of the Caspian Sea. To protect the troops in that main attack, part of the German army was to capture the city of Stalingrad. German troops pushed into Stalingrad in September 1942. There, however, Soviet fighting grew stronger. Hitler now

---

DAILY LIFE

The Eastern Front
In the four years following the German invasion of Russia in 1941, some of the worst fighting of the war took place on the eastern front. The Germans particularly suffered from the bitter Russian winters. They had assumed that the bulk of the campaign would be over in weeks and so had not prepared equipment and supplies for winter conditions. **How did the weather influence the fighting on the eastern front?**

These photographs show women on the eastern front coping with the devastation of war.

LEVEL 3: Have selected students form a panel with two or three in the role of Japanese diplomats, two or three as American and British diplomats, and a moderator. The diplomats should use their textbooks and other resources to determine their attitudes about the growing crisis in the Pacific in 1939–1941. In the panel discussion, the moderator should question each side about its goals in Asia and its differences with the other side, and should explore possible areas of accommodation or compromise among the diplomats.

CLOSE

Ask the class how Americans felt when they heard about the Japanese attack on Pearl Harbor. Ask them how it might affect the views of Americans who were isolationists in the 1930s. Ask whether the United States might have stayed out of the war if it had not been attacked. Have students defend their viewpoints.

made capture of Stalingrad the main objective of the offensive. Stalin ordered that the city be held at all costs. The battle of Stalingrad had begun.

✔ **READING CHECK: Sequencing** How did Hitler try to gain control of the Soviet Union, and how did the Soviets defend themselves? invaded Soviet Union, marched to Stalingrad; scorched-earth methods, guerrilla attacks

Japanese Aggressions in the Pacific

The struggle against the Axis Powers took another important turn in December 1941 when events in the Pacific drew the United States into the war. Japanese militarism and aggression had increased throughout the 1930s. Japanese armies pushed farther and farther into China, although the Chinese continued to resist. Early in 1939, with the situation in Europe growing increasingly tenser, Japan saw a chance to extend its control over Southeast Asia. Japan first captured several small islands off the coast of French Indochina. The effect was to cut off the British sea route between Hong Kong and Singapore. Neither France nor Great Britain could act in time to prevent this move.

The Japanese used fighter planes like the ones shown here to expand their empire in the Pacific.

After both the Netherlands and France fell, Japan made further aggressive moves in East Asia. The Japanese government announced that the Netherlands East Indies was under Japanese "protective custody." The Japanese also forced the Vichy government to allow French Indochina to become a Japanese protectorate.

In September 1940 Japan formed an alliance with Germany and Italy. In April 1941 Japan and the Soviet Union signed a five-year nonaggression treaty. Soon after, the Japanese moved farther south to occupy lands in French Indochina.

The United States responded to Japanese aggressions in three ways. First, it protested Japan's violations of the Nine-Power Pact of 1922. Second, it provided assistance to Chinese Nationalists. Third, it placed an embargo on the sale to Japan of steel and scrap iron, and then of oil. These actions made Japan even more intent on expanding in East Asia. Now only the American-held Philippines and the Hawaiian Islands threatened Japanese rule in the Pacific. The United States, meanwhile, had already moved a large part of its Pacific Fleet to Hawaii.

Relations between the United States and Japan continued to worsen. An even more militaristic government came to power in Japan under Premier **Hideki Tōjō.** Early in 1941 the Japanese government realized that their most dangerous potential enemy was the United States. Believing that their best chance for victory was to knock out the U.S. Pacific Fleet quickly, the Japanese commanders began to plan a surprise attack on the U.S. fleet, based at Pearl Harbor in Hawaii.

✔ **READING CHECK: Analyzing Information** How did relations between Japan and the United States worsen between 1939 and 1941? Japanese alliance with Germany and Italy, U.S. embargo on oil and scrap iron

Interdisciplinary Connection

LITERATURE. In an excerpt from his book *At Dawn We Slept,* historian Gordon Prange relates an eyewitness account of the attack on Pearl Harbor:

"When the attack began, . . . the explosion of bombs, the whine of bullets, the roar of planes, the belching guns of aroused defenders, the acrid smell of fire and smoke—all blended into a nerve-racking cacophony [sound] of chaos. . . . Bombardiers still dropped their torpedoes, while dive bombers pounced like hawks. . . . Far above, high-level bombers rained their deadly missiles as fighters shuttled in and out, weaving together the fearful tapestry of destruction."

ACTIVITY: Ask students what makes this eyewitness account so vivid. Then ask them to draw or paint the scene on the basis of this description. They should use colors and shapes to convey the feeling of the scene. Their art may be somewhat abstract.

REVIEW

Have students complete the Section 4 Review on p. 800.

ASSESS

Have students complete Daily Quiz 30.4. As Alternative Assessment, you may want to use the Allied- and Axis-controlled countries exercise in this section's lessons.

RETEACH

Have students complete Main Idea Activity for English Language Learners and Special-Needs Students 30.4. Then have students make a list of the major headings within Section 4 and the important details under each heading. **ENGLISH LANGUAGE LEARNERS**

EXTEND

Have students interview older family members or members of the community about their memories of the attack on Pearl Harbor. Then have students write a short article using their interviews and other information they can find about Pearl Harbor. **BLOCK SCHEDULING**

‹SECTION›
4 REVIEW ANSWERS

❶ Identify
- Erwin Rommel, p. 797
- Hideki Tōjō, p. 799

❷ Eastern Europe: Germans occupied Balkans, were stopped at Stalingrad in Russia; Middle East: British and Free French drove Vichy French from Lebanon and Syria, crushed pro-Axis coup in Iraq; North Africa: British drove Italians from Ethiopia and British Somaliland, defeated Rommel at El Alamein, Axis forces retreated to Tunisia

❸ a. Germans moved toward Moscow and Leningrad; Soviets retreated with scorched-earth methods; Germans moved toward Stalingrad; Soviets fought to hold Stalingrad

b. to destroy United States ability to challenge Japan in the Pacific; knocked out U.S. fleet before U.S. entered the war

❹ By 1942 Germany controlled most of Europe and the Soviet Union as far as Stalingrad, Italy's actions had little lasting effect, there was a stand-off in North Africa, and Japan controlled most of the South Pacific.

800

American Entry into the War

On December 7, 1941, the Japanese launched a surprise bombing raid on the American naval base at Pearl Harbor, Hawaii. They planned to strike such a severe blow that the United States would be unable to fight the Japanese in the Pacific. Several U.S. battleships were sunk. Others were badly damaged. American military dead totaled more than 2,300.

On December 8, 1941, Congress declared war on Japan, as did the British Parliament. Three days later, Germany and Italy declared war on the United States, and Congress replied with its own declaration of war. The Japanese quickly took advantage of American unreadiness. On the same day as the attack on Pearl Harbor, Japan captured the American island of Guam. They also began aerial attacks on the Philippines. Soon afterward, Japan took control of Luzon, Burma, Thailand, and Malaya.

Japan went on to conquer what became a widespread island empire. Most of the Netherlands East Indies (Indonesia), the Philippines, and the Gilbert Islands came under Japanese rule. Australia was the last stronghold of resistance in the southwest Pacific. The landing of the Japanese on New Guinea and the Solomon Islands threatened to cut off Australia's important supply routes from Hawaii.

✔ **READING CHECK: Identifying Cause and Effect** How did Japan's goals in the Pacific lead to war with Britain and the United States? Japan's expansion in Southeast Asia and the Pacific threatened U.S. and British interests.

INTERPRETING THE VISUAL RECORD

Pearl Harbor Americans were shocked and outraged by the Japanese attack on Pearl Harbor. *What do these headlines suggest about public concern over the bombing?*

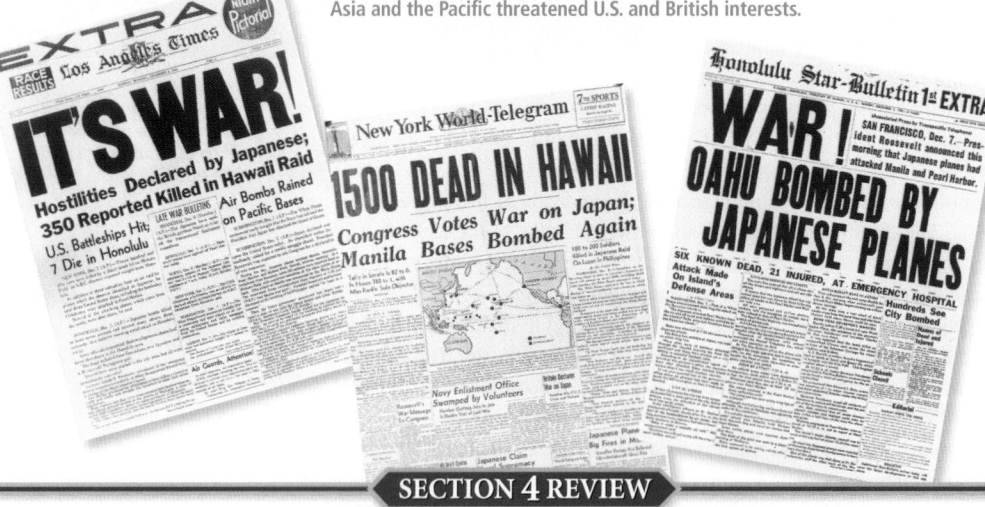

◄ SECTION 4 REVIEW ►

1. **Identify** and explain the significance:
   Erwin Rommel
   Hideki Tōjō

2. **Identifying Cause and Effect** Copy the graphic organizer below. Use it to describe the results of the Axis attacks on eastern Europe, the Middle East, and North Africa.

   Axis attacks → Eastern Europe → Results
   → Middle East → Results
   → North Africa → Results

3. **Finding the Main Idea**
   a. What steps did Hitler take to gain control over the Soviet Union, and how did the Soviets respond?
   b. Why did the Japanese attack Pearl Harbor, and what was the result?

4. **Writing and Critical Thinking**
   Sequencing Describe the results of Axis aggressions from late 1940 through 1942.
   Consider:
   • Italy's actions
   • Germany's expansion
   • Japan's actions in the Pacific

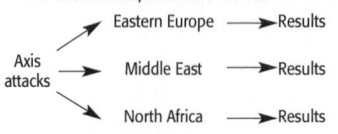
Homework Practice Online
keyword: SP3 HP30

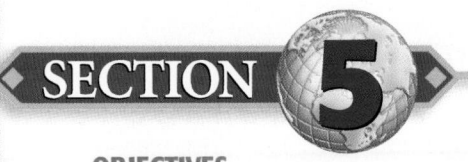

SECTION 5

OBJECTIVES

1 **Explain how the Final Solution was developed.**

2 **Describe conditions in the concentration camps.**

3 **Identify ways different people resisted the Holocaust.**

LET'S GET STARTED!

As students enter the classroom, send those with blond hair to the back of the room. Say that a new policy declares blond students are inferior and may not interact with other students. Ask all students how they would feel about such a policy. Tell students that in Section 5 they will learn what happened when the Nazis treated Jews and other people as inferior.

SECTION 5

READ TO DISCOVER

❶ How was the Final Solution developed?

❷ What were conditions like in concentration camps?

❸ In what ways did different people resist the Holocaust?

IDENTIFY

"New Order"
Final Solution
Heinrich Himmler
SS
Wannsee Conference
Auschwitz
Holocaust
Anne Frank

▶ WHY IT MATTERS TODAY

The oppression and persecution of people based on ethnicity or race continues today. Use CNN News .com or other **current event** sources to find at least two recent examples of racial or ethnic discrimination in the world. Record your findings in your journal.

CNN Student News.com

The Holocaust

The Main Idea
Hitler led the Nazi effort to kill all European Jews and others who were not members of the "Aryan race."

The Story Continues *Holocaust survivor Elie Wiesel remembered his arrival at the death camp Auschwitz. "A German officer gave the order: 'Men to the left! Women to the right!' Eight words spoken quietly, indifferently, without emotion. . . . I walked on with my father and the other men. And I did not know that in that place, at that moment, I was parting from my mother and [sister] Tzipora forever."*

Hitler's "New Order"

The invasion of the Soviet Union was part of Hitler's master plan for a European **"New Order."** Hitler wanted to make the European continent into a single political and economic system. He planned to gain "living space" in Eastern Europe. Then his pure "Aryan race" could colonize the new area. According to Hitler's plan, the land in the Soviet Union would supply Germany with food and raw materials. Hitler expected tens of millions of Russians to starve to death. According to Nazi beliefs, all Slavs were "racially inferior."

The Nazis increasingly practiced anti-Semitism during the 1930s. Then in 1941 Hitler ordered the destruction of Europe's entire Jewish population. The Nazis called this program the **Final Solution** to the "Jewish question." In Germany this genocide was made possible by the passionate racist beliefs of some people. Hitler used past genocides that had gone unpunished as examples. Some of Hitler's officers had witnessed the Armenian genocide in Turkey. As Hitler sent his generals to run the death camps in Poland, he said, "Go, kill without mercy . . . who today remembers the annihilation [total destruction] of the Armenians?"

Heinrich Himmler, the head of the the Schutzstaffel, or **SS,** the military branch of the Nazi Party, headed the Final Solution. At first the SS simply rounded up Jews and shot them in large groups. Soon, however, they turned to using poison gas as a more efficient method of execution. At a January 1942 conference in Wannsee, Germany, officials met to formalize their plans. The **Wannsee Conference** set out a systematic plan for exterminating Jews in concentration camps.

✔ **READING CHECK: Evaluating**
How was the Final Solution an extension of Nazi philosophy?
racist beliefs that Aryan race was superior

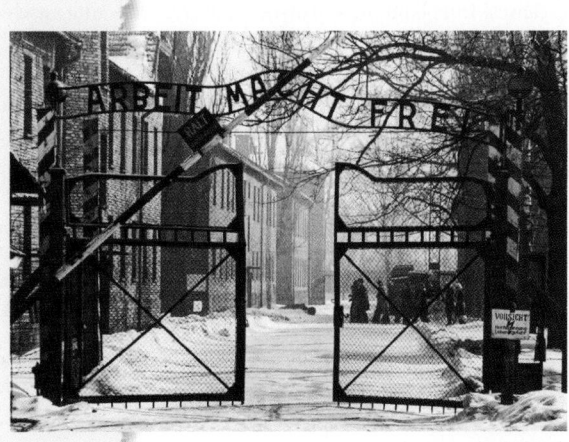

The sign over the gate of this concentration camp translates to "Work makes you free."

SECTION 5 RESOURCES

REPRODUCIBLE RESOURCES

▶ Guided Reading Strategy 30.5

▶ Readings in World History 107: The Discovery of Anne Frank's Hiding Place

TECHNOLOGY RESOURCES

▶ One-Stop Planner 30.5

▶ Holt Researcher: World History: Fania Fenelon

▶ Religions of the World Video Series: Judaism

▶ Homework Practice Online

REINFORCEMENT, REVIEW, AND ASSESSMENT

▶ Section 5 Review, p. 803

▶ Daily Quiz 30.5

▶ Main Idea Activity 30.5

▶ English Audio Summary 30.5

▶ Spanish Audio Summary 30.5

TEACH OBJECTIVE 1

LEVEL 1: Tell students that Hitler's wish for "living space" for his "pure Aryan race" led him to kill Jews and others he considered inferior. Have students make a cause-and-effect chart of the Final Solution.
ENGLISH LANGUAGE LEARNERS

TEACH OBJECTIVE 2

LEVEL 3: Have students read a description of concentration camp life by a survivor such as Elie Wiesel or Primo Levi. Have them write an essay and report to the class.

TEACH OBJECTIVE 3

ALL LEVELS: Ask students to consider why people might not act to help those who are being threatened and killed. (*denial, blaming the victims, sense of helplessness, fear of punishment*) Ask how those who did help showed courage. (*risked their lives*)

HOMEWORK Have students write an essay about what responsibility people have, if any, when they see others treated unfairly. Would students' opinions change if they knew it was dangerous to intervene?

Daily Life

In many occupied cities, the Nazis crowded Jews into small areas called *ghettos*. The Warsaw ghetto was surrounded by a wall topped with barbed wire and held 500,000 Jews in a small, cramped area. As the Germans began to deport Jews from the Warsaw ghetto to the death camps, thousands of Jews hid in underground rooms and bunkers. German troops tried to enter the ghetto, only to be driven out by Jewish resistance forces. Starting in April 1943, armed with little more than pistols, about 700 Jews battled 2,000 German soldiers and tanks for 27 days.

internet connect

TOPIC: Anne Frank
GO TO: go.hrw.com
KEYWORD: SP3 WH30

Have students access the Internet through the HRW Go site to conduct research on the history and legacy of Anne Frank. Then have students write an informative report about Anne Frank. Students may wish to use the interactive template provided to write their reports.

MAP ANSWER
most labor camps: Germany; most death camps: Poland

Holt Researcher

go.hrw.com
KEYWORD: Holt Researcher
FreeFind: Fania Fenelon
After reading more about Fania Fenelon on the Holt Researcher, write a diary entry about her experiences at Auschwitz.

Analyzing Primary Sources

Drawing Inferences What does Primo Levi's account reflect about the methods of the SS? Arbitrary choices determined life and death.

Concentration Camps, 1933–1945

Interpreting Maps As the German army invaded surrounding countries, Hitler ordered the construction of concentration camps, which became sites of enforced labor and death.

■ **Skills Assessment: Locate** Which European country contained the most labor camps? The most death camps?

Concentration Camps

The Nazis moved Jews by the hundreds of thousands to concentration camps in Germany and Poland. Dachau and Buchenwald in Germany were two of the largest labor camps. In Poland the Germans built Treblinka and **Auschwitz**—huge death camps in which people were systematically murdered. At first the Nazis buried their victims in mass graves. Eventually they used huge ovens to cremate the dead.

Not everyone who arrived at the camps was killed immediately. As prisoners arrived, SS officers sorted them into groups by age, health, and sex. Some groups, especially those unable to do much physical work, were immediately sent to "showers" for cleaning. These "showers" were really gas chambers. Primo Levi, a survivor of Auschwitz, recalled the selection process when he arrived at the camp.

❝The SS man . . . judges everyone's fate, and in turn gives the card to the man on his right or his left, and this is the life or death of each of us. . . .
Even before the selection is over, everybody knows that the left was effectively the 'schlechte Seite,' the bad side.❞

Primo Levi, from *Survival in Auschwitz*

CLOSE

Have students create a flier asking for help for European Jews. The fliers should describe conditions and try to motivate U.S. readers to help. **ENGLISH LANGUAGE LEARNERS**

REVIEW

Have students complete the Section 5 Review on p. 803.

ASSESS

Have students complete Daily Quiz 30.5. As Alternative Assessment, you may want to use the essay exercises in this section's lessons.

RETEACH

Have students complete Main Idea Activity for English Language Learners and Special-Needs Students 30.5. Then ask students what Hitler meant by the "New Order" and the Final Solution. Ask what the Nazis did to carry out the Final Solution and how some people resisted. **ENGLISH LANGUAGE LEARNERS**

EXTEND

If possible, invite a survivor of the Holocaust or another atrocity to speak to the class. Otherwise, have students view and discuss the movie *Schindler's List*. **BLOCK SCHEDULING**

Those Jews who were not killed soon after arrival lived in unspeakable conditions. The combination of forced labor, brutal treatment, starvation, filth, and disease killed thousands of other people in the camps.

During the war, people in some western European countries tried to protect Jews. In eastern Europe, however, a long tradition of anti-Semitism made the Nazi program easier to carry out. Its results there were even more devastating. By the time the Nazi government fell, its leaders and its followers had murdered 6 million European Jews. The Nazi genocide of the 1930s and 1940s is called the **Holocaust.** Millions of Slavs, Gypsies, and others who did not conform with the Nazi idea of "purity" were also murdered.

✔ **READING CHECK: Making Generalizations** What was life like in concentration camps during the Holocaust? unspeakable conditions: forced labor, brutality, starvation, filth, disease

Resisting the Holocaust

At first most Jews obeyed the orders of the SS. Some went into hiding, including the family of **Anne Frank,** a teenager who kept a diary of her experiences during the Holocaust. As many people began to realize what the Nazis were doing, some Jews fought back. The fiercest resistance came from those in the Jewish ghetto in Warsaw, Poland. A band of Jews resisted Nazi efforts to evacuate the ghetto to concentration camps. In the end, however, the poorly armed group could not hold off the German forces. Eventually the Jewish rebels were killed and the ghetto was destroyed.

Many other Europeans quietly ignored what was happening to the Jews. Some non-Jews, however, did try to help save some people from the Holocaust. After the Germans occupied Denmark, for example, Danes helped some 7,000 Jews escape into neutral Sweden. In Hungary, Swedish diplomat Raoul Wallenberg saved countless Jews by declaring them under the protection of the Swedish embassy. In Poland and Czechoslovakia, German industrialist Oskar Schindler saved many Jews by employing them in his factories.

✔ **READING CHECK: Summarizing** How did some people resist the Holocaust? went into hiding, fought, escaped with help of non-Jews

HISTORY MAKER

Anne Frank (1930–1945)

One of the most powerful and haunting documents of World War II is the diary of teenager Anne Frank. Anne's diary, containing her thoughts and feelings, has come to represent for many the horrors of the Holocaust.

Anne's German-Jewish family fled Nazi Germany for Amsterdam, where they hid in a friend's home. Eventually, however, the Nazis found the Franks' hiding place and sent the entire family to a concentration camp, where Anne later died. **What does Anne Frank's diary symbolize?**

The Nazis forced Jews to wear the Star of David (shown here) to identify themselves.

SECTION 5 REVIEW ANSWERS

❶ **Identify**
• "New Order," p. 801
• Final Solution, p. 801
• Heinrich Himmler, p. 801
• SS, p. 801
• Wannsee Conference, p. 801
• Auschwitz, p. 802
• Holocaust, p. 803
• Anne Frank, p. 803

❷ The "New Order" would have Aryans dominate Europe. Nazi aggression aimed to achieve that domination. People other than Aryans (Jews, Slavs, Gypsies, and others) were despised as inferior.

❸ a. mass murder, first by shooting, later by gas in concentration camps

b. forced labor, brutality, starvation, filth, disease

❹ Students should mention that Jews were being taken from the ghetto to be killed in concentration camps.

HISTORY MAKER ANSWER
the horrors of the Holocaust

SECTION 5 REVIEW

1. **Identify** and explain the significance:
"New Order"
Final Solution
Heinrich Himmler
SS
Wannsee Conference
Auschwitz
Holocaust
Anne Frank

2. **Evaluating** Copy the graphic organizer below. Use it to show the role of aggression and anti-Semitism in the Nazis' "New Order."

3. **Finding the Main Idea**
a. How did the Nazis carry out the Final Solution?
b. What were concentration camps like?

4. **Writing and Critical Thinking**

Identifying a Point of View Imagine you are a resistance fighter in the Warsaw ghetto. Write a letter to a friend explaining why you are fighting the evacuation of the ghetto, even though you realize that you have little chance of defeating the Germans.
Consider:
• why the ghetto was evacuated
• what the fate of the fighters would be if they complied with German orders
• the odds of succeeding

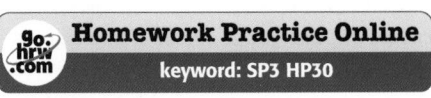

Homework Practice Online
keyword: SP3 HP30

OBJECTIVES

1 **Identify the outcomes of Allied military actions in the Soviet Union, North Africa, Italy, and the Atlantic.**

2 **Describe how the Allies were able to achieve victory in Europe.**

3 **List the steps the Allies took to end the war with Japan.**

⊚)) LET'S GET STARTED!

As students enter the classroom, ask them what may go wrong when one side in a fight involves many different participants. *(People or countries may disagree among themselves; one may drop out and leave the others at a disadvantage.)* Tell them that leaders of 26 Allied nations agreed in 1942 to keep fighting the Axis and not to make a separate peace. Ask why the Allied leaders made that agreement. *(Countries could be assured of one another's continuing support.)* Tell students that in Section 6 they will learn how the Allies fought to victory over Italy, Japan, and Germany.

SECTION 6 RESOURCES

REPRODUCIBLE RESOURCES

▸ Guided Reading Strategy 30.6

▸ Creative Teaching Strategy 30: Mapping a Global War

TECHNOLOGY RESOURCES

▸ One-Stop Planner 30.6

▸ World History and Cultures Video Program 25: The Lessons of World War II

▸ CNN Presents World Cultures: Yesterday and Today Segment 29: Rosie the Riveter

▸ Homework Practice Online

▸ Online Maps, Charts, and Graphs: Invasion of Normandy, June 6, 1944

REINFORCEMENT, REVIEW, AND ASSESSMENT

▸ Section 6 Review, p. 809

▸ Daily Quiz 30.6

▸ Main Idea Activity 30.6

▸ English Audio Summary 30.6

▸ Spanish Audio Summary 30.6

SECTION 6

▶ READ TO DISCOVER

❶ What were the outcomes of Allied military actions in the Soviet Union, North Africa, Italy, and the Atlantic?

❷ How were the Allies able to achieve victory in Europe?

❸ What steps did the Allies take to end the war with Japan?

▶ DEFINE

"soft underbelly of the Axis" island hopping

▶ IDENTIFY

Battle of Stalingrad
Dwight D. Eisenhower
Battle of Midway
Operation Overlord
D-Day
V-E Day
V-J Day
Bataan Death March

▶ WHY IT MATTERS TODAY

Today the United States and Japan have a much different relationship than the one they had during World War II. Use CNN or other **current event** sources to determine the kind of relationship the former enemies share. Record your findings in your journal.

CNN student News.com

The End of the War

The Main Idea
Allied victories in North Africa, Europe, and the Pacific led to the end of World War II.

The Story Continues *After France fell, French generals had predicted that Britain would "have her neck wrung like a chicken" in three weeks. Churchill later commented: "Some chicken! Some neck!" The British had survived Hitler's aggression. Now, with the help of the United States, they stood ready to turn the tide of war in the Allies' favor.*

Important Offensives

Representatives of 26 nations came together in Washington, D.C., in January 1942. Each nation promised to use all its resources to defeat the Axis. They also agreed to not sign any separate peace treaties and to follow the Atlantic Charter.

In the summer of 1942, the Germans pushed the Soviets back to Stalingrad. The **Battle of Stalingrad** went on for six long and bloody months. German forces pushed inside the city, suffering terrible losses on the way. Instead of falling back, the determined Soviets defended the city street by street and house by house. In November 1942 the Soviets began a counterattack. They circled around the German troops, trapping them in Stalingrad. Those who were left of Hitler's troops surrendered on February 2, 1943. Stalingrad became a major turning point in the war as the Germans never fully recovered from their defeat.

The Allies also made progress in North Africa during 1942. General **Dwight D. Eisenhower** of the United States landed his American and British troops in Africa in November 1942. Eisenhower's army and British General Bernard Montgomery's forces in Tunisia trapped Rommel's army between them. By the middle of May 1943, the Axis forces in North Africa were forced to surrender. As a result of Rommel's defeat, North Africa was completely under Allied control. Italy's African empire disappeared. Control of the French colonies in Africa passed to the Free French government. Moreover, the Allies had kept control of the Suez Canal. This made the Mediterranean safer for Allied navies.

After the Allied victory in North Africa, Stalin demanded that British and American troops open a second front in Europe. He wanted to lessen the German pressure on the Soviet Union. Churchill suggested attacking what he called the **"soft underbelly of the Axis"**—through Italy and the Balkans. American and British forces took the island of Sicily in the summer of 1943. Then they made plans to invade the Italian mainland. When the Allies landed on Sicily, Mussolini was forced to resign. Marshal Pietro Badoglio (bah·DOHL·yoh) became premier. His first act was to dissolve the Fascist Party. Then he began secret talks with the Allies. When the Allied army landed on the southwestern tip of Italy in September 1943, the Italians agreed to stop fighting the Allies. In fact Italy declared war on Germany. German troops still present in Italy, however, continued to resist Allied troops.

✔ **READING CHECK: Summarizing** What did the Allies gain as a result of their victories in the Soviet Union, North Africa, and Italy? *saved Stalingrad, made Mediterranean safe for Allies, gained Sicily*

LEVEL 1: Ask students why the Soviets wanted Britain and the United States to attack the Germans from the west or south. (*so Germany could not use all its troops against Russia*) Ask where the Allies attacked the Germans in 1942 and 1943. (*North Africa, then Sicily and Italy*) Ask why they moved into Europe from the south instead of the west. (*Italy and the Balkans were less well-defended than the Atlantic coast.*) Make sure students understand the concept of opening a second front and the meaning of "soft underbelly."

ENGLISH LANGUAGE LEARNERS

Teacher to Teacher

Alfred J. Hamel of Worcester, Massachusetts, suggested the following activity: To help students understand the strategy of island hopping, have them research the topic and draw a map or model showing which islands were taken by the Allies and how that related to the range of aircraft used by Allied forces.

The War at Sea and in the Air

During 1943 American and British bombing attacks against Germany and the occupied countries increased. The Allies bombed nearly every German city. Many were greatly damaged. The Allies were also gaining strength in the Atlantic. Beginning in 1939, German submarines had sunk many Allied ships. In the spring of 1943, however, destroyers and other armed ships safely led troop and supply ships from the United States. Planes also protected the shipping routes. Improved sonar technology located submarines. This took away much of their advantage.

The Japanese advance in the Pacific took its first loss in May 1942. In the Battle of the Coral Sea, American and Australian air and naval forces defeated a Japanese fleet headed for Australia. Soon afterward an American fleet met a larger Japanese fleet pushing eastward to try to capture Midway Island, northwest of Hawaii. The Americans defeated the Japanese in the important **Battle of Midway** in June. With these two victories, the United States Navy began to turn the tide in the war against Japan.

In August 1942 American marines took the airfield on Guadalcanal. This was the first invasion of Japanese-held territory. Winning control of Guadalcanal was important because it protected the Australian supply line. It also gave the Americans a huge lift in confidence. As Japan tried to reclaim the territory during the next three months, both sides suffered great losses. In 1943 the Allies took the offensive in the Pacific. Forces from Australia and New Zealand helped those from the United States. Together they fought to drive the Japanese out of the Solomon Islands. Then they began a strategy called **island hopping.** Under this policy, only certain Japanese islands were captured. Others were skipped and left without supplies.

During 1944 the Americans cleared the Japanese from the Marshall Islands, New Guinea, and the Marianas. In October 1944 an American army under General Douglas MacArthur landed in the Philippines. Shortly afterward, the Japanese suffered a crushing defeat in a great air and sea fight, the Battle of Leyte Gulf. In six months the Allies gained control of the Philippine Islands.

✔ **READING CHECK: Analyzing Information** What victories did the Allies achieve at sea, and what was the turning point in the war in the Pacific? Coral Sea, Guadalcanal, Solomon Islands, Marshall Islands, New Guinea, Marianas; Midway was turning point

Victory in Europe

British and American troops slowly fought their way up the Italian Peninsula. However, most German troops remained locked in bloody battles with the Soviet Union. It was clear that another, larger invasion of Europe was needed to create the hoped-for "second front." Plans were started for **Operation Overlord,** the invasion of northwest France.

On June 6, 1944—**D-Day** as the military called it—the long-awaited landing began on France's Normandy coast. Within a month, more than 1 million Allied troops had landed. After heavy fighting Allied troops moved into northern France. Shortly afterward, Allied forces landed on the Mediterranean coast of France and fought their way northward. On August 25, 1944, Allied troops entered Paris. By September they faced the strongly fortified Siegfried Line along Germany's western edge.

INTERPRETING THE VISUAL RECORD

Midway The U.S. victory in the Battle of Midway crippled the Japanese navy. *From the painting, what can you determine about the type of fighting that took place during the Battle of Midway?*

Global Relations

After the United States declared war against Japan, Roosevelt and Churchill agreed they would fight to end the war in Europe first, while simply trying to defend their positions in the Pacific. Late in 1941, however, Admiral Chester W. Nimitz was appointed to command the U.S. Pacific fleet. He initiated a complex, multi-part strategy. U.S. submarines would attack Japanese shipping to cut off Japan's oil supply in the East Indies. Also, U.S. naval and land forces would seize one Pacific island after another, advancing ever closer to Japan.

Critical Thinking

Why did Nimitz plan to seize islands closer and closer to Japan?

ANSWER: He wanted islands near Japan as bases for bombing and ultimately invading Japan.

VISUAL RECORD ANSWER

It involved airplanes, bombs, and ships.

LEVEL 3: Have students use the process of historical inquiry to find information about each of the five D-Day landing sites: Omaha, Utah, Gold, Juno, and Sword. Individually or in small groups, have them create an illustrated map to show what happened at each site. Encourage them to find photographs and other supporting material.

ALL LEVELS: Form students into four groups to conduct military press briefings on Operation Overlord, the surrender of Italy, the piercing of the Siegfried Line, and the Battle of the Bulge. Each briefing will need a press officer to coordinate it; officers to brief the press on tactics, locations, and other geographic aspects; and troops to recount their experiences. **ENGLISH LANGUAGE LEARNERS, COOPERATIVE LEARNING**

internet connect

TOPIC: D-Day
GO TO: go.hrw.com
KEYWORD: SP3 WH30

Have students access the Internet through the HRW Go site to learn more about D-Day. Assign each student one of the five landing sites: Utah, Omaha, Gold, Juno, or Sword. Have each student create a report that includes a map, a description of what happened, pictures, eyewitness accounts, and other interesting information.

SKILLS PRACTICE ANSWERS

1. Yes, Gilbert admired Churchill.

2. "gifts," "mastery," "finest hour," "courage"

3. Reviews will vary.

Technology **Resources**

World History Teaching Transparency: Geography and History 25: World War II in the Pacific, 1941–1945

SKILL-BUILDING STRATEGIES

Reading About History: Understanding a Biographical Account

Winston Churchill: Symbol of Wartime Britain

The quality of its leadership, as well as its military and industrial might, help to explain why a nation wins or loses a war. During World War II, the personalities of Allied and Axis leaders played a major role in the war's outcome. Under the exceptional leadership of Prime Minister Winston Churchill, Great Britain was able to overcome staggering odds as it battled the concentrated power of the German war machine. Churchill inspired his nation to victory. His greatest service may well have been his ability to symbolize—through speeches and personal actions—the characteristics of courage, endurance, and determination that his nation so badly needed in the face of German aggression.

Reading biographical accounts of Churchill's life helps us to understand this important man. A biographical account is a secondary source that describes all or part of an individual's lifetime. The source represents the opinions of the writer, and readers must be alert for evidence of bias—either for or against the individual whose life and work is being described. A biographical account is one of several sources that can be used to gather information about a historical figure. The reliability of a biographical account depends upon the biographer's approach—careful or careless, objective or subjective—to the subject. One of the best ways to determine the value of the account is to analyze several different types of evidence, primary and secondary alike, to develop as complete a picture of the subject as possible.

Churchill made clear his vision of Britain's wartime aims in a speech broadcast to the nation during the darkest days of the war.

> "You ask what is our policy? I will say: It is to wage war, by sea, land and air, with all our might and with all the strength that God can give us . . . You ask, What is our aim? I can answer in one word: Victory—victory at all costs, victory in spite of all terror, victory, however long and hard the road may be; for without victory, there is no survival."
>
> Winston Churchill,
> Speech to the House
> of Commons,
> May 1940

Churchill as a Symbol—A Biographer's View:

"One of Churchill's greatest gifts . . . was his ability to use his exceptional mastery of words and love of language to convey detailed arguments and essential truths; to inform, to convince, and to inspire. . . . His dislike of unfairness, of victimization, and of bullying—whether at home or abroad—was the foundation stone of much of his thinking. His finest hour was the leadership of Britain when it was most isolated, most threatened, and most weak; when his own courage, determination, and belief in democracy became one with that of a beleaguered [threatened with destruction] nation."

Martin Gilbert, "Churchill, Winston," *The Oxford Companion to Politics of the World*

Churchill's bulldog appearance, coupled with his gift of oratory and his unswerving determination to defeat the "monstrous tyranny" of Hitler's Germany, symbolized Britain's dedication to victory. He became the visible image of Allied determination.

Skills Reminder

To understand a biographical account, carefully assess the account to identify the writer's underlying bias. Is the biographical account balanced in its treatment? Does it provide a complete picture, placing equal emphasis on the subject's strong and weak points, contributions and failures, and positive and negative traits? Note what kind of language—positive, negative, or neutral—the writer uses to describe the subject. Are descriptors chosen to build a certain "image" of the subject?

Skills Practice

❶ Analyze Martin Gilbert's description of Churchill above. Can you infer Gilbert's general opinion of Churchill based on the excerpt?
❷ What clues regarding Gilbert's view of Churchill can you identify?
❸ Read a biography of a person mentioned in this chapter, then write a book review assessing its value in understanding the person and their importance to history.

ALL LEVELS: Draw students' attention to the map on page 807 of their textbook and have them find the two principal lines of Allied advance. Have them work in pairs to draw a graphic organizer showing each line of advance.

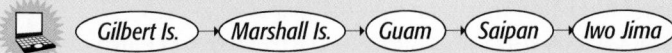
Gilbert Is. → Marshall Is. → Guam → Saipan → Iwo Jima

Above and below each island or battle, have students include related information such as date or significance.

ENGLISH LANGUAGE LEARNERS, COOPERATIVE LEARNING

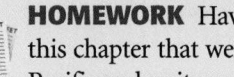

HOMEWORK Have students choose three events from this chapter that were critical to the Allies' victory in the Pacific and write a paragraph justifying each choice.

Several weeks after D-Day, the Soviets began a major drive against Germany from the east. By the end of 1944, they had taken Finland, Estonia, Lithuania, Latvia, Romania, and Bulgaria. After five weeks of fighting, the Americans broke through the Siegfried Line in October. After a costly 10-day battle—the Battle of the Bulge—the Allies turned back the German drive. Finally, in early spring 1945, German defenses fell apart. At the end of April, the German army in Italy surrendered. The Soviet and American armies made their first contact in eastern Germany in April of 1945. It was agreed that the Soviets would take Berlin. On April 30—two days before the Soviets captured the ruined city—Hitler committed suicide. Within a week the German high command surrendered unconditionally. May 8, 1945 became **V-E Day,** the day of victory in Europe.

✔ **READING CHECK: Sequencing** What events led to the Allied victory in Europe?
D-Day, Battle of the Bulge

World War II in the Pacific, 1941–1945

Interpreting Maps In 1943 the Allies waged a series of battles against the Japanese in the Pacific.

■ **Skills Assessment: The World in Spatial Terms** Where did the two northernmost Pacific battles take place?

Citizenship

A famous photograph shows United States servicemen raising the American flag on Iwo Jima after winning one of the bloodiest battles of the war. The tiny, 8-mile-square island was honeycombed with caves and tunnels, and its natural terrain protected many guns. After attacking the island for more than two months with shells and bombs, some 30,000 United States marines stormed ashore in February of 1945.

Japanese resistance was so fierce that after three days of combat, the marines had advanced only about 700 yards inland. Although about 110,000 American troops opposed fewer than 25,000 Japanese, it took more than 30 days of fighting to secure Iwo Jima. Approximately 1000 Japanese defenders survived to be taken prisoner.

ACTIVITY: Have students imagine they were in the Battle of Iwo Jima and were present when the American flag was raised. Have them write a diary entry for the day they saw this scene.

MAP ANSWER
Attu and Kiska

Reproducible Resources
PS Readings in World History 108: The Morning of the 500-Ton Bomb

TEACH OBJECTIVES 1 and 2

LEVEL 2: Have students script a dialogue between Churchill and Stalin about opening a second front against Germany. Stalin should push for a second front to reduce pressure on Russia. Churchill should resist attacking in the west but suggest attacking southern Europe, which is less well-defended. Make sure students understand why Stalin wanted a second front and why Churchill preferred to attack the south. *(take pressure off Soviet Union; easier to invade Italy, particularly after Allies control North Africa)*

TEACH OBJECTIVES 1, 2, and 3

ALL LEVELS: Organize the class into five groups to prepare and present 10-minute summaries of the course of World War II in North Africa, southern Europe, eastern Europe, western Europe, and the Pacific. Suggest they illustrate their presentations with time lines, flowcharts, or regional maps.
ENGLISH LANGUAGE LEARNERS, COOPERATIVE LEARNING

CLOSE

Ask students whether they think the United States was right to drop the atomic bomb. Have students defend their views.

Linking Past to Present

The agreement at Yalta provided that countries the Allies liberated from Nazi control should hold free elections. Stalin did not keep his side of the promise. The long-promised free elections in eastern Europe finally began in 1989, as the Soviet Union was collapsing.

Critical Thinking

How did the war strengthen the Soviet Union as a world power?

ANSWER: Students may answer that it forced the United States and Britain to cooperate with Stalin and offer concessions, and that Soviet troops moved into much of eastern Europe in their advance toward Germany.

VISUAL RECORD ANSWER

serious, thoughtful, determined

Victory Over Japan

Although the war had ended in Europe, it continued in the Pacific. American marines captured the island of Iwo Jima after a month of the most bitter fighting in the war. The Allies took the island of Okinawa next. One marine later remembered his dreadful experience in the battle.

History Makers Speak

“The mud beneath our feet was deeply veined with blood. It was slippery. Blood is very slippery. So you skidded around, in deep shock, fighting as best you could until one side outnumbered the other. The outnumbered side would withdraw for reinforcements and then counterattack.”

William Manchester, *The New York Times Magazine*

In this battle about 263 Allied ships were sunk or damaged by suicide attacks of Japanese pilots. The only goal for these young kamikaze pilots was to find a good target and dive into it. The Japanese continued their resistance under heavy Allied bombing. Japan's ports were blocked and their navy could not move. The Japanese refused to surrender, however, and the Allies prepared for a major invasion of the home islands.

Yalta and Potsdam. In February 1945, Roosevelt and Churchill met with Stalin at Yalta, in the Soviet Union. They agreed that Germany would be divided and occupied by Allied troops. The Soviets agreed to enter the war against Japan. In return for their help, the Soviet Union would receive several Japanese territories. Another meeting began on July 17, 1945, at Potsdam, Germany. Roosevelt had died in April and Harry Truman was now president of the United States. Britain's new prime minister, Clement Attlee, had replaced Churchill. The leaders planned for the occupation of Germany and demanded an unconditional surrender from Japan.

INTERPRETING THE VISUAL RECORD

The "Divine Wind" The Japanese believed that pilots who promised to die for the emperor would save the empire, just as the kamikaze, or "divine wind" had saved Japan from the Chinese-Mongol attack in 1281. *What mood is suggested by the expressions on the faces of the pilots shown below?*

Japanese surrender. When Japan again refused to surrender, President Truman made an important decision—to use the atomic bomb against Japan. On August 6, 1945, an American B-29 bomber dropped the deadly weapon on the city of Hiroshima. The impact of the bomb demolished everything in the area and started a spontaneous fire that destroyed the city. About 80,000 people were killed instantly, with many more injured. Countless more people later died from radiation sickness. The effects of the bomb were unlike anything ever seen before. In Tokyo, government officials at first had difficulty comprehending the scale of the damage.

On August 8, the Soviet Union declared war on Japan. Soviet armies swept into Manchuria, meeting little resistance. On August 9, an American plane dropped a second atomic bomb on Japan. This time the target was Nagasaki, where 40,000 people died instantly. Finally, on August 14, the Japanese surrendered unconditionally, asking only that the emperor be allowed to retain his title and authority. The Allies agreed, on the condition that the emperor accept the orders of the top Allied commander in the Pacific, General Douglas MacArthur. On September 2, 1945, known as **V-J Day,** both sides signed the Japanese surrender documents.

Costs of the war. World War II was the most destructive war in history. More than 22 million military personnel died and more than 34 million were wounded. In Europe and Asia,

REVIEW

Have students complete the Section 6 Review on p. 809.

ASSESS

Have students complete Daily Quiz 30.6. As Alternative Assessment, you may want to use the graphic organizer exercise in this section's lessons.

RETEACH

Have students complete Main Idea Activity for English Language Learners and Special-Needs Students 30.6. Then have students divide a piece of paper into five columns, headed *North Africa, southern Europe, eastern Europe, western Europe,* and *Pacific.* Under each heading have them list the major events of the war in sequence. **ENGLISH LANGUAGE LEARNERS**

EXTEND

Have students assume the role of a soldier or a citizen during the war. Have them write five diary entries for dates at different phases during the war, telling what is happening and describing their feelings about it. **BLOCK SCHEDULING**

---

upward of 16 million civilians died. As the war progressed, weapons and tactics became more devastating. People began to feel that killing civilians was acceptable if it weakened the enemy.

The war also violated human rights on a scale never before seen. The Nazi Holocaust was only the most extreme of the war's atrocities. The Japanese and Soviets also committed acts of cruelty. Viewing conquered enemies as people without honor, Japanese troops often treated soldiers and civilians alike with great brutality. When the Japanese occupied the Chinese city of Nanjing in 1937, they burned stores and homes, eventually massacring about 250,000 people. In the Philippines in 1942, Japanese soldiers forced some 78,000 prisoners of war to march more than 55 miles up the Bataan Peninsula, killing more than 600 Americans and as many as 10,000 Filipinos. The incident became known as the **Bataan Death March.**

Soviet policy in occupied Poland was similar to that of the Nazis. The Soviets did not single out Jews, but instead attacked specific groups including landowners, local officials, clergy, teachers, and intellectuals. The Soviets sent about 1.5 million Poles to labor camps. When the Soviets retreated during the German invasion of 1941, they simply began shooting many of the imprisoned Poles. Close to 100,000 of those prisoners were executed.

The American use of nuclear weapons ushered in the atomic age and with it, many new questions and fears. How would the world deal with these powerful new weapons? What effect might they have on future wars? In the aftermath of World War II, leaders throughout the world struggled with these questions.

✔ **READING CHECK: Summarizing** How was World War II like no other war? most destructive, use of nuclear weapons

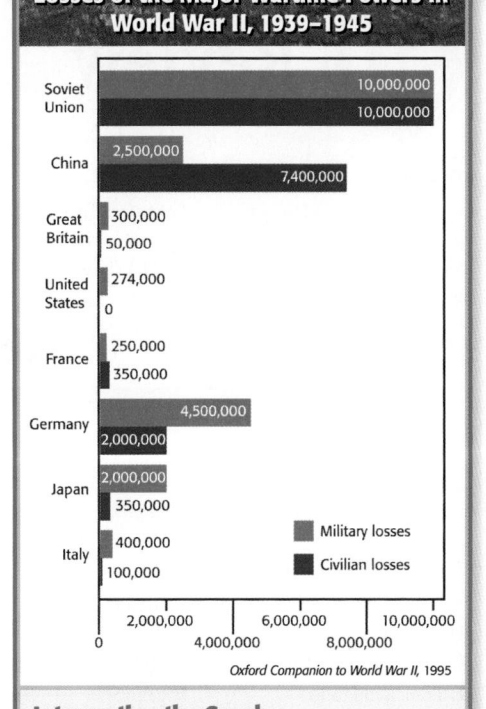

Losses of the Major Wartime Powers in World War II, 1939–1945

Country		
Soviet Union	10,000,000	10,000,000
China	2,500,000	7,400,000
Great Britain	300,000	50,000
United States	274,000	0
France	250,000	350,000
Germany	4,500,000	2,000,000
Japan	2,000,000	350,000
Italy	400,000	100,000

Military losses / Civilian losses

Oxford Companion to World War II, 1995

Interpreting the Graph
More than 50 million people were killed during World War II. Overall, more civilians were killed than soldiers.
What three countries had the highest civilian losses? What factors do you think contributed to these losses?

SECTION 6 REVIEW

1. **Define** and explain the significance:
   "soft underbelly of the Axis"
   island hopping

2. **Identify** and explain the significance:
   Battle of Stalingrad
   Dwight D. Eisenhower
   Battle of Midway
   Operation Overlord
   D-Day
   V-E Day
   V-J Day
   Bataan Death March

3. **Sequencing** Copy the graphic organizer below. Use it to show the events that led to the Allies' victory in World War II.

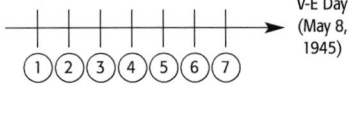
V-E Day (May 8, 1945)
① ② ③ ④ ⑤ ⑥ ⑦

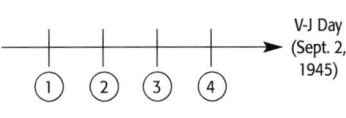
V-J Day (Sept. 2, 1945)
① ② ③ ④

4. **Finding the Main Idea**

   a. Why were Allied victories in the Soviet Union, North Africa, Italy, and the Atlantic necessary to win World War II?

   b. Why were the American victories in the Battle of the Coral Sea and the Battle of Midway important?

   c. Why was an Allied invasion of Europe necessary for achieving victory in Europe?

   d. What was unique about World War II?

5. **Writing and Critical Thinking**

   Supporting a Point of View Do you think the Allies were right to use the atomic bomb on Japan? Why or why not?
   Consider:
   • the benefits of getting Japan to surrender more quickly
   • the great destruction and loss of civilian life caused by the two atomic bombs

Homework Practice Online
keyword: SP3 HP30

INTERPRETING THE GRAPH ANSWERS
Soviet Union, China, Germany; bombing, atrocities

SECTION 6 REVIEW ANSWERS

❶ **Define**
• "soft underbelly of the Axis," p. 804
• island hopping, p. 805

❷ **Identify**
• Battle of Stalingrad, p. 804
• Dwight D. Eisenhower, p. 804
• Battle of Midway, p. 805
• Operation Overlord, p. 805
• D-Day, p. 805
• V-E Day, p. 807
• V-J Day, p. 808
• Bataan Death March, p. 809

❸ V-E Day: 1 defeat Rommel in Africa, 2 land in Italy, 3 D-Day, 4 Soviet offensive, 5 Battle of the Bulge, 6 Soviet capture of Berlin, 7 German surrender; V-J Day: 1 Battle of Midway, 2 island hopping, 3 atomic bombs, 4 Japanese surrender

❹ a. stop German eastward offensive at Stalingrad; make Mediterranean and Atlantic safe for Allied ships

b. turning point, stopped Japanese advance in Pacific

c. to create a second front

d. nuclear weapons, most destructive war ever

❺ Students' views will vary.

REVIEW AND ASSESSMENT RESOURCES

REPRODUCIBLE RESOURCES
▶ Vocabulary Activity 30

TECHNOLOGY RESOURCES
▶ Chapter 30 Test Generator (on the One-Stop Planner)
▶ Global Skill Builder CD–ROM
▶ HRW Web Site

REINFORCEMENT, REVIEW, and ASSESSMENT
▶ Chapter 30 Review, pp. 810–811
▶ Chapter 30 Tutorial for Students, Parents, Mentors, and Peers
▶ Chapter 30 Test (Form A or B)
▶ Alternative Assessment Handbook
▶ Chapter 30 Test for English Language Learners and Special-Needs Students

REVIEW
Have students complete the Chapter 30 Review on pages 810–811.

ASSESS
Use one of the chapter tests to assess students' understanding of the content. For Alternative Assessment, see the Portfolio Activities and Alternative Assessment Handbook.

CHAPTER 30 REVIEW ANSWERS

Understanding Main Ideas

1. lack of military or enforcement power, unwillingness to risk war

2. let Hitler take Sudetenland; unwilling to risk war

3. from neutrality to active support for Britain, Lend-Lease

4. goal to dominate Asian Pacific; bombing Pearl Harbor brought United States into the war

5. Jews in ghettos tried to defend themselves against Nazis; non-Jews hid Jews and helped them escape to neutral countries.

6. took islands near enough to Japan as bases for bombing Japan; dropped atomic bombs

Reviewing Themes

1. Alliances brought nations into war.

2. He told Germans they were racially superior and had a right to take land from "inferior" peoples.

3. Airplanes and bombs did great damage. Radar saved lives by forewarning of enemy planes.

CHAPTER 30 Review

Creating a Time Line

Copy the time line below onto a sheet of paper. Complete the time line by filling in events, individuals, and dates from the chapter that you think were significant. Pick three events and explain why you think they were significant.

| 1921 | 1933 | 1945 |

Writing a Summary

Using standard grammar, spelling, sentence structure, and punctuation, write an overview of the chapter.

Identifying People and Ideas

Identify the following terms or individuals and explain their significance:

1. Kellogg-Briand Pact
2. Francisco Franco
3. Munich Conference
4. Winston Churchill
5. Atlantic Charter
6. Hideki Tōjō
7. genocide
8. Holocaust
9. Dwight D. Eisenhower
10. D-Day

Understanding Main Ideas

Section 1 *(pp. 782–785)*
Threats to World Peace
1. Why was the League of Nations unable to keep Japan and Italy from taking over other countries?

Section 2 *(pp. 786–790)*
Hitler's Aggressions
2. How and why did Great Britain and France follow a policy of appeasement with Hitler?

Section 3 *(pp. 791–795)*
Axis Gains
3. How did the U.S. role in World War II change between the late 1930s and the fall of 1941?

Section 4 *(pp. 796–800)*
The Soviet Union and the United States
4. What were Japan's goals in the Pacific and how did they affect the United States?

Section 5 *(pp. 801–803)*
The Holocaust
5. How did some people try to resist the Holocaust?

Section 6 *(pp. 804–809)*
The End of the War
6. How did the Allies win the war with Japan?

Reviewing Themes

1. **Global Relations** How did regional conflicts grow to involve many nations in World War II?
2. **Government** How did Hitler use prejudice as a tool?
3. **Science, Technology & Society** How was the technology of World War II both beneficial and destructive?

Thinking Critically

1. **Making Generalizations** How was the era from 1939 to 1945 unique?
2. **Identifying Cause and Effect** How did the rise of nazism, fascism, and militarism in Germany, Italy, and Japan, as well as communism in the Soviet Union, contribute to the outbreak of World War II?
3. **Summarizing** What violations of human rights took place during World War II?

Writing About History

Problem Solving Review the failure of the League of Nations to end Italian and Japanese aggression during the 1930s. Then use a problem-solving process to write a peace-keeping plan for a new organization that would make it better equipped to keep international peace. Use the following diagram to organize your thoughts before you begin writing.

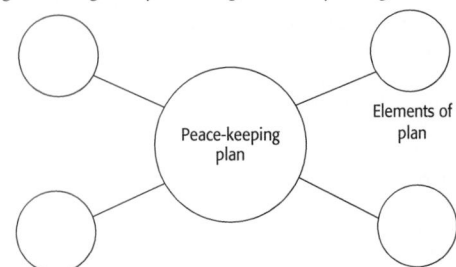

Peace-keeping plan

Elements of plan

CLOSE

Ask how 1939–1945 was a turning point in world history. *(dates signify World War II, nuclear age, emergence of United States and Soviet Union as world powers, leading to Cold War)*

RETEACH

Have students write two questions related to major points in each section.

ENGLISH LANGUAGE LEARNERS,
COOPERATIVE LEARNING

Portfolio Extensions

Link to TODAY

1. Have students write an editorial about the horrors and atrocities of the war and the importance of making sure such things never happen again. Their descriptions should include specific examples, suggestions for preventing such events in the future, and an explanation of why war-prevention efforts after World War I were unsuccessful.

2. Have groups of students draw a large illustrated map of World War II, showing the major fronts and battles.

3. Have students imagine they are members of the French resistance. Have them write a biographical essay covering the period from the time Germany attacked Poland until after the Allies liberated Paris. The essay should describe their changing activities and feelings over the course of the war.

Thinking Critically

1. beginning of the nuclear age; years of WW II.

2. They deepened the differences between opposing sides.

3. Jews, Slavs, Gypsies, and others were murdered by Nazis during the Holocaust. Victims in concentration camps suffered forced labor, starvation, brutality, filth, and disease.

Writing About History

Plans will vary but might include armed peacekeepers and procedures to enforce self-determination.

Building Social Studies Skills

1. d

2. U.S. drops atomic bombs on Japan. Japan surrenders in the same year.

3. c

4. invasion of Poland, Battle of Britain

Building Your Portfolio

Students' interviews will vary.

Building Social Studies Skills

Reading a Chart

Study the chart below. Then answer the questions that follow.

Major Stages of World War II

Date	Europe and North Africa	The Pacific Theater
1939	Germany invades Poland.	—
1940	"Battle of Britain" occurs.	—
1941	U.S. enters war against the Axis.	Japan attacks Pearl Harbor.
1942	Allies invade North Africa.	U.S. lands on Guadalcanal.
1944	Allies land in Normandy.	U.S. lands in Philippines.
1945	Germany surrenders to the Allies.	U.S. drops atomic bombs on Japan. Japan surrenders.

1. Which statement correctly describes a relationship shown on the chart?
   a. The war in Europe and North Africa was shorter than the war in the Pacific.
   b. Hitler invaded Poland two years after Japan attacked Pearl Harbor.
   c. The U.S. landed in the Philippines one year after the Allies invaded North Africa.
   d. The war in the Pacific started two years after the war began in Europe.

2. Which of the events that occurred in 1945 was most responsible for Japan's surrender to the Allies? Give specific reasons to support your view.

Identifying Bias

Read the following quote from a message that Winston Churchill sent to Franklin Roosevelt in February, 1941. Then answer the questions.

> "Some believe that Japan in her present mood would not hesitate to court an attempt to wage war both against Great Britain and the United States. Personally, I think the odds are definitely against that, but no one can tell. Everything that you can do to inspire the Japanese with fear of a double [two-front] war may avert the danger. If however they come in against us and we are alone, the grave character of the consequences cannot easily be overstated."

3. Which of the following best describes how Churchill's experience influenced his viewpoint?
   a. Churchill had experience dealing with the Japanese, and he thought they feared a two-front war.
   b. Churchill welcomed the chance to show the world that Britain could defeat Japan.
   c. He had seen the war damage in his country, and he knew that Britain could not hold off Japan alone.
   d. Churchill was a soldier and wanted to command the Allied troops.

4. What events of World War II had Churchill already witnessed before he sent this message? Give specific examples.

Alternative Assessment

Building Your Portfolio

Link to TODAY

Global Relations

Interview a friend or relative who remembers the World War II years. Ask this person to explain the meaning of the following words or phrases: victory garden, ration books, blackouts, dog tags, Rosie the Riveter, war bonds, C-rations, and black market. During your interview, try to discover other World War II terms that you might add to the list.

☑ **internet** connect

Internet Activity: go.hrw.com
KEYWORD: SP3 WH30

Choose a topic on World War II to:
- write a biography of Raoul Wallenberg.
- write a report on the historical information and legacy of Anne Frank.
- write a report about a landing beach on D-Day that includes a map, a description of what happened there, photographs, and eyewitness accounts.

Spotlight on LITERATURE

A diary is a record of events that ranges from personal to public in nature. The terms *diary* and *journal* are frequently interchangeable. Personal diaries tell of the inner thoughts and feelings of the writer. They are often private and sometimes kept secret. In public diaries, or journals, the writer records and reacts to things happening in the world. Diaries of famous writers and artists have often given valuable information about their lives and the times in which they lived.

Spotlight on LITERATURE

The film *From Here to Eternity* (1953) was adapted from James Jones's best-seller about life in a Pearl Harbor army barracks before World War II. The movie won eight Academy Awards™, including best picture, screenplay, and director. Frank Sinatra and Donna Reed won Academy Awards™ for their roles in the film. Actual battle footage was incorporated into the unforgettable action scenes of the Japanese attack on Pearl Harbor. Have students use primary and secondary sources to learn more about Pearl Harbor and the global effects it had.

Interdisciplinary Connection

LITERATURE. A monologue is a piece of writing that expresses the words of a person speaking alone. Monologues include the following: monodrama, a play or story with only one character; soliloquy, as when a character in a play or story "thinks aloud"; solo addresses to an audience in a play or to readers of a story, as when a character speaks directly to the audience or reader to explain some plot point; and dramatic monologue, a poem in which an imaginary speaker addresses an imaginary audience.

Critical Thinking

Which type of monologue appears in the excerpt from *All Quiet on the Western Front* on page 812?

ANSWER: The novel has many characters, so it is not a monodrama. The character is not speaking directly to the reader, so it is not a solo address. The excerpt is not a poem, so it is not a dramatic monologue. Therefore it must be a form of soliloquy— the speaker is alone, he is thinking aloud, although directing his words to a dead body.

UNDERSTANDING LITERATURE ANSWER

Both writings give examples of people clinging to hope under severe circumstances. Frank's diary in particular has remained popular as an inspirational example to young people everywhere.

CROSS-CULTURAL *Literature*
CONNECTIONS

Hope Amid Turmoil

Erich Maria Remarque (1898–1970) wrote All Quiet on the Western Front *to overcome his depressing memories of trench warfare in World War I. In the excerpt below, German Paul Baumer has stabbed a French soldier after he fell on top of Baumer in a shell-hole. Later, Baumer regrets his enemy's death. Despite Remarque's hopes for a peaceful future, the world was soon at war again. As Allied armies advanced toward Germany in World War II, eight Jews hiding above a Dutch factory hoped for liberation. One of them was Anne Frank (1929–1945), who had received a diary for her 13th birthday. She hoped her diary would one day become a record of the Holocaust. Twenty days after the excerpt below was written, the Germans found the Frank's hiding place. Sent to the Bergen-Belsen concentration camp, Anne died of typhoid just weeks before the camp's liberation in April 1945.* The Diary of a Young Girl *has sold millions of copies since Anne's father published her diary in 1947.*

All Quiet on the Western Front
by Erich Maria Remarque

The silence spreads. I talk and must talk. So I speak to him and say to him: "Comrade, I did not want to kill you. If you jumped in here again, I would not do it, if you would be sensible too. But you were only an idea to me before, an abstraction that lived in my mind and called forth its appropriate response. It was that abstraction I stabbed. But now, for the first time, I see you are a man like me. I thought of your hand-grenades, of your bayonet, of your rifle; now I see your wife and your face and our fellowship. Forgive me, comrade. We always see it too late. Why do they never tell us that you are just poor devils like us, that your mothers are just as anxious as ours, and that we have the same fear of death, and the same dying and the same agony— Forgive me, comrade; how could you be my enemy? If we threw away these rifles and this uniform you could be my brother just like Kat and Albert."

The Diary of a Young Girl
by Anne Frank

Anyone who claims that the older folks have a more difficult time in the Annex doesn't realize that the problems have a far greater impact on us. We're much too young to deal with these problems ... It's difficult in times like these: ideals, dreams and cherished hopes rise within us, only to be crushed by grim reality. It's a wonder I haven't abandoned all my ideals, they seem so absurd and impractical. Yet I cling to them because I still believe, in spite of everything, that people are truly good at heart. It's utterly impossible for me to build my life on a foundation of chaos, suffering and death. I see the world being slowly transformed into a wilderness, I hear the approaching thunder that, one day, will destroy us too, I feel the suffering of millions. And yet, when I look up at the sky, I somehow feel that everything will change for the better, that this cruelty too shall end, that peace and tranquility will return once more.

Understanding Literature

How do Remarque's and Frank's writings reflect hope? Why do you think Frank's diary has remained a bestseller for more than 50 years?

Economics

Have students work with partners to list the main characteristics of fascism and communism. Then have them work together to compare and contrast ways that proponents of these two political systems attempted to solve economic and social problems. Students should list similarities and differences, consider advantages and disadvantages, and compare results. Have them write an essay explaining their conclusions.

Global Nationalism

Write the following concept web on the board, and have students fill in the blanks to correctly summarize nationalist efforts in Egypt, India, and the Middle East—all parts of the British Empire.

India

British Empire

Egypt

Middle East

UNIT 7

BUILDING YOUR Portfolio

Economics

The Great Depression of the 1930s not only influenced the world economy, it also played an important role in shaping political events. Imagine that you are a German student living in Berlin. You have faithfully kept a journal throughout your life, taking special care to note the changing economic and political trends in Germany. Create seven journal entries detailing national events taking place in 1933. You can write entries for seven consecutive days or select seven dates from throughout the year. Remember to consider the state of the German economy and its influence on German political life during the early 1930s.

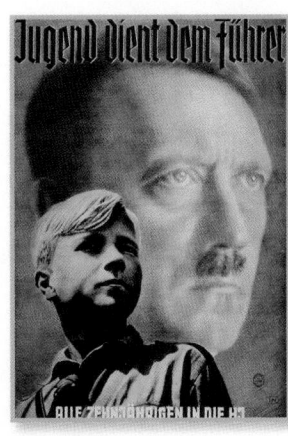

Hitler youth propaganda poster

Global Nationalism

Nationalist movements brought about change in many parts of the world, including Africa, Asia, and Latin America, during the early 1900s. The influence of strong leaders inspired calls for independence, modernization, and other political, social, and economic change. Imagine that you are an international correspondent assigned to interview a nationalist leader for a feature article on revolutions. Create a list of questions you would ask. The questions should indicate your understanding of the conditions in the country as well as the goals and methods of the person you are interviewing.

Chinese leader Chiang Kai-shek, shown here in about 1935, was head of the Chinese Nationalist Army. He later became president of Taiwan.

Further Reading

Holliday, Laurel, ed. *Children in the Holocaust and World War II: Their Secret Diaries.* New York: Simon and Schuster, 1995. First-person accounts of events during the Second World War as seen by young people.

Lang, Sean. *The Second World War: Conflict and Co-Operation.* London: Cambridge University Press, 1993. Presents an overview of the people, places, and events of the war.

Terkel, Studs. *Hard Times: An Oral History of the Great Depression in America.* New York: New Press, 2000. Classic featuring the voices of Americans who lived during the Great Depression.

Wepman, Dennis. *Africa: The Struggle for Independence.* New York: Facts on File, 1994. A history of African responses to imperialism and colonial rule.

Winter, J. M. *The Experience of World War I.* New York: Oxford University Press, 1989. A survey history of the First World War.

Culture

Propaganda is presenting information for the purpose of trying to influence public opinion. Propagandists present facts, arguments, half-truths, and lies in order to have the greatest effect on reaching a specific goal. During World War I all governments used propaganda to keep up morale and sway the opinions of neutrals. Germans depicted Russians as barbarians. The French and British identified atrocities of the "Huns" (Germans). The Allies, promoting democracy and national self-determination, were better at psychological warfare than the Germans, who only had national appeal.

ACTIVITY: Have students work in groups to research propaganda techniques during World Wars I and II and the Cold War. Suggest that students identify characteristics of propaganda and explain how to evaluate messages of propaganda.

internet connect

go.hrw.com

Internet Activity
KEYWORD: SP3 U7

In assigned groups, develop a multimedia presentation about the era from World War I to World War II. Choose information from the chapter Internet Connect activities and the Holt Researcher that best reflects the major topics of the period. Write an outline and a script for your presentation, which may be shown to the class.

EXAMINING THE VISUAL RECORD

❶ *Based on this picture, what is a mural?*

ANSWER: a large painting

Most murals are large works painted directly on a wall in a public place and intended to be viewed by a wide audience. The Mexican muralists, including Diego Rivera, Jose Clemente Orozco, and David Alfaro Siqueros, expressed revolutionary or socially conscious themes.

❷ *What is the theme of this mural?*

ANSWER: the modernization of medicine in Mexico

Diego Rivera worked in fresco, which is paint applied to wet plaster. His flattened, stylized figures are set in crowded, shallow spaces and enlivened by bright colors. Many of his murals depict Mexican history from pre-Columbian times to modern.

ACTIVITY: Ask students to use primary and secondary sources, including computer software, to learn more about the Mexican muralists and their art. Have students present their findings to the class. Then have students create small-scale murals of their own.

UNIT 8 The World Since 1945

1945–Present

ern leaders were determined to break free from European domination. The nation of Israel was created, apartheid ended in South Africa, and tensions escalated in the Middle East.

CHAPTER 34 **Latin America Since 1945**
Latin America nations struggled to establish economic and political stability. Mexico made progress toward democracy, while other nations' dictators were overthrown by communist revolutionaries. Fidel Castro established a communist state in Cuba.

CHAPTER 35 **The Superpowers in the Modern Era**
New tensions surfaced as the political and economic battles of the Cold War began. The United States and the U.S.S.R. emerged as the world's superpowers with opposing ideologies. With the breakup of the Soviet Union, the United States became the world's sole superpower.

CHAPTER 36 **The Modern World**
New styles in the arts reflected a rapidly changing world. Science, technology, and a new commitment to human rights brought about many of these changes, which included the new world of the Internet.

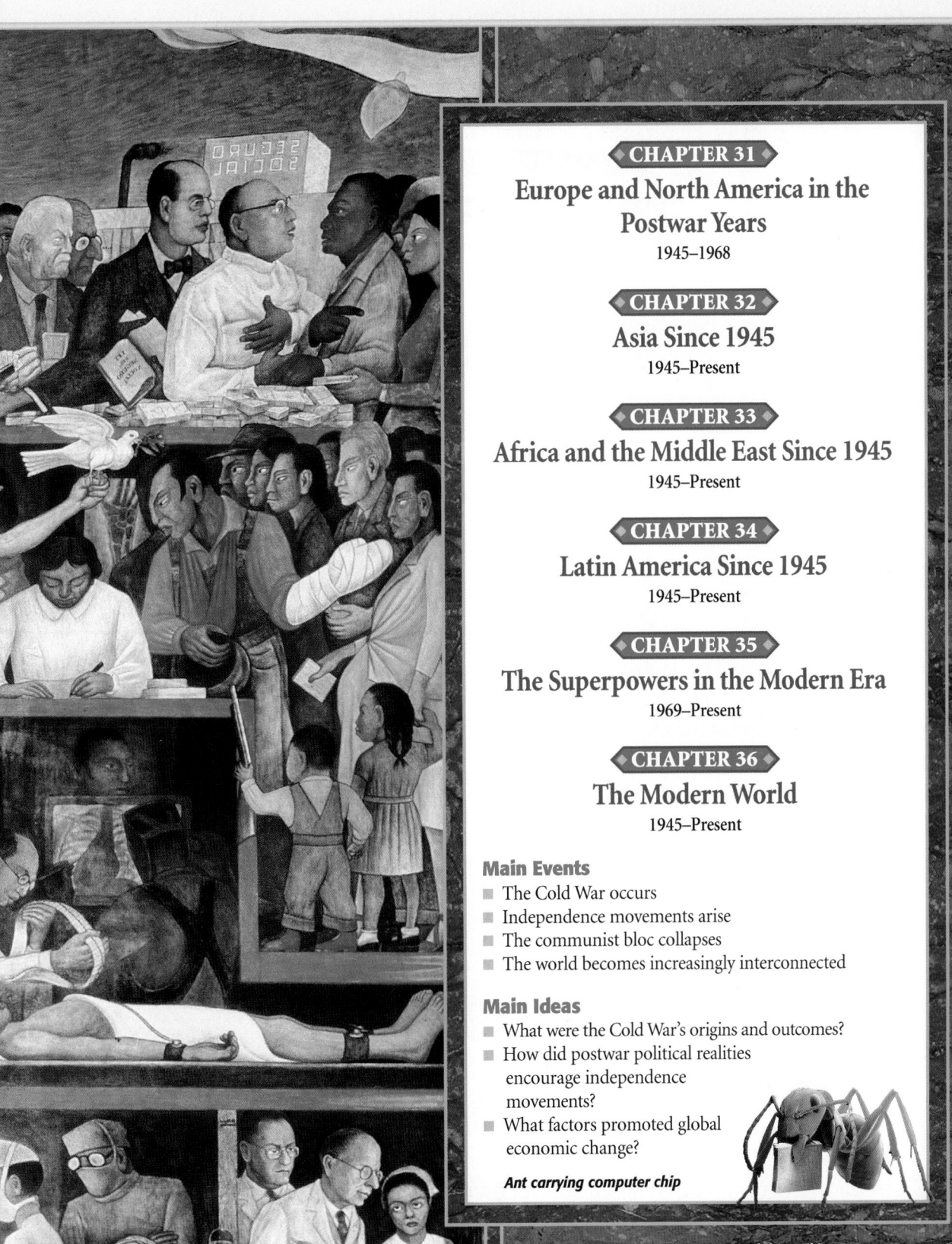

Mexican muralist Diego Rivera created this striking composition, entitled The History of Medicine in Mexico, in 1953.

◆ CHAPTER 31 ◆
Europe and North America in the Postwar Years
1945–1968

◆ CHAPTER 32 ◆
Asia Since 1945
1945–Present

◆ CHAPTER 33 ◆
Africa and the Middle East Since 1945
1945–Present

◆ CHAPTER 34 ◆
Latin America Since 1945
1945–Present

◆ CHAPTER 35 ◆
The Superpowers in the Modern Era
1969–Present

◆ CHAPTER 36 ◆
The Modern World
1945–Present

Main Events
- The Cold War occurs
- Independence movements arise
- The communist bloc collapses
- The world becomes increasingly interconnected

Main Ideas
- What were the Cold War's origins and outcomes?
- How did postwar political realities encourage independence movements?
- What factors promoted global economic change?

Ant carrying computer chip

815

🔊 LET'S GET STARTED!

As students enter the classroom, ask them to think about different ways in which the people of the modern world are connected. Have students keep their thoughts in mind as they read Cross-Cultural Connections. Tell students that in this unit they will learn how recent changes in politics, economics, and technology have changed our lives.

Citizenship

Disobeying a law because of moral principles is an act of civil disobedience. Successful civil disobedience can change society. It is nonviolent but can involve actions such as street demonstrations or peaceful occupation of premises. It is different from other forms of rebellion because the civil disobeyer is willing to be arrested or punished for his or her actions. In his book, *On the Duty of Civil Disobedience*, Henry David Thoreau said that when the laws and a person's conscience clash, that person must follow his or her conscience. The most famous examples of mass civil disobedience were those of Mahatma Gandhi and Martin Luther King, Jr. Gandhi led the campaign for Indian independence. King was the leader of the civil rights movement of the 1960s. Civil disobedience stems from the idea that there are times when law and justice do not coincide and that obeying the law at such times is both morally unjust and politically ineffective.

Critical Thinking

What are some social or political issues that you feel strongly about and for which you would be willing to be arrested in expressing your beliefs?

ANSWER: Answers will vary.

CROSS-CULTURAL CONNECTIONS

Focus On: Citizenship

Main Idea **What are the rights of citizens?** A citizen is a member of a political community. He or she enjoys certain rights and privileges, such as the right to vote, and certain responsibilities, such as the defense of the community. The nature of citizenship changed dramatically in many nations after 1945.

Asia
Europe and North America
Latin America
Africa and the Middle East

1945   *present*

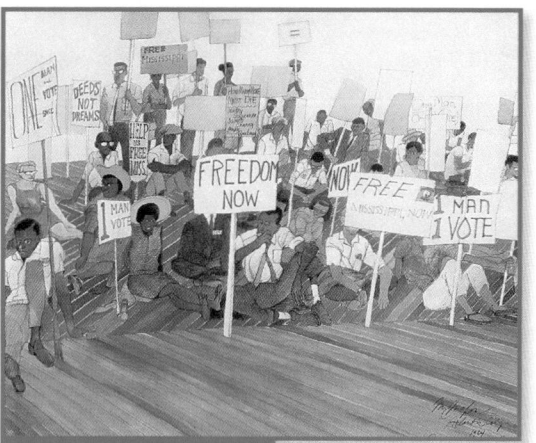

United States, 1945–present

◀ **Civil Rights Movement** Although thousands of African-Americans fought for freedom in Europe and the Pacific during World War II, they returned to a nation that still practiced segregation in schools, stores, and jobs. During the postwar years African-Americans began a nationwide crusade for civil and political rights. The 1950s and the 1960s were particularly turbulent. This painting by Franklin McMahon, entitled *Civil Rights Protestors at the 1964 Democratic National Convention,* captures a moment in the long struggle for equality.

Communist China On October 1, 1949, Communist leader Mao Zedong proclaimed the new People's Republic of China. Mao used the Soviet Union as a model to begin a series of socialist actions designed to redistribute land, eliminate rural landlords, and promote industrial production. When Mao's policies failed, he silenced his critics by launching the Cultural Revolution in 1966. During this period Mao brutally suppressed political opposition by mobilizing youth in the Red Guards, such as those pictured here, to attack his enemies. In the years following Mao's death in 1976, however, demands for democratic reform began to be heard in China.

China, 1945–present

Statue of "Goddess of Democracy" erected in 1989 in Tiananmen Square during demonstrations for reform

Have students review the information in the chart on page 816. Ask them to use standard grammar, spelling, sentence structure, and punctuation to answer the questions in "Why It Matters Today" and to share their answer with the class.

Have students complete their answer to the question in "Why It Matters Today" and add it to their portfolio. As Alternative Assessment, you may want to use the web exercise in the lesson.

Have students work in groups of three or four to create a poster that explains a recent technological innovation. Tell students to use information from their textbooks, the library, computer software, and any other available resources to determine how the innovation came about, how it functions, and what it does. Posters may include illustrations, charts, or graphs. Allow time for students to explain their poster and display it in the classroom.

Creating Israel The nation of Israel was created on May 14, 1948. Eight months later, in January 1949, Israelis held their first general election to establish the new nation's government. Political leaders, including the prime minister, who heads the government, and members of the Israeli Knesset, the nation's legislature, are elected by popular vote. Representatives to the Knesset meet in the starkly impressive building pictured at right. The Knesset has supreme political authority in Israel, including the power to oust the prime minister and dissolve the government.

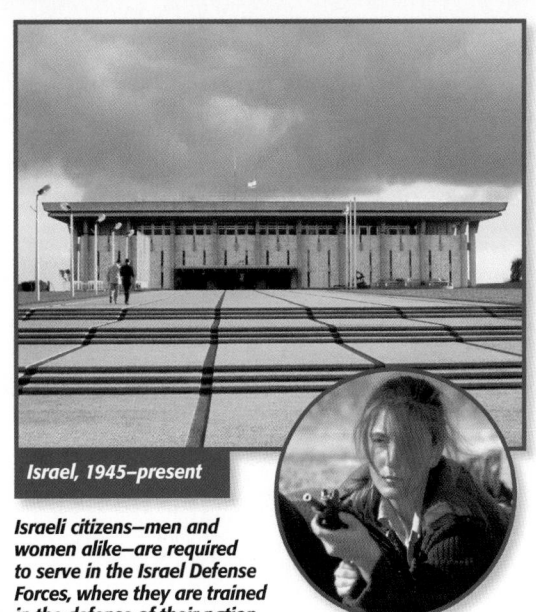

Israel, 1945–present

Israeli citizens—men and women alike—are required to serve in the Israel Defense Forces, where they are trained in the defense of their nation.

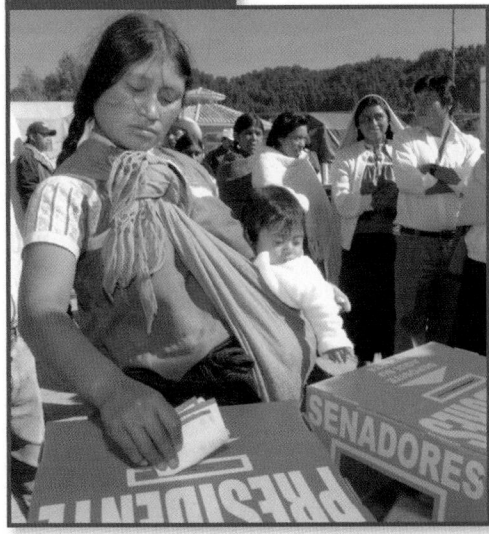

Mexico, 1945–present

Mexico's Peaceful Revolution On July 2, 2000, Mexican citizens brought an end to the 71-year rule of the PRI—the Institutional Revolutionary Party. By electing Vicente Fox president of Mexico, citizens sought to rid their country of a corrupt government. Some Mexicans compared Fox's election in 2000 to the storming of the Bastille in 1789, when French citizens overthrew their unjust monarchy. The Totzil Mayan woman pictured here voting in Mexico's 2000 elections is exercising the citizen's power to choose political representatives.

Why It Matters Today

After World War II people around the globe experienced many different forms of citizenship. As political transformations took place in the late 1900s, the nature of citizenship changed in many countries. **In what countries has citizenship recently changed? Where are people continuing to fight for rights as citizens?**

Government

The process of voting today is almost always by secret ballot. In the past, a person's choice was indicated by a show of hands, by announcing one's vote aloud, or by putting colored ballots into a ballot box. Under U.S. law, the ballot must be available only at polling places where people vote in private booths and must list all candidates legally entitled to have their names included. In the United States, paper ballots have been mostly replaced by voting machines. Some places have switched to electronic balloting, in which voters mark cards that are run through a machine for rapid counting.

Critical Thinking

Why is voting so important in a democratic society?

ANSWER: Voting is the way citizens in a democracy choose the members of the government and express their ideas about the nation's policies and laws.

WHY IT MATTERS TODAY ANSWER

Citizenship issues continue in the nations that made up the former Soviet Union, in Israel and other nations of the Middle East, and in the Indonesian nation of East Timor, among many others. In all these areas, people are fighting to gain citizenship rights or to prevent others from doing so.

Europe and North America in the Postwar Years

CHAPTER RESOURCE MANAGER

	Objectives	Pacing Guide	Reproducible Resources
SECTION 1 **Aftermath of the War in Europe** (pp. 820–824)	• Describe the origins of the postwar settlement for Europe. • Explain why Germany was divided into four occupation zones and what developed as a result. • Explore how the United Nations is organized. • Identify the problems the Allies faced in keeping the peace.	**Regular** 1.5 day / **Block Scheduling** 1 day *Block Scheduling Handbook with Team Teaching Strategies, 31.1*	**RS** Guided Reading Strategy 31.1 **PS** Readings in World History 109: The Universal Declaration of Human Rights **PS** Readings in World History 110: George Marshall Outlines the Need for a European Rehabilitation Program
SECTION 2 **Origins of the Cold War** (pp. 825–830)	• Examine how and why the alliance between the Western Allies and the Soviet Union ended. • Investigate how the United States attempted to stop the spread of communism and aid Europe. • Describe how Germany became two separate countries. • Identify the Cold War alliances that developed in Europe.	**Regular** 1.5 day / **Block Scheduling** 1 day *Block Scheduling Handbook with Team Teaching Strategies, 31.2*	**RS** Guided Reading Strategy 31.2 **RS** Graphic Organizer Activity 31: Cold War Alliances **PS** Readings in World History 112: Soviet Dissidents Decry the Invasion of Czechoslovakia **E** Creative Teaching Strategy 31: A Cold War Era Atlas
SECTION 3 **Reconstruction, Reform, and Reaction in Europe** (pp. 831–836)	• Describe the West German "miracle." • Explain why the British met with mixed success in stimulating economic growth. • Explore how France maintained an independent position in European affairs. • Analyze how the Soviet Union changed under new leadership. • Identify the problems Eastern European nations faced.	**Regular** 1.5 day / **Block Scheduling** 1 day *Block Scheduling Handbook with Team Teaching Strategies, 31.3*	**RS** Guided Reading Strategy 31.3 **SM** Geography Activity 31: The Berlin Wall **PS** Readings in World History 111: The Battle of the Sorbonne
SECTION 4 **The United States and Canada** (pp. 837–841)	• Examine the major domestic problems the United States faced in the postwar era. • Investigate how the policy of containment led to foreign conflicts. • Identify the challenges the Canadian people responded to in the postwar era.	**Regular** 1.5 day / **Block Scheduling** 1 day *Block Scheduling Handbook with Team Teaching Strategies, 31.4*	**RS** Guided Reading Strategy 31.4 **E** Hands-on History Activity 31: The New Consumer Culture

Chapter Resource Key

PS Primary Sources	**A** Assessment	Music	
RS Reading Support	**REV** Review	Video	
IC Interdisciplinary Connections	**ELL** Reinforcement and English Language Learners	Internet	
E Enrichment	Transparencies	Holt Presentation Maker Using Microsoft® PowerPoint®	
SM Skills Mastery	CD-ROM		

 One-Stop Planner CD-ROM

See the ***One-Stop Planner*** for a complete list of additional resources for students and teachers.

One-Stop Planner CD-ROM

It's easy to plan lessons, select resources, and print out materials for your students when you use the *One-Stop Planner* CD–ROM with *Test Generator.*

Technology Resources	Reinforcement, Review, and Assessment
One-Stop Planner 31.1 Homework Practice Online	Daily Quiz 31.1 Main Idea Activity 31.1 English Audio Summary 31.1 Spanish Audio Summary 31.1 REV Section 1 Review, p. 824
One-Stop Planner 31.2 Holt Researcher: World History: Harry Truman World History and Cultures Video Program 26: Television and the Cold War CNN. Presents World Cultures: Yesterday and Today Segment 30: NATO at 50 World History Teaching Transparency: Geography and History 26: Cold War Defenses Homework Practice Online Online Maps, Charts, and Graphs: Communist Europe in 1949	Daily Quiz 31.2 Main Idea Activity 31.2 English Audio Summary 31.2 Spanish Audio Summary 31.2 REV Section 2 Review, p. 830
One-Stop Planner 31.3 Holt Researcher: World History: Nikita Khrushchev World History Teaching Transparency: Everyday Life 25: Russian Tanks in Berlin Homework Practice Online Online Maps, Charts, and Graphs: Europe	Daily Quiz 31.3 Main Idea Activity 31.3 English Audio Summary 31.3 Spanish Audio Summary 31.3 REV Section 3 Review, p. 836
One-Stop Planner 31.4 World History Teaching Transparency: Everyday Life 26: Segregation in the United States, 1960 World History Teaching Transparency: Art and History 26: Return of the Prodigal Son Homework Practice Online Online Maps: The United States and Canada Online Maps: The Threat of Cuban Missiles, 1962	Daily Quiz 31.4 Main Idea Activity 31.4 English Audio Summary 31.4 Spanish Audio Summary 31.4 REV Section 4 Review, p. 841

internet connect

HRW ONLINE RESOURCES
GO TO: go.hrw.com
Then type in a keyword.

TEACHER HOME PAGE
KEYWORD: SP3 Teacher

CHAPTER INTERNET ACTIVITIES
KEYWORD: SP3 WH31
Choose an activity to:
- research the Cold War and look for elements of popular culture that reflect Cold War anxieties.
- assess how human rights and democratic ideals have been advanced by the United Nations.
- learn about McCarthyism and its effect on the United States.

CHAPTER ENRICHMENT LINKS
KEYWORD: SP3 CH31

ONLINE ASSESSMENT
Homework Practice
KEYWORD: SP3 HP31
Standardized Test Prep
KEYWORD: SP3 STP31
Rubrics
KEYWORD: SS Rubrics

ONLINE MAPS, CHARTS, AND GRAPHS
KEYWORD: SP3 MCG

CONTENT UPDATES
KEYWORD: SS Content Updates

HOLT PRESENTATION MAKER
KEYWORD: SP3 PPT31

ONLINE READING SUPPORT
KEYWORD: SS Strategies

CURRENT EVENTS
KEYWORD: S3 Current Events

Meeting Individual Needs

Ability Levels

Level 1 Basic level activities designed for all students encountering new material

Level 2 Intermediate level activities designed for average students

Level 3 Challenging activities designed for honors and gifted and talented students

English Language Learners These activities address the needs of students with Limited English Proficiency.

Chapter Review and Assessment

IC Vocabulary Activity 31
 Global Skill Builder CD–ROM
 HRW Web Site
REV Chapter 31 Tutorial for Students, Parents, Mentors, and Peers
REV Chapter 31 Review, pp. 842–843
A Chapter 31 Test Generator (on the One-Stop Planner)
A Chapter 31 Test (Form A or B)
A Alternative Assessment Handbook
A Chapter 31 Test for English Language Learners and Special-Needs Students

Section 1   Aftermath of the War in Europe

Section 2   Origins of the Cold War

Section 3   Reconstruction, Reform, and Reaction in Europe

Section 4   The United States and Canada

Build on What You Know

Ask students to answer the following questions:

What threats to world peace occurred in the 1930s?

Consider:

- Japanese occupation of Manchuria
- Italy's invasion of Ethiopia
- German rearmament under Adolf Hitler

How did the Allies achieve victory during World War II?

Consider:

- Soviet victory at Stalingrad
- Allied invasions of North Africa and Italy
- Germany's surrender
- the dropping of the atomic bomb on Hiroshima and Nagasaki

CHAPTER
31

1945–1968

Europe and North America in the Postwar Years

1945
Global Events
The United Nations is established.

1950
The Arts
Construction begins on Le Corbusier's Notre Dame du Haut.

1953
Politics
Joseph Stalin dies.

1955
Global Events
The Warsaw Pact is established.

1955
Business and Finance
Egypt agrees to trade cotton with Romania and the Soviet Union.

1945

1945
The Arts
Jazz saxophonist Charlie Parker popularizes "bebop."

1945–1946
Global Events
The Nürnberg trials are held.

1950

1949
Global Events
NATO is formed.

1949
Politics
The Federal Republic of Germany is founded.

1948
Global Events
The Berlin blockade and airlift begin.

1955

1954
Daily Life
U.S. Supreme Court bans school segregation.

1953
Science and Technology
Biologists discover the double helix structure of DNA.

1956
The Arts
Spanish poet Juan Ramón Jiménez receives the Nobel Prize for literature.

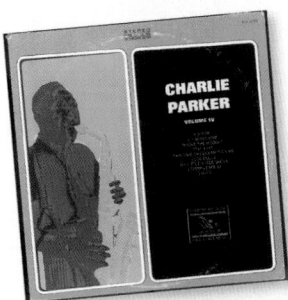

Cover of a Charlie Parker album

DNA molecule

Build on What You Know

*I*n order to defeat the Axis Powers in World War II, Western nations had allied themselves with the Soviet Union. This alliance proved effective, and in 1945 Soviet troops entered Berlin, bringing the fighting in Europe to an end. With the war over, however, prewar differences that had divided the Western European democracies from the communist Soviet Union reemerged. Moreover, much of Europe had been devastated in the fury of World War II. In this chapter, you will learn about economic and political conditions in Europe and North America in the decades following World War II.

What's Your Opinion?

 To help students create their Themes Journal entries, provide the following examples of appropriate **agree**/**disagree** *statements.*

Economics

Agree Government control of all economic decisions is the best way to achieve rapid national economic growth.

Disagree A nation prospers when the government does not take an active role in controlling the economy.

Government

Agree Citizens in every nation should have the right to elect their leaders and participate in democratic government.

Disagree Sometimes a leader must seize power and implement a government without the people's approval in order to stabilize society and the economy.

Citizenship

Agree When citizens of a democracy engage in public protest, they are often successful in bringing about positive changes in society.

Disagree Public protests are an ineffective means of bringing about change and progress in a democracy.

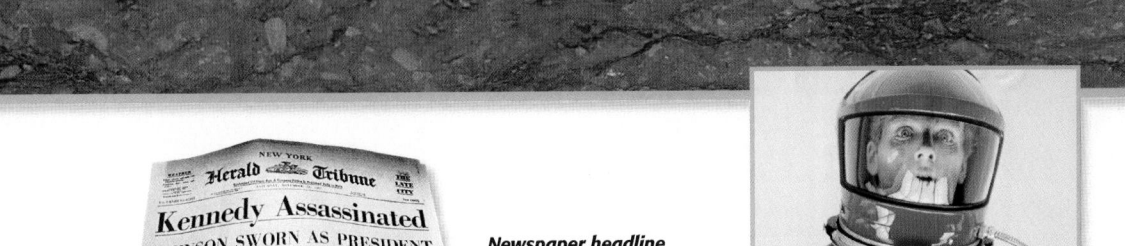

Newspaper headline following the 1963 Kennedy assassination

A still from the movie 2001: A Space Odyssey

1957
Business and Finance
The Common Market is created.

1957
Science and Technology
The Soviets launch *Sputnik I.*

1959
Politics
The Cuban government falls to Marxist rebels.

1959
Science and Technology
The St. Lawrence Seaway is completed.

1964
Politics
Soviet leader Nikita Khrushchev is forced to resign.

1964
Daily Life
Martin Luther King Jr. receives the Nobel Peace Prize.

1964
The Arts
The Beatles make their first tour of the United States.

1968
Global Events
Warsaw Pact troops invade Czechoslovakia, ending the Prague Spring.

1968
The Arts
Stanley Kubrick's film *2001: A Space Odyssey* is released in Britain.

1960

1965

1958
Business and Finance
West Germany is the leading industrial power in Western Europe.

1961
Global Events
The Berlin Wall is built.

1963
Politics
Lyndon Johnson becomes president after John F. Kennedy is assassinated.

1968
Science and Technology
The Soviet *Zond* becomes the first spacecraft to fly around the moon.

1968
Daily Life
Vietnam War protesters clash with police in the streets of Chicago.

Antiwar protesters face troops at the 1968 Democratic Party Convention in Chicago.

What's Your Opinion?

 Do you **agree** *or* **disagree** *with the following statements? Support your point of view in your journal.*

Economics National economies grow more quickly when all economic decisions are made by the government.

Government People should always be allowed to determine who governs them and what kind of government they have.

Citizenship Public protests can be an effective way to bring about change and progress in a democracy.

OBJECTIVES

1 Describe the origins of the postwar settlement for Europe.

2 Explain why Germany was divided into four occupation zones and what developed as a result.

3 Explore how the United Nations is organized.

4 Identify the problems the Allies faced in keeping the peace.

LET'S GET STARTED!

As students enter the classroom, ask them to recall the Allies' policies regarding Germany after World War I. (*included disarmament, territorial losses, enormous reparations, little economic aid*) Ask students how this treatment affected Germany. (*It helped cause inflation, resentment toward the Allies, disenchantment with the Weimar government, and ultimately led to the rise of the Nazi government.*) Tell students that in Section 1 they will learn about the Allies' post-WWII policies toward Germany.

SECTION 1 RESOURCES

REPRODUCIBLE RESOURCES

▸ Guided Reading Strategy 31.1

▸ Readings in World History 109: The Universal Declaration of Human Rights

▸ Readings in World History 110: George Marshall Outlines the Need for a European Rehabilitation Program

TECHNOLOGY RESOURCES

▸ One-Stop Planner 31.1

▸ Homework Practice Online

REINFORCEMENT, REVIEW, AND ASSESSMENT

▸ Section 1 Review, p. 824

▸ Daily Quiz 31.1

▸ Main Idea Activity 31.1

▸ English Audio Summary 31.1

▸ Spanish Audio Summary 31.1

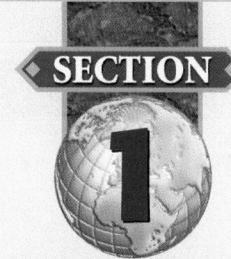

SECTION 1

READ TO DISCOVER

1 What were the origins of the postwar settlement for Europe?

2 Why was Germany divided into four occupation zones and what developed as a result?

3 How is the United Nations organized?

4 What problems did the Allies face in keeping peace in Europe?

DEFINE

veto power

IDENTIFY

United Nations
Nürnberg trials
Eleanor Roosevelt
General Assembly
Security Council

▶ WHY IT MATTERS TODAY

The United Nations remains active today in efforts to promote peace. Use CNN or other **current event** sources to learn more about United Nations peacekeeping efforts today. Record your findings in your journal.

CNNstudentNews.com

Aftermath of the War in Europe

The Main Idea
At the end of World War II, the Allied nations had trouble determining how to keep peace in Europe.

The Story Continues *Harry Hopkins, an American who attended the Yalta Conference, later recalled participants' optimism. "We were absolutely certain we had won the first great victory of the peace—and, by 'we,' I mean all of us, the whole human race." The dangerous waters of the postwar world, however, proved far more difficult to navigate than Hopkins or others imagined.*

Wartime Conferences and Postwar Problems

Victory over the Axis powers brought on a whole new set of problems for Allied leaders. To a degree, these problems were the result of decisions they had made during the war.

In November and December of 1943, the "Big Three" Allied leaders—Churchill, Roosevelt, and Stalin—had met at Tehran, the capital of Iran. At this meeting, they decided to defeat Germany by carrying on the war on two fronts. Western Allied forces would attack Germany from the west, while Soviet forces would attack from the east. This decision meant that Western forces would meet the Soviets somewhere in the middle of Germany.

In February 1945, Churchill, Roosevelt, and Stalin had met at the Black Sea resort town of Yalta. With victory clearly in sight, the three leaders agreed to divide Austria and Germany into zones of military occupation. Armies from each of the Allied nations would be responsible for the territories they liberated from Nazi control. Berlin would lie entirely within the Soviet zone, but it would be divided into four parts. The Soviets would control East Berlin, and the Western Allies would create their own zones in West Berlin. Vienna was to be divided in a similar manner. The Allied leaders regarded the division of Germany as only a temporary measure, however. They foresaw that a final peace settlement would be arranged later.

The Allies seemed to reach agreement on Poland and territories that the Soviets had already taken in Eastern Europe. Churchill and Roosevelt believed these countries should be allowed to determine their own futures. They obtained Stalin's promise that

Two months after the Yalta Conference, President Roosevelt died. Millions in the United States and around the world mourned his death.

LEVEL 3: Copy the following chart onto the board or overhead projector, leaving out the italicized answers. Have students complete the chart.

	Purpose	Result
Yalta Conference	*ensure lasting peace, decide how to deal with defeated nations*	*decided to establish UN and to partition Germany*
Allied Control Council	*to oversee temporary German government*	*members deadlocked on decisions; each ended up governing its own zone*
United Nations	*to prevent another war*	*41 nations drafted charter; members worked together to avoid conflict*

he would allow free elections and the establishment of democratic governments. In return, they agreed with Stalin that governments in these eastern countries must be friendly to the Soviet Union. Each side left Yalta believing its viewpoint had won.

For Stalin, however, friendly governments meant governments under Soviet control. In addition, he believed that free elections could take place only after eastern Europeans had learned socialist principles. As a result, Stalin's promise of free elections was meaningless from a Western point of view.

The three leaders also considered how to prevent another war. They disagreed considerably on this issue. Churchill and Stalin wanted the Allies to divide the world into spheres of influence. Roosevelt, however, called for an internationalist approach similar to that used for the League of Nations after World War I. He proposed a **United Nations** organization that would keep the peace through collective security arrangements. The initial plans for such an organization had already been worked out at a 1944 conference. At Yalta, the three leaders discussed the proposed charter for the organization and agreed on voting procedures to be followed.

✔ **READING CHECK: Identifying Cause and Effect** How did decisions made during the war affect the situation in postwar Europe? military occupation, plans for United Nations

The Occupation of Germany

After Germany's surrender in 1945, the Allies occupied their military zones and established temporary military governments. In July Allied leaders met at Potsdam, outside Berlin, to discuss a postwar settlement. Churchill, and later Clement Attlee, who had replaced Churchill as prime minister, represented Great Britain. Harry Truman, who became president after Roosevelt's death in April 1945, represented the United States. Stalin remained the Soviet representative.

Decisions at Potsdam. At Potsdam, the three leaders agreed on several basic principles: (1) Germany should remain a single country, although for the time being it would be divided, (2) Germany must be demilitarized, (3) the Nazi party must be outlawed, (4) German political structure should be rebuilt on a democratic basis, and (5) individuals responsible for war crimes should be brought to trial.

To oversee the occupation governments, the Allied leaders established the Allied Control Council. They also agreed that a Council of Foreign Ministers representing China, France, Great Britain, the Soviet Union, and the United States should write the peace treaties. As the councils began their work, however, it became clear that the Western democracies and the Soviet Union had very different plans for a postwar settlement. The major disagreements centered on two points: the boundaries of postwar Germany and war reparations.

Occupied Germany, 1945–1955

Interpreting Maps The Allies decided to divide Germany into zones of military occupation after the war.

■ **Skills Assessment:** **Using Geography** Why did the Soviet Union control the eastern portion of Germany?

Government

The secretary-general is the leader of the United Nations. He or she is elected every five years by the members of the General Assembly. During World War II, former members of the League of Nations drew up these guidelines for the type of person who should hold the position of secretary-general in the future United Nations: "[The person should be] young [and have] political or diplomatic experience, but not necessarily great fame or eminence." In addition, they said the person should at all times have "common sense, courage, integrity, and tact."

Critical Thinking

Ask students what type of person they think usually gets the Security Council's approval and nomination.

ANSWER: Successful candidates would be largely politically neutral and not very outspoken about volatile issues.

MAP ANSWER

Allied leaders had agreed that armies from each allied nation would be responsible for the territories they liberated from Nazi control.

TEACH OBJECTIVE 2

LEVEL 2: Ask students to explain why Germany was divided into four occupation zones. *(to defeat Germany)* Then have students list the decisions made at Potsdam. *(Germany should remain a single country, although for the time being it would be divided. Germany must be demilitarized. The Nazi party must be outlawed. German political structure should be rebuilt on a democratic basis. Individuals responsible for war crimes should be brought to trial.)*

TEACH OBJECTIVE 3

LEVEL 1: Direct students' attention to the "Organization of the United Nations" chart on page 823. Have students list the six main bodies of the UN. *(General Assembly, Security Council, Trusteeship Council, International Court of Justice, Economic and Social Council, Secretariat)* Then ask students to list and explain the purposes of the United Nations. *(maintain international peace and security; foster international cooperation to solve cultural, economic, and social problems)* **ENGLISH LANGUAGE LEARNERS**

Global Relations

The principles established in the Nürnberg trials were further developed and later became part of international law. In 1950 the International Law Commission outlined certain guiding principles and definitions of criminality. War crimes include violations of traditional treatment of civilians and prisoners in time of war. Crimes against peace include plans to begin a war of aggression. Crimes against humanity include extermination, enslavement, deportation, and other persecutions.

Critical Thinking

Ask students how war crimes differ from other crimes.

ANSWER: Students should answer that war crimes are committed through governmental policy against large numbers of people.

THEN & NOW ANSWER
murder and mistreatment of civilians, theft, racial or religious persecution, the killing of hostages

---

War Crimes

A "war crime" refers to any crime that violates the laws of war. Murder and mistreatment of a nation's civilian population are usually considered war crimes. Others include theft, racial or religious persecution, and the killing of hostages. The Nürnberg trials of 1945 helped nations agree on how to try suspected war criminals. International war crimes trials were held in 1996, when Bosnian Serb Dusko Tadic was sentenced to 20 years in prison for the torture and murder of prisoners of war. In 1999 former Yugoslav leader Slobodan Milošević was also indicted for war crimes in the Balkans. Milošević was taken into UN custody in June of 2001 and his trial began in 2002. **What actions taken during a war would be considered crimes?**

Redrawing borders. Stalin now insisted that the Soviet Union would retain territories in Poland and on the Baltic Sea gained as a result of the Nazi-Soviet Pact. To make up for lost territory, Poland should receive German territory to its west. The Allies agreed to the new western border for Poland. Both Poland and the Soviet Union took parts of East Prussia. This transfer of territory stripped Germany of one fourth of its land.

These territorial adjustments also led to a large increase in Germany's population. The Poles and Soviets evicted Germans from the lands they acquired. In addition, Czechoslovakia insisted that Sudeten Germans who had supported Hitler's invasion in 1938 must leave the country. The burden of feeding, housing, and employing these refugees fell on a shrunken and divided postwar Germany.

Demilitarization and reparations. The Allies swiftly disbanded all German land, air, and sea forces. They also demanded that all factories used in the war industry be dismantled. This plan proved difficult to enforce. The Allies had to determine what constituted a war industry. For example, a factory that manufactures tractors can easily be converted to produce tanks.

The Allies disagreed on German economic recovery. The United States and Britain concluded that German industry must be revived if Europe was to become prosperous again. France initially preferred to keep German industry weak to prevent future rearmament. The Soviets saw reparations as more important than reviving German industry. They demanded that Germany pay them $10 billion in reparations.

In the end, Western leaders agreed that the Soviets could claim reparations, mostly in the form of industrial equipment from all the military zones. The Soviets dismantled and moved hundreds of industrial plants from Germany to the Soviet Union. This practice severely hurt German industry's chances to recover. Eventually, the Western Allies halted the flow of reparations to the Soviet Union.

With such problems, the Allied Control Council found it increasingly difficult to reach decisions. The occupation governments soon began to ignore it and administered their territories as they saw fit.

The Nürnberg trials. After the war the full horror of the German concentration camps and the terrible consequences of Nazi racial purification were revealed to the world. Although Hitler was dead and many high-ranking Nazi officials had fled to South America, many Nazi leaders had been captured. The Allies were determined to bring them to trial. In 1945 and 1946, a special international court met at Nürnberg, Germany (also known as Nuremberg). At the **Nürnberg trials** the court charged 22 Nazi leaders with crimes against peace and humanity. In the end, 12 were sentenced to death, 7 were sentenced to life imprisonment, and 3 were acquitted. The court also declared the Nazi Party a criminal organization.

✔ **READING CHECK: Making Predictions** What might result from the temporary division of Germany? increase in population

This October 1946 photo was taken at the Nürnberg trial of the Nazi leaders.

TEACH OBJECTIVE 4

ALL LEVELS: Ask students why the Western Allies disagreed with Soviet plans for the future of Europe. (*Soviets wanted to establish communist governments, unlike the Allies who wanted free elections and representative governments.*) Have students explain under what condition Austria was restored as an independent, sovereign republic. (*It had to agree to remain neutral.*) Then ask students what happened to the division of Germany into eastern and western parts. (*It became a formal division into two countries.*)
ENGLISH LANGUAGE LEARNERS

HOMEWORK Ask students how the Allies treated Germany after World War II. Then ask students to compare this treatment with that following World War I.

CLOSE

Ask students to describe the actions taken by the Allies to deal with the atrocities committed during the war.

The United Nations

In April 1945 representatives from 51 nations met in San Francisco. This General Assembly agreed on a charter for the United Nations (UN). By October 1945, enough nations had ratified the charter to establish the UN. The primary purpose of the UN was to maintain international peace and security. It was also designed to foster international cooperation to solve cultural, economic, and social problems. A UN official explained why the organization's headquarters would be in the United States.

 History Makers Speak

“It was of paramount importance that the nerve-centre [of the United Nations] be located as close as possible to the new economic and political centre. . . . The challenging question of the future was how to secure the fullest possible U.S. participation in whatever international organizations might emerge.”

Trygve Lie, from *A History of the United States*

Even so, many Americans looked with skepticism at the UN. One person responsible for persuading many skeptics to support the new organization was former First Lady **Eleanor Roosevelt.**

The two most important bodies within the UN were the **General Assembly** and the **Security Council.** Any nation that wished to join would be admitted to the General Assembly. Each nation in the Assembly, regardless of its size or power, would have the same rights and voting power as any other nation. The Assembly was responsible for drawing up the UN budget and determining each member's share of the cost. The General Assembly also elected the secretary-general and the judges of the International Court of Peace.

The Security Council included 10 temporary members elected from the General Assembly for two-year rotating terms. Five nations—Britain, China, France, the Soviet Union, and the United States—were permanent members. Each permanent member could prevent the council from taking action by using its **veto power**—the power to defeat a measure with a single vote. The Security Council was designed to satisfy those who felt some members should have more influence than others.

✔ **READING CHECK: Drawing Inferences** Why did the planners of the United Nations make some nations permanent members of the Security Council? to give them more influence

Analyzing Primary Sources

Decision Making What two reasons did Lie offer for deciding to locate the UN headquarters in the United States? to be near the economic and political center, to secure U.S. participation

HISTORY MAKER

Eleanor Roosevelt (1884–1962)

As the niece of one president of the United States and the wife of another, Eleanor Roosevelt grew up with politics in her blood. Her willingness to tackle tough issues made Roosevelt one of the most admired first ladies ever.

Roosevelt also wrote more than a dozen books and a weekly newspaper column. She later served as the U.S. delegate to the United Nations. Her good works and compassion earned her the nickname "First Lady of the World." **Why was Eleanor Roosevelt admired?**

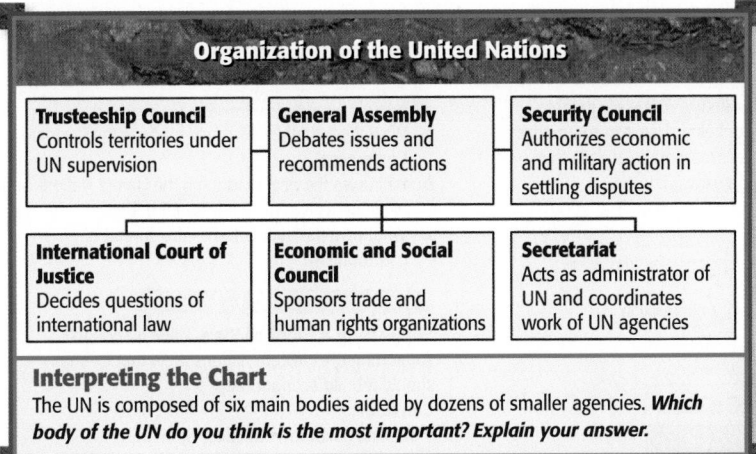

Organization of the United Nations

Trusteeship Council Controls territories under UN supervision	**General Assembly** Debates issues and recommends actions	**Security Council** Authorizes economic and military action in settling disputes
International Court of Justice Decides questions of international law	**Economic and Social Council** Sponsors trade and human rights organizations	**Secretariat** Acts as administrator of UN and coordinates work of UN agencies

Interpreting the Chart
The UN is composed of six main bodies aided by dozens of smaller agencies. *Which body of the UN do you think is the most important? Explain your answer.*

REVIEW

Have students complete the Section 1 Review on p. 824.

ASSESS

Have students complete Daily Quiz 31.1. As Alternative Assessment, you may want to use one of the chart activities in this section's lessons.

RETEACH

Have students complete Main Idea Activity for English Language Learners and Special-Needs Students 31.1. Then have students list the main ideas of each heading and subheading in the section. **ENGLISH LANGUAGE LEARNERS**

EXTEND

Have each student write a letter to the editor of a fictional 1945 newspaper commenting on the Nürnberg trials. Students may write in the roles of Americans or Europeans. The point of view expressed in each letter should be realistic and should be supported by historical facts. **BLOCK SCHEDULING**

Peacemaking Problems

The war undermined or destroyed many governments in Europe. As they emerged from the shambles of the war, many European states established new forms of government. In 1946 the Italian people voted to abolish the monarchy and become a republic. In France Charles de Gaulle headed a temporary government until a new constitution was adopted in 1946.

In Eastern Europe the Soviets established temporary governments in the countries they had liberated. These governments were dominated or controlled outright by communists, despite the anticommunist feelings of the majority of the population. It soon became clear that the Soviet Union and the Western Allies had conflicting goals for postwar Europe.

In February 1947 the Council of Foreign Ministers reached agreement on several peace treaties. Italy gave up claims in countries it had invaded during the war and lost other territory. Its colonies were placed under the authority of the United Nations. Bulgaria, Finland, Hungary, and Romania also had to return territory and accept changes to their prewar boundaries. In addition, they had to reduce their armed forces and pay reparations to invaded nations.

As the Red Army rolled across Eastern and Central Europe, Stalin insisted on placing governments friendly to Soviet interests in power in the liberated nations.

The peace negotiations exposed growing differences between the Soviet Union and the Western Allies. The Soviets insisted that communists control the governments of Eastern European nations so that the Soviet Union would be safe from future invasion. The Western Allies wanted free elections and representative governments. In the end, a compromise was reached. The Soviets agreed to allow a few representatives of noncommunist parties to participate in the new Eastern European governments.

The Allies could not reach agreements on the most important treaties. The four-way occupation of Austria continued until 1955. That year a treaty restored Austria as an independent, sovereign republic within its 1930 boundaries. For its part, Austria had to agree to remain neutral. In the case of Germany, the Allies never reached a final settlement. The division of Germany into eastern and western parts eventually became a formal division into two countries.

✔ **READING CHECK: Contrasting** How did Soviet plans for the future of Europe differ from those of the Western Allies? Soviets wanted communist-controlled governments.

SECTION 1 REVIEW

1. **Define** and explain the significance:
   veto power

2. **Identify** and explain the significance:
   United Nations
   Nürnberg trials
   Eleanor Roosevelt
   General Assembly
   Security Council

3. **Summarizing** Copy the graphic organizer below. Use it to summarize the agreements made at Yalta that affected postwar Europe.

4. **Finding the Main Idea**
   a. What were the key decisions made at the Postdam Conference?
   b. What was the goal in forming the United Nations and what are its two most important bodies?
   c. What postwar events led to the spread of communism?

5. **Writing and Critical Thinking**
   Supporting a Point of View Write an editorial supporting the Western nations' view that Germany should rebuild economically.
   Consider:
   • the Allied plan for rebuilding Germany
   • the conflict over territorial adjustments and reparations

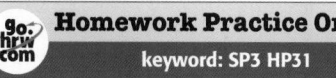

Homework Practice Online
keyword: SP3 HP31

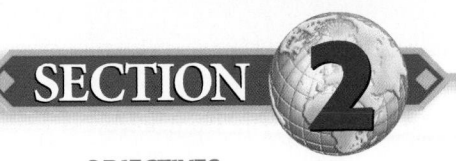

SECTION 2

OBJECTIVES

1 **Examine how and why the alliance between the Western Allies and the Soviet Union ended.**

2 **Investigate how the United States attempted to stop the spread of communism and aid Europe.**

3 **Describe how Germany became two separate countries.**

4 **Identify the Cold War alliances that developed in Europe.**

🔊 LET'S GET STARTED!

As students enter the classroom, ask them what they know about the Truman Doctrine, the Marshall Plan, NATO, and the Warsaw Pact. Some students may not know anything about them; others may be able to provide some information. List responses on the board. Then tell students that in Section 2 they will learn about these plans and agreements.

SECTION 2

READ TO DISCOVER

1 How and why did the alliance between the Western Allies and the Soviet Union end?
2 How did the United States attempt to stop the spread of communism and aid Europe?
3 How did Germany become two separate countries?
4 What Cold War alliances developed in Europe?

DEFINE

containment

IDENTIFY

Cold War
Truman Doctrine
Marshall Plan
Cominform
Berlin Airlift
NATO
Warsaw Pact

WHY IT MATTERS TODAY

The North Atlantic Treaty Organization still exists today. Use [CNN Student News.com] or other **current event** sources to learn which nations currently belong to NATO and what recent actions it has taken. Record your findings in your journal.

[CNN Student News.com]

Origins of the Cold War

The Main Idea
The wartime alliance between the Soviet Union and Western powers ended, leading to a Cold War.

The Story Continues *At one meeting during the 1943 conference in Tehran, President Roosevelt teased Winston Churchill so much that Joseph Stalin laughed. Roosevelt recalled, "From that day on our relations were personal. . . . The ice was broken and we talked like men and brothers." Friendly relations between the United States and the Soviet Union, however, soon proved impossible to maintain.*

The End of the Alliance

Disagreements between the Soviet Union and the Western Allies eventually caused the alliance that had defeated the Axis Powers to dissolve. In its place, a new rivalry emerged. On one side was the Soviet Union, supported by the communist nations of the world. The Soviet Union and its allies were sometimes called the Eastern bloc. On the other side was the United States, supported by the Western democracies and other noncommunist nations.

This struggle between communism and democracy occasionally led to bloody local wars. For the most part, however, it was a war of ideas and worldviews waged by the two superpowers, the Soviet Union and the United States. As a result, the struggle quickly became known as the **Cold War.**

The two sides in the Cold War had completely different economic and political systems. Each side naturally believed that its own system should be the model for European reconstruction. In addition, each side was concerned with its own future security. The Soviet Union was determined to protect itself from any future attack from the West. Thus, Stalin created a buffer zone of communist nations along the western frontier of the Soviet Union.

The Western powers regarded Stalin's buffer zone as evidence that the Soviets hoped to expand and one day dominate all of Europe. Soviet actions fueled their fears. Stalin insisted that the Soviet Union retain territories it had gained in the Nazi-Soviet Pact, and he installed a pro-Soviet government in Poland. This seemed to violate the agreement Stalin made at Yalta regarding free elections.

ВСЁ ДЛЯ ФРОНТА!

ДАДИМ КРАСНОЙ АРМИИ БОЛЬШЕ
ТАНКОВ, САМОЛЕТОВ, ОРУДИЙ, ПУЛЕМЕТОВ
ВИНТОВОК, СНАРЯДОВ, ПАТРОНОВ!

Shown here is a Soviet propaganda poster from the mid-1940s. The theme of this poster reflects the military and industrial buildup that would continue throughout the Cold War.

SECTION 2 RESOURCES

REPRODUCIBLE RESOURCES

▶ Guided Reading Strategy 31.2
▶ Graphic Organizer Activity 31: Cold War Alliances
▶ Readings in World History 112: Soviet Dissidents Decry the Invasion of Czechoslovakia
▶ Creative Teaching Strategy 31: A Cold War Era Atlas

TECHNOLOGY RESOURCES

▶ One-Stop Planner 31.2
▶ Holt Researcher: World History: Harry Truman
▶ CNN Presents World Cultures: Yesterday and Today Segment 30: NATO at 50
▶ Homework Practice Online
▶ Online Maps: Communist Europe in 1949

REINFORCEMENT, REVIEW, AND ASSESSMENT

▶ Section 2 Review, p. 830
▶ Daily Quiz 31.2
▶ Main Idea Activity 31.2
▶ English Audio Summary 31.2
▶ Spanish Audio Summary 31.2

ALL LEVELS: Organize students into groups of three and have each triad develop an illustrated time line of the events that contributed to the development of the Cold War. Time lines should cover the years 1945 through 1968, though you might wish to encourage students to go back as far as the Russian Revolution and as far forward as the fall of the Iron Curtain. **ENGLISH LANGUAGE LEARNERS, COOPERATIVE LEARNING**

LEVEL 3: Have students read the subsection "The Truman Doctrine" on pages 826–827. Ask students to define *containment. (the policy of restricting the spread of communism wherever possible)* Then ask them what they think might have been different if the United States had not instituted the Truman Doctrine. *(Answers will vary but most will probably say that countries like Turkey and Greece would have fallen quickly under communist aggression, and the Iron Curtain would have continued to expand across a weakened Europe.)* Have students create two political cartoons commenting on the Truman Doctrine from opposing points of view.

Global Relations

Although most of Europe was divided between the communist and democratic camps, some nations remained neutral. These nations, which included Sweden, Switzerland, and Austria, maintained a foreign policy of nonalignment in peace and neutrality in war. They worked to maintain independence from alliances with either side by defending their territory against all opponents. This stance resulted in dissuasion, a policy that deterred potential opponents from invading while reassuring those same opponents that their enemies would be similarly discouraged.

Critical Thinking

Ask students to name a disadvantage of the policy of armed neutrality.

ANSWER: Students might answer that if an enemy invaded a neutral country, the armed neutral could not count on other countries to help it.

Technology Resources

 World History and Cultures Video Program 26: Television and the Cold War

In 1947 President Truman speaks to Congress.

go.hrw.com
KEYWORD: Holt Researcher
FreeFind: Harry Truman
After reading more about Harry Truman on the Holt Researcher, analyze one of his controversial political decisions, taking historical context into account.

Analyzing Primary Sources

Contrasting How did Truman summarize the different ways of life of communist and democratic countries? will of the majority and will of the minority

More militaristic actions followed. Stalin massed troops along the border of Turkey. He demanded the return of territory in Caucasia that had once been taken by the czars. Stalin also insisted upon joint Soviet-Turkish control over the straits that connected the Black Sea to the Aegean and Mediterranean Seas. Such control would guarantee the Soviet Union's naval fleet an outlet to the Mediterranean. In February 1946 Stalin announced that the communist struggle for worldwide revolution would continue. In March Soviet forces that had occupied Iran during the war refused to withdraw. Instead, they supported the establishment of a communist party in Iran.

To the West, Soviet policy seemed to be based on expansion, not self-defense. Pressure from the United States and Britain forced Stalin to back down from his positions on Turkey and Iran. When a political crisis broke out in Greece in 1947, the United States finally decided to intervene.

✔ **READING CHECK: Summarizing** What actions led Western nations to believe that the Soviets wanted to dominate Europe? created buffer zone of communist nations on western frontier of Soviet Union

The United States Aids Europe

By 1944 the Nazis had withdrawn from Greece. A civil war then broke out between communists and conservatives loyal to the monarchy. Great Britain, which supported the royalists, negotiated a truce in 1945. In the summer of 1946, however, the communists renewed the civil war. They received aid from the new communist governments in Albania, Bulgaria, and Yugoslavia. The Greek government turned once again to the British for help.

Britain was exhausted and almost bankrupted by the war. In February 1947 the British informed the United States that they would end financial aid to Greece and Turkey and withdraw their troops from Greece. Britain hoped the United States would come to aid those countries to prevent communist domination of the region.

The Truman Doctrine. On March 12, 1947, President Harry Truman spoke before Congress. He offered his perception of the postwar world.

 ❝At the present moment in world history nearly every nation must choose between alternative ways of life. . . . One way of life is based upon the will of the majority, and is distinguished by free institutions, representative government, free elections, guarantees of individual liberty, freedom of speech and religion, and freedom from political oppression. The second way of life is based upon the will of a minority forcibly imposed upon the majority. It relies upon terror and oppression, a controlled press and radio, fixed elections, and the suppression of personal freedoms.❞

Harry Truman, from *Public Papers of the Presidents*

Truman went on to set forth a policy that is called the **Truman Doctrine.** He declared that the United States must consider the continued spread of communism to be a threat to democracy. He argued that the United States must "support free peoples who are resisting attempted subjugation [takeover] by armed minorities or by outside pressures." Truman asked Congress to provide $400 million to help defend Greece and

The Marshall Plan emphasized the need for European countries to agree on a plan of action before the United States stepped in. Discuss reasons why the United States placed restrictions on the assistance it offered. *(Answers will vary. One reasonable response would be that the United States hoped to solve the economic problems in Europe rather than simply offer a temporary fix. The conditions associated with economic aid were designed to restore what the U.S. government hoped would be longterm peace and prosperity.)*

Turkey from communist aggression. Congress agreed. With U.S. technical and financial assistance, the Greek government ended the rebellion.

To carry out the Truman Doctrine, the United States would not try to stamp out communism in countries where it already existed. If a country requested assistance to prevent a communist takeover, the United States would offer materials, money, and technical knowledge. Thus, the United States committed itself to contain, or restrict, the spread of communism. This policy became known as **containment.**

The Marshall Plan. Western leaders feared that ongoing poverty in war-torn Europe would drive Europeans into communist parties. Thus, the United States announced a new plan of massive economic assistance. Called the **Marshall Plan** after U.S. Secretary of State General George Marshall, the European Recovery Program also encouraged European nations to work together. They were to determine their needs and remove trade barriers so that goods could flow freely across the continent. Eventually, 17 European nations participated in the Marshall Plan. The United States also offered aid to the Soviet Union and Eastern European nations under Soviet control, but those nations rejected the offer.

Between 1948 and 1952, the United States spent over $13 billion on the Marshall Plan. By 1952 European farm and industrial production was above prewar levels. Europe was on the road to prosperity. The United States also benefited from the Marshall Plan, as it supplied export goods to the recovering European economies.

In 1949 as a response to the Marshall Plan, the Soviet Union founded the Council for Mutual Assistance, COMECON, to develop economic cooperation among Eastern European nations. Because the Soviet Union could not adequately fund the program, it did not suceed.

✔ **READING CHECK: Finding the Main Idea** In what ways did the United States aid Europe after the war? Marshall Plan provided economic aid

The Cold War in Europe

The Soviets regarded the Truman Doctrine as an effort to encircle and undermine the Soviet Union. They denounced the Marshall Plan as an American capitalist effort to dominate Europe economically. In September 1947 the Soviets established the Communist Information Bureau, or **Cominform,** to oppose the Marshall Plan. This organization included all European communist parties. The Cominform, however, was unsuccessful in opposing Marshall Plan aid. Its major effect was to create tension between communist and noncommunist parties in Europe.

Eastern and Central Europe. As the West put its containment policy into place, the Soviets tightened their grip on Eastern and Central Europe. In 1948 communists overthrew the democratic government of Czechoslovakia. They turned the nation into a one-party communist state and a member of the Eastern bloc. Only one break appeared in the division between East and West. Marshall Tito of Yugoslavia, a devoted communist, objected to Soviet domination. He announced that Yugoslavia would follow an independent path. By June 1948 Yugoslavia was expelled from Cominform.

INTERPRETING THE VISUAL RECORD

The Marshall Plan The photo below shows a shipment of sugar provided under the Marshall Plan arriving in London. *What does this image tell you about the types of aid needed by people in European countries?*

Economics

In order to convince Congress to supply $400 million in aid to Greece's efforts to withstand communist aggression, Truman stated his belief in the probability of a domino effect taking place in the Middle East. If Greece were to fall, he argued, then a weakened Turkey would soon follow. And if Turkey toppled, the Middle East would be open to a communist takeover and formerly pro-Western nations would be absorbed into the Communist bloc. So members of Congress who were skeptical of the need for U.S. intervention in trouble spots around the globe were persuaded to support not only immediate aid to Greece and Turkey but also the Truman Doctrine in general.

Critical Thinking

Ask students why the domino theory was a particularly effective persuasive device in getting Congress to approve the Truman Doctrine.

ANSWER: Although most Americans would probably have little real interest in one or two nations falling under communist rule, most feared a widespread communist takeover because it would mean a loss of potential allies while the enemy grew stronger.

VISUAL RECORD ANSWER

needed food

EUROPE AND NORTH AMERICA IN THE POSTWAR YEARS **827**

LEVEL 1: Ask students to describe the Berlin airlift. *(provided food and supplies to the inhabitants of the western part of the city)* Ask them what consequence resulted from the Berlin blockade. *(the division of Germany)* Have students explain why the division of Germany was symbolic of the Cold War in general. *(It symbolized the division between communism in the East and democratic government in the West.)* **ENGLISH LANGUAGE LEARNERS**

HOMEWORK Ask students if they think the Truman Doctrine and the Marshall Plan were appropriate and effective actions at the time they were instituted. Have students write a paragraph that explains their opinions.

That's Interesting!

The term *cold war* was coined by American journalist Herbert Bayard Swope. However, its usage was popularized by journalist and political commentator Walter Lippmann.

☑ internet connect

TOPIC: Cold War
GO TO: go.hrw.com
KEYWORD: SP3 WH31

Have students access the Internet through the HRW Go site to learn more about the Cold War. Tell them to look for elements of popular culture that reflect Cold War anxieties and attitudes and to collect three to five examples. For each example, have students write a paragraph that explains how it reflects a Cold War attitude.

Problems in Germany. By 1948 it was clear that joint government in Germany by the four former Allies was impossible. The three Western powers had taken steps to reunite their zones economically and to revive democracy in Germany. It became clear that they were moving toward a unified German state.

The Soviets bitterly opposed reunification. In June 1948 they blockaded the East German border to all land and water traffic into Berlin from the west. The people of West Berlin soon faced starvation. Western nations reacted swiftly. The United States and Great Britain organized an airlift to supply West Berlin. The **Berlin Airlift** provided food and supplies daily to the inhabitants of the western part of the city. One inhabitant of West Berlin recalled those times:

Analyzing Primary Sources

Drawing Inferences According to this West Berliner, what did the Berlin Airlift do for the residents besides just providing supplies?
provided certainty that they were not alone

History Makers Speak

❝Early in the morning, when we woke up, the first thing we did was listen to see whether the noise of aircraft engines could be heard. That gave us the certainty that we were not alone, that the whole civilized world took part in the fight for Berlin's freedom.❞

Anonymous Berliner, quoted in *Bridge in the Sky,* by Frank Donovan

The airlift operated so efficiently that raw materials were also supplied to West Berlin factories. As a warning to the Soviets, the United States also stationed long-range bombers in Great Britain. The Soviets made no real efforts to stop the airlift and in May 1949 lifted the blockade.

The division of Germany. The Berlin blockade might be seen as the "official" beginning of the Cold War. It also had one immediate and important consequence—the division of Germany. With the approval of the Western Allies, in May 1949 a constitutional assembly declared the Federal Republic of Germany. Popularly known as West Germany, the nation had its capital in Bonn. The Soviet Union followed suit, establishing the German Democratic Republic—also known as East Germany—in October 1949. The division of Germany became a symbol of the East-West division of the Cold War.

✔ **READING CHECK: Problem Solving** Was the division of Germany the best solution to disagreements over its future? Explain. Students might note that East-West tensions continued.

Supplies were airlifted into an isolated West Berlin by the United States and Great Britain.

During the airlift, each child's ration consisted of just a slice of dark bread and margarine.

LEVEL 2: Draw the following Venn diagram on the board or overhead projector, leaving out the italicized sample answers. Ask students to help you fill in the similarities and differences between NATO and the Warsaw Pact.

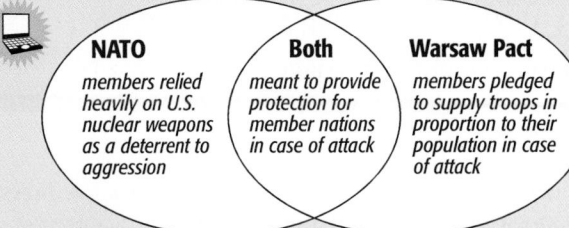

NATO
members relied heavily on U.S. nuclear weapons as a deterrent to aggression

Both
meant to provide protection for member nations in case of attack

Warsaw Pact
members pledged to supply troops in proportion to their population in case of attack

CLOSE

Ask students to describe the functions of NATO and the Warsaw Pact. Then have them explain why these alliances were formed.

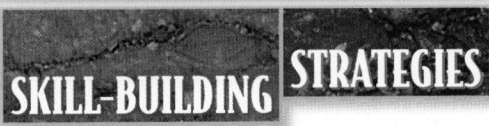

SKILL-BUILDING STRATEGIES
Transferring Information from One Medium to Another

Cold War Alliances

When the United States and its allies formed NATO, an alliance for mutual protection, the Soviet Union and its allies did the same through the Warsaw Pact. As the United States became more important to global defense, the country wound up spending more money on military defense even during times of relative peace.

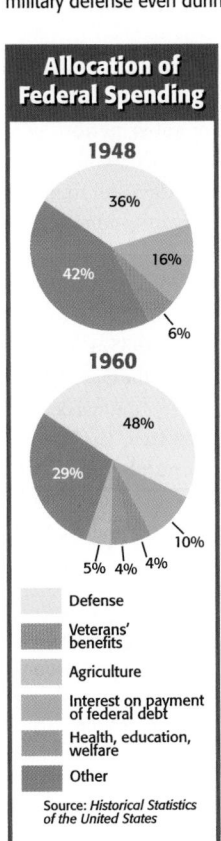

Allocation of Federal Spending

1948
36%
42%
16%
6%

1960
48%
29%
10%
5% 4% 4%

- Defense
- Veterans' benefits
- Agriculture
- Interest on payment of federal debt
- Health, education, welfare
- Other

Source: *Historical Statistics of the United States*

European Alliances, 1955

Skills Reminder

Information about a complicated historical topic such as the Cold War is often conveyed through various media: verbal, visual or graphic, and statistical. The ability to transfer information from one form to another—writing a paragraph to summarize a chart or graph, for example—will help you more easily comprehend and remember the information. To transfer information from one medium to another, identify the main idea. Choose the necessary details appropriate for the medium you are going to use. Create the new form of information. In making charts, maps, or graphs, use the steps you have learned. Finally, evaluate the new medium. Make sure you have accurately and clearly conveyed the original information.

Skills Practice

❶ Study the map above. Make a chart that lists the members of NATO and the Warsaw Pact by 1955.
❷ Study the graph above. Why do you think the portion of U.S. spending devoted to defense increased so much between 1948 and 1960?
❸ Using databases on the Internet, find information about Soviet defense spending in the late 1940s and 1950s and create a graph that illustrates this information.
❹ Using all the information you have gathered, write a short essay explaining how the formation of NATO and the Warsaw Pact affected government spending in the United States and the Soviet Union.

Government

Friendship, mutual assistance, and cooperation were the foundation of the Warsaw Pact. This agreement allowed the Soviet Union to maintain a military presence in surrounding nations. Defense treaties were designed to promote cooperation, but in this pact, national armies were limited to internal security tasks while military power was retained by the Soviet armed forces.

Critical Thinking

Ask students why the Soviets wanted to maintain command of other nations' armed forces.

ANSWER: to control military forces on their borders and crush opposition to communism in Eastern bloc countries

SKILLS PRACTICE ANSWERS

1. NATO: Norway, Denmark, Netherlands, United Kingdom, Northern Ireland, Belgium, Luxembourg, France, Portugal, Italy, Greece, Federal Republic of Germany; Warsaw Pact: German Democratic Republic, Poland, Czechoslovakia, Hungary, Romania, Bulgaria, Soviet Union, Albania

2. Cold War caused the U.S. to spend more on defense.

3. Students' graphs will vary.

4. Students' essays will vary.

REVIEW

Have students complete the Section 2 Review on p. 830.

ASSESS

Have students complete Daily Quiz 31.2. As Alternative Assessment, you may want to use the time line or Venn diagram exercises in this section's lessons.

RETEACH

Have students complete Main Idea Activity for English Language Learners and Special-Needs Students 31.2. Then have students

compile a Cold War glossary. Their glossaries should contain and define abbreviations such as the UN and NATO, as well as Cold War terms such as the Marshall Plan.
ENGLISH LANGUAGE LEARNERS, COOPERATIVE LEARNING

EXTEND

Have students work individually or in pairs to write encyclopedia entries for the Truman Doctrine, the Marshall Plan, the Berlin airlift, NATO, and the Warsaw Pact. **BLOCK SCHEDULING, COOPERATIVE LEARNING**

SECTION 2 REVIEW ANSWERS

❶ Define
- containment, p. 827

❷ Identify
- Cold War, p. 825
- Truman Doctrine, p. 826
- Marshall Plan, p. 827
- Cominform, p. 827
- Berlin Airlift, p. 828
- NATO, p. 830
- Warsaw Pact, p. 830

❸ Students' charts should include Truman Doctrine, Marshall Plan, Cominform, and division of Germany.

❹ a. to create a buffer zone; as evidence that the Soviets hoped to expand and dominate all of Europe

b. They both provided aid to other countries in an attempt to stop the spread of communism.

c. divided into East and West

❺ Paragraphs should include the goals and purposes of the alliances.

Technology Resources

World History Teaching Transparency: Geography and History 26: Cold War Defenses

NATO and the Warsaw Pact

The division of Germany was one of a series of events in 1949 and 1950 that made clear the split between East and West. In the summer of 1949, the Soviets detonated their first atomic bomb. In October 1949 armies of the Chinese Communist Party defeated the Chinese Nationalist Government, driving the Nationalists off the mainland to the island of Taiwan. In 1950 North Korean communist forces invaded South Korea. These events reminded the world that the Cold War might all too quickly grow hot.

Because of the East-West split, new political and military alliances formed. In April 1949 twelve Western nations signed the treaty creating the North Atlantic Treaty Organization (**NATO**). Signers agreed that if one member nation were attacked, all members would take united action against the aggressor. Greece and Turkey joined NATO in 1952, and West Germany followed in 1955. All member nations contributed to a NATO military force. Eventually the organization came to rely heavily on U.S. nuclear weapons to deter Soviet invasion of Western Europe.

After West Germany joined NATO, the Soviet Union responded by creating a formal alliance of its own. In May 1955 a meeting was held with representatives of the Eastern bloc. These nations adopted a 20-year mutual defense agreement called the **Warsaw Pact.** The Warsaw Pact troops greatly outnumbered NATO troops in Europe. The overwhelming difference in ground troops between NATO and the Warsaw Pact reinforced the Western powers' reliance on using nuclear weapons as a deterrent.

In this picture U.S. President Harry Truman signs the North Atlantic Pact, which created NATO. Shown above is the NATO emblem.

✔ **READING CHECK: Identifying Cause and Effect** Why did Western nations and nations of the Eastern bloc form alliances? for mutual protection against aggression

SECTION 2 REVIEW

1. **Define** and explain the significance:
   containment

2. **Identify** and explain the significance:
   Cold War
   Truman Doctrine
   Marshall Plan
   Cominform
   Berlin Airlift
   NATO
   Warsaw Pact

3. **Sequencing** Make a flowchart like the one below to sequence the main events that led to the Cold War.

4. **Finding the Main Idea**
   a. Why did Stalin want to control Eastern Europe? How did Western nations perceive his actions?
   b. How were the Truman Doctrine and the Marshall Plan part of the containment policy?
   c. What happened in Germany as a result of the Cold War?

5. **Writing and Critical Thinking**
   Identifying a Point of View Write a paragraph explaining why NATO and the Warsaw Pact were formed.
   Consider:
   • the goal of NATO
   • the purpose of the Warsaw Pact

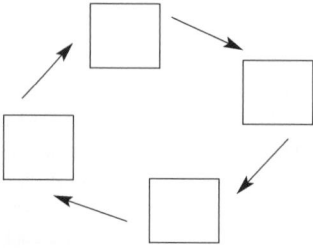
Homework Practice Online
keyword: SP3 HP31

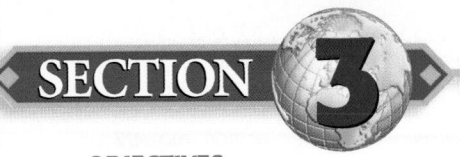

SECTION 3

OBJECTIVES

1 **Describe the West German "miracle."**

2 **Explain why the British met with mixed success in stimulating economic growth.**

3 **Explore how France maintained an independent position in European affairs.**

4 **Analyze how the Soviet Union changed under new leadership.**

5 **Identify the problems Eastern European nations faced.**

LET'S GET STARTED!

As students enter the classroom, ask them to recall the primary economic policy adopted worldwide after World War I. *(economic nationalism—high protective tariffs and trade restrictions)* Then ask them to discuss the results of this policy. *(failure and global depression—nearly every country that practiced it was hurt by it)* Tell students that in Section 3 they will examine how countries around the world tried to avoid a similar economic catastrophe after the second world war.

SECTION 3

READ TO DISCOVER

❶ What was the West German "miracle"?

❷ Why did the British meet with mixed success in stimulating economic growth?

❸ How did France maintain an independent position in European affairs?

❹ How did the Soviet Union change under new leadership?

❺ What problems did Eastern European nations face?

DEFINE

welfare state

IDENTIFY

Berlin Wall
Common Market
European Community
Nikita Khrushchev

WHY IT MATTERS TODAY

European integration remains an important issue today. Use ![CNN Student News.com] or other **current event** sources to learn about recent efforts at cooperation and integration between European nations. Record your findings in your journal.

Reconstruction, Reform, and Reaction in Europe

The Main Idea
While many Western European nations prospered after World War II, Eastern Europe faced difficulties.

The Story Continues *Author Marion Dönhoff described the devastation he witnessed in Germany as the war came to an end. "We spent the nights around camp fires on the road or else in the barns of abandoned farmyards; every dawn brought the same scene: dying children and old people closing their eyes which reflected the fear and anxiety and suffering of generations." Would it be possible for a nation in such ruin to rebuild after the war?*

The West German "Miracle"

After the war the Western Allies remained committed to democracy and the principle of majority rule. Economically, they continued to accept the basic principles of capitalism. They believed in some form of a market economy. In a market economy, competition among private businesses and individuals determines what goods will be produced, how they will be produced, and what they will cost.

West German economic recovery. West Germany followed this free-market policy. The reconstruction and industrial development of the nation progressed at a remarkably rapid rate. In fact, some people called it the German "miracle."

During the postwar years, the West German government provided housing and jobs to many refugees from East Germany and other Eastern European nations. The labor of these refugees contributed to West Germany's rapidly growing economy. German industry flourished, thanks to technological innovation, a commitment to quality, and few labor troubles. The West German unit of currency, the Deutsche mark, became one of the most stable in the world. By 1958 West Germany was the leading industrial nation in Western Europe.

The West German automobile industry was one of the business successes that helped boost economic recovery after World War II.

SECTION 3 RESOURCES

REPRODUCIBLE RESOURCES

▶ Guided Reading Strategy 31.3

▶ Geography Activity 31: The Berlin Wall

▶ Readings in World History 111: The Battle of the Sorbonne

TECHNOLOGY RESOURCES

▶ One-Stop Planner 31.3

▶ Holt Researcher: World History: Nikita Khrushchev

▶ World History Teaching Transparency: Everyday Life 25: Russian Tanks in Berlin

▶ Homework Practice Online

▶ Online Maps, Charts, and Graphs: Europe

REINFORCEMENT, REVIEW, AND ASSESSMENT

▶ Section 3 Review, p. 836

▶ Daily Quiz 31.3

▶ Main Idea Activity 31.3

▶ English Audio Summary 31.3

▶ Spanish Audio Summary 31.3

LEVEL 3: Organize students into groups and assign each group one of the following topics: West Germany, Great Britain, France, or Other Western European Nations. Have students work in their groups to fill in the following chart. Then have each group evaluate the effectiveness of each policy or program and summarize their opinions for the class. If students feel that a nation's policies were lacking, encourage them to offer alternative ideas that might have been more effective.

COOPERATIVE LEARNING

	Economic policies	Results
West Germany	free market economy	"miracle" recovery
Great Britain	welfare state	slow economic growth, low productivity
France	help from Marshall Plan	slow recovery, political instability
Other Western European Nations	varied; generally focused on free-enterprise systems	varied; differing rates of political and economic stability

Culture

India had been a British colony since the 1700s. After World War II, the Indian nationalist movement led by Mohandas Gandhi and Jawaharlal Nehru found success when the new, more liberal, Prime Minister Clement Attlee announced that India would be granted full independence. In 1947 India became independent but was plunged into even more turmoil as religious factions began fighting for dominance. Now one of the largest democracies in the world, India still faces widespread poverty and the continuing bitter religious rivalry between Muslims and Hindus.

Critical Thinking

Ask students why the conflict between Muslims and Hindus came to the forefront only after India was granted independence.

ANSWER: Before India gained independence the two factions may have been united in their efforts to end British rule; after India became independent, the two groups may have begun fighting for dominance.

In 1961 more than 1,000 East Germans were fleeing to West Berlin every day. To halt the flow, East Germany built the Berlin Wall. After its construction, more than 170 people died trying to escape over it.

Clement Attlee (front row, center) is surrounded by supporters after his Labour Party wins the 1945 election and Attlee becomes prime minister.

Politics. West Germany had also become one of the world's most stable democracies. In the postwar era two parties, the Christian Democrats and the Social Democrats, dominated West German politics. The first West German chancellor, Konrad Adenauer, was a Christian Democrat. Adenauer was committed to a market economy and establishing the rule of law as a principle of the German state.

A dedicated anticommunist and anti-Soviet, Adenauer also closely aligned with the West. Under his guidance, Germany joined NATO in 1955. He also encouraged Germans in the Soviet bloc to escape to the West. Many did so, particularly in Berlin. In response, in 1961 the East German government erected a wall separating the two halves of the city. Anyone caught trying to escape over the wall was shot. The **Berlin Wall,** with its cap of barbed wire, became a major symbol of the Cold War.

Adenauer retired from office in 1963. Another Christian Democrat, Ludwig Erhard, became chancellor. Erhard had in many ways been the architect of the free-market polices that produced the "German miracle." Under Erhard's leadership, West Germany continued to prosper, but the rate of economic growth slowed. In 1966 the country experienced a mild recession, or economic slowdown. Worries over the economy and the Christian Democrat's foreign policy of complete alignment with the United States caused many Germans to turn to the Social Democrats. In 1969 the Social Democrats won a national majority under their leader, Willy Brandt.

✔ **READING CHECK: Analyzing Information** What elements of Adenauer's leadership helped economic growth and democracy in West Germany? commitment to market economy, rule of law, aligned with West

Postwar Britain

As West Germany pursued free-market polices, Great Britain moved in the opposite direction. In 1945 British voters rejected Winston Churchill's Conservative Party. The Labour Party, a moderate socialist party, formed Britain's postwar government.

Under Labour Party leadership, Great Britain became a **welfare state**—a state in which the government takes primary responsibility for the social welfare of its citizens. The British government provided free medical care for everyone. It nationalized the Bank of England, coal mines, railroads, and utilities. It did not, however, interfere with most industry, which remained privately owned.

For years after the war, Great Britain faced economic problems. Its industrial equipment was inefficient and outdated. Many workers had died in the war. Some scientists and managers had emigrated to Australia, Canada, or the United States. After the war Great Britain lost valuable colonies and possessions. The cost of its remaining overseas commitments was a heavy burden.

In 1951 voters elected a new Conservative government to power. As prime minister once again, Winston Churchill reversed some of the Labour government's nationalization policies. However, the general outlines of the British welfare state remained in place under the Conservatives.

Britain continued to lag behind the rest of Europe in economic recovery. Industrial growth was much slower than in other countries. In fact, in the 1960s Great Britain's industrial productivity fell to one of the lowest national levels in the industrialized world.

LEVEL 1: Ask students to describe France's position in European affairs after the war. *(remained independent)* Have them list steps France took to maintain this position. *(withdrew French forces from NATO command; opposed U.S. and British influence in Europe)* **ENGLISH LANGUAGE LEARNERS**

 HOMEWORK Have students explain why economic cooperation among European countries was imperative after World War II.

One cause of this decline was the shift in the world economy from coal to oil and nuclear power as energy resources. Britain's strength had long been its coal reserves. The Labour Party blamed the Conservatives for the poor economy, but it did no better when holding the majority itself.

✔ **READING CHECK: Identifying Cause and Effect** Why did the British economy face continuing difficulties in the postwar era? loss of workers and colonies, cost of overseas commitments, shift from coal to oil and nuclear power

New Republics in France

Postwar France also faced difficulties. During the war France had suffered considerable damage. Towns and cities were destroyed; farmlands were ravaged. At war's end inflation caused even more hardship for the French people. Jean Monnet, a French economist, crafted policies to revive the economy. In addition the Marshall Plan provided economic assistance. Slowly French agriculture and industry began to recover and even modernize.

After the war French voters adopted a new constitution and proclaimed the Fourth Republic. However, this government was politically unstable. It fell during the late 1950s over a crisis that brought France to the brink of civil war. The crisis involved the French army's attempt to restore its prestige after the defeat of 1940.

The French considered Algeria, in northern Africa, an important part of France. In 1954, however, Algerian nationalists began a bloody war for independence. After several years of extreme violence, many people in France wanted to let Algeria go, but others strongly opposed such a course. In 1958 the French legislature turned to General Charles de Gaulle to save the nation from civil war. De Gaulle was authorized to write a new constitution and to rule by decree until its ratification. The new constitution created France's Fifth Republic and a strong presidency.

De Gaulle became the first president of the Fifth Republic. To the surprise of the army, he accepted Algerian independence. He also moved to peacefully transform the French empire into a voluntary association of self-governing nations known as the French Community.

In foreign policy de Gaulle was a nationalist. He believed Europe would prosper only as an alliance of strong nations with individual identities and freedom of action. Although France remained a political member of NATO, de Gaulle withdrew French forces from NATO command. He opposed U.S. and British influence in Europe and established close relations with West German Chancellor Adenauer to offset it.

In the late 1960s political conditions within France became unstable. Militant students demanded reforms in the educational system. Workers held strikes, calling for higher wages and better working conditions. To meet the crisis, de Gaulle dissolved the National Assembly and called for general elections. In April 1969 the French people rejected de Gaulle's proposed reforms, and de Gaulle resigned from office.

✔ **READING CHECK: Sequencing** What events led to de Gaulle's rise and fall from power in France? new constitution created strong presidency, political instability led people to reject reforms

Western Europe and Integration

Recovery in other Western European nations took many different paths. To solidify economic health, some nations sought cooperation within the European community.

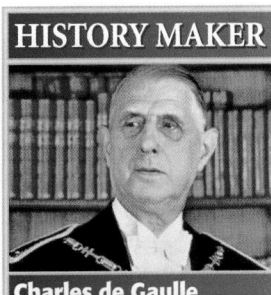

HISTORY MAKER

Charles de Gaulle (1890–1970)

Charles De Gaulle was one of the great military heroes of France during World War I. Between the wars, he pushed for a small, but more mobile and technically advanced, army. After France fell to the Germans in World War II, de Gaulle led the Free French forces. Upon liberation, he helped rebuild the French government.

De Gaulle retired from politics in 1946, but was called back into service during the crisis of the late 1950s. As a politician, he believed in strong national government, with as few alliances as possible. He also granted independence to 12 French territories in Africa. **How might de Gaulle's treatment of French territories in Africa have related to his views about alliances?**

TEACH OBJECTIVE 4

ALL LEVELS: Ask students the following questions: Who succeeded Stalin as the Soviet leader? *(Nikita Khrushchev)* What was the policy of "destalinization?" *(condemned Stalin for crimes against the Soviet people; lifted restrictions on intellectuals and artists; freed many political prisoners; ended some of the terrorism of the secret police)* What was Khrushchev's primary economic goal? *(to make more consumer goods available to the Soviet people)* What were the results of his economic policies? *(economy expanded; living conditions improved; became a modern industrialized society)*

ENGLISH LANGUAGE LEARNERS

History Maker

KONRAD ADENAUER. As chancellor of the Federal Republic of Germany (West Germany), Konrad Adenauer became the architect of its astounding economic recovery. He also negotiated the West German peace treaty and gained recognition of West Germany's political sovereignty. He promoted his country's membership in various organizations that led to the European Union. Adenauer was a great authority in West German public life from the 1940s to the early 1960s.

Critical Thinking

Ask students why Adenauer promoted West Germany's membership in European organizations.

ANSWER: to strengthen ties with the West

CONNECTING TO ART ANSWER

Its upward curves may be seen as offering hope.

CONNECTING TO *Art*

Architecture: Chapel by Le Corbusier

World War II damaged or destroyed numerous European works of art, including many old and beautiful churches. Many Europeans, then, hailed the construction of a new church that was built from 1951 to 1955 and designed by renowned architect Charles-Édouard Jeanneret, better known as Le Corbusier. Called Notre Dame du Haut, the chapel (at right) is located on a mountaintop in Ronchamp, France. Its massive walls seem to curl like paper. Its doors are almost concealed. According to one art historian, its interior evokes "a nostalgia for the certainties of a faith that is no longer unquestioned. Ronchamp mirrors the spiritual condition of the modern age."

Understanding the Arts

How does Le Corbusier's construction give an impression of hope?

Analyzing Primary Sources

Identifying a Point of View Why did Adenauer see European integration as necessary? Individual countries could not achieve aims.

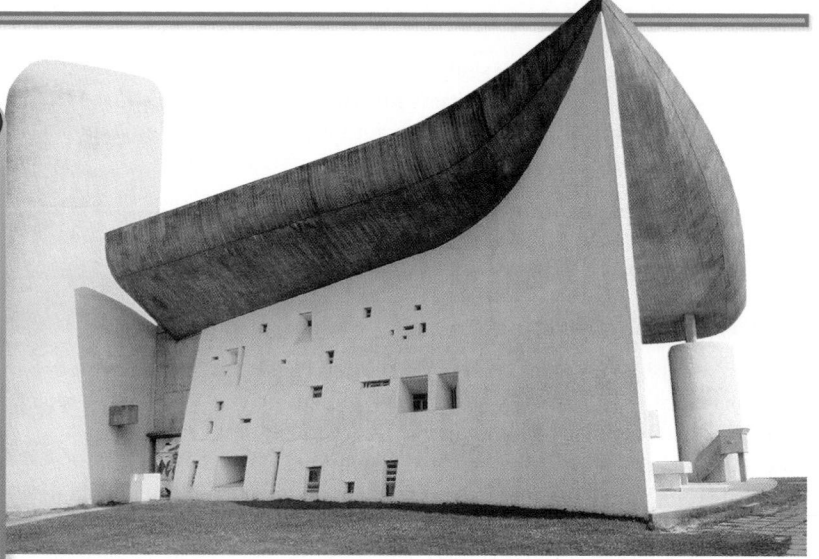

Recovery elsewhere in Europe. Denmark, Norway, and Sweden had strongly entrenched democracies and greater political stability than other countries. Their economies prospered during the 1950s and 1960s. This prosperity allowed them to establish extensive welfare states. In Italy the Christian Democratic Party dominated politics during the 1950s and 1960s and the country experienced major agricultural and industrial growth. By the 1960s, however, the communist and socialist parties had gained considerable strength because of labor unrest. By the end of the 1960s, Italy's economic growth declined sharply. This decline led to political instability.

Greece, Portugal, and Spain all developed free-enterprise systems. Their economic programs, however, met with varying degrees of success. Portugal and Spain were the only Western European nations that did not establish democratic governments after the war. Governments in the two nations remained authoritarian.

Economic integration. In the 1950s the French proposed that the nations that produced most of Western Europe's coal and steel unite their facilities. In 1952 Belgium, France, Italy, Luxembourg, the Netherlands, and West Germany formed the European Coal and Steel Community (ECSC). A central authority regulated production and prices. Member nations did not charge each other tariffs on coal or steel. Konrad Adenauer explained the reason for the international cooperation.

History Makers Speak

“These West European countries are no longer in such a position that each can defend itself on its own; they are no longer in such a position that each can save European culture by itself. These aims, which are common to all of us, can only be attained, if West European countries join together, politically, economically, and culturally . . .”

Konrad Adenauer, from *The Adenauer Era*

In 1957 the same six nations established the European Economic Community (EEC)—usually called the **Common Market.** The six members agreed to gradually abolish import quotas and tariffs within the Common Market. They also agreed to a common tariff on goods coming into the market from nonmember nations.

LEVEL 2: Have students prepare a compare and contrast chart. One column should be labeled *Western Europe* and the other column should be labeled *Eastern Europe*. Have each student list aspects of postwar reconstruction in the appropriate columns. After students have completed their charts, as a class use the lists to determine categories for the aspects of postwar reconstruction. *(for example, Western Europe established market economies; Eastern Europe had government-controlled economies; category for these aspects of postwar reconstruction is economic systems)* Then have students analyze the successes and failures of Western and Eastern Europe in their reconstruction attempts.

Ask students which European nation demonstrated the most marked and rapid economic recovery. Then ask students which European nation experienced the slowest or most problematic recovery.

In 1967 the Common Market adopted a five-year plan to provide greater price and wage stability and more uniform tax levels among member nations. That same year, the EEC merged with the ECSC and another multinational group, the Atomic Energy Community, to form the European Communities. Later called the **European Community,** or EC, the organization was headquartered in Belgium.

In the 1950s Britain had refused to join the EEC. In the 1960s, however, the EEC prospered, while Britain lagged behind. Eventually the British applied for admission. Still worried about British influence in Europe, French president Charles de Gaulle vetoed Britain's application. Not until de Gaulle's retirement and death did Britain gain admission to the EEC in 1973.

✔ **READING CHECK: Problem Solving** Why did Western European nations seek to integrate economically? to provide price and wage stability, more uniform tax levels

The Soviet Union After Stalin

In 1953 Joseph Stalin, who had ruled the Soviet Union with an iron hand for three decades, died. His death led to a power struggle for control of the Soviet government. Eventually **Nikita Khrushchev** (kroosh·CHAWF), former secretary of the Communist party in the Ukraine, emerged as Stalin's successor.

In a 1956 speech, Khrushchev shocked the Soviet leadership when he denounced Stalin's policies. He condemned Stalin for the murder of hundreds of thousands of innocent Soviet citizens and a host of other crimes against the Soviet people. This speech marked the beginning of the policy of "destalinization." Khrushchev lifted restrictions on intellectuals and artists, freed many political prisoners, and ended some of the terrorism of the secret police.

Khrushchev also enacted economic reforms. He loosened somewhat the central government's tight grip on the economy. Local factory and farm managers were given more control to help meet production quotas. Khrushchev's primary economic goal was to make more consumer goods available to the Soviet people. Continued spending on heavy industry and the military prevented any substantial increase in consumer goods, however. In addition, Soviet industry had been rebuilt after the war, but largely with prewar technology. The only real Soviet innovations were in military and space technology. In 1957 the Soviets launched the first orbiting satellite, *Sputnik I.*

Despite problems, the Soviet economy did expand, and living conditions of the people rose considerably. The Soviet Union gradually became a modern industrial society.

For a time Khrushchev attempted to improve relations with Western powers. This thaw in East-West relations lasted until 1960, when the Soviets shot down a U.S. spy plane. The building of the Berlin Wall in 1961 and a crisis over Soviet missiles in Cuba in 1962 worsened relations even further. After Khrushchev's economic reforms also failed to produce results, he was forced to resign from office. His successor, Leonid Brezhnev, tightened domestic and foreign polices once more.

✔ **READING CHECK: Drawing Inferences** Why did Khrushchev criticize Stalin's rule? crimes against the Soviet people, restrictions, terrorism

Eastern Europe

Like the rest of Europe, the new satellite countries of the Eastern bloc also had to rebuild after World War II. Communist bloc leaders accepted the Marxist-Leninist

Holt Researcher
go.hrw.com
KEYWORD: Holt Researcher
FreeFind: Nikita Khrushchev
After reading more about Nikita Khrushchev on the Holt Researcher, write a newspaper article describing U.S. reactions to his policies.

The successful launch of the Sputnik I satellite (shown above) by the Soviet Union helped spark the international race to put a man on the moon.

Science, Technology & Society

Mechanized agriculture, particularly the use of tractors, led to what is sometimes called the "Green Revolution" in Western Europe. Advances in animal husbandry, irrigation techniques, and seed production also contributed to the agricultural boom. Before World War I, about half of all Europeans worked in agriculture. By 1955, the percentage had fallen to about 24 percent and has continued to decline. Because more farm work could be done by fewer people, many former farmers moved to cities in search of other careers. The cities grew, and the economy expanded as people were freed for new pursuits and production increased in many different areas.

Critical Thinking

Ask students how the Green Revolution helped many European nations to recover from the war.

ANSWER: Greater agricultural production meant many countries could export food; farmers were able to move to the cities to add to the urban workforce; and the land was revitalized and rebuilt by more efficient farming techniques.

REVIEW

Have students complete the Section 3 Review on p. 836.

ASSESS

Have students complete Daily Quiz 31.3. As Alternative Assessment, you may want to use the chart activity in this section's lessons.

RETEACH

Have students complete Main Idea Activity for English Language Learners and Special-Needs Students 31.3. Then ask students to

write a question and answer that covers the main idea for each subsection in the section. **ENGLISH LANGUAGE LEARNERS**

EXTEND

Ask students to imagine what kinds of stories the Berlin Wall could tell if it could speak. What kinds of suffering and turmoil did it see before it was brought down in 1989 and 1990? How might it have felt about the events it witnessed? Have students write creative stories from the point of view of the wall. They should base their stories on historical facts and actual events. **BLOCK SCHEDULING**

VISUAL RECORD ANSWER

broken it and defaced it with writing

◄ SECTION 3 REVIEW ANSWERS

❶ Define
• welfare state, p. 832

❷ Identify
• Berlin Wall, p. 832
• Common Market, p. 834
• European Community, p. 835
• Nikita Khrushchev, p. 835

❸ Market: competition determines the production and cost of goods, West Germany, rapid economic growth; Command: government makes the economic decisions, Soviet Union, slower economic expansion

❹ a. government takes primary responsibility for the social welfare of its citizens; free medical care

b. formed European Coal and Steel community and eventually the European Economic Community to abolish tariffs and import quotas

c. continued spending on heavy industry and the military, reliance on prewar technology

❺ Students' analyses will vary.

INTERPRETING THE VISUAL RECORD

The Hungarian revolt In these photos Hungarians in Budapest topple a statue of Stalin during the 1956 uprising. *What have the protesters done with the statue?*

doctrine that ordinary people did not always know what was best for society. In keeping with this principle, communist countries practiced a command economy, in which the government made all economic decisions.

The Soviet-controlled governments in Eastern Europe attempted to implement collective farming. Bulgaria collectivized over half its available farmland. The Poles, however, resisted collectivization so forcefully that most land remained in private hands. Collectivization delayed economic recovery in Eastern Europe.

Soviet-style Five-Year Plans and central planning made the industrialization of Eastern Europe more successful. East Germany became the leading industrial power in the region. Consumer goods remained a low priority, however. Living standards rose in Eastern Europe, but remained low when compared with those in the West.

During the early postwar years, the Communist bloc seemed a solid group of nations with common goals. However, rifts soon appeared. Yugoslavia's growing independence from the Soviet Union inspired people in other satellite countries. In 1953 Soviet forces put down a revolt in East Germany. Poland threatened a revolt in 1956, and as a result gained a small amount of independence in domestic affairs. Hungarians revolted against Soviet domination in 1956. Soviet troops violently repressed the revolt.

Dissatisfaction with communism and Soviet domination continued in Eastern Europe throughout the 1960s. In 1968 Alexander Dubcek (DOOB·chek) began a program of reforms in Czechoslovakia. Dubcek promised civil liberties and democratic political reforms. This short-lived period of freedom became known as the Prague Spring. Warsaw Pact troops invaded Czechoslovakia, seized reform leaders, and replaced them with pro-Soviet people.

✔ **READING CHECK: Drawing Conclusions** Why did the Soviets suppress political freedoms in Eastern Europe? establish communist control

SECTION 3 REVIEW

1. Define and explain the significance: welfare state

2. Identify and explain the significance:
Berlin Wall
Common Market
European Community
Nikita Khrushchev

3. Categorizing Copy the chart below. Use it to explain the economic policies of Western and Eastern European nations and the Soviet Union.

	Market economy	Command economy
Defined		
Example nations		
Results		

4. **Finding the Main Idea**

a. What is a welfare state? What welfare program did the British government establish?

b. What moves toward economic integration did some European nations take in the 1950s?

c. Why did Khrushchev's efforts to reform the Soviet economy meet with limited success?

5. **Writing and Critical Thinking**

Contrasting Write an economic analysis contrasting the West German "miracle" with the performance of the Soviet economy.
Consider:
• the differences between a command economy and a market economy
• the type of goods that each nation produced

go.
hrw
.com
Homework Practice Online
keyword: SP3 HP31

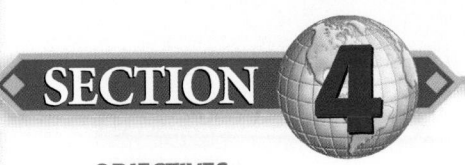
OBJECTIVES

1 **Examine the major domestic problems the United States faced in the postwar era.**

2 **Investigate how the policy of containment led to foreign conflicts.**

3 **Identify the challenges the Canadian people responded to in the postwar era.**

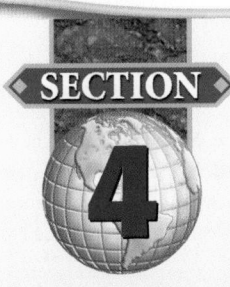

SECTION 4

The United States and Canada

READ TO DISCOVER

❶ What major domestic problems did the United States face in the postwar era?

❷ How did the policy of containment lead to foreign conflicts?

❸ What challenges did the Canadian people respond to in the postwar era?

IDENTIFY

Joseph McCarthy
John F. Kennedy
Lyndon Johnson
NAACP
Martin Luther King Jr.
Southeast Asia Treaty
  Organization
Cuban missile crisis
DEW Line

WHY IT MATTERS TODAY

The United States and Canada remain close allies today. Use CNN or other **current event** sources to learn more about relations between the United States and Canada. Record your findings in your journal.

CNN Student News.com

The Main Idea
The United States and Canada prospered in the postwar era, but both nations faced internal difficulties.

The Story Continues *On January 20, 1961, the new president John F. Kennedy spoke to the American people. Kennedy declared, "Ask not what your country can do for you; ask what you can do for your country. . . . Ask not what America will do for you, but what together we can do for the freedom of man." Kennedy's call for dedication and sacrifice inspired many Americans as they faced a difficult period in their history.*

Domestic Challenges Face the United States

During the postwar era, the United States had a strong economy and a leading role in world affairs. However, the nation still faced difficulties. Internal conflicts, political problems, and the growing realization that there are limits to economic growth marked the years following the war.

Between 1945 and 1968 three Democrats and one Republican served as president of the United States. These four presidents often had similar goals, but they differed on how to achieve those goals. The decisions they made shaped the way in which the American people viewed both the world and themselves during a critical period in American history.

The economy and the Cold War at home. After World War II the U.S. economy reached new peaks of productivity, with huge new industries and rapid growth of new construction. Several minor recessions, in which business slowed and unemployment increased, occurred during the 1940s and 1950s. The 1960s, however, were a period of continuous economic growth. Only toward the end of the decade did rising inflation foreshadow economic problems to come.

Economic prosperity led to a rising standard of living in the United States. However, the Cold War made some Americans feel anxious and insecure. Many people did not understand why the United States allowed the Soviet Union to dominate Eastern Europe. Eventually a climate of anticommunist hysteria developed. Some Americans came to believe that Soviet gains occurred because certain people in the United States were sympathetic to communism.

Senator **Joseph McCarthy** of Wisconsin became the leading spokesman for this conspiracy belief. Between 1950 and 1954 McCarthy questioned the loyalty of some government officials. Without presenting any real evidence, he accused people of communist activities. In the process he ruined the careers and destroyed the reputations of many Americans. A Senate

This Time *magazine cover from 1954 reveals the great impact Senator Joseph McCarthy had on the politics of his day.*

ALL LEVELS: Have students work individually or in small groups to create collages that represent the people, issues, and events that shaped the United States between 1945 and 1968. Students should include images that represent aspects of domestic policy, the economy, McCarthyism, and the civil rights movement. **ENGLISH LANGUAGE LEARNERS, COOPERATIVE LEARNING, BLOCK SCHEDULING**

Teacher to Teacher

Mattie P. Collins of Pine Bluff, Arkansas, suggested the following activity: Have students research more information about the U.S. civil rights movement and create a time line of the major events in the movement.

---

internet connect

TOPIC: McCarthyism
GO TO: go.hrw.com
KEYWORD: SP3 WH31

Have students search the Internet through the HRW Go site for more information about the McCarthy era and its effects on the United States. Have them locate information on people whose reputations were damaged during this time. Ask students to choose one and write a biography that includes how that person was affected by McCarthyism.

Technology Resources

World History Teaching Transparency: Everyday Life 26: Segregation in the United States, 1960

Dr. Martin Luther King Jr. delivered his "I Have a Dream" speech at the Lincoln Memorial in Washington, D.C.

subcommittee in 1950 found the charges false. Although he had a large following, the senator was again investigated. In late 1954 the Senate voted 67–22 to condemn McCarthy's conduct. He soon lost influence, but the Cold War, especially the threat of nuclear conflict, continued to concern many Americans.

Domestic reforms and civil rights. Following the example of the New Deal, postwar presidents created new programs to address social problems. President **John F. Kennedy** introduced a broad program of domestic reforms. Before Congress passed much of his proposed legislation, however, Kennedy was assassinated on November 22, 1963.

Kennedy's successor, **Lyndon Johnson,** offered an even more sweeping vision of social reform. Johnson hoped to create what he called the Great Society. His program included a war on poverty and other major reforms, including important civil rights legislation.

As the United States grew more affluent, minorities began to demand equal civil rights with the rest of the population. For example, African Americans lived under many political, economic, and social restrictions. In parts of the United States, black Americans could not vote or obtain decent educations, jobs, and housing. In response to racial discrimination, African Americans had formed organizations in the early 1900s, such as the National Association for the Advancement of Colored People (**NAACP**), to secure civil rights.

A turning point in the civil rights movement took place in 1954. In the landmark case *Brown v. Board of Education of Topeka*, the U.S. Supreme Court declared that state laws requiring black children to attend separate schools were unconstitutional. The court ordered states that had such laws to integrate their schools. This important decision encouraged the growing civil rights movement of the late 1950s and 1960s. In the 1960s Congress passed several civil rights and voting rights acts that guaranteed political equality for African Americans and other minorities.

The best-known civil rights leader of this time was **Martin Luther King Jr.,** a Baptist minister. King called for the use of nonviolent methods, such as boycotts, marches, and sit-ins, to bring about change. African Americans and their supporters held peaceful demonstrations and mass protests against discrimination. For his efforts, King received the Nobel Peace Prize in 1964. Four years later he died violently at the hands of an assassin. His murder dealt a severe blow to the civil rights movements and sparked a wave of riots across the country.

The U.S. civil rights movement had global effects as well. People protesting for their rights throughout the world found inspiration from the civil rights movement. One Catholic woman in Northern Ireland compared the struggles of her people to African Americans. "Like . . . the blacks [in the United States], we were poor, virtually disenfranchised, and very angry." Some Irish Catholics tried to emulate the style of African American civil rights activists, even borrowing their use of the African American spiritual "We Shall Overcome." When Martin Luther King Jr. was killed, he was mourned throughout the world.

✔ **READING CHECK: Identifying Cause and Effect** How did the civil rights movement affect the world? inspiration for similar movements

LEVEL 1: Have students fill in the following chart to illustrate the results of the policy of containment.

ENGLISH LANGUAGE LEARNERS

Policies and Actions	Purpose	Results
police action in Korea	*to stop spread of communism*	*nuclear arms competition*
SEATO		
Eisenhower Doctrine		*fear and discontent within the U.S.*
invasion of Cuba		
involvement in Vietnam		

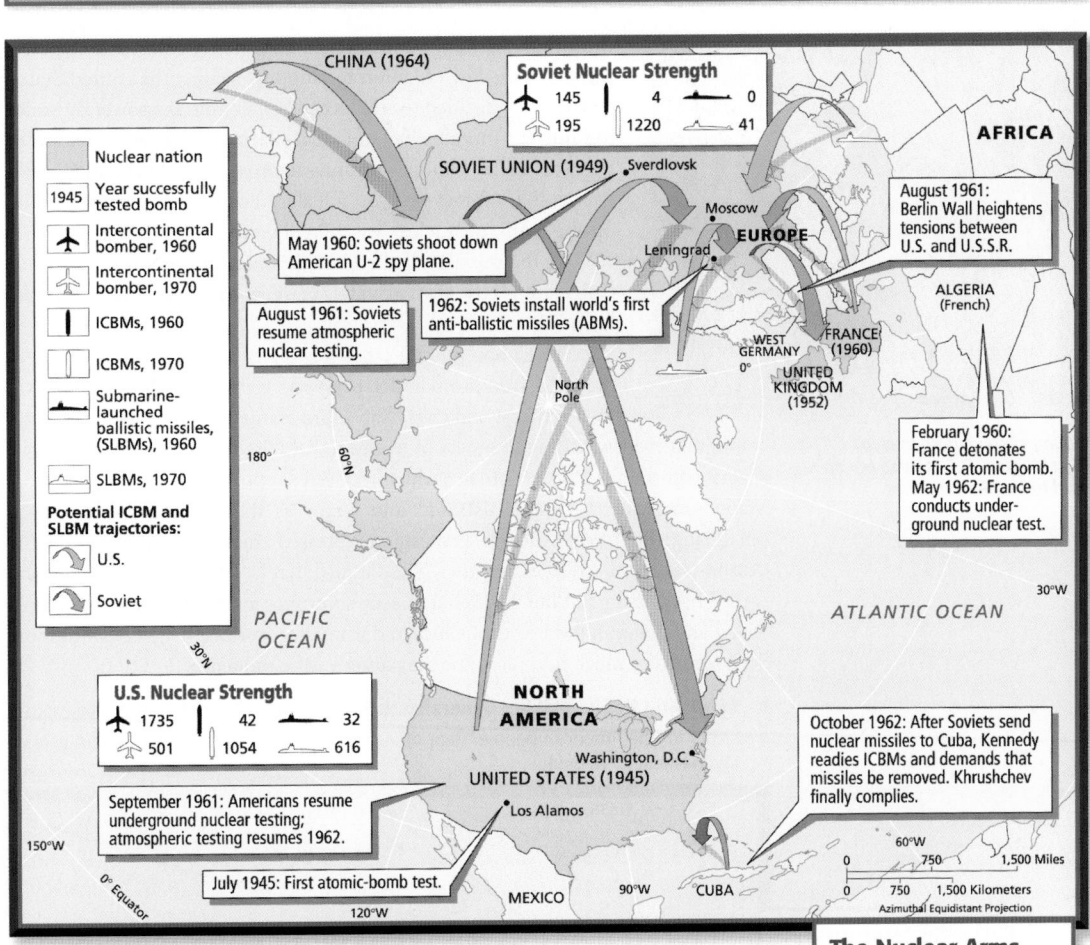

The Nuclear Arms Race, 1945–1970

Foreign Policy and the Cold War

For the most part U.S. foreign policy during the postwar period focused on the containment of communism. In Asia the United States sent troops to South Korea in a "police action" to stop North Korean Communists from taking over the country. President Dwight D. Eisenhower created the **Southeast Asia Treaty Organization** (SEATO) in an attempt to halt further communist advances in the region. He also announced the Eisenhower Doctrine, which provided economic and military assistance to noncommunist nations in the Middle East. Efforts to ease Cold War tensions during this period failed. In 1961 the construction of the Berlin Wall made it clear that the Cold War would continue in full force. The greatest fear was that the war would turn hot and result in nuclear conflict.

In 1959 a Marxist named Fidel Castro led rebel forces that overthrew the corrupt government of Cuba. The Eisenhower administration feared that a communist Cuba would become a base of Soviet operations. In April 1961 newly elected President Kennedy authorized an invasion of Cuba by anti-Castro forces who received training and equipment from the Central Intelligence Agency (CIA). However, U.S. air support for the invasion was canceled, and Cuban forces

Interpreting Maps
Throughout the postwar era, the United States and the Soviet Union were locked in a deadly nuclear arms competition. Flashpoints, such as the U-2 spy plane crisis in 1960, increased global tensions and spurred ongoing weapons development and deployment.

■ **Skills Assessment:**
Using Geography How did Soviet nuclear arms strength compare to that of the United States in 1960? In 1970?

Citizenship

The civil rights movement was not limited to African Americans. Many other groups began to fight in earnest for their full rights as citizens during this time. Women, Hispanics, American Indians, and people with disabilities, among others, formed groups to struggle for fairness and equality in American society. Prominent groups included the United Farm Workers and the Chicano movement, the American Indian Movement, and a more active women's rights movement. These groups succeeded in getting legislation passed that has greatly improved their situations, but many people are still fighting for fair treatment and their full rights as American citizens.

Critical Thinking

Ask students why so many rights movements were born or gained momentum during the 1960s.

ANSWER: the nation was economically stable, young people were willing and able to voice their opinions, television made it possible to gain widespread publicity and support

---

MAP ANSWER
1960: United States had greater strength; 1970: Soviets had more ICBMs

TEACH OBJECTIVE 3

LEVEL 3: Ask students to list the major changes that took place in Canada during the postwar years. *(Canada experienced tremendous economic growth and enjoyed a close relationship with the United States. The two countries cooperated to build the Distant Early Warning Line. Postwar problems included the risk of separatism in Quebec.)* Then have students work in pairs to write personal letters as if they were American and Canadian pen pals who enjoy writing to each other about their respective countries. They should exchange a total of four letters—two each—that discuss events during a particular year in their countries. For example, a pair might discuss events during the Cuban missile crisis.

COOPERATIVE LEARNING, BLOCK SCHEDULING

HOMEWORK Ask students to list the reasons why the relationship between the United States and Canada has largely been a close one.

CLOSE

Have students list and describe the domestic policy concerns of the United States from 1945 to 1968.

Linking Past to Present

For more than a quarter of a century after World War II, the United States enjoyed an unparalleled economic boom. Consumerism rose dramatically, and people bought automobiles, houses, and household items. In addition, they were moving to the suburbs and having babies in unprecedented numbers. This rise in the birthrate during the 1950s is called the "baby boom." This huge generation will soon be reaching retirement age, and the U.S. government is facing the challenge of stretching the Social Security program and other resources to handle the strain of aging baby boomers.

Critical Thinking

Ask students what other problems American society might encounter as its largest generation ages.

ANSWER: meeting healthcare needs, rising prices of care for the aging, higher taxes to help pay for Social Security and other government programs, the possible collapse of the Social Security program

MAP ANSWER

It stretches across the northern border of North America.

Young citizens gathered in Washington, D.C., to call for an end to the Vietnam War.

captured or killed the invaders. After the failed invasion, Castro turned to the Soviet Union for support against the United States. Khrushchev decided to strengthen Soviet military power by building nuclear missile sites in Cuba. Alarmed, Kennedy demanded that the Soviet Union withdraw its missiles. NATO and Warsaw Pact military forces went on full alert. For 13 days the world stood on the brink of nuclear war. Finally, the Soviet Union agreed to remove the missiles, if the United States promised not to invade Cuba. Kennedy also privately agreed to remove U.S. missiles from Turkey.

The **Cuban missile crisis** was the most dangerous moment of the Cold War. From a U.S. perspective, however, the Vietnam War in Southeast Asia was far more damaging. The United States committed ever-increasing numbers of troops to help South Vietnam in its struggle against communist North Vietnam, which received support from the Soviet Union. Many Americans became frustrated and angry as the Vietnam War dragged on during the 1960s. Antiwar protesters expressed their discontent by staging demonstrations on college campuses. They argued that U.S. involvement in Vietnam caused needless loss of life. In 1968 a violent confrontation broke out between protesters and police in the streets of Chicago during the Democratic Party Convention. Such scenes did much to undermine the nation's self-confidence.

✔ **READING CHECK: Making Generalizations** What problems did Cold War tensions create for the American people? fear of nuclear war, frustration and discontent over involvement in Vietnam

Radar Systems and Defenses in North America, 1959–1964

Interpreting Maps During the Cold War the United States invested enormous amounts of money to build nuclear warning and defense systems. Many of these systems ran through Canada.

■ **Skills Assessment: The World in Spatial Terms** Why was the DEW Line considered to be America's first line of defense against a Soviet nuclear attack?

REVIEW

Have students complete the Section 4 Review on p. 841.

ASSESS

Have students complete Daily Quiz 31.4. As Alternative Assessment, you may want to use the collage exercise in this section's lessons.

RETEACH

Have students complete Main Idea Activity for English Language Learners and Special-Needs Students 31.4. Then have students create a chart with the headings *U.S. Domestic Challenges, U.S. Foreign Policy Challenges,* and *Canada's Challenges* and summarize each of those categories. **ENGLISH LANGUAGE LEARNERS**

EXTEND

Have students find out more information about the civil rights movement for one of the following groups in the United States: African Americans, American Indians, women, disabled individuals, or Hispanics. Ask them to write a paragraph summarizing the postwar goals and activities of the movement they choose. **BLOCK SCHEDULING**

Canada's Challenges

For more than a century, Canada and the United States had maintained a close relationship. During and after World War II this relationship grew stronger, especially with regard to economic and military affairs. Canada relied heavily on the United States for its national defense. Together the two nations built a line of radar installations called the Distant Early Warning Line, or **DEW Line,** designed to give early warning of air attacks. Together, Canada and the United States also established the North American Air Defense Command.

Active participation in two world wars ended the isolation policy that Canada had maintained for many years. After World War II, Canada became a vigorous supporter of the United Nations and NATO. Canadians loaned billions of dollars to other countries and welcomed refugees from Europe. Like the United States, Canada experienced considerable economic development after World War II. Much of the country remained agricultural, producing corn, feed grains, and wheat. However, industry also grew after the war. The large Canadian forests provided wood products, and the wood pulp and paper industries expanded. Development of electrical power and improvements in transportation stimulated the mining of coal, iron, and uranium. Oil and gas production increased. Aircraft, automobile, and electrical industries developed in the provinces of Quebec and Ontario.

During the 1960s a new challenge appeared in Canadian life. Many French-speaking Canadians, particularly those living in the province of Quebec, desired to separate from the rest of Canada. Feelings of French nationalism were not new, but grew more intense at this time. The movement received a boost from the 1967 visit of French president Charles de Gaulle. A new political party, the Parti Quebecois, (par•TEE kay•bay•KWAH) called for secession from the Canadian Confederation. The party gained 24 percent of the vote in Quebec in the 1970 elections, and in 1976 won control of Quebec's government. In 1980 the Parti Quebecois put the issue of separation to voters. The referendum failed, but in 1995 a similar vote showed 49.4 percent of Quebecois in favor of separation, indicating that the challenge to Canadian unity will not vanish soon.

✔ **READING CHECK: Making Predictions** What challenges might a separatist movement create for a nation such as Canada? loss of labor force, natural resources

CONNECTING TO
Civics

Separatism

Quebec's separatist movement is just one of many that have occurred throughout history. Over time, various ethnic, national, cultural, and religious groups have expressed a desire to be free from the larger groups to which they belong. Because of their wish to separate from this larger group, they are often referred to as separatists. Separatist movements continue throughout the world today. The Kurds, a Middle Eastern cultural group of 20 to 25 million people, want their own nation. The Basque people, a small cultural group in Spain, have turned to violence in their bid to be free from Spanish control.

Understanding Civics

Why might political leaders oppose separatist movements in their nations?

CONNECTING TO CIVICS ANSWER

They might believe such movements would weaken their nation internally.

SECTION 4 REVIEW ANSWERS

❶ **Identify**
- Joseph McCarthy, p. 837
- John F. Kennedy, p. 838
- Lyndon Johnson, p. 838
- NAACP, p. 838
- Martin Luther King, Jr., p. 838
- Southeast Asia Treaty Organization, p. 839
- Cuban missile crisis, p. 840
- DEW Line, p. 841

❷ economic boom, anticommunist hysteria, increased defense spending, civil rights movement

❸ a. social problems, civil rights movement

b. ended its isolation policy

c. its heterogeneous population and the determination of the people of Quebec to retain their own identity

❹ Essays should point out the effects of the movements in the United States and throughout the world.

SECTION 4 REVIEW

1. **Identify** and explain the significance:
   Joseph McCarthy
   John F. Kennedy
   Lyndon Johnson
   NAACP
   Martin Luther King Jr.
   Southeast Asia Treaty Organization
   Cuban missile crisis
   DEW Line

2. **Identifying Cause and Effect** Copy the graphic organizer below. Use it to explain the effect that the Cold War had on domestic concerns in the United States.

Effects of the Cold War	
Economic	
Political	
Security	
Civil Rights	

3. **Finding the Main Idea**
   a. What domestic issues caused conflicts in the United States during the postwar era?
   b. How did Canada's foreign policy change in the postwar era?
   c. What did the separatist movement reflect about Canada?

4. **Writing and Critical Thinking**
   Finding the Main Idea Write an essay about the importance of the U.S. civil rights movement.
   Consider:
   • the effect of the movement on the United States
   • how it affected other movements throughout the world

Homework Practice Online
keyword: SP3 HP31

CHAPTER 31

REVIEW AND ASSESSMENT RESOURCES

REPRODUCIBLE RESOURCES
▶ Vocabulary Activity 31

TECHNOLOGY RESOURCES
▶ Chapter 31 Test Generator (on the One-Stop Planner)
▶ Global Skill Builder CD–ROM
▶ HRW Web Site

REINFORCEMENT, REVIEW, and ASSESSMENT
▶ Chapter 31 Review, pp. 842–843
▶ Chapter 31 Tutorial for Students, Parents, Mentors, and Peers
▶ Chapter 31 Test (Form A or B)
▶ Alternative Assessment Handbook
▶ Chapter 31 Test for English Language Learners and Special-Needs Students

REVIEW

Have students complete the Chapter 31 Review on pages 842–843.

ASSESS

Use one of the chapter tests to assess students' understanding of the content. For Alternative Assessment, see the Portfolio Activities and Alternative Assessment Handbook.

CHAPTER 31 REVIEW ANSWERS

Understanding Main Ideas

1. Stalin did not fulfill his promise to allow free elections.

2. Germany lost land but gained population to feed, house, and employ.

3. It provided help to countries threatened by communism.

4. Soviets opposed the reunification of Germany; the division of Germany

5. rapid reconstruction and industrial development under free market policies

6. slower growth; living standards rose but remained low compared to the West

7. political, social, and economic equality for minorities

8. to help South Vietnam in its struggle against communist North Vietnam

Reviewing Themes

1. They were not as effective in promoting rapid economic expansion as were free market economies.

2. rights of minorities to form their own government

3. boycotts, marches, sit-ins, peaceful demonstrations, mass protests

842

CHAPTER 31 Review

Creating a Time Line

Copy the time line below onto a sheet of paper. Complete the time line by filling in the events, individuals, and dates from the chapter that you think were significant. Pick three events and explain why you think they were significant.

| 1940 | 1950 | 1960 | 1970 |

Writing a Summary

Using standard grammar, spelling, sentence structure, and punctuation, write an overview of the events in the chapter.

Identifying People and Ideas

Identify the following terms or individuals and explain their significance:

1. United Nations
2. Cold War
3. containment
4. Marshall Plan
5. NATO
6. European Community
7. Nikita Khrushchev
8. Joseph McCarthy
9. John F. Kennedy
10. Martin Luther King Jr.

Understanding Main Ideas

SECTION 1 *(pp. 820–824)*
Aftermath of the War in Europe

1. How did unresolved issues following World War II contribute to postwar tensions between the United States and the Soviet Union?
2. How did territorial adjustments affect the German economy?

SECTION 2 *(pp. 825–830)*
Origins of the Cold War

3. How did the Truman Doctrine reflect the goal of containment?
4. What were the causes and effects of the Berlin blockade?

SECTION 3 *(pp. 831–836)*
Reconstruction, Reform, and Reaction in Europe

5. What was the West German "miracle" and what produced it?
6. What was the economic situation in the Soviet Union and Eastern Europe after the war?

SECTION 4 *(pp. 837–841)*
The United States and Canada

7. What was the goal of the civil rights movement in the United States?
8. Why did the United States become involved in the conflict in Vietnam?

Reviewing Themes

1. **Economics** How effective were command economies in the postwar era?
2. **Government** What problems regarding democracy did the separatist movement in Canada raise?
3. **Citizenship** What sort of protests did civil rights activists rely upon in the 1960s?

Thinking Critically

1. **Summarizing** What are the responsibilities of the UN Security Council and the General Assembly?
2. **Identifying Cause and Effect** How did American political ideas shape events in the postwar era?
3. **Evaluating** Why did Nikita Khrushchev denounce Stalinism?
4. **Contrasting** How were the market economies of most Western European nations different from the command economies of the Soviet Union and Eastern European nations?

Writing About History

Summarizing Suppose you are a foreign correspondent in Europe after the war. Write a report that informs about economic and political development in Europe and the Soviet Union after World War II. Use the following chart to organize your thoughts before you begin writing.

	Economics	Politics
Germany		
Great Britain		
France		
Eastern Europe		
Soviet Union		

CLOSE

Ask students to list and describe the postwar developments that increased tensions between the Soviet Union and Western nations.

RETEACH

Have students who had difficulty with the test rewrite each question that they missed and then use their textbooks and notes to answer the questions in complete sentences. When they are ready, have students take the Form B Test to assess their mastery of the material. **ENGLISH LANGUAGE LEARNERS**

Portfolio Extensions

Link to TODAY

1. Ask students to choose one protest movement, such as the civil rights movement, the equal rights movement for women, or the movement for human rights in Eastern Europe. Have them research their movements, making sure to look at both written and visual material, and create an illustrated time line of the major events in the movement and major changes that this movement generated.

2. Have students use the *Dictionary of American Biography* or other biographical references to find information about a leader of one of the protest movements of the 1950s and 1960s. Then ask them to create a visual presentation, using computer software as appropriate.

Building Social Studies Skills

Interpreting a Chart

Study the chart below. Then use the information on the chart to answer the questions that follow.

Growth in World Energy Demand, 1940-1970*

Year	Form of energy			
	Coal	Oil	Natural Gas	Hydroelectric
1940	1.0	0.33	0.1	0.25
1950	1.0	0.5	0.25	0.15
1960	1.5	1.0	0.5	0.15
1970	1.75	2.25	1.0	0.25

*Values are approximate and expressed as "thousand million tons oil equivalent."

1. Which statement correctly describes a relationship shown on the chart?
   a. In 1940 the demand for coal was greater than for oil, but by about 1960 the demand for both was the same.
   b. Between 1960 and 1970 the demand for natural gas and hydroelectric was greater than for coal or oil.
   c. In the 1950s the demand for coal was about the same as it had been in the 1940s.
   d. In the 1940s the demand for hydroelectric became greater than the demand for natural gas.

2. What trends account for the difference in world energy demand between 1940 and 1970? Give specific examples.

Drawing Inferences

Read the following comment made by Robert McNamara in 1988 on the Cuban missile crisis. McNamara had been the United States Secretary of Defense during the crisis. Answer the questions that follow.

> "At the time, we had 5,100 nuclear weapons that we could deliver onto the Soviet Union and they had only 300 they could deliver onto the U.S. We knew that, and we knew our knowledge was reliable. And that was strategic parity. We were prevented from using our 5,100 nuclear weapons because we knew that whatever damage we did to you, you would have enough left to inflict unacceptable damage on the United States. So that was parity."

3. Which of the following is the best statement of what the author's comment implies?
   a. The U.S. could not afford to use all of its nuclear weapons.
   b. The U.S. looked for ways other than using nuclear weapons to solve the crisis.
   c. The U.S. was not concerned about the 300 nuclear missiles the Soviets had.
   d. The U.S. did not like the concept of "strategic parity."

4. Why is the Cuban missile crisis considered by many to have been the most dangerous period of the Cold War? Give specific reasons.

Alternative Assessment

Building Your Portfolio

Link to TODAY

Citizenship

The right to assemble and to protest are long-standing rights enjoyed by Americans. The civil rights movement of the late 1950s and 1960s was just one area of protest in U.S. history. Research to find out what other movements have inspired large-scale protests in recent history and how successful these protest have been. Compile your findings in a chart.

internet connect

Internet Activity: go.hrw.com
KEYWORD: SP3 WH31

Choose a topic on Europe and North America in the Postwar Years to:
- research the Cold War and look for elements of popular culture that reflect Cold War anxieties.
- assess how human rights and democratic ideals have been advanced by the United Nations.
- learn about McCarthyism and its effects on the United States.

go.hrw.com

Thinking Critically

1. Security Council: authorizes economic and military action in settling disputes; General Assembly: debates issues and recommends actions

2. containment influenced Cold War, involvement in Vietnam

3. His foreign policy and economic reforms ultimately failed.

4. Competition, rather than the government, determined production and cost in Western Europe.

Writing About History

Students' reports will vary.

Building Social Studies Skills

1. c

2. increase in defense measures, increase in population, increase in car and television ownership

3. b

4. The world stood on the brink of nuclear war.

Building Your Portfolio

Students' charts will vary.

CHAPTER 32

Asia Since 1945

CHAPTER RESOURCE MANAGER

Objectives	Pacing Guide	Reproducible Resources
SECTION 1 **South Asia After Empire** (pp. 846–851) • Explain how differences between Hindus and Muslims led to a divided India. • Identify problems that India faced after independence. • Describe how Pakistan and Bangladesh developed after the partition of India.	**Regular** 1.5 day **Block Scheduling** 1 day *Block Scheduling Handbook with Team Teaching Strategies, 32.1*	**RS** Guided Reading Strategy 32.1 **PS** Readings in World History 115: A New Leader for Pakistan
SECTION 2 **Communist China and Its Influence** (pp. 852–858) • Describe how Mao Zedong's government tried to rebuild China after World War II. • Identify what happened at Tiananmen Square and what the consequences were for China. • Explain why Korea was divided and how the two Koreas have developed since 1953. • Explain why China and Taiwan have been in conflict.	**Regular** 1.5 day **Block Scheduling** 1 day *Block Scheduling Handbook with Team Teaching Strategies, 32.2*	**RS** Guided Reading Strategy 32.2 **SM** Geography Activity 32: Agriculture in China **PS** Readings in World History 113: Rewriting History in China
SECTION 3 **The Japanese Miracle** (pp. 859–862) • Identify the factors that allowed Japan to recover effectively after World War II. • Describe the economic and social changes that occurred in Japan from the 1950s onward. • Explain how the relationship between Japan and the United States changed in the years since World War II.	**Regular** 1.5 day **Block Scheduling** 1 day *Block Scheduling Handbook with Team Teaching Strategies, 32.3*	**RS** Guided Reading Strategy 32.3 **PS** Readings in World History 114: The Japanese Passion for Comics
SECTION 4 **Independence Struggles in Southeast Asia** (pp. 863–869) • Describe the causes and effects of dictatorships in the Philippines and Indonesia. • Explain how the Vietnam War affected Vietnam, Laos, and Cambodia. • Identify the problems that the nations of Southeast Asia faced as they struggled to create stable governments.	**Regular** 1.5 day **Block Scheduling** 1 day *Block Scheduling Handbook with Team Teaching Strategies, 32.4*	**RS** Guided Reading Strategy 32.4 **PS** Readings in World History 116: The Filipinos Celebrate the Fall of President Marcos
SECTION 5 **Asian Paths to Prosperity** (pp. 870–873) • Explain what led Asian governments to impose tight controls in their countries. • Describe the problems Asian countries faced as they tried to develop their economies and how they solved those problems. • Explain how economic success in Asian countries affected the West.	**Regular** 1.5 day **Block Scheduling** 1 day *Block Scheduling Handbook with Team Teaching Strategies, 32.5*	**RS** Guided Reading Strategy 32.5 **RS** Graphic Organizer Activity 32 **E** Hands-on History Activity 32 **E** Creative Teaching Strategy 32:

Chapter Resource Key

PS Primary Sources	**A** Assessment	Music
RS Reading Support	**REV** Review	Video
IC Interdisciplinary Connections	**ELL** Reinforcement and English Language Learners	Internet
E Enrichment	Transparencies	Holt Presentation Maker Using Microsoft® PowerPoint®
SM Skills Mastery	CD–ROM	

 One-Stop Planner CD-ROM

See the *One–Stop Planner* for a complete list of additional resources for students and teachers.

One-Stop Planner CD-ROM

It's easy to plan lessons, select resources, and print out materials for your students when you use the *One-Stop Planner* CD–ROM with *Test Generator.*

Technology Resources	Reinforcement, Review, and Assessment
One-Stop Planner 32.1 Holt Researcher: World History: Mother Teresa World History Teaching Transparency: Geography and History 27: The Economy of South Asia Homework Practice Online Online Charts: Population and Population Projections, Asia	Daily Quiz 32.1 Main Idea Activity 32.1 English Audio Summary 32.1 Spanish Audio Summary 32.1 REV Section 1 Review, p. 851
One-Stop Planner 32.2 Holt Researcher: World History: Jiang Qing World History and Cultures Video Program 31: North Korea Turns 50 Homework Practice Online Online Maps, Charts, and Graphs: China's Urban Centers	Daily Quiz 32.2 Main Idea Activity 32.2 English Audio Summary 32.2 Spanish Audio Summary 32.2 REV Section 2 Review, p. 858
One-Stop Planner 32.3 World History and Cultures Video Program 27: Planning Japan's Future World History Teaching Transparency: Art and History 27: Two Bridges for Peace Park Homework Practice Online	Daily Quiz 32.3 Main Idea Activity 32.3 English Audio Summary 32.3 Spanish Audio Summary 32.3 REV Section 3 Review, p. 862
One-Stop Planner 32.4 Holt Researcher: World History: Corazon Aquino Holt Researcher: World History: Ho Chi Minh Homework Practice Online Online Maps, Charts, and Graphs: East and Southeast Asia	Daily Quiz 32.4 Main Idea Activity 32.4 English Audio Summary 32.4 Spanish Audio Summary 32.4 REV Section 4 Review, p. 869
One-Stop Planner 32.5 CNN Presents Geography: Yesterday and Today Segment 30: The Highway to Prosperity World History Teaching Transparency: Everyday Life 27: A Factory in Hong Kong Homework Practice Online	Daily Quiz 32.5 Main Idea Activity 32.5 English Audio Summary 32.5 Spanish Audio Summary 32.5 REV Section 5 Review, p. 873

internet connect

HRW ONLINE RESOURCES
GO TO: go.hrw.com
Then type in a keyword.

TEACHER HOME PAGE
KEYWORD: SP3 Teacher

CHAPTER INTERNET ACTIVITIES
KEYWORD: SP3 WH32

Choose an activity to:
- create a chart comparing the population growth of the United States and India by analyzing factors such as death rates, birth rates, and immigration statistics.
- research the Association of Southeast Asian Nations (ASEAN) and write a persuasive report on why or why not to join the association.
- write a biography of an Asian leader.

CHAPTER ENRICHMENT LINKS
KEYWORD: SP3 CH32

ONLINE ASSESSMENT
Homework Practice
KEYWORD: SP3 HP32
Standardized Test Prep
KEYWORD: SP3 STP32
Rubrics
KEYWORD: SS Rubrics

ONLINE MAPS, CHARTS, AND GRAPHS
KEYWORD: SP3 MCG

CONTENT UPDATES
KEYWORD: SS Content Updates

HOLT PRESENTATION MAKER
KEYWORD: SP3 PPT32

ONLINE READING SUPPORT
KEYWORD: SS Strategies

CURRENT EVENTS
KEYWORD: S3 Current Events

Meeting Individual Needs

Ability Levels

Level 1 Basic level activities designed for all students encountering new material

Level 2 Intermediate level activities designed for average students

Level 3 Challenging activities designed for honors and gifted and talented students

English Language Learners These activities address the needs of students with Limited English Proficiency.

Chapter Review and Assessment

IC Vocabulary Activity 32
Global Skill Builder CD-ROM
HRW Web Site
REV Chapter 32 Tutorial for Students, Parents, Mentors, and Peers
REV Chapter 32 Review, pp. 874–875
A Chapter 32 Test Generator (on the One-Stop Planner)
A Chapter 32 Test (Form A or B)
A Alternative Assessment Handbook
A Chapter 32 Test for English Language Learners and Special-Needs Students

Build on What You Know

Ask students to answer the following questions:

How did postwar Western Europe encourage economic development?

Consider:

- how a stable society promotes economic growth
- the ways a nation's people contribute to its development
- how government policies can affect a nation's economy

What factors make the transition from colony to nation difficult?

Consider:

- the impact of ethnic and religious diversity on national unity
- how the economy and standard of living affect politics in a nation
- the people's level of experience with self-government

EXPLORING THE TIME LINE
GLOBAL EVENTS

CHAPTER 32

1945–Present

Asia Since 1945

Sitar musician Ravi Shankar of India

1945
Global Events
The United Nations is established.

1947
Politics
India gains independence from Britain.

1950
Daily Life
Mother Teresa founds a religious order in Calcutta.

1968
The Arts
Japanese writer Yasunari Kawabata wins the Nobel Prize for literature.

1968
Business and Finance
The United States relaxes trade restrictions with China.

1971
Politics
Bangladesh becomes independent from Pakistan.

1950	1960	1970

1946
Science and Technology
The electric rice saucepan revolutionizes Japanese cooking.

Poster advertising the Japanese movie classic, The Seven Samurai

1954
The Arts
The Japanese movie *The Seven Samurai* becomes popular in the West.

1954
Politics
The Geneva Accord divides Vietnam.

1961
Daily Life
China's population reaches 650 million.

1960
The Arts
Indian musician Ravi Shankar becomes popular in the West.

1960
Business and Finance
A Tokyo company introduces the world's first felt-tip pen.

1965
Daily Life
Pakistan and much of India suffer starvation because of drought.

1967
Global Events
Israel wins the Six-Day War in the Middle East.

1969
Science and Technology
The *Apollo 11* mission lands Americans on the moon.

1972
Business and Finance
Indian entrepreneur Ravi Tikkoo founds Globtik Tankers.

Build on What You Know

Before World War II most of the countries of Asia were colonies of European powers. During the war, some Asian countries provided supplies or arms to the war effort. Some sent troops to join the fighting. Some, because of their strategic locations, were invaded and occupied. After World War II the Asian world changed greatly. The European empires in Asia began to crumble as nationalist sentiments grew and new political parties gained influence. In this chapter, you will learn how the nations of Asia made the transition from colonial possession to independent statehood.

What's Your Opinion?

Government

Agree Whenever government controls people's actions, it is limiting their civil rights.

Disagree People are most free to enjoy their rights when government controls have created a stable society.

Global Relations

Agree History shows that communists are committed to spreading their ideas to other nations.

Disagree There is no reason that communist and noncommunist neighbors cannot peacefully coexist.

Economics

Agree A nation's economy must grow if the standard of living of its citizens is to improve.

Disagree The people of a nation can be content even if the economy does not grow.

Chinese students celebrate as Hong Kong returns to Chinese control.

1976
Daily Life
The World Health Organization reports Asia is free of smallpox for first time in history.

1986
Science and Technology
The Chernobyl nuclear disaster occurs in USSR.

1986
Politics
Corazon Aquino is elected president of the Philippines.

1991
Global Events
The Soviet Union breaks up.

1997
Global Events
The former British colony of Hong Kong is returned to Chinese control.

1998
Business and Finance
Economic problems in Japan spread to other Asian economies and to markets worldwide.

1998
The Arts
The Petronas Twin Towers, the world's tallest buildings, are completed in Kuala Lumpur, Malaysia.

1980

1990

2000

1984
The Arts
Chinese writers call for greater artistic freedom.

1989
Politics
A pro-democracy movement is repressed in China.

2001
Global Events
A mid-air collision between a U.S. intelligence-gathering aircraft and a Chinese jet fighter creates new international tensions.

2000
Daily Life
Two pandas on loan from China arrive at the National Zoological Park in Washington, D.C.

A lone man stands before a line of tanks as Chinese troops move toward student demonstrators in Tiananmen Square in 1989.

Chinese pandas relax at the National Zoological Park in Washington, D.C.

What's Your Opinion?

*Do you **agree** or **disagree** with the following statements? Support your point of view in your journal.*

Government The more controls a government puts in place, the fewer civil rights the people have.

Global Relations Communist and noncommunist countries clash whenever they are located near each other.

Economics A new or developing nation can only succeed if its economy grows.

The Geneva Accords resulted from a conference held in Switzerland from April to July 1954. Delegates attended from Cambodia, China, France, Great Britain, Laos, the Soviet Union, and the United States. Two Vietnamese delegations attended, one from the south and the other representing northern Communist guerrillas, the Viet Minh.

The agreements that were reached dealt with Laos, Cambodia, and Vietnam. They called for elections in all three countries under Canadian, Polish, and Indian supervision. Communist guerrillas were to leave Laos and Cambodia and withdraw to north of the 17th parallel in Vietnam.

Most participants agreed to honor these accords, but the Americans and the South Vietnamese refused to make such a pledge. Therefore, the conference's Final Declaration was not signed by any nation.

Critical Thinking

Ask students why they think the United States refused to sign the Geneva Accords.

ANSWER: Students might suggest that the United States did not trust the Communists to hold to their agreements, or it feared the Communists would win elections in Laos, Cambodia, and Vietnam.

SECTION 1

OBJECTIVES

1 Explain how differences between Hindus and Muslims led to a divided India.

2 Identify problems that India faced after independence.

3 Describe how Pakistan and Bangladesh developed after the partition of India.

LET'S GET STARTED!

As students enter the classroom, ask each to make a list of reasons that neighbors might not get along. *(feuds over property, lifestyle or personality differences)* Then have students use their lists to create a class list on the chalkboard. Then ask volunteers to explain how the items on the list might apply to relations between neighboring nations. Tell students that in Section 1 they will learn how some of the reasons on the list have shaped the history of South Asia since the mid-1900s.

SECTION 1

READ TO DISCOVER

❶ How did differences between Hindus and Muslims lead to a divided India?

❷ What problems did India face after independence?

❸ How did Pakistan and Bangladesh develop after the partition of India?

DEFINE

nonalignment
mixed economy

IDENTIFY

Muslim League
Muhammad Ali Jinnah
Jawaharlal Nehru
Indira Gandhi
Mother Teresa
Dalai Lama
Awami League
Benazir Bhutto

WHY IT MATTERS TODAY

India, Pakistan, and Bangladesh regularly experience natural disasters. Use CNN.com or other **current event** sources to find recent examples. Record your findings in your journal.

CNN Student News.com

South Asia After Empire

The Main Idea
India and Pakistan emerged from British control as independent nations divided along religious lines.

The Story Continues *In the years following World War II, India and Pakistan gained their independence from British rule. The change, however, was not an easy one. Two months after Independence Day, Mohandas K. Gandhi commented sadly, "What sin have I committed that He should have kept me alive to be witness of these horrors?"*

The End of British Rule

The movement for Indian self-rule grew after World War I. Many Indians agreed with the nationalists. They wanted complete freedom from British rule. The nationalists continued to work for self-rule throughout World War II.

Wartime developments. Many Indians refused to back Britain in World War II. They were angry because Great Britain would not meet their demands for self-rule. Also, the British had said that India was at war with Germany without asking the Indian National Congress. Ministers of the Congress resented this action, and the entire Congress resigned in 1939. They called for immediate self-rule.

When Japan entered the war on the side of Germany, the Allies needed India as a base. The pressure on Britain to reach a settlement with India increased. In March 1942, Britain sent Sir Stafford Cripps to work out the terms for India's independence. This would only happen, though, once the war ended. The Indian National Congress rejected his plan. So did the **Muslim League,** a group of Muslim leaders formed to protect the rights of Indian Muslims.

Soon after the Cripps plan failed, nationalist leader Mohandas Karamchand Gandhi started the "Quit India" movement. He insisted that complete separation was the only answer. Great Britain should leave India at once. Britain treated the "Quit India" campaign as a rebellion. Gandhi and some 60,000 of his followers were arrested.

While the Hindus continued to resist the British, the Muslim League made different demands. Led by **Muhammad Ali Jinnah,** they wanted a Muslim state separate from India. This new state would be Pakistan. They believed a separate country would better protect the interests of India's Muslims. The Muslim League wanted Britain to divide the country and then leave. Talks between Gandhi and Jinnah failed to resolve the differences. By 1946 bloody riots had broken out between Hindus and Muslims.

Indian statesman Muhammad Ali Jinnah was the driving force in the creation of the independent Muslim state of Pakistan.

TEACH OBJECTIVE 1

LEVEL 1: Copy the following chart on the chalkboard, omitting the italicized answers. Work with the class to fill in the chart. Then ask students whether the British solution was a good one. *(Answers should note the dislocation of people and the tensions between India and Pakistan that followed.)*

ENGLISH LANGUAGE LEARNERS

Independence Movements in India		
Group	**Hindus**	**Muslims**
Leader	*Mohandas Gandhi*	*Muhammad Ali Jinnah*
Organization/ Motivation	*"Quit India"*	*Muslim League*
Goal for India	*independence for India*	*partition of India*
Outcome	*creation of India*	*creation of Pakistan*

HOMEWORK Have students write letters to the editor of a fictional newspaper in the role of Hindu or Muslim Indians before independence telling why they support or oppose the partition of India.

The partition of India. In March 1947, Lord Louis Mountbatten became British viceroy in India. His strategy was to set a short deadline for Britain to grant independence and force the leaders to reach agreement. The decision to partition, or divide, India was made difficult by the fact that the Muslim and Sikh minorities lived next to Hindus in some areas. Division of the minorities would cause dislocation and tension. Police and military forces would have to be divided, weakening these forces when they would be needed most. In the Punjab, nationalist Sikhs wanted their own state.

Independence was declared in August according to the borders defined by a British-led commission, but without enough preparation for keeping the peace. The celebrations were hardly over before the tragedy began. Citizens fled their homes in the chaos that followed. Violence and massacres erupted. Millions, primarily Muslims, lost their homes or were killed in the following months.

On August 15, 1947, the two nations of India and Pakistan were born. Just before midnight **Jawaharlal Nehru,** India's first prime minister, rose to speak.

History Makers Speak

❝At the stroke of the midnight hour, when the world sleeps, India will awake to life and freedom. A moment comes, which comes but rarely in history, when we step out from the old to the new, when an age ends, and when the soul of the nation, long suppressed, finds utterance. . . .❞

Jawaharlal Nehru, "Tryst with Destiny"

Less than six months later, Mohandas Gandhi was assassinated. The assassin was a Hindu extremist who resented Gandhi for his tolerant attitude toward Muslims.

✔ **READING CHECK: Identifying Cause and Effect** What caused the violence in India after partition? religious divisions

Independent India

In 1950 India's new constitution went into effect. The government became a republic. It has an elected president and parliament. Although the president is the head of state, the prime minister and cabinet members hold the real power.

Government leaders and policies. Jawaharlal Nehru faced a difficult task as the first prime minister of India. Many forces divided his country from the start. There were several religions, many languages, and the caste system. Nehru hoped to unite India. He wanted to separate religion from government and give people more individual rights. Nehru also set India on its path of **nonalignment.** This meant that India did not ally with either the United States or the Soviet Union.

Nehru died in 1964. Two years later his daughter, **Indira Priyadarshini Nehru Gandhi,** became the prime minister. Her goal was to carry out her father's ideas. Indira Gandhi ran the Indian government for nearly 20 years. Some of her actions, however, angered people. Many Indians turned against her. In 1977 they voted her out of office. Three years later voters elected her prime minister again.

Analyzing Primary Sources

Analyzing Information What did Nehru mean when he said "the soul of the nation, long suppressed, finds utterance"? now have a free voice in their own affairs

India's first prime minister, Jawaharlal Nehru, and his daughter, Indira Gandhi, made a state visit to the United States in December 1956.

Government

The constitution created under Nehru brought significant social changes to India. For one thing, it outlawed the long-standing practice of untouchability, which relegated members of India's lowest caste to inferior positions in society. Enforcement of these new rules helped former untouchables get better jobs and obtain an education.

The new constitution also gave Hindu women many rights, such as the right to vote and to hold office. Later, Hindu women also won the right to divorce and to inherit property. Muslim women retained their rights under Islamic law.

Critical Thinking

What other constitutional provisions might have been added to benefit Indian society and lessen social problems?

ANSWER: Answers will vary, but might include freedom-of-religion guarantees and provisions for more regional autonomy.

TEACH OBJECTIVE 2

ALL LEVELS: Write the following four headings on the chalkboard: *Social Problems, Economic Problems, Political Problems,* and *Foreign Relations Problems.* Call on students to identify a problem India has faced since independence and list it under one of the chalkboard headings. When the lists are complete, have students work in pairs to decide which category of problem presents the most serious challenge for India. Have each pair explain its conclusion to the class. **COOPERATIVE LEARNING**

LEVEL 3: Organize students into small groups to assume the roles of economic advisers to India's prime minister. Each group should decide whether India should pursue a socialist, free market (capitalist), or mixed economy. Each group should draft a memo for the prime minister stating their recommendation and explaining why they think it is the best course for India to follow. **COOPERATIVE LEARNING**

Geography

Sikhism, founded in the Punjab in the late 1400s, combines the Muslim belief in one eternal and all-powerful god with the Hindu concepts of karma and reincarnation. However, unlike Hindus, Sikhs reject the caste system and believe in the equality of humankind.

Sikhism is a global religion today, due largely to Sikh emigration from India. Significant Sikh communities can be found in Great Britain, Canada, South Africa, and the United States. However, some 80 percent of the world's 14 million Sikhs still live in the Punjab, where Sikh separatism has become a militant political movement and another divisive force in India.

Critical Thinking

Why might Sikh settlement patterns lead to a movement for separatism?

ANSWER: The concentration of Sikhs in the Punjab could weaken that region's feelings of attachment and loyalty to the nation of India.

MAP ANSWER
Muslim and Hindu

INTERPRETING THE GRAPH ANSWER
Hindu

Religious Divisions and the Partitioning of India, 1947
Interpreting Maps The partitioning of India created conflicts among the country's main religious groups.
■ **Skills Assessment: Human Systems** Which two religious groups were fighting for control of Kashmir?

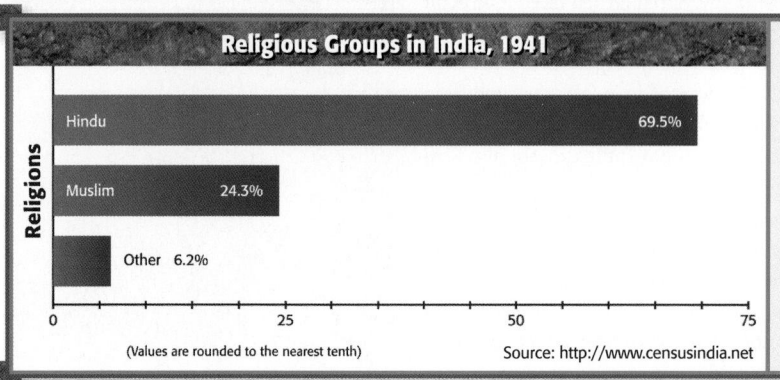

Religious Groups in India, 1941
(Values are rounded to the nearest tenth)   Source: http://www.censusindia.net

Interpreting the Graph
Religious groups in India identified by the 1941 British census included Hindu, Muslim, Christian, Sikh, Buddhist, and Jain faiths. Most of the former British colony's Muslims became citizens of Pakistan as a result of the partition of 1947. *Which religious group probably dominated India's political scene following independence?*

848

LEVEL 1: Ask students to create flowcharts showing the sequence of events that led to Pakistan becoming two nations. *(Pakistan holds elections; Awami League wins most East Pakistan seats in assembly, favors self-rule for East Pakistan; Pakistan's government rejects election results; riots break out in East Pakistan; Pakistan's government sends troops to put down riots and arrest Awami League leaders; civil war breaks out; India sends arms and troops to aid East Pakistan; East Pakistan defeats West Pakistan and becomes nation of Bangladesh)* After students have completed their flowcharts ask them what challenges Bangladesh faces today. *(political unrest, natural disasters, famine)*

ENGLISH LANGUAGE LEARNERS

Gandhi faced a difficult problem on her return. Sikhs from the province of Punjab were fighting for self-rule. They had killed a number of government officials. In 1984 Gandhi ordered the Indian army to storm the Sikh base, which was the Golden Shrine in Amritsar, their holiest place of worship. About 1,000 people died in the attack. The Sikhs promised to get revenge. A few months later, two of Gandhi's Sikh bodyguards assassinated her. Her son, Rajiv Gandhi, took over as prime minister. He was a popular leader, but his party lost power.

In 1989 a new prime minister, V. P. Singh, was elected. He wanted to improve the rights of the lower castes. Violent protests forced him to resign in 1990. Most people thought voters would return Rajiv Gandhi to power. Before the election, though, Gandhi was assassinated. Several years of unrest followed as more than 20 political parties fought for power. In 1998 Atal Bihari Vajpayee was elected prime minister. Vajpayee, like his predecessors, expressed his desire for better relations with Pakistan. In spite of this, clashes between troops from both countries continued. By 2000 the fighting between India and Pakistan had taken a frightening turn. Both countries had built and tested nuclear weapons.

Social and economic problems. Nehru followed socialist ideas for India's economy. From 1947 onward, India has had a **mixed economy.** This occurs when private companies own some industries and the government owns the rest. To help the economy grow, India followed a series of Five-Year Plans. These plans worked very well. By the end of the 1980s, Indian farms were growing more food. The textile and steel industries were strong. The country also was exporting many finished products, such as clothing and bicycles.

In spite of this growth, India still had a huge problem. Its population was growing too fast. In 1950 the Indian population was about 360 million. Within about 30 years, it had grown to about 685 million. The nation's economy could not keep up with the population increase. By the late 1980s, the average annual income was $300. Millions of Indians had no jobs. Cities were crowded and housing was short. Many millions barely managed to stay alive from day to day.

In the 1990s, India tried to find new solutions to its problems. As the government became more open to foreign investors and trade, the economy grew. At the same

HISTORY MAKER

**Indira Gandhi
(1917–1984)**

Indira Gandhi was involved in India's political scene for most of her life. Gandhi was the daughter of Jawaharlal Nehru. Like her father, she became involved in nationalist activities while India was fighting for its independence.

Indira Gandhi followed in her father's footsteps when she became India's prime minister in 1966. She surprised many people who believed she was incapable of doing the job. Instead, Gandhi showed herself to be a powerful ruler whose leadership helped India to become a key force in world affairs. **How might Indira Gandhi's childhood have prepared her for political leadership?**

Linking Past to Present

India's most common agricultural pattern has been small-scale peasant farming. After independence, India's population growth put increased pressure on land resources. Today, India continues to struggle with this problem. The urban growth that has occurred is due more to economic pressure driving people from the land than it is to available opportunities in the cities.

internet connect

TOPIC: India's Population
GO TO: go.hrw.com
KEYWORD: SP3 WH32

Have students access the Internet through the HRW Go site to find information on the populations of the United States and India. Ask students to research birth rates, death rates, and immigration statistics for the two countries. Then ask them to create charts to present their findings. Ask them to write a brief paragraph that explains their findings.

HISTORY MAKER ANSWER
observing and talking with her father

Indira Gandhi, India's prime minister from 1966 to 1977 and again from 1980 to 1984, bridged the country's transition from colony to independent republic.

Rudy Martinez of San Antonio, Texas, suggested the following activity: Have students write a short essay to answer this question: "What might be the consequences of the build-up of nuclear weapons in India and Pakistan?" After students have completed their essays, select answers to be compared and discussed by the class.

CLOSE

Ask students to cite various ways in which people in South Asia are divided. List responses on the chalkboard. *(religion, nationality, urban/rural, caste, culture, language)* Then call on volunteers to explain which of these divisions they believe to be the biggest obstacle to progress in the region.

History Maker

MOTHER TERESA. Mother Teresa was born in Albania in 1910. She was the daughter of a grocer. In 1928 she went to Ireland to join a Roman Catholic religious order. Six weeks later she was sent to India. Soon afterward she began her work with the destitute of India.

Mother Teresa founded the Missionaries of Charity about 20 years later. She had made India her home and adopted Indian citizenship. In 1963 the Indian government gave her a special award for her services to the Indian people. She was also awarded the 1979 Nobel Peace Prize. Mother Teresa continued to work, in spite of health problems, until her death in 1997.

Critical Thinking

Why was Mother Teresa so revered in India and worldwide?

ANSWER: Answers will vary but should include her efforts to address intractable problems.

DAILY LIFE ANSWER
provides nursing care and education for the poor in India

Technology Resources
World History Teaching Transparency: Geography and History 27: The Economy of South Asia

DAILY LIFE

Helping India's Poor
Today more than 40 percent of the world's poor live in India. To provide aid for so many people is an overwhelming task. But help comes from a variety of groups that assist India's poor with food, clothing, shelter, and other services. Among the most famous of these groups are the nuns of the Missionaries of Charity, founded in 1950 by an Albanian nun known as **Mother Teresa.** The nuns provide nursing care for the ill and educational programs for children. Volunteers from around the world also come to India to aid the poor.

How does the organization founded by Mother Teresa help India's poor?

Holt Researcher go.hrw.com

go.hrw.com
KEYWORD: Holt Researcher
FreeFind: Mother Teresa
After reading more about Mother Teresa on the Holt Researcher, analyze her influence on events of the 20th century.

time, though, the population continued to grow. By 2000 India had over 1 billion people. If this rate continues, India will have more people than any other country by 2050. These people will live on just 2 percent of the world's land area.

✔ **READING CHECK: Making Predictions** What effect do you think India's population growth will have on the nation's future? increased poverty, disease, pollution

Foreign relations. In world affairs, India tried to build friendships with both communist countries and the West. This nonalignment became a model for other countries. A number of new African and Asian nations followed India's lead. By staying neutral, these countries hoped to get aid from both sides.

India's foreign policy did not solve all its problems. In 1950 China occupied Tibet. The Tibetans rebelled, but the Chinese crushed the revolt. For a long time before this, India had backed the **Dalai Lama,** Tibet's Buddhist religious leader and political head. When the Chinese took control of Tibet, the Dalai Lama and some of his Buddhist followers fled to India. There they formed a government in exile. During the next few years, relations between India and China became even more difficult.

India began to move away from nonalignment in the 1970s and established close ties with the Soviet Union. Then, in the 1980s, India became interested in better relations with the United States. Even so, India would not take sides in the Cold War. By the 1990s, India's policies had changed, and it began to take a more open approach to foreign affairs.

The continuing problem of Kashmir. India and Pakistan faced a difficult problem in the northern state of Kashmir. The problem began with partition in 1947. Kashmir's ruling prince, who was Hindu, at first tried to avoid joining either country. On the one hand, Pakistan claimed Kashmir because three quarters of its people were Muslim. On the other hand, Nehru's family was from Kashmir and he had ties with the area. He sent Indian troops to back the Hindu prince.

Muslims and Hindus in Kashmir fought each other for control. This led to fighting between Indian and Pakistani soldiers. In 1949 the United Nations set a cease-fire line. At that point, India held two thirds of Kashmir. Still, the question of Kashmir's nationality was not answered. India and Pakistan continued to fight on and off throughout the 1950s and 1960s. In the late 1980s, border clashes and other violence between rebel groups became more common. Such flare-ups continued into the early 2000s. By 2004, more than 20,000 people had been killed.

✔ **READING CHECK: Finding the Main Idea** What challenges with foreign affairs did India face? maintaining relations with East and West, problem of Kashmir

The Division of Pakistan

When British rule ended, Pakistan became a two-part country. West Pakistan and East Pakistan were separated by India. The two parts were about 1,000 miles from each other. The differences between them were huge. They had different languages, cultures, and geography. It was almost impossible to govern the two parts as one country. Although Pakistan started out as a republic, the government soon lost control to a series of military leaders.

Independence for Bangladesh. When Pakistan held elections in 1970, the **Awami League** won the majority of the East Pakistani seats in the assembly. The Awami League

REVIEW

Have students complete the Section 1 Review on page 851.

ASSESS

Have students complete Daily Quiz 32.1. As Alternative Assessment, you may want to use the chart activity or the homework assignment in this section's lessons.

RETEACH

Have students complete Main Idea Activity for English Language Learners and Special-Needs Students 32.1. Then have students work in pairs to answer each of the Read To Discover questions at the beginning of this section.
ENGLISH LANGUAGE LEARNERS, COOPERATIVE LEARNING

EXTEND

Organize two groups of students, one representing colonial India's Hindus and the other its Muslims. Have each group prepare a written proposal, including maps or diagrams, for how India could function as a single nation if granted independence from Great Britain. Then have each group review the other group's plan and negotiate to see if they can arrive at a mutually acceptable proposal. **BLOCK SCHEDULING, COOPERATIVE LEARNING**

was a political party that wanted self-rule for East Pakistan. When Pakistan's central government refused to accept the election result, riots broke out in East Pakistan. The central government sent troops to put down the riots. They arrested the leaders of the Awami League. The situation soon became a civil war in which thousands of people were killed. India sent arms and troops to help East Pakistan. Ten million people from East Pakistan fled to India. Late in 1971 the West Pakistanis were defeated and East Pakistan became the new nation of Bangladesh.

Bangladesh and Pakistan today. Bangladesh had been torn apart by war. It also suffered famines, floods, and tropical storms. The new government was not equal to the huge task of rebuilding the country. In the mid-1970s, it was taken over in a military coup. In the 1991 elections, the Bangladesh National Party (BNP) won a victory over the Awami League. The BNP leader, Khalida Zia, became the country's first woman prime minister. In 1996 new elections brought the Awami League back into power. Bad feelings between the two parties continued, and the country faced huge challenges. In 1998 floods covered almost all of Bangladesh. More than 1 million people died, and at least 30 million people lost their homes.

Pakistan, too, faced political unrest. In 1977 General Mohammed Zia ul-Haq took control of the government. He had the prime minister, Zulfikar Ali Bhutto, arrested. Bhutto was put to death two years later. Zia finally allowed elections in 1988. **Benazir Bhutto,** the daughter of Ali Bhutto, was elected prime minister. She became the first woman to serve as head of a Muslim nation. The army removed her from office in 1990, but she was elected again in 1993. Three years later she was defeated. In 1999 the army took control, and General Pervez Musharraf became prime minister. General Musharraf has been active in removing Taliban allies from the Pakistani military forces and in 2002, Pakistan's participation in the war against terrorism led to the repeal of U.S. economic embargoes imposed on the country in 1998.

✔ **READING CHECK: Contrasting** In what ways are Pakistan's current problems different from those of Bangladesh? Bangladesh faces problems of war and natural disasters; Pakistan faces political unrest

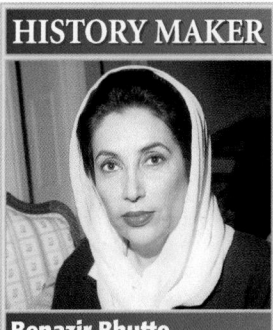

HISTORY MAKER

Benazir Bhutto (1953–)

Benazir Bhutto graduated from Radcliffe College, in the United States. When she was sworn in as the prime minister of Pakistan, she became the first woman to govern a Muslim country. **How do the experiences of Benazir Bhutto reflect the changing roles and influence of women in modern Asia?**

HISTORY MAKER ANSWER
Women are gaining status and rights in Muslim society.

SECTION 1 REVIEW ANSWERS

❶ Define
- nonalignment, p. 847
- mixed economy, p. 849

❷ Identify
- Muslim League, p. 846
- Muhammad Ali Jinnah, p. 846
- Jawaharlal Nehru, p. 847
- Indira Gandhi, p. 847
- Mother Teresa, p. 850
- Dalai Lama, p. 850
- Awami League, p. 850
- Benazir Bhutto, p. 851

❸ India: Hindus demand independence, Muslims demand separate state, Britain partitions along religious lines; Pakistan: Britain creates East and West Pakistan from Muslim areas in India; Bangladesh: Awami League wants self-rule for East Pakistan, wins majority in assembly, civil war breaks out, India aids East Pakistan, East Pakistan wins independence and becomes Bangladesh

❹ a. boundaries of two countries drawn along religious lines

b. tried to build friendships with both communist countries and the West

c. population growth, political unrest, natural disasters

❺ Answers will vary but should include the conditions that led to the decision as well as the result.

SECTION 1 REVIEW

1. **Define** and explain the significance:
   nonalignment
   mixed economy

2. **Identify** and explain the significance:
   Muslim League
   Muhammad Ali Jinnah
   Jawaharlal Nehru
   Indira Gandhi
   Mother Teresa
   Dalai Lama
   Awami League
   Benazir Bhutto

3. **Summarizing** Make a chart like this one to summarize how India, Pakistan, and Bangladesh became independent nations.

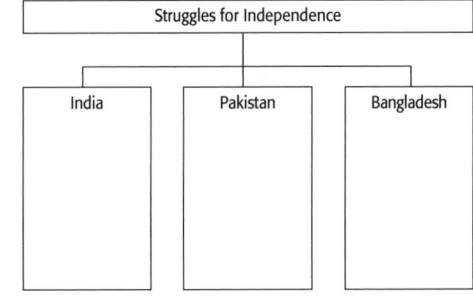

Struggles for Independence

India	Pakistan	Bangladesh

4. **Finding the Main Idea**
   a. What effect did religion have on the way India and Pakistan were established?
   b. How did nonalignment affect India's foreign relations?
   c. What have been the greatest domestic challenges for India, Pakistan, and Bangladesh?

5. **Writing and Critical Thinking**
   Supporting a Point of View Write a paragraph explaining why you think it was a good or bad idea to divide India before independence.
   Consider:
   • the fighting between Hindus and Muslims
   • relations between India and Pakistan since partition

Homework Practice Online
keyword: SP3 HP32

SECTION 2

OBJECTIVES

1 Describe how Mao Zedong's government tried to rebuild China after World War II.

2 Identify what happened at Tiananmen Square and what the consequences were for China.

3 Explain why Korea was divided and how the two Koreas have developed since 1953.

4 Explain why China and Taiwan have been in conflict.

LET'S GET STARTED!

As students enter the classroom, ask them whether they would rather live in a society where everyone's standard of living is roughly the same, regardless of how much or how little work they did, or in a society where they have a chance to become very rich or very poor. Discuss students' opinions. Then tell students that in Section 2 they will learn how other people's feelings about these choices have affected China and Korea.

SECTION 2

READ TO DISCOVER

❶ How did Mao Zedong's government try to rebuild China after World War II?

❷ What occurred at Tiananmen Square, and what were the consequences for China?

❸ Why was Korea divided, and how have the two Koreas developed since 1953?

❹ Why have China and Taiwan been in conflict?

IDENTIFY

Great Leap Forward
Cultural Revolution
Red Guards
Jiang Qing
Gang of Four
Deng Xiaoping
Tiananmen Square Massacre
Kim Il Sung
Syngman Rhee

WHY IT MATTERS TODAY

The pro-democracy movement in China is still active today. Use CNN fyi.com or other **current event** sources to find out what has happened to the movement since 2000. Record your findings in your journal.

CNN Student News.com

Communist China and Its Influence

The Main Idea
China and North Korea became communist, while South Korea and Taiwan remained non-communist.

The Story Continues *Unlike India, China did not have to fight for self-rule. In the 1930s, however, conflicts inside China had grown into a bloody civil war. According to one observer, "We need only look at . . . the uprisings by the peasants, the mutinies of soldiers and the strikes of students . . . to see that it cannot be long before a 'spark' kindles 'a prairie fire.'" By the time the civil war ended, China was devastated.*

China Under Mao Zedong

During World War II, the Chinese Nationalists and Chinese Communists had agreed to temporarily stop their civil war in the face of the common threat posed by Japanese aggression. Throughout the war years, the Nationalists and the Communists joined in an uneasy alliance against the Japanese. Their combined forces fought an effective guerrilla campaign until Japan surrendered in 1945. Following the war, however, bitter fighting broke out once again as China's destructive civil war resumed.

In 1949 the Communists under the leadership of Mao Zedong finally drove the Nationalists from power. Chiang Kai-shek, the Nationalists' leader, fled with his supporters to the island of Taiwan. Chiang and the Nationalists formed a government there. On the Chinese mainland Mao Zedong's Communists formed the People's Republic of China. About 1 million Chinese were killed during the communist takeover. The United States, which had supported the Nationalists, refused to recognize the new Chinese Communist government.

The People's Republic of China. The Communists wanted to turn China into a modern, industrialized nation. Because of the damage from the civil war, this was a huge task. In 1953 the Communists began their first Five-Year Plan for economic growth. It was modeled on similar Soviet plans. Part of the plan was to build up China's industry. Another part was land reform. The Communists forced landlords to give their land to the peasants. Millions of people were killed during this violent change. The peasants organized their new land into collective farms. The government operated state farms on much of the land that was left. The first Five-Year Plan was a success, as both agricultural and industrial output increased.

The flag of the People's Republic of China, designed after the communist takeover of the Chinese mainland in 1949.

LEVEL 1: Call on students to identify the three major programs undertaken by Mao Zedong to change China in the 1950s and 1960s. *(first Five-Year Plan, Great Leap Forward [second Five-Year Plan], Cultural Revolution)* Then put the chart on the chalkboard, including one example in each column as shown. Have students add to each column to complete the chart. Then have them decide which program was the most beneficial and which was the most harmful to China.

ENGLISH LANGUAGE LEARNERS

How Mao's Programs Affected China		
First Five-Year Plan	**Great Leap Forward**	**Cultural Revolution**
1. transferred farm-land from landlords to peasants	1. threatened Mao's leadership	1. had a disastrous effect on China's economy
2. collective farms and state farms	2. people's communes	2. Red Guard rampages
3. agricultural and industrial output increase	3. industrial output decrease, food shortages	3. agricultural and industrial production falls

Revolution in China, 1945–1949

Interpreting Maps Communists gained control over China over a four-year period.

■ **Skills Assessment: Places and Regions** What city was a communist capital until 1949?

Geography

Land along the Chang River, west of Chongqing, is exceptionally rich and productive. But before the Communists imposed land reform in the 1950s, some 80 percent of the region's peasants were not able to raise enough food for their families. Many people starved, and life expectancy in the region was only 40 years. When the Communists redistributed the land there and throughout China, each farmer had about the same amount of land. They labeled the program "the land returning home." Previous landowners were allowed to keep some of their former holdings—exactly as much as everyone else.

Critical Thinking

Ask students if they think most landlords would have been pro- or anticommunist and why.

ANSWER: likely anticommunist because land reform took their land and thus their source of income

MAP ANSWER
Yan'an

The Great Leap Forward. To speed up progress, in 1958 Mao's government announced a second Five-Year Plan called the **Great Leap Forward.** The Chinese government hoped to increase industrial output to the point where it matched that of the West. To reach this goal, China bought modern machinery and ran it almost continuously. The government encouraged people to produce their own iron and steel in small backyard blast furnaces.

The Great Leap Forward created huge farm communities called people's communes. These included farms and small industries. Single people lived in dormitories, meals were served in mess halls, and children were cared for in nurseries while their parents worked long hours in the fields and factories. Workers were paid based on "work points," which were set based on gender, age, skills, type of job, and region.

Spotlight on ECONOMICS Ask students to identify and explain the term *Four Modernizations* found on page 855. *(late 1970s plan to reform China's economy)* Ask students what was different about the Four Modernizations plan that helps explain its success. *(moved China toward a market economy)* Ask students to speculate about why private ownership of business has promoted economic growth in China. *(possible response: the profit incentive encourages people to work harder)*

Interdisciplinary Connection

ART. The Chinese Communist Party viewed all art as simply another tool to be used by the revolution. The most extreme form of communist art occurred during the Cultural Revolution, when virtually all forms of art, including painting, opera, and literature were scrutinized for their "socialist content."

Traditional art forms, such as landscape painting, had to portray some aspect of socialism. A waterfall, for example, may have been painted as running a hydroelectric plant or serving some other useful function for the revolution. Operas written during the Cultural Revolution often portrayed loyal Communists in action, waving huge red banners and quoting Chairman Mao while attacking capitalist "imperialism."

Critical Thinking

What might Chinese artists have thought of this system?

ANSWER: Students may respond that some artists probably disliked it because it restricted creative freedom, but that others might have been glad to have state support.

YOUNG PEOPLE IN HISTORY ANSWER

by attempting to destroy all remnants of China's "old way"

YOUNG PEOPLE IN HISTORY

The Red Guards

In 1966 almost 11 million Chinese students from all across China banded together to form a political group known as the Red Guards. The students marched to the capital of Beijing, where they held mass demonstrations in support of the Communist Party. According to Chinese officials, the aim of the Red Guards was to "purify" China's political scene by ridding it of opponents to the rule of Mao Zedong. The Red Guards were responsible for the execution of thousands of Chinese who disagreed with Mao and his government. The group did not last long. By 1968 the Red Guards had diminished in power and prestige. **How did the Red Guards show their support for the Communist government?**

Holt Researcher
go.hrw.com
KEYWORD: Holt Researcher
FreeFind: Jiang Qing
After reading more about Jiang Qing on the Holt Researcher, create a chart comparing China under her influence with China under Mao.

At a 1966 rally, thousands of Red Guards wave Mao Zedong's "little red book," which was a collection of his political ideas.

The Great Leap Forward was a terrible failure. Industrial output decreased, and there were constant food shortages. As many as 20 million people starved to death between 1958 and 1960. The government abandoned the program in the early 1960s.

The Cultural Revolution. After the failure of the Great Leap Forward, Mao's leadership of the Communist Party was in question. He fought back in 1966 by launching the **Cultural Revolution,** a violent attempt at social change. Mao aimed to rid China of its old customs, habits, and thoughts. He wanted to replace them with a new socialist culture. Mao's ideas were collected in a little red book. For example, Mao spoke against intellectuals.

 History Makers Speak   **❝The . . . intellectuals who are hostile to our state . . . will stir up trouble and attempt to overthrow the Communist Party and restore the old China. . . . Such people are to be found in political circles and in . . . educational, scientific . . . and religious circles, and they are extremely reactionary.❞**

from Mao Zedong, *Quotations from Chairman Mao*

Mao chose China's young people to lead this revolution. These radical students soon became known as the **Red Guards.** They went on rampages throughout China. They ruined ancient works of art, burned books, and destroyed anything from the "old way." They also beat, tortured, or killed some people who did not follow Mao's teachings completely.

The Cultural Revolution and the mass murders it involved had a disastrous effect on China. Agricultural and industrial production fell sharply. Chinese society was in chaos. In late 1968 Mao took control and broke up the Red Guards.

✔ **READING CHECK: Summarizing** What did Mao do to try to solve China's problems?
Five-Year Plans, Great Leap Forward, Cultural Revolution

China After Mao

Mao Zedong died in 1976. After his death, a struggle began between moderate Communists and a radical group led by Mao's widow, **Jiang Qing** (jee·AHNG CHING), who was sometimes known as Madame Mao. The moderates wanted to restore order and economic growth. Jiang Qing's group, known as the **Gang of Four,** wanted to continue the Cultural Revolution. In time, the moderates won control and placed the Gang of Four on trial for numerous crimes, including treason. They were found guilty and given life sentences.

TEACH OBJECTIVE 2

ALL LEVELS: Organize students into groups to decide whether the events at Tiananmen Square in 1989 were good or bad for China. Have each group explain its reasoning to the class.
COOPERATIVE LEARNING

HOMEWORK Have students write journal entries as if they were Chinese students in Tiananmen Square in May 1989. They should explain their reasons for being there and their feelings about their government.

By the late 1970s, **Deng Xiaoping** (DUHNG SHOW·PING) had become leader of the moderates. He directed a complete reform of the economy. Deng's plan was called the Four Modernizations. The goal was to improve agriculture, industry, science and technology, and national defense. China began to move toward a market economy. This led to a more open society in which there were cultural and scientific exchanges with Western countries. China also began importing technology from the West. This new direction led to major economic gains. From the mid-1980s to the early 1990s, China had one of the world's fastest-growing economies.

The new direction encouraged many Chinese to speak out. Some called for a "fifth modernization"—democracy. In the spring of 1989, hundreds of thousands of pro-democracy demonstrators occupied Tiananmen Square, Beijing's central gathering place. They wanted an end to corruption in the ruling party, a greater say in government, and better conditions in the universities.

Thousands of students staged a hunger strike and ignored government orders to leave. In early June tanks and armed troops began to move toward Tiananmen Square, opening fire on the protesters. Hundreds were killed and thousands wounded. This incident became known as the **Tiananmen Square Massacre,** and it stunned the West. Most Western nations and international aid agencies stopped or cut back on loans to China. Tourism halted. Since China needed to replace this lost income, Jiang Zemin, China's president from 1993 to 2003, proposed a new plan. In 1997 the government turned over control of thousands of failing state-owned businesses to private owners. Although few of the companies made money at first, the plan did give China some much-needed income. As memories of the Tiananmen Square Massacre faded, foreign investment revived and foreign trade surged to new highs. By 2003 China had become the world's second-largest economy. Even so, many of China's economic problems persisted. Unemployment remained high and millions of people continued to live in poverty.

Foreign relations since 1949. In the early 1950s the Soviet Union and China were allies, but before long, the two nations developed differences. China began to view the Soviet Union as a threat, and during the 1960s the two countries clashed along their common border. As the split with the Soviet Union deepened, China turned to the United States. Following President Nixon's visit to China in 1972, the two nations began to allow exchanges, increasing travel back and forth. In 1979 the United States officially recognized the People's Republic of China and ended recognition of Taiwan. China's improving relations with the West through the 1980s led to trade agreements with several countries and increased financial aid and technical help.

By the late 1990s China had largely recovered from the results of Tiananmen Square. In 1997, neighboring Hong Kong, which had been a British colony since the 1840s, was returned to Chinese rule. Although China's human rights record and the status of Taiwan, which has resisted reunification efforts, are issues of disagreement between the United States and China, relations between the two countries have improved since President Hu Jintao and Premier Wen Jiabao were elected in 2003.

✔ **READING CHECK: Drawing Inferences** Why did the Chinese government crack down on the students in Tiananmen Square? Democratic reforms would have threatened their power.

Chinese human-rights demonstrators and uniformed soldiers mingle during a 1989 protest in Beijing's Tiananmen Square.

What If? How would U.S. relations with China be different if the Chinese had not been in conflict with the Soviet Union?

Economics

Deng Xiaoping incorporated elements of the free-enterprise system into the Chinese economy. He allowed peasant farmers to have individual control over and responsibility for their production and profits. As a result agricultural production greatly increased during the 1980s. Deng also strengthened China's trade with the West and opened Chinese enterprise to foreign investment.

Critical Thinking

How might the new prosperity have affected the attitudes of the Chinese people toward their government?

ANSWER: Answers may vary. Some might predict that prosperous people are less inclined to complain about their government. Others might suggest that gaining economic control leads to a desire for political control.

WHAT IF? ANSWER

Students might suggest that Chinese leaders would have had less need of allies and thus would have been less interested in forming better relations with the United States.

That's Interesting!

North Korean TV consists mostly of musical shows that praise the qualities of Kim Jong Il and his late father Kim Il Sung, the first leader of Communist North Korea. Kim Il Sung became the subject of an extreme personality cult that continues to this day.

MAP ANSWERS

1. near the 38th parallel

2. little territory changed hands

Korean War, 1950–1953

Interpreting Maps North Korea and South Korea were initially divided along the 38th parallel.

■ **Skills Assessment: 1. Locate** Where was the cease-fire line established? **2. Drawing Conclusions** What does this indicate about the effect of the war on the geographic boundary of the two countries?

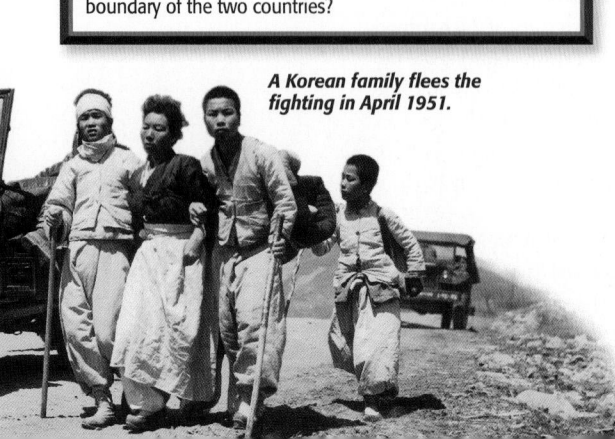

A Korean family flees the fighting in April 1951.

A Divided Korea

Relations between China and the United States were tense in the 1950s and 1960s. A major cause of the tension was Korea. After World War II Korea had been divided at the 38th parallel (north latitude). The Soviet Union occupied the area north of this line. American troops controlled the southern part. The division was meant to be temporary. The two powers agreed that a government should be formed to rule the entire country. That never happened, and Korea remained divided. In North Korea, a communist government led by **Kim Il Sung** took power. In South Korea a republic was created with **Syngman Rhee** as president. Both leaders wanted to reunite Korea, by force if necessary. In June 1950 North Korea invaded South Korea. The Communists quickly captured Seoul (SOHL), the South Korean capital. The United Nations Security Council condemned the attack. It called on UN members to furnish troops and supplies to stop the invasion. Most of the troops came from the United States. In September the United States and South Korea launched an attack. The North Koreans fell back behind their border, with U.S. troops in pursuit.

As the U.S. troops approached the border between Korea and China, China felt threatened. It sent several hundred thousand Chinese soldiers to join those of North Korea. This combined force drove the U.S. troops back south of the 38th parallel. In response, some U.S. military leaders wanted to bomb China directly. President Harry Truman opposed these actions. He thought it might lead to a third world war. Bitter fighting continued for two more years. The two sides finally signed a cease-fire agreement in July 1953. The dividing line was almost exactly where it had been before the war.

Although South Korea was a republic, it was not democratic. Syngman Rhee and the leaders who followed him ran the country as dictators. They used their power, however, to promote economic growth. Both industry and foreign trade increased. South Korea had one of the fastest-growing economies in the world from the 1960s to the 1990s. At the same time, South Koreans had little political freedom.

In 1998 Kim Dae Jung was sworn in as president of South Korea. Kim placed great importance on bringing democracy to South Korea. He also made a point of reaching out to North Korea.

North Korea had severe problems. Terrible famines plagued the nation. The United States and other nations sent massive amounts of food aid to North Korea. Faced with famine and economic collapse, North Korea finally agreed to a meeting with South Korea.

Have two panels of students take the roles of Chinese and Taiwanese diplomats to debate the status of Taiwan. One panel should represent the position of the Chinese government regarding Taiwan and the other the Chinese Nationalist position. Have the rest of the class act as observers and direct questions to each panel about its position. At the end of the debate, have students vote on whether Taiwan should be part of China or remain independent. **COOPERATIVE LEARNING**

Ask students which person they would prefer to be if they lived in China: government official, rural peasant, industrial worker, soldier, or business person. Then ask which person they would *least* like to be. Repeat the process for North Korea and South Korea. Have students explain the reasons for their choices.

SKILL-BUILDING STRATEGIES Conducting Research

The Two Koreas

On June 14, 2001, North Korea and South Korea observed the first anniversary of the Korea Summit. At this important summit, leaders of the two nations signed the North Korea-South Korea Joint Declaration, beginning a new phase in the history of the divided peninsula. Here is how one reporter described the mood at the summit in June of 2000:

> "The Korea Summit appears to have gone better than most had hoped. No one expected such genuine warmth to be generated between the two presidents. Reunification of Korea is still on a distant horizon, and the journey to that day will not be smooth and easy. But the fact that reunification is now discussed as a tangible possibility instead of an abstract dream is significant. Almost as significant is the impact this new relationship will have on the United States. . . .
>
> Less than a year ago [June 1999] there was a confrontation between North Korea and South Korea on the high seas. The conflict ended with the sinking of a North Korean ship. Less than two years ago [August 1998] North Korea tested a missile which could threaten South Korea, Japan, and other neighbors. . . .
>
> Now the president of North Korea and president of South Korea are meeting in Pyongyang, the North Korean capital. This is the first inter-Korean summit since a 1953 cease-fire put the Korean War on hold."

The North Korea-South Korea Joint Declaration, with the two leaders' signatures

South Korean President Kim Dae Jung (left) and North Korean leader Kim Jong Il (right) raise their arms together before signing the joint declaration.

Skills Reminder

Students today have more ways to find information than ever before. One traditional way of finding information is by consulting books and periodicals in a library. Check the library's card catalog or computerized records to find out how the library organizes its materials. The World Wide Web can also be a great research tool. Search engines can provide you with a list of Web sites that contain keywords relating to your topic. Use the skills you have developed for evaluating sources to judge the validity of any Web site you access.

Skills Practice

Consult three or more reference sources to answer the following questions.
1 What types of information about the two Koreas can you get from a library's card catalog, whether traditional or electronic?
2 What kinds of references contain information about the geography and political boundaries of the Korean Peninsula?
3 Where would you look to find the most recent coverage of developments in the relationship between North Korea and South Korea?

Daily Life

North Korean society is built on a rigid "estates" system. The population is grouped into three categories: loyal, wavering, and hostile. Classification in the first category is necessary for advancement. Those considered "hostile"—usually Christians and the children of former landlords or Koreans who fled to the South—have almost no rights. Daily life is strictly regulated. Women make up more than half the workforce and are required to run the home as well. The political elite, about 200,000 of the nation's more than 23 million people, enjoy a privileged lifestyle. This is a source of great resentment among average North Koreans.

ACTIVITY: Ask students to imagine they live in North Korea. Have them write letters to relatives in South Korea describing what daily life is like in North Korea.

SKILLS PRACTICE ANSWERS
1. titles and summaries of books about the topics, dates of publication, authors

2. atlases, electronic or bound

3. newspapers and newspaper indexes, encyclopedia yearbooks, current periodicals, and electronic databases of current events

REVIEW

Have students complete the Section 2 Review on page 858.

ASSESS

Have students complete Daily Quiz 32.2. As Alternative Assessment, you may want to use the homework assignment or the graphic organizers in this section's lessons.

RETEACH

Have students complete Main Idea Activity for English Language Learners and Special-Needs Students 32.2. Then have them write

EXTEND

Organize students into two groups. One group should portray Chinese Communists loyal to the original principles of Mao. The other group should represent Chinese Communists who are moderate reformers. Then hold a "party congress" to debate who is responsible for the unrest in China. **BLOCK SCHEDULING, COOPERATIVE LEARNING**

SECTION 2 REVIEW ANSWERS

❶ Identify
- Great Leap Forward, p. 853
- Cultural Revolution, p. 854
- Red Guards, p. 854
- Jiang Qing, p. 854
- Gang of Four, p. 854
- Deng Xiaoping, p. 855
- Tiananmen Square Massacre, p. 855
- Kim Il Sung, p. 856
- Syngman Rhee, p. 856

❷ 1953: first Five-Year Plan; 1958: Great Leap Forward; 1966: Cultural Revolution; 1976: Mao Zedong dies; 1989: Tiananmen Square Massacre, economy hurt; 1997: government gives up state-owned businesses, Hong Kong returned

❸ a. Great Leap Forward failed to increase industrial and farm output, led to Cultural Revolution; farm and industrial production fell more; by 2003, China had the world's second-largest economy, but unemployment and poverty levels remained high

b. Korea divided between Soviet-dominated Communist North and U.S.-dominated pro-West South

c. China considers Taiwan a wayward province; Taiwan considers itself independent.

❹ Pamphlets will vary but should express a desire for democratic government even if government response is harsh.

Since World War II, Taiwan has become a leading nation in the shipbuilding industry.

In June 2000 Kim Jong Il of North Korea and Kim Dae Jung of South Korea held a summit meeting. They agreed that families who had been separated could visit each other. The leaders also made plans for future meetings. In October Kim Dae Jung was awarded the 2000 Nobel Peace Prize for his efforts to reunify Korea.

✔ **READING CHECK: Comparing and Contrasting** What were the similarities and differences between North Korea and South Korea after the Korean War? North was communist, South was a republic, but there was little political freedom in either place.

The Nationalists in Taiwan

The Chinese Nationalists had fled to Taiwan in 1949 and formed a new government. Although China considered Taiwan a Chinese province and most countries never recognized it as an independent nation, Taiwan was generally allowed to govern itself. The government formed on the island seemed to be democratic, but actually Chiang Kai-shek and other Nationalist Party members held all the power. In spite of this, the United States gave aid to Taiwan for many years. The United States also had army and navy bases on the island and kept social and economic ties with Taiwan. By the 1990s Taiwan had become a leading economic power in Asia, even though the island had few natural resources. Instead, the island became one of the world's major producers of manufactured goods, many of which went to the United States. The people of Taiwan enjoyed a high standard of living.

In the early 1980s the Nationalists agreed to allow other parties to form. In 1989 Taiwan had open elections for the first time. Then in 2000 the Nationalist Party lost the election to another party. The new president was Chen Shui-bian, whose party strongly believed that Taiwan should become an independent nation. China, though, insisted that Taiwan was a Chinese province. This position has been a key part of China's foreign policy since the late 1940s. The status of Taiwan continues to cause tension between China and the United States.

✔ **READING CHECK: Drawing Conclusions** Why might the United States keep military and economic ties with Taiwan? to have an ally near China

---

SECTION 2 REVIEW

1. Identify and explain the significance:
Great Leap Forward
Cultural Revolution
Red Guards
Jiang Qing
Gang of Four
Deng Xiaoping
Tiananmen Square Massacre
Kim Il Sung
Syngman Rhee

2. Sequencing Make a chart like the one below. Use it to list in chronological order the main events that happened in China since 1949.

Date	Event
1949	Communists form People's Republic of China

3. **Finding the Main Idea**

a. How did the Great Leap Forward and the Cultural Revolution affect China?

b. How did Cold War politics affect the future of Korea after World War II?

c. What is the main reason for tensions between Taiwan and China?

4. **Writing and Critical Thinking**

Making Generalizations Imagine that you are a student protesting in Tiananmen Square. Write a pamphlet explaining why you are protesting despite government calls to stop.

Consider:
• the issues that concerned students
• the possible response of the government
• the views of the outside world

Homework Practice Online
keyword: SP3 HP32

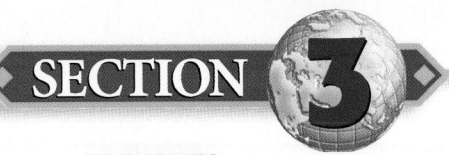
OBJECTIVES

1 **Identify the factors that allowed Japan to recover effectively after World War II.**

2 **Describe the economic and social changes that occurred in Japan from the 1950s onward.**

3 **Explain how the relationship between Japan and the United States changed in the years since World War II.**

SECTION 3

READ TO DISCOVER

❶ What factors allowed Japan to recover as effectively as it did after World War II?

❷ What economic and social changes occurred in Japan from the 1950s onward?

❸ How has the relationship between Japan and the United States changed in the years since World War II?

DEFINE

zaibatsu

IDENTIFY

SCAP
"MacArthur Constitution"
Liberal-Democratic Party

▶ WHY IT MATTERS TODAY

The emperor is still the official head of state in Japan. Use CNN News.com or other **current event** sources to find out who the emperor is and what his role is in modern Japan. Record your findings in your journal.

CNN student News.com

The Japanese Miracle

The Main Idea
Japan grew into a major international and economic power after recovering from World War II.

The Story Continues *After World War II Japan was in ruins. Many homes and factories had been destroyed. There were severe shortages of food, clothing, and fuel. The Japanese emperor told his people that they should pave the way for future generations by "enduring the unendurable and suffering what is insufferable." Much of their help would come from their former enemies.*

The Occupation of Japan

After World War II American troops occupied Japan under the command of General Douglas MacArthur, the Supreme Commander for the Allied Powers. His offices became known as **SCAP,** after his title. MacArthur's first task was to demilitarize Japan. He removed the people who had been powerful in government and business during the war. Some top leaders were tried for war crimes. Several were executed for their crimes. More than 5 million troops were disarmed and released from military service.

At first SCAP had planned to take over the war industries that were still left in Japan. Taking the factories, however, would have created difficulties. The Allied Powers did not want to support Japan indefinitely. The Japanese had to be given the chance to provide for themselves. In the end, the Japanese were allowed to keep most of their factories and switch them to peacetime activities.

SCAP's second task was to create a new Japanese government. Under MacArthur's direction, the Japanese set up a nonmilitary and democratic government. The "**MacArthur Constitution**" created a parliamentary democracy that called for the direct election of the Diet, or parliament. All Japanese adults now had the right to vote. It also made it clear that the emperor was not divine. He was now a symbol of state who had little power. Finally, the constitution included an important clause that said the Japanese people gave up war as a natural right of their country. The Japanese adopted their new constitution in 1947.

General MacArthur and Emperor Hirohito, c. 1945

✔ READING CHECK:
Summarizing What were the two main tasks SCAP undertook at the beginning of the occupation of Japan? demilitarize Japan, create new government

LEVEL 1: Write the following on the chalkboard: *Japan's recovery after World War II was a result of changes in its (1) government (2) economy (3) society.* Divide students into pairs. Assign each pair one of the three categories listed. Have pairs use their texts to find examples that belong in their assigned category. Call on pairs to share their findings with the class. **ENGLISH LANGUAGE LEARNERS, COOPERATIVE LEARNING**

TEACH OBJECTIVE 2

ALL LEVELS: Copy the graphic organizer on the chalkboard, omitting the italicized words. Have students complete the diagram.

Social Changes in Japan after World War II
- longer work hours
- women join workforce
- higher standard of living
- importance of family declines
- increased pollution
- more household appliances and cars
- land and housing price increases
- greater freedom for women

Linking Past to Present

The zaibatsu, which means "financial clique" in Japanese, arose during the Meiji emperors' industrialization of Japan in the late 1800s. After the government ceased playing a direct role in economic development, the zaibatsu stepped in to fill the gap. They gained control of interrelated mining, transport, industrial, commercial, and financial concerns.

Many owners and leaders of the zaibatsu were descended from the Japanese samurai class. They extended its traditions, particularly *bushido* or "the way of the warrior," to business dealings.

After a 1948 SCAP decree banned members of traditional zaibatsu families from holding official positions in their companies, the influence of the zaibatsu declined. However, they continue to provide the pattern for large industrial organizations in Japan today. They are now referred to as keiretsu instead of zaibatsu.

Critical Thinking

Why did SCAP want to dismantle the zaibatsu?

ANSWER: Answers will vary, but students might suggest SCAP feared the zaibatsu would resist the democratizing of Japan.

Japanese women in the electronics industry contributed to their country's economic revival after World War II.

Postwar Developments

Before World War II Japan had been the most industrialized of the Asian nations. Afterwards, its economy was badly damaged. Japan, however, made a surprisingly rapid recovery.

Economic development. Several SCAP policies helped Japan recover after the war. One important program was land reform. For the first time, many small farmers were able to own the land they worked. New farm machinery and improved seeds helped them grow and harvest more. Farm output increased very quickly.

Another SCAP program broke up some of the **zaibatsu.** These were huge industrial firms controlled by powerful families. They were so big they prevented free trade. Some of the zaibatsu, such as Mitsubishi and Mitsui, survived the breakup. None, however, had the power they had before the war.

In the 1960s Japan changed its economic focus and started to take advantage of its highly skilled work force. It began to produce advanced technology for the world market. With government support, the new approach was very successful. By the 1980s Japan had become Asia's leading economic power.

In the 1990s the pace of Japan's economic growth slowed. Some companies had grown too fast and had financial problems. Also, there was more competition from other countries. The government tried to revive the economy, but it had only limited success.

Social changes. The economic growth after World War II brought Japan a much higher standard of living. Most families had lived modestly before the war. Now they were able to buy modern household appliances and new automobiles. Also, more women began to join the workforce. This caused a major shift in Japanese society. Women won greater legal, political, and social freedom. At the same time, the importance of the family began to decline. It was no longer the center of all Japanese life.

The higher standard of living did not always mean a better quality of life. The Japanese worked longer hours than people in the West, and the cost of living was much higher. Both the number of factories and the number of people grew. Land to build on became very scarce. From the 1960s onward, prices for land and housing soared. Factories created another problem—pollution. Many Japanese called on their government to pay more attention to quality of life and less to economic growth. In 1974 a young political party member told an American reporter:

Analyzing Primary Sources

Identifying Bias How did the young person's attitude toward the quality of life in Japan affect his comments? made him more critical

History Makers Speak

❝If we get too rich, prosperous, and materialistic, all we do is create more unhappiness. We must therefore return to the true Japanese moral standards, including respect for our ancestors, compassion, gratitude, courage, cooperation, and obligation—all virtues neglected since the war. Only in this way will we regain the confidence of the people.❞

from "Letter from Tokyo," *The New Yorker,* May 1974

✔ **READING CHECK: Finding the Main Idea** What effect did economic growth have on Japanese society? led to higher standard of living, more women in workplace, more pollution

TEACH OBJECTIVE 3

LEVEL 3: Divide students into groups of four or five. Have each group decide whether or not the United States is still the dominant partner in the Japanese-U.S. relationship. When all groups have reached a consensus, have a class discussion about their conclusions. **COOPERATIVE LEARNING**

 HOMEWORK Ask students to write a short essay explaining why they think Japan would or would not be hurt more than the U.S. by a future worldwide recession. Select essays to read and discuss with the class.

CLOSE

Ask students to compare and contrast daily life in 1945 Japan with that of the United States in 1945. Then have them discuss how living in Japan today would be similar to and different from life in the United States.

Foreign Relations and Political Life

The "MacArthur Constitution" had limited Japanese armed forces and military production. In addition, the Japanese had signed a treaty agreeing to renounce war as a political tool. Within a few years, however, the Cold War between the United States and the Soviet Union led to a reversal in U.S. policy toward Japan. The communist victory in China and the stalemate in North Korea had changed the balance of power in Asia. The United States viewed these communist states as a threat. The U.S. government felt that Japan should be able to defend itself in case of war and urged Japan to increase its armed forces.

The Japanese did not want a return of the militaristic governments of prewar days. They had no wish to rearm. They spent their money to build peacetime industries and to increase exports. Raising the standard of living was more important than raising an army. In spite of pressure from the West, Japan resisted increased military spending. Finally in 1997 the United States and Japan reached an agreement. In case of a conflict near Japan, Japan would provide the United States with supplies and assistance, but not armed forces.

A more independent stance. After World War II Japan and the United States kept friendly ties. At times, there was stress between the two countries. For example, the Japanese resented the U.S. pressure to build up their armed forces. Many Japanese also disliked having American troops stationed in Japan. The U.S. forces on the island of Okinawa had been a sore point since the 1960s. Toward the end of 2000, the United States finally began to reduce the number of troops stationed there.

During the 1980s Japan began to follow its own course in world affairs and make decisions apart from the United States. Japanese leaders wanted the country to become the economic and political leader in Asia. Part of their plan was to help developing countries by giving them large amounts of money and technical aid. By the end of the 1980s, Japan was giving more aid than any other country in the world.

In the early 1990s Japan began to rethink its relations with the nations of the former Soviet Union. In 1996 the leaders of Japan and Russia met for talks. Even after the meetings, however, relations between the two countries were strained. Japan and Russia had an ongoing dispute over the Kuril Islands. The Soviet Union had occupied the islands after World War II, and Russia still claimed them. Japan insisted that four small islands in the southern Kuril chain belonged to Japan because they were part of the Japanese-controlled island of Hokkaido. The Russians insisted the islands were part of the Kurils and thus fell under their control. The Japanese were not willing to give Russia any aid until the problem was solved.

Toshiki Kaifu and Mikhail Gorbachev signed a joint declaration in April 1991.

Global Relations

In recent years, Japan has begun to take a more active role in world affairs. Although this course is controversial, many Japanese feel that their country's economic importance justifies a leadership position in international affairs.

Government leaders took a step toward this goal in 1995. Japanese forces became part of a UN peacekeeping mission in Cambodia—the first appearance of Japanese troops on foreign soil since World War II. The action caused vigorous protests among Japanese who fear a resurgence of militarism in their country.

Japan's quest for an increased global role is also burdened by public opinion throughout Asia. Feelings of bitterness and distrust remain from Japanese actions during World War II and before. Today, however, Japan continues to be the world's largest aid donor, most of its aid going to countries in Asia and the Pacific.

Critical Thinking

Why does Japan direct so much of its foreign aid to countries in Asia?

ANSWER: to be a leader in the region, to develop markets for its products, to regain good standing with its Asian neighbors

REVIEW

Have students complete the Section 3 Review on page 862.

ASSESS

Have students complete Daily Quiz 32.3. As Alternative Assessment, you may want to use the graphic organizer or homework assignment in this section's lessons.

RETEACH

Have students complete Main Idea Activity for English Language Learners and Special-Needs Students 32.3. Then have them use the section's headings and subheadings to create an outline. **ENGLISH LANGUAGE LEARNERS**

EXTEND

Invite students to learn more about postwar Japan by researching one of the following subjects: U.S. aid to Japan following World War II, the Japanese war crimes trials, U.S. military presence in Japan, or Japanese defense forces today. Ask students to make presentations of their findings to the class. **BLOCK SCHEDULING**

SECTION 3 REVIEW ANSWERS

❶ Define
- zaibatsu, p. 860

❷ Identify
- SCAP, p. 859
- "MacArthur Constitution," p. 859
- Liberal-Democratic Party, p. 862

❸ Economics: land reform, increased farm output, advanced technology for world market, leading economic power, growth slows; Society: higher standard of living, women in workforce, social freedoms for women, importance of family declines; Foreign Relations: military limited, resists U.S. pressure to increase military, follows independent foreign policy, becomes leader in Asia, rethinks relations with former Soviet Union and U.S.

❹ a. constitutional and parliamentary democracy, all adults can vote, emperor has little power, active political parties

b. higher living standard, role of women changed, housing costs high, declining quality of life

c. U.S. forces in Japan and on Okinawa; U.S. pressure on Japan to build up its armed forces

❺ Predictions should consider postwar destruction, devastated economy, and traditional economic and political structures.

Japan's national legislature, the Diet, meets in this impressive building in Tokyo.

Politics in Japan. After World War II a large number of political parties were active in Japan. The most powerful was the **Liberal-Democratic Party** (LDP), which controlled the government from the 1950s until the 1990s. The Socialists and others strongly disagreed with LDP policy and voiced their dislike of Japan's defense agreement with the United States. They also were against having American armed forces stationed in Japan.

In 1989 Japan faced a government crisis when a financial scandal rocked the LDP. It involved many top LDP members. A few months after the scandal broke, Toshiki Kaifu became prime minister. People trusted him even though he was a member of the LDP. By 1991, however, he had been forced out of office. In the 1993 elections, the LDP lost its majority in the Diet, ending the party's almost 40-year rule. Political turmoil continued, however.

In 1998 Keizo Obuchi, a member of the LDP, was chosen to be prime minister. Obuchi focused on ways to revive the economy and his programs had some success. After Obuchi died in early 2000, Yoshiro Mori became prime minister. When Mori resigned a year later, Junichiro Koizumi was elected prime minister. Koizumi promised to thoroughly reform the government and bring an end to political corruption. Although he has had only limited success in his efforts, he was re-elected in 2003.

✔ **READING CHECK: Identifying Cause and Effect** How did the Liberal-Democratic Party's policies affect Japanese relations with the United States? made defense agreement

SECTION 3 REVIEW

1. **Define** and explain the significance: zaibatsu

2. **Identify** and explain the significance: SCAP "MacArthur Constitution" Liberal-Democratic Party

3. **Categorizing** Copy the chart below. Use it to organize the changes that occurred in Japan after World War II.

Changes in Japan after WWII		
Economics	Society	Foreign Relations

4. **Finding the Main Idea**

   a. What were the characteristics of the postwar Japanese government?

   b. How did the life of an average Japanese person change after World War II?

   c. What have been the main causes of tension between Japan and the United States in the postwar years?

5. **Writing and Critical Thinking**

   Making Predictions Describe what the results might have been if the Allied Powers had not helped Japan after World War II.

   Consider:
   • the destruction in Japan after the war
   • land ownership and the control of industry
   • the social structure of Japan

Homework Practice Online
keyword: SP3 HP32

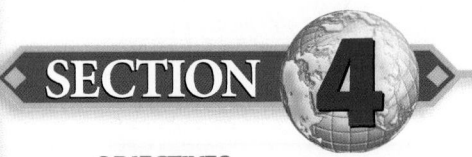
OBJECTIVES

1 Describe the causes and effects of dictatorships in the Philippines and Indonesia.

2 Explain how the Vietnam War affected Vietnam, Laos, and Cambodia.

3 Identify the problems that the nations of Southeast Asia faced as they struggled to create stable governments.

As students enter the classroom, ask them to write a paragraph explaining how economic conditions might cause unrest in a nation. Call on volunteers to read their explanations to the class. Then ask students if a government has a right to limit citizens' freedoms in order to achieve a peaceful and stable society. Ask those who say "no" if their opinion would be different if Communists were behind the unrest. Tell students that in Section 4 they will learn how concern about communism has shaped the history of Southeast Asia since World War II.

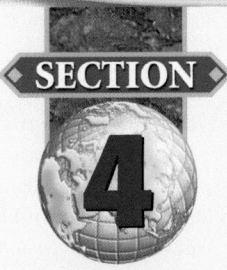

SECTION 4

READ TO DISCOVER

1 What were the causes and effects of dictatorships in the Philippines and Indonesia?

2 How did the Vietnam War affect Vietnam, Laos, and Cambodia?

3 What problems did the nations of Southeast Asia face as they struggled to create stable governments?

DEFINE

domino theory

IDENTIFY

Ferdinand Marcos
Corazon Aquino
Aung San Suu Kyi
Ho Chi Minh
Geneva Accord
Tet Offensive
Paris Peace Accords
Ho Chi Minh Trail
Khmer Rouge
Pol Pot

◢WHY IT MATTERS TODAY

Each Southeast Asian country has had ongoing political problems. Use CNNnews.com or other **current event** sources to find out about the political situation in one of these countries. Record your findings in your journal.

CNN student News.com

Independence Struggles in Southeast Asia

The Main Idea
After World War II all the former colonies in Southeast Asia became independent countries.

The Story Continues *Almost all the countries in Southeast Asia were once colonies. After World War II these countries gained their independence. Some did so peacefully, while others resorted to violent means. An interviewer asked one revolutionary leader how his people could expect to win against a well-armed Western power. He replied, "Our secret weapon is nationalism. To have nationhood…is greater than any weapons in the world."*

The Philippines

The United States controlled the Philippines from the time of the Spanish-American War in 1898 until early 1946. Then, on July 4, 1946, the Philippines became an independent nation with a government modeled after that of the United States. The new nation had an elected president and congress. Economic and political relations between the Philippines and the United States continued to be close, and the Philippines continued to play a key role in U.S. policy toward Asia.

In the 1970s the Philippines were in turmoil. Communists were rioting in some areas. Muslims were fighting for self-rule. Philippine president **Ferdinand Marcos** needed to gain control. He placed the country under martial law and had hundreds of his enemies arrested. In 1973 Marcos put a new constitution in place that gave him even more powers. Although these were the actions of a dictator, U.S. officials continued to support Marcos because of his anticommunist and pro-Western policies.

Ferdinand Marcos gained much wealth through his corrupt government. He and his wife, Imelda, lived extravagantly while the country was mired in poverty. One example of their wasteful lifestyle was Imelda Marcos's collection of over 1,000 pairs of shoes.

REPRODUCIBLE RESOURCES

▶ Guided Reading Strategy 32.4

▶ Readings in World History 116: The Filipinos Celebrate the Fall of President Marcos

TECHNOLOGY RESOURCES

▶ One-Stop Planner 32.4

▶ Holt Researcher: World History: Corazon Aquino

▶ Holt Researcher: World History: Ho Chi Minh

▶ Homework Practice Online

▶ Online Maps, Charts, and Graphs: East and Southeast Asia

REINFORCEMENT, REVIEW, AND ASSESSMENT

▶ Section 4 Review, p. 869

▶ Daily Quiz 32.4

▶ Main Idea Activity 32.4

▶ English Audio Summary 32.4

▶ Spanish Audio Summary 32.4

LEVEL 1: Have students work in pairs to create two diagrams. One diagram should show the power relationship between the government and the people during the Marcos and Sukarno regimes. The other diagram should show the power relationship in a democracy. Select pairs to replicate their diagrams on the chalkboard and explain the similarities and differences to the class. **ENGLISH LANGUAGE LEARNERS, COOPERATIVE LEARNING**

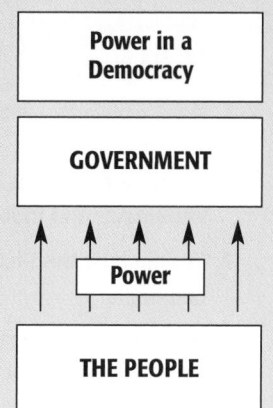

Power under Marcos/Sukarno — GOVERNMENT → Power → THE PEOPLE

Power in a Democracy — GOVERNMENT ↑ Power ↑ THE PEOPLE

HISTORY MAKER ANSWER
restored democracy in the Philippines

Global Relations

Today, the biggest benefactor Burma (Myanmar) has is China. China supports Myanmar's military rulers with modern weapons. It also provides various forms of economic aid. In return, Myanmar gives China access to the Indian Ocean.

The famous Burma and Silk Roads, both of which lead into China, are being rebuilt with Chinese aid. This construction has military as well as commercial ramifications. Myanmar's neighbors fear that the close ties between the two nations might ultimately destabilize the entire region. Therefore they too have cultivated relations with Myanmar, despite concerns about its human rights record. Myanmar was accepted for membership in ASEAN (see page 872) in 1997.

Critical Thinking

Why would China benefit from having access to the Indian Ocean?

ANSWER: gives China access to East Africa, the Middle East, and Europe via the Suez Canal

HISTORY MAKER

Corazon Aquino (1933–)

When political enemies killed her husband, Corazon Aquino stepped into the political arena herself as a candidate for president. Although well-educated, Corazon Aquino had little political experience. Until her husband's death, she had been a full-time homemaker.

The election was close. At first it looked as if Aquino had lost. But when her supporters uncovered voter fraud, they challenged the results. Even after taking office, Aquino faced challenges from people who wanted to destroy democracy. She survived no fewer than six coup attempts. **How did Corazon Aquino affect politics in the Philippines?**

Holt Researcher

go.hrw.com
KEYWORD: Holt Researcher
FreeFind: Corazon Aquino
After reading more about Corazon Aquino on the Holt Researcher, assess how she helped advance democratic ideals in the 20th century.

Under Marcos the Philippine economy weakened and protests against his rule began to grow. In 1983 the leader of an opposing party, Benigno Aquino, was assassinated. His death sparked riots all over the country. In 1986 Aquino's widow, **Corazon Aquino,** ran against Marcos in a special election. Although Marcos claimed that he won the election, it soon became clear that Aquino was the real winner. Marcos and his family were forced to leave the country.

When Aquino took office, the economy was very weak, and many people were living in poverty. Aquino was able to make some gains. She did bring democracy back after the Marcos years. She also promoted new business. Aquino, however, was not able to carry out all of her programs. Her government began to lose power as it failed to manage the nation's huge debt and poor economy.

In 1992 Fidel Ramos became president. While he was president the economy finally began to improve. Then in 1998 former movie actor Joseph Estrada was elected president. Within two years his government was in deep trouble as Estrada was accused of taking large sums of money in bribes. By 2000 the Philippines were torn by mass protests once again.

✔ **READING CHECK: Comparing and Contrasting** What were the similarities and differences between the presidencies of Ferdinand Marcos and Corazon Aquino? economy remained poor under both, but Aquino restored democracy

Burma (Myanmar)

Since medieval times the area known as Burma has been a strategically important region, an area of important trade routes. During World War II the British colony served as an important route for getting supplies to China until the Japanese occupied the region in 1942. In 1948 Great Britain gave Burma its independence. The new nation faced difficulties that included the lack of a strong central government, a scarcity of trained civil servants, tribal and political dissension, and communist attempts to seize the country. The first premier, U Nu, headed a coalition government that brought some order to the country. However, the coalition soon broke into factions and the army, led by General Ne Win, seized control of the government.

Ne Win ruled Burma from 1962 to 1988. His government took total control of the economy, a move that almost destroyed Burma's economy. Farm production fell, and consumer goods became scarce. In 1988, violent riots forced Ne Win to resign, but other military leaders seized power. To show that they wanted to make a fresh start, the new leaders renamed the country Myanmar.

The first free elections in 30 years took place in 1990. When the opposing party won, the military refused to give up power. Instead it cracked down on everyone it considered a threat. In 1991 **Aung San Suu Kyi** won the Nobel Peace Prize for her efforts to reform her country. She was kept under house arrest for several years. Many of her supporters were killed or put in prison. The government's crackdown only added to the unrest in Burma. Still, the military ruled the country throughout the 1990s.

The United States limited its contact with Myanmar during this period. In other Western nations, many criticized Myanmar's poor record in human rights. Though some political prisoners were released from house arrest in 2003, the U.S. and some Asian countries continue to push for the reform of Myanmar's government.

✔ **READING CHECK: Supporting a Point of View** What evidence would you give to show that people in Myanmar have few civil rights? military control, crackdowns, opposition leader under house arrest

LEVEL 2: Tell students that both the Philippines and Indonesia underwent a period of authoritarian rule after they achieved self-rule. Have half the class create *Before, During,* and *After* charts for the Philippines and the other half for Indonesia. Charts should list the factors that led to authoritarian rule; the country's key problems during authoritarian rule; how this rule was overthrown; and the country's subsequent progress.

HOMEWORK Have students research and report on political developments in Thailand or Malaysia since the end of World War II compared with those in the Philippines or Indonesia. Ask students to prepare written reports or make presentations.

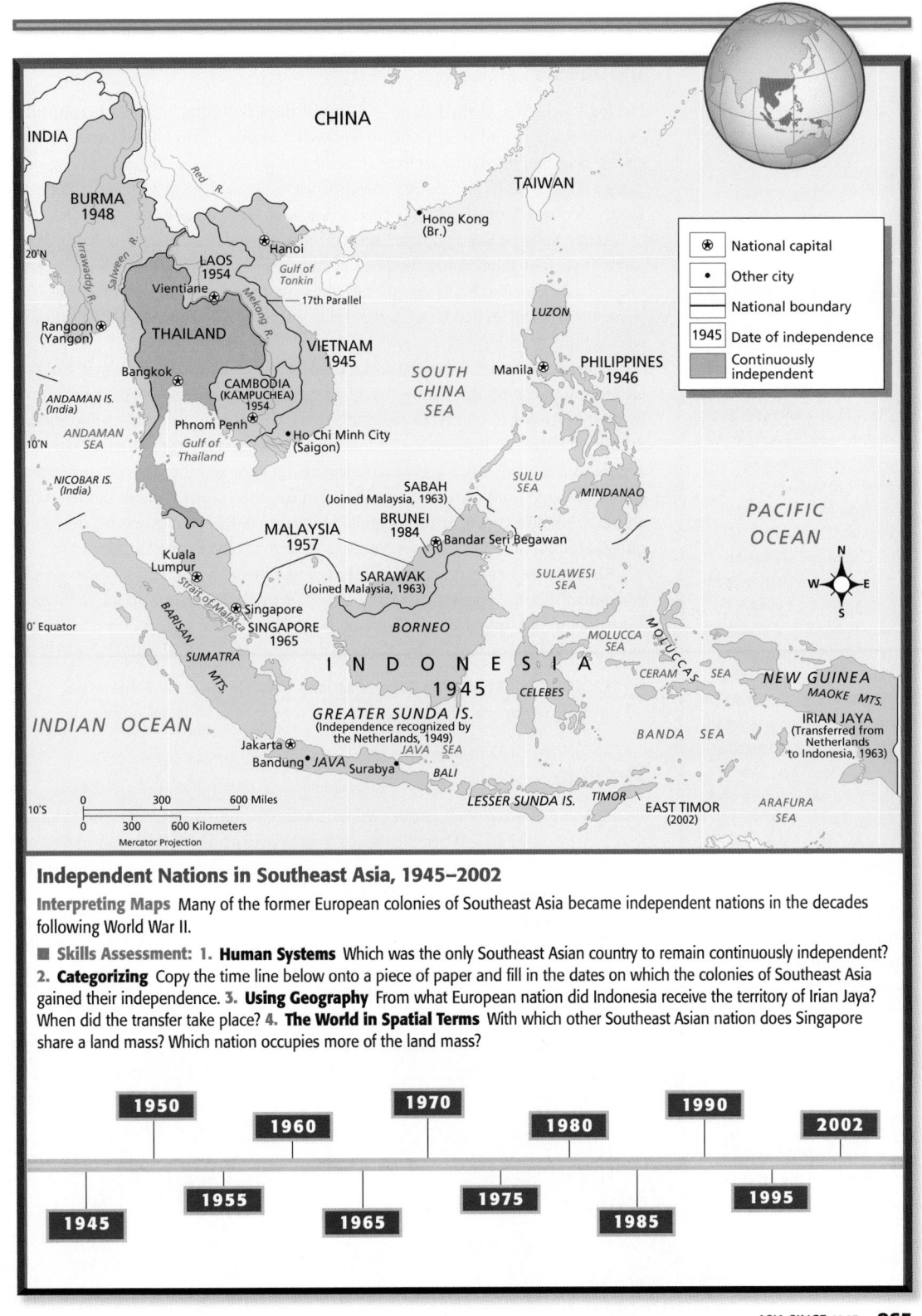

Independent Nations in Southeast Asia, 1945–2002

Interpreting Maps Many of the former European colonies of Southeast Asia became independent nations in the decades following World War II.

■ **Skills Assessment: 1. Human Systems** Which was the only Southeast Asian country to remain continuously independent? **2. Categorizing** Copy the time line below onto a piece of paper and fill in the dates on which the colonies of Southeast Asia gained their independence. **3. Using Geography** From what European nation did Indonesia receive the territory of Irian Jaya? When did the transfer take place? **4. The World in Spatial Terms** With which other Southeast Asian nation does Singapore share a land mass? Which nation occupies more of the land mass?

1945 • 1950 • 1955 • 1960 • 1965 • 1970 • 1975 • 1980 • 1985 • 1990 • 1995 • 2002

Historical Sidelight

Hassanal Bolkiah, the Sultan of Brunei, is among the world's richest persons. His fortune, estimated at about $16 billion in 2001, comes from the large oil deposits in his small country.

The sultan rules by decree. However, Brunei's standard of living, one of the highest in the world, keeps public discontent to a minimum. Health care and education are free for all citizens. Workers, who receive high wages, pay no taxes, and Bruneians are major consumers of high-tech audio and video equipment and designer-label Western clothes. The nation also shares its wealth through foreign aid. Among the recipients are Bosnia's Muslims and homeless people in New York.

ACTIVITY: Have students write a paragraph explaining why they would or would not like to be citizens of Brunei.

MAP ANSWERS
1. Thailand

2. Vietnam, 1945; Philippines, 1946; Burma, 1948; Indonesia, 1949; Cambodia, Laos, 1954; Malaysia, 1957; Singapore, 1965; Brunei, 1984; East Timor, 2002

3. the Netherlands; 1963

4. Malaysia; Malaysia

CONNECTING TO Art

Weaving: Ikat Cloth
The woven cloth shown here is from Bali, Indonesia. It was made by an ancient method of dyeing and weaving known as ikat. Several Southeast Asian countries use the ikat method, which may have originated in India.

Cotton and silk are the most common fibers used for ikat. Before the thread is woven, bundles of threads are tied tightly at certain points. Then the bundles are dyed. Most of the thread will absorb the dye, but the places where the strands are tied together do not absorb color. After it is dyed, the yarn is woven on a loom. Ikat is a long, difficult process. One cloth takes many hours to complete.

Ikat cloths have been an important part of Indonesian culture for centuries. They are sometimes given as wedding gifts between families. Because of the long process to make them, they are often saved for special ceremonies.

Understanding the Arts

What does the process of ikat weaving imply about the weavers?

Indonesia

During World War II the Japanese occupied the East Indies, an island group that includes Sumatra and Java. The Dutch expected to take control again when the war ended. They had ruled the East Indies since the 1600s. Instead, an Indonesian engineer named Sukarno led a successful independence movement against them. In 1949 the East Indies became the Republic of Indonesia, with Sukarno as its first president.

At first Sukarno was a popular leader able to unite the Indonesian people and make some important gains in health and education. In the early 1960s, Sukarno became more of a dictator, but his severe rule failed to solve Indonesia's growing problems. The government's policies had brought the country close to bankruptcy, and Communists were fighting for control of some areas.

General Suharto, head of the army, acted against Sukarno. He took over the government and in 1968 was named president. Suharto planned to reform the economy by creating closer ties with the West and using Western aid to build up Indonesia's industry. By the late 1980s, many Indonesians had turned against Suharto. They were angry about the growing gap between the rich and poor and thought the government was mismanaged and corrupt. Several Western countries worried about human rights abuses by the Indonesian army and police. In early 1998 a major economic downturn plunged the country into turmoil. President Suharto finally resigned in May 1998.

After two of Suharto's successors failed to win the trust of the Indonesian people, parliament named Megawati Sukarnoputri—Sukarno's daughter—president in 2001. Sukarnoputri has struggled to lead a diverse nation and revive an economy damaged by terrorist bombings carried out by Islamic extremists in Bali in 2002 and Jakarta in 2003.

✔ **READING CHECK: Making Generalizations** What effect did the Sukarno and Suharto governments have on Indonesia? economy suffered, unrest increased

Vietnam

France had colonized Vietnam in the late 1800s. During World War II the Japanese took control of the area. When the French tried to return after the war, they met resistance from a group of communist guerrilla fighters. These were the Viet Minh, led by **Ho Chi Minh.** Ho declared Vietnam independent in 1945.

In 1946 fighting broke out between the French and the Viet Minh. The war dragged on for years. In 1954 the French suffered a major defeat at Dien Bien Phu (dyen byen FOO). The Viet Minh captured thousands of French troops. After this defeat, the French agreed to peace talks.

HOMEWORK Ask students to imagine it is 1965. They are foreign policy experts in the governments of Cambodia or Laos. Have them write a memo to their nation's top government official making one of these recommendations: their country should remain neutral; their country should side with North Vietnam; or their country should side with South Vietnam and the United States. Tell students that their memos must also explain the reasons for their recommendation.

TEACH OBJECTIVES 2 and 3

ALL LEVELS: Ask students to list ways that the Vietnam War affected the people of North and South Vietnam. Write responses in two columns on the chalkboard. Then ask students which country suffered more as a result of the war, North Vietnam or South Vietnam. Ask students to justify their opinions. Conclude by asking the class whether the people of the former South Vietnam are better off today under a communist government than they were during the war, when South Vietnam was fighting a communist takeover.

Division and war. The **Geneva Accord,** signed in 1954, ended the war. After the French withdrew their forces, Vietnam was divided into two zones at the 17th parallel. Elections were planned for 1956 to select one government for the whole country. With Chinese and Soviet help, Ho Chi Minh began to build a communist state in the north zone. Ngo Dinh Diem was president of the non-communist government in the south. Diem put down all opposition to his government. He showed little interest in reforms or in fixing government corruption. He refused to participate in the elections planned for 1956. As a result, no elections were ever held.

By the late 1950s the Viet Minh had formed the National Liberation Front (NLF). The NLF soon became known as the Viet Cong, or Vietnamese Communists. Their goal was to overthrow Diem and reunite Vietnam. The Viet Cong began a guerrilla war in rural South Vietnam. Diem's answer was to crack down on the Viet Cong and anyone else who opposed him. In 1963 a military group assassinated Diem and took control of the government.

American involvement. American leaders did not want South Vietnam to fall to communism. If that happened, they thought all of Southeast Asia would follow. This idea was called the **domino theory.** The United States government decided to get directly involved in the war. In January 1965 President Johnson ordered air attacks on North Vietnam. By the late 1960s more than 500,000 U.S. troops were in Vietnam.

At the beginning of 1968, North Vietnam launched a major attack called the **Tet Offensive,** named for the Vietnamese New Year on which it began. Although American and South Vietnamese forces drove the Communists back, many Americans who saw the fierce fighting on television began to openly oppose U.S. involvement in the war.

The **Paris Peace Accords** of 1973 ended American involvement in the war. The South Vietnamese army could not hold back the enemy after the United States pulled out its troops. In April 1975 South Vietnam surrendered to North Vietnam. More than 1.3 million Vietnamese and nearly 58,000 Americans had lost their lives during the war.

A reunited Vietnam. In 1976 the two Vietnams united as one country, with Hanoi in the north as the capital. The former southern capital, Saigon, was renamed Ho Chi Minh City. After Saigon fell, more than 1 million Vietnamese fled their country. Some left because they feared the North Vietnamese. Most left because they did not want to live under a communist government. These refugees faced a dangerous sea voyage to one of the other Southeast Asian countries. Many of these "boat people" died at sea. Those who survived spent months in crowded camps. They had to wait for permission to settle in another country. The largest number, about 725,000, came to the United States.

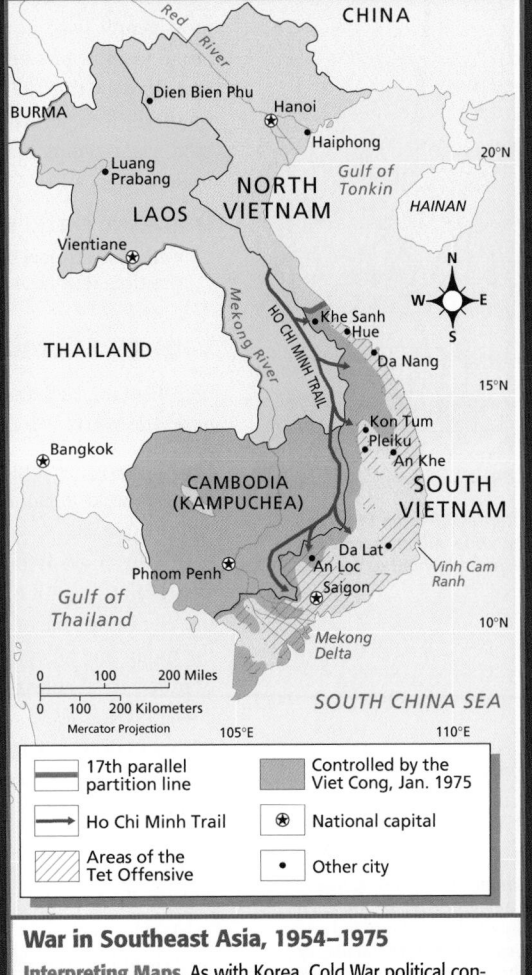

War in Southeast Asia, 1954–1975

Interpreting Maps As with Korea, Cold War political concerns led to the division of Vietnam and eventually to war.

Skills Assessment: Physical Systems Through what countries did the Ho Chi Minh Trail run?

Global Relations

U.S. actions in the Vietnam War left Americans divided over what the nation's basic values and role in the world should be. It also left some Americans with an attitude of distrust toward their government and political leaders that continues to be felt today.

The effects of the Vietnam War on U.S. foreign policy have been equally significant. The level of American involvement in the Middle East, Africa, and the Balkans has been constrained by the Vietnam experience. Because of its broad global and domestic impact, many historians consider the Vietnam War to be the defining event in American history since World War II.

ACTIVITY: Have students research primary sources such as letters, newspapers, and magazines from the Vietnam War era and present their findings to the class. Have students compare and discuss the different feelings and opinions expressed in the sources.

MAP ANSWER
from North Vietnam through Laos and Cambodia to South Vietnam

Holt Researcher
go.hrw.com
KEYWORD: Holt Researcher
FreeFind: Ho Chi Minh
After reading more about Ho Chi Minh on the Holt Researcher, write a pamphlet describing his views on Vietnamese independence.

TEACH OBJECTIVE 3

ALL LEVELS: Ask students to identify problems that the nations of Southeast Asia had in common. List responses on the chalkboard. *(unstable governments, authoritarian regimes, recent colonial histories, internal violence and insurgency, communist takeover attempts, economic problems)* Then ask which country, since World War II, has the most unusual history and why. *(Vietnam because of its partition, large-scale war, and reunification.)*

CLOSE

Have students form groups to evaluate which Southeast Asian nation seems most likely to overcome its problems in the next 30 years. Call on representatives from each group to present its conclusion to the class, summarizing the reasons for its choice.
COOPERATIVE LEARNING

Government

The 1954 Geneva Accords allowed the Pathet Lao, Laotian Communists, to operate in Laotian provinces adjacent to North Vietnam. The rest of Laos was to be ruled by the royal government.

By 1959 hostilities had broken out between the two Laotian factions. In 1962 a coalition government was formed. It consisted of leftists (the Pathet Lao), rightists (supported by Thailand and the United States), and neutrals (led by Prince Souvanna Phouma). This coalition fell apart in 1964 when the Vietnam War engulfed Laos.

Critical Thinking

How were the governments of Laos and Vietnam different in the 1950s and early 1960s?

ANSWER: Vietnam was formally divided; it had no coalition government as in Laos.

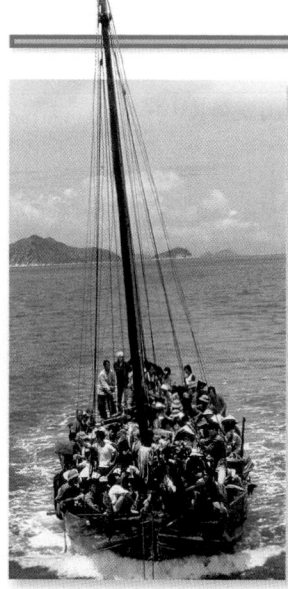

After the Vietnam War, more than one million people left Vietnam by boat as refugees.

Human skulls were gathered as a memorial in the Cambodian city of Phnom Penh. The grisly display honors the victims of Khmer Rouge genocide that took place during the mid-1970s.

After 1975 Vietnam struggled financially. The country was deeply in debt and most people lived in poverty. To solve its problems, the Vietnamese government began to allow private businesses to develop. At first, progress under this program was slow. In the 1990s, though, the economy boomed as the country started to attract foreign investors and open diplomatic ties. In 1995 the United States even restored diplomatic relations with Vietnam. In 2000 the two nations signed a trading pact.

✔ **READING CHECK: Identifying Cause and Effect** What were the main causes of the Vietnam War? How did it change the country? Viet Cong desire to reunite country, American resistance to the spread of communism

Laos and Cambodia

Like Vietnam, Laos and Cambodia were French colonies that gained their independence after World War II. Later, both nations were drawn into the Vietnam conflict.

Laos. Laos gained independence from France in 1954. Almost immediately, however, civil war broke out among the country's political factions. This turmoil continued for almost 20 years.

In the midst of this internal chaos, Laos began to feel the effects of the Vietnam War, even though it officially was neutral in the conflict. The **Ho Chi Minh Trail,** the Viet Cong's major supply route from North to South Vietnam, wound through the mountain valleys of eastern Laos. To break this supply line, the United States bombed the Laotian countryside, causing heavy property damage and many civilian casualties.

In 1975 the struggle for power in Laos ended when the Pathet Lao set up a communist government called the Lao People's Democratic Republic. Although the Pathet Lao tried to follow a policy of nonalignment, this proved impossible in the complicated politics of Asia. Laos had to call on the Vietnamese for help in controlling anticommunist factions in its northern provinces. In return it allowed Vietnam to station 50,000 troops on Laotian soil. These troops were not withdrawn until 1989. Then in the early 1990s Laos began to go its own way as Laotian leaders worked to improve relations with Thailand and China. They also signed trade and financial aid agreements with the United States, Japan, and Russia. By the mid-1990s, Laos had attracted a significant amount of foreign investment, which helped its economy grow.

Cambodia. Cambodia gained its independence from France in 1953. As with Laos, Cambodia tried to remain neutral in the Vietnam War but was drawn into it because the Ho Chi Minh Trail ran inside its eastern border. Also, Viet Cong troops had established supply lines in Cambodia. In response the United States bombed the Ho Chi Minh Trail and sent troops into Cambodia.

During the war, the Viet Cong began arming and training a group of Cambodian Communists called the **Khmer Rouge.** In 1975 the Khmer Rouge seized the Cambodian capital of Phnom Penh and set up a new Cambodian government under their leader, **Pol Pot.**

The Khmer Rouge enforced a brutal plan that resulted in a massive genocide of Cambodia's population. The government emptied all the cities and forced people to do manual labor on farms. No one had any tools or farming experience, however, and many of these former city dwellers died of starvation. The Khmer Rouge also undertook a systematic program to execute almost all of Cambodia's government officials, army officers, teachers, and intellectuals. This survivor describes the constant fear.

Primary Source

"Angkar [the name of Cambodia's Communist party] was everywhere, a pervasive presence that none could escape.... Husbands and wives spoke . . . only in private, in a whisper, fearful of being overheard.... No one criticized Angkar in public; even the minimally critical passing allusion could be enough to ensure arrest, interrogation and subsequent disappearance for re-education.**"**

M. Stuart-Fox, *The Murderous Revolution*

Analyzing Primary Sources

Drawing Inferences What did this survivor mean by the phrase "disappearance for re-education"?
removal to labor farm

Between 1975 and 1977, more than 1 million Cambodians—one fifth of the population—died under Pol Pot's regime. Thousands more fled to makeshift refugee camps in neighboring Thailand.

Border disputes that were centuries old soon brought Cambodia into conflict with Vietnam. In 1978 Vietnam invaded Cambodia. Although China threw its support to the Khmer Rouge, in 1979 the Vietnamese overthrew Pol Pot's government and installed one friendly to them. With Pol Pot in exile, fighting continued throughout the 1980s. Finally, in 1991 the UN brought an end to the fighting and the leading parties agreed to share power. Free elections were held in 1993, but the government continued to be unstable. By the late 1990s, however, opposition from the Khmer Rouge began to weaken. The group weakened even further after it was announced in 1998 that the notorious Pol Pot had died.

This former Khmer Rouge soldier defected to Cambodian government forces during fighting in 1998.

✔ **READING CHECK: Evaluating** What led to mass murder in Cambodia? government effort to purge dissent

SECTION 4 REVIEW

1. Define and explain the significance:
domino theory

2. Identify and explain the significance:
Ferdinand Marcos
Corazon Aquino
Aung San Suu Kyi
Ho Chi Minh
Geneva Accord
Tet Offensive
Paris Peace Accords
Ho Chi Minh Trail
Khmer Rouge
Pol Pot

3. Identifying Cause and Effect Use a chart like this one to organize details of times when existing governments in Southeast Asia were taken over without consent or election.

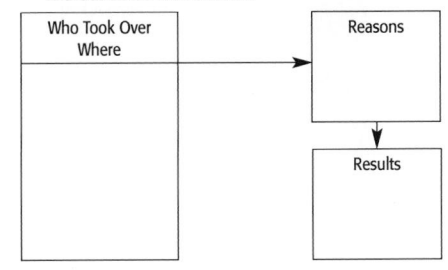

Who Took Over Where		Reasons
	→	
		Results

4. **Finding the Main Idea**

a. What effect did government have on the economic growth of the Philippines and Indonesia?

b. What effect did the Vietnam War have on countries other than Vietnam?

c. How does Cambodia's history differ from other Southeast Asian countries?

5. **Writing and Critical Thinking**

Decision Making Decide whether you agree or disagree with U.S. involvement in the Vietnam War. Write a short article explaining your position.
Consider:
• the domino theory
• the number of U.S. troops involved and the loss of life
• how the war ended

Homework Practice Online
keyword: SP3 HP32

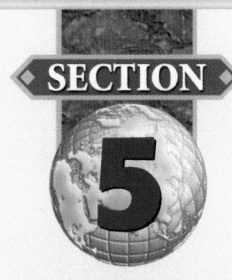

SECTION 5

OBJECTIVES

1 **Explain what led Asian governments to impose tight controls in their countries.**

2 **Describe the problems Asian countries faced as they tried to develop their economies and how they solved those problems.**

3 **Explain how economic success in Asian countries affected the West.**

🔔 *LET'S GET STARTED!*

As students enter the classroom, ask them to compile lists of items they can buy in the United States that are produced in Asian countries. Then begin a master list on the chalkboard, calling on students to add to it from the lists that they have prepared. Tell students that in Section 5 they will learn about the tremendous economic growth and development that has occurred in Asia in recent years.

SECTION 5

READ TO DISCOVER

1 What led Asian governments to impose tight controls in their countries?

2 What problems did Asian countries face as they tried to develop their economies, and how did they solve those problems?

3 How has economic success in Asian countries affected the West?

IDENTIFY

ASEAN
"Four Tigers"

▶ WHY IT MATTERS TODAY

Many products we use every day are made in Asia. Use or other **current event** sources to trace an Asian product you own from the place it was made to the store where you bought it. Record your findings in your journal.

CNN student News.com

Asian Paths to Prosperity

The Main Idea
By the year 2000 some of the fastest-growing economies in the world were in Asia.

The Story Continues *The newly independent Asian nations were soon in the midst of great changes. As one Asian leader told young people at a conference, "You have tilled the earth the way your ancestors have always done and eked out a living of some sort. . . . And the world has, meanwhile, passed you by. Then, all of a sudden, you decide that you must also join this race to the moon. . . ."*

Political Development

Many of the new Asian nations set up democratic governments. As time passed, however, democracy faded and some governments became communist. Others were highly authoritarian. Loss of human rights was a constant threat. This tight government control was common in Asia for three main reasons.

First, most Asian nations faced conflicts between people of different ethnic backgrounds. Most Asian countries have populations of different races and cultures. In Malaysia, for example, there are Malays, Chinese, and Indians. Often there had been hatred between one group and another for centuries. From time to time these tensions erupted into fighting. Government leaders relied on their armies and police forces to maintain control. Usually this meant loss of civil rights.

Second, governments worried about their national security. Some leaders in the Philippines, Indonesia, and other countries opposed communism. Some of these leaders did little to restrain violence against people who were thought to be communists, and many people were killed. In communist countries it was the reverse. Leaders of these countries fought anticommunists within their own borders. Their strong central governments allowed little talk of reform.

Third, the Asian countries wanted rapid economic growth. Many Asian leaders thought a democratic government was slow and inefficient in promoting economic growth. They believed that government control would allow their countries to grow faster.

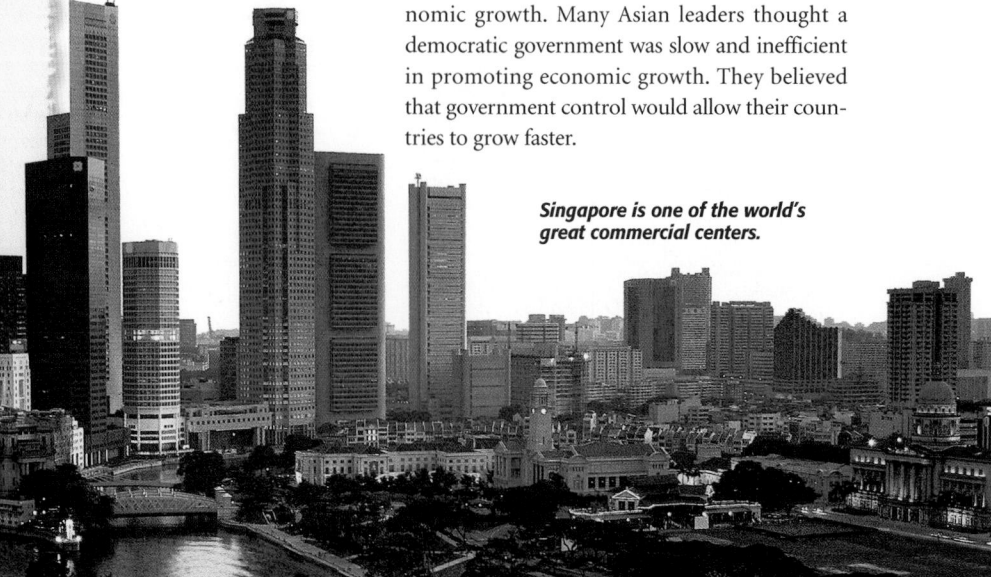

Singapore is one of the world's great commercial centers.

LEVEL 1: Copy the chart on the chalkboard, omitting the check marks. Have students copy and complete the chart by checking the reasons that apply for each country.
ENGLISH LANGUAGE LEARNERS

HOMEWORK Have students write a letter to the editor as a citizen of one of the Southeast Asian countries. The letter should explain why the writer supports or opposes authoritarian government.

Why Governments Limited Civil Rights			
	Ethnic/Religious Conflicts	Oppose or Protect Communism	Promote Economic Developments
Burma	✔	✔	
Cambodia		✔	
China		✔	✔
Indonesia		✔	
Laos		✔	
Malaysia	✔		
Philippines	✔	✔	✔
Singapore			✔
South Korea		✔	✔
South Vietnam		✔	

An example of the effect of these ideas was Singapore. From the time Singapore became independent in 1965, one man ran the government. He was Prime Minister Lee Kuan Yew. Throughout his time in office, Lee imposed strict controls on labor unions, political activity, and the media. When Lee stepped down in 1990, he left Singapore with one of the world's most stable governments. It was also one of the wealthiest countries in Asia. Lee described his government this way.

History Makers Speak

❝We have departed in quite a number of material aspects . . . from the principles of justice, and the liberty of the individual. . . . We have had to adjust, to temporarily deviate from ideas and norms. This is a heavy price. . . . So let us always remember . . . the price we have had to pay in order to maintain normal standards in the relationship between man and man, [and] man and authority . . .❞

from a speech by Lee Kuan Yew, Singapore, 1967

Analyzing Primary Sources

Evaluating Does Lee Kuan Yew think individual rights are important or unimportant? unimportant

✔ **READING CHECK: Summarizing** What were the three reasons Asian countries imposed tight government controls? ethnic divisions, government security, economic growth

Economic Development

By the year 2000, more than 3.5 billion people lived in Asia. That was 60 percent of the world's total population. Although millions of Asian people still lived in poverty, the continent was home to some of the fastest-growing economies in the world.

Barriers to economic development. With a few exceptions, the economies of most Asian countries started their postwar growth slowly. In part, this was because many Asian countries emerged from the colonial era with little wealth of their own. It took huge amounts of money to develop industry. They needed machinery, factories, and transportation networks. Some Asian countries did not have the money needed to bring their industries up to the level of the world's more advanced nations.

The Asian countries had two ways to get the money they needed. They could get loans from international agencies and other countries and encourage investment by foreign individuals or foreign corporations. Or, they could export their agricultural goods and natural resources. They could sell tea, spices, timber, rubber, minerals, and other goods. In the 1950s and 1960s, however, these items brought low prices in the world markets. Sometimes, too, their trading partners would have economic downturns. Then demand for Asian goods would drop. Reliance on foreign investment could also cause economic downturns. Just as capital could come in, financial investors would withdraw it suddenly when they lost confidence in a country. Such dependence on foreign capital helped to bring about a major crisis for Asian economies during the 1990s.

In the years immediately following World War II, most Asian countries lacked managers and skilled workers. To solve this problem,

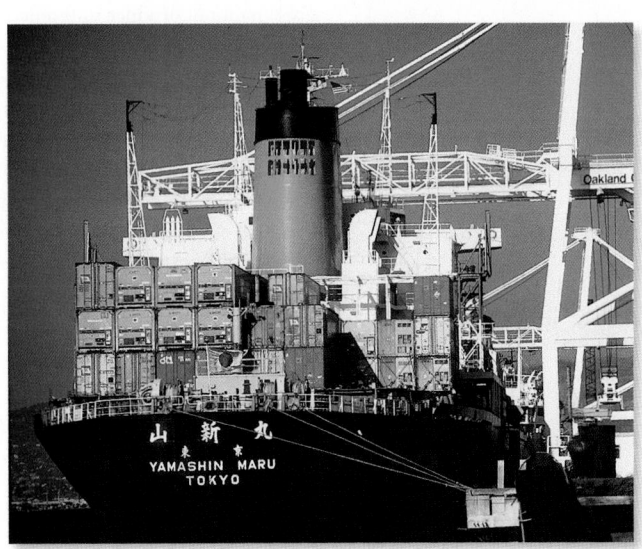

The containers stacked on the deck of this Japanese freighter hold just a fraction of the billions of dollars worth of goods that the United States imports every year from Asian countries.

YAMASHIN MARU
TOKYO

That's Interesting!

Government control in Singapore has been intense. Official campaigns to improve public behavior are common. Chewing gum, for example, is illegal. Even the smallest offenses, such as spitting in public, carry severe punishments.

Economics

During the 1990s Indonesia experienced firsthand the danger of relying on outsiders for economic growth. Indonesia's Muslim and Hindu populations shun pork and beef. Foreign investors decided to develop a poultry industry. They estimated that Indonesians, who ate only one chicken per capita annually, would each consume 60 chickens a year if they were available.

Foreign companies built commercial chicken farms and processing plants, and encouraged Indonesia's farmers to raise chickens. However, chicken feed could not be produced profitably in Indonesia, so farmers had to buy expensive imported feed. Then the price of feed doubled during the Asian financial crisis of the late 1990s. This drove up the price of chickens and cut demand. As the chicken market collapsed, the foreign companies closed. Indonesian chicken farmers were bankrupted.

ACTIVITY: Have students research other foreign companies operating in Asian nations today.

ALL LEVELS: Ask students to cite obstacles that stood in the way of economic development in many Asian countries. *(lack of money, poor transportation network, few factories, lack of managers and skilled workers, political unrest, labor unrest, low-priced exports)* As students respond, make a list on the chalkboard. Then discuss why each was an obstacle. Conclude by having students identify which obstacles might encourage foreign investment and which might discourage it.

LEVEL 3: Provide students with the following quotation from turn-of-the-century British writer and poet Rudyard Kipling (1865–1936): "East is East and West is West and never the twain shall meet." Ask students to what extent Kipling's observation applies to today's world. *(To argue that it is no longer valid, students should cite such developments as immigration, international investment, trade, and other examples of economic and cultural ties between the two regions.)*

Economics

Huge conglomerates called *chaebol* emerged in South Korea in the late 1900s. They enjoyed preferential government support. Few small and medium-sized companies could compete with the *chaebol.* Democratic reform greatly weakened the power of the *chaebol.* In 1996 *chaebol* leaders were put on trial and found guilty of having bribed two South Korean presidents in return for government favors.

Critical Thinking

Why did democratic reform lead to an attack on the power of the *chaebol?*

ANSWER: The power and influence of the *chaebol* led to social inequality.

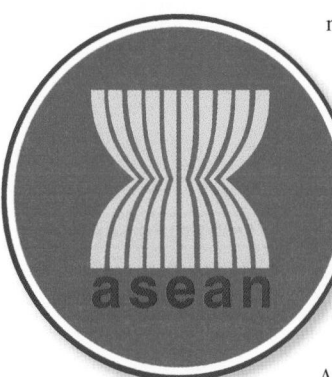

The logo of the Association of Southeast Asian Nations symbolizes ASEAN's goals of unity, growth, and peace.

many nations completely reformed their education systems. They opened vocational schools to train workers and started on-the-job training programs.

Cooperating for development. In the 1970s, some Asian countries began to find answers to their problems. They began to form loose economic groups among themselves. This helped them get higher prices for their exports. Asian countries also joined with developing nations in other parts of the world. Together they were able to get better loan terms. Most of these loans were from agencies such as the World Bank and the International Monetary Fund.

In 1967 Southeast Asian countries joined together in an association to develop trade and economic policies for the whole region. They started the Association of Southeast Asian Nations (**ASEAN**). Its goals were to promote economic growth and social progress in Southeast Asia. In addition, ASEAN hoped to improve peace and security in the area.

Several Asian nations tried to speed up economic growth through greater government control. Some governments took over and ran important industries. For example, the Indonesian government took over the oil industry. These governments wanted to see that the profits went back into the country's development. Other countries passed laws against labor unions and strikes. They wanted to make sure that nothing would stop work in the factories. In some cases these actions might have led to more rapid economic growth. The growth, however, was at the expense of individual rights.

Economic expansion. By the beginning of the 1990s, some Asian countries had made a great deal of progress. Japan, for example, ranked as one of the world's major economic powers. South Korea, Taiwan, Singapore, and Hong Kong all had very strong economies. They played important roles in the world markets. Together, these four became known as the **"Four Tigers."**

By the mid-1990s, all of Asia was a region of powerful economic growth. Observers began to call this growth "the Asian miracle." Many Asian nations were growing at annual rates of 6 percent to 10 percent. China's growth was dramatic. Its gross national product multiplied by four in just twenty years. Even so, millions of Asian people still lived in poverty. The numbers of poor, though, had decreased. In East and Southeast Asia, the number dropped by 50 percent between 1975 and 1995.

Nevertheless, there are significant problems in the region, including political instability, overpopulation, and a growing gap between rich and poor. In 1997 a financial crisis in Thailand began to spread to neighboring nations. By 2000 many Asian economies were experiencing economic crises. However, many experts predict that Asia will continue to gain strength. Some expect that by about 2025 China may surpass the United States as the largest economy in the world.

✔ **READING CHECK: Making Generalizations** How did Asia become a region of powerful economic growth? economic cooperation between Asian nations, greater government control

Asian Cultural Diffusion

For hundreds of years, Asia has exercised a powerful influence over the West. The ancient religions, philosophies, and martial arts of China and Japan have long fascinated many Westerners. Exhibits of ancient Asian porcelain, carpets,

CLOSE

Have students discuss whether authoritarian governments or democratic ones create a better climate for economic growth.

REVIEW

Have students complete the Section 5 Review on page 873.

ASSESS

Have students complete Daily Quiz 32.5. As Alternative Assessment, you may want to use the chart in this section's lessons.

RETEACH

Have students complete Main Idea Activity for English Language Learners and Special-Needs Students 32.5. Then have them list the main idea of each heading and subheading in the section.
ENGLISH LANGUAGE LEARNERS

EXTEND

Invite students to research the current political or economic situation in one of the "Four Tigers" and to report their findings to the class. **BLOCK SCHEDULING**

manuscripts, and other arts and crafts have drawn huge crowds to Western art galleries. More recently, Asia has exerted an economic influence on Western consumers through Asian-made products. Asian electronics, for example, own a large share of the world market. Many Asian televisions, computers, cameras, and video equipment are in American stores. Asian cars and trucks, too, find ready markets in Western countries. A few Asian companies have opened automobile factories in the West. Asia has also supplied parts to Western companies. A great number of products constructed in the West have been made from Asian parts.

This economic competition from Asia has both alarmed and fascinated Western business leaders. Since the late 1970s, Western economists have traveled throughout Japan trying to discover why Japanese goods sell so well in world markets. Many economists have suggested that the answer lies in the cooperative relationship between management and workers. Others have noted that government assistance and low-interest business-development loans enable Japanese companies to buy the latest machinery. Still others have pointed out that the Japanese educational system emphasizes the study of science and math. This focus has produced a force of scientists and engineers who have been able to develop better, more competitive products.

✔ **READING CHECK: Analyzing Information**
How has Asian economic success influenced the West? alarmed some business leaders; model for others

This skilled Japanese worker uses high-technology tools and instruments to assemble and test cameras.

SECTION 5 REVIEW

1. **Identify** and explain the significance:
   ASEAN   "Four Tigers"

2. **Categorizing** Copy the chart below. Use it to organize the economic problems Asian countries had and how they were solved.

Economic problems in new Asian countries
1.
2.
3.

Solutions to economic problems
1.
2.
3.

3. **Finding the Main Idea**
   a. In general, what have been the effects of tight government controls and restrictions on individual human rights in many Asian countries since the end of World War II?
   b. In what ways did efforts to build cooperation and alliances among the countries of Southeast Asia help to promote economic development and growth throughout the region?
   c. In what ways have the United States and other countries of the West been influenced by Asian nations' economic growth and competition since the end of World War II?

4. **Writing and Critical Thinking**
   Supporting a Point of View Imagine that you are a journalist working in today's Asia. Write a newspaper editorial in which you analyze the loss of individual rights in some Asian nations, and explain why you think this is an important issue.

   Consider:
   • what actions resulting in the loss of individual rights have taken place in the region
   • why some Asian governments have moved to put tight controls in place in their countries
   • why many people in Asia see a need for increased individual rights
   • what these people might do to promote the growth of individual political and human rights

go.hrw.com **Homework Practice Online**
keyword: SP3 HP32

SECTION 5 REVIEW ANSWERS

❶ **Identify**
• ASEAN, p. 872
• "Four Tigers," p. 872

❷ Economic Problems: slow economic growth, reliance on foreign investment, low prices for their exports, lack of managers and skilled workers; Solutions: greater government economic controls, loans from World Bank and IMF, provide vocational schools and on-the-job training, joint cooperation, formation of ASEAN

❸ a. They tended to limit human rights.

b. got higher prices for their exports and better terms on international loans

c. many Asian products for sale in United States, components part of United States products, competition for United States businesses, adopted Asian ideas of organizational theory

❹ Editorials should consider that rights may be lost in the interest of national growth, and whether or not individual rights are more important than what is best for the nation as a whole.

REVIEW AND ASSESSMENT RESOURCES

REPRODUCIBLE RESOURCES
▸ Vocabulary Activity 32

TECHNOLOGY RESOURCES
▸ Chapter 32 Test Generator (on the One-Stop Planner)
▸ Global Skill Builder CD–ROM
▸ HRW Web Site

REINFORCEMENT, REVIEW, and ASSESSMENT
▸ Chapter 32 Review, pp. 874–875
▸ Chapter 32 Tutorial for Students, Parents, Mentors, and Peers
▸ Chapter 32 Test (Form A or B)
▸ Alternative Assessment Handbook
▸ Chapter 32 Test for English Language Learners and Special-Needs Students

REVIEW
Have students complete the Chapter 32 Review on pages 874–875.

ASSESS
Use one of the chapter tests to assess students' understanding of the content. For Alternative Assessment, see the Portfolio Activities and Alternative Assessment Handbook.

CHAPTER 32 REVIEW ANSWERS

Understanding Main Ideas
1. to separate religious groups

2. physically divided, cultural diversity, political unrest, East Pakistan independence movement

3. move toward market economy, more open society, privately-owned businesses

4. North Korea: communist dictatorship, famine, economic collapse; South Korea: move to democracy, economic growth

5. demilitarized, new constitution, democratic government, breakup of zaibatsu, land reform

6. built industry, increased exports, gave foreign aid, independent foreign policy

7. communism suppressed, loss of civil rights, economic problems

8. Causes: Vietnam divided, political oppression in South Vietnam, communist insurgency, U.S. concerns; Results: Vietnam reunited under communist rule

9. internal unrest, lack of money and infrastructure, lack of skilled workers and managers

Reviewing Themes
1. Tiananmen Square Massacre; Aung San's arrest in Burma; tight controls in Singapore

2. Korean War; Vietnam War; North Vietnam's intervention in Laos and Cambodia

3. South Korea, Singapore, Japan, Taiwan

874

CHAPTER 32 Review

Creating a Time Line
Copy the time line below onto a sheet of paper. Complete the time line by filling in the events, individuals, and dates from the chapter that you think were significant. Pick three events and explain why you think they were significant.

1945	1960	1975	Present

Writing a Summary
Using standard grammar, spelling, sentence structure, and punctuation, write an overview of the events in the chapter.

Identifying People and Ideas
Identify the following terms or individuals and explain their significance:

1. nonalignment
2. Indira Gandhi
3. Red Guards
4. Tiananmen Square Massacre
5. SCAP

6. MacArthur Constitution
7. domino theory
8. Ho Chi Minh
9. Tet Offensive
10. Khmer Rouge

Understanding Main Ideas

SECTION 1 (pp. 846–851)
South Asia After Empire
1. Why did Great Britain partition India before independence?
2. What problems did Pakistan face after it became independent?

SECTION 2 (pp. 852–858)
Communist China and Its Influence
3. How did life in China differ after Mao Zedong's death from what it had been before?
4. In what ways have the histories of the two Koreas differed?

SECTION 3 (pp. 859–862)
The Japanese Miracle
5. What happened in Japan during the Allied occupation following World War II?
6. What steps did Japan take to become a major world economic power?

SECTION 4 (pp. 863–869)
Independence Struggles in Southeast Asia
7. What were the results of strong government control in the Philippines and Indonesia?
8. What were the causes and results of the Vietnam War?

SECTION 5 (pp. 870–873)
Asian Paths to Prosperity
9. What problems did the Asian countries face as they worked toward economic development?

Reviewing Themes
1. **Government** What evidence is there that people had fewer civil rights in Asian countries that had strong controlling governments?
2. **Global Relations** List examples of clashes between neighboring communist and noncommunist Asian nations.
3. **Economics** What are examples of Asian countries whose economic growth has led to outstanding success?

Thinking Critically
1. **Summarizing** What problems did the new independent nations of Asia have in common?
2. **Comparing** What are the similarities and differences between the Korean and Vietnam wars?
3. **Drawing Inferences** How do the World Bank and the International Monetary Fund affect Asian growth?
4. **Supporting a Point of View** What evidence would you give that a democratic government does not slow economic progress as some Asian leaders thought?

Writing About History
Comparing Write a short essay comparing events in China and Cambodia in the late 1900s, noting how their policies violated political, economic, social, and human rights. Use the chart below to help organize your thoughts.

	China	Cambodia
Political rights		
Economic rights		
Social rights		
Human rights		

CLOSE

Ask students what they think the biggest challenge facing Asia is today. List responses on the chalkboard. Then discuss how and why the challenges on the list are related.

RETEACH

Pair students who had difficulty with the test. Have each pair use their textbooks to correct their tests. Then have them create flashcards and quiz each other on the chapter content. When they are ready, have students take the Form B Test to assess their mastery of the material. **ENGLISH LANGUAGE LEARNERS, COOPERATIVE LEARNING**

Portfolio Extensions
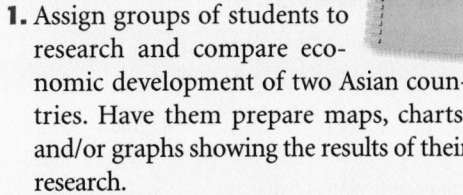

1. Assign groups of students to research and compare economic development of two Asian countries. Have them prepare maps, charts, and/or graphs showing the results of their research.
2. Have students collect information about the Tet Offensive and the reaction to it in the United States. Then have them write a report describing how it affected attitudes in the United States toward the Vietnam War.
3. Ask students to imagine they live in one of the countries discussed in the chapter. Have them pick a political or economic issue in that country and create a political cartoon that expresses an opinion on the issue they have chosen.

Building Social Studies Skills

Determining Chronological Sequences

Study the chronological data below.

The Vietnam Conflict: Selected Events

1967—389,000 U.S. troops in Vietnam by end of year
1967—Anti-war protests increase in the U.S.
1968—North Vietnam launches the Tet Offensive
1969—First withdrawals of U.S. troops announced
1970—U.S. troops move into Cambodia
1973—U.S. Congress prohibits further U.S. military activity in Indochina

1. Determine if each of the statements that follows is true, false, or unknown based on the information provided by the data only.

   a. Anti-war protests in the United States grew until the early 1970s.

   b. The number of U.S. troops in Vietnam was never greater than 350,000.

   c. U.S. troops moved into Cambodia about two years after the Tet Offensive.

   d. After 1976 U.S. military activity in Indochina was prohibited by the U.S. Congress.

2. Today, some Americans believe that the United States should work to build closer cultural and economic ties with the people of Vietnam. What factors do you think might limit or prevent the growth of such ties?

Identifying a Point of View

Read the following description by a North Vietnamese soldier about using elephants to improve the Ho Chi Minh Trail. Then answer the questions.

> "Thuan, the commander of the unit, sent men to fell trees in the forest to fill up the swamp. The elephant quickly understood: it grabbed hold of the logs with its forelegs and gradually pulled itself from the mud and out of danger. We were all overjoyed and set off immediately . . . but somehow we were detected and our convoy was shelled. We were worried that our animals, because of their size, were not safe. . . . I still wonder how no elephants were hit."

3. Which of the following statements best describes the author's perspective toward the situation?

   a. He was most comfortable in the forests and swamps along the trail.

   b. He would rather have been fighting than working with elephants.

   c. He was more focused on building the trail and caring for elephants than on fighting a war.

   d. He was surprised the convoy was shelled.

4. Why might the North Vietnamese have been improving the Ho Chi Minh Trail? Give specific reasons.

Alternative Assessment

Building Your Portfolio

Government

Loss of individual rights is still a problem in the world today. Use your textbook and other sources to find examples of countries where strong government control has meant loss of civil rights. Then write a newspaper article about your findings. Illustrate your article with drawings, photographs, or maps.

🖥 internet connect

Internet Activity: go.hrw.com
KEYWORD: SP3 WH32

Choose a topic on Asia Since 1945 to:

- create a chart comparing the population growth of the United States and India by analyzing factors such as death rates, birthrates, and immigration statistics.
- research the Association of Southeast Asian Nations (ASEAN), and write a persuasive report on why or why not to join the association.
- write a biography of an Asian leader.

Thinking Critically

1. civil unrest, communist insurgencies, poor economies

2. Similarities: partitioned, north invades south, United States sends troops; Differences: communists win in Vietnam and lose in Korea, Vietnam unified, Korea remains divided

3. help by making loans for economic development

4. events in Japan

Writing About History

Students' essays should include specific examples of rights violations.

Building Social Studies Skills

1. a. unknown, b. false, c. true, d. false

2. lingering hostility and distrust

3. c

4. to get troops and supplies to South Vietnam

Building Your Portfolio

Articles will vary but might focus on recent developments in China, Cambodia, Vietnam, Indonesia, Latin America, or Africa.

CHAPTER
33

Africa and the Middle East Since 1945

CHAPTER RESOURCE MANAGER

Objectives	Pacing Guide	Reproducible Resources
SECTION 1 **African Independence After World War II** (pp. 878–885) • Identify the factors that led to a rise of African nationalism after World War II. • Explain how the processes that ended colonial rule in British, French, Belgian, and Portuguese colonies differed. • Explain how South Africa's move to independence was different from that of other African nations.	**Regular** 1.5 day **Block Scheduling** 1 day *Block Scheduling Handbook with Team Teaching Strategies, 33.1*	**RS** Guided Reading Strategy 33.1 **RS** Graphic Organizer Activity 33: Independence for Africa **PS** Readings in World History 117, 118
SECTION 2 **Africa Since Independence** (pp. 886–890) • Identify the challenges—political, ethnic, economic, and environmental—that newly independent African countries faced. • Explain how rivalry between the superpowers of the Cold War affected Africa. • Explain the ways in which Africa experienced a revival of African culture.	**Regular** 1.5 day **Block Scheduling** 5 day *Block Scheduling Handbook with Team Teaching Strategies, 33.2*	**RS** Guided Reading Strategy 33.2 **SM** Geography Activity 33: Population in Modern Africa
SECTION 3 **Nationalism in the Middle East and North Africa** (pp. 891–897) • Explain how France's position in the Middle East and North Africa changed after World War II. • Explain how Britain's position in the Middle East and Egypt changed after World War II. • Identify the political and social changes that independence brought to Egypt and the Middle East. • Identify the major issues that Iran and Turkey faced after World War II.	**Regular** 1.5 day **Block Scheduling** 1 day *Block Scheduling Handbook with Team Teaching Strategies, 33.3*	**RS** Guided Reading Strategy 33.3 **E** Hands-on Activity 33: New Countries in Africa and the Middle East
SECTION 4 **War, Revolution, and Oil in the Middle East and North Africa** (pp. 898–905) • Explain how Arab-Israeli conflicts have shaped the recent history of North Africa and the Middle East. • Explain how the presence of rich oil fields affected the Middle East. • Describe the revolution in Iran and explain why it occurred. • Explain the types of leadership that emerged in the Arab world in the 1960s and after.	**Regular** 1.5 day **Block Scheduling** 1 day *Block Scheduling Handbook with Team Teaching Strategies, 33.4*	**RS** Guided Reading Strategy 33.4 **PS** Readings in World History 119: The Meaning of the *Intifada* **PS** Readings in World History 120: Beirut Diary **E** Creative Teaching Strategy 33: Family Histories

Chapter Resource Key

PS Primary Sources	**A** Assessment	Music	
RS Reading Support	**REV** Review	Video	
IC Interdisciplinary Connections	**ELL** Reinforcement and English Language Learners	Internet	
E Enrichment	Transparencies	Holt Presentation Maker Using Microsoft® PowerPoint®	
SM Skills Mastery	CD-ROM		

 One-Stop Planner CD-ROM

See the ***One-Stop Planner*** for a complete list of additional resources for students and teachers.

One-Stop Planner CD-ROM

It's easy to plan lessons, select resources, and print out materials for your students when you use the **One-Stop Planner** CD–ROM with **Test Generator.**

Technology Resources	Reinforcement, Review, and Assessment

 One-Stop Planner 33.1
Holt Researcher: World History: Desmond Tutu, Nelson Mandela
World History and Cultures Video Program 28
CNN. Presents World Cultures: Yesterday and Today Segment 32
CNN. Presents Geography: Yesterday and Today Segment 27
Homework Practice Online
Online Maps: Colonialism in Africa, 1945

Daily Quiz 33.1
Main Idea Activity 33.1
English Audio Summary 33.1
Spanish Audio Summary 33.1
REV Section 1 Review, p. 885

One-Stop Planner 33.2
CNN. Presents Geography: Yesterday and Today Segment 24: The Women of Nigeria
World History Teaching Transparency 28: Everyday Life: A Literacy Class in Africa
World History Teaching Transparency 28: Art and History: Kumasi Market
Homework Practice Online

Daily Quiz 33.2
Main Idea Activity 33.2
English Audio Summary 33.2
Spanish Audio Summary 33.2
REV Section 2 Review, p. 890

One-Stop Planner 33.3
Regions of the World Music Audio CD Program 12, 13
World History Teaching Transparency 35: Regional and World Maps: Southwest Asia
Religions of the World Video Series: Judaism, Islam
Homework Practice Online
Online Maps, Charts and Graphs: Southwest Asia

Daily Quiz 33.3
Main Idea Activity 33.3
English Audio Summary 33.3
Spanish Audio Summary 33.3
REV Section 3 Review, p. 897

One-Stop Planner 33.4
Holt Researcher: World History: Golda Meir
Regions of the World Music Audio CD Program 11
CNN. Presents World Cultures: Yesterday and Today Segment 33
CNN. Presents Geography: Yesterday and Today Segment 22
Homework Practice Online
Online Maps, Charts, and Graphs: Iran-Iraq War, 1980–1988

Daily Quiz 33.4
Main Idea Activity 33.4
English Audio Summary 33.4
Spanish Audio Summary 33.4
REV Section 4 Review, p. 905

internet connect

HRW ONLINE RESOURCES
GO TO: go.hrw.com
Then type in a keyword.

TEACHER HOME PAGE
KEYWORD: SP3 Teacher

CHAPTER INTERNET ACTIVITIES
KEYWORD: SP3 WH33
Choose an activity to:
• write a biography of Desmond Tutu which highlights his influence on events in South Africa during the 1900s.
• create a time line sequencing the major events of apartheid in South Africa.
• learn about recent developments in the Israeli-Palestinian peace process.

CHAPTER ENRICHMENT LINKS
KEYWORD: SP3 CH33

ONLINE ASSESSMENT
Homework Practice
KEYWORD: SP3 HP33
Standardized Test Prep
KEYWORD: SP3 STP33
Rubrics
KEYWORD: SS Rubrics

ONLINE MAPS, CHARTS, AND GRAPHS
KEYWORD: SP3 MCG

CONTENT UPDATES
KEYWORD: SS Content Updates

HOLT PRESENTATION MAKER
KEYWORD: SP3 PPT1

ONLINE READING SUPPORT
KEYWORD: SS Strategies

CURRENT EVENTS
KEYWORD: S3 Current Events

Meeting Individual Needs

Ability Levels

Level 1 Basic level activities designed for all students encountering new material

Level 2 Intermediate level activities designed for average students

Level 3 Challenging activities designed for honors and gifted and talented students

English Language Learners These activities address the needs of students with Limited English Proficiency.

 Chapter Review and Assessment

IC Vocabulary Activity 33
Global Skill Builder CD-ROM
HRW Web Site
REV Chapter 33 Tutorial for Students, Parents, Mentors, and Peers
REV Chapter 33 Review, pp. 906–907
A Chapter 33 Test Generator (on the One-Stop Planner)
A Chapter 33 Test (Form A or B)
A Alternative Assessment Handbook
A Chapter 33 Test for English Language Learners and Special-Needs Students

875b

Section 1 *African Independence After World War II*

Section 2 *Africa Since Independence*

Section 3 *Nationalism in the Middle East and North Africa*

Section 4 *War, Revolution, and Oil in the Middle East and North Africa*

Build on What You Know

Ask students to answer the following questions:

What purposes did the major treaties and alliances serve after World War II?

Consider:

- the United Nations
- the North Atlantic Treaty Organization
- the Warsaw Pact
- the Southeast Asia Treaty Organization

What challenges did India face after the end of British rule?

Consider:

- political instability
- social and economic problems
- foreign relations
- conflict over Kashmir

EXPLORING THE TIME LINE
GLOBAL EVENTS

■ internet connect ≡≡≡

TOPIC: Hominid Footprints
GO TO: go.hrw.com
KEYWORD: SP3 WH33

Have students access the Internet through the HRW Go site to conduct research on the findings of hominid footprints in archaeological research. Have each student assume the role of an archaeologist who has recently visited the site in Tanzania where Mary Leakey discovered hominid foot-prints in 1975. He or she should collect information from similar reports and write a letter to a friend or relative describing the find-ings and his or her opinion of their significance.

CHAPTER
33

1945–Present

Africa and the Middle East Since 1945

Rough, uncut diamond from Sierra Leone

1956
Politics
The Suez Crisis erupts in Egypt.

Late 1950s
Business and Finance
Oil is discovered in the Niger Delta of Nigeria.

1967
Politics
Civil war erupts in Nigeria.

1967
Global Events
Israel fights the Six-Day War against Arab neighbors.

1975
Science and Technology
Mary Leakey discovers hominid footprints in Tanzania that are estimated to be more than 3.6 million years old.

1976
Politics
Violence erupts in Soweto, South Africa.

1950

1960

1970

1948
Global Events
The state of Israel is declared; war begins with neighboring Arab states.

Abebe Bikila

1960
Business and Finance
OPEC is formed.

1960
Daily Life
Abebe Bikila of Ethiopia wins the first of two Olympic gold medals in the marathon.

1960
Science and Technology
Jane Goodall begins research on chimpanzees in Tanzania.

1965
Politics
Joseph Mobutu takes full control of the Congo.

Jane Goodall

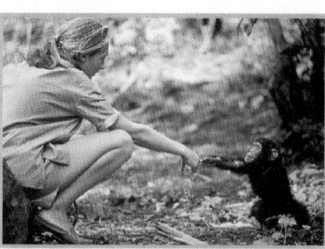

1972
Business and Finance
History's third largest diamond is discovered in a Sierra Leone mine.

1979
Politics
The shah of Iran is overthrown.

1979
Global Events
The Iran hostage crisis begins.

1979
Daily Life
Strict Islamic customs are enforced in Iran.

1979
Global Events
Israel and Egypt sign the Camp David Accords.

Build on What You Know

World War II produced great political, economic, and social change throughout Europe, Asia, and the Americas. The formation of the United Nations brought with it the hope that further wars could be avoided through peaceful negotiation. The nationalist movements that had begun in Africa and the Middle East after World War I increased after World War II. In Africa, radical young leaders demanded independence from European colonial powers. New Middle Eastern leaders were determined to break free from European domination. In this chapter, you will learn how Africa and the Middle East have changed since 1945.

What's Your Opinion?

 To help students create their Themes Journal entries, provide the following examples of appropriate **agree**/**disagree** *statements.*

Government

Agree Even if a country gains its independence peacefully, it may still face violent political and ethnic conflict in the future.

Disagree The method in which a country gains its independence has a great impact on its future development.

Culture

Agree A country's ethnic diversity has little impact on its government.

Disagree A government should equally represent all ethnic groups within a country.

Economics

Agree A country's economy is affected more by the economic policies of its leaders than by its natural resources.

Disagree Sometimes the discovery of an important resource can cause a country to experience rapid economic growth.

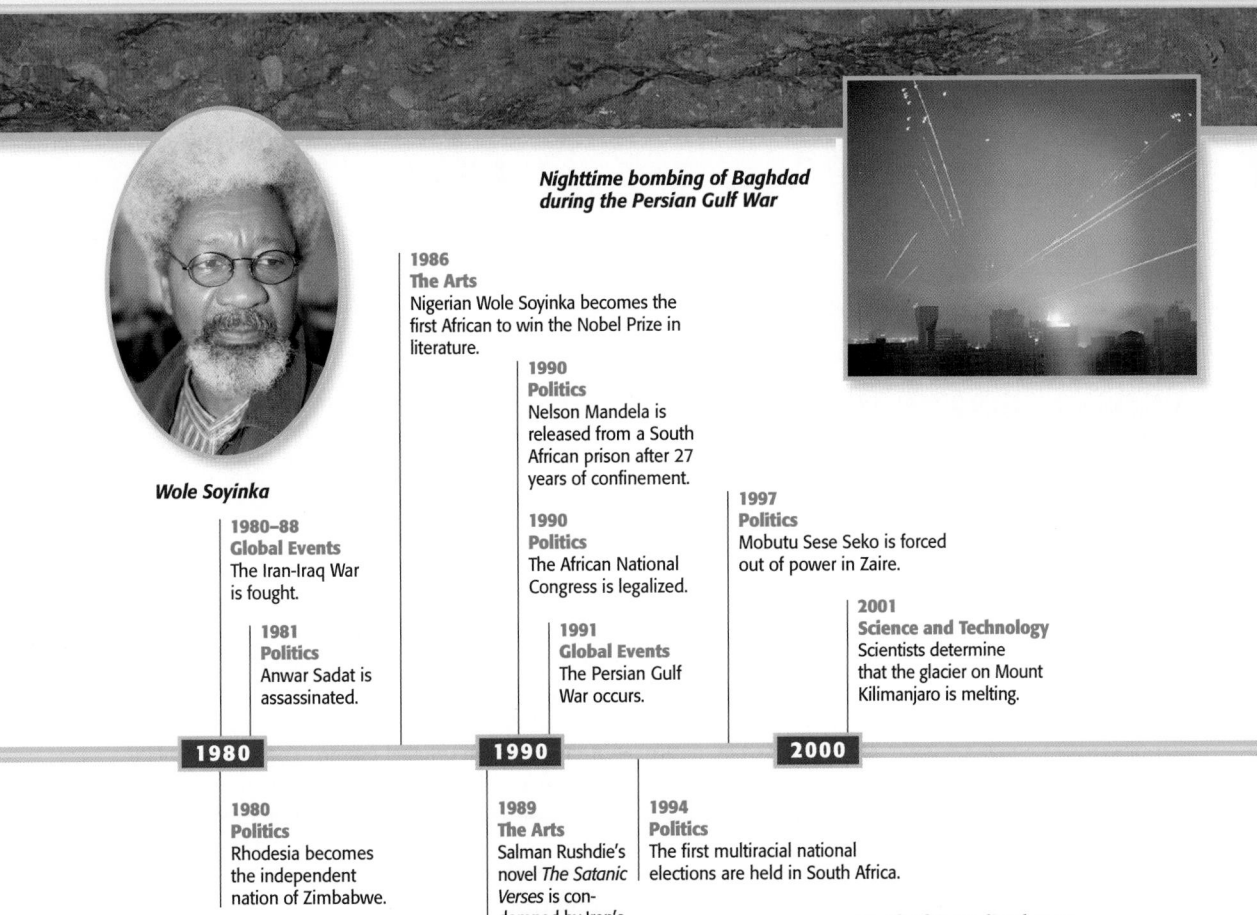

Wole Soyinka

Nighttime bombing of Baghdad during the Persian Gulf War

1986
The Arts
Nigerian Wole Soyinka becomes the first African to win the Nobel Prize in literature.

1990
Politics
Nelson Mandela is released from a South African prison after 27 years of confinement.

1980–88
Global Events
The Iran-Iraq War is fought.

1990
Politics
The African National Congress is legalized.

1997
Politics
Mobutu Sese Seko is forced out of power in Zaire.

1981
Politics
Anwar Sadat is assassinated.

1991
Global Events
The Persian Gulf War occurs.

2001
Science and Technology
Scientists determine that the glacier on Mount Kilimanjaro is melting.

| 1980 | 1990 | 2000 |

1980
Politics
Rhodesia becomes the independent nation of Zimbabwe.

1989
The Arts
Salman Rushdie's novel *The Satanic Verses* is condemned by Iran's Ayatollah Khomeini.

1994
Politics
The first multiracial national elections are held in South Africa.

South Africans lined up to cast their votes in 1994.

EXPLORING THE TIME LINE
GLOBAL EVENTS

Since the end of the Cold War, several African nations have become electoral democracies. These changes in government resulted from internal pressure as well as support from the international community. Democratic nations, such as Botswana and Mauritius, have shown economic growth and political stability.

Critical Thinking

Ask students to suggest ways the United States could help encourage democracy in Africa.

ANSWER: Students' answers will vary but might include providing advice about democratic policies or sending monitors to ensure that elections are fair.

What's Your Opinion?

 Do you **agree** *or* **disagree** *with the following statements? Support your point of view in your journal.*

Government The process that a country uses to achieve its independence has little effect on its later history.

Culture The presence of different ethnic groups within a country has little effect on that country's government.

Economics The discovery of an important resource in a country has little effect on the development of the country's economy.

◆ SECTION ❶ ▶

OBJECTIVES

1. **Identify the factors that led to a rise of African nationalism after World War II.**

2. **Explain how the processes that ended colonial rule in British, French, Belgian, and Portuguese colonies differed.**

3. **Explain how South Africa's move to independence was different from that of other African nations.**

📻 LET'S GET STARTED!

As students enter the classroom, ask them how they would feel if the United States was ruled by another nation thousands of miles away. Ask if it would make any difference if those rulers were of a different culture and looked down on Americans as inferior. Then tell students to suppose that those rulers refused to grant the "inferior" Americans any degree of self-rule. Ask students if such a situation would justify civil disobedience to achieve reforms. Would it justify terrorism? Revolution and independence? Tell students that in Section 1 they will learn about similar issues that Africans had to deal with in the decades following World War II.

SECTION ❶ RESOURCES

REPRODUCIBLE RESOURCES

▶ Guided Reading Strategy 33.1

▶ Readings in World History 117, 118

TECHNOLOGY RESOURCES

▶ One-Stop Planner 33.1

▶ Holt Researcher: World History: Desmond Tutu, Nelson Mandela

▶ World History and Cultures Video Program 28

▶ CNN Presents World Cultures: Yesterday and Today Segment 32

▶ CNN Presents Geography: Yesterday and Today Segment 27

▶ Homework Practice Online

REINFORCEMENT, REVIEW, AND ASSESSMENT

▶ Section 1 Review, p. 885

▶ Daily Quiz 33.1

▶ Main Idea Activity 33.1

▶ English Audio Summary 33.1

▶ Spanish Audio Summary 33.1

SECTION ❶

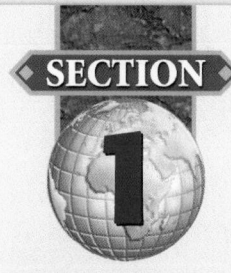

READ TO DISCOVER

❶ What factors led to a rise of African nationalism after World War II?

❷ How did the processes that ended colonial rule in British, French, Belgian, and Portuguese colonies differ?

❸ How was South Africa's move to independence different from that of other African nations?

DEFINE

apartheid

IDENTIFY

Pan-Africanism
Kwame Nkrumah
Mau Mau
Robert Mugabe
Nelson Mandela
Desmond Tutu
Steven Biko
F. W. de Klerk

▶WHY IT MATTERS TODAY

Some African nations are still experiencing problems in achieving democratic government and peaceful rule. Use or other **current event** sources to identify the present areas of conflict. Record your findings in your journal.

CNN Student News.com

African Independence After World War II

The Main Idea
African nationalists demanded freedom from European colonial powers after World War II.

The Story Continues *"The social and economic development of Africa will come only within the political kingdom, not the other way around."* With these words, Kwame Nkrumah expressed the belief that political unity in Africa was the key to success. Before unity could come, however, Africans had first to satisfy their growing desire for independence.

Nationalism

The 1930s had seen Africans increasingly demand independence from the European colonial powers. This movement strengthened when colonial governments cut back wages for African civil servants during the Great Depression. It was fueled even more by the 1935 Italian invasion of Ethiopia, the last great independent African state.

World War II was a turning point in African history. During the war thousands of Africans served in the armies of the European colonial powers. The continent itself became a source and a route for supplies. At the same time declarations such as the Atlantic Charter seemed to promise self-determination for all peoples after the war. When the war finally ended, many Africans were no longer satisfied to remain under European control. A new wave of nationalism began to sweep the continent. A group of young African leaders headed movements to end colonial rule.

These African nationalists were heavily influenced by the Pan-African movement. **Pan-Africanism** promoted the cultural unity of people of African heritage in their struggle for freedom. It began among people of African descent in North America and the West Indies, but the movement sought equality for black people throughout the world. Ending African colonial rule was central to this goal. Many young Africans were drawn by the Pan-African call "Africa for the Africans at Home and Abroad." In 1945 a Pan-African Congress was held in Manchester, England. Some of its delegates would go on to lead independence movements.

Africans expected that their demands for freedom would soon be met. The colonial powers did not plan to give up their empires in Africa easily, however. Some colonies followed a slow constitutional process with popular elections and a peaceful transfer of power. Others suffered long wars of national liberation.

✔ **READING CHECK:**
Summarizing What were some reasons that Africans demanded independence after World War II? wage cuts, invasion of Ethiopia

These Congolese soldiers fought for the Allies in World War II.

878

LEVEL 3: Have students work in pairs to create a dialogue on self-rule between an African and a European colonist. Roles from which students may choose should include a European plantation or mine owner, missionary, or colonial government official and an African worker, farmer, or Western-educated nationalist leader. Tell students that in each dialogue the European should explain his or her reasons for supporting continued control of the colony. The African should state his or her view on colonialism and on self-government versus independence. Select pairs to present their dialogues to the class.
COOPERATIVE LEARNING

HOMEWORK Have students imagine that they are Western-educated Africans living under European rule in the years following World War II. Ask them to write letters to the editor arguing either for self-government in their colony or for independence. Have students representing each alternative read the letters to the class.

The British Colonies

In February 1960 British prime minister Harold Macmillan addressed the South African Parliament. He warned that "winds of change" sweeping through Africa would blow away colonialism. In fact, the British had been the first to recognize this change. The first sub-Saharan colony to gain independence under majority rule was the British colony of the Gold Coast. When it became independent, the country was given a historically African name—Ghana.

Ghana. One young nationalist leader was **Kwame Nkrumah** (en·KROO·muh) of the Gold Coast. Nkrumah received his higher education in the United States and worked in Great Britain. In 1945 he attended the Pan-African Congress in Manchester. In late 1947 he returned to the Gold Coast to become general secretary of the United Gold Coast Convention. This was a political party of the westernized African upper class. From this position Nkrumah began to build a national following. He believed that political unity in Africa was the key to liberation.

Soon Nkrumah called on people to begin a campaign of civil disobedience, including strikes and boycotts of British goods. In this charged atmosphere in 1948, riots broke out in Accra, the colony's capital city. They soon spread to other towns. It took colonial authorities several days to restore order. The riots did much to convince the British that they must make some concessions to nationalist demands.

Nkrumah's radical tactics and demands alarmed more conservative African leaders. After they expelled him from his post, Nkrumah founded his own political party, the Convention People's Party. The CPP was dedicated to achieving immediate self-government. Under Nkrumah's guidance, it soon became a major political party.

Under constant pressure from the CPP, the British agreed to hold a national election in the Gold Coast in 1951. Nkrumah's party won a huge victory, but Nkrumah continued to press for full independence. In 1957 the Gold Coast achieved that status. Nkrumah renamed the newly independent nation Ghana to commemorate the ancient African kingdom of Ghana.

Kenya. The example of Ghana became an inspiration to African nationalists in other colonies. In some, however—particularly those with significant numbers of white settlers—the movement toward independence was more difficult and complicated. Kenya in East Africa, for example, took a very different road to independence.

By the early 1950s, the British government was willing to grant an increasing political role for Africans in the East African colony of Kenya. Many white settlers there, however, rejected any kind of reform. They feared that African self-government would threaten their ownership of huge fertile tracts of land in the central highlands on which they grew valuable cash crops like coffee.

Rapid population growth after World War II had led to land shortages. As a result, Africans demanded to settle in the highlands, although they were not allowed to own land there.

CONNECTING TO GEOGRAPHY

Pan-Africanism

Pan-Africanism refers to the movement whose goal has been to improve the lives of all people of African descent. The word *Pan-Africanism* was chosen to describe the movement because it means "all African." American intellectual W. E. B. Du Bois and Jamaican Marcus Garvey were leaders of the movement. While Pan-Africanism sought to end colonial control of Africa, it had as its larger goal the unification of people of African descent throughout the world. It was, then, a movement that went beyond geographical boundaries. The Organization of African Unity (OAU) was founded in 1963 to promote Pan-Africanism. It had 53 member nations by the year 2000.

Understanding Geography

How is Pan-Africanism different from a single nation's independence movement?

The flag of the Organization of African Unity

Global Relations

In addition to fighting in Europe and in Allied armies in all the African campaigns, thousands of African troops served with the British in Asia, in the war against Japan. Then, after the fall of the Dutch and British colonies in the Far East, Africa became a vital source of tin, rubber, and other materials vital to the Allies' war effort. Many of these goods were produced by forced labor. To assure a steady flow of essential supplies, colonial governments required Africans to cultivate certain crops and requisitioned other needed materials. In addition, they established price controls on African goods in order to keep the costs of their purchases below world market prices. All of these behaviors influenced postwar political developments in Africa.

Critical Thinking

Ask students what effect such wartime events inside the African colonies likely had on African nationalism.

ANSWER: Students should suggest that Africans likely felt abused by their wartime treatment, causing their desire for equality to grow.

CONNECTING TO GEOGRAPHY ANSWER

It goes beyond geographical boundaries with a goal of improving the lives of all people of African descent.

LEVEL 2: Create a two-column table on the chalkboard, headed *Ghana* and *Kenya*. Down the side of the table, write the following labels: *Nationalist Leader, Africans' Issues, Independence Methods,* and *Date of Independence.* Have students work in pairs to copy and fill in the table. Next, call on pairs to provide information from their tables for each cell of the chalkboard table. As you enter the "issues" and "methods" information in each column, ask class members to explain how it strengthened the movement for independence in each country. Then have students work individ-ually, using information from the chalkboard table, to write a paragraph comparing and contrasting the independence movements in Ghana and Kenya. **COOPERATIVE LEARNING**

History Maker

W.E.B. DU BOIS. W.E.B. Du Bois was the first African American to be awarded a Ph.D. from Harvard University. One of the founders of the National Association for the Advancement of Colored People (NAACP) in 1909, Du Bois spent more than a half-century fighting for African American rights. In 1961, at the age of 93, he immigrated to Ghana, where he was made a citizen shortly before his death in 1963.

Critical Thinking

Explore students' knowledge of the American civil rights movement in the 1950s and 1960s. Ask them to speculate on how the growth of that movement might have influenced events in Africa.

ANSWER: Students might suggest that the American civil rights movement strengthened African nationalism.

MAP ANSWERS
1. Western Sahara; Morocco

2. 1960

Technology Resources

Online Maps: Colonialism in Africa, 1945

African Independence, 1946–2000

Interpreting Maps Within 15 years of the end of World War II, many colonial powers had granted independence to their African colonies. By the 1990s all of Africa was free from colonial rule.

■ **Skills Assessment: 1. Locate** What country remained a dependency in 1993? Of what colonial power was it a dependency? **2. Making Generalizations** What year seems to have been a watershed for independence for western and central African nations?

ALL LEVELS: Have students locate Zambia, Malawi, and Zimbabwe on the map on page 880. Ask them by what names these countries were known when they were British colonies. *(Northern Rhodesia, Nyasaland, and Southern Rhodesia respectively)* Have students note the independence dates on the map and ask why Zimbabwe gained independence so much later than the other two British colonies. *(delayed by breakaway white minority government and guerrilla war)* Conclude by having each student create a flowchart showing the course of events leading to independence for all three countries in British central Africa.

ENGLISH LANGUAGE LEARNERS

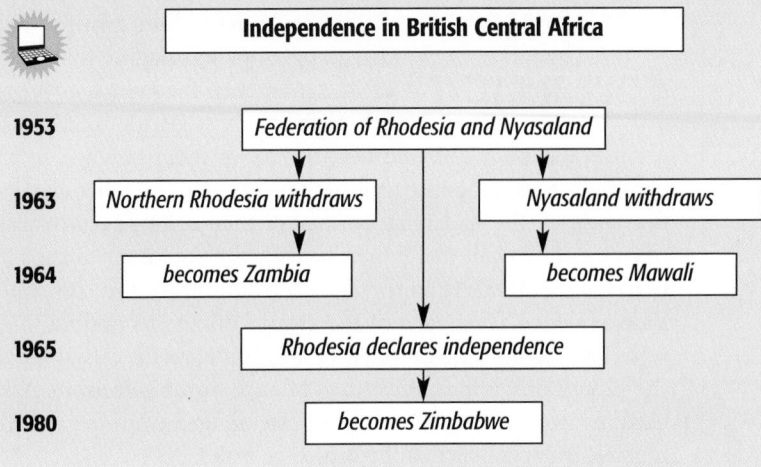

Independence in British Central Africa

1953	Federation of Rhodesia and Nyasaland
1963	Northern Rhodesia withdraws / Nyasaland withdraws
1964	becomes Zambia / becomes Mawali
1965	Rhodesia declares independence
1980	becomes Zimbabwe

The Kikuyu, Kenya's largest ethnic group, saw this area as their ancestral homeland. Kikuyu leader Jomo Kenyatta explained:

History Makers Speak

❝It is the key to the people's life; it secures them that peaceful tillage [cultivation] of the soil which supplies their material needs and enables them to perform their magic and traditional ceremonies in undisturbed serenity [happiness].❞

Jomo Kenyatta, *Facing Mount Kenya: The Tribal Life of the Gikuyu*

The Kikuyu continued to be excluded, however. The situation exploded into violence in the early 1950s. In a four-year guerrilla campaign, a secret Kikuyu organization known as the **Mau Mau** brought terror and destruction to the central highlands. About 100 Europeans and at least 2,000 Africans loyal to the British government were killed. When the British took military action against the movement, more than 11,500 Kikuyu were killed. Thousands more were jailed in detention camps. Although the British had put down the rebellion, they had not ended the drive for Kenyan independence.

In 1961 Kenyatta, who had been jailed as a suspected Mau Mau leader, was freed. He emerged as a popular and forceful leader of the independence movement. Despite ethnic rivalries, Kenyatta created a shared sense of Kenyan nationalism. He won an easy victory in national elections held in May 1963. Later that year Kenya gained its independence and Jomo Kenyatta became its first prime minister. In 1964 he became president and held that position until his death in 1978.

British central Africa. British colonies in central Africa also experienced both guerrilla warfare and peaceful constitutional change. Southern Rhodesia's large white population had achieved internal self-government in the 1920s. Northern Rhodesia and Nyasaland were governed by the British.

In an attempt to create a multiracial state, the British created the Federation of Rhodesia and Nyasaland. Many white settlers had lobbied for this set-up. However, African nationalist leaders saw the federation as a way for white settlers to continue to control the black majority populations of the territories. After 10 years, in 1963, the African majorities in Northern Rhodesia and Nyasaland voted to withdraw from the federation. In 1964 these areas became the independent states of Zambia and Malawi. Both were under majority African rule. Although Britain tried to force Southern Rhodesia toward majority rule, the white population, led by Prime Minister Ian Smith, refused to cooperate.

In 1965 Smith declared Rhodesia an independent state. Great Britain and much of the rest of the world refused to recognize this illegal act and cut off trade relations. Smith still refused reforms, and guerrilla warfare broke out. Eventually Smith was forced to work with moderate African leaders to form a new government under African leadership. However, the privileged status of whites was still guaranteed.

The guerrilla warfare therefore continued. The Rhodesian government finally agreed to hold free elections open to all, including the guerrilla leaders. **Robert Mugabe,** considered the most radical of the candidates, won. In April 1980 Rhodesia became the new nation of Zimbabwe—after the ancient southern African kingdom of Great Zimbabwe.

✔ **READING CHECK: Making Generalizations** What kinds of changes occurred in British Africa? guerrilla warfare, independence

---

Analyzing Primary Sources

Identifying a Point of View Why were the Kikuyu willing to fight for the right to occupy Kenya's central highlands? need for farmland, traditional culture

Jomo Kenyatta, a member of the 1945 Pan-African Congress in England, was jailed on charges of leading the Kenyan Mau Mau rebellion of 1951. He became the prime minister of Kenya in 1963 and president a year later.

Daily Life

British policy toward the native peoples of Kenya resembled the reservation system the United States imposed on Native Americans in the West. By 1895, when Britain established a protectorate over Kenya, the agricultural Kikuyu and the pastoral Masai were being forcibly crowded onto "reserves," and their ancestral lands sold at low prices to encourage white settlement. Reduced to subsistence agriculture on the poor land they were given, many Africans left the reserves to work as low-wage laborers on the British-owned farms, plantations, and ranches that occupied their former homelands. Later, the British imported large numbers of Indian workers to the region to build a railroad. They too were forbidden to purchase land in the "white highlands." Not until 1959 did Africans gain the right to buy land in this region.

Critical Thinking

Ask students to suggest a possible effect of forbidding land ownership to a group of people.

ANSWER: Students might suggest that it discourages economic advancement.

Reproducible **Resources**

RS Graphic Organizer Activity 33: Independence for Africa

Organize students into groups. Tell half the groups to imagine that they are the cabinet of the French government. They have to decide whether to grant France's African colonies self-rule or independence, or to continue resisting the African nationalists. Tell the other groups that they are the leadership council of their colony's nationalist movement. Explain that France has asked their colony to choose between membership in the French Community and complete independence. Have each of the groups discuss its options and report its decision and rationale to the class. Have the class discuss the practicality and implications of each group's decision. Ask class members how the French process differed from the attainment of independence in the British colonies.

History Maker

FELIX EBOUÉ. Born in French Guinea in 1884, Felix Eboué was educated in a French colonial school. After rising through the colonial service, in 1936 he became governor of the West Indies colony of Guadeloupe, making him the first black French colonial governor. In 1939 he became governor of Chad. He soon developed a reputation as an innovative colonial administrator.

Eboué was well known for his support of African political development. During World War II he played a crucial role in rallying French Equatorial Africa to the side of General de Gaulle and Free France. He raised troops from the areas he administered and supplied materials for the war effort. Eboué died in 1944.

Critical Thinking

Ask students why Felix Eboué was effective in recruiting African troops to fight for France.

ANSWER: Students might suggest that Eboué's efficiency as a governor, his respect for African peoples, or the fact that a non-European had risen to a high level in the French government made Africans feel they would be better off if the Allies won the war.

This **Time** *magazine cover from 1959 demonstrates the worldwide attention that African independence movements drew.*

Analyzing Primary Sources

Decision Making Do you agree with Touré's decision to become independent? Why or why not? need for freedom to preserve dignity; isolated from other French colonies

The French Colonies

French colonies in Africa took a somewhat different path toward independence than British colonies. Unlike the British, the French had always insisted that their goal was to incorporate their African colonies into France itself.

Before World War II most of France's African colonies had been organized in two administrative units. These were French West Africa and French Equatorial Africa. The colonial governors of French West Africa remained loyal to Vichy during the war. French Equatorial Africa, led by Chad's governor Félix Éboué, supported the Free French forces of General Charles de Gaulle. In 1944, with de Gaulle's approval, the governors of French Equatorial Africa met to announce liberal reforms. The Brazzaville Declaration also made it clear, however, that the colonies should not expect independence.

After the war France adopted a new constitution. Under this constitution the French empire became the French Union. The vote was extended to more Africans, who were now eligible to elect African representatives to the French National Assembly in Paris. Other Africans were also elected to the Assembly of the French Union.

Although this system provided many Africans with political experience, it fell short of true independence. Many Africans felt that their interests were second to those of France. In response, African leaders such as Léopold Senghor of Senegal, Felix Houphouet-Boigny of the Ivory Coast, and Sékou Touré of Guinea began to develop the same kind of popular parties that were emerging in British colonies. At first the new political parties only sought self-government within the French Union. As it became increasingly clear that France was not interested in granting anything but limited control over the colonies, however, many African nationalists became more radical in their demands.

In 1958 French president de Gaulle gave the African colonies a choice. They could be members of a new organization called the French Community and accept French control of their foreign affairs. Or they could become independent. By remaining with the French, they would continue to receive French aid. Those that chose independence would be immediately cut off from all aid and contacts with France. Only Guinea, under Sékou Touré, chose complete independence.

 History Makers Speak

❝We have to tell you bluntly, Mr. President, what the demands of the people are. . . . We have one prime and essential need: our dignity. . . . But there is no dignity without freedom. . . . We prefer freedom in poverty to opulence [wealth] in slavery.❞

Sékou Touré, quoted in *Africa Since 1875: A Modern History,* by Robin Hallett

The other French colonies accepted de Gaulle's new French Community. Guinea was immediately isolated, both politically and economically. It turned to the Soviet Union for help. Alarmed, de Gaulle reversed his position. Two years later, in 1960, the African colonies that had accepted membership in the French Community were granted independence without losing their close French ties.

✔ **READING CHECK: Drawing Conclusions** Why did many African colonies decide against accepting France's offer of complete independence? so they could continue to receive French aid

LEVEL 3: Have students work in groups to create "op-ed" pages that might have appeared in a Belgian Congo newspaper in early 1960. Each group's page should contain editorials and pundits' columns supporting and attacking Belgium's decision to grant independence. It should include at least one political cartoon on the subject and a feature article to give readers a background on the controversy. Each page should also contain letters to the editor from white colonists and Africans, expressing their views on impending independence. Post each group's page in the classroom. **COOPERATIVE LEARNING**

Belgian and Portuguese Colonies

Unlike Britain and France, Belgium and Portugal at first opposed any form of self-rule in their African colonies. As a result, the struggle for African nationalism in these colonies was more difficult. Perhaps the most frightful journey to independence occurred in the Belgian Congo.

The Belgian Congo. Belgium opposed independence because of its colony's great wealth in timber and mineral resources. It therefore provided little opportunity for Africans to develop skills in self-government.

The Congo was home to many groups of people, with different languages and customs. Belgian rule reinforced these differences. During World War II, however, many Congolese left their villages and flocked to the cities to help produce goods for the war effort. There they met other Congolese and established cultural clubs.

The Congo was a Belgian colony from 1908 until 1960. Violence broke out across the country after independence. Here UN troops arrive in the Congo in 1961.

In the 1950s events in neighboring British and French colonies introduced nationalistic ideas into the Congo. After 1955 Belgian authorities even allowed new political parties to form. Most remained committed to their local regions, but a few parties encouraged national unity. At first the Belgian government resisted. It proposed a gradual 30-year timetable to prepare the Congo for independence. In 1959, however, violent protests erupted in the capital city of Léopoldville. Alarmed, Belgian authorities announced that the Congo would become independent on June 30, 1960.

African leaders were not prepared for independence to come so quickly. Various political parties—representing different ethnic groups, geographical regions, and political beliefs—participated in the first elections. Patrice Lumumba (lu·MUHM·buh), an outspoken critic of European influence, became premier. The vast majority of Belgian technicians and experts feared his anti-European views and left the country. With few trained Africans to replace them, the Congo descended into chaos.

In July 1960 Congolese soldiers mutinied against their Belgian officers. A period of violence, aimed mostly at white people, followed. To make matters worse, the copper-rich province of Katanga seceded from the Congo. As civil war broke out, first Belgium and then the United Nations intervened. The Congolese army, under Colonel Joseph Mobutu, overthrew Lumumba, who was assassinated in 1961.

Fighting wracked the country until 1965, when Mobutu himself took full control. He established a ruthless military dictatorship that lasted into the 1990s. His long rule was due in part to the Cold War. Western countries supported Mobutu as a counterweight against other African countries that were leaning toward the Communists. In 1971 Mobutu Africanized the name of the country to Zaire and his own name to Mobutu Sese Seko.

The Portuguese colonies. While many African colonies were winning their independence, Portugal continued to oppose it for Portuguese Guinea, Portuguese West Africa, and Portuguese East Africa. In desperation, African leaders in these colonies organized "liberation armies." Long, bloody wars, in which nationalists gained control of much of the countryside, followed.

Economics

Before 1940, the Portuguese considered Angola to be fit for settlement only by convicts. However, a boom in coffee-growing after 1950 brought about 300,000 new immigrants in the next two decades, most from Portugal and the Cape Verde Islands. Rising coffee prices led to a rapid expansion of Angola's plantation system, which squeezed African small farmers out of the business and off their land. A similar situation developed in Mozambique, where cotton, sugar, and coffee plantations became the backbone of the economy. In the 1960s, an influx of about 160,000 white immigrants competed with Africans for jobs as well as for land. Within a decade, whites, who comprised just 1 percent of the farmers, occupied some 40 percent of the productive land. The growing disparity in opportunities for Africans that resulted from the situation in both colonies, combined with nationalism and the inspiration of independence in neighboring countries, caused rebellions to break out in Angola in 1961 and in Mozambique in 1964.

ACTIVITY: Have students work in groups to research events leading up to the rebellions in Angola in 1961 and in Mozambique in 1964. Then have students write brief reports and report on their findings to the class.

LEVEL 1: Ask students to identify ways in which South Africa developed differently from the rest of colonial Africa. List responses on the chalkboard. *(long history of self-rule, industrialization, and apartheid)* Then ask how South Africa's history was similar to the rest of Africa. *(white control, racism, development of African nationalist groups)* Have class members explain how apartheid differed from racism in the rest of colonial Africa. Tell students that when the Union of South Africa was formed, the British allowed the white colonists to decide if Africans should have the right to vote. Have the class speculate on how South Africa's history might have been different if the whites had said yes. **ENGLISH LANGUAGE LEARNERS**

CLOSE

Ask students if they think it was in the best interests of the Europeans in Africa to resist the demands of Africans for a greater voice in their government.

That's Interesting!

In 1960 South African Zulu chief Albert Luthuli became the first African to receive the Nobel Peace Prize for his nonviolent struggle against racial discrimination. In 1984 Desmond Tutu received the prize for his anti-apartheid work. Nelson Mandela and F. W. de Klerk shared a Nobel Peace Prize in 1993 for their efforts to transform South Africa into a multiracial democracy.

internet connect

TOPIC: Apartheid
GO TO: go.hrw.com
KEYWORD: SP3 WH33

Have students access the Internet through the HRW Go site to conduct research on apartheid in South Africa. Ask students to create a time line sequencing the major events of apartheid in South Africa. Ask them to include information on the origins, growth, opposition, and policy changes of apartheid.

HISTORY MAKER ANSWER
first black Anglican bishop of South Africa, first black archbishop, Nobel Peace Prize

Holt Researcher
go.hrw.com
KEYWORD: Holt Researcher
FreeFind: Desmond Tutu
Nelson Mandela
After reading more about Desmond Tutu and Nelson Mandela on the Holt Researcher, analyze their influence on events of the 20th century.

HISTORY MAKER

Desmond Tutu (1931–)

Although he originally wanted to be a doctor, Desmond Tutu could not afford the tuition. Instead, he became a teacher and, later, a priest. He also became the first black Anglican bishop of South Africa and the first black archbishop.

Tutu knew firsthand what it was like to live under apartheid. His opposition to apartheid earned him the Nobel Peace Prize in 1984. **What were some of Desmond Tutu's accomplishments?**

The wars ended only when the military in Portugal staged a coup in 1974 and announced that Portugal would withdraw from Africa. Within months the three former colonies became the independent nations of Guinea-Bissau, Angola, and Mozambique. None had the time to build firm foundations for their economies or governments. Portugal, the first European power to establish colonies in Africa, was also the last to give them up. Enormous pressure was now placed on the last remaining holdout of minority white rule in Africa, the Republic of South Africa.

✔ **READING CHECK: Identifying Cause and Effect** Why did the Congo and Portuguese colonies have a difficult time with independence? Belgium and Portugal opposed any form of self-rule in their colonies.

South Africa

South Africa was created in 1910 from the union of two British and two Boer territories. It was a white-ruled nation with dominion status, linked to Great Britain only in foreign affairs. Internally, it ruled itself as it saw fit.

Apartheid. Before World War II English-speaking whites dominated the South African government. By custom, whites and nonwhites were segregated socially. Nonwhites had fewer educational opportunities. By law, they could get only low-paying manual work. Africans made up about 75 percent of the population, but were restricted by law to just 13 percent of the land.

In 1948 the National Party—dominated by Afrikaans-speaking descendants of the original Dutch settlers—came to power. Segregation and economic exploitation became a government policy called **apartheid**—the Afrikaans word for "apartness." Separate tribal states, known as homelands, were founded for Africans. After a brief period of self-government, these homelands were supposed to become independent. Afrikaaner leaders insisted that under apartheid each race would develop separately. However, the homelands were in the most barren areas of the country. Even after independence, they remained completely dependent on South Africa.

Protests against apartheid. The African National Congress (ANC) was just one group that fought apartheid, but it was the best-known group. In the 1950s it launched a campaign of civil disobedience in which ANC members openly violated apartheid laws. The South African government responded swiftly and brutally. In 1960 police fired on peaceful demonstrators in Sharpeville. More than 60 died and more than 180 were wounded. World opinion condemned the massacre. Some ANC leaders—among them black lawyer **Nelson Mandela**—now felt that they would have to confront violence with violence. In response, the government banned the ANC.

In 1961 Prime Minister Hendrik Verwoerd proclaimed South Africa a republic, and it withdrew from the British Commonwealth. The government arrested Mandela and other ANC leaders in 1962. Found guilty of treason, they all received life jail terms. Yet the ANC continued to operate, primarily from bases outside South Africa. Inside the country leaders such as **Desmond Tutu, Steven Biko,** and others continued to speak out against apartheid. Some, such as Biko, paid with their lives. An increasing number of white South Africans joined the antiapartheid movement.

Meanwhile the government continued its policy of repression. In 1976 it passed a law that Afrikaans must be spoken in all South African schools. Black schoolchildren in Soweto were peacefully marching in protest when police fired on them, killing many.

REVIEW

Have students complete the Section 1 Review on p. 885.

ASSESS

Have students complete Daily Quiz 33.1. As Alternative Assessment, you may want to use the flowchart exercise in this section's lessons.

RETEACH

Have students complete Main Idea Activity for English Language Learners and Special-Needs Students 33.1. Then ask them to create a chapter glossary that includes the vocabulary and significant people, places, and events from the section. ENGLISH LANGUAGE LEARNERS

EXTEND

Have students imagine they are ANC supporters and create anti-apartheid posters or political cartoons. Display students' work in the classroom. BLOCK SCHEDULING

Over the next months outraged Africans rioted all over the country. Many were no longer willing to wait for change.

In the 1980s, faced with protests at home and abroad, the government began to retreat from its strict apartheid policies. Constitutional reforms gave some political voice to "Colored," or mixed race, and Asian South Africans. Black Africans, however, were still denied any political participation. To pressure South Africa to change its racist policies the international community imposed economic sanctions.

A change of direction. In September 1989 **F. W. de Klerk** was elected president of South Africa. De Klerk lifted a 30-year ban on antiapartheid rallies and legalized the ANC and other banned organizations. He also ordered the release of Nelson Mandela. On his release Mandela repeated the words he had spoken at his trial:

66 I have cherished the ideal of a democratic and free society in which all persons live together in harmony and with equal opportunities. It is an ideal which I hope to live for, and to see realized. But . . . if needs be, it is an ideal for which I am prepared to die. **99**

Nelson Mandela, quoted in *Higher than Hope,* by Fatima Meer

De Klerk hoped that Mandela and other opposition leaders would meet with him to discuss ways to build a new South Africa. The promise of reform, however, did not end the violence. A fight for leadership of the black population broke out between the ANC and the largely Zulu Inkatha Freedom Party. Thousands of black South Africans died in the next 15 months. In addition, not all whites supported de Klerk.

In 1994 South Africa held its first all-races elections. Nelson Mandela was elected president. He called on the people to "heal the wounds of the past." However, Mandela's government faced the challenges of desperate poverty and an AIDS epidemic. Mandela retired in 1999 and was succeeded by Thabo Mbeki.

✔ **READING CHECK: Evaluating** How did reforms in South Africa expand civic participation by citizens? *extended political rights to some non-whites*

HISTORY MAKER

Nelson Mandela (1918–)

After serving 27 years in prison for his activism, Nelson Mandela became the first black president of South Africa. **How did the slogan on Mandela's campaign button reflect the expansion of democracy in South Africa?**

HISTORY MAKER ANSWER
It reflected the power of the people to choose their leaders.

SECTION 1 REVIEW ANSWERS

❶ **Define**
• apartheid, p. 884

❷ **Identify**
• Pan-Africanism, p. 878
• Kwame Nkrumah, p. 879
• Mau Mau, p. 881
• Robert Mugabe, p. 881
• Nelson Mandela, p. 884
• Desmond Tutu, p. 884
• Steven Biko, p. 884
• F. W. de Klerk, p. 885

❸ Ghana: civil disobedience led by Nkrumah; Kenya: Mau Mau uprising; British central Africa: creation of new colonial states, guerrilla warfare; French colonies: development of French Community; Belgian Congo: violent protests; South Africa: apartheid, protests at home and abroad

❹ a. promoted by the Pan-African movement because many Africans were no longer satisfied to remain under European control

b. See answers in Number 3.

c. government-sponsored apartheid

❺ Students' lists will vary.

SECTION 1 REVIEW

1. **Define** and explain the significance:
   apartheid

2. **Identify** and explain the significance:
   Pan-Africanism
   Kwame Nkrumah
   Mau Mau
   Robert Mugabe
   Nelson Mandela
   Desmond Tutu
   Steven Biko
   F. W. de Klerk

3. **Sequencing** Make a cluster drawing like the one below. Use it to identify the events leading to African independence.

4. **Finding the Main Idea**
   a. How and why did African nationalism grow after World War II?
   b. In what different ways did British, French, Belgian, and Portuguese colonies achieve their independence?
   c. Why was South Africa's experience of independence different from that of other African nations?

5. **Writing and Critical Thinking**

   Supporting a Point of View Many people within the African nations were willing to face imprisonment or violence to achieve independence. Write a list of reasons that either support these actions or argue against them.
   Consider:
   • the failure of colonial governments to keep promises of independence made to African nations
   • the resistance of white settlers to black Africans occupying lands the Africans considered sacred
   • repression of nationalist movements by colonial governments
   • the legalization of segregation and other apartheid laws in South Africa

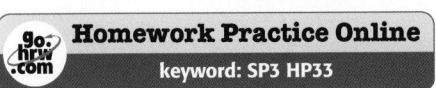
Homework Practice Online
keyword: SP3 HP33

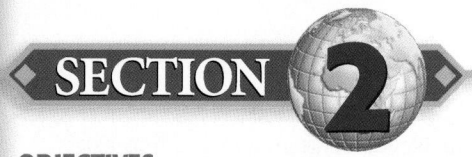

SECTION 2

OBJECTIVES

1 **Identify the challenges—political, ethnic, economic, and environmental—that newly independent African countries faced.**

2 **Explain how rivalry between the superpowers of the Cold War affected Africa.**

3 **Explain the ways in which Africa experienced a revival of African culture.**

🔊 LET'S GET STARTED!

As students enter the classroom, ask them to imagine they live in a region that has long been ruled as the colony of another country. Tell them that they worked for many years to attain self-government but, failing that, were finally successful in attaining independence. Ask them what hopes they would have for the future of their new country and how they would expect things to improve. Ask what challenges they would expect their new country to face. Tell students that in Section 2 they will learn about the hopes and challenges newly independent African nations experienced.

SECTION 2 RESOURCES

REPRODUCIBLE RESOURCES

▶ Guided Reading Strategy 33.2

▶ Geography Activity 33: Population in Modern Africa

TECHNOLOGY RESOURCES

▶ One-Stop Planner 33.2

▶ CNN Presents Geography: Yesterday and Today Segment 24: The Women of Nigeria

▶ World History Teaching Transparency 28: Everyday Life: A Literacy Class in Africa

▶ World History Teaching Transparency 28: Art and History: Kumasi Market

▶ Homework Practice Online

REINFORCEMENT, REVIEW, AND ASSESSMENT

▶ Section 2 Review, p. 890

▶ Daily Quiz 33.2

▶ Main Idea Activity 33.2

▶ English Audio Summary 33.2

▶ Spanish Audio Summary 33.2

SECTION 2

READ TO DISCOVER

1 What challenges did newly independent African countries face?

2 How did rivalry between the Cold War superpowers affect Africa?

3 In what ways did Africa experience a revival of African culture?

DEFINE

desertification

IDENTIFY

Jerry Rawlings
Laurent Kabila
Shaaban Robert
Wole Soyinka

▶ WHY IT MATTERS TODAY

Since African nations achieved independence, there has been a great surge of interest in the cultures of Africa. Use CNN or other **current event** sources to identify some of the African art forms and cultural practices that have become popular. Record your findings in your journal.

CNN Student News.com

Africa Since Independence

The Main Idea
After achieving independence African nations faced many political and economic problems.

The Story Continues *In the 1960s Obafemi Awolowo, a political leader from western Nigeria, spoke about human rights in his newly independent homeland: "Every member of any human association has rights, intangible though they are, which are sacred and inalienable, and which must be protected against any invasion, at all costs." Awolowo believed that it was the duty of the state to preserve these rights. However, in newly independent African nations, that was more easily said than done.*

Political Challenges

Africans greeted independence with high hopes. The end of colonial rule, however, brought with it many serious problems. New African leaders were inexperienced in politics and in governing the new states. When they failed to improve conditions as quickly as people wanted, the military often stepped in. Soon many African countries were being ruled by military dictatorships.

Ghana is a good example of the pattern that emerged in many African states after independence. During the early years of Kwame Nkrumah's rule, Ghana's main cash crop—cocoa—sold for high prices on world markets. The resulting prosperity helped make Nkrumah popular. He used that popularity to gain absolute power.

In 1964 a new constitution made Ghana a one-party state, and any challenge to Nkrumah was seen as treason. "All Africans know that I represent Africa," Nkrumah said, "and that I speak in her name. Therefore no African can have an opinion that differs from mine." That did not stop people from criticizing, particularly when the price of cocoa dropped on the world market. This drop, combined with government debt and corruption, caused Ghana's economy to collapse. Nkrumah became more and more ruthless and his popularity fell rapidly. In 1966 he was ousted in a military coup. Over the next 12 years Ghana shifted between civilian and military rule. Political instability was linked to shifts in the economy that resulted from changing cocoa prices.

Kwame Nkrumah reviews an honor guard in 1961. He led Ghana to independence, but his thirst for power resulted in his eventual removal from office.

TEACH OBJECTIVE 1

LEVEL 1: Create a four-column chalkboard table titled *Problems the New African Nations Faced.* Label the columns *Political, Ethnic, Economic,* and *Environmental.* Then call on class members to identify the challenges of each type that Africa has faced since independence and enter the information in the appropriate column of the table. As some students suggest entries for the table, call on others to cite examples of how these problems have affected specific nations.

ENGLISH LANGUAGE LEARNERS

Problems the New African Nations Faced			
Political	**Ethnic**	**Economic**	**Environmental**
inexperienced leaders, military coups, corruption and mismanagement	civil wars, ethnic tensions	only one or two major exports, lack of balance between industry and agriculture, vulnerable to changes in global economy, heavy debt	population growth, land overuse, drought, desertification, starvation, epidemic viruses

In 1979 a young air force pilot, **Jerry Rawlings,** led a takeover. Rawlings claimed that the present military leaders were corrupt and had to go. After public trials several leading military officers were executed. Rawlings then allowed elections to take place, and the country returned to civilian rule.

A little more than a year later, Rawlings dissolved the civilian government. He claimed it was worse than the military junta it had replaced. Rawlings tried socialist policies to improve the economy, but they too failed. A new course toward free enterprise worked. By 1990 Ghana's rate of economic growth was one of the highest in Africa.

To achieve this success, however, the people of Ghana had to pay high import, sales, and income taxes. Subsidies on food and fuel were reduced. The currency was devalued to stimulate exports. Ghanaians grew tired of these measures and of Rawlings's rigid governing style. A new constitution was adopted, and civilian rule was established. Resigning from the military, Rawlings ran for the presidency and won.

✔ **READING CHECK: Making Generalizations** What kinds of political problems—exemplified by Ghana—did new African nations face? instability, military rule, failing economy

Ethnic Violence

Ghana's political experience was typical of many African nations. Some nations, however, had to deal with special problems left over from colonial rule. National boundaries had been drawn by imperialist powers for their own convenience. People of similar cultural backgrounds were often separated, while people of different cultures were grouped together. In some places, such as Nigeria, this led to civil war.

Nigeria. By 1963, four years after independence, Nigeria was a federation of four regions. Each had a large degree of local independence. The government hoped that this loose federation would satisfy people's ethnic and regional differences and prevent conflicts. It did not.

In 1966 the military took over the government but still could not overcome the ethnic and regional tensions. In 1967 the Eastern Region seceded from the federation and declared itself the independent Republic of Biafra. A two-year civil war followed that resulted in the deaths of several million Biafrans from starvation and disease. After Biafra surrendered, the Nigerian government gradually restored stability. Ethnic and regional tensions continued, however.

The Nigerian civil war showed what ethnic conflict could do within a country. Such violence also spilled over national borders and threatened whole regions.

Rwanda, Burundi, and Zaire. In the 1990s in Rwanda and Burundi, tensions between the two major ethnic groups, the Tutsi and the Hutu, exploded into violence. In late 1993 about 50,000 Burundians—mostly Hutu—lost their lives in violence following a Tutsi-sponsored coup attempt. Marie Kaboinja, a survivor of the massacres, told of the violence:

❝Tutsis charged us with spears and pangas [machetes].... We ran away with my family. But many of us were killed, including my grandfather, father, mother, aunt and my three children.❞

Marie Kaboinja, quoted in "Burundi Still Bleeding," *The Economist*

During the Nigerian civil war with Biafra, millions of people like the refugees shown here died of starvation and disease.

Global Relations

Many African countries have formed trading blocs to encourage African unity, promote economic growth, and counter the ethnic divisions related to their European-set borders. In west Africa, 16 former British and French colonies formed the Economic Community of West African States (ECOWAS) in 1975 to promote industry, agriculture, telecommunications, and free trade. The organization also has involved itself in regional politics, sending a joint force into Liberia in 1990 to intervene in that country's civil war. In 1980 the countries of southern Africa formed what is now called the Southern Africa Development Community (SADC). The eastern and central states have formed themselves into a Preferential Trade Area (PTA) to promote interstate trade and integrated industrial development. Like the European Union, on which it is modeled, the PTA is working toward a uniform currency for all member nations.

Critical Thinking

Ask students why it is important for African nations to form such alliances and communities.

ANSWER: Students might suggest that it allows them to act as a more powerful force in global politics and that they can help each other develop economically.

LEVEL 3: Organize students into six groups to represent intelligence task forces of the American CIA or the Soviet KGB. Assign one pair of groups to be specialists on Angola, another pair to Ethiopia, and the third pair to Somalia. Have each group prepare a briefing for its nation's leaders that assesses the crisis in its assigned country, explains the country's importance to the United States or USSR, analyzes the other superpower's involvement in the country, and makes a recommendation regarding its own nation's involvement. Have each task force present its briefing to the class. **COOPERATIVE LEARNING**

HOMEWORK Ask students if the United States would have taken such an interest in helping African nations if the Soviet Union had not. Have students use sources such as computer software and media and news services to find out what changes have occurred in the level of American foreign aid to Africa since the collapse of the Soviet Union and write a paragraph reporting their findings.

Economics

Perhaps the greatest problems accompanying African independence were economic. As elsewhere in the developing world, many African socialist leaders came to believe that the path to prosperity lay in industrialization. Consequently, many of the new states neglected agricultural development in favor of industrial projects that were not always successful.

Critical Thinking

Ask students why many African governments might have favored industrial projects over agricultural development.

ANSWER: Students might suggest that industrial projects carried greater prestige value than agricultural efforts or that governments wanted to diversify their economies.

These Rwandan refugees are shown here waiting to cross the border into Zaire to escape the ethnic civil war in their own country.

In 1994 an estimated 500,000 Rwandans were killed. Most were Tutsi slaughtered by Hutu. A Tutsi army then captured the capital of Rwanda. About 2 million people fled to refugee camps in Zaire and in other neighboring countries. Many refugees died of disease and starvation. The killing in Rwanda continued.

The presence of so many Rwandan refugees destabilized Zaire. In 1995 the government stood by as Hutu refugees forcibly expelled Tutsi whose ancestors had settled in the eastern Congo as early as the 1700s. The Tutsi responded with force. It was feared that the Tutsi-Hutu conflict would engulf the entire central African lakes region. The Tutsi rebels were joined by forces who opposed Zaire's Mobutu Sese Seko. The Tutsi and the anti-Mobutu forces, led by **Laurent Kabila,** marched on the capital city of Kinshasa. In May 1997 they forced Mobutu to flee the country. Kabila renamed Zaire the Democratic Republic of the Congo. He promised to rebuild the country and halt foreign interference. After Kabila was assassinated in a failed coup attempt in 2001, his son Joseph took his place as head of the government.

✔ **READING CHECK: Problem Solving** How might ethnic conflicts have been reduced in Africa? consider cultures when establishing national boundaries

Economic and Environmental Problems

Almost all new African nations experienced economic difficulties. Their colonial economies had been tied to their imperialist rulers. After independence, they lacked the balance between agriculture and industry that is needed for economic stability.

Limited economies. Many new African nations depended on a single crop or mineral resource. For example, Ghana depended on cocoa, Zambia on copper, Sudan on cotton, Zaire on cobalt, and Nigeria on oil. All these products were subject to large price swings in the world market. Dependence on one product puts an economy at risk. When prices for that product drop, the whole economy—and therefore the nation—suffers. This is what happened in Ghana when cocoa prices dropped. A similar situation occurred in Nigeria.

By 1979 Nigeria had returned to a democratically elected civilian government. Because of the country's oil wealth, Nigerians had the chance to escape the poverty that threatened most other African nations. Industrialization looked promising. Then in the 1980s the international price of oil dropped. Oil had accounted for 95 percent of Nigeria's export revenues. With the drop in oil prices, the country's economy faltered. As in Ghana, the military took over in 1983 and introduced strict new measures to try to turn the economy around. In 1985 this government was itself overturned by Major General Ibrahim Babangida. He introduced bold reforms to restore economic and political stability. Babangida renegotiated the country's foreign loans and applied for assistance from international financial organizations. In the 1990s he and other generals tried to return the country to civilian rule.

Nigerians voted in a 1992 election, as the military government tried to return the country to civilian rule after an economic crisis.

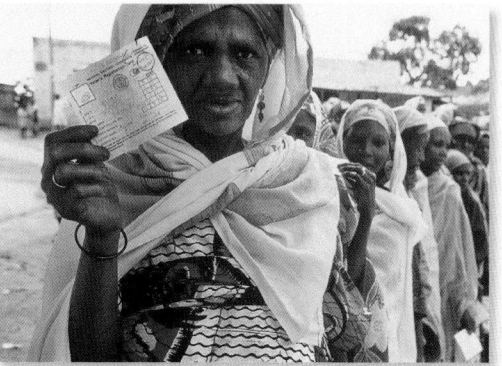

Like Nigeria, many new African countries turned to international organizations such as the World Bank for loans. However, bad planning, poor management, and corruption often left the countries worse off than before. Soon most African countries were deeply in debt. In addition, their economies

ALL LEVELS: Ask students to speculate about the effects colonialism and white minority rule would have had on African art and culture. *(Students may suggest a repressive effect, citing the Western orientation of many early African leaders and the European disdain for African culture.)* Ask students to deduce from this relationship the effect that independence would have on African culture. *(Responses should suggest an African cultural revival.)*
ENGLISH LANGUAGE LEARNERS

Ask students to explain how ethnic diversity contributed to problems in the independent countries of Africa.

---

remained highly vulnerable to changes in the global economy. Rising prices often forced Africans to pay huge amounts for imported goods.

Population and environment. Under colonial rule improvements in health care, disease control, and nutrition led to population growth. After independence this growth continued. To provide food farmers overused their land and planted crops on dry areas where fierce winds stripped away the topsoil. Acres of trees were cut down for firewood. The combined effect of these practices was **desertification**—the spread of the desert. In addition, severe droughts have brought starvation to millions.

Beginning in the 1970s and 1980s, new diseases emerged and new strains of viruses appeared. AIDS, for example, spread rapidly through many regions of the African continent. By 2003 approximately 30 million Africans were infected with HIV or AIDS. In 1995 the deadly Ebola virus struck in Zaire, causing the government to close the borders of an entire province.

✔ **READING CHECK: Identifying Cause and Effect** What has been one of the main causes of economic problems in Africa nations since their independence? lack of balance between agriculture and industry

Superpower Rivalries

As African nations pursued peace and stability, they sought assistance from both the Soviet Union and the United States. The Cold War between these two superpowers added to Africans' problems.

When civil war broke out in Angola after independence in 1975, the United States, the Soviet Union, and Cuba rushed military support to the rival factions. For the next 12 years, Angola became a battleground, or "hot war," for the Cold War. When tensions between the two superpowers eased, attempts were made to end the Angolan civil war. A regional agreement linking the independence of Namibia to the withdrawal of Cuban troops was reached in 1988. In 1991 the rival sides agreed to hold free elections the following year. Tensions still remain, however.

Soviet-American rivalry was even more complex in the Horn of Africa, the area that includes Ethiopia and Somalia. The Horn borders the Red Sea as well as the Indian Ocean sea-lanes to the oil-rich Persian Gulf.

When Ethiopian emperor Haile Selassie was overthrown in 1974, a Marxist regime came to power. The Soviet Union provided military aid. Ethiopia's traditional enemy, Somalia, was also a socialist country supported by the Soviet Union. When Somalia invaded Ethiopia in 1977, the Soviet Union sided with Ethiopia. Somalia was defeated by Cuban troops with Soviet weapons.

African nations, however, often sought aid for practical reasons rather than ideological beliefs. A worldwide relief effort tried to help Ethiopia during a severe drought in 1984. Somalia, also devastated by drought, called on its Arab neighbors as well as the United States for aid.

In 1991 after the Cold War had ended, the military dictatorships in both Somalia and Ethiopia collapsed. Somalia descended into civil war as different clans and rival warlords fought for power. The fighting prevented aid from reaching victims of the drought. In 1992 a United Nations force intervened. Unable to stop the bloodshed, it

INTERPRETING THE VISUAL RECORD

Desertification Slash-and-burn techniques used to clear land for agriculture contribute to erosion and desertification. **Based on the picture, what problems might this practice have for the future of the land?**

Economics

Violence in Angola resumed shortly after the 1992 elections, when the National Union for the Total Independence of Angola (UNITA) restarted the civil war. Some 200,000 Angolans died in the renewed fighting before another peace accord was reached in November 1994. Under UN supervision, UNITA agreed to disarm, to surrender the regions of Angola that it controlled, and to participate in Angola's government. UNITA continued to hold areas of the country, and in 1998 Angola was once again plunged into crisis. The dominant Marxist Popular Movement for the Liberation of Angola government expelled the UNITA delegates from the country's national assembly, and UNITA suspended all cooperation with government authorities. Although UN observers remained in Angola, in 1998 the country was again plunged into civil war. In 2002 a cease fire with UNITA took effect; however, fighting continued between government forces and separatist guerrillas.

Critical Thinking

Ask students why communist aid to Angola in the 1970s and 1980s included troops, while U.S. aid did not include troops.

ANSWER: Students may suggest that American public opinion might not have tolerated that level of involvement, especially so soon after the Vietnam War.

VISUAL RECORD ANSWER

The land may become infertile.

ASSESS

Have students complete Daily Quiz 33.2. As Alternative Assessment, you may want to use the African challenges table exercise in this section's lessons.

RETEACH

Have students complete Main Idea Activity for English Language Learners and Special-Needs Students 33.2. Then have students

write the section's headings and subheadings on a sheet of paper, leaving a space between each. Ask students to list the main ideas of each heading and subheading in the appropriate space.
ENGLISH LANGUAGE LEARNERS

EXTEND

Have students conduct research to find African literature that represents the continent's cultural diversity. Ask students to select one aspect of African literature to explore in depth and to write a short paper that summarizes what they have learned.
BLOCK SCHEDULING

SECTION 2 REVIEW ANSWERS

❶ Define
• desertification, p. 889

❷ Identify
• Jerry Rawlings, p. 887
• Laurent Kabila, p. 888
• Shaaban Robert, p. 890
• Wole Soyinka, p. 890

❸ Ghana: one-party state, economic collapse, military rule; Nigeria: military rule, civil war, starvation, disease, ethnic tension; Angola: civil war, Cold War battleground; Somalia: Soviet-American rivalry, military dictatorship; Rwanda: ethnic tension and violence, disease, starvation; Zaire: ethnic tension and violence, influx of refugees

❹ a. economic: depended on a single crop or mineral resource, drop in oil prices, debt, rising prices; environmental: population growth, desertification, drought, spread of disease

b. As Cold War rivals, they wanted to limit each others' influence

c. renewed interest in African literature, music, sculpture

❺ Students' explanations will vary.

---

withdrew in frustration in 1995. Although warring factions reached agreement in 1998, fighting continued. Many Somalis have sought refuge in other countries.

✔ **READING CHECK: Drawing Inferences** What are some reasons that the world's powerful nations have taken an interest in Africa? Soviet-American rivalry, humanitarian aid

Revival of African Culture

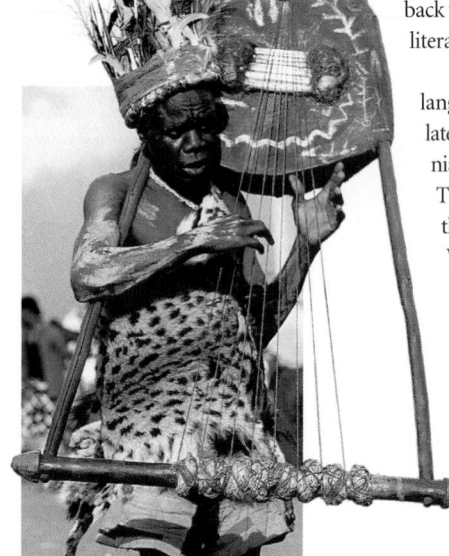
This Kenyan harpist is one of many musicians and artists keeping the traditional arts of Africa alive.

Despite the political and economic problems that followed independence, the people of Africa have experienced a rebirth of cultural self-confidence. During the colonial era, some Africans adopted European attitudes toward their own cultures. African art and music were considered primitive and crude. The literature of Africa—a treasury of oral traditions including myths, proverbs, and folktales—was of little interest.

Not all Africans turned away from their own history and cultural heritage, however. Written records of Swahili poetry and tales in this Bantu language go back to the 1600s. Swahili has continued to evolve. The father of modern Swahili literature was **Shaaban Robert,** a Tanzanian poet, essayist, and novelist.

In West Africa a new literary tradition developed using the colonial languages of English and French. The poems of Léopold Senghor, who later became president of independent Senegal, described the hardships of colonialism. Senghor celebrated his deep sense of pride in being a black African. The works of Senghor, novelist Camara Laye, and others also proudly point to the deep spiritual traditions of Africa. In 1986 Nigerian playwright and poet **Wole Soyinka** became the first African to win the Nobel Prize in literature.

Similarly, an interest in African music and sculpture was reawakened. African artists began to produce traditional pieces—ceremonial masks, decorated weapons, traditional musical instruments, wood and bronze statues—for a growing world market. In many places African artists combined age-old techniques with new materials and artistic ideas. In addition, a film industry has developed. Throughout the continent, this mixture of African and outside influences has revitalized African art.

✔ **READING CHECK: Drawing Conclusions** Why would some Africans lose their pride in their culture and artistic traditions? adopted European attitudes

---

SECTION 2 REVIEW

1. **Describe** and explain the significance:
   desertification

2. **Identify** and explain the significance:
   Jerry Rawlings
   Laurent Kabila
   Shaaban Robert
   Wole Soyinka

3. **Categorizing** Copy the diagram below. List some of the factors that caused problems for African countries after independence.

Ghana	Nigeria	Angola
Somalia	Rwanda	Zaire

Homework Practice Online
keyword: SP3 HP33

4. **Finding the Main Idea**
   a. What economic and environmental challenges did some of the newly independent African countries face?
   b. Why were the superpowers eager to help some of the African nations?
   c. How has African culture revived in the last half of the 1900s?

5. **Writing and Critical Thinking**
   Identifying Cause and Effect Explain how ethnic conflicts contributed to problems in the independent countries of Africa.
   Consider:
   • the problems in Nigeria left over from colonial rule
   • the rivalry between the Tutsi and Hutu
   • battles for power between rival warlords and clans in Somalia

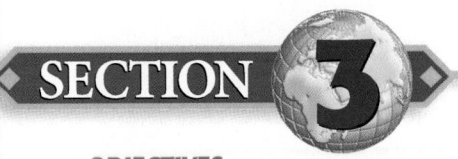
OBJECTIVES

1 **Explain how France's position in the Middle East and North Africa changed after World War II.**

2 **Explain how Britain's position in the Middle East and Egypt changed after World War II.**

3 **Identify the political and social changes that independence brought to Egypt and the Middle East.**

4 **Identify the major issues that Iran and Turkey faced after World War II.**

SECTION 3

Nationalism in the Middle East and North Africa

READ TO DISCOVER

1 How did France's position in the Middle East and North Africa change after World War II?

2 How did Britain's position in the Middle East and Egypt change after World War II?

3 What political and social changes did independence bring to Egypt and the Middle East?

4 What major issues did Iran and Turkey face after World War II?

DEFINE

kibbutz

IDENTIFY

Menachem Begin
Gamal Abdel Nasser
Suez Crisis
Mohammad Mosaddeq

WHY IT MATTERS TODAY

Tensions continue in the Middle East. Use CNN fyi.com or other **current event** sources to identify the conflicts that exist between Israelis and Palestinians today. Record your findings in your journal.

CNNstudentNews.com

The Main Idea
Nationalist pressures created conflicts in the Middle East and North Africa after World War II.

The Story Continues *New nations emerging in the Middle East after World War II confronted a host of regional problems. One of the greatest ongoing conflicts was between the newly formed state of Israel and its Arab neighbors. In 1948 Azzam Pasha, the secretary of the Arab League, predicted, "This will be a war of extermination and momentous [extraordinary] massacre." Israeli extremists responded with their own threats. "We intend to attack, conquer and keep [territory] until we have the whole of Palestine," declared one group.*

The French Withdraw

Even before the French colonies in sub-Saharan Africa gained their independence, France was confronted with independence struggles in other colonies. In fact, the first successful challenges to French colonialism came in Syria and Lebanon in the Middle East.

France had gained control of Syria and Lebanon as a mandate after World War I. During World War II British and Free French troops had taken control of both countries from the Vichy government. After the war, despite promises of independence, French troops remained. After British pressure and several bloody battles with Arab nationalists, French troops withdrew. Syria and Lebanon became fully independent republics in the mid-1940s.

The heart of the French colonial empire in Africa was Algeria. In fact, Algeria was more than a colony. It had been assimilated, or legally absorbed, into France, like other parts of West Africa. Algerian voters elected representatives to the French National Assembly in Paris. However, voting restrictions were placed on the large majority of Muslim Arabs. Algeria had a community of Europeans known as *colons*. The *colons* accounted for about 10 percent of the population but owned most of Algeria's industries and its best land.

The success of Arab nationalism in Syria inspired many Algerians, who began to demand independence. When both the *colons* and the French authorities resisted these demands, nationalists formed the Algerian National Liberation Front (the French initials are FLN) to fight for independence. The FLN launched its revolution on November 1, 1954.

French police troops occupied streets in Algiers during a 1961 demonstration. The Algerian Revolution ended with the 1962 referendum on independence.

SECTION 3 RESOURCES

REPRODUCIBLE RESOURCES
▶ Guided Reading Strategy 33.3
▶ Hands-on Activity 33

TECHNOLOGY RESOURCES
▶ One-Stop Planner, Lesson 33.3
▶ Regions of the World Music Audio CD Program 12, 13
▶ World History Teaching Transparency 35
▶ Religions of the World Video Series: Judaism, Islam
▶ Homework Practice Online
▶ Online Maps, Charts and Graphs: Southwest Asia

REINFORCEMENT, REVIEW, AND ASSESSMENT
▶ Section 3 Review, p. 897
▶ Daily Quiz 33.3
▶ Main Idea Activity 33.3
▶ English Audio Summary 33.3
▶ Spanish Audio Summary 33.3

LEVEL 1: Ask students what similarities Algeria shared with other French-held territories in North Africa and the Middle East at the end of World War II. *(predominantly Arab, rising nationalism)* Next, have them cite ways in which Algeria was different. *(a longtime colony, whereas others were recent protectorates; large European population with representation in French National Assembly)* Call on volunteers to explain why rising Arab nationalism in Algeria would have inspired desires for independence in other French holdings. *(Responses should recognize Algeria's influence as "most secure" and favored of the French Empire.)* Ask students if they think problems in Algeria and elsewhere could have been avoided if France had given Arabs the right to elect representatives to the French National Assembly. *(Answers will vary.)* **ENGLISH LANGUAGE LEARNERS**

Global Relations

As the extent and horror of the Holocaust became public knowledge after World War II, Zionist demands for a Jewish state in Palestine increased. Massive numbers of Jews immigrated to Palestine illegally, while some extremist groups such as the Irgun waged a terrorist war against the British. In 1947 the United Nations voted to partition Palestine into two states—one Jewish, the other Arab—and an internationally administered territory around Jerusalem. In 1948 the British mandate collapsed under economic and political pressure. As the British withdrew, David Ben-Gurion, a leading Zionist, proclaimed the state of Israel on May 14, 1948.

Critical Thinking

Ask students why it was important for Jewish people to have their own state in Palestine after the Holocaust.

ANSWER: Students might answer that they had just suffered horrible atrocities and needed a place of safety.

CONNECTING TO ART ANSWER

He used stained glass windows to represent the twelve tribes of Israel and tell Jewish stories.

CONNECTING TO
Art

Stained Glass: Windows in Jerusalem

As Jews settled in Palestine and, later, in the Jewish state of Israel, they constructed houses, schools, and other facilities. One of these was a hospital in Jerusalem. Shown in the picture are stained-glass windows from the hospital's synagogue. There are 12 windows in all, each devoted to one of the 12 tribes of Israel. Marc Chagall, a Russian Jewish artist who settled in France, designed the windows. By Jewish law, images of people cannot appear in synagogues. The artist therefore cleverly used symbols of animals, birds, plants, and fish to tell Jewish stories and convey his faith.

Understanding the Arts

How did Marc Chagall convey his faith through his art?

The Algerian war became brutal as both sides committed atrocities and used torture. The FLN waged a campaign of terror against both the French and the less radical Algerian Arabs who opposed independence. The war was so severe that in 1958 an uprising among the *colons* in Algiers contributed to the downfall of the French Fourth Republic. In France Charles de Gaulle returned to power.

The *colons* and the military leaders who supported them expected de Gaulle to crush the rebels. Instead he chose to negotiate with them. Despite resistance, including attempts on his life, de Gaulle granted Algeria independence in 1962.

The Algerian war influenced French colonialism elsewhere. In 1958 it motivated de Gaulle to offer terms for independence to the French colonies south of the Sahara. It was also partly responsible for independence in its two Muslim neighbors, Morocco and Tunisia.

Tunisia had become a French protectorate in 1883. Morocco had only become a protectorate in 1912. In 1954 nationalists from both countries launched guerrilla campaigns to drive out the French. In 1956, while fighting the war in Algeria, France gave in. Morocco became a constitutional monarchy, and Tunisia became a republic.

✔ **READING CHECK: Identifying Cause and Effect** How did events in Syria and Lebanon affect French colonialism in Africa? inspired others to demand independence

British Withdrawal

At the end of World War II, Britain's control over the Middle East seemed solid. During the war the British had stationed huge numbers of troops in Egypt to protect their interests. With their allies, they had occupied much of Iran to keep supply lines to the Soviet Union open. They had forced Reza Shah Pahlavi to step down and placed his son, Mohammad Reza Pahlavi, on the throne. British troops had occupied Syria along with the Free French and had established control over Iraq. In addition, the British still held their mandate for Palestine, despite opposition from both Jews and Arabs. Britain's control over the Middle East, however, was about to slip away.

The creation of Israel. In 1939 the British reversed the Balfour Declaration, which had pledged to secure a Jewish national homeland. Instead they favored an end to Jewish immigration and the creation of an Arab Palestinian state. The Jewish Agency, which oversaw the affairs of the Jewish community in Palestine, supported increased Jewish immigration as survivors of the Nazi Holocaust fled Europe. The Holocaust had left hundreds of thousands of Jewish refugees stranded. Once the war was over, the Jewish Agency withdrew its support for the British mandate because Britain refused to allow Holocaust survivors to resettle in Palestine.

Meanwhile extremist Zionist groups waged a terrorist campaign against British authorities. In 1946 a group called the Irgun, led by **Menachem Begin** (BAY·guhn), blew up the King David Hotel in Jerusalem. Eventually a virtual state of war existed between the British and the Zionists.

In 1947 Britain gave up its Palestinian mandate and referred the entire problem to the United Nations. In November of that year the UN voted to partition Palestine into separate Jewish and Arab states. Jerusalem would be an international city. The Arabs unanimously rejected the UN plan, while the Zionist leaders accepted it. In May 1948 Israel declared its independence as a sovereign Jewish state. Chaim Azriel Weizmann became its first president and David Ben-Gurion its first prime minister.

The establishment of a Jewish nation infuriated Palestinian Arabs. As soon as British troops withdrew from the area, armies from neighboring Arab countries moved against Israel. Although outnumbered, the determined Israelis won. When the war ended in early 1949, Israel had won more territory than it had been given in the UN partition plan. The Arabs accepted a cease-fire, but UN-sponsored efforts to negotiate permanent peace failed.

One Arab nation gained land from the 1948 war. What remained of the proposed Palestinian state was officially annexed by Transjordan (now Jordan) in 1950. Other Arabs, including many Palestinians, bitterly opposed this action. Hundreds of thousands of Palestinians who had been expelled from the land claimed by Israel were living as refugees in camps. The Israeli government would not allow the return of the Palestinians, nor would it pay the Palestinians for lands seized. Palestinian lands were given to Jewish immigrants. Most Arab countries refused to resettle the Palestinians, arguing that such a move would justify the seizure of their lands or lessen the pressure on Israel to return the lands.

From 1948 to 1960 Israel absorbed about 1.3 million immigrants. That number almost tripled the Jewish population of the country. The use of the **kibbutz,** a type of collective farm that exists in Israel, helped turn desert areas into productive land.

Egypt. In addition to their problems in Palestine, the British also faced Egyptian demands for true independence. The presence of large numbers of British troops in Egypt after the war angered many Egyptian nationalists. So, too, did Britain's continuing control of the Sudan, which Egypt considered an Egyptian province. Between 1945 and 1952, efforts to negotiate a complete British evacuation from Egypt failed.

Meanwhile King Farouk I of Egypt headed a corrupt and inefficient government that came under fire from both nationalists and reformers. In 1952 a group of army leaders toppled the monarchy and made Egypt a republic. A popular young officer, **Gamal Abdel Nasser**, emerged as Egypt's new leader.

Nasser decided to rid Egypt of foreign domination once and for all. In 1954 Great Britain agreed to evacuate the Suez base and to allow free elections in the Sudan. Sudan chose independence rather than union with Egypt. In domestic affairs Nasser emphasized land reform, industrialization, greater government control over the economy, and expanded rights for women. His development projects to modernize Egypt were expensive, and he soon decided to seek aid from both the East and West. His efforts led to a crisis over the Suez Canal.

What If? If the Holocaust had not occurred during World War II, do you think the United Nations would have supported the creation of Israel? Why or why not?

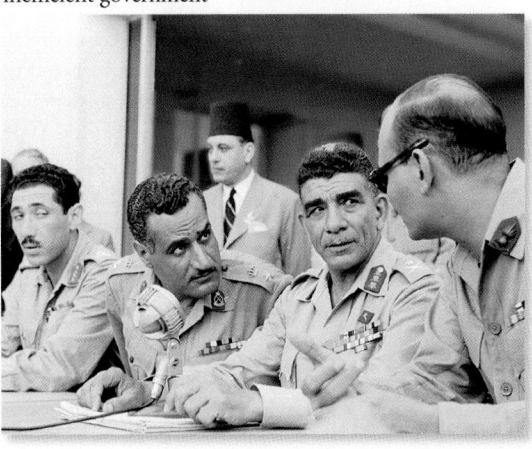

General Gamal Abdel Nasser (seated second from left) invited members of the world's media to see Egypt celebrate the first anniversary of the 1952 revolution that deposed King Farouk.

Government

The Anglo-Egyptian Sudan was a condominium, or jointly controlled area, ruled by Britain and Egypt as equal powers. In practice, however, the territory was ruled by a series of British governors-general. Nevertheless, because of its condominium status, the British Union Jack and the flag of Egypt flew together over Sudan until 1956, when both were replaced by the new flag of the independent republic of Sudan.

Critical Thinking

Ask students if they think Britain or Egypt held actual power in the Sudan.

ANSWER: Students should suggest that Britain actually controlled the Sudan, since the governors-general and most of the administrators were British.

TEACH OBJECTIVE 2

LEVEL 2: Ask students what comprised the region known as Palestine. *(Israel and Jordan)* Have them make a chart to explain the roles that the British, Jews, Arabs, and United Nations all played in the division of Palestine in 1947. Ask students how the territory granted to the Arabs in Palestine ended up being controlled by Israel and Jordan. *(as a result of Arab-Israeli wars)*

Division of Palestine	
Jews and Arabs	*rejected a joint state*
British	*gave up mandate*
United Nations	*partitioned Palestine into Arab and Jewish sections*

Geography

The Aswan High Dam was built to improve Egypt's economic situation. The dam captures the flow of the yearly Nile flood and allows that water to be used for irrigation. Over a million acres have been converted to farmland since the dam's construction. The storage capacity of the dam, more than 150 billion cubic meters of water, provides a tremendous reservoir for use in periods of drought. Turbines in the dam also supply part of Egypt's electricity needs.

The dam has caused problems, however. The absence of the yearly flood means that farmland in the Nile Valley is not fertilized by silt. This forces farmers to use chemical fertilizers. Silt is constantly building up in the lake above the dam.

Critical Thinking

Ask students if they think the benefits of the Aswan High Dam outweigh the costs.

ANSWER: Students' answers will vary.

VISUAL RECORD ANSWER

Students might suggest that the canal would need to be reopened to allow passage.

INTERPRETING THE VISUAL RECORD

The Suez Crisis The picture shows ships blocking the Suez Canal during the Suez Crisis. *What problems would sinking these ships create for both sides when the crisis finally ended?*

The Suez Crisis. In 1955 Nasser announced an arms agreement between Egypt and Czechoslovakia (acting for the Soviet Union). The United States and Britain became alarmed over the possibility of an alliance between Egypt and the Eastern bloc. They offered funds for Nasser's most ambitious project—the construction of a dam at Aswan on the Nile. The Aswan High Dam would irrigate new lands for farming and produce hydroelectric power. United States and British leaders hoped that this offer would keep Egypt from slipping further under Soviet influence.

Nasser hesitated, hoping for a better offer from the Soviets. He also recognized the communist People's Republic of China. When he finally agreed to the U.S. and British offer, he was told it had been withdrawn. Nasser viewed this as an insult to Egyptian national dignity. In response, he nationalized the Suez Canal in 1956.

The canal had been controlled primarily by British and French shareholders since the 1800s. This control had long been resented by Egyptians, whose labor had built the canal. Many felt that foreign funding of the canal had cost the country its independence. Nasser planned to use the revenues from the canal to fund the Aswan High Dam. His action was also a public way to assert his independence from European domination of Egypt. To Arabs and anticolonial nationalists, Nasser became a great hero. To the West, he became a demon. Nationalization of the canal led to a confrontation with old colonial powers.

Britain, France, and Israel felt the most threatened by the move. The Egyptians refused to allow Israeli ships to pass through the canal. Britain and France were outraged because they both had a stake in the company that built the canal. They worried that Egypt, which was friendly to the Soviet Union, now controlled a waterway through which much of the world's trade passed.

Israel, Britain, and France conspired to overthrow Nasser and take control of the canal. They agreed that Israel should launch a lightning attack across the canal into Egypt. Britain and France would then intervene, supposedly to separate the Israelis and Egyptians. In reality, they would help destroy the Egyptian armed forces and reestablish European control over Suez.

At first the plan went well. Israel advanced through the Gaza Strip and into the Sinai Peninsula, moving toward the canal. Great Britain and France demanded an Egyptian cease-fire and insisted on temporary control of the Canal. When Egypt refused, British and French troops seized the Mediterranean end of the canal. Both sides sank ships in the canal to block it.

The United States, under President Dwight Eisenhower, worried that the Soviets would be drawn into the crisis. With that fear in mind, the United States intervened. Privately, Eisenhower threatened to cut off all U.S. aid to Britain unless the invasion ended and the Anglo-French forces withdrew. The British agreed, and the invasion collapsed.

In a UN-negotiated settlement, Britain and France withdrew their forces. The Israelis withdrew after gaining a vague guarantee that Egypt would allow Israeli ships through the canal. Later, however, Egypt blockaded the canal. A UN force was sent to patrol the cease-fire line between the Israelis and the Egyptians in the Sinai Desert. The **Suez Crisis** was seen as the final defeat of European imperialism. Nasser became

LEVEL 3: Have students locate the Suez Canal on the map on page 900 and note its proximity to Israel. Ask students why control of the canal was so important to Britain. *(shortened water route to Asia)* Have them speculate on what effect the canal's importance, combined with Britain's loss of Palestine, might have had on British policy toward Egypt. *(more determined not to give up its presence)* Then have students work in groups to answer the following question: Would the Suez Crisis have occurred if Israel had not gained independence? *(Groups' responses should recognize that Arab-Israeli conflict created instability in the region but that other issues were also involved.)* **COOPERATIVE LEARNING**

the most popular leader in the Arab world. Many Middle Eastern countries now turned toward their political and social development.

✔ **READING CHECK: Sequencing** What were the major events in the British sphere of influence in the Middle East and North Africa from the end of World War II to Egypt's victory in the Suez Crisis? creation of Israel, independence for Sudan and Egypt

Political and Social Change

In Africa younger, Western-educated leaders had led the movements for independence. In contrast, most of the new Middle Eastern states became independent under an older, traditional, upper-class or even royal generation. Iraq and Jordan became Arab kingdoms under the sons of Sharif Husayn of Mecca. They had been installed as monarchs by the British after World War II. Saudi Arabia was a traditional Arab kingdom ruled by the house of Ibn Sa'ud. Syria and Lebanon were both ruled by wealthy landowning and merchant elites. Only in Egypt, where army officers overthrew King Farouk and negotiated Britain's withdrawal, did revolution precede independence.

Nasser developed a political ideology that bound together not only Egypt but also the entire Arab world. Nasser always made his appeals for support in Islamic terms that would appeal to the people. However, he insisted that modernization along socialist lines was the key to independence.

> *History Makers Speak* **❝Revolution is the way in which the Arab nation can free itself of its shackles, and rid itself of the dark heritage which has burdened it. . . . [It] is the only way to overcome underdevelopment which has been forced on it by suppression and exploitation . . . and to face the challenge awaiting the Arab and other underdeveloped nations; the challenge offered by the astounding scientific discoveries which help to widen the gap between the advanced and backward countries. . . . Freedom today means that of the country and of the citizen. Socialism has become both a means and an end: sufficiency and justice.❞**
>
> Gamal Abdel Nasser, quoted in *A History of Arab Peoples,* by Albert Hourani

A common practice in Egypt was absentee land ownership, in which wealthy city people owned rural farmland and made fortunes from tenants who actually worked the land. Under Nasser the Egyptian government ended this system. It took control of most industries and businesses such as banks and insurance companies. The government also passed laws limiting work hours, establishing a minimum wage, and creating many social services. Education was extended, and the government tried to improve the status of women.

Similar reforms were embraced by the Ba'ath Party, which first emerged in Syria. Initially the Ba'athists emphasized a kind of Pan-Arab nationalism. By the mid-1950s, however, they had also adopted socialism. This party appealed primarily to the new generation of Western-educated Arab intellectuals.

Ba'athism, whose name means rise or rebirth, took on many characteristics of dictatorial rule as it spread to neighboring countries such as Iraq and Lebanon.

Analyzing Primary Sources

Identifying a Point of View By which means did Nasser feel Arab nations could overcome underdevelopment and meet the challenge of scientific advances? revolution

'Abd al-'Aziz Ibn Sa'ud unified Arabian domains into the Kingdom of Saudi Arabia in 1932.

TEACH OBJECTIVE 4

ALL LEVELS: Have students work in pairs to identify one issue facing Turkey and one issue facing Iran in the 1950s. Call on pairs for responses until all significant issues are listed on the chalkboard. Then ask the class how each of the issues was resolved. Ask students whether they believe the resolution of each of these issues was in the best interest of the Iranian or Turkish people.
ENGLISH LANGUAGE LEARNERS, COOPERATIVE LEARNING

CLOSE

Ask students if they think the Middle East might be called the "Balkans" of Asia and to explain the significance of this comparison.

Global Relations

In response to growing Soviet influence in the Middle East, the growth of Marxist-oriented Ba'th parties in several countries, and the growth of Pan-Arab nationalism, President Eisenhower acted following the Suez Crisis to protect American interests in the region. In early 1957 he announced what became known as the Eisenhower Doctrine, stating the intent of the United States to extend economic and military aid to any Middle Eastern nation asking for help that was threatened by international communism. The following year, communists in Lebanon tried to force that country to join Egypt and Syria in the newly formed United Arab Republic. To protect the pro-Western government, Eisenhower ordered 15,000 U.S. Marines into Lebanon. At the same time, Great Britain sent troops into neighboring Jordan, which was under similar pressures from pro-Nasser elements.

Critical Thinking

Ask students what vital American interests the United States sought to protect in the Middle East.

ANSWER: Students might suggest access to Middle Eastern oil or to block communist expansion during the Cold War.

In 1957 a Ba'athist government took over in Syria, and in 1958 a Ba'athist-inspired coup took place in Iraq. A new generation of leaders emerged in the Middle East and North Africa that believed in socialism as the best way to modernize their countries. The socialism practiced by these governments, however, proved to be the first step toward dictatorship.

Meanwhile Nasser began to preach a new brand of Pan-Arabism combined with socialism. In 1958 he persuaded Syria to merge with Egypt in the United Arab Republic, or UAR. As new Arab leaders emerged in Syria and Iraq, their fears of Egyptian domination grew. In 1961, despite all the talk of Pan-Arabism, Syria broke away from the UAR. The only point of agreement between Egypt and Syria was their opposition to Israel.

✔ **READING CHECK: Drawing Inferences** Why did changes occur in Egypt differently from in other Middle Eastern states? Revolution preceded independence.

Iran and Turkey

Unlike other Middle Eastern nations, Iran and Turkey had strong ties to the West. They also faced challenges after World War II.

Iran. At the end of World War II, Great Britain and the Soviet Union occupied Iran. Although U.S. and British pressure eventually forced the Soviet Union to withdraw, Iran remained under heavy British influence. Britain owned the majority of the Anglo-Iranian Oil Company, which controlled Iran's oil industry. Iranian nationalists resented British domination of their country. They believed that Iranian development could be achieved through democratic, constitutional means.

Iranians cheer as their flag is raised over an oil company nationalized by the Iranian government in 1951.

In 1951 the popular Iranian nationalist leader **Mohammad Mosaddeq** (MOHS·ad·dek) became Iran's prime minister. Mosaddeq's two goals were to establish constitutional government in Iran and to free Iran from foreign interference. He tried to limit the power of the shah and to strengthen the Majlis, the Iranian parliament. He also established Iran's sovereignty over the country's primary source of income, the oil industry. Shortly after coming to power, he nationalized the Anglo-Iranian Oil Company. These moves outraged both the British and Iranian conservatives, who supported a strong monarchy.

The British called the nationalization illegal and organized a worldwide boycott of Iranian oil. United States officials were alarmed by claims that Mosaddeq accepted political support from Iranian communists. They feared that the Soviet Union might gain control of Iran. For this reason, in 1953 the U.S. Central Intelligence Agency helped Mosaddeq's opponents engineer a coup and restore power to Mohammad Reza Pahlavi. The young shah of Iran worked to reestablish his power and to modernize Iran rapidly. He relied on close ties with the United States and on his army and secret police. By the early 1960s the shah controlled Iran and ran it as a dictatorship.

REVIEW

Have students complete the Section 3 Review on p. 897.

ASSESS

Have students complete Daily Quiz 33.3. As Alternative Assessment, you may want to use the French colonialism or Suez Canal exercises in this section's lessons.

RETEACH

Have students complete Main Idea Activity for English Language Learners and Special-Needs Students 33.3. Then ask students to write a question and answer that covers the main idea for each subsection in the section. **ENGLISH LANGUAGE LEARNERS**

EXTEND

Organize the class into groups to create and present 10-minute "news broadcasts" summarizing the Algerian revolt, the creation of Israel, the Suez crisis, and the overthrow of the Mosaddeq government in Iran. **BLOCK SCHEDULING, COOPERATIVE LEARNING**

Turkey. Following World War II the secular and progressive policies of Turkey's leader, Mustafa Kemal, were continued under his successor, Ismet Inönü (i·nuh·NOO). Through careful diplomacy, Inönü kept Turkey neutral during the war. Turkey declared war on Germany and the other Axis Powers only when it became clear that they were going to lose.

After the war Turkey came under increased pressure from the Soviet Union, which continued to push south just as imperial Russia had done. In response, Turkish leaders allied themselves more closely with the United States and the Western world. In 1952 Turkey joined NATO.

Meanwhile Inönü moved away from Kemal's autocratic rule toward a more democratic government. In 1945 he announced the end of the one-party state and allowed other political parties to form. In May 1950 the first free elections brought the opposition party to power under its leader, Adnan Menderes. After Menderes began to lose support, he restricted groups that opposed him, and threatened to undo some of the reforms made by Kemal. In 1960 the Turkish army overthrew Menderes, who was later executed. The army soon restored civilian rule. It also made it clear that it would resist any attempts to stray from the path of reform begun by Kemal and Inönü.

Turkey continued to industrialize like European nations. Education continued to be extended, and the Turkish economy generally prospered. One source of conflict, however, was continued restrictions on religion. Eventually some Turks organized in an attempt to lift the restrictions and restore Islam to a central role in national life.

Ismet Inönü, president of Turkey

✔ **READING CHECK: Contrasting** Why were events in Iran and Turkey after the war different from those in other Middle Eastern countries?

had strong ties to the West

SECTION 3 REVIEW

1. **Define** and explain the significance:
   kibbutz

2. **Identify** and explain the significance:
   Menachem Begin
   Gamal Abdel Nasser
   Suez Crisis
   Mohammad Mosaddeq

3. **Sequencing** Copy the flowchart below. Use it to identify the events leading up to the Arab-Israeli war of 1948–1949.

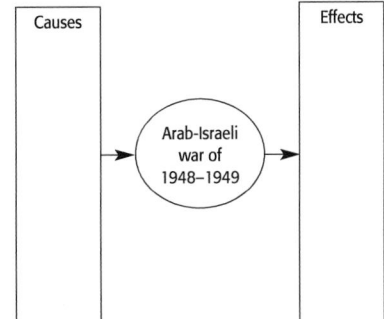

Causes → Arab-Israeli war of 1948–1949 → Effects

4. **Finding the Main Idea**
   a. How did nationalism in the Middle East influence French colonialism in Africa?
   b. How did Israel and Egypt come to be independent nations?
   c. Why did the United States support a monarchy instead of a democratic, constitutional government in Iran?

5. **Writing and Critical Thinking**
   Evaluating Of the changes described in this section, which do you think has had the greatest impact on the rest of the world? Explain your reasoning.
   Consider:
   • the liberation movement in Algeria that led to war
   • the UN decision to create an Israeli state within Palestine
   • Nasser's actions in ridding Egypt of European domination
   • the Iranian nationalization of the Anglo-Iranian Oil Company

Homework Practice Online
keyword: SP3 HP33

SECTION 3 REVIEW ANSWERS

❶ **Define**
• kibbutz, p. 893

❷ **Identify**
• Menachem Begin, p. 893
• Gamal Abdel Nasser, p. 893
• Suez Crisis, p. 894
• Mohammad Mosaddeq, p. 896

❸ Causes: Holocaust survivors immigrated to Palestine, Zionist groups waged terrorist campaign against British authorities, UN voted to partition Palestine, Arab countries moved against Israel; Effects: Israel won more territory, many Palestinian refugees

❹ a. The French were forced to withdraw.

b. Israel was created when the UN partitioned Palestine; Britain and France withdrew their forces from Egypt after the UN negotiated a settlement.

c. They feared the Soviet Union might gain control of Iran.

❺ Students' answers will vary but should be supported with evidence from the chapter.

AFRICA AND THE MIDDLE EAST SINCE 1945 **897**

SECTION 4

OBJECTIVES

1 Explain how Arab-Israeli conflicts have shaped the recent history of North Africa and the Middle East.

2 Explain how the presence of rich oil fields affected the Middle East.

3 Describe the revolution in Iran and explain why it occurred.

4 Explain the types of leadership that emerged in the Arab world in the 1960s and after.

LET'S GET STARTED!

As students enter the classroom, ask them to imagine that the United States was structured so that only members of a certain religion could hold leadership positions in government and that all laws were based on that religion's beliefs. Call on class members to suggest social and political problems that might arise from such an arrangement. Ask students if they would like to live in such a society, and to explain why or why not they feel as they do.

SECTION 4

READ TO DISCOVER

1 How have Arab-Israeli conflicts shaped the recent history of North Africa and the Middle East?

2 How did the presence of rich oil fields affect the Middle East?

3 What was the revolution in Iran and why did it occur?

4 What types of leadership emerged in the Arab world in the 1960s and after?

DEFINE

intifada

IDENTIFY

PLO
Yasir Arafat
Anwar Sadat
Golda Meir
Camp David Accords
OPEC
Ayatollah Khomeini
Saddam Hussein

WHY IT MATTERS TODAY

OPEC, the Organization of Petroleum Exporting Countries, sets the prices for much of the oil used in the world. Use [CNN] or other **current event** sources to find out how OPEC actions have affected the United States in the past and recently. Record your findings in your journal.

Jerusalem has historical significance for Judaism, Christianity, and Islam.

898 CHAPTER 33

War, Revolution, and Oil in the Middle East and North Africa

The Main Idea
Bitter ethnic, religious, and political disputes continued to disrupt peace throughout the Middle East.

The Story Continues *The Arab-Israeli war of 1948–1949 was only the beginning of postwar conflict and upheaval in the Middle East. In August 1990 the Iraqi army of Saddam Hussein launched a major attack against other Middle Eastern states. Yet it, too, was not the last disturbance in this turbulent area of the world.*

The Arab-Israeli Confrontation

After the breakup of the union between Egypt and Syria in 1961, Gamal Abdel Nasser worked to keep his country's leadership role in the Arab world. He faced a difficult choice when tension arose along Israel's border with Syria and Jordan in the late 1960s. If Nasser supported his Arab neighbors, he risked war with a powerful Israeli military. If he held back, he risked his leadership standing.

In May 1967 Nasser made his choice. He demanded the withdrawal of UN troops that had been policing the Egyptian-Israeli border since the end of the Suez Crisis in 1956. He also blockaded the Gulf of Aqaba to cut Israel's direct sea route to Africa and Asia. In mid-May Egyptian troops began mobilizing in large numbers near Israel's southern border. Syrian forces mobilized along the Golan Heights at Israel's northern frontier.

The Six-Day War. Realizing the danger of delay, Israel launched an attack, on June 5, 1967. In six days of fighting, Israel captured the Sinai Peninsula and the Gaza Strip from Egypt. Driving back Syrian and Iraqi armies on its northern border, Israel seized the Golan Heights from Syria. It pushed back invading Jordanian forces and took the entire West Bank of the Jordan River from Jordan. Israel also captured East Jerusalem, which had been occupied by Jordan since the 1948 war.

The events of the Six-Day War radically changed Middle Eastern politics. Many displaced Palestinians lost faith in the Arab governments' ability to recapture what had

LEVEL 3: Organize the class into groups to represent senior officials in the Israeli or Egyptian government. Tell the groups to imagine that it is 1974, and they must decide whether the time has come to seek some compromise settlement in the conflict over Palestine. After groups gather information, identify options, predict consequences, and decide on what action to take, have each report its conclusion to the class. Ask each group what factors it weighed in making its decision.

COOPERATIVE LEARNING

---

been Palestine. They began to rely on their own guerrilla organization, the Palestine Liberation Organization (**PLO**), led by **Yasir Arafat.** The United States and the Soviet Union realized that they might be drawn into an Arab-Israeli conflict. Both therefore actively sought peace in the Middle East. Egypt, Syria, and Jordan wished to regain lost territory. Mutual suspicions and fears, however, doomed peace efforts.

Egypt under Sadat. When Nasser died in September 1970, **Anwar Sadat** succeeded him. Under Sadat's leadership, Egypt and Syria began a war against Israel on October 6, 1973, the Jewish holy day of Yom Kippur. The attack caught Israeli prime minister **Golda Meir** and her military off guard. At first the Arabs pushed Israeli troops back. Then Israel rallied to cross the Suez Canal and occupy Egyptian land.

All sides had reason to seek a settlement. U.S. Secretary of State Henry Kissinger used shuttle diplomacy—trips back and forth between Egypt and Syria—to obtain an agreement. He eventually achieved two, one between Israel and Egypt and one between Israel and Syria. Then moves toward peace stalled.

In November 1977, however, Sadat surprised the world. He went to Israel to speak in person to the Israeli parliament and to then Israeli prime minister Menachem Begin. In his speech, Sadat explained that peace must be won by all:

> **History Makers Speak** "It is not my battle alone. Nor is it the battle of the leadership in Israel alone. It is the battle of all and every citizen in all our territories, whose right it is to live in peace. It is the commitment of conscience and responsibility in the hearts of millions."
>
> Anwar Sadat, *In Search of Identity: An Autobiography*

Supported by the United States, many months of delicate negotiations followed. In September 1978 U.S. president Jimmy Carter invited the two leaders to Camp David, the presidential retreat in Maryland. Sadat and Begin eventually agreed on the framework for a peace settlement. The **Camp David Accords** were followed by a peace treaty signed by Egypt and Israel in March 1979.

Many people doubted that this breakthrough would end the Arab-Israeli confrontation. Palestinian terrorist attacks and calls by the Palestinian leadership for Israel's demise continued. As a result, Israelis resisted any idea of a Palestinian state. Sadat's opponents claimed that he sold out the Palestinians to regain Egyptian territory. In 1981 peace hopes dimmed when Sadat was assassinated.

The conflict continues. The Camp David Accords established peace on Israel's western border, but they did not address the problem of Palestinian refugees in neighboring countries or Israel's occupation of the West Bank and Gaza Strip. From bases in Lebanon the PLO launched guerrilla attacks on northern Israel. Israel retaliated by invading Lebanon in 1982. For two months Israel bombed Lebanon's capital, Beirut, where the PLO had its headquarters. After a settlement the PLO withdrew its forces to Tunisia. However, the Israeli invasion was not successful politically, and resulted in enormous suffering by Palestinians and Lebanese. It actually strengthened the PLO's standing among Palestinians and intensified an already bitter civil war in Lebanon. Although the Palestinians were exiled to Tunisia, they were not removed as a political force. Because many Israelis had opposed the invasion, it also caused a deep split within Israeli society.

Israelis also disagreed on how to handle the territories acquired during the Six-Day War. Since the 1970s Israelis had been establishing settlements in these zones. Palestinians living there demonstrated against the settlements. In December 1987 they

---

HISTORY MAKER

Golda Meir (1898–1978)

Golda Meir immigrated to Palestine as a young woman. She was a leader of the Zionist movement in the 1920s. By 1946 she had established herself as one of the leaders of the Jewish Agency. Meir signed Israel's Declaration of Independence. In 1956 she became the nation's foreign minister and in 1969 was elected as its first female prime minister. During her time as leader, she tried to form lasting peace agreements with Arab countries. The outbreak of the Yom Kippur War in 1973 put an end to her efforts. **What kind of role did Golda Meir play in founding Israel?**

Holt Researcher

go.hrw.com
KEYWORD: Holt Researcher

FreeFind: Golda Meir
After reading more about Golda Meir on the Holt Researcher, write a diary entry by her explaining her feelings about the peace process.

History Maker

GOLDA MEIR. The only woman to lead Israel in its half century as a nation was former American schoolteacher Golda Meir. Born as Goldie Mabovitch to a poor Jewish family, at age 8 she emigrated with her parents from Kiev, Russia, to Milwaukee, Wisconsin. In 1917 she graduated from the local teacher's college and married Morris Myerson. The couple left the United States for Palestine in 1921. For the next several years she and her husband worked as farm laborers on a kibbutz, where she became active in the Zionist labor movement and held a seat on the Women's Labor Council until 1949. In 1948 she became Israel's first ambassador to the Soviet Union and later served as labor minister and foreign minister in the Israeli cabinet. Her husband died in 1951, and in 1956 she took the more Hebrew-sounding name Meir. Becoming prime minister in 1969, she held the post until criticism in the aftermath of the Yom Kippur War forced her to resign in 1974.

Critical Thinking

Ask students to speculate about why she changed her name to the Hebrew-sounding Meir.

ANSWER: Students might suggest she used her name to reflect her connection to her heritage.

HISTORY MAKER ANSWER
leader of the Zionist movement, signed Israel's Declaration of Independence

---

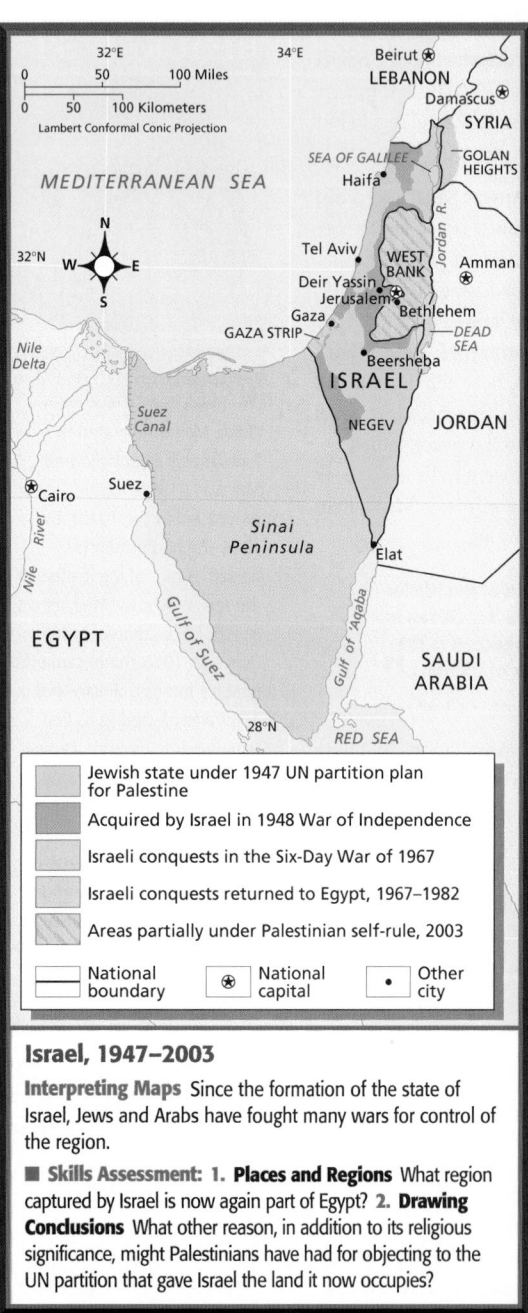
MAP ANSWERS

1. Sinai Peninsula

2. easy access to the Mediterranean Sea

Israel, 1947–2003

Interpreting Maps Since the formation of the state of Israel, Jews and Arabs have fought many wars for control of the region.

■ **Skills Assessment: 1. Places and Regions** What region captured by Israel is now again part of Egypt? **2. Drawing Conclusions** What other reason, in addition to its religious significance, might Palestinians have had for objecting to the UN partition that gave Israel the land it now occupies?

began a violent uprising called the **intifada** (Arabic for "shaking"). Young Palestinians threw rocks, bottles, and homemade weapons at army patrols and other Israeli authorities. The Israeli army responded with arms. In the first year alone, the intifada claimed more than 300 Palestinian lives. Another 20,000 were wounded; almost 12,000 were imprisoned. Although some Israelis supported these harsh measures, others believed that the Israelis should withdraw from the occupied zones and exchange land for a peace settlement with the Palestinians.

Moves toward peace. Despite the continuing intifada, a growing Israeli peace movement and the Israeli election of 1992 shifted the situation. Yitzhak Rabin (rah·BEEN), a former army chief who had led Israeli forces in the Six-Day War, became prime minister. Rabin authorized secret negotiations with Palestinian leaders.

After negotiations in Oslo, Norway, during 1993, Israeli foreign minister Shimon Peres met with PLO Chairman Arafat. Israel agreed to Palestinian self-government in the West Bank and Gaza Strip. The PLO officially recognized Israel's right to exist. On September 13, 1993, Rabin, Peres, and Arafat met in Washington, D.C., to sign a preliminary agreement.

Extremists on both sides opposed parts of the peace process. Many Israelis who had settled on the West Bank feared violence at the hands of the self-governing Palestinian Authority. In 1994 a radical Israeli settler killed 29 Palestinians in the West Bank city of Hebron. At the same time, a radical Palestinian organization known as Hamas launched a terrorist campaign within Israel.

An Israeli radical opposed to giving land to Palestinians assassinated Rabin in 1995, further disrupting the peace plans. In 2001 Israeli military leader Ariel Sharon was elected prime minister. His reputation for harsh treatment of Palestinians in previous wars, however, led to more Palestinian violence, which Israeli troops met in return. In April 2003, the United States, Russia, the European Union, and the United Nations presented a joint peace plan to the Israelis and Palestinians. Nicknamed the "road map," the plan spells out steps for the two sides to take to work toward a final peace settlement. Although both sides have pledged to follow the plan, each continues to blame the other for a lack of progress. In the meantime Palestinian suicide bombers continue to blow themselves up in Israel in an effort to kill Israelis. Israeli security forces respond by targeting suspected terrorists for assassination.

✔ **READING CHECK: Making Generalizations** What are the major reasons why efforts to bring about an Arab-Israeli peace failed? terrorism, assassination of Rabin, opposition to Sharon, suicide bombings, Israeli response to bombings

ALL LEVELS: Create two columns on the chalkboard, headed *Israeli Viewpoint* and *Arab Viewpoint*. Invite students to imagine first that they are Israeli settlers in the occupied territories and then that they are Palestinian residents of refugee camps. Ask students to explain, in each role, what rights they have in the territories, what rights the other side has, and why. List Palestinian and Israeli points in the appropriate columns on the chalkboard. Then ask students to explain how radical elements on each side have undermined hopes for a peaceful settlement of the dispute. *(riots, bombings, assassinations, and other terrorist acts)* Have them speculate about why these radicals seek and are able to perpetuate tension and conflict in the region. *(Responses may point to the*

frustration level of Palestinian and Israeli residents, each side's fervent belief in the justness of its cause, each side's fear of the other and of what the future holds, and the radicals' ability to exploit these factors in a self-serving way to maintain their power and status among their peers.)

Mideast Oil and World Energy Needs

During the early 1900s the manufacture of cars, ships, and aircraft increased greatly. These vehicles relied on petroleum for fuel. The demand for petroleum threatened to outrun production from existing oil fields. New sources of oil were needed, and the Middle East was where oil prospectors looked. Many countries in this region granted prospecting companies—mostly from Britain or the United States—land-use permits called concessions to search for oil. Beginning in the early 1900s, major oil fields were discovered in countries around the Persian Gulf and then in Libya in North Africa.

The rulers of these countries—many of them monarchies established by colonial powers under protectorates—received a share of the oil companies' profits. After World War II oil production increased, and the rulers and many of their subjects became very rich. Some critics pointed out that oil profits, called petrodollars, mainly increased the personal fortunes of local rulers. However, much of the money did go to improve the lives of the citizens. Petrodollars paid for social welfare systems and huge economic developments throughout the Persian Gulf region. They provided funds to build roads, schools, and desalinization plants to supply precious fresh water to desert regions.

As nationalism grew following World War II, many oil-producing countries demanded a larger share of the profits. Foreign companies were often unwilling to grant their demands. When the Iranian government nationalized the country's oil industry in 1951, the Anglo-Iranian Oil Company organized an international boycott of Iranian oil. Because oil from other countries was plentiful, the world market did not suffer from the loss of Iranian oil.

Iran's experience showed oil-producing countries that, individually, they had little power in dealing with the oil companies. In 1960 Middle East and Latin American oil-producing nations such as Venezuela created the Organization of Petroleum Exporting Countries (**OPEC**). Other oil-producing nations later joined the organization. As the bargaining agent for oil-producing nations, OPEC worked to set oil production levels and world oil prices. Its power soon became apparent. During the Arab-Israeli War of 1973, Arab OPEC members used oil as an economic weapon. They temporarily cut off shipments to the United States as punishment for supporting Israel. The price of oil rose sharply, from about $3 to more than $12 a barrel. This boycott was later eased, partly because it also hurt OPEC members.

The discovery and development of new oil fields in Alaska and the North Sea helped Western nations reduce their dependency on Middle Eastern oil after 1973. The Persian Gulf oil fields, however, remain the world's largest. They are a critical source of energy for the industrialized world. Production is expected to decline in oil fields outside the Middle East. Experts therefore predict that oil produced in Iran, Iraq, Kuwait, Saudi Arabia, and the United Arab Emirates will become even more important to the world economy. There may also be huge oil reserves in the newly independent Central Asian states, which are close to the Middle East in religion and culture.

✔ **READING CHECK: Finding the Main Idea** How is the oil produced in the Middle East important to Arab countries? How is it important to the rest of the world? funds social and economic development; critical source of energy

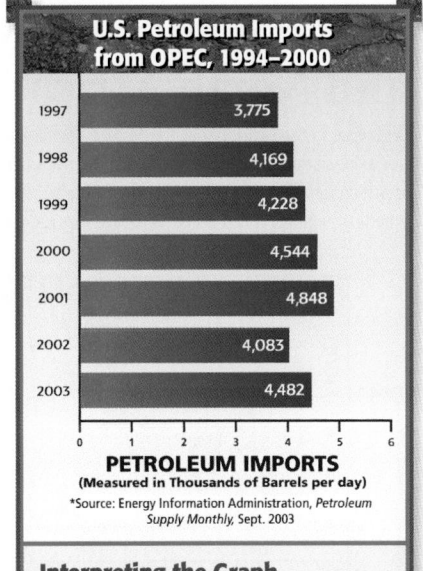

U.S. Petroleum Imports from OPEC, 1994–2000

Year	Imports
1997	3,775
1998	4,169
1999	4,228
2000	4,544
2001	4,848
2002	4,083
2003	4,482

PETROLEUM IMPORTS
(Measured in Thousands of Barrels per day)
*Source: Energy Information Administration, *Petroleum Supply Monthly,* Sept. 2003

Interpreting the Graph
The United States, like other highly industrialized nations, consumes a great deal of petroleum to meet its energy needs. Much of the oil that drives the American economy is purchased from OPEC nations. *What trend in U.S. petroleum consumption is shown by the graph, and how does this trend influence U.S. relations with the nations of OPEC?*

LEVEL 2: Write the terms *OPEC* and *petrodollars* on the chalkboard and call on volunteers to define each. Then have the class identify the major oil-producing countries in the Middle East and compare the standard of living in those nations with life in neighboring countries that lack such resources. *(Responses should recognize the social and economic benefits that petrodollars have brought to the citizens of oil-rich nations.)* Ask students how the OPEC nations obtain their petrodollars. *(sale of oil to industrial nations)* To illustrate how important oil is to the industrial nations, have students create a web diagram showing the effects of an oil embargo.

That's
Interesting!

In response to OPEC's cutbacks in oil production in the 1970s, nations around the world took measures to conserve energy. The United States, Europe, and Japan raised fuel taxes. Europeans switched to cars that used lower-cost diesel fuel. The United States lowered speed limits from 70 to 55 miles per hour and placed a tax on big, gas-guzzling automobiles. American manufacturers significantly improved automobile fuel economy. As a result, Americans paid $4.51 to drive 100 miles in 1991 compared to $6.28 in 1973.

SKILLS PRACTICE ANSWERS

1. to show the oil deposits in the Middle East and North Africa in the 1970s

2. Students might note that some countries, like Yemen, which have little or no oil, would be poorer than their neighbors and for that reason perhaps less politically stable.

3. Students might predict that oil exports out of the Persian Gulf would be slowed.

4. Answers will vary.

SKILL-BUILDING STRATEGIES Using a Special-Purpose Map

Oil Deposits in the Middle East and North Africa, 1970s

Oil is vital to the economy of the Middle East as well as to the world economy. It is possible to use a special-purpose map to understand how vital it is. A special-purpose map provides data about factors such as natural resources. It also shows the relationship of these factors to geographical regions. It can be used to visualize data, to draw conclusions, and to make predictions.

OPEC Member Nations in the Middle East and North Africa, 1970

Skills Reminder

To read a special-purpose map, first determine the purpose of the map. Is it designed to give you information on troop movements? Resources? Land use? Then formulate conclusions about the information presented on the map. For example, if the map shows troop movements, can you learn why the troops took the particular routes they did?

Skills Practice

❶ Study the map above. What is the purpose of the map?
❷ What conclusions can you draw from the map?
❸ Use the map to predict what might happen if the Strait of Hormuz were blocked.
❹ Identify another map in this book as a special-purpose map and explain what conclusions you can draw from it.

ALL LEVELS: Have students work in pairs to create time lines of developments in Iran and Iraq since 1968. Suggest that they plot Iranian events on one side of the time line and Iraqi events on the other. Have students refer to their time lines as they review the events since the formation of Iran's Islamic republic and discuss whether the benefits of Iran's revolution have outweighed the difficulties that it has faced. Then have them repeat the process for Iraq. **ENGLISH LANGUAGE LEARNERS, COOPERATIVE LEARNING**

The Iranian Revolution

By 1971 Britain had withdrawn most of its troops from the Persian Gulf region, leaving Iran as the leading power in the area. Western nations, including the United States, looked to the shah of Iran, Mohammad Reza Pahlavi, to guarantee the region's security. Discontent, however, was growing in Iran.

Socialists and Islamic traditionalists opposed the shah's ties with the West. In addition, an economic slump in the 1970s frustrated millions of Iranians who had moved from the countryside to the cities to look for work. The brutality of the shah's secret police only increased anger against his rule.

Many of those who opposed the shah took a renewed interest in Islam. Conservative Islamic leaders led by the **Ayatollah Khomeini** (koh·MAY·nee) opposed the shah's modernization efforts. Banished from Iran since 1964, the 76-year-old religious leader had continued to speak out against the shah. By 1978 discontent with the shah's rule erupted in riots and demonstrations. Unable to contain the unrest, the shah left Iran in early 1979. Khomeini returned in February. He demanded abolition of the monarchy and the establishment of an Islamic republic. Iranians elected a president in January 1980, but Khomeini held the real power. His supporters eliminated other political forces in the country.

Meanwhile the shah had entered the United States for medical treatment. On November 4, 1979, Iranian militants captured the U.S. embassy in Tehran and seized more than 60 American hostages. They demanded that Mohammad Reza Pahlavi be returned to Iran to stand trial. The shah quickly left the United States. He died in Egypt in 1980, but the Iranians continued to hold the hostages until January 1981.

Trouble for Iran came in September 1980, when its neighbor Iraq attacked. Iraq wanted to control a waterway between the two countries. A bitter war raged. Both sides suffered heavy casualties but made little territorial gain. The war posed a serious threat to the Persian Gulf region until a cease-fire was agreed upon in 1988.

Khomeini died in 1989, and more moderate leaders took over. However, Iran continued to call for Islamic revolution in other Middle East countries. Relatively liberal Islamic leaders were elected in 1997, but relations with the United States remained strained. Following a devastating earthquake in the city of Bam in December 2003, however, the United States sent relief supplies and lifted some economic sanctions against Iran. The moves raised hopes for improved relations between the two countries.

✔ **READING CHECK: Sequencing** List the events that led up to and followed the revolution in Iran. Khomeini took control, American hostages seized, war with Iraq; continued difficult relations with the United States.

Struggle for Leadership in the Arab World

After the Camp David Accords, most Arabs rejected Anwar Sadat and Egypt's leadership. A struggle over which country would lead the Arab world began.

Syria. In 1970 General Hafiz Asad took control in Syria. He ruthlessly put down any challenges to his authority. After Syria's defeat in the Yom Kippur War, Asad turned his attention to building his influence in the Arab world. He aided and helped train Palestinian guerrilla groups. During the civil war in Lebanon in 1975, he first acted as mediator and then sent a large peacekeeping force to Lebanon. These troops gave the Lebanese people real hope for a lasting peace. Some wondered, however, what Asad

INTERPRETING THE VISUAL RECORD

The hostage crisis Images of the Ayatollah Khomeini were posted outside the U.S. embassy in Tehran, where Iranian revolutionaries held 60 Americans hostage. *What does this picture tell you of the Iranian revolutionaries' view of Khomeini?*

LEVEL 1: Write the following quotation by Gamal Abdel Nasser on the chalkboard: "Within the Arab circle is a role wandering aimlessly in search of a hero." Have students identify Nasser and query them about the meaning of his statement. (*The Middle East has great potential but lacks a great leader.*) Ask them who Nasser had in mind to be the "hero" of which he spoke. (*himself*) Call on volunteers to evaluate how well Nasser filled that role. Ask students if today's Arab leaders are more similar or dissimilar to Nasser in terms of background and goals for their country and region. Discuss the goals and methods of those who are similar to Nasser and compare them to the goals and methods of those who are not. **ENGLISH LANGUAGE LEARNERS**

CLOSE

Ask students what difficulties continue to challenge the Middle East.

That's Interesting!

An unstated reason that Saddam Hussein had for annexing Kuwait was a direct result of the Iran-Iraq War. Kuwait had made more than $7 billion in loans to help Iraq fight the war, a sum that war-torn Iraq appeared unlikely to be able to repay. Conquering his creditor relieved Saddam of the need to repay the money he owed to Kuwait.

MAP ANSWER
Saudi Arabia

Technology Resources

 CNN Presents Geography: Yesterday and Today Segment 22: Kuwait— Restoring the Environment

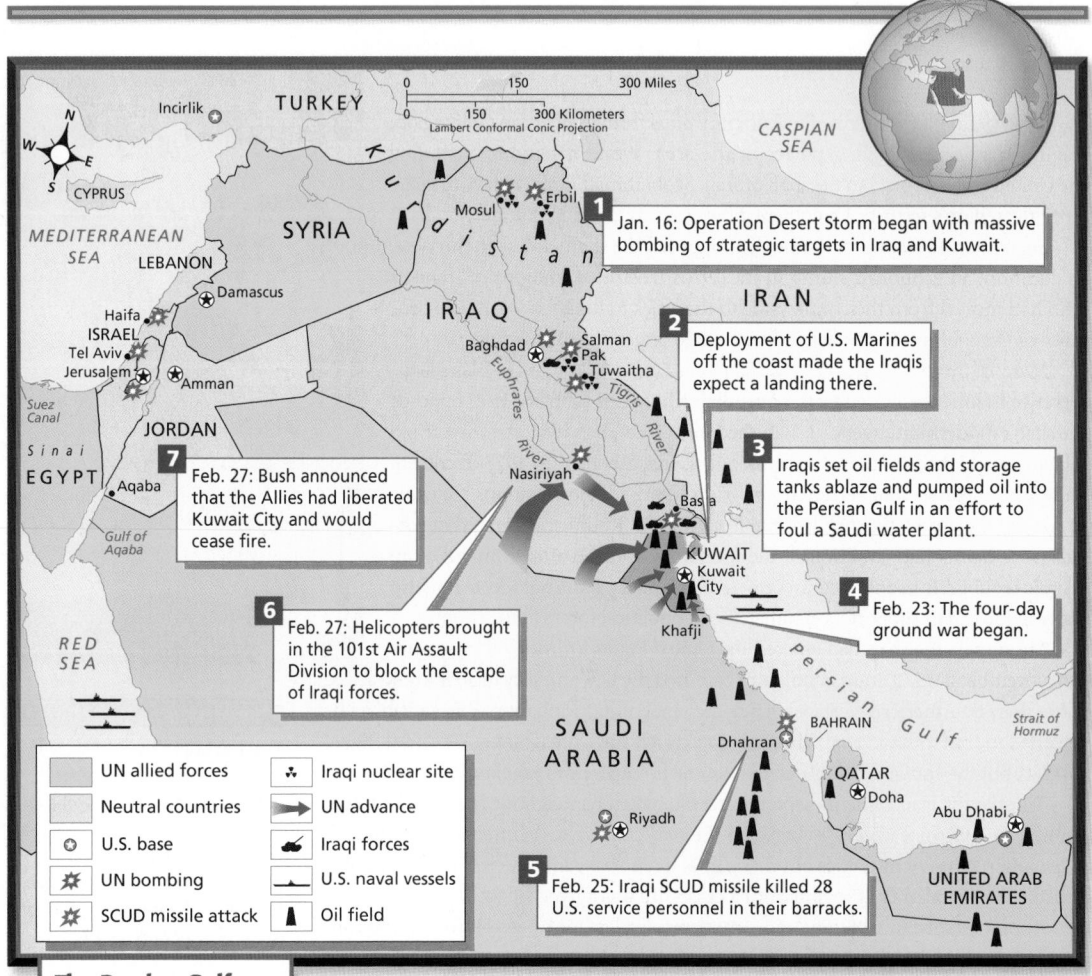

The Persian Gulf War, 1991

Interpreting Maps Iraq's attack on Kuwait brought about a quick response from UN allied forces.

■ **Skills Assessment: Places and Regions** From what country did most UN allied troops advance during the ground war?

would ask in return. In 1980 Asad supported Iran in the Iran-Iraq War. In 1990 he again opposed Iraq when it invaded Kuwait. After Asad's death in 2000, his son Bashar Al-Asad became president, maintaining the policy of little tolerance for any opposition.

Iraq. When the nationalist Ba'ath Party seized power in Iraq in 1968, **Saddam Hussein** was one of the driving forces. Using execution and imprisonment, Saddam removed anyone who threatened the party. In 1979 he took control of the government. When the Kurds, a minority group in northern Iraq, called for a degree of self-rule, he used chemical weapons against them. When the Iran-Iraq War ended in 1988, Iraq had the largest and best-equipped army in the Arab world. It also had enormous debts and economic problems because Iran had destroyed Iraqi oil facilities during the war. Saddam began a program of reconstruction. In August 1990 Saddam attacked Kuwait. He charged the Kuwaitis with pumping Iraq's share of oil from a jointly owned oil field. Kuwait's high level of production was driving down the price of oil. Iraq quickly took possession of the smaller country and formally annexed Kuwait on August 8.

World opinion was solidly against the Iraqi invasion. When Iraq seemed poised to invade Saudi Arabia, a coalition of about 30 nations launched Operation Desert Shield. They sent more than 600,000 troops to defend Saudi Arabia. The UN imposed economic

REVIEW

Have students complete the Section 4 Review on p. 905.

ASSESS

Have students complete Daily Quiz 33.4. As Alternative Assessment, you may want to use the OPEC or time line exercises in this section's lessons.

RETEACH

Have students complete Main Idea Activity for English Language Learners and Special-Needs Students 33.4. Then have students compile a section glossary with definitions, abbreviations, and significant individuals. **ENGLISH LANGUAGE LEARNERS, COOPERATIVE LEARNING**

EXTEND

Have students bring in current newspaper and magazine articles on recent developments in the Middle East. Call on students to summarize their articles and place the events they report on in historical perspective. **BLOCK SCHEDULING**

sanctions on Iraq and set a date for Iraqi withdrawal. If Iraq failed to withdraw, military action would result. The deadline passed, and the next day Desert Shield became Desert Storm. Coalition forces led by the United States launched an air attack. Iraq launched missile attacks against Saudi Arabia and Israel. Coalition air attacks continued for nearly 40 days. Then ground forces began to move into Kuwait and southern Iraq.

Worn down by weeks of bombing, and surrounded by Allied forces, the Iraqi soldiers retreated from Kuwait City across the desert. Kuwait was liberated within weeks. Hoping that Saddam would fall, Iraqis in the south and the north rebelled. The rebellions failed, however, and Saddam remained in power. To prevent Iraq from launching another war, stiff sanctions on oil and other goods continued. The UN ordered Iraq to stop producing weapons of mass destruction. When UN inspectors arrived to see that Saddam had complied, the Iraqis made inspections difficult.

Iraq's continued resistance to inspections, repeated violations of UN sanctions, and suspected development of prohibited weapons led the United States in 2002 to threaten an invasion of the country to force its compliance with the UN sanctions program. Saddam's delay in allowing unobstructed inspections to resume convinced the U.S. government that the Iraqi ruler would never fully comply with the sanctions program and would continue to pose a threat to neighboring countries and to the United States.

As a result, the United States led a coalition of forces in an invasion of Iraq in March 2003. Major combat was declared over in early May after Iraq's armed forces had been defeated and Saddam had fled from power. In December 2003, Saddam was located in hiding and captured by U.S. troops. The U.S.-led coalition remains in Iraq and is working to maintain order until a democratically chosen government is ready to assume the administration of the country.

While many women in the Middle East today wear the traditional body veil demanded by some Islamic leaders, others have adopted Western-style clothes.

✔ **READING CHECK: Summarizing** What reasons led the United States and its coalition partners to invade Iraq in 2003? unequal distribution of wealth, overpopulation

---

SECTION 4 REVIEW

1. **Define** and explain the significance:
   intifada

2. **Identify** and explain the significance:
   PLO
   Yasir Arafat
   Anwar Sadat
   Golda Meir
   Camp David Accords
   OPEC
   Ayatollah Khomeini
   Saddam Hussein

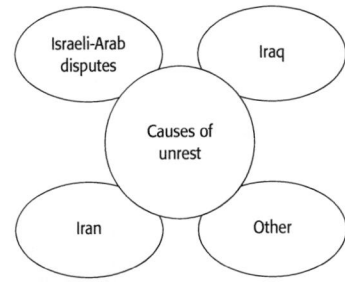

3. **Categorizing** Copy the web diagram below. Use it to identify the causes of unrest in each of the areas shown.

   Israeli-Arab disputes — Iraq — Causes of unrest — Iran — Other

4. **Finding the Main Idea**
   a. How did conflicts between Arabs and Israelis influence the history of North Africa and the Middle East?
   b. How did the presence of rich oil fields in the Middle East affect the region?
   c. What were the causes and effects of the revolution in Iran?
   d. How has the leadership of countries in the Middle East and North Africa changed since World War II?

5. **Writing and Critical Thinking**
   Comparing and Contrasting Write an article comparing the ways Iran and Iraq developed after World War II.
   Consider:
   • the political and economic issues that each country dealt with
   • the type of leadership each country had
   • the results of internal dissent

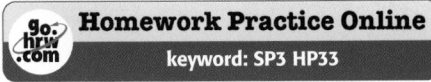

Homework Practice Online
keyword: SP3 HP33

SECTION
4 REVIEW ANSWERS

❶ **Define**
• intifada, p. 900

❷ **Identify**
• PLO, p. 899
• Yasir Arafat, p. 899
• Anwar Sadat, p. 899
• Golda Meir, p. 899
• Camp David Accords, p. 899
• OPEC, p. 901
• Ayatollah Khomeini, p. 903
• Saddam Hussein, p. 904–05

❸ Israeli-Arab disputes: Nasser demanded withdrawal of UN troops, blockade; Iraq: chemical weapons used against Kurds, attacked Kuwait, U.S. and allied forces removed Saddam from power; Iran: socialists and Islamic traditionalists opposed shah, economic slump; Other: Syria aided Palestinian guerrilla groups

❹ a. caused war, reliance on guerrillas, terrorism, border conflicts, intifada

b. nations joined together into a powerful organization

c. causes: political divisions, shah's modernization programs, autocratic methods, revived interest in Islam, economic slump; effects: shah left Iran, Khomeini held power and eliminated political forces

d. The rise of religious fundamentalism has challenged traditional leadership. There is movement toward democracy in some countries.

❺ Students' articles will vary.

REVIEW AND ASSESSMENT RESOURCES

REPRODUCIBLE RESOURCES

▶ Vocabulary Activity 33

TECHNOLOGY RESOURCES

▶ Chapter 33 Test Generator (on the One-Stop Planner)
▶ Global Skill Builder CD–ROM
▶ HRW Web Site

REINFORCEMENT, REVIEW, and ASSESSMENT

▶ Chapter 33 Review, pp. 906–907
▶ Chapter 33 Tutorial for Students, Parents, Mentors, and Peers
▶ Chapter 33 Test (Form A or B)
▶ Alternative Assessment Handbook
▶ Chapter 33 Test for English Language Learners and Special-Needs Students

REVIEW

Have students complete the Chapter 33 Review on pages 906–907.

ASSESS

Use one of the chapter tests to assess students' understanding of the content. For Alternative Assessment, see the Portfolio Activities and Alternative Assessment Handbook.

CHAPTER 33 REVIEW ANSWERS

Understanding Main Ideas

1. They were no longer satisfied to remain under European control.

2. It was a white-ruled nation with dominion status, linked to Great Britain only in foreign affairs. Internally, it ruled itself as it saw fit.

3. When new, inexperienced African governments failed to improve conditions, the military began to rule as in many other African countries.

4. ethnic tension often led to political turmoil and violence

5. They were forced to withdraw from most of their colonies.

6. Turkey: Soviet imperialism, autocratic rulers, military coup, restrictions on Islam; Iran: British domination, political unrest, control of oil industry

7. borders, blockades, armed attacks, refugees, guerrilla attacks

8. Many conflicts remain unresolved, making it a volatile region.

Reviewing Themes

1. Independence came so quickly that African leaders were not fully prepared and a military dictatorship was eventually established.

2. Nigeria, Rwanda, Burundi, Zaire

3. It has brought both wealth and power to the region.

CHAPTER 33 Review

Creating a Time Line

Copy the time line below onto a sheet of paper. Complete the time line by filling in the events, individuals, and dates from the chapter that you think were significant. Pick three events and explain why you think they were significant.

Writing a Summary

Using standard grammar, spelling, sentence structure, and punctuation, write an overview of the events in the chapter.

Identifying People and Ideas

Identify the following terms or individuals and explain their significance:

1. Pan-Africanism
2. apartheid
3. Nelson Mandela
4. desertification
5. Gamal Abdel Nasser
6. PLO
7. Camp David Accords
8. OPEC
9. Ayatollah Khomeini
10. Saddam Hussein

Understanding the Main Ideas

SECTION 1 *(pp. 878–885)*

African Independence After World War II

1. How did nationalists after 1945 differ from earlier African leaders?

2. How did South Africa's experience of colonialism and independence differ from that of other nations of Africa?

SECTION 2 *(pp. 886–890)*

Africa Since Independence

3. How does Ghana represent the post-independence experience of most African countries?

4. How did ethnic diversity contribute to political instability in independent African nations?

SECTION 3 *(pp. 891–897)*

Nationalism in the Middle East and North Africa

5. How did the rise of Arab nationalism affect France's and Britain's positions in North Africa and the Middle East?

6. What major issues confronted Turkey and Iran after World War II?

SECTION 4 *(pp. 898–905)*

War, Revolution, and Oil in the Middle East and North Africa

7. What were the causes of Arab-Israeli disputes?

8. Why is the Middle East still a source of major concern?

Reviewing Themes

1. **Government** How did the way the people of the Belgian Congo achieved their independence affect their nation?

2. **Culture** In which countries have the presence of different cultures contributed to unrest and civil wars?

3. **Economics** How have the rich oil fields of the Middle East and North Africa affected the lives of people there?

Thinking Critically

1. **Comparing and Contrasting** Compare and contrast the way colonial rule ended in British, French, and Belgian colonies after World War II.

2. **Summarizing** What factors have troubled the Middle East and North Africa?

3. **Sequencing** Trace the events leading to the rise and fall of apartheid in South Africa.

4. **Identifying Cause and Effect** What were the causes and results of the Arab-Israeli war of 1948–1949?

Writing About History

Supporting Points of View Many problems that still exist in Africa and the Middle East stem from differences in cultures. The civil wars in Kenya and Nigeria, apartheid in South Africa, the Arab-Israeli disputes, and the rise of Islamic fundamentalism all have a basis in cultural and religious differences. Select one of these issues. Write a dialogue between two persons on opposite sides in which they try to explain and resolve their differences. Use the following chart to organize your thoughts before you begin writing.

What the culture on one side of the dispute believes	
What the culture on the other side of the dispute believes	
Previous results of attempts to reach an agreement	
Action to be taken	

CLOSE

Ask students to explain how the history of Ghana is representative of the post-independence experience of most African nations.

RETEACH

Organize students who had difficulty with the test into groups. Assign each group a section of the chapter and have them develop several questions about the information in its section. Then have each group use its questions to quiz the other groups. When they are ready, have groups take the Form B Test to assess their mastery of the material.

Portfolio Extensions

1. Tell students OPEC is prominent in world affairs. Organize students into groups to research how OPEC conducts its meetings. Then have students conduct a mock OPEC meeting in which the ministers discuss how to raise the price of oil and how to enforce their decisions.

2. Have interested students research traditional or modern art forms of the nations of Africa and pick one on which to do an in-depth report. Have students include images of examples in their reports.

3. Have students prepare a debate on the following topic to present to the class. Resolved: The world community of nations should agree never to meet any terrorist demands. As students prepare their debates, they will find it useful to research some of the terrorist incidents that have taken place in the world in recent years.

Building Social Studies Skills

Using Art to Understand History

Study the painting below. Then answer the questions that follow.

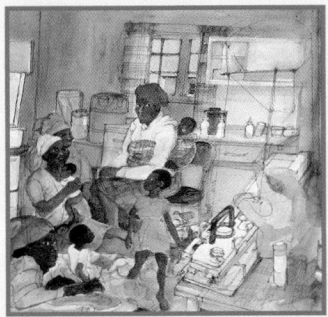

South African Family at Home, by Franklin McMahon

1. Which statement best describes what you can conclude from the painting about contemporary daily life in South Africa?

a. Most South Africans live in one-room houses.

b. In South Africa, women live separately from men.

c. Everyone in South Africa is very poor.

d. Some South African women are very poor and struggle to care for their children.

2. Why do you think the artist chose the subject he did for his painting? Give specific reasons to support your point of view.

Analyzing Primary Sources

Read the following quote. Then answer the questions.

> "In a large desert tent in war-torn Ajeip, Sudan, doctors and nurses . . . hover over starving Sudanese children, administering high-calorie biscuits and sugar water in an effort to revive them. . . . Half a world away, patients arrive at the cardiac ward of Mt. Sinai hospital in Manhattan, many complaining of chest pains. Doctors and nurses prepare some for open-heart surgery, . . . In contrast to the Sudanese children, many of whom will not pull through, most of the New Yorkers will survive."

3. Which of the following statements best describes the issue introduced in the excerpt?

a. People are dying from not enough food and from too much food, and both situations are preventable.

b. Children in the Sudan are dying of starvation, while people in New York are surviving heart disease.

c. The money spent on heart surgery in New York could be used to feed the children in the Sudan.

d. Doctors and nurses in both the Sudan and New York should have more recognition for saving lives.

4. Do you think the issue presented in the quote is an important one? Give specific reasons for your viewpoint.

Alternative Assessment

Building Your Portfolio

Economics

America's dependence on foreign oil makes this country vulnerable to disputes in oil-producing countries. Some possible solutions are developing more of the oil resources on U.S. land and using energy sources that do not require oil. Use the Internet and other sources to find out the pros and cons of each solution. Make a chart that displays your results.

internet connect

Internet Activity: go.hrw.com
KEYWORD: SP3 WH33

Choose a topic on Africa and the Middle East Since 1945 to:

• write a biography of Desmond Tutu which highlights his influence on events in South Africa during the 1900s.

• create a time line sequencing the major events of apartheid in South Africa.

• learn about recent developments in the Israeli-Palestinian peace process.

Thinking Critically

1. British: civil disobedience in Ghana, Mau Mau uprising in Kenya, guerrilla warfare in central Africa; French: development of African nationalism, became part of the French Community; Belgian: formed new political parties, violent protests

2. economic instability, terrorism, ethnic conflict, environmental problems

3. Afrikaaners came to power; segregation and economic exploitation became a government policy; protests against apartheid; government began to retreat from its policies in the 1980s; de Klerk helped end apartheid

4. causes: Holocaust survivors immigrated to Palestine, Zionist groups waged terrorist campaign against British authorities, UN voted to partition Palestine, Arab countries moved against Israel; effects: Israel won more territory, Palestinian refugees

Writing About History

Students' dialogues will vary.

Building Social Studies Skills

1. d

2. Students might suggest to show the injustice of poverty.

3. b

4. Students' answers will vary.

Building Your Portfolio

Students' charts will vary.

Latin America Since 1945

CHAPTER RESOURCE MANAGER

Objectives	Pacing Guide	Reproducible Resources
SECTION 1 **Facing New Challenges** (pp. 910–914) • Identify the steps Latin American nations took and what problems they faced as they sought to develop their economies. • Analyze the effect industrialization had on Latin American nations. • Identify the political and social forces that have emerged in Latin American nations.	**Regular** 1.5 day / **Block Scheduling** 1 day *Block Scheduling Handbook with Team Teaching Strategies, 34.1*	RS Guided Reading Strategy 34.1 RS Graphic Organizer Activity 34: Latin America and Trade SM Geography Activity 34: New Directions in Latin America PS Readings in World History 121: Daily Life in a Mexican Shantytown
SECTION 2 **Mexico and Central America** (pp. 915–921) • Explain how Mexico's fortunes rose and fell after World War II. • Describe how economic conditions influenced political events in Central America. • Explain how Central American nations have moved toward democracy.	**Regular** 1.5 day / **Block Scheduling** 1 day *Block Scheduling Handbook with Team Teaching Strategies, 34.2*	RS Guided Reading Strategy 34.2 PS Readings in World History 123: Objectives of the Contradora Process
SECTION 3 **Nations of the Caribbean** (pp. 922–928) • Explain how Fidel Castro's rule affected Cuba. • Identify the key issue that has caused ongoing debate in Puerto Rico. • Identify problems the smaller Caribbean nations have faced.	**Regular** 1.5 day / **Block Scheduling** 1 day *Block Scheduling Handbook with Team Teaching Strategies, 34.3*	RS Guided Reading Strategy 34.3 PS Readings in World History 135: Bringing Democracy to Haiti E Hands-on Activity 34: Economy and Revolution in Latin America
SECTION 4 **South America** (pp. 929–935) • Explain how the economy of Brazil first prospered, then stumbled. • Identify the political and economic troubles Argentina had. • Describe how Peru was affected by the drug trade and terrorism. • Describe how Columbia was affected by the drug trade. • Identify what led to Chile's continuously strong economy.	**Regular** 1.5 day / **Block Scheduling** 1 day *Block Scheduling Handbook with Team Teaching Strategies, 34.4*	RS Guided Reading Strategy 34.4 PS Readings in World History 122, 124 E Creative Teaching Strategy 34: Eye on Latin America

Chapter Resource Key

PS	Primary Sources	A	Assessment	Music
RS	Reading Support	REV	Review	Video
IC	Interdisciplinary Connections	ELL	Reinforcement and English Language Learners	Internet
E	Enrichment		Transparencies	Holt Presentation Maker Using Microsoft® PowerPoint®
SM	Skills Mastery		CD-ROM	

 One-Stop Planner CD-ROM

See the ***One-Stop Planner*** for a complete list of additional resources for students and teachers.

One-Stop Planner CD-ROM

It's easy to plan lessons, select resources, and print out materials for your students when you use the **One-Stop Planner** CD–ROM with **Test Generator**.

Technology Resources	Reinforcement, Review, and Assessment
One-Stop Planner 34.1 World History Teaching Transparency: Geography and History 29; Regional and World Map 32 Homework Practice Online Online Maps, Charts, and Graphs: Latin American Foreign Debts, 1986, 1989; Latin American Governments; Latin American Economic Growth, 1980–1989; Urban Population of Latin American	Daily Quiz 34.1 Main Idea Activity 34.1 English Audio Summary 34.1 Spanish Audio Summary 34.1 REV Section 1 Review, p. 914
One-Stop Planner 34.2 Holt Researcher: World History: Violeta Barrios de Chamorro CNN Presents World Cultures: Yesterday and Today Segment 34 CNN Presents Geography: Yesterday and Today Segments 4, 10 Homework Practice Online Online Maps, Charts, and Graphs: United States Trade with Canada and Mexico	Daily Quiz 34.2 Main Idea Activity 34.2 English Audio Summary 34.2 Spanish Audio Summary 34.2 REV Section 2 Review, p. 921
One-Stop Planner 34.3 Holt Researcher: World History: Jean-Bertrand Aristide CNN Presents World Cultures: Yesterday and Today Segment 35: The History of Haiti Homework Practice Online	Daily Quiz 34.3 Main Idea Activity 34.3 English Audio Summary 34.3 Spanish Audio Summary 34.3 REV Section 3 Review, p. 928
One-Stop Planner 34.4 Holt Researcher: World History: Eva Perón World History and Cultures Video Program 29: Brazil's Changing Horizon CNN Presents Geography: Yesterday and Today Segments 11, 12, 13 World History Teaching Transparency: Everyday Life 29 Homework Practice Online	Daily Quiz 34.4 Main Idea Activity 34.4 English Audio Summary 34.4 Spanish Audio Summary 34.4 REV Section 4 Review, p. 935

⬜ internet connect

HRW ONLINE RESOURCES
GO TO: **go.hrw.com**
Then type in a keyword.

TEACHER HOME PAGE
KEYWORD: **SP3 Teacher**

CHAPTER INTERNET ACTIVITIES
KEYWORD: **SP3 WH34**
Choose an activity to:
- learn about current events in Latin America.
- analyze Mexico's political choices and decisions since 1945 and how they are reflected in Mexico today.
- research current statistics and create a database for comparison.

CHAPTER ENRICHMENT LINKS
KEYWORD: **SP3 CH34**

ONLINE ASSESSMENT
Homework Practice
KEYWORD: **SP3 HP34**
Standardized Test Prep
KEYWORD: **SP3 STP34**
Rubrics
KEYWORD: **SS Rubrics**

ONLINE MAPS, CHARTS, AND GRAPHS
KEYWORD: **SP3 MCG**

CONTENT UPDATES
KEYWORD: **SS Content Updates**

HOLT PRESENTATION MAKER
KEYWORD: **SP3 PPT34**

ONLINE READING SUPPORT
KEYWORD: **SS Strategies**

CURRENT EVENTS
KEYWORD: **S3 Current Events**

Meeting Individual Needs

Ability Levels

Level 1   Basic level activities designed for all students encountering new material

Level 2   Intermediate level activities designed for average students

Level 3   Challenging activities designed for honors and gifted and talented students

English Language Learners   These activities address the needs of students with Limited English Proficiency.

Chapter Review and Assessment

IC   Vocabulary Activity 34
 Global Skill Builder CD–ROM
 HRW Web Site
REV   Chapter 34 Tutorial for Students, Parents, Mentors, and Peers
REV   Chapter 34 Review, pp. 936–937
A   Chapter 34 Test Generator (on the One-Stop Planner)
A   Chapter 34 Test (Form A or B)
A   Alternative Assessment Handbook
A   Chapter 34 Test for English Language Learners and Special-Needs Students

Section 1   *Facing New Challenges*

Section 2   *Mexico and Central America*

Section 3   *Nations of the Caribbean*

Section 4   *South America*

Build on What You Know

Ask students to answer the following questions:

Why did World War II mark a turning point in world history?

Consider:

- **the new world order that was created by the upheaval**
- **the new balance of economic power**
- **the new balance of political power**

What challenges did the countries of Asia and Africa struggle with?

Consider:

- **economic instability**
- **the struggle for independence**
- **attempts to overcome the long-term effects of colonialism**

EXPLORING THE TIME LINE

GLOBAL EVENTS

internet connect

TOPIC: The Nobel Prize
GO TO: go.hrw.com
KEYWORD: SP3 WH34

Have students access the Internet through the HRW Go site to learn about the Nobel Prize in various fields of endeavor. Ask the student to prepare an oral presentation about the history of this prestigious award. The report should include a brief statement about the two winners for Literature mentioned in the time line of this chapter, as well as some information about Rigoberta Menchú, who won the award for Peace in 1992. Other well-known persons who have won in any category could be included.

CHAPTER

34

1945–Present

Latin America Since 1945

Eva Perón

1963
Daily Life
A hurricane kills more than 4,000 people in the Caribbean.

1945
Global Events
World War II ends.

1948
Global Events
The OAS is founded.

1952
Politics
Eva Perón dies.

1959
Global Events
Fidel Castro becomes the leader of Cuba.

1963
Politics
Fidel Castro visits the Soviet Union.

1967
The Arts
One Hundred Years of Solitude by Gabriel García Márquez is first published.

1945   **1955**   **1965**

1946
Politics
Juan Perón is elected president of Argentina.

1946
Daily Life
Brazil's population reaches 45 million.

1950
Science and Technology
Mario Pani and Enrique del Moral begin designing University City, Mexico.

1958
Daily Life
Pelé helps Brazil win the first of three World Cup soccer championships.

1961
Global Events
The Bay of Pigs invasion occurs.

BRASIL CORREIO
10 CTS

University City building in Mexico

Brazilian postage stamp celebrating soccer star Pelé's 1,000th career goal in 1969.

Build on What You Know

The end of World War II marked a turning point in world history. The upheaval caused by the war resulted in a new world order and a new balance of economic and political power. While Europe struggled to rebuild its shattered cities and towns, the countries of Asia and Africa tried to address fundamental challenges by revamping their struggling economies, fighting for independence, and overcoming the long-term effects of colonialism. In this chapter, you will learn how the nations of Latin America struggled to establish and gain economic and political stability after World War II.

What's Your Opinion?

Economics

Agree Economic stability leads to political stability.

Disagree The strength of a government is not dependent upon the strength of its economy.

Government

Agree If citizens were allowed basic freedoms in some countries, their governments would not be able to run efficiently.

Disagree The opportunity for a government to run efficiently is not an acceptable excuse for restricting basic freedoms.

Global Relations

Agree When its vital interests are at stake, one nation has the right to interfere in the affairs of another nation.

Disagree One nation never has the right to interfere in the affairs of another nation.

Vicente Fox

Cover of Gabriel García Márquez's
One Hundred Years of Solitude

1972
Daily Life
A Nicaraguan earthquake kills more than 10,000.

1974
Business and Finance
Worldwide inflation occurs.

1976
Politics
Isabel Perón is overthrown in Argentina.

1976
Business and Finance
Argentina devalues the peso.

1982
Politics
The British battle Argentina for the Falkland Islands.

1983
Global Events
The United States invades Grenada.

1987
Science and Technology
A portion of Ecuador's main oil pipeline is destroyed in an earthquake.

1990
The Arts
Mexican poet Octavio Paz wins the Nobel Prize for literature.

1992
Business and Finance
The United States increases trade sanctions against Cuba.

1992
Science and Technology
Brazil hosts a world environmental conference.

1994
Business and Finance
NAFTA goes into effect.

1999
Business and Finance
Panama takes over control of Panama Canal.

2000
Politics
Vicente Fox is elected president of Mexico.

1975 **1985** **2000**

Former U.S. president Jimmy Carter turns over control of Panama Canal to Panamanian President Mireya Moscoso.

What's Your Opinion?

 *Do you **agree** or **disagree** with the following statements? Support your point of view in your journal.*

Economics Strong economies make strong governments.

Government In order to run the government efficiently, some governments must restrict basic freedoms.

Global Relations One nation has the right to interfere in the affairs of another nation.

EXPLORING THE TIME LINE
GLOBAL EVENTS

While one of the prevailing cultural norms in Latin America has been *machismo*—the glorification of masculine power and virility—another has been *marianismo*—the exaltation of the role of women as the keepers of virtue and propriety in society. *Marianismo* has become a powerful political force. In 1958, for example, Chilean women voters were largely responsible for electing a conservative president rather than a radical. Women were also highly influential in the Perónist movement in Argentina—taking their cue from Evita Perón.

Critical Thinking

Ask students how *marianismo* might be a disadvantage to Latin American women.

ANSWER: Students might suggest that *marianismo* limits women to roles such as motherhood and caregiving, which may prevent them from gaining full political power.

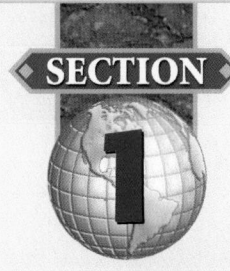
OBJECTIVES

1 **Identify the steps Latin American nations took and what problems they faced as they sought to develop their economies.**

2 **Analyze the effect industrialization had on Latin American nations.**

3 **Identify the political and social forces that have emerged in Latin American nations.**

🔔 LET'S GET STARTED!

As students enter the classroom, tell them that most Latin American countries supported the Allies against the Axis Powers during World War II. When the Allies emerged victorious, most Latin Americans felt proud and optimistic, expecting a period of growth and prosperity in the decades to come. Tell students that in Section 1 they will learn that long-term prosperity proved to be elusive and the next several decades were difficult ones for Latin America.

SECTION 1 RESOURCES

REPRODUCIBLE RESOURCES

▶ Guided Reading Strategy 34.1

▶ Graphic Organizer Activity 34

▶ Geography Activity 34

▶ Readings in World History 121

TECHNOLOGY RESOURCES

▶ One-Stop Planner 34.1

▶ World History Teaching Transparency: Geography and History 29; Regional and World Map 32

▶ Homework Practice Online

▶ Online Maps, Charts, and Graphs: Latin American Governments; Latin American Economic Growth, 1980–1989; Urban Population of Latin America

REINFORCEMENT, REVIEW, AND ASSESSMENT

▶ Section 1 Review, p. 914

▶ Daily Quiz 34.1

▶ Main Idea Activity 34.1

▶ English Audio Summary 34.1

▶ Spanish Audio Summary 34.1

SECTION 1

READ TO DISCOVER

❶ What steps did Latin American nations take and what problems did they face as they sought to develop their economies?

❷ What effect did industrialization have on Latin American nations?

❸ What political and social forces have emerged in Latin American nations?

DEFINE

multinational corporations
monoculture
import substitution

IDENTIFY

NAFTA
Mothers of the Plaza de Mayo
Organization of American States

▶ WHY IT MATTERS TODAY

Economics often plays a role in deciding who gains political power in a nation. Use CNN.com or other **current event** sources to find out how the Latin American nations are faring economically today. Record your findings in your journal.

CNN Student News.com

Facing New Challenges

The Main Idea
The nations of Latin America have struggled to establish stable economies since 1945.

The Story Continues *Industrialization in Latin America was a mixed blessing. Carolina Maria de Jesus, a Brazilian slum dweller, supported her three children by recycling trash. In a diary entry she summed up her plight: "I returned home, or rather to my shack, nervous and exhausted. I thought of the worrisome life that I led. Carrying paper, washing clothes for the children, staying in the street all day long. Yet I'm always lacking things."*

Developing New Economies

Before World War II Latin America had been dominated by rural, agricultural societies. During the war the region provided a steady flow of raw materials and foods to the Allies. After the war the demand for these goods increased. Even so, many Latin American nations found it difficult to become economically stable.

Economic instability. Most Latin American political leaders thought the way to solve the region's economic problems was for each nation to develop its own national industries. Such industrial development would provide jobs and consumer goods for the growing population, and it would make the nations less dependent on foreign goods. To pay for industrial development, Latin American governments obtained loans from foreign countries and commercial banks.

Another way to develop economically was to invite foreign corporations to do business in Latin America. Leaders believed these corporations would bring capital and technology into their nations and spur industrialization. Relations between these foreign-owned businesses, known as **multinational corporations,** and their host countries soon became strained, however. Many Latin Americans resented that

Traditionally, most agricultural workers in Latin America, like these coffee bean harvesters, have received little compensation for their labor.

ALL LEVELS: Ask students to define *monoculture*. *(the reliance of an entire region or country on a single crop for export)* Then ask students why monoculture was a poor foundation for a national economy. *(Only plantation owners and managers profited; plantation workers and small farmers often lived in poverty. In addition, the nation's dependence on a single crop made the economy unstable.)* Ask students to create a chart showing problems Latin American countries faced after World War II and what steps these countries have taken to improve economic conditions. Have students write two to three paragraphs evaluating the effectiveness of such efforts.
ENGLISH LANGUAGE LEARNERS

Problems	Solutions
poverty	*diversified exports*
international debts	*trade agreements, protective tariff*
high inflation	*raised taxes cut spending*

foreigners owned important factories. In addition, the foreign corporations often took their profits back home instead of investing them in the host nations.

Monoculture. One reason that Latin American economies were unstable was their basis in **monoculture.** In other words, almost every country in the region relied on just one or two crops or minerals for exporting. Venezuela and Mexico relied on oil. Colombia and Central American nations relied on coffee. When world prices for these products rose or fell, the economies of the countries rose or fell. The nations rode an economic roller coaster.

Latin American monocultures favored crops grown on large commercial plantations. Many plantation workers were families who came to the plantation only at harvest time. Writer Rigoberta Menchú, a Maya Indian of the Quiché group, described the childhood experience of being a coffee-bean picker:

> **History Makers Speak**
>
> ❝When I turned eight, I started to earn money on the finca [plantation]. I set myself to the task of picking 35 pounds of coffee a day. In those days, I was paid 20 centavos for that amount. . . . It was very hard on me. I remember very well never wasting a single moment, mainly out of love for my parents and so that they could save a little of their money, although they couldn't really. . . .❞

Rigoberta Menchú, *I, Rigoberta Menchú: An Indian Woman in Guatemala*

Import substitution. You have already read how Latin American nations followed a policy of economic nationalism in the 1930s. They tried to encourage their own industries and reduce foreign imports. After the war the nations took this policy one step further. They tried to identify certain imported goods and replace them with their own manufactured goods. This policy is known as **import substitution.** To make the policy work, Latin American governments granted favors to businesses to encourage them to manufacture these goods. They also imposed tariffs on imported goods, making them more expensive.

This approach worked well in larger nations like Mexico, Argentina, and Brazil because they had enough resources. These countries began to produce steel, heavy machinery, pharmaceuticals, cars, and many consumer goods. From 1950 to 1978 manufacturing grew in Latin America at a steady rate, even among smaller nations like Chile and Guatemala. Industrial growth slowed by the mid-1980s, however. Many Latin Americans did not earn enough money to purchase consumer goods in substantial quantities. In addition, a worldwide recession had begun to affect the region.

Debt problems. In the 1980s Latin America faced another economic problem: debt. Nations such as Argentina, Brazil, and Mexico had borrowed huge sums of money from foreign nations and commercial banks to help them industrialize. Many of these loans were made in the 1970s, when interest rates were rising. When their economies began to decline in the early 1980s, the nations had a hard time making their loan payments. The lenders of the money took steps to make it easier for the nations to repay the money they owed. Even so, the nations still owed hundreds of billions of dollars.

This huge debt led to inflation. The Latin American nations had to pay interest on foreign loans as well as keep their industries and governments running. To do this they printed more and more money. When too much money is in circulation, its value decreases and more money is needed to buy the same goods. In other words, prices rise and inflation occurs. By the 1980s several Latin American countries had annual inflation rates of over 1,000 percent.

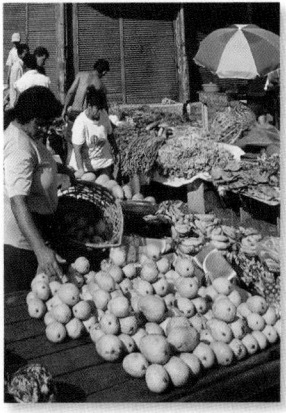

Guatemalan writer and civil rights activist Rigoberta Menchú received the Nobel Peace Prize in 1992.

Analyzing Primary Sources

Drawing Inferences Is 20 centavos a day a small or large amount of money? How can you tell?
small; very hard on worker, couldn't save money

Geography

Geography has in large part shaped the history of Latin America. The vastness, fertility, and overwhelming beauty of the lands of the Americas are what initially impressed European explorers and Spanish conquistadors. Europeans immediately set about finding and removing valuable resources such as gold and silver, frequently to the detriment of indigenous peoples. The struggle to control the rich resources and fertile land of Central and South America has generated conflict in that region for centuries.

Critical Thinking

Ask students in what other ways the geography of Latin America has influenced its history.

ANSWER: Answers will vary. Students might mention the Isthmus of Panama, which has been a focus of international interest and conflict for over a century due to its strategic location across the narrowest point between the two oceans.

INTERPRETING THE VISUAL RECORD

Markets Street vending is common in many Latin American countries and helps to keep consumer prices down. *How do markets such as this help consumers?*

LEVEL 3: Organize students into four groups and assign each group one of the following topics: *population growth, urbanization, poverty,* or *environmental problems.* Have each group use the textbook and other sources that you provide to put together a brief oral presentation about its assigned topic. Presentations should define and explain the problem, elaborate on its repercussions, outline attempted solutions, and evaluate the effectiveness of such solutions. If students find the attempted solutions to be insufficient, tell them to propose other ideas for solving the problem. Tell them to use visual aids during their presentations. Tell audience members to take notes on each other's presentations.
COOPERATIVE LEARNING

HOMEWORK After the presentations are complete, have each student use the information in their notes to complete a four-column chart titled *Problems Facing Latin America,* with the following heads: *Population Growth, Urbanization, Poverty,* and *Environmental Problems.*

Economics

In some Latin American countries, the debt crisis contributed to a rethinking of economic policies. In Chile and Argentina, government officials abandoned protectionism and adopted free-market theories in an effort to stop inflation and stimulate growth. Although at first this led to recession and hardship, by the 1990s both economies had again begun to prosper.

Critical Thinking

Ask students to suggest other results of ending protectionism.

ANSWER: The move could provide new markets.

CONNECTING TO ECONOMICS ANSWER
advantages: fewer trade barriers, availability of goods to Mexico; disadvantages: Mexico could become too dependent on U.S. agricultural products

CONNECTING TO Economics

NAFTA
The North American Free Trade Agreement was designed to promote free trade between the United States, Canada, and Mexico. NAFTA officially went into effect on January 1, 1994. By dropping trade barriers such as tariffs, the agreement makes it easier for the three nations to buy and sell their products to each other. For example, Mexico now purchases 75 percent of its agricultural products from the United States. Special NAFTA rules promote the purchase and use of home-grown North American products.

Understanding Economics

What might be the advantages and disadvantages of NAFTA?

A migrant farmworker from Mexico harvests apples on a farm in the United States.

To combat such high inflation, most nations raised taxes, cut spending, and stopped aiding industries. They also reduced the number of government workers and controlled their wages. The nations still had high inflation rates, however, and the actions taken to cut inflation slowed down economies. Hardest hit was the working class.

Economic alliances. After World War II Latin American countries explored new forms of economic relations. They wanted to lessen their dependence on industrialized countries and achieve greater cooperation in areas of tariffs and trade. In 1969 the nations of Bolivia, Chile, Colombia, Ecuador, and Peru put into effect the Andean Pact. This agreement was designed to restrict foreign investment, improve tariff coordination, and increase economic cooperation among these nations. Many Latin American countries strengthened their economies in the 1990s by making agreements with the United States and establishing regional free-trade alliances with each other. For example, the North American Free Trade Agreement, or **NAFTA,** which took effect in 1994, economically united Mexico with Canada and the United States, creating a large free-trade zone. Argentina, Brazil, Paraguay, and Uruguay formed a similar alliance known as Mercosur, which took effect in 1995. In Miami at the end of 2003, trade ministers from 34 nations in North, Central, and South America participated in talks to set up a Free Trade Area of the Americas (FTAA).

✔ **READING CHECK: Identifying Cause and Effect** What factors affected the economies of Latin American nations? debt, high inflation; free-trade zones

Changes and Challenges of Industrialization

Industrialization created higher standards of living and better health care for some Latin Americans. It also created many new challenges.

Population growth and poverty. When nations industrialize, their populations show a typical pattern of change. Before industrialization a nation's birthrate and death rate are usually high. Industrialization lowers the death rate because it brings better living conditions, sanitation, nutrition, and health care. Eventually birthrates will lower too, as women have fewer babies. During the period of transition, however, when death rates lower but birthrates stay high, a population boom occurs. Since World War II the Latin American population has skyrocketed. By the mid-1990s the population had tripled to nearly 470 million people. It is expected to continue growing through the year 2025.

An increasing percentage of Latin Americans live in poverty. More than one-third of the people in Latin America were poor in 1997. That figure was an increase of almost 60 million in 10 years. This situation was made worse by widespread unemployment. At the same time the gap between rich and poor grew, leading to much discontent. Many Latin Americans moved to the United States and to cities in search of better jobs and better lives.

Urban growth. In addition to overall population growth, Latin American cities began to grow as more and more people moved to them to find work. The cities also offered schools, social services, hospitals, and entertainment. Since 1945 urban populations have grown much faster than national populations, often twice as fast. The largest cities, such as Lima, Mexico City, and São Paulo, have grown the most.

TEACH OBJECTIVE 3

ALL LEVELS: Have students read the section titled "New Political and Social Forces" on pages 913 and 914. Then have them work individually or in pairs to come up with a slogan for each of the following groups that represented an emerging political force in Latin America: women, labor, and the Roman Catholic Church. Slogans should indicate the political aims of each group and might promote membership or support for the group as well. Then have students create logos and make promotional posters using the slogan and logo for each group. Display the posters and encourage students to constructively comment on each other's work. **ENGLISH LANGUAGE LEARNERS, COOPERATIVE LEARNING**

CLOSE

Ask students to speculate about why organizations such as the OAS have generally failed to achieve their goals of good relations among the nations of the Western Hemisphere.

As Latin American cities grew, governments had to install sewage systems, water mains, electrical lines, roads, and public transportation. These projects often caused financial burdens. Also, severe housing and job shortages existed. Governments were able to provide only a limited amount of housing, and most of the migrants who did find work in the cities did not make enough money to pay for housing. People began to live on empty land without permission. They built shacks of scrap metal and other cast-off materials. Many newcomers to Latin American cities today end up living in these shantytown slums. Because the urban slums have inadequate sewer systems and no running water, they are ideal places for diseases to spread. A cholera outbreak in Peru in 1991 spread to Brazil, Chile, Colombia, and Ecuador, killing more than 3,000 people.

Environmental problems. Growing urban populations cause environmental damage too. Mexico City's many cars and factories, for example, have led to high levels of pollution, endangering health and life. Many infants there have harmful levels of toxins in their blood.

In addition to the pollution caused by urban growth, the development of resources has led to other environmental problems. Millions of acres of land—including valuable rain forests—have been cleared to make room for buildings, roads, industry, and farms. In Central America alone more than two thirds of the rain forests have been destroyed. Many plant and animal species have become extinct, and there has been significant soil erosion. Also, dangerous pesticides, many of which have been banned in the United States, are still being used in Latin America.

✔ **READING CHECK: Problem Solving** What did Latin American leaders need to do in response to the problems caused by growing cities and industrialization? provide sewage systems, water mains, electric lines, roads, and public transportation

New Political and Social Forces

As Latin American nations changed and developed, so too did their political structures. By the mid-1990s most of the nations had democratic governments, and increasingly people began to make their voices heard in government.

Women, workers, and the Catholic Church. In Latin America today women are emerging as a political force. They began their struggle for the right to vote around World War I, but were not successful region-wide until 1961. Though their voting power has increased their influence in society, they still struggle for full equality. In southern Latin American countries, women have led the fight against military dictatorships and abuses of human rights. In Argentina a group of women whose family members had disappeared due to government-sanctioned violence formed **Mothers of the Plaza de Mayo** to oppose abuses of government and military power.

To gain land for agriculture and development, some Latin American rain forest lands have been cleared.

Population Growth in Selected Latin American Countries, 1900–2025

Legend: ■ Argentina ■ Mexico ■ Brazil ■ Peru ■ Chile

Y-axis: 0, 50,000,000, 100,000,000, 150,000,000, 200,000,000, 250,000,000
X-axis: 1900, 1950, 1988 2000 *2025
*Projected figures

Source: Population Reference Bureau

Interpreting the Graph
The populations of Latin American countries have grown dramatically, in part because of better nutrition and health care for some in the region. *In addition to having more people than the other countries shown, what else is different about the population projections for Brazil and Mexico?*

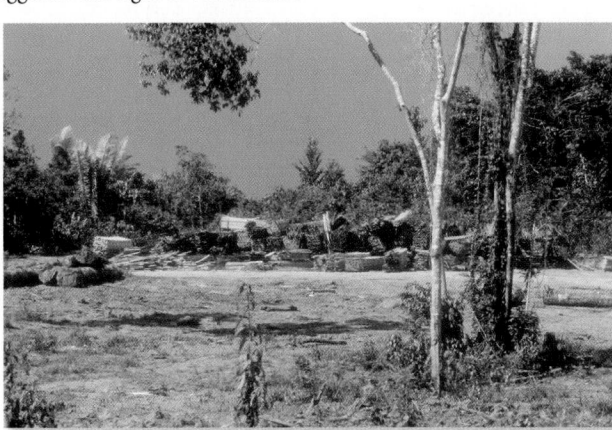

REVIEW

Have students complete the Section 1 Review on p. 914.

ASSESS

Have students complete Daily Quiz 34.1. As Alternative Assessment, you may want to use the oral presentation exercise in this section's lessons.

RETEACH

Have students complete Main Idea Activity for English Language Learners and Special-Needs Students 34.1. Then have students write the section's headings and subheadings on a sheet of paper and list the main ideas in the appropriate space.
ENGLISH LANGUAGE LEARNERS

EXTEND

Have students choose a Latin American country and conduct research on its economy. They should research the nation's GNP, per capita income, industrial growth rate, population growth rate, major exports, balance of trade, and major occupations. Have students summarize the information in brief oral presentations. **BLOCK SCHEDULING**

SECTION 1 REVIEW ANSWERS

1 Define
- multinational corporations, p. 910
- monoculture, p. 911
- import substitution, p. 911

2 Identify
- NAFTA, p. 912
- Mothers of the Plaza de Mayo, p. 913
- Organization of American States, p. 914

3 Attempts at economic development: loans for industrial developments, multinational corporations, import substitution, economic alliances; Economic problems experienced: economic instability, debt, poverty, urban growth, environmental problems

4 a. went into debt to develop national industries, allowed multinational corporations to do business in Latin America, engaged in import substitution

b. People came to look for work.

c. women: fought against military dictatorships and abuses of human rights; workers: fought for better working conditions by striking; the church: supported political change; fought for social justice

5 Students' letters will vary.

Union members demonstrate in protest of worker lay-offs by a Brazilian auto-making plant in January 1999.

Workers have gained power also. As industrialization spread and immigration declined, workers began to organize into unions. They fought for better working conditions by striking. Today a significant portion of the workforce belongs to unions.

The Roman Catholic Church, which has always been a strong presence in Latin America, has increasingly supported political change in Latin America. Following a meeting of Catholic bishops in 1968, church leaders began to oppose certain governments on issues such as welfare and human rights. They fought for social justice against oppressive economic and political systems.

International alliances. During and just after World War II, Western nations entered into several mutual defense pacts. Many political leaders viewed such pacts as necessary to prevent communist powers from gaining more territory. Inter-American cooperation was taken a step further in 1948. In that year delegates from the nations of the Western Hemisphere met in Bogotá, Colombia and founded the **Organization of American States** (OAS). The organization's aim was to foster economic, military, and cultural cooperation among the hemisphere's nations. The OAS works to prevent outside states from intervening in the Western Hemisphere and to maintain peace among member nations. The group currently has 35 members, including most of the independent nations in the hemisphere.

The founding of the OAS represented a continuation of the Good Neighbor Policy, through which the United States sought cooperation with its southern neighbors. This ideal, however, proved difficult to achieve. For example, in 1965 the U.S. intervened in a revolution in the Dominican Republic. The OAS gave its approval to this military action. Despite this official support, however, the incident caused some local resentment and soured U.S.-Latin American relations.

✔ **READING CHECK: Finding the Main Idea** Which groups have gained political influence in Latin America? women, workers, Roman Catholic Church

SECTION 1 REVIEW

1. **Define** and explain the significance:
   multinational corporations
   monoculture
   import substitution

2. **Identify** and explain the significance:
   NAFTA
   Mothers of the Plaza de Mayo
   Organization of American States

3. **Categorizing** Copy the chart below. Use it to categorize the positive and negative effects of industrialization on Latin American countries.

Attempts at economic development	Economic problems experienced

4. **Finding the Main Idea**
   a. What economic measures did Latin American leaders take to industrialize?
   b. Why did the populations of Latin American cities increase?
   c. What role do women, workers, and the church play in Latin American politics?

5. **Writing and Critical Thinking**
   Decision Making Pretend you are writing to a poor friend who is moving to a Latin American city to find work. Tell your friend whether he or she is making a good decision. Explain your reasoning.
   Consider:
   - what the housing is made of
   - what sewage and water systems they have
   - what the countryside can and cannot offer

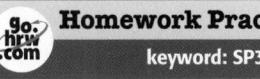
Homework Practice Online
keyword: SP3 HP34

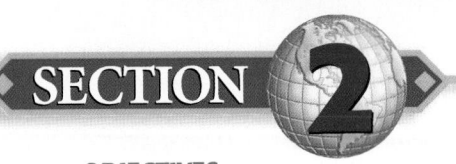

SECTION 2

OBJECTIVES

1 **Explain how Mexico's fortunes rose and fell after World War II.**

2 **Describe how economic conditions influenced political events in Central America.**

3 **Explain how Central American nations have moved toward democracy.**

SECTION 2

READ TO DISCOVER

❶ How did Mexico's fortunes rise and fall after World War II?

❷ How did economic conditions influence political events in Central America?

❸ How have Central American nations moved toward democracy?

DEFINE

contras

IDENTIFY

PRI
Carlos Salinas de Gortari
Vicente Fox
Sandinistas
Daniel Ortega
Violeta Barrios de Chamorro
Contadora Principles
Oscar Arias

WHY IT MATTERS TODAY

The Central American nations have worked toward peace and democracy since the 1990s. Use CNN News.com or other **current event** sources to find out which Central American nations are democracies today. Record your findings in your journal.

Mexico and Central America

The Main Idea
Mexico and the nations of Central America have experienced political and economic problems.

The Story Continues *Mexico rang in a new millennium with a new president and a new, more hopeful attitude about the future. Launching the New Development Plan, government spokeswoman Martha Sahagun said it called for "good government, healthy public finances, a revolution in education and great social development." These advances, she said, would "permit each Mexican to have a dignified life" by at least the year 2025.*

Mexico

Mexico was a stable nation right after World War II. The Institutional Revolutionary Party (its initials are **PRI** in Spanish) had firm control over the civilian government. A succession of presidents ran the nation effectively. The party, however, became entrenched in power. It refused to allow opposition and resisted demands for reform.

By the late 1960s student protests racked Mexico, just as they did in many nations at that time. There were numerous confrontations between protesters and police. In 1971 an anti-government guerrilla campaign began. The government hunted down the guerrillas, ending the threat by the late 1970s.

Economic problems. Mexico experienced economic ups and downs after World War II. Its leaders tried to remedy these problems by lowering the value of the currency, the peso, and cutting back on government spending. Then in the 1970s the economy was boosted significantly when huge oil reserves were discovered. Mexico's earnings from petroleum and petroleum-based products soared from about $544 million in 1976 to more than $16 billion in 1981. Believing its economic problems were over, the nation borrowed great sums of money to fund development projects.

Things took a turn for the worse, however, in the 1980s. Financial problems in the state-owned oil company, PEMEX, led the government to reduce investments in the company. Then the world oil market slumped, reducing Mexico's income. The nation still had major debts from the money it had borrowed, and inflation skyrocketed.

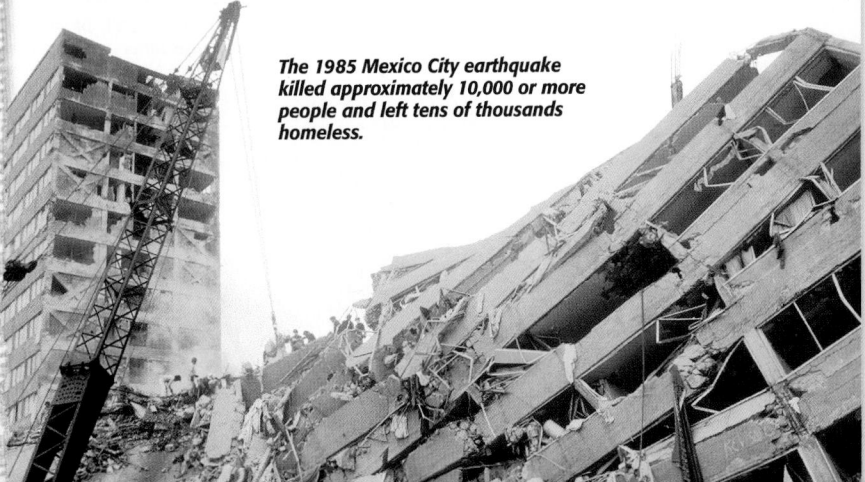

The 1985 Mexico City earthquake killed approximately 10,000 or more people and left tens of thousands homeless.

TEACH OBJECTIVE 1

LEVEL 1: Have students use the textbook subsection "Mexico" to create a table showing the effects of Mexican problems since World War II.

ENGLISH LANGUAGE LEARNERS

Problems	Effects
guerrilla campaign	*suppression of rebels*
slump in oil market	*huge foreign debt, rapid inflation*
earthquake	*shattered capital, homeless people*
unemployment	*illegal migration, strained relations with U.S.*

Linking Past to Present

Illegal immigration continues to trouble relations between Mexico and the United States. In California, Governor Pete Wilson sponsored a law, known as Proposition 187, restricting the provision of social services, including education, to illegal aliens and their children. Although approved by California voters, the law created much bitterness and anger.

Worried that the growing backlash against illegal immigration would be aimed at anyone of Hispanic descent, leading Hispanic politicians challenged the law's constitutionality in the courts. In 1999 Governor Gray Davis stated he would not appeal the decision of an appellate court judge, who ruled Proposition 187 was unconstitutional.

Critical Thinking

Ask students why voters might pass laws like Proposition 187.

ANSWER: Students should answer that some voters feel that they are spending tax revenues to support illegal aliens.

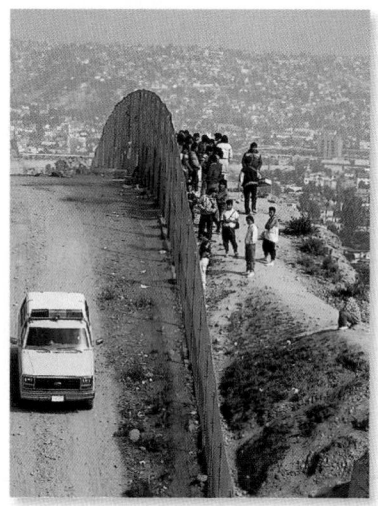

In Tijuana, Mexico, a group of would-be immigrants waits for nightfall to cross the fence into the United States.

Another blow came in 1985, when a massive earthquake rocked Mexico City. The nation needed to rebuild the shattered capital as well as provide for the thousands of citizens who were now homeless.

President **Carlos Salinas de Gortari** took office in 1988. He tried to solve the economic crisis by loosening government controls on the economy and selling some government-owned businesses to encourage foreign investors. He also encouraged free trade, working hard for NAFTA. He hoped it would lead the United States and Canada to invest in Mexico and stimulate economic growth.

Salinas's plan to decrease government control over the economy did not improve the situation, however. In December 1994 the next president, Ernesto Zedillo Ponce de León, lowered the value of the peso again. Confidence in the Mexican economy plummeted and many questioned Mexico's ability to repay its loans. U.S. president Bill Clinton pulled together a multibillion-dollar aid package, but the Mexican economy remained in trouble. Inflation rose roughly 50 percent, and Mexico suffered its worst recession in its history. Finally, with government-ordered spending cuts, the economy began to recover in 1996.

Emigration. Another problem in Mexico was unemployment. The economy did not grow as quickly as the population, and too many people could not find jobs. As a result, thousands of Mexicans began entering the United States illegally to look for work. Relations between the two countries suffered. In 1986, however, the United States granted legal status to some who had entered illegally. Tensions eased. Illegal immigration into the United States has continued, however, in part because of Mexico's economic problems.

Political consequences. Mexico's problems in the 1980s and 1990s had political consequences for the PRI. Despite having held power since 1929, the party began to lose its grip on Mexico. More groups opposed the party in elections, and many observers felt that President Salinas had won the presidency in 1988 only through fraud.

In 1994 an uprising of peasant farmers in Chiapas led to clashes with government troops. That same year the PRI presidential candidate was assassinated. By 1997 the PRI's hold was broken. For the first time other political parties took control of Mexico's congress. In the 2000 election, the PRI lost the presidency after holding it for more than 70 years, when opposition candidate **Vicente Fox** was victorious. Fox ushered in a new approach to governing.

✔ **READING CHECK: Finding the Main Idea** How did the political domination of the PRI affect Mexico after 1945? What finally broke the power of the party? put down opposition, resisted reform; peasant uprising, assassination of candidate

Mexico's oil deposits, processed at refineries such as this, are found along the Gulf of Mexico from Tampico to Campeche.

916

916 CHAPTER 34

SKILL-BUILDING STRATEGIES   Using Multimedia Resources

Recent Mexican History

Multimedia resources are sources of information that incorporate words, sounds, and images in a single package. They include, among other things, television documentaries, CD-ROMS, and Internet presentations. Multimedia resources often include ideas and data on historical topics from a variety of primary and secondary sources. Such resources can help you better understand events like the recent political changes in Mexico.

Television is symbolic of the endless possibilities of modern multimedia technology. TV can inform, entertain, and educate us.

This compact disc can store and deliver huge quantities of data in many different forms.

This small television camera is a marvel of optical, electronic, and audio performance.

Skills Reminder

To use a multimedia resource, take note of its title, publication date, and the people or organization that produced it. Study the resource, listening, watching, and reading carefully. Identify the main ideas and the specific means it uses to convey each piece of information. As you examine the information, use the skills you have developed in evaluating sources of evidence and identifying bias. This will help you identify any factual inaccuracies or general biases. Then put the information to use. Use the results of your analysis to form generalizations and draw conclusions based on the multimedia resources.

Skills Practice

In your local library or through the Internet, examine a multimedia source on recent Mexican history. Answer the following questions about the multimedia source you examined.
1. What was its title? Who produced or created it? When?
2. What types of evidence does the source provide to convey its main ideas?
3. How does the source handle any differing points of view? What biases, if any, does the source display?
4. How does the source contribute to your understanding of the topic you chose?

Interdisciplinary Connection

LITERATURE. After World War II many Latin American writers became interested in exploring the problems of human alienation in the modern world. Jorge Luis Borges of Argentina, for example, was highly praised around the world for his poems, stories, and essays dealing with the problems individuals encountered as they faced uncertainty in their lives. Meanwhile, poets like César Vallejo of Peru and Pablo Neruda of Chile developed a new surrealistic style as they sought to express the subconscious in creative imagery.

Critical Thinking

Ask students why Latin American writers might have become concerned with alienation and uncertainty.

ANSWER: Students might answer that as Latin American society became increasingly violent, uncertainty and alienation were more and more part of people's lives.

SKILLS PRACTICE ANSWERS

1–4. All answers will vary according to the multimedia source chosen by the student.

Central American Conflicts

After World War II Central America enjoyed economic growth. From 1950 to 1970 the nations cooperated, allowing industry to grow and highways and other trade routes to be built. People began to move to the cities in great numbers. Urban populations grew steadily in the 1970s and 1980s.

This economic growth, however, benefited only a small section of the population. Campesinos, the region's poor peasants, did not enjoy the prosperity. In many cases, the best farmlands stayed in the hands of the rich, while the number of landless farm workers grew. Then even more poor citizens became homeless when devastating earthquakes and hurricanes struck the region.

Nicaragua. One nation where people joined efforts in a revolutionary movement was Nicaragua. By the late 1970s much of the nation had risen up against its oppressive dictator, Anastasio Somoza Debayle.

The anti-Somoza revolution was led by a Marxist group called the **Sandinistas.** When Somoza fled the country in 1979, the Sandinistas took control of the government. Led by **Daniel Ortega,** they set up a ruling council, or junta.

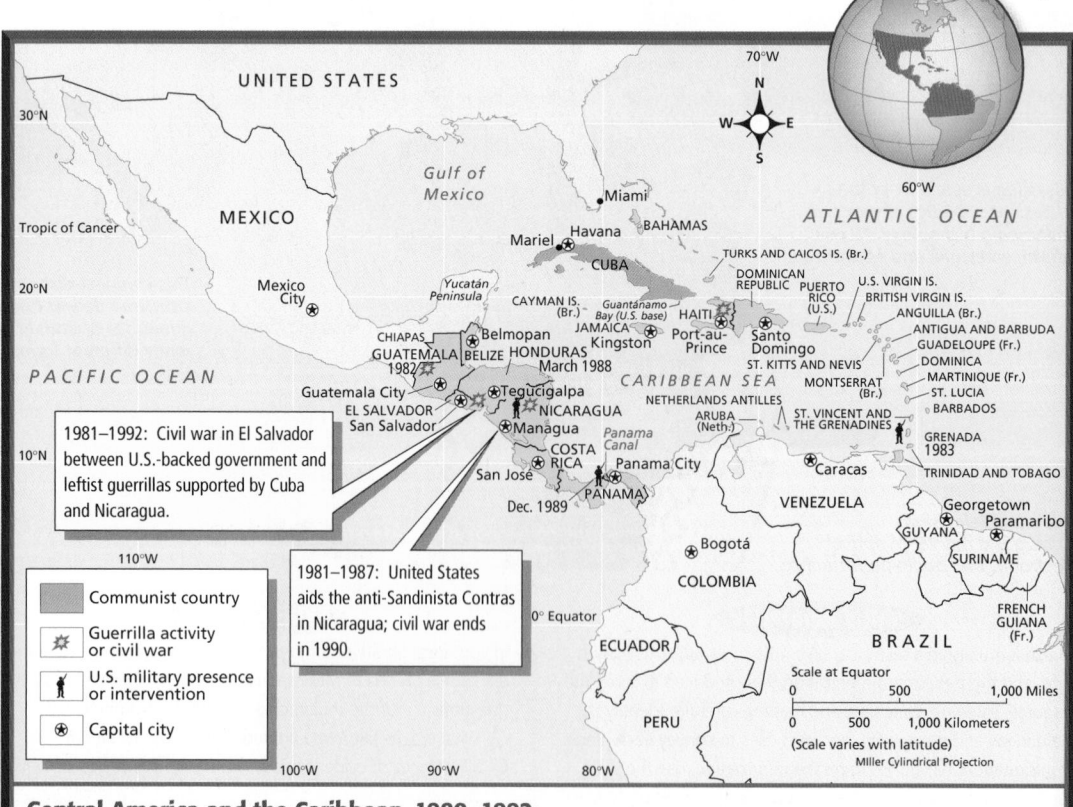

Central America and the Caribbean, 1980–1992

Interpreting Maps The Central American and Caribbean nations faced political and economic difficulties in the 1980s.

Skills Assessment: Locate In which nations did the United States maintain a military presence or intervene?

TEACH OBJECTIVE 3

LEVEL 1: Ask students the following questions: What were the Contadora Principles? *(document that promoted negotiations rather than violence to settle disputes)* Which countries agreed to them? *(Colombia, Mexico, Panama, and Venezuela)* What did Oscar Arias believe was the only thing that would secure peace in the region? *(democracy)* **ENGLISH LANGUAGE LEARNERS**

HOMEWORK Ask students why they think some people considered the 1990s a decade of hope for Central America. Have them write a few sentences that explain whether they agree or disagree with them and why.

The Sandinistas forged close ties with Cuba and began to move Nicaragua toward communism. They adopted programs to help the poor and spent money on health and education. They also restricted civil rights and limited political opposition.

In the early 1980s opposition to the Sandinistas grew inside Nicaragua. In addition, the United States under President Ronald Reagan charged that the Sandinistas were aiding other Marxist rebels in Central America. A U.S.-funded group called the **contras** began a guerrilla war to overthrow the Sandinistas. Although they were aided by the Soviet Union and Cuba, the Sandinistas had to devote more and more government money to their army. As the civil war raged, the economy of the country suffered severely. Shortages of goods were common. The fighting wore on and cost many lives.

Faced with trade embargoes and a weak economy, the Sandinistas could no longer carry on the fight. In 1990 the fighting between the Sandinistas and the contras ended when Daniel Ortega conducted free elections. He gave up power peacefully after losing the election to **Violeta Barrios de Chamorro.** The United States quickly lifted the trade embargo it had placed on Nicaragua in 1985. The new government also received foreign economic aid.

The change of government, however, did little to help Nicaragua. Under Barrios de Chamorro the country faced political instability, foreign debt, and high inflation and unemployment. The Sandinistas in the National Assembly challenged many of her reforms. The presidents who followed Barrios de Chamorro also had to deal with high inflation, unemployment, and other continuing problems.

El Salvador. Northwest of Nicaragua lies El Salvador. From the 1940s to the 1970s, this Central American nation was ruled by wealthy citizens or military dictatorships. In the 1970s guerrilla groups began to mobilize people to demonstrate against the government. Some Catholic clergy supported these protests.

In 1979 civil war broke out between the government and a leftist guerrilla group called the Farabundo Martí National Liberation Front (its initials are FMLN in Spanish). The FMLN waged a campaign of urban terrorism and fierce battles against government forces. In response, right-wing "death squads"—many of them backed by the army—attacked anyone who expressed any kind of support for the FMLN's aims. In 1980 Catholic archbishop Oscar Romero was assassinated, and three American nuns and a volunteer were murdered.

José Napoleón Duarte was appointed president in December 1980 and elected in 1984. Throughout most of the 1980s, his government was supported and aided by the United States. Duarte was a civilian and a moderate who tried to enact reforms. The violence continued during his administration, however.

The right-wing ARENA party won control of the government in the late 1980s. The FMLN responded with even more violence. Guerrillas attacked urban centers, including the capital of San Salvador, in 1989. Right-wing death squads reacted. In November 1989 one such squad murdered six Catholic priests. By 1992 more than 80,000 Salvadorans had been killed in the continuing violence.

Alfredo Cristiani succeeded Duarte as president in 1989. Cristiani and FMLN leaders took steps toward peace. A peace agreement, reached through UN mediation, was signed in 1992. The first postwar elections were held in 1994. The ARENA candidate, Armando Calderón Sol, became president. In the 1997 elections ARENA maintained a strong presence in the national legislature, even though FMLN showed strength among the voters. ARENA candidate Francisco Flores won the presidency in 1999.

HISTORY MAKER

Violeta Barrios de Chamorro (1929–   )

When the husband of Violeta Barrios de Chamorro was killed—probably by agents of Somoza—she took a leading role in the struggle against Somoza. Barrios de Chamorro was part of the government that took power after Somoza fled. She became unhappy with the Sandinistas, however. When she won the presidency in 1990, she became a symbol of the triumph of democracy. Barrios de Chamorro also promoted peace when she declared amnesty for many who had fought in the civil war. **Why would Barrios de Chamorro declare amnesty after the civil war?**

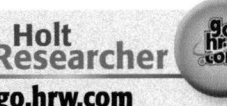

Holt Researcher

go.hrw.com
KEYWORD: Holt Researcher
FreeFind:
  Violeta Barrios de Chamorro
After reading more about Violeta Barrios de Chamorro on the Holt Researcher, create a campaign poster for her explaining why she is a symbol of democracy.

History Maker

OSCAR ROMERO. An outspoken critic of human rights violations, Archbishop Oscar Romero was assassinated while celebrating mass. He had recently written to Jimmy Carter, then president of the United States, requesting that the U.S. not provide military assistance to El Salvador that might perpetuate human rights violations. Despite investigation by the Truth Commission, no one has been brought to justice for the killing. Before his assassination, Romero helped create the Commission on Human Rights of El Salvador (CDHES). The aim of the organization was to promote human rights, but several members of the group have been killed or have "disappeared" because of their involvement and work on behalf of victims of human rights violations.

Critical Thinking

Ask students why people might risk membership in groups like CDHES.

ACTIVITY: Students might suggest commitment to a cause or belief in human rights.

HISTORY MAKER ANSWER

Students might suggest that she wanted to return the country to peace and stability and not reopen old wounds.

TEACH OBJECTIVE 4

LEVEL 3: Organize students into seven groups and assign each group one of the following countries: Mexico, El Salvador, Nicaragua, Panama, Guatemala, Costa Rica, or Honduras. Have them use the textbook, the library, computer software, and other sources to find information about daily life in their assigned country and then create a scrapbook that might belong to an average family living in its assigned country in the present day.
COOPERATIVE LEARNING, BLOCK SCHEDULING

CLOSE

Read to the class the quotation from Oscar Arias on page 921. Ask

students to make suggestions about how peace and stability might be achieved in the region.

Teacher to Teacher

Rudy Martinez of San Antonio, Texas, suggested the following activity: Working in groups or independently, have students research the history of the Panama Canal, including why it was built, how the United States came to build it, what controversies have been associated with it, and why the United States turned it over to Panama.

internet connect

TOPIC: Latin American Statistics
GO TO: go.hrw.com
KEYWORD: SP3 WH34

Search the Internet through the HRW Go site for recent statistics on gross domestic product, major exports, and major imports of these countries: Belize, Costa Rica, El Salvador, Haiti, Honduras, Mexico, and Nicaragua. Then assemble the information you have gathered into a chart to display.

Panama. The nation of Panama endured its own political and economic problems. One complicating factor there was that the United States controlled the Panama Canal and the land around it. The two nations signed a treaty in 1978 that would give Panama control of the area by the end of 1999. Many Americans, though, were concerned that U.S. interests would be threatened if Panama controlled the canal.

By the late 1980s relations between the two nations had deteriorated. United States officials believed that Manuel Noriega, the Panamanian dictator, was helping South American nations bring drugs into the United States. President Ronald Reagan urged Noriega to resign, but he refused. To pressure him further, the Reagan administration cut off aid to Panama. Later, when Panamanian soldiers killed a U.S. soldier and harassed others, President George Bush sent U.S. troops in to restore order. Noriega was captured, convicted of drug trafficking, and sentenced to 40 years in prison.

Panama had its first democratically elected government in years, after the U.S. invasion in 1989. The country worked hard to maintain its democracy and avoid a return to military dictatorship. Major economic and social problems, though, persisted. In 1999 Mireya Moscoso became Panama's first female president. As promised by the United States, the Panama Canal was turned over to Panama that same year.

✔ **READING CHECK: Identifying Cause and Effect** How did economic factors play a role in the conflicts that took place in Central America? widened gap between rich and poor

A freighter in the Miraflores Locks of the Panama Canal

REVIEW

Have students complete the Section 2 Review on p. 921.

ASSESS

Have students complete Daily Quiz 34.2. As Alternative Assessment, you may want to use the Mexico problems exercise in this section's lessons.

RETEACH

Have students complete Main Idea Activity for English Language Learners and Special-Needs Students 34.2. Then have students

compile a section glossary containing abbreviations and significant individuals. **COOPERATIVE LEARNING, BLOCK SCHEDULING**

EXTEND

Have students write a biographical profile of a Mexican or Central American leader from 1945 to the present. Tell them to include information about the person's personal and political life in their profiles. Call on volunteers to share some of the information they found and have the class take notes.
BLOCK SCHEDULING

Moves Toward Peace and Democracy

After years of turmoil in Central America, several Latin American countries tried to find a peaceful solution to the region's problems. In 1983 Colombia, Mexico, Panama, and Venezuela agreed to the **Contadora Principles.** This document promoted negotiations rather than violence as the way to settle regional conflicts. It also called for a reduction in foreign military presence.

In 1987 representatives from throughout Central America met in Guatemala for a regional peace conference. Costa Rican president **Oscar Arias** proposed a peace plan that called for an end to all fighting in the region, an end to foreign aid to rebels, and economic reforms. As the following excerpt from a speech by Arias shows, he believed that there would be no peace in the region without democracy:

Oscar Arias's peace plan was endorsed by five Latin American nations.

 History Makers Speak

❝Freedom works miracles. For free men everything is possible. The challenges confronting us can be overcome by an America which is democratic and free. When I assumed the Presidency of Costa Rica, I called for an alliance for freedom and democracy in the Americas. I said then, and I repeat today, that we cannot ally ourselves either politically or economically with governments which oppress their peoples. Latin America has never known a single war between two democracies. That is reason enough for every person of good faith, for every government with good intentions, to supports the efforts to stamp out tyranny.❞

Oscar Arias, "Nobel Peace Prize Acceptance Speech"

Costa Rica, El Salvador, Guatemala, Honduras, and Nicaragua all supported the proposal. For his efforts, Arias received the Nobel Peace Prize in 1987. Political instability, however, caused in part by deeply rooted social and economic divisions, continued to plague parts of Central America throughout the 1980s. Peace would not seem to be a likely prospect in the region until the 1990s.

✔ **READING CHECK: Making Generalizations** What political changes swept through Central America in the 1990s? movement toward peace and democracy

Analyzing Primary Sources

Identifying a Point of View
Would military dictators agree with Arias's viewpoint? no, because Arias believed in democracy

---

SECTION 2 REVIEW

1. **Define** and explain the significance:
   contras

2. **Identify** and explain the significance:
   PRI
   Carlos Salinas de Gortari
   Vicente Fox
   Sandinistas
   Daniel Ortega
   Violeta Barrios de Chamorro
   Contadora Principles
   Oscar Arias

3. **Sequencing** Make a flowchart like the one below. Complete it to show how world oil prices affected Mexico.

Mexico has economic problems

Oil is discovered

4. **Finding the Main Idea**
   a. What events showed that the PRI was losing its political hold on Mexico?
   b. How did the United States influence events in Nicaragua and Panama in the 1980s?
   c. What did Oscar Arias propose in his plan?

5. **Writing and Critical Thinking**
   Supporting a Point of View Pretend you are an editor of a newspaper in Central America in the 1980s and are opposed to your nation's dictatorship. Write an editorial explaining why you believe the government must be changed.
   Consider:
   • what the economy and society of the nation are like
   • what life is like under a dictatorship

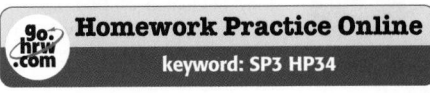
Homework Practice Online
keyword: SP3 HP34

SECTION 2 REVIEW ANSWERS

❶ **Define**
• contras, p. 919

❷ **Identify**
• PRI, p. 915
• Carlos Salinas de Gortari, p. 916
• Vicente Fox, p. 916
• Sandinistas, p. 918
• Daniel Ortega, p. 918
• Violeta Barrios de Chamorro, p. 919
• Contadora Principles, p. 921
• Oscar Arias, p. 921

❸ Mexico has economic problems; oil is discovered; borrows great sums of money to fund development projects; oil market slumps; inflation skyrockets

❹ a. student protests; anti-government guerrilla campaign

b. Nicaragua: funded the contras; Panama: cut off aid and sent troops to restore order

c. an end to all fighting in the region; an end to foreign aid to rebels; economic reforms

❺ Students' editorials will vary but should consider what the economy and society of the nation are like and what life is like under a dictatorship.

OBJECTIVES

1 **Explain how Fidel Castro's rule affected Cuba.**

2 **Identify the key issue that has caused ongoing debate in Puerto Rico.**

3 **Identify problems the smaller Caribbean nations have faced.**

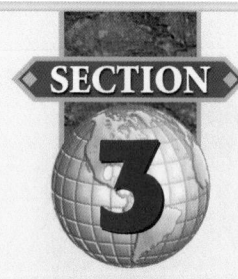

Nations of the Caribbean

The Main Idea
Political affairs in Caribbean nations have been strongly influenced by the United States.

The Story Continues *The nations of the Caribbean experienced their own political upheavals, revolutions, and attempted rebellions. When young revolutionary Fidel Castro was on trial in Cuba for his raid on a military barracks, he stated confidently, "History will absolve me."*

The Cuban Revolution

Fulgencio Batista was a Cuban army officer who had taken control of the island nation of Cuba. In 1959 Batista was overthrown in the Cuban revolution, one of the greatest political upheavals in Latin American history.

Fidel Castro. The leader of the Cuban revolution was **Fidel Castro.** Castro's anti-Batista campaign began in 1953, when he led an attack on a military barracks. Castro was jailed, but later went into exile in Mexico, where he trained a group of revolutionaries. He returned to Cuba with a band of followers in 1956. Along with his brother Raúl and a young Argentine revolutionary named **Ernesto "Che" Guevara,** Castro led guerrilla operations against the corrupt Batista government.

Batista responded with brutal and oppressive measures. As a result, many Cubans began to support the revolutionaries. In 1958 the United States decided to cut off its support of Batista, and stopped shipping arms to his government. Realizing he had no chance of surviving, Batista fled Cuba in 1959. Castro took control of the government. A young schoolgirl described the scene as Fidel Castro led his victorious troops into the Cuban capital of Havana:

History Makers Speak ❝Out in the street all the cars were flying pennants, people sang and whistled, strangers embraced each other, and everybody was shouting, 'Viva Cuba libre!' [Long live free Cuba!]❞

from *Four Women: Living the Revolution*, by Oscar Lewis et al.

Life under Castro. The lower and middle classes at first supported Castro. They approved of his promises to reform education and agriculture, improve health care, restore civil liberties, and hold open elections. His desire to build a new Cuba free of American influence was welcomed by many Cubans.

INTERPRETING THE VISUAL RECORD

Castro Huge crowds welcomed Fidel Castro upon his arrival in the town of Cienfuegos. *Does this picture support the schoolgirl's account of the people's response to Castro?*

ALL LEVELS: Organize the class into two groups and have them conduct a debate of the following statement: Fidel Castro's government and policies were more harmful than beneficial to the Cuban people.

ENGLISH LANGUAGE LEARNERS, COOPERATIVE LEARNING

Soon, however, the new government veered toward communism and the Soviet bloc. By the end of 1959 Castro's openly communist regime became dictatorial. Freedom of the press was denied, and some of Castro's opponents were executed. Castro began to make Marxist land reforms that redistributed income and property. His government took control of U.S.-owned agricultural estates and businesses. Castro did make many of his promised social reforms. His education policy boosted Cuba's literacy rate to 96 percent, the highest in Latin America.

Although the poor generally supported Castro, he lost the backing of many upper- and middle-class Cubans. Businesspeople and landowners were angry that their property had been seized. Middle-class intellectuals and liberal politicians were shocked by Castro's authoritarianism. In time more and more Cubans began to flee the country. Many settled in Florida.

The Bay of Pigs. Cuba's growing relationship with the Soviet Union troubled the U.S. government. Concerns about this relationship grew in 1960, when Castro ordered U.S.-owned oil companies in Cuba to process fuel supplied by the Soviets. The companies refused, and Castro seized their refineries. To strike back, the United States refused to import sugar from Cuba. Castro responded by seizing other U.S. properties in Cuba. Relations between the countries took a turn for the worse. In January of 1961 President Eisenhower broke off U.S. diplomatic relations with Cuba.

The U.S. Central Intelligence Agency (CIA) began to provide support for Cuban exiles in Guatemala and to train them for an uprising against Castro. A rebel invasion landed at the Bay of Pigs in April 1961. However, the U.S. military support that was key to the invasion never came. Nor did the expected anti-Castro uprising among Cubans. The invasion failed miserably. Castro's forces killed or captured many rebels, several of whom were Batista supporters. The failed invasion only pushed Castro even closer to the Soviets.

Cuba and the Cold War. After the Bay of Pigs invasion, Castro was concerned that the United States would attempt another attack on Cuba. He therefore allowed the Soviets to build nuclear missile sites on the island. The crisis that followed brought the world to the brink of nuclear war. The two superpowers eventually agreed the missile sites would be removed if the United States promised not to invade Cuba.

HISTORY MAKER

**Fidel Castro
(c. 1927–   )**

Fidel Castro was the son of a sugar plantation owner. He graduated with a law degree in 1950. In 1952 he ran for election to the Cuban congress, but troops led by Batista stopped the election, and Batista himself took control of the government.

Castro then began his revolution against the Batista dictatorship. When he landed from Mexico with his small band of rebels in December 1956, many were killed. Castro and the survivors fled to the mountains, where other Cuban rebels joined them. About two years later, Castro took over the government. **How did Castro come to power?**

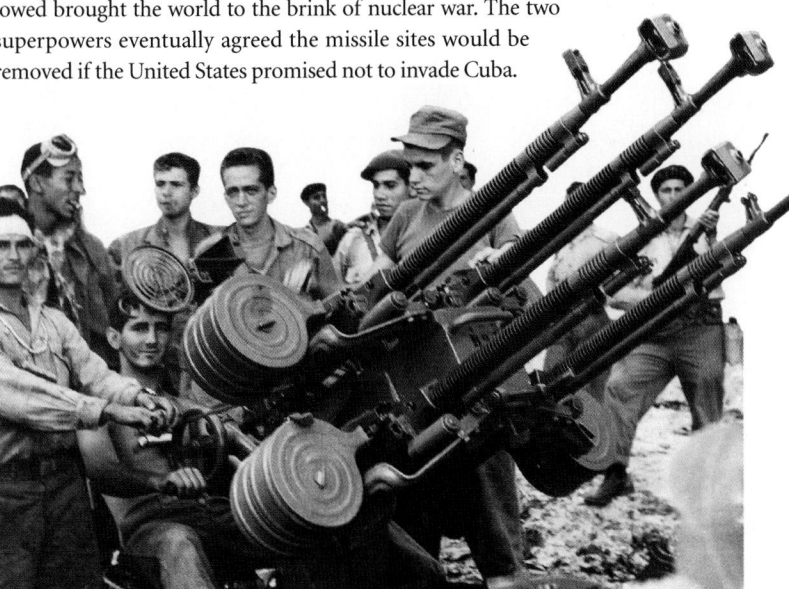

Castro's Cuban troops easily repelled the Bay of Pigs invasion force.

What If? Would Fidel Castro have been able to retain control of Cuba if the Bay of Pigs invasion had been successful? How would Cuban-American relations have changed if the invasion had toppled Castro?

Government

In 1952 Fidel Castro was a member of the *Ortodoxo* Party and a candidate for the Cuban House of Representatives. It is believed that he almost certainly would have won if the election had taken place. Instead, the election was cancelled by dictator Fulgencio Batista. As a result, an angered Castro vowed to force Batista from office and set out to raise a military force to do so. After an initial failure, Castro was imprisoned for about two years before he fled to Mexico to build a revolutionary force. When he returned, he rapidly gained support for his revolution. He represented for the people a champion against the corruption and cruelty of the Batista regime.

Critical Thinking

Ask students how they think the history of Cuba might have been different if Batista had not called off the election of 1952.

ANSWER: Responses will vary, but many students will probably suggest that Castro would have won the election and used his career as a politician to institute reform measures.

HISTORY MAKER ANSWER
took over the government through revolution

WHAT IF? ANSWER
probably not; Cuba might have developed a democratic government

HOMEWORK Have students use their textbooks to create time lines of the events leading up to, during, and following the Cuban Revolution. Then have them use their time lines to write narrative summaries and analyses of the Cuban Revolution.

History Maker

FIDEL CASTRO. After Castro graduated from the University of Havana, he became committed to communism. A turning point in his life occurred in 1948 in Bogotá, Colombia, when a popular leftist politician, Jorge Eliécer Gaitán, was assassinated. For two days, the entire city rioted in reaction. Eventually, as the mobs took over the city, the authorities fled.

Critical Thinking

Ask students why the assassination and riots in Colombia might have been a turning point for Castro.

ANSWER: The riots showed Castro that the power of large groups of people affected the government.

Economics

More than 1 million Cuban refugees fled to the United States during the 1960s. A large part of this exodus was fueled by Castro's economic policies. Those policies proved disastrous for the Cuban economy, causing a negative growth rate in some years.

Critical Thinking

Ask students what type of people probably fled to the United States.

ANSWER: educated and skilled workers who could foresee the coming problems

Che Guevara was an Argentine doctor who became a revolutionary after witnessing a U.S.-backed overthrow of the Guatemalan president in 1954. He served in various posts under Fidel Castro and was killed while leading a guerrilla attack in Bolivia.

In the mid-1960s Castro began a program to assist communist revolutions in other nations. He sent arms, soldiers, and military advisers to Latin American countries such as the Dominican Republic and Nicaragua, and to African countries such as Angola and Ethiopia.

As he had with the revolution in Cuba, Che Guevara helped Castro in these efforts. While leading a guerrilla operation in the mountains of Bolivia in 1967, he was killed by Bolivian rangers.

Because of Cuba's efforts to "export" revolution, the United States urged the Organization of American States to expel Cuba. It also encouraged other nations in the region to participate in an economic boycott of Cuba. The boycott isolated Cuba and its economy from the United States.

Problems at home. Cuba's economy was hurt as a result of this isolation. Industrialization did not proceed as planned. Production of Cuba's main crop, sugar, fell. As a result, Cuba became more dependent on aid from the Soviet Union.

The economic difficulties and shortages of goods created dissatisfaction and unrest. Many Cubans sought political asylum in other countries. The number of **dissidents**—those who disagree with a government—grew. Castro agreed to let anyone who wanted to leave Cuba do so, as long as the authorities were informed. About 125,000 people left, most of them on boats provided by Cuban exiles in Miami. Castro used the opportunity to empty Cuba's prisons and mental hospitals, forcing the inmates onto boats heading to the United States.

The recent past. Despite being isolated, Cuba maintained its support of revolutions. Throughout the 1980s it aided communist regimes in Angola and Ethiopia and remained opposed to the United States.

Cuba also remained economically dependent on the Soviet Union. In the late 1980s, however, the Soviets drastically reduced aid to Cuba. With little aid and with the economic boycott still in effect, the Cuban economy nearly collapsed in the early 1990s. Basic goods were in short supply. The Cuban government began a rationing program and imposed restrictions on the purchase of consumer goods.

In the face of economic disaster, Castro insisted that Cuba would remain a communist nation. In the mid-1990s, however, he allowed a limited number of private businesses. He also enacted other economic reforms. The Cuban economy slowly

Thousands of Cubans took advantage of the opportunity to leave their country when Castro loosened emigration restrictions. These people fled in 1994.

TEACH OBJECTIVE 2

LEVEL 3: Go over the subsection on Puerto Rico on page 925 with students. Then have them take on the roles of modern Puerto Ricans to write letters to the editor of a Puerto Rican newspaper arguing the merits of either remaining a commonwealth or becoming a state. Encourage students to edit each other's work for standard grammar, spelling, sentence structure, and punctuation before they submit it. **COOPERATIVE LEARNING**

began to show signs of recovery due to increased tourism and foreign investment. In 1998 Pope John Paul II visited Cuba. He called for an end to U.S. trade sanctions and asked Castro to allow religious freedom and social justice in Cuba. The United States eased trade restrictions on agricultural products in 2000, and Cuba began purchasing U.S. farm goods in 2001.

READING CHECK: Summarizing What kind of economic relationship does Cuba have with the United States and other capitalist countries? one of isolation; suffers under U.S. trade restrictions; tourism and foreign investment are increasing

Puerto Rico

The island of Puerto Rico has been associated with the United States since 1898. In that year the United States took control of the island following the Spanish-American War. By 1917 the U.S. Congress had made Puerto Rico a U.S. territory and given all Puerto Ricans U.S. citizenship. In the early 1930s Puerto Ricans led by **Luis Muñoz Marín** began to call for greater autonomy from the United States. The United States granted Puerto Rico a degree of self-government in 1947, and Muñoz Marín became the island's governor one year later.

This was not enough for Muñoz Marín. He pushed for even greater freedom for Puerto Rico. The U.S. Congress responded in 1950 by allowing Puerto Rico to write its own constitution. Two years later Puerto Rico was given commonwealth status.

Muñoz Marín had worked since the 1940s to boost Puerto Rico's economy. His plan for outside investment and industrialization was called **Operation Bootstrap.** Aided by tax breaks for investors from the United States, it was a great success. The economy thrived over the next two decades. Once-poor Puerto Rico raised its per capita income—the amount of money each person earns on average—dramatically.

Good economic times did not last, however. There were not enough jobs for the island's growing population. Many Puerto Ricans left for the continental United States to find work. More than 2 million Puerto Ricans live on the U.S. mainland today.

There has been constant debate in Puerto Rico about whether the island should become one of the states in the United States or remain a commonwealth. In a 1993 nonbinding vote on the issue, about 48 percent preferred to stay a commonwealth, while about 46 percent favored statehood. A small percentage—less than 5 percent— voted for independence.

READING CHECK: Making Predictions Based on what you know, do you think Puerto Ricans will ever choose U.S. statehood? Why or why not? strong ties to United States, but slightly fewer voters favor statehood

Luis Muñoz Marín (shown with hands raised) initially supported independence for Puerto Rico. He was later elected governor of the U.S. commonwealth and made economic and social reforms on the island.

Citizenship

Strained relations between the United States and Cuba were affirmed when a child custody case became an international debate. On Thanksgiving Day in 1999, six-year-old Elian Gonzalez was found clinging to an inner tube off the Florida coast during a failed attempt to reach U.S. shores from Cuba. His mother and others had died when their boat capsized near Fort Lauderdale. After his rescue, Elian was placed in the custody of distant relatives in Miami, who began a fight to keep him in the United States. However, Elian's father, who remained in Cuba, began a legal battle to have Elian returned to him in Cuba.

Elian's relatives and anti-Castro Cuban-Americans in the U.S. argued that returning Elian to Cuba would be "irreparably harmful" under Castro's communist rule. Cuba, in the meantime, charged America with "kidnapping" and held anti-American protests. Although most Americans supported the return of Elian to his father, many Cuban-Americans resisted his return. Eventually, Elian was returned to his father and went back to Cuba seven months after his rescue at sea.

ACTIVITY: Have students debate whether Elian should have been returned to Cuba or not.

LEVEL 1: Go over the subsections on the Dominican Republic and Haiti. Point out that the most overwhelming problem faced by these two nations during the latter half of the 1900s was a high poverty rate. Ask students to complete a flowchart showing the effects of poverty. Then ask them how a high poverty rate can affect other aspects of society and politics in a nation. (*Answers will vary, but students should point out that great numbers of people suffering under the poverty line are likely to support revolutions and other violent means of achieving change quickly. They also may turn to crime out of anger and frustration in order to feed themselves.*)

ENGLISH LANGUAGE LEARNERS

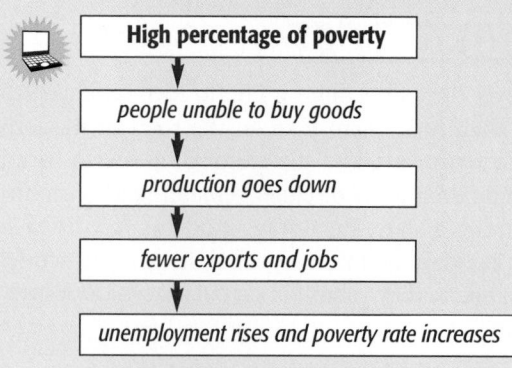

High percentage of poverty

↓

people unable to buy goods

↓

production goes down

↓

fewer exports and jobs

↓

unemployment rises and poverty rate increases

That's Interesting!

In 1967, when Puerto Ricans were asked to vote on becoming a state, 60 percent chose to continue as a commonwealth. In a nonbinding vote taken in 1993, 48.4 percent preferred commonwealth status and 46.2 favored statehood, while a small percentage voted for independence. The debate over Puerto Rico's future political status continued into the turn of the century.

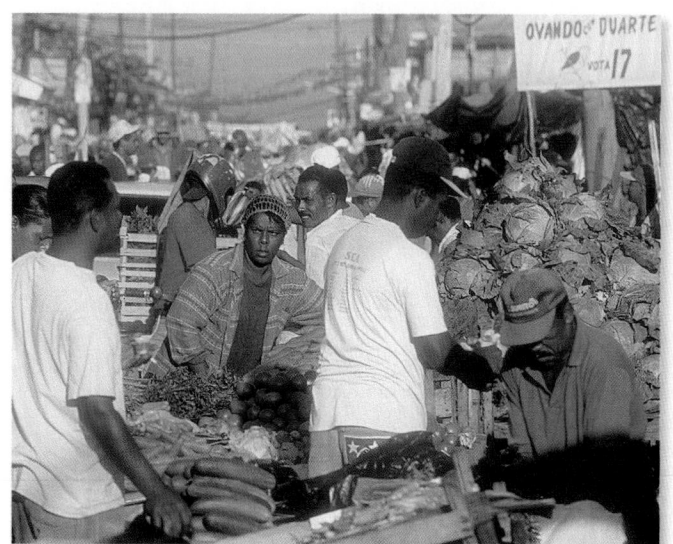

The Mercado Nuevo is the main fruit and vegetable market in Santo Domingo, Dominican Republic.

Other Caribbean Nations

Cuba was not the only troubled island nation in Latin America. In the 1960s in particular other Caribbean islands faced political changes, challenges, and violence.

The Dominican Republic. The Dominican Republic occupies two thirds of the Caribbean island of Hispaniola. Haiti occupies the other third. The country occupies a strategic position on major sea routes leading from Europe and North America to the Panama Canal. The Dominican Republic, despite its name, was for many years ruled as a dictatorship. A constitutional government had been set up in 1924 after a period of occupation by U.S. forces who had been sent to maintain stability in the troubled nation. In 1930, however, the dictator Rafael Trujillo overthrew this government. Trujillo's military dictatorship lasted until he was assassinated in 1961. Trujillo was succeeded by Juan Bosch, the first democratically elected president in over 30 years.

A coup overthrew Bosch in 1963. Military leaders formed a three-member ruling junta. Bosch's followers, some of whom were said to be communists, started an uprising to return him to power. U.S. president Lyndon Johnson feared that the Dominican Republic would become, like Cuba, another communist nation in the Western Hemisphere. In 1965 he sent thousands of U.S. marines to the Dominican Republic to support the military government in case of an attempted communist takeover.

After 1965 the nation's political situation and economy saw some degree of improvement. A new constitution was introduced in 1966. Democracy began to advance again within the country. Throughout the 1970s and 1980s, the island was stable. Although the economy depended heavily on sugar exports, the government also developed some tourism and light industry.

The Republic's economy declined slightly in the 1970s, fluctuated during the 1980s, and then took a downturn in the early 1990s, as the nation suffered through an energy crisis. The utilities that provided power could generate just a fraction of what the country needed. Business and industry were disrupted. Unemployment and inflation soared.

By the mid-1990s, however, the economy had improved somewhat. More and more people visited the island as tourists. The inflation rate was down well below earlier levels. The Republic's unemployment rate, however, was still high. Millions of Dominicans lived in poverty. Democratic elections were held in 1996, and Leonel Fernandez Reyna became president without incident. The country still had major economic problems to be solved, and anti-government feelings persisted. In May 2000 Hipólita Mejía Domínguez was elected president. He promised to fight corruption and expand the economy.

Haiti. The nation of Haiti occupies the western third of the island of Hispaniola. Haiti originally became an independent nation in 1804 after the island's population of

LEVEL 2: Have students take on the roles of individuals living in Cuba, Puerto Rico, Haiti, or the Dominican Republic. In these roles, have them write several journal entries that discuss aspects of their daily lives and significant events that have affected them and their families.

slaves successfully rebelled against the French. However, the history of republican government in Haiti has often been interrupted. From 1957 to 1971 the country was dominated by President François Duvalier, who ruled with an iron hand. He was succeeded by his son, **Jean-Claude Duvalier,** who declared himself "President for Life." Jean-Claude was forced into exile in 1986 and the military took power.

The rule of the Duvalier family had left Haiti the poorest country in the Western Hemisphere. The Haitian people hoped that a new government would help improve their lives. However, the military regime that had forced Duvalier out of power was reluctant to hold elections. It finally agreed to do so in 1987, but when violence flared between rival political groups the elections were canceled. Free elections in 1988 brought a civilian government council to power, but they in turn were followed by a series of military coups and more violence.

The government remained in the hands of the military until 1990, when elections were held. In December of 1990 **Jean-Bertrand Aristide** became the nation's first democratically elected president. Aristide, a former Catholic priest, did not last long, however. In September of 1991 rebel troops took over the government, forcing Aristide to flee the nation. International aid was suspended and trade sanctions imposed against the new government of Haiti. The United States intervened, and nearly four years later Aristide was able to return to Haiti and take office.

In the 1995 election René Préval was elected president. It marked the first time in Haiti's history that one elected Haitian official, Aristide, had completed his term in office and peacefully passed power on to his successor. In 2000 Aristide's party, the Lavalas Political Organization, swept parliamentary elections that many argued were marred by fraud. Although opposition parties protested by boycotting the presidential elections later that year, Aristide won the vote. As Haiti continued to suffer from poverty, crime, and corruption, however, opposition to the president grew. When armed rebels advanced on the capital in February 2004, Aristide was forced to resign.

Smaller nations of the Caribbean. After being colonized by European powers more than 200 years ago, most Caribbean islands today have their own governments. Many are independent nations.

Democratic elections brought Jean-Bertrand Aristide to Haiti's presidency in 1990. Although he was re-elected in 2000, armed opposition to his rule forced Aristide to resign in early 2004.

go.hrw.com
KEYWORD: Holt Researcher
FreeFind:
      Jean-Bertrand Aristide
After reading more about Jean-Bertrand Aristide on the Holt Researcher, write a memo by a U.S. official explaining why the United States intervened to help him take office.

In the 1990s the presence of U.S. troops in Haiti helped restore Haitian president Jean-Bertrand Aristide to power.

Economics

The U.S. plan in 1995 for economic recovery in Haiti depended heavily on reactivating the private sector. Haiti's private sector had reduced its involvement with the formal economy, and during the Aristide government, had sent millions of dollars abroad without repatriating the funds. This might have been the result of the private sector remaining unconvinced of the sincerity of the Aristide government to win over the business community. Of the $162 million in U.S. assistance scheduled for Haiti in 1995, $58 million was intended to go toward economic stabilization programs—payments of overdue foreign debt; programs in agriculture, education, environment; and private-sector development. Private-sector development would focus on telecommunications, power generation, light assembly manufacturing, arts, and handicrafts.

Critical Thinking

Why is the involvement of the private sector important to Haiti's economy?

ANSWER: Students might suggest that Haiti needs to decrease its economic dependence on other countries.

CLOSE

Ask students to describe how the revolution in Cuba has affected U.S. relations with Caribbean nations over the past three decades.

REVIEW

Have students complete the Section 3 Review on p. 928.

ASSESS

Have students complete Daily Quiz 34.3. As Alternative Assessment, you may want to use the Castro or Puerto Rico exercises in this section's lessons.

RETEACH

Have students complete Main Idea Activity for English Language Learners and Special-Needs Students 34.3. Then ask students to write a question and answer that covers the main idea for each subsection in the section. **ENGLISH LANGUAGE LEARNERS**

EXTEND

Have students read a book about the Cuban missile crisis. Then have them summarize the main points of the book in a one- to two-page written report. **BLOCK SCHEDULING**

SECTION 3 REVIEW ANSWERS

❶ Define
- dissidents, p. 924

❷ Identify
- Fidel Castro, p. 922
- Ernesto "Che" Guevara, p. 922
- Luis Muñoz Marín, p. 925
- Operation Bootstrap, p. 925
- Jean-Claude Duvalier, p. 927
- Jean-Bertrand Aristide, p. 927

❸ charts should include economic slowdown, shortages of goods, trade embargoes, isolationism, population growth, job shortages, energy crisis

❹ a. The poor tended to support him while the middle and upper classes did not.

b. degree of self-government, own constitution

c. cancelled elections, military coup

❺ Students' memos will vary but should consider what economic conditions the Latin American nation faced and what effect communism had on the U.S. government's thinking.

In 1958 most of the British islands of the Caribbean were joined together into a country called the West Indies Federation. The federation was dissolved in 1962, after Jamaica seceded. Jamaica was then granted status as an independent dominion within the Commonwealth of Nations, an association consisting primarily of former members of the British Empire. Soon afterward Barbados and Trinidad and Tobago also became independent nations. In 1967 some nations attempted to create a Federation of the East Caribbean. When these efforts failed, some smaller islands temporarily became "associated states of the United Kingdom." However, a number of small islands have gained their independence in recent decades. For example, Grenada became independent in 1974, Antigua and Barbuda in 1981, and St. Kitts and Nevis in 1983. Other new members of the Commonwealth include Dominica, Saint Vincent and the Grenadines, and Saint Lucia.

In 1983 a coup overthrew the Marxist government of Grenada. The rebels themselves were also communists. Neighboring Caribbean nations asked the United States to help restore order. President Ronald Reagan sent troops on October 25. Aided by small numbers of troops from several Caribbean nations, the U.S. forces quickly took control of Grenada. A democratic government was restored in 1984.

The invasion of Grenada was an unusual instance of cooperation among Caribbean nations. Despite sharing certain physical, historic, and economic traits, the islands have not developed much cohesiveness. In the late 1980s regional groups and associations such as the Caribbean Community and Common Market (Caricom) did begin to advance island trade and business. This organization now has 14 members. Agriculture and tourism are important to the economies of many Caribbean nations.

The invasion of Grenada was carried out by a multinational force led by U.S. troops to restore order after a bloody coup.

✔ **READING CHECK: Making Generalizations**
What role has the military played in many Caribbean nations since the end of World War II?
control by military governments, intervention of U.S. military

---

SECTION 3 REVIEW

1. **Define** and explain the significance:
   dissidents

2. **Identify** and explain the significance:
   Fidel Castro
   Ernesto "Che" Guevara
   Luis Muñoz Marín
   Operation Bootstrap
   Jean-Claude Duvalier
   Jean-Bertrand Aristide

3. **Summarizing** Copy the graphic organizer below. Complete it to show the economic problems Central American and Caribbean nations faced after World War II.

   Nations

4. **Finding the Main Idea**
   a. Which Cuban citizens tended to support Castro, and which did not?
   b. What political freedoms has Puerto Rico won from the United States since 1898?
   c. How did the Haitian military respond to attempts at democracy in the 1980s and 1990s?

5. **Writing and Critical Thinking**
   Problem Solving Imagine you are a U.S. government adviser in the 1960s. Write a memo to the president explaining how the United States can support democracy in Latin America.
   Consider:
   • what economic conditions the Latin American nations faced
   • what effect communism had on the U.S. government's thinking

Homework Practice Online
keyword: SP3 HP34

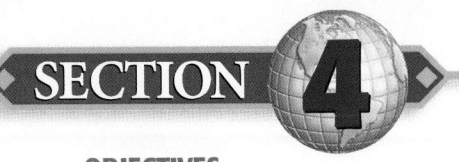

SECTION 4

OBJECTIVES

1 **Explain how the economy of Brazil first prospered, then stumbled.**

2 **Identify the political and economic troubles Argentina had.**

3 **Describe how Peru was affected by the drug trade and terrorism.**

4 **Describe how Columbia was affected by the drug trade.**

5 **Identify what led to Chile's continuously strong economy.**

LET'S GET STARTED!

As students enter the classroom, ask them to list some basic human rights and record them on the chalkboard. *(possible responses include freedom of expression, freedom of association, due process of law, equality before the law, and the right to human treatment)* Explain to students that in many Latin American countries where political and social upheaval created instability, one of the first casualties was usually human rights. Tell students that in Section 4 they will learn about political turmoil in South America.

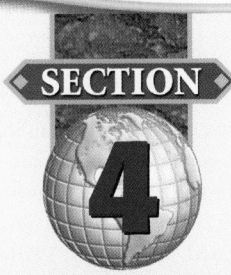

SECTION 4

READ TO DISCOVER

1 How did the economy of Brazil first prosper, then stumble?
2 What political and economic troubles did Argentina have?
3 How was Peru affected by the drug trade and terrorism?
4 How was Colombia affected by the drug trade?
5 What led to Chile's continuously strong economy?

DEFINE

desaparecidos

IDENTIFY

Fernando Henrique Cardoso
Eva Perón
Juan Perón
Shining Path
Alberto Fujimori
Salvador Allende
Augusto Pinochet

WHY IT MATTERS TODAY

To increase industrialization and agriculture, Brazil has allowed parts of the Amazon rain forest to be cleared. Use CNN student News.com or other **current event** sources to find out how this has affected Brazil both economically and environmentally. Record your findings in your journal.

CNN student News.com

South America

The Main Idea
Revolution and political turbulence swept the continent of South America in the years after World War II.

The Story Continues *As in the Caribbean and Central America, military control of the government became common in South American nations. Marcio Moreira Alves, a Brazilian citizen, described the frightening aspects of military rule: "The military could rule by decree, arrest whom they pleased, abolish political rights and electoral posts. Their acts could not be examined by the courts."*

Brazil

The Brazilian dictator Getúlio Vargas, who had taken power in 1930, was ousted by the army at the close of World War II in 1945. He was elected president again in 1950 and again was ousted by the military, four years later. His successor continued Vargas's policy of industrialization and modernization. He also borrowed heavily from foreign banks to build a splendid new capital in the interior called Brasília.

In 1961 João Goulart became president of Brazil with strong support from the labor movement. The military distrusted Goulart because they believed he sympathized with left-wing causes. Inflation grew and industrialization slowed under Goulart's rule. To improve the economy and head off a threat from the political left, the army overthrew Goulart in 1964.

The military government forced wages down and pressured labor unions to cooperate in the effort to cut production costs. In addition, foreign corporations were encouraged to invest in Brazil. This policy worked. The nation's economy grew so fast that it was called "the Brazilian Miracle." People migrated to the cities to get jobs. However, civil rights were lost amid the economic prosperity. The government suppressed all dissent and banned political parties. It also went heavily into debt. By the late 1980s Brazil had the highest foreign debt of all the developing nations in the world.

A civilian government took office in 1990. President Fernando Collor tried to strengthen the Brazilian economy by reducing government spending, selling state-owned industries to private businesses, and even freezing most savings and checking accounts. His actions, however, pushed Brazil into a recession. Collor resigned in 1992, and his vice president, Itamar Franco, took over. President for 24 months, Franco could not turn the economy around, either. Meanwhile, corruption and crime flourished.

Brazilian president Goulart fled to Uruguay after he was ousted from power in 1964. His overthrow was an example of authoritarian rule replacing democratically elected leaders in South America in the several decades after World War II.

SECTION 4 RESOURCES

REPRODUCIBLE RESOURCES

▶ Guided Reading Strategy 34.4
▶ Readings in World History 122, 124
▶ Creative Teaching Strategy 34: Eye on Latin America

TECHNOLOGY RESOURCES

▶ One-Stop Planner 34.4
▶ Holt Researcher: World History: Eva Perón
▶ World History and Cultures Video Program 29: Brazil's Changing Horizon
▶ CNN Presents Geography: Yesterday and Today Segments 11, 12, 13
▶ World History Teaching Transparency: Everyday Life 29
▶ Homework Practice Online

REINFORCEMENT, REVIEW, AND ASSESSMENT

▶ Section 4 Review, p. 935
▶ Daily Quiz 34.4
▶ Main Idea Activity 34.4
▶ English Audio Summary 34.4
▶ Spanish Audio Summary 34.4

LEVEL 1: Ask students to answer the following questions: How did the Brazilian government improve the country's economy? *(forced wages down and pressured labor unions to cooperate in the effort to cut production costs; foreign corporations were encouraged to invest in Brazil)* To what did the "Brazilian Miracle" refer? *(the rapid growth of the economy)* What drawbacks did this economic prosperity have? *(Civil rights were lost; the government was heavily in debt.)* Why did the economy stumble? *(The actions of Collor pushed the economy into a recession.)* **ENGLISH LANGUAGE LEARNERS**

Interdisciplinary Connection

THE ARTS. Under President Juscelino Kubitschek, one of Vargas's successors, the Brazilian government fostered a new sense of national pride through architecture. He ordered the building of a new capital city in the interior of Brazil. Brasília was dedicated in 1960. Kubitschek hoped that the new capital would open up Brazil's interior to further economic development. The city was a model of modern architecture, with gleaming futuristic buildings that inspired admiration and enthusiasm outside Brazil.

Critical Thinking

Ask students how this new city would foster a sense of national pride in Brazil.

ANSWER: Students should reply that the progressive look of the capital would give Brazilians a sense of pride in their progress.

Brazil's new postwar capital, Brasília, boasts examples of stark modern architecture.

Juan and Eva Perón in a procession through Buenos Aires

Analyzing Primary Sources

Comparing How had Eva Perón changed from 1946 to 1951? *appearance, style, illness*

Holt Researcher

go.hrw.com
KEYWORD: Holt Researcher
FreeFind: Eva Peron
After reading more about Eva Perón on the Holt Researcher, write a magazine article explaining why so many people in Argentina mourned her death.

Then in 1994 Franco's finance minister, **Fernando Henrique Cardoso,** devised economic reforms so successful that in 1995 Cardoso himself went on to become president. Under his government economic production increased and inflation decreased. In the late 1990s changes in world markets challenged Brazil's ability to maintain this economic progress.

✔ **READING CHECK: Identifying Cause and Effect**
How did the state of Brazil's economy affect the nation's politics? *changes in government were based on economic policies*

Argentina

Like Brazil, Argentina had political and economic problems. Yet a powerful, popular woman added a bit of glamour to Argentina's post–World War II difficulties. Her name was **Eva Perón.**

The Peróns. Colonel **Juan Perón** steadily rose to power in Argentina in the 1940s with strong support from lower-class workers and the growing middle class. He became Argentina's president in 1946. Perón, however, was greatly overshadowed by his wife, Eva. "Evita," as she was called, was a former film and radio actress. Through her skillful political use of the media, she developed a huge following and was considered the hero of the working class. Juan Perón held the title of president, but it was Evita who was loved by the people.

The Peróns helped the working class and soon had the support of much of Argentina. With little opposition, they built up a dictatorship. Political dissent was suppressed. By the early 1950s, Argentina had developed many economic troubles. Even so, the adoration for Evita did not wane. In 1951, an ill Eva Perón made a public appearance to decline the nomination of vice president. The following is a description of the event:

> **History Makers Speak**
> ❝The woman who mounted the steps and looked out upon the frenzied crowd was a far cry from the fledgling first lady of 1946, or the glamorous queen of the Rainbow Tour. The blonde curls and gaudy attire had long since given way to what one scholar called 'the streamlined, eternally classic style which was to be hers—and uniquely hers at that time—until her death.' Her hair was pulled back severely, accentuating the growing gauntness of her features. Tears flooded her eyes. She raised her arms in response to the delirium, and a look of uncertainty clouded her expression.❞
>
> *from Péron: A Biography, by Joseph A. Page*

When Evita died of cancer in 1952, Juan Perón lost his greatest political weapon. While Evita's popularity became legendary after her death, Juan's fell dramatically. By 1955 he was forced into exile after a military coup.

For the next 18 years Argentina endured a series of military and civilian governments struggling against both political and economic difficulties. A terrorist campaign waged by leftist guerrillas added to the chaos. By the early 1970s the Argentines had begun to look back fondly on the Perón years as a time of peace and prosperity. Juan Perón seized the opportunity and in 1973 returned from exile. He won a landslide victory and become Argentina's president once more. His third wife, Isabel, was his vice president.

ALL LEVELS: Tell students that in El Salvador, Guatemala, Cuba, Argentina, Brazil, and many other Latin American countries, human rights violations became a matter of course when military rule or harsh authoritarian governments took control. Tell them that it was common practice in many countries to suppress any antigovernment literature or press, to persecute or even assassinate members of rival parties or factions, and to imprison individuals arbitrarily and without trial. This was particularly true of South America; in virtually every South American country at one time or another during the past five decades human rights violations have occurred. Ask students what types of human rights violations occurred in Argentina. *(Political dissent was suppressed; desaparecidos were tortured and killed.)* Ask students, as they read the section, to think about ways to stop such violations and to evaluate South Americans' efforts to do so.

ENGLISH LANGUAGE LEARNERS

Juan Perón immediately set out to wage war against the leftist guerrillas and to improve Argentina's poor economy. He died before he was able to make any progress, however. Isabel succeeded him, becoming the first woman president in the Americas. Her government was incapable of dealing with Argentina's many problems and was overthrown in 1976. The military seized control once again.

Two wars. To end the guerrilla attacks once and for all, the military regime launched an all-out assault on its opponents. The army and police arrested and imprisoned not only opposition leaders but also anyone who criticized the government. As many as 15,000 people or more were taken away in the night and never seen again. Most of these **desaparecidos,** or "disappeared persons," were tortured before being killed. The military government's campaign became known as the "dirty war."

Because of the dirty war, as well as ongoing economic problems, public support for the military government weakened. To regain its popularity, the military decided in 1982 to invade the Falkland Islands off the coast of Argentina. These islands were owned by Great Britain, but Argentina had long laid claim to them. The Argentine military leaders thought the British would not bother to defend them. They anticipated an easy victory that would be popular among the Argentines.

The generals were wrong. The British sent an armada of ships and thousands of soldiers to reclaim the islands. In a matter of weeks, the British had won decisively. The Argentines were embarrassed by the defeat.

A return to democracy. The Falklands defeat was the end of the military government. Free elections were held in 1983, and Raúl Alfonsín was elected president. He promised to bring to justice all those who had been involved in the dirty war. Hundreds of military personnel were put on trial. Three former presidents and several high-ranking officials were convicted. This unkept promise, as well as ongoing economic problems, hurt Alfonsín's party. Its presidential candidate lost the 1989 election.

Carlos Menem became president and faced massive problems. Inflation was high. The country had difficulty making its foreign payments. The threat of still another military takeover was constant. To aid the economy, Menem set wage and price controls and sold state-owned businesses to private owners. To soothe the military, he pardoned many of those found guilty of crimes during the dirty war. This last act angered some Argentines, but Menem was reelected in 1995. His economic policies helped return Argentina to economic growth. Fernando de la Rua became the new president in 1999.

✔ **READING CHECK: Summarizing** What role did the military play in Argentina's recent past? controlled government, dirty war, invaded Falkland Islands, defeated by British

Then & Now

The Falklands
The Falkland Islands have remained an object of dispute for many years. In 1764 and 1765 the French and the British made rival claims to parts of the island group. When British priorities changed, however, the islands were abandoned. Spain also had a small settlement in the island group until 1811. The new nation of Argentina took over in 1820, but in 1833 the British reclaimed the islands, an action the Argentines have long considered to be illegal. This disputed claim of ownership set the stage for the Falkland Islands War of 1982. With the Argentine defeat, the islands remain in British hands. **What ongoing dispute led to the Falkland Islands War?**

Port Howard settlement on East Falkland is one of the two main islands of the Falklands.

Culture

As Eva Perón demonstrated by the power she wielded so effectively in Argentina, Latin American women found new avenues for expressing themselves and becoming involved in politics. Although Evita was not an elected official, most historians agree that she had more power with the public than her husband, the dictator. Similarly, women across the region acted in unofficial roles, alone or in groups, to affect politics and society. After Evita's death, the group calling itself "Las Madres" (the mothers) of the Plaza de Mayo became the conscience of the nation by carrying photos of their relatives who had become *desaparecidos*. Many women organized in movements like this one to make their voices heard.

Critical Thinking

Ask students how effective they think such organized women's movements were.

ANSWER: Students might suggest very effective because, like Evita, women were able to assert indirect power and to influence politics.

THEN & NOW ANSWER
Argentines consider British possession of the islands illegal.

931

LEVEL 3: Organize students into groups and tell them to research the guerrilla groups in Peru known as the Tupac Amarú Revolutionary Movement (MRTA) and Sendero Luminoso (Shining Path). Have students discuss the effects of the groups' terrorism on Peruvian society and include information on their involvement in drug trafficking. Then have groups write brief essays and report their findings to the class.

BLOCK SCHEDULING, COOPERATIVE LEARNING

Culture

The leaders of Latin American countries demonstrate the tremendous diversity of ethnic representation and mixing in the region. Carlos Menem of Argentina is of Arab descent. Brazilian leader Kubitschek has Slavic roots. Guatemala's Kjell Lagerud is of Scandinavian heritage. Chile's Aylwin has British forebears, and his predecessor, Pinochet, comes from French stock. Peruvian leader Fujimori's family emigrated from Japan. Haiti's Aristide and Trinidad's Williams both boast an African heritage.

For centuries, waves of immigrants from all over the world have contributed to the polyglot culture and ethnicity of Latin America. Indeed, contrary to the beliefs of many in the United States, Spanish is not universally spoken throughout Latin America. Rather, 10 principal languages—European, Indian, and African in origin—dominate various areas.

Critical Thinking

Ask students what the ethnic and linguistic diversity of Latin America indicates about the region's history.

ANSWER: Students might suggest that it indicates that the area was subject to many waves of conquest, colonization, and/or immigration; that the various groups value the input of the cultures that contribute to their societies and work to preserve languages and traditions.

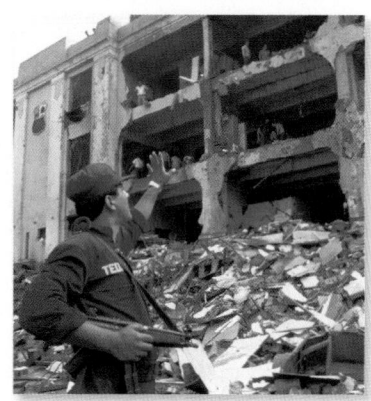

This Peruvian police building was bombed by Shining Path guerrillas protesting government actions.

Peru

Peru was similar to other Latin American nations during this time period. The nation had economic problems—soaring inflation, unemployment, crushing poverty, and increasing foreign debt. It suffered an economic depression in the 1980s. The government was run by either military dictators or conservative civilians. Another threat to democracy in Peru came from communist guerrilla groups that waged war against the government.

Guerrillas. There were two major groups of guerrillas. The Tupac Amarú Revolutionary Movement (its initials are MRTA in Spanish) was an urban group. It bombed public buildings and utility companies in cities and assassinated police and other public officials. A second group, *Sendero Luminoso,* or **Shining Path,** carried out its terrorist campaign in the rural highland areas. Shining Path was a Maoist group. Like Mao Zedong of China, they believed that Peruvian society must be destroyed and a new, socialist society built on its ruins.

Drug trafficking complicated Peru's situation even more. The country is Latin America's leading producer of coca, the plant from which cocaine is made. The MRTA and Shining Path both accepted money and weapons in exchange for helping protect the profitable cocaine business.

Alberto Fujimori. Things began to change in 1990, when the son of a Japanese immigrant was elected president. **Alberto Fujimori** took over a country in chaos. His austere economic measures lowered the astronomically high inflation rate (7,650 percent in 1990) to a manageable level. By the end of 1994, terrorism and violence had also decreased. With a growing economy, Fujimori easily won reelection in 1995.

By mid-1996, however, Fujimori's popularity was on the decline. Economic growth had slowed. Charges of corruption were leveled at his government. Then in December of that year, MRTA guerrillas invaded the Japanese embassy in Lima, Peru. For months, they held people hostage inside. The crisis did not end until April 1997, when Fujimori ordered Peruvian soldiers to storm the embassy. All the guerrillas were killed, along with two soldiers. One hostage died of heart failure. Fujimori's popularity rose again, at least for a time. Then, in November 2000 Fujimori fled the country amid a growing corruption scandal. A few months later the Peruvian congress charged him with crimes against humanity for his involvement with death squads in the early 1990s.

✔ **READING CHECK: Comparing and Contrasting** How did MRTA and Shining Path differ? In what ways were they similar? MRTA: urban, bombed cities; Shining Path: rural terrorists, Maoist; both communist guerrillas

Colombia

Colombia was a nation in turmoil immediately following World War II. A series of military and civilian dictators ruled. Civil strife and economic problems plagued the nation. Fighting between political factions was so intense that Colombians call this time *La Violencia,* meaning "The Violence."

In 1957 the situation was so bad that the two major political parties agreed to form a coalition government. They shared political offices and alternated holding the office of president. By the early 1970s the economy had stabilized. Colombia's future appeared brighter. In fact, the country was considered one of the models of democracy in Latin America.

ALL LEVELS: Tell students to create a flowchart such as the following to illustrate the effects of Columbian drug trade. Ask students if they see any hope of the government regaining order. *(Answers will vary.)* Then ask students how the situation in Columbia affects the United States. *(The United States has worked with the Colombian government to try to break the drug cartels. Also, tons of narcotics originating from the Colombian cartels make their way illegally into the United States each year, so the United States must fight against drug smuggling, selling, and use at home as well.)* **ENGLISH LANGUAGE LEARNERS**

Effects of Colombian Drug Trade

violent rival groups compete to control the drug trade	→	Medellín becomes headquarters of the cartel	→	cartel gains control of law enforcement agencies	→
Colombian authorities declare war on drug cartels; enlist U.S. involvement	→	open street warfare ensues	→	corruption maintains the cartels' power on drug trafficking	→
economic and political problems continue in the late 1990s					

The drug trade. Drugs, however, changed Colombia's fortunes. When illegal drug use in the United States and Europe increased in the 1970s, Colombians realized they could make money growing marijuana and coca. Drug producers and dealers began making huge profits. More and more marijuana and coca were grown. As rival groups tried to control the drug trade, violence and crime soared. The industrial city of Medellín became the headquarters of the Medellín cartel, a group that ran the Colombian drug trade. The cartel used assassination and other threats to gain control of law enforcement agencies. Lower-level officials were bribed or threatened until they cooperated with the cartel.

Adding to Colombia's problems were terrorist campaigns waged by both political sides. Left-wing groups such as M-19 kidnapped and sometimes murdered public officials. Right-wing death squads, many connected with the army, killed people who sympathized with the leftists. Politically and economically motivated murder and intimidation became commonplace in Colombia. Behind this political violence stood the drug lords, who financed it.

The war on drugs. In the late 1980s Colombian authorities declared war on the drug cartels. They asked U.S. law officers and the military to help them. They also promised to turn over to the United States any drug traffickers they captured. The result was open warfare on the streets of Medellín and Cali, headquarters of another drug cartel.

Despite efforts by the government to end drug trafficking, it continued into the 1990s. By 1995 the Cali cartel was believed to control perhaps 70 percent of the world trade in cocaine. Part of the problem was extensive corruption, as drug lords continued to funnel large sums of money in the form of "campaign contributions" into the hands of selected political leaders. Colombian president Ernesto Samper himself was accused of having accepted millions of dollars from the Cali cartel for his 1994 election campaign. In 1996 the Colombian legislature considered impeaching Samper, but chose not to.

Colombia's economic and political problems continued into the late 1990s. In June 1998 Andrés Pastrana Arango succeeded Samper as president.

✔ **READING CHECK: Summarizing** How did the Colombian drug cartels affect the government? used threats and bribes to control law enforcement

Economics

By the 1980s a dangerous new problem had arisen in Latin America—the enormous expansion of the illegal drug trade. Some experts have estimated that the drug trade was worth over $110 billion by the mid-1980s. Peru, Bolivia, Colombia, and Mexico became major producers of narcotics, from marijuana to cocaine and heroin.

Critical Thinking

Ask students why they think some Latin American countries have become heavily involved in the drug trade.

ANSWER: Students might suggest that economic problems make many citizens of these Latin American countries eager to earn money, even if it is by selling illegal drugs. Students might also suggest that the unstable governments have difficulty stopping the drug dealers, so the trade persists.

Colombian drug enforcement officers patrol fields and destroy illegal crops.

LEVEL 1: Ask students how Pinochet strengthened the economy of Chile. *(allowed it to operate under free-market forces of supply and demand; increased foreign investment)* Then ask students the following questions: How did Pinochet respond to civil unrest? *(with repressive measures; eventually allowed elections and stepped down)* Despite a continuously strong economy, with what problems did Chile struggle? *(poverty and widespread pollution)*

ENGLISH LANGUAGE LEARNERS

Ask students to list the major challenges confronting the countries of South America.

Geography

Many people around the world are concerned about the rate of deforestation in South America—particularly in Brazil, which is dominated by the vast Amazon rain forest. Although Brazilian leaders share concerns for the environment, the issue is more complex for them than simply stopping the deforestation. In recent years, the rain forest has been opened to clearing and settlement by over half a million landless poor in Brazil, who have gratefully claimed the land to farm. Although the soil is soon exhausted under farming, to people who have nothing, the rain forest opens opportunities they otherwise would not have. Respected Brazilian environmentalist Jacques Marcovitch summed up the situation eloquently when he said, "You can not talk about ecology to people who are struggling to survive." Brazilian leaders are seeking strategies for development that are both economically productive and environmentally sound.

Critical Thinking

Ask students if they agree with Marcovitch's assessment of the situation, and why.

ANSWER: Students' responses will vary.

MAP ANSWERS

1. Paraguay

2. nations in the northern region

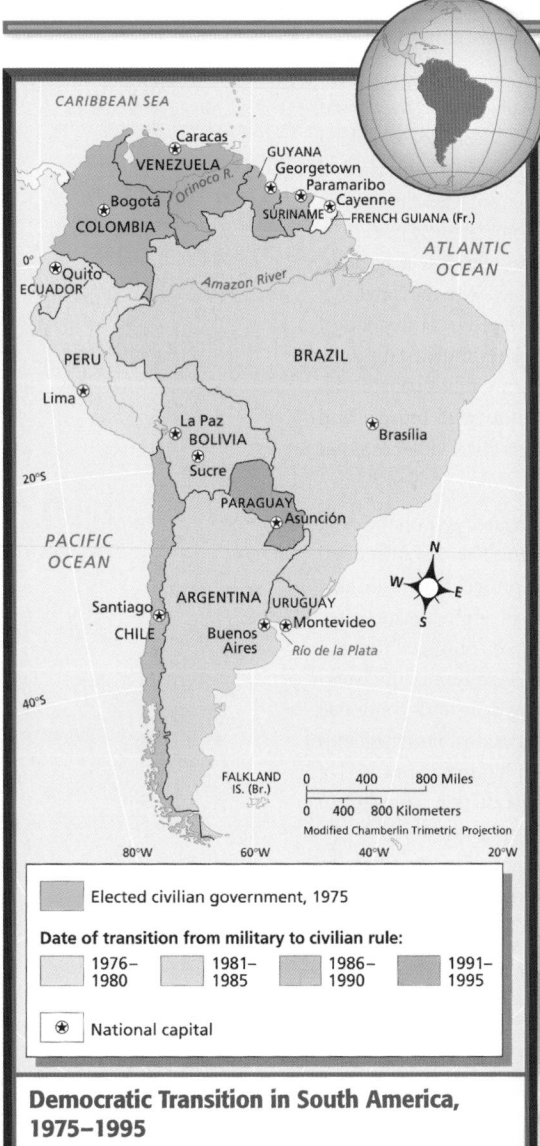

Elected civilian government, 1975

Date of transition from military to civilian rule:
1976–1980 1981–1985 1986–1990 1991–1995

⊛ National capital

Democratic Transition in South America, 1975–1995

Interpreting Maps During the postwar period, many South American countries underwent military coups. Beginning in 1975, however, the nations gradually moved from military to civilian rule.

Skills Assessment: 1. Human Systems What was the last South American country to end military rule? **2. Making Generalizations** In general, which nations first adopted civilian rule?

Chile

Chile had long been noted as a model of stable democracy in Latin America. In the 1970s and 1980s, that changed. In 1970 Chileans elected **Salvador Allende** as president. Allende was the first Marxist to come to power peacefully in the Western Hemisphere. As a socialist, Allende nationalized the country's copper mines and other industries, broke up large estates, and increased wages across the board. His more radical followers seized farms and factories. Before long the Chilean economy was in a dramatic decline, and food shortages had spread. Hard pressed for funds, Allende's government printed more money to meet its needs. By 1972 inflation was rampant. All segments of the Chilean population suffered.

As the economy worsened, discontent and unrest spread. In 1973 military leaders who opposed Allende overthrew the government, with the support of the United States. Allende died in the bloody coup.

Once in control, the military worked quickly to crush opposition. The government jailed or executed many who had opposed the coup. Fearing for their lives, thousands fled into exile. The leader of the coup, **Augusto Pinochet,** dissolved the national legislature, outlawed all political parties, and restricted civil liberties.

The beauty and geographic diversity of Chile is illustrated in this striking image of the Torres del Paine National Park.

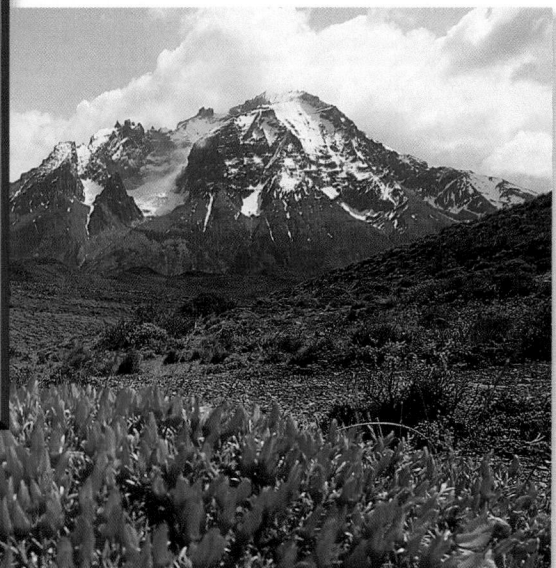

REVIEW

Have students complete the Section 4 Review on p. 935.

ASSESS

Have students complete Daily Quiz 34.4. As Alternative Assessment, you may want to use the flowchart exercise in this section's lessons.

RETEACH

Have students complete Main Idea Activity for English Language Learners and Special-Needs Students 34.4. Then ask them to cre-

ate a chapter glossary that includes the vocabulary and significant people, places, and events from the section.
ENGLISH LANGUAGE LEARNERS

EXTEND

Have interested students select a piece of Latin American art to analyze, for example, a painting, story, or poem. Then have students write three to five paragraphs evaluating the work, explaining its themes, and pointing out what it implies about society or politics in its creator's country. **BLOCK SCHEDULING**

Pinochet also ended all government interference in the nation's economy. He allowed it to operate under free-market forces of supply and demand. The high inflation that was common under Allende declined significantly, but unemployment rose. During the early 1980s unemployment ranged at or near 20 percent throughout Chile. At the same time, however, increased foreign investment helped Pinochet's economic program to take hold. By the late 1980s prosperity had returned to Chile.

Even so, civil unrest plagued the country. Pinochet responded with repressive measures. Then, to strengthen his hold on power, he called for a plebiscite, or special vote, in 1988 to determine whether he should remain in power. Pinochet expected to win, but nearly 55 percent of the voters called for him to step down. Accepting defeat, Pinochet set an election for 1989. A coalition candidate, Patricio Aylwin Azócar, was elected president. Pinochet, however, remained in control of Chile's army until 1998.

The nation's economy continued to grow under Aylwin Azócar and his successor, Eduardo Frei Ruiz-Tagle. Although the nation struggled with poverty and widespread pollution, the Chilean economy grew for 14 straight years and became one of the strongest in Latin America. In January 2000 Ricardo Lagos Escobar, a socialist, became president. He was the nation's first socialist president since Allende. Two years earlier Pinochet had been arrested in Great Britain on charges of torture and human rights abuses. A Chilean court found Pinochet unfit to stand trial, however, and few people expected that the aging former dictator would ever be tried for his role in violating the rights of his people.

Salvador Allende (top) was killed in a military coup that brought Augusto Pinochet (below) to power.

✔ **READING CHECK: Analyzing Information** What measures helped make the Chilean economy one of the most prosperous in Latin America? end of government interference, free-market forces, foreign investment

SECTION 4 REVIEW

1. **Define** and explain the significance: desaparecidos

2. **Identify** and explain the significance:
   Fernando Henrique Cardoso
   Eva Perón
   Juan Perón
   Shining Path
   Alberto Fujimori
   Salvador Allende
   Augusto Pinochet

3. **Sequencing** Copy the chart below. Complete it to show the order of Brazil's leaders and the dates they took power.

Leader	Leader	Leader	Leader
Jaõa Goulart			Fernando Cardoso
Year	Year	Year	Year
1961			1994

4. **Finding the Main Idea**
   a. Why did the Argentine military's "dirty war" occur?
   b. What did MRTA and Shining Path hope to achieve in Peru?
   c. What role did Augusto Pinochet play in recent Chilean history?

5. **Writing and Critical Thinking**
   Identifying Cause and Effect Imagine you are a reporter. Write an article detailing the reasons for and the effects of the drug trade in Colombia.
   Consider:
   • why Colombians started growing crops for drugs
   • what has happened in Colombia as a result
   • how the Colombian government has been affected

Homework Practice Online
keyword: SP3 HP34

SECTION 4 REVIEW ANSWERS

❶ **Define**
• desaparecidos, p. 931

❷ **Identify**
• Fernando Henrique Cardoso, p. 930
• Eva Perón, p. 930
• Juan Perón, p. 930
• Shining Path, p. 932
• Alberto Fujimori, p. 932
• Salvador Allende, p. 934
• Augusto Pinochet, p. 934

❸ Fernando Collor, 1990; Itamar Franco, 1992

❹ a. The military launched an all-out assault on its opponents to end guerrilla attacks.

b. the destruction of Peruvian society and a new socialist society built on its ruins

c. led a coup; brought economic prosperity; charged with human rights abuses

❺ Students' articles will vary.

REVIEW AND ASSESSMENT RESOURCES

REPRODUCIBLE RESOURCES
▶ Vocabulary Activity 34

TECHNOLOGY RESOURCES
▶ Chapter 34 Test Generator (on the One-Stop Planner)
▶ Global Skill Builder CD–ROM
▶ HRW Web Site

REINFORCEMENT, REVIEW, and ASSESSMENT
▶ Chapter 34 Review, pp. 936–937
▶ Chapter 34 Tutorial for Students, Parents, Mentors, and Peers
▶ Chapter 34 Test (Form A or B)
▶ Alternate Assessment Handbook
▶ Chapter 34 Test for English Language Learners and Special-Needs Students

REVIEW
Have students complete the Chapter 34 Review on pages 936–937.

ASSESS
Use one of the chapter tests to assess students' understanding of the content. For Alternative Assessment, see the Portfolio Activities and Alternative Assessment Handbook.

CHAPTER 34 REVIEW ANSWERS

Understanding Main Ideas

1. women: fought against military dictatorships and abuses of human rights; workers: organized into unions, fought for better working conditions by striking; the church: supported political change, fought for social justice against oppressive economic and political systems

2. large debt, inflation, wage controls

3. Mexicans entered the United States illegally to look for work.

4. upper classes had most of the wealth; number of poor landless farm workers grew

5. Puerto Rico: democracy; Cuba: under communist rule

6. dictatorship, coups, political violence, energy crisis, unemployment, inflation, suspension of international aid

7. successes: helped the working class; failures: political dissent suppressed, economic troubles

8. poor economy; terrorist campaigns, violence, corruption

Reviewing Themes

1. Poor economies led to political instability.

2. suppression of dissent; torture; sometimes murder

3. to prevent spread of communism and to protect its interests in the region

---

CHAPTER 34 Review

Creating a Time Line
Copy the time line below onto a sheet of paper. Complete the time line by filling in the events, individuals, and dates from the chapter that you think were significant. Pick three events and explain why you think they were significant.

| 1945 | 1975 | present |

Writing a Summary
Using standard grammar, spelling, sentence structure, and punctuation, write an overview of the events in the chapter.

Identifying People and Ideas
Identify the following terms or individuals and explain their significance:

1. monoculture
2. NAFTA
3. Sandinistas
4. contras
5. Oscar Arias
6. Fidel Castro
7. Operation Bootstrap
8. Eva Perón
9. desaparecidos
10. Augusto Pinochet

Understanding the Main Ideas

SECTION 1 (pp. 910–914)
Facing New Challenges
1. What political forces emerged in Latin America after World War II, and how did they affect each region?
2. What economic struggles did the nations face after World War II?

SECTION 2 (pp. 915–921)
Mexico and Central America
3. How did Mexico's economic problems affect emigration?
4. How was wealth distributed in Central America? Who had it and who did not have it?

SECTION 3 (pp. 922–928)
Nations of the Caribbean
5. How have Cuba and Puerto Rico differed since World War II?
6. What economic and political problems have affected Haiti and the Dominican Republic since World War II?

SECTION 4 (pp. 929–935)
South America
7. What were the successes and failures of Juan Perón's first presidency?
8. What caused the Colombian drug trade to increase, and how did it affect the country?

Reviewing Themes
1. **Economics** How did poor economic conditions affect political events in Latin America?
2. **Government** What methods did Latin American dictators use to retain their control of a country?
3. **Global Relations** Why has the United States sometimes gotten involved in Latin American political situations?

Thinking Critically
1. **Identifying Cause and Effect** What caused the general population increase in Latin America, and what were its consequences?
2. **Comparing and Contrasting** How were the revolutions in Cuba and Nicaragua similar? How were they different?
3. **Problem Solving** How did Fidel Castro deal with the large number of dissidents in Cuba? Was this a successful approach?
4. **Evaluating** What economic reforms seemed to work best in Latin America? Which seemed to be least effective?

Writing About History
Evaluating Violeta Barrios de Chamorro declared amnesty for many involved in the Nicaraguan civil war. Carlos Menem in Argentina pardoned many of those found guilty of crimes during his country's "dirty war." Write an essay analyzing the effects of these actions and whether they were proper given the historical context. Use the following chart to organize your thoughts before you begin writing.

	Negative	Positive
Effects of amnesty/ pardons		

CLOSE

Ask students to describe the results of the United States involvement in Nicaragua, Cuba, and the Dominican Republic.

RETEACH

Pair students who have had difficulty with the test. Have each pair outline the chapter and compile a chapter glossary. From the outline and glossary, have the pair create flash cards and quiz each other on the chapter content. Then have students take the

Form B Test to assess their mastery of the material. **ENGLISH LANGUAGE LEARNERS**

Portfolio Extensions

1. Tell students that although the Brazilian economy grew rapidly in the 1960 and 1970s, many Brazilians still lived in poverty. Have students find out about living conditions in the slums and present an oral report to the class.

2. Organize students into groups to find more information on how the nations of Latin America are dealing with low rates of economic growth, high rates of unemployment and population growth, and burgeoning foreign debts. Then students should use the information they have collected to prepare a panel discussion detailing possible solutions to these problems.

Building Social Studies Skills

Interpreting a Chart

Study the chart below. Then use the information to answer the questions that follow.

Populations of Selected Latin American Nations, 2003

Nation	Population, 2003 (est.)	Population Growth Rate (est.)
Argentina	38.7	+1.0%
Brazil	182.0	+1.1%
Chile	15.7	+1.0%
Mexico	104.9	+1.4%
Peru	28.4	+1.6%

(All figures are projected, shown in millions, rounded to nearest 100,000)

1. Which statement is most accurate based on the information in the chart?
  a. Peru is the fastest-growing nation in Latin America.
  b. Chile is growing at a faster rate than is Peru.
  c. Brazil's population is more than twice as large as Mexico's population.
  d. Not all the nations shown experienced increased population growth between 2000 and 2001.

2. What impact might population growth in Latin America have on the developing economies of the region? Give specific examples.

Identifying a Point of View

Read the following quote by anthropologist Jason Clay about indigenous—or native—people living in Brazil. Then answer the questions.

> "Modern technology in the form of helicopters, satellite surveys, and telecommunications equipment has enabled states and corporations to make detailed surveys of the Earth. Even the most isolated indigenous societies are now being probed in a one-sided, involuntary exposure to the rest of the world. . . . For example, in late 1987 gold was found on the lands of the 8,000 forest-dwelling Yanomami Indians of northern Brazil. Within eight months nearly 30,000 Brazilian prospectors had invaded the region to seek their fortunes."

3. Which of the following statements best describes the author's point of view?
  a. He is against the use of helicopters, satellite surveys, and telecommunications equipment.
  b. He does not like the fact that modern society is destroying the land and lifestyles of indigenous people.
  c. He is against states and corporations surveying the Earth.
  d. He thinks Brazil allowed too many prospectors into the region where the Yanomami live.

4. Why might the Brazilian government have a viewpoint different from the author's concerning indigenous people? Give specific reasons.

Alternative Assessment

Building Your Portfolio

Government

Political power has changed hands frequently in Latin America. Using your textbook and other sources, find out how many governments in the region came to power from coups or revolutions, whether these governments are secure, and if any are dictatorships. Make a chart that shows the nations, their leaders, how they gained power, and whether or not they are dictatorships.

internet connect

Internet Activity: go.hrw.com
KEYWORD: SP3 WH34

Choose a topic on Latin America Since 1945 to:
• learn about current events in Latin America.
• analyze Mexico's political choices and decisions since 1945 and how they are reflected in Mexico today.
• research current statistics on per capita gross domestic product, major exports, and major imports of Mexico, Honduras, El Salvador, Belize, Costa Rica, Nicaragua, and Haiti. Create a database for comparison.

Thinking Critically

1. industrialization; consequences: slums, disease, environmental damage

2. similar: violent overthrow of government; different: Nicaragua eventually held elections while Cuba did not

3. repressed it; students may answer yes because he is still in power

4. Gradual reform and free market economies seemed to work best. Rapid industrialization, which led to huge debt and government-controlled economies, was least effective.

Writing About History
Students' essays will vary.

Building Social Studies Skills
1. a

2. Students might answer that it could hinder growth because of high unemployment and shortages of goods.

3. b

4. Students might answer that such activities bring wealth to the region.

Building Your Portfolio
Students' charts will vary.

CHAPTER
35

The Superpowers in the Modern Era

CHAPTER RESOURCE MANAGER

Objectives	Pacing Guide	Reproducible Resources
SECTION 1 **The Industrial Powers of North America** (pp. 940–947) • Explore how the Vietnam War and the Watergate scandal affected political attitudes in the United States. • Analyze the changes that have occurred in the economy of the United States since 1970. • Explain how American foreign policy changed in the 1970s, 1980s, and 1990s. • Identify the major challenges Canada faced in the late 1900s.	**Regular** 1.5 day / **Block Scheduling** 1 day *Block Scheduling Handbook with Team Teaching Strategies, 35.1*	RS Guided Reading Strategy 35.1 RS Graphic Organizer Activity 35 SM Geography Activity 35 PS Readings in World History 125, 134, 137 E Hands-on History Activity 35
SECTION 2 **Europe** (pp. 948–955) • Describe how Margaret Thatcher's leadership affected Britain. • Explain the challenges European nations faced in the late 1900s. • Identify the steps European nations took toward unity in the late 1900s.	**Regular** 1.5 day / **Block Scheduling** 1 day *Block Scheduling Handbook with Team Teaching Strategies, 35.2*	RS Guided Reading Strategy 35.2 PS Readings in World History 126: A Child of the Troubles PS Readings in World History 131: The Opening of the Berlin Wall
SECTION 3 **The Fall of Communism** (pp. 956–963) • Explain what events led to the fall of the Soviet Union. • Explore how Russia fared under Boris Yeltsin. • Describe how Eastern Europe was affected by the fall of communism.	**Regular** 1.5 day / **Block Scheduling** 1 day *Block Scheduling Handbook with Team Teaching Strategies, 35.3*	RS Guided Reading Strategy 35.3 PS Readings in World History 127: Glasnost and Journalism PS Readings in World History 128: The Communist Roller Coaster PS Readings in World History 133: Russia After Communism
SECTION 4 **A Day That Changed the World** (pp. 964–969) • Explain how the United States was attacked on September 11, 2001, and how people responded. • Describe how the events of September 11, 2001, affected the U.S. economy. • List the immediate steps that U.S. leaders and their allies took to find those responsible for the attacks and bring them to justice.	**Regular** 1.5 day / **Block Scheduling** 1 day *Block Scheduling Handbook with Team Teaching Strategies, 35.4*	RS Guided Reading Strategy 35.4 E Creative Teaching Strategy 35: Emergency Response Team

Chapter Resource Key

PS Primary Sources	A Assessment	Music	
RS Reading Support	REV Review	Video	
IC Interdisciplinary Connections	ELL Reinforcement and English Language Learners	Internet	
E Enrichment	Transparencies	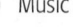 Holt Presentation Maker Using Microsoft® PowerPoint®	
SM Skills Mastery	CD-ROM		

 One-Stop Planner CD-ROM

See the **One-Stop Planner** for a complete list of additional resources for students and teachers.

One-Stop Planner CD-ROM

It's easy to plan lessons, select resources, and print out materials for your students when you use the **One-Stop Planner** CD–ROM with **Test Generator.**

Technology Resources

 One-Stop Planner 35.1

 Holt Researcher: World History: George W. Bush

 World History and Cultures Video Program 30: A New Era

 Regions of the World Music Audio CD Program 2: Canada: Folk Songs of France and French Canada

 World History Teaching Transparency: Regional and World Map 31: The United States and Canada

 Homework Practice Online

 One-Stop Planner 35.2

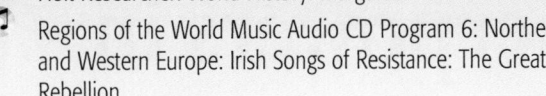 Holt Researcher: World History: Margaret Thatcher

 Regions of the World Music Audio CD Program 6: Northern and Western Europe: Irish Songs of Resistance: The Great Rebellion

 World History Teaching Transparency: Regional and World Maps 33: Europe

Homework Practice Online

 One-Stop Planner 35.3

 Holt Researcher: World History: Mikhail Gorbachev

 Regions of the World Music Audio CD Program 9

 CNN Presents World Cultures: Yesterday and Today Segment 36

 CNN Presents Geography: Yesterday and Today Segments 1, 17, 19

Homework Practice Online

 One-Stop Planner 35.4

 World History Teaching Transparency: Regional and World Maps 35: Southwest Asia

 Homework Practice Online

 Online Maps, Charts, and Graphs: Southwest Asia

Reinforcement, Review, and Assessment

Daily Quiz 35.1

Main Idea Activity 35.1

English Audio Summary 35.1

Spanish Audio Summary 35.1

REV Section 1 Review, p. 947

Daily Quiz 35.2

Main Idea Activity 35.2

English Audio Summary 35.2

Spanish Audio Summary 35.2

REV Section 2 Review, p. 955

Daily Quiz 35.3

Main Idea Activity 35.3

English Audio Summary 35.3

Spanish Audio Summary 35.3

REV Section 3 Review, p. 963

Daily Quiz 35.4

Main Idea Activity 35.4

English Audio Summary 35.4

Spanish Audio Summary 35.4

REV Section 4 Review, p. 969

Meeting Individual Needs

Ability Levels

Level 1   Basic level activities designed for all students encountering new material

Level 2   Intermediate level activities designed for average students

Level 3   Challenging activities designed for honors and gifted and talented students

English Language Learners   These activities address the needs of students with Limited English Proficiency.

Chapter Review and Assessment

IC   Vocabulary Activity 35

 Global Skill Builder CD–ROM

 HRW Web Site

REV   Chapter 35 Tutorial for Students, Parents, Mentors, and Peers

REV   Chapter 35 Review, pp. 970–971

A   Chapter 35 Test Generator (on the One-Stop Planner)

A   Chapter 35 Test (Form A or B)

A   Alternative Assessment Handbook

A   Chapter 35 Test for English Language Learners and Special-Needs Students

Build on What You Know

Ask students to answer the following questions:

What were some of the postwar conflicts in the Middle East?

Consider:

- the Arab-Israeli Confrontation
- the Iranian Revolution
- the Gulf War

What were some of the challenges faced by postwar Latin America?

Consider:

- economic instability
- population growth and poverty
- environmental problems

EXPLORING THE TIME LINE

GLOBAL EVENTS

internet connect

TOPIC: Space Program 1969–2001

GO TO: go.hrw.com

KEYWORD: SP3 WH35

Have students access the Internet through the HRW Go site to research the history of the Space Program from 1969 to the present. Have each student develop a time line of the important events and missions during this time period and record them into a log. Ask him/her to choose at least 2 (or more) missions and at least 5 of the discoveries as the most important. The student should be prepared to discuss why he/she thinks these are the most significant.

CHAPTER

35

1969–Present

The Superpowers in the Modern Era

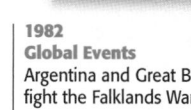

Apollo *and* **Soyuz** *crew members during docking.*

1970
Politics
National Guard troops fire on students protesting the Vietnam War at Kent State University.

1973
Global Events
U.S. combat troops withdraw from Vietnam.

1973
Business and Finance
An OPEC oil embargo leads to a U.S. energy crisis.

1976
Daily Life
The United States celebrates its bicentennial.

c. 1978
The Arts
"Disco" music and dancing are popular.

1980
Politics
Ronald Reagan becomes president of the United States.

1982
Global Events
Argentina and Great Britain fight the Falklands War.

1970

1980

1970
The Arts
Russian writer Aleksandr Solzhenitsyn wins the Nobel Prize for literature.

1972
Politics
The Watergate break-in occurs.

1975
Science and Technology
The *Apollo* and *Soyuz* spacecraft dock in orbit.

1974
Politics
Richard Nixon resigns as U.S. president.

c. 1979
Global Events
Diplomatic relations officially open between China and the United States.

1979
Politics
Margaret Thatcher becomes prime minister of Great Britain.

Vietnam War Memorial

President Richard M. Nixon

Build on What You Know

As the nations of Latin America struggled to develop their economies after World War II, they endured political upheaval. In this chapter, you will learn how the final decades of the 1900s were also turbulent times in the industrialized nations of North America and Europe. The Soviet Union, formerly one of the world's superpowers, dissolved into separate states. The nations of Western Europe moved closer toward union, and the fall of communism reawakened ethnic divisions in Eastern Europe. The United States and Canada confronted challenges at home.

What's Your Opinion?

Themes Journal

To help students create their Themes Journal entries, provide the following examples of appropriate **agree**/**disagree** *statements.*

Economics

Agree In a fair and just society, wealth is shared equally by all citizens.

Disagree A society is typically more stable if it has multiple economic classes and an unequal distribution of wealth.

Government

Agree A nation's strength is measured by the amount of control it is able to exert over its citizens.

Disagree Citizens should not be subjected to a government that exerts strong control over their lives.

Global Relations

Agree It is good for a weak nation to be dominated by a stronger nation. The weaker nation will experience progress and improvement.

Disagree It is not permissible for a nation to dominate another nation, even if it is for the weaker nation's own good.

Russian president Boris Yeltsin at a Moscow rally, 1993

Newspaper headline announcing the election of George W. Bush

1991
Global Events
The Soviet Union dissolves.

1991
Global Events
The United States leads the Persian Gulf War against Iraq.

1986
Science and Technology
The Chernobyl nuclear accident occurs in the Soviet Union.

1992
Politics
Bill Clinton becomes the president of the United States.

1995
Science and Technology
The U.S. space shuttle *Atlantis* docks with the Russian space station *Mir*.

2001
Politics
George W. Bush becomes president of the United States after a disputed election.

1990

2000

1990
Global Events
East and West Germany reunite.

1993
Business and Finance
The nations of the European Economic Community implement the Maastricht Treaty, ending trade barriers.

2001
Global Events
On September 11, terrorists attack the World Trade Center and the Pentagon.

New York City's Manhattan Island following the terrorist attack on September 11, 2001

What's Your Opinion?

Themes Journal

Do you **agree** *or* **disagree** *with the following statements? Support your point of view in your journal.*

Economics Wealth should be shared equally by all members of a society.

Government A nation that maintains strong government control over the people is a strong nation.

Global Relations It is permissible to dominate another country for its own good.

OBJECTIVES

1 **Explore how the Vietnam War and the Watergate scandal affected political attitudes in the United States.**

2 **Analyze the changes that have occurred in the economy of the United States since 1970.**

3 **Explain how American foreign policy changed in the 1970s, 1980s, and 1990s.**

4 **Identify the major challenges Canada faced in the late 1900s.**

🔔 LET'S GET STARTED!

As students enter the classroom, have each student write on a sheet of paper what he or she considers to be the five biggest problems or issues facing the United States today. Call on students to read their lists to the class, and write these responses on the chalkboard. Tell students that in Section 1 they will learn about issues that affected the United States in the late 1900s.

SECTION 1

READ TO DISCOVER

❶ How did the Vietnam War and the Watergate scandal affect political attitudes in the United States?

❷ What changes have occurred in the economy of the United States since 1970?

❸ How did American foreign policy change in the 1970s, 1980s, and 1990s?

❹ What major challenges did Canada face in the late 1900s?

DEFINE

détente
weapons of mass destruction

IDENTIFY

Richard Nixon
Vietnamization
Watergate scandal
Jimmy Carter
Ronald Reagan
Iran-contra affair
Bill Clinton
George W. Bush
Carter Doctrine
Pierre Trudeau
Meech Lake Accord

▶ WHY IT MATTERS TODAY

Watergate was only one scandal to affect American presidents in recent times. Use CNNews.com or other **current event** sources to find out about investigations the U.S. Congress conducted during the Reagan and Clinton administrations. Record your findings in your journal.

CNN student News.com

The Industrial Powers of North America

The Main Idea
The United States and Canada faced challenging political, economic, and foreign policy issues in the 1970s, 1980s, and 1990s.

The Story Continues *"Our constitution works. Our great republic is a government of laws and not of men. Here the people rule."* With these words, President Gerald Ford tried to renew the American people's faith in their government following a national scandal. The next few decades would see the United States confront other challenges both within and outside its borders.

Ending the Vietnam War

The war in Vietnam was still raging when Republican **Richard Nixon** became President in 1969. Hoping to avoid complete defeat, Nixon searched for ways to end America's involvement in the conflict "with honor."

Nixon planned to withdraw American forces from Vietnam. In a process called **Vietnamization,** he planned for the South Vietnamese to take over the fighting as American troops gradually withdrew. By 1973 there were only about 40,000 American troops left in Vietnam. At the same time Nixon used military pressure to force communist leaders to accept peace on American terms. He ordered the invasion of Cambodia in 1970 and increased the bombing of North Vietnam. On January 27, 1973, communist leaders accepted an agreement called the Paris Peace Accords. This agreement stated that all U.S. and allied forces would leave Vietnam in exchange for the release of all prisoners of war. Within months all major combat units were back home, although some troops remained until 1975.

The Vietnam War had a negative impact on the United States. It cost many lives and strained the nation's economy. Moreover, communist forces won control of South Vietnam in 1975. Thus the United States failed to achieve its main goal in the war—preventing the unification of a communist Vietnam.

The war also divided the American people. During the Nixon administration the antiwar movement gained strength. Actions such as the invasion of Cambodia appeared

to contradict Nixon's promise to end the war. Demonstrations against the war at college campuses became common. Some of these protests turned violent or even deadly. In 1970 National Guard troops fired on students at Kent State University in Ohio, killing four people. Eleven days later two more students were killed in a protest at Jackson State

The image of young woman crying over the body of a student killed at Kent State University expressed the horror of the event.

TEACH OBJECTIVE 1

LEVEL 1: Ask students why the United States sought to end its involvement in Vietnam. *(The war was unpopular with many Americans, and it was also economically burdensome. President Nixon also hoped to avoid outright defeat.)* Then ask students to classify the effects the Vietnam War had on American society by writing them in a chart under the following headings: *Economy, Society, Global Influence. (Economy: burdensome to the United States; Society: inflicted heavy human toll, divided the American people, led to violent antiwar protests, led Americans to distrust the government leaders; Global Influence: indicated failure of the United States as a leading power)*
ENGLISH LANGUAGE LEARNERS

College in Mississippi. The government's claims of success in Vietnam proved to be exaggerated. Many Americans began to question the trustworthiness of their leaders.

✔ **READING CHECK: Problem Solving** How did Nixon attempt to end American involvement in Vietnam? withdraw troops

Watergate and Its Legacy

After Vietnam many Americans had become disillusioned with their government. This situation worsened as a result of a major political scandal involving President Nixon.

In 1972 burglars were caught breaking into the headquarters of the Democratic National Committee at the Watergate hotel in Washington, D.C. The *Washington Post* newspaper charged that officials of President Nixon's reelection campaign had planned the break-in. A U.S. Senate investigation revealed that an illegal secret fund had been used to conceal the burglary's connection to high-level White House aides. It soon became clear that Nixon had known about and approved this cover-up. Facing impeachment by Congress, Nixon resigned his office in August of 1974. His vice president, Gerald R. Ford, took power.

The **Watergate scandal** shook many Americans' faith in their government. President Ford's decision to pardon Nixon did not help restore public confidence. As a result of Watergate, many people began to associate Washington politics with dishonesty and corruption. To combat this perception several candidates for the presidency after Watergate campaigned as "outsiders" with no ties to Washington. They promised to clean up corruption in the political system. In 1976 Democrat **Jimmy Carter,** a former governor of Georgia, was elected president. Carter proved to be a man of high integrity, but his presidency was troubled. The U.S. economy remained sluggish, and Carter suffered setbacks in foreign policy. In 1979 Muslim militants seized the American embassy in Iran, leading to a lengthy hostage crisis.

In 1980 Carter lost to another Washington outsider—conservative Republican **Ronald Reagan,** the former governor of California. Reagan's optimistic slogans lifted the spirits of many Americans, helping him win reelection in 1984. However, during Reagan's second term a scandal known as the **Iran-contra affair** came to public attention. Members of Reagan's National Security Council staff had arranged the sale of weapons to Iran in exchange for the release of U.S. hostages in Lebanon. Money from these sales was then used to fund Nicaraguan rebels called contras, against the wishes of Congress.

CONNECTING TO
Art

Architecture: The Vietnam Veterans Memorial

The Vietnam Veterans Memorial was dedicated in 1982 to help heal the divisions over the war. It was designed by a 21-year-old student at Yale University named Maya Ying Lin. Her design, comprised of two long black granite walls that rise out of the earth and meet at an angle, contains the names of the 58,000 Americans who died in the war. Lin decided the wall should be black granite, because black is the traditional color of mourning in the United States. The monument is located near the Constitutional Gardens on the Mall in Washington, D.C.

Understanding the Arts

What kind of mood does the Vietnam Veterans Memorial convey?

At left, a man reads names of fallen soldiers inscribed on the Vietnam Veterans Memorial. Shown above is a close-up of the wall.

Global Relations

Many Americans believed the United States should not have been fighting in Vietnam. This pervasive belief continued to have an influence on foreign policy. Former Defense Secretary James Schlesinger concurred with thoughts on foreign policy written by General Bruce Palmer in his book on the Vietnam War. Schlesinger quoted from Palmer's book: ". . . our failure in Vietnam lay in the simple fact that the United States had lost the battle for international opinion. . . . one might also trace the erosion of public and congressional support."

Critical Thinking

Ask students how public opinion could affect foreign policy.

ANSWER: Students may suggest popular opinion against the war could cause dissension and disunity.

CONNECTING TO ART ANSWER

Students may suggest somber due to the black granite and stark list of names inscribed on the wall.

Reproducible **Resources**

PS   Readings in World History 134: Young Americans in Vietnam

ALL LEVELS : Ask students to explain how the Watergate scandal unfolded. *(Burglars broke into the Democratic National Committee headquarters; they were found to be acting under orders from President Nixon's re-election campaign leaders; the Senate discovered that Nixon's White House staff had concealed the incident's connection to the president; it was learned that Nixon knew about the cover-up.)* Then ask students to sum up how the Watergate scandal affected Americans' political attitudes. *(It shook the faith many Americans had in the political system; people began to believe that politicians lacked integrity; and people lost confidence in the government.)* Then have students write a response to the Water-

gate scandal, as if they had lived through this difficult period in American history. Students may choose their own form of written response, such as a letter to the president or Congress, an editorial, or an essay. **ENGLISH LANGUAGE LEARNERS**

Government

Soon after Ford took office, he gave Nixon "a full, free, and absolute pardon." Many Americans, however, did not agree with this decision. Ford believed that he had done the right thing. His popularity decreased dramatically, and he lost his bid for re-election in 1976.

Critical Thinking

Ask students if they agree with Ford's decision to pardon Nixon, and to explain why or why not.

ANSWER: Answers will vary.

Technology Resources

World History and Cultures Video Program 30: A New Era

Holt Researcher go.hrw.com

go.hrw.com
KEYWORD: Holt Researcher
FreeFind: George W. Bush
After reading more about George W. Bush on the Holt Researcher, write an outline for a campaign commercial explaining how his background prepared him for the presidency.

Reagan's vice president, George Bush was elected in 1988. Although Bush won praise for his leadership during the Persian Gulf War, an economic recession caused growing concern among voters. In 1992 **Bill Clinton,** the Democratic governor of Arkansas, became president. Clinton proved popular with the public and won a second term in 1996. However, his image was harmed by questionable financial dealings and accusations of sexual misconduct. In December 1998 the Senate voted to impeach Clinton for lying to a grand jury. In February 1999 the Senate acquitted Clinton of the charges against him, but the scandal had weakened Clinton's administration. In November 2000 Bush's son, **George W. Bush,** ran against Clinton's vice president, Al Gore. After a closely disputed election that took several weeks to resolve, Bush won the presidency.

✔ **READING CHECK: Identifying Cause and Effect** How did the Watergate scandal affect American politics? shook Americans' faith in government, resulted in election of "outsiders"

The U.S. Economy

During the late 1960s government spending soared to finance the Great Society programs and the Vietnam War. At the same time energy costs and prices for other goods were rising. This led to inflation—a general increase in prices and a decline in the buying power of the dollar. The instability of the U.S. economy became a cause for concern in the 1970s.

Attempts to stabilize the economy. Efforts made throughout the 1970s to stabilize the economy were unsuccessful. President Nixon tried to stimulate the economy with tax changes. However, his policies led to stagflation, a combination of decreased economic activity, high unemployment, and rising prices. Presidents Ford and Carter tried to fight stagflation through tax cuts, but the problem persisted throughout the 1970s.

A recession in the early 1980s finally brought inflation down as Ronald Reagan took office. To increase economic activity Reagan called for tax cuts that would encourage consumer spending and business investment while borrowing heavily from the national debt. By the mid-1980s unemployment had dropped and the economy began a period of sustained growth. However, the debts of the U.S. government had grown greatly. Until the late 1980s the government spent more money than it took in through taxes. To make up the difference the government had to borrow money, often

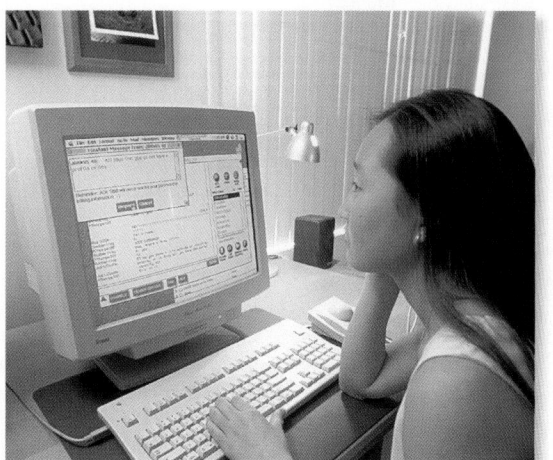

The computer industry helped fuel the economic boom of the 1990s.

from foreign lenders. As the debt and interest on it grew, many American leaders became increasingly concerned.

Finally in the late 1990s, economic growth made a balanced budget possible for the first time in almost 30 years. After a brief downturn in the early 1990s, the economy stayed strong for the rest of that decade. Boosted by growth in technology industries and a record rise in the stock market, the boom of the 1990s marked one of the longest and strongest periods of economic growth the country had ever seen.

The changing U.S. economy. Changes in the world economy significantly affected the U.S. economy. In the 1970s and 1980s, the United States began to lose its lead in heavy industry. American shipbuilders, automakers, and steel companies found it more difficult to compete with

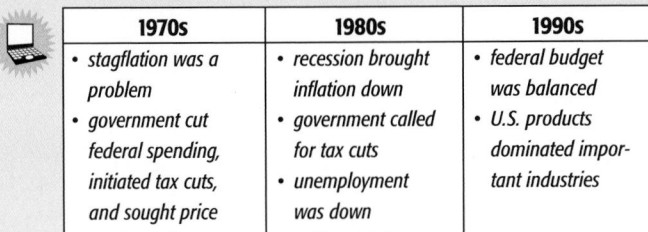

ALL LEVELS: Tell students that the U.S. economy has undergone some significant changes since the 1970s. Have students create a graphic organizer that lists the key characteristics of the U.S. economy in the 1970s, 1980s, and 1990s. For example:

1970s	1980s	1990s
• stagflation was a problem • government cut federal spending, initiated tax cuts, and sought price and wage freezes	• recession brought inflation down • government called for tax cuts • unemployment was down • national debt rose	• federal budget was balanced • U.S. products dominated important industries

1970s	1980s	1990s
• economy showed little improvement • U.S. began to lose its lead in heavy industry • U.S. first experienced a trade deficit	• U.S. began to lose its lead in heavy industry • U.S. products dominated important industries • U.S. products pioneered the revolution in computers and information technology	• U.S. products remained the leaders in the computer and information technology fields • new jobs were created

Then ask students how the changes in the U.S. economy reflect an economic transformation. Remind students of the economic impact of the war on terror and the economic downturn following September 11, 2001. **ENGLISH LANGUAGE LEARNERS**

companies in countries such as Germany and Japan, resulting in job loss in the 1980s. The decline in heavy industry meant that the United States had to import more goods than it exported, creating a trade deficit. Through the 1980s and 1990s, American products dominated the fields of aerospace engineering, pharmaceuticals, and information technology, creating new jobs that outpaced the loss of jobs in heavy industry.

By the end of 2000 a downturn in Asian economies affected the U.S. economy, and worried investors sold off stocks, leading to a decline in U.S. stock market prices. A slowdown in growth among technology companies marked a gradual end to the boom and despite high expectations among Internet entrepreneurs, the "dot-com" bubble burst, weakening the economy and causing widespread job loss.

As unemployment and corporate fraud rose, consumer confidence and the stock market dropped in 2002. Two multi-billion dollar companies, Enron and WorldCom, were forced to declare bankruptcy when the discovery of illegal accounting practices in their operations caused their stock prices to plummet. The stock market climbed back up by the end of 2003 as economic growth improved and business profits rose. The unemployment rate, however, remained stubbornly high.

✔ **READING CHECK: Comparing** How did the U.S. economy of the 1970s compare with the U.S. economy of the 1990s? unstable in 1970s, strong in 1990s

Energy. The cost and availability of energy plays a large role in the U.S. economy. Fossil fuels such as coal, natural gas, and oil have generally been the nation's main sources of energy. By the 1970s the United States was importing much of its oil, particularly from the Middle East. This created problems. An embargo by oil-producing countries in 1973 and the Iranian revolution of 1979 each caused oil shortages and price hikes. These events added to U.S. economic instability in the years following Vietnam.

Americans began to look to other sources of energy. Greater use of coal was one possibility, but would cause further air pollution. Some Americans pushed for the development of clean, renewable sources of energy, such as solar and wind power. Nuclear power was considered as an alternative to oil, but critics worried about its safety. After serious accidents at the Three Mile Island power plant in Pennsylvania and the Chernobyl plant in the Soviet Union, support for nuclear energy eroded.

In the 1990s oil companies began to tap into new oil deposits in Alaska, the Gulf of Mexico, and the Caspian Sea. Oil remained the main source of energy for the United States and the world. Despite concerns over dependency on foreign oil, American consumption of oil continued to increase. The economic prosperity of the 1990s did little to encourage energy conservation and sales of sport utility vehicles that got very poor gas mileage increased. In 2001 gas prices soared to record levels. This increase, coupled with the slowing economy, may have led some people to trade in their large vehicles for more fuel-efficient cars.

While gasoline prices for vehicles increased, some parts of the country experienced power outages due to a shortage of energy sources. To save power, California instituted "rolling blackouts," planned power outages designed to preserve the overall amount of energy available. In August 2003, an overloaded electrical grid in the eastern United States caused a power surge that resulted in a blackout in the country's northeast region and portions of Canada.

✔ **READING CHECK: Problem Solving** How should U.S. leaders deal with energy concerns in the coming years? promote conservation, seek alternative sources

The U.S. Energy Crisis: Oil Prices, 1973–1981

Source: *World Energy: The Facts and the Future*

Interpreting the Graph
Throughout the 1970s the U.S. government struggled to ease problems caused by skyrocketing oil prices. *During which two-year period did the United States experience its biggest increase in oil prices?*

Gasoline Consumption 1970 vs. 2000

Total gas consumption
Then 92.3 billion gallons
Now 162.3 billion gallons

Average annual consumption per car
Then 688 gallons
Now 547 gallons

Average gas mileage
Then
cars 13.5 miles per gallon
trucks 5.5 miles per gallon
Now
cars 22.0 miles per gallon
trucks 5.8 miles per gallon

Interpreting the Chart
Despite concerns over dependency on oil, total American gasoline consumption for vehicles increased between 1970 and 2000. *What does the chart imply about the reasons why gasoline consumption has increased?*

Economics

Reagan's economic program, often called Reaganomics, was based on a theory known as supply-side economics. This theory argued that lowering the income taxes for wealthy Americans and corporations would spur economic growth because people would invest their tax savings in businesses. These new businesses, in turn, would create new jobs, increase consumer spending, and generate more tax dollars for the U.S. government. Critics debated the success of supply-side economics and many still hold conflicting opinions.

Critical Thinking

Ask students if they believe that practicing supply-side economics would likely spur the economy, and have them explain their answers.

ANSWER: Answers will vary.

INTERPRETING THE GRAPH ANSWER
1977–1979

INTERPRETING THE CHART ANSWER
More vehicles on the road would explain why consumption actually increased despite better gas mileage.

LEVEL 2: Draw a time line on the chalkboard that extends from the 1970s to the present day. Tell students to copy this time line on a sheet of paper and then fill it in with 10 significant events in the United States's relationship with foreign countries. Tell students to annotate their time line by explaining the significance of each event. (Also remind students they may place events on their time line even if they do not have an exact date of occurrence, such as if the text states something happened in the late 1970s.) After students have completed their time line, call on volunteers to share their time line entries with the class. Use these to launch a discussion on the important events and changes that occurred in U.S.

foreign policy. Close by asking students what events they believe most threatened U.S. safety and what measures were the most important to U.S. stability. *(Answers will vary.)*

Historical Sidelight

When the Soviets increased their military presence in Afghanistan, the U.S. Olympic Committee voted to boycott the games. The decision was not universally popular, and some U.S. athletes and coaches attempted to block the boycott with a class action suit that was eventually dismissed. Ultimately, 44 additional nations refused to send athletes to compete in the Moscow Games.

internet connect

TOPIC: U.S.-Soviet Relations
GO TO: go.hrw.com
KEYWORD: SP3 WH35

Have students access the Internet through the HRW Go site to find information on U.S.-Soviet relations after WWII. Have students choose several key people and events to create a sequence chart that details the relationship of these two superpowers. Ask students to explain why they chose the events they did.

CONNECTING TO GEOGRAPHY ANSWER

They hope to find signs of water and discover whether other planets can sustain life.

CONNECTING TO GEOGRAPHY

Beyond Planet Earth
During the 1960s and 1970s, both the United States and the Soviet Union sent out deep-space probes to explore the solar system. The *Viking* probes landed on Mars. The *Voyager* vehicles flew by Jupiter, Saturn, and Uranus, and the *Venera* explorations studied the surface of Venus.

In 1973 the United States built the first successful space station, *Skylab*. A space station is a manned outpost in orbit where astronauts can conduct scientific experiments. In 1986 the Russians sent up the space station *Mir*.

Other U.S. unmanned explorations of Mars include the *Pathfinder*, the rover vehicles *Sojourner* in 1997, and *Spirit* and *Opportunity* in 2004. In 2003, China launched its first manned spacecraft.

Understanding Geography

What can scientists learn from studying the geography of places beyond the earth?

Changes in American Foreign Policy

American foreign policy underwent several changes in the late 1900s. In the 1970s, American leaders sought to ease the tensions of the Cold War by improving relations with communist countries.

U.S.-Soviet relations. In 1972 President Nixon became the first American president to visit Moscow. During that visit Nixon and Soviet leader Leonid Brezhnev signed the Strategic Arms Limitation Treaty, or SALT. This treaty limited each nation's nuclear weapon supplies. The two nations also agreed to cooperate in other areas. This general improvement in Soviet-American relations became known as **détente,** a French word meaning "easing of strain."

Presidents Ford and Carter continued the policy of détente throughout the 1970s. By the end of that decade, however, tensions flared again. President Carter, who felt strongly about human rights, protested the harsh way that the Soviet government treated those who opposed its policies. He also criticized Soviet and Cuban involvement in civil wars in Angola and Ethiopia. In December 1979 the Soviets invaded nearby Afghanistan. This invasion threatened the security of the oil-rich Persian Gulf. In 1980 President Carter made a statement called the **Carter Doctrine.** He declared that the United States would regard any attempts by outside forces to control the Persian Gulf as an assault on U.S. interests. The United States, he said, might even respond with military force. Carter then limited trade with the Soviets and called for a boycott of the 1980 Olympic Games in Moscow.

Détente came to an end. Some Americans believed the reduction in U.S. military forces after Vietnam had encouraged Soviet aggression. In the early 1980s President Reagan increased military spending, updated the U.S. nuclear arsenal, and boosted aid to anticommunist forces overseas. The Soviet Union tried to keep up with U.S. military spending.

By the mid-1980s new Soviet leadership pursued a friendlier relationship with the United States. American and Soviet leaders met several times and finally agreed to eliminate certain nuclear weapons. The Soviet Union reduced its military presence around the world, withdrawing from Afghanistan in 1989. When the Soviet Union officially dismantled in 1991, the United States was left as the world's only superpower.

The "new world order." Threats to world security existed throughout the world. Iraq and other countries tried to acquire **weapons of mass destruction**—nuclear, chemical, and biological weapons. The spread of such weapons remained a major concern throughout the 1990s. President George Bush urged the United Nations to work toward a "new world order," in which nations would cooperate to defend weaker countries.

The United States played an active role in world politics in the mid-1990s. Presidents George Bush and Bill Clinton both attempted to settle the ongoing Arab-Israeli dispute. U.S. policy also concerned itself with the international issues of trade, terrorism, and the environment.

Earth, as viewed from the space shuttle

Shown at left is a photo of the damaged U.S. spy plane that landed in the Hainan province of China in 2001. Below, members of the crew describe their experience during a press conference after their return to U.S. territory.

Relations with China. U.S. relations with the People's Republic of China improved steadily during the 1970s and 1980s. In 1972 President Nixon visited China, beginning a new period of diplomacy. By 1979 the U.S. had established full diplomatic relations with China. Many Americans saw opportunities for investment and trade in China's rapidly growing economy. The fact that China and the United States both distrusted the Soviet Union also helped bring the two nations together.

By the late 1980s, however, the nations found themselves at odds over China's treatment of its own citizens. Many Americans criticized China's record on human rights, especially after the Chinese government killed and wounded perhaps thousands of pro-democracy demonstrators at Tiananmen Square in 1989. Moreover, China continued to sell advanced weapons to potentially hostile nations like Iran, while building up its own military. Such issues became part of a larger debate among U.S. politicians. Some wanted to improve trading relations between the two countries, while others wanted to wait until China had improved its human rights record.

Tensions between China and the United States spiked in 2001 when a U.S. spy plane collided with a Chinese fighter jet, killing the Chinese pilot. After the United States apologized for the incident, relations improved. They continue to do so, despite ongoing differences over human rights, trade, missile defense, and the status of Taiwan.

✔ **READING CHECK: Identifying Cause and Effect** What issues affected U.S. foreign policy from the 1970s through the year 2001? Cold War tensions, threats to world security, human rights

Canada

Geographically, Canada is the world's second-largest country. It possesses a wealth of raw materials, and its citizens enjoy a high standard of living. Still, Canada faced political and economic challenges in the late 1900s.

The leader of the Liberal Party, **Pierre Trudeau,** was prime minister of Canada from 1968 to 1979, when he was defeated by Joseph Clark, a Progressive Conservative. Trudeau won re-election in 1980. Trudeau focused on maintaining Canada's federal union. In the early 1980s a recession led many Canadians to call for economic reforms. In 1984 the Progressive Conservative Party won a general election. The new prime minister, Brian Mulroney, attempted to strengthen the economy, but the recession deepened into the early 1990s. In 1993 the Conservatives replaced Mulroney with Kim Campbell, Canada's first woman prime minister. Later that year, the Conservatives lost a general election and Jean Chrétien of the Liberal Party became Canada's new prime minister. Chrétien served for 10 years and in 2003 was succeeded by Paul Martin, leader of the Liberal Party.

TEACH OBJECTIVE 4

LEVEL 3: Ask students to name the two most important issues facing Canadians in the 1990s. *(French Canadian separatism and relations with the United States)* Ask students to write a brief paragraph explaining the concerns and demands that surround each issue. *(Paragraphs on separatism should emphasize the failure of the Meech Lake Accord and the referendum of 1995; paragraphs on Canada's relationship with the United States should emphasize U.S. interference in the Canadian economy.)* After students have completed their paragraphs, ask them which of these issues they believe has found more resolution with Canadians. *(Students will probably answer the Canadian-U.S. relationship because NAFTA*

was signed, whereas the referendum of 1995 was not passed but almost half of the population was in favor of it.)* Close by asking students to predict future events or issues that will concern many Canadians.

CLOSE

Have students work in two groups to debate the views of French Canadian separatists and those opposed to separation of Quebec from the rest of Canada.

History Maker

PIERRE TRUDEAU. This charismatic prime minister came into power in 1968. United States President Richard Nixon and Trudeau did not like each other, although Trudeau admired chief foreign policy adviser Henry Kissinger. "Living next to you is like sleeping with an elephant; no matter how friendly and even-tempered is the beast, one is affected by every twitch and grunt," Trudeau told an American audience in 1969. Canada's relationship with the United States remained tense during the 1960s and 1970s. Nixon claimed the special relationship between Canada and the United States was dead. "It is time for us to recognize," he stated, "that we have very separate identities; that we have significant differences; and that nobody's interests are furthered when these realities are obscured."

ACTIVITY Have students compare trade between Canada and the United States during the Trudeau years with trade relations that exist today between the two countries.

VISUAL RECORD ANSWER

Signs are written in French. The flags have French emblems.

Technology **Resources**

Regions of the World Music Audio CD Program 2: Canada: Folk Songs of France and French Canada

Analyzing Primary Sources

Analyzing Information What sort of relationship does the Parti Quebécois envision between Canada and an independent Quebec? complete separation

INTERPRETING THE VISUAL RECORD

Independence for Quebec Despite the failure of the Meech Lake Accord, many people in Quebec continue to push for separation from Canada. *What evidence in this photo reflects Quebec's French-based culture?*

Separatism. One of the major issues facing Canada was that of French Canadian separatism. Most Canadians are of English-speaking descent. However, in the province of Quebec, French-speaking Canadians form the majority. Throughout Canada's history this group has struggled to preserve its distinct culture, which is based heavily on French traditions.

In the 1960s French Canadians began to demand cultural recognition, as well as more power in local and national government. Prime Minister Trudeau promised to protect French Canadian culture while still keeping Canada united. In 1969 he helped pass the Official Languages Act, making both French and English official languages of Canada.

For many French Canadians this was not enough. The Parti Québécois wanted complete separation of Quebec from Canada. In 1976 this party won control of the government of Quebec. The Parti Québécois explains their goals in the following way:

 Primary Source **❝Our program proposed two elements of association between Quebec and Canada [after independence]: first a customs union, then a monetary union.**
The customs union recognizes simply that Quebec exports an important part of its production to the other Canadian provinces and that these provinces have essential markets in Quebec. Nothing would be more ridiculous than to begin independence with a tariff war between the two countries....In the event of a monetary union.... [all] that is required is that, when Quebec becomes independent, the two new countries—each with its own monetary institutions—agree to coordinate their policies closely....❞

Pierre Vallieres, *The Revolutionary Process in Quebec*

Canadian leaders met at Meech Lake in 1987. In an agreement known as the **Meech Lake Accord,** they agreed to accept Quebec as a "distinct society" within Canada. However, the accord failed to become part of Canada's constitution. Many Canadians felt that it gave too much power to Quebec. The separatists renewed their efforts and in 1995 held a referendum on separation. The result was very close—

REVIEW

Have students complete the Section 1 Review on p. 947.

ASSESS

Have students complete Daily Quiz 35.1. As Alternative Assessment, you may want to use economy or foreign policy exercises in this section's lessons.

RETEACH

Have students complete Main Idea Activity for English Language Learners and Special-Needs Students 35.1. Then ask students to

write a question and answer that covers the main idea for each subsection in the section. Have the class try to answer each question. **ENGLISH LANGUAGE LEARNERS**

EXTEND

Have students research Watergate and the Iran-contra affair and use the information to create a compare-and-contrast chart about these events. Students should also write a paragraph summing up their findings and expressing which event they feel was more harmful to the American public and why. **BLOCK SCHEDULING**

just under 50 percent of the people of Quebec voted in favor of separation. French Canadian separatism remains a hotly debated issue.

Relations with the United States. Most Canadians live within several hundred miles of the border with the United States. This border is the longest undefended international frontier in the world. Relations between Canada and the United States became very close during the 1900s. The flow of trade across the Canadian-United States border remains the heaviest bilateral trade in the world.

Even so, the two countries have at times had disagreements. Disputes sometimes arise over fishing rights in the Atlantic and Pacific. Environmental concerns were raised when pollution from American smokestacks was found to be contributing to acid rain in northeastern Canada. The greatest strain, however, stems from Canada's concern about U.S. involvement in its economy.

Many Canadians have been unsure about free trade. In 1988 the United States-Canada Free Trade Agreement proposed to eliminate almost all tariff barriers between the two nations. Opponents worried that the agreement would give the United States too much control over the Canadian economy. The debate grew even more heated in the early 1990s, when the United States suggested adding Mexico to the agreement at a time when Canada had just gone into a deep recession. In the end Canada joined with the United States and Mexico in 1992 to sign the North American Free Trade Agreement (NAFTA). This agreement went into effect on January 1, 1994.

Officials from Mexico, the United States, and Canada sign the North American Free Trade Agreement (NAFTA) in 1992.

✔ **READING CHECK: Summarizing** How have U.S.-Canadian relations been throughout the 1990s? How can you tell? good; signed free trade agreement

---

SECTION 1 REVIEW

1. **Define** and explain the significance:
   détente
   weapons of mass destruction

2. **Identify** and explain the significance:
   Richard Nixon
   Vietnamization
   Watergate scandal
   Jimmy Carter
   Ronald Reagan
   Iran-contra affair
   Bill Clinton
   George W. Bush
   Carter Doctrine
   Pierre Trudeau
   Meech Lake Accord

3. **Categorizing** Copy the chart below. Use it to describe the U.S. economy during the 1970s, 1980s, and 1990s.

	1970s	1980s	1990s
Economic activity			

4. **Finding the Main Idea**
   a. How did many Americans feel about political leaders after Watergate?
   b. What actions of the Chinese government have created tension with the United States?
   c. Why were the Meech Lake Accords not approved in Canada?

5. **Writing and Critical Thinking**
   Supporting a Point of View Imagine that you are a Canadian citizen who opposes the separatist movement in Quebec. Write a newspaper editorial explaining your opposition to independence for Quebec.
   Consider:
   • why many French Canadians seek independence
   • why many Canadians oppose Quebec independence
   • how Quebec's independence would affect Canada

Homework Practice Online
keyword: SP3 HP35

SECTION 1 REVIEW ANSWERS

❶ **Define**
• détente, p. 944
• weapons of mass destruction, p. 944

❷ **Identity**
• Richard Nixon, p. 940
• Vietnamization, p. 940
• Watergate scandal, p. 941
• Jimmy Carter, p. 941
• Ronald Reagan, p. 941
• Iran-contra affair, p. 941
• Bill Clinton, p. 942
• George W. Bush, p. 942
• Carter Doctrine, p. 944
• Pierre Trudeau, p. 945
• Meech Lake Accord, p. 946

❸ 1970s: stagflation, tax cuts; 1980s: recession, tax cuts, boom, increasing national debt; 1990s: economic growth, balanced budget

❹ a. They lost confidence in them.

b. human rights violations; sale of weapons to potentially hostile nations; building its own military; collision with U.S. spy plane

c. Many Canadians felt the accords gave too much power to Quebec.

❺ Students' editorials will vary.

OBJECTIVES

1 Describe how Margaret Thatcher's leadership affected Britain.

2 Explain the challenges European nations faced in the late 1900s.

3 Identify the steps European nations took toward unity in the late 1900s.

🔊 *LET'S GET STARTED!*

As students enter the classroom, ask students what they know about Margaret Thatcher. *(Some students will not recognize the name; others will know that she was Britain's first female prime minister.)* Then ask students when they think the first woman will be elected to the U.S. presidency. *(Responses will vary.)* Tell students that in Section 2 they will learn more about Thatcher's administration in Great Britain.

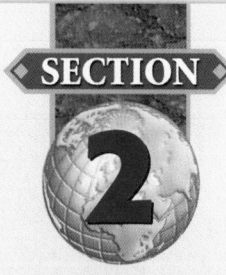

SECTION 2

READ TO DISCOVER

1 How did Margaret Thatcher's leadership affect Great Britain?

2 What challenges did European nations face in the late 1900s?

3 What steps did European nations take toward unity in the late 1900s?

IDENTIFY

Margaret Thatcher
Tony Blair
Georges Pompidou
François Mitterand
Willy Brandt
Ostpolitik
Helmut Kohl
Juan Carlos
Helsinki Accords
Maastricht Treaty

▶ WHY IT MATTERS TODAY

The European Union has stirred controversy. Use CNNStudentNews.com or other **current event** sources to find out how Europeans today feel about the union. Record your findings in your journal.

CNN Student News.com

Europe

The Main Idea
Many nations in Europe moved toward political and economic integration in the late 1900s.

The Story Continues *By the end of the 1960s, Great Britain faced severe economic problems. Outdated factories and low productivity made it hard to compete with other industrialized nations. The economy was further strained as the government raised taxes and increased borrowing. Unemployment and inflation remained high throughout the 1970s. Into this situation came a new leader with a new vision for Britain. "Let me give you my vision," Margaret Thatcher once said, "A man's right to work as he will, to save what he earns, to have property, to have the state as a servant and not as a master; these are the British inheritance."*

Great Britain

With a decisive victory in the 1979 election, the Conservative Party came to power. The party's leader, **Margaret Thatcher,** became the first female prime minister in Britain's history. Thatcher argued that the government regulated industry too closely and taxed people too heavily. She worked to reduce the role of the government in the economy.

Thatcherism. Thatcher reduced government funding of many social programs, and eliminated some completely. This prompted her critics to charge that her real goal was to abolish the British welfare system. Thatcher continued to ease government controls on business, converting many government-owned industries into private companies. She also reduced the power of labor unions in the economy.

The economy had begun to improve by the mid-1980s, especially in southern England. The development of new oil fields in the North Sea helped in this recovery. However, many areas of northern England did not benefit from the economic rebound. In this industrial region unemployment remained very high. This was partly the result of the same economic shift seen in the United States, from heavy industry to an economy based on services. Thatcher's critics charged that her policies favored the wealthy and created an unequal society.

Thatcher brought the same tough approach to her foreign policy. In 1982 she ordered troops to defend the British-held Falkland Islands after Argentina invaded them. She maintained close ties to the United States. In 1990 she played an important role in forming the international coalition that forced the Iraqi army out of Kuwait.

Prime Minister Margaret Thatcher and President Ronald Reagan were similar in their approaches to politics and economics.

LEVEL 3: Tell students to read the section under "Great Britain" beginning on page 948–949. Then have students construct diagrams to illustrate effects of Thatcherism. Students should list Thatcher's policies, describe their positive and negative outcomes, and identify outcomes that could be characterized as either positive or negative, depending upon one's point of view. Place the sample diagram on the right on the chalkboard to provide guidance. Then facilitate a class discussion of Thatcher's approach to government.

```
                  ┌─────────────────────────┐
                  │  Reduced government      │
                  │  economic role           │
                  └─────────────────────────┘
         ┌──────────────┼────────────────────────┐
┌────────────────┐                      ┌──────────────────────────┐
│   Positive     │                      │ Either positive or negative│
│  Lower taxes   │                      │  less government social    │
└────────────────┘                      │        spending            │
                                         └──────────────────────────┘
              ┌───────────────────────────┐
              │        Negative           │
              │ less support for unemployed│
              └───────────────────────────┘
```

In the late 1980s Thatcher began to lose support as the British economy weakened. Her downfall came when she implemented the so-called poll tax. This tax replaced property taxes as the source of funds for local government. The poll tax charged all taxpayers the same percentage, regardless of their income level. The tax proved very unpopular with the British people. Opponents within her own Conservative Party challenged Thatcher's leadership. Realizing she could not win reelection, Thatcher resigned in November 1990.

To replace Thatcher the Conservatives chose John Major, a member of her cabinet. On many issues Major was more moderate than Thatcher. He believed in forging closer ties with Europe. The British economy began to pick up again. However, scandals and incompetence in the government led many in Britain to seek new leadership. In 1997 the Labour Party, led by **Tony Blair,** came to power. Blair faced many challenges, such as the ongoing conflict in Northern Ireland and the 2003 war in Iraq.

Northern Ireland. When the Republic of Ireland gained independence in 1922, only the territory of Northern Ireland remained part of Britain. People hoped that the ancient ill will between Ireland and Britain would diminish. However, new disagreements emerged. Within Northern Ireland Protestants are in the majority. Over time this majority came to control the government and the economy of Northern Ireland. Lack of political power and economic opportunity created resentment among the Northern Irish Catholics.

In the late 1960s Catholic protests began to turn violent. In the early 1970s the British government sent troops to Northern Ireland to keep the peace. The presence of British soldiers in Northern Ireland soon became permanent.

Throughout the 1970s Catholic and Protestant groups used violence to further their causes. The Irish Republican Army (IRA) has been the most active group. Almost entirely Catholic, the IRA wanted to drive the British out of the north and unite all of Ireland. The IRA took its war beyond Irish borders, staging bombings in British cities and attacking British soldiers in other parts of Europe.

Aside from military force, the British tried to resolve the conflict through political means. The Republic of Ireland gained a voice in the affairs of Northern Ireland with the Anglo-Irish Agreement of 1985, but over time both Protestants and Catholics opposed the pact. In 1993 the British and Irish prime ministers pledged to give Northern Ireland the right to decide its own fate. The IRA declared a cease-fire the following year. Peace talks followed, and in 1998 the Good Friday Peace Accords were signed. Despite efforts to instill power sharing in Northern Ireland, Catholic-Protestant government has been suspended several times since the transfer of power from London in 1999.

✔ **READING CHECK: Summarizing** What caused Margaret Thatcher to lose her political support in Great Britain? poll tax

HISTORY MAKER

Margaret Thatcher (1925–   )

Margaret Thatcher was the first woman to be elected prime minister of any European country. She won a record three general elections, serving longer than any other British prime minister of the 1900s. She had a reputation for being very strong and sticking by her convictions, including opposing communism and supporting a free market economy. Thatcher was so tough that she earned the nickname "the Iron Lady." **What did Margaret Thatcher's nickname reflect about her style of leadership?**

Holt Researcher

go.hrw.com
KEYWORD: Holt Researcher
FreeFind: Margaret Thatcher
After reading more about Margaret Thatcher on the Holt Researcher, create a chart listing her successes and failures in office.

INTERPRETING THE VISUAL RECORD

IRA violence The IRA claimed responsibility for this bus bombing, which occurred in London. **What does the damage seen here suggest about IRA methods?**

Government

Once a week, for about half an hour, the British prime minister faces the House of Commons and answers whatever questions the members of Parliament choose to ask. Critics believe that "Question Time" is merely political theater, while supporters believe that it demonstrates the government's accountability to Parliament.

☑ internet connect

TOPIC: Margaret Thatcher
GO TO: go.hrw.com
KEYWORD: SP3 WH35

Have students access the Internet through the HRW Go site to research the life of Margaret Thatcher. Then ask students to create a biography of this former Prime Minister of Great Britain. Students may wish to use the interactive template provided.

HISTORY MAKER ANSWER
her strength and conviction

VISUAL RECORD ANSWER
They are violent and destructive.

LEVEL 2: Assign to each student either Chirac, Mitterand, Giscard d'Estaing, or Pompidou. Have students summarize their leader's main ideas about domestic, foreign, social, and economic policy. Use students' work to launch a discussion on the positive and negative effects of each leader's rule. Then students should write a sentence describing what they think was the most important problem that faced each of these leaders.

History Maker

GEORGES POMPIDOU. Georges Pompidou was honored with the building of the Georges Pompidou National Center of Art and Culture in Paris. Inaugurated in 1977, the Pompidou Center has generated some controversy over its design. On the outside of the building are piping and ventilation ducts painted in red, blue, yellow, and green. Escalators to get from one level to the next are also on the outside, as are steel support bars. Inside the Pompidou Center is the National Museum of Modern Art and a large library. More visitors per year visit the Pompidou Center than any other museum or monument in France.

Critical Thinking

Ask students if they think the Pompidou Center is an apt monument to Pompidou.

ANSWER: Students might suggest it is because Pompidou strove to make Paris a major tourist attraction.

François Mitterand, the first socialist president of France, served for two six-year terms.

France

In 1969 **Georges Pompidou** replaced Charles de Gaulle as president of France. Because the two men had worked together for years, they viewed French interests somewhat similarly. De Gaulle had seen France as a major player in world affairs. Pompidou worked to widen French trade involvement overseas and focused on domestic issues.

Pompidou believed that France should continue to cooperate with its traditional allies. He strengthened ties with the United States and ended French opposition to British membership in the European Economic Community, or EEC. Pompidou also introduced social programs designed to ease the problems that had led to widespread protests in the 1960s. He began an ambitious plan of renovation for the city of Paris. However, he had to curb many of his plans due to an economic crisis brought on by the OPEC oil embargo of 1973.

Pompidou died unexpectedly in 1974, and Valery Giscard d'Estaing became president. He continued Pompidou's foreign policy of cooperation with other countries. Domestically, Giscard d'Estaing reduced state controls on the economy. However, high inflation and unemployment made it impossible for him to implement his programs for social change.

Disappointed with Giscard d'Estaing's failure to bring about prosperity and social change, in 1981 the French people elected socialist **François Mitterand.** France still faced severe economic problems—high inflation, trade deficits, and rising unemployment. Mitterand sought to strengthen the economy by increasing the role of government. Several industries and banks were nationalized, and taxes on the wealthy were raised. Mitterand also expanded government programs for the unemployed. However, by the 1990s Mitterand had moved away from traditional socialist policies.

French foreign policy once again became aggressive under Mitterand. France often provided military assistance to its former colonies in Africa. Mitterand contributed troops to peacekeeping missions in Lebanon and Bosnia in the 1980s and 1990s. French troops also participated in the Gulf War coalition against Iraq.

However, uncertainty about the future affected French voters in the 1990s. Economic problems such as unemployment and recession remained. Immigration of Arabs from North Africa into France became a source of social tension. The French also worried about their ability to compete with the new, powerful Germany. In 1995 Jacques Chirac, the conservative mayor of Paris, became president. Chirac promised a fresh approach to France's economic problems, but encountered difficulty. Many people feared the loss of jobs and income as France dropped barriers to trade with other European countries. Moreover, in 1996 Chirac provoked international protests by testing nuclear weapons in the South Pacific. Chirac's party suffered a setback in the elections of 1997, and as a result a coalition government was formed. Chirac, a conservative, remained president, while Lionel Jospin, a socialist, became prime minister

✔ **READING CHECK: Finding the Main Idea** What was the main factor preventing French leaders from attaining their goals for the country? economic problems

Read aloud each set of statements below. Then have students write a conclusion that can be drawn from these statements. Use students' conclusions to discuss the development of Germany since the 1960s.

1. Unemployment was widespread in the former East Germany. West Germans became disillusioned at the cost of reunification. Reunification placed a burden on the German economy. (*The reunification of Germany had serious economic costs.*)

2. Willy Brandt worked to improve relations with the East through *Ostpolitik*. In 1973 East and West Germany officially recognized each other. Helmut Schmidt continued the policy of *Ostpolitik*. (*The policy of Ostpolitik was successful and brought East and West Germany to better terms.*)

3. In 1982 the Christian Democrats came to power after more than 12 years out of power. Helmut Kohl strongly reaffirmed West Germany's commitment to NATO in the 1980s. Talks about German reunification began in 1989. (*West Germany underwent many significant changes in the 1980s.*)

Germany

By the late 1960s West Germany had become a major economic power. Even so, it faced political problems. Relations with East Germany, the Soviet Union, and other communist countries posed challenges.

A member of the liberal Social Democratic Party, **Willy Brandt** was elected Chancellor in 1969. He believed West Germany had to stay allied with the rest of Western Europe and the United States. However, he also wanted to reduce tensions between his country and the communist nations of Eastern Europe. His effort to improve these relations was called **Ostpolitik,** German for "Eastern Policy." This policy led to treaties with Poland and the Soviet Union in 1970, and to other agreements. In 1974 Helmut Schmidt succeeded Brandt and continued Ostpolitik. He also pursued closer political and economic ties with Western Europe. In the early 1980s, however, an economic recession hit West Germany. The people faced rising unemployment and inflation.

The economic troubles led to political change. In 1982 the Christian Democrats, led by **Helmut Kohl,** took power. Kohl promised to return the country to prosperity by following conservative policies like those of Ronald Reagan and Margaret Thatcher. He also made changes in foreign policy, committing more firmly to the NATO alliance and strengthening relations with the United States.

Kohl's greatest challenge was the reunification of Germany. After the Berlin Wall fell in 1989, talks were held between the two Germanies, Britain, France, the Soviet Union, and the United States. In October of 1990 East and West Germany became one nation again. The goodwill generated by this great change helped Kohl win reelection two months later. However, Kohl began to lose popularity as German citizens faced the difficult realities of reunification. Revitalizing the former East Germany became a great burden on the German economy in the 1990s. Kohl remained in power until 1998, when he was defeated by Gerhard Schroeder of the Social Democratic Party. Schroeder pledged to reduce unemployment and stimulate the economy.

✔ **READING CHECK: Summarizing** What was the goal of the policy of Ostpolitik?
to improve relations with communist nations in Eastern Europe

Young people in Berlin wave German flags in celebration as the reunification of Germany takes effect in October of 1990.

Global Relations

German reunification has not been an easy process for western Germans, known as "Wessies," or eastern Germans, known as "Ossies." Many former government-owned businesses in eastern Germany have gone private, often into western hands. Many Wessies continue to be unhappy with the monetary cost of reunification. Some feel that it is time for eastern Germany to take care of itself, and some Ossies actually agree that too many eastern Germans rely on government assistance. One thing that both the Wessies and the Ossies do agree on: although the Berlin Wall has come down, the so-called mental wall between west and east still remains.

Critical Thinking

Ask students to share their opinions on the problems between eastern and western Germans.

ANSWER: Answers will vary.

LEVEL 1: Write the names Willy Brandt and Helmut Kohl on the chalkboard. Then read aloud with students the text under "Germany" on page 951. During the course of reading, invite students to point out important actions taken by each of the leaders. Write students' suggestions on the chalkboard, under the appropriate name. After students have finished reading the textbook, have them look at the completed lists. Ask students which leader they believe helped the German people more, and why.

ENGLISH LANGUAGE LEARNERS

ALL LEVELS: Have students match each of the following statements to the country(ies) which they describe. Write *I* for *Italy, S* for *Spain, P* for *Portugal,* and *G* for *Greece.*

1. became a republic in the 1970s
2. was at odds with some of its neighbors in the 1990s
3. experienced high unemployment and inflation in the late 1990s
4. joined the EEC

(1: S, P, G; 2: G; 3: I, S; 4: I, S, P, G)

ENGLISH LANGUAGE LEARNERS

Linking Past to Present

Francois Grimaldi took power of the Monaco fortress on January 8, 1297, an event that signaled the turning point in the history of the tiny European principality located near the south of France. Grimaldi, disguised as a monk, obtained entrance onto the enclosed grounds. He overthrew the guards, and his troops, who had been hiding outside in the darkness, forced the gates open and attacked. The Grimaldi family has ruled Monaco ever since. Prince Rainier III succeeded to the throne in 1949. The principality is economically driven by its hospitality sector, modern tourism, and facilities to host international conferences. The growth of the industrial and business services sectors also provides a major portion of the national income. The 700th anniversary of the arrival of the Grimaldi family to the rock of Monaco was commemorated in 1997. Prince Rainier III celebrated the 50th anniversary of his succession to the throne in 1999. Next in hereditary line is Prince Albert.

ACTIVITY: Have students research the principality of Liechtenstein and compare it to Monaco.

CONNECTING TO CIVICS ANSWER
royals lack unlimited power

CONNECTING TO
Civics

The Decline of European Monarchies
Louis XIV of France summed up the power of absolute monarchies in Europe when he said, "I am the state." Powerful European monarchies, however, have declined dramatically over the centuries, due to wars and democratic movements. They have largely been replaced by constitutional monarchies. In constitutional monarchies, royals lack the unlimited power of kings and queens of the past. Instead, they serve in a ceremonial or charitable capacity while a written constitution sets the legal framework for rule. In most of these countries the true head of government is the prime minister.

Understanding Civics

In what ways does constitutional monarchy differ from absolute monarchy?

Juan Carlos is the king of Spain, but his power is limited by parliament and a constitution.

Northern and Southern Europe

The other nations of Europe confronted their share of problems brought on by the postwar period, the Cold War, and economic instability. The late 1900s brought prosperity to the smaller nations of northern Europe.

Northern Europe. The tiny principalities of Monaco and Liechtenstein kept their autonomy. Belgium, Luxembourg, and the Netherlands worked together to foster European unity. During the Cold War, NATO members Denmark, Iceland, and Norway played an important role in helping defend Western Europe. The nations of Finland, Sweden, Austria, and Switzerland chose to remain neutral throughout the Cold War, but stayed on good terms with the rest of Western Europe.

Italy. The worldwide economic recession of the 1970s hit Italy hard, leading to high unemployment and runaway inflation. This created great political turmoil. Of the 14 political parties, none could gain a majority in the Italian parliament. Therefore governments had to be formed through coalitions. Few of these coalitions lasted very long, making it difficult to solve the nation's problems. A wave of terrorism at the end of the decade only added to Italy's problems.

Italy's situation improved during the 1980s. Many terrorist organizations were defeated, and free-market reforms stimulated the economy. However, the economy was also strained by Italy's huge national debt. Moreover, a huge gap in wealth existed between the industrialized north and the poor, mostly rural south. Political instability continued into the 1990s. Corruption scandals, some involving organized crime, shook the government. By 1997 reforms in parliament had restored some stability to Italian politics.

Portugal. Portugal made the transition from dictatorship to democracy in the late 1900s. In 1974 a military coup led by Antonio de Spinola ousted dictator Marcello Caetano. Spinola granted independence to most of Portugal's remaining colonies, including Angola and Mozambique. He then resigned, calling for free elections. Portugal faced serious political and economic instability over the next several years. In 1986 Portugal joined the EEC and implemented a series of free-enterprise reforms. These measures helped spur economic growth. Lisbon mayor Jorge Sampaio won the presidency in 1996, and the strong economy continued into the late 1990s.

Spain. When dictator Francisco Franco died in 1975, **Juan Carlos** became king. He began restoring democracy to Spain. In 1977 Spain held its first free democratic elections in 40 years. Moderate political parties led by socialists won most of the seats in the Cortes, or Spanish parliament. In 1981 a group of army officers tried to seize control of the government. The attempt failed, but demonstrated the fragility of the new democracy.

Another challenge came from the ongoing separatist movement in the Basque region of Spain. The Basque people, with their own distinct culture and language, have long pushed for independence. In 1980 they won self-government within Spain, but some separatists remain unsatisfied. The Basque separatist group ETA demanded complete independence and used terrorism throughout the 1980s.

HOMEWORK Have interested students find out more about the Basque people. Assign to students different aspects of Basque history, such as cultural background, beginning of the separatist movement, self-government, continuing problems, the ETA's use of terrorism, and Basque dissenters. Then have students share their findings with the rest of the class.
BLOCK SCHEDULING

Spain faced the same economic problems as other European nations—high inflation and unemployment. Spanish leaders sought to improve their economy through trade. In 1986 Spain joined the EEC. Despite the ongoing Basque separatist issue and lingering economic problems, Spain has become one of the leading democracies in Europe. Conservative Prime Minister José Maria Aznar's Popular Party won a majority in the Cortes in March 2000.

Greece. Greece endured a dark political period during the late 1900s. In 1967 a repressive military group known as the "Colonels" overthrew King Constantine II in a coup. In 1974 the Colonels supported a revolt against the democratically elected government of nearby Cyprus. When this revolt failed, however, the rule of the Colonels in Greece collapsed. In 1974 Greek voters chose to make their country a republic rather than return to monarchy. Andreas Papandreou, a socialist, was elected prime minister in 1981. That same year Greece joined the EEC, but economic problems persisted. Also, in the 1990s Greece's relations with its neighbors Turkey and Macedonia worsened. Papandreou resigned in 1996 due to ill health, and Costas Simitis became prime minister. His new, more conservative government promised closer cooperation with the West.

✔ **READING CHECK: Summarizing** What major political changes took place in Italy, Greece, Spain, and Portugal during the late 1900s? democracy, economic stability

European Cooperation

In the years after World War II, cooperation between the nations of Europe increased. Organizations such as NATO and the European Economic Community grew in strength and membership. Political changes within Europe in the late 1900s created the possibility for even greater cooperation and union.

The Helsinki Accords. In 1975 some 35 nations—including the United States and the Soviet Union—met in Helsinki, Finland. They discussed topics of security and cooperation in Europe. The meeting resulted in a series of agreements known as the **Helsinki Accords.** These accords gave European nations a new framework for

Living in the Pyrenees Mountains on both sides of the French-Spanish border, the Basque people maintain their own culture and government.

Global Relations

The Conference on Security and Cooperation in Europe met for the first time in 1973. Two years later, the representatives of the countries involved signed a declaration outlining the international policies they intended to follow, known as the Helsinki Accords.

An excerpt from the document states, "The participating States will respect human rights and fundamental freedoms, including the freedom of thought, conscience, religion or belief, for all without distinction as to race, sex, language or religion . . . The participating States on whose territory national minorities exist will respect the right of persons belonging to such minorities to equality before the law, [and] will afford them the full opportunity for the actual enjoyment of human rights and fundamental freedoms."

Critical Thinking

Ask students to think about the other issues the Helsinki Accords addresses and then create a brief paragraph that might have been included in the document.

ANSWER: Paragraphs will vary but might deal with economic and technological cooperation and the settlement of boundary disputes.

LEVEL 1: Ask students to name the major treaties or agreements made between European countries since the 1970s. *(the Helsinki Accords, the North Atlantic Treaty Organization, the Maastricht Treaty, the European Union)* Ask students to briefly characterize the main goals of each treaty or agreement. *(Helsinki: improve economic and technological cooperation between the East and West and use peaceful means to settle international disputes; NATO: create military alliances; Maastricht: create the European Union; EU: ease trade barriers between member countries, accept a common currency, and pursue closer cooperation in defense and foreign relations)* **ENGLISH LANGUAGE LEARNERS**

Hold a class debate that argues the following topic: "Margaret Thatcher's government brought great economic improvements to Britain." Remind students that they may consider any information they have learned from the text in their arguments.

Economics

The strength of the EU was tested in 1996, when sales of British beef were banned because of mad cow disease. Britain vowed to paralyze EU business until the ban was lifted. However, the crisis was averted when a British plan for the eradication of the disease was approved. The ban was lifted in 1999. However, the French still refused to allow the sale of British beef until October 2002. The restriction on beef imports caused strains in the relationship between Britain and France.

Critical Thinking

Ask students why it was important for Britain to have the EU lift the ban on British beef.

ANSWER: Students may suggest that disallowing sale of British beef would put Britain at a severe economic trade deficit.

MAP ANSWER
Sweden, Finland, Ireland, United Kingdom, Denmark, Netherlands, Belgium, Germany, Luxembourg, France, Portugal, Spain, Austria, Italy, Greece

economic and technological cooperation, and provided a peaceful means for settling certain boundary disputes. The agreements also called on all nations to respect basic human rights, such as freedoms of speech and worship. The Helsinki Accords were largely symbolic. However, they provided an important foundation for the democratic movements that swept across Eastern Europe in the 1980s.

NATO. The North Atlantic Treaty Organization (NATO), which had kept Western Europe safe during the Cold War, remained the cornerstone of security in the region as the 1900s drew to a close. However, the organization's policies and future role increasingly came into question. Tensions between Greece and Turkey, both NATO members, eventually led to Greece quitting NATO in 1974. Greece later rejoined, but its relations with other NATO countries remained strained. The United States provoked controversy by deploying nuclear weapons within Europe during the Cold War. Many European nations did not want American nuclear weapons on their soil. At the same time, the United States demanded that other NATO nations pay a larger share of the expense of defending Europe.

NATO's future grew uncertain following the collapse of the Soviet Union in the early 1990s. With no great military threat from the East, critics charged that NATO was no longer needed. Eastern European countries, however, were eager to join NATO to protect against any possible Russian effort to reassert control in the region. Poland,

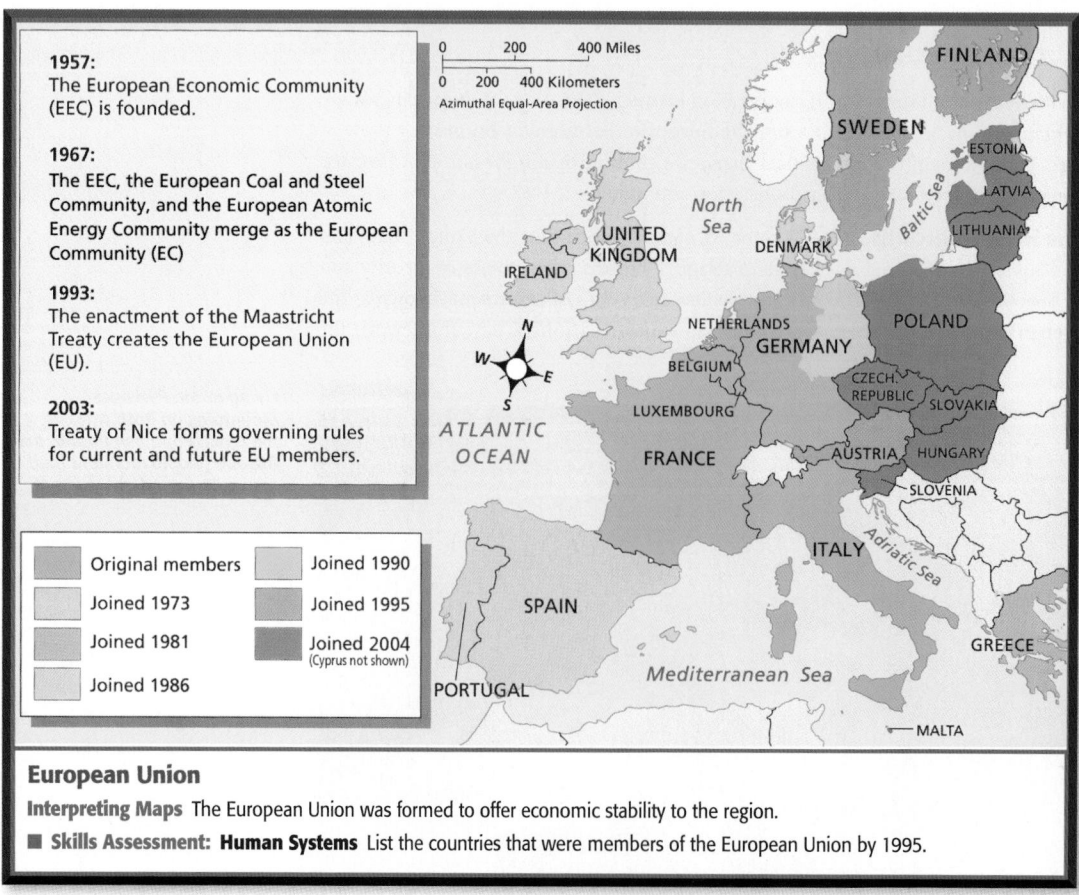

1957:
The European Economic Community (EEC) is founded.

1967:
The EEC, the European Coal and Steel Community, and the European Atomic Energy Community merge as the European Community (EC)

1993:
The enactment of the Maastricht Treaty creates the European Union (EU).

2003:
Treaty of Nice forms governing rules for current and future EU members.

Original members
Joined 1973
Joined 1981
Joined 1986
Joined 1990
Joined 1995
Joined 2004 (Cyprus not shown)

European Union
Interpreting Maps The European Union was formed to offer economic stability to the region.
■ **Skills Assessment: Human Systems** List the countries that were members of the European Union by 1995.

REVIEW

Have students complete the Section 2 Review on p. 955.

ASSESS

Have students complete Daily Quiz 35.2. As Alternative Assessment, you may want to use the diagram exercise in this section's lessons.

RETEACH

Have students complete Main Idea Activity for English Language Learners and Special-Needs Students 35.2. Ask students to list the main ideas of each heading and subheading in the appropriate space. **ENGLISH LANGUAGE LEARNERS**

EXTEND

Organize students into three groups, and assign each group to be supporters of the Helsinki Accords, NATO, or the EU. Then tell students to develop convincing arguments that show the agreement you are in favor of is the best one for European nations to follow. Have students present their arguments to the class. **BLOCK SCHEDULING**

Hungary, and the Czech Republic were welcomed into the alliance in 1999. In 2002, three ex-Soviet republics—Estonia, Latvia, and Lithuania—along with Bulgaria, Romania, Slovakia, and Slovenia were invited to join in 2004.

From EEC to EU. In the 1990s the European Economic Community evolved into the more closely knit European Union (EU). During the 1970s and 1980s, the EEC grew from 6 members to 12. Britain joined, after lengthy negotiations, in 1973, as did Ireland and Denmark. They were followed by Greece in 1981, Spain and Portugal in 1986, and Austria, Finland, and Sweden in the early 1990s. As the EEC grew, members began to work toward common practices regarding taxation, credit, trade, and monetary policy.

In 1993 the EEC countries implemented an agreement called the **Maastricht Treaty,** creating the European Union. With the Maastricht Treaty, members ended trade barriers between their countries, agreed to pursue closer cooperation in defense and foreign relations, and accepted the idea of a common currency. Implementation of the treaty in the 1990s proved difficult, however. Several members of the EEC worried that the EU would undermine their sovereignty. British leaders were especially concerned. Voters in Denmark just barely ratified the Maastricht Treaty, and in Norway EU membership was rejected. By 1995, however, 15 nations had joined the EU. In 2004, 10 more countries joined the EU, bringing the number of member nations to 25. Europe continues to achieve a remarkable degree of unity as it moves forward in the new century.

✔ **READING CHECK: Finding the Main Idea** What were the goals of the Maastricht Treaty? end trade barriers, cooperate in defense and foreign relations, common currency

Shown here are some of the coins and bills of the European Union's currency system.

SECTION 2 REVIEW ANSWERS

❶ **Identify**
- Margaret Thatcher, p. 948
- Tony Blair, p. 949
- Georges Pompidou, p. 950
- François Mitterand, p. 950
- Willy Brandt, p. 951
- Ostpolitik, p. 951
- Helmut Kohl, p. 951
- Juan Carlos, p. 952
- Helsinki Accords, p. 953
- Maastricht Treaty, p. 955

❷ EEC, membership increased, Maastricht Treaty, EU, Treaty of Nice

❸ **a.** rise: economic improvement, tough foreign policy; fall: weakening economy, poll tax

b. economics, trade, defense, foreign relations

c. no great military threat from the East; disputes over new members

❹ Students' dialogues will vary but should demonstrate both support of the EU and opposition to it.

SECTION 2 REVIEW

1. **Identify** and explain the significance:
   Margaret Thatcher
   Tony Blair
   Georges Pompidou
   François Mitterand
   Willy Brandt
   Ostpolitik
   Helmut Kohl
   Juan Carlos
   Helsinki Accords
   Maastricht Treaty

2. **Sequencing** Copy the chart below. Use it to explain how the move toward European cooperation led from the European Economic Community (EEC) to the European Union (EU).

   EEC →

3. **Finding the Main Idea**
   a. What issues led to the rise and fall of Margaret Thatcher's party?
   b. What issues universally concerned European countries in the late 1900s?
   c. What problems did NATO encounter in the late 1900s?

4. **Writing and Critical Thinking**
   Contrasting Write an imaginary dialogue between someone who supports the EU concept and someone who opposes it.
   Consider:
   • what European countries can gain from membership in the Union
   • what many Europeans fear losing

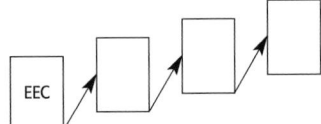

Homework Practice Online
keyword: SP3 HP35

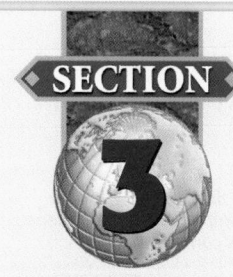

SECTION 3

OBJECTIVES

1 Explain what events led to the fall of the Soviet Union.

2 Explain how Russia fared under Boris Yeltsin.

3 Describe how Eastern Europe was affected by the fall of communism.

SECTION 3

READ TO DISCOVER

❶ What events led to the fall of the Soviet Union?

❷ How did Russia fare under Boris Yeltsin?

❸ How was Eastern Europe affected by the fall of communism?

DEFINE

perestroika
glasnost
ethnic cleansing

IDENTIFY

Leonid Brezhnev
Brezhnev Doctrine
Mikhail Gorbachev
Boris Yeltsin
Commonwealth of Independent States (CIS)
Lech Walesa
Vaclav Havel
Dayton Accord

WHY IT MATTERS TODAY

When the Soviet Union dissolved, the former republics were left to fend for themselves economically. Use CNN or other **current event** sources to gather information about economic conditions in former Soviet territories. Record your findings in your journal.

The Fall of Communism

The Main Idea
After influencing international politics for half a century, communism lost its hold in Eastern Europe.

The Story Continues *During the 1980s widespread political protests in Poland brought about radical change. As one reporter commented, "Communist reforms, prodded by popular pressure, have moved even faster there than in the Soviet Union. Just weeks ago, Poland's Solidarity union was illegal. Now, [the president of Poland] is ready to ask Solidarity to lead the next government."* Similar reforms swept other Eastern European countries at a rapid pace, bringing both promise and risk.

The Soviet Union Under Brezhnev

Throughout the 1970s **Leonid Brezhnev** led the Soviet Union. He proved to be a forceful leader. With the invasion of Czechoslovakia in 1968, Brezhnev demonstrated that the Soviet government would tolerate no dissent among its satellite nations. He issued the **Brezhnev Doctrine,** stating that the Soviet Union would intervene in any satellite nation that seemed to be moving away from communism. As a result, no satellite government attempted reforms on the scale of the Prague Spring during the Brezhnev years. Brezhnev also suppressed dissent at home. He restricted such basic human rights as freedom of speech, worship, and movement.

While seeking to crush all opposition both domestically and in the Soviet satellites of Eastern Europe, Brezhnev worked to strengthen his country's position in the balance of world power. Through the policy of détente, he tried to stabilize relations with the United States. However, world leaders found it difficult to believe the Soviet Union was working toward peace when it continued to build up its military and support anti-Western movements. The 1979 Soviet invasion of Afghanistan further strained relations with the West.

Meanwhile, the Soviet economy remained inefficient and troubled. Most Soviets experienced a decline in their standard of living under Brezhnev. Agricultural failures, inadequate transportation, and outdated factories all contributed to the dire state of the Soviet economy. Heavy military spending compounded the problem severely. By the time Brezhnev died in 1982, the need for economic reform had become clear and relations with the United States had substantially deteriorated.

Brezhnev and Nixon in 1973

ALL LEVELS: Ask students to describe the reforms that Gorbachev initiated in the Soviet Union. *(relaxing of government controls on the economy, easing restrictions on dissent, allowing citizens to speak their minds and read whatever they like)* Then discuss with students the way various people, such as average Soviet citizens, U.S. officials, or hardline Soviet Communists, reacted to these reforms and how they contributed to the fall of communism. You may choose to assign these roles to your students and have them speak from this point of view during the discussion. **ENGLISH LANGUAGE LEARNERS**

Teacher to Teacher

Rudy Martinez of San Antonio, Texas, suggested the following activity: Working in groups or independently, have students create cause-and-effect graphic organizers showing how the fall of communism came about and what the effects of the fall have been for various countries.

A new debate about the future ensued after Brezhnev died. Older Soviet leaders worried that reform would weaken the nation. They sought to improve the economy without abandoning communism. They named Yuri Andropov, former head of the secret police, to succeed Brezhnev. In poor health, Andropov held office for only about 15 months and was replaced by the aging Konstantin Chernenko, who lasted for little more than a year. After Chernenko's death, a younger generation of leaders finally gained control of the government.

✔ **READING CHECK: Summarizing** What problems did the Soviet Union face under Leonid Brezhnev? strained relations with the West, poor economy, agricultural failures, outdated factories

Gorbachev and Reform

In 1985 **Mikhail Gorbachev** became the new leader of the Soviet Union. Gorbachev had a background in agricultural and economic affairs. He began to overhaul the Soviet political and economic systems.

Perestroika and glasnost. Gorbachev began a series of reforms known as **perestroika** (per-uh-STROY-kuh), or "restructuring," and **glasnost** (GLAZ-nohst), meaning "openness." Gorbachev relaxed government control of the economy and eased restrictions on dissent, allowing people to speak freely and read whatever they liked. Recognizing the burden that military spending placed on the Soviet economy, he planned to reduce the size of the armed forces. He also looked for a way to end the unpopular Soviet occupation of Afghanistan.

Gorbachev's reforms won him international praise. Relations improved with the United States, and Gorbachev met with President Reagan. The two signed several arms-reduction agreements. In 1989 Soviet forces withdrew from Afghanistan. At home, however, Gorbachev's programs were slow to take effect and sometimes caused hardship. Perestroika made more consumer goods available, but there were still shortages of basic necessities. In 1990 Gorbachev introduced a plan for a mixed economy, combining private ownership with government control. Hard-line communists, though, pressured him to drop the plan. In 1991 conservative members of the government and military attempted a coup. They arrested Gorbachev, but the president of Russia, **Boris Yeltsin,** raised opposition to the coup. The coup failed, but Gorbachev never recovered his former popularity. Yeltsin emerged as the new leader of reform.

The end of the Soviet Union. Keeping the Soviet Union together became increasingly difficult as Gorbachev's reforms took effect. The freedom of speech provided by glasnost increased tensions between the various Soviet ethnic groups and nationalities. Rival groups could now express opinions they would otherwise have kept to themselves. Ethnic fighting broke out between the Muslim Soviet republic of Azerbaijan and the Christian Soviet republic of Armenia.

Some Soviet republics began to demand independence. In 1990 the Baltic republics—Latvia, Lithuania, and Estonia—tried to secede from the Soviet Union. Gorbachev attempted an

---

Holt Researcher

go.hrw.com
KEYWORD: Holt Researcher
FreeFind: Mikhail Gorbachev
After reading more about Mikhail Gorbachev on the Holt Researcher, write a memo as an American diplomat noting how he is different from previous Soviet leaders.

 What If? What might have happened if Gorbachev had achieved his goals and had not been forced to resign in 1991? How might the Soviet Union and Eastern Europe be different?

Mikhail Gorbachev won the Nobel Peace Prize in 1990 for his reform work in the Soviet Union. He is shown here with his wife, Raisa.

Global Relations

In August 1991, Mikhail Gorbachev and his wife traveled to his summer retreat in Crimea where he expected to meet with four Soviet officials. The officials, who felt threatened by the demands of greater independence for Soviet republics, insisted that Gorbachev declare a state of emergency. When Gorbachev refused, he was placed under house arrest for several days. The next day the national Soviet news agency announced that Gorbachev was ill, and his vice president would act as president. A ruling committee quickly banned all political opposition, declared martial law, and sent hundreds of tanks to Moscow. Within a week, however, the coup had collapsed, and Gorbachev was back in office.

Critical Thinking

Ask students why they think the coup was unsuccessful.

ANSWER: Students might guess that the leaders of the coup were not able to gain widespread support.

WHAT IF? ANSWER
The Soviet people might have accepted a hybrid form of communism, one that allows more political and economic freedom; the Eastern European countries might have retained closer ties to communism.

LEVEL 3: Have students write journal entries as if they were average Soviet citizens. Students should write a "Before" entry, chronicling life before Gorbachev's reforms, and then an "After" entry. Then discuss whether most Soviet citizens likely thought their lives were better under Brezhnev or under Gorbachev.

History Maker

YELTSIN AND GORBACHEV.
Boris Yeltsin was actually Mikhail Gorbachev's protégé. Gorbachev had appointed Yeltsin head of the Communist Party organization in Moscow in 1985, but Yeltsin had held the post for only about two years before he began to criticize conservative policies, including Gorbachev's. Still, during the attempted coup in 1991, Yeltsin urged on Gorbachev's supporters, even calling on Soviets across the country to go on strike until Gorbachev was returned to power. Although there were numerous political upheavals in the Russian government, Yeltsin remained president until 1999. He was succeeded by Vladimir Putin.

ACTIVITY: Organize students into small groups and have each group create a compare-and-contrast chart on the Yeltsin and Gorbachev governments.

Technology Resources
Regions of the World Music Audio CD Program 9: Russia, Ukraine, and Belarus: Russian Choral Music

Technology Resources
CNN Presents Geography: Yesterday and Today Segment 19: Cossacks Return to Power

In May of 1990, Boris Yeltsin (center, holding papers) became the first popularly elected leader in the history of Russia.

economic and military crackdown, drawing criticism both at home and abroad. In 1991 more and more Soviet republics demanded independence. It soon became clear that the Soviet Union could not last. In December of 1991 Gorbachev stepped down as president of the Soviet Union. By the end of the year the Soviet Union had ceased to exist.

✔ **READING CHECK: Identifying Cause and Effect** How did Gorbachev's reforms lead to the breakup of the Soviet Union? Freedom of speech increased tensions among ethnic groups.

Russia's New Leadership

After the breakup of the Soviet Union, the Federation of Russia emerged as the largest and most powerful of the newly independent states. Under Boris Yeltsin's leadership, Russia began to make the transition to democracy, though high inflation and unemployment strained the Russian economy. Yeltsin privatized many industries and opened Russia to foreign investment, but Russia's economic troubles continued throughout the 1990s.

Political and social troubles. The ongoing economic problems led to political turmoil. In the early 1990s Yeltsin was strongly challenged by the Russian legislature, which still included many communists. When Yeltsin attempted to dissolve the legislature in 1993, its members declared the move unconstitutional and announced a new government. Yeltsin kept power only by ordering a military assault against the legislative building.

At the same time, Yeltsin's nationalist and communist opponents began to win more support. The military became increasingly dissatisfied over low pay and poor living conditions. There was danger of a coup. Amid questions about his health, Yeltsin faced a strong challenge in the election of 1996. Only by making concessions to the conservatives did Yeltsin manage to win reelection.

Russia's diverse challenges continued. The Orthodox church experienced renewed growth and power and did not always agree with democratic reformers. In addition, the fall of communism sparked an increase in organized crime in Russia, with criminal gangs dealing in illegal enterprises such as drugs, prostitution, and black-market goods.

Another challenge came from increased separatist movements among Russian minority groups. The most serious case involved the small southern region of Chechnya. The Chechens, a Muslim people, had long fought their Russian conquerors. With the breakup of the Soviet Union, Chechnya declared its independence. Yeltsin, however, refused to let the oil-rich region break away, and in 1994 sent in the army. The brutal war provoked international criticism and caused heavy casualties on both sides. In 1996 a peace treaty was signed and Russian and Chechen leaders pledged to work out the final status of Chechnya in later negotiations. After these negotiations faltered and Chechen rebels were blamed for a series of bombings in Moscow and other cities in 1999, Russian troops again invaded. The renewed fighting has degenerated into a stalemate. Russian forces are not strong enough to defeat the Chechen fighters, and the Chechens are too weak to turn back the Russians.

TEACH OBJECTIVE 2

LEVEL 1: Write the following chart on the chalkboard, omitting the answers shown in italics. Then, using these categories, discuss with the class Russia's development after the breakup of the Soviet Union. Encourage students to come up with a generalization for each category that describes Russia and then provide a few specifics. For example, students might characterize the economy as unstable and note that many Russians suffered severe hardships. **ENGLISH LANGUAGE LEARNERS**

Russia's Development				
Economy	**Politics**	**Religion**	**Domestic Difficulties**	**Foreign Relations**
• *high inflation and unemployment* • *food and housing in short supply* • *slow to improve* • *new class of entrepreneurs became wealthy*	• *political turmoil* • *Yeltsin struggled for power with legislature* • *danger of a coup* • *Putin elected president*	• *new growth and power for Orthodox church*	• *increase in organized crime* • *increased separatist movements among Russian minority groups such as Chechnya*	• *cooperated with the West* • *reached arms reduction agreements with the U.S.* • *opposed expansion of NATO* • *Western leaders concerned over security of Russian nuclear weapons*

Russia and the world. The breakup of the Soviet Union created 15 independent republics. To coordinate defense and economic policies for the new nations, Russia established the **Commonwealth of Independent States (CIS).** Relations between Russia and the republics were often strained. A major concern was the perception that Russia was trying to dominate the new republics near the oil-rich Caspian Sea.

Needing financial assistance, Yeltsin's government cooperated with the West and reached important agreements with the United States on arms reduction. NATO expansion into eastern Europe and Western fears over the security of Russia's nuclear weapons caused some tension, but Russia and the West tried to focus on matters of agreement.

When Yeltsin resigned in late 1999, Prime Minister Vladimir Putin became acting president. The following March, Putin was formally elected to the presidency. His hard line against Chechnya and his efforts to further reform a once again growing Russian economy have been the focus of his term in office.

✔ **READING CHECK: Categorizing** What types of problems did Russia face under Boris Yeltsin? high inflation, unemployment, political unrest, problems with Chechnya

Economics

By the late 1990s, the Russian economy was in ruins. There was little cash money in the country. Rather than fail, small banks rushed to merge with large banks.

Critical Thinking

Ask students to explain what factors contributed to Russia's economic ruin.

ANSWER: Students should mention high inflation and unemployment as well as a shortage of food and housing.

MAP ANSWER

12

Reproducible Resources

PS Readings in World History 127, 128: Glasnost and Journalism; The Communist Roller Coaster

Eastern Europe, 1991

The Breakup of the Soviet Sphere

Interpreting Maps In 1989 many Soviet republics began to demand independence.

■ **Skills Assessment: Analyzing Information** How many of the Soviet satellite nations became part of the Commonwealth of Independent States?

Government

The first free elections in Poland since the 1960s were held in 1989. After much negotiation with Solidarity, the government agreed to allow the Polish people to vote for their officials, including a non-Communist president, if they so desired. In the weeks leading up to these elections, Solidarity literature could be found throughout the streets of Polish cities. Candidates campaigned with posters that displayed the word *Solidarnosc* (the Polish word for "Solidarity") emblazoned in red letters. Passersby were encouraged to vote. Poles everywhere celebrated the return to democracy.

Critical Thinking

Ask students what they think the literature passed out by Solidarity supporters might have said.

ANSWER: Students might guess it promoted democracy and encouraged people to vote.

VISUAL RECORD ANSWER

Students might guess frustration and anger.

HISTORY MAKER ANSWER
imprisoned

INTERPRETING THE VISUAL RECORD

Berlin Wall The Berlin Wall, which had divided East and West Germany for nearly 30 years, came down in 1989. *What feelings are expressed in the grafitti and artwork on the wall?*

HISTORY MAKER

**Vaclav Havel
(1936–   )**

Playwright, poet, and political activist Vaclav Havel had long opposed the communist government in Czechoslovakia. The government, calling Havel a threat to national security, banned his plays and put him in jail. In fact, Havel was still in prison only a few weeks before becoming president in 1989. **What happened to Havel as a result of his political views?**

Dissent and Revolution in Eastern Europe

During the 1960s and 1970s, the Brezhnev Doctrine had prevented any real dissent in nations under Soviet control. Gorbachev's reforms, however, gave encouragement to democratic movements in Eastern Europe. In 1989 a tide of democratic reform swept communist governments from power across Eastern Europe.

Growing dissent. The announcement of the Helsinki Accords in the late 1970s improved the climate for dissidents in Eastern European countries. Those who opposed totalitarian rule called on their governments to abide by the human rights articles of the accords. In Poland economic troubles also fueled the growth of dissent. Huge price increases in 1980 sparked massive labor strikes. Led by an unemployed electrician named **Lech Walesa** (LEK vah·LEN·suh), the strikers demanded political and economic reforms. They formed an independent trade union called Solidarity. Aided by glasnost, the Solidarity protests continued throughout the 1980s and eventually led to the downfall of Poland's communist government.

Initially, both communist governments and dissidents were skeptical of Gorbachev's reforms. Despite their economic problems, Eastern European governments were perhaps uneasy about restructuring along Soviet lines. Dissidents may have at first expressed disbelief, but finally came to support glasnost and perestroika as the best hope for winning freedom.

The 1989 revolutions. In 1989 Poland became the first Eastern European country to throw off communist rule. In April of that year the government legalized Solidarity. Poland's first non-communist prime minister in forty years was elected. In 1990 the Communist Party was dissolved and replaced by two social democratic parties.

Other nations followed Poland's example. In Czechoslovakia, protesters took to the streets to demand reform. When they lost the support of the workers, who went on a national strike, the government quickly gave in. Shortly thereafter the national legislature selected **Vaclav Havel,** a writer and former dissident leader, as the country's new president. The transition to democracy was so smooth in Czechoslovakia that people called it the "Velvet Revolution."

The transition to noncommunist rule was less peaceful in Romania. People there had long suffered under the repressive rule of dictator Nicolae Ceausescu (chow·SHES·koo). A brief civil war broke out as pro-reform demonstrators clashed with Ceausescu's secret police. By the end of 1989, pro-democracy forces captured and executed the dictator.

In East Germany the government came under increasing pressure to open its borders. Many East Germans had been traveling to Czechoslovakia or Hungary and from there escaping to West Germany. As protests grew, the East German government agreed to open the country's borders at midnight on November 9, 1989. That night thousands of Berliners from both East and West Germany gathered at the infamous Berlin Wall. On the stroke of midnight, they raced to break holes in the wall or climb over it. The fall of the Berlin Wall became the most powerful symbol of the collapse of communism.

✔ **READING CHECK: Comparing and Contrasting** How did dissidents and government leaders in Eastern Europe view Gorbachev's reforms? disbelief, then support as best hope for winning freedom

LEVEL 2: Ask students how Gorbachev's reforms affected the Communist satellites. *(They gave encouragement to democratic forces in the satellites.)* Then ask students to write a few sentences explaining how democratic governments arose in Poland, Czechoslovakia, Romania, and East Germany. Ask students to compare the events in each of these countries. Which country would they have held up as the best example?

HOMEWORK Have students look in newspapers or newsmagazines or watch the national news on television to find at least one contemporary event from around the world that reminds them of some of the problems experienced in Eastern Europe in the late 1980s and 1990s. *(for example, ethnic cleansing or uprisings against governments)* Then have students write a brief report explaining the event and why it happened. Ask students to present their reports to the class.

The Aftermath of Communism

The end of communism in Eastern Europe promised new prosperity. The new governments of Eastern Europe adopted democratic policies and free-market reforms. Many hoped for closer cooperation with the West.

The challenges of change. However, change was not easy. The Eastern European countries had lost their largest trading partner, the Soviet Union. Their inefficient industries could not compete with those of the West. Furthermore, the years of communist rule had left Eastern Europe one of the world's most polluted regions.

The new freedoms gained in Eastern Europe also released old ethnic tensions. In 1992 Czechoslovakia peacefully split into two separate countries, as Slovak nationalism grew. This created the more prosperous Czech Republic and the poorer country of Slovakia. Other countries, such as Albania, experienced more violent unrest.

Yugoslavia's breakup. In Yugoslavia, ethnic tensions led to one of the bloodiest civil wars of modern times. Yugoslavia was made of six republics and many different ethnic groups, including Serbs, Croats, Slovenians, Macedonians, and Albanians. The Serbs were mainly Eastern Orthodox, and Croats and Slovenians Roman Catholic. In the republic of Bosnia and Herzegovina, Muslims were the largest group.

As communism fell, Serbia, under President Slobodan Milošević (SLOH•buh•dahn muh•LOH•suh•vich), tried to dominate the rest of Yugoslavia. This inspired intense nationalism among the Croats and Slovenians. In 1991 Croatia and Slovenia declared their independence. Fighting broke out between Serbia and Croatia, ending in a truce mediated by the United Nations and enforced by UN peacekeepers. Croatia and Slovenia had won their freedom. In 1992 Bosnia similarly declared its independence.

Strife in Bosnia. Bosnia's greatest challenge was its diverse ethnic and religious mix. Muslims formed the largest single group, but still did not make up a majority of the entire population. Nearly one third of Bosnia's population identified themselves as Serbian, while about one fifth claimed Croatian descent. Many Bosnian Serbs wished to remain part of Serbian-dominated Yugoslavia. Receiving aid from the Yugoslavian government in Belgrade, Bosnian Serbs began a program of **ethnic cleansing**—a campaign of terror and murder intended to drive the Muslims out of areas the Bosnian Serbs claimed.

In an effort to end the fighting, the United Nations stopped the flow of weapons into the region. However, this only made it harder for the Muslim-controlled Bosnian government to fight off the better-armed Serbs. As Serb attacks continued, the UN set up certain protected "safe haven" areas. This did not stop the Serbs, who continued to bomb the Bosnian capital of Sarajevo as well as UN "safe havens." NATO responded by bombing Serbian targets in 1995.

The Bosnian Serbs finally agreed to enter into U.S.-led peace talks in Dayton, Ohio. These talks resulted in the **Dayton Accord.** This

Children are seen here playing in a suburb of Sarajevo. This area was surrounded by Serb forces for at least six months during the campaign of ethnic cleansing.

In 1992 Serb nationalist forces attacked the Oriental Institute in Sarajevo, which housed important collections of Islamic manuscripts. Flames consumed the contents of the library. Tens of thousands of Ottoman-era documents and 5,263 bound manuscripts in Arabic, Persian, Turkish, Hebrew, and local *alhamijado,* were lost in the attack. Many other libraries and archives in Bosnia and Herzegovina suffered similar losses during the ethnic cleansing. A group of scholars and librarians in the United States and Canada are attempting to reassemble part of the destroyed collections by locating copies of the Bosnian material taken abroad in the form of microfilm or photocopies.

Critical Thinking

Why would libraries be targeted during an ethnic cleansing campaign?

ANSWER: Students may suggest to eliminate references to a particular culture and its beliefs or to control information's availability.

Reproducible Resources

PS Readings in World History 133: Russia After Communism

LEVEL 3: Present to students the following scenario: *You live in a country where most people have no say in the government or its policies. All your life you have been told what to do, what to study, what kind of job to have, what to read, what to say, and even what to think! Then, one day, your country's government resigns. You and your fellow citizens must rebuild and reinvent your government and develop a good way to run your country. What kind of problems do you think you would face?* Ask students to respond to you promptly, and discuss these responses. Link any responses that are similar to the problems or challenges faced in Eastern European countries after the fall of communism back to the text.

Have each student write a paragraph that describes how the fall of communism contributed to the resurgence of ethnic tensions in Eastern Europe.

That's Interesting!

Vaclav Havel, who used elements of the Theater of the Absurd in his work, may very well have felt he was a character in one of his own plays. Only a few months before becoming the president of Czechoslovakia, he had been languishing in prison due to involvement in protests against the government.

SKILLS PRACTICE ANSWERS

Students' research papers will vary but should demonstrate the process of historical inquiry.

SKILL-BUILDING STRATEGIES Writing a Research Paper

Transition to Democracy

After throwing off communist rule, Eastern European countries faced a sometimes rough road to economic and social recovery. In his first presidential address to the people of Czechoslovakia, Vaclav Havel did not hide the truth from them:

> "Our country is not flourishing. . . . Entire branches of industry are producing things for which there is no demand while we are short of things we need. . . . We have spoiled our land, rivers and forests, inherited from our ancestors, and we have, today, the worst environment in the whole of Europe. . . . If we accept [the heritage of the last 40 years] in such a way, we shall come to understand it is up to all of us to do something about it."

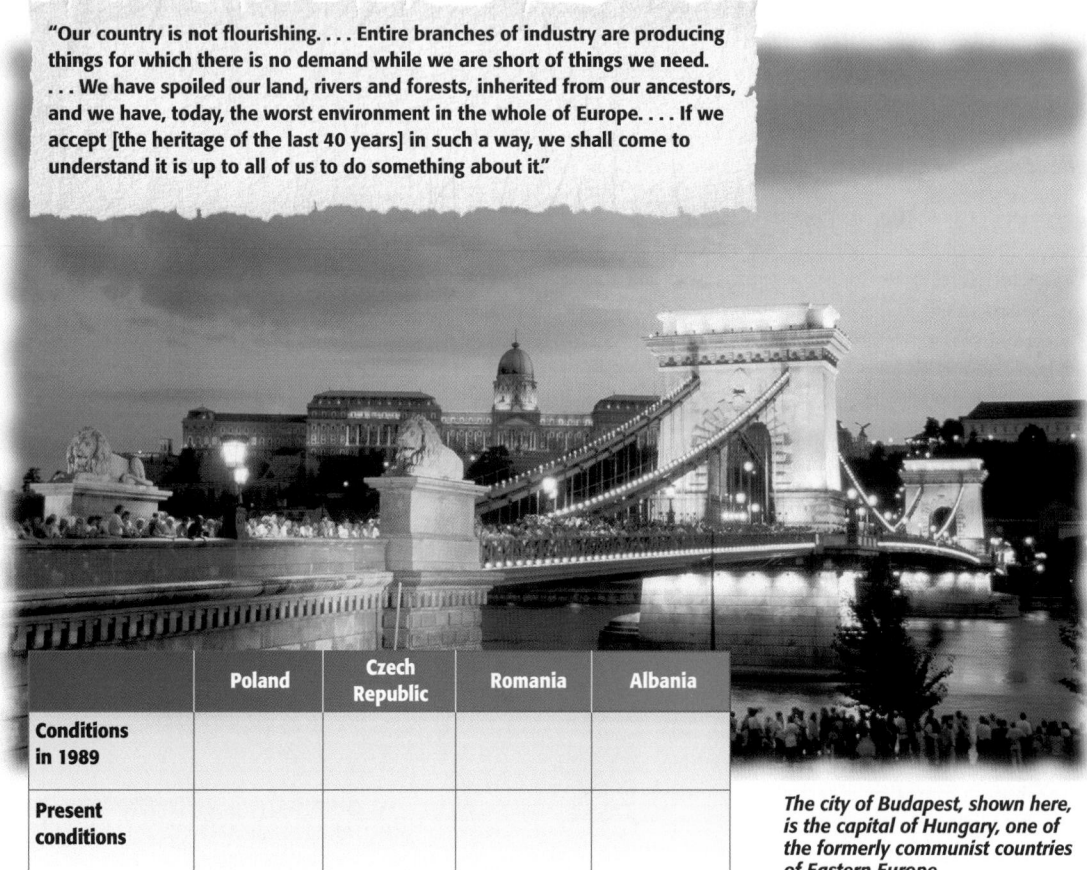

	Poland	Czech Republic	Romania	Albania
Conditions in 1989				
Present conditions				

The city of Budapest, shown here, is the capital of Hungary, one of the formerly communist countries of Eastern Europe.

Skills Reminder

Before writing a paper, choose a topic of interest. Determine what you wish to describe, explain, or prove. Decide what questions you hope to answer.

Begin to collect facts about the topic. Then use the information you have gathered and your stated purpose to formulate a thesis statement.

Determine what ideas and evidence you will need to use to support your thesis statement. Organize the collected facts and discard those that have no bearing on the general statement.

Skills Practice

Pick one of the following Eastern European countries and use the process of historical inquiry to research it. Use and interpret multiple sources of evidence about the country. Then write a five-page research paper on its progress since achieving independence. Maintain standard grammar, spelling, sentence structure, and punctuation in your report. Use the graphic organizer above to help prepare your outline before you begin writing.

- Poland
- Czech Republic
- Romania
- Albania

REVIEW

Have students complete the Section 3 Review on p. 963.

ASSESS

Have students complete Daily Quiz 35.3. As Alternative Assessment, you may want to use the chart exercise in this section's lessons.

RETEACH

Have students complete Main Idea Activity for English Language Learners and Special-Needs Students 35.3. Then ask them to create a chapter glossary that includes the vocabulary and significant people, places, and events from the section.
ENGLISH LANGUAGE LEARNERS

EXTEND

Tell students to imagine they are UN workers in 1994. Organize the class into small groups, and have them brainstorm ideas for bringing peace to the Balkans. After all the ideas have been presented, discuss the positive and negative aspects of each plan.
BLOCK SCHEDULING

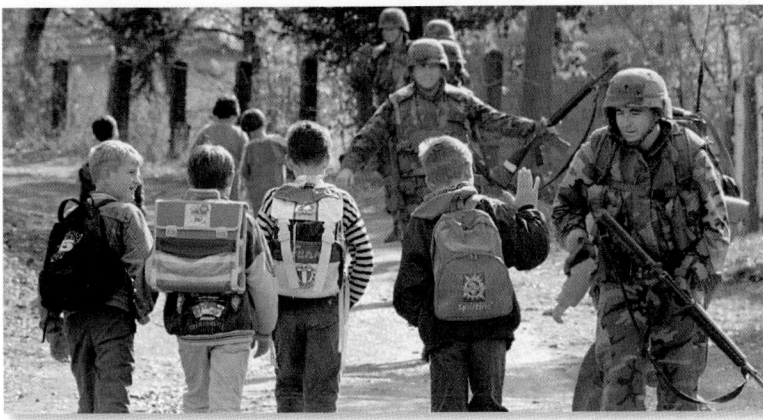

U.S. troops were part of the UN peacekeeping force sent to Bosnia to enforce the Dayton Accord.

agreement gave the Bosnian Serbs control over certain areas while still recognizing the overall sovereignty of Bosnia's Muslim-led government. The UN sent a joint military Implementation Force to Bosnia in December 1995 to enforce the new peace.

In 1998, however, the Yugoslav government cracked down on ethnic Albanian rebels seeking independence for the province of Kosovo. NATO responded to Yugoslavia's actions with air strikes in March 1999. After 11 weeks of bombing, the Yugoslavian government finally allowed a NATO peacekeeping force into Kosovo and withdrew its own troops from the province. Kosovo now operates under UN rule.

Following protests over fraudulent elections in Serbia in 2000, Slobodan Milošević was forced to resign as president. The following year he was turned over to international authorities to face trial on charges of crimes against humanity for his role in directing the wars in Bosnia and Kosovo. In 2003, Yugoslavia dropped its old name and adopted the name of the only two republics that still make it up—Serbia and Montenegro.

✔ **READING CHECK: Identifying Cause and Effect** How did the fall of communism contribute to the resurgence of ethnic tensions in Eastern Europe? led to civil wars among ethnic and religious groups

---

SECTION 3 REVIEW

1. **Define** and explain the significance:
   perestroika
   glasnost
   ethnic cleansing

2. **Identify** and explain the significance:
   Leonid Brezhnev
   Brezhnev Doctrine
   Mikhail Gorbachev
   Boris Yeltsin
   Commonwealth of
     Independent States (CIS)
   Lech Walesa
   Vaclav Havel
   Dayton Accord

3. **Identifying Cause and Effect** Copy the chart below. Use it to explain the causes and results of the fall of communism.

4. **Finding the Main Idea**
   a. Compare and contrast the reforms that Gorbachev and Yeltsin implemented.
   b. How did Eastern European countries throw off communist rule?
   c. What factors led to strife in Bosnia?

5. **Writing and Critical Thinking**
   Supporting a Point of View Write a speech to be given by Mikhail Gorbachev in 1985, telling why perestroika and glasnost will benefit the nation.
   Consider:
   • the purpose of the reforms
   • what problems the Soviet Union had at the time
   • effect on international relations

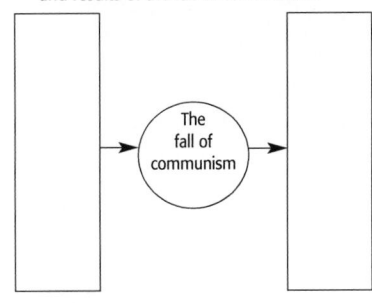

Homework Practice Online
keyword: SP3 HP35

THE SUPERPOWERS IN THE MODERN ERA **963**

---

❶ **Define**
• perestroika, p. 957
• glasnost, p. 957
• ethnic cleansing, p. 961

❷ **Identify**
• Leonid Brezhnev, p. 956
• Brezhnev Doctrine, p. 956
• Mikhail Gorbachev, p. 957
• Boris Yeltsin, p. 957
• Commonwealth of Independent States (CIS), p. 959
• Lech Walesa, p. 960
• Vaclav Havel, p. 960
• Dayton Accord, p. 963

❸ Students' charts should include causes: economic troubles, revolutions, strained relations with the West; effects: economic changes, instability, political challenges, break up of Czechoslovakia and Yugoslavia

❹ a. Gorbachev: relaxed government control of the economy, eased restrictions on dissent, planned to reduce size of armed forces, ended Soviet occupation of Afghanistan; Yeltsin: began transition to democracy, privatized many industries, opened Russia to foreign investment

b. appealed to their government, engaged in labor strikes, protested, started revolutions

c. diverse ethnic and religious mix; Serbs wanted to drive the Muslims out of certain areas

❺ Students' speeches will vary.

OBJECTIVES

1. Explain how the United States was attacked on September 11, 2001, and how people responded.

2. Describe how the events of September 11, 2001, affected the U.S. economy.

3. List the immediate steps that U.S. leaders and their allies took to find those responsible for the attacks and bring them to justice.

🔔 LET'S GET STARTED!

As students enter the classroom, ask them to write a paragraph discussing past cases in which wars or battles have been fought on U.S. soil. *(War of 1812, Civil War, Pearl Harbor)* Have volunteers share their responses with the class. Tell students that in Section 4 they will learn about the terrorist attacks of 2001 and ways in which they affected the U.S. and the world.

SECTION 4

READ TO DISCOVER

1. How was the United States attacked on September 11, 2001, and how did people respond?

2. How did the events of September 11, 2001 affect the U.S. economy?

3. What immediate steps did U.S. leaders and their allies take to find those responsible for the attacks and bring them to justice?

IDENTIFY

World Trade Center
Pentagon
Rudolph Giuliani
Tom Ridge
Donald Rumsfeld
Colin Powell

WHY IT MATTERS TODAY

The terrorist attacks of September 11, 2001, continue to affect American life and U.S. foreign policy. Use CNNfyi.com or other **current events** sources to learn about the latest issues and events stemming from this national tragedy.

CNN Student News.com

A Day That Changed the World

The Main Idea
The United States suffered a devastating terrorist attack by Islamic extremists on September 11, 2001.

The Story Continues *On Tuesday morning, September 11, 2001, it was business as usual in the downtown financial district of New York City. In the World Trade Center complex, some of the 50,000 employees were starting their workday, most of them within the Twin Towers that dominated the Manhattan skyline. Others were still on their way to work. On Fifth Avenue a group of pedestrians noticed a large airplane pass by. "We all looked up," recalled one man. "We all thought it would be unusual for a plane to be flying so low over the city." Moments later they witnessed a terrible disaster unfold.*

The Attack

At 8:45 A.M., the daily routine of a city and a nation was shattered when an American Airlines passenger jet crashed into the north tower of the **World Trade Center.** The impact was devastating, as though a bomb had struck the 110-story building. Lynn Simpson, who was working on the 89th floor, recalled, "I heard an enormous crash. The ceiling fell in, the lights went out and the sprinklers went on. . . . I told everyone to get out." Stunned men and women began evacuating the building as emergency crews rushed to the scene. Then at about 9:00 A.M. a second plane—United Airlines Flight 175—slammed into the south tower of the WTC complex.

Shocked Americans began to realize that these were deliberate attacks when it was learned that both planes had been hijacked by terrorists. Moreover, it was soon clear that New York was not the terrorists' only target. At approximately 9:40 A.M. a third plane, American Airlines Flight 77, hit the west side of the Pentagon. Located just outside Washington, D.C., the **Pentagon** is the headquarters of the U.S. military leadership. The impact of the crash caused massive damage and started fires deep within the huge, five-sided building. Hundreds of military personnel and civilians were killed.

At the World Trade Center complex, hundreds of rescue workers struggled to aid victims and firefighters tried to control the raging fires. In the midst of their efforts, further disaster struck. At 10:00 A.M. the south tower suddenly collapsed, followed half an hour later by the fall of the north tower. "It [the south tower] just fell down in perfect symmetry, one floor, then another

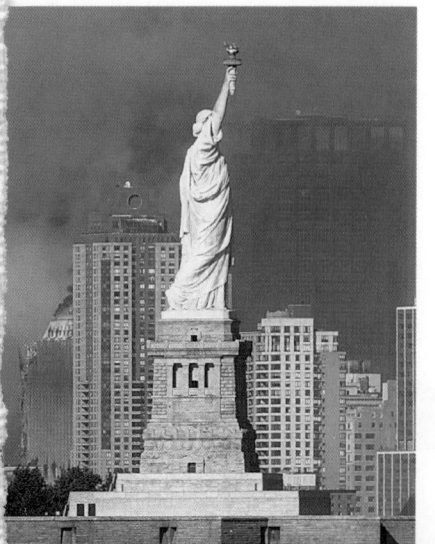

Columns of thick smoke billow from the wreckage of the World Trade Center's twin towers on September 11, 2001, after hijacked commercial airliners piloted by Islamic extremists dove into the buildings, killing thousands.

LEVEL 1: Ask students to summarize the events that took place on September 11, 2001. Then have them discuss the results of the events. Have students write brief essays discussing ways in which the U.S. government and people responded to the events, and ways in which the events may have changed U.S. citizens' attitudes about their own nation and the world. (*Essays should include mention of the way the events unified the American people.*) **ENGLISH LANGUAGE LEARNERS, COOPERATIVE LEARNING**

floor, then another," said a stunned witness. The collapse of the massive buildings killed or trapped thousands of people still inside or near the towers, including hundreds of firefighters, police officers, and other rescuers.

A fourth plane—United Airlines Flight 93—was also hijacked and still in the air over southern Pennsylvania. Cell phone calls from passengers aboard the plane indicate that they learned of the other attacks and decided to stop the terrorists on board from hitting their next target. Flight 93 crashed southeast of Pittsburgh sometime around the time of the collapse of the World Trade Center's towers.

In downtown New York City, clouds of smoke, dust, and ash drifted through the streets along with thousands of battered and dazed survivors. Thousands more people were unaccounted for in the wreckage. Meanwhile, emergency teams battling fires in the Pentagon were unable to search for survivors. As many as 266 passengers and crew aboard the four hijacked flights had been killed. Americans everywhere were shocked, wondering what was to come.

✔ **READING CHECK: Sequencing** In what order did the events of the morning of September 11, 2001, take place? (1, 2) Hijacked planes slammed into the WTC towers and (3) the Pentagon. (4) A fourth airliner crashed in Pennsylvania.

The World Responds

Government officials raced to mount rescue efforts and placed the U.S. military on full alert. The Federal Aviation Administration temporarily grounded air traffic nationwide and closed airports. Key government centers, such as the White House, were briefly evacuated.

Rescue and relief. New York hospitals mobilized hundreds of doctors but found, tragically, that there were relatively few survivors to care for. Within hours, firefighters and other rescue workers from across the nation came to New York to join state and city emergency personnel searching the rubble for survivors. Their efforts were hampered by the tons of unstable debris and by the intense heat from underground fires. Three weeks after the attack there were still more than 5,900 people missing, all presumed dead. New York mayor **Rudolph Giuliani** said of the final death toll, "It will be more than we can bear." In all, about 2,500 people were killed at the World Trade Center, including more than 300 firefighters and many other rescue workers. At the Pentagon, 184 military and civilian personnel, including those on the hijacked plane, had been killed.

Congress swiftly approved a $40 billion relief package to help the nation recover from the attacks. The money would fund emergency assistance and national security measures. The government also passed legislation that provided compensation to the families of victims. Democrats and Republicans displayed an unusual degree of cooperation in pushing through such measures. "I think the message is very simply we are united . . . when it comes to a national threat as great as this," said Senate Majority Leader Tom Daschle of South Dakota.

People unite. Political leaders also tried to rally Americans' spirit on the day of the attack. Mayor Giuliani assured fellow New Yorkers, "We're going to rebuild and rebuild stronger." President George W. Bush, who had been in Florida visiting an elementary school, was moved to a safe location. From there, he

In the aftermath of the terrorist attacks, members of New York City's fire and police departments mounted a heroic effort to rescue victims trapped in the rubble of the World Trade Center.

Americans such as these middle school students from Burnet, Texas, united to demonstrate patriotism and support for the victims of the September 11 terrorist attacks.

Citizenship

Tell students that a crisis can often bring people together in their efforts to help and comfort others. Examples of such a crisis might be natural disasters such as floods or earthquakes, or acts of war and terror such as Pearl Harbor, the Oklahoma City bombing, or the terrorist attacks of September 11, 2001. When such a crisis occurs, many ordinary people are moved to acts of bravery, generosity, or sacrifice that might seem unusual in everyday life.

Critical Thinking

Ask students why crises often bring out the best in people.

ANSWER: Answers will vary but students will probably say that this phenomenon is a demonstration of the essential goodness of human beings.

That's Interesting!

Rising to a height of 110 stories, the twin towers of the World Trade Center were the second tallest structures in the United States. They held 13 million square feet of office space—enough to house about 50,000 workers. In 1993, the explosion of a bomb in the underground garage killed six people, injured one thousand more, and caused $600 million worth of damage. Like the attack of September 11, that bomb was planted by members of a radical Islamic group.

ALL LEVELS: Begin by reading the quote from James Earl Jones on page 966. Ask students to list ways in which U.S. citizens are united and ways in which they are different. Help students understand that U.S. citizens reacted to the attacks by immediately setting aside their differences and uniting to help one another and show their unity and strength. Ask students what the headline in the French newspaper *Le Monde*, "We Are All Americans," means, and discuss with students the concept of what it is to be a citizen of the world. **ENGLISH LANGUAGE LEARNERS, COOPERATIVE LEARNING**

HOMEWORK Ask students to write a brief essay explaining why they think traditional opponents of the U.S., such as Cuba and Iran, expressed sympathy and regret for the September 11 tragedy. (*They may have been sincerely shocked by the barbarity of the act; they may have wanted to distance themselves from the terrorists; they may have wanted to maintain stable relations with the U.S.*)

Culture

Remind students that actors, musicians, and athletes all contributed to the effort to help after the attacks by holding benefit shows and concerts or by donating money to the cause. Tell students that entertainers and artists have tried to help keep spirits high and patriotism strong in past times of emergency, such as the Great Depression and World War II.

Critical Thinking

Ask students if they think the efforts of entertainers and artists during times of crisis are effective, and if so, why.

ANSWER: Answers will vary but most students should recognize that the great deal of money to be raised by benefit shows helps in many ways and that entertainment is an important way of lifting spirits and recovering from grief.

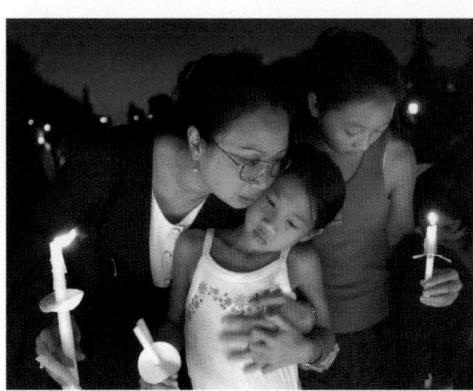

In the days following the terrorist attacks, Americans across the nation came together in a series of interfaith memorial services to honor the victims and to demonstrate unity and faith.

gave a brief speech to the nation. "Freedom itself was attacked this morning by a faceless coward," he declared. Republican and Democratic members of Congress issued a joint declaration to the country from the Capitol steps. They said that the United States would not be intimidated by terrorism. The members then sang a chorus of "God Bless America."

The tragic events of September 11, 2001, drew sympathy and support from around the world. Citizens of more than 40 countries were among the missing. The European Union declared September 14 a day of mourning throughout its 15 member states. British prime minister Tony Blair called the terrorist acts "an attack on the free and democratic world everywhere." The French newspaper *Le Monde* ran a headline saying, "WE ARE ALL AMERICANS." Russian and Chinese leaders gave their condolences. Even traditional opponents of the United States, such as Cuba and Iran, expressed their sympathy and regret. U.S. leaders gave thanks for these gestures and worked to form an active coalition against terrorism.

Perhaps the greatest show of unity came from the American people themselves. Many were inspired to displays of charity and patriotism. Within two days Wal-Mart, the nation's largest retail chain, had sold its entire stock of half a million American flags. Charitable groups across the country moved swiftly to raise funds for relief efforts. Thousands of people went to Red Cross centers to donate blood. "It's just amazing," said one nurse in New York. "There'll be a three- or four-hour wait, and just look at all of these people standing here." Actors and musicians held a special telethon, "America: A Tribute to Heroes," on September 21. The effort raised some $150 million to benefit the families who had lost loved ones in the attacks.

People also came together in public to heal their wounds and show their strength. When professional sports leagues resumed their schedules, stadiums were filled with patriotic tributes and fans waving flags. Actor James Earl Jones drew cheers as he opened a mass prayer service held in New York City's Yankee Stadium.

History Makers Speak

❝Our spirit is unbroken. In fact, it is stronger than ever. Today we reaffirm our faith in the essential dignity of every individual. What we share as Americans and as human beings is far greater than what divides us.❞

James Earl Jones, September 23, 2001

Spiritual leaders representing many faiths led prayers for the victims and called for unity as a nation. The Boys and Girls Choir of Harlem sang a stirring rendition of "We Shall Overcome," with its refrain, "We are not afraid. . . . We shall live in peace."

✔ **READING CHECK: Finding the Main Idea** In what ways did Americans first respond to the terrorist attacks? shock, followed by displays of patriotism, charity, and unity

The Investigation

Immediately after the attacks, the largest criminal investigation in U.S. history began. Within 48 hours the Federal Bureau of Investigation (FBI) placed more than 4,000 special agents on the case. The FBI soon released the names of 19 suspected hijackers from several Middle Eastern nations. Investigators gathered evidence suggesting that

LEVEL 2: Begin by discussing the role air travel plays in U.S. and world society. Ask students to brainstorm services that commercial airlines provide. *(carry business people from place to place, tourists to their vacation spots, goods and products to markets; employ many people)* Then ask students to describe how the terrorist attacks damaged the airline industry and other industries. *(airlines shut down for days, expense of increased security, people fearful of flying; business people and products could not reach destinations, vacationers canceled trips)* Tell students that the government's purpose in providing $15 billion dollars for the airline industry was to try to help the economy stay strong and active.

COOPERATIVE LEARNING

LEVEL 3: Copy the following chart on the chalkboard, omitting the italicized answers. Have each student complete the diagram by filling in the effect for each cause listed.

The Stock Market	
Cause	**Effect**
people worry about how war will affect stock prices	*stock prices fall*
stock prices fall	*people lose money*
people lose money	*people sell stocks*
people sell stocks	*companies lose money*
companies lose money	*people lose jobs*

Explain to students that this downward spiral effect can lead to a bad economy known as a "recession."

---

each group of hijackers included trained pilots and that some of these men had been living and training in the United States for months. Even more crucial was the identity of those who had planned these acts of terror.

A prime suspect surfaced almost immediately—Osama bin Laden. This wealthy Saudi Arabian exile was already wanted for his suspected role in earlier terrorist attacks against U.S. forces overseas. A supporter of an extreme form of Islamic fundamentalism, bin Laden had publicly called for attacks on the United States, which he claimed had corrupted and oppressed Muslims. Officials believed that bin Laden's global terrorism network, known as al Qaeda, or "the Base," was one of the few terrorist groups with the resources and organizational structure to have carried out the attacks.

Experts also agreed that the attacks of September 11 probably involved the cooperation of more than one terrorist group. Investigators from a broad range of federal agencies, with assistance from other nations, began a global manhunt for anyone with knowledge of the attacks. They sifted through debris at the crash sites to find physical evidence and tracked airline, telephone, credit card, and other financial records to trace terrorists' movements. Several hundred suspects were detained at home and abroad for questioning. Although the complexity of the task and the need to protect security and sources forced officials to be cautious, the Bush administration pledged to release conclusive evidence about the attacks as soon as it was feasible to do so.

✔ **READING CHECK: Summarizing** What early conclusions did investigators draw about the source of the attacks, and how did they investigate them? FBI investigators analyzed physical evidence and telephone, airline, and financial records to conclude that Osama bin Laden's al Qaeda network was responsible.

The Economic Impact

The terrorist strikes on the World Trade Center had a high cost in economic terms as well as in lives. The costs related to the immediate physical damage were estimated at $25 billion. In addition, the New York Stock Exchange (NYSE) had to shut down operations for four days following the attack. When the stock market reopened, concerns about a potential war and poor economic indicators combined to cause one of the worst weeks in the history of the NYSE. European and Asian stock markets also suffered heavy losses. Although stock prices made a modest rally the following week, concerns about the health of the national and global economy remained. "The insecurity is still there," commented one German trader. "There is no way to tell what is going to happen," explained an American trader. The Federal Reserve quickly cut interest rates in an effort to help the economy.

One area of particular concern was the airline industry. Forced to shut down operations for days and facing greatly increased security expenses and a public reluctance to fly, major airlines took heavy financial losses. They laid off thousands of workers, and at least one smaller carrier went out of business. The air-travel crisis caused wider problems as well. Tourism declined severely around the nation, and companies relying on supplies shipped by air endured shortages. Congress and the president rushed to pass a $15 billion bail-out package to help keep the nation's airlines operating.

One of the most difficult economic problems for the government to address was falling consumer confidence. Many Americans had been concerned by the weakness of the economy before the terrorist attacks. Uncertainty and fear raised by

The stock market tumbled sharply when exchanges such as the NASDAQ, pictured here, reopened six days after the September 11 terrorist attacks. National economies around the world were hard hit by the attacks and the threats they posed to global peace.

967

ALL LEVELS Have students select some aspect of the steps taken by the U.S. government in locating and apprehending the terrorists to study in more depth. They might investigate the freezing of assets, diplomatic efforts, the military campaign, or humanitarian aid to the Afghan people. Ask each student to find out something interesting about their chosen topic and share it with the class. They might watch a TV news report and summarize it for the class; they might read and report on books about the longstanding conflicts in the Middle East. Encourage students to spend about three to five minutes on their presentations to the class. **ENGLISH LANGUAGE LEARNERS, COOPERATIVE LEARNING**

Have students work in groups to develop a multimedia presentation covering the September 11, 2001, terrorist attacks. Suggest to students that each member of the group specialize in one aspect of the crisis or its aftermath. Have students use their textbooks, the library, computer software, television, and any other sources that are available to complete their work. **COOPERATIVE LEARNING**

Geography

The nation of Afghanistan is known for its harsh, rugged, and forbidding terrain. The Afghan people know their land better than anyone else. They are also renowned for being brave and formidable soldiers. In recent history they have defeated both British and Soviet forces attempting to invade their nation.

ACTIVITY: Have students research Afghanistan to discover what makes it a formidable terrain and what kinds of problems a military campaign in that country might encounter.

History Maker

GEORGE W. BUSH. George W. Bush, the 43rd president of the United States, was born July 6, 1946. He served in the Texas Air National Guard, worked in the oil and gas business, and was a managing partner of the Texas Rangers baseball team before being elected governor of the state of Texas. He was the first governor in Texas history to be elected to consecutive four-year terms. His father, George Herbert Walker Bush, was the 41st president.

ACTIVITY: Have students research and make a time line of the actions taken by President Bush after the attack on New York and Washington, D.C.

President George W. Bush addressed a joint session of Congress on September 20, during which he pledged to utilize the full might of the nation in a war on international terrorism.

Analyzing Primary Sources

Identifying a Point of View
What did President Bush call on other nations to do? determine if they supported the U.S. or the terrorists

---

the events of September 11 made many Americans believe the country was headed for a recession. "We do have to fear fear itself, it matters, it affects consumer spending," stated one economist. Government officials responded to such concerns by emphasizing that the long-term health of the economy was strong, even if difficult times lay ahead.

✔ **READING CHECK: Identifying Cause and Effect** What immediate effect did the terrorist attacks have on the U.S. economy?
huge costs of damage, falling stock prices, declining consumer confidence

A Call to Action

In a national address on September 20, President George W. Bush called the attacks on the World Trade Center and the Pentagon "an act of war." He promised that the United States would bring those responsible to justice.

A war on terrorism. The president also declared that the United States would wage war on terrorism itself. Bush emphasized that U.S. efforts would be aimed not only against terrorist organizations but also against national governments that supported and protected terrorists. "Either you are with us, or you are with the terrorists," he declared.

 History Makers Speak

"Tonight we are a country awakened to danger and called to defend freedom. Our grief has turned to anger, and anger to resolution. Whether we bring our enemies to justice, or bring justice to our enemies, justice will be done. . . . The enemy of America is not our many Muslim friends; it is not our many Arab friends. Our enemy is a radical network of terrorists, and every government that supports them. . . . Every nation, in every region, now has a decision to make. Either you are with us, or you are with the terrorists. From this day forward, any nation that continues to harbor or support terrorism will be regarded by the United States as a hostile regime. . . . Great harm has been done to us. We have suffered great loss. And in our grief and anger we have found our mission and our moment. Freedom and fear are at war. The advance of human freedom—the great achievement of our time, and the great hope of every time—now depends on us. Our nation—this generation—will lift a dark threat of violence from our people and our future. We will rally the world to this cause by our efforts, by our courage. We will not tire, we will not falter, and we will not fail."

George W. Bush, September 20, 2001

In his speech the president singled out one government—the Taliban regime of Afghanistan—as a key sponsor of terror. The Taliban emerged in the mid-1990s as a splinter group of fundamentalist Muslims. Many members had fought against the Soviets during their occupation of Afghanistan. Its leaders had developed ties to Osama bin Laden, whom they later sheltered.

Domestic security. President Bush appointed Governor **Tom Ridge** of Pennsylvania to head the Office of Homeland Security. This office was created to coordinate the domestic national security efforts of various government agencies.

Key goals included improving airport security and protecting vital systems such as transportation and power networks from attack. Proposed airline security measures included background checks on passengers and employees, more-thorough

REVIEW

Have students complete the Section 4 Review on p. 969.

ASSESS

Have students complete Daily Quiz 35.4. As Alternative Assessment, you may want to use the graphic organizer or the essay exercise in this section's lessons.

RETEACH

Have students complete Main Idea Activity for English Language Learners and Special-Needs Students 35.4. Then, as a group, have the class discuss what they might do to assist the victims of the terrorist attacks and their families. Ask students to prepare a plan of action to help the U.S. recover from the tragedy.
ENGLISH LANGUAGE LEARNERS, COOPERATIVE LEARNING

EXTEND

Have students imagine that they are a young person growing up in an Islamic nation. Ask them to write essays about how they would react to the terrorist attacks on the United States. Encourage students to be as imaginative as possible. Muslim students may wish to express their actual feelings. **BLOCK SCHEDULING**

baggage searches, and restricted access to airport facilities. Political leaders such as U.S. Attorney General John Ashcroft also called for expanded law-enforcement powers to combat terrorism.

A difficult mission. Administration officials, including Secretary of Defense **Donald Rumsfeld,** agreed that striking at terrorists outside the United States would be a lengthy and difficult task. Success would require identifying the proper targets as well as finding ways to destroy them.

The Bush administration sought to fight terrorism using economic, diplomatic, and military means. The president froze the assets of individuals, groups, and companies with suspected terrorist ties. Secretary of State **Colin Powell** led U.S. efforts to build an international coalition against terrorism and to isolate the Taliban regime. The leaders of nations such as Great Britain and Russia pledged their support of antiterrorist efforts. For the first time in its existence, NATO invoked Article 5 of its original treaty, under which NATO members are required to come to the defense of an alliance member under attack. Even former allies of the Taliban regime, such as Pakistan and Saudi Arabia, were convinced to support U.S. efforts.

The United States also began mobilizing military forces such as aircraft-carrier groups and ground troops in preparation for attacks on terrorism. Less than one month after the terrorists' attacks, the United States and its allies began their offensive. On October 7, the first in a series of powerful air strikes hit al Qaeda bases and Taliban sites in Afghanistan. At the same time, food, medicine, and other supplies were air-dropped to the country's impoverished civilian population. The Northern Alliance, an Afghan group that had fought against the Taliban since the early 1990s, provided ground support. The United States and Great Britain also sent ground troops. The troops slowly drove out the Taliban and captured members of al Qaeda. On December 17, the American flag was raised at the U.S. embassy in Kabul for the first time since 1989. Four days later a new Afghan government was established.

In the days immediately following the attacks of September 11, 2001, the United States began deploying its military arsenal in preparation for a long and difficult struggle against global terrorism. Pictured here is the U.S. aircraft carrier Theodore Roosevelt.

✔ **READING CHECK: Summarizing** What early steps did U.S. leaders take to respond to the terrorist attacks on the United States? government leaders declared war on terrorism, mobilized military forces

SECTION 4 REVIEW

1. **Identify** and explain:
   World Trade Center
   Pentagon
   Rudolph Giuliani
   Tom Ridge
   Donald Rumsfeld
   Colin Powell

2. **Analyzing Information** Copy the graphic organizer below. Use it to explain some of the ways in which the U.S. government responded to protect the United States and bring its attackers to justice.

   Economic → Military
   Government Actions
   Social → Diplomatic

3. **Finding the Main Idea**
   a. Who did investigators initially suspect of carrying out the terrorist attacks of September 11, 2001, and how did they pursue the investigation?
   b. How did the attacks affect the economy?

4. **Writing and Critical Thinking**
   Evaluating Imagine that you are first learning of the attacks on September 11, 2001, and want to help however you can. Write a paragraph describing possible actions you could take to assist those in need.
   Consider the following:
   • the efforts of relief agencies to help victims
   • the need for national unity
   • the importance of tolerance

Homework Practice Online
keyword: SP3 HP35

❶ **Identify**
• World Trade Center, p. 964
• Pentagon, p. 964
• Rudolph Giuliani, p. 965
• Tom Ridge, p. 968
• Donald Rumsfeld, p. 969
• Colin Powell, p. 969

❷ Economic: froze and seized assets of terrorists and their supporters; Diplomatic: created international coalition against terrorism and the Taliban; Military: attacked Taliban sites and al Qaeda bases in Afghanistan; Social: provided food and other relief to Afghan civilians

❸ a. Osama bin Laden; by hunting for people with knowledge of the attacks, by checking financial records to trace terrorists' movements, by inspecting debris at crash sites, by questioning suspects

b. caused $25 billion in physical damage, forced the New York Stock Exchange to close, damaged the airline industry, weakened consumer confidence

❹ Answers will vary.

REVIEW AND ASSESSMENT RESOURCES

REPRODUCIBLE RESOURCES
▶ Vocabulary Activity 35

TECHNOLOGY RESOURCES
▶ Chapter 35 Test Generator (on the One-Stop Planner)
▶ Global Skill Builder CD–ROM
▶ HRW Web Site

REINFORCEMENT, REVIEW, and ASSESSMENT
▶ Chapter 35 Review, pp. 964–965
▶ Chapter 35 Tutorial for Students, Parents, Mentors, and Peers
▶ Chapter 35 Test (Form A or B)
▶ Alternative Assessment Handbook
▶ Chapter 35 Test for English Language Learners and Special-Needs Students

REVIEW
Have students complete the Chapter 35 Review on pages 964–965.

ASSESS
Use one of the chapter tests to assess students' understanding of the content. For Alternative Assessment, see the Portfolio Activities and Alternative Assessment Handbook.

CHAPTER 35 REVIEW ANSWERS

Understanding Main Ideas
1. dissent over Vietnam; presidential scandals

2. nations would cooperate to defend weaker countries

3. They want to preserve their distinct culture.

4. tough approach to foreign policy, close ties to U.S., helped form national coalition against Iraqi army; reduced government funding of many social programs, eased government control on business, reduced power of labor unions

5. economic recession prevented any political party from gaining a majority in Parliament

6. They worried the EU would undermine their sovereignty.

7. repressed attempted reforms in satellite nations

8. overhaul the Soviet economic system

9. ethnic tensions; Serbia tried to dominate Yugoslavia; Serbia and Croatia declared independence

10. Islamic terrorists destroyed the World Trade Center in New York City and seriously damaged the Pentagon in Washington, D.C.

11. The attacks caused the U.S. to increase security measures and did serious damage to the U.S. economy.

Reviewing Themes
1. It exerted more control over the economy.

970

Review

Creating a Time Line
Copy the time line below onto a sheet of paper. Complete the time line by filling in the events, individuals, and dates from the chapter that you think were significant. Pick three events and explain why you think they were significant.

| 1969 | 1985 | present |

Writing a Summary
Using standard grammar, spelling, sentence structure, and punctuation, write an overview of the events in the chapter.

Identifying People and Ideas
Identify the following terms or individuals and explain their significance:

1. Watergate scandal
2. détente
3. Margaret Thatcher
4. Helmut Kohl
5. Helsinki Accords
6. European Union
7. Mikhail Gorbachev
8. glasnost
9. ethnic cleansing
10. World Trade Center

Understanding the Main Ideas
SECTION 1 *(pp. 940–947)*
The Industrial Powers of North America
1. What political problems plagued the United States in the 1970s and 1980s?
2. What did President Bush mean by "new world order"?
3. Why do many people in Quebec desire autonomy?

SECTION 2 *(pp. 948–955)*
Europe
4. What was Margaret Thatcher's approach to foreign and economic policy?
5. What led to coalition governments in Italy?
6. Why did some European nations oppose entry into the European Union?

SECTION 3 *(pp. 956–963)*
The Fall of Communism
7. How did the Brezhnev Doctrine affect Eastern Europe?
8. What were perestroika and glasnost intended to do?
9. What factors led to war in the former Yugoslavia?

SECTION 4 *(pp. 964–969)*
A Day That Changed the World
10. What events took place in the United States on September 11, 2001?
11. How did these events affect U.S. security and the economy?

Reviewing Themes
1. **Economics** How did the government's role in the economy differ in the Soviet Union as compared with Western nations?
2. **Government** How did the communist states suppress dissent?
3. **Global Relations** What political and economic concerns did leaders in the West have regarding Russia after the fall of communism?

Thinking Critically
1. **Comparing and Contrasting** Compare and contrast the political changes that took place in Great Britain and West Germany in the 1970s and 1980s.
2. **Analyzing Information** How did human rights affect U.S. policies toward China and the Soviet Union?
3. **Identifying Cause and Effect** How was the Soviet Union affected by perestroika and glasnost?

Writing About History
Summarizing Not all of the former Soviet republics have joined the Commonwealth of Independent States. Write a brief essay that explains which nations have joined the commonwealth and what the costs and benefits are of joining. Use the following chart to organize your thoughts before you begin writing.

Benefits of joining CIS	Costs of joining CIS

CLOSE

Ask students to describe the progress the EU has made toward political unity in Europe.

RETEACH

Pair students who have had difficulty with the test. Have each pair compile a chapter glossary. From the glossary, have the pair create flash cards with a definitional sentence on the back and quiz each other. When they are ready, have students take the Form B Test to assess their mastery of the material.

ENGLISH LANGUAGE LEARNERS

Portfolio Extensions

1. Have students research the ideas and circumstances that influenced revolution and reform in the former Soviet Union. Ask them to write a report that details the rise of democratic ideals in Russia and the former Soviet satellites.
2. Relations between Canadians who speak English and Canadians who speak French have occasionally been tense. Ask students to present an oral report on the differences between these two cultural groups. Their reports should include a discussion of recent trends toward separatism and away from it.
3. Have students use resources in the library to gather information on the economies of the nations of Eastern Europe. Note each nation's major industries, leading imports and exports, and chief trading partners. Ask students to construct a chart showing their findings.

Building Social Studies Skills

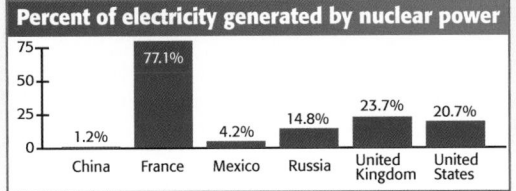

Interpreting a Graph

Study the graph below. Then use the information on the graph to answer the questions that follow.

Nuclear Electricity Generation in Selected Countries (2003)

Percent of electricity generated by nuclear power

China	1.2%
France	77.1%
Mexico	4.2%
Russia	14.8%
United Kingdom	23.7%
United States	20.7%

1. Which of the following is a correct general statement about the data shown on the graph?
   a. The more lakes and rivers a country has, the more nuclear power it uses.
   b. The amount of electricity generated by nuclear power has no relationship to the size of the country.
   c. Electricity generated by nuclear power is expensive.
   d. Some nuclear reactors generate more electricity than can be used by its customers.

2. Of the 32 countries that use nuclear power, some have cut back on their nuclear energy programs. Why do you think the countries cut back? Give specific reasons to support your view.

Understanding Frames of Reference

Read the following excerpt from a speech given by historian Barbara Tuchman in 1966. Then answer the questions.

"I know very little . . . about laboratory science, but I have the impression that . . . from a given set of circumstances a predictable result should follow. The trouble is that in human behavior and history it is impossible to isolate or repeat a given set of circumstances. . . . Tides are so obedient to schedule that a timetable for them can be printed like that for trains, though more reliable. In fact, tides and trains sharply illustrate my point: One depends on the moon and is certain; the other depends on man and is uncertain."

3. Which of the following probably best describes Tuchman's approach to understanding human behavior?
   a. Tuchman sees little difference between the study of history and the study of science.
   b. Patterns of human behavior are predictable.
   c. Tuchman believes that history repeats itself.
   d. Tuchman follows a historical—rather than a purely scientific—approach toward understanding human behavior.

4. Explain your choice of statements in question 3. Give specific examples to support your point of view.

Alternative Assessment

Building Your Portfolio

Government

Political systems of the superpowers are based on philosophies and ideas developed throughout history. Use the library and other sources to compile a list of such ideas, including Judeo-Christian ethics and the rise of secularism and individualism in Western civilization, beginning with the Enlightenment. Then write a report that analyzes how at least one of these ideas has influenced governments, institutions, or societies.

☑ internet connect

Internet Activity: go.hrw.com
KEYWORD: SP3 WH35

Choose a topic on the Superpowers in the Modern Era to:
• create a chart about U.S. and Soviet relations after World War II.
• write a biography of former British prime minister Margaret Thatcher.
• create a newspaper of Quebec.

The Modern World

CHAPTER RESOURCE MANAGER

Objectives	Pacing Guide	Reproducible Resources
SECTION 1 **The Arts and Literature** (pp. 974–980) • List trends that occurred in painting, sculpture, and architecture after World War II. • Identify the major themes of music, dance, film, and drama after 1945. • Explain how poetry and novels expressed the mood of the times. • Describe how public support of cultural activities changed after World War II.	**Regular** 1.5 day **Block Scheduling** 1 day *Block Scheduling Handbook with Team Teaching Strategies, 36.1*	**RS** Guided Reading Strategy 36.1 **E** Creative Teaching Strategy 36: A Look at the Future: The Movie
SECTION 2 **Science and Technology** (pp. 981–989) • List the advances in travel and space exploration that have occurred since 1945. • Explain the effect miniaturization and computerization have had on modern life. • Describe the technological improvements that have been made in medical science. • Discuss the environmental concerns scientists have identified.	**Regular** 1.5 day **Block Scheduling** 1 day *Block Scheduling Handbook with Team Teaching Strategies, 36.2*	**RS** Guided Reading Strategy 36.2 **RS** Graphic Organizer Activity 36: Technological Innovations and Challenges **SM** Geography Activity 36: The Expanding Sahara **PS** Readings in World History 129: A Message from the *Apollo XI* Astronauts **PS** Readings in World History 130: Books, Gadgets, and Freedom **PS** Readings in World History 136: People 3.1: The Ethics of Human Cloning
SECTION 3 **Human Rights and the Spread of Democratic Ideals** (pp. 990–993) • List some recent examples of human rights abuses. • Explain how the nations of the world have dealt with human rights violations. • Discuss how democratic ideals and practices spread in the late 1900s.	**Regular** 1.5 day **Block Scheduling** 1 day *Block Scheduling Handbook with Team Teaching Strategies, 36.3*	**RS** Guided Reading Strategy 36.3 **PS** Readings in World History 132: Rock Music and Politics **PS** Readings in World History 138: A Lebanese Woman Speaks **E** Hands-on History Activity 36: Looking Into the Future

Chapter Resource Key

PS	Primary Sources	**A**	Assessment	Music	
RS	Reading Support	**REV**	Review	Video	
IC	Interdisciplinary Connections	**ELL**	Reinforcement and English Language Learners	Internet	
E	Enrichment		Transparencies	Holt Presentation Maker Using Microsoft® PowerPoint®	
SM	Skills Mastery		CD-ROM		

 One-Stop Planner CD-ROM

See the ***One–Stop Planner*** for a complete list of additional resources for students and teachers.

One-Stop Planner CD-ROM

It's easy to plan lessons, select resources, and print out materials for your students when you use the **One-Stop Planner** CD–ROM with **Test Generator**.

Technology Resources	Reinforcement, Review, and Assessment
One-Stop Planner 36.1	Daily Quiz 36.1
Holt Researcher: World History: Maya Angelou, Toni Morrison	Main Idea Activity 36.1
Regions of the World Music Audio CD Program 1: The United States: Doc Evans and his Dixieland Jazz Band	English Audio Summary 36.1
World History Teaching Transparency: Art and History 30: Freeway Mural in Los Angeles	Spanish Audio Summary 36.1
Homework Practice Online	REV Section 1 Review, p. 980
One-Stop Planner 36.2	Daily Quiz 36.2
CNN Presents World Cultures: Yesterday and Today Segment 37	Main Idea Activity 36.2
CNN Presents Geography: Yesterday and Today Segments 3, 5, 7	English Audio Summary 36.2
World History Teaching Transparency: Geography and History 30, 40; Everyday Life 30	Spanish Audio Summary 36.2
Homework Practice Online	REV Section 2 Review, p. 989
Online Maps: The World; The Global Problem of Acid Rain	
Online Graphs: Green Revolution in Mexico and India	
One-Stop Planner 36.3	Daily Quiz 36.3
Holt Researcher: World History: Aung San Suu Kyi	Main Idea Activity 36.3
Homework Practice Online	English Audio Summary 36.3
	Spanish Audio Summary 36.3
	REV Section 3 Review, p. 993

HRW ONLINE RESOURCES

GO TO: go.hrw.com
Then type in a keyword.

TEACHER HOME PAGE
  KEYWORD: SP3 Teacher

CHAPTER INTERNET ACTIVITIES
  KEYWORD: SP3 WH36
Choose an activity to:
- investigate global warming.
- learn more about modern world literature by studying contemporary novelists and poets.
- write a biography about one of the artists mentioned in this chapter.

CHAPTER ENRICHMENT LINKS
  KEYWORD: SP3 CH36

ONLINE ASSESSMENT
  Homework Practice
  KEYWORD: SP3 HP36
  Standardized Test Prep
  KEYWORD: SP3 STP36
  Rubrics
  KEYWORD: SS Rubrics

ONLINE MAPS, CHARTS, AND GRAPHS
  KEYWORD: SP3 MCG

CONTENT UPDATES
  KEYWORD: SS Content Updates

HOLT PRESENTATION MAKER
  KEYWORD: SP3 PPT36

ONLINE READING SUPPORT
  KEYWORD: SS Strategies

CURRENT EVENTS
  KEYWORD: S3 Current Events

Meeting Individual Needs

Ability Levels

Level 1 Basic level activities designed for all students encountering new material

Level 2 Intermediate level activities designed for average students

Level 3 Challenging activities designed for honors and gifted and talented students

English Language Learners These activities address the needs of students with Limited English Proficiency.

Chapter Review and Assessment

- IC Vocabulary Activity 36
- Global Skill Builder CD–ROM
- HRW Web Site
- REV Chapter 36 Tutorial for Students, Parents, Mentors, and Peers
- REV Chapter 36 Review, pp. 994–995
- A Chapter 36 Test Generator (on the One-Stop Planner)
- A Chapter 36 Test (Form A or B)
- A Alternative Assessment Handbook
- A Chapter 36 Test for English Language Learners and Special-Needs Students

Build on What You Know

Ask students to answer the following questions:

What have human beings accomplished since 1945?

Consider:

- developments in art
- advancements in science and technology
- changes in the area of human rights

What are improvements humans could make?

Consider:

- importance of creative expression
- health needs
- safety needs
- opportunities for international cooperation

EXPLORING THE TIME LINE

GLOBAL EVENTS

🎵 **internet** connect

TOPIC: Television: Its History

GO TO: go.hrw.com

KEYWORD: SP3 WH36

Have students access the Internet through the HRW Go site to learn about the beginning of television in the twentieth century—its history and the effect it has had on our culture. Have students prepare a poster or skit to teach the rest of the class what they have learned.

CHAPTER 36

(1945–Present)

The Modern World

1947
Daily Life
More than 1 million U.S. war veterans enroll in colleges under the "G.I. Bill of Rights."

This stamp was issued by the U.S. Postal Service to commemorate the G.I. Bill.

Apollo mission patch

1950
Daily Life
The UN reports that more than half the world's children are undernourished.

1961
Global Events
The UN General Assembly condemns apartheid.

1952
Business and Finance
Germany becomes a member of the World Bank.

1961
Science and Technology
Soviet cosmonaut Yury Gagarin becomes the first person to travel in space.

1969
Science and Technology
The *Apollo 11* mission lands on the moon and Neil Armstrong takes the first human steps there.

1950 | **1960** | **1970**

1949
The Arts
American playwright Arthur Miller wins the Pulitzer Prize for *Death of a Salesman.*

1954
Science and Technology
Jonas Salk's polio vaccine is released for general use.

1965
The Arts
The Beatles' song "A Hard Day's Night" is popular.

1975
Politics
Russian scientist Andrey Sakharov wins the Nobel Peace Prize for his humanitarian efforts.

1963
The Arts
New York's Guggenheim Museum holds a show of pop art, including works by Andy Warhol.

1946
The Arts
Russian immigrant George Balanchine directs the *Nightshadow* ballet in New York City.

1970
Daily Life
About 231 million television sets are in use around the world.

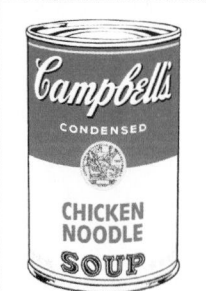

1946
Politics
The UN General Assembly holds its first session in London.

One of Andy Warhol's signature soup can paintings

Build on What You Know

uring World War II, many nations suffered from economic hardship, ruined property, and loss of life. After the war's end, nations struggled to rebuild their cities and economies. New tensions surfaced as the political and economic battles of the Cold War began. In this chapter, you will learn how the everyday lives of most of the world's citizens changed dramatically in the years following World War II. Exciting and thoughtful new styles in the cultural arts reflected the world's rapidly changing society. Science, technology, and a new commitment to human rights brought about much of this transformation.

What's Your Opinion?

 To help students create their Themes Journal entries, provide the following examples of appropriate **agree**/**disagree** *statements.*

Culture

Agree Economic prosperity provides more leisure time for people to pursue the arts.

Disagree The arts flourish in hard times when people express emotions and concerns.

Science, Technology & Society

Agree Overall health and living standards have improved in the developed world with advances in science and technology.

Disagree Human rights and values have been threatened by advances in science and technology.

Citizenship

Agree Local initiative is more effective than outside pressure in resolving human rights violations.

Disagree The nations of the world are interdependent and cannot ignore abuses of citizens anywhere.

Compact discs became popular in the 1980s.

In 2003 China sent Yang Liwei, its first astronaut, into outer space.

1983
Business and Finance
The compact disc is marketed for the first time.

1989
Politics
Czechoslovakia's communist government falls, and playwright Vaclav Havel becomes president.

2001
Global Events
United States invades Afghanistan after terrorist attacks on September 11.

1980

1990

2000

1978
Daily Life
The world population is 4.4 billion, with 200,000 people added each day.

1982
The Arts
Colombian author Gabriel García Márquez wins the Nobel Prize for literature.

1986
Science and Technology
An explosion at the Chernobyl nuclear power plant spreads radiation over parts of the Soviet Union and Europe.

1990
Science and Technology
World Wide Web is created.

2000
Global Events
A joint American and Russian crew begin living on the new international space station.

2003
Global Events
United States invades Iraq, and Saddam Hussein is captured.

2003
Science and Technology
China launches its first manned spacecraft.

1976
Business and Finance
The world's first supersonic passenger jet service begins when two Concorde jets take off at the same time from London and Paris.

NASA's rover, Spirit, landed on Mars in 2004.

What's Your Opinion?

 Do you **agree** *or* **disagree** *with the following statements? Support your point of view in your journal.*

Culture The arts flourish during times of economic prosperity.

Science, Technology & Society Technological developments and advances always improve society.

Citizenship Citizens of one country cannot stop human rights violations in another country.

GLOBAL EVENTS

Since prehistoric times people have used art to express themselves and to reveal their views of life around them. Have students study the prehistoric cave painting on page 5, Michelangelo's work on page 357, and the Jackson Pollock painting on page 974.

ACTIVITY: Ask students to compare and contrast art through the ages. Have students work in pairs to make a compare-and-contrast chart that illustrates the similarities and differences between the cave painter's view, Michelangelo's view, and Jackson Pollock's view. Include the qualities of each artist's world in the chart. Students might compare the materials each artist used, the purpose of the artwork, and the mood created by each work.

OBJECTIVES

1 List trends that occurred in painting, sculpture, and architecture after World War II.

2 Identify the major themes of music, dance, film, and drama after 1945.

3 Explain how poetry and novels expressed the mood of the times.

4 Describe how public support of cultural activities changed after World War II.

🔊 LET'S GET STARTED!

As students enter the classroom, divide them into pairs and have them look at the photo from the musical *Cats* on page 978. Have them list adjectives that describe the mood of the musical as shown in the picture. *(exuberant, exotic, daring)* Then have them list adjectives that describe the music of the modern world. *(lively, rhythmic, multicultural)* Tell students that in Section 1 they will learn how trends and themes of artistic works reflect life in the period from World War II to the present.

REPRODUCIBLE RESOURCES

▸ Guided Reading Strategy 36.1

▸ Creative Teaching Strategy 36: A Look at the Future: The Movie

TECHNOLOGY RESOURCES

▸ One-Stop Planner 36.1

▸ Holt Researcher: World History: Maya Angelou, Toni Morrison

▸ Regions of the World Music Audio CD Program 1: The United States: Doc Evans and his Dixieland Jazz Band

▸ World History Teaching Transparency: Art and History 30: Freeway Mural in Los Angeles

▸ Homework Practice Online

REINFORCEMENT, REVIEW, AND ASSESSMENT

▸ Section 1 Review, p. 980

▸ Daily Quiz 36.1

▸ Main Idea Activity 36.1

▸ English Audio Summary 36.1

▸ Spanish Audio Summary 36.1

SECTION 1

READ TO DISCOVER

1 What trends occurred in painting, sculpture, and architecture after World War II?

2 What were the major themes of music, dance, film, and drama after 1945?

3 How did poetry and novels express the mood of the times?

4 How did public support of cultural activities change after World War II?

DEFINE

abstract expressionism
pop art
op art
conceptual art
performance art
theater of the absurd

IDENTIFY

Jackson Pollock
George Balanchine
Martha Graham
Federico Fellini
Akira Kurosawa
Bertolt Brecht
Beats
Toni Morrison
Maya Angelou

▸ WHY IT MATTERS TODAY

Artistic styles are continuously changing. Use CNNfyi.com or other **current event** sources to find out what some popular styles of art are today. Record your findings in your journal.

CNNstudentNews.com

The Arts and Literature

The Main Idea
After World War II the arts and literature reflected the political and social changes of the time.

The Story Continues *During the late 1940s Jackson Pollock started a bold new style of painting. He explained why the floor was the best place to create his drip-and-splash art. "On the floor, I am more at ease," he said. "I feel nearer, more a part of the painting, since this way I can walk around in it, work from the four sides and be literally 'in' the painting." Such experimentation was a major trend in the art world after World War II.*

Visual Arts

The period since 1945 has been one of constant change and experimentation in the arts. This experimentation has even led to an expansion of what it means to be an artist.

Painting and sculpture. After 1945 New York City became one of the liveliest centers of new ideas and painting styles. Many painters began to use a new style that came to be known as **abstract expressionism.** American **Jackson Pollock** was one of the leading abstract expressionists. Pollock expressed himself by dripping different colors of paint onto a canvas spread out on the floor. He believed art was a personal expression that came from the artist's unconscious mind.

During the 1950s artists expressed themselves in different ways. Some realists in the United States and Great Britain developed a new style called **pop art.** These artists, such as Andy Warhol, used everyday items such as soup cans, comic strips, or road signs in their art. Experimentation also occurred in sculpture. The American sculptor Louise Nevelson created large wooden sculptures, often as wall units. Her sculpture *Black Chord* is filled with objects placed within boxed compartments.

In the late 1950s and 1960s another group of artists began painting **op art.** Painters of this style worked with brilliant colors and shapes to create optical illusions. Painting realistic scenes, objects, and people, became more common during the 1970s and 1980s. German artist Anselm Keifer, for example, dealt with the moral problems of Nazism.

This painting by Jackson Pollock, Silver Over Black, White, Yellow, and Red (1948), exemplifies the abstract expressionist style.

TEACH OBJECTIVE 1

LEVEL 1: Have students work in pairs to find pictures that suggest the post-1945 trend toward experimentation or technology in the arts. Call on class members to present their pictures to the class. Have them identify images that exemplify abstract expressionism, pop art, op art, conceptual art, or new techniques in architecture.

ENGLISH LANGUAGE LEARNERS

New types of visual art. As artistic experiments continued, many different kinds of art came to be accepted. One trend of the modern age has been **conceptual art.** Often conceptual art focuses on "environments" made up of relationships among objects and people. Conceptual artists believe that the act of creating the art is more important than the actual art object. In **performance art,** the artist actually becomes a living work of art. The German artist Joseph Beuys, for example, spent a week caged in a New York gallery with a coyote.

Architecture. Architects continued to search for new ideas and techniques after 1945. One popular material was reinforced concrete. French architect Charles-Édouard Jeanneret, known as Le Corbusier, used this material in his buildings. One of the most influential architects of the 1900s, he used clean, precise forms in his designs. Many architects used smooth, polished materials, such as glass. Le Corbusier and a committee of others employed this idea in designing the UN headquarters in New York City. New shapes also appeared in architectural designs. The Sydney Opera House in Australia is one example of an unusually shaped building. American architect Frank Gehry's wildly innovative Guggenheim Museum in Bilbao, Spain, and his Walt Disney Concert Hall in Los Angeles, California, are two others.

New engineering techniques led to the creation of domed stadiums, such as the Astrodome in Houston, Texas. Cities built structures with unique designs, large areas of glass, or shining mirrored tiles. Some homes combined attractive designs with new technologies to save fuel, such as solar panels. However, no single design has been the most popular architecture since 1945. Experimentation has resulted in many different styles standing side by side.

✔ **READING CHECK: Comparing** How were developments in painting, sculpture, and architecture similar? characterized by change and experimentation

Music and Dance

Experimentation has also been common in the world of music. After 1945 new kinds of sound were created in serious music. Composers wrote new music that included synthesizers—sounds created by computers. Composers such as John Cage wrote music that gave the performer—and even the audience—a major role in determining how a piece would sound. Other composers, such as Dmitry Shostakovich, wrote important music based on traditional forms. Although he lived under Stalin's repressive rule in the Soviet Union, Shostakovich's orchestral music expressed great emotion. His symphonies continue to attract listeners worldwide.

Popular music broke new ground in the 1950s when a style called rock 'n' roll developed in the United States. Rock music had a heavy, accented beat and a simple, repetitive melody. It grew out of many different styles, including African American rhythm and blues. During the 1960s a rock band of four young men from Liverpool, England, became enormously popular. In their creative style, the Beatles sang about love and finding one's place in the world. These universal themes made the Beatles popular around the world. Other forms of rock also developed, including folk rock, hard rock, punk rock, and disco. Country-western and African American music such as soul, rhythm and blues, and rap were also popular music forms.

The Beatles' creative style had a major influence on popular music in the 1960s.

🖳 **internet** connect

TOPIC: Contemporary Artists and Writers
GO TO: go.hrw.com
KEYWORD: SP3 WH36

Have interested students search the HRW Go site for information about one of the artists mentioned in this chapter. Have them locate an interview or other information about the person and write a biography that tells what they learned about the person and his or her art or writings. Students may use the interactive template provided.

That's Interesting!

When the Beatles appeared at New York's Shea Stadium in August of 1965, they were greeted by a crowd of about 55,000 fans and a deafening wall of screams so loud that most people could not hear the concert.

ALL LEVELS: Ask class members to pose and answer questions about whether performance art is truly art. Then ask students if photographers, glassblowers, dancers, and others are producing art. Require students to use standard English to explain their answers. *(sample responses: No, art is more than original personal expression; it has to have a lasting impact on society; Yes, art is any form of creative personal expression that makes a statement that is important to society, whether it affects society now, later, or never.)*
ENGLISH LANGUAGE LEARNERS

SKILLS PRACTICE ANSWERS

1. Queen's Hall: Roman, imposing, grandiose; Walt Disney Concert Hall: soaring, imaginative, innovative

2. similarities: welcoming, attractive, big; differences: one named for monarch, a single hall; one named for its donor; innovative engineering design

3. 100 years ago: art supported by the queen; art supported by the public

4. Students' answers will vary.

Interdisciplinary Connection

ARCHITECTURE. The Guggenheim Museum in New York City was designed by Frank Lloyd Wright to display Solomon R. Guggenheim's modern art collection. The building represents a radical departure from traditional museum design. The exterior shows smoothly sculpted, round layers of white concrete. The interior contains a spiral ramp that encircles the inside of the building for six stories. Many of the paintings are "floated" from the interior wall on concealed metal arms.

Critical Thinking

Ask students to tell how the architecture of the building reflects its purpose.

ANSWER: The building was meant to display a modern art collection. The building itself is an example of modern art.

976

SKILL-BUILDING STRATEGIES Connecting Architecture to History

How Architecture Reflects Society

Architecture often reflects cultural values, environmental characteristics, and historical realities. For example, the Sears Tower in Chicago and the Empire State Building in New York City are symbols of metropolitan society. In the same way, the Cathedral of Notre Dame in Paris reflects the religious focus of medieval society. Linking architecture to history helps historians to explain societies and their environments. Historians can also study architectural styles to analyze people's reactions to their environment and thus to better understand the society's values and the historical conditions in which it existed. By comparing different architectural styles for the same type of structure over time, historians can spot changes in social norms and values.

The Queen's Hall in London (right) presented its first performance in 1893. The hall featured an elaborate and ornate interior (above).

Known for his inventive architectural style, American architect Frank Gehry designed the Walt Disney Concert Hall, which opened in Los Angeles, California, in 2003. The new hall, which is home to the Los Angeles Philharmonic Orchestra, boasts state of the art acoustics and a highly sculptured pipe organ.

Skills Reminder

To link architecture to history, first establish the historical context of the piece of architecture. Identify the society that built the structure. Identify the major characteristics of the piece of architecture. Then describe the characteristics of the environment. Relate the environmental characteristics to the historical context in which the piece of architecture was built. Finally, identify the values expressed by linking the historical context of the piece of architecture with its environmental characteristics.

Skills Practice

❶ Carefully study the two buildings shown above. What do the images reveal about the societies that built them?
❷ What are their most evident similarities and differences?
❸ What do the images tell you about changes in public performance halls and the societies that support them?
❹ Using the library or Internet, research information about another piece of architecture you have seen in this book. Then write a short analysis of what it reflects about the society that built it.

In the 1980s and 1990s music videos became increasingly popular. This spread popular music and created fans worldwide for many musicians. Interest also grew in the music of different cultures. Many Western artists took their ideas from the music of Africa, the Caribbean, South America, and other parts of the world.

The world of dance also followed new directions after 1945. Artists who left Russia after its revolution particularly influenced ballet. Russian exile **George Balanchine** became founder, artistic director, and chief choreographer/director of the New York City Ballet. In the 1960s and 1970s, young ballet stars such as Rudolf Nureyev, Mikhail Baryshnikov, and Nataliya Makarova defected from the Soviet Union. They made new homes and careers in the West. After 1945 the freer and looser forms of modern dance began to affect ballet. As in all the performing arts, new forms of individual expression and experimentation took the place of traditional uniformity. **Martha Graham,** an American, became a leader in modern dance. In the late 1900s American choreographers such as Alvin Ailey Jr., Twyla Tharp, Paul Taylor, and Alwin Nikolais were powerful figures in the world of dance.

✔ **READING CHECK: Summarizing** What universal themes were expressed in music and dance, and who were the most influential figures in these fields after 1945? love, finding one's place in the world; Beatles, George Balanchine, Martha Graham

Motion Pictures

Most filmmakers used traditional subjects after 1945. These included adventures, comedies, and social drama. Spectacular productions—costing millions of dollars—continued to be popular. Other films tried to break free of traditional restrictions. In the 1940s and 1950s, Italian directors such as **Federico Fellini** produced films that sharply criticized social and political injustice.

At the end of the 1950s, a group of young French directors known as the "New Wave" further revolutionized film. New Wave directors included Louis Malle and Jean-Luc Godard. They believed that the director should act as the *auteur,* or author, of a film. That is, a film should reflect one person's idea, rather than be a commercial package put together by a movie studio. The New Wave directors often used nontraditional filmmaking methods, such as hand-held cameras. They also edited their films in new ways. As a result they created a particular visual style for the film, which they believed was more important than the storyline.

Some of the most interesting but disturbing films of the 1960s and 1970s came from Japan. **Akira Kurosawa** and other Japanese directors used violence and a dark atmosphere to create startling and frightening new effects. Meanwhile director Lina Wërtmuller was making deeply satirical films about Italian politics and society as well as the relations between men and women.

Technical skill became an important part of Aemrican films after the 1970s. George Lucas's *Star Wars* series, Steven Spielberg's *E.T., The Extraterrestrial* (1982), and James Cameron's *Titanic* (1997) all depended heavily on visual effects. The creative use of computer technology was shown in *Jurassic Park* (1993), *Toy Story* (1995), and *Shrek* (2001). Meanwhile, independent moviemakers took film in a new direction. Largely free of ties to the big studios, they made films with strong

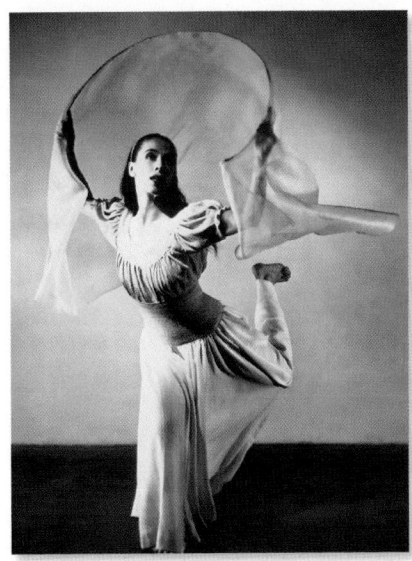

INTERPRETING THE VISUAL RECORD

Modern dance Martha Graham's dance choreography expressed powerful emotions. *Why do you think Graham's dancing was influential during this period?*

Daily Life

Emile Jaques-Dalcroze was a Swiss musician who developed eurythmics, a system of musical education based on bodily movements, ear training, and improvisation. Rather than teaching music theory on paper, Jaques-Dalcroze used physical reaction to respond to music. For example, a quarter note is represented by a single step.

Jaques-Dalcroze developed this system in about 1905 and first applied his method to elementary-school children. In 1910 he established an institute near Dresden, Germany. Today eurythmics is considered an important influence on twentieth-century modern dance and continues to have influence on creative movement and rhythmic gymnastics.

ACTIVITY: Have students choose from a variety of musical selections, from classical to modern, and improvise movements based on the rhythm of the music.

TEACH OBJECTIVE 3

LEVEL 3: Have students work in pairs to create tables of major postwar writers. Provide this format, omitting words in italics.

COOPERATIVE LEARNING

Literary form	Name	Country	Theme
Poetry	Allen Ginsburg	U.S.	protest commercialism
	Maya Angelou	U.S.	black experience in South
	Octavio Paz	Mexico	loneliness
Novel	Jack Kerouac	U.S.	protest materialism
	Kurt Vonnegut, Jr.	U.S.	protest insensitivity
	Laura Esquivel	Mexico	Hispanic experience

TEACH OBJECTIVE 4

LEVEL 2: Ask students what factors boosted public support of cultural activities after World War II. *(more education, leisure time, cultural awareness because of television)*

🖥 **internet** connect

go.hrw.com

TOPIC: World Literature
GO TO: go.hrw.com
KEYWORD: SP3 WH36

Have students access the Internet through the HRW Go site to learn more about modern world literature by studying contemporary novelists and poets. Have students prepare short oral reports about one author and his or her writings.

Interdisciplinary Connection

LITERATURE. Both Arthur Miller and John Steinbeck wrote about men in families. In the play *Death of a Salesman*, Miller focuses on salesman Willy Loman's relationship with his grown sons. In Steinbeck's novel *East of Eden*, two brothers of opposite temperament (like Cain and Abel) are at the center of the story's conflict.

Critical Thinking

What primary sources might you use to help you find out about Miller and Steinbeck?

ANSWER: letters, copies of original manuscripts, interview transcripts

---

social commentary. Director Spike Lee, for example, addressed the experiences of urban African Americans, forcing audiences to think about race relations.

The American filmmaking industry suffered financial setbacks during the 1980s when widespread use of VCRs, videotape rentals, and cable television in private homes gave movie theaters increasing competition. More recently, the influx of DVDs and the ability to download films has raised issues involving copyright law and piracy.

✔ **READING CHECK: Categorizing** Which countries influenced filmmaking the most after 1945? Italy, France, Japan, United States

Drama

Important new developments also occurred in the theater. In East Germany the company founded by playwright **Bertolt Brecht** staged plays that brought attention to their artificiality. Audience members were constantly reminded that they were watching a play. Perhaps the most powerful new outlook on the modern age was the biting social commentary of the playwrights of the so-called "**theater of the absurd.**" Its leaders were Samuel Beckett, an Irishman, and Eugene Ionesco, a Romanian. Both playwrights lived in France. Puzzlement and absurdity run throughout Beckett's works. His most famous play is *Waiting for Godot* (1953).

Other playwrights of the period made more realistic but no less sharp attacks on modern society. The most notable of these dramatists were John Osborne, an Englishman, and Arthur Miller, an American. Osborne wrote about the cruel lives of the British working class. Miller's powerful dramas—particularly *Death of a Salesman* (1949)—explored human weaknesses and the tensions in families. Social themes also entered the world of American musical theater. For example, *West Side Story* (1957), based on Shakespeare's *Romeo and Juliet*, focused on inner-city gangs divided by race and turf wars. Similarly, the hit Broadway musical *Rent* breathed new life into a classic story in the late 1990s. This modernized version of Puccini's opera *La Bohéme* dealt with topics such as drug use and AIDS.

While on Broadway for nearly 18 years, the musical Cats *was performed 7,485 times.*

Other "blockbuster" musicals appeared in the 1980s and 1990s, featuring impressive sets and musical arrangements. Shows by British composer Andrew Lloyd Weber, including *Phantom of the Opera* and *Cats,* enjoyed much success and longevity on Broadway stages. *Cats,* based on a collection of works by British poet T.S. Eliot, closed in 2000 after the longest run in Broadway history. In addition, motion pictures served as inspiration for some Broadway musicals, such as *The Lion King,* based on the popular Disney film, and Mel Brooks's hit musical *The Producers,* which won a record-breaking 12 Tony Awards.

✔ **READING CHECK: Analyzing Information** How did plays and musicals of the postwar years reflect the histories of the cultures in which they were produced? *Waiting for Godot criticized absurdity and confusion of modern age; Death of a Salesman explored modern family tensions; West Side Story addressed gang issues*

Poetry and Novels

Protest was a major theme of leading writers in the postwar years. Many poets and novelists took a stand against the comfortable self-satisfaction they saw in the world around them.

Writers. A group of writers called the **Beats** criticized wealthy citizens and their values. Beat novelist Jack Kerouac and poet Allen Ginsberg began writing in the 1950s. Like many Beat writers, they attacked the commercialism, materialism, and insensitivity they saw in the American way of life. With anger and sadness, Ralph Ellison and James Baldwin each wrote about the life of African Americans in the United States. Nigerian novelist Chinua Achebe examined the effects of colonial rule on his native land. Boris Pasternak and Aleksandr Solzhenitsyn addressed the oppression of the Soviet system. Writers from Eastern Europe wrote about the hardships of life under communism. These "underground" works were often the only source of truth for many Eastern Europeans.

Scientific and technological advances after World War II boosted interest in science fiction. Writers filled the imaginations of millions of readers with tales of space travel, robots, and distant planets. Ray Bradbury, Robert Heinlein, and Isaac Asimov were leading science fiction authors. A character in one of Bradbury's short stories gave voice to the excitement many people felt as humans came closer to breaking out of Earth's gravitational field.

> **Primary Source** ❝All I know is it's really the end of the beginning. The Stone Age, Bronze Age, Iron Age; from now on we'll lump all those together under one big name for when we walked on Earth and heard the birds at morning and cried with envy [jealousy]. Maybe we'll call it the Earth Age, or maybe the Age of Gravity.❞
>
> Ray Bradbury, "The End of the Beginning"

Other writers such as American Kurt Vonnegut, Jr. created new views of the real world. These stories and novels also criticized the cold and heartless attitudes of the times. Mexican author Octavio Paz used haunting, lonely images of people in his dreamlike poems. Colombian Gabriel García Márquez wrote dark, mystical stories about everyday subjects. These two Latin American authors won Nobel Prizes for their work.

In recent years the voices of minority women have become increasingly powerful in the United States. Alice Walker (*The Color Purple*) and **Toni Morrison** (*Beloved*) won Pulitzer Prizes for their work. Morrison also won the Nobel Prize for literature. Walker and Morrison wrote about the issues African Americans faced from the period of slavery through the late 1900s. African American writer **Maya Angelou** wrote books and poetry that explored the black experience in the South. In her novels, Laura Esquivel looked at the experience of being a Hispanic woman in her native Mexico.

Criticism. Some writers provoked controversy. For example, in 1988 Western critics hailed Anglo-Indian author Salman Rushdie's satirical novel *The Satanic Verses*. Many Muslims, however, thought the book was extremely offensive. Some governments banned the book, and the Ayatollah Khomeini of Iran issued a death sentence against Rushdie. As a result the writer was forced into hiding. Violent demonstrations against *The Satanic Verses* occurred in Pakistan and other countries.

Controversy led to violence elsewhere as well. In 1994 Egyptian author Naguib Mahfouz became the first Arab writer to win the Nobel Prize. Mahfouz was attacked by an assailant who objected to the author's treatment of Islam in his works.

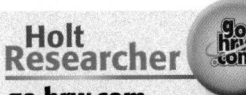

Holt Researcher

go.hrw.com
KEYWORD: Holt Researcher
FreeFind: Maya Angelou
Toni Morrison
After reading more about Maya Angelou and Toni Morrison on the Holt Researcher, assess how their personal experiences influenced their writing.

Analyzing Primary Sources

Analyzing Information How does this excerpt from Bradbury's science fiction story reflect the time in which it was written? excitement about new technology

---

HISTORY MAKER

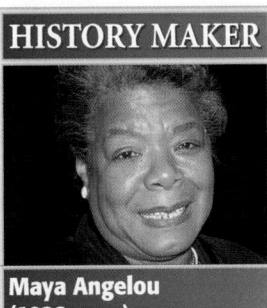

Maya Angelou (1928–)

Maya Angelou grew up in Arkansas. During her childhood, she experienced constant abuse and crushing poverty. Today she is celebrated as one of America's foremost writers and poets. Her books and poems explore racism and oppression of all kinds. **What topics form the focus of Maya Angelou's works?**

Linking Past to Present

The controversies around Salman Rushdie and Naguib Mahfouz show that some writing can offend members of one group while being well regarded by most other critics.

ACTIVITY: Help students use information in earlier chapters of the textbook to identify similarities between Christianity and Islam. *(single deity, single prophet, profession of faith, prayer, charity, fasting, pilgrimages)* Have the class discuss what kind of writing about either religion might offend people of that religion while winning praise from other critics around the world. *(Students' answers will vary.)*

SECTION 1 REVIEW ANSWERS

❶ Define
- abstract expressionism, p. 974
- pop art, p. 974
- op art, p. 974
- conceptual art, p. 975
- performance art, p. 975
- theater of the absurd, p. 978

❷ Identify
- Jackson Pollock, p. 974
- George Balanchine, p. 977
- Martha Graham, p. 977
- Federico Fellini, p. 977
- Akira Kurosawa, p. 977
- Bertolt Brecht, p. 978
- Beats, p. 979
- Toni Morrison, p. 979
- Maya Angelou, p. 979

❸ Beat generation: poet Ginsberg, novelist Kerouac; African Americans: poet Angelou, novelists Ellison, Baldwin, Walker, Morrison; Science Fiction: novelists Bradbury, Heinlein, Asimov; Fantasy/Social commentary: poet Paz, novelists García Márquez, Vonnegut, Esquivel, Rushdie, Mahfouz; Women: poet Angelou, novelists Walker, Morrison, Esquivel

❹ a. abstract expression, pop art, op art, realism (70s and 80s)

b. reinforced concrete, more glass, domed stadiums

c. music: synthesizers, rock 'n' roll; dance: Russian ballet, modern dance

d. director as artist, special effects, theater of the absurd

❺ Answers will vary.

In 1988 Naguib Mahfouz became the first Arab writer to be awarded the Nobel Prize for literature.

At the end of the 1900s and as the next century began, novelists and poets continued to share their unique insights and personal experiences with readers around the world. Many of these writers produced works that expressed social commentary and powerful emotions. Some of the most influential writers today include Japanese novelist Kenzaburo Oe, American novelist John Updike, and Irish poet Seamus Heaney.

✔ **READING CHECK: Finding the Main Idea** What themes were important to postwar writers? protest, science fiction, mystical stories

The Audience for the Arts

The excitement of postwar artistic and literary activity created great public interest. This was particularly true in the United States. More than half of the existing American museums today were founded since 1970. More Americans pay to go to museums, concerts, operas, ballets, and theaters each year than to attend sporting events.

Around the world today, people's average level of education continues to increase. People also have more time for leisure activities, particularly in industrialized nations. Television allows millions of viewers to see films, plays, concerts, and a wide range of other cultural activities. Many people continue to pursue similar interests outside the home. Thus education, increased leisure time, and expanding cultural awareness have combined to give the arts and literature greater exposure and support than ever before.

✔ **READING CHECK: Analyzing Information** What evidence suggests that more people participated in cultural activities after World War II? many museums founded since 1970; high attendance at cultural events

SECTION 1 REVIEW

1. Define and explain the significance:
abstract expressionism
pop art
op art
conceptual art
performance art
theater of the absurd

2. Identify and explain the significance:
Jackson Pollock
George Balanchine
Martha Graham
Federico Fellini
Akira Kurosawa
Bertolt Brecht
Beats
Toni Morrison
Maya Angelou

3. Categorizing Copy the chart below. Use it to identify the leading poets and novelists after 1945.

Theme/Category	Poets	Novelists
Beat generation		
African Americans		
Science Fiction		
Fantasy/Social commentary		
Women		

4. Finding the Main Idea
a. What have been the major developments in painting and sculpture since 1945?
b. What new techniques and designs have architects used since 1945?
c. How have music and dance changed since the end of World War II?
d. What trends developed in film and drama after 1945?

5. Writing and Critical Thinking
Making Generalizations What overall trends have developed in the arts since 1945?
Consider:
- the visual arts
- the performing arts
- architecture
- literature
- public participation

 Homework Practice Online
keyword: SP3 HP36

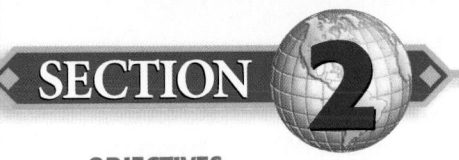

SECTION 2

OBJECTIVES

1 **List advances in travel and space exploration that have occurred since 1945.**

2 **Explain the effect of miniaturization and computerization on modern life.**

3 **Describe the technological improvements that have been made in medical science.**

4 **Discuss environmental concerns scientists have identified.**

⏰ LET'S GET STARTED!

As students enter the classroom, divide them into groups of four in which each student will assume the role of an astronaut, a doctor, a forest ranger, or a software engineer. Ask the groups to discuss the issues raised by science and technology in the modern world from the perspective of their roles. Tell students that in Section 2 they will learn how advances in science and technology since 1945 have dramatically changed the quality of life and the view of the future.

SECTION 2

READ TO DISCOVER

1 What advances in travel and space exploration have occurred since 1945?

2 What effect have miniaturization and computerization had on modern life?

3 What technological improvements have been made in medical science?

4 What environmental concerns have scientists identified?

DEFINE

miniaturization
supercomputers
laser
antibiotics
DNA
genetic code
cloning
urbanization
biodiversity
acid rain
greenhouse effect

IDENTIFY

Yury Gagarin
Alan Shepard
Neil Armstrong
Columbia
Alpha
Rachel Carson

▶ WHY IT MATTERS TODAY

The United States continues to lead the world in space exploration. Use CNN or other **current event** sources to learn about current NASA programs. Record your findings in your journal.

CNN student News.com

Science and Technology

The Main Idea
Dramatic advances in science and technology after World War II affected all the nations of the world.

The Story Continues *As astronaut Neil Armstrong climbed out of the lunar module and onto the surface of the moon, he spoke to Mission Control in Houston, Texas. "That's one small step for a man, one giant leap for mankind." Armstrong's words described the amazing achievement of putting humans on the moon. His words also speak to the whole of humans' extraordinary achievements in science and technology after World War II.*

Faster Travel

After World War II improvements in airplanes changed travel throughout the world. The first jetliner began passenger service between the United States and Europe in 1958. By the mid-1960s jetliner travel had become commonplace. The first jumbo jet began passenger service in 1970, traveling at speeds of more than 400 miles per hour. Air travel became the most popular and convenient way to visit distant places.

Meanwhile other forms of transportation also advanced rapidly. Trains in Japan and Europe sped through the countryside at more than 150 miles per hour. Automobile use increased throughout the world. In 1994 the Channel Tunnel, nicknamed the "Chunnel," connected Great Britain and France underneath the English Channel.

✔ **READING CHECK: Identifying Cause and Effect** When did the technology for jet airplanes develop, and how did it affect travel in the 1900s? *1950s, faster travel to nearly anywhere in the world*

Space Exploration

The United States and the former Soviet Union led the world in space exploration. However, other countries such as Canada, Japan, and several Western European nations also developed space programs. In 2003, China launched its first manned spacecraft and the United States sent rovers to further Mars exploration.

Advances in air travel were a direct result of World War II. Engineers took the technology developed to build fighter jets in the war and changed it to fit the needs of civilian travel.

SECTION 2 RESOURCES

REPRODUCIBLE RESOURCES

▶ Guided Reading Strategy 36.2

▶ Graphic Organizer Activity 36

▶ Geography Activity 36

▶ Readings in World History 130

TECHNOLOGY RESOURCES

▶ One-Stop Planner 36.2

▶ CNN Presents Geography: Yesterday and Today Segments 3, 5, 7

▶ Homework Practice Online

▶ Online Graphs: Green Revolution in Mexico and India

REINFORCEMENT, REVIEW, AND ASSESSMENT

▶ Section 2 Review, p. 989

▶ Daily Quiz 36.2

▶ Main Idea Activity 36.2

▶ English Audio Summary 36.2

▶ Spanish Audio Summary 36.2

ALL LEVELS: Have students work in pairs to create time lines of the "space race," beginning with the launching of *Sputnik* in 1957. (might include *1957* Sputnik; *1958 U.S. satellite; 1961 Gagarin, Shepard; 1969 moon landing; 1971 space station; 1973 Pioneer 10 flies by Jupiter; 1976 Viking 1 and Viking 2 land on Mars; 1981 Columbia space shuttle; 1986 Challenger explosion, Voyager 2 passes Uranus; 1989 Voyager 2 passes Neptune,* Magellan *maps Venus; 1990 Hubble Space telescope; 1995* Galileo *orbits Jupiter; 1997* Pathfinder *finds water on Mars; 1998 sixteen nations begin ISS construction; 2004,* Spirit *and* Opportunity *land on Mars)* Encourage pairs to illustrate their time line. Display students' time lines in the classroom.

ENGLISH LANGUAGE LEARNERS , COOPERATIVE LEARNING

Science, Technology & Society

The film *October Sky* tells the true story of four boys in a West Virginia mining town inspired by *Sputnik* to build a real rocket.

ACTIVITY: Have students use a decision-making process to choose something they could invent from free or inexpensive materials. Have them do research, list options and resources (used machine parts or clothing remnants, talented friends), and predict consequences.

Reproducible **Resources**

PS Readings in World History 129: A Message from the *Apollo XI* Astronauts

Technology **Resources**

 CNN Presents World Cultures: Yesterday and Today Segment 37: Mission to Mars

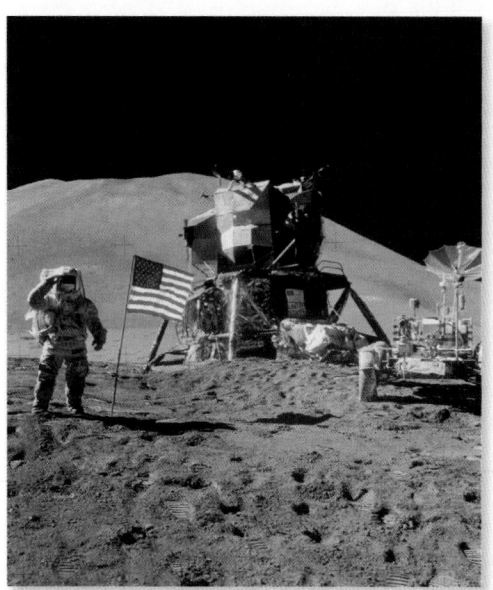

On July 20, 1969, the United States won the intense race to put the first person on the moon.

Early successes. The space age began on October 4, 1957, when the Soviet Union launched *Sputnik*—the world's first space satellite—into orbit around Earth. Then the Soviets built a rocket with enough power to put a person into orbit. Soviet cosmonaut **Yury Gagarin** became the first person to orbit Earth. The United States' progress in space exploration closely followed the Soviets. In 1958 the U.S. successfully launched an unmanned satellite into space. **Alan Shepard** became the first American to travel in space in 1961.

Lunar landing. In July 1969 the United States sent three Americans to the moon. They traveled aboard the spaceship *Columbia*. The astronauts on this *Apollo 11* mission were **Neil Armstrong,** Edwin "Buzz" Aldrin, Jr., and Michael Collins. On July 20, Armstrong and Aldrin boarded the lunar module, the *Eagle*. Collins stayed aboard the spaceship to help manage the mission. As the lunar module set down safely on the moon's surface, the crew told Mission Control, "The Eagle has landed." Mission Control responded, "Be advised, there are lots of smiling faces in this room and all over the world."

For the next two hours the astronauts took photographs and collected lunar soil and rocks. They also planted a U.S. flag on the moon's surface and conducted experiments. About 22 hours after the *Eagle* had landed, the astronauts left the moon and returned to the command module. On July 24, 1969, they returned to Earth.

✔ **READING CHECK: Sequencing** Identify the major events in the space race between the United States and the Soviet Union. *Sputnik, space flights by Yury Gagarin and Alan Shepard, moon landing by Armstrong and Aldrin*

Unmanned spacecraft. The United States completed several manned moon landings from 1969 to 1972. Then the U.S. space program began to shift its focus to unmanned spacecraft. These missions explored the solar system. Late in 1973 *Pioneer 10* became the first spacecraft to fly by Jupiter. In mid-1976, *Viking 1* and *Viking 2* landed on Mars, the "red planet." For several years they sent information back to Earth that helped scientists understand the planet's makeup. *Voyager 1* and *Voyager 2,* launched in 1977, explored the more distant planets of the solar system. Both made flybys of Jupiter and Saturn between 1979 and 1981. They sent spectacular photographs back to Earth. Then *Voyager 2* continued to the outer reaches of the solar system. It passed the planet Uranus in 1986 and by 1989 had reached Neptune.

After a break of some years, the United States restarted its unmanned space exploration program in 1989 with the *Magellan* and *Galileo* missions. *Magellan* mapped nearly the entire surface of Venus. *Galileo* went into orbit around Jupiter in 1995, sending back information about the planet and its moons. One of the most exciting accomplishments in the mid-1990s was the landing of another U.S. spacecraft on Mars. The *Pathfinder,* which touched down on July 4, 1997, gave scientists strong proof that there had once been water on Mars. Water is the key item needed to create and sustain life. Scientists launched *NEAR Shoemaker* (Near Earth Asteroid Rendezvous) in 1996. This spacecraft was the first to study asteroids, or deep space geology. *NEAR* spent one year taking 160,000 photographs of the asteroid Eros. At the end of the mission, NASA successfully landed the spacecraft on Eros. This gave scientists even more detailed photographs of the asteroid's surface.

TEACH OBJECTIVE 2

LEVEL 3: Ask students to pose and answer questions about the process of miniaturization and how it has stimulated computerization. (*The chips and wafers in calculators, automatic cameras, microwaves, automobiles, and so on, are tiny, powerful, and highly specialized computer processors.*) Encourage students to use standard English and correct terminology. **COOPERATIVE LEARNING**

 HOMEWORK Have students create a cartoon expressing their opinion about whether the trend toward computerization is good or bad for society.

Satellites. Satellites are spacecraft that orbit Earth and include several types—communications, weather, Earth observation, navigation, and military. Communications satellites receive radio signals from one location on Earth and then send the signals to a different location. Recent improvements in this technology have made satellite radio possible, giving listeners far more choices in audio entertainment than available on traditional radio. Advances in navigation satellite technology have resulted in widespread availability of global positioning systems (GPS). Originally designed for military use, GPS technology now allows people to determine their precise location when operating a GPS-equipped car, boat, plane—or even cell phone or wristwatch.

New frontiers in space. A new period of space exploration began in 1981. That year the United States launched the first space shuttle, *Columbia.* By 1986 these reusable shuttles had made two dozen successful missions, so the launch of the *Challenger* on January 28, 1986, seemed routine. However, 73 seconds after liftoff the shuttle burst into flames, killing its seven crew members. The disaster halted U.S. manned space flights until the launch of the space shuttle *Discovery* in 1988. In 1990 the *Discovery's* crew placed the Hubble Space telescope into orbit, allowing astronomers to look deeper into space than ever before.

The United States and the Soviet Union also built space stations. The Soviets led the way with the launch of *Salyut 1* in 1971. Two years later, the United States followed with *Skylab.* These space stations allowed astronauts to do experiments in geography, engineering, medicine, and many other fields. After the Cold War ended, the United States and the former Soviet Union joined some of their space exploration efforts. In 1995 the United States space shuttle *Atlantis* docked with the Russian space station *Mir.* The United States, Russia, and 14 other nations began building an International Space Station (ISS) in 1998. In November 2000 one U.S. astronaut and two Russian cosmonauts began a four-month stay on the ISS. They named their new home *Alpha.*

On February 1, 2003, tragedy struck the U.S. space program. That morning, the space shuttle *Columbia* disintegrated upon re-entering Earth's atmosphere after a successful space mission. All seven astronauts aboard were killed. Athough U.S. manned space flights were once again suspended until safety improvements could be made, the United States and Russia reaffirmed their commitment to continue work on the ISS.

Sixteen nations worked together to build the International Space Station—now one of the brightest objects in the night sky.

✔ **READING CHECK: Summarizing** How did scientists learn about the solar system after the moon landing? exploration by unmanned spacecraft

Miniaturization and Computerization

Advances in air and space travel often involved making machines smaller and lighter. This process is known as **miniaturization.** One of the most helpful products of miniaturization was a tiny electronic device called the transistor, invented in 1947. It took the place of the much larger vacuum tube and could do many times as much work. Within 25 years, many transistors and other components could be placed on an integrated circuit—a tiny wafer of material such as silicon.

Interdisciplinary Connection

SCIENCE. Unmanned spacecraft had been in orbit for years before reaching the outer planets of our solar system. These spacecraft, as well as the Hubble Space Telescope, send data and pictures from deep space to scientists on Earth.

Critical Thinking

Based on information in the textbook about unmanned spacecraft, how long did *Voyager II* take to reach Neptune?

ANSWER: It was launched in 1977 and arrived in 1989—12 years.

Linking Past to Present

On May 29, 1953, Tenzing Norgay (Nepalese) and Edmund Hillary (New Zealander) became the first persons to reach the peak of Mount Everest, 29,028 feet above sea level.

Critical Thinking

Was the Everest team's accomplishment more or less significant an achievement than the International Space Station project?

ANSWER: Students may say *more* (humans did it with almost no technological support) or *less* (it did not lead to a way that humans could live on top of Mount Everest).

LEVEL 2: Write the words *genetics* and *cloning* on the chalkboard. Ask volunteers to explain each term. Have students pose and answer questions about the potential benefits of cloning for humankind. *(improving farm animals and crops to produce more food, human organs for transplant, and so on)*

COOPERATIVE LEARNING

Interdisciplinary Connection

SCIENCE. X-ray technology remained unchanged for nearly a century until, in 1996, the Xerox Corporation and the University of Michigan produced the first digital X-ray machine. Using computer technology, they developed a machine that produces images electronically rather than on conventional X-ray film. After X-rays from the new device pass through a patient's body, they are converted to electric signals that a computer uses to construct the image.

ACTIVITY: Have students use databases to investigate the advantages of digital X-ray machines over the old system. *(easier to store, copy, and send; computer can enhance poor-quality images)*

ENIAC formally started working in February 1946. The computer contained 18,000 tubes, and its power source was half as large as the machine itself.

Miniaturization made possible dozens of new products that affect the activities of people around the world. Portable radios, pocket calculators, digital watches, and automatic cameras developed from this process. At first these products were expensive and not widely used. However, costs fell quickly as technology advanced and the demand for such products increased.

History of the computer. The most remarkable result of miniaturization was the modern computer. In the 1600s the French scientist Blaise Pascal invented the first automatic calculator. It worked with wheels linked to each other by gears. The idea interested scientists and engineers for the next 300 years. In the 1830s Charles Babbage designed a mechanical calculating machine that he called the "analytical engine." His machine had all of a modern computer's basic parts. These include data storage, memory, a system for moving between the memory and storage components, and an input device. Babbage was not, however, able to build the machine he designed.

ENIAC—Electronic Numerical Integrator and Calculator—was an enormous computer built in 1946. It took up a whole room at the University of Pennsylvania. The discovery of transistors helped make possible much smaller machines that could store and rapidly process information. The later development of integrated circuits also allowed for smaller machines. As scientists improved computers year after year, the new machines quickly began to influence society. Computers became faster and more efficient. Meanwhile they needed less and less space to store gigantic amounts of information. As a result, products ranging from automobiles to self-focusing cameras to microwave ovens began using computers.

Computer uses. Computers made it easier for doctors to diagnose diseases. They also improved patients' treatment. Devices such as CAT (computerized axial tomography) scanners and MRI (magnetic resonance imaging) machines allow doctors to view the human body in incredible detail. These diagnostic tools reduce the need for surgery. Outside the medical field, tasks assigned to computers range from guiding spacecraft, to printing newspapers, to constructing maps. In addition, large and powerful **supercomputers** help to solve complex scientific and engineering problems. Solutions to these problems would have been impossible a short time ago. Supercomputers have more than one processing unit. This means they can do billions of computations per second. Supercomputers have revolutionized the way products are developed, experiments are conducted, and research is performed.

Today computers increasingly affect people's daily lives. Desktop and lightweight laptop computers are common in offices, homes, schools, and libraries. Businesses use computers to process and store enormous amounts of financial and administrative information. The range of activities affected by computers grows daily. Meanwhile, computers continue to increase in power and speed while shrinking in size and cost.

✔ **READING CHECK: Making Generalizations** How have miniaturization and computerization affected modern life? made new products possible, revolutionized ways of solving problems, storing and processing information, performing research

Some people believe that audiovisual communication is more easily controlled and manipulated, and is more limiting to the imagination, than the printed word. Have students debate this statement, explaining and defending their positions: "Audiovisual culture is a threat to freedom." (*Agree: Audiovisual culture overstimulates the senses and keeps the reader from following his or her own thoughts on the reading. Disagree: Audiovisual culture allows readers to access quickly the ideas that most interest them.*)

Communications

After World War II technological advances made radio and then television affordable to more people. Radio and television made it possible to spread ideas and information faster and to more people than ever before.

The Internet. The development of computers further extended the information revolution. The Internet allows computers to communicate with one another over telephone lines. By connecting computer networks, the Internet creates a global network. People all over the world can exchange information—words, pictures, and sound—nearly instantaneously. About 250 million personal computers had access to the Internet by 2000. People spent an average of one hour per day online. Many now communicate with each other through e-mail—electronic messages delivered in a matter of seconds.

In the 1990s companies began using the Internet to do business, market and sell products, and carry out research. As a result, the number of Internet-related jobs in 1999 doubled from the previous year to 2.5 million. The high-tech industry was responsible for nearly a third of real U.S. economic growth in the late 1990s. The fastest growing part of Internet business was the sale of products online, often called e-commerce.

In the 1990s and the years that followed, the Internet (at left) came into worldwide use as both a business and educational tool. Below, women in Somalia use computers.

Other innovations. In addition to desktop computers, many other important methods of communication came into use in the late 1900s. In the 1970s photocopiers became essential business machines. In the 1980s and 1990s fax machines became affordable and widely used. Cellular phones became common in the mid-1990s. Fiber-optic cables also improved communications. These cables use light instead of electricity or radio waves to send information. In 1960 an American scientist built the first **laser.** A laser concentrates light and releases it in an intense beam that travels in a straight line. Lasers are used in communications as well as medicine and industry. Radio, television, and telephone signals are sent with lasers. Doctors use lasers to repair damaged tissue in the eye and to burn away unhealthy tissue. Lasers help manufacturers accurately cut into hard substances, such as metal or diamonds. They can even be used to clean delicate pieces of art.

✔ **READING CHECK: Finding the Main Idea** What new communication tools were developed after World War II? computers, Internet, photocopiers, fax machines, cellular phones, fiber-optic cables, lasers

Medical Science

Not all advances that followed World War II involved physics or electronics. Biologists and other scientists made large gains in their battle against disease.

Treatment of diseases. In 1928 the British scientist Alexander Fleming discovered a substance he called penicillin. He noted that it stopped the growth of many types of bacteria. Fleming believed penicillin could help cure illnesses caused by those bacteria.

Economics

In the early 1990s, when many Asian countries experienced phenomenal economic growth, nations around the globe saw investment opportunities and sank money into the region. In the late 1990s, when markets in Japan, Hong Kong, and other Asian countries suffered serious financial setbacks, the global economy reeled. Markets in North America, Europe, and Latin America experienced losses of varying degrees.

ACTIVITY: Have students use various resources to select a nation or group of nations where one might expect a high return on investment. Students should support their point of view in relation to factors such as the region's natural resources, political and economic stability, and trade agreements. Ask students to identify bias, if any, in their sources.

LEVEL 1: Tell students that scientists are learning how to identify and replace defective genes. Write these questions on the chalkboard to start a class discussion: Will insurance companies refuse coverage based on genetic information? Can criminals blame their criminal behavior on a gene for excessive aggression? Should people be allowed to create "designer babies" by selecting hair color, eye color, or musical ability? *(Answers will vary but should be supported with logical reasoning.)*

Historical Sidelight

In Edinburgh, Scotland, Dr. Ian Wilmut cloned the famous sheep Dolly in 1997.

Critical Thinking

How might scientists learn more from Dolly about cloning?

ANSWER: long-term observation of Dolly and her clone

UNDERSTANDING SCIENCE AND TECHNOLOGY ANSWER

positive: food sources, cures for diseases; negative: ethical issues such as "designer babies"

Reproducible **Resources**

PS Readings in World History 136: People 3.1: The Ethics of Human Cloning

Technology **Resources**

 World History Teaching Transparency: Everyday Life 30: The AIDS Quilt Project, 1980s

CONNECTING TO
Science and Technology

Genetic Engineering

During the 1980s scientists began to use genetic engineering to alter genes in plants and animals. A major goal of this effort was to produce bigger and better food sources.

Today scientists have identified genes that cause or contribute to Alzheimer's disease, breast cancer, skin cancer, and other devastating illnesses. In the photo below, lab technicians analyze a film showing part of a DNA sequence. Scientists are also learning how to use gene therapy—replacing defective genes with normal genes—as a major new approach to medicine.

Our increasing control over the human genetic makeup raises important moral and ethical questions. For example, will people be able to create "designer babies" by selecting specific characteristics such as hair color, eye color, or musical ability? If so, what would the implications be for society? Bioethicists are struggling with such questions as our ability to control our genetic structures continues to increase.

Understanding Science and Technology

What are some potentially positive and negative effects of genetic engineering?

Penicillin and similar substances that can kill or limit bacterial growth are called **antibiotics.** After 1945 these "wonder drugs" transformed the fight against disease. Antibiotics cured some illnesses, such as tuberculosis, that previously had no cure. Medical researchers also made great progress in preventing disease. Jonas Salk's polio vaccine was released for general use in 1954. As a result, polio has been all but wiped out in developed countries. Similarly, a worldwide campaign against smallpox nearly eliminated the disease by the 1980s. Elsewhere, however, overuse of antibiotics for conditions that antibiotics cannot cure (such as the cold or flu) has begun to limit their effectiveness in treating some conditions for which they were designed (various viruses, for example).

The worldwide AIDS (acquired immunodeficiency syndrome) epidemic began in the early 1980s. By the end of 2001 the United Nations UNAIDS program had recorded nearly 22 million deaths from AIDS since the beginning of the epidemic. In 2003, 40 million people were living with HIV/AIDS. Of these cases, Sub-Saharan Africa had about 25 million. There is no known vaccine or cure for AIDS. However, researchers have had increasing success in treating AIDS with a powerful combination of drugs. Making these often-expensive drugs available to poor AIDS patients in Africa and Asia, where the disease continues to accelerate, has proven a major challenge. Fighting the disease requires continuing research and education programs. AIDS education teaches people how HIV, the virus that causes AIDS, is spread and how it can be prevented.

Genetics. In 1953 scientists discovered the structure of **DNA** (deoxyribonucleic acid). DNA is a basic part of genes—the small units of chromosomes that determine hereditary characteristics, such as eye and hair color. In 2001 an international team called the Human Genome Project mapped the chemical structure of DNA. This sequence of DNA's chemical "letters" provides a "recipe" for human life, called the **genetic code.** Understanding this genetic code may lead to new cures for cancer, heart disease, and other illnesses. One scientist involved in the project explained its importance.

History Makers Speak **❝[Mapping human DNA] has been compared with putting a man on the moon, but I believe it is more than that. This is the outstanding achievement not only of our lifetime but perhaps in the history of mankind.❞**

Michael Dexter, "Human Genome to go Public," www.cnn.com

Scientists' knowledge of DNA raised new questions about what could be done with their findings. The process of making a genetically identical copy of an animal's cell is called **cloning.** In 1997 researchers at the Roslin Institute in Edinburgh, Scotland, successfully cloned a sheep. Since then, other species of mammals have been cloned. Some experts believe that within the next decade scientists might have the ability to clone humans.

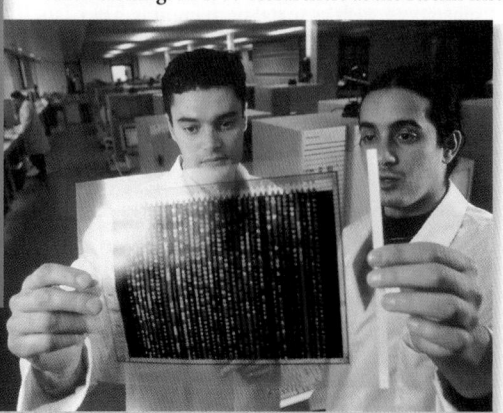

✔ **READING CHECK: Evaluating** What is the significance of developments in medical science and genetic research since 1945? eliminated some diseases, helped fight or prevent diseases

ALL LEVELS: Draw a circle and write the phrase *Environmental Problems* within it. Have students create a web diagram in which they identify at least six environmental problems the world faces today. Then have students pose and answer questions about each problem. **ENGLISH LANGUAGE LEARNERS, COOPERATIVE LEARNING**

Technology

With increasingly powerful instruments, physical scientists were able to look at the tiny particles within the atom. They soon learned how to use the energy released when the structure of the atom is changed. Atomic energy was first used to make more powerful bombs. Later it was used to produce electricity for a growing population. Whenever atomic energy is created, dangerous radiation, known as radioactivity, is released. When carefully controlled, radioactivity can have very helpful medical uses. For example, cancer can be treated with radiation. Uncontrolled exposure, however, can be deadly.

An explosion at the Chernobyl nuclear power plant in the Soviet Union in 1986 made radiation's dangers clear. Chernobyl was the world's worst nuclear accident. The explosion spread radioactive material over areas in the Soviet Union and Europe. Many people later died of radiation-related illnesses. Cancer rates and the number of birth defects jumped. Doctors believed these trends would continue for decades. The Chernobyl accident increased opposition to nuclear power. However, researchers continued to find helpful uses for radiation, including treatment of disease and food preservation.

Chemists developed the first synthetic substances—materials that do not occur in nature—in laboratories in the 1800s. It was not until the 1940s, however, that these synthetic substances, called plastics, began to appear in every area of life. Plastics completely changed the way products looked. They also changed how products were manufactured. By the 1990s plastics were being used to create automobiles, desktop computers, clothing, and many other products.

Since 1945 technological advances have dramatically changed the world. Devices such as telephones and refrigerators existed before 1945. However, only after the war were they made cheaply enough for millions of people to buy them. New technological products are more common in industrialized nations. However, they have also had a great influence on life in developing nations. New industries, such as television and computer manufacturing, sprang up. Millions of people were employed in new kinds of jobs. World trade also grew as nations exchanged new products.

Tens of thousands of people living near Chernobyl had to be evacuated after a nuclear accident in 1986.

✔ **READING CHECK: Identifying Cause and Effect** How did technology affect people's lives in the late 1900s? new products and sources of energy, new industries, increased employment and trade

Science and the Environment

Many scientists are looking at ways to preserve the world's environment. Some scientific advances have had unexpected effects on the natural world. Scientists are helping to find ways to balance human needs with the earth's delicate environment.

History Maker

RACHEL CARSON. By the mid-1800s scientific researchers had begun to use new chemicals to eliminate harmful insects. Biologist Rachel Carson worried about the effects of the new chemicals on the natural environment. In *Silent Spring* she warned that overuse of the pesticide DDT was killing wildlife. Although Carson died in 1964, her efforts inspired major investigations into the effects of DDT. In 1972 the U.S. Environmental Protection Agency banned the use of DDT, although other countries continued to use it. *Silent Spring* encouraged a new movement of environmental activism that spread to Europe and other parts of the world.

Critical Thinking

What other books have affected attitudes about the environment or other issues?

ANSWER: Students' answers will vary. If they cannot think of books that have had a public impact, ask them to think of something they have read that affected their personal attitudes on any issue.

Technology Resources

 Online Maps, Charts, and Graphs: The World

CLOSE

In 1960 per capita income in the world's richest 20 percent of nations was 30 times per capita income in the poorest 20 percent of nations. By 1994, that ratio had more than doubled, to 78:1. Have students use a problem-solving process to consider ways advances in technology and health care might have contributed to this situation or might be used to help address it.

REVIEW

Have students complete the Section 2 Review on p. 989.

ASSESS

Have students complete Daily Quiz 36.2. As Alternative Assessment, you may want to use the space race time line exercise in this section's lessons.

Global Relations

The United States and Canada use almost twice as much energy as Europe and 10 times more than Africa.

Critical Thinking

What consequences of economic development would increase a nation's energy use?

ANSWER: Students might cite increases in employment, transportation use, production, and income.

MAP ANSWER

Brazil

Technology Resources

 World History Teaching Transparencies: Geography and History 30, 40: The Global Environment; World Biomes

Technology Resources

 Online Maps: The Global Problem of Acid Rain

INTERPRETING THE GRAPH ANSWER

(from page 989)
Antarctica has the most severe ozone depletion but almost no humans or pollutants.

Deforestation Around the World, c. 1940–1995

Interpreting Maps In recent years many of the world's tropical rain forests have experienced deforestation, or the loss of trees, due to numerous factors.

■ **Skills Assessment: Places and Regions** What country has the world's largest remaining area of rain forest?

Rachel Carson raised awareness of the effects of pesticides on the environment.

Population issues. An important development in the postwar period was the rapid growth in world population. Between 1930 and 1950, world population grew by about 23 percent. In the next four decades, however, population rose by 112 percent. It reached almost 6.3 billion people in 2003 as medical advances and improvements in health and sanitation lowered death rates. Scientific advances also helped feed people.

Migration from the countryside to the city—a process known as **urbanization**—has swelled urban populations around the world. From Mexico City to Cairo to Calcutta, overcrowding has added to environmental problems such as pollution in those areas. Limiting the birth rate and improving food production are two of the ways people are trying to ease the effects of population growth.

Population growth and industrialization increase the need for land and other natural resources. As a result, forests, wetlands, and other areas are sometimes destroyed, causing the loss of plant and animal habitats. This situation has been a particular problem in the world's rain forests. Some scientists argue that this reduction in **biodiversity**—the variety of plants and animals that naturally occurs in the environment—could have damaging effects on humans as well as the environment. Industrialization and population also increase the amount of waste humans create. Government and industry leaders in many nations continue searching for ways to reduce waste, encourage recycling, and safely dispose of dangerous materials.

Effects of pollution. Air pollution also became an environmental concern. Motor vehicles and factories pollute the air with toxins when they burn fossil fuels. When rain falls through these toxins in the air, **acid rain** is created. Recently many nations have worked together to reduce the production of toxins. After 1945 many farmers began to use pesticides to decrease crop damage caused by insects. **Rachel Carson** warned in her 1962 book, *Silent Spring*, that some pesticides had harmful effects on the environment. As a result, certain pesticides were banned from use. Scientists now pay closer attention to the long-term environmental effects of pesticides.

RETEACH

Have students complete Main Idea Activity for English Language Learners and Special-Needs Students 36.2. Then have pairs of students take turns reading the section's headings and subheadings. Ask students in turn to say the main idea of each heading and subheading, using standard English and correct terminology.
ENGLISH LANGUAGE LEARNERS , COOPERATIVE LEARNING

EXTEND

Have students choose a region of the world and write a brief essay about ways technological advances have affected that region. Suggest that students find primary source material, copies of letters, interviews, photographs, and so on, to support the ideas they present in the essay. **BLOCK SCHEDULING**

According to many scientists, the burning of oil, coal, and natural gas has increased the amounts of carbon dioxide and other gases in the earth's atmosphere. At normal levels these gases allow the sun's rays to warm the planet and keep the earth's heat from escaping. This **greenhouse effect** helps keep the earth's temperature at the right levels for plants and animals to live. When the level of greenhouse gases increase, more heat is trapped and global temperatures rise. Scientists do not agree on just how great a danger global warming is, but they are closely monitoring changes in the earth's temperature. The United Nations has also held summits addressing this issue.

Some scientists argue that pollution is causing the ozone layer in the earth's atmosphere to become thinner. Ozone is a gas that shields the earth against the sun's ultraviolet rays. These dangerous rays can cause skin cancer in humans and damage plant and animal life. Some scientists believe that a leading cause of ozone thinning is the use of chemicals called chlorofluorocarbons (CFCs). CFCs are used in aerosol sprays, coolants, and to make electronic parts and plastics. Many countries began to phase out or ban the use of CFCs in the 1980s and 1990s.

✔ **READING CHECK: Categorizing** What environmental problems have scientists been concerned about in recent years? acid rain, greenhouse effect, thinning of ozone layer

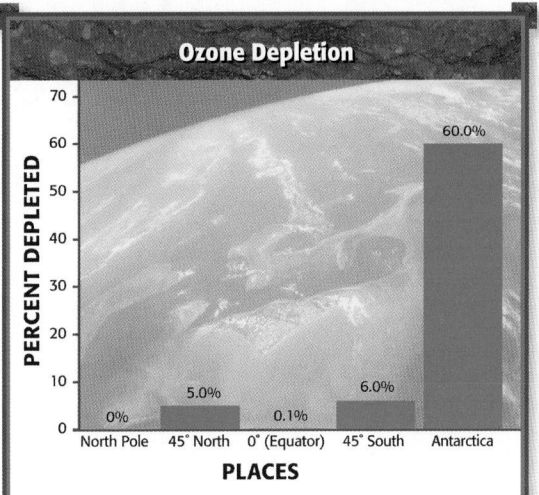

Ozone Depletion

Interpreting the Graph
Many scientists believe that ozone depletion in the atmosphere has been caused by pollution. *How might a person use these same statistics to argue that ozone depletion is not caused by pollution?*

SECTION 2 REVIEW

1. **Define** and explain the significance:
   miniaturization
   supercomputers
   laser
   antibiotics
   DNA
   genetic code
   cloning
   urbanization
   biodiversity
   acid rain
   greenhouse effect

2. **Identify** and explain the significance:
   Yury Gagarin
   Alan Shepard
   Neil Armstrong
   Columbia
   Alpha
   Rachel Carson

3. **Identifying Cause and Effect**
   Copy the graphic organizer below. Use it to identify the effects of World War II and U.S.-Soviet competition on travel and space exploration.

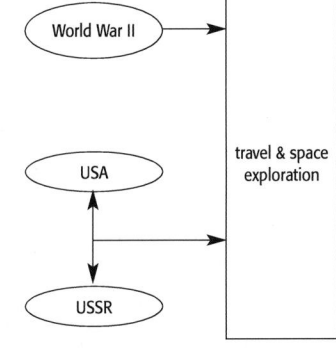

4. **Finding the Main Idea**
   a. Describe the influence of miniaturization and computerization on life in the late 1900s.
   b. List three medical or technological advances made since 1945 and their importance.
   c. How has the rate of growth of the world population changed during the 1900s? What effect might this have on the environment?
   d. What were some of the causes of pollution during the 1900s, and what were some of the solutions scientists proposed for dealing with pollution?

5. **Writing and Critical Thinking**
   Making Generalizations Select one of the technological advances discussed in this chapter and explain ways in which it could have positive and negative effects.
   Consider:
   • genetics
   • nuclear science
   • the environment

Homework Practice Online
go.hrw.com
keyword: SP3 HP36

THE MODERN WORLD **989**

SECTION 2 REVIEW ANSWERS

❶ **Define**
• miniaturization, p. 983
• supercomputers, p. 984
• laser, p. 985
• antibiotics, p. 986
• DNA, p. 986
• genetic code, p. 986
• cloning, p. 986
• urbanization, p. 988
• biodiversity, p. 988
• acid rain, p. 988
• greenhouse effect, p. 989

❷ **Identify**
• Yury Gagarin, p. 982
• Alan Shepard, p. 982
• Neil Armstrong, p. 982
• *Columbia*, p. 983
• *Alpha*, p. 983
• Rachel Carson, p. 988

❸ World War II: aviation technology modified for commercial use; U.S.-Soviet competition: race to put up satellites, humans in space, moon landing

❹ a. led to smaller components, making computers more prevalent

b. laser: telecommunications, surgery, and manufacturing; DNA mapping: cures for cancer, heart disease, mental illness, animal cloning; space stations: space communities; rovers on Mars

c. doubled between 1950 and 1990; urbanization reduces access to shelter, clean water and air, fresh food

d. causes: urbanization, pesticides, burning fossil fuel; proposed solutions: banning certain pesticides, monitoring Earth's temperature, phasing out use of CFCs

❺ Answers will vary.

989

SECTION 3

OBJECTIVES

1 **List some recent examples of human rights abuses.**

2 **Explain how the nations of the world have dealt with human rights violations.**

3 **Discuss how democratic ideals and practices spread in the late 1900s.**

SECTION 3 RESOURCES

REPRODUCIBLE RESOURCES

▶ Guided Reading Strategy 36.3

▶ Readings in World History 132: Rock Music and Politics

▶ Readings in World History 138: A Lebanese Woman Speaks

▶ Hands-on History Activity 36: Looking Into the Future

TECHNOLOGY RESOURCES

▶ One-Stop Planner 36.3

▶ Holt Researcher: World History: Aung San Suu Kyi

▶ Homework Practice Online

REINFORCEMENT, REVIEW, AND ASSESSMENT

▶ Section 3 Review, p. 993

▶ Daily Quiz 36.3

▶ Main Idea Activity 36.3

▶ English Audio Summary 36.3

▶ Spanish Audio Summary 36.3

🔊 LET'S GET STARTED!

As students enter the classroom, divide them into pairs to discuss what they know about human rights abuses around the world. Have each pair compile a list of countries with recent abuses (*Guatemala, China, Iraq, South Africa, Rwanda, Northern Ireland, Bosnia*) and support their point of view by listing the kind of abuse in each country. Tell students that in Section 3 they will learn how citizens and governments reacted to human rights abuses in the late 1900s.

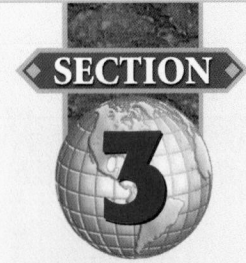

SECTION 3

READ TO DISCOVER

1 What are some recent examples of human rights abuses?

2 How have the nations of the world dealt with human rights violations?

3 How did democratic ideals and practices spread in the late 1900s?

IDENTIFY

Universal Declaration of Human Rights
Convention on the Rights of the Child

▶ WHY IT MATTERS TODAY

Abuses of human rights continue today. Use or other **current event** sources to find out what countries are currently abusing human rights and what people are doing to combat it. Record your findings in your journal.

CNN Student News.com

Human Rights and the Spread of Democratic Ideals

The Main Idea
In many parts of the world, respect for human rights and democracy spread after World War II.

The Story Continues *"I have a dream that one day . . . all of God's children . . . will be able to join hands and sing in the words of the old Negro spiritual, 'Free at last! Free at last! Thank God Almighty, we are free at last!'"* Martin Luther King, Jr. spoke these words as he led the fight for African American equality in the United States. Around the world many people worked to protect and advance basic human rights.

Human Rights Issues

The horrors of World War II demonstrated the need to protect human rights around the world. To advance support of human rights, in 1945 the newly formed United Nations made a strong statement.

> **Primary Source**
> ❝We the people of the United Nations, determined . . . to reaffirm faith in fundamental human rights, in the dignity and worth of the human person, in the equal rights of men and women and of nations large and small, . . . have resolved to combine our efforts to accomplish these aims.❞
>
> from the Preamble to the United Nations Charter

In 1948 the UN adopted the **Universal Declaration of Human Rights.** This document outlined the basic human rights that the international community agreed every person should have. However, the UN did not have any way to enforce the declaration or later agreements on human rights. Indeed, most countries argued that any attempt at enforcement would violate their national sovereignty. This opposition to outside influence remains a major problem for international human rights protection.

Human rights abuses. Even though the United Nations continues to address human rights abuses around the world, such abuses remain all too common. Human rights violations often have political, ethnic, racial, or religious roots. For example,

These refugees fled Bosnia to avoid the ethnic cleansing in that country.

TEACH OBJECTIVE 1

LEVEL 1: Have students brainstorm about human rights abuses that exist in the world today. Write their responses, and use them to compile a class list on the chalkboard. *(ethnic cleansing in Bosnia and Rwanda; terrorist acts in Northern Ireland; imprisonment, torture, and execution of people who speak out against repressive governments)*

ENGLISH LANGUAGE LEARNERS

TEACH OBJECTIVE 2

ALL LEVELS: Ask students to identify ways that human rights have been protected. *(international pressure, political changes, United Nations activity, Amnesty International reports, criminal trials of abusive officials)* Then ask students to identify difficulties in defining human rights. *(Non-Western countries favor community interests over individual rights; Islamic countries define women's rights by the Qur'an; poverty affects human rights.)*

ENGLISH LANGUAGE LEARNERS

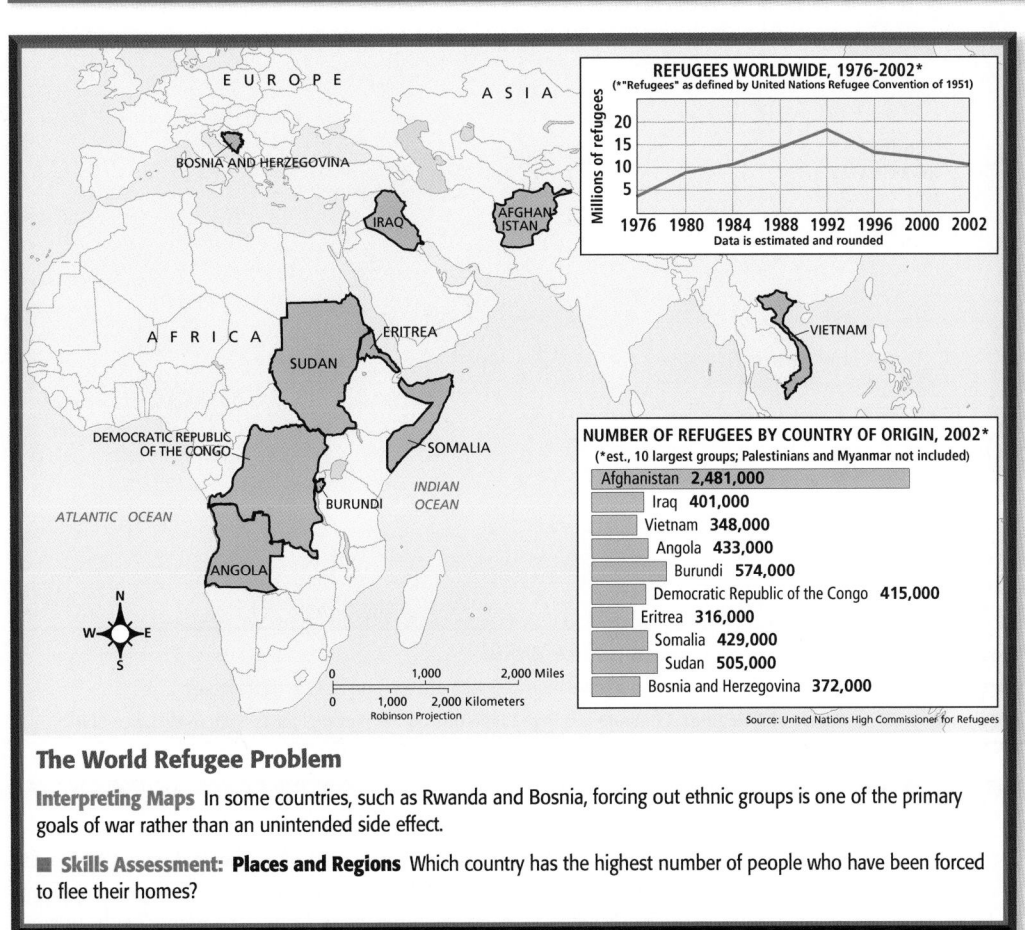

REFUGEES WORLDWIDE, 1976–2002*
(*"Refugees" as defined by United Nations Refugee Convention of 1951)

1976 1980 1984 1988 1992 1996 2000 2002
Data is estimated and rounded

NUMBER OF REFUGEES BY COUNTRY OF ORIGIN, 2002*
(*est., 10 largest groups; Palestinians and Myanmar not included)

Country	Refugees
Afghanistan	2,481,000
Iraq	401,000
Vietnam	348,000
Angola	433,000
Burundi	574,000
Democratic Republic of the Congo	415,000
Eritrea	316,000
Somalia	429,000
Sudan	505,000
Bosnia and Herzegovina	372,000

Source: United Nations High Commissioner for Refugees

The World Refugee Problem

Interpreting Maps In some countries, such as Rwanda and Bosnia, forcing out ethnic groups is one of the primary goals of war rather than an unintended side effect.

■ **Skills Assessment: Places and Regions** Which country has the highest number of people who have been forced to flee their homes?

brutal "ethnic cleansing" during the civil war in Bosnia resulted in thousands of deaths. In addition to interethnic war crimes in Kosovo and Rwanda, terrorist acts in Northern Ireland have also killed many innocent people. Elsewhere, repressive governments have imprisoned, tortured, and executed people who have spoken out against them.

✔ **READING CHECK: Summarizing** What are some recent examples of human rights abuses? "ethnic cleansing" in Bosnia and Rwanda, terrorist acts in Northern Ireland

Protecting human rights. Still, there has been some progress. International pressure helped bring an end to apartheid in South Africa. In 1994 that nation held its first truly democratic election. Political changes in the former Soviet Union also led to improved human rights and tensions have eased in Northern Ireland. In addition to the United Nations, many other organizations work to protect human rights. For example, Amnesty International, a private organization, investigates and reports on human rights abuses around the world. International organizations have pressed for officials who abuse human rights to be tried for war crimes. In addition to human rights in general, people in many countries have actively supported the rights of specific groups, such as women and children.

MAP ANSWER
Afghanistan

Economics

In 1970 more than one in three people in the developing world were found to be chronically undernourished. By 1990 that number had been reduced to one in five. The most spectacular success occurred in China, where 46 percent of the people were undernourished in 1970 and only 16 percent just 20 years later. In the Middle East and North Africa, the figure dropped from 23 percent to just 5 percent in the same time period, the lowest hunger rate in the developing world. However, the incidence of malnutrition in sub-Saharan Africa grew to 37 percent of its people by 1990.

Critical Thinking

What relationship might there be between authoritarian governments and hunger?

ANSWER: Students may say authoritarian governments can use national resources for the benefit of the rulers, or that people who have too little food have little energy to devote to political change.

TEACH OBJECTIVE 3

LEVEL 3: Have students design, research, and fill in a chart or other graphic organizer listing at least five nations that have become more democratic since 1970, with the date and nature of the transition.

Nation	Steps to Democracy
South Africa	1994: from apartheid to first elections open to all races

HOMEWORK Have students write one to three paragraphs describing one human rights organization and its work.

CLOSE

Discuss differences between the pre-World War II and post-World War II human rights approaches. Discuss what human rights the international community might agree every person should have.

That's Interesting!

Large-scale migrations occur for many reasons, including war, famine, political changes, a search for fertile soil, and ethnic rivalries. In the Middle East in the early 1990s, many people migrated to find safety in Turkey, Iran, and other countries during the Persian Gulf War. In Rwanda in the mid-1990s a bloody civil war between the country's two major ethnic groups caused the movement of large numbers of people. In Afghanistan, civil strife and war have caused many to flee the country.

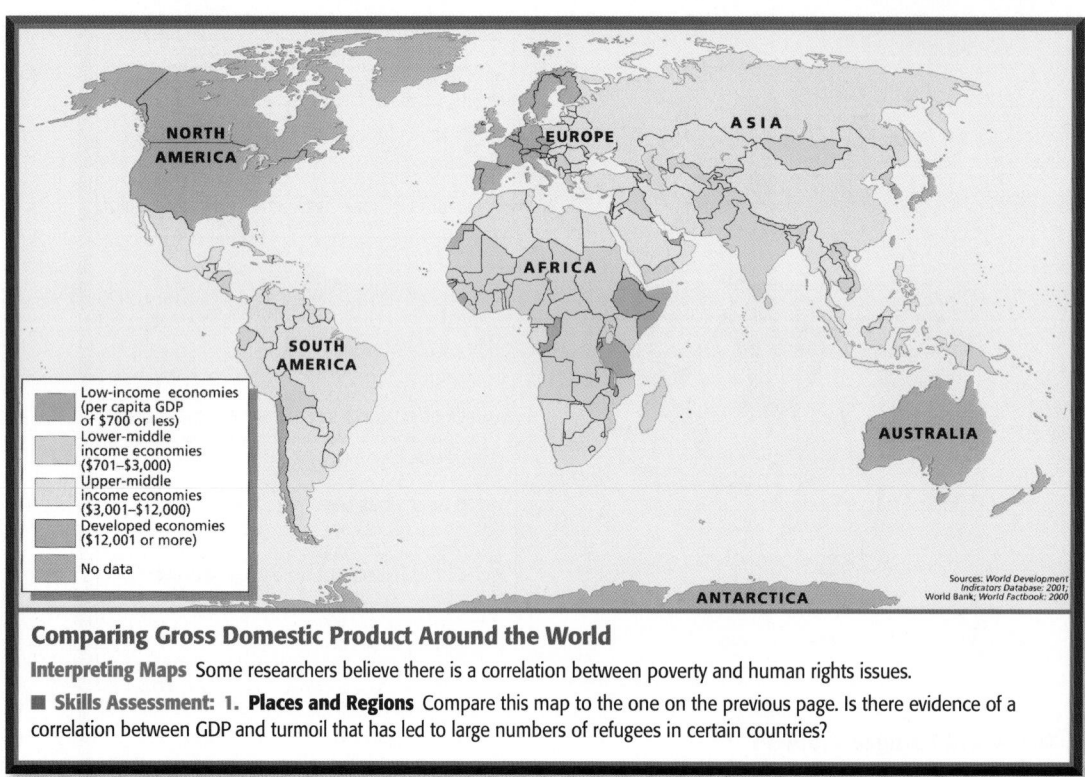

Comparing Gross Domestic Product Around the World

Interpreting Maps Some researchers believe there is a correlation between poverty and human rights issues.

■ **Skills Assessment: 1. Places and Regions** Compare this map to the one on the previous page. Is there evidence of a correlation between GDP and turmoil that has led to large numbers of refugees in certain countries?

One challenge to addressing human rights is that the concept does not have a single, universal meaning. Different cultures look at human rights in different ways. Some people, particularly in non-Western countries, place greater importance on the interests of the community than on the rights of the individual. Many of these people criticize Western nations for expecting other nations to follow their values. Similarly, such concepts as women's rights have different meanings in different societies. In the Islamic world, women's rights are viewed within the context of the Qur'an, the holy book of Islam. Others argue that allowing people to live in extreme poverty is a violation of human rights. They argue that one way to combat human rights abuses is to try to help improve the overall Gross Domestic Product (GDP) of poorer nations.

✔ **READING CHECK: Finding the Main Idea** What are some ways that people have successfully advanced human rights? international pressure, political changes, support by individuals and organizations

The Spread of Democratic Ideals

During the 50-year period after World War II, communism spread to many nations. Then in the early 1990s, the Soviet Union and its former satellite states in Eastern Europe rejected communism. These countries were actually part of a larger trend in world politics that began in the mid-1970s. Authoritarian regimes began to lose control of many countries and democracy began to take hold. For example, after decades of dictatorship in Portugal, a constitutional government finally began in 1976.

In 1975 Spanish dictator Francisco Franco died. Spain returned to democracy under the restored constitutional monarch, King Juan Carlos I. This trend toward democracy continued in the 1980s and grew after the fall of communism in the Soviet Union and Eastern Europe.

Democratic gains. Democracy made significant gains in Asia. South Korea and Taiwan both allowed more popular participation in politics. Democracy returned to the Philippines after nearly 15 years of autocratic rule by Ferdinand Marcos. In Pakistan and Bangladesh, military rulers stepped aside, if not very far and not always for very long. Latin America also experienced a shift toward democracy. Nicaragua, Chile, Brazil, Argentina, Peru, and Mexico moved from various levels of dictatorship and authoritarian rule to greater democracy. In South Africa the formerly powerless black majority elected a government headed by Nelson Mandela. In 1998 Indonesians forced President Suharto to leave office after 32 years of authoritarian rule. In 2002, East Timor won its independence from Indonesia and established democratic rule.

Holdouts on democracy. While many nations moved toward democracy, a few governments continued authoritarian rule. The People's Republic of China began economic reforms to move towards a free market. At the same time, however, hard-line communists cracked down on a growing pro-democracy movement. Living standards in Cuba dropped dramatically after Soviet economic support dried up in the early 1990s. Nevertheless, Fidel Castro continued to hold on to power. Communist rule also continued in North Korea, even though longtime dictator Kim Il Sung died in 1994.

Some other countries also chose not to follow the trend toward democracy. Muslim revolutionaries limited democratic participation in Iran and Sudan. Revolutionary dictatorship passed from father to son in Syria. Saudi Arabia remained under the autocratic rule of the Saudi royal family. A military junta continued to repress democracy in Burma. Human rights activist Aung San Suu Kyi lived under house arrest in Burma from 1989 to 1995. Suu Kyi was not allowed to attend the presentation ceremony for her Nobel Peace Prize in 1991. However, she never stopped working for democratic reforms.

✔ **READING CHECK: Finding the Main Idea** What made the spread of democratic ideals and practices possible? fall of communism in the Soviet Union and Eastern Europe, loss of control by dictators

YOUNG PEOPLE IN HISTORY

Children's Rights

Within a century children have gone from having almost no legal rights to having most of the same legal rights as adults. In 1989 the United Nations passed the **"Convention on the Rights of the Child."** This agreement outlines the legal, social, and economic guidelines that each country must follow to protect children. The accord has won support worldwide. **How have views of children's rights changed?**

Holt Researcher

go.hrw.com
KEYWORD: Holt Researcher
FreeFind: Aung San Suu Kyi
After reading more about Aung San Suu Kyi, assess how she helped to advance human rights and democratic ideals.

SECTION 3 REVIEW

1. **Identify** and explain the significance:
   Universal Declaration of Human Rights
   Convention on the Rights of the Child

2. **Making Generalizations** Copy the graphic organizer below. Use it to identify countries that moved toward democracy in the late 1900s.

   Democratization after 1970

3. **Finding the Main Idea**
   a. What areas of the world are still struggling with human rights issues?
   b. How has the international community worked to protect human rights?

4. **Writing and Critical Thinking**
   Supporting a Point of View Imagine you are the U.S. ambassador to the United Nations. Write a speech arguing that nations must work together to advance human rights and democratic ideals.
   Consider:
   - where human rights violations have occurred
   - how knowledge of human rights issues has spread
   - how democracy has spread

Homework Practice Online
keyword: SP3 HP36

REVIEW AND ASSESSMENT RESOURCES

REPRODUCIBLE RESOURCES

▸ Vocabulary Activity 36

TECHNOLOGY RESOURCES

▸ Chapter 6 Test Generator (on the One-Stop Planner)
▸ Global Skill Builder CD–ROM

REINFORCEMENT, REVIEW, and ASSESSMENT

▸ Chapter 36 Review, pp. 994–995
▸ Chapter 36 Tutorial for Students, Parents, Mentors, and Peers
▸ Chapter 36 Test (Form A or B)
▸ Alternative Assessment Handbook
▸ Chapter 36 Test for English Language Learners and Special-Needs Students

REVIEW

Have students complete the Chapter 36 Review on pages 994–995.

ASSESS

Use one of the chapter tests to assess students' understanding of the content. For Alternative Assessment, see the Portfolio Activities and Alternative Assessment Handbook.

CHAPTER 36 REVIEW ANSWERS

Understanding Main Ideas

1. art as expression of unconscious mind; new architectural materials and techniques

2. social commentary, science fiction, mystical stories

3. new products, new ways to process information and do research

4. antibiotics (other than penicillin), polio and smallpox vaccines, AIDS drugs, mapping chemical structure of DNA, cloning

5. Repressive governments silence dissidents; non-Western countries prize community interests over individual rights; some Islamic governments view women's rights according to their interpretation of the Qur'an; poverty abuses human rights.

6. Soviet Union rejected communism; authoritarian regimes lost control to democracies

Reviewing Themes

1. more freedom; fewer standards

2. ideas/information transmitted quickly across social boundaries

3. ways to combat disease, effects of genetic engineering, dangers of pollution, effects of population growth and industrialization

---

CHAPTER 36 Review

Creating a Time Line

Copy the time line below onto a sheet of paper. Complete the time line by filling in events, individuals, and dates from the chapter that you think were significant. Pick three events and explain why you think they were significant.

| 1945 | 1985 | present |

Writing a Summary

Using standard grammar, spelling, sentence structure, and punctuation, write an overview of the chapter.

Identifying People and Ideas

Identify the following terms or individuals and explain their significance:

1. abstract expressionism
2. George Balanchine
3. Maya Angelou
4. Yury Gagarin
5. *Alpha*
6. miniaturization
7. genetic code
8. urbanization
9. biodiversity
10. Rachel Carson

Understanding Main Ideas

Section 1 *(pp. 968–974)*

The Arts and Literature

1. What were the major themes in painting, sculpture, and architecture after World War II?
2. How did poetry and novels written in the years after 1945 reflect postwar society around the world?

Section 2 *(pp. 975–983)*

Science and Technology

3. How have major trends and developments in modern technology, such as miniaturization and computerization, changed modern life?
4. What major advances in medical science have taken place since 1945?

Section 3 *(pp. 984–987)*

Human Rights and the Spread of Democratic Ideals

5. Why are human rights difficult to protect?
6. What evidence suggests that democracy has spread in the late 1900s?

Reviewing Themes

1. **Culture** What direction did developments in the arts and literature follow in the years after World War II?
2. **Science, Technology & Society** How can technological change affect ideas and behavior?
3. **Citizenship** What challenges to well-being can people expect in the future?

Thinking Critically

1. **Comparing** How were early successes of the space exploration programs of the United States and the Soviet Union similar?
2. **Evaluating** How might rapid population growth in a developing country slow down other types of growth and development?
3. **Drawing Inferences** What are some of the positive and negative results of genetic engineering?
4. **Identifying Cause and Effect** How did lifestyles in America change after World War II, and what factors caused these changes?

Writing About History

Problem Solving Imagine that you are a journalist who specializes in developing articles about modern issues and challenges. Choose a current environmental problem and write a short paper that describes several ways the world community might deal with the issue. Then predict what the outcomes of your suggested actions might be. Analyze which interest groups might favor your recommendations and which might oppose them, and explain why. Use the following diagram to organize your thoughts before you begin writing.

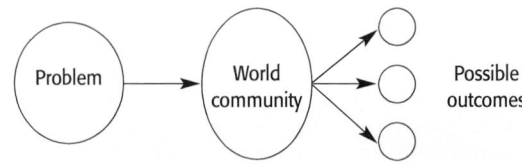

CLOSE

Ask students to name three major challenges of post-World War II civilization. Have them explain how life in the United States today reflects each of these characteristics.

RETEACH

Group students who had trouble with the test into pairs. Have them use their textbook to correct their tests. Ask them to create flash cards and then quiz each other on the chapter content. Then have students take the Form B Test to assess their mastery of the material. **ENGLISH LANGUAGE LEARNERS, COOPERATIVE LEARNING**

Portfolio Extensions

Link to TODAY

1. Ask students to imagine they are art curators a hundred years from now, looking for icons of the late 1900s. Have them create a list of artists and art objects that symbolized the challenges of this era. Have them write an explanation of each item.

2. Ask students to make a chart showing challenges to life on Earth in the late 1900s. For each challenge, have them list ways that technology has resolved the problems or could possibly resolve the situation.

3. Have students assess the degree to which human rights and democratic ideals and practices have been advanced throughout the world during the 1900s.

Building Social Studies Skills

Comparing and Contrasting

Study the list of modern sources of information below. Then use the information from the list to answer the questions that follow.

Some Typical Sources of Information in Today's World

- The Internet
- Information passed by word of mouth
- Newspapers and magazines
- Public library
- Television and radio

1. Which of the statements below is the most accurate?

   a. The most important source of information among the sources listed above is "The Internet."

   b. Public libraries are the best single source of information because they are so easy to use.

   c. All of the sources listed above are important, and all take different approaches to information sharing.

   d. Television and radio are most important because they rely upon sight and sound.

2. Information is more available in greater quantities today than ever before. Write a brief paragraph explaining why this might actually pose a disadvantage to those who seek information.

Identifying Cause and Effect

Read the following quote from a report about information technology. Then answer the questions.

> "In June 1999, reporters from around the world flocked to Bhutan to watch the tiny Himalayan kingdom officially enter the information age. Bhutan's rulers had long tried to protect the nation's traditional Buddhist culture from outside influence with limits on tourist traffic and bans on satellite television receivers. But now King Wangchuck was . . . inaugurating Bhutan's first Internet hookup and addressing his subjects during the nation's first television broadcast. . . . Bhutan has joined a diverse and rapidly expanding global network."

3. Which of the following correctly states the reason so many reporters went to Bhutan in 1999?

   a. Reporters had not been allowed to visit the small nation of Bhutan for many years, but now they were allowed in to cover this event.

   b. Many of the reporters wanted to see the Himalayas.

   c. This was an important news story because Bhutan's king had rejected Buddhism.

   d. This was an important news story because Bhutan had successfully resisted outside influence for so long.

4. Do you think it is important for all countries to be part of the global information network? Give specific reasons.

Alternative Assessment

Building Your Portfolio

Link to TODAY

Citizenship

Democratic ideals and practices spread to new countries in the late 1900s. Select one country that changed to a democratic government after 1970. Research the reasons for and consequences of this change. Is everyday life for citizens of this country better or worse since democracy took hold? Make an oral presentation of your findings to your class.

internet connect

go.hrw.com

Internet Activity: go.hrw.com
KEYWORD: SP3 WH36

Choose a topic on the Modern World to:
- investigate global warming.
- learn more about modern world literature by studying contemporary novelists and poets.
- write a biography about one of the artists mentioned in this chapter.

Thinking Critically

1. satellites, people in space

2. put more demand on limited resources

3. medical gains; ethical issues such as "designer babies"

4. more education, more leisure time, television, faster transportation and communications technology

Writing About History

Students' papers will vary but should describe the specific issue; suggested actions and outcomes in the paper should correspond to those on the diagram.

Building Social Studies Skills

1. c

2. information overload, hard to sort out what's important

3. d

4. yes: can get education, access to changing information, less control by dictators; no: outside influences may not be beneficial, privacy may be invaded

Building Your Portfolio

Students should focus on a specific country, describe its change to democracy, and compare and contrast the country before and after the change.

THE MODERN WORLD **995**

995

Spotlight on LITERATURE

Originally, a lyric was a poem intended for musical accompaniment. We still refer to the words of a song as "lyrics." The term also refers to subjective and emotional poems that are melodious in meter and rhythm. Lyric poems are often distinguished from two other broad categories of poetry—narrative and dramatic. Even so, long narrative poems and verse plays often include lyrical passages.

Spotlight on LITERATURE

Frantz Fanon wrote several important books on racism and colonial liberation. He was born in Martinique and educated as a psychiatrist. He took a psychiatric post in an Algerian hospital in 1953. Fanon joined the liberation movement and became editor of its newspaper. In 1960 the rebel Algerian government appointed him ambassador to Ghana. In 1961 he published *The Wretched of the Earth*, in which he called for revolutions to liberate developing countries from colonialism.

Interdisciplinary Connection

LITERATURE. A metaphor is a figure of speech in which a word referring to one object is applied to another. A metaphor creates a new image that incorporates characteristics of the two entities. Many words that were once metaphors, such as the "leg" of a table or the "hood" of a car have come to be accepted as literal descriptions. Such expressions are called dead metaphors. Metaphor is often distinguished from simile, which is a comparison containing the words *like* or *as*. Both metaphor and simile are used in literature to evoke likenesses between different objects or areas of experience.

Critical Thinking

What examples of metaphor can you find in the literary selections on page 996?

ANSWER: Senghor: tied to us at the navel, give their lives like the poor man his last garment, rebirth of the world, deadened by machines, wake the dead; Allende: with the vocation of a true apostle; we live in a jungle.

UNDERSTANDING LITERATURE ANSWER

Lines like "we are men of dance" show evidence of cultural pride as does the idealism of the character, Jaime, in the Allende piece. People of other cultures read literature such as this for inspiration and to gain understanding.

CROSS-CULTURAL *Literature* CONNECTIONS

Cultural Pride

Léopold Senghor and Isabel Allende find inspiration for their literature in their cultural heritage. Born in Senegal and educated in France, Léopold Sédar Senghor explains that many of his poems echo African dance rhythms while they tell of African nations' struggles to overcome hatred of the colonial powers that once ruled them. After leading Senegal's independence movement, Senghor served as the country's first president from 1960 to 1980. Novelist Isabel Allende was forced to leave Chile in 1973 after her uncle, President Salvadore Allende, was assassinated in a military coup. Allende's novel The House of the Spirits *tells the story of several generations of a Latin American family led by Esteban Trueba. Allende uses the conflicts in Trueba's family to mirror issues dividing Latin America in the late 1900s.*

"Prayer to the Masks" by Léopold Senghor

The Africa of empires is dying–it is the agony
Of a sorrowful princess
And Europe, too, tied to us at
    the navel.
Fix your steady eyes on your
    oppressed children
Who give their lives like the
    poor man his last garment.
Let us answer "present" at the
    rebirth of the World
As white flour cannot rise without
    the leaven.
Who else will teach rhythm to the world
Deadened by machines and cannons?
Who will sound the shout of joy at daybreak to wake orphans
    and the dead?
Tell me, who will bring back the memory of life
To the man of gutted hopes?
They call us men of cotton, coffee, and oil
They call us men of death.
But we are men of dance, whose feet get stronger
As we pound upon firm ground.

The House of the Spirits by Isabel Allende

Jaime practiced his profession with the vocation of a true apostle. ... [H]e spent his strength working in the clinic and treating the poor without charge in his spare time.

"You're a hopeless loser, son," Trueba would say, sighing. "You have no sense of reality. You've never taken stock of how the world really is. You put your faith in utopian values that don't even exist."

"Helping one's neighbor is a value that exists."

"No. Charity, like Socialism, is an invention of the weak to exploit the strong and bring them to their knees."

"I don't believe in your theory of the weak and the strong," Jaime replied.

"That's the way it is in nature. We live in a jungle."

"Yes, because the people who make up the rules think like you! But it won't always be that way."

"Oh, yes, it will. Because we always win. We know how to move around in the world and how to use power. Listen to me, son. Pull yourself together and open your own clinic. I'll help you. But cut out your Socialist nonsense!"

Understanding Literature

What evidence of cultural pride can you find in Senghor's and Allende's literature? Why do you think their writings are widely read outside their cultures?

Citizenship

Have students select one of the regions discussed in the unit and use their textbooks and other primary and secondary resources to create a detailed time line of events in the region since 1945. Then have them use their time line to write a summary of ways in which the region has changed and to express their opinion of whether the change has been for the better or for the worse. (Example: *Nicaragua: late 1970s—opposition to dictator; 1979—Sandinistas, led by Ortega, take control; early 1980s—move toward communism, opposition grows; 1990—Ortega conducts free elections*)

Global Relations

Have students work with partners to learn more about two world leaders since 1945. Then have them work together to compare and contrast these two individuals—their goals, their successes, their failures. Students should list similarities and differences, consider external circumstances, and compare results. Have them write an essay explaining their conclusions.

UNIT 8 — BUILDING YOUR Portfolio

Citizenship

The nature of citizenship changed for many Europeans, Asians, and Latin Americans during the last decades of the 1900s. Imagine that you are an artist living in Buenos Aires, Argentina, in 1983. You have been asked to create a mural for a new civic building. Your task is to create a series of images that depict the new meaning of citizenship in your country compared to other countries. What kinds of images would you show, and what would they reveal about the nature of citizenship in the 1980s?

Miniature flags from some of the world's nations

Global Relations

During the second half of the 1900s, sweeping political changes took place in many countries around the world. As a result, our world is a far different place today than it was in the 1950s. Imagine that you are a historian at work on a biographical dictionary. The dictionary will contain entries describing significant political figures on the world stage between the years 1945 and 2000. Your task is to prepare individual sample entries discussing five political figures whom you consider the most important leaders of the period. Which figures would you include? Ask yourself which world leaders had the greatest global impact during the years after World War II. Explain your selections.

Demolition of the Berlin Wall

Further Reading

Fireside, Harvey and Bryna J. Fireside. *Young People From Bosnia Talk About War.* New York: Enslow Publishing, 1996. First-person accounts from teenagers living in Bosnia during the civil war.

Matthews, John R. *The Rise and Fall of the Soviet Union.* San Diego: Lucent Books, 2000. A comprehensive survey from the beginning of the Soviet Union to its collapse.

Pietrusza, David. *The Chinese Cultural Revolution.* San Diego: Lucent Books, 1997. A history of China focusing on the period between the rise of the Chinese Communist Party and the Tiananmen Square demonstration in 1989.

Roberts, J. M. *The Illustrated History of the World: Volume 10, The Global Age.* New York: Oxford University Press, 2000. A survey of world events from the period 1945 to the present.

Winkler, Alan M. *The Cold War: A History in Documents.* New York: Oxford University Press, 2001. A history of the Cold War told through first-person accounts and government documents.

---

internet connect

Internet Activity
KEYWORD: SP3 U8

In assigned groups, develop a multimedia presentation about the world from 1945 to the present. Choose information from the chapter Internet Connect activities and the Holt Researcher that best reflects the major topics of the period. Write an outline and a script for your presentation, which may be shown to the class.

History Maker

V. S. NAIPAUL. The novelist and essayist Sir Vidiadhar Surajprasad Naipaul is considered to be one of the greatest living writers of English. He was born in Trinidad to Indian parents but lived in England. His early novels focused on West Indian life. Later novels, such as *The Mimic Men* and *In a Free State,* dealt with themes of expatriate alienation. *A Bend in the River* is a grim description of life in postcolonial Africa. Some of Naipaul's essays are collected in *India: A Wounded Civilization, The Return of Eva Peron,* and *Among the Believers: An Islamic Journey. Way in the World* is an autobiography that includes a tribute to Trinidad. Naipaul was knighted in 1990 and received the Nobel Prize for Literature in 2001.

ACTIVITY: Have students read brief excerpts from Naipaul's works. Then challenge them to write essays discussing the works, their meaning, and Naipaul's writing style.

The War on Terrorism: A Global View

OBJECTIVES

1 **Discuss the nature of terrorism around the world.**

2 **Analyze the United States and allied response to the events of September 11, 2001.**

3 **Explain why the United States and its allies went to war in Afghanistan and Iraq.**

4 **Discuss the international efforts to combat terrorism.**

Geography

BOMBING IN BUENOS AIRES, ARGENTINA. The central image on this page is from the car bombing of the Israeli embassy in Buenos Aires, Argentina. In the attack, which was traced to Hezbollah, 29 people were killed, and 242 were injured. Hezbollah claimed that the bombing was in retaliation for an Israeli attack that killed a leader of Hezbollah and his family.

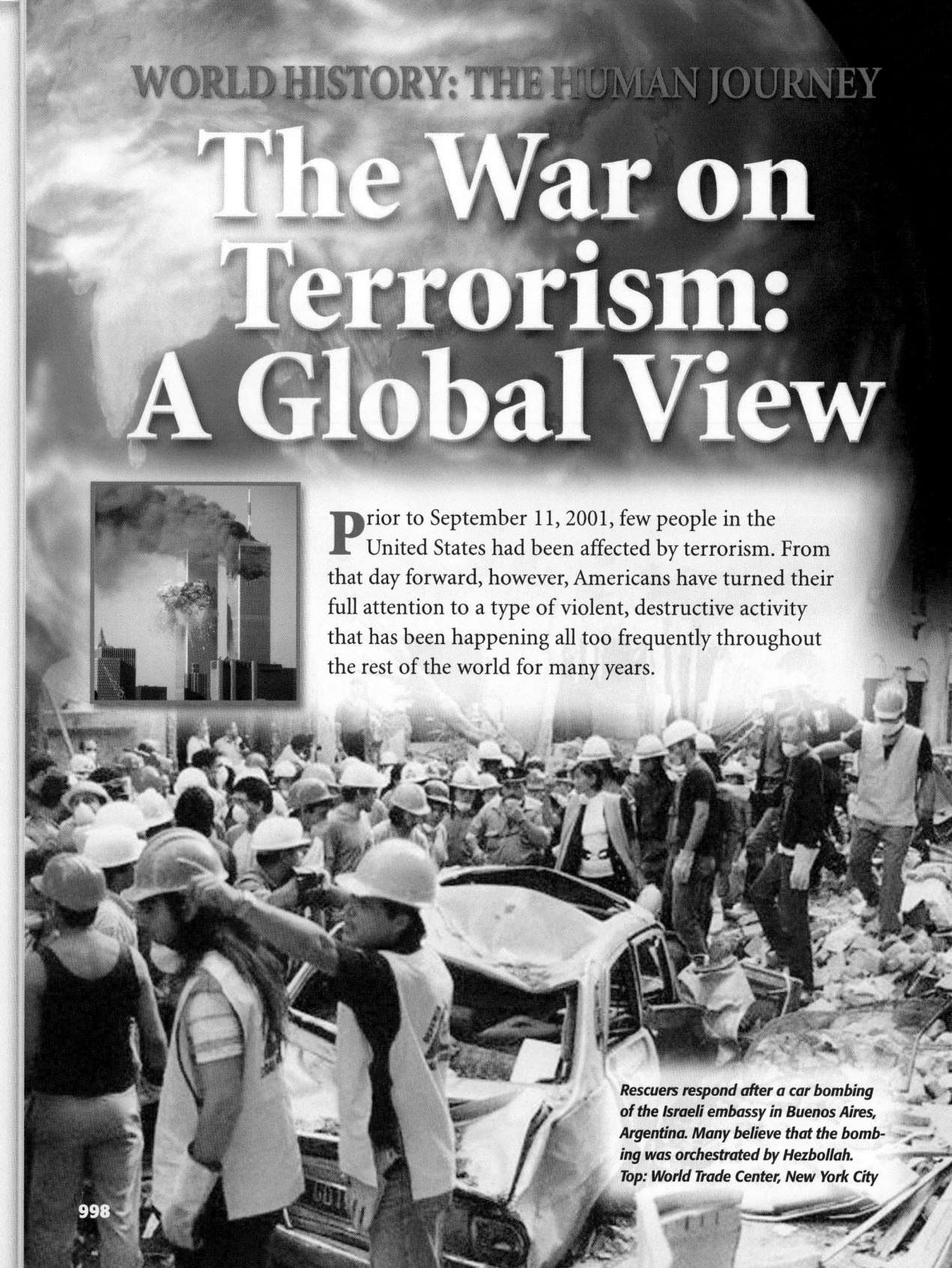

WORLD HISTORY: THE HUMAN JOURNEY

The War on Terrorism: A Global View

Prior to September 11, 2001, few people in the United States had been affected by terrorism. From that day forward, however, Americans have turned their full attention to a type of violent, destructive activity that has been happening all too frequently throughout the rest of the world for many years.

Rescuers respond after a car bombing of the Israeli embassy in Buenos Aires, Argentina. Many believe that the bombing was orchestrated by Hezbollah. Top: World Trade Center, New York City

998

Have students copy the two definitions. Ask them to write their own definitions, and have volunteers share these definitions with the class.

Guide the class in a discussion of what terrorism is, how it differs from civil insurrection, and reasons that groups resort to terror as a means of achieving their goals.

Terrorism Around the World

As of early 2004, the U.S. State Deparment had identified over 70 terrorist organizations in various parts of the world. These groups have planned and executed wide-scale attacks on public buildings, guerrilla raids on villages, kidnappings, suicide bombings, and airplane hijackings. Between 1998 and 2002 there were over 1,600 terrorist attacks worldwide, and more than 17,000 people lost their lives as a result of terrorist activities.

Terrorism in Latin America and Africa

Since 1998, more than 650 terrorist attacks have been recorded in Latin America. In Colombia, the terrorist groups Revolutionary Armed Forces of Colombia (FARC) and the United Self-Defense Forces of Colombia (AUC) have kidnapped over 3,000 people since 2000. In February 2003, alone, FARC took responsibility for more than 53 deaths.

In Peru, the Sendero Luminoso, or Shining Path, has been active since the 1960s trying to establish a Communist regime. Over 30,000 Peruvians have lost their lives as a result of this group's activities. In the southern Mexican state of Chiapas, the Zapatista National Liberation Army has been waging a campaign against the Mexican government since 1994.

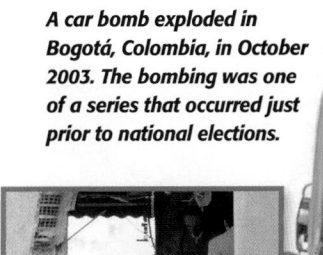

Investigators inspect debris after a terrorist bomb ripped through a busy café in Ankara, Turkey.

This group considers itself a national movement whose goals are to gain land, work, shelter, and respect for indigenous peoples and protection for their cultures.

In Africa, terrorist groups are active in more than 20 countries. Some of the rebel groups, such as the Lord's Resistance Army in Uganda, are well armed, well organized, and have been active for years. Other terrorist groups are smaller bands operating within individual nations or across borders. Terrorist activities in Africa have claimed approximately 6,000 lives since 1998.

Terrorism in Europe

Europe has not been free of terrorist activities. For example, over the past few years Chechen rebels have claimed responsibility for numerous terrorist attacks in various Russian cities. Among these was

A car bomb exploded in Bogotá, Colombia, in October 2003. The bombing was one of a series that occurred just prior to national elections.

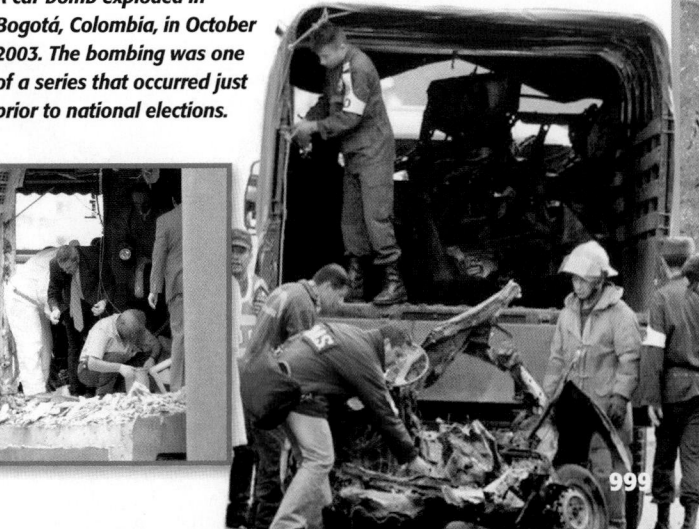

the highly publicized occupation of the Dubrovka Theater in Moscow in 2002, which led to the deaths of 170 people. The attacks are part of Chechnya's effort to secede from Russia, which has fought a military campaign in Chechnya for most of the last decade to prevent the breakup.

In the Basque region of northern Spain, the Basque Fatherland and Liberty group, ETA, has waged a violent campaign to establish an independent Basque homeland. More than 800 people have been killed as a result of ETA bombings and assassinations. Many hundreds more have been injured.

Various groups continue to commit terrorist attacks in the struggle over whether Northern Ireland should remain part of the

ALL LEVELS: The United States has long been the world's leader for ensuring personal freedoms, especially speech, religion, and privacy rights. Among the first reactions of the U.S. government to the events of 9/11 was passage of the PATRIOT Act. Guide students in a discussion of the PATRIOT Act, and review why some provisions of the act were considered to be in violation of the Bill of Rights. Have students research the act and prepare a chart listing its major provisions.

LEVELS 2 AND 3: Have students write editorials or create political cartoons about the PATRIOT Act. Students should either defend the PATRIOT Act as necessary to ensure the safety of Americans or suggest ways to reform the PATRIOT Act to ensure that the constitutional rights granted to Americans in the Bill of Rights are guaranteed and safeguarded. Have students share their editorials and political cartoons with the class.

Linking Past to Present

AL QAEDA. You may wish to provide students with background information on al Qaeda. Al Qaeda is an Arabic word meaning "the base."

Al Qaeda is an international terrorist group that was founded in the late 1980s by Osama bin Laden and others. It brought together Arabs who had fought against the Soviet Union in the war in Afghanistan, and its mission was to oppose non-Islamic governments through the use of force and violence. One of al Qaeda's principal goals was to drive U.S. armed forces out of Saudi Arabia and Somalia. Al Qaeda had ties to other terrorist organizations, including Hezbollah and the al Jihad in Egypt. Al Qaeda was a well-financed, well-organized organization with cells throughout the Middle East, Africa, and Europe.

ANSWERS TO THINK ABOUT IT

1. Non-violent demonstrations, civil disobedience, economic boycotts, and mediation have proven to be more successful than terrorism.

2. Student answers may include that poverty, repression, social injustice, and the lack of democratic means to express one's opinions lead some people to turn to terrorism. These conditions are more prevalent in Africa and Latin America.

United Kingdom. Over the past thirty years, more than 3,500 civilians and soldiers have been killed in the conflict over the territory's fate.

One of the most tragic acts of terrorism in Europe occurred in 1988. That year, PanAm Flight 103 was brought down over Lockerbie, Scotland, by Libyan terrorists who had planted a bomb in a suitcase loaded onto the plane. Two hundred and seventy people lost their lives—259 passengers and crew and 11 people on the ground. Among the 270 dead, 189 were Americans.

Terrorism in the Middle East

In the Middle East, Palestinian groups such as Hamas, Abu Nidal, the Al-Aqsa Martyrs, and Hezbollah continue to conduct terrorist attacks against Israel. These attacks, and Israeli retaliations, have complicated efforts to build a lasting peace and have been a major source of tension in the region. The ongoing conflict between Israel and Palestine has been used by some to justify the horrendous acts of terrorism committed by a few fanatics. Despite

U.S. efforts to bring all the parties to negotiations to work toward a peaceful solution, suicide bombings and retaliations continue.

Al Qaeda

Few, if any, terrorist groups have carried out attacks in as many different parts of the world as al Qaeda and its allies. In October 2002, a group with links to al Qaeda bombed a nightclub on the Indonesian island of Bali, a popular vacation spot. More than 200 people were killed, including many young Australians. In May 2003, bombings in Morocco attributed to

Two nightclubs on the beach in Bali were bombed in October 2002. Rescuers helped search for survivors, but more than 200 people were killed in the blasts.

al Qaeda took 41 lives. In August of that same year, bombings at a Marriott hotel in Jakarta, Indonesia, killed 10 and wounded 150. Soon after, in Ankara, Turkey, two synagogues, the British consulate, and a British bank were bombed. Turkish authorities arrested al Qaeda sympathizers for their suspected role in the plot.

It was the tragic results of al Qaeda's attacks on the United States on September 11, 2001, however, that triggered worldwide outrage over terrorism. The United States was quick to respond to the attacks, both at home and abroad. Buoyed by international sympathy, the United States declared war on terrorism.

THINK ABOUT IT

1. What alternatives to terrorism provide a better means of achieving social change?

2. Why are there many more terrorist incidents in Africa and Latin America than in Europe and North America?

An armed member of Fatah marches at the funeral of a Hamas suicide bomber in Gaza City, Palestine.

1000

ALL LEVELS: One of the first steps taken by the U.S. government following 9/11 was to establish a new executive-level department. The U.S. Department of Homeland Security is organized into five main divisions: Border and Transportation Security; Emergency Preparedness and Response; Science and Technology (Chemical, Biological, Radiological and Nuclear Countermeasures); Information Analysis and Infrastructure Protection; and Administration. Twenty-two domestic agencies fall under the umbrella of the department. Have students research this department and create large-scale charts of the agencies that belong within the Homeland Security administration.

LEVELS 2 AND 3: Ask students to examine the divisions of the department that would interact with law enforcement or intelligence agencies of other countries. Have students present their findings to the class.

Fighting Terrorism in the United States

Following the events of 9/11, the United States took a number of steps to help prevent further terrorist attacks within the nation.

The USA-PATRIOT Act

In October 2001, Congress passed the USA-PATRIOT Act. This sweeping law, a first step in U.S. homeland security, gave the government added powers to investigate persons suspected of planning terrorist acts. It permitted the Department of Justice to intercept e-mail messages, wiretap telephones, search private residences, and even check library users' computer records. Following passage of the act, the Justice Department detained and questioned more than a thousand persons living in the United States.

Stringent security checks mean long lines for passengers at airports.

Imprisoning al Qaeda Suspects

Many al Qaeda suspects, mostly of Middle Eastern origin, were imprisoned at Guantánamo, the U.S. military base in Cuba. By 2004, an estimated 650 prisoners from forty-two countries were being held.

Most of these prisoners were in a legal limbo, being held with no charges filed against them and no trials scheduled. In May 2003, Secretary of State Colin Powell urged the Pentagon to decide quickly which Guantánamo prisoners could be released and which prisoners would be charged and tried. Later that year, a federal appeals court ruled that the prisoners should be tried in U.S. civil courts, not by military tribunals as the Pentagon desired. The ruling highlighted America's struggle to protect individual rights while ensuring security.

Airport Security

The 9/11 attackers had used airplanes to carry out their terrible deeds, so airport security in the United States became a high government priority. Congress tightened inspection procedures and imposed stricter standards for security personnel. Most air travelers accepted the resulting long lines. They understood the importance of strengthened air security.

In late 2003 and early 2004, many international flights to the United States were cancelled due to suspected terrorist activity. In addition, the Department of Homeland Security began photographing and fingerprinting visitors from many countries as an additional security precaution.

THINK ABOUT IT

1. Why did Congress pass the USA-PATRIOT Act?
2. The attacks of September 11, 2001, "horrified the nation," as well as people throughout the world. What other one-day events in world history have resulted in worldwide sympathy and reaction?

Linking Past to Present

GUANTÁNAMO BAY. In 1898, during the Spanish-American War, U.S. Marines established camp at the harbor known as Guantánamo Bay. The United States acquired the land from Spain at the end of the war. In 1903 President Theodore Roosevelt was able to obtain a permanent lease on the land from Cuba; Franklin Delano Roosevelt ordered that the base be expanded in 1939. It has served as a maintenance port for U.S. ships and as a facility to house Cuban and Haitian refugees intercepted at sea while trying to reach the United States. The base was also used to house suspected al Qaeda and Taliban prisoners.

ANSWERS TO THINK ABOUT IT

1. to help ensure better sharing of information, consolidate agencies involved in disaster relief and prevention, help ensure that terrorist activities do not recur in the United States

2. Students might include the assassination of Archduke Francis Ferdinand; the sinking of the *Lusitania;* Germany's invasion of Poland; the dropping of atomic bombs on Hiroshima and Nagasaki, Japan; assassination of President John F. Kennedy.

ALL LEVELS: Remind students that immediately following the events of 9/11, global condemnation of the tragedy was tremendous. Around the world, people reacted immediately and with sympathy. The headline of the French newspaper *Le Monde* proclaimed in response to that day, "We are all Americans!" You might wish to have students prepare a bulletin board with the international outcry that followed the 9/11 attacks on the United States.

The United States had little difficulty recruiting international support for its efforts to remove the Taliban from power in Afghanistan, and 26 nations were involved in the war effort.

Have students write a brief essay explaining why it was crucial for the United States and its allies to move quickly and forcefully to remove the Taliban from power in Afghanistan. Have students share their essays.

Geography

AFGHANISTAN AND PAKISTAN.
Using the map as a reference, discuss the location of Kabul in relation to the Pakistani border. Have students measure the distance from Kabul to the border (approximately 100 km, or 60 miles). Ask students how this closeness would help and hinder both al Qaeda terrorists and allied forces working to eradicate the terrorists.

MAP ANSWER
The mountains provide excellent coverage; they are riddled with caves where terrorists can hide; terrorists could easily cross into the villages of Pakistan for supplies and to escape military patrols.

Geography

THE AFGHAN LANDSCAPE.
Ask students to examine the image on the bottom of the page. What does it reveal about the landscape of this region of Afghanistan? Guide students in a discussion of how warfare in a flat desert area differs from warfare conducted in the mountains or jungles.

Fighting Terrorism in Afghanistan

Shortly after the 9/11 attacks were linked to al Qaeda forces operating in Afghanistan, under the protection of the Afghan government, U.S. and allied troops invaded the country. The U.S.-led coalition forces destroyed al Qaeda strongholds and worked with local leaders to begin the process of establishing a stable, democratic government.

Battling al Qaeda and the Taliban
By late 2001, the U.S.-led military operations in Afghanistan had killed or captured many suspected al Qaeda fighters and destroyed their bases and training camps. These military operations also overthrew the Taliban, which had ruled Afghanistan since 1996.

The coalition's efforts left al Qaeda severely weakened, but still a threat. Some al Qaeda loyalists hid out in rugged eastern Afghanistan, where the mountains are riddled with caves. Others slipped across the border into Pakistan.

Searching for Osama bin Laden
The leader of al Qaeda, Osama bin Laden, eluded capture in the initial military operations in Afghanistan. Continuing into 2004, an Arabic-language TV network even broadcast videotapes in which bin Laden urged continued struggle against the United States. His responsibility for the 9/11 attacks became absolutely clear when U.S. forces in Afghanistan discovered a videotape on which he boasted of planning the attacks.

Born around 1957, bin Laden was the son of a fabulously rich Saudi Arabian construction contractor. Over the years, bin Laden had developed a fanatical hatred of the United States. As a strict Muslim fundamentalist, he saw America as morally corrupt and in violation of Islamic law, including the requirement that women be veiled. He was outraged that U.S. troops operated bases in Saudi Arabia, home of the sacred shrine

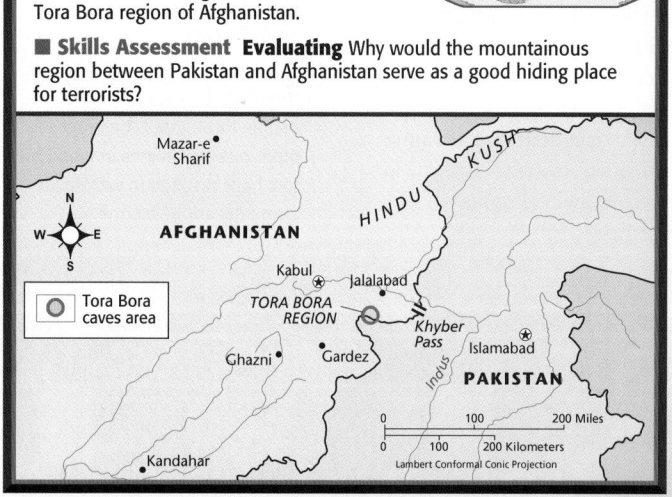

Afghanistan-Pakistan Border Region

Interpreting Maps Osama bin Laden and members of his al Qaeda forces were believed to be hiding in the caves within the Tora Bora region of Afghanistan.

■ **Skills Assessment Evaluating** Why would the mountainous region between Pakistan and Afghanistan serve as a good hiding place for terrorists?

Mazar-e Sharif

HINDU KUSH

AFGHANISTAN

Kabul • Jalalabad
Tora Bora caves area
TORA BORA REGION
Khyber Pass
Islamabad
Ghazni • Gardez
Indus
PAKISTAN

Kandahar

0   100   200 Miles
0   100   200 Kilometers
Lambert Conformal Conic Projection

The U.S. military relied heavily on Black Hawk helicopters to move troops throughout Afghanistan. The troops in these helicopters were on a mission to clear caves of terrorists and their weapons.

Afghanistan's *loya jirga*

Write the following question on the board: *What is the* loya jirga *and who are its members?* Have students work in pairs or small groups to answer the question and have them share their responses with the class. Point out to students that the *loya jirga* is unique to Afghanistan. It is a grand council comprised of political and tribal leaders and elders; it includes Pashtuns, Tajiks, Hazaras, Uzbeks, and representatives from the other tribes and groups within Afghanistan, including nomads. The institution has existed for hundreds of years and is similar to the Islamic *shura*, or consultative assembly. In the past, *loya jirgas* have been organized when it was necessary for tribal elders to come together to settle affairs in the country, to settle international disputes, or to discuss possible social reforms. In this *loya jirga*, 160 seats were reserved for women. Guide students in a discussion of the ways that the backgrounds of these leaders would help and hinder the establishment of a democratically elected government.

Right: Delegates of the loya jirga *met in Kabul, Afghanistan, in January 2004 to discuss the country's new constitution.*

Osama bin Laden

of Mecca. American support for the Jewish nation of Israel infuriated him as well.

Even before 9/11, federal courts had indicted bin Laden for terrorist crimes, including the 1998 bombing of U.S. embassies in Tanzania and Kenya. After the 1998 attacks, President Clinton had ordered missile attacks on al Qaeda camps in Afghanistan.

An Afghan man watches a group of U.S. soldiers inspect a local bazaar.

A New Government in Afghanistan

With the Taliban defeated, U.S. authorities and Afghan leaders worked on plans for a new government. However, conflicts among Afghanistan's regional warlords complicated the task. So did hostility between the country's two major ethnic groups, the Pashtuns and the Tajiks.

In 2002, an assembly of regional Afghan leaders, called the *loya jirga*, chose Hamid Karzai as president. Early in 2004, after months of wrangling, the *loya jirga* agreed on a new constitution providing for a democratically elected government, an independent judiciary, and more rights for women and minorities.

The capital, Kabul, remained dangerous, however, with assassination attempts against President Karzai and other officials. Outside the capital, local warlords and diehard Taliban supporters controlled some areas. Soldiers and civilians continued to suffer casualties. Some *loya jirga* members even feared to return home because of death threats. The new constitution was a big step forward, but the future of this troubled land remained uncertain.

THINK ABOUT IT

1. Why did Osama bin Laden focus his hatred on the United States?
2. What problems make it difficult for the new Afghan government to function effectively?

History Maker

HAMID KARZAI. Hamid Karzai was born in Kandahar, Afghanistan, in 1957. During Afghanistan's struggle against the Soviet invasion in the 1980s, Karzai provided arms and money to the mujahadeen, and he later served as deputy foreign minister in the post-Soviet government. Following the ouster of the Taliban, Karzai led the interim government and was then elected president by the *loya jirga*.

In February 2003, Karzai addressed the United States Senate, saying: "Afghanistan will, by the grace of God, stand on its own feet in three to five years time. Till then, of course, we need strong support from the international community, including the United States, to stay with us and support us fully."

Critical Thinking

What was Karzai hoping to achieve in this speech? *(garner U.S. support)*

ANSWERS TO THINK ABOUT IT

1. The U.S. represented moral corruption; the American way of life violates Islamic law; the U.S. has military bases in Saudi Arabia; the U.S. has been a staunch ally of Israel.

2. Afghanistan faced social problems and remained dangerous; there was hostility among ethnic groups and conflicts among the warlords.

ALL LEVELS: In 1988 Iraq used chemical warfare on Iraqi Kurds, killing 200,000 in that year alone. Therefore, it was documented that Iraq possessed and had used chemical weapons. Following Iraq's defeat in the Persian Gulf War, a UN coalition forced Iraq to agree to an inspections and monitoring regime to ensure that the country had dismantled its WMD program. The UN Special Commission on Iraq was established and continued its arms inspection work until 1998. In 2002, in response to calls from various nations, particularly the United States and Britain, to resume the arms inspection program, the UN established UNMOVIC (UN Monitoring, Verification, and Inspections Commission), and Iraq agreed to accept the UN inspectors. Searches for WMDs resumed in November 2002. No WMDs were ever found by the UN Commission, nor were WMDs found by the U.S. Iraq Survey Group led by David Kay following the ouster of Saddam.

History Maker

HANS BLIX. Hans Blix had worked for many years with the United Nations prior to his appointment to the UN Monitoring, Verification, and Inspection Commission. From 1961 until 1981, Dr. Blix served as a member of Sweden's delegation to the UN General Assembly; from 1962 to 1978, he was a member of the Swedish delegation to the Conference on Disarmament in Geneva, Switzerland. In January 2000 Dr. Blix was asked to serve as executive chairman of the UN Monitoring, Verification, and Inspection Commission, and he began his work in March of that year. In June 2003, in his position as the UN chief weapons inspector, Hans Blix addressed the UN Security Council concerning the search for weapons of mass destruction in Iraq: "The Commission has not at any time during the inspections in Iraq found evidence of the continuation or resumption of programs of weapons of mass destruction or significant quantities of proscribed items, whether from pre-1991 or later." Dr. Blix retired as head of UNMOVIC the next month, July 2003.

Guide students in a discussion of the reasons the United States and Britain continued to press for an ongoing search for WMDs in Iraq.

The War in Iraq

With al Qaeda on the run in Afghanistan, the Bush administration and its allies identified Iraq as the next battlefield in the war on terrorism.

Background of the Iraq War

During a war between Iran and Iraq in the 1980s, the United States had supported Iraq and its ruler Saddam Hussein. At that time, Iran, which had held American citizens hostage from 1979 to 1981, seemed the more dangerous foe.

This changed in 1990, when Iraq invaded Kuwait. A multinational coalition drove the Iraqis from Kuwait, but Saddam remained in power. Under the cease-fire terms, however, Saddam agreed to admit UN inspectors to make sure he was not building weapons of mass destruction, or WMDs—chemical, biological, or nuclear weapons capable of killing enormous numbers of people.

The cease-fire also restricted Iraq's oil exports, and "No Fly" zones were imposed in northern and southern Iraq to prevent Saddam from attacking opposition groups: Kurds in the north and Shiite Muslims in the south. U.S. and British warplanes enforced these "No Fly" zones. When fired upon, they bombed Iraqi antiaircraft sites.

Despite obstruction from Saddam, the UN inspectors generally concluded that Iraq had halted its WMD programs. Many U.S. officials disagreed, however, suspecting that Saddam was simply hiding these programs. From 1998 to 2001, U.S. and British bombing of Iraqi military targets increased.

The Bush Administration Focuses on Iraq

In his January 2002 State of the Union address, President Bush accused three nations—Iraq, Iran, and North Korea—of forming an "axis of evil." The phrase stirred memories of World War II, when Germany, Japan, and Italy had been called the "Axis powers."

Of the three countries that Bush named, Iraq topped the list. Saddam's record of aggression and obstructing the weapons-inspection program was clear. In addition, key administration figures believed that Saddam should have been overthrown in the Persian Gulf War. They urged Bush to complete this "unfinished business" from his father's presidency.

Others argued that the United States, as the world's only superpower, should use that power to promote democracy in the Middle East. Ending Saddam's dictatorship, they insisted, could transform the region.

Supporters of overthrowing Saddam also contended that his removal from office could create better conditions for resolving the disputes between Israel and its Arab neighbors and promote peace in the region. The war on terrorism presented an opportunity to pursue all these goals.

Thousands of anti-war demonstrators marched through many cities in Europe protesting the war in Iraq.

ALL LEVELS: Ask students to review what they know from their study of history about declarations of war. Ask: *In the United States, who has the power to declare war? (Congress).* When the U.S. Congress voted to go to war in Iraq, the war resolution passed the House with a vote of 296-133 and the Senate in a 77 to 23 vote. A number of leading Democrats, including John Kerry of Massachusetts and Hillary Clinton of New York, voted for the resolution. Senator Robert Byrd of West Virginia opposed the war resolution.

LEVELS 2 AND 3: Ask students to imagine that they are members of Congress or the British Parliament. Have them write letters to their constituents explaining the necessity of committing troops to the war in Iraq.

Americans Debate War with Iraq

President Bush, Vice President Dick Cheney, and other administration leaders made the case for war. Saddam had links to al Qaeda, they asserted, and had played a role in the 9/11 attacks. They also claimed that Saddam possessed WMDs that endangered America.

For these reasons, they said, the United States was justified in launching a preemptive war—that is, a war against a nation that had not attacked the United States. Cheney declared, "The risks of inaction are greater than the risks of action."

Many Americans, however, did not believe that the administration had offered convincing proof of Saddam's ties to al Qaeda, or of his continuing WMD programs. The critics agreed that Saddam was a brutal tyrant, but they questioned whether this justified a preemptive war against his regime.

Despite these differences, on October 11, 2002, the Congress passed a war resolution authorizing President Bush to "use the Armed Forces of the United States as he determines to be necessary and appropriate" to deal with "the continuing threat" posed by Iraq.

Bush Seeks International Support

President Bush urged America's NATO allies to join in a war to overthrow Saddam Hussein. After initial reluctance, he also sought UN support. Addressing the United Nations in September

British Prime Minister Tony Blair spoke with many world leaders, including Jacques Chirac, the president of France, to try to enlist their support for the war.

2002, the president called on the world body to act decisively against Saddam for violating UN resolutions.

After this speech, Saddam pledged full cooperation with the UN weapons inspectors. The inspectors reported better cooperation and asked for more time to complete their task. UN Secretary-General Kofi Annan supported this position. The United States dismissed Iraq's hasty about-face as mere propaganda, however, and continued to press for war.

France, Germany, and other U.S. allies did not agree with the U.S. government's assessment or its call for war. They favored continued diplomatic pressure and UN arms inspections. Russia and China opposed the war as well. "France and Germany have the same point of view on this crisis. Any decision belongs to the Security Council and the Security Council alone," argued Jacques Chirac, president of France. The differences over Iraq severely frayed

American relations with these countries.

A wave of sympathy for America had swept much of the world after 9/11, but world opinion on the war differed. Massive antiwar rallies filled the streets in Rome, Paris, London, and other cities.

Approximately thirty governments did support the United States, however, including Great Britain, Spain, Italy, and Poland. British Prime Minister Tony Blair strongly backed Bush, despite heavy domestic opposition. The Bush administration called these supporters "the coalition of the willing."

Prime Minister Tony Blair addresses members of the British House of Commons.

TONY BLAIR. Tony Blair became prime minister of Britain in 1997 and became the youngest British prime minister since Lord Liverpool in 1812. Blair studied law at Oxford and is a barrister. A member of the Labour Party, he is a moderate centrist, and with his support, the government began to invest heavily in health and education. Tony Blair once said, "I did not come into politics to change the Labour Party. I came into politics to change the country."

Blair was a staunch supporter of the United States' plan to oust Saddam Hussein from power. Blair focused much of his support for the war on the human rights abuses that had occurred in Iraq under Saddam Hussein. In 2003 Blair addressed the U.S. Congress: "As Britain knows, all predominant power seems for a time invincible, but, in fact, is transient. The question is: What do you leave behind? And what you can bequeath to this anxious world is the light of liberty."

Critical Thinking

Why did Prime Minister Blair say that Britain in particular knew that power seems invincible, but is not?

(Students should recognize that for centuries Britain ruled the seas and the British Empire stretched from one continent to another.)

International Support for the War in Iraq

Although some European nations did not support the war in Iraq, many did. Spain was a staunch supporter of the war and sent a medical support vehicle that held nuclear, biological, and chemical treatment facilities. Poland and Romania sent noncombat troops; Portugal allowed allied forces to use its airbase in the Azores. Denmark sent a submarine, and Italy allowed the United States to use its airspace and ports. Bulgaria and Croatia allowed allied forces to use their airspace and airports. The Czech Republic sent noncombat troops that specialized in chemical warfare decontamination. Other countries around the world lent support, including Kuwait, Jordan, Bahrain, Saudi Arabia, and Australia. Have students work in small groups to create charts or maps showing the countries that assisted in the war efforts and the contributions of each country.

That's Interesting!

The term "shock and awe" refers to a particular military doctrine; it is an attempt to change the enemy's will to fight, view of the battlefield, and understanding of what is happening. Intended to demoralize an opposing army, its purpose is to "break the enemy's will to fight." "Shock and awe" has been called the official strategy of the war in Iraq, and it was very effectively coupled with superior military equipment used by allied forces to overwhelm Iraqi forces.

Have students examine the photos on these two pages carefully. They represent just a sampling of the military armaments that the United States, Britain, and other allies sent to fight the war in Iraq. Have students identify the following from left to right:

* F/A-18 Hornet
* Bradley armed fighting vehicles
* fast combat support ship USS *Arctic*
* aircraft carrier USS *Enterprise*
* British Royal Air Force Tornado fighter bomber

History Makers Speak

"This is not the time to falter. This is the time . . . to show that we will stand up for what we know to be right, to show that we will confront the tyrannies and dictatorships and terrorists who put our way of life at risk, to show at the moment of decision that we will have the courage to do the right thing."

British Prime Minister Tony Blair, in a speech to the House of Commons, March 18, 2003

Assembling troops, planes, and ships in the Middle East, the United States prepared to act without UN or NATO backing. In February 2003, Secretary of State Colin Powell presented the case for war to the UN General Assembly, but few minds were changed.

Senator Robert C. Byrd, a West Virginia Democrat, criticized the administration's decision to proceed without UN authorization or support from key allies. Said Byrd, "Before committing our nation to war with Iraq and the years of

The UN Security Council at UN headquarters in New York City

occupation that will surely follow, we should repair the damage to our relations with our allies. . . . Our rhetoric has gone over the top, from giving an indication of our strength to giving an indication of recklessness."

Critics recalled how the first President Bush in 1990 had patiently built strong international support for ousting Iraqi troops from Kuwait. They urged the current President Bush to do the same, rather than adopting a go-it-alone approach.

"I'm still in a war mode, and the war is terrorism."
—George W. Bush

America Goes to War

On March 19, 2003, the first air strikes of "Operation Iraqi Freedom" hit targets in and around Baghdad. The following night, U.S. and British ground forces invaded Iraq from the south. While the British secured the oil center of Basra, U.S. forces proceeded north toward Baghdad.

The American troops included Army and Marine forces, as well as reservists and National Guard members called to active duty.

International Reaction to the War

Senator Robert C. Byrd of West Virginia was one of the 23 senators who opposed the war in Iraq. In one of his addresses, he said the following: "The American people have serious questions [about the war in Iraq]. The nation's allies have serious questions. Members of this body [the Senate] have serious questions. These must be answered before going to war, and it is not now, nor was it ever, unpatriotic to ask questions."

France and Germany, generally considered to be American military allies, did not support the war. Nor did a number of other nations that belong to the United Nations. Have students research and report on statements given by the leaders of countries that did not support the war, and have students compare and contrast international opinions about the war in Iraq.

Many left family and jobs behind. Among those called to action were a significant number of women, reflecting the fact that the U.S. military is about 15 percent female.

On March 22, Iraqi troops attacked a U.S. convoy, killing several Americans. Private Jessica Lynch from Palestine, West Virginia, suffered two broken legs and was captured. A few days later, U.S. soldiers rescued her from an Iraqi hospital. Publicized by the Pentagon, Lynch's story caught the nation's imagination. She denied that she was a hero and paid tribute to her fallen comrades. One of these was Private Lori Piestewa, the first American-Indian woman killed in action fighting for the U.S. Army.

Iraqi resistance proved weak, and after three weeks of sporadic fighting, Baghdad was captured. American troops occupied government buildings and Saddam's palaces, pulled down a massive statue of Saddam, and found mass graves of victims of Saddam's murderous regime.

By the end of this stage of the conflict, 140 coalition soldiers had been killed, including 109 Ameri-

Soldiers carry the flag-draped coffins of Italian servicemen who were killed in a terrorist attack in Iraq.

cans. Although precise figures are unknown, more than 2,300 Iraqi military troops had also been killed in the fighting. In addition, over 6,300 Iraqi civilians had died or suffered injuries, despite extensive coalition efforts to spare noncombatants.

On May 1, President Bush, wearing an Air Force flight suit, flew to the U.S. aircraft carrier *Abraham Lincoln* off the coast of San Diego to declare

major combat operations in Iraq completed. In front of a banner proclaiming "Mission Accomplished," the president said, "In the battle of Iraq, the United States and our allies have prevailed." Saddam remained at large, however, and more difficulties lay ahead.

THINK ABOUT IT

1. Why did the United States decide to go to war in Iraq without UN support?
2. What role should the UN play in settling international conflicts?

British Tornado fighter bomber

With "shock and awe," American and allied forces invaded Iraq and removed Saddam Hussein from power. Iraqi forces were overwhelmed, and within four weeks, the war was over.

"America fights wars, but America does not start wars."
—Robert Byrd

The Long Aftermath in Iraq

Major combat was over, but establishing a lasting peace and reconstructing Iraq proved a long and demanding task.

The High Cost of Reconstruction

The United States at once set out to rebuild Iraq's oil industry and restore long-neglected public services, such as telephones, electricity, water, and health care. The U.S. administrator in Iraq, L. Paul Bremer, led this effort.

Reconstruction contracts went to major U.S. companies, such as the Halliburton Corporation and the Bechtel Group. Some critics objected that political influence helped these businesses win the contracts. Vice President Cheney was a former head of Halliburton, and President Reagan's secretary of state, George P. Schultz, was a director of Bechtel. The government official responsible for awarding these contracts denied this charge. "The notion that any of us . . . manipulated the process is ridiculous," he said.

The occupation and reconstruction of Iraq involved massive costs. Late in 2003, Bush asked Congress to appropriate $87.5 billion for Iraq-related expenditures. He compared this project to the

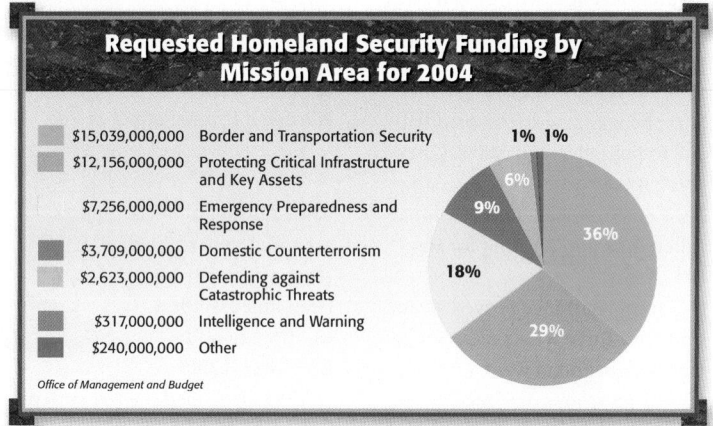

Requested Homeland Security Funding by Mission Area for 2004

Amount	Mission Area	Percent
$15,039,000,000	Border and Transportation Security	36%
$12,156,000,000	Protecting Critical Infrastructure and Key Assets	29%
$7,256,000,000	Emergency Preparedness and Response	18%
$3,709,000,000	Domestic Counterterrorism	9%
$2,623,000,000	Defending against Catastrophic Threats	6%
$317,000,000	Intelligence and Warning	1%
$240,000,000	Other	1%

Office of Management and Budget

Marshall Plan, which had helped rebuild Europe after World War II. The costs would likely mount even higher in future years, he warned.

Congress approved the request, but the total shocked even legislators who had supported the war. With federal deficits mounting because of rising Medicare,

Medicaid, and social-security expenses, as well as military costs unrelated to Iraq, years of massive spending in Iraq would further strain the budget.

Bush Seeks Other Nations' Assistance

The administration asked other nations to help in the reconstruction effort. Japan pledged $5 billion. Most countries, however, argued that the UN should be more involved in the process.

In December 2003, Bush sent former Secretary of State James Baker abroad to persuade other nations to cancel Iraq's debts to them, or to at least stretch out the time allowed for repayment. These debts totaled $125 billion. Several nations agreed, including some that had opposed the war. Baker's task was complicated, however, by a Department of Defense announcement that only nations that had supported the Iraq war would be permitted to bid on reconstruction contracts. After several nations expressed their concerns, the United States revised its policy, and companies from other nations were allowed to bid on the second round of contracts.

Following the ouster of Saddam, U.S. soldiers and Iraqis worked together to remove giant statues of the tyrant that had adorned his Republican Palace in Baghdad.

Sunnis, Shiites, and Kurds

Iraq's population is divided into three major groups: Sunnis, Shiites, and Kurds. Shiite Muslims form a majority in Iraq (there are approximately 15 million Shiites in Iraq, 60 percent of the country's population), and in 2004, the spiritual leader of the Shiite Muslim majority was the 73-year-old Grand Ayatollah Ali Sistani. The oppression of the Shiites by the Sunnis has a long history. It began around 1638 when an Ottoman sultan captured Baghdad.

Before the war, the Sunnis controlled the government and the army, and it was well known that the Shiites were brutally repressed under Saddam's regime.

The Kurds, a non-Arabic people, form about 23 percent of Iraq's population, and the majority are Sunni Muslims. The Kurds supported Iran in the 1980-88 Iran-Iraq war; Saddam retaliated against them, murdering thousands.

The Sunnis and the Kurds, both minority groups, feared that a Shiite majority in the new Iraqi government might not honor their minority rights.

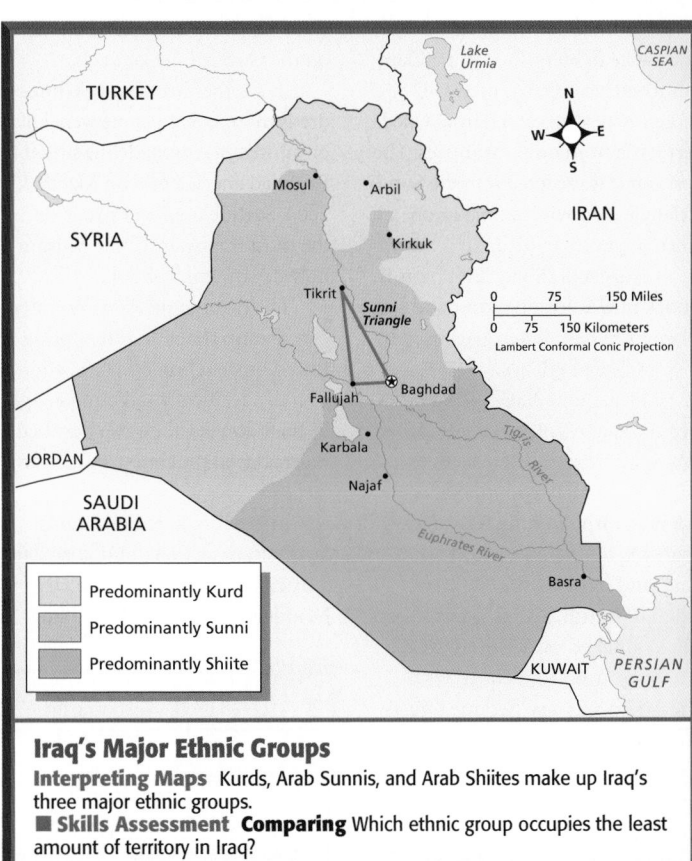

Iraq's Major Ethnic Groups

Interpreting Maps Kurds, Arab Sunnis, and Arab Shiites make up Iraq's three major ethnic groups.
■ **Skills Assessment Comparing** Which ethnic group occupies the least amount of territory in Iraq?

30, 2004, for handing over power to a new Iraqi government. This task proved difficult, however. No census records existed that could establish a list of eligible voters. Furthermore, deep hostilities divided the country's ethnic and religious groups.

Iraq is a predominantly Arab, Islamic nation, but Islam is split into two major groups, the Sunnis and the Shiites. The Sunnis are generally more liberal and more prosperous. The Shiites, numerous among the urban poor, strictly enforce Islamic law and are more hostile to non-Muslim "infidels." Iraq's Arab Shiites, centered in the south and comprising about two-thirds of the population, were oppressed by Saddam and his Arab Sunni supporters in the north. In addition, approximately 5 million Kurds live in northeastern Iraq. Although mostly Sunni, the Kurds are a fiercely independent non-Arab ethnic group. Shiites, Sunnis, and Kurds had very different ideas about Iraq's future government.

Establishing a New Government

After Saddam's overthrow, the United States set up a Governing Council drawn from Iraq's major ethnic and religious groups. At first, however, this body accomplished little and was divided by internal disputes.

In November 2003, amid growing violence in Iraq, President Bush instructed Paul Bremer to move quickly toward creating an Iraqi government, police force, and army to take over security responsibilities and permit coalition forces to withdraw. The administration set a goal of June

Continued Resistance in Iraq

Before the war, top Bush administration officials had predicted that the Iraqis would greet American troops as liberators. As it turned

In March 2004, Iraq's Governing Council, some of whom are shown here, agreed on an interim constitution to govern the country.

Bombing of the UN and Red Cross Headquarters

The bombing of the Canal Hotel, headquarters for the UN mission in Iraq, was a stunning blow to the international community, and it resulted in worldwide condemnation. Seventeen people were killed and 100 were wounded. One of those killed in the bombing was Sergio Vieira de Mello. De Mello had taken a four-month leave of absence from his position as UN High Commissioner for Human Rights to serve in Iraq as Special Representative of the Secretary-General.

Kofi Annan, Secretary-General of the United Nations, spoke of the men and women who lost their lives, saying: "The brave men and women we lost in Baghdad on 19 August—UN staff and others—were free spirits and free thinkers and also soldiers of humanity and of peace."

The bombing of the Red Cross, which occurred on the first morning of the month of Ramadan, resulted in 12 deaths. A delegate from the International Committee of the Red Cross, Nada Doumani, spoke of the bombing: "We believe we have to stay here because we do have an important job to do here for the Iraqis."

Guide students in a discussion of the role of relief agencies during wartime. Ask students if they believe these organizations should stay or remain when their staffs are under attack.

Culture

THE NATIONAL MUSEUM AND LIBRARY. Iraq's national museum in Baghdad was looted during the war. Among the many items stolen were a 5,000-year-old golden vessel that had been found at Ur, an Akkadian statue, and an Assyrian statue. According to one specialist from the British Museum in London, England, it was "like stealing the Mona Lisa."

Dr. Dony George, head of Iraq's national museum, said, "I believe they were people who knew what they wanted…they must have been specialists." Dr. George also said, "It's the crime of the century, because it affects the heritage of all mankind."

Although many of the artifacts were later found and returned to the museum, many priceless items have not yet been recovered.

The House of Wisdom, the National Library of Iraq, was also looted. Rare, centuries-old illuminated copies of the Qur'an were taken, along with exquisite examples of Islamic calligraphy and historical documents from the Ottoman Empire. The library building was then set on fire, and many more documents were destroyed.

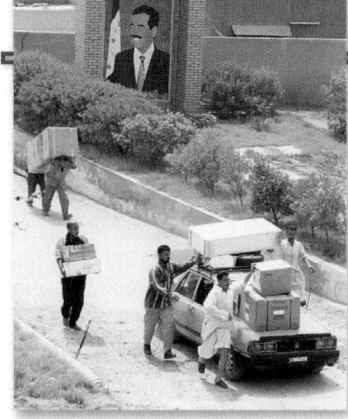

Looters took whatever supplies and equipment they could find.

out, most Iraqis did indeed welcome Saddam Hussein's overthrow, but many also resented the presence in Iraq of 132,000 U.S. troops, 10,000 British soldiers, and 14,000 armed service personnel from approximately thirty other nations.

With Iraq's police forces in disarray, ordinary criminals operated freely for some time. After Baghdad's fall, looters broke into the national museum, stealing priceless objects. Although many of the objects were later returned, lawlessness remained a major problem in Baghdad and other cities.

In addition, insurgents, or resistance fighters, loyal to Saddam launched a campaign of anti-U.S. violence, perhaps aided by al Qaeda terrorists from other countries. The resistance was centered in the Sunni Triangle, a heavily Sunni region northwest of Baghdad.

Insurgents shot at U.S. patrols, attacked U.S. installations, and planted mines along roads used by U.S. military vehicles.

Throughout 2003, such attacks produced a mounting toll of casualties. From May 1, when President Bush declared an end to major combat, through early 2004, more than 400 U.S. GIs were killed in Iraq, and more than 2,000 were injured. British, Spanish, and Italian forces suffered casualties as well.

Iraqis who cooperated with the Americans also became targets. An Iraqi woman on the Governing Council was assassinated, and Iraqi police were often targeted in bombings. Shiites, too, fell victim to Sunni insurgents. A leading Shiite cleric, Mohammed Baqir al-Hakim, was killed when a bomb exploded outside a sacred Shiite shrine in Najaf, taking the lives of 125 worshippers. The cleric's brother was on the Governing Council.

In another brutal attack, hundreds of innocent people were killed or injured in simultaneous strikes in Baghdad and Karbala on March 2, 2004. Suicide bombers struck on the most important Shiite Muslim holy day of year, Ashura.

The insurgents were also intent on creating chaos and disrupting the reconstruction effort. In addition to specifically targeting people in their attacks, they also bombed railroads, oil pipelines, and electric facilities.

International organizations faced attack as well. In August 2003, a truck bomb destroyed the UN headquarters in Baghdad, killing

A car bombing destroyed the Canal Hotel, UN headquarters, in Baghdad.

PRIMARY SOURCE

Following the bombing of UN headquarters in Baghdad, Kofi Annan gave the following statement:

"Nothing can excuse this act of unprovoked and murderous violence against men and women who went to Iraq for one purpose only: to help the Iraqi people recover their independence and sovereignty, and to rebuild their country as fast as possible, under leaders of their own choosing."

EXTEND

The Capture of Saddam Hussein

Saddam Hussein was also known as the Glorious Leader, Direct Descendant of the Prophet, the Lion of Babylon, the Father of the Two Lion Cubs, the Anointed One, the Successor of Nebuchadnezzar, and the Butcher of Baghdad. The hunt for him had been a long, trying ordeal for the military forces in Iraq, but when he was found, he was easily taken. No one was hurt, no bullets were fired. Following his capture, members of the Iraqi Governing Council were allowed to question Saddam. He was held as a prisoner of war in Iraq and, under the Geneva Conventions concerning the welfare of prisoners of war, he received official visits from the Red Cross. Have interested students research and report on what happened to Saddam during his initial imprisonment and afterward.

---

twenty-three people, including the UN's top envoy to Iraq, Sergio Vieira de Mello. Secretary-General Kofi Annan withdrew the UN mission, citing security concerns.

In October 2003, insurgents bombed the International Red Cross's Baghdad office.

Saddam Is Captured

In the months following the war, Saddam remained at large, and many Iraqis feared that he might return to power.

Then, in December 2003, Saddam was captured. He was found hiding in a hole in a building near his hometown of Tikrit. Paul Bremer announced the capture to the press in simple words: "Ladies and gentlemen, we got him."

Most Iraqis wanted Saddam tried by an Iraqi tribunal because the people of Iraq had suffered so heavily under his regime. Others favored a trial by a UN-appointed tribunal, so that Saddam's punishment would have international authority behind it.

Even with Saddam in custody, Iraq remained turbulent and violent. The attacks on GIs continued, as did the bombings designed to disrupt Iraqi society. The reconstruction effort went forward steadily, but under great difficulties.

President Bush offered assurances that as living conditions improved and a new Iraqi government took power, Iraq would be a better and safer place, and the hopes of those who had planned

the war would be fulfilled. In addition, he continued to emphasize that the war in Iraq had reduced the threat of terrorism in the United States. "In 2003, we've become a safer nation," he said.

However, the debate continued. Opponents of the Bush strategy argued that the war in Iraq may have strengthened support for terrorism in the Muslim world, and in fact made the nation less safe.

Searching for Weapons of Mass Destruction

President Bush had justified the war by claiming that Saddam had links to al Qaeda and, especially, by warning that Iraq possessed weapons of mass destruction that endangered American security. After Saddam's fall, 1,200 U.S. inspectors entered the country to search for WMDs. In January 2004, the team's leader, David Kay, testified before the

This photo of Saddam was taken following his capture in Tikrit. He was the "Ace of Spades" within the deck of cards representing the United States' most wanted list.

Senate Intelligence Committee that no evidence of WMDs had been discovered. "It turns out that we were all wrong, . . . and that is most disturbing."

Critics immediately demanded that an independent panel study why intelligence on Iraq's WMDs had been so flawed. President Bush responded by naming a blue-ribbon panel to investigate U.S. intelligence.

THINK ABOUT IT

1. Does the United States have an obligation to help rebuild Iraq? What previous historical events might serve as a guide?
2. Why would insurgents bomb both the UN and Red Cross headquarters in Baghdad?

Iraqi insurgents repeatedly blew up Iraq's oil pipelines, railroads, electric lines, and police stations.

ANSWERS TO THINK ABOUT IT

1. Student answers will vary, but most students may agree with the U.S. Congress that the United States had a moral obligation to help Iraq rebuild its infrastructure. Having toppled the existing government, the United States had an obligation to protect Iraqi citizens against further insurgencies and help ensure that civil war did not erupt in the country. Students may recall the Marshall Plan, which helped European countries following World War II.

2. Student answers will vary but may include that the mission of these organizations is to help promote peace, safety, and stability. By bombing their headquarters and forcing a pullout, the insurgents continued to push for instability within the country.

ALL LEVELS: Because terrorist groups operate throughout the world, terrorism continues to be an international problem. Countries have joined together to fight international terrorist groups, and they have begun to share information to stop these international groups from attacking. The U.S. State Department has listed a number of worldwide terrorist groups. Among the groups listed are Abu Nidal, Aum Shinrikyo, Basque Fatherland and Liberty, Hamas, Hezbollah, National Liberation Army, the Revolutionary Armed Forces of Colombia, and Shining Path.

Have students research and report on international terrorist groups and international cooperative efforts to fight terrorism.

Science, Technology & Society

NUCLEAR PROLIFERATION. The Nuclear Non-Proliferation Treaty (NPT), signed in 1968 by 188 nations, restricted the possession of nuclear weapons to the United States, the United Kingdom, France, Russia, and the People's Republic of China. These five nations possessed nuclear weapons when the treaty was adopted. These five countries are also the five permanent members of the United Nations Security Council, and they have agreed not to transfer nuclear weapons technology to other nations. Pakistan, India, and Israel also possess nuclear weapons. In addition, North Korea allegedly announced to U.S. diplomats that it possessed several nuclear weapons. Have students research and report on efforts to control nuclear proliferation and have them prepare a map showing the countries that are suspected of possessing or of developing nuclear weapons.

Fighting Terrorism Worldwide

The effort to combat terrorism and eliminate WMDs was global in scope. A series of attacks, arrests, and diplomatic initiatives made clear the worldwide nature of the danger and the effort to combat it.

Continued Dangers

Many governments have cooperated in the effort to unearth the secretive terrorist networks that are plotting and carrying out terrorist attacks. The governments have worked to trace and shut down these groups' funding sources. The effort, however, has often been frustrating.

Nonetheless, international forces have had some success. In March 2003, Khalid Sheikh Mohammad, an alleged planner of the 9/11 attacks, was captured in Pakistan, and in February 2004, Iraqi police captured Muhammad Ziman Abd al-Razzaq al-Sadun, a wanted senior member of the toppled Ba'ath Party. However, al Qaeda and other terrorist groups continue to wreak havoc in the Middle East and elsewhere.

Combatting Nuclear Threats

A major concern in the battle against terrorism was the increased threat of nuclear weapon proliferation. For example, the creator of Pakistan's first nuclear bomb, Dr. Abdul Qadeer Khan, admitted in 2004 to leaking nuclear weapon information to Iran, Libya, and North Korea. In addition, the United States had long suspected Iran of pursuing nuclear-weapons research. When late in 2003, Iran agreed to inspections by the UN's International Atomic Energy Agency, Washington welcomed the development.

North Korea, an impoverished Communist nation ruled by the unpredictable Kim Jong Il, openly boasted of its nuclear program. Although a North Korean nuclear attack on the United States was unlikely, many feared that North

North Korea's leader, Kim Jong Il, oversaw North Korea's military buildup, including the development of a nuclear program.

New Ways of War

The "war on terrorism" differed from other U.S. wars, such as World War I and World War II. In those conflicts, Congress had declared war against specific nations for specific attacks. German U-boats had sunk U.S. ships before America declared war in 1917. The Japanese had attacked Pearl Harbor in 1941. When these nations surrendered, the wars ended. In the new kind of war that followed the 9/11 attacks, the enemy—"terrorism"—was shadowy and elusive. Small groups operated across national boundaries and chose targets throughout the world, often with little coordination. No single moment of victory could be declared. This war could last indefinitely, the president warned, and could take many different forms.

Pakistani scientist Dr. Abdul Qadeer Khan created an underground network that sold nuclear secrets and equipment to countries such as Syria, Libya, and North Korea.

TEACH OBJECTIVE 4

ALL LEVELS: Have students carefully examine the chart and map on this page. Ask students to identify the region that has had the most terrorist attacks. *(Latin America)*. Ask students to suggest possible reasons why Latin America has had almost twice as many terrorist attacks as any other region. Then ask students to identify the region that has had the most deaths due to terrorist activities. *(Africa)*. Again, ask students to suggest reasons.

Guide students in a discussion of the information presented in this chart, and have interested students research and report on data for the current year. Compare and contrast the data. Is the number of terrorist attacks increasing or decreasing? Which region or which countries have been subject to the most terrorist activity?

CLOSE

Organize a class debate on the following topic: "Military might, not mediation, is the best way to fight terrorism."

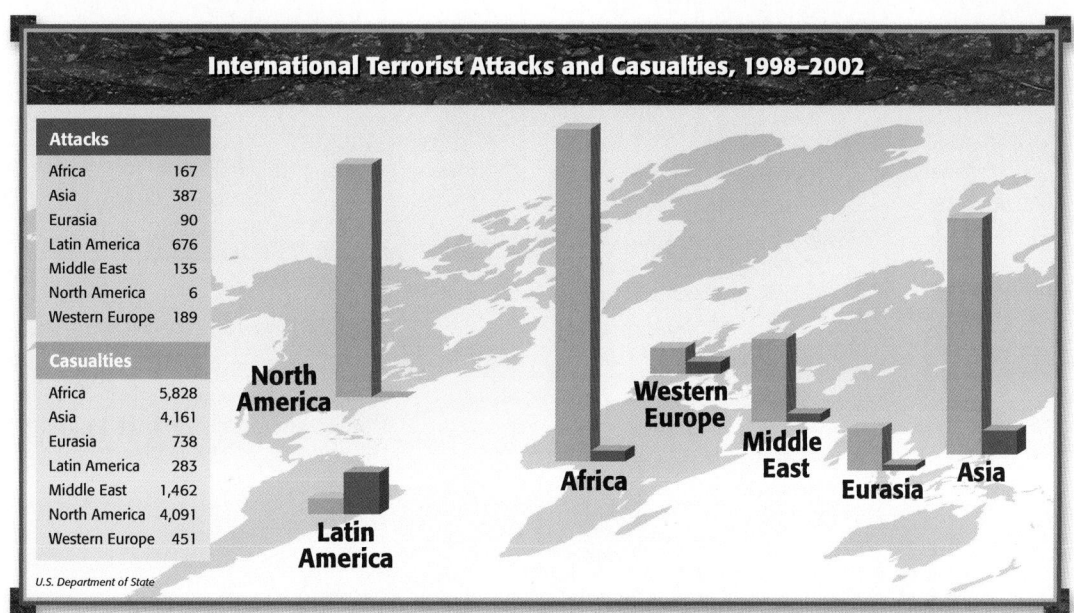

International Terrorist Attacks and Casualties, 1998–2002

Attacks	
Africa	167
Asia	387
Eurasia	90
Latin America	676
Middle East	135
North America	6
Western Europe	189

Casualties	
Africa	5,828
Asia	4,161
Eurasia	738
Latin America	283
Middle East	1,462
North America	4,091
Western Europe	451

U.S. Department of State

Korea's nuclear weapons or materials might fall into the hands of terrorists.

Joining with South Korea, Japan, Russia, and China, the Bush administration pursued diplomatic negotiations with the North Koreans. Progress was slow, but North Korea did express willingness to end its nuclear-weapons program in return for economic aid and security guarantees against attack.

In December 2003, President Bush announced that Mu'ammar Gadhafi of Libya had agreed to UN inspections to verify that he had no WMDs. This, too, was welcome news.

In his statement of U.S. goals for 2004, Secretary of State Colin Powell wrote, "The war on terrorism remains our first priority, but success in that war depends on constructive ties among the world's major powers. These we pursue without respite." Achieving that goal, in societies that are very different from America's, and in regions of the world torn by conflict and inflamed by hatred and resentment, poses enormous challenges not just for the United States, but for all nations of the world.

THINK ABOUT IT

1. Is it possible to wage a successful international war on terrorism?
2. What steps can a country take to help ensure that terrorist groups do not receive funding from groups inside or outside of the country?
3. What steps should the international community take to prevent terrorist groups from acquiring nuclear technology and weapons?

Providing reconstruction and humanitarian aid was a major goal of the allied forces in Iraq. Many soldiers were warmly welcomed, and their efforts greatly appreciated.

Geography

EURASIA. Some students may not be familiar with the term *Eurasia*. Point out to students that because of cultural differences between Europe and Asia, they have been considered separate continents. Some earth scientists, however, consider Eurasia to be a continent in and of itself. The U.S. Department of State considers that the following nations comprise Eurasia: Armenia, Azerbaijan, Belarus, Georgia, Kazakhstan, Kyrgyzstan, Moldova, Russia, Tajikstan, Turkmenistan, Ukraine, and Uzbekistan.

ANSWERS TO THINK ABOUT IT

1. Student answers may include that countries can work together to successfully combat the threat of terrorism.

2. Student answers will vary but may include that countries need to monitor the flow of large sums of money that pass in and out of the country's banks or that banks should be held accountable for flowing large sums into questionable accounts.

3. Student answers will vary but may include the necessity to share information, to share military resources, to organize international monitoring groups, and to provide financial aid to other countries to help track groups that might be purchasing nuclear weapons or technology and supplies to produce weapons of mass destruction.

TEACHER'S EDITION

HOLT

World History

The Human Journey

Reference Section

Almanac

Standard Time Differences Among Selected Cities

At 12:00 noon Eastern Standard Time in Washington, D.C., it is . . .

1:00 p.m. in Santiago, Chile
5:00 p.m. in London, United Kingdom
6:00 p.m. in Madrid, Spain
7:00 p.m. in Athens, Greece
7:00 p.m. in Tel Aviv, Israel

8:00 p.m. in Moscow, Russian Republic
8:00 p.m. in Nairobi, Kenya
1:00 a.m. the following day in Beijing, China
2:00 a.m. the following day in Seoul, Korea
3:00 a.m. the following day in Melbourne, Australia

Major World Languages[1]

[1]Figures include estimated total number of native and non-native speakers of a given language. A "native" speaker is defined as one for whom the language is his or her first language.

Heights of Selected World Mountains, in Feet

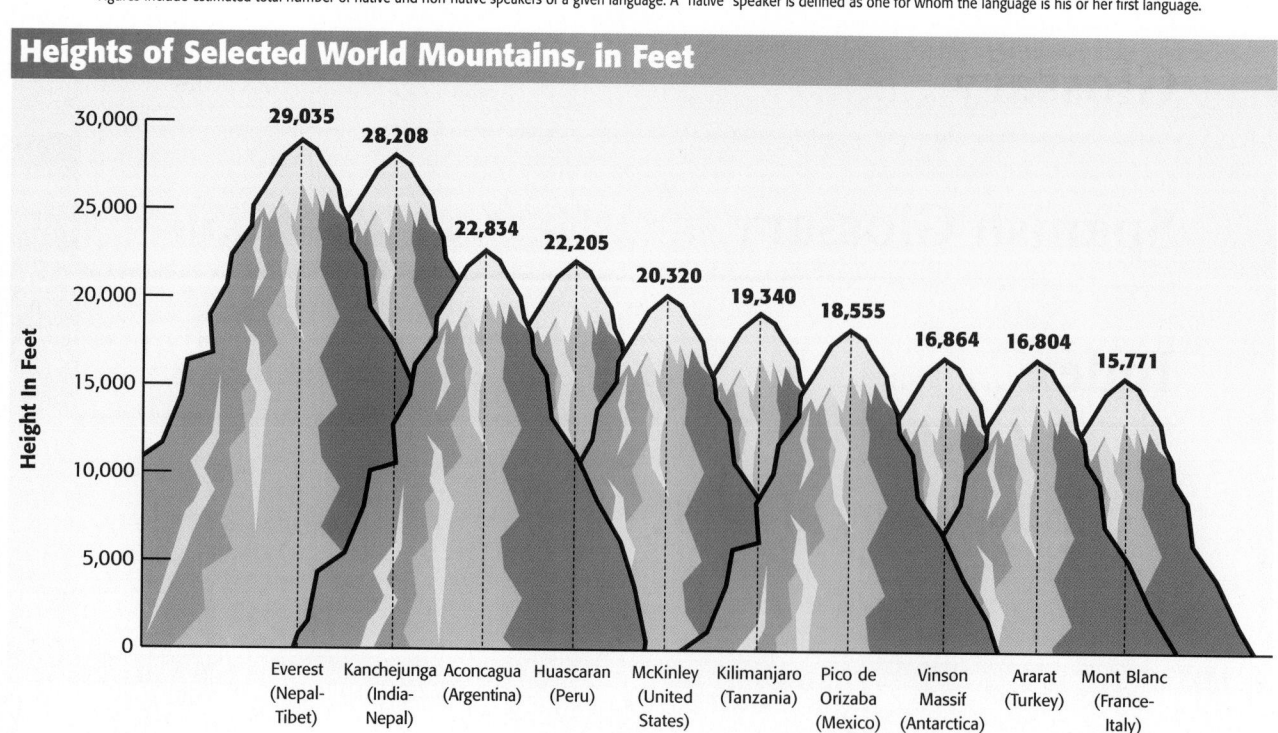

Selected Major Rivers of the World

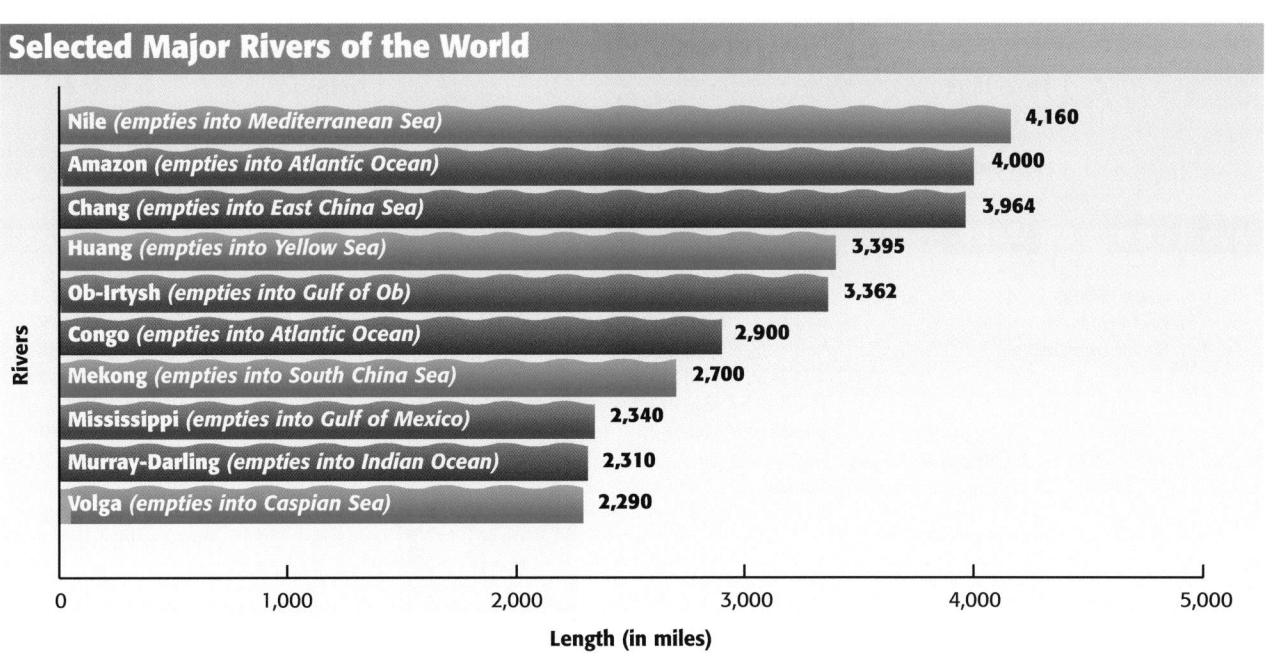

River	Length (in miles)
Nile *(empties into Mediterranean Sea)*	**4,160**
Amazon *(empties into Atlantic Ocean)*	**4,000**
Chang *(empties into East China Sea)*	**3,964**
Huang *(empties into Yellow Sea)*	**3,395**
Ob-Irtysh *(empties into Gulf of Ob)*	**3,362**
Congo *(empties into Atlantic Ocean)*	**2,900**
Mekong *(empties into South China Sea)*	**2,700**
Mississippi *(empties into Gulf of Mexico)*	**2,340**
Murray-Darling *(empties into Indian Ocean)*	**2,310**
Volga *(empties into Caspian Sea)*	**2,290**

Rivers — Length (in miles): 0, 1,000, 2,000, 3,000, 4,000, 5,000

Continental Highs and Lows

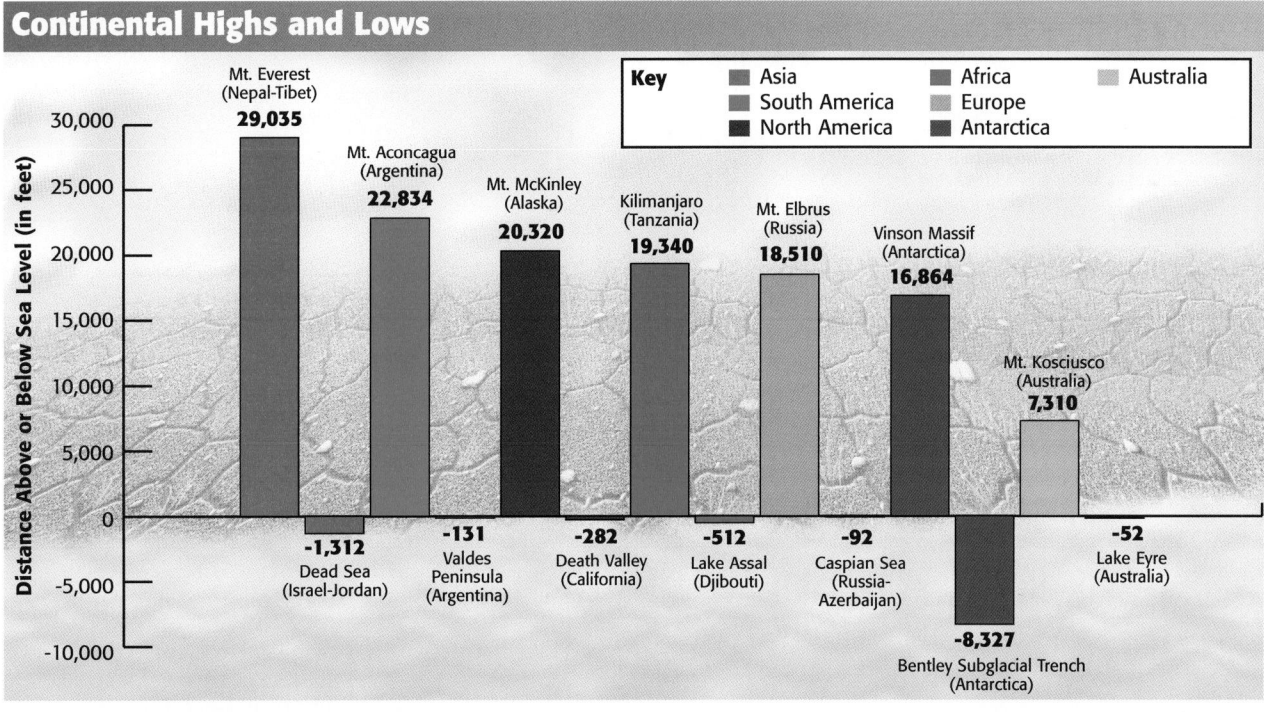

Key: Asia, South America, North America, Africa, Europe, Antarctica, Australia

Distance Above or Below Sea Level (in feet)

- Mt. Everest (Nepal-Tibet) **29,035**
- Mt. Aconcagua (Argentina) **22,834**
- Mt. McKinley (Alaska) **20,320**
- Kilimanjaro (Tanzania) **19,340**
- Mt. Elbrus (Russia) **18,510**
- Vinson Massif (Antarctica) **16,864**
- Mt. Kosciusco (Australia) **7,310**
- Dead Sea (Israel-Jordan) **-1,312**
- Valdes Peninsula (Argentina) **-131**
- Death Valley (California) **-282**
- Lake Assal (Djibouti) **-512**
- Caspian Sea (Russia-Azerbaijan) **-92**
- Bentley Subglacial Trench (Antarctica) **-8,327**
- Lake Eyre (Australia) **-52**

The World's Largest Natural Lakes

Sea or Lake (Continent)	Area (Sq. Mi.)	Max. Depth (ft.)	Sea or Lake (Continent)	Area (Sq. Mi.)	Max. Depth (ft.)
Caspian Sea (Asia-Europe)	143,244	3,363	Lake Michigan (North America)	22,300	923
Lake Superior (North America)	31,700	1,330	Lake Tanganyika (Africa)	12,700	4,823
Lake Victoria (Africa)	26,828	270	Lake Baikal (Asia)	12,162	5,315
Aral Sea (Asia)	24,904 (est.)	220	Great Bear Lake (North America)	12,096	1,463
Lake Huron (North America)	23,000	750	Lake Malawi (Africa)	11,150	2,280

Some Early Explorers of the Western Hemisphere

1513
Vasco Núñez de Balboa
Panama, Pacific Ocean

1492–1502
Christopher Columbus
West Indies

1539–41
Hernando de Soto
Mississippi River

1576
Sir Martin Frobisher
Frobisher's Bay, Canada

1603–09
Samuel de Champlain
Canadian interior

A.D. 1000

1500

1550

1600

C. A.D. 1000
Leif Ericsson
Newfoundland

1534
Jacques Cartier
Canada, Gulf of St. Lawrence

1609–10
Henry Hudson
Hudson River, Hudson Bay

1519–20
Ferdinand Magellan
Straits of Magellan

1497–98
Vasco da Gama
Cape of Good Hope, India

1595
Sir Walter Raleigh
Orinoco River

1497–99
Amerigo Vespucci
Coastal South America

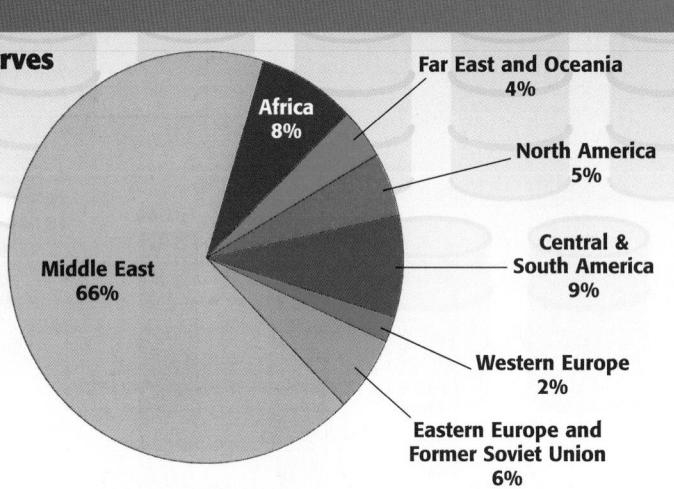

Ferdinand Magellan

World Energy Facts

Estimated World Crude Oil Reserves by Region, January 2002
(Expressed as approximate percent of estimated world total, rounded)

Far East and Oceania
4%

Africa
8%

North America
5%

WORLD TOTAL
100%

Central & South America
9%

Middle East
66%

Western Europe
2%

Eastern Europe and Former Soviet Union
6%

Some Great Milestones in Medicine

1890
Robert Koch
Tuberculin diagnosis

1909
Charles Nicolle
Typhus transmission

1842
Crawford Long
Ether (anesthesia)

1867
Joseph Lister
Antiseptic surgery

1892
Emil von Behring
Diptheria antitoxin

1650

1850

1900

1676
Antoni van Leeuwenhoek
Description of bacteria

1885
Louis Pasteur
Anti-rabies treatment

1909
Paul Ehrlich
Chemotherapy

1895
Wilhelm Röntgen
X–ray

Louis Pasteur

1673
Jacques Marquette,
Louis Joliet
Mississippi River

1727–29
Vitus Bering
Bering Strait, Alaska

1804–06
Meriwether
Lewis,
William Clark
Missouri River,
Rocky Mountains

| **1700** | **1750** | **1800** |

1789
Sir Alexander
Mackenzie
Northwestern Canada

Henry Hudson

Estimated World Population in 2000

(Approximate populations are shown and rounded)

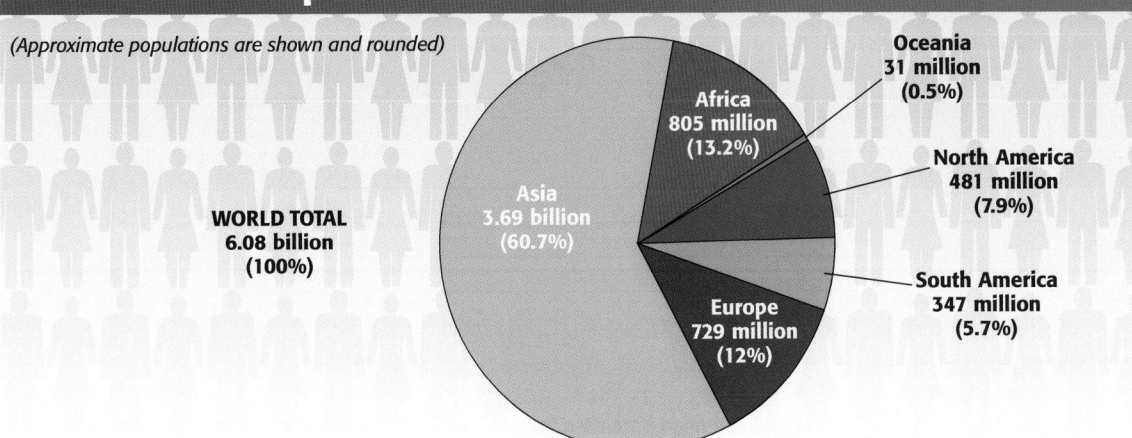

Oceania
31 million
(0.5%)

Africa
805 million
(13.2%)

North America
481 million
(7.9%)

Asia
3.69 billion
(60.7%)

WORLD TOTAL
6.08 billion
(100%)

South America
347 million
(5.7%)

Europe
729 million
(12%)

Model of the
"double helix"
of DNA

1951
Francis Crick, James Watson,
Maurice Wilkins
Structure of DNA

2001
Joint research effort:
U.S. government
agencies and private
institutions
Human Genome
Project

1928
Alexander Fleming
Penicillin

1963
John Enders
Measles vaccine

| **1950** | **2000** |

1922
Frederick Banting,
Charles Best,
John Macleod
Insulin

1940
Charles Drew
Storage of
blood plasma

1954
Jonas
Salk
Polio
vaccine

1979
U.N. World Health
Organization
Smallpox eradication

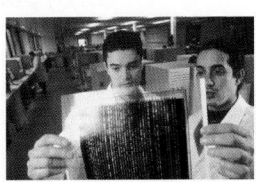

The Human Genome
Project—DNA sequencing

Glossary

This Glossary contains many of the terms you need to understand as you study world history. After each term there is a brief definition or explanation of the meaning of the term as it is used in world history. The boldfaced page number after each definition refers to the page on which the term is boldfaced in the textbook. A phonetic respelling is provided to help you pronounce many of the terms.

Phonetic Respelling Guide

Many of the key terms in the textbook have been respelled to help readers pronounce them. The following Phonetic Respelling and Pronunciation Guide has been adapted from several common dictionaries. Using the guide along with the text respellings will allow readers to pronounce difficult terms, including biographical and place names.

Mark	As In	Respelling	Example
a	alphabet	a	*AL·fuh·bet
ā	Asia	ay	AY·zhuh
ä	cart, top	ah	KAHRT, TAHP
e	let, ten	e	LET, TEN
ē	even, leaf	ee	EE·vuhn, LEEF
i	it, tip, British	i	IT, TIP, BRIT·ish
ī	site, buy, Ohio	y	SYT, BY, oh·HY·oh
	iris	eye	EYE·ris
k	card	k	KAHRD
kw	quest	kw	KWEHST
ō	over, rainbow	oh	OH·vuhr, RAYN·boh
ū	book, wood	ooh	BOOHK, WOOHD
ō	all, orchid	aw	AWL, AWR·kid
aù	out	ow	OWT
ə	cup, butter	uh	KUHP, BUHT·uhr
ü	rule, food	oo	ROOL, FOOD
yü	few	yoo	FYOO
zh	vision	zh	VIZH·uhn

*A syllable printed in small capital letters receives heavier emphasis than other syllables in a word.

A

abbess Head of a convent who served a role similar to an abbot. **302**

abbot Head of a monastery who controlled and distributed all property. **302**

Aborigines Original inhabitants of Australia. **608**

abstract expressionism Style of painting after 1945 that involved a personal expression from the artist. **974**

acid rain Rainfall that contains toxins produced from burning fossil fuels. **988**

acropolis Hill or mountain in Greece that included a fort as well as temples and other public buildings. **109**

Acropolis A high hill that marked the center of ancient Athens. **130**

acupuncture Chinese medical practice of inserting needles into certain areas of the body. **95**

adobe Sun-dried brick used for building purposes by the Pueblo Indians. **205**

aerodynamics Scientific principles governing the movement of air around objects. **575**

Afrikaans Language of the Boers in South Africa. **673**

agora Marketplace in a city-state in Greece. **109**

agriculture Raising of crops for food. **9**

Allied Powers Alliance that included Great Britain, France, Russia (later, the Soviet Union), the United States, and other countries during World Wars I and II. **705**

almanacs Books that predict the weather and the prospects for growing crops, and also contain such things as calendars, maps, and medical advice. **375**

Alpha First international space station, as named in November 2000. **983**

Analects Collection of the ideas and teachings of Confucius. **90**

anarchists Political extremists who oppose all government. **619**

Anglo-Egyptian Treaty Treaty in 1936 between Egypt and Britain that gave Egypt greater independence. **758**

animism Belief that spirits inhabit everything. **82**

antibiotics Substances that can kill or limit bacterial growth. **986**

Anti-Comintern Pact Agreement between Japan and Germany pledging to stop the spread of Russian communism. **786**

antisepsis Use of chemicals to kill disease-causing germs. **579**

apartheid Government policy of segregation and economic exploitation in South Africa. **884**

appeasement Policy of trying to avoid war by accepting some demands of the aggressor. **787**

apprentice One who learns a skill under a master. **328**

aqueducts Bridgelike structures that carry water. **166**

arch Curved structure over an opening. **32**

archons Rulers in ancient Athens who served one-year terms. **115**

aristocracies Greek city-states controlled by nobles. **111**

aristocracy Government ruled by an upper class. **134**

armistice Agreement signed by leaders of warring nations to stop fighting. **715**

Articles of Confederation Plan ratified by the American states in 1781 that set up a central government with a one-house Congress in which each state had a single vote. **502**

artifacts Objects made and used by early humans. **6**

artisans Skilled workers. **12**

ASEAN Association of Southeast Asian Nations; organization formed to promote economic growth. **872**

Ashikaga Family of shoguns who ruled in Japan for nearly 250 years. **278**

assimilation Process in which people give up their own culture and adopt another culture. **674**

astrolabe Instrument used to calculate latitude by looking at stars. **251**

Atlantic Charter Statement created by Winston Churchill and Franklin Roosevelt that declared their two countries' intentions in 1941. **795**

atrocities Brutal crimes of war, often committed against civilians. **710**

Auschwitz Nazi death camp in which people were systematically murdered. **802**

autocracy Government in which the ruler holds absolute power. **86**

autocrat Ruler who holds absolute power. **648**

Awami League Political party dedicated to East Pakistan's independence. **850**

Axis Powers Alliance including Germany, Italy, and Japan. **786**

Aztec Wandering warriors who gradually came to rule central Mexico. **210**

B

Babylonian Captivity Years that the pope lived in Avignon, France, instead of Rome, Italy (1309-1377). **342**

balance of power Principle in which countries have equal strength in order to prevent any one country from dominating the others. **457**

Balfour Declaration Statement written by the British foreign secretary to a Zionist leader in Palestine. **760**

Balkan "powder keg" State of unrest in the Balkans that allowed the assassination of the heir to the Austro-Hungarian throne and led to World War I. **701**

Balkan League Balkan nations of Bulgaria, Serbia, Greece, and Montenegro that declared war on the Ottoman Empire. **657**

Bantu Family of closely related African languages. **184**

barter Exchange of one good or service for another. **43**

barter economy Economy of exchanging goods and services for other goods and services without using money. **325**

Bataan Death March Forced march by the Japanese of prisoners of war in the Philippines in 1942. **809**

Battle of Britain Nonstop German air raids on Britain during 1940 and 1941. **794**

Battle of Marathon Battle during the Persian Wars when Persia invaded Greece. **121**

Battle of Midway Important battle in which the Americans defeated the Japanese in 1942. **805**

Battle of Stalingrad Battle between Germany and the Soviets in Stalingrad in the summer of 1942; Soviet victory greatly weakened Germany's forces. **804**

Battle of Thermopylae Battle during the Persian Wars in which Spartan troops fought to the death against a much larger Persian force. **121**

Beats Group of writers in the post–World War II years that criticized wealthy citizens and their values. **979**

bedouins Nomadic Arab herders of sheep and camel. **240**

belligerents Warring nations. **702**

Beringia Land bridge during the Ice Age that provided the means for Asians to travel to the Americas. **200**

Berlin Airlift System of dropping food and supplies by air into West Berlin by the United States and Britain. **828**

Berlin Wall Wall constructed to separate East and West Berlin, to prevent East Germans from escaping to West Berlin. **832**

Bhagavad Gita Last 18 chapters of the Mahabharata, stressing the idea of proper conduct for one's status. **60**

Bill of Rights Ten amendments of the U.S. Constitution that protect the freedoms and rights of individuals. **503**

biodiversity Variety of plants and animals that naturally occurs in the environment. **988**

biological sciences Sciences that deal with living organisms, such as biology and genetics. **576**

bishops Heads of the Catholic Church in major cities. **171**

Black Death Terrible plague that swept through Europe, beginning in 1347. **330**

Black Shirts Fascists who conducted a violent campaign against their opponents. **744**

Black Tuesday October 29, 1929, when stock investors rushed to sell their shares, resulting in a major financial collapse. **735**

blitzkrieg German for "lightning war"; fast, forceful style of fighting used by Germany during World War II. **791**

"Bloody Mary" Nickname for Mary I of England. **470**

bobbies Nickname for London police. **588**

Boers Descendants of the original Dutch settlers in South Africa. **673**

Boer War War between the Boers and the British for control in the Transvaal in 1899. **673**

Bolsheviks Radical faction of Russia who won over the Mensheviks for control, led by Lenin. **712**

bourgeoisie (boorzh·wah·zee) Urban middle class, including merchants, manufacturers, and professionals. **509**

Boxer Rebellion Uprising in China in which foreigners were attacked and anything connected with outsiders was destroyed. **765**

boyars Nobles who advised the prince in each Kievan city. **231**

Brahmins Special priests of the Indo-Aryan society who knew the proper forms and rules of their complicated religious rituals. **57**

Brezhnev Doctrine Doctrine stating that the Soviet Union would intervene in any satellite nation that seemed to be moving away from communism. **956**

broadsides Single printed news sheets sold to the public. **375**

buffalo Primary animal that roamed the Great Plains of the United States; hunted by the Plains people. **205**

Bundesrat Upper house of the legislative branch of the united German states. **642**

bureaucracy Government organized into different levels and tasks. **81**

burgesses Merchants and professional people from towns and cities. **472**

Bushido "Way of the warrior"; code of behavior of the samurai, stressing bravery, loyalty, and honor. **278**

business cycle Alternating periods of prosperity and decline. **558**

C

cabinet Heads of government departments who advise the head of state. **488**

caliph Title meaning "successor to the Prophet" used in government and religion in Islamic society. **243**

calligraphy Chinese art of writing. **83**

Camp David Accords Peace agreement between Egypt and Israel, mediated by the United States. **899**

canon law The code of law in the Catholic Church. **302**

capital Wealth that is earned, saved, and invested to make profits. **326**

capitalism Economic system in which individuals, rather than governments, control the factors of production. **555**

caravans Groups of people traveling together for safety over long distances. **29**

Carbonari Secret society of Italian nationalists in the early 1800s. **632**

cardinals Catholic officials ranking next below the pope. **301**

Carolingians Line of Frankish rulers established by Pepin III's coronation in A.D. 751. **289**

cartels Corporate combinations that control entire industries. **557**

Carter Doctrine Statement declaring that the United States would regard any attempts by outside forces to control the Persian Gulf as an assault on U.S. interests. **944**

caste system Complex form of social organization that began to take shape after the Indo-Aryan migration. **61**

Cavaliers Those who supported the king in the English Civil War; also known as royalists. **480**

censors Roman officials who registered citizens according to their wealth. **152**

Central Powers World War I alliance of Germany, Austria-Hungary, Bulgaria, and the Ottoman Empire. **704**

Chavín Earliest people of Andean South America. **209**

checks and balances System of government that prevents any one part of the government from becoming too powerful. **152**

Children's Crusade Short-lived failed crusade in 1212 by young people from Europe who marched on the Holy Land to regain it for Christianity. **321**

chinampas Raised fields made by the Aztec with mud taken from the bottoms of lakes. **210**

chivalry Code of conduct that dictated knights' behavior toward others. **298**

citadel Strong central fortress of a city. **53**

city-state Form of government that includes a town or city and the surrounding land controlled by it. **32**

civil service Centralized system that runs the day-to-day business of government. **87**

civilization Complex culture that can produce a surplus of food, establish large towns with a government, and has people who perform different jobs. **11**

cloning Process of making a genetically identical copy of an animal's cell. **986**

coalitions Political groups organized to support a common cause. **620**

Cold War Suspicion and hostility between the communist and Western democratic nations, waged primarily by political and economic means rather than with weapons. **825**

collaborators People who are willing to help their country's enemies. **791**

collective bargaining Process of negotiation between management and union representatives. **563**

collective farms Land pooled into large farms on which people work together as a group. **749**

Columbia Spaceship used for travel for the first United States mission to the moon. **983**

Columbian Exchange Massive exchange of goods, plants, animals, and diseases that took place between the Western and Eastern Hemispheres following Columbus's voyage. **394**

Cominform Communist Information Bureau established by the Soviets to oppose the Marshall Plan. **827**

Comintern Communist International, an organization founded by Lenin to spread the communist revolution throughout the world. **753**

command economy Economy in which the government controls all economic decisions. **750**

commercial capitalism Early economic system in which most capitalists were merchants who bought and sold goods. **555**

Commercial Revolution Era between 1400 and 1750 when Europeans made major changes to their economies due to new exploration. **389**

commodities Goods that have value, especially relating to barter economies. **43**

common law Law based upon customs and judges' decisions rather than upon written codes. **307**

Common Market Officially called the European Economic Community, an organization of six Western European

nations established in 1957 for international economic cooperation. **834**

commonwealth A republic. **480**

Commonwealth of Independent States (CIS) Commonwealth established to coordinate defense and economic policies for the new independent republics following the breakup of the Soviet Union. **959**

Communards Paris council members who wanted a decentralized government, separation of church and state, and other socialist reforms. **619**

communism Authoritarian socialism; economic and political system in which governments own the means of production and control economic planning. **566**

Communist Party New name of the Russian Bolsheviks who dissolved the constitutional assembly in 1918. **713**

compass Navigational instrument created in the 1300s that uses a magnetized piece of metal that points to the north. **388**

conceptual art Style of art in which the act of creating the art is more important than the actual art object. **975**

Concordat Agreement between Napoléon and the pope recognizing Catholicism as the religion of most French citizens. **524**

conscription Military draft. **518**

conservatives Group that does not want to change existing conditions. **515**

constitution Document outlining the basic laws and principles that govern a nation. **481**

consulates Foreign diplomatic offices headed by consuls. **427**

consuls Chief executives elected to run the government in ancient Rome. **152**

Contadora Principles Agreement promoting negotiations rather than violence as a way to settle regional conflicts in Latin America. **921**

containment Policy aimed at restricting the spread of communism. **827**

contraband War materials supplied by a neutral nation to a belligerent one. **710**

contras Group seeking to overthrow Nicaragua's Sandinista government. **919**

Convention on the Rights of the Child An agreement passed by the United Nations in 1989 that outlines the legal, social, and economic guidelines each country must follow to protect children. **993**

corporations Businesses that allow people to buy stock in the company. **557**

corporatist state Nation in which the major economic activities, such as agriculture, transportation, manufacturing, and commerce, are organized into syndicates that resemble corporations. **745**

Council of Trent Meeting of church leaders in the 1500s to clearly define Catholic doctrines for the Counter-Reformation. **369**

Counter-Reformation Attempt by the Catholic Church, following the Reformation, to return the church to an emphasis on spiritual matters. **368**

counterrevolutionary Activities aimed against, or counter to, a revolution, organized by supporters of the Old Regime. **518**

coup d'état (koo day·tah) Seizure of power by force; in French, a "stroke of state." **522**

covenant Solemn agreement. **45**

craft guilds Associations of skilled workers that set standards for working conditions. **328**

creoles White people born in Spanish or Portuguese colonies. **622**

Crimean War War waged by France, Great Britain, and the Ottoman Empire against Russia. **617**

Cro-Magnons Group of early people appearing about 35,000 years ago in Europe. **8**

crop rotation The practice of alternating crops of different kinds to preserve soil fertility. **544**

Crusades Expeditions by Christians to regain the Holy Land from the Muslims. **318**

Cuban missile crisis Situation during the Cold War in which the Soviet Union built nuclear missile sites in Cuba. **840**

cubism Artistic style that emphasizes geometric designs, using shapes such as cubes, flat planes, and spheres. **731**

cultural diffusion Spread of culture from one area of the world to another. **12**

Cultural Revolution Violent attempt at social change in China, launched by Mao Zedong in 1966. **854**

culture Beliefs, knowledge, and patterns of living that a group of people acquire by living together. **6**

cuneiform (kyoo·nee·uh·fawrm) Sumerian writing made by pressing a wedge-shaped tool into clay tablets. **31**

curia Group of advisers to the pope drawn from the highest ranks of clergy. **301**

czar Title taken by Ivan the Terrible; Russian for "caesar." **234**

dadaists Group of artists who used random images to reflect what they considered the insanity of war. **731**

daimyo (dy·mee·oh) Powerful local lords in feudal Japan. **280**

Dao De Jing Compilation of Laozi's teachings on Daoism. **91**

Dayton Accord Agreement mediated by the United States that gave Bosnian Serbs a degree of autonomy while recognizing the sovereignty of the Muslim-led government. **963**

D-Day June 6, 1944, the day Allied troops began the invasion on France's Normandy coast. **805**

Delian League Alliance of city-states in ancient Greece, with Athens as a leader. **123**

democracy Government in which citizens take part. **112**

democratic socialism Political system in which the government takes over the means of production peacefully; people retain basic human rights and partial control over economic planning. **567**

departments Administrative districts in France. **513**

dependent colonies Colonies in which a few officials from one country (usually European) rule (non-European) people of another country. **662**

depression Period in which the decreased demand of goods causes the entire economy to sink. **558**

desaparecidos "Disappeared" people in Argentina who criticized the government and were killed by the military government's campaign. **931**

desertification Spread of the desert. **889**

détente (day·tahnt) Era of improved Soviet-American relations. **944**

DEW Line Radar installations built by the United States and Canada to give early warning of air attacks. **841**

dialects Variations of a language. **82**

Diamond Sutra World's first known printed book, a Buddhist text produced in China in A.D. 868. **270**

dictator Absolute ruler. **151**

Diet Japan's two-house national legislature. **676**

dikes Earthen walls built along a river to protect from floods. **78**

Diplomatic Revolution Major reversal of alliances in Europe in the mid-1700s. **467**

direct democracy Form of democracy in which all citizens participate directly in making decisions. **117**

dissidents People who disagree with a government. **924**

divine right of kings Belief that God chooses kings to rule nations. **456**

division of labor Characteristic of civilizations in which different people perform different jobs. **12**

DNA Deoxyribonucleic acid; the small units of chromosomes that convey characteristics from parent to child. **986**

domestic system Method of production that takes place in the worker's home rather than in a shop or factory. **325**

domestication Taming of animals such as cattle, goats, sheep, and pigs. **9**

domino theory Idea that if one country falls to communism, surrounding countries will soon follow. **867**

dowry Money or goods a wife brings to a marriage. **222**

dramas Plays containing action or dialogue and usually involving conflict and emotion. **136**

Duma Elected parliament for Russia. **652**

dynamo Electric generator. **572**

dynasty Family of rulers whose right to rule is hereditary. **22**

Easter Rising April 24, 1916, when Irish nationalists revolted against Britain. **740**

economic nationalism Policy that a nation uses to try to improve its economic well-being by limiting trade. **734**

economic sanctions Refusal to trade with an offending nation. **723**

Emancipation Edict Proclamation by Czar Alexander in 1861 that freed all Russian serfs. **649**

Emancipation Proclamation Decree issued by President Abraham Lincoln in 1863 that effectively ended slavery at the end of the Civil War. **611**

emigrations Movements of people away from their native lands. **586**

émigrés Nobles who fled France during the Revolution. **513**

empire Form of government that unites different territories and peoples under one ruler. **24**

enclosure movement Practice of fencing or enclosing common lands into individual holdings. **544**

Encyclopedia, The Reference book describing the ideas of the Enlightenment. **494**

English Bill of Rights Document in 1689 that declared the powers of Parliament and protected private citizens. **485**

enlightened despotism System of government in which an absolute monarch ruled according to the principles of the Enlightenment. **496**

Enlightenment Period in the 1700s when philosophers believed that they could apply the scientific method and use reason to explain human nature logically. **494**

ephors Five officials in ancient Sparta who were elected for one-year terms to make sure the king stayed within the law. **114**

epics Long poems based on historical or religious themes. **60**

equites Class of business people and landowners in ancient Rome who had wealth and power. **157**

ethical monotheism Religion believing in one god, emphasizing ethics. **47**

ethics Study of what is good and bad, and of moral duty. **120**

ethnic cleansing Campaign of terror and murder intended to drive out certain ethnic groups from a region or an area. **961**

European Community Multinational European economic organization headquartered in Belgium. **835**

evolution Belief that organisms develop through change over time. **577**

excommunication Official edict that bars a person from church membership. **226**

executive branch Branch of government that enforces the laws and is headed by the president. **502**

Exodus Escape of the Hebrews from Egypt. **44**

export Good or service sold to another country or region. **118**

extraterritoriality Exemption of foreigners from the laws of the country in which they live or do business. **419**

 F

factors of production Basic resources for industrialization, such as necessary land, capital, and labor. **545**

factory system Production of goods in a factory through the use of machines and a large number of workers. **546**

Falange Spanish fascist party. **784**

fascism Governmental doctrine that relies on dictatorial rule and a totalitarian regime, in which the state maintains rigid control of the people through force and censorship. **743**

Fashoda crisis Conflict between France and England in the Sudan. **669**

favorable balance of trade Situation that exists when a country sells more goods than it buys. **390**

federal system of government System of government in which power is divided between a central, or federal, government and individual states. **502**

feudalism Political system of local government based on the granting of land in return for loyalty, military assistance, and other services. **294**

fief Grant of land given to a vassal from a lord. **294**

Final Solution Name given to the Nazi attempt to destroy the Jewish population of Europe. **801**

Five Classics Texts used to train scholars and civil servants in ancient China. **94**

Five Good Emperors Five rulers who led Rome for almost 100 years during the Pax Romana. **161**

Five-Year Plan Plan of Stalin's government for economic growth during the 1920s. **750**

flappers Young women who challenged the social norms of the 1920s by wearing short hair and skirts and going out to jazz clubs. **733**

Flemish school Group of painters who perfected the technique of oil painting on canvas. **361**

Fourteen Points President Woodrow Wilson's plan for a just world based on the Allies' aims to end World War I. **714**

"Four Tigers" South Korea, Taiwan, Singapore, and Hong Kong; noted for their strong economic growth. **872**

Franco-Prussian War War between France and Prussia that ended in France's defeat in 1871. **618**

free enterprise System in which economic forces work automatically and naturally, without mercantilist laws and regulations. **560**

free trade Practice based on the belief that government should not restrict or interfere with international trade. **418**

frescoes Paintings done on wet plaster walls. **107**

Fujiwara First family to gain control over the central government in Japan; had power from the mid-800s to the mid-1100s. **278**

functionalism Style of architecture in which a building is designed for its specific use rather than according to a particular style. **731**

G

Gang of Four Madame Mao's radical communist group who wanted to continue the Cultural Revolution in China. **854**

genealogy Record of a family history. **93**

General Assembly One body of the United Nations, comprised of any nation that wishes to join. **823**

general strike Refusal by workers in various industries to work until their demands are met. **739**

genetic code Sequence of DNA's chemical "letters" that determines the characteristics for each human life. **986**

genetics Study of the ways in which inborn characteristics of plants and animals are inherited by their descendants. **577**

Geneva Accord Agreement signed in 1954 that called for French withdrawal from Vietnam and division of the country into two zones. **867**

genocide Systematic extermination of a people. **721**

gentry Landowners in England who had social positions but no titles. **472**

geocentric theory Theory according to Hellenistic thinker Ptolemy that Earth is the center of the universe. **383**

German-Soviet nonaggression pact 1939 agreement dividing eastern Europe into spheres of influence. **789**

ghazis Warriors for Islam; Turkish soldiers who were the first Ottomans. **432**

gladiators Trained fighters, usually slaves, who fought in arenas as entertainment. **165**

glasnost (glaz·nohst) Soviet policy of openness under which government controls on the economy were relaxed and restrictions on dissent were eased. **957**

Glorious Revolution Bloodless transfer of power to William and Mary of England in 1688. **484**

golden age Era of cultural progress in Greece in the 400s B.C. **130**

Golden Horde Name given by Europeans to the Mongol invaders of the 1200s due to the golden color of their tents. **273**

Good Neighbor Policy U.S. policy during the 1930s that stressed cooperation among Latin American nations. **776**

Gothic Style of church architecture characterized by tall spires and flying buttresses that was developed by master builders during the mid-1100s. **334**

Goths One of a group of Germanic tribes who flooded into the Roman Empire and later revolted, weakening the empire. **174**

Gracchi, the Two brothers, Tiberus and Gaius Gracchus, who saw the need for reform in the Roman Republic. **158**

Grand Canal Canal constructed during the Sui dynasty that linked northern and southern China for the first time. **266**

Great Depression Worldwide depression in the early 1930s when prices and wages fell, business activity slowed, and unemployment rose. **735**

Great Elector Nickname for Frederick William, one of the greatest Hohenzollern rulers. **466**

Great Leap Forward Mao Zedong's second Five-Year Plan for China in 1958, intended to speed progress. **853**

Great Schism Period of church history from 1378 to 1417 when the church was divided into opposing groups. **342**

Great Wall of China Wall built and expanded upon by early rulers of China to protect from invasions. **86**

Greek fire Flammable liquid used as a weapon by the Byzantine navy. **224**

greenhouse effect Warming of the earth's surface. **989**

Grimm brothers German brothers who collected fairy tales that continue to be well known. **592**

guerilla warfare Military technique relying on swift raids by small bands of soldiers. **403**

habeas corpus Legal right protecting individuals from arbitrary arrest and imprisonment. **485**

Habsburg Powerful family of European rulers in the 1200s. **340**

haciendas (hah·see·en·duhz) Large self-sufficient farms in Spanish America. **621**

Hagia Sophia Great, decorative Byzantine church in Constantinople. **227**

Han Dynasty of rulers that ruled a centralized and growing empire in China. **84**

heliocentric theory Theory developed by Copernicus that the sun is the center of the universe. **383**

Hellenistic culture "Greek-like" way of life that combined ideas and values drawn from the Mediterranean and Asia. **141**

helots (HEL·uhts) Conquered people of the Peloponnesus, who became the lowest class in Spartan society. **113**

Helsinki Accords Series of agreements in 1975 that gave European nations a new framework for economic and technological cooperation, among other democratic agreements. **953**

heresy Opinion that conflicts with official church beliefs. **226**

heretics People who denied the truth of the official church's principles or who preached beliefs not approved by the church. **302**

hieroglyphics (hy·ruh·gli·fiks) Form of ancient writing developed by Nile River valley people by about 3000 B.C. **22**

hijrah (hi·jy·ruh) Migration of Muhammad and his followers in A.D. 622, marking the first year in the Muslim calendar. **241**

Ho Chi Minh Trail Viet Cong's major supply route through Laos from North to South Vietnam. **868**

Hohokam Group of people who lived in the southwestern United States who abandoned their communities in the 1300s or 1400s. **203**

Holocaust Systematic elimination of European Jews and others by the Nazis. **803**

hominids Early humans and other humanlike creatures. **6**

Hopewell Group of people who settled in the Ohio Valley region sometime from about 300 B.C. to 200 B.C. **207**

hoplites Heavily armed Greek infantry who carried long spears and fought in closely spaced rows. **112**

Huguenots French people, including high-ranking nobles, who converted to Calvinism. **367**

humanists People who specialize in studying the humanities, which includes grammar, history, poetry, and rhetoric. **355**

humanitarians People who work to improve the conditions of others. **561**

Hundred Years' War War between France and England for the French throne that continued from 1337 to 1453, and introduced the use of new weapons. **336**

Huns Nomadic people from Asia who attacked the Roman Empire. **175**

hunter-gatherers Early people who lived by hunting animals and gathering plants for food. **10**

Hyksos Group of people who arrived in ancient Egypt from Asia and introduced new war tools. **23**

icon Holy picture of Jesus, the Virgin Mary, or a saint. **224**

Iconoclastic Controversy Debate between opponents and defenders of icons in the Byzantine Church; one of the issues that led to the split of the Christian church in 1054. **226**

iconoclasts People who opposed the use of icons in worship. **224**

Iliad Homer's great epic that tells the story of the Trojan War. **110**

imams Spiritual leaders who, according to some Shi'ah Muslims, should be direct descendants of Muhammad. **244**

imperialism Ambition of a powerful nation to dominate the political, economic, and cultural affairs of another nation or region. **662**

import Good or service bought from another country or region. **118**

import substitution Economic policy of replacing certain imported goods with a country's own manufactured goods produced inside the country. **911**

impressionists Group of painters who developed a type of realism by studying light and color to create vivid impressions of people and places. **596**

Inca Civilization in the Andes Mountains in South America that by the end of the 1400s included much of what is now Peru, Ecuador, Bolivia, and Chile. **211**

indemnity Compensation paid to a nation for damage inflicted on it. **530**

Indo-Aryans Indo-European tribes who moved in slow waves into India in about 1750 B.C. **56**

indulgences Paid pardons from punishment for sin. **363**

industrial capitalism Type of capitalism that began during the Industrial Revolution when capitalists were involved in producing and manufacturing goods themselves, often using mechanized and industrialized methods of production. **555**

Industrial Revolution Term for changes beginning in the 1700s, when power-driven machines began to do much of the work that people had done before. **545**

inflation Rise in prices caused by a decrease in the value of the medium of exchange. **172**

influenza pandemic Flu-like epidemic that killed more than 20 million people worldwide during 1918 and 1919. **728**

inoculation Practice of infecting people with a mild form of a disease to protect them from more serious illness. **71**

Inquisition Institution of the Roman Catholic Church that sought to eliminate heresy by seeking out and punishing heretics. **303**

Intendants Regional administrators and representatives of the crown in the provinces of France. **455**

interchangeable parts Identical parts that can replace each other. **556**

interdict The Catholic Church's punishment of a region, involving closing churches and withholding sacraments. **302**

International Brigades Antifascist volunteers from France, Britain, and the United States who participated in the Spanish Civil War. **785**

international style Style of architecture that included uninterrupted expanses of steel and glass. **732**

intifada Violent uprising by Palestinians in the late 1980s. **900**

Iran-contra affair Scandal in which members of President Reagan's national security staff sent money from the sale of weapons to Iran in exchange for hostages to the Nicaraguan contras. **941**

Irish Republican Army (IRA) The military branch of the Irish nationalist group Sinn Fein. **741**

irrigation System of ditches and canals that transports water from a source into an agricultural field. **12**

Islam Religion based on Muhammad's teachings and ideas that began spreading throughout Arab tribes in the A.D. 600s. **241**

island hopping Military strategy of capturing only certain islands of a country and bypassing the others. **805**

isolationists Persons who believe that their own country should not become involved in relations with other nations, especially alliances. **794**

Janissaries Highly trained troop of slave soldiers for Ottoman sultans. **432**

jazz New form of music that originated in the 1920s among the African American communities in New Orleans. **731**

Jesuits Catholic religious order founded by Ignatius de Loyola in 1534. **369**

jihad (ji·hahd) Teaching of Islam to defend the faith. **242**

joint-stock company Business organization developed during the Commercial Revolution in which owners raised money by selling shares, or stock, in the company. **389**

journeyman Skilled worker who was paid wages by a master. **328**

Judeo-Christian ethics Values first established by the Hebrews that contribute greatly to Western civilization. **47**

judicial branch Branch of government that interprets and applies the laws. **502**

Julio-Claudian Emperors Relatives of Caesar who ruled for 54 years of the Pax Romana following the death of Augustus. **160**

jungle Thick growth of plants found in a tropical rain forest. **182**

Junkers Group of aristocratic landowners who campaigned for abolishing tariffs in the early 1800s. **638**

junks Large Chinese ships. **412**

Justinian Code Collection of laws that formed the basis for Byzantine law under Emperor Justinian. **222**

kaiser Title of the German emperor. **641**

kami Japanese gods or nature spirits. **277**

Kellogg-Briand Pact Agreement made between the United States and France in 1928 that made war "illegal." **782**

Khmer Rouge Cambodian Communists trained by the Viet Cong who took over the government and enforced a massive genocide of the Cambodian population. **868**

kibbutz Collective farm in Israel. **893**

kizilbash Military army developed by the Safavids to fight for political power. **436**

Kulturkampf An anti-Catholic program started by Bismarck in Germany in the late 1800s. **643**

Kuomintang Chinese Nationalist Party that grew out of the nationalist desire for reform. **766**

laissez-faire (le·say·far) Belief that government should not interfere with the operations of businesses. **560**

laser Device that concentrates light and releases it in an intense beam that travels in a straight line. **985**

League of Nations World organization formed after World War I to maintain peace. **716**

Legalism School of Chinese philosophy concerned with politics. **91**

legislative branch Branch of government that makes the laws. **502**

legitimacy Principle involving restoring former ruling families to their thrones. **529**

Lend-Lease Act 1941 legislation allowing the United States to supply war materials to Great Britain on credit. **794**

leveling Policy in which government uses price controls to balance the economic effects of farm surpluses or shortages. **87**

Liberal-Democratic Party Most powerful political party in Japan after World War II, which controlled the government from the 1950s to the 1990s. **862**

liberalism Political movement believing in representative government protecting individual rights and the rule of law; also refers to movements to reform government. **533**

limited constitutional monarchy Government in which the monarch remains head of the state, but the king or queen is required to consult Parliament. **489**

limited evidence Evidence, such as artifacts, about which little information is given, requiring scientists to make educated guesses. **6**

linguists Scholars who study languages. **184**

Locarno Pact Number of treaties signed in Locarno by delegates of seven European countries in 1925. **739**

loess (les) Fertile yellow soil. **78**

Long March 6,000-mile journey by Communist Chinese to escape Nationalist troops. **768**

Long Parliament English Parliament elected in 1640 that convened on and off for 20 years. **479**

Lost Generation Group of American writers whose writings reflected a generation that lost its moral grounding during World War I. **729**

Loyalists American colonists who opposed independence from England. **498**

Luftwaffe German air force in World War II. **793**

Maastricht Treaty Treaty that created the European Union. **955**

"MacArthur Constitution" U.S.-imposed constitution adopted by Japan in 1947. **859**

Maginot Line France's fortifications along the borders of Germany and Luxembourg. **738**

Magna Carta "Great Charter," English document that made the law the supreme power and became a cornerstone of constitutional government. **306**

Magyars Nomadic group who invaded Europe; eventually settled in what is now Hungary. **292**

Maine U.S. battleship that exploded in Havana harbor in 1868, contributing to the Spanish-American War. **683**

mandate Area, usually a former colony, to be administered by the government of another nation. **723**

manorialism Economic system during the Middle Ages that revolved around self-sufficient farming estates where lords and peasants shared the land. **297**

Maori Original inhabitants of New Zealand. **608**

maquis Members of a French underground resistance movement. **793**

market economy Economy in which land, labor, and capital are controlled by individual persons. **326**

market speculations Risky investments in the stock market. **734**

Marshall Plan Massive economic assistance program to European countries by the United States. **827**

martyrs Persons put to death for their beliefs. **170**

mass production System of producing large numbers of identical items. **556**

matrilineal Describes a society in which people trace their ancestors and inherited property through their mothers rather than through their fathers. **186**

Mau Mau Kikuyu organization that waged a guerilla campaign against British presence in Kenya. **881**

Maya One of the most advanced early people in the Americas, occupying most of the Yucatán Peninsula. **209**

maya Illusory world of the senses, according to Hinduism. **61**

means of production Everything used to produce and exchange goods. **564**

mechanization Use of automatic machinery to increase production. **546**

medieval Term that describes the period of western European history known as the Middle Ages. **288**

Meech Lake Accord Failed agreement between Canadian leaders to accept Quebec as a "distinct society" within Canada. **946**

Meiji Restoration Change when a group of samurai overthrew the Tokugawa shogunate and restored the emperor to power. **676**

Mensheviks Moderate faction of Russia who fought for control during the early 1900s. **712**

mercantilism Economic theory stating that there is a fixed amount of wealth in the world and that in order to receive a larger share, one country has to take some wealth away from another country. **390, 493**

merchant guild Association of merchants and workers created to protect their rights to trade and to help out members and their families. **327**

Merovingians Clovis and his successors, who were generally weak Frankish rulers who left the job of governing to palace officials. **288**

mestizos People of American Indian and European descent. **622**

metics People living in Athens who were not Athenian citizens, who could work and who paid taxes but were not allowed to own land or take part in government. **115**

Middle Ages Period in western European history between the collapse of the Roman Empire and the Renaissance. **288**

middle class Class of skilled workers between the upper class and the poor and unskilled workers. **328**

Middle Passage Second stage of the triangular trade system, which involved the shipping of slaves across the Atlantic to the Americas. **398**

militarism Glorification of armed strength. **698**

millets Separate, self-governed religious minorities within the Ottoman Empire. **434**

Minamoto Clan reigning in Japan beginning in 1156; changed the way governments were run by introducing the shogun control. **278**

minaret Tower attached to the outside of a mosque, from where a crier would call Muslims to worship. **253**

miniaturization Process of making machines smaller and lighter. **983**

Minoans Earliest Greek civilization that had developed on the island of Crete by 2000 B.C. **107**

Mississippians Group that lived in the Eastern Woodlands of North America from about A.D. 700 to A.D. 1550. **207**

mixed economy Economy in which private companies own some industries, and the government owns the rest. **849**

mobilize Act of preparing a nation's army and other resources for war. **698**

moderates Persons who do not hold extreme political views. **515**

monasticism Way of life in convents and monasteries where nuns and monks withdraw from the world and its temptations. **301**

money economy Economic system based on the use of money as a measure of value and a unit of account. **43**

monism Belief in the unity of God and creation. **61**

monoculture Country's reliance on one crop. **911**

monopoly Complete control of the production or sale of a single good or service by a single firm. **557**

monotheism Belief in one god. **25**

Monroe Doctrine Doctrine in 1823 stating that the United States would not interfere in European affairs or with Europe's remaining colonies in the Western Hemisphere, as long as the Europeans did not try to regain or create new colonies in the region. **625**

monsoons Winds that mark the seasons in India. **52**

Moors Muslims who made Spain their home in the A.D. 700s. **245**

mosaic Picture or design made from small pieces of enamel, glass, or stone. **227**

mosques Muslim places of worship. **242**

Mothers of the Plaza de Mayo Group of Argentine women whose family members disappeared due to government-sanctioned violence and abuses that they opposed. **913**

mulattoes People of European and

African ancestry in the Spanish American colonies. **622**

multinational corporations Foreign-owned businesses in a host country. **910**

mummification Process of preserving the body with chemicals after death. **28**

Munich Conference Meeting called by Hitler in 1938 to discuss the Czech problem, which led to the annexation of the Sudetenland by Germany. **787**

Muslim League Political group of Indian Muslims, formed to protect their rights. **846**

Muslims Followers of the religion of Islam. **242**

Mycenaeans Civilization on the Greek mainland that conquered the Minoans in Crete in about 1400 B.C. **107**

myths Traditional stories about gods, goddesses, and heroes. **111**

NAACP National Association for the Advancement of Colored People; group that worked for civil rights. **838**

NAFTA North American Free Trade Agreement, linking Mexico, Canada, and the United States in a large free-trade zone. **912**

Nalanda Famous Buddhist university of ancient India. **71**

Napoléonic Code System of French law under Napoléon's direction. **524**

Nazi Party Extremely nationalistic, anti-Semitic, and anticommunist party that rose to power in Germany in the 1920s. **745**

nationalism Love of one's country rather than of one's native region. **526**

nationalization Act of placing an industry under government control. **739**

NATO North Atlantic Treaty Organization; an alliance of twelve Western nations formed in 1949. **830**

naturalists Realists who took the approach one step further to show the ugly or unpleasant aspects of everyday life. **596**

Navigation Act of 1651 Law that required imported goods to be carried in English ships or ships of the country making the goods. **481**

Neanderthals Early people who lived during the Old Stone Age. **8**

Neolithic agricultural revolution Shift in human history from food gathering to food producing. **10**

Neutrality Acts Legislation passed between 1935 and 1937 in the United States that stated its wish to stay neutral in future wars. **794**

New Deal Programs by President Franklin D. Roosevelt in which the federal government established public works to create jobs and granted money to each state to provide for the needy. **737**

New Economic Policy Lenin's policy to deal with the economic collapse in Russia that allowed some free trade. **749**

New Model Army Cromwell's powerful army that defeated King Charles in the English Civil War. **480**

"New Order" Adolf Hitler's plan for organizing Europe into a single political and economic system ruled by Germany. **801**

nihilists Political group that believes in abolishing the existing political, economic, and social structures. **650**

nirvana Perfect spiritual peace, as taught in Hinduism. **62**

nomads People who wander from place to place. **9**

nonalignment Nation's policy of refusing to ally with either the United States or the Soviet Union. **847**

Northwest Ordinance Law passed by the U.S. Congress to provide government for the Northwest Territory. **609**

Nürnberg trials Nuremberg trials; postwar trials of Nazi leaders charged with crimes against peace and humanity. **822**

Odyssey Homer's epic that tells the story of the Greek hero Odysseus on his way home from the Trojan War. **110**

Olmec Earliest culture of Mexico, beginning in about 1200 B.C. **209**

Olympic Games Originally, ancient Greek festival including contests of sports, music, and literature; the modern revival of these games as international athletic competitions. **111**

op art Art of the 1950s and 1960s in which artists used brilliant colors and shapes to create optical illusions. **974**

OPEC Organization of Petroleum Exporting Countries, created in 1960 to set oil prices and world oil production levels. **901**

Open Door Policy Right of all foreign nations to trade equally in China. **765**

Operation Bootstrap Plan for outside investment and industrialization to boost Puerto Rico's economy. **925**

Operation Overlord Code name for the Allied invasion of northwest France. **805**

Opium War Conflict from 1839 to 1842 between China and Britain that arose due to Britain's export of opium to China. **419**

oracle bones Cattle bones or tortoise shells on which Chinese priests would write questions and then interpret answers from the cracks that formed when the bones were heated. **82**

oracles Special places where the ancient Greeks believed gods spoke through priests and priestesses. **111**

oral traditions Poems, songs, and stories passed by word of mouth from one generation to another. **184**

orators Public speakers. **139**

Organization of American States (OAS); group designed to foster military, economic, and cultural cooperation among nations of the Western Hemisphere. **914**

Ostpolitik Term used to describe Willy Brandt's efforts to improve relations between East and West. **951**

Ottoman Turks Asian people who conquered Constantinople in the 1300s and established a large empire. **228**

Pan-Africanism Movement promoting the cultural unity of people of African heritage in their struggle for freedom. **878**

Panama Canal Canal completed in 1914 that connects the Atlantic and Pacific Oceans. **684**

Panchatantra Fables from the Gupta period of ancient India. **70**

Pan-Slavism Unity of all Slavic peoples under Russian leadership. **648**

papyrus Kind of paper made by Egyptians from the stem of the papyrus plant. **22**

Paris Peace Accords 1973 cease-fire agreement calling for withdrawal of U.S. troops from South Vietnam. **867**

Paris Peace Conference Meeting of victorious nations to write terms for the peace following World War I. **716**

Parthenon White marble temple built in ancient Athens in honor of Athena. **130**

passive resistance Nonviolent civil disobedience. **761**

pasteurization Process of heating liquids to kill bacteria and prevent fermentation. **579**

paternalism System of governing colonies in much the same way that parents guide their children. **673**

patriarchs Bishops of the administrative centers for the church in the last years of the Roman Empire. **171**

patricians Powerful landowners who controlled Roman government and society. **153**

Patriots American colonists who favored independence from England. **498**

Pax Romana Period of Roman peace

from the beginning of Augustus's reign until the death of Marcus Aurelius. **160**

pedagogue In ancient Greece, a male slave who taught a young boy manners. **119**

Peloponnesian War War between Sparta and Athens that broke out in 431 B.C. and lasted for 27 years. **124**

peninsulares Europeans who were born on the Iberian Peninsula of Spain or Portugal. **622**

Pentagon Headquarters of the United States military leadership, located near Washington, D.C., and the scene of a terrorist attack on September 11, 2001. **964**

People's Will Russian movement that tried to use violence and intimidation to bring about reform. **650**

perestroika (per·uh·stroy·kuh) Soviet restructuring policy designed to overhaul the Soviet political and economic systems. **957**

performance art Art form in which the artist becomes a living work of art. **975**

Persian Wars Conflicts between Greece and Persia. **121**

perspective Art technique that involves making distant objects smaller than those in the foreground and arranging them to create the illusion of depth on a flat canvas. **356**

Petition of Right Petition stating four ancient liberties presented to Parliament by Charles I. **478**

phalanx (fay·langks) Military formation composed of rows of soldiers standing shoulder to shoulder, carrying pikes or heavy spears. **138**

pharaoh "Great House"; Egyptian ruler's title. **22**

philology History of literature and language. **415**

philosophes (fee·luh·zawfs) Thinkers of the Age of Enlightenment. **494**

philosophy Study of basic questions of reality and human existence. **133**

Phoenician alphabet Alphabet developed by the Phoenicians that became the model for later Western alphabets. **42**

"phony war" Early phase of World War II marked by little activity in western Europe. **791**

physical sciences Sciences concerned with energy and mostly nonliving matter, such as astronomy, geology, physics, and chemistry. **576**

Platt Amendment Provision of the Cuban constitution giving the United States the right to intervene in Cuba. **683**

plebeians Farmers and workers who made up most of the Roman population. **153**

plebiscite (pleb·uh·syt) Procedure used to submit the constitution of a new government to the people for a yes-or-no vote. **523**

PLO Palestine Liberation Organization; Palestinian guerilla organization led by Yasir Arafat. **899**

pogroms (poh·gruhmz) Riots in which Jews were massacred in Russia in the 1880s. **651**

polis Greek word for city-state, which developed around a central fort. **108**

Politburo Political Bureau of the Communist Party that held most of the power in the Soviet Union. **752**

Polovtsy Turkish people who after 1055 controlled the area south of Kiev in Russia. **233**

polygymy Practice in which a man is allowed to have more than one wife. **69**

polytheism Belief that many gods exist. **25**

polytheistic Based on a belief in many gods. **62**

pop art Style used by artists who painted common objects such as soup cans, pictures from comic books, or road signs. **974**

pope Title assumed by the patriarch of Rome and head of the Catholic Church; from the Latin word meaning "father." **171**

Popular Front Left-wing coalition government of France in the late 1930s. **739**

popular government Idea that people can and should rule themselves. **112**

popular sovereignty Governmental principle based on just laws and on a government created by and subject to the will of the people. **496**

potlatches Ceremonial gatherings of Native Americans of the Pacific Northwest. **203**

praetors (preet·uhrz) Elected Roman officials who helped the consuls. **152**

Pragmatic Sanction Statement made by Charles VI, urging European leaders to allow Maria Theresa to inherit Habsburg lands. **465**

Pravda Russkia Russia's first law code, created by Yaroslav I. **231**

predestination Belief that at the beginning of time God decided who would be saved. **366**

PRI Mexico's Institutional Revolutionary Party. **915**

prime minister Head of government in Great Britain. **488**

primogeniture (pry·moh·je·nuh·choohr) System of inheritance from father to eldest son for ownership or possession of land. **294**

prohibition Policy forbidding the manu-facture, sale, and transportation of alcoholic beverages. **733**

proletariat (proh·luh·tayr·ee·uht) Name given by Karl Marx to the working class. **566**

propaganda Ideas, facts, or rumors spread deliberately to further one's cause or to damage an opposing cause. **706**

protectorates Colonies in which the native rulers keep their titles, but officials of the foreign power actually control the regions. **663**

psychiatry Study and treatment of mental illness. **585**

psychoanalysis Process of revealing and analyzing the unconscious. **585**

Pueblo Group of people who lived in permanent settlements in the southwestern United States. **205**

Punic Wars Three costly conflicts between Romans and Carthaginians over control of the Mediterranean and overseas expansion. **155**

purge A large-scale elimination of people from an organization or area. **752**

Puritans People who objected to the Anglican Church maintaining some Catholic practices; they wanted to further "purify" the English Church. **471**

Q

Qin Dynasty that came to power in China in 221 B.C. under which the first true empire of China was created. **84**

quantum theory Max Planck's theory stating that energy can only be released in definite "packages," or quanta. **581**

Quechua Inca language, still spoken today by millions in South America. **211**

queue Single braid that characterized the hairstyle that all Chinese men were required to wear during the Qing dynasty. **414**

quipu (kee·poo) Kind of knotted string used as a memory aid by the Inca. **211**

Qur'an Holy book of Islam. **242**

R

rabbis Religious scholars of Judaism. **168**

radicals Persons who want broad changes made in government. **515**

radioactivity Process in which atoms of certain elements constantly break down and release energy. **581**

raja Prince who ruled an Indo-Aryan city-state. **57**

Rajputs Indian warrior princes who began challenging Turkish Muslim control in India in the 1500s. **439**

rationalism Belief that truth can be determined solely by logical thinking. **494**

reaction Period of time during which people in authority want a return to the conditions of an earlier time. **530**

reactionaries Extremists who not only oppose change, but also want to undo certain changes. **530**

realism A method of dealing with the realities of everyday life and expressing a keen observation of social settings, characteristic of literature and art in the mid-1800s. **596**

reaya Masses of ordinary subjects in Ottoman society. **434**

Red Army Communist forces. **713**

Red Guards Radical students chosen by Mao Zedong to lead the Cultural Revolution. **854**

Reformation Religious revolution that split the church in western Europe and created a number of new churches. **363**

regionalism Form of realism that focuses on everyday life in particular places. **596**

Reichstag Lower house of the German legislature. **642**

Reign of Terror Period during the French Revolution when the National Convention worked to suppress all opposition. **519**

reincarnation Belief in the rebirth of souls. **61**

Renaissance Movement following the Middle Ages that centered on revival of interest in the classical learning of Greece and Rome; French word meaning "rebirth." **354**

reparations Payment for war damages. **716**

representative democracy Form of government in which citizens elect representatives to run the government for them, rather than each citizen serving directly in the government. **117**

republic Form of government in which voters elect officials to run the state. **151**

Restoration Period of the reign of Charles II of England when the monarchy was restored; also the rebirth of English culture during that time. **483**

rhetoric Study of public speaking and debating. **120**

risorgimento Italian word for "resurgence"; used as a name for the Italian nationalist movement of the 1800s. **632**

romanticism Trend followed by many writers of the early 1800s whose work appealed to sentiment and imagination and dealt with the romance of life. **592**

Rome-Berlin Axis 1936 alliance formed

between Mussolini in Italy and Hitler in Germany. **748**

Roosevelt Corollary Extension of the Monroe Doctrine stating that the United States would guarantee that Latin American nations would meet their international obligations. **685**

Rosetta Stone Black basalt stone found in 1799 that bears an inscription in hieroglyphics, demotic characters, and Greek; gave the first clue to deciphering Egyptian hieroglyphics. **22**

Roundheads Those who supported Parliament in the English Civil War. **480**

Rump Parliament Parliament controlled by Oliver Cromwell that abolished the monarchy and proclaimed England a republic. **480**

Rus People led by Rurik who came to rule Keiv and the Slavic tribes along the Dnieper River. **230**

"Russification" Program by Czar Nicholas I in the 1830s that forced non-Russian peoples to adopt the Russian language, religion, and culture. **648**

Russo-Japanese War War between Japan and Russia for Manchuria that began with Japan's unannounced attack in 1904. **771**

sacraments Ceremonies at which participants receive God's direct favor, or grace, to ward off the consequences of sin. **300**

samurai Japanese warriors hired for protection by wealthy landlords in feudal Japan. **278**

Sandinistas Marxist group who led the revolution against the dictator of Nicaragua. **918**

Sanskrit Indo-Aryan language. **56**

savannas Dry grasslands south of the Sahara Desert in Africa. **182**

SCAP "Supreme Commander of the Allied Powers," General Douglas MacArthur and his offices in occupied Japan. **859**

scholasticism Medieval philosophy attempting to bring together faith and reason. **334**

scientific method Method of inquiry that includes carefully conducted experiments and mathematical calculations to verify the results of experiments. **383**

Scientific Revolution Transformation in thinking that occurred during the 1500s and 1600s caused by scientific observation, experimentation, and the questioning of traditional opinions. **382**

scorched-earth policy Tactic of burning or destroying crops and anything else of value to an invading army. **527**

scribes Egyptian clerks who read or wrote for those who could not do so for themselves. **27**

sea dogs Adventurous group of English sea captains who lived in the late 1500s. **490**

secede Withdraw from a union. **611**

sectionalism Competition among sections or regions of a country. **611**

sects Religious societies of a few people, usually with a preacher as their leader. **365**

Security Council Body of the United Nations that includes temporary members elected from the General Assembly for two-year rotating terms. **823**

Seljuq Turks Muslim people from central Asia who gained control of Palestine, or the Holy Land to Christians, during the late 1000s. **318**

seppuku (se·poo·koo) Form of ceremonial suicide of defeated or disloyal samurai to avoid dishonor; also known in the West as hari-kari. **278**

serfs Peasants who were bound to the land where they worked for a lord. **298**

settlement colonies Large groups of people from one country living together in a new country. **662**

Seven Years' War War from 1756 to 1763 that involved almost all of Europe; the fighting began in North America as the French and Indian War. **468**

Shang Invaders of the Huang River valley who came to power sometime between 1750 B.C. and 1500 B.C. and established the first dynasty in China. **81**

Shi'ah Branch of Islam formed in the A.D. 600s that believed only imams should decide religious and worldly matters. **244**

Shining Path Maoist guerilla group in Peru that carried out its terrorist campaign in the rural highland areas. **932**

Shinto "Way of the kami"; indigenous religion of Japan involving rituals and prayers to appease nature spirits, and veneration of the emperor. **277**

shires Governmental districts in early England; governed by a shire-reeve (sheriff). **304**

shogun Chief military and governmental officer in feudal Japan. **278**

Shona People who migrated onto the plateau of what is known today as Zimbabwe. **192**

Sikh Religion based on the teachings of Nānak, an Indian mystic in the 1500s, who tried to unite the Hindu and Muslim religions. **441**

Silk Road Trade route stretching from China to the Mediterranean. **88**

simony (sy·moh·nee) Practice of buying high positions in the Catholic Church, common during the Middle Ages. **303**

Sinn Fein Irish nationalist party that in 1918 declared themselves the representative government for an independent Irish republic. **741**

Sino-Japanese War War between China and Japan over Korea in 1894, resulting in a Japanese victory. **677**

social Darwinism Theory developed by Herbert Spencer that applies Darwin's theories to the evolution of human societies. **584**

Social Democratic Labor Party Russian socialist party formed in 1898. **651**

Social Democratic Party German socialist party formed in the late 1800s. **644**

social sciences Branches of knowledge that scientifically study people as members of society, covering such areas as economics, political institutions, history, and relations among people. **583**

Social Security Act U.S. law providing for unemployment and old-age benefits. **737**

socialism Political and economic system in which the government owns the means of production. **564**

"soft underbelly of the Axis" Region of Italy and the Balkans that Churchill believed to be the weak part of the Axis Powers. **804**

Sophists Athenian men who opened schools for boys to study government, mathematics, ethics, and rhetoric. **120**

Southeast Asia Treaty Organization SEATO; organization created by President Dwight D. Eisenhower to halt communist advances in Southeast Asia. **839**

Spanish Armada Impressive fleet of ships launched by Philip II of Spain; defeated by England in 1588. **471**

Spanish Civil War War between Falangist Nationalists of Spain and the Republicans during the 1930s. **784**

special theory of relativity Einstein's theory that no particle of matter can move faster than the speed of light and that motion can be measured only relative to a particular observer. **582**

spheres of influence Areas in which one country has a special interest, and other nations agree to respect that interest. **663**

SS Schutzstaffel, or military branch of the Nazi Party. **801**

Stamp Act Law passed by Parliament in 1765 that imposed a tax, in the form of a stamp, on special documents for American colonists. **498**

standard of living Measure of the quality of life. **376**

steppe Large, grassy plain stretching

across eastern Europe and central Asia that is ideal for agriculture. **229**

strait Narrow strip of water that connects two larger bodies of water. **200**

strike Refusal of workers to work until their demands are met. **562**

subsidies Government grants of money. **390**

suburbs Residential areas on the outskirts of a city. **588**

Suez Canal Canal that goes through the Isthmus of Suez to connect the Mediterranean Sea and the Red Sea. **668**

Suez Crisis Conflict between primarily Western powers and Egypt over the possession of the Suez Canal in the 1950s. **894**

suffrage Right to vote. **602**

suffragettes Women who fought for all women's right to vote. **605**

Sufi Muslim mystics who tried to live simple lives. **245**

sultan Ruler of the Turks who claimed to serve the Muslim caliph. **247**

Sunni Branch of Islam formed in the A.D. 600s who believed agreement among Muslim people should settle religious and worldly matters. **244**

supercomputers Powerful computers that help solve complex scientific and engineering problems. **984**

surrealism Artistic style that brings conscious and unconscious ideas together to portray life in a dreamlike way. **730**

suttee Ancient Indian practice of a woman committing suicide after her husband's death. **69**

Swahili African society that emerged in the late 1100s along the East African coast and combined elements of African, Asian, and Islamic cultures. **191**

taiga (ty·gah) Russian region north of the steppe having great forests, much rainfall, and cold, long winters. **231**

Taiping Rebellion Revolt in China from 1850 to 1864, led by Hong Xiuquan who, influenced by Christian teachings, declared a mission to establish a new dynasty. **421**

Taj Mahal Building constructed under Shah Jahan as a tomb for his wife, which remains one of the architectural wonders of the world. **441**

Tale of Genji, The Story of courtly life in Japan written by Murasaki Shikibu in about A.D. 1000; generally considered the world's first novel. **278**

tariffs Import taxes on foreign goods. **390**

tepees Cone-shaped tents made of buffalo hide. **205**

tenements Cramped, shabby apartment buildings where workers lived during the Industrial Revolution in England. **552**

terracing Carving small, flat plots of land from hillsides to use for farming. **118**

terrorism Bombings, kidnappings, and other acts of violence by political groups or governments, sometimes against innocent people, to force governments to grant their demands. **650**

Tet Offensive Major attack launched on the South Vietnamese by North Vietnam and the Viet Cong in 1968. **867**

theater of the absurd Type of theater characterized by biting social commentary. **978**

theocracy Government ruled by religious leaders claiming God's authority. **367**

Third Reich Adolf Hitler's name for his regime meaning the "third empire." **748**

third Rome Moscow; Russian Orthodox interpretation of the city's leading role in bringing spiritual light to the world. **235**

Thirty Years' War War beginning in Prague in 1618 as a Protestant rebellion against the Holy Roman Empire. **455**

Thousand and One Nights, The Popular collection of Muslim folktales. **253**

Tiananmen Square Massacre Incident in which students staged a hunger strike in Tiananmen Square and ignored government orders to leave, resulting in the death of hundreds. **855**

tithe Church tax collected from Christians in early times that represented one tenth of their income; later became a gift to the church representing one tenth of a person's income. **302**

Toleration Act 1689 act of British Parliament granting some religious freedoms to non-Anglican Protestants. **487**

Toltec People who invaded central Mexico from the north in about A.D. 800. **210**

Torah Jewish scriptures that include the first five books of the Old Testament of the Bible. **46**

Tories Political party that supported the monarchy in England in the 1600s. **484**

total war Strategy in which the enemy's military and civilian resources are attacked. **611**

tragedies Forms of Greek drama in which the main character struggles against fate or events. **137**

Treaty of Kanawaga Negotiations between Matthew Perry and Japan in 1854 that permitted trade between the two countries. **427**

Treaty of Nanjing Treaty following the Opium War in which China gave Hong

Kong to Britain and opened ports to British trade. **419**

Treaty of Portsmouth Agreement that ended the Russo-Japanese War. **771**

Treaty of Prague Agreement at the end of the Seven Weeks' War in 1866 between Prussia and Austria. **640**

Treaty of San Stefano Treaty that forced the defeated Turks to grant independence to Romania, Serbia, and Montenegro. **656**

Treaty of Shimonoseki 1895 treaty forcing China to recognize independence of Korea and make concessions to Japan. **677**

Treaty of Tordesillas Agreement between Spain and Portugal that moved west the line determining the land each country could claim in the Atlantic. **394**

Treaty of Versailles Treaty between Germany and the Allied Powers at the end of World War I. **718**

triangular trade System of trade involving three stages, one of which was the transatlantic slave trade. **398**

tribunes Officials elected by Rome's popular assemblies. **152**

Triple Alliance Alliance between Germany, Austria-Hungary, and Italy. **699**

Triple Entente Alliance between France, Russia, and Great Britain in the early 1900s. **699**

triumvirate Political alliance of three rulers. **159**

tropical rain forests Vast forests that have a great amount of rainfall and vegetation. **182**

troubadours Traveling singers who entertained people during the Middle Ages. **332**

Truman Doctrine Policy declaring that the United States must consider the continued spread of communism as a threat to democracy. **826**

Twelve Tribes of Israel Twelve sons of Abraham's grandson Jacob (Israel), from whom modern Jews trace their heritage. **44**

tyrants In ancient Greece, rulers who seized power by force but who ruled with the people's support; later came to refer to rulers who exercise brutal and oppressive power. **112**

U-boats German submarines used in World War I. **705**

ultimatum Demand in which one party threatens harmful action to another party if the other party rejects its proposals. **701**

"unequal" treaties Trade treaties

that China signed under pressure of invasion, giving Western powers trade benefits. **419**

unions Associations of workers that combine forces and demands of different workers. **563**

United Nations Organization of nations to keep peace through collective security arrangements. **821**

Universal Declaration of Human Rights Document adopted by the United Nations in 1948 that outlined the basic human rights every person should have. **990**

universal manhood suffrage Policy that every adult male could vote, whether he owned property or not. **517**

Upanishads Written explanations of the Vedic religion. **60**

urbanization Migration from the countryside to the city. **988**

usury (yoo·zhuh·ree) Policy of charging high interest on loans. **326**

utilitarianism Belief that a law was useful if it led to "the greatest happiness of the greatest number" of people. **561**

utopian socialists Persons who believe that people can live at peace with each other if they live in small cooperative settlements, owning all of the means of production in common and sharing the products. **565**

Vandals One of a group of Germanic tribes who invaded and destroyed territory in the Roman Empire. **174**

varnas Social classes in Indian society. **61**

vassal Person granted land from a lord in return for services. **294**

V-E Day May 8, 1945, the day of Allied victory in Europe in World War II. **807**

Vedas Great literature of the Indo-Aryan religion. **56**

Vedic Age Period of India's history from 1500 B.C. to 1000 B.C. **56**

vernacular languages Everyday speech that varies from place to place. **331**

veto Refuse to approve, as in a bill or law. **152**

veto power Power to defeat a measure with one single vote. **823**

viceroys Spanish officials who represented the monarchy in Spain's colonial empire. **401**

Vietnamization Process of preparing the South Vietnamese to take over the fighting of the Vietnam War to allow for the withdrawing of U.S. troops. **940**

Vikings Germanic people from Scandinavia who often raided western Europe during the A.D. 800s and 900s. **292**

V-J Day September 2, 1945, the day the Japanese surrendered to the United States in World War II. **808**

vulcanization Process of treating rubber to make it more useful. **547**

Wafd Party Egyptian nationalist party that led a revolt against the British in 1919. **758**

Wannsee Conference Meeting of German officials to plan for systematically exterminating Jews. **801**

war of attrition Slow wearing-down manner of warfare in which each side tries to outlast the other. **709**

War of the Roses War between the York and Lancaster families of England in 1455. **337**

War of the Spanish Succession War in which European countries battled Louis XIV to avoid Bourbon rule in both France and Spain. **457**

Warsaw Pact Mutual defense agreement between the Soviet Union and countries of the Eastern bloc. **830**

Watergate scandal The break-in at the Democratic National Committee headquarters in 1972 that led to President Nixon's resignation. **941**

weapons of mass destruction Nuclear, chemical, and biological weapons of great power. **944**

welfare state State in which the government undertakes primary responsibility for the social welfare of its citizens. **832**

Whigs Political party in England that rebelled against the monarchy, wanted a strong Parliament, and opposed having a Catholic ruler. **484**

White Lotus Rebellion Peasant rebellion against the Qing dynasty led by the Buddhist cult known as the White Lotus Society. **416**

"White Man's Burden, The" Poem by Rudyard Kipling that expressed the European attitude toward non-Western people during the imperialist era. **664**

World Court Permanent Court of International Justice, located at The Hague in the Netherlands. **722**

World Trade Center New York City office complex that was struck by a devastating terrorist attack on September 11, 2001. **964**

Xia Line of kings ruling over a late Neolithic people in the Huang River region of China starting in about 2000 B.C. **80**

yang Force that is male, bright, and active; part of the Chinese belief of dualism or balance in life. **89**

Yi Korean dynasty founded in 1392 when Koreans drove out the Mongols; lasted until Korea was annexed by Japan in 1910. **281**

yin Force that is female, dark, and passive; part of the Chinese belief of dualism or balance in life. **89**

Young Italy movement Group of Italian patriots dedicated to spreading ideas of nationalism. **632**

zaibatsu Huge industrial firms controlled by powerful families in Japan. **860**

Zen Sect of Buddhism that stresses meditation as a means of enlightenment. **269**

Zhou People who overthrew the Shang dynasty of China in 1122 B.C. **83**

ziggurats Sumerian temples made of sun-dried brick. **32**

Zionism Nationalist movement to build a homeland for the Jews in Palestine. **760**

Zollverein Customs union of most German states in 1834. **638**

Glosario

Este GLOSARIO contiene muchos de los términos que necesitas entender cuando estudias la historia mundial. Cada palabra tiene una breve definición o explicación de su significado, según su uso en historia mundial. El número entre paréntesis al lado de cada definición, se refiere al número de página en la cual esa palabra está marcada en el libro de texto.

A

abbess/abadesa Dirigente de un convento, quien ejerce un rol similar al de un abad. **302**

abbot/abad Dirigente de un monasterio, quien controla y distrubuye la propiedad. **302**

Aborigines/Aborígenes Habitantes originarios de Australia. **608**

abstract expressionism/expresionismo abstracto Estilo de pintura a partir de 1945 que envuelve la expresión personal del artista. **968**

acid rain/lluvia ácida Lluvia que contiene toxinas producidas por el consumo de petróleos fósiles. **982**

acropolis/acrópolis Monte o montaña en Grecia, que incluye un fuerte, así como también templos y otros edificios públicos. **109**

Acropolis/Acrópolis Monte alto que marcó el centro de la antigua Atenas. **130**

acupuncture/acupunctura Práctica medicinal china que consiste en insertar agujas en ciertas partes del cuerpo. **95**

adobe/adobe Ladrillo de barro secado al aire, usado para la construcción por los Pueblos Indígenas. **205**

aerodynamics/aerodinámica Principios científicos que regulan el movimiento de aire alrededor de los objetos. **575**

Afrikaans/Afrikaans Aficaans. Lenguaje de los Bóers en Sudáfrica. **673**

agora/ágora Plaza pública en las ciudades griegas. **109**

agriculture/agricultura Cultivo y cosecha de alimentos. **9**

Allied Powers/potencias aliados Gran Bretaña, Francia, Rusia, y otros aliados que lucharon unidos durante la Primera Guerra Mundial. **705**

almanacs/almanaques Libros que pronostican el tiempo y las probabilidades de creci-miento de los cultivos, y también contienen cosas como calendarios, mapas, y consejos médicos. **375**

Alpha/Alfa Primer estación espacial internacional, nombrada en noviembre del 2000. **977**

Analects/Analectas, Las Colección de ideas y enseñanzas de Confucio. **90**

anarchists/anarquistas Extremistas políticos que se oponen al gobierno. **619**

Anglo-Egyptian Treaty/Tratado Anglo-Egipcio tratado entre Egipto e Inglaterra que le entregó a Egipto una mayor independencia, en 1936. **758**

animism/animismo Creencia de que los espíritus habitan todas las cosas. **82**

antibiotics/antibióticos Substancias que pueden matar o limitar el crecimiento de bacterias. **980**

antisepsis/antisepsia Uso de químicos que destruyen los microbios que causan enfermedades infecciosas. **579**

apartheid/apartheid Política de gobierno, de segregación y explotación económica en Sudáfrica. **884**

appeasement/pacificación Política que intentar evitar guerras, por medio de la aceptación de algunas de las demandas del atacante. **787**

apprentice/aprendiz El que aprende alguna destreza de su maestro. **328**

aqueducts/acueductos Construcciones para la conducción de agua. **166**

arch/arco Estructura curva que está sobre una entrada. **32**

archons/arcontes Dirigentes en la antigua Grecia, que servían durante períodos de un año. **115**

aristocracies/aristocracias Ciudades griegas controladas por nobles. **111**

aristocracy/aristocracia Gobierno controlado por la clase alta. **134**

armistice/armisticio Acuerdo firmado por países en guerra para detener su lucha. **715**

Articles of Confederation/Artículos de la Confederación Plan ratificado por los estados Americanos en 1781, que establece un gobierno central con un solo Congreso en el cual cada estado tiene un voto. **502**

artifacts/artefactos Objetos fabricados y utilizados por los primeros humanos. **6**

artisans/artesano Los que trabajan alguna técnica o arte manual. **12**

ASEAN/ASEAN Asociación de Naciones Sudasiáticas. Organización formada para promover el crecimiento economico. **872**

Ashikaga/Ashikaga Familias de shogunes quienes gobernaron Japón durante cerca de 250 años. **280**

assimiliation/asimilación Proceso en el cual una persona renuncia a su propia cultura y adopta una cultura diferente **674**

astrolabe/astrolabio Instrumento usado para calcular la latitud, por medio de la observación de estrellas. **251**

Atlantic Charter/Carta del Atlántico Declaración creada por Winston Churchill y Franklin Roosevelt que declaró las intenciones de sus dos países en 1941 **795**

atrocities/atrocidades Crímenes brutales de guerra, cometidos a menudo contra los ciudadanos. **710**

Auschwitz/Auschwitz Campo de concentración nazi donde las personas eran asesinadas sistemáticamente. **802**

autocracy/autocracia Gobierno en el cual la persona al mando tiene el poder absoluto. **86**

autocrat/autócrata Dirigente con el poder absoluto. **648**

Awami League/Liga Awami partido político dedicado a la independencia de Pakistan del Este. **850**

Axis Powers/potencias del Eje Eje Roma-Berlín. Alianza entre Alemania, Italia, y Japón. **786**

Aztec/Aztecas Guerreros viajantes quienes gradualmente llegaron a gobernar el centro de México. **210**

B

Babylonian Captivity/Cautiverio Babilónico Años durante los cuales El Papa vivió en Avignon, Francia, en lugar de Roma, Italia. (1309–1377) **342**

balance of power/balance de poder Principio en el cual los países tienen igualdad de fuerza para prevenir que un país trate de dominar a los otros. **457**

Balfour Declaration/Declaración Balfour Declaración escrita por el Ministro Británico de Asuntos Exteriores a un líder Sionista en Palestina. **760**

Balkan "powder keg"/Balkan "powder keg" Estado de desasosiego en los Balcanes que provocó el asesinato del heredero del imperio Austro-Húngaro e inició la guerra (I Guerra Mundial). **701**

Balkan League/Guerra de los Balcanes Las naciones Balcánicas de Bulgaria, Servia, Grecia, y Montenegro que declararon la guerra en el Imperio Otomano. **657**

Bantu/Bantú Familia de lenguas africanas. Relativo bantúes, pueblos del centro y sur de África. **184**

barter/trueque Intercambio de un bien y servicio por otro. **43**

barter economy/economía de trueque Economía basada en el intercambio de bienes y servicios, sin usar dinero. **325**

Bataan Death March/Marcha de la Muerte Marcha impuesta por los japoneses a los prisioneros de guerra en las Filipinas, en 1942. **809**

Battle of Britain/Batalla de Inglaterra Enfrentamientos aéreos entre la aviación británica y la alemana en 1940 y 1941. **794**

Battle of Marathon/Batalla de Maratón Batalla durante la guerra persa, cuando Persia invadió Grecia. **121**

Battle of Midway/Batalla de Midway Importante batalla en la cual los Norteamericanos derrotaron a los Japoneses en 1942. La victoria soviética debilitó grandemente las fueras germanas. **805**

Battle of Stalingrad/Batalla de Stalingrado Batalla entre alemanes y soviéticos en Stalingrado, en el verano de 1942 **804**

Battle of Thermopylae/Batalla de Termópilas Batalla durante las Guerras Persas en la cual un reducido ejército espartano peleó hasta la muerte contra fuerzas persas mucho más grandes que ellos. **121**

Beats/Beats Pertenecientes a la Generación Beat. Grupo de escritores que en los años de la Post-Guerra (Segunda Guerra Mundial) criticaban a los ciudadanos ricos y sus valores. **973**

bedouins/beduinos Árabes nómadas del desierto, que llevan manadas de camellos y ovejas. **240**

belligerents/beligerantes Naciones en guerra. **702**

Beringia/Estrecho de Bering Camino o puente que permitía el paso entre Asia y América durante la Edad de Hielo. **200**

Berlin Airlift/Ayuda aéreade Berlín Sistema de aerotransporte de los Estados Unidos e Inglaterra, de arrojar comida y otros víveres desde el aire, en el sector occidental de Berlín. **828**

Berlin Wall/Muro de Berlín Muro construido para separar el este del oeste de Berlín, para prevenir que los alemanes del este escaparan al oeste de Berlín. **832**

Bhagavad Gita/Bhagavad Gita Últimos 18 capítulos del Mahabharata, que enfatizan la idea de conducta apropiada según la posición o status de uno. **60**

Bill of Rights/Carta de Derechos Diez enmiendas o modificaciones de la Constitución de los Estados Unidos, que protegen la libertad y los derechos de los individuos. **503**

biodiversity/biodiversidad Variedad de plantas y animales que se dá naturalmente en el ambiente. **982**

biological sciences/ciencias biológicas Ciencias que estudian a los organismos vivientes,como la biología y la genética. **576**

bishops/obispo Dirigente de la Iglesia Católica en una ciudad importante. **171**

Black Death/muerte negra Terrible plaga que devastó Europa a principios de 1347 **330**

Black Shirts/camisas negras Fascistas que dirigieron una violenta campaña contra sus oponentes. **744**

Black Tuesday/martes negro 29 de octubre de 1929, cuando inversionistas de valores se lanzaron a vender sus acciones y esto tuvo como resultado un gran colapso financiero. **735**

blitzkrieg/blitzkrieg Guerra Relámpago que tiene lugar con una gran fuerza y velocidad, empleado por los alemanes durante la Segunda Guerra Mundial. **791**

"Bloody Mary"/"Bloody Mary" Sobrenombre utilizado para Mary I de Inglaterra. **470**

bobbies/bobbies Apodo que recibe la policía de Londres. **588**

Boers/Bóers Sudafricanos de origen holandés. **673**

Boer War/Guerra Bóer Guerra entre los Bóers y los británicos por el control en Transvaal en 1899 **673**

Bolsheviks/bolcheviques Facción radical de Rusia dirigida por Lenin, que ganaron el control contra los Mencheviques. **712**

bourgeoisie/burguesía Clase media urbana, que incluye comerciantes, industriales y profesionales. **509**

Boxer Rebellion/Rebelión de los Bóxers Levantamiento en China en el cual fueron atacadas personas ajenas a esta sociedad secreta y todo lo conectado con ajenos fué destruido. **765**

boyars/boyardos Nobles que aconsejaban al príncipe en cada ciudad Kievan. **231**

Brahmins/Brahmins Sacerdote especial de la sociedad Indoaria, quien sabía las formas y reglas apropiadas de sus complicados rituales religiosos. **57**

Brezhnev Doctrine/Doctrina Brezhnev Doctrina que establece que la Unión Soviética puede intervenir cuando alguna de las naciones satélites parece estar alejándose del comunismo. **956**

broadsides/broadsides Hojas de papel impreso con noticias, vendidos al público. **375**

buffalo/búfalo Animal que andaba en las Grandes Planicies de los Estados Unidos, y eran cazados por la gente de las planicies. **205**

Bundesrat/Bundesrat Cámara legislativa de Alemania. **642**

bureaucracy/burocracia Gobierno organizado en dife-rentes niveles y tareas. **81**

burgesses/burgueses Mercaderes y profesionales de pueblos y ciudades. **472**

Bushido/Bushido Código de conducta del samurai, que enfatiza valentía, lealtad y honor. **280**

business cycle/ciclo comercial Ciclo de los negocios. Períodos alternos de prosperidad y declinamiento **558**

cabinet/gabinete Cabecillas de los departamentos de gobierno, quienes aconsejan al jefe de Estado. **488**

caliph/califa Título que significa "sucesor del Profeta" usado en el gobierdo y religión de la sociedad Islámica. **243**

calligraphy/caligrafía Arte de escritura china. **83**

Camp David Accords/Acuerdos de Campo David Acuerdo de paz entre Egipto e Israel, mediadas por los Estados Unidos. **899**

canon law/ley canónica Código de derecho de la Iglesia Católica. **302**

capital/capital Dinero ganado, ahorrado e invertido para conseguir ganancias. **326**

capitalism/capitalismo Sistema económico en el cual los individuos, en vez del gobierno, son quienes controlan los factores de la producción. **555**

caravans/caravanas Grupos de personas que por seguridad viajaban juntos, recorriendo largas distancias. **29**

Carbonari/Carbonari Sociedad secreta de italianos nacionalistas, a principios de los años 1800. **632**

cardinals/cardenales Rangos oficiales de la Iglesia Católica, que siguen detrás del Papa. **301**

Carolingians/Carolingios Dinastía relativa a Carlomagno, establecida con la coronación de Pipino III como"rey por la gracia de Dios" desde el 751 D.C. **289**

cartels/carteles Combinaciones corporativas que controlan industrias enteras. **557**

Carter Doctrine/Doctrina de Carter Declaración que establece que los Estados Unidos vigilaría cualquier intento de fuerzas ajenas por controlar el Golfo Pérsico, como un asalto a los intereses de Estados Unidos. **944**

caste system/sistema de castas Compleja forma de organización social que comienza a tomar forma después de la migración Indoaria. **61**

Cavaliers/Cavaliers Partidarios del Rey Carlos I en la Guerra Civil Inglesa; también conocidos como "monárquicos". **480**

censors/censores Oficiales romanos que registraban a los ciudadanos de acuerdo con su fortuna. **152**

Central Powers/potencias centrales Alianza entre Alemania, Austria-Hungría, Bulgaria,y el Imperio Otomano, en la Primera Guerra Mundial. **704**

Chavín/Chavín Primeros habitantes andinos en Suramérica. **209**

checks and balances/revisión y balance
Sistema de gobierno que impide que
alguna parte del gobierno se convierta
demasiado poderosa. **152**

Children's Crusade/Cruzada de los Niños
Efímera cruzada en 1212, donde jóvenes
de Europa marcharon en la Tierra Santa
para recuperar el Cristianismo. **321**

chinampas/chinampas Terrenos levantados
construidos por los Aztecas, hechos con
barro tomado del fondo de los lagos. **210**

chivalry/Caballería Código o sistema
medieval de caballería. **298**

citadel/ciudadela Fortaleza central en una
ciudad. **53**

city-state/ciudad-estado Forma de gobierno que incluye una ciudad o pueblo,
y las áreas que la rodean y que son
controladas por ella. **32**

civil service/servicio civil Sistema centralizado que se encarga de los asuntos del
gobierno día a día. **87**

civilization/civilización Cultura compleja
que puede producir un excedente de
comida, establecer grandes poblaciones
con un gobierno, y tener personas que
realizan diferentes labores. **11**

cloning/clonación Proceso de hacer una
copia genéticamente idéntica, a partir de
una célula animal **986**

coalitions/coaliciones Grupos políticos
organizados para apoyar una causa
común. **620**

Cold War/guerra fría Sospecha y hostilidad
entre las naciones comunistas y las
naciones occidentales democráticas, que
se libró primordialmente, usando medios
políticos y económicos, en lugar de
armas. **825**

collaborators/colaboradores Personas
dispuestas a ayudar a los enemigos de
su nación. **791**

collective bargaining/pacto colectivo
proceso de negociación entre dirigentes
y representantes sindicales. **563**

collective farms/fincas colectivas Tierras
mancomunadas en grandes fincas, donde
las personas trabajan juntas como un
grupo. **749**

Columbia/Columbia Nave espacial usada
para el viaje de la primera misión de los
Estados Unidos a la luna. **976**

**Columbian Exchange/intercambio
colonista** Intercambio masivo de bienes,
plantas, animales, y enfermedades, que
tuvo lugar entre los hemisferios Oriente
y Occidente, que siguieron a los viajes
de Colón. **394**

Cominform/Cominform Oficina de Información Comunista establecido por los Soviéticos para oponerse al Plan Marcial. **827**

Comintern/Comintern Comunismo Internacional,una organización fundada por
Lenín para esparcir la revolución comunista alrededor del mundo. **753**

command economy/economía de mando
Economía en la cual el gobierno controla
todas las decisiones económicas. **750**

**commercial capitalism/capitalismo com-
ercial** Sistema económico temprano,
en el cual la mayoría de los capitalistas
eran comerciantes que compraban y
vendían bienes. **555**

**Commercial Revolution/Revolución Com-
ercial** Época entre 1400 y 1750 cuando
los europeos hicieron cambios mayores
a sus economías debido a las nuevas
exploraciones. **389**

commodities/mercancías Bienes que
tienen valor, especialmente relacionados
con economías de trueque. **43**

common law/ley común Ley basada en las
costumbres y decisiones de jueces, en
vez de lo escrito en los códigos. **307**

Common Market/Mercado Común
Llamado oficialmente la Comunidad
Económica Europea, una organización
de seis naciones de Europa Occidental,
establecida en 1957 para la cooperación
económica internacional. **834**

commonwealth/república Régimen político
en Inglaterra. Forma de gobierno. **480**

**Commonwealth of Independent
States/Comunidad de Estados Inde-
pendientes** (CIS) Sistema establecido
para coordinar políticas económicas y de
defensa para las nuevas repúblicas inde-
pendientes, después de la ruptura de la
Unión Soviética. **959**

Communards/Comuneros Miembros del
concejo local en París quienes querían
un gobierno decentralizado, separando
la Iglesia del Estado, y otras reformas
socialistas. **619**

communism/comunismo Sistema
económico y político en el cual los gob-
iernos poseen los medios de produccción
y controlan el planeamiento de la
economía. **566**

Communist Party/Partido Comunista
Nombre nuevo de los rusos Bolcheviques,
que disolvieron la asamblea constitucional en 1918. **713**

compass/brújula Instrumento de nave-
gación creado en 1930, que utiliza una
pieza de metal magnetizada que apunta
al norte. **388**

conceptual art/arte conceptual Estilo de
arte en el cual el acto de crear arte es
más importante que el mismo objeto
artístico. **969**

Concordat/Concordato Acuerdo entre
Napoleón y el Papa, reconociendo al
Catolicismo como la religión de la may-
oría de los ciudadanos franceses. **524**

conscription/reclutamiento Reclutamiento
militar. **518**

conservatives/conservadores Grupo que
no desea cambiar las condiciones exis-
tentes. **515**

constitution/constitución Documento que
contiene las leyes y principios básicos
que gobiernan una nación. **481**

consulates/consulados Oficinas diplomáti-
cas en el extranjero, dirigidas por un
cónsul. **427**

consuls/cónsul Jefes ejecutivos elegidos para
dirigir el gobierno en la antigua Roma. **152**

**Contadora Principles/Principios de Con-
tadora** Acuerdo promoviendo negociaciones en lugar de violencia, como una
manera de apaciguar conflictos regionales
en América Latina. **921**

containment/contención Política de con-
tención, dedicada a restringir la expansión
del comunismo. **827**

contraband/contrabando Materiales béli-
cos suplidos por una nación neutral a una
nación beligerante. **710**

contras/contras Grupos que buscan sustituir
el gobierno Sandinista en Nicaragua. **919**

**Convention on the Rights of the
Child/Declaración de los Derechos
del Niño** Acuerdo de las Naciones
Unidas, en 1989, que apunta las directri-
ces legales, sociales y económicas que
cada país debe seguir para proteger a
los niños y las niñas. **993**

corporations/corporaciones Negocios en
crecimiento desde los años 1800, que
permiten a la gente comprar acciones en
una compañía. **557**

corporatist state/estado corporativo
Nación en la cual la mayor parte de las
actividades económicas, como la agricultura, transporte, industria y comercio,
están organizadas en sindicatos similares
a las corporaciones. **745**

Council of Trent/Concilio de Trento
Reunión de líderes de la Iglesia en los años
1500, para definir claramente las doctrinas
católicas para la Contrareforma. **369**

Counter-Reformation/Contrareforma
Intento de la Iglesia Católica, luego de la
Reforma, por devolver a la Iglesia a un
énfasis en asuntos espirituales. **368**

**counterrevolutionary/contrarrevolu-
cionario** Actividades en contra de una
revolución,organizadas por los que
apoyan el Viejo Régimen. **518**

coup d'état/coup d'état Toma de poder
por la fuerza; en francés, un "ataque al
Estado". **522**

covenant/alianza Acuerdo solemne. **45**

craft guilds/gremios de artesanos Asociación de trabajadores manuales para
establecer las condiciones de trabajo. **328**

creoles/creoles Personas caucásicas nacidas
en colonias españolas o portuguesas. **622**

Crimean War/Guerra de Crimea Guerra
declarada por Francia, Gran Bretaña y el
Imperio Otomano, contra Rusia. **617**

Cro-Magnons/Cromañones Grupo de los
primeros hombres aparecidos hace cerca
de 35,000, en Europa. **8**

crop rotation/rotación de cultivos La práctica de alternar cultivos de diferentes tipos, para preservar la tierra fértil. **544**

Crusades/Cruzadas Expediciones hechas por los cristianos para recuperar la Tierra Santa de los musulmanes. **318**

Cuban missile crisis/Crisis de los misiles Cuba Situación durante la Guerra Fría en la cual la Unión Soviética construyó zonas de misiles nucleares en Cuba. **840**

cubism/cubismo Estilo artístico que enfatiza diseños geométricos, usando formas como cubos, superficies planas y esferas. **731**

cultural diffusion/difusión cultural Expansión de una cultura de un área del mundo a otra. **12**

Cultural Revolution/Revolución Cultural Intento violento de un cambio social en China, encabezado por Mao Zedong en 1966. **854**

culture/cultura Creencias, conocimiento, y patrones de vida, que un grupo de personas adquiere al vivir juntas. **6**

cuneiform/cuneiforme Escritura sumeria en forma de cuñas. **31**

curia/curia Grupo de consejeros del Papa, llevados desde los más altos rangos del clero. **301**

czar/zar Título tomado por Iván el Terrible; pala-bra rusa para "caesar" o "césar". **234**

dadaists/dadaístas Grupo de artistas que usaban imágenes al azar para reflejar lo que ellos consideraban la insensatez de la guerra. **731**

daimyo/daimyo señores o amos feudales en Japón. **282**

Dao De Jing/Dao de Jing Compilación de las enseñanzas de Laozi en el Daoismo. **91**

Dayton Accord/Acuerdo de Daytona Acuerdo mediado por los Estados Unidos, mediante el cual se le otorga a los Bosnios–Serbios un grado de autonomía y a la vez se reconoce la soberanía del gobierno de Mahoma. **961**

D-Day/día D 6 de junio, 1944, el día que las tropas aliadas iniciaron la invasión de la costa de Normandía. **805**

Delian League/Liga Delian Alianza de ciudades y estados en la antigua Grecia, con Atenas como líder. **123**

democracy/democracia Gobierno en el cual los ciudadanos forman parte de él. **112**

democratic socialism/socialdemocracia Sistema político en el cual el gobierno toma posesión pacíficamente de los bienes de producción, la gente conserva los derechos humanos básicos y control parcial de la economía. Tránsito del capitalismo al socialismo por medio de reformas graduales. **567**

departments/departamentos Distritos administrativos en Francia. **513**

dependent colonies/colonias dependientes Colonias en las que unos pocos oficiales de un país (generalmente europeo), gobierna o dirige a otro país no-europeo. **662**

depression/depresión Período en el cual la poca demanda de bienes causa que la economía de un país se hunda. **558**

desaparecidos/desaparecidos Desaparecidos en Argentina, quienes criticaron el gobierno, y fueron asesinados por la campaña del gobierno militar. **931**

desertification/desertificación Expansión del desierto. **889**

détente/détente Era de mejorías de las relaciones Soviético-Americanas. **944**

DEW Line/DEW límite Radares instalados por los Estados Unidos y Canadá, que advierte sobre ataques aéreos. **841**

dialects/dialectos Variaciones de un lenguaje. **82**

Diamond Sutra/Diamond Sutra Primer libro impreso del mundo, un texto Budista producido en China en el año 868 A.C. **272**

dictator/dictador Gobernante absoluto. **151**

Diet/Dieta Cámaras legislativas en Japón. **676**

dikes/diques Muros de tierra construidos a lo largo de un río para evitar innundaciones. **78**

Diplomatic Revolution/Revolución Diplomática Transformación de alianzas en Europa a mediados de los años 1700. **467**

direct democracy/democracia directa Forma de democracia en la que todos los ciudadanos participan directamente en la toma de decisiones. **117**

dissidents/disidentes Personas que no están de acuerdo con el gobierno. **924**

divine right of kings/derechos divinos de los reyes Creencia de que Dios elige a los reyes que reinarán una nación. **456**

division of labor/división de labores Característica de las civilizaciones en la cual diferentes personas realizan diferentes trabajos. **12**

DNA/ADN Ácido desoxirribonucléico, pequeñas unidades de cromosomas que transportan características de padre a hijo. **980**

domestic system/sistema doméstico Método de producción que tiene lugar en la casa del trabajador, y no en una tienda o fábrica. **325**

domestication/domesticación Amansar animales como cabras, ovejas y cerdos. **9**

domino theory/teoría dominó Idea de que si un país cae en el comunismo, los países que lo rodean, eventualmente caerán en él. **867**

dowry/dote Dinero y bienes que una esposa brinda al matrimonio. **222**

dramas/dramas Piezas o representaciones de teatro que contienen acciones y diálogos y que usualmente involucran conflicto y emoción. **136**

Duma/Duma Parlamento elegido por Rusia. **652**

dynamo/dínamo Generador eléctrico. **572**

dynasty/dinastía Familia de gobernantes que reinan en forma hereditaria. **22**

Easter Rising/Rebelión del Este 24 de abril de 1916, cuando nacionalistas irlandeses se rebelaron en contra de los británicos. **740**

economic nationalism/nacionalismo económico Política económica que usa una nación para tratar de mejorar su economía, por medio de limites en el comercio. **734**

economic sanctions/sanciones económicas Negativa de co-merciar con una nación ofensiva. **723**

Emancipation Edict/Edicto de Emancipación Proclamación del Zar Alexander en 1861 que liberó a los siervos rusos. **648**

Emancipation Proclamation/Proclamación de Emancipación Decreto emitido por el presidente Abraham Lincoln en 1863 que acabó efectivamente con la esclavitud, a final de la Guerra Civil. **611**

emigrations/emigraciones Personas que se alejan de su tierra natal **586**

émigrés/émigrés Nobles que dejaron Francia durante la Revolución **513**

empire/imperio Forma de gobierno que une dife-rentes territorios y poblaciones, bajo el mando de un mismo gobernante. **24**

enclosure movement/movimiento de encercamiento Práctica de cercar territorios comunes y convertirlas en propiedades individuales. **544**

Encyclopedia, The/Enciclopedia, La Libro de referencia de las ideas de la Ilustración. **494**

English Bill of Rights/Cesión Inglesa de Derechos Documento en 1689 que declaró los poderes del Parlamento y protegía a los ciudadanos particulares. **485**

enlightened despotism/despotismo ilustrado Sistema de gobierno en el cual un monarca absoluto dirigía de acuerdo con la Ilustración o Iluminación. **496**

Enlightenment/Ilustración Período en los años 1700, cuando los filósofos creían que podían aplicar el método científico y el uso de la razón para explicar de manera lógica la naturaleza humana. **494**

ephors/éforos Cada uno de los cinco magistrados que elegía el pueblo todos los años en Esparta. **114**

epics/épicas Largos poemas basados en temas históricos o religiosos. **60**

equites/équites Clase de gente de negocios y dueños de propiedades que tenían el poder en la Antigua Roma. **157**

ethical monotheism/monoteísmo ético Religión que cree en un sólo Dios, y enfatiza la ética. **47**

ethics/ética Estudio de lo que es bueno y malo, y del deber moral. **120**

ethnic cleansing/limpieza étnica Campaña de terror y muerte que intentaba sacar ciertos grupos étnicos de una región. **961**

European Community/Comunidad Europea Organización multinacional europea, con sede en Bélgica. **835**

evolution/evolución Creencia de que los organismos se desarrollan y cambian a través del tiempo. **577**

excommunication/excomulgación Edicto oficial que expulsa a una persona como miembro de la Iglesia. **226**

executive branch/poder ejecutivo Sección administrativa de gobierno, que refuerza las leyes, y está encabezado por el presidente. **502**

Exodus/éxodo Escape de los hebreos de Egipto. **44**

export/exportación Bienes y servicios vendidos a otro país. **118**

extraterritoriality/inmunidad Exoneración de extranjeros de las leyes del país en el cual viven o trabajan. **419**

factors of production/factores de producción Recursos básicos para la industrialización, tales como tierra necesaria, capital y mano de obra. **545**

factory system/sistema de factoría Producción de bienes en una fábrica, utilizando maquinaria y un gran número de trabajadores. **546**

Falange/Falange Partido fascista español **784**

fascism/fascismo Doctrina gubernamental que se basa en reglas dictatoriales y en un régimen totalitario, en el cual el Estado mantiene control rígido de la población, por medio de la fuerza y de censura. **743**

Fashoda crisis/crisis Fachoda Conflicto entre Francia, Inglaterra y Sudán. **669**

favorable balance of trade/balance favorable de comercio Situación favorable que existe cuando un país vende más bienes de los que compra. **390**

federal system of government/sistema de gobierno federal Sistema de gobierno en el cual el poder está dividido entre un poder central, uno federal, gobierno, y estados individuales. **502**

feudalism/feudalismo Sistema de gobierno local basado en la concesión de tierras como pago por lealtad, ayuda militar y otros servicios. **294**

fief/feudo Concesión de tierras de un amo a su vasayo. **294**

Final Solution/Solución Final Nombre dado al intento de los Nazis por destruir la población judía de Europa. **801**

Five Classics/Cinco Clásicos Textos usados para entrenar alumnos y servidores civiles en la antigua China. **94**

Five Good Emperors/Cinco Emperadores Buenos Cinco gobernantes que dirigieron Roma por casi 100 años durante la Pax Romana. **161**

Five-Year Plan/Planes Quinquenales Plan del gobierno de Stalin para el crecimiento económico durante los años 1920. **750**

flappers/agitadoras mujeres jóvenes que desafiaron las normas sociales en los 1920, usando cabello corto, y faldas cortas, y saliendo a clubes de jazz. **733**

Flemish school/escuela Flamenca Grupo de pintores que perfeccionaron la técnica de pintura sobre lienzo. **361**

Fourteen Points/Catorce Puntos Plan del Presidente Woodrow Wilson por un mundo justo basado en los objetivos de los Aliados por terminar la Primer Guerra Mundial. **714**

"Four Tigers"/"Cuatro Tigres" Korea del Sur, Taiwan, Singapur, y Hong Kong; llamados así por el fuete crecimiento de sus economías. **872**

Franco-Prussian War/guerra Francopprusiana Guerra entre Francia y Prusia, que terminó con la derrota de Francia en 1871 **640**

free enterprise/libre empresa Sistema en el cual las fuerzas económicas trabajan automática y naturalmente, sin leyes mercantilistas ni regulaciones. **560**

free trade/libre comercio Práctica basada en la creencia de que el gobierno no debe restringir o interferir con el comercio internacional. **418**

frescoes/frescos Pinturas en paredes y muros hechas con yeso mojado. **107**

Fujiwara/Fujiwara Primer familia en ganar control sobre el gobierno central en Japón, desde mediados de los años 800 hasta mediados de los 1100. **280**

functionalism/funcionalismo Estilo arquitectónico en el que un edificio es diseñado basado en su uso específico, y no en un estilo en particular. **731**

Gang of Four/bandade de los cuatro Grupo comunista radical de Madame Mao, que querían continuar con la revolución cultural China. **854**

genealogy/genealogía Récord de la historia de una familia. **93**

General Assembly/Asamblea General Colectivo de las Naciones Unidas, que consta de cualquier nación que desee unirse a él. **823**

general strike/huelga general Trabajadores de varias industrias, que se niegan a trabajar hasta que sus demandas sean cumplidas. **739**

genetic code/código genético Secuencia o cadena de información genética que determinan las características de cada vida humana. **980**

genetics/genética Estudio de cómo las características de plantas y animales sin nacer, son heredadas por sus descendientes. **577**

Geneva Accord/Convención de Ginebra Acuerdo firmado en 1954, que puso fin a la guerra colonial entre Francia e Indonesia. **867**

genocide/genocidio Exterminación sistemática de personas. **722**

gentry/alta burguesía Terratenientes en Inglaterra que tenían una buena posición social pero no tenían un título. **472**

geocentric theory/teoría geocéntrica Teoría de acuerdo con el pensador Helenístico Tolomeo, de que la Tierra es el centro del universo. **383**

German-Soviet nonaggression pact/pacto Germanosoviético de no agresión Acuerdo en 1939 dividiendo Europa del este en esferas de influencia. **789**

ghazis/ghazis Guerreros del Islam; soldados turcos quienes fueron los primeras Otomanos. **432**

gladiators/gladiadores Luchadores entrenados, usualmente esclavos, que peleaban en arenas para entretenimiento. **165**

glasnost/glásnost Política soviética de apertura bajo el cual el gobierno controla que la economía fuera desahogada y las restricciones en desacuerdo fueran disminuidas. **957**

Glorious Revolution/Revolución Gloriosa Traspaso de poder de Guillermo y María de Inglaterra en 1688. **484**

golden age/epoca dorada Era de progreso cultural en Grecia en los años 400 A.C. **130**

Golden Horde/Horda Dorada Nombre dado por los europeos a los invasores mongoles de 1200, debido al color dorado de sus tiendas. **273**

Good Neighbor Policy/Política del Buen Vecino Política esta dounidense durante los años 30, que promulga la cooperación entre las naciones de América Latina. **776**

Gothic/gótico Estilo arquitectónico de iglesias, caracterizado por arcos apuntados y la bóveda sobre crucería de ojivas. Este estilo fué desarrollado por los maestros constructores de mediados de los 1100. **334**

Goths/Godos Individuos de un antiguo pueblo germano, que se estableció en la desembocadura del Vístula en el siglo I A.C. **174**

Gracchi, the/Gracchi, los Dos hermanos, Tiberus y Gaius Gracchus, quienes vieron la necesidad de reforma en la República Romana. **158**

Grand Canal/Gran Canal Canal construido durante la dinastía Sui que unió el norte con el sur de China por primera vez. **266**

Great Depression/Gran Depresión Depresión mundial a principios de los años 1930, cuando los salarios cayeron, la actividad comercial bajó y hubo mucho desempleo. **735**

Great Elector/Gran Elector Sobrenombre dado a Frederick William, uno de los grandes gobernantes Hohenzollern. **466**

Great Leap Forward/Gran Salto Adelante Segundo Plan Quiquenal de Mao Zedong para China, en 1958, para acelerar el progreso. **853**

Great Schism/Gran Escisión Período de la historia de la Iglesia, de 1378 a 1417 cuando ésta fué dividida en dos grupos opuestos. **342**

Great Wall of China/Gran Muralla China Muro construido y expandido alrededor de China, construido por antiguos gobernantes para proteger a China de las invasiones. **86**

Greek fire/combustible Griego Líquido inflamable usado como arma por la marina bizantina. **224**

greenhouse effect/efecto invernadero Calentamiento de la superficie terrestre. **983**

Grimm brothers/hermanos Grimm Hermanos alemanes que publicaron una famosa colección de cuentos infantiles. **592**

guerilla warfare/guerrilla Técnica que cuenta de invasiones repentinas por parte de pequeñas bandas de soldados. **403**

habeas corpus/habeas corpus Derecho legal que protege a los individuos de un arresto arbitrario. **485**

Habsburg/Habsburg Poderosa familia de gobernantes europeos en los años 1200. **340**

haciendas/haciendas Largas fincas autosu-fucientes en América Española. **621**

Hagia Sophia/Hagia Sophia Iglesia deco-rativa Bizantina en Constantinopla. **227**

Han/Han Dinastía de gobernantes que dirigieron un imperio creciente y centralizado en China. **84**

heliocentric theory/teoría heliocentrista Teoría desarrollada por Copérnico, que dice que el Sol es el centro del universo. **383**

Hellenistic culture/cultura Helénica Cultura que mezcló ideas griegas con características de otras culturas de la región Mediterránea. **141**

helots/helots Pueblos conquistados del Peloponeso, que se convirtieron en la clase más baja de la sociedad Espartana. **113**

Helsinki Accords/Acuerdo Helsinki Serie de acuerdos en 1975 que dió a las naciones europeas nuevos esquemas de trabajo para la cooperación económica y tecnológica entre otros acuerdos democráticos. **953**

heresy/herejía Opinión que la Iglesia considera contra la fé católica. **226**

heretics/herejes Personas que negaban la veracidad de los principios de la Iglesia, o que predicaban creencias que la Iglesia no aprobaba. **302**

hieroglyphics/hieroglíficos Forma antigua de escritura, desarrollada por los habi-tantes del valle del Río Nilo, alrededor de los 3000 B.C. **22**

hijrah/hijrah Migración de Muhammad y sus seguidores en 622 D.C., marcando el primer año en el calendario Musulmán. **241**

Ho Chi Minh Trail/Sendero Ho Chi Minh Nombre de la. mas importante ruta de abastecimiento de Viet Cong, a través de Laos, del norte al sur de Vietnam. **868**

Hohokam/Hohokam Grupo de personas que habitaron en el suroeste de Estados Unidos, y que abandonaron sus comu-nidades en 1300 o 1400. **203**

Holocaust/Holocausto Eliminación sis-temática de los judíos en Europa, por parte de los Nazis. **803**

hominids/homínidos Primeras criaturas similares al hombre. **6**

Hopewell/Hopewell Grupo de personas asentados en el Valle de Ohio, aproxi-madamente entre los años 300 y 200 A.C. **207**

hoplites/hoplites Infantería griega fuerte-mente armada, que llevaban largas lan-zas, y peleaban formados en líneas muy estrechas. **112**

Huguenots/Hugonotes Franceses, entre ellos nobles de alto rango, que se con-virtieron al Calvinismo. **367**

humanists/humanistas Personas que se especializan en el estudio del Human-ismo. Este incluye gramática, historia, poesía y retórica. **355**

humanitarians/humanitarios Personas que trabajan para mejorar las condiciones de otros. **560**

Hundred Years' War/Guerra de los Cien Años Guerra entre Francia e Inglaterra por el trono francés, que continuó desde 1337 a 1435, e introdujo el uso de nuevas armas. **336**

Huns/Hunos Población nómada de Asia, que atacó el Imperio Romano. **175**

hunter-gatherers/cazadores-recolectores Pobladores tempranos que vivían de la caza. **10**

Hyksos/Hyksos Grupo de personas que lle-garon de Asia al antiguo Egipto, e introdu-jeron nuevas herramientas de guerra. **23**

icon/ícono Imagen sacra de Jesús, la Vírgen María, o de algún santo. **224**

Iconoclastic Controversy/Controversia Iconoclástica Debate entre oponentes y defensores de iconos en la Iglesia Bizantina. Uno de los motivos que llevó a la división de la Iglesia Cristiana en 1054. **226**

iconoclasts/iconoclastas Personas que se oponían al culto de las imagenes. **224**

Iliad/Iliada La gran épica de Homero, que cuenta la historia de la guerra Troyana. **110**

imams/imamíes Líderes espirituales, quienes de acuerdo con algunos musul-manes, son descendientes directos de Muhammad. **244**

imperialism/imperialismo Ambición de una nación poderosa por dominar los asuntos políticos, económicos y culturales de otra nación o región. **662**

import/importación Bienes y servicios comprados a otra nación. **118**

import substitution/sustitución de importaciones Política económica de reemplazar ciertos bienes importados con bienes fabricados por otra nación, producidos dentro del país. **911**

impressionists/impresionistas Grupo de pintores que desarrollaron un tipo de realismo, mediante el estudio de la luz y el color, para crear vívidas impresiones de personas y lugares. **596**

Inca/Inca Civilización en los Andes en América del Sur, que para fines de 1400 D.C., incluía gran parte de lo que hoy día es Perú, Ecuador, Bolivia y Chile. **211**

indemnity/indemnización Compensación pagada a una nación por algún daño causado a ella. **530**

Indo-Aryans/Indoarios Tribus Indo-Euro-peas que se mudaron gradualmente a la India, alrededor de 1750 D.C. **56**

indulgences/indulgencias Perdonar un castigo o pecado. **363**

industrial capitalism/capitalismo indus-trial Tipo de capita-lismo ocurrido durante la revolución Industrial, cuando los capitalistas estaban involucrados en la producción y manufactura de bienes, utilizando métodos mecanizados e indu-trializados de producción. **555**

Industrial Revolution/Revolución Indus-trial Cambios producidos a principios de los años 1700, cuando las maquinarias empezaban a hacer mucho del trabajo que las personas tenían que hacer antes. **545**

inflation/inflación Alza de precios causada por el decrecimiento del valor de la moneda. **172**

influenza pandemic/influenza pandémico Epidemia de este tipo de gripe, que mató 20 millones de personas alrededor del mundo, entre 1918 y 1919. **728**

inoculation/inoculación Práctica de infectar personas con una forma leve de enfer-medad, para protegerlos de padecimientos más serios. **71**

Inquisition/Inquisición Institución de la Iglesia Católica Romana que perseguía y eliminaba herejes y castigaba las herejías. **303**

Intendants/Intendentes Administradores regionales y representantes de la corona en las provincias de Francia. **455**

interchangeable parts/partes intercambiables Partes idénticas que pueden ser sustituidas entre ellas. **556**

interdict/interdicto Castigo de la Iglesia Católica de una región, que involucra la clausura de iglesias y la negación de sacramentos. **302**

International Brigades/Brigadas Internacionales Voluntarios antifascistas de Francia, Inglaterra y los Estados Unidos, que participaron en la Guerra Civil Española. **785**

international style/estilo internacional Estilo de arquitectura que incluye continuas extensiones de acero y vidrio. **732**

intifada/intifada Violento levantamiento de Palestinos en 1980 **900**

Iran-Contra affair/Asunto Irán-Contras Escándalo en el cual miembros del consejo de Ronald Reagan, vendían ilegalmente armas a Irán como intercambio por los rehenes. **941**

Irish Republican Army (IRA)/Ejército Republicano Irlandés Rama militar del grupo nacionalista irlandés Sinn Fein. **741**

irrigation/irrigación Sistema de diques y canales que transportan agua de una fuente a un campo de agricultura. **12**

Islam/islam Religión basada en las enseñanzas e ideas de Muhammad que comenzaron a expandirse a través de las tribus Árabes en los años 600 D.C. **241**

island hopping/salto de islas Estrategia militar de capturar solo ciertas islas de un país y saltar las otras. **805**

isolationists/aislacionistas Personas que creen que su propio país no debe involucrarse en relaciones con otras naciones, especialmente alianzas. **794**

Janissaries/Janissaries Tropa de soldados esclavos altamente entrenada por los sultanes Otomanos. **432**

jazz/jazz Nueva forma de música originada en los años 1920 entre los afroamericanos en Nueva Orleans. **731**

Jesuits/Jesuitas Orden de religiosos católicos fundada por Ignacio de Loyola en 1534. **369**

jihad/jihad Enseñanzas del Islam de defender la fé. **242**

joint-stock company/sociedad anónima Organización de negocios desarrollada durante la Revolución Comercial en la que sus dueños acumulan dinero con la venta de acciones en la compañía. **389**

journeyman/jornalero Trabajador especializado al que se le pagaba un salario. **328**

Judeo-Christian ethics/ética judaicocristiana Valores establecidos por los hebreos, que contribuyeron enormemente con la cultura Occidental. **47**

judicial branch/poder Judicial Sector del gobierno que interpreta y aplica las leyes. **502**

Julio-Claudian Emperors/Emperadores Julios-Claudios Parientes de César quienes gobernaron 54 años del Pax Romana, seguidos de la muerte de Augusto. **160**

jungle/jungla Espeso crecimiento de plantas encontrado en un bosque tropical lluvioso. **182**

Junkers/Junkers Grupo de terratenientes aristócratas quienes querían que se aboliera el pago de aranceles a principios de los años 1800. **638**

junks/juncos Grandes embarcaciones chinas. **412**

Justinian Code/Código de Justiniano Colección de leyes que formaban las bases de la ley Bizantina, en el imperio de Justiniano. **222**

kaiser/kaiser Título del emperador Alemán. **642**

kami/kami Dioses japoneses o espíritus naturales. **279**

Kellogg-Briand Pact/Pacto Kellogg-Briand Acuerdo hecho en 1928 entre los Estados Unidos y Francia, que hizo la guerra "ilegal". **782**

Khmer Rouge/Khmers Rojos Comunistas camboyanos que instauraron un régimen de terror, tomando el gobierno y realizaron un genocidio masivo de la población camboyana. **868**

kibbutz/kibbutz Finca colectiva en Israel. **893**

kizilbash/kizilbash Ejercito militar de los Safavids para luchar por el poder político. **436**

Kulturkampf/Kulturkampf Programa anticatólico ini-ciado por Bismarck en Alemania a finales de 1800. **643**

Kuomintang/Kuomintang Partido Nacionalista Chino que nació del deseo nacionalista de una reforma. **766**

laissez-faire/laissez-faire En francés "dejad hacer". Creencia de que el gobierno no debe interferir con las operaciones de negocios. **560**

laser/láser Aparato que concentra luz y la libera en un intenso rayo que viaja en línea recta. **985**

League of Nations/Liga de Naciones Organización mundial formada después de la Primer Guerra Mundial para mantener la paz. **716**

Legalism/Legalismo Escuela de filosofía china concerniente a la política. **91**

legislative branch/poder legislativo Área del gobierno que hace las leyes. **502**

legitimacy/legitimidad Principio que envuelve el restablecimiento de anteriores familias gobernantes a sus tronos. **529**

Lend-Lease Act/Ley de préstamos En 1941, legislación que permite a los Estados Unidos suplir materiales de guerra a crédito a Gran Bretaña. **794**

leveling/nivelación Política en la que el gobierno hace control de precios para equilibrar la economía cuando hay exceso o escasez en la producción. **87**

Liberal-Democratic Party/Partido Liberaldemócratico El mas poderoso partido político en Japón después de la Segunda Guerra Mundial, que controló el gobierno de 1950 a 1990. **862**

liberalism/liberalismo Movimiento político que cree en un gobierno representativo que defiende los derechos del individuo frente al Estado y la supresión de trabas a la actividad económica. **533**

limited constitutional monarchy/monarquía constitucional limitada Gobierno en el cual el monarca permanece a la cabeza del Estado pero el rey o reina son requeridos en el Parlamento. **489**

limited evidence/evidencia limitada Cuando los científicos cuentan con poca información o evidencia de artefactos, para hacer una conclusión adecuada o documentada. **6**

linguists/lingüistas Especialistas que estudian lenguas. **184**

Locarno Pact/Pacto de Locarno Número de tratados firmados por delegados de siete países de Europa, en Locarno, en 1925. **739**

loess/loes Suelo fértil de color amarillento. **78**

Long March/Gran Marcha Viaje de 6,000 millas hecho por los comunistas chinos para escapar de las Tropas Nacionalistas. **768**

Long Parliament/Parlamento Largo Parlamento Inglés seleccionado en 1640 y que entraban y salían de él por 20 años. **479**

Lost Generation/Generación Perdida Grupo de escritores americanos cuyos escritos reflejaba la experiencia de una generación que perdió los fundamentos de su moral durante la Primera Guerra Mundial. **729**

Loyalistas/Leales Colonistas americanos que se oponían a independización de Ingalterra. **498**

Luftwaffe/Luftwaffe Fuerza aérea Alemana en la segunda Guerra Mundial. **793**

M

Maastricht Treaty/Tratado Maastricht
Tratado que creó la Unión Europea. **955**

"MacArthur Constitution"/"Constitución MacArthur" Constitución impuesta por Estados Unidos, adoptada por Japón en 1947. **859**

Maginot Line/Línea Maginot Sistema defensivo francés, en la frontera con Alemania, construido entre 1927-1932. **738**

Magna Carta/Carta Magna Documento inglés que hizo de la ley un poder supremo y la convirtió en la piedra angular del gobierno constitucional. **306**

Magyars/Magyars Grupo nómada que invadió Europa; eventualmente se establecieron en lo que hoy día es Hungría. **292**

Maine/Maine Barco de guerra estadounidense, que explotó en el puerto de la Habana en 1868, y que sirvió a Estados Unidos para declararle la guerra a España. **683**

mandate/mandato Territorio bajo mandato, usualmente una colonia previa que sería administrada por el gobierno de otra nación. **723**

manorialism/sistema feudal Sistema económico durante la edad Media, desarrollado alrededor de fincas autosuficientes donde los dueños y los campesinos compartían la tierra. **297**

Maori/Maori Habitantes originarios de Nueva Zelanda. **608**

maquis/maqués Miembros de un movimiento encubiero de resistencia francés. **793**

market economy/economía de mercado Economía en la que la tierra, trabajo y capital, son controlados por personas individuales. **326**

market speculations/especulación de mercado Inversiones riegosas en el mercado de valores. **734**

Marshall Plan/Plan Marshall Programa de reconstrucción europea, adoptado en Estados Unidos en 1948. **827**

martyrs/mártires Personas que han padecido muerte, persecución o torturas por mantenerse fiel a sus ideas o creencias. **170**

mass production/producción en serie Sistema de producción de grandes cantidades de productos idénticos. **556**

matrilineal/materno Describe la forma de transmitir la propiedad, la herencia o el nombre por línea materna. **186**

Mau Mau/Mau Mau Organizanción Kikuyu que agitó una campaña de guerilla en contra de la presencia británica en Kenya. **881**

Maya/Maya Una de las más avazadas poblaciones de las Américas, que ocuparon gran parte la Península de Yucatán. **209**

maya/maya Mundo ilusorio de los sentidos, de acuerdo con el hinduismo. **61**

means of production/medios de producción Todo lo utilizado para producir e intercambiar bienes. **564**

mechanization/mecanización Uso de maquinaria automatizada para acelerar la producción. **546**

medieval/medieval Término que describe el período de la historia de Europa occidental, conocido como la Edad Media. **288**

Meech Lake Accord/Acuerdo de Meech Lake Acuerdo fallido entre líderes canadienses de aceptar a Québéc como una "sociedad distinta". **946**

Meiji Restoration/Restablecimiento de Meiji Cambio cuando un grupo de samurai derrocó el shogunato Tokugawa y restableció el emperador al poder. **676**

Mensheviks/Mencheviques Facción moderada rusa que luchó por el poder a principios de los 1900. **712**

mercantilism/mercantilismo Sistema económico vigente en los siglos XVII y XVIII que atiende en primer término al desarrollo del comercio con intervención del Estado, y que considera la posesión de metales preciosos como signo de riqueza. **390, 493**

merchant guild/gremio mercantilista Asociación de mercaderes y trabajadores, para proteger sus derechos de comerciar y para ayudar a los miembros de su familia. **327**

Merovingians/Merovingios Dinastía de los primeros reyes de Francia. Clodoveo, hijo de Meroveo extendió sus dominios a casi toda la Galia. **288**

mestizos/mestizos Pesonas descendientes de amerindios y europeos. **622**

metics/meticos Personas que vivían en Atenas pero no eran ciudadanos atenienses, que podían trabajar y pagaban impuestos, pero no tenían derecho de poseer tierra propia ni a formar parte del gobierno. **115**

Middle Ages/edad media Período de la historia occidental de Europa, comprendido entre la caída del Imperio Romano y el Renacimiento. **288**

middle class/clase media Clase formada por comerciantes, patronos de pequeña y mediana industria y profesiones liberales. Está entre la clase noble y la clase campesina en la Edad Media. **328**

Middle Passage/Pasaje Medio Segunda etapa del sistema de comercio triangular, el cual envolvía el transporte de esclavos a las Américas a través del Atlántico. **398**

militarism/militarismo Glorificación del poder armado. **698**

millets/millets Minorías religiosas separadas y autogobernadas en el Imperio Otomano. **434**

Minamoto/Minamoto Clan que reinaba en Japón en 1156; introdujo el control shogun, y cambió el la forma en que el gobierno era llevado. **278**

minaret/minarete Alminar, torre de la mezquita. **253**

miniaturization/miniaturización Proceso de hacer máquinas más pequeñas y livianas. **983**

Minoans/Minóicas La más temprana civilización griega, que se desarrolló en la isla de Creta alrededor del 2000 A.C. **107**

Mississippians/Mississippianos Grupo que vivía en los bosques del Este en Norteamérica alrededor del 700 al 1500 D.C. **207**

mixed economy/economía mixta Economía en la cual empresas privadas son dueñas de algunas compañías y el gobierno es el dueño de las demás. **849**

mobilize/movilizar Acción de preparar el ejército de una nación y otros recursos de guerra. **698**

moderates/moderados Personas que no mantienen un punto de vista político extremo. **515**

monasticism/monasticismo Modo de vida en conventos y monasterios donde las monjas y monjes eran alejados del mundo y sus tentaciones. **301**

money economy/sistema monetario Sistema económico basado en el uso de la moneda como una medida de valor y una unidad de cuentas. **43**

monism/monismo Creencia en la unidad de Dios y la creación. **61**

monoculture/monocultura Cuando un país depende de un solo tipo de cultivo. **911**

monopoly/monopolio Control completo de la producción o venta de un solo bien o servicio, por una firma en particular. **557**

monotheism/monoteísmo Que cree en un solo Dios. **25**

Monroe Doctrine/Doctrina Monroe Doctrina en 1823 que establecía que los Estado Unidos no deberían interferir en los asuntos europeos o en las colonias europeas en el hemisferio oeste. **625**

monsoons/monzones Vientos que marcan las estaciones en la India. **52**

Moors/Moros Musulmanes que hicieron de España su hogar en los años 700 D.C. **245**

mosaic/mosaico Pintura o diseño hecho de pequeñas piezas de esmalte, vidrio o piedra. **227**

mosques/mezquita Edificio que los mahometanos usaban para la oración y las ceremonias religiosas. **242**

Mothers of the Plaza de Mayo/Madres de la Plaza de Mayo Grupo de mujeres argentinas cuyos familiares desaparecieron debido a las sanciones violentas y los abusos del gobierno a los que ellos se opusieron. **913**

mulattoes/mulatos Personas de antepasados europeos y africanos, en las colonias españolas en América. **622**

Q

Qin/Qin Dinastía que llegó al poder en China en 221A.C., bajo la cual el primer imperio chino verdadero fué creado. **84**

quantum theory/teoría cuántica Teoría de Max Planck que dice que la energía solo es liberada en grupos determinados, o quanta. **581**

Quechua/Quechua Lenguaje Inca, aún hablado hoy día por millones de personas en América del Sur. **211**

queue/queue Trenza de cabello que caracterizaba el estilo de peinado que todos los hombres chinos debían usar durante la dinastía Qing. **414**

quipu/quipu tipo de cuerdas con nudos y de colores usados para suplir la falta de escritura por los Incas. **211**

Qur'an/Corán libro sagrado del Islam. **242**

R

rabbis/rabinos Religiosos expertos del Judaísmo. **168**

radicals/radicales Personas que propugnan grandes reformas en distintos órdenes. **515**

radioactivity/radioactividad Proceso en el que los átomos de ciertos elementos constantemente se separan y liberan energía. **581**

raja/rajá Príncipe que reinaba en una ciudad indoaria. **57**

Rajputs/Rajputas Príncipes guerreros indios que empezaron a retar el control turco musulmano en la India en 1500. **439**

rationalism/racionalismo Creencia de que la verdad puede ser determinada solamente por el pensamiento lógico. **494**

reaction/reacción Tendencia tradicionalista que se opone a lo nuevo. Cuando una persona con autoridad desea restablecer lo abolido. **530**

reactionaries/reaccionarios Extremistas que se oponen al cambio, y desean deshacer ciertos cambios. **530**

realism/realismo Doctrina o sistema de los filósofos de atribuir realidad a las ideas gene-rales; atribuido a la literatura, arte y sociedad desde 1800. **596**

reaya/reaya Masas de sujetos ordinarios en la sociedad Otomana. **434**

Red Army/Ejército Rojo Fuerzas comunistas. **713**

Red Guards/Guardia Roja Estudiantes radicales elegidos por Mao Zedong, para dirigir la Revolución Cultural. **854**

Reformation/Reforma Revolución religiosa que dividió la Iglesia en Europa occidental, y creó una cantidad de iglesias nuevas. **363**

regionalism/regionalismo Forma de realismo que se enfoca en la vida diaria de lugares particulares. **596**

Reichstag/Reichstag Casa de la legislatura alemana. **642**

Reign of Terror/Régimen de Terror Período durante la Revolución Francesa cuando la Convención Nacional trabajó para suprimir toda oposición. **519**

reincarnation/reencarnación Creencia del renacimiento de las almas. **61**

Renaissance/Renacimiento Movimiento que precedió a la Edad Media, es el renacer del interés en las enseñanzas clásicas de Grecia y Roma. **354**

reparations/reparaciones Pago por el daño causado por guerras. **716**

representative democracy/democracia representativa Forma de gobierno en el que los ciudadanos eligen el representante para llevar el gobierno, en vez de que cada ciudadano le sirva directamente al gobierno. **117**

republic/república Forma de gobierno representativo en que la soberania reside en el pueblo. **151**

Restoration/Restauración Período en que reinó Carlos II de Inglaterra, cuando la monarquía fué restablecida; se refiere también al nacimiento de la cultura inglesa en ese tiempo. **483**

rhetoric/retórica Estudio de debates y discursos públicos. **120**

risorgimento/risorgimento Palabra italiana para resurgimiento, usada como el nombre del movimiento nacionalista italiano en 1800. **632**

romanticism/romanticismo Corriente seguida por muchos escritores a principios de 1800, cuyos trabajos apelaban al sentimiento e imaginación y el romance en la vida. **592**

Rome-Berlin Axis/Axis Roma-Berlín (Eje Roma-Berlín) Alianza formada en 1936, entre Mussolini en Italia y Hitler en Berlín. **748**

Roosevelt Corollary/Consecuencia Roosevelt Extensión de la Doctrina de Monroe, que dicta que los estados Unidos garantizarían que las naciones de Latinoameerica cumplirían con sus obligaciones internacionales. **685**

Rosetta Stone/Roseta Piedra negra encontrada en 1799 cuya inscripción trilingue fué el punto de partida de la egiptología. **22**

Roundheads/Roundheads Cabezas redondas. Aquellos que apoyaron al Parlamento en la Guerra Civil Inglesa. **480**

Rump Parliament/Parlamento Remanente Parlamento controlado por Oliver Cromwell, que abolió la monarquía y proclamó a Inglaterra como república. **480**

Rus/Rus Región bajo el control de Rurik quines llegaron a gobernar Kiev y las tribus Eslavas a lo largo del Río Dneiper. **230**

"Russification"/"Rusificación" Programa del zar Nicolás I en 1830 que forzó a los pueblos no-rusos a adoptar el lenguaje, religión y cultura rusa. **648**

Russo-Japanese War/Guerra Ruso-Japonesa Guerra entre Japón y Rusia que empezó con un ataque sorpresivo de Japón en 1904 **771**

S

sacraments/sacramentos Ceremonias en las que los participantes reciben la gracia de Dios para salvarse de las consecuencias de pecar. **300**

samurai/samurai Guerreros japoneses contratados para proteger el bienestar de los terratenientes en Japón feudalista. **278**

Sandinistas/Sandinistas Grupo marxista que dirigió la revolución contra el dictador de Nicaragua. **918**

Sanskrit/Sánscrito Lenguaje indo-ario. **56**

savannas/sabanas Llanuras secas al sur del desierto del Sahara en África. **182**

SCAP/SCAP "Comandante Supremo de las Potencias Aliadas" General Douglas MacArthur, en la ocupación de Japón. **859**

scholasticism/escolasticismo Filosofía medieval que intentara juntar la fé y la razón. **334**

scientific method/método científico Método de investigación que incluye cuidadosos experimentos conducidos y cálculos matemáticos para verificar el resultado de los experimentos. **383**

Scientific Revolution/Revolución Científica Transformación de pensamiebnto ocurrido durante 1500 y 1600, causada por la observación científica, la experimentación, y el cuestionamiento de las opiniones tradicionales. **382**

scorched-earth policy/política militar de quemar la tierra Táctica de quemar o destruir cultivos y tierras de valor. **527**

scribes/escriba Clérico egipcio que leía y escribía para aquellos que no podían hacerlo por sí mismos. **27**

sea dogs/perros marinos Grupo de aventureros capitanes marinos, que vivieron a finales de 1500. **490**

secede/separarse Retiro de una unión o nación. **611**

sectionalism/seccionalismo Competencia entre secciones o regiones de un país. **611**

sects/sectas Sociedades religiosas de pocas personas, usualmente con un sacerdote como líder. **365**

Security Council/Consejo de Seguridad Cuerpo de las Naciones Unidas que incluye miembros temporales elegidos por la Asamblea General, por términos de dos años. **823**

Seljuq Turks/turcos Saljuq Musulmanes de Asia central quienes le ganaron el control de Palestina o Jerusalem a los cristianos, a finales de los 1000. **318**

seppuku/seppuku Forma ceremonial de suicidio de samurais derrotados o desleales, para salvar el honor. También conocidos en Occidente como hari-kari. **278**

serfs/siervos Campesinos que debían vivir en la tierra en la que trabajaban para un amo. **298**

settlement colonies/colonias Grandes grupos de personas de un país, que viven en un país diferente. **662**

Seven Years' War/Guerra de los Siete Años Guerra desde 1756 a 1763 que involucró a casi toda Europa; la pelea empezó en Norteamérica como una guerra entre indios y franceses. **468**

Shang/Shang Invasores del valle del río Huang que llegaron al poder entre 1750 y 1500 A.C., y establecieron la primer dinastía China. **81**

Shi'ah/Shi'ah Rama del Islam formada en los 600 D.C., que creía que solo los imams deberían decidir sobre asuntos religiosos y terrenales. **244**

Shining Path/Sendero Luminoso Grupo de guerrilla Maoísta que llevó su campaña terrorista a las zonas altas rurales. **932**

Shinto/Shintoísmo o Sintoísmo Religión indígena de Japón que envuelve rituales y oraciones para apaciguar espítitus de la naturaleza y venerar al emperador. **277**

shires/condados Distritos gubernamentales en la vieja Inglaterra. **304**

shogun/shogun Jefe militar y oficial gubernamental en Japón feudal. **280**

Shona/Shona Pueblo que emigró al lugar que hoy día es conocido como Zimbabwe. **192**

Sikh/Sikh Religión basada en las enseñanzas de Nañak, un místico hindú en 1500, quien trató de unir las religiones hinduista y la musulmana. **441**

Silk Road/Ruta de seda Ruta de comercio que se extiende desde China hasta el Mediterráneo. **88**

simony/simonía Práctica de comprar altos puestos en la Iglesia, actividad común en la Edad Media. **303**

Sinn Fein/Sinn Fein Partido nacionalista Irlandés que en 1918 se declararon a sí mismos, el gobierno representante de una república irlandesa independiente. **741**

Sino-Japanese War/Guerra Sino-Japonesa Guerra entre China y Japón por Corea, en 1894, cuyo resultado fué la victoria de Japón. **677**

social Darwinism/darwinismo social Teoría desarrollada por Herbert Spencer que aplica la teoría de Darwin de la evolución de las sociedades humanas. **584**

Social Democratic Labor Party/Partido Laboral Socialdemócrata Partido socialista ruso formado en 1898. **651**

Social Democratic Party/Partido Social Demócrata Partido socialista alemán formado a finales de 1800. **644**

social sciences/ciencias sociales Rama del conocimiento que estudia científicamente a las personas como miembros de la sociedad; cubren áreas tales como la economía, las instituciones políticas, historia, y relaciones entre los individuos. **583**

Social Security Act/Ley de seguridad social Leyes que proveen beneficios a personas desempleadas y a personas mayores en los Estados Unidos. **737**

socialism/socialismo Sistema político y económico en el que el gobierno posee los medios de producción. **564**

"soft underbelly of the Axis"/"la parte vulnerable del Axis" Región de Italia y los Balcanes que según Churchill, era la parte débil del Poder Axis. **804**

Sophists/Sofistas Hombres atenienses que abrieron escuelas para que jóvenes estudiaran política, matemática, ética y retórica. **120**

Southeast Asia Treaty Organization/Organización de Tratados Sudasiáticos (SEATO) Organización creada por el presidente Dwight D. Eisenhower para detener los avances del comunismo en el sureste de Asia. **839**

Spanish Armada/Armada española Impresionante flota de naves enviadas por Felipe II de España para invadir Inglaterra y que fueron derrotados por Inglaterra en 1588. **471**

Spanish Civil War/Guerra Civil Española Guerra entre los Falangistas Nacionalistas de España y los Republicanos durante 1930. **784**

special theory of relativity/teoría general de la relatividad Teoría de Einstein, que proporciona la ley de la gravitación y sus relaciones con otras fuerzas de la naturaleza. **582**

spheres of influence/esferas de influencia Áreas en las cuales un país tiene un interes particular y otras naciones respetan ese interés. **663**

SS/SS Schutzstaffel, o rama militar del Partido Nazi. **801**

Stamp Act/Ley del timbre Ley pasada por el Parlamento en 1765, que impuso un impuesto en forma de sello, en documentos especiales, para los americanos colonistas. **498**

standard of living/estándares de vida Medición de la calidad de vida. **376**

steppe/estepa Llanura muy extensa ideal para la agricultura, en el este de Europa y el centro de Asia. **229**

straight/estrecho Angosta faja de agua que conecta dos masas de agua más grandes. **200**

strike/huelga Cuando los trabajadores se niegan a trabajar hasta que sus demandas sean aceptadas. **562**

subsidies/subsidios Concesiones de dinero del gobierno. **390**

suburbs/suburbios Áreas residenciales en las afueras de la ciudad. **588**

Suez Canal/Canal de Suez Canal que va desde el Istmo de Suez y conecta con el Mar Mediterráneo y el Mar Rojo. **668**

Suez Crisis/Crisis de Suez Conflicto entre potencias Occidentales y Egipto, por la posesión del Canal de Suez en 1950. **894**

suffrage/sufragio Derecho al voto. **602**

suffragettes/sufragistas Mujeres que lucharon por el derecho de las mujeres de votar. **605**

Sufi/Sufi Místicos mahometanos que trataban de vivir una vida simple. **245**

sultan/sultán Título del emperador de los Turcos. Príncipe o gobernador mahometano. **247**

Sunni/Sunní Nombre que se le da en el islamismo a los ortodoxos seguidores de la Sunna. **244**

supercomputers/supercomputadoras Potentes computadoras que ayudan a resolver complicados problemas científicos y tecnológicos. **978**

surrealism/surrealismo Estilo artístico que junta ideas conscientes e inconscientes para retratar la vida en forma de sueño. **730**

suttee/suttee Antigua práctica hindú en que una mujer cometía suicidio después de la muerte de su marido. **69**

Swahili/Swahili Sociedad africana que emergió a finales de los años 1100 a lo largo de la costa Este africana. Combinaba elementos de las culturas africana, asiática e islámica. **191**

taiga/taiga Región rusa muy lluviosa, al norte de las estapas, con largos y fríos inviernos. **231**

Taiping Rebellion/Rebelión de Taiping Revuelta en China entre 1850 a 1864, guiada por Hong Xiuquan, quien influenciado por las enseñanzas del cristianismo, declaró una misión para establecer una nueva dinastía. **421**

Taj Mahal/Taj Mahal Palacio construido bajo Shah Jahan, como una tumba para su esposa. Actualmente es una de las maravillas arquitectónicas del mundo. **441**

Tale of Genji, The/La Aventura de Genji Historia escrita por Murasaki Shikibu, en Japón, alrededor del año 1000 D.C. Considerada generalmente como la primer novela en el mundo. **280**

tariffs/tarifas Impuestos a la importación de productos extranjeros. **390**

tepees/tepees Tiendas de forma cónica, hechas de piel de búfalo. **205**

tenements/viviendas Edificios de apartamentos, muy juntos y en mal estado donde los trabajadores vivían, durante la Revolución Industrial en Inglaterra. **553**

terracing/parcelar Cavar pequeñas parcelas de tierra en las colinas, para la agricultura. **118**

terrorism/terrorismo Bombardeos, secuestros, y otro actos de violencia, llevados a cabo por grupos políticos, muchas veces realizados contra gente inocente, para forzar a un gobierno a conceder demandas. **650**

Tet Offensive/Ofensiva del Tet Ataque iniciado en el sur de Vietnam, por el norte de Vietnam y el Viet Cong en 1968. **867**

"theater of the absurd"/"teatro del absurdo" Tipo de teatro caracterizado por hacer sarcásticos comentarios sociales. **972**

theocracy/teocracia Gobierno dirigido por líderes religiosos, que proclaman la autoridad de Dios. **367**

Third Reich/Tercer Reich Nombre dado por Adolfo Hitler a su régimen, significa "tercer imperio" **748**

third Rome/tercera Romana Interpretación rusa ortodoxa de su rol principal de traer la luz espiritual al mundo. **235**

Thirty Years' War/Guerra de los Treinta Años Guerra inicia-da en Praga en 1618, como una rebelión de los Protestantes contra el Santo Imperio Romano. **455**

Thousand and One Nights, The/Las Mil y Una Noches Colección de cuentos populares musulmanes. **253**

Tiananmen Square Massacre/Masacre de la Plaza Tianamen Incidente en el que estudiantes iniciaron una huelga de hambre en la Plaza Tianamen, e ignoraron las órdenes del gobierno de retirarse, resultó en la muerte de cientos de personas. **855**

tithe/diezmo Impuesto recogido por los cristianos para la Iglesia en los viejos tiempos, que representaba una décima parte de sus ganancias. **302**

Toleration Act/Ley de tolerancia Acta del Parlamento Británico en 1689, concediéndo algunas libertades religiosas a los no-protestantes. **487**

Toltec/tolteca Pueblo que invadió el centro de México desde el norte, alrededor de los 800 D.C. **210**

Torah/Torá Escrituras judías que incluyen los primeros cinco libros del Viejo Testamento de la Biblia, que incluyen el libro de las leyes hebreas. **46**

Tories/Tories Partido político que apoyaba la monarquía en Inglaterra en los 1600. **484**

total war/guerra total Estrategia en la que la milicia enemiga y los recursos civiles son atacados. **611**

tragedies/tragedia Forma de drama griego en el cual el personaje principal luchaba contra el destino y los eventos. **137**

Treaty of Kanagawa/Tratado de Kanagawa Negociaciones entre Matthew Perry y Japón en 1854 que permitió comerciar entre los dos países. **427**

Treaty of Nanjing/Tratado de Nanjing Tratado que siguió la Guerra del Opio en la cual China cedió Hong Kong a los británicos y abrieron puertos para el comercio británico. **419**

Treaty of Portsmouth/Tratado de Portsmouth Acuerdo que terminó con la guerra ruso-japonesa. **771**

Treaty of Prague/Tratado de Praga Acuerdo para terminar la Guerra de las Siete Semanas entre Prusia y Austria. **640**

Treaty of San Stefano/Tratado de San Stefano Tratado que obligó a los turcos derrotados a conceder la independencia a Rumanía, Serbia y Montenegro. **656**

Treaty of Shimonoseki/Tratado de Shimonoseki Tratado en 1895 obligando a China a reconocer la independencia de Korea y hacer concesiones a Japón. **677**

Treaty of Tordesillas/Tratado de Tordesillas Acuerdo entre España y Portugal que movió hacia el oeste el límite del territorio que cada país podía reclamar en el Atlántico. **394**

Treaty of Versailles/Tratado de Versalles Tratado entre Alemania y los Países Aliados para ponerle fin a la Primer Guerra Mundial. **718**

triangular trade/comercio triangular Sistema de comercio que involucra tres etapas, una de las cuales es la trata de esclavos a traves del Atlántico. **398**

tribunes/tribuna Oficiales elegidos por las asambleas populares romanas. **152**

Triple Alliance/Alianza Triple Alianza entre Alemania, Austria- Hungría e Italia. **699**

Triple Entente/Triple Entente Alianza entre Francia, Rusia y Gran Bretaña, a principios de 1900. **699**

triumvirate/triunvirato Alianza política de tres dirigentes. **159**

tropical rain forests/bosque tropical lluvioso Bosques de vasta vegetación donde llueve mucho. **182**

troubadours/trovadores Cantantes que viajaban entreteniéndo gente en la Edad Media. **332**

Truman Doctrine/Doctrina Truman Política que declara que los Estados Unidos considera que el continuar con la expansión del comunismo es una amenaza a la democracia. **826**

Twelve Tribes of Israel/Las Doce Tribus de Israel Doce hijos de Israel, nieto de Abraham, de quienes los judíos modernos siguieron su herencia. **44**

tyrants/tiranos En la Grecia antigua, gobernantes que medían el poder por la fuerza, pero eran gobernantes con el apoyo del pueblo; más adelante este término se refería a gobernantes que ejercían poder brutal y opresivo. **112**

U-boats/U-boats Submarinos alemanes usados en la Primer Guerra Mundial. **706**

ultimatum/ultimátum Demanda en la que una parte amenaza a la otra si esta no acepta sus propuestas. **701**

"unequal" treaties/trueque desigual Intercambio de bienes que China firmó bajo amenaza de invasión, dándole a las potencias Occidentales los beneficios del intercambio. **419**

unions/uniones Asociaciones de trabajadores, que combinan fuerzas y demandas de diferentes trabajadores. **563**

United Nations/Organización de las Naciones Unidas Organización de naciones para mantener la paz a traves de acuerdos colectivos. **821**

Universal Declaration of Human Rights/Declaración Universal de los Derechos Humanos Documento adoptado por las Naciones Unidas en 1948, que resume los derechos humanos básicos que cada persona debe tener. **984**

universal manhood suffrage/sufragio universal de los hombres Política de que todo hombre adulto podía votar, sin importar si poseía propiedades o no. **517**

Upanishads/Upanishad Escritura sagrada que explica la religión Védica. **60**

urbanization/urbanización Migración del campo a la ciudad. **982**

usury/usura Política de cobrar altos intereses por un préstamo. **326**

utilitarianism/utilitarismo Creencia de que una ley funcionaba si llevaba a "la mayor felicidad al mayor número de personas posible". **561**

utopian socialists/socialistas utópicos Personas que creen que se puede vivir en paz los unos con los otros, si se vive en pequeñas colonias cooperativistas que poseen todos los bienes de producción en común, y comparten los productos. **565**

Vandals/Vándalos Que pertenece a un grupo de tribus germánicas que invadieron y destruyeron territorio en el Imperio Romano. **174**

varnas/varnas Clases sociales en la sociedad de la India. **61**

vassal/vasallo Persona a la que un amo le concedía tierras, como pago por sus servicios. **294**

V-E Day/Día V-E 8 de mayo de 1945, el día de la victoria Aliada en Europa en la Segunda Guerra Mundial. **806**

Vedas/Vedas Los más antiguos textos religiosos de la India. **56**

Vedic Age/Edad Védica Período histórico de India, de 1500 al 1000 A.C. **56**

vernacular languages/lenguaje vernácular Lenguaje doméstico, nativo, propio de un país. **331**

veto/veto Derecho de vedar o impedir una cosa, tal como un proyecto de ley. **152**

veto power/poder de veto Poder de derrotar una medida con un solo voto. **823**

viceroys/virrey El que con ese título gobierna en nombre y con autoridad del rey. Oficiales españoles que representaban a la monarquía en el imperio colonial español. **401**

Vietnamization/vietnamización Proceso de preparación de los sudvietnamitas para tomar el control de la lucha en la Guerra de Vietnam y permitir la retirada de las tropas de Estados Unidos. **940**

Vikings/Víkingos Pueblo germánico de Escandinavia que atacaban frecuentemente el oeste de Europa durante los años 800 y 900. **292**

V-J Day/Día V-J 2 de setiembre de 1945, el día que los japoneses se rindieron ante los Estados Unidos en la Segunda Guerra Mundial. **807**

vulcanization/vulcanización Proceso de tratar el hule para hacerlo mas usable. **547**

Wafd Party/Partido Wafd Partido nacionalista egipcio que llevó a una revuelta contra los británicos en 1919. **758**

Wannsee Conference/Conferencia Wannsee Reunión de oficiales alemanes para externinar la raza judía. **801**

war of attrition/guerra de desgaste Lenta manera de debilitar el bienestar en la que que cada parte trata de sobrevivir a la otra. **709**

War of the Roses/Guerra de las Rosas Guerra entre las familias York y Lancaster de Inglaterra en 1455. **337**

War of the Spanish Succession/Guerra de Sucesión Española Guerra en la que países europeos combatieron a Luis XIV para evitar el dominio Bourbon en Francia y España. **457**

Warsaw Pact/Pacto de Varsovia Acuerdo de mutua defensa entre la Unión Soviética y países del bloque del Este. **830**

Watergate scandal/Escándalo de Watergate La entrada a los cuarteles del Comité Democrático Nacional en 1972 que llevó a la renuncia de Nixon. **941**

weapons of mass destruction/armas de destrucción masiva Armas nucleares, químicas y biológicas de gran poder. **945**

welfare state/estado benefactor Estado en el que el gobierno se hacía responsable primordialmente del bienestar social de sus ciudadanos. **832**

Whigs/Whigs Partido político en Inglaterra, que defendían los derechos del Parlamento y de los sectores protestantes frente a la monarquía. **484**

White Lotus Rebellion/Rebelión de Lotos Blancos Rebelión campesina contra la dinastía Qing, liderada por el culto budista conocido como la Sociedad de Lotos. **416**

"The White Man's Burden"/"La Carga del Hombre Blanco" Poema de Rudyard Kipling que expresó la actitud de los europeos hacia personas no-occidentales durante la era imperialista. **664**

World Court/Tribunal Internacional de Justicia Corte de justicia internacional, ubicada en La Haya, en Holanda. **722**

World Trade Center/Centro de Comercio Internacional (WTC) Complejo de oficinas en la ciudad de Nueva York, que fué destruido por un devastador ataque terrorista el 11 de septiembre del 2001. **664**

Xia/Xia Línea de reyes que estuvieron a lo largo un Neolítico tardío y vivían en la región del río Huang en China, comenzando alrededor del 2000 antes de cristo. **80**

yang/yang Fuerza masculina. Brillante y activa, y es parte de la creencia china de dualismo o balance en la vida. **89**

Yi/Yi Dinastía coreana en 1392, cuando los coreanos sacaron a los mongoles, y duró hasta que Corea se anexó a Japón en 1910. **282**

yin/yin Fuerza femenina, oscura y pasiva, y es parte de la creencia del dualismo o balance en la vida. **89**

Young Italy movement/movimiento joven italiano Grupo de patriotas italianos dedicados a extender las ideas del nacionalismo. **632**

zaibatsu/zaibatsu Enormes firmas industriales controladas por familias poderosas en Japón. **860**

Zen/Zen Secta del Budismo que se enfoca en la meditación como método de ilustración. **271**

Zhou/Zhou Los que derrocaron la dinastía china Shang, en 1122 A.C. **83**

ziggurats/zigurats Templos sumerios hechos de ladrillo secado al sol. **32**

Zionism/Sionismo Movimiento nacionalista para construir un hogar para los judíos en Palestina. **760**

Zollverein/Zollverein Unión aduanera de los Estados alemanes creada en 1834 **638**

Index

Common Market (European Economic Community), 819, 834–835, 950, 953
commonwealth, 480–481
Commonwealth of Australia, 608
Commonwealth of Independent States (CIS), 959
Communards, 619
communications, *f*14, 274, 387, 572, 574, 589–590, 983
Communications Revolution, 548
communism, 566–567, 712, 749–753, 825–827, 983; art depicting life under, 979; Cuba and, 923; fall of, 956–961; in Nicaragua, 919; in the Soviet Union, *f*749; as variation of socialism, 566
Communist Information Bureau. *See* Cominform
Communist Manifesto (Marx and Engels), 543, 565
Communist Party, Soviet Union and, 713, 716, 749–753
compass, 287, 388, 412
competition, law of, 559, 569
compurgation, 295, 297
computers, 975, 977, 983–984
Comte, Auguste, 584
concentration camps, 748, 801, 802–803, *m*802
conceptual art, 975
concert halls, 590
Concert of Europe, 531, 532, 533
Concordat, 524
Concordat of Worms, 311–312
Concorde jets, 973, *p*973
Confederate States of America, 611
Conflict of the Orders, 153
Confucianism, 90, *f*90, 91, 92, 256, 260, 269; four classes under, 413; restored in China, 413; Vietnam and, 282
Confucius (K'ung Ch'iu), 90, *f*90, *p*90, 260, *f*260, *p*260, 267, 269, 282
Congo, 671, 883. *See also* Democratic Republic of the Congo
Congo River, 182
Congress of Berlin, 631, 656–657, 701
Congress of Vienna, 529–532, *m*531, 533, 615, 632, 698
conquistadors, 621
Conrad III (king of Germany), 320
conscription, 518

conservation of matter, law of, 387
Conservative Party, 603
conservatives, 515
Constable, John, 594
Constantine (emperor of Rome), 149, 171, 173–174
Constantine II (king of Greece), 953
Constantinople, 173, *p*173, *p*220, 221, *f*222, 224, *m*224, 430; captured by Crusaders, 221; as center of Christian church, 171; Muslim attempted conquest of, 243; Ottoman conquest of, 221, 433, 434; Russian attack of, 229
Constantius (Roman emperor), 173
constitution, defined, 481
Constitution of the United States, 450, 477, 480, *p*480, 502, 611
constitutionalism, *f*450, 451, *f*478, 481, *f*481
consulates, 427
consuls, Roman, 152
consumer culture, 732–733
Contadora Principles, 921
containment, 827
Continental System, 524–525
contraband, 710
contras, 919
"Convention on the Rights of the Child", 987, *f*993
Convention People's Party, 879
Cook, Captain James, 607
Cooper, James Fenimore, 592
cooperative movement, 565. *See also* Owen, Robert
Copernicus, Nicolaus, 380, 383, *f*383, *p*383
copper, 15
Coptic art, 220
Coral Sea, Battle of, 805
Corday, Charlotte, 518–519
Córdoba, 239, 248, 249, 250–251, 252
Corinth, agora of, *p*109
corn, 207
Corn Laws, 603
corporations, *f*555, 557
corporatist state, 745
Cortés, Hernán, 400, *p*400, 401
cosmologists, 133
Cossacks, 459, 464
Costa Rica, *m*A1, *m*A7, 624, 921
cotton, 28–29, 350
cotton gin, 542, *p*542, 546
Council of Constance, 342, 343
Council of Elders (Sparta), 114
Council of Five Hundred, 117

Council of Foreign Ministers, 821, 824
Council of the Indies, 401
Council of People's Commissars, 752
Council of Trent, 369, *p*369
Counter-Reformation, 368–371, 386, 402, 470
counterrevolutionary, 518
country-western music, 975
coup d'état, 522, 775
Courbet, Gustave, 596
court jesters, 316
Court of Common Pleas, 307
Court of the Exchequer, 307
Court of the King's Bench, 307
covenant, 45–46
Covenant of the League of Nations, 722–723
cowpox, 578
craft guild, 328
Crane, Stephen, 683
Cranmer, Thomas (archbishop of Canterbury), 470
creation myths, 200, 201
credit buying, 733
creoles, 622, 627
Crete, 104, 106, 796
Crimean Peninsula, 435
Crimean War, 601, 617–618, 660
Cripps, Stafford, 846
Crisis of Church & State: 1050–1300, The (Tierney), 312
Cristiani, Alfredo, 920
Croatia, *m*A2, *m*A9, 655, 721, 961
Cro-Magnon people, 4, 8; carving of, *f*8; mammoth-bone shelters of, *p*2
Cromwell, Oliver, 480–482, *p*482
Cromwell, Richard, 482
crop rotation, 544
crossbow, 287
Crusades, 221, 316, *f*319, *m*319; Byzantine Empire and, 318, 321; causes of, 318; Children's Crusade, 321; Crusader states, *m*321; economic impact, 320, 322; First Crusade, 319–320; Fourth Crusade, 321; papal prestige and, 322; political impact, 320, 321, 322; results of, 321–322; Second Crusade, 320; social impact, 320, 322; Third Crusade, 320–321; trade and, 322; weaponry and, 322
Cuba, *m*A1, *m*A7, 685, 908, 909, 922–925, 993; economic boycott of, *f*922, 924; Marxist overthrow of

government, 819, 839–840; Nicaraguan Sandinistas and, 919; social and political disorder in, 776–777; Spain and, 625; Spanish-American War and, 683
Cuban missile crisis, 835, 840
cubism, 731
Cuicuilco, Mexico, 198
Cullen, Countee, 182
cultural diffusion, 12, *f*138
Cultural Revolution, 816, 854
culture, defined, 6, *f*218
Cunard, Samuel, 548
cuneiform, 31, *p*31
curia, 301
Curie, Irene, 581
Curie, Marie and Pierre, 581, *f*581, *p*581
Cuzco, 211
Cynicism, 143
Cyprus, 796, 953
Cyril, 226, *p*226
Cyrillic alphabet, 226
Cyrus the Great, 39, *f*39, 46, 121
czar, 234
Czech Republic, *m*A2, *m*A9, 955, 961
Czechoslovakia, 721; arms agreement with Egypt, 894; democratic government overthrown, 827; division of, 961; fall of communism, 960, 973; Germany and, 786–788, 822; invaded by Warsaw Pact troops, 819; Locarno Pact and, 739; Prague Spring, 836; Soviet invasion of, 956

da Gama, Vasco, 392, *p*393, 413
da Vinci, Leonardo, 353, 358, 380, 385
Dachau, 802
dadaists, 731
Daguerre, Louis-Jacques-Mande, 594
daguerreotype, 594
Dahl, Hans, 594
Daimler, Gottlieb, 575
daimyo, 279, 280
Daladier, Édouard, 787
Dalai Lama, 850
Dali, Salvador, 727, 731, *f*731
Dalton, John, 570, 580
Damascus, 320
dams, 573
dance, 696, 977
Danish War, 639
Dante. *See* Alighieri, Dante
Danton, Georges-Jacques, 517–519

119; geography of, 106, *m*107; geography study in ancient Greece, 145; German control of, 796; golden age of, 128, 130–137, *f*147; government of ancient Greece, *f*106, 111–112, *f*115; "Greek fire," 222, *p*221, 224; Hellenistic Age, 129, 141–145; Homeric Age, 110–111; independence and, 533, 655; influence on Muslim culture, 250; mathematics in ancient Greece, 135, 143; medicine in ancient Greece, 135, 145; military service in ancient Greece, 120; money, 43; NATO and, 830, 954; neighboring countries and, 953; Ottoman Empire and, 430, 533, 655, 657; painting in ancient Greece, 131; Peloponnesian War, 124–125, *m*124; Pericles, 123–124, 125; Persian invasion of, 39; Persian Wars, 105, 121–123; philosophy in ancient Greece, 128, 133–135, 143; post–World War II recovery, 834; religion in ancient Greece, 110–111, 143; Renaissance interest in, 354–356; Roman conquest of, 129, 141; science in ancient Greece, 135, 143–145; sculpture in ancient Greece, 131; Sparta, 112, 113–114, 128; territorial gains after World War I, 721; theater in ancient Greece, 136–137, *p*136; Thebes, 128; trade in ancient Greece, 118, *m*118; trade with Egypt, 104; Turkey and, 954; tyrannical rule in, 105; written history in ancient Greece, 136

"Greek fire", 221, 222, 224
greenhouse effect, 989
Greenland, *m*A1; Vikings and, 293
Gregory VII (pope), 311, *p*311, 312
Gregory XI (pope), 342, 352
Grenada, *m*A1, *m*A7, 909, 928
Grimm brothers, 592
griots, 185
Gropius, Walter, 732
gross domestic products, *m*991
Group, The (Warren), *f*536
Guadalcanal, 805
Guam, *m*A12, 681, 683, 800
Guangzhou, 270, 411
Guantánamo Bay, 683

Guatemala, *m*A1, *m*A7, 624, 911, 921
Guernica (Picasso), 781, *f*784, *p*784
Guevara, Ernesto "Che", 922, 924, *p*924
Guggenheim Museum, 972
Guiana, bauxite and, 774
guilds, 327–328, 333
guillotine, *p*506, 517, *p*517
Guinea, *m*A1, *m*A10, 882
Guinea-Bissau, *m*A1, *m*A10, 883–884
Gulag Archipelago, The (Solzhenitsyn), 753
gulags, 753, *f*753
Gulf of Aqaba, 898
Gulf of Mexico, 943
gunpowder, 270, 295, 322, 337, 660
guns, introduced to the Americas, 400
Gupta Empire, 51, 68, *m*68
Gurkhas, 663
Gutenberg, Johannes, 353, 359–360
Gutenberg Bible, *p*359
Gypsies, 803

habeas corpus, 485
Habeas Corpus Act, 485, 489
Habsburg family, 340, 402, 530, 637, 715, 720
haciendas, 621
Hadar (Ethiopia), 6
Hades, 111
Hadrian (Roman emperor), 161, 169
al-Hafid, Moulay Abd, 667
Hagia Sophia, 227, *p*227, 228, 430
Hague, The, 701, 722
haiku, *f*446
Haiti, *m*A1, *m*A7, 458, 600, 624, 685, 776, 926–927
Hakluyt, Richard, 491
Hall of Private Audience, 441
Halley's Comet, 570
Hamas, 900
Hamburg, 323
Hamlet (Shakespeare), 359, 361
Hammurabi, 36, *f*36, *p*36
Han dynasty, 75, 87–88; approach to government, 87; civil service system and, 87; economic leveling and, 87–88; trade and, 75, 88
Hanging Gardens of Babylon, 38
Hangzhou, 267, 268, 269
Hannibal, *p*148, 155–156
Hanseatic League, 316, 317, 323–324, *f*323

Hanukkah, 257
hara-kiri, 278
Harappa, 53, *m*53
Harappan civilization, 50, 53–55, *f*54, *m*53
hard rock music, 975
Hargreaves, James, 546
Harold of Wessex, 305
Harvey, William, 381, 385
Hatshepsut, 24, *f*24, *p*24
Havana, 661
Havel, Vaclav, 960, *f*960, *p*960, 962, 973
Hawaiian Islands, *m*A1, *m*A5, *m*A12, 681, 799, 800
Hawaii's Story (Liliuokalani), *f*690
Hawkins, Sir John, 490
health insurance, 605
Heaney, Seamus, 980
Hebrews, 19, 44–47
Hebron, 900
Heian-kyo, 278
Heinlein, Robert, 979
heliocentric theory, 383
Hellenistic Age: breakup of Alexander the Great's empire, 141; learning and commerce during, 142; religion and philosophy in, 143; science in, *f*142, 143–145; spread of Greek culture, 141
Hellenistic culture, 141
helots, 113, 123
Helsinki Accords, 953–954, 960
Hemingway, Ernest, 727, 729–730
Henrietta (wife of Charles I), *p*478
Henry I (king of England), 306
Henry II (king of England), 306
Henry III (Holy Roman emperor), 311
Henry III (king of England), 307
Henry IV (Holy Roman emperor), 311
Henry IV (king of France), 367, 454
Henry VII (king of England), 317, 337, 470, 490
Henry VIII (king of England), 353, 360, 365–366, *p*366, 452, 470
Henry the Navigator (prince of Portugal). *See* Prince Henry
heresy, 226, 302, 303, 343
heretics, 302, 303, 364
Herodotus, 21, 136, 188
Herophilus, 145
Hertz, Heinrich Rudolph, 574
Herzegovina, 657, 721. *See also* Bosnia and Herzegovina

Hessians, 500
Hidalgo y Costilla, Miguel, 624
hieroglyphics, 22, 209
High Renaissance, 358
hijackers, 966
hijrah, 238, 241
Hildegard of Bingen, *f*302
Himalayas, 52
Himmler, Heinrich, 801
Hindu Kush, 67
Hinduism, 60, 61–62, 256, 258, 284–285
Hipparchus, 145
Hippocrates, 129, *p*129, 135
Hippocratic oath, 135
Hiroshima, 808
Hispanic literature, 979
Hispaniola, *p*380, 624, 926
Histories, The (Herodotus), 21
Histories, The (Moore), 156
History of Japan, A (Totman), 278
History of Medicine in Mexico, The (Rivera), *p*814–815
History of Rome (Livy), 151
History of the Decline and Fall of the Roman Empire, The (Gibbon), 176
History of the Peloponnesian War (Thucydides), 116, 124, 136
History of the United States, A (Lie), 823
Hitler, Adolf, *p*695, 727, 745–748, *f*746, *p*746, *f*747, *p*747, *p*780; as chancellor of Germany, 746, 780; Emergency Decree, 747; "New Order," 801; orders Final Solution, 781, 801; suicide of, 807
Hitler Youth, 789; propaganda poster, *p*813
Hittite Empire, 37, *m*37
HIV/AIDS, 986; in Africa, 877, 885, 889
Ho Chi Minh, 866–867, *f*867
Ho Chi Minh City, 867. *See also* Saigon
Ho Chi Minh Trail, 868
Hobbes, Thomas, 485, *f*486, *p*486
Hohenzollerns, 466–467
Hohokam people, 203
Hokkaido, 861
Holbein, Hans, 362, 366
Holiday, Billie, 731
Holocaust, 801, 803, 809, 892, *f*893. *See also* Final Solution
Holstein, 639, 640
Holy Alliance, 531
Holy Land, 318–322, *f*318
Holy Roman emperor, Habsburg family and, 637

572–573; Ten Hours Act, 562; textile industry, 546; transportation and, 540, 548; union movement, 563; wage system, 551–552. *See also* Industrial Age

industrialism: in Germany, 644; growth of cities and, 775; imperialism and, 663–664; in Japan, 677

industrialization, effects of, *f*549

inflation, 172, 376, 909, 911–912, 930, 942

influenza pandemic, 726, 728, *m*729

information revolution, 985

information technology, 943

inheritance, theory of, 577

Inkatha Freedom Party, 885

Innocent III (pope), 312–313, *f*312, *p*312, 321, 341

inoculation, in ancient India, 71

Inönü, Ismet, 897, *p*897

Inquisition, 303, 368, 369, *f*369, 402

Institutes of the Christian Religion, The (Calvin), 366

Institutional Revolutionary Party (PRI), 915, 916

Instrument of Government of 1653, 481

insulin, 580

integrated circuit, 977

integration, 838

intendancy system, 622

intendants, 455

interchangeable parts, 556

interdict, 302

internal combustion engine, 575

International Brigades, 785

International Court of Peace, 823

International Justice. *See* World Court

International Monetary Fund, 872

International Space Station (ISS), 973, 983

international style, 732

International Working Men's Association, 567

Internet, 985

intifada, 900

Intolerable Acts, 498

investing, 326

Ionesco, Eugene, 978

Ionian Sea, 106

Iran, *m*A2, *m*A11, 39, *f*436, 763, 892, 896; hostage crisis, 876, 903, *p*903, 941; Iran-contra affair, 941; Iran-Iraq War, 877, 903, 904; limited democracy in, 993; national-

ization of oil companies, 896, 901; oil and, 896, *p*896, 901; revolution in, 903; shah overthrown, 876

Iraq, *m*A2, *m*A11, 247, 722, 760, 892, 895; Iran-Iraq War, 877, 903, 904; Islamic conquest of, 243; oil and, 901; Persian Gulf War and, 877, 904–905; weapons of mass destruction, 944; in World War II, 796

Ireland, *m*A2, *m*A9; Act of Union and, 604; Christianity and, 302; Easter Rising, 740–741, *p*740; home rule movement, 741; Irish Free State, 741; "Irish question," 604; Northern Ireland, 741; potato famine, *f*604; poverty in, 536; rebellion of 1641, 479; Republic of Ireland, 741, 949; terrorism in, 991

Irish Republican Army, 741, 949

iron, 15, 51, 547, 558

Iron Age, 5, 15, 180

"Iron Chancellor" (Bismarck), 641

iron law of wages, 560

ironmaking: in Africa, 180; in Asia, 15

ironworking, 188

irrigation: in American Southwest, 203; in development of civilizations, 12, 22; in Egypt, 21; and the Inca, 211; in Indo-Aryan economy, 50, 58; and Shang, 81

Irving, Washington, 592

Isabella of Castile (queen of Spain), 317, 338, 393, *f*393, *p*393

Isfahan. *See* Eṣfahān

Isis, 28

Islam, 241, *f*255, 262; Abraham and, 257, *p*257; in Africa, 191; beliefs of, 242; caliphs, 243, 244, 247, 249, 253; calligraphy and, 218, *p*218; civilization of, 248–255; division of, 238, 244–245; expansion of, 243, *f*246; family and, 249; Five Pillars of Islam, 242; holy places of, 194; Muhammad and, 238, 241, 243, 248, 252, 262, *p*262; pilgrimage to Mecca, 241, 242; prayer rugs, 253, *p*262; Qur'an and, 242, 243, 249; Ramadan, 262; Shi'ah Muslims, 244–245; slavery and, 249; spread of, 245–246; Sunni Muslims, 244–245; Turks and, 247; women of, 905, *p*905, 986

Islam in Practice: Religious Beliefs in a Persian Village (Loeffler), 245

Islamic Arabs, competition with Aksum, 190

Islamic extremists, 964

island hopping, 805

isolationists, 794, 795

Israel, *m*A2, *m*A11, 41, 876, *m*900; creation of, 817, 892–893; founding of, 45; Israel Defense Forces, 817, *p*817; Knesset, 817, *p*817; kingdom of, 45, *m*45; Six-Day War, 844, 898–899, *m*900

Istanbul. *See* Constantinople

Isthmus of Panama, 4, 394, 401, 684

Isthmus of Suez, 30

Italy, *m*A2, *m*A9; Africa and, 636; Anti-Comintern Pact, 786; building as a nation, *f*635; Byzantine Empire and, 310; Carbonari, 632; Christian Democratic Party, 834; cities of, *f*310; conquest of Libya, 636; as corporatist state, 745; Crusades and, 319, 321; declares war on France and Great Britain, 793; declares war on Germany, 804; declares war on United States, 800; economic recession, 952; expansion (1935–1941), *m*788; fascism in, 743–745, 783; geography of, 150, *m*150; Holy Roman Empire and, 310–312; invasion of Albania, 787; invasion of Ethiopia, 782, 783–784; League of Nations and, 722; Libya and, 666; Locarno Pact and, 739; Lombard settlement in, 228; Napoléon and, 521, 525; plebiscites in, 636; political instability, 952; postwar recovery, 834; Prussian alliance, 640; Renaissance in, 354–358, *m*354; risorgimento, 632; Rome-Berlin Axis, 748; South Africa and, 674; in Spanish Civil War, 784; taxation in, 635; territorial rule by Austria, 632; terrorism, 952; trade and, 323; Treaty of Prague and, 640; unification of, 632–636, *m*636, 699; war with Austria, 633–634; war with Ottoman Empire, 636; in World War I, 703, 716; in World War II, 796, 804; Young Italy movement, 632

Itō Hirobumi, 677

Iturbide, Agustín de, 624

Ivan I (Great Prince), 234

Ivan III (Ivan the Great), 221, 234

Ivan IV (Ivan the Terrible), 234, *f*234, *p*234, 452, 459

Ivanhoe (Scott), 592

ivory, 42, *p*42, 218

Iwo Jima, *p*695, 808

Jabal Ṭāriq, 245

"J'accuse" (Zola), 620

Jackson, William, 594

Jackson State College, 940

Jacobins, 517–519, 520

Jade Buddha Temple (Shanghai), 92, *p*92

Jahān, Shah, 441, 443

Jahāngīr, 439

Jainism, 258

Jamaica, *m*A1, *m*A7, 928

James I (king of England), 452, 473, *p*473, 478, 479

James II (king of England), 484

Jamestown, 381, 476, 492

Janissaries, 432, 435

Japan, *m*A2, *m*A11, *f*422; alliance with Germany and Italy, 799; alliance with Great Britain, 770–771; annexation of Korea, 756; Anti-Comintern Pact, 786; atomic bombings of, 807; attack on Pearl Harbor, 781; Buddhism in, 65, 277–278, 280; China's influence on, 266, 277, 278; Christianity and, 424; civil war in, 427; daimyo, 279, 280, 422, 423, 424, 426; Diet, 676, 859, 862; Dutch traders and, 403, 425; early history of, 277–278; economic development, 860, 872, 873; education system of, 873; emigration from, 771; expansion of, 770–771, 782, *m*783; feudal, 278–279, *c*279, *f*279, 422; foreign relations, 861; Fujiwara family and, 278; industrialization and, 677; invasion of China, 782; isolation of, 422, 424, 426–427; Jesuit mission in, 370, 424; Kabuki theater, 425; Kamakura period, 219; Korea and, 423, 770, 771; League of Nations and, 722; Liberal-Democratic Party, 862; "MacArthur Constitution," 859, 861; Manchuria and, 770–771, 782; Meiji Empire, 427; Meiji

Menelik II (emperor of Ethiopia), 674, p674
Menem, Carlos, 931
Menes (first known king of Egypt), 5, 22
Menominee, 214
Mensheviks, 712, 713
mental illness, 585
mercantilism, 390, 493, f493, 559
mercenaries, 500
merchant guild, 316, 327
merchants, in China, 413, 414–415
Mercia, 304–305
Meroë, 180, 188
Merovingians, 288–289
Mesolithic Age, 9. *See also* Middle Stone Age
Mesopotamia, 18–19, 30–31, 35, 135, 140, 247
Messiah (Handel), 453
mestizos, 622, 627
metals/metalworking, 5, 15, f22, f81, 210, 280, f649
Metamorphoses (Ovid), 149, 167, f214
Methodius, 226, p226
metics, 115
metric system, 520
Metternich, Prince, 532–533, p533, 653
Mexican Cession, 610
Mexican Revolution, 661, 686–687
Mexico, mA1, mA7, 908–909, 912, 915–917, f917; Aztec civilization, 199, 210, 400; Contadora Principles, 921; democratic gains in, 993; earthquake of 1985, 915–916, p915; economic problems in, 915–916; emigration from, 916; empires of, 208–210, m208; European explorers and, 400–401; France and, 618; Institutional Revolutionary Party (PRI), 817, 915, 916; Maya civilization, 198–199, 209–210, 400; Mexican Revolution, 661, 686–687; oil and, 757, 774, 777, 911, 915, p916; Olmec peoples in, 198; revolution in, 624; single-party political system in, 775; Toltecs and, 199, 210; war with United States, 610
Mexico City, 400, 621, 774, p774, 775, 912–913, 915–916
Michelangelo, 353, 358, f358, 362
Micrographia (Hooke), 476, p476

microscopes, p381, 383, 576, p576
Middle Ages, f315, f345; architecture of, 219, p219, 316, 334–335, p335, p347; art and culture of, 331–333; banking and investment in, 326; Black Death and, 317, 329–330, p317; chivalry in, 298–299; church and, 302–303; compared to modern civilizations, 297–299, 312; compared to previous civilizations, 295; Crusades, 316, p316, 318–322; development of nations, 336–339; education and, 333; England and, 304–305, 336–337; feudalism in, 294–297, c296; France, 308–309, 337–338; games of, f374; guilds, 327–328; Holy Roman Empire in, 310–311, 339–340; language and literature in, 331–333; Magna Carta, 306–307; manorial system, 297–299; manufacturing in, 325; market economy and, 324–326; mathematics in, 334; middle class and, 328; Norman conquest, 305; philosophy in, 334; Roman Catholic Church in, 300–303, 341–343; science in, 334; Spain and, 338–339; towns and, 327–330; trade and, 323–325; warfare and weaponry in, 295, 336
middle class: emergence in Middle Ages, 328; in France, 509; Industrial Revolution and, 553; Reform Bill of 1832 and, 603
Middle East: Arab-Israeli confrontation, f891, 898–900; British withdrawal from, 892–894; French withdrawal from, 891–892; oil and world energy needs, 901–902, g901, m902; political and social change, 895–896. *See also under specific countries of the Middle East*
Middle English, 333
Middle Kingdom (Egypt), 23
Middle Passage, 398
Middle Stone Age, 8. *See also* Mesolithic Age
Middlemarch (Eliot), 596
Midway, Battle of, 805
migration, human, 7, 8
Milan, 312, 355
militarism, 698

military satellites, 983
military techniques, Napoléon and, 521–522, 524–528
Mill, John Stuart, 551, 561
Miller, Arthur, 972, 978
Millet, François, 617
millets, 434
Milton, John, 476, p477
Minamoto (clan), 278
Minamoto Yoritomo, 278
minaret, 253
Ming dynasty, 351, 410, 412–415, m412
miniaturization, 977
minimum wage, 737
Minoans, 104, 107–108, p106
Minos (king of Crete), 107
Mir, 939, 983
miracle plays, 286, 332
missi dominici, 290
missionaries, 665, f764
Mississippi River, 200
Mississippians, 207
Mitterand, François, 950
mobilize, 698
Mobuto Sese Seko (Joseph Mobuto), 876, 877, 883
Moctezuma I (Aztec ruler), 199
Moctezuma II (Aztec ruler), f210, 400, p400
Model T Ford, 697
model towns, 565
Modena, 633–634
moderates, 515
Modern Times, 727, f732, p732
modernization, of colonies, f762
Modest Proposal, A (Swift), f536
Mogadishu, 191
Mohács, Battle of, 55, 435, p435
Mohenjo Daro, 50, 53–54, m53, p53, p73
Molina, Rafael Trujillo, 776
Moluccas islands, 395
Mona Lisa (da Vinci), 358, 380
Monaco, mA2, mA9, 952
monarchy: absolute monarchy, 450, 478, 484; democratic, f110; English, 470–473; in Europe, f475, f512, f952; limited constitutional monarchy, 489; West African, 193
monasteries, 231, 333
monasticism, 301–302
Mondrian, Piet, 731
Monet, Claude, 597
money: coined, 43, 115; in Indus River valley, 51; invention of by Lydians, 19; standard system of, 389
money changers, 325

money economy, 43, f43
Mongkut (king of Siam), 679, f679, p679
Mongol Empire: Baghdad and, 247; China under, 274–275; conquests of, 272–274; defeat of by Ming Empire, 413; Genghis Khan and, 272–273; Golden Horde, 273, 275; influence on Slavic society, 233; Kievan Russia under, 233; Korea and, 281; Kublai Khan and, 273–275, p274; Mongol threat to northeastern China, 273; Qidan, 269; warriors of, p221, p233
Mongolia, mA2, mA11, 76, 272, 414
Mongols, invasions by: Asia, 273; Hungary, 233; India, 430; Poland, 233
monism, 61
monks, 316
Monnet, Jean, 833
monoculture, 911
Monomakh, Vladimir, 233
monopoly, 557
monotheism, 25, 61
Monroe, James, 625
Monroe Doctrine, 625
monsoons, 52
Monte Cassino, 301
Montenegro, mA2, mA9, 656, 657, 721
Montesquieu, Baron de, 495
Montevideo, 776
Montgomery, Bernard, 804
Monticello, 450, p451
moon exploration, 982
Moors, 238, 245, 289, 332, 338
moral relativism, 729
morality plays, 332
morality tales, 214
More, Thomas, 360, 361, 452, p452, 565
Morelos y Pavón, José María, 624
Morgan, J. P., 557
Mori Ogai, 757
Moriscos, 407
Morocco, mA1, mA10, 666–668, 892
Morrison, Toni, 979, f979
Morse, Samuel, 548
Morse code, 548
Morton, "Jelly Roll," 731
Mosaddeq, Mohammad, 896
mosaic, p148, p220, 227, 231
Mosaic law, 46
Moscoso, Mireya, 920
Moscow, 234–235, 459–460, 527
Moses, p19, 44
Mosque of Córdoba, 238, p252

mosques, *p*194, *p*238, *p*241, 242, *p*245, 252–253, *p*431
mosquito, 661, 684
Mother Teresa, 844, *f*850, *p*850
Mothers of the Plaza de Mayo, 913
motion, laws of, 385
motion pictures, *f*728, 732, 977–978
Mott, Lucretia, 614
Mount Fuji Seen Below a Wave at Kanagawa (Hokusai), 660
Mount Kenya, 184
Mount Kilimanjaro, 184, 877
Mount Sinai, *p*44
Mount Vesuvius, 149
Mountbatten, Lord Louis, 847
movable type, 270, 353, 359
movies, 977–978
Mozambique, *m*A2, *m*A10, 884, 952
Mozart, Wolfgang Amadeus, 381
MRI (magnetic resonance imaging) machines, 978
MRTA. *See* Tupac Amarú Revolutionary Movement (MRTA)
Mu'awiyah, 244–245
Mugabe, Robert, 881
Mughal Empire, 351, 431, 439–443, *m*440, 491
Muhammad, 238, 241–243, *f*241, 246, 248, 252, 262, *f*262
Mukden, 771
mulattoes, 622
Mulroney, Brian, 945
multinational corporations, 910
mummification, 28
Munich Conference, 787
Muñoz Marín, Luis, 925, *p*925
al-Muqaddasī, 322
Murad II (Ottoman sultan), 433
Murasaki Shikibu, Lady, 265, *p*265, 278
Murderous Revolution, The (Stuart-Fox), 869
murex, 42
museums, 590, 591
Musharraf, Pervez, 851
music: African, 185, *f*185; African American, 975; Arab influence in Europe, 239; concerts, 590; in Japan, 426; jazz, 731; opera, 593–594; post–World War I, 730–731; ragtime jazz, 571; rock music, 975; romanticism and, 593; synthesized, 975; "troubadour" tradition in France, 287; videos, 977

Muslim countries, limited democracy in, 993
Muslim Empire, *f*250, conquest of Syria, Palestine, and North Africa, 228
Muslim influence, on Byzantines, 243
Muslim League, 846
Muslims, 242–255, *f*243, *f*248, 318–322, 338, 676, 847, 850, 968
Mussolini, Benito: Ethiopia and, 695, 783–784; growth of fascism and, 726, 743, 780; Hitler and, *p*695, *f*745, 748, *p*786; invasion of Albania, 787; Rome-Berlin Axis, 695, 781, 786
Myanmar, *m*A2, *m*A11, 65, 282, 864
Mycenaeans, 104, 107–108, *p*108
Myron, 131
mystery plays, 332
mystery religions, 143
myths, *f*80, 98, 111, 214; creation myths, 200, 201

NAACP (National Association for the Advancement of Colored People), 838
NAFTA (North American Free Trade Agreement), 909, 912, *f*912, 947
Nagasaki, 403, 807–808
Nalanda, 71, *p*71
Namib Desert, 183
Namibia, *m*A2, *m*A10, 889
Nānak, 441
Nanjing, 413, 809
Nanjing, Treaty of, 419
Nanna, 34
Napata, 187, 188
Naples, 355, 634
Napoléon I. *See* Bonaparte, Napoléon
Napoléon II, 526
Napoléon III, 633, 640. *See also* Louis-Napoléon
Napoléonic Code, 524, 526
Napoléonic Wars, 521
NASDAQ, 967
Nasser, Gamal Abdel, 893–894, *p*893, 895–896
Natal, 673
National Association for the Advancement of Colored People. *See* NAACP
National Covenant, 479
National Liberation Front (NLF), 867
National Socialist German Workers' Party. *See* Nazi Party

nationalism, *f*523, 526, 541, *f*640, *f*659, 663, 676, 716, *f*779
nationalization, 739
Native Americans: attempted enslavement of, 395; children of, *f*205; creation myths of, 200, 201, *f*214; diseases from Europe, 401; European explorers and, 394; Spanish missionaries and, *p*406
NATO (North Atlantic Treaty Organization), 818, *f*825, 829, 830, 833, 897, 954–955, 969
natural disasters, *f*846
Natural History of Animals (Lamarck), 507
natural philosophers, 382
natural resources, 988
natural selection, 577, 584
naturalists, 596
nature gods, 231
naval stations, 663, 680
Navarre, 454
Navigation Act of 1651, 476, 481
navigation instruments, 388–389
navigation map, 380
navigation satellites, 983
Nazi Party: in Austria, 786; in Czechoslovakia, 787; outlawed after World War II, 821; rise to power, 745–748
Nazi-Soviet Pact, 789, 791, 822, 825
Neanderthals, 8
NEAR Shoemaker (Near Earth Asteroid Rendezvous), 982
Nebuchadnezzar, 19, 38
Nehru, Jawaharlal, 847, *p*847
Nelson, Horatio, 524
Neman River, 229
Neo-Confucianism, 269
Neolithic Age, *p*4, 9, 10, 182. *See also* New Stone Age
Neolithic agricultural revolution, 8–10
Nepmen, 749
Netherlands, *m*A2, *m*A9, 323, 455, 952; American Revolution and, 501; battles with France, 457, 527; Calvinists and, 367, 403; colonial empire of, 403; Congress of Vienna and, 529; Dutch East India Company, 403; Dutch East Indies, 679; German invasion of, 792; Napoléon and, 525; religious wars in, 371; revolt against Spain, 403; society of, 403; stock exchange opens in, 353; War of the

Austrian Succession and, 467
Netherlands East Indies (Indonesia), 799, 800
Neutrality Acts, 794
Nevelson, Louise, 974
Nevis, 928
New Amsterdam, 403, 483
New Brunswick, 607
New Deal, 737
New Economic Policy (NEP), 749
New France, 497
New Guinea, 800, 805
New Kingdom (Egypt), 24–25, *m*24
New Model Army, 480
"New Order", 801
New South Wales, 607
New Stone Age, 8, 9. *See also* Neolithic Age
New Testament, 169
"New Wave" film directors, 977
New York, *m*A6, 483
New York City, 964, *p*964
New York Herald, 670
New York Stock Exchange (NYSE), 543, 735, 968
New Zealand, *m*A2, *m*A12, 601, *m*607, 608, 631, 761, 805
Newcomen, Thomas, 547
newspapers, 589, 590, 617
Newton, Isaac, 385, 386, 476
Ngo Dinh Diem, 867
Nibelungenlied, *f*346
Nicaea, 171
Nicaragua, *m*A1, *m*A8; authoritarian government in, 776; democratic gains in, 993; earthquake in, 909; peace plan and, 921; revolution in, 918–919; Roosevelt Corollary and, 685; United Provinces of Central America and, 624
Nice, 633
Nicholas I (czar of Russia), 648, 654
Nicholas II (czar of Russia), 539, 651
Niger River, 182
Nigeria, *m*A2, *m*A10, 184, 887, 888
Nightingale, Florence, 618, *f*618, *p*618
Nightshadow ballet, 972
nihilists, 650
Nika Revolt, 223
Nikolais, Alwin, 977
Nile River, 2, 20–21, *p*20, *m*21, 184, 200
Nile River valley: annual flooding of, 11, *p*11, 21,

Acknowledgements

For permission to reproduce copyrighted material, grateful acknowledgment is made to the following sources:

About.Com, Inc.: From "The Korea Summit" June 13, 2000 by Keith Porter, accessed July 19, 2001, from http://worldnews.about.com/library/weekly/aa061300a.htm?terms=korea+summit. Copyright © 2000 by Keith Porter. All rights reserved.

American Heritage Magazine, a division of Forbes Inc.: Quotes by Al-Bakri and Ibn Battuta from *The Horizon History of Africa*, edited by Alvin M. Josephy, Jr. Copyright © 1971 by American Heritage Publishing Co. Inc.

Biblioteca Persica: From *Persian Heritage Series, No. 2: The Epic of Kings: Shah-Nama, the national epic of Persia* by Ferdowsi, translated by Reuben Levy. Copyright © 1967 by Center for Iranian Studies.

Cambridge University Press: From Chapter XVII from *The Prince* by Niccolo Machiavelli, edited by Quentin Skinner and Russell Price. Copyright © 1988 by Cambridge University Press.

Carcanet Press Limited; electronic format by permission of A. P. Watt, Ltd. on behalf of the Trustees of the Robert Graves Copyright Trust: From "Julius Caesar" from *The Twelve Caesars* by Suetonius , translated by Robert Graves, revised with an introduction by Michael Grant. Copyright © 1957 by Robert Graves; copyright © 1979 by Michael Grant Publication Limited. Users must not reproduce, download, store in any medium, distribute, transmit or retransmit, or manipulate any text reproduced on web site www.apwatt.co.uk.

Peter Coan: From "Esther Gidiwicz" from *Ellis Island Interviews: In Their Own Words* by Peter Morton Coan. Copyright © 1997 by Peter Morton Coan.

Columbia University Press: From "The Russian Law" from *Medieval Russian Laws*, translated by George Vernadsky. Copyright 1947 by Columbia University Press.

Doubleday, a division of Random House, Inc., www.randomhouse.com: From *The Diary of a Young Girl: The Definitive Edition* by Anne Frank, edited by Otto H. Frank and Mirjam Pressler, translated by Susan Massotty. Copyright © 1995 by Doubleday, a division of Random House, Inc.

Grove/Atlantic, Inc.: From "The Book of Songs" and from "A Song of War Chariots" by Du Fu, translated by Witter Bynner, from *Anthology of Chinese Literature: From Early Times to the Fourteenth Century*, edited by Cyril Birch. Copyright © 1965 by Grove Press. Inc. From *The Book of Songs*, translated by Arthur Waley. Copyright 1937 by Arthur Waley.

HarperCollins Publishers, Inc.: No. 47: "Without Even Going out the Door" from *The Essential Tao*, translated and presented by Thomas Cleary. Copyright © 1991 by Thomas Cleary.

David Higham Associates Ltd.: From *The Song of Roland*, translated by Dorothy L. Sayers (Penguin Classics, 1937). Copyright © 1957 by Executors of Dorothy L. Sayers. Originally published by Penguin Books Ltd.

Hill and Wang, a division of Farrar, Straus & Giroux, LLC: From *Night* by Elie Wiesel, translated by Stella Rodway. Copyright © 1958 by Les Editions de Minuit; English translation copyright © 1960 by MacGibbon & Kee, renewed © 1988 by The Collins Publishing Group. Originally published as *La Nuit*. All rights reserved. Electronic format by permission of **Georges Borchardt, Inc., for Les Editions de Minuit.**

Johns Hopkins University Press: From "Book VIII" from *The Metamorphoses of Ovid*, translated by David R. Slavitt. Copyright © 1994 by The Johns Hopkins University Press.

The Heirs to the Estate of Martin Luther King, Jr., c/o Writers House, Inc. as agent for the proprietor, New York, NY: From "I Have a Dream" by Martin Luther King, Jr. Copyright © 1963 by Martin Luther King, Jr.; copyright renewed © 1986 by Coretta Scott King.

Alfred A. Knopf, a division of Random House, Inc.: From "The Epoch of Decline" from *The House of the Spirits* by Isabel Allende, translated by Magda Bogin. Translation copyright © 1985 by Alfred A. Knopf, Inc., a division of Random House, Inc.

National Geographic Society: From "Viking Trail East" by R. P. Jordan from *National Geographic*, March 1985. Copyright © 1985 by National Geographic Society.

The New York Times Company: Quote by Vaclav Havel from "Speech by the Czech President" from *The New York Times*, January 2, 1990. Copyright © 1990 by The New York Times Company.

Oxford University Press: From "The Period of Civil Wars" from *The Sumerians* by C. Leonard Woolley. Copyright 1928 by Oxford University Press.

Raimon Panikkar: From Part III, Chapter B "Sacrifice" from *The Vedic Experience*, edited and translated with introductions and commentary by Raimon Panikkar. Copyright © 1977 by The University of California Press.

Penguin Books Ltd.: From *The Nibelungenlied* translated by A. T. Hatto (Penguin Classics, 1965, revised edition, 1969). Translation copyright © 1965, 1969 by A. T. Hatto. From *Utopia* by Thomas More, translated by Paul Turner (Penguin Classics, 1965). Copyright © 1965 by Paul Turner. From *The Secret History* by Procopius, translated by G. A. Williamson (Penguin Classics, 1966). Copyright © 1966 by G. A. Williamson.

Penguin Books Ltd.; electronic format by permission of The Random House Group Limited: From *The Peloponnesian War* by Thucydides, translation by Rex Warner (Penguin Classics, 1954). English translation copyright 1954 by Rex Warner. Published by Bodley Head.

Estate of Erich Maria Remarque: From *All Quiet on the Western Front* by Erich Maria Ramarque. Copyright 1929, 1930 by Little, Brown and Company; renewed © 1957, 1958 by Erich Maria Remarque. "Im Westen Nichts Neues." Copyright 1928 by Ullstein A.G.; renewed © 1956 by Erich Maria Remarque. All rights reserved.

Charles E. Tuttle Co., Inc., Boston, MA, and Tokyo, Japan: Haiku death poem by Banzan from *Japanese Death Poems: Written by Zen Monks and Haiku Poets on the Verge of Death*, compiled by Yoel Hoffmann. Copyright © 1986 by Charles E. Tuttle Co., Inc. From *Hawaii's Story* by Hawaii's Queen by Liliuokalani. Copyright © 1964 by Charles E. Tuttle Co., Inc.

University Press of Virginia: From "Prayer to the Masks" from *The Collected Poetry* by Léopold Sédar Senghor, translated by Melvin Dixon. Copyright © 1991 by the Rector and Visitors of the University of Virginia.

The University of California Press: From "Fragment #17: Sleep, darling" from *Sappho: A New Translation* by Mary Barnard. Copyright © 1958 by The Regents of the University of California; copyright renewed © 1984 by Mary Barnard.

The University of Chicago Press: From "The Fundamental Characteristics of European Feudalism" from *Feudal Society* by Marc Bloch, translated by L. A. Manyon. Copyright © 1961 by The University of Chicago Press.

Verso: From *I, Rigoberta Menchu: An Indian Woman in Guatemala*, edited and introduced by Elisabeth Burgos-Debray, translated by Ann Wright. Copyright © 1983 by Editions Gallimard and Elisabeth Burgos; translation copyright © 1984 by Verso.

Sources Cited:

From *The Murderous Revolution: Life & Death in Pol Pot's Kampuchea* by Martin Stuart-Fox. Published by Alternative Publishing Co-operative Ltd., Chippendale, New South Wales, 1985.

From "The Bucolic Mode" from *Pharaoh's People* by T. G. H. James, Published by Bodley Head Ltd., London, 1984.

From *The Tomb of Tutankhamen* by Howard Carter. Published by Cassell and Company Ltd., London, 1923.

From "Eastern Asia and Oceania: Mohenjo-Daro, Pakistan" from *The Atlas of Past Worlds: A Comparative Chronology of Human History 2000 BC-AD 1500* by John Manley. Published by Cassell Publishers Limited, 1993.

Quote from "Letter from Tokyo" from *The New Yorker*, May 20, 1974. Published by The Condé Nast Publications, Inc., New York, 1974.

From "To Feed My People: The Coming of Corn—Zuñi" from *American Indian Mythology* by Alice Marriott and Carol K. Rachlin. Published by Thomas Y. Crowell Publishers, a division of HarperCollins Publishers, Inc, New York, 1968.

From "Unity in Diversity" by Walter Gropius from *Four Great Makers of Architecture: Gropius, Le Corbusier, Mies van der Rohe, Wright*. Published by Da Capo Press, a division of Perseus Books, New York, 1970.

Quote by automobile consumer from *Middletown: A Study in Modern American Culture* by Robert S. Lynd and Helen Merrell Lynd. Published by Harcourt, Inc., Orlando, 1929.

Quote by Carmelite cleric from "Half the World (1450-1750)" from *Crossroads of Civilization: 3000 Years of Persian History* by Clive Irving. Published by HarperCollins Publishers, Inc., New York, 1979.

Quote from "A Relativistic World" from *Modern Times: The World from the Twenties to the Nineties*, Revised Edition by Paul Johnson. Published by HarperCollins Publishers, Inc., New York, 1991.

From "Poets, Scholars, and Physicians" from *Islam, from the Prophet Mohammed to the Capture of Constantinople, Part II: Religion and Culture*, edited and translated by Bernard Lewis. Published by HarperCollins Publishers, Inc., New York, 1974.

From account regarding Russian collective farming from *The Gulag Archipelago 1918-1956* by Aleksandr I. Solzhenitsyn, translated by Thomas P. Whitney. Published by HarperCollins Publishers, Inc., New York, 1973, 1974.

From funeral oration by the Archbishop of Novgorod, Feofan Prokopovich, from "The Heroic Tsar" (Retitled: "The Great Czar") from *Peter the Great Changes Russia*, Second Edition, edited by Marc Raeff. Published by D. C. Heath and Company, Lexington, MA, 1972.

Quote from Bernabe Cobo's account regarding worship of the sun god from *Latin American Civilization: The Colonial Origins*, Vol. 1, Third Edition edited by Benjamin Keen. Published by Houghton Mifflin Company, Boston, 1974.

Exodus 20:1–7 from *JPS Hebrew-English Tanakh*. Translated and published by Jewish Publication Society, Philadelphia, PA, 1999.

From "The End of the Beginning" by Ray Bradbury from *The Stories of Ray Bradbury*. Published by Alfred A. Knopf, a division of Random House, Inc., New York, 1980.

From granite inscription by Ezana, King of Aksum, from *An Introduction to the Economic History of Ethiopia from Early Times to 1800* by Richard Pankhurst. Published by Lalibela House, London, 1961.

From *The Guns of August* by Barbara Tuchman. Published by Macmillan Publishing Company, a division of Simon & Schuster, New York, 1962.

From *The Ramayan: A "Telling" of the Ancient Indian Epic*, adapted by Larry Tominberg. Published by The Maxwell School of Syracuse University, Syracuse, NY, 1997.

Quote by Guglielmo Marconi from "The First Radio Signal Across the Atlantic, 12 December 1901" from *Scrapbook 1900-1941* by Leslie Bailey. Published by Frederick Muller, 1957.

From "The Bloodiest Battle of All" by William Manchester from *The New York Times Magazine*, June 14, 1987.

From "The Communist Roller Coaster" from *The New York Times*, August 18, 1989.

From "Churchill, Winston" by Martin Gilbert from *The Oxford Companion to Politics of the World*, edited by Joel Krieger. Published by Oxford University Press, New York, 1993.

From military account from "Events of the Year 932" from *The Baburnama: Memoirs of Babur, Prince and Emperor*, edited, translated and annotated by Wheeler M. Thackston. Published by Oxford University Press, New York, 1996.

From "Book One" from *Livy, The History of Early Rome*, translated by Aubrey de Sélincourt. Published by Penguin Books Ltd., London, 1960.

From "Twentieth-Century Architecture" from *The History of Art* by H. W. Janson and Anthony F. Janson. Published by Prentice Hall and Harry N. Abrams, Inc., 1997.

From account of exodus of German citizens in January 1945 from "From Collapse to Re-creation" from *Foe into Friend: The Makers of the New Germany from Konrad Adenauer to Helmut Schmidt* by Marion Dönhoff, translated by Gabriel Annan. Published by St. Martin's Press, Inc., New York, 1982.

Quote by Ammianus Marcellinus, translated by W. Hamilton from "The Huns" from *Readings in the Classical Historians*, selected and introduced by Michael Grant. Published by Scribner, a division of Simon & Schuster, New York, 1992.

From Native American myth regarding the disappearance of the Paleo-Indians from "The Big Game Vanishes" from *Kingdoms of Gold, Kingdoms of Jade: The Americas Before Columbus* by Brian M. Fagan. Published by Thames & Hudson Ltd., London, 1991.

From writing on an ancient clay tablet from "The First Case of Juvenile Delinquency" from *The Sumerians* by Samuel Noah Kramer. Published by The University of Chicago Press, 1963.

Quote by Legalist Han Fei Tzu and from Dao de Jing by Laozi from *Chinese Thought: From Confucius to Mao Tso-Tung* by Herrlee G. Creel. Published by The University of Chicago Press, 1953.

From description of the Petrograd riots by Alexandra Rodionova from "Working-Class and Peasant Women in the Russian Revolution" from *Signs: Journal of Women in Culture and Society*, No. 2, Winter 1982. Published by the University of Chicago Press, 1982.

From "Paris During the Hundred Years' War" from *The Portable Medieval Reader*, edited by James Bruce Ross and Mary M. McLaughlin. Published by Viking Penguin, a division of Penguin Putnam Inc., New York, 1949.

From *The Epic of Gilgamesh, Tablet IX*, translated by Yanita Chen. Published by www.MythHome.org, Toronto, ON, Canada, 1994.

From poem from *Shang Civilization* by Kwang-Chih Chang. Published by Yale University Press, New Haven, 1980.

Ezekiel 37:32–33 and Luke 6:20-22 from *The Holy Bible, New International Version*. Published by Zondervan Bible Publishers, Grand Rapids, MI, 1984.

Photo Credits

Positions are shown in abbreviated form as follows: t-top, b-bottom, c-center, l-left, r-right.

v (l) Erich Lessing/Art Resource, NY, (r) Dilip Mehta/Woodfin Camp & Associates; vi (l) George Grigoriou/Stone, (c) The Michael C. Rockefeller Memorial Collection/Gift of Nelson A. Rockefeller, 1972/Metropolitan Museum of Art; vi–vii Leo Keeler/Animals Animals; vii (c) Paul Dupuy Museum, Toulouse, France/Lauros-Giraudon,Paris/SuperStock, (r) Bildarchiv Steffens/Bridgeman Art Library; viii (l) Gail Mooney/Corbis, (c) Alinari/Art Resource, NY; viii–ix Werner Forman Archive/Art Resource, NY; ix (cl) Bonhams, London, UK/Bridgeman Art Library, (cr) Magdalen College, Oxford/Bridgeman Art Library, (r) Dave G. Houser/Corbis; x (l) North Wind Picture Archives, (c) Christie's Images/Bridgeman Art Library, (r) Corbis; xi (l) AKG London, (r) Richard T. Nowitz/Corbis; xii (l) American Stock/Hulton Archive by Getty Images, (cl) Hulton Archive by Getty Images, (cr) Brown Brothers, (r) Lawrence Migdale/Stock Boston/PictureQuest; xiii (l) Wolfgang Kaehler, (r) ©European Communities; xvi SuperStock; xviii (tl) Bojan Breceli/Corbis, (tr) The British Museum, (bl) Eileen Tweedy/Victoria & Albert Museum, London/The Art Archive, (br) Douglas Peebles/Corbis ; xix Giraudon/Art Resource, NY; xx (t) Werner Forman Archive/Art Resource, NY; (b) Bridgeman Art Library; xxii Elio Ciol/Corbis; xxvii HRW Photo; xxxi (t) Michael Dibari Jr./AP/Wide World Photos, (b) E. Rooraid/PhotoEdit, (frame) MetaTools; xxxii (t) Erich Lessing/Art Resource, NY; xxxii (bl) Réunion des Musées Nationaux/Bridgeman Art Library, (br) Werner Forman Archive/Treasury of St. Mark's, Venice/Art Resource, NY; xxxiii (t) Réunion des Musées Nationaux/Art Resource, NY, (b) HRW Photo; xxxiv Hugh Sitton/Stone; S1 (l) Dagli Orti/Musée du Chateau de Versailles/The Art Archive, (r) David Parker/Science Photo Library/Photo Researchers; S2 (t) Scala/Art Resource, NY, (b) Laurie Platt Winfrey /Woodfin Camp & Associates; S3 (t) North Wind Picture Archives, (bl) Bettmann/Corbis, (br) HRW Photo; S4, S5 HRW Photo; S6 (t) HRW Photo (b) HRW Photo; S8 (t, c) HRW Photo, (b) AKG London; S9, S12, S14 HRW Photo; 1 Sisse Brimberg/NGS Image Collection, (b) Corbis; 2 (l) Courtesy Mammoth Site Museum, Hot Springs, SD, (r) Scala/Art Resource, NY; 3 (tl) Scala/Art Resource, NY, (tr) Werner Forman Archive/Art Resource, NY; (u) Joseph Needham (*Science and Civilisation in China*, Vols. 1–6, Cambridge University Press), (br) Genius of China Exhibition/The Art Archive; 4 (tr) Shelly Grossman/Woodfin Camp & Associates, (rc) Archivo Iconographico, S.A./Corbis, (bl) Robert Campbell/NGS Image Collection, (br) Martha Avery/Asian Art & Archaeology, Inc./Corbis; 5 (tl) Erich Lessing/Art Resource, NY, (tr) Erich Lessing/Art Resource, NY, (b) Richard T. Nowitz/Corbis; 6 Nik Wheeler/Corbis; 7 Dr. Owen Lovejoy and students, Kent State University. Photo © 1985 David L. Brill; 8 Ronald Sheridan/Ancient Art & Architecture Collection; 10 Zafer Kizilkaya/Atlas Geographic; 11 Paul Almasy/Corbis; 14 Winfield I. Parks/NGS Image Collection; 15 Sisse Brimberg/NGS Image Collection; 17 Gianni Dagli Orti/Corbis; 18 (tl) Gianni Dagli Orti/Corbis, (tr) Erich Lessing/Art Resource, NY, (b) Gianni Dagli Orti/Corbis; 19 (t) Dagli Orti/Archaeological Museum Spalato/The Art Archive, (bl) AKG London, (b) Gianni Dagli Orti/Corbis; 20 Robert Caputo/Stock Boston/PictureQuest; 22 Pix 2000/FPG International; 23 Jim Zuckerman/Corbis; 24 (t) Carmen Redondo/Corbis, (b) Erich Lessing/Art Resource, NY; 25 Erich Lessing/Art Resource, NY; 26 Hugh Sitton/Stone; 27 (t) Zefa/H. Armstrong Roberts, (b) Scala/Art Resource, NY; 28 (l) The British Museum/DK Images, (r) Harvey Lloyd/FPG International; 29 Erich Lessing/Art Resource, NY; 31 Gianni Dagli Orti/Corbis; 32 Nik Wheeler; 33 (t) Hulton-Deutsch Collection/Corbis, (b) R. Sheridan/Ancient Art & Architecture Collection; 34 (t) The British Museum/Compass, (b) Gianni Dagli Orti/Corbis; 36 Gianni Dagli Orti/Corbis; 37 Dagli Orti/Musée du Louvre, Paris/The Art Archive; 40 Hulton Archive by Getty Images; 42 (t) Dagli Orti/The British Museum/The Art Archive, (b) R. Sheridan/Ancient Art & Architecture Collection; 43 (l, c) Scala/Art Resource, NY, (r) Erich Lessing/Art Resource, NY; 44 O. Alamany & E. Vicens/Corbis; 46 Gene Plaisted, OSC, The Crosiers; 47 R. Sheridan/Ancient Art & Architecture Collection; 50 (t) Angelo Hornak/Corbis, (bl) Archivo Iconografico, S.A./Corbis; 50–51 Christophe Boisvieux/Corbis; 51 (tl) Victoria & Albert Museum, London/Art Resource, NY; (r) Jeremy Horner/Corbis; 53 Paul Almasy/Corbis; 54 (t) Archivo Iconografico, S.A./Corbis, (b) Robert Harding/Corbis; 55 Dilip Mehta/Woodfin Camp & Associates; 57 Scala/Art Resource, NY; 59 Gable/Sylvia Cordaiy Photo Library; 60 Luca I. Tettoni/Corbis; 61 Peter Baker/Leo de Wys; 62 (t) Erich Lessing/Art Resource, NY, (b) Reuters NewMedia Inc./Corbis; 64 Bill Gallery/Viesti Associates; 67 Hulton Archive by Getty Images; 69 Dagli Orti/Biblioteca Nazionale Marciana Venice/The Art Archive; 70 Alison Wright/The Image Works; 71 (b) Imtiaz Dharkas/The Image Works, (t) Lindsay Hebberd/Woodfin Camp & Associates; 73 Diego Lezama Orezzoli/Corbis; 74 (tl) Philadelphia Museum of Art/Corbis, (tr) Dagli Orti/The Art Archive, (b) O. Louis Mazzatenta/NGS Image Collection; 75 (b) Dennis Cox/ChinaStock, (tl, tr) Werner Forman Archive/Art Resource, NY, (c) Martha Avery/Asian Art & Archaeology, Inc./Corbis; 76 Wang Lu/ChinaStock; 77 Dennis Cox/ChinaStock; 78 Julia Waterlow/Eye Ubiquitous/Corbis; 79 Michel Setboun/Stone; 81 Freer Gallery of Art, Smithsonian Institution, Washington, D.C.; 82 The British Museum/Bridgeman Art Library; 83 British Museum/Bridgeman Art Library; 84 Wang Lu/ChinaStock; 86 Bibliothèque Nationale, Paris/The Art Archive; 87 Giraudon/Art Resource, NY; 88 (l) Wan-go Weng/from the Collection of the National Palace Museum, Taipei, Republic of China (r) Ancient Art & Architecture Collection; 89 The British Museum/The Art Archive; 90 Bibliothèque Nationale, Paris/Bridgeman Art Library, London/SuperStock; 91 Giraudon/Art Resource, NY; 92 Dennis Cox/ChinaStock; 93 Keren Su/Corbis; 94 Bob Rowan/Progressive Image/Corbis; 95 Dennis Cox/ ChinaStock; 98 (l) Dagli Orti/Archaeological Museum Aleppo/The Art Archive, (r) Angelo Hornak/Corbis; 99 (t) Robert E. Murowchick/Photo Researchers, (bowl) Erich Lessing/Art Resource, NY, (tools) Gianni Dagli Orti/Corbis; 100–101 Scala/Art Resource, NY; 101 (b) Borromeo/Art Resource, NY; 102 (tl) Araldo de Luca/Corbis, (tr) John Hios/AKG London; 102–103 (b) Scala/Art Resource, NY; 103 (t) Fitzwilliam Museum, University of Cambridge, UK/Bridgeman Art Library, (cr) North Carolina Museum of Art/Corbis, (cl) Werner Forman Archive/Art Resource, NY; 104 (tl) Archaeological Museum of Heraklion, Crete, Greece/Bridgeman Art Library, (tc, tr) Ashmolean Museum, Oxford, UK/Bridgeman Art Library, (b) National Archaeological Museum, Athens, Greece/Bridgeman Art Library; 105 (tl, tr) Scala/Art Resource, NY, (b) Erich Lessing/Art Resource, NY; 106 National Archaeological Museum, Athens, Greece/Bridgeman Art Library; 108 (l) National Archaeological Museum, Athens, Greece/Bridgeman Art Library, (r) Archaeological Museum of Chora, Greece/Bridgeman Art Library; 109 SEF/Art Resource, NY; 111 (t) SuperStock, (b) Walter Schmid/Stone; 112 Gianni Dagli Orti/Corbis; 113 Gian Berto Vanni/Art Resource, NY; 114 Robert Harding/Corbis; 115 The Brooklyn Museum, Charles Wilbour Fund; 116 Phyllis Picardi/Stock South/PictureQuest; 119 Erich Lessing/Art Resource, NY; 120 The British Museum, London, UK/Bridgeman Art Library; 121 Wolfgang Kaehler; 123 (t) Scala/Art Resource, NY, (b) George Grigoriou/ Stone; 125 Nimatallah/Art Resource, NY ; 127 Ashmolean Museum, Oxford, UK/Bridgeman Art Library; 128 (t) Private Collection, Milan/Canali PhotoBank, Milan/SuperStock, (bl) Gian Berto Vanni/Corbis, (br) Yann Arthus-Bertrand/Corbis; 129 (tl) Réunion des Musées Nationaux/Art Resource, NY, (tr) Erich Lessing/Art Resource, NY, (b) Jeremy Horner/Corbis; 130 Charles O'Rear/Corbis; 131 National Museum, Athens/Art Resource, NY; 132 Scala/Art Resource, NY; 134 (t) Museo Archeologico Nazionale, Naples/Bridgeman Art Library, (b) Roger-Viollet, Paris/Bridgeman Art Library; 136 Scala/Art Resource, NY; 137 The Lowe Art Museum, The University of Miami/ SuperStock; 138 Bettmann/Corbis; 139 Fitzwilliam Museum, University of

Cambridge/Bridgeman Art Library; 140 Erich Lessing/Art Resource, NY; 141 (t) Art Resource, NY, (b) Staatliche Glypothek, Munich, Germany/ET Archive, London/SuperStock; 142 Michael Holford; 143 Erich Lessing/Art Resource, NY; 145 Réunion des Musées Nationaux/Art Resource, NY; 151 AKG London; 152 VCG/FPG International; 153 (t, b) Erich Lessing/Art Resource, NY; 154 Erich Lessing/Art Resource, NY; 155 Scala/Art Resource, NY; 157 Réunion des Musées Nationaux/Art Resource, NY; 159 Giraudon/Art Resource, NY; 160 Robert Emmett Bright/Photo Researchers; 161 Bettmann/Corbis; 162 (t) Florence Bargello/Bridgeman Art Library, (bl) National Museums of Scotland/Bridgeman Art Library, (br) Victoria & Albert Museum, London/Art Resource, NY; 164 Archivo Iconografico, S.A./Corbis; 165 Roger Wood/Corbis; 166 Jose Fuste Raga/Corbis Stock Market; 167 Index/Bridgeman Art Library; 168 Scala/Art Resource, NY; 169, 170, 171 Gene Plaisted, OSC/The Crosiers; 172 Scala/Art Resource, NY; 173 Robert Frerck/Stone; 175 Courtesy The Bancroft Library; 176 (t) Archäologisches Landesmuseum der Christian-Albrechts-Universität, Schloss Gottorf, Schleswig, Germany, (b) Elio Ciol/Corbis; 177 Dallas and John Heaton/Corbis; 180 (t) Mike Yamashita/Woodfin Camp & Associates, (bl) Stephen Studd/Stone, (br) The British Museum, London/Bridgeman Art Library/SuperStock; 181 (tl) MIT Collection/Corbis, (tr) The Michael C. Rockefeller Memorial Collection, Gift of Nelson A. Rockefeller, 1972, Metropolitan Museum of Art, (b) Réunion des Musées Nationaux/Art Resource, NY; 184 (t) Gallo Images/Corbis, (b) M & E Bernheim/Woodfin Camp & Associates; 185 (t) Boltin Picture Library, (b) Ebet Roberts; 186 Trip/M Jelliffe/The Viesti Collection; 187 Mike Yamashita/Woodfin Camp & Associates; 189 (l, c, r) Werner Forman Archive/Art Resource, NY; 190 Salim Amin/Camerapix Ltd, Kenya; 191 Cordaiy Photo Library Ltd./Corbis; 192 Barbara Maurer/Stone; 193 Museum of Mankind, London/Bridgeman Art Library; 194 (t) Giraudon/Art Resource, NY, (b) Sandro Vannini/Corbis; 195 Dagli Orti/Musée des Arts Africains et Océaniens/The Art Archive; 198 (t) Kevin Schafer/Corbis, (bl) Runk/Schoenberger/Grant Heilman Photography, (br) PhotoDisc, Inc.; 199 (t) Dr. S. Coyne/Ancient Art & Architecture Collection, (bl) Patti Murray/Earth Scenes, (br) Courtesy, National Museum of the American Indian, Smithsonian Institution (T189306). Photo by David Heald; 200 Tom McHugh/Photo Researchers; 202 Werner Forman Archive/Art Resource, NY; 203 Wild Country/Corbis; 205 Leo Keeler/Animals Animals; 206 (totem pole) HRW Photo, (salmon, evergreens) Corbis, (buffalo) Courtesy Department of Library Services, American Museum of Natural History, (cactus, acorns) PhotoDisc, Inc., (clovis points) Steve Elmore/Tony Stone/AllStock, (corn) HRW Photo by Sam Dudgeon, (t) Johan Adlercreutz/Ancient Art & Architecture Collection; 207 Richard A. Cooke/Corbis; 209 Jose Fuste Raga/Corbis Stock Market; 210 (t) Werner Forman Archive/National Museum of Anthropology, Mexico City/Art Resource, NY, (b) Ancient Art & Architecture Collection; 211 Stephen L. Alvarez/NGS Image Collection; 213 Bettmann/Corbis; 214 (l) AKG London, (r) Werner Forman Archive/Art Resource, NY; 215 (r) Werner Forman Archive/Art Resource, NY, (l) Erich Lessing/Art Resource, NY; 216–217 Burstein Collection/Corbis; 217 (b) Victoria & Albert Museum, London/Art Resource, NY; 218 (l) Andrea Jemolo/Corbis, (cl) Bojan Brecelj/Corbis, (cr) The British Museum; 219 (t) Peter M. Wilson/Corbis, (bl) Dagli Orti/The Art Archive, (br) Paul Almasy/Corbis; 220 (l) Church of San Vitale, Ravenna, Italy/Canali PhotoBank, Milan/SuperStock, (r) British Library, London, UK/Bridgeman Art Library; 221 (tl) The British Museum, London, UK/Bridgeman Art Library, (r) Scala/Art Resource, NY, (b) Erich Lessing/Art Resource, NY; 222 Werner Forman Archive/Treasury of St. Mark's, Venice/Art Resource, NY; 224 Scala/Art Resource, NY; 225 (t, b) Church of San Vitale, Ravenna, Italy/Canali PhotoBank, Milan/SuperStock; 226 Jose F. Poblete/Corbis; 227 Robert Frerck/Stone; 228 Scala/Art Resource, NY; 229 Werner Forman Archive/Art Resource, NY; 231 Bridgeman Art Library; 232 Giraudon/Art Resource, NY; 233 Art Resource, NY; 234 Tretjakov Gallery, Moscow/AKG London; 235 Geoff Johnson/Stone; 238 (tl) Giraudon/Art Resource, NY, (tr) Owen Franken/Corbis, (b) Sylvain Grandadam/Stone; 239 (tl) AKG London, (tr) Dagli Orti/National Museum Damascus, Syria/The Art Archive, (b) Réunion des Musées Nationaux/Art Resource, NY; 241 Nabeel Turner/Stone; 245 (t) Printed by permission from the International Association of Sufism, (b) SuperStock; 246 (t, l) AKG London, (r) Werner Forman Archive/Art Resource, NY, (b) Reprinted courtesy the Rare Book Department, The Free Library of Philadelphia, Philadelphia, PA; 247 Bibliothèque Nationale, Paris, France/Bridgeman Art Library; 248 Sonia Halliday Photographs; 249 Bibliothèque Nationale, Paris/AKG Berlin/SuperStock; 250 (t) Giraudon/Art Resource, NY, (b) Roland & Sabrina Michaud/Woodfin Camp & Associates; 251 (l) Roland & Sabrina Michaud/Woodfin Camp & Associates, (r) Paul Dupuy Museum, Toulouse, France/Lauros-Giraudon, Paris/SuperStock; 252 (t) Bridgeman Art Library, (b) Index/Bridgeman Art Library; 253 Dreweatt Neate Fine Art Auctioneers, Newbury, Berkshire, UK/Bridgeman Art Library; 255 Archivo Iconografico, S. A./Corbis; 257 (tl) Lisa Quinones/Black Star Publishing/PictureQuest, (tc) Jewish Museum, London/Bridgeman Art Library, (tr) Art Resource, NY, (c) Richard Nowitz/Words & Pictures/PictureQuest, (b) Annie Griffiths Belt/Corbis; 258 (tl) Dinodia/Trip Photo Library, (tc) Milind A. Ketkar/ Dinodia Picture Agency, (tr) Mark Downey/Viesti Associates, Inc., (c) Lindsay Hebberd/Corbis, (b) Gian Berto Vanni/Corbis; 259 (tl) AFP/Corbis, (tc) Luca I. Tettoni/Corbis, (tr) Josef Beck/FPG International, (cl) SOA/Dinodia, (b) ML Sinibaldi/Corbis Stock Market; 260 (t) Bridgeman Art Library, (tc) Bohemian Nomad Picturemakers/Corbis, (tr) Courtesy of Information Division, Taipei Economic and Cultural Office in Chicago, (c) Alan Thornton/Stone, (b) Courtesy of Information Division, Taipei Economic and Cultural Office in Chicago; 261 (t) Scala/Art Resource, NY, (tc) PhotoDisc, Inc., (tr) Erich Lessing/Art Resource, NY, (c) Elio Ciol/Corbis, (b) Mark Thiessen/Corbis; 262 (tl) Ronald Sheridan/Ancient Art & Architecture Collection, (tc) Werner Forman Archive/Art Resource, NY, (tr) Bonhams, London/Bridgeman Art Library, (c) AFP/Corbis, (b) Reuters NewMedia Inc./Corbis; 263 Gael Cornier/AP/Wide World Photos; 264 (t) Erich Lessing/Art Resource, NY, (bl) Victoria & Albert Museum, London/Art Resource, NY, (br) British Library, London/Bridgeman Art Library; 265 (t) Sakamoto Photo Research Laboratory/Corbis, (b) The Art Archive; 266 Michael Bodycomb/Kimbell Art Museum/Corbis; 266 Musée Guimet, Paris, France/Lauros-Giraudon, Paris/SuperStock; 267 Liu Xiaoyang/ChinaStock; 269 The British Library/The Art Archive; 271 (t) The Metropolitan Museum of Art, A.W. Bahr Collection, Fletcher Fund, 1947. (47.18.1) Photography © 1978 The Metropolitan Museum of Art, (b) Photograph Courtesy Peabody Essex Museum; 272 Werner Forman Archive/Art Resource, NY; 274 (t) National Palace Museum, Taiwan/ET Archive, London/SuperStock, (b) Giraudon/Art Resource, NY; 275 Bibliothèque Nationale, Paris, France/Bridgeman Art Library; 276 Janette Ostier Gallery, Paris, France/Giraudon, Paris/SuperStock; 278 Werner Forman Archive/Victoria & Albert Museum, London/Art Resource, NY; 280 Chris Lisle/Corbis; 281 Ronald Sheridan/Ancient Art & Architecture Collection; 282 Boltin Picture Library; 283 (t) Dan McCoy/Rainbow/PictureQuest, (b) Pictor International/Pictor International, Ltd./PictureQuest; 286 (t) Dagli Orti/University Library Heidelberg/The Art Archive, (bl) Eirik Irgens Johnsen/University Museum of National Antiquities, Oslo, Norway, (br) The Pierpont Morgan Library/Art Resource, NY; 287 (t) Musée de la Tapisserie, Bayeux, France/Bridgeman Art Library, (bl) Bibliothèque Nationale, Paris/AKG London, (br) Erich Lessing/Art Resource, NY; 288 Pierre Belzeaux/Photo Researchers; 289 (t) AKG London, (b) Bildarchiv Steffens/Bridgeman Art Library; 290 Giraudon/Bridgeman Art Library; 293 Knudsens-Giraudon/Art Resource, NY; 294 Bettmann/Corbis; 295 (t) AKG London, (b) Robert W. Madden/National Geographic Image Collection; 297 Bridgeman Art Library/SuperStock; 298 Bibliothèque Nationale, Paris/AKG London; 299 (l) The Pierpont Morgan Library/Art Resource, NY; (r) The New York Public Library/Art Resource, NY; 300 AKG London; 301 British Library/Bridgeman Art Library; 302 Michael Teller/AKG London; 303 Dagli Orti/The Art Archive; 304 Winchester Cathedral, Hampshire, UK/Bridgeman Art Library; 305 Michael Freeman/Corbis; 306 Bettmann/Corbis; 309 AKG London; 310 Erich Lessing/Art Resource, NY; 311, 312 AKG London; 313 HarperCollins Publishers/The British Library/The Art Archive; 316 (t) Archivio Iconografico, S.A./Corbis, (bl) Erich Lessing/Art Resource, NY, (br) The British Library/The Art Archive; 317 (tl) Bibliothèque Royale de Belgique, Brussels, Belgium/Bridgeman Art Library, (tr) Réunion des Musées Nationaux/Art Resource, NY, (b) Bill Bachmann/ Index Stock Imagery/PictureQuest; 318 Bridgeman Art Library; 320 Bibliothèque Nationale, Paris, France/Bridgeman Art Library; 322 Ancient Art & Architecture Collection; 325 Giraudon/Art Resource, NY; 326 British Library, London/Bridgeman Art Library, London/SuperStock; 328 Victoria & Albert Museum, London/Art Resource, NY; 329 Mary Evans Picture Library; 330 Giraudon/Art Resource, NY; 331 Giraudon/Art Resource, NY; 332 Archivio Iconografico, S.A./Corbis; 333 (t) Mary Evans Picture Library, (b) Archivio Iconografico, S.A./Corbis; 334 Archivio Iconografico, S.A./Corbis; 335 (t) Mimmo Jodice/Corbis, (b) Massimo Listri/Corbis; 336 Bibliothèque Nationale, Paris/AKG London; 338 Christie's Images/Corbis; 340 Dagli Orti/Musée du Chateau de Versailles/The Art Archive; 341 Giraudon/Art Resource, NY; 342 Gail Mooney/Corbis; 343 Dagli Orti/University Library Prague/The Art Archive; 346 (l) Archivio Iconografico, S.A./Corbis, (r) Eileen Tweedy/Victoria & Albert Museum London/The Art Archive; 347 (t) Dagli Orti/Tiroler Landesmuseum, Innsbruck/The Art Archive, (cl) von Linden/AKG London, (cr) Dagli Orti/The Art Archive; 348–349 Library of Congress, Washington, D.C./Bridgeman Art Library; 349 Eileen Tweedy/The Art Archive; 350 (tl) Alinari/Art Resource, NY, (tr) Victoria & Albert Museum/Art Resource, NY, (b) Erich Lessing/Art Resource, NY; 351 (t) Royal Ontario Museum/Corbis, (bl) Dagli Orti/Palace of Chihil Soutoun Isfahan/The Art Archive, (br) Victoria & Albert Museum, London/ Bridgeman Art Library; 352 (t) Dagli Orti/Galleria degli Uffizi, Florence/The Art Archive, (b) Gary Yeowell/Stone; 353 (tl) Bettmann/Corbis, (tr) Réunion des Musées Nationaux/Art Resource, NY, (b) Scala/Art Resource, NY; 355 Ali Meyer/Bridgeman Art Library; 356 Musée Des Beaux-Arts de Lille, Jardin du Muss/Giraudon/Art Resource, NY; 357 (t) Scala/Art Resource, NY, (b) Araldo de Luca/Corbis; 358 Réunion des Musées Nationaux/Art Resource, NY; 359 The Pierpont Morgan Library/Art Resource, NY; 360 Erich Lessing/Art Resource, NY; 362 Erich Lessing/Art Resource, NY, (bl, br) Erich Lessing/Art Resource, NY; 363 The Art Archive; 364 Scala/Art Resource, NY; 365 Index/Bridgeman Art Library; 366 Belvoir Castle, Leicestershire/Bridgeman Art Library; 367 British Library, London/Bridgeman Art Library; 368 Erich Lessing/Art Resource, NY; 369 Giraudon/Art Resource, NY; 371 Bridgeman Art Library; 372 Peter Willi/Bridgeman Art Library; 373 Bridgeman Art Library; 374 Kunsthistorisches Museum Vienna, Austria/Bridgeman Art Library; 376 (t) Phillips, The International Fine Art Auctioneers, UK/Bridgeman Art Library, (b) Francis G. Mayer/Corbis; 377 Giraudon/Art Resource, NY; 379 Eilo Ciol/Corbis; 380 (t) Corbis, (tr) Dagli Orti/The Art Archive, (b) Scala/Art Resource, NY; 381 (tl) Dave Bartruff/Corbis, (tr) Bettmann/Corbis, (bl) Library of Congress, Washington, D.C./Bridgeman Art Library, (br) Bettmann/Corbis; 382 Scala/Art Resource, NY; 383 (t) Erich Lessing/Art Resource, NY, (b) Alinari/Art Resource, NY; 385 Nimatallah/Art Resource, NY; 386 Sheila Terry/Science Photo Library/ Photo Researchers; 387 Giraudon/Art Resource, NY; 388 Réunion des Musées Nationaux/Bridgeman Art Library; 389 David Parker/Science Photo Library/Photo Researchers; 390 Lauros-Giraudon/Bridgeman Art Library; 391 PhotoDisc, Inc.; 393 (l) Bettmann/

Corbis, (r) Bridgeman Art Library; 395 Royal Geographical Society, London/Bridgeman Art Library; 398 Bettmann/Corbis; 400 Historical Picture Archive/Corbis; 401 Bettmann/Corbis; 402, 403 Francis G. Mayer/Corbis; 406 (l) Art Resource, NY, (r) Museum of the City of New York/Corbis; 407 Archivo Iconografico, S.A./Corbis; 410 (t) Grafica/Pacific Stock, (b) Werner Forman Archive/Art Resource, NY; 411 (tl) Richard Powers/Corbis, (tr) Paul Freeman/Bridgeman Art Library, (b) Fitzwilliam Museum/ University of Cambridge, UK/Bridgeman Art Library; 413 Pierre Colombel/Corbis; 414 Stock Montage; 415 Victoria & Albert Museum, London/Art Resource, NY; 416 Archivo Iconografico, S.A./Corbis; 417 Royal Geographical Society, London/Bridgeman Art Library; 418 (t) AKG London, (b) Paul Freeman/Bridgeman Art Library; 419 Hulton-Deutsch Collection/Corbis; 421 Historical Picture Archive/Corbis; 423 (t) The Art Archive, (b) Palubniak Studios; 424 Victoria & Albert Museum, London/Art Resource, NY; 425 Réunion des Musées Nationaux/Art Resource, NY; 426 Palubniak Studios; 427 The British Museum/Bridgeman Art Library; 430 (t) Victoria & Albert Museum, London/Art Resource, NY, (b) Elio Ciol/Corbis; 431 (tl) Magdalen College, Oxford/Bridgeman Art Library, (tr) Erich Lessing/Art Resource, NY, (bl) Madar-i-Shah Madrasa, Isfahan, Iran/Bridgeman Art Library, (br) Bibliothèque Nationale, Paris, France/ Bridgeman Art Library; 432 Dagli Orti/Topkapi Museum, Istanbul/The Art Archive; 434 (t) Erich Lessing/AKG London, (b) Giraudon/Art Resource, NY; 435, 436 Ronald Sheridan/Ancient Art & Architecture Collection; 438 Bonhams, London, UK/Bridgeman Art Library; 439 The British Library/The Art Archive; 441 Chris Haigh/Stone; 442 Chester Beatty Library & Gallery of Oriental Art, Dublin/ Bridgeman Art Library; 443 Metropolitan Museum of Art, New York/Bridgeman Art Library; 446 (l) Werner Forman Archive/Art Resource, NY, (r) Dagli Orti/Musée du Chateau de Versailles/The Art Archive; 447 (l) Dagli Orti/Musée Ceramique Sevres/The Art Archive, (r) Bjorn Landstrom/NGS Image Collection; 448–449 Giraudon/Art Resource, NY; 449 (b) Lee Snider/Corbis; 450 (tl) The Art Archive, (tr) Historical Picture Archive/Corbis, (b) Alison Wright/ Corbis; 451 (t) Giraudon/Art Resource, NY, (c) Hulton Archive by Getty Images, (bl) Bettmann/Corbis, (br) David Muench/Corbis; 452 (tl) Jarrold Publishing/The Art Archive, (tr) Victoria & Albert Museum, London/The Art Archive, (b) Yale Center for British Art, Paul Mellon Collection, USA/Bridgeman Art Library; 453 (tl) Adam Woolfitt/ Corbis, (tr) Dagli Orti/Russian Historical Museum, Moscow/The Art Archive, (b) Wolfgang Kaehler/Corbis; 454 AKG London; 455 Erich Lessing/Art Resource, NY; 456 SuperStock; 457 Dave G. Houser/Corbis; 458 Superstock; 459 Sovfoto/Eastfoto; 461 (t) Collection of Countess Bobrínskoy/ Michael Holford, (b) Hulton Archive by Getty Images; 462 Dagli Orti/Musée de Versailles/The Art Archive; 464 (t) Dagli Orti/Russian Historical Museum, Moscow/ The Art Archive, (b) Sovfoto/Eastfoto; 465 Palace of Versailles, France/Lauros-Giraudon, Paris/SuperStock; 466 (t) Musée du Louvre, Paris/SuperStock, (b) AKG London; 467 AKG, Berlin/SuperStock; 469 AKG London; 470 Richard Glover/Corbis; 471 Dagli Orti/Pinacoteca di Siena/The Art Archive; 472 (t) Art Resource, NY, (r) Robert Harding Picture Library; 473 (t, b) Erich Lessing/Art Resource, NY; 476 (l) Erich Lessing/Art Resource, NY, (r) Bettmann/Corbis; 477 (tl) Bettmann/Corbis, (tr) Giraudon/Bridgeman Art Library, (bl) The Huntington Library, Art Collections, and Botanical Gardens, San Marino, California/SuperStock, (br) Colonial Williamsburg Foundation; 478 Alinari/Art Resource, NY; 479 Houses of Parliament, Westminster, London, UK/Bridgeman Art Library; 480 Bridgeman Art Library; 482 National Portrait Gallery, London/SuperStock; 483 Dreweatt Neate Fine Art Auctioneers, Newbury/Bridgeman Art Library; 484 Victoria & Albert Museum, London, UK/Bridgeman Art Library; 485 AKG London; 486 (t, b) Stock Montage/SuperStock; 487 Bettmann/Corbis; 489 The British Museum, London, UK/Bridgeman Art Library; 490 Stock Montage/SuperStock; 491 Michael Holford; 492 (l) New York Historical Society, New York, USA/Bridgeman Art Library, (r) SuperStock; 493 (4 left coins) Eileen Tweedy/The British Museum/The Art Archive, (r) Fitzwilliam Museum, University of Cambridge, UK/Bridgeman Art Library; 493 Eileen Tweedy/The British Museum/The Art Archive; 494 Louvre, Bibliothèque, Paris, France/Erich Lessing/Art Resource, NY; 495 Erich Lessing/Art Resource, NY; 496 Tate Gallery, London/Art Resource, NY; 498 (t) Stock Montage, (b) Library Company of Philadelphia; 499 SuperStock; 503 Christie's Images/SuperStock; 506 (t) Ronald Sheridan/Ancient Art & Architecture Collection, (b) Paul Almasy/Corbis, (b) Dagli Orti/Post and Telecommunications Museum Rome/The Art Archive; 507 (t) Réunion des Musées Nationaux/Art Resource, NY, (bl) John Lawrence/Stone, (br) Todd Gipstein/Corbis; 508 Bettmann/Corbis; 509 (t) Erich Lessing/Art Resource, NY, (b) Hulton-Deutsch Collection/Corbis; 510 (t) Ali Meyer/Corbis, (b) Robert Holmes/Corbis; 511 Giraudon/Art Resource, NY; 512 AKG, Berlin/SuperStock; 513 Dagli Orti/Musée Carnavalet, Paris/The Art Archive; 514 Giraudon/Art Resource, NY; 516 Dagli Orti/Musée de l'Affiche, Paris/The Art Archive; 517 Dagli Orti/Musée Carnavalet, Paris/The Art Archive; 518 Museo del Prado, Madrid/The Art Archive; 519 Dagli Orti/Musée Carnavalet, Paris/The Art Archive; 520 (t) Gianni Dagli Orti/Corbis, (b) Giraudon/Art Resource, NY; 521 Scala/Art Resource, NY; 522 Dagli Orti/Musée de Versailles/The Art Archive; 523 Erich Lessing/Art Resource, NY; 524 Giraudon/Art Resource, NY; 526, 527, 528 Archivo Iconografico, S.A./Corbis; 529, 530 AKG London; 532 Bettmann/Corbis; 533 AKG London; 536 (l) Philip Mould, Historical Portraits Ltd, London, UK/Bridgeman Art Library, (tr) Bequest of Winslow Warren/Courtesy Museum of Fine Arts, Boston, MA, (br) Library Company of Philadelphia; 537 (cr) AKG London, (tr) Stock Montage, (l) Harris Museum and Art Gallery, Preston, Lancashire, UK/Bridgeman Art Library; 538–539 Yale Center for British Art, Paul Mellon Collection, USA/Bridgeman Art Library, (b) Forbes Collection, New York City/Bridgeman Art Library, London/SuperStock; 540 (t) Royal Holloway and Bedford New College, Surrey, UK/Bridgeman Art Library, (c) Gianni Dagli Orti/Corbis, (b) Bettmann/Corbis; 541 (t) Dagli Orti/Civiche Raccolte Museo L. Bailo Treviso/The Art Archive, (bl) M. & E. Bernheim/Woodfin Camp & Associates, (br) Bridgeman Art Library; 542 (t, br) Bettmann/Corbis (bl) Christie's Images/Corbis; 543 (t) Stock Montage, (br) Philip Mould, Historical Portraits Ltd, London, UK/Bridgeman Art Library, (bl) Bettmann/Corbis, (bc) Library of Congress/Corbis, (br) Hulton-Deutsch Collection/Corbis; 546 Library of Congress/Corbis; 547 AKG London; 548 Palubniak Studios; 550 Andrew Russell/Culver Pictures; 552 Bridgeman Art Library; 553 Slater Mill Historic Site/PRC Archive; 554 (t) Snark/Art Resource, NY, (b) North Wind Picture Archives; 555 Steidle Collection, College of Earth and Mineral Sciences, Pennsylvania State University/Steidle Art Collection/SuperStock; 556 From the Collections of Henry Ford Museum and Greenfield Village; 558 New York Historical Society, USA/Bridgeman Art Library; 559 The British Museum/The Art Archive; 560 (t, b) North Wind Picture Archives; 561 Hulton Archive by Getty Images; 562 Bettmann/Corbis; 563 Pinacoteca di Brera, Milan, Italy/Bridgeman Art Library, (b) Bettmann/Corbis; 565 AKG London; 566 Archivo Iconografico, S.A./Corbis; 567 Sovfoto/Eastfoto; 569 Schenectady Museum, Hall of Electrical History Foundation/ Corbis; 570 (t) Stock Montage, (b) Bettmann/Corbis; 571 (t, bl) Hulton Archive by Getty Images, (br) Blank Archives/Hulton Archive by Getty Images; 572, 574 Hulton Archive by Getty Images; 575 Bettmann/Corbis; 576 John D. Cunningham/Visuals Unlimited; 577 (t) South African National Gallery, Cape Town, South Africa/Bridgeman Art Library, (b) Stock Montage; 578 (l) Culver Pictures, (r) The Museum of Modern Art/Film Stills Archives; 579 Gernsheim Collection, Harry Ransom Humanities Research Center, The University of Texas at Austin; 580 Steve Raymer/NGS Image Collection; 581 Archive Photos/PictureQuest; 582 Library of Congress/Corbis; 584 Osa & Martin Johnson Safari Museum/Hulton Archive by Getty Images; 585 Bettmann/Corbis; 586 Edwin Levick/Hulton Archive by Getty Images; 588 Brown Brothers; 589 (t) Culver Pictures, (bl) New York Journal, Jan 5, 1896, Courtesy OldNews, Inc., (br) New York World, 1883, Courtesy OldNews, Inc.; 590 Francis G. Mayer/Corbis; 591 Winslow Homer, American, 1836–1910, Croquet Scene, oil on canvas, 1866, 15 7/8 x 26 1/16in, Friends of American Art Collection, 1942.35, photograph ©1998, The Art Institute of Chicago, All Rights Reserved.; 593 Scala/Art Resource, NY; 594 Christie's Images/SuperStock; 595 (l) Clore Collection, Tate Gallery, London/Art Resource, NY, (r) Erich Lessing/Art Resource, NY, (frame) Image Farm; 596 Giraudon/Art Resource, NY; 597 Christie's Images/Bridgeman Art Library; 599 Philip De Bay/Historical Picture Archive/Corbis; 600 (t) North Wind Picture Archives, (b) White House Collection, Courtesy White House Historical Association, (bc) The Granger Collection, (c) George Rinhart/Underwood & Underwood/Corbis; 601 (tl) Francis G. Mayer/Corbis, (tr) Laurie Platt Winfrey/Woodfin Camp & Associates, (b) Bettmann/Corbis; 603 Mansell Collection/TimePix; 604 (t) AKG London, (b) Corbis; 605 Hulton-Deutsch Collection/Corbis; 607 Bettmann/Corbis; 608 Mansell Collection/TimePix; 609 North Wind Picture Archives; 613 Brown Brothers; 614 Seneca Falls Historical Society; 615 AKG London; 616 Gianni Dagli Orti/Corbis; 617 Musée d'Orsay, Paris, France/Réunion des Musées Nationaux/ Bridgeman Art Library; 618 (t) Bettmann/Corbis, (b) Bridgeman Art Library; 619 Giraudon/Art Resource, NY; 620 Leonard de Selva/Corbis; 621 Giraudon/Art Resource, NY; 622 Bettmann/Corbis; 624 Topham/The Image Works; 625 Bettmann/Corbis; 627 Art Resource, NY; 630 (t) Bridgeman Art Library, (b) National Portrait Gallery, London/SuperStock; 631 (t) Courtesy of the Red Cross, (tr) Scala/Art Resource, NY, (b) Dagli Orti/The Art Archive, (tr) Musée d'Orsay, Paris/Giraudon, Paris/SuperStock; 632 A. Marc/Mary Evans Picture Library; 633 (t) SEF/Art Resource, NY, (b) Museo Civico del Risorgimento, Bologna, Italy; 634 (t) Hulton-Deutsch Collection/Corbis, (b) Archivio Iconografico, S.A./Corbis; 635 Christie's Images/SuperStock; 637, 638 AKG, London; 639 AKG Berlin/SuperStock; 640 (t) AKG London, (b) A. Liebert/Hulton-Deutsch Collection/Corbis; 642 AKG, London; 643 Giraudon/Art Resource, NY; 644 AKG London; 645 Dave Bartruff/Corbis; 646 Culver Pictures; 647 Fine Art Photographic Library, London/Art Resouce, NY; 648 (t) Christel Gerstenberg/Corbis, (b) Steve Raymer/Corbis; 649 (bl) Walters Art Gallery, Baltimore, Courtesy of Robert Forbes Collection; 650 SuperStock; 652 Dagli Orti/Domenica del Corriere/The Art Archive; 653 AKG London; 655 Francoise de Mulder/Corbis; 657 Hulton-Deutsch Collection/Corbis; 660 (t) Dreweatt Neate Fine Art Auctioneers, Newbury, Berkshire, UK/Bridgeman Art Library, (b) Explorer, Paris/SuperStock; 661 (tl) PhotoDisc, (tr) National Portrait Gallery, London/SuperStock, (bl) SuperStock, (br) Brown Brothers; 662 A Dawson Gallery Image/Annapolis Maryland; 663 (t) The Granger Collection, (b) Eileen Tweedy/Lords Gallery/The Art Archive; (b) Michael Maslan Historic Photographs/Corbis; 664 North Wind Picture Archives; 665 Brown Brothers; 666 Culver Pictures; 667 (t) Brown Brothers, (b) Hulton Archive by Getty Images; 668 Hulton Archive by Getty Images; 669 Stock Montage; 671 Granger Collection; 673 Bettmann/Corbis; 674 Brown Brothers; 675 Hulton Deutsch Collection/ Woodfin Camp & Associates; 676 Topham/The Image Works; 677 Bridgeman Art Library; 679 (t) Robert Harding Picture Library, The Metropolitan Museum of Art, The Helena Woolworth McCann Collection, Winfield Foundation Gift, 1958. (58.52) Photograph © The Metropolitan Museum of Art.; 681 Bettmann/Corbis; 682 Brown Brothers; 683 Culver Pictures; 684 Brown Brothers; 686 Robert Frerck/Woodfin Camp & Associates; 687 (l) Library of Congress, (r) Bettmann/Corbis; 690 (l) Archivo Iconografico, S.A./Corbis, (r) Douglas Peebles/Corbis; 691 (t) The Art Archive, (cl) Gianni Dagli Orti/Corbis, (cr) Science Museum London/The Art Archive; 692–693 Bridgeman Art Library; 693 (t) Minnesota Historical Society/Corbis, (b) Library of

Congress/Corbis; 694 (t) Imperial War Museum/ The Art Archive, (b) AP/Wide World Photos; 695 (t) Scheufler Collection/Corbis, (c) Dagli Orti/The Art Archive, (b) PhotoDisc, Inc.; 696 (t) Musée National du Château de Malmaison, Rueil-Malmaison/Lauros-Giraudon, Paris/SuperStock, (b) Sovfoto/Eastfoto; 697 (tl) Stock Montage, (tr) Hulton-Deutsch Collection/Corbis, (bl) AKG London, (br) Brown Brothers; 698 Hulton Archive by Getty Images; 699 Brown Brothers; 701 Leonard de Selva/ Corbis; 702 The Burns Collection; 703 (t) Leonard de Selva/Corbis, (b) Bain News Services/Corbis; 706 Hulton Archive by Getty Images; 710 National Archives and Records Administration, Records of the Department of State (RG59); 713 Sovfoto; 714 Culver Pictures; 716 Bettmann/Corbis; 717 Culver Pictures; 720, 721, 722, 723 Bettmann/Corbis; 726 (t) Bettmann/Corbis, (bl) W.W. Norton & Company, New York. Cover artwork, Saint-Severin by Robert Delaunay, 1909. © L&M Services B.V. Amsterdam 201101, (br) Richard T. Nowitz/Corbis; 727 (t) SuperStock, (bl) Brown Brothers, (br) AKG London; 729 (t) Lloyd Arnold/Hulton Archive by Getty Images, (b) Hulton Archive by Getty Images; 730 Topham/The Image Works; 731 Ezra Stoller/Esto Photographics; 732 Chaplin/United Artists/Kobal Collection; 733 George Rinhart/Underwood & Underwood/Corbis; 735 AP/Wide World Photos; 737 SuperStock; 738 Bettmann/Corbis; 739 AKG London; 740 (l) Michael St. Maur Sheil/Corbis, (r) Topham/The Image Works; 742 Culver Pictures; 743 AKG London; 744 (t) Mary Evans Picture Library, (b) AP/Wide World Photos; 745 AKG London; 746 (l) Bettmann/Corbis, (r) AKG London; 747 AKG London; 748 Corbis; 749 Morton Beebe, S.F./Corbis; 750 (t, b) AKG London; 751 (t) AKG London, (b) Paul Almasy/Corbis; 753 Staffan Widstrand/Corbis; 755 Neil Rabinowitz/Corbis; 756 (tl) Bettmann/Corbis, (tr) AKG London, (b) Brown Brothers; 757 (tl) Hulton-Deutsch Collection/Corbis, (tr)Wolfgang Kaehler/Corbis, (b) Keren Su/Corbis; 758 Photri; 759 Hulton Archive by Getty Images; 760 Hulton-Deutsch Collection/Corbis; 762 Brown Brothers; 766 AKG London; 767 (t) Bettmann/Corbis, (b) Hulton Archive by Getty Images; 768 Corbis; 770 The Art Archive; 771 AKG London; 772, 773 Bettmann/Corbis; 774 Brown Brothers; 775 Schalkwijk/Art Resource, NY; 776 AP/Wide World Photos; 777 Kal Muller/Woodfin Camp & Associates; 780 (tl, tc) New World Music Corporation, (tr) AKG London, (bl) PhotoDisc, Inc., (br) SuperStock; 781 (tl) Bettmann/Corbis, (tr) Michael St. Maur Sheil/ Corbis, (b) Warner Brothers/Kobal Collection; 782 Norsk Press Service/Getty News Services; 784 Giraudon/Art Resource, NY; 785, 786 Hulton-Deutsch Collection/Corbis; 787 UPI/Bettmann/Corbis; 789 (l) AP/Wide World Photos, (r) Bilderdienst Suddeutscher Verlag; 790 Hulton-Deutsch Collection/Corbis; 792 (b) AKG London; 792, 793 Bettmann/Corbis; 794 Imperial War Museum/Hulton Archive by Getty Images; 795 (l) Stock Montage, (r) AP/Wide World Photos; 796 Culver Pictures; 798 (l, r) AKG London; 799 George Hall/Check Six; 800 (l) American Stock/Hulton Archive by Getty Images, (c, r) Hulton Archive by Getty Images; 801 Hulton Archive by Getty Images; 803 (t) Loomis Dean/TimePix (b) Bridgeman Art Library; 805 Division of Political History, Smithsonian Institution, Washington, D.C.; 806 Carl Mydans/TimePix; 808 (t) TimePix, (b) Nicolas Reynard/Getty News Services ; 812 (l) Cover courtesy Little, Brown, and Company, (r) AKG London; 813 (l) AKG London, (r) Hulton-Deutsch Collection/Corbis; 814–815 Schalkwijk/Art Resource, NY; 815 (b) Andrew Syred/Science Photo Library/Photo Researchers; 816 (t) Franklin McMahon/Corbis, (bl) Bettmann/Corbis, (br) Robin Moyer/TimePix; 817 (t) Hanan Isachar/Corbis, (c) Rina Castlenuovo/Contact Press Images/PictureQuest, (b) Reuters NewMedia Inc./Corbis; 818 (bl) 2002 Aubrey Mayhew under license authorized by CMG Worldwide, Inc., Indianapolis, IN 46256 www.cmgww.com. Record cover courtesy Everest Records Archive of Folk & Jazz Music. (br) Ken Eward/Biografx/Science Source/Photo Researchers; 819 (tl) Bettmann/Corbis, (tr) MGM/Kobal Collection, (b) Rick Winsor/Woodfin Camp & Associates; 820 Corbis; 822 FPG International; 823 SuperStock; 824 AKG London; 825 Leonard de Selva/Corbis; 826 Bettmann/Corbis; 827 Hulton-Deutsch Collection/Corbis; 828 (l) AP/Wide World Photos, (r) Tony Vaccaro/AKG London; 830 (t) Courtesy of NATO, (b) Corbis; 831 AKG London; 832 (t) AP/Wide World Photos, (b) UPI/Bettmann/Corbis; 833 Bettmann/Corbis; 834 IPA/The Image Works; 835 Novosti/Science Photo Library/Photo Researchers; 836 (t) UPI/Bettmann/Corbis, (b) Erich Lessing/AKG London; 837 TimePix; 838 AP/Wide World Photos; 840 Wally McNamee/Corbis; 844 (t) John Reader/TimePix, (b) The Everett Collection; 845 (t) Katsumi Kasahara/AP/Wide World Photos, (bl) Stuart Franklin/Magnum Photos, (br) Jeff Tinsley/AP/Wide World Photos; 846 Hulton Archive by Getty Images; 847 AP/Wide World Photos; 849 (t) Dilip Mehta/Contact Press Images/PictureQuest, (b) Nadirsh Naoroji/Dinodia Picture Library; 850 Plinio Lepri/AP/Wide World Photos; 851 Robin Nowacki/AP/Wide World Photos; 852 Lawrence Migdale/Stock Boston/PictureQuest; 854 (l) Sovfoto/ Eastfoto/PictureQuest, (r) Macduff Everton/Corbis; 855 Michael Coyne/Black Star Publishing/Picture Quest; 856 Brown Brothers; 857 (t) AFP/Corbis, (b) Pool Yonhap/AP/Wide World Photos; 858 Robin Moyer/Getty News Services; 859 Hulton Archive by Getty Images; 860 Alan Levenson/Stone; 861 Reuters/Bettmann/Corbis; 862 Eye Ubiquitous/Corbis; 863 AFP/Corbis; 864 Bettmann/Corbis; 866 HRW photo by Sam Dudgeon; 868 (t) Magnus Bartlet/Woodfin Camp & Associates, (b) Lori Grinker/Contact Press Images/PictureQuest; 869 Toru Yokota/AP/Wide World Photos; 870 Greg Girard/Contact Press Images; 871 Frank Wing/Stock Boston; 872 Courtesy ASEAN; 873 H. Armstrong Roberts; 876 (t) Getty News Services, (bl) Hulton Archive by Getty Images, (br) Hugo Van Lawick/NGS Image Collection; 877 (tl) Sean Gallup/Getty News Services, (tr) Dominique Mollard/AP/Wide World Photos, (b) Dennis Farrell/AP/Wide World Photos; 878 AP/World Wide Photos; 879 Courtesy Organization of African Unity; 881 John Moss/Black Star; 882 TimePix; 883 Robinson/Black Star; 884 Reuters NewMedia Inc./Corbis; 885 Paul Velasco/Gallo Images/Corbis; 886 Black Star; 887 Kurt Strumpf/AP/Wide World Photos; 888 (t) Howard Davies/Corbis, (b) Betty Press/Woodfin Camp & Associates; 889 Trygve Bolstad/Panos Pictures; 890 Marc & Evelyn Bernheim/Woodfin Camp & Associates; 891 Bettmann/Corbis; 892 David Rubinger/Corbis; 893, 894, 895 Hulton Archive by Getty Images; 896 Graebli/Black Star; 897 George Pickow/Hulton-Deutsch Collection/Corbis; 898 Steve Vidler/SuperStock; 899 Dennis Brack/Black Star; 903 Reza/SIPA Press; 905 Robert Azzi/Woodfin Camp & Associates; 907 Franklin McMahon/Corbis; 908 (t) Mireille Vautier/Woodfin Camp/PictureQuest, (bl) Leonard de Selva/Corbis, (br) Carl & Ann Purcell/Corbis; 909 (tl) Cover illustration by Fernando Botero/Courtesy Grupo Anaya, Adiciones Catedra, Madrid (tr) Wesley Bocxe/Getty News Services, (b) John Davenport/Getty News Services; 910 Russell Gordon/Odyssey Productions; 911 (t) Getty News Services, (b) Wolfgang Kaehler/Corbis; 912 Kelly Gillin/The Wenatchee World/AP/Wide World Photos; 913 Stephen Ferry/Getty News Services; 914 Marie Hippenmeyer/AFP/Corbis; 915 Raphael Gaillarde/Getty News Services; 916 (t, b) Alon Reininger/Contact Press Images; 917 (tr, cr, br, tv) PhotoDisc, Inc., (cl) Reuters NewMedia Inc./Corbis, (bc) Robert Fried; 919 J.B. Diederich/Contact Press Images; 920 Dave G. Houser/Corbis; 921 Bleibtreu/Sygma; 922 Hulton Archive by Getty Images; 923 (t) Piko/SIPA Press, (b) Hulton Archive by Getty Images; 924 (t) Hulton Archive by Getty Images, (b) AP/Wide World Photos; 925 AP/Wide World Photos; 926 Robert Nickelsberg/Getty News Services; 927 (t) Starr/Stock Boston, (b) A. Ramey/ Stock Boston; 928 Lochon/Getty News Services; 929 AFP/Hulton Archive by Getty Images; 930 (t) Daniel Aubry/ Odyssey Productions, (b) Bettmann/Corbis; 931 Adam Woolfitt/Woodfin Camp & Associates; 932 Vera Lentz/Black Star Publishing/PictureQuest; 933 AFP/Corbis; 934 Wolfgang Kaehler; 935 (t) Raymond Depardon/Magnum Photos, (b)AFP/Corbis; 938 (t) Hulton Archive by Getty Images, (bl) Todd Gipstein/Corbis, (br) Bettmann/Corbis; 939 (tl) Klaus Reisiniger/Black Star, (tr) Getty News Services, (b) Stuart Ramson/AP/Wide World Photos; 940 John Filo; 941 (t) Todd Gipstein/Corbis, (b) James P. Blair/ Corbis; 942 David Young-Wolff/PhotoEdit; 944 NASA; 945 (l) AFP/Corbis, (r) Reuters New Media, Inc./Corbis; 946 Steve Liss/TimePix; 947 Bettmann/Corbis; 948 Getty News Services; 949 (t) David Levenson/Black Star, (b) Lionel Cherruault/Sipa Press; 950 Archive Photos/PictureQuest; 951 Bruno Barbey/Magnum/PictureQuest; 952 Julian Martin/AP/Wide World Photos; 953 Galen Rowell/Corbis; 955 ©European Communities; 956 Dennis Brack/Black Star Publishing/ PictureQuest; 957 Getty News Services; 958 Sovfoto/Eastfoto; 960 (t) B. Annebicque/Sygma, (b) Getty News Services; 961 M. L. Corvetto/The Image Works; 962 David Sutherland/Stone; 963 Amel Emric/AP/Wide World Photos; 964 Daniel Hulshizer/AP/Wide World Photos; 965 Bob Daemmrich/Corbis Sygma; 966 AFP/Corbis; 967 Spencer Platt/Getty Images; 968 Mark Wilson/Getty Images; 969 Adrin Snider/Daily Press/Corbis Sygma; 972 (tl) Courtesy of the United States Postal Service, (tr) Corel Corporation, (b) The Andy Warhol Foundation for the Visual Arts/Art Resource, NY; 973 (tl) PhotoDisc, Inc., (tr) ©Lin Hui/Xinhua Photo/Corbis, (b) EPA/NASA/Landov; 974 © 1999 Pollock-Krasner Foundation/Artists Rights Society (ARS) New York/Musée National d'Art Moderne, Paris, France/Giraudon/Art Resource, NY; 975 Hulton Archive by Getty Images; 976 (tr, cr) Hulton Archive by Getty Images, (cl) © Ted Soqui/Corbis, (b) Courtesy L.A. Music Center/ Tom Bonner; 977 Corbis; 978 Reuters NewMedia Inc./Corbis; 979 Mitchell Gerber/Corbis; 980 Jean-Claude Aunos/Getty News Services; 981 Hulton Archive by Getty Images; 982, 983 NASA; 984 UPI/Bettmann/Corbis; 985 Liba Taylor/Panos Pictures; 986 H. Raguet/Phototake; 987 (t, b) AFP/ Corbis; 988 Erich Hartmann/Magnum Photos; 990 Enrico Dagino/Cosmos/Woodfin Camp & Associates; 996 (r) Eric Risberg/AP/Wide World Photos; 996 (l) Bettmann/Corbis; 997 (l) AFP/Corbis; 997 (r) W. Cody/Corbis; 998 Kunsthistorisches Museum, Vienna, Austria/Bridgeman Art Library; R4 Royal Geographical Society, London/ Bridgeman Art Library, (b) Bettmann/Corbis; R5 (t) SuperStock, (bl) Ken Eward/Biografx/Science Source/Photo Researchers, (br) H. Raguet/Phototake.

Maps

All maps created by MapQuest.com, Inc.

Illustrations

58, 144, 209, 279, 296 Nenad Jakesevic; 375 UHL Studios; 705 Craig Attebery.